International Conference on Electronic, Information and Computer Engineering 2016

MATEC Web of Conferences Volume 44 (2016)

Hong Kong, China
26 - 27 April 2016

Editors:

Wen-Pei Sung
Jimmy Chih-Ming Kao

ISBN: 978-1-5108-2210-8

Printed from e-media with permission by:

Curran Associates, Inc.
57 Morehouse Lane
Red Hook, NY 12571

Some format issues inherent in the e-media version may also appear in this print version.

Printed by Curran Associates, Inc. (2016)

For additional information, please contact EDP Sciences – Web of Conferences
at the address below.

EDP Sciences – Web of Conferences
17, Avenue du Hoggar
Parc d'Activité de Courtabœuf
BP 112
F-91944 Les Ulis Cedex A
France

Phone: +33 (0) 1 69 18 75 75
Fax: +33 (0) 1 69 28 84 91

contact-edps@webofconferences.org

Additional copies of this publication are available from:

Curran Associates, Inc.
57 Morehouse Lane
Red Hook, NY 12571 USA
Phone: 845-758-0400
Fax: 845-758-2633
Email: curran@proceedings.com
Web: www.proceedings.com

TABLE OF CONTENTS

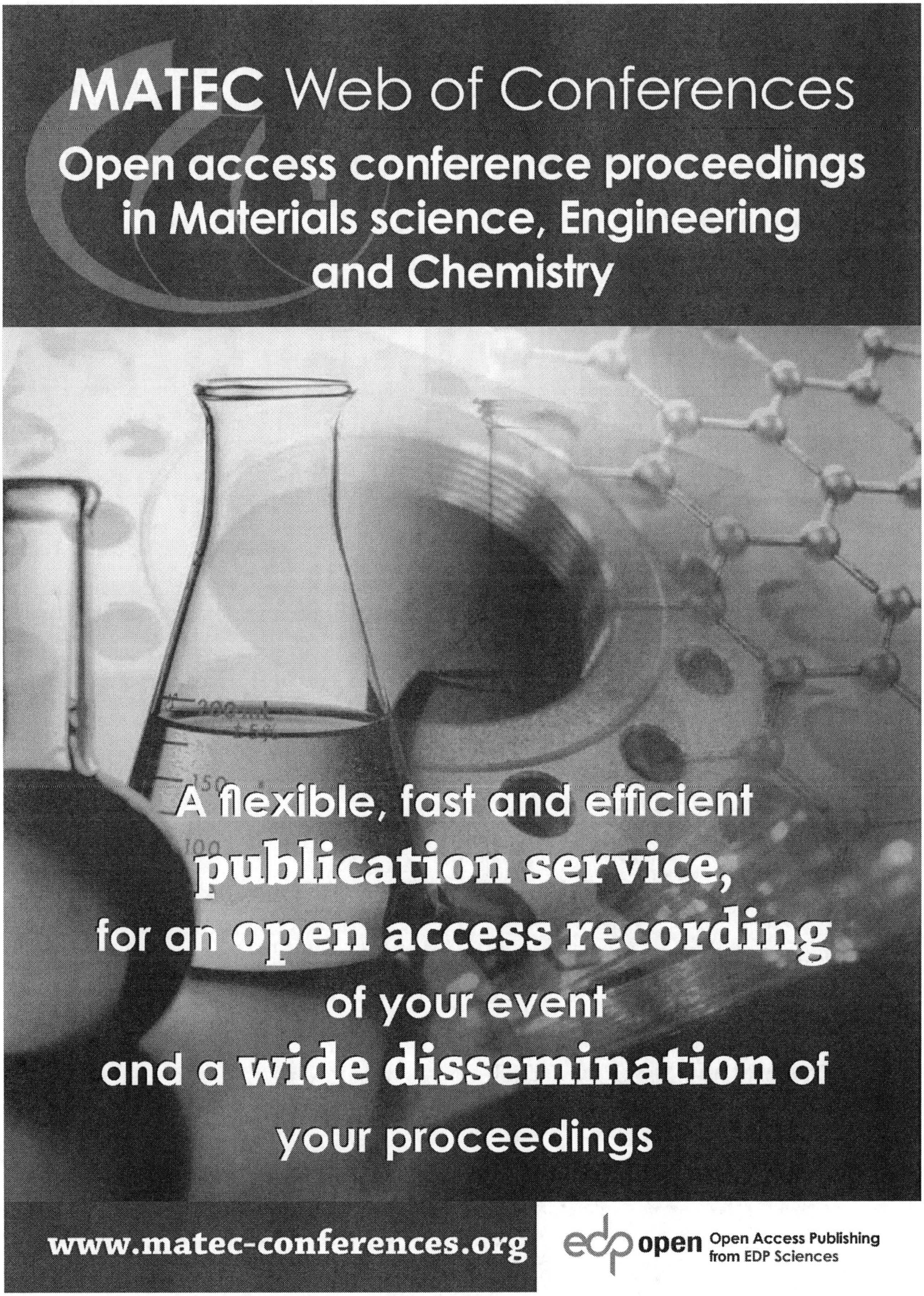

Aims & scope

MATEC Web of Conferences is an open-access journal devoted to the publishing of conference proceedings dealing with Materials science, Engineering and Chemistry.

The journal aims to make conference proceedings visible, citable and widely usable by the scientific community. It offers outstanding services for the publication and dissemination of contents in order to ensure long-term archiving and maximum exposure of scientific events.

Coverage includes all engineering disciplines: civil, naval, mechanical, chemical, and electrical engineering as well as nanotechnology and metrology. The journal also deals with the physical-chemical characterization of materials, their implementation, their resistance in their environment, etc. Others subdisciplines of chemistry, such as analytical chemistry, petrochemistry, organic chemistry, etc., and even pharmacology, are also welcome.

Why publish with MATEC Web of Conferences?

- **Open access:** conference papers available worldwide.
- **Fast publication:** less than 3 months.
- **Total flexibility:** no page restrictions, free unlimited use of colour in the online version, any kind of scientific document welcomed (traditional articles, posters, abstracts and slideshows).
- **High visibility:** all documents indexed in main databases and easily found online.
- **Fair author rights:** CC-BY Creative Commons license.
- **Range of additional publishing options:** printed proceedings, CD-ROMs, copy-editing, etc.

Contact: Isaline Augusto
matec@webofconferences.org

ISSN (electronic edition): 2261-236X

www.matec-conferences.org

edp open Open Access Publishing from EDP Sciences

MATEC Web of Conferences 44, 00001 (2016)
DOI: 10.1051/matecconf/20164400001

Preface

2016 International Conference on Electronic, Information and Computer Engineering (ICEICE 2016) will be held in Hong Kong, during April 26-27, 2016. The conference will bring together leading researchers, engineers and scientists in the domain of interest from around the world. We warmly welcome previous and prospected authors submit your new research papers to ICEICE2016, and share the valuable experiences with the scientist and scholars around the world.

In this conference, we received more than 500 submissions from email and electronic submission system, which were reviewed by international experts, and about 188 papers have been selected for presentation, representing 8 national and international organizations. I think that ICEICE 2016 will be the most comprehensive Conference focused on the Computer Application Engineering, Information Science and Engineering Application.

We would like to thank the conference chairs, organization staff, the authors and the members of International Technological Committees for their hard work.

We hope that ICEICE 2016 will be successful and enjoyable to all participants.

Jan, 2016

Wen-Pei Sung
National Chin-Yi University of Technology

Article available at http://www.matec-conferences.org or http://dx.doi.org/10.1051/matecconf/20164400001

ICEICE 2016 Committee

Conference Chairman

Prof. Jimmy C.M. Kao, National Sun Yat-Sen University
Prof. Wen-Pei Sung, National Chin-Yi University of Technology

Program Committee

Ghamgeen Izat Rashed, Wuhan University, China
Andrey Nikolaevich Belousov, Prof. Andrey Belousov, Head Laboratory of Applied Nanothechnology, Ukraine
Krupa Ranjeet Rasane, Department of Electronic Communications Engineering KLE Society's College of Engineering, India
Sajjad Jafari, Semnan University, Iran
Ahmed N. Abdalla, Universiti Malaysia Pahang, Malaysia
BUT ADRIAN, ELECTROMOTOR company, Timisoara, Bulevardul, Romanian
Yan Wang, The University of Nottingham, UK
Prof. Yu-Kuang Zhao, National Chin-Yi University of Technology, Taiwan
Yi-Ying Chang, National Chin-Yi University of Technology, Taiwan
Darius Bacinskas, Vilnius Gediminas Technical University, Lithuania
Viranjay M. Srivastava, Jaypee University of Information Technology, Solan, H.P., India
Chenggui Zhao, Yunnan Normal University, China
Hsiang-Chuan Liu, Asia University
Hao-En Chueh Yuanpei University
Zhou Liang, Donghua University, China
Liu Yunan, University of Michigan, USA
Wang Liying, Institute of Water Conservancy and Hydroelectric Power, China
Chenggui Zhao, Yunnan University of Finance and Economics, China
Rahim Jamian, Universiti Kuala Lumpur Malaysian Spanish Institute, Malaysia
Lixin Guo, Northeastern University, China
Wen-Sheng Ou, National Chin-Yi University of Technology
Mostafa Shokshok, National University of Malaysia, Malaysia
Ramezan ali Mahdavinejad, University of Tehran, Iran
Wei Fu, Chongqing University, China
Anita Kovač Kralj, University of Maribor, Slovenia
Tjamme Wiegers, Delft University of Technology, Netherlands
Gang Shi, Inha University, South Korea
Bhagavathi Tarigoppula, Bradley University, USA

Co-sponsor

International Frontiers of science and technology Research Association
HongKong Control Engineering and Information Science Research Association
National Chin-Yi University of Technology

edp sciences

MATEC Web of Conferences

Statement of Peer review

In submitting conference proceedings to MATEC Web of Conferences, I certify to the Publisher that I adhere to the **Policy on Publishing Integrity** of the journal in order to safeguard good scientific practice in publishing.

1. All articles have been subjected to peer review administered by the proceedings editors.
2. Reviews have been conducted by expert referees, who have been requested to provide unbiased and constructive comments aimed, whenever possible, at improving the work.
3. Proceedings editors have taken all reasonable steps to ensure the quality of the materials they publish and their decision to accept or reject a paper for publication has been based only on the merits of the work and the relevance to the journal.

Title, date and place of the conference

2016 International Conference on Electronic, Information and Computer Engineering (ICEICE 2016)
April 26-27, 2016
Hong Kong

Proceedings editor(s):

Wen-Pei Sung, National Chin-Yi University of Technology
Jimmy Chih-Ming Kao, National Sun Yat-Sen University

Date and editor's signature

2016. 1.21

MATEC Web of Conferences 44, 01001 (2016)
DOI: 10.1051/matecconf/20164401001

RESEARCH for face detection on improved algorithm of AdaBoost

Hong CHEN

Department of Engineering Technology and Information, Guang'an vocational and technical college, Guangan 638000,China

Abstract. Face detection is basic research in computer visual field, it has important application value in the fields of cameras and surveillance and Automatic face recognition. Because traditional algorithm of AdaBoost has the problem that it needs more features and the detection speed is slow when it is used to detect face, so a improved algorithm of AdaBoost is presented. The experiment results shows that compared with traditional algorithm of AdaBoost, lower features are used in the improved algorithm and higher accuracy rate can be get and the speed of detection is improved Significantly.

keywords: face detection; algorithm of AdaBoost;double threshold

1 introduction

With the quick development and wide application of computer,face detection is more and more attented by Science and technology personnels, it is widely used in the fields of Real-time monitoring, identification and Image database retrieval.Face detection is the key step in the system of face automatic recognition,certain strategy is used to search some of the pictures or videos,and as a result, it can be judged that if there is face.If the faces exit then their position,size and pose will be ensured[1].

Viola and his friends[2] used algorithm of AdaBoost to establish cascading face detector,the method is important progress on face detection.The basic ideology is on the training set that is given,important classification characteristics are selected to expanse the weak classifier through repeated training,and finally the strong classifier can be get afer the weak classifier through a course of linear combination.After each round of training, AdaBoost must resolve two core problems that how to update sample weight and how to choose appropriate weak classifier to constitute strong classifier. The traditional AdaBoost exists a certain problem that the algorithm weight update rule will be handled well when difficult samples appear.But sample weight becomes very big if very few difficult samples exist,as a result,the weigh will be distorted and the trainning will be stop.The search strategy of AdaBoost is ordered to go forward, local optimal principle is used to every iteration,but the weak classifier and coefficient that constitute strong classifier is not the most optimal,as a result,the face detection effect is reduced.

2 improved AdaBoost

Additional AdaBoost has some insufficient,a improved AdaBoost is proposed in the article,the improved AdaBoost changes single threshold value weak classifier to double threshold value weak classifier.There are many factors are considered in the course of selecting characters,for example,the classification ability of characteristics of their own. Information relevance is used to measure the degree of correlation among

characters and redundant information is reduced among characters.

Supposing f1,f2,⋯,fm are selected in the course of selecting characters. In order to avoid redundant information among selected characters and will be selected, relevance should be evaluated from selected characters and will be selected. Supposing x is a character that will be selected,the relevance of R(x) with character which is selected is as follows:

$$R(x)=\max(x,fi)\ i\text{-}1,2,\cdots,m \quad (1)$$

A appropriate threshold value of ε is assumed,if R(x)>ε ,it will be considered that there exists very big relevance between x and selected character,new information will not generate and x can't be selected as character.On the contrary,the relevance between x and selected character is small and it can generate enough new information,x can be selected as character.

Contraposing the defects of traditional AdaBoost, some improvements are arised in the article.Improved algorithm main bring in character relevance and is used to chatacer selection,the method reduces the redundant information among selected characters to minimum. A certain number of sample(label to Positive or negative) are selected as training set,then improved Adaboost is used to be feature selection. The following steps are used to set up strong classifier:

(1) Sample training set{(x1,y1),⋯,(xn,yn)} is input,n is number of sample,xi is NO. of i in the Sample training set,yi is the category lable(1 or 0,their mean are positive samples or Negative samples);{h1(x),h2(x),⋯,hk(x)} has k number of weak classifier,each weak classifier has a character that will be choosed, t is the number of characters which will be choosed, ε is the Correlation threshold.

(2)Sample weigh is initialized:

$$w1,j=1/n. \quad (2)$$

(3)Character is choosed and classifier is established:if the number of character which is choosed less than t then the circulation occurs:

①Sample weigh is normalized:

$$Wt,i \leftarrow pt,i=\frac{Wt,i}{\sum_{j=1}^{N} Wt,i} \quad (3)$$

Weak classifier which is h(j) is designed for each character:

$$h(j)=\begin{cases}1 & \delta 1 < fj(x) < \delta 2\\ 0 & \text{others}\end{cases} \quad (4)$$

In the formula (4),fj(x)is the character value of sample. Weighted classification error is:

$$\varepsilon_t=\sum_{i=1}^{N} Wt,i|ht(xi)-yi| \quad (5)$$

The minimum of ε_t and δ1 and δ2 should be computed.

②Among the all weak classifiers,the h*m* whose Weighted classification error is minimum is choosed,it's character value is f*m*.If M(f*m*)> δ then it will exit the current cycle,otherwise f*m* is the character of the current cycle.

③Output:

$$H(x)=\begin{cases}1 & \sum_{t=1}^{T} atht(x) \ge \frac{1}{2}\sum_{t=1}^{T} at\\ 0 & \text{others}\end{cases} \quad (6)$$

In the formula (6),$at=\log(1/\beta t)$.

X is extracted from image that is detected input into the classifier and get discriminant set,the result in the discriminant set is voted and the final classification result is get.

3 Experimental environment and the simulation results

In order to verify the improved algorithm's feasibility,the training sample relevant data which is choosed when the simulation result is carryed through:there are 3486 pieces of face sample. There are 1686 pieces of positive face images are selected from Feret face database,these face images have been Image processed.There are 5590 piecesof image that are not face,they are from Internet and 45898 Harr features are extracted from each image.There are 4605 pieces of face images and 6415 pieces of images that are not face when test,these images are from Internet and the size are set to be 240×320 pixel.The test environment are Visual c++.NET,4G internal storage, Inter(R) Core(TM) i5-3230M 2.60 GHz.True Positive Rate(TPR) and False Positive Rate(FPR) are used to be test standards.The test result is follows in figure 1 and figure 2.

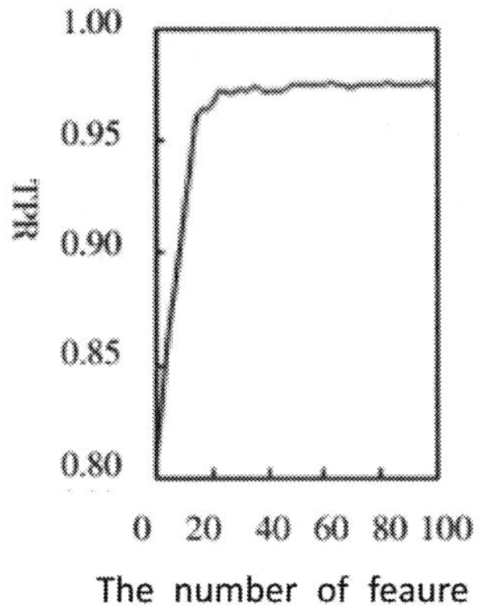

Figure 1. the ratio that face divide to be non-face

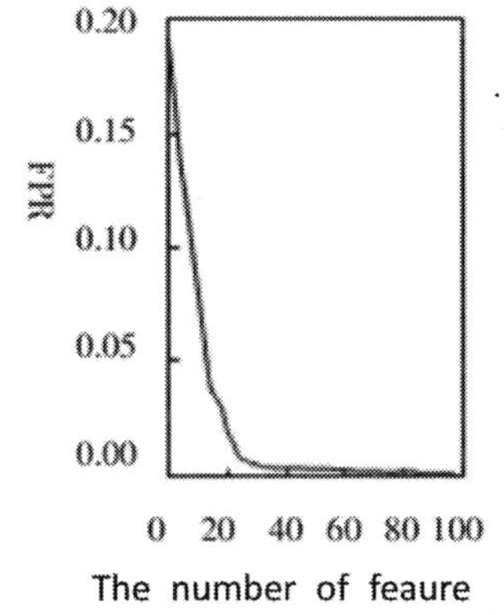

Figure 2.the ratio that non-face divide to be face

It shows from the figure 1 that good effect is get if the selected feature number reach 25,the reason is that the accuracy rate is stable afer feature number reach 25.

The same experimental samples that in the simulation results are used to be compared,they direct at the algorithm in the article,traditional AdaBoost algorithm, the algorithms in reference[3]and in reference [4].Same training set is used and Harr feature is extracted,the four method are used to trained and same testing set is used to test.The threshold value of feature relevance is ε =0.28.The judgement of the four algorithms's property is described by ROC curve.It is assumed that sample is described by two method: positive(face) and feminine(non-face). Positive sample is named true positive if it is classified to positivity, otherwise it is named false feminine. Negative sample is named true feminine if it is classified to Negativity ,otherwise it is named false positive.ROC curve of four al-gorithms is in figure 2, false positive ratio is expressed by x axis,true positive ratio is expressed by y axis.The data of feature number,TPR,FPR,test time is given in table 1 when the four algorithms's property is stable.

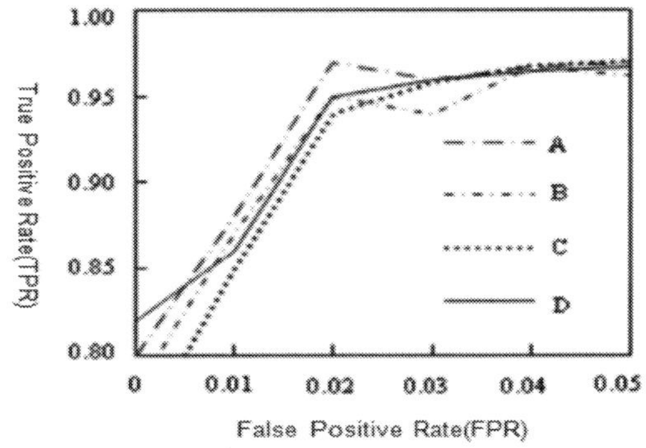

Figure 3. ROC curve of four algorithms

Table 1.experimental result comparation of four algorithms

Algori-thm	**AdaBoost**	**Reference [3]**	**Reference [4]**	**the algorithm in the article**
Feature number	90	60	50	25
True Positive Rate(%)	97.0	96.8	97.0	97.1
False Positive Rate(%)	2.6	3.3	2.7	2.4
Average time(s)	0.309	0.209	0.168	0.094

It shows from figure 3 that the detection performance are same to four algorithms,but it shows from table 1 that the four algorithms need feature number are 90,60,50,25 if stable detection accuracy is reached. The algorithm in the article needs minimum of feaure,so the detection rate is fastest.

4 Conclusion

Traditional AdaBoost algorithm of face detection has some defection,so improved algorithm of AdaBoost is created.The simulation result shows that improved algorithm of AdaBoost can reduce the feature number which is used to detection,so the detect rate is improved Significantly,the accuracy rate of face detection improved obviously.

Referance

1. Yang Ming-Hsuan David J Kriegman, Narendra

Ahuja.Detecting Faces in Images ASurvey [J]. IEEE Transactions on Pattern Analysis and Machine Intelligence,2002,**24** (1):34~58

2.P Viola M Jones Rapid Object Detection using a Boosted Cascade of Simple Features [C]. IEEE Proceedings of the Computer Vision and Patton Recognition Conference December 11~13, Hawaii USA,2001.

3.Tian jian Liu.the improved AdaBoost algorithm that base on character selection of entropy[J].Min jiang academic journal, 2009,4,**30**(2): 60~64

4. Rongye Liu. An Unsupervised Feature Selection Algorithm:Laplacian Score Combined with Distance -Based Entropy Measure, Third International Symposium on Intelligent Information Technology Application, 2009. Nov.21~22 2009, 65~68

MATEC Web of Conferences **44**, 01002 (2016)
DOI: 10.1051/matecconf/20164401002

MQAM Modulation Recognition Based on AP Clustering Method[1]

Qiang Li[1,a], Dong Shen[1] and Fei Wang[1]

[1]*School of Electronic and Information Engineering, Lanzhou Jiaotong University, Lanzhou, China*

Abstract. For signal analysis in the management and monitoring of the radio spectrum, it is need to automatically identify the modulated signal. This paper performs clustering algorithm on signal constellation diagram after equalization through AP clustering method, and proposes a clustering method for limited problem of modulation recognition type. After normalizing the shape of the constellation diagram, the size of the constellation diagram, and signal AP clustering, it realizes the matching recognition of the constellation diagram. The simulation results show that the AP clustering has efficient recognition ability.

1 Introduction

With the rapid development of modern communication technology, in the civil, modulation recognition of communication signals is mainly applied to software radio [1], spectrum monitoring and management, cognitive radio and so on [2-3]. In the increasingly complicated signal environment, some of the illegal users interfere and utilize the wireless spectrum, affecting the normal communication of legitimate users seriously. Spectrum resources management departments need to detect the interference of illegal radio and identify the modulation type of the interference signal, so as to having better monitoring and management of radio resources. For achieving all of these, modulation identification technology must be used.

In the military, electronic warfare has become the main form in the future. The battlefield information mainly is transmitted by radio, so the communication signal detection has become the important content of electronic warfare, which is an important premise to implement the communication countermeasure [4-6]. Communication signal detection firstly is to monitor the enemy signal, and using the receiver to intercept the enemy signal, and then the intercepted signal will be analyzed and processed, obtaining the communication signal modulation type and finally the useful information. Modulation recognition technology is helpful in choosing the optimal jamming technology in electronic warfare. While taking effective suppression and destruction to enemy signals, the communication of friendly parts will be ensured. In addition, the modulation recognition technology can also be used for radiating source recognition [7]. According to the modulation type of the received signal and some other measurement parameters, the type of enemy detector will be detected, distinguishing the kind of radar signal and analyzing the threat level, so as to improve the survival ability of the platform.

In recent years, with the rapid development of digital modulation techniques, the modulation method of communication signals are more complicated and diversity. M-ary quadrature amplitude modulation is a

[a] Corresponding author: Liqiang_fly@163.com

kind of commonly used digital modulation mode of modern wireless communication system which is widely used in satellite communication, network communication, microwave communication and cable TV networks. At the same time, the MQAM has also become the modulation way for broadband access network technology-ADSL, VADSL and modern CATV network. Comparing with other modulation techniques, MQAM modulation technology has the characteristics of flexible modulation modes, strong anti-noise performance and so on. In addition, MQAM is especially suitable for occasions of limited spectrum resources [8]. So researching on MQAM modulation mode recognition technology has very important application value.

There are two main methods of signal modulation recognition, one is inter-class recognition, such as the recognition between MPSK and MQAM; another is within-class recognition that is different modulation order recognition to the same signal, such as between different hexadecimal identification of MQAM [9]. This paper focuses on the inter-class recognition which is based on constellation diagram modulation type, the premise is: if a digital modulation signal can be only expressed by its constellation diagram, then it can also be identified by restoring the constellation diagram at the receiver.

2 Signal model

Given the signal received by the receiver is:

$$r(t) = \mathrm{Re}[s(t) + n(t)] \quad (1)$$

where $s(t)$ is modulation signal, the expression is:

$$s(t) = \mathrm{Re}[\sum_n A_k g(t-nT_s)\cos(2\pi f_c t + \varphi_n) + n(t)] \; 0<t<T=NT_s \quad (2)$$

A_k is the amplitude of the kth symbol, T_S is the symbol width, f_c is the carrier frequency, φ_n is the phase error, N is the receiving characters in T, $g(t-nT_s)$ is the baseband pulse, $n(t)$ is the white Gaussian noise.

2.1 Constellation graphical shape normalization

In order to make the constellation diagram got fits to the constellation diagram model in the database, constellation diagramical shape must be normalized. The center of the constellation diagram can be obtained by the mean of all cluster centers. In order to calculate conveniently, the constellation diagram center can be takes as the origin of coordinate. Due to the angle θ of phase error is a random variable, so the position relationship between the clustering centers obtained can judge if the constellation has deflection or not. If there is a deflection, then the deflection angle is estimated, further more the standard form constellation diagram can be got with the constellation diagram rotating reversely by the same angle.

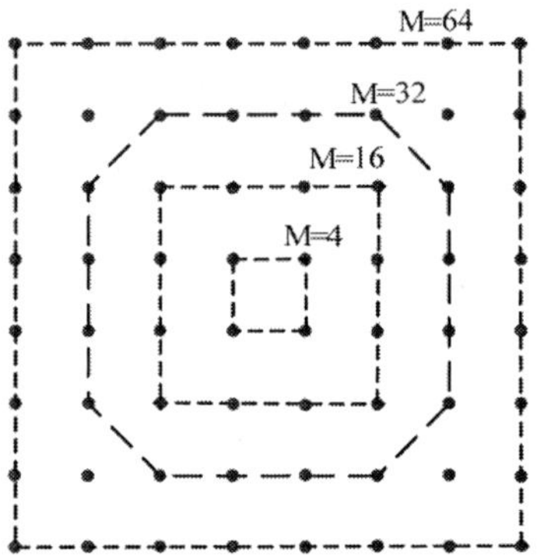

Figure 1. Constellation diagram of rectangular MQAM modulation signal

As shown in Fig.1, in the constellation diagram of the rectangular MQAM, regardless of how much the value of M is, the constellation points for $M = 4$ are fixed. According to the distribution of these four points, the rotation angle of the signal constellation diagram can be obtained. The specific approach is: in the standard signal constellation diagram, the minimum positive angle value in the four points is $\pi/4$. The minimum positive angle of four points having smaller radius in all the points in constellation diagram minus $\pi/4$, the obtained minimum positive value is the reverse rotation angle. Considering the distribution of the information carried on the periphery of the point symbol energy greater than the inner point of the information carried by the symbol of energy, that is in the same SNR condition, influence of the interference at the periphery points is relatively small. So for high order MQAM signal, using peripheral vertex information as far as possible, the influence of noise will be reduced. The above steps achieve the constellation

reverse rotation which may not be synchronized in the carrier phase, namely the constellation graphical shape normalization.

2.2 Constellation graphical size normalization

AP clustering will get the constellation diagram in the [-1, 1] plane. In order to match with the model in constellation library, the constellation diagram needs to be mapped to the 64×64 plane. As long as adjusting constellation diagram abscissa and ordinate respectively, constellation diagram size normalization can be realized [10]. Given the adjusting parameters of abscissa is mul_x, adjusting parameters of ordinate is mul_y, mul_ratio is $mul\_ratio = \frac{mul\_x}{mul\_y}$. For symmetric constellation diagram, the value of mul_ratio is 1.

$$mul\_x = mul\_y = \frac{k}{\max(y) - \min(y)} \tag{3}$$

$\max(y)$ represents the maximum value, $\min(y)$ represents the minimum value. The K value has the relationship with the structure of the histogram, each cluster center is moved to the plane center of size 16×16. With 16QAM, K is 48, for different M, the value of K is also different, specifics seen in reference [11].

In order to realize constellation diagram model, the shape of signal constellation diagram must be represented discretely. So we need to mesh the constellation diagram plane, the size of meshes affects the amount and accuracy of calculation. If the meshes are too large, the recognition accuracy will decline. The meshes are too small, the amount of calculation for the algorithm is great. The following method is to use Parzen window to grid [12].

Still with 16QAM signal as an example, Constellation diagram is composed of 16 vertices generated by the clustering module. In order to easy representation, the whole constellation diagram is mapped to a discrete grid with size 64×64, each modulation state is a pixel of image with size 64×64. The initial size V_0 of resolution unit should be able to meet enough detail to obtain the probability density function of the constellation diagram shape.

$$V_0 \le \frac{64^2}{M} \tag{4}$$

where M is the constellation diagram modulation state. For the 16QAM signal constellation diagram in grid with size 64×64, the initial V_0 of the kernel function base is the unit size 64×64. Obtained from the Parzen window method, each resolution unit must be further divided to obtain the details of each vertex distribution. When 4096 data points from each constellation, i.e. each vertex has 256 data points, the kernel function base [13]:

$$\rho = \frac{V_0}{\sqrt{n}} \qquad n = 256 \tag{5}$$

Therefore, for each vertex of the density function to obtain the Parzen window is a unit with size 4×4. At the same time, the Parzen window of 4QAM signal is a unit with size 2×2, the Parzen window of 64QAM signal is a unit with size 8×8.

3 Constellation diagram matching

Taking the constellation diagram matching as the classification process, according to the clustering results, the points of constellation diagram in choosing modulation set are assigned to each class, the specific method is:

Based on Euclidean distance, the similarity matrix $s(i,j)$ of these data points is defined as:

$$s(i,j) = -\left\|(x_i - x_j)^2 + (y_i - y_j)^2\right\| \tag{6}$$

All the data points in original sample set are potentially paradigm samples, so all the $s(m,m)$ initialization is the same. In the clustering process, there are two variables, the degree of attraction $r(i,j)$ and the degree of membership $a(i,j)$, which need to be updated by the competition mechanism. The update rules are:

$$r(i,j) = s(i,j) - \max_{j' s.t. j' \ne j} \{a(i,j') + s(i,j')\} \tag{7}$$

$$r(j,j) = s(j,j) - \max_{j' s.t. j' \ne j} \{a(j,j') + s(j,j')\} \tag{8}$$

$$a(i,j) = \min\{0, r(j,j) + \sum_{i' s.t. i' \ne i,j} \max\{0, r(i',j)\}\} \tag{9}$$

$$a(j,j) = \sum_{i' s.t. i' \ne j} \max\{0, r(i',j)\} \tag{10}$$

By the updating rules above [14], the information is exchanged between the sample points, finally the function chosen achieves minimum. The

AP algorithm can be terminated by a fixed number of iterations or changing extent in the local. The symbol numbers here $N = 400$ ·

The specific algorithm flowchart is:

To compute the similarity between the $N = 400$ points values, the value is placed in the similarity matrix $s(i, j)$, where s is $N \times N$ matrix.

Diagonal value of the similarity matrix S is selected as the value of the P parameter. After the iterative process begins, the R value and a value are computed at each time.

With the value of $r(j,j)+a(j,j)$ to determine whether is the clustering center or not, the calculation will be terminated when the clustering center value do not change after 100 times iteration.

4 Simulation analysis

Under the hypothesis of not account for blind equalization and after constellation graphical shape normalization, from the AP algorithm above, the number of symbols is $N = 400$, the number of iterations is 100, the reconstruction figure of the rectangular 16QAM constellation diagram are shown as follows. Fig.2 and Fig.3 represent the performance of AP algorithm respectively under different SNR. From the figures below, it can be seen that AP clustering can basically identify the positions of constellation points when SNR=12. When SNR=18, AP clustering can accurately identify the positions of constellation points.

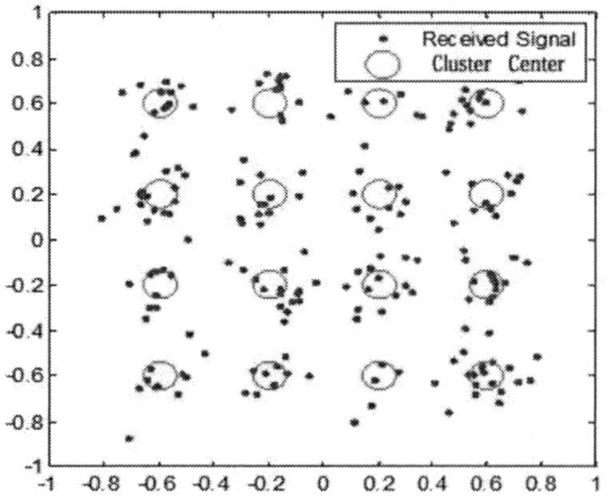

Figure 2. 16 QAM clustering when SNR=12

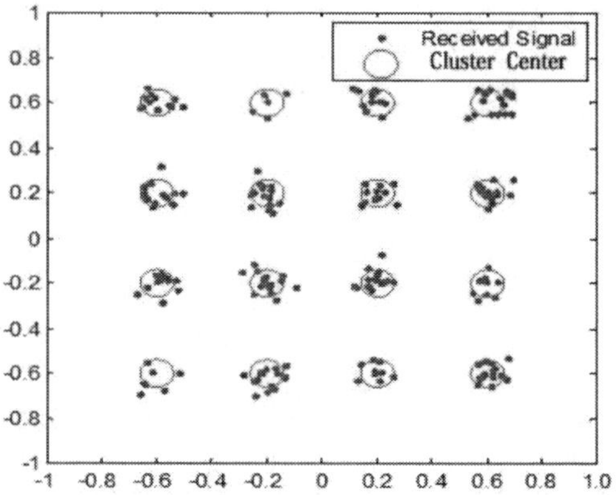

Figure 3. 16 QAM clustering when SNR=18

Fig.4 is the recognition success rate of QAM signal from M hexadecimal modulation, the symbol length is 400, it can be seen that AP clustering recognition rate has reached 90% when the SNR=12. But the recognition rate curve is nonlinear, modulation recognition has the threshold effect. If the ideal results need to be got, the requirements for the SNR should be more than 12.

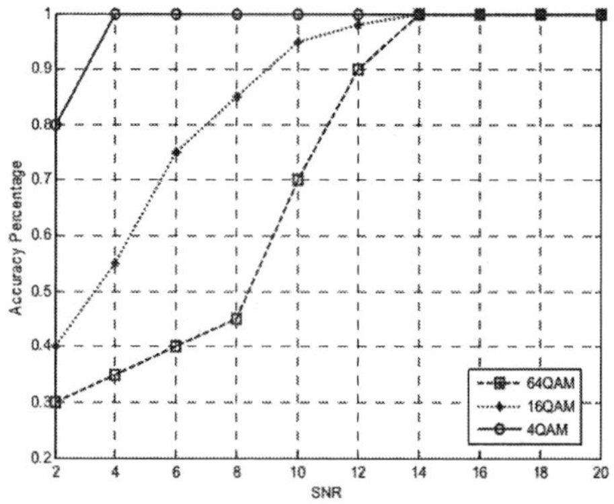

Figure 4. the recognition success rate of QAM signal from M hexadecimal modulation (the symbol length is 400)

5 Conclusions

This paper mainly studies the recognition of MQAM signals which has important application value in modern communications. The method of AP clustering reconstruction constellation diagram matching is used here to recognize the MQAM signals, cluster center is extracted by the constellation diagram clustering which is got by constellation graphical shape normalization by using

the clustering methods, and then identification is used here. The simulation results show that the algorithm can basically identify the positions of modulation signals when SNR=12. For different modulation mode from M value, the modulation recognition success rate has reached 90% when the SNR=12. The modulation recognition success rate is greater than 99% when SNR=16.

The method of AP cluster reconstruction constellation diagram matching has good practicability for MQAM signals recognition.

Acknowledgement

This work was supported by Gansu Natural Science Foundation (No.148RJZA033) and Youth Foundation of Lanzhou Jiaotong University with grant No. 2012002.

References

1. P. Pinto, S. Silva, H. Miranda, An adaptive software radio receiver architecture for linear bidimensional modulations, The Sixth Baiona Workshop on Signal Processing in Communications, Baiona, Spain, 2003, pp. 211-216.
2. L. C. Freitas, C. Cardoso, F. C. Muller, et al, Automatic modulation classification forcognitive radio systems: Results for the symbol and wave domains, 2009 IEEE Latin-American Conference on Communications, Brazil, Sep. 2009, pp. 1-6.
3. B. Ramkumar, Automatic modulation classification for cognitive radios using cyclicfeature detection, IEEE Circuits and systems Magazine, **2** (2009).
4. D. P. Zhang, Y. F. Chen, X. F. Li, QAM modulation recognition based on constellation diagram,Communication Countermeasures, **1** (2006).
5. The group of Technology and application of electronic war-communication countermeasures, Technology and application of electronic war- communication countermeasures, China, Publishing House of Electronics Industry, 2005: pp. 10-13.
6. S. X. Guo, L. X. Zhang, G. X. Hua, Research on the key techniques in communication countermeasures,Telecommunications Technologies, **6** (2005).
7. M. J. He, Research on sub-set recognition of the MPSK and QAM,Cheng Du: University of Electronic Science and technology, Jan. 2006.
8. C.X. Fan, L. N. Cao, *The principle of communication* (National Defence Industry Press, 2009).
9. Y. L. Gao, Z. Z. Zhang, Modulation recognition based on combined feature parameter and modified probabilistic neural network, In Proc of the Sixth World Congress on Intelligence Control and Automation, Dalian, China, Jun. 2006, pp. 2954-2958.
10. J. X. Wang, H. Song, Digital modulation recognition based on constellation diagram,Journal of China Institute of Communications, **25** (2004).
11. B. G. MOBASSERI. Digital modulation classification using constellation shape, Signal Processing, **80** (2000).
12. Z. Q. Bian, X. G. Zhang, Pattern recognition, (2nd ed. Tsinghua University press, 1999).
13. A. Swami, B. M. Sadler, Hierarchical digital modulation classification using cumulates,IEEE Trans. Communications, **48** (2000).
14. B. J. Frey, D. Dueck, Clustering by passing messages between data points,Science, **315** (2007).

MATEC Web of Conferences 44, 01003 (2016)
DOI: 10.1051/matecconf/20164401003

Research of MOOC Platform Based "Internet +"

Guang Xing Wang[1,a], Yan Chen[1]

[1]Technology Center of Jiujiang University, 332005, Jiujiang, Jiangxi, China

Abstract. This paper is devoted to examining the construction of MOOC platform based "Internet +". It firstly introduced the "Internet+" model, the "Internet + education" influence and the significance of education. Then, it analyzed the existing problems in the development of the current MOOC, and put forward the model of "Internet + MOOC" through the method of software engineering. It explored the advantage of "Internet + MOOC" mode and promoting the function to the education teaching. This paper put forward the framework of "Internet + MOOC platform model, and point out the problems need attention in the construction of the platform.

1 "Internet +" model

In recent years, with the rapid development of computer technology, people's work and life more convenient. The changing of the Internet technique makes the transmission of information increasing rapidly, the Internet changed the way people's work and life. Distance education based on Internet technology, online education, online college education mode booming, has a huge impact on traditional classroom education. The age of the Internet is known as the era of knowledge explosion.

1.1 "Internet +" concept

"Internet +" is the Internet to develop new patterns, new form of innovation 2.0 environment, and it is a form of Internet evolution, driven by the knowledge society and innovation 2.0 birth of new patterns of economic and social development. "Internet +" is to further the practice of thinking of the outcome of the Internet, it represents a kind of advanced productive forces, promote the evolution of economic patterns occurs continuously, thus boosting social and economic vitality entity, reform, innovation and development and provide a vast network platform.[1] Popular, "Internet +" is the Internet + various traditional industries. It is the use of modern information technology and the Internet platform that enables Internet and depth of integration of traditional industries, creating new ecological development. E-commerce, e-government, Internet banking, online travel, online open class and so on, are the "Internet +" and the depth of integration of the results of traditional industries.

1.2 The concept of "Internet + education"

The 21st century is the information into the main features of the knowledge economy. Along with the rapid development of computer technology, network technology, multimedia technology, mobile communications technology and Internet technology, each industry is under "Internet +" engaged in promoting the reform and development, the education sector as well. The first generation of education in the book as the core, the second generation of educational materials for the core to the third generation of education in counseling and case mode appears, now the fourth generation of education, is the real student-centered. Chinese education is moving towards 4.0 era.[2] A school, a teacher, a classroom, which is the traditional education. An educational private network, a mobile terminal, hundreds of millions of students, selecting any schools and teachers, this is the "Internet + education". This model can be truly student-centered learning, you can learn anywhere, anytime. In MOOC represented, such as micro-lessons, flipped classroom, online classrooms, mobile classroom, e-learning platforms are the result of the "Internet + Education". "Internet +" Time triggered mode of education reform wave has arrived, and the competition has broken borders, worth thinking about how to respond.

2 MOOC development history

2.1 MOOC introduction

MOOC is a massive open online courses, is a newly emerged an online curriculum model. Unlike traditional online courses, MOOC idea is to open education in communication theory and network-based learning, a large-scale, open courses and online courses three characteristics. MOOC with students as the center,

[a] Corresponding author: wanggxrs@163.com

quality-based curriculum resources, rich network resources, supplemented by the use of a gradual approach MOOC offer different courses for different learners, and the use of real-time communication and under classroom after school to discuss the combination. MOOC establish performance through classes and homework curriculum evaluation system, and promote teachers to improve teaching and learning materials and improve the quality of teaching, and ultimately improve student learning efficiency and learning.

2.2 MOOC development

MOOC emergence and development manager of a short but long-term process of birth, to be exact, it can be traced back to the 1960's. In 1962, as American inventor and innovator knowledge, Douglas Engelbart presented a project called "Enhancing human intelligence: a conceptual framework for the Stanford Research Institute". In this research project, he stressed the possibility of the computer as a tool to enhance collaboration wisdom be applied.[3] In 2008, MOOC name is a senior fellow at Wagner Gennaro, director of communication and innovation with the National Institute of Humanistic Education Technology University of Prince Edward Island jointly proposed, the main purpose is to use the Internet to offer online courses, drew a large number of learners cited.[4] In 2011, Stanford University's "Introduction to Artificial Intelligence" course online free MOOC get established as a representative of a breakthrough development. Subsequently, by the famous university participation, the impact so far of Udacity, Coursera, edX have established, they opened the curtain MOOC education reform. 2012 has been called MOOC year.

MOOC formally entered China in 2013. In 2013, Tsinghua University and Peking University in May announced it has joined the online education platform edX, the same year in July, Shanghai Jiaotong University and Fudan University have announced to join Coursera. July 2013, Online Education Development (MOOCs) International Forum held in Shanghai Jiao Tong University, and Shanghai Jiao Tong University announced to build China MOOC with Peking University, Tsinghua University and other C9 universities such as Tongji University, Dalian University of Technology, Chongqing University.[5] MOOC is a new form of education, the rise and development of wave MOOC positive impact on the traditional mode of education, speed up the pace of education reform in our education.

2.3 MOOC problems in development

MOOC is a massive open online courses, and is a new route of knowledge transmission that traditional courses of education through the Internet opens and IT support. It is an attempt educational reform. This educational reform is successful which has been proved by practice. Its rich teaching resources, task-based learning, forms of learning pathways and relatively complete evaluation mechanism, MOOC attracted many learners participate.

However, after a recent period of development, MOOC drawbacks are gradually revealed, in particular in the following aspects. First, MOOC still complement and expand the traditional teaching, both teachers and students adaptation it need a relatively long time. MOOC current form of teaching is still not out of network learning platform, network classroom education mode. Educational exchange student interaction than traditional classroom network has improved greatly, but only limited exchange of text, images exchange, hardly intuitive expression, emotional feelings, pan situation still lack education, teachers and students it is difficult to establish friendship. Secondly, the current process MOOC courses learners are not knowledge-based systems. Because learners MOOC courses are mostly based on need or interest, in the absence of credit constraints and other conditions, as time goes on, probably because the learner has mastered the skills needed, or interest in learning subside and give up learning. Third, the evaluation mechanism is still not perfect course. MOOC current curriculum evaluation is still a teacher to learner tests and homework assignments online case evaluation means, there is a replacement that plagiarism, on behalf of homework and other defects. Fourth, MOOC courses not yet out of a pile of such information, courseware display and other features network classroom. Currently, there are still some cases MOOC courses taught video, courseware and other information displayed, and curriculum instructional videos rational knowledge is not strong, the quality of teaching is not high. "Internet + MOOC" mode can effectively solve these problems.

3 "Internet + MOOC" advantage

In the era of knowledge explosion, the spread of knowledge and innovation is inseparable from the development of the Internet. The development of mobile communications technologies such as 2G, 3G, 4G, WLAN, WIFI and other network technology, combined with the Internet, is boosting the dissemination of knowledge and innovation. A new wireless network technology IEEE802.11ax being developed, the use of this technology can achieve 8 seconds to download complete 10GB of capacity.[6] IEEE802.ax not only use the MU-MIMO (Multi-User Multiple-Input Multiple-Output) technology, but also the use of OFDMA (Orthogonal Frequency Division Multiple Access), that is orthogonal frequency-division multiple access technology, which is the next-generation high-speed wireless. Therefore, the "Internet + MOOC" mode is Internet-based, with 2G, 3G, 4G and WLAN, WIFI wireless network communications technology. In this mode, it is possible to achieve a smooth access MOOC systems used such as PC, laptop, IPAD, PDA, smart phones and other intelligent mobile terminals. Thus we will build three-dimensional forms of the "Internet + MOOC" Education mode. In this mode, MOOC courses are transparent to the learner, allowing the learner to access the Internet using a smart device and

authenticated, learner can achieve learning MOOC courses. "Internet + MOOC" network frame shown in Figure 1.

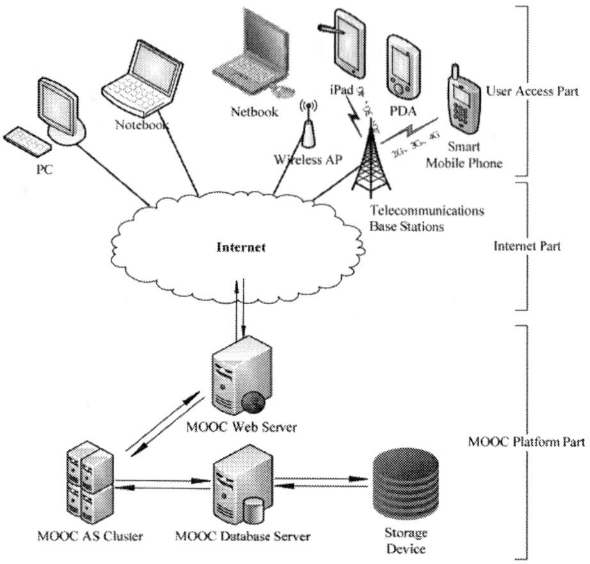

Figure 1. "Internet + MOOC" Network System Frame Chart.

Advantage "Internet + MOOC" mode is mainly reflected in the following aspects. First, this model breakthrough time and geographical constraints, to achieve a student-centered autonomous learning. "Internet + MOOC" mode Internet-based learners only need to use smart devices to access the Internet, will be able to achieve self-learning anytime, anywhere. Learners can choose their own time to arrange live classroom learning or video-on-demand learning. Second, it can achieve webcast experimental classes and operations Course. Currently, it has achieved a webcast SD or HD video, but also to achieve a multi-screen display technology. Therefore, teachers interspersed with some aspects of experimental operation has been able to achieve during the theoretical lectures. Such interludes labs, both to strengthen the students' understanding of the theory, improve the ability, but also regulates classroom teaching atmosphere, achieve a good situational teaching. Third, this model is conducive to integration and optimization of educational resources, improve teaching quality. Under the "Internet + MOOC" mode, teacher focused on the design and development of the MOOC courses, improve teaching methods. Using this model, teacher can break the regional restrictions, to achieve inter-school cooperation forum set up teacher or team of teachers hired well-known university lectures, which effectively integrates the teaching resources for learners to provide a more extensive knowledge feast. Fourth, it is well to eliminate the gap between urban and rural education resources to achieve educational equity. Based on the Internet MOOC education can breakthrough the limitation of time and place. In this way, learners that in remote villages can be accessed high-quality educational resources of developed areas via the Internet, and to carry out independent study, to some extent, to eliminate the gap between urban and rural education resources and achieve educational equity.

In addition, the "Internet + MOOC" mode compared to traditional network teaching has significant advantages, mainly in the learning process monitoring, learning evaluation, data analysis and other aspects of learning, it helps learners to long-term learning and lifelong learning.

4 "Internet + MOOC" platform model

4.1. "Internet + MOOC" platform framework design

In learner-centered "Internet + MOOC" mode, learner can achieve self-learning, mobile learning, learning process monitoring, learning exchanges under the results of the evaluation, as well as teachers and students, between students interact online and offline. Teachers focus on curriculum development and improve teaching methods, and do not care about technical issues. This model implements the scene of teaching and effective integration of educational resources, and it is good to make up for the shortcomings of traditional education process. Therefore, the framework of the "Internet + MOOC" platform we designed shown in Figure 2.

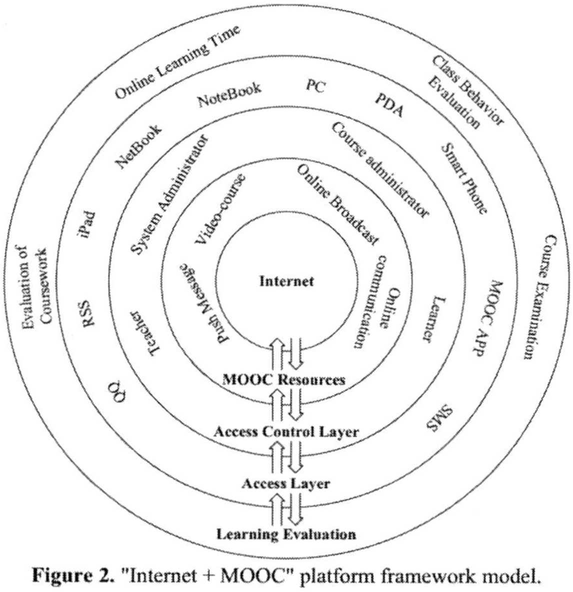

Figure 2. "Internet + MOOC" platform framework model.

We designed the "Internet + MOOC" platform framework is divided into five layers. The first layer is called the internet layer, and that is the base layer of the "Internet + MOOC" platform. The second layer is called the resource layer, including MOOC courses application server, database server, learning to monitor servers, which is the core layer of the "Internet + MOOC" platform. The third layer is called the access control layer, including user identity and user equipment identification. User identification is used to determine the user's identity and assign the appropriate access right, the user identity is divided into four categories of people: system administrators, curriculum administrators, teachers and students. Identify the user equipment is

mainly based on the user terminal equipment used by the access control server automatically transferred to the corresponding application server MOOC courses, to achieve a seamless connection of users, enhance the user experience. The fourth layer is the access layer (also called the user layer). In this layer, the user can use desktop computers, notebook computers, IPAD, smart phones and other mobile terminal to access a variety of intelligent MOOC learning courses via the Internet. Users can also RSS, Email, curriculum exchange forum, course text messaging, network cameras and even real-time interaction with teachers, with other learners to communicate online. Users can also receive through MSN, QQ, MOOC APP and other social, learning tools curriculum, job scheduling, and other timely information to answer more reasonable arrangements for their own learning plan to achieve personalized learning. The fifth layer is called learning assessments layer. At this level, teacher build learning evaluation model through a plurality of evaluation points time online learning, classroom performance, course work, final examination, etc., to achieve the learning outcomes of learners overall rating. Finally, the teacher combines course management, credit management, and comprehensive evaluation of academic degree awarded system to decide whether to grant the learner corresponding degrees. Of course, degree granting and recognition has yet to be further research and exploration.

4.2 The main technologies

"Internet + MOOC" development platform need to use techniques include: software development technology, production technology curriculum, skills of the teacher's teaching. Software development technology including Internet technology, database technology, cloud computing, mobile development technology, network security, data storage technology. Courses production technology including multimedia technology, video production technology, courseware production technology. Skills of the teacher's teaching mainly in lecture style, well-organized and the convergence of knowledge, and grasp the extent of classroom rhythm. In these three technologies, the difficulty and the focus should lecture Art and style in teachers. Therefore, make good MOOC courses for teachers put forward higher requirements, but also to attract more learners to participate.

4.3 Platform development matters needing attention

"Internet + MOOC" platform development is not a leap into the sky, but also the need for a process of continuous improvement. Especially in the beginning of the construction, it requires a certain personnel, capital investment, but also need to support certain policies. Therefore, in the course of implementation should be noted that several aspects. First, staging, implementation batches. Stage, implemented in batches MOOC construction, easy to identify problems promptly corrected, but also conducive to the rational use of personnel and funds. Second, the recommended way to select excellent curriculum, and building high quality courses. Build quality courses in the form of courses match, innovation projects, to determine the "Internet + MOOC" course content, and ultimately launch on-line. Third, increase personnel training investment. Encourage young teachers to participate in various lectures competitions, training and learning, improve their own quality and lectures levels. Finally, from the leadership to the staff of one mind, using a variety of ways to actively promote MOOC courses.

"Internet + education" is just rising, "Internet + MOOC" is undoubtedly an important road to reform education. "Internet + MOOC" pay more attention to learner-centered learning, long-term learning and lifelong education, but also pay more attention to the learning process of learners systematic knowledge and learning situational. Looking to the future, with the development of Internet technology and computer technology, based on education in the form of "Internet + MOOC" mode will be more perfect. With the virtual reality equipment, teacher (by the virtual reality device configuration teacher model) will stand in front of the learner extremely rich teaching knowledge, answering questions.

5 Conclusion

The article from the "Internet +" concept paper introduces the development status of the "Internet + education", and as an entry point MOOC, elaborated MOOC development, advantages and problems. Then, the article on the problems MOOC depth analysis, with the current "Internet +" trends, elaborated the "Internet + MOOC" advantage, proposed the "Internet + MOOC" platform frame and analyzed. The paper further describes the "Internet + MOOC" platform model, implementation techniques and problems that need attention. Finally, we have the "Internet + MOOC" platform in the future. "Internet + education" must be of educational reform is the way, the "Internet + MOOC" is the implementation of educational reform, it is learn from each other with the traditional education, learn from each other until the final fusion.

References

1. Xinglei. "Internet +" new form of innovative development of the Internet in 2.0. Information & Communications.2015(9) :200-201
2. Internet + education to promote Chinese education towards 4.0 times. China Daily, 2015.6
3. Caifuhong. MOOC on the design of higher vocational education. China Education Network, 2014(5) :71-72
4. Xiajuping. Thoughts on open courses MOOC of large scale network. Education Circle. 2013(25):166,149
5. Online Education Development international forum held in Shanghai. China Education Network. 2013(8) :10

6. DJ Deng, KC Chen, RS Cheng.IEEE 802.11ax: Next generation wireless local area networks. International Conference on Heterogeneous Networking for Quality,Reliability,Security&Robustness2014:77-82

MATEC Web of Conferences **44**, 01004 (2016)
DOI: 10.1051/matecconf/20164401004

The Quality Prediction in Small-batch Producing Based on Weighted Least Squares Support Vector Regression

Sheng Bo Zhang and Qing Ling Dai

Jiujiang University, Jiujiang, Jiangxi, 332005, China

Abstract. A novel quality prediction method with mobile time window is proposed for small-batch producing process based on weighted least squares support vector regression (LS-SVR). The design steps and learning algorithm are also addressed. In the method, weighted LS-SVR is taken as the intelligent kernel, with which the small-batch learning is solved well and the nearer sample is set a larger weight, while the farther is set the smaller weight in the history data. A typical machining process of cutting bearing outer race is carried out and the real measured data are used to contrast experiment. The experimental results demonstrate that the prediction accuracy of the weighted LS-SVR based model is only 20%-30% that of the standard LS-SVR based one in the same condition. It provides a better candidate for quality prediction of small-batch producing process.

1 Introduction

For small batch production, it is unrealistic to make trial runs for the determination of suitable values of the variables in machining operations [1,2]. This problem becomes even worse with the increasing requirements of product accuracy, the more frequent application of new materials and new machining operations, as, for instance, high-speed and precision machining of hardened steel components [3].

Many methods of quality prediction with the techniques are proposed such as liner predicting model, generalized liner predicting model, memory-based predictor [4] and neural networks [5,6]. Recently, support vector machines proposed by Vapnik have become a key machine learning technique [7]. They have strong theoretical foundation and show excellent empirical success in supervised learning framework [8]. Quality prediction can attribute to supervised learning framework. So support vector machines such as SVR, LS-SVR are applied to deal with quality prediction [9,10].

However, in actual production, quality parameters change constantly with process. The short-term impact, in future, on producing accuracy mainly comes from not history parameters but the latest processing parameters. We call the rule as "nearer data weigh heavier and farther data weigh lighter". The concept of membership was introduced into the article, and a weight LS-SVR prediction model based time-domain membership was presented. This model put different memberships according to the impact extent of history data. It reduces the impact of early data to the current producing process, and improves the accuracy of real-time prediction. The model was researched in the producing process of bearing's outer ring, and compared prediction accuracy with the traditional model. The research demonstrates that the model is applicable and reasonable to small-batch producing process.

Zhang Shengbo : E-mail: B761127@tom.com

2 Principle of Wighted LS-SVR

2.1 Conventional LS-SVR

Consider a given training set of n data points $\{x(i), y(i)\}_{i=1}^{n}$ with input $x(i) \in R^m$ and output $y(i) \in R$. In feature space SVR models take the form as

$$y = \omega^T \varphi(x) + b, \tag{1}$$

where the nonlinear function $\varphi(\cdot)$ maps the input data into a higher dimensional feature space. Note that the dimension of ω is not specified. The training is to estimate the optimal parameters ω, b in the regression function (1).

LS-SVR is a tool based on statistical learning theory and selects squared error ξ_t as the loss function [11]. Therefore, the following optimization problem is formulated as

$$\min_{\omega,\xi} J(\omega, \xi) = \min \frac{1}{2}\omega^T \omega + \frac{1}{2}\gamma \sum_{i=1}^{n} \xi_i^2, \tag{2}$$

subject to the equality constraints

$$y(i) = \omega^T \varphi(x(i)) + b + \xi_i, \ i = 1,2,\ldots,n, \tag{3}$$

where γ is a positive constant parameter used to control the tradeoff between the training error and the model complexity. The larger γ is, the less error of regression model will make. This is the only free parameter in the LS-SVR formulation.

The parameter ω can be evaluated according to objective function (2) and constraints (3). This corresponds to a form of ridge regression and Lagrange function is given by

$$L(\omega,b,\xi,a)=\frac{1}{2}\omega^T\omega+\gamma\sum_{i=1}^{n}\xi_i^2 -\sum_{i=1}^{n}a_i\left(\omega^T\varphi(x(i))+b+\xi_i-y(i)\right), \quad (4)$$

with Lagrange multipliers a_i, $i=1,\dots,n$.

The optimal $\boldsymbol{a}=[a_1,\dots,a_N]^T$ can be solved on Karush-Kuhn-Tucke conditions [2], which for optimality are

$$\begin{cases} \frac{\partial L}{\partial\omega} & \to\quad \omega=\sum_{i=1}^{n}a_i\varphi(x(i)) \\ \frac{\partial L}{\partial b} & \to\quad \sum_{i=1}^{n}a_i=0 \\ \frac{\partial L}{\partial\xi_i} & \to\quad a_i=\gamma\xi_i \\ \frac{\partial L}{\partial a_i} & \to\quad \omega^T\varphi(x(i))+b+\xi_i-y(i)=0 \end{cases} . \quad (5)$$

After elimination of ξ_i, ω, the solution is solved by the following set of linear equations

$$\begin{bmatrix} 0 & \boldsymbol{\Theta}^T \\ \boldsymbol{\Theta} & \boldsymbol{\Omega}+\gamma^{-1}\boldsymbol{I} \end{bmatrix}\begin{bmatrix} b \\ \boldsymbol{a} \end{bmatrix}=\begin{bmatrix} 0 \\ \boldsymbol{Y} \end{bmatrix}, \quad (6)$$

where $\boldsymbol{I}$ is the identity matrix, $\boldsymbol{\Theta}=[1,\dots,1]^T$, $\boldsymbol{a}=[a_1,\dots,a_n]^T$ and the Mercer condition

$$\boldsymbol{\Omega}_{ij}=\varphi(x(i))^T\varphi(x(j))=\psi(x(i),x(j)), \quad (7)$$

has been applied.

Lagrange multiplier $\boldsymbol{a}$ and model offset b could be solved in formula (6), which could also be expanded as

$$\boldsymbol{\Theta}^T\boldsymbol{a}=0,$$
$$b\boldsymbol{\Theta}+\left(\boldsymbol{\Omega}+\gamma^{-1}\boldsymbol{I}\right)\boldsymbol{a}=\boldsymbol{Y},$$

namely,

$$\hat{\boldsymbol{a}}=\left(\boldsymbol{\Omega}+\gamma^{-1}\boldsymbol{I}\right)^{-1}\left(Y-b\boldsymbol{\Theta}\right). \quad (8)$$

Substituting formula (8) into formula (6), and

$$\boldsymbol{\Theta}^T\boldsymbol{a}=0\to\boldsymbol{\Theta}^T\left(\boldsymbol{\Omega}+\gamma^{-1}\boldsymbol{I}\right)^{-1}\left(Y-b\boldsymbol{\Theta}\right)=0$$

$$\to\hat{b}=\frac{\boldsymbol{\Theta}^T\left(\boldsymbol{\Omega}+\gamma^{-1}\boldsymbol{I}\right)^{-1}\boldsymbol{Y}}{\boldsymbol{\Theta}^T\left(\boldsymbol{\Omega}+\gamma^{-1}\boldsymbol{I}\right)^{-1}\boldsymbol{\Theta}}. \quad (9)$$

The finally results into the following LS-SVR model for function estimation

$$y=\sum_{i=1}^{n}\hat{a}_i\psi(x,x(i))+\hat{b}. \quad (10)$$

2.2 Weighted LS-SVR

In this paper, we introduced the weight into standard LS-SVR. That is to introduce the weight terms w_i into each sample of LS-SVR to change the importance of input sample $\{x(i),y(i),w_i\}_{i=1}^{n}$, where, $0\le w_i\le 1$. Thus, the optimization objective function of Equation (2) is re-expressed as

$$\min_{\omega,\xi} J(\omega,\xi)=\min\frac{1}{2}\omega^T\omega+\frac{1}{2}\gamma w_i\sum_{i=1}^{n}\xi_i^2. \quad (11)$$

The Lagrange function is re-structured as

$$L(\omega,b,\xi,a,w)=\frac{1}{2}\omega^T\omega+\gamma\sum_{i=1}^{n}w_i\xi_i^2 -\sum_{i=1}^{n}a_i\left(\omega^T\varphi(x(i))+b+\xi_i-y(i)\right). \quad (12)$$

According to the optimum conditions, the matrix is also re-structured as

$$\begin{bmatrix} 0 & \boldsymbol{\Theta}^T \\ \boldsymbol{\Theta} & \boldsymbol{\Omega}+\gamma^{-1}\boldsymbol{WI} \end{bmatrix}\begin{bmatrix} b \\ \boldsymbol{a} \end{bmatrix}=\begin{bmatrix} 0 \\ \boldsymbol{Y} \end{bmatrix}, \quad (13)$$

where $W=\left[w_1^{-1},w_2^{-1},\dots,w_N^{-1}\right]$ is the weight vector.

Estimation function of weighted LS-SVR can be obtained by solving the weighted matrix (13) as

$$\hat{\boldsymbol{a}}=\left(\boldsymbol{\Omega}+\gamma^{-1}\boldsymbol{WI}\right)^{-1}\left(Y-b\boldsymbol{\Theta}\right),$$
$$\hat{b}=\frac{\boldsymbol{\Theta}^T\left(\boldsymbol{\Omega}+\gamma^{-1}\boldsymbol{WI}\right)^{-1}\boldsymbol{Y}}{\boldsymbol{\Theta}^T\left(\boldsymbol{\Omega}+\gamma^{-1}\boldsymbol{WI}\right)^{-1}\boldsymbol{\Theta}}. \quad (14)$$

3 Quality Prediction Using Weighted LS-SVR

Let $x(t_0+\tau)$, $x(t_0+2\tau)$, …, $x(t_0+n\tau)$ be a measured quality series with sampling time τ in a machining process. Our objective is to predict the future quality of the piecework from the series $x(t)$ according to the history quality data. However the quality series data are single-dimension usually, it is different to be used to the regression modeling directly.

For this problem, we apply the technique of mobile time window (MTW) of nonlinear quality series, the width of which is set to include m+1 data points [8]. In the model building, move the MTW on time series from the anterior to posterior, and the process of data extraction is shown as Figure 1.

The relationships in the MTW between $x(t_0+k\tau)$ and $x(t_0+(k-1)\tau)$ are supposed to be a nonlinear map

$$x(t_0+k\tau)=f\{x(t_0+(k-1)\tau),\dots,x(t_0+(k-m)\tau)\} \quad (15)$$

where m is MTW width and also called embedding dimension. If m is small, the past values are not enough to predict the future value; however, if m is high, the training is hard.

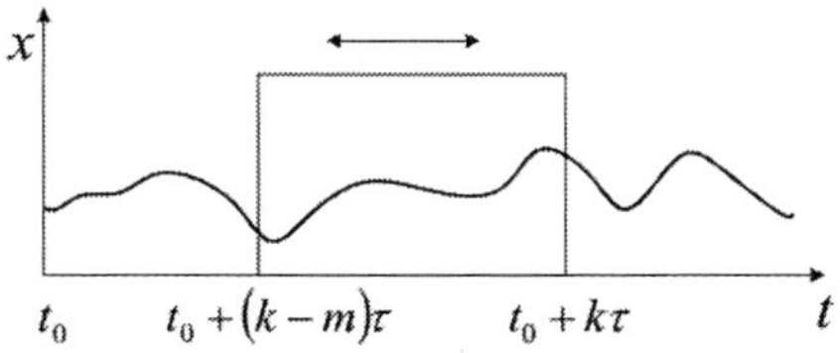

Figure 1. The process of MTW data extraction

Supposing that the current position of MTW is i, the input vector x_i are the data from $i-1$ to $i-m$ on the quality series where x_i denotes $x(t_0+(i-1)\tau),\dots,x(t_0+(i-m)\tau)$, and the output $y(i)$ is $x(t_0+i\tau)$. When the MTW moving, the next training sample $\{x(i+1),y(i+1)\}$ can be produced continually.

The training sample set are input into weighted LS-SVR to get the regression parameters $\boldsymbol{a}$ and b. When the future value is predicted using the weighted LS-SVR-based model, the parameters $\boldsymbol{a}$ and b are substituted in model (3) and the MTW is also shifted to the corresponding position. The history quality data $x(t_0+(i-1)\tau),\dots,x(t_0+(i-m)\tau)$ are taken as input data $\boldsymbol{x}(i)$ to obtain the model responses $\hat{y}(i)$, which are the prediction value of $x(t_0+i\tau)$. The modeling process of quality series prediction with weighted LS-SVR is shown as Figure2.

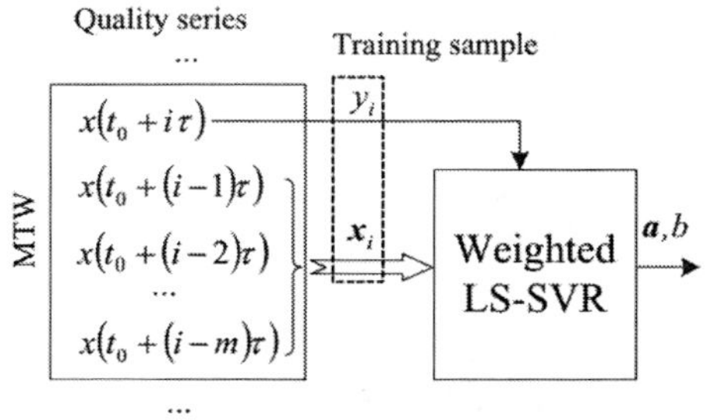

Figure 2. Quality series prediction modeling with wighted LS-SVR

The degree of importance and the impact on the future quality data by history data is increasing from far to near. Different membership to history samples according to its difference positions in the time domain are observed. That is to say, nearer data samples are given larger weight, while further data samples are given smaller weight. Through this weight, in the quality series, the nearer samples are enhanced and the farther ones are weakened.

We apply the index distribution as the weight, and the actual weight of index distribution is available as follows

$$w_i=\alpha(1-\alpha)^{n-i}, \quad (16)$$

where α is index coefficient, $0<\alpha<1$ and $i=1,2,\dots,N$.

Form (16), the sum of weights is

$$\lim_{n\to\infty}\sum_{i=1}^{n} w_i=\lim_{n\to\infty}\sum_{i=1}^{n}\alpha(1-\alpha)^{n-i}=1. \quad (17)$$

The index coefficient α in time domain is very important to solve multivariate linear equation (15). It impacts on the accuracy of results obviously. Under normal circumstances, if the time sequence is stable, linear distribution and less value of α can be selected; if the data sequence fluctuates more seriously, index distribution and lesser value of α can be selected. The value of α can also be selected through optimized calculation with the least fitting error.

4 Experiments

An automatic turning process has been observed, and the real deviation sequence for outer ring of bearings size is shown in Table I. The tolerance of the outer ring is $90^{+0.45}_{+0.30}$ where, $\Delta D_{s\,max\,s}$ is the largest deviation of the outer ring's diameter by measurement. In the turning process, there are system factors (such as tool wear, thermal deformation, etc.) and random factors (such as system vibration, rough material, etc.) impacting the turning quality.

Table 1. Real deviation sequence for outer ring size

UNIT: MM

No.	1	2	3	4	5	6	7
$\Delta D_{s\,max\,s}$	0.38	0.37	0.38	0.39	0.42	0.41	0.40
$\Delta D_{s\,min\,s}$	0.35	0.33	0.32	0.35	0.37	0.37	0.36
No.	**8**	**9**	**10**	**11**	**12**	**13**	**14**
$\Delta D_{s\,max\,s}$	0.38	0.36	0.42	0.44	0.40	0.37	0.40
$\Delta D_{s\,min\,s}$	0.35	0.32	0.39	0.40	0.35	0.33	0.34
No.	**15**	**16**	**17**	**18**	**19**	**20**	**21**
$\Delta D_{s\,max\,s}$	0.42	0.45	0.42	0.41	0.40	0.42	0.41
$\Delta D_{s\,min\,s}$	0.38	0.41	0.38	0.36	0.38	0.39	0.36
No.	**22**	**23**	**24**	**25**	**26**	**27**	**28**
$\Delta D_{s\,max\,s}$	0.44	0.43	0.43	0.42	0.43	0.44	0.46
$\Delta D_{s\,min\,s}$	0.38	0.37	0.40	0.38	0.36	0.40	0.41

Firstly, different prediction models using three-order polynomial regression, four-order polynomial regression, BP neural network, standard LS-SVR, and weighted LS-SVR were set up respectively, with the first twenty-five data in Table 1. Then the values of the 26th, 27th, 28th work pieces were predicted and the results were compared with the real ones.

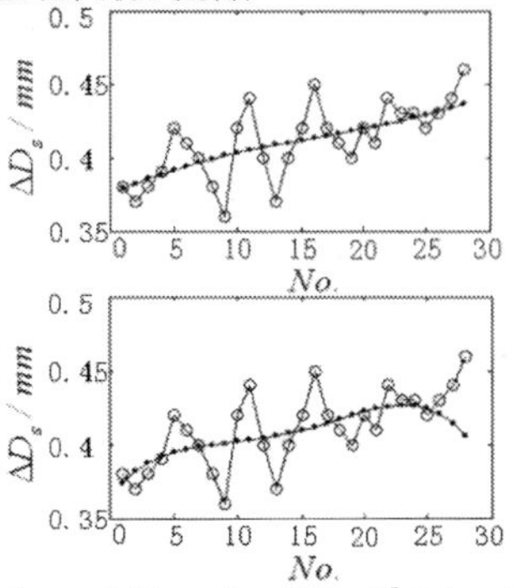

(a) 3-order polynomial based model; (b) 4-order polynomial based model;

Figure 3. Prediction using polynomial based model

In the experiments, the width of time was all set as 5. The polynomial and BP neural network are realized with the polynomial function and artificial neural network toolbox in Matlab6.5, respectively. In the BP neural network based model, the learning rate $a = 0.1$, hidden layer neurons were taken 6 and training steps is 10000. The prediction results using polynomial based model are shown in Figure 3.

In the testing, the data from 3th to 25th are taken as regression checking, and the data from 26th to 28th are taken as the testing. From Figure 3, it is obvious to see that polynomial model can predict quality deviation caused by system factors but cannot predict those by random factors in turning process.

Standard LS-SVR and weighted LS-SVR algorithm were achieved by matrix function in matlab6.5, with the parameter adjusting constant valued 500. RBF was chosen as Kernel function of above two models with the parameter $\sigma = 0.1$, and in the weighted LS-SVR based model, the distribution parameters $\alpha = 0.3$. The predicted deviations of LS-SVR and weighted LS-SVR based model are shown in Figure 4.

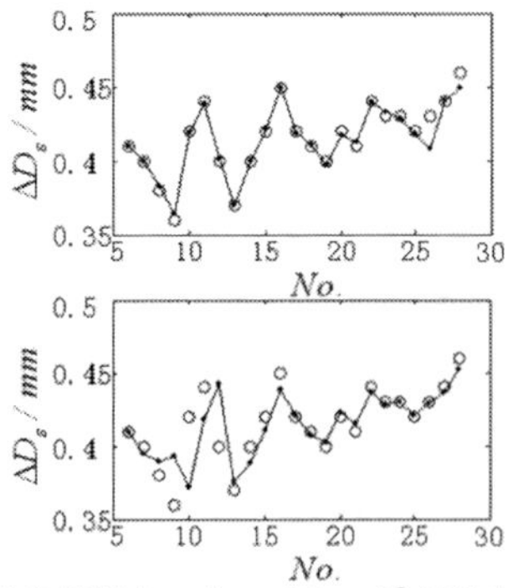

(a) Standard LS-SVR based model; (b) Weighted LS-SVR based model;

Figure 4. Prediction results using different LS-SVR based model

As seen from Figure 4, LS-SVR model has high regression precision for training samples. Output sequence of the LS-SVR model almost coincides with the real deviation sequence. There are more regression errors on the first half of sample sequence based on weighted LS-SVR model but much higher precision on the second half of the sample sequence. It's better to predict the three future data by weighted LS-SVR based model.

Mean square error $MSE = \sum_{i=1}^{n} (\hat{y}_i - y_i)^2 / n$ was introduced to compare the prediction precision of each model, where $\hat{y}_i$, y_i and n are output of models, output of training sample sets, and the number of training samples, respectively. The prediction precisions of each model are shown in Table II.

Table 2. Prediction precision of different model

Method		26th	27th	28th	MSE
Real value		0.43	0.44	0.46	/
3-order polynomial	Prediction	0.431	0.434	0.437	0.010
	Error	0.001	0.006	0.023	/
4-order polynomial	Prediction	0.421	0.415	0.406	/
	Error	0.009	0.025	0.054	0.029
Standard LS-SVR	Prediction	0.408	0.441	0.450	/
	Error	0.022	0.001	0.010	0.011
Weighted LS-SVR	Prediction	0.429	0.436	0.452	/
	Error	0.001	0.004	0.008	0.004

Analyzing the prediction results shown in Table III, we can contend that in all these experiments, weighted LS-SVR based model outperforms its main competitors – polynomial and standard LS-SVR based models. The MSE of weighted LS-SVR prediction model is only 20%-30% that of standard ones. That proves the rule: "nearer data weigh heavier and farther data weigh lighter".

5 Conclusions

The main benefits of this presented prediction model are that it could be applied to quality prediction of small-batch producing process well and make history data 'nearer is more weight' through using the index distribution as the weight in time domain.

The testing result of weighted LS-SVR based prediction model is very competitive in comparison with the other models. Thus the presented prediction model is demonstrated to be capable of describing the variety of quality with time.

References

1. C.A. Van Luttervelt, and J. Peng, "Symbiosis of modelling and sensing to improve the accuracy of workpieces in small batch machining operations,"

International Journal of Advanced Manufacturing Technology, 1999, **vol. 15,** no. 10, pp. 699-710.

2. D.M. Hawkins, and K.D. Zamba, "On Small Shifts in Quality Control," Quality Engineering, Sep. 2003, **vol. 16**, no. 1, pp. 143-149.
3. H.A. Kishawy, "An experimental evaluation of cutting temperatures during high speed machining of hardened D2 tool steel", Machining Science and Technology, 2002, **vol. 6**, no. 1, pp. 67-79.
4. E.S. Chng, S. Chen, and B. Mulgrew, "Gradient radial basis function networks for nonlinear and nonstationary time series prediction," IEEE Transactions on Neural Networks, **vol. 7**, no.1, pp. 190-194, 1996.
5. Y. Becerikli, and Y. Oysal, "Modeling and prediction with a class of time delay dynamic neural network," Applied Soft Computing Journal, Aug. 2007, **vol. 7**, no. 4, pp. 1164-1169.
6. E. Gomez-Ramirez, and K. Najim, E. Ikonen, "Forecasting time series with a new architecture for polynomial artificial neural network," Applied Soft Computing Journal, Aug. 2007, **vol. 7**, no. 4, pp. 1209-1216.
7. V.N. Vapnik, The nature of statistical learning theory. New York: Spring-Verlag, 1999.
8. V.N. Vapnik, "An overview of statistical learning theory," IEEE Transaction Neural Networks, 1999, **vol. 10**, no.5, pp. 988–999.
9. J. A. K. Suykens, and J. Vandewalle, "Least squares support vector machine classifiers," Neural Processing Letters, 1999, **vol. 9,** no. 3, pp. 293-300.
10. J. A. K. Suykens, J. Vandewalle, "Sparse least squares support vector machine classifiers," European Symposium on Artificial Neural Networks, 2000, Bruges Belgium, 37-42.
11. J.A.K. Suykens, L. Lukas, and J. Vandewalle, "Sparse approximation using least squares support vector machines," Proceedings - IEEE International Symposium on Circuits and Systems, Geneva, **vol. 2**, pp. 757-760, 2000.

MATEC Web of Conferences 44, 01005 (2016)
DOI: 10.1051/matecconf/20164401005

An Agent Framework of Tourism Recommender System

Zhi Yang Jia[1,a], Wei Gao[2] and Yi Jin Shi[1]

[1]Yunnan University, Tourism and Culture College, 674100 Lijiang, China
[2]Yunnan Normal University, School of Information Science, 650500 Kunming, China

Abstract. This paper proposes the development of an Agent framework for tourism recommender system. The recommender system can be featured as an online web application which is capable of generating a personalized list of preference attractions for tourists. Traditional technologies of classical recommender system application domains, such as collaborative filtering, content-based filtering and content-based filtering are effectively adopted in the framework. In the framework they are constructed as Agents that can generate recommendations respectively. Recommender Agent can generate recommender information by integrating the recommendations of Content-based Agent, collaborative filtering-based Agent and constraint-based Agent. In order to make the performance more effective, linear combination method of data fusion is applied. User interface is provided by the tourist Agent in form of webpages and mobile app.

1 Introduction

Over the last few years, communication services via the Internet are springing up at an amazing rate. The world is revolving around information which can be easily access to a massive load of information [1] through the Internet. The big data era [2], despite all its competitive advantages and extensive prospect, also comes with the disadvantage of information overload, making the search of precise information an overwhelming and time consuming task [3]. A personal recommender system [4] is considered as the effective way to overcome this problem by supporting people in daily choices and pointing out alternatives.

For the tourism suppliers, the Internet and mobile communication technology provides multiple ways to globally sell their products and services to potential tourists at any time. The suppliers can remotely manage their Web & WAP servers to display their marketing content at a high speed. For tourists, the Internet enables them to communicate directly with tourism suppliers to obtain information, and to search and purchase services at any time and any place online [5].Now recommender systems are partially applied in the travel industry helping tourists to make personalized vacation plans. Personal preferences of people and their interests play a decisive role in choosing their supplier considering the fact that on vacations. In such a customer sensitive industry the application of personal travel recommender systems become a necessity, not a luxury. This has become more important for survival of tourism companies for the fact that economic slowdowns have curtailed excursion budgets of people. Moreover, demand for package travel has declined and people prefer personalized trips, therefore recommender systems have attracted attention of business and academic community.

Conventional recommendation techniques, content-based filtering and collaborative filtering [6], for instance, are particularly well suited for the recommendation of quality and taste products such as books, movies, or pop music. However, for products from other categories such as cars, computers, apartments or tourist attractions these conventional approaches are not as efficient. The reasons are many, for example, tourist attractions are not visited very frequently which makes it rather infeasible to collect numerous ratings for one specific item. Ratings from users and similar data are required by collaborative recommendation algorithms. Furthermore, customers who use recommendation applications would not be satisfied with recommendations based on years-old item preferences.

The two major alternative knowledge-based recommender systems are called case-based and constraint-based recommendation systems [7]. In both approaches the principles of exploiting knowledge are similar: User requirements are collected, and recommendation results are explained. The major difference between them is in the method solutions are calculated. Knowledge-based approaches have the advantage of direct inclusion and mapping of expert's knowledge, for that neither a cold-start phase nor large user communities is required. As with all knowledge-based systems however, the development of such a knowledge intensive application requires some additional ramp-up effort in both knowledge acquisition and engineering, as well as in the development of an interactive user interface.

[a] Corresponding author: jdyjazz@gmail.com

An agent-based model [8] is one of a class of computational models for simulating the actions and interactions of autonomous agents with a view to assessing their effects on the system as a whole. In artificial intelligence, an intelligent agent is an autonomous entity which observes through sensors and acts upon an environment using actuators and directs its activity towards achieving goals. Multi-agent based frameworks [9] are considered as potential effective solutions for tourism recommender system. A series of knowledge-based agents that include a knowledge base and an inference system can be parts of the multi-agent framework.

2 Architecture of the Agent framework

The framework proposed in the paper integrates Collector Agent, Tourist Agent, Content-based Agent, Collaborative Filtering-based Agent and Constraint-based Agent into a multi-agent system through the Internet to providing tourism recommender service. The design of this mechanism is based on three kinds of recommendation system [10], which can perform respective recommendation filtering algorithm. The framework can integrated the recommendations generated by the three Agents, and then presents the results to the tourist. The Framework is depicted in Figure 1.

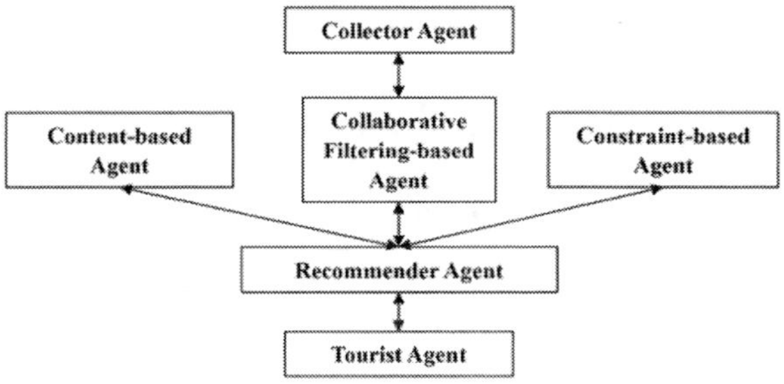

Figure 1. Agent framework for attraction recommendations.

3 Developments of the Agents

3.1 Collector Agent

The Collector Agent of the framework is consisted of some web crawlers [11] that follow hyperlinks throughout a Web site, retrieving and indexing pages to document the site for collecting tourist information. In other words, it is an intelligent topic crawler focusing on the tourist field. Based on the tourist ontology designed for parsing the unstructured Web, the Collector Agent can also discover emerging Web pages related to tourism on the Web, and extract the text information after downloading the Webpages.

3.2 Recommender Agent

As shown in Figure 1, Recommender Agent can generate recommender information by integrating the recommendations of Content-based Agent, Collaborative Filtering-based Agent and Constraint-based Agent. And then the recommender information can be transferred to the Tourist Agent. In order to make the performance more effective, linear combination method of data fusion [12] is applied.

Assumed that, the recommendations sent to the tourists is specified as $List_n$, where n is the amount of the total items. And $List_{n1}$ is the recommendation generated by Content-based Agent; And $List_{n2}$ is the recommendation generated by Collaborative Filtering-based Agent; And $List_{n3}$ is the recommendation generated by Constraint-based Agent. So that the final recommendation $List_n$ can be:

$$List_n = \alpha \cdot List_{n1} + \beta \cdot List_{n2} + \gamma \cdot List_{n3} \quad (1)$$

Where α , β and γ are weights, and they are set to be 1/3 initially.

Depending on the feedback of Tourist Agent, the three weights which stored in the Tourist Agent can be updated dynamically according to the preferences of the tourists.

Neighbour tourists generated mainly based on the similarity between each user. However, a larger number of users have become null and void, so the system needs to pre-process [13] the user data before generating neighbours. The pre-processing process consists of data cleaning, data integration, data conversion and data reduction. The system then can get a more streamlined and representative list of users which are usually often logged on and recently recorded users, which are recognized as active users. For users already have travel records, the system can use the visiting history of tourist attractions to calculate the similarities between users. For the user there is no travel records, the system can use the user's basic information (such as logging times, sex, professional, vehicle, etc.) as the basis for the calculation of similarity [14].

3.3 Content-based Agent

Items that can be recommended to the tourist are represented by a set of features, also called attributes or properties. For example, in a tourist attraction recommendation application, features adopted to describe a movie are: actors, directors, genres, subject matter. When each item is described by the same set of attributes, and there is a known set of values the attributes may take, the item is represented by means of structured data. In this case, many ML algorithms can be used to learn a user profile. In most content-based filtering systems, item descriptions are textual features extracted from Web pages, emails, news articles or product descriptions. Unlike structured data, there are no attributes with well-defined values. Textual features create a number of complications when learning a user profile, due to the natural language ambiguity. The problem is that traditional keyword-based profiles are unable to capture the semantics of user interests because they are primarily driven by a string matching operation. If a string, or some morphological variant, is found in both the profile and the

document, a match is made and the document is considered as relevant. The result is that, due to synonymy, relevant information can be missed if the profile does not contain the exact keywords in the documents while, due to polysemy, wrong documents could be deemed relevant.

Most content-based recommender systems use relatively simple retrieval models, such as keyword matching or the Vector Space Model (VSM) with basic TF-IDF weighting [15]. VSM is a spatial representation of text documents. In that model, each document is represented by a vector in an n-dimensional space, where each dimension corresponds to a term from the overall vocabulary of a given document collection.

Formally, every document is represented as a vector of term weights, where each weight indicates the degree of association between the document and the term. Let $D=\{d_1,d_2,...,d_n\}$ denote a set of documents or corpus, and $T=\{t_1,t_2,...,t_n\}$ be the dictionary, that is to say the set of words in the corpus. T is obtained by applying some standard natural language processing operations, such as tokenization, stop words removal, and stemming [16]. Each document d_j is represented as a vector in an-dimensional vector space, so $d_j=\{w_{1j},w_{2j},...,d_{nj}\}$, where w_{kj} is the weight for term t_k in document d_j.

Document representation in the VSM raises two issues: weighting the terms and measuring the feature vector similarity. The most commonly used term weighting scheme, TF-IDF (Term Frequency-Inverse Document Frequency) weighting, is based on empirical observations regarding text :

- Rare terms are not less relevant than frequent terms (IDF assumption),
- Multiple occurrences of a term in a document are not less relevant than single occurrences (TF assumption),
- Long documents are not preferred to short documents (normalization assumption).

In other words, terms that occur frequently in one document (TF=term-frequency), but rarely in the rest of the corpus (IDF=inverse-document-frequency), are more likely to be relevant to the topic of the document. In addition, normalizing the resulting weight vectors prevent longer documents from having a better chance of retrieval. These assumptions are well exemplified by the TF-IDF function [17]:

$$TF-IDF(t_k,d_j)=TF(t_k,d_j)\cdot\log\frac{N}{n_k} \quad (2)$$

Where N denotes the number of documents in the corpus, and nk denotes the number of documents in the collection in which the term tk occurs at least once.

$$TF(t_k,d_j)=\frac{f_{k,j}}{\max_z f_{z,j}} \quad (3)$$

Where the maximum is computed over the frequencies fz,j of all terms tz that occur in document dj .

In order for the weights to fall in the [0,1] interval and for the documents to be represented by vectors of equal length, weights obtained by

Equation (2) is usually normalized by cosine normalization [18]:

$$w_{k,j}=\frac{TF-IDF(t_k,d_j)}{\sqrt{\sum_{s=1}^{|T|}TF-IDF(t_k,d_j)^2}} \quad (4)$$

As stated earlier, a similarity measure is required to determine the closeness between two documents. Many similarity measures have been derived to describe the proximity of two vectors; among those measures, cosine similarity is the most widely used:

$$sim(d_i,d_j)=\frac{\sum_k w_{ki}\cdot w_{kj}}{\sqrt{\sum_k w_{ki}^2}\cdot\sqrt{\sum_k w_{kj}^2}} \quad (5)$$

The Content-based agent is relying on VSM where as both tourist profiles and items are represented as weighted term vectors. Predictions of a tourists' interest in a particular item can be derived by computing the cosine similarity.

3.4 Collaborative filtering-based Agent

The starting point of collaborative filtering-based agent is: Suppose that tourists with similar interests should favourite to the same items as each other. So, as long as the maintenance of a database on the tourists' preference, the neighbour tourists with similar interests can be calculated by analysing the stored preference, and then it can be recommended to the tourist based on the neighbour tourists' interests.

On the basis of collaborative filtering principle, the recommendation process of tourist attractions can be divided into three steps [19].

- The representation of tourist information. Tourist visiting history of attractions needs to be analysed and modelled.
- The generation of neighbour tourists. The similarity of tourists can be computed according to the visiting history data and the collaborative filtering algorithm presented by us. A neighbour tourist list can be calculated on the basis of known similarities.
- The generation of attraction recommendations. Top-N attractions will recommended to the tourist according to the visiting history of his neighbours.

According to above steps, user's basic information and past travel history can be used to calculate the user list of neighbours which are recorded in the corresponding record in the user database. When users log into the system, the recommendations of tourist attractions can be presented based on the travel experiences of his neighbours.

The process of recommendation is shown in Figure 1. In order to increase the efficiency of the system, the system calculated users' neighbours when offline for each tourist, and calculated at regular intervals

Neighbour users generated mainly based on the similarity between each user. However, a larger number of users have become null and void, so the system needs to pre-process the user data before generating neighbours. The pre-processing process consists of data cleaning, data integration, data conversion and data reduction. The system then can get a more streamlined and representative list of users which are usually often logged

on and recently recorded users, which are recognized as active users. For users already have travel records, the system can use the visiting history of tourist attractions to calculate the similarities between users. For the user there is no travel records, the system can use the user's basic information (such as logging times, sex, professional, vehicle, etc.) as the basis for the calculation of similarity [20].

Suppose that the set of all tourists $T=\{T_1, T_2...T_n\}$, for each tourist T_i (i=1, 2...n), the system can calculate the neighbours list including the top N tourists which similarity is higher than the given threshold θ.

The core of collaborative filtering algorithms is the calculation of users' similarity. The similarity between the tourist T_i and T_j is measured as follows: First the system needs to retrieval all the ratings of tourist T_i and T_j over the attractions, and then calculate the similarity between the tourist T_i and T_j through different similarity models, denoted as $sim(T_i,T_j)$. There are mainly three ways to measure the similarity between tourists, including Cosine method, Correlation similarity method and Adjusted Cosine method. We have adopted the Cosine method in this paper. Tourist ratings are viewed as a vector of n-dimensional term space. If the tourist has ever visited the attraction, the rating is set to 1, otherwise set to 0. And the cosine similarity between tourists is computed by the angle between vectors. The similarity between tourist T_i and T_j can be calculated by:

$$sim(\mathrm{T}_i, \mathrm{T}_j) = \frac{R_{T_i} \bullet R_{Tj}}{\left\|R_{T_i}\right\| \times \left\|R_{Tj}\right\|} \quad (6)$$

When computing recommendations for a particular tourist, the very basic approach is to select the objects favoured by other tourists that are similar to the target tourist. When new tourists enter the system, there is usually insufficient information to produce recommendation for them, because there is no visiting history of the new tourists. The usual solution of the cold start problem is similarity calculation between each user by profile information, such as age, sex, professional, vehicle, income, etc.

3.5 Constraint-based Agent

Main objective of constraint-based agent is to generate tourist attraction recommendations, and the task is viewed as a constraint satisfaction problem (CSP) [21]. Formally, a constraint satisfaction problem is defined as a triple of $\langle V, D, C\rangle$, where:

- $V = \{V1,...,Vn\}$ is a set of variables,
- $D = \{D_1,..., D_n\}$ is a set of the respect domains of values, and,
- $C = \{C_1,..., C_m\}$ is a set of constraints.

Each variable V_i can take on the values in the nonempty domain D_i. Every constraint $C_j \in C$ is in turn a pair $\langle t_j, R_j\rangle$, where $t_j \subset X$ is a subset of k variables and R_j is an k-ary relation on the corresponding subset of domains d_j. An evaluation of the variables is a function from a subset of variables to a particular set of values in the corresponding subset of domains. An evaluation v satisfies a constraint $\langle t_j, R_j\rangle$ if the values assigned to the variables t_j satisfies the relation R_j.

An evaluation is consistent if it does not violate any of the constraints. An evaluation is complete if it includes all variables. An evaluation is a solution if it is consistent and complete; such an evaluation is said to solve the constraint satisfaction problem.

Constraint Satisfaction Solutions for constraint satisfaction problems are calculated on the basis of search algorithms that use different combinations of backtracking and constraint propagation.

For the particular issue of recommendation task, we could define [22]:

$V = V_C \cup V_P$, where V_C is a set of single-valued or multiple-valued variables that represent the tourists' requirement, and V_P is a variable set represent the properties of tourist attraction.

D contains the domain definitions for variables in V.

$C = C_P \cup C_I \cup C_F \cup C_O$, where C_P is the constraints set of the values in V_P that describe the available tourist attractions; C_I is the constraints (capturing tourist requirements) set of the values in V_C; C_F is the set of filters' constraints; C_O is the set of other constraints (inconsistency constraints).

3.6 Tourist Agent

The Tourist Agent mainly acts as the intermediary service provider between the framework and tourists.

The emergence of the World Wide Web and mobile networks has given even the most mundane of applications a spiffy GUI. The Tourist Agent provides webpage UI and mobile APP UI to the tourist.

Tourist Agent saves the profile, preferences, Agent weights, and the use history of the tourist. It can send browse and enquiry request of tourist information to the Recommender Agent. The Recommender Agent response the Tourist Agent by recommendations based on the linear combination calculation. The tourist can feedback or rate the result recommendations presented by the Tourist Agent UI.

4 Conclusions

Traditional technologies of classical recommender system application domains, such as collaborative filtering, content-based filtering and content-based filtering are effectively adopted in the framework. In the framework they are constructed as Agent that can generate recommendations respectively. Recommender Agent can generate recommender information by integrating the recommendations of Content-based Agent, Collaborative Filtering-based Agent and Constraint-based Agent. In order to make the performance more effective, linear combination method of data fusion is applied. User interface is provided by the Tourist Agent in form of webpages and mobile app.

The emergence of the World Wide Web and mobile networks has given even the most mundane of applications a spiffy GUI. The Tourist Agent provides webpage UI and mobile APP UI to the tourist.

References

1. WP Eveland Jr, S Dunwoody. Examining information processing on the World Wide Web using think aloud protocols. MEDIAPSYCHOLOGY, **2** (2000)
2. B Brown, M Chui, J Manyika. Are you ready for the era of 'big data'. McKinsey Quarterly, **11** (2011)
3. Tuan-Dung Cao, Quang-Minh Nguyen. Semantic approach to travel information search and itinerary recommendation. International Journal of Web Information Systems, **8**, 3 (2012)
4. Paolo Cremonesi, Franca Garzotto, Sara Negro et al.. Comparative evaluation of recommender system quality. CHI '11 Extended Abstracts on Human Factors in Computing Systems, (ACM, New York, 2011)
5. GI Alptekin, Gülçin Büyüközkan. An integrated case-based reasoning and MCDM system for Web based tourism destination planning. Expert Systems with Applications,**38**,3(2011)
6. Xiaoyuan Su, Taghi M. Khoshgoftaar. A survey of collaborative filtering techniques. Advances in Artificial Intelligence, (2009)
7. Adomavicius, G., Tuzhilin, A.. Toward the next generation of recommender systems: a survey of the state-of-the-art and possible extensions. IEEE Transactions on Knowledge and Data Engineering, **17**, 6(2005)
8. Linden, G., Smith, B., York, J. Amazon.com recommendations: item-to-item collaborative filtering. IEEE Internet Computing, (IEEE Computer Society Press, Los Alamitos, 2003)
9. Jonathan L. Herlocker, Joseph A. Konstan, John Riedl. Explaining collaborative filtering recommendations. Proceedings of the 2000 ACM conference on Computer, (ACM, New York, 2011)
10. W. R. Gilks and P. Wild. Adaptive Rejection Sampling for Gibbs Sampling. Journal of the Royal Statistical Society. Series C (Applied Statistics), **2**, 41 (1992)
11. Badrul Sarwar, George Karypis, Joseph Konstan, and John Riedl. Application of Dimensionality Reduction in Recommender System - A Case Study. Technical Report, (2000)
12. Robin Burke. Hybrid Recommender Systems: Survey and Experiments. User Modeling and User-Adapted Interaction, **4**, 12(2002)
13. Lu, E.H.-C. ,Chih-Yuan Lin, Tseng, V.S.. Trip-Mine: An Efficient Trip Planning Approach with Travel Time Constraints. 2011 12th IEEE International Conference on Mobile Data Management (MDM) (IEEE Computer Society Press, Los Alamitos, 2007)
14. G. D. Abowd, C. G. Atkeson, J. Hong, S. Long, R. Kooper and M.Pinkerton. Cyberguide: A Mobile Context Aware Tour Guide. Wireless Networks, **5**, 3 (1997)
15. T. Horozov, N. Narasimhan, V. Vasudevan. Using Location for Personalized POI Recommendations in Mobile Environments. Proceedings of International Symposium on Applications on Internet, (IEEE Computer Society Press, Los Alamitos, 2006)
16. Y. Zheng, X. Xie. Learning Travel Recommendations from User-Generated GPS Traces. ACM Transactions on Intelligent Systems and Technologies, **2**, 2 (2011)
17. V.-W. Soo, S.-H. Liang. Recommending a Trip Plan by Negotiation with a Software Travel Agent. Cooperative Information Agents(Springer Berlin Heidelberg , 2001)
18. Makoto Yokoo. Constraint Satisfaction Problem. Distributed Constraint Satisfaction, Springer Series on Agent Technology,(Springer Berlin Heidelberg , 2001)
19. Dietmar Jannach, Markus Zanker, Matthias Fuchs. Constraint-based recommendation in tourism: A multi-perspective case study, Information Technology & Tourism, 11 (2009)
20. Tsang, E. Foundations of Constraint Satisfaction, (Academic Press, London and San Diego, 1993)
21. A. Felfernig, G. Friedrich, D. Jannach, M. Zanker. Developing Constraint-based Recommenders, Recommender Systems Handbook, (Springer Berlin Heidelberg , 2011)
22. Ricci, F., Mirzadeh, N., Bansal, M.. Supporting user query relaxation in a recommender system. In: Proceedings of the 5th International Conference in E-Commerce and WebTechnologies - EC-Web, 2004:31-40.WP Eveland Jr, S Dunwoody. Examining information processing on the World Wide Web using think aloud protocols. MEDIAPSYCHOLOGY, **2** (2000)

MATEC Web of Conferences **44**, 01006 (2016)
DOI: 10.1051/matecconf/20164401006
© Owned by the authors, published by EDP Sciences, 2016

Application of AHP-Ansoff Matrix Analysis in Business Diversification: The case of Evergrande Group

Nan Yin [1,a]

[1]*Business School, Nanjing Xiaozhuang University, Nanjing City, China*

Abstract. A new method of enterprise strategic research, the AHP—Ansoff Matrix analysis method, is put forward in this paper for the first time and applied in the enterprise practices. By using this research method, the development strategy of enterprise diversification is analyzed scientifically and reasonably with Evergrande group as the example. And finally, main procedures of the method are summarized.

1 INTRODUCTION

Diversified development strategy is a kind of enterprise development strategy chosen by the enterprise in order to maximize profit and occupy more market, which is generally suitable for large enterprises with great financial strength, large scale of development and significant market share. Regarded as one aspect of the enterprise strategic decision research, the study of enterprise diversification strategy is currently studied by several domestic experts and scholars in the following aspects:(1)the relationship between enterprise diversification strategy and business performance. Zhao Feng[1], the scholar from Harbin Industrial University concluded that the enterprise diversification strategy had a significant negative effect on business performance of enterprises based on sample data of the real evidence; With the method of questionnaire survey, Zou Hao[2], the scholar from Northeastern University concluded that the diversification strategy was as a function of enterprise business performance, different analytical functions could be acquired according to different types of diversification strategy, and then on the basis of the function, the corresponding enterprise performance value could be found.(2)the relationship between diversification strategy and enterprise's technological capabilities. Liu Hongwei[3], the scholar form Xiangtan University has conducted empirical research on the related samples, the results of which showed that enterprise diversification strategy went against the promotion of enterprise's technological capabilities, and the negative effect brought by can by diversification strategy could be weakened by enhancing the technological research and development.(3)the relationship between diversification strategy and characteristics of entrepreneurs. Cheng Chuanming[4], the scholar from Nanjing University verified the relationship between entrepreneurs' personal background characteristics and diversification strategy based on the panel data of public companies, the results indicating that educational background of the entrepreneur was in positve correlation with the degree of enterprise diversification, the degree of enterprise diversification would be higher if entrepreneur had a technical background, and the degree of enterprise diversification would be lower if entrepreneur had a financial background.(4)the relationship between enterprise diversification strategy and the choice of target industry. Lan Weiguo[5], the scholar from Beijing University of Technology studied the correlation of diversification strategy and industry life cycle, and methods to recognize and evaluate enterprise diversification industry.

Above all, nowadays, the study of enterprise diversification strategy conducted by domestic experts and scholars were mainly limited to the relevance of enterprise diversification development strategy and enterprise business performance, enterprise technological capabilities and entrepreneurs' characteristics, lacking of relevant research methods about how to implement the strategy of diversifying effectively and how to choose suitable diversification strategy for the enterprise's development. This paper puts forward a new method of enterprise strategic research, the AHP—Ansoff Matrix analysis method that is innovative and practical. This method was applied in the enterprise practices, and can effectively analyze the enterprise diversification development strategy.

2 THE PRINCIPLE OF ANSOFF MATRIX ANALYSIS

Ansoff Matrix, also named Product Market Expansion Grid or Growth Vector Matrix, is a research method applied in the analysis of products and markets, which was proposed by Ansoff, the father of strategic

[a] Corresponding author: kitupfor@163.com

Article available at http://www.matec-conferences.org or http://dx.doi.org/10.1051/matecconf/20164401006

management in 1975[6]. This method can be used to analyze the thoughts for enterprise to expand the market and develop new products more objectively and accurately, and is extensively applied in enterprise strategic management. The matrix analysis is composed of four research strategies——new products strategy, existing products strategy, new market strategy and the existing market strategy. For an enterprise implementing diversification strategy, it is faced with fierce competition in terms of market and products both. Therefore, the analysis of the four research strategies has an important significance on the enterprise strategy.

Table1 Ansoff Matrix

	existing market	new market
new products	products expansion strategy	combination strategy
existing products	market penetration strategy	market development strategy

Table 1 is the base form of Ansoff Matrix. Ansoff matrix can help enterprise manager to implement strategy mode in a scientific and effective way, and the basic application procedures of Ansoff Matrix are as follows:

Enterprises consider whether the existing products in the existing market can get more market share (market penetration strategy);

Enterprises consider whether new market can be developed for the existing products (market development strategy)

Enterprises consider whether new products can be developed for the existing market to satisfy the need of more customers (products expansion strategy);

Enterprises consider whether new products and new market can be developed by making full use of the advantages in products, technology and market, which is a comprehensive strategy to enable enterprise to develop in multi-levels and all aspects (combination strategy).

3 ESTABLISHMENT OF ANSOFF MATRIX ANALYSIS

Evergrande group is a large enterprise implementing the strategy of diversified development, with real estate as the main business. According to its website (http://www.evergrande.com), Evergrande group is an enterprise group with the integration of residential buildings, cultural tourism, fast-moving consumer products, health and sports, covering extensive diversified development business. So, Evergrande group is taken as an example in this paper to conduct relevant research on diversified business development strategy, which has certain feasibility and practical significance.

The strategy of diversified development carried out by enterprises is counter to the single specialized business strategy implemented by other enterprises. According to the principle of Ansoff Matrix analysis, table 2 establishes diversification business development strategy for Evergrande group based on four research strategies of Ansoff Matrix .

Table 2 Ansoff analysis matrix of diversification business development strategy for Evergrande group

Target hierarchy	Criterion hierarchy	Index hierarchy
diversification business development strategy for Evergrande group（A）	new products（B1）	X1 fast-moving consumer products X2 health and medical products X3 The internet community service products X4 video and musical products X5 sports related products
	exsiting products（B2）	X6 products of residential buildings X7 products of commercial real estate X8 products of hotel industry X9 products of cultural tourism
	new market（B3）	X10 market of fast-moving consumer products X11 market of high-end health industry X12 market of internet community service X13 market of film and television relevant industry X14 market of football and volley industry
	exsiting market（B4）	X15 market of residential buildings X16 market of commercial real estate X17 market of hotel industry X18 market of cultural tourism

The above is the establishment of Ansoff analysis matrix of diversification business development strategy for Evergrande group, the relative importance of each factor in each hierarchy can be judged with the combination of Analytic Hierarchy Process (AHP) and the AHP method is adopted to calculate the coefficient of relative importance.

4 HIERARCHICAL RANKING AND CONSISTENCY TEST ON THE BASIS OF AHP

4.1. The principle of AHP method

Proposed by American operations researcher A.L.Saaty in the 1970s, Analytical Hierarchy Process (the AHP method) is a combinative method of qualitative and quantitative decision analysis. It is a type of modelizing and quantifying process for complex decision-making thoughts of the decision maker. The basic procedures of analysis are as follows [7]:

(1) Establishment of hierarchical structure model. On the basis of in-depth analysis of the actual problems, all the relevant factors are decomposed into several hierarchies from top to bottom according to different attributes and are concluded into groups according to whether sharing some common characteristics. The common characteristics between them are considered as factors in the new hierarchy of the system, and according to additional characteristics, these factors themselves are integrated to form factors of a higher hierarchy, until factors of the single highest hierarchy are finally formed.

(2) Establishment of judgment matrix。 Judgment matrix compares the relative importance between the certain unit (element) of the previous hierarchy and the related unit of this hierarchy. The value of each element in the judgment matrix is determined by 1~9 digit scale method[8] and obtained mainly through expert evaluation or historical data (experience). Quantity scale of assessment in different situation is given and the basic rules are shown in table 3.

Table 3 1~9 scale method

Scale	Definition and Explanation
1	two elements have equal importance to certain attribute
3	two elements compare, and one element is slightly more important than the other
5	two elements compare, and one element is obviously more important than the other
7	two elements compare, and one element is much more important than the other
9	two elements compare, and one element is extremely more important than the other
2,4,6, 8	representing the scale compromised between two standards above
$1/b_{ij}$	converse comparison of two elements

(3) Weight vector is calculated and consistency test is conducted. The relative weight of each factor in every judgment matrix to its criterion is calculated. The correspondent eigenvector W of judgment matrix A to maximum eigenvalue is normalized to obtain importance rank weights of the correspondent factors in the same hierarchy to the certain factor in previous hierarchy. To avoid interference of other factors on the judgment matrix, in reality, the judgment matrix is required to meet the general consistency and a consistency test is needed. Only by passing the test, the judgment matrix is proved to be reasonable in logic, and the results can be further analyzed.

To test the consistency of judgment matrix, calculate:

$$CR = CI / RI \qquad (1)$$

In formula (1), CR represents consistency ratio. If CR<0.10, the consistency of judgment matrix is acceptable. Otherwise, the judgment matrix should be adjusted properly. CI represents consistency index and is calculated as the follow formula:

$$CI = (\lambda max - n) / (n - 1) \qquad (2)$$

In formula (2), λmax is the maximum eigenvalue of the judgment matrix; n is the number of the comparative factor in pairs; RI represents random index.

4.2. analysis and calculating process

(1) Establishment of hierarchy structure model

As table 2 illustrates, establishment of hierarchy structure model for diversification business development strategy of Evergrande group could be descried as follows:

The target hierarchy (the highest hierarchy): diversification business development strategy of Evergrande group (A);

The criterion hierarchy (the middle hierarchy): new products (B1), existing products (B2), new market (B3), existing market (B4);

The index hierarchy (the bottom hierarchy): index X1 to X18 in table 2.

(2)Establishment of judgment matrix and consistency test

The judgment matrix is established and the four factors in the target hierarchy and the criterion hierarchy are compared in pairs. The four factors in the criterion hierarchy are compared with their factors in the index hierarchy in pairs, and through calculation the weights of the four factors in the criterion hierarchy——new products (B1), existing products (B2), new market (B3), existing market (B4) versus the target hierarchy——diversification business development strategy of Evergrande group (A) are 0.125, 0.250, 0.125 and 0.500, respectively. And the calculation results of weights of the other indexes versus their factors in the criterion hierarchy are shown in Table 4, and pass the consistency test with the result of CR<0.10.

Table 4 single ordering weight value of hierarchies

Matrix	W_1	W_2	W_3	W_4	W_5	CR test
A	0.125	0.250	0.125	0.500		0
B_1	0.455	0.181	0.195	0.099	0.070	0.022
B_2	0.437	0.210	0.220	0.133		0.020
B_3	0.341	0.130	0.325	0.123	0.081	0.032
B_4	0.422	0.152	0.236	0.190		0.059

According to the results of single ordering weight value of hierarchies in Table 4 and the importance degree of the evaluation ability, the relative importance degree of all factors versus total target is calculated from top to bottom hierarchy by hierarchy and the results are shown in table 5. The diversification business development strategy of Evergrande group is analyzed systematically

with Analytic Hierarchy Process method and the ranking of importance degree of each factor in index hierarchy (X1 to X18) versus the target hierarchy is shown in Figure 1.

Table 5 total ordering weight value of hierarchies

Matrix	W_1	W_2	W_3	W_4	W_5
B_1	0.050	0.007	0.020	0.032	0.016
B_2	0.092	0.104	0.035	0.019	
B_3	0.042	0.012	0.028	0.014	0.029
B_4	0.213	0.098	0.131	0.058	

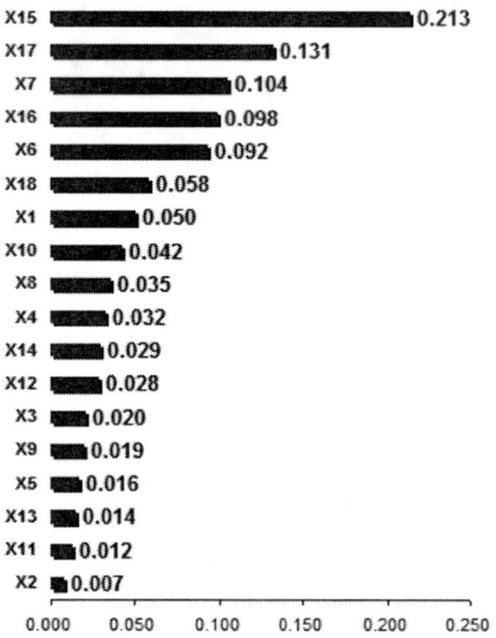

Figure 1 the weight ranking of each factor in the index hierarchy

5 Diversification business development strategy and measures of Evergrande group

Based on the results of calculation and analysis above, the diversification business development strategy of Evergrande group is analyzed systematically. The relative importance of all factors in the process of diversification business development of Evergrande group is ranked; the ranking results indicate that the effect degree of each factor in the process of diversification business development of Evergrande group is of great difference. To highlight the major factors, four factors in the criterion hierarchy——new products (B1), existing products (B2), new market (B3), existing market (B4) is integrated with four research strategies in the Ansoff Matrix analysis diagram to figure out the maximum importance of each research strategy, namely to find out the highest index value of weight for each index of the four factors in the criterion hierarchy, and the results are X1=0.050, X7=0.104, X10=0.042, X15=0.213. The representative results of total ranking of these hierarchies are marked in the Ansoff Matrix analysis diagram and are linked into a quadrangle in sequence and in the form of coordinate axis, as shown in Figure 2.

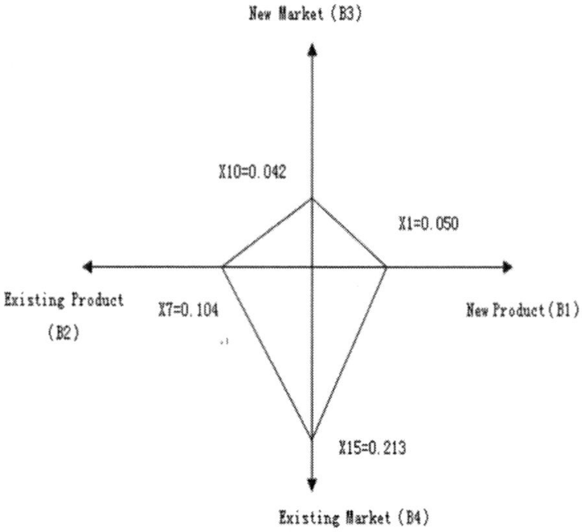

Figure 2 Ansoff Matrix analysis methods for diversification business development strategy of Evergrande group

The calculation results of triangle size of each quadrant in the coordinate axis of figure 2 are: triangle size of B1-B3 quadrant=0.00105, triangle size of B2-B3 quadrant =0.002184, triangle size of B2-B4 quadrant=0.011076, and triangle size of B1-B4 quadrant=0.005325. The triangle size of each quadrant is compared and the result indicates that triangle size of B2-B4 quadrant>triangle size of B1-B4 quadrant>triangle size of B2-B3 quadrant>triangle size of B1-B3 quadrant. Combined with Ansoff Matrix analysis method, the sequence for diversification business development strategy of Evergrande group is market penetration strategy, products expansion strategy, market development strategy and combination strategy.

In accordance with the calculation results and Ansoff Matrix analysis method in figure 2, further analysis could be conducted on the four diversified development strategies chosen by Evergrande group.

(1) Market penetration strategy. Market penetration strategy is an enterprise development strategy to fully develop its existing market potential based on the existing main products. It is the most important strategy for Evergrande group since Evergrande group started as a real estate company and then grew into an enterprise of diversified development and real estate industry remains the main business and major source of profits. Therefore, when adopting diversified development strategies, the main business direction is still to attach great importance to the existing products, such as products of residential buildings and products of commercial real estate; meanwhile, develop the potential of existing market, for example, the major markets of Evergrande group are still first-tier cities like Beijing, Shanghai, Guangzhou and Shenzhen ect.. Some commercial real estate projects

could be developed in the suburb with development potential in the future which is far from the main urban zone.

(2) Products expansion strategy. The products expansion strategy is to expand the scale of sales by improving existing products or developing new products in the existing market. It is the second important strategy after market penetration strategy for diversification development strategy of Evergrande group. When Evergrande group applies diversification business development strategy, it will strengthen its main market of real estate industry and develop some new products based on the industry to maintain of the main market on the one hand and expand the sales scale of the main market. For example, Evergrande group launched new product of mineral water, Evergrande spring, and introduced it into the supply system of direct drinking water for Evergrande Real Estate, thus sales of residential building industry was promoted.

(3) Market development strategy. Market development strategy is that enterprises develop new markets with existing products. When Evergrande group chooses diversification business development strategy, it can develop new markets with existing products on the basis of strengthening its main market. By applying this strategy, Evergrande group could expand the sales scale for existing products and find opportunity for profits in the new market. The existing products of Evergrande group are mainly related to real estate industry, such as products of residential building, products of commercial real estate and products of hotel industry ect.. Under the condition that real estate industry of first-tier cities likes Beijing, Shanghai, Guangzhou and Shenzhen ect. is trending towards saturation gradually, Evergrande group could march into the second-tier and third-tier cities to develop the markets of residential building and commercial real estate in these medium and small-sized cities.

(4) Combination strategy. Combination strategy is that enterprises develop new products in new market to maximize the profit. Since this strategy means developing new products in new market to satisfy target consumers, so enterprises should consider carefully and conduct adequate preliminary market research before implementing this enterprise development strategy. Owing to the great financial strength of Evergrande group, when taking the diversified development strategies it develop several new products that are not relevant to its main business in many potential emerging markets, for example, Evergrande group has acquired one of South Korea's largest plastic surgery hospital to march into the market of plastic surgery in China, and now Evergrande group has opened up its first plastic surgery hospital in the city of Tianjin.

6 Conclusions

This paper utilizes a new research method of enterprise strategy——AHP—Ansoff Matrix analysis method to analyze the possible strategy decision for Evergrande group to carry out diversification business development strategy scientifically with Evergrande group as the example. Based on the analytical results above, this research method for enterprise strategy is proved to be effective and the results indicate that when Evergrande group develop diversified business, the diversified business strategy to choose is to focus on the main business of real estate industry and gradually develop other markets and new products. And the enterprise's development strategy should focus on market penetration strategy and products expansion strategy and gradually implement market development strategy and combination strategy.

For the analysis procedures above, the application steps of AHP—Ansoff Matrix analysis method can be summarized as follows: (1) Establish Ansoff Matrix analysis for enterprise diversification business development strategy. (2) Establish hierarchy structure model for enterprise business development strategy on the basis of Analytic Hierarchy Process (AHP). (3) Judge the importance of each factor in every hierarchy to obtain the total ordering weight value of hierarchies and rank the orders of each factor in the criterion hierarchy. (4) Integrate with four research strategies in the Ansoff Matrix analysis diagram to figure out the maximum importance of each research strategy, namely to find out the highest index value of weight for each index of the four factors in the criterion hierarchy. (5) The representative results of total ranking of these hierarchies are marked in the Ansoff Matrix analysis diagram and are linked into a quadrangle in sequence and in the form of coordinate axis. (6) Obtain the results to choose for enterprise business strategy and conduct further analysis.

References

[1]Zhaofeng, Wang Tienan, Zhangliang. The Effect of Diversification Strategy on Enterprise's Performance Based on Study with Real Evidence. China Soft Science,2012, (11):111-122.

[2]Zouhao, Yang Xihuai, Cai Jinzheng. The Relationship between Diversification Strategy and Enterprise's Performance. Economic Management,2007,29(11):12-16.

[3]Liu Hongwei, He Meili. Effect Study of Diversification Strategy on Enterprise's Technological Capabilities. Soft Science,2015,29(8):61-65.

[4]Chen Chuanming, Sun Junhua. Entrepreneurs' Personal Background Characteristics and the Choice of Diversification Strategy. Management World,2008, (5):124-188.

[5]Lan Weiguo, Zhang Yongan, Yangli. Study on Enterprise's Diversification Strategy and the Choice of Target Industry. Soft Science,2009,23(4):7-12.

[6]Igor Ansoff. Strategy Management.Beijing: China Machine Press,2013.

[7]Qian Songdi. Operations Research (the third edition). Beijing: Tsinghua University Press,2005.

[8]Zhang Bingjiang. Analytic Hierarchy Process and Application Cases. Beijing: Publishing House of Electronics Industry,2014.

MATEC Web of Conferences 44, 01007 (2016)
DOI: 10.1051/matecconf/20164401007

The Analysis of the Development of Futures Investment Funds in China

Zhe Jing Zhang[1]

[1]A teacher with a lectureship in Langfang Polytechnic Institute, Hebei Province, China

Abstract. This paper introduces the futures investment fund, elaborates on its functions and puts forward its problems in China. It also comes up with some personal suggestions for reference based on the measures for its development.

1 An overview of futures investment funds

In the 1940's, futures investment funds appeared in the United States market. As time goes by, they have greatly developed in the United States and has a stable scale. With the continuous progress made in the world financial market, the development of the futures investment fund has reached a higher level in the United States. In recent years, with the development of social economy in China, Chinese economy continues to improve and the financial market has been fully developed, which provides opportunities for the development of the futures investment funds in China that has become an inevitable trend in China's financial market.

The so-called futures investment fund, from a broad sense, is "the management of futures". It means that investors make use of financial management provided by professional fund managers, the global futures market and option market for investment. Investors can carry out physical commodities trading in the investment market. They can also carry out futures or option contract trading; from a limited sense, futures investment fund is also known as "mutual futures fund". It is a kind of innovation of the investment fund and is mainly used in futures investment. Its operating process is similar to the public fund.

2 Functions of futures investment funds

2.1 To control transaction exposure and ensure the return on investment

Compared with traditional investment portfolios, the advantages of adding futures investment funds into the investment portfolio are very prominent, which can effectively control price fluctuations in the traditional investment portfolio, investment risk can be reduced, and increase the return on investment.

2.2 To use short-selling mechanism to resist the economic downturn

Investors face a variety of investment risks in the futures investment market which can be summarized as "high risks, high profits". Due to the high risk in the futures investment market, they have to choose a reasonable investment portfolio in order to effectively avoid the investment risk and guarantee the profitability of investment. Investment risks brought by futures investment funds can be effectively avoided in the futures market by reasonable investment portfolio strategies which can increase investment income. Compared to stock investment and bond investment, futures investment funds are much more flexible and unstable. If the economic cycle is in a recession or on the edge of a recession, it will cause the stock price to fall and economic collapse. But futures investment funds can remain profitable in this case. The reasons are due to the flexible operation of futures investment funds. Investment is controlled by the price fluctuations to guarantee that it makes profits and resist the economic recession.

2.3 To optimize the investment structure and improve the market system

In terms of the global financial market, futures business and futures investment funds have been fully developed in the United States. It also has the most perfect construction of regulatory system. In the United States, the construction of the regulatory system of the futures

Article available at http://www.matec-conferences.org or http://dx.doi.org/10.1051/matecconf/20164401007

investment funds includes three aspects: the legal framework for regulating the futures investment fund, its regulatory system and its regulatory measures. China's futures business started late. Futures investment funds occupy an important position. During the regulatory process, successful experience of the United States should be actively learned and used. And the development of China's futures investment funds needs to be analyzed in detail in order to construct a reasonable regulatory mechanism. With the continuous improvement of the financial business, every investment group plays an important part. According to different types of futures funds, investors are also different. The rapid development of futures investment funds makes the role of institutional investors in the market more important. Therefore, institutional investors have to be further developed and the investment structure of the futures market should be constantly adjusted and improved in order to reduce the investors' risks and investment risks and to further optimize the investment structure to promote the development and progress of the futures market.

3 Problems of china's futures investment funds

With the continuous development of the futures market, although underground futures investment funds in China have developed for a long period of time, they still have some problems compared to the futures market in some developed countries. Specific problems can be shown from the following aspects:

3.1 Lack of relevant legislation

Although China's futures market develops rapidly and improves greatly in terms of the scale, the futures investment funds are lack of standardization and have certain defects in many aspects. To promote the standardization and development of futures investment funds should strengthen the construction of legal system. The improved legal system will guarantee the development of futures investment funds. At present, China still has a lot of problems in the legislation system of futures investment funds, and it has not promulgated the relevant regulations on futures investment funds. Due to the lack of effective laws and regulations, the development of futures investment funds has been severely restricted. In addition, the lack of relevant policies in the development of the China's futures investment fund has affected its development. While the underground futures investment funds in China develop relatively faster, the reason is lacking legislation, leading to the deviation from the direction of developing the futures investment fund.

3.2 Lower professional level of managing financial affairs

Currently, underground futures investment funds in China have few types. Underground futures investment managers mainly use a single type, and their main types of investment are speculation, arbitrage and hedging. Compared with some developed countries, these types of investment are too simple and lack of flexibility. Investment management personnel make use of investment tools, but their simple investment behavior, a lower design level and lack of effective usage of different investment tools result in the ineffective usage of investment tools. The investment behavior is difficult to fully play the role of investment tools. While the United States and other western countries use a variety of investment tools for futures investment. They combine various investment tools, and make a thorough analysis of the characteristics of the investment clients to design the most suitable investment products for the clients, which can improve the reasonability of investment products and also have a very positive impact on the development of futures investment funds.

3.3 Client groups have limitations

With the continuous development of China's futures investment funds, requirements for the investors become higher and higher. According to different futures investment funds, the choice of investors is also different, which makes the investment clients have limitations. At present, futures investment groups are limited to individuals, enterprises and listed corporations in China's futures market. Compared to some developed countries, there is a large gap between investors in China's futures market in terms of investment scope, operability and technologies. At the present stage, there are a lot of investors in the futures market in the United States-all types of investment institutions and individual investors can be involved in the investment of the futures investment funds, which can further promote the development of futures investment funds.

3.4 Higher credit risks

At present, there is a large number of private fund managers in China's futures investment market who have some investment experience. But compared to developed countries, China's financial market is not fully developed in many aspects for lacking perfect market and competitive mechanisms. And some private fund managers are lack of professional qualities and professional ethics, which makes private fund managers for the underground futures lack enough credibility and brings higher credit risks.

3.5 The unsatisfied construction of the internal and external regulatory mechanism

Currently, underground futures investment funds still account for a large proportion in China's futures investment funds and the underground investment activity is not legitimate. Fund managers are lack of independence and relevant national departments don't make enough efforts for supervision, which results in a higher rate of internal transactions and other illegal operating acts. At present, with the development of China's futures investment funds, the risk brought by illegal operating acts has a great impact on the standardized development of the futures investment fund. Therefore, it's necessary to strengthen the construction of the legal system in order to ensure its development, which provides a powerful legal protection. Relevant national departments should actively guide the futures investment fund and give guidance to its right developmental directions. In order to achieve this goal, regulatory authorities must pay more attention to the development and supervision of futures investment funds.

4 Measures to develop the futures investment fund

4.1 To constantly improve laws and regulations

At present, China has to constantly improve laws and regulations of the futures investment fund in order to realize its fast and better development and provide a powerful institutional guarantee. It needs to strengthen the construction of the legal system in the market of the futures investment fund during the process of legislation and makes detailed analysis of the development of futures investment funds in our country based on which management regulations of the futures investment fund are formulated to guarantee its development and promote its legitimate and standardized development. In addition, it should take the development of the futures market into consideration and adjust the measures for managing futures investment funds. The restrictions to develop futures investment funds have to be canceled gradually, and the proportion of futures investment funds in the futures market should be expanded constantly in order to create a good environment for the market to promote the development of futures investment funds.

4.2 To strengthen supervision and management

There are a lot of futures investment funds in China's futures investment market which can also be called underground private funds. This kind of futures investment fund has no legitimacy. Investors face big investment risks and the investment income is not higher. Therefore, private funds of the underground futures have to be brought into the legal system of the futures market to realize the standardized development of the private funds. Now China's private funds have been fully developed. According to the development of the underground futures fund, laws and regulations have to be strengthened to further improve its development and reasonable measures should be taken to guarantee its legitimacy and standardization. With the continuous development of China's futures market, the investors' demand for futures investment will grow bigger and bigger. Therefore, China has to strengthen supervision and management and the construction of the regulatory authorities to promote the development of China's financial business.

4.3 To strengthen the construction of professional teams for investment

In China's futures market, the development of the futures investment funds is very promising. Futures investment managers, as a major force to invest futures investment funds, their professional level and investment experience directly determine whether the futures investment funds can make profits and make a great value. Therefore, it is very important to strengthen the construction of professional teams for investment and improve the comprehensive ability of the managers for futures investment funds, so as to effectively make up for the shortage of talents in the futures investment fund market. With the continuous development of China's futures investment market, the demand for futures investment funds is growing bigger and bigger. However, lack of professional talents with high quality and high level has become an important issue in the development of China's futures investment market. Therefore, the construction of the talent team for futures investment funds should be strengthened in order to continuously improve the development. Specific measures are as follows: Firstly, to introduce foreign talents and learn from foreign successful experience. In the development of futures investment funds, outstanding fund management personnel have to be gathered together. The introduction of talents will alleviate the problem of talent shortage in China's futures market; secondly, to improve talent training mode and cultivate financial talents to meet the requirements of the China's financial market; thirdly, to take the method of vocational training and effectively improve investment fund managers' ability.

5 Conclusion

All in all, the development of the futures investment fund is of great significance for the development of China's financial market. In-depth study about it needs to be

carried out to find problems and put forward effective measures so as to promote the development and progress of China's futures investment funds.

References

1. Xiao Duan, Jia Yuhe. 2004. "Ideas on developing China's futures investment funds," *J. South China Finance*, 6: 41-42, 40.
2. Liu Peng, Zhu Guohua. 2012. "Analysis on the necessity of developing the futures investment funds in China," *J. Modern Management Science*, 7: 28-30.
3. Wu Liping, Li Mei. 2009. "Strategic conceptions on the development of China's futures investment funds in the new period," *J. Financial World*, 1: 14-16.

MATEC Web of Conferences 44, 01008 (2016)
DOI: 10.1051/matecconf/20164401008

The Analysis of the Refined Financial Management of Modern Enterprises

Ran Li

[1]*Ran Li, a teacher with a lectureship in Langfang Polytechnic Institute, Hebei Province, China*

Abstract. This paper briefly introduces the concept of the refined financial management, elaborates on its characteristics and puts forward some main points about it. It also comes up with some personal suggestions for reference on effective ways of refining financial management.

1 The concept of the refined financial management

The refined financial management means that the responsibilities for financial management should be fully fulfilled by refining the management responsibilities to make them specific and clear. It requires relevant people must fulfill their duties to complete their work in the shortest time and to check it seriously. Once they find problems, they have to immediately take corresponding measures to make it right. The specific concept of the refined financial management include the following three aspects: Firstly, comprehensive management should be emphasized. The refined financial management requires enterprises to achieve an overall refinement. Secondly, the refined financial management requires enterprises to realize all-personnel management to finish their financial work together, which will achieve the working efficiency and optimal quality of the financial management. Thirdly, the refined financial management attaches importance to the management of the process. Financial management should fully reflect the characteristics of refinement, and follow-up management should strictly control the details in order to improve them.

2 The characteristics of the refined financial management

Firstly, the enterprise's refined financial management must make significant changes in all aspects to fully reflect the value of the enterprise's economic activities. Its primary goal is to improve the financial management. It will change the implementation of the financial management, including financial functions, financial work and the transformation of the financial working style. In order to realize the refined financial management, enterprises have to adopt the operating and management mode, and control their financial activities in the entire process. Besides, they should change the nature of their work to achieve its service functions.

Secondly, the refined financial management requires to refine financial management to expand its field. Financial management and work quality can be greatly improved by refining and integrating financial management. To expand the field of financial management is good for the implementation of the "huge financial" strategy inside the enterprise. The procedures of the financial management should be constantly standardized and financial management has to be used for production management. Each department should actively cooperate with one another to complete the enterprise's financial management which makes the enterprise's management more flexible and makes it complete its work effectively.

Thirdly, the realization of the refined financial management of modern enterprise should depend on scientific management means and strict management system. Job responsibilities and internal management system have been continuously improved by establishing work norms and supervision mechanism, which realizes a change from the rule of man to the rule of law and guarantees the fairness and objectivity of the financial management.

Fourthly, the goal of the refined financial management should be to improve the efficiency of enterprises. Its implementation needs to further expand the working field in order to realize the potential value of production and operating activities. The high added value of financial activities can be achieved which can increase economic benefits of the enterprises to the utmost.

Article available at http://www.matec-conferences.org or http://dx.doi.org/10.1051/matecconf/20164401008

3 The practical significance of the refined financial management

With the increasingly fierce market competition, modern enterprises have to realize the refinement of financial management in order to adapt to the development of the times. The implementation of the refined financial management can improve its financial management level, which has a very positive impact on the overall development of enterprises. From the perspective of the enterprise, its management should focus on the refined financial management which requires the enterprise not only expands its operating management, but also strengthens the enterprise's internal financial management. It should have dynamic control and management of the enterprise's finance and realize the transformation of the financial management mode. The enterprise should transform its post-accounting to pre-budget, during-the-process control and post-supervision and further constructs its refined financial management system in order to realize centralized management, to further standardize financial accounting procedures, to improve the scientificity and reasonability of the internal control system, and to comprehensively improve the financial analysis system. The implementation of the refined financial management can have a dynamic control over the financial management and make costs get optimal precontrol which enhances the core competitiveness of enterprises.

4 Main contents of the enterprise's refined financial management

4.1 To reinforce the construction of the enterprise's internal control system

With the continuous development of social economy and the increasingly fierce market competition, modern enterprises are confronted with more and more risks in their operating and management, which has had a great impact on their development. In order to realize an effective control of the enterprise's financial risk, it is necessary for the enterprise to establish a scientific and reasonable internal control system. The refined financial management enables to establish the internal control system which will improve the enterprise's risk control level. However, it is necessary to emphasize that the enterprise's refined financial management may have a negative impact on the establishment of the internal control system. Therefore, the enterprise's internal control system must take this problem into consideration and take positive measures to avoid financial risks.

4.2 To reinforce the construction of informatization

The enterprise's refined financial management makes higher requirements for the efficiency of the financial management, and details should be controlled. To reinforce the construction of informatization is good for the realization of the refined financial management. The construction of financial informatization requires to improve both hardware facilities and software. On the one hand, enterprises have to define the scientificity of the informatization content, including decision-making, business and resources and so on. They should also sort out the procedures of informatization construction, specify information analysis, collection and transmission path, etc. On the other hand, enterprises should pay attention to the financial personnel construction. Personnel who have participated in the construction of the informatization system must enhance their training to better improve their comprehensive ability.

4.3 To promote a comprehensive budget management

The realization of the enterprise's management goal requires to improve and promote the construction of a comprehensive budget management mode, which can make the enterprise proactive and realize an effective control of costs. The comprehensive budget management includes the budget management of the asset income and the budget management of the assets investment expenditure. Enterprises need to make a detailed analysis of their planning and assets investment income of the previous year when carrying out investment system budget. They should also assess the achievement of investment projects and market. The assets share and expenditure of the incremental assets can be determined. Stock assets can be adjusted. Adjusting the scale and direction guarantees the enterprise's operation and production. The effective implementation of the enterprise's financial management is based on the scientific assets budget. A specific revenue target must be formulated and then refined. Relevant tasks and responsibilities fall on specific departments and individuals, which will increase the possibility of achieving the enterprise's target.

4.4 To reinforce the construction of the activity-based management system for the refined costs

Compared with the traditional cost accounting method, the activity-based costing method has its advantages-it can be used to accurately share mutual cost by tracking and looking for motives. Enterprises should implement activity-based costing method and carry out research on their process activities, costs items, services and products.

They should also provide scientific and reasonable criteria for the design of the cost model. The enterprise's activity-based costing method makes it possible to achieve cost sharing. In order to make an effective analysis of the enterprise's activities, it is necessary to determine the center of their costs. The establishment of the cost center should consider the enterprise's sectors actual conditions. Some sectors have a direct connection with the products. Their possession of resources and costs have to be calculated. Under normal circumstances, primary-level sectors don't produce excessive costs. They should adhere to the principle of efficiency and avoid separating cost center which can't be separated into more than three ones. The activity-based sharing should choose major tasks to participate regularly in the activities; and some minor tasks can be ignored.

5 Effective methods for the implementation of the enterprise's refined financial management

5.1 To strengthen the construction of the financial management personnel

The financial management personnel are the principal force to carry out financial management. Their comprehensive ability directly determines the efficiency and quality of financial management. Therefore, enterprises must strengthen their internal team construction and improve the overall comprehensive ability of the financial management personnel in order to achieve sustainable development and improve their core market competitiveness. The enterprise should speed up the construction of financial team and improve the quality of personnel according to its financial conditions. The primary task for the enterprise is to cultivate the professional ethics of financial management staff. It should enhance their sense of responsibility and risk awareness and improve their professional responsibility which will be helpful for effectively implementing the enterprise's measures and policies. The enterprise should also improve the enthusiasm of the staff and continuously improve their service awareness. Besides, the enterprise should strengthen the construction of its working style for financial management and correct the working attitude of the financial management personnel. It should cultivate a cautious and careful working style in order to improve the working efficiency and quality. In addition, it should also strengthen the construction of the responsibility system and specify the financial management staff's work and responsibilities fallen on specific sectors and individuals.

5.2 To standardize the procedures of the financial work

The procedures of the financial work have to be standardized in order to achieve the enterprise's refined financial management. The enterprise's management personnel must refine the procedures of the financial management work of each sector which need to be fully grasped and controlled in order to realize the financial management targets. Enterprises can formulate relevant regulations and standards to strengthen supervision and make up for the deficiency of the financial management work which can guarantee the normal operation of the enterprise's economic activities. Thus, the enterprise must refine its procedures of the financial management work in order to achieve the refined financial management. The financial procedures can be optimized to improve the efficiency and quality of financial management.

5.3 To actively change the management concept

Enterprises must actively change their management concepts, establish the concept of refined management, and put forward effective measures in the daily financial management work in order to effectively implement the refined financial management. At present, some enterprises have some misunderstanding about the refined financial management. They regard the financial work as the accounting work, which causes their functions and roles to be not fully played and hinders their development. Therefore, enterprises must change their dated management mode, and make careful analysis of the refined financial management. They should realize the importance of the refined financial management for their development, and change the focus in their operating and management to improve the efficiency and quality of their financial work.

5.4 To promote the construction of informatization of financial management

The realization of the refined financial management must promote the construction of informatization of financial management and strengthen the control of the financial information system. It can be achieved by the following steps: firstly, the enterprise should strengthen the internal auditing control and increase the reliability and authenticity of financial information; secondly, the enterprise should improve the security of information system and restrict the behavior of the personnel who have nothing to do with informatizaion; thirdly, the enterprise should increase the control of financial organizations and strengthen the construction of management system. It should also specify job

responsibilities of the financial management staff and improve its internal organization; fourthly, the enterprise should standardize the procedures of its financial management work; fifthly, the enterprise should strengthen its control over financial accounting to carry out its financial activities perfectly.

6 Conclusion

In summary, it is necessary for the enterprise to realize its refined financial management which is good for carrying out its financial work. At present, there are many problems in the financial management of modern enterprises, which lead to many financial risks in the enterprise's operating and management. So to further study the refined financial management and put forward effective methods will improve the financial management and promote the sustainable development of enterprises.

References

1. Cao Jian. Exploration of the enterprise's refined management. J. Technology wind, 2011, (24): 265-266.
2. Zhang Jingjun. Research on the enterprise's refined management. J. Management and Research on Scientific & Technological Achievements, 2010, (8): 100-101.
3. Zhang Baoding. The refined management of enterprises and the refinement of financial management. J. Contemporary Economic, 2008, (22): 59-60.

MATEC Web of Conferences **44**, 01009 (2016)
DOI: 10.1051/matecconf/20164401009

The methodology of multicriterial assessment of Petri nets' apparatus

Dmitry Pashchenko[1a], Dmitriy Trokoz[2], Galina Sovetkina[3], Ekaterina Nikolaeva[4], Michael Sinev[5], Aleksey Dubravin[6] and Nikolas Konnov[7]

[1234567]*Department of Computer Science, Penza State University, Penza, Russia*

Abstract. This article emphasizes the effectiveness and relevance of the using of the apparatus of Petri nets for modeling of complex computing systems. Due to the fact that the methods of analysis existing in this theory do not allow estimating the resources required to build the desired model of the system, there is a problem of shortage of criteria for its evaluation in terms of the complexity of the construction. In the article we consider the method of analysis of a random Petri net based on the complexity of its building and relationships of internal units - subnets. The purpose of this article is a software implementation of such an assessment within the theory of PN structures. Due to the fact, that structural approach allows to perform the operation of decomposition of the original system, this model can be divided into subnets of minimal dimension, that will allow to make its quantitative assessment - ranking. To determine the total assessment of the input and output data of the system we will perform the analysis of head and tail positions of the net taking into account the weights of the input and output arcs of these positions. In order to identify an extent of the cost required to build the system, the number of operations of union of subnet transitions and positions. These subnets have minimal dimension in the original PN. Thus, the article demonstrates the formal implementation of assessment technique modules with using of algebra of sets, and the rules of splitting the PN structure into elementary blocks are formulated. The example of a comparative assessment of the two Petri nets based on the proposed complexity criteria is given; the plots of PN in different coordinate systems are displayed. The article presents the results of the research - a plot of PN structures in three-dimensional space, implemented using described software. It demonstrates the accuracy of PN assessment by structural analysis in comparing with a non-automated visual one. This approach can be applied for comparative assessment of computer systems in terms of complexity of their construction and size of input and output data.

1 Introduction

The development of modern information technology has already determined the effectiveness of the application of mathematical abstractions in order to identify the properties and behavioral states of complex computing systems. The theories of graphs [1, 2], finite automata [3], as well as the apparatus of Petri nets may be the tools of such research. The article will consider the apparatus of Petri nets which has a powerful formal expressiveness in describing and modelling of computing systems.

In addition, works [4, 5] show the effectiveness of using of the PN theory as a tool to track the system response to the manifestation of various cause-effect relationships, which are widely used in the model description of parallel processes, in sharing of critical resources, in the search for security, persistence, accessibility and vitality of the system. There are several types of PN: time, scholastic, inhibitory, colored and hierarchical ones. The using of the particular specie of net determines the functionality of the system being modeled. For example, the inhibitory nets [6, 7] are used in order to ensure the protection and security of information system, hierarchical ones [8] are to perform the analysis of complex dynamic systems containing embedded nets, scholastic ones [9] are used when it is necessary to provide the random length of the trigging of net transitions.

There are three main groups of methods for analyzing the properties of Petri nets: methods based on the construction of tree of reachable markings and tree of covering markings; matrix methods using the fundamental equation of the net and invariants; reduction methods [10]. It should be noted that the reduction is a complementary research tool and it is a special case of equivalent transformations, reducing the dimension of the net [10].

2 Statement of the problem

The mentioned analysis methods do not allow to characterize the system in terms of the complexity and difficulty of its construction.
Let's consider the example in Figure 1.

[a] Corresponding author: dmitry.pashchenko@gmail.com, dmitriy.trokoz@gmail.com, sovetkina-galja@rambler.ru

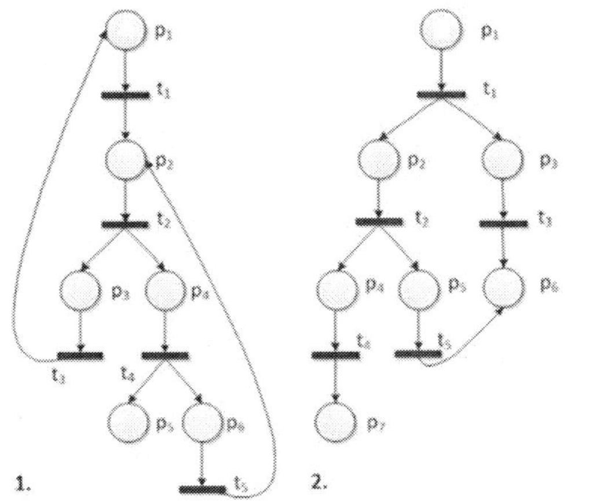

Figure 1. The arbitrary Petri nets.

The nets have the same number of transitions, however, net 1 is composed of 2 cycles, and the network 2 has one position more. It is not possible to determine which of them is more difficult, and with non-automated analysis of bulky computer systems it would be practically impossible.

In order to solve the optimization and verification problems, the concept of structural analysis of system is used; it provides a mechanism of identification of the subsystems of different levels, their relations and connections. Application of the decomposition operation to a discrete system would divide it into several functional parts, which can then be reorganized in order to increase its effectiveness.

Under the grant of RNF for conducting of the fundamental scientific research and exploratory scientific research involving young researchers on the theme "Analysis and synthesis of net structures of complex systems based on tensor and transformational techniques," the task of performing the structural analysis of Petri nets (PN) using the methodology tensor transformations was given. As it is known, tensor calculating [11, 12], is widely used in mechanics (elasticity theory), electrodynamics and in the theory of relativity.

During the work it is planned to find numerous alternative variants of primitive PN by dividing it into partial elements, thereby implementing the conversion of model from one coordinate system to another, using the tensor methodology by introducing space, dimension, defining of the coordinate system, and methods for their conversion. The elementary blocks obtained after decomposition are proposed to be under the operations of union, without breaking the rules of the original system known previously. As a result of the synthesis of the simplest structures we obtain a PN space of varying degree of equivalency to the original net. For the analysis of the obtained structures we will perform the introduction of the assessment system for the apparatus of Petri nets, given below, in order to select the net with a less complex structure.

Taking into account the mentioned facts, it is planned to implement plotting, that displays a set of synthesized PN as points in space, using the software.

3 The formal implementation

The program will be a set of modules; each of them calculates the index of a particular scale.

3.1. Module 1. The scale of number of the simplest elements.

3.1.1 The input data

Petri net *P*, described by the generalized matrix.

3.1.2 Calculating

Let's divide *P* into a set of elementary nets

$$E = \{ e_1, e_2, \dots, e_k \} \quad (1)$$

Elementary net is a net with one input position, one output position and one transition (Figure 2).

Figure 2. The elementary Petri net.

First we hold the decomposition of the net into linear base fragments (LBF) - cycles and chain sequences of transitions and positions, and we get the simplest ones of them. Splitting into linear base fragments (LBF) will be produced with using of the following rules:

1) We perform the splitting of transitions, which have more than one input or output position. The original net is given in the Figure 3 (a), and the net with divided transitions t_1 and t_3 is given in the Figure 3 (b).

2) We exclude the cycles from the obtained net (if there are cycles in the net), dividing positions and transitions if it is necessary, without breaking of existing links. A net element (transition or position) will be divided in case when it has more than one output element or input element (Figure 3c).

3) We isolate the linear sequences of transitions, performing the dividing of positions, if it is necessary, as in the previous step (Figure 3d).

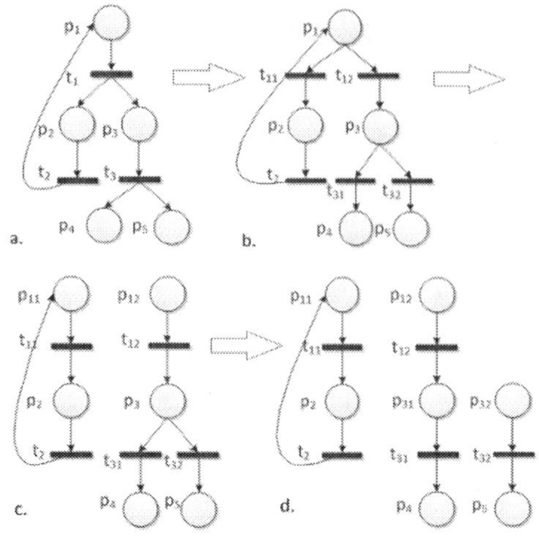

Figure 3. The example of dividing PN into LBF.

To formalize the process of dividing into elementary blocks we introduce the operator J(*P*), which returns a set of elementary elements of the net P. Thus, the value of the scale will be the power of the resulting set:

$$f_1(P) = |J(P)| \quad (2)$$

3.1.3 The characteristic of system

It allows defining the rank of the system.

3.2 The scale of positions' weights

3.2.1 The input data

The incidence matrix D of the net, s_1, s_2 - weights of the head and tail positions, respectively.

3.2.2 Calculating

To find the sum of the weights of positions let's use the formula:

$$f_2(D) = s_1 K_1 + s_2 K_2, \quad (3)$$

where K_1 is the number of head positions, K_2 is the number of tail positions. The values of K_1, K_2 are defined by the incidence matrix. The incidence matrix D has a dimensionality of $m \times n$, where m is a number of positions, n is a number of transitions, and it represents the difference between the input and output matrices:

$$D = D^+ - D^- \quad (4)$$

It is clear that element $d_{i,j}$, $0 \leq i \leq m$, $0 \leq j \leq n$ of matrix D, determines the ratio of the position and the transition in such a way: $d_{i,j} > 0$, if the position belongs to the set of input position of transition, $d_{i,j} < 0$, if the position belongs to a set of output positions of transition, $d_{i,j} = 0$ if the position does not belong to any of these sets or belongs to two sets simultaneously, forming a loop. In this formalism we do not take into account the structures of PN which have loops. It follows that for finding of the tail positions of PN, it is necessary to search for such a row of a matrix, in which for $\forall d_j$ the condition $d_j \geq 0$ would be performed. Similarly, for determining of the head position of the structure it is necessary to search for such a row of matrix in which for $\forall d_j$ the condition $d_j \leq 0$ would be performed.

3.2.3 The characteristic of system

The scale allows to make the total assessment of the input and output data that is interesting in terms of the investigation of the behavior of the whole system, and it can be applied to the models of the "black box" type.

3.3 The scale with the number of operations performing transitions and positions union

3.3.1 The input data

Petri net P described by the generalized matrix.

3.3.2 Calculating

On the stage of the calculation in the module 1, we obtain the sum of the number of dividing of transitions and positions, which in this case will be similar to the sum of the number of union of transitions and positions $f_3(P)$.

3.3.3 The characteristic of system

It allows to define the complexity of a system.

The assessment of the scales all together allows to analyze such criteria as:

1) The complexity of the overall system. It allows to get the most comprehensive assessment of the complexity of the synthesized PN structure.

2) The effectiveness of parallelization. It allows tracking the degree of parallelism of processes.

3) The assessment of the dimension of the system. The ranking of the system.

To determine the optimal element of discrete set of received net, it is necessary to take into account the original model of the system and tasks that it performs. At this stage, the optimal element of the PN set is the one that has the shortest length of the vector:

$$R = \sqrt{f_1^{\,2}(P) + f_2^2(D) + f_3^2(P)} \quad (5)$$

Taking into account the available data, a three-dimensional space is supposed to be built, but there is the prospect of working with hyperspaces. The result of the work is a plot showing a set of PN as points in space, which allows to allocate the nets with the most simple structure and equivalent to the original network.

4 An example

Let's hold the comparative analysis of the complexity of Petri nets presented in Figure 1. For this purpose, we calculate the values for each of them using scales.

4.1 Scale 1

The process of dividing of nets into the linear basic fragments is shown in the figures 4 and 5.

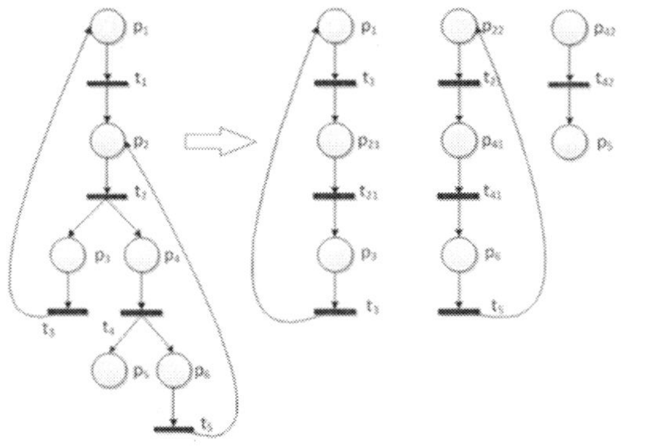

Figure 4. Petri net 1. Dividing into LBF.

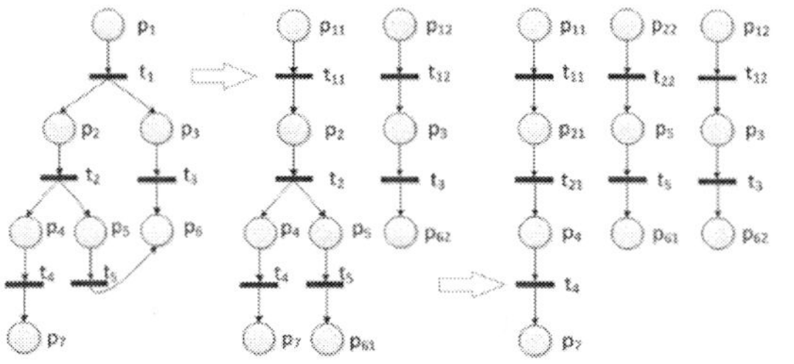

Figure 5. Petri net 2. Dividing into LBF.

We divide the obtained elements into elementary blocks. For the first we obtain a set $E = \{ e_1, e_2, \ldots, e_k \}$ of elementary Petri nets, each of them is described by a variety of positions and transitions.

Table 1. A set of elementary nets E_1 for Petri net 1.

PN e_i	Set of positions	Set of transitions
e_1	$\{p'_1, p'_{21}\}$	$\{t_{11}\}$
e_2	$\{p''_{21}, p'_3\}$	$\{t_{21}\}$
e_3	$\{p''_3, p''_1\}$	$\{t_3\}$
e_4	$\{p'_{22}, p'_{41}\}$	$\{t_{21}\}$
e_5	$\{p''_{41}, p'_6\}$	$\{t_{41}\}$
e_6	$\{p''_6, p''_{22}\}$	$\{t_5\}$
e_7	$\{p_{42}, p_5\}$	$\{t_{42}\}$

Table 2. A set of elementary nets E_2 for Petri net 2.

PN e_i	Set of positions	Set of transitions
e_1	$\{p_{11}, p'_{21}\}$	$\{t_{11}\}$
e_2	$\{p''_{21}, p'_4\}$	$\{t_{21}\}$
e_3	$\{p''_4, p_7\}$	$\{t_4\}$
e_4	$\{p_{22}, p'_5\}$	$\{t_{22}\}$
e_5	$\{p''_5, p_{61}\}$	$\{t_5\}$
e_6	$\{p_{12}, p'_3\}$	$\{t_{12}\}$
e_7	$\{p''_3, p_{62}\}$	$\{t_3\}$

We calculate the capacity of each of obtained sets: $f_1(P_1) = |J(P_1)| = |E_1| = 7, f_1(P_2) = |J(P_2)| = |E_2| = 7.$

From these calculations, it follows that for the construction of both net, the same number of blocks is required.

4.2 Scale 2

$$f_2(D) = s_1 + K_1 + s_2 K_2 \quad (6)$$

We take the coefficients s1 and s2 equaling 1 for both nets.

Let's find the quantity of head and tail positions of net 1, using the incidence matrix D_1.

Table 3. The incidence matrix D_1.

	t_1	t_2	t_3	t_4	t_5
p_1	1	0	-1	0	0
p_2	-1	1	0	0	-1
p_3	0	-1	1	0	0
p_4	0	-1	0	1	0
p_5	0	0	0	-1	0
p_6	0	0	0	-1	1

Table 4. The incidence matrix D_2.

	t_1	t_2	t_3	t_4	t_5
p_1	1	0	0	0	0
p_2	-1	1	0	0	0
p_3	-1	0	1	0	0
p_4	0	-1	0	1	0
p_5	0	-1	0	0	1
p_6	0	0	-1	0	1
p_7	0	0	0	-1	0

$K_1 = 1, K_2 = 1, f_2(D_2) = 2.$

From the obtained values it can be concluded that the Petri net 2 exceeds Petri net 1 in the total amount of input and output data.

4.3 Scale 3

Online references will be linked to their original source, only if possible. To enable this linking extra care should be taken when preparing reference lists.

For calculating the value on the scale it is necessary to know how many unions of positions and transitions of elementary nets we need to make to get the original Petri net. Obviously, the number of unions is identical to the number of dividing of positions and transitions. Let's find such positions and transitions for the first net:

$p_1 = p'_1 + p''_1$
$p_2 = p_{21} + p_{22}$
$p_{21} = p'_{21} + p''_{21}$
$p_{22} = p'_{22} + p''_{22}$
$p_3 = p'_3 + p''_3$
$p_4 = p_{41} + p_{42}$
$p_{41} = p'_{41} + p''_{41}$
$p_6 = p'_6 + p''_6$
$t_2 = t_{21} + t_{22}$
$t_4 = t_{41} + t_{42}$

We have $f_3(P_1) = 10$. We make the similar equations for the second net:

$p_1 = p_{11} + p_{12}$
$p_2 = p_{21} + p_{22}$

$p_{21} = p'_{21} + p''_{21}$
$p_3 = p'_3 + p''_3$
$p_4 = p'_4 + p''_4$
$p_5 = p'_5 + p''_5$
$p_6 = p_{61} + p_{62}$
$t_1 = t_{11} + t_{12}$
$t_2 = t_{21} + t_{22}$
We have $f_3(P_2) = 9$.

The conclusion: the complexity of net 1 building is higher.

The following values were obtained as results of calculations:

Table 5. Results of calculations.

	f_1	f_2	f_3
P_1	7	1	10
P_2	7	2	9

The assessment of PN structures in different coordinate systems is given below. Figure 6 shows the dependence of a structure rank of the total weights of the input and output data, Figure 6 b shows the dependence of the structure rank of the number of operations of transitions and positions union in the elementary PN. After analyzing the comparative characteristics charts, we can conclude that the system described by PN 1, operates with a smaller total amount of input and output data than PN 2. A system described by PN 2, requires less work intensity for its construction.

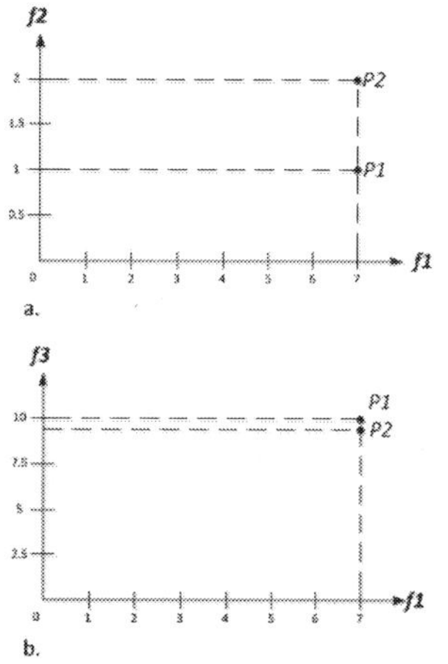

Figure 6. PN in different systems of coordinates.

For the convenience of the visual analysis of structures let's combine axes f_1 and get a chart of the comparative characteristics in three-dimensional space, shown in Figure 7.

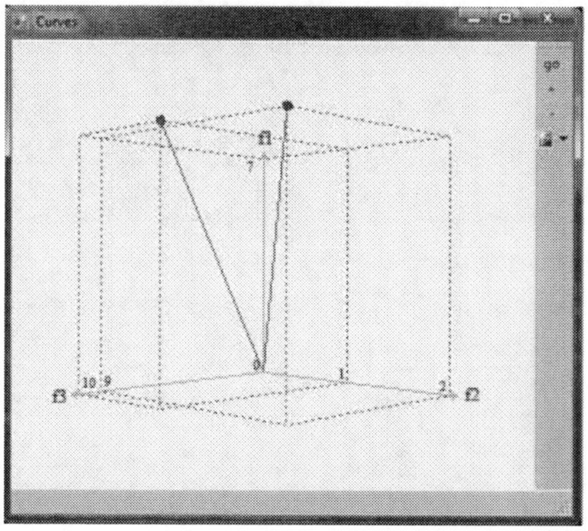

Figure 7. Displaying of PN in three-dimensional space.

This graph is the result of the program described above, which performs a calculating of values for each Petri net using scales and graphically displays the received values as points in three-dimensional space.

Let's calculate the length of the obtained vectors:

$|\overline{P_1}| \approx 12{,}2$, $|\overline{P_2}| = 11{,}5$.

$|\overline{P_1}| > |\overline{P_2}|$, then the first net is more complex than the second one, taking into account the total assessment in all the criteria of complexity.

5 Conclusion

A formalized methodology for quantifying assessment of the complexity of arbitrary Petri nets is described.

During the further research it is planned to develop an algorithm that determines the effectiveness of the assessment system for structures and the extent of the need to introduce new scales.

Acknowledgements

This work was performed as part of the RNF grant for conducting the fundamental scientific research and exploratory scientific research involving young researchers on the theme "Analysis and synthesis of complex net structures of complex systems based on tensor and transformational methods" (convention № 15-11-10010).

References

1. V.P. Kulagin, Automatic Control and Computer Sciences, **23**, 55-61, (New York , 1989)
2. B. Bollobas, *Graph theory: an introductory course*, **63**, (2012)
3. H. Straubing, *Finite automata, formal logic, and circuit complexity*, (2012)
4. T. Agerwala, Computer, 12, 85-94, (1979)
5. T. Agerwala, M. Flynn, ACM SIGARCH Computer Architecture News, **2**(4), 81-86, (1973)

6. D. Pashchenko, D. Trokoz, N. Konnov, and M. Sinev, Procedia Computer Science, 2015, 99-103, (2015)
7. D.A. Zaitsev. Systems Research and Information Technologies, 2, 26–41, (2012)
8. K. Jensen, G. Rozenberg, (Eds.), *High-level Petri nets: theory and application*, (2012).
9. F. Tüysüz, C. Kahraman, Expert Systems with Applications, **37**,5, (2010)
10. D.A. Zaitsev, Cybernetics and Systems Analysis, **42**, 1, 126-136, (2006)
11. W. Hackbusch, *Tensor spaces and numerical tensor calculus*, **42**, (2012)
12. A.J. McConnell, *Applications of tensor analysis*, (2014)

MATEC Web of Conferences 44, 01010 (2016)
DOI: 10.1051/matecconf/20164401010

Construction features of procedural simulator for objective control expert systems management devices of rocket and space technology ground infrastructure objects

Dmitry Pashchenko[1a], Michael Sinev[2], Dmitriy Trokoz[3], Mary Sineva[4], Andrey Tokarev[5] and Aleksey Dubravin[6]

[123456] *Penza State University, Department of Computer Science, Russia*

Abstract. Paper refers to the construction of procedural simulators for expert systems management devices of rocket and space technology ground infrastructure objects. A classification of courses, which allows to realize the development of skills with both hardware and software components of a diagnostic expert systems. A method of calculating the integrated assessment of the student mastery of the material.

Acknowledgements

This paper is made in the framework of the Federal Targeted Programme "Research and development in priority areas of elaboration of the science and technology complex of Russia for 2014-2020" (agreement of 06.19.2014 №14.574.21.0045 UIN:RFMEFI57414X0045)

Introduction

One of the main problems encountered during testing and operation of the devices that control the ground infrastructure objects of rocket and space technology (RST) is to provide tracking of process of their performance [1]. Therefore, the complex includes means of objective control (MOC), providing analysis of complex hardware and operator's actions.

Using of technology of expert systems (ES) allows extending the functionality of the MOC information, documented by management system [2]. However, the ES itself is a complex technological system, and it is required to have certain skills to work with it. Therefore, along with the development of diagnostic ES, there is a research aiming to build their procedural simulators [3].

The aim of the article is to study ways of building of procedural simulators for diagnostic expert systems of devices controlling ground infrastructure RST objects.

1. Classification of training courses

As it is known, there are several classifications of training methods, one of which is the division taking into account the degree of awareness of the perception of educational material: passive, active and interactive. There is also a division into the methods for monitoring the effectiveness, promotion and organization of training process. However, despite the presence of multiple approaches to training, it is difficult to identify a methodology that would become a basis for designing of a simulator with assessment tools for hardware and software complex MOC for military and civilian applications. The procedural trainer (PT) should ensure the acquisition of the trainees the necessary competencies in the form of practical skills of working with ES during the objective monitoring of the results of application of devices which control ground infrastructure of RST using information registered by registration device, as well as a maintenance of technical servicing of ES hardware and software [4].

Taking into account structural features of the hardware-software complex ES performing objective monitoring of devices managing objects of RST ground infrastructure, it is not possible to implement training in all modes using only interactive courses. The mastering of such competencies as setting of ES hardware and software installation requires the using of modern multimedia tools that can be used in videos and tests [5].

In accordance with the classification of training methods [6], we divide them into active and interactive training courses, presented in Figure 1.

[a] Corresponding author: dmitry.pashchenko@gmail.com, mix.sinev@gmail.com, dmitriy.trokoz@gmail.com, mary.sineva@gmail.com, ant19@mail.ru, radamsa@gmail.com

Article available at http://www.matec-conferences.org or http://dx.doi.org/10.1051/matecconf/20164401010

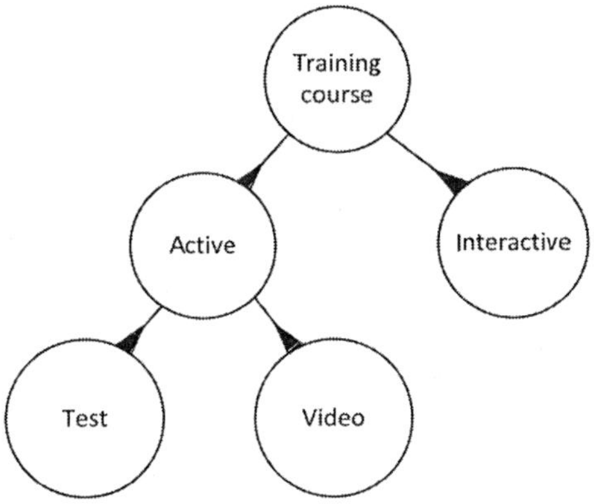

Figure 1. Diagram of training courses classification

Using this classification, it is possible to go to the construction of standard models of training courses.

2. Stages of training

The compositional scheme of the organization of training courses for the PT diagnostic ES for analysis of results of using devices controlling objects of ground infrastructure of RST in terms of ontology language IDEF5 is presented in Figure 2.

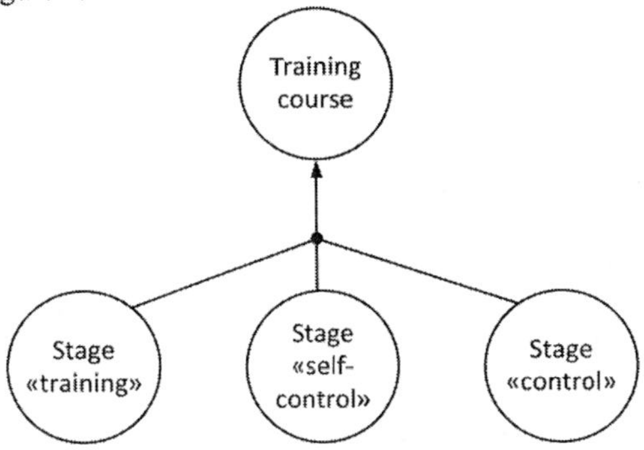

Figure 2. Composite scheme of training course

According to the composite scheme, the mastering of competencies includes the following stages:

- training (direct learning in interactive mode);
- self-control;
- control of the knowledge gained.

The proposed system of construction of training courses using the standard of ontological research IDEF5 [7,8], allows to construct a diagram of trainee's state during mastering of the competencies, that is shown in Figure 3.

Stage of training should be carried out by including the PT into the mode "TRAINING". Thus the trainee has one or several available courses for practical courses, including a variety of scripts and tasks different in structure and content of codes [9]. Courses given by the instructor should be formed on the principle "From simple to complex." PT must provide interactive training mode with the issuance of the necessary clues to the trainee [10].

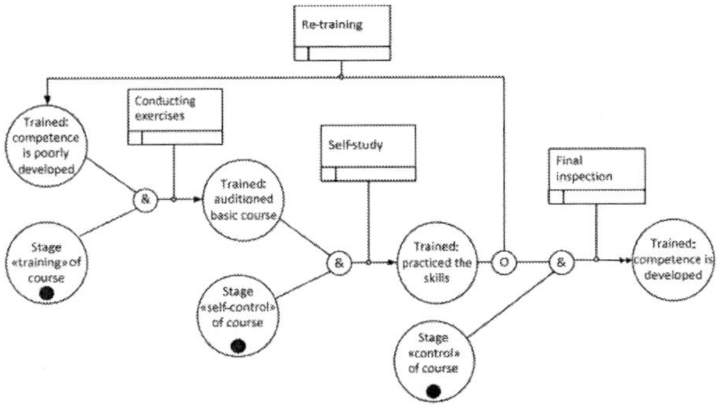

Figure 3. The diagram of the trainees' state during the mastering of competencies

After passing the course, trainee using the "SELF-CONTROL" mode should be offered to solve the test (without giving tips in the normal mode) task on the basis of the passed course. During the self-control mode, practical skills of trainee should be evaluated. Marks obtained by the trainees during the self-control mode aren't taken into account.

Stage of practical skills monitoring should be implemented by turning on "CONTROL" mode in PT. At the same time instructor gives trainee testing courses. Testing courses in their structure and tasks to perform should be similar to courses offered for training. In content, they can differ. In the "CONTROL" mode acquired practical skills of a trainee should be evaluated [11]. Student's mark, formed in the "CONTROL" mode can be corrected by the instructor. This mark comes as a credit for this course.

3. The methodology for calculating the integrated rating of material mastering degree

As a result of a full course of training a certificate with the integrated rating of the material mastering degree is given.

Method of calculation of integral rating is following: for each employee having training courses' marks are selected, they evaluate the quality of his training. For each course, its weight is taken into account, relative to the others, as well as normalization of rating scales occurs, if marks do not match (e.g., 5-point rating system and 100-point system). The formula for calculating the average mark for each trainee is following:

$$Q_{av} = \frac{\sum_{i=1}^{N}(P_i \times f_{norm}(q_i, scale_i, Scale))}{N}, \qquad (1)$$

where P_i is the proportion of the course;

N is a total number of courses;

f_{norm} is a function converting of value q_i of rating scale $scale_i$ to the value of the total scale $Scale$.

In order to determine the proportion of the competence the method by V. A. Blumberg can be used [12. 146]. For doing this, a group of experts is created

(management interested in training), which compares the pairs of courses but does not give any quantitative assessment to these courses. Comparing each time only two of the courses, the expert determines the relationship between them as "more than" (>), "less than" (<) or equal to (=). On the basis of the system of equations represented by experts, the averaged system of comparisons is constructed. Then a square matrix is made using the accepted system.

$$A = \|a_{ij}\|, \qquad (2)$$

where

$$a_{ij} = \begin{cases} 1{,}5 \text{ when } x_i > x_j \\ 1 \text{ when } x_i = x_j \\ 0{,}5 \text{ when } x_i < x_j \end{cases}.$$

Here a_{ij} is a numerical measure that determines the degree of superiority of the course *i* over the course *j*.

Determining of the significance of each course (the value of its priority) is made in such a way:

1. the sum of the elements a_{ij} of rows of the matrix for each course is founded and the total sum of the column is calculated (sum of partial sums obtained in the rows of the matrix);

2. calculation of relative assessments P_i of courses, as the ratio of the sum of the row to the total sum, is made.

Let us consider the following example of calculating the average degree of mastering of the material in the specialization "Engineer" of documenting and displaying console (DDC engineer). For this specialization the courses listed in Table 1 are offered.

Table 1. Training courses in "DDC Engineer"

Number	Name of competence	Rating Scale
1	Installing of general software DDC	5-point
2	Installing of functional software DDC	5-point
3	Technical maintenance of PDO	5-point
4	Comprehensive objective control	5-point
5	Work with the passport of the experiment and the input information, work with menus and basic operations and XML files	passed-not passed (2-point)

5-point rating scale is looking like this:

E[-2] - one does not meet the requirements;

D[-1] - one poorly meets the requirements;

C[0] – one possesses them on an average level;

B[+1] - one meets the requirements;

A[+2] - one meets the requirements perfectly.

The averaged matrix of assessment has the form:

$$A = \begin{bmatrix} 1 & 1{,}5 & 0{,}5 & 0{,}5 & 1 \\ 0{,}5 & 1 & 1 & 1{,}5 & 1{,}5 \\ 1{,}5 & 1 & 1 & 0{,}5 & 1{,}5 \\ 1{,}5 & 0{,}5 & 1{,}5 & 1 & 1{,}5 \\ 1 & 0{,}5 & 0{,}5 & 0{,}5 & 1 \end{bmatrix}$$

Let us find the sum of elements in each row of the matrix *S* and the total sum S_{sum}:

$$S = \begin{bmatrix} 4{,}5 \\ 5{,}5 \\ 5{,}5 \\ 6 \\ 3{,}5 \end{bmatrix};$$

$$S_{sum} = \sum S_j = 4{,}5+5{,}5+5{,}5+6+3{,}5=25;$$

Then, we find the proportion of each course:

$$P = \begin{bmatrix} 0{,}18 \\ 0{,}22 \\ 0{,}22 \\ 0{,}24 \\ 0{,}14 \end{bmatrix}.$$

As it can be seen in Table 1, there are two types of rating scales that are used to evaluate the degree of mastering of the material: 5-point rating system and 2-point rating system (passed-not passed). Therefore, it is necessary to introduce the function of values' convention:

$$f_{norm}(q,2,5) = \begin{cases} -2, \text{ when } q=\text{not-passed} \\ +2, \text{ when } q=\text{passed} \end{cases} \qquad (3)$$

Thus, for the trainee who has got the following marks on the results of the courses:

- installing of general software DDC - B[+1];
- installing of functional software DDC - B[+1];
- technical maintenance of DDC - C[0];
- comprehensive objective control - A[+2];
- work with the passport of the experiment and the input information, work with menus and basic operations and XML files - passed

the average mark will be calculated in such a way:

$$Q_{av} = \frac{1*0{,}18+1*0{,}22+0*0{,}22+2*0{,}24+2*0{,}14}{5} = 1{,}16$$

In accordance with the rating criteria that were introduced previously, the resulting value can be defined as "satisfactory".

4. The interaction between the trainees' workstation and instructor workstation

The interaction between the trainees' workstation and instructor workstation is carried out by the overhead commands with information about the actions of the trainee, the state of the complex, tips, test results, etc.

During the test the instructor controls the correct sequence of commands for a specific time. Thus, there is the concept of exercises scenario. It consists of a set of instructions, in the form of a mandatory and specific sequence occurs in the trainee and the time in which passes the test.

The scenario file is described in a format xml, file encoding of *UTF*-8. Structure description of the scenario workshops on language *XMLSchema* shown in Figure 4.

Where the description string of a single operator action contains the following mandatory attributes:

- *comand* - action of the operators;
- *passing* - fuzzy sequence may wedging other teams prior to this (true, false);
- *itemnum* – item number of sequence;

- *comment* – text comment.

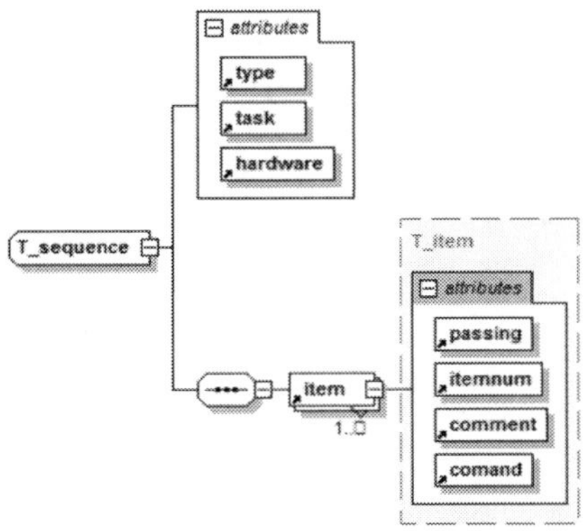

Figure 4. Structure description of the scenario workshops

Order of interaction of trainee and the instructor when passing TRAINING exercises presented using UML sequence diagram in Figure 5.

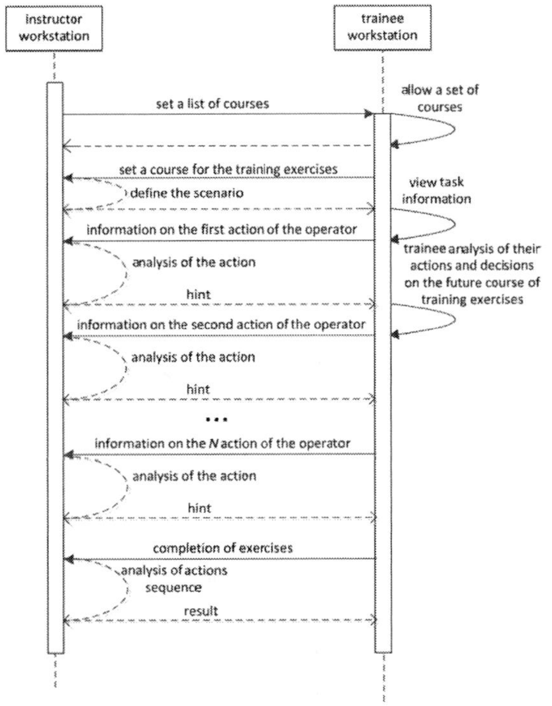

Figure 5. Order of interaction of trainee and the instructor when passing TRAINING exercises

Order of interaction of trainee and the instructor when passing CONTROL exercises presented using UML sequence diagram in Figure 6.

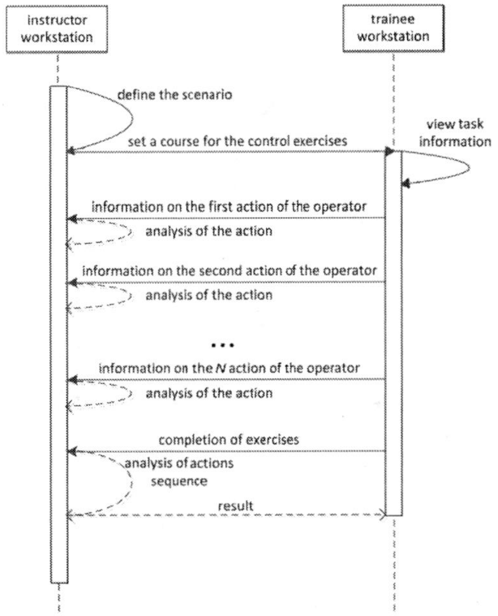

Figure 6. Order of interaction of trainee and the instructor when passing CONTROL exercises

Presented system of training scenarios construction allows the instructor to easily modify existing training courses descriptors, as well as to introduce new courses, thus not requiring a deep knowledge in the field of information technology and programming.

Conclusion

The proposed way of organizing the procedural simulators allows holding multi-user and multi-mode training how to work with the ES devices controlling objects of ground infrastructure of RST and with similar in their functional purpose hardware-software complexes.

References

1. Spaceport in Siberia." Airliners & airports magazine 29.2 (2014).
2. Pashchenko D. V., Sinev M. P. Metodika postroeniya system ob'ektivnogo kontrolya aviatsionnyh radiolokatsionnyh kompleksov // Izvestiya vysshyh uchebnyh zavedeniy. Povolzhskiy region. Technicheskiye nauki. 2009. № 1. P. 49-59.
3. ZHOU, Hui-feng, et al. "Cosmodrome Fault Diagnosis System Based on Case-Based Reasoning." Journal of Sichuan Ordnance 5 (2013): 005.
4. Cencetti, Marco, et al. "SARRIM: A tool to follow the rocket releases used by the CNES Environment and Safety Division on the European Spaceport of Kourou (French Guyana)." International Journal of Environment and Pollution 44.1-4 (2011): 87-95.
5. Bobrova, Ludmila Vladimirovna, and Olga Aleksandrovna Marinova. "Methodological Problems in Organization of Educational Process for

Remote Audience." World Applied Sciences Journal 20.20 (2012): 78-83.

6. Stone, Robert J., Peter B. Panfilov, and Valentin E. Shukshunov. "Evolution of aerospace simulation: From immersive Virtual Reality to serious games." Recent Advances in Space Technologies (RAST), 2011 5th International Conference on. IEEE, 2011.
7. Mayer R.J. Information Integration for Concurrent Engineering (IICE) IDEF3 Process Description Capture Method Report. 1995.
8. Ping J., Peng Z., Wei X. Research on business process simulation method of architecture based on IDEF3 // Management Science and Industrial Engineering (MSIE), 2011 International Conference on. , 2011. PP. 1130–1133.
9. de Winter, Joost CF, Dimitra Dodou, and Max Mulder. "Training effectiveness of whole body flight simulator motion: A comprehensive meta-analysis." The International Journal of Aviation Psychology 22.2 (2012): 164-183.
10. Newman, Michael C., et al. "The role of perceptual modeling in the understanding of spatial disorientation during flight and ground-based simulator training." AIAA modeling and simulation technologies conference and exhibit, AIAA. Vol. 5009. 2012.
11. Chaudron, Jean-Baptiste, et al. "Real-time aircraft simulation using HLA standard." (2011): 1-28.
12. Blumberg V. A., Glushchenko V. F. Primeneniye ekonomiko-matematicheskih metodov dlya upravlencheskih i proizvodstvennyh resheniy. Mashinostroitel'. 1972.

MATEC Web of Conferences 44, 01011 (2016)
DOI: 10.1051/matecconf/20164401011

Scheduling queues in the Ethernet switch, considering the waiting time of frames

Evgeniy Kizilov[1], Nikolas Konnov[1], Kirill Nikishin[1], Dmitry Pashchenko[1,a], and Dmitriy Trokoz[1]

[1]Penza State University, Departmen of Computer Engineering, 40, Krasnaya street, Penza, 440026, Russia

Abstract. Authors proposes an algorithm to scheduling queues with temporal selection of frames in the Ethernet switches with QoS support, which is based on the waiting time of frames in the queues of different classes. Evaluation of the effectiveness of this algorithm compared to the classical cyclic algorithms by simulation with hierarchical temporal coloured Petri nets using CPN Tools package was conducte.

1 Introduction

A necessary requirement to modern networks is the support quality of service (QoS), which enables various network applications to coexist on the same network, without consuming the bandwidth of other applications. Among the mechanisms to ensure quality (marking and traffic classification, Scheduling queues, congestion control, bandwidth control) is the most important mechanism for Scheduling queues, i.e. the selection rules of the queue to read data which directly determine the frame delay, its variation (jitter) and the probability of their loss [1,2].

In the intelligent Ethernet switches with QoS support for queuing the cyclic algorithms are widely used that provide traffic prioritization and allocation of guaranteed bandwidth to individual classes: Weighted Round Robin (WRR) and Deficit Round Robin (DRR). In these algorithms for each traffic class its own queue is allocated in the buffer of the output port. Queues are serviced in order of ascending of their numbers, if there is the absence of frames in some queue, the algorithm switches to another queue.

The amount of data sent from each queue during one session of servicing, is set by its assigned weight which determines allocated for the corresponding traffic class bandwidth of an output port.

In the algorithm WRR weight specifies the maximum number of frames transmitted from the queue in one session, and in the algorithm DRR weight specifies number of bytes of data. Difference between DRR and WRR algorithm is that if a situation arises when the band of queue has not been developed, but it is not sufficient for transmission of the next packet, then the problem frame packet is transmitted, but the amount of information which exceeded the allocated band is subtracted from the newly allocated for this queue bandwidth in the next cycle of servicing. This allows you to select more accurately the desired band with a significant spread of sizes of frames in queues [3].

An advantage of cyclic algorithms is an exception of the monopolization of channels and the ease of implementation, and the disadvantage of cyclic algorithms is the uncontrolled size of jitter of switched frames from the spread waiting time of frames in different queues, which is caused by the deterministic order of service. Besides, the delay of frames of a certain class of QoS and the size of the corresponding queue depend on the allocated bandwidth for a specific class. It leads to increasing of delay of frames and congestion of queues in channels with small assigned bandwidth when there is the pulsating character of the traffic, as the round robin algorithms do not effectively redistribute unused bandwidth underutilized channels to extend the overloaded bandwidth

2 The principle of queuing with time selection of frames

To solve this problem, the authors propose a new algorithm queue control, called "Time Selection Service" (TSS), which is based on the waiting time of frames in the queues of different classes.

The TSS algorithm works in such a way:

- each frame sent in the appropriate class QoS queue, is supplied the attribute, marking time of setting in queue;
- after the end of the servicing the next queue the controller of switch analyzes the attributes of frames which are in the queues and selects for the further servicing of queue with its smallest value, i.e., the queue with the most "old" frame at the moment;
- from the analysis of queues the last serviced one is eliminated (except when all other queues are empty);

[a] Corresponding author: dmitry.pashchenko@gmail.com

- to regulate the bandwidth of each traffic class the standard methods of weighting (WTSS) or deficit (DTSS) are used.

3 Modeling by Petri nets

Evaluating the effectiveness of the TSS-algorithms compared with WRR and DRR algorithms is implemented by their simulation modeling in CPN Tools package, using the mathematical apparatus of hierarchical temporal coloured Petri nets. Freeware CPN Tools package was selected as tool system, which due to a rich set of extensions allows simulating various aspects of the behavior of telecommunication systems [4].

The structure of the Petri net modeling TSS-algorithms is built on the principles defined in [5] and in many respects is similar to the previously developed networks, modeling the WRR and DRR algorithms [6,7]. Within developing of the model the methodology of top-down design was used. Model Petri net of the switch on the top level of the hierarchy is shown on Figure 1, it actually follows the structure of the switch [5] and includes:

- Subnet "Bufer", which simulates a frame buffer directed to the corresponding output port of the switch. This subnet actually implements QoS mechanisms, so it will be considered further.

- Subnet "Outport", which simulates the switch ports that provide access to the Ethernet communication lines. This subnet generates the delay serialization during the transmitting of frames, the duration of which depends on the size of the preamble and interval of frames.

- Subnet "SetTrafGenerator" that simulates the flow of frames belonging to different QoS classes and following through the time intervals distributed according by a given law [8].

-The position of "Outport", containing the tokens that imitate the frames of switched traffic.

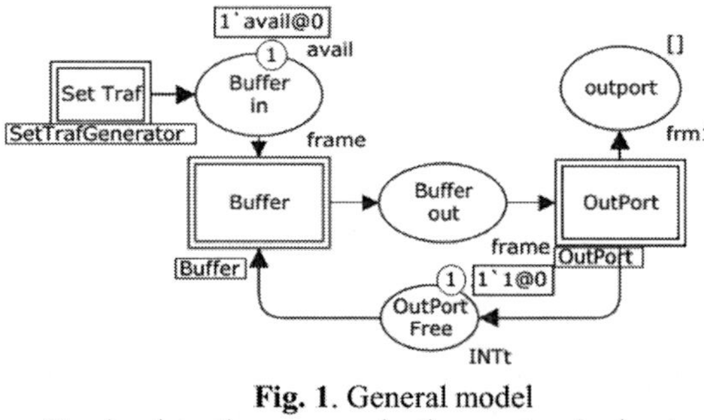

Fig. 1. General model

To simulate the communication protocol of network devices it is very important to effectively use the apparatus of color tokens. Network traffic is modeled by a sequence of tokens received at the input ports and leaved from the output ports, colours of which form a tuple frm of fields corresponding to the frame format Ethernet 802.1 q/p [9]: source and destination addresses, the field tag with information about belonging to a specific priority level, a field indicating the length of the payload of the frame, as well as servicing time field the parish and the outcome of the frame (used to collect statistics). The variety of colors frame is also used, it is the bearer, which may be either busy sending a frame frm, or free avail, that allows to detect and handle events related to the presence or absence of the frame. Additionally, the tokens are introduced, they reflect the colour characteristics of the utility model (queue size, amount of transferred data, the attribute of queue cleaning et al.).

The model of "Buffer" (fig.2) serves queue of 4 QoS classes and contains the following elements:

- "Buffer in" and "Buffer out" - input and output positions of subnet;

- "Classifier" – subnet of classifier, which analyzes the token of input frame and sends it to one of four queues, simultaneously sending to "Count time" the token the colour of which is set in equal to the value of model time of arrival of the token frame (attribute);

-"Queue1", ... "Queue4" - subnets of queues containing frame tokens, waiting for servicing. Subnet is also formed in the positions "indicator1", ... "indicator4" the colour of the token that reflects the time of admission to queue of the frame located at the head of the appropriate queue, and in the positions of the "Size Queue1", ... "Size Queue14" the colour of the token indicating the size of the queue is formed;

- "Scan" – is subnet, which implements the TSS-algorithm of queuing, forming the token for one of the positions "Start selection1", ... "Start selection4";

- "bend1", ... "bend4" – is subnet, allocating bandwidth for the traffic of each queue;

-"Number Queue" - position that contains the number of the queue that was last serviced;

="Holder" – position the token of which synchronizes the operation of the subnet "Scan" and "bend";

-"OutPortFree" - position reflecting the state of the output port.

After classification the next incoming frame token is transmitted to one of the queues "Queue", each of which contains two FIFO buffer for token of frames and their attributes. Let's note that to describe the queue the language CPN ML is used, which allows to represent the queue by one token, which is a list of frames. In the initial marking the list is empty.

The size of the buffers can be defined in frames or in bytes, depending on the method of bandwidth control. Work of the buffers during writing and reading is synchronized, so that the head token of queue of attributes is always placed in the position "Indicator". The subnet "Queue" is also counting the current size of the queue displayed in the token position "Size Queue", and is resetting the tokens when the queue is full.

Reading from the queues is performed on arrival of the authorizing token at the position "Start selection" from the subnet "Scan", which selects the served queue as follows:

- when there is the releasing of an output port, it writes the corresponding position "OutPortFree" the authorizing token, if there is the token then a subnet "Scan" analyzes the colour of the token in "Holder";

- if it is 0, it means that the session of service the previous queue, the number of which defines the colour of the token at position "Number Queue", is finished, the

subnet "Scan" comparing attribute values in the positions "indicator" defines the queue attribute of which has the smallest value and sends it to position "Start selection4" of the tokens. Thus if there are multiple active queues it prevents duplicate service of previously served queue, which will eliminate the monopolization of the output port of any queue.

- if token color is 1, the subnet "Scan" sends a permissive reading in position "Start selection4" of the queue, the number of which specifies the colour of the token at position "Number Queue", so the session of servicing of selected before queue is continued.

Subnet "Bend" implements the allocation of bandwidth for each queue by setting a quota of data transferred in one session of service. For the WTSS algorithm weight set for queues 1, 2, 3 and 4 that sets a quota in the frames and for the DTSS algorithm sizes of a quota are set to 1500, 3000, 4500 and 6000 byte.

In addition to the calculation of transferred data while promoting in the "Buffer out" of each frame, subnet sets the colour of the token in the position "Number Queue", equal to the number of the served queue, and the colour of the token in the position "Holder" is set to 1 during transmitting of all frames except the last one in the servicing session, which is zero colour of this token.

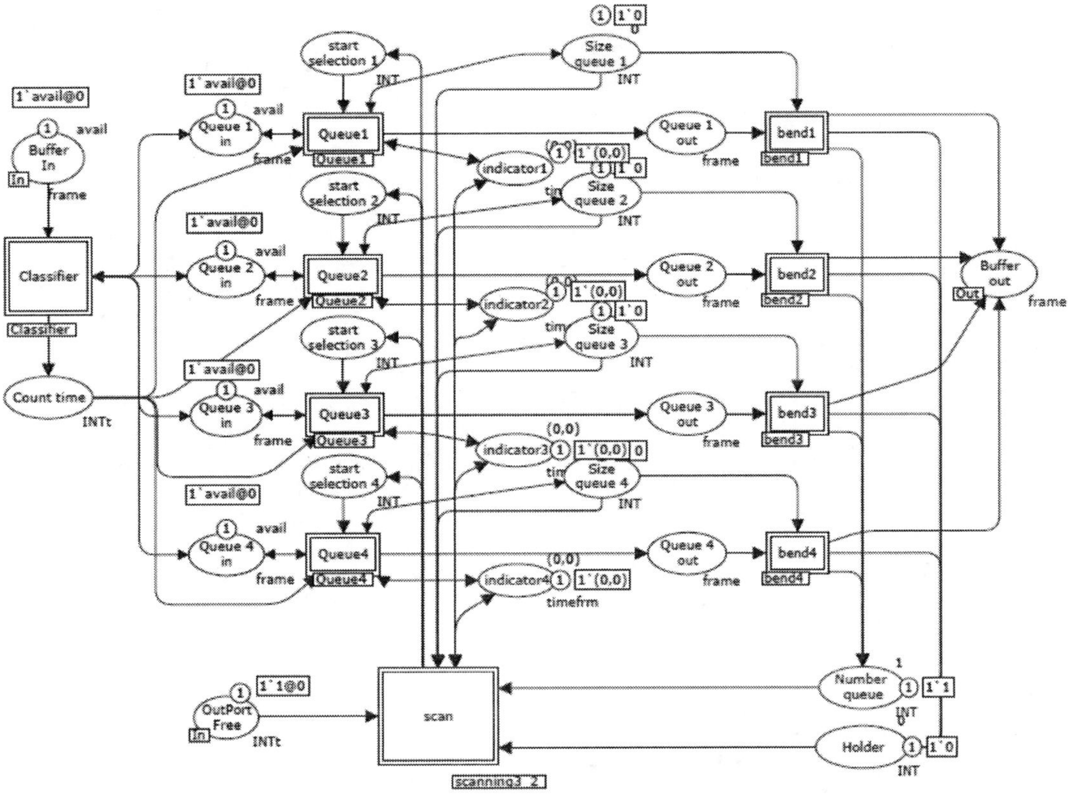

Fig.2. Subnet of the Buffer of Output Port

4. Discussing of modeling results

The proposed model allows to investigate the probabilistic-temporal characteristics (average delay, jitter, percentage of packets lost) of mixed traffic, switched to the Ethernet.

As an example of using of the proposed model, the results of the evaluation of the distribution function of the jitter of frames with different QoS classes with algorithms queuing WRR, DRR [6,7] and WTSS, DTSS are shown below.

The input traffic is modeled with using of special Petri nets [8] and represents a combination of stream of frames belonging with equal probability to 4 QoS classes and following through the time intervals distributed exponentially with an average value of the delivery period, and quasi-regular steam with rare frames of the maximum duration. Model time is expressed by clock intervals TI, which is equal to 100 ns for Ethernet or 10 ns for Fast Ethernet. The random frame length has the following distribution corresponding to real networks [10]: 25% of all frames have a minimum and maximum length (512 and 12176, respectively), length of remaining ones is evenly distributed in the remaining range.

Noticeable difference in the statistical characteristics of the jitter frames RR- and TSS-algorithms is occurred when the load factor of the channel is greater than 0.5. The following data for the load factor of the channel is equal to 0.8. The frames have uniform QoS labels from 0 to 7. 4 classes of traffic are formed, the appropriate queues are allocated for them, and the following values of the bandwidth are set:

- queue with QoS 0-1 – 10% of the output bandwidth;

- queue with QoS 2-3 – 20% of the output bandwidth;
- queue with QoS 4-5 – 30% of the output bandwidth;
- queue with QoS 6-7 – 40% of the output bandwidth;

As well, the generated traffic of class QoS 0-1 exceeds the allocated bandwidth in 2 times, QoS 2-3 is agreed with the allocated bandwidth and QoS 4-5 and 6-7 – underutilize the allocated bandwidth.

The average values of frame delay for each class, received during the simulation are presented in Table 1, show that the TSS-algorithms reallocate unused bandwidth, in order to reduce the delay in overloaded queues at the expense of the most underutilized ones.

Table 1. Average values of frame delay (jitter)

QoS class	Average delay (TI)			
	WRR	DRR	WTSS	DTSS
0-1	55601	45788	45544	28279
2-3	27631	28429	26554	32967
4-5	20688	25676	24634	30710
6-7	21817	26018	29094	33807
All	31434,3	31477,8	31456,5	31440,8
Variation of average delay	34913	20112	20910	5528

Using algorithms posravneniyu EYY QC reduces the variation of the average delay for the different classes of traffic qo 1.68 to 3.64 times.

The fact that the redistribution of unused bandwidth graphs illustrate the probability distribution functions of jitter for classes QoS 0-1 (overloaded), and QoS 6-7 (underused) are shown in Fig. 3.

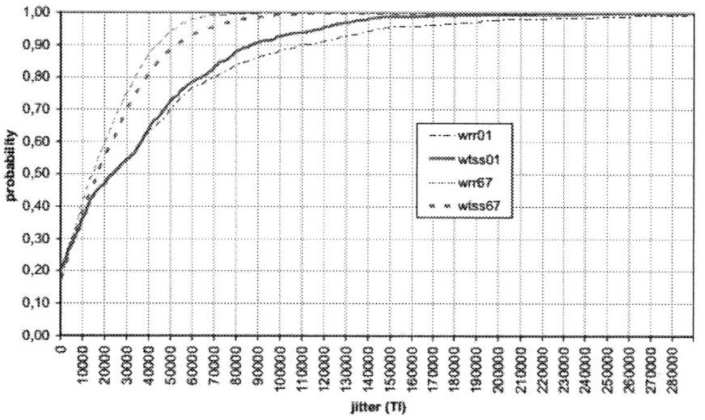

Fig.3. The probability distribution functions of jitter for classes QoS 0-1 QoS 6-7 и scheduling algorithms WRR and WTSS .

5.Conclusions

Thus, it can be considered that TSS-algorithms provide a range of delays in the promotion of traffic of different classes, as well as more comfortable conditions for the transferring of traffic with different classes in case of imbalance of bandwidth allocated to them, at the expense of more fair and effective redistribution of unused resource.

Acknowledgements

This paper is made in the framework of the Federal Targeted Programme "Research and development in priority areas of elaboration of the science and technology complex of Russia for 2014-2020" (agreement of 06.19.2014 №14.574.21.0045 UIN:RFMEFI57414X0045).

References

1. N. Olifer, V. Olifer. *Computer Networks: Principles, Technologies and Protocols for Network Design,* Wiley E-Text, (2007)
2. Miguel Barreiros, Peter Lundqvist *QOS-Enabled Networks: Tools and Foundations*. (2011)
3. S. Vegesna. *IP Quality of Service.* Cisco Press,(2001)
4. K. Jensen, L. Kristensen. *Coloured Petri Nets: modelling and validation of concurrent systems.* (2009)
5. D.A. Zaitsev. Mathematics and Computers in Simulation. 65, 245-249 (2004)
6. V.B. Mehanov, E.A. Kizilov. *Novyie informatsionnyie tehnologii i* sistemyi, **1**. 67-73 (Penza, PGU, 2010)
7. E. Kizilov, N., Konnov, D Pashchenko, D. Trokoz, *2015 5th International Workshop on Computer Science and Engineering: Information Processing and Control Engineering,(WCSE 2015-IPCE), 185-*190. (Moscow, 2015)
8. K.I. Nikishin, N.N. Konnov, A.L. Domnin. *Sovremennyie problemyi kompyuternyih nauk (SPKN-2013).* 120-123 (Penza, PGU, 2013)
9. E. Niclas. IEEE 802.1 P,Q - QoS on the MAC level, http://www.tml.tkk.fi/Opinnot/Tik110.551/1999/papers/08IEEE802.1QosInMAC/qos.html
10. R. Sinha, C. Papadopoulos, J. Heidemann. Internet Packet Size Distributions: Some Observations. Technical Report ISI-TR-2007-643, USC/Information Sciences Institute, (2007). http://netweb.usc.edu/ rsinha/pkt-sizes

MATEC Web of Conferences **44**, 01012 (2016)
DOI: 10.1051/matecconf/20164401012

The methodology for constructing the linear and linear-cyclic basic fragments by means of decomposition of PN-model

Dmitry Pashchenko[1,a], Dmitriy Trokoz[1], Nikolas Konnov[1], Andrew Krasnov[1], Paul Chechel[1] and Tania Pashchenko[1]

[1] *Penza State University, Department of Computer Science, 440000 Penza Krasnaya 40, Russia*

Abstract. This article gives a brief analysis of the subject area and the approaches to the analysis and synthesis of models of complex systems structures were discussed. A number of problems occurred; these problems can be effectively solved with using of the method generally considered in this article. This article describes an approach to the construction of a system of linear and linear-cyclic basic fragments as a part of the method for obtaining the equivalent PN-model with tensor methods by decomposition of initial one. The rules describing the implementation of the various stages of the construction of a system of linear and linear-cyclic base fragments were introduced. An alternative method of vertical division of transitions in the PN-structure was suggested, it allows saving all available links.

1 Introduction

Currently, there is a continuous increase in the complexity of computing systems for information processing in all modern human activities. Each computing system has a number of parameters, and importance of which varies in different fields of application. The tendency to optimize the parameters of operation of a finite computing system requires the developers to do hard work in the modeling stage, where a fundamental working model of functional processes of developed system is constructed [1-6].

There are many methods of analysis and synthesis of models of complex systems' structures, based on a structured approach [7], the methods of the upstream and downstream designing, metamodelling and others. However, as it is noted by Kulagin [8], the contradiction between the complexity made by modern systems and traditional approaches to their designing, today one of the main issues of the theory of systems is defined, it is development of a methodology and the designing of systems of computer-aided design, solving not support, but the main task of synthesis.

The requirements described above have led to the emergence and development of the system approach to the design of complex systems, the concept of which does not contradict the classical structural approach. In accordance to it, there are the following stages:

1. the development of a number of hypotheses concerning the structure of the subsystems of which the projected system will consist of;
2. the formation of the finished candidate structures from the given sub-systems;
3. analyzing of each structure in order to determine the characteristics that allows reducing the number of candidate structures and ultimately selecting the final structure.

In his works V. P. Kulagin is considering described above method for the analysis of complex systems, based on the synthesis of a variety of candidates, and offers the following way for practical implementation: to use Petri nets as structure models of systems.

2 Way to build alternatives

The approach defining the mechanism for constructing alternative variants (the equivalent PN-models) is presented below.

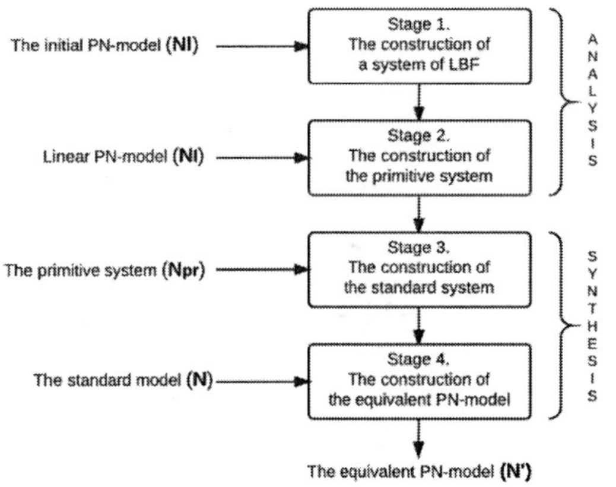

[a] Corresponding author: dmitry.pashchenko@gmail.com

Figure 1. The scheme of stages of constructing the equivalent PN-model.

The following definitions are introduced:

• *The initial PN-model* (**N$_I$**) – is a model, for which it is necessary to do an analysis;

• Linear PN-model (**N$_l$**) – is PN, obtained by decomposition of the initial PN-model (**N$_I$**) and given by the set of linear and linear-cyclic basic fragments (LBF);

• The primitive system (**N$_{pr}$**) – is a set of elementary nets, the power of which is defined by the number of transitions of linear PN-model (**N$_l$**);

• *The standard model* (N) – is PN, obtained from a primitive system by union of a set of vertices given in advance *(by performing of a program of synthesis);*

• The equivalent PN-model (**N'**) – is PN, obtained from the standard model by means of tensor of transformation;

As part of this article the first stage is considered, the problems and an implementation details - decomposition of the initial PN-model and the construction of a system of linear and linear-cyclic basic fragments (LBF) in the example of the initial structure of Petri net and the vector of initial marking given below.

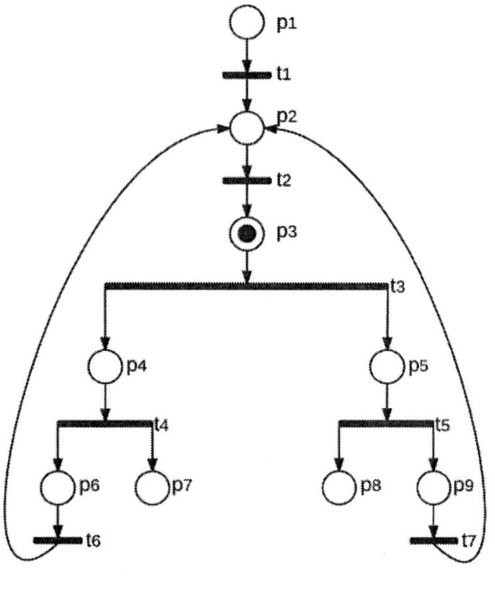

Figure 2. The initial PN-structure.

Table 1. The initial vector of marking.

P1	P2	**P3**	P4	P5	P6	P7	P8	P9
0	0	**1**	0	0	0	0	0	0

For the decomposition of the initial PN-model and the construction of a system of linear and linear-cyclic basic fragments it is required:

1. to identify sequentially and separate the shortest cycles;
2. to select alternately the branches with the maximum length.

As a result, the initial PN-model is transformed into a non-connected graph consisting of a system of linear and linear-cyclic base fragments.

Let's prepare an initial PN-model for convenient selection of cycles, dividing vertically all the transitions that have more than one input or (and) one output position. The method described below is an alternative one - in contrast to one proposed by Kulagin [2], it allows to split the transition without losing any links.

3 The vertical dividing of transition

If for a transition t_i the following conditions are true:

$$\mathrm{pre}(t_i) = \{p_{11}, p_{12,\dots,}p_{1m}\}, \mathrm{post}(t_i) = \\ = \{p_{21}, p_{22,\dots,}p_{2n}\}; \quad (1)$$

and

a) $$\mathrm{pre}(t_i) = \{p_{11}, p_{12,\dots,}p_{1m}\}, \mathrm{post}(t_i) = \\ = \{p_{21}, p_{22,\dots,}p_{2n}\};\ m > n, \quad (2)$$

• when n > 1 the transition is divided into transitions t_i^1, t_i^2, for which it is true that:

$$\mathrm{pre}(t_i^1) = \{p_{11}, p_{12,\dots,}p_{1m}\}, \mathrm{post}(t_i^1) = \{p_{21}\} \quad (3)$$

$$\mathrm{pre}(t_i^2) = \{p_{11}, p_{12,\dots,}p_{1m}\}, \mathrm{post}(t_i^1) = \\ =\{p_{22}, p_{23,\dots,}p_{2n}\}; \quad (4)$$

• when n = 1 the transition is divided into transitions $t_i^1, t_i^2, \dots, t_i^n$, for which it is true that:

$$\mathrm{pre}(t_i^1) = \{p_{11}\}, \mathrm{post}(t_i^1) = \{p_{21}\}$$
$$\mathrm{pre}(t_i^2) = \{p_{12}\}, \mathrm{post}(t_i^2) = \{p_{21}\} \quad (5)$$
$$\dots$$
$$\mathrm{pre}(t_i^n) = \{p_{1n}\}, \mathrm{post}(t_i^n) = \{p_{21}\}$$

b) m < n ,

• when n > 1 the transition is divided into transitions t_i^1, t_i^2, for which it is true that:

$$\mathrm{pre}(t_i^1) = \{p_{11}\}, \mathrm{post}(t_i^1) = \{p_{21}, p_{22,\dots,}p_{2n}\}; \quad (6)$$

$$\mathrm{pre}(t_i^2) = \{p_{12}, p_{13,\dots,}p_{1m}\}, \mathrm{post}(t_i^1) = \\ =\{p_{21}, p_{23,\dots,}p_{2n}\}; \quad (7)$$

• n = 1; then the transition is divided into transitions $t_i^1, t_i^2, \dots, t_i^n$, for which it is true that:

$$\mathrm{pre}(t_i^1) = \{p_{11}\}, \mathrm{post}(t_i^1) = \{p_{21}\}$$
$$\mathrm{pre}(t_i^2) = \{p_{11}\}, \mathrm{post}(t_i^2) = \{p_{22}\} \quad (8)$$
$$\dots$$
$$\mathrm{pre}(t_i^n) = \{p_{11}\}, \mathrm{post}(t_i^n) = \{p_{2n}\}$$

After vertical dividing of all the transitions, which have more than one input or (and) one output position the initial PN-model was transformed to the following form.

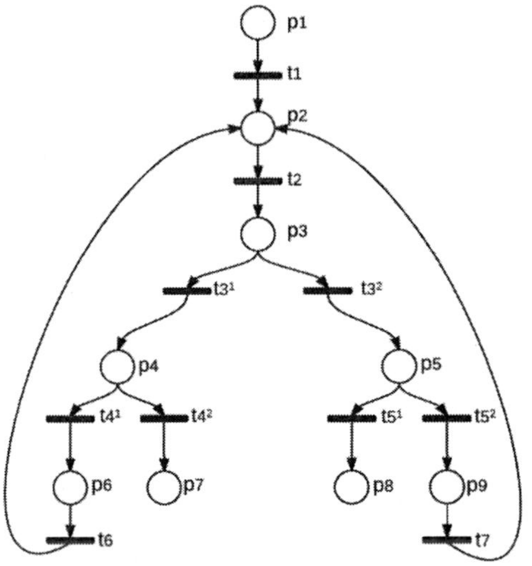

Figure 3. PN-structure after the vertical dividing of transitions.

In next step we will select all the cycles in the transformed PN-structure. We construct the adjacency matrix of transitions from the row-vertex to the column-vertex:

Table 2. The adjacency matrix.

	P_1	P_2	P_3	P_4	P_5	P_6	P_7	P_8	P_9
P_1	0	**1**	0	0	0	0	0	0	0
P_2	0	0	**1**	0	0	0	0	0	0
P_3	0	0	0	**1**	**1**	0	0	0	0
P_4	0	0	0	0	0	**1**	**1**	0	0
P_5	0	0	0	0	0	0	0	**1**	**1**
P_6	0	**1**	0	0	0	0	0	0	0
P_7	0	0	0	0	0	0	0	0	0
P_8	0	0	0	0	0	0	0	0	0
P_9	0	**1**	0	0	0	0	0	0	0

Let us use the following algorithm:

If a vertex has only input or only output arcs, then it obviously does not occur in any cycles. You can remove all such vertices from the graph with all the related arcs.

As a result, new vertices will occur, having only input or only output arcs. They are also to be removed. The iterations are repeated as long as the graph does not stop changing. The absence of any changes indicates the absence of cycles, if all the vertices have been removed. Otherwise, all the remaining vertices necessarily belong to cycles.

Table 3. The adjacency matrix after the applying of algorithm for cycles searching.

	P_2	P_3	P_4	P_5	P_6	P_9
P_2	0	**1**	0	0	0	0
P_3	0	0	**1**	**1**	0	0
P_4	0	0	0	0	**1**	0
P_5	0	0	0	0	0	**1**
P_6	**1**	0	0	0	0	0
P_9	**1**	0	0	0	0	0

As a result of the applying of algorithm, two cycles have been selected in the converted PN-structure:

- $\{P_2, P_3, P_4, P_6, P_2\}$
- $\{P_2, P_3, P_5, P_9, P_2\}$

In the next step we alternately separate the shortest cycles of the PN-structure. Due to the fact that the resulting cycles have equal length, we separate the first obtained cycle from the PN-structure.

During the separating of vertices cycle, transitions that intersect with the rest of the PN-structure (with more than one input or output position or transition) also will be divided taking into account copying of token if it presents there.

In this case, after separating of the first cycle, the second one exists no longer - as the transition **t2** remained in the first cycle.

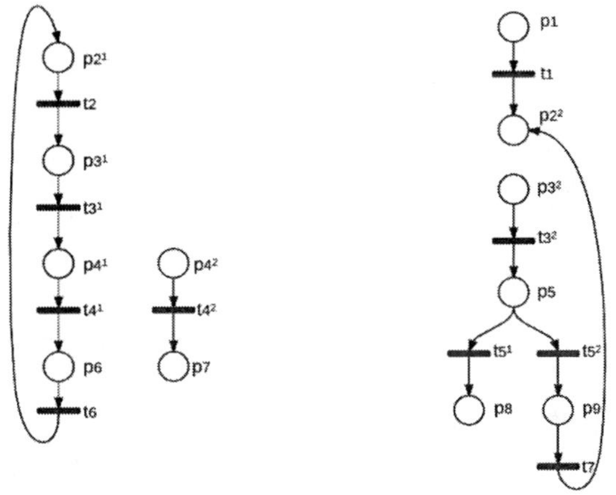

Figure 4. PN-structure after the separating of a cycle.

Because of the fact that all the cycles were separated from the PN-structure, we go to the final stage of the transformation of the initial PN-structure to the system of linear and linear-cyclic basic fragments – we select linear fragments, taking into account the requirement to minimize redundancy and condition for the separation of only those vertices and transitions that have more than one input and output position or transition, as well as rule for copying of token, taking into account its presence.

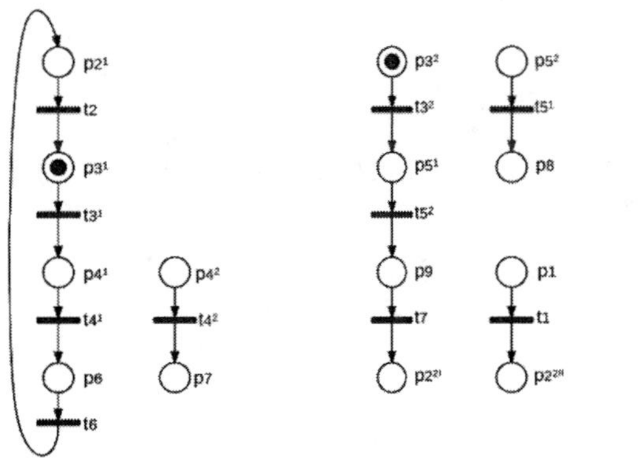

Figure 5. The system of LBF of the initial PN-structure.

The system of LBF obtained taking into account the introduced rules, is the minimal possible one, and it is

equivalent to the initial PN-structure due to the using of an alternative method of vertical dividing of transitions with saving of all the initial links. This LBF system can be used in the following stages of the algorithm of *constructing an equivalent model* [9-10].

The example illustrating the algorithm for *constructing the LBF system* was based on a relatively simple initial PN-structure. To work with PN-structures organized more complexly, software for automation of constructing of LBF system is required [11-12]. Further it is supposed to integrate software for the automation of constructing of LBF-systems with the software products designed to automate the following stages of the algorithm for constructing the equivalent PN-models in a common comprehensive software solution for the user.

Acknowledgment

The development of software for automating of the construction of LBF system is performed within RSF grant to conduct fundamental scientific research and exploratory scientific research involving young researchers on the theme "Analysis and synthesis of complex net systems based on tensor and transformational methods" (convention № 15-11-10010).

References

1. D. A. Zaitsev. IEEE Transactions on Systems, **44**, 1–12 (2013)
2. M. Beccutti, E. Bibbona, A. Horvath, R. Sirovich, A. Angius, G. Balbo. App. and Theory of Petri Nets and Con., 273–293 (2014)
3. T. Chatain, S. Haar. Transact. on Petri Nets and Other Models of Con. IX, 83–98 (2014)
4. K. S. Cheung. *Augmented Marked Graphs* (2014)
5. S. Y. Li, A. M. An, Y. Wang. Journal of Intelligent Manufact., **24**, 1157–1173 (2013)
6. S. Li, Y. Che, W. Liu, H. Wu, Y. Cai. Inform. Science and Manag. Engineer. II, **3**, 19–28 (2015)
7. D. Pashchenko, D. Trokoz, N. Konnov, M. Sinev. Procedia Computer Science, **49**, 99–103 (2015)
8. V. P. Kulagin. *Razrabotka teoreticheskih osnov i instrumental'nyh sredstv avtomatizirovannogo proektirovanija struktur parallel'nyh vychislitel'nyh sistem na osnove tenzornogo ischislenija setevyh modelej* (1995)
9. W. Reisig. *Understanding Petri Nets: Modeling Techniques, Analysis Methods, Case Studies* (2013)
10. M. Diaz. *Petri Nets: Fundamental Models, Verification and Applications* 656 (2013)
11. E. Kizilov, D. Pashenko, D. Trokoz, N. Konnov 5th International Workshop on Computer Science and Engineering Information Processing and Control Engineering, WCSE 2015-IPCE, 185-190 (2015)
12. A. V. Dubravin, S.A. Zinkin, D. V. Paschenko. Int. Siberian Conf. on Control and Communic., (2015)

MATEC Web of Conferences **44**, 01013 (2016)
DOI: 10.1051/matecconf/20164401013

Applying an e-PBL Platform to Develop a Storytelling-Based Arithmetic Card Game

Li Ling Hu[1, a] and Shian Shyong Tseng[2]

[1]*Department of Computer Science and Information Engineering, Asia University, Taiwan (R.O.C.); Department of Digital Media Design, Tatung Institute of Technology, Taiwan (R.O.C.)*
[2]*Department of M-Commerce and Multimedia Applications, Asia University, Taiwan (R.O.C.)*

Abstract. Mathematics is a very important learning subject. Mathematical knowledge can be learned by traditional or distance learning, but the mathematical problem solving ability is hard to improve without experiences through practice. Therefore, developing an interesting learning game to enhance students' problem solving ability is the major concern in this paper. Since the storytelling strategy has been proved to be useful to enhance the students thinking ability, we develop a storytelling-based arithmetic card game to encourage and guide students to speak out their thinking process of problem solving, where the e-Project-Based Learning (e-PBL) platform has been applied to brainstorm the characteristics of the game and construct the storytelling script. Thus, the misconceptions can be easily diagnosed. To evaluate the performance of our approach, 40 5-grade primary school students have participated in the storytelling-based arithmetic card game experiment. The experimental result shows that the storytelling-based learning can enhance the mathematical problem solving ability via playing the game.

1 Introduction

Mathematics is a very important learning subject which can be directly or indirectly applied to solve a lot of real problems in our daily life. In addition to mathematical concepts or knowledge, problem solving ability including inference ability, abstract ability, and calculating ability is also very important [1]. Mathematical concepts or knowledge can be learned by traditional or distance learning, but the problem solving ability is hard to improve without experiences through practice. As we know, game-based learning is a promising approach to enhance the students learning interest and motivation. Therefore, developing an interesting learning game to enhance students' problem solving ability is the major concern in this paper.

There are a lot of mathematical games to assist and enhance students' mathematical knowledge or ability, such as 2048, Decimal Number Puzzles, Sum Tracks, and so on. But, the traditional arithmetic games rarely diagnose players' misconception in mathematics. Since the storytelling strategy has been proved to be useful to enhance the students thinking ability, it will be adopted to encourage and guide students to speak out their thinking process of problem solving. Thus, the misconceptions can be easily diagnosed.

The e-Project-Based Learning (e-PBL) platform can be applied to brainstorm the characteristics of the game and construct the storytelling script in game developing [3-4]. Therefore, our idea is to use it to develop an arithmetic card game to enhance students' mathematical problem solving ability. But, applicable techniques are still needed to construct the storytelling script, including scenes and interactive dialogues, to guide students speak out and improve the learning effectiveness [5-6]. For finding the way of student's thinking, we need to find the strategy used by students in problem solving. As we know, problem decomposition strategy, the basic one for reducing the problem difficulty, could be recursively applied to decompose the original problem into several simple sub-problems, and therefore the backward reasoning can be embedded in the storytelling script construction as the scaffolding for learning. The 24 Game, an arithmetical card game, consists of four cards and combines them to 24 with addition, subtraction, multiplication, or division operations [2]. Since it can be easily decomposed into sub-problems, it will be used as an example to illustrate our idea. Firstly, we define *X-card Y game* to represent the arithmetical card game consisting of X cards and combining them to Y with addition, subtraction, multiplication, or division operations. And then, the 4-card 24 game can be decomposed to a 3-card game or a 2-card game according to whether some card being used as an operand of the chosen last arithmetic operation. Similarly, the 3-card game can be further decomposed to a 2-card game. Accordingly, the students can enhance the inference ability, abstract ability, calculating ability, and recursive concept via the arithmetic card game.

The backward reasoning ability of students can be trained to infer the solution of the 4-card 24 game and

[a] Corresponding author: jasmine819@gmail.com

their misconceptions in mathematical problem solving ability can then be diagnosed. In this paper, we focus on developing a storytelling-based arithmetic card game.

Based on the e-PBL platform, the arithmetic card game development consists of game analysis phase, storytelling construction phase, and game developing phase, where each phase consists of four steps, case inquiry, brainstorming, collaborating and discussing, to provide appropriate case scaffolding. The students brainstorm and achieve the storytelling-based game collaboratively in each phase. The students' learning path will be stored as their learning portfolio.

To evaluate the effectiveness of our approach, 40 5-grade primary school students have played the arithmetic card game to enhance the mathematical problem solving ability, and 34 students got the good learning performance in the assessment. It means that the storytelling-based learning can enhance the mathematical problem solving ability via playing the game.

2 Related works

2.1 Learning by storytelling

Since 2010, storytelling has been widely used in learning knowledge and skills. Storytelling allows students to collect information, to stimulate ideas, and to encourage students organize their knowledge structure from the storyline [7]. It is a good approach for improving students' learning motivation and establishing self-confidence [8-14]. Hung et al. [15] claimed that the storytelling can improve students' learning motivation, problem-solving ability, and learning achievement.

As mentioned above, many tools have been proposed in enhancing students' learning. However, it is required to construct storytelling script for learning by storytelling. Moreover, problem decomposing strategy will be applied in this paper to help students inferring the solution of the 24 Game and then enhancing students' mathematical problem solving ability. Thus, how to construct storytelling scenes and interactive dialogues for students learning becomes an important and interesting issue.

2.2 e-PBL

PBL has been proved to be an effective learning strategy [16]. With the progress of new era, e-PBL (PBL joins the IT technology) is used as a powerful tool to simulate the dangerous or expensive projects and provide scaffolding assist students learning [17-18]. However, without good platform, the previous cases cannot be properly stored and reused, and the achievement cannot be easily assessed. PBL platform using CBR (Case Base Reasoning) techniques is a good e-PBL platform to provide the case scaffoldings and reserve the learning portfolio [19]. The e-PBL platform is a multi-spiral learning model. In the spiral learning model, the learning objectives can be gradually achieved from outside to inside, each of which can be beneficial from the e-PBL platform using CBR techniques.

Therefore, e-PBL using CBR techniques can provide appropriate learning scaffolding to assist students and improve learning performance.

3 Applying e-PBL to Develop a Storytelling-Based Arithmetic Card Game

3.1 e-PBL Platform for Arithmetic Card Game

The e-PBL platform in Hu et al. [19] has been modified for developing arithmetic card game using problem decomposition strategy, as shown in Figure 1. It consists of game analysis phase, storytelling construction phase, and game developing phase. The e-PBL platform is a multi-step spiral model, each spiral of e-PBL platform corresponds to a phase, each phase consisting of four steps: case inquiry, brainstorming, collaborating and discussing.

Step1. *Case inquiry*: CBR case retrieve technique is used to inquire appropriate case scaffoldings.

Step2. *Brainstorming*: CBR case reuse or case revise technique is used to assist student to brainstorm.

Step3. *Collaborating*: Students collaborate to stimulate the brainstorming outcome.

Step4. *Discussing*: CBR case retain technique is used to assist student to discuss experiences.

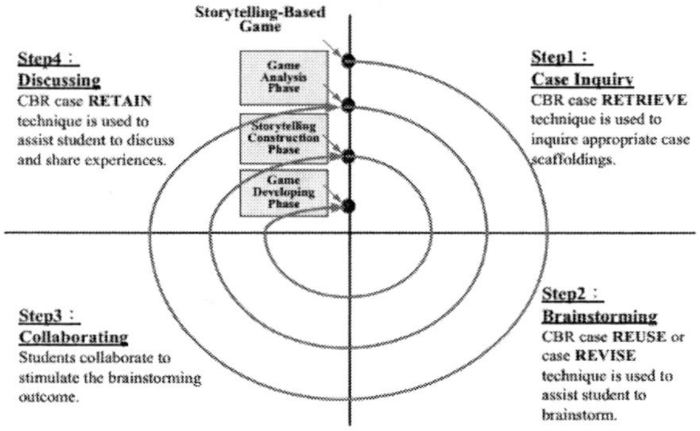

Figure 1. The multi-step spiral e-PBL platform for developing arithmetic card game.

3.2 Phases on e-PBL Platform

For illustrate our idea, the formal definition of the game is given as below.

Definition: **X-card Y game** is an arithmetic card game consists of X cards and combines them to Y with addition, subtraction, multiplication, or division operations, where X=2, 3, 4 and Y=1, 2, … , 24.

We use the 4-card 24 game as an example to elaborate the application of e-PBL platform to develop a storytelling-based arithmetic card game for assisting students to enhance mathematical problem solving ability, including inference ability, abstract ability, and calculating ability. The development of the storytelling-based arithmetic card game can be divided into game analysis phase, storytelling construction phase, and game developing phase.

3.2.1 Game Analysis Phase

In case inquiry step, the CBR case retrieve technique is used to inquire appropriate case as the case scaffoldings. In brainstorming step, the CBR case reuse or case revise technique is used to assist student to analyse the characteristics of 4-card 24 game. As shown in Figure 2, the AND/OR tree, which is a tree structure of the reduction of problems to conjunctions and disjunctions of sub-problems, can be used to represent the decomposition process of the 4-card 24 game. It can be seen that the 4-card 24 game can be decomposed to three cases according to whether some card being used as an operand of the chosen last arithmetic operation:

(1). If some card is used as the first operand, the 4-card 24 game is decomposed to 3-card game.

(2). If some card is used as the second operand, the 4-card 24 game is decomposed to 3-card game.

(3). Otherwise, the 4-card 24 game is decomposed to two 2-card games.

The 3-card game can be further decomposed to a 2-card game. Therefore, the students can learn the recursive concept in the arithmetic card game. In collaborating step, students collaborate to stimulate the brainstorming outcome. In discussing step, the students discuss and clarify the learning process of the phase and share their experiences with each other.

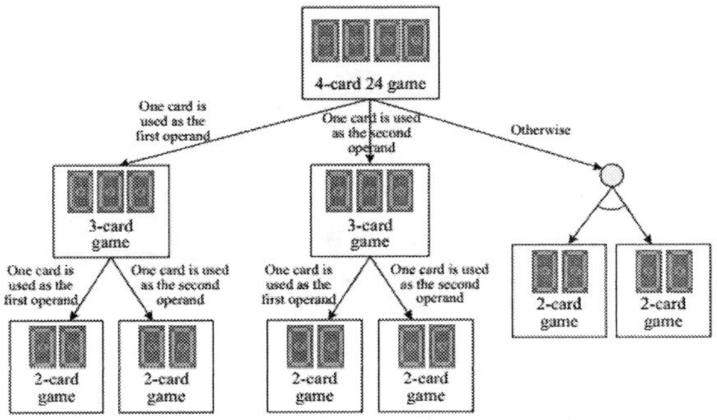

Figure 2. The characteristics of 4-card 24 game.

3.2.2 Storytelling Construction Phase

In case inquiry step, the CBR case retrieve technique is used to inquire appropriate case as the case scaffoldings. In brainstorming step, the CBR case reuse or case revise technique is used to assist student to brainstorm the storytelling script and assessment framework; the storytelling script consists of scenes and interactive dialogues; the assessment framework consists of the concept index and ability index. As mentioned in analysis phase, the storytelling script can be composed of the dialogues and the scenes of solving 4-card game, 3-card game, and 2-card game, as shown in Figure 3, Figure 4, and Figure 5, respectively, where the backward reasoning method is used to guide students to infer the solution in each scene. According to mathematics education target [1], the mathematical problem solving ability consists of inference ability, abstract ability, and calculating ability. The relationship between the scenes of the game and the problem solving abilities is shown in Table 1 for helping the diagnosis of the students' misconception in mathematics. In each scene, students brainstorm with the interactive dialogues, as shown in Table 2. Some game rules which can assist students to infer whether the final operation could be a multiplication are shown in Table 3. The collaborating and discussing steps are the same as those in the previous phase.

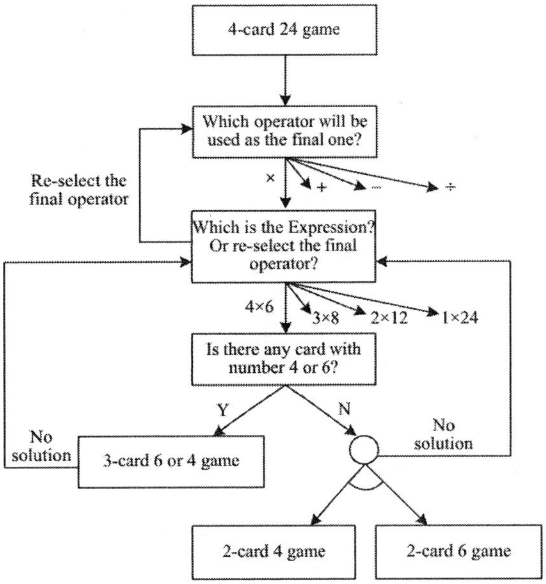

Figure 3. The dialogues and the scenes of solving 4-card game.

(a). The final operator is "+" or "-"

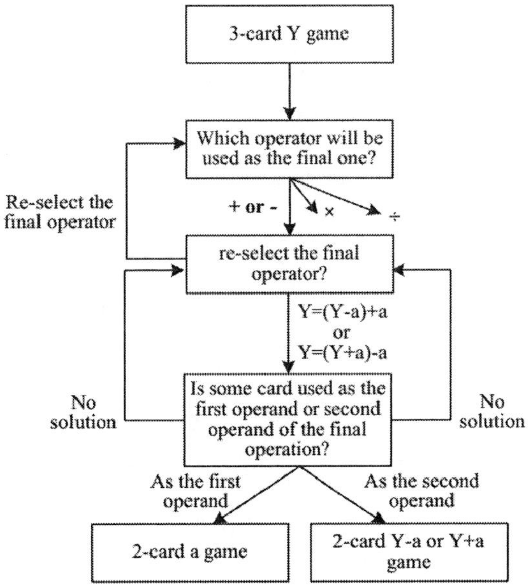

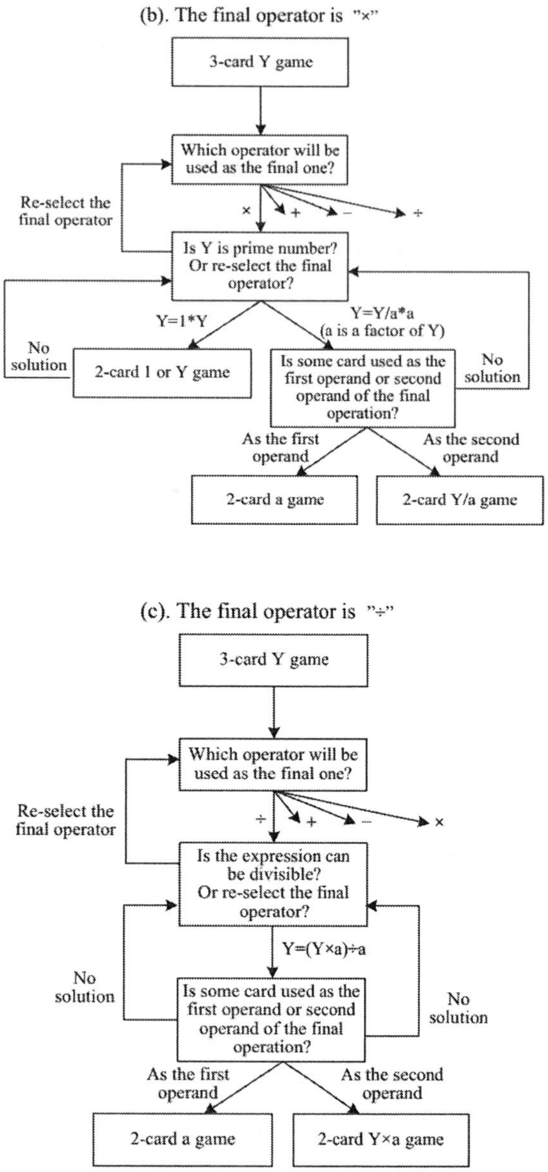

Figure 4. The dialogues and the scenes of solving 3-card game.

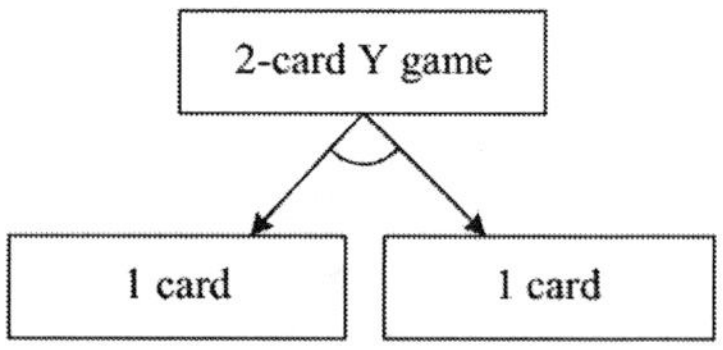

Figure 5. The scenes of solving 2-card game.

Table 1. The relationship between the scenes and abilities.

Scene \ Ability	Problem solving ability
4-card scene	Inference ability
3-card scene	Abstract ability
2-card scene	Calculating ability

Table 2. The storytelling interactive dialogues.

Scene \ Dialogues	Storytelling interactive dialogues
4-card game	1. Which operator will be used as the final one? 2. Which is the expression? Or re-select the final operator? 3. Is there any card with number ( )?
3-card game	1.Which operator will be used as the final one? 2.Is ( ) a prime number? Or re-select the final operator? 3.Is the expression can be divisible? Or re-select the final operator? 4.Is some card used as the first operand or second operand of the final operation?

Table 3. The game rules.

Game rules
If there exist two cards with two consecutive numbers, then these cards can be combined to 1.
If there exist two cards with the same number, then these cards can be combined to 0 or 1.
If there exist three cards with three consecutive numbers, then these cards can be combined to any one of three numbers.
If there exist three cards with the same number, then these cards can be combined to the number.

3.2.3 Game Developing Phase

In case inquiry step, the CBR case retrieve technique is used to inquire the similar case as case scaffoldings. In brainstorming step, the CBR case reuse or case revise technique is used to assist student to brainstorm the context of the game. In collaborating step, students develop the storytelling-based arithmetic card game collaboratively. In discussing steps is the same as those in the previous phase.

4 Experiment

With the storytelling-based arithmetic card game, students can accumulate the experiences through practice and enhance their mathematical problem solving ability during playing the game. When the game started, if the students did not solve the problem by themselves, the interactive dialogues will be provided to assist and guide them to solve the problem.

40 5-grade primary school students can enhance the mathematical problem solving ability through the arithmetic card game. Before the game playing, we firstly introduce the 24-card game to the students, and showed them related website arithmetic learning games. As shown in Figure 6, 34 students have the high learning performance. It means that the storytelling-based learning system can enhance students' mathematical problem solving ability.

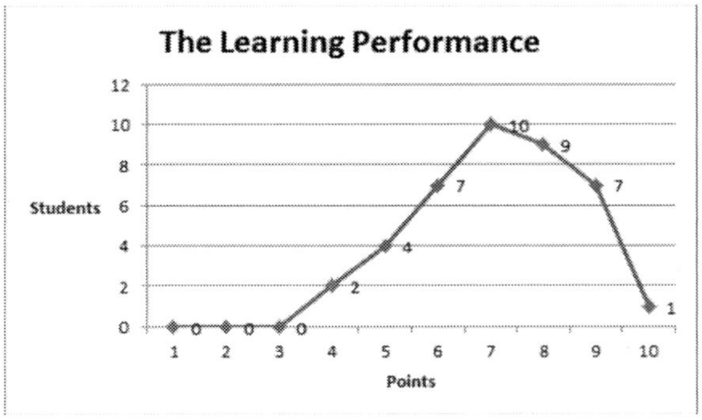

Figure 6. The learning performance of 40 5-grade students.

5 Conclusions

For accumulating students' experiences through practice, we apply an e-PBL platform to develop a storytelling-based arithmetic card game to assist students to enhance mathematical problem solving ability. Applying the e-PBL platform, students brainstorm the characteristics of the game and the storytelling interactive dialogues. The experimental result shows the backward reasoning method combining the recursive problem decomposition strategy can guide students to infer the solution of 4-card 24 game. In the near future, we will focus on finding players' frequent error pattern from their learning portfolio in order to analyse the students' misconception.

Acknowledgements

This work was partially supported by the National Science Council of the Republic of China under grants MOST 104-2511-S-468-002-MY2 and MOST 104-2511-S-468-005-MY2.

References

1. Information on http://teach.eje.edu.tw/data/files/class_rules/math.pdf, (2015)
2. Information on https://en.wikipedia.org/wiki/24_Game, (2015)
3. P.H. Hung, G.J. Hwang, Y.H. Lee, T.H. Wu, B. Vogel, M. Milrad, E. Johansson, A Problem-based Ubiquitous Learning Approach to Improving the Questioning Abilities of Elementary School Students, *Educational Technology & Society*, 17(4) (2014) 316-334
4. H.S. Barrows, Problem-based learning in medicine and beyond: A brief overview, *New Directions for Teaching and Learning*, 68 (1996) 3-12
5. G.J. Hwang, Y.R. Shih, H.C. Chu, A concept map approach to developing collaborative Mind-tools for context-aware ubiquitous learning. *British Journal of Educational Technology*, 42(5) (2011) 778-789
6. C.E. Mora Luis, J.M. Gutierrez, A.M. González Marrero, Using mobile devices and internet technologies in problem-based learning: Design of a suitable active and collaborative learning environment in engineering education, *Frontiers in Education Conference (FIE)*, 2014
7. L. Malita, C. Martin, Digital Storytelling as web passport to success in the 21st Century, *Procedia-Social and Behavioral Sciences*, 2(2) (2010) 3060-3064
8. T. Grisham, Metaphor, poetry, storytelling and cross-cultural leadership, *Management Decision*, 44(4) (2006) 486-503
9. C. Haigh, P. Hardy, Tell me a story - a conceptual exploration of storytelling in healthcare education, *Nurse Education Today*, doi: 10.1016/j.nedt.2010.08.001, (2010)
10. P.R. Lowenthal, Digital storytelling: An emerging institutional technology? In K. McWilliam & J. Hartley (Eds.), Story circle: Digital storytelling around the world, *Oxford: Wiley-Blackwell*, (2009) 252-259
11. P.R. Lowenthal, J.C. Dunlap, From pixel on a screen to real person in your students' lives: Establishing social presence using digital storytelling, *The Internet and Higher Education*, 13(1-2) (2010) 70-72
12. G. Stacey, P. Hardy, Challenging the shock of reality through digital storytelling, *Nurse Education in Practice*, 11(2) (2011) 159-164
13. K. Gyabak, H. Godina, Digital storytelling in Bhutan: A qualitative examination of new media tools used to bridge the digital divide in a rural community school, *Computers & Education*, 57(4) (2011) 2236-2243
14. Y. T. C. Yang, W. C. I. Wu, Digital storytelling for enhancing student academic achievement, critical thinking, and learning motivation: A year-long experimental study, *Computers & Education*, 59(2) (2012) 339-352
15. C. M. Hung, G. J. Hwang, I. Huang, A Project-based Digital Storytelling Approach for Improving Students' Learning Motivation, Problem-Solving Competence and Learning Achievement, *Educational Technology & Society*, 15(4) (2012) 368-379
16. P.C. Blumenfeld, E. Soloway, R.W. Marx, J.S. Krajcik, M. Guzdial, A. Palincsar, (1991). Motivating Project-Based Learning: Sustaining the Doing, Supporting the Learning, *Educational Psychologist*, 26(3-4) (1991) 369-398
17. B. Rienties, B. Giesbers, D. Tempelaar, S. Lygo-Baker, M. Segers, W. Gijselaers, The role of scaffolding and motivation in CSCL, *Computers & Education*, 59(3) (2012) 893-906.
18. H.C. Chu, G.J. Hwang, Development of a project-based cooperative learning environment for computer programming courses, *International Journal of Innovation and Learning*, 8(3) (2010) 256-266.
19. L.L. Hu, S.S. Tseng, J.F. Weng, Building Project-Based Learning Platform for the Capstone Project, *23rd International Conference on Computers in Education*, Nov 2015.

MATEC Web of Conferences 44, 01014 (2016)
DOI: 10.1051/matecconf/20164401014

Third-party Reverse logistics platform and method Based on Bilateral Resource Integration

Hong Zhen Zheng[1,a], Dian Hui Chu[2] and Ming Shun Shao[3]
[123]*Department of Computer Science & Technology Harbin Institute of Technology Weihai, 264209, China*

Abstract. Dispersion of reverse logistics resources makes it difficult to create relationships between demanders and providers, thereby the personalized demand for the construction of enterprise reverse logistics cannot be satisfied and the service quality cannot be guaranteed. Aiming at these problems, this paper presents a platform and method of enterprise reverse logistics based on bilateral resource integration (RLBRI). The method creates a third-party reverse logistics platform to accumulate a mass of reverse logistics demanders and providers together. And the platform integrates bilateral resources and acts as an intermediary to establish relationships between two sides. Through the platform, a complete and high-quality business chain for enterprise reverse logistics will be built efficiently. Finally put forward an effective strategy of non-defective reverse logistics depends on the integrity checking service provided by third-party logistics. By using this strategy it can short the distance of non-defective reverse transportation. Computational tests validate the strategy.

1 Introduction

There is an increasing trend toward sustainable and green supply chain design and management in today's business world. In terms of execution and practice, reverse supply chain management is an effective way for enterprises to achieve sustainability and become green and lean. Reverse supply chains deal with products that have reached the end of their life cycles or the ones returned by the final users. Furthermore, reverse supply chain management can reduce the negative environmental impacts of waste disposal and resource extraction, and reduce production costs. It considers a generic electronic product that can be remanufactured or recycled at the end of its life cycle to generate new profit. Amy Z. Zeng [6] explores a revenue-sharing coordination mechanism which generate insights on how to manage an efficient consumer-retailer-manufacturer reverse supply chain, as well as on the feasibility of simplifying such a three-stage chain structure. More and more enterprises have recognized the importance of reverse logistics on enterprise's competitive advantages, ultimate issue of profitability, environment-friendly image and better consumer service [2,7]. However, reverse logistics is actually very involved and can be extremely complex, which severely constrains the development of the enterprise reverse logistics. BIRIS [4], a new service application mode designed by our lab ICES, is proposed for solving the difficulties to create relationships among a large number of suppliers and demanders and to guarantee the service quality. In this mode, a third-party platform was imported to accumulate a mass of customers and providers together, and it could collect customer resources to providers and integrate service resources to customers. At present, our laboratory has done some researches on BIRIS-based forward logistics which proves BIRIS can better solve the problems of logistics field. In addition, gathering and integrating reverse logistics resources reasonably, and building relationships between suppliers and demanders of the reverse logistics efficiently [3] are two key steps to establish enterprise reverse logistics. So this paper will combine BIRIS with reverse logistics to better serve the enterprise.

The rest of the paper is structured as follows. Section 2 is devoted to presenting the current status of enterprise reverse logistics and their problems. Section 3 proposes a third-party reverse logistics platform based on bilateral resource integration to build enterprise RL and outlines its core issues, business analysis, functional design and technical architecture. Section 4 presents five advantages of this platform. Section 5 gives an example about RL of an electronic company on the platform. Finally a conclusion and future research is outlined.

[a] Hongzhen Zheng: hithongzhen@163.com

Article available at http://www.matec-conferences.org or http://dx.doi.org/10.1051/matecconf/20164401014

2 Current operation modes and industry practices of enterprise reverse logistics

2.1 Current operation modes of enterprise reverse logistics

Enterprise reverse logistics generally involves events like collection, classification, transportation and disposing of goods. These goods are moved backward from consumers to enterprises. In general, there are three common operating modes of enterprise reverse logistics [2,7].

(1) Self-managed. Enterprises take the whole responsibilities of investment, cost and administration under procedures of collection, classification, transportation and disposal. The enterprise must have its own reverse logistics management systems, recycling facilities and technology, related personnel, etc. However, goods in reverse logistics are relatively low value and the volumes in reverse logistics are much less than in foreword logistics. So it is difficult for an individual enterprise to run a self-managed reverse logistic to reach economies of scale.

(2) Alliance of enterprises. Enterprises alliance is built by several companies who produce same or similar products. They could share facilities on recycling, reusing, disposal, repairing or remanufacturing and therefore reduce the investment. Compared with the former, the alliance of enterprises reduces the cost and makes the risk shared between companies. But these two operation modes above both require independent reverse logistics management system more or less, which is not under the control of those business-oriented enterprises. In addition, most of the enterprises are unable to handle the complex networking necessary to have an efficient reverse logistics links such as collection, classification, transportation and warehousing.

(3) Outsourcing. Enterprises outsource all or part of their reverse logistics to the third-party logistics service providers (3PL). Alliance of 3PLs [5] serve similar industries or have complementary businesses has been built to reduce costs and risk and expand the economies of scale. This mode is undoubtedly the best choice for enterprises to build reverse logistics. However, from a long-term perspective, there are some disadvantages. Firstly, not all of the 3PLs can provide a complete and professional reverse logistics businesses, and then available selections for enterprises are even fewer. Secondly, during the cooperation, it is hard for enterprises to get feedbacks quickly and even difficult to monitor the process of reverse logistics. Finally, with the rapid development of forward logistics, a large majority of 3PLs are unwilling to devote all of the resources to reverse logistics.

A construction method of enterprise reverse logistics based on bilateral resource integration proposed next will not only inherits the advantages of these three operation modes, but also avoids and improves their drawbacks to some extent.

2.2 Current operation industry practices reverse logistics

Most of the online store in order to improve the competitiveness provides "7/15 days no reason to return", "free shipping insurance", "free postage return" and other services like that. Ghazaleh Tajik [1] proposed a method improves the purchase rate as well as the returns, the additional reverse logistics process brings great pressure to the third party logistics (3PLs) providers. Most free-return policy supports unconditional return within the limited time, thus consumers may return the product due to its appearance, model or other personal reasons. This is called non-defective return which plays an important role in reverse logistics. And the following is the conventional process of non-defective return:

Step 1 Consumer B apply for non-defective returns
Step 2 Seller A allows return request and notify the return address addr1
Step 3 Consumer B sent goods to addr1 through 3PLs
Step 4 Seller A receives the goods and checks the integrity
Step 5 Seller A confirms refund
Step 6 Consumer C place an order
Step 7 Seller A sends goods to C's address addr2

There is twice cargo transportation in that process. Step 3: From consumer B to seller A, Step 7: From seller A to consumer C. The second time transportation is the forward logistics' process, the first time transportation is to check the integrity of the goods (assume that all non-defective return items will be sold again), so if the integrity check work was transferred to the logistics business, the second time transportation can be omitted.

3 Third-party reverse logistics platform based on bilateral resource integration

In order to overcome the existing drawbacks and break the bottlenecks of enterprise reverse logistics development, the idea of BIRIS [4] was applied to reverse logistics.

As a result, this paper proposes to build a third-party reverse logistics platform based on bilateral resource integration in which the third-party reverse logistics providers (3PRL) provide one or more parts of the reverse logistics links and enterprises are demanders to build their own reverse logistics business chains. Core issues of enterprise reverse logistics based on bilateral resource integration need to be solved are as follows:

(1) How to solve the difficulties to create relationships among a large number of reverse logistics providers and demanders.

(2) 3PRLs, as individuals, can only support a small part of links on reverse logistics. But after the effective integration of their resources, an all-around and personalized reverse logistics business links can serve demanders.

(3) Collections of reverse logistics demands from enterprises should be provided to reverse logistics providers.

(4) Monitoring the whole process of reverse logistics from both providers' side and demanders' side will improve the service quality of reverse logistics and the value of reverse logistics.

3.1 Business analysis of the third-party reverse logistics platform

The third-party reverse logistics platform consists of three main parts: reverse logistics demanders, reverse logistics providers and third-party centre. A large amount of demanders and providers connect to the platform. The former express their personalized demands, the latter provide a variety of heterogeneous resources, and the platform acts as an intermediary to establish relationships between two sides. As it is shown in Fig.1.

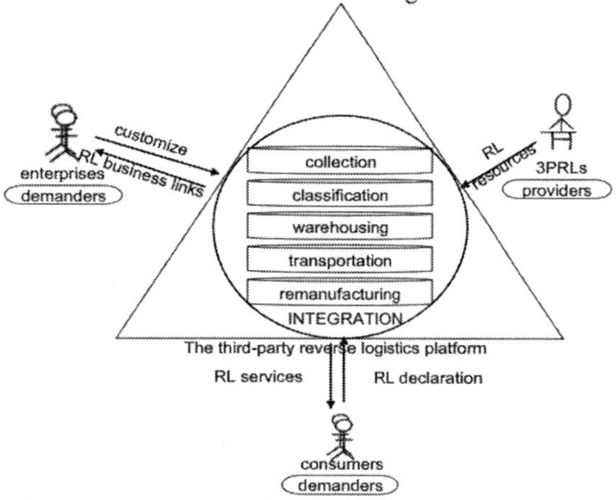

Fig.1 Business analysis of third-party reverse logistics service platform

The core businesses of reverse logistics are collection, classification, warehousing, transportation, and remanufacturing, and these functional links are all provided by registered 3PRLs. 3PRLs is composed by many kinds of agencies. Like agencies of collection, classification, warehousing or transportation and agencies of recycling, remanufacturing or maintenance. All these providers can provide all or just a small part of the functional businesses in reverse logistics. Finally, the platform takes a management of large numbers of decentralized reverse logistics resources, then integrates and publishes them.

As an enterprise-type reverse logistics demander, you need to first describe your products and choose which part of the reverse logistics functional links you want to subscribe. As your own original services, you can choose to connect it to the platform through an interface and publish it or not. After the collection of the enterprise-type demander's personalized needs, the platform will recommend an existing integrated business chain of reverse logistics to the enterprise. Only accepted schemes audited by platform will build up suitable reverse logistics business chains. At the same time, the enterprise can publish its business chains to seek corporate allies. In addition, a reverse logistics platform without terminal products consumers likes a smart machine without power unit. Therefore, in order to design a perfect third-party reverse logistics platform, it is crucial to consider how to make product consumers participate into the platform. The reverse behaviours of consumers, like product scrapped, maintenance, unconditional return or product trial, are the sources of reverse logistics. Through the platform, recycling sites for specific products have already been announced by enterprises. For example, a tablet purchased by a consumer has some quality problems. First of all, the consumer logs on to the platform, enters the name of the company and the SN of the product. Then the platform will show a list of recycling sites at the consumer's city. Consumers can send the product to the recycling site. Finally, based on the invoice number of reverse logistics, consumers can query or monitor the dealing progress of products at home through the platform.

Under the bilateral resources integration, the platform not only establishes better relationships between providers and demanders, but also gives more chances to small enterprises even 3PRLs to develop their reverse logistics.

3.2 Functional design of the third-party reverse logistics platform

Combined with the business analysis described, we design a functional diagram of the platform. It is shown in Fig.2.

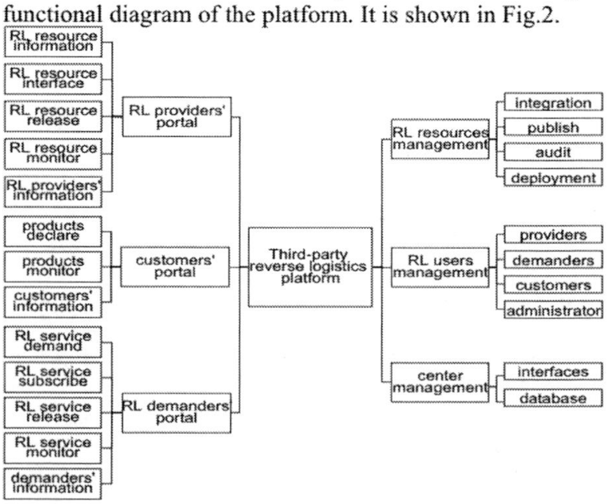

Fig.2 Functional design of third-party reverse logistics service platform

The third-party reverse logistics platform has two main parts, management and portal. The management part consists of resources management, user management and

centre management. And portal part consists of providers' portal, demanders' portal and consumers' portal.

(1) Management module. First, we must clearly ensure the users of the platform and preserve their information. Providers, demanders, consumers, and administrators are listed in the "user management" module. Then the platform has the responsibility to manage all the resources provided by providers, like integrating the resources, publishing the integrated business links, auditing the demanders' schemes and then deploying resources for them. Finally, in order to maintain the stability, the platform needs to check the interfaces linked by the demanders' or providers' business systems and maintain the database.

(2) Portal module. The platform provides three portals to our three main users, including providers, enterprise-type demanders and product consumers. Providers have access to register reverse logistic resources which includes resource information and resource interfaces, publish and monitor their resources. Second, demanders have access to subscribe reverse logistics business links, publish and monitor them as well. Finally, terminal product consumers could surf the platform, declare the recycling requirements and monitor the process.

3.3 Technical architecture of third-party reverse logistics platform

Based on the idea of bilateral resource integration, the third-party reverse logistics platform needs to consider the coordination and interoperability between reverse logistics resource and reverse logistics businesses with the specific information technology, as shown in Fig.3.

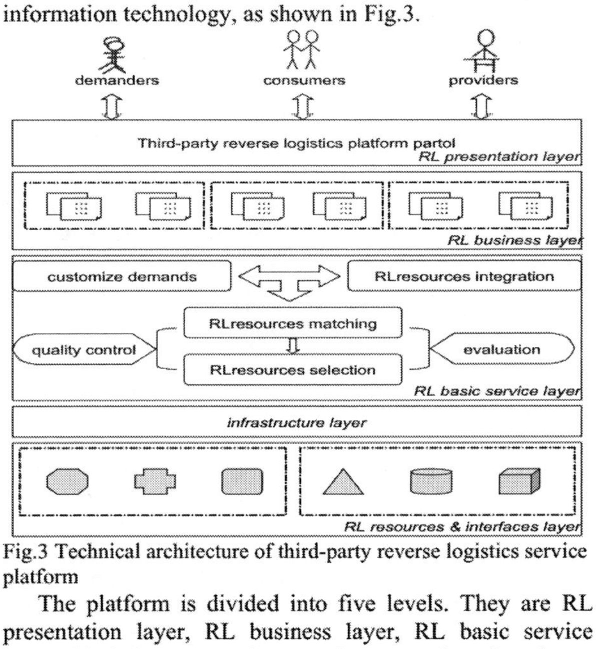

Fig.3 Technical architecture of third-party reverse logistics service platform

The platform is divided into five levels. They are RL presentation layer, RL business layer, RL basic service layer, RL infrastructure layer and resource/interface layer. This is a typical SOA-based architecture. The detailed description of a certain technology can be found in literature [4].

3.4 Method of enterprise reverse logistics, RLBRI

In order to build high-quality reverse logistics for enterprises in a quicker and more efficient way, this paper proposes to design a third-party reverse logistics platform. And its five advantages need to be outlined.

(1) Integrating decentralized reverse logistics resources to virtual resources. In the traditional cooperation between enterprises alliances and 3PL alliances, there are only a limited number of 3PLs for enterprises to choose from. In addition, in the traditional 3PL alliances, most 3PLs are professional reverse logistics providers which can provide most parts even all parts of reverse logistics businesses. But in the platform proposed in this paper, providers with only one part of the reverse logistics businesses can also register their resources. The platform collects decentralized reverse logistics resources and then integrates them to virtual resources with higher added value.

(2) An adaptive solution of enterprise reverse logistics is supported. In the forward logistics, except that some goods need special treatment like frozen food and chemicals, most goods are suitable for standard processes. While in the reverse logistics, situations are more complicated. The solutions of reverse logistics always change among different types of products or even sometimes among the same type of products. Therefore, simply relying on the platform to integrate resources and publish functional links is not flexible and applicable enough. So our platform allows enterprise-type demander to customize its own reverse logistics businesses according to its products. This complete personalized reverse logistics business chain is also a new chain for the platform.

(3) Value addition among providers, demanders and consumers. Providers in the platform will make a better management of their resources. They can get more businesses, reach economies of scale and make more profits.

Enterprise-type demanders will customize their reverse logistics through the platform. Under the proper regulation, the reverse logistics of enterprise works fluently and gains more competitive advantages, more businesses, more profits and better environment-friendly image.

(4) It is beneficial for the combination between forward logistics and reverse logistics. Providers in our platform maybe only support a small part of functional links in reverse logistics, which is relatively easy for them to combine businesses between forward logistics and reverse logistics.

(5) Credit accumulation and evaluation between providers and demanders makes a higher-quality enterprise reverse logistics. In the process of reverse logistics, demanders and providers can choose each other based on their credit data. Credit data can be obtained from two ways.

One asks the two sides to score each other. Another asks the platform to monitor some key points of processes in reverse logistics. In the end, the credit history will be used to recommend, select, supply or set the price of the reverse logistics functional links.

3.5 RL of typical electronic company on the platform

Electronic product recovery has always been an issue of concern. The construction process of electronic company RL through the platform is described as follow:

(1) Enterprises register to the platform. Our third-party reverse logistics platform has already accumulated a mass of reverse logistics providers which provide reverse logistics resources. Company A deals in office computer products, such as desktop computer, server computer, laptop computer is going to build its own reverse logistics business. As the first step, company A has to register to the platform, describes its business and puts forward its individual demands.

(2) Establishing reverse logistics business chain. As company A is a typical electronic company, it can not only choose an existing business chain about electronic products recovery recommended by the platform, but also select functional units

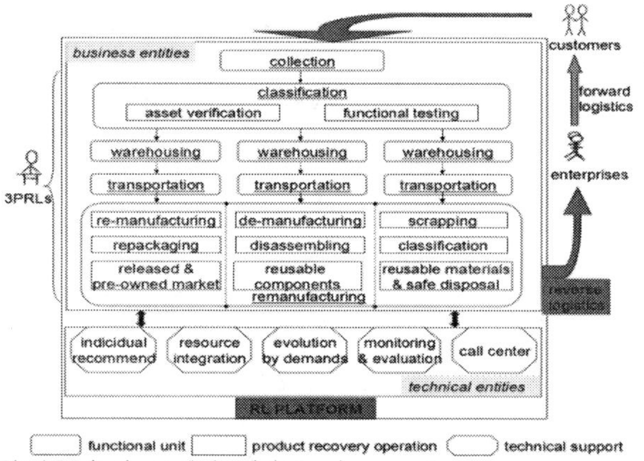

Fig.4 RL business chain of electronic company

Separately according to its' budget or special situations. The RL business chain of electronic company A is illustrated in Fig.4. The returned products are accumulated firstly in the process of collection. Products are either for repairmen or for returning. The process of assets verification is to ensure products are in good and ordered conditions and a bill for cost of replacing missing or non-functional items will be sent to the consumers. By functional testing, the returned products are classified into three categories, i.e., re-manufacturing, de-manufacturing and scrapping. Warehousing and transportation are two necessary links.

Functional links mentioned above are all supported by registered RL providers of the platform. Furthermore, resources integration, business construction and process monitoring are supported by RL platform. The platform collects and monitors the data generated in each step of execution process.

4 Non-defective reverse logistics

Section2 has described the process of non-defective reverse logistics; Step 3: From consumer B to seller A, Step 7: From seller A to consumer C. The second time transportation is a common forward logistics process which we won't be taken into consider in this paper. And the significance of the first time transportation is to check the integrity of the goods (assume that all non-defective return items will be sold again), so if the integrity check work was transferred to third party logistics' business, the second time transportation can be omitted.

Fig5 is the simulation map of forward and reverse logistics process. Star icon represents seller's address (assume delivery address correspond with return address).

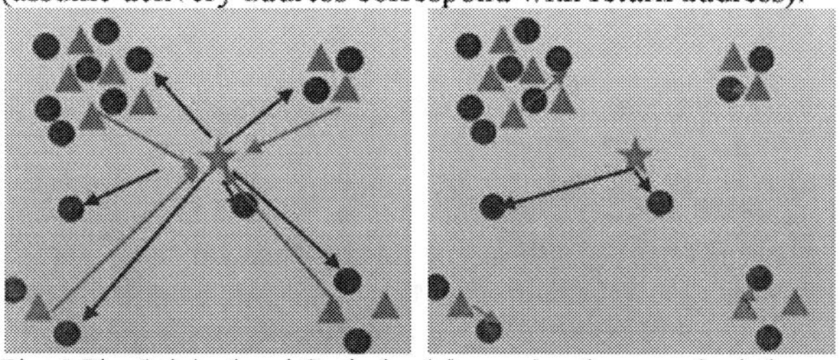

Fig. 5 The Original and Optimized forward and reverse logistics simulation map.

Based on the above analysis, in this paper we will introduce a new strategy for non-defective reverse logistics. This strategy optimized the flow of non-defective returns process which has been described in section2. After the optimization of the strategy, Step 3 and Step 7 in section2 can be integrated into third-party logistics providers send goods to add2. Fig5 left was changed to Fig5 right. The arrow indicates reverse returns are sent from consumer to consumer. The total transportation length in Optimized forward and reverse logistics is shorter than half of the length in Original, thereby reduced transportation costs and waste.

5 Computational tests

In this section optimized transportation distance is compared with previous transportation distance which was described in Section 4 and Section 2. The sales data of U-shape pillow is used as test data, for the sake of authenticity we use the real data provided by Alibaba. And this data comes from Taobao Index. Consumers' geographical distribution screenshot of U-shape pillow (from 2013-11-01 to 2014-04-26) is show as Fig6, circles represents the

consumer position and the size of these circle represents the number of consumers who bought the U-shape pillow.

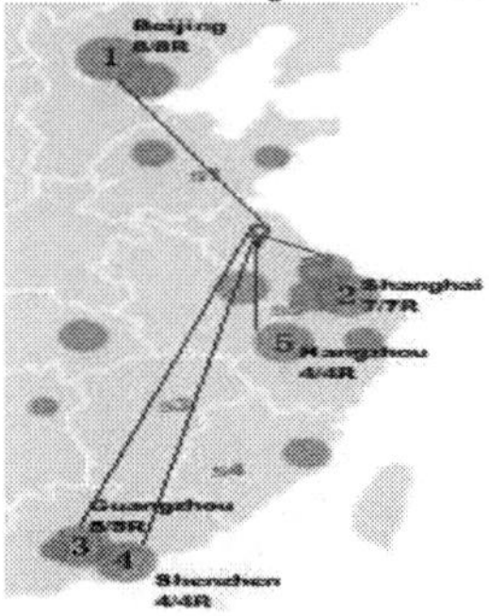

Fig.6 Consumer geographical distribution of U-shape pillow.

For seller, a return process and a delivery process is a circle unit. In Fig6, the figures show that in every 100 sold U-shape pillows there are 8 pillows has shipped to Beijing, 7 to Shanghai, 5 to Guangzhou, 4 to Shenzhen and 4 to Hangzhou. $S_{total} = S_{forward} + S_{return}$ represents the straight-line distance between seller address with Beijing, Shanghai, and Guangzhou and so on. The total transportation distance in one circle unit is defined as below:

$$S_{forward} = 8 \times s_1 + 7 \times s_2 + 5 \times s_3 + 4 \times s_4 + 4 \times s_5 \quad (5\text{-}1)$$

$$S_{return} = R \times S_{forward}, 0 \leq R \leq 1 \quad (5\text{-}2)$$

$$s_1 = 1040KM, s_2 = 310KM, s_3 = 1378KM, s_4 = 1383KM, s_5 = 270KM \quad (5\text{-}3)$$

(5-1) is the distance of forward logistics, (5-2) is the distance of reverse logistics. The data in (5-3) comes from Google Map. Based on section4, the optimized total transportation distance in one circle unit is defined as follows:

$$S'_{forward} = (1 - R) \times S_{forward} \quad (5\text{-}4)$$

$$S'_{return} = R \times (8 \times l_1 + 7l_2 + 5l_3 + 4l_4 + 4l_5) \quad (5\text{-}5)$$

l_1, l_2, l_3, l_4, l_5 Represents the average distance between any two points [4-5] within a city, as the general north-south length and east-west length is not greater than 100KM, so $l = 50km$ can be used instead of l_1, l_2, l_3, l_4, l_5. Then the final result is as below:

$$S'_{total} / S_{total} \approx 0.908, R = 0.1 \quad (5\text{-}6)$$

(5-6) means if the return rate is 0.1 then the sellers' transportation expenses will cutting to former's 90%. For consumers, the total transportation distance is cutting from s_1, s_2, s_3, s_4, s_5 to l_1, l_2, l_3, l_4, l_5. Then the result is:

$$\frac{l_1}{s_1} = 0.048, \frac{l_2}{s_2} = 0.161, \frac{l_3}{s_3} = 0.036, \frac{l_4}{s_4} = 0.036, \frac{l_5}{s_5} = 0.185$$

That means consumer's transportation expenses can be cutting to former's 3.6%~19% by using the strategy introduced in section4.

6 Conclusion

In this paper, we propose a construction platform and method of enterprise reverse logistics based on bilateral resource integration and a third-party platform is imported in it. The platform collects decentralized reverse logistics resources and then integrates them to virtual resources with higher added value. It accumulates a mass of demanders and providers together and creates relationships between them quickly. Through the platform, enterprises could create their own service chains of reverse logistics with low cost, low risk, high profit, direct feedback and real-time monitoring according to their individual demands. Last, this paper proposes an effective strategy, which can choose another customer's delivery address as consumer's return address to shorten the distance of return transportation. Simulation and computation test show that by using the proposed strategy, the consumer's return transportation expenses can be cut to former's 3.6%~19%.

The idea of bilateral resource integration is a new concept proposed in recent years. And most of the researches are about to combine it with forward logistics in a certain field. Further research would be on field of the combination between forward logistics and reverse logistics through the platform.

Acknowledgment

The paper is supported by National Science and Technology Support Program (2014BAF07B02) and Natural fund (ZR2015FM006).

References

[1] Ghazaleh Tajik, Amir Hossein Azadnia, "*A Hybrid Fuzzy MCDM Approach for Sustainable Third-Party Reverse Logistics Provider Selection,*" Advanced Materials Research Vol. **845**, (2014) pp.521-526.

[2] Hernandez-Hernandez, Helga J.Design of multi-product / multi-period closed-loop reverse logistics network using a genetic algorithm. Source: IEEE Proceedings Symposium on Computational Intelligence in Production and Logistics Systems, January 12, (2015), pp 40-47.

[3] Li-xia Su, Zhao-hua Wang and Li Su, "*The impact of information sharing on reverse logistics performance based on Canonical Correlation Analysis,*" Information Management, Innovation Management and Industrial Engineering (ICIII), (2012), pp 167-170.

[4] WANG Zhong-jie and XU Xiao-fei, "*Bilateral resource integration service mode for value innovation,*" Computer Integrated Manufacturing Systems, Vol. **15**, No.11, (2009), pp 2216-2225.

[5] Weidong Guo, "*Selection Model of Third-party Reverse Logistics Service Providers Under supply chain management,*" Control and Decision Conference (CCDC), (2012), pp 1761-1764.

[6] Zeng, Amy Z Coordination mechanisms for a three-stage reverse supply chain to increase profitable returns. Source: Naval Research Logistics, February, v **60**, n 1, (2013), pp31-45.

[7] Zhao Jian guang, "*Basic research on reverse logistics implemented by enterprise,*" Mechatronic Science, Electric Engineering and Computer (MEC), (2011), pp 807-810.

MATEC Web of Conferences 44, 01015 (2016)
DOI: 10.1051/matecconf/20164401015

A Chinese text classification system based on Naive Bayes algorithm

Wei Cui [1]

[1]Department of Information Technology , Luzhou Vocational&Technical College, Sichuan Luzhou, 646005

Abstract. In this paper, aiming at the characteristics of Chinese text classification, using the ICTCLAS(Chinese lexical analysis system of Chinese academy of sciences) for document segmentation, and for data cleaning and filtering the Stop words, using the information gain and document frequency feature selection algorithm to document feature selection. Based on this, based on the Naive Bayesian algorithm implemented text classifier , and use Chinese corpus of Fudan University has carried on the experiment and analysis on the system.

Keywords: Chinese word segmentation. Text categorization; Information gain; Naive Bayes algorithm

With large network retrieval system, document management, information filtering system, such as wide application , thc growing importance of text categorization have been increasingly emerging。The common method to text classification are mainly Support Vector Machine method, the K-Nearest Neighbor , Naive Bayes theorem, Neural Net, etc. These methods in the English and European languages, automatic text classification had extensive research and achieved good results. However Chinese than English in word formation is more complicated, so the Chinese text classification and English text categorization in text preprocessing phase, there is a certain difference. This article is based on Naive Bayes algorithm and Chinese lexical analysis system ICTCLAS, design a suitable Chinese text categorization system.

1. Chinese text preprocessing.

We first for Chinese text preprocessing, including structure processing, word processing, to stop words and so on. Extract on behalf of the text characteristic of metadata (characteristics), saved in a structured form, as the center of the document representation.

1.1 segmentation preprocessing

In the organization of the text, Chinese is very different to the European and American language which is Represented by English. In western languages, the word and the word was separated by Spaces, don't need word processing. In the Chinese text, words are joined together.

Therefore, word segmentation is difficult. Chinese word segmentation technology is facing two biggest problems, the ambiguous segmentation and the unknown word recognition[1].

In this paper, use ICTCLAS(Institute of Computing Technology, Chinese Lexical Analysis System) [2] to finish the job . The system adopts the combination of, statistical method and rule method, based on N - the shortest path to unambiguous text at the beginning of Chinese text segmentation, then through multiple hidden markov model algorithm to identify the word which is not log in, very good segmentation results have been achieved. System segmentation accuracy is as high as 97% above, not on word recognition recall rate is as high as 90%.

1.2 Data cleaning

After word segmentation processing of text, not all of the features are helpful to structure vector space model and classification, on the contrary, will make the word which without help for text classification as a feature , can cause great influence to the precision of classification. In addition, take out of stop words can largely reduce the number of feature item, has great help for text dimension reduction, so in front of the vector space model , to clean up the words thoroughly which are without help for classify. This system is based on the part-of-speech tagging for data cleaning. After dealing with the word segmentation, for punctuation w, partical u, conjunctions, prepositions p c, quantifier q cleaning, etc.

1.3. Take out the Stop words

Stop words mainly refers to the utterances, adverbs, conjunctions, pronouns, prepositions, interjection, quantifier, numerals etc, in the text . For example: the auxiliary "di, di, de, ba "; The adverb "very, very, very, all".

To get rid of the Stop words in technology implementation is not complicated, just build a stop words dictionary, will stop at each word after word segmentation and matching words in dictionary entry, if the match is successful, will remove the word.

2. the text feature selection

Feature selection is to improve the efficiency of text classification, reduce the computational complexity . Text feature selection is usually through the judgment of key . The commonly used methods are: document frequency, information gain cross entropy, mutual information, statistics and expectations, and so on . This paper uses the information gain and document frequency method of key judgment.

2.1 the information gain

Information gain is an evaluation method based on entropy, is defined as a feature in text information entropy difference before and after.

For the characteristics of w and c document category, the IG considered the appear frequency of w in document c to measure the information gain of w for c, the greater W for c information gain, the most important characteristics for category c items w, the greater the contribution. Information gain evaluation function definitions as shown in formula 1[3].

Among them, m said category number , $P(c_i)$ refers the probability of c_i such documents in the corpus , $P(w)$ said corpus contained in the feature item w document frequency, $P(c_i \mid w)$ said document contains feature when w belongs to the conditional probability of class c_i, $P(\overline{w})$ said the item does not contain features from the corpus of w document frequency, $P(c_i \mid \overline{w})$ said document does not contain feature when w belongs to the conditional probability of class c_i.

2.2 document frequency

Document frequency is the number of text feature item。The idea is: the DF value below a certain threshold of entry is low frequency words, they contain less or no category information. And get rid of the low-frequency

words from the feature space, reducing space dimension to improve the accuracy of classification.

3 text classification

Text classification use a tagged category of text data sets to train a classifier , this text data set is called the training set , then use the trained classifier of unmarked categories of text classification. Text classification algorithms, which are frequently used KNN algorithm, the SVM algorithm and Bayesian algorithm, etc.

On many occasions, Naïve Bayes classification algorithm is comparable to obtained with the decision tree classification algorithm and neural network, the algorithm can be applied to large databases, and the method is simple, high classification accuracy and speed. Theoretically, compared with all other classification algorithms, Bayesian classification has the smallest error rate, in its class under the premise of conditional independence assumption was set up, it is the best classification algorithm. In many cases, however, its class conditions independent simple assumption is not established, but the practice has proved that even so, it in many areas are still able to obtain better classification results.

Naive Bayes method [3] will break down training document into eigenvector and decision class variables. Assumed the characteristic vector of each weight relative to the decision variables is relatively independent, that is to say, each component independently on the decision variables. Naive Bayesian conditional independence assumption between attributes greatly simplify the calculation of joint probability, formula as shown in (2).

To construct a classifier module is the key to the training process module, using Bayes classification algorithm, structure specific classifier. Training process is generally more time-consuming, the system will training all text once, the characteristics of related information in the file. In training once, testing directly from the configuration file read relevant information without the need for training again, to save time.

Assume that the training corpus containing N text $D=\{D_1,D_2,\cdots D_n\}$, these texts are now owned by M text category $C=\{C_1,C_2,\cdots C_m\}$, training corpus set consists of L key text $W=\{W_1,W_2,\cdots W_L\}$.

When text D_i belongs to the category C_j, there is $P(C_j \mid D_i)=1$, Otherwise $P(C_j \mid D_i)=0$. If a given category variable text, the text category of prior probability is estimated according to the formula (3).

If use $F(W_k,D_i)$ expressing the number of occurrences of key word W_k in the text D_i, the key word W_k in the category C_j's probability estimation according to the formula (4).

Total number of key + frequently number of the eigenvalues in class C_j

Any text can be seen as a collection of a series of orderly arrangement of key, in the Naive Bayes model assumes that feature vector relative to the decision variables between each component is relatively independent, the category C_j generated in the probability of text D_i according to the formula (5).

According to the test text belongs to the text characteristic data computing the probability of each category, and in accordance with the largest probability to test text classification. Test text D_i belongs to the category C_j of probability according to the formula (6).

4. Experiments and analysis

The corpus for the experiments is Fudan university's Chinese corpus (part), divided into two parts, training corpus and test corpus. Training set is composed of a set of completed classification of text , used to summing up the characteristics of each category to construct classifiers . The classification of the test set is used to test the classifier effect is a collection of documents. The number of the training set and testing set text basic is a 2:1 ratio, such as table 1.

There are a total of 170 training document, system characteristic value of a total of more than 6000 after training. Feature extraction using information gain (IG), the dimensions of the feature extraction for 3000 d, the classes of recall, check, and the comparison of F1 value as shown in table 2.

As you can see, "traffic" and "sports" two categories of recall, precision and F1 value is 100%. "Economic" recall only at 77.8%, is relatively low. "Education" only 71.4% of precision, also is the lowest in all categories. This result is due to the two categories of training and test text similarity is relatively low.

Test documentation to extract 1000 d, 2000 d, 3000 d when the experimental comparison results as shown in table 3.

Visible, the classification effect of classifier with the increase of dimension increased after decreased first. Document the eigenvalue extraction dimension at 3000 d classifier classification effect is best.

Feature extraction using information gain (IG) and document frequency (DF) extract 3000 d experimental results as shown in table 4..

Visible, the classification of the document frequency (DF) effect to lag behind the information gain (IG) classification effect. In order to verify the effects of the feature selection algorithm for classification will be effected according to the characteristics of DF and IG choose after 30 words out before analysis.

Feature selection algorithm adopts DF, the organization form of word for < word: document frequency>, the result is:

"China:10 / the national:6 / protection:5 / environment:4 / Beijing:4 / American:4 / Britain:3 / Iraq:3 / Baghdad:3 / East Asia:3 / railway:3 / text:3 / word:3 / computer:3 / education:3 / japan:2 / continuous:2 / correct:2 / Shanghai:2 / involve:2 / correct:2 / transportation:2 / military:2 / Guangdong province,:2 / data:2 / World Cup:2 / bus:2 / Brazil:2 / sport:2 / Finance and economics:2"。

Feature selection algorithm USES the IG, the organization form of word is > < word: information gain, the result is:

"The national :0.0227 / protection:0.0210 / China:0.0183 / Baghdad :0.0174 / Iraq :0.0174 / Railway:0.0170 / East Asia:0.0165 / environment:0.0159 / text:0.0151 / education :0.0118 / aviator:0.01145 / navy:0.0114 / battlefield:0.0114 / military :0.0114 / world:0.0114 / ritain:0.0113 / teaching :0.0112 / international:0.0112 / traffic:0.0112 / Water transport:0.0112 / The World Cup :0.0109 / sports :0.0109 / Brazil :0.0109 / prosperity :0.0109 / International Monetary Fund:0.0109 / football team:0.010906 / Guangdong:0.01090 / operation:0.0107 / bleeding:0.0107 / solid :0.0107 / calculator :0.0106".

By comparison with the former 30 words, it can be seen that DF based text categorization effect to lag behind the IG based on the text classification effect. The lack of DF in that on the whole, the rare words may not rare in one type of text, and contains important information.

References

[1] Chen ping .svm-based Chinese text classification research and implementation of relevant algorithm [D] .at northwestern university in 2008

[2] The ICTCLAS official website http://ictclas.org/ 2010 6

[3]Yu fang .a web text classification system based on Naive Bayes method: web CAT computer engineering and application, 2004

[4] Wenhua, Dai .text classification and clustering based on genetic algorithm research of Beijing: science press, 2008

$$IG(w) = -\sum_{i=1}^{m} P(c_i)\lg P(c_i) + P(w)\sum_{i=1}^{m} P(c_i \mid w)\lg P(c_i \mid w) + P(\bar{w})\sum_{i=1}^{m} P(c_i \mid \bar{w})\lg P(c_i \mid \bar{w}) \quad (1)$$

$$P((w_1, w_2, \cdots, w_n) \mid C_j) = \prod_{i=1}^{n} P(w_i \mid c_j) \tag{2}$$

$$P(C_j) = \frac{\sum_{i=1}^{N} P(C_j \mid D_i)}{N} \tag{3}$$

$$P(W_k \mid C_j) = \frac{1 + \sum_{i=1}^{N} F(W_k, D_i) P(C_j \mid D_i)}{L + \sum_{s=1}^{L} \sum_{i=1}^{N} F(W_s, D_i) P(C_j \mid D_i)} \tag{4}$$

$$P(D_i \mid C_j) = P((w_1, w_2, \cdots, w_n) \mid C_j) = \prod_{k=1}^{n} P(W_k \mid C_j) \tag{5}$$

$$P(C_j \mid D_i) = \frac{P(C_j) P(D_i \mid C_j)}{\sum_{j=1}^{M} P(C_j) P(D_i \mid C_j)} \tag{6}$$

Table 1. Experiment training set and test set

Classes	Enviro-nment	Comp-uter	Trans-portation	Edu-cation	Eco-nomic	Mil-itary	Sports	Med-ical
Training set	22	26	22	20	21	20	22	22
test set	11	12	11	10	9	9	11	10

Table 2. The results of classification algorithm

Evaluation	Category							
	environment	computer	traffic	education	economic	military	sports	medicine
recall ratio	81.8%	92.3%	100%	100%	77.8%	100%	100%	81.8%
precision ratio	100%	100%	100%	71.4%	100%	75%	100%	100%
F1value	90%	96%	100%	83.3%	87.5%	85.7%	100%	90%

Table 3. The extraction of different dimensional results more classification algorithm.

Dimension.	micro recall rate	Micro accuracy	Macro recall rate	Macro accuracy	Macro F1 value
1000	85.37%	85.37%	84.43%	87.39%	84.27%
2000	87.8%	87.8%	87.32%	89.60%	87.31%
3000	91.46%	91.46%	91.72%	93.3%	91.57%
4000	90.24%	90.24%	90.58%	92.17%	90.44%

Table 4 different performance comparison method to extract features

proposed method	micro recall rate	Micro accuracy	Macro recall rate	Macro accuracy	Macro F1 value
Information gain	91.46%	91.46%	91.72%	93.3%	91.57%
Document frequency	81.71%	81.71%	79.84%	84.75%	78.33%

MATEC Web of Conferences 44, 01016 (2016)
DOI: 10.1051/matecconf/20164401016

A game-theory approach to manage decision errors

Chuan Xi Cai[1], Shu E Mei[1,a] and Wei Jun Zhong[1]

[1]Department of School of Economics and Management, Southeast University, Nanjing, Jiangsu Province, China

Abstract. With the fast development of modern computer and networks, information communication between firms and users becomes more complex. Recently, a game-theory approach has been widely used to investigate this issue. However, for firms and users, inaccuracies (defined as decision errors) persist in the gap between strategic decisions and actual actions. This paper, based on game theory, analyses the effects of decision errors on optimal equilibrium strategy of the firm and the user. Precisely speaking, we analysed how the firm and the user adjust their strategy accordingly to compensate for the mistakes caused by decision errors. Besides, we demonstrated that decision errors are not necessarily bad for the firm, and put forward the optimal methods of managing decision errors.
Keyword: Intrusion detection system (IDS) ; Game-theory; Decision Errors

1 Introduction

With the development of computers and networks, information security problems become increasing important in the key management area. Detection software (i.e., an intrusion detection system, IDS) provides effective supports for security management of information system, but fails to resolve the security problem of information system effectively by only relying on technology, since the environment of information system becomes more complex. Therefore, the economics of information security from the perspective of economics and management theory has developed rapidly in recent years. In the field of economics of information security, game theory has been used as a key research approach. For example, Cavusoglu & Raghunathan, Cavusoglu et al. and Levitin & Hausken give a game-theory analysis of the optimal configurations for security devices [1-3], Gao et al. and Hausken provide a game framework to discuss the investment of information security [4-5].

This paper attempts to discuss how to adjust the optimal strategy in the information system that has decision errors, and how to manage the decision errors. Decision errors are the inaccuracies between strategic decisions and actual actions, which is shown in Figure.1. Zhuang discusses the effect of decision errors by the agents on the social optimal investment in system security [6]. The work (Alpcan & Basar, Nguyen et al.) analyzes the decision errors of firms and users in the field of information security [7-8]. Our work is closely related to a seminal study [9], who analyzes the impact of the firms' and the users' decision errors on the equilibrium strategies and optimal configurations of the IDS.

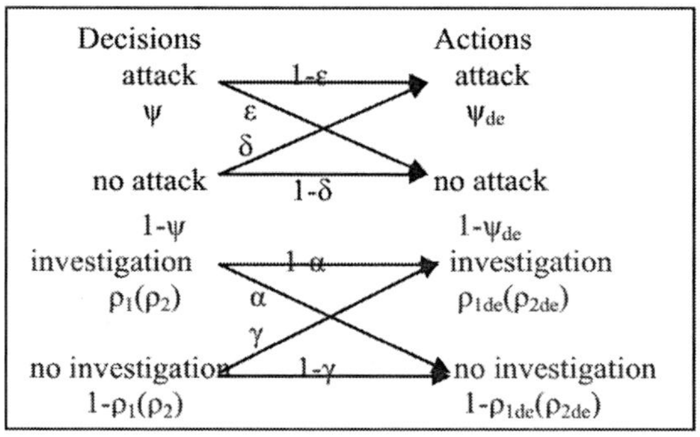

Figure.1. Decision errors of the firms and the users

In this paper, we developed a game-theory framework for the interaction between firms and users that include decision errors, analyzed the impact of decision error on equilibrium strategies and how the firm and the user adjust their strategy accordingly to compensate for the mistakes caused by decision errors. This paper proceeds as follow: section 2 provides a game model of the interaction between the firm and the user. Section 3 derives the equilibrium strategies, the adjustment strategies and the optimal methods of managing decision errors. Section 4 concludes this paper.

2 Model description

2.1 Strategies and notations

Probability of detection is P_D, probability of false negative is $1-P_D$; Probability of false positive is P_F.
$P_D = P$ (classified as attacker | attacking transaction);
$P_F = P$ (classified as attacker | normal transaction);

[a] Corresponding author: meishue@seu.edu.cn

Article available at http://www.matec-conferences.org or http://dx.doi.org/10.1051/matecconf/20164401016

$P_F = (P_D)^L$ (L>1) [10].

Because of the inaccuracy inherent in the IDS, manual investigations from a human security expert are necessary to verify the signal given by the IDS. It is assumed that manual investigations always succeed. We assume that a user's strategy is $S^U \in \{A, NA\}$, in which A is attacking transaction, NA is normal transaction; a firm's strategy is $S^F \in \{(I,I), (I,NI), (NI,I), (NI,NI)\}$, in which I is to investigate, NI is not to investigate, and the first element in each ordered pair is the firm's action when the IDS raises a signal, while the second element is the firm's action when the IDS does not raise a signal. The mixed strategy pair of the firm is given by $(\rho_1, \rho_2) \in [0,1] \times [0,1]$, it is reasonable to assume $\rho_1 \geq \rho_2$, ρ_1 denotes the actual probability of a manual investigation in the presence of a signal, and ρ_2 denotes the actual probability of a manual investigation in the absence of a signal. Similarly, the mixed strategy of the user is given by the actual probability of attacking, $\psi \in [0,1]$.

Now, following [7-8], decision errors are introduced. Assume that parameter ε (parameter δ) denotes the probability that the user decides (not) to attack but ends up not attacking (attacking); and that parameter α (parameter γ) represents the probability that the firm intends (not) to implement manual investigation but ends up not implementing manual investigation (implementing manual investigation) regardless of whether the IDS generates a signal. ψ_{de} is the user's actual probability of attacking. ρ_{1de} (ρ_{2de}) denote the firm's actual probabilities of manual investigation when the IDS (dose not) generates a signal.

When the user attacks, it gains benefit of μ if not caught but receives a penalty of β if caught. The manual investigations incur a cost of c because the firm exerts some effort each time, and the necessary analysis software may be used. If an attack is undetected, the firm incurs a loss of d. If the firm successfully detects the attack, a fraction, $0 \leq \varphi \leq 1$, of d will be recovered. It is reasonable to assume that $c \leq d\varphi$, so that the firm's cost of investigation is not higher than its benefit if it detects an attack.

2.2 The model

The effect of decision errors can be described by the following equations:

$$\psi_{de} = (1-\varepsilon-\delta)\psi + \delta \quad (1)$$

$$\rho_{1de} = (1-\alpha-\gamma)\rho_1 + \gamma \quad (2)$$

$$\rho_{2de} = (1-\alpha-\gamma)\rho_2 + \gamma \quad (3)$$

The following probability computations are used in deriving the equilibrium.

$$P(signal) = P_F + \psi_{de}(P_D - P_F) \quad (4)$$

$$P(no\ signal) = 1 - P_F - \psi_{de}(P_D - P_F) \quad (5)$$

$$\eta_1 = P(attack \mid signal) = \frac{\psi_{de} P_D}{P_F + \psi_{de}(P_D - P_F)} \quad (6)$$

$$\eta_2 = P(attack \mid no\ signal) = \frac{\psi_{de}(1-P_D)}{1 - P_F - \psi_{de}(P_D - P_F)} \quad (7)$$

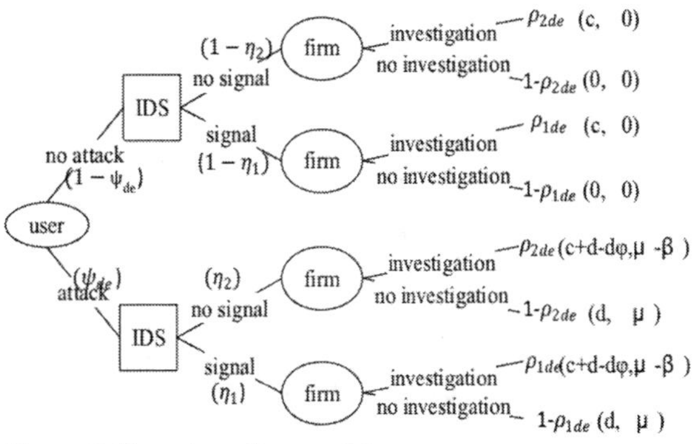

Figure 2. Game tree of our model

The game tree of our model is shown in Figure.2. The firm's expected costs when the IDS generate a signal and does not take the form:

$$M_s(\rho_1, \psi) = c\rho_{1de} + \eta_1(d - d\varphi\rho_{1de}) \quad (8)$$

$$M_{ns}(\rho_2, \psi) = c\rho_{2de} + \eta_2(d - d\varphi\rho_{2de}) \quad (9)$$

So, the firm's overall expected cost is

$$M(\rho_1, \rho_2, \psi) = M_s(\rho_1, \psi)P(signal) + M_{ns}(\rho_2, \psi)P(no\ signal) \quad (10)$$

Similarly, the user's expected benefits when the IDS generates a signal and does not take the form:

$$H_s(\rho_1, \psi) = \eta_1(\mu - \beta\rho_{1de}) \quad (11)$$

$$H_{ns}(\rho_2, \psi) = \eta_2(\mu - \beta\rho_{2de}) \quad (12)$$

Thus the overall expected benefits is

$$H(\rho_1, \rho_2, \psi) = H_s(\rho_1, \psi)P(signal) + H_{ns}(\rho_2, \psi)P(no\ signal) \quad (13)$$

3 Model analysis

3.1 The optimal strategies

In this section, assume that a simultaneous game is played between the firm and the user. The Nash equilibrium strategies of this game can be solved, in which neither the firm nor the user can improve its utility by unilaterally deviate its strategy.

Proposition 1: The following mixed strategy profiles constitute the Nash equilibrium in the presence of decision errors. Due to the limitation of space, the proof is omitted.

If $\mu > \gamma\beta + (1-\alpha-\gamma)\beta P_D$, then

$$\rho_1^* = 1, \rho_2^* = \frac{1}{1-\alpha-\gamma}\left[\frac{\mu-(1-\alpha)\beta P_D}{\beta(1-P_D)} - \gamma\right],$$

$$\psi^* = \frac{1}{1-\varepsilon-\delta}\left[\frac{c(1-P_F)}{c(P_D-P_F)+d\varphi(1-P_D)} - \delta\right];$$

If $\mu < \gamma\beta + (1-\alpha-\gamma)\beta P_D$, then

$$\rho_1^* = \frac{1}{1-\alpha-\gamma}\left[\frac{\mu-\beta\gamma}{\beta P_D}\right], \rho_2^* = 0,$$

$$\psi^* = \frac{1}{1-\varepsilon-\delta}\left[\frac{cP_F}{d\varphi P_D - c(P_D-P_F)} - \delta\right].$$

By substituting $\alpha=\gamma=\varepsilon=\delta=0$ in proposition 1, the equilibrium without decision errors is obtained.

Proposition 2: The following mixed strategy profiles constitute the Nash equilibrium without decision errors.

If $\mu > \beta P_D$, then

$$\rho_1^* = 1, \rho_2^* = \frac{\mu - \beta P_D}{\beta(1-P_D)}, \psi^* = \frac{c(1-P_F)}{c(P_D-P_F)+d\varphi(1-P_D)};$$

If $\mu < \beta P_D$, then

$$\rho_1^* = \frac{\mu}{\beta P_D}, \rho_2^* = 0, \psi^* = \frac{cP_F}{d\varphi P_D - c(P_D-P_F)}.$$

Low detection rates of IDS result in a high level of attacking, and therefore, the firm will not only inspect any users who raise a signal, but also a fraction of the users that do not raise a signal. On the other hand, sufficiently high detection rates of IDS reduce attacking. Therefore, the firm will not inspect any users who do not raise a signal, and, it can only inspect a fraction of the users that raise a signal.

3.2 The optimal configurations

Proposition 3: Decision errors have a great influence on the optimal strategies, and it is not necessary bad for the firm. With the change of decision errors, the firm and the user need to adjust their strategy accordingly to compensate for the mistake, which are illustrated by Table 1.

Table 1. The firm's and the user's adjustment to the strategy because of the decision errors

If	ρ_2^* ψ^*	$\frac{\mu}{\beta} > \frac{\gamma}{\alpha+\gamma}$	$\frac{\mu}{\beta} < \frac{\gamma}{\alpha+\gamma}$
Case1 $\rho_1^*=1$	$\frac{c(1-P_F)}{c(P_D-P_F)+d\varphi(1-P_D)} > \frac{\delta}{\varepsilon+\delta}$	A1 (↑, ↑)	B1 (↑, ↓)
	$\frac{c(1-P_F)}{c(P_D-P_F)+d\varphi(1-P_D)} < \frac{\delta}{\varepsilon+\delta}$	C1 (↓, ↑)	D1 (↓, ↓)
If	ρ_1^* ψ^*	$\frac{\mu}{\beta} > \frac{\gamma}{\alpha+\gamma}$	$\frac{\mu}{\beta} < \frac{\gamma}{\alpha+\gamma}$
Case2 $\rho_2^*=0$	$\frac{c(1-P_F)}{c(P_D-P_F)+d\varphi(1-P_D)} > \frac{\delta}{\varepsilon+\delta}$	A2 (↑, ↑)	B2 (↑, ↓)
	$\frac{c(1-P_F)}{c(P_D-P_F)+d\varphi(1-P_D)} < \frac{\delta}{\varepsilon+\delta}$	C2 (↓, ↑)	D2 (↓, ↓)

The proof is as follow:

Compare proposition 1 with proposition 2, we get:

Case1: If $\mu > \gamma\beta + (1-\alpha-\gamma)\beta P_D$, then $\rho_1^* = 1$,

$$\rho_2^* : \frac{1}{1-\alpha-\gamma}\left[\frac{\mu-(1-\alpha)\beta P_D}{\beta(1-P_D)} - \gamma\right] > \frac{\mu-\beta P_D}{\beta(1-P_D)} \Leftrightarrow \frac{\mu}{\beta} > \frac{\gamma}{\alpha+\gamma},$$

$$\psi^* : \frac{1}{1-\varepsilon-\delta}\left[\frac{c(1-P_F)}{c(P_D-P_F)+d\varphi(1-P_D)} - \delta\right] > ;$$

$$\frac{c(1-P_F)}{c(P_D-P_F)+d\varphi(1-P_D)} \Leftrightarrow \frac{c(1-P_F)}{c(P_D-P_F)+d\varphi(1-P_D)} > \frac{\delta}{\varepsilon+\delta}$$

Case2: If $\mu < \gamma\beta + (1-\alpha-\gamma)\beta P_D$, then $\rho_2^* = 0$,

$$\rho_1^* : \frac{1}{1-\alpha-\gamma}\left[\frac{\mu-\beta\gamma}{\beta P_D}\right] > \frac{\mu}{\beta P_D} \Leftrightarrow \frac{\mu}{\beta} > \frac{\gamma}{\alpha+\gamma},$$

$$\psi^* : \frac{1}{1-\varepsilon-\delta}\left[\frac{cP_F}{d\varphi P_D - c(P_D-P_F)} - \delta\right] > .$$

$$\frac{cP_F}{d\varphi P_D - c(P_D-P_F)} \Leftrightarrow \frac{cP_F}{d\varphi P_D - c(P_D-P_F)} > \frac{\delta}{\varepsilon+\delta}$$

According to Figure.1, when δ is low or ε is high ($\frac{c(1-P_F)}{c(P_D-P_F)+d\varphi(1-P_D)} > \frac{\delta}{\varepsilon+\delta}$, $\frac{cP_F}{d\varphi P_D - c(P_D-P_F)} > \frac{\delta}{\varepsilon+\delta}$), the user needs to increase his decision probability of attacking (ψ), because decision errors cause the user's actual probability of attacking (ψ_{de}) to be decreased. This is shown in section A1, B1, A2 and B2. When δ is high or ε is low ($\frac{c(1-P_F)}{c(P_D-P_F)+d\varphi(1-P_D)} < \frac{\delta}{\varepsilon+\delta}$, $\frac{cP_F}{d\varphi P_D - c(P_D-P_F)} < \frac{\delta}{\varepsilon+\delta}$), the user needs to decrease his decision probability of attacking (ψ), because decision errors cause user's actual probability of attacking (ψ_{de}) to be increased. This is shown in section C1, D1, C2 and D2.

When γ is low or α is high, that is, $\mu/\beta > \gamma/(\alpha+\gamma)$, the firm needs to increase his decision probability of manual investigation (ρ_1 or ρ_2), because decision errors cause the firm's actual probability of manual investigation (ρ_{1de} or ρ_{2de}) to be decreased. This is shown in section A1, C1, A2 and C2. When γ is high or α is low that is, $\mu/\beta < \gamma/(\alpha+\gamma)$, the firm needs to decrease his decision investigation rate (ρ_1 or ρ_2), because decision errors cause the firm's actual investigation rate (ρ_{1de} or ρ_{2de}) to be increased. This is shown in section B1, D1, B2 and D2.

To further understand the effect of decision errors on firm's strategies, we compare the firm's expected cost with decision errors and without decision errors. According to Proposition 1 and (10), we have:

If $P_D < (\mu-\gamma\beta)/((1-\alpha-\gamma)\beta)$, then

$$M(\rho_1^*, \rho_2^*, \psi^*) = c - c\alpha + \frac{[d-(1-\alpha)d\varphi]c(1-P_F)}{c(P_D-P_F)+d\varphi(1-P_D)},$$

$$\frac{\partial M}{\partial \alpha} = \frac{c(d\varphi-c)(P_D-P_F)}{c(P_D-P_F)+d\varphi(1-P_D)} > 0$$

If $P_D > (\mu-\gamma\beta)/((1-\alpha-\gamma)\beta)$, then

$$M(\rho_1^*, \rho_2^*, \psi^*) = c\gamma + \frac{(d-\gamma d\varphi)cP_F}{d\varphi P_D - c(P_D-P_F)},$$

$$\frac{\partial M}{\partial \gamma} = \frac{c(d\varphi-c)(P_D-P_F)}{(d\varphi-c)P_D + cP_F} > 0.$$

The firm's loss is composed of two components (investigation cost and expected damage). The investigation cost is increasing in the investigation rate, and the damage cost is increasing in the attacking probability. The value of IDS not only comes from improved detection of attackers, but also from increased deterrence of attackers [2]. With the increase of parameter α, decision errors cause the actual investigation rate to be decreased. It decreases the deterrence of

attackers, so the attacking probability increases. Therefore, with the increase of parameter α, decision errors decrease investigation cost, but increase damage cost. Compared to parameter α, parameter γ has opposite effect. With the increase of parameter γ, decision errors decrease damage cost, but increase investigation cost.

When P_D is low, the firm not only inspect any users who raise a signal, but also a fraction of the users that do not raise a signal. Actual probability of manual investigation is changing with parameter α and γ. If P_D is low, when the firm inspect the users who do not raise a signal, with the change of actual investigation rate, the change of damage cost offset the change of investigation cost, causing the firm's total cost no change; when the firm inspect the users who raise a signal, with the decrease of actual investigation rate (with the increase of α), the increase of damage cost more than offset the saving realized in investigation cost, causing the firm's total cost to be increased.

When P_D is high enough, the firm will not inspect any users who do not raise a signal, and, it can only inspect a fraction of the users that raise a signal. If P_D is high, when the firm inspect the users who raise a signal, with the change of actual investigation rate, the change of damage cost offset the change of investigation cost, causing the firm's total cost no change; when the firm inspects the users who do not raise a signal, with the increase of actual investigation rate (with the increase of γ), the increase of investigation cost more than offset the damage cost, causing the firm's total cost to be increased.

Based on the above analysis, it is obvious that decision errors are not necessary bad for the firm except two cases. First is when P_D is low, decision errors cause the actual investigation rate to be decreased. Second is when P_D is high, decision errors cause the actual investigation rate to be increased. Decision errors are not neglected in practice, it will take firm a lot of money to decrease the decision errors. Therefore, the firm needs to decrease the decision errors only in the two cases above.

4 Conclusions

Decision errors should not be neglected in practice. In this paper, we investigate the effects of decision errors on the optimal strategies by developing a game theory framework between the firm and the users. We discuss the effect of decision errors on the optimal configurations and the firm's expected cost, and the adjustment strategy of both the firm and the user. That is how the firm and the user adjust their strategy accordingly to compensate for the mistakes caused by decision errors. Besides, we demonstrate that decision errors are not necessarily bad for the firm, and put forward the optimal methods of managing decision errors.

This paper assumes that both the firm and the user have complete knowledge about decision errors. But both firms and users have imperfect information about decision errors in practice. The optimal methods of managing decision errors is the problem that needs further research in this case.

References

1. H. Cavusoglu, S. Raghunathan. Configuration of detection software: A comparison of decision and game theory approaches. DATA ANAL *Decision Analysis,* **1(3):** 131-148(2004).
2. H. Cavusoglu, B. Mishra, S. Raghunathan. The value of intrusion detection systems (IDSs) in information technology security. INF SYSTEMS RES, **16(1):**28–46(2005)
3. G. Levitin, K. Hausken. Resource distribution in multiple attacks with imperfect detection of the attack outcome. RISK ANAL, **32(2):** 304-318(2012)
4. X. Gao, W. Zhong, S. Mei. Security investment and information sharing under an alternative security breach probability function. INF SYST FRONT, **17(2):** 423-438(2013)
5. K. Hausken. Information sharing among firms and cyber attacks. J ACCOUNT PUBLIC POL, **26(6):** 639-688(2007)
6. J. Zhuang. Impacts of subsidized security on stability and total social costs of equilibrium solutions in an n-player game with errors. ENG ECONOMIST, **55(2):**131–49(2010)
7. T. Alpcan, T. Başar. Network security: A decision and game-theoretic approach. CAMBRIDGE UNIV Press.(2010)
8. K. C. Nguyen, T. Alpcan, T. Basar. Security games with decision and observation errors. *ACC2010* (pp. 510-515). IEEE:(2010)
9. X. Gao, W. Zhong, S. Mei. A game-theory approach to configuration of detection software with decision errors. RELIAB ENG SYST SAFE, **119**, 35-43(2013)
10. H. Cavusoglu, S. Raghunathan. Configuration of and interaction between information security technologies: the case of firewalls and intrusion detection systems. INF SYSTEMS RES, **20(2):**198–217(2009)

MATEC Web of Conferences 44, 01017 (2016)
DOI: 10.1051/matecconf/20164401017

Research on GPS Receiver Autonomous Integrity Monitoring Algorithm In the Occurrence of Two-satellite Faults

Er Shen Wang [1,2,a], Xiao Dong Yue[1] ,Tao Pang[1] and Zhi Xian Zhang[1]
[1] *Shenyang Aerospace University, Shenyang 110136, China*
[2] *Liaoning General Aviation Key Laboratory, Shenyang 110136,China*

Abstract. *Reliability is an essential factor for GPS navigation system. Therefore, an integrity monitoring is considered as one of the most important parts for a navigation system. GPS receiver autonomous integrity monitoring (RAIM) technique can detect and isolate fault satellite. Based on particle filter, a novel RAIM method was proposed to detect two-satellite faults of the GPS signal by using hierarchical particle filter. It can deal with any system nonlinear and any noise distributions. Because GNSS measurement noise does not follow the Gaussian distribution perfectly, the particle filter can estimate the posterior distribution more accurately. In order to detect fault, the consistency test statistics is established through cumulative log-likelihood ratio (LLR) between the main and auxiliary particle filters (PFs).Specifically, an approach combining PF with the hierarchical filter is used in the process of two-satellite faults. Through GPS real measurement, the performance of the proposed GPS two-satellite faults detection algorithm was illustrated. Some simulation results are given to evaluate integrity monitoring performance of the algorithm. Validated by the real measurement data, the results show that the proposed algorithm can successfully detect and isolate the faulty satellite in the case of non-Gaussian measurement noise.*

Keywords: *Global positioning system (GPS), Receiver autonomous integrity monitoring (RAIM), Hierarchical Particle filter, Fault detection, Fault isolation*

1. INTRODUCTION

Integrity of global navigation satellite system (GNSS) is important for safety-critical applications, such as aircraft and missile applications. With the development of GNSS and the increasing requirements for satellite navigation and positioning performance, the integrity monitoring is an inseparable part of GNSS. Integrity monitoring can be able to detect and exclude faults satellite that could cause risks to the accuracy and reliability of GNSS positioning, so that GNSS receivers can operate continuously without any degradation in performance[1]. Because it needs a long time for satellite fault monitoring to alarm through the satellite navigation system itself, usually within 15 minutes to a few hours, that can't meet the demand of air navigation. As a result, to monitor the satellite fault rapidly, namely the receiver autonomous integrity monitoring (RAIM) has been researched a lot. At present, with multiple GNSSs development, there is a need for RAIM to identify multiple outliers. The multiple outliers are more frequent due to the additional affects of non line of sight multipath[2-3]. Therefore, the RAIM needs to be able to detect and exclude multiple biases. It is difficult to detect simultaneous multiple faults using conventional snapshot RAIM algorithms, and therefore various filter algorithms have been studied for reducing the measurement noise level so that GNSS receiver can estimate its position more accurately and reliably[4]. However, for example, Kalman filter presumes that the measurement error follows a Gaussian distribution, the performance can degrade if this assumption is not correct. Because GNSS measurement error does not follow a Gaussian distribution perfectly[5], Kalman filter will use an inaccurate error model that may cause performance degradation. Particle filters have been researched over the last few years as an alternative for solving nonlinear/non-Gaussian problems. And, the particle filter for fault detection has been widely used[6-7].

Based on the particle filter, the two-satellite faults detection and isolation algorithm was designed. The new integrity monitoring algorithm for RAIM using hierarchical particle filter was proposed. The proposed algorithm estimates a distribution of a measurement residual from the posterior density and detects large residuals to satisfy a false alarm rate. With a non-Gaussian measurement error, the algorithm can estimate the distribution of the state more accurately. The work focused on the effect of a non-Gaussian error distribution of the GPS measurement on the integrity monitoring. The paper is organized as follows. First, a theory of a particle filter is briefly reviewed. Then the general scheme of the approach followed by a hierarchical particle filtering based log likelihood ratio (LLR) approach to fault detection and isolation (FDI) are presented. And the consistency test statistics is derived and established. The next section is a description of the system and measurement equation of GPS receiver. Finally, the GPS receiver autonomous integrity monitoring and its usefulness are presented with numerical simulation and experiment.

[a] Ershen Wang: wanges_2016@126.com

2. PARTICLE FILTER ALGORITHM

In this section, the principle of PF algorithm will be given. Particle filter is a method based on sequential monte carlo method and sequential importance sampling (SIS). It has a good filtering effect for non-linear and non-Gaussian system state estimation problem by obtaining sampling from the probability density function (PDF) in the state space. These sampling are called particles. Each of the particles has an assigned weight, and the state variable's distribution can then be approximated by a discrete distribution that depends on each of the particles. The probability assigned to each particle is proportional to the weight. These particles are random samples from the priori PDF. With the increasing of number of particles, a good approximation to the required PDF is effectively provided. Through the system state equation and measurement equation, the collection of sampling for approximating random Bayesian estimation of nonlinear system can be predicted and updated. Gordon, first proposed an algorithm of PF. The algorithm is known as the SIR (sampling importance resampling) [8-9]. At present, the particle filter has been widely used in location tracking, robot localization, signal estimation and detection, speech recognition and enhancement, dynamic fault detection system and satellite navigation[10], and so on. Let's consider the PF dynamic state space model below.

$$x_k = f(x_{k-1}, v_{k-1})$$
$$z_k = h(x_k, n_k)$$

Where x_k is a state vector, z_k is an output measurement vector. $f(\cdot,\cdot)$ and $h(\cdot,\cdot)$ are state transition function and measurement function respectively. v_k is the process noise vector independent of current state, and n_k is a measurement noise vector independent of states and system noise.

The basic flow of particle filter algorithm can be described as the following steps.

(1).Initialized

According to the priori probability distribution $p(x_0)$, the initial particles $\{x_0(i)\}_{i=1}^{N_s}$ from the pdf $(x_{k-1}|Z_{k-1})$ are generated, and the weight of the particles is $1/N_S$.

(2).Prediction

Using these particles to generate new samples $(x^i_{k/k-1}, i=1,...,N)$,which is approximated the predicted PDF $p(x_k|Z_{k-1})$.

Where,

$$x^i_{k/k-1} = f(x^i_{k-1}, v^i_{k-1})$$

(3). Update

After the measurement z_k attained, the weight of each particle at time k instant is updated. The weights are given by the following equation.

$$w^i_k = w^i_{k-1} p(z_k | x^i_{k|k-1}) = w^i_{k-1} p(z_k - h(x^i_{k|k-1}))$$

Where, $i = 1,2,3,\cdots,N$ .The weights are normalized by.

$$w^i_k = w^i_k \Big/ \sum_{i=1}^{N} w^i_k$$

(4). Resampling

From a set of particles $(x^i_{k/k-1}, w^i_k)$, according to the value of the importance resampling, a new set of particles $(\tilde{x}^i_{k/k-1}, i=1,...,N)$ can be gotten.

(5). Estimation

The set of particles can be used to approximate the posterior PDF, that is $p(x_k|Z_k)$ and the estimated value is as follows.

$$\hat{x}_k \approx \sum_{i=1}^{N_s} w^i_k \tilde{x}^i_{k/k-1}$$

Then, k=k+1, go to step (2).

3. HIERARCHICAL PARTICLE FILTER FOR TWO-SATELLITE FAULTS DETECTION

The problem of fault detection (FD) consists of making the decision on the presence or absence of faults for GPS monitored system, and the problem of fault isolation (FI) consists of deciding the present faulty mode among a number of possible modes. In this paper, a fault detection and isolation (FDI) method is designed for GPS integrity monitoring using hierarchical PF algorithm to detect the consistency of GPS system measurements, and then make the consistency of the test statistic. Finally, the consistency of changes caused by fault compares with the detection threshold to determine the moment of fault and fault satellite. In the algorithm, calculating each time the accumulated LLR function, according to the characteristic of the accumulated LLR function, the characteristic is that under normal circumstances the function curve is smooth with time. When the data fluctuates, it will produce a negative drift before the change and after the change it will produces a positive drift[11]. So the fault detection is to decide a model shift or detecting a jump from the normal model.

This particle filter combining with LLR is used to detect and isolate satellite faults, namely, through PF generating the state estimates, the LLR at each time is calculated. Among the window time, the cumulative LLR is gotten. The consistency is checked. Then the satellite faults are detected and isolated. Therefore, the MAIN PF and auxiliary PF particle normalized weights are calculated in every moment, which is easy to do for PF algorithm[12]. Accumulated LLR can be gotten for consistency test to detect whether there is fault satellite.

The fundamental schemes of RAIM are the same, whether multiple-satellite faults or a single-satellite fault using hierarchical PF based on LLR is achieved to FDI. Thus, given the standard deviation of the pseudo-range errors and false alarm probability, the detection thresholds are the same for both situations. The RAIM method to detect two-satellite faults of the GPS is

adapted by using hierarchical particle filter based probability test.

1) First, after calculating system state estimation with all N measurements, the corresponding state estimation with remaining N-1 measurements is calculated. Then LLR consistency checking is evaluated, if it exceeds the detection threshold, fault alarm is set, or no fault.

2) If there is a fault, the corresponding state estimation with remaining N-2 measurements is calculated. Then LLR consistency checking is evaluated, if it exceeds the detection threshold, second fault alarm is set, or no fault.

3) Using the method, after two iterations, the detection of two-satellite faults can be implemented. According to the principle of the method, it can also detect multi- satellite faults.

4. EXPERIMENT TESTING AND RESULTS ANALYSIS

The experimental raw measurement data are collected by GPS receiver N220 (positioning accuracy is 2.5 meters (RMS)), the measurement data including the position information of satellites and the pseudoranges were generated for each epoch for 418 epochs. The user's position outputs at a frequency of 1Hz. During the period of this collected data, there are six satellites used for PVT solution, the number of GPS satellites is 3, 15, 18, 19, 21, 26 respectively, and the corresponding pseudorange value can be expressed as $Y=(y_1, y_2, y_3, y_4, y_5, y_6)$. At the same time, another RCB-4H receiver produced by the ublox company is used to monitor whether the satellite is working normally. In order to simulate the fault satellite, the biases were intentionally injects into the pseudorange of two satellites. Here, the 50m bias was added to No.19 and No.26 satellites at time 90～120(k=90～120). In the simulated experiment, the particle number is chosen as N=100, the calculated decision function of window length is selected as U=30, the simulated experimental data measurement noise obeys Gaussian kernel Laplace distribution. Some results of applying the proposed FDI algorithm for GPS integrity monitoring were shown as follows.

In order to conduct fault testing, the bias was added into the pseudoranges measurements. And the detection of anomalies with the proposed FDI method for GPS integrity monitoring was tested. Firstly , by inserting errors into nominal GPS data. In this work, the pseudorange measurements of satellites No.19 and No.26 were modified. Then these modified pseudorange measurements were put back into the FDI system for hierarchical filter. The results of first hierarchical PF are shown as figure 1 and figure 2.

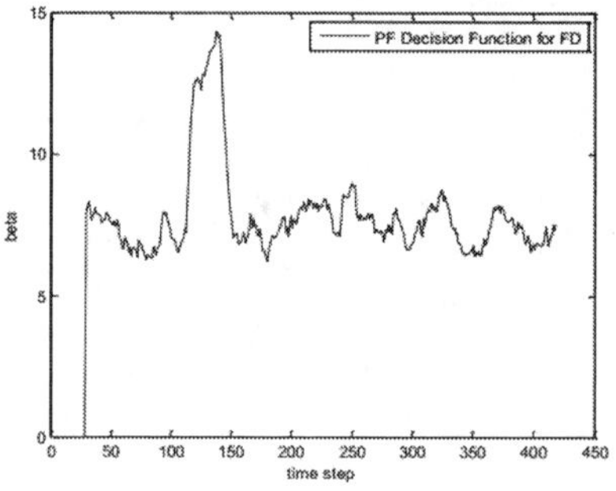

Figure 1. Decision function for fault decision for first hierarchical PF under two-satellite faults condition isolation

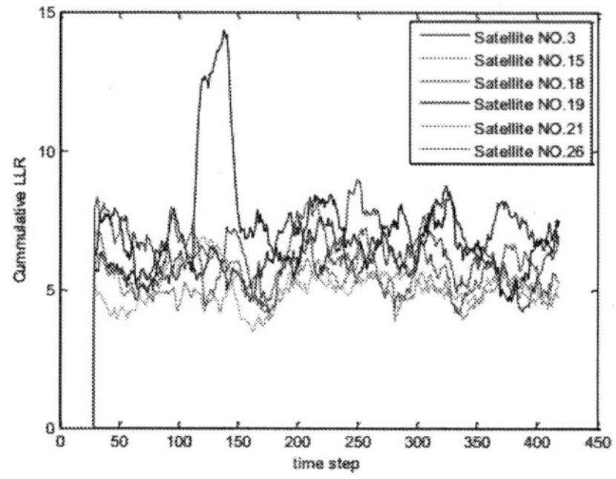

Figure 2. Cumulative LLR for fault for first hierarchical PF under two-satellite faults condition

Figure 1 and Figure 2 show the experimental results of the hierarchical particle filter for GPS RAIM under the first hierarchical PF under two-satellite faults conditions. From figure 1 and figure 2, it can be seen that the decision function β_k appeared a significant jump at k=95 that has over the detection threshold. According to the principle of fault detection of the above described, it can be judged that the first satellite No.19 exists fault. When calculating the PVT (position velocity and time) using the data, among the measurement data of the first hierarchical PF, the satellite No.19 should be abandoned. Then the second hierarchical PF continues to detect the other fault satellite. The results of second hierarchical PF are shown as figure 3 and figure 4.

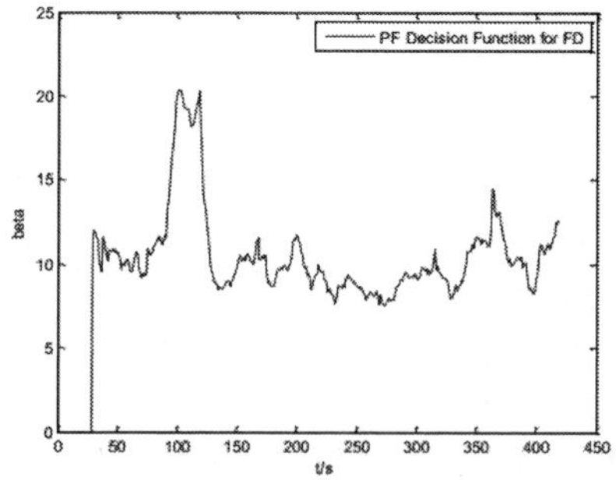

Figure 3. Decision function for fault decision isolation for second hierarchical PF under failure condition

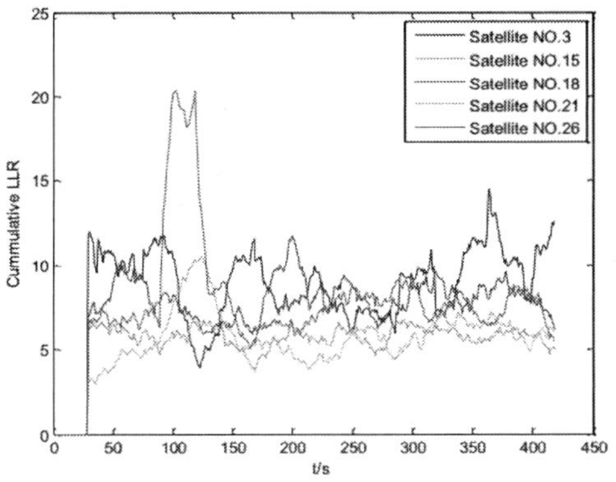

Figure 4. Cumulative LLR for fault for second hierarchical PF under failure condition

Figure 3 and Figure 4 shows the experimental results of the hierarchical particle filter for GPS RAIM under the second of two-satellite faults conditions. From figure 3 and figure 4, it can be seen that the decision function β_k appeared a significant jump at k=95 that has over the detection threshold. According to the principle of fault detection of the above described, it can be judged that the satellite No.26 exists fault. When calculating the PVT using the satellite data, the satellite No.26 should be abandoned. So far, two-satellite faults are both abandoned. And the purpose of two-satellite fault detection for GPS integrity monitoring is achieved. The method based on hierarchical PF for GPS RAIM is feasible and effective.

5. CONCLUSIONS

A new FDI method for GPS integrity monitoring by using the hierarchical particle filter was proposed. The proposed method makes it possible to detect two-satellite faults for GPS receiver. The hierarchical PF is executed in turn for detecting and isolating two-satellite faults. The test statistics is established .The likelihood function is established and tested by integrating state estimate from both the main PF and auxiliary PFs. Furthermore, the LLR test is used to detect fault, which compares the consistency of the measurement between the main PF and auxiliary PFs. The evaluation of FDI is conducted through simulation using the real GPS measurement data. The measured data from GPS receiver are deliberately contaminated with the bias. Based on the simulation result, the proposed approach demonstrated that it can successfully detect GPS measurement fault under non-Gaussian measurement noise, and particularly showed its outstanding performance in the aspects of processing multi-satellite faults. The proposed RAIM algorithm has certain reference value for BeiDou navigation receiver autonomous integrity monitoring.

Acknowledgments

This research was supported by the National Natural Science Foundation of China (No.61571309,61101161), The Aeronautical Science Foundation of China (No. 2011ZC54010) and the Joint Funds of the Natural Science Foundation of Liaoning Province(2013024003),and Shenyang Aerospace University Doctor start-up fund(15YB23).

References

1. Ling Yang, Nathan L. Knight, Yong Li, etc, Optimal Fault Detection and Exclusion Applied in GNSS Positioning, JOURNAL OF NAVIGATION, 66, 683–700(2013).
2. JUAN BLANCH,TODD WALTER,PER ENGE,RAIM with Optimal Integrity and Continuity Allocations Under Multiple Failures,IEEE TRANSACTIONS ON AEROSPACE AND ELECTRONIC SYSTEMS, VOL. 46, NO. 3,1235-1247(2010).
3. J. Liu, M. Lu and Z. Feng,Theoretical analysis of RAIM in the occurrence of simultaneous two-satellite faults,IET Radar Sonar Navig.,1, (2), pp. 92–97(2007).
4. Nathan L. Knight and Jinling Wang,A Comparison of Outlier Detection Procedures and Robust Estimation Methods in GPS Positioning, JOURNAL OF NAVIGATION, 62, 699–709(2009).
5. I.Sayim,B. Pervan, S. Pullen,etc,"Experimental and theoretical results on the LAAS sigma overbound", Proceedings of the ION GPS, Portland, Oregon:29-38(2002).
6. YUN Y, KIM D, " Integrity monitoring algorithms using filtering approaches for higher navigation performance:consideration of the non-gaussian gnss measurements " ,Proceedings of ION GNSS 20th International Technical Meeting of the Satellite Division, Fort Worth, TX:3070-3081(2007).
7. Rosihan, Arif Indriyatmoko, Sebum Chun,etc, " Particle Filtering Approach to Fault Detection and Isolation for GPS Integrity Monitoring " , Proceedings of ION GNSS 19th International Technical Meeting of the Satellite Division, Fort Worth, TX:873-881(2007).
8. GORDONN J, ALMOND S, D J, et al,Novel approach to nonlinear/non-Gaussian Bayesian state estimation,IEEE Proceedings F Radar and Signal Processing, 140(2):107-113(1993).
9. M. S. Arulampalam,S.Maskell,N.Gordon,etc, A tutorial on particle filters for online nonlinear/non-Gaussian Bayesian tracking,IEEE Transactions on Signal Processing,50(2):174–188(2002).
10. Fredrik Gustafsson, Fredrik Gunnarsson,etc,Particle filters for positioning, navigation, and tracking,IEEE Trans. on Signal Processing,50(2): p 425-437(2002).
11. LI P , KADIRKAMANATHAN V,Particle filtering based likelihood ratio approach to fault diagnosis in nonlinear stochastic systems,IEEE Trans. Syst., Man,Cybern. C, 31(3):337-343(2001).
12. E Kaplan, C Hegarty,Understanding GPS: Principles and Applications,Second Edition. MA, US:Artech House, Inc, 239-264(2006).

MATEC Web of Conferences **44**, 01018 (2016)
DOI: 10.1051/matecconf/20164401018

Design and Simulation of PID parameters self-tuning based on DC speed regulating system

Wei Jie Feng[a], Dong Xia Xu and Zhong Yu Hu

Automation and Mechanical Engineering College of Kunming University, Kunming 650214, China

Abstract. The DC speed regulating system has many difficult issues such as system parameters and PID control parameters are difficult to determine. On the basis of model for a single closed-loop DC speed regulating system, this paper puts forward a method of PID parameters self-tuning based on the step response detection and reduced order equivalent. First, detect system step response and get response parameters. Then equal it to a second order system model, and achieve optimal PID control parameters based on optimal second order system to realize of PID parameters self-tuning. The PID parameters self-tuning process of DC speed regulating system is simulated with the help of MATLAB/Simulink. The simulation results show that the method is simple and effective. The system can obtain good dynamic and static performance when the PID parameters are applied to DC speed regulating system.

1 Introduction

DC motor is widely used because that it has wide speed range, high characteristics, and can be controlled easily. While the control of DC motor speed is the key to meet different applications. PID controller is widely used in DC speed regulation system because of its advantages of simple structure, good stability and reliable operation [1]. There are many methods of PID, including position, increment, integral separation, anti integral saturation, variable speed integration, band filter etc. Tuning of PID parameters all depends on the system parameters in these algorithms[2]. The speed control system can be influenced by many factors, such as friction disturbance, delay of PWM transform, speed measurement delay, etc, so it is difficult to tune PID parameters because that system parameters are difficult to determine in practically.

In this paper, the step response parameters of the system are obtained by measuring the step response of the DC speed regulation system.The equivalent system model parameters are obtained by using the two order system to equivalent original system, and the self tuning of PID parameters is realized based on the optimal two order system.The method can get the PID parameters which meet the requirements of the control system with one measurement in the case of unknown system parameters.

2 Mathematical model of single closed loop DC speed control system

Figure 1 is a single closed-loop DC motor speed control systemwith speed feedback in which the amount of adjustment is speed n, the given quantitation is given rotational speed n*. The speed encoder tests motor speed n, then the speed deviation Δn is obtained by comparing the n with the n*, which can generate the required voltage U_c of PWM control through PID controller. The PWM controller outputs control voltage U_g, which then controls the PWM converter to output motor control voltage U_d.

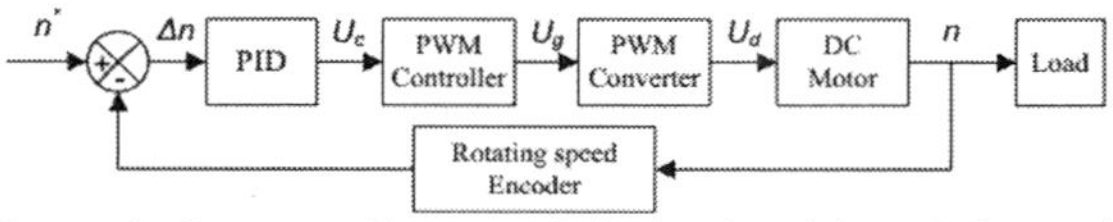

Figure 1. Structure diagram of single closed loop DC speed control system

2.1. Mathematical model of DC motor

When the excitation is rated and the DC motor is no-load, its transfer function is[3]

$$W_m(s) = \frac{n(s)}{U_{d0}(s)} = \frac{1/C_e}{T_m T_l s^2 + T_m s + 1} \tag{1}$$

In the type:

T_m — System electromechanical time constant,

T_l— Armature circuit electromagnetic time constant,

C_e — Motor potential constant.

It is known that the DC motor of the rated excitation is a two-step linear link by (1), in which the parameters C_e, Tl are determined by the motor used in the system and Tm is determined by the motor and load used in the system.

[a] Corresponding author: fwiejie@163.com

2.2. Mathematical model of PWM control converter

Whatever the PWM control converter, its drive voltage is all emitted by the PWM controller which can be simulated or digital. The structure diagram of PWM control inverter is shown in Figure 2. As shown in the figure, when the control signal U_c is changed, the duty cycle of $U_g$varies with the U_c, then the output voltage of the PWM converter is also changed by the linear law, but there will be a certain delay, whose maximum value is a switching period T.The whole PWM control converter can be considered as a lagging link, whose transfer function is

$$W_{pwm}(s) = \frac{U_d(s)}{U_c(s)} = K_{pwm}e^{-T_{pwm}s} \tag{2}$$

In the type:

K_{pwm}— Amplification factor of PWM device,

T_{pwm}— Delay time of PWM device.

When the switching frequency is 10kHz, T= 0.1ms, the time constant is small. It can be approximated as a first-order inertia link in the general electric drive system[4]. Its transfer function is

$$W_{pwm}(s) = \frac{U_d(s)}{U_c(s)} \approx \frac{K_{pwm}}{T_{pwm}s+1} \tag{3}$$

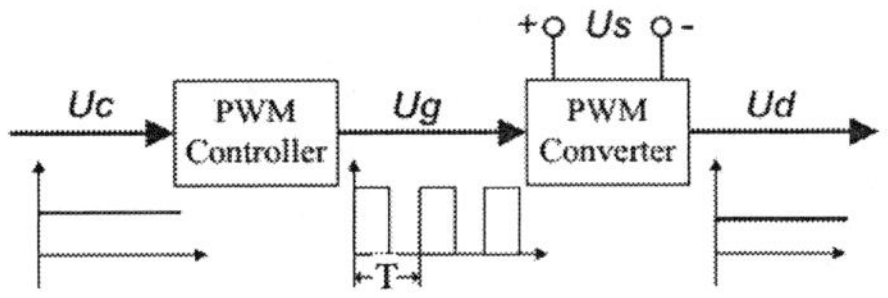

Figure 2. Structure diagram of PWM control converter

2.3. Mathematical model of speed detection link

The speed detection link is composed of a speed encoder and a speed control algorithm. If the M/T method is adopted, the principle is shown in Figure 4 in which the sampling clock and the high frequency clock are all generated by the system timer. The following type can be got according to the principle of M/T method.

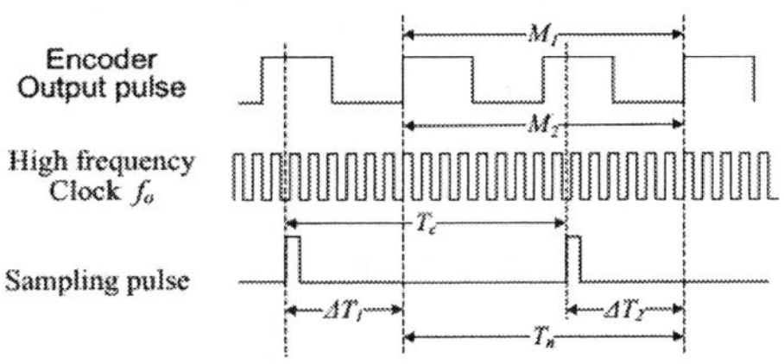

Figure 3. M/T method for velocity measurement

$$n = \frac{60M_1}{ZT_c} = \frac{60M_1f_o}{ZM_2}(r/\min) \tag{4}$$

In the type:

Z —Encoder grating number,

f_o—Frequency of high frequency clock.

The detection period Tnis determined by the edge of the output pulse of the first encoder after the Tc, that is

$$T_n = T_c - \Delta T_1 + \Delta T_2 \tag{5}$$

So the M/T method can be regarded as a lagging link whose transfer function is

$$W_n = \frac{C_n(s)}{n(s)} = K_n e^{-T_n s} \tag{6}$$

In the type, $K_n = \dfrac{60M_1f_o}{ZM_2}$.

The number of encoder grating Z is relatively large generally, so the motor speed is high, then ΔT_1 and ΔT_1 are relatively small and can be ignored. So $T_n \approx T_c$. In addition, the selection of Tc is small in order to improve the response speed of the speed control system, so the speed detection is simplified as a first-order inertia link whose transfer function is

$$W_n(s) = \frac{C_n(s)}{n(s)} = \frac{K_n}{T_n s+1} \tag{7}$$

2.4. Mathematical model of digital PID controller

PID controller is one of the most commonly used controller in automatic control system. When the sampling frequency is high enough in computer numerical control system, the controller can be designed according to analog controller firstly. Then the algorithm of digital controller can be obtained after being discrete.

The transfer function of the PID controller is shown in type (8) or (9).

$$W_{PID}(s) = K_P(1+\frac{1}{T_i s}+T_d s) \tag{8}$$

Or

$$W_{PID}(s) = K_P + K_i\frac{1}{s} + K_d s \tag{9}$$

In the type:

T_i —Integral time constant,

T_d —Differential time constant,

K_p —Proportional coefficient,

$K_i = K_p / T_i$ —Integral coefficient,

$K_d = T_d K_p$ —Differential coefficient.

In summary, the speed feedback closed-loop DC speed control system mathematical model is shown in Figure 4. The DC speed control system is a 4 order linear systemin the case of no introduction of PID control.

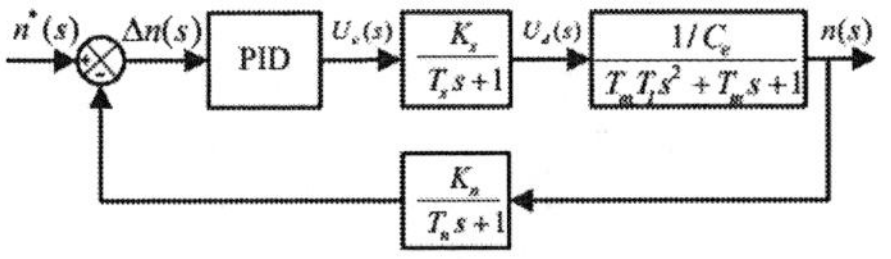

Figure 4. Dynamic structure diagram of single closed loop DC speed regulation system

3 Parameter detection of DC speed

regulation system

The system can be regarded as a black box in order to detect system parameters. The step response sequence $n(k)$ can be obtained from the output of the sampling system after adding step excitation to the system.

3.1. System type discrimination

The forward peak sequence $VF_{max}(k)$ and valley sequence $VF_{min}(k)$ can be obtained according to time. Then the reverse peak sequence $VR_{max}(k)$ and valley sequence $VR_{min}(k)$ can be obtained after reversing. We can identify the system type according to the number of peak and valley value of both forward and reverse. The discriminant method is shown in Table 1.

Table 1. Table of discriminating of system type

$\lvert VF_{max}\rvert$	$\lvert VF_{min}\rvert$	$\lvert VR_{max}\rvert$	$\lvert VR_{min}\rvert$	Response type
=1	=1	=1	=1	Damping
>1	>1	=1	=1	Under damping
<=2	<=2	>1	>1	Self excited oscillation
$\lvert VF_{max}\rvert=\lvert VR_{max}\rvert$ OR $\lvert VF_{min}\rvert=\lvert VR_{min}\rvert$				Equal amplitude oscillation

Figure 5 and Figure 6 illustrates the distribution of peak and valley value of both forward and reverse in the under damped system or self excited system respectively.

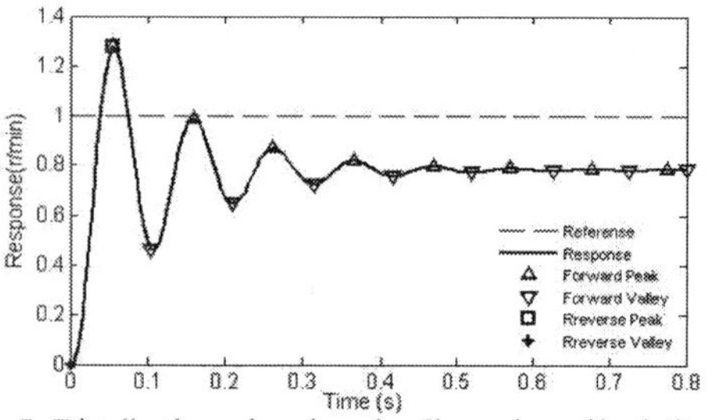

Figure 5. Distribution of peak and valley value of both forward and reverse.in the under damped system

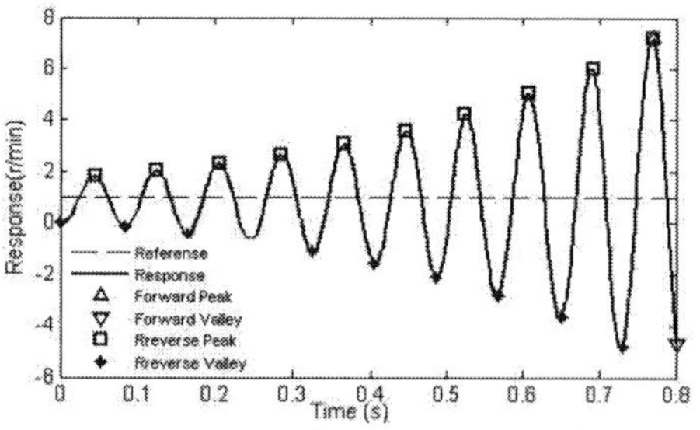

Figure 6. The distribution of peak and valley value of both forward and reverse.in the self excited system

We only discuss the under damped system in this paper. The system parameters can be properly adjusted to make other types of systemsbe a under damped system.

3.2. Determination of step response parameter

Setting the sampling period of the system as T_s and the sampling time as T, the step response parameters can be obtained by $n(k)$[5].

Peak response $n_p = \max[n(k)]$

Steady state value $n(\infty) = n(\frac{T}{T_s})$

Maximum relative overshoot $M_p = \frac{n_p - n(\infty)}{n(\infty)} \times 100\%$

Solutions obtained by $M_p = e^{-\frac{\zeta\pi}{\sqrt{1-\zeta^2}}} \times 100\%$ is

Damping coefficient $\zeta = \sqrt{\frac{\ln^2(100/M_p)}{\ln^2(100/M_p)+\pi^2}}$

Damping frequency $\omega_d = \frac{2\pi}{(k_{i+1}-k_i)T_s}$, k_i and k_{i+1} are the number of adjacent peaks or valleys.

Natural frequency $\omega_n = \frac{\omega_d}{\sqrt{1-\zeta^2}}$

4 System equivalence of two order systems

We use two order system shown in Figure 7 to equal the DC speed regulation system shown in figure 4 in this paper.

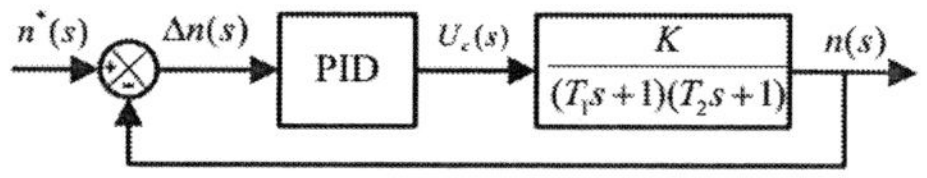

Figure 7. Dynamic structure diagram of equivalent two order system

PID regulation is not used firstly(K_p=1, K_i=0, K_d=0). At this time, the open-loop transfer function of two order equivalent system is

$$W_{EK}(s) = \frac{K}{(T_1s+1)(T_2+1)} = \frac{K}{T_1T_2s^2+(T_1+T_2)s+1} \quad (10)$$

Closed loop transfer function is

$$W_{EB}(s) = \frac{K}{(T_1s+1)(T_2+1)+K} = \frac{K/T_1T_2}{s^2+\frac{T_1+T_2}{T_1T_2}s+\frac{K+1}{T_1T_2}} \quad (11)$$

In the type, K, T_1 and T_2 are all Greater than 0.

If step excitation is set as R(s)=A/s,in which A represents excitation amplitude, the closed loop step response C(s) is

$$C(s) = R(s)W_{EB}(s) = \frac{AK}{s[(T_1s+1)(T_2+1)+K]} \quad (12)$$

Steady state value of step response $C(\infty)$ is

$$C(\infty) = \lim_{s\to 0} sC(s) = \frac{AK}{1+K} \quad (13)$$

Making $C(\infty) = n(\infty)$, the solution is

$$K = \frac{n(\infty)}{A-n(\infty)} \quad (14)$$

Comparing the standard form (15) of the closed-loop transfer function of the unit feedback two order system with type (11), type (16) can be obtained.

$$W_{2B}(s)=\frac{\omega_n^2}{s^2+2\zeta\omega_n s+\omega_n^2} \tag{15}$$

$$\begin{cases}\dfrac{T_1+T_2}{T_1T_2}=2\zeta\omega_n\\ \dfrac{K+1}{T_1T_2}=\omega_n^2\end{cases} \tag{16}$$

T_1 and T_2 can be obtained by the type (16).

$$\begin{cases}T_1=\dfrac{\zeta+\sqrt{(K+1)[\zeta^2(K+1)-1]}}{\omega_n}\\ T_2=\dfrac{(K+1)}{\omega_n(\zeta+\sqrt{(K+1)[\zeta^2(K+1)-1]})}\end{cases} \tag{17}$$

5 PID parameter tuning

Starting from the fast and stability of the system, we use the optimal parameters of the two order system as the basis for tuning the PID parameters, which requires that the open-loop transfer function of the system has basic form of the two order optimal design (18)[6]

$$W_{gK}(s)=\frac{1}{\sqrt{2T_g}s(1+\frac{1}{2}\sqrt{2T_g}s)} \tag{18}$$

Setting $T=\frac{1}{2}\sqrt{2T_g}$, type (8) can be equal to

$$W_{gK}(s)=\frac{1}{2Ts(1+Ts)} \tag{19}$$

The open-loop transfer function of the system withthe introduction of PID is

$$PID(s)W_{EK}(s)=PID(s)\frac{K}{(T_1s+1)(T_2s+1)} \tag{20}$$

In order to make (20) into (19), the PI regulator should be selected.Meanwhile, for the system to have a fast response, $\frac{K_P}{K_i}=\max(T_1,T_2)$ is selected to offset the large time constant of the system. If $T_1>T_2$, type (19) can be equal to

$$PID(s)W_{EK}(s)=\frac{K_iK}{s(T_2s+1)} \tag{21}$$

Following type can be got by comparing the coefficient of type (21) and (19).

$$\begin{cases}K_p/K_i=T_1\\ 1/(K_iK)=2T_2\end{cases}$$

Solution is

$$\begin{cases}K_p=T_1K_i=T_1/(2T_2K)\\ K_i=1/(2T_2K)\end{cases} \tag{22}$$

We can determine K by PID normalized parameter tuning method. According to the empirical formula (23) of PID normalized parameter tuning method[7]

$$\begin{cases}T\approx 0.1T_s\\ T_i\approx 0.5T_s\\ T_d\approx 0.125T_s\end{cases} \tag{23}$$

And the relationship (24) between coefficient of PID controller and time constant

$$\begin{cases}K_i=K_p/T\\ K_d=T_dK_p\end{cases} \tag{24}$$

Solution is

$$K_d=\frac{0.25K_p^2}{K_i}=0.125\frac{T_1^2}{T_2K} \tag{25}$$

K_p, K_i, K_d can be obtained from type (22) and (25) to act as the parameters of the PID controller in the original system. Then the tuning of PID parameters is completed.

6 System simulation

Speed feedback single loop DC motor speed control system can be built in the MATLAB/Simulink environment, which is shown in Figure 8. The system parameters is supposed as follows.K_{pwm}=1.8, T_{pwm}=0.002s, C_e=0.5,T_m=0.05s, T_l=0.02s, K_n=1, T_n=0.002s. The sampling period is T_s=0.005s. Simulation time is T=0.8s. Step excitation is 100rpm. The PID control is not used at first. The PID parameter is K_p=1, K_i=0, K_d=0.

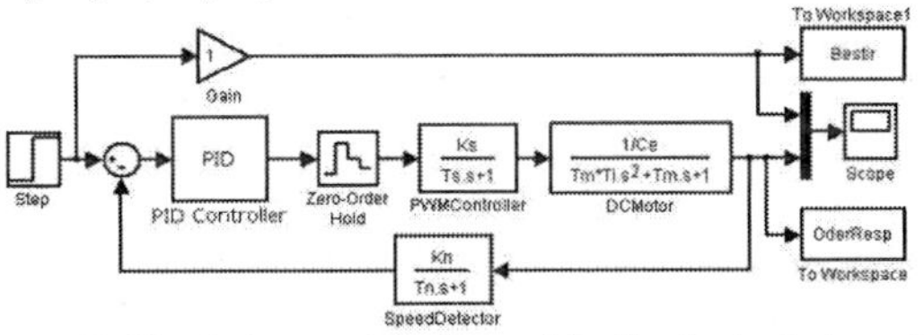

Figure 8. Simulation model of speed feedback single loop DC speed regulation system

The simulation model of equivalent two order system is shown in Figure 9.The PID control is not used at firstsimilarly. The PID parameter is K_p=1, K_i=0, K_d=0. Other parameters are to be determined.

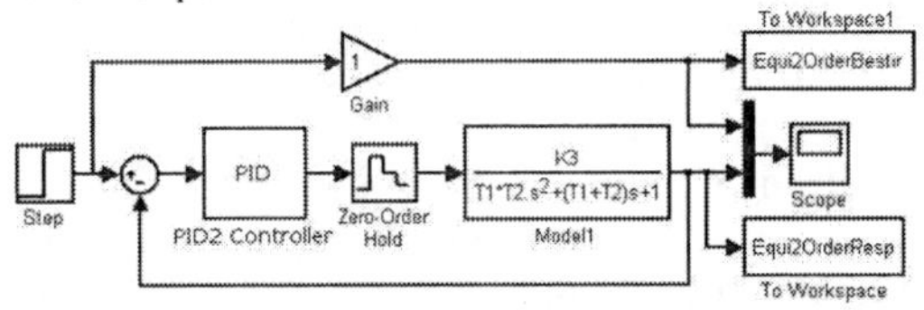

Figure 9. Simulation model of equivalent two order system

At first, the step response of the DC speed regulating system is obtained before PID correction which is shown in Figure 10. The step response parameters of DC speed regulation system can be obtained according to O(t). The steady state is $n(\infty)$=78.3375r/min. The natural frequency is ω_n=61.4782rad/s.The damping frequency is ω_d=61.0865rad/s.The damping coefficient is ξ=0.1460. The overshoot is M_p=62.8975%.

Secondly, the equivalent two order system parameterscan be calculated according to the parameters of the step response of the DC speed regulation system. K_3=3.6159, T_1=0.0354s, T_2=0.0342s. Its step response is shown in figure 10. Then the PID parameters can be obtainedbased on this.

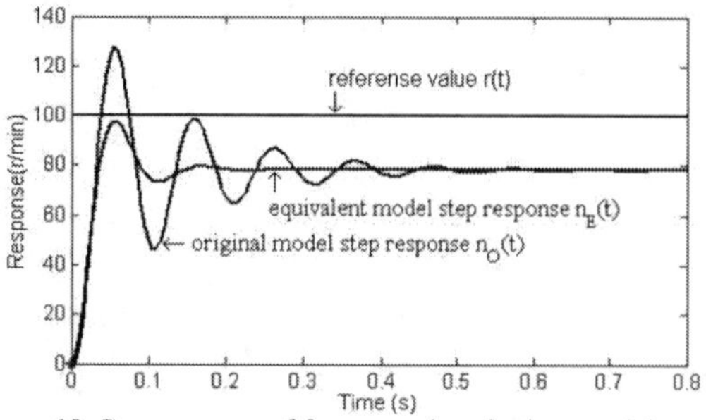

Figure 10. Step responseof former and equivalent model

$$\begin{cases} K_p = 0.1432 \\ K_i = 4.0437 \\ K_d = 0.0013 \end{cases} \quad (26)$$

Finally, applying the PID parameters to the equivalent two order system and the original DC speed control system for simulation , can get the PID correction step response curveof the equivalent two order system $E_{PID}(t)$ and of the original DC speed control system $O_{PID}(t)$, which are shown in Figure 11.

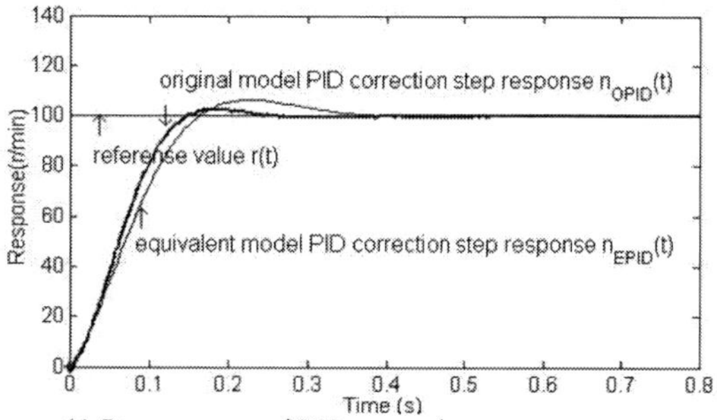

Figure 11 Step responseof PID correction

The step response parameter of the two models can be calculated according to the step response parameter of the PID correction which is shown in Table 2.

According to the simulation results, the PID parameters which are obtained by using two order equivalent and based on the optimal two order system, can make the speed feedback single closed loop DC speed control system to obtain better control effect. It has the characteristics of good dynamic performance and high steady precision.

In addition, it also can realize the self tuning of PID parameters.

Table 2. Step response parameter of PID correction

Response parameters	Equivalent two order system	DC speed regulation system
Steady state value $n(\infty)$	100.0171	100.1362
Natural frequency ω_n	18.2022	62.8114
Damping coefficient ζ	0.6610	0.7632
Rising time T_r	0.1660	0.1183
Peak time T_p	0.2263	0.1800
Super tone M_p	6.2839	2.4472

7 Conclusion

The PID parameter tuning is difficult in speed feedback DC speed control system because that system parameters are difficult to obtain and are easy to change, which makes the speed control system difficult to obtain good dynamic and static performance. This paper uses the two order system to equal the original system by measuring the step response of a DC speed regulating system, and then realizes the self tuning of PID parameters based on optimal two order system. The Simulink /MATLAB is used to simulate the self tuning method. The simulation results show that the tuning method has a strong ability of self tuning. The DC speed regulation system after being tuned has good dynamic and static performance, which can meet the requirements of engineering application.

References

1. Yadong Chen, Zhifeng Li, Design and implementation of the single closed loop DC speed control system based on PID algorithm, Micro machine and application,**32**,77-79 (2013)
2. Junrong Wang, Research and simulation of digital PID control algorithm, Popular science and technology, **4**, 27-28 (2008)
3. Yi Ruan, Boshi Chen, *Motion control system for electric drive automatic control system(the Fourth Edition)*(Machinery Industry Press, 2010)
4. Li Mei, Xiaoyan Ye, Design of PWM speed controller for DC motor based on MSP430, China test, **36**, 63-65 (2010)
5. Shousong Hu, *Automatic control principle(the Fifth Edition)*(Science Press, 2012)
6. Shouhong Lai, *Microcomputer control technology*(. Machinery Industry Press, 2013)
7. Jianhua Wang, *Computer control technology*(Higher Education Press, 2009)

MATEC Web of Conferences 44, 01019 (2016)
DOI: 10.1051/matecconf/20164401019

Transport Logistics Optimization Model Of Passenger Car Based On Heuristic Algorithm

Juan Zhou [1,2] , Mao Sheng Zhong [3] Dao Lei Cheng [1] and Xie Xin[3]

1.School of Software

2.Intelligent Optimization & Information Processing Lab

3.School of Information Engineering,East China Jiaotong University, Nanchang 330013

Abstract Passenger car logistics transportation problem is at the primary stage of development in China, great economic loss and waste of resources caused in the process of logistics transportation,because most of enterprises in China rely on artificial experience for guidance at present.And use of a particular genetic algorithm to solve this problem by previous also exist many defects ,such as programming complexity, instability and low efficiency etc.In view of this,The heuristic algorithm designing based on the greedy thought and the 0-1 knapsack thought was proposd, according build a universal model of the logistics transportation to the passenger car.Experimental results show, this model not only recording the concrete scheme of loading,also can make the optimization by changing the loading sequence.etc.This model is applicable to solve similar problems of transport logistics,and containing great practical application value and economic value.

Keywords Passenger car logistics transportation problem The greedy thought The 0-1 knapsack thought

1 INSTRUCTIONS

Passenger transport logistics problem refers to the production of passenger cars off the assembly line after finished, By means of transport, and distribution to all distribution warehouse, and finally to a series of storage and transportation process in the hands of consumers.How to use the limited means of transport, and to minimize the cost of [1] to be complete this process is a thorough study of the problems.At present, most of China's passenger car stowage scheduling logistics companies mainly rely on manual operation, depending on experience dispatchers, the prevalence of the following questions:1) lack of scientific methods to guide; 2) work-intensive, low efficiency; waste 3) car carriers capacity, high cost.For car carriers stowage plan and the lack of in-depth study of the lack of strong support software tools lead to the root cause of this problem.

Passenger transport logistics problems can be divided into loading problem and vehicle routing problem two sub-problems to solve.Loading Problem belong combination [2-3] Mathematics category, the paper loading problem based on rules that CLP (Container Loading Problems) issues.To solve this problem, heuristic algorithm foreign scholars have George & Robinson (referred to as the G & R) algorithm [4], Ngoi algorithm [5] and Loh & Nee algorithm [6].Domestic, He Dayong [7] Based on Space Decomposition layout heuristic genetic algorithm processing container loading problem;Wanch [8] proposed a hybrid genetic algorithm based on stereotypes and adaptive heuristic techniques to solve the actual operation of the most common weak heterogeneous container loading problem;Guo Hongwei [9] proposed the concept of "spatial layout point", and are using heuristic algorithms, genetic algorithms and simulated annealing algorithm.They common drawback of programming complexity, instability, and the solution process is slow.The difficulty of the problem is how to resolve the issue as one-dimensional multi-dimensional problem and how to solve the ultimate problem of sub-problems, which requires the use of dynamic programming.

This article based on ideology and greed 0-1 knapsack [10-12] dynamic programming ideas to construct heuristic algorithm to construct logistics model, and find the corresponding reprint and distribution programs to passenger transport and logistics issuesIt is converted to P class of problems, and accurately solved in polynomial time.The paper is arranged as follows: Section I introduces the background passenger transport and logistics problems, research status and the purpose and significance of the study; Section introducing practical problems to set forth the proposed

modeling scheme; s three, elaborated on the establishment and solution models, and details the corresponding algorithm; the fourth quarter, this model is summarized.

2 issues into

Through modeling and solving a practical problem as an example,to elaborate modeling of the model solution process, the question summarized as follows: passenger car manufacturer according to the customer's purchase orders nationwide (Table 1):

Table1 list the distribution of passenger cars needs NOTE: A representation A land demand

NO:	Brand	Long (mm)	Width (mm)	High (mm)	A	B	C	D	E
1	Benz	4610	1826	1763	4	2	0	3	1
2	Benz	5015	1880	1475	2	3	0	4	2
3	Benz	4310	1693	1480	12	6	5	10	7
4	modern	4747	1820	1440	15	8	4	9	6
5	Honda	3460	1618	1465	12	8	7	21	6

Transportation logistics company issued to passenger cars to the task throughout the country, the logistics companies plan to develop transport and distribution in accordance with the mandate issued by these passenger cars.To this end, the logistics company first they were selected from a number of vehicle car carriers can call "car carriers" (Table 2 below):

Table 2 has a list of car carriers

No.	type	long (m)	Width (m)	High(m)	Owners hip
1	1-1type	19	2.7	4.35	21
2	1-2type	23.7	2.8	3.9	10
3	2-2type	19	3.5	3.4	5

Which gives each passenger a car transport car loading programs and destinations, in order to ensure the completion of the transport task, the paper involved in car carriers in three models: the next upper each load a passenger, remember 1-1 type; in the upper load 1,2 respectively column, referred to as 1-2 type; in upper various load 2, recorded as 2-2.

Load requirements are as follows: Each car transport car, the lower the loading area can be considered equivalent to a rectangle, each longitudinal row of passenger cars were placed longitudinally and transversely between adjacent passenger cars are at least as safe distance between vehicles 0.1 m, lower strive to fill the upper two symmetrical strive to ensure a smooth ride car carriers, the line shown in Figure 1.

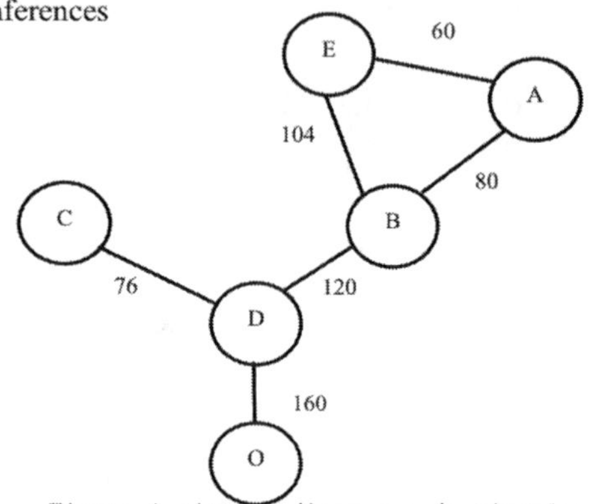

Figure 1 circuit diagram a destination

3 Examples of Modeling

Previous section details the problems to be solved, this section will establish the corresponding mathematical model of the problem.First, the modeling process need to make the following assumptions: (1) car carriers on standby after arrival, without emptying return; (2) the cost per Unloading almost negligible; and (3) that the cost per unit distance simplify and model-independent; (4) does not consider the special circumstances that occurred during the actual transport; (5) car carriers can not turn back.

3.1 Model analysis

This problem has several different types of car carriers and a number of different models of cars, and there is a triangular network path shown in Figure 1 [13]. Because of the limited number of car carriers, and therefore should be the first consideration is to be able to hold all the goods vehicles, followed by the total distance before considering the issue, the node D is a key node problem.In order to simplify the problem, trying to FIG divided into two lines, but because of too many models of goods vehicles and not be able to enumerate how to assign to two branch road, so it can be divided into two sub-path path directly to the point and the point together transport, after transport direction before going to demand, as shown in Figure 2.

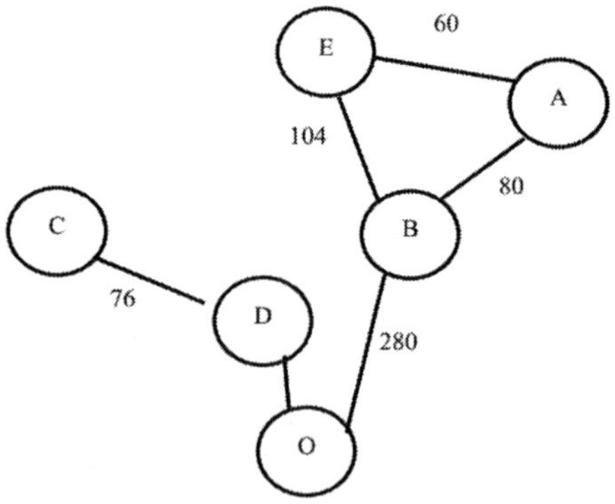

Figure 2 Figure II line destination

Then you can start with the first one first car carriers, according to the order for loading, and the first shipment of direction, until demand for

passenger cars and a variety of point all 0, and then further direction for shipment.During shipment, due to the size of the car models are different, so the vehicle when installed, should determine the size meets the requirements, and then decide to install or not install.After all the goods vehicles Bahrain, according to backpack load process the recorded program, the calculation of specific per car carriers actual distribution lines.First principle and point to stop at car carriers allocated, allocation: go after the order enumerate direction of the car, according to various distribution shipment demand for passenger cars, all to meet the farthest point, the remaining amount of car all will be docked at the D point.But there are some car though docked in point, but there is remove the part of the goods at the point, this may count for each item separately vehicles remaining amount, which in turn find the point after the previous, with the remaining amount of demand for this point subtraction, if they oversupply, will continue to find its former relay node.Since the backpack obtained during shipment program must be just to meet shipment demand, so eventually will find its most start unloading point.

Obtaining the specific distribution plan, we got the number in each node docked car carriers, then you can calculate the total distance of the program.

3.2 Model establish

Simplified diagram of the transport and two independent directions OC and OA, the definition y_i represents OC the kind of i demand for passenger cars, empathy x_i is defined OA demand for passenger cars, said first kind i, and $car_i(n)$ is defined as a passenger n point of the first species on the passenger the demand for the kind of i car, thereby obtaining the following equation:

$$y_i = car_i(\mathrm{C}) + car_i(\mathrm{D}) \tag{1}$$

$$x_i = car_i(\mathrm{A}) + car_i(\mathrm{B}) + car_i(\mathrm{E}) \tag{2}$$

OC hypothesis needs direction k cars car carriers need to accomplish this k cars car carriers may include three models, In order to meet the needs of its car carrier below filled with as much as possible, let's start from the lower load, in order to meet the requirements for the bottom of the two columns to symmetric, we try to fill up the columns, maximize space utilization. Therefore, the introduction of the 0-1 knapsack algorithm to solve this problem, and with the idea of dynamic programming to solve this problem. Definition methods: $solution(s, T_i, l, w, h)$, That the use of a given car carriers loaded the remaining i-type passenger car program. Where s is currently used model car carriers, T_i represents the number of the remaining need to be loaded i-type ride transport vehicles, l、w、h car carriers currently using the length and breadth. But this is only the loading program car carriers in a column position. So for the 1-1 type car carriers, adjustment shall be co-loaded sequence twice from bottom to top: $2*solution(s, T_i, l, w, h)$; 1-2 basis having car from bottom to top, from left to right and then co-loaded three times: $3*solution(s, T_i, l, w, h)$; 2 - 2 type car as from bottom to top, from left to right in all loading four times: $4*solution(s, T_i, l, w, h)$. G were used car transport car, you can get the following formula:

$$R = \sum_{i=1}^{k} solution(s, x_i, l, w, h)*t + \sum_{j=k}^{g} solution(s, y_i, l, w, h)*t \quad ,t \in \{2,3,4\} \tag{3}$$

T from the value of the s. As $solution(s, T_i, l, w, h)$ is a single single loading problem, so the car transport the position the lower single aspect high value can be determined according to l、w、h. We will be the car car carrier single row as a container for l long, with the given passenger car filled according to the specific space requirement.Let $dp(v) = 1$ to v represents the size of the space has been filled, to obtain the following formula:

$$dp(v) = dp(v - v_i) > 0 ? 1 : 0 \tag{4}$$

If the size is expressed $v - v_i$ space has been filled, then the passenger i load length of v_i, v space size will also be filled Note that initially $dp(0) = 1$.

In the calculation of the loading process, the need to record the specific circumstances of each of the next load.After that, according to the route problem solving concrete delivery vehicle specific programs, including the initial program loading, and unloading volume intermediate stops, as well as the final stops.Let $number(n_i)$ represents the final stop in n_i number of car carriers, it can be calculated, the total number of miles traveled by car carriers to obtain the following formula:

$$S = \sum_{i=A}^{D} dis(n_i, O) * number(n_i) \tag{5}$$

Where S represents the total number of miles traveled, $dis(n_i, O)$ represents the shortest

distance O of n_i .Requirements $dis(n_i, O)$, according to the following formula (Floyd algorithm):

$$dis(i,j) = Min(dis(i,k) + dis(k,j), dis(i,j)) \quad (6)$$

3.3 Algorithm Description

Algorithm 1 Loading process of the algorithm is described as follows:

1) The cumulative total for each model of each destination passenger demand OC direction;

2) Enumeration of the i-th car carriers j-cars, its loading vehicles. According to the i-th model car carriers, the election of the corresponding load means (such as described in 3.2);

3) Enumerate each task is not yet complete loading of the passenger, assuming k numbers v_k passenger cars left, try to mount the first i kind of car carriers j-cars. And record the loading programs;

4) Analyzing the i-th car carriers j-vehicle whether there is space, if there is, the implementation of $k = k+1$, skip to Procedure 3), and if not, skip to process 5);

5) Determine the direction of the loading task is completed, if not yet complete, execute $j = j+1$, if j exceeds a given range, execution jumps to $i = i+1$, process 2) If you have completed skip to 6);

6) To determine whether there is a path did not complete loading, if there is, skip to procedure 7), otherwise skip to process 8);

7) Accumulated OA direction of each destination the total demand for passenger cars for each model, the Executive $j = j+1$, if j exceeds a given range, execution $i = i+1$, skip to Procedure 2);

8) The loading program records, calculates per car carriers transport path and calculate the final number of car carriers docked at each destination, the statistical total distance.

Algorithm 2 According stowage plans, calculate specific delivery routes algorithm is described as follows:

1) per enumeration packed car carriers, starting from the current path farthest destination stowage, provided the current destination $node$;

2) i enumerate car carriers loaded passenger j, set up a total of v_j vehicles;

3) Analyzing the current v_j passenger cars exceeds n-point demand for j passenger cars, if not exceed, home $need[n].car[j] = 0$, execute $j = j+1$, skip to Procedure 2); otherwise, the process jumps to 4);

4) n calculated point before a node $pre[n]$, update $v_j = v_j - need[n].car[j]$, which $need[n].car[j]$ represents node of n demand for passenger car j,put $need[n].car[j] = 0$;

5) Print out the distribution record n nodes, and set $n = pre[n]$, such as $n = pre[n]$ does not exist, skip to procedure 7);

6) Analyzing v_j is 0, and if yes, then execute $j = j+1$, the process jumps to 10); if not, skip to Procedure 4);

7) Determine whether there are car carriers useless statistics, if there is, do $i = i+1$, skip process 2), otherwise the algorithm ends.

3.4 model solution

According to the above models and algorithms to obtain results as shown in Table 3:

Table 3 car carriers specific distribution pla

Vehicle order	Car name	models	Car layer	Loading mode (a, b) A passenger car number b	Unlouading capacity in middle point (X, Y, Z) which unlouding Z vehiccles of Y types in place X	termini
1	1	1-1	Upper layer	(3,2)、(5,3)		C
			Lower	(3,2)、(5,3)		
2	1	1-1	Upper layer	(3,2)、(5,3)	(D,3,3),(D,5,5)	C
			Lower	(3,2)、(5,3)		
3	1	1-1	Upper layer	(3,2)、(5,3)	(D,3,4), (D,5,6)	D
			Lower	(3,2)、(5,3)		
4	1	1-1	Upper layer	(4,4)	(D,3,2), (D,5,3)	C
			Lower	(3,2)、(5,3)		

5	1	1-1	Upper layer	(4,4)		D
			Lower	(4,4)		
6	1	1-1	Upper layer	(1,1)、(2,2)、(3,1)		D
			Lower	(1,2)、(2,1)、(4,1)		
7	1	1-1	Upper layer	(5,3)		D
			Lower	(2,1)、(5,4)		
8	1	1-1	Upper layer	(3,2)、(5,3)		E
			Lower	(3,2)、(5,3)		
9	1	1-1	Upper layer	(3,2)、(5,3)	(A,3,1),(A,5,6)	E
			Lower	(3,2)、(5,3)		
10	1	1-1	Upper layer	(3,2)、(5,3)	(A,3,4),(A,5,6)	A
			Lower	(3,2)、(5,3)		
11	1	1-1	Upper layer	(3,2)、(5,3)	(A,3,4),(B,5,6)	A
			Lower	(3,2)、(5,3)		
12	1	1-1	Upper layer	(4,4)	(A,4,2)	E
			Lower	(4,4)		
13	1	1-1	Upper layer	(4,4)	(A,4,8)	A
			Lower	(4,4)		
14	1	1-1	Upper layer	(4,4)	(A,4,5) ,(B,4,3)	A
			Lower	(4,4)		
15	1	1-1	Upper layer	(1,2)、(2,1)、(4,1)	(A,1,1)、(A,4,5)	E
			Lower	(4,4)		
16	1	1-1	Upper layer	(1,1)、(2,2)、(3,1)	(A,1,2)、(A,2,2)、(A,3,2) 、(B,2,1),	E
			Lower	(1,1)、(2,2)、(3,1)		
17	1	1-1	Upper layer	(1,2)、 (3,2)	(B,1,2) 、(B,2,2)、(B,3,2)	A
			Lower	(1,1)、(2,2)、(3,1)		
18	1	1-1	Upper layer	(5,2)		B
			Lower	(3,4)		
Total distance				5520		

By adjusting the car carriers loading order, you can get a different load transport programs, the following comparison between different options of its exemplar 4 is as follows:

Table 4 car carriers adjustment sequence loading program obtained Compare

Program	Sequence	Number of car carriers	Total distance
1	1 2 3	18	5520
2	1 3 2	18	5520
3	2 1 3	20	5940
4	2 3 1	19	5660
5	3 1 2	15	4668
6	3 2 1	15	4668

Through Table 4 we found that the program loading sequence 5 and 6 can be used to make car carriers number and total distance are relatively small. Thus show that the model can adjust the load order to achieve the effect of optimization models.

4 Conclusion

The time complexity of the model analysis as follows: Suppose a total of M cars need to use car carriers and distribution N cars, car carriers which length is L, then every - time during loading time complexity is $O(NL)$, Assuming a positive integer $2 \le k \le 4$, the complexity of the whole loading process there is $O(\sum_{i=1}^{M} kNL)$. A number n for the middle of the unloading point, and then calculate its car carrier consumed by a specific distribution path time complexity is $O(nM)$. Let the path a total of Z sites, if $Z \le 100$,Algorithm *Floyd* [14] to solve the shortest path between points, time

complexity $O(Z')$; If Z, algorithm SPFA [15-16] Solving the shortest time complexity is O (ZE), where E is the figure of the total number of edges, So the algorithm's time complexity is $O(\sum_{i=1}^{N} kNL) + O(nM) + \min(O(Z'), O(ZE))$, the model is suitable for large-scale car car carrier load distribution scheme.

The proposed model can be solved to a certain extent in our asked the passenger vehicle logistics transportation problem today. In the future work, will do the further research on the model, the improvement and optimization, and the corresponding software system, and its promotion to the commercial market.

Acknowledgments

This work was supported by the National Natural Science Fund of China (No.61462027, No. 61163055, No. 61165004), and by science& technology pillar program of Jiangxi province (20151BBE50055), and by Science Fund of ECJT University(No.13RJ04).

References

[1] Li Da,Capital University of Economics and Business,Beijing,2012.

[2] Zhang Jiangjin, Combinatorial Packing Problem: Models and Algorithms[D].Shanghai Jiao Tong University,2012.

[3] ZHANG Jiangjing,CHEN Feng.One-dimensional Packing Problem with Loading Combination Contraints.Industrial Engineering and Management.2012,17(3):90-96.

[4] Eberhard E.Bischoff ,Michael D.Marriott.A comparative evaluation of heuristics for container loading[J].European Journal of Operational Research 1990,44(2):267-27.

[5] B.K.A.Ngoi, M.L.Tay, E.S.Chua.Applying spatial representation techniques to the container packing problem[J].International Journal of Production Research,1994,32(1): 111-123.

[6] T. H. Loh, A. Y. C. Nee.A packing algorithm for hexahedral boxes[C].In:Proceedings of the Conference of Industrial Automation, Singapore ,February 1992: 115–126.

[7] HE Dayong,E Mingcheng,CHA Jianzhong,WANG Chun Xi,JIANG Yi Dong.A Heuristic Approach to Container Loading Problem Based on Space Decomposition and A Rule for Usage Rate of Packing Space, Journal of Computer-Aided Design & Computer Graphics. 2000,12 (5) :367-370.

[8] Huang Chuan.The Research of the Optimization Algorithm of the Container Loading Problem.Fujian Normal University 2005.

[9] Guo Hongwei, Development of airborne packing scheme and software development of the logistics system.qingdao,qingdao University, 2005.

[10] Shan Xiaojun ,Wu Suping. Solving 0-1 Knapsack Problems with Genetic Algorithm Based on Greedy Strategy,Computer Applications and Software,2010,27(12):238-240.

[11] SHI Lan,LV Jian-hui.New optimization algorithm of 0-1 knapsack problem.Application Research of Computers,2014,31(4):997-1000.

[12] YU Juan,HE Yuyao. Hybrid algorithm based on Genetic Algorithm and estimation of distribution algorithm for 0-1 knapsack problem. Computer Engineering and Applications, 2014,50 (9) :12-16.

[13] SONG Wenfeng.The Research of Finished Vehicle Logistics Based on Tirangle Distribution Network[D].Hefei University of Technology,2012.

[14] WANG Hua,A mixed algorithm of shortest path in logistics and distribution. Science of Surveying and Mapping, 2014.39 (9) : 135-137.

[15] SHEN Hai-lan,WANG Yu-bin,CHEN Zai-liang,CA,Zi-wen Improved SPFA Algorithm Based on Layered Graph,Computer Engineering, 2012,38 (13) :251-253.

[16] WU Xiao-zhen,LI Biao-kui,DONG Zi-yan,LI Bo-xing ZHAN Jun The Optimization and Solving of Vehicle Logistics Transport Routes and the Mode of Transportation Based on SPFA. Logistics Engineering and Management, 2014,36 (5) :176-178.

Zhou Juan is a full lecture of School of Software at East China Jiaotong University, female,born on September, 1977.She is the instructor of the Mathematical Contest in Modeling and the coach of ACM ICPC(International Collegiate Programming Contest).Her current research interests include design and analysis of computer algorithms and Graph Theory.

MATEC Web of Conferences 44, 01020 (2016)
DOI: 10.1051/matecconf/20164401020

The effect of sediment content to fluid - solid interface time-domain waveform

Li Hua Qi[1], Qing Bang Han [1,2,a], Xue Ping Jiang[1], Zi Wei Tong[1], Yu Zhang[1] and Chang Ping Zhu[1]

[1]College of IOT Engineering, Hohai University ,Changzhou, Jiangsu, 213022,China

[2]Huaian Research Institute, Hohai University, Huaian 223001, China

Abstract: A model was established for the fluid - solid interface of semi-infinite medium, and the characteristic equation was established using the potential function. Applying line source at the fluid-solid interface, transform solution of displacement could be obtained, and time-domain solution could be evaluated through the inverse Fourier transform. Two kinds of ultrasound suspension model, UA and HT, were used to study and discuss the effect of sediment content to fluid-solid interface time-domain waveform. The results of two models have a good consistency. The sediment content have a great impact on the Scholte wave. With the increase of the sediment content, for Scholte wave, the velocity increases and the attenuation decreases.

1 Introduction

The research on the effect of sediment content to fluid-solid interface time-domain waveform has profound theoretical and practical significance. In large projects, sediment content plays a key role on the implementation of the project. Since the ultrasonic wave penetrating effectively, there are obvious advantages in the detection of sediment contained of two-phase fluid[1]. In recent years, there are more and more application of ultrasonic testing. In this paper, we obtained the fluid-solid interface time-domain waveform by potential function. As early as 1948, Urick first proposed the form of velocity when the ultrasonic propagates in the suspension. Urick model is an ideal suspension model. Since then, a comprehensive model, Urick-Ament model, in which transmitted and reflected waves are considered. Then Harker and Temple proposed the Harker-Temple model based on the view of hydrodynamic. This paper mainly uses Urick-Ament model (UA model) and coupling phase model (HT model) to study and discuss the effect of sediment content to fluid-solid interface time-domain waveform.

[a] Corresponding author:hqb0092@163.com

2 Establishment of potential function

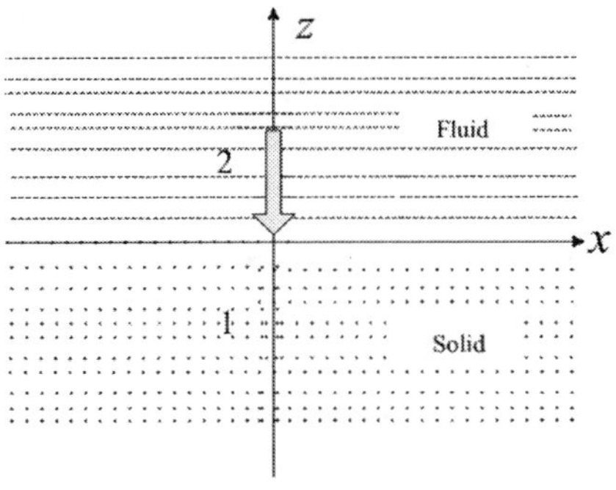

Figure1 Semi-infinite fluid-solid interface schematic

As shown in Figure 1, $Z>0$ for the semi-infinite fluid space, $Z<0$ for the semi-infinite solid space, $Z=0$ indicates the fluid - solid interface. The potential function of solid can be

expressed as ϕ_1 ψ_1. The potential function of fluid medium can be expressed as ϕ_2. The displacement potential obeys the Helmholtz equation[2].

$$\begin{cases}\nabla^2\phi = \dfrac{\partial^2\phi}{c_L{}^2\partial^2 t^2} \\ \nabla^2\psi = \dfrac{\partial^2\psi}{c_S{}^2\partial^2 t^2}\end{cases} \tag{1}$$

where c_L is the velocity of longitudinal wave, c_S is the velocity of shear wave. Carrying out Fourier transform to space x and time t

$$G(k) = \int_{-\infty}^{+\infty} g(x)e^{ikx}dx \qquad F(\omega) = \int_{-\infty}^{+\infty} f(t)e^{-i\omega t}dt \tag{2}$$

For the semi-infinite solid medium

$$\begin{cases}\overline{\phi_1}^* = A_1 e^{-k_{a1}z} \\ \overline{\psi_1}^* = C_1 e^{-k_{b1}z}\end{cases} \tag{3}$$

where, $k_{a1} = \sqrt{k^2 - \dfrac{\omega^2}{c_{L1}{}^2}}$ $k_{b1} = \sqrt{k^2 - \dfrac{\omega^2}{c_{S1}{}^2}}$

Displacement, stress can be expressed by potential function as

$$\begin{cases}\overline{\mu_{z1}}^* = -k_{a1}e^{-k_{a1}z}A_1 + ike^{-k_{b1}z}C_1 \\ \overline{\sigma_{zz1}}^* = \mu_1\left(2k^2 - \dfrac{\omega^2}{c_{S1}{}^2}\right)e^{-k_{a1}z}A_1 - 2\mu_1 ikk_{b1}e^{-k_{b1}z}C_1 \\ \overline{\sigma_{zx1}}^* = -\mu_1\left(2k^2 - \dfrac{\omega^2}{c_{S1}{}^2}\right)e^{-k_{b1}z}C_1 - 2ikk_{a1}e^{-k_{a1}z}A_1\end{cases} \tag{4}$$

For the semi-infinite fluid medium

$$\overline{\phi_2}^* = B_2 e^{k_{a1}z} \tag{5}$$

where, $k_{a2} = \sqrt{k^2 - \dfrac{\omega^2}{c_{L2}{}^2}}$

Displacement, stress can be expressed by potential function as

$$\begin{cases}\overline{\mu_{z2}}^* = k_{a2}e^{k_{a2}z}B_2 \\ \overline{\sigma_{zz2}}^* = -\lambda_2\dfrac{\omega^2}{c_L{}^2}e^{k_{a2}z}B_2 \\ \overline{\sigma_{zx1}}^* = 0\end{cases} \tag{6}$$

At z=0, According to the boundary conditions:

$$\begin{cases}\overline{\mu_{z1}}^* = \overline{\mu_{z2}}^* \\ \overline{\sigma_{zz1}}^* - \overline{\sigma_{zz2}}^* = G(k)F(w) \\ \overline{\sigma_{zx1}}^* = \overline{\sigma_{zx2}}^* = 0\end{cases} \tag{7}$$

we can get the characteristic equation:

$$\begin{bmatrix} m_{11} & m_{12} & m_{13} \\ m_{21} & m_{22} & m_{23} \\ m_{31} & m_{32} & m_{33}\end{bmatrix}\begin{bmatrix}A_1 \\ B_2 \\ C_1\end{bmatrix} = \begin{bmatrix}0 \\ G(k)F(w) \\ 0\end{bmatrix} \tag{8}$$

$m11 = -k_{a1}$ $m12 = k_{a2}$ $m13 = ik$

$m21 = -\mu_1\left(2k^2 - \dfrac{\omega^2}{c_{S1}{}^2}\right)$

$m22 = -\lambda_2\dfrac{\omega^2}{c_{L2}{}^2}$ $m23 = 2ik\mu_1 k_{b1}$

$m31 = 2ikk_{a1}$ $m32 = 0$ $m33 = 2k^2 - \dfrac{\omega^2}{c_{S1}{}^2}$

By the formula (8), coefficients A_1 B_2 C_1 can be obtained, then the transform solution of displacement of solid can be obtained.

$$\overline{\mu_{z1}}^* = -k_{a1}A_1 + ikC_1 \tag{9}$$

Inverse transform yields the solution of displacement

$$\mu_{z1} = \int_{-\infty}^{+\infty}\left(\int_{-\infty}^{+\infty}\overline{\mu_{z1}}^* e^{-ikx}dk\right)e^{i\omega t}d\omega \tag{10}$$

Formula(8), $G(k)$ $F(\omega)$ are obtained from transformed $g(x)$ $f(t)$

$$G(k) = \int_{-\infty}^{+\infty} g(x)e^{ikx}dx \qquad F(\omega) = \int_{-\infty}^{+\infty} f(t)e^{-i\omega t}dt \tag{11}$$

This passage selects $G(k) = 1$ $F(\omega) = e^{\frac{-(f-f_0)^2}{b^2}}$

3 Theoretical models of the suspension

3.1 Urick and Ament model

It is a true model of fluid[3-4], taking into account the refraction, reflection and other complex situations which occur during the propagation of the wave. The complex propagation equation of k_s^2, which describes both the velocity and attenuation in the suspension is:

$$k_s^2 = k^2\frac{\beta_{eff}}{\beta_c}\times\left[1 + \frac{3\varphi\xi(bR(2bR+3)+3i(bR+1))}{bR(4\xi bR+6bR+9)+9i(bR+1)}\right] \tag{12}$$

Where $b=\left(\frac{\omega\rho}{2\alpha}\right)^{1/2}$, $\xi=\frac{\rho^{'}-\rho}{\rho}$, α is viscosity of water, R is the radius of suspended sediment particles, k is real wave number of the pure liquid. k_s is the plural wave number, whose real part represents real wave number, imaginary part denotes attenuation.

Substituting equation(12) into.(8), the time-domain waveforms of different sediment content can be obtained.

3.2 Hanker-Temple model

Harker and Temple[5-6]considered suspension of wave phenomena from hydrodynamics, and deduced the viscous drag equation, momentum and mass conservation equations. The plural wave number equation of the Harker-Temple model could be obtained by solving these differential equations:

$$k_l^2=\beta_{eff}\omega^2\left[\frac{\rho\{\rho^{'}+(\varphi\rho^{'}+(1\text{-}\varphi)\rho)S(\omega)\}}{(\varphi\rho+(1\text{-}\varphi)\rho^{'})+\rho S(\omega)}\right] \quad (13)$$

Where $S(\omega)=\frac{1+2\varphi}{2(1\text{-}\varphi)^2}+\frac{1}{1\text{-}\varphi}\frac{9\varepsilon_v}{4}\left[1+(1+\frac{\varepsilon_v}{R})\mathrm{i}\right]$, ρ is the density of continuous phase medium, $\rho^{'}$ is the density of particle phase, φ is the solid volume fraction, β_{eff} is effective density volume compressibility factor, R is the radius of suspended sediment particles, $\varepsilon_v=\sqrt{2\eta/\omega\rho}$ is viscous shin depth, η is viscosity.

The velocity c_{l1} of the fluid can be obtained through the equation $k_l=\omega/c_{l1}$. Then substituting c_{l1} in to Eq(5), the time-domain waveforms of different sediment content can be obtained.

4 Numerical results

Parameters of Semi-infinite medium and sediment are listed in Table 1 and Table 2.Numerical results are shown in Figure 2 to Figure 7.

Table 1. Material parameters

Media	Longitudinal wave velocity/(m·s^{-1})	Shear wave velocity/(m·s^{-1})	Density /(kg· m^{-3})
Aluminum	6260	3080	2700
water	1500	--	1000

Media	Density /(kg· m^{-3})	Longitudinal wave velocity/(m·s^{-1})	Shear wave velocity/(m·s^{-1})
water	1000	1500	--
Sediment	2640	6600	2750

Media	volume compressibility /(10^{10}pa)	Thermal conductivity /(W/mK)	Specific heat capacity /(J/kgK)
water	10^{-9}/2.25	0.595	4178.5
Sediment	10^{-9}/88.378	0.269	920

Table 2. The physical parameters of sediment suspension

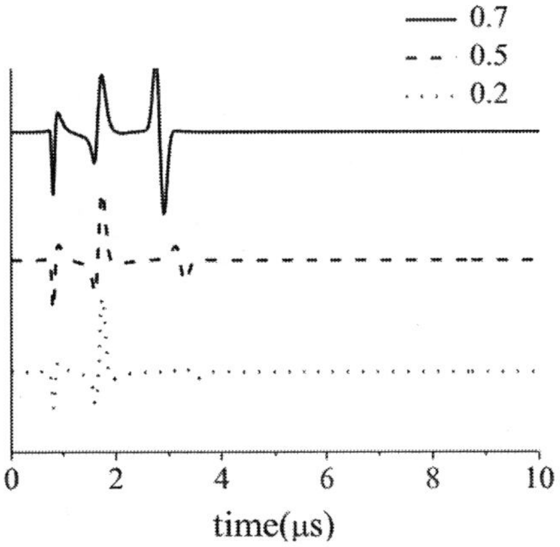

Figure 2. Interface waveforms of different sediment content at 5mm of UA model

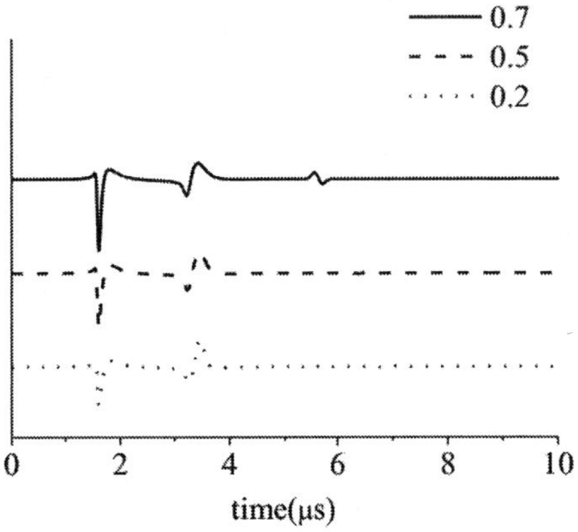

Figure 3. Interface waveforms of different sediment content at 10mm of UA model

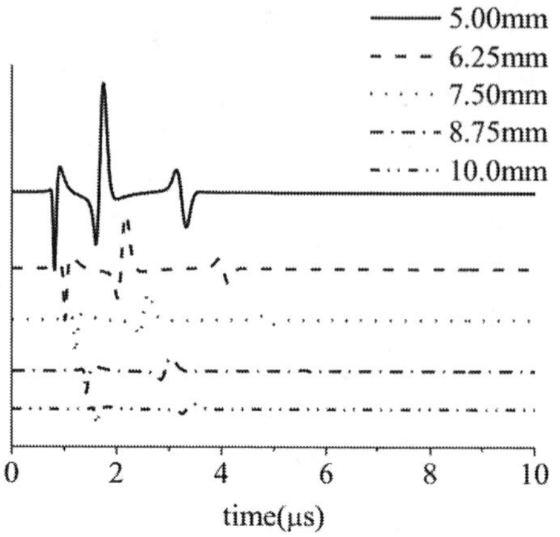

Figure4. UA model interface waveforms of different location (The sediment content is 0.5)

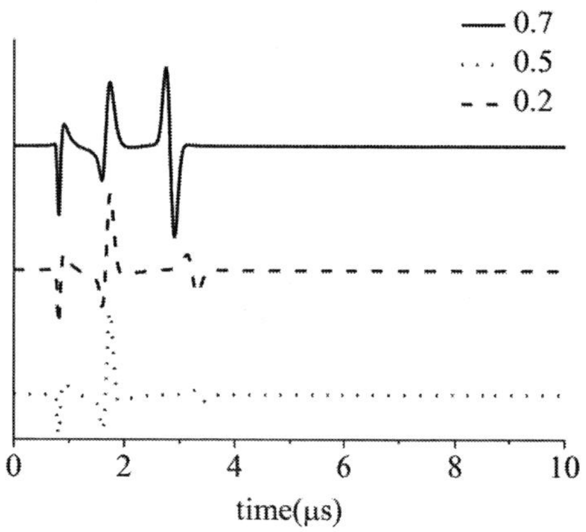

Figure 5. Interface waveforms of different sediment content at 5mm of HT model

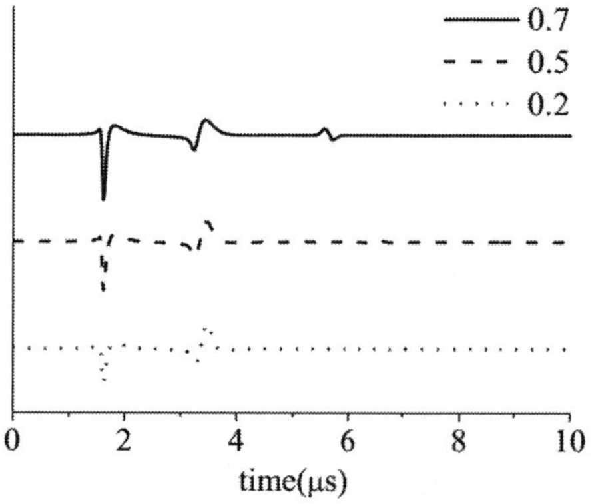

Figure6. Interface waveforms of different sediment content at 10mm of HT model

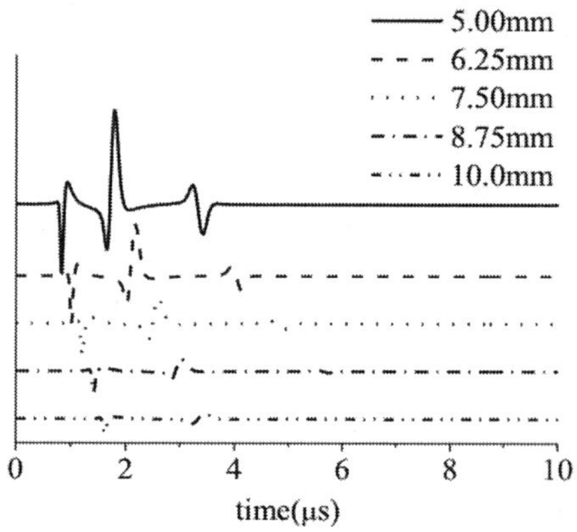

Figure7. HT model interface waveforms of different location (The sediment content is 0.5)

From Figure 2 and Figure 3, we can obtain the interface waveforms of different sediment content at 5mm and 10mm of UA model. We can find that the velocity and energy of Scholte wave increases when the sediment content grows. From Fig4, we can observe the waveforms of different locations when the sediment content is 0.5. From the waveforms, we can find that the energy of each waveform declines, when the propagation distance increases.

From Figure5 to Figure7, we can find the propagation characteristics of HT model are in good agreement with UA model.

5 Conclusions

In this paper, based on two models of suspension which are UA model and HT model, we get the fluid-solid interface time-domain waveform[7-9]. From the numerical results, the time-domain waveforms of UA model and HT model have a good consistency. By analyzing the influence of the sediment content, we can get the conclusion that the sediment content have a great impact on the Scholte wave and have little effect on the propagation of other waves. With the increase of the sediment content, for Scholte wave, the velocity increases and the attenuation decreases. Besides, in the same sediment content, with the distance of propagation increases, the energy of all the waves attenuate.

Acknowledgements

This work is supported by the Natural Science foundation of China Grant No.11274091,11574072 and the Fundamental Research Funds for the Central Universities of Hohai

University No:2011B11014

References

1. Mingxu Su, Xiaoshu Cai, Progress and Status ultrasonic particle detection technology and its applications in two-phase flow measurement,J. Journal of Northeastern University. **21(S1)**,96~99(2000).
2. Jianguo Shen, Applied Acoustics basis: the real axis integration method and two-dimensional spectroscopy (Tianjin University Press, 2004)
3. J.S. Tebbutt, R.E.Challis, Ultrasonic wave propagation in colloidal suspensions and emulsions:a comparison of four models,J. Ultrasonics.**34**,363-368(1996).
4.]R.J.Urick, J.Acoust.Soc.Am.,**20**,283(1948).
5. Harker A H, Temple J a G, Velocity and attenuation of ultrasound in suspensions of particles in fluidsJ. J Phys D.Appl Phys, **21**,1576~1588(1988)
6. Riebel U,KytoemaaH K,Theory of Sound Propagation in Suspensions:A Guide to Partical Size and Cncentration Characterization,J Powder Technol,**82,**115~121(1998)
7. J. G. Scholt. The range of existence of Rayleigh and Stoneley Waves[J]. Mo. Not. Roy. Astronomical Soc, **5**,120-126(1947).
8. Zhu JY, Popovics JS, Analytical study of excitation and measurement of fluid-solid interface wave,J. Geophysical research letter,**33(11)**,09~14(2006).
9. Favretto-Anres N, Rabau G. Excitation of the Stoneley-Scholte wave at the boundary between an ideal fluid and a viscoelastic solid, J. Journal of sound and vibration, **203(2)**, 193-208(1997)

MATEC Web of Conferences 44, 01021 (2016)
DOI: 10.1051/matecconf/20164401021

Application of genetic algorithm in target image processing of TV guided missile

Jing Feng He, Ru Liang Xiao, Ming Ji and Guang Zhen Zhang
College of Control Engineering, Xijing University, NO.1 Xijing Road, Xian,China

Abstract. Target image processing requirements of the TV guided missile is high, and the speed is fast, and the quality of target image segmentation is high.In this paper, an improved genetic algorithm based on genetic algorithm is introduced, which is used in the image segmentation of the TV guided missile, and the processing effect is good and the calculation speed is fast.Simulation results show that the algorithm is effective.

KeyWord. Image segmentation; Inter class variance method; Genetic algorithm

1 PREFACE

TV guided missile is widely used in one aspect of attack of air-to-ground because of having the characteristics of flexibility, rapid response, without geographical influence.After missile seeker intercepts the target ,Its track starts to work, and Calculates on the image to complete real-time tracking of the target. The segmentation of target directly impact on identification and track of target,so the study on segmentation of target is of great significance to combat effects of TV guided missile.

2 DEVELOPMENT STATUS OF THE IMAGE SEGMENTED METHOD

At present,there are many methods of image segmentation,and common segmented method consists of edge detection type,regional tracking,threshold type[1].Threshold type is a method that is simple and effective,simple to calculation , fast,and is a preferred method for image processing,Because the TV-guided missiles in recognition of the target tracking has a high demand on quality, speed and unity of the divided regions of target image segmentation.In this paper,we using inter class variance method based on high quality image segmentation in Threshold as foundation, and propose an improved Inter class variance method based on genetic algorithm .

3 AN IMPROVED INTER CLASS VARIANCE METHOD BASED ON GENETIC ALGORITHM

3.1 The principle upon image segmentation of threshold type

Order the grayscale range of the image that captured by seeker as $G=\{0,1,\dots,l-1\}$,$t\in G$as a limit, $B=\{b_0 b_1\}$ as one pair of binary gray,and $b_0 b_1\in G$ .The threshold settings of t can be obtained by a binary image of f_t,that is,

$$f_t(x,y)=\begin{cases} b_0 & f(x,y)<t \\ b_1 & f(x,y)\ge t \end{cases} \quad (1)$$

Threshold method of image segmentation is a process in accordance with the nor that select the most appropriate t in the range of possible values .Threshold method is divided into global threshold and local threshold . Global threshold to the whole image only sets a threshold segmentation, however, local threshold to the whole image is divided into several sub-graph, and each sub is set a threshold of segmentation.Local threshold has been more widely used, and inter-class variance method (Otsu) is one kind of representative of algorithm in local threshold.

3.2 The basic principle of inter class variance method

Threshold setting of inter class variance method divides image into target class C_0 and background class C^1 [2].and $c_0=\{0,1,\dots,t\}$, $c_1=\{t+1,\dots,l-1\}$ .Set $\sigma_b^2(t^*)$ as inter class variance method ,and the choice of optimum threshold t^* is the gray level which the maximum of σ_b^2 is corresponding to.This is:

$$\sigma_b^2(t^*)=\max_{t=G}\sigma_b^2(t\ ) \quad (2)$$

among

$$\sigma_b^2(t) = \omega_0(m_0 - m)^2 + \omega_1(m_1 - m)^2 = \omega_0\omega_1(m_1 - m_0)^2 \quad (3)$$

$$\omega_0 = \Pr(c_0) = \sum_{i=0}^{t} p_i \quad (4)$$

$$\omega_1 = \Pr(c_1) = \sum_{i=t+1}^{l-1} p_i = 1 - \omega_0 \quad (5)$$

$$m_0 = \sum_{i=0}^{t} i\Pr(c_0 \mid i) = \sum_{i=0}^{t} ip_i / \omega_0 \quad (6)$$

$$m_1 = \sum_{i=t+1}^{l-1} i\Pr(c_1 \mid i) = \sum_{i=t+1}^{l-1} ip_i / \omega_1 \quad (7)$$

$$m = \sum_{i=0}^{l-1} ip_i \quad (8)$$

Pi the rate of occurrence of Grayscale i and the graph of i are called gray histogram.

3.3 Concrete realization of of improved Otsu

Otsu method will eventually need to determine the optimal threshold value t^* to make the σ_b^2 biggest.How to choose t^* directly relate to the quality of image segmentation.For TV-guided missile, its onboard computer speech is slow, but seeker has higher requirement on the target image.The original method of optimization is not only time consuming but also requires a lot of math, not suitable for use in TV-guided missile,therefore, we need a fast and efficient method to find the optimal threshold.Based on this request, we propose the genetic algorithm optimization algorithm is introduced into the Ostu, in search of a suitable space, use a genetic algorithm to find the optimal value [3].

Genetic algorithm[4] (Genetic Algorithm abbreviated GA)is a new kind of simulation of the evolution of life mechanism and optimization ,and is a optimization equation that is with the natural genetics and computer science.It is a probabilistic search algorithm, uses some coding technique called chromosome acting on index string and simulate evolutionary process of group including these strings,using some kind of effect on the index string encoding technique called chromosome evolution simulation string composed from these groups, in order to find the best individual that suitable for a specific problem.

In our algorithm, we must first determine the decision variables and the various constraints that determine the individual's phenotype X and solution space of problem.Decision variables are the optimal threshold required of t^*.The image captured by TV-guided missile seeker of is a 256 grayscale image[5],and each pixel is an integer, and the range is 0 to 255,so the optimal threshold should be within this range, and is integer.Second, the optimal model, which determines the form of the mathematical description of the objective function and quantification methods.The specific design of fitness function uses the value of σ_b^2 as the standard, and the theory of genetic algorithms are generally established on the basis of looking at the minimum, therefore, function equation of σ_b^2 should be transformed , this is:

order

$$g(t) = -\sigma_b^2(t) = -\omega_0\omega_1(m_1 - m_0)^2 \quad (9)$$

Since $\sigma_b^2(t)$ is a non-positive, we transform $g(t)$ into minimum issue.Third, determine to represent the coding method of feasible solution of chromosome. For the coding of optimal threshold t^* can represent binary coded 0,1, its value ranges from 0 to 255, with eight of the code strings, ie 00000000-1111111. Fourth, Fourth, determine the method of quantitative evaluation of individual fitness. Since $\sigma_b^2(t)$ is a non-positive,So take the minimum individual of $g(t)$ as criteria. Fifth, design genetic operator and designing the specific operating methods of determining Selection operator, crossover operator, mutation operator.In order to meet the onboard computer and seeker needs to achieve better segmentation results in the shortest possible time in our algorithm ,So we choose the simpler operator in terms of operator.Wherein the selection operation to select proportional selection operator, crossover operator to select a single point of crossover, probability is set to 0.8, mutation operation selection uniform mutation (Uniform Mutation) operator, the probability is set to 0.008.Sixth,to determine the operating parameters relating to genetic algorithms and stop criterion.In the calculation taking into account the impact of the onboard computer speed,and evolution algebra and a large population can not be set, we taken 20,10. Stop algebraic criterion set an upper limit, namely stopping operation when reach the maximum algebraic.

Experiments show that the use of this class of genetic algorithm can get the global optimal solution of the optimal threshold t^* in a very short time. This fully meets the speed requirements onboard computer, and a better image segmentation.

4 The simulation analysis

The experiment is completed on the ground simulated projectile of TV-guided missile.First,we through seeker to capture two images of ground targets,which is transmitted to the onboard computer as an image segmentation original picture, and then by the onboard computer for image processing, image process after the original image and are fed to the type ground surveillance computer simulated projectile.The following is a target image of the original image of ground targets and the use of based on improved genetic algorithm between class variance law division.

（a） Goal one artwork

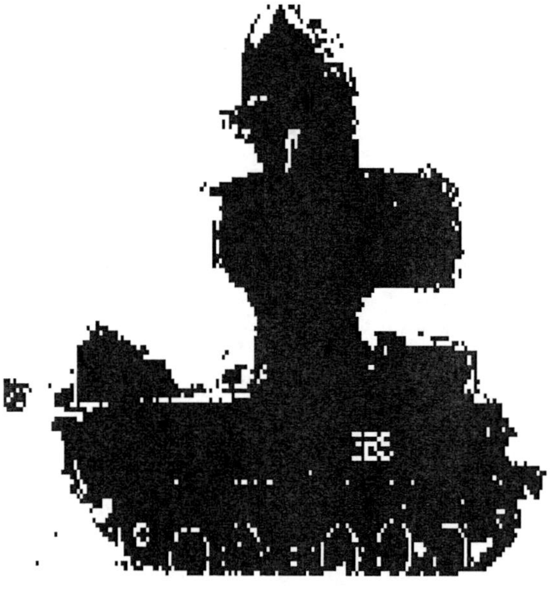

（b） Goal two segmented image

Figure I target- image segmentation

（a）Goal two artwork

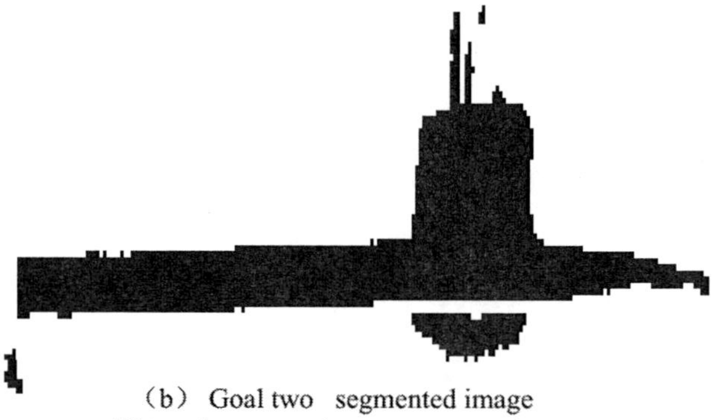

（b） Goal two segmented image

Figure 2 target- image segmentation

From the segmented image can be seen,two target image used inter class variance method have a good segmentation results.The target is clearly separated from the background, and the basic characteristics of the target is also well demonstrated.

5 Conclusion

Experiments show that, based on the type of TV-guided missiles of this approach can distinguish, track targets very good and always with the goal keep the range of allowable deviation.This shows that the target image segmentation In this method not only has a good segmentation effect, while the requirements for the onboard computer of the TV-guided missile, which provides a good research methods in the study of television guided missiles in.

References

[1]Zhon Ming,Sun Shudong.The principle and application of the genetic algorithm [M] 。Beijing:national defense industry press,2002
[2]Hou Gexian.Genetic algorithm and its application in tracking system [D],Xi'an：Xi'an university of electronic science and technology, 1998
[3]Cui Yi.The technology and application of digital image process[M].Beijing:electronic industry press,2001
[4]Peng Xuan.Genetic algorithm and its application in image segmentation [D].Changchun: Jilin university graduate thesis, 2006
[5]Le Zhongxin.Digital image process [M] Beijing: national defense industry press, 2003.

MATEC Web of Conferences 44, 01022 (2016)
DOI: 10.1051/matecconf/20164401022

Multi-channel Dual Clocks three-dimensional probability Random Multiple Access protocol for Wireless Public Bus Networks based on RTS/CTS mechanism

Sheng Jie Zhou[1], Hong Wei Ding[1,a], Meng Yao Wang[1], Qian Lin Liu[1] and Zhi Jun Yang

[1] School of Informaton, Yunnan University, Kunming, 650091, China.

Abstract. A MAC protocol for public bus networks, called Bus MAC protocol, designed to provide high quality Internet service for bus passengers. The paper proposed a multi-channel dual clocks three-demission probability random multiple access protocol based on RTS/CTS mechanism, decreasing collisions caused by multiple access from multiple passengers. Use the RTS/CTS mechanism increases the reliability and stability of the system, reducing the collision possibility of the information packets to a certain extent, improves the channel utilization; use the multi-channel mechanism, not only enables the channel load balancing, but also solves the problem of the hidden terminal and exposed terminal. Use the dual clocks mechanism, reducing the system idle time. At last, the different selection of the three-dimensional probabilities can make the system throughput adapt to the network load which could realize the maximum of the system throughput.

1 Introduction

Intelligent Transportation Systems (Intelligent Traffic System, referred ITS), is the advanced science and technology (information technology, computer technology, data communication technology, sensor technology, electronic control technology, automatic control theory, operations research, artificial intelligence, etc.) to effectively apply the integrated transport, service control and vehicle manufacturing, to strengthen ties vehicles, roads, among users, creating a safety, improve efficiency, improve the environment, energy conservation integrated transport system [1].

With the development of intelligent transportation systems technology, intelligent transportation system will be more widely used in the transportation industry. Therefore, Internet access by bus achieves growing demand. In major cities, every day about the millions of people travel by bus and often takes several minutes or even one hour in traffic.

Compared to other networks, providing Internet services have its obvious channel for the bus access features. Buses usually have more than one passenger. These passengers as a group of mobile node moves and each passenger simultaneously produce different types of Internet service request, for example, news browsing, e-mail access and streaming media data services [2].

Combined bus communication characteristics, the paper proposed a multi-channel dual clocks three-demission probability random multiple access protocol based on RTS/CTS mechanism.

Before the site first sends a request to send a packet transmission frame RTS (Request to Send) to the target site, waiting for the response from the target site CTS (Clear to Send) frame after, it began to transfer packets. If the transmitting station does not receive CTS, then perform a binary exponential backoff algorithm delay retransmission RTS. In this process, we listen to the other node RTS to be delayed for some time to send, in order to ensure the sending node capable of successfully received CTS. Use RTS/CTS handshake (handshake) mechanism, it can ensure that the next transmission packet, no collision, since the RTS/CTS frame while very small, so that the invalid transmission overhead becomes small [3].

Above is the RTS/CTS mechanism. Based on the three-dimensional probability random multiple access protocol, we resolve the "hidden terminal" and "exposed terminal" problem, decreasing collisions caused by multiple access from multiple passengers [4].

Also to reduce the system idle time, we adopt the dual clocks mechanism. When the system is idle, we use continue-time control strategy; when the system is busy, we use the discrete-time control strategy [5].

Last to achieve the multiple business access and improve the system throughput, we join the multi-channel mechanism realization the channel load balancing, meet the different priorities business with different QoS requirements by taking advantage of the priority control of multi-channel multi-service [6].

2 The analysis of the proposed protocol

[a] Corresponding author: *dhw1964@163.com*

2.1 The analysis of RTS/CTS mechanism

The channel model of three-dimensional random multiple access protocol is shown in Figure 1.

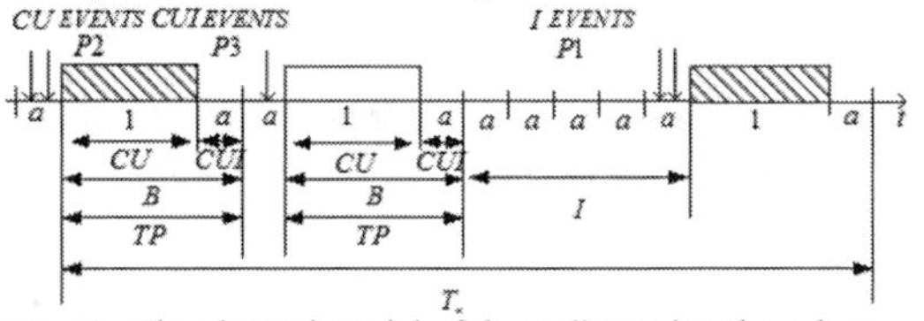

Figure 1. The channel model of three-dimensional random multiple access protocol

In this model, there will be three random events:

● Event that information packets are sent successfully (U events).

● Event that information packets collide with each other (the collision appears, C events).

● Event that there are no information packets in the channel arrive, the channel is idle (I events) [7].

These three events are forced into: the channel is idle (I events) event, the channel is busy (CU events) and the channel is idle following the CU events (CUI events); the packet is sent successfully or unsuccessfully (combined C events with U event, denoted by CU event); force the CU events and the CUI events into B events [8].

According to the new protocol, if the channel is idle, then the user decides to send an information packet probability P_1; if the channel is in transmission time, the user listens to the channel with probability P_2 and P_3 repectively in time 1 and a. This control strategy, P_1, P_2 and P_3 by three-dimensional selection enables the system utilization and throughput is guaranteed under different load.

The channel model of three-dimensional random multiple access protocol based on RTS/CTS mechanism is shown in Figure 2.

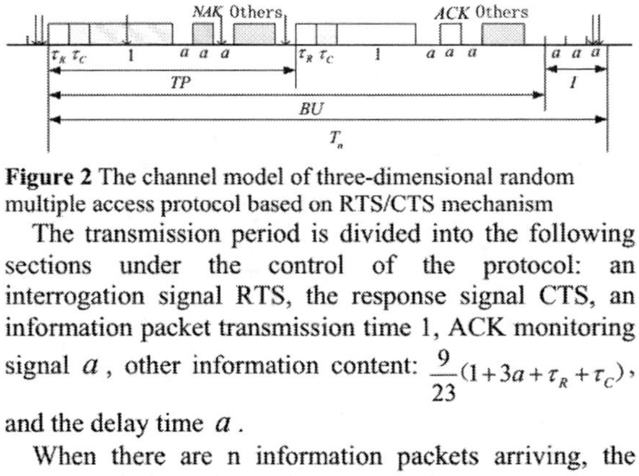

Figure 2 The channel model of three-dimensional random multiple access protocol based on RTS/CTS mechanism

The transmission period is divided into the following sections under the control of the protocol: an interrogation signal RTS, the response signal CTS, an information packet transmission time 1, ACK monitoring signal a, other information content: $\frac{9}{23}(1+3a+\tau_R+\tau_C)$, and the delay time a.

When there are n information packets arriving, the process of channel satisfying the Poisson process, the probability is:

$$P(n)=\frac{(aG)^n e^{-aG}}{n!} \tag{1}$$

In I events, at idle time slot a, if there is no information packets to be sent, its possibility is:

$$q_1^0=e^{-ap_1G} \tag{2}$$

In I events, at idle time slot a, if there is only one information packet to be sent, its possibility is:

$$q_1^1=ap_1Ge^{-ap_1G} \tag{3}$$

At the transmission period, if there is no information packets to be sent, its possibility is:

$$q_2^0=e^{-\{p_2+[\frac{32}{23}(3a+\tau_R+\tau_C)+\frac{9}{23}]p_3\}G} \tag{4}$$

In the transmission period, if there is only one information packet to be sent, its possibility is:

$$q_2^1=\{p_2+[\frac{32}{23}(3a+\tau_R+\tau_C)+\frac{9}{23}]p_3\} Ge^{-\{p_2+[\frac{32}{23}(3a+\tau_R+\tau_C)+\frac{9}{23}]p_3\}G} \tag{5}$$

In a cycle, the possibility of continuous i idle events is:

$$P(N_I=i)=(e^{-ap_1G})^{i-1}e^{-\{p_2+[\frac{32}{23}(3a+\tau_R+\tau_C)+\frac{9}{23}]p_3\}G} \tag{6}$$

In a cycle, the possibility of continuous j B events is:

$$P(N_B=j)=(1-e^{-ap_1G})(1-e^{-\{p_2+[\frac{32}{23}(3a+\tau_R+\tau_C)+\frac{9}{23}]p_3\}G})^{j-1} \tag{7}$$

In a cycle, the possibility of continuous i I events and j B eventsis:

$$P(N_I=i,N_B=j)=(e^{-ap_1G})^{i-1}(1-e^{-ap_1G}) (1-e^{-\{p_2+[\frac{32}{23}(3a+\tau_R+\tau_C)+\frac{9}{23}]p_3\}G})^{j-1}e^{-\{p_2+[\frac{32}{23}(3a+\tau_R+\tau_C)+\frac{9}{23}]p_3\}G} \tag{8}$$

The averages number of i continuous I events in a cycle is:

$$\begin{aligned}E(N_I)&=\sum_{i=1}^{\infty}\sum_{j=1}^{\infty}iP(N_I=i,N_B=j)\\&=\sum_{i=1}^{\infty}\sum_{j=1}^{\infty}i(e^{-ap_1G})^{i-1}(1-e^{-ap_1G})\\&\quad(1-e^{-\{p_2+[\frac{32}{23}(3a+\tau_R+\tau_C)+\frac{9}{23}]p_3\}G})^{j-1}e^{-\{p_2+[\frac{32}{23}(3a+\tau_R+\tau_C)+\frac{9}{23}]p_3\}G}\\&=\frac{1}{1-e^{-ap_1G}}\end{aligned} \tag{9}$$

The average number of j continuous B events in a cycle T_n is:

$$\begin{aligned}E(N_B)&=\sum_{i=1}^{\infty}\sum_{j=1}^{\infty}jP(N_I=i,N_B=j)\\&=\sum_{i=1}^{\infty}\sum_{j=1}^{\infty}j(e^{-ap_1G})^{i-1}(1-e^{-ap_1G})\\&\quad(1-e^{-\{p_2+[\frac{32}{23}(3a+\tau_R+\tau_C)+\frac{9}{23}]p_3\}G})^{j-1}e^{-\{p_2+[\frac{32}{23}(3a+\tau_R+\tau_C)+\frac{9}{23}]p_3\}G}\\&=\frac{1}{1-e^{-\{p_2+[\frac{32}{23}(3a+\tau_R+\tau_C)+\frac{9}{23}]p_3\}G}}\end{aligned} \tag{10}$$

To the discrete time three-dimensional probability random multiple access protocol with RTS/CTS mechanism, the information packets are sent successfully in two cases.

Firstly the number of information packet transmitted successfully in I events are:

$$E(N_{U_1})=\frac{q_1^1}{1-q_1^0}=\frac{ap_1Ge^{-ap_1G}}{1-e^{-ap_1G}} \tag{11}$$

The average length of information packet transmitted successfully in I events is:

$$E(U_1)=E(N_{U_1})\times 1=\frac{ap_1Ge^{-ap_1G}}{1-e^{-ap_1G}} \tag{12}$$

Secondly the average length of continuous K U events in the TP time in a cycle is:

$$E(U_2)=\sum_{i=1}^{\infty}\sum_{j=1}^{\infty}\sum_{K=0}^{i-1}KP(N_I=i,N_B=j)\times 1$$
$$=\sum_{i=1}^{\infty}\sum_{j=1}^{\infty}\sum_{K=0}^{i-1}K(e^{-ap_1G})^{i-1}(1-e^{-ap_1G})$$
$$(1-e^{-\{p_2+[\frac{32}{23}(3a+\tau_R+\tau_C)+\frac{9}{23}]p_3\}G})^{j-1}e^{-\{p_2+[\frac{32}{23}(3a+\tau_R+\tau_C)+\frac{9}{23}]p_3\}G}$$
$$=\{p_2+[\frac{32}{23}(3a+\tau_R+\tau_C)+\frac{9}{23}]p_3\}G \tag{13}$$

In a cycle, the average length of time slot that information packet has been successfully sent is:

$$E(U)=E(U_1)+E(U_2)$$
$$=\frac{ap_1Ge^{-ap_1G}}{1-e^{-ap_1G}}+\{p_2+[\frac{32}{23}(3a+\tau_R+\tau_C)+\frac{9}{23}]p_3\}G \tag{14}$$

The average length of B event in is:

$$E(B)=E(N_B)\times\frac{32}{23}(1+3a+\tau_R+\tau_C)=\frac{\frac{32}{23}(1+3a+\tau_R+\tau_C)}{1-e^{-\{p_2+[\frac{32}{23}(3a+\tau_R+\tau_C)+\frac{9}{23}]p_3\}G}} \tag{15}$$

The average length of I event is:

$$E(I)=E(N_I)\times a=\frac{a}{1-e^{-ap_1G}} \tag{16}$$

The throughput of the three-dimensional probability random multiple access protocol with RTS/CTS mechanism is:

$$S=\frac{E(U)}{E(B)+E(I)}$$
$$=\frac{\frac{ap_1Ge^{-ap_1G}}{1-e^{-ap_1G}}+\{p_2+[\frac{32}{23}(3a+\tau_R+\tau_C)+\frac{9}{23}]p_3\}G}{\frac{\frac{32}{23}(1+3a+\tau_R+\tau_C)}{1-e^{-\{p_2+[\frac{32}{23}(3a+\tau_R+\tau_C)+\frac{9}{23}]p_3\}G}}+\frac{a}{1-e^{-ap_1G}}} \tag{17}$$

2.2 The analysis of dual clocks mechanism

When the system is idle, the system uses continuous-time control strategy. And if the system is busy, the system uses discrete-time control strategy.

Since the number of idle slots I within the geometric distribution with the mean: $E(N)=\frac{1}{1-e^{-Gp_1a}}$, an information packet arrive in a time slot with normalized probability: $p_{I1}=\frac{Gp_1ae^{-Gp_1a}}{1-e^{-Gp_1a}}$, more than an information packet arrives in a time slot with the normalized probability: $p_{I2}=\frac{1-Gp_1ae^{-Gp_1a}-e^{-Gp_1a}}{1-e^{-Gp_1a}}$.

Then we get:

$$E(I)=(\frac{1}{1-e^{-Gp_1a}}-1)a+\frac{Gp_1a^2e^{-Gp_1a}}{2(1-e^{-Gp_1a})}+\frac{(1-Gp_1ae^{-Gp_1a}-e^{-Gp_1a})a}{1-e^{-Gp_1a}} \tag{18}$$

The throughput of the dual clocks three-dimensional probability random multiple access protocol with RTS/CTS mechanism is:

$$S=\frac{E(U)}{E(B)+E(I)}$$
$$=\{\frac{ap_1Ge^{-ap_1G}}{1-e^{-ap_1G}}+\{p_2+[\frac{32}{23}(3a+\tau_R+\tau_C)+\frac{9}{23}]p_3\}G\}$$
$$/[\frac{\frac{32}{23}(1+3a+\tau_R+\tau_C)}{1-e^{-\{p_2+[\frac{32}{23}(3a+\tau_R+\tau_C)+\frac{9}{23}]p_3\}G}}+(\frac{1}{1-e^{-Gp_1a}}-1)a$$
$$+\frac{Gp_1a^2e^{-Gp_1a}}{2(1-e^{-Gp_1a})}+\frac{(1-Gp_1ae^{-Gp_1a}-e^{-Gp_1a})a}{1-e^{-Gp_1a}}] \tag{19}$$

2.3 The analysis of multi-channel mechanism

Assuming that nodes have different service requirement have different priorities, setting N traffic channels in the system, the node occupies the channel according to their business priorities. Assume that each priority unlimited the number of users, the priority from low to high in order is priority 1, priority 2... priority N.

Priority 1 occupies the channel 1, priority 2 occupies channel 1 and channel 2... priority i occupies channel 1 to channel i. The arrival information packets on the channel i subject to the *Poisson* distribution with arriving rate G_i, the arrival packets of priority r on the channel i subject to the *Poisson* distribution with arriving rate $\lambda_i=G_i/(N-i+1)$. The multichannel mechanism owning N channels is showed in Figure 3.

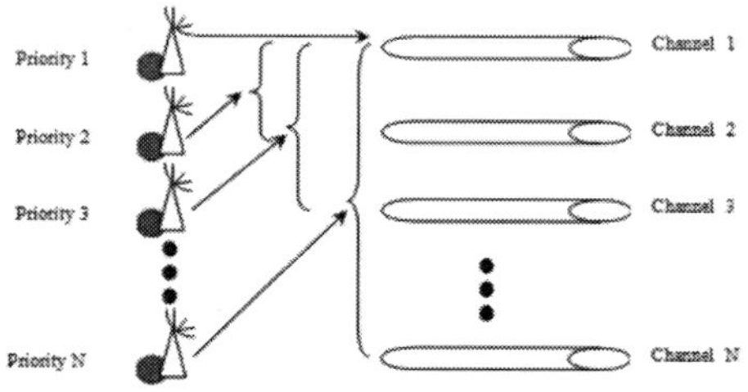

Figure 3 The multichannel mechanism owning N channels

In the N channels of wireless communication system, because this channel model is a load equilibrium model, so the arrival probabilities of each channel are the same, that is to say:

$$G_1=G_2=G_3=\cdots=G_i=\cdots=G_N=G \tag{20}$$

Basing on the above analysis and computational formula of the systemic throughput, the system total throughput is:

$$S'=NS$$
$$=N\{\frac{ap_1Ge^{-ap_1G}}{1-e^{-ap_1G}}+\{p_2+[\frac{32}{23}(3a+\tau_R+\tau_C)+\frac{9}{23}]p_3\}G\}$$
$$/[\frac{\frac{32}{23}(1+3a+\tau_R+\tau_C)}{1-e^{-\{p_2+[\frac{32}{23}(3a+\tau_R+\tau_C)+\frac{9}{23}]p_3\}G}}+(\frac{1}{1-e^{-Gp_1a}}-1)a$$
$$+\frac{Gp_1a^2e^{-Gp_1a}}{2(1-e^{-Gp_1a})}+\frac{(1-Gp_1ae^{-Gp_1a}-e^{-Gp_1a})a}{1-e^{-Gp_1a}}] \tag{21}$$

Then according to the above analysis, we can get the throughput with the priority l:

$$S_{pl}=(\sum_{i=1}^{l}\frac{1}{N-i+1})S$$
$$=(\sum_{i=1}^{l}\frac{1}{N-i+1})\{\frac{ap_1Ge^{-ap_1G}}{1-e^{-ap_1G}}+\{p_2+[\frac{32}{23}(3a+\tau_R+\tau_C)$$
$$+\frac{9}{23}]p_3\}G\}/[\frac{\frac{32}{23}(1+3a+\tau_R+\tau_C)}{1-e^{-\{p_2+[\frac{32}{23}(3a+\tau_R+\tau_C)+\frac{9}{23}]p_3\}G}}+(\frac{1}{1-e^{-Gp_1a}}-1)a$$
$$+\frac{Gp_1a^2e^{-Gp_1a}}{2(1-e^{-Gp_1a})}+\frac{(1-Gp_1ae^{-Gp_1a}-e^{-Gp_1a})a}{1-e^{-Gp_1a}}] \tag{22}$$

3 Experimental classification results and analysis

Based on the above analysis, with the use of simulation tool: MATLAB R2010a, the simulation results are shown as following. During the simulation, transmission delay time: $a = 0.1$, $\tau_R = \tau_C = 0.1$, packet length is: $\frac{32}{23}(1+3a+\tau_R+\tau_C)$.

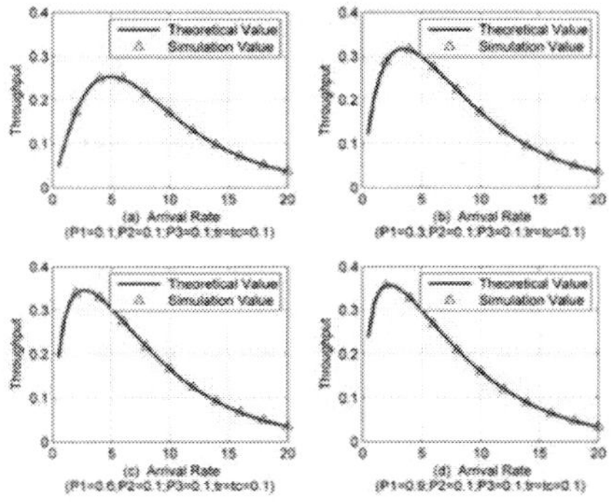

Figure 4 The throughput of the new protocol with different P1.

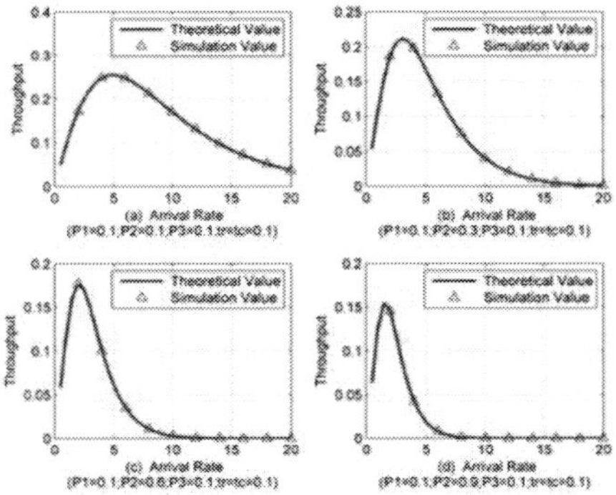

Figure 5 The throughput of the new protocol with different P2.

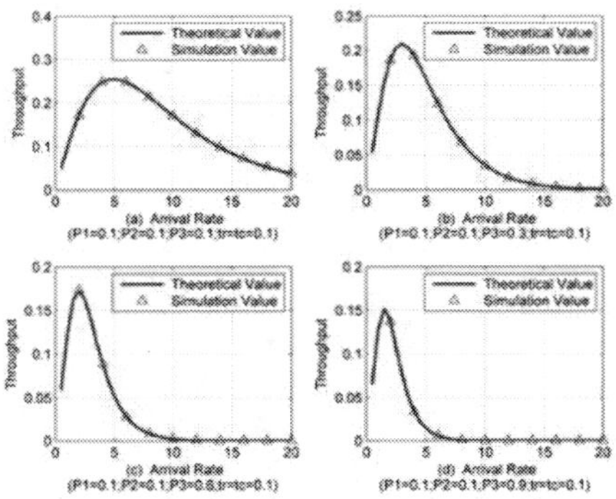

Figure 6 The throughput of the new protocol with different P3.

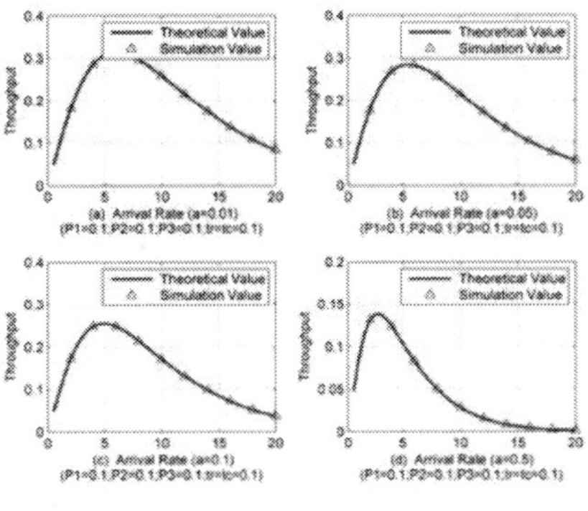

Figure 7 The throughput of the new protocol with different a.

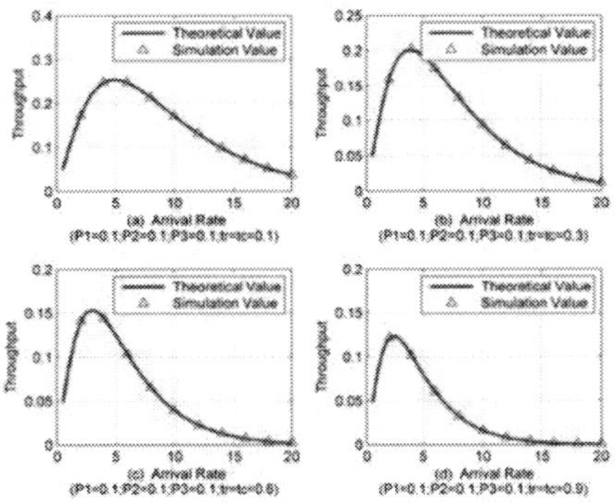

Figure 8 The throughput of new protocol with different tr, tc.

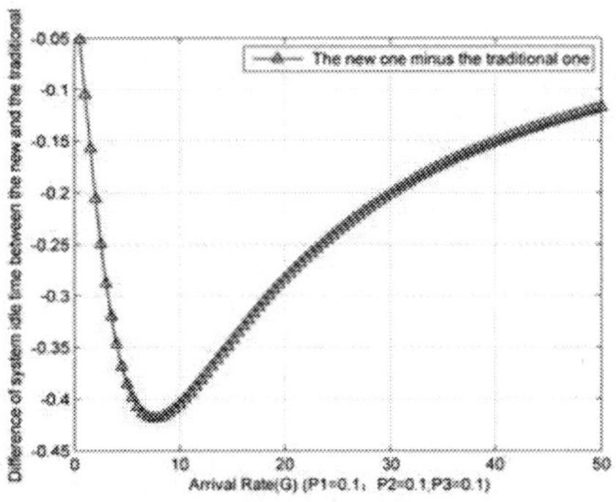

Figure 9 The difference of system idle time between the new protocol and the traditional one.

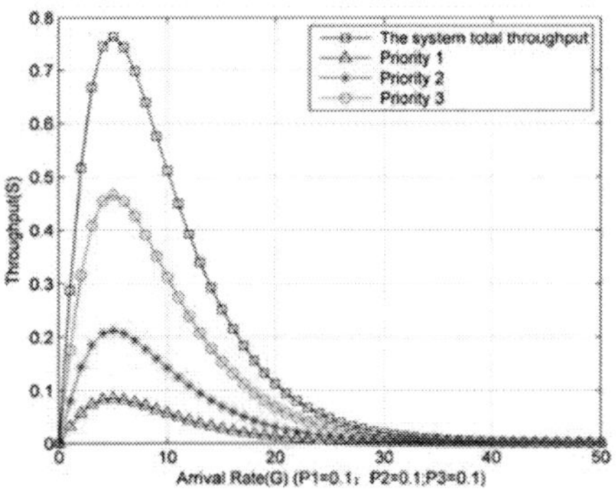

Figure 10 The throughput of the new protocol with 3 channels.

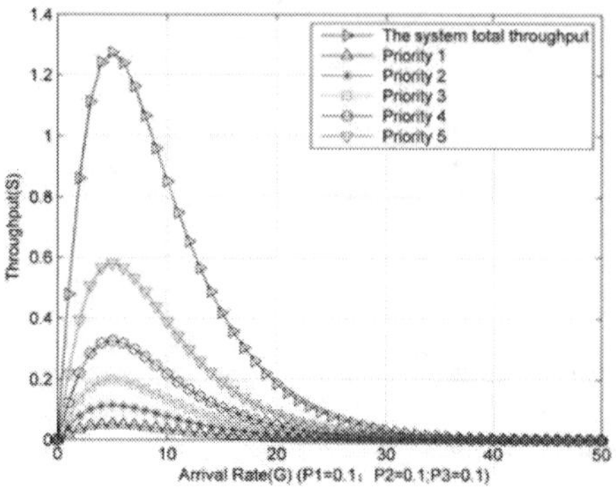

Figure 11 The throughput the new protocol with 5 channels.

Through the above simulation results, we can draw the following conclusions:

1, system simulation coincides with the theoretical value higher degree of consistency proved the theoretical derivation, and proves the accuracy of the simulation.

2, through P1, P2 and P3, we achieve regulation on the system throughput. At low load, P1 increases system throughput can be improved; however, at a high load, P1 increases will reduce the throughput. Because of the low load increases the transmission probability may increase the probability of successfully transmitted packets, and transmit high load increases the probability it will cause more serious conflict. Similarly, when a low load, P2 make a small increase system throughput will increase; a high load, increasing the probability P2 collisions will increase dramatically reduces system throughput. Therefore, we can make the probability of a combination of P1, P2 and P3 at optimum circumstances mentioned in the throughput is greater.

3, by introducing the dual clock mechanism, it can really reduce the idle rate of the system, especially at low load, idle rate of the system is reduced by a big margin; because at high load, the system is idle rate already high, so the capacity of the mechanism at a high load reducing system idle rate weakened; and in different combinations of probability, idle rate of the system is reduced rates are not the same.

4, and finally through a multi-channel mechanism, not only improves the overall throughput of the system, but also to achieve the different priorities for different bus passengers, providing a different throughput access to multiple services.

4 Conclusions

With the development of intelligent transportation systems technology, for providing high quality Internet service in public buses, combined bus communication characteristics, the paper proposed a multi-channel dual clocks three-demission probability random multiple access protocol based on RTS/CTS mechanism. By introduction of the RTS/CTS mechanism increases the reliability and stability of the system, reducing the collision possibility of the information packets to a certain extent, improves the channel utilization; by the use of the multi-channel mechanism, not only enables the channel load balancing, but also solves the problem of the hidden terminal and exposed terminal. By introduction of the dual clocks mechanism, reducing the system idle time. The different selection of the three-dimensional probabilities can make the system throughput adapt to the network load which could realize the maximum of the system throughput. At last, system simulation coincides with the theoretical value higher degree of consistency proved the theoretical derivation, and proves the accuracy of the simulation.

Acknowledgements

This work was supported by the National Natural Science Foundation of China (61461053, 61461054, 61072079); Natural Science Foundation of Yunnan Province (2010CD023); The Financial Support of Yunnan University (No.XT412004).

References

1. Shengjie Zhou, Hongwei Ding, Yifan Zhao, Zhijun Yang and Qianlin Liu. Research on the discrete time three-dimensional probability csma protocol in ad-hoc network [J]. International Journal of Recent Scientific Research, 2015, 6(5): 4257-4262.
2. Xuming. Research and development of mobile Ad Hoc network [J]. Data Communications, 2003 (4): 15-18.
3. Conti M, Giordano S. Mobile ad hoc networking: milestones, challenges, and new research directions [J]. Communications Magazine, IEEE, 2014, 52(1): 85-96.
4. Gandhi C, Arya V. A Survey of Energy-Aware Routing Protocols and Mechanisms for Mobile Ad Hoc Networks [M]. Intelligent Computing, Networking, and Informatics. Springer India, 2014: 111-117.
5. Xiaoping Wu. Research on the hidden and exposed terminal problem in the Ad Hoc network [J]. Microcomputer Information, 2006 (10X): 35-37.
6. Jayasuriya A, Perreau S, Dadej A, et al. Hidden and exposed terminal problem in ad hoc networks[D]. ATNAC 2004.
7. Wang L, Wu K, Hamdi M. Attached-RTS: Eliminating an Exposed Terminal Problem in Wireless Networks [J]. IEEE Transactions on Parallel and Distributed Systems, 2013, 24(7): 1289-1299.
8. Dongfeng Zhao. Study on A New Method for Continuous-time Systems of Random Access Channel [J]. Journal of Electronics, 1999, 21(1): 37-41.

MATEC Web of Conferences **44**, 01023 (2016)
DOI: 10.1051/matecconf/20164401023

The discrete time multichannel three-dimensional probability CSMA with function of monitoring based IoT

Sheng Jie Zhou[1], Hong Wei Ding[1*], Zhi Jun Yang[1], Qian Lin Liu[1], Meng Yao Wang[1]
[1]Information Academic, Yunnan University, Cuihu North Road NO.2, Kunming, China
*dhw@163.com

Abstract: Currently, with the rapid development of Internet of Things (IoT), users demand more and more personalized and diversified business categories, radio spectrum increasingly tense. With the exploiting of Transmission Control Protocol/Internet Protocol (TCP / IP) protocol, network achieves the objects of the intelligent identifying, locating, tracking, monitoring and managing a network. Multichannel random access mechanism maximizes the utilization of constrained spectrum resources and allocating scarce channel resources to disparate hierarchical according to business priorities with various qualitiy of service (QoS) requirements. In this paper, we propose a MAC design combining them together in one unit system under three-dimensional probability CSMA (Carrier Sense Multiple Access) adopting the average cycle analysis method to analysis. Through the paper, precise mathematical value of system throughput is got by rigorous derivations under many circumstances. The correctness of the theory and model is demonstrated with simulation results and effectiveness illustrated. In the offline phase, simulation results verify that the proposed algorithm can improves the controllability of the system, the channel utilization, system security, and reliability of packet transmission and meet the different priorities of different QoS requirements.
Keywords: Three-dimensional probability, CSMA, multichannel, IoT, throughput.

1. Introduction

Things to be considered as use of the Internet expansion, the application of innovation is the core of the development of things to the user experience as the core of the innovation is the soul of the development of things. IoT (Internet of Things) is an important part of the new generation of information technology [1]. Thus, by definition, "things that material objects connected to the Internet." "Things" refers to the various information sensing equipments, such as: radio frequency identification, infrared sensors, global positioning systems, laser scanners, various other devices and the Internet combine to form a huge network. The aim is to have all the items are connected to the network to facilitate the identification and management. This has two meanings: First, the core and foundation of things is still the Internet, is based on the Internet extension and expansion of the network; second, to extend and expand its client to any goods and items of information exchange and communication [2].

The role of the MAC layer is to provide fair, reliable, efficient scheduling mechanism to allocate radio channel resources, MAC protocol performance is directly related to the performance of the wireless channel utilization and the entire network [3]. It has always been important and difficult research among scholars.

And the most common MAC layer protocol is carrier sense multiple access (CSMA) with varieties of other mechanisms.

There are many sites in the wireless communication network, so the channel resource is limited. If the site sends a message according to no law, then the probability that information packets come into the collision will be greatly increased[4]. Then if we use the CSMA (Carrier Sense Multiple Access) protocol, a site listens to the status of the channel first, and then decides whether to send a message or not[5]. With the mechanism, the probability of such a collision would be significantly reduced.

During the process of information exchange and communication, in order to achieve the objects of the intelligent identify, locate, track, monitor and manage a network, then TCP / IP (Control Protocol/Internet Protocol) come into use [6, 7].

For TCP / IP protocol, if the recipient successfully receives the data, it will return an ACK. ACK signals usually have their own fixed format, the length of size, to reply to the sender by the recipient. The format depends on which kind of the network protocol is taken [8]. When the sender receives the ACK signal, it can send the next data. If the sender does not receive a signal, then the sender may retransmit the current data package, data transfer may stop. The process is depending on the network protocol used.

Currently, with the rapid development of IoT, users demand more and more personalized and diversified business categories, radio spectrum increasingly tense. Multichannel random access protocol can maximize the utilization of

spectrum resources and to allocate resources according to business priorities various QoS (qualitiy of service) requirements. On the future development of mobile communications, it will play an important role.

To achieve the above functions we propose the multichannel three-dimensional probability CSMA with function of monitoring (MMTDP-CSMA). The agreement not only enables the function of intelligent identify, locate, track, monitor and manage a network, but also realizes maximizing the utilization of spectrum resources and allocating resources according to business priorities various QoS requirements.

The rest of this paper is organized as follows: Section 2 describes the based protocol three-dimensional probability CSMA. Section 3 presents our MMTDP-CSMA protocol in detail. To evaluate the performance of the MMTDP-CSMA protocol, simulation setup and results are presented in Section 4. Finally, Section 5 concludes the paper.

2. Three-dimensional probability CSMA

The basic idea of CSMA is that before a site attempts its transmission, it needs to infer the channel condition by sensing the channel. If it infers that its transmission will upset (or be upset by) any receiver's ongoing transmissions (including its own receiver), then it defers its transmission. In addition, to prevent two sites from beginning their transmissions at the same time (given that they both sense the channel to be safe for transmission), each transmitter undergoes a random back-off countdown period before transmission .

For three-dimensional probability CSMA, there will be three random events appearing repeatedly: a packet is sent successfully (U events), transmission is done unsuccessfully namely two or more packets are sent at one time (C events), no packets need to be transmitted that channel is idle (I events), these three events are forced into: channel is idle (I events) event, channel is busy (CU events) and channel is idle following the CU events (CUI events); packet is sent successfully or unsuccessfully(combined C events with U event, denoted by CU event); force CU events and CUI events into B events. A cycle period is T_n. TP is transmission period. Use three-dimensional probability: P1, P2, P3 to control the period of I events, CUI events and CU events separately. At I events phase, a site send a packet at probability P1. During the CU events, the site senses channel status with probability P2. Similar to CU events, while a site is in CUI events, it senses channel status at probability P3.

Basic unit of the system control clock is a , the information packets arrived at time a will transmit at the starting time of the next slot;

Channel propagation delay is a ,the packet length is unit length and is an integral multiple of a ;

Packets need to be sent at the first slot in the transmission period can always sense the state of channel at last moment;

During the transmission period of information packets, the phenomenon of packet collisions occur inevitably, and continues to be sent after a random time delay, it sends will not produce any adverse effects on the arrival process channel

In a cycle, the average length of time slot that information packet has been successfully sent in a cycle is:

$$E(U)=E(U_1)+E(U_2)=\frac{ap_1Ge^{-ap_1G}}{1-e^{-ap_1G}}+(ap_2+p_3)G \tag{1}$$

Average length of B event is:

$$E(B)=E(N_B)\times(1+a)=\frac{1+a}{1-e^{-(ap_2+p_3)G}} \tag{2}$$

Where $(1+a)$ represents the length of information packet whether it transmitted successfully or not in the TP cycle.

Average length of I event is:

$$E(I)=E(N_I)\times a=\frac{a}{1-e^{-ap_1G}} \quad 3$$

System throughput of three-dimensional probability CSMA is:

$$S=\frac{E(U)}{E(B)+E(I)}=\frac{\frac{ap_1Ge^{-ap_1G}}{1-e^{-ap_1G}}+(ap_2+p_3)G}{\frac{1+a}{1-e^{-(ap_2+p_3)G}}+\frac{a}{1-e^{-ap_1G}}} \quad 4)$$

3. MMTDP-CSMA

With the multi-channel mechanism, there is more than one channel; we assume it owns N channels.

Thus considering the system having N channels and N priorities, the nodes are accessed to the channel resources randomly by the business priorities of themselves which is depicted in Fig.2.

Assume that the priority sequence is arranged from low to high as priority 1, priority 2... priority N. The service with priority i occupies channel 1 to i (i=1, 2... N), that is the service with priority 1 occupies channel 1, priority 2 occupies channel 1 and channel 2, and the service with priority N occupies channel 1 to channel N .

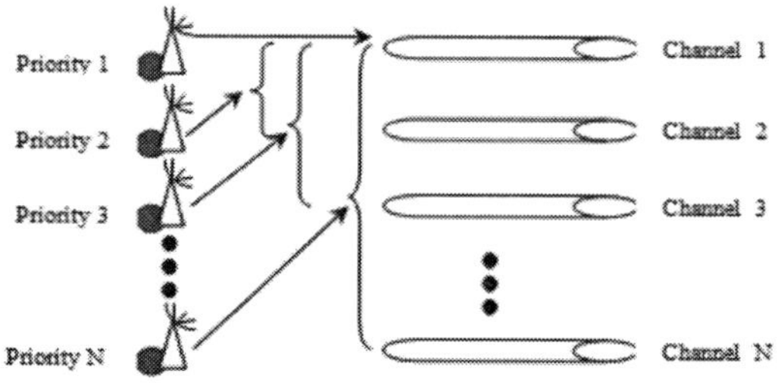

Fig. 1. Structure of multichannel mechanism with N channels

For a single channel, assuming channel i , under the MMTDP-CSMA mode, packet transmission and retransmission phase is the same as three-dimensional probability CSMA. Unlike the above B events scenarios, when during the transmission interval, the time is added to $(1+3a)$ while the previous is $(1+a)$, the addition time slot $2a$ is exploited to transmit ACK or NCK information.

Before analysis, do assumptions as before while adding one more: the access method of number $i(i=1,2,...,N)$ channel is timeslot three-dimensional probability CSMA, and the arrival process of number i channel satisfy the Poisson

process whose independent parameter is G_i, each arrival process on the channel is independent of each other.

For channel i, in a cycle, the average length of time slot that information packet has been successfully sent in a cycle is:

$$E(U_i)=E(U_{1,i})+E(U_{2,i})=\frac{ap_1G_ie^{-ap_1G_i}}{1-e^{-ap_1G_i}}+(3ap_3+p_2)G_i$$

(5)

Average length of B event in channel i is:

$$E(B_i)=E(N_{B_i})\times(1+3a)=\frac{1+3a}{1-e^{-(3ap_3+p_2)G_i}}$$

(6)

Where $(1+3a)$ represents the length of information packet whether it transmitted successfully or not of channel i in the TP cycle.

Average length of I event in channel i is:

$$E(I_i)=E(N_{I_i})\times a=\frac{a}{1-e^{-ap_1G_i}} \quad (7)$$

For channel i, system throughput of MMTDP-CSMA is:

$$S_i'=\frac{E(U_i)}{E(B_i)+E(I_i)}=\frac{\frac{ap_1G_ie^{-ap_1G_i}}{1-e^{-ap_1G_i}}+(3ap_3+p_2)G_i}{\frac{1+3a}{1-e^{-(3ap_3+p_2)G_i}}+\frac{a}{1-e^{-ap_1G_i}}}$$

(8)

Basing on the above analysis and computational formula of the systemic throughput.

systemic throughput of MMTDP-CSMA is:

$$S=NS_i' \quad (9)$$

Assuming that the length of information packet sent by the business with priority l successfully in average cycle period of channel i is: $E(U_i^{(pl)})(i\le l)$.

Then according to the above analysis, we can get the throughput of the MMTDP-CSMA with the priority l:

$$S_{pl}=(\sum_{i=1}^{l}\frac{1}{N-i+1})S_i' \quad (10)$$

4. Simulation results and analysis

From the above analysis, the expression of the system throughput under the discrete time three-dimensional probability CSMA protocol with multichannel mechanism is got. With the simulation tool-MATLAB R2010a, the simulation results are shown in Figure 4 to Figure 7. If not specified $a=0.01$.

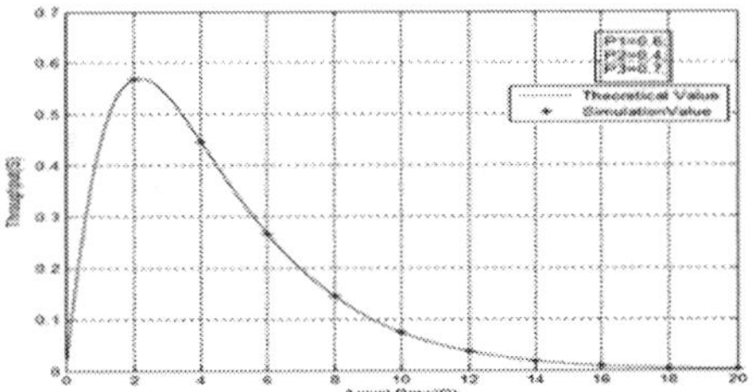

Fig. 2. The throughput of the new protocol for channel i

As it can be seen from the Fig. 2, the simulation values of system throughput under the new protocol are consistent with the theoretical ones. At the beginning, when the arrival rate increases, the system throughput also increased; then throughput reaches its maximum under the condition. Finally, with the increasing amount of the arrival rate, the system throughput decreases. The simulation values of system throughput under the new protocol are consistent with the theoretical ones.

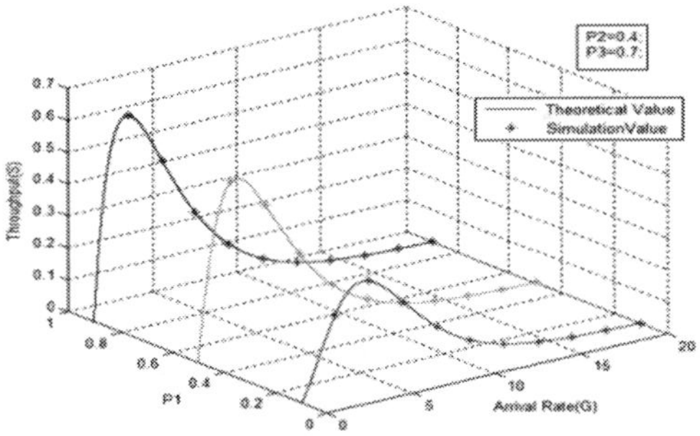

Fig. 3. The throughput of the new protocol with variable parameter P1

Can be seen from the Fig. 3, the simulation values of system throughput are consistent with the theoretical ones. We can find that with the $P1$ increases, the system throughput is increases too. This is laying that when the arrival rate is small, if the probability of arrival information sent is too small at the I events, the channel resource is not fully utilized. Thus, if we increase the probability of the arrival information transmitted at this time, we can improve the efficiency of channel resources and increase the value of the system throughput.

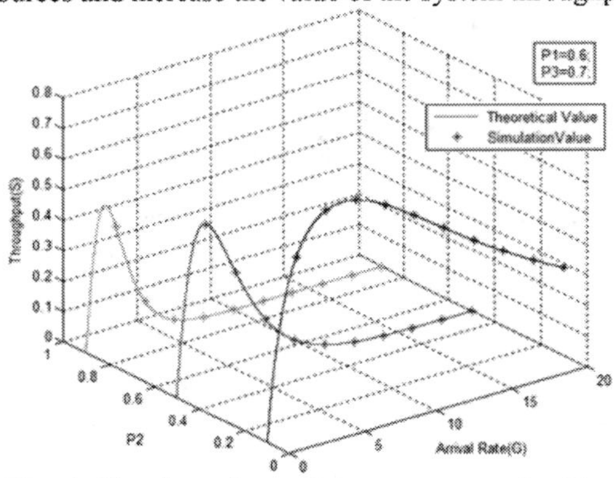

Fig. 4. The throughput of the new protocol with variable parameter P2

In the Fig. 4, the simulation values of system throughput under the new protocol are consistent with the theoretical ones. As can be understood from the figure, when $P2$ becoming bigger, the throughput will decrease; because when the

channel is busy sending the packet, the more new arrival information packets to send at the CU events the more collisions will be.

So we can change variable $P3$ to control the process of the CUI events. Not only this, we can change the variable of $P1$, $P2$ and $P3$ at the same time to get value of the system throughput needed.

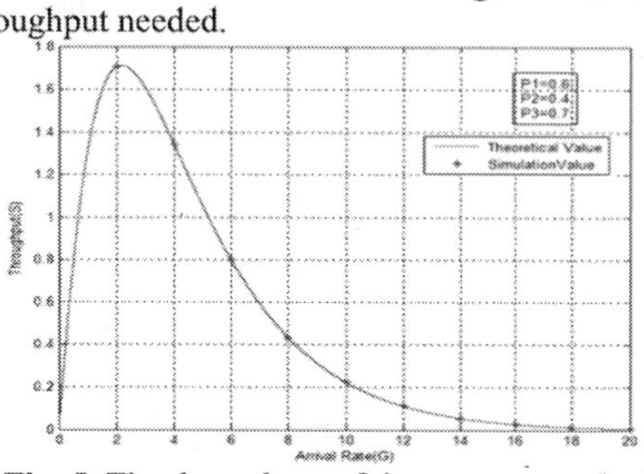

Fig. 5. The throughput of the new protocol with 3 channels

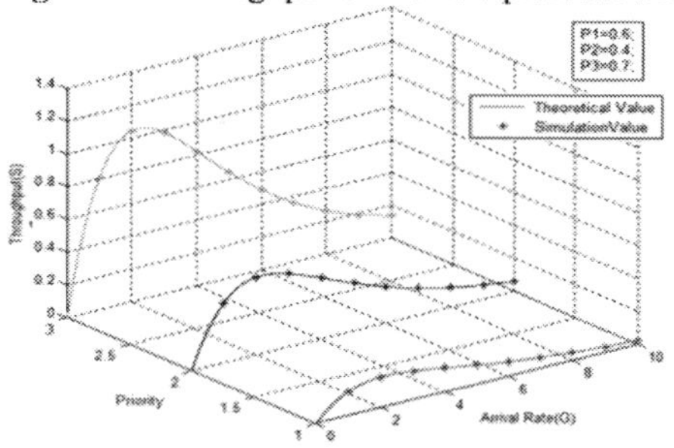

Fig.6. The comparison of system throughput owning 3 channels with different priorities

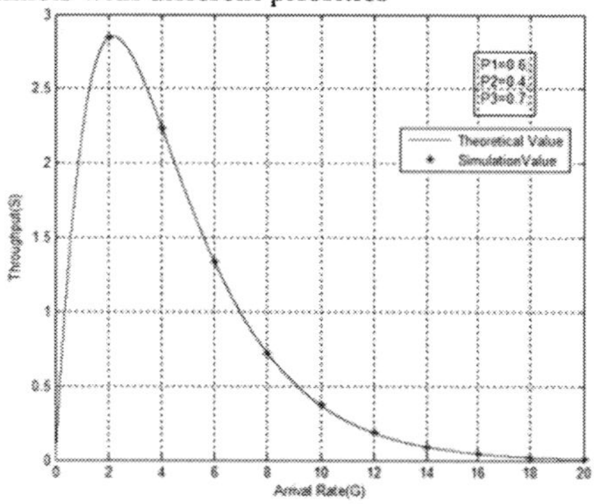

Fig. 7. The throughput of the new protocol with 5 channels

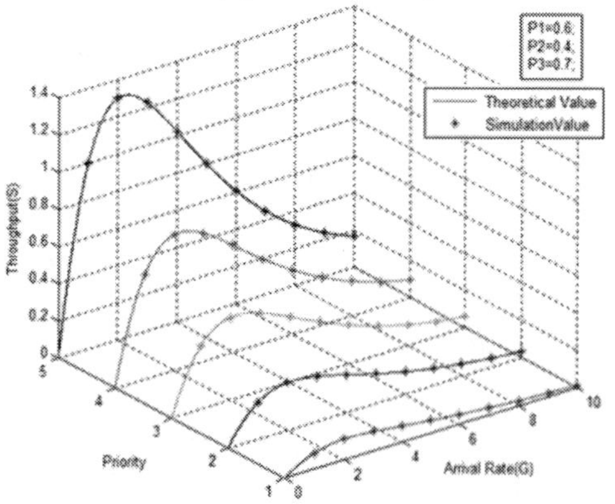

Fig. 8. The comparison of system throughput owning 5 channels with different priorities

As can be understood from Fig. 5 to Fig. 8, the simulation values of system throughput under the new protocol are consistent with the theoretical ones. With the total number of channels increases, the value of the new protocol's total system throughput will increases; the channel resources can distribute to every channel according to their priority according to their own priority separately; when the priority is higher, the corresponding single channel will get more network resources than the lower priorities; thus the value of throughput with higher priority channel is bigger than others with lower priorities. With the multi-channel mechanism, the network resources utilization has been improved significantly.

Conclusions

With radio spectrum increasingly tense, to satisfy the users' demand of more personalized and diversified business categories. To realizing the functions the intelligent identify, locate, track, monitor and manage a network. Using the average cycle analysis method to analysis the proposed protocol of the discrete time multichannel three-dimensional probability CSMA protocol with function of monitoring, realizing the functions above at the same time; during the paper, through the vigorous deviations obtains the accurate mathematical expressions of the system throughput. The correctness of the theory and model is demonstrated with the simulation tool-MATLAB and its effectiveness is illustrated.

References

[1] Yuhong, Z., Wei, L.: 'Modeling and energy consumption evaluation of a stochastic wireless sensor network ', EURASIP Journal on Wireless Communications and Networking, 2012, 4, (1), pp.79-82

[2] Dongfeng, Z.: 'Study on A New Method for Continuous-time Systems of Random Access Channel', Journal of Electronics, 1999, 21, (1), pp.37-41

[3] Hongwei, D., Yingying, G., Yifan, Z., et al.: 'Sensor Lett',2015, 13, pp.143-146

[4] E. A, B.: 'Towards robust distributed systems ACM New Method for the Slotted Access Channel, Journal of Electronics, 1997, 19, (6), pp.814-819

[5] Wenmiao, S., Yanming, L.: 'Research on S-MAC protocol for WSN', IEEE Wireless Communications, 2008, pp.779-782

[6] Dongfeng, Z., Bihai, L.., Sumin, Z.: 'Study on a New Method for the Slotted Access Channel', Journal of Electronics, 1997, 19, (6), pp.814-819

[7] Dongfeng, Z.: 'Study on the Average Cycle Method for Slotted Multiple-Access Communications', Journal of China Institute of Communications, 1999, 20, (8), pp.80-85

[8] Dongfeng, Z.: 'Study on A New Method for the Slotted Access Channel', Journal of Electronics,1997, 19, (6), pp.814-819

MATEC Web of Conferences 44, 01024 (2016)
DOI: 10.1051/matecconf/20164401024

Energy Efficiency Analysis of the Discrete Time Three-Dimensional Probability CSMA Protocol in WSN

Sheng Jie Zhou[1], Hong Wei Ding[1,2], Zhi Jun Yang[1], Qian Lin Liu[1] and Meng Yao Wang[1]
[1] *School of Information, Yunnan University, Kunming, Yunnan, China*
[2] *E-mail:dhw1964@163.com*

Abstract: In the wireless sensor network, energy supply and consumption is the main factors to affect survival time. Introducing the three-dimensional probability CSMA protocol, the paper analyses the system throughput, system delay and energy efficiency with using the average cycle analysis methods. For this protocol, the system time is slotted into a time slot with high channel utilization realized by the choice of three parameters P1, P2 and P3. The correctness of the theory is verified through the simulation.
Keywords: WSN, three-dimensional probability, CSMA, throughput.

1. Introduction

Wireless sensor networks (Wireless Sensor Networks, WSN) are deployed in the detection zone through a lot with network nodes which have the wireless communication and computing capabilities. It is able to complete the assigned task of distributed intelligent network system consisting of self-organization of nodes. Between the nodes of a wireless sensor network is a short distance; the general multi-hop wireless communication. The network can be run in a standalone environment. You can also connect to the Internet through a gateway in remote access. Wireless sensor networks originated in military applications, and now, wireless sensor networks are increasingly used in environmental and ecological monitoring, health monitoring, home automation and traffic control, and many other civilian areas [2].

Typically wireless sensor nodes in the network are widely distributed at a larger number, which cannot rely on supplemental batteries as an energy source. In many cases due to constraints, maintenance personnel inaccessible, battery replacement is very difficult or even impossible to replace. And requirements of lifetime for the network are months or even years. So the energy supply has become a major factor affecting network effective survival time and overall network performance. How in the existing energy supply conditions, without affecting system functionality premise, as far as possible to reduce energy consumption, save battery power, maximizing network lifetime wireless sensor networks has become the core issue.

Since each node sends a packet random, in order to reduce collisions, the MAC layer protocol necessary to establish a shared channel access mechanism. Efficient MAC layer protocol is a hot topic for the Ad-hoc networks; the most common MAC layer protocol is carrier sense multiple access (CSMA) and a variety of other mechanisms.

2. The three-dimensional probability CSMA protocol

In the proposed protocol, there will be three random events:

a) Event that information packets are sent successfully (U events).
b) Event that information packets collide with each other (the collision appears, C events).
c) Event that there are no information packets in the channel arrive, the channel is idle (I events) [3].

These three events are forced into: the channel is idle (I events) event, the channel is busy (CU events) and the channel is idle following the CU events (CUI events); the packet is sent successfully or unsuccessfully (combined C events with U event, denoted by CU event); force the CU events and the CUI events into B events [4].

A cycle period is T_n . The three events above continuously staggering circulate on the time axis and the cycle is variable T_n [5]. TP is the transmission period. Use three-dimensional probability: $P1$, $P2$, $P3$ to control the period of I events, CU events and CUI events separately.

Article available at http://www.matec-conferences.org or http://dx.doi.org/10.1051/matecconf/20164401024

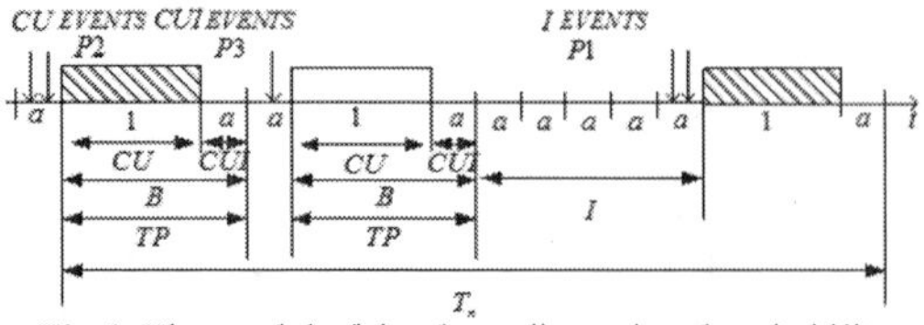

Fig.1. The model of the three-dimensional probability CSMA protocol

According to the protocol, if the channel is idle, then the user decides to send an information packet probability $P1$; if the channel is busy, the user listens to the channel at probability $P2$ in the CU events; in the transportation period, if the channel is the first idle following the CU events, then the user listens to the channel at probability $P3$ [6]. This control strategy, $P1$, $P2$ and $P3$ by three-dimensional selection enables the system under different load utilization and throughput is guaranteed.

3. Analysis of the model

3.1 The Analysis of System Throughput

Before analyze the system performance, first do the following assumptions:

a) The channel is ideal with no noise and interference;
b) The basic unit of the system control clock is a, the information packets arrived at time a will transmit at the starting time of the next slot;
c) The channel propagation delay is a ,the packet length is unit length and is an integral multiple of a;
d) The arrival process of channel satisfies the Poisson process whose independent parameter is G, each arrival process on the channel is independent of each other;
e) The channel using three-dimensional probability CSMA protocol, the information packets need to be sent at the first slot in the transmission period can always detecting the state of the channel at last moment;
f) During the transmission of information packets, the phenomenon of packet collisions occur inevitably, and continues to be sent after a random time delay, it sends will not produce any adverse effects on the arrival process channel [7].

In a cycle, the average length of time slot that information packet has been successfully sent in a cycle is:

$$E(U) = E(U_1) + E(U_2) = \frac{ap_1Ge^{-ap_1G}}{1-e^{-ap_1G}} + (ap_3 + p_2)G \qquad (1)$$

The average length of B event is:

$$E(B) = E(N_B)\times(1+a) = \frac{1+a}{1-e^{-(ap_3+p_2)G}} \qquad (2)$$

Where $(1+a)$ represents the length of information packet whether it transmitted successfully or not in the TP cycle [8].

The average length of I event is:

$$E(I) = E(N_I)\times a = \frac{a}{1-e^{-ap_1G}} \qquad (3)$$

The throughput of the new protocol in channel i is:

$$S = \frac{E(U)}{E(B)+E(I)} = \frac{\frac{ap_1Ge^{-ap_1G}}{1-e^{-ap_1G}} + (ap_3+p_2)G}{\frac{1+a}{1-e^{-(ap_3+p_2)G}} + \frac{a}{1-e^{-ap_1G}}} \qquad (4)$$

3.2 The Analysis of System Delay

First do the following assumptions before analyze the system delay: the monitoring signal can always being transmitted correctly; the time generating monitoring signal can be ignored; R is the average delay of a packet to be transmitted twice, then R is formed by four parts: the time that information packet transmitted 1, round-trip propagation delay a, and the average retransmission delay δ [9].

The average delay of information packets for the three-dimensional probability CSMA protocol is:

$$D = \left[\frac{\frac{(1+a)G}{1-e^{-(3ap_3+p_2)G_i}} + \frac{aG}{1-e^{-ap_1G_i}}}{\frac{ap_1G_ie^{-ap_1G_i}}{1-e^{-ap_1G_i}} + (3ap_3+p_2)G_i} - 1\right]R + 1 + \tau_A \qquad (5)$$

3.3 The Analysis of Energy Efficiency

Assuming the transmitting power of sensor node is P_{tx}, receiving power is P_{rx}, the power of detection channel is P_{dd}.

1) Energy consumption analysis

The detecting duration of all service nodes in the idle time is:

$$t_d(I) = \frac{a^2}{2}GE(I)\frac{a}{1-e^{-GP_1a}} \qquad (6)$$

Then the sensing consumption in the next T_i is:

$$W_d = (t_d(B) + t_d(I))\ P_{lsm} \qquad (7)$$

Therefore, the average operating power of channel i is:

$$P(S) = \frac{W_t + W_{rec} + W_d}{E(B)\ + E(I)} \qquad (8)$$

2) The life cycle of node

For the terminal nodes, assuming it sleeps 1 at a time, then it sleeps a within time a, the average

power of the node which priority is l in the N nodes is:

$$P_d = \frac{W_t + W_d}{E(B) + E(I) + [q_2^0 + q_{\tau_A}^0 \tau_A + a q_1^0]\dfrac{E(B)}{1 + a + \tau_A}} \qquad (9)$$

Where, $q_{\tau_A}^0$ is the definition of the probability that there is no packet to be sent within time τ_A in a transmission period, $q_{\tau_A}^0 = e^{-GP_3\tau_A}$.

For the aggregation nodes, the average power is:

$$P_s = \frac{W_{rec} + P_{lsm}\dfrac{E(I) + E(B)}{T_s}a}{2E(B) + E(I) + \dfrac{E(I)}{a}} \qquad (10)$$

Since the energy consumption is constant in the transmission process, therefore, for the terminal nodes under the control of MCPDCSMA/ACK protocol, the lifecycle T_d is:

$$T_d = \frac{E}{24 \times 365 \times P_d + 0.1E} \qquad (11)$$

For the aggregation node, the lifecycle T_s is:

$$T_s = \frac{E}{24 \times 365 \times P_s + 0.1E} \qquad (12)$$

4. Simulation

From the above analysis, the expression of the system throughput under the discrete time three-dimensional probability CSMA protocol is got. With the simulation tool-MATLAB R2010a, the simulation results are shown in Figure 2 to Figure 6.

Before the simulation, assume that:

a) The channel is ideal with no noise and interference;
b) The basic unit of the system control clock is a, the information packets arrived at time a will transmit at the starting time of the next slot;
c) The channel propagation delay is a , the packet length is unit length and is an integral multiple of a;
d) The arrival process of the channel satisfy the Poisson process whose independent parameter is G, each arrival process on the channel is independent of each other;
e) The P is the probability of the discrete timeslot P-detection CSMA protocol which is proposed by Dongfeng Zhao professor;
f) The packet length is 1.
g) $a = 0.01$.

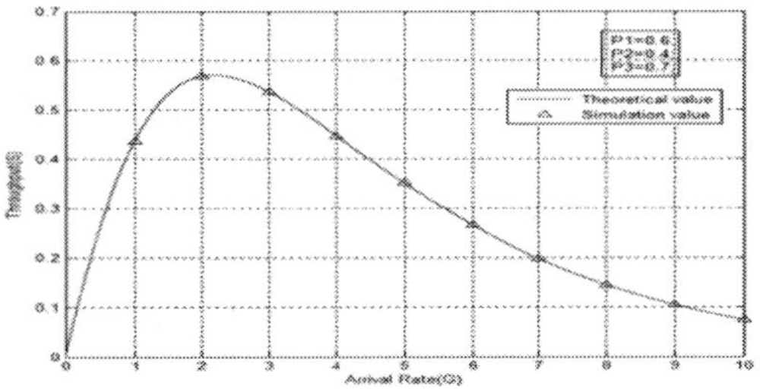

Fig.2. The throughput of the new protocol

In Fig.2, the simulation values of system throughput under the new protocol are consistent with the theoretical ones, verified the correctness of mathematical derivation done before.

When G becomes bigger, the system throughput is increase; especially when G is near 1.5, the system throughput is very high; next when G is bigger, the system throughput decreases.

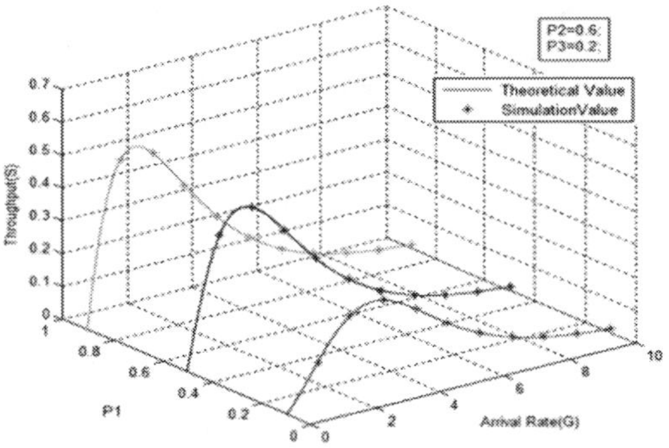

Fig.3. The throughput of new protocol with variable P1

In the Fig.3, the simulation values of system throughput under the new protocol are consistent with the theoretical ones, verified the correctness of mathematical derivation done before.

When $P1$ becoming bigger, the throughput will increase, especially with small value of G; because when the channel is idle, the probability of an information packet sent successfully will increases; the utilization of channel resources is improved.

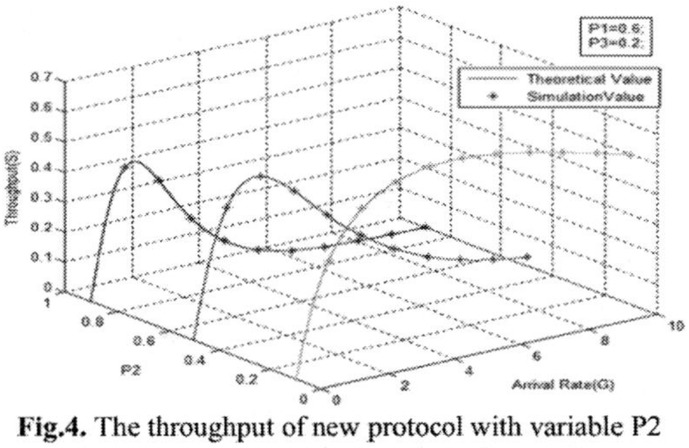

Fig.4. The throughput of new protocol with variable P2

In the Fig.4, the simulation values of system throughput under the new protocol are consistent with the theoretical ones, verified the correctness of mathematical derivation done before.

When $P2$ becoming bigger, the throughput will decrease; because when the channel is busy sending the packet, if the more new arrival information

packets the more collisions will be; the utilization of channel resources decreases.

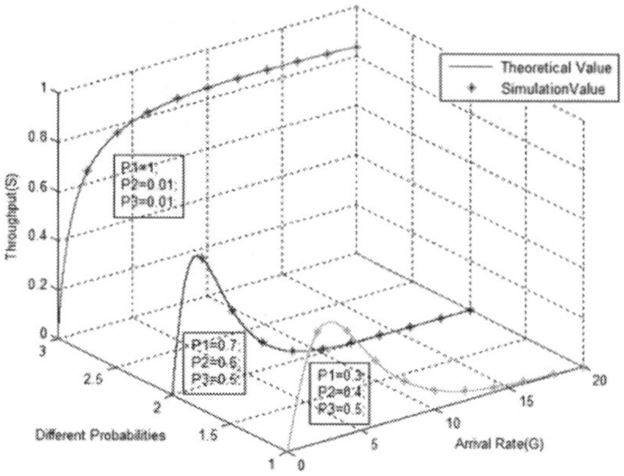

Fig.5. The comparison of system throughput under the new protocol with different probabilities

In the Fig.5, the simulation values of system throughput under the new protocol are consistent with the theoretical ones, verified the correctness of mathematical derivation done before.

From the figure, we can find that changing the variable $P1$, $P2$ and $P3$ at the same time to get value of the system throughput needed.

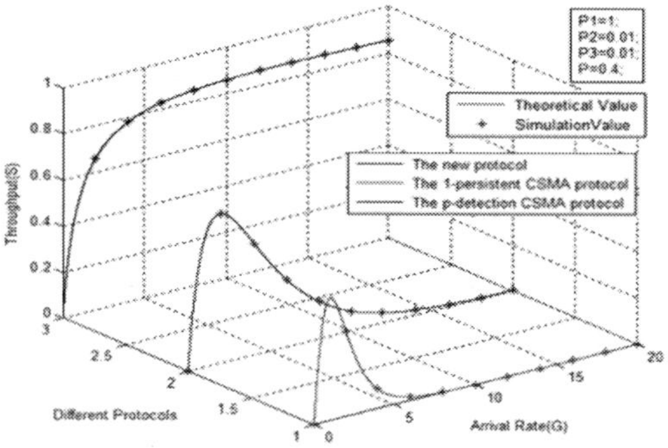

Fig.6. The comparison of system throughput under the different protocols

In the Fig.6, the simulation values of system throughput under the new protocol are consistent with the theoretical ones. When $a=0.01$ $P=0.4$ $P1=1$ $P2=P3=0.01$, the throughput of the system under new protocol is bigger than the ones using the non-persistent CSMA protocol or the P-detection CSMA protocol, showing the priority than other protocols. On the whole, throughput of system using three-dimensional probability CSMA protocol can increases to a certain extent.

Through the above figures, we can find that when $a=0.01$ $P1=1$ $P2=P3=0.01$, the throughput of the system under new protocol is approaching 1. If we need the system throughput to get the value, we can set the parameters just as above.

5. Conclusions

At present, wireless sensor mainly uses the battery without uncharged ability as the power source. In the present technical conditions, there are still certain difficulties to improve the battery capacity per unit volume. So whether we can make reasonable use of the existing energy resources is the main factors of the network lifetime. The discrete time three-dimensional probability CSMA protocol, using the average cycle method, gets the precise mathematical expressions of system throughput, system delay and energy efficiency by rigorous mathematical derivation. The correctness of the theory is verified through the simulation.

With the continuous development of technical conditions, the environmental protection of the power supply technology such as solar power, wind power generation has gradually mature, use of these skills will also gradually mature. There is reason to believe that in the near future, energy supply problems will no longer become a bottleneck restricting the development of wireless sensor network, wireless sensor network will feed into every aspect of our lives. To the progress of the society as a whole development, it will play a more and more important role.

References

[1].Jinyang Li, Charles Blake, Douglas S. J. De Couto, Hu Imm Lee, and Robert Morris, Capacity of Ad Hoc Wireless Networks, in the proceedings of the 7th ACM International Conference on Mobile Computing and Networking, Rome, Italy, July 2001.

[2].Yuhong Zhang, Wei Li. Modeling and energy consumption evaluation of a stochastic wireless sensor network[J]. EURASIP Journal on Wireless Communications and Networking, 2012(1): 79-82.

[3].Hongwei Ding , Yingying Guo, Qianlin Liu and Shengjie Zhou. The Multichannel Pd-Csma With 3-Way Handshake Based On Conflict Resolution Algorithm In Wsn. International Journal of Recent Scientific Research Vol. 6, Issue, 4, pp.3714-3718, April, 2015.

[4].Zhao Dongfeng. Study on A New Method for Continuous-time Systems of Random Access Channel [J]. Journal of Electronics, 1999, 21(1): 37-41.

[5].Hung LeHong and J. Fenn. Garnter Report. "Hype Cycle for Emerging Technolo-gies", July 2012. [Online]. Available: http://www.gartner.com/newsroom/id/2124315.

[6].Hongwei Ding, Yingying Guo, Yifan Zhao, Shengjie Zhou, and Qianlin Liu. Sensor Lett. 13, 143-146 (2015).

[7].D. Vesset and B. Woo et al. "Worldwide Big Data Technology and Services2012-2015 Forecast," IDC Report 233485, March 2012. [Online]. Available: http://www.idc.com/getdoc.jsp?containerId=233485.

[8].E. A. Brewer."Towards robust distributed systems,"inProc. 19th Annual ACM New Method for the Slotted Access Channel [J]. Journal of Electronics, 1997, 19(6):814-819.

[9].Zhao Dongfeng, Li Bihai, Zheng Sumin. Study on a New Method for the Slotted Access Channel [J]. Journal of Electronics, 1997, 19(6):814-819.

[10].Yi Shang, Hongchi Shi. Flexible Energy Efficient Density Control on Wireless Sensor Networks[J]. International Journal of Distributed Sensor Networks, 2007, 3(1): 101-120.

[11].Muaz Niazi, Amir Hussain (March 2009). "Agent based Tools for Modeling and Simulation of Self-Organization in Peer-to-Peer, Ad Hoc and other Complex Networks, Feature Issue" (PDF). IEEE Communications Magazine. 47 No.3. Cs.stir.ac.uk. pp. 163–173.

MATEC Web of Conferences **44**, 01025 (2016)
DOI: 10.1051/matecconf/20164401025

The Application of The Double Queue Asymmetric Gated Service Polling Control Theory in Intelligent Traffic System

Yi Fan Zhao[1,a],Hong Wei Ding[1,a],Meng Yao Wang[1,b],Zhu Guan Liang[1,b],
[1] School of Informatics,Yunnan University,China
[a,b]hw1964@163.com,byakazo@163.com

Abstract: This paper presents a new use of double queues asymmetric gated service polling system in the intelligent traffic light control system.Usually there are more vehicles in main road than minor road,so there are more green light time be needed in the main road.From the computer simulation and theory analysis,we can find that the application of double queues asymmetric gated service polling theory in intelligent traffic system can balance intersections load and set suitable passing time for vehicles to assure the roads open.

Keywords:gated service; intelligent traffic; polling; arrive rate; waiting time;

1 Introduce

Withing the development of urban economy, the city scale expands unceasingly,the vehicles also become more and more,but when people enjoying the convenient that vehicles bring,at the same time,also meet more and more problems,such as air pollution,noise pollution and traffic congestion. The traffic light in intersections is a very important role to maintain the traffic order, guarantee the road clear. The development of urban lead to more and more vehicles. Ordinary traffic system can not meet the requirement today. So in order to Alleviate the increasing traffic pressure， the intelligent traffic system[1] come.

Intelligent traffic system including the detection of road traffic, according to the intersection traffic flow characteristics and queuing delay, effectively, design a more advanced traffic signal timing scheme in order to improve the efficiency of intersection and so on.The appropriate traffic lights control strategy which can alleviate the traffic congestion is the most important topic in intelligent traffic system.

In this paper we apply the theory of double queues asymmetric gated service polling[2] to intelligent traffic system. Designing a traffic lights system which can adjust the timekeeping time of the traffic light according to the change of the traffic volume. To alleviate traffic pressure, and can save transportation resources.Through reasonable design, the system can realize control length of red,green,yellow light time reasonably and automatically with different arrival rate.

2 Specific design

we design a traffic light system which the light time can be adjusted intellectually according to the change of the vehicles arrive rate[3].

Specific design is installing ground loop[4] in all directions 80 meters away from the intersections to count the number of vehicles,and then enter data into the computer central control system to analyze the data and calculate the waiting time through the polling model with the current arrive rate.This result of the calculation been seem as the green light time in this direction.

In this intelligent system,because the application of double queues asymmetric gated service polling theory,the load of main road which has higher arrive rate and minor road which has lower arrive rate balancing well.Considering that there are more vehicles arrive in the main road,so there need longer pass time in main road.

3 Polling system

Polling system model[5] consists of a server and N queues[6].The queues arrival process and the service time are random process in queuing mode.

The double queues asymmetric gated service polling control system made up of a server,a high arrive rate queue1 and a low arrive rate queue2.The queue1 and queue2 adopt the rule which is gated service.Whatever the queue1 and queue2,the server services the current gated information packet with gated service,only,and turn to service anther queue after a conversion time.The information packet arrive during the service time of the queue would be serviced in the nextpollingcycle.This is the principle of double queues asymmetric gated service polling control system.The asymmetry beem bodiedin different arrive rate of the queue1 and queue2

4 The double queue asymmetric gated service polling model of intelligent traffic lights control system

This intelligent traffic lights control system is seem as a double queues asymmetric gated service polling control system.For practical purposes,suppose,the main road be seem as a queue with the higher arrival rate of vehicles which is λ_h,the minor be seem as a queue with the lower arrival rate of vehicles which is λ_o.The main road and minor road both adopt the rule which is gate service polling strategy.The β means the service rate of the traffic light system.In this intelligent system β is 1,mean there is one vehicle spend 1s to pass the waiting line.The conversion rate of traffic light system is the length of yellow light time in this system,and there γ=10 means that there are 10s yellow light.

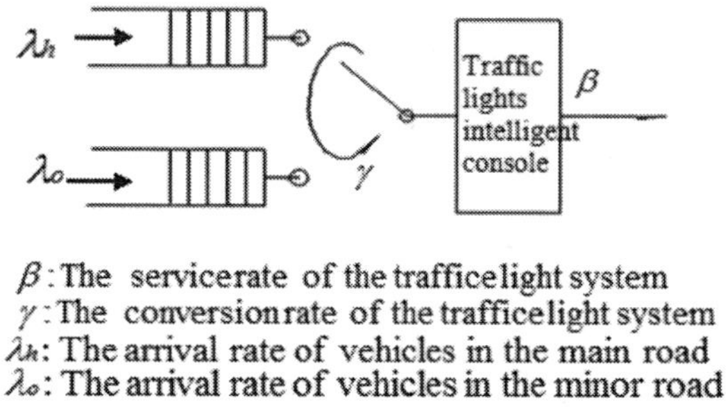

Fig 1. The double queues asymmetric gated service polling model of intelligent traffic lights control system

5 Queuing model and operation mode

There are 2 queues serviced by one traffic lights console in this intelligent traffic lights control system.Due to the queuing system is a solving process under the discrete time state,so the time axis is divided in time slot τ (To make analysis into concise,we take τ as the unit of time)

5.1 Assumptions

Each queues has the vehicles arrived into their queue space with independent and identically probability distribution at any time slot the distribution of probability generating function,the mean and variance are $A_i(Z)$、$\lambda = A_i'(1)$、and $\delta_\lambda^2 = A_i''(1) + \lambda - \lambda^2$ respectively.

The random variable of query conversion time between the two queues is subject to a probability distribution which is mutually independent and identically distributed, the distribution of probability generating function, the mean and variance are $R(Z)$, $\gamma = R'(1)$ and $\delta_\gamma^2 = R''(1) + \gamma - \gamma^2$ respectively.

The random variable of the time that each vehicles pass the crossroads is subject to a probability distribution which is mutually independent and identically distributed, the distribution of probability generating function, the mean and variance are $B(Z)$ 、 $\beta = B'(1)$ and $\delta_\beta^2 = B''(1) + \beta - \beta^2$ respectively.

The queue space is big enough. The number of vehicles would not more than the queue space.

For the vehicles that in the each queue, according to the principle of first-in-first-out.

5.2 Mean queue length

Define the variable $g_1(1)$ as the number of vehicles in the minor road and main road waiting for passing the interaction while there is the green light in the minor road and the variable $g_2(2)$ as the number of vehicles in the minor road and main road waiting for passing the interaction while there is the green light in the main road.then,

$$g_1(1) = \frac{2r\lambda_1}{1-\rho_1-\rho_2} \qquad (1)$$

$$g_2(2) = \frac{2r\lambda_2}{1-\rho_1-\rho_2} \qquad (2)$$

5.3 Mean waiting time

Then, define the variable $E(W_i)$ as mean waiting time of the vehicles in the minor road and main road(i=1,2).According to queue theory, the mean waiting time $E(W_i)$ are expresses as follows:

$$E(W_1) = \frac{(1+\rho_1)g_1(1,1)}{2\lambda_1 g_1(1)} - \frac{A_1''(1)}{2\lambda_1^2} \qquad (3)$$

$$E(W_2) = \frac{(1+\rho_2)g_2(2,2)}{2\lambda_1 g_2(2)} - \frac{A_2''(1)}{2\lambda_2^2} \qquad (4)$$

6 The simulation

The simulation calculation and theoretical calculation take the same parameters.

Because the main objective in this paper is find a traffic lights control strategy to balance load and alleviate traffic pressure, so the simulations is simulating peak-time road condition that the main road load ρ_1 is the double of load ρ_2 in the minor road.

In this system, there has a rang which is stable region. The stable region means in this rang of load, this system is working properly and steadily, would not occur traffic congestion and end up with the traffic system collapse. And there has a rule of the stable region is $\rho_1 + \rho_2 < 1$ .So, in the simulation of peak-time($2\rho_1 = \rho_2$)as the Fig.2,Fig.3 and Fig.4,the stable region is less than 0.25.

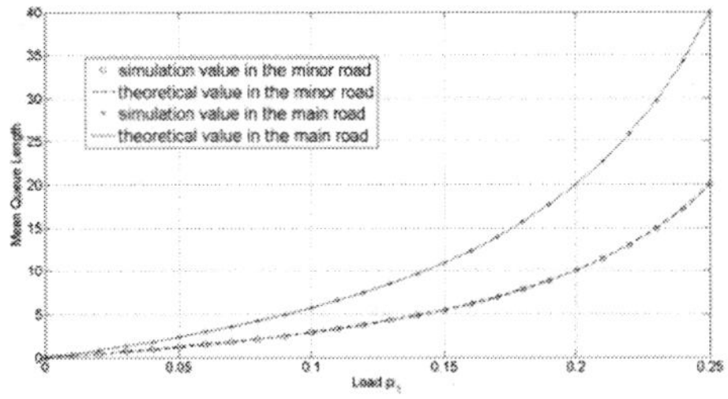

Fig.2 The mean queue length with the system

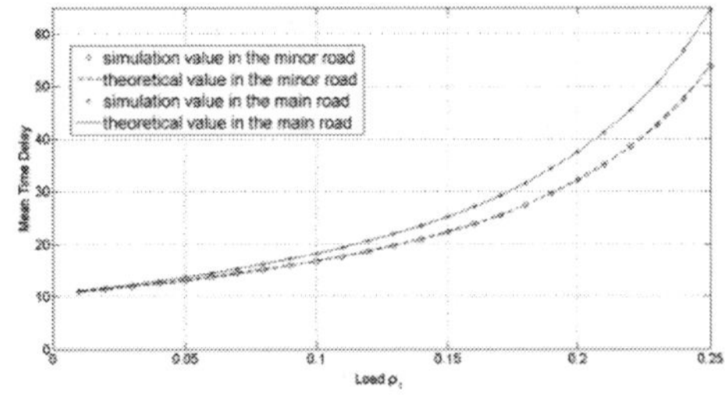

Fig.3 The mean waiting time with the system

The Fig2 and Fig3 reflect the theoretical value and the simulation values are the same.In those two diagrams we can find that the mean queue length and the mean time delay are proportional to load. Compare main road condition and minor road condition we can find that the mean queue length and the mean time delay of main road is longer than the mean queue length and the mean time delay of minor road under the assumed condition that $2\rho_1 = \rho_2$ .So, considering the mean queue length and the mean time delay the longer green light time be need in the main road.

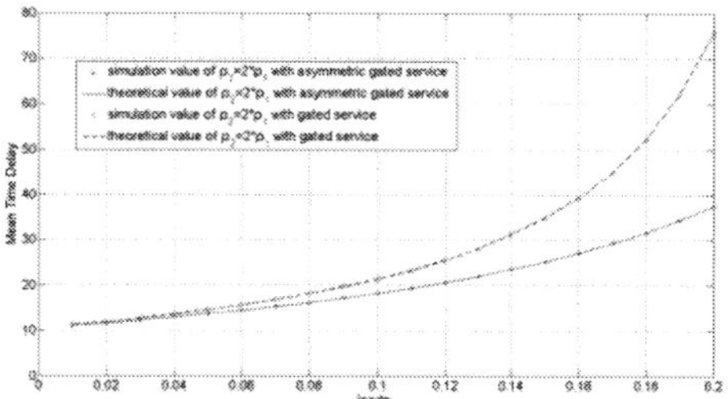

Fig.4 Compare with normal gated service polling

The Fig4 contrasts the mean waiting time under double queues asymmetric gated service polling theory to mean waiting time under normal gated service polling theory. In the main road which $2\rho_1 = \rho_2$ the double queues asymmetric gated service polling theory manifests the superiority. The double queues asymmetric gated service polling theory has the shorter waiting time and greater reliability than normal gated service polling theory with the same load (simulate $2\rho_1 = \rho_2$).In a real world application ,the intelligent traffic system which adopt the double queues asymmetric gated service polling theory can ensure the smooth road better.

7 Conclusions

Different road has different arrival rate. Whatever in the main road which has higher load or in the minor road which is low load, the mean queue length and mean time delay increase over the system load.Compared to main road and minor road,because the main road has the higher arrive rate so there has longer waiting time and the longer green light time would be need in the real world application. And by contrasting the simulation of double queues asymmetric gated service polling theory to normal gated service polling theory ,the former is presenting advantages in the heavy load. Compute simulating result are consistent with theoretical analyses. Through above analysis, the intelligent traffic light control system which using double queues asymmetric gated service polling theory can do improve the road capacity .

References

[1]Dimitrakopoulos, G. (2011) Intelligent transportation systems based on internet-connected vehicles: Fundamental research areas and challenges. 11th International Conference on ITS Telecommunications (ITST), Saint Peterburg , 23-25 August 2011, 145-151.

[2]Ding Hongwei, Zhao Dongfeng, Zhao Yifan. Packet delay analysis of continuous-time polling system with M-gated services[A]. Chengdu, P.R.China, August, 2010, Page(s):408-411.

[3] Jan-Pieter Dorsman, S. Borst, O. Boxma, Maria Vlasiou,Markovian polling systems with an application to wireless random-access networks[J].IEEE Trans. Eurandom Prepront Series, 2014, 5(6):1389-2355.

[4]Dimitrakopoulos, G. (2011) Intelligent transportation systems based on internet-connected vehicles: Fundamental research areas and challenges. 11th International Conference on ITS Telecommunications (ITST), Saint Peterburg, 23-25 August 2011, 145-151.

[5] Giambene, G.,Hadzic-Puzovic, S. Nonsaturated Performance Analysis for WiMAX Broadcast Polling Access[J]. IEEE Transactions on Vehicular Technology, 2013, 62(1):306-325.

[6] Qianlin Liu, Dongfeng Zhao, Dongming Zhou. An analytic model for enhancing IEEE 802.11 coordination function media access control protocol[J]. European Transactions on Telecommunications, 2011, 22(6):332-338.

MATEC Web of Conferences 44, 01026 (2016)
DOI: 10.1051/matecconf/20164401026

Extraction for fetal ECG using single channel blind source separation algorithm based on multi-algorithm fusion

Peng Ju He, Xiao Meng Chen, Yan Liang, Hua Zhi Zeng

Department of Automation, Northwestern Polytechnical University, Xi'an 710129, China
Corresponding author: Pengju He
E-mail: hepengju@nwpu.edu.cn

ABSTRACT: Nowadays, detecting fetal ECG using abdominal signal is a commonly used method, but fetal ECG signal will be affected by maternal ECG. Current FECG extraction algorithms are mainly aiming at multiple channels signal. They often assume there is only one fetus and did not consider multiple births. This paper proposed a single channel blind source separation (SCBSS) algorithm based on source number estimation using multi-algorithm fusion to process single abdominal signal. The method decomposed collected single channel signal into multiple intrinsic mode function (IMF) utilizing Empirical Mode Decomposition (EMD), mapping single channel into multiple channels. Four multiple channel source number estimation (MCSNE) methods (Bootstrap, Hough, AIC and PCA) were weighting fused to estimate accurate source number and the particle swarm optimization algorithm (PSO) was employed to determine weighted coefficient. According to source number and IMF, nonnegative matrix was constructed and nonnegative matrix factorization (NMF) was employed to separate mixed signals. Experiments used single channel signal mixed by four man-made signals and single channel ECG mixed by two to verify the proposed algorithm. Results showed that the proposed algorithm could determine number of independent signal in single acquired signal. FECG could be extracted from single channel observed signal and the algorithm can be used to solve separation of MECG and FECG.

Key words: Fetal ECG, Single channel blind source separation, Empirical mode decomposition, Multi-algorithm weighting fusion, Nonnegative matrix factorization

1. INTRODUCTION

Fetal ECG (FECG) has an important significance for fetal monitoring. The commonly used method to detect FECG is using abdominal signal. However, the obtained FECG is easy to be affected by maternal ECG (MECG) and noise and pure FECG cannot be acquired [1][2].

In order to eliminate the interference of MECG and noise and extract accurate FECG, many scholars have proposed methods to solve this problem, such as, autocorrelation techniques, adaptive filtering and wavelet transform. Recently, blind source separation (BSS) method has been introduced into FECG extraction domain. Especially, single channel blind source separation (SCBSS) has attracted attention because of its less require for observed signal. Singular value decomposition (SVD) and analysis based on the singular value ratio (SVR) spectrum was applied, followed by an iterated application of independent component analysis (ICA) on the principle components [3]. But SVD method requires that decomposition path must be orthogonal. And the selection for separated signals needs prior knowledge. Method combined wavelet decomposition with BSS algorithm independent component analysis (ICA) to extract FECG based on single-channel recordings was developed [4][5]. But the selection of mother wavelet in wavelet analysis is needed, and mother wavelet determination is difficult with lack of prior knowledge. Reference [6] proposed to adopt ensemble empirical mode decomposition (EEMD) to decompose single-channel abdominal signal, and applied FastICA to obtain recovered FECG. But FastICA in this method is sensitive to initial value, and it could not converge if selection of initial value is not proper. Meanwhile, all above algorithms only consider one fetus, without considering multiple births, having poor practicability.

This paper proposed a single channel blind source separation algorithm to separate maternal and fetal ECG. The method employs the principle of multiple channels mapping, uses Empirical Mode Decomposition (EMD) to map single channel signal into multiple intrinsic mode function (IMF) adaptively; four different source number estimation method for multiple channels are applied to estimate independent component number, and four obtained number are fused utilizing Particle Swarm Optimi-

zation (PSO) to determine accurate number; according to independent component number and IMF, nonnegative matrix is constructed and blind source separation is achieved using Nonnegative Matrix Factorization (NMF). This method is advantageous since it is based only on the analysis of one abdominal signal, in contrast to other methods which need a large number of abdominal ECG recordings. And this algorithm could accurately determine number of baby, not limited to one birth.

2. MATHEMATIC MODEL OF SCBSS

Lathauwer had proved separation of FECG is blind source separation problem based on linear instantaneous mixed model [7]. Under such model, received single channel mixed signal *x(t)* is composed of *N* independent sources. The mathematical model can be expressed as:

$$x(t)=\sum_{i=1}^{N}\lambda_i s_i(t)+n(t) \tag{1}$$

Where *si(t)*,(i=1,2,...,N) is *ith* source signal, n(t) is additive noise with a mean of zero, variance of σ^2, mixing coefficient λ_i and N the number of source signals. If the observation is single channel signal (signal collected by single sensor), equation (1) can be rewritten as:

$$x(t)=\sum_{i=1}^{N}s_i(t)+n(t) \tag{2}$$

SCBSS denotes recovering every original signal *si(t)* only according to the received mixed single signal *x(t)* under the condition that original signal and mixing coefficients are unknown.

3. SOURCE NUMBER ESTIMATION FOR SINGLE CHANNEL SIGNAL

It is commonly known that a signal is a function of time, and is thus considered dynamic. The acquisition system is a dynamic system when multiple sources are sampled by one sensor. Single channel dynamic signal can be mapped into multiple channels signal based on dynamical systems theory [8]. In this way, methods for multiple channels source number estimation can be used to effectively determine the number of single-channel mixed signals.

3.1 Multiple channel mapping based on empirical mode decomposition

EMD is a self-adaptive signal decomposition method based on local features [9]. EMD assumes that signals are composed of different and simple non-sine signals. EMD acts to decompose a signal into a series of linear, steady intrinsic mode functions (IMF) adaptively. IMF must meet the following two conditions: (1) the mean value of the envelope defined by local maxima and the envelope defined by the local minima is zero at any point; and (2) the number of extrema and number of zero crossings must either equal or differ only by one in the entire data set.

Given an observed signal *x(t)*, the main EMD procedure is [10][11]:

1. Identify all extrema of *x(t)*.

2. Estimate the upper envelope *xu(t)* and the lower *xl(t)* by extrema and calculate the mean envelope *xm(t)=(xu(t)+xl(t))/2*.

3. Extract the detail *h(t)=x(t)-xm(t)*.

4. Set *x(t)=h(t)* and iterate the process to meet IMF requirements.

Employing EMD on a single channel signal may produce multiple IMF with different frequencies. Utilizing one IMF as a signal, single channel can then be mapped into multiple channels.

3.2 Source number estimation methods for multiple channels signal

Bootstrap, AIC, Hough, and PCA are MCSNE methods, considering signal characteristics in the time domain and frequency domain.

3.2.1 Bootstrap Method Based on Hypothesis Testing

Bootstrap method takes resample on actual data to acquire samples. It can estimate the confidence intervals of the statistics under the condition where statistic distribution is unknown, doing judgment on hypothesis testing. Bootstrap method was applied on multi-hypothesis test and a method for estimating the source number was proposed [12]. Multi-hypothesis test $H_k=\bigcap_{i,j}K_{i,j}$ can be defined as:

$$\begin{aligned}&H_k:\lambda_{k+1}=\cdots=\lambda_M\\&\quad\vdots\\&H_{M-2}:\lambda_{M-1}=\cdots=\lambda_M\end{aligned} \tag{3}$$

Hk represents that source number is *k* when eigenvalues of latter *M-k* are same. Where $K_{i,j}:\lambda_i=\lambda_j, i=k+1,\cdots,M-1, j=i+1$. The process is described in detail as follows:

(1) Take resample on data for B times in time domain.

(2) Calculate eigenvalues $l^*(b)$ of covariance matrix $R^*(b)$ in frequency domain. Estimate eigenvalue source (useful signal or noise signal) according to the value of $T^*_{ij}(b)=l_i^*(b)-l_j^*(b)\ ,b=1,\cdots,B$.

(3) Set α as the confidence level of *ki,j*, and $P_{ij}=\frac{1}{B}\sum_{b=1}^{B}I(|T_{ij}|\le|Q_{ij}(b)|)$ as the significant function, where $Q_{ij}(b)=T^*_{ij}(b)-T_{ij}$.

(4) If the significant of *Hk* satisfies $P_k\ge\alpha/k$, assumption *Hk* is accepted, otherwise, refused. Then continue to test *Hk-1* until estimating the source number.

Source number estimation based on Bootstrap always is combined with hypothesis testing, which will be affected by subjective factors, resulting in unstable results. There is great difference between estimated number and real source number with poor practicability.

3.2.2 Hough Transform Method

The next method is based on Hough transform. Sorted eigenvalues of covariance matrix for observed signal can be transformed into Hough parameter space using equation (4). Source number is determined according to detecting accumulated peaks in parameter space [13].

$$\rho = x\cos\theta + y\sin\theta \tag{4}$$

(1) Calculate the covariance matrix and its eigenvalues of observation data, and eigenvalues are arranged in descending order (*l1>...>lq...>lp*), forming the characteristic point *(k,lk)* *(k=1,...,p)*.

(2) Discretize the plane (ρ,θ) and determine the search range $0 \le \theta \le \pi/2$, $0 \le \rho \le \rho_0$, where $\rho_0 = \max_{k\in\{1,\cdots,p\}} \sqrt{k^2 + l_k^2}$. Divide the Hough plane into several small squares (an equally divided part of θ and ρ is *N1* and *N2* respectively,) and set *AN1* ×*N2* be 0.

(3) Use Eq. (4) to calculate ρ_{ik} , which corresponds to the midpoint of small squares for each sinusoid. If $\rho(j) \le \rho_{ik} < \rho(j+1), (j = 1,\ldots, N_2)$, *A(i,j)=A(i,j)+1* ,where $\rho(j) = (j-1)\rho_0 N_2, (j = 1,\ldots, N_2 + 1)$.

(4) For *k=1,...,p*, repeat the step (3). The original number of source signals is obtained according to $\hat{q} = p - \max\{A(i,j)\}, i \in [1, N_1], j \in [1, N_2]$.

The method based on Hough transform performs better than AIC with low SNR. But maximum number estimation is restricted and it cannot be more than *P-3* (*P* is the number of array elements).

3.2.3 Akaike Information Criteria

Recently, the information theory approach used for source number estimation was proposed [14]. A related estimation model commonly applied is AIC expressed as follows:

$$AIC = -2\log f(X|\hat{\Theta}) + 2\phi \tag{5}$$

$$AIC(k) = -2N(m-k)\ln\Lambda(k) + 2k(2m-k) \tag{6}$$

$$\Lambda(\mathrm{k}) = \frac{\frac{1}{m-k}\sum_{i=k+1}^{m}\lambda_i}{(\prod_{i=k+1}^{m}\lambda_i)^{\frac{1}{m-k}}} \tag{7}$$

Where, *N* is sampling points, m is the number of array elements, and k is the source number to be estimated. *2k(2m-k)* is the penalty function that ensures unbiased estimation. The main steps are as follows:

(1) Calculate the covariance matrix *S=(sij), p* ×*p* of sampled data, where $s_{ij} = \frac{1}{n-1}\sum_{k=1}^{n}(x_{ki} - \bar{x}_i)(x_{ki} - \bar{x}_j), i, j = 1,\cdots,p$.

(2) Calculate the eigenvalues $\lambda_1, \lambda_2, \ldots, \lambda_p$ of S.

(3) Calculate the value of Eq. (6) according to log-likelihood function. The optimal number k is obtained when the value of Eq. (6) reaches its minimum.

AIC compensates for weaknesses in hypothesis testing, and performs well in engineering applications. Estimation error exists in results, though, when SNR (Signal to Noise Ratio) is low.

3.2.4 Principal Component Analysis

PCA is used to reduce the dimensions of data [15]. Because the multidimensional vector is composed of sample characteristics that some elements is similar, elements with large variance must be identified and elements with little change must be eliminated. Thus, all remaining characteristics are useful. The main steps of the process are as follows:

1) Calculate the covariance matrix $S = (s_{ij})_{p\times p}$ of sample data, where $s_{ij} = \frac{1}{n-1}\sum_{k=1}^{n}(x_{ki} - \bar{x}_i)(x_{ki} - \bar{x}_j), i, j = 1,\cdots,p$

2) Calculate the eigenvalues $\lambda_1 \ge \cdots \ge \lambda_p > 0$ and corresponding orthogonal unit eigenvectors *a1,a2,...,ap* of covariance matrix *S*.

3) Select r principal components from determined p principle components to achieve the final evaluation. Variance devoting rate $\partial_i = \lambda_i \Big/ \sum_{j=1}^{p}\lambda_j$ is generally used to explain amount of information that principle component Fi reflects. The determination of number r is based on the principle that cumulative contribution rate $G(r) = \sum_{j=1}^{r}\lambda_j \Big/ \sum_{j=1}^{p}\lambda_j$ is big enough (generally larger than 90%).

4) Calculate the score of n samples on principal component r using equation (8):

$$F_i = a_{1i}X_1 + \cdots + a_{pi}X_P (i = 1,\ldots,r) \tag{8}$$

PCA mainly depends on the cumulative contribution rate of the characteristics to determined source number, which means that human error will quite easily affect its accuracy.

In above four methods, Bootstrap and Hough transform methods estimate source number based on covariance in frequency domain, while AIC and PCA are based on time domain covariance. In order to make more efficient use of the characteristics in time and frequency domains, this study uses the weighted fusion method described in the next section.

3.3 Weighted fusion of multiple algorithms

The advantages and disadvantages of above estimation methods have been discussed. This work proposes a new method based on multi-algorithm weighted fusion to estimate the number of sources.

3.3.1 Mathematical Model

After studied above four methods, we can obtain the optimal solution by optimizing the estimation error for the optimization problem.

The objective function is:

$$\min f_0 = (S - \hat{S})^2 \tag{9}$$

The constraint function is:

$$\begin{cases} f_i = \sum_{i=1}^{m} \partial_i = 1, \ i = 1, \cdots, m \\ \partial_i \geq 0 \end{cases} \tag{10}$$

Where S is the real source number, $\hat{S}$ is the estimate of S. ∂_i is the weighted factor of algorithm S_i, and $\hat{S} = \sum_{i=1}^{m} \partial_i S_i \quad i = 1, \cdots, m$.

3.3.2 Particle swarm optimization algorithm

In this study, the weighted coefficient in the mathematical model above can be optimized by PSO, which regards a particle as an available solution [16], then guides the particle to its optimal position using itself and its neighboring particles' information.

A. Definition of Position and Speed

In PSO, position of every particle represents an available scheme for optimizing weights. *xij* is the weight that algorithm *Sj* have in fusion algorithm, where the sum of all weights must be equal to 1. Speed is used to calculate the probability of particle positions transformation. The speed of the particle i is *V={vij}*, where $v_{ij} \in [-v_{\max}, v_{\max}]$.

B. Update of Position and Speed

In PSO, the position and speed are updated as follows:

$$v_{ij}^{k+1} = w * v_{ij}^{k} + c_1 * rand_1 * (pb - x_{ij}^{k}) + c_2 * rand_2 * (gb - x_{ij}^{k}) \tag{11}$$

$$x_{ij}^{k+1} = x_{ij}^{k} + v_{ij}^{k+1} \tag{12}$$

where *c1, c2* are learning factors, *w* is the weighted parameter, *rand()* are random numbers, and x_{ij}^{k} is the current position.

C. Specific procedure of PSO

(1) Initialize every particle, particle number, maximum iteration number and maximum speed, randomly generate initial position and initial speed;

(2) Generating a new position of each particle according to current position and speed;

While (Iterations < maximum iterations) do

(3) Compute fitness function value for every particle according to f0, current fitness value of particle is compared with the most optimized value and individual optimal value pb is updated;

(4) According to the pb of each particle, update the group optimal value gb;

(5) According to formal (11), update new speed, this is limited within maximum speed;

(6) According to formal (11), update new position;

End

As discussed above, the proposed source number estimation algorithm for single channel based on algorithm fusion can be described as Algorithm 1.

Algorithm 1 Estimating the Number of Single Channel Source (ENSCS)

1. Input: single channel signal *x(t)*.
2. Empirical mode decomposition is used to map the single channel signal *x(t)* into multi-channel *{x1(t),x2(t),...,xn(t)}*.
3. AIC, PCA, Hough transform, and Bootstrap methods are employed to obtain the source number *{r1,r2,r3,r4}*.
4. The proposed weighted fusion method is utilized: $\hat{S}_n = \sum_{i=1}^{4} w_i r_i$.
5. PSO is used to determine the weighted coefficient *wi (i=1,2,3,4)*.
6. Output: source number of single-channel signal is $r = \hat{S}_n$.

4. NONNEGATIVE MATRIX RECONSTRUCTION AND SEPARATION

4.1 Nonnegative multiple channels signal reconstruction

Following independent components estimation in a single channel signal, combined with IMF, multiple channel signals reconstruction is required for transforming underdetermined blind source separation into a well-posed problem.

The signal based on IMF and the number of independent components r is constructed, as follows:

$$x_1(t) = (c_1, c_2, \cdots, c_{r-1}, c_r + c_{r+1} + \ldots + r_{1n})^T \tag{13}$$

As negative value will appear in EMD results, the constructed matrix is not a nonnegative matrix and cannot meet the requirements for input of NMF, thus a positive

matrix must be added to allow the reconstructed matrix to become a nonnegative matrix $x_2(t)$, that is,

$$x_2(t) = x_1(t) + positive\ value.*ones(r, l) \quad (14)$$

Where r is the number of independent components, and l is the length of data.

This method only increases the amplitude of signals while not influencing signal information and results of separation.

4.2 Nonnegative matrix factorization

NMF was proposed by Lee and Seung as a new method to factorize the matrix. NMF seeks two nonnegative matrices $W \in R^{m \times r}$ and $H \in R^{r \times n}$ for a nonnegative matrix $V = [v_1, v_2, \dots, v_m]^T \in R^{m \times n}$ to meet equation:

$$V = WH \quad s.t. W, H \geq 0 \quad (15)$$

Where W is basis matrix, H is coefficient matrix, r is the rank of matrix factorization, generally $r \leq \min(m,n)$.

NMF can be described as following optimization problem:

$$\min D(V \| WH) \quad s.t. W_{ik}, H_{ik} > 0, \sum_i W_{ik} = 1, 1 \leq k \leq n \quad (16)$$

Where $D(V \| WH)$ is distance function between V and WH, that is reconstruction error. Function model based on Frobinus-norm is defined as follows [17]:

$$D(V \| WH) = \frac{1}{2} \| A - WH \|_F^2 \quad (17)$$

Thus, optimization problem can be transformed into nonlinear programming problem with constraints. If standard NMF algorithm is used to solve blind source separation problem without any constraint on W and H, it is difficult obtaining desired separation results. This paper employs determinant constraint [18] on basis matrix W, and applies minimum correlation constraint on coefficient matrix H [19].

A. Determinant constraint

Firstly, let us explain a definition. Let $P(W)$ is a space which is spanned with w1,w2,…,wn. If W is square matrix, volume of $P(W)$ can be described as:

$$vol(P) = |\det(W)| \quad (18)$$

If W is not a square matrix, then,

$$vol(P) = |\det(WW^T)| \quad (19)$$

Then determinant constraint can be defined as: if the space $P(W)$ is spanned with vector $w1, w2, \dots, wn$, and the volume $vol(P)$ of this space is minimum, then vectors $w1, w2, \dots, wn$ have uniqueness.

B. Minimum correlation constraint

When NMF is applied to solve BSS problem, coefficient matrix H represents sources in BSS problem. If source signal is not related to each other, absolute value of correlation coefficients between mixed signals is larger than source signals. That is, if mixed signals are not separated completely, every row of coefficient matrix will contain components of other source signals. Comparing completely separated signal with not completely separated signal, the absolute value of correlation coefficients for the former is less than the latter. So minimum correlation constraint can be applied to coefficient matrix H, making correlation coefficient of separated signals the least. Expression of correlation coefficient is:

$$R(H) = \frac{1}{2}\left[\sum_{i=1}^{n} \log(HH^T)_{ii} - \log|HH^T|\right] \quad (20)$$

Where $H=[h1, h2, \dots, hn]^T$, when $\langle h_i, h_j \rangle = 0$, $\forall i, j, i \neq j$, correlation coefficient $R(H)$ is the minimum value.

Determinant constraint on W and minimum correlation constraint on H are introduced simultaneously into Eq. (17), a new cost function can be obtained:

$$F(V \| WH) = \alpha_D D(V \| WH) + \alpha_W vol(P(W)) + \alpha_H R(H) \quad (21)$$

Where $vol(P(W))$ is determinant constraint on W, $R(H)$ is minimum correlation constraint on H. α_D, α_W and α_R are weight coefficients, $\alpha_D = 1$, $\alpha_W = 1$, $\alpha_R = 0.01$. The equation above is convex in either W or H, but not in both W and H. Gradient descent method is utilized to update W and H alternately and calculate the optimal solution for optimization problem. Updating rule of NMF is as follows:

$$\begin{cases} W_{ik} = W_{ik} - \eta_W \dfrac{\partial F(V \| WH)}{\partial W_{ik}} \\ H_{kj} = H_{kj} - \eta_H \dfrac{\partial F(V \| WH)}{\partial H_{kj}} \end{cases} \quad (22)$$

$$\begin{cases} \dfrac{\partial \det(WW^T)}{\partial W_{ik}} = \det(WW^T)[(WW^T)^{-1}W]_{ik} \\ \dfrac{\partial R(H)}{\partial H_{kj}} = \dfrac{1}{(h_k h_k^T)H_{kj}} - [(HH^T)^{-T}H]_{kj} \end{cases} \quad (23)$$

η_W and η_H in above equation is iteration speed, they can be set as:

$$\begin{cases} \eta_W = \dfrac{W_{ik}}{[WHH^T]_{ik}} \\ \eta_H = \dfrac{H_{kj}}{[W^T WH]_{kj}} \end{cases} \quad (24)$$

From above three equations, we can drive new updating rules:

$$\begin{cases} W_{ik} = W_{ik}\left[\dfrac{[VH^T]_{ik}}{[WHH^T]_{ik} + \varepsilon} - \alpha_W \det(WW^T)\dfrac{[(WW^T)^{-1}W]_{ik}}{[H^T HW]_{ik} + \varepsilon}\right] \\ H_{kj} = H_{kj}\dfrac{[W^T V]_{kj} - \alpha_R(\dfrac{h_{kj}}{(h_k h_k^T)} - [(HH^T)^{-T}H]_{kj})}{[W^T WH]_{kj} + \varepsilon} \end{cases} \quad (25)$$

Where ε is little enough to avoid denominator in equation (25) being zero. In the process of iteration, negative values in W and H should be set to zero and every row

of W should be normalized, that is $W_{ik} = W_{ik} / \sum_k W_{ik}$. The algorithm converges when $F(V||WH)$ is less than a threshold value.

Algorithm 2:SCBSS algorithm

---

1. Single channel observed signal is x(t);
2. Single channel signal x(t) is decomposed by EMD into many IMFs: ximf=(c1,c2,…,cn,r1n)T;
3. Estimate source number according to algorithm based on multi-algorithms fusion proposed above, the result is r;
4. Construct nonnegative matrix based on r and IMFs. Reconstruct the multiple channels signal according to equation (14), then construct nonnegative matrix x2(t) according to equation (15);
5. Perform NMF on new nonnegative multiple channel signals x2(t) to derive original source signals.

---

5 EXPERIMENTS AND RESULTS

5.1 Experimental setup

Two experiments were designed to verify the effectiveness of proposed algorithm and are described as follows:

(1) Experiment one utilized four man-made signals to verify the correctness of EMD-NMF algorithm. The four man-made signals (Figure. 1) are: a square signal $s_1 = 1 + sign(\cos(50 \times pi \times t / f_s))$, two sinusoidal signals of different frequency $s_2 = 1 + \sin(90\pi t / f_s)$, $s_3 = 1 + \sin(10\pi t / f_s)$, and a modulating signal $s_4 = 1 + \sin(10\pi t / f_s)\sin(300\pi t / f_s)$, at sampling frequency of $f_s = 5000$. Sampling point is 4000. The four original signals are mixed as s=s1+s2+s3+s4, shown in Figure. 2.

(2) Two ECG signals were chosen from MIT-BIH database [20] to verify the feasibility of proposed algorithm. Amplitude of signal is *mV*, sampling point is 2048 (Figure. 5). These two signals were instantaneous linearly mixed with a randomly generated matrix as a single observed signal, shown in Figure. 6.

Experiments were simulated in MATLAB R2010a by a personal computer with Pentium (R) T4400 2.20GHz CPU and 2GB RAM.

5.2 Experimental results

A. Four channels man-made signal experiment

Four channels man-made signal s1,s2,s3 and s4 described in experimental setup are original signals. They are mixed to obtain a single channel observed signal. The waveform of original signals and mixed signal are presented in Figure.1 and Figure.2 separately.

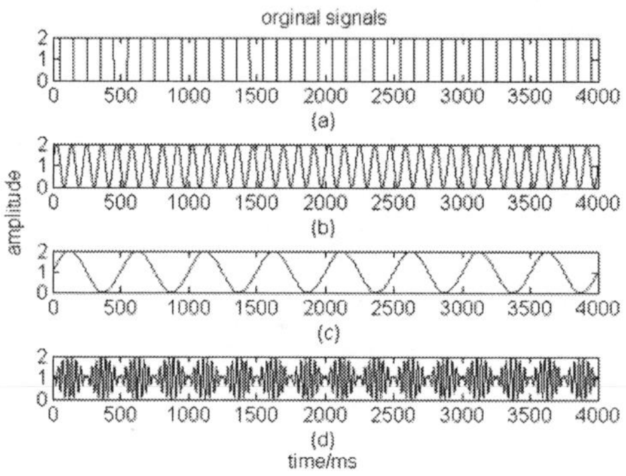

Figure.1 four channels man-made signal, (a) square signal, (b) and (c) sinusoidal signals with different frequency, (d) modulating signal

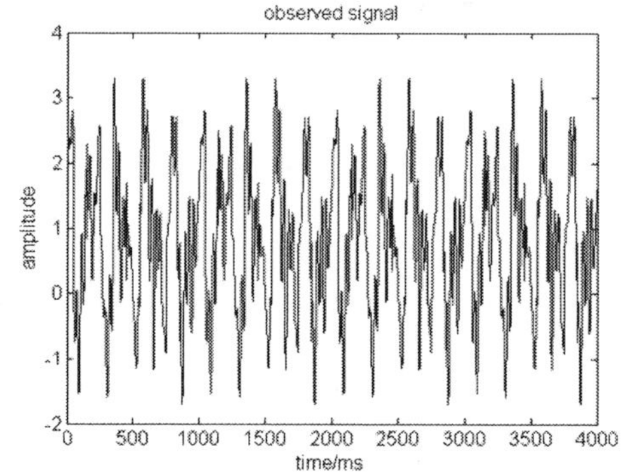

Figure.2 single channel mixed signal, which is obtained by adding four man-made

Estimation of the independent component number: EMD decomposed single channel signal into a set of IMF with results presented in Fig.3.

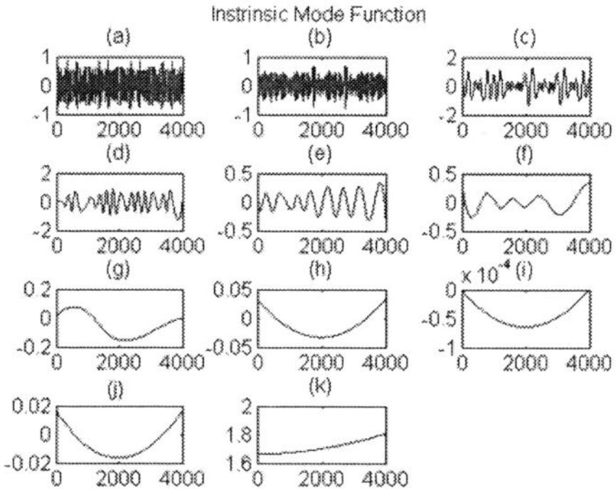

Figure.3 result of empirical mode decomposition on single channel mixed signal. Eleven IMFs are arranged from high frequency to low frequency, from left to right, and from top to bottom

Four multiple channels source number estimation algorithms AIC, PCA, Bootstrap and Hough trans-form are applied to estimate source number in single channel signal, obtaining the results 5, 3, 2, and 4 separately. Then four results are weighted fused based on PSO algorithm to de-

rive accurate number in single channel signal. The source number calculated with this method is 4 which agrees with the experimental setup.

Results of AIC, PCA, Bootstrap, Hough transform and fusion algorithm proposed in this paper are shown in Table.1.

Tab.1 source number estimation for single channel signal mixed with four man-made signals using four traditional algorithm and proposed fusion algorithm

AIC	PCA	Bootstrap	Hough	Fusion value
5	3	2	4	4

Table.1 indicates that source number estimation based on multi-algorithm fusion method can determine the source number in single channel signal accurately and it performs better than other four algorithms.

Four channels signal were reconstructed according to nonnegative matrix construction principle described above. NMF was employed to separate reconstructed signals and the results are shown in Fig.4.

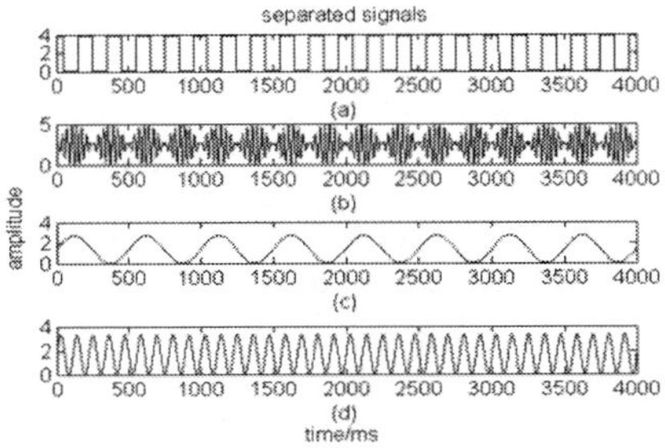

Figure.4 four channels separated signal from single channel mixed signal using NMF

The four channel man-made signals experiment revealed the algorithm proposed in this paper could determine source number accurately and achieve single channel signal separation with more than two channel sources.

B. ECG experiment

This section selected two channels ECG signal from MIT-BIH to verify the feasibility of proposed algorithm. The two ECG signals are added together as a single observed signal. The waveform of original and mixed signal is shown in Figure.5 and Figure.6 separately.

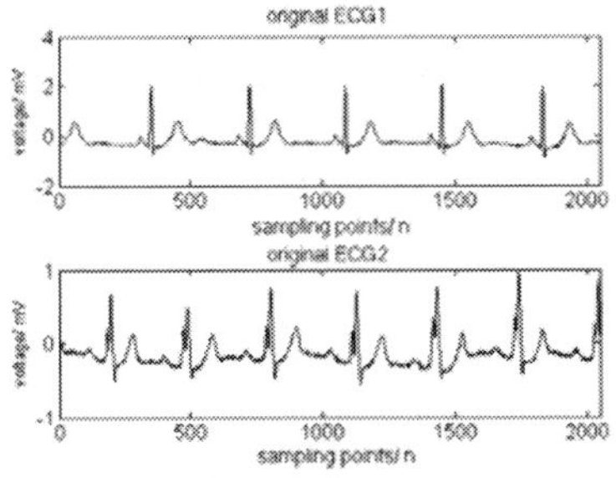

Figure.5 waveform of two channels ECG signal

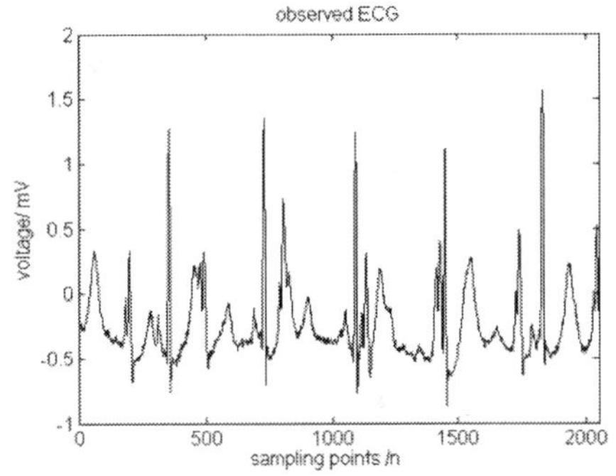

Figure.6 single channel mixed ECG signal, which is obtained by adding two ECG signals in Figure.5 together

Estimation of number for independent component: firstly, EMD was employed to single channel signal to derive a set of IMF whose results are depicted in Fig. 7.

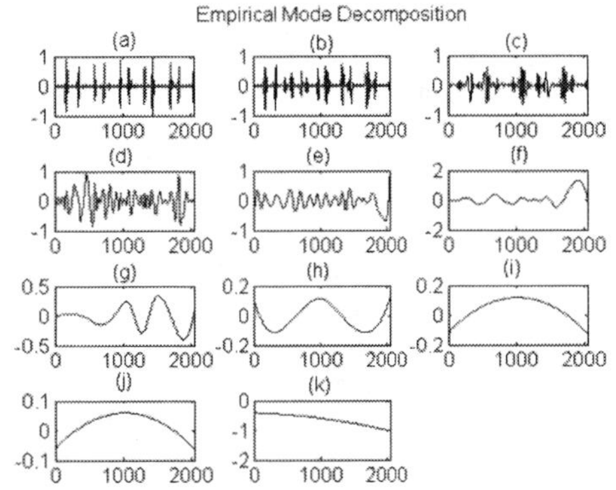

Figure.7 a set of IMFs obtained using empirical mode decomposition. They are arranged from high frequency to low frequency, from left to right, and from top to bottom

Then AIC, PCA, Bootstrap and Hough were utilized to estimate source number in single channel signal, deriving the result 2, 2, 1, 3 respectively.

At last, the four results were used to do weighted fusion to determine the accurate source number is 2 which is no difference with the experimental setup. During the weighted fusion, weighting coeffi-cient was determined by PSO.

Number estimations of AIC, PCA, Bootstrap and Hough are compared with fusion algorithm result in Table.2.

Tab.2 number estimation results for single channel signal mixed with two ECG using AIC, PCA, Bootstrap, Hough and Fusion algorithm

AIC	PCA	Bootstrap	Hough	Fusion value
2	2	1	3	2

We can conclude from Table.2 that fusion algorithm proposed in this paper can estimate source number in single channel signal accurately compared with traditional four algorithms.

Two channels signal were reconstructed according to nonnegative matrix construction principle described above. NMF was employed to separate reconstructed signals and the results are shown in Fig.8.

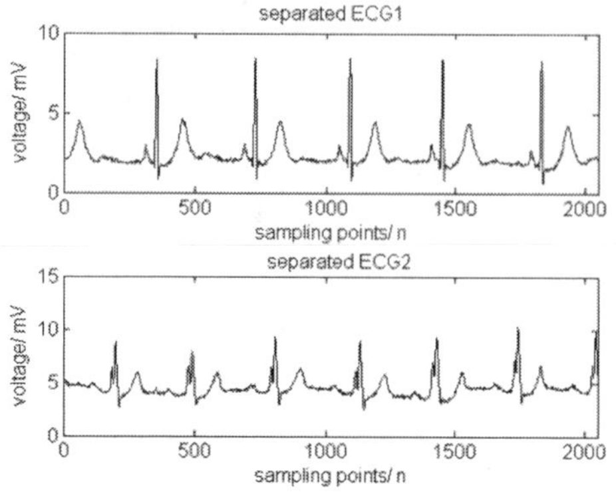

Figure.8 recovered two channels ECG from single channel mixed signal using proposed algorithm

The experiment revealed the algorithm proposed in this paper can be used to separate ECG signals and it can determine source number in single ECG signal, having practical application value.

Typical man-made signals and ECG signals are chosen as experimental objects to verify the effectiveness and practicability of proposed SCBSS algorithm based on source number estimation using multi-algorithm fusion. Results show that proposed algorithm could estimate source number accurately in single channel mixed signal and could solve blind source separation with two or more sources, which can be applied in engineering practices. The deficiency exists in this algorithm is construction of nonnegative matrix will affect amplitude of signals. Corresponding disposal, however, under specific amplitude requirement circumstances, may act to eliminate these defects.

6 CONCLUSION

A single channel blind source separation algorithm based on source number estimation using multi-algorithm fusion was proposed in this paper, which is used to solve signal mixture problem for maternal and fetal ECG exists in clinical fetal monitoring. The algorithm employed EMD to decompose single channel signal into multiple IMF, mapping single channel into multiple channels. Then AIC, PCA, Bootstrap and Hough transform were utilized to estimate source number in single channel signal, and PSO was employed to optimize weight during weighted fusion, deriving accurate number of independent components. Multiple channel signals were reconstructed and NMF was used to achieve separation of signals. Experiments utilized single channel speech whose source is two and single channel man-made signal whose source is four to verify the feasibility of proposed algorithm. Results indicate that proposed algorithm could determine source number in single channel signal accurately, and it could separate fetal ECG from single channel collected abdominal signal. Meanwhile, the proposed algorithm is suitable for multiple births and provides a total solution for separation of maternal and fetal ECG.

REFERENCES

[1] Hasan, M. A., et al. (2009). Detection and processing techniques of FECG signal for fetal monitoring', Biological procedures online. 11: 263-295.

[2] Sameni, Reza, and Gari D. Clifford. (2010). A review of fetal ECG signal processing; issues and promising directions. The open pacing, electrophysiology & therapy journal. 3: 4-20.

[3] Gao P, Chang E C, Wyse L. (2003). Blind separation of fetal ECG from single mixture using SVD and ICA. In Information, Communications and Signal Processing, 2003 and Fourth Pacific Rim Conference on Multimedia. Proceedings of the 2003 Joint Conference of the Fourth International Conference on IEEE. 3: 1418-1422.

[4] Azzerboni, B., La Foresta, F., Mammone, N., & Morabito, F. C. (2005). A new approach based on wavelet-ICA algorithms for fetal electrocardiogram extraction. ESANN. 193-198.

[5] La Foresta, F., N. Mammone, and F. C. Morabito. (2005). Independent component and wavelet analysis for fECG extraction: the stwaveform evaluation. Computational Intelligence for Measurement Systems and Applications, CIMSA. 2005 IEEE International Conference on. IEEE. 86-90.

[6] Mijovic, Bogdan, et al. (2010). Source separation from single-channel recordings by combining empirical-mode decomposition and independent component analysis. Biomedical Engineering, IEEE Transactions on. 57: 2188-2196.

[7] De Lathauwer L, De Moor B, Vandewalle J. (2000). Fetal electrocardiogram extraction by blind source subspace separation. IEEE transactions on biomedical engineering, 47: 567-572.

[8] Luenberger, David. (1979). Introduction to dynamic systems: theory, models, and applications. John Wiley & Sons. New York.

[9] Huang N E, Shen Z, Long S R, et al. (1998). The empirical mode decomposition and the Hilbert spectrum for nonlinear and non-stationary time series analysis. Proceedings of the Royal Society of London. Series A: Mathematical, Physical and Engineering Sciences. 454: 903-995.

[10] Rilling G, Flandrin P, Goncalves P. (2003). On empirical mode decomposition and its algorithms. IEEE-EURASIP workshop on nonlinear signal and image processing, NSIP-03, Grado (I). 3: 8-11

[11] Xu, Z., B. Huang, and F. Zhang. (2009). Envelope approach based on special knots for empirical mode decomposition. Electronics letters. 45: 480-481.

[12] Wang L, Yin J H, Chen T Q. (2007). Frequency domain bootstrap method for source number estimation of wideband signals. CHINESE JOURNAL OF RADIO SCIENCE. 22: 130-132.

[13] Zhang Y F, Guan J, Wang J et al. (2006). A Novel Method for Determination of the Number of Signal

Sources Based on Hough Transform. Journal of Detection & Control. 28: 26-28.

[14] Ye Z F, Xiang L, Xu X. (2007). Improvement of source number estimation based on information theoretic criteria. CHINESE JOURNAL OF RADIO SCIENCE. 22: 593-598.

[15] Gu Q W, Jin W D, Yu Z B. (2014). Blind source separation of single channel train signal based on EEMD and ICA. Application Research of Computers. 31: 1551-1553.

[16] Feng J Z, Song L, Huo X M, Yang X K, Zhang W J. (2014). An Optimized Pixel-Wise Weighting Approach for Patch-Based Image Denoising. IEEE Signal Processing Letter. 22: 115-119.

[17] Lee D D,Seung H S. (1999). Learning the parts of objects by non-negative matrix factorization. Nature. 401: 788-791.

[18] Schachtner, Poppel G, Tom A M,et al. (2009). Minimum determinant constraint for non-negative matrix factorization. Lecture Notes in Computer Science. 5441: 106-113.

[19] Y Zhang,Y Fang. (2007). A NMF algorithm for blind separation of uncorrelated signals. Wavelet Analysis and Pattern Recognition, 2007, ICWAPR'07. International Conference on. IEEE. 3: 999-1003.

[20] Goldberger AL, Amaral LAN, Glass L, Hausolorff JM,et al.. (2000). Components of a New Research Resource for Complex Physuologic Signals, Circulation 101(23): e215-e220 [Circulation Electronic Pages; http:// circ. Ahajournals.org/cgi/content/full/101/23/e215].

MATEC Web of Conferences 44, 01027 (2016)
DOI: 10.1051/matecconf/20164401027

The Study and Simulation of Multi-interface Extension for OLSR Protocol

Hui Zhong[1,a], Xu Bin Wang[2]

[1] *Shenyang Jianzhu University, Faculty of Information & Control Engineering, 110168, Shenyang, China*
[2] *Shenyang Jianzhu University, Faculty of Information & Control Engineering, 110168, Shenyang, China*

Abstract. The way to improve the performance of the throughput in the wireless Mesh network is nodes with multiple interfaces. In view of the problem of multi-interface multi-channel extension for OLSR protocol, multi-interface multi-channel OLSR protocol is proposed. Nodes can have multiple network interfaces, but each node has only one IP, using the index of interface to distinguish the multiple interfaces of the node. Selected the receiving interface according to the channel, modified the message delivery method and introduces the protocol implementation and technology. Finally, the simulation is carried out by using the extended NS2. Simulation results show that extended OLSR protocol has high network performance, and improve the network throughput. What is new and original in this paper is adding multiple physical interface support for proactive protocol OLSR.

1 Introductions

Wireless Mesh Network (WMN) [1], has the characteristics of high performance ratio, scalability, and high reliability, etc. However, in general, the nodes in the network have only one single interface. Single interface affects the data transmission between nodes, which limits the throughput of the network. One of the most effective ways to solve the problem is to equip nodes with multiple interfaces [2]. Wireless Mesh networks with multiple interfaces can improve the data processing speed of nodes; improve the network throughput .

In order to achieve the goal, it is necessary to expand the NS2. The well-known scheme is the method of Ramon multi-interface extension in the AODV protocol [3]. However, there is no extension of the OLSR protocol. In this paper, we refer to the method of the Ramon scheme and modify it, then expand the OLSR protocol to the multi-interface multi-channel OLSR.

2 NS2 multi-interface multi-channel expansion

It needs to modify the MobileNode model in order to extend the NS2 to multi-interface multi-channel [4]. The original MobileNode model has only one component, which is the link layer, ARP, interface queue, MAC, network interface and channel. The modified MobileNode model for each interface has a set of components, as shown in figure 1. The number of interfaces and the distribution of the channels can be easily controlled in the simulation scripts.

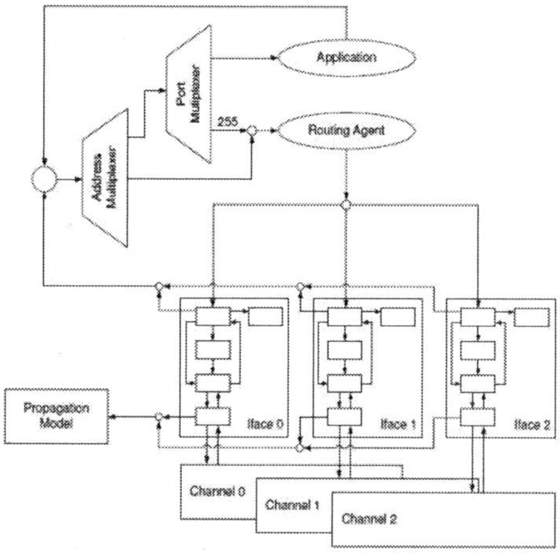

Figure 1. Modified MobileNode architecture.

3 Multi-interface multi-channel AODV

Ramon scheme is extended the AODV protocol under NS2. The main idea of the scheme is to increase the number of interfaces and channels, increase the number of channels under the AODV protocol, and modify the protocol itself, so that AODV can support multi-interface [5].

Ramon scheme has been modified in three ways, which is to modify Tcl, modify C++ code and modify AODV routing agent. The modification of Tcl is mainly to complete the expansion of MobileNode model, and the modification of C++ file is used to adapt to the new framework, and most of the changes are affecting the simulator to deal with the MobileNode class. The last part

[a] Corresponding author: syzhonghui@sina.com

Article available at http://www.matec-conferences.org or http://dx.doi.org/10.1051/matecconf/20164401027

of the change is the implementation of the AODV protocol. The way to transmit message (RREP, RRER, RREQ and HELLO) is different between Multi-interface AODV and the original AODV, and it also needs to add some new parameters to the routing agent to manage the corresponding interface information. So this part has made some changes from two aspects: routing finding and routing maintenance [6].

With the increase of the number of effective network interfaces, the multi-interface multi-channel AODV, which improves the throughput of the network, reduces the end-to-end delay, and the network also becomes more stable [7].

4 OLSR protocol

OLSR routing protocol is a kind of the optimal link state routing protocol which is driven by the MANET IETF (Mobile Ad hoc Net-work) working group, especially suitable for large and scale mobile network [8].

The operation of the OLSR protocol relies on the various types of data table of the nodes[9]. The node broadcasts HELLO messages periodically, and forms a Link Set based on the HELLO messages, then forms a Neighbor Set based on the Link Set. The TC messages are broadcasted to the whole network by MPR nodes. Each node maintains a Topology Set. If the node contains multiple interfaces (each interface is only assigned one IP address), an interface Association Set table is formed. Finally, the routing table of the node is obtained by calculating these data tables.

Interface Association Set

I_iface_addr	I_main_addr	I_time

Figure 2. Interface Association Set.

This set is used to store the relationship between the main address of the node and the OLSR interface addresses of a node. I_iface_addr represents t the OLSR interface addresses, I_main_addr is the main address of the node, and I_time represents the effective time of the event.

Link Set

L_local_iface_addr	L_neighbor_iface_addr	L_SYM_time	L_ASYM_time	L_time

Figure 3. Link Set.

Link Set is used to store the link information of the node. L_local_iface_addr represents the local interface address of the link, L_neighbor_iface_addr represents the link's neighbor interface address, and L_SYM_time represents the time when the link is symmetry, L_ASYM_time indicating that the time when the link is asymmetric, and L_time is an effective time for the event.

Neighbor Set

N_neighbor_main_addr	N_status	N_willingness

Figure 4. Neighbor Set.

This set is used to store information about a neighbor node. N_neighbor_main_addr for the main address of the neighbor node. N_status is the state of a neighbor node. N_willingness for the forwarding value of the neighbor node.

2-hop Neighbor Set

N_neighbor_main_addr	N_2hop_addr	N_time

Figure 5. 2-hop Neighbor Set.

This set stores the information of the 2-hop neighbor nodes. N_neighbor_main_addr represents the main address of the neighbor node. N_2hop_addr represents the main address of the 2-hop neighbor node. N_time is a valid time for the event.

Topology Set

T_dest_addr	T_last_addr	T_seq	T_time

Figure 6. Topology Set.

By exchanging TC messages periodicity, the topology set recorded the network topology. T_dest_addr represents the main address of the destination node, T_last_addr is the main address of the last hop of the destination node, T_seq is the sequence number of the event, and T_time is the effective time of the event.

Routing Set

R_dest_addr	R_next_addr	R_dist	R_iface_addr

Figure 7. Routing Set.

R_dest_addr is the interface address of the destination node, R_next_addr is the interface address of the next hop neighbor node, R_dist is the number of hops to the destination node, R_iface_addr is the address of the local interface to the next hop.

5 Multi-interface multi-channel OLSR extension scheme

OLSR is a proactive protocol, each node in the OLSR network needs to maintain a routing table. Therefore, the routing table is the extraction of the link state, neighbor state and topology information. That is to say, when the corresponding event is changed, the routing table also needs to be calculated.

Node builds and updates their own network topology by exchanging control messages periodically. Among them, there are three types of control messages. First, the HELLO message, which is used for link sensing and populating neighbor; Second, the TC message, which is used to declare the topology; Third, the MID message is used to declare the relationship between OLSR interface addresses and main addresses. The Interface Association Set is formed according to the MID message, and the Topology Set is formed according to the TC message. The formation of the Link Set depends on the HELLO message. After the formation of the Link Set, the neighbor populating process is completed according to the Link Set and the HELLO messages, format the Neighbor Set and 2-hop Neighbor Set.

In order to realize the multi-interface multi-channel extension of OLSR protocol, a new approach is proposed, which a node can have multiple interfaces. But each node

has only one IP address. Which interface is used to send and receive messages is distinguished by the index of the interface. Since each node has only one IP address, MID message will be lost.

L_local_iface_addr	L_local_iface	L_neighbor_iface_addr	L_SYM_time	L_ASYM_time	L_time

Figure 8. Modified Link Set.

The main process of link sensing is to maintain a local Link Set using HELLO messages that are exchanged between nodes periodically. When a node has multiple interfaces (only one IP address), it needs to know which interface the node has is formed a link with its neighbor. Therefore, the paper is expanded based on the original Link Set, add an index of local interface L_local_iface after the L_local_iface_addr, and record the interface which is used, as shown in Figure 8.

Routing tables are also involved in the Neighbor Set, 2-hop Neighbor Set and Topology Set. The Neighbor Set and 2-hop Neighbor Set is forms by the Link Set and HELLO message. Each node maintains a Link Set, we need to add the index of interface to the Routing Set when the routing table is calculating, the Neighbor Set and the 2-hop Link Set do not need to change. Topology Set shows that the topology of the entire network, and do not need to save the interface information, so it is not necessary to modify it.

R_dest_addr	R_next_addr	R_dist	R_iface_addr	R_iface

Figure 9. Modified Routing Set.

In order to enable nodes to transmit data with the the added interface, an interface index is required to added during the calculation of the routing table. The protocol only needs to know which interface the data need to be sent from, so we add the index of local interface R_iface into the routing table after the local interface address, as shown in Figure 9. Then we can get the corresponding index by looking up the Link Set.

6 Multi-interface multi-channel OLSR implementation

Based on the above-mentioned programme, the NS2 related components can be modified. In order to make NS2 more suitable for multi-interface multi-channel model, we have modified the Tcl script, C++ source code and routing protocol.

6.1 Modify the Tcl script

The first needs to make changes to the tcl/lib/ns-lib.tcl file and tcl/lib/ns-mobilenode.tcl file. In ns-lib.tcl, the code in the original NS2 is not defined the corresponding multi-interface multi-channel parameters, which only supports single interface single channel, thus creating the four new program to achieve the goal. The change-numifs creates an interface for the node; add-channel adds the corresponding channel for the interface. The ifNum process is used to set the number of interfaces, and get-numifs is used to get the number of interfaces. In addition, it is also required to initialize the corresponding variables in the node configuration process.

For ns-mobilenode.tcl, the first need to modify the add-target, call get-numifs to get the number of interface, while the process of routing agent if-queue has been modified to adapt to the multi interface. Secondly, it needs to modify the add-target-rtagent. This program uses the get-numifs to get the number of interfaces, and then uses the variable to connect the routing agent and the link layer. The next one need to be modified is add-interface. Since the previous process created one ARP per node, we need to create one ARP per interface, so the arptable_ is modified as an array arptable_ ($i). The last change affects the way the MobileNode is created and reset.

6.2 Modify the C++ source code

The purpose of this section is to adapt the new framework. Most of the changes affect how the simulator deals with the MobileNode class.

After creating the multi-interface architecture for a mobile node, it is required to connect to the appropriate channel properly. Therefore, the modification in Mobilenode.h is to manage the channel with two pointers nextX_[MAX_CHAN] and prevX_[MAX_CHAN]. However, after the redefinition of prevX_ and nextX_ the getLoc function errors, so we redefinition getLoc method. In addition, we need to add a new definition of getLoc in mobilenode.cc file.

Since the previous definition of two array pointers need to be used in the channel.cc file in order to manage the list of nodes, it is necessary to modify the nextX_ to nextX_[this->index()] and the prevX_ to prevX_[this->index()] through the entire file. In addition, when a packet is sent, the first need to evaluate is which node is close enough to the source node, and is connected to the channel. Then packets can be sent to the interface of node. This is meaningless, however, because the packets can only be received from the interface with the appropriate channel. In this case, we need to inspect whether the sender and the receiver of the interface is using the same channel. "if (rifp->channel () ==this) " was added to the code.

The last one need to be modified is the mac-802_11.cc. In order to recognize the interface, we need to add " hdr->iface ()=addr ();"into it.

6.3 Modify the routing protocol

The first two parts of the changes is to do the preparation for using the multi-interface, routing protocol itself is also modified to adapt to this change. In the OLSR_repositories.cc, the iface_ and the Iface () are added to the struct OLSR_rt_entry. The index of local interface is saved in the variable iface_ in the routing table, and the return value of the function iface() is iface_. In the struct OLSR_link_tuple, added the variable local_iface_ and the function local_iface() , which is used to store the interface index of the local node.

In the OLSR_state.cc, the operation of Link Set is required to add a function find_link_tuple, so the Link Set entries corresponding to the interface address and

interface index are found by using this function, and then return it.

In the OLSR_rtable.cc, we need to modify the add_entry method. Add interface index entry->iface() = iface_ after the local interface address. Since the original add_entry method using the map container, the key and value is one to one relationship, so we change the map to multimap. This allows for a destination address with multiple routing tables that can be present.

In order to achieve the OLSR protocol interface extensions, we need to change the routing proxy implementation. In OLSR.h , the first one need to declare is a global variable numIfaces. It used to store the number of interfaces owned by the node. Now we need to declare two arrays: targetlist[] and ifqueuelist[]. The targetlist[] is used to store all the interfaces of the link layer model in a particular node, the ifqueuelist[] is used to store the corresponding queue. At the same time, it also needs to define a new constant MAX_IFACE, which is used to manage those two arrays.

In the OLSR.cc, it needs to modify the command method of the OLSR routing agent class, and completes the initialization of the above variables. In order to use the Tcl script in the simulation, we also need to implement the distribution of Tcl commands.

The role of the method send_pkt is to generate enough OLSR packets according to the cached OLSR message, and then send it out. Since the node may contain two or more interfaces, it is required to determine whether the node has multi-interface. If it is multi-interface, the OLSR packets are broadcast on all interfaces. Otherwise, keep the original behavior unchanged.

Method recv_olsr is used to process the received OLSR packets. In the recv_olsr method, we need to define a local variable recv_iface. This variable is used to store the index of the interface that used by the node to receive packets. According to the index, we can learn which interface is connected with its neighbor node. Therefore, in the case of multi-interface, we need to calculate the index. We can use the recv_iface=ch->iface()-((Mac *)ifqueuelist[0]->target())->addr() to calculate it. Among them, the ch->iface ()is the number of interface which receive packets, and the second part is the first number of interface. In the case of a single interface, the index is not required, so we set recv_iface to -1, an invalid value. After we get the index of the receiving interface, we pass the index to the process_hello method.

Method process_hello is used for processing HELLO message, including link sensing, populate neighbor and 2-hop neighbor, and MPR computation. The index recv_iface will be used for the link sensing process, and finally form the Link Set. In the Link Set, add the local interface index local_iface () after the local interface address, and assign recv_iface to it.

When the destination address of the packets received by the node is not itself, the node calls the forward_data method to forward the packet. Different with send_pkt method, the destination address of the forwarding packets have already been learned, so the forwarding is unicast. Lookup the routing table, get the interface address to the next hop and the index, and then put packets into the scheduler.

The calculation of the routing table contains in rtable_computation method. Under the multi-interface extension, modification Link Set of will take effect. We get the index of the interface in Link Set, add it to routing table by add_entry method, and select the interface when the packet is sent.

7 The simulation and results of experiment analysis

In order to verify the multi-interface multi-channel expansion, we need to write Tcl script for simulation. Then the simulations compare single-interface OLSR with multi-interface OLSR, and multi-interface OLSR with multi-interface AODV.

Simulation 1: single-interface OLSR and multi-interface OLSR.

Create such a scene, 5 wireless nodes, numbered from 0 to 4. Node 0 sends packets to node 4 by nodes 1, 2 and 3. The single-interface OLSR protocol created only one channel per node, while the multi-interface OLSR protocol creates two different channels per node. Using the UDP connection and CBR flows, and packet size is 500 bytes, send interval is 0.005 seconds, the simulation lasts 60 seconds.

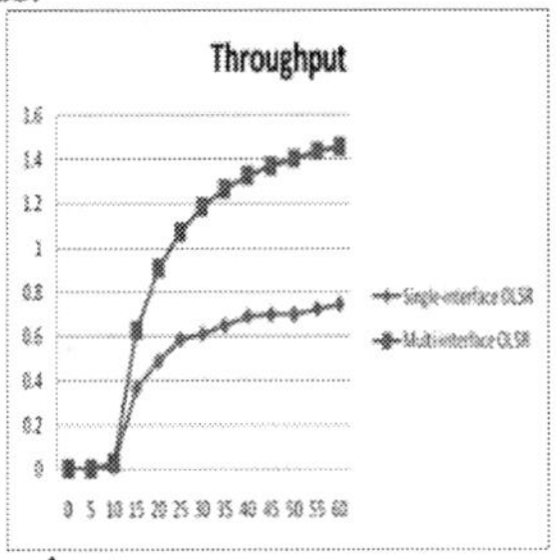

Figure 10. Throughput.

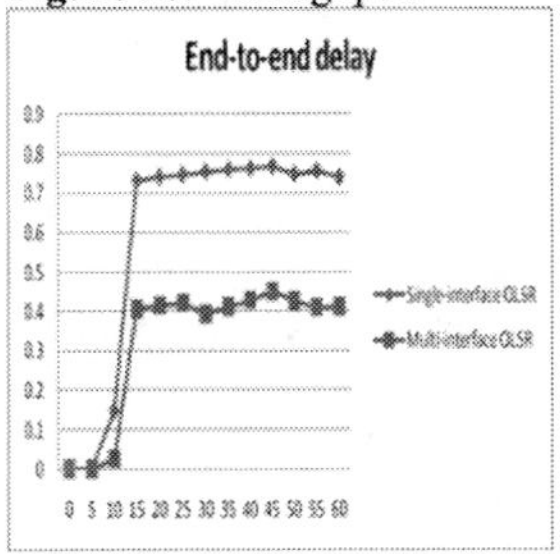

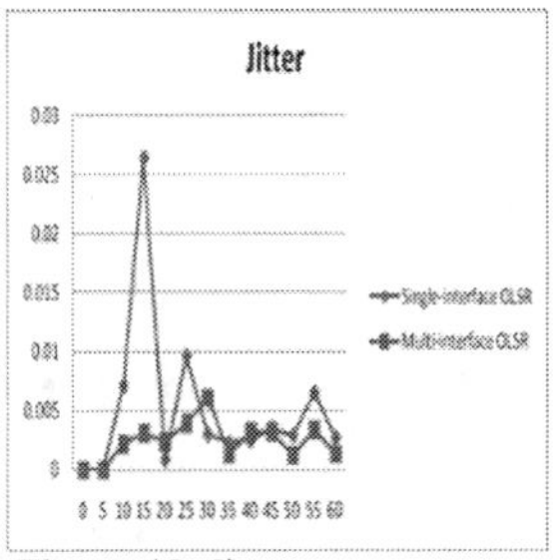

Figure 11. End-to-end delay. **Figure 12.** Jitter

Throughput is the number of successful delivery of data within a unit time. Figure 10 shows that with the start of simulation, the throughput of the single-interface and multi-interface OLSR protocols are all start to rise, and the rise of the extended multi-interface OLSR protocol is significantly faster. This indicates that the throughput of the extended OLSR protocol is better than single-interface OLSR.

End-to-end delay is the delay time of the CBR packet to the end. From Figure 11 it can be seen that after 10 seconds the end to end delay is basically stable, and the

extended OLSR protocol is lower than the original OLSR protocol.

Jitter means the delay variance. Because of the state of network changes and the traffic is always changing. So the data may be queued in the queue, waiting for transmission. The time of each packet from the source node to the destination node is not necessarily the same. This time difference is Jitter. As can be seen from Figure 12, the jitter of the single interface OLSR protocol is much bigger than the multi-interface OLSR, so it is shown that the multi-interface OLSR protocol is more stable than the original OLSR protocol.

Simulation 2: multi-interface OLSR and multi-interface AODV.

To build a simulation with 5 nodes, node 0 send data to node 4 by nodes 1, 2 and 3. Both two scripts are used the multi-interface protocol, and each node creates two different channels. Use the UDP connection and the CBR flows, the packet size is 500 bytes, send interval is 0.005 seconds; the simulation time is 60 seconds. Nodes start sending and receiving data from 1.0 seconds.

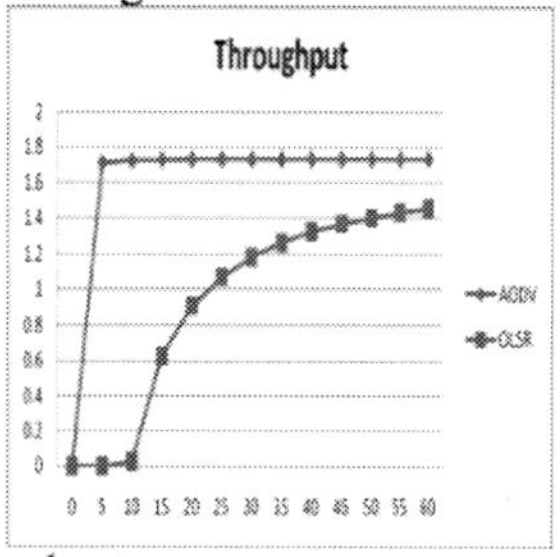

Figure 13. Throughput.

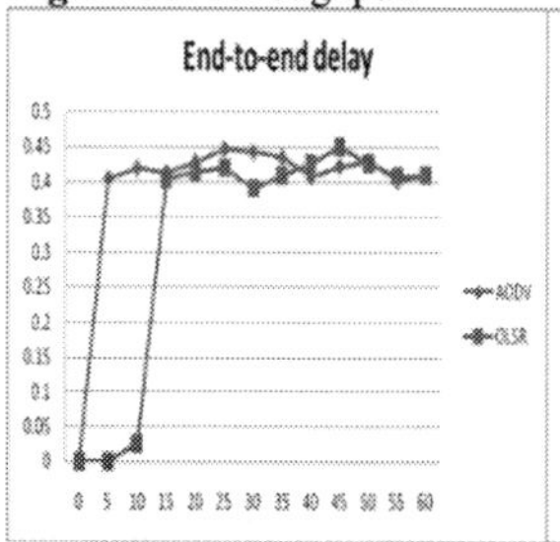

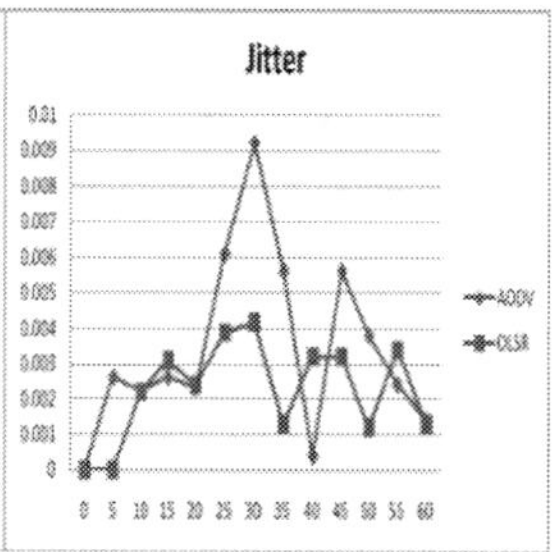

Figure 14. End-to-end delay. **Figure 15.** Jitter.

As s By Figure 13, in the same scenario, Throughput of multi-interface AODV is growing rapidly, and the multi-interface OLSR protocol is slowly improving. This may have relations with the network environment, the number of nodes and the different operation modes of the reactive routing protocols and the prior routing protocols.. In the case of small number of nodes, the throughput of multi-interface AODV is better than the multi-interface OLSR.

As can be seen from Figure 14, with the beginning of the simulation, the end to end delay of the two protocols are beginning to rise, and eventually stabilized in a range. It can be known that, in the case of small number of nodes, the performance of multi interface OLSR and multi interface AODV is similar.

As shown in Figure 15, in most of the time, the jitter of the multi-interface AODV is bigger than the multi-interface OLSR. Therefore, it can be concluded that the stability of the multi-interface OLSR protocol is better than multi-interface AODV.

8 Conclusions

In recent years, the research of multi-interface multi-channel wireless Mesh networks has been an active research topic. In NS2, the simulation of wireless network is a very complex process, it is necessary to understand the working mechanism of each component in the simulator, which requires a lot of time and work. The original OLSR defined the multiple network interfaces, but because of the characteristics of the simulator architecture, it cannot be used. This paper presents a method to implement multi-interfaces and multi-channels on NS2, complete the multi-interface multi-channel OLSR protocol, and improve the throughput of wireless network. However, the existing interface switching strategy is not very good; it can't fully play the advantages of multi-interface and multi-channel. Therefore, the next step will be to make further improvements to the OLSR, so that it can play the advantages of multi-interface performance better.

References

1. XU Tong, YANG Shou-bao, HU Yun. P2P Super Node Selection Strategy Based on Physical Characteristic of WMN[J]. Computer Engineering, 2009, 35(1):101-104.
2. ZHONG Hui;LANG Bing. Research on Link Redundancy Abstract Model for Multi-radio Mesh Network [J]. Journal of Chinese Computer Systems, 36(6):1255-1260.
3. Calvo R A, Campo J P. Adding multiple interface support in NS-2[J]. University of Cantabria, 2007.
4. XIE Peng-yu,SONG Ling,CHEN Yan. Research of AODV Extension for Multi-interface Multi-channel WMN[J]. Computer Engineering, 2011, 37(13): 74-76.
5. YOU Xiao-qian, WEI Yong-lin. (2009).AODV Routing Protocol Supporting Multi-interface. Computer Engineering,35(23), 109-111.
6. FU Qi, CHEN Zhi-gang,JIANG Yun-xia. (2013). Research on Multi-interface Multi-channel Simulation Model Extension Based on NS-2. Computer Engineering, 39(4), 113-117.
7. LAI Cai-hua, TAO Yang. Research on multipath routing algorithm in Wireless Mesh Networks [J]. GUANGDONG Communication Technology, 2010, 30:10-14.
8. ZHAO Jian, SUN Jun-suo. (2008). Simulation and Analysis of an improved OLSR Routing Protocol Based on NS2 . Computer Simulation, 25, 161-163.
9. CHEN Ji-tong. (2006). Design and implementation scheme of OLSR routing protocol for multi-hop wireless ad hoc networks [D](Doctoral dissertation, University of Electronic Science and Technology of China).

MATEC Web of Conferences 44, 01028 (2016)
DOI: 10.1051/matecconf/20164401028

Answer Card Identification Method Based on Pattern Recognition Technology

Jing Xu[1,a], Kun Fang Zhang[1]

[1]The College of Information and Electric Engineering Shenyang Agricultural University, 110866, China

Abstract. The traditional answer card reading method using OMR (Optical Mark Reader), most commonly, OMR special card special use, less versatile, high cost, aiming at the existing problems proposed a method based on pattern recognition of the answer card identification method. Using the method based on Line Segment Detector to detect the tilt of the image, the existence of tilt image rotation correction, and eventually achieve positioning and detection of answers to the answer sheet .Pattern recognition technology for automatic reading, high accuracy, detect faster.

1 Introduction

Examination questions include two types: objective and subjective questions, which objective standard, specification format can through the answer card answer, batch marking by computer systems.The traditional answer card automatic marking system, often adopts the photoelectric reader and a special card reader, can greatly improve the efficiency of the checking work, but at the same time, there are complicated operation,high cost and other shortcomings.With the development of digital image processing and pattern recognition techniques, the use of relatively inexpensive digital camera or scanner as the image data input device to capture the answer sheet image pattern recognition technology to achieve automatic marking the answer sheet, it can greatly reduce equipment costs, and can also identify a variety of types of answer sheet, which has good versatility.

2 Answer card image recognition

Answer card image recognition processing components, to achieve the picture adjustment, cutting, recognition and associated with the data, the bulk of the answer sheet for the recognition process.

The examination system transmits answer card picture information, paper information, student number, after answer sheet image processing component processing,required to achieve:

(1)The picture of answer card is associated with the student number;

(2)Divided the picture into several parts by object answer area,every sub-picture is associated with corresponding papers questions.

(3)If the test questions is for the choice questions, the judge, then the corresponding answer card picture of the segmentation image need to identify the corresponding option.

Answer card image recognition work flow shown in figure 1:

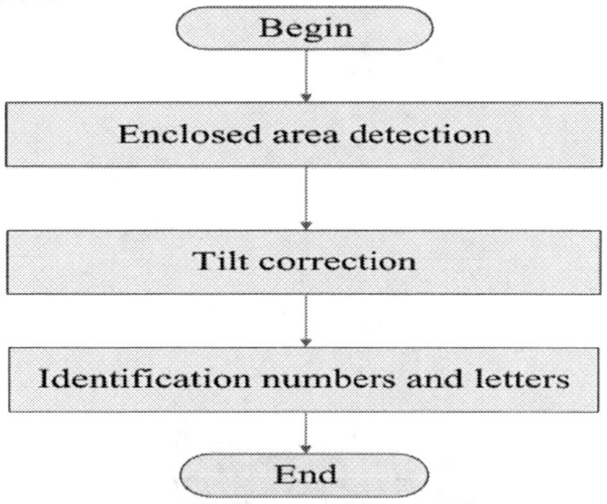

Figure 1. Image recognition work flow.

3 Closed area detection

Detailed algorithm description of the contour region.

(1)From top to bottom, from left to right traverse figure 2 successively.

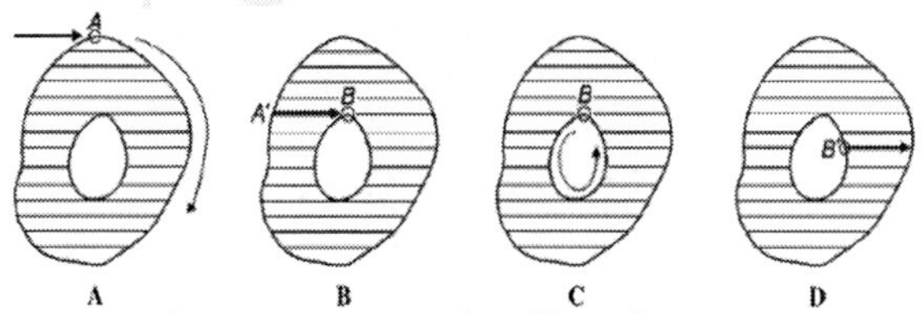

Figure 2. Demonstration of legend.

(2)As shown in figure2A, A is experiencing an outer contour point(in fact, white spots on the traversal of the

[a] Corresponding author: syauxj@163.com

first encounter is the outer contour point),and it has not been marked, then give A a new tag number.Started from point A, in accordance with certain rules(the rules in detail later) of the outer contour point A where the whole track to, and then back to point A, points on the path of all marked label A.
(3)As shown in figure2B, if you have already encountered the outer contour point A 'which has been marked , from A' to the right, it would point to the right are labeled A 'label, until it encounters a black pixel up.
(4)As shown in figure2C, if you encounter a point B, which has been labeled, and is the inner contour of the point(which is black pixel and not outside the contour), then start from the B point, tracking inner contour, the point on the path is set to B label, because B has been labeled with A same, so the inner and outer contour will be labeled with the same label.
(5)As shown in figure2D, if the point on the inner contour is traversed, it also mark the point on the right side of the right side with the contour until the black pixels are encountered.
(6)End of traversal.As shown in figures 3 and figures 4:

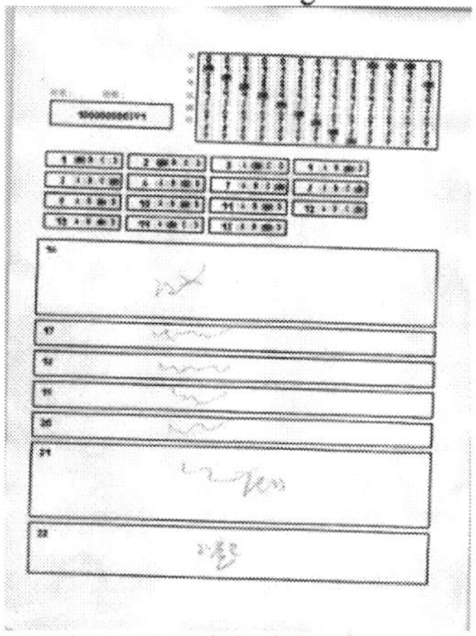

Figure 3. Original drawings.

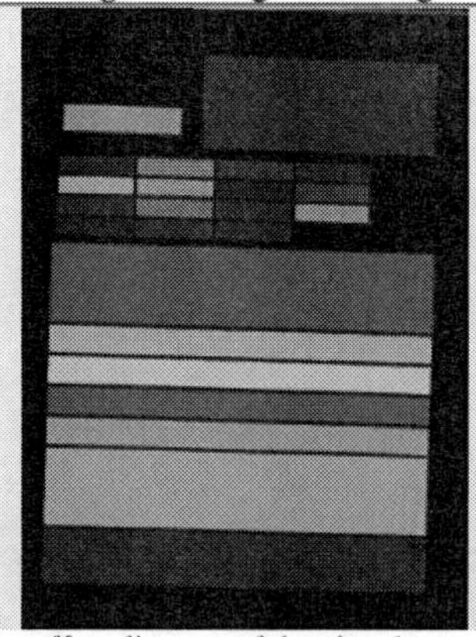

Figure 4. The effect diagram of the closed contour is identified.

4 Image slope detection and rotation correction

In the process of image acquisition, the answer card may produce image tilt for a variety of reasons, and to properly identify must be corrected.Tilt correction, including the following two steps
(1)Tilt angle detection
(2)Image rotation correction

4.1 Image tilt angle detection

Using the Line Segment Detector (LSD) Line Segment detection method to detect whether the image is tilted.LSD is the core of pixels merging in error control.LSD is in linear time that the accuracy of sub-pixel level line segment detection algorithm.LSD in the actual use, the need to set the sampling rate and determine whether the two pixels are merged in the directional difference. Actually detection in the image line is looking for the larger pixel in the image gradient change.For a pair of images i and a rectangular r, denoted k (i, r) for the number of aligned points,n(r) is the total number of pixels within the rectangular r.Then hope to be able to see:

$$N_{test}\cdot \bullet P_{H0}[k(r,I)\rangle = K(r,i)] \qquad (1)$$

Among them, Ntest is the number of rectangles to be considered.PH0 is a probability.I is a random image in the H0 model.In this paper, adopting H0 model,which mainly has the following two properties:
(1){LLA(j)}, J is the pixel, is composed of a set of random variables;
(2)LLA (j) uniform distribution on [0, 2 PI].
So, Determine whether a pixel is not point aligned can be recorded as probability:

$$p = \tau / \pi$$

Thus,then through error control, finally for line segment detection results are shown in figure 5.

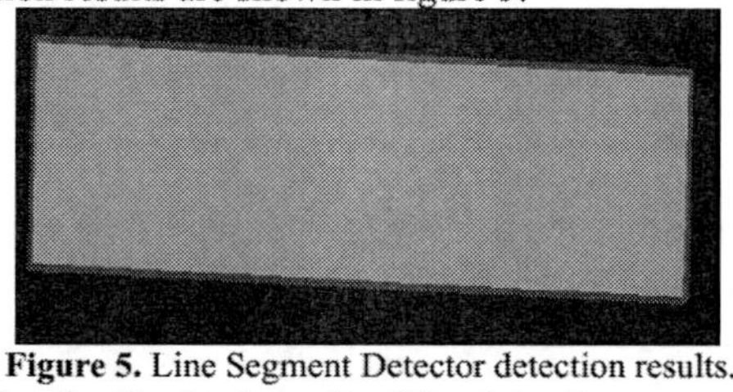

Figure 5. Line Segment Detector detection results.

Red line for the final result of the detection , we can get the coordinates, the starting point of the line segment, the end point coordinates, indirectly calculated the straight line and the horizontal Angle and so on.

4.2 Image rotation correction

For tilting the image, three steps are needed to complete the rotation transformation.
(1)Translation of x'o'y' coordinate system to xoy;
(2)Rotation transformation under xoy coordinate system;
(3)After transformation, the coordinate system is translated back to the original position.
By matrix:

$$(x1 \;\; y1 \;\; 1) = (x0 \;\; y0 \;\; 1)TRT^{-1}$$

R representation of rotation transformation matrix.When the rotation doesn't change the image size, T and T 'are inverse matrix; When the rotating image becomes large, the T and T' are not the inverse matrix, because the image becomes larger, the first and second translation coordinates translation distance is not the same department.Since the algorithm implementation process is the formula we need the inverse transform, so we just write the inverse transform expression,as figure 6:

$$(x0\ \ y0\ \ 1)=(x1\ \ y1\ \ 1)(T_{old}RT_{new}^{-1})^{-1}=(x1\ \ y1\ \ 1)T_{new}R^{-1}T_{old}^{-1}$$

$$=(x1\ \ y1\ \ 1)\begin{pmatrix}1 & 0 & 0\\ 0 & 1 & 0\\ -0.5wn & -0.5hn & 1\end{pmatrix}\begin{pmatrix}\cos a & \sin a & 0\\ -\sin a & \cos a & 0\\ 0 & 0 & 1\end{pmatrix}\begin{pmatrix}1 & 0 & 0\\ 0 & 1 & 0\\ 0.5wo & 0.5ho & 1\end{pmatrix}$$

$$=(x1\ \ y1\ \ 1)\begin{pmatrix}\cos a & \sin a & 0\\ -\sin a & \cos a & 0\\ -0.5wn\cos a+0.5hn\sin a+0.5wo & -0.5wn\sin a-0.5hn\cos a+0.5ho & 1\end{pmatrix}$$

Figure 6. Inverse transform expression.

Thus, the new figure for each point, we can find the corresponding point in the original basis of the inverse transformation formula above, get it gray.If beyond the original scope, set to the background color.Figure 7 gives a collection of the original image, figure 8 is the image after correction.

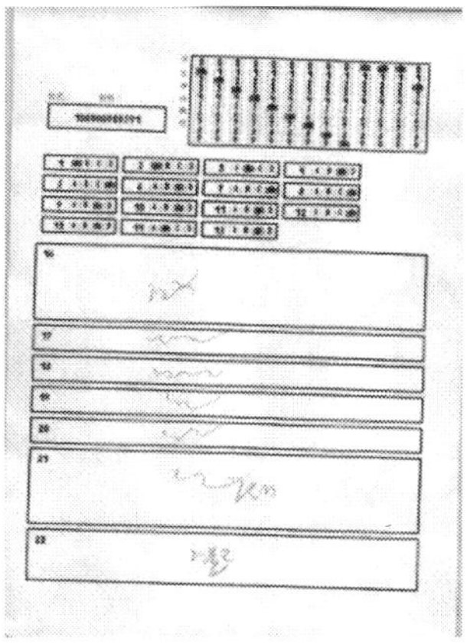

Figure 7. Original image.

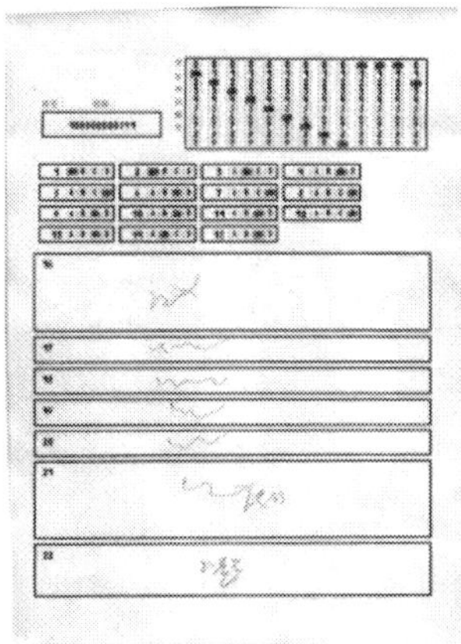

Figure 8. Image after correction

5 Identification Numbers and letters

Digital and letter recognition algorithms are random forests. Random Forest(s), is called Random Trees, it is a combined forecasting model, which is composed of multiple decision trees, which can be used as a fast and effective multi class classification model. Every decision tree of the RF is composed of numerous split and node: the split by entering the test values give direction to output (left or right); Node as the leaf nodes, decided to final output of the single decision tree and probability distribution of the genus for the class in the classification problem or maximum probability category, for the value function in regression problems.The output of the whole RT is determined by the number of common tree, argmax or avg, as figure 9.

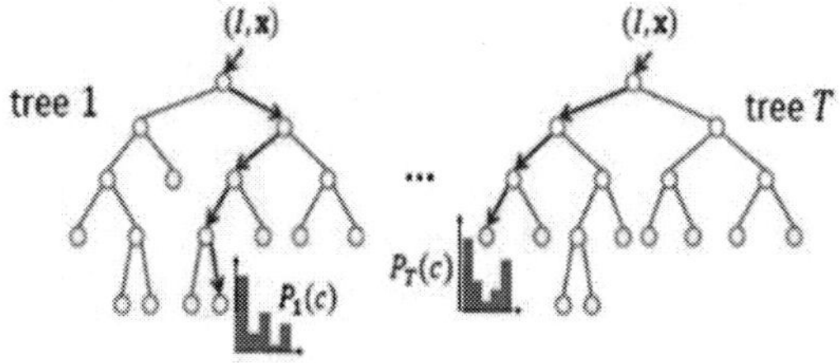

Figure 9. Random Forest(s).

Using random forest algorithm, generating training documents, as shown in figure 10, the results of the training to identify letters and figures, the results are shown in figure 11.

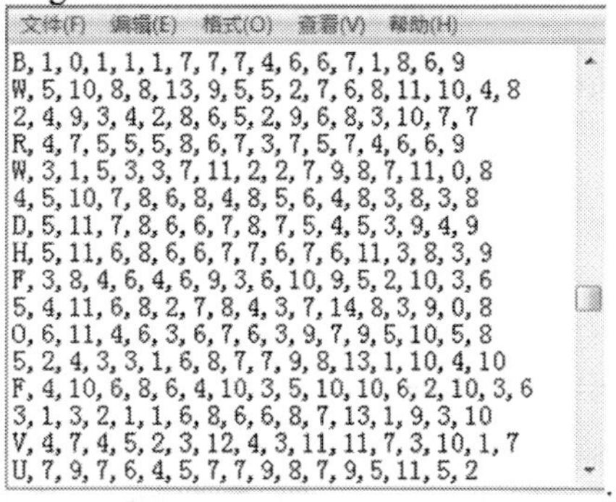

B, 1, 0, 1, 1, 1, 7, 7, 7, 4, 6, 6, 7, 1, 8, 6, 9
W, 5, 10, 8, 8, 13, 9, 5, 5, 2, 7, 6, 8, 11, 10, 4, 8
2, 4, 9, 3, 4, 2, 8, 6, 5, 2, 9, 6, 8, 3, 10, 7, 7
R, 4, 7, 5, 5, 5, 8, 6, 7, 3, 7, 5, 7, 4, 6, 6, 9
W, 3, 1, 5, 3, 3, 7, 11, 2, 2, 7, 9, 8, 7, 11, 0, 8
4, 5, 10, 7, 8, 6, 8, 4, 8, 5, 6, 4, 8, 3, 8, 3, 8
D, 5, 11, 7, 8, 6, 6, 7, 8, 7, 5, 4, 5, 3, 9, 4, 9
H, 5, 11, 6, 8, 6, 6, 7, 7, 6, 7, 6, 11, 3, 8, 3, 9
F, 3, 8, 4, 6, 4, 6, 9, 3, 6, 10, 9, 5, 2, 10, 3, 6
5, 4, 11, 6, 8, 2, 7, 8, 4, 3, 7, 14, 8, 3, 9, 0, 8
O, 6, 11, 4, 6, 3, 6, 7, 6, 3, 9, 7, 9, 5, 10, 5, 8
5, 2, 4, 3, 3, 1, 6, 8, 7, 7, 9, 8, 13, 1, 10, 4, 10
F, 4, 10, 6, 8, 6, 4, 10, 3, 5, 10, 10, 6, 2, 10, 3, 6
3, 1, 3, 2, 1, 1, 6, 8, 6, 6, 8, 7, 13, 1, 9, 3, 10
V, 4, 7, 4, 5, 2, 3, 12, 4, 3, 11, 11, 7, 3, 10, 1, 7
U, 7, 9, 7, 6, 4, 5, 7, 7, 9, 8, 7, 9, 5, 11, 5, 2

Figure 10. Random forest training file.

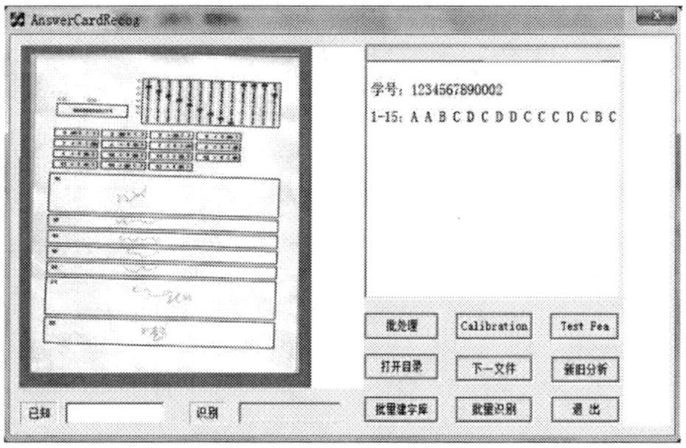

Figure 11. Final identification results.

6 Conclusion

The server is 64 bit Linux system, support as a component integrated into the platform, also support independent release application. Pictures from uploaded successfully start time, adjusted, cutting, recognition to the output paper number, student id as a result, the processing speed is not less than 200 pieces of sheet per minute;After abnormal data processing to complete the confirmation of the beginning of the time, after cutting, identification to the output of the test results, processing speed shall not be less than 60 per minute;Image processing, should not affect the normal use of docking system, the use of 4 core processor 16G memory server, it is recommended that the CPU share of no more than 10%, memory usage is not more than 20%.The other component needs to support multi-threaded processing, processing speed to provide parameters adjustment. Image is divided into normal and abnormal images images, for the picture of the normal scope of cutting accuracy of 100%, image recognition accuracy of 100%;For abnormal image output image type is abnormal. Abnormal image is defined as: scan the answer sheet because the occurrence of wrinkles, deformation, missing picture critical information.

Acknowledgement

This research was financially supported by the science foundation of Liaoning Province (L2014265) and science and technology project of Liaoning Province (2014104017).

References

1. Rafael Grompone von Gioi, Jeremie Jakubowicz, Jean Michel Morel, Gregory Randall. LSD:a Line Segment Detector.
2. J. Shotton, A. Fitzgibbon, M. Cook, T. Sharp, M. Finocchio, R. Moore, A. Kipman, and A. Blake. Real-Time Human Pose Recognition in Parts from a Single Depth Image. In CVPR 2011.
3. L. Breiman. Random forests. Mach. Learning, 45(1):5 - 32, 2001.
4. T. Hastie, R. Tibshirani, J. H. Friedman. The Elements of Statistical Learning. ISBN-13 978-0387952840, 2003, Springer.

MATEC Web of Conferences 44, 01029 (2016)
DOI: 10.1051/matecconf/20164401029

Interactive Safety Analysis Framework of Autonomous Intelligent Vehicles

You Xiang Cui[1,2], Lei Sun[a], Li Hui Sui, Jun Kang, Yong Jiang[2]
[1] *Department of Quality Management Engineering, Businness School, Shanghai Dianji University No.1350 Ganlan Road, Lingang New City, Pudong District, Shanghai 201306, China*

[2] *Shanghai Connected & Automated Vehicles Industrial Promotion Center*

Abstract. More than 100,000 people were killed and around 2.6 million injured in road accidents in the People's Republic of China (PRC), that is four to eight times that of developed countries, equivalent to 6.2 mortality per 10 thousand vehicles—the highest rate in the world. There are more than 1,700 fatalities and 840,000 injuries yearly due to vehicle crashes off public highways. In this paper, we proposed a interactive safety situation and threat analysis framework based on driver behaviour and vehicle dynamics risk analysis based on ISO26262. .

1 Introduction

Safety is one of the key issues of future automobile development. New functionalities not only in areas such as driver assistance, propulsion, in vehicle dynamics control and active and passive safety systems increasingly touch the domain of system safety engineering. Development and integration of these functionalities will strengthen the need for safe system development processes and the need to provide evidence that all reasonable system safety objectives are satisfied.

Automobile safety is the study and practice of design cars, construction, equipment and regulation to minimize the occurrence and consequences of traffic collisions. Road traffic safety more broadly includes roadway design. Improvements in roadway and automobile designs have steadily reduced injury and death rates in all first world countries. Nevertheless, auto collisions are the leading cause of injury-related deaths. In the United States a pedestrian is injured by an automobile every 8 minutes, and are 1.5 times more likely than a vehicle's occupants to be killed in an automobile crash per outing.

The field of intelligent vehicles has become a major research theme in intelligent transportation systems since traffic accidents are serious and growing problems all over the world. The goal of an intelligent vehicle is to augment vehicle autonomous driving either entirely or partly for the purposes of safety, comfortable, and saving energy. Indeed, many technologies of intelligent vehicles root in autonomous mobile robots.

For systems that operate continuously (continuous mode) the allowable frequency of failure must be determined. For systems that operate more than once a year (high demand) the allowable frequency of failure must be determined. For systems that operate intermittently (less than once a year / low demand) the probability of failure is specified as the probability that the system will fail to respond on demand. ISO 26262 is an adaptation of the Functional Safety standard IEC 61508 for Automotive Electric/Electronic Systems. ISO 26262 defines functional safety for automotive equipment applicable throughout the lifecycle of all automotive electronic and electrical safety-related systems

Safety is NHTSA's number one priority. It's mission is to reduce the number of deaths and injuries on nation's roadways by getting drivers, pedestrians and cyclists to change their behaviors once they get behind the wheel or on the streets. NHTSA(National Highway Traffic Safety Administration) Defines 5 Levels of Vehicle Automation in May 2013.

Level 0: No-Automation

The driver is in complete and sole control of the primary vehicle controls (brake, steering, throttle, and motive power) at all times

Level 1:Function-specific Automation

Automation at this level involves one or more specific control functions if multiple functions are automated, they operate independently from each other.

Level 2:Combined Function Automation

This level involves automation of at least two primary control functions designed to work in unison to relieve the driver of control of those functions.

Level 3: Limited Self-Driving Automation

The vehicle is designed to ensure safe operation during the automated driving mode but can determine when the system is no longer able to support automation and then signals to the driver to reengage in the driving task, providing the driver with an appropriate amount of transition time to safely regain manual control.

[a] Lei Sun: Sunlei@sdju.edu.cn

Article available at http://www.matec-conferences.org or http://dx.doi.org/10.1051/matecconf/20164401029

Level 4: Full Self-Driving Automation

The vehicle is designed to perform all safety-critical driving functions and monitor roadway conditions for an entire trip.

2 Passive Safety and Active Safety

The terms "active" and "passive" are simple but important terms in the world of automotive safety. "Active safety" is used to refer to technology assisting in the prevention of a crash and "passive safety" to components of the vehicle (primarily airbags, seatbelts and the physical structure of the vehicle) that help to protect occupants during a crash[8,9]. As Fig. 1 show.

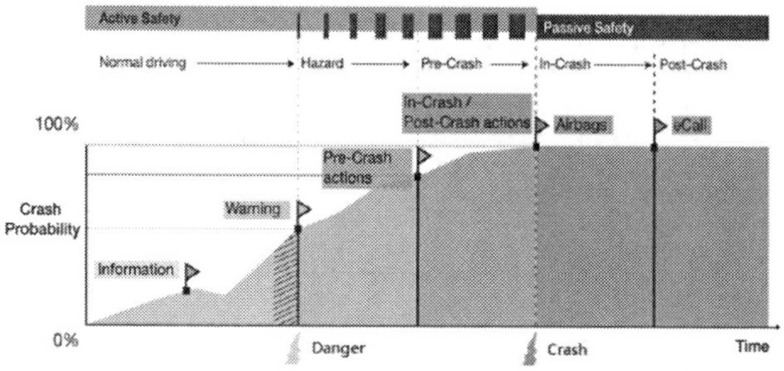

Figure 1. Active safety and Passive safety during a crash

A passive safety system has a passive safety device mounted on a vehicle, and a passive safety control means having an acceleration sensor detecting acceleration caused by an impact at the time of collision. The passive safety control means receives input an impact acceleration detection signal from the acceleration sensor and operates controllably the passive safety device. Further, the passive safety control means computes a physical quantity based on the impact acceleration detection signal inputted from the acceleration sensor, sets maximum and minimum reference values of the physical quantity in normal driving, performs a computation with respect to addition of a present acceleration inputted from the acceleration sensor to an integrated acceleration value at this point in time when the physical quantity crosses a range defined between the maximum and minimum reference values, and performs a computation with respect to a reset process of the integrated acceleration value when the physical quantity remains within the range defined between the maximum and minimum reference values[10]

Active safety system make vehicles and drivers more aware of the situation around them. Addressing the front, sides, rear and even the interior of vehicles, these systems are designed to help drivers avoid crashes and reduce the effects if a crash can't be avoided.

As industry rushes towards the goal of automated vehicles, the driver-control to system-only narrative becomes more and more critical.

3 Safety Analysis Framework of ISO26262

ISO 26262 is a Functional Safety standard, titled "Road vehicles – Functional safety". Functional safety features form an integral part of each automotive.

System safety is achieved through a number of safety measures, which are implemented in a variety oftechnologies (e.g. mechanical, hydraulic, pneumatic, electrical, electronic, programmable electronic) and applied at the various levels of the development process. Although ISO 26262 is concerned with functional safety of E/E systems, it provides a framework within which safety-related systems based on other technologies can be considered. ISO 26262:

a) Provides an automotive safety lifecycle (management, development, production, operation, service,decommissioning) and supports tailoring the necessary activities during these lifecycle phases;

b) provides an automotive-specific risk-based approach to determine integrity levels [Automotive Safety Integrity Levels (ASIL)];

c) uses ASILs to specify applicable requirements of ISO 26262 so as to avoid unreasonable residual risk;

d) provides requirements for validation and confirmation measures to ensure a sufficient and acceptable level of safety being achieved;

e) Provides requirements for relations with suppliers.

Functional safety is influenced by the development process (including such activities as requirements specification, design, implementation, integration, verification, validation and configuration), the production and service processes and by the management processes.

Safety issues are intertwined with common function-oriented and quality-oriented development activities and work products. ISO 26262 addresses the safety-related aspects of development activities and work products.

Figure 2 shows the overall structure of ISO 26262

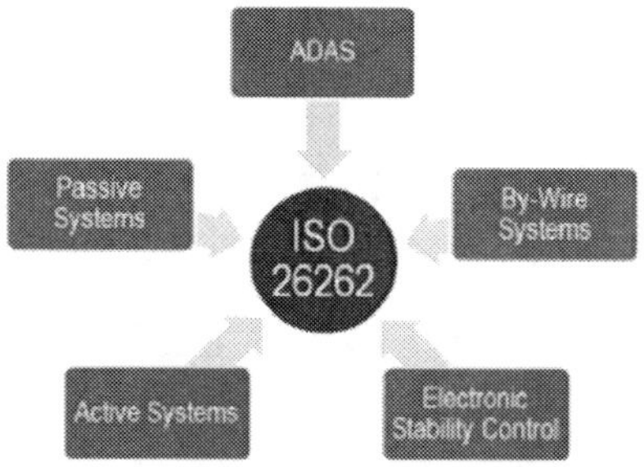

Figure 2. The overall structure of ISO 26262

With the trend of increasing technological complexity, software content and mechatronic implementation, there are increasing risks from systematic failures and random hardware failures. ISO 26262 includes guidance to avoid these risks by providing appropriate requirements and processes. Automated functionalities are very complex and can take quite some time to reach, as Figure 3 shows.

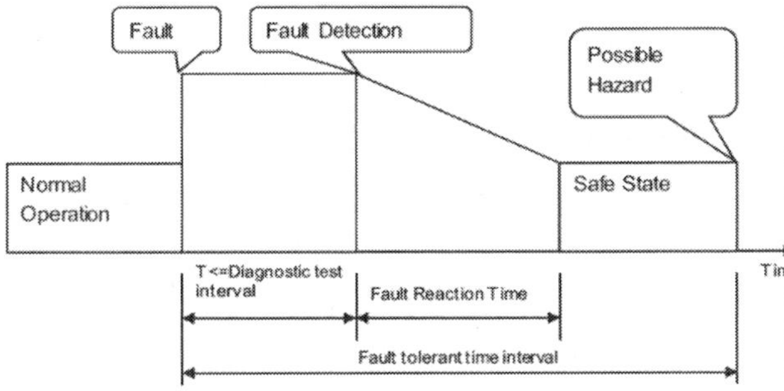

Figure 3. Fault reaction time and fault tolerant time interval

The ISO 26262 safety framework (see Figure 4) encompasses the principal safety activities during the concept phase, product development, production, operation, service and decommissioning. Planning, coordinating and documenting the safety activities of all phases of the safety lifecycle are key management tasks.

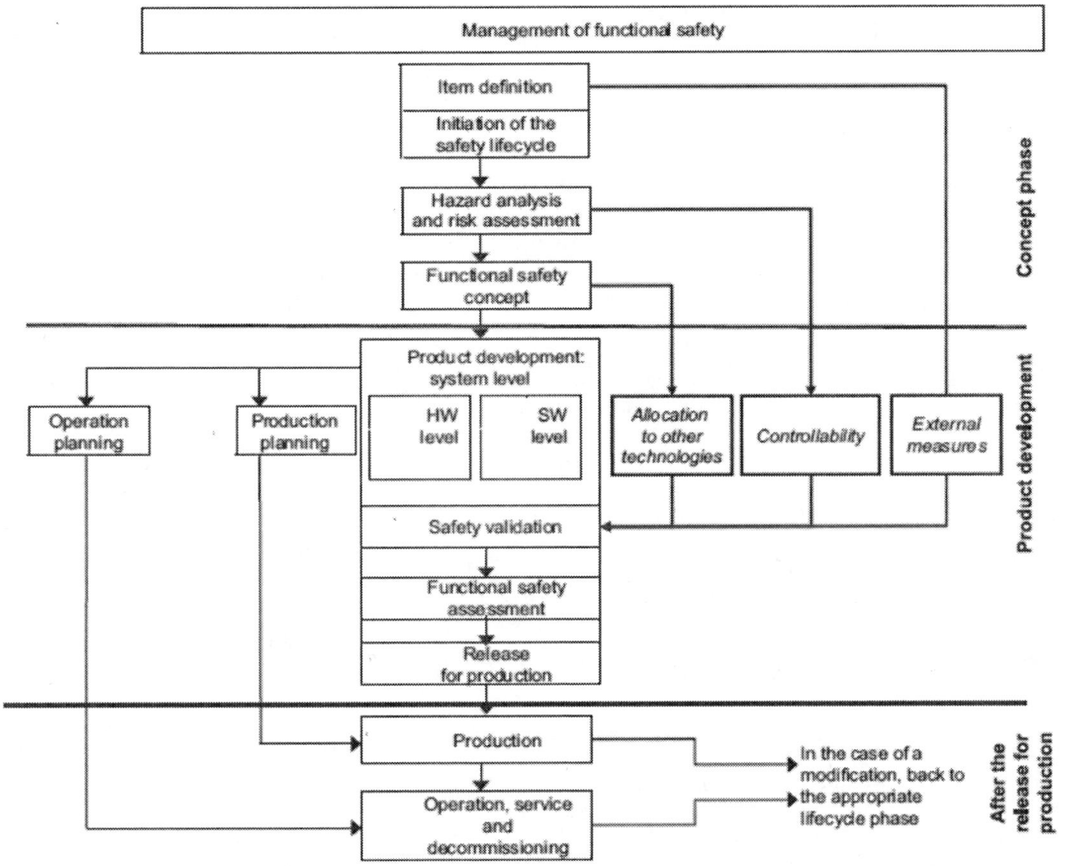

Figure 4 Safety framework of ISO 26262

The following descriptions explain the definitions of the safety framework.

a) The subphase: item definition

The initiating task of the safety lifecycle is to develop a description of the item with regard to its functionality, interfaces, environmental conditions, legal requirements, known hazards, etc. The boundary of the item and its interfaces, as well as assumptions concerning other items, elements, systems and components are determined.

b) The subphase: initiation of the safety lifecycle

Based on the item definition, the safety lifecycle is initiated by distinguishing between either a new development, or a modification of an existing item.

c) The subphase: hazard analysis and risk assessment

After the initiation of the safety lifecycle, the hazard analysis and risk assessment is performed as given in ISO 26262-3:2011. First, the hazard analysis and risk assessment estimates the probability of exposure, the controllability and the severity of the hazardous events with regard to the item. Together, these parameters determine the ASILs of the hazardous events. Subsequently, the hazard analysis and risk assessment determines the safety goals for the item, with the safety goals being the top level safety requirements for the item. The ASILs determined for the hazardous events are assigned to the corresponding safety goals.

During the subsequent phases and subphases, detailed safety requirements are derived from the safety goals. These safety requirements inherit the ASIL of the corresponding safety goals.

d) The subphase: functional safety concept

Based on the safety goals, a functional safety concept is specified considering preliminary architectural assumptions. The functional safety concept is specified by functional safety requirements that are allocated to the elements of the item. The functional safety concept can

also include other technologies or interfaces with external measures, provided that the expected behaviours thereof can be validated. The implementation of other technologies is outside the scope of ISO 26262 and the implementation of the external measures is outside the scope of the item development.

e) The phase: product development at the system level

After having specified the functional safety concept, the item is developed from the system level perspective, as given in ISO 26262-4. The system development process is based on the concept of a V-model with the specification of the technical safety requirements, the system architecture, the system design and implementation on the left hand branch and the integration, verification, validation and the functional safety assessment on the right hand branch.

The hardware-software interface is specified in this phase.

The product development at the system level incorporates validation tasks for activities occurring within other safety lifecycle phases, including the validation of the aspects of the functional safety concept that are implemented by other technologies.

4 Conclusions and prospects

To maximize the potential and achieve an optimal ITS ecosystem that supports safety, mobility, increased transportation efficiency, and environmental applications, we must have a clear and implementable ITS privacy and security strategy and framework which harnesses both connected and autonomous technologies.

The Interactive Safety Analysis Framework must include technical and policy solutions, namely a fully secured connected vehicle network and adequate consumer privacy protections that evoke trust from drivers and passengers traveling on roads and highways as fellows:

- Required Technologies to be realized in 2014-2020
- Detect exact location of a vehicle (sub cm)
- Detect surrounding obstacles and their next move (sec)
- Stop or determine collision avoidance routing
- Additional Key Factors
- Research of Human Factors

i.e. Evaluate override requirements such that the driver can always or when appropriate over ride the automated systems and regain control Computational algorism to perceive, understand and judge vehicle and environmental status in place of a human brain

- Need test of Level 3 vehicles in real life situation to identify answers to many of technical and human factors questions.
- Analyze sensor data from various operating scenarios (traffic dynamics), driver capabilities, environmental variations (rain, snow, etc.), and roadway types/configurations.
- Apply Big Data Analysis on Cloud
- Cyber-security and Privacy issues need to be addressed

Acknowledgment

This research was financially supported by think tank construction project of equipment manufacturing industry development research center: intelligent manufacturing (15AR01) and the Leading Academic Discipline Project of (10XKJ01) in Shanghai Dianji University.

References

1. Gereon Meyer Sven Beiker. Road Vehicle Automation, April 2015 Springer.
2. http://www.nhtsa.gov/Driving+Safety
3. Ogiela M R, Hachaj T. Advances in Computer Vision and Pattern Recognition[M]// Advances in computer vision and pattern recognition. Springer, 2015:1-70.
4. Manawadu U, Ishikawa M, Kamezaki M, et al. Analysis of Individual Driving Experience in Autonomous and Human-Driven Vehicles using a Driving Simulator[C]// Advanced Intelligent Mechatronics (AIM), 2015 IEEE International Conference on. IEEE, 2015.
5. Mladenovic M N, Abbas M M. Self-organizing Control Framework for Driverless Vehicles[C]// Intelligent Transportation Systems - (ITSC), 2013 16th International IEEE Conference on. IEEE, 2013:2076-2081.
6. Cheng, Autonomous Intelligent Vehicles (Advances in Computer Vision and Pattern Recognition)[M]//DOI 10.1007/978-1-4471-2280-7 Springer, 2011
7. http://auto.huanqiu.com/news/2014-10/5161704.html
8. Yazzie T J, Zhang G, Tarefder R, et al. Autonomous Vehicle System-Driven Innovative Traffic Control and Management Strategy Review[C]// Transportation Research Board 94th Annual Meeting. 2015.
9. "American Honda safety page". Corporate.honda.com. 2006-03-02. Retrieved 2011-09-20.
10. Jump up Gladwell, Malcolm (2004-01-12). "BIG AND BAD: How the S.U.V. ran over automotive safety." (PDF). The New Yorker. Retrieved 2009-07-24.
11. Yamashita T. Passive safety system: US, US6636794 B2[P]. 2003.

MATEC Web of Conferences 44, 01030 (2016)
DOI: 10.1051/matecconf/20164401030

Control System Design of a DSP-based Real-time Leveling Platform

Jin Ming Zhang[1,a], He Zhang[2]

[1] School of Mechanical Engineering, Nanjing University of Science and Technology, Nanjing210094, China

Abstract. Since platform working in the sea is badly influenced by the wave, leveling control system is researched to control the leveling platform, so as to prevent the device which is fixed on the platform from being affected. TMS320F2812 chip is set as the control core, and serial communication module, gyroscope etc. are adopted to design real-time leveling control system. Gyroscopes are used to measure the angular speed of the carrier and the angle of the platform, filtering processing is done to the data collected by the gyroscopes and PID algorithm is adopted to calculate the real-time speed of motor ,in order to control the leveling platform. Tests are conducted to prove that the system can well control the leveling platform, in which the shake range of the platform is (-12 °, +12 °), while the shake range of carrier is only about (-0.5 °, +0.5 °).

1 Introduction

Leveling platform can effectively isolate the carrier movement, and ensures that the device fixed on the platform can work well without being affected by disturbs. Both in the military field and civilian field, is the real-time leveling platform popular[1]. The platform researched in my paper freely floats on the sea, and it will generate posture deflection under the continuous interference caused by the wave and currents. To provide that the device on the platform can work preciously, we need to insulate the environment disturbs. This paper designs a control program to control the leveling by using DSP, so that we can control the electrical machine to keep the platform stable[2].

2 System Function and Project Design

2.1 System functional analysis

The control system of the leveling mechanism contains several functions, such as driving electrical machine, displaying angle status, communicating with sensors and PC, and storing data[3]. According to the system function that we need to realize, we break down the hardware circuit into several different parts and design the parts one by one. The different parts are shown as following: DSP minimum system, motion control module, status display module, communication module, SD card read/write module[4].

2.2 System solutions

2.2.1 Motion control module

The main job of motion control module is to send signal from TMS320F2812 chip to the servo controller, so as to drive the motor , control the steering , speed, position . And we can control the rolling and pitching motion of platform to reach the dynamic balance of platform and guarantee the stability. There are two event managers (EVA and EVB) in the TMS320F2812. Each event manager is made up of 2 general timer, 3 whole comparing unit , 3 capture unit and 1 orthogonal coded pulse circuit, which can generate four independent PWM waveform and 6pairs of complementary PWM waveform[5]. It is particularly suitable for motor control field. The control of position and speed of motor is realized by using pulse control mode, directly through the DSP to produce PWM wave to control the actuator. The DSP chip communicates with the servo motor actuator through 1 pulse transmit pin, 2 direction pins and 2 receiving feedback pulse pins, thus accomplishes the position and speed of motor control.

2.2.2 Status display module

Status display module is used to remind us of the error which appears in the working process, and it can display angles of deflection Angle and angles of the motor turns. To design the Status display module, we select a relatively common device named HS12864-12, which is one kind of HS12864-15 series produced by HanSheng limited company. The status display module is composed of liquid crystal display, control chip ST7920 and drive chip ST7921. There is word stock inside the device and it can programme, display characters and letters. This module uses standard data and provide control interface and the controller instructions for other devices. When we use it, we only need to write the required controller

[a] Jinming Zhang: 819068820@qq.com

data into the module's built-in buffer so as to realize its basic function.

2.2.3 Communication module

There are two serial communication interface (SCIA and SCIB) inside TMS320F2812 chip that uses receiving, sending two-wire system[6]. Each SCI has a receiver and transmitter, and each receiver and transmitter which are double buffer are equipped with a 16 FIFO queue so that the SCI can complete half-duplex and full-duplex communication mode. SCI continuous monitors and checks the data received to ensure integrity of the data by checking timeout error and frames error. This paper uses MAX232 to design the RS232 serial communication interface made up of two serial communication interface designed SCIA and SCIB, so that we can realize the communication between DSP and sensors, PC.

2.2.4 SD card read/write module

The internal storage space of TMS320F2812 is small, but our sensors will produce a large amount of data when the platform are leveling, including angle, speed and leveling status data. We need these data to analysis the effects of the algorithm, so we need to store the data in the process of research. Here, we choose widely used memory SD card which is a storage device based on semiconductor flash memory device and popular for its small size and large storage.

3 Principle diagram of system and circuit design

3.1 Principle diagram of system

Real-time leveling platform sets DSP chip TMS320F2812 as the core, and connects with angle sensor and speed angle through RS232 serial port. After receiving data from the sensors, we will filter the data and get the angle of leveling platform and swing angular velocity. After the data calculated by the DSP chip, we can get motor control signals, including motor rotation angle, direction and speed. The DSP chip will send two lines of the pulse signals which is boosted by the step-down circuit into the two motor drivers respectively, to drive the motor. And the motor driver will send back the real-time state of motor to TMS320F2812 via step-down circuit. Then, the system gives the following instructions based on the feedback data. PC can be connected to the control system via the JTAG emulator, so as to debug program, download program and observe some data. It can also be connected to the motor driver through RS232 to set the start state of driver and monitoring motor state real-timely.SD card storage module can store sensors measured data, so as to facilitate our debugging for data analysis, and status display module can display the system state of leveling. The figure 1 is the principle diagram.

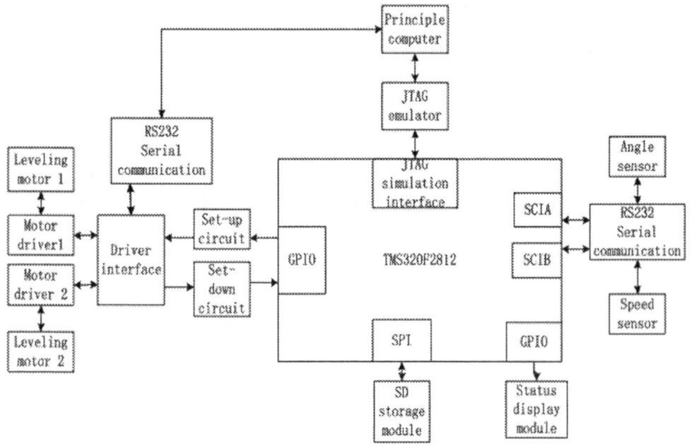

Figure 1. Real-time leveling control system composition diagram

3.2 Circuit design

3.2.1 Step-up and Step-down Circuit

Since the pin voltage of TMS320F2812 is + 3.3 V, the pin voltage of actuator is + 5 V, so we need to design a voltage conversion interface circuit between the two, including step-up circuit while sending signals and step-down circuit while receiving feedback signals.

The step-up circuit consists of NPN silicon triode, and the base current changes will affect the collector current . Even the base current changes very small, it will lead the collector current change a lot which fit a certain proportion relations. Based on the triode amplifier principle, the circuit can raise the 3.3V signal to 5.0V to drive the motor actuator. The circuit is shown in figure 2.2: PWM1 and PWM2 are the direction signals of rolling motor, and T1PWM is used to control the motor position and speed ;similarly, PWM7and PWM8 are the direction signals of pitching motor, and T3PWM is used to control motor position and speed.

Each motor sends back two-way feedback signal, and the signal was received into the DSP chip to calculate after its voltage was reduced by step-down circuit, to get the motor speed and position. Here , we designs the step-down circuit for simplification and convenience by adopting resistive subdivision method. Resistive subdivision is often used in weak current that needs to reduce voltage. When determining the divider resistance , we need to follow the wanted current to make sure that the power of the divider resistance fits the maximum power of the circuit to prevent the resistance from burned. As shown in figure 2.3, the circuit reduce the 5V rotating transformer feedback signal to 3.3V.

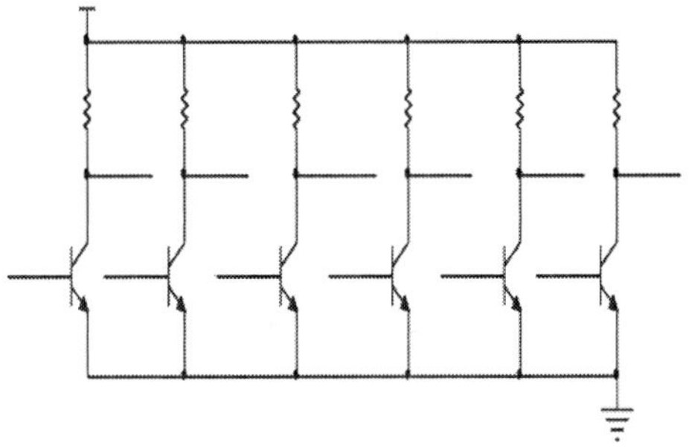

Figure 2. Step-up circuit

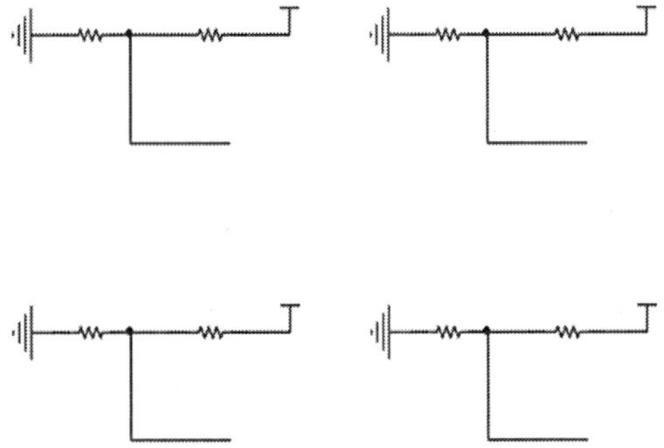

Figure 3. Step-down circuit

3.2.2 Status display circuit

Display used in this system adopts the 2-wire serial connection mode, for the aim of reminding us of the operation error and displaying the deflection angle detected by angle sensor and the deflection angle of motor. The connection between display module circuit and DSP chip is shown in figure 2.4. DSP sends data through the SID (serial data input port) to HS12864-12. When serial synchronous clock SCLK is rising , the display module will read the data from SID port. For the mode chosen in the paper is serial mode ,PSB pin should be connected to high level. And VL pin can connect a slide rheostat to adjust the contrast of the screen, which is shown in figure 4. Because this article choose the serial mode, so the PSB directly lead to high level, pick up the VL pin a slide rheostat to adjust the contrast of the screen.

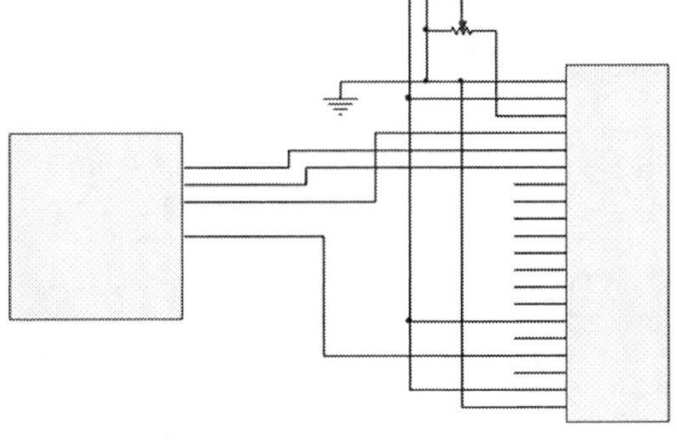

Figure 4. Status display circuit

4 Software design of control system

4.1 The whole block software diagram design of real-time leveling control system

Control system program is written by C language, and uses the idea of modularization while programming. The control program mainly includes the main monitoring program, system initialization program, motion control program, data processing program, status display program, SD card storage program and communication program.

Among them, the motion control program can be divided into motor drive module, leveling algorithm and position feedback module. The concrete block diagram is shown in figure 5.

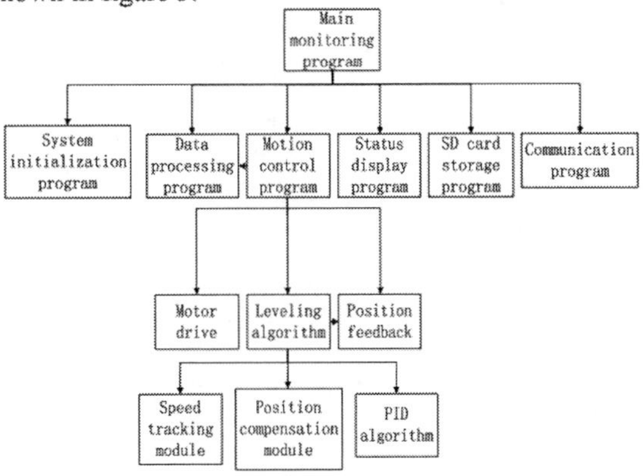

Figure 5. Main body of control system

4.2 The program design of motion control

Motion control program is mainly used for driving motor, receiving and dealing with feedback data and finishing the leveling algorithm. The motor driver module and position feedback module form the motor position servo control.

4.2.1 Motor driver module program

DSP2812 event manager module is a typical extension function module, especially suitable for motion control and motor control field[7]. Event manager module mainly includes the general timer, comparison PWM unit circuit, the capture unit and orthogonal coded pulse (QEP) circuit. When the motor drive is controlled by PWM pulse, the only thing we need to do is to configurate the event manager EVA and EVB. Each general contains four counting modes, including timer continuous incremental, continuous increment / decrement, directional increment / decrement and stop / keep. This article selects the continuous increment / decrement count mode to produce square wave pulse signal, and configurates duty ratio to create the PWM wave that we need. Figure 6 is the program flow char to produce PWM pulse.

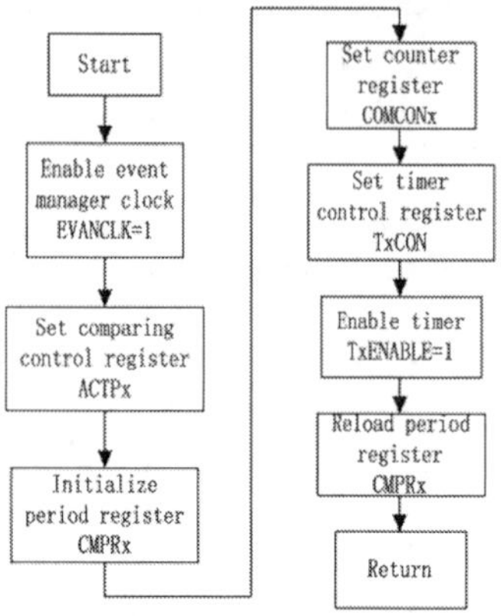

Figure 6. Flow chart of PWM pulse generating set

4.2.2 Position feedback module program

Feedback data is received into the control system through the orthogonal coded pulse circuit of the event manager. Two feedback signals of each motor are respectively received into the QEP circuit through the two pins of the event manage[8]. After resolving by the decoder of the circuit, we can get the number of motor feedback pulse by using which we can calculate and get the current position, speed of the motor. When QEP circuit is working, the timer works in directional increase/decrease count mode, and the setup program flow chart (figure7) is shown as follows.

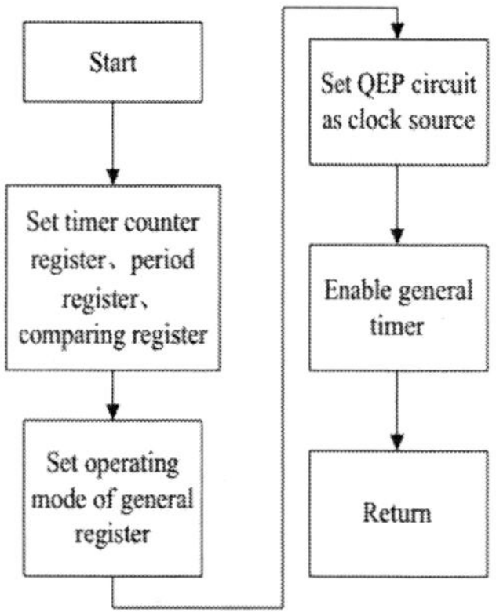

Figure 7. Flow chart of enabling QEP

4.2.3 Leveling module program

Leveling process mainly includes the speed tracking and position compensation module, and PID algorithm module. In which , the speed tracking program can drive the motor running at the same speed with the swaying platform while in the opposite direction, so as to realize the coarse leveling motion. And the position compensation program can improve the leveling accuracy and reduce the dynamic error[9]. PID algorithm ensures that the motor can respond real-timely and change the motion situation quickly according to the swaying speed of the system.

1) In the speed tracking program, we can calculate the speed PID value after filtering processing the sampling speed, and then we can get the motor speed according to the transfer relationship. According to the motor speed required, we calculate to get the setting value of the event manager cycle register, and then update the cycle register values to control signals of the motor speed. Among them, the motor speed and cycle register values satisfy the following relations:

$$V = \frac{SYSCLKOUT}{CMPRx \cdot NPR \cdot 4}$$

In the relationship, V is the motor speed, NPR is the pulse number required while the motor rotates for a round, $CMPRx$ is the setting value of cycle register, and $SYSCLKOUT$ is the system clock frequency.

The principle of position compensation program is similar as speed tacking program, which converts angle error to the speed of motor. The two program flow is shown in figure 8.

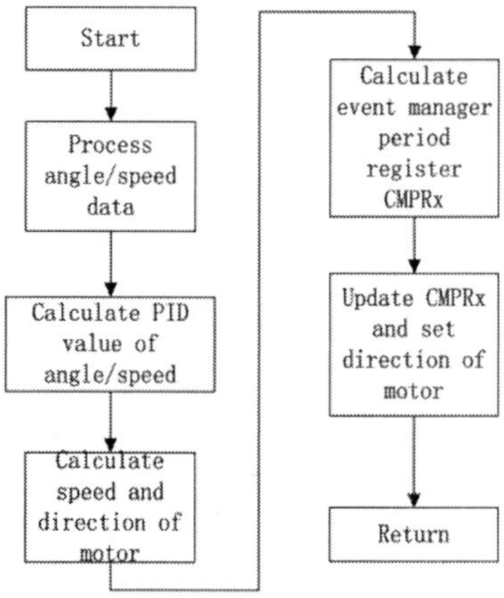

Figure 8. Flow charts of speed tracking module and position compensation module

2) PID algorithm is the core of the whole motor driver. It realizes the ability that the motor can change the speed according to the tested real-time data. After filtering processing, the data measured by sensor is calculated by PID algorithm. The percentage deviation is calculated first, and if the ratio deviation is greater than the set value, we conduct the integral and differential calculation.

5 Test results

When doing the stable tracking test to test the two degree of freedom control performance of the platform, we need to make the platform fixed on the swing platform rotate around its ' shaft for a degree to simulate rocking movement caused by incident wave of any angle, because our swing device can only provide a degree of freedom. Figure 9 and 10 are the figures of the angle tracking of platform. Figure 9 represents the angle tracking of roll axis while figure 10 represents the angle tracking of pitch axis. Figure 11 and 12 stand for the figures of angle tracking of the device fixed on the platform. Figure11

represents the angle tracking of roll axis while figure 12 represents the angle tracking of pitch axis.

From the figures, we can find that the shake range of the platform is (-12 °, +12 °), while the shake range of device is only about (-0.5 °, +0.5 °). The leveling platform can well isolate the shock of the wave.

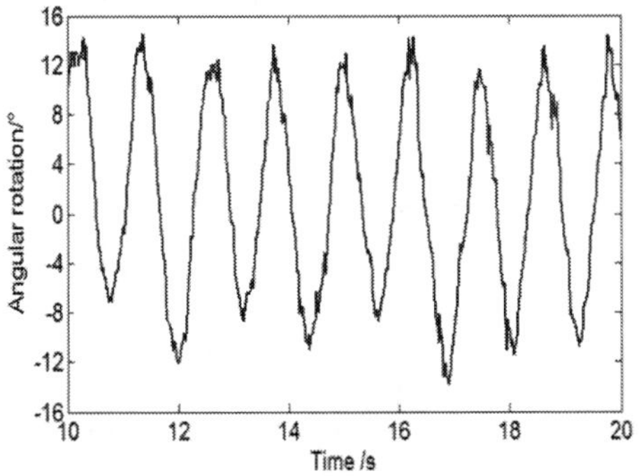

Figure 9. Angle tracking of roll axis of the platform

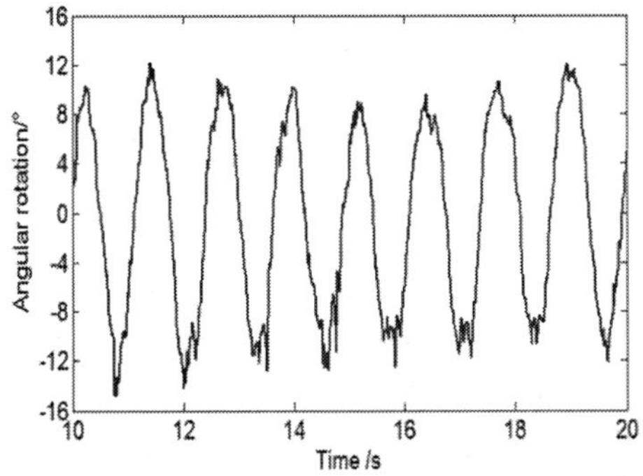

Figure 10. Angle tracking of pitch axis of the platform

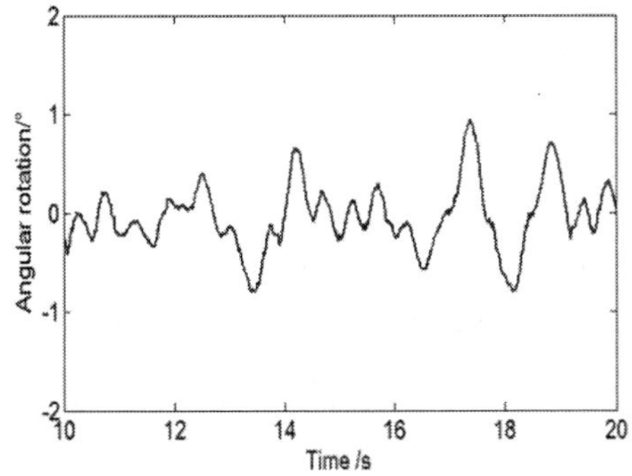

Figure 11. Angle tracking of the roll axis of the device

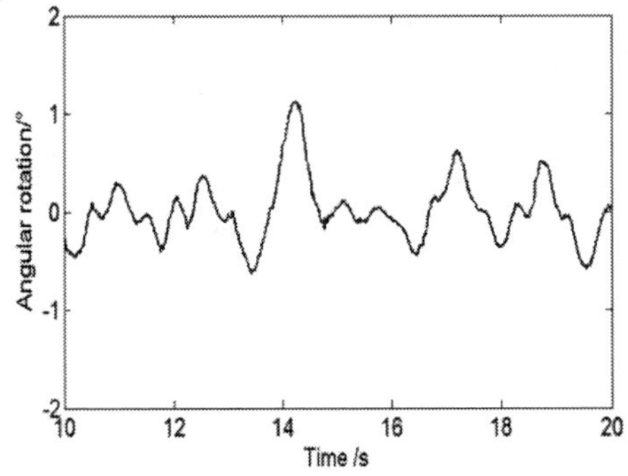

Figure12. Angle tracking of the pitch axis of the device

6 Conclusion

The control system of a leveling system is designed in this paper to realize the self-leveling of the platform. Both the design of hardware circuit and the software programming are conducted in the event that the TMS320F2812 chip is set as the core, and the test of leveling ability is done finally. The test proves that the control system can well control the leveling platform to perform self-leveling, and insure that the device fixed on the platform can work steadily. The research result provides a general solution for the real-time leveling platform whose swing period is irregular or swing angle is irregular.

References

1. Y. Shang. Technology Foundation of National Defense, **1**, 40-43(2009)
2. X. Guo. *Stabilized platform test system research* (NJUST, Nanjing,2010)
3. F. Xiao. *Key technology of stabilized platform*(NJUST, Nanjing: , 2013)
4. X. Pang . *A study on key technology of digital control of airborne electro-optical stabilization platform system*(NUDT,Changsha,2007)
5. W. Gu . *Teach you how to use DSP——based on TMS320F2812* (BUAA press, Beijing, 2011)
6. F. Pan . Modern electrical technology, **35**, 69-71(2012)
7. S. Yu . *The research on servo control system for AC PMSM based on DSP* (NUAA, Nanjing, 2012)
8. L.Chen, J. Li , M. Zhu . Electrical Design Engineering , **18**, 103-105 (2010)
9. M. Zhu, J. Li, D. Luan, Z. Mo. Electrical Design Engineering, **19**, 74-76(2011)

MATEC Web of Conferences 44, 01031 (2016)
DOI: 10.1051/matecconf/20164401031

Sliding mode control of photoelectric tracking platform based on the inverse system method

Zong Chen Yao[1,a], He Zhang[1,b]

[1]School of Mechanical Engineering, Nanjing University of Science and Technology, Nanjing 210094, China

Abstract. In order to improve the photoelectric tracking platform tracking performance, an integral sliding mode control strategy based on inverse system decoupling method is proposed. The electromechanical dynamic model is established based on multi-body system theory and Newton-Euler method. The coupled multi-input multi-output (MIMO) nonlinear system is transformed into two pseudo-linear single-input single-output (SISO) subsystems based on the inverse system method. An integral sliding mode control scheme is designed for the decoupled pseudo-linear system. In order to eliminate system chattering phenomenon caused by traditional sign function in sliding-mode controller, the sign function is replaced by the Sigmoid function. Simulation results show that the proposed decoupling method and the control strategy can restrain the influences of internal coupling and disturbance effectively, and has better robustness and higher tracking accuracy.

1 Introduction

Photoelectric tracking platform is a two-axis gimbal system equipped with photoelectric detection equipment, can capturing and real-time tracking of moving target in the air or on the ground, has been widely used in military and civil areas.

During tracking, small angle errors can cause big deviation of target position. However, Due to the presence of strong coupling and nonlinear factors in the platform, the tracking performance and accuracy will be affected. Obviously, the problem of coupling and nonlinear need to be resolved urgently and the key lies in the decoupling method. As a nonlinear coupling system, previous literature[1] did not pay enough attention to the coupling factors of the system, it usually treated as disturbances and use the disturbance observer to compensate.

In recent years, various types of decoupling method have been proposed. One is the Intelligent decoupling method which does not depend on the precise mathematical model, such as neural network decoupling[2], sliding mode decoupling[3] and fuzzy decoupling[4] etc. When a system is unable to modeling, theoretically, is more suitable for the use of intelligent decoupling method. However, all the intelligent decoupling method requires a lot of computer resources on practical application, for example, neural network decoupling requires a large amount of measurement data and repeated experiments to optimize the parameters. Another kind of decoupling method is linearization and decoupling (L&D) method, including inverse system method and differential geometry method. Compared with the differential geometry method, the inverse system method does not need complex nonlinear coordinate transformation, also does not need to transform the nonlinear control problems into the "geometric domain"[5]. Based on these advantages, the inverse system method is more available in practical application.

The tracking accuracy and robust performances can adversely affected by the exist of uncertainties and model errors[6] as well. Therefore, the introduction of a control strategy is required to overcome the shortcomings. Sliding mode control with advantages of whole robustness on external disturbance and uncertainty which satisfy the matching conditions, has been widely used in air vehicle, robot control field and many other complex system control with disturbance and uncertainty[7,8]. The introduction of integral can decrease the steady-state error caused by traditional sliding mode, and improve the transient performance of the system[9].

In this paper, a sliding mode control strategy based on inverse system decoupling method for the photoelectric tracking platform with nonlinear coupling, parameter uncertainties and unknown disturbances is proposed. Kinematic relations of the photoelectric tracking platform is analyzed first, and the electromechanical system model of the photoelectric tracking platform is established by using the traditional Newton – Euler method. Based on the inverse system method, the coupling and nonlinearity in system dynamic are resolved, such that the dynamics of two gimbals can be regulated independently. Based on the decoupled pseudo linear system, the integral sliding mode control is applied to reject the influence of uncertainties and disturbances. Moreover, the symbolic function is replaced by the proposed Sigmoid function to

[a] yaozongchen@gmail.com [b] hezhangz@njust.edu.cn

Article available at http://www.matec-conferences.org or http://dx.doi.org/10.1051/matecconf/20164401031

restrained the chattering phenomenon of sliding-mode controller. At last, the stability of the proposed control strategy is verified by the Lyapunov criterion. Simulation results demonstrate the effectiveness and reliability of the proposed control strategy.

2 Modeling of the photoelectric tracking platform

2.1 Kinematic relations

The structure of the photoelectric tracking platform is a two-axis gimbal system. Figure 1 shows the coordinate systems of the photoelectric tracking platform. Three coordinate frames have been introduced as:

1) The base coordinate system $\{C_1\}$ is fixed on the base or ground.
2) The azimuth gimbal coordinate system $\{C_2\}$ can rotate around the axis of OZ_2 (OZ_1) and the relative azimuth angle is defined as ξ.
3) The elevation gimbal coordinate system $\{C_3\}$ can rotate around the axis of OY_3 (OY_2) and the relative elevation angle is defined as η.

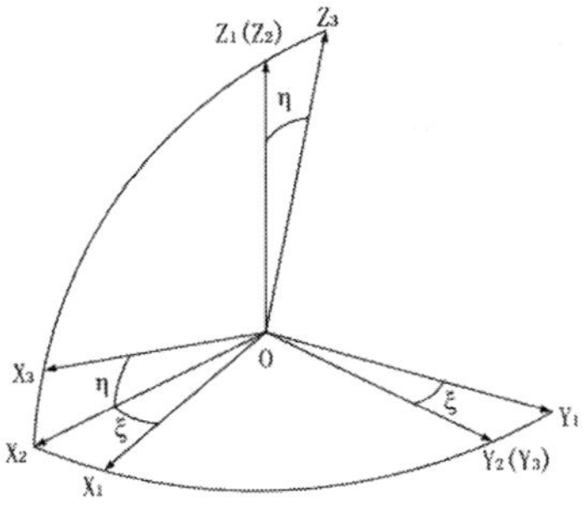

Figure 1. Coordinate systems of the photoelectric tracking platform

By using Euler matrix, transformation matrix from $\{C_3\}$ to $\{C_2\}$ become

$$\mathbf{C}_{ea} = \begin{bmatrix} \cos\eta & 0 & \sin\eta \\ 0 & 1 & 0 \\ -\sin\eta & 0 & \cos\eta \end{bmatrix} \tag{1}$$

The relative angular rate of azimuth gimbal and elevation gimbal can be described as:

$$\boldsymbol{\omega}_{aa} = [0 \quad 0 \quad \dot{\xi}]^T \tag{2}$$

$$\boldsymbol{\omega}_{ee} = [0 \quad \dot{\eta} \quad 0]^T \tag{3}$$

By using transformation matrix $\mathbf{C}_{ea}$, absolute angular rate of azimuth gimbal and elevation gimbal becomes:

$$\boldsymbol{\omega}_a = \begin{bmatrix} \omega_{ax} \\ \omega_{ay} \\ \omega_{az} \end{bmatrix} = \boldsymbol{\omega}_{aa} = \begin{bmatrix} 0 \\ 0 \\ \dot{\xi} \end{bmatrix} \tag{4}$$

$$\boldsymbol{\omega}_e = \begin{bmatrix} \omega_{ex} \\ \omega_{ey} \\ \omega_{ez} \end{bmatrix} = \mathbf{C}_{ea}\boldsymbol{\omega}_a + \boldsymbol{\omega}_{ee} = \begin{bmatrix} -\dot{\xi}\sin\eta \\ \dot{\eta} \\ -\dot{\xi}\cos\eta \end{bmatrix} \tag{5}$$

Where subscript e stands for the elevation gimbal and subscript a stands for the azimuth gimbal; subscripts x, y and z stand for the components in direction of axis x, axis y and axis z of the variables respectively.

2.2 Dynamical model

Assuming that each gimbal can be regarded as a rigid body, based on the traditional Newton-Euler equations[10] , the dynamic model of photoelectric tracking platform can obtained:

$$\mathbf{M} = \mathbf{J}\dot{\boldsymbol{\omega}} + \boldsymbol{\omega} \times (\mathbf{J}\boldsymbol{\omega}) \tag{6}$$

Where $\mathbf{M}$ stands for the external torque applied to each gimbal; $\mathbf{J}$ stands for the inertia moments; $\boldsymbol{\omega}$ stands for absolute angular rate ; $\dot{\boldsymbol{\omega}}$ stands for absolute angular acceleration.

The equation also can be written as:

$$\mathbf{M} = \begin{bmatrix} M_x \\ M_y \\ M_z \end{bmatrix} = \begin{bmatrix} J_x\dot{\omega}_x \\ J_y\dot{\omega}_y \\ J_z\dot{\omega}_z \end{bmatrix} + \begin{bmatrix} (J_z - J_y)\omega_y\omega_z \\ (J_x - J_z)\omega_x\omega_z \\ (J_y - J_x)\omega_y\omega_x \end{bmatrix} \tag{7}$$

Because each gimbal respect to their coordinate axes is axisymmetric, so the product of inertia in inertia moments matrix of each gimbal is zero[11], then the inertia moments $\mathbf{J}$ becomes:

$$\mathbf{J} = diag[J_x \quad J_y \quad J_z] \tag{8}$$

The inertia moments respect to the rotation axis of elevation gimbal and azimuth gimbal are given by

$$J_{Oey} = J_{ey} \tag{9}$$

$$J_{Oaz} = J_{az} + J_{ex}\sin^2\eta + J_{ez}\cos^2\eta \tag{10}$$

2.2.1 *Elevation gimbal*

The external torque of elevation gimbal can be expressed as

$$\mathbf{M}_e = \begin{bmatrix} M_{ex} \\ M_{ey} \\ M_{ez} \end{bmatrix} = \begin{bmatrix} M_{ex} \\ T_e - M_{de} \\ M_{ez} \end{bmatrix} \tag{11}$$

Where M_e stands for coupling torque between the azimuth gimbal and the elevation gimbal in directions of each axis; T_e is the motor torque of the elevation gimbal; M_{de} represent uncertainties and disturbance including friction torque, unmodeled dynamics, wire torque etc.

By combination of (7) and (11), the dynamic model of the elevation gimbal can obtained

$$\begin{bmatrix} M_{ex} \\ T_e - M_{de} \\ M_{ez} \end{bmatrix} = \begin{bmatrix} J_{ex}\dot{\omega}_{ex} \\ J_{ey}\dot{\omega}_{ey} \\ J_{ez}\dot{\omega}_{ez} \end{bmatrix} + \begin{bmatrix} (J_{ez} - J_{ey})\omega_{ey}\omega_{ez} \\ (J_{ex} - J_{ez})\omega_{ex}\omega_{ez} \\ (J_{ey} - J_{ex})\omega_{ey}\omega_{ex} \end{bmatrix} \tag{12}$$

The elevation gimbal only has rotational freedom in direction of axis y, therefore, take its component of axis y, and the dynamic model of elevation gimbal become

$$T_e - M_{de} = J_{ey}\dot{\omega}_{ey} + (J_{ex} - J_{ez})\omega_{ex}\omega_{ez} \tag{13}$$

2.2.2 *Azimuth gimbal*

Due to the reaction moment from the elevation gimbal, the dynamic model of the azimuth gimbal become

$$\mathbf{M}_a = \mathbf{J}_a\dot{\boldsymbol{\omega}}_a + \boldsymbol{\omega}_a \times (\mathbf{J}_a\boldsymbol{\omega}_a) + \mathbf{M}_{ae} \tag{14}$$

Where $\mathbf{M}_{ae}$ stands for the reaction moment from the elevation gimbal, and it can be obtained by using the transformation matrix $\mathbf{C}_{ea}$:

$$\mathbf{M}_{ae} = \mathbf{C}_{ea}^{-1}\mathbf{M}_e \tag{15}$$

The external torque of azimuth gimbal can be expressed as

$$\mathbf{M}_a = \begin{bmatrix} M_{ax} \\ M_{ay} \\ M_{az} \end{bmatrix} = \begin{bmatrix} M_{ax} \\ M_{az} \\ T_a - M_{da} \end{bmatrix} \quad (16)$$

By combination of (14) and (16), the dynamic model of the azimuth gimbal can obtained:

$$\begin{bmatrix} M_{ax} \\ M_{az} \\ T_a - M_{da} \end{bmatrix} = \begin{bmatrix} J_{ax}\dot{\omega}_{ax} \\ J_{ay}\dot{\omega}_{ay} \\ J_{az}\dot{\omega}_{az} \end{bmatrix} + \begin{bmatrix} (J_{az} - J_{ay})\omega_{ay}\omega_{az} \\ (J_{ax} - J_{az})\omega_{ax}\omega_{az} \\ (J_{ay} - J_{ax})\omega_{ay}\omega_{ax} \end{bmatrix} + \mathbf{M}_{ae} \quad (17)$$

The azimuth gimbal only has rotational freedom in direction of axis z, therefore, take its component of axis z, and the dynamic model of azimuth gimbal become

$$T_a - M_{da} = J_{az}\dot{\omega}_{az} + (J_{ay} - J_{ax})\omega_{ay}\omega_{ax} + M_{aez} \quad (18)$$

2.2.3 Driving torque of motors

The pivoting movement of each gimbal were achieved by torque motors, therefore, the dynamic model of torque motors[12] for azimuth gimbal and elevation gimbals can be described as

$$\begin{cases} T_a = \frac{K_{Ta}}{R_a}(U_a - n_a K_a \dot{\xi}) \\ T_e = \frac{K_{Te}}{R_e}(U_e - n_e K_e \dot{\eta}) \end{cases} \quad (19)$$

Where T stand for the electromagnetic torque generated by motor; K_T stand for the torque coefficient of the motor; R stand for the armature resistance of the motor; U stand for the input driven voltage of the motor. n stand for the reduction ratio of the reducer; K stand for back EMF constant.

Finally, the electromechanical dynamic model of the photoelectric tracking platform can obtained

$$\begin{cases} \frac{K_{Ta}}{R_a}(U_a - n_a K_a \dot{\xi}) - M_{da} = J_{Oaz}\ddot{\xi} - 2(J_{ex} - J_{ez})\dot{\eta}\dot{\xi}\sin\eta\cos\eta \\ \frac{K_{Te}}{R_e}(U_e - n_e K_e \dot{\eta}) - M_{de} = J_{Oey}\ddot{\eta} - (J_{ex} - J_{ez})\dot{\xi}^2\sin\eta\cos\eta \end{cases} \quad (20)$$

3 Decoupling control

Before decoupling design, the dynamic model should be transformed to a form of state space representation.

By substituting the inertia moments and motor parameters value from [13], the differential equation of the system can be obtained:

$$\begin{cases} \ddot{\xi} = -6.03\dot{\xi} - 0.16\dot{\eta}\dot{\xi}\sin\eta\cos\eta + 0.52U_a + d_1(t) \\ \ddot{\eta} = -47.98\dot{\eta} - 0.67\dot{\xi}\sin\eta\cos\eta + 3.26U_e + d_2(t) \end{cases} \quad (21)$$

Assuming that :

$$\begin{cases} \mathbf{x} = [x_1 \;\; x_2 \;\; x_3 \;\; x_4]^T = [\xi \;\; \dot{\xi} \;\; \eta \;\; \dot{\eta}]^T \\ \mathbf{u} = [U_a \;\; U_e]^T \\ \mathbf{y} = [x_1 \;\; x_3]^T \end{cases} \quad (22)$$

Where $\mathbf{x}$ is a 4-dimensional state vector; $\mathbf{u}$ stand for the control input; $\mathbf{y}$ stand for the control output.

The state space of original system s_0 can be described as:

$$s_0 = \begin{cases} \dot{\mathbf{x}} = f(\mathbf{x}) + b(\mathbf{x})\mathbf{u} + g(\mathbf{x}) \\ \mathbf{y} = h(\mathbf{x}) \end{cases} \quad (23)$$

Where $b(\mathbf{x})$ stands for the input matrix, $h(\mathbf{x})$ stands for the output matrix:

$$f(\mathbf{x}) = \begin{bmatrix} x_2 \\ -0.63x_2 - 0.16x_2x_4\sin x_3\cos x_3 \\ x_4 \\ -47.98x_4 - 0.67x_2\sin x_3\cos x_3 \end{bmatrix},$$

$$b(\mathbf{x}) = \begin{bmatrix} 0 & 0 \\ 0.52 & 0 \\ 0 & 0 \\ 0 & 3.26 \end{bmatrix}, \; h(\mathbf{x}) = [x_1 \;\; x_3]^T \quad (24)$$

It is observed that the photoelectric tracking platform is a 2-input 2-output system with characteristics of strong coupling and nonlinearity.

3.1 Decoupling and linearization

Based on the system model (23), take the derivative of the output y with respect to the time t until the control variables U_a and U_e is explicitly included, which can get the following equation:

$$J(\mathbf{u}) = \begin{bmatrix} \ddot{y}_1 \\ \ddot{y}_2 \end{bmatrix} = \begin{bmatrix} \dot{x}_2 \\ \dot{x}_4 \end{bmatrix} = \begin{bmatrix} -0.63x_2 - 0.16x_2x_4\sin x_3\cos x_3 + 0.52U_a \\ -47.98x_4 - 0.67x_2\sin x_3\cos x_3 + 3.26U_e \end{bmatrix} \quad (25)$$

The Jacobi matrix of $J(\mathbf{u})$ with respect to the control input vector $\mathbf{u}$ can be calculated as follows:

$$\mathbf{D} = \frac{\partial J(\mathbf{u})}{\partial \mathbf{u}^T} = \begin{bmatrix} 0.52 & 0 \\ 0 & 3.26 \end{bmatrix} \quad (26)$$

According to (26), det($\mathbf{D}$)$\neq$0. Moreover, the relative degrees of the system are $\boldsymbol{\alpha} = (\alpha_a, \alpha_e) = (2, 2)$, which satisfy $\alpha_a + \alpha_e = 4 \leq n$, where n is the dimensions of the state vector $\mathbf{x}$. Based on the inverse system theory [14], the original system is invertible.

Define the new input variables

$$\boldsymbol{\varphi} = \begin{bmatrix} \varphi_1 \\ \varphi_2 \end{bmatrix} = \begin{bmatrix} \ddot{y}_1 \\ \ddot{y}_2 \end{bmatrix} \quad (27)$$

By substituting (26) into (24) and make $\mathbf{u} = [U_a \;\; U_e]^T$ as output can get the inverse system s_0^{-1}

$$s_0^{-1} = \begin{cases} \dot{\mathbf{x}} = f(\mathbf{x}) + b(\mathbf{x})\mathbf{u} + g(\mathbf{x}) \\ \mathbf{u} = \mathbf{D}^{-1}[\boldsymbol{\varphi} - \bar{f}(\mathbf{x})] \end{cases} \quad (28)$$

If the inverse system s_0^{-1} in series with the original system s_0 (see Figure 2(a)), two pseudo-linear subsystems can be formed (see Figure 2(b)).

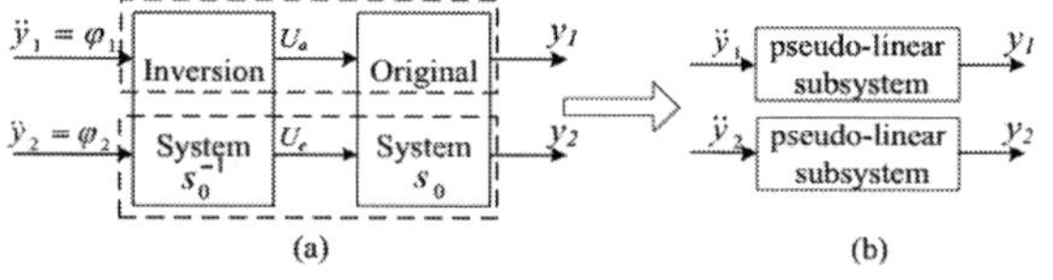

Figure 2 decoupling and linearization

3.2 Controller design

For the pseudo-linear subsystem, the system uncertainties and external disturbance should be considered, then (27) can be written as:

$$\boldsymbol{\varphi} = \begin{bmatrix} \varphi_1 + d_1 \\ \varphi_2 + d_2 \end{bmatrix} = \begin{bmatrix} \ddot{y}_1 \\ \ddot{y}_2 \end{bmatrix} \quad (29)$$

Where d_1 and d_2 are the equivalent parameter of system uncertainties and external disturbance, unknown but bounded.

Define the tracking error $\mathbf{e}=\begin{bmatrix} e_a \\ e_e \end{bmatrix}=\begin{bmatrix} x_1-r_1 \\ x_3-r_3 \end{bmatrix}$, in which r_1 and r_3 represents the reference trajectory.

Accordingly,

$$\dot{\mathbf{e}}=\begin{bmatrix} \dot{e}_a \\ \dot{e}_e \end{bmatrix}=\begin{bmatrix} \dot{x}_1-\dot{r}_1 \\ \dot{x}_3-\dot{r}_3 \end{bmatrix} \quad \ddot{\mathbf{e}}=\begin{bmatrix} \ddot{e}_a \\ \ddot{e}_e \end{bmatrix}=\begin{bmatrix} \ddot{x}_1-\ddot{r}_1 \\ \ddot{x}_3-\ddot{r}_3 \end{bmatrix}=\begin{bmatrix} \varphi_1-\ddot{r}_1+d_1 \\ \varphi_2-\ddot{r}_3+d_2 \end{bmatrix}$$

Then the sliding mode surface with integral actions[15] is designed as follows

$$\mathbf{S}=\begin{bmatrix} S_a \\ S_e \end{bmatrix}=\begin{bmatrix} (c_1+c_2)\mathrm{e}_a+c_1c_2\int_0^t e_a d\tau+\dot{e}_a \\ (c_3+c_4)\mathrm{e}_e+c_3c_4\int_0^t e_e d\tau+\dot{e}_e \end{bmatrix} \tag{30}$$

And the control input $\boldsymbol{\varphi}$ is designed as

$$\begin{bmatrix} \varphi_1 \\ \varphi_2 \end{bmatrix}=\begin{bmatrix} \ddot{r}_1-(c_1+c_2)\dot{\mathrm{e}}_a+c_1c_2e_a-k_1S_a-k_2 sign(S_a) \\ \ddot{r}_3-(c_3+c_4)\dot{\mathrm{e}}_e+c_3c_4e_e-k_3S_e-k_4 sign(S_e) \end{bmatrix} \tag{31}$$

Where c_1 c_2 c_3 and c_4 are positive constant, k_1 and k_3 are fixed gain which satisfied with $k_1>0$ and $k_3>0$, k_2 and k_4 are switching gain which satisfied with $k_2>|d_1|$, $k_4>|d_2|$. The control block diagram is shown in Figure 3.

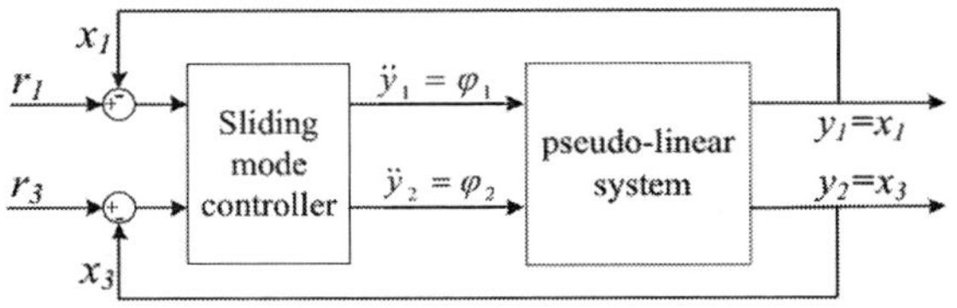

Figure 3. Control block diagram

3.3 Stability analysis

For the stability analysis of the system dynamics, select a Lyapunov function as

$$V=\frac{1}{2}S^2 \tag{32}$$

The time derivative of V is

$$\begin{aligned}\dot{V}&=\mathbf{S}^{\mathrm{T}}\dot{\mathbf{S}}=S_a[(c_1+c_2)\dot{e}_a+c_1c_2e_a+\ddot{e}_a]+S_e[(c_3+c_4)\dot{e}_e+c_3c_4e_e+\ddot{e}_e]\\&=S_a[(c_1+c_2)\dot{e}_a+c_1c_2e_a+\varphi_1-\ddot{r}_1+d_1]\\&\quad+S_e[(c_3+c_4)\dot{e}_e+c_3c_4e_e+\varphi_2-\ddot{r}_2+d_2]\end{aligned} \tag{33}$$

Substituting (31) into (32), (32) becomes

$$\begin{aligned}\dot{V}&=\mathbf{S}^{\mathrm{T}}\dot{\mathbf{S}}=S_a[-k_1S_a-k_2 sign(S_a)+d_1]+S_e[-k_3S_e-k_4 sign(S_a)+d_2]\\&\le -k_1S_a^2-(k_2-d_1)|S_a|+(-k_3S_e^2-(k_4-d_2)|S_e|)\le 0\end{aligned} \tag{34}$$

From Lyapunov stability theory, it means the designed control system is stable, and the system can reach the sliding mode surface in finite time.

3.4 Chattering restrain

We can see from (31) that the control law $\boldsymbol{\varphi}$ contains the symbolic function *sign()*. Although due to the existence of it can ensure the robustness of sliding mode control, it can also led to the chattering phenomenon of sliding mode control, affecting the convergence precision of the system, even can inspiring the unmodeled dynamics and make the system unstable. In order to weaken the chattering phenomenon and strengthen the robustness of system at the same time, the Sigmoid function[16] is designed to replace the symbolic function as:

$$Sig(x)=\frac{2}{1+\exp(-ax)}-1 \tag{35}$$

Where a is positive constant, it determines the convergence rate of the sigmoid function.

4 Simulation results

To verify the effectiveness and reliability of the decoupling control strategy proposed in this paper, simulations have been carried out on the photoelectric tracking platform.

The initial position of two gimbals is set as $\mathbf{x}_0=[0 \quad 0]^T$, the tracking signals are given as $r_1=\pi-\pi\sin(2\pi\times 0.3t)$, $r_3=\pi/4-\pi/4\sin(2\pi\times 0.2t)$, and assuming that the disturbance torque of two gimbals are $d_1=0.5\sin(\pi t)$, $d_2=0.1\sin(\pi t)$ respectively.

The simulation results are shown in Figure 4 ~ 9:

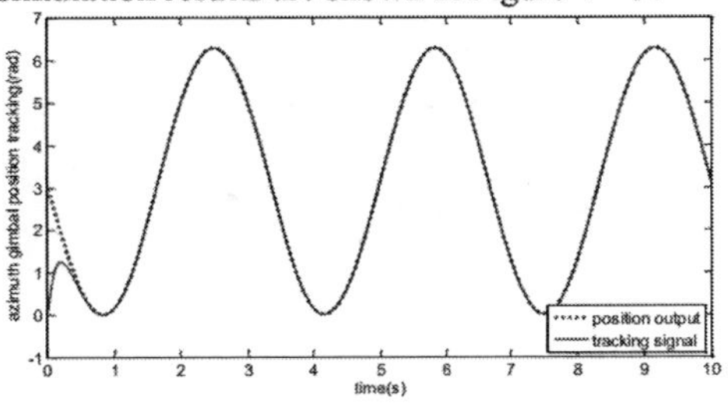

Figure 4. Position tracking of azimuth gimbal

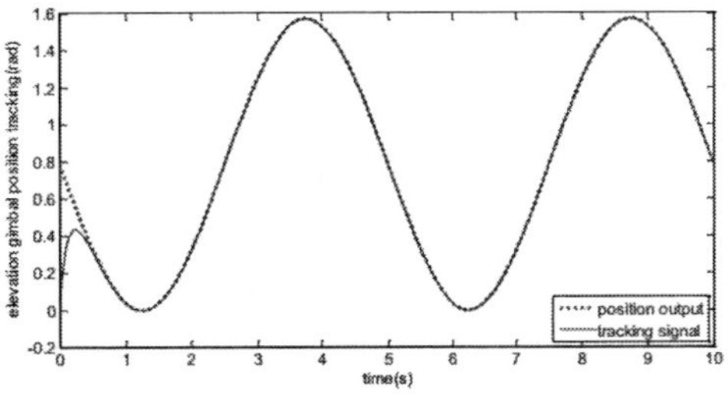

Figure 5. Position tracking of elevation gimbal

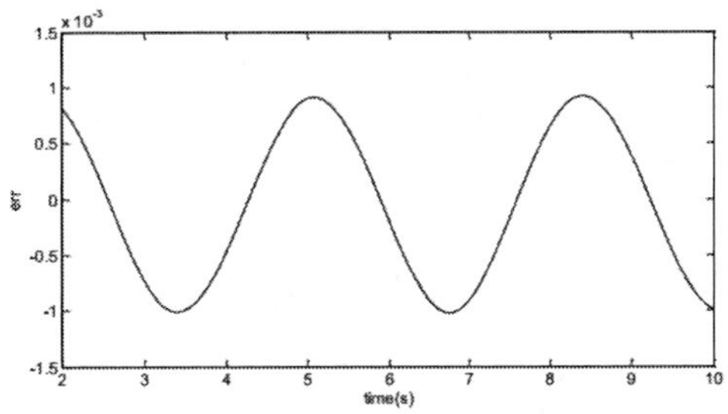

Figure 6. Tracking error of azimuth gimbal(2s~10s)

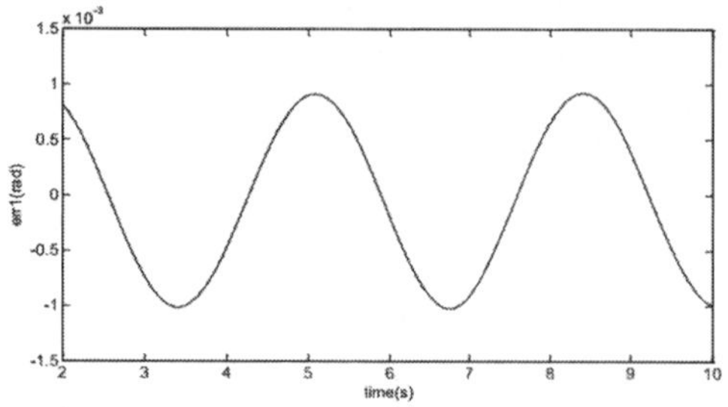

Figure 7. Tracking error of elevation gimbal(2s~10s)

Figure 4 and 5 are position tracking curves of azimuth gimbal and elevation gimbal respectively, it is observed that the system state can be reaching and perfect tracking to the desired state within 1s Figure 6 and 7 are tracking error curves from 2s to 10s of azimuth gimbal and elevation gimbal respectively, it is observed that the tracking error of both gimbals are less than 1mrad. It can be concluded that the system has fast convergence speed and dynamic response, can effectively reduce the influence of system uncertainties and disturbance torque, and satisfying the requirements of control precision.

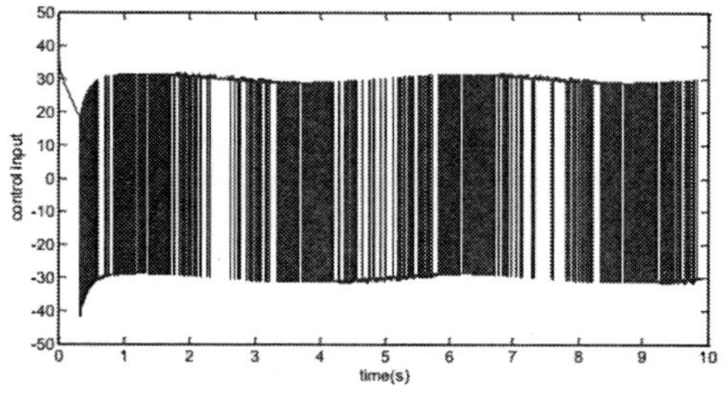

Figure 8 control input signal (using traditional *sign(x)*)

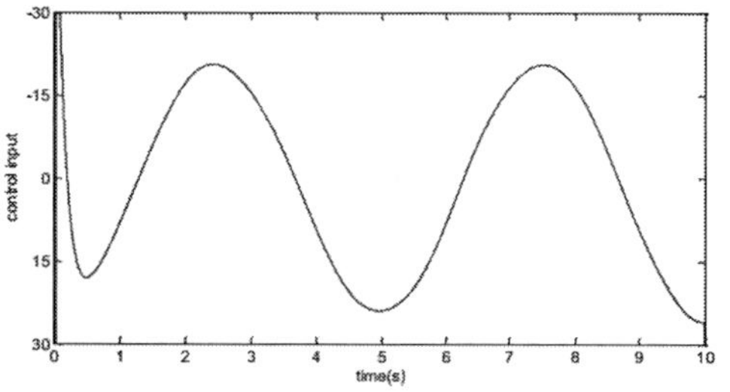

Figure 9. Control input signal (using *Sig(x)*)

From Figure 8, it is found that the controller which using the traditional symbolic function *sign(x)* has strong chattering phenomenon, and its amplitude can reach more than 30. Figure 8 is control input signal of which the controller using the Sigmoid function *Sig(x)*. Compared with Figure 9, the chattering phenomenon in Figure 8 has decreased significantly, and its amplitude was controlled at about 2. It can be concluded that the proposed Sigmoid function is able to reduce the chattering phenomenon effectively and ensure the robustness of the system.

5. Conclusions

An integral sliding mode control strategy based on inverse system decoupling method is proposed for the photoelectric tracking platform. The kinematic relations is analyzed and the dynamic model is developed based on multi-body system theory and Newton-Euler method. The electromechanical system model are linearized and decoupled into two pseudo linear subsystems and the strong coupling and nonlinearity of the system are resolved. the integral sliding mode controller is designed for the pseudo linear subsystems to reject the influence of system uncertainties and disturbance. By adopting the proposed Sigmoid function, The chattering phenomenon of sliding-mode controller is restrained. The performance of the proposed decoupling control strategy is studied in simulation. It is observed that the proposed decoupling control strategy can effectively restrain the influences of coupling and disturbance, and has satisfactory tracking performance.

References

1. T. Bhagyashri, S. Kurode, P. Parkhi, *12th International Conference on Control, Automation and Systems* 1358 (2012)
2. R.L. McMillen, J.E. Steck, K.Rokhsaz, J. Aircraft, **32**, 1088 (1995)
3. S.J. Dodds, A.B. Walker, Int. J. Control, **54**, 737 (1991).
4. J. Nie, IEEE T. Fuzzy. Syst. **5**, 304 (1997)
5. J. Fang, Y. Ren, IEEE T. Ind. Electron. **58**, 4331 (2011)
6. J Fang, Y. Ren IEEE-ASME T. Mech. **17**, 1133 (2012)
7. J.K. Liu, F.C. Sun, Control Theory & Applications, **23**, 407 (2007)
8. W. Lu, C. Li, C. Xu, Int. J. Elec. Power, **57**, 39 (2014)
9. J.H. Lee, Automatica, **42**, 929 (2006)
10. P.J. Kennedy, R.L. Kennedy. IEEE T. Contr. Syst. T. **11**, 3(2003)
11. H. Khodadadi, M.R.J. Motlagh, M. Gorji. *International Conference on Electrical, Control and Computer Engineering*, 223 (2011)
12. B. Kou, S. Cheng, *AC servo motor and its control* (China Machine Press, Beijing, 2008)
13. K. Li. *Research on Dynamics Modeling and Attitude Stability for Floating Unmanned Platform* (Nanjing University of Science&Technology, Nanjing, 2014)
14. X. Dai, D. He, X. Zhang, et al. IEE P-Contr. **148**, 125 (2001)
15. V. Utkin, J. Guldner, J. Shi. *Sliding mode control in electro-mechanical systems* (CRC press, Boca Raton, 2009)
16. H. Kim, J. Son, J. Lee, IEEE T. Ind. Electron. **58**, 4069 (2011)

MATEC Web of Conferences **44**, 01032 (2016)
DOI: 10.1051/matecconf/20164401032

An RSA Scheme based on Improved AKS Primality Testing Algorithm

Han Wei Wu [a], Cai Mao Li, Hong Lei Li, Jie Ding, Xiao Ming Yao

College of Information Science and Technology, Hainan University, Haikou ,China 570228

Abstract. In applied cryptography, RSA is a typical asymmetric algorithm, which is used in electronic transaction and many other security scenarios. RSA needs to generate large random primes. Currently, primality test mostly depends on probabilistic algorithms, such as the Miller-Rabin primality testing algorithm. In 2002, Agrawal et al. published the Agrawal–Kayal–Saxena (AKS) primality testing algorithm, which is the first generic, polynomial, deterministic and non-hypothetical algorithm for primality test. This paper proves the necessary and sufficient condition for AKS primality test. An improved AKS algorithm is proposed using Fermat's Little Theorem. The improved algorithm becomes an enhanced Miller-Rabin probabilistic algorithm, which can generate primes as fast as the Miller-Rabin algorithm does.

Keywords: RSA, Miller-Rabin, AKS algorithm, Primality testing

1 Introduction

The RSA algorithm is a typical asymmetric algorithm, which is used for security applications in the information society, including ID authentication and electronic transaction in electronic transaction scenarios [1]. Compared with other public key algorithms, RSA is slow but its strength is its ability to be used for encryption and digital signature. Its key generation principle states that it should first choose two large primes P and Q, computing $n=P*Q$. Then, it will calculate the Euler function $\phi(n) = (P-1)*(Q-1)$, and randomly select a positive integer e so that $1 < e < \phi(n)$. Meanwhile, they need to be coprime, i.e. $gcd(\phi(n), e) = 1$. Later on, the private key d needs to be computed via $d * e = 1 \bmod \phi(n)$, where n and e are public keys. The security of RSA depends on the difficulty in decomposing the large integer n.

From the procedures above, it can be seen that the RSA key scheduling algorithm needs to generate two large primes. To ensure security strength, the two generated large primes are usually longer than 512 bits. In December 12, 2009, the large integer with a number of RSA-768 (768-bit key) was decomposed successfully [2]. This event poses threats against the security of existing 1024-bit key, highlighting the need for general users to upgrade to keys of 2048- or longer bits. Rapid generation of large primes is essential for RSA. The current approach for generation of large primes is to randomly generate a large integer, and then perform the primality test. Common approaches for primality test include the probabilistic Miller-Rabin test method [3], Solovay-Strass test method [8], and the Lucas-Lehmer N-1 and N+1 deterministic test methods [10][11]. Agrawal, Kayal and Saxena [4] successfully addressed the worldwide problem of testing primality in polynomial time by proposing an algorithm called AKS. Their algorithm determines the input integer is a prime or a composite number. It is the first published generic, polynomial, deterministic and non-hypothetical algorithm for primality test. All of the previous primality test algorithms can have at most three of the four properties above.

Despite its ability to perform primality test in polynomial time, the overheads that it incurs during operation in terms of transport and storage complexity are so large that it is infeasible in practice. Major improvements achieved include the improved algorithm by Bernstein [5] and the optimized algorithm by Jin Zhengping based on that of Bernstein [6]. The algorithm by Bernstein is more efficient. For positive integers 3640471 and 4295884871, the running time of the original AKS and Bernstein algorithms is dozens or hundreds of hours. The improved algorithm by Bernstein still costs tens of seconds. For primes as long as 40 plus digits, the improved version still requires several hours. After a thorough analysis of the improved version by Bernstein, Jin Zhengping et al. demonstrated not only enormous improvements over other algorithms but also some problems that it has. Meanwhile, they stated that it needs to be further improved for practical applications of primality test. None of existing AKS algorithms are useful for practical security applications, because algorithm completeness cannot be achieved without enormous computing and storage overheads.

[a] Corresponding author: wuhanwei@hainu.edu.cn
This work is supported by National Natural Science Foundation of China (No. 61462023), Natural Science Foundation of Hainan Province (No. 614231, 613158, 20156250).

This paper begins with the necessary and sufficient condition for AKS primality test, and does not compute the congruent polynomial as the original algorithm does. The proposed algorithm is rendered non-deterministic by choosing smaller test sets. It is proved strictly that the proposed algorithm is equal to the strong-constraint Miller-Rabin test. Prime generation of the proposed algorithm achieves a substantial speedup. A complete example of RSA based on the improved AKS test algorithm is implemented on computer using Python (64-bit Windows 7, Python 3.4.3, 8G memory, AMD FX8300@3.30G, 256 G solid-state drives). Comparison shows that the executing efficiency of the improved AKS algorithm can rival the industry-standard Miller-Rabin algorithm. Therefore, the proposed algorithm is useful for practical applications.

2 Common Primality Testing Algorithms

2.1 Fundamental concepts and principles of AKS

AKS primality test is mainly based on the following theorem: the integer n ($\geq$2) is a prime when and only when

$$(x-a)^n \equiv (x^n - a)\ (mod\ n) \qquad (1)$$

This congruent polynomial is true for all integers a which are coprime with n. This theorem is a generic representation of Fermat's Little Theorem.

Proof:

1. First prove that (1) holds when n is a prime.

Based on Fermat's Little Theorem $a^{n-1} \equiv 1\ (mod\ n)$, where n is a prime, it can be deduced that

$$(x-a)^n \equiv (x-a)^{n-1} \cdot (x-a) \equiv (x-a)\ mod\ n$$

$$(x^n - a) \equiv (x^{n-1} \cdot x - a) \equiv (x-a)\ mod\ n$$

Therefore, (1) is true.

2. Proceed to prove that if (1) holds, then n is a prime.

For each $0 < i < n$, we have

$$(x-a)^n = x^n + \sum_{i=1}^{n-1} \binom{n}{i} x^i (-a)^{n-i} + (-a)^n$$

The number of interest, n, is either composite or prime. If n is prime, then $n | \binom{n}{i}, 0 < i < n$. The conclusion is true.

If n is composite, then there must exist a prime divisor of n, denoted with q. Consider that $q^k \parallel n$, i.e. $q^k | n$. But $q^{k+1} \nmid n$. Then, it can be proved that $q^k \nmid \binom{n}{q}$, where $\binom{n}{q} = \frac{n(n-1)\cdots(n-q+1)}{q!}$.

Because $\binom{n}{q} = \frac{n(n-1)\cdots(n-q+1)}{q!}$, we can let $n = q^k m$ and *gcd(m, q)*=1. Thus, $1 \leq i \leq q-1$ for $1 \leq i \leq q-1$. Otherwise, $q | n-(n-i) = i$. Therefore, $q | n-(n-i) = i$, it can be deduced that

$$\binom{n}{q} = \frac{n}{q} \frac{(n-1)\cdots(n-q+1)}{(q-1)!}$$
$$= q^{k-1} m \frac{(n-1)\cdots(n-q+1)}{(q-1)!}$$

But

$$\gcd\left(m\frac{(n-1)\cdots(n-q+1)}{(q-1)!}, \mathrm{q}\right) = 1$$

Hence, we have $q^k \nmid \binom{n}{q}$. The largest common divisor of n and a can be obtained quickly using the extended Euclidean algorithm. If the two numbers are not coprime, then it can be inferred directly that n is composite. Thus, $gcd(n = q^k, a)$=1 is requested. Then, the coefficient module of x^q is not zero. $(x-a)^n - (x^n - a)$ modulo n is not always equal to zero. (1) is false and contradictory to the original condition. Therefore, if (1) is true, then n is prime.

Although the primality test can be done based on the defined formulation, the time needed increases exponentially. To reduce computational complexity, AKS switches to the following congruent polynomial.

The steps of the algorithm are as follows:

Input: integer n>1

① If there exist a > 0 and b > 1, and $n = a^b$; then output the composite number.

② Find the smallest r such that $ord_r(n) > \log^2(n)$.

③ If 1 < *gcd(a,n)* < n is true for some a ≤ r, then output the composite number. (gcd represents the largest common divisor of a and n.)。

④ If n ≤ r, output the prime number.

⑤ For all a from 1 to$\lfloor\sqrt{\varphi(r)}log\ (n)\rfloor$, if $(x+a)^n \neq x^n+a$ (mod n, $x^r - 1$), output the composite number.

⑥ Output the prime number.

Here, $ord_r(n)$ is the order of n mod r. In addition, log represents the logarithm with 2 as the base, $\varphi(r)$ represents the Euler function of r. If n is prime, then the algorithm can always return prime number. Due to primality of n, Steps 1 and 3 will never return composite number. Neither will Step 5, because (2) is true for all primes n. Hence, there is no doubt the algorithm steps 4 and 6 will return prime number. Correspondingly, if n is composite, then the algorithm will undoubtedly return composite number. If the algorithm returns prime number, then it is returned from Steps 4 or 6. In the former case, considering n ≤ r, it is certain that n has divisor a ≤ r such that 1 < gcd(a, n) < n. So composite number will be returned. The remaining case is Step 6, which is impossible, because the several equations tested in Step 5 can ensure that the output number is composite.

Many works have been done later to propose variants of the original algorithm. The best examples of improved algorithms include the method by Bernstein in [5]. Its complexity is $O(log^{4+o(1)}(n))$. A large prime number of n is requested for practical applications. In RSA, n usually has a binary length of over 1024 bits. So the improved version are unsuited for practical security applications.

2.2 Miller-Rabin algorithm

Primality test algorithms are classified into the probability-based method and the deterministic method. The probability-based method is fast but its misjudgment probability is high. The greatest property of the deterministic method is its ability to prevent misjudgment.

But its test speed is so low that it is not as feasible as the probability-based method in practical applications.

The Miller-Rabin algorithm achieves improvements by using Fermat's Little Theorem. It incorporates square root decision into Fermat's Little Theorem [3][7]. In the Miller-Rabin primality test, strong psedoprime decision is made by elegantly combining Format test with square root test, achieving a misjudgment probability of 1/4 per time. Choosing multiple base numbers in the test, the misjudgment probability can be reduced to an extremely low level. For example, choosing 64 base numbers in the test can lead to a misjudgment probability of 1/(464). In the test, n-1 is represented with the product of an odd number m and 2.

$$n - 1 = m \times 2^k$$

Fermat test of the base number a can be written as

$$a^{n-1} = a^{m \times 2^k} = [a^m]^{2^k}$$

Note that $a^{n-1}\,(mod\,n)$ is computed through k+1 steps rather than in a single step. In this way, square root test can be done in each step. If square root test fails, it means that n is composite. If each step is correct, then it can be known for sure that not only Fermat test but also all square root tests are passed.

Algorithm is summarized using Python in Fig.1.

```
def Miller_Rabin(n, count=33):
    testnum = [2, 3, 5, 7, 11, 13, 17, 19, 23, 29, 31, 37, 41,
               43, 47, 53, 59, 61, 67, 71, 73, 79, 83, 89, 97]
    if n in testnum:
        return True
    if 0 in [n%i for i in testnum]:
        return False
    neg_one = n - 1

    k, m = 0, neg_one
    while not m & 1:
        k, m = k + 1, m >> 1
    #assert 2 ** k * m == neg_one and m & 1

    for _ in range(count):
        a = random.randrange(2, neg_one)
        x = pow(a, m, n)
        if x in (1, neg_one):
            continue
        for _ in range(k - 1):
            x = pow(x, 2, n)
            if x == 1:
                return False
            if x == neg_one:
                break
        else:
            return False
    return True
```

Figure 1. Miller-Rabin algorithm.

Algorithm steps:

①. Choose primes below 100. If n belongs to this list, return true。If n is divisible by primes below 100, return the conclusion that n is composite.

② . Randomly choose a base number a and compute$T = a^m$, where m $= (n-1)/2^k$.

③. If T is either 1 or -1 and all subsequent square root tests can be passed, it means that n is a strong pseduprime, and return to Step 2, choose a new base number to test. If T are other numbers, go to the following step.

④. Conduct the worst-case test through K-1 steps. First compute $T = T^2 \bmod n$. If T=1, because the original value of T are other numbers, based on the square root test rule, if n is composite, then $T = \sqrt{1} = \pm 1$ or other numbers. Thus when T=1, return the conclusion that n is composite.

⑤. In Step 4, if T= -1, based on the square root test rule, if n is prime, then $T = \sqrt{1} = \pm 1$. So n will pass the test definitely. T= -1 for this step and 1 for the next step. Return the conclusion that n is prime。

⑥. If in Step 4, T is other numbers, compute k=k-1, and then jump to Step 4.

⑦. If primality of n cannot be determined when k=0, return the conclusion that n is composite.

3 Result and Analysis of the Improved AKS Algorithm

3.1. Miller-Rabin-based improved algorithm

Based on the Fermat's Little Theory, if n is prime, then (1) is true definitely. (1) can be rewritten as

$$(x-a)^{n-1}(x-a) \equiv (x^n - a)\,(mod\,n)$$

If n is prime, then it can undoubtedly justify gcd($(x-a)$,n)=1. That is, $(x-a)$ has an inverse element $(x-a)^{-1}$. It can be further deduced that

$$(x-a)^{n-1} \equiv (x^n - a)(x-a)^{-1}\,(mod\,n) \quad (2)$$

It can be derived from using Fermat's Little Theory again that the left and right sides of (2) mod n are invariably equal to 1.

Consider the left side of (2). If x is set to a fixed number and the value of the base number a is changed only

Rabin primality test. That is, for the base number $(x-a)$,

$$(x-a)^{n-1} = (x-a)^{m \times 2^k} = [(x-a)^m]^{2^k}$$

Consider the right side of (2). It is requested to justify gcd($(x-a)$,n)=1 and $(x^n - a) = (x-a)$. Further simplifying it yields $x^{n-1} = 1(mod\,n)$. Thus, by using Fermat's Little Theory many times to narrow the range of the base number a, AKS can be expressed as a Miller-Rabin test algorithm with two additional constraints.

For an input large integer n of interest, the Miller-Rabin testing algorithm jointly performs a Fermat's test and a square root test. The newly added constraints introduce an additional Fermat's test and an additional greatest common divisor test. Neglecting the test for greatest common divisor, the improved AKS has a misjudgment probability of 1/8 per time. For a given misjudgment probability, the set of base numbers in the improved AKS algorithm is two thirds of that in the Miller-Rabin test algorithm.

Algorithm steps:

①. Choose primes below 100. If n belongs to this list, return true。If n is divisible by primes below 100, return the conclusion that n is composite.。

②. Randomly choose a base number a and then choose a fixed value for x. Compute gcd($(x-a)$,n)=1. If

the condition is not met, return the conclusion that n is composite. If it meets the condition, go to the next step.

③. Compute to check whether $x^{n-1} = 1(mod\ n)$ is true。If not, return the conclusion that n is composite. Otherwise, go to the next step.

④. Test $(x-a)$ using the Miller-Rabin algorithm. If the result is true, it means that n is prime. Otherwise, return the conclusion that n is composite.

Major Python codes of the algorithm are given in Fig.2. In this algorithm, the extended Euclidean algorithm is used to check whether two numbers are coprime. The built-in modulo operating function in Python is directly utilized for code complicity. Note that the Miller-Rabin algorithm is changed into Miller-Rabin-Base, where the division test for primes below 100 is omitted.

```
def Aks_Miller_Rabin(n, count=22):
    testnum = [2, 3, 5, 7, 11, 13, 17, 19, 23, 29, 31, 37, 41, \
               43, 47, 53, 59, 61, 67, 71, 73, 79, 83, 89, 97]
    if n in testnum:
        return True
    if 0 in [n%i for i in testnum]:
        return False
    neg_one = n - 1

    k, m = 0, neg_one
    while not m & 1:
        k, m = k + 1, m >> 1
    #assert 2 ** k * m == neg_one and m & 1

    for _ in range(count):
        a = random.randrange(13, neg_one)
        x = [5] #[3,4,5,7,8,11]
        for i in x:
            if pow(i-a, n-1, n)!=1 or ex_euclid(i,n)[1]!=1:
                return False
            if Miller_Rabin_Base(n,a):
                continue
            else:
                return False
    return True
```

Figure 2. The improved AKS algorithm.

3.2 Correctness and efficiency of the improved AKS algorithm

Multiple large random numbers are generated in larger ranges to demonstrate correctness of the proposed algorithm. Tests are done on the Miller-Rabin algorithm and the proposed algorithm, respectively. Discrepancy between test results is defined as an erroneous output. The results are given in Tab.1.

Table 1. Correctness test for the improved AKS algorithm

Length of N	Test numbers	Primes	Test time(s)	Errors
$2^{32} < n < 2^{64}$	10000	219	0.7082	0
$2^{80} < n < 2^{128}$	10000	106	1.0046	0
$2^{130} < n < 2^{180}$	10000	82	1.2839	0
$2^{256} < n < 2^{512}$	10000	34	5.3189	0
$2^{1024} < n < 2^{1028}$	10000	23	26.1501	0

Consider a random range in Tab.1, such as $2^{130} < n < 2^{180}$. A total of 10,000 random numbers is chosen. Each random number is subject to a Miller-Rabin test and an improved AKS test. 82 of the 10,000 numbers pass the primality test, costing 1.2839s. All 50,000 tests over different ranges of n show that the two algorithms provide the same results.

Executing efficiency comparison is then performed between the Miller-Rabin and the improved AKS algorithms. The set of base numbers has 33 base numbers for the Miller-Rabin algorithm and 22 base numbers for the improved AKS algorithm. The test time is shown in Fig.3.

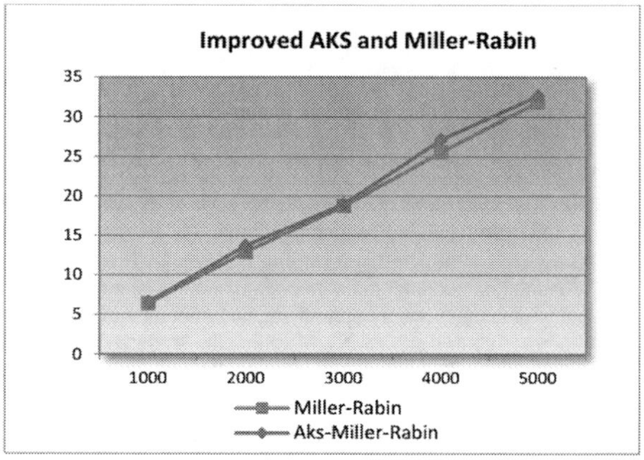

Figure 3. The execution efficiency of improved AKS algorithm.

4 Conclusion

AKS provides an effective approach for the worldwide problem of checking primality in polynomial time. Many improvements have been made on the original algorithm. The complexity of the computation procedures necessary to ensure algorithm completeness is too heavy. Great security strength can be achieved by using the public key scheme based on the elliptic curve discrete logarithm when the number n of interest has a length of 200 bits. The improved Bernstein algorithm can be used on the supercomputer to check the primality of n. But this type of complete algorithms is infeasible for RSA in electronic transaction.

This paper starts with analyzing the necessary and sufficient conditions for AKS and performs equivalence transformation on the algorithm's equations using Fermat's Little Theory. It is proven that this algorithm can be expressed as the Miller-Rabin testing algorithm with two additional constraints when the set of base numbers is narrowed. Experimental results show that the executing efficiency of the improved AKS algorithm can rival that of the Miller-Rabin algorithm. So the proposed algorithm is of value for practical applications.

References

1. RIVEST R, SHAMIR A, ALDEMAN L. A method for obtaining digital signatures and public-key cryptosystems[J].Communications of the ACM, 1978, 21(2):120-126

2. Thorsten Kleinjung, Kazumaro Aoki, Jens Franke, Arjen K Lenstra, Emmanuel Thomé, Joppe W Bos, Pierrick Gaudry, Alexander Kruppa, Peter L Montgomery, Dag Arne Osvik, Herman te Riele, Andrey Timofeev, and Paul Zimmermann. Factorization of a 768-bit RSA modulus[G]. // Advances in Cryptology-CRYPTO 2010. Santa Barbara:Springer, 2010: 333-350

3. Rabin M O. Probabilistic algorithm for testing primality[J]. Number Theory, 1980, 12(1):128-138

4. Manindra Agrawal, Neeraj Kayal and Nitin Saxena. PRIMES is in P [J]. Annals of Mathematics, 2004, 160(2):78-793

5. Bernstein D J. Proving primality in essentially quartic random time[J] . Math Comp , 2007 , 76(257):389-403

6. JIN Zheng-ping , WEN Qiao-yan. Implementations of the Improved AKS Primality Testing Algorithm[J]. Journal of Sichuan University Natural Science Edition, 2009, 41 (1):147-152 (in Chinese)

7. Miller, Gary L. Riemann's Hypothesis and Tests for Primality[J]. Journal of Computer and System Sciences ,1976,13 (3): 300-317

8. R. Solovay and V Strassen. A fast Monte-Carlo test for primality[J]. SIAM Journal on Computing, 1977, 6(1):84–86

9. Bruce, J W. A Really Trivial Proof of the Lucas-Lehmer Test[J]. The American Mathematical Monthly, 1993, 100(4): 370-371

10. SHAFI GOLDWASSER and JOE KILIAN.Primality Testing Using Elliptic Curves[J]. Journal of the ACM, 1999, 46(4): 450-472

11. Atkin, AOL and Morain F. Elliptic Curves and Primality Proving[J]. Mathematics of Computation, 1993, 61(203): 29-68

MATEC Web of Conferences **44**, 01033 (2016)
DOI: 10.1051/matecconf/20164401033

Field-Effect Phototransistors Based on Graphene-Quantum Dot Hybrids

Heng Zhang[1], Ya Ting Zhang[1,a]
[1]Institute of Laser & Opto-Electronics, College of Precision Instruments and Opto-electronics Engineering, Tianjin University, Tianjin 300072, people's Republic of China

Abstract. Field effect photo-transistors (FEpTs) based on graphene-PbSe quantum dot (QD) hybrids have been designed and fabricated. By electrical and photoelectrical measurements, the carrier mobilities reached to 1621 $cm^2V^{-1}s^{-1}$ for electrons and 1228 $cm^2V^{-1}s^{-1}$ for holes, the photoresponsivity (R) achieved to 1 AW^{-1}, and the photoresponse time (τ_1) was 0.7 s when the photocurrent came to about 80%. Therefore, the FEpTs based on graphene-QD hybrids have shown broad application prospects.

1 Introduction

Field effect phototransistors based on graphene-semiconductor quantum dot (QD) hybrids have achieved high performances, and have attracted great attention for a number of near infrared (NIR) detector applications because of their low cost and low energy consumption, increased flexibility, and easy fabrication and easy integration [1]. The photoconductive gain of FEpTs based on graphene-QD hybrids has reached up to 10^8 and was several orders of magnitude larger that of any graphene FETs or QD FETs reported before [2-5]. The excellent performance of extra high mobility and responsivity of FEpTs based on graphene-quantum dots is mainly attributed to the large absorbance of PbSe QDs and the fast transport in graphene [6]. The intrinsic properties of these two materials provide an opportunity for FEpTs to achieve ultrahigh performances. Recently, some architecture of FEpTs have been designed and fabricated based on graphene-QD hybrids, and the electrical and optical characteristics have been studied. The results exhibited high mobilities, high photoconductive gain and high responsivities. Here, we designed and fabricated the structure of FEpTs based on graphene-PbSe QD hybrids. With the experiment and theory calculation, the carrier mobilies were measured to be 1621 $cm^2V^{-1}s^{-1}$ for electrons and 1228 $cm^2V^{-1}s^{-1}$ for holes, the photoresponsivity R ~ 1 AW^{-1}, and the photoresponse time 0.7 s when the photocurrent reached to almost 80%. Therefore, the FEpTs based on graphene-QD hybrids will have broad application prospects.

2 Experiments

2.1 Structural design

Graphene provides a channel that can transport carriers effectively (high mobility) yet with weak capacity of photo absorption. On the other hand, QDs serve as providers of photo-induced carriers with low mobility. Thus the device designed with QDs as light absorption layer and graphene as charge transfer layer can achieve ultrahigh photoresponsivity.

PbSe QDs were synthesized using a wet chemical method, and a typical synthesizing process was detailed in reference [7].The absorption and photoluminescence (PL) spectrum of QDs is shown in figure 1(a), according to which the absorption and PL peaks were 1616 nm and 1645 nm correspondingly. And the architecture is given by figure 1(b).

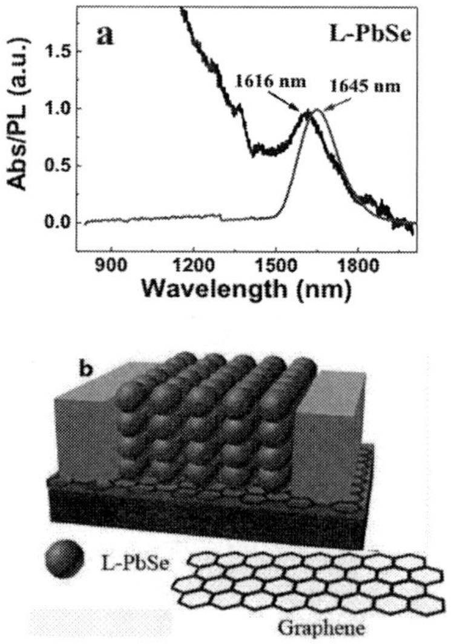

Figure 1.(a) The absorption and PL spectra of PbSe QDs. (b) Schematic diagram

[a] Ya-Ting Zhang: yating@tju.edu.cn

2.2 Device fabrication and measurements

2.2.1 Electrodes

The contact between metallic electrode and graphene not only changes the doping of graphene but also affects its electronic structure and Fermi energy. Therefore the contact have an impact on graphene's electrical characteristics near the electrode, eventually altering the property of devices. Researches have shown that Au is the only one whose forbidden band between graphene is 0 among several choices such as Cu, Ag, Al and so on [8]. Thus Au was utilized as the electrode material to reduce the influence to the device.

2.2.2 Fabrication of devices

FEpTs were fabricated on heavily doped, n-type Si substrate with a 300 nm thick SiO_2 capping layer on top and a predefined back gate electrode at the bottom. The graphene sheet was grown by chemical vapor deposition (CVD) and was transferred to the substrate [9]. Then, Au source and drain electrodes with a thickness of 500 nm were thermally evaporated using a shadow mask. Subsequently, four layers of PbSe QDs were deposited by using a layer-by-layer method. Each layer was prepared as follows: one drop of PbSe QD solution (30 mg ml^{-1}) was deposited on a spinning substrate at a speed of 2000 rpm for 60s and left for 20s to dry. Three drops of 2% (vol.) ethanedithiol (EDT) solution were then deposited on the rotating substrate at the same spin speed for ligand exchange, followed by two drops of acetonitrile and two drops of toluene.

2.2.3 Measurements

In the electrical measurements, a bias voltage (V_{SD}) was applied over the source (ground connection) and drain electrodes using a Keithley 2400. The channel current flowing into the drain is I_D, which was also measured by the Keithley 2400. An applied gate voltage (V_G) electrically connected the gate electrode to the source using HP6030A. During the photo electrical measurement, an 808 nm continuous-wave (cw) laser was used to provide incident light.

3 Results and discussion

3.1 Transfer characteristics

To illustrate the role of graphene, a comparison measurement in conductivity was performed on the FEpTs with a single layer of graphene and that without it. Figure 2 shows the increments in channel current as the bias voltage increases gradually for 300s. Figure 2 (a) displays the FEpTs conductivity without a layer of graphene and the I_D rose from $4.24 \times 10^{-4} \mu A$ to $0.0123\ \mu A$, the increments is several nA while the V_{SD} increased from 5V to 150V. Figure (b) shows the FEpTs conductivity with a graphene layer, the V_{SD} increased from 5V to 25V, while the I_D increased from 5.97mA to 35.54mA, the increments have reached to several mA, which is five orders higher than the former FEpTs. The results demonstrate that the graphene have a great contribution on conductivity of FEpTs.

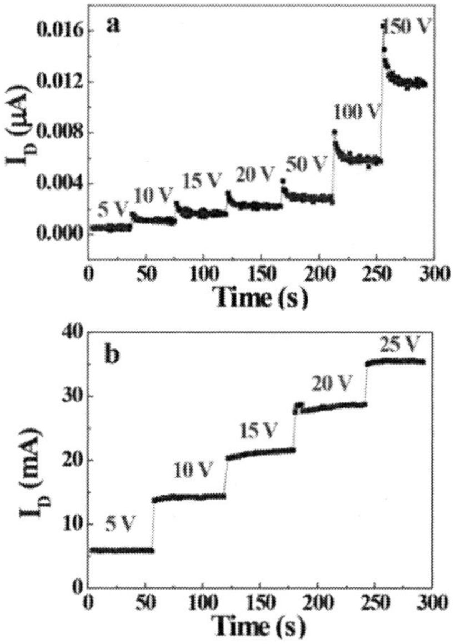

Figure 2. Conductivity respone to bias voltages, (a) QDs FEpTs without graphene, (b) QDs FEpTs with a layer of graphene.

3.2 Electrical properties of the FEpTs

Electrical measurements were performed at ambient conditions at room temperature.

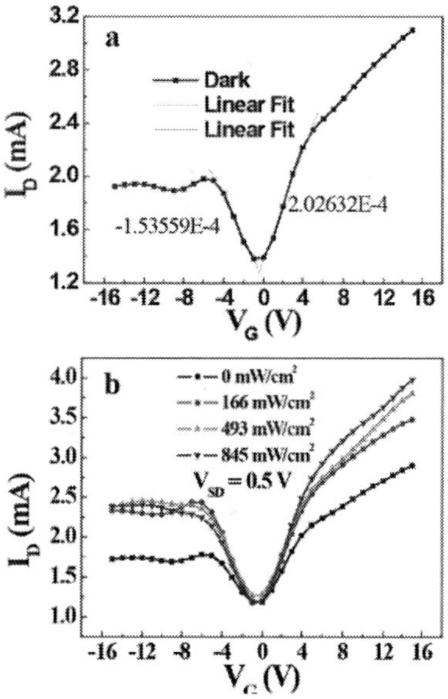

Figure 3. (a) Transfer characteristics (I_D versus V_G) in the dark with a constant V_{SD} =0.5V and fitting curves. (b) transfer characteristics (I_D versus V_G) with a constant V_{SD} =0.5V with illumination of 0 $mWcm^{-2}$, 166 $mWcm^{-2}$, 493 $mWcm^{-2}$, 845 $mWcm^{-2}$.

Figure 3 exhibits the transfer characteristics of FEpTs at the bias voltage of 0.5V. The bipolarity is observed.

Based on FET theory, when $V_G >> V_{SD}$, the transfer characteristics is in the linear region because of the constant hole mobility (in the third quadrant) and electron mobility (in the first quadrant) as shown in figure 3 (a). The minimum point in a transfer curve corresponds to the Dirac point of graphene [6]. After modified by QDs, the minimum point slightly shifted. We attributed the slight shift to the internal barrier formed by the capping ligands, which prevented carriers from transferring from the QDs to graphene.

The relation between the current change of ΔI_D and the light-induced gate voltage ΔV_G [9] can be shown as:

$$\Delta I_D = \frac{W\mu C_{OX}}{L} \cdot V_{SD} \cdot \Delta V_G \quad (1)$$

Where W and L are the width and length of the channel, respectively and C_{OX} is the capacitance of the gate dielectric per unit area. μ is the mobility of the carrier. The μ can be deduced from the equation (1):

$$\mu = \frac{L}{WC_{OX}V_{SD}} \cdot \frac{\partial I_D}{\partial V_G} \quad (2)$$

The slope of $\partial I_D / \partial V_G$ can be obtained by linearly fitting the transfer characteristics at low V_{SD} and the mobility can be calculated according to equation (2). For W=2.5mm, L=0.1mm, V_{SD} =0.5V, C_{ox}~100pFcm^{-2}, the hole mobility and electron mobility were calculated to be 1228.0 cm^{2}V^{-1}s^{-1} and 1621.0 cm^{2}V^{-1}s^{-1}.

Figure 3 (b) shows the transfer characteristics of FEpTs at the bias voltage of 0.5V with the irradiance of 0 mWcm^{-2}, 166 mWcm^{-2}, 493 mWcm^{-2}, 845 mWcm^{-2}. The profile of the transfer curves kept to the same with and without the illumination of laser. When the device was under illumination, QDs absorbed the light to generate the photo-induced carriers. And when the illumination increased, more photo-induced carriers were generated and separated into holes and electrons in the electric field.

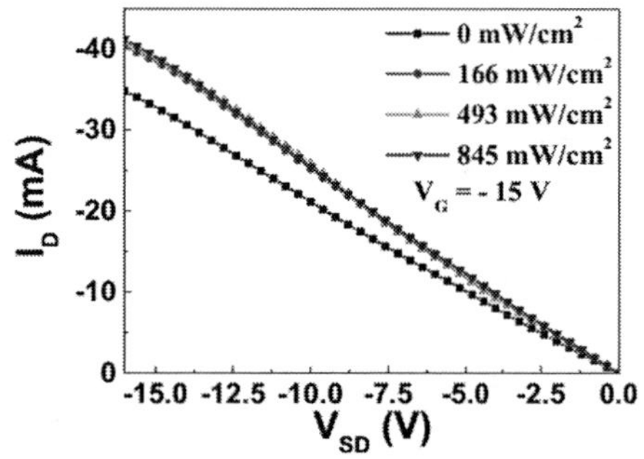

Figure 4. Output characteristics (I_D versus V_{SD}) at the gate voltage of −15 V with illuminations of 0 mWcm^{-2}, 166 mWcm^{-2}, 493 mWcm^{-2}, 845 mWcm^{-2}.

Figure 4 shows the output characteristics of FEpTs, at gate voltage of −15V in the third quadrant, with irradiance of 0 mWcm^{-2}, 166 mWcm^{-2}, 493 mWcm^{-2}, 845 mWcm^{-2}. The channel current went up with the bias voltage increasing, as the field generated by bias voltage drives the electrons and holes in the graphene to flow, forming the current. And the current was increasing with the rise of irradiance. Little increase of channel current, when the irradiance rose from 166 mWcm^{-2} to 845 mWcm^{-2}, is attributed to a saturation region the channel current reaches.

The physical mechanism of light sensing is described as follows. Under illumination, photo-induced excitons were generated in PbSe QDs and then separated into free electrons and holes. Because of the driving effect of the gate voltage, holes (or electrons depending on gate voltage) transferred from the QDs to graphene where carriers were transported effectively. Equal numbers of electrons (or holes) remaining in the QDs formed an electric field in the direction opposite to the gate electric field. This additional photo-induced gate voltage is termed the 'light gating effect'. Because of this effect, horizontal shifts in the ΔV_G can be used for FEpTs to calibrate the irradiance(E_e) [10]:

$$\Delta V_G = \alpha E_e^{\beta} \quad (3)$$

Where α and β are constants which reflected the situation of carriers transporting from QDs to graphene. The responsivity (R) of a FEpT is defined using ΔI_D and is

$$R = \frac{I_{ill} - I_{Dark}}{P} = \frac{\Delta I_D}{P} \quad (4)$$

Where I_{ill} and I_{Dark} are the channel current values under light and dark, respectively, P = AE_e is the incident optical power, and A is the illumination area. Substituting equation (2) into (4) gives

$$R = \frac{\alpha C_{ox} V_{sd} \mu}{L^2} E_e^{\beta - 1} \quad (5)$$

$$log(R) = log\left(\frac{\alpha C_{ox} V_{sd} \mu}{L^2}\right) + (\beta - 1) log\,(E_e) \quad (6)$$

According to the calculation of theory, the R is in the order scale of 1 AW^{-1}.

3.3 Photoresponse time

Though the responsivity of graphene-QDs based FEpTs has been measured experimentally, the photoresponse time is an important parameter as well.

The transient photocurrent response of the FEpTs to on/off illumination was measured as shown in figure 5 (a) where the irradiance was 845 mWcm^{-2}, at the wavelength of 808 nm, under V_{SD} = 0.01 V, V_G = 3 V, and the on/off time were both 24s.

The channel current increased sharply once the light was switched on, then the increase slowed down during the illuminating time. On the contrary, when the light was switched off, the current dropped exponentially to the initial state.

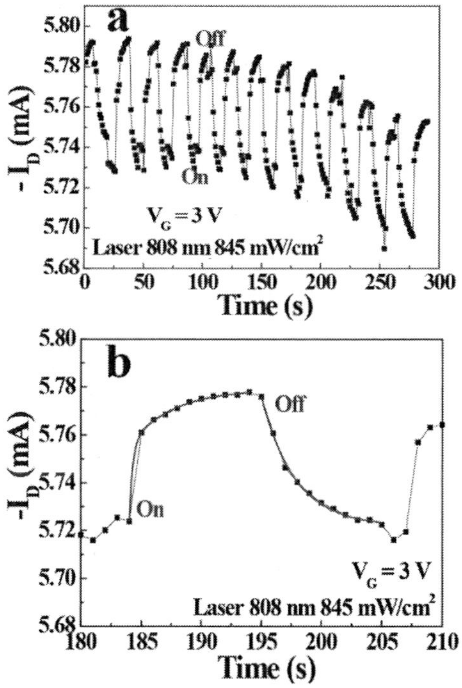

Figure 5. (a) The photocurrent of FEpTs to on/off illumination for various cycles where V_{SD} =0.01V and V_G =3V. The irradiance was 845 mWcm^{-2}, the wavelength was 808 nm and the on/off time was 24s. (b) The fitting result of a cycle.

The process of on/off illumination could be fitted using the exponential equation:

$$I_D = \begin{cases} \Delta I_1 \, exp\left(-\frac{t}{\tau_1}\right) + \Delta I_2 \, exp\left(-\frac{t}{\tau_2}\right) + I_{Dark} \\ \Delta I_1 \, [1 - exp\left(-\frac{t}{\tau_3}\right)] + I_{Dark} \end{cases} \quad (7)$$

Where the physical meaning of τ refers to the time of carriers transferring between the QDs and graphene sheets, that is, relaxation time. Figure 5 (b) shows the fitting result of a cycle according to the exponential function. The time constants τ_1 and τ_2 were calculated to be 0.7s and 2.4s respectively. As the photocurrent has taken the proportion of almost 80% during the time of τ_1=0.7 s, the photoresponse property of the FEpTs based on graphene and QDs is remarkable.

4 Conclusions and summary

We combined the advantages of graphene with high carrier mobility and quantum dots with large absorbance at the same time, designed the structure of graphene-based FEpTs with four layers of PbSe QDs. Then its electrical and optical properties were studied, the output and transfer curves were plotted, and the photoresponse characteristics were analyzed. Furthermore, we calculated the mobility, photoresponsivity and relaxation time: $\mu_e = 1621.0\ \text{cm}^2\text{V}^{-1}\text{s}^{-1}$, $\mu_h = 1228.0\ \text{cm}^2\text{V}^{-1}\text{s}^{-1}$, R~1AW^{-1}, $\tau_1 = 0.7s$, $\tau_2 = 2.4s$. Through the data, it can be concluded that FEpTs based on the graphene and PbSe QDs achieved excellent performances with high mobility of electrons and holes and great light responsivity. It is ensured that the FEpTs based on graphene-quantum dot hybrids will have a promising future.

References

1. X. Song, Y. Zhang, R. Wang, M. Cao, Y. Che, J. Wang, H. Wang, L. Jin, H. Dai, X. Ding, G. Zhang, J. Yao, Bulk- and layer-heterojunction phototransistors based on poly 2-methoxy-5-(2 '-ethylhexyloxy-p-phenylenevinylene) and PbS quantum dot hybrids. *Applied Physics Letters* **106**, (2015); published online EpubJun 22 (10.1063/1.4922917).
2. S. Yigen, V. Tayari, J. O. Island, J. M. Porter, A. R. Champagne, Electronic thermal conductivity measurements in intrinsic graphene. *Physical Review B* **87**, (2013); published online EpubJun 27
3. C. P. Church, E. Muthuswamy, G. M. Zhai, S. M. Kauzlarich, S. A. Carter, Quantum dot Ge/TiO2 heterojunction photoconductor fabrication and performance. *Applied Physics Letters* **103**, (2013); published online EpubNov 25
4. D. Reddy, L. F. Register, G. D. Carpenter, S. K. Banerjee, Graphene field-effect transistors. *J Phys D Appl Phys* **44**, (2011); published online EpubAug 10
5. G. Konstantatos, I. Howard, A. Fischer, S. Hoogland, J. Clifford, E. Klem, L. Levina, E. H. Sargent, Ultrasensitive solution-cast quantum dot photodetectors. *Nature* **442**, 180-183 (2006); published online EpubJul 13
6. Y. Zhang, X. Song, R. Wang, M. Cao, H. Wang, Y. Che, X. Ding, J. Yao, Comparison of photoresponse of transistors based on graphene-quantum dot hybrids with layered and bulk heterojunctions. *Nanotechnology* **26**, (2015); published online EpubAug 21 (10.1088/0957-4484/26/33/335201).
7. Y. Zhang, M. Cao, X. Song, J. Wang, Y. Che, H. Dai, X. Ding, G. Zhang, J. Yao, Multiheterojunction Phototransistors Based on Graphene–PbSe Quantum Dot Hybrids. *The Journal of Physical Chemistry C* **119**, 21739-21743 (2015)10.1021/acs.jpcc.5b07318).
8. A. Varykhalov, M. R. Scholz, T. K. Kim, O. Rader, Effect of noble-metal contacts on doping and band gap of graphene. *Physical Review B* **82**, (2010); published online EpubSep 1
9. R. Wang, Y. T. Zhang, J. Q. Yao, Abnormal Temperature Dependence of Mobility in a Disordered System With Traps: Experiment and Theory. *IEEE Photonics Journal* **7**, 1-8 (2015)10.1109/jphot.2015.2423561).
10. Z. H. Sun, Z. K. Liu, J. H. Li, G. A. Tai, S. P. Lau, F. Yan, Infrared Photodetectors Based on CVD-Grown Graphene and PbS Quantum Dots with Ultrahigh Responsivity. *Adv Mater* **24**, 5878-5883 (2012); published online EpubNov 14

MATEC Web of Conferences 44, 01034 (2016)
DOI: 10.1051/matecconf/20164401034

Design of the adaptive log-domain low-pass filter

Sheng Qian Ma[1,a], Li Rong Zheng[1], Yong Jie Ma[1], Wei Zhao Zhang[1] and Zhi Feng Ma[2]

[1]College of Physics and Electronic Engineering, Northwest Normal University, Lanzhou, China
[2]College of Zhixing, Northwest Normal University, Lanzhou, China

Abstract. This paper presents the structure and realization method of the current-controlled adaptive low-pass filter which based on the design of LC ladder network. After amplifying, amplitude limiting and shaping, the input voltage signal was converted into frequency signal. Then by the broadband frequency-current conversion circuit it was converted into current signal which has a linear relationship with input frequency. The current signal was as the bias current to adjust the cut-off frequency of the log-domain low-pass filter. So that frequency of the filter can automatically track the input signal frequency. In this paper, the design principle was introduced in detail, the design formulas were derived and the circuit of adaptive second order log-domain low-pass filter was given. The filter can realize the scope of the cut-off frequency up to 30MHz. The tracking range for the input frequency is from 1MHz to 30MHz. The simulation results show the effectiveness of design method.

1 Introduction

Filter has a wide range of applications in the fields of the signal processing, the data transmission and interference suppression [1-2]. Especially, adaptive filter plays an important role in the field of the adaptive signal processing and has the distinctive features of filter frequency following the change of input signal frequency automatically [3-4]. When signal processing, the test signal will inevitably be doped with noise. The filter which has fixed frequency can only realize signal filtering within a small frequency range. However, the adaptive filter can change the filter frequency according to the change of the signal, it is good to suppress the noise, and it has good filtering performance.

At present, there are many kinds of methods to implement analog adaptive filter. The first is the state variable method which can realize low-pass, high-pass, band-pass, band-stop and all-pass filter simultaneously, but the design and debug are troublesome and difficult to control, and besides the components are discrete and the non-linear effects are large [5-7]. The second method is the voltage-controlled method. Using this method, the offset voltage and drift will directly affect the stability of the low frequency [8-9]. The third method is using existing integrated filter chip. This method does not require to know the signal frequency in advance, the stability is better and cut-off or central frequency is controllable, but there are some large circuit noise and signal aliasing problems in the course of the use, even through clock frequency or pin programming is difficult to achieve the filter cut-off frequency or central frequency continuous change [10-12]. If the signal frequency changes in a wide range, the above three tracking methods are unable to achieve the fast tracking of the signal frequency. Log-domain filter is a current mode circuit in the true sense, which has been widely used in electronic systems by virtue of the advantages of power supply voltage, low power consumption, wide dynamic range, high frequency, wide tuning range and good linearity, and improves signal processing accuracy further [13-14]. This paper presents a design method of analog adaptive filter which use high-performance broadband frequency current converter (F/I) circuit, combined with the log-domain filter with transistors as the core elements to achieve the analog filter whose cut-off frequency can fast adapt the change of processed signal frequency automatically. The design of log-domain adaptive filter compared to other adaptive filters, it has the advantages of a low power consumption, high filtering frequency, wide dynamic range and low distortion. It can be applied in these cases: a wide range of signal frequency changing, a high-speed of the filtering, and filter frequency is not fixed.

2 Working principle

The principle diagram of the adaptive log-domain low-pass filter is shown in figure 1. The input voltage signal V_i gets through the amplifier to output voltage signal V_x .Then the voltage signal V_x is divided into two paths, the first will get through the limiting circuit and over-voltage comparison circuit which MAX903 is the core component to be shaped to send signal into the broadband F/I circuit, and then the bias current signal I_B output from

[a] Corresponding author: s.q.ma@163.com

F/I circuit is sent to the log-domain low-pass filter to control the cut-off frequency. The other one will get through the voltage current conversion (V/I) circuit to send current signal i_i into the logarithmic compression circuit to be pre-processed, and then the logarithmic compression circuit output current signal i is as the input signal of the log-domain low-pass filter.

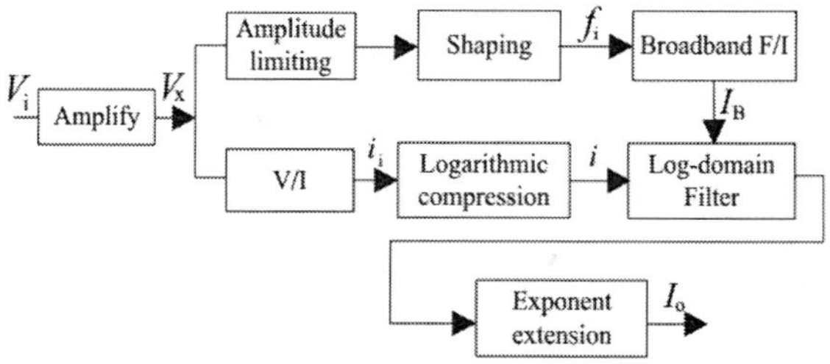

Figure 1. The diagram of adaptive log-domain low-pass filter.

2.1 Broadband frequency current conversion(F/I) circuit

The principle diagram of the broadband F/I circuit is shown in figure 2, which consists of the main control circuit, the frequency division circuit, the F/I circuit and the current amplification circuit. Since the chip AD650 which in the F/I circuit maximum switching frequency is 1MHz, so the high frequency signal to be processed first need dividing frequency after shaping. The principle of realizing broadband F/I circuit is the processed frequency signal f_i after shaping first gets through 400 frequency division circuit to send signal f_{i1} into main control circuit in which control chip is 89s52. Main control circuit calculates and compares parameters in its internal to choose the appropriate frequency division multiple, and then controls frequency division circuit to re-divide frequency for the signal after shaping. Meanwhile, it controls current amplification circuit to generate the corresponding magnification. The re-divided frequency signal gets through F/I circuit to convert frequency signal to current signal, and it will go into current amplification circuit. The I_B is output current of broadband F/I circuit.

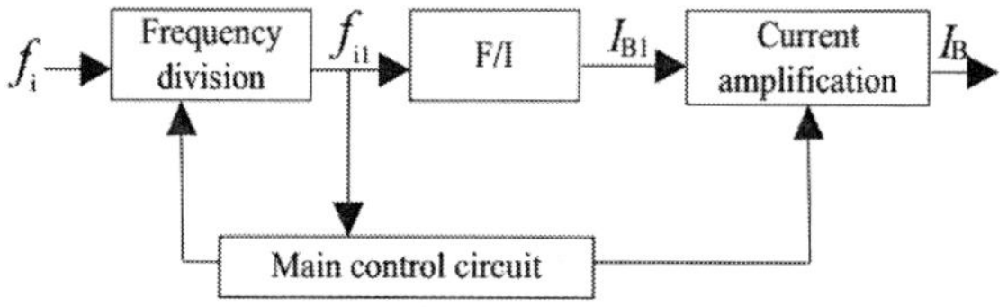

Figure 2. The diagram of broadband frequency-current conversion circuit.

The F/I of figure 2 is shown in figure 3, it converts input pulse signal into current signal. Input pulse frequency has a linear relationship with output current value, so it is possible to measure the input pulse frequency indirectly by measuring the output current value. F/I circuit is composed of the frequency voltage (F/V) conversion chip AD650, operational amplifier OP37 and a small amount of resistors and capacitors.

In figure 3, the input pulse f_{i1} through the coupling capacitor C_1 to be sent into AD650 internal comparator, when its potential is low to the comparator reference potential (-0.6V), internal current switch to end of integral capacitor C_{INT} and charge for it. When the leakage current on R_4 and the charging current on C_{INT} is equal, the voltage on the C_{INT} is stability. The output voltage U_i of pin 1 is proportional to the input frequency f_{i1}, that is

$$U_i = t_{OS}\times R_{INT}\times f_{i1} = (C_{OS}\times 6.8\times 10^3 + 3.0\times 10^{-7})\times R_4\times f_{i1} \quad (1)$$

Then input U_i into the subsequent V/I circuit in which operational amplifier OP37 is as the core component.

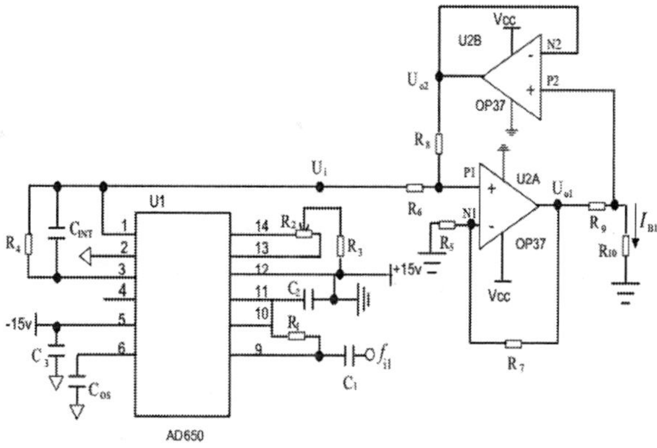

Figure 3. F/I circuit.

For the op-amp U2A and U2B, it can obtain

$$U_{O1} = (R_7 / R_5 + 1)U_{P1} \quad (2)$$

$$U_{P1} = U_i R_8 / (R_6 + R_8) + U_{P2} R_6 / (R_6 + R_8) \quad (3)$$

The voltage on R_9 is $U_{R9} = U_{o1} - U_{P2}$, the eqution (2) and (3) are substituted into U_{R9}, it can deduce

$$U_{R_9} = (1 + R_7 / R_5)[U_i R_8 / (R_6 + R_8) + U_{P2} R_6 / (R_6 + R_8)] - U_{P2} \quad (4)$$

When taking $R_5 = R_6 = R_7 = R_8 = 47K$, then $U_{R9} = U_i$, it can deduce

$$I_{B1} = U_{R_9} / R_9 = U_i / R_9 \quad (5)$$

The eqution (1) is substituted into eqution (5), and due to $I_B = mI_{B1}$, $f_i = mf_{i1}$, in figure 2, m=400. it can deduce

$$I_B = [(C_{OS}\times 6.8\times 10^3 + 3.0\times 10^{-7})\times R_4 / R_9]\times f_i \quad (6)$$

It can be seen from eqution (6) the output current will change linearly with input frequency as long as adjusting the value of resistors and capacitors reasonably.

2.2 Log-domain filter

There is a strict logarithmic relationship between the input voltage and output current of the transistor $v_{BE} = V_T \ln(I_C/I_S)$. According to the characteristics, people use

transistors as core component to build the log-domain filter circuit, so as to realize linear circuits by using nonlinear components. Compared with the traditional filter, log-domain filter has advantages in the frequency characteristic, processing speed, and signal bandwidth. It can meet the requirements of wide tuning range and good linearity when the modern electronic products work under the condition of low voltage.

Log-domain filter is composed of logarithmic compression circuit, the state space of nonlinear filter circuit and the exponent extension circuit, its composition block diagram is shown in figure 4. Input current signal gets through the logarithmic compression circuit to be processed and converted into a logarithmic domain. Weak signals are amplified to a much greater than the noise signal level, and strong signals are compressed to less than distortion level, thus preventing signal distortion and expanding the dynamic range of the circuit. After logarithmic compression circuit processing, the output voltage signal is processed by the state space nonlinear filtering circuit realized by bipolar transistors, so can make the system achieve a particular filtering function. The signal after filtering is decompressed by the exponent extension circuit and converted into a linear domain. Namely process signal nonlinearly again, the weak signal is attenuated, and the strong signal is amplified, so as to restore the proportion of the original signal, making the system into a linear system.

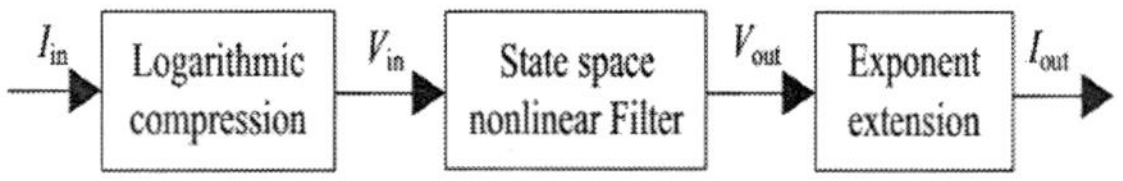

Figure 4. The diagram of log-domain filter.

3 Design of adaptive second-order log-domain low-pass filter

The proposed adaptive second-order log-domain low-pass filter is designed based on LC ladder network, mainly using the broadband F/I circuit, V/I circuit, the transistors, and a small amount of resistors and capacitors. The low-pass LC ladder prototype circuit is shown in figure 5.

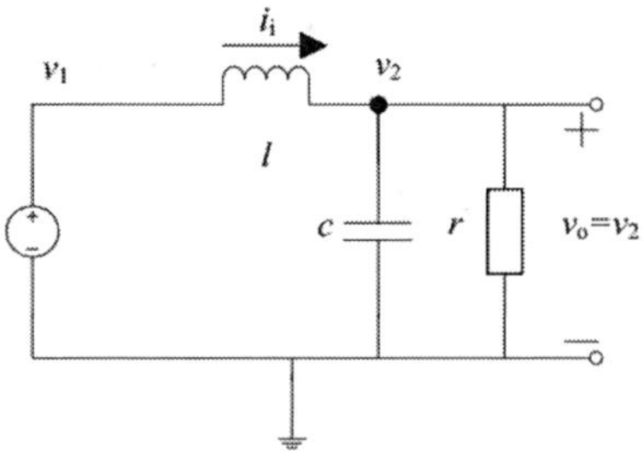

Figure 5. Prototype circuit of low-pass LC ladder.

The transfer function of the LC ladder prototype circuit is:

$$H(s)=V_o(s)/V_i(s)=[1/(lc)]/[s^2+s/(rc)+1/(lc)] \qquad (7)$$

And the transfer function of the standard low-pass filter is:

$$H(s)=K\omega_0^2/(s^2+s\omega_0/Q+\omega_0^2) \qquad (8)$$

Comparing the eqution (7) with (8), it can deduce cut-off frequency ω_0 of LC ladder filter:

$$\omega_0=1/\sqrt{lc} \qquad (9)$$

quality factor $Q=r\sqrt{c/l}$ and dc gain K=1.

The log-domain filter corresponding to the LC ladder filter is shown in figure 6, it is made up of transistors and a small amount of capacitors.

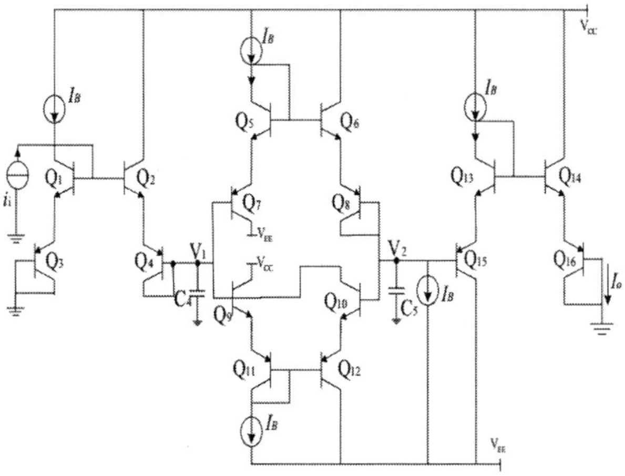

Figure 6. The circuit of log-domain filter.

The in-phase integrator which is composed by transistors Q1-Q4 and capacitor C_4 implement in-phase integral operation and logarithmic operation for the input current i_i. Transistors Q9-Q12 and capacitor C_5 realize inverse integral operation to voltage V_2. Transistors Q13-Q16 controlled by the bias current compose exponent extension circuit. I_B is produced by figure 2, which is as the bias current control end of the log-domain filter.

According to Kirchhoff's law for capacitor C_4 node, we can obtain:

$$C_4dV_1/dt=i_ie^{-V_1/2V_T}+I_Be^{-V_1/2V_T}-I_Be^{(V_2-V_1)/2V_T} \qquad (10)$$

On both ends of eqution (10) multiplied by $e^{V_1/2V_T}$ at the same time and adjust the order, it can deduce

$$2C_4V_T/I_B\cdot[d/dt(I_Be^{V_1/2V_T}-I_B)]=i_i-I_Be^{V_2/2V_T}+I_B \qquad (11)$$

In addition, the LOG and EXP mapping function is:

$$\mathrm{LOG}(x)=2V_T\ln[(I_B+x)/I_B] \quad \mathrm{EXP}(x)=I_Be^{x/2V_T}-I_B \qquad (12)$$

The eqution (12) is substituted into eqution (11), it can deduce

$$\mathrm{EXP}(V_1)=I_B/(2V_TC_4)\cdot\int[i_i-\mathrm{EXP}(V_2)i_i]dt \qquad (13)$$

From figure 5, we can obtain:

$$\text{EXP}(V_1) = 1/l \cdot \int [i_i - \text{EXP}(V_2)] dt \tag{14}$$

Comparing the eqution (13) with eqution (14), it can deduce

$$l = 2V_T C_4 / I_B \tag{15}$$

By the same token, writing KCL equation of capacitor C_5 node and using the LOG and EXP mapping function, we can get:

$$\text{EXP}(V_2) = I_B / (2V_T C_5) \cdot \int [\text{EXP}(V_1) - \text{EXP}(V_2)] dt \tag{16}$$

From figure 5, we can obtain:

$$\text{EXP}(V_2) = 1/c \cdot \int [\text{EXP}(V_1) - 1/r\text{EXP}(V_2)] dt \tag{17}$$

When taking r = 1Ω, comparing the eqution (16) with eqution (17), it can deduce

$$c = 2V_T C_5 / I_B \tag{18}$$

The eqution (15) and (18) are substituted into eqution (9), it can obtain

$$\omega_0 = I_B / (2V_T \sqrt{C_4 C_5}) \tag{19}$$

quality factor $Q = \sqrt{C_5 / C_4}$ and dc gain K=1.

so the cut-off frequency of log-domain filter is:

$$f_0 = \omega_0 / 2\pi = I_B / (4\pi V_T \sqrt{C_4 C_5}) \tag{20}$$

The eqution (6) is substituted into eqution (20), it can deduce

$$f_0 = [(C_{OS} \times 6.8 \times 10^3 + 3.0 \times 10^{-7}) \times R_4] / (4\pi V_T R_9 \sqrt{C_4 C_5}) \times f_i \tag{21}$$

It can be seen from eqution (21) that the cut-off frequency of the filter designed will change linearly with input frequency as long as adjusting the value of capacitors and resistors reasonably.

4 Experimental result

Design frequency range of the filter from 1MHz to 30MHz. When taking C_{OS} = 53pf, $C_4 = C_5$ = 1010pf, R_4 = 100Ω, R_9 = 200KΩ, R_1 = 2.2KΩ, R_2 = 20KΩ, R_3 = 250KΩ, C_1 = 1000pf, $C_2 = C_3$ = 0.1uf, C_{INT} = 3.3pf, R_{10} = 500Ω, then according to eqution（21）, it can deduce

$$f_0 = f_i \tag{22}$$

The above parameters are substituted into the eqution (20), it can deduce $f_0 = 3.03\times10^9 I_B$. The input current signal is taken 500uA, the control bias current I_B are taken 330uA, 990uA, 3300uA, 6600uA, 9900uA, the simulation results with ORCAD are shown in figure 7.

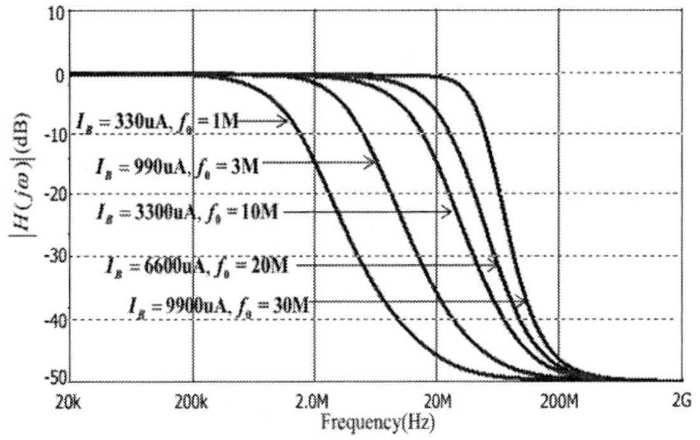

Figure 7. The amplitude-frequency responses of the log-domain second-order low-pass filter.

According to figure 7, the analysis of second-order low-pass log-domain filter performance is shown in table 1, including the bias current corresponding to the input frequency, cut-off frequency and stop-band attenuation rate.

Table 1. The performance of the filter.

Input frequency (f_i / MHz)	Bias current (I_B / uA)	Cut-off frequency (f_0 / MHz)	Stop-band attenuation rate(dB/decade)
1	330	1	40
3	990	3	40
10	3300	10	45
20	6600	20	45
30	9900	30	45

Analysis the experimental results, it can obtain: the cut-off frequency f_0 of the designed second-order low-pass log-domain filter changes along with the change of the input bias current I_B, and has a linear relationship with I_B. When the frequency of the input signal is small, the attenuation of amplitude frequency characteristics of the filter in stop-band is not very good. When the input frequency increasing, the cut-off frequency of low-pass filter also increases accordingly, the amplitude frequency characteristics within the pass-band is relatively flat, in the stop-band attenuation rate is also increasing, the attenuation is very good. Transformation precision of the transistor is the main affecting factor. Can be seen from the overall result, the cut-off frequency of second-order low-pass log-domain filter can vary with the change of the input signal frequency, namely realizing automatic adjustment of the cut-off frequency to the input signal frequency.

5 Conclusion

The design method of this paper is to convert the signal frequency into current value through the broadband F/I

circuit. The current signal, which is input into the bias current control end of the log-domain filter, controls the cut-off frequency of filter, so as to achieve automatic adaptation of the filter's frequency. The actual circuit structure is designed. When the input signal changes in frequency range from 1MHz to 30MHz, the cut-off frequency of the adaptive second-order low-pass filter can automatically adapt to the change of the input signal frequency. From software simulation test of the circuit, it can see the waveform is good, and the filter amplitude-frequency characteristics within the pass-band is relatively flat, the attenuation in stop-band is good, proved the correctness of the circuit and the validity of the design. In this paper, the designed adaptive second-order log-domain low-pass filter is mainly composed of the broadband F/I circuit, V/I circuit, transistors and a small amount of resistors and capacitors. The structure of circuit is simple and easy to adjust. And the filter system has broad filtering bandwidth, good real-time dynamic characteristics, and can be widely used in all aspects of the sensor data processing. It resolves the problem of the measured signal frequency changing in a wide range.

Acknowledgement

The authors are thankful to the Natural Science Foundation of China (61162017) and Northwest Normal University NWNU-LKQN-13-16.

References

1. D. Yang, J.Y. Wang, F. Cai. Journal of detection and control, **32(3)**: 79-82 (2010)
2. S.Q. Ma, X.P. Ran, M.H. Fan. Piezoelectric and light, **35(2)**: 245-249 (2013)
3. Rola A, Mourad N. IEEE Journal of solid-state circuits, **38(2)**: 205–215 (2003)
4. T.F. Wang, T.S. Wang, Z.Y. Zhang. Mechanical and electrical engineering, **32(9)**:1267-1270 (2015)
5. H.L. Cheng, W.Z. Ge. Semiconductor integrated circuit, **38(3)**: 173-188 (2013)
6. L. Cai, X.K. Ma. Journal of xi 'an jiaotong university, **37(10)**: 1075-1078 (2003)
7. J.J. CHU, Z.Y. Xiao, H. Li. Journal of Shanghai university (natural science edition), **20(1)**: 1-8 (2014)
8. L. Zhang, Y.C. Zeng, H.J. Yang. Microelectronics, **39(3)**: 380-384 (2009)
9. C. Kasimis, G. Souliotis, C. Psychalinos. International journal of electronics, **99(2)**: 197-209 (2012)
10. M. Li, Z. Wang, Y.Q. Shao. Laboratory research and exploration, **33(8)**: 89-92 (2014)
11. N.A. Shah, S.Z. Iqbal, N. Parveen. Analog integrated circuits and signal processing, **67(1)**: 85-88 (2011)
12. X.Y. Wang, H.G. Yang, T. Yin. Microelectronics and computer, **29(7)**: 18-22 (2012)
13. A.U. Cam. Analog integr circ sig process, **60**: 221-229 (2009)
14. S.M. Maria Cristina Piccirilli. Circuits syst signal process, **30**: 371-389 (2011)

MATEC Web of Conferences **44**, 01035 (2016)
DOI: 10.1051/matecconf/20164401035

Design of Self-tracking High-pass Filter

Wei Zhao Zhang[1,2,a], Jin Long Li[3], Man Hong Fan[1,2] and Sheng Qian Ma[1,2]

[1]*College of Physics and Electronic Engineering, Northwest Normal University, 730070 Lanzhou, China*
[2]*Key Laboratory of Atomic and Molecular Physics & Functional Materials of Gansu Province, 730070 Lanzhou, China*
[3]*College of Electronic Engineering, Lanzhou Institute of Technology, 730050 Lanzhou, China*

Abstract. A novel self-tracking high-pass filter by using analog multiplier and current feedback op-Amp (CFA) is proposed in this paper. The frequency-voltage (F/V) converter transforms the input pulse signal into the voltage, and then the output of F/V converter controls the cut-off frequency of voltage controlled high-pass filter. Thus, the cut-off frequency of designed filter is linear with the frequency of input signal in case that resistors and capacitors are reasonable adjusted. The experiment and simulation results show that the cut-off frequency of designed filter is 1 kHz-100 kHz.

1 Introduction

Filters are widely used in information processing, automatic control, communications, and other fields. In the process of signal transmission, the signal is usually contaminated by noise. Using filtering technology can extract the useful signal, while suppressing the noise. The fixed cut-off frequency filter can be used in the situation of narrow range of the signal frequency. The frequency of the input signal often changes with the time. Therefore, the fixed cut-off frequency of the filter is difficult to meet the requirements. A self-tracking high-pass filter is proposed in this paper, and its cut-off frequency follows the frequency of the input signal.

There are three ways to regulate the cut-off frequency of filter. Firstly, the cut-off frequency of filter can be adjusted by variable resistors and capacitors [1, 2]. In these filters, the cut-off frequency can only take the limited discrete value. What's more, variable resistors and capacitors may be cause unpredictable effects on signal amplitude and phase. Secondly, filter can be realized by the current mode technique, the cut-off frequency can be adjusted by bias current [3-6]. In these circuits, floating capacitor is used, and X terminal of the CCII is connected with a capacitor, which is easy to cause the circuit self-oscillates. Thirdly, the monolithic active filter chip, such as MAX26X, MAX29X, MAX27X, can be used [7, 8]. Although the cut-off frequency of these chips can be programmed (generally less than 1MHz), it is difficult to realize the continuous adjustment of the cut-off frequency. In this paper, a new self-tracking high-pass filter is proposed. It is based on the high performance of F/V converter LM331, the analog multiplier MLT04 and CFA (AD8001). The cut-off frequency of filter can automatically follows the frequency variation of input signal.

[a] Corresponding author: zhangweizhao163@163.com

2 The principle of self-tracking high-pass filter

The principle of self-tracking high-pass filter is shown in figure 1, which is composed of six parts: signal conditioning circuit, shaping circuit, F/V converter, programmable gain amplifier, control circuits based on FPGA and voltage controlled high-pass filter. At first, the input signal (V_{in}) amplified by signal conditioning circuit is converted into rectangular wave by shaping circuit. Since the bandwidth of F/V converter is no more than 3MHz, the frequency dividing circuit is designed, which scales down the frequency of input signal to the bandwidth range of F/V converter. Then the output voltage of F/V converter (V_f) multiplied frequency dividing coefficients is frequency-voltage conversion of the input signal. At last, the cut-off frequency of high-pass filter is continuously controlled by adjusting V_f. In order to realize the fast and real-time measurement, the frequency measurement circuit and frequency dividing circuit are designed by FPGA.

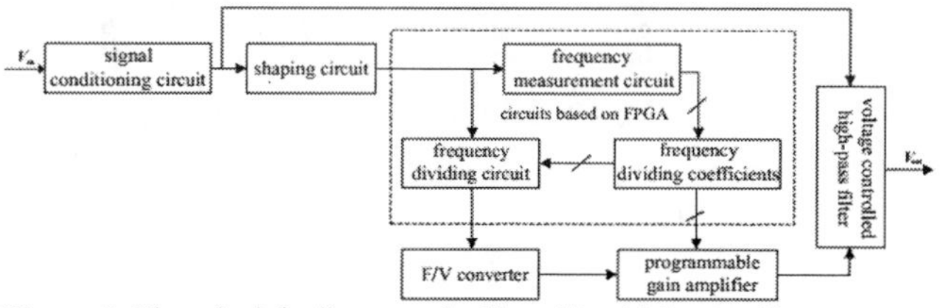

Figure 1. The principle diagram of self-tracking high-pass filter

2.1 Wide-band signal conditioning circuit

The wide-band signal conditioning circuit mainly realizes the gain adjustment of the input signal, including the

variable gain control circuit and the fixed gain control circuit. The circuit diagram is shown in figure 2(a) and figure 2(b). The AD603 is a low noise, voltage-controlled amplifier for using in RF and IF AGC systems. It provides accurate, pin-selectable gains of −11 dB to +31 dB with a bandwidth of 90 MHz or 0~+40dB with a bandwidth of 30 MHz or +9 dB to 51+ dB with a bandwidth of 9 MHz. The variable gain control circuit consists of two pieces of cascaded AD603 at the gain of −11 dB to +31 dB with a bandwidth of 90 MHz. Thus, the voltage gain of -20dB~60dB can be realized by adjusting the voltage of VREF1_0 and VREF2_0. The gain of the fixed gain control circuit is 12db.

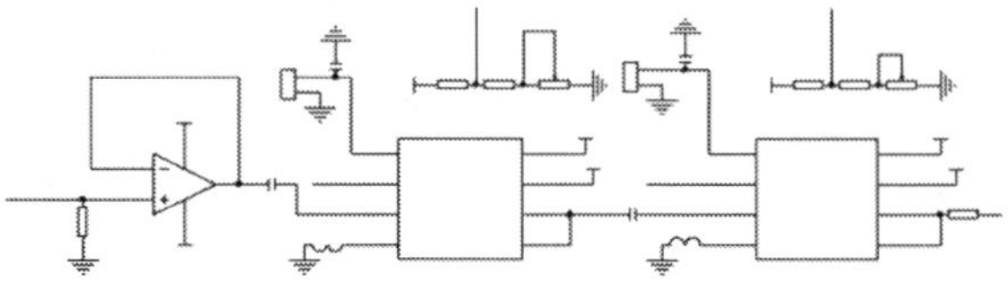

Figure 2(a). The variable gain control circuit

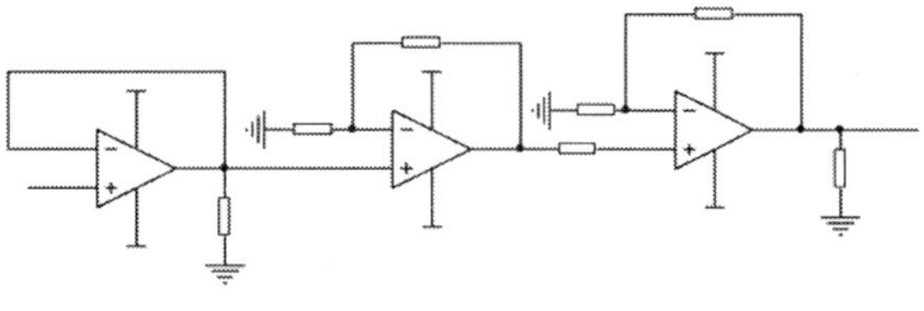

Figure 2(b). The fixed gain control circuit

The Amplitude-frequency characteristic curve of signal conditioning circuit measured by the 3577A HP network analyzer is shown in figure 3. The analysis shows that the 3dB cut-off frequency of signal conditioning circuit can reach 70MHz with the 55dB gain of voltage.

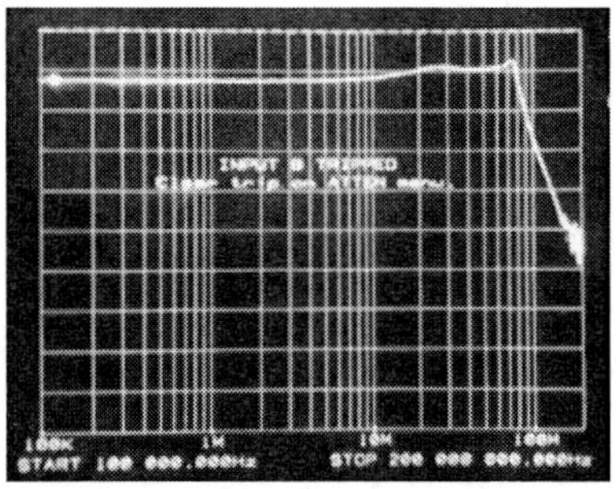

Figure 3. The Amplitude-frequency characteristic curve of signal conditioning circuit

2.2 F/V converter

F/V converter transforms the input pulse signal into voltage output. The output voltage is linear with the frequency of input pulse signal. Thus, the frequency of input pulse signal can be measured indirectly by measuring the output voltage of F/V converter. The F/V converter consists of LM331, a few resistors and capacitors [9].

The relationship between the output voltage V_f and the input frequency f_i of F/V converter can be expressed as:

$$V_f = \frac{2.09 * R_L * R_t * C_t}{R_s} * f_i \tag{1}$$

Where $R_s = R_{s1} + R_{s2}$.From (1) the output voltage V_f is linear with the input frequency f_i in case that resistors and capacitors are reasonable adjusted.

2.3 Analog multiplier

The MLT04 is a complete, four-channel, voltage output analog multiplier. The input voltage range of MLT04 is -2.5V ~ +2.5V, DC and AC is allowed. Without considering of the nonlinearity of MLT04, the output voltage of MLT04 can be given as:

$$V_w = 0.4V_x * V_y \tag{2}$$

The combination of MLT04 and operational amplifier can also constitute analog divider as shown in figure 4:

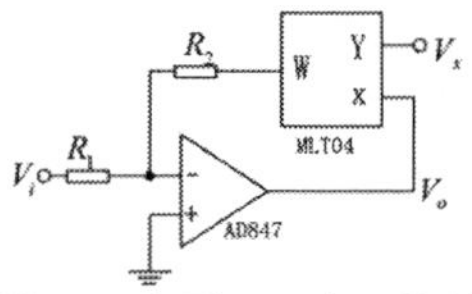

Figure 4. The analog divider

Defining equation can be given as:

$$V_0 = -\frac{2.5R_2V_i}{R_1V_x} \tag{3}$$

Here, $R_1 = R_2$ is chosen, the equation can be written as:

$$V_o = -\frac{2.5V_i}{V_x} \tag{4}$$

3 The principle and design of self-tracking filter

3.1 The self-tracking first-order filter

As shown in figure 5, the self-tracking first-order high-pass filter circuit consists of F/V converter, an analog divider, an operational amplifier, a few resistances and capacitances. U3 (MLT04), U4 (AD8001), a few capacitances and resistances constitute first-order voltage controlled high-pass filter. U1 (AD847) and U2 (MLT04) constitute divider. The control voltage V_f is from the output of F/V converter [10].

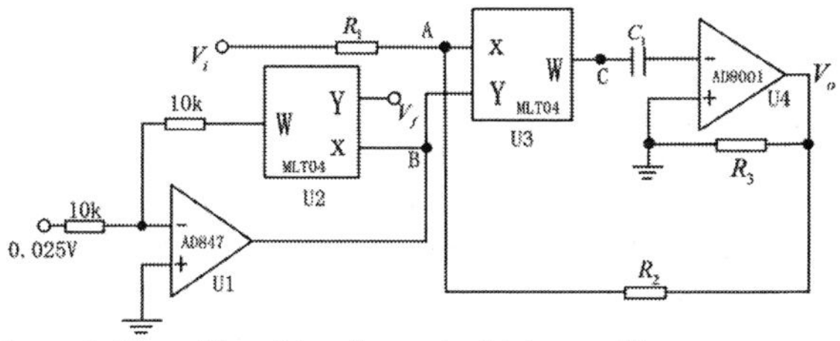

Figure 5. The self-tracking first-order high-pass filter

According to Kirchhoff's law and figure 5, the transfer function can be expressed as:

$$H(s)=\frac{V_o}{V_i}=\frac{\frac{R_2}{R_1}s}{s+\frac{40V_f(R_1+R_2)}{R_1R_3C_1}} \quad (5)$$

Therefore, the 3dB cut-off frequency f_0 and the gain factor a_0 of this transfer function can be given as:

$$f_0=\frac{20V_f(R_1+R_2)}{\pi R_1R_3C_1} \quad (6)$$

$$a_0=\frac{R_2}{R_1} \quad (7)$$

The sensitivity of components is $S_{R_1}^{f_0}=0$, $S_{R_2}^{f_0}=1$, $S_{R_3}^{f_0}=S_{C_1}^{f_0}=-1$. It shows that the change of component value has little effect on the performance of filter. Here, $R_1=R_2=R_3=R$ is chosen, the equation (6) can be written as:

$$f_0=\frac{40V_f}{\pi RC_1} \quad (8)$$

The equation (9) can be derived from equation (8) and equation (1):

$$f_0=\frac{40*2.09R_tR_LC_tf_i}{\pi RC_1R_s} \quad (9)$$

From (9), it can be known that the 3dB cut-off frequency f_0 is linear with the input frequency f_i in case that resistors and capacitors are reasonable adjusted.

3.2 The self-tracking second-order filter

As shown in figure 6, a second-order voltage controlled high-pass filter is implemented by using three AD8001s, two MLT04s, a few resistances and capacitances. The control voltage V_f is from the output of F/V converter.

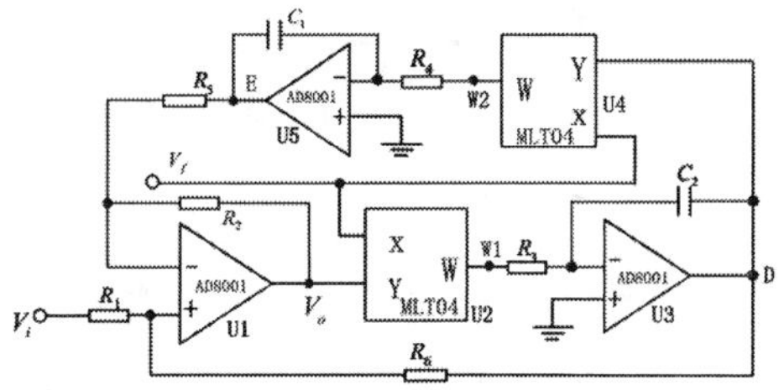

Figure 6. The self-tracking second-order high-pass filter

According to Kirchhoff's law and figure 6, the transfer function can be expressed as:

$$H(S)=\frac{\frac{R_6(R_2+R_5)}{R_5(R_1+R_6)}s^2}{s^2+\frac{V_fR_1(R_2+R_5)s}{2.5R_3R_5(R_1+R_6)C_2}+\frac{V_f{}^2R_2}{(2.5)^2R_3R_4R_5C_1C_2}} \quad (10)$$

Therefore, the 3dB cut-off frequency f_0 and the gain factor a_0 of this transfer functions can be given as:

$$f_0=\frac{V_f}{5\pi}\sqrt{\frac{R_2}{R_3R_4R_5C_1C_2}} \quad (11)$$

$$a=\frac{R_6(R_2+R_5)}{R_5(R_1+R_6)} \quad (12)$$

The sensitivity of components is $S_{R_2}^{f_0}=\frac{1}{2}$, $S_{R_3}^{f_0}=S_{R_4}^{f_0}=S_{R_5}^{f_0}=S_{C_1}^{f_0}=S_{C_2}^{f_0}=-\frac{1}{2}$. It shows that the change of component value has little effect on the performance of filter. Here, $R_2=R_3=R_4=R_5=R$, $C_1=C_2=C$ is chosen, the equation (11) can be written as:

$$f_0=\frac{V_f}{5\pi RC} \quad (13)$$

The equation (14) can be derived from equation (13) and equation (1):

$$f_0=\frac{2.09R_tR_LC_tf_i}{5\pi RCR_s} \quad (14)$$

From (14), it can be known that the 3dB cut-off frequency f_0 is linear with the input frequency f_i in case that resistors and capacitors are reasonable adjusted.

4 Simulation result

As the maximum input voltage of MLT04 is 2.5V, the 3dB cut-off frequency of filter is 1 kHz-100 kHz. As to first-order high-pass filter, when taking $C=C_t=10nF$, $R_t=910\Omega$, $R_L=18.73k\Omega$, $R_s=14.25k\Omega$ and $R=31.84k\Omega$, the equation (9) becomes to be : $f_0=f_i$.

When taking the frequency of input signal is 1kHz, 5kHz, 10kHz, 50kHz, 100kHz, the amplitude-frequency characteristic curve of first-order high-pass filter is shown in figure 7 by the PSPICE simulations.

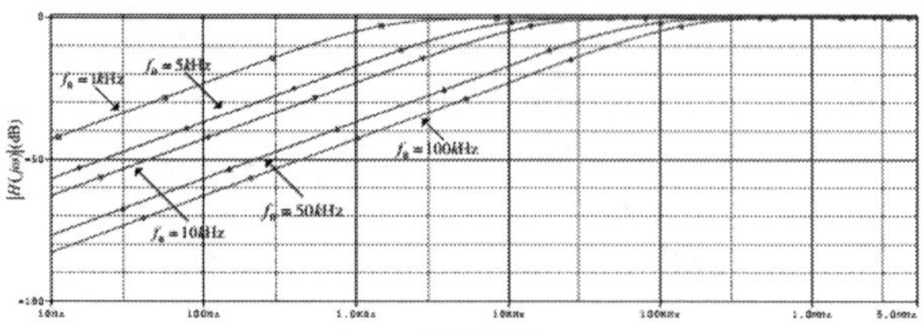

Figure 7. The amplitude-frequency characteristic curve of first-order high-pass filter

When taking the frequency of input signal is 1kHz, 5kHz, 10kHz, 50kHz, 100kHz, the experiments comparison of f_i and f_0 of first-order high-pass filter is shown in table 1, δ is the relative error.

Table1. The experiments comparison of f_i and f_0 of first-order high-pass filter

f_i (kHz)	1	5	10	50	100
f_0 (kHz)	0.991	4.898	9.887	49.885	99.882
δ (%)	0.9	2.04	1.13	0.23	0.12

As to the second-order high-pass filter, when taking $C = C_t = 10nF$, $R_t = 910\Omega$, $R_L = 18.73k\Omega$, $R_s = 14.25k\Omega$ and $R = 159\Omega$, the equation (14) becomes to be : $f_0 = f_i$.

When taking the frequency of input signal is 1kHz, 5kHz, 10kHz, 50kHz, 100kHz, the amplitude-frequency characteristic curve of second-order high-pass filter is shown in figure 8 by the PSPICE simulations.

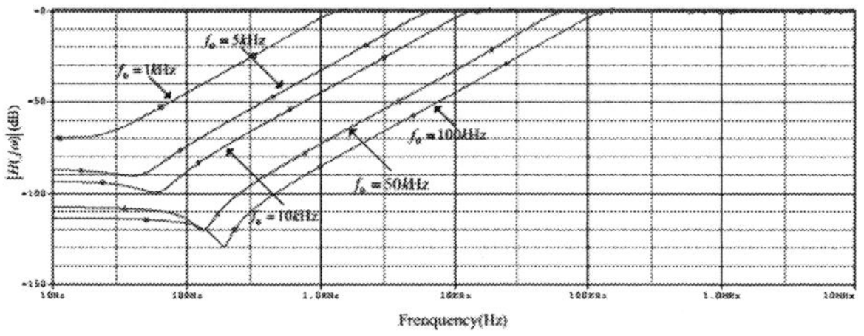

Figure 8. The amplitude-frequency characteristic curve of second-order high-pass filter

When taking the frequency of input signal is 1kHz, 5kHz, 10kHz, 50kHz, 100kHz, the experiments comparison of f_i and f_0 of second-order high-pass filter is shown in table 2, δ is the relative error.

Table2. The experiments comparison of f_i and f_0 of second-order high-pass filter

f_i (kHz)	1	5	10	50	100
f_0 (kHz)	0.989	4.892	9.881	49.878	99.872
δ (%)	1.10	2.16	1.19	0.24	0.13

From the above simulation and experiment results, it can be seen that the cut-off frequency of designed filter can be adjusted automatically according to the input signal frequency.

5 Conclusion

In this paper, a self-tracking high-pass filter by using analog multiplier and CFA is proposed. Firstly, the F/V converter transforms the input pulse signal into output voltage V_f . Then the cut-off frequency of voltage controlled high-pass filter is controlled by V_f . The simulation and experiment results show that the cut-off frequency of designed filter is 1 kHz-100 kHz. If using the higher frequency characteristics of analog multiplier (i.e., AD835), the cut-off frequency of filter can be extended 30MHz.

Acknowledgement

The authors are thankful to the Natural Science Foundation of China (61162017) and Northwest Normal University NWNU-LKQN-13-16.

References

1. W. Z. Zhang , S. Q. Ma, X. P. Ran. Application of Electronic Technology, **37**(07), 97-99 (2011).
2. J. Guo, Y. Jia, J. Teng, Q. Li. Chinese Journal of Scientific Instrument, **3**(3), 295-297 (2006).
3. W. Sa-Ngiamvibool, B. Srisuchinwong. AEU - International Journal of Electronics and Communications, **61**(5), 307-313 (2007).
4. Z. Ali, T. Ali. International Journal of Electronics, **89**(12), 913-923 (2002).
5. L. Y. Peng, Y. He, M. C. Huang, J. WU. Acta Electronica Sinica,**31**(8), 1234-1236 (2003).
6. A. M. Soliman. International Journal of Circuit Theory & Applications, **35**(4), 463–467 (2007).
7. S. M. Yin, B. Ji, H. L. Bao. J. L. Liu, J. G. Zhang. Application of Electronic Technology, **1**(1), 54-56 (2012).
8. W. S. Wang. *University of Electronic Science and Technology of China.* (2010).
9. S. Q. Ma, X. P. Ran, M. H. Fan, W. Z. Zhang. Piezoelectrics & Acoustooptics, **46**(10), 969-971 (2013).
10. X. P. Ran, S. Q. Ma, J. F. Liu, W. Z. Zhang. *Unifying Electrical Engineering and Electronics Engineering.* Springer New York **4**,1733-1741 (2014).

MATEC Web of Conferences 44, 01036 (2016)
DOI: 10.1051/matecconf/20164401036

Analysis of Location Ambiguity, GDOP and Station Layout of Three-station in Multilateration

Zi Li Xu[1], Dong Lin He[1], Jing Li[1,a], Yong Tang[1] and Jian Hong Yang[1]

[1]R&D Center, the 2nd Research Institute of Civil Aviation Administration of China(CAAC),Chengdu, Sichuan Province, China

Abstract. In practice, the two-dimensional TDOA source location in the case of three stations would encounter the ambiguity problem of dual solutions. The relationship between distributions of location curve intersections, GDOP and receiving station layout is numerically analyzed, namely the distributions of location curve intersections and GDOP are determined by the receiving station layout, and the areas of two curve intersections are consistent with these of larger GDOP. These analysis results could serve as reference for avoiding or dealing with the ambiguity problem when multilateration is in application.

1 Introduction

When the multilateration system is applied to actual target positioning, it will inevitably cause that three receiving stations are only used for two-dimensional target positioning no matter in consideration of cost-effectiveness or actual environmental limitation. Even for three-station positioning of three-dimensional target not complying with the positioning principle, as target barometric altitude can often be obtained in practice[1,2], three-dimensional positioning equation can be reduced to two-dimensional positioning equation to realize accurate positioning of target[3], therefore, three-station target positioning has a important place in actual application of multilateration technology.

In hyperbolic multilateration system, target position is obtained through the intersection of hyperbolic curve determined by solving positioning equation. Under the situation of only three receiving stations receiving the target signal, the positioning curve intersection situation is also different due to different relative location between the target and the receiving stations, namely, the positioning curves may generate a point of intersection and also may generate two points of intersection. If the positioning curves generate two points of intersection, it is very difficult to judge which point of intersection is the target's actual position without any prior verification information of the target, in other words, ambiguity appears in solving the target position. However, through analysis on the relationship between three-station positioning curve intersection point distribution, GDOP distribution and stations layout, three-station positioning ambiguity problem can be effectively avoided and target positioning accuracy can be improved by reasonably selecting stations layout.

2 Numerical simulation analysis of three-station positioning curves intersections point distribution

For multilateration three-station positioning two-dimensional target, the target position can be obtained by the point of intersection determined by the positioning equation

$$\sqrt{(x_i-x)^2+(y_i-y)^2}-\sqrt{(x_j-x)^2+(y_j-y)^2}=c\cdot TDOA_{ij},\quad i,j=1,2,3,\ i\neq j \qquad (1)$$

Where, (x,y) is position coordinates of the target to be positioned, (x_i,y_i) is position coordinates of the receiving stations, $TDOA_{ij}$ is time difference of arrival (TDOA) between the target signal reaching station i and station j , c is signal velocity. Equation (1) determines two independent positioning equations, corresponding to two independent positioning hyperbolic curves. Besides it may result in no point of intersection between two positioning curves due to too large measurement error of Time Difference of Arrival (TDOA) of the signal in practice, with different relative position between the target and the receiving stations, the positioning curve may generate one point of intersection, and also may generate two points of intersection. Two intersection situations of the pointing curves are as shown in Fig. 1.

[a] Corresponding author: jfm1113@163.com

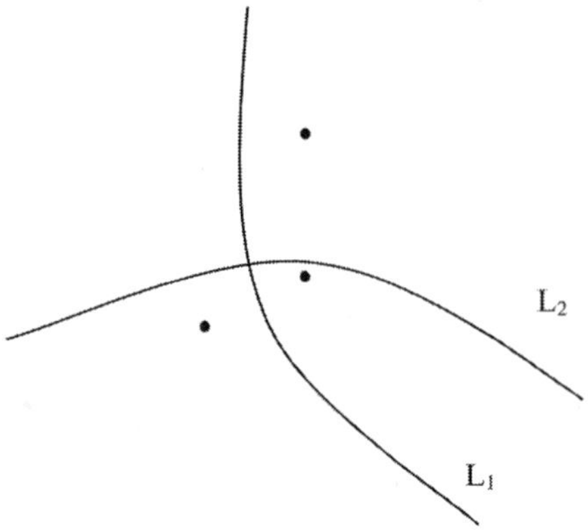

(a)

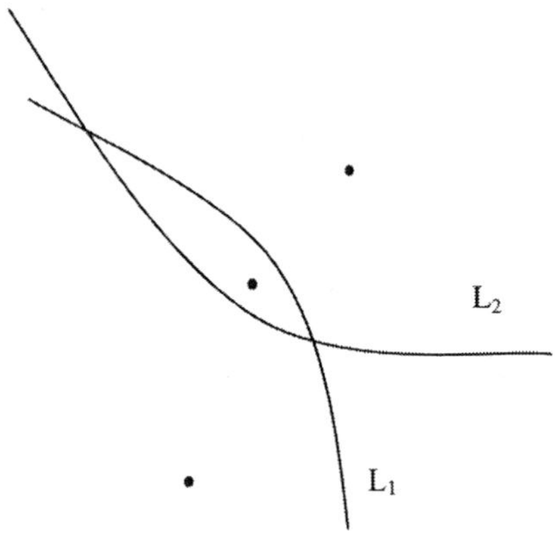

(b)

Figure 1. Schematic diagram of intersection of three-station positioning curves
(a) Positioning curves only with one point of intersection
(b) Positioning curves with two points of intersection
'●'Receiving station 'L' Positioning curve

It is relatively complicated to carry out analytical analysis for intersection situation of positioning curves and it is difficult to intuitively see the specific distribution of curve intersection situation if directly in accordance with equation (1), therefore, numerical simulation method is used to conduct analysis for intersection situation of positioning curves. For ideal regular triangle layout of three receiving stations, the distribution situation of intersection point of target positioning curves are as shown in Fig. 2(a). In the figure, white region means that when the target lies in the regional, the positioning curves determined by the target and the stations only has one point of intersection (namely, the target position); shadow area means that when the target lies in the area, the positioning curves determined by the target and the stations have two points of intersection (namely, target position calculation generates ambiguity). For the determined layout of receiving stations, if the target monitored is located at the white area where the positioning curves only have one point of intersection, positioning result selection problem doesn't exist. However, if the target is located at the shadow area where the positioning curves have two points of intersection, the positioning result will generate ambiguity. About how to deal with or avoid such situation, such problem is related to GDOP and stations layout. Thus further analysis will be made as below.

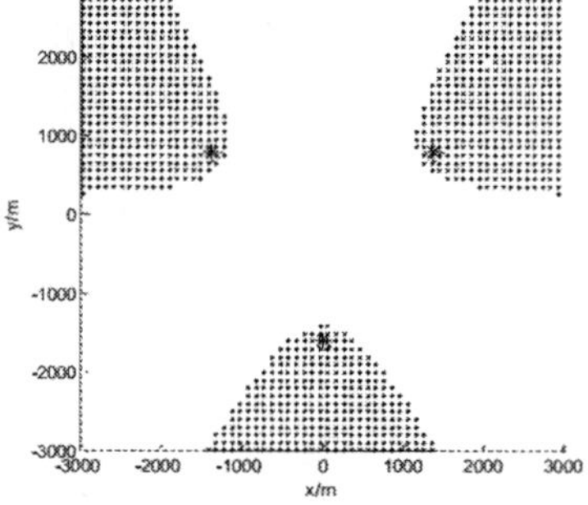

(a)

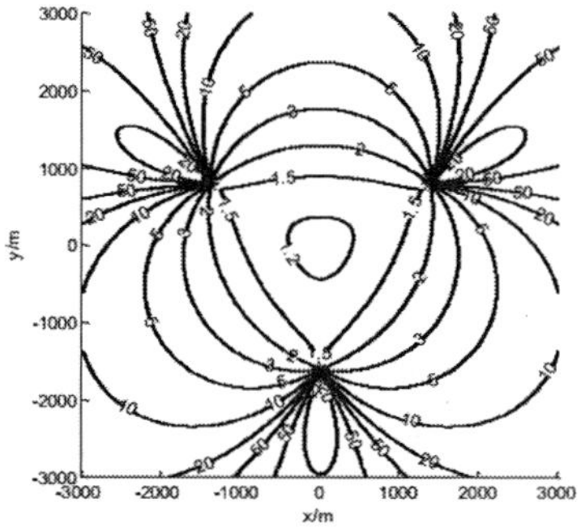

(b)

Figure 2. Intersection point distribution of three-station positioning curve and GDOP distribution (Three stations in the form of regular triangle)
(a) Intersection point distribution of positioning curve
(b) GDOP distribution
'*'Receiving station

3 Numerical simulation analysis of three-station positioning curve intersection point, GDOP and station layout

GDOP is a factor establishing relationship between target positioning error and measurement accuracy of time of arrival of the receiving stations realizing target positioning (assuming that measurement error of TOA of target signal of each receiving station realizing target positioning has the same statistics characteristics). GDOP factor describes the influence of the position relationship between multilateration system stations layout and the positioned target on the target positioning accuracy. Assuming that measurement error of TOA of target signal of receiving stations is σ , target positioning relative standard error in horizontal direction is σ_x , σ_y and target positioning relative standard error in vertical direction is σ_z , GDOP is as following [4] :

$$GDOP = \sqrt{\sigma_x^2 + \sigma_y^2 + \sigma_z^2} / (c \cdot \sigma) \quad (2)$$

Under the situation of two-dimensional positioning, GDOP is:

$$GDOP = \sqrt{\sigma_x^2 + \sigma_y^2} / (c \cdot \sigma) \quad (3)$$

Obviously, for determined TOA measurement accuracy, the smaller GDOP, the smaller corresponding target positioning error is:

$$GDOP = \sqrt{\sigma_x^2 + \sigma_y^2 + \sigma_z^2} / (c \cdot \sigma) \quad (2)$$

GDOP distribution situation of three stations layout shown in Fig. 2(a) is as shown in Fig. 2(b). It can be seen from Fig. 2(b) that central area of triangle formed by three stations is an area with relatively small GDOP, namely, for TOA measurement accuracy of determined receiving station target, target positioning error in such area is relatively small. By comparing Fig. 2(a) with Fig. 2(b), it can be seen that the area where three-station positioning curves have two points of intersection is basically identical with the area with relatively large GDOP, this indicates that the area where three-station positioning curves have two points of intersection not only will generate position calculation error, but also generate relatively large target positioning error even if correct target position can be selected out. In practice, if target TOA measurement accuracy of receiving stations is relatively low, target positioning in such area may lead invalid result due to too large positioning error even.

Fig. 2 is an analysis result under the situation of regular triangle layout of three receiving stations. In order to analyze the influence of stations layout change to positioning curves intersection point distribution and GDOP, the station position can be changed to make qualitative analysis for target positioning curves intersection point distribution and GDOP.

Firstly, move coordinates of one station in Fig. 2 towards inside of the triangle, corresponding target positioning curves intersection point distribution and GDOP are as shown in Fig. 3. It can be seen from Fig. 3 that, with movement of a station towards inside of the triangle, the triangle area surrounded by the stations are reduced and the area where three-station positioning curves have single intersection point and the area with relatively small GDOP are also reduced. However, it can be seen that by comparing Fig. 3(a) and Fig. 3(b), the area where three-station positioning curves have two points of intersection is still basically the area with relatively large GDOP.

Secondly, move coordinates of one station in Fig.2 towards outside of the triangle, corresponding target positioning curves intersection point distribution and GDOP are as shown in Fig. 4. It can be seen from Fig.4 that, with movement of a station towards outside of the triangle, the triangle area surrounded by the stations are increased and the area where three-station positioning curves have single intersection point and the area with relatively small GDOP are also increased. However, it can be seen that by comparing Fig. 4(a) and Fig. 4(b), the area where three-station positioning curves have two points of intersection is still basically the area with relatively large GDOP.

Through the above analysis, the relationship between positioning curves intersection point distribution, GDOP distribution and stations layout at the time of three-station positioning can be qualitatively determined, namely stations layout determines positioning curves intersection point distribution and GDOP, and the area where three-station positioning curves have two points of intersection is basically identical with the area with relative large GDOP. According to the analysis result, when three stations are used for target positioning in practice, please pay attention to select a reasonable stations layout to make the area under monitoring is located at the center of the triangle surrounded by the three stations and the triangle shall "expand" as far as possible, so as to maximize the area where positioning curves have single point of intersection and the area with relatively small GDOP; for the target appearing at the area where the positioning curves have two points of intersection, the positioning result can be given up because it is difficult to judge correct target position and positioning error is relatively large, so as to reduce handling difficulty.

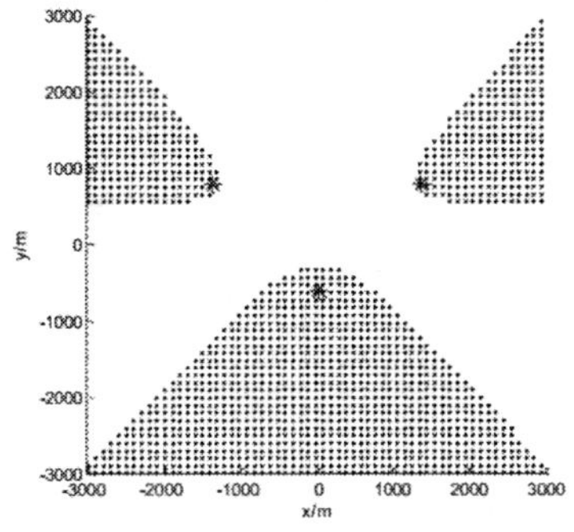

(a)

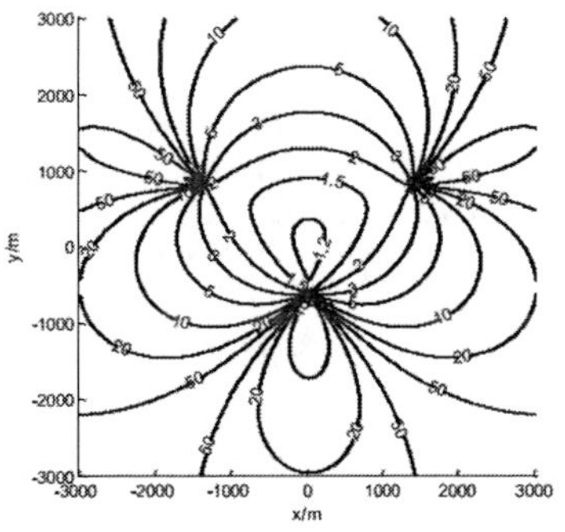

(b)

Figure 3. Three-station positioning curves intersection point distribution and GDOP distribution (one station moves towards inside of the triangle)
(a) Positioning curves intersection point distribution
(b) GDOP distribution
'*'Receiving station

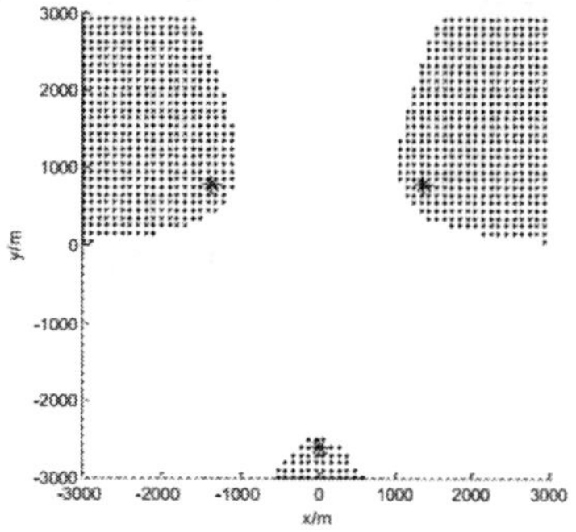

(a)

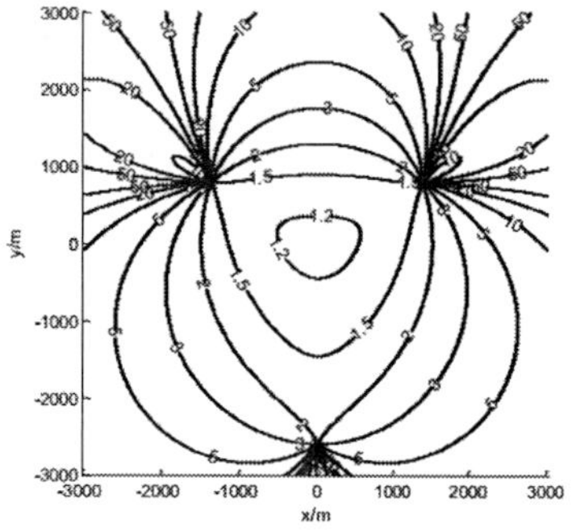

(b)

Figure 4. Three-station positioning curves intersection point distribution and GDOP distribution (One station moves towards outside of the triangle)
(a) Positioning curves intersection point distribution
(b) GDOP distribution
'*'Receiving station

4 Conclusions

The multilateration system will encounter the positioning ambiguity problem if three stations are used for two-dimensional target positioning in practical application. The relationship between three-station positioning ambiguity, GDOP and stations layout is numerically analyzed. The qualitative analysis result shows that the distributions of positioning curve intersections and GDOP are results of the stations layout, and the area where the positioning curves have two intersections is basically identical with the area with relative large GDOP. The analysis results can be used as references to avoid and deal with the position calculation ambiguity problem of three-station multilateration positioning target.

Acknowledgment

This paper is supported by the National Natural Science Foundation of China (Grant No.61079006), and the National Natural Science Foundation of China (Grant No. U1433129).

References

[1]. International Civil Aviation Organization. ICAO Annex 10 - Aeronautical Telecommunications, Volume IV - Surveillance Radar and Collision Avoidance Systems. International Civil Aviation Organization (2002).
[2]. MH/T4010.Technical standards for ATC secondary surveillance radar (2006).
[3]. Xu zili, Liu Changzhong, He Donglin, et al. Positioning solution using target barometric altitude. Communications Technology (2011).
[4]. H. B. Lee. A novel procedure for assessing the accuracy of hyperbolic multilateration systems. IEEE Trans. Aerospace and Electronic Systems (1975).

MATEC Web of Conferences **44**, 01037 (2016)
DOI: 10.1051/matecconf/20164401037

The Design Of Colleges And Universities Education Resource Platform Based On Cloud Computing

Hong Qin Zhu [1,a], Zhi Mei Cheng[1], You Lin Cai [1]

[1]*East China University of Technology,Fuzhou,jiangxi,344000,China*

Abstract—With the rapid growth of colleges and universities education resources, people access to those resources on the network more frequently, but the distribution of resources is too loose and the repeat of resources is too high, people need a lot of time to get information from those resources and constantly jump from one site to another for some information. According to this situation, this paper designed a system of colleges and universities education resource based on cloud computing. With this system, people get resources do not need to find everywhere, people can directly find all of the educational resources on the system platform, it not only save a lot of time, but also save the brain; With this system, resource managers or information publishers can pass the information in the shortest time, eliminating the need for duplication of labor

1 Introduction

With the rapid development of information technology, network technology and communication technology, Colleges and Universities education resources are becoming more and more abundant, many Colleges and Universities have produced some quality courses, many big website appeared MOOC course. In order to promote the teachers to master the latest information technology to hold all kinds of competitions, such as the micro lesson competition, the information technology teaching competition, etc. Education resources in colleges and universities is expansive growth, therefore, when you need to find and collect information, but the amount of information is too lager, then it will spend you a lot of time to differentiate and filter.

The higher authorities cascaded down issued a notice, when the notice come to school, the end date is approaching, so teachers are in a hurry to execution notice.

When people want to apply postgraduate or doctoral exam, they need to find the school first, and then find The graduate department , and then find whether there is a recruit professional, that bother people very much.

All the above problems, is due to large amount of information, and the information is not concentrate, and there is no convenient tool to filter the information. With the emergence of cloud computing, it can convenient the scattered resources by the network to form a shared pool of resources, then based on shared resource pool, to realize the resources classification and on-demand lookup.

2 Cloud computing applications in the fields of education

Cloud computing applications in the field of education is called Educational cloud,it includes Cloud Computing Assisted Instructions (CCAI) and Clouds Computing Based Education(CCBE).

CCAI means that the school and teachers using education cloud services supported by the cloud computing to build personalized teaching information environment. It Supports teacher's effective teaching and students' active learning, promotes the students' advanced thinking ability and swarm intelligence development, improves the quality of education.CCBE means that , In various fields of education, using cloud computing services to assist the education teaching activities.

CCBE is a new discipline concept, belongs to the cross field of computer science and education science, Mainly to explore the application rule of cloud computing services in the education teaching , Studies education teaching resources and the process of design and management based on The dominant theory of learning.

[a] Zhu hongqin: zhq@ecit.cn

Article available at http://www.matec-conferences.org or http://dx.doi.org/10.1051/matecconf/20164401037

This paper is concerned with the integration of college education resources based on cloud computing to provide a convenient platform for teachers and students.

3 Platform design

Because of educational resources are too rich,the user of educational resources are to much, and education platform should follow the characteristics of education. This article only pays attention to the public part of the Colleges and universities education resources, the private education resources of Colleges and universities not included in the platform .

This paper designed system running environment and system composition, which is divided into three parts, they are information platform construction, the overall framework of the Colleges and Universities education resource system, and system platform module of colleges and universities education resource. The following are described.

3.1 Information platform construction

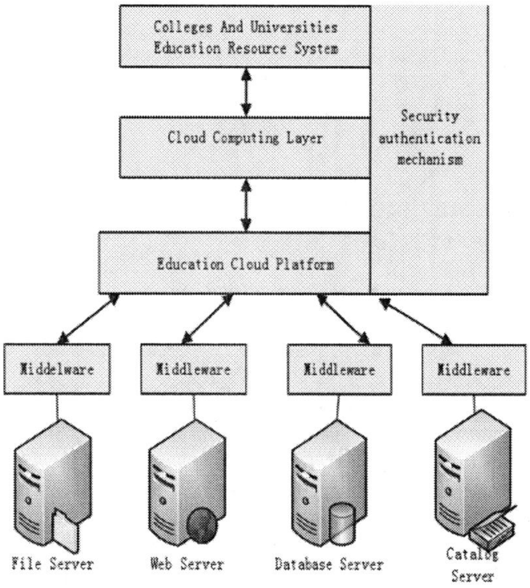

Figure1. Information platform construction

- Cloud computing layer: mainly used to calculate the location of resources, balance network load, allocate resources
- Education cloud platform: the hardware resource platform of cloud computing
- Middleware: Shield inconsistent of the database server, the operating system and the file system
- Security authentication mechanism: the combination of cloud computing authentication mechanism (Keystone), from the users login to the system to access the cloud platform ,in the whole process, every step of the resource access requires authentication. To ensure the security of information and correctness, and non-repudiation.

3.2 The overall framework of the colleges and universities education resource system

Colleges and universities education resources system is composed of three kinds of users: ordinary users, system users, cloud client users. As shown in Figure 2.

- Ordinary users: Users can be students, teachers and other people, do not need to be certified, they access to the system with the web browser, they can browse resources, download resources.
- System users: This user has only a few people, they have the ability to manage and monitor the whole system, such as the platform service directory configuration, adding and deleting a user, etc
- Cloud client users: the users are mainly the platform management of colleges and universities, education administrative department of colleges and universities. They use the web browser or web application to access the platform to publish information and manage the resources, If a publishing information needed to multistage audit , When information release, it automatically transfer to superior for approval, When all the approval is completed, the information can be presented in the web client.

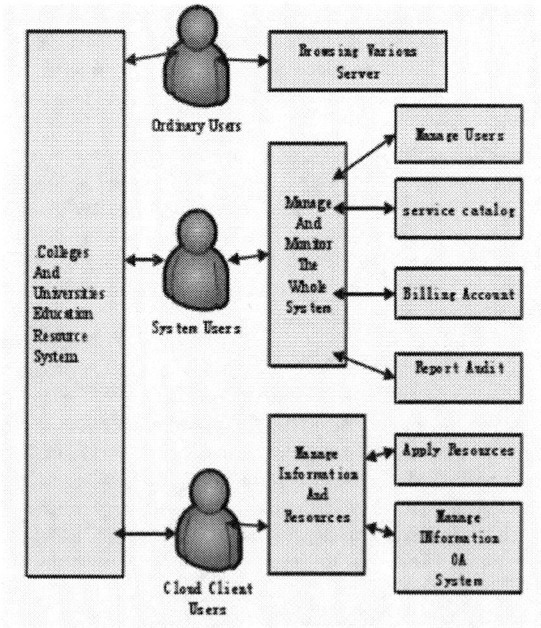

Figure2. The Overall Framework Of The Colleges And Universities Education Resource System

3.3 The Design on system platform module of Colleges and Universities education resource .

In Colleges and universities, the school mainly attaches to scientific research, competition, policy news, propaganda, enrollment; teachers are keen to focus on research, competition, policy news; students pay attention to the course, enrollment information. Around these aspects, the system module of the college education resource as shown in figure 3.

If the higher authorities publish scientific research, competition, news and other information, there is no need to issued the information to every school, then the school load the information on their official website. The higher authorities can directly publish the information on the platform ,then all the schools can bower the information. With this platform, Message passed with the fastest speed.

With this platform, students and teachers can be very conveniently to find the courses they want to learn, they can easily find enrollment information to prepare for further education.

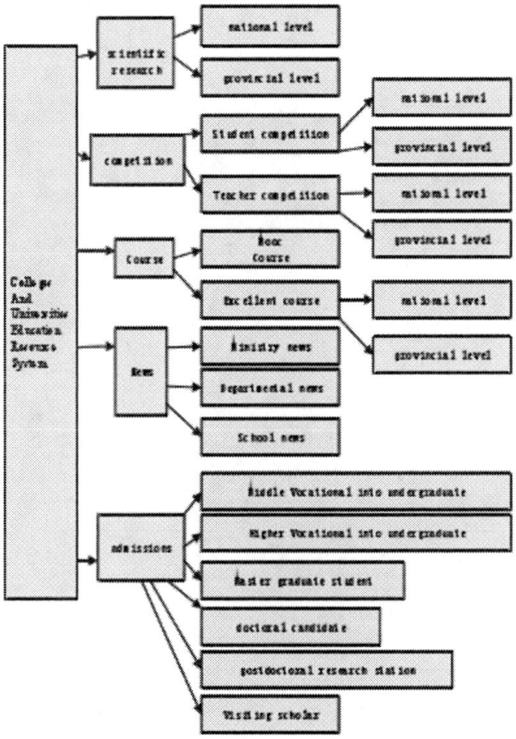

Figure3. System Platform Module of Colleges and Universities Education Resource .

- Scientific research module:it is divided into national level and provincial level, national research institutions directly send the information to the platform, then all provinces, all teachers and researchers can see; Provincial scientific research institutions directly send the information to the platform, then all schools, all teachers and researchers can see. On the platform you can also know that other schools or research institutions are studying in which field, it is conducive to information sharing, and avoiding plagiarism.
- Competition module: it is divided into student competiton and teacher competion. For students, the ability of the students could not have been discoveried and excavated by the teacher, students best know themselves, but students lack of competition information.If students use this platform, they can immediately get their interested competition, ahead of time to prepare for the work. For the teacher, the competition information comes from the school related departments to publish the information, if the relevant departments do not have the first time to obtain information, or information can not be released in time, the teacher would not be enough time to paraper the competition. The result is that the teacher is not satisfied with the results of the competition,it will influence teacher's enthusiasm.If teachers use this platform,they can obtain information immediately, and make full preparations to improve the quality of the competition.
- Course modules: with the development of information, the teacher and the students need to continue to learn, This platform collects curriculum quality resources , to eliminat the time for teachers and students to find resources. Teachers and students can better plan their own learning plan by the concentration of resources.
- News module: when school won prizes such as news , the school will announce the news on its official website, to praise the award-winning teacher, at the same time, encourage other teachers to progress. Through this platform, the message can be maximize propaganda.Once the news release, all school teachers can see.
- Admissions module: in order to adapt higher vocational education connect with the middle vocational, undergraduate education connect with the higher vocational ,the platform collect all admission policy, the student can learn about admissions policy in advance on this platform, determine their own learning plan. Students make their own planning more accurate and more specific with the centralized and the integrated information resources.

4 Summary

In this paper a platform is designed , which is divided into three parts, they are information platform construction, the overall framework of the colleges and universities education resource system, and system platform module of colleges and universities education resource .

Information platform construction is that education cloud platforms integrates the various information systems by middleware; the overall framework of colleges and universities education resource system is designed for user, the system platform module of colleges and universities education resource is designed for the functional of system. It is discussed on the system platform that the user convinence and platform benefit, In this paper, If the designed system can be implemented, it will bring a lot of benefits for the management department, school, teacher and scientific research departments and the students .

References

[1] Caifeng Zou,Huifang Deng, and Qunye Qiu, "Design and Implementation of Hybrid Cloud Computing Architecture Based on Cloud Bus," 2013 IEEE Ninth International Conference on Mobile Ad-hoc and Sensor Networks (MSN), 2013,pp:289-293.

[2] Junggab Son, Hussain, R., Hunmin Kim, Heekuck Oh,"2 SC-DVR: a secure cloud computing based framework for DVR service "2014 IEEE Transactions on Consumer Electronics,2014, Volume: 60, Issue: 3 ,Pages: 368 – 374.

[3] Zhuang Wu," Study and realization of automatic supply solution for enterprise IT basic facility based on cloud computing,"World Automation Congress (WAC), 2012 ,Pages: 1 - 4 .

[4] Zhidong Shen, Li Li, Fei Yan, Xiaoping Wu,"Cloud Computing System Based on Trusted Computing Platform ,"Intelligent Computation Technology and Automation (ICICTA), 2010 International Conference on ,Year: 2010, Volume: 1 ,Pages: 942 – 945.

[5] Cui Yun-fei, Li Yi, Zhu Ji-lu, Wang Peng," The research on cloud computing architecture for campus-based networks," 2013 IEEE Conference on Anthology , 2013,Pages: 1 – 4.

[6] Haijun Gu, Yufeng Diao, Wei Liu, Xueqian Zhang,"6 The design of smart home platform based on Cloud Computing "Electronic and Mechanical Engineering and Information Technology (EMEIT), 2011 International Conference on ,Year: 2011, Volume: 8 ,Pages: 3919 – 3922.

MATEC Web of Conferences **44**, 01038 (2016)
DOI: 10.1051/matecconf/20164401038

The Key Solution Algorithm of Linear Programming Model

Jun Liu [1,a] , Chuan Cheng Zhao[1] , Zhi Guo Ren[1] , Zhong Yi Feng[1] , Zheng Ping Zhu [1]

1. Lanzhou City University, School of Information Science and engineering, Lanzhou 730070, P.R.China

Abstract. Linear programming problem is a common problem, and to solve the linear model is more plagued. The paper generating algorithm is based on mathematical theory and composition. The design of feasible solution algorithm illustrates key linear programming model, then we can find a better way to solve the linear programming model solutions.

1 Introduction

According to mathematical theory of linear programming model[1-2] (1):

$$\max \quad z=\sum_{i=1}^{n} c_i x_i$$

$$s.t\begin{cases}\sum_{j=1}^{n} a_{ij}x_j \le a_{in+1}(i=1,2,\cdots,m) \\ x_i \ge 0(i=1,2,\cdots,n)\end{cases} (m\ge n)$$

S,t condition of the equation

$$\sum_{j=1}^{n} a_{ij}x_j = a_{in+1}(i=1,2,\cdots,m)$$

And $x_i = 0(i=1,2,\cdots,n)$ $m+n$ equations form an optimal solution *m+n* plane (side) closed set *Ω*, the linear programming model (1) on the closed set *Ω* border on the objective function s,t condition of the equation:

$$z=\sum_{i=1}^{n} c_i x_i$$

From (0,0, ···, 0) (z = 0) moving along the surface normal direction, so that the value of *z* is gradually increased until the value of the maximum, then getting a linear programming model (1) of the optimal solution $(x_1,x_2,\cdots,x_n)$ and the corresponding *z* maximum. This method is theoretically established, but in practice it would be inconvenient to solve over three-dimensional linear programming model[3].

This paper designs the key feasible solution algorithmsof computer of graphic linear programming model.

2 The Combination Generation Algorithm

In the key feasible solution algorithms of computer of graphic linear programming model, it is supposed to discuss the combination generation algorithm of C_n^m, C_n^m linear equations are generated from m + n equations[4].

Let$C_n^0=\emptyset$, $C_n^n = 1,2,3,\cdots,n$. When generating the combination of C_n^m, *n* numbers of the generated combination, each and all combinations are arranged by the dictionary order.

2.1 The Generation of Combination C_n^1

The combination of C_1^1 is 1, C_2^1 is 1,2, C_3^1 is 1,2,3..., and the combination of C_n^1 is 1,2,3, ...,n. Combination can be expressed as follows (to be expressed simply, writtenC_n^m *as* $\Delta(n,m)$),borrowing documents[2] to discuss the digital triangles and trigonometric operations and "⊕" and the triangular numbers counted by "∘"):

$\Delta(1,1)=(1)^T$,

$\Delta(2,1)=(1 \quad 2)^T$,

$\Delta(3,1)=(1 \quad 2 \quad 3)^T$,

…,

$\Delta(n,1)=(1 \quad 2 \quad 3 \quad \cdots \quad n{-}1 \quad n)^T$

[a]authore-mail: 527876625@qq.com
This studywas supported by Lanzhou City University Ph.D. Research Fund (21265099,41361013,GS[2013]GHB1084, LZCU-BS2013-09 and LZCU-BS2013-12).

(To write conveniently, matrix form is used above.)

2.2 The Generation of Combination C_n^2

The combination of $C_2^2$is 12,$C_3^2$is 12,13,23, …, $C_n^2$is 12,13,14, …, $1n$; 23,24,…$2n$; ……; $n-2n-1, n-1n$; $n-1n$.

It can be expressed by digital triangle as follows:

$\Delta(2,2) = 12 = \Delta(1,2) \oplus \Delta(1,1) \circ 2$,

$$\Delta(3,2) = \begin{array}{cc} 12 & 13 \\ & 23 \end{array} = \Delta(2,2) \oplus \Delta(2,1) \circ 3,$$

$$\Delta(4,2) = \begin{array}{ccc} 12 & 13 & 14 \\ & 23 & 24 \\ & & 34 \end{array} = \Delta(3,2) \oplus \Delta(3,1) \circ 4,$$

…,

$$\Delta(n,2) = \begin{array}{cccccc} 12 & 13 & 14 & \cdots & 1n\text{-}1 & 1n \\ & 23 & 24 & \cdots & 2n\text{-}1 & 2n \\ & & 34 & \cdots & 3n\text{-}1 & 3n \\ & & & & \cdots & \cdots \\ & & & & (n-2)(n-1) & (n-2)n \\ & & & & & (n-1)n \end{array}$$

$= \Delta(n-1,2) \oplus \Delta(n-1,1) \circ n$

2.3 The Generation of Combination C_n^3

Similarly, itcan get the digital triangle indicating the combinations of $C_3^3, C_4^3, C_5^3, \ldots, C_n^3$.

$\Delta(3,3) = 123 = \Delta(2,3) \oplus \Delta(2,2) \circ 3$,

$$\Delta(4,3) = \begin{array}{ccc} 123 & 124 & 134 \\ & & 234 \end{array} = \Delta(3,3) \oplus \Delta(3,2) \circ 4,$$

$$\Delta(5,3) = \begin{array}{cccccc} 123 & 124 & 134 & 125 & 135 & 145 \\ & & 234 & & 235 & 245 \\ & & & & & 345 \end{array}$$

$= \Delta(4,3) \oplus \Delta(4,2) \circ 5$,

…,

$$\Delta(n,3) = \begin{array}{ccccccc} 123 & 124 & 134 & 125 & 135 & 145 & \cdots \\ & 234 & & & 235 & 245 & \cdots \\ & & & & & 345 & \cdots \end{array}$$

$$\begin{array}{cccccc} 12n & 13n & 14n & \cdots & 1(n-2)n & 1(n-1)n \\ & 23n & 24n & \cdots & 2(n-2)n & 2(n-1)n \\ & & 34n & \cdots & 3(n-2)n & 3(n-1)n \\ & & & & \cdots & \cdots \\ & & & & (n-3)(n-2)n & (n-3)(n-1)n \\ & & & & & (n-2)(n-1)n \end{array}$$

$= \Delta(n-1,3) \oplus \Delta(n-1,2) \circ n$

2.4 The Generation of Combination $\Delta(n,m)$ (C_n^m)

Similarly, itcan obtain the combination of $\Delta(n,m)$.

Thus, itcan get the $\Delta(n,m)$ of combination C_n^m generating algorithm theorem.

Theorem: the combination of $C_n^m (m \le n/2, m \ge 2)$ is $\Delta(n,m) = \Delta(n-1,m) \oplus \Delta(n-1,m-1) \circ n$.

3 The Design of Key Feasible Solution Algorithm

From the foregoing, if the feasible solutions of linear programming model (1) is the closed setΩ, and the optimal solution is in the boundary of this closed set Ω, and the possible case is unique (a vertex of closed set Ω) or infinite (an edge or a surface of closed set Ω). So it only need to find each vertex of the closed set Ω when calculating.These vertices of the closed set $\Omega(x_1, x_2, \cdots, x_n)$are called key feasible solutions, then determining the optimal solution of the linear programming model (1) from key feasible solution[5-10].

To find the key feasible solution on the closed set Ω, changing the restrictions of linear programming model to:

$$\begin{cases} \sum_{j=1}^{n} a_{ij}x_j = a_{in+1} (i = 1,2,\cdots,m) \\ x_i = 0 (i = 1,2,\cdots,n) \end{cases}.$$

This is a linear equation containing n variables and m + n equations, the key feasible solution of the closed set Ω is the intersection from m + n equations obtained C_{m+n}^n equations. The intersection satisfies the points of restrictions in model (1),and it corresponds to the value of the objective function z. Finding the maximum value from these values, there may be three cases, one (unique), two (an edge) or three (a surface).

Computer algorithm as following:

(1) Let max=0;

(2) Generating $m+n$ equations to C_{m+n}^n equation groups by the algorithm of generated combination and solving it;

(3) Substituting the linear programming model (1) restrictions, judging whether it is the key feasible solution on the closed set Ω, if so, calculating the value of objective function z;

(4) Judging whether $z > \max$ is established, if so, $\max = z$ returningthe key feasible solution of equation groups is $(x_1, x_2, \cdots, x_n)$. If $z = \max$ is satisfied, keeping the key feasible solution of equation groups as $(x_1, x_2, \cdots, x_n)$;

(5) Returning to 1,until getting the solution of C_{m+n}^nequation groups;

(6) Outputting the value of z and the optimal solution $(x_1, x_2, \cdots, x_n)$;

With this algorithm, we can easily calculate the optimal solution of linear programming model (1) $(x_1, x_2, \cdots, x_n)$.

4 The Advantages of Algorithm

This algorithm is based on the principle of the

existence of the optimal solution on the closed set Ω, directly calculating the intersection and determining whether it is the key feasible solution of the closed set Ω, and immediately seeking z, greatly reducing the number of calculations, and occupying less memory as a fast and effective way. Meanwhile, it will have a good reference for the algorithm of integer programming by improving this algorithm. This section will be discussed about the pull-off algorithm of the solutions of integer programming model in another text.

References

1. Prof. Dr. T. Gal. Homogene mehrparametrische lineare Programmierung[J]. Zeitschrift für Operations Research . 1972 (3)
2. K. -H. Borgwardt. The Average number of pivot steps required by the Simplex-Method is polynomial[J]. Zeitschriftfür Operations Research . 1982 (1)
3. Wolfgang Temelt. The parameter space of the general linear programming problem[J]. Soviet Mathematical Journal . 1967 (3)
4. The ellipsoid method and its consequences in combinatorial optimization[J]. Combinatorica . 1981 (2)
5. N. Karmarkar. A new polynomial-time algorithm for linear programming[J]. Combinatorica . 1984 (4)
6. Yamamura K,TanakaS.Performance evaluation of the LPtest algorithm for finding all solutions of piecewise-linearresistive circuits. International Journal of CircuitTheory and Applications . 2000
7. H. P. Benson,D. Lee. Outcome-based algorithm for optimizing over the efficient set of a bicriteria linear programming problem[J]. Journal of Optimization Theory and Applications . 1996 (1)
8. F. P. Vasil'ev,M. Yachimovich. Discrepancy method for the lexicographic linear programming problem[J]. Computational Mathematics and Modeling . 1995 (1)
9. J. Fülöp,L. D. Muu. Branch-and-Bound Variant of an Outcome-Based Algorithm for Optimizing over the Efficient Set of a Bicriteria Linear Programming Problem[J]. Journal of Optimization Theory and Applications . 2000 (1)
10. Adi Ben-Israel. A ℤ-Simplex Algorithm with partial updates[J]. BIT . 1987 (1)

6 C language source code

```
#include <stdio.h>
#include <stdlib.h>
#include <string.h>
#include <math.h>
#define N 100
#define OK 1
#define ERROR 0
double a[N][N],c[N][N];
typedefstruct
{
double number[N];
doublereasult;
}
SeqList;
typedefstruct
{
    SeqListrecord[N];
    intNsize,Size;
}Node;
int Print(double b[][N],intn,int m)
{
    inti,j;
    for(i=1;i<=n;i++)
    {
        for(j=1;j<=m;j++)
            printf(" %lf ",b[i][j]);
        printf("\n");
    }
    return OK;
}
void Print1(Node *L)
{
    inti,j;
    for(i=1;i<=L->Size;i++)
    for(j=1;j<=L->Nsize;j++)
    {
        printf("i=%d    %lf",i,L->record[i].number[j]);
printf("\n");
        printf("\n");
    }
    printf("\n");
}
void Print2(Node *L)
{
    inti,j;
    for(i=1;i<L->Size;i++)
    {
    for(j=1;j<=L->Nsize;j++)
        printf(" %e ",L->record[i].number[j]);
        printf(" The sult is:%lf ",L->record[i].reasult);
printf("\n");
        printf("\n");
      }
    printf("\n");
}
intCreat(Node *L,intn,int m)
{
    inti;
    int c1=1,c2=1;
    printf("未知数的个数 Nsize:");
    scanf("%d",&L->Nsize);
    for(i=n;i>1;i--)
```

```
        c1*=i;
      for(i=m-1;i>1;i--)
        c2*=i;
      for(i=n-(m-1);i>1;i--)
        c2*=i;
      L->Size=c1/c2;
      return OK;
}
int meet(Node *L,intfirst,intnumber,int m)
{
   FILE *fp;
inti,j,ok=0;
doubley,sum;
for(i=first,j=1;j<=L->Nsize;j++)
      if(L->record[i].number[j]<0
L->record[i].number==-0)
            return ERROR;
fp=fopen("wang.txt","rt");
if(fp==NULL)
   {
      printf("Can't Open!");
      exit(0);
   }
for(i=1;i<=number;i++)
   {
      sum=0;
for(j=1;j<=L->Nsize;j++)
      {
            fscanf(fp,"%lf",&y);
            sum+=L->record[first].number[j]*y;
      }
fscanf(fp,"%lf",&y);
      if(sum>y+1)
      return ERROR;
   }
fclose(fp);
return OK;
}
int Sub(Node *L,int m)
{
      inti,j,number;
      double x;
      FILE *fp;
      printf("pleaser enter s.t number:");
scanf("%d",&number);
      for(i=1;i<=L->Size;i++)
      {
      if(meet(L,i,number,m))
         {
            fp=fopen("zhu.txt","rt");
            if(fp==NULL)
             {
                  printf("Can't open!");
                  exit(0);
             }
             L->record[i].reasult=0;
            for(j=1;j<=L->Nsize;j++)
             {
                  fscanf(fp,"%lf",&x);

L->record[i].reasult+=L->record[i].number[j]*x;
             }
                  fclose(fp);
             }
         else L->record[i].reasult=0;
         }
return OK;
}
int Memory(double b[][N],Node *L,int m)
{
int j;
staticinti=1;
for(j=1;j<=L->Nsize;j++)
      {
            L->record[i].number[j]=b[j][m];
      }
i++;
return OK;
}
intTackback(double b[][N],Node *L,intn,int m)
{
         inti,j,k;
         double s;
         for(i=1;i<=n;i++)
         {
         if(b[i][i]==0) break;
              s=1.0/b[i][i];
         for(j=1;j<=m;j++)
         b[i][j]=s*b[i][j];
         }
         for(i=n;i>=1;i--)
         {
         for(j=i-1;j>=1;j--)
            {
                  s=b[j][i]/b[i][i];
               if(s==0) break;
               for(k=i;k<=m;k++)
                     b[j][k]=(-1*s)*b[i][k]+b[j][k];
            }
         }
Memory(b,L,m);
         return OK;
}
int change(double b[][N],inttime,intn,int m)
{
         inti,j,max;
         doublet,x,y;
         max=time;
         for(i=time+1;i<=n;i++)
         {
                  x=b[max][time];
                  y=b[i][time];
               if(fabs(x)<fabs(y))
                     max=i;
         }
         if(max!=time)
         {
               for(j=1;j<=m;j++)
               {
                     t=b[time][j];
b[time][j]=b[max][j];
                     b[max][j]=t;
               }
         }
```

```
return OK;
}
intuptriangle(double b[][N],Node *L,intn,int m)
{
      inti,j,k;
      double s;
for(i=1;i<=n;i++)
      {
            change(b,i,n,m);
            for(j=i+1;j<=n;j++)
            {
                  s=b[j][i]/b[i][i];
                  if(s==0) break;
                  for(k=1;k<=m;k++)
                     {
                        b[j][k]=(-1*s)*b[i][k]+b[j][k];
                     }
            }
      }
Tackback(b,L,n,m);
return OK;
}
int Assemble(double b[][N],Node *L,intn,int m)
{
      inti,j,k,elem[100];
      i=1; elem[i]=1;
      while(i!=0)
       {
if(elem[i]>n)
             {
                  i--;
                  elem[i]++;
             }
            else if(i==m-1)
             {
for(j=1;j<=m-1;j++)
            for(k=1;k<=m;k++)
                  c[j][k]=b[elem[j]][k];
uptriangle(c,L,m-1,m);
                  memset(c,0,sizeof(c));
            elem[i]++;
             }
            else
             {
                  i++;
                  elem[i]=elem[i-1]+1;
             }
      }
      return OK;
}
int main()
{
      FILE *fp;
      inti,j,m,n;
      Node list;
      printf("pleaser enter n and m:");
      scanf("%d%d",&n,&m);
      fp=fopen("wang.txt","rt");
      if(fp==NULL)
      {
            printf("Can't open!");
            exit(0);
      }
for(i=1;i<=n;i++)
            for(j=1;j<=m;j++)
            {
                  fscanf(fp,"%lf",&a[i][j]);
            }
creat(&list,n,m);
            assemble(a,&list,n,m);
            sub(&list,m);
            print2(&list);
return 0;
}
```

MATEC Web of Conferences 44, 01039 (2016)
DOI: 10.1051/matecconf/20164401039

Robust Face Recognition via Occlusion Detection and Masking

Tan Guo[1,a], Xiao Heng Tan[1] and Chao Chen Xie[1]
[1]College of Communication Engineering, Chongqing University, 400044, Chongqing, China

Abstract. Sparse representation-based classification (SRC) method has demonstrated promising results in face recognition (FR). In this paper, we consider the problem of face recognition with occlusion. In sparse representation-based classification method, the reconstruction residual of test sample over the training set is usually heterogeneous with the training samples, highlighting the occlusion part in test sample. We detect the occlusion part by extracting a mask from the reconstruction residual through threshold operation. The mask will be applied in the representation-based classification framework to eliminate the impact of occlusion in FR. The method does not assume any prior knowledge about the occlusion, and extensive experiments on publicly available databases show the efficacy of the method.

1 Introduction

Face recognition (FR) is one of the most intensively investigated topics in biometrics. It has a wide range of applications, e.g., information security, access control, smart payment and law enforcement [1]. A common face recognition system mainly consists of two modules, namely feature extraction and classifier design. In the past decades, many algorithms have been proposed for the two aspects. For feature extraction, classical dimensionality reduction methods include Principle Component Analysis (PCA) [2] and Linear Discriminative Analysis (LDA) [3]. These methods aim to construct projections that can map the high-dimensional face image into a lower-dimensional space to get a compact representation of face image. The most used classifiers are Nearest Neighbor (NN) and Nearest Feature Subspace (NFS) [4].

Generally speaking, occlusion poses a significant obstacle in a robust, real-world face recognition system [5-6]. This difficulty is mainly due to the error in query sample incurred by occlusion. In recent years, representation based methods for classification [6, 11, 14] has attracted much attention due to their powerful performance in FR. The most representative approach is sparse representation-based classification (SRC). Wright et al. [6] exploited the discriminative nature of sparse representation via l1-norm regularization. The method has shown great potential in handling various occlusions, such as real disguise, continuous occlusion, random pixel corruption, etc. SRC triggers many following works, including the l1-graph for image classification [7], kernel based SRC [8], Gabor feature based SRC [9], and robust sparse coding [10]. Meanwhile, Naseem et al. [11] proposed a linear regression classification (LRC) algorithm using the concept that patterns from a single-object class lie on a linear subspace. Luan et al. [12] indicated that error image derived from the LRC was a better choice than original image to identify occluded regions, and presented an appearance-based method for face recognition based on LRC and level set method to deal with contiguous occlusion. Sparse error of Robust PCA was also extracted for FR under varying illumination and occlusion [13].

Zhang et al. [14] indicated that it is the collaborative representation but not the l1-norm sparsity that makes SRC powerful for face classification, and present a collaborative representation based classification (CRC) method. CRC aims to represent the query sample using all the training samples with a weaker l2-norm regularization, and then perform classification according to the contribution of each class in representing the query sample. Nevertheless, the estimated coefficients of an occluded test sample may be corrupted and unstable.

In this paper, we present a novel method for robust face recognition in the presence of occlusion, such as block occlusion, pixel occlusion and real disguise. As introduced above, CRC actually performs a separation of query sample into the parts similar and dissimilar with the training set. The occlusion part in query samples is considered to be heterogeneous with the training samples, and thus can not be well reconstructed by the training samples, and is left in the reconstruction residual. We exploit the reconstruction residual to detect occlusion, and get a mask for the test sample. The mask will be used in the CRC scheme to

[a] Corresponding author: tanguo@cqu.edu.cn

Article available at http://www.matec-conferences.org or http://dx.doi.org/10.1051/matecconf/20164401039

isolate the side effect of occlusion in FR.

The remainder of this paper is organized as follows: In section 2, we introduce the CRC and the proposed method. Section 3 presents the experimental results. The conclusion is drawn in Section 4.

2 CRC and Proposed method

2.1. CRC

CRC was proposed by Zhang et al. [14]. The work argued the function of collaborative representation in SRC [6], and empirically showed that the non-sparse l2-norm regularization could outperform the state-of-the-art SRC based on l1-norm regularization, both in computational complexity and classification accuracy. We first review the typical CRC algorithm.

Assume there are C distinguished training classes with n_i samples in each class. Let $\boldsymbol{D} = [\boldsymbol{D}_1, \boldsymbol{D}_2 \ldots \boldsymbol{D}_C]$, where $\boldsymbol{D}_i \in R^{m \times ni}$ is the data matrix of the ith class. Each column of $\boldsymbol{D}_i$ denotes a training sample of the ith class. For a test sample $\boldsymbol{y} \in R^m$, CRC uses all the samples in the training set to collaborative represent it as

$$\boldsymbol{y} = \boldsymbol{D}\boldsymbol{X} \quad (1)$$

Considering that the dictionary $\boldsymbol{D}$ can be under-determined, they use l_2-norm to regularize the solution. The CRC aims to solve the following problem.

$$\boldsymbol{X} = \arg\min_{\boldsymbol{X}} \{\|\boldsymbol{y} - \boldsymbol{D}\boldsymbol{X}\|_2^2 + \mu\|\boldsymbol{X}\|_2^2\} \quad (2)$$

The solution of (2) can be analytically derived as $\boldsymbol{X} = (\boldsymbol{D}^T\boldsymbol{D}+\mu \cdot \boldsymbol{I})^{-1}\boldsymbol{D}^T\boldsymbol{y}$. The class-specified representation residual $\|\boldsymbol{y}-\boldsymbol{D}_i\boldsymbol{X}_i\|_2$ together with the coefficient $\boldsymbol{X}_i$ are used for classification.

$$identity(\boldsymbol{y}) = \arg\min_i \{\|\boldsymbol{y} - \boldsymbol{D}_i\boldsymbol{X}_i\|_2 / \|\boldsymbol{X}_i\|_2\} \quad (3)$$

Where $\boldsymbol{X}_i$ is the representation coefficient vector in $\boldsymbol{X}$ associated with training class $\boldsymbol{D}_i$.

2.2 Proposed method

As mentioned earlier, the goal of the proposed method is to detect and eliminate the occlusion part in test sample. Firstly, we need to detect the occlusion part in test sample. As discussed in [6, 12, 14], in representation based classification methods, such as LRC, the reconstruction residual was a better choice than original image to identify occluded regions. Similarity, the reconstruction residual in CRC also has such property. The occluded parts in query sample are always heterogeneous with the training samples, highlighting the occlusion part in query sample. Figure 1 shows an example for distribution of intensity values of reconstruction residual by CRC. We can find most of the values are near 0, in the interval [-0.005, 0.005]. The large values in the reconstruction residual are known to be outliers in query sample that can not be well fitted by the training samples. Based on this, we propose to extract the occluded parts in query sample from the reconstruction residual of CRC model.

Firstly, we use all the training samples to represent the test sample, and solve the following problem

$$\hat{\boldsymbol{X}} = \arg\min_{\boldsymbol{X}} \{\|\boldsymbol{y} - \boldsymbol{D}\boldsymbol{X}\|_2^2 + \eta\|\boldsymbol{X}\|_2^2\} \quad (4)$$

Notably, we set η a relatively large value to relax the regularization on the reconstruction fidelity, which helps for the extraction of occlusion part. Then we get the reconstruction residual ($\boldsymbol{y}$-$\boldsymbol{D}\boldsymbol{X}$) of $\boldsymbol{y}$. The pixels whose value meet the condition in (5) is assigned as 1, otherwise 0.

$$\boldsymbol{m} = \left|\boldsymbol{y} - \boldsymbol{D}\hat{\boldsymbol{X}}\right| < \sigma \quad (5)$$

σ in (5) is a threshold needed to be specified. This way, we can get a mask of the test sample. The zero entities in $\boldsymbol{m}$ indicate the outliers in test sample. Figure 2.shows an example of this case. Figure 2(b) is a mask extracted from the reconstruction residual of Figure 2(a), and Figure 2(c) shows the test sample with mask, from which we can see that the occlusion part is well eliminated.

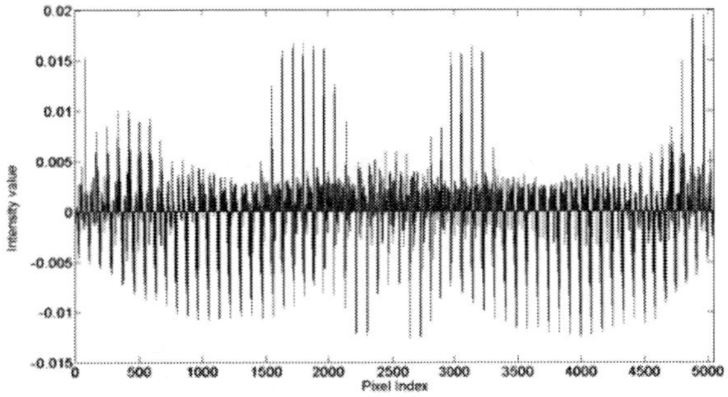

Figure 1. An example for distribution of intensity values of reconstruction residual in CRC.

Once the binary mask of test sample obtained, we solve the following regularized least square problem with mask.

$$\hat{\boldsymbol{X}} = \arg\min_{\boldsymbol{X}} \{\frac{1}{2}\left(\|diag(\boldsymbol{m})(\boldsymbol{y} - \boldsymbol{D}\boldsymbol{X})\|_2^2 + \lambda\|\boldsymbol{X}\|_2^2\right)\} \quad (6)$$

Let $\boldsymbol{M} = diag(\boldsymbol{m})$, we have

$$\hat{\boldsymbol{X}} = \arg\min_{\boldsymbol{X}} \{\frac{1}{2}(\|\boldsymbol{M}(\boldsymbol{y} - \boldsymbol{D}\boldsymbol{X})\|_2^2 + \lambda\|\boldsymbol{X}\|_2^2)\}$$

The closed form solution of above equation can be derived by taking partial derivations and setting them equal to **0** as

$$-(\boldsymbol{M}\boldsymbol{D})^T(\boldsymbol{M}\boldsymbol{y} - \boldsymbol{M}\boldsymbol{D}\hat{\boldsymbol{X}}) + \lambda\hat{\boldsymbol{X}} = \boldsymbol{0} \quad (7)$$

The solution is

$$\hat{\boldsymbol{X}} = (\boldsymbol{D}^T\boldsymbol{M}^T\boldsymbol{M}\boldsymbol{D} + \lambda \cdot \boldsymbol{I})\boldsymbol{D}^T\boldsymbol{M}^T\boldsymbol{M}\boldsymbol{y} \quad (8)$$

Decision is made in favor of the class with the minimum regularized residual.

$$identity(\boldsymbol{y}) = \arg\min_i \{\left\|\boldsymbol{M}(\boldsymbol{y} - \boldsymbol{D}_i\hat{\boldsymbol{X}}_i)\right\|_2 / \left\|\hat{\boldsymbol{X}}_i\right\|_2\} \quad (9)$$

In summary, the main steps of our method are as follows.

Setp1. Input: matrix of training samples $\boldsymbol{D} \in R^{m \times n}$, a test sample with occlusion $\boldsymbol{y} \in R^m$.

Setp2. Normalize the columns of $\boldsymbol{D}$ and $\boldsymbol{y}$ to have unit l_2-norm.

Setp3. Use Eq. (4) and Eq. (5) to estimate the pixels shaded in $\boldsymbol{y}$, and get a mask for it.

Setp4. Solve the regularized least square problem with binary mask in Eq. (6).

Setp5. Give the identity of the test sample y on the basis of Eq. (9).

The essence of our method is to detect and eliminate the impact of occlusion in query sample, and use the clear part to perform classification.

Figure 2. (a) A test sample with sunglass. (b) the binary mask extracted from (a). (c) test sample with mask.

3 Experiments

To verify the performance of our algorithm in dealing with occlusion, we use four state-of-the-art algorithms for comparison. They are the Nearest Neighbor (NN), LRC [11] and CRC [14] and SRC [6]. All the Matlab implementations are on a PC with Intel core i5 3.3GHz CPU, 8 GB RAM, and Windows 7 operating system.

3.1 Recognition with random pixel occlusion

In this experiment, we test the robustness of the proposed method in the presence of pixel corruption. We use the Extended Yale B database for this experiment. The Extended Yale B database [15] consists of 2414 frontal face images of 38 individuals under various laboratory-controlled lighting conditions. Subset 1 consists of 266 images (seven images per subject) under normal lighting conditions. Subsets 2 includes 12 images per subject, characterize slight illumination variations (as shown in Figure 3). For Subset 2, we replace 10%~60% of its pixels by uniformly distributed random values within [0,255] (as shown in Figure 4).The corrupted pixels are randomly chosen for each query image and the location are unknown to the algorithm. All images are cropped and resized to 64×56. Table 1 reports the recognition results of each algorithm. From this table, one can see our method classifies all the test samples correctly even in the case of 60% of the pixels are occluded.

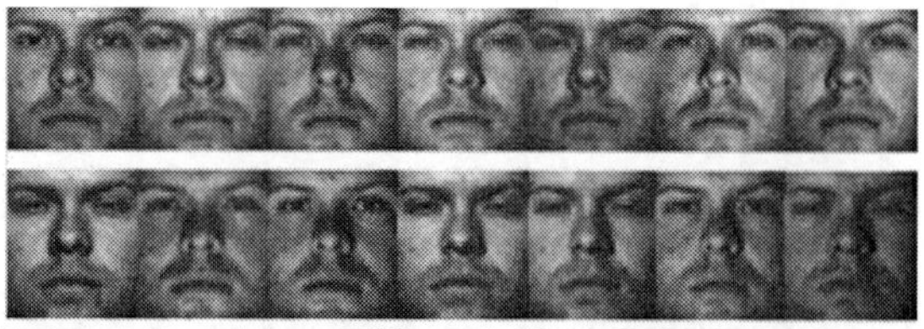

Figure 3. Two Subsets of Extended Yale B database. First row illustrates images from Subset 1, and second row Subset 2.

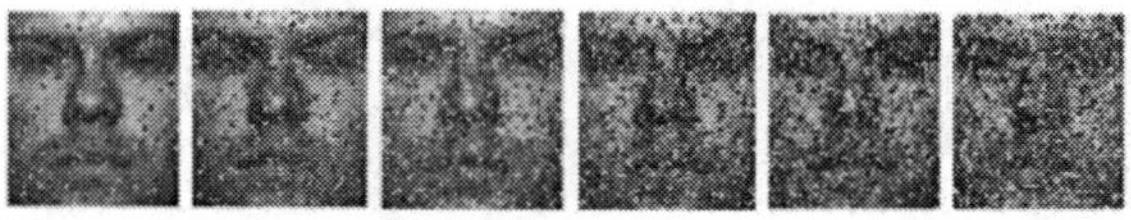

Figure 4. Test samples under varying level of random pixel occlusion, from left 10% to right 60%.

Table 1. Recognition results on the Extended Yale B database under varying level of random pixel occlusion using Subset 1 as training set.

	0%	10%	20%	30%	40%	50%	60%
NN	99.3	99.3	99.1	98.6	95.6	84.6	79.2
LRC [11]	100	100	100	100	99.1	94.3	87.7
CRC [14]	100	100	100	100	100	99.6	99.1
SRC [6]	**100**	**100**	**100**	**100**	**100**	**100**	**100**
Ours	**100**	**100**	**100**	**100**	**100**	**100**	**100**

3.2 Recognition with contiguous occlusion

The Extended Yale B database is used in this experiment. We use Subset 1 for training and Subsets 2 for testing. Various levels of contiguous occlusion are simulated by replacing a square block of each query image with an unrelated image (as shown in Figure 5.). The location of occlusion is randomly chosen and is unknown to the algorithms. Compared to random pixel corruption, contiguous occlusion is certainly a worse type of errors. As reported in Table 2, our algorithm outperforms other competing methods in the presence of contiguous occlusion.

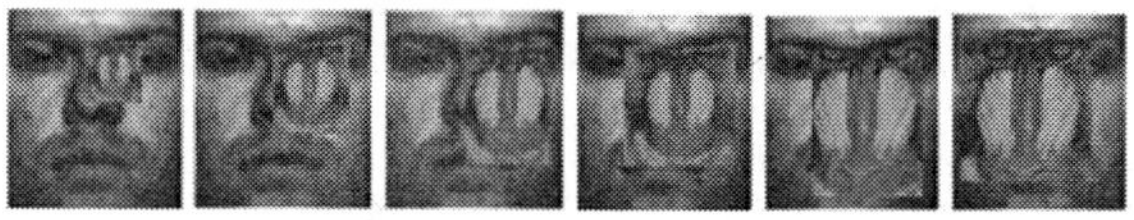

Figure 5. Test samples under varying level of contiguous occlusion, from left 10% to right 60%.

Table 2. Recognition results on the Extended Yale B database under varying level of contiguous occlusion using Subset 1 as training set.

	0%	10%	20%	30%	40%	50%	60%
NN	99.3	99.1	96.3	96.3	84.9	73.9	45.6
LRC [11]	**100**	**100**	99.8	99.1	89.5	77.2	49.1
CRC [14]	**100**	**100**	99.6	98.9	93.0	77.6	28.5
SRC [6]	**100**	**100**	**100**	**100**	**100**	90.1	67.1
Ours	**100**	**100**	**100**	**100**	**100**	**92.3**	**68.4**

3.3 Recognition with real disguise occlusion

In this section, experiments are carried out using a subset from the AR database [16] consisting of 100 individuals, 50 male and 50 female. 799 images of non-occluded frontal views with various facial expressions are used for training, while two separate sets of 200 images are selected for testing [12]. The first test set contains images of the subjects wearing sunglasses, which occlude roughly 25% of the face image. The second test set considered includes images of the subjects wearing a

scarf, which occludes roughly 40% of the face image. All images are cropped and resized to 84×60 (as shown in Figure 6).

We also present the recognition accuracy of SRC and LRC using partition scheme [6,11]. Each test sample was partitioned into 8 regions. From the recognition results in Table 3, It can be seen that our algorithm has a higher recognition rate comparing with other contrastive methods.

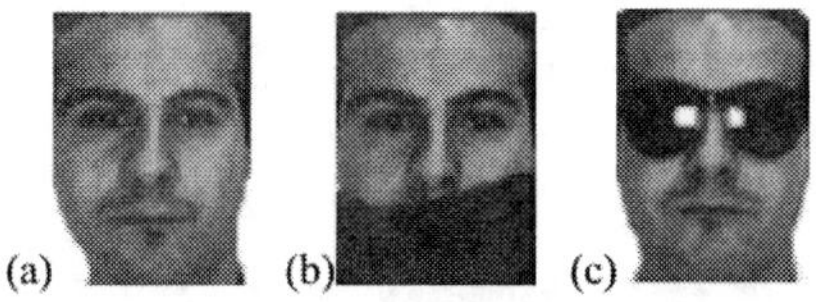

Figure 6. The training and test samples with sunglasses and scarf in AR database. (a) is the training sample, and (b)-(c) for test.

Table 3. Recognition results on the AR database with real disguise occlusion

	Scarf	Sunglasses
NN	12.0	69.0
CRC	90.0	66.5
LRC	11.5	68.0
LRC(partitioned)	73.0	93.0
SRC	60.5	87.0
SRC(partitioned)	**92.0**	94.0
Ours	**92.0**	**99.5**

4 Conclusions

In this paper, we present a novel method for robust face recognition in the presence of occlusion. We exploit the reconstruction residual of CRC model to detect the occlusion in test sample, and get a binary mask of the occlusion. Then the mask is used in the CRC scheme to isolate the side effect of occlusion in FR. Experimental results on Extended Yale B and AR database demonstrate that our algorithm performs well in dealing pixel occlusion , block occlusion and real disguise. The method does not assume any prior knowledge about the occluded regions, and can be analytically solved, and thus can be applied in a robust, real-time face recognition system.

Acknowledgments. This work is supported by National Nature Science Foundation of China (No.61571069), the open research fund of Chongqing key Laboratory of Emergency Communications and Chongqing University Postgraduates' Innovation Project (No.CYB15030).

References

1. Jafri, R., Arabnia, H. R. A survey of face recognition techniques. Jips, 11(19) (2009) 29-33
2. Turk, M., Pentland, A, Eigenfaces for recognition. Journal of Cognitive Neuroscience, 3 (**1**) (2007) 71-86
3. Belhumeur, P. N., Hespanha, J. P., Kriegman, D. J. Eigenfaces vs. fisherfaces: recognition using class specific linear projection. IEEE Trans. on Pattern Analysis and Machine Intelligence, 19 (**7**) (1997) 711-720
4. Chien, J. T., Wu, C. C, Discriminant waveletfaces and nearest feature classifiers for face recognition. IEEE Trans. on Pattern Analysis and Machine Intelligence, 24 (**12**) (2002) 1644-1649
5. Fidler, S.,Sko aj, D., Leonardis, A. Combining reconstructive and discriminative subspace methods for robust classification and regression by subsampling. IEEE Trans. on Pattern Analysis and Machine Intelligence, 28 (**3**) (2006) 337-350
6. J.Wright, A.Y.Yang, A.Ganesh, S.S. Sastry, Y. Ma, Robust face recognition via sparse representation, IEEE Trans. on Pattern Analysis and Machine Intelligence, 31 (**2**) (2009) 210–227
7. B. Cheng, J. Yang, S. Yan, Y. Fu, and T. Huang. Learning with l1-graph for image analysis. IEEE Trans. Image Processing, 19 (4) (2010) 858-866
8. S. Gao, I. Tsang, L. Chia, Kernel sparse representation for image classification and face recognition. In ECCV, 6314 (2010) 1-14
9. M. Yang, L. Zhang. Gabor feature based sparse representation for face recognition with Gabor occlusion dictionary. In ECCV, 6316 (2010) 448-461.
10. M. Yang, L. Zhang, J. Yang, D. Zhang. Robust sparse coding for face recognition. IEEE, 42(7) (2011) 625-632
11. Naseem, I., Togneri, R., Bennamoun, M. Linear regression for face recognition. IEEE Trans. on Pattern Analysis and Machine Intelligence, 32 (**11**) (2010) 2106-2112.
12. X. Luan, B. Fang, Face recognition with contiguous occlusion using linear regression and level set method. Neurocomputing, 122 (2013) 386–397
13. X. Luan, B. Fang, Extracting sparse error of robust PCA for face recognition in the presence of varying illumination and occlusion. Pattern Recognition, 47 (2) (2014) 495-508
14. L. Zhang, M. Yang, X. Feng, Sparse representation or collaborative representation: Which helps face recognition? Proceedings of the 2011 International Conference on Computer Vision IEEE Computer Society, (2011) 471-478
15. A. Georghiades, P. Belhumeur, D. Kriegman, From few to many: Illumination cone models for face recognition under variable lighting and pose, IEEE Trans. on Pattern Analysis and Machine Intelligence, 23 (2001) 643-660
16. A. Martinez, R. Benavente, The AR face database, CVC Tech. Report. 24, 1998.

MATEC Web of Conferences 44, 01040 (2016)
DOI: 10.1051/matecconf/20164401040

Research of the Technology and Application of Spacecraft Assembly Data-package Construction Based on MBD

Bi Le Wan [1], Chang Yu Chen [1] and Wen Xing He [1,a]

[1] *1Beijing Institute of Spacecraft Environment Engineering, Beijing 100094, China*

Abstract. In order to implement spacecraft assembly based on MBD, this article proposes a method to construct data-package automatically based on 3D model. First, an Assembly Digital Mock-up (ADMU) is constructed. Second, we propose the way of assembly process design based on 3D structural process design. Third, we construct the product data-package automatically based on the relationship among ADMU, the process files and production parameters Finally, the paper describes the application of the technology, and analyses the effect of the scheme during a satellite development. The technology and systems should be applied on other sophisticated products development, with some essential modifications.

1 Introduction

For international aerospace companies, Product Data-package is an assemblage of product data, specification and form, and its management is also an important work for product quality. For example, the ECSS (Europe Cooperation for Space Standardization) requires that the data-package must include manufacture data, assembly data, test data and event record, and the data-package is the foundation of the product delivery. Meanwhile, other companies or organizations propose similar requirements [1].

Traditionally, with two-dimensional drawings and files, people design in Computer Aided Process Planning (CAPP), and all product data need to deliver manually among departments, specialties, and careers, especially between the design department and the assembly department. So traditionally the data-package is constructed manually, but the development of Model Based Definition technology makes it possible to construct the data-package automatically [2].

Researchers have made much research on about Model Data Definition [3-4], Digital Mock-up construction [2] [5-6], Process Planning and Alteration Control [7-11]. But those papers didn't describe the technology of Data-package Construction Based 3D model and related systems. Scheme of 3d structural process design shown in Fig. 1.

In order to fulfill the requirement of the spacecraft assembly, the paper proposes 3D Data-package Construction scheme based on Assembly Process Digital Mock-up (APDM) and 3D Structural Process Design. The paper defines a special parameter named as Structural Assembly Parameter, and proposes the 3D Data-package Construction scheme based on it. The paper describes the workflow and introduces the application of a satellite development.

[a] Corresponding author: hewenxing@163.com

2 The Status of Spacecraft Digital Assembly

Currently, the spacecraft digital assembly has already realized structural process design based on three-dimension. The general idea is using process digital mock-up which inherits and refactors design digital mock-up as the only data source. Firstly, we conduct the design and simulation of process planning. After that, we conduct process explicit design and edition after the process of simulation verification. Materiels such as manufacturing resources, manufacturing information and design information can be acquired directly from process digital mock-up. Then the relevant process files, including media such as models, videos and pictures, are delivered to MES as production basis after approval. After that, the staff responsible for dispatch, quality or production conduct work and record production parameters through MES system. After executing that, relevant production data will be uploaded to process design system as data resources of assembly data-package.

3 The Definition and Construction of Spacecraft Assembly data-package

Before you begin to format your paper, first write and save the content as a separate text file. Keep your text and graphic files separate until after the text has been formatted and styled. Do not use hard tabs, and limit use of hard returns to only one return at the end of a paragraph. Do not add any kind of pagination anywhere

in the paper. Do not number text heads-the template will do that for you.

Finally, complete content and organizational editing before formatting. Please take note of the following items when proofreading spelling and grammar.

3.1 The definition of spacecraft assembly data-package

According to 'The quality and reliability data package space product and its application' and 'Research on the basic theory of product data-packages and product maturity', China's space industry defines data package as the product quality and reliability data-packages. It was born from the process of whole satellites and parts in the aerospace products from the design to the delivery, and it mainly record the product quality and reliability of the relevant documents and process information. The space product data packages are reflected in the whole process of the design, manufacture, testing and delivery of the product data and integrated into results of quantitative control of all technical activities. At the same time, product data-package is the object record of product realization process and the realization result.

In summary, spacecraft assembly data-package type faces to spacecraft system design, assembly and test, test and launchment and assembly of the entire process, including the overall design data, process design data, production data, test data and objective record data.

3.2 Constituent elements of spacecraft assembly data-package

With the development of 3D, the 3D data-packages of spacecraft can be divided into design data, process design data, production data, test data and objective data. The design data generally includes three-dimensional design data (such as three-dimensional model, structured data), technical documents, etc., as well as the relevant alteration of design data, technical notice and technical problem bills. Process design data including process planning (including formal process files and temporary process files), the implementation of change records, simulation video, workflow, process route, drawings and process alternation etc. Production data including production status data, executed production parameters, material data and the person who implemented. The inspection data includes the actual measurement parameters, the executor and the re-inspection information. The objective record data mainly includes the data of the objective state of the product, such as photos, video and so on.

All kinds of data in the three-dimensional assembly data exist in the form of electronic data, or a small amount of paper data (such as product transfer, review records, etc.). But comparing with the traditional assembly data-packages, the electronic data of three-dimensional assembly data-packages has the character of bidirectional correlation, such as the relation among counting machine and process digital mock-up, process digital mock-up and process rules, process rules and production data, production data and the implementation process, which makes the application of three-dimensional assembly data-packages convenient and proficient.

4 The Construction Scheme of Three-dimensional Assembly Data-packages

On the basis of constructing the digital mock-up and the 3D structural process design, the basic frame of the Built BOM is using Process BOM constructing the frame of Built BOM (known as three-dimensional assembly data-package). After that, it gradually builds a Built BOM with the implement. Then the Executed Process File BOM is constructed by combining the Process File BOM with the production data, and we can build a complete Built BOM through the real process tree and the bidirectional association of Process BOM. The general plan is shown as below. Assembly data-package construction shown in Fig. 1.

4.1 Definition of assembly structural parameter (ASP)

In the process of constructing 3D assembly data-package, the ASP is key to achieve this object. According to figure 1 and figure 2, the ASP is defined in the process file, which include three elements, the type of keywords, the main object product or related product, technical requirement and executed parameters.

Type keywords is the basis to determine the execution record type, including "install, remove and record", such as "XX product has been installed in place", "XX product has been removed" and "the insulation resistance of XX product is --". The type of installation and remove are critical to generate Built BOM, while the record type is the supplement of these two types. The keyword is determined when the system uses the definition of a record template.

Main object or relational object is the keyword to judge the ASP, and make it associated with the Process BOM, which determines the state or parameter of Built BOM. The keywords are determined by the process designer during process design.

Technical requirements are keywords of process requirements, and it is used to determine the type of production parameters. The keywords are determined by the process designer in the process design.

The production parameters are used to record the total actual production data, which are filled by inspectors, and automatically feedback to Built BOM after finishing the corresponding completion.

4.2 Assembly data-packages construction process based on ASP

The workflow as shown:

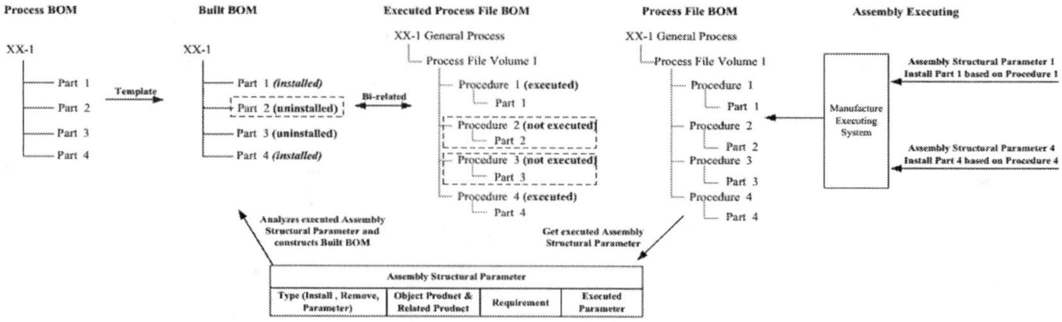

Fig.1 Assembly Data-package Construction

• Operation or inspection personnel in the MES check the three-dimensional process files and implement the assembly operation based on the process requirements. After that, they sign in the execution record of the three-dimensional process files and the implementation of the process in the MES system.
• Pending the completion of the process or procedure (i.e. completed deployment), MES will return process or step file that contain production data and ASP to the three-dimensional assembly data package system. In addition, photos and other objective data are returned by the inspection personnel through the MES tools after associating the photograph with process.
• Analysis the returned ASP (record of implementation of execution) and determine its type. Specifically, it is judged whether it belongs to the installation, removal or record.
• If it belongs to installation, first constructs Executed Process File BOM according to Process File BOM and analyzes main object of ASp. After that, connect the corresponding product to Built BOM. Besides, connects ASP with its parameters, and connects objective record data connected with implementation process files, such as photos, with Built BOM.
• If it belongs to demolition, removes corresponding product from Built BOM after generating the main BOM and analyzes main object. Then connects ASP.
• If it belongs to record, record ASP and its parameters to the corresponding product of Built BOM after generating the main tree and analyzes main object.

4.3 The Frame of 3D Assembly Data-packages System

3D assembly data-packages system contains Interface layer, Data flow, and Application layer, and the overall framework is shown in the following figure. The acquisition of the data is collected through the integration of MES and Webservice interface, and production data analysis is achieved by collecting the XML file returned through integration of the interface. Framework of 3D assembly data-package system shown in Fig. 2.

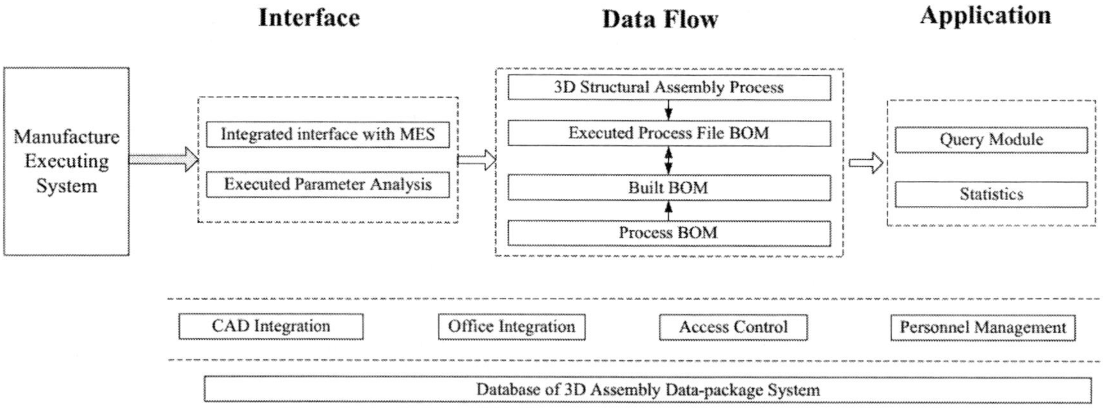

Fig.2 Framework of 3D Assembly Data-package System

5 Application

In the process of 3D assembly, automatic creation of 3D assembly data is realized on a certain type of product based on the construction of the digital prototype and the completion of the three-dimensional structure of the process design:
• Complete the association of design digital prototype, process digital prototype, process documents and production implementation of the relationship, and realize the traceable query of association, as shown in the following figure

• Realize the construction of digital experimental prototype shown in the form of tree structure, in which products have been installed tare represented in white, the uninstalled or dismantled products is shown in red .Besides, implementation of product model and types of real are consistent.
• Realize the association query of product object, implementation process and objective record of data and personalized comprehensive query and data statistics based on template.

6 Conclusion

This paper introduces the construction and application of spacecraft assembly data based on MBD. On the base of construction of the digital prototype of the model and the 3D structure design, this paper propose the construction scheme and process of 3D assembly data ,and illustrate the application effect by the case of model application.

Acknowledgement

This research is supported by Natural Science Foundation of China (51405025).

References

1. Hongtao Liu. Research on commercialization management evaluation in aerospace enterprise [D]. Hebei University of Technology. 2012.
2. Wenxing He, Bile Wan, Bin Zhang, Xinghui Wu. Research of the technology and application of process digital mock-up for spacecraft assembly. Advanced Materials Research. 2014(1037):447-452.
3. Yuqing Fan. Model Based Definition Technology and Its Practices. Aeronautical Manufacturing Technology. 2012(06):42-47.
4. Quintana V, Rivest L, Prellerin R, et al. Will Model-Based Definition replace engineering drawings throughout the product lifecycle? A global perspective from aerospace industry [J]. Computers in Industry. 2010, 61(5):497-508.
5. Zorriassatine F, Wykes C, Parkin R, et al. A survey of virtual prototyping techniques for mechanical product development [J]. Proceedings of the Institution of Mechanical Engineers, Part B (Journal of Engingeering Manufacture). 2003, 217(B4):513-530.
6. sebastien Gagne, Clement Fortin. Application of the CMII Model to an integrated engineering and manufacturing development environment. Ingt J Ineract Des Manuf. 2007(1):5-13.
7. Alemanni M, Destefanis F, Vezzetti E. Model-based definition design in the product lifecycle management scenario [J]. International Journal of Advanced Manufacturing Technology. 2011,52(1-4):1-14
8. Lihong Qiao, Jin Zhang. Some Key Issues in Three-Dimensional Digital Process Planning and Their Research. Aerospace Manufacturing Technology. 2010(1):29-32.
9. Tao Yang, Zhongyi Mei. Aircraft Full Three-Dimensional Implementation Technology Based on Mbd. Aerospace Manufacturing Technology. 2013(08):26-31.
10. Yuqing Fan, Yan Liang, Guocheng Feng. Data Organization of MBD-Based Assembly and Its Implementation, Aviation Maintenance & Engineering .6(2010)56-59.
11. In-Ho Song, Sung-Chong Chung. Synthesis of the digital mock-up system for heterogeneous CAD assembly. Computers in Industry. 2009(60):285-295.
12. Jiajun Yuan. Study of Aerospace Product Maturity. Spacecraft Engineering. 2011(20):1-7.

MATEC Web of Conferences 44, 01041 (2016)
DOI: 10.1051/matecconf/20164401041

Research and Progress on Virtual Cloud Laboratory

Jian Wei ZHANG[2], Zhi Hui SHANG[1], Chen YUAN[1], Lin Lin MA[1], Zeng Yu CAI[1], Chun Hui HU[2]

[1]*School of Computer and Communication Engineering, Zhengzhou University of Light Industry, Zhengzhou 450002, China*
[2]*Software Engineering College, Zhengzhou University of Light Industry, Zhengzhou 450002, China*

Abstract. In recent years, cloud computing technology has experienced continuous development and improvement, and has gradually expanded to the education sector. First, this paper will introduce the background knowledge of the current virtual cloud laboratory; by comparing the advantages and disadvantages between traditional laboratory and virtual cloud laboratory, and comparing the application, advantages and disadvantages, and development trend of OpenStack technology and VMWare technology in safety, performance, design, function, use case, and value of virtual cloud laboratory, this paper concludes that application based on OpenStack virtual cloud laboratory in universities and research institutes and other departments is essential.

1 Introduction

Many universities worldwide have numerous high laboratory teaching resources but low resource-sharing capability, which leads to the problem that laboratory teaching resources in universities often require multiple configurations to meet the need of laboratory teaching, or teaching resources cannot be effectively shared, resulting in a serious waste of teaching resources. Application of the virtual cloud computing platform is of great significance, having a great impact on integrating the hardware and software laboratory teaching resources in universities and improving the automation, networking and digitization of teaching. Typical universities are as follows: South China University of Technology mainly focuses on the service end design of OpenStack system; Sun Yat-Sen University mainly pays attention to the application of OpenStack in virtual classroom, and the major of Beijing University of Posts and Telecommunications is the research on OpenStack resource monitoring technology. The main purpose of those researches is to carry out secondary development on OpenStack, so that it can serve the school's teaching and research. By comparing the advantages and disadvantages between traditional laboratory and virtual cloud laboratory, and comparing the application, advantages and disadvantages, and development trend of OpenStack technology and VMWare technology in safety, performance, design, function, use case, and value of virtual cloud laboratory, this paper concludes that application based on OpenStack virtual cloud laboratory in universities and research institutes and other departments is essential.

2 Overview of Virtual Cloud Laboratory

2.1 Overview

Cloud computing[1]is based on the increase, use and delivery model of internet-related service, usually involving in providing dynamic, scalable and often virtualized resources via the Internet. The definition by National Institute of Standards and Technology (NIST) is widely accepted currently: cloud computing[2]is a pay-per-use model that supplies available, convenient, and on-demand network access, and gets into the shared pool of configurable computing resources (resources include network, server, storage, application, service), these resources can be provided quickly, and simply needs little management effort or little interaction with the service provider.

Thus,cloud computing mainly uses a distributed manner to reallocate computing resources, and and make distributed nodes work together to as to achieve simultaneous working. So in accordance with the form of service, the cloud is divided into services of the following three levels[3-4]: Infrastructure as a Service (IaaS), Platform as a Service (PaaS) and Software as a Service (SaaS), as shown in figure 1:

[a] Jian-wei ZHANG: 1126483520@qq.com

Article available at http://www.matec-conferences.org or http://dx.doi.org/10.1051/matecconf/20164401041

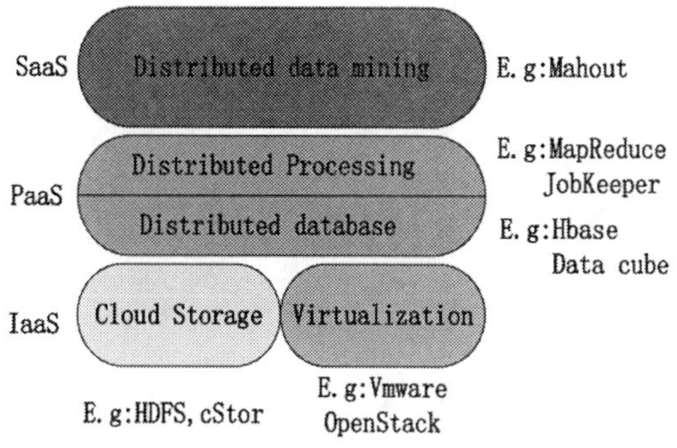

Figure 1. level of cloud computing services

Virtualization is to create a virtual version for some objects. It is an abstract method to represent computer resources. Through virtualization, abstracted resources can be accessed by the same way before the abstraction; a set of similar resources can be provided with a common abstract interface set, thereby hiding the differences between attribute and operation; a common way is allowed to view and maintain resources, including server virtualization, storage virtualization, application virtualization, platform virtualization, and desktop virtualization. Virtualization technology is a key technology that fully integrates and effectively uses a variety of computing and storage resources.

Cloud storage actually is also an application in teaching informatization cloud laboratory. For one thing, cloud storage can effectively arrange the teaching resources in laboratory so as to avoid the waste of teaching resources, and teachers and students can query related teaching resources through cloud storage. For another, cloud storage can integrate a variety of related teaching resources while investing in the construction of teaching resources, and provide multiple versions of teaching resources in different periods, so that teachers and students can make comparisons. Currently cloud storage technology in many colleges and universities has taken the lead, wherein the personal cloud storage services (jucbe) of Shanghai Jiaotong University run in 2012 has set us an example.

2.2 Introduction of OpenStack architecture

First, the role of each module in OpenStack architecture diagram will be introduced: the role of Heat is to arrange the required cloud user-defined OpenStack service, Horizon provides UI to other cloud services, Ceilometer is responsible for collecting the data of other services for monitoring, charges and other uses, another program that conducts authentication by Keystone to achieve the core of cloud computing is a virtual machine. In OpenStack, Nova is responsible for creating virtual machines, Glance provides mirror image for virtual machines, Cinder provides block storage for virtual machines, and Neutron is responsible for the network activity service of virtual machines. In addition, the object storage of OpenStack is in the charge of Swift, the image file of Glance and the backup volume of Cinder are stored on Swift. The overall architecture is shown in Figure 2:

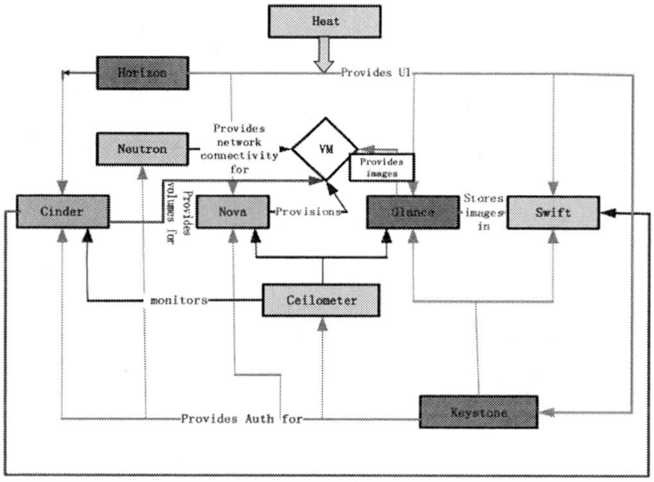

Figure 2. Architecture of OpenStack components

3 Classification of Laboratory

3.1 Traditional Laboratory

For the first time, Colleges and universities make a breakthrough in laboratory informatization teaching, which is a huge progress of the education sector. It is convenient for practical management and maintenance, as well as observation of failures and other problems. But with the gradual expansion of the scale of computer laboratory in universities, computer ownership is also on the increase. Many universities have the problem of large number of PC, high energy consumption, low resource utilization, management and maintenance difficulties and other issues, specifically in the six areas: tense funding, high energy consumption, difficult management and maintenance, low efficiency, low resource sharing, and difficult software update.

3.2 Virtual Cloud Laboratory

We will use cloud computing technology to build a private cloud of laboratory based on existing infrastructure, take advantage of virtualization to simulate rare hardware, build required experimental simulation environment, establish greater teaching and research platform, and provide large-scale reliable, scalable environment for software. In laboratory construction and management, laboratory built with the virtual cloud technology has the advantages that a traditional laboratory does not: less investment, high efficiency, high utilization, high experiment resource sharing, and convenient, fast and efficient management and maintenance of laboratory.

Compared with conventional laboratory, although virtual cloud laboratory boosts incalculable advantage, it also has its own drawbacks and shortcomings: Firstly, it

has difficulties in management and maintenance; different from the traditional laboratory management, all the resources of virtual cloud computer laboratory is virtualized on the server, and configuration and management of virtual resources are relatively difficult, therefore, familiarity of management personnel with virtualization and cloud computing technology determines the management and maintenance effectiveness of virtual computer laboratory. Secondly, the three-dimensional image processing capacity is limited; three-dimensional image processing capability of virtualized server hardware resources is poor; professional 3D graphic image testing software 3Dmark is applied for testing; a CPU-intensive hardware can only bring 30% of the performance into play, thus, it can be seen that a virtual computer lab cannot complete experiments which require a lot of three-dimensional image processing such as 3Dmax, AutoCAD and other three-dimensional graphic softwares. Table 1 is a comparison of the advantages and disadvantages between traditional laboratory and virtual cloud laboratory.

Table 1. comparison of the advantages and disadvantages between traditional laboratory and virtual cloud laboratory

	Traditional Laboratory	Virtual Cloud Laboratory
Advantages	For the first time, informatization teaching is achieved which facilitates effective management and maintenance, as well as observation of failures and other problems.	Less investment, high efficiency, high utilization, high experiment resource sharing, and convenient, fast and efficient management and maintenance of laboratory.
Disadvantages	Tense funding, high energy consumption, difficult management and maintenance, low efficiency, low resource sharing, and difficult software update.	Difficult management and maintenance, limited three-dimensional image processing capability, poor three-dimensional image processing capability of virtualized server hardware resources.

4 Development of Virtual Cloud Laboratory Technology

In the cloud computing ecosystem, there are two types of users that need to use cloud computing resources: Traditional IT applications and Cloud-aware applications gradually rising in the tide of the Internet. The cloud computing Vision, function, feature comparison or trend of VMWare and OpenStack will give you a vivid portrayal. Applied architecture in the future should be treated the same as virtual machines: compared with cloud computing application pattern, "care" of VMware and various functions to protect the virtual machine become increasingly less important.

4.1 Introduction of Virtual Cloud Laboratory based on OpenStack

OpenStack [5] is a Apache-licensed free software and open source project co-developed and initiated by NASA and Rackspace, which is designed to provide software for the construction and management of public and private clouds. Private cloud of Rackspace based on OpenStack revenues $ 700 million per year, an increase of more than 20%. It creates an opportunity to enter the field of cloud computing for hosting providers who wish to provide customers with cloud services. The project can help enterprises and service providers to achieve the infrastructure services similar to Amazon EC2 and S3, and change the actual server resources into computing resources changing according to demand so as to provide services to users in the form of a virtual machine. In addition, it can also help companies or institutions to establish their own private cloud, integrate the internal computing resources to provide services for sectors. The main purpose of the current considerable research on OpenStack of domestic colleges and universities is to carry out secondary development, enabling it to serve the teaching and research of the school. Virtual cloud laboratory is to carry out secondary development through OpenStack open source so as to achieve the application in teaching.

Features:

(1)OpenStack is an open source project, which facilitates the development and utilization of virtual cloud laboratory.

(2)OpenStack private cloud business growth rate has been increased.

(3)Computing resources changing according to demand can provide services to users in the form of a virtual machine.

(4)Pace of cloud construction can be promoted; IT operating cost can be reduced; business agility can be increased, energy can be conserved, industrial upgrading can be promoted.

4.2 Introduction of Virtual Cloud Laboratory based on VMW

Virtual Machine ware is a "virtual PC" software company, and products of the company can provide solutions to server and desktop virtualization. Products of its virtualization platform include players; VMware life cycle management can provide control over the virtual environment, realizing multi-performance of computers. The method provided by VMware can speed up the transition to cloud computing while retaining existing investments and improving security and control.

It allows you to run two or more Windows, DOS, LINUX systems simultaneously on a single machine. Compared with the "multi-boot" system, VMWare uses a completely different concept. Multi-boot system can only run one system at a time and should re-start the machine when one system switches into another. VMWare really runs "simultaneously"; multiple operating systems can switch into each other on the platform of the main system, like standard Windows application. Each operating

system can have a virtual partition and configuration without affecting the real hard drive data, and several virtual machines can be connected into a local area network with the network cards, which is extremely convenient. Performance of the operating system on VMware is lower than that directly on the hard disk, therefore, it is more suitable for learning and testing.
Features:
(1) providing solutions to server and desktop virtualization.
(2)accelerating the transition to cloud computing.
(3) conducting virtual partition and configuration.
(4) starting multiple systems simultaneously.

4.3 Contrast between OpenStack technology and VMware technology

In Cloud area,contrast between OpenStack and VMware is discuss most. The contrast content can be completed by comparing the key point of the two cloud computing products in the data center application. The contrast content specifically includes the following six sections: safety, performance, design, function, customer use case and value.

4.3.1 From the point of view of security

The openness of OpenStack open source cloud platform allows us to quickly identify and fix security vulnerabilities, which can reduce the possibility of overflow, and has flexibility and compatibility. Generally speaking. open source project has a good track record, but they also have holes and vulnerabilities, OpenStack is still an emerging area. VMware has high safety, which can be viewed as two separate computers to use. If the network in virtual machines is set only for the host, external network can not access the internal network of the virtual machine.

4.3.2 From the point of view of performance

OpenStack lacks practicality. Currently most scientific research institutes, businesses and other organizations are using its open source for secondary development, so many of the functions need to perfect himself. However, the code is more flexible and has strong compatibility. VMware performance is not high, and support of some hardware is not good, which is mainly shown in some peripherals linked in the virtual machine. CPU performance of VMware virtual system have some losses compared with the real system, but the performance has not been not significantly attenuated. Performance of register operation, integer operation, floating-point operation and many other operations are varied compared with that of the real system.

4.3.3 From the point of view of design

OpenStack is an open source system, and no one single company is in control of the development path of OpenStack. Many companies are supporting the development of OpenStack, because it has great market power, and the development of OpenStack is diversified. However, some problems have occurred; implementation and maintenance of OpenStack deployment and infrastructure costs much more than those of VMware. At the same time, due to the relatively fast pace of version updates, technical support document cannot keep up the pace.

The advantages of VMware product is in the robustness of its architecture, and users of high-profile have used it in a multi-scale data center environment. The drawback of VMware is that the software system is closed, and software development route is in full compliance with VMware's own development goals; users or consumers do not have any control in this regard.

4.3.4 From the functional point of view

Among OpenStack, KVM supports block storage migration, and dynamic migration of KVM allows a virtual machine to migrate from one virtual machine manager to another. OpenStack scheduler includes scheduling for the compute and volume; through a series of rule parameters and filters set by the administrator, OpenStack scheduler deploys a virtual machines to an appropriate host. In terms of filter, the scheduler is very flexible; users can complete a filter with JSON format themselves and the filter also contains a number of predefined filters. Although OpenStack scheduler is very flexible, it still cannot completely replace DRS.

VMware fault tolerant mechanism monitors the state of the virtual machine and all changes, these changes will be synchronized to the second backup ESX (i) server. The concept of fault tolerance is that whether it is the main host or the minor host that has a problem, as long as one can work, the virtual machine on the host maintains normal operation. VMware already does not require shared storage to achieve dynamic migration. When a virtual machine is migrated from one host to another, the virtual machine's memory status and data migration should be synchronized. If the case is a shared memory, in fact, the data does not need to be migrated, only the link pointing to the data storage should be changed. This can reduce the network load during replication while accelerating the migration speed.

4.3.5 From the functional point of use case

Cloud computing application is not required. When a virtual machine has a problem, a new virtual machine will replace it. OpenStack inherited this advantage. Although VMware has many functions that OpenStack does not, for cloud computing applications, these functions become less important. In future, you probably will pay for the uncontrollable additional functions of VMware, which is of little use. Compared with cloud computing applications, the maintenance of VMware, and the protection of the various functions of virtual machines become increasingly less important.

4.3.6 From the functional point of value

It is still not clear whether OpenStack is more valuable than VMware, and the answer depends on the size of the deployment. Although OpenStack is free to use, it needs numerous engineering resources and experts, as well as a lot of effort in architecture and construction. As it supports many deployment scenarios, and the installation processes are different. VMware needs some funds to purchase rights, and is relatively easier to install and run; in addition, compared with the command line, the learning cost of VMware is lower.

Generally speaking, OpenStack has high barrier to entry, but with the expansion of the scale of the project, you will benefit from it, because you do not need to pay high copyright fees. Although VMware is relatively easy to install in a small scale, but with the expansion of the scale, things have changed. That is, with the large-scale expansion of cloud application, we are more familiar with OpenStack, so barrier to entry into OpenStack is much lower. Not long ago, the CEO of OpenStack Foundation, Jonathan Bryce, said at the OpenStack summit in Vancouver, Canada that it was OpenStack that made the software more meaningful and things became more modular and easier with OpenStack. At the same time, he also clearly showed that the deep integration of that OpenStack community and the Docker community has entered a substantive stage, which is the direction of future development.

4.3.7 Comparison Results between OpenStack and VMware Shown in the Figure

Thus, VMware is better than OpenStack in safety, design and function, but worse than it in performance, use case and value. If the full point is 10 in safety, performance, design and other aspects, then the gap among those comparison trend can be seen in the bar chart, as well as the comprehensive comparison trend between VMware and OpenStack. The comprehensive comparison between VMware and OpenStack is shown in Figure 3.

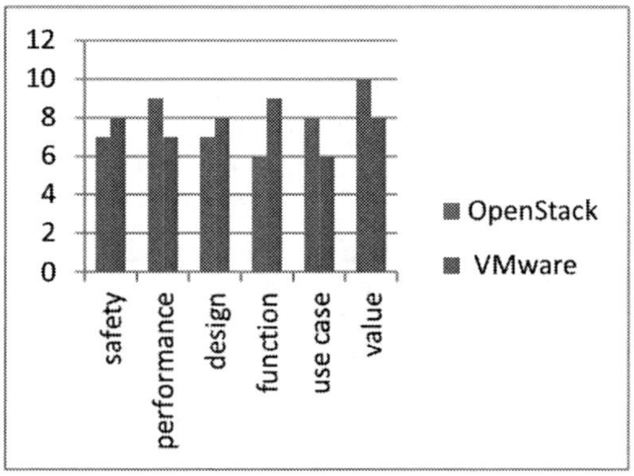

Figure 3. The comprehensive comparison chart between OpenStack and VMware

Conclusion:

1 OpenStack technology takes an advantage over VMware technology in overall.
2 Virtual cloud laboratory based on OpenStack technology is the future development direction of the laboratory.

5 Conclusion

In summary, through the discussion of cloud computing, cloud storage, and virtual cloud of virtual cloud laboratory, the advantages and disadvantages of traditional laboratory and virtual cloud laboratory can be found, and finally we come to the conclusion that virtual cloud lab will be the development trend of laboratory in the information age. Through the comparison between OpenStack technology and VMware technology, the advantages of OpenStack technology in virtual cloud laboratories can be seen. Application of virtual cloud platform based on OpenStack technology will be the development direction in the next few years, and it can further improve the digitalization, networking , and automation of virtual experiment teaching.

Acknowledgements

This work is Supported by 2016 Outstanding Innovation Science and Technology Youth Project of the Innovation Scientists and Technicians Plan of Henan Province: research of the macro scenario fitting routing technology centering on content. Zhengzhou 2015 science and technology development plan (key science and technology): research on virtual cloud desktop scheduling key technology based on OpenStack（153PKJGG26）. the Graduate's Scientific Research Foundation of Zhengzhou University of Light Industry.

References

1. Zhang Q,Cheng L,Boutaba R.Cloud computing: state-of-the-art and research challenges[J]. Journal of internet services and applications , vol.1,no.1, 7-18 (2010).
2. Armbrust M, Fox A, Griffith R, et al. A view of cloud computing[J]. Communications of the ACM, vol.53,no.4, 50-58(2010).
3. Mell P, Grance T. The NIST Definition of Cloud Computing[J]. NIST Special Publication,145(2011).
4. Luo J Z,Jin J H, Song A B, et al. Cloud computing: architecture and key technologies[J].Journal of China Institute of Communications, vol.32,no.7,3-21(2011).
5. OpenStack Cloud Administrator Guide[J]. docs.openstack.org, (2014).
6. Cao Wei. Application of cloud computing platform based on OpenStack in university teaching. Hei Longjiang Information Technology,vol..26,183-184(2014).
7. Wan Hongfeng. Construction and application of teaching cloud computing platform based on

OpenStack.China High Technology Enterprises,No.20,45-46(2015).
8. Lv Site. Virtualization, A Beginner's Guide. Bei Jing: China Machine Press, (2011).
9. Ren Yu, Li Qingrong. Research on virtualization resource management platform based on VMware vSphere. Computer Applications and Software.vol.5,219-223(2012).
10. Sun Tao, Qiao Zhihe, Li Juan. Application of virtual cloud technology in computer laboratory construction management. Journal of Daqing Normal University,vol33,no.3,139-141(2013).
11. Zhang Jianwei, Wang Lu, Cai Zengyu,et al. System design and implementation of college graduation project whole-process management based on Web. Journal of Zhengzhou University of Light Industry: natural science edition,vol.24,no.5,54-58(2009).

Jian-wei ZHANG,born in April, 1971, Henan, P R china Current position, grades: Professor at Zhengzhou University of Light Industry, China University studies: PhD degree from The PLA Information Engineering University in China Scientific interest: broadband information network and network security .

Zhi-hui SHANG, born in November, 1989, Henan, grades: A graduate student at Zhengzhou University of Light Industry, Scientific interest: Cloud computing and computer network .

MATEC Web of Conferences 44, 01042 (2016)
DOI: 10.1051/matecconf/20164401042

A Cigarette Surface Defect Detection System Based on Data Acquisition Card

Jun Li Cao[1a], Ju Feng Li[1], Teng Da Lu[1]

[1]*School of Mechatronics Engineering and Automation, Shanghai University, Shanghai 200072,China*
[a]*caojunli1009@163.com*

Abstract. The author introduces a self-learning control system used in cigarette surface defect detection system. The database, data acquisition card and industrial computer are used to realize high speed detection of cigarette surface defects. The results show that the advantages compared with the traditional measurements are as follows: Firstly, realize the detection of entire cigarette surface; Secondly, achieve the unmanned operation with no manual operation needed from the beginning to the end; Thirdly, save the qualified and unqualified testing data, convenient to historical retrospection and data statistics.

1 Introduction

The traditional method of surface defects detection mainly relies on the artificial observation which is inefficient and not comprehensive. Even if there are some manufacturers using automatic detection system, most of them aim at the detecting the shape of the seal, rather than the position of the seal and other defects on the cigarette[1]. Therefore, this paper introduces a work piece surface defect detection system based on the data acquisition card and database in improving the work piece machining process with high measurement accuracy and efficiency.

2 Overview

System works as shown in Figure 1,the programming language of the system is C# based on Visual Studio software. And the program includes the information of measuring point on work piece surface and the database of measurement information. Firstly, the system controls the motion of work piece and the detection of defect by servo motor and optical encoder. Then, the DAQ-2010 data acquisition card collects signal and realizes analogue-to-digital conversion[3]. Thirdly, IPC processes and stores the data, and sends the results to PLC. Finally, PLC issues an instruction to remove the non-qualified cigarettes according to the test results. For Human–Computer Interaction, the operators can set the parameters and adjust the historical data manually through the user interface.

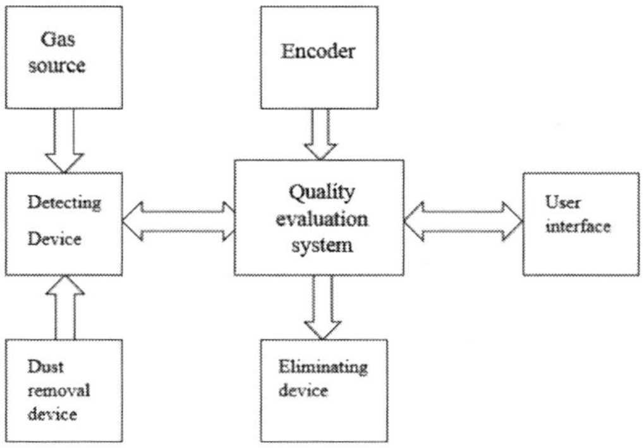

Figure 1. Schematic diagram of cigarette defect detection system

3 Detection System constitution

3.1. Data acquisition card selection and control

DAQ-2010 is the data acquisition card in Ling China. It can simultaneously collect the four circuit voltage signal based on PCI bus. The work performance of DAQ-2010 data acquisition card is as follows: supporting 32-bit 3.3 V or 5 V PCI bus;4 channel differential analog input; synchronous sampling rate up to 2 Ms/s;14 A/D resolution; up to 8 K sampling A/D FIFO; double or single polarity analog input range; programmable gain:x1,x2,x4,x8. DAQ - 2010 data acquisition card also provides secondary development of file based on a variety of programming languages such as VB, VC, VC + +, c # and so on[4,10].

[a] Corresponding author: caojunli1009@163.com

The control process of PC software based on C# programming language and data acquisition card is as follows:

1) Install driver, then automatically generate dynamic link library files D2K-Dask.dll on disk c;

2) Call the library function of the data acquisition card;

3) Initialize the data acquisition card;

Firstly, there will be a card number after registering the card using the function D2K_Register_Card;

Then, set the acquisition voltage range and acquisition mode of each card using the function D2K_AI_CH_Config and D2K_AI_Config.For this project ,the voltage range is -10V~10V,the acquisition mode is external trigger, and the external trigger signal is A pulse in Optical encoder. The data acquisition card collects data once the A pulse detected. The optical encoder is installed on the motor which is used for production. There are 256 pulses in one revolution of the optical encoder. And the length of each 64 pulses is as long as one detected cigarette.

Thirdly, set the acquisition channel using the function D2K_GCTR_Reset.Set the acquisition mode using the function D2K_GCTR_Setup and D2K_GCTR _Control. The acquisition of A pulse is on the service of the detecting production rate[6].

Finally, set the cache. Create the double cache using the function D2K_GCTR_Reset to insure the speed of operation and the data security. For the double cache, one is used to handle the cached data, the other is used for data acquisition. And set the cache to 256 bytes, the same size as 4 cigarettes.

That is all the work for the initialization of the data acquisition card.

4)Enable and close the data acquisition card;

Enable the data acquisition card using the function D2K_AI_ContReadChannel.It begins to acquit data once receiving the external trigger signal. After using the acquisition card, release the cache using the function D2K_AI_AsyncClear, and close the data acquisition card using function D2K_Release_Card.

3.2 Optical Detection

Optical detection device is composed of photoelectric diode, lens, LED lamp and amplifying circuit. Optical detection has the advantages of fast measurement, high sensitivity, simple operation, low price and so on[2,9] .The optical detection operating diagram is shown in Figure 2 as follows. This optical detection system is divided into eight channels, each channel with two LED lights. LED lights on the surface of the cigarette, and the light is focused on the photodiode by spectacle lenses after the reflection .

The voltage signal generated on the photodiode is amplified by the amplifying circuit and then outputted .Then the data acquisition card acquits the voltage signal to distinguish the surface colour on the cigarette.

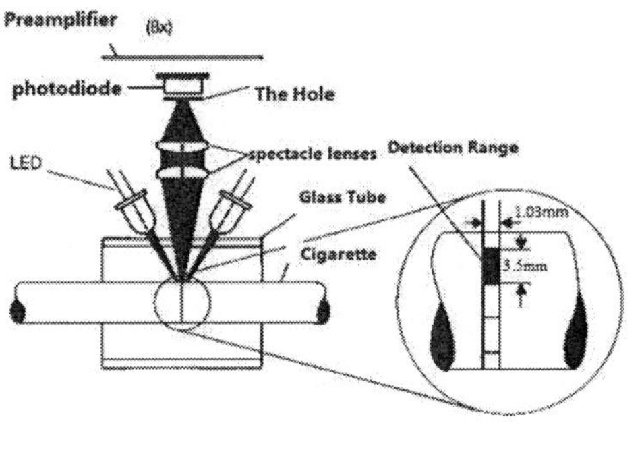

Figure 2. The optical detection principle

3.3 Self-learning and Data storage

3.3.1 self-learning system

The program starts to run automatically after the computer powered- on. The multithreading technology is used in the program because of the need for high-speed acquisition and processing. Among these threads, the acquisition card monitoring thread ,velocity measurement thread, A pulse counting thread and learning thread are related to the self-learning system.

The velocity measurement thread starts running after the program begins working . The principle of velocity measurement is to collect the number of A pulse in Optical encoder. When the number of A pulse reaches the requirement, the system starts to execute the self-learning mode. The operating diagram of velocity measurement thread is shown in Figure 3 as follows:

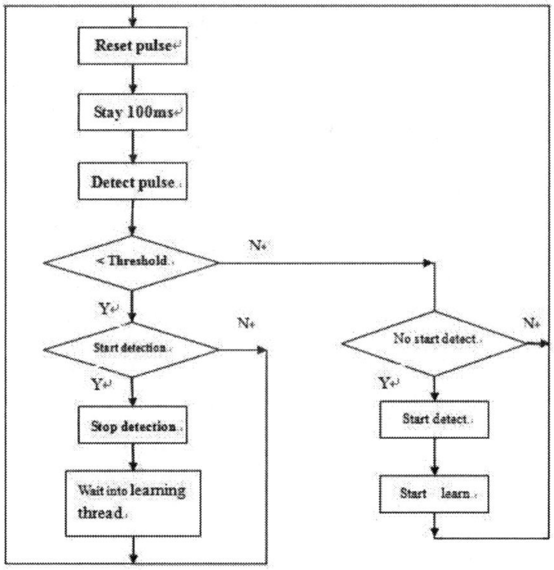

Figure 3. The optical detection principle

The number of A pulse is counted by the A pulse counter. The data acquisition monitoring thread card starts detecting the state of the card. When half full (one buffer of the double is full), extract data and transform the data into standard voltage value using the function

D2K_AI_ContVScale. Then, the learning thread will collect 20 sets of data, and compute a standard template using these data. The learning thread functional diagram is shown as figure 4. In this system, the learning thread starting signal is provided by velocity thread; the half full signal that a set of data detected is provided by monitoring thread. For the leaning process, the first step is saving the acquitted data; then find the Z pulse generated by the motor when it turns a turn. The third step is alignment data. The number of pulses may be more than 256 in one revolution of the optical encode because of mechanical vibration. So it is absolutely important to align data based on the Z pulse when detecting the position of seal on the cigarette.

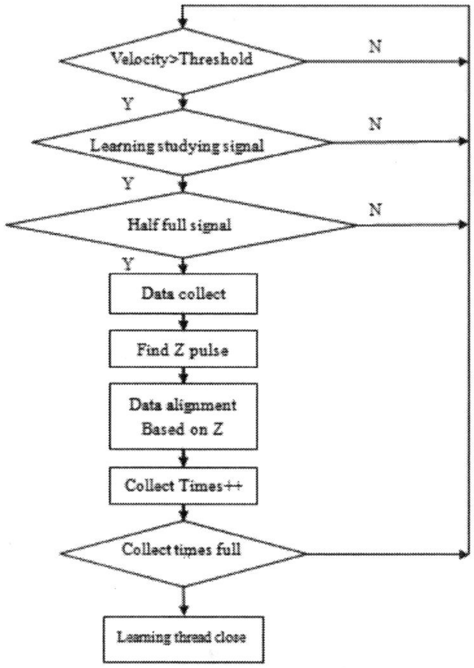

Figure 4. The learning thread principle

Acquisition times are set up in the program. The initial value is 20 which can be also changed manually. When the acquitted times comes to the initial value, the system stops collecting data and begins processing data. And the processing mainly includes calculating the average curve and envelope. The average curve is calculated by the average value of the test points in 20 sets of data. Then calculate the upper and lower envelope according to the average curve. The average curve and envelope are as shown in figure 5, where the X-axis is the length of detected cigarette and the Y-axis is the voltage value acquitted.

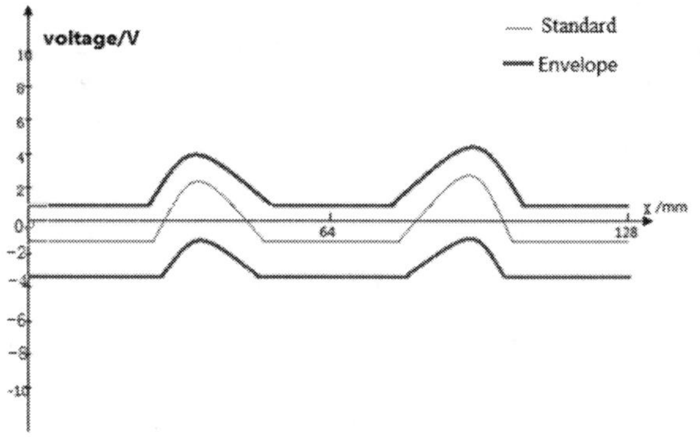

Figure.5. The learning thread figure

In figure 5,the standard curve is the average curve .And the length of a standard cigarette is 64mm. As long as the value of detected point is within the envelope, the result is qualified. After learning ,the learning thread is closed and detected thread starts. The self-learning system reduces the intensity of work caused by different varieties of cigarette .

3.3.2 Data storage

C# provides a variety of interface technology such as ODBC,DAO,OLE/DB and ADO to support database programming. Through these interfaces, the database such as Microsoft Access, SQL Server can be operated directly. But we find that these databases can not store such the fast update data, so we use txt to store these data using Stream Writer. Because the storage speed will be lower and lower with the increase of file memory, the program creates 600 txt files one day such as 1.txt, 2.txt, 3.txt……600.txt to reduce the size of every single file. Once comes the half full, the data is put into one txt in the program. In this way, the error in program and data missing can be avoided . The following is a storage code for qualified data:

```
if (count > 1 && Write)//Write is the signal for
//starting
{
saving = true;
Write = false;
if (fileNo == 600)
{ fileNo = 1; }//fileNo is the no. for file
else
{
fileNo++;
}
Settings.Default.fileno = fileNo;// Save the current
//file number
Settings.Default.Save();
string time =
System.DateTime.Now.ToString("hh:mm:ss.fff");
string C1, C2, C3, C4, C5, C6, C7, C8, D;
wlog =
File.AppendText(@"d:\\Adlink\DataBase\TXTDATA\" +
name + "\\" + classNo + "\\" + fileNo.ToString() + ".txt");
for (int i = 0; i < ANo/2; i++)
{
```

```
...... // storage code for qualified data:
wlog.Write("{0}", sqlStr + "\r\n");
wlog.Flush();
}
wlog.Close();
saving = false;
}
```

Wlog is a new Stream Writer method .The program specifies the file path, and opens the file using the function File.Appendtext();The function wlog.Write() is used to write data ; The function wolg.Flush() is used to save the file. Then wlog.Close() is used to close the connection.

The problem of data high speed memory is solved by txt which is convenient to historical data tracing and statistics.

4 Conclusion

This is a self-learning control system used in a cigarette surface defect detection system. When the machine is powered, the computer and program start automatically. The self-learning and detection can be finished automatically without any manual operation. The cigarette is full rang detected by optical measurement .The program includes all kinds of defect statistics. And the unqualified cigarette will be eliminated by the eliminating valve.

Acknowledgements

This work was supported by Chang De cigar mill. The authors would also like to express their thanks to the associate professor Li

References

1. Liu Yong, Cheng, Xiao, Zhang Long, Zhu Zhen, Wang An. Design of Cigarette Circumference Gauge based on DSP. Measurement & Control Technology, 2008,No.7:p38-39(in Chinese)
2. Hong Jie. Design of Online Cigarette's Circumference Detection based on Laser Sensor. Journal of Hunan University of Arts and Science (Natural Science Edition), 2012,Vol. 24, No. 3
3. Yu Jinbin. The Application of High-speed Acquisition Card. Computer CD Software and Applications,No.14, 2012(in Chinese)
4. Zhang Guangjun. Machine Vision[M].Beijing: Science Press ,2005
5. Long jie, Zhao Qiuming, Jia Leilei. he Application of Acquisition Card in Industry based on PCI Bus. Journal of Changchun institute of Technology (National Sciences Edition.) , 2011,Vol. 12. No.1(in Chinese)
6. Yin Xiuyan. Application of programmable control technology[M].Beijing: Publishing House of Electronics Industry
7. Liu Cheng, Zeng Fanjun. The Research and Application of Cigarette Circumference Measurement System on Cigarette Making Machine. Equipment Manufacturing Technology, 2011,No.7
8. Nanko. Possibility of machine vision in the pulp and paper industry. Kami Pa Gikyoshi/Japan Tappi Journal. 2009, v 63, n 3: p 28-31
9. Field, Jim. SMD Placement Using Machine Vision. Electronic Packaging and Production. 1986, v26, n1:p128-129
10. Gao Xuefei, Zhu Kaiyu, Su Zhen. Design of Ion-coating Monitoring System Based on Advantech Data Acquisition Card and MCGS Software. Control and Instruments in Chemical Industry, 2012,NO.2

MATEC Web of Conferences 44, 01043 (2016)
DOI: 10.1051/matecconf/20164401043

Analysis and Implement of Broadcast Program Monitoring Data

Jin Bao Song [1,a], Lun Lun Huang[1]

[1]Information Engineering School, Communication University of China, Beijing, China

Abstract. With the rapid development of the radio and TV industry and the implementation of INT (the integration of telecommunications networks, cable TV networks and the Internet), the contents of programs and advertisements is showing massive, live and interactive trends. In order to meet the security of radio and television, the broadcast of information have to be controlled and administered. In order to master the latest information of public opinion trends through radio and television network, it is necessary research the specific industry applications of broadcast program monitoring. In this paper, the importance of broadcast monitoring in public opinion analysis is firstly analysed. The monitoring radio and television programs broadcast system architecture is proposed combining with the practice, focusing on the technical requirements and implementation process of program broadcast, advertisement broadcast and TV station broadcast monitoring. The more efficient information is generated through statistical analysis, which provides data analysis for radio and television public opinion analysis.

1 Introduction

The program analysis of broadcasting and television public opinions is the analysis of public opinion in essence. Public opinion is people's social and political attitudes on the social management surrounding the occurrence, development and change of the intermediary social events in the certain social space. It is the sum of the performance of beliefs, attitudes, opinions and emotions and so on expressed by the more public about the various phenomena in the society[1]. Public opinions form rapidly and have the huge influence to the society. Not only Party and government cadres at all levels need to pay close attention to public opinions, but also the all sectors of society need pay great attention to public opinions[2]. In general, the broadcast television public opinion analysis is an important part of radio and television industry.

Newspapers, broadcasting, television, network is the main channel reflects the social public opinion. Compared to newspapers and network, it determines that broadcasting and television has the characteristics of public opinion:

1) timeliness; through the cable and satellite transmission, they can quickly cover nationwide.

2) authority; It reports and publicizes the policies of the government.

3) popularity; Broadcasting's coverage rate is 98% .Television's coverage rate is 92%. They are the most common direct access to information sources for people[3].

Along with the development of broadcasting and television, broadcasting television public opinion analysis is taken seriously more and more, and become an important and hot research topic[4]. As the mainstream, the authoritative media, broadcasting and television public opinion analysis hasn't been researched on due to the restrict of one-way transmission. Lack of the situation analysis and statistics of broadcasting and television, it restricts the further development of broadcasting and TV industry[5].

In order to make the public opinion analysis system can be more complete and the concluded analysis data can be more standard, the national radio and television broadcasting must be monitored[6]. In order to improve the quality and level of radio and television broadcast and transmission, ensure the safety of radio and television broadcast and transmission quality and prevent the radio and television fault broadcasting, bad broadcasting even off the air, we must strictly monitor the radio and television signal[7]. We should not only investigate users viewing behaviour, but also monitor the broadcast content of radio and TV station and cable TV in every district in cities in order to understand the national radio and television broadcasting[8].

The study of this topic in the information society and the media, under the background of the accurate diagnoses in national broadcasting and television, promotes the influence and approval of radio and television broadcasting a healthy and orderly, harmonious development.

2 The monitoring radio and television programs broadcast system architecture

[a] Corresponding author: songjinbao@cuc.edu.cn

Article available at http://www.matec-conferences.org or http://dx.doi.org/10.1051/matecconf/20164401043

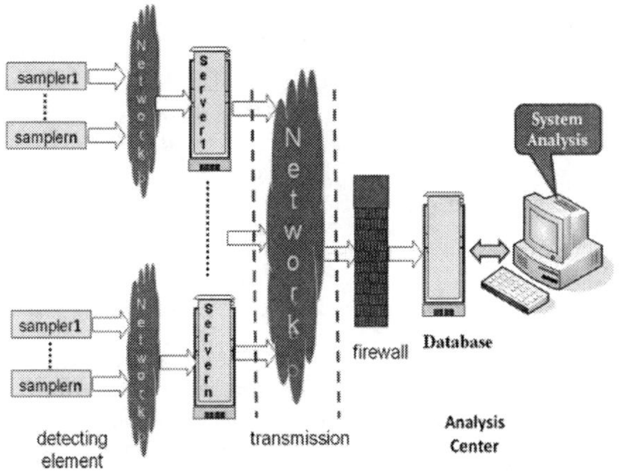

Figure 1. The monitoring radio and television programs broadcast system architecture

The show program source is gained from detecting cities. There are two types of program, type Ⅰ superimposed by watermarking, type Ⅱ without any watermarking. The pictures of each shown program are sampled from cable television network using frame samplers. Then the data is stored in the disk, encrypted and transmitted back to analysis center using the Internet at night when network isn't busy. All the information enters the data storage structure through the Internet according to frame dispatching mechanism in the analysis center. For type Ⅰ, watermark is decoded. For type Ⅱ, it is treated with image matching retrieval. The formation of the actual radio and television broadcast programs data and audience rating data is produced by the two ways. Then all the information data entries processing and management system. In management system, through radio and television broadcast content analysis software will do data mining and statistical analysis of various content[3].

The concrete modules of the monitoring radio and television programs broadcast system are as follows:

- frame sampler module
- frame sampler dispatching module
- television content watermark superimposition and recognition module
- image matching and recognition module
- program background information data module
- storage structure, database module
- broadcasting and television public opinion analysis software modules

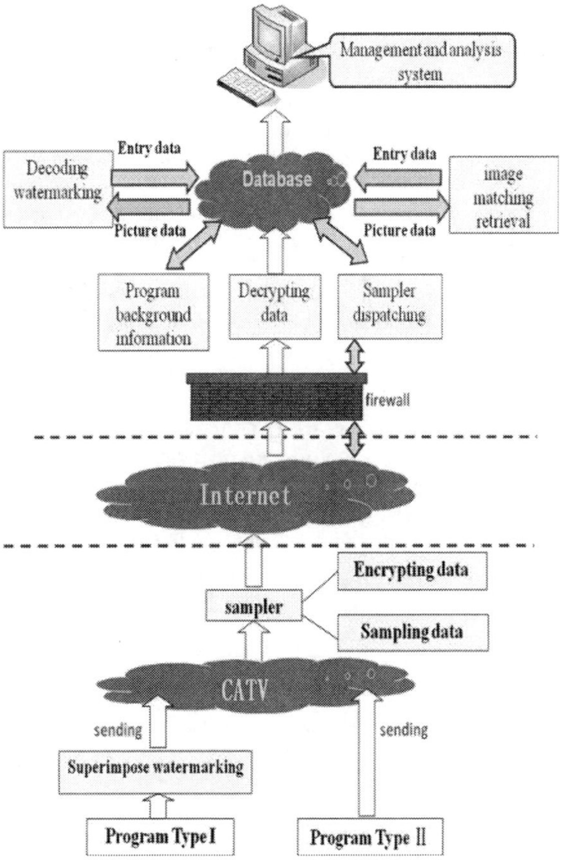

Figure 2. The concrete modules of the monitoring radio and television programs broadcast system

3 Program monitoring analysis

As is known to all, now broadcasting and making program are divided. The program production company makes program. Then, the program is broadcast by television station. The company of program production will receive payment from TV station. But a lot of television stations, especially at county level, use a way of recorded broadcast from province station program or CCTV and broadcast within the scope of the county in reality. A lot of royalties have been seriously lost by company of program production. Therefore program monitoring analysis is being researched by us. The above functions will be achieved in program monitoring analysis module. It is necessary to filter data in the database, including city, broadcasting television station, broadcasting time, broadcasting duration, program categories, keywords of program, program production company, broadcasting date. Graphics drawing pattern is set when statistical graphics are drawn after filtering data, which makes the final result of the statistical analysis more practical.

3.1. Statistical analysis based on program production company

Many of the high audience ratings programs broadcast by television stations are purchased from some high level program production companies. The audience ratings of program are the important indicator of television stations. So more and more television stations begin to pay more and more attention to program production companies of high level. At the same time, along with the increasingly competition among the program production companies, it is particularly important to show the ranking information of the production companies generated by the statistics of broadcast data. The ranking information of the program production company can be generated by the program monitoring analysis system through filtering broadcast data. The following example is the ranking information of program production companies in the statistical analysis of CCTV 1 channel, as shown in figure 3. It can be seen through the graphic that China TV drama production center has established nearly a quarter of the broadcast television program in the program production companies in China central television (CCTV) - 1.

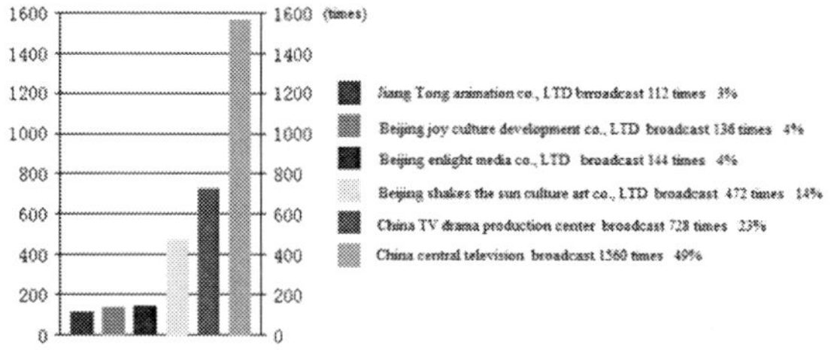

Figure 3. The ranking information of program production companies broadcast on CCTV-1

The broadcast data can also be firstly selected depending on the type of programs. And then the ranking information is carried out in accordance with the programme production company list. So you can know the strength of some program production company in the field of the special program production. For instance, statistical analysis to the ranking information of program production companies in cultural entertainment programs broadcast on CCTV-1 and CCTV-4 channel as shown in figure 4.

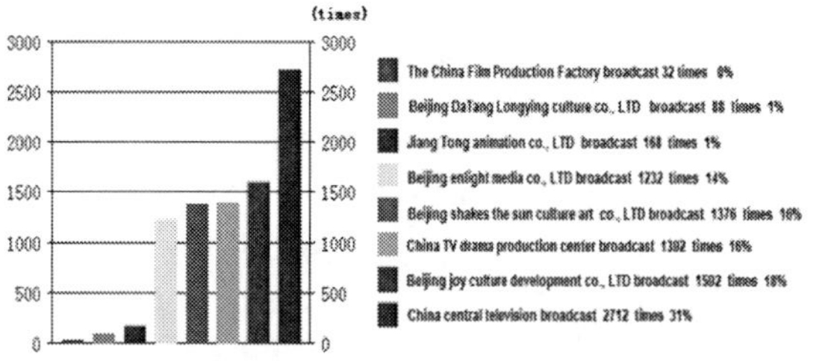

Figure 4. The ranking information of program production companies in cultural entertainment programs broadcast on CCTV-1 and CCTV-4

Through the above statistical analysis, the purpose is to serve TV station and the company of program production. For television station, through the list statistics, one can choose the power program production companies for their production program. Besides, the station chooses people loved program in order to improve its audience rating. For company, it can know its rankings in the companies of program production and also can learn from this list of different production department of program company performance. The department with poor performance should be adjusted or eliminated. It provides the company decision-maker favourable adjustment accordance.

3.2 Statistical analysis based on program type

CCTV and the provincial satellite television stations establish a variety of non-integrated channels, such as economic channels, entertainment channels, news channels. Some satellite TV channels don't achieve the result of professional channel due to economic interests. For instance, in order to increase ratings and advertising revenue, the science and technology education programs are few in the education channel in broadcasting every day. These phenomena show that it is necessary to supervise the professional channels. At the same time, the state administration of radio, film and television also has corresponding measures with the establishment of these special channels, such as assuming that the proportion of economic programs in all broadcasting programs should not be less than 30% in the economic channels. So this analysis module can provide analytical data for government regulators. For example, the statistical analysis of the proportion of each type of program shown in CCTV-3 channel, as shown in figure 5. Through the figure we can see very clearly that among all programs broadcast by CCTV-3, cultural entertainment programs together with music programs common occupy nearly 73% proportion, which belongs to the normal range of broadcasting.

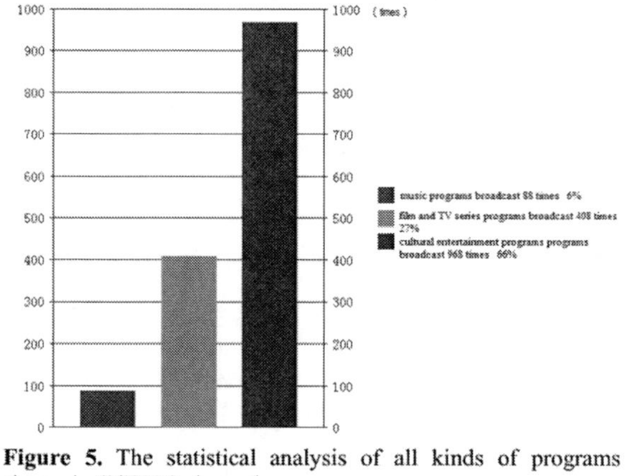

Figure 5. The statistical analysis of all kinds of programs shown in CCTV-3 channel

4 Advertisement monitoring analysis

The service object of advertisement monitoring analysis is the advertisement owner and the advertisement company. We know that advertisement owner that are mainly the manufacturers entrust the advertisement company to make advertisement. The advertisement will

be shown on television. The ad-rate depends on five factors:

(1) the broadcast channels. BTV's ad-rate and CCTV's ad-rate are obviously discriminating. Different TV ad-rate is determined by the TV audience rating.

(2) the advertisement's broadcasting time. Prime-time ad-rate and non prime-time ad-rate are a great difference.

(3) the broadcasting duration. 9 seconds ad-rate and 15 seconds ad-rate are different.

(4) the advertisement's broadcasting times. Three times advertisement and one time advertisement have different ad-rate.

(5) the broadcast order. This is the most neglected advertisement monitoring analysis of factors. For example, when television ad time begins, expenses of the first ad and of the third ad will also be different. The audience may change to other channels when the third advertisement begins. The similar product advertising affects advertisement effect each other if similar advertisements broadcast one by one. So advertisements sequence also need to include into public opinion analysis[3].

4.1 Statistical analysis based on the advertisement company

An important index that advertisement owner chooses the advertisement company is to check the occupancy of the advertisement market. By means of the statistical list of advertisement companies of advertising information broadcast in a channel or an area, the advertisement company's market share can be analysed within a specified channel or regional. For example, through the statistical analysis of advertisement broadcast on CCTV-2, advertisement companies share can be carried out in all entry broadcasting advertisement information, as shown in figure 6.

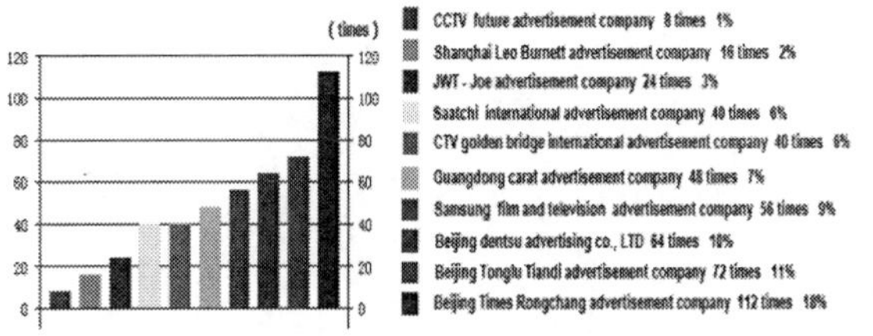

Figure 6. The statistical analysis of advertisement companies share shown on CCTV-2

In addition, the advertisement monitoring analysis also includes various ranking list statistics and comparison of statistics of similar products advertisement. Purpose is to serve the advertisement owner and the advertisement company.

For the advertisement owners, through the list statistics and comparative statistics of similar products, one can choose the power advertisement company to make advertisement. The advertisement owners also can understand their products in the same products in position. The company can understand relationship of the sales of its products in the different regions and its advertisement in different areas. Then, the company can adjust its advertisement strategy.

For the advertisement company, it can know its rankings in advertisement and also can learn from this list of different production department of the advertisement company performance. The department with poor performance should be adjusted or eliminated. It provides the company decision-maker favourable adjustment accordance.

4.2 Statistical analysis based on the advertisement broadcasting

Advertisement owners generally advertise on television for profit, which makes the enterprise occupy a broader market, sell production and take advantage with the competitors of similar products. The competition doesn't just exist in the market. There is competition in the advertising. The advertisement owners can get competitors' advertising information in order to make the next step of advertising strategy.

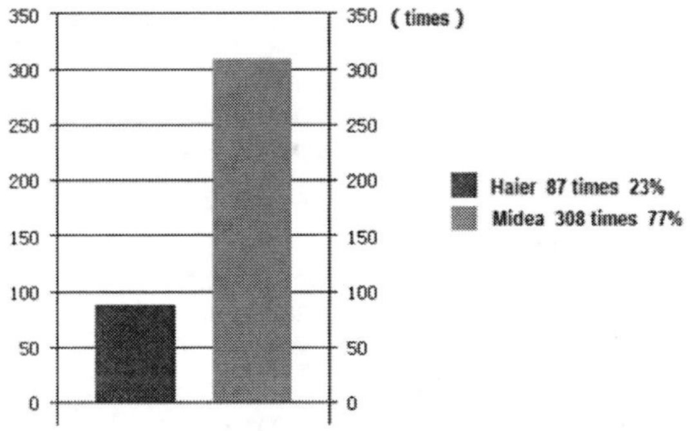

Figure 7. The contrast situation of Haier and Midea air-conditioning advertising

Advertising is also pay attention to broadcasting time. No matter how good the advertisement is produced and how many the advertisements are delivered, it will be nothing if you can't arrange the broadcasting time well. It also cannot achieve the desired effect. So the advertisement owner must do market research ahead when advertising and analyse the effect of time factors on the advertisement effect. At the same time, the advertisement owner can also get statistics data of the successful advertising companies in the industry for reference.

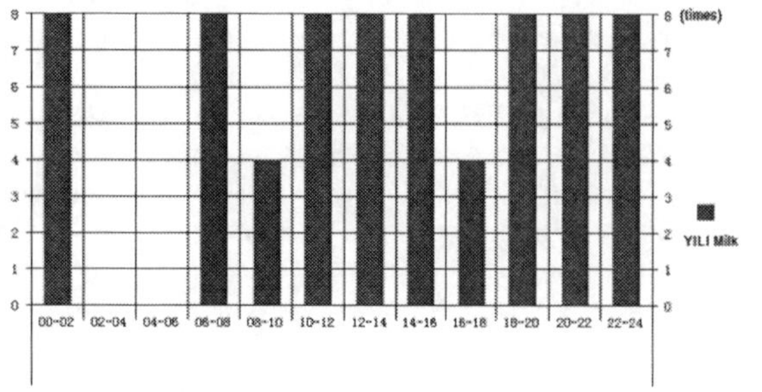

Figure 8. The broadcasting situation of YILI milk advertisement for one day

5 Summary

The broadcast program monitoring analysis system presents multiple analysis methods and realizes the combination of the monitoring and analysis in the exploration. The statistical analysis services are provided for television stations, program production companies, advertising companies, advertising owners, government, and so on. The television broadcast information is made good use of. The research and application of this topic have wide development prospects.

References

1. L.H. Wang. Public Opinion Overview: theory, method and realistic hot . Tianjin: tianjin academy of social science press, 2003.
2. Xu Xin, Zhang Zhicheng. Research on Application and analysis of Internet Mediated Public Sentiment[J]. Information Science, No 8,2008,1194-1201.
3. Song Jinbao, Chai Jianping. An Analysis System of Broadcasting and Television Public Opinions[J]. Proceedings-International Conference on Management and Service Science(MASS2009),2009,9,923-927.
4. K.L.ZHANG. National Decision: mechanism and public opinion. Tianjin: tianjin academy of social science press, 2004.
5. Qian Aibing. A Model for Analyzing Public Opinion Under the Web and Its Implementation[J].Xiandai Tushu Qingbao Jishu, No 4,2008.
6. Y.S.CHEN. Colony Accidents and Public Opinion.Tianjin: tianjin academy of social science press, 2005.
7. J.BE. Try to Spread the Era of High Technology.journal of early experiments in 2006, News Journalists, (4) : 29-31.
8. G.LIU. in public opinion. The Function of Media Collection and Analysis of the Mechanism.Journal of Chinese reporters, 2005, (9) : 14-16.

MATEC Web of Conferences **44**, 01044 (2016)
DOI: 10.1051/matecconf/20164401044

Some Equal Degree Graph Edge Chromatic Number

Jun Liu[1,a] , Zhi Guo Ren[1] , Qiu Ju Yue[1] , Zhong Yi Feng[1] and Cai Hui Lan[1]

1. Lanzhou City University, School of Information Science and engineering, Lanzhou 730070, P.R.China

Abstract. Let $G(V, E)$ be a simple graph and k is a positive integer, if it exists a mapping of f, and satisfied with $f(e_1) \neq 6{=}f(e_2)$ for two incident edges $e_1,e_2 \in E(G)$, $f(e_1) \neq 6{=}f(e_2)$, then f is called the k-proper-edge coloring of G(k-PEC for short).The minimal number of colors required for a proper edge coloring of G is denoted by $X'(G)$ and is called the proper edge chromatic number. It exists a k-proper edge coloring of simple graph of G, for any two adjacent vertices u and v in G, the set of colors assigned to the edges incident to u differs from the set of colors in cident to v, then f is called k-adjacent-vertex-distinguishing proper edge coloring, is avvreviated k-$AVDEC$, also called a adjacent strong edge coloring. The minimal number of colors required for a adjacent-vertex-distinguishing edge coloring of G is denoted by $X'_{ad}(G)$ and is called adjacent-vertex-distinguishing edge chromatic number. The new class graphs of equal degree graph are be introduced, and this class graphs adjacent-vertex-distinguishing edge chromatic numbers of path ,cycle, fan, complete graph, wheel, star are presented in this paper.

1 Introduction

The coloring problem of graphs is a extremely difficult problem, widely applied in practice. In [1], some conditional coloring problems are introduced. Some network problems can be converted to the edge coloring[2–9] and adjacent strong edge coloring.

Definition 1[10] For a graph$G(V, E)$, if a proper coloring f is satisfied with $C(u) \neq C(v)$ for $u, v \in V(G)(u \neq v)$ and $uv \in E(G)$ then f is called k-adjacent-vertex- distinguishing edge coloring of G, is abbreviated k-$AVDEC$, and

$$X'_{ad}(G) = \min\{k \mid k - AVDECofG\}$$

is called the adjacent-vertex-distinguishing edge chromatic number of G[6] , where $C(u) = \{f(uv) \mid uv \in E(G)$

Conjecture [2] Let G be a connected graph with $|G| \geq 3$, and $G \neq C_5(5-cycle)$, then

$$X'_{ad}(G) \leq \Delta(G) + 2$$

where $\Delta(G)$ is the maximum degree of graph G.

Definition 2[5] Let$G(V, E)$ be a simple graph, $M(G)$ is called the equal degree graph of G, where

$$V(M(G)) = V(G) \bigcup V' \bigcup \{W\};$$

$$E(M(G)) = E(G) \bigcup \{uv' \mid u \in V(G),$$
$$v' \in V', d(u) = d(v)\} \bigcup \{wv' \mid v' \in V'\}$$

Where as

$$V' = \{v' \mid v \in V(G)\}, \{w\} \bigcap (V(G) \quad \vee V') = \varphi.$$

2 Main result

Lemma 1 For $n \geq 2$, then

$$\Delta\ (M(P_n)) = \begin{cases} 3, n = 2, 3; \\ n, n \geq 4. \end{cases}$$

Lemma 2 For $n \geq 3$, then

$$\Delta\ (M(P_n)) = n + 2$$

Lemma 3 For $n \geq 3$, then

$$\Delta(M(F_n)) = \begin{cases} 5, n = 2, 3; \\ n+1, n \geq 4. \end{cases}$$

Lemma 4 For $n \geq 2$, then

$$\Delta(M(K_n)) = \begin{cases} 3, n = 2 \\ 5,\ \ N = 3; \\ 2n - 1 \geq 4. \end{cases}$$

Lemma 5 For $n \geq 3$, then

$$\Delta(M(W_n)) = \begin{cases} 7, n = 3; \\ n+3, n \geq 4. \end{cases}$$

[a]authore-mail: 527876625@.qq.com
This studywas supported by Lanzhou City University Ph.D. Research Fund (21265099,41361013,GS[2013]GHB1084, LZCU-BS2013-09 and LZCU-BS2013-12).

Article available at http://www.matec-conferences.org or http://dx.doi.org/10.1051/matecconf/20164401044

Lemma 6 For $n \geq 3$, then

$$\Delta(M(S_n)) = \begin{cases} 3, n = 1,2; \\ n+1, n \geq 3. \end{cases}$$

Lemma7 [2] Let G be a connected simple graph with $|V(G)| \geq 3$, if $uv \in E(G)$ and $d(u) = d(v) = \Delta(G)$, then

$$X'_{ad}(G) \geq \Delta(G)+1$$

Theorem 1 For $n \geq 2$, then

$$X'_{ad}(M(P_n)) = \begin{cases} 5, n = 3; \\ n+1, n \geq 4. \end{cases}$$

Proof Let

$V(P_n) = \{u_1, u_2, \cdots, u_n\}, V' = \{v_1 v_2, \cdots, v_n\}$, there are two cases to be discussed as follow:

Case1 When $n=2$, $\Delta(M(P_2)) = 3$ from lemma 1. However u_1, u_2, v_1, v_2 are vertices which are maximum degree of $M(P_2)$ and all adjacent, $X'_{ad}(M(P_2)) \geq \Delta(M(P_n)) = 4$ from lemma 7. If $M(P_2)$ exists *4-AVDEC*, because four vertices of maximum degree are adjacent each other, and $\binom{4}{3} = 4$, the set are $\{1,2,3\}$, $\{1,2,4\}$, $\{1,3,4\}$, $\{2,3,4\}$. Let every set correspond a vertex, we can obtain the vertices of coloring same color are odd, but the vertices of coloring same color are even by graph theory, so $M(P_2)$ don't exists 4-AVDEC. In order to prove the conclusion be true, we only need construct a map f from $E(M(P_2))$ to $\{1,2,3,4,5\}$:

$f(u_1v_2) = f(u_2v_1) = 1;$

$f(u_1v_1) = 2;$

$f(u_2v_2) = 3;$

$f(u_1u_2) = 4;$

$f(wv_1) = 3;$

$f(wv_2) = 5$

Then we have

$\overline{C}(u_1) = \{3,5\};$

$\overline{C}(u_2) = \{2,5\};$

$\overline{C}(v_1) = \{4,5\};$

$\overline{C}(v_2) = \{2,4\};$

Obviously, the f is *5-AVDEC* of $M(P_2)$, the conclusion is true.

When $n=3$, $\Delta(M(P_3)) = 3$ from lemma 1. But $M(P_2) \subset M(P_3), M(P_3) \geq 5$ from n=2. It is obviously to prove exists *5-AVDEC* of $M(P_3)$, we only need to construct a map f from $E(M(P_3))$ to $\{1,2,3,4,5\}$:

$f(u_1u_2) = f(u_3v_3) = 1;$

$f(u_1v_1) = f(u_2u_3) = 2;$

$f(u_1v_3) = f(wv_2) = 3;$

$f(u_1uv_2) = f(wv_1) = 4;$

$f(u_3v_1) = f(wv_3) = 5;$

Then we have

$\overline{C}(u_1) = \{4,5\};$

$\overline{C}(u_2) = \{3,5\};$

$\overline{C}(u_3) = \{3,4\};$

$\overline{C}(v_1) = \{1,3\};$

$\overline{C}(v_2) = \{1,2,5\};$

$\overline{C}(v_3) = \{2,4\};$

Obviously, the f is *5-AVDEC* of $M(P_3)$, the conclusion is true.

Case2 When $n \geq 4$, $\Delta(M(P_n)) = n$ from lemma 1. However the vertices of $u_2, u_3, \cdots, u_{n-1}$, w are vertices which are maximum degree, and exist some are adjacent, $X'_{ad}(M(P_n)) \geq n+1$ from lemma 7. It is obviously to prove exists *(n+1)-AVDEC* of $M(P_n)$, we only need to construct a map f from $E(M(P_n))$ to $\{1,2,\cdots, n,0\}$:

$f(u_iu_{i+1}) = i-1, i = 1,2,\cdots,n-1;$

$f(u_1v_1) = 1; f(u_1v_n) = 2;$

$f(u_iv_j) = i+j-2(\bmod n),$

$i = 2,3,n-1; j = 2,3,n-1;$

$f(u_nv_1) = n; f(u_nv_n) = 0;$

$f(wv_i) = i-1, i = 1,2, \cdots, n.$

So we have

$\overline{C}(v_i) = \{0,1,2\};$

$\overline{C}(u_2) = \{n\};$

$\overline{C}(u_i) = \{i-3\}, i = 3,4,\cdots,n-1;$

$\overline{C}(u_n) = \{0, n-2, n-1\};$

$\overline{C}(v_1) = \{0,1,n\};$

$\overline{C}(v_i) = \{i-1, i, \cdots, n+i-3\}(\bmod n+1),$

$i = 2,3,\cdots,n-1;$

$\overline{C}(v_n) = \{0,2,n-1\}.$

Obviously, the f is *(n+1)-AVDEC* of $M(P_n)$, the conclusion is true.

From all of above two cases, the conclusion is true.

Theorem 2 For $n \geq 3$, then

$$X'(M(C_n)) = n+3.$$

Proof Let

$V(C_n) = \{u_1, u_2, \cdots, u_n\}, V' = \{v_1, v_2, \cdots, v_n\}, u_1, u_2, \cdots, u_n$ are vertices of maximum degree andexists some adjacent, $X'_{ad}(M(C_n)) \geq n+3$ from lemma 2 and 7. It is obviously to prove exists *(n+3)-AVDEC* of $\geq M(C_n)$, we only need to construct a map f from $E(M(C_n))$ to $\{1,2,\cdots, n+2,0\}$:

$f(u_iu_{i+1}) = i-1, i = 1,2,\cdots,n-1;$

$f(u_1u_n) = 0;$

$f(u_iv_j) = i+j(\bmod n+3),$

$i = 1,2,\cdots,n-1; j = 1,2,\cdots n;$

$f(u_nv_j) = n+j, j = 1,2;$

$f(u_nv_j) = j-2, j = 3,4,\cdots,n;$

$f(wv_j) = j-1.$

So we have

$\overline{C}(u_1) = \{n+2\};$

$\overline{C}(u_i) = \{i-1\}, i = 2,3,\cdots,n-1;$

$\overline{C}(u_n) = \{n\}.$

Obviously, the f is (n+3)-*AVDEC* of $M(C_n)$, the conclusion is true.

Theorem 3 For $n \geq 3$, then

$$X'(M(F_n)) = \begin{cases} 6, n = 2,3; \\ n+2, n \geq 4. \end{cases}$$

Proof Let $V(F_n) = \{u_0, u_1, u_2, \cdots, u_n\}$, $V' = \{v_0, v_1, v_2, \cdots, u_n\}$, there are three cases to be discussed as follow:

Case1 When n=2,$M(F_2)$ =$M(C_3)$, so we can obtain $X'(M(F_3)) = X'(M(C_3)) = 6$, then the conclusion is true.

Case2 When n= 3, $\Delta(M(F_3))$ = 5 from lemma 3, and $M(F_3)$ exists two vertices of maximum degree are adjacent, so X'_{ad} $(M(F_3))$ ≥ 6 by lemma 7. It is obviously to prove exists 6-*AVDEC* of $M(F_3)$, we only need to construct a map f from $E(M(F_3))$ to $\{1,2,\cdots,5,0\}$:

$f(u_0u_i) = i-1, i = 1,2,3;$

$f(u_iu_{i+1}) = i+1, i = 1,2;$

$f(u_0v_0) = 3;$

$f(u_0v_2) = 4;$

$f(u_1v_1) = 3;$

$f(u_3v_1) = 4;$

$f(u_3v_3) = 5;$

$f(wv_i) = i-1, i = 0,1,2,3.$

The we have

$\overline{C}(u_0) = \{5\};$

$\overline{C}(u_2) = \{0\}.$

Obviously, the f is 6-*AVDEC* of $M(F_3)$, the conclusion is true.

Case3 When $n \geq 4$, $\Delta(M(F_n))$ = n+ 1 from lemma 3,$M(F_n)$ exists some vertices of maximum degree are adjacent, X' $(M(F_n))$ $\geq \Delta(M(F_n))+1=n+2$ by lemma 3,7. It is obviously to prove exists (n+2)-*AVDEC* of $M(F_n)$, we only need to construct a map f from $E(M(F_n))$ to $\{1,2,\cdots, n+1,0\}$:

$f(u_0u_i) = i-1, i = 1,2,\cdots,n;$

$f(u_iu_{i+1}) = i+1, i = 1,2\cdots,n-1;$

$f(u_0v_0) = n;$

$f(u_1v_1) = 3;$

$f(u_1v_n) = 4;$

$f(u_iv_j) = i + j(\bmod n+2),$

$i = 2,3,\cdots,n-1; j = 2,3,\cdots,n-1;$

$f(u_nv_1) = 1;$

$f(u_nv_n) = 2;$

$f(wv_i) = i+1, i = 0,1,\cdots,n.$

So we have

$\overline{C}(u_0) = \{n+2\};$

$\overline{C}(u_i) = \{i-2\}, i = 2,3,\cdots,n-1;$

$\overline{C}(w) = \{0\}.$

Obviously, the f is (n+2)-*AVDEC* of $M(F_n)$, the conclusion is true.

From all of above, the conclusion is true.

Theorem 4 For $n \geq 2$, then

$$X'(M(K_n)) = \begin{cases} 5, n = 2; \\ 6, n = 3; \\ \Delta(M(K_n))+1, n \geq 4. \end{cases}$$

Proof Let $V(F_n) = \{u_1, u_2, u_2, \cdots, u_n\}, V' = \{v_1, v_2, \cdots, u_n\}$, there are three cases to be discussed as follow:

Case 1 When n= 2,$M(K_2)$ =$M(P_2)$, so we can obtain X' $(M(K_2))$ = X' $(M(P_2))$ = 5, the conclusion is true.

Case 2 When n= 3,$M(K_3)$ =$M(C_3)$, so we can obtain X' $(M(K_3))$ = X' $(M(C_3))$ = 6, the conclusion is true.

Case 3 When $n \geq 4$, $\Delta(M(K_n))$ = $2n-1$ from lemma 4,$M(K_n)$ exists some vertices of maximum degree are adjacent, X' $(M(K_n))\geq\Delta(M(K_n))+1=2n$ by lemma 4,7. It is obviously to prove exists $2n$-*AVDEC* of $M(K_n)$,we only need to construct a map f from $E(M(K_n))$ to $\{1,2,\cdots,2n-1,0\}$:

$f(u_iu_j) = i + j,$

$i = 1,2,\cdots,n-1; j = i+1, i+2\cdots,n-1;$

$f(u_iv_j) = i + j + n - 3(\bmod 2n),$

$i = 1,2,\cdots,n; j = 1,2,\cdots,n-1;$

$f(v_nu_1) = 2n-1;$

$f(v_nu_i) = 2(i-1)-1, i = 2,3,\cdots,n;$

$f(wv_n) = i, i = 1,2,\cdots,n-1;$

$f(wv_n) = n, n \equiv 0(\bmod 2);$

$f(wv_n) = n+1, n \equiv 1(\bmod 2).$

The we have

$\overline{C}(u_i) = \{2n+i-3\}(\bmod 2n), i = 1,2,\cdots,n.$

Obviously, the f is $2n$-*AVDEC* of $M(K_n)$, the conclusion is true.

From all of above, the conclusion is true.

Theorem 5 For $n \geq 3$, then

$$X'(M(W_n)) = \begin{cases} 8, n = 3; \\ n+4, n \geq 4. \end{cases}$$

Proof Let $V(W_n) = \{u_0, u_1, u_2, \cdots, u_n\}, V' = \{v_0, v_1, v_2 \cdots, u_n\}$, there are two cases to be discussed as follow:

Case1 When n= 3,$M(W_3)$ =$M(K_4)$, so we can obtain X' $(M(W_3))$ = X' $(M(K_4))$ = 8, the conclusion is true.

Case2 When $n \geq 4$, $\Delta(M(W_n))$ = n+ 3 from the lemma 5,$M(W_n)$ exists some vertices of maximum degree are adjacent, X' $(M(W_n))$ $\geq$ $\Delta(M(W_n))+1=n+4$ by lemma 5,7. It is obviously to prove exists (n+4)-*AVDEC* of $M(W_n)$, we only need to construct a map f from $E(M(W_n))$ to $\{1,2,\cdots, n+3,0\}$:

$f(u_0u_i) = i-1, i = 1,2,\cdots,n;$

$f(u_0v_0) = n;$

$f(u_iv_j) = i + j - 1(\bmod n+4),$

$i = 1,2,\cdots,n-1; j = 1,2,\cdots n;$

$f(u_nv_1) = n;$

$f(u_nv_j) = n + j(\bmod n+4), j = 2,3,\cdots,n-1;$

$f(u_nv_n) = n-3;$

$f(u_iu_{i+1}) = n + i + 1(\bmod n + 4),$

$i = 1, 2, \cdots, n-1;$

$f(u_1u_n) = n + 1;$

$f(wv_i) = n + 2 + j(\bmod n + 4), i = 0, 1, \cdots n,.$

Then we have

$\overline{C}(u_i) = \{n + i + 2\}(\bmod n + 4), i = 1, 2, \cdots, n.$

Obviously, the f is (n+3)-*AVDEC* of $M(W_n)$, the conclusion is true.

From all of above, the conclusion is true.

Theorem 6 For $n \geq 1$, then

$$X'(M(S_n)) = \begin{cases} 5, n = 1, 2; \\ n + 3, n \geq 3. \end{cases}$$

Proof Let $V(S_n) = \{u_0, u_1, u_2, \cdots, u_n\}$, $V' = \{v_0, v_1, v_2 \cdots, u_n\}$,there are three cases to be discussed as follow:

Case 1 When n=1,$M(S_1)$=M(P_2), so we can obtain X' ($M(S_1)$)= X' ($M(P_2)$)=5, the conclusion is true.

Case 2 When n=2,$M(S_2)$=$M(P_3)$, so we can obtain X' ($M(S_2)$)= X' ($M(P_3)$)=6, the conclusion is true.

Case 3 When $n \geq 3$, $\Delta(M(S_n))$=n+1 by lemma 6,$M(S_n)$ exists some vertices of maximum degree are adjacent, X' ($M(S_n)$) $\geq \Delta(M(S_n))$+1=n+2 by lemma 6,7. If $M(S_n)$ exists n+2-*AVDEC*, then

$\overline{C}(u_0) = \overline{C}(u_i) = \overline{C}(v_i) = 1, i = 1, 2, \cdots n.$

$$\begin{cases} \overline{C}(u_0) \in \overline{C}(u_1) \cup \overline{C}(u_2) \cup \cdots \cup \overline{C}(u_n); \\ \overline{C}(u_1) \in \overline{C}(v_1) \cup \overline{C}(u_2) \cup \cdots \cup \overline{C}(v_n) \\ \overline{C}(u_2) \in \overline{C}(v_1) \cup \overline{C}(v_2) \cup \cdots \cup \overline{C}(v_n) \\ \cdots \\ \overline{C}(u_n) \in \overline{C}(v_1) \cup \overline{C}(v_2) \cup \cdots \cup \overline{C}(v_n) \end{cases}$$

from (1) and (2), we can obtain

$|\overline{C}(u_0) + \overline{C}(u_1) + \overline{C}(u_2) + \ldots + \overline{C}(u_n) + \overline{C}(v_1) + \overline{C}(v_2) + \ldots + \overline{C}(v_n)| > n+2.$

It is obvious that $M(S_n)$ don't exists n+2-*AVDEC*. In order to prove the conclusion be true, we only need to construct a map f from $E(M(S_n))$ to {1,2,· · ·, n+2,0}:

$f(u_0u_i) = i - 1, i = 1, 2, \cdots, n;$

$f(u_0v_0) = n;$

$f(u_iv_j) = i + j(\bmod n + 3),$

$i = 1, 2, \cdots, n; j = 1, 2, \cdots n;$

$f(wv_i) = i - 1, i = 0, 1, \cdots, n$

Then we have

$\overline{C}(u_0) = \{n + 1, n + 2\};$

$\overline{C}(u_i) = \{1, n + 2\};$

$\overline{C}(u_i) = \{i - 2, i\}, i = 2, 3, \cdots, n;$

$\overline{C}(v_1) = \{0, n + 2\};$

$\overline{C}(v_i) = \{i - 2, i - 1\} i = 2, 3, \cdots n;$

Obviously, the f is (n+3)-*AVDEC* of $M(S_n)$, the conclusion is true.

From all of above, the conclusion is true.

From the conclusions of Theorem 1,2,3,4,5,6, the Conjecture is true for equal degree graph.

References

1. Harary F, Conditional colorability in graphs, In Graphs and Applications,Proc Graph theory Fist Colorado symp,John Wilh & Sons, New York, 1985;
2. J.cerny M.hornak and R.sotak Observability of a graph, Math. Slovaca 46, 1996,21-31;
3. Burris A C and Schelp R H, Vertex-distinguishing Proper Edge-colorings, J of Graph Theory, 1997, 26(2):73-82;
4. Bazgan C Harkat-Benhamdine A, Li H, etc. On the Vertex-distinguishing Proper Edge-coloring of Graph, J Combin Theory Ser B, 1999, 75:288-301;
5. Balister P N, Bollob'as B, Schelp R H, Vertex distinguishing coloring of graphs with Δ(G)=2, Discrete Mathematics,2002,252(2):17 29;
6. Balister P N,Riordan O M and Schelp R H, Vertex-distinguishing edge coloring of graphs, J. Graph Theory 42(2003)95-109;
7. Zhongfu Zhang, Linzhong Liu, Jianfang Wang, Adjacent Strong Edge Coloring of Graphs, Applied MathematicsLetters, 2002, 15:623-626;
8. Wang shudong, Li chongming, Xu Ji, et, On the adjacent strong edge coloring of some graphs, J of Mathematical Research and exposition, Vo1.22, No 4, 2002, 412-417;
9. Balister P N, Gyori and Schelp R H , On the adjacent-strong edge coloring of graphs with Δ(G)≤3, J.G.T to appear;
10. Bondy J A and Marty U S R, Graph Theory with Applications, The Macmillan Press Ltd, New York, 1976;
11. Chartrand G, Linda L F, Graphs and diagraphs, Ind edition wadsirth Brokks/cole, Monterey, CA(1986).

MATEC Web of Conferences 44, 01045 (2016)
DOI: 10.1051/matecconf/20164401045

Design and Realization of Network Teaching System

Shan Shan Ji [1]
Department of Computer Engineering, DongGuan Polytechnic, DongGuan GuangDong,523808, China

Abstract: Since 21 century, with the wide spread in family and public, network has been applied in many new fields, and the application in classes is of no exception. In traditional education, teachers give lessons to students face to face. Hence, the teaching quality depends largely on the quality and initiative of the individual teacher. However, the serious disadvantages of this mode are that teachers completely dominate the classroom and may ignore the subjective cognition role of the students, which may be bad for the growth of creativity and the innovative thinking ability. Obviously, traditional education mode cannot meet the requirements of the this new era which leads to the booming developing tendency of the network. As a new teaching measure, scientifically combining modern information technology and teaching practice, network teaching not only changes the traditional education by the means and form, but even also gives new meanings to teaching concept, process, method as well as teacher-student role and other deep levels. With the help of network teaching system, on-line classroom learning, relevant information systematization, standardization and automation, this system provides students with an efficient online learning method with high quality. This also helps to solve the disadvantages of the traditional teaching mode and promote the teaching methods to a new stage. It improves the network teaching platform, enriches the network teaching resources, and establishes a network teaching system, so as to improve information quality of teachers and students and assist in improving teaching quality of schools.

[1] Author profile: Ji Shanshan (1985-), female, computer lecturer and network engineer in Dongguan Polytechnic, research direction: computer education
Corresponding author: jss060@163.com

In order to comprehensively implement the Scientific Outlook on Development and focus on quality improvement in developing higher education in an earnest manner, the Ministry of Education and the Ministry of Finance decide to implement quality engineering in universities and colleges. One of the requirements in implementing the quality engineering is to strengthen the excellent network resource construction of courses, take information technology as an important method to improve teaching quality, widely use information technology, change talent cultivation mode of universities and colleges, and constantly promote common construction and sharing of teaching resources, to gradually achieve the grand objective of networking and digitization of teaching and management.

From the current situation in China, the teaching mode in the 21st century is basically teacher-centered. The advantages of this mode are that it is helpful for teachers to play the leading role and easy for teachers to organize and monitor the process of the whole teaching activity, which is convenient for emotion exchange between teachers and students, thus this mode is beneficial to systematically pass on scientific knowledge and it fully considers the important role of emotion factors in learning process. However, the serious disadvantages of this mode are that teachers completely dominate the classroom and ignore subjective cognition role of students, which is bad for growth of creative talent with innovative thinking and innovative ability.

Therefore, network teaching will certainly become a development trend in modern education. Network teaching system pays more attention to width, depth and effectiveness, achieving all-round integration of information technology and classroom. The basis of integration and application is to construct a perfect network teaching platform, while constructing a network teaching system with strong functions and good safety is the only way for network teaching, and it is also a fundamental method to solve the disadvantages in modern education.

1. System Development Background

The role of the teacher-centered teaching mode in the cause of education is indeed ineffaceable, but its serious disadvantages are that its basis in terms of learning theories is behaviorism. If this teaching mode dominates in the classrooms of various schools at all levels in China for a long term, the learning theories of behaviorism will have deep-rooted effects on the schools. As a new teaching form scientifically combining modern information technology and teaching practice, network teaching not only changes the traditional teaching from the means and form, but even also gives new meanings to teaching from concept, process, method, teacher-student role and other deep levels. All this originates from three basic characteristics of network teaching: creativity of teachers' labor, integration of knowledge information and cooperation of teaching processes. Thus, development of the network teaching system is just conforming to urgent hope of all the teachers and students.

2. System Function Description

Network teaching system is a system oriented to teachers and students, which takes students as core and provides humanized functions as much as possible, such as online teaching support system, network course development tools and online teaching resource management system. In this system, analysis and design of the system adopt UML as the modeling tool, using asp.net as the development platform, visual c# as the programming language and sql as the database support. The system can adopt the object-oriented design and encapsulate database operations in categories, making program structure clear and easy to maintain. In the meantime, the system adopts a four-layer architecture where interface and business logic are separated, and encapsulates business logic in components, greatly improving safety, reliability, reusability and expansibility of the system.Functional requirements of network teaching system mainly include the followings:

(1) "Online class" function: teachers prepare courseware before class and store it on the server; students can enter corresponding "classroom" to watch the courseware to study (or download corresponding resources). This system adopts "asynchronous teaching mode": teachers provide online teaching courseware, students can carry out massed learning in online classrooms through the Internet, or separately carry out self-learning on demand with the teaching courseware on the computer, and communicate and discuss with teachers and students through the network. The schematic diagram of the online classroom is as shown in Figure 2.1:

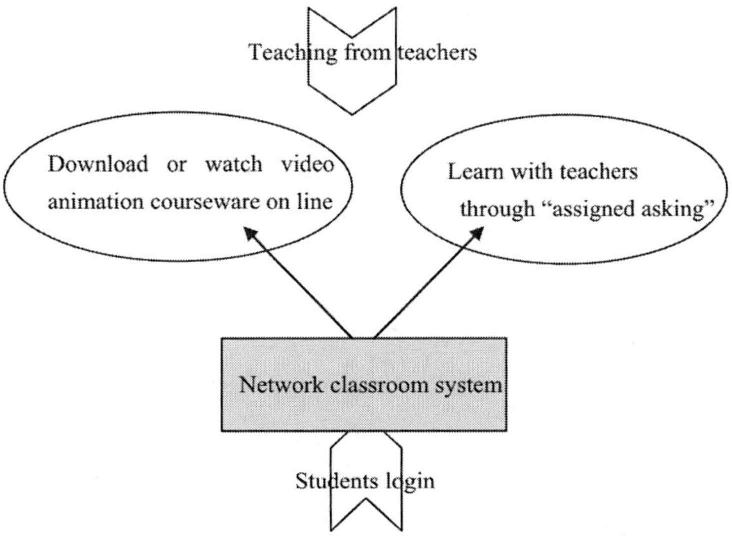

Figure 2.1 Schematic Diagram of "Online Class"

(2) "Raising hands to speak" function: this function is divided into two kinds: one is ordinary speak where students can express their thoughts, learning experience and others in the form of BBS, and the other is assigned asking where students can assign a teacher for asking questions which will be displayed on the "desktop" of the corresponding teacher.

(3) "Online signing up" function: students register a user name on line to log in the system; they can browse classrooms, and click "signing up" to submit the application to background, which will be seen by administrator.

(4) "My desk" function: personal information of students will be displayed on their own "my desk"; teachers can see "assigned asking" of the students on his/her "my desk"; students can see the "assigned answers" provided by the teachers on their own "my desk".

(5) E-business module: it handles sign-up sheet of students and opens classes; all the tuition revenue of the previous month and the current month are clear.

(6) Background management module: all the function parameters of the system can be configured; it manages the authorization of the users and user groups; it can manage each classroom and online courseware.

3.System Objective

The general task of developing this system is to achieve systematization, standardization and automation of various information related to online classroom learning. This system provides an efficient online learning method with high quality for students and solves disadvantages of the traditional teaching mode, promoting the teaching to a new stage. It improves the network teaching platform, enriches the network teaching resources, and establishes a network teaching system, so as to improve information quality of teachers and students and assist in improving teaching quality of schools.

4.System Working Principle

This system adopts a four-layer architecture design including database storage, database access, business logic and user interface, which are mutually independent. Its working principle is as shown in Figure 4.1:

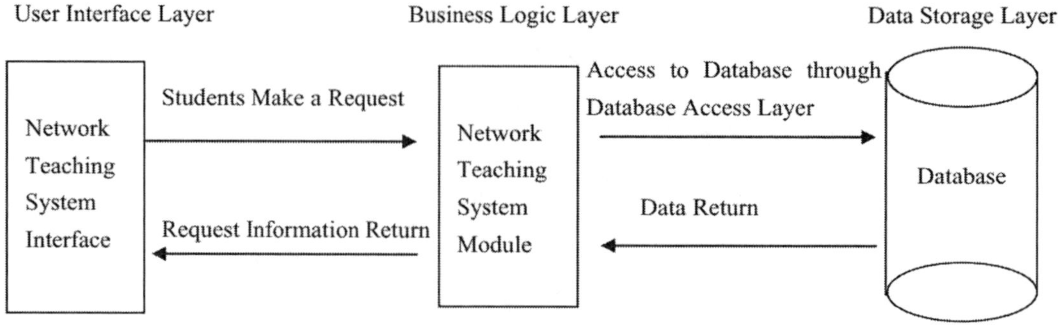

Figure 4.1 System Working Principle Diagram

The network teaching system has the following characteristics:

(1) Four-layer architecture design: this system adopts the four-layer architecture design, that is, the program logic structure is composed of user interface layer, business logic layer, database access layer and data storage layer. All the layers are mutually independent in the actual physical structure. The business logic is separated from the database access and the user interface is separated from the business logic, which greatly improves safety, maintainability, reusability and expansibility of the system.

(2) Object-oriented design: the system encapsulates the students and teachers into categories, and each category has its own corresponding collection class, thus improving the safety of the database operation and the expansibility of the program.

(3) More excellent stability: since B/S is adopted, as long as your company has a browser (IE5.5 or above is recommended), you can use this system. 80% of the stability performance of the system on the client depends on the server performance, so it is unnecessary to consider the barrier set by the old C/S installation method to the client performance.

(4) Faster speed: it adopts ASP.Net language (C#), the newest product of Microsoft. If you have heard ASP, please don't say that ASP.Net is the updated version of ASP. As a matter of fact, ASP.NET and ASP are two completely different concepts, and their working principles are different. ASP only provides explanation of the server, while ASP.NET also has compiling function whose caching can greatly increase your access speed to the network.

5.Conclusion

Through test, we find that the system still has some imperfect problems, such as encoding test. These corrections need to be further improved and refined in our subsequent researches. Generally, the system function is comparatively complete with stable and reliable running, simple operation and convenient maintenance.

This system has the following highlights:

(1) With the B/S method, students can learn any time at any place. Unlimited by region and time, students can access to the Internet and open the browser to learn without installing a client, no matter you are on business trip, go out or are travelling.

(2) It has no any requirements for hardware of student client.

(3) An E-business module is built in the system, making it simple and easy for students to pay tuition fees.

Acknowledgments

This research is supported by Guangdong Province Outstanding Young Teachers Training program Funded Project (Grant No. 2015S02 – Jianfeng Luo). the Guangdong Science and Technology Department of High Tech Industrialization Project (Grant No. 2012B010100050 - Jianfeng Luo) and the Special

Funds for Demonstration Projects of Dongguan Polytechnic College (Grant No. ZXHQ2014d001 - Jianfeng Luo). Educational research subject （professional education category） of Education Research Institute of Guangdong Province(project number：GDJY2015Bb060- Shanshan Ji)

References

1. Liu Yanling. Improve Computer Classroom Effect by Using Network Technology. Modern Aggregation. 2009, (2)
2. Zhang Yueting and Gu Yanling. ASP.NET Step by Step. Tsinghua University Press. 2008
3. Translated by Li Minbo. C# Advanced Programming. Tsinghua University Press, 2006, (1)
4. Wang Fengmao and Guo Shuyan. SQL Server 2000 Practical Development Tutorial. China Electric Power Press. 2006
5. Dong Jing. Design and Realization of ASP.NET-based Alumni Record System. China Science and Technology Information, 2011, (3)
6. Wu Ping, Liu Yimin and Chen Heping. Unreadable Codes of ASP.NET Cross-page Value-passing and Solution. Information Science, 2011, (5)
7. Translated by Li Minbo. C# Advanced Programming. Tsinghua University Press, 2006, (1)

MATEC Web of Conferences 44, 01046 (2016)
DOI: 10.1051/matecconf/20164401046

Modelling of technological reliability in traffic logistic networks in urban areas

Reiner Keil[1], Frank Hedrich[2], Iveta Kremenova[3] and Radovan Madlenak[3, a]

[1]Saxon Telecommunications Center, Faculty of Transportation and Traffic sciences, Technical University of Dresden, 01062 Dresden, Germany
[2]Technical University of Dresden, Faculty of Transportation and Traffic sciences, 01062 Dresden, Germany
[3]University of Zilina, The Faculty of Operation and Economics of Transport and Communications, 01026, Zilina, Slovakia

Abstract. The trend of growing parcel numbers with the customer's desire for shorter delivery times as a result of increasing online trade and economic specialization requires an adjustment of transport systems. The share of transportation costs per postal item depends mainly depends on costs for employees and vehicles, in addition are still the costs of processing in the sorting centers. There are only predictions and experiences for the amount of postal item are available for the tour in advance. The difficult planning leads, in addition to the high cost share and the key feature of a high quality of service to a large relevance to the total transportation process. It is presented an analytical model of the transport process. This includes models to forecast the number of postal items, for capacity-oriented planning of tours and a determination of the current vehicle usage and the volume of transported parcels.

1 Introduction

Scientific based organization of transport processes relies on elaboration of analytic or heuristic models. This paper deduces a model for uniform analysis of traffic organization processes based on traffic theory [4] using the parcel pickup process in urban area for model validation. Operating data cannot be acquired prior to stationary processing in sorting centers [5]. The initial lack of accurate raw data requires statistical data treatment of operating data for tour design. Explicit data on pickup tours, for example utilization of letterboxes or vehicles, is liable to subjective errors, hence constrained in use for modelling purposes.

2 Basic model for analytic description of transport logistic processes

Initial step for analytic modelling of transport logistic processes is deduction of fundamental processes based on universal operation process definition used in logistics and telecommunication [4]:

Operate = serving, maintenance and monitoring

A traffic-logistic process can be described by the following basic processes, which run off at the same time and relatively independently:

- Traffic object input and output, consisting of the **traffic process** with the characteristic random variables traffic object quantity X and the **entrance process** with the random variable entrance time T_E, the exit process is not explicitly regarded,
- Technological process, handling and transportation processes - modelled as **serving process**,
- Operating disturbance – modelled as a **failure process**,
- Maintenance - modelled as a **recovery process**.

Modelling of the afore mentioned processes was carried out using the specific probability model in [4] and can be characterized by the figure 1.

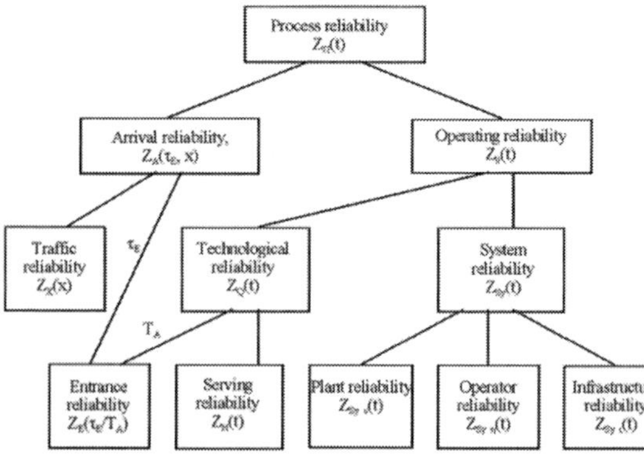

Figure 1. Reliability model

Process reliability $Z_\Pi(t)$ is defined as the probability of a system configuration SY using maintenance method IM during the time period t being able to fully serve the amount of traffic objects X at a point in time T_E.

[a] Corresponding author: radovan.madlenak@fpedas.uniza.sk

$$Z_{\Pi}(t) = P\left[T_Q \middle| \left(X \middle| T_E \wedge SY \wedge IM\right) \leq t\right] = P\left[T_Q \middle| \left(X \middle| T_E \cap T_\lambda \middle| T_\mu \geq t\right) \leq t\right] \quad (1)$$

Within this model, technological reliability describes the **operation reliability** $Z_Q(t)$ - characterizing the operation process in nodes and edges with the **inbound probability** $Z_E(\tau_E / T_A)$ - characterizing the inbound process by using the inbound point in time τ_E or the arrival interval T_A depending upon operation process.

Utilizing **traffic reliability** $Z_X(x)$, corresponds the traffic objects′ distribution function,

$$Z_X(x) = F_X(x) \quad (2)$$

includes the stochastic of the amount of traffic object. In this instance, the traffic objects are given by letters and parcels. Using an Erlang - k distribution to model the traffic objects quantity [3], the following distribution formula applies

$$F_X(x) = \int_0^x \frac{\lambda^k \xi^{k-1} e^{-\lambda\xi}}{(k-1)!} d\xi \quad (3)$$

Parameters λ and k are calculated using the estimates for expected value and variance

$$\lambda = \frac{E(X)}{D^2(X)}, \quad k = \frac{E^2(X)}{D^2(X)} \quad (4)$$

Raw data has to be gathered and edited to determine expected value and variance.

3 Data collection and preparation

3.1 Collection of the amount of traffic objects

Transport process planning depends on knowledge about estimated amount of traffic objects to ensure high capacity utilization via suitable vehicle selection and adjusted tour planning. On the other hand, backlog must not occur. Those result from a discrepancy between vehicle capacity and current amount of traffic objects. With the complete recording of traffic objects during stationary processing in sorting centers, the distribution function of traffic objects can aid the probability of backlog P_R.

With calculation utilizing formula (2)

$$P_R = 1 - F_X(x = C_{Fzg}) \quad (5)$$

Truncate the distribution function on the upper ceiling oft the amount of traffic objects $x_o = C_{Fzg}$ yields vehicle utilization η_{Fzg}. Truncate in the distribution function within a interval $\alpha \leq u \leq \beta$ are calculated according to [4]

$$\tilde{F}_U(u) = \frac{F_U(u) - F_U(\alpha)}{F_U(\beta) - F_U(\alpha)} \quad (6)$$

Applying formula (3) with $F_X(\alpha = 0) = 0$ to Erlang - k distribution results

$$\eta_{Fzg} = \tilde{F}(x) = \frac{F_X(x)}{F_X(C_{Fzg})} \quad (7)$$

During stationary processing in outbound hubs, the amount of traffic objects is measured by counting the unique kinds of traffic objects, for example standard letters, large letters, small parcel and packages. Thus said, tour design is primary limited by volume and mass of traffic objects. Acquisition of traffic object data in outbound hubs limits conclusions of tour specific load and ratio of traffic object types. For instance, tours serving mainly letterboxes or mayor parcel customers vary greatly. In addition, the measured amount of traffic objects underlies fluctuations of various causes requiring the tour design and vehicle assignment furthermore to rely on estimates.

3.2 Time series analysis

The time sequence of daily traffic objects can mathematically be described as time series with components for trend, business cycle, seasonal and residual figure. In this instance particularly focusing on the estimation of trend and seasonal components.

The trend component reflects long term change of the examined feature discarding short term and small periodic fluctuations. Presuming the trend component as deterministic allows extrapolation of the trend function to forecast. Long term development is crucial for strategic shaping of the transportation system.

Elimination of irrelevant fluctuations and outliers via smoothing is advisable for long term analysis. Smoothing is a piecewise local adjustment replacing the observations with weighted means of the surrounding observed values. The number of included values and their weighting characterize smoothing methods.

Smoothing of letter and parcel time series aims for balancing the influence of business days and decommission days. At the same time a small smoothing period is advantageous for to keep distortions to the subsequent seasonal analysis low. In order to eliminate business day fluctuations at least a one-week period has to be span. For smoothing the method of a moving average is sufficient. By using the actual, the three prior and subsequent values for the smoothing the smoothing method can be formally described as follows:

$$y_t = \frac{1}{7} \sum_{i=-3}^{3} y_{t+i} \quad (8)$$

To illustrate the moving average smoothing method an extract of the letter time series is shown below.

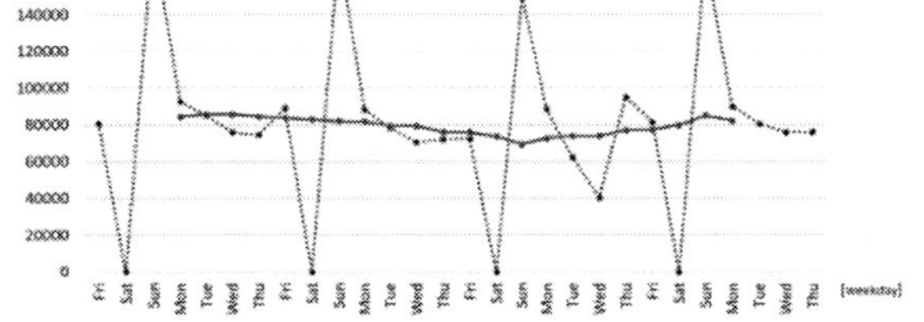

Figure 2. Extract of the letter time series [2]

Trend regression is used to describe the long term monotone progression of time series in a mathematical manner. With the available raw data, a rather small forecast period, the flat gradient and good regression a linear function of the following type is used to characterize the trend function.

$$g(t) = a_0 + a_1 \cdot t \qquad (9)$$

The parameters a_0 and a_1 are estimated using least square minimization. Once the trend function is determined, trend adjustment is carried out by subtracting the trend figure from the initial time series. This allows for further analysis without interference of the trend function. Another periodic fluctuation in quantity of traffic objects occurs at the end of the year. Those fluctuations are equal in strength and depend in the base amount of traffic objects. This insight is incorporated into the regression model by linking the seasonal figure multiplicatively to the base amount, given by the trend function, using a coefficient.

The seasonal component reflects the fluctuations within a year's period. Through sorting the values of the time series by their calendar date enables calculation of the average seasonal figure. Lacking correlation between calendar date and weekdays furthermore independence of seasonal figure and long term development allows to using the smoothed, detrended time series. Due to the complex nature of the seasonal figure a five zone spline was used to capture the specific regression functions individually providing seamless transitions between spline zones. Figure 3 illustrated the seasonal figure and upon based spline modelling of the letter time series.

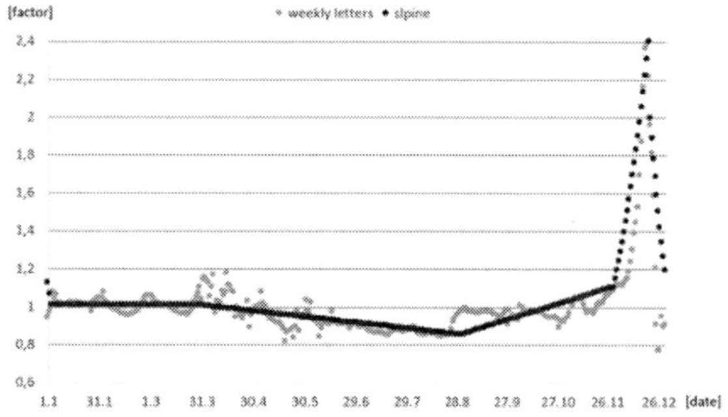

Figure 3. Seasonal figure of letter time series [2]

3.3 Weekday factor analysis

Calculation of weekday coefficients is carried out through the ratios of daily quantity of traffic object compared to the weekly moving average. Furthermore, variance analysis is used to examine the separation of weekdays to each other. All values without processed traffic objects, e.g. holydays, are excluded leaving the letter final day coefficients below:

Table 1. Final letter day coefficients [2].

	Mon	Tue	Wed, Thu, Fri	Sun
Day coefficient	1,087	0,986	0,931	2,262

3.4 Transport volume enquiry

The current capacity planning acts on the judgement of the responsible transport planner with circumstantial feedback regarding capacity shortage or lack of service quality by carriers and customers. Ideally vehicle deployment and provided transport capacity with buffer should comply with the expected amount of traffic units. Approaching the coupling of transport volume and quantity of traffic objects through a mean traffic object size is not sufficient given that:

- lack of numerical acquisition of transported letters and parcels in vehicles,
- volume of letters and parcels varies greatly,
- lack of knowledge about share between investigated area and covered total influence area,
- lack of knowledge about share between combined letter and parcel transportation compared to covered total influence area,

A survey of the transported letters and parcels in vehicles serving within the investigation area and the knowledge enable prognosis of the expected transport volume [6].

3.5 Load state classification

Connecting transport planning to extrapolated transport volume leads to a variety of loads of the transport system. The introduction of discrete load states can minimize the transport planning effort. Further advantages are:

- ability to forecast due to connection between tour planning and extrapolated transport volume,
- reduction in planning effort through pooling of similar load states,
- stable transport schedules through reuse of planned tours for similar transport loads,
- estimation of consignment load and transportation load of accumulative haul tours through linkage to transport volume aiding planning process of alternative transportation concepts,
- short reaction time to adopt fluctuations in transport volume via premade tour plans.

In contrast to commonly used approach for capacity planning are improvements by linking vehicle assignment and operating data based extrapolation of transport volume likely. Figure 4 presents 12 load states with their respective transport volume and occurrence within a year. The classification of those 12 load states yields the needed number of vehicles.

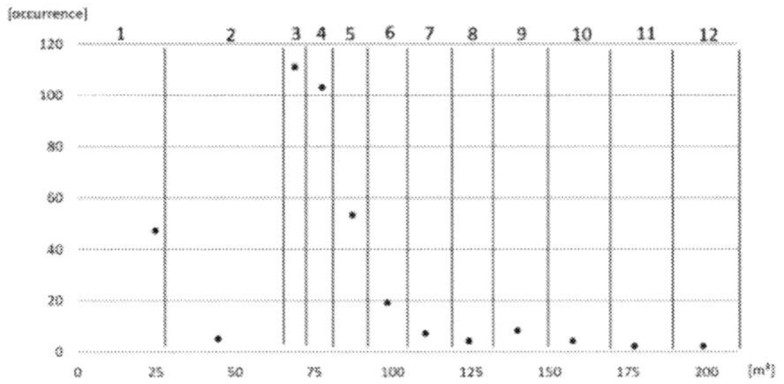

Figure 4. Classification of load states [2]

3.6 Localization of transport volume

Final data acquisition step is assignment of transported transport volume to individual locations, e.g. letterboxes, stores or customers. Attention is specially paid to letterboxes due to potentially multiple approaches daily. Localization utilizes geographic coordinates of corresponding address data. Particular urban environments with limited size allow for the simplification of the geographic coordinate system as orthogonal.

4 Tour planning

4.1 Clustering of service area

After gathering and preparing all planning data, tour planning can be executed. Beginning with the clustering of the service area to allow for individual tour planning within the clusters. In this case the investigation area spreads 500 km^2 including 589 relevant locations. Locations concentrate in the center of the investigation area. Clustering is based on the spatial separation of the locations.

4.2 Calculation of travelled distance

Calculation of total driven distance distinguishes two types of tours; direct transport for locations with high, vehicle filling transport volume and collection tours with several locations to fill up vehicle capacity. Further investigation additionally evaluated the option of transshipment. Distance calculation for direct transport, routes between terminal and hub likewise route between hub and cluster uses beeline distance and infrastructure based detour factor. Distance travelled within the clusters is based on analogy to Travelling Salesman Problem [1] using regression of solved TSP samples between location count and saved mileage in comparison to a star network. Infrastructure is also represented using detour factors.

4.3 Travelled distance of load states

Calculation of distance driven is based on the clustering of locations. The leg between starting point and the first location is called pass way. By estimating the distance travelled within clusters based on analogy to the Travelling Salesman Problem, the estimated distance travelled is independent of the chosen locations to anchor the pass way. This is also advantageous for the calculation of the total travelled distance consisting of circular tour within clusters and the pass way because different start points for the pass way can comparably be evaluated. Minimizing total distance, the nearest location to a start point within a cluster is chosen figure 5 illustrated the afore mentioned by means of two different start points as well as a circular tour within the cluster. Not changing the result of the TSP round tour estimation, different start points with corresponding path optimized cluster locations yield identical TSP estimates. The difference among both cases being the difference in pass way distance (blue and red line). The total distance driven for collection tours consists of the circle tour estimate and two times the pass way for approach and return. For direct transport, the circle tour is dispensed, leaving two times the pass way distance.

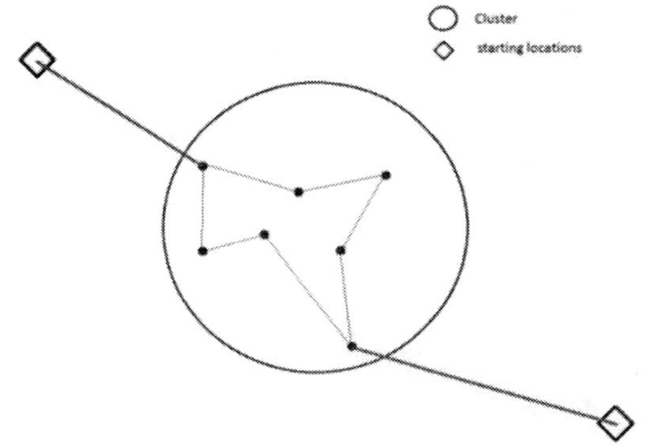

Figure 5. Pass ways of different start points [2]

Distance travelled of each load state is based on three calculated load states and uses interpolation for residual load states. For vans, vehicles mass not exceeding 3500 kg, correlation between transport volume and travelled distance is presented in figure 6.

Technological reliability of the transport process's finishing time requires the assumption of independent singular trips across the product over transportation durations distribution function of each tour. In this context applies:

$$Z_Q(t_S)=\prod_k Z_{Q_k}(t_{S_k})=\prod_k F_{T_{T\eta}}(t_{S_k}) \tag{10}$$

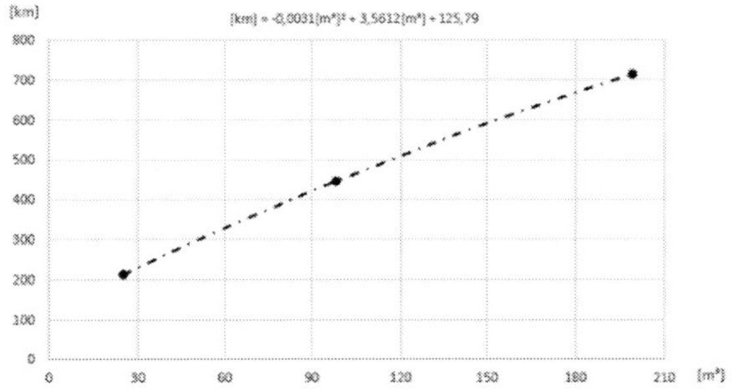

Figure 6. Distance travelled in conjunction with transport volume [2]

5 Conclusion

The introduced technique enables to determine traffic cost for letter and parcel transportation of postal carriers in urban areas. Insufficient data for planning of the initial transportation process – collection of mail and parcel with transportation to sorting centers – and restriction to subjective measurements result in low data quality. The lack in data quality can be compensated through systematic application of mathematical statistical methods.

Time series analysis of processed letters and parcels allows for to forecast the transport volume and promises benefits for capacity planning in sorting centers. Knowledge of estimated parcels and letters allows to adjust the deployment of personnel and set the start of stationary processing. In reverse uncritical processing load allows later start of stationary processing widening the time frame for parcel and letter transportation. Both business areas interact and leave potential for improvement by integrating transportation planning and processing planning.

References

1. W. Domschke, A. Drexel, *Logistik: Rundreisen und Touren*. (München: R. Oldenburg Verlag, 1997)
2. F. Hedrich, *Modellierung der technologischen Zuverlässigkeit in Verkehrsnetzen der stofflichen Kommunikation*. (Dresden, Germany. Technische Univeresität, 2015)
3. R. Keil, *Beschreibung des Zeitverhaltens informationslogistischer Prozesse*, (Schriftenreihe des Sächsischen Telekommunikationszentrums, 2/2006, Dresden, 2006)
4. R. Keil, *Analytische Ansätze zur Modellierung verkehrslogistischer Prozesse – Teil 1 Modellierung* (Schriftenreihe des Sächsischen Telekommunikationszentrums, 11/2011, Dresden, 2011)
5. T. Corejova, E. Imriskova, *Convergence at the postal market*. Eksploatacja i Niezawodnosc. Vol. **39/3**, p. 74-76, 2008
6. L. Madleňáková, *Layer model of the postal system*. (University of Zilina, Zilina, 2013)

MATEC Web of Conferences **44**, 01047 (2016)
DOI: 10.1051/matecconf/20164401047

The Applied Research on Computer Aided Design in Art Design

Yong Min Cui[1], Xin Guang Ren[2,a]

[1] Rongcheng College,Harbin University of Science and Technology,Rongcheng;Shandong,China
[2] Rongcheng College,Harbin University of Science and Technology,Rongcheng;Shandong,China

Abstract. Aiming at constant improvement of computer technology development, the paper proposes the specific applications and prospects of Computer Aided Design(CAD) in the art design field by considering applied research background of CAD in art design, investigating and analyzing superiority and status of CAD, and reinforcing important significance of CAD on art design development. Only to create the CAD continuously and promote applied skills of CAD in art design field can make art design assist CAD to development continuously and satisfy pursuits of material progress and spirit civilization.

In today's society with rapid development of technology and continuous improvement of computer technology, computer technology has been applied to numerous fields and also has been widely applied in art design. Computer technology is equipped with sufficient superiority in price and performance, owing to continuous development of network communication technology, so computer technology performs a huge potential in the art design field. Speaking of computer design, Hearst Randolph once said that "computers impact thinking modes of users. It has compulsive demands for logical analysis, accurate formula and quantitative expressions". Computers can help people to have rationalized thinking, analyze and process all kinds of logical information rapidly. Thus, art design is established on the basis of modern science to constitute assisted design, and such a mode is the feature of modern art design and also opens up a new research field for us to engage in art design career.

1 Features of Computer-assisted Art Design

1.1 Superiority of Computer-assisted Art Design

With the deep development of computer technology, the status of CAD in art design field is increasingly important. For example, industrial design, advertising design, webpage design and animation design, etc., various art design fields concentrate on embodying ability of CAD. One of prominent advantages of computers is to provide greater degree of freedom for designers, who can apply computers to switch and combine pictures at will, as well as attempt various different configurations to create unexpected effects. In this way, it not only can seek for the most excellent and satisfactory works, but also stimulate creative inspiration of designers simultaneously. Secondly, applications of computers improve design precision and speed effectively, reduce labor intensity of designers, and reduce tedious process of some complicated design works. For instance, CAD system can make data of interior design become accurate and reliable and avoid from unnecessary losses caused by errors in the construction project. For some animation design, computers can give simulation preview, and virtuality of real technology makes design performance intuitive and vivid, so that animation drawing will be more accurate. Nowadays, with the constant occurrence of computer three-dimensional software, designers generally can perform their creativity and inspiration by using computers. For example, they draw a three-dimensional spatial model to express shape, structure and size of design products, stimulate color and texture of product surface under the lighting, shorten deign time greatly, and promote design quality effectively. Another advantage of computer technology refers to user-friendly control. It can bring great convenience to designers and change malpractice of time-consuming handwork drawing effectively. In the design working process, it inevitably will appear more or less problems. A simple cancel command of computers can change wrong steps and offer largely free alternation space to designers.

In addition, many computer-assisted manufacturing operations can't be handled by traditional handicraft. For example, crystal laser art engraving uses a model with good three-dimensional software design and graves by using a laser engraving machine to generate complicated, miraculous and distinctive three-dimensional laser engraving graphs. The development of rapid science and technology brings new revolution in art design, and this is the new beginning of better combining technology and art.

[a] Xin Guang Ren:renxinguang12@163.com

1.2 Status of CAD

At present, software development of CAD changes quickly, and functions are increasingly strong and become widely in various fields. It has moved towards life and work of humans gradually and unconsciously and also becomes an indispensable part in the design industry. Therefore, it almost can say that all design industries apply CAD, commonly including CAD in the building field, which generally is embodied in two forms: on the one hand, it is about production software of effect pictures represented by 3DStudioVIZ to make houses or stimulate interior finishing effects. On the other hand, it refers to CAD in interior design represented by AutoCAD and can complete accurate construction drawing design and structure analysis.

As for the CAD in print advertisement, modern printing technology has changed inflexible and typing, etc., traditional technology completely to finish through computer operation from design to output. Under the assistance of Photoshop and InDesign, etc., software, people have already realized the working mode that what you see is what you get. Our thinking can outline rudiment on a computer easily. After repeated modification, perfection and special-effect combination, these productions will be better expressed.

1.3 Significance of CAD on Art Design

Art design is a kind of technological means. It refers to inartistic (especially for non-pure artistic) material product design and also has certain aesthetic property. Art design is an important constituent part of human civilization and mainly constructs material and spiritual civilization. The art design aesthetics still is the bridge to communicate with two major civilized fields, while main research object of technological aesthetics can be objected only by virtue of object production. From the perspective of social meaning, art design always makes progress with technological level synchronously. Design objects, means, thinking or even designers have huge changes due to powerful intervention of technology. Art design depends on technology, so the relationship between computer technology and art design is not opposite, but is interdependent and indivisible.

Computer technology performs art design, while art design needs computer technology to serve for modern market. The core of art design is to innovate and create. CAD is the most advanced and effective tool in our design, is another way of exploiting design thinking and also is an essential advanced brush in modern design. Designers are design subjects, while computers are tools. As a result, in the process of design creation, it not only cultivates innovation consciousness consciously, enriches the ability of artistic appreciation, exploits and enriches design methods and innovation, and improves artistic culture and design ability, but also reinforces the application ability of CAD. Art design has bright fashionability, so it means that it need to integrate knowledge of modern science technology into it and from synchronous development of times culture and social knowledge.

2 Applications of Computer Technology in the Art Design Field

In recent years, the applied range of computer technology is increasingly extensive in the art design field, such as building art design, animation design, and graphic art design, which are contributed to CAD.

2.1 Applications of CAD in the Building Art Design

CAD has widely extensive applications in the building art design and mainly reflects in the following two aspects: First of all, it refers to design building effect pictures. When designing building effect pictures, it needs to use CAD, so it not only can shorten design time effectively, but also can perfect design effects and improve goodness of fit between designed buildings and building effect pictures and viewing value of building effect pictures. Secondly, it refers to animation design. By virtue of CAD, it can present effects of buildings vertically in the form of three-dimensional animation, so people can observe achievements after completing construction of buildings intuitively. Recently, with the rapid development of social economy and continuous development of technology, art design of buildings also applies CAD greatly and improves artistic effects of buildings.

2.2 Applications of CAD in the Animation Design

With the constant development of social economy, the national investments of cultural industry are enlarged increasingly, especially for recent years. Thus, the nation also enlarges the supporting strength of domestic animation industries, such as Boonic Bears, and Radiant and Wolf, etc., which are deeply welcomed by the public. The animation art gives full play to advantages of CAD. In other words, animation industry is arisen with the development of computer technology. The future development of animation industry also must depend on computer industry, For example, by using computer technology, three-dimensional animation is made. In three-dimensional animation, it can set up many three-dimensional figures, animals, scenes, trees and houses, or even sea waves, sands, blues sky and white cloud etc., which have higher authenticity. In the animation art design, designers can make abundant and colorful animation in line with demands and by virtue of computer technology and computer software. Meanwhile, it is also beneficial to continuous development of animation artistic industry.

The constant deepness of CAD has already exceeded the range of easy production internationally. It will be widely applied to television ads and film/television film titles. Due to integration of CAD, techniques, which can't be performed in the past, also can be realized. For instance, Jurassic Park, which has broken box office in America, has been made by special effects using computer-assisted animation technology. With the publication of excellent films and television programs, such as Star Wars, it can be seen everything by using

computer animation design technology to make advertising production. Thus, reliable computer technology and design software with powerful functions can image and develop in the limited thinking space by designers.

2.3 Applications of CAD in the Animation Design

In the art design field, graphic design is a basic art major, so if CAD wants to fully being applied to building art design and animation design, it must has a wide application in graphic design. Using computer technology in graphic design not only can process graphic images, but also can change the way of graphic design. In the past, the production process of graphic design is very completed, while after using CAD, it can realize systematization and simplification of graphic design. Moreover, design effects and efficiency also will be very prominent. For example, when designing graphic images, computer graph and image processing can be used to transit, incise and process lots of graphic pictures, so as to create an extremely fantastic image world and create more refinement of graphic design images. The visual impact goes without saying and fully satisfies aesthetic demands of the public.

3 The Development Tendency of CAD in the Art Design

3.1 Combination of Art Design and Multidisciplinary

Differing from pure fine arts, art design is developed with the development of social economy and technology and is the intersection and integration of technology and aesthetics. The core of art design is "people first", so designers not only should have good foundation of fine arts, but also know about knowledge in multiple aspects, such as knowledge of materials, psychology and economics. CAD also should perform in this way. As for webpage design, it not only requires designers to have certain foundation of fine arts, but also requires designers to have the ability to apply network design language to program. This is a necessary skill to develop dynamic and interactive webpage. For another example, packing design should know about features of different packing materials and characteristics of different packing structure.

3.2 Development, Professional and Intelligence of Design Software

At present, the reason for surviving mainstream design software mainly benefits from development. For example, over 10 companies develops plug-in filter for photoshop, so special effects and corresponding applications of filters obtained by several changes can be completed in a time. For another example, AUTOCAD provides ADS, VBA, Java and Visuallisp, etc., multiple secondary development languages, so commercial corporations can use corresponding language development based on the plug-in platform of AUTOCAD, and designers also can use secondary development languages to complete effects which are hard to reach by using traditional computer design methods. Meanwhile, MAYA, etc., some large-scale professional dimensional design software also has been spread to the domestic.

In order to make artists and designers to accept the tool—CAD, design software also become increasingly intelligent. Painter software stimulates features of a great number of traditional tools and it lengthens the traditional painting experience. In the Painter software, plenty of tools of imitating traditional brushwork and various painting materials can stimulate oil painting, watercolor and traditional Chinese painting, etc., effects easily. Moreover, it is sensitive to texture of painting materials and drawing of designers, so artworks are rich in expressive force.

To sum up, the paper mainly analyzes and discusses art design and applications of CAD simply. The research finds that applying CAD in the art design field is beneficial to ensure quality of art design and improve art design level. Moreover, it is good for designers to apply more modern information technology, improve effects of art design, enhance market competitiveness, and promote constant development of art design industry.

References

[1] Muzi Li, The Study on CAD in Decorative Design [D], Harbin Normal University, 2010.6

[2] Wei Tan, Discussion on CAD and Art Design [J], Teaching Research, 2008(9)

[3] Yongning Zhang, Dongsheng Chen and Xiangning Zhang, Status and Prospect of CAD [J], 2003, (9);

[4] Xiaochuan Fu, Applied Research of CAD in Landscape Performance [D], Northwest Agriculture & Forestry University, 2010.11;

[5] Yanhua Li, Applications and Exploration of CAD in Design Construction [J], Computer Knowledge and Technology, 2015(3);

[6] Jiming Wang, Applied Research on CAD [J], Science and Innovation, 2014(21);

[7] Yang Yang, Development and Applications of CAD [J], Information System Engineering, 2014(2).

MATEC Web of Conferences **44**, 01048 (2016)
DOI: 10.1051/matecconf/20164401048

An applicable approach for performance auditing in ERP

Jian Guo Wan[1,a], Ting Liao Li[2]

[1]*School of Economic and Management, Southeast University, 210008 Nanjing, China, PRC*
[2]*Southeast University, Nanjing Audit University, 211815 Nanjing, China, PRC*

Abstract. This paper aims at the realistic problem of performance auditing in ERP environment. Traditional performance auditing methods and existing approaches for performance evaluation of ERP implementation could not work well, because they are either difficult to work or contains certain subjective elements. This paper proposed an applicable performance auditing approach for SAP ERP based on quantitative analysis. This approach consists of 3 parts which are system utilization, data quality and the effectiveness of system control. In each part, we provide the main process to conduct the operation, especially how to calculate the online settlement rate of SAP system. This approach has played an important role in the practical auditing work. A practical case is provided at the end of this paper to describe the effectiveness of this approach. Implementation of this approach also has some significance to the performance auditing of other ERP products.

1 Introduction

In the 1990 of the 20th century, according to the development of information technology and enterprise's demand for supply chain management, based on enterprise's management information systems in the era of information on future development trend forecast, the United States computer technical advisory and evaluation group (Gartner Group) first proposed the concept of Enterprise Resource Planning (ERP). After more than 20 years of development, ERP has been widely used all over the world. ERP is widely recognized as a kind of advanced concept of enterprise management. Supply chain management is the core idea of ERP.

From the perspective of management science, ERP is an integration of business processes, data, human resources, computer hardware and software. It acts as an enterprise resource management system based on the advanced concept of ERP. It not only provides decision support for enterprise decision management, but also provides operation means for the end users. From the perspective of information technology, ERP is a consolidated information system, in which enterprise's logistics, capital flow and information flow are comprehensive integrated. Business modules of ERP can be applied not only to the manufacturing enterprise, but also to other types of businesses and organizations.

In the field of ERP products, from Germany's SAP is the most representative. SAP is known as management gurus behind successful enterprise, occupies an extremely important market share in ERP products. SAP industry solutions covering almost all the major sectors, at present, such as Sinopec, Petro China, national grid and many large enterprises have implemented SAP.

[a] Corresponding author: wanjianguo2002@hotmail.com

As an integrated computer information system, it brings great deal of benefits to many enterprises. Widespread use of ERP systems has fundamentally changed the way of business data processing. The complexity of ERP systems has brought new challenges to performance audit under ERP environment. Many traditional performance auditing methods could not work well in ERP environment because they are difficult to work. Due to the lack of quantitative evaluation method, performance audit under ERP environment has remained stagnant. In order to meet the new demands of ERP, we have to find new performance auditing method in an applicable way. This paper proposed a quantitative performance audits method for SAP based on the audit work. We believe that the implementation of this approach also has some significance to the performance auditing of other ERP product.

2 Literature review

Current study literatures on the performance auditing methods under ERP environment is generally little. Current research focuses on performance evaluation of ERP systems implementation. Performance evaluation of ERP systems implementation is multi-layered complex systems, which has multiple indicators. There are many system evaluation methods from different ways, such as the commonly used ABCD checklist, the balanced scorecard, the weighted average method, fuzzy comprehensive evaluation and Data Envelopment Analysis (DEA), the Analytic Hierarchy Process (AHP). These assessment methods are generally using a combination of quantitative and qualitative methods.

Article available at http://www.matec-conferences.org or http://dx.doi.org/10.1051/matecconf/20164401048

Zhang Hui, Mou Yankui (2009) performed metric analysis from multiple angles on the results of ERP implementation, using ABCD check table. They provided assessment scores to the running situation of enterprise's ERP system according to 4 aspects and 25 questions respectively. These aspects contain technology, data integrity, education and training, and system usage. According to the degree of performance for each items, different scores are given (excellent 4 points, good 3 points, medium 2 points, poor 1 points, not implementation 0 points). The cumulative total 90 points above of determine for A level, 71~90 points determine for B level, 50~70 identified as C level, less than 50 points identified as D level. According to different levels of results (ABCD), a qualitative description and conclusions can be provided. Ma Guangqing (2009) using the weighted average method which is simple and intuitive, from technical capacity, managerial capacity and elements of efficiency evaluation, construct a set of index system of performance evaluation for ERP system implementation. The evaluation model and its solution are given on this basis. This method uses AHP method to determine the relative weight of each index based on experts' scores. Zou Mingxin, and Xu Xuejun (2006) proposed a three-layer index system based on the balanced scorecard to evaluate the performance of ERP implementation combined with the overall goals of ERP implementation. They also used expert comprehensive evaluation method for example of application. Sun Yuefan, Zhang Zhenhao (2007) conducted a quantitative research on how investment of ERP affects the economic efficiency and competitive of enterprises based on DEA model. This provides a possible idea for study on performance evaluation of ERP investment. Analytic Hierarchy Process (AHP) is a common method of performance evaluation of ERP, which is discussed in many literatures. The key point of Analytic Hierarchy Process is to establish the index system and determine the standard points of each indicator. It is a subjective and an objective, quantitative and qualitative methods.

There are some empirical researches on ERP performance. Zheng Chende, Chen Jinyong, and WangYan (2008) took listed enterprises which implemented ERP as samples to study the impact of ERP implementation on the performance of State-owned enterprises. Empirical results show that ERP systems can improve the operation of State-owned enterprises. Inventory turnover, accounts receivable turnover, turnover and total assets turnover were all increased significantly after the ERP implementation. ERP system can effectively improve the productivity of workers, reducing the number of employees; but the profitability of State-owned enterprises is not increased after the implementation of ERP system. Xu Ming (2010) took manufacturing listed companies in Shanghai and Shenzhen as the research object, conducting an empirical research on how the implementation of ERP systems affects the performance of listed companies. Research showed that, implementation of ERP does help to improve enterprise's operating performance, and affect financial performance index such as assets turnover and inventory turnover. Improved performance of enterprise through the implementation ERP has time lag effect. It always needs 3 to 4 years of using to gain the effect of ERP. In short-term view, enterprise using domestic ERP system would improve its benefits faster than enterprise using foreign ERP systems, but from long-term view, Indicators of enterprises using foreign ERP systems is superior to the using domestic ERP systems. Li Benbo, ChenSheng, and Qiang Haitao (2006) used 87 valid questionnaires from 30 small and medium enterprises in Chongqing for empirical research. Results showed that quality of members in project team, budget, enterprise management, ERP project implementation are significant factors of the performance of ERP implementation. Quality of project members is the fundamental factor, and software selection and performance of ERP implementation has no significant positive relationship.

Existing approaches for performance evaluation of ERP implementation can be little help to performance auditing under ERP environment. First of all, because these approaches contain certain subjective elements (such as the construction of index system), and even adopt the experts' advice cannot eliminate subjectivity. On the contrary, audit evidence is required to be objective. Therefore, these methods are rarely used. Secondly, these methods are systematic evaluation method, which needs large collection of information, and has a long period of data acquisition and processing. It is difficult to meet the requirements of the time limit for the field audit. An objective, quantitative audit approach is urgently needed in the performance audit process under ERP environment.

3 Applicable performance auditing approach of SAP

Through the study of auditing work, we summarized 3 parts of the performance indicators in ERP system according to the feature of SAP. Quantitative performance audit methodology for SAP consists of system utilization, data quality and the effectiveness of system control. System utilization consists of 2 aspects, which are the condition of user login and online settlement rate. Data quality consists of master data quality and interface data quality. Effectiveness of system control consists of the achievement of key business controls and the validity of control data.

3.1 System utilization

System utilization is the most intuitive judgment of the application performance of ERP system. If an ERP system has a low utilization rate after the completion of implementation, and a large number of businesses are conducted without ERP system, the performance is clearly low. The indicator of system utilization can be divided into two indexes, one is the condition of user login, and the other is the online settlement rate.

User login condition reflects to what extent the SAP users rely on the ERP system. Users of SAP will be charged by license fee. The license fee for each user in China will be USD 2300 to USD 3000. One license is generally for one user. In order to save money and

improve the efficiency, enterprises should give full play to each user role to minimize the occurrence of idle users during the implement and application of ERP. ERP generally records the user information and login information in the database. During the process of audit, we downloaded the user table of SAP (USR01, USR02, USR04, and USR21 etc.) to query the last login date of each SAP user. If the value of last login date is null, then indicate the user has never login the system. If the date of last login is several months ago, it also indicate the idle user of the system. If there are large numbers of idle users, not only illustrates the waste may exist in the process of ERP implementation, but also indicates that ERP system may not play as expected. For example, Part of the users who never (up to year 2009) login SAP system is shown as table 1.

Table 1. Part of the users never login SAP system

User	User group	Create date	Last login date
BAIBG	CNOOC_USER	2007-5-11	null
CAIHY1	JD_CJF_USER	2009-4-22	null
CAONONG	COSL_USER	2007-7-27	null
CHENGC2	OIL&GAS_DX	2006-7-3	null
CHENYH	CHEMICAL_USR	2006-6-29	null

Online settlement rate refers to the proportion of the business which are conducted and settled by ERP system in an online manner. High online settlement rates indicate the business functions of the ERP system have been fully utilized, and the system performance is high. Conversely, it indicates that ERP system has not been fully utilized. Therefore, the online settlement rates can act as an important index which reflecting the effect of ERP application.

In order to calculate the online settlement rate, we have to find the differences of vouchers between online settlement and off-line settlement. In SAP, for example, the voucher header data is stored in the SAP table "BKPF", and the type of business transaction is stored in the field GLVOR, which indicates the business type of the voucher. For example, if the field has the value of "RMRP", it means that the voucher is generated by the MM module of invoice verification transactions. Take the business of procurement as another example, to calculate the accounting entries which have the credit account as accounts payable can calculate the settlement amount of purchase. The online settlement amount for the purchase consists of the accounting entries which has the content "RMRP" in the field "GLVOR".

Online settlement rate calculation also needs to consider the business process in ERP. In the procurement process, for example, assume that procurement in the SAP business settlement meets the following prerequisites:

• Accounts payable change the error using the red write-off method;
• Accounting methods of the receipt or acceptance of services through the ERP Material Module is as follows:
 - Receipt / service acceptance:
  Debit: material / cost
  Credited: GR / IR
 - When invoices are received:
  Debit: GR/IR
  Credited: accounts payable (212100*-212101*)
 - If invoice could not arrive at the end of the month:
  Debit: GR / IR adjustment
  Credited: payable provisional estimate (212,102 *)
• Accounting methods of the receipt or acceptance of services not through the ERP Material Module is as follows:
 - Estimates at the end of the month:
  Debit: material / cost
  Credited: Accrued expenses (2191 *)
 - Early next month Reversal (both reverse reversal and red letter are available):
  Debit: Material / Costs - The red letter
  Credited: Accrued expenses (2191 *) - The red letter

The calculation formula of online settlement rate is as follows (calculation of 01-12 accounting period, not including the adjustment period):

Settlement amount of Procurement = credit amount of accounts payable (2121000000, 2121010000) current year + online prepaid balance, namely amount of GR/IR account (1201000000-1201000010) current year (credit amount- debit amount) + amount of accrued expense account (2191*) current year (credit amount- debit amount)

Online settlement amount = credit amount of accounts payable (2121000000, 2121010000) current year, which has the RMRP type in account (that is, fields of business transactions for "RMRP" indicates online vouchers of settlement) + current year amount of GR/IR account (credit amount- debit amount)

Online settlement ratio = amount of online settlement current year / amount of procurement settlement current year

If the online calculation is low, this indicates the utilization of ERP system is poor, and system performance is not good. It also implies that there is a lot of off-line settlement of business which can result in control risk. Therefore, the online settlement rate is an important indicator reflects the system utilization and performance. For example, Part of the online settlement ratio of each branch in year 2009 is shown as table 2.

Table 2. Online settlement ratio of each branch in year 2009

Company name	Business amount	online settlement amount	online settlement rate
Beijing	2593485785	0	0
Jiangsu	355823563.8	350108875	98.39%
Tianjin	4057447397	2222236533	54.77%
Zhejiang	1235129867	769696329.7	62.32%
Shenzhen	737475062.6	55704875.09	7.55%
Shanghai	20190673.76	17422760.33	86.29%

3.2 Data Quality

There are 3 ways through which data come into ERP system: manual input, system interfaces and migration of

legacy data. Data in ERP can be divided into master data and transaction data. Master data is the foundation of shared data between systems, such as customer, vendor, material, organization, and so on. These data entrance the system only once, for common use of each module, and will be maintained in a unified manner by the system. If the master data information is inaccurate, then an error will be diffused in the system, resulting in a significant impact on data quality. For example, if the vendor's bank account information could not be updated timely in the master data, it may cause failure of payment. Therefore, the quality of master data is particularly important for system data integrity and reliability. We can start from the following point of view to analysis the quality of master data using technical means:

- If key information about the master data exists vacancy,
- If master data which describe the same object is consistent,
- If information about master data in the parent company and its subsidiary or between subsidiaries is consistent,
- Whether the master data redundancy.

Interface data quality is another important aspect of ERP data quality. ERP does not cover all aspects of the enterprise production and management. Most enterprises in the ERP environment integrates a variety of external systems, such as procurement bidding systems, customer relationship management systems, financial systems, and weighbridge system and so on. These external systems generally exchange data with the core modules of ERP. For example, the results of the procurement bidding system (procurement of goods name, code, quantity, price, the successful vendor information, delivery and payment conditions, etc.) will pass to ERP to form procurement orders. Customer relationship management system is in charge of the customer information, and with the ERP customer master data to interact in real-time or on a regular basis so as to maintain the timeliness of customer information. Weighbridge system will transmit metering information of materials to ERP inventory management module.

These data is an important data source of external systems to ERP system, and is important to the accuracy, reliability and integrity of system data. The interface between ERP and external system has important implications for data quality. In the SAP audit process, we can evaluate the data quality of ERP by checking the master data tables in relevant modules and the tables imported from the interface of external systems.

3.3 Effectiveness of the system control

Traditional means of controls are usually replaced by information system controls in ERP. Information system controls consist of those internal controls that are dependent on information systems processing. Many control criteria and procedures of internal control have been previously develop and embedded in ERP modules or achieved by control data configuration. When business activities occur, the information system may automatically initiate transactions or perform processing functions. Relevant information is recorded and stored in the central database of ERP.

General controls and business process application controls are highly integrated in ERP. These controls can be divided into programmed controls, parameterized controls and other controls. Programmed control refers to control activities embedded in a computer program. Parameterized control means control activities implemented by configuring the parameters in ERP. These parameters can also be called control data.
Business process is controlled by business rules in ERP system. Business rules are basic and important business process application controls in ERP. ERP system may automatically initiate transactions or perform processing functions according to pre-defined business rules. Processing steps and related controls may be set in business rules, which are a kind of critical control data.

Control data can be set in the period of ERP system implementation. Necessary adjustments should be made during system running. The effectiveness of the programmed control depends on the quality of programming. If the program does not work or contains an error, the control failure is likely to exist for a long time. The effectiveness of the parameterized control depends on the accuracy and the timeliness of control data setting. If a control data is not properly set for a long time, the control failure may also exist for a long time. Because information systems process groups of identical transactions consistently, any misstatements arising from erroneous computer programming or control data will occur consistently in the same types of transactions. Therefore, it is necessary to assess the state of control data, and to review the history of control data, in order to assess the potential impact of the changes, and ensure control data set or changed by appropriate personnel at the appropriate time in a timely manner.

Control data play a significant role in ERP's internal control system. It is generally set in the system configuration during the period of system implementation. Necessary adjustments are also needed during the system running. Auditors may evaluate the effectiveness of the controls implemented through the use of ERP's configuration management tools. For example, in SAP, transaction code SPRO can be used to configure the control data during the system configuration. Control data is generally stored in the central database of ERP. Some control data can be retrieved directly and easily through database queries, while others are stored in a special format which can only be read and set by specific configuration management tools.

4 Application case

In the audit of a petroleum corporation in year 2010, we used quantitative method described above to evaluate the performance of the corporation, and found the following problems:

4.1 Idle users

According to statistics, to the start date of auditing, the petroleum corporation has created about 5,000 SAP users, including more than 300 users never logged, accounting for about 6%. More than 1,000 users have not logged in the ERP system for more than 60 days, about 22%.

The creation of ERP users is usually according to business process requirements. User idle indicated that resources in ERP system have not been fully used. In addition, the petroleum corporation needs to purchase SAP user licenses, each ranging from approximately USD 2300 to USD 3000, and have to pay an annual service charge 17% of the purchase price. By the end of year 2009, the petroleum corporation has paid license fees and service charges more than USD 13.9 million. A large number of idle users created losses and waste to some extent.

4.2 Low utilization of core business processes

The most advantage of ERP systems is the integration of logistics, capital flow and information flow. This makes the enterprise management more efficient. The audit found that to the procurement management processes, one of the core processes in ERP system, usage of subordinate enterprises is not high. According to statistics, in 2009, only about 60 subordinate companies deployed the procurement management module, accounting for 21% of the total companies which implemented ERP. To those companies which deployed the procurement management module, 5 subordinate units simply unused, 16 companies had the online settlement rate of 60% or less, the lowest online settlement rate is only 5.1%.

4.3. Lack of system control

After audit analysis on the ERP system of the petroleum corporation, we found that about 1500 items of sales contract have the final execution exceeds 10% of the amount. There are more than 100 crude oil sales transactions which have the ultimate shipments exceeded the sales contracts and orders 10000 barrel or more. There are more than 1000 orders which have a total of receiving exceeding the amount of orders by 5%. There are more than 10 sales records of urea, which have the quantity of 1 ton and the price from USD 6165 to USD 1.54 million, whereas the normal price at around USD 262. After verification, we found that these companies are in this way to improve the prices of the whole batch of fertilizer in order to skirt state limits on factory price of chemical fertilizer. We also found a large number of incomplete master data and data error problems of ERP data interface, which affected the cost accounting of ERP system seriously.

5 Conclusions

Many traditional performance auditing methods could not work well in ERP environment because they are always time-consuming and difficult to work. Existing approaches for performance evaluation of ERP implementation can be little help to performance auditing under ERP environment because these methods contains certain subjective elements, while audit evidence is required to be objective. This paper proposed an applicable performance audit approach for SAP ERP based on quantitative analysis, which could help auditor to gain substantial audit evidence with quantitative results. This approach can minimize the subjective judgment of the ERP in the performance audit process. Believe that the implementation of this approach also has some significance to the performance auditing of other ERP product.

References

1. Cheng de.Chen Jinyong.Wang Yanguo, Study on the enterprise ERP system implementation performance, Statistics and decision, 19 (2008)
2. Sun Yuefan.Zhang Zhenhao, In China based on DEA model study on the performance evaluation of enterprise ERP investment, Shanghai Journal of Economics. 5(2007)
3. Zou Ming.Xu Xuejun, Study on performance evaluation of ERP implementation based on BSC. Management and information technology, 13(2006)
4. Ma Guangqing.Zhang Yanping.Xu Rui Yuan.Zhou Shugong, Study on ERP implementation performance evaluation system, Journal of Hebei University of Science and Technology, 1(2009)
5. Zhang Jianguang.Zhang Junrui.Wang Lina, ERP implementation performance of foreign research, Finance and accounting monthly, 7(2009)
6. Zhang Hui.Mouyankui, Discussion on ERP performance measurability, Silicon Valley, 22(2009)
7. Xu Youjia, Research on the performance evaluation of enterprise's ERP system, Enterprise economy. 11(2008)
8. Tan Jiu, ERP implementation performance studies: Retrospect and prospect, The Theory and Practice of Finance and Economics (bi-monthly), 27(2006)
9. Lee Benbo.ChenSheng.Qiang Haitao, Empirical research on the influencing factors of ERP implementation performance of Chinese enterprises, Modern Finance and Economics. 6(2005)
10. Xu Ming, ERP system implement effect on the performance of listed companies: an empirical study, Guangdong University of Finance & Economics Master's degree thesis, 2010

MATEC Web of Conferences 44, 01049 (2016)
DOI: 10.1051/matecconf/20164401049
© Owned by the authors, published by EDP Sciences, 2016

A Real-Time Renewable Plastic Particles Sorting Algorithm Based on Image Processing

Zhi Jiao [1,a], Yan Sun [1]

[1]North China Institute of Aerospace Engineering, 133 Aimin East Road, Hebei Langfang 065000, China

Abstract. According to the demand of harmonia renewable particles sorting in domestic plastics recycling industry,mainly for white and gray recycled plastic particles,a mathematical model is built in RGB color space and a kind of high accuracy, real-time sorting algorithm based on image processing is proposed.This algorithm is intended to use related multiplication, addition and comparison operations of particles pixels R, G, B component,,instead of sorting algorithm based on the difference and threshold processing commonly used in domestic products,and verify its effectiveness through simulation.

1 Introduction

Waste plastics contains huge renewable resources, waste plastic for recycling and processing into recycled plastic is significant: Firstly, recycling can compensate for raw material consumption, and saving energy ; Secondly, it can reduce the white pollution formed by the discarded plastic trash to protect the environment;Thirdly,you can take advantage of recycled plastic as a raw material in manufacturing of plastic products to create considerable economic benefits for related industries.Since entering twenty-first Century,waste plastic recycling has received heightened attention from the world. To make better use of recycled plastics and generate more economic benefits, we need to sort particles of different colors, and achieve a certain sort of purity.Therefore, recycled plastic particles (hereinafter referred to as renewable particles) sorting industry has broad market prospects. Figure 1 shows the renewable particles.

Figure 1. Renewable Particles

At present, some foreign countries such as Switzerland, Germany, the United States have been using high-precision digital cameras and automatic identification technology to produce Plastic color separation machine for automatic sorting of renewable particles. However, the high price (RMB 200-400 million) of foreign-related products is not acceptable to the plastic products industry in china. Currently,in our country,utilization of waste plastics recycling is not high, waste plastic recycling plant is not much, especially uneven distribution;on the other hand, in recent years, domestic manufacturing has been developed rapidly and the market is very prosperous, the number of large plastics markets is more than ten .Renewable particles has been in short supply,and Prices have been rising,so renewable particles process will be Hot spot in the future development[1].The few large-scale plastics recycling companies in China use self-developed sorting device to realize renewable particles sorting.As the Renewable particles sorting algorithm is the core technology of sorting device,it determines the sorting accuracy and real-time sorting speed.

2 RGB color space model of white renewable particles

At present, most of the domestic renewable particles sorting device (color separation machine) use CCD camera acquisition capture renewable particles color information, calling sorting algorithm to achieve real-time sorting recycling particles base on the DSP or FPGA hardware platform.Mainstream sorting algorithms are based on image processing techniques to construct a three-dimensional mathematical model in the RGB color space, then use difference and threshold algorithm to complete sorting process [2-3].

For white and gray recycling particles,the sorting algorithm based on the difference and the threshold operation is treated the qualified renewable particle image as a gray image, the image captured by the CCD camera is basically white,which means that the three component value of R, G, B are substantially equal in the renewable particles image data.In the RGB three-dimensional color space,such image data points located substantially on the main diagonal (Gray axis) which has the same angle with three axes,as shown in Figure 2.In the filming process,we capture the particles information through the reflected light,but the particles reflect light intensity is different at different angles,so the particles of the gray image data has a certain range.

Considering the factors of light,raw material itself characteristic, the front plastic particles renewable technology and so on,making the white and gray renewable particles image is not gray scale image entirely,that is the value of the three components of RGB particles pixels may not exactly equal------- In the RGB color space, the data points of the regenerated particles are not only distributed in the gray level, but also in a certain range of the gray axis. When collecting a large number of qualified white renewable particles for image

[a] Zhi Jiao: lfjaozhi@126.com

acquisition, image data in the RGB color space formed a "mallet" shape, the main in gray axis which has the same angle with RGB three axes,as shown in Figure 3.This is the model characteristic of the white renewable particles in RGB three-dimensional color space.Thus,if only based on the difference and threshold operation to make the harmonia sorting algorithm ,it will affect the sorting accuracy and especially when sorting smaller particle size, that will bring great error.

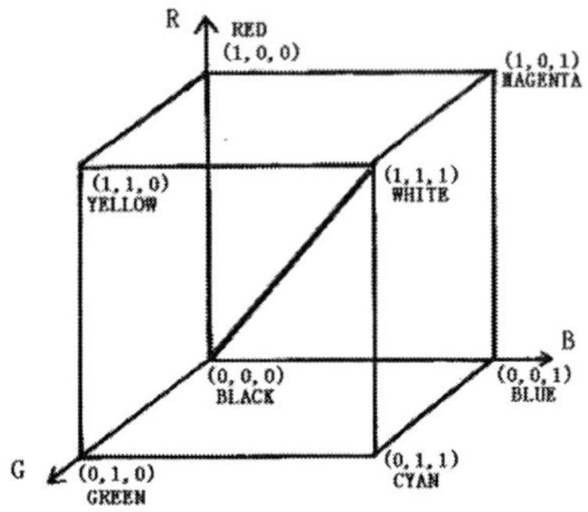

Figure 2. RGB 3D Color Space

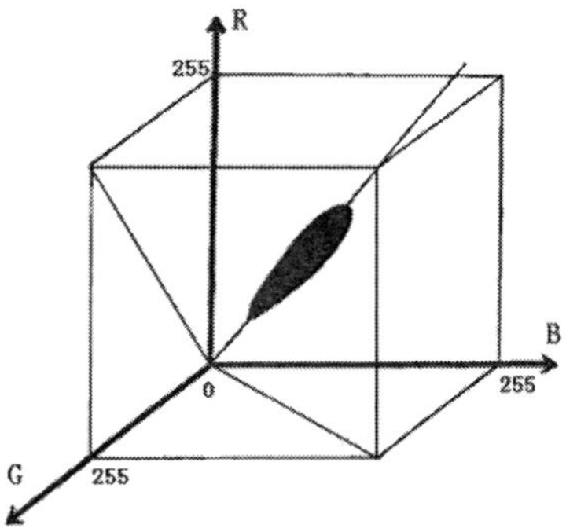

Figure 3. White Renewable Particles Data Distributed in the RGB Color Space

When collected a sufficient number of standard white renewable particles,then we can be sure this is the qualified renewable particles space range,the remaining are heterochromatic particles which to be picked out .Foreign fiber detection work is making use of the algorithms to determine the spatial extent and judge the image point is within this range or not.

Through the observation of renewable particles, you will find harmonia particles generally have the following three categories.

1) Black particles - including renewable black particles and the large black impurities which do not be filtered by the filter during the regeneration process,the color is nearly black,the brightness is low in the particle image and locate in the end of the gray axis.

2) Harmonia particles - refers to the particles whose color"is obviously not black and white," maybe blue, yellow, red and so on.

3) Color- impured particles - the main is white,but in poor quality.Data points fall out of the "mallet" range formed by the white renewable particles,but the deviation is in a narrow range.

In summary, these types of major heterochromatic particles in RGB color space,do not overlap with the white particles space,so this feature models has already met the sort requirements.

3 Renewable particles sorting algorithm

Combined research experience in similar projects completed by author with the proposed white particles feature model, renewable particles sorting algorithm is proposed.

3.1 Determine the Scope of Qualified Particle Data

Gathering a large number of qualified white renewable particles image data, depict these data points in the RGB color space,and determine the symmetry axis of "mallet".

Reexamining the qualified white particle image RGB space model from an engineering point, we find that the deviation between the "mallet" symmetry axis and the RGB cube space gray axis is not large,in the introduction of error conditions,under the conditions of certain errors,view the two axes as one. After thus approximation,use some plane which are perpendicular to the gray axis to cut the “mallet”, then we can get a series of concentric circles. Then, theorem 1 can be proved based on the previous approximation , that is :

Theorem 1 - the value of (R+G+B) which is the summation of R, G and B coordinates for every image pixel in a given plane that is perpendicular to the symmetry axis of the 3D stick is equal to each other, this uniform summation can be recorded as a constant 3m [4] , which can be expressed as below:

$$R+G+B=3m \quad (1)$$

Then, we can use the added value of R, G, B coordinate components of the particles data point to determine circular section of the "mallet".As in the case of 3m,establish a mapping table which includes all qualified circular section . Obviously,by determining the minimum value of 3m,we can regard the min as the threshold(At the low end of the gray axis) sorting the first category harmonia particles(black).In real-time sorting process ,compared the added three coordinate value of actual regeneration of particle image data point 3m with the min,then make the judgment:if $3m < min$, particles are first category harmonia particles.

As the circular cross-section is determined by the calculated value of 3m, another theorem can be proved based on strict researching and demonstrating , that is:

Theorem 2 - the cross-sectional radius of the circle is approximately equal in value to the average of the difference between maximum and minimum of R,G and B coordinates in the section multiplied by a constant[4].

So,the circle radius can be approximately figured out listed below:

$$radius = \frac{\sqrt{6}}{12}[(R_{max} - R_{min}) + (G_{max} - G_{min}) + (B_{max} - B_{min})] \quad (2)$$

Furthermore,we can determine the maximum distance r from each point on the section of qualified particle space "mallet"to the RGB color space coordinate origin:

$$r = \sqrt{3m^2 + (radius)^2} \quad (3)$$

The actual distance from the renewable particle image data points to the RGB coordinate origin is:

$$D = \sqrt{R^2 + G^2 + B^2} \quad (4)$$

While real-time sorting, compare D with r value to make a certain judgement based on the comparison result – if $D \le r$, the actual particle being detected is qualified renewable particle ; if $D > r$, the actual particle being detected belongs to the second or third harmonia particle. The schematic of renewable particles mallet cross section is shown in Figure 4. For the convenience of DSP and other chips for real-time processing, we can compare D^2 and r^2 to increase sorting speed.

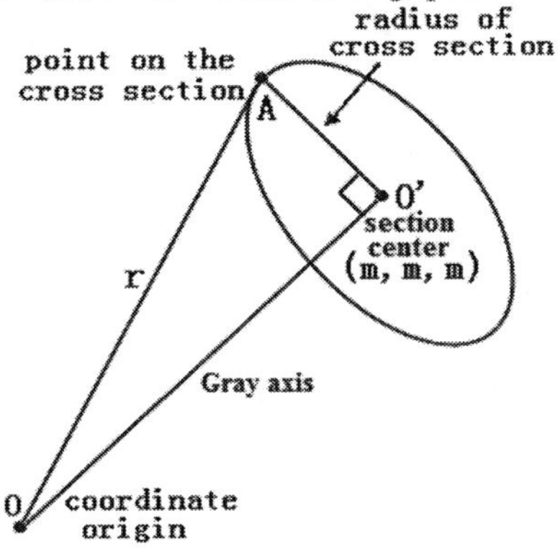

Figure 4. The Schematic of Renewable Particles Mallet Cross Section

In summary, in order to get qualified particle data range,we can calculate(and storage) the value of 3m(to determine the circular section,meanwhile ,we can obtain the min as the threshold sorting the first category harmonia particles);then make 3m to be the index, calculate (and storage) the maximum distance r (as the comparison threshold to determine the second or third harmonia particles)from point of each section in the qualified particle space mallet body to the RGB color space coordinate origin.

3.2 Renewable Particle Real-time Sorting Algorithm

Real time sorting for renewable particles may start after the data range of qualified particles is obtained . Real-time sorting algorithm steps are listed as follows:

1) Capture an image point of the particles to be picked with CCD camera.

2) Calculate the sum of the three R, G, B coordinates $3m$ and D^2.

3) Compared $3m$ with $\min$, if $3m < \min$, it is belongs to the first category harmonia particles;if not, compared D^2 with r^2 : if $D^2 \le r^2$, it is qualified particles; on the contrary, it is belongs to the second or the third harmonia particles.

The algorithm flow is shown as Figure 5.

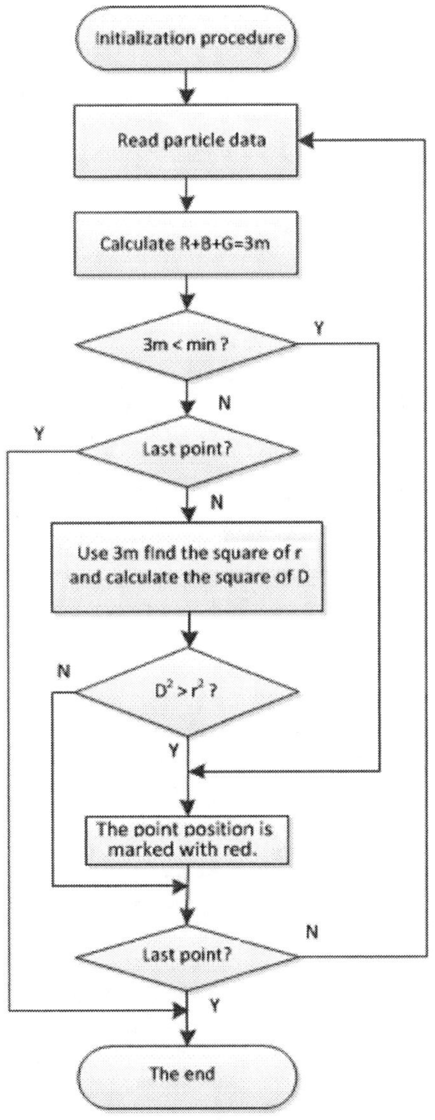

Figure 5. The Flow Chart of Real-time Renewable Plastic Particles Sorting Algorithm

4 Algorithm Validation

To visualize verify the validity of the algorithm, we can verify the validity of the algorithm by observing the renewable particles image which is processed through the renewable particles sorting algorithm.The picture (the background is under smooth processing)of qualified white renewable particles is shown as figure 6.The picture of renewable particles mixed with harmonia particles is shown as figure 7. Processing the figure 7 using the algorithm-------marking the harmonia particles pixels with striking dark color,and the verification results is shown in Figure 8.

Figure 6. Qualified White Regenerated Particles

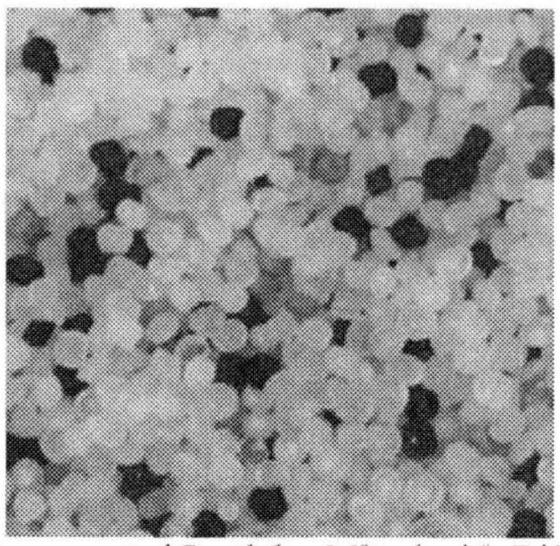

Figure 7. Regenerated Particles Mixed with Different Color Particles

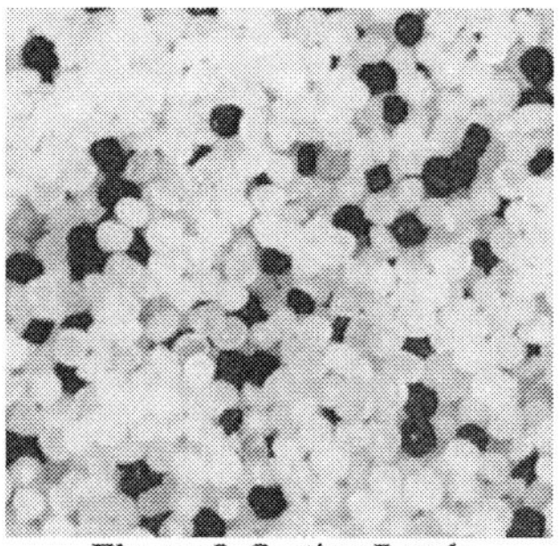

Figure 8. Sorting Result

From the experimental results we can know that the algorithm can effectively pick harmonia particles from the mixed white particles.Compared the number of picked harmonia particles through the algorithm with the number of manually sorted,we can verify that this algorithm sorting rate is more than 95%,and the algorithm is effective.

At the same time, it must be pointed out that the accuracy of the algorithm depends largely on the accuracy of the data range of qualified particles .In practical engineering applications, we should strive to select a large number of different types of qualified particles for analyzing in the process of determining qualified particle data range,thus we can guarantee the accuracy and the validity of the algorithm.

5 Conclusion

After the analysis and data simulation experiments,we can prove the proposed renewable particles particles sorting algorithm which aims at improve the accuracy of real-time sorting,uses the pixel R, G, B components related multiplication, addition and comparison operations instead of domestic common sorting algorithm that based on the difference and threshold process, is a feasible sorting algorithm.In this paper ,the mathematical model and sorting algorithms can be applied and transplanted to other related projects.

References

1. Zhu Yu-hong, Status and Development Trend of Waste Plastic Recycling and Utilizing [J],Technology Information , Issue **16**,pp:395-396 (2011)
2. Zhang Yin-hui, Bao Neng-sheng, Xie Rong-sheng,The Application of Image Processing Technology in Renewable Plastic Particles Sorting Device[J],Light Industry Machinery,**27**(5),pp:90-91(2009)
3. Huang Dong-hai,Fang Rui-ming,Zheng Li-Xin, DSP Application in Multi-Channel Color Sorting Machine Sorting System[J] , Electric Automation, **26**(2),pp:119-120(2006)
4. Jiao Zhi, Research and Implement on Foreign Fiber Detection Algorithm [D], Beijing University of Technology Master's Degree Thesis, pp. 12-33(2006)
5. Ma Chang-song,Color Sorter Signal Processing System Based on HSI Colorspace[J],Equipment ManufacturingTechnology, Issue**9**,pp:177-178 (2013)

MATEC Web of Conferences **44**, 01050 (2016)
DOI: 10.1051/matecconf/20164401050

Application of Markov chain Monte carlo method in Bayesian statistics

Qi Zhao

Department of Foundation, Shandong Yingcai University, Jinan 250104, China

Abstract. In statistical inference methods, bayesian method is a method of great influence . This paper introduces the basic idea of the bayesian method . However, the widespread popularity of MCMC samplers is largely due to their impact on solving statistical computation problems related to Bayesian inference. Markov chain Monte Carlo method is essentially a Monte Carlo synthesis procedure. The random sample of it is related to a Markov chain. It is a widely used stochastic simulation method. This paper mainly introduces Gibbs sampling,and its application in Bayesian statistics. We use a simple example to illustrate how to tackle a typical Bayesian problem via the MCMC method

1 Introduction

Bayesian statistical originated in the eighteenth century British scholar Bayesian. His method was later developed into a system of statistical inference method. By the 1930 s has formed a bayesian school of thought, To 50 ~ 60 s has developed into an influential school of statistics, the effects are still growing. An important unfavorable factors hampering the bayesian method widely used in the further, that is obtaining the posterior distribution is often complex, high dimension, no standard form, the function on the integral calculation is often very difficult. Recently,several approaches short of direct integration have been proposed . we focus here on Markov Chain Monte Carlo methods. Markov chain monte carlo method, the basic idea is through the establishment of a stationary distribution $\pi(x)$ for markov chains to get the samples, And then based on these samples can do all kinds of statistical inference.

.

2 Bayesian statistical inference method and bayesian formula

The basic point of bayesian school is: Any unknown quantity θ can be regarded as random variables, A probability distribution is available to describe it, this distribution as prior distribution, denoted by $\pi(\theta)$ .suppose $p(x\mid\theta)$ is conditional density function depend on the parameters θ. Our mission is to make statistical decision for θ ,According to the bayesian school point of view that should be divided into the following steps

1. Produce the sample $X=(X_1,...,X_n)$ needs to be done in two steps: First of all a observed value θ generated by the prior distribution $\pi(\theta)$. Then from the conditions of density function $p(x\mid\theta)$ to produce sample observations $x=(x_1,...,x_n)$. then the joint conditions density function of the sample as follows

$$p(x\mid\theta)=\prod_{i=1}^{n}p(x_i\mid\theta) \qquad (1)$$

the joint distribution comprehensive sample information, referred to as the likelihood function.

2. $\pi(\theta)$ is prior distribution of the θ. Synthetic a priori information and samples after get sample joint distribution of X and θ.

$$h(x,\theta)=p(x\mid\theta)\pi(\theta) \qquad (2)$$

3. In order to make statistical decision to θ, decompose the joint distribution

$$h(x,\theta)=\pi(\theta\mid x)m(x) \qquad (3)$$

here $m(x)$ is the marginal density function of x

$$m(x)=\int_{\Theta}h(x,\theta)d\theta=\int_{\Theta}p(x\mid\theta)\pi(\theta)d\theta \qquad (4)$$

The parameter space of θ is Θ

the $m(x)$ does not contain θ any priori information. Therefore can be used to make statistical decision to θ is only conditional distribution of $\pi(\theta\mid x)$. Its computation formula is

$$\pi(\theta\mid x)=\frac{h(x,\theta)}{m(x)}=\frac{p(x\mid\theta)\pi(\theta)}{\int_{\Theta}p(x\mid\theta)\pi(\theta)d\theta} \qquad (5)$$

This is a density function of the bayesian formula. This is under the condition of the given samples, the conditional distribution of θ, Called the posterior distribution of θ .It focus on the sample and all information related to the θ in the prior distribution. It is more close to the actual situation than prior distribution $\pi(\theta)$ .So using posterior distribution $\pi(\theta\mid x)$ to make statistical decision may be improved.

Example 1 Gelfand and Smith, consider the following example. Set a test may have five as a result, the probability of their occurrence, respectively

$$\frac{\theta}{4}+\frac{1}{8},\frac{\theta}{4},\frac{\eta}{4},\frac{\eta}{4}+\frac{3}{8},\frac{1}{2}(1-\theta-\eta)$$

It contains two unknown parameters θ and η, and between 0 and 1. The existing 22 test results observed value as follows. $y=(y_1,...,y_5)=(14,1,1,1,5)$, y_i denotes the number of occurrences of the ith a result. $i=1,...,5$. Now, put the x, y is decomposed into two

E-mail addresses: zaho231200@163.com

parts,respectively.let

$y_1 = z_1 + (y_1 - z_1), y_4 = z_2 + (y_4 - z_2)$,such that

$(Z_1, Y_1 - Z_1, Y_2, Y_3, Z_2, Y_4 - Z_2, Y_5) \sim M[22; \frac{\theta}{4}, \frac{1}{8}, \frac{\theta}{4}, \frac{\eta}{4}, \frac{\eta}{4}, \frac{3}{8}, \frac{1}{2}(1-\theta-\eta)]$

M denotes the multinomial distribution. z_1 and z_2 are not observed, Can be seen as defect data, (θ, η) are assumed to be evenly distributed. i.e.

$$\pi(\theta, \eta) \propto 1$$

Let $z = (z_1, z_2)$ is the value of $Z = (Z_1, Z_2)$,then , (θ, η) likelihood function and posterior distribution, respectively

$$L(y, z \mid \theta, \eta) \propto (\frac{\theta}{4})^{z_1+y_2} (\frac{1}{8})^{y_1 - z_1} \times (\frac{\eta}{4})^{y_3+z_2} (\frac{3}{8})^{y_4 - z_2} (\frac{1-\theta-\eta}{2})^{y_5}$$

$$\pi(\theta, \eta \mid y, z) \propto \theta^{z_1+y_2} \eta^{y_3+z_2} (1-\theta-\eta)^{y_5}$$

3 Markov Chain Monte Carlo method

Markov chain monte carlo method is essentially a monte carlo comprehensive program. The generation of random sample is associated with a markov chain. The basic idea of this method is to create a stationary distribution is $\pi(x)$ markov chain, Samples of $\pi(x)$ is obtained by the markov chain, Then based on these samples can do all kinds of statistical inference, In summary is divided into the following three steps

1. To construct a "suitable" markov chains,its transition kernel is $P(\cdot,\cdot)$, "suitable" is refers to the meaning of $\pi(x)$ is its corresponding stationary distribution
2. Starting from a point $X^{(0)}$, creating a point sequence $X^{(1)}, \ldots\ldots, X^{(n)}$ using the markov chains
3. for a certain number of m and a big enough number n, the expectations of any function $f(x)$ is estimated as follows

$$\hat{E}_\pi f = \frac{1}{n-m} \sum_{t=m+1}^{n} f(X^{(t)})$$

Using MCMC methods, construct transition kernel is crucial, different MCMC method often is the transition kernel structure is different

Based conditional distribution of iteration sampling is a kind of important markov chain monte carlo method. A special case of the most famous is the Gibbs sampling, Now has become the standard of statistical computing tools, Its potential of markov chains is established by decomposition a series of conditional distribution, It's the most appealing features. Here to use conditional distribution, Especially with full conditional distribution. The so-called full conditional distribution is shaped as the conditional distribution of $\pi(x_T \mid x_{-T})$ .among them $x_T = \{x_i, i \in T\}, x_{-T} = \{x_i, i \notin T\}, T \subset N = \{1, \ldots, n\}$ .take notice, In the conditional distribution of the above, All variables appears(either appear in conditions or in the variable). Because the Gibbs sampling involves only a single variable sampling, it is the most attractive. The following will introduce the Gibbs sampling method

Let $\pi(x_1, \ldots, x_m)$ denotes m-dimensional joint distribution, constructor the transition nuclear in Gibbs sampling as follows

$$P_{x,y} \triangleq P(x, y) = \prod_{k=1}^{m} \pi(y_k \mid y_1, \ldots, y_{k-1}, x_{k+1}, \ldots, x_m)$$

Among them

$$x = (x_1, \ldots, x_m), y = (y_1, \ldots, y_m), x_i \in D, y_i \in D$$

$\pi(y_k \mid y_1, \ldots, y_{k-1}, x_{k+1}, \ldots, x_m)$ is the conditional distribution. Verifiable $(P_{x,y})$ is indeed a transfer matrix

i.e. $\sum_y p_{x,y} = 1$

$$\sum_{y_1} \pi(y_1 \mid x_2, \ldots, x_m) = \sum_{y_1} \frac{\pi(y_1, x_2, \ldots, x_m)}{\pi(x_2, \ldots, x_m)} = \frac{\pi(x_2, \ldots, x_m)}{\pi(x_2, \ldots, x_m)} = 1$$

$\sum_y p_{x,y} =$

$$\sum_{y_m} \sum_{y_{m-1}} \cdots [\sum_{y_1} \pi(y_1 \mid x_2, \ldots, x_m)] \pi(y_2 \mid y_1, x_3, \ldots, x_m) \ldots \pi(y_m \mid y_1, \ldots, y_{m-1}) = 1$$

Verifiable, $\pi(x_1, \ldots, x_m)$ is stationary distribution, it's probability transition matrix is $p(x, y)$

$$\sum_{(x_1, \ldots, x_m)} \pi(x_1, \ldots, x_m) p((x_1, \ldots, x_m), (y_1, \ldots, y_m)) =$$

$$\sum_{x_m} \sum_{x_{m-1}} \cdots \sum_{x_1} \pi(x_1, \ldots, x_m) \pi(y_1 \mid x_2, \ldots, x_m) \pi(y_2 \mid y_1, x_3, \ldots, x_m) \ldots \pi(y_m \mid y_1, \ldots, y_{m-1})$$

$=$

$$\sum_{x_m} \sum_{x_{m-1}} \cdots \sum_{x_1} \pi(x_1, \ldots, x_m) \cdot \frac{\pi(y_1, x_2, \ldots, x_m)}{\sum_{x_1} \pi(x_1, \ldots, x_m)} \pi(y_2 \mid y_1, x_3, \ldots, x_m) \ldots \pi(y_m \mid y_1, \ldots, y_{m-1})$$

$=$

$$\sum_{x_m} \sum_{x_{m-1}} \cdots \sum_{x_2} \pi(y_1, x_2, \ldots, x_m) \pi(y_2 \mid y_1, x_3, \ldots, x_m) \ldots \pi(y_m \mid y_1, \ldots, y_{m-1})$$

$= \ldots\ldots$

$=$

$$\sum_{x_m} \pi(y_1, \ldots, y_{m-1}, x_m) \frac{\pi(y_1, \ldots, y_m)}{\sum_{x_m} \pi(y_1, \ldots, y_{m-1}, x_m)} = \pi(y_1, \ldots, y_m)$$

Gibbs sampling specific steps are as follows

By markov chain $X_n(\omega)$ sample, a sample $(y_1, \ldots, y_m)$ of $X_{n+1}(\omega)$ can be obtained according to the following procedure

1 first , y_1 is obtained by a random variable $X_{n+1,1}(\omega)$, $X_{n+1,1}(\omega)$ obey the distribution of $\{\pi(y_1 \mid x_2, \ldots, x_m), y_1 \in D_1\}$ ($x_2, \ldots, x_m$ from $X_n(\omega)$)

2 secondly, y_2 is obtained by a random variable $X_{n+1,2}(\omega)$, $X_{n+1,2}(\omega)$ obey the distribution of $\{\pi(y_2 \mid y_1, x_3, \ldots, x_m), y_2 \in D_2\}$,In this down, $y_k (k = 1, \ldots, m-1)$ is obtained by a random variable $X_{n+1,k}(\omega)$, $X_{n+1,k}(\omega)$ obey the distribution of $\{\pi(y_k \mid y_1, \ldots, y_{k-1}, x_{k+1}, \ldots, x_m, y_k \in D_k\}$

In the end , y_m is obtained by a random variable $X_{n+1,m}(\omega)$, $X_{n+1,m}(\omega)$ obey the distribution of $\{\pi(y_m \mid y_1,\dots,y_{m-1}), y_m \in D\}$

Definition $y \triangleq (y_1,\dots,y_m)$ is a sample of $X_{n+1}(\omega)$

Now, Take an initial value $X_0(\omega)=y^{(0)}$, $y^{(1)}$ is obtained by the random variable $X_1(\omega)$ According to the above methods. To get the sample $y^{(2)},\dots,y^{(n)}$ from $X_2(\omega),\dots,X_n(\omega)$ .When n is large, the distribution of $X_n(\omega)$ approximation of $\pi(x_1,\dots,x_m)$,Can approximate thought, $y^{(n)}$ is a sample obey the distribution of $\pi(x_1,\dots,x_m)$

Example 2 from example 1,can obtained full conditional distribution of (θ,η) from its Posterior distribution

$$\pi(\theta \mid y,z,\eta) \propto \theta^{z_1+y_2}[(1-\eta)-\theta]^{y_5} \propto \left(\frac{\theta}{1-\eta}\right)^{z_1+y_2}\left(1-\frac{\theta}{1-\eta}\right)^{y_5}$$

$$=(1-\eta)Be(z_1+y_2+1,y_5+1)$$

$$\pi(\eta \mid y,z,\theta)=(1-\theta)Be(y_3+z_2+1,y_5+1)$$

$$\pi(z_1 \mid y,\theta,\eta)=\pi(z_1 \mid y_1,\theta)=b(y_1,\frac{2\theta}{2\theta+1})$$

$$\pi(z_2 \mid y,\theta,\eta)=\pi(z_2 \mid y_4,\eta)=b(y_4,\frac{2\eta}{2\eta+3})$$

the Gibbs sampling can be carried out on the full conditions of distribution.

Let The initial value $\theta=0.5,\eta=0.5$, Iterative sampling program compiled with MATLAB, Below is the first 1000 θ and η values draw the image

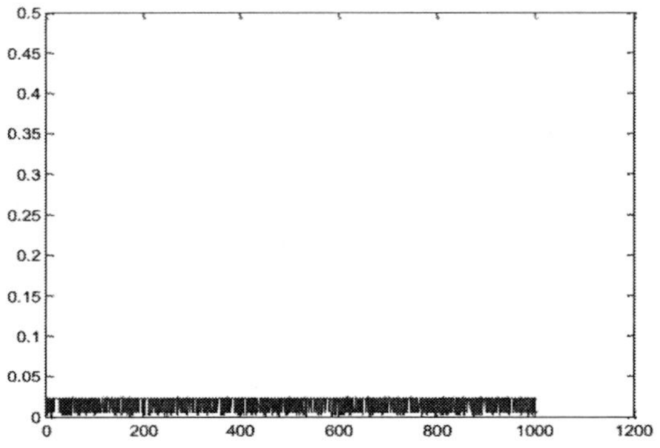

Figure 1 **Figure of θ**

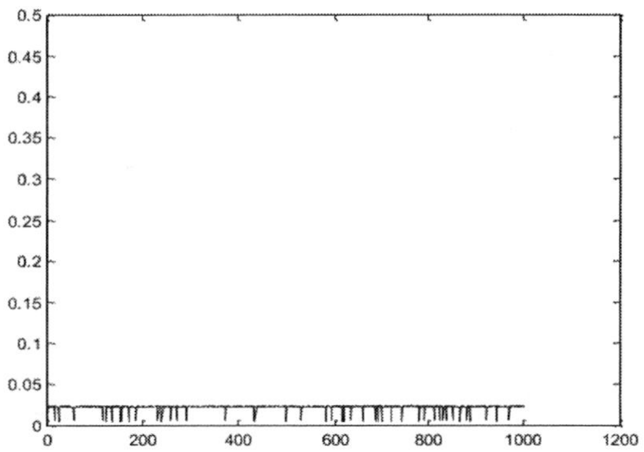

Figure 2 **Figure of η**

4 On the convergence of Markov chains

To make the markov chain monte carlo method is applied to practical problems, to determine Markov chains when to converge to the stationary distribution. convergence of markov chains is a property in theory,i.e. There is always a time t,

Markov chains convergence to a stationary distribution when $t^{'}>t$. We generally through a special markov chains to judge whether the convergence, but state is usually high dimension, and so it is difficult to estimate. Most judge convergence of the method is based on the monitoring of one or some state the number of functions, The most common way is as time increases, simply draw these functions, and then on intuitive determine when to stationary distribution

Example 3 Gelfand and Smith to Gibbs sampling data in case 1. they judge convergence adopt the mean value of ergodic, Every 10 data in the markov chain, take a sample, Calculate a traverse the mean every 20 sample. After 5000 times of the calculation, the Gibbs sampling has converged, Get the following estimate

$$E(\theta \mid y)=0.520$$

$$E(\eta \mid y)=0.123$$

$$Var(\theta \mid y)=0.018$$

$$Var(\eta \mid y)=0.0065$$

Gelfand and Smith still calculated $E(\theta \mid y)=0.520$ and $E(\eta \mid y)=0.123$ use quadratic gaussian integral method, Both consistent

Conclusion

to integrate complex and high dimensional functions is extremely difficulty in Bayesian statistics, however,the Markov chain Monte Carlo method provides a good way, we sample from the posterior directly,and obtain sample estimates of the quantities of interest,thereby performing the integration implicitly.This method is also applicable to other fields, has the widespread application prospect

References

[1] G. L. Gong , M. P. Qian. The application of stochastic process . Tsinghua University press, Beijing, 2004

[2].Sh.S.Mao,J.L.Wang,X.L.Pu. Advanced Mathematical Statistics,_Higher education press,Beijing,1998

[3] Y.Q. Li, Ch. Liu, Q. Wang. stochastic process. National Defense Industry Press, Beijing, 2009

[4] Gelfand A E, Smith A F M. samling based approaches to calculating marginal densities. J Amer Statist Assoc,1990,85:398~409

[5] Gelfand A E, Smith A F M. Gibbs sampling for marginal posterior expections.Communications in Statistics A,1991,20:1747~1766

[4] Walsh, B. (2004). Markov Chain Monte Carlo and Gibbs Sampling. Lecture Notes for EEB 581, version 26 April 2004.

[5] Gareth O. Roberts , Jeffrey S . Rosenthal., General state space Markov chains and MCMC algorithms, Probability surveys Vol.1 (2004) 20-71

MATEC Web of Conferences **44**, 01051 (2016)
DOI: 10.1051/matecconf/20164401051

Analytical Research on Upstream Channel Noise Monitoring

Jin Bao Song [1,a]

[1]Information Engineering School, Communication University of China, Beijing, China

Abstract. The Hybrid Fiber Coax (HFC) network of CATV has tremendous advantages as the platform of B-ISDN. In practical application, the upstream channel noise and the special tree-and-branch topology will make it difficult to transmit data. Hence it's necessary to monitor and analyse the real-time characteristics of the upstream channel noise and bit-error-rate (BER), and understand present and historical situation of noise. In the paper, the cause and characteristics of each kind of noise especially the noise in the upstream channel are studied. Based on this, the formula to calculate the BER of QPSK and 16QAM signal in various environment of upstream channel noise is developed respectively. The imitation of system is made. And the performance comparison between them is given.

1 Introduction

The broadband network based on two-way HFC cable network has the advantages of wide users, low cost, wide band and good compatibility and therefore has a broad development prospects. But there's a lot of noise in upstream channel of HFC network, combined with the funnel effect of the noise of coax cable distribution network, which seriously influences the upstream transmission of digital signal and limits the development of two-way HFC network[1]. So effective measures should be taken to suppress the noise in return path. To suppress noise, the characteristics of the noise must be firstly deep understood. The noise of actual network must be tested and analysed. So that the method of being targeted to suppress noise will be generated. This paper is based on this consideration. A set of real-time monitoring test system of cable TV upstream channel noise is designed and set up. And the test data is analysed scientifically[2]. The noise characteristics are extracted. The historical information of noise is stored. The digital transmission characteristics and noise performance of upstream channel as well as their change trend can be timely understood by the user. Thus reasonable suggestions to two-way network maintenance and upstream business can be put forward[3].

HFC upstream channel monitoring systems that can be seen on the market at present are basically the company's products, such as TRILITHIC Company's GUARDIAN / 9580 reverse maintenance system, ACTERNA PathTrak performance monitoring system and so on. These systems generally have the function of real-time monitoring upstream channel noise spectrum and adopt their own software to analyse noise spectrum in order to achieve the alarm function[4]. Also a lot of long-term historical data are stored for the researchers. But the existing monitoring systems only simply collect and record the noise data for simple alarm. They don't give the user an intuitive, simple and clear illustration about upstream channel. Only very professional and technical personnel can understand the channel condition through analysing these data. This is obviously not conducive for the normal network management personnel to do the upstream channel monitoring and timely maintenance. In order to solve this problem, we hope to develop the noise test system of cable back analysis software in this paper, which realizes the comprehensive analysis of the test data. And the results of the analysis feedback to the user in the most practical way. The nonprofessional users can also understand the general operation of the network and other useful information of network maintenance in the present condition[5].

2 The integral design of the monitoring system

The main purpose for monitoring system is to understand the noise characteristics of HFC network upstream channel. The real-time situation and historical situation of the noise are analysed. The real-time monitoring of the whole upstream system is realized. The corresponding reports and recommendations are put forward.

In order to measure the noise of the transmission network, the generally adopted method is to send a test signal, pass the network transmission and receive the signal. By comparing the difference between the signals before and after the network transmission, the network noise's influence on the signal is analysed. In HFC network, this method means that a digital signal for test is launched by the user, passes the upstream channel of HFC network transmission, the signal is received on the

[a] Corresponding author: songjinbao@cuc.edu.cn

front end. By comparing with the known test signal, it is concluded that the upstream channel noise effect on the digital signal transmission. This is the method used by all current HFC upstream channel monitoring system. But this test method has the certain shortcomings. First of all, the cost of the whole test system would be high if the client launch test signal and compare on the front end. Secondly, the operability of the test system will be greatly reduced. In order to overcome the above shortcomings, considering the accuracy, operability and the overall cost of the test system, an improved testing method is adopted in this system. All of the measuring instruments will be put in the front end, through the corresponding processing, to simulate the digital signal transmission in HFC network upstream channel.

Based on the above consideration, the test system is designed as shown in Figure 1. The whole test system is divided into the following five parts: the noise import part, the spectrum test part, reverse modem part, the error test part and test result analysis part.

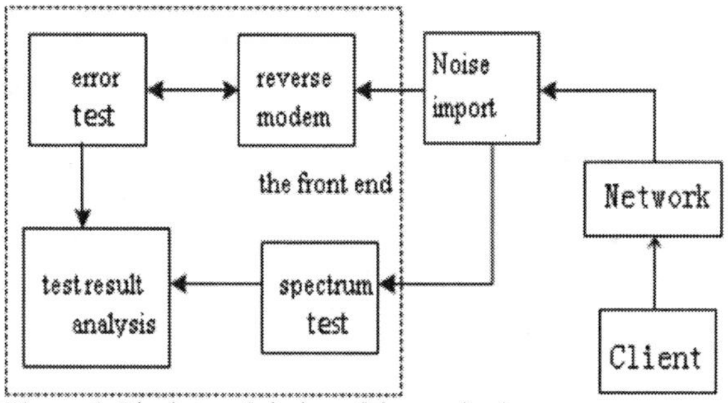

Figure 1. The integral design of the monitoring system

The noise import part is introduced to analyse the noise function. In this scheme, all of the test equipments including signal source equipment are on the front end. So the test signal does not actually pass through the upstream channel transmission of HFC network. In order to make the test result manifests the influence on transmission signal of the upstream channel noise, noise interference to signal transmission in HFC network must be imitated by adopting corresponding way. We usually think that HFC network upstream channel noise belongs to the additive noise. So signal and noise can be separated. On the one hand, the signal modulation in the client is implemented on the front end. On the other hand, the noise of the client is introduced into the front end. The demodulation test is made after adding noise to the modulation signal through the coupler. In this way, the test system can imitate signal transmission in actual HFC network. The role of the noise import part is to introduce the upstream channel noise into our test system.

The function of the spectrum test part is to use a dedicated cable analyser to monitor the frequency spectrum characteristic of the upstream channel noise in non-business state. The noise signal can be introduced by the noise import part. Because we need to know the upstream channel frequency range (5 ~ 65 MHZ) noise distribution. Therefore, parameter setting and measurement of cable TV analyser is different from the downstream channel. The test result of cable analyser to is transmitted to the computer through GPIB cable. The corresponding analysis and the test data processing are carried out by the computer.

The function of reverse modem part is modulation and demodulation to digital signal in some way. Because the digital signal from the source is a baseband signal, which can't transfer in the upstream channel of cable TV system. So the signal modulation and demodulation must be firstly made when error characteristics of upstream signals is measured. And the modem method is different from the process of signal transmission in downstream channel. So it is called reverse modulation and demodulation.

The error test part is to do the digital signal bit error rate test by using a dedicated error analyser. The error analyser is put as signal source to send baseband digital signal. Baseband digital signal passes through reverse modulator, superimpose upstream channel noise introduced from the former part, passes through the reverse demodulator and arrives at the receiving end of the analyser. So that the error characteristics of upstream channel can be concluded. Error test result of error analyser is transmitted to computer via RS232 cable. Further analysis of the data is carried out by computer.

Test result analysis part belongs to the software. The computer statistically analyses error and noise characteristics and obtains the corresponding analysis results according to the test data transmitted from the error analyser and cable TV analyser. If performance deterioration of the upstream channel happens, the system will generate real-time alarm information, put forward corresponding suggestions and notify the manager timely troubleshooting. At the same time, the analysis software also will store the historical information of the system, analyse the long-term trend the upstream channel performance and put forward practical suggestions for the network maintenance and business configuration problems.

3 The implement of the monitoring system

The schematic diagram of HFC upstream channel noise monitoring system is shown in Figure 2.

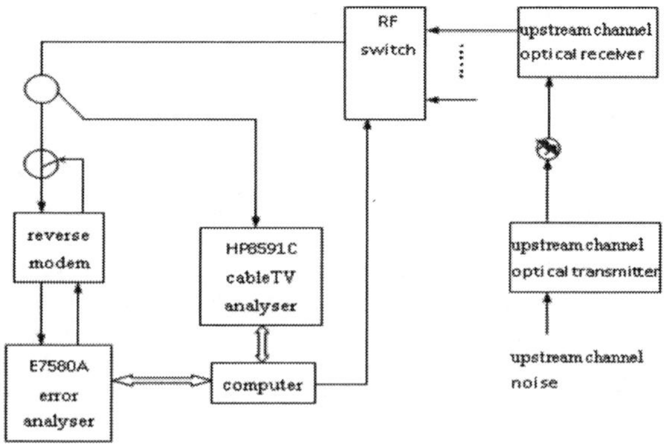

Figure 2. The schematic diagram of HFC upstream channel noise monitoring system

In this paper, the monitoring system are simulated by using the MATLAB software. The way is as follows:

(1)A random testing signal is sent.

(2)The random testing signal passes through QPSK and 16 QAM modulation respectively in two ways.

(3) The random testing signal passes through the network.

(4) Gaussian noise, narrowband continuous wave noise and impulse noise signals are introduced respectively.

(5) QPSK and 16 QAM demodulation are accordingly made.

(6) Bit error rate and other indicators are given by the monitoring system.

(7) The noise's influence on the signal in the network is analysed by comparing the difference between the signals before and after the transfer.

In HFC network, this method means that a digital signal for test is launched by the user, passes the upstream channel of HFC network transmission, the signal is received on the front end. By comparing with the known test signal, it is concluded that the upstream channel noise effect on the digital signal transmission. By comparing differences of various indicators of different types of noise in different signal under different modulation mode, the best way of modulation and demodulation adopted to different upstream channel noise are determined. This test method through MATLAB simulation is the current method of all HFC upstream channel monitoring systems use. The various cable TV systems upstream channel test data and indicators of this test system are required for every cable channel statistics. In addition, the research on the upstream channel cable TV system performance in this paper is somewhat superficial, but also carries on the beneficial attempt for the future development and reconstruction of the cable television.

4 The simulation of HFC network upstream channel

In HFC network, general transmission general transmission the upstream channel is the digital signal. Therefore, BER should be chosen as main indicators to evaluate its transmission performance. But in fact, the analog signal is in the process of transmission. All kinds of noise has a direct effect on the analog signal, which in turn affect the analog signal correctly received on the front end. Therefore, the requirement of digital signal transmission error rate can be attributed to the requirement of the analog signal carrier to noise ratio on the receiving end. In the test system, the carrier to noise ratio largely reflects the channel noise, with the characteristics of real time measurement. The error rate measured by the error analyser has only a posteriori. So we need to further study the relationship between the carrier to noise ratio and the error rate and analyse channel noise influence on BER. Due to the different modulation mode, the relationship between BER and carrier to noise ratio is different. So the main content of this paper is to discuss the most commonly used two kinds of modulation: QPSK and 16 QAM mode in HFC network upstream transmission mode and all kinds of noise influence on signal bit error rate. The corresponding simulation is carried out by using MATLAB software.

4.1 Upstream channel BER of QPSK modulation

In QPSK modulation, baseband signal waveform, the waveform and spectrum of modulated signal, as well as the signal constellation diagram are shown in the case of not setting the output parameters, as shown in Figure 3.

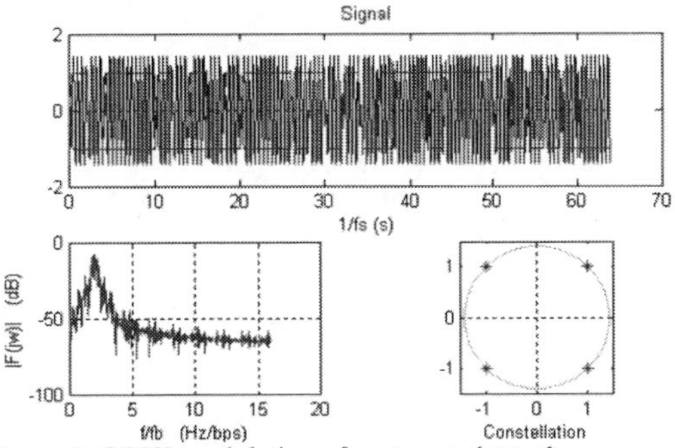

Figure 3. QPSK modulation of upstream channel

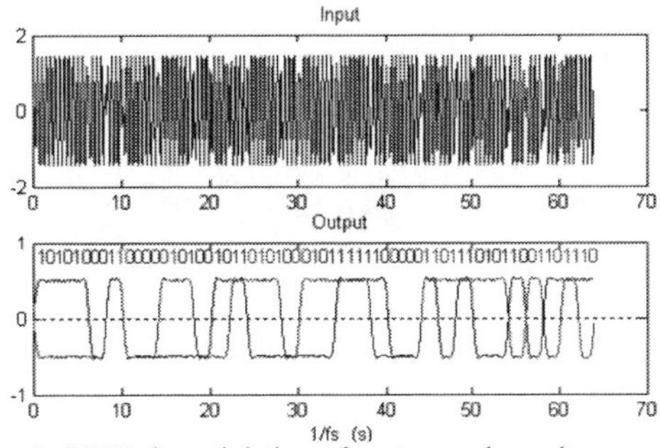

Figure 4. QPSK demodulation of upstream channel

Based on the analysis of HFC network upstream channel noise effects, noise actually always is introduced into the main categories: Gaussian noise, narrowband continuous wave and impulse noise. The following analysis is according to the characteristics of these three kinds of noise.

(1) Gaussian noise

After Gaussian noise superimposed on the transmission signal in upstream channel passes by receiving filter, it becomes a narrowband Gaussian noise, which can be represented as:

$$n(t) = n_i(t)\cos\omega_c t - n_q \sin\omega_c t \tag{1}$$

Gaussian noise and its spectrum are shown in Figure 5.

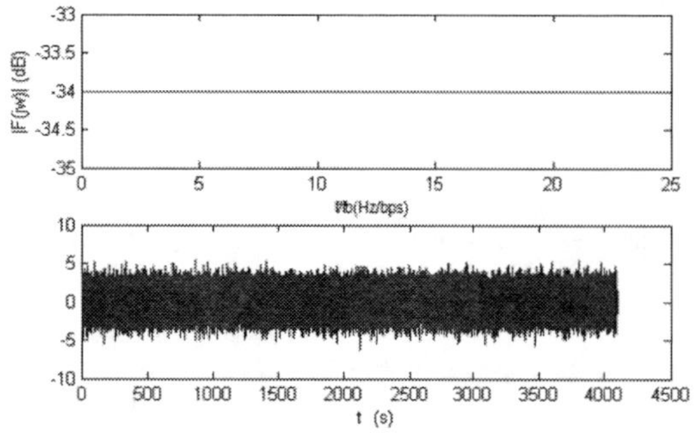

Figure 5. Gaussian noise and spectrum in upstream channel

(2) Narrowband continuous wave noise

After continuous wave noise superimposed on the transmission signal in upstream channel passes by receiving filter, it becomes a narrowband continuous wave noise, which can be represented as:

$$c(t) = a\cos(\omega_c t + \Delta\omega t + \theta) \tag{2}$$

Narrowband continuous wave noise and its spectrum are shown in Figure 6.

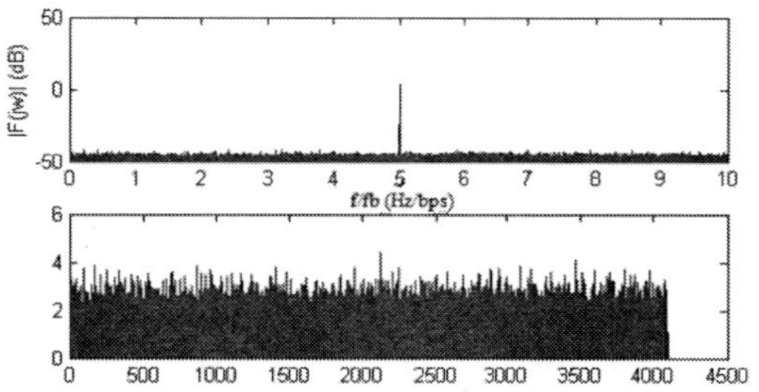

Figure 6. Narrowband continuous wave noise and spectrum in upstream channel

(3) Impulse noise

Hypothesis is as follows: Impulse noise model is the Poisson impact sequence. Random arrival. Each impulse area is independent and obeys the Rayleigh distribution. The sample is expressed as:

$$i(t) = \sum_{i=0}^{\infty} a_i \delta(t - t_i) \tag{3}$$

Impulse noise and its spectrum are shown in Figure 7.

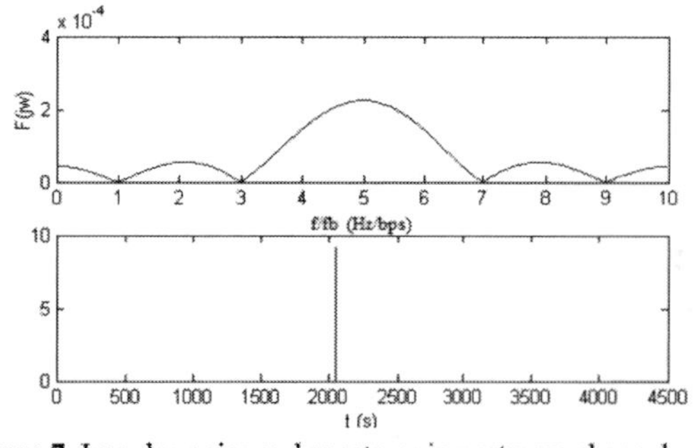

Figure 7. Impulse noise and spectrum in upstream channel

Random binary signal generated by a random binary signal generator and its spectrum are shown in Figure 8.

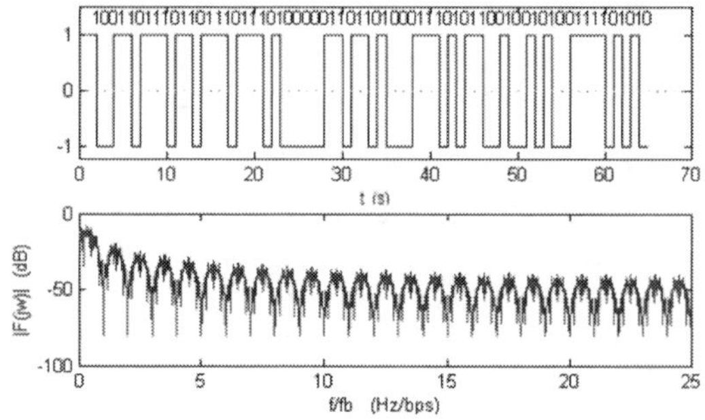

Figure 8. Random binary signal and spectrum in upstream channel

The simulation waveform, spectrum and the constellation diagram of the random binary signal after QPSK modulation are shown in Figure 9.

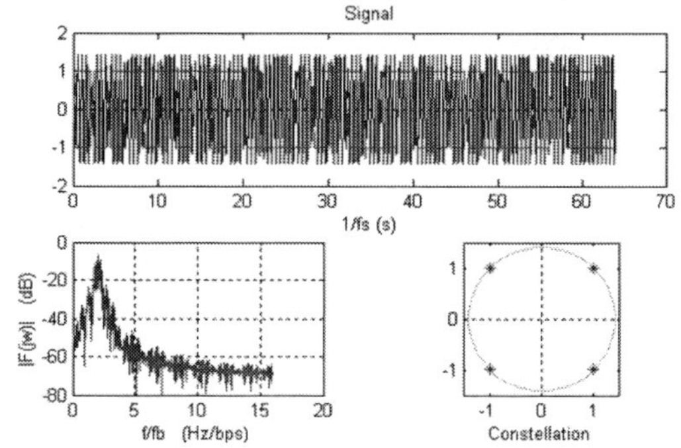

Figure 9. Random binary signal after QPSK modulation in upstream channel

Gaussian noise shown in Figure 5 is introduced into upstream channel.

The waveform after QPSK demodulation is shown in Figure 10.

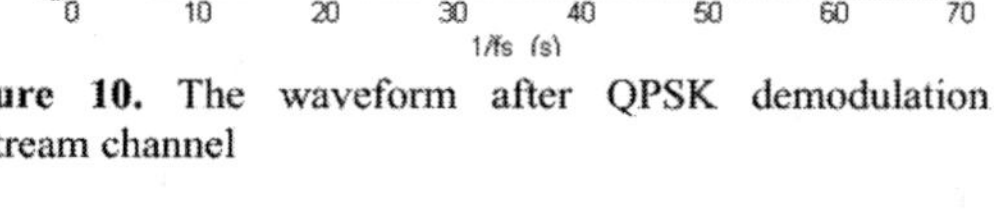

Figure 10. The waveform after QPSK demodulation in upstream channel

The comparison between the original input signal and the final output signal is shown in Figure 11.

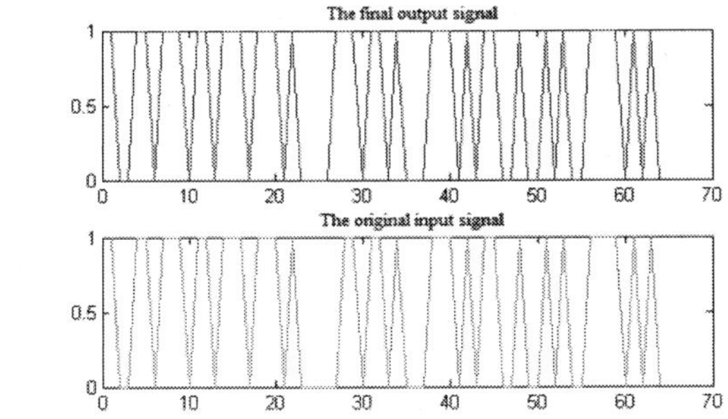

Figure 11. The comparison between the original input signal and the final output signal in upstream channel

4.2 Upstream channel BER of QAM modulation

In 16QAM modulation, baseband signal waveform, the waveform and spectrum of modulated signal, as well as the signal constellation diagram are shown in the case of not setting the output parameters, as shown in Figure 12.

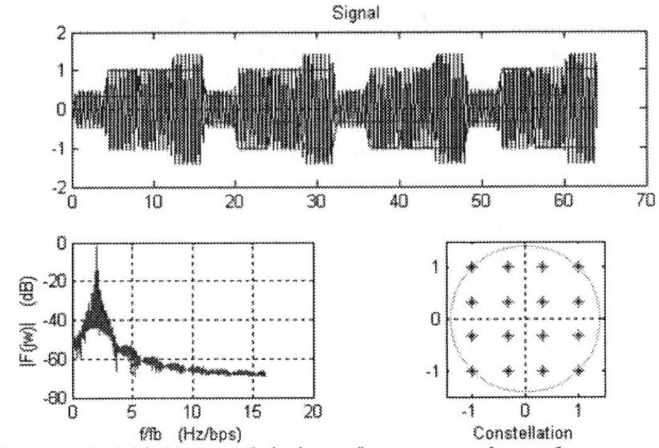

Figure 12. 16QAM modulation of upstream channel

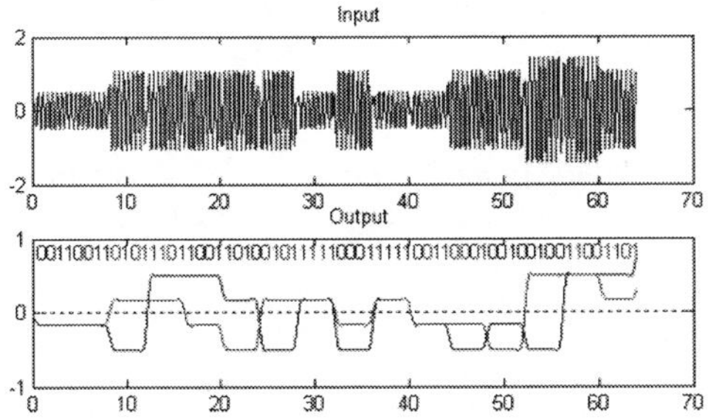

Figure 13. 16QAM demodulation of upstream channel

Random binary signal generated by a random binary signal generator and its spectrum are shown in Figure 8. The simulation waveform, spectrum and the constellation diagram of the random binary signal after 16QAM modulation are shown in Figure 14.

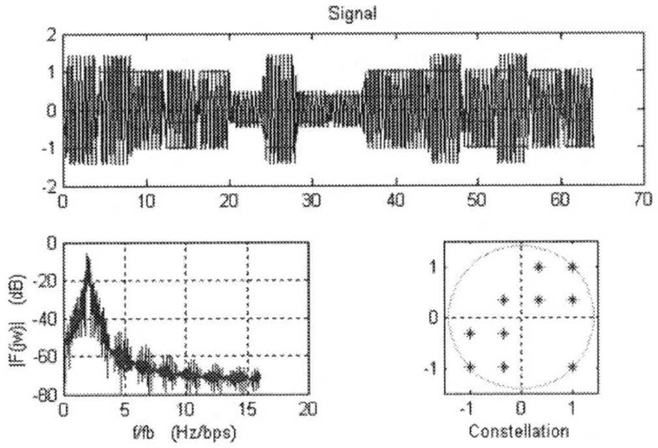

Figure 14. Random binary signal after 16QAM modulation in upstream channel

Gaussian noise shown in Figure 5 is introduced into upstream channel. The waveform after 16QAM demodulation is shown in Figure 15.

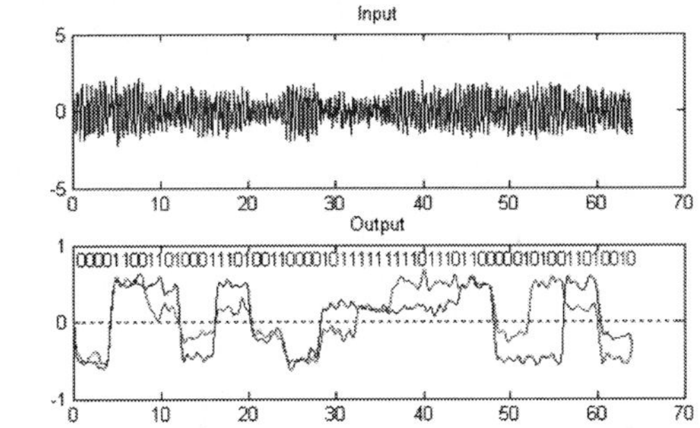

Figure 15. The waveform after 16QAM demodulation in upstream channel

5 Summary

In practical application, the upstream channel noise and the special tree-and-branch topology will make it difficult to transmit data. Hence it's necessary to monitor and analyse the real-time characteristics of the upstream channel noise and BER. In the paper, the cause and characteristics of each kind of noise especially the noise in the upstream channel are studied. The research and application of this topic have wide development prospects.

References

1. Paul T S. Two-Way Cable Television System Characterization. SPIE Proc, Vol 2609, Philadelphia, Oct, 2009, 94-104.
2. Eldering C A. CATV Return Path Characterization for Reliable Communications. IEEE Commun Mag, 2010, 33(8):62-69.
3. Wolters R P C. Characteristics of Upstream Channel Noise in CATV-network. IEEE Trans. On Broadcast, 2011, 42(4):328-332.
4. Kapoor S. Mitigating Impulse Noise over HFC Network For Telephony-Over-Cable. IEEE GLOBECOM, SESSION 28, 2012, 967-971.
5. Campos L A, Krinsky D. Effects of Upstream Channel Distortion in HFC Networks.SPIE Proc,Vol 2609, Philadelphia, Oct,2009:203-214.

MATEC Web of Conferences 44, 01052 (2016)
DOI: 10.1051/matecconf/20164401052

A heterogeneous network choice algorithm based on dynamic

Hong Yu Gao, Yi Jiang and Yang Zou

Chongqing University of Posts and Telecommunications, School of computer science and technology, Chongqing, China

Abstract. To enhance the user experience and quality of service about wireless heterogeneous networks,I presented a dynamically selected heterogeneous network algorithm.The algorithm considereed the variability of the real-time network property and user demanded for real-time multi- business.The algorithm added weight between the right multi-business on the basis of AHP.And it introduced dynamic index matrix by calculating in GRA algorithm,thereby selecting the optimal access network.Simulation results show that the improved algorithm can effectively reduce the switching frequency and blocking rate, enhance the user experience QoS to some extent.

1 Introduction

With the popularity of intelligent terminals, users have demand more and more diverse. So synergy between heterogeneous networks, integration interoperability can give users better communication service. The best access to the network could maximize the quality of service and users satisfaction[1]. The choice of wireless network needs to comprehensive include users experience and network performance, and many other characteristics or requirements. Including bandwidth, delay, jitter, cost, business type, user policies, etc..Also it constitute a multi-attribute decision making problems[2].

In the heterogeneous network selection, the more common type of network is about MADM algorithm. For example, [1] proposed user level using AHP, the network using objective weighting method and deviation minimization method. Finally it use the TOPSIS determine the optimal network. [3] shows that by the integration to a variety of subjective and objective results with weighting method, it use of consistent criteria to determine the weight vector of consistency, and to determine the final network through TOPSIS method. The factors above algorithms are integrated user and network multifaceted. But in reality, the user's business is changing, network property is also changing in real time, both do not consider the multi-business and attribute dynamic situation. This affects the accuracy of the optimal network selection, as well as ping-pang effect and have other adverse circumstances. To solve these problems, this paper proposes a heterogeneous network dynamic selection algorithm based on the present view.The algorithm adds user multi-business priority weights on the basis of AHP in subjective level and reflects the user's dynamic nature. In the network, the use of GRA process each judgment indicators, while using a mathematical way to determine the dynamics of the judgment indicators over time and in conjunction with the GRA, in order to determine the optimal network. Examples and simulation results demonstrate the effectiveness of the algorithm.

2 Dynamic selection algorithm

The algorithm join multi-business priorities in subjective weight, then according to the dynamic of index judgment,it calculate the index of dynamic change weight matrix in a period of time, and combined with gray relational analysis to select the best network.

2.1 Analytic Hierarchy Process

Analytic Hierarchy Process (AHP) is proposed by TLSatty in operations research expert from the United States in the 1970s and has become one of the most popular multi-attribute decision problem and most important method to effectively solve multi-attribute decision problem.AHP can well reflect the impact of user needs,preferences and other subjective attributes[5-8].

2.1.1 Establish a hierarchy model

According to business type have requirements for QoS property, so the paper choose delay, jitter, bandwidth, packet loss rate as QoS setting parameters.

In order to better reflect the needs of users,in addition to the relevant parameters of QoS attributes, it choose cost,security,network load,historical preference and other

Fund Project:Chongqing Municipal Education Commission scientific and technological research projects(KJ1400414);Chongqing University of Posts and Telecommunications, Dr. startup fund, A2015-18.Author: Hongyu Gao,male,graduate,e-mail:578515622@qq.com.Yi Jiang,male,master instructor,mobile Internet research.Yang Zou,male,graduate,lecturer.

attributes as judged parameters.According to the hierarchy of AHP,namely the target layer,criterion layer,project layer construct hierarchical model of the algorithm shown in Figure 1.

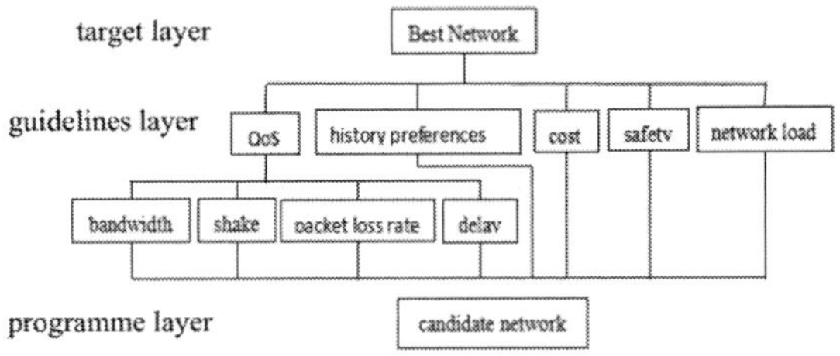

Figure.1. Hierarchical model

2.1.2 Determine the weights

In AHP,Satty and others recommend that referencing 1 to 9 scale method and the inverse indicate both the attributes of importance,so that construct judgment matrix[9-11].Its scale value and meaning as shown in Table 1.

Table1. 1~9 Scale method

The importance of scale	The importance of the ratio between elements
1	Equally important
3	The former is slightly more important than the latter
5	The former obviously more important than the latter
7	The former than the latter is very important
9	The former than the latter is extremely important
2、4、6、8	Intermediate values adjacent to judgment

According to property element use the above 1 to 9 scale method to construct a judgment matrix A :

$$A=(a_{ij})_{n\times n},a_{ii}=1,a_{ji}=1/a_{ij},a_{ij}>0,i,j=1,2,\cdots,n.$$

Wherein a_{ij} represents the same time the importance of the two types of business correspondence ratio between the properties, n as the number of elements.

According to the method of characteristic root and root calculate weights, then weight vectors can be obtained by normalization process.

Assume $Aw=\lambda_{\max}w$ available

$$w_i=\prod_{j=1}^{n}a_{ij},\quad i=1,2,\cdots,n \tag{1}$$

A where $\lambda_{\max}$ is the greatest characteristic root, w is the corresponding feature vectors, n is the number of evaluation parameters, A is element values in a_{ij} matrix .

Compute w_i n -th root $\overline{w_i}$,

$$\overline{w_i}=\sqrt[n]{\prod_{j=1}^{n}a_{ij}},\quad i=1,2,\cdots,n \tag{2}$$

$\overline{w_i}$ is normalization process,which is

$$u_i=\overline{w_i}=\sum_{i=1}^{n}\overline{w_i},\quad i=1,2,\cdots,n \tag{3}$$

Consistency check. Because the judgment matrix is obtained by the user subjectively,it is necessary for consistency check. $C.I.=\frac{\lambda_{\max}-n}{n-1},C.R.=\frac{C.I.}{R.I.}$,

Wherein $C.I.$ is the consistency index, n is the judgment matrix order, $C.R.$ is the consistency ratio, $R.I.$ is the Mean Random Consistency Index ,it can look-up table available. When $C.R.<0.1$, it considered to have a satisfactory consistency, otherwise A judgment matrix need to correction, until a satisfactory consistency.

Can be obtained from the above that the right decision attribute parameters of each weight vector is $\vec{U}=\{u_1,u_2,\cdots,u_n\}$.

2.2 Priority right multi-business weight

3G business is divided into four types by 3GPP, including streaming type, background type, conversation type,interactive type. Users business conducted in constant change, and users of the different service types have certain preferences.But also there is a certain conflict and competition between a variety of business .This requires that the user wants to prioritize the various business when it generates the conflict between the business according to their preferences or actual situation and give priority to certain types of business[10,12].

According to the above AHP, the priority for all types of business construct the judgment matrix $B=(b_{ij})_{n\times n},i,j=1,2,\cdots n$,n is the number of businesses.In accordance with the calculation method described above AHP right weight vector can be drawn judgment matrix B weight vector $\vec{V}=\{v_1,v_2,\cdots,v_n\}$.

Both the calculated weight vector $\vec{U}$ by the front of the decision property parameters and business type priority weight vector $\vec{V}$ are to combine as subjective weight vector. According to equation (4) can be obtained $\vec{W}=\{w^1,w^2,\cdots,w^n\}$ with the reunification of the right weight vector as the subjective weight vector finalized, n is the number of operations.

$$w^i=u_iv_i\Big/\sum_{i=1}^{n}u_iv_i \tag{4}$$

2.3 Dynamic decision Indexes

Because of the instability of network, the decision indicators are real-time dynamic changes.To reflect the dynamic of the decision indicators for the impact of network selection, it choose the parameter value over a period of time more than one time decision indicators.By the corresponding calculation,it reflect the degree of dispersion and volatility of each candidate network parameter values in this period of time.And thus it calculate the dynamic matrix judgment indicators, as the optimal network selection factors.

2.3.1 Decision matrix

Assume that dynamic multiple index decision set for candidates network is $s=\{s_1,s_2,\cdots s_m\}$, m is the number of candidates network,decision index set is $p=\{p_1,p_2,\cdots,p_n\}$, n is the number of indicators,time sample point is $T_t(t=1,2,\cdots,k)$, k is the number of sample points,time weight vector is $\lambda=\{\lambda_1,\lambda_2,\cdots,\lambda_k\}^T,0\le\lambda_t\le 1,\sum_{t=1}^{k}\lambda_t=1$. Candidate network s_i respect to the property index p_j value is b_{ij}^t in the period of T_t .In the period of T_t ,candidate network for the index set of decision matrix is $B^t=(b_{ij}^t)_{m\times n},t=1,2,\cdots k$.

Under normal circumstances indicators divided efficiency, costs and interval.Efficiency of the indicators is more larger and more better;costs of the indicators is more smaller and more better; interval index whose value falls within a certain range for the best.In order to eliminate unfairness by a different dimension,it need to do standardization process to decision matrix,so that standardized analysis and processing of data.Equation (5) and (6) are the normalized process about costs and efficiency indicators.

$$c_{ij}^t=\frac{(b_{ij}^t)_{\max}-b_{ij}^t}{(b_{ij}^t)_{\max}-(b_{ij}^t)_{\min}} \quad (5)$$

$$c_{ij}^t=\frac{b_{ij}^t-(b_{ij}^t)_{\min}}{(b_{ij}^t)_{\max}-(b_{ij}^t)_{\min}} \quad (6)$$

After the normalization process of decision matrix is $C^t=(c_{ij}^t)_{m\times n}$ 。

2.3.2 Dynamic matrix

To reflect the changing trends of the indicators, it introduce a dynamic matrix.Equation(5) reflects the average of the decision index in period of corresponding time.Equation (6) reflects the degree of dispersion about corresponding index in the period of time, the larger value, the larger volatility index, the more unstable.Structure dynamic matrix $D^t=(d_{ij}^t)_{m\times n},t=1,2,\cdots,k,$ among them $d_{ij}^t=D(c_{ij}^t-c_{ij}^{t-1})$ 。 $c_{ij}^t-c_{ij}^{t-1}$ is growth degree about indicators for sample point T_t .

$$E(x)=\sum_{i=1}^{n}x_i p_i \quad (7)$$

Where,x is the value of the corresponding judgment index,p is the probability of emergence about x, n is the number of sample values for judgment index the.

$$D(x)=\sum_{i=1}^{n}p_i\cdot(x_i-\mu)^2,\mu=E(x) \quad (8)$$

2.3.3 Comprehensive evaluation decision matrix

After normalization the decision matrix C^t and dynamic matrix D^t is binding, we can get a comprehensive evaluation decision matrix:

$$V^t=(v_{ij}^t)_{m\times n},v_{ij}^t=E(c_{ij}^t)c_{ij}^t+d_{ij}^t,t=2,3,\cdots,k \quad (9)$$

$E(c_{ij}^t)$ reflects network parameters the current state.

2.4 Grey Relational Analysis

Grey Relational Analysis(GRA) refers to the trend of development and change in things which a quantitative description and method of comparison.The basic idea is to determine the geometry of the similarity about reference data columns and the several of comparative data columns to judge which contact is tight.Curve is more closer,between the correlation degree of the corresponding sequence is more larger,the contrary is more smaller,it reflects the degree of association between the curves[13-15].

This article will be applied GRA to dynamic multiple index decision, gray correlation were calculated for each available network with over networks and non-ideal network.Finally, according to the comprehensive evaluation value of the network is to sort,and determine the best access network.

According to matrix V^t define period T^t's the ideal and not ideal network: $H^t=\{\max v_{i1}^t,\max v_{i2}^t,\cdots,\max v_{in}^t\}$, $L^t=\{\min v_{i1}^t,\min v_{i2}^t,\cdots,\min v_{in}^t\}$. According to Gray Correlation Theory,in the period T^t candidate network s_i and over the network H^t and not over network L^t grey correlation coefficients about indicators p_j were:

$$\xi_{ij} = \frac{\min_i \min_j |v_{ij}^t - h_j^t| + \rho \max_i \max_j |v_{ij}^t - h_j^t|}{|v_{ij}^t - h_j^t| + \rho \max_i \max_j |v_{ij}^t - h_j^t|} \tag{10}$$

$$\xi_{ij} = \frac{\min_i \min_j |v_{ij}^t - l_j^t| + \rho \max_i \max_j |v_{ij}^t - l_j^t|}{|v_{ij}^t - l_j^t| + \rho \max_i \max_j |v_{ij}^t - l_j^t|} \tag{11}$$

Wherein, ρ is discrimination coefficient, $\rho \in [0,1]$, there $\rho = 0.5$.

Obtained weights vector $\overrightarrow{W} = \{w^1, w^2, \cdots, w^n\}$ by the AHP, according to equation (10) and (11) can obtain gray correlation about candidate network with positive and negative ideal network.

$$\xi_i = \sum_{i=1}^{k} \lambda_t \sum_{j=1}^{n} w_j \xi_{ij}^t, i = 1,2,\cdots,m \tag{12}$$

$$\eta_i = \sum_{i=1}^{k} \lambda_t \sum_{j=1}^{n} w_j \eta_{ij}^t, i = 1,2,\cdots,m \tag{13}$$

Among them, $0 \le \xi_i \le 1, 0 \le \eta \le 1$.

Comprehensive evaluation value is $\gamma_i = \frac{\xi_i}{\xi_i + \eta_i}$。

(14)

Finally, depending on the size of γ_i to sort candidate network, it choose the largest network of its value as the best network.

3 Simulation and Analysis

This paper is simulation in Matlab environment, in order to verify the feasibility and effectiveness of the algorithm.

3.1. Simulation

It assumes that there are four types of wireless network environment, including the UMTS, GSM, WLAN, multi-mode terminal is located in the four kinds of wireless network environment at the same time. When user uniform motion within the range, the terminal select the appropriate network .Analog simulation scene as described below, users need to undertake a variety of business services in a heterogeneous network coverage area, such as type session (IP telephone), interactive type (web), streaming media (such as FTP download). Among them, the various of business according to the parameters forλ poisson distribution reache overlapping coverage of the network, the duration of the various types of business is to obey exponential distribution with meanμ . Draw four time points t1, t2, t3, t4, including t1 < t2 < t3 < t4. The corresponding time weight vector is set toλ = {1/3, 1/3, 1/3}.

In the above-mentioned AHP ,it set attribute parameters and these three categories network about UMTS, GSM, WLAN s'the actual situation of corresponding attribute.Under the above emulation scenario assumes that multimode terminal monitored network parameters such as table2,4 times sample points attribute parameters as shown in Table 3.

Table2. Network attribute parameter settings

Network parameters	UMTS	GSM	WLAN
Bandwidth	4	6	8
Cost	0.8	0.4	0.2
Security Level	8	6	7
Network Load	0.4	0.7	0.6
History Preferences	1	1	1

Table3. Network dynamic attribute parameter settings

Candidate network		Delay	Shake	Packet loss rate
UMTS	t1	20	6	0.08
	t2	18	6	0.07
	t3	18	7	0.06
	t4	17	8	0.06
GSM	t1	30	7	0.05
	t2	28	8	0.06
	t3	27	8	0.05
	t4	25	9	0.04
WLAN	t1	45	12	0.06
	t2	44	11	0.05
	t3	46	11	0.04
	t4	43	13	0.03

3.2 Results and analysis

Based on the above assumptions simulation scenarios and parameter values,this paper makes experimental comparison with the dynamic selection algorithm and original static AHP, GRA algorithm. The simulation results shown in Figure 2- 3.

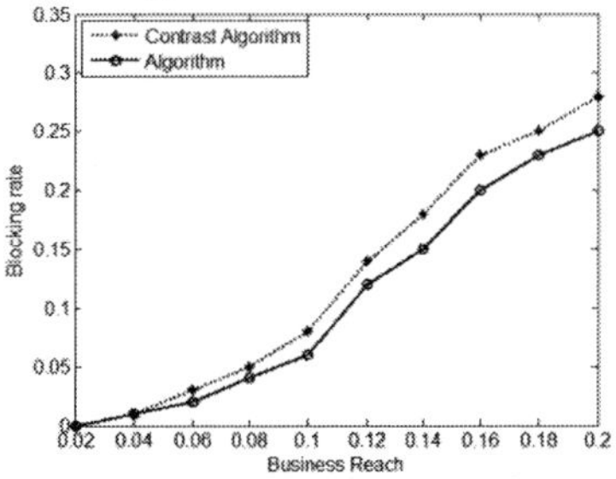

Figure.2. Blocking rate comparison

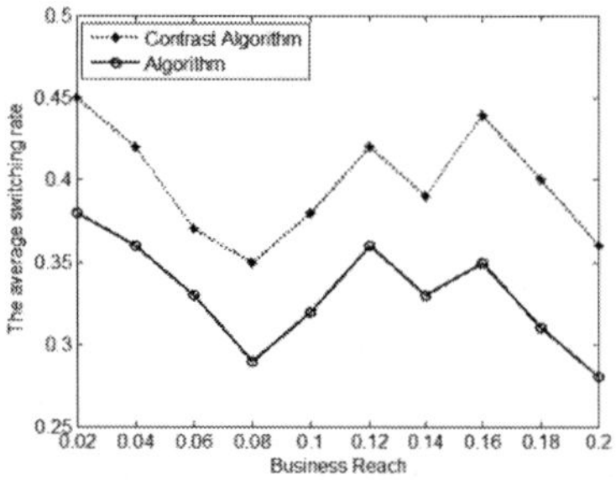

Figure.3. The average switching rate comparison

From figure 2 shows, when the business arrival rate increases, blocking rate are constantly increasing, but the dynamic selection algorithm blocking rate is lower than static selection algorithm. The figure 3 shows that ,with the increasing arrival rate of business, two algorithms for comparing the average switching rate has different amplitude fluctuations, but the dynamic selection algorithm on the average switching rate overall value has a certain reduce than static selection algorithm.

From the above experimental results and analysis can be concluded that when users is using business services in a heterogeneous network environment ,dynamically selects algorithm selecting the best network than static network algorithms have obtained better performance with the best results. In terms of switching rates, blocking rates, etc. have been some optimization , enhance the QoS experience in a certain extent .

4 Conclusion

In this paper,for heterogeneous networks indicators with dynamic, it presents a heterogeneous network access algorithm based on dynamic selection.The core idea is to use AHP to calculate the subjective weight of user level, and combined with real-time multi-business priority weight.When selecting the optimal network,it bind with properties' dynamic matrix based on the GRA , on this account reflect the decision indicators dynamic for influence of network selection.Through compares with the static multi-attribute network selection algorithm,the proposed algorithm reduces the number of network switching, reduces the ping-pong effect, improve the accuracy of network selection and effectively improve the QoS.

References

1. Wang JunXuan,Wang Lei.Selection algorithm based on subjective and objective weights of heterogeneous networks[J]. Electronic Technology,2014,27(11).
2. Zhang Yu,Liu ShengMei.Network based on multi-attributed ecision algorithm[J]. computer science,2015.6,42(6):120-124.
3. Wu Ping,Lv Lu.Heterogeneous network selection algorithm based on decision fusion[J].Guilin University of Electronic Technology,2013.10,33(5):384-389.
4. Song JianFeng,Li JianDong.Heterogeneous network game selection policy by maximize cost-effective[J].Xi'an University of Electronic Technology,2014.2,41(1):18-22.
5. Zhao YaNan,Zhu XiaoRong.Selection algorithm based on heterogeneous network access user experience research[J].Nanjing University of Posts and Telecommunications. 2014.8,34(4):72-78.
6. Qin YongGang,Dou ZhuMei,Hu Gang. Dynamic selection algorithm weights based on heterogeneous wireless networks[J].Computer and IT,53-59.
7. Liu Bo.Study on Heterogeneous Network Access Selection Algorithm based on Analytic Hierarchy and Prediction[D].Xi'an:Xidian University,2011.
8. He Xin,Lin Bin.Handoff technology for heterogeneous wireless network[M].Beijing:Publishing House of Beijing University of Posts and Telecommunications.2008.
9. Ma ShaoJuan,Zhang JiRong.Network selection algorithm based on analytic hierarchy processand entropy theory[J].Shanxi University of Science and Technology, 2014.6,32(3):162-167.
10. Qi XinGuang,Liang Jun,Xiao Nan,Dai Shuai.Selection algorithm based on fuzzy multiple attribute comprehensive weight Based on a heterogeneous network[J].Modern defense technology,2013.12,41(6):76-82.
11. Zeng XuBin,Yuan Lin.Based on multi-dimensional dynamic network selection algorithm[J].Computer engineering and applications,2014,50(1):83-86.
12. Zhang YuanYuan,Xiao ChuangBai,Wang Jian.A new user-oriented multi-service QoS demand network access selection algorithm[J].computerscience,2015.3,42(3):55-59.
13. Liu SiFeng,Guo TianBang,Dang YaoGuo.Grey system theory and its applications[M].Beijing:Science Press,1999:40 -70.
14. Wang YaNan,Feng ChunYan,Xia HaiLun.Based on dynamic grey multiple attribute decisionheterogeneous network selection[J].Information systems and networks,2009,39(11):1-4.
15. Li Jun,Fang YaDing,Song Mei.Heterogeneous network based on gray associated dynamic access selection policy[J].Beijing University of Posts and Telecommunications,2006(29):174-177.

MATEC Web of Conferences 44, 01053 (2016)
DOI: 10.1051/matecconf/20164401053

Research on Wireless Sensor Network Intrusion Detection Technology

Qing Gang Fan[1,a], Li Wang[2], Yun Jie Zhu[1], Yan Ning Cai[1] and Yong Qiang Li[1]

[1] *Computer Staff Room, Xi'an Research Institute of High Technology, 710025 Xi'an, China*
[2] *Library, Xi'an Research Institute of High Technology, 710025 Xi'an, China*

Abstract. With the development of science and technology, wireless sensor network (WSN) has been widely used in all walks of life. The security problem of WSN has become a research hotspot. Intrusion detection technology has an important position in the network security. In this Paper, firstly, the intrusion and intrusion detection are introduced, secondly, the WSN intrusion detection system and its classification are analyzed. The main study is to analyze the current WSN intrusion detection technology and their respective advantages and disadvantages. The development direction of WSN intrusion detection technology is put forward finally.

The related research on Wireless sensor network (WSN) has become research hotspot at home and abroad at present stage [1-4]. Compared with the common wireless network, WSN has the following characteristics: the self-organizing network, the dynamic change of network topology, the distributed control, multiple wireless network, the node functional limitations, the limitations of wireless network, poor safety, quantity, size, data redundancy and the convergence and so on.

Studies and history suggests that no matter how advanced security measures in the network, the attacker always could find weaknesses in the network system, to carry out attacks. Used alone prevention technology (such as encryption, authentication, etc.) is difficult to achieve the desired security objectives, these technologies can reduce the possibility of network attack, but can't completely put an end to attacks. therefore, the security defensive measures is also indispensable, intrusion Detection System (IDS) is a new network security technology in recent years, it made up for the inadequacy of the preventive measures, can provide real-time intrusion Detection for network security and take appropriate protection.

In this paper, the intrusion detection systems and intrusion detection technology are introduced and analyzed at present stage mainly, then compared their respective advantages and disadvantages, finally put forward his prospect to the development of wireless sensor network intrusion detection technology.

1 Intrusion and intrusion detection

Intrusion detection system in WSN, through collecting and analyzing information of sensor nodes, check the illegal behavior of security policy and the signs of being attacked, and timely report to system administrator. In order to achieve this goal, the WSN intrusion detection system model should be build, the model should include the following three necessary function modules: information collection module, detection engine module, response module, as shown in Figure 1.

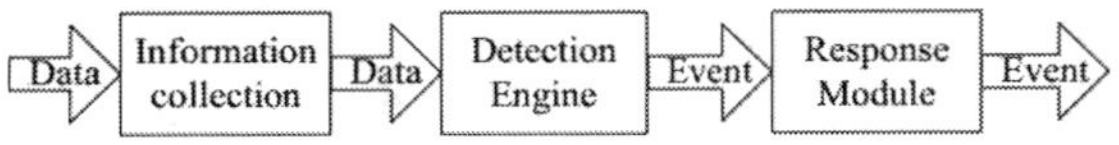

Figure 1. WSN intrusion detection system structure

2 The classification of the intrusion detection system

2.1 According to the distribution system running way

Centralized intrusion detection: the model has a center computer, which is in charge of monitoring, detection and response. It is suitable for the relatively simple network.

Distributed intrusion detection: the model monitor and test the network with a mobile agent, each node has the response analysis ability.

2.2 According to the response way

Active response IDS: if detected after the invasion, to take the initiative to reconfigure the firewall, close the appropriate service or against invaders, then known as the active response.

Passive response IDS: if given only after detected intrusion alarm or log, is a passive response.

[a] Qinggang Fan: fangang3232@126.com

2.3 According to the data sources

Host-based IDS: to test the attack in operating systems, applications, or kernel level. System to get the data on the basis of the system is running to the host, the protection of the target host lies the system running, through monitoring and analysis of host audit records and log files to intrusion detection.

Network-based IDS: the system data source is the original packet of network transmission, NIDS placed in key areas of the network infrastructure, usually using a network adapter running in random mode to real-time monitor and analyze all communication through the network business, in order to protect the network operation.

Hybrid IDS: it is combination system based on the host and the intrusion detection based on network, in the network NIDS is established to detect the network security situation, at the same time HIDS is established on those key host. Better secure protection can be provided than using a single intrusion detection scheme.

2.4 According to analysis method

Anomaly intrusion detection: the method sums up the characteristics of normal operation firstly, then to monitor the subsequent operations. If the normal operating modes of deviation statistical significance are found, the model report to the police immediately.

Misuse intrusion detection: the method collect abnormal operation behavior characteristics firstly, to establish related the feature library, in the subsequent detection process, the collected data and features will be compared to the library code, then come to the conclusion that whether the invasion.

Hybrid intrusion detection: the combination with anomaly detection and misuse detection, intrusion detection based on anomaly can find some unknown attacks, the dependence of specific system is relatively lower, but rate of false positives is high, configuration and implementation is relatively difficult. Intrusion detection based on misuse can detect more accurately identified intrusion behavior, but the dependence of specific system is relatively higher, portability is poor, and can't detect new attack types. Therefore, only combine the two sides, to achieve the best performance of the system.

3 INTRUSION DETECTION TECHNOLOG -Y

The resource limitations and applications correlation characteristics of sensor networks indicate, the study of intrusion detection is a challenging task. An effective sensor network intrusion detection system must have three features, simplicity, accuracy and real-time. Next the wireless sensor network intrusion detection methods and their respective advantages and disadvantages are mainly introduced:

3.1 Intrusion detection based on multi-agent.

Wang Pei in the literature [5] proposed intrusion detection method based on multi-agent for clustering type wireless sensor network, and its system structure is shown in Figure 2.

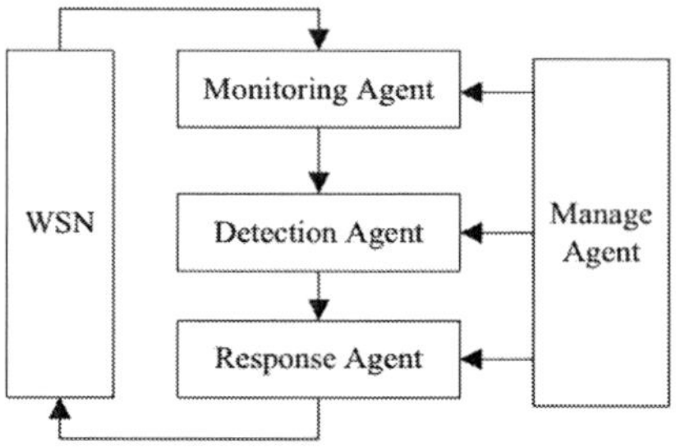

Figure 2. Intrusion detection system based on multi-agent

By having the nodes and the cluster head respectively carry out different detection tasks, combine with the local inspection and joint inspection, use the multiple agent module respectively to realize data collection, analysis, detection and intrusion response and agents management tasks, in order to make the system has simple operation, easy to expand, reduce energy consumption, to enhance the security features. But each node in the scenario, which needs to be equipped with monitoring Agent, inspection Agent, Agent and management Agent, will take up a large amount of storage space of the node, also increase the energy consumption of nodes.

This method can reduce the network load and overcome network latency and good scalability, high security, but each node has more than one proxy function, large energy consumption, in the process of testing activities overlap, the accuracy will be much lower.

3.2 Intrusion detection based on SVM.

In literature [6], anomaly detection based on immune genetic algorithm is put forward, eavesdropping on beacon node from its neighbor node package and extract known as antigens, the key parameters of the number of antigen in if the match is in the life of a probe predefined threshold value is high, the probe will fail and generate a new detector. On the other hand, if the amount of antigen matching threshold, than the life of the detector probe will trigger the intrusion alarm, update mechanism for the detector, make suggestion of IDS more robust. In literature [7], anomaly detection based on support vector machine (SVM) was proposed for selective forwarding attack, using the SVM for intrusion data of robust classification method.

SVM overcome the defects of large sample traditional machine learning methods, based on limited sample

information, in the complexity and the ability to learn of the model, find the best compromise, can obtain the best Fan Hua ability.

Intrusion detection system based on SVM as shown in Figure 3.

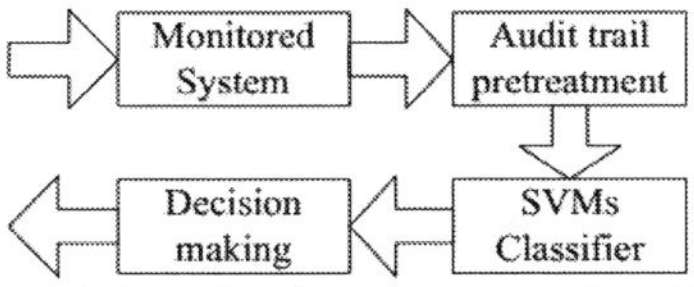

Figure 3. Intrusion detection system based on SVM

This approach to anomaly detection for classification or clustering problems, using machine learning effective learning ability, establish anomaly detection model having certain accuracy. The model has high accuracy, but the disadvantage is too large sample size and too long training time.

3.3 Intrusion detection based on network traffic analysis

The basic structure of intrusion detection model based on flow analysis as shown in Figure 4.

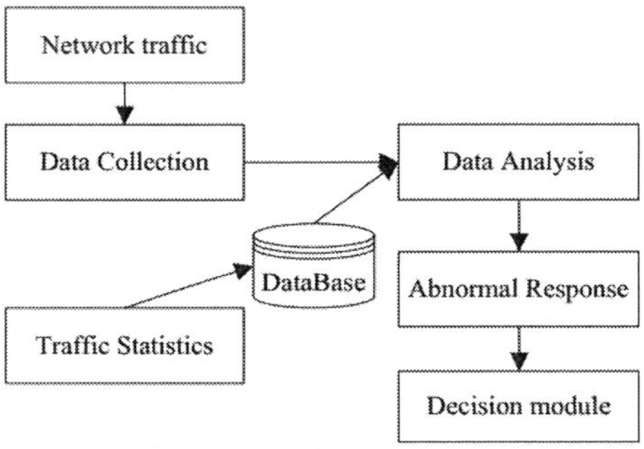

Figure 4. Intrusion detection model structure based on flow analysis

In literature [8], a denial service attack detection scheme based on traffic prediction – MPDD, is designed using Markov linear prediction model for wireless sensor network. In the scenario, each node judgment and detect abnormal network flow based on traffic, without special hardware support and cooperation between nodes. A warning assessment mechanism is put forward, effectively improve the detection accuracy of solutions. Reduce the prediction error or channel error caused by the false positives.

Literature [9], such as intrusion detection scheme based on flow analysis was proposed, based on the statistical analysis of the behavior of the neighbor node threshold technical analysis, and then applied to the selected parameters, namely, under a certain length of time window of the number of packets received and the time interval between packets, it does not require any additional hardware installation and additional communication cost, its computational cost is low.

This method is relatively simple, intuitive, high real-time performance, but requires traffic input to have certain statistical properties, therefore does not have versatility, high rate of false positives.

3.4 Intrusion detection based on the game theory model.

The basic model of intrusion detection system based on game theory is shown in figure 6. Intrusion detector distributed in the network audit network data in some detection methods, detecting intrusion, and submit the test results. Then the game model to simulate the attack and defense both sides of the interactive behavior, and weigh from intrusion detector test results and the test efficiency, reach Nash equilibrium to the secondary IDS make response strategies.

Mohsen Estiri and others in the literature [10] puts forward the theory of repeated game model for intrusion detection for wireless sensor network packet loss against intrusion detection scheme. In this model, the attacker in wireless sensor networks and intrusion detection system as a collaboration, not zero-sum game of both sides, and the average discount factor income is used to display the node at the current stage of game, more valuable than the next phase of. And eventually the system will reach the Nash equilibrium, the formation of wireless sensor network defense strategy.

This method can help managers to weigh the detection efficiency and network resources, but the detection of human intervention is necessary, and has a poor system adaptability.

3.5 Intrusion detection based on the trust mechanism.

Min Lin [11] and put forward the dynamic intrusion detection scheme based on trust model, using the node with higher credibility to alternately testing within the cluster nodes, non-parametric CUSUM detection algorithm was proposed, alarm response also differentiate with the aid of the trust level of trust model, effectively reduce the node energy consumption, reduce the computational overhead of node. Long Ju [12], such as intrusion detection method was proposed based on weighted trust mechanism, at the beginning of the system is assigned to each sensor node weights, each cycle when the node to send with other different report is updated, so that when the node weight below a certain threshold is detected is malicious act.

The advantages of this method has low power consumption, high safety, but when the cluster head nodes invasion, or meet with Sybil attack detection accuracy is reduced, and the threshold setting will affect the precision of the algorithm, and how to find a suitable threshold is a thorny problem.

4 CONCLUSION

From what has been discussed above, the accuracy and real-time performance of intrusion detection technology is not enough to detect all kinds of intrusion behavior.The main challenge of wireless sensor network (WSN) in intrusion detection has the following several aspects. (1) The new type of attack emerge in endlessly. How to improve the ability of intrusion detection system to detect the unknown attack is the need to solve the problem. (2) The resources, which include storage, computing power, energy and bandwidth, are poor. The intrusion detection system based on knowledge learning is not only required to store large amounts of intrusion pattern characteristics, but also with the increase of intrusion type, of the storage space. Limited computing power and energy means that nodes can't run complex intrusion detection algorithm. The algorithm of lightweight should be studied in terms of WSN intrusion detection, in order to adapt to the characteristics of the wireless sensor network (WSN), prolong the life cycle of the network.

References

1. F. Ian, Akyildiz, S. Weilian, S. Yogesh, Computer Net-works, **38**:393-442, 2002.
2. C.C. Mai, Computer knowledge and Technology, 11:29-33, 2015
3. L.X. Chen, Wireless sensor network technology and application, 12-13,2009.
4. I. Onat, A. Miri, Proceedings of the IEEE International Conference on Wireless and Mobile Computing, Networking and Communications253-259, 2005.
5. P. Wang, X.W. Zhou, CHINESE JOURNAL OF SENSORS AND ACTUATORS, **20**, 677-681, 2007.
6. Y. Liu, F.Q. Yu, Proc Int Jt Conf Neural Networks, 439-444, 2008.
7. J.W. Tian, M.J. Gao,S.R. Zhou, Proceedings of the 2009 IEEE International Conference on Information and Automation, 1217-1221,2009.
8. Z.J. Han,W.W. Zhang, Z.G. Chen, Engineering and computer science, **32**,27-29,2010.
9. Y. Ponomarchuk, D.W. Seo, 19th nnual Wireless and Optical Communications Conference, 2010.
10. M. Estiri, A. Khademzadeh, A, Electrical and Computer Engineering (CCECE), 2010 23rd Canadian Conference on, 1-5, 2010.
11. L. Min, N. Shi, Internet Technology and Applications, 2010 International Conference on, 1-4, 2010.
12. L. Ju, H.J. Li, Ubiquitous Information Technologies and Applications (CUTE), 2010 Proceedings of the 5th International Conference on, 1-6, 2010.

MATEC Web of Conferences 44, 01054 (2016)
DOI: 10.1051/matecconf/20164401054

Software Reuse of Mobile Systems based on Modelling

Ping Guo[1,a], Ming Liu[1]

[1]Computing Center, Kunming University of Science and Technology, Kunming, China

Abstract. This paper presents an architectural style based modelling approach for architectural design, analysis of mobile systems. The approach is developed based on UML-like meta models and graph transformation techniques to support sound methodological principals, formal analysis and refinement. The approach could support mobile system development.

1 Introduction

Reuse is a common practice in software development, and it is critical for both cost savings and quality assurance. When properly done, reuse of artefacts (e.g., architectural styles, design patterns, source code) often improves productivity, in turn leading to cost savings. More importantly software reuse improves the quality of software, due to the reuse of quality code components and makes it possible to leverage the collective wisdom of numerous seasoned software designers and software engineers who faced similar challenges and found optimal solutions widely accepted by the software developer community.

Types of reusable software artefacts vary ranging from those found in the requirements phase to design phase to implementation and testing phases. They include domain requirements, architectural styles and design patterns, Commercial Off-The-Shelves (COTS), code reuse, reusable tests, etc.

A number of architectural styles [1] for distributed systems have been identified, such as "client-server system", "message-passing protocols ", "event-based systems" etc. Architectural styles are often developed systematically to solve difficult architectural problems on the conceptual level. When designing a new software, the engineers can select and reuse an appropriate style(s) as the basis for further design and improvement.

With the fast development of wireless communication technologies, and the increasing popularity of portable computing devices, many [4, 5, 6] platforms and paradigms for mobile systems have been created to deal with the new requirements brought by mobility and provide better service to applications. At the same time, the design and development of mobile systems is a difficult task. Problems arise from the complexity of the mobility and the lack of abstractions, services, and tools for designing, analyzing, implementing, and testing it. However, the previously mentioned architectural styles and approaches are designed for distributed systems, and they are very hard to be used for mobile systems, since mobility has created additional complexity for computation and coordination. The current architectural approach [12] offers only a logical view of change; it does not take into account the properties of the "physical" distribution topology of locations and communications. It relies on the assumption that the computation performed by individual components is irrelative to location of the component, and the coordination mechanisms through connectors can be always transmitted successfully by the underlying communication network. In order to support mobility, the architectural approach needs to be adjusted in different abstract layers of modelling and specification languages.

We propose to use styles for mobile systems to capture the properties of a certain class of mobile computing middleware platforms. Such a style should provide high-level abstractions for the structure, behaviour, and key properties of the platforms.

We present a methodology for developing complicated software systems based on architectural styles in this paper. The approach is developed based on graph transformation systems to support sound methodological principals, formal analysis and refinement. We illustrate the approach through the modelling and simulation of architectural styles for nomadic networks.

The rest of the paper is organized as follows. Sect. 2 introduces the framework of our approach, which includes two parts: modelling and simulation. Sect. 3 illustrates the approach through the modelling of

[a] Corresponding author: guoping29@yeah.net

architectural styles for mobile computing middleware. Related work is discussed in Sect. 4.

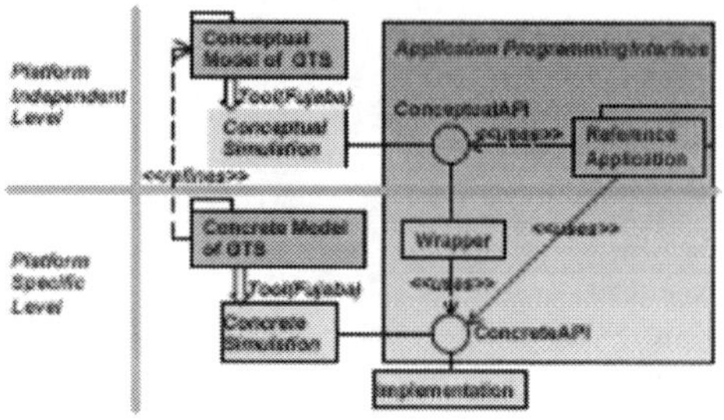

Fig.1. The modelling framework based on GTS

2 The modelling based on GTS

Graphs are often used as abstract representation of diagrams, e.g., UML class diagrams. Graph transformation is defined by the application of graph transformation rules that model the permitted actions on graphs representing system states. Such transformation defines a relation on state graphs that can be iterated arbitrarily yielding the transformation process. In this way, a graph grammar consisting of a start graph and a set of rules gets an operational semantics.

A GTS (Graph Transformation System) [13] is a system using the techniques of graph transformation. Providing visual representation and formal semantics, GTSs are exploited for modelling distributed systems, mobile systems and other complex software systems. Especially, a TGTS (Typed Graph Transformation System) is used for modelling functional requirements, software architectures, and architectural styles. We will use the TGTS [14] G = (TG,C,R) to define architectural styles. TG is here meta models (or, UML class diagrams) that define architectural elements. C is a set of constraints restricting their possible compositions. Simple constraints, already included in the class diagrams, are cardinalities that restrict the multiplicity of links between the elements. More complex restrictions can be defined by OCL (Object Constraint Language) constraints. R is a set of graph transformation rules (given by pairs of object diagrams).

In order to help the design and development of complicated software system, we develop an approach based on the GTS modelling and simulation (in Fig. 1). The approach is driven by a stepwise refinement between GTS-based models on different abstract levels. As shown in Fig. 1, a conceptual model is smaller and easier to understand; a concrete model reflects more design or implementation concerns. Starting from an abstract description of the systems, stepwise refinements yield more and more concrete specifications that should finally be directly implementable.

The definition of the model as platform-independent or platform-specific is rather relative. The conceptual model in Fig. 1 is platform-independent compared to the concrete model. The concrete model is platform-specific since it has a more specific design and realization. On the other hand, the conceptual model is also platform independent in the sense that it is independent of specific programming languages, hardware platforms and concrete implementation methods. Besides this, the number of the abstract levels is not fixed as only two levels. More or less levels can be defined according to the complexity of the system and requirements of the models.

For example, we define three-level abstract models in Sect. 3 in order to decrease the complexity of the styles. The operational semantics of the GTS allows us to execute the models and thus analyzing the system through simulation and model checking. Due to the well known state explosion problem with model checking, we prefer using simulation for analysis. Simulating the dynamic behaviour of a high level architecture can implement the system in a quicker, cheaper, and more flexible way. Some desired information and properties can be gotten through the simulation of the architecture. The programmers can execute the system and have a direct feeling how the system works.

3 Architectural styles for mobile systems

In this section, we will illustrate the proposed approach through an example of how to specify architectural styles for mobile systems. The main aspects of the mobile systems are explained in Sect. 3.1. Sect. 3.2. illustrates how to separate the aspects into different abstract levels of styles. Afterwards, we explain an example: styles of mobile systems for nomadic network to show how to get a complete specification of a style by starting from a very abstract conceptual style (in Sect. 3.3).

3.1. Main characteristics of mobile systems

When building architectural styles for mobile systems, we need to identify the main properties to be modelled. Two important aspects: dynamic change and component interaction are explained here.

3.1.1. Dynamic change Supporting for runtime modification is a key aspect of mobile systems. Mobility represents a total meltdown of the stability assumptions (e.g. network structure, network connection, power supply, CPU, etc.) associated with traditional distributed computing. The main differences are caused by the possibility of roaming and wireless connection. Roaming implies that, since devices can move to different locations, their context (network access, services, permissions, etc.) may change, and that mobile hosts are resource limited, for example, in computation power, memory capacity, and electrical power. Wireless connections are generally less reliable, more expensive, and provide smaller bandwidth, and they come in a variety of different technologies and protocols. This results in a very dynamic software architecture, where configurations and

interactions have to be adapted to the changing context and relative location of components.

3.1.2. Component interaction

One important purpose of a mobile system is facilitating component interaction, and enabling the cooperation of distributed components. More specifically, component interaction covers component communication, collaboration, and coordination. These different aspects are not orthogonal and there is no clear boundary. For example, components need a method to communicate with each other through the network. The method can be message based, transactional based, event based, etc. The communication requires the coordination and synchronization between different actions and components, and the components collaborate with each other in order to perform a task.

A mobile system can be distinguished through the supported component interaction patterns and paradigms, e.g., RPC (Remote Procedure Call) pattern, message-based pattern, event-based pattern, etc. The static assumption of network structure, network connection and execution context in distributed systems makes the component interaction quite static. The components involved for interactions are generally fixed. Such fixed configurations will not change till a dynamic change happens. And the messages for communication are always supposed to be successfully transmitted by the network. In a mobile setting, the components involved in an interaction change dynamically due to their migration or connectivity patterns. This results in dynamic changes and reconfigurations among the components interaction.

3.2 The modelling framework for the styles

In order to define the style clearly and decrease the complexity brought by mobility, we will separate the styles into three abstract levels, i.e, the conceptual style and concrete styles in Fig. 2. The identified two properties: dynamic change and component interaction will be modelled on different abstract levels. The conceptual style will specify only the dynamic change of the components in the presence of mobility, but not the component interaction, for the reason that dynamic change is more general and abstract, while component interaction is more design specific. Different mobile systems can support the same model of dynamic change, whereas the applied interaction models can be very different.

For example, the conceptual style of mobile systems for nomadic networks (in Fig. 2) can be refined into concrete styles that support different component interaction models, such as RPC and publish-subscribe model. Besides this, the conceptual model should answer the following questions: What functionalities can be provided by such mobile systems? What application scenarios can be implemented on the system? On the concrete level, the conceptual style is refined into a concrete style, where more and more design-specific aspects like component interaction protocols and patterns are integrated into the core functionality. The concrete style also specifies dynamic changes of components involved in an interaction due to their migration or connectivity patterns.

As a result, the dynamic change specified on the conceptual level will be associated with component interaction on the concrete level. The concrete style can be refined into a platform-specific style to add more implementation specific aspects. For example, the platform-independent concrete style based on RPC (in Fig. 2) can be refined into a platform-specific concrete style of Wireless CORBA, while the concrete style based on Publish-Subscribe can be refined into a concrete style of REBECA. We will explain the three-layer modeling approach through specifying the architectural styles of mobile computing middleware for nomadic networks. The corresponding three abstract layers will be illustrated in the following three sections.

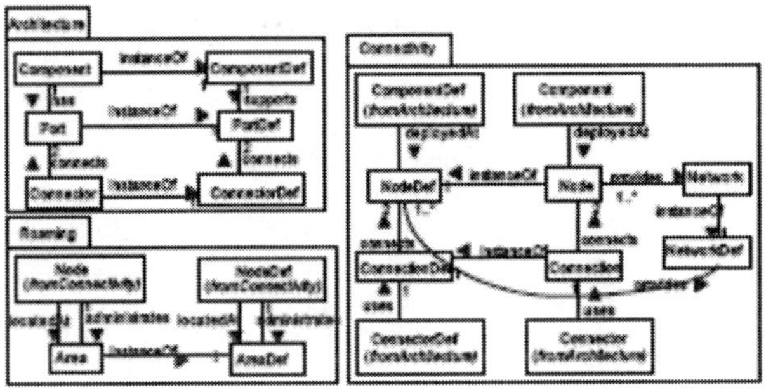

Fig.2. Conceptual style

3.3 Conceptual style

The conceptual style should define dynamic changes and main functionalities of a class of mobile computing middleware for nomadic networks. Nomadic networks utilize the infrastructure as access points to establish connectivity among mobile application components and to coordinate their transmissions. The nomadic network has a structured space where components are allowed to move inside the scope of areas covered by access points. Examples for such network are WLAN and telecommunication networks as GSM, GPRS, UTMS. The mobile computing middleware for nomadic network focuses on how to provide continuous connectivity and other services when components move across the structured spaces where handover protocols are often used.

Recalling the definition of the TGTS, G = (TG,C,R). The meta model (TG) of the style is shown in Fig. 2. We use a meta model structured into three packages. This allows us to separate different concerns, like software architecture, distribution, and roaming, while at the same time retaining an integrated representation.

Our meta models capture these relations in the three packages Architecture, Connectivity and Roaming to present different viewpoints of the systems [7]. The structured space of nomadic network is modeled as AreaDef in Roaming package. An area is defined by an administrative domain, like a cell managed by a GSM base station, or aWireless LAN domain. The wireless connection is modeled as Connection in Connectivity package. Connection is a physical network link which delivers communication services to Connectors at the

software level. The typing ConnectionDef means that we can distinguish, for example, between Ethernet, WLAN, or GSM-based connections.

The Architecture package defines the architectural view, containing both a definition of an architectural model (meta classes ComponentDef, ConnectorDef, PortDef) and an individual configuration (meta classes Component, Connector, and Port), related by the meta association instanceOf. It defines the architectural elements and constraints, and it represents the TG(type graph) in a TGTS. The style includes architectural model which is defined through meta classes, e.g., ComponentDef, ConnectorDef, PortDef) as well as of an individual configuration (meta classes Component, Connector, and Port), related by the meta association instanceOf.

The conceptual style is focussed on the roaming and connectivity of mobile hosts, i.e., hosts can change location and possible connections may vary according to their relative location to each other. Naturally, architectural components and behaviour of applications depend on the connectivity and location of their host computers. A node is a (real or virtual) machine, accessible through bridges via connections. The typing means that we can distinguish, for example, between Ethernet, WLAN, or GSM-based connections, or between different kinds of machines like PCs, laptops, cell phones, etc.

A Connection is a physical network link which delivers communication services to Connectors at the software level. An area is defined by an administrative domain, like a cell managed by a GSM base station, or a Wireless LAN domain. Thus, there are different types of areas which may be overlapping. An area can have an administrative Node who serves the connectivity in this Area. This node does not need to be located inside the same area. We do not separate mobile from stationary hosts at this level. A node is mobile if it changes its location to a different area, a fact that is part of the dynamics of the model. This allows the added flexibility of considering, e.g., a laptop that does not move as a stationary device.

The Connectivity package presents the distributed view of the system in terms of the concepts Node and Connection, paired as above with corresponding type-level concepts. a (real or virtual) machine. distinguish, for example, between Ethernet, WLAN, or GSM-based connections, or between different kinds of machines like PCs, laptops, cell phones, etc. The package uses the elements Component, ComponentDef from the Architecture package to be able to specify deployment using the deployedAt association. A Connection is a physical network link which delivers communication services to Connectors at the software level.

The Roaming package defines the location and mobility of Nodes in terms of Areas, i.e., places where Nodes can be located. area is defined by an administrative domain, like a cell managed by a GSM base station, or aWireless LAN domain. Thus, there are different types of areas which may be overlapping. An area can have an administrative Node who serves the connections in this Area. This node does not need to be located inside the same area. We do not separate mobile from stationary hosts at this level. A node is mobile if it changes its location to a different area, a fact that is part of the dynamics of the model. This allows the flexibility of considering, e.g., a laptop that does not move as a stationary device.

We define graph transformation rules (R): moveIn, moveOut, connect, disconnect and handOver. These rules are used to describe the dynamic changes and reconfigurations of the style in the presence of mobility. moveIn, moveOut model the movement of components, connect, disconnect model the connection and disconnection of wireless networks, and handOver models the main functionality handOver.

As examples, we will introduce the rule handOver here, where the pre-conditions of the rule describe the situation must be satisfied when reconfiguration happens, and the post-conditions describe the results after the reconfiguration. The rule handOver (in Fig. 3) explains how to maintain connectivity between administrative domains. It requires that node n1 is located in two areas served by two administrative nodes n2 and n3. Connector cr uses connection c1 between node n1 and n2. The connection is replaced by c2 of type ConnectionDef which, according to the types declaration, is permitted between nodes of type NodeDef nd1 and nd2. The uses relation of the connector is transferred to the new connection.

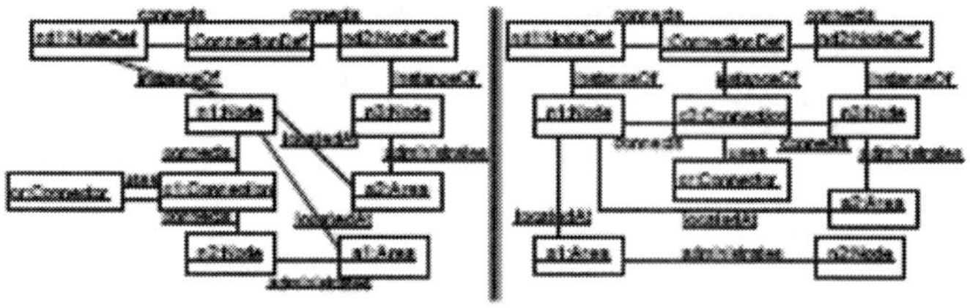

Fig. 3. HandOver rule

4 Related work

A number of different process calculi have been proposed to describe the interaction and movement of mobile processes, mostly by extending the calculus [3, 6, 8]. In order to express runtime properties of mobile systems, some of these calculi have been complemented by logics [10, 11]. Apart from the fundamentally different appearance and style which, in our opinion, makes them harder to grasp for the average software engineer than our meta model-based approach, these process calculi with their associated logics have a complementary focus: they provide means for programming mobility in terms of the processes driving individual components or devices, rather than for its high-level conceptual modelling in terms of global pre- and post-conditions. In this sense, our model defines requirements, e.g., for handOver, while the actual protocol implementing the operation is more easily specified (and verified) in a process calculus.

There exist different specification and modelling methods of mobility in the software architecture area. Some of the techniques proposed by the AGILE project [2] are closer to our approach. AGILE develops an architectural approach by extending existing specification languages and methods to support mobility: UML stereotypes are used to extend UML class, sequence and activity diagrams in order to describe how mobile objects can migrate from one host to another, and how they can be hosts to other mobile objects. Graph transformation systems are proposed as a means to give operational semantics to these extensions.

Other extensions are based on architectural description languages, like the parallel program design language CommUnity using graph transformation to describe the dynamic reconfiguration; Klaim is a programming language with coordination mechanisms for mobile components, services and resources; The specification language CASL as a means for providing architectural specification and verification mechanisms. While Klaim and CASL are more programming and verification-oriented, the approaches based on UML and CommUnity are at a level of abstraction similar to ours, but the goals are different: our focus is to model a style of mobile systems, while the focus in the cited approaches is on the modeling of applications within a style that is more or less determined by the formalisms.

References

1. G. D. Abowd, R. Allen, and D. Garlan. Formalizing style to understand descriptions of software architecture. In ACM Transactions on SoftWare Engineering and Methodology, volume 4(4), pages 319–364, Oct. 1995.
2. L. Andrade, P. Baldan, and H. Baumeister. AGILE: Software architecture for mobility. In Recent Trends in Algebraic Develeopment, 16th Intl. Workshop (WADT 2002), volume 2755 of LNCS, Frauenchiemsee, 2003. Springer-Verlag.
3. L. Caires and L. Cardelli. A spatial logic for concurrency (part I). Information and Computation, 186(2):194–235, November 2003.
4. L. Capra, C. Mascolo, andW. Emmerich. Middleware for mobile computing. In Q. Mahmoud, editor, Middleware for Communications. John Wiley, 2002.
5. L. Cardelli and A. Gordon. Anytime, anywhere. model logics for mobile ambients. In 27th ACM Symposium on Principles of Programming Languages, pages 365–377. ACM, 2000.
6. L. Cardelli and A.D. Gordon. Mobile ambients. In Foundations of Software Science and Computation Structures: First International Conference, FOSSACS '98. Springer-Verlag, Berlin Germany, 1998.
7. R. Heckel and P. Guo. Conceptual modeling of styles for mobile systems: A layered approach based on graph transformation. In IFIP TC8 Working Conference on Mobile Information Systems(MOBIS) and IFIP International Federation for Information Processing, pages 65–78. Kluwer and Springer Verlag, Sept. 2004.
8. M. Hennessy and J. Riely. A typed language for distributed mobile processes. In Proc. ACM Principles of Prog. Lang. ACM, 1998.
9. H. J. Koehler, U. Nickel, J. Niere, and A. Z undorf. Integrating uml diagrams for production control systems. In 22nd International Conference on Software Engineering (ICSE), pages 241–251. ACM Press, 2000.
10. S. Merz, M.Wirsing, and J. Zappe. A spatio-temporal logic for the specification and refinement of mobile systems. In Mauro Pezz`e, editor, Proc. Fundamental Approaches to Software Engineering, 6th International Conference (FASE 2003), volume 2621 of LNCS, pages 87–101. Springer-Verlag, 2003.
11. R. Milner, J. Parrow, and D. Walker. A calculus of mobile processes. Information and Computation, 100:1–77, 1992.
12. G.-C. Roman, G. P. Picco, and A. L. Murphy. Software engineering for mobility: A roadmap. In A. Finkelstein, editor, Proc. ICSE 2000: The Future of Software Engineering, pages 241–258. ACM Press, 2000.
13. G. Rozenberg, editor. Handbook of Graph Grammars and Computing by Graph Transformation, Volume 1:Foundations. World Scientific, 1997.

MATEC Web of Conferences **44**, 01055 (2016)
DOI: 10.1051/matecconf/20164401055
© Owned by the authors, published by EDP Sciences, 2016

A granular computing method for nonlinear convection-diffusion equation

Ya Lan Tian[1,2], Guo Yin Wang[1,2,a], Jian Jun Xu[2] and Ji Xu[2]

[1]1Chongqing Key Laboratory of Computational Intelligence, Chongqing University of Posts and Telecommunications, Chongqing 400065, China
[2] Institute of Electronic Information & Technology, Chongqing Institute of Green and Intelligent Technology, Chinese Academy of Sciences, Chongqing 401122, China

ABSTRACT: This paper introduces a method of solving nonlinear convection-diffusion equation (NCDE), based on the combination of granular computing (GrC) and characteristics finite element method (CFEM). The key idea of the proposed method (denoted as GrC-CFEM) is to reconstruct the solution from coarse-grained layer to fine-grained layer. It first gets the nonlinear solution on the coarse-grained layer, and then the function (Taylor expansion) is applied to linearize the NCDE on the fine-grained layer. Switch to the fine-grained layer, the linear solution is directly derived from the nonlinear solution. The full nonlinear problem is solved only on the coarse-grained layer. Numerical experiments show that the GrC-CFEM can accelerate the convergence and improve the computational efficiency without sacrificing the accuracy.

1 Introduction

As a key branch of PDEs, the convection-diffusion problem plays an important role in the field of theoretical as well as applied research.

In this paper, we consider the following NCDE in $\mathbb{R}^2$:

$$\begin{cases} c\cdot u_t + b\cdot\nabla u - \nabla\cdot(a\nabla u) = f(u), & in\ \Omega\times(0,T] \\ u(x,t)=0, & \text{on } \partial\Omega\times(0,T] \\ u(\cdot,0)=u_0, & \text{on } \Omega\times\{0\} \end{cases} \quad (1.1)$$

Where $\Omega\subset\mathbb{R}^2$ is a bounded domain with boundary $\partial\Omega$, $\nabla=(\partial/\partial x_1,\partial/\partial x_2)^T$, $x=(x_1,x_2)^T$, $a=(a_1,a_2)^T$ and $b=(b_1,b_2)^T$ is a vector function, $f(u)=f(u,x,t)$ is a nonlinear function.

$W^{m,p}(\Omega)$ is Sobolev Space[1] on Ω, m is non-negative integer, the Sobolev Space norm is:

$$\|v\|_{W^{m,p}} = \begin{cases} \left(\sum_{|\alpha|\le m}\|D^\alpha v\|^p_{L^p(\Omega)}\right)^{\frac{1}{p}}, & 1\le p\le\infty \\ \max_{|\alpha|\le m} ess\ sup|D^\alpha v|, & p=\infty \end{cases} \quad (1.2)$$

We write: $W^{m,2}(\Omega)=H^m(\Omega)$, $\|v\|_{L^2(\Omega)}=\|v\|_0=\|v\|$, $\|v\|_{H^m(\Omega)}=\|v\|_m$.

Supposing problem (1.1) satisfies the following assumptions:

a) $0<c_*\le c\le c^*<+\infty$, $0<a_*\le a\le a^*<+\infty$, $\max|a|<\max|b|<c_1$

b) $|b/c|+|\nabla\cdot(b/c)|\le c_2$

c) $|\partial f(s)/\partial s|+|\partial^2 f(s)/\partial s^2|\le c_3$

d) $u\in L^\infty(0,T;H^{r+1}(\Omega))$

e) $u_t\in L^2(0,T;H^{r+s}), r=1\ if\ s=1 \text{ and } r\ge 2\ if\ s=0$

f) $\partial^2 u/\partial t^2\in L^2(0,T;L^2(\Omega))$

where $c_*,c^*,a_*,a^*,c_1,c_2,c_3$ are positive constant.

In most applications, PDEs are often difficult to get the analytic solutions. Therefore, numerical methods must be applied. At present, the major numerical methods are finite element methods(FEM)[2][3][4][5], finite difference methods (FDM)[6][7], finite volume methods(FVM)[8][9][10]. However, when the FEM or FDM are used to solve the NCDE, it exhibits excessive numerical diffusion and nonphysical oscillation[11]. To address this issue, we use the modified method of CFEM developed by Douglas-Russell[12]. But it is of high computational complexity and low efficiency.

Originally, in 1965, Zadeh, proposed the GrC. GrC is a natural mode to simulate human thinking and solve the large-scale problem [13]. For many practical problems, we cannot get the exact solution. Instead of searching for the exact solution, one may search for good approximate solutions. The basic components of GrC include granule, granulated views and levels, hierarchies, and granular structures [14].

As far as we know GrC theory is not applied to the NCDE. In this paper, we consider the GrC for NCDE, and focus on the reconstruction of solution from coarse-grained layer to fine-grained layer. We first gets the nonlinear solution on the coarse-grained layer, and then the function $f(x)$ is applied to linearizing the NCDE. Switch to the fine-grained layer, the linear solution is directly derived from the nonlinear solution. The full nonlinear problem is solved only on the coarse-grained layer. The new way of GrC-CFEM can accelerate the convergence and improve the computational efficiency

[a] Corresponding author: wangguoyin@cigit.ac.cn

Article available at http://www.matec-conferences.org or http://dx.doi.org/10.1051/matecconf/20164401055

without sacrificing the accuracy.

The rest of this paper is organized as following. In Section 2, the general theories of Characteristic finite element discretization and Granular computing are described. In Section 3, we illustrate the applications of GrC-CFEM method to the NCDE. Section 4 gives convergence analysis and time complexity analysis. Section 5 presents a numerical experiment. Finally, conclusions are given in Section 6.

2 Preliminaries

2.1 Characteristic finite element discretization

The concept of CFEM is now generally well understood, this article only provides a brief introduction. Let

$$\psi(x)=\sqrt{c^2(x)+b^2(x)}\,, \tag{2.1}$$

and let the characteristic direction associated with the operator $c(x)\frac{\partial u}{\partial t}+b(x)\frac{\partial u}{\partial x}$ be denoted by $\tau=\tau(x,t)$, where

$$\frac{\partial}{\partial \tau}=\frac{c(x)}{\psi(x)}\frac{\partial}{\partial t}+\frac{b(x)}{\psi(x)}\frac{\partial}{\partial x}. \tag{2.2}$$

Then Eq. (1.1) can be put in form

$$\begin{cases}\psi\cdot u_\tau-\nabla\cdot(a\nabla u)=f(u), & in\ \Omega\times(0,T]\\ u(x,t)=0, & \text{on } \partial\Omega\times(0,T]\\ u(\cdot\,,0)=u_0, & \text{on } \Omega\times\{0\}\end{cases} \tag{2.3}$$

Sobolev space $V=H_0^1(\Omega)$, let $A(u,v)=(a\nabla u,\nabla v)$, and the notation $(u,v)=\int_\Omega u(x)v(x)dx,\ \forall u,\ v\in V$. Then, applying Green formula, (2.3) can be written in the equivalent variations:

$$\begin{cases}(\psi\cdot u_\tau,v)+A(u,v)=(f(u),v), & v\in V\\ A(u(0)-u_0,v)=0, & v\in V\end{cases} \tag{2.4}$$

We consider a time step $\Delta t=T/N$ and approximate the solution at times $t^n=n\cdot\Delta t,\quad n=1,2,\cdots,N$. The characteristic derivative is approximated in the following way at $t=t^n$:

$$(\psi\cdot u_\tau)^n\approx\psi\frac{u(x,t^n)-u(\bar{x},t^{n-1})}{\sqrt{(x-\bar{x})^2+\Delta t^2}}=c(x)\frac{u(x,t^n)-u(\bar{x},t^{n-1})}{\Delta t}. \tag{2.5}$$

Where $\bar{x}=x-[b(x)/c(x)]\Delta t$ is the foot (at level t^{n-1}) of the characteristic corresponding to x at the head (at level t^n).

We denote the grid by Δh whose grid size is h, V_h be a finite-element subspace of $V\cap W^{1,\infty}(\Omega)$. So, the CFEM for (2.4) is defined:

for $n=1,2,\cdots,N$ find $u_h^n\in V_h$ such that

$$\begin{cases}\left(c\frac{u_h^n-\bar{u}_h^{n-1}}{\Delta t},v\right)+A(u_h^n,v)=(f(u_h^n),v), & v\in V_h\\ A(u_h^0-u_0,v)=0, & v\in V_h\end{cases} \tag{2.6}$$

The initial approximation u_h^0 in V_h can be defined as any reasonable approximation of u_0 such as the interpolation of in V_h. The (2.6) determines $\{u_h^n\}$ uniquely in terms of the data u_0.

2.2 Granular computing

This paper focuses on the reconstruction of solution based on the transformation between granule spaces [16]. In figure 1, fine-grained layer and coarse-grained layer are different from granular partitions on the same domain. $u(x,t)$ is NCDE. s and s' are numerical solutions of the function $u(x,t)$ on the domain with different granular partitions, respectively.

As we know, it is difficult to directly solve NCDE, furthermore, the acquisition of numerical solution maybe too costly. So, we explore GrC-CFEM to get s'. The key idea of the proposed method is to reconstruct the solution from coarse-grained layer to fine-grained layer. The full nonlinear problem is solved only on the coarse-grained layer. Comparing with the traditional method, the new method is faster and at a smaller cost. The new way can accelerate the convergence and improve the computational efficiency without sacrificing the accuracy.

3 Description of the GrC-CFEM

In this section, describe the new method. We combine GrC with CFEM to accelerate the solving process.

The method consists of two major steps:

Step1. On the coarse-grained ΔH, solve the following nonlinear system for $u_H^n\in V_H$:

$$\begin{cases}\left(c\frac{u_H^n-\bar{u}_H^{n-1}}{\Delta t},v\right)+A(u_H^n,v)=(f(u_H^n),v), & v\in V_H\\ A(u_H^0-u_0,v)=0. & v\in V_H\end{cases} \tag{3.1}$$

Step2. Switch to the fine-grained $\Delta h,\ h=H^2$, (2.6) is linearized according to $f(\hat{u}_h^n)=f(u_H^n)+f'(u_H^n)(\hat{u}_h^n-u_H^n)$, the solution is reconstructed as follows:

$$\begin{cases}\left(c\frac{\hat{u}_h^n-\bar{\hat{u}}_h^{n-1}}{\Delta t},v\right)+A(u_h^n,v)=(f(\hat{u}_h^n),v), & v\in V_h\\ A(u_h^0-u_0,v)=0. & v\in V_h\end{cases} \tag{3.2}$$

This linearization is efficient without sacrificing the accuracy associated with the fine-grained solution u_h^n.

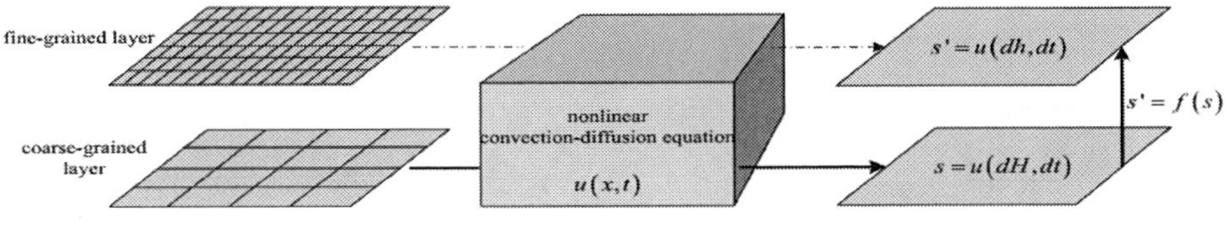

Figure 1. The flow chart of GRC-CFEM

4 Convergence analysis and time complexity analysis

In this section, the convergence analysis of algorithm are performed.

4.1 Convergence analysis

First, we briefly introduce a convergence analysis for the CFEM. Base on it, we give the GrC-CFEM.

We consider (1.1) on Ω . For $v \in V_H$ the following approximation property holds:

$$\inf_{v_h \in V_h}(\|v-v_h\|+h\|v-v_h\|_1) \le Ch^{r+1}\|v\|_{r+1}, \tag{4.1}$$

where $r \ge 1$. Let $w_h:[0,T] \to V_h$, satisfy

$$A(u-w_h,v)=0 \ , v \in V_h \ . \tag{4.2}$$

Set $\eta = u - w_h$, $\xi = u_h - w_h$, then $u - u_h = \eta - \xi$. It is well known that[18], for $p = 2,\infty$ and $1 \le s \le r+1$,

$$\|\eta\|_{L^p(0,T;L^2(\Omega))} + h\|\eta\|_{L^p(0,T;H^1(\Omega))} \le Ch^s\|u\|_{L^p(0,T;H^s(\Omega))}. \tag{4.3}$$

For $r \ge 2$ and $1 \le s \le r+1$

$$\left\|\frac{\partial\eta}{\partial t}\right\|_{L^2(0,T;H^{-1}(\Omega))} + h\left\|\frac{\partial\eta}{\partial t}\right\|_{L^2(0,T;L^2(\Omega))} \le Ch^s\left\|\frac{\partial u}{\partial t}\right\|_{L^2(0,T;H^{s-1}(\Omega))}. \tag{4.4}$$

The inverse property on V_h holds [19], namely, for $v_h \in V_h$,

$$\|v_h\|_\infty \le h^{-1/2}\|v_h\| . \tag{4.5}$$

And we also have the approximation property:

$$\|u^n - w_h^n\|_\infty \le \|u^n\|_{r+1,\infty} h^{r+1} . \tag{4.6}$$

Let u and u_h be the respective solutions of (2.4) and (2.6). Under assumptions (a-f) and Δt is sufficient small. To derive the following main result, some useful lemmas are needed [20][21].

When $s=1, r=1$ and $s=0, r \succ 1$ we have the error estimate:

$$\max_{1\le n\le N}\|u^n - u_h^n\| \le C(\Delta t + h^{r+1}). \tag{4.7}$$

When $r \ge 2$, we have the error estimate:

$$\max_{1\le n\le N}\|u^n - u_h^n\|_1 \le C(\Delta t + h^r). \tag{4.8}$$

Let u and $\hat{u}_h$ be the respective solutions of (2.4) and (3.2). Under assumptions (a-f), and also assume that Δt is sufficient small, $r \ge 1$. We have:

$$\max_{1\le n\le N}\|u^n - \hat{u}_h^n\| \le C(\Delta t + h^{r+1} + \mathrm{H}^{2r+3/2}) . \tag{4.9}$$

Proof: Let $\eta^n = u^n - w_h^n$, $\hat{\xi}^n = \hat{u}_h^n - w_h^n$ at $t = t^n$. By (2.4),(3.2), choosing $v = \hat{\xi}^n$, we have

$$\begin{aligned}&(c\frac{\hat{\xi}^n-\hat{\xi}^{n-1}}{\Delta t},\hat{\xi}^n)+A(\hat{\xi}^n,\hat{\xi}^n)\\&=(\psi\frac{\partial u^n}{\partial\tau}-c\frac{u^n-\bar{u}_h^{n-1}}{\Delta t},\hat{\xi}^n)+(c\frac{\eta^n-\eta^{n-1}}{\Delta t},\hat{\xi}^n)+(c\frac{\eta^{n-1}-\bar{\eta}^{n-1}}{\Delta t},\hat{\xi}^n)\\&-(c\frac{\hat{\xi}^{n-1}-\bar{\hat{\xi}}^{n-1}}{\Delta t},\hat{\xi}^n)+((f(u^n)-f(u_H^n)-f'(u_H^n)(\hat{u}^n-u_H^n)),\hat{\xi}^n)\end{aligned} \tag{4.10}$$

By $f(u^n)=f(u_H^n)+f'(u_H^n)(u^n-u_H^n)+\frac{1}{2}f''(\tilde{u})(u^n-u_H^n)^2$ for some function $\tilde{u}$. From (4.10), we have

$$\begin{aligned}&(c\frac{\hat{\xi}^n-\hat{\xi}^{n-1}}{\Delta t},\hat{\xi}^n)+A(\hat{\xi}^n,\hat{\xi}^n)\\&=(\psi\frac{\partial u^n}{\partial\tau}-c\frac{u^n-\bar{u}_h^{n-1}}{\Delta t},\hat{\xi}^n)+(c\frac{\eta^n-\eta^{n-1}}{\Delta t},\hat{\xi}^n)+(c\frac{\eta^{n-1}-\bar{\eta}^{n-1}}{\Delta t},\hat{\xi}^n)\\&-(c\frac{\hat{\xi}^{n-1}-\bar{\hat{\xi}}^{n-1}}{\Delta t},\hat{\xi}^n)+(f'(u_H^n)\eta^n,\hat{\xi}^n)-(f'(u_H^n)\xi^n,\hat{\xi}^n)\\&+(\frac{1}{2}f''(\tilde{u})(u^n-u_H^n)^2,\hat{\xi}^n)=\sum_{i=1}^{7}T_i^{'}.\end{aligned} \tag{4.11}$$

Using (c) and $a(a-b) \ge \frac{1}{2}(a^2-b^2)$. From (4.11), we get

$$(c\frac{\hat{\xi}^n-\hat{\xi}^{n-1}}{\Delta t},\hat{\xi}^n)+A(\hat{\xi}^n,\hat{\xi}^n)\ge\frac{1}{2\Delta t}\left[(c\hat{\xi}^n,\hat{\xi}^n)-(c\hat{\xi}^{n-1},\hat{\xi}^{n-1})\right]+\frac{a_0}{2}\|\hat{\xi}^n\|_1^2 \tag{4.12}$$

Using arguments similar to [22], plugging (4.12) in to equation (4.11), we can get

$$\begin{aligned}&\frac{1}{2\Delta t}\left[(c\hat{\xi}^n,\hat{\xi}^n)-(c\hat{\xi}^{n-1},\hat{\xi}^{n-1})\right]+\frac{a_0}{2}\|\hat{\xi}^n\|_1^2\\&\le C\left[\|\hat{\xi}^n\|^2+\|\hat{\xi}^{n-1}\|^2+\Delta t\left\|\frac{\partial^2 u}{\partial\tau^2}\right\|_{L^2(t^{n-1},t^n;L^2)}^2+\frac{1}{\Delta t}\left\|\frac{\partial u}{\partial t}\right\|_{L^2(t^{n-1},t^n;H^{-1})}\right.\\&\left.+\|\eta^n\|^2+\|\eta^{n-1}\|^2+\|(u^n-u_H^n)^2\|^2\right].\end{aligned} \tag{4.13}$$

Now multiplying both sides of (4.13) by $2\Delta t$, summing over n and applying the discrete Gronwall lemma. Note that $\hat{\xi}^0 = 0$, we have:

$$\max_{1\le n\le N}\|\hat{\xi}^n\|\le C\left[\Delta t\left\|\frac{\partial^2 u}{\partial\tau^2}\right\|_{L^2(0,T;L^2)}^2+\left\|\frac{\partial\eta}{\partial t}\right\|_{L^2(0,T;H^{-1})}+\|\eta\|_{L^\infty(0,T;L^2)}+\max_{1\le n\le N}\left\|(u^n-u_H^n)^2\right\|\right] \tag{4.14}$$

Let $h = H$ in (4.7) and using (4.5) (4.6), we get

$$\begin{aligned}\left\|(u^n-u_H^n)^2\right\|&\le\|u^n-u_H^n\|_\infty\|u^n-u_H^n\|\\&\le\left(\|u^n-w_H^n\|_\infty+\|w_H^n-u_H^n\|_\infty\right)\|u^n-u_H^n\|\\&\le C\left(H^{r+1}+H^{-1/2}\left(H^{r+1}+\Delta t\right)\right)\left(H^{r+1}+\Delta t\right)\\&\le C\left(H^{2r+3/2}+\Delta t\right).\end{aligned} \tag{4.15}$$

Note that $u^n - \hat{u}_h^n = \eta^n - \hat{\xi}^n$. This together with (4.3), (4.4) (4.14) and (4.15) yields (4.9).

Let u and $\hat{u}_h$ be the respective solutions of (2.4) and (3.2). Under assumptions (a-f) and Δt is sufficient small, $r \ge 2$, we have:

$$\max_{1\le n\le N}\|u^n - \hat{u}_h^n\|_1 \le C(\Delta t + h^r + \mathrm{H}^{2r}) . \tag{4.16}$$

Proof: An optimal order estimate for $u^n - \hat{u}_h^n$ in $H^1(\Omega)$ can be derived in a similar fashion of the first proof.

4.2 Efficiency analysis

4.2.1 Time complexity analysis for the CFEM

We will analyze the basic calculation method of CFEM about Eq.(2.6):

The pseudo-code for CFEM is as follows:

The CFEM Algorithm

```
Input:  //initial-boundary value
    u(x,t)=0, on ∂Ω×(0,T];  u(·,0)=u_0, on Ω×{0}
    m  // m=Ω/h . Ω is a bounded domain, h is spatial step
    n  // n=T/Δt . T is total time, Δt is time step
Output:  u_h  // Solutions of NCDE
for i ← 1 to n do
  for j ← 0 to m do
      u_h[i,j] ← Eq. (2.6) ;
return u_h
```

The input size of this algorithm is $n\times m$. The key step to solve Eq. (2.6) is to solve nonlinear equation $f(u_h^n)$. We have following equation by Thayer Series Expansion:

$$f(x)=f(x_0)+f'(x_0)(x-x_0)+\frac{f''(x_0)(x-x_0)^2}{2!}+\cdots+\frac{f^p(x_0)(x-x_0)^p}{p!}+R_p(x) \quad (4.17)$$

The basic operation of solving Thayer Series Expansion is derivation, exponentiation and factorial. Based on input size, the computation times of basic operation is:

$$C_1=n\times m\times(1+2+\cdots+(p-1)+p)=\frac{1}{2}(p^2+p)(n\times m) \quad (4.18)$$

During the calculation process of solving Thayer Series Expansion, considering p is limited. So the time complexity of CFEM is $o(n\times m)$.

4.2.2 Time complexity analysis for the GrC-CFEM

We will analyze the basic calculation method of GrC-CFEM about Eq. (3.1) and (3.2):

According to the Eq. (3.1) and (3.2), this algorithm has following pseudo-code:

```
The GrC-CFEM Algorithm
Input:  // initial-boundary value
    u(x,t)=0, on ∂Ω×(0,T];  u(·,0)=u_0, on Ω×{0}
M // M=Ω/H , H is spatial step, h=H^2
n // n=T/Δt . T is total time, Δt is time step
Output:  û_h  // Solutions of NCDE
for i ← 1 to n do
  for j ← 0 to M do
      u_H[i,j] ← Eq. (3.1) ;
for i ← 1 to n do
  for j ← 0 to M do
      û_h[i,j] ← Eq. (3.2) ;
return û_h
```

CFEM directly solves the nonlinear problem on fine-grained space, but GrC-CFEM can linearize the nonlinear problem. GrC-CFEM involves a nonlinear solution on the coarse-grained space and a linear solution on the fine-grained space.

The input size of this algorithm is $n\times M$. Based on input size, the computation times of basic operation is:

$$C_2=(n\times M\times(1+2+\cdots+(p-1)+p))+(n\times M)=\frac{p^2+p+2}{2}(n\times M). \quad (4.19)$$

During the calculation process of solving Thayer Series Expansion, considering p is limited. So the time complexity of GrC-CFEM is $o(n\times M)$.

So, the GrC-CFEM is faster than the CFEM by one order of magnitude, because there is quadratic relation between m and M.

5 Numerical experiments

In this section, we provide numerical experiments to demonstrate the efficiency of the GrC-CFEM.

Example1: NCDE with constant coefficients:

$$\begin{cases} c\cdot u_t+b\cdot\nabla u-\nabla\cdot(a\nabla u)=f(u), & in\ \Omega\times(0,T] \\ u(x,t)=0, & \text{on } \partial\Omega\times(0,T] \\ u(\cdot,0)=0, & \text{on } \Omega\times\{0\} \end{cases} \quad (5.1)$$

where $f(u)=-u^2+G(x,t)$ is a nonlinear function, $G(x,t)$ is determined by the exact solution of the $u(x,t)=tx_1x_2(1-x_1)(1-x_2)e^{x_1+x_2}$, $x=(x_1,x_2)$, $c=1$, $b=(1,1)^T$, $a=0.001$, $\Omega=[0,1]\times[0,1]$, $\Delta t=1.25\times10^{-4}$.

Figure2 and Figure3 are the solution $\hat{u}_h^n$ of (5.1) and its contour-line. The solution $\hat{u}_h^n$ obtained by the GrC-CFEM method. The graph shows us how the concentration varies with time and how the concentration varied in space. Figure 4 is the coarse-grained ($H=1/4$, $h=1/16$) and fine-grained ($H=1/8$, $h=1/64$) solution $\hat{u}_h^n$ of example1 obtained by the GrC-CFEM at $t=0.125$.

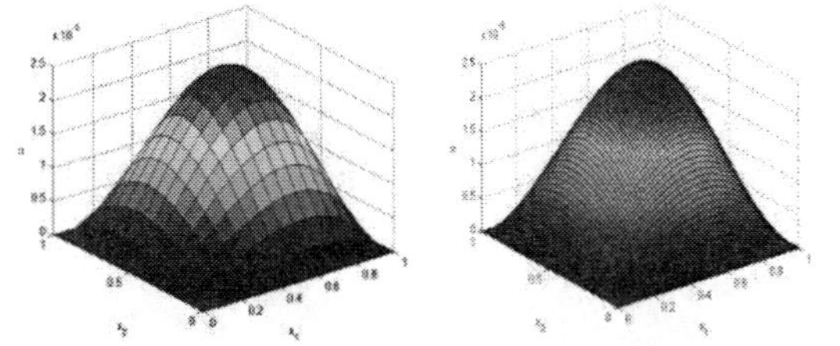

Figure 4. The coarse-grained solution (left) and fine-grained solution (right) $\hat{u}_h^n$ at $t=0.125$ for example1 (GrC-CFEM)

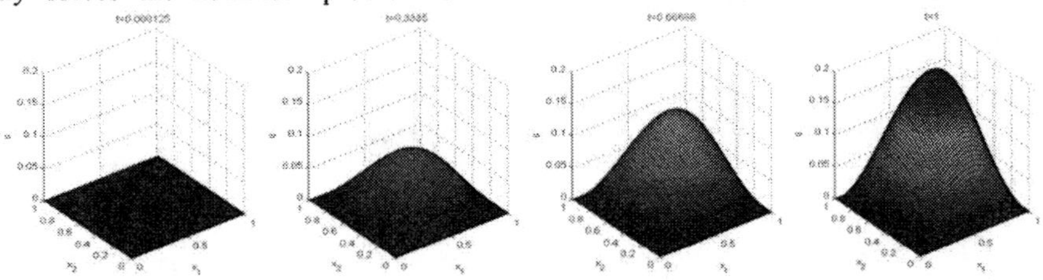

Figure 2. The numerical solution $\hat{u}_h^n$ at different time with $H=1/8, h=1/64$ for example1

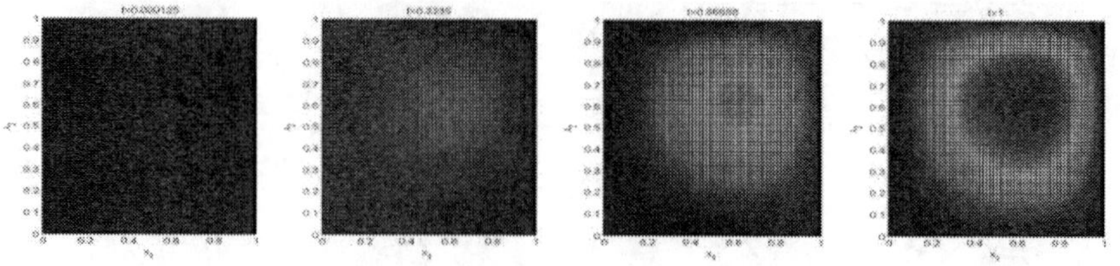

Figure 3. The contour-line of $\hat{u}_h^n$ at different time with $H = 1/8, h = 1/64$ for example1

Table 1. L^2 errors of u_h at $t = 0.125$ for example1 (CFEM)

h	$\|u_h - u\|/\|u\|$	CPU seconds
1/16	3.1163×10^{-4}	1.9052×10^{2}
1/64	1.2161×10^{-5}	2.5273×10^{4}

Table 2. L^2 errors of $\hat{u}_h$ at $t = 0.125$ for example1 (GrC-CFEM)

H	h	$\|\hat{u}_h - u\|/\|u\|$	CPU seconds
1/4	1/16	3.2151×10^{-4}	3.2916×10^{1}
1/8	1/64	2.1826×10^{-5}	6.4819×10^{3}

Table1 shows the L^2 errors of u_h and the CPU time for CFEM over the range of fine-grained Δh . Table2 shows the L^2 errors of $\hat{u}_h$ and the CPU time for GrC-CFEM when $h = H^2$.

Figure 2-4 and Table 1-2 shows that the solution $\hat{u}_h$ and u_h have the same order of accuracy. GrC-CFEM uses less computation time than CFEM.

Example2: In this example, we consider two-dimensional NCDE with anisotropic diffusion and a source term [23]:

$$\frac{\partial u}{\partial t}+\frac{\partial u^m}{\partial x}+\frac{\partial u^n}{\partial y}=D\left[d_1\frac{\partial^2 u}{\partial x^2}+d_2\frac{\partial^2 u}{\partial y^2}+2d_3\frac{\partial u}{\partial x\partial y}\right]+F. \quad (5.2)$$

The problem has the following analytical solution with proper initial and boundary conditions:

$$u(x,y,t)=\text{sech}\left[2(x+y-t)\right]. \quad (5.3)$$

and the source term F is defined as

$$F = 2\vartheta\left(u - mu^m - nu^n\right) - 4Du\left(d_1 + d_2 + 2d_3\right)\left(2\vartheta^2 - 1\right). \quad (5.4)$$

Where $\vartheta = \tanh\left[2(x+y-t)\right]$, $m = n = 2$, $d_1 = 1$, $d_2 = 2$, $d_3 = 0\ or\ 1$ .The computational domain is fixed in $[-5,5]\times[-5,5]$.

In our simulation, the global relative error (GRE) is used to test the accuracy of the model, and defined by

$$GRE = \frac{\sum_j \left|\phi(X_j,t) - \phi^*(X_j,t)\right|}{\sum_j \left|\phi^*(X_j,t)\right|}. \quad (5.5)$$

where $\phi(X_j,t)$ and $\phi^*(X_j,t)$ are the numerical and analytical solutions, respectively.

Example2 solved by the GrC-CFEM. We present the results in Figure 5 where $D = 0.01$, $dx = 0.05$, $c = 10$, $d_3 = 1$, $t = 0.5$. we can see the distribution and contour-line of numerical solution for example2.

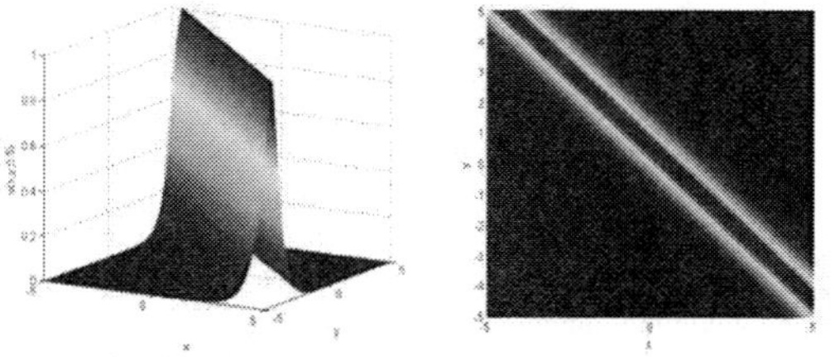

Figure5. the distribution(left) and contour-line(right) of numerical solution for example2

Furthermore. from Figure6, it can be seen that the numerical result also agrees well with the corresponding analytical solution. In addition, a straight comparison between GrC-CFEM and RLBM is presented in Table3.

We can find that, the accuracy of GrC-CFEM could reach the same order of magnitude as the RLBM.

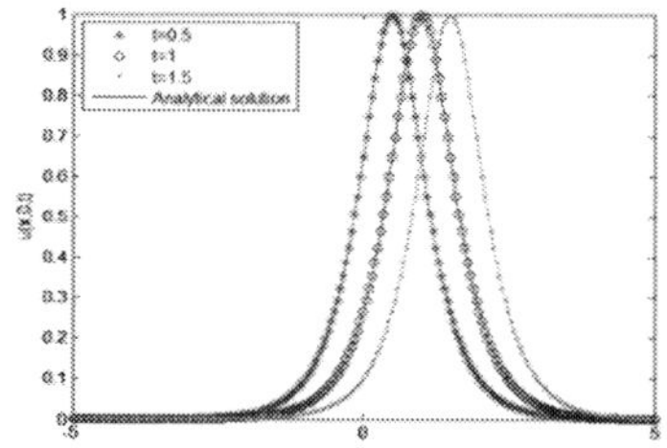

Figure6. The numerical and analytical solution of example2 at different time

Table 3. The distribution and contour-line of numerical solution for example2 (Blank mean that the model is unstable)

				D=0.1		D=0.01	
dx	c	Method	t	d_3=0	d_3=1	d_3=0	d_3=1
0.1	10	GrC-CFEM	0.5	6.7245×10^{-3}	5.8131×10^{-3}	1.1016×10^{-2}	2.0251×10^{-2}
			1.0	1.8240×10^{-2}	1.5024×10^{-2}	2.9481×10^{-2}	4.6162×10^{-2}
			1.5	3.0216×10^{-2}	2.4672×10^{-2}	4.6104×10^{-2}	6.7225×10^{-2}
		RLBM	0.5	6.5691×10^{-3}	5.4372×10^{-3}	1.1138×10^{-2}	2.0670×10^{-2}
			1.0	1.7245×10^{-2}	1.5144×10^{-2}	2.8303×10^{-2}	4.5020×10^{-2}
			1.5	2.8083×10^{-2}	2.5276×10^{-2}	4.4329×10^{-2}	6.5755×10^{-2}

	15	GrC-CFEM	0.5	7.5312×10^{-3}	7.9412×10^{-3}	1.1802×10^{-2}	2.6115×10^{-2}
			1.0	2.5512×10^{-2}	2.7514×10^{-2}	3.5456×10^{-2}	6.4008×10^{-2}
			1.5	3.8412×10^{-2}	4.0215×10^{-2}	4.7145×10^{-2}	6.9541×10^{-2}
		RLBM	0.5	7.4175×10^{-3}	7.8539×10^{-3}	1.1749×10^{-2}	2.3511×10^{-2}
			1.0	2.0575×10^{-2}	2.2402×10^{-2}	3.0116×10^{-2}	6.4079×10^{-2}
			1.5	3.4330×10^{-2}	3.8004×10^{-2}	4.7029×10^{-2}	
0.05	10	GrC-CFEM	0.5	6.8154×10^{-4}	9.5479×10^{-4}	2.9004×10^{-3}	4.9214×10^{-3}
			1.0	1.4515×10^{-3}	2.0154×10^{-3}	7.0845×10^{-3}	9.0415×10^{-3}
			1.5	7.5124×10^{-4}	2.9054×10^{-3}	9.7145×10^{-3}	9.6418×10^{-3}
		RLBM	0.5	6.5523×10^{-4}	9.8464×10^{-4}	2.7444×10^{-3}	4.5346×10^{-3}
			1.0	1.2211×10^{-3}	1.9854×10^{-3}	6.5336×10^{-3}	8.9663×10^{-3}
			1.5	1.8660×10^{-3}	2.9241×10^{-3}	9.9516×10^{-3}	1.2648×10^{-2}
	15	GrC-CFEM	0.5	8.5012×10^{-4}	7.2148×10^{-4}	1.9152×10^{-3}	3.8415×10^{-3}
			1.0	2.7081×10^{-3}	1.1040×10^{-3}	4.8415×10^{-3}	6.7147×10^{-3}
			1.5	3.4243×10^{-3}	2.1017×10^{-3}	7.0145×10^{-3}	9.9621×10^{-3}
		RLBM	0.5	8.4940×10^{-4}	7.4292×10^{-4}	1.7846×10^{-3}	3.1030×10^{-3}
			1.0	2.1072×10^{-3}	1.2356×10^{-3}	4.2660×10^{-3}	6.7396×10^{-3}
			1.5	3.5255×10^{-3}	2.1970×10^{-3}	6.9221×10^{-3}	9.9502×10^{-3}

6 Conclusions

The key feature of the GrC-CFEM is that it can accelerate the solving process without sacrificing the order of accuracy. Solving the nonlinear problems on the fine-grained layer is reduced to solving a nonlinear system on coarse-grained layer and a linear system on the fine-grained layer. The GrC combined with the CFEM cannot only decreases the numerical oscillation caused by dominating convection, but also saves much computational time for solving the NCDE.

Acknowledgements

This work is supported by National Science and Technology Major Project (2014ZX07104-006).

References

[1] Attouch H, Buttazzo G, Michaille G. *Variational analysis in Sobolev and BV spaces: applications to PDEs and optimization* [M]. Society for Industrial and Applied Mathematics: Mathematical Optimization Society, 2014.

[2] Deckelnick K, Elliott C M, Ranner T. Unfitted finite element methods using bulk meshes for surface partial differential equations [J]. Siam Journal on Numerical Analysis, 2013, 52.

[3] Wacher A. A comparison of the String Gradient Weighted Moving Finite Element method and a Parabolic Moving Mesh Partial Differential Equation method for solutions of partial differential equations[J]. Central European Journal of Mathematics, 2013, 11(4):642-663.

[4] Ford N, Xiao J, Yan Y. A finite element method for time fractional partial differential equations [J]. Fractional Calculus & Applied Analysis, 2011, 14(3):454-474.

[5] Tang Y, Xiang J, Xu J, et al. Adaptive Wavelet Finite Element Method for Partial Differential Equation [J]. Advanced Science Letters, 2011, volume 4:3151-3154(4).

[6] Mohanty R K. An unconditionally stable finite difference formula for a linear second order one space dimensionalhyperbolic equation with variable coefficients [J]. Applied Mathematics & Computation, 2005, 165(1):229–236.

[7] Fan C, Yeih P L W. Generalized finite difference method for solving two-dimensional inverse Cauchy problems [J]. Inverse Problems in Science & Engineering, 2014:1-23.

[8] Shakeri F, Dehghan M. A high order finite volume element method for solving elliptic partial integro-differential equations [J]. Applied Numerical Mathematics, 2013, 65(2):105-118.

[9] McCorquodale P, Dorr M R, Hittinger J A F, et al. High-order finite-volume methods for hyperbolic conservation laws on mapped multiblock grids [J]. Journal of Computational Physics, 2015, 288.

[10] Feng L B, Zhuang P, Liu F, et al. Stability and convergence of a new finite volume method for a two-sided space-fractional diffusion equation[J]. Applied Mathematics & Computation, 2015, 257:52–65.

[11] Chen Z, Chou S, Kwak D Y. Characteristic-mixed covolume methods for advection-dominated diffusion problems [J]. Numerical Linear Algebra with Applications, 2006, 13(9):677–697.

[12] Douglas J, Russell A T F. Numerical Methods for Convection-Dominated Diffusion Problems Based on Combining the Method of Characteristics with Finite Element or Finite Difference Procedures[J]. Siam Journal on Numerical Analysis, 1982, 19(5):871-885.

[13] Guoyin Wang, Qinghua Zhang, Jun Hu. An overview of granular computing [J].CAAI Transactions on Intelligent Systems, 2008, 2(6): 8-26.

[14] Yao Y Y. Granular Computing: basic issues and possible solutions [J]. Proceedings of Joint Conference on Information Sciences, 2002:186--189.

[15] Qian Y, Zhang H, Li F, et al. Set-based granular computing: A lattice model [J]. International Journal of Approximate Reasoning, 2014, 55(3): 834-852.

[16] Ji Xu, Guoyin Wang, Hong Yu. Review of Big Data Processing Based on Granular Computing [J]. Chinese Journal of Computers, 2015(8):1497-1517.

[17] Gacek A. Granular modelling of signals: a framework of granular computing [J]. Information Sciences, 2013, 221: 1-11.

[18] Douglas J, Russell T F. Numerical Methods for Convection-Dominated Diffusion Problems Based on Combining the Method of Characteristics with Finite Element or Finite Difference Procedures[J]. Siam Journal on Numerical Analysis, 1982, 19(5):871-885.

[19] Pasciak J E. The Mathematical Theory of Finite Element Methods (Susanne C. Brenner and L. Ridgway Scott)[J]. Siam Review, 1995, 37(3):472-473.

[20] Fu H. A characteristic finite element method for optimal control problems governed by convection-diffusion equations [J]. Journal of Computational & Applied Mathematics, 2010, 235(3):825-836.

[21] Ciarlet P G. *The finite element method for elliptic problems* [M]// Society for Industrial and Applied Mathematics, 2002:460.

[22] Kaitai Li. *The finite element method and its application* [M]// XI'AN Jiaotong University Press, 1984.

[23] Wang L, Shi B, Chai Z. Regularized lattice Boltzmann model for a class of convection-diffusion equations[J]. Physical Review E, 2015, 92(4)

MATEC Web of Conferences **44**, 01056 (2016)
DOI: 10.1051/matecconf/20164401056

Hybrid Electric Vehicle Motor Power Operation Control Analysis

Min Wei[1, a], Bing Li[1] and Juan Wei[2]

[1]*School of Electronic Engineering, Xi'an Shiyou University, 710065 xi'an, Peoples R China*
[2]*School of Telecommunications Engineering, Xidian University, 710071 xi'an, Peoples R China*

Abstract. The design of hybrid electric vehicle drive motor is based on the premise of meeting the electric requirement. As the power generation and the regenerative braking are in operation state, it can not charge the battery when the normal generating voltage of motor is lower than that of the battery. In view of the problem, the hybrid electric vehicle driving motor control system is designed. In this system, the boost operation of pulse-width modulation (PWM) method of half controlled rectifier is used to improve the power voltage, as the speed is the main measure of the feedback current and voltage. The fuzzy PID control strategy can optimize the frequency and duty cycle of PWM pulse width, and then with the generating efficiency is greatly improved. The power generation principle, control strategy and software implementation are analyzed in the paper, and its rationality is verified by experiments.

1 Introduction

Hybrid electric vehicle (HEV) is the mainstream of the development of electric vehicles as it combines many advantages of the traditional fuel vehicle and pure electric vehicle [1] and the development of battery is the bottle-neck issue. For China, which has a vast territory but has a slow popular in charging station, the development of HEV is the first choice.

At present, the investment of the parallel hybrid electric vehicle (PHEV) is much more than other forms at home and abroad [2]. PHEV ensures the coordination of the internal combustion power source and the electric power source, so it can achieve the best energy distribution. To achieve the purpose, the running car motor, as the electromotor and engine, is used. The engine is always operated in the optimal efficiency state point by Clipping Fill Valley effect of the motor. At the same time in the automobile braking process, even if the speed is low, it is hoped that the motor's power generation voltage is higher than the battery voltage, which can normally charge the battery. Therefore, the vehicle system can achieve the highest efficiency.

The rest of the paper is organized as follows. Section 1 presents a brief overview of the system composition of the motor. Section 2 describes the power operation control strategy. Section 3 shows the software implementation. Section 4 provides some result and test data. Section 5 is the conclusion.

2 System composition

As the main control chip, DSP [3-4] (TMS320F2812) is the core design of the motor digital system. It is the most powerful and the strongest real-time system, and its high-speed can achieve the complex control strategy and make the cost reduction. The stator of the magneto of the control system is connected with Y shape three-phase windings. The main power circuit is the three-phase inverter bridge composed of large IGBT power modules. The structure diagram of the system is shown in Fig.1.

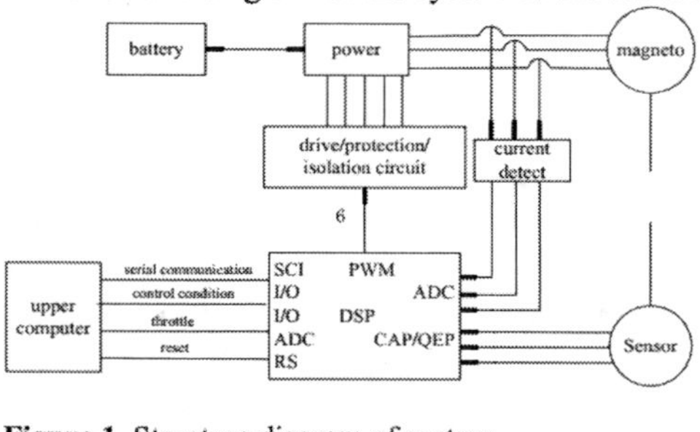

Figure 1. Structure diagram of system

3 Power operation control analysis

The design of the PHEV drive motor is to ensure that the output voltage of the maximum speed power is not greater than the battery rated voltage (U_N), so that the electric energy can be outputted. The half bridge chopper principle is employed to control the generator, where three power tubes of the half bridge are closed by the main control panel signal and the other 3 power tubes are regularly controlled by the PWM. Thus, the boost voltage

[a] Corresponding author: weimin_pb@163.com

is produced. The signal waveform of the power operation control is shown in Fig.2.

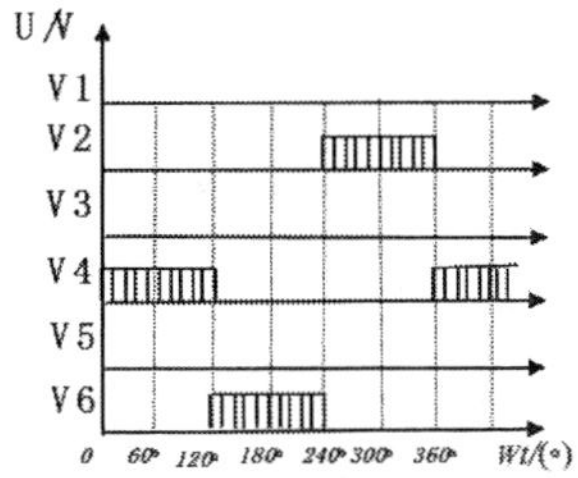

Fig.2 Signal waveform of power operation control

As shown in Fig.2, by using V_4 during a PWM switch state period (T) the voltage, current and energy of the power operation are analyzed, where the current waveform, the conducted and stopped power operation circuit are shown in Fig.3, Fig.4 and Fig.5, respectively.

In Fig.3, the circuit is in the storage state during the conducted circuit, as [t0, t1] shows, where t0 is equal to zero. The reason is that the loop current rises as the winding inductance saves the magnetic field energy in the period. The circuit is in the charging state during the stopped circuit, as [t1, t2] shows. The reason is that the loop current decreases as the winding inductance releases the magnetic field energy in the period.

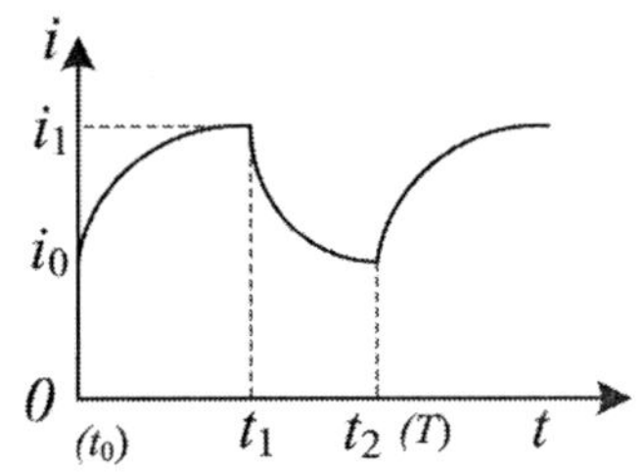

Fig.3 Current waveform in a PWM period

V_4 is conducted during [0， t1], and its circuit is described in Fig.4. When the pressure drop of V_4 and D_6 is ignored, $u_A - u_B = 0$, and $i = i_B = -i_A$, the loop voltage is obtained as Eq.1 shows.

$$2(L-M)\frac{di}{dt} + 2Ri - (e_A - e_B) = 0 \qquad (1)$$

where $2(L-M)$ is the value of the motor inductance.

According to the three-factor method [5], we obtain the Eq.2 and the Eq.3.

$$i_{(\infty)} = \frac{e_A - e_B}{2R} \qquad (2)$$

$$\tau = \frac{L-M}{R} \qquad (3)$$

Setting $i_{(0+)} = i_0$, and combining with the Eq.2 and the Eq.3, the loop current is obtained as Eq.4.

$$i = \frac{e_A - e_B}{2R} + (i_0 - \frac{e_A - e_B}{2R})e^{-tR/_{L-M}}, \quad 0 \le t \le t_1 \qquad (4)$$

The magnetic energy stored in the motor inductance can be representing as Eq.5.

$$\begin{aligned} W_L &= \int_0^{t_1} i u_L dt \\ &= \int_0^{t_1} (e_A - e_B - 2Ri) i dt \end{aligned} \qquad (5)$$

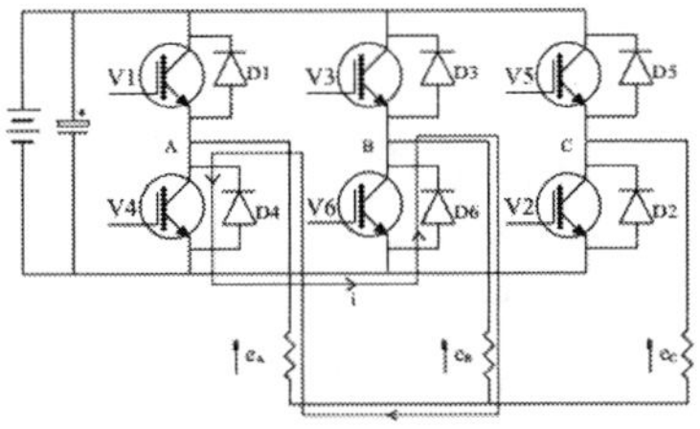

Fig.4 Conducted power operation circuit

V_4 is stopped during [t1， t2], and its circuit is described in Fig.5. When the pressure drop of D_1 and D_6 is ignored, $U_d = u_A - u_B$, and $i = i_B = -i_A$, the loop current is obtained as Eq.6.

$$U_d = -2(L-M)\frac{di}{dt} - 2Ri + (e_A - e_B) \qquad (6)$$

According to the three-factor method, we obtain the Eq.7 and the Eq.8.

$$i_{(\infty)} = \frac{e_A - e_B - U_d}{2R} \qquad (7)$$

$$\tau = \frac{L-M}{R} \qquad (8)$$

Setting $i_{(0+)} = i_1$, and combining with Eq.7 and Eq.8, the loop current is obtained as Eq.9 shows.

$$\begin{aligned} i &= \frac{e_A - e_B - U_d}{2R} \\ &+ (i_0 - \frac{e_A - e_B - U_d}{2R})e^{-(t-t_1)R/_{L-M}}, \quad t_1 \le t \le T \end{aligned} \qquad (9)$$

The storage battery is representing as Eq.10 shows.

$$\begin{aligned} W_d &= \int_{t_1}^{T} u_{AB} i dt = \int_{t_1}^{T} U_d i dt \\ &= \int_{t_1}^{T} (e_A - e_B) i dt - \int_{t_1}^{T} 2Ri^2 dt + \int_{t_1}^{T} (-u_L i) dt \\ &= W_e - W_R + W_L' \end{aligned} \qquad (10)$$

where W_L' is magnetic energy, which is equal to the energy by motor inductance released during [t1， t2(T)].

Assuming that the energy stored in the motor inductance during [0， t1] is equal to that released by the motor inductance during [t1， T]. Substituting the Eq.5 into the Eq.10, we obtain the Eq.11.

$$\begin{aligned} W_d &= W_e - W_R + W_L' = W_e - W_R + W_L \\ &= \int_{t_1}^{T}(e_A - e_B)idt - \int_{t_1}^{T} 2Ri^2 dt \\ &\quad + \int_0^{t_1}(e_A - e_B - 2Ri)idt \\ &= \int_0^{T}(e_A - e_B - 2Ri)idt \end{aligned} \tag{11}$$

And then according to the Eq.11, we can obtain the Eq.12.

$$\int_{t_1}^{T} u_{AB} idt - = \int_0^{T}(e_A - e_B - 2Ri)idt \tag{12}$$

Ignoring the impulse of the current (i) and the voltage (u_{AB}), the Eq.13 can be obtained according to the Eq.12.

$$u_{AB} = \frac{1}{1-\alpha}(e_A - e_B) \tag{13}$$

where α is the PWM duty cycle and its value is equal to t_1/T.

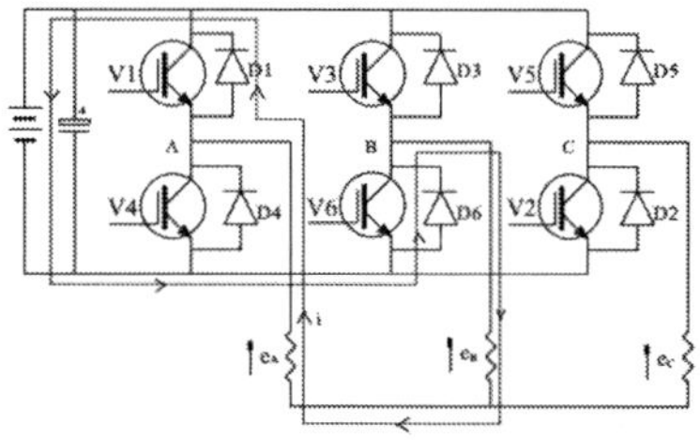

Fig.5 Stopped power operation circuit

4 Software Implementation

4.1 Power operation mode

In the case of the same system hardware, the power operation control is achieved by software and the mode is shown in Fig.6.

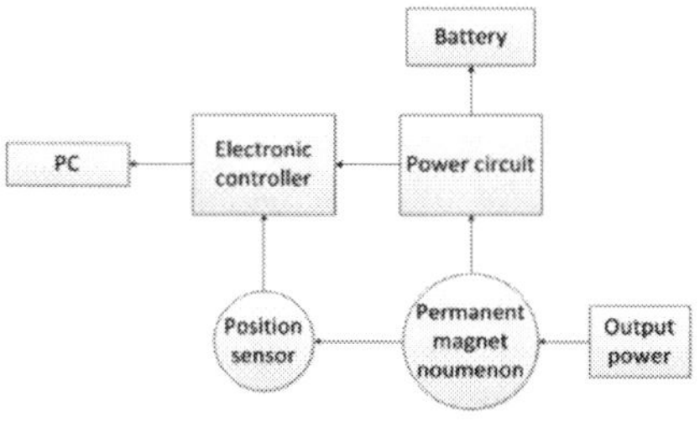

Fig.6. Power operation mode

4.2 Power Operation Control Strategy

The control system optimizes the frequency and duty cycle of the PWM pulse width by a fuzzy PID control strategy. The PID control algorithm is an incremental control algorithm. The PWM signal generates in the adjustment process of the voltage and current. And then the average value of voltage and current can be contained by adjusting the frequency and duty cycle (α) of PWM signal. When the voltage satisfies $u_{AB} \geq U_d$, the battery is charged, where u_{AB} should be not greater than the maximum charging voltage of the battery and the current should be not greater than the maximum charging current of the battery.

The software of the power operation control employs a combination of the query and interruption. The core components of the software are the motor commutation, the generating voltage and the adjustment current, and they are completed by the capture interruption subroutine and A/D converter interruption subroutine, respectively. The software flow chart of the power operation is described in the Fig.7.

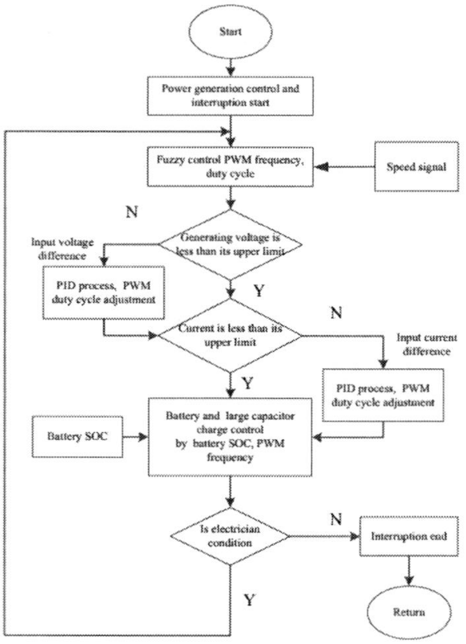

Fig.7. Software flow chart of power operation

5 Experimental results

Based on the HEV, a rare-earth permanent magnet brushless DC motor prototype is made by using the DSP control chip. The rationality of the motor is verified by debugging and testing the prototype. The result describes as follows.

(1) Rated voltage: 336 V (DC);
(2) Motor/generator power: 20kW/5kW;
(3) Motor weight ratio power: 1.37kW/kg;
(4) Maximum motor speed: 5000 r/min;
(5) System maximum efficiency: 89%;
(6) Motor weight: 16.5kg;
(7) Controller Weight: 6.6kg

6 Conclusions

The result shows that the design for the control system based on TMS320F2812 is very feasible. The system

provides a complete digital control scheme. In the case of the same motor structure and control circuit hardware, it ensures that the motor generates and operates, normally. Therefore, the system has a great reliability and security.

Acknowledgments

This study is supported by grants from the Xi 'an science and technology plan projects (CXY1515(1)), Science and technology fund in shaanxi province department of education (2013JK1047), Xi'an Shiyou University Student Research Training Program(1027) and Shaanxi science and technology research and development projects (2012GY2-41).

References

1. C.H.Zhang, K.LI, etc., Shandong Univ. J. **41**, 5(2011)
2. Y.H. Ge. Internal Combustion Engine Powerplant. **121,1**(2011)
3. L.N.Duan, J.Zhao, Micromotors.**47,** 3 (2014)
4. Z.Y.Wang, E.Q.Chen,TMS320F2812 *Principle and application of DSP*(Electronic Industry Press, Beijing,2010)
5. Qin Zeng huang, *Electrotechnics*(higher education press, Beijing,2008)

MATEC Web of Conferences **44**, 01057 (2016)
DOI: 10.1051/matecconf/20164401057

Coordination Control Strategy for Compound Fault of MMC-HVDC

Ming Guang Zhang[1], Zhao Yu Zhang[1,a], Li Jie Qiu[2] and Xi Chen[1]

[1]*School of Electrical and Information Engineering, Lanzhou University of Technology, Lanzhou, China*

[2]*Lanzhou Petrochemical Company Power Plant, Lanzhou, China*

Abstract. Single-line to ground fault of DC side and sub-module fault are typical faults of MMC-HVDC. When each of the above faults occurs, the system will give a signal for circuit-breaker releasing, this will result in interruption of power delivery, the stability of the system is greatly reduced. When these two faults occur simultaneously, research on control strategy for compound fault will help to improve the reliability of the system. While single-line to ground fault of DC side happens, only the electric potential auxiliary point of DC side is changed, system's power transport normally. When sub-module is fault, redundancy fault-tolerated control strategy is presented, which replace the failed sub-modules with equal number of redundant sub-modules, it can restrain the fluctuation of direct current. A double terminals and 21 voltage-level MMC-HVDC system simulation model is set up in PSCAD/EMTDC. From the computation and simulation results, it is concluded that the proposed control strategy is correct for above compound fault, it can achieve rapid recovery after faults, effectively improve fault tolerance of the system, develop the stability and reliability of the system.

1 Introduction

Modular Multilevel Converter is a VSC topology proposed by Marquardt and Lesnicar of the University of the Bundeswehr Munich in 2002, And researcher of the power electronics laboratory of the school developed a prototype in 2004 [1]. Compared to the traditional two-level or three-level voltage source converter topology, MMC has obvious advantages such as reducing switching losses, upgrading capacity, electromagnetic compatibility, fault management, etc[2-3]. TBC (Trans Bay Cable) project of the United States, Nanhui wind farm demonstration project of China's Shanghai, Nan'ao three-terminal HVDC flexible engineering(the world's first multi-terminal VSC engineering)has been put into operation in the MMC-HVDC projects[4].

With the growing shortage of fossil fuels, and the use of fossil fuels brings problems such as environmental pollution, the concerns must be transferred to the development and utilization of clean renewable energy. Liu Zhenya, chairman of the China State Grid Corp, in his book, "Global Energy Internet," a profound point is proposed: The alternative of clean energy and electric energy will become the inevitable trend of global energy development. MMC-HVDC is more flexible, and it has the technology features of economic and environmental protection. According to the operational status of the on-site project, MMC is suitable for grid-connected of the renewable energy and distributed generation , and its research will become a hot spot. At home and abroad, the control and protection research of MMC-HVDC is mostly aimed at single fault modeling and simulation analysis of two-terminal or multi-terminal system, in addition, DC bus fault and sub-module fault is the typical fault of MMC-HVDC. The DC side bus fault is divided into single pole ground fault, the pole-to-pole short circuit fault and the break line fault [5]. The reference[6] analyzes three kinds of DC-side faults qualitatively for MMC-HVDC, designs their respective control and protection strategies. The reference [7] establishes a circuit model under pole-to-pole short circuit fault, a detailed analysis of fault characteristic is done for it. In addition, the reference carries out overcurrent stress analysis, provides the basis for designing the electrical element of sub-module. The reference [5] analyzes the effects of three kinds of DC-side faults on the system, presents the corresponding control protection strategies and protection timing sequence for MTDC technology based modular multi-level converter. Tang, Xu, and Zhou (2014) analyzes the transient stability of three MMC-HVDC topology under DC-side fault, the result of analysis and simulation shows that LCC-D-MMC-HVDC topology performance is the most superior[8]. Tang and Xu (2014)analyzes the fault clearance capability when a LCC and MMC hybrid HVDC topology with DC line fault, It pointed out that the DC line fault can be cleared by delaying the trigger angle of LCC and changing high power diode which installed at the overhead line close to the inverse[9]. Sub-module faults include power electronic devices (IGBT or with anti-parallel diode) fault, capacitor fault and trigger signal fault [10]. The reference[11-12] pointed out that during the switching of

[a] Corresponding author: zzy411010283@163.com

sub-module, the maximum current flowing through the sub-module is much higher than RMS, and the change rate of the current relatively high. The reference [13] points out a single sub-module fault will lead to DC voltage and current's oscillations, meanwhile proposes sub-module fault redundancy protection method. Hu et al.(2013) analyzes and compares the advantages and disadvantages of three sub-module redundant fault-tolerant solutions, basic mathematical model derived from MMC running in redundant state. On the basis of mathematical expression derived from bridge-arm energy, proposes redundant fault-tolerant solution to restrain direct current fluctuations[10]. This paper introduces the sub-module redundancy protection method of the reference[13], taking into account that when the monopolar grounding fault occurs, the system can still transmit power normally, if the sub-module fault occurs at same time, research in this compound fault is necessary.

2 Structure and operation mechanism of MMC-HVDC

2.1 Topology of MMC-HVDC

MMC-HVDC's one-terminal topology is shown in Figure 1. Each phase has two bridge-arms, every bridge-arm consists of several sub-modules(SM) and with a serial reactors L_s. DC side voltage between the two poles is U_d, positive voltage is $U_d/2$, negative voltage is $-U_d/2$, $i_{pj}(j=a,b,c)$ is the current of each upper bridge-arm, $i_{nj}(j=a,b,c)$ is the current of each lower bridge-arm, v_a, v_b, v_c and i_a, i_b, i_c are voltage and current at the AC side' outlet of converter. The structure of a sub-module is shown in Figure 2, it is consisted by two IGBT and corresponding anti-parallel diodes, then, with a shunt capacitors.

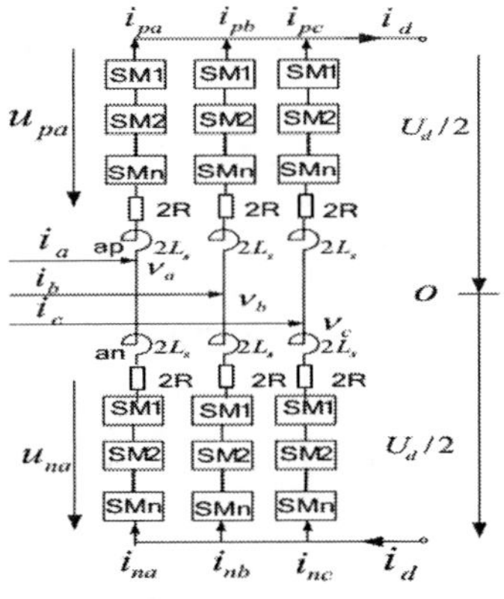

Figure 1. MMC-HVDC one-end topology.

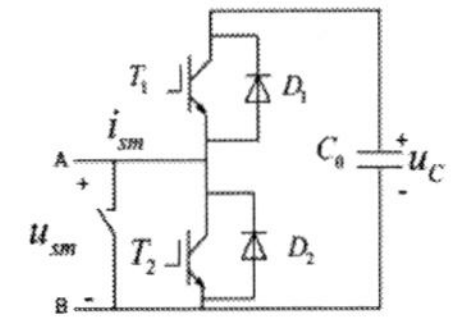

Figure 2. The sub-module's topology.

2.2 Mathematical model of MMC-HVDC

According to Kirchhoff's current law, current of phase $k(k=a,b,c)$ can be expressed as $i_k = i_{pk} + i_{nk}$, application of Kirchhoff ' s voltage law.

$$v_k - (\frac{U_d}{2} - u_{pk}) = 2L_s \frac{di_{pk}}{dt} + 2Ri_{pk} \quad (1)$$

$$v_k - (u_{nk} - \frac{U_d}{2}) = 2L_s \frac{di_{nk}}{dt} + 2Ri_{nk} \quad (2)$$

(1)+(2), considering $u_k = (u_{nk} - u_{pk})/2$,

$$v_k - u_k = L_s \frac{di_k}{dt} + Ri_k \quad (3)$$

The three-phase form of formula (3) is:

$$\begin{cases} L_s \dfrac{di_a(t)}{dt} + Ri_a(t) = v_a(t) - u_a(t) \\ L_s \dfrac{di_b(t)}{dt} + Ri_b(t) = v_b(t) - u_b(t) \\ L_s \dfrac{di_c(t)}{dt} + Ri_c(t) = v_c(t) - u_c(t) \end{cases} \quad (4)$$

For use of converter transformer, it will block the path of zero sequence current, in asymmetrical grid fault condition, it will contain negative sequence component, same as formula (4).

2.3 Control strategy of MMC-HVDC

Converter's control use DQ decoupling control strategy, state variable is i_d^+ and i_q^+, disturbance component is v_d^+ and v_q^+, input variable is u_d^+ and u_q^+. $i_d^{+*}, i_q^{+*}, i_d^{-*}$ i_q^{-*} are given reference values. Introducing voltage coupling compensation items $\omega L_s i_d^+$ and $\omega L_s i_q^+$, proportional-plus-integral control, then, input value of positive sequence current controller is shown in formula (5) and (6):

$$u_d^{+*} = v_d^+ + \omega L_s i_q^+ - \left[k_{p1}\left(i_d^{+*} - i_d^+\right) + k_{i1}\int\left(i_d^{+*} - i_d^+\right)dt\right] \quad (5)$$

$$u_q^{+*} = v_q^+ - \omega L_s i_d^+ - \left[k_{p2}\left(i_q^{+*} - i_q^+\right) + k_{i2}\int\left(i_q^{+*} - i_q^+\right)dt\right] \quad (6)$$

Similar to positive sequence parameters, input value of negative sequence current controller is shown in formula (7) and (8):

$$u_d^{-*} = v_d^- - \omega L_s i_q^- - \left[k_{p3}\left(i_d^{-*} - i_d^-\right) + k_{i3}\int\left(i_d^{-*} - i_d^-\right)dt\right] \quad (7)$$

$$u_q^{-*} = v_q^- + \omega L_s i_d^- - \left[k_{p4}\left(i_q^{-*} - i_q^-\right) + k_{i4}\int\left(i_q^{-*} - i_q^-\right)dt\right] \quad (8)$$

we can get the dynamic expression of positive sequence d-q axis current component, which has been decoupled. It is shown in formula(9):

$$\begin{cases} L_s \dfrac{di_d^+(t)}{dt} + Ri_d^+(t) = k_{p1}\left(i_d^{+*} - i_d^+\right) + k_{i1}\int\left(i_d^{+*} - i_d^+\right)dt \\ L_s \dfrac{di_q^+(t)}{dt} + Ri_q^+(t) = k_{p2}\left(i_q^{+*} - i_q^+\right) + k_{i2}\int\left(i_q^{+*} - i_q^+\right)dt \end{cases} \quad (9)$$

We can get the dynamic expression of negative sequence d-q axis current component similarly, they all make the coupling system decoupled. The control block diagram of positive sequence inner current decoupling controller is as follows[14].

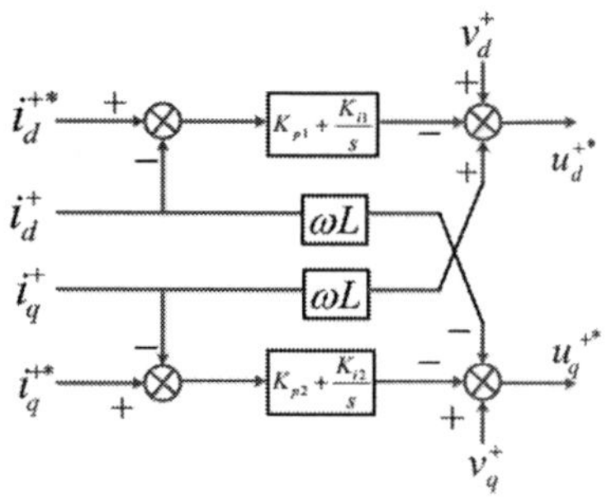

Figure 3. Structure of positive sequence inner current decoupling controller.

Modulation strategy using nearest level modulation(NLM)[15], Capacitor voltage balance control strategy is to monitor the capacitor voltage, then determine putting into or removing sub-modules according to capacitor voltage value[16].

3 Faults and its control strategy analysis

3.1 Control strategy of MMC-HVDC

DC Pole-to-Pole fault and break line fault are generally permanent fault, when detecting these two faults, the inverters must be closed, and the AC circuit breaker tripped, out of operation. When use overhead line as the DC transmission line, monopolar grounding fault has the maximum probability of occurrence, and it is usually a temporary fault. To prevent clamp capacitor will discharge through the ground and have a greater surge current, DC side use the structure of two large grounding resistance, the single-phase structure is shown in Figure 4. Firstly, this structure can clamp the voltage of pole-to-pole, secondly, it can provide a electric potential auxiliary point for positive and negative bus.

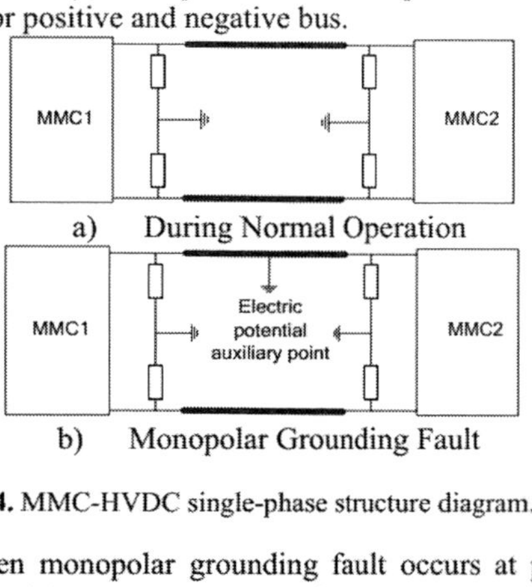

Figure 4. MMC-HVDC single-phase structure diagram.

When monopolar grounding fault occurs at positive pole, positive voltage $U_+ = U_d/2$ becomes zero, due to the large clamp resistance, negative voltage becomes twice of the original($U_- = -U_d$), however, the voltage U_d between two poles is constant, therefore, the system can transmit power continuously, and due to the large resistance, the capacitor in operating sub-module hasn't discharge path, capacitor voltage remains stable, this is beneficial to the fast recovery of system under the fault is cleared. All this characteristic is shown in Figure 5-6.

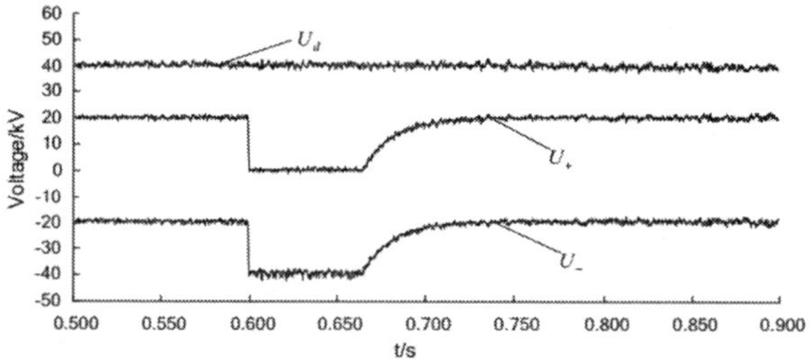

Figure 5. DC side voltage under the situation of monopolar grounding fault.

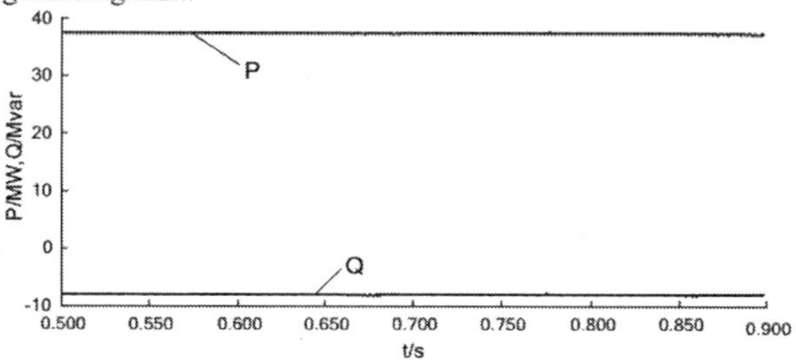

Figure 6. Active and reactive power at rectifier.

3.2 MMC-HVDC Sub-module fault

While monitoring the sub-module fault, we should bypass the faulted sub-modules. at this time, the converter station works in asymmetrical status, voltage deviation of fault phase and another two phases increases, this would increase the internal circulation. DC voltage and current, bridge-arm current will start to oscillate, it will impact the rest of normal working sub-modules. Without quick action, this situation will eventually make the system out of operation, but if after bypassing fault sub-modules, same amount of redundant sub-modules are input, through a process to charge the capacitor, the system can transmit power normally. However, bypassing the fault sub-modules, inputting standby redundancy sub-module and charging the capacitor to reach equilibrium, this process will take some time. During this time, to minimize fluctuations in voltage and current, bridge-arm energy of each phase should be balanced. Order the number of sub-module on each phase before the fault occurs totally is N, number of fault sub-module is N_f, Pre-fault voltage across each sub-module is U_c, voltage across each sub-module after the fault is U_f,then, the bridge-arm energy before and after fault is:

$$W = \frac{1}{2}\frac{C}{N}(NU_c)^2 \tag{10}$$

$$W_f = \frac{1}{2}\frac{C}{N-N_f}\left[(N-N_f)U_f\right]^2 \tag{11}$$

$W = W_f$, then $NU_c^2 = (N-N_f)U_f^2$, thereby pushed out:

$$\sqrt{\frac{N}{N-N_f}U_c} = U_f \tag{12}$$

And considering $U_c = {}^{U_d}\!/_{N}$,then:

$$\sqrt{\frac{1}{N(N-N_f)}U_d} = U_f \tag{13}$$

With this control strategy can avoid large fluctuations, smooth DC voltage waveform. Combining redundant sub-module, it will be a smooth transition to the original operating state.

4 Compound fault and its simulation

Establish the model of two-terminal MMC-HVDC system in PSCAD/EMTDC, the parameters is show in Table 1, the primary side of converter transformer adopts star type connection, and the secondary side adopts delta connection. Reference direction of active and reactive power is from the AC side to the DC side, set value of rectifier for D-Q decoupling control is: DC voltage=40kV, reactive power=-8Mvar, active power at inverter side=36MW, reactive power=8Mvar.

Table 1. Simulation parameters.

Variables	Symbol	Value
Rated AC voltage	U_s	10 kV
AC reactor	L	1.5 mH
AC circuit resistance	R	0.2ohm
Rated capacity of converter transformer	-	40MVA
Converter transformer ratio	-	10kV/23kV
Rated frequency	f	50 Hz
Rated DC voltage	U_d	40 kV
Bridge-arm buffer reactance	L_s	8 mH
Number of SM of single bridge-arm	N	20
The number of redundant sub-module at each bridge-arm	N_r	1
Number of fault SM at bridge-arm	N_f	1
Capacitor voltage of SM	U_c	2 kV
Capacitance value of SM	C	9mF

The settings of rectifier fault protection sequence are as follows: at 0.6s, the monopolar grounding fault at positive pole in DC side is switched in, 0.605s,the sub-module fault occurs, 0.61s, put redundant sub-module into operation, entire fault persists 0.065s.

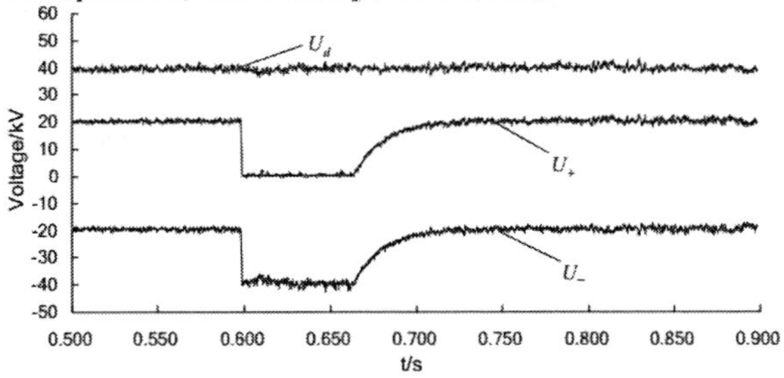

Figure 7. DC voltage when compound fault occurs.

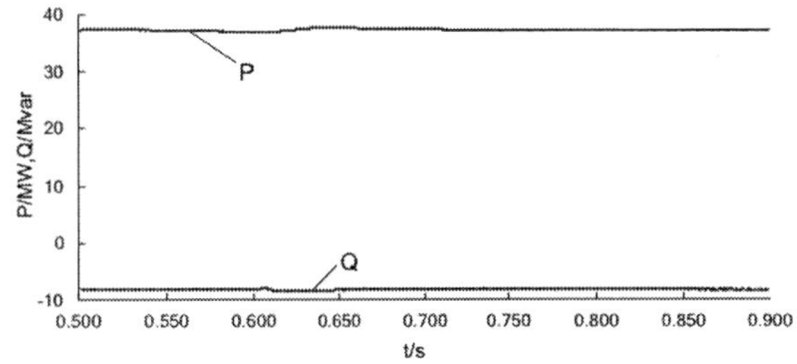

Figure 8. Active and reactive power at the rectifier when compound fault occurs.

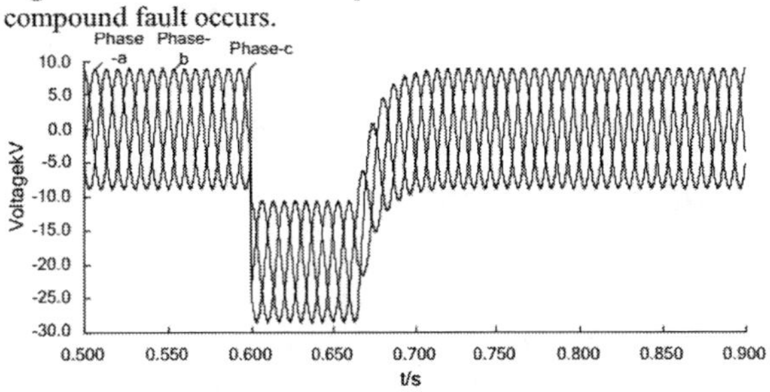

Figure 9. The voltage of converter station at ac side.

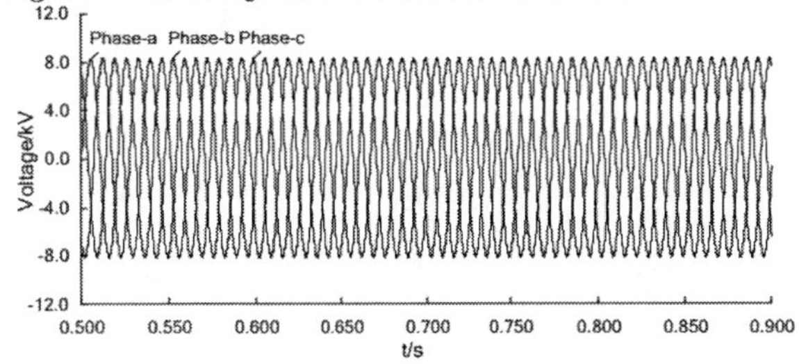

a) The voltage of converter transformer in its AC side.

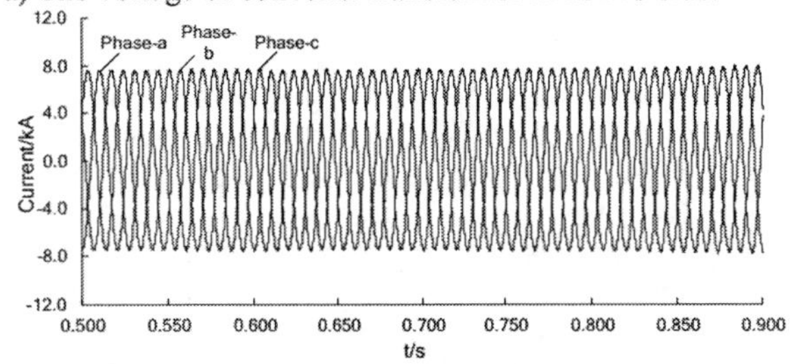

b) The current of converter transformer in its AC side.

Figure 10. The AC waveform when compound fault occurs.

As can be seen from the above simulation waveform, DC voltage and its active and reactive power shown in Figure 7 and Figure 8. DC voltage waveform is similar to the situation of monopolar grounding fault. At 0.61s, due to inputting the redundant sub-modules, after a brief shock, the system resume normal operation. In the fault and its recovery process, the active and reactive power will fluctuate, but the fluctuation will limit within the allowable range. Figure 9 is the voltage waveform at converter station AC outlet, when monopolar grounding fault occurs, because positive pole is grounding, positive voltage is zero, electric potential auxiliary point is changed, voltage will drop a original positive voltage which is 20kV, so we need to improve the insulation level of the AC bus. Voltage and current of line-side

converter transformer is shown in Figure 10, the fault basically has no effect on the voltage and current at converter transformer of line-side.

5 Conclusion

As can be seen from the simulation waveform, fault characteristics are as follows:

1) Coordination control strategy is not only good for voltage balance control, but also for quickly recovery after fault. As the AC system, when monopolar grounding fault occurs, if meet the insulation requirement, MMC-HVDC system will allow transient operation.

2) During the charging time of the redundant modules, the redundancy fault-tolerated control strategy based on energy balance of bridge-arms can reduce the voltage and current fluctuation.

3) On the basis of the monopolar grounding fault protection and control of sub-module fault, compound fault protection can be achieved easily, there is no need to add additional protective measures.

From the above, the coordination control strategy for compound fault can improve the reliability and fault tolerance of MMC-HVDC system. The control strategy is feasible, simulation results verify it.

Acknowledgements

The work is supported in part by the National Science Foundation of China under grant No.51567016.

References

1. R. Marquardt and A. Lesnicar, "New Concept for High Voltage–Modular Multilevel Converter", Proceedings of the 2004 IEEE Power Electronics Specialists Conference, Aachen, Germany, (2004) June 25-26.
2. M. Hagiwara, K. Nishimura and H. Akagi, "A Medium-voltage Motor Drive with a Modular Multilevel PWM Inverter", IEEE Trans on Industrial Electronics, vol. 25, no. 7, (2010), pp. 1786-1799.
3. J. Dorn, H. Huang and D. Retzmann, "A New Multilevel Voltage-sourced Converter Topology for HVDC Applications", CIGRE Session: International Council on Large Electric Systems, Paris, France (2008).
4. C. Y. Zhao, T. Li, L. J. Yu, Y. Huang, L. F. Li and X. L. Li, "DC Pole-to-ground Fault Characteristic Analysis and Converter Fault Recovery Strategy of MMC-HVDC", Proceedings of the CSEE, vol. 34, no. 21, (2014), pp. 3518-3526.
5. X. N. Zhang, C. Y. Zhao and H. Pang. "A Control and Protection Scheme of Multi-terminal DC Transmission System Based on MMC for DC Line Fault", Automation of Electric Power System, vol. 37, no. 15, (2013), pp. 140-145.
6. C. Y. Zhao, X. F. Chen, C. G. Cao and H. B. Jing, "Control and Protection Strategies for MMC-HVDC under Faults", Automation of Electric Power Systems, vol. 35, no. 23, (2011), pp. 82-87.
7. S. S. Wang, X. X. Zhou, G. F. Tang, Z. Y. He, L. T. Teng and H. L. Bao, "Analysis of Submodule Overcurrent Caused by DC Pole-to-pole Fault in Modular Multilevel Converter HVDC System", Proceedings of the CSEE, vol. 31, no. 1, (2011), pp. 1-7.
8. G. Tang, Z. Xu and Y. Z. Zhou, "Impacts of Three MMC-HVDC Configurations on AC System Stability Under DC Line Faults", IEEE TRANSACTIONS ON POWER SYSTEMS, vol. 29, no. 6, (2014), pp. 3030-3040.
9. G. Tang and Z. Xu, "A LCC and MMC Hybrid HVDC Topology with DC Line Fault Clearance Capability", INTERNATIONAL JOURNAL OF ELECTRICAL POWER & ENERGY SYSTEMS, vol. 62, no. 11, (2014), pp. 419-428.
10. P. F. Hu, D. Z. Jiang, Y. B. Zhou, Z. Y. Lin, Y. Q. Liang and J. Guo, "Redundancy Fault-tolerated Control Strategy for Sub-module Faults of Modular Multilevel Converters", Automation of Electric Power Systems, vol. 37, no. 15, (2013), pp. 66-70.
11. L. G. Franquelo, J. Rodriguez, J. I. Leon, S. Kouro and R. Portillo, "The Age of Multi-level Converters Arrives", IEEE Industrial Electronics Magazine, vol. 2, no. 2, (2008), pp. 28-39.
12. J. Dorn, H. Huang and D. Retzmann, "Novel Voltage Source Converters for HVDC and FACTS Applications", CIGRE International Symposium Conference, Osaka, Japan, (2007) pp. 1-8.
13. M. Y. Guan and Z. Xu, "Redundancy Protection for Sub-module Faults in Modular Multilevel Converter", Automation of Electric Power Systems, vol. 35, no. 16, (2011), pp. 94-99.
14. M. Y. Guan and Z. Xu, "Modeling and Control of Modular Multilevel Converter-based HVDC Systems under Unbalanced Grid Conditions", IEEE Transactions on Power Electronics, vol. 27, no. 12, (2012), pp. 4858-4867.
15. M. Y. Guan, Z. Xu, Q. R. Tu and W. Y. Pan, "Nearest Level Modulation for Modular Multilevel Converters in HVDC Transmission", Automation of Electric Power Systems, vol. 34, no. 2, (2010), pp. 48-52.
16. M. Y. Guan, Z. Xu, "Optimized Capacitor Voltage Balancing Control for Modular Multilevel Converter Based VSC-HVDC System", Proceedings of the CSEE, vol. 31, no. 12, (2011), pp. 9-14.

MATEC Web of Conferences 44, 01058 (2016)
DOI: 10.1051/matecconf/20164401058

Research of the path optimization in agricultural water-saving irrigation and canal system water distribution in Ant colony algorithm

Lei Lei DENG[1], Zi Tong WANG[1]

[1]*College of Information Technology, Ji lin Agricultural University ,Chang chun 130118*

Abstract:To realize the management and control of the water-saving irrigation of the path pipeline distribution in field plots,get the terrain information through remote sensing technology and analyze the path and the amount of the water in the field plots by the ant colony algorithm according to the matter of the low generality in most parts in China.The result shows that the rules were put forward with shorter path,smaller cost and the most utilization of water eventually.It can be widely used in most areas which is lack of water and scientific technology.

Key word: ant colony algorithm,optimization of water allocation, pheromone ,water-saving irrigation

The ant colony algorithm was applied in saving data mining, network routing optimization, logistics distribution, and other issues as the development of the bionic engineering .The effect in agricultural irrigation has been known recently,therefore,how to design the Scientific and reasonable path and deployment plan is imperative.This article aimed to analyze several shorter path and distribution plans by the Positive feedback phenomenon of ant colony algorithm,by which the higher pheromone concentration the ants secret,the shorter path would be.According to the reasonable path,the aim to save water and increase production by using the Advanced science and technology can be reached.This research can provide new Ideas and methods for the

implementation and management in water-saving irrigation with the data source in plot coordinates.

1 methods and technology of agricultural water-saving irrigation

1.1 Test plan

This test is based on the field plot in Shuang Yashan,Hei Longjiang Province where the Regional differentiation is obvious, the land is trapezoidal orderly and the soil types are various that is suitable for the design of deployment of water-saving pipeline.Choose a coordinate point in the experimental plot area of the high terrain ,calculate the approximate optimal solution by the ant colony algorithm and then set the line path optimization.Soil moisture monitoring equipment uses the GPRS wireless communication mode and the lower soil can reach the humidity without the hydrovalve directly when the higher soil humidity is set. Relief map of Shuang Yashan is as shown in the figure.

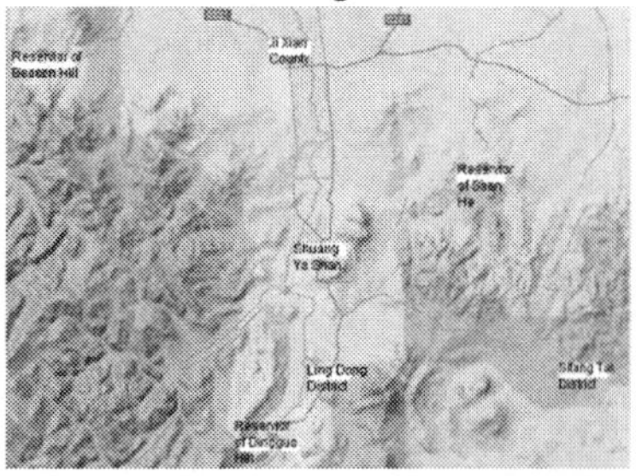

Figure 1. Relief map of Shuang Yashan

1.2 Technology of the test

The ant colony algorithm was raised connecting to the research of TSP, which was called the traveling businessman matter. It can be described that if a businessman would visit n cities, he must choose the corresponding path whose qualification is each city must be visited only once and when he return to the first city, the calculating distance is the shortest among all the tries.

This paper simulates the phenomenon of ants foraging and several mathematical symbols were brought to introduce easily.

C is the collection of cities,and C=(1,2，……,n).d_{ij} stands for the distance between two cities.$b_i(t)$means the number of ants in city i at t,let m be the total number of ants,so $m=\sum_{i=1}^{n} b_i(t)$ means the amount of pheromone on (i,j)， $V\tau_{ij}$ means the increment, $V\tau_{ij}^{k}$ means the pheromone of Number K ant on the way i to j. ρ is the residual factor，and make $\rho \in (0,1]$. L_k is the distance of Number K ant walks， p_{ij}^{k} is the probability of the first k ant moving direction.

The initial state， $\tau_{ij}(0)=\tau_0$, τ_0 is a constant， $V\tau_{ij}=0$ .The update of pheromone follows the principles:

$$\tau_{ij}(t+n)=\rho\tau_{ij}(t)+\nabla\tau_{ij} \quad (1)$$

$$\nabla\tau_{ij}=\sum_{k=1}^{n}\nabla\tau_{ij}^{k} \quad (2)$$

This paper research the information increment of the K ant moves a cycle by the model of Ant-cycle,when the ants appear,the number is

$$\nabla\tau_{ij}^{k}(t)=\begin{cases}\dfrac{Q}{L_k} & \\ 0 & else\end{cases} \quad (3)$$

The ants are controlled by directions of probabilities,we set the route at t as $allowed_k$,the tabu table is $tabu_k$. There is $allowed_k=\{0,1,\ldots,n-1\}-tabu_k$ 。 Construct the following probability expressions by introducing information stimulating factor and expect stimulating factor

$$p_{ij}^{k}=\begin{cases}\dfrac{[\tau_{ij}(t)]^{\alpha}[\eta_{ij}(t)]^{\beta}}{\sum_{s\in allowed_k}[\tau_{ij}(t)]^{\alpha}[\eta_{ij}(t)]^{\beta}} & if\ j\in allowed_k \\ 0 & else\end{cases} \quad (4)$$

Therefore,ant colony algorithm can make sure the action mode and path and get the process disorderly to orderly by the pheromone.M ants start from a city,and then come to the next judging by (4) and put $tabu_k$ .The pheromone will be changed according to (1)(2)(3) and the change can affect the construction of (4).After the repeated cycle,the optimal solution will be put forward.

2 The simulation test for water-saving irrigation

2.1 Inspection of field

This paper selects some fields plots in Shuang Yashan as the coordinates.The specific coordinates are as followed.

x=[1.67 ,1.41,3.54,3.29,4.41,7.01,7.98,1.99,2.98,4.56,3.46,3.96,5.55,6.73,7.69].

y=[5.5,4.32,6.01,7.68,0.75,1.00,3.21,1.11,7.01,2.87,3.87,5.42,3.00,3.134.59].

The scatter diagram is shown in the figure.

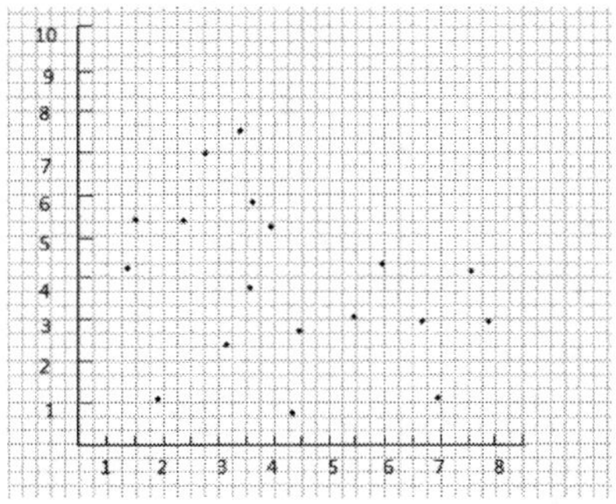

Figure2.The scatter diagram of the data

Calculate the processes and code them by Matlab,the route is 4-12-7-9-1-3-7-5-6-11-8-13-17-16-2-12-14-15-18 , and the summation of them is

$$\sum Dtao(ij)=171$$

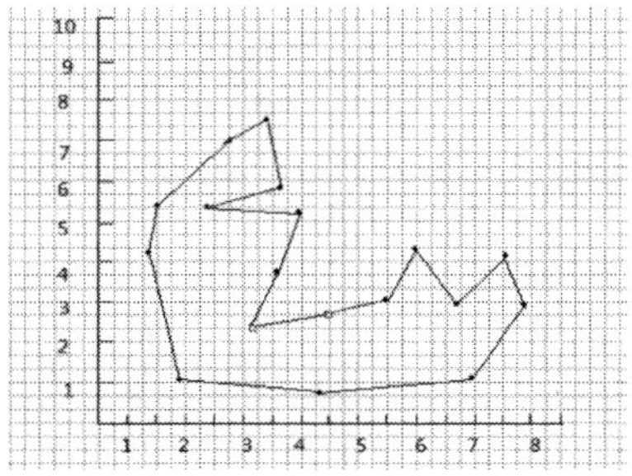

Figure 3.The path of the scatter

This paper compares 3 irrigation methods with ant colony algorithm, make the conclusion of total irrigation water by irrigating in different times when the area is insured. The result shows that using the ant colony algorithm can save more water and the results of comparing shows in the figure.

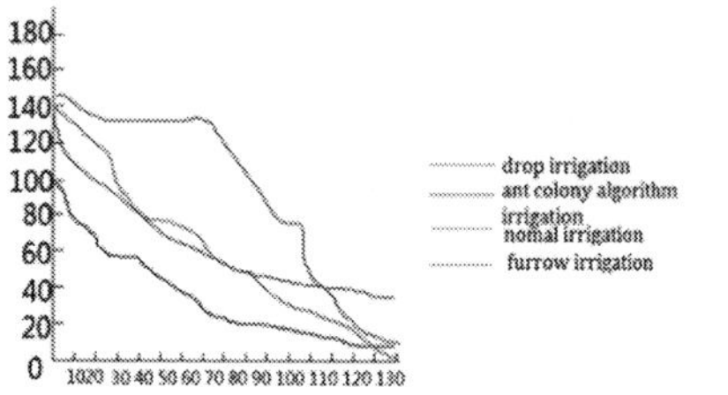

Figure4.different ways for irrigation

3 Analyze the optimization path and data by remote sensing

Assuming that the outlet of canal M=14,the coefficient of main outlet is 0.86 and the branch is 0.80,moreover there are 2 species plants ,apples and vegetables,so N=2,and the day for irrigation T=15,the amount of canal Q=3.0m³/s,so the first time of water diversion of main canal is 1728000m³ .We set the initial amount of ants is 100. $\alpha=0.1,\beta=0.2,\beta_0=0.1,\beta_1=0.1,q_0=0.5$,the interaction is 1000.

We can get the water consumption of different plants, the average water quantity and other data by calculating with the ant colony algorithm. Data is shown in the figure.

sequence number	Total area/hm^2	Amount of irrigation/m^3	vegetables			apples		
			area/hm^2	Amount of need/m^3	Average of quota/$m^3 \cdot hm^{-2}$	area/hm^2	Amount of need/m^3	Average of quota/$m^3 \cdot hm^{-2}$
1	167.18	155162.25	104.48	72927.00	600.25	62.69	82237.50	1128.15
2	376.88	279546.75	235.55	152084.25	555.27	141.33	127462.50	775.63
3	225.00	111125.25	140.63	85423.50	522.41	84.38	25701.75	261.97
4	110.25	130977.00	68.91	32523.75	405.92	41.34	98453.25	2047.95
5	358.43	341698.50	224.02	150347.25	577.19	134.41	191351.25	1224.33
6	119.93	136356.75	74.95	35100.00	402.73	44.97	101256.75	1936.34
7	368.10	201424.50	230.06	109570.50	409.59	138.04	91854.00	572.27
8	112.50	71032.50	70.31	45742.50	559.48	42.19	25290.00	515.54
9	408.83	214029.00	255.52	121997.25	410.61	153.31	92031.75	516.26
10	378.90	306364.50	236.81	166657.50	605.23	142.09	139707.00	845.59
11	636.08	614216.25	397.55	288681.75	624.50	238.53	325534.50	1173.70
12	56.93	54045.00	35.58	23672.25	572.21	21.35	30150.00	1214.65
13	326.25	383944.50	203.91	126702.00	534.38	122.34	257242.50	1808.25
14	114.08	110479.50	71.30	41982.75	506.41	42.78	68496.75	1377.04
Σ	3759.30	3110402.25	1283.04	1453412.25	7286.18	2138.40	1656769.50	662.99

most increasing product in the case,the vegetables need 1453412.25 m³ while the apples need 1656769.50m³.Although the area of apples is just as 60% as the vegetables,the water distribution tends to apples,that's because the apples are high economic crop.

4 Conclusion

This paper mainly takes out a method tending to get the most optimized result of only one path that can get to every point by using the ant colony algorithm.Meanwhile, the best effect of the way to water irrigation can be reached and the utilization of water is used in maximization. The method can solve the problems of serious water waste causing by uncertain path and low universalization of the deployment of canal water irrigation. It is

worth to promote and employ especially in the areas where lack of water.

References

[1]LAN Y B, THOMSON S J, HUANG Y B, et al. Computers and Electronics in Agriculture. Current status and future directions of precision aerial application for site—specific crop management in the USA [J] . 34—38 , 7(2010).

[2]ZHU H, LAN Y B, WU W F, et al. Journal of Bionic Engineering. Development of a PWM precision spraying controller for unmanned aerial vehicles [J] . 276—283, 7(2010).

[3] THOMSON S J, HUANG Y B, HANKS J E, et al. Computers and Electronics in Agriculture. Improving flow response of a variable —rate aerial application system by interactive refinement [J].99—104. 73(2010).

[4] YU LI, LIANG MA.Journal of Shanghai University of science and technology.With quantum ant colony algorithm to solve the large-scale traveling salesman problem[J]. 354—358.34(2012)..

[5] RINA S,YU W.Computer Engineering and Application.Quantum ant colony algorithm based on grid task scheduling research [J] .44—49.47(2011).

[6]WENCHUAN W,XIAOFENG L,DONGMEI X. China Rural Water and Hydropower. Large-scale water-saving reform comprehensive benefit evaluation method research[J].119—123,1(2012).

[7]Fang Chong, Zhang Chunle, Lu Mingben. Water saving Irrigation .Application of TOPSIS method based on entropy weight coefficient in comprehensive evaluation of water saving reconstruction benefit in you irrigation district[J]. 52—54 ,2(2011).

[8] Yuan Yao, Liu Chao. Transactions of the Chinese Society for Agricultural Machinery. Pump operation optimization and projection pursuit evaluation strategy based on ant colony optimization[J]. 38—44. 44(2013).

MATEC Web of Conferences 44, 01059 (2016)
DOI: 10.1051/matecconf/20164401059

The Application of Asphalt Cold Recycling Technology in Lower Yellow River Flood Control Project

Yu Kun ZHAO[1], Qing An LI[2]

[1] Engineering Construction Center, Yellow River Shandong Bureau, Jinan, 250011, China

[2] Reconnaissance, Design and Research Institute of Yellow River Shandong, Jinan, 250013, China

Abstract: Asphalt cold recycling technology has many advantages, such as rapid construction, energy saving, and environmental protection. In this article, the works based on the flood control dike road repair of lower Yellow River flood control project and cold asphalt recycling technology. Combined with the current flood control dike road in Liaocheng, the old pavement rehabilitation program was designed and the program was successfully implemented. It provided a successful reference cases for application of asphalt cold recycling technology for flood control dike road repair in the lower Yellow River flood control project.

1 THE PURPOSE AND SIGNIFICANCE OF ASPHALT RECYCLING TECHNOLOGY

Asphalt recycling technology was asphalt pavement material recycling technology, it was the entire process technology that the old asphalt pavement needed to overhaul or abandoned was added in the right amount of new aggregate, new asphalt after scarifying, recycling, crushing, screening, and then re-mixed into a good road performance of recycled asphalt mix, for pavement surface or substrate.

Recycled asphalt pavement materials, could save a lot of asphalt and gravel material, thus saving engineering investment. At the same time, it was beneficial to handling of waste, energy conservation, environmental protection, which had a significant economic and social benefits.

2 THE MECHANISM AND TECHNICAL REQUIREMENTS OF ASPHALT RECYCLING TECHNOLOGY

The key of recycled asphalt pavement materials was regenerated asphalt. Recycled asphalt was the reverse process of asphalt aging. In the aging old asphalt, adding a certain component of low viscosity oil (regeneration agent), or adding an appropriate consistency of bituminous materials, with scientific and rational process, recycled asphalt having a suitable viscosity and meeting the performance requirements of pavement was deployed out. Contrasting old asphalt, the composite fluidity of recycled asphalt had improved greatly, and the rheological properties was greatly improved.

The technical requirements for regenerated catalyst were Ⅰ a softening penetration, that had the appropriate viscosity, Ⅱ good rheological properties, that showed Newtonian liquid nature, Ⅲ the ability to disperse and dissolve asphaltenes, which had rich aromatic phenol, Ⅳ a high surface tension, Ⅴ good heat resistance and weather resistance.

According reproduction mode, regeneration sites, the use of mechanical devices, the asphalt recycling technology could be divided into hot or cold mix

recycling technology, artificial or mechanical mixing technology, mixed in factory or field.

3 PROJECT OVERVIEW

Landforms of lower Yellow River were plains, hills and mountains, the main topography was plain. The implementation of the project object was the road on certain flood control dike of Liaocheng left bank facing Lower Yellow River. Earth's surface of project area was consistent with the loose deposits composition of Quaternary, geotechnical properties was mainly decided by light loam, silt, clay and other components. The thickness was uniformity, and the layer was stable. Engineering regional was belongs to the warm temperate monsoon climate zone, it was a semi-humid continental climate.

The damaged road flood control dike located between embankment Stake 9 + 800 to 59 + 200, the total length was 6.24km. Road situation was showed in Figure 1. In this project, the flood control dike road damaged by construction was to be repaired.

Figure 1. Road situation

4 ASPHALT RECYCLING TECHNOLOGY DESIGN IN ENGINEERING PROJECTS

4.1 Survey for old Road[1-2]

After site survey, asphalt pavement diseases of flood control dike road was mainly longitudinal cracks, transverse cracks, network cracks and other diseases. Pavement condition detection for flood control dike road applied pavement deflection tests, coring test, flatness and breakage detection. The detection was sampling test. The total detection length was 5.2km.

After testing, the damage extent of pavement had been assessed as poor, the road flatness was evaluated as a secondary, the structural strength of pavement was evaluated as poor, surface layer thickness was in the range 4.0-5.0cm. The base material was lime stable detritus soil, the gravel particle size was larger. The conjugates of lime, soil and gravel failed to form a base layer with a certain intensity, most of the core sample was fragmented.

4.2 Pavement repair design

Because of the original dike road renovations, the dike road grade was surveyed and designed according to original flood control dike standards. Consider the characteristics such as less daily traffic on flood control dike road, a sudden increase traffic in flood season, alarge tonnage of emergency vehicles, and relatively slow speed of traffic, the road design referenced in plain three road standards. However, due to the irregularity of dike line layout, flat route could not meet the requirements of tertiary roads, the graphic design made appropriate adjustments by lower standards combined with the specific circumstances. The design of pavement structure type was refered to builted highway in the project area, and accorded with the principles of local conditions, a reasonable selection, convenient construction and convenient conservation.

For the renovation of the road surface, first poured process for the cracks in the original pavement structure, then cleared road surface dust, debris and brushing sticky asphalt, hot mix asphalt concrete was paved 5cm finally.

For general grassroots renovated sections(old asphalt surface was 5cm thickness, lime stable detritus soil was 8 ~ 10cm thickness, gravel aggregate increase was 6 ~ 8cm thickness), the 20cm-cement cold recycling was constructed and then 5cm-hot mix asphalt concrete was paved.

Considering project cost, construction technology, construction period, energy saving, construction equipment, etc. the program was that the project cost was lower, the construction technology is mature, the construction period was moderate, the pavement strength was better. Those were well done, waste treatment, energy conservation and environmental protection. There was no the problem of random release of old asphalt and waste arbitrary.

The used equipments were WR2500S type Wirtgen cold recycling machine, motor graders, rollers, water tankers, hot asphalt mixing station and hot asphalt paver.

5 THE IMPLEMENTATION OF ASPHALT RECYCLING TECHNOLOGY IN THE PROJECT[3-5]

5.1 Construction preparation

5.1.1 Traffic

Since the road along the flood control dike crossed numerous local roads, the outbound traffic was in good condition. Stone, oilseeds, living materials and others directly accessed to the construction area. Use of existing flood control dike road, construction and traffic road in construction zone could be built temporary roads as needed. During construction, the construction section was closed to traffic. Construction plan should be reasonable organization by segmented construction approach. Vehicles can bypass the construction area by the upstream or downstream Voeux Road of the construction segment and construction detour.

5.1.2 Material

The cement applied in regeneration mix is used ordinary portland cement. The initial setting time of the cement was required more than 3h, and the final setting time 6h above. The rapid hardening cement, early strength cement and damp cement should not be used. The cement should be loose and dried, no lumps and damp cement. The cement strength class of 32.5 or 42.5 can be chose. The aggregates and water should meet the specifications. When the cement stabilized CIR layer used as a base layer, the maximum diameter of the individual particles should not exceed 37.5mm.

When the cement stabilized CIR layer used as a base layer, the minimum dose of cement should not be less than 4%. But the strength of the cement regenerated mixture can not be got by increasing the cement content, cement doses should not exceed 5.5%.

5.1.3 Equipment

The used equipments were one dedicated in-situ cold recycling equipment for Wirtgen WR2000 / WR2500S Cold Recycling Machine, two water tankers, two single drum compactor, one motor grader, one sprinkler, one rubber tire roller above 20t with spray function intact.

5.2 Construction technology

After the preparatory work, the formal construction was officially started. The cement stabilized in situ cold recycling process should be carried out in the order of FIG. 2.

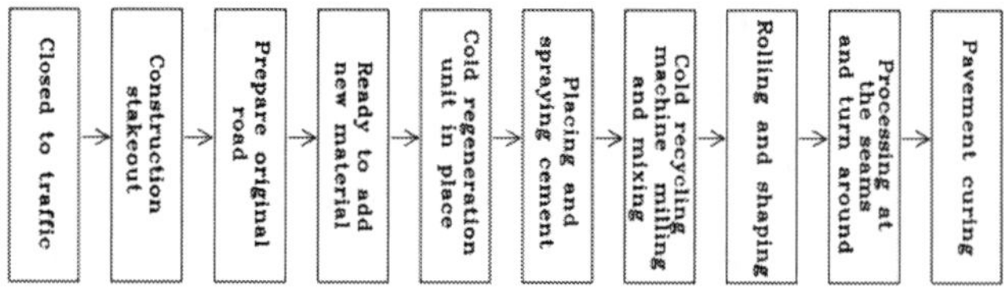

Figure 2. Cement stabilized cold recycling process

5.2.1 Cold recycling machine milling and mixing

The water content of regeneration mixture should be controlled in range 0.5% to 1.0% of optimum moisture content. The cold recycling machine pushed slurry or tankers traveling on the old pavement. The travel speed of the cold recycling machine is controlled within the 6m / min ~ 12m / min range.

After the recycling machine, professionals control the construction quality. The professionals always checked the regeneration depth, cement content and water content, and recycling machine operator adjusted operating the machine with the inspection results. In order to prevent the influence of vertical joints, horizontal joints, flatness and compactness of recycled materials, it was better that 4-5 people should be arranged to handle edges, clean-up the impurities of mixture and the excess material of the first cut after the recycling machine.

The best length of each regeneration was that the follow-up operations can be definitely and normally performed. Construction should be carefully organized so that the length of regeneration was implemented as long as possible, in order to reduce lateral seams. A (non-stop) regeneration length is generally 150m ~ 250m.

5.2.2 Rolling and forming

Drum vibratory rollers should immediately follow the regeneration machine to initially roll. Roller used the high amplitude-low frequency manner to roll, and the compaction passes should be sufficient to ensure that the degree of compaction within the bottom two-thirds thickness range of the reproduction layer meet the requirements. The working speed of the drum compactor could not exceed 3km / h.

After completion of the initial roll, motor grader should be immediately applied shaping. In line segment, motor graders calibrated from both sides of the road to center. In the flat curve segment, motor graders performed calibrating from the inside to the outside. For topical low-lying areas, the surface was harrowed by tooth harrow more than5cm, and with a fresh mix for leveling.

When shaping, high material should be directly blew way out, the phenomenon of a thin layer subsidies should not be formed. In the shaping process, vehicular traffic was prohibited, and no significant segregation of thick or thin aggregate was hold.

After shaping, when the water content of the mixture was at optimum moisture content, light wheel roller compacted immediately with the mode of high amplitude low frequency vibration mode firstly and then a low amplitude high frequency mode. In the straight line and no ultra flat curve segment, roller should overlap 1/2 wheel width from the shoulder to the center of rolling Road, and rear wheels must cover two sections seams. When the rear wheels rolled full width of the surface, one rolling was completed. It generally took six to eight times rolling. Roller's rolling speed, was appropriate with the speed of 1.5 ~ 1.7km / h at first and second times, and then 2.0 ~ 2.5km / h.

5.2.3 Pavement curing and traffic control

Each section of the road was completed rolling and the compaction degree was inspection and approval, it should immediately begin to cut off traffic and curing. When using mulch curing method, the cover must be cleaned after the curing. The curing period of grassroots should not be less than 7d.

After the curing period, the grass roots should be cleaned, and asphalt penetration oil layer and asphalt adhesive oil layer were immediately sprayed. After spraying penetration oil layer or adhesive oil layer of asphalt, small pieces or gravel with diameter of 5-10mm should be evenly spread, and the amount of the stone was about the 60% -70% of the amount of whole layer of stone. After the curing of the regeneration layer, surface construction was completed before open traffic.

Figure 3. Flood control road situation after the restoration

6 CONCLUSION

Ⅰ This project of the asphalt pavement cold recycling technology was first applied for road repairing in Shandong Yellow River flood control dike. Compared with traditional methods of renovation, cold recycling technology has obvious advantages. The application was successful, it can provided a reference for dike road repair construction in lower Yellow River flood control dike.

Ⅱ Asphalt cold recycling technology was constructed on base or sub base. Through the old asphalt pavement crushing, mixing, shaping, and rolling, asphalt cold recycling technology accelerated the construction schedule and reduced environmental pollution. In today's emphasis on sustainable development, asphalt recycling technology has particular significance for the development of highway construction.

REFERENCES

1. JTG F41-2008, Technical Specifications for Highway Asphalt Pavement Recycling [S].
2. JTJ 034-2000, Technical Specifications for Construction of Highway Roadbases [S].
3. YI Qigui. Application of Cement Stabilized Macadam Base Cold in-palce Recycling Technology and Its Economical Efficiency[J]. Highway Construction & Maintenance, 2011 (3/4) : 91-95.
4. FENF Yinfu, ZHU Haizhe. The Research on Cement Full Deep Cold in-place Recycling Base Application[J]. Shanxi Science & Technology of Communications, 2013(3):3-5.
5. JIN Fang, LIU Yue, XUE Liang. The Application of Cold Recycling Technology in-Place to Municipal Road Reconstruction [J]. Shanxi Science & Technology of Communications, 2013(1):20-21,24.

MATEC Web of Conferences 44, 01060 (2016)
DOI: 10.1051/matecconf/20164401060

A GSM-Based Remote Temperature and Humidity Monitoring System for Granary

Xiao Xi Zheng[1], Lian Rong Li[1] and Shuai Fei Shao[2]

[1]*Zhengzhou Technical College, Zhengzhou, Henan, China*

[2] *Sippr engineering group CO.LTD, Zhengzhou, Henan, China*

Abstract. A remote temperature and humidity monitoring system is designed based on the GSM technology and MSP430. With the digital sensor DSB1820 and SHT11, the temperature and humidity of the granary are detected, and these parameters can be adjusted with the controlling system to adapt various working conditions. Through the GSM system, the detected data could be sent to various monitoring devices, such as cellphones and laptops. These data can be used for data display, inquiry, controlling and storage at the remote terminals. The experimental results show that the system is convenient and concise, which meets the remote monitoring demand for the modern granary.

1 Introduction

Safe storage of grain is a big problem of people's livelihood, in the process of grain storage, easy to affected by storage environment temperature and humidity conditions, easy to fever, mildew and insect pests, etc.while improper granary of temperature or humidity control, , thus resulting in loss of food, to ensure the storage of food in good condition, must make the granary of the temperature and humidity control in a certain range.In order to improve the reliability of the system, GSM mobile communication network of wireless data transmission technology is applied to the granary monitoring system, which has less investment, quick opening, simple operation, low communication cost, and the advantages of reliability and coverage guaranteed, very suitable for small granary monitoring system of data transmission.

Based on a small grain granary as the research object, with high reliability, perfect function, strong anti-jamming capability, higher cost performance advantage of MSP430 MCU as the core controller, using the granary of temperature and humidity and the temperature and humidity of the grain in pile testing and the value passed to the single chip microcomputer, and then compared with the temperature and humidity of the preset threshold to decide whether to start the alarm circuit, by controlling the motor start-stop control of the temperature and humidity. Granary to make use of PC monitor and store data, the system uses the free GSM network as a way of information transmission, users can check to the food temperature and humidity data conveniently on the computer or mobile phone, realize the real-time remote monitoring of the temperature and humidity of a small Granary.

2 The overall structure and function of the control system

The granary intelligent monitoring system consists of the microcontroller core controller, real-time detection of temperature and humidity, GSM transmission of information of temperature and failure. MSP430 microcontroller as control core, through the external keyboard can easily set the telephone number and the monitoring center temperature and humidity, using temperature and humidity sensors to detect the monitoring point temperature and humidity inside the granary, using a temperature sensor to collect grain temperature, and the temperature and humidity data sent to the single-chip microcomputer software system for data processing, single chip digital output of the D/A conversion into A suitable analog to drive actuators to adjust temperature and humidity, so as to ensure the temperature and humidity of granary and grain are within the scope of the set.

The real time Temperature and humidity information is displayed through the LCD, Using GSM technology to transfer information to PC or mobile phone, it can be convenient to monitor information of granaries by PC or mobile phone. At the same time, fan open and alarm prompt system with related by administrators in the PC software and mobile phone can be convenient to monitor granaries. At the same time, the system with a fan and alarm prompt function, when the temperature exceeds the limit of the set automatically adjust temperature and

[a] Corresponding author:zxx20028@163.com

Article available at http://www.matec-conferences.org or http://dx.doi.org/10.1051/matecconf/20164401060

humidity, and sound and light alarm. Control system overall structure block diagram as shown in figure 1.

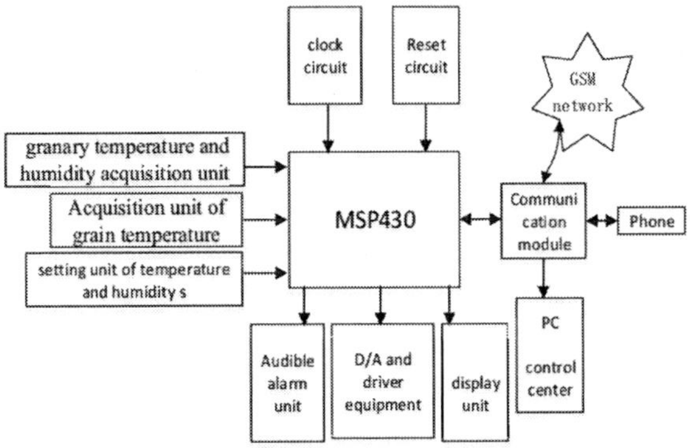

Figure 1. Control system overall structure block

3 Hardware selection and design

3.1 Core controller

MSP430 MCU by TI company launched a series of ultra-low power consumption microprocessor, it has the characteristics of ultra-low power consumption, there are five modes to choose from, low power consumption and wake up of time is very short, only need 6 mu s, at the same time also has a strong processing capacity, rich on-chip peripheral modules, flexible clock system, stable working condition, convenient and efficient way of development, etc. The above features make it become the preferred microprocessor. The system selects the MSP430F449 as the core controller, its minimum system diagram as shown in figure 2.

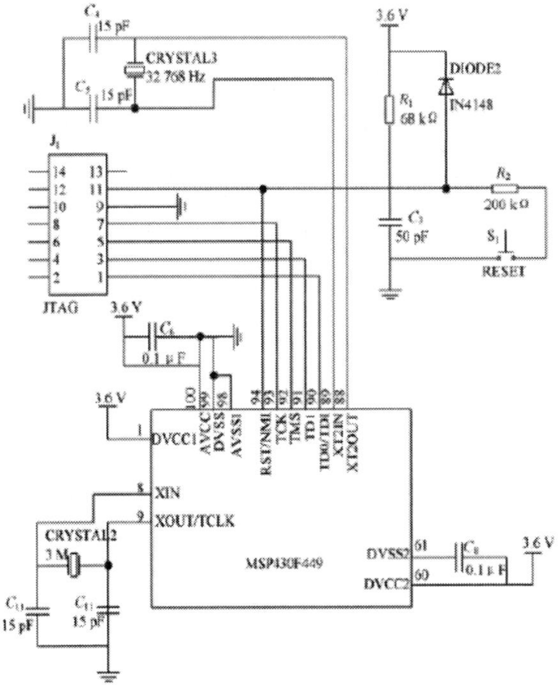

Figure 2. Minimum system diagram of MSP430

3.2 Temperature and humidity acquisition unit of Granary

Granary data acquisition module is responsible for the internal temperature and humidity information collection and data conversion, the system uses the temperature and humidity sensors SHT11 which was launched by sensirion company, the chip including temperature and humidity sensor, signal amplification processing, A / D conversion and I2C bus interface. Sensor SHT11 temperature range for - 40 ~ 123.8 ℃, for the resolution of the 14 is 0.01 ℃, humidity measurement range is 0 ~ 100% RH. Supply voltage of 2.4-5.5V, using two wire serial interface. Temperature and humidity data, temperature and humidity sensitive element respectively will converted to electrical signals, after the signal amplification, using A/D converter into digital signal, Then, through the bus interface and output to MSP430, MSP430 process and send signal. In order to avoid the signal conflict, one pull-up resistors in DATA access, at the same time one decoupling capacitor in the VCC & gnd access. SHT11 and MSP430 interface circuit as shown in Figure 3.

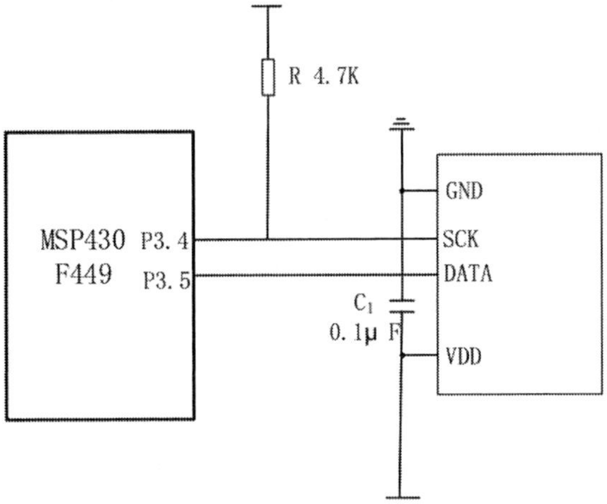

Figure 3. SHT11 and MSP430 interface circuit

3.3 Acquisition unit of temperature in Grain bulk

Using intelligent digital temperature sensor DS18B20 of Dallas to detecting the temperature of grain, can easily achieve multi-point temperature measurement, temperature measurement circuit as shown in Figure 4. DS18B20 temperature detection range of -55℃~ + 125℃, the maximum resolution of 12, the detection accuracy of ± 0.5℃. DS18B20 read and write information requires only one bus (ie, single-bus interface). the required energy of Temperature conversion is provided by bus, no external power supply. the temperature of the collected signal is converted to A digital output by DS18B20, directly connected to the microcontroller, don't need A/D conversion module, , which greatly simplifies the design of the circuit. Meanwhile, DS18B20 itself with the command set and memory, microcontroller by issuing

control commands to read and write memory DS18B20 complete temperature measurement.

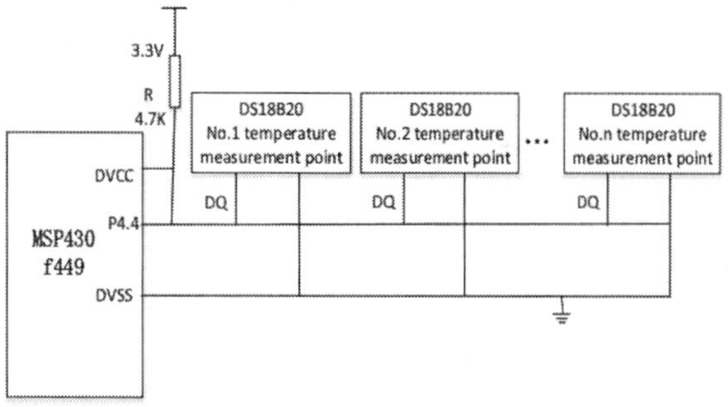

Figure 4. Temperature measurement circuit of Temperature sensor

3.4 Design of GSM wireless communication module

This design adopts common GSM wireless communication network as a data transmission channel, its coverage, transmission distance is not restricted. This design uses wireless transmission module of TC35i, which is composed of power supply module (ASIC), ZIF connectors, flash memory, antenna interface, etc. It's internal composition as shown in figure 5.

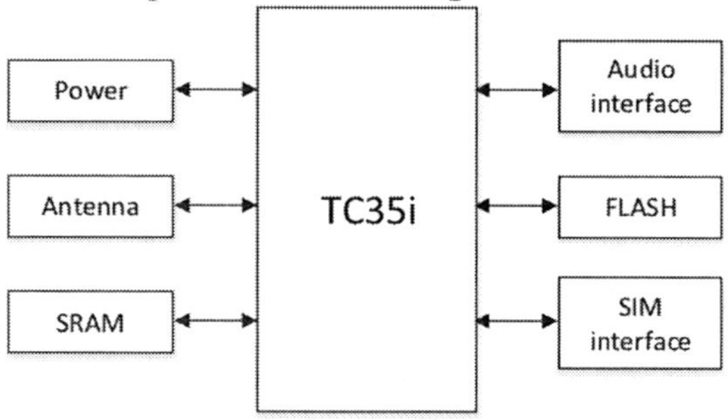

Figure 5. Internal component of TC35i module

Siemens TC35i module is to support Chinese short message and Work in EGSM900 and GSM1800 dual band, can carry both voice and data signals, this system is mainly to transmit data information. TC35i module connect SIM card reader and antenna respectively through the interface connector and antenna. TC35i data interface (CMOS level) can be two-way transfer instructions and data by the AT command, which supports Text and PDU format of the SMS (Short Message Service, Short Message), can be achieved on or off to restart and recovery by signal AT commands. TC35i for dc power supply range from 3.3 V to 4.8 V, power supply circuit diagram as shown in figure 6. Design, in order to reduce interference in the input point connected to filter capacitance; In order to reduce the output voltage stability, on the output side connected to three capacitance.

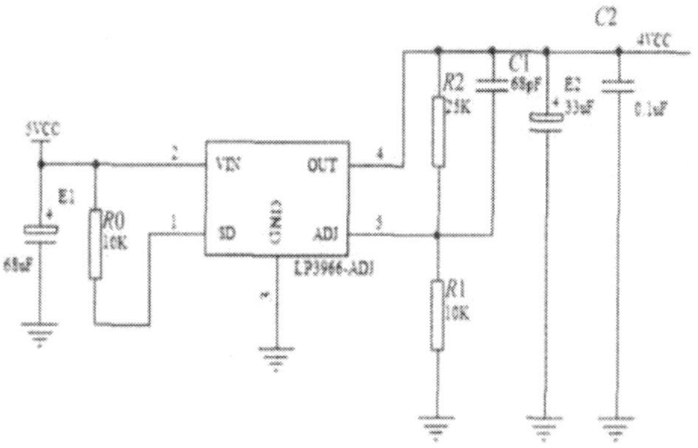

Figure 6. Power supply circuit diagram

TC35i has 40 pins, through a ZIF (zero resistance) socket connector leads. The 40 pin can be divided into power supply, input/output data, SIM card, audio interface and control 5 classes. Among them, 1 ~ 5 for positive power input pins, voltage of 3.3 V. 6 ~ 10 pin for power line ground;11, 12 pin for charging pins, to external rechargeable battery; 13 pin for output voltage to external circuit; 14 pins for BATTTEMP which connect the negative temperature coefficient thermistor, 15 pin is to start foot IGT, which connecting MCU P3.0 pin, through P3.0 making low pulse, to start the TC35i module; 16 ~ 23 pin for data input/output, conforms to the ITU - TRS232 interface standards; 24 to 29 pins connect with SIM card; 30~ 32 for control pin; 33 ~ 40 pin for the voice interface, used to connect the speaker, mike, headphones, etc. Unused pins of TC35i should be hung up as output, the input should be on, such as 21, 22 pin; SYNC instructions working condition of TC35i; power supply is connected, grounding and grounding; IGT pull up resistor connected to the microcontroller, can control the work state by MSP430. TC35i module interface circuit as shown in figure 7. The work level of serial port pin of TC35i is CMOS level, while the single chip computer is TTL level, using 74F07 to convert level to connect the TC35i serial port, only when the connection even good serial transceiver and TC35i diode lamp control side. It only need to do serial transceiver and TC35i diode lamp control when connecting both.

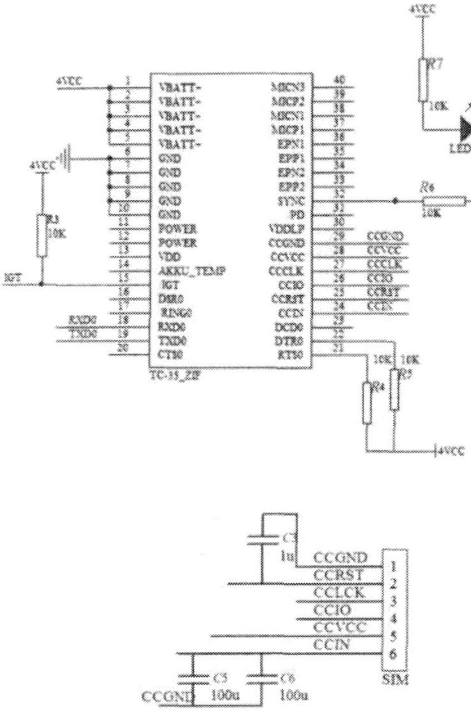

Figure 7. TC35i module interface circuit

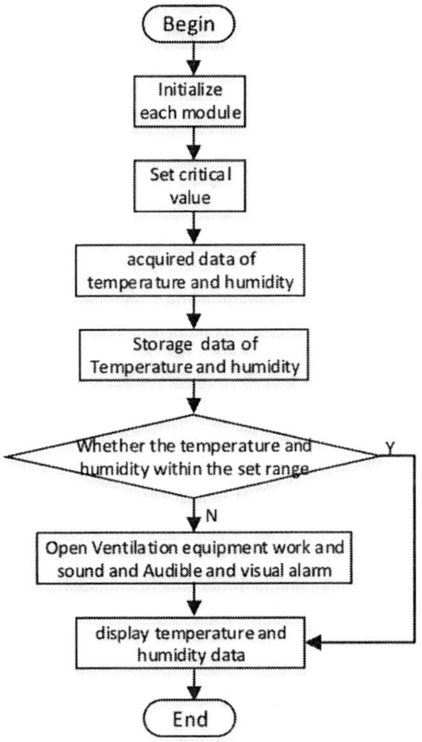

Figure 8. Program flow chart

4 Software design of the system

4.1 Main program design of granary monitoring

The function of main program for granary monitoring system are data analysis and processing. The design of system software is mainly composed of Initialization, temperature and humidity data acquisition and signal display device driver, signal processing, keyboard processing, data communication, etc. Program flow chart as shown in figure 8. The initialization completed the functional configuration of the initial state of single-chip, open watchdog; Real-time data acquisition of temperature, humidity, alternating with single-chip computer transmission data , after data communication unit to complete communication. between the control system of temperature - humidity measurement and PC machine (or phone) .When the measurement data detected by Single-chip is greater than the set threshold, single-chip send control signal in time,driving circuit control fan equipment such as opening and closing, when the temperature and humidity is not in the normal range, start the audible and visual alarm at the same time.

4.2 Software design of monitoring center

Monitoring software is developed using vc + + 6.0, software has friendly interface, convenient operation, the control and monitoring center connect wireless communication circuit to complete information transmission through GSM module TC35i. System is mainly composed of the communication control part ,the parameters of the serial port and the number set parts of SMS service center, collecting data to database, data display and alarm display part, send controlling instruction parts and database maintenance, etc. The monitoring center software is equipped with the temperature display function, the query point to point, temperature anomaly prompt, remote temperature setting, system configuration, and other functions, printing, historical data query, temperature curve shows, etc.

5 Conclusion

This paper make full use of the public mobile communication GSM network resources, designed the MSP430 MCU as the core, using temperature and humidity sensor of intelligent detection of granary environmental and food temperature detector, To communicate with wireless monitoring terminal communications composed of TC35i, can control the TC35i send short message to the monitoring center computer, realized the remote monitoring system of granary temperature and humidity, greatly reduces the

cost. Making grain storage quality guaranteed, this design has wide application prospect and value in the granary storage.

References

1. Xiao ling XU, Shaobiao Li, Fuqiang Zhang.Design of Granary Temperature and Humidity Control System Based on ZigBee. Journal of Guangdong University of Petrochemical Technology[J].2011(21)
2. LiuYang, Zhihuai Mao, Zhijie Jiang,etc.The granary temperature and humidity remote monitoring system based on wireless transmission.Transactions of the Chinese Society of Agricultural Engineering[J].2012(04)
3. Juncai,Hu hua Hou,HouYao. A Digital Temperature and Humidity Monitoring System for Grain Storage.Journal of Agricultural Mechanization Research[J].2012(09)
4. Wuli Wang, Hua Yang. Design of Granary Temperature and Humidity Measurement and Control System Basedon SHT11Instrument Technique and Sensor [J].2010(09)
5. Chaoze Huang， Qiyi Guo， Zhong-ya Mao.The Design and Implementation of Sending and Receiving SMS Based on MSP430G2231 and TC35i. Electrical Automation[J].2013(01)
6. Fuquan Wang,Pin,Feng Wan,miao Kong. Application of DS18B20 in the temperature collect module of air detection system.Application of Electronic Technique[J].2011(08)
7. Xin Zan; Zhongde Yu. Design of the remote monitoring system of food cold storage based on GSM technology.Journal of Dalian Polytechnic University[J].2014(06)

MATEC Web of Conferences **44**, 01061 (2016)
DOI: 10.1051/matecconf/20164401061

Railway automatic safety protection system based on GPS

Hai Juan Fu[1,a]

Ji'nan,Shandong province Chinese Lishan North Road No.2,Shandong Vocational College of Foreign Affairs Translation

Abstract: The automatic protection system of railway safety is designed for the railway construction workers to protect alarm, and the safety protection device by using GPS satellite positioning system to acquire location information of the operating point, through the CTC/TDCS system and computer monitoring system for the running of the train position and the arithmetic distance. Achieving timely and continuously forecasts about the distance of the train which is apart from the operating point to prompt the voice alarm of the approaching train. Using digital technology to realize the function of the traditional analog interphone, eliminates the quality problems of the call. With the GSM-R, mobile wireless transmission channel and terminal technology, it overcomes the restrictions of the analog interphone which influenced by communication distance and more problems of blind areas. Finally to achieve practical, convenient, applicable and adaptable design goals.

1 Introduction

The increase of the train speed has greatly increased the capacity and service quality of the transport, and greatly promoted the national production. However, the speed upgrade brings some security risks, and the train crash people happened frequently which seriously threat the personal safety of personnel, the personnel crossing through the railway and the others on the railway running through.

Especially in railway construction workers on the job, the main works, electricity, train inspection, shunting, power supply, construction and other units of the workers. The main means of communication is by wire or wireless walkie talkie to inform each other, and this dozens years old notification method has been difficult to adapt to the speed and density after speed increase. The first is due to the long time interval operation notice made workers form the paralysis of thought in mind, that they can also do it in a few minutes; The second is the personnel who is responsible for informing that often forget the risk of accidents and notify the operating personnel factors, and even sometimes occurred the problems telephone channel and other reasons not to operating personnel; The third is the phone notice because of language expression, the field operation personnel can't hear the uplink, downlink and several road trips clearly; The forth is due to bad weather, such as line curve look bad, and lead to adult injury accident[1].

How to improve the safety index and reduce the incidence of accidents is the all cadres and workers are most concerned after the increased speed, it is also an important issue which needs to be solved. This paper discusses the issues and put forward the technical scheme of railway safety automatic protection system.

[a] fuhaij@hotmail.com

2 System structure

2.1 System features

This system is to provide protection alarm to the railway operation personnel ,requiring system has the high reliability and stability. This system has the following characteristics: independent of geographical location which can realize the full range alarm; independent of climate, which can be used normally in all weather conditions delay in short time, the alarm delay can be controlled to 3 seconds; support people voice alarm information can be used in or out the station[2].

2.2 System structure

The system consists of the ground signal acquisition terminal, I alarm terminal, II alarm terminal, alarm center server and monitoring terminal. The system architecture is shown in Figure 1.

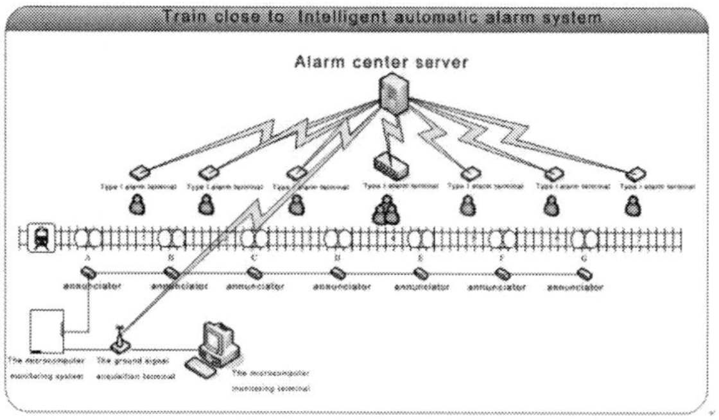

Figure 1. System architecture diagram

2.3 Introduction of the function of each part

The ground signal acquisition terminal is responsible for collecting the train signal and operation information to the alarm center server; I alarm terminal is applied to the construction personnel to wear which can automatically the coming track and be self checking to give abnormal alarm automatically. It can also get their own position by GPS, and sent its location to the alarm center server. The server can in voiced and light alarm after receiving the alarm, with voice calls and video transmission function; The function of II and I alarm terminal is similar, but the double GPS and double GPRS channel receiver is more suitable for the construction of the team alarm; alarm center server installed on the mobile room, according to the size, it can be worked in cluster which can track the I type and II type alarm position information of the terminal, converted to latitude, longitude and kilometer, communicate with the ground signal acquisition terminal, which can obtain the information of the train operation to analyze the alarm terminal which into the warning area and notify the alarm; computer monitoring terminal is responsible for monitoring the construction personnel on the railway station, monitoring the alarm notification information check, alarm history, and is responsible for notifying the attendant to a dangerous situation for manual alarm, which can be done by the computer control center.

3 System working principle

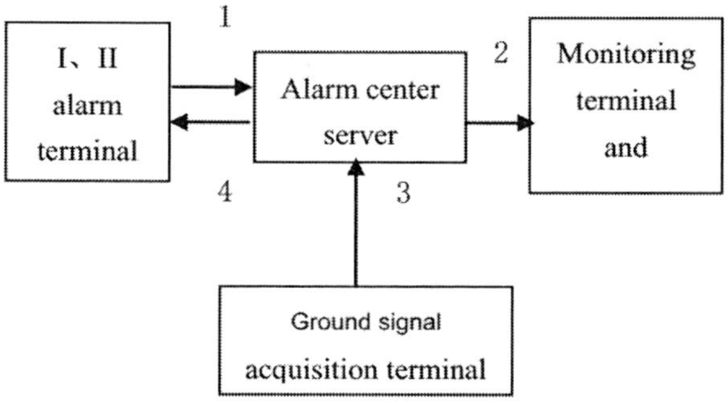

Figure 2. Schematic diagram

I, II type of alarm terminal real-time acquisition of their position, and sending alarm center server. The alarm center server notifies the distribution of operations personnel to monitoring terminal, when the ground signal acquisition terminal receives a train passing through the insulating section information, notifying the alarm center server the train location, speed, up and down. The alarm center server through calculation, obtained 1, 2, 3 level alarm device, and to alarm. The alarm center server received alarm equipment identification information, and sends the result to the PC monitoring terminal display.

3.1 Working principle of ground signal acquisition terminal

The terminal can communicate through RS232 interface and control center, and upload them to the central server. Meanwhile, the server receives the alarm notification.

As shown in Figure 3, the wireless module receives the alarm center server send alarm notification data through the asynchronous serial port UART is sent to the CPU terminal. The data checking and decrypting by sending a RS485/RS232 communication interface to the computer monitoring terminal. Signal information to the CPU for data encryption by sending a RS485/RS232 communication interface, while the formation of cyclic redundancy check code packaged with the CRC16 data, the formation of a data frame, and then by the asynchronous serial port UART is sent to the wireless module is transmitted to the alarm center server, complete the network data transmission.

Each terminal has a fixed address, which is to identify the word recognition of the terminal. The terminal in the data processing of the first is to detect whether the packet is a local address. If it is the local address for data processing, or drop the packet in order to ensure the accuracy of the data to the terminal; the data package will be packaged together to address the data.

3.2 Working principle of the alarm terminal

I alarm terminal for construction personnel to work independently of the train approaching alarm. The terminal start the GPS module to self-test when the power is supported. At the same time to prepare the ready alarm lights. After satellite synchronous open GPRS connection to the server and report the location and status. The server received confirmation is not ready for the lights, work lights (green) light, this time into the construction state. When the alarm terminal server received the alarm, it will according to the alarm level to open the corresponding level horn sound. At the same time the vibration motor vibration alarm, flashing lights. When receiving the alarm termination notice, stop all alarm. After receiving alarm notification, it's no more than 1 minute which stopped alarm automatically when overtime. Enhanced terminal with two-way voice and video transmission function.

II alarm terminal is used for train approaching alarm by construction personnel working. Compared to I type terminal, it reduces vibration alarm function which increase the speaker power and driving ability. In order to ensure the reliability of the system, the system adopts double parallel working mode.

3.3 The call function of railway safety automatic protection system

The call function of railway safety automatic protection system by using digital technology to achieve the functions of the traditional analog interphone, one click you can call. To solve the limited blind spot of traditional analog interphone communication distance, but also can solve the problem that the traditional telephone to dial 11 digits to wait several seconds or longer to call, if the other is a calling also do not know when to call, no matter how much you urgent things, you can only wait patiently.

The voice of railway safety automatic protection system call function has the following characteristics:

3.3.1 Emergency

The voice function of railway safety automatic protection system set up time is short (less than 500ms), to achieve a real push to talk. In the face of unexpected events, to group cooperative work which must be timely communication between groups to jointly cope with a sudden event in question. If there is a push to talk, not to the user level which will be unable to command the command into a group action and it will delay the time and result in significant loss. Emergency is the main voice characteristics of railway safety automatic protection system call function.

3.3.2 Group

The voice of railway safety automatic protection system call function not only to achieve a single call, more important can do group group call, group call, broadcast, and call the different professional groups of users, in order to achieve the group cooperative work.

3.3.3 Controllability

The voice of railway safety automatic protection system call function is the use of hierarchy, which is provided with a dispatch command center, which can monitor the user state within the system, it can adjust the user call according to the needs of the work to achieve reasonable

allocation of personnel and effective working state[3].

3.3.4 Special function

As the voice of railway safety automatic protection system call function is used in the hierarchical, network users are not equal, it has a strong, demolition, emergency alarm, and other functions, to ensure the effective work of the command center. The waiting, as long as the user initiates a call, temporarily not connected, it will no longer need to call the control center, according to the operation of the system, at any time to call back call tips, improve the professional network efficiency. The system of voice calls through dynamic reorganization of function, directing work mode (DMO) is an indispensable function of railway safety automatic protection system function.

4 Summary

The safety protection device by using the GPS to obtain the location information for the operating point location and the running position of the train through the CTC/TDCS system and computer monitoring system for operation, find out the distance. Achieving timely continuous prediction of train operating point of the distance from the voice alarm of a train approaching,. Realize the function of traditional analog interphone by using digital technology and eliminating the call quality problems existing in analog radios. Due to the adoption of the GSM-R, the mobile wireless transmission channel and terminal technology to overcome the analog radio communication distance limitations and there are many blind spots, and ultimately to achieve the design goals of practice, convenience, appliance and strong adaptability.

References

1. Jian zhen Liu, Science & Technology Ecnony Market，8(2010)
2. Han wu Sun， SWJTU，(2008)
3. Xiao he Li，BUPT，(2009)

MATEC Web of Conferences 44, 01062 (2016)
DOI: 10.1051/matecconf/20164401062

Audible Noise Measurement and Analysis of the Main Power Apparatus in UHV GIS Substations

Nian Guang Zhou[1], Qi Tang[2,a], Xiao Wen Wu[1] and Sheng Hu[1]

[1]*State Grid Hunan Electric Power Corporation, Electric Power Research Institute, 410007 Changsha, China*
[2]*Hunan Electric Experiment Research Institute, Environmental Protection Department, 410007 Changsha, China*

Abstract. Investigation of audible noise characteristics of the main power apparatus in UHV GIS substations provides essential statistics for the noise prediction and control. Noise pressure level, spectrum and attenuation characteristics of the main transformers and high voltage (HV) reactors are measured and analyzed in this paper. The result shows that the main transformer and HV reactor have identical A-weighted equivalent sound pressure level. The medium- and low-frequency noises are the primary components in the spectral. More attention should be paid to the low-frequency bands in the noise control process. The noise of cooling fan has a large influence on that of the main transformer. Without the consideration of corona noise, the average A-weighted sound pressure level shows an overall decreasing trend with the increase of the propagation distance. Obvious interference phenomenon of the noises at 100 and 200Hz exists in the noise propagation process.

1 Introduction

Audible noise has become the attention focus of the inhabitants around the substations. The research on the characteristic of UHV substation noise is particularly important and has practical significance in UHV power transmission project [1-3]. GIS equipment has numerous advantages, such as high reliability, less environmental impact and anti-electromagnetic interference. Besides, another significant advantage of GIS lies in that it has no audible corona noise, which reduces the noise emission level of substations [4].

The main noise of the UHV GIS substation comes from the transformer and HV reactor in operation. Compared with the conventional UHV substations, the noise characteristics of the GIS substation have some certain particularity. Hitherto, the noise characteristics of UHV substations are studied by some researchers [5]. However, few research reports are observed about the noise characteristics of UHV GIS substations.

In this paper, the audible noise characteristics of 1000 kV GIS substation in Anhui province of China has been investigated. The spectrum distribution and attenuation characteristics generated by transformers and reactors were analyzed in detail, which can provide reference to the acoustic environment impact prediction and assessment of different types of UHV substation.

2 Description of tests

The rated capacity of 1# transformer in the substation is 1000/1000/334 MVA with the size of transformer is 11 m*12 m*5.5 m and the cooling mode of oil-immersed forced oil circulation air cooling(OFAF). Each phase of the transformer has 8 sets of cooling fans. There is a 17 m long and 9 m high firewall between two adjacent transformers. The distance from the firewall to the transformer is 8.5m and 2.5m, respectively. In the test process, the active power of 1# transformer is -671.03 MW, meanwhile, the reactive power is 98.65 Mvar.

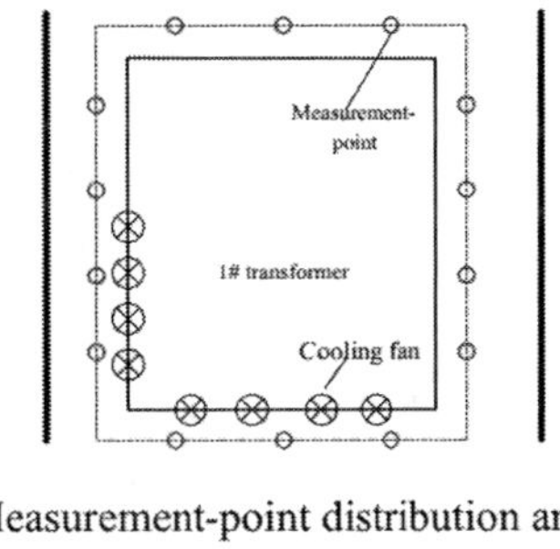

Figure 1. Measurement-point distribution around the transformer

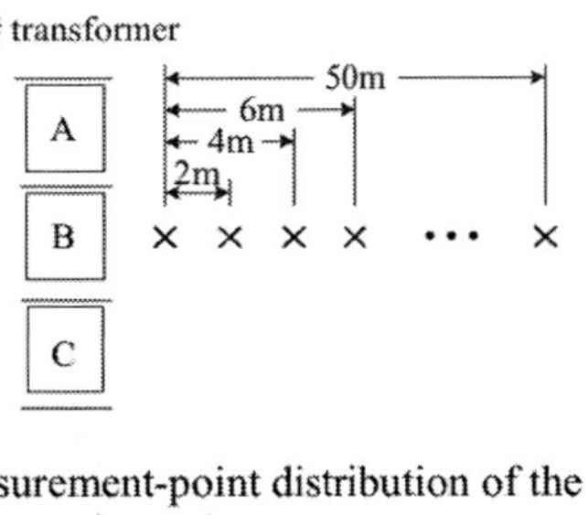

Figure 2. Measurement-point distribution of the transformer attenuation noise

[a] Corresponding author: tqi081@163.com

The measurement-point distribution around the transformer is shown in Figure 1. Figure 2 gives the measurement-point distribution of the transformer attenuation noise. The measurement section is located in the middle of the three phase transformers. The distance between the measurement points is 2m. Subjected to space constraints, 26 points are set in the measurement process.

Hu'An and Huai'Wu HV reactors are of the same type, of which the rated capacity is 240 000 kvar. The size of reactor is 12 m*10 m*5.5 m, and cooling mode adopts oil-immersed air cooling (ONAF). There is a 17 m long and 9 m high firewall between the two neighboring reactors. During the test, the active power of Hu'An line I is 1135.05 MW and the reactive power is 247.78 Mvar. Meanwhile, the active power of Huai'Wu line II is -1670.34 MW and the reactive power -27.15 Mvar. The measurement-point distribution of the reactors and the reactor attenuation noise are identical to that of the transformer, as shown in Figure 3 and Figure 4, respectively.

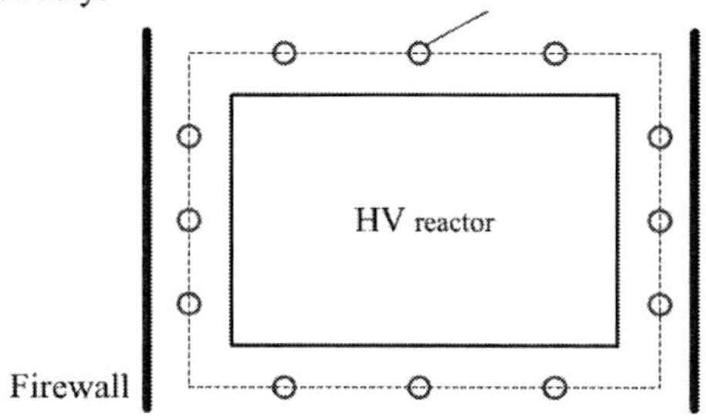

Figure 3. Measurement-point distribution around the reactor

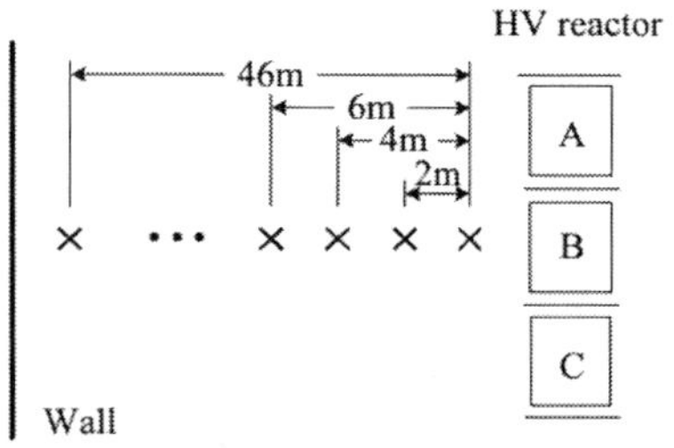

Figure 4. Measurement-point distribution of the reactor attenuation noise

3 Results and discussion

3.1 Transformer Noise

The test result of A-weighted equivalent sound pressure level (L_{Aeq}) around each phase transformer is shown in Table 1. Because no noise sources are in the northern open-space of the main transformer and the only single cooling fan is shut down when the measurement is conducted, the minimum L_{Aeq} of each transformer appears in the northern direction. The lowest sound pressure level of the three transformers is observed in A-phase, which is 67.2 dB (A).

On the south side, two sets of cooling fans are running in the noise test process. Compared with the northern side, it is found that the operation of cooling fans makes the main transformer noise increases over 3 dB (A). Highest noise level appears in the west side of the transformer, which is 3.2~6.3 dB (A) higher than that of the northern side. This is attributed to the reason that the west side of the transformer is only 2.5 m away from the firewall, and the reflection phenomenon of the wall makes the noise of the side further enhanced to a large degree. On the other hand, there are 4 sets of cooling fans in the west side, one of which in operation. As the noise level of transformer is much affected by that of the wind turbine. Thus, in order to improve the calculation accuracy while predicting the noise distribution of UHV substations, the cooling fan of main transformers should be treated as independent sound source. A large calculation error will be caused if only take the transformer as area noise source with equivalent sound pressure level distribution. Moreover, in order to reduce the noise emission level, the low-noise fan should be considered as much as possible in the equipment selection process before the substation is put into service.

Table 1. Test results of average L_{Aeq} around the main transformer

Phase	L_{Aeq}/dB(A)			
	East	South	West	North
A	73.3	73.4	73.5	67.2
B	72.8	73.9	74.3	71.0
C	70.6	72.1	72.9	69.7

The 1/3-OCT spectrum distribution of the main transformer noise is shown in Figure 5. The spectrum distribution shows that A-weighted sound pressure level (L_A) of the main transformer in the range of 100~1600 Hz is relatively high. The maximum L_A is in the 315Hz band, which belongs to the transformer body noise. The L_A decreases gradually as the frequency increases over 500 Hz. Influenced by the noise of cooling device, the middle- and high-frequency sound pressure level of the main transformer is relatively high.

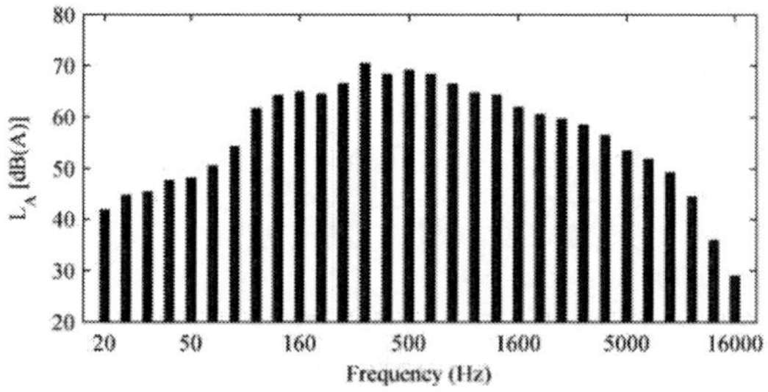

Figure 5. Spectrum distribution of the main transformer noise

The L_{Aeq} was detected according to measurement-points in Figure 2. The noise attenuation process of main transformer is shown in Figure 6. As the northern and southern side of the main transformer is relatively open, the sound pressure level is not affected by the corona noise generated on the power transmission structures

such as the transmission lines, fittings and insulators compared with traditional UHV substations. Therefore, the noise attenuation processes of principal frequency components show the trend of decreasing gradually with the increase of the transmission distance. However, due to the phase difference of the transformer noises, interference phenomenon is observed in the noise transmission process. The noise level goes up and down to a certain degree depending on the distance other than a monotonous decline [5]. Thus, in order to improve the accuracy of noise prediction, the phase of main power transformers needs to be considered in the substation noise simulation model.

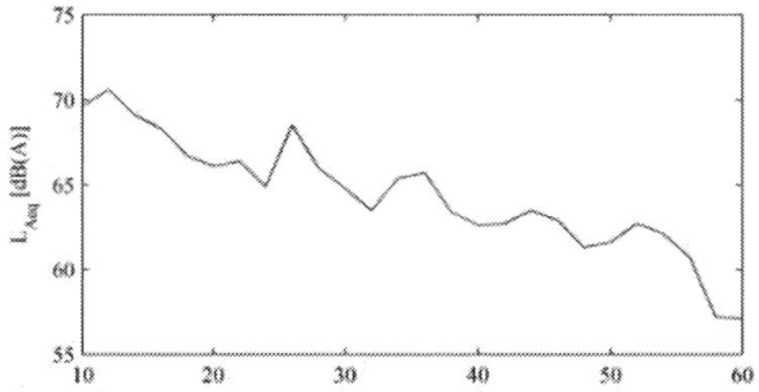

Figure 6. Noise attenuation process of the main transformer

The noise attenuation of the main transformer at various frequencies is shown in Figure 7. It is shown that in the noise propagation process, the fluctuations of the noise pressure level below 500 Hz are more obvious than that of 800 and 1000 Hz. The noise fluctuations of 100 and 200 Hz are most significant. The largest fluctuation appears at the location of 50 m away from the main transformer. The above analysis shows that in the frequency range of 1000 Hz the noise propagation distance of 100 and 200 Hz frequency band in UHV substations is much further and the interference is the most serious. Thus, more attention should be paid to the low-frequency noises while controlling the transformer noises.

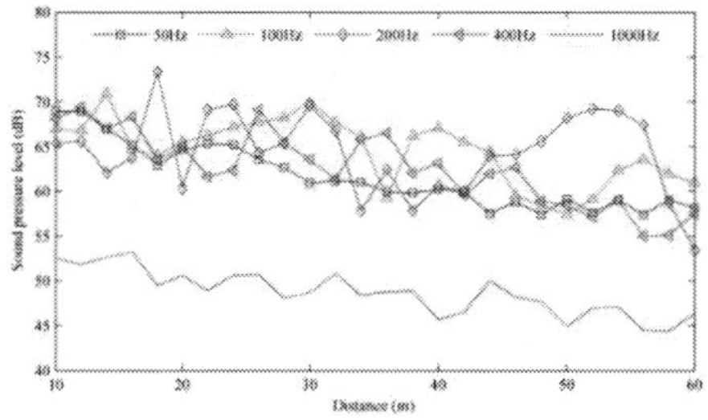

Figure 7. Noise attenuation of the main transformer at various frequencies

3.2 HV reactor noise

The result of L_{Aeq} around the reactor of Hu'An line I and Huai'Wu line II is given in Table 2 and Table 3, respectively. It can be seen that the noise of HV reactors in UHV substation and that of transformers is at the same level. Reflected by the firewall, the noise level of reactor near the firewall is much higher. In the two reactor groups, the highest L_{Aeq} (78.2 dB (A)) appears in the phase-C reactor of Huai'Wu line II, while the minimum L_{Aeq} (70.1 dB(A)) appeared in the phase-A reactor of Hu'An line I.

Table 2. Test results of average L_{Aeq} around the reactor of Hu'An line I

Phase	L_{Aeq}/dB(A)			
	East	South	West	North
A	74.2	70.3	72.6	70.1
B	73.4	72.9	73.8	75.8
C	75.3	72.1	74.3	73.0

Table 3. Test results of average L_{Aeq} around the reactor of Huai'Wu line II

Phase	L_{Aeq}/dB(A)			
	East	South	West	North
A	71.6	75.0	71.2	72.2
B	73.2	71.8	71.0	73.0
C	78.2	74.2	72.5	76.5

The spectrum distribution of the HV reactor noise is shown in Figure 8 and Figure 9, respectively. Different from the frequency distribution characteristics of UHV transformer noise, the high noise level of the reactor mainly concentrates in the 100Hz band, which is mainly caused by the expansion of core lamination and electromagnetic force of the winding. Therefore, the body noise should be considered in priority when controlling the HV reactor noise.

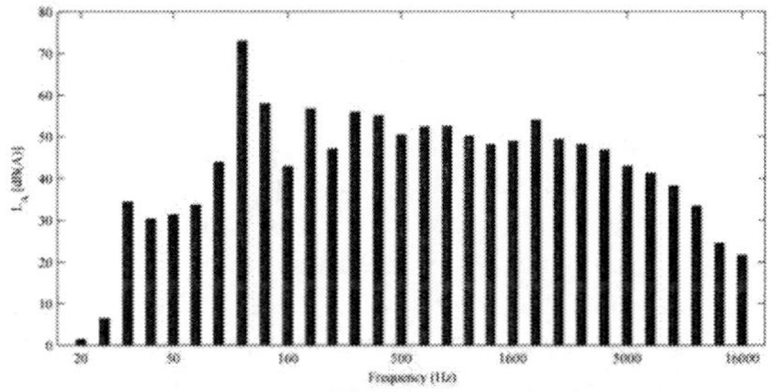

Figure 8. Spectrum distribution of the HV reactor (Hu'An line I)

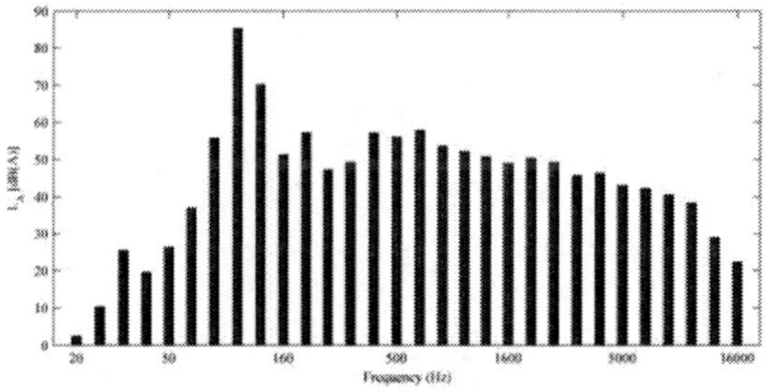

Figure 9. Spectrum distribution of the HV reactor (Huai'Wu line II)

The noise attenuation process of the two sets of HV reactors is shown in Figure 10. It can be seen that the noise attenuation process of the HV reactor is similar to the process of transformer. There is obvious interference in the propagation process of HV reactor noise [9]. Except that the sound pressure level near the wall increases due to reflection, the sound pressure level of

Hu'An line I within the range of 30 m shows a monotonically decreasing trend. Compared with the reactor of Hu'An line I, the noise fluctuation of Huai'Wu line II is more significant. The noise pressure level, which locates at 14 and 36 m away from the HV reactor, is close to that of the measurement-point near the HV reactor. The overall trend of sound pressure level within the scope of 50 m doesn't decrease gradually. The reason for this phenomenon may be that the west and south of Huai'Wu line II are surrounded by high wall, and the distance is pretty close. The distance between the reactor and the west wall is only 30.5 m. Owing to the reflection of the wall and the interference between acoustic waves, the noise on that side maintains a high level and the attenuation process is relatively slow.

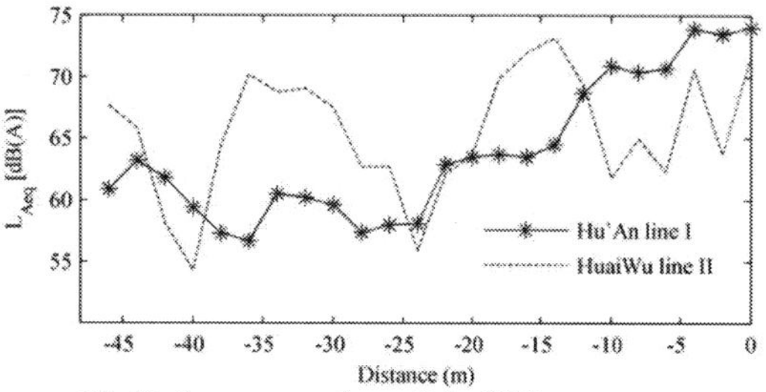

Figure 10. Noise attenuation of the HV reactors

In general, the location of HV reactors in UHV substation is near the wall. Because of the low frequency and the long propagation distance, the wall reflection and the interference between acoustic waves usually lead to the noise emission level in the region can't meet the specified value in the standards. Hence, in the planning and designing stage of UHV substations, the position of noise-sensitive point and the layout of HV reactor should be take into account.

The noise attenuation processes of HV reactors in different frequency band are shown in Figure 11 and Figure 12, respectively. It is shown that, the fluctuations of sound pressure levels at 100 and 200Hz is most obvious in the process of sound transmission. Moreover, the noise of 1000 Hz decreases with the increase of the propagation distance. It can be concluded that the noise attenuation process of HV reactors is similar to that of transformers, and the noise interference at 100 and 200Hz is most obvious. In order to realize accurate prediction of the sound field distribution of the reactor, phase information of each noise source needs consideration in the calculation.

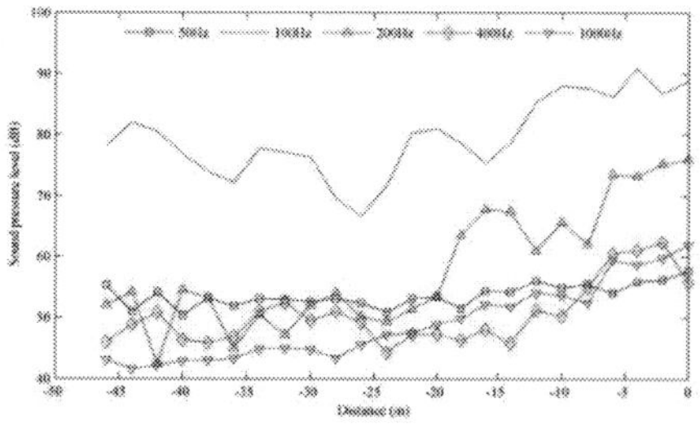

Figure 11. Noise attenuation of the HV reactor at various frequencies (Hu'An line I)

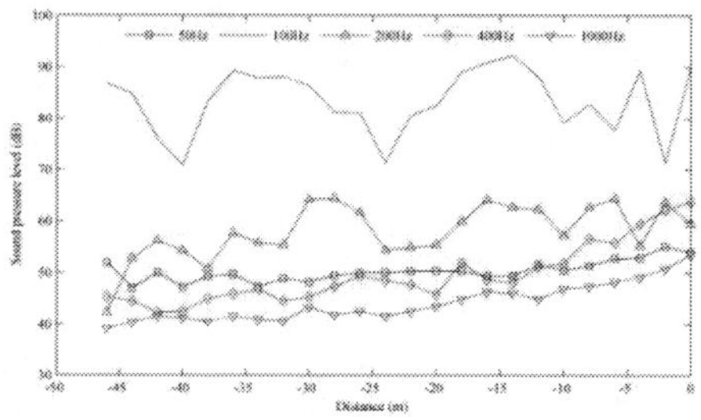

Figure 12. Noise attenuation of the HV reactor at various frequencies (Huai'Wu line II)

4 Conclusions

In this paper, the noise pressure level, spectrum and attenuation characteristics of Wuhu UHV GIS substation are measured and analyzed. The following conclusions can be drawn:

(a) The noise of the main transformers and HV reactors in UHV GIS substations are mainly in middle- and low-frequency. However, the noise level of the HV reactor is relatively higher than that of main transformer. The cooling fan has a large effect on the noise of main transformer.

(b) Since the noise source of the UHV GIS substation does not include the corona noise generated on the power transmission structures, the average L_{Aeq} shows an overall decreasing trend with the increase of the propagation distance.

(c) Interference phenomenon exists in the noise propagation process of the main transformers and HV reactors, and the interference of 100 and 200Hz is most obvious. Layout optimization of the HV reactors could reduce the noise emission level at the substation boundary.

References

1. Y. Chen, H. Xie and Y. Zhang. High Voltage Engineering, **38**, 2189-2194 (2012)
2. G. Di, X. Zhou and X. Chen. Applied Acoustics, **91**, 40-46 (2015)
3. J. Zhou, L. Li and Y. Du. Electric Power, **42**, 75-78 (2009)
4. R. Nagarsheth, S. Singh. International Journal of Electrical Power & Energy Systems, **55**, 481-485 (2014)
5. B. Zhou, C. Pei and Y. Ni. High Voltage Engineering, Vol. **39**, 1447-1453 (2013)
6. H. Ma, J. He and Q. Chen. High Voltage Engineering, **34**, 1599-1604 (2008)
7. J. Mo, X. Zhang and J. Yuan. Advanced Technology of Electrical Engineering and Energy, **34**, 76-80 (2015)
8. Y. Yu, B. Chen. Transformer, **44**, 23-44 (2007)
9. Y. Ni, B.Zhou and C.Pei. High Voltage Engineering, **40**, 3926-3932 (2014)

MATEC Web of Conferences **44**, 01063 (2016)
DOI: 10.1051/matecconf/20164401063

Performance Analysis of SIFT Feature Extraction Algorithm in Application to Registration of SAR Image

Yan Li SUN, Jie WANG
Department of basic experiment, Naval Aeronautical and Astronautical University, Yantai264000,China

Abstract. Exactly extracting the stable feature of high resolution SAR image as well as matching it are two critical steps for the Antomatic regiestation systems. It is suggested that the Scale Invariant Feature Transform (SIFT) algorithm can be applied in the optical image registration systems and four representative experiments were performed to test its validity. It is found that SIFT can accurately register the high resolution SAR images than the traditional Harris in applicability and precision.

Keywords: SAR Imagery, SIFT, Harris, Automatic Registration.

1. Introduction

Image registration [1,2] is the process of aligned two or more images in space from different time, different perspectives and different sensors, and it is a key step of multi-source image fusion or change detection. It can be divided into semi-automatic and automatic image registration according to people's participation. Semi-automatic registration extract feature based on human-computer interaction, and then match the feature, transformation and re-sampling using the computer. Automatic registration accomplishes registration by computer directly without consumer's participation.

Automatic registration of SAR image especially High-resolution SAR image has not been well solved for a long time, sub-pixel registration accuracy is often required to achieve in practical applications. It put forward higher requirements to feature extraction and feature matching algorithm. The method Based on regional correlation applies more in optical remote sensing image registration. However, it is difficult to apply in the high-resolution SAR images, because it is more sensitive to image gray, rotation and objectives' increase or decrease, and its high complexity computation of using all points of regional information. The key of another registration method based feature is to establish the key points, lines or other geometric corresponding relationship. As the SAR image of special imaging modalities and imaging mechanism, in particular a large number of speckle noise, some feature extraction algorithm take good performance in optical image registration but failed in SAR image. Some more robust feature extraction algorithm need to be introduced.

This article discusses the application of SIFT feature extraction algorithm in high resolution SAR image registration. SIFT algorithm is aimed to the SAR image's in four representative designed experiments. It is compared with traditional Harris corner point in running time, the correct rate of the matching and the accuracy of the key points . According to qualitative and quantitative analysis, SIFT can accurately register the high resolution SAR images were acquired in the same ascending orbit, and it is better than

Harris in applicability and precision, and analysis limitations of the two algorithms.

2. Registration of SAR Image based on feature matching

First extract feature point by feature extraction operators in the reference image and the registration image, and then match the feature point using a similarity measure, at last use two-way relevance method and the RANSAC to remove external point to improve the registration accuracy. As shown in Fig. 1.

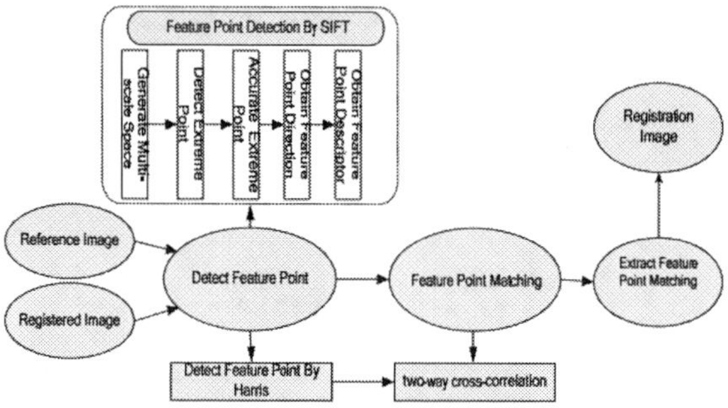

Figure 1. Flow chart of SAR Image Registration based on feature matching

2.1 Image registration based on Harris

Harris operator is Proposed by C.Harris[6] that based on extraction operator of signal point feature. Even if there is image rotation, gray change, noise and viewpoint change and so on in the optical image, Harris is also the most stable operator of point feature extraction operator. Fu Kun[7]register SAR image by hand first then by Harris operator and at last using small panel to make registration accuracy better than 1 pixel.

This operator inspirited by the autocorrelation function of the signal processing ,given the matrix M associated with the autocorrelation function. Eigen values of matrix M is first-order curvature of the autocorrelation function, the point is the feature points if the two curvature values are high. The operator expression of Harris:

$$R = \det(M) - ktr^2(M)$$

$$M(x,y) = \begin{bmatrix} I_u^2(x,y) & I_{uv}(x,y) \\ I_{uv}(x,y) & I_v^2(x,y) \end{bmatrix}$$

where $I_u(x,y)$ and $Iv(x,y)$ are the partial derivative of the pixel gray value of point (x, y) in the direction of u and v, $Ivu(x,y)$ is mixed partial derivative of second order; det is the determinant of matrix, tr is the trace of matrix, k is determined by experience, usually take 0.04 .If R exceeds a certain threshold, the point is considered the corner point. Realize matching by normalized cross correlation of the center intensity of the local image after the extraction of same feature point.

2.2 The registration based on SIFT

SIFT is a algorithm that can extract local feature, the core idea is to find extreme points in scale space, extract invariant when location, scale, rotation, illumination changed. The algorithm is proposed by David Lowe [3] [4] in 1999 and to be completed in 2004. The algorithm is robust with scale, rotation, brightness, affine, and so is invariant noise, increase or decrease in the target and blocks. Mikolajczyk [5] do experiment and compare the performance with most representative descriptors (10 descriptors such as SIFT, matrix invariants, cross correlation and so on) under different scenes. The results show that, the performance of SIFT descriptor is best. SIFT method includes three steps: detection of extreme point in scale space, the formation of feature point descriptor and feature point matching.

2.2.1 Detection Extreme point in scale space

SIFT algorithm usually form a pyramid by down-sampling the original image, build filter images group by each image convolute with Gaussian kernel convolution of different scales. To detect the stability of the feature points, minus each layer image of each group is required to form a difference of Gaussian scale space (DOG). Each pixel compared with the adjacent eight pixels of the same scale and around the scale 9 × 2 pixels surrounding neighborhood to ensure that local extremum can be detected in the scale of space and two-dimensional image space. Sub-pixel level positioning with quadratic functions, while removing some of the edge point of instability.

2.2.2 The formation of feature points descriptor

Determine the main direction of feature points through the gradient direction distribution characteristic of neighborhood pixel, the 16*16 window of the center of feature points is divided into 4 * 4 sub-windows, each sub-window calculate gradient direction histogram of 8 directions by Gaussian-weighted, form the 4 * 4 * 8vector that is the feature point descriptor.

2.2.3 Feature points matching

Take a feature point of reference image, find out the feature points in the registration image that Euclidean distance between them is smallest and second smallest. If the value that divide the nearest distance by second nearest distance is less than a certain threshold that is the right match. In order to ensure the accuracy of matching points, two-way matching is used.

2.3 Purifying matching point by RANSAC

Although the right rate of matching point is high by using two-way nearest neighbor method in SIFT algorithm, but then the mismatch is inevitable. The basic idea of RANSAC algorithm is: select two points randomly, determine a straight line by two points, the points within a certain distance in this line called the interior point, the rest called external point. Select repeat times randomly, the straight line with the most interior points is recognized as a sample point set and to exclude external point.

2.4 Construction of polynomial realize the registration

Model parameters of spatial transformation can be get by extracting feature points using polynomial equation of least squares:

$$Xc = a0 + a1xr + a2yr + a3xryr + a4x2r + a5y2r$$

$$Yc = b0 + b1xr + b2yr + b3xryr + b4x2r + b5y2r \quad (1)$$

The coordinate of registration points is expressed as(Xc; Yc), and the coordinate of reference points is expressed as(Xc; Yc). Images will be transformed in space and registered using equation (1).

3. Experiment and Analysis

In order to analysis and compare application performance of two feature extraction operators comprehensive, we selected four pairs of typical SAR images, The first major is the change in brightness and rotation angle and a small number of target changes (Figure 2).The second not only brightness changes greatly、 screen on different directions but also a large number of targets changes (Figure 3).the main difference of the third is resolution (Figure 4). The fourth pair is obtained by exactly the opposite direction of flight (Figure 5).

The accuracy and time of SIFT and Harris extract feature points is shown in Table Ⅰ. Precision of feature points in the first pair SAR images that detected by two method is compared particularly in Table Ⅱ. It can be seen, the scope of classic Harris corner detection algorithm is very narrow in SAR images, and time-consuming is long.

In the first pair images Harris can extract enough feature points, but usually use maximum mutual correlation as similarity measure to find matching points, and it is sensitive with the rotation angle, resulting many errors in matching point pairs. Complete the registration after using RANSAC to remove error matching point pairs but the average accuracy only reached 2.12 pixels. The SIFT not only can extract enough feature points but also its' correct matching rate can reach 100% by the method of two-way the largest neighboring matching (Figure 6). Accuracy can reach 0.52 pixels on average after the image registration. In the second pair images, only a small amount of feature point is extracted by SIFT because of big perspective (Figure 3), However, registration accuracy can still achieve sub-pixel, the average deviation in horizontal direction is 0.928 pixels, in vertical direction is 0.7 pixels. But Harris can not extract the correct feature points that can be used to match, particularly in the target changed area, so indicates that SIFT is stable with the increase or reduction of the target. In the third pair Harris can not extract the correct feature points because it is not invariant on the scale changed. But SIFT not only extract a large number of feature points but also

matching feature points absolutely right (Figure 4),so confirms its scale invariant.

There is difference between SAR image and ordinary optical image. There will be a completely different texture features of SAR image obtained by entirely different angle, so can not get satisfactory results using SIFT. In the fourth pair of images, SIFT also fails to extract sufficient amount of correct registration points (Figure 5), this indicates that the SIFT is not robust on the flight in the opposite direction or big change in perspective.

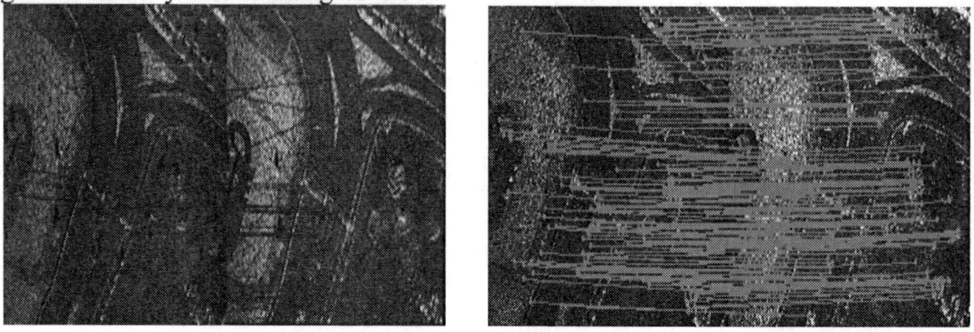

Figure 2. Matching points on the first image by Harris and SIFT (Image size is 2510*1638)

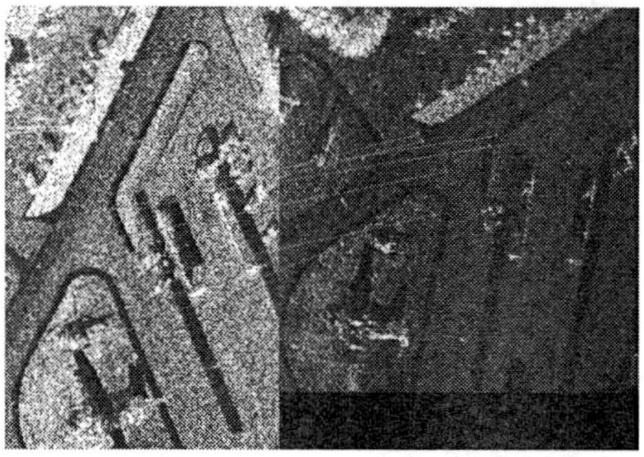

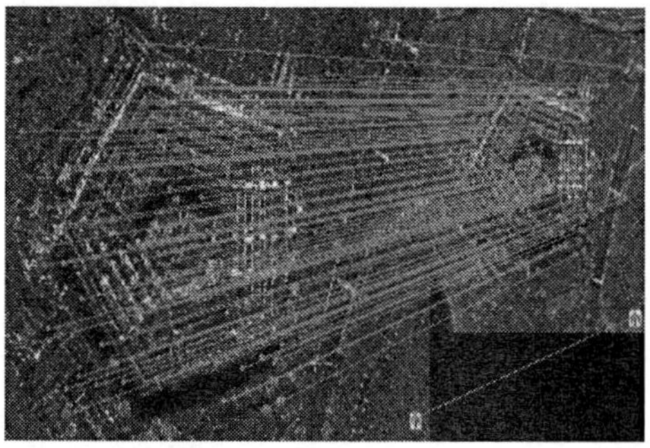

Figure 3. Matching points on second image by SIFT (750*1150 1000*1000) **Figure4.**Matching points on third image by SIFT (1200*800 600*600)

Figure 5. Matching points on the fourth image by SIFT (Image size is 2510*1638)

TABLE 1. Compared SIFT algorithm with the Harris

Image	SIFT			Harris		
	Matching Points	Accuracy Rate	Time	Matching Points	Accuracy Rate	Time
1	150pairs	100%	50.328s	32 pairs	53.1%	629.71s
2	7 pairs	100%	10.207s	0 pair	0%	935.12s
3	63 pairs	100%	8.251s	34 pairs	0%	516.72s
4	17 pairs	17.6%	53.178s	0 pair	0%	985.62s

TABLE 2. the accuracy of feature point extraction compared SIFT with Harris in the first pair of SAR images

Algorithm	NO.	Coordinate Of Reference Image	Registration value	True value	Horizontal Vertical Deviation
SIFT	1	(1922.6,924)	(1926,886.19)	(1925.8,885.04)	(-0.2,-1.15)
	2	(769.32,1534.3)	(840.68,1579.3)	(840.4,1579.4)	(-0.28,0.1)
	3	(1652,1056.2)	(1671,1035.4)	(1670.6,1036.9)	(-0.4,0.1)
	4	(2152.4,1453.2)	(2208,1396.8)	(2208.6,1396.3)	(0.6,-0.5)
	5	(1198.5,1030.6)	(1216.8,1043.1)	(1216.7,1044.9)	(-0.1,1.8)
Harris	1	(2118.7,1459.9)	(2176.7,2208)	(2179.2,2211.1)	(2.5,3.1)
	2	(2152.4,1453.2)	(1402.5,1396.8)	(1403.8,1394.2)	(1.3,-2.6)
	3	(881.91,938.09)	(893.67,975.6)	(895.6,973.1)	(1.93,-2.5)
	4	(1633.4,1210.6)	(1665.8,1402.5)	(1666.2,1401.2)	(0.4,-1.3)
	5	(1140.3,970.14)	(1155.7,991.04)	(1152.6,993.5)	(-3.1,2.46)

4. Conclusion

In this paper, the SIFT algorithm is proposed and compared with Harris in high resolution SAR image registration. The result of experiments shows that SIFT can accurately register the high resolution SAR images that acquired in the same ascending orbit with different translation、rotation、scaling、brightness、the increase or reduction of the targets and view angle changes. The precision of registration can reach sub-pixel. The Harris can not extract the correct feature points in scaling or perspective changing image, and is also sensitive to increase or reduction of the targets. Thus SIFT is better than Harris in applicability and precision. SIFT can not extract invariant feature in SAR images that acquired in the different ascending orbit. How to solve this type of image registration issues will be the focus of future research.

References

[1] L G Brown. A survey of image registration techniques[J]. ACM Computing Surveys (S0360-0300),1992,24(4):326-376.

[2] B Zitová, J Flusser. Image registration methods: a survey [J].Image and Vision Computing(S0262-8856),2003,21(11):977-1000.

[3] Lowe D G. Object recognition from local scale-invariant features[A].International Conference on Computer Vision[C], Cor-fu, Greece, Sep 1999: 1150~1157.

[4] Lowe D G. Distinctive image features from scale-invariant key-points[J].International Journal of Computer V ision,2004,60(2): 91~110.

[5] Mikolajczyk K, Schmid C. A Performance Evaluation of Local Descriptors[J].IEEE Trans. Pattern Analysis and Machine Intelligence,2005,27(10): 1615—1630.

[6] HarrisC G, StephensM J. A Combined Corner and EdgeDetector[A]. Proceedings Fourth Alvey Vision Conference[C].Manches-ter, 1988

[7] Kun Fu,Hongjian You.Precise research about matching technology of multi-temporal spaceborne SAR images[J]. Remote Sensing Technology and Application,2007,10(5):37-05

MATEC Web of Conferences 44, 01064 (2016)
DOI: 10.1051/matecconf/20164401064

Estimation of Source Number for Single-Channel Received Signal

Zhen Zuo[1], Jun Peng Hu[1,a], Zhi Ping Huang[1] and Yi Meng Zhang[1]

[1]College of Mechatronics and Automation, National University of Defense Technology, Changsha, Hunan Province, China.

Abstract. A single-channel source number estimation method is presented. The single-channel received signal is firstly decomposed into several intrinsic-mode functions (IMFs) by empirical mode decomposition (EMD). Then the information theoretic criteria (ITC) based methods, MDL and AIC, are introduced to realize the source number estimation. And the diagonal loading technique is used to smooth the fluctuation of the eigenvalues. Compare with the previous works, the proposed method can effectively improve the source number detection performance.

1 Introduction

Blind source separation (BSS) has aroused a large number of researchers interest in it during the resent years because of its wide range of application. Accurate estimation of the source number is a vital issue for BSS. In the array signal process, the source number estimation has been well learned and a plethora of algorithms have been proposed [1-9].

Restricted by the cost and the limited fix space, only one receiver can be installed in some situation. The BSS problem is reduced to a single-channel blind source separation (SCBSS) problem[10]. In such cases, the conventional source separation methods can not be used directly. Many approaches have been introduced to realize the SCBSS[11, 12]. But most of them are built upon the precondition that the number of source has been known already. Without the precise estimation of the source number, the performance of the BSS or SCBSS algorithms will be severely impacted.

Various methods have been proposed to solve the source number estimation, such as the methods based on hypothesis testing [7, 9], information theoretic criteria (ITC) based approaches[1-3] and Gerschgorin's disk estimation (GDE) method[6]. The ITC based approaches are represented by Akaike Information Theory (AIC)[1] and minimum description length (MDL)[2, 3] criteria. The MDL estimator is known to be a consistent estimator[13], whereas the AIC principle is not consistent and in most cases overestimates the number of signals[14]. The ITC based methods are in essence estimating the source number by the differences of eigenvalues between the signal and the noise. They can not be used for the single-channel signal directly.

Transforming the single-channel signal to multi-channel form is a feasible way. The empirical mode decomposition (EMD) has recently gained reputation as a method for analyzing non-linear and nonstationary time series data[15]. The EMD is a signal-analysis tool that is able to decompose any time series into a set of spectrally independent oscillatory modes, called intrinsic-mode functions (IMFs)[16]. Accordingly, the EMD tool can be used to transform the single-channel signal to multi-channel.

The purpose of this paper is to solve the sources number estimation under single-channel signal condition. The EMD technique is firstly used to decompose the single-channel data into multi-channel form. And the ITC based methods, MDL and AIC, are used to estimate the source number. Then the diagonal loading technique is introduced to reduce the fluctuation of eigenvalues caused by noise.

The rest of this paper is organized as follows. Section 2 presents the single-channel received signal model. And the review of the EMD decomposition is introduced in section 3. Section 4 describes the source number estimation algorithm and the improvement realized by this paper. The experiment results show performance of the proposed algorithm in section 5, followed with the conclusions in section6.

2. Signal Model

For the single-channel received signal, only one data can be observed at every time point. The signal model can be described as follow.

$$X(t) = AS(t) + N(t) \tag{1}$$

Where $X(t) = [x(1), x(2), ..., x(m)]$ represents the observed data and t indicates the observation time. $\mathbf{A} = [a_1, a_2, ..., a_m]$ is the mixing matrix. $S(t) = [s_1(t), s_2(t), ..., s_m(t)]^T$ is a source signal matrix. Noise and signal are independent. The parameter estimation of single-channel signal is an underdetermined

[a] Corresponding author: hujunpeng332@163.com

problem. It is difficult to process the single-channel signal directly.

3. EMD Decomposition

EMD is a signal processing tool for decomposing signal into oscillating components by empirically identifying the physical time scales intrinsic to the data[15]. The EMD decomposes the mixture signal into a collection of IMFs[17].

$$y(t) = \sum_{n=1}^{N} c_n(t) + r_N(t) \quad (2)$$

$c_n(t)$ is the nth IMF and N is the total number of IMFs. $r_N(t)$ is the final residue. The IMFs satisfy two fundamental conditions[15]: firstly, in the whole dataset, the number of extrema (minima and maxima) and the number of zero crossing must be same or differ at most by one. Second, the mean value of envelop defined by the local minima is always zero.

4. Source Number Estimation Method

Assuming that the noise and the source signals are mutually independent and $X(t)$ represents the multi-dimension recording data, the covariance matrix of the observed signal can be expressed as

$$R_X = E\left\{X(t)X^T(t)\right\} = AR_S A^T + \sigma^2 I \quad (3)$$

Where $R_S = E\left\{S(t)S^T(t)\right\}$ is the signal covariance matrix. $\sigma^2 I$ represents the covariance matrix contains the noise signal. Transform R_X by eigenvalue decomposition (EVD).

$$R_X = \sum_{i=1}^{p} \lambda_i u_i u_i^H \quad (4)$$

$\lambda_i, i = 1,..., p$ are the eigenvalues of R_X in descending order, $\lambda_1 > \cdots > \lambda_q > \lambda_{q+1} = \cdots \lambda_p = \sigma_n^2$. $u_i, i = 1,..., p$ stand for the corresponding eigenvectors.

Since the noise and signal are independent, it can be deduced that $\lambda_1 = \mu_1 + \sigma^2$, $\lambda_2 = \mu_2 + \sigma^2$,..., $\lambda_n = \mu_n + \sigma^2$, $\lambda_{n+1} = \lambda_{n+2} = \cdots = \lambda_m = \sigma^2$. Under normal circumstances, the signal eigenvalues are far greater than the noise one. Setting an appropriate threshold, the source number is equal to the amount of the eigenvalues which are bigger than threshold.

In real application, due to the limited number of snapshots, eigenvalues of noise and signal are difficult to distinguish. It is impossible to directly determine the number of sources according to the size of the eigenvalues. Some criteria need to be taken to further estimate the number of sources. The ITC has been proved to be useful mean to solve the source number estimation problem. There are two parts in the ITC. The first part is the likelihood function representing the information gained from the recording data which are dependent on the assumed number of sources. The second part is the penalty term, a function of the number of snapshots[18].

AIC is a ITC method for model order selection, introduced by Akaike[1]. MDL is used to select the model based on the concept of the shortest code length, proposed by Rissanen[3, 19]. AIC and MDL estimation function can be show as follow.

$$AIC = -2\log f(\mathbf{X}|\hat{\boldsymbol{\theta}}) + 2k \quad (5)$$

$$MDL = -\log f(\mathbf{X}|\hat{\boldsymbol{\theta}}) + \frac{1}{2} k \log N \quad (6)$$

$\hat{\boldsymbol{\Theta}}$ represents the maximum likelihood estimation of the parameters $\boldsymbol{\Theta}$. k is freedom degrees of the parameter vector $\boldsymbol{\Theta}$. N is the number of samples and $f(\mathbf{X}|\hat{\boldsymbol{\theta}})$ indicates the joint probability density of X . The first term of the right end in Equation (9) and (10) denote model parameter estimation function. The second term represents the penalty function. When AIC and MDL are applied as source number estimate criteria, the model is expressed as follows[4]

$$AIC(k) = -2N(M-k)\log f(k) + 2k(2M-k) \quad (7)$$

$$MDL(k) = -N(M-k)\log f(k) + \frac{1}{2} k(2M-k)\log N \quad (8)$$

Where

$$f(k) = \left(\prod_{i=k+1}^{M} \lambda_i\right)^{\frac{1}{M-k}} \left(\frac{1}{M-k} \sum_{i=k+1}^{M} \lambda_i\right) \quad (9)$$

And the number of source can be yielded by minimizing the corresponding criterion of AIC and MDL.

$$\hat{q}_{AIC} = \arg\min_k AIC(k) \quad (10)$$

$$\hat{q}_{MDL} = \arg\min_k MDL(k) \quad (11)$$

The AIC and MDL criteria get the sources number via the eigenvalues of data covariance matrix R_X . Owing to its properties of simplicity and consistency, the MDL estimator has become the standard tool for estimating the number of sources[20]. However, on account of the impact of noise and limited snapshots of received data, the eigenvalues of R_X are fluctuant. This will affect the estimation performance. To reduce the impact of the noise, a diagonal loading technique is proposed to modify the eigenvalues of the data covariance matrix [21-23].

$$\mu_i = \lambda_i + \lambda_{DL}, i = 1,2,..., p \quad (12)$$

$\lambda_i, i = 1,2,..., p$ are the eigenvalues of R_X , and λ_{DL} is the loading value. μ_i are the final eigenvalues with diagonal loading. Diagonal loading produces little affect to the bigger eigenvalues corresponding to source signals. And the smaller eigenvalues corresponding to the noise will convergence near the loading value λ_{DL} . Therefore, by diagonal loading technique, the noise eigenvalues are approximately equal and the noise is smoothed.

The selection of loading value λ_{DL} makes a great impact to this method. It can be inferred that a small value of λ_{DL} play little improvement to the estimation, and an oversize λ_{DL} may bring effect to the signal eigenvalues and destroy the difference of eigenvalues between noise and signal. Remarkable improvement of the diagonal loading technique needs an appropriate selection of λ_{DL} .

The loading value λ_{DL} should satisfy the follow equations.

$$\lambda_N \ll \lambda_{DL} \ll \lambda_S \tag{13}$$

Where λ_N relates to the noise eigenvalue, and λ_S relates to the signal eigenvalue. To meet this condition, a feasible selection of λ_{DL} is described as[21]

$$\lambda_{DL} = \sqrt{\sum_{i=1}^{p} \lambda_i} \tag{14}$$

Then the eigenvalues of R_X are transformed to follow by diagonal loading.

$$\mu_i = \lambda_i + \sqrt{\sum_{i=1}^{p} \lambda_i}, i = 1, 2, ..., p \tag{15}$$

Then λ_i in equation (9) are replaced with μ_i in equation (15).

5. Experiments

Consider the single-channel recording signals which are collected from a single sensor. The received data contains three source signals with different frequencies and initial phase. The source signals can be expressed in the form as follow.

$$\begin{cases} s_1(t) = \cos(2\pi f_1 t + \theta_1) \\ s_2(t) = \cos(2\pi f_2 t + \theta_2) \\ s_3(t) = \cos(2\pi f_1 t + \theta_1)\cos(2\pi f_2 t + \theta_2)) \end{cases} \tag{16}$$

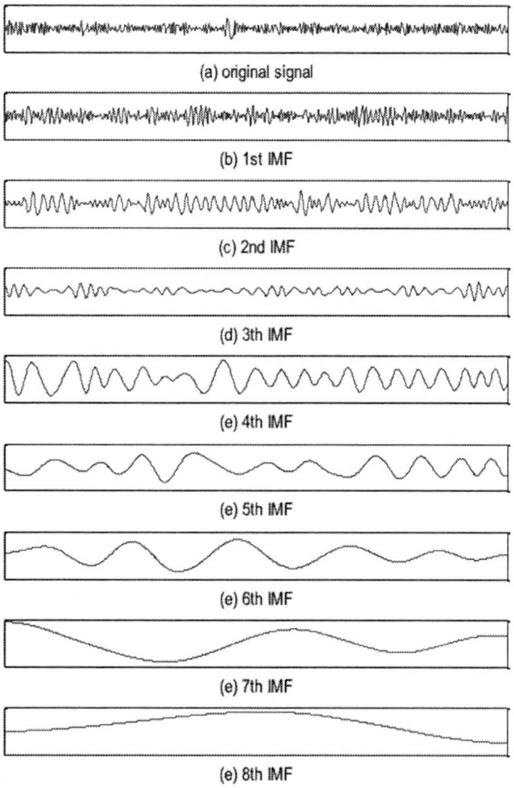

Figure 1. The single-channel signal and its IMFs component

The mixed signal is acquired by a single sensor and converted to discrete form with snapshots $L = 1000$. Noise is added to the signal, making SNR increase from -10 dB to 60dB. Then the mixed signal is analyzed by EMD decomposition as discussed in section 3. The decomposed and original signals are shown in Fig 1.

It can be implied that a single-channel received signal has been transformed to multi-dimension form by EMD, that is $X = [y(n); c_1(n); c_2(n); ...; c_N(n); r_N(n)]$. $y(n)$ is the original signal. $c_1(n), c_2(n), ..., c_N(n)$ are the IMFs with total number of N and $r_N(n)$ is the final residue signal. Then the covariance matrix R_X can be calculated as follow.

$$R_X = XX^H \tag{17}$$

The sources number of the received signal is estimated by AIC and MDL criteria based on the eigenvalues of R_X . Fig 2 describes the estimation performance of the method with and without diagonal loading. Due to the fluctuation of the eigenvalues caused by the added noise, the method without diagonal loading can no longer estimate the source number correctly. By diagonal loading technique, the AIC and MDL estimators obtain a good estimation performance.

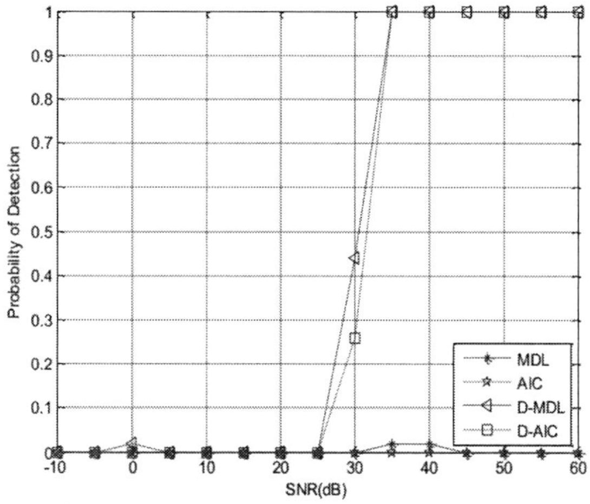

Figure 2. estimation performance comparing of MDL and AIC method and the method improved by diagonal loading technique

6. Conclusion

Accurately estimating of the sources number is essential for the blind source separation (BSS). Many algorithms have been proposed to estimate the sources number with multi-channel received signal, but not applicable for the single-channel recording data.

This paper has proposed a source number estimation method based on empirical mode decomposition (EMD), dealing with the single-channel received signal. The single-channel recording data is firstly decomposed into many intrinsic mode functions (IMFs) by EMD. The ITC based methods, AIC and MDL, are used to calculate the

source number, which obtain well performance at high SNR. The diagonal loading technique is introduced to smooth the fluctuation of the eigenvalues to reduce the effect of noise. After computing the mix matrix, this paper proposed an improved method which calculates the source number by the inner product of the eigenvectors and the mix matrix, instead of eigenvalues. The experiments results show that the improved method gets a better performance than the conventional method at low SNR.

References

1 H. Akaike. *IEEE Trans on Automatic Control*, **19**:716-723 (1974).
2 G. Schwartz. *The Annals of Statistics*, **6**:461-464 (1978).
3 Rissanen J. *Automatica*, **14**:465-471 (1978).
4 Wax M., Kailath T. *IEEE TRANS Acoustic, Speech, and Signal Process*, **ASSP-33**:387-392 (1985).
5 Wax M, Ziskind I. *IEEE Trans on Acoustics Speech Signal Processing*, **37**:1190-1196 (1989).
6 Wu H T, Yang J F, Chen F K. *IEEE Trans on Acoustics Speech Signal Processing*, **4**:261-264 (1994).
7 R.F. Brcich, A.M. Zoubir, P. Pelin. *IEEE Trans Signal Process*, **50**:20-215 (2002).
8 Gu J.-F., P.Wei, Tai H.-M. *IET Signal Process*, **1**:2-8 (2007).
9 Xiao Manlin, Wei Ping, Tai Heng-Ming. *journal of communications and networks*, **14** (2012).
10 Wang Dong, Tse Peter W. *Journal of Sound and Vibration*:4956-4970 (2012).
11 QuanWei CAI, Ping WEI, XianCi XIAO. *SCIENCE CHINA*, **53**:147-157 (2010).
12 Tengtrairat N., Gao Bin, Woo W. L., Dlay S. S. *IEEE TRANSACTIONS ON NEURAL NETWORKS AND LEARNING SYSTEMS*, **24**:1722-1735 (2013).
13 Fishler Eran, Poor H. Vincent. *IEEE TRANSACTIONS ON SIGNAL PROCESSING*, **53**:3543-3553 (2005).
14 Valaee S., Kabal P. *Ieee Transactions on Signal Processing*, **52**:1171-1178 (2004).
15 Gao Bin, Woo W. L., Dlay S. S. *IEEE TRANSACTIONS ON AUDIO, SPEECH, AND LANGUAGE PROCESSING*, **19**:961-976 (2011).
16 Mijovic Bogdan, Vos Maarten De, Gligorijevic Ivan, Taelman Joachim, Huffel Sabine Van. *IEEE TRANSACTIONS ON BIOMEDICAL ENGINEERING*, **57**:2188-2196 (2010).
17 Wu B.Z., Huang N.E. A study of the characteristics of white noise using the empirical mode decomposition method. Proc R Soc London A2004. p. 1597-1611.
18 Bai X. X., He B. *Ieee Transactions on Biomedical Engineering*, **53**:1883-1892 (2006).
19 Cheng W., Lee S., Zhang Z. S., He Z. J. *Journal of Sound and Vibration*, **331**:5153-5167 (2012).
20 Xiao M. L., Wei P., Tai H. M. *Journal of Communications and Networks*, **14**:481-486 (2012).
21 Jiling Xie, Xicai Si. *Systems Engineering and Electronics*, **30**:46-49 (2008).
22 D. Calson B. *IEEE Transactions on Aerospace and Electronic Systems*, **24**:397-401 (1988).
23 Ma Ning, Goh Joo Thiam. *Acoustics Speech and Signal Processing*, **15**:341-344 (2003).

MATEC Web of Conferences 44, 01065 (2016)
DOI: 10.1051/matecconf/20164401065

Design and Experiment of Flight Path Control System of Unmanned Autogyro

Song Wang[1,a], Wan Li Chen[2], Wen Qiang Dun[2], Liang Liang Bu[2] and Fang Chen Dong[2]

[1]*UAV Research Institute, Beihang University, Beijing 100191, China*
[2]*Robotics Institute, School of Mechanical Engineering & Automation, Beihang University, Beijing, 100191, China*

Abstract. This paper presents the architecture of flight tracking control system for unmanned autogyro, and designs the control law based on the control characteristics of unmanned autogy-ro. To reduce the lift force loss during turning and maintain the altitude, the feedforward control method of pitching rudder for propeller is adopted (dur-ing rolling); To reduce the influence of propeller anti-twisting effect on the roll at-titude and course, feedforward control method of the propeller rolling rudder (during throttle changing) is adopted; to reduce the slide slipping and achieve coordinated turning, a hybrid control strategy of the yaw rudder and rolling rud-der of propeller is developed. The flying platform is built to verify the flying. It is proved that this control system can effectively control the altitude and horizontal path of the unmanned autogyro, the control accuracy is better than ±5m.
Keywords. Autogyro UAV; flight path control; control law; feedforward control; flight verification

1 Foreword

The autogyro is an aircraft which gains the lift force via the main rotor of the free rotation, and gains the thrust from the propeller; it features short take-off and landing distance, simple structure, low cost, high safety and other advantages. In recent years, as the UAV (Unmanned Aerial Vehicle) industry booms, the unmanned autogyro becomes a new research focus.

United States Navy once conducted the research on unmanned autogyro and the wind tunnel test; scholars of University of Maryland conducted the relevant test and study on the run-up mechanism and characteristics of nonmotile rotor of the autogyro, and achieved certain results [1]; Sweden also developed a midget unmanned autogyro to equip the Sweden Armed Forces [2]. Comparatively, domestic study on autogyro UAV is rare. The Aviation Simulation and Control Laboratory of Nanjing University of Aeronautics and Astronautics once used a prototype as the platform to conduct the research regarding flight control [3]; Wang Deshuang and other experts of AVIC Aerodynamics Institute have designed a semi-physical simulation system for autogyro flight control [4].

The development of flight control technologies of unmanned autogyro in China is basically at the phase of theoretical and semi-physical simulation. The actual flight has not been reported yet, which poses an opportunity and challenge for the work in this paper. This paper presents a design for flight path control system that suits autogyro characteristics, and conducts flight verification on the small-scale test prototype, which achieves the altitude control and flight path tracking and can provide reference for the flight control system design of medium and large unmanned autogyro in the next stage.

2 Control system architecture

The unmanned autogyro control system achieves the attitude stabilization, position tracking and velocity tracking of the gyroplane via the control of the propeller horizontal rolling rudder, pitching rudder [9], yaw rudder and throttle. The horizontal rolling and pitching are achieved via the linkage of the two steering engines.

When the two controlling steering engines work with counter actions, they complete the horizontal rolling function, which is similar to the aileron of the fixed wing UAVs; when the two control steering engines work with equidirectional actions, they complete the pitching function, which is similar to the elevator of the fixed wing UAVs.

The flight control requirement of gyroplane is similar to the fixed wing UAVs, but the customized controller structure and control laws should be specially designed according to the characteristics of gyroplane.

The flight path control system for autogyro includes the sensor system, master control system and servo actuation system etc. Its system architecture is shown in Figure 1.

[a] Song Wang: wsongking@126.com

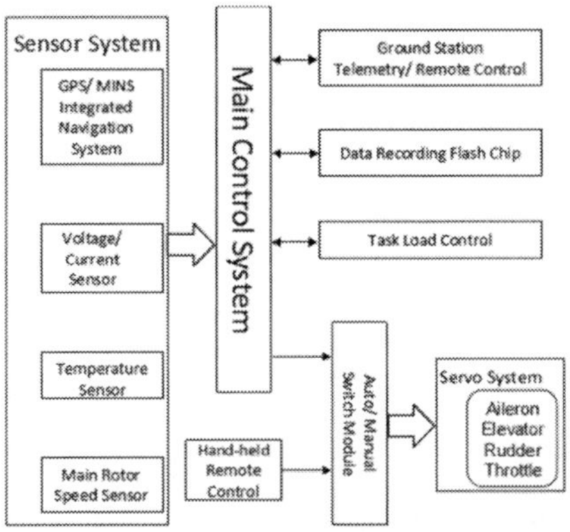

Figure 1. Autogyro flight path control system architecture

In this architecture, the master control system is at the core position, which links the other parts closely to jointly achieve the following functions [5]:

- Real-time measurement of the posture, position, altitude, velocity, angular rate and acceleration etc. of the gyroplane and the navigation computing;
- Real-time monitoring of the voltage of the main power supply, steering engine voltage, main rotor rotation speed and machine room temperature and other signal information related to the flight safety as well as complete malfunction alarm and emergency protection mechanism;
- Online adjusting the paraments of control law via the ground station;
- Synchro recording the key state variables and the operating instruction during the flight;
- Switches between the manual and auto mode via the remote controller;
- Controlling of the output of horizontal rolling rudder and pitching rudder of the propeller, the yaw rudder, throttle, etc.

The physical figure and the technical parameters of the flight path control system is shown in Figure 2 and Table 1.

Figure 2. Physical map of the gyroplane flight tracking control

Table 1. Specifications of the autogyro flight tracking

Size	110mm×58mm×53mm
Weight	200g
Power consumption	700-1350mW

3 The design of control law

The control channels of autogyro include the longitudinal channel, lateral passage, speed channel, etc. The longitudinal channel controls the angle of pitch and altitude via the propeller pitching rudder; the lateral passage controls the roll position, course and horizontal position via the horizontal rolling rudder and the yaw rudder; the speed channel controls the speed by adjusting the propeller rotation speed [6].

Control laws for each channel are designed in this paper based on the flight control characteristics of the autogyro, with details expounded as follows:

3.1 Longitudinal channel

The longitudinal channel adopts the cascade PID controller, with which outer loop controls altitude, and inner loop controls pitch attitude. The control method is based on the altitude difference, the altitude controller calculates the target pitch angle, and inputs it to the pitch stabilization and control circuit, and calculates and outputs the pitching rudder factor to control the gyroplane pitch attitude and correct the altitude.

The characteristic of longitudinal channel control is that the gyroplane altitude falls due to the fact that the propeller vertical pulling force cannot offset the counterweight force, and the propeller pitches laterally during the bank-and-turn in the forward flight process of the gyroplane [7].

To reduce the lifting force loss during the turning and maintain the altitude, this paper adopts the pitching rudder feedforward control method of the propeller (during rolling), the controller structure is shown in Figure 3:

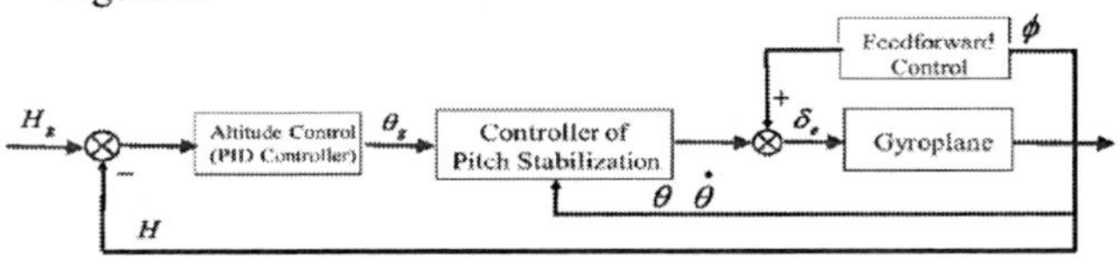

Figure 3. Structure of longitudinal channel controller

In Figure 3, H_g is the given target altitude; H is the actual altitude; θ_g is the calculated target pitch angle; θ and $\dot{\theta}$ are the true angle of pitch and true angle of pitch rate respectively; ϕ is the actual roll angle; δ_e is the pitching rudder output factor of the propeller.

3.2 Lateral channel

The lateral channel also adopts cascade PID controller, with which the external loop controls the level position, and the inner loop controls the roll position and course. The external loop control adopts the lateral deviation guidance method..

The control characteristics of the lateral channel of gyroplane are as follows:

- When controlling the gyroplane to turn, if the yaw rudder only is operated, the gyroplane will have outward slipping; if the rolling rudder of the propeller only is operated, the gyroplane will have inward slipping. To

reduce the lateral slipping and achieve the coordinated turning, a hybrid control strategy for the rolling rudder is developed by the authors: based on the lateral deviation and the lateral deviation speed, the lateral deviation controller calculates the target course angle and the target rolling angle. The target course angle plus the forward course angle is input to the course stabilization and control circuit, which will calculate and output the yaw rudder value; the target rolling angle are input to the roll stabilization and control circuit, which will calculate and output the rolling rudder value [8]. The yaw rudder and roll rudder of the propeller jointly complete the rolling posture and course control of the gyroplane and correct the lateral deviation.

- The gyroplane generally adopts the back-push propeller, with untwisting effect greater than the front-pull type. In addition, the throttle change may result in the untwisting force change on the gyroplane, which further causes the rolling posture and course fluctuation. Therefore, this paper adopts the rolling rudder feedforward control method (during throttle changing) to offset the untwisting torque.

Based on the above study, the controller structure of the lateral channel of autogyro is shown in Figure 4.

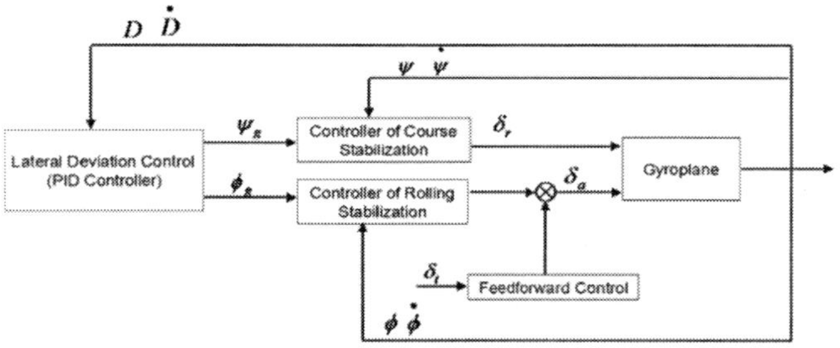

Figure 4. Structure of lateral channel controller

In Figure 4, D and $\dot{D}$ are the lateral deviation and lateral deviation speed respectively; ψ_g and ϕ_g calculate the target course angle and target rolling angle separately; ψ, $\dot{\psi}$, ϕ and $\dot{\phi}$ are the true course angle, the actual course angular rate, actual rolling angle and the actual rolling rate respectively; δ_t is the throttle rudder value; δ_r and δ_a are output yaw rudder value and the rolling rudder value respectively.

3.3 Speed channel

The structure of the speed channel controller is shown in Figure 5:

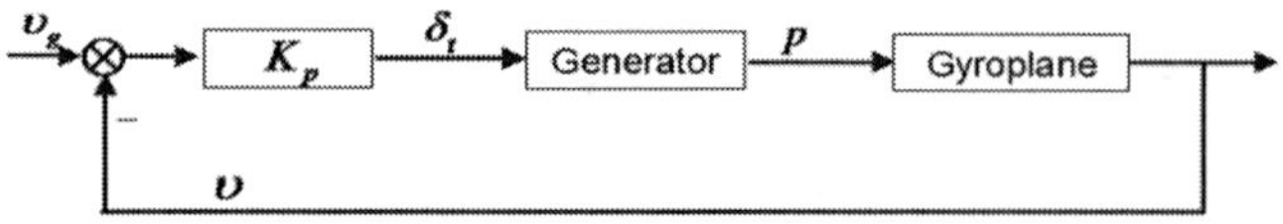

Figure 5. Structure of speed channel controller

In Figure 5, v_g is the target airspeed; K_g is the proportional component gain; δ_t is the throttle rudder value; p is the propeller thrust; v is the true air speed.

The small-scale test prototype studied in this paper is not installed with the airspeed sensor, so a simplified speed controller is applied during the flight test.

As the main rotor of the autogyro is nonmotile wind power rotor, it has such disadvantages as obvious lagging and non-linearity in driving the rotor [9]. The control strategies for speed channel accordingly developed in this paper are as follows:

$$\begin{cases} \delta_t = \delta_{t0}, when\theta_g < 0 and\theta < 0 \\ \delta_t < \delta_{t2}, when\theta_g > 0 and\theta > 0 \\ \delta = \delta_{t1}, other \end{cases} \quad (1)$$

In the above formula, δ_{t0}, δ_{t1} and δ_{t2} are the diving throttle, cruise throttle and climbing throttle respectively, which are given during calibration; θ_g and θ are target pitch angle and true angle of pitch respectively.

4 Experiment verification

During the experiment of this paper, a minitype electric drive gyroplane is installed with the flight path control system and data transmission module. The physical figure and the technical parameters of this prototype is shown in Figure 6 and Table 2:

Figure 6. Physical map of the prototype

Table 2. Specifications of the prototype

Rotor DIA.	1840mm
Body length	1048mm
Body height	600mm
Propeller	13inch×6.5inch
TOW.	3500g
Flying speed	10-100km/h
Take-off mode	Taxi take off (Distance≤10m)
Landing mode	Taxi landing (Distance≤10m)

The experimental process followed in this paper is: first, the ground station uploads the flight course via the wireless link circuit; then manually controls the gyroplane to take off; after reaching certain altitude, it switches to auto flight mode, and the gyroplane completes the auto flight as per the scheduled course via the flight path control system; during the flight, the ground station sends the flight course change instruction to test the various performance factors.

This experiment includes altitude control performance test, horizontal path control performance test and quadrilateral flight course test.

4.1 Performance test of altitude control

The performance test of altitude control is conducted by switching between two flight courses. One is 80m-high quadrilateral flight course, and the other is 105m-high quadrilateral flight course. This link consists of altitude tracking of climbing and descending branch stage, with the test results shown in Figure 7 and 8:

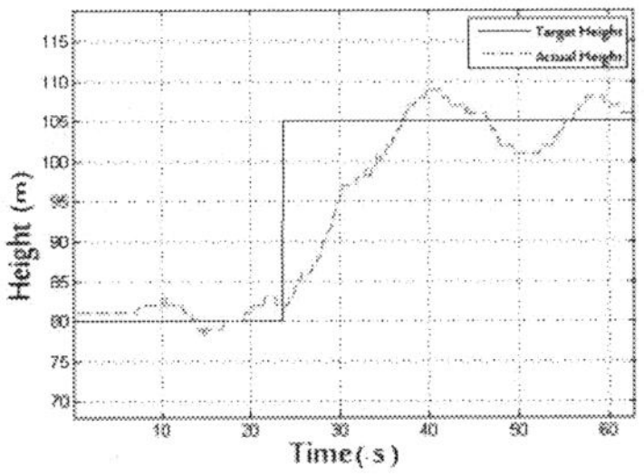

Figure 7. Height tracking curve in climbing test

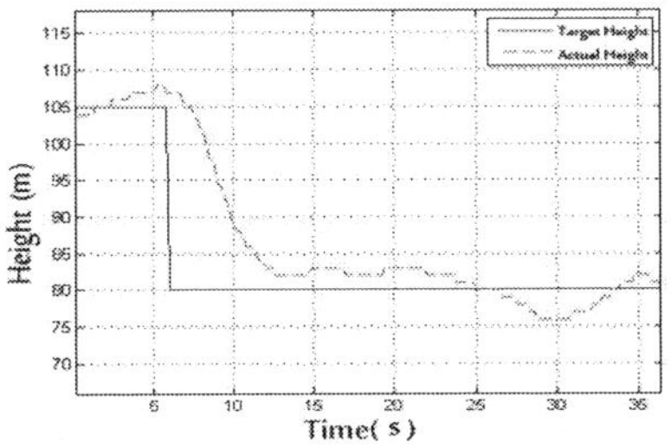

Figure 8. Height tracking curve in diving test

4.2 Performance test for horizontal path control

In this test, the gyroplane starts to converge to the planned flight course at the 45m lateral deviation point; the lateral deviation convergence curve is shown in Figure 9:

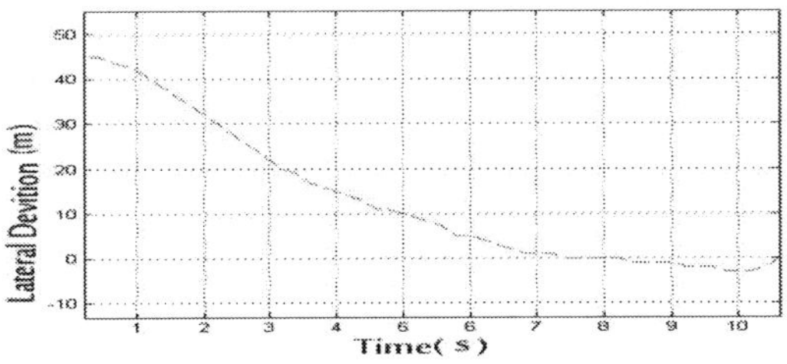

Figure 9. Lateral offset convergence curve

It can be seen that, the convergence procedure is smooth, from 45m to 0, it only takes about 7s, and the speed of convergence is about 6.5m/s. After it is on the planned flight course, the lateral deviation curve is smooth and the control accuracy is better than ±5m, but the lateral deviation is more of the flight course, which is due to the small scope of the flight course, and the lateral deviation has not reached the steady state during the gyroplane turning.

4.3 Quadrilateral flight course test

Based on the above control performance tests, a quadrilateral flight course is proposed by the authors, which is 80m high, 200m long and 80m wide. The gyroplane will fly 12 circles under the auto mode, with the total journey of 7km, and the flight time about 6 minutes. Taking the small battery capacity into consideration, this test is conducted in 3 missions each with 4 flights.

Certain session of test data is selected for analysis, and the results are shown in Figure 10 and 11:

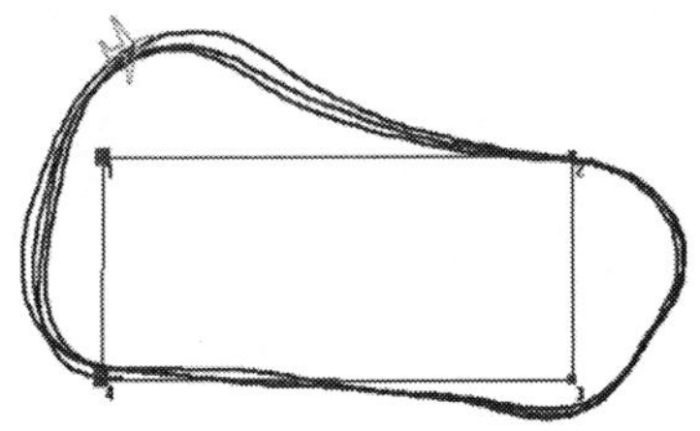

Figure 10. Track map in circular route test

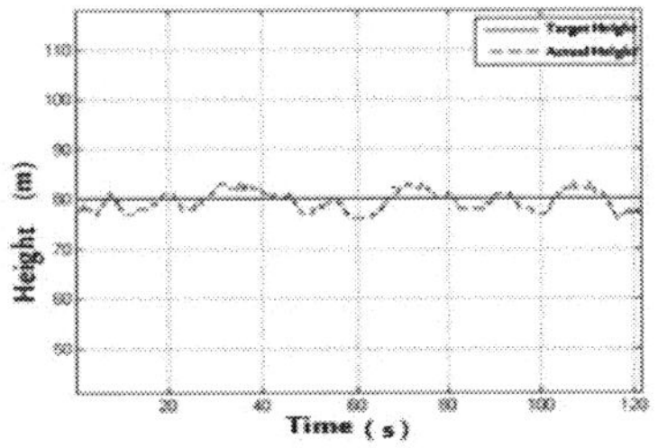

Figure 11. Height tracking curve in circular route test

In it, the rectangle is the planned flight course and the curve is the flight path.

From Figure 10 and 11, it can be seen that the unmanned autogyro can achieve the auto flight as per the planned flight course, with average speed about 20m/s; the horizontal path fluctuation is less than 10m, with high overlap ratio; the altitude control accuracy is better than ±5m, which shows cyclical changes, due to the fact that the gyroplane turns frequently, and the turning altitude is not stable yet.

There is a big lateral deviation during the switch between navigation point 2 and 4, which is due to the following reasons:

- The gyroplane is incapable of steep turn during the flight;
- The flight course is small; the lateral deviation does not converge to 0 when the gyroplane switches between navigation points.

5 Conclusion and prospect

This paper mainly presents the design of flight path control system of unmanned autogyro, and conducts the auto flight of the experimental prototype. It is concluded that this system can effectively control the altitude and

horizontal path of unmanned autogyro, which has a high degree of precision and reliability.

The key study in the next step is to enhance the sensor precision, further adjust the control laws and other work with a view to achieve the flight control of large and medium unmanned autogyro.

References

1. Chen M. Research on flight control technologies for unmanned gyroplane [D] Nanjing: Nanjing University of Aeronautics and Astronautics, 2011(in Chinese).
2. Wei K, Li Z G, Ma C W. Technology and development prospects of unmanned gyroplane [J]. Aerodynamic Missile Journal, 2012, (12):37-40 (in Chinese).
3. Chen J. Research on flight control and simulation technology of unmanned gyroplane [D]. Nanjing: Nanjing University of Aeronautics and Astronautics, 2013 (in Chinese).
4. Wang D S, Li G, Yang N. Semi-physical simulation system of a certain type of unmanned gyroplane [J]. Ordnance Industry Automation, 2014, 33 (4):22-25 (in Chinese).
5. Wang S. Study of the integrated flight control system for miniature fixed-wing unmanned aerial vehicles [D]. Beijing: Beihang University, 2010 (in Chinese).
6. Xu H, Zhang B H, et al. Research on control system of small unmanned gyroplane [J]. Science, 2011, (12):145-147 (in Chinese).
7. Hao C J. Research on control technology of unmanned gyroplane [D]. Nanjing: Nanjing University of Aeronautics and Astronautics, 2011 (in Chinese).
8. Chen J, Wang D B, et al. Turning flight control of unmanned gyroplanes based on deviation correction [J]. Ordnance Industry Automation, 2012, 31 (1):57-60 (in Chinese).
9. Chen M, Wang D B, et al. Study on navigation control of turning flight for unmanned rotorcraft [J]. Electronics Optics & Control, 2012, 19 (3):6-11 (in Chinese).
10. Gilbert L. Crouse. Conceptual design of an unmanned gyroplane for an endurance mission[C]//45th AIAA Aerospace Sciences Meeting and Exhibit. Reno, Nevada: AIAA, 2007.
11. Liu W D, Wang D L, et al. MATLAB/Simulink and process control system [M]. Beijing: China Machine Press, 2012:127-143 (in Chinese).

MATEC Web of Conferences **44**, 01066 (2016)
DOI: 10.1051/matecconf/20164401066

Teacher's Roles in Computer Based College English Collaborative Learning

Zhuo Ma

Foreign Languages and Cultures Department, 10049 Beijing Wuzi University, China

Abstract. With computer and network as setting in collaborative learning, due to the changes on learning environment and mode, the roles of teachers online are faced with challenges. This study is to examine functions of online teachers' roles in computer based college English collaborative learning. In the test carried in college English writing course, teachers perform roles of guide, assistant, facilitator, coordinator, etc. in collaborative learning procedure, namely the steps of Imputing, Drafting, Revising, Final drafting and Final evaluation. For functions of teachers' online and effects of the test, questionnaires on students' recognition, understanding, satisfaction and expectations of teachers' roles are employed respectively. From results of questionnaires and interviews, students' response prove that most learners' have already confirmed online teachers' roles, yet to fully realize their responsibilities, adequate measures and strategies must be taken to enrich teachers' online serving experiences.

1 Introduction

Collaboration is "a coordinated, synchronous activity that is the result of a continued attempt to construct and maintain a shared conception of a problem" [1]. And collaborative writing involves active participation of the project members, shared editing, reading and group writing strategies, revisions, peer-review, and group evaluations of contributions [2].

Foreign languages collaborative learning under computer environment has become an innovative learning mode these years. It refers that language learners employ online communicative media and tools, by way of group interaction, with help of computer technology, to carry out language learning experience and achieve knowledge construction. Students may participate into group activities to learn collaboratively in different time and place, instead of being confined to traditional classrooms. As a result, learners' abilities of language communication, autonomous and collaborative learning are effectively fostered. The new learning strategy embodies students-centered teaching methodology; however, it cannot work well without teachers' support and aid.

With the development of online teaching, studies on teachers' roles in computer based instruction have been increasing. Generally speaking, teachers under computer based collaborative learning, directly communicate with students via computer and websites, to support and facilitate individual learning and process of group study. For conventional teaching, the role of teachers is to design lessons, devise tasks and objectives, guarantee quality of class and arrange process of lectures. While with online learning, the role of teachers has changed greatly, from instructing to guiding, from teaching center to students-focused stimulator, assistant and facilitator. However, in practical collaborative learning, there is still gap between teacher's roles and learners' expectations. Teachers' functions haven't been fully realized, and teachers' managing skills are to be enhanced. Therefore, the study on teacher's role in computer based collaborative learning, is the indispensable perspective for online education. This paper is to examine role of teachers in a computer aided college English writing course, and learners' satisfaction and expectations upon this role, by following detailed composing procedure and investigating results of questionnaires. It is expected that this study would provide online teachers with necessary guidance and training, so as to raise the quality of online collaborative learning.

2 Teacher's roles in computer based writing course

College English writing course based on collaborative learning under computer environment, takes multimedia and websites as platform, adopts process-oriented teaching methodology, and instructs students to fulfill writing tasks by group participation, division of labor, sharing resources and community intelligence. To meet the objective of English online and collaborative writing, the corresponding writing mode is devised. In this approach, teachers perform roles of guide, participant and aid, whose main duty is to assign writing tasks, introduce writing strategy, analyze students' characters and abilities so as to group them, guide and involve in group

[a] Corresponding author: mazhuo@bwu.edu.cn

discussions, evaluate final drafts, timely send feedbacks, and interact with learners' through email or Blog. Students are center of whole teaching process, as well as active learning participants, cooperators, explorers of problems solving, donators and sharers of community intelligence and resources. They are expected to take on writing tasks, play roles in groups, collect and assort information, take part in discussing, commenting and editing, perfect drafts, till summit final drafts. The whole writing procedure takes four steps and teacher's roles are presented likewise.

2.1 Imputing step

Firstly, brainstorming is adopted so students could freely exchanges opinions in pleasant, casual and relaxing atmosphere, in which the collective intelligence can be brought out, and the originality and inspiration of learners are hence stimulated. In this phase, teachers as guide and instructor, encourage students to think actively and critically, communicate with them to dig out any relevant message to all kinds of writing subjects, so as to formulate flow of thoughts and outline in written form.

Teachers then release a topic and have students in groups talk about it. A student in charge in each group is appointed to coordinate discussions, persuade members to speak, generalize collective viewpoints, and note down key points. Teachers themselves also join in students' activities in order to monitor and guarantee learner's involvement. This group discussion as communication can stimulate writers' creative desire, and help them to correctly express ideas.

When computer and websites are available for writers to search, store and internalize related writing information, it is responsibility of teachers to introduce helpful writing training websites, or any useful reading pages. At the same time, they should recommend students browse e-magazines or e-book to cultivate good sense of language, take in more amounts of inputs, enhance competence of sentences making and vocabularies selecting.

2.2 Drafting step

After class and online activities, students are pretty clear about writing objectives, and move into drafting period. Teachers need to inform writers of synthesizing all useful materials to sort out flow of thoughts and set up specific writing contents. While in writing, teachers advise students to take down whatever occurring in minds, without stopping to pick up such mistakes as grammar, spelling, or punctuation. Besides, instructors will remind them that the faster and quicker they write, the better, because checking will interrupt thoughts and destroy its fluency. After the first draft is completed, writers then may examine whether their ideas are clear, writing objectives are definite, as well as contents and style are coordinated.

2.3 Revising step

Peers feedback ensued since the first draft comes out. Teachers proceed to organize students to exchange drafts online, through email or QQ, and direct them to read others with patience and send feedbacks by underlining or commenting. For the first time evaluation, teachers suggest readers focus checking perspective on general aspects, e.g. ideas, structure, contents, and writing techniques.

Under computer environment, it is convenient for students to manipulate such functions as cutting, pasting, adding, mistakes checking, searching, etc. Teachers now serve as technicians, teaching and assisting computer users to apply all necessary functions to revising exercises.

2.4 Final drafting step

Accordingly writers read others' feedbacks online and rewrite the first draft, which may be homework after class since students would spend considerable amount of time on it. Yet before leaving language labs, teachers need to propose certain guidance and directions. For example, typical revising samples are exhibited through multi-media approach, including peer feedbacks and teacher feedbacks, for both students and tutors to analyze, discuss and explore the contents, structure, sentence patterns, and language usage. In this procedure, instructors should build up active class atmosphere, encourage learners to talk frankly and sincerely, and confirm positive aspects of samples in order to raise students' writing enthusiasm. Final drafts are then submitted to online discussion board of Blogs, or any other online space to upload, paste, store, edit, and delete messages. For instance, for New Horizon College English Online Learning System, *Discussion Board for Teachers and Students* provide room for anyone involved in this task to donate resources, edit, and submit final drafts.

2.5 Final evaluation step

Teachers and peers will respond online in time to students' finals by underlining proper corrected points and suitable employment of language. Besides, under the final version, teachers' comments and suggestions should be adequate and inspiring enough to maintain students' composing energy and spirits. At last, all excellent products and typical problems are submitted online on *Appreciation Corpus*, for the former to be followed, and the latter to be avoided. One thing that teachers ought to be aware of is that models are to be coupled with teachers' feedbacks, while typical errors couldn't be tied with students' identity. Otherwise learners' writing motivation and passion would be greatly stricken.

3 Questionnaires and discussions

The computer based English writing collaborative mode is utilized by 85 first-year non-English majors from Beijing Wuzi University for a whole semester. Right after the course drew to end, students were asked to fill out

two pieces of questionnaire, respectively on recognition and understanding of teacher's roles, and students' satisfaction and expectation of such roles.

Table 1. Frequency on Students' Recognition and Understanding of Teacher's Roles

Questions	SA%	A%	U%	D%	SD%
1.I believe online teacher's roles are greatly different from those in traditional classrooms.	43	33	6	9	9
2.Teacher online plays important roles in computer based collaborative learning	41	27	11	11	10
3. In online collaborative study, the roles of teacher online are greatly challenged	35	36	14	7	8
4. I am still not clear about roles of teacher online.	29	21	15	17	18
5. I believe teacher online is one member of group, therefore should join in team discussion and study	46	33	9	8	4
6. I believe teacher online should mainly afford support and aid, and could only involve in our discussions when needed.	55	21	12	7	5

SA=Strongly Agree, A=Agree, U=Unclear, D=Disagree, SD=Strongly Disagree.

For statistics drawn from the above questionnaire, it is obvious that compared to old writing mode held in classrooms in which teacher's role is simply to assign writing tasks and give written feedbacks, majority of students (43%+33%=76%) could feel teacher's participation and help in process of writing. As for the significance of teacher's roles in collaborative learning, 68%(41%+27%=68%) students have realized the reason why collaboration benefits whole procedure of writing is mainly due to teacher's coordination and facilitation, while 21% students haven't recognized such roles. From interviews carried afterwards, it is learned that occasionally some inactive students are neglected so that group activities cannot run smoothly. Similarly, when asked whether teacher's roles are challenged immensely for online learning, 71% (35%+36=71%) students vote for positive answer, which indicates that for a trial of online learning, there is still certain space for teacher to strive and develop. From Question 4, it is gathered that half subjects are not aware of definite roles of online teacher. For one side, the figure shows different expectations on teachers; for the other, the recognition of collaborative learning and teacher's roles are not impressive enough for learners after the first round of experiment. Contrary to students' discussions, computer aided collaborative communications take teacher as a group member who listens, argues, thinks, and comments as students do, which is welcomed and accepted by overwhelming students. And the fact that 55% students is in strong agreement to Question 6 once more prove that teacher is only expected to perform role of participator instead of instructor or organizer in collaborative activities. In other words, they would neither act as onlookers nor controllers, but serve when needed.

In Table 2, statistics of frequency of students' satisfaction and expectation on teacher's roles are presented.

Table 2. Frequency of Students' Satisfaction and Expectation on Teacher's Roles

Questions	SA%	A%	U%	D %	SD %
1. Teacher online adopts so many effective methods in our collaboration and discussion, that collaborative discussion run smoothly.	21	25	17	20	17
2. The timely response from teacher online encourages me to actively take part in online communication.	45	25	11	12	7
3. In group cooperation, teacher is the authority and leader of discussion.	16	19	15	24	26
4. In group cooperation, teacher is the onlooker and intervener.	12	15	19	24	30
5. I wish teacher online is like our friends to study together.	77	14	5	2	2
6. I wish teacher online can evaluate my work positively and fairly so I won't give up the practice.	69	21	5	3	2

SA=Strongly Agree, A=Agree, U=Unclear, D=Disagree, SD=Strongly Disagree.

Generally speaking, for students' opinion on variety of coordinative approaches invented by teachers, nearly half of students (21%+25%=47%) express their satisfaction, while 37% (20%+17%=37%) students feel disappointed with teacher's performance, which shows

that there is still distance between functions of teachers online and students' expectations. As for practical roles teacher online plays in group interaction, 70% (45%+25%=70%) students believe teachers' immediate reply is the force and support to maintain enthusiasm in collaboration. Though online learning is asynchronous, learners still expect direct communications with teachers and face-to-face reactions in traditional classrooms. Since students haven't adjusted to new online writing mode, teacher's fast online feedback is crucial especially for the first phase of collaborative study. According to the computer assisted writing methodology, the role of teacher online should be directed from the unique lecturer to supplementary duties. However, 35% (16%+19%=35%) subjects hold that in their online writing course, teacher still takes control of whole procession instead of providing chances for learners to take charge, which is a sign that further training and practice for teachers is a must. Similarly, teachers also cannot act as absolute outsider or strict intervener, but to participate at proper time, which is convinced by over half students (24%+30%=54%). As for students' expectation on teachers, students overwhelmingly wish their tutors can be friendly, easygoing and generous enough to afford help. For the last item in this questionnaire, altogether 90% students regard teachers' positive and just feedback as a drive sticking to online writing activity. Likewise, it could be seen that some online teachers are not considerate enough in judging students' efforts, or indifferent to certain inactive learners, who would be definitely disheartened.

4 Conclusions

In computer based online teaching, teachers should take hold of measures with which their roles extend or withdraw. When learners feel free to try and explore in collaborative cognition, teachers need to play six roles, namely the deviser of context (to design tasks closely related to learners' life, challenging, and worthy to investigate), the provider of information and clues (to guarantee efficient online surfing), the guide of division of workload in collaboration (to distribute duties reasonably and properly to ensure quality of group work), the facilitator of knowledge inquiry (to keep learners follow set goals without disorientation, and to stimulate them to explore deeply rather than superficially), the organizer of exchanging opinions and feedbacks (to keep communications on right way), and the evaluator (to inspire, motivate and encourage learners) [3]. All in all, with computer and network as setting in collaborative learning, due to the changes on learning environment, mode, and its features, the roles of teachers are faced with challenges, therefore are multiple and comprehensive. For variety of roles endowed, teachers should be able to timely shift roles according to different steps of learning, and problems and difficulties students encounter in collaboration. From results of questionnaires and interviews, students' response on recognition, understanding, expectation and satisfaction on teacher's roles prove that, most learners' have already confirmed online teachers' roles, yet to fully realize their responsibilities, adequate measures and strategies must be taken to enrich teachers' online serving experiences.

References

1. J. Roschelle & S. D.Teasley. The construction of shared knowledge in collaborative problem solving. *Computer Supported Collaborative Learning*. 69-97(1995)
2. T. Judd et G. Kennedy et S. Cropper. Using wikis for collaborative learning: Assessing collaboration through contribution. *Australasian Journal of Educational Technology*, 26(2010)
3. On College English Writing Teaching under Online Environment. *Journal of Mudanjiang Teachers University (Philosophy Social Sciences Edition,5:21),*.

MATEC Web of Conferences 44, 01067 (2016)
DOI: 10.1051/matecconf/20164401067

A new type of mass structured data duplicate data check

Wen Qi Huang[1,a], Hua Jun Chen[1], Xiao Bin Guo[1], Li Peng[1]

ElectricPowerResearchInstitute,ChinaSouthernPowerGrid,China, 510080.

Abstract. In this study, the data processing method of a large-scale isoface is used to reduce the storage space of internal memory, improve data structure, and achieve predictability. The design of an algorithm mainly includes the following tasks: increasing the operation speed by improving the parallel granular of the GPU, finishing the segmentation of the adaptive tetrahedral octree, calculating the dual points through the quadric error function in four-dimensional space, searching for the minimum edge as well as finishing the data structure of the edge and the design of the octree node, and proposing that the algorithm be constantly performed until all levels of the minimum edge are found. The result of the algorithm design for the large-scale data is that the speed of parallel algorithms improves and the effect becomes more obvious. Research on large-scale data access high-speed ratio and structure improvement have experimental and theoretical reference value.

0 Introduction

The mode of computer storage and data organization is called data structure. Data structure refers to a set of one or more relationships between data elements. Generally, the selected data structure must lead to a higher operating or storage efficiency. The data structure is related to retrieval algorithm and index technology. The structure experience of large-scale systems verify that the degree of difficulty in achieving the quality and system configuration depends largely on the optimality of the data structure. In most cases, the algorithm is easy to obtain after the data structure is determined Occasionally, data structures are chosen in accordance with the specific algorithm. In other words, choosing the data structure that fits is crucial. In this study, a large-scale mesh simplification and an adaptive isoface-generating algorithm are investigated. Rossignac, Borrel, and Kok-Lim proposed a mesh resampling method that deals with any form of grid data. DeFlorianie et al. proposed that simplifying a triangle set with the same boundary by replacing it with a triangle set in an adjacent grid. Lindstrom proposed an algorithm that processes triangular patches by batches. In the current study, we propose the use of a large-scale isoface based on streaming simplified thought and saving on the global optimal queue.

1 Design of adaptive octree algorithm

Most adaptive isoface algorithms are not guaranteed to produce a mesh manifold. To solve this problem, we propose a sorting method that simplifies and reduces the error produced by the volume data function. This method can be improved by exploiting the parallel granular and operating speed dynamic increase.

1.1 Tetrahedral generation of adaptive octree

First, we consider how to obtain a manifold without a self-intersecting isoface from an adaptive octree data. In an adaptive octree data, every node has eight child nodes or none. The parent nodes are divided equally by all child nodes. The vertex of every node corresponds to a sampling point of the original volume data. All nodes are either a unit cubic voxel of the original data or contain it. All child nodes are filled with the entire volume data. We use the quadtree in a two-dimensional plane to explain this problem. This quadtree includes three-layer nodes. The lower right of the first layer has no child nodes. The other has 4 child nodes and constitutes the second-layer node, which includes 12 nodes. Four nodes in the second-layer node have child nodes and constitute a third layer, which includes 16 nodes. The third layer is a voxel of the

[a] Corresponding author: xuyunfei902@163.com

original volume data and cannot be divided. This quadtree has 25 child nodes, the first layer has 1, the second layer has 8, and the third layer has 16. Where nodes intersect at different layers of volume data, the edge of the node of the high layer adjacent to the lower nodes is split, so that higher-layer nodes no longer take a quadrilateral form.

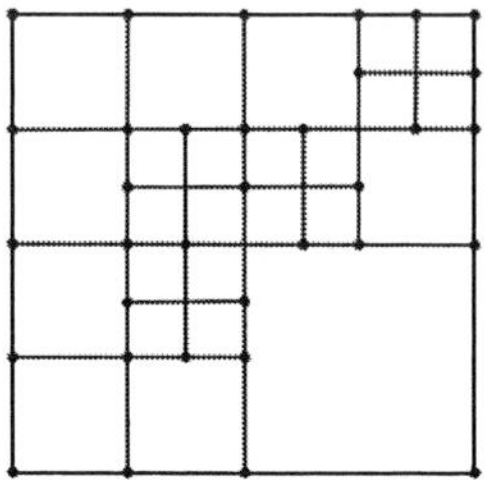

(a)

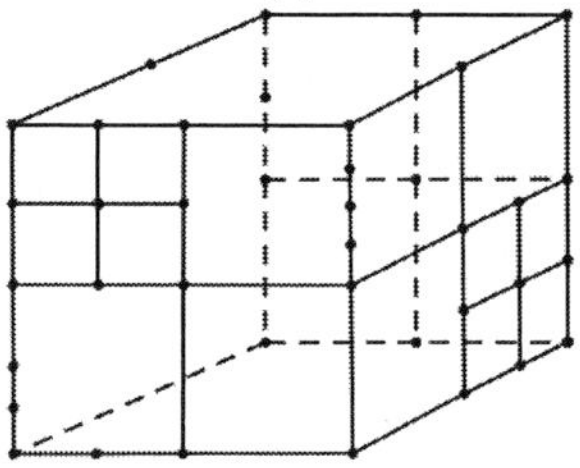

(b)

Figure 1: (a) adaptive quadtree in two-dimensional space and (b) divided higher-layer nodes of the octree

The octree in three-dimensional space is based on this intersection. Where the octree nodes intersect at different layers, the edge of the high-layer nodes is split, thereby resulting in a polygon. At the same time, the face is split and the high-layer nodes become a polyhedron. Figure 1(b) shows the splitting of the high-layer nodes of the octree. In the figure, this node becomes a polyhedron and a portion of the face becomes a polygon. The separation of the face and that of the edge both begin from this node adjacent to the lower-layer nodes. When the face is split, it produces a dual point. This dual point consists of four vectors (x, y, z, and w), where x, y, and z are the coordinates of the three-dimensional space, and w is the density value of the volume data. The dual points are connected to each edge of the face and form multiple triangles. The triangular segmentation of the outside surface of Figure 1(b) is presented in Figure 2.

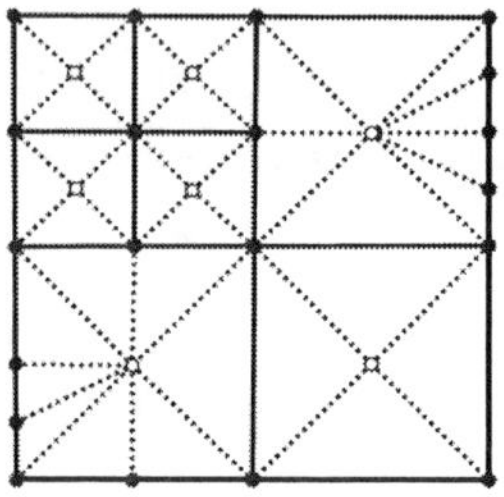

Figure 2: A divided triangle facing outside (white color point indicates the dual point, and dotted lines connect the octree and the dual vertex)

The splitting of the body follows a similar method. Each polyhedron generates a dual point. The triangle is obtained from the dividing face connected with this dual point.

1.2 Search for minimum edge

In the octree, the minimum edge cannot be divided and is significant for the formation of the tetrahedral. The storage structure of the minimum edge is similar to that of an octree. The data structure of the edge includes the direction of edge and the level and index of the octree node. To obtain it, we divide the edge into x, y, and z axes. Figure 3 illustrates the data structure of the edge.

```
struct OctEdge {
    EdgeDir dir;
int level1, level2, level3,
    level4;
int node1, node2, node3,
    node4;
      }
```

Figure 3 Data structure of edge

node1	node2
node4	node3

Figure 4 Position of adjacent nodes

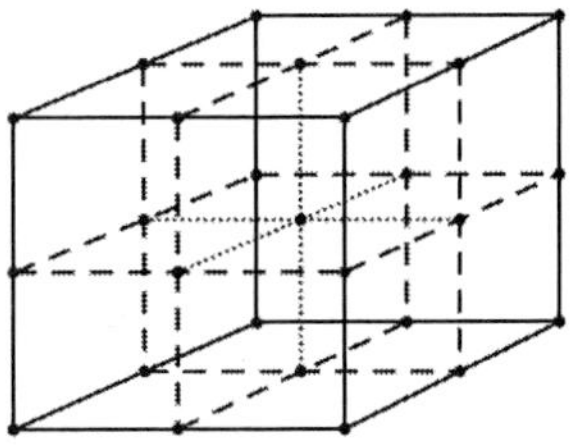

Figure 5 New edge introduced from the octree nodes (dashed line indicates the new edge on the top and dotted line indicates the edge of the nodes)

Figure 4 shows the position of the nodes. These four nodes are grouped into four faces: (node1, node2), (node2, node3), (node3, node4), and (node4, node1). If we assume that all edges of one layer are known, the edge is called the split edge. The process in which the current split edge produces the subsequent split edge may be described as follows. The number of segmentations of the current split edge is checked. The edge with zero segmentation and the edge with non-vanishing number of segmentations are considered as a parallel array segmentation. Then, the minimum edge is copied into the minimum edge array. At the same time, we store the edge with non-vanishing number of segmentations into the next layer array. The edge of the next layer to be split includes the new edge introduced when the octree nodes of the current layer are expanded. These new edges are included in the octree nodes and in the face (see Figure 5).

For the new edges of the octree nodes, the algorithm is parallel to the achieved number of new edges, in which each octree node has expanded. Then, new edges are written into the array to be split.

```
struct OctFace {
    FaceDir dir;
    int level1, level2;
    int node1, node2;
}
```

Figure 6 Data structure of face

We have to solve the edges of every layer face. This face is the face to be segmented. The data structure of the face includes the direction of the face and the layers and index of the nodes adjacent to the face. The direction of the face includes the xy, yz, and xz planes. Figure 6 shows the data structure of the face. As it is similar to the edge to be segmented, we have to know the number of the next layer segmentation. We add the results into the array of the next layer face. The next face to be segmented contains the new face expanded from the nodes of the current layer. The method of adding new edges into the face involves computing the number of new edges and offsetting it through parallel scanning. Then, we add the new edge into the next layer array to be segmented, which includes three sections. These sections are the segmented edge of the last layer, the expanded edge of the last layer nodes, and the expanded edge of the last layer face. To obtain the pseudocode of every segmented layer, we conduct the following procedure. The segmented number of the current layer edge is obtained in parallel. The edge array is segmented in parallel according to the segmented number of the minimum edge, which is zero at the front. The minimum edge is stored into the current layer minimum edge array. The non-vanishing segmented number undergoes SCAN in parallel and is offset. The number of the new parallel edges and faces is obtained. The new edges from the expanded nodes undergo SCAN and are offset in parallel. The new faces from the expanded face undergo SCAN in parallel and are offset in parallel. The number of new edges and faces from every segmented parallel face is obtained and offset. The segmentation number of the surface undergoes SCAN and is offset. The next layer array of the edge to be segmented is entered in the graphics memory. The three parts of the edges to be segmented are added into the array. The next layer array of the face to be segmented is entered in the graphics memory. The tow parts of the edges to be segmented are added into the array.

At the start, we produce the edge and the face of the first layer. Through continuous and iterative execution of

the algorithms, the minimum edges are found.

2 Execution results of algorithm design

For different models, we use the adaptive isosurface and large-scale isosurface. We test the speed of the parallel algorithm, implementation results, and execution time,see table 1 and Fig 7. In the test, the simplified algorithm of the unified cache size is set to 20,000.

Table 1 the serial algorithm and implementation time speedup of different models

Model	Size	Iso	Sl	Et	Sides
Teapot	256x256x178	60	5	4000	293042
Engine	256x256x110	127.5	5	1000	1044735
CT_	256x256x106	100	6	103500	183630
HKugel	64x64x64	100	3	990	32592
blunt	256x128x64	90	3	5000	9206

Teapot	0.0803	0.0547	0.166	0.426	13.198	30.9
Engine	0.118	0.125	0.523	0.866	16.614	19.18
CT_	0.102	0.0574	0.191	0.443	4.352	9.82
HKugel	0.0259	0.0106	0.0242	0.141	0.406	2.88
blunt	0.0345	0.0376	0.0673	0.219	0.343	1.57

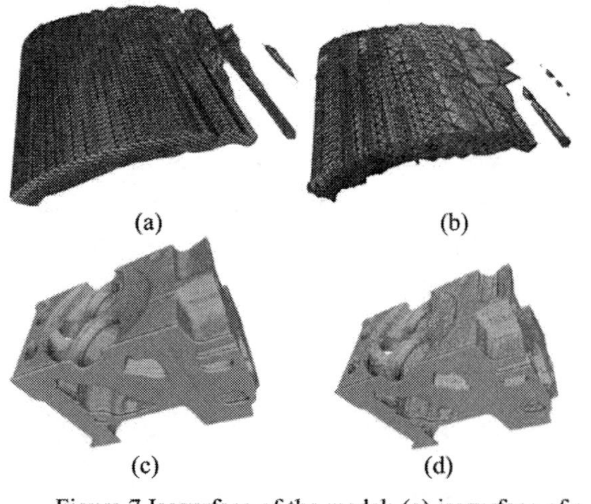

Figure 7 Isosurface of the model: (a) isosurface of a Blunt model using a marching tetrahedron, (b) isosurface of a Blunt model using this algorithm, (c) isosurface of an engine model using a marching tetrahedron, and (d) isosurface of an engine model using this algorithm.

The results indicate that for the large-scale data, the speed of the parallel algorithm is larger and its effect is more obvious. In addition, the simplified model shows that the effect of this algorithm is better on smoother surfaces.

3 Summary

Most adaptive isosurface algorithms cannot be guaranteed to produce a grid manifold without self-intersection. However, a sequential algorithm based on volume data simplex segmentation can solve this problem. This study is based on sequential simplex segmentation. The method of segmentation is simplified to reduce the approximate error of the volume function. Furthermore, the method is improved and is made to fully exploit the use of the parallel granular of GPU, which increases the operating speed. We propose a complete set minimum edge search method. According to the minimum edge, the nodes of the octree undergo tetrahedral segmentation, and the tetrahedral uses a marching tetrahedron to obtain the isosurface of the volume data. In practical tests, the algorithm can produce a high-quality adaptive isosurface.

MATEC Web of Conferences 44, 01068 (2016)
DOI: 10.1051/matecconf/20164401068

Study on Compensation Control of STATCOM Based on MMC

Yan Xie[1,a] , Mu LI[2]

[1]School of Electrical and Electronic Engineering, Wuhan Polytechnic University, Wuhan 430023, China
[2]Wuhan Nari Limited Liability Company of State Grid Electric Power Research Institute, Wuhan 430074, China

Abstract. This paper introduced modular multi-level converter (MMC), which could enhance the voltage and power level by sub-converter modules in series and was easy to extend to any level of output. Its structure and working mechanism were described. By analyzing the energy transfer performance of STATCOM based on MMC working conditions in the compensation, a comprehensive compensation control strategy was proposed based on direct current control mode. By analyzing the higher harmonic components circulation generated by the inconsistencies in the three-phase upper and lower arm voltage, a loop control strategy is proposed for the suppression of the circulation in the arms of the M-STATCOM. The simulation results show the strategy has a better tracking precision and response speed for the compensation control.

1 Introduction

With the development of power electronics technology, a variety of high-power switching devices was used widely. In the high-voltage high-power application fields, the demand for advanced power electronic devices has become increasingly urgent, such as in the field of power transmission and distribution, voltage source converter(VSC) has be widely used. VSC can have various forms of topology, and now commonly used the two-level VSC and three-level VSC in practice. There are the main problems for two-level VSC , which are static voltage balance, dynamic voltage balance and electromagnetic interference (EMI) caused by the insulated gate bipolar transistor (IGBT) series, and excessive switching losses caused by the high switching frequency. For multi-level voltage source converter, common topologies include diode clamped, capacitor clamped and cascaded H-bridge type.

From the point of industrial production and demand for services, it is essential that the main inverter circuit is strictly modular structure. In 2002, a new topology of modular multi-level VSC is proposed by Germany Bundeswehr Munich University. The new modular multi-level VSC (MMC) satisfies the modular functional requirements, and it will capacitance and switching device as a whole to build a sub-module, to enhance the voltage and power level by sub-converter modules in series, easy to extend to any level of output, and it can be used to reduce switching loss and improve transmission efficiency with low harmonic distortion and lower switching frequency.

With all the above its advantages, the study on MMC is become a hot research. In this paper the structure and working mechanism of the MMC are described, and an MMC bridge armbands flow control strategy is given to achieve the effective suppression of the circulation of the high-frequency component and verify the effect of the control.

2 Structure and working principle of MMC

Three-phase MMC converter structure is shown in Figure 1(a). It has a modular structure. Each phase includes upper and lower bridge, and each bridge consists of n sub-modules and current limiting reactor L in series. Udc is the DC side voltage. In order to maintain a constant DC output voltage, at any time into each phase of MMC is equal to the total number of sub-modules. So each phase of the MMC sub-module has 2n, the number of output level is n+1. The sub-module structure is shown in Figure 1(b). Each sub-module structure is the same. It includes: T1 and T2 (insulated gate bipolar transistors, IGBT), D1 and D2 (diodes for the continued flow) and C (the sub-module capacitor). u_C is the voltage of the sub-module capacitor C.

By controlling the switch IGBT T1 and T2, it can make the capacitor C into or removed from the bridge, and the corresponding output voltage u_{SM} is equal to u_c or 0.The work state of new modular multi-level converter (MMC) is changed by controlling its sub-modules (Fig.1). According to current direction of the bridge arm, switches T1 and T2 of sub-module are controlled on or off, and the capacitor C is achieve to be charged, discharged, or bypass, so the sub-module output voltage u_{sm} varies between zero and u_c. When the operating switches T1 and T2, it is equivalent to a DC power input

[a] Yan Xie: limimimm@163.com

Article available at http://www.matec-conferences.org or http://dx.doi.org/10.1051/matecconf/20164401068

or removal from the bridge. Through balancing the sub-module's capacitor voltage, it is considered the capacitor voltage as the voltage source u_c.

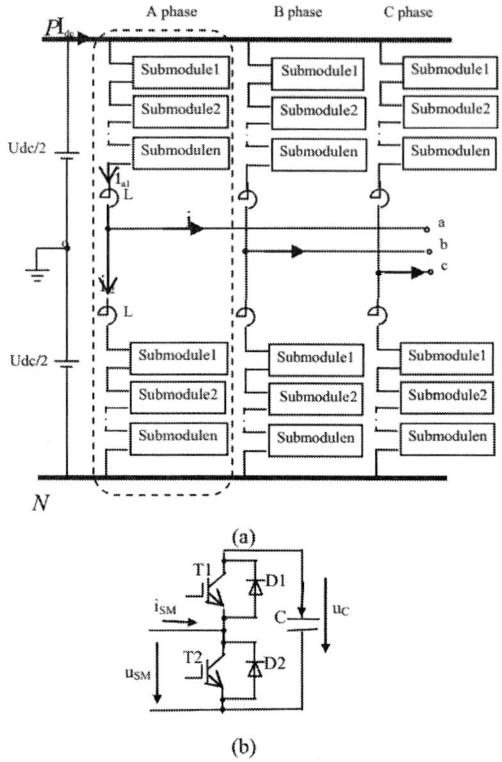

Figure 1. The circuit structure of MMC system (a) and MMC sub-module (b)

MMC used as STATCOM in China is at an early research stage, and there is a lot of research work needed. Existing studies show that the three-phase M-STATCOM system (i.e. the STATCOM system based on MMC) is at run time, there will be a high-order harmonic component circulation in the bridge arm. The circulation will not have any impact for external AC system, but it will increase requirements for the flow capacity of the MMC bridge arm power module. Therefore, in order to reduce the MMC power module current stress requirements, it is necessary on the effective circulation suppressed.

3 Control of STATCOM based on MMC

When the M-STATCOM operates on comprehensive compensation for the negative sequence current according to the load changing, the equivalent circuit is shown in Figure 2.

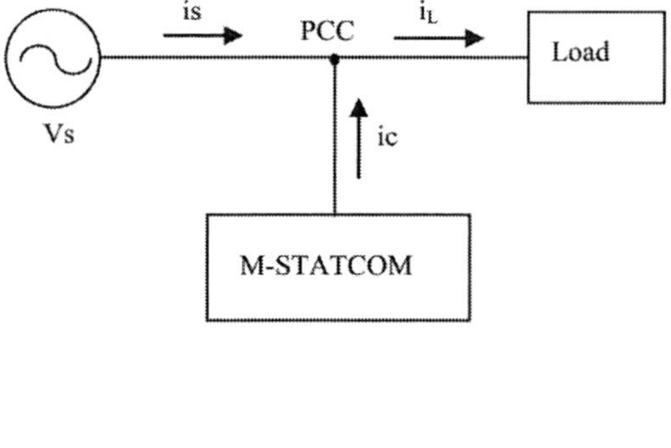

Figure 2. Equivalent circuit diagram of the system when M-STATCOM working in unbalance compensation condition

3.1. Unbalance compensation control

When the M-STATCOM working in imbalance compensation control state, it can be seen as a the ideal current source parallel with the grid based on the direct current control theory.The control objective is the output current of M-STATCOM system being fast-tracked to compensate for the desired harmonics, negative sequence and reactive current components of uneven load side and ensuring the current supplied by the grid containing only the fundamental positive sequence active current component. By M-STATCOM system compensation, the grid current and voltage are in same phase and symmetrical three-phase. The direct current control strategy can meet the requirements for fast dynamic response speed and small steady-state error.

Figure 3 shows the control block diagram of the M-STATCOM system unbalance compensation, which uses d-q model decoupling control method based on the synchronous rotating coordinate system.

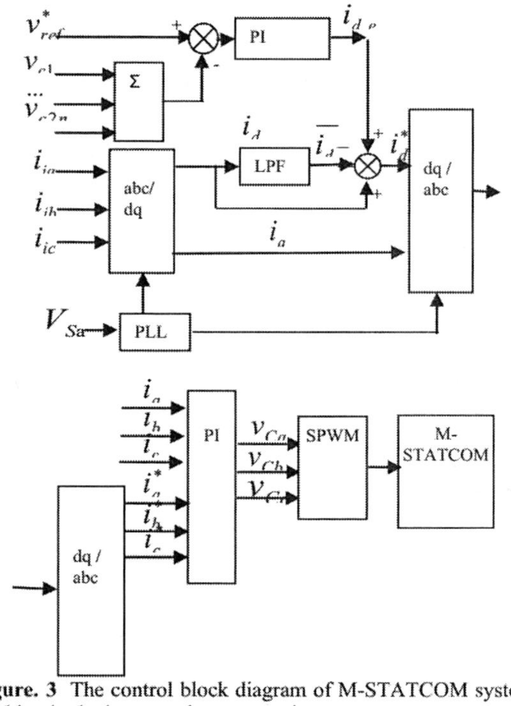

Figure. 3 The control block diagram of M-STATCOM system working in the integrated compensation

3.2 Circulation control

These higher harmonic components circulation is essentially due to the inconsistencies in the three-phase upper and lower arm voltage, and they flows between MMC three-phase bridge arm balanced in order to achieve the energy between each phase leg.

Figure 4 shows M-STATCOM single-phase circuit and its equivalent circuit with three-phase inductive load phase. Based on the idea of balance each phase leg

voltage, an MMC bridge armbands flow control strategy is given to achieve the effective suppression of the circulation of the high-frequency component and verify the effect of the control.

According to their working principle, there are:

$$V_{a'o} = V_{po} - V_p \tag{1}$$

$$V_{a''o} = -V_{on} + V_n \tag{2}$$

And so

$$V_{a'a''} = V_{a'o} - V_{a''o} = V_{po} + V_{on} - V_p - V_n \tag{3}$$

To a point in figure 2, there are:

$$i_{a1} = i_{a2} + i_a \quad V_{a''o} = -V_{on} + V_n \tag{4}$$

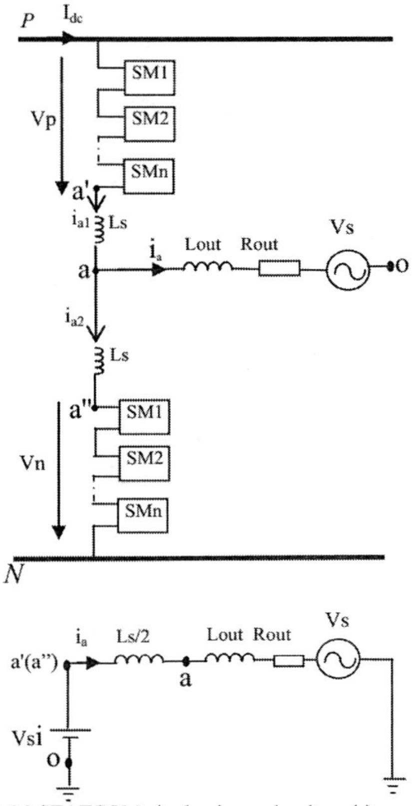

Figure 4. M-STATCOM single-phase circuit and its equivalent circuit diagram

Let a phase bridge arm in circulation are as follows:

$$i_Z = \frac{i_{a1} + i_{a2}}{2} \tag{5}$$

So the upper and lower arms of the current are:

$$i_{a1} = i_Z + \frac{i_a}{2} \text{ , and } i_{a2} = i_Z - \frac{i_a}{2} \tag{6}$$

The corresponding voltage and current relationship is as follows:

$$V_{a'a} = V_{aa''} = -\frac{V_{a'a''}}{2} \tag{7}$$

Take the reference value of upper-arm power module output the control voltage and the lower-arm power module output control voltage, respectively are:

$$V^*_{pa'} = -V^*_{ao} - \frac{V^*_{a'a''}}{2} + V_{po} \tag{8}$$

$$V^*_{a''n} = V^*_{ao} - \frac{V^*_{a'a''}}{2} + V_{on} \tag{9}$$

Therefore, the control block diagram of the circulation controller can be gotten as figure 5.

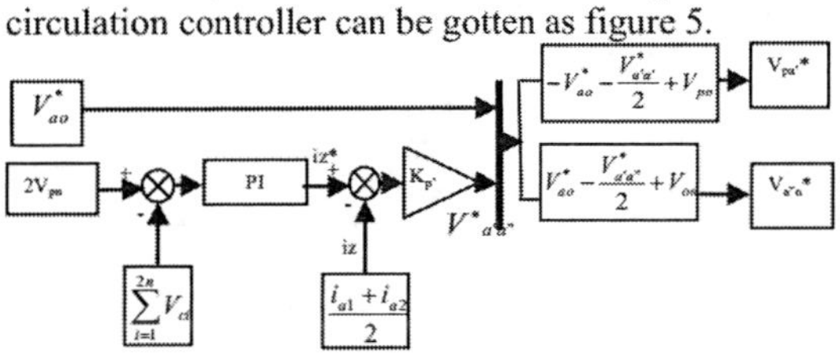

Figure 5. Single-phase M-STATCOM devices circulation control relationship diagram

4 Simulation results

According to the control strategy (Figure 3), the grid system voltage is 10kV, and a resistive inductive load Z=10+j0.63Ω is connected between the B and C phases. The second and third harmonic currents are superimposed on the load side, and it makes the load unbalance and containing harmonic current component. In t1 (= 0.1s) time, M-STATCOM system has been put in to achieve integrated compensation for the grid negative sequence harmonics and reactive. For compensation control system, the PI control parameters of controlling the DC-side voltage value is taken as : Kp = 2, Ki = 5, and PI control parameters of controlling AC current value is taken as :Kp = 800, Ki = 1.

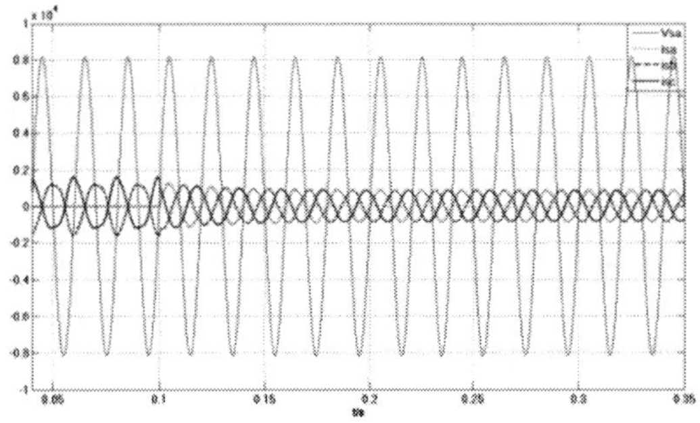

(a) A phase voltage and three-phase current waveforms

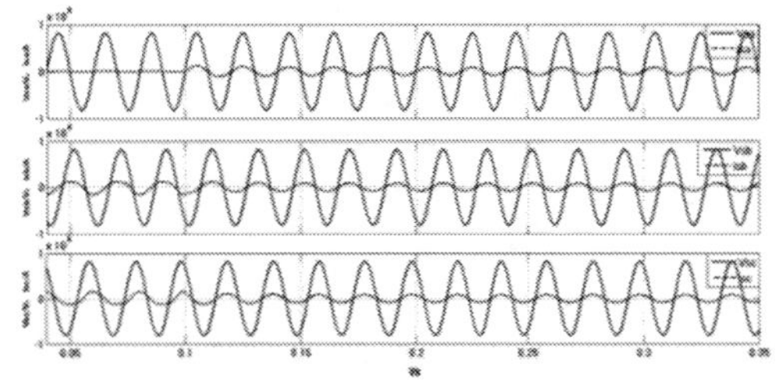

(b) Three phase voltages and three phase corresponding currents waveforms

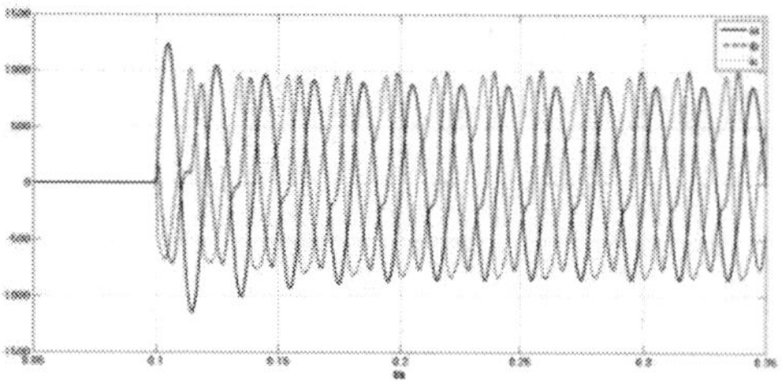

(c) M-STATCOM three-phase bridge arm output current waveforms

Figure 6. The simulation waveform of M-STATCOM system working in the current imbalance compensation

From figure 6(a), it show that the output current of the grid exist serious distortion due to load imbalances and low order harmonic currents, and the voltage and the output current exist phase difference due to the presence of the reactive load current.

In t1, M-STATCOM device has been put in to the grid, and the grid three-phase output current waveform has been improving rapidly. The current total harmonic distortion rate decreased rapidly, the three-phase output current waveform close to the ideal symmetrical three-phase sine wave, and its phase have been corrected to achieve unity power factor output of the grid control(Fig.6(b)).Compensating for the unbalanced load currents imbalance, its output currents are unbalanced (Fig.6(c)).

According to the loop control strategy (Figure 5), PI regulator control parameters of per phase DC bus regulator control is taken as: Kp = 0.001, Ki = 0.01, Kp '= 1000. This circulation suppressor is in operation at t2 (t2 = 0.2s), and the current waveforms are as shown in Figure 7.

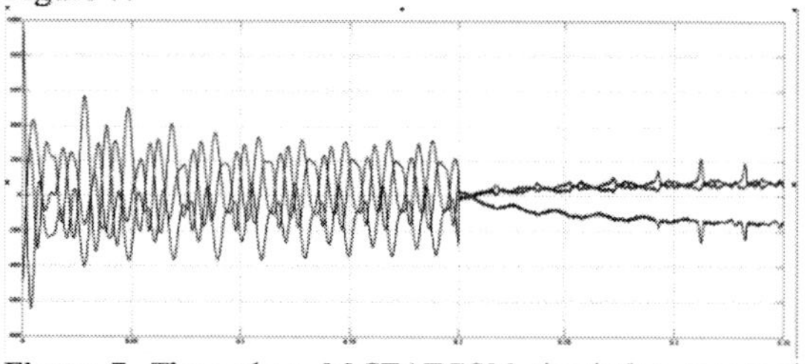

Figure 7. Three-phase M-STATCOM circulation suppression current simulation waveform

5 Conclusion

Recently, a modular multi-level converter (MMC) has been proposed and widely studied. So its structure and working principle has been described in detail. MMC used as STATCOM in China is at an early research stage. By analyzing the energy transfer performance of STATCOM based on MMC, this paper studied compensation control theory in complex conditions. To obtain compensation control response speed faster and better compensation effect, a comprehensive compensation control strategy was proposed based on direct current control mode. By analyzing the higher harmonic components circulation generated by the inconsistencies in the three-phase upper and lower arm voltage, a loop control strategy is proposed for the suppression of the circulation in the arms of the M-STATCOM. It can not only help to reduce the working current of the switching device of the sub-module, and can also reduce the power loss of the M-STATCOM system. The simulation results show the strategy has a better tracking precision and response speed for the control.

References

1. Veenstra M. , Rufer , A. Control of a hybrid asymmetric multi-level inverter for competitive medium-voltage industrial drives. *IEEE IAS Conf. Rec.* 190-197(2003).
2. G.J.Ding, M.Ding, G.F.Tang, Z.Y. He: Submodule capacitance parameter and voltage balancing scheme ofa new multilevel VSC modular [J]. *Proceedings of the CSEE,* **29** (30): 1-6 (in Chinese)(2009).
3. Q.R.Tu, Z.Xu, X.Zheng, M.Y.Guan, Mechanism Analysis on the Circulating Current in Modular Multi level Converter Based HVDC[J]. *High Voltage Engineering,* **36** (2): 547-552(2010).
4. Q.R.Tu, Z.Xu, M.Y.Guan, X.Zheng, J.Zhang. Design of circulating current suppressing controllers for modular multilevel converter[J]. *Automat ion of Electric Power Systems,* **34** (18): 57-61(2010).
5. S.S.Wang, X.X.Zhou, G.F.Tang, Z.Y.He, L.T.Teng, H.L.Bao. Analysis of sub module over current caused by DC pole-to-pole fault in modular multilevel converter HVDC system[J]. *Proceedings of the CSEE,*31 (1): 1-7(in Chinese)(2011).

MATEC Web of Conferences **44**, 01069 (2016)
DOI: 10.1051/matecconf/20164401069

ANALYSES the application of multimedia and network technology in College English Teaching

Chun Yan TENG

Department of English lecturer, Guang'an vocational and technical college, Guangan 638000,China

Abstract. with the development of the times and scientific progress, multimedia and network has been widely used in College English teaching. This paper analyzes the advantages of network and multimedia technology in College English teaching practice, and puts forward that teachers should use network teaching method in College English teaching, to enhance the efficiency of English learning and students' English ability and improve the quality of College English teaching.

Key words: network and multimedia technology; College English teaching; application

1 cited

In September 2007, the Ministry of Education issued 《College English curriculum teaching requirements》 (Referred to 《the curriculum requirements》) It is pointed out that universities should make full use of modern information technology, computer and classroom teaching mode to improve teachers -centered single teaching mode. based on modern information technology,especially network technology ,to a certain extent,English teaching and learning can not be limited by time and place.and should walk towards the direction of personalized and autonomous learning.The notice make full use of the necessity and importance of network multimedia teaching. With the rapid development of computer network technology, network technology in College English teaching plays a more and more important role, under the network environment, the use of multimedia network is student-centered, and regard the language skill training as the main content of the English teaching, the combination practicality, knowledge and interest is beneficial to arouse the teachers and students' 'enthusiasm, and reflect leading role of students in the teaching process and the dominant position of the teachers in the teaching process, which is beneficial to enhance the efficiency of English learning and improve the quality of College English teaching.

2 The advantages of network and multimedia in College English teaching

2.1 Network multimedia teaching can stimulate students' interest in learning English, give full play to our imagination

Bruneo once said: "Interest is the best teacher". with the widespread use of the network, now the students are very interested computers,the same as saying: "love me, love my dog,"because they like the network best, the students who are not interested in English would like to learn English Online. The visualization of multimedia network English teaching,Interesting and Diversity make the abstract, boring learning content into vivid, interesting, visual, audible dynamic content. Not only arouse the

students' interest in English Learning, provide students with the virtual and real image of the scene, but also create a pleasing to eyes ,ears and heart's English communicative situations, in visual and auditory interleaving of three-dimension space, stimulate student's brain and imagination,according to what they have learned in English, they create and explore.

2.2The teaching of network and multimedia can expand scope of teaching and add to students' knowledge

The network is updated and instantaneous, it can let the students read the English teaching resources such as ESL and EFL conveniently, and read the new ideas, new developments and new trends in various academic fields. British and American newspapers and magazines such as 《the New York times》、《China Daily》、《USA today》 Let the students keep pace with the times, expand learning time and space and enlarge their knowledge.

2.3The teaching of network and multimedia can afford interactive communication platform to the students

With the development of English teaching reform, oral English become more and more important. For students who are from higher vocational colleges,they don't have a good command of English,The base of English is poor.so they are reluctant to speak English in the class. Through usage of multimedia and network ,the students can speak English freely, imitate dialogue and practice virtual session, so that they can build up the fluid flow and musical sense of language, improve English oral expression ability and use English at the same time, in addition to discussion on BBS board (web page) ,Students can also express their opinion, to guarantee to find the object of the communicate in English between students and teachers as well as among students at any time, They can discuss oral English and written communication, in order to provide the corpus resources and interactive platform for students and teachers.

3 The application of multimedia and network technology in College English Teaching

The Multimedia and network technology utilized in College English teaching is a kind of multimedia information which provides the advanced teaching means. The network multimedia teaching refers to a kind of teaching activity which can make use of multimedia information. Network..computer to comprehensively deal with and control some multimedia information such as animation, audio,text .symbols, and video etc .it also carry on the organic combination between the multimedia and network in accordance with the requirements for teaching so as to form a reasonable teaching structure and and appear on the screen, then complete a series of human-computer interactive operations.to make the students study in optimizing the learning environment .More and more people agree with the advantage of the network multimedia in college English teaching As a college English teacher ,we should take advantage of the new concept and the development view, to explore the integration of multimedia and network teaching,research the new method about the Network and multimedia applied in college English teaching, make it give full play to its advantages ,to promote the teaching reform process,Now we will talk about practical application of network and multimedia in college English the teaching :

3.1 The use of multimedia and network in classroom enrich learning resources

One of advantage of network and multimedia applied in teaching is rich in resources, information on the Internet is an inexhaustible source of "information ocean", it can be a steady stream of enriching the students' and Teachers' knowledge ,In the classroom, teachers search the related information,find links related to the theme of the textbooks of each unit cultural background knowledge through the network ,such as pictures, audio and video processing, tab ,according to the teaching contents, teachers work out the course-ware, make the corresponding PPT, display in the student's field of vision vividly ,to provide students with relevant to the theme of the unit of cultural knowledge and the latest developments, in order to cultivate students' cultural awareness, thus it can have the students accumulate to enrich them cultural knowledge, form objective, open cultural viewpoint from the point to the surface day by

day .It also make the teaching contents become rich and vivid, stimulate students' interest, enhance the memory effect. Especially the master of lexical phrases and accumulation has been considered by many students as a dull, difficult process, In the explanation of the words and phrases in the text ,the network and multimedia used in teaching let students see the explanation When they click on the words and phrases which can appear before the example simple text interpretation and related pictures, The use of multimedia and network in classroom Intuitive reflects its significance and lets students think of how to use the words or phrases scenario, guide the student to look at the picture to make a sentence .and then Presents a detailed explanation and example for students to test the output corpus including collocation rules and words.In this way, it can not only stimulate students actively to participate in the output of the sexual activity and self examination process in making sentence according to the pictures, but also enriches rendering method, reduces students' boredom so as to give the students feel more intuitive, therefore it improves the students' interest of learning lexical phrases, understanding level and application ability, farther more optimizes teaching contents in the classroom, and enhance the teaching effect as well.

3.2 The use of multimedia and network build up open communication platform online after class

The application of multimedia and network technology in College English Teaching is the most advanced means of modern educational technology, The English level of students in higher vocational has a certain foundation, but the English level of students is different. In order to stimulate students' interest in learning English ,develop their ability to learn English, cultivate good habits of learning English, in addition to the daily teaching, the teacher in the class can also make full use of campus the network and multimedia to teach students in school. Such as the multimedia and network assisted with computer Instruction opened BBS. in this forum, At the same time students can make use of their spare time to prepare their studying contents in multimedia and network computer room fully , or in dormitory where they can exchange in Chinese and English ,They can speak with fervour and assurance in the English BBS,Teachers may design some topics in advance that students are concerned about current affairs and campus life, students can fully express their views in the preparation,Teachers show respect, care, appreciation and affirmation and encouragement for the students in words and attitudes, Help them to build confidence, to establish an equal and harmonious relationship between teachers and students, democratic cooperation. In the BBS forum, students can talk freely in condition that they can conceal their identity. They think themselves safely . Students and teachers can also ask some questions and send emails by one-to-one or one-to-many; teachers must promptly respond to student by email, treat every communication with the students seriously, put forward to the constructive suggestions as much as possible,.and do a good job of coordination. So all express their views, many questions are open for discussion of the individual learning subject ,teachers will unite separate studying subject into a group fully interactive to construct harmonious platform.

3.3 The application of multimedia and network technology in the procession of College English Teaching management can cultivate students' ability of autonomous learning

The teaching management Online can mainly provide for the functions of learning process and basic information which used to manage class , monitor the learning process and give feedback function to teachers ,according to assignments online or on BBS, In the procession of teaching management,teachers make the corresponding PPT associated with the teaching contents to hang on the Internet, Set the corresponding problem sets that can test studying effect when students are active to join in learning and finish the exercise on the Internet. After Students who complete submit permission correctly can enter the unit standard like the game stage mode to control the learning process ,teachers can view and modify the class basic information,Such as members, members of the account and password, class, etc, The teacher may arrange exercises outside of the online homework and test; only in this way ,teacher can monitor the students' learning, view the members' record each member in each unit,including learning time, answers in all operation and accuracy and the situation of set of exercises. According to the management of Internet on

BBS, teacher also can delete some speech on BBS , or make a post top, Generally they cannot change the structure of the BBS or increase or decrease contents in columns, In order to improve the students' ability of analyzing quickly and judging the problems involved in reading comprehension after accepting the language, teachers should design the corresponding the corresponding comprehension, vocabulary, translation online and so on. At first ,teacher consider to set a time limit, When time is up to date, exercises disappear automatically ,students who participate in the teaching have a feeling of pressing challenges at the beginning, In the whole teaching process, We develop the students' individuality and cultivate students' autonomous learning ability as well.

4 Conclusion

In a word, The essence of multimedia and network technology is to share resources on the internet, As a saying:"Everyone is equal before the network", everyone can enjoy powerful features and rich resources which was brought by the network . The integration of modern network and Multimedia together with English teaching is an unstoppable reforming trend . All of us make full use of multimedia and network applied in teaching larger and more effective to construct an open, interactive, personalized, autonomy of college English multimedia teaching platform, we also make English teaching become scientific, practical, informative, interesting, toward the healthy, rapid and coordinated development.

References

1.Higher Education Department of the Ministry of education.College English curriculum teaching requirements [M] Beijing foreign language teaching and Research Press, 2007

2.Zhou Fuqiang, Internet and foreign language teaching: opportunities and challenges[J] .Foreign language and foreign language teaching ,2000 (11) .

3.Liu Wenyu,Xiang Bihua. Network and College English Teaching[J] . Foreign language and foreign language teaching,2000 (10)

4.He Kekang.Application of multimedia courseware and network course in Teaching[J].Teaching in Chinese Universities.2007(7)

MATEC Web of Conferences **44**, 01070 (2016)
DOI: 10.1051/matecconf/20164401070

The Design and Implementation of Financial System Architecture based on J2EE

Dan Niu, Chun Ming An[a]

School of Economic Management, Beihua University, Jilin City, China

Abstract. With the rapid development of information technology and economical globalization, the traditional financial system can no longer adapt the great change in e-ecommerce environment. Then new advanced financial administration is needed. In this paper, the way how to perform and improve the functionality of financial system architecture based on J2EE is going to be the focal points in the realm of financial management.

1 General instruction

Internet to promote business system digital "Internet enterprises have become a node global J2EE of supply chain, business and system information are run electronically, enterprise system objects and system processes can be digitized, system becomes calculable activity" System computability facilitate system automation, enabling digital system "changes the Internet has brought corporate form" in the Internet, driven by the new enterprise systems began to appear, the ecological environment such as online businesses, Internet businesses, virtual enterprises and other "corporate also changed, namely from the original suppliers, manufacturers, vendors to the customer's level of string-type mode to J2EE-based non-hierarchical parallel mode "Internet further promote the internationalization of enterprises, while at the macro promote the integration of the global economy, as well as the formation of new economic forms, namely: direct economic, J2EE economy."

Internet business to promote e-commerce, "the Internet is the second PC, occurred in the global IT industry in the field of the second wave, which brought major changes in the IT industry and the global economy and society. Impact on business is the most direct and far-reaching the "no matter how large or small businesses, the Internet is unavoidable, it pushes business to e-commerce. E-commerce will become one way and the way of life of the Internet age important commercial enterprises.

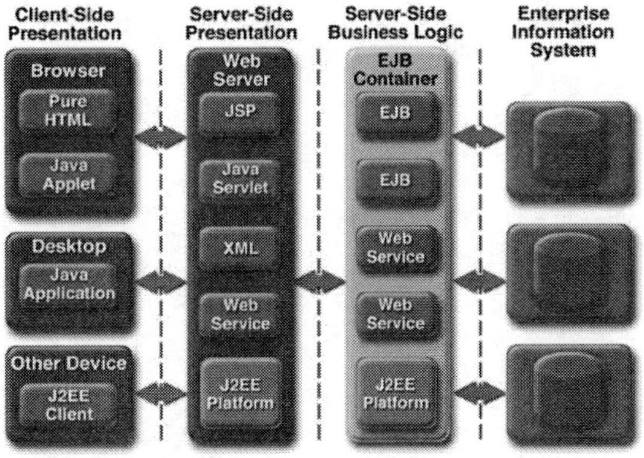

Figure 1. Java 2 Platform, Enterprise Edition (J2EE) Overview

2 Overview of financial system E-commerce environment

First, the sale of e-commerce is a way of using advanced IT "transaction parties will own all kinds of input supply and demand of e-commerce J2EE in accordance with the wishes of a certain format, e-commerce J2EE will be based on the user's requirements, and to find relevant information available to the user Choose a variety of trading "Once the user confirms, e-commerce will help complete the signing of the contract, classification, transfer and payment services, such as full payment. This provides a very good way for sellers to sell products at a higher price, the buyer purchases at lower prices for goods and raw materials.

Second, e-commerce is essentially formed a virtual swap market place "it can transcend time and space, in real time to provide users with all kinds of goods and services supply. Development and buyers and sellers, so that buyers and sellers can more easily study the market, more

[a] Corresponding author: chunmingan70@126.com

accurate understanding of the market and grasp the market.

Third, the understanding of e-commerce should be "modern information technology" and "business" two considerations. On the one hand, "electronic commerce" included the concept of "modern information technology" should cover a variety of techniques based on the use of electronic means of communication: the other hand, for the term "commercial" should be interpreted broadly, to include both contract or non-contractual relationship between the various matters of a commercial nature, all caused by "If the" modern information technology "seen as a subset of" business "seen as another subset, the scope of e-commerce should be covered by the two formed by the intersection of subsets, namely under the "e-commerce" title may be widely involved in the Internet, intranet and electronic data interchange for various purposes in the trade.

Fourth, e-commerce is not equal. E-commerce is much more than a real business enterprise foreground electronic, more importantly, the whole operation is a comprehensive information technology system, including the background, including, as well as the optimization and reorganization of business processes of the enterprise as a whole, "that is, to establish a comprehensive enterprise information, based on the implementation of comprehensive control by electronic means of the production, sales, inventory, service and other aspects of human resources is the e-commerce in the true sense.

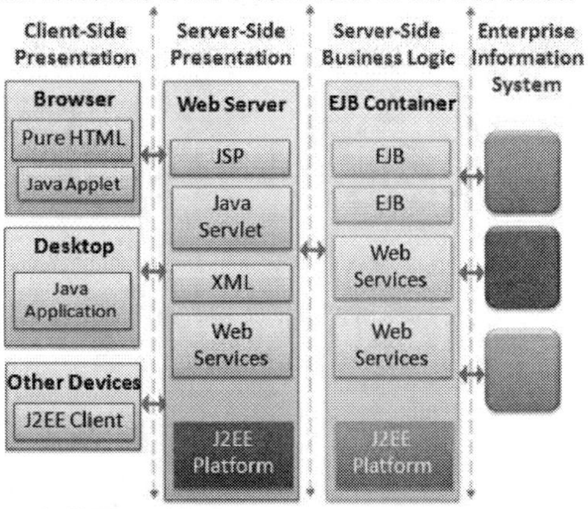

Figure 2. J2EE Architecture

3 The financial impact of strategic decisions

Many factors influence the formation of a strategic decision, and the impact of each factor in the decision-making has particularity. This makes the enterprise a lot of careful analysis of internal and external environment become a key strategic decision, "the financial impact of strategic decisions environmental factors, including the following aspects:

(1) Social, political, regulatory and public interest "Broadly speaking, the strategy must first meet the requirements of relevant laws and administrative regulations, is community-wide acceptance and is recognized by the public.

(2) Industry attractiveness and competitive conditions, "industry attractiveness is a key factor in strategic decision-making" business valuation industry and the competitive environment will directly determine its position in the industry and the basic means of competition taken.

(3)External opportunities and threats, enterprises must fully consider and seize good opportunities when they face strategic decisions, especially those that can improve the opportunities for its long-term competitive position and profitability, at the same time, we must try to avoid those that will weaken its various external threat competitive position and future operating results.

(4) Internal strengths. Weaknesses and core competitiveness, the company's strengths can attract more opportunities, weaknesses and current competitive position in the market can make some risky strategy does not even set up a decisive factor in the formation of a strategic decision is whether a company has or is likely to create a key factor in strategic decision-making as a distinctive characteristic competitiveness of enterprises to take advantage of its unique ability to seize a special opportunity, and have a competitive advantage in the marketplace.

(5)Personal ambitions of senior system, business philosophy and moral beliefs "strategic decisions are rarely made entirely through objective analysis by managers, managers of personal ambition, values, Philosophy, Attitudes to risk and so on strategic decisions has a significant impact.

E-commerce refers to the enterprise corporate financial strategy in order to seek long-term development strategy based on the overall movement of capital requirements and business trends in the analysis of internal and external environmental factors and the basis of the impact on the financial activities of the business done by global capital flows long-term, systematic and decisive plan.

Financial strategy focus of e-commerce business is the development direction of the company's future financial activities. Goals and objectives of the basic approaches and strategies of course, but also consider some of the new features is different from traditional e-commerce business. Overall e-business strategy, corporate finance goal is reasonable to mobilize, allocation and utilization of resources, to seek a balanced enterprise funds, effective flow, build their core competitiveness, and ultimately maximize enterprise value. several aspects of this goal is interrelated, "in the long run it performance of enterprise financial resources for sustainable growth and the ability to achieve capital appreciation and corporate enterprise financial ability sustained, rapid and healthy growth and development of enterprises to maintain a competitive advantage.

Specific objectives of e-commerce enterprise financial strategy is to achieve the overall goal of corporate financial strategy developed, which provides the direction of business operations and financial strategy to achieve the goal of basic approaches and strategies, e-commerce businesses funding strategic goal is to make companies funds can be provided to meet the needs of investment, and the lowest cost of capital; investment strategy objective is to pursue a satisfactory return on investment and cash flow, market share and so satisfying enterprise financial system by the overall objective of the strategic objectives and sub-objectives. Financial strategy the overall objective is to dominate the strategic objectives in the financial system, play a leading role in the goal, because the enterprise value maximization is the ultimate expression of enterprises of all economic, strategic financial theory therefore be established as the overall objective of the financial strategy. Sub-goal is to serve the overall goal, guidance to the financial activities of a particular area of the locality of goals, including the financing of strategic goals, investment strategy and asset system objectives strategic objectives. Specific target layer is about one aspect of specific goals, such as the most appropriate scale of investment, optimal capital structure, and lowest overall cost of capital, most reasonable profit distribution rate, and so on.

According to the views of modern finance, e-commerce should also exist optimal financing structure "and traditional business, as well financing structure depends on the cost of long-term funding needs of the enterprise." We know that when the cost of debt capital is less than the cost of capital when sovereignty , debt system can obtain the appropriate financial leverage, thereby increasing the sovereign capital gains enterprise; but when leverage reaches a certain limit, continue to increase debt funding could have the opposite effect, because people will realize that bonds continue to invest risks increase, a change in the solvency of the enterprise, which requires compensation expense to take this extra risk should be obtained, therefore, will increase the cost of debt capital and financial leverage may cause the loss of "optimal capital structure should be a company's stock price can reach the largest proportion of long-term funds, and meet the conditions of this ratio is: weighted average cost of capital to a minimum.

The beginning of e-commerce development, access to finance is important, but considering the cost of financing. Attention is also critical financing structure. Debt should be generally appropriate choice, after all, in the case of a moderate increase in risk for shareholders or increased benefits. Moreover, as e-commerce and gradually into the normal track profit, tax effect is more prominent bond financing, then further reduce the risk of J2EE industries, and appropriately increase the proportion of debt financing to bring positive effects will exceed the negative effects.

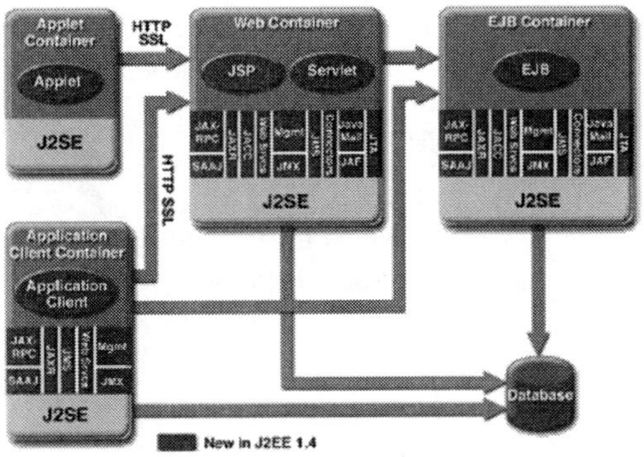

Figure 3. j2ee platform and the j2se enterprise apis

4 The financial system is the core

The main function of the J2EE of financial system is:

(1) to achieve the integration of supply and marketing business and financial system, "the implementation of procurement operations, automatically generates the corresponding single storage, inventory system, warehousing and other processing modules while automatic inventory costing, and transferred to the general ledger accounting vouchers modules based on the integration of the new moon brings source tracking function, can realize from the general ledger to ledger voucher to the original documents to the penetration of the query, and fully synchronized financial processing and business processes.

(2) The effective control of costs. Online financial software data imputation in terms of cost, design comprehensive data source automatically "cost system module from the inventory accounting, payroll, fixed asset system and general ledger automatically extract cost data. Each cost data will be synchronized automatically generated during" in terms of cost planning, you can prepare a comprehensive cost plan, after the end of the cost accounting and cost variance analysis results for this program automatically generate "cost forecasting and analysis, can be made to predict the cost and product cost sector forecast.

(3) Effective control of financial operations risk. Online financial software by implementing financial business integration, making the occurrence of any business will be immediately reflected in the financial account, which truly reflects the number of changes in inventory and inventory costs, and a true reflection of scattered information on the distribution channel inventory and sales information to more effectively control operational risks.

(4) Provides enterprise-level analysis of decision-making information. Online financial software is a cross-sectored, cross-regional application software system, systems store a large number of financial and business information, users can meet fully understand the business situation, the need to develop prospects and business risks, and provide predictive analysis for managers and scientific decision

Analysis. The beginning of e-commerce development, access to finance is important, but considering the cost of financing. Attention is also critical financing structure. Debt should be generally appropriate choice, after all, in the case of a moderate increase in risk for shareholders or increased benefits. Moreover, as e-commerce and gradually into the normal track profit, tax effect is more prominent bond financing, then further reduce the risk of J2EE industries, and appropriately increase the proportion of debt financing to bring positive effects will exceed the negative effects.

This site provides ASP services can be divided into free browsing, paid downloads, and the general Internet, as the Internet of the costs and expenses the same. As for entering the site-specific information services and downloaded the software being selected, according to their complexity. Workload service pays the prescribed fee. Such costs will create complex than corporate accounting information systems. Purchased or developed accounting software to be much smaller. As a registered membership of the way, also known as club membership, that is to give full play to the advantages of a good J2EE of financial various ways, member companies can get the site fixed various information services, to build their own pages on the site; released they think need to publish information they need to download any software provided by the site; You can also use its website has commissioned software companies need to complete an accounting and financial system tasks: the website each Member companies kinds of information exchange and access to counselling and training and other educational services website.

5 Conclusions

The rise of e-commerce has brought to the development of new business opportunities, financial services will no longer be confined to one country or one region, but will toward internationalization, precise, computerized, J2EE-oriented development "in the new environment, the study of financial system will be more valued and developed, so e-commerce based financial system research has particular practical significance.

At present, domestic and foreign research focuses on the financial system of e-commerce on the J2EE financially J2EE technology introduction to the original financial system, mainly the need for use of the J2EE in order to solve the financial problems have been studied from a J2EE application functions of financial systems (especially J2EE of financial applications) to study such consolidated statements, analysis of financial condition, remote data processing, functional analysis data storage, J2EE security solutions, etc. "in fact, the J2EE of financial electronic commerce just under a financial system mode, the current study did not conduct systematic financial system theory analysis of the new era, nor build the Financial System.

References

1. Ding Yuan Bamboo volunteerism function in building a socialist core value system. Beijing: Peking University Press, 67(2008)
2. Yan Lv. On the impact of e-commerce and innovation of financial system. Chengdu Westernization University, 46(2004)
3. Yang Fuqiang. Enterprise financial system of e-commerce era. Ningbo Vocational and Technical College, 33(2004)
4. HU Guo Liu. Corporate Financial Strategy and Financial Control. Tsinghua University Press, 195(2002)
5. Wong Jing. After the 2004 Chinese e-commerce into the financing of the times. Computer Knowledge and Technology, 979(2004)
6. Hao Liren. Practical statistical analysis. China Water Power Press, 356(2009)
7. Yang Xiaoming. SPSS Statistics in Education. Higher Education Press, 97(2004)
8. Chang Dayong, Zhang Lili. Economic System Fuzzy Mathematics. Beijing Economic Publishing House, 78(2005)
9. Zhang Wei. AHP and fuzzy theory in research evaluation. Ningxia University, 230(2002)
10. Comprehensive evaluation method HUANG Ti-yun multi-factor Fuzzy economic growth in e-commerce applications. Quantitative and Technical Economics Research, (495)2008

MATEC Web of Conferences 44, 01071 (2016)
DOI: 10.1051/matecconf/20164401071

Research on Application to College Study in Organic Chemistry Teaching based on Computer Software

Jing Wang

Teacher's College, Beihua University, Jilin City, China

Abstract. In order to give more accurate response to some basic chemical problems, it relates to the theoretical analysis and calculation, so the computer chemistry has been developed rapidly. The computational chemistry software has its unique properties, and it can achieve human-computer interaction, showing vividness and intuitiveness, etc. the effect is significant, which concrete teaching case analysis, and in chemistry teaching by making good use of computer chemistry software so as to improve the actual effect of classroom teaching, enrich the teaching contents in class, animate the classroom atmosphere and enhance students enthusiasm of learning chemistry.

1 General instruction

Development of computer technology in many fields and opportunities in the field of chemical, more specialized computer software into use these the use of software, by the chemical symbol or chemical formula for the expression of the image, etc., these symbols belong to the plane of the traditional symbols, but it is these symbols and chemical structures of all chemical information can express object of study can also be described in the microscopic world of chemical, chemical microscopic world is more esoteric, using computer software can well reveal because these two advantages, computer software is widely used not only in the scientific community, but also become one of the popular university teaching tools, and even become an essential teaching tool. Traditional teaching methods are mainly chemical Chemistry, models and slides, the disadvantage of this kind of teaching methods that can not be vividly describes the chemical issues to be told, and computer software chemistry teaching methods are able to solve this problem, the chemical when combining software with multimedia, vivid display the content to be described, some of the more abstract issues concrete, simplified, thereby reducing the difficulty of teaching students to understand abstract chemistry problem, no longer as difficult as using traditional methods, and can range from simple concrete steps begin to understand and improve their interest in chemistry learning, encourage them to continue in-depth understanding of chemistry microscopic world.

So far, the popular software on the market a variety of chemical, computational chemistry software, which is more commonly used are three categories, namely Caucasian developed Caucasian, Hypercube developed and developed by Cambridge Soft. Writer mainly from the actual teaching case of view, the computer software used in university chemistry organic chemistry teaching briefly described, and discuss issues related to the chemical for software design.

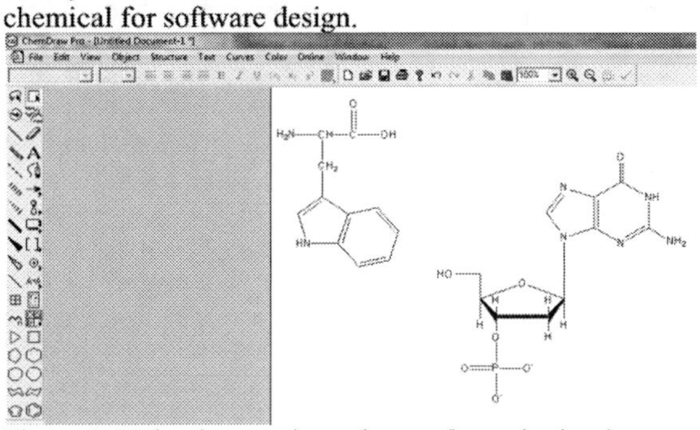

Figure 1. Molecular mapping software of organic chemistry

2 The traditional higher mathematics education

In traditional organic chemistry teaching, about three-dimensional structure of the molecule to explain, just by Molecular Structure to show, but due to insufficient visual image, three-dimensional structure of the molecule for students is still obscure, difficult for students to imagine its structure and thus can not understand, but the structure of molecules of organic compounds is the focus of teaching, its three-dimensional geometry of the reaction mechanism and constitute the physical and chemical nature of the relationship to the molecule, etc. with the evolution of modern technology, there are many software can molecule three-dimensional structure of the simulation demonstration, teachers can use it for

secondary education, so that students can clearly recognize intuitively structural model molecules, such as ChemOffice, Hyperchem, Gaussian 03 and so on chemically assisted instruction software, can be achieved by molecular stereoscopic 3D technology simulation demonstration structure for various models can simulate the structure of the molecule, such as stick models, metal bond model and sticks models, etc. Such software can not only enhance students 'understanding of molecular structure, but also improve students' spatial thinking ability and imagination.

For example, when teaching against ethane molecule conformation can be Gaussian 03 software to assist teaching, through its operation, it is conceivable molecular conformation, and can be associated with the energy of its molecules to their specific operation is as follows: the first step in the establishment of an ethane molecule model and optimize its molecular structure. Second step, in order to rotate 360 degrees CC, is necessary for the H4-C3-C2-H1 dihedral angle change for the third step, input scan to scan for potential energy curves of the rotation process. fourth step variation from CC rotation curve analysis of molecular potential energy conformation, and the lowest point potential energy curves corresponding conformation is stable conformations, also known as cross-type conformation ; while the highest point of the potential energy curves corresponding conformation is overlapping conformation when teachers during teaching, but also to assist by designing courseware, these conformations shots, made a dynamic picture and set these figures too and potential energy curve movements simultaneously, so that students will be able to grasp very clearly understand the various conformations of ethane its corresponding potential relationship through these animations.

Analysis of the characteristics of organic matter

For some properties of organic compounds, such as physical and chemical properties, related chemical auxiliary software can simulate and predict, to help students achieve the image of intuitive understanding. For example, when studying the molecular orbital theory, can assist the relevant chemical teaching software to overcome difficult problems in the past, with the help of chemical auxiliary software to help students understand abstract theory of knowledge, so that students clearly observed by the shape of the molecule reaches orbit HOMO understand and grasp the concepts so abstract image of the theoretical knowledge into knowledge the approach not only reduces the burden on teachers teaching, but also reduces the difficulty students understand, you can clearly see the three-dimensional shape of the molecular orbital grasp. Hyperchem software also can be achieved by drawing on the molecular orbital, including its level presented the sketch; the specific steps are as follows:

First, the establishment of a molecular model is proper optimization. Secondly, by Compute following Orbital option to automatically generate the molecular orbital and the energy level schematic. Third in the schematic generated randomly select a track, come on its three-dimensional models show this intuitive, obvious effect of three-dimensional hierarchical diagram fully demonstrated the conjugated π bond-dimensional structure helps students improve learning efficiency.

The basic parameters for the structure of organic compounds and analysis of relevant physical and chemical properties, can also be related to chemical auxiliary software to achieve, for example, learning characteristics for acetyl salicylic acid, you can use the Chem Office software to assist its specific operation steps are as follows: first, first by Chem Draw molecular Structure to describe a second step, by clicking on the View menu option to let it calculate the corresponding compounds of critical pressure, critical temperature, critical volume, boiling point, melting point. Molecular weight generates heat and so on.

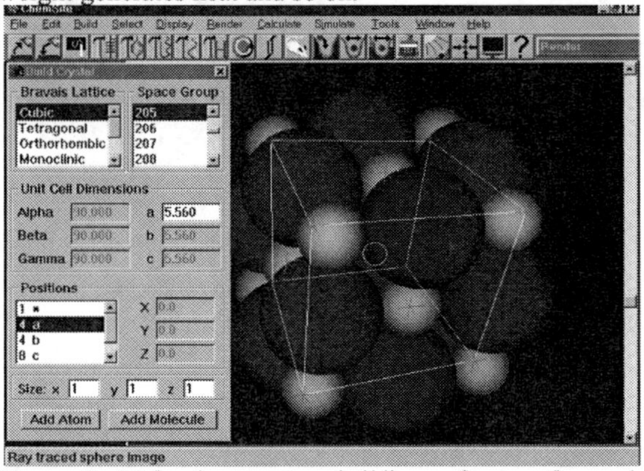

Figure 2. Molecular structure building software of organic chemistry

3 The keyword computational design

In organic chemistry teaching, the compound is also the focus of organic reactions, the mechanism and impact is very complex species are also very large, very abstract and difficult, often difficult for students to grasp the depth of their understanding, but for it to learn help students grasp the future synthesis process and the choice of a reasonable method to improve students' scientific research ability, so learning organic reactions is of great significance for students. Gaussian 03 software appears a good solution to this problem, so that students can easily understand and master this theory, for example, for learning bimolecular nucleophilic reactions, the specific steps are: a first step, to establish the appropriate CH3CL + BR- and CH3CL + Br- molecular model, and its optimization the second step, by using the form QST2 related to the reaction, and the keyword corresponding computational design third step, to render the IRC by calculating the energy variation of the molecular structure and in the course of the reaction. After their reactions via software demo can be observed, the nucleophilic reagent, leaving the evolution of the group, between the central carbon atom, when the nucleophile bypass leaving group and slowly approaching the central carbon atom, it will forming Br-C, when the leaving group is Chemistry her away from the central carbon atom, then the C-Cl presentation will slowly break phenomenon causes the central carbon atom and the corresponding changes occur, according to which hydrogen atoms leaving groups

appear direction deflection when the reaction carried out as described above to the transition state, then the central carbon atom structure will change, mostly showing sp2 hybrid phenomenon, and it will work with a leaving group and the pro-nucleophile is on the same line, the other atom or a group will also appear in a plane perpendicular to this line until at last completely away leaving group other atoms, as an independent product and independent of, the nucleophilic reagent will combine to form a bond with the central carbon atom of these processes are through GaussView software image presentation and observed.

After their reactions via software demo can be observed, the nucleophilic reagent, leaving the evolution of the group, between the central carbon atom, when the nucleophile bypass leaving group and slowly approaching the central carbon atom, it will forming Br-C, when the leaving group is fChemistry her away from the central carbon atom, then the C-Cl presentation will slowly break phenomenon causes the central carbon atom and the corresponding changes occur, according to which hydrogen atoms leaving groups appear direction deflection when the reaction carried out as described above to the transition state, then the central carbon atom structure will change, mostly showing sp2 hybrid phenomenon, and it will work with a leaving group and the pro-nucleophile is on the same line, the other atom or a group will also appear in a plane perpendicular to this line until at last completely away leaving group other atoms, as an independent product and independent of, the nucleophilic reagent will combine to form a bond with the central carbon atom of these processes are through GaussView software image presentation and observed, the use of this chemical auxiliary software for student learning plays a great role in improving student can therefore more in-depth understanding to grasp the concept of the transition state as well as organic reaction principle.

4 The understanding of molecular spectroscopy analysis

Learn about the molecular spectral characteristics of organic compounds can encourage students to be more flexible in order to analyze the perspective of molecular material world in modern society, the scientists want to achieve for the understanding of molecular spectroscopy analysis, usually by modern instruments molecule organics accurate analysis of the structure to achieve, but it is difficult for this type of instrument referenced test in real classrooms. while Gaussian 03 software can be easily implemented in the classroom to simulate and predict the molecular spectra, such as infrared spectroscopy for organic molecules and vibration when the mode of learning can refer to the software, the specific steps are as follows: a first step, to establish and optimize the corresponding molecular model the second step, to calculate the molecular vibration frequency table by Freq keyword. The third step is to identify the corresponding calculation result output file and open the fourth step, click Vibrations option to choose a pop of molecular vibration frequency, can be obtained through the StChemistry vibration modes corresponding amount of audio, and the molecular compound infrared spectra can be obtained by clicking on the spectrum. Such intuitive display vibration compounds through animation, to obtain the corresponding infrared spectra, etc. for students, it is very easy to learn to master.

In addition, the software can also ChemOffice mass to charge ratio of organic compounds and NMR spectra prediction and simulation, for example, for the simulation and prediction of the benzophenone, the specific steps are as follows: a first step, the establishment of appropriate in ChemDraw the molecular structure and optimize a second step, by clicking Predict 1H NMR Shifts derived 1H NMR chemical shift spectra and the corresponding form. Third step, by clicking Show Analysis Windows to get the corresponding compound of the mass to charge than the students by observing the software forecast shows more easily grasp the content to improve learning efficiency.

5 Conclusions

The overall goal of chemistry education, new curriculum standards referred to "the learning process of students in chemistry , rich visual, tactile and aesthetic experience, access to chemistry of enduring interest in learning, form the basic chemistry literacy", "improve the aesthetic ability to understand chemistry the unique role of cultural life and social development." Here is more clearly explained the ultimate goal of chemistry courses. In the "targets" in the four fields of study made specific teaching requirements, these instructional purposes basically not much difference with older versions of curriculum standards. It is worth mentioning that in the "comprehensive exploration of the area," the teaching objectives, calling for "understanding the relationship between chemistry and nature, chemistry and life, chemistry and culture, between chemistry and technology, to explore and comprehensive chemistry activities, and to published in various forms of learning outcomes ", where clearly pointed out a comprehensive exploration of objects and methods, while the new curriculum standards also require our chemistry curriculum to make students feel a sense of pleasure and success.

As we all know, in today's education, discipline increasingly fine division. Such an increase implies something the students want to learn more and more, but their time is fixed. As a result, the constant increase in core subjects or other subjects only make students more overwhelmed. For this reason, the development trend of the moment the best education is infinitely split from discipline to a new integration. Chemistry education in this, should implement the existing curriculum standard, advocated chemistry ability is to train students and humanities integration development. It is an integrated aesthetic intuition all sense and sensibility to chemistry ability into aesthetic activity. Therefore, how people perceive the aesthetic intuition, how to understand the

process of aesthetic intuition in chemistry education's role, and what kind of approach to training is worth exploring issues such as students' aesthetic intuition.

See some natural or man-made works of chemistry , we tend to happen on an emotional excitement, perhaps pleasant excitement, perhaps sad passionate, whether it is the former or the latter, in short, we were moved, so emotional the excitement, called appreciation, that is, we are looking at things from the beauty. Education is when a person learned in school has forgotten the rest of the stuff. Into their own behaviours within that chemistry of the way of thinking is not visible knowledge is permanent. No matter what kind of chemistry education means education methods, we want to achieve the ultimate goal is to train a person's right or even aesthetic intuition is a national beauty bright positive psychological intuition and aesthetic.

Because aesthetic intuition without hesitation and a look that is beautiful aesthetic phenomenon, people tend to go for the emotional behaviours aesthetic intuition, put it on the shelf, and scientific and rational opposition. As Freud and psychoanalysis, led by western modernist chemistry is the chemistry expression of this anti-rational. After careful thought is not difficult to find, aesthetic intuition itself is permeated with a rational component, bears deep and rich social and cultural connotations, this intuition has all the ability to think. It has a rational component, needs to be guided chemistry education and promotion. Aesthetic intuition is an important measure of the strength of the aesthetic capacity through chemistry training of chemistry generally has relatively strong aesthetic intuition.

References

1. Chee Soon Juan, Zhang Yong, Zhao Yang, a chemical commonly used software, such as research and development of multimedia teaching software. Computers and Applied Chemistry, 45(2010)
2. Liu Xiaodong, Zong ball .GaussView some applications in chemistry teaching. University Chemistry, 37(2009)
3. Zheng Wenrui computational chemistry applications in chemistry and chemical engineering. Shanghai Chemical12(2010)
4. Chee Soon Juan, Zhang Yong, Zhao Yang, a chemical commonly used software, such as research and development of multimedia teaching software. Computers and Applied Chemistry, 34(2009)
5. Xiao Ying. Aesthetic strategies of Contemporary Aesthetic Culture. Academic Monthly58(2002)
6. Chen Meimin. Aesthetic under Contemporary Aesthetic Culture. Hainan Radio and Television University, 89(2005)
7. Lu Chang. On the relationship between Chemistry s education and aesthetic education. Theory and practice of education, 75(2002)
8. Chen Chi-yu. Chinese modern aesthetics and Chemistry theory . Central China Normal University, 124(2000)

MATEC Web of Conferences **44**, 01072 (2016)
DOI: 10.1051/matecconf/20164401072

Study on Teaching Strategies in Mathematics Education based on CAI

Yan Feng Wei

Teacher's College, Beihua University, Jilin City, China

Abstract. With the development of information technology and the popularization of internet, mobile phone, new media represented is gradually influencing and changing people's study and life, become the centre and social consensus of cultural information, according to the China Internet Network Information centre, the youth is the main use of CAI(Computer Assisted Instruction), which is the most active group of customers, fully understand the impact of the new media environment for students, higher mathematics education of college students in CAI. In this paper, the CAI is proposed for mathematics education of college students.

1 General instruction

according to "Report of China Internet Development Statistics" in July 2013 by the China Internet Network Information Centre released 32nd (CNNIC) data show that "As of the end of June 2013, the scale of China reached 591 million Internet users, Internet penetration rate of 44.1%, where 20-year-old to 29-year-olds accounted for 29.5% of all Internet users among the largest proportion of high school students, to 26.8 percent." Internet, mobile phones and other new media appear to accelerate the rhythm of people's lives, so that students become very con-fused and impetuous; in the new media environment presents information uneven, Western countries control the discourse of new media, these phenomena to the development of higher mathematics education has brought many new problems, while the higher mathematics education of college workers is also a great challenge.

With the development of information technology to the Internet, mobile phones represented by the new media has gradually come into our lives, as our access to information, interpersonal communication and entertainment were an indispensable tool in different disciplines and researchers are beginning to focus on this one issue, the higher mathematics education is an important social practices, should continue to meet the development needs of modern society.

How to carry out higher mathematics education in the new media environment is the higher mathematics reality we must face university educators and historic mission. The term "new media" comes from the West, the Western countries to study new media has 40 years of history, our focus on new media is only in recent years things, mostly general, introductory study, not yet formed complete theoretical system of systematic, so contemporary to the higher mathematics education in the context of new media continue research in order under the guidance of Marxism, and in a correct understanding of the basis of new media theory, combined with the actual situation of China's college students proposed countermeasures for our own education.

Figure 1. Computer assisted instruction

2 The traditional higher mathematics education

New media to expand the dissemination of spatial information, people can at any time, anywhere access to information through new media, and according to their needs and preferences, to form their own independent media space, while traditional media often do not have this feature. Traditional media are unidirectional linear propagation, is a little on the multi-faceted communication, new media, communication style are spread, you can achieve "many to many" communication, is spread by everyone, everyone can be among the audience and interchange the AC content. The traditional news media no longer dominate the mathematics', more and more of the audience began to mathematics in the

dissemination of information, and even become a source of information and the publisher, the mainstream media no longer grasp the absolute right to speak, many of whom are involved in college students. The emergence of new media has changed the past, people tuning in via radio and television programs must be synchronized features, at any time to obtain information the audience can select according to their own circumstances, if you are interested you can repeatedly watch the same programs.

The development of digital technology, the economy, politics, culture and society have had a profound impact on the application and research of new media mathematics to get people's attention, especially in recent years, with the development of 3G technology, some scholars have begun to attention to the relationship between the new media environment and the higher mathematics education among college students, recognizing the rapid development and application of new media to bring new development opportunities to the higher mathematics education in colleges and universities, research new media applications in the higher mathematics education activities, and made some useful results.

2009 Ministry of Education, Social Science Centre hosted "in the new media technology background of higher mathematics education of college students' seminars, conferences, studies the" contemporary college students use new media tools of the status quo and development trend of ideological and new media environment, learning and life the impact of new media to enhance the method by means of higher mathematics education. "the meeting noted that the new media technology platform to broaden the higher mathematics education, higher mathematics means to enrich education, provide a new perspective for the traditional higher mathematics education workers, is conducive to enhancing the practical effect of the higher mathematics education, but also should be noted that under the new media environment impact of a flood of information on college students, is apt to cause physical and psychological double crisis college students, college is not conducive to the formation of a correct world outlook, outlook on life and values. Higher mathematics Education Workers in the actual teaching work to change the educational ideas to improve the understanding of new media, and actively explore ways and laws of the higher mathematics education of college students in the new media environment, strengthen the construction of university networks, active occupation Ideological new Media positions of political education.

Figure 2. Computer Assisted Instruction scene renderings

3 Computer multimedia technologies in mathematics foundation course

Computer multimedia technology in mathematics foundation course in computer applications in mathematics teaching universities are generally placed in specialized courses designed mathematics lesson, rarely involves basic course, most teachers believe that the traditional mathematics of teaching is the key to solving the shape of basic skills students. But the study, we found that the traditional teaching of basic courses in computer multimedia teaching should be assisted. In this regard, we can learn on the computer and briefly studied mathematics analysis. We know that the traditional mathematics of teaching is mainly on the basis of sketches and colour teaching, teaching in the sketch is mainly to solve our modelling capabilities, modelling training, perspective, anatomy, sense of space, texture, composition and other content; colour teaching in our main solution hue contrast, colour contrast, complementary colour contrast and colour space and colour contrast and well-being and so on. We discuss these issues now can be done in a number of software, ie for colour sketch studies can be carried out entirely in the computer. Such teaching and research can save a lot of time, avoiding the production of hand-painted dull duplication of effort. Take a colour mosaic effect work constitutes an example, if you want to complete a form, you need to repeatedly create and modify, wasting a lot of time and effort. The application of computers to complete simply enters an image in Photoshop software, and then performs Filter- Pixy elate- Mosaic command, a mosaic work done in an instant.

We also found that there are some modern software can simulate the effect of a variety of drawing tools, has now developed software such as Fractal Design Painter is good painting software. It provides a lot of painting tools, such as pens, pencils, brushes, watercolour pen, oil paints, airbrush, crayons, etc., but also offers a wide variety of strokes, to a certain extent, truly mimics the effect of freehand drawing. Such as when using painting tools, mimic Van Gogh, Cezanne and other masters of the brush strokes; when the brush tool, combined with wet drawing paper, the effect of Mathematics on rice paper for the imitable. Although it can not fully replace the painting, the painting can be used as a research method and means. In this way, students can save a lot of freehand drawing practice time, students can also develop visual thinking and analytical skills, help cultivate innovation ability.

Computer multimedia technology in mathematics appreciation class application is an important mathematics' of mathematics class mathematics teaching content. The purpose of mathematics appreciation, mainly in fine mathematics s teaching in two ways: first, through the appreciation of works of mathematics, to understand the history of mathematics development, grasp the law of development of fine mathematics s; second, through appreciation, inspire students' creative thinking, and thus create outstanding works. Through

appreciation teaching courses on pictures or slides are operations due to the complexity of the fuzzy, often not very efficient. Using computer multimedia teaching, mathematics appreciation class effect is greatly changed. As long as teachers have a multimedia computer, there is mathematics appreciation information and data to a disc loaded into the optical drive (CDROM), students in the appreciation of classical works, a little mouse, a painter's masterpiece and biographies will appear, not only can get a glimpse of picture works, you can also zoom in mathematics observation; not only a comprehensive view of the works, you can also choose to enjoy or have a work print.

Students in the classroom can break time, space, geographical restrictions, and foreign gallop across the ancient and modern, mathematics gallery stroll. Appreciate the mathematics of architecture, when not only the usual way to appreciate the buildings form of visual perception in the stationary state, but also can do dynamic display, allowing the building to spin up, enjoy the multiple sides of the building. You can also incomplete, or damaged historic buildings were restored. Enjoy a graphic design or cover design time, but also can be altered according to their preferences, but it is also indispensable for students to creative material. These are the traditional appreciation class unmatched.

Computer multimedia technology in computer is professional courses in mathematics, as a modern tool, first used in mathematics class in design teaching. It is widely used in the design, liberated the previous complex design work, improve work efficiency, the designer's right-hand man.

The accuracy is concerned, with the computer to produce an object the size of an absolute right, almost no errors. Such as the use of CAD software or 3DMAX produced graphics, with an accuracy of less than 0. 1mm, it can show the most delicate mathematics' of the design, which is the traditional hand-painted difficult to achieve, but its camera angles, pleasant to the eye point of view, depending on from fully simulate the real, not the existence of handmade randomness and imprecision. Therefore, the authenticity of computer design by the majority of designers agrees. In recent years, the development of software used in graphic design software is gradually increasing, a common two-dimensional CorelDraw, Photoshop, AutoCAD, and three-dimensional 3DMAX other software.

In painting courses teaching, there must be a lot of painting techniques require students to master, every teacher of painting styles, techniques have their own characteristics. The instructor is necessary to allow students to expand their horizons, to absorbing. Application of multimedia technology, breaking the teachers' knowledge of this one-way transmission of information sources, expanding the scope of information exchange teaching, breaks the teaching space, so that unrestricted access to information and delivery time and space. For example the Central Academy of Fine Mathematics s masters editing techniques textbooks, covering drawing, painting, oil painting techniques, such as content, teachers can combine curriculum content for teaching demonstration, in the classroom so that students can see the famous painter's lecture demonstrations, but the key place to repeat Play, learn to understand the true meaning of painting masters. Similarly, professional instructors techniques can also be made from their own multimedia courseware demonstration teaching, improve teaching effectiveness.

4 Mathematics educations is basically synchronized

Mathematics as a symbol of Chinese mathematics, has developed a number of years, has experienced a long history. Its development and development of traditional mathematics education is basically synchronized. Traditional mathematics education model for studying the development of self-contained mathematics provides a strong guarantee, but the crisis has brought to the development of Mathematics, Mathematics may lead to the development of stagnation and rigid.

With the introduction of Western culture, contemporary mathematics education has been given a new content and features, traditional mathematics education has been seriously challenged, and Mathematics is no exception. Chinese and Western cultures fierce collision, given the contemporary mathematics education conform to the trend of the times, and the Chinese have a tendency to weaken the function of painting, we can see the impact on Mathematics contemporary mathematics education development is enormous. Therefore, Mathematics to have sustainable development, we must look for a path.

Given the cultural heritage and cultural traditions there are significant differences among different ethnic, fusion of contemporary mathematics education and the presence of significant challenges, mainly as follows: Western contemporary mathematics education curriculum is based on the theory, although trying to achieve Western reconcile, western system in order to mark the traditional mathematics education is based on the poetry of learning-based, it is trying to achieve a comprehensive innovation in the original basis. Since the mathematic sing point of contemporary mathematics education and traditional mathematics education, the focus is different. Should contrary to objective laws, not according to the actual situation of contemporary mathematics education and the development of Mathematics, blindly impose two very different systems together, will generate a lot of negative impact, but we should make an objective assessment, can not ignore the contemporary the positive role of mathematics education for the development of Mathematics.

Contradictions are opposites, we study the impact of Chinese contemporary mathematics education in the process of painting effects, specifically requires an objective analysis of contemporary mathematics education teaching, writing produced. This mathematics from the aspect of two dimensions, the use of comparative approach, in teaching, through the teaching objectives, teaching methods, teaching materials, teaching content, teaching evaluation analysis of

differences in traditional and contemporary mathematics education mathematics education; in the creative aspects of , will be an inspiration on Mathematics, technique, emotion comparative study, summed up the pros and cons of contemporary mathematics education for the development of mathematics, but overall, pros and cons, more harm than good.

Because of our long-term in a feudal society, and the ancient social, political, cultural and systems are designed to meet the needs of the ruling class. The prevalence of the traditional hierarchy is mathematics education, just to satisfy the interests of the ruling class and the service. In this case, the role of mathematics education is major with a strong "into enlightenment, helping Fallon," the. In this historical context, the traditional mathematics education does not have a complete and standardized education system. In mathematics oculars the teaching process, the main idea is to master personal education based, then painting learners main objective things through observation and copying works of the classical way to achieve the purpose of drawing creation.

Visible, education has become the most basic rights of every person, and not a few aristocratic privileges, which will benefit the construction of a socialist harmonious society. Contemporary mathematics education teaching objectives conducive to the development of our comprehensive quality education, improve the overall level of China's national mathematics knowledge. For the construction of a beautiful home that has everything to gain but no harm. However, we also see the shortcomings can not be ignored him an objective reality. Universality corresponds to the peculiarities of contemporary mathematics education is universal knowledge for all students in the mathematics of Mathematics teaching goal setting, and not as a traditional mathematics education that, according to each student's specific conditions, can amount tailor the most appropriate teaching painting learning objectives and teaching goals at any time to adjust according to the needs of learning. Contemporary Mathematics by differences in education and Mathematics teaching objectives analysis, summed up contemporary mathematics education exists on the pros and cons of teaching objectives. We can see that they are closely related, the latter is dependent on the former, while drawing on Western mathematics education.

5 Conclusions

Computer mathematics multimedia technology in teaching, not only to speed up the progress of the mathematics of teaching, improve learning outcomes, more important is that it can give students a more novel stimuli, resulting in the best area of the cerebral cortex related development, so as to stimulate their creative evolving thinking. To innovative works are mathematics majors. The information age, computer multimedia teaching the mathematics of teaching is the direction of development, however, stressed the role of modern teaching media is not to deny the traditional teaching, but rather calls attention to a combination of both in teaching practice, flexible use. Contemporary mathematics teaching focus on the integrated is use of multimedia in order to continuously improve the quality and efficiency of the mathematics of teaching. The main trends in the mathematics of teaching is the traditional teaching media development and integration of modern teaching media, and gradually form a complete, current information society to adapt to the development of mathematics education system.

The concept of new media technology director of the Institute was first proposed by Mark P. Gold by the American television network CBS (CBS) in 1967, the concept of new media, academia is also formed without a fully unified conclusion, current consensus view is that new media is relying on network technology and digital technology, the Internet, mobile phones and digital television media representatives, to the public to provide personalized information and entertainment services spread form.

References

1. Sun Zhuanbo, Guan Hui. Decided to investigate the factors basketball shooting overcast. Harbin Institute of Physical Education, 26(2006)
2. Yuan Ting Gang. A comparative study of two EMG muscle strength training methods and the characteristic parameters. State Sports General Administration of Sports Science Research Thesis. Beijing: State Sports General Administration of Sports Science Institute, 155(2000)
3. Xu honest, Bing-Hong, Wen-Hai Liu. And so on. A comparative study of vibration when the vibration strength training with non-EMG changes. Xi'an Institute of Technology, 54(2004)
4. YANG Haiping. Basketball players of different positions and excellent pitcher perception characteristics. Guangzhou Physical Education Institute. 52(2005)
5. Lu Aiyun. Biomechanical characteristics under different weight men snatch action. Shanghai Institute of Physical Education, 61(2000)
6. Liu Yajun. EMG Tennis basic technology research. Tianjin Institute of Physical Education. 18(2005)
7. Cao Hui. Speed skating leg muscle coordination synchronized EMG analysis grieved. Tsinghua University. 45 (2005)

MATEC Web of Conferences 44, 01073 (2016)
DOI: 10.1051/matecconf/20164401073

Rearch on Remote Video Monitoring Technology in Industry based on Zigbee

Li Wei Wang

Teacher's College, Beihua University, Jilin City, China

Abstract. ZigBee is a recent rise of wireless network technology, with low-rate, low cost, low power, network capacity and other characteristics, to organize their own network, and network recovery ability, very suitable for wireless sensor networks. In this paper, the industrial production environment, systematic study of the ZigBee technology, video compression technology, as well as data communication principle, the development of the industrial video monitoring and control system based on ZigBee protocol.

1 General instruction

With the development, technological advances, modern industrial production scale expanding rapidly update production equipment, production technology becomes more advanced, accompanying the increasingly complex production environment, production monitoring and control technology which made more high requirements. Traditional wired network monitoring and control system by wiring, maintenance and scalability limitations, cannot better adapt to modern industrial production environments, requiring more advanced industrial monitoring and control system to meet the needs of modern industrial production. Wireless sensor network is a major trend of modern communication development, has a certain application basis, and in the continuing efforts of researchers, more advanced and mature, is an alternative to a wired network the best choice.

Figure 1. ZigBee wireless Network Protocol chart

2 Wireless communications in early industrialization

The first generation of wireless communications in early industrialization, from war needs, people use smoke signals, fire, semaphore, gestures to fellow transmit information. Of course, the amount of information and complexity is low, and information transmission is within visible distance range. In order to achieve a greater amount of information transmission, richer, more distant, it is encoded in the form of information, the formation of the original signal. Set up observatories in line of sight and at receiving the message transmitted to the distance again, that the relay-style messaging. Until 1838, the United States • Samuel Morse (Samuel Finley Breese Morse) invented the Morse code (also known as the Morse code), electricity yard pass digital message, the digital and the word corresponding to realize the complex information pass, and is the earliest form of digital communication, the end of the original forms of information transmission. Subsequently, the Americans Bell invented the telephone in 1876, replacing the telegraph. It took another ten years, in 1895, Italy's Galileo Stockholm • Marconi in his father's estate began his experiment, successfully received a radio signal from the 1.5 miles (about 2.4km) outside realization the world's first wireless telegraph transmission, thus, the birth of modern wireless communications.

As of 1934, the United States nearly 200 city police monitoring system, fifty-eight state police used AM (Amplitude Modulation, AM) technology for wireless communication system so that public safety be better protected. According to statistics, the mid thirties of the last century, there are about more than five thousand mobile devices installed radio receiver, based mainly in the vehicle, for the purposes of these early radio device mounted on a vehicle, the noise of the vehicle is a major obstacle. Later, an American radio engineer Edwin• Howard Armstrong (Edwin Howard Armstrong) invented the frequency modulation (Frequency Modulation, FM)

technology; its powerful features make it the world's communications major modulation techniques.

World War II accelerated the development of manufacturing and micro technology, and has been used in a large number of one-way and two-way radio communication systems and television systems. With the advancement of technology, the development, wireless communication technology has been extended too many fields such as business, agriculture, industry, etc., and the depth and breadth of applications evolving.

Figure 2. zigbee and Bluetooth match results demonstrate

3 State of the art industrial monitoring and control

Currently widely used industrial monitoring and control technology is a network monitor; it evolved from earlier centralized monitoring technology came. Centralized monitoring technology mainly through the central control platform for industrial production of core equipment for centralized monitoring; monitoring equipment is used in large-scale instrumentation. With the expansion of production scale, in the 1950s, sixties, used in industrial production, a special control room for centralized control of production parameters, such as current signal (0~10mA, 4~20mA of DC current signal) and voltage signals (1~5VDC voltage signal), and other analogy signals are processed in a centralized control room. The 1960s and 1970s, due to the development of computer technology, cost and operational monitoring equipment limitations, encourage people to try to use a computer to replace the traditional test instrumentation and control terminal, so the digital monitoring and control system began to develop. In the initial stage, the stability, the computer system is limited to the use of computer system architecture to achieve centralized monitoring and control of the production process has not been accepted. A failure occurs because the computer will cause the entire monitoring system failures, causing serious losses to the production, which is very dangerous.

In recent years, with the rapid development of information technology and network technology, Ethernet has become one of the most widely used network technology information, which has been applied to a large area of industrial monitoring and control, Industrial Ethernet is based on the IEEE 802.3 powerful regional and cell networks using TCP / IP communications protocol. By designing real-time communication methods and high stability industrial application network, Ethernet can meet the needs of real-time industrial data communications, industrial control functions to achieve the top-level data and the underlying control integrated together. Industrial Ethernet relative to the early industrial automation technology, transmission speed, construction costs, ease of formation and compatibility and so there are a lot of advantages. But established on which the monitoring and control system for real-time communication, network stability, system security, and data integrity have high demands, because monitoring technology Industrial Ethernet is for industrial production processes.

Wireless communication technology is following the industrial Ethernet and fieldbus, used in industrial production monitoring and control of another hot technology is the development trend of industrial automation production. Wireless communication technology to avoid the traditional wired network defects, wired network needs a conductor media for data transmission, resulting in a series of work and transmission pathways, such as planning the wiring, the default port, line testing, line expansion and so on. With the accompanying destruction of buildings, waste interfaces, maintenance difficulties, difficulties in expansion and other ills. In addition, in some special production environment (such as the petrochemical industry as well as hydrological monitoring, environmental monitoring, oil, coal, street surveillance, meter monitoring, etc.), a wired network coverage and network support is limited, there is high cost. The wireless communications transmission medium is not required in the industrial production environment; you can send data to the space, by installing a network access device in the networking area, wireless Internet connection, high flexibility, scalability, and convenient operation advantage.

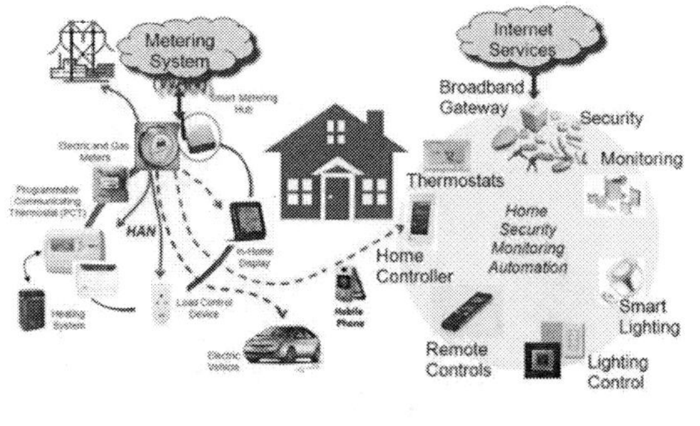

Figure 3. Zigbee remote monitoring system Demo

4 ZigBee and image compression coding technology

ZigBee is a wireless network in recent years, the rise of communications technology, the technology alliance by British Invensys, Japan's Mitsubishi Electric, Motorola USA, the Netherlands, Philips Semiconductors and other companies in the development of a network, security and application software protocol layer, cost, power

consumption, speed, complexity is relatively low, when the word is used to notify the pollen from the honey bees companion way location, is a simple, effective "Wireless Communications" in the form of.

ZigBee technology is mainly used in short-distance data transmission between a variety of electronic devices, the lower its data transfer rate, and therefore suitable for industrial production environments wireless transmission of video data. Its main features are as follows has several areas:

(1) The rate is low. ZigBee network in all the different bands work data transfer rates are at a low level, but also for different working frequencies corresponding rate is adjusted, so that work more in line with the principle of energy distribution.

(2)Low power Because the transmission rate is low, the transmission power is only 1mW, and the use of sleep mode (when required data is received, only wake up by a network of "coordination" on them), so the ZigBee technology is very low power consumption, for energy security network to run a small, usually two AA batteries can support up to two years of operation of the network.

(3)Low cost Compared to other short-range communication technology, ZigBee technology research and development costs low, because of its simple design protocol stack. Moreover, program development is also very convenient; eight microprocessors will be able to meet the needs of ordinary network. With the application and development of the product, is expected to further reduce costs.

(4) Reliable data transmission. Using CSMA-CA (Carrier Sense Multiple Access-Collision Avoidance) mechanism to avoid a collision, and dedicated time to leave gaps for the fixed-band communications to provide protection, but also the establishment of independent network, data communication between nodes in the network have robust path transmission security, because the transmission path is not fixed, the flexibility to choose the best communication path through a router.

(5)Short delay for latency applications optimized data communication with a relatively short delay and a short wake-up delay.

(6)The network capacity ZigBee network can be employed, such as a star, the number of state and mesh network structure, can form large networks with a hierarchical network structure.

(7)Network security ZigBee technology uses a common encryption algorithms, and provides a complete data packet check function (available on the quality of data packet inspection, such as redundancy and integrity), thus ZigBee network has very good security.

5 Requirements ZigBee network transmissions of video compressed data

ZigBee is a low-rate wireless data transmission network, and the content of the original uncompressed video data is the large number of successive image frames, which have higher bandwidth data transmission requirements, so the transmission of video in low transmission rate of ZigBee networks the data must be through efficient compression, otherwise, is not complete real-time video monitoring tasks. Video compression is by deleting unnecessary video data (such as duplicate colors, color changes, repeating image frames, etc.), so as to achieve the purpose of reducing the amount of data. Video compression is divided into loss and lossless compression, loss compression of video information deleted when decompression is unrecoverable, but it can greatly reduce the amount of video data, and lossless compression during decompression can restore the original video data, the picture quality can be good assurance, but its share of the memory space will not be reduced. This article video application environment for production and management industry, the core purpose is to monitor and control, so the picture quality requirements can be appropriately lowered, no need to reach the TV, movies, etc. to quality requirements, so the use of loss compression is most appropriate.

Compressed video data is a measure of the effectiveness and versatility compression method selection criteria. Moment, major international organizations to develop video coding standard is the International Telecommunication Union Telecommunication Standardization Organization (ITU-T for ITU Telecommunication Standardization Sector) and the International Organization for Standardization/ International Electro technical Commission (ISO/IEC, International Organization for Standardization/ International Electro technical Commission) , MPEG-x and H.26x series of video compression standard is developed by the two, two series of compression encoding technology is relatively similar, including MPEG-4 and H.264 compression technology is the most studied and most widely used. MPEG-4 may be employed according to the different objects of different coding algorithm, coding algorithm is more flexible, more targeted, thus making the compression rate, encoding target independent and allows reuse of video data, in addition, MPEG-4 encoding in different objects The rate can be flexibly assigned, which can be assigned to match the byte coded according to the degree of importance, the important objects of points on the object of little minor points, so you can achieve good results at low bit rates. The H.264 encoding technology used is more advanced than the MPEG-4, but it's relatively complex computing, technology is not mature enough, the risk of instability exists in the coding system. In summary, to meet ZigBee network video transmission, the paper selected coding technology MPEG-4 format, industrial surveillance video compression.

6 Image compression coding algorithm

MPEG-2 technology has been developed MPEG-4, MPEG-4 compression algorithm uses a large number of

efficient algorithms, but also provides specialized tools for the operation and the coded video data, so the MPEG-4 video standard than the earlier of a higher compression ratio, better scalability advantages, MPEG-4 not only uses such as motion estimation and motion compensation and some other traditional methods, but also uses a video extraction, classification and other advanced video encoding technology, based on manipulation of the image frame is not again limited. In addition, flexible rate control video object is achieved in accordance with the importance of the distribution rate, even if the bandwidth is not ideal, but also to ensure picture quality, picture frames no longer limited by the low bit rate. Therefore, the full bandwidth utilization is better quality.

MPEG-4 video standard introduces the video object (Video Object, VO) concept can be based on content access, high efficient video data compression. A video sequence is split into one or a group of VO, VO can be any shape in the video area (such as Portrait, things like), the user can be obtained and image manipulation entity, it is flexible and no longer limited to the traditional rectangular frame, VO has a moving object, the object shape and texture objects 3 types. Furthermore, MPEG-4 also introduces a video object plane (Video Object Plan, VOP) concept, VOP is a VO successive frames having image frame, such as VO is defined as a ball beating, then the VOP is the ball in the beating during a time of the image. VOP is the basis for MPEG-4 encoding, encoding or interpolation can be independently encoded, i.e. estimated or motion picture compensation did not occur. VOP before the MPEG-4 coding needs to be defined.

References

1. Li Xinrong overall intelligent building control system design [J] Technology Information, 63(2007)
2. Jiang Xiaolin, Miao Yu design and development of intelligent building monitoring system. Security Technology, 23(2006)
3. Wang Shuang application and development of video surveillance systems in industrial production. Network and Information, 25(2009)
4. Sun school on behalf of the development and application of "video surveillance system. Jiangxi Communication Technology, 38(2009)
5. Ruan Weihua common indoor wireless location technology introduction. Science and Technology Information, 90(2009)
6. Liang Guangsheng, Liudan Juan, Haofu Zhen based on CC2430 ZigBee wireless network nodes. Electronic Design Engineering, 18(2010)
7. Mengzhen Fei, Ya Ling, Hou Yi handsome design is based on ZigBee technology wireless module. Electronic Component Applications, 39(2010)
8. Baozhao Wei, Wang Lin, Xu Qideng design USB-RS232 converter module FT232R. Computer Knowledge and Technology, 1204(2008)
9. Wang LonWorks technology based on LabVIEW and iLab remote experiment system design. Dalian: Dalian University of Technology 251(2009)

MATEC Web of Conferences **44**, 01074 (2016)
DOI: 10.1051/matecconf/20164401074

Application of Multimedia Technology in Business English Interactive Teaching

Xi Wen Zhang[1], Da Peng Wang[2]

[1] *Foreign Languages' College, Beihua University, Jilin City, China*
[2] *Financial Information Center, Jilin City, China*

Abstract. The CALLS (Computer Assisted Language Learning System) is an effective method in business English writing teaching, particularly for students which are non-speaking countries. The CALLS is suited to self-learning because of the Rich scenario module design. Application results are examined by using the methods of group experiments, questionnaires, examinations and others. The CALLS is especially suited to creating a better studying atmosphere among students in the process of business English writing teaching than other methods.

1 General instruction

Business English Writing course in higher most difficult packages to considerable deliver in Business Vocational College has always been one of the English teachings. Though both teachers and students spend time and make great efforts, the results are too often far from satisfactory. In Business English Writing, many students are: 1) too often unfamiliar with the writing form of daily Business English; 2) only able to write material that baffles those who are engaged in business activities.

Many of the students who major in Business English are, unexpectedly, unable to write a resume or an application letter in English upon graduation. Such students would be defeated in the fierce job-hunting competition. In my view, this phenomenon occurs because of the defective methods and scarce knowledge involved in traditional Business English Writing teaching. With widespread application of multimedia in education, more and more educators are trying to apply modern education tools to English teaching to improve results. However, such researches often concentrate on listening, speaking and reading of Basic and College English while Business English Writing is seldom involved.

With reference to the findings of experts' research in the relevant field both at home and abroad, the writer of this paper introduces the multimedia computer into Business English Writing as an auxiliary teaching method. Application results are examined by using the methods of group experiments, questionnaires, examinations and others. Analysis of questionnaires, final examination papers and teacher-and-student forums and checks conducted by the Human Resources Departments of related enterprises show that the multimedia computer applied in Business English Writing teaching can help to remedy the deficiency of traditional teaching methods. The computer is especially suited to creating a better studying atmosphere among students in the process of Business English Writing teaching than other methods.

Figure 1. Interactive video transforming teaching and learning

2 Computer-assisted language learning and effective

With the rapid development of higher vocational education scale and continue to improve the education system and structure, there is a growing awareness of the importance of profound reform of special and vocational education in teaching and learning activities. Computer-assisted language learning as a hotspot of educational reform, reform has become one of the traditional way of teaching and learning the most important factor. How to use the advanced vocational education in computer-assisted language learning and effective use of a variety of modern educational technology to promote the improvement of the efficiency and effectiveness of higher vocational education has become an important issue that every vocational education teachers must concern.

Computer Assisted Language Learning concern not only IT, but also pay attention to improving the teaching design, teaching methods, teaching resources and build teaching environment. We strive at the latest educational theory to guide, to explore business English writing in higher vocational colleges teaching how to more effectively use computer-assisted language learning design new teaching models and methods, create excellent teaching resources and the environment, hope to the majority of English teachers between vocational colleges and higher vocational computer-assisted teaching practice English Teaching Business English Writing to bridge.

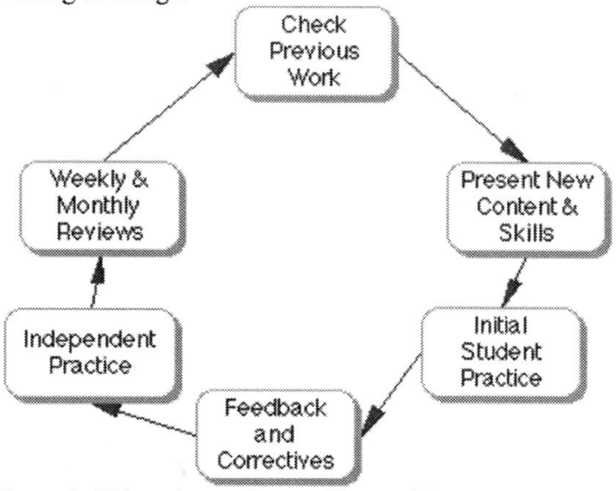

Figure 2. 3Direct-interactive teaching model

3 Subject characteristics of business English

Business English is the business environment in the application of English, English for Specific Purposes one belongs (ESP) of. ESP actually formed in the 1960s, but after World War II had begun germination. A time when many countries are struggling to get rid of the dilemma caused by the war, to revive the economy, the development of science and technology, to strengthen international exchanges. Because the United States at the time has a strong economic and technological strength, and is in the position of a superpower, so it uses the language - English shows its unique value in international exchanges. Many people also see that learning English learning English is no longer in order to complete a course of school education, but a way to give a job, doing business as well as the convenience of an important scientific communication tools or media. 60 years before is the English curriculum more emphasis on teaching grammar, sentence knowledge. Due to the continuous development of applied linguistics, linguists began to focus from the study of language in the form of steering the actual exchange of language law research and analysis. So people will come to realize that the same is a language, its meaning and role differences exist in different areas and situations of use. As pilot, businessman, engineer, etc., because of their profession difference, the language it uses is different. ESP is characterized emphasize teaching content rather than on teaching methods, emphasizing the teaching must meet the needs of learners and language learning practicality, as well as emphasizing the combination of vocational training and language training.

4 Features information on teaching mode

With the comprehensive application of information technology in the teaching field of education, profound changes in the way teaching and learning occurs. Many colleges and universities to establish a multimedia projector classroom, multimedia computer network classrooms, electronic reading room, campus paperless office platform and teaching platform and other modern teaching environment. These information technology equipment and resources must be the concept of modern education and teaching of integration, we must directly serve the Course, and penetrated into all aspects of teaching, namely improving teaching models and teaching methods in order to achieve optimal teaching effectiveness and efficiency. Meanwhile, the development and application of modern information technology for the development of new teaching model provides a unique condition.

Information on teaching models based on modern educational thought as a guide, make full use of functional advantages of modern educational technology, and give full play to the students' initiative, enthusiasm and creativity, to optimize the structure of a stable form of teaching effectiveness and efficiency of the teaching process. Typical information technology teaching mode: observable phenomena - exchange phenomena - Computer Aided imagine - clear discovery - using discovery. Among them:

1. observable phenomena: the basic principles of natural phenomena in macroscopic or microscopic implied by the experimental demonstration to students, the main form of demonstration experiments for teachers, teachers focused on organizing students to observe experiments, let them discover scientific principles inherent in the experimental phenomena, and with try to resolve their existing knowledge observed.

2. AC phenomenon: Students will observe some found that to be wrong, then, to organize students to share their discoveries, by teachers and students to discuss the essence of which derives from it.

3. Computer-aided imagine: organizing students' prior knowledge combined bold imagination macroscopic or microscopic natural phenomena, and ask students to tell the reason of their own imagination, that imagination is based on scientific analysis, rather than fantasy, combined with student teachers imagine corresponding computer simulation of the phenomenon, and gradually rationalized.

4. Clearly found that: Teachers organize students to use scientific language to explain the phenomenon.

5. The use of discovery: the practical application of organizing students to contact their findings, to solve some practical problems.

5 Classified information teaching mode

Various factors interact to form the teaching process of teaching mode, teaching mode information is to contact the teaching process of modern information technology environment in a number of factors each other, mutual restraint and completely constituted a stable, systematic and theorized teaching mode. Teaching modern IT environment consists of four factors: teachers, students, information technology teaching resources and information technology teaching environment. In support of information technology, the teaching can be for the individual, team and organizational forms in three classes. In the characteristics of IT application for the division basis, information can be divided into three teaching mode of teaching.

Rich source of information, knowledge, capacity, and strong interactive function, help to improve learners' learning initiative, enthusiasm, help students and higher-order thinking skills. Because of multimedia and network technology to provide user-friendly, visually interactive learning environment, capable of maps, text, sound, image and integrated multi-sensory stimulation Mao, but also by hypertext, hyperlinks, organize and manage a variety of subject knowledge teaching information, not only help to stimulate students' interest in learning and consultation sessions, collaborative learning, help students take the initiative to found the initiative to explore, acquire and maintain a situation conducive to the creation and extensive knowledge of the development of associative thinking and the establishment of the establishment of new and old knowledge contact, but also on the formation and development of students 'cognitive structure, namely, to promote students' current knowledge about the significance of the construction of the school is very favorable, but also in other instructional media or other learning environment cannot be compared.

Teaching activities, teaching methods can be more flexible, to more fully meet the learning needs of learners. With the support of multimedia and network technology, learners can study at home or in the office, you can also learn on the go, every learner in the learning process are acceptable information for their own learning abilities and learning needs.

In recent years, the use of higher vocational colleges multipurpose room and two-way control system of classroom teaching has been more widespread, multi-purpose classrooms is an integrated multimedia computers, large-screen projectors, video Showcase, DVD players, video recorders and microphones and other equipment for one classroom teaching system, using the full power of teaching, computer aided teaching and demonstration tool, is currently the most popular, easy to use, the effect is the best form of teaching. This multi-purpose classroom for teachers of higher vocational college's computer-aided instruction provides a good teaching environment.

Universities from the current status of view, the use of computer-aided Microsoft Office PowerPoint lectures increasingly common form of teaching that the use of electronic teaching slides complete the task of teaching in the classroom. Teachers can be prepared in advance their own good Microsoft Office PowerPoint courseware into the multi-purpose classrooms for playback. Microsoft Office PowerPoint as an intuitive and convenient multimedia authoring tool, so that front-line teaching staff can easily create their own ideas to meet the actual needs of educational software. But note that, first of all, Microsoft Office PowerPoint courseware is part or a fragment of the content of classroom teaching; it should not be the entire contents of a class.

Second, it can have voice commentary language, but do not have full voice; again, it has some interactivity, but the main function is to demonstrate; and finally, in general, it does not interact directly with students occur. These features are by such courseware position in the application of the decision; it cannot replace nor should replace the leading role of teachers in the classroom teaching. In addition, the multi-purpose classroom, teachers also can directly use CAI courseware classroom presentations. Generally, this type of CAI courseware content suitable for the performance, but it is somewhat different with Microsoft Office PowerPoint courseware, such as CAI courseware microscopic phenomena show is difficult to demonstrate by other means, the real danger of the phenomenon of the experiment, the real experiment to a very long or very short time in order to see the phenomenon, process or event in the past, we need dynamic phenomenon repeatedly observed.

6 Virtual labs

Virtual Lab (Virtual Laboratory) is actually a simulation using virtual reality technology or fictitious certain situations, for students to observe, manipulate and construct the objects, so that they get the experience or discoveries. In using virtual reality technology to build a variety of virtual labs, students can do all kinds of dangerous in real life, or because of space-time interval completely impossible experiments. Virtual laboratory can be immersive, by increasing the number of helmet-mounted display, data gloves and the like sensing devices; it allows students to experiment with the operation in almost real virtual environment. From now, most schools usually is through the keyboard and mouse operation to perform virtual experiments, computer software can simulate a realistic three-dimensional laboratory, on the monitor students can see their operating procedures and experimental phenomena changes in real time, if the software is relatively high degree of interaction, students can operate controlled experimental details more similar to the real test, then the student to appreciate more from the experimental laws and practices. Virtual laboratory can provide students with a non-hazardous, non-expensive way to interact with the real world.

For my country, online education (or online teaching), after all, still a novelty, follow what educational theory, how to design and develop online courses, teaching how to implement the network, how to give the learner with the necessary assistance and guidance on how to network education (or online teaching) evaluation, etc., many questions that we should seriously think about and deal with problems. Colleges and universities on the current situation in terms of teaching, collaborative inquiry-based resource-based and collaborative inquiry process is very important, network teaching platform in which plays an extremely important role. Collaborative network teaching platform to explore is to life and life and provide a space for the exchange of teachers and students or carrier. On the network teaching platform, through which teachers can present their own point of view, through which students can present their own views; network teaching platform provides a place with a clear theme of the exchange activities for teachers and students: teachers and students can mutually ideas exchange, teachers and students can agree on a topic or task consensus learning objectives, teachers can provide active environment to students, and make or receive feedback on a topic destination; network teaching platform can enhance the interaction between teachers and students; Students must be reached through the activities of the mission objectives, teachers must provide meaningful feedback on the inherent nature of the relationship between mission objectives activities; network teaching platform can provide feedback on activities, so that students can adjust according to the feedback learning activities.

7 Computer aided business English writing teaching model

Teacher training and student training combined. To make better use of computer-assisted language learning, teachers and students should be short-term training, to make clear teaching objectives, basic grasp of operation of the device, effectively solve technical problems. If you do not go through the training, students spend a lot of time to figure out how to operate the device, it is a waste of limited time and anxiety, and even computer-assisted learning would be bored.

Using advanced teaching equipment and training of the students' interest combined. Regardless of any kind of teaching methods, the dominant position of the students cannot be ignored. If the student is not interested in learning, lack of motivation, it is difficult to achieve good learning outcomes. Therefore, the use of advanced teaching equipment should also pay attention to cultivate students' interest in learning.

Man-machine communication and interpersonal combined. The computer cannot replace teachers; online teaching cannot replace classroom teaching. In autonomous learning ability is not ideal situation, teachers organize the classroom is the key. The author will be introduced to computer-assisted language learning business English writing teaching, teaching effectiveness effective. But the age of vocational college students to learn basic features and it is worthy of further discussion and study. For example, in a network environment, some students keen to chat, play games, do not put effort into learning them completely. Thus, computer-assisted language learning applications to Business English Writing Course in Vocational Schools cannot be completely ignored lectures, in teaching business terms, knowledge can use traditional teaching methods, while a strong practical content can use computer-aided, two complementary kinds of teaching methods in order to better use to improve teaching effectiveness. Computer-assisted language learning resources are abundant, and the prospects are bright, as an English teacher to new ideas and knowledge. Traditional teaching resources cannot meet the demands of the times. English teachers will be in the ever-changing information age, the computer-assisted language learning research and practice to new heights.

References

1. Inch Xiane Authorware interactive multimedia CAI courseware production method of Dali University 32(2007)
2. Wu Fang, HONGKONG "Business Communication" Foreign Language Teaching and Research Press, 111(2002)
3. Zhang Jianfei Development and application of "rules of the game of Table Tennis" Multimedia CAI Wuhan Institute of Physical Education Thesis, 22(2007)
4. Niehong Ling multimedia courseware evaluation to explore the basic framework of China Educational Technology Academy • Master of Education (Chemistry) Thesis, 22(2005)
5. Liu multimedia courseware development and integration of the material prepared in Kunming Metallurgy College,30(2002)

MATEC Web of Conferences **44**, 01075 (2016)
DOI: 10.1051/matecconf/20164401075

Study on Distance Education to Adult Students in New Media Background based on Computer Technology

Ying Pan

Adults and Continuing Education, Beihua University, Jilin, China

Abstract. In the context of new media, traditional adult students' distance education has been an unprecedented challenge to the current distance education of adult students to fully understand the importance of the use of new media, necessity, and through new media the student population is widely popular media to develop and strengthen distance education of adult students, so as to continuously improve the effectiveness of distance education, and improve the quality of personnel training. In this paper, the characteristics of the new media, the impact of new media and how to use distance education of adult students as well as to strengthen the distance education of adult students three elaborate.

1 General instruction

With the continuous development of China's market economy, improve, life-long learning the knowledge economy has been widely recognized under social, adult higher education should once again usher in the spring of rapid development, but students of Adult Higher Continuing Education has reduced year by year, adult recognition of higher education community to continue declining. Analysis of the reasons is the following aspects: (1) college enrollment, self-examination of the shunt. (2) Continuing education and training of adult higher goals are not clear, unscientific; resulting in no significant effect of continuing education training, training of personnel can not meet the needs of socialist modernization. Deal with the problems, scholars have put forward correct school of thought, insist on serving the community and training of personnel to perform functions; flexible school system, and effectively meet the social needs of adults continue to learn; to achieve academic education and job training to improve the quality changes. From the academic point of view than the macro-level analysis of the Adult Higher Education and General Higher Education continues reasonable division of labor discussed the essential attribute of adult higher education and continuing training objectives, from the point of view of the basis of the quality of personnel training of adult higher education continues to present problems and solutions.

In cultivating innovative educational and cultural backgrounds innovative thinking talent, the Chinese Adult Education also shoulder the heavy responsibility of innovation and social development. Innovation is the soul of national progress, "Gou Nisshin, Japan Nisshin also Nisshin" culture of innovation is an important connotation of advanced culture, a culture of innovation and create an atmosphere conducive to innovative activity is generated in the production activities associated with the social value system as a whole and its results innovative forms combined. This article continues to follow the basic rules of adult higher education, in line with the content of education and innovation, education concept innovation, education and means of communication in the form of innovation and innovative ideas put forward in the context of the whole social innovation, the core content of adult higher education is continuing students innovative consciousness and ability to target, according to the development trend of adult higher education continues, in fact, made possible the development of ideas to help the development of our country for the development of adult higher education institutions to continue.

Figure 1. Online college

2 Adult higher educations continues to achieve the diversification

Since the founding of adult higher education continues to achieve the diversification of higher education, improve the structure of the system of higher education. Access to higher education meets the aspirations of the people, while actively promoting the popularization of higher education process. Our Adult Higher Education for Adult Continuing Education, to enhance the level of knowledge provides an important way to meet the diversified market economy, the development process of the educational needs of different groups of people, train outstanding talent as a market economy of China's socialist construction and reform made great contribution. However, the development of adult higher education has continued, but there are still many problems.

Since the Department of Adult Education Adult Education formerly responsible for managing the development of functional differentiation Planning Division, Basic Education, Department of Higher Education, Division after college students, resulting in higher fuzzy adult continuing education status, resulting in the management process prone to blind spots, affecting healthy and orderly development of adult education. In addition, China to develop a complete no adult education laws, with the continuous progress of adult higher education popularization process for the new high-level job training in the form of adult higher education, age education, leisure and education does not correspond to adult education, lifelong education law guide, specification, build lifelong education, public vision of a learning society will not really implemented.

Adult higher education community on the utilitarian value orientation is mainly reflected in the pursuit of one-sided and one-sided pursuit of academic skills in two ways. If the adult learners to pursue higher education for the purpose of Adult Continuing Education, the adult learners in the learning process will be to re-examination by getting educated, to improve their quality in the second. The adult higher education organizations continue to need income to meet the needs of the candidate's access to educational qualifications, in terms of personnel training and examination process reduces the standard. The adult higher education as a single continuing technical education, the educational process as a way to get to work, thus ignoring the humanities enhance adult learners, resulting in reduced quality of training Adult Higher Education. In addition, continuing adult higher education did not really get the same higher education and general social acceptance, is widely recognized that the presence of adult higher education entrance requirements, low quality of training, strict examination requirements and other issues. These cognitive biases are the direct cause of the social reality of adult higher education continues to doubt and negative outcomes.

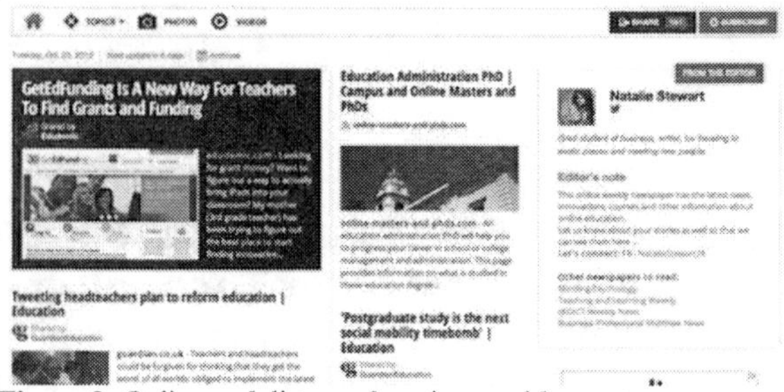

Figure 2. Online and distance learning weekly

Revenue in the heavy, light management, heavy quantity of light training under the guidance of the school tendencies, whether TV is an independent, and dependent adult education colleges (Continuing Education) School of Continuing Education in Adult Higher regarded as a way to generate income. Under the guidance of this distortion educational philosophy, the school principal continuing adult higher education setting unrealistic professional, blind expansion of enrolments, reducing teaching inputs. Teaching process of copying or imitating general higher education, "Pu enlightenment" mode, completely out of the training objectives of adult higher education to cultivate application continues skilled personnel. In addition, China Adult Higher Education shared teaching resources to continue running colleges and universities, with enrolments in colleges and universities, students in adult higher education can not continue the same teachers, experimental resources and library resources and teaching college students. Coupled with the lack of full-time teachers for adult students to understand, are not familiar with the laws of teaching adult higher education, it is difficult to achieve the desired training goal.

3 Adult higher educations is importance of continuing education

Traditional concepts of education will be divided into everyone's life and work of the learning period of two parts, higher education is recognized as the highest stage of life education, the adult higher education as higher education continues to supplement academic education. Adult higher education is importance of continuing education basic value orientation, resulting in higher adult continuing education with strong utilitarian overtones, ignoring the human learning process. With the social and economic changes in the structure and social changes in the population structure, increased leisure time and improvement in the level of information presented continuing education lifelong adult higher requirements, and it has the conditions for implementation. Lifelong education is not only a new concept of education, but it is also a new education system. The dominant ideology of lifelong education believes that education should relate to all aspects of life that emphasize lifelong learning educational content intrinsic link between education and the standard of living and quality of leisure education, life education is one of the higher content of continuing education for adults. Lifelong Education everyone that

education should provide the necessary skills and knowledge in the best way, to abandon the idea of lifelong education selection of traditional education, out of action, to achieve a higher education is open to adult education recipients to meet their education the goal. Lifelong Education stressed that human life should be constantly learning and education, continue to update their knowledge structure, the idea is completely realistic needs of social development and personal growth. Lifelong Education to achieve a positive guidance for continuing adult higher education, higher sublimation adult continuing education and social development in the modernization process of the value and role of adult higher education is bound to continue to follow the traditional academic education to change the law of life-long education.

Caption is the Adult Higher the right direction. Under the lifelong learning and learning society background, higher education will be highlighted in supply and demand, it is due to the time, energy, and economic and other reasons, can not be carried out through the normal channels, improve general higher education qualifications, and then choose the adult higher education. With the advancement of the process of popularization of higher education, enrollment ongoing work, along with the private higher education, professional and independent colleges and higher education abroad into the country, so that people can get personal qualifications to improve education through different forms of higher education. Currently, the domestic Adult Higher Education although there is some room for development, but has been unable to account for the same as before the main position, enrollment in colleges and universities to expand the number of students will inevitably affect the adult higher education continues. In addition, with the further development of the market economy, the educational needs of the public have been transformed from a single diploma to pursue the improvement of the capacity and quality. Continuing education and academic qualifications in improving education faced with dwindling situation actively carry out academic education at the same time, efforts to job training, continuing education after college, age education and leisure education and other non-academic education, continuing education is the Adult Higher the right direction.

There are two folds sound, so each one and the same at a level surface. Each sound folds itself divided down into two parts, the upper part is called the plicate, also called false vocal cords, the following section is called the lower folds, folds under what we call the usual sense of the vocal cords. False vocal cord in the normal pronunciation is not closed; it does not have a real sense of sound effects. The main role is to assist the true vocal cords false vocal cord closure.

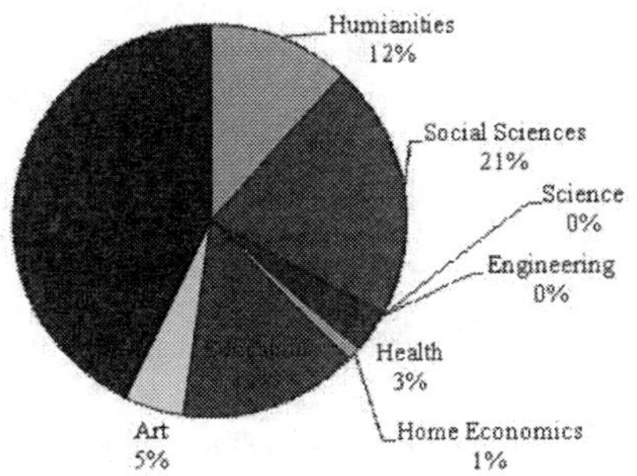

Figure 3. Distance education resource Map

Longitudinal development of adult higher education continues, countries continue to adult higher education have gone to focus on general education, vocational education and then to the core, and the development of occupational and non-occupational continuing education process. "Occupational" is inherent property of adult higher education continues, but the essential attribute of "occupation" of not continuing adult higher education. In the course of development of adult higher inertia is continuing education, occupational just important manifestation in the form of a stage. Adult Higher Education clients are mainly working, unemployed and retirees, is typical of post-secondary vocational education. Vocational education services are mainly working, unemployed adults or full-time students. In addition, adult continuing education, not only were higher employment-oriented adult vocational education, including leisure education, universities and other non-elderly "vocational" education. With the improvement of the socio-economic, cultural progress and material living standards, to meet the material needs of people on the basis of the level of spiritual life put forward a new goal. At this point, people want to accept more than is career-oriented education, but to meet the personal feelings, hobbies, leisure education and other needs of self-cultivation. Although the object of education and higher education continuing education adult content are not the same, but with adult higher education continuing education professional nature of the current and future development trends for a long period of time, but not the ultimate direction of development of adult higher education continues . With the development of society, people's living standards improve, career-oriented education will gradually move toward the edge of Adult Higher Education. At present, the overall level of development of difficult compared with developed countries, economic restructuring and industrial restructuring still need to rely on people to improve their professional competence and level to support. So, even though the ultimate goal of career-oriented adult higher education is not continuing adult higher education, but still has a special meaning of its existence in the future for a long period of time.

For a long time, much of adult higher education continue to condemn and controversy in the implementation process, in pursuit of academic qualifications for the final values reflect the utilitarian type of education, ignoring

the needs of the people of internal development, but also affect the quality of personnel training. The career-oriented adult higher education continuing education, although a period of time to adapt to social development, but the same people did not pay attention to the needs of comprehensive development, in which case it becomes an adult higher education career development tools. In fact, in the context of a learning society, adult continuing higher education is an important way to promote universal enter a learning society, full of learning, building a learning society is the ultimate direction of development of adult higher education continues. In the future, adult higher education will continue to raise the overall quality of education goals, to conduct a full range of contact through extensive educational and social approach to actively penetrate the rural areas, communities and businesses. Therefore, changes in academic education into learning not only to build a learning society inexorable law, but also the objective requirements of adult higher education continue their own development.

Adult higher education is an effective means to manage and control the development of education. Legislation can clear the status of Adult Higher Education in Adult Higher Education in the education system, with a sense of guidance in the specification and management of adult higher education run, therefore, to promote the legislation with the help of Adult Higher Education Adult Continuing Education out of development difficulties, promote lifelong an important way of learning process. Government should pay attention to changes in general higher education, continuing to ignore the practice of adult higher education, should continue to adult higher education management as job duties related to education through increased funding, to provide policy support and other forms of adult higher education continue to guide and support, avoid adult higher education continue to continue to develop in the direction of quick success.

After merging the former Department of Adult Education explicit adult education specifically to deal with the functions, so that the development of Adult Higher Management Planning Division of Continuing Education, Basic Education, Department of Higher Education, Division of college students a clear responsibility, truly standardize management of adult education. Continue to strengthen adult higher education institutions, and encouraging private capital founded an independent adult higher education institutions continue. This adult higher education funding to ensure continuing education to some extent, dependent adult higher education colleges and universities to avoid the tendency to Cape enlightenment drawbacks. Establish a scientific and feasible, adult continuing education evaluation system of higher complex continuing adult higher education law, and by evaluating hardware and software and the quality of adult higher education institutions, such as continuing education, in the form of assessment continued to promote adult higher education institutions reform and development.

4 Conclusion

In the knowledge economy, higher adult continuing education course content will be constantly updated according to the social development needs, while achieving academic education function, but also to meet people's needs comprehensively improve. Modern enterprise education, community education, vocational education, knowledge and skills to improve the short-term training updates and content-rich education, rural populations will continue our Adult Higher Education new development space. Adult Higher Education is also a concrete manifestation of lifelong continuing education in the form of continuing education after the University can undertake work to provide educational opportunities for people to have to get a college degree, and is willing to continue to receive relevant education. Therefore, adult higher education needs to continue to improve the level of training, on the basis of steady development, college education, and gradually develop job postgraduate education. In today's highly developed information technology, relying on remote technology actively, improve remote mode adult higher education continues to regional economic and social development in rural areas requires knowledge of the economic development of agriculture, rural and remote areas to train practical talents.

References

1. Should Wangjiang China Education Reform and Development for 30 years. Shanghai: Shanghai University of Finance and Economics Press, 105(2008)
2. Maoyuan China popularization of higher education structures and systems. Guangzhou: Guangdong Higher Education Press, 14(2009)
3. Du to Germany, Yaoyuan Feng, Li Xing-Dong Toward Development of Adult Education. Beijing: China Renmin University Press, 267(2007)
4. He Qizong new era of education - theory and practice of lifelong education. Beijing: People's Publishing House, 23(2008)
5. Zhao new study occupational characteristics of the Adult Higher Education - Xiamen five universities, for example the status of implementation of Adult Higher Education. Xiamen University, master's thesis, 251(2007)
6. High Zhimin, Cai Baotian social transition adult education, lifelong education and research. Beijing: Capital Normal University Press, 112(2007)

MATEC Web of Conferences **44**, 01076 (2016)
DOI: 10.1051/matecconf/20164401076

Study on Teaching Reformation of Contemporary Art Teaching to University Students on Corel Painter Software

Mei Ni Xiong, Bao Quan Pan[a]

College of Fine Arts, Beihua University, Jilin City, China

Abstract. Contemporary art education started late in China on the basis of western teaching theories formed its own unique system, which has a great influence on Corel Painter software. This paper explores that contemporary art education is analyzed advantages and disadvantages of the influence on the development of Chinese painting, and the solutions are found out to the existing problems, summed up the reality enlightenment of that the contemporary art on the impact of education on Chinese painting development.

1 General instruction

On the contemporary art education teaching materials, mainly from the West, the system is only a product of modern times. Since the early 1950s, the introduction of "Soviet model", the "sketch teaching system" long-term dominant position, which makes the development of Chinese painting to a certain extent, too much emphasis on the infected 'Western realism based "colours. Eighties and nineties change the status quo of contemporary art education and teaching methods make "student-cantered" has become the consensus of the majority of school education. And in the final analysis, the development of Chinese painting and contemporary art education on how mutual integration, how to seek common ground, how to learn from each other, the development of both what constraints they are facing a series of problems have become more apparent, prompting the inheritance and development of Chinese painting has become the most contemporary art education one of the important issues.

On the subject of correlation, the author of the information is available and rare. Correlation of the current works are mostly to be an analysis of the development of Chinese painting from the perspective of traditional art education, lack of breath new era. Influence of contemporary art education for the development of Chinese painting is to better summarize now able to meet the needs of the development of socialism with Chinese characteristics, and promote national love of national culture and develop.

Figure 1. Corel painter X3 download free version for windows and mac

2 The basic idea of contemporary art education

With the changing times, contemporary art education has been given a new era of more spirit and values in heritage and inheritance will appear in many of the vitality and new understanding. Ming Dong Qichang in the "painting Chanshi Essay," also said: "The painter Kamijina pole for the case, another to add to Kamijina Yiping over who said natural then for God." Zhuangzi also think simple and natural as the highest realm. He proposed "both carved both clumsy, reverted to the Park," "simple and indisputable beauty of the world Mo 'point of view. That is, he is not opposed to artificial artistic process, but the goal is still to reach the return process simple and natural realm, which is the high degree of unity between man and nature realm, namely "World and I, and students, all things with me as a" to enter into the realm of Heaven. Huang landscape painting throughout profound works,

[a] Corresponding author: baoquanpan@126.com

Shi Qi pen ink out of the poor, and each time he gave the next dye dyed leaving gaps.

The entire screen layout, tend to put the picture of a mountain, although black ink round, but it does not make people feel choking. The actual situation in which the secret lies is in the handling of the screen, revealing a little bit of virtual white. Only the saints, "Road", "reason" with their spirit of harmony, trigger the unlimited mental state. The ancients also realized in the form of landscape view of the "Road" and on the "truth" of deep understanding. Landscape scenery of the gas is to borrow the influence of the mind can be detached in order to enter the realm of Takashi more elegant.

Overall, the four basic schools of Chinese classical aesthetics point of view, although somewhat different, but there is a very obvious thing in common. That are advocating Heaven, things I harmony, harmonious people I do not emphasize the antagonistic relationship between man and nature. The formation of this ideology is affected by the ideology of ancient society. From primitive society to rely on the natural slave class division, agriculture and light industry and then re-feudal society, the traditional subsistence peasant economy of production, backward social system so that people have a natural nature admiration, any resistance to natural disasters mean humans, and therefore the relationship between man and nature was the ancient Chinese spontaneously as one unified relationship; and now, with the progress of society, the advent of the industrial age machines, productivity is greatly improved, production expanded rapidly diminishing reliance on nature. The social economical and extremely underdeveloped, people of the world, has been deeply Confucian aesthetic values, the impact of the Taoist aesthetics, aesthetics of Chug, Buddhist aesthetics thought.

In summary, the Confucian aesthetic beauty in the pursuit of unity, they pursue personal beauty, and ultimately for life and art; Taoist pursuit of truth and beauty of unity. Their pursuit of natural beauty is the ultimate realization of art and life. Chu Sao aesthetic and moral is unity throughout the pursuit, the pursuit of beauty and Zen Buddhist aesthetic unity. When aesthetic ideology of Confucianism, Taoism, Chu, Buddha, although there are many differences in their philosophy and awareness, but they are exploring the aesthetic image of Chinese painting, but also the similarities together to form ideas from contemporary art education to a very important role. So that in the contemporary art education background, shaping the personality characteristics of different artists.

We should admit that Chinese painting is the beginning of self-reliance in the Western impact and modernization. Contemporary art education is neither a Westernized, nor is along the natural development of the traditional track, but the Chinese people with advanced culture as the reference, the development of individual creative thinking, discover and create their own value. In order to play as the main driving force of subjective creativity, school education for learning pathways, inheriting Chinese traditional education on the basis of ideology, from Western educational model, starting from China's basic national conditions, to develop a number of professional painting, oil painting, printmaking, design, sculpture, etc. for the community to cultivate outstanding talents specialized art education, improve with distinct Chinese characteristics art education system.

Figure 2. People face renderings

3 Chinese painting as a symbol of Chinese art

Chinese painting as a symbol of Chinese art, has developed a number of years, has experienced a long history. Its development and development of traditional art education is basically synchronized. Traditional art education model for studying the development of self-contained Chinese painting provides a strong guarantee, but the crisis has brought to the development of Chinese painting, Chinese painting may lead to the development of stagnation and rigid.

With the introduction of Western culture, contemporary art education has been given a new content and features, traditional art education has been seriously challenged, and Chinese painting is no exception. Chinese and Western cultures fierce collision, given the contemporary art education conform to the trend of the times, and the Chinese have a tendency to weaken the function of painting, we can see the impact on Chinese painting contemporary art education development is enormous. Therefore, Chinese painting to have sustainable development, we must look for a path.

Given the cultural heritage and cultural traditions there are significant differences among different ethnic, fusion of contemporary Chinese painting art education and the presence of significant challenges, mainly as follows: Western contemporary art education curriculum is based on the theory, although trying to achieve Western reconcile, western system in order to mark the traditional Chinese painting art education is based on the poetry of learning-based, it is trying to achieve a comprehensive innovation in the original basis. Since the starting point of contemporary art education and traditional art education, the focus is different. Should contrary to objective laws, not according to the actual situation of contemporary art education and the development of Chinese painting, blindly impose two very different systems together, will generate a lot of negative impact, but we should make an objective assessment, can not ignore the contemporary the positive role of art education for the development of Chinese painting.

Contradictions are opposites, we study the impact of Chinese contemporary art education in the process of painting effects, specifically requires an objective analysis of contemporary Chinese painting art education teaching, writing produced. This article from the aspect of two dimensions, the use of comparative approach, in teaching, through the teaching objectives, teaching methods, teaching materials, teaching content, teaching evaluation analysis of differences in traditional and contemporary art education art education; in the creative aspects of , will be an inspiration on Chinese painting, technique, emotion comparative study, summed up the pros and cons of contemporary art education for the development of Chinese painting, but overall, pros and cons, more harm than good.

Because of our long-term in a feudal society, and the ancient social, political, cultural and systems are designed to meet the needs of the ruling class. The prevalence of the traditional hierarchy is art education, just to satisfy the interests of the ruling class and the service. In this case, the role of art education is major with a strong "into enlightenment, helping Fallon," the. In this historical context, the traditional art education does not have a complete and standardized education system. In particular the teaching process, the main idea is to master personal education based, then painting learners main objective things through observation and copying works of the classical way to achieve the purpose of drawing creation. Contemporary Art education is committed to the community to cultivate creative talents, and the fine arts education in the country gaining in popularity, becoming a national art education. Up to now, we have been gradually achieving the transformation of quality education by exam-oriented education to the "moral, intellectual, physical, aesthetic, labour" comprehensive development.

Visible, education has become the most basic rights of every person, and not a few aristocratic privileges, which will benefit the construction of a socialist harmonious society. Contemporary art education teaching objectives conducive to the development of our comprehensive quality education, improve the overall level of China's national art knowledge. For the construction of a beautiful home that has everything to gain but no harm. However, we also see the shortcomings can not be ignored him an objective reality. Universality corresponds to the peculiarities of contemporary art education is universal knowledge for all students in the art of Chinese painting teaching goal setting, and not as a traditional art education that, according to each student's specific conditions, can amount tailor the most appropriate teaching painting learning objectives and teaching goals at any time to adjust according to the needs of learning. Contemporary Art by differences in education and Chinese painting teaching objectives analysis, summed up contemporary art education exists on the pros and cons of teaching objectives. We can see that they are closely related, the latter is dependent on the former, while drawing on Western art education.

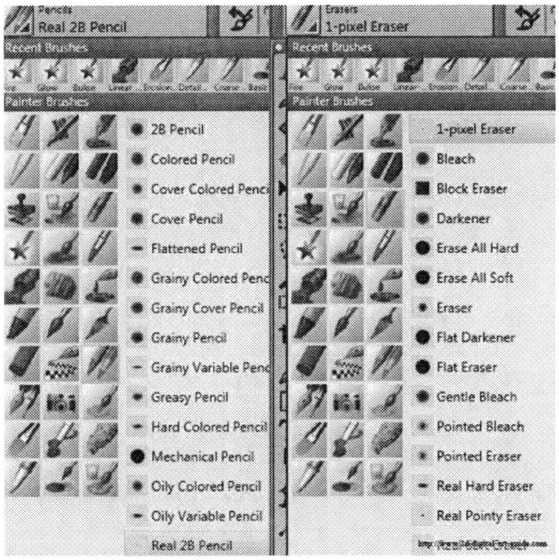

Figure 3. Different pen selection panel

4 Perfect entrance painting system

Perfect entrance painting system is established by the test subjects mainly market-oriented to meet the spiritual needs of the national culture as a starting point, the establishment of mechanisms to match the talent of our modern society.

First, adjust the fine arts enrolments appraisal system. We must correct the student selected the correct professional life and values. Put an end to the culture results due to lower admission line, and were blindly irrational choice. Second, the development of relevant is personnel green channel mechanism. For talented people, low scores may be due to cultural studies, and lose the opportunity to further studies. To avoid loss of talent, we can be relaxed too rigid mandatory. Third, to ensure the standard of Fine Arts entrance painting is marking a serious scientific unity.

First, compulsory and elective hours arrangements should be reasonable clear relationship between primary and secondary. Ensure the completion of required courses on the basis of content, complemented by select electives to enrich students' extracurricular knowledge. Secondly, reducing college English, computer, Marxism philosophy and curriculum is such as Introduction to Mao in proportion. In high school, students have to spend a lot of time to learn common subjects of Chinese painting has been selected for professional students, definitely should concentrate on drawing learning Chinese painting. Again, increase appreciation for literature class curriculum arrangements. Development of Chinese painting is based on a comprehensive knowledge of Chinese classical literature, history, philosophy, calligraphy, and other cultural compile engraved based bedding. To truly comprehend the essence of Chinese paintings, we must fully understand its surrounding culture.

How to adjust the structure of teachers, the paper be summarized in the following three aspects. First, the

rational use of contemporary art education resources. Outstanding art teachers, most choose to stay at the front line state, second-tier cities, thus resulting in a remote area art teacher resource deprivation. For the economically backward areas, should improve conditions for running schools, art teachers to improve the treatment, add some additional financial subsidies to attract relevant professional talent. Second, to improve the art teacher is professionalism of teachers including the character, professional two aspects. Confucian school representative spring and Autumn Period Confucius said: "The body is not to make the trip, its body is not correct, although that is not from." A way to explain is the importance of teachers to teach by example to explain in words. Learn all the prerequisite knowledge is a noble culture of ideological and moral qualities. The so-called style is the man, drawing as it were true. In contemporary art education system, the state in the form of laws requiring teachers to implement lifelong learning system. Through a lot of reading articles, appreciate the works, schools, and other ways to organize collectively to promote teachers' knowledge and constantly updated.

Aesthetic pursuit of Chinese painting is one of the nation's most ethnic characteristics of performance. It leads people to enjoy the beauty; they also placed a love for life is infinite. Song period Sushi once said: "On the painting to the shape, see neighbours' and children", this sentence sharply revealed the aesthetic characteristics of traditional Chinese painting. Depicted object is to pursue the objective nature quite similar, but the shape is quite similar to do the groundwork for the performance of foreshadowing. Process is an evolving aesthetic pursuit of development,, development of Chinese painting is supposed to reflect the people's living conditions in different periods and aesthetics. Look, unlike Song Tang painting paintings, but also different from the Song, Ming and Qing, a generation a generation of style, this style different times, although by the time the political, economic constraints, but for contemporary art education Chinese painting still play an important role can not be ignored.

However, the twenty-first century we modern people really understand our own aesthetic pursuit of it? For the current Chinese painting aesthetic criteria to evaluate the messy nature, which requires us to use the development of a comprehensive, materialist view links to see the world. Always respect the objective laws of development of things, the use of advanced thinking with the times to analyze the problems encountered. Mr. Shi Taolao borrows the words: "When the ink with the times", shows that aesthetic pursuit of Chinese painting should change with the times and constantly evolving.

5 Conclusions

Impact of contemporary art education in the 21st century the development of Chinese painting is multifaceted, deep-seated. This influence is reflected not only in terms of teaching methods of Chinese painting, but also in the creative aspects of Chinese painting. Art Education bears important historical role in the inheritance and development of Chinese traditional culture in. Diverse artistic language is an inevitable trend in the context of traditional Chinese painting new era of development. Theoretical basis of traditional and contemporary art education art education is completely different. Contemporary art education is not only developed on the ideological basis of Confucian philosophy of Chinese classical aesthetics, Taoist aesthetics of Chu on aesthetics and Zen aesthetics, but also by the Western aesthetic thought impressionism, realism, romanticism, neo-impressionist, post-impact of Impressionism and other aesthetic thoughts.

Because of the theoretical basis is different, leading to the existence of a series of discord between the contemporary Chinese painting and art education with a strong ethnic colour issues. Inheritance and development of Chinese painting in the contemporary art education system is facing serious challenges. Where the way contemporary Chinese painting art education development is is an issue that we need to seriously consider. Teaching and writing are two aspects of my departure from traditional Chinese painting made in-depth analysis, pointed out that the healthy development of Chinese painting need to focus on pioneering form of language, aesthetic intention of innovation, creativity and subjective thinking of abandoning traditional culture.

Acknowledgements: Jilin Province Department of Education Projects [2012-344]

References

1. ZHANG Yao-guang. Lilley. Chinese modern art education in the "Western painting" Complex. Grand Art. 09(2011)
2. Lee slip down modern art education model and the concept of cultural and ecological harmony - of Our universities Normal Art Education in the 21st Century. "Inner Mongolia Normal University (Educational Science Edition). 11(2006)
3. Reflections by Lisa Shuai. Contemporary art trends in China. "Industry and Technology Forum." 2012.
4. Zhang Bing. Explore the aesthetic perspective of Art Education. China-school education, 15(2010)
5. Li Si Hui. On Myth and Art Education of College Students Comprehensive. Heilongjiang Science and Technology Information. 25(2008)
6. Liangtai Sheng. Reform of university teaching of Chinese painting Rethinking. Zong Tai'an College of Education Science, 45(2003)
7. Han Jing. Confront contemporary art education principal institutions of higher art China Forum on -- 2010. Art Watch, 78(2010)
8. Zhang Jun to stay. On Chinese painting teaching traditional culture. Arts education research, 47(2011)

MATEC Web of Conferences 44, 01077 (2016)
DOI: 10.1051/matecconf/20164401077

Research on Tactics of English Teaching to College Students by Modern Media Technology

Gang Zhou

College of Foreign Language Education, Beihua University, Jilin City, China

Abstract. Modern colleges are faced with the dual pressures of university reform and international competition, how to overcome difficulties, to play the role of modern English teaching in colleges and colleges to enhance the core competitiveness of colleges, colleges and colleges modern English teaching problems to be solved. Based on the current situation of modern colleges in the premise of the Modern media platform fully demonstrated the characteristics and viability of the Modern media English teaching, the necessity of modern English teaching of college Modern media. Discusses the Modern media targeting English teaching and important role is in the English teaching to guide the development of modern colleges modern media.

1 General instruction

Today, with the computer network at the core of modern science and technology has provided us with an unprecedented opportunity and great potential for development; it is the people and people, people and information together. As China's papermaking and printing changed the human civilization spread the same way, the computer revolution has brought people to process and disseminate information in English teaching. IT influence and impact on education has quietly begun, and thus produce a modern form of education. English teaching with modern technology education is also linked to together.1994 proposed a modern definition of educational technology Educational Communications and Technology Association of American technology and modern media technology education, once again caused a big discussion about China's educational technology development and positioning. Our audio-visual sector that "AVE" is China's educational technology; audio-visual education means "the use of modern media, the media, and with the right combination of traditional educational media, educational information transfer in order to achieve optimal education."

But with the development of education and in-depth understanding of educational technology, obviously, AVE's This definition has not properly summarize the connotation and denotation, need not meet the educational development of the representation of educational technology, because: AVE focus on media the lack of a systematic approach, and education is a big system, many of its elements, including audio-visual education, not only in the study of media, including elements of teachers, students, teaching content, just the study of the use of the media, it is impossible to achieve optimal education; galvanic Education refers to the definition of media generated by the media after the fourth revolution in education, does not contain the information revolution appeared fifth multimedia computer and network technology, virtual reality and other digital information technology, some people mistakenly believe that is the traditional slide AVE projection, movies and other media technology applications, is a traditional audiovisual media education; not easy international academic exchanges. Since it is not a substitute AVE modern media technology, then, modern media technology how to define what should be? First let's understand a few concepts related.

Figure 1. 21st century classroom

2 Evolution of technology in the field of education and awareness

Evolution of technology in the field of education and awareness is the definition of educational technology linked with people's practical work, the impact of some of the other disciplines of the field theory (such as cognitive

psychology, systems theory, etc.) are closely linked to the development of other aspects of the Department a. Since the beginning of this century to the present audio-visual teaching, educational technology has been rapid development, has in 1963, 1970, 1972, 1977 and 1994 five times to give the definition of educational technology. This five defined according to statements can be divided into three categories, the first category (1963, 1994 definition) expresses the main object of study of educational technology, content, research methods and disciplines category; second class (1970 definition) expresses the education technology is both a specific expertise or specific means and methods that educational technology is a media technology, but also a system technology, namely the design, implementation and evaluation of learning and teaching throughout the technology; the third category (1972, 1977 definition) expresses the definition of educational technology in the field, indicating that this area is a some kind of theory-based, learner-cantered, with the resources, the use of a systematic approach to analyze and solve the problem of human learning an integrated complex process.

These definitions from different angles describes the meaning of educational technology, together, we can consider: Educational technology is the sum of all the technical means and methods of human activity employed in education, which is divided into physical and chemical form and intelligent form of two categories, physical and chemical forms of technology refers to the solidification and embodied in a tangible object of scientific knowledge, intelligent forms of technology are those abstract forms, in order to function in the role of scientific knowledge in the form of educational practice. Fred Percival and Henry Ellington in the "Educational Technology Handbook," a book is divided into more specific education technology an integral three parts: First, the hardware, refer to the appropriate technical equipment and teaching systems: software, refers to hardware implementation and design materials: Three pieces of latent means theoretical concepts and research findings related disciplines. 1994 American Association for Educational Communications Technology (AECT) on the modern definition of educational technology as: "Instructional technology is the learning process and learning resources for the theory and practice of design, development, utilization, management and evaluation of" Here, teaching techniques broader sense of educational technology, clearly outlines the study is to learn the process of educational technology and learning resources.

Based on the above analysis, we can see that the three basic attributes of educational technology: (1) Educational technology is the application of a systematic approach to analyze and solve problems in the process of human learning, its purpose is to pursue education optimization: (2) Educational technology division technology for tangible and intangible technology into two categories, tangible technology refers to the use of natural science, engineering and technology achievements, the physical and chemical forms of technology in education, in order to improve teaching efficiency technology that aids ranging from traditional blackboard, chalk, etc. to multimedia computers and networks can be used for education of all equipment, facilities, equipment, etc., and the corresponding software: invisible technology mainly refers to the use of the results of education, psychology, systems science, communication and other aspects of the educational process in order to optimize the technology. (3) Educational technology relies on the development and utilization of all learning resources to achieve their own ends. Learning resources into information, personnel, materials, equipment, techniques and environments, these resources come from two aspects, one is specifically designed for the purpose of learning out of resources, such as teachers, textbooks, instructional television, computer courseware, chalk board , projectors, classroom, playground, lectures, classroom discussions, and the other aspect is the real resources that can be utilized in the world and some of the Central Plains, for example, all walks of life experts, modern sappers, film, exhibitions, museums, production site, games, contests and so on.

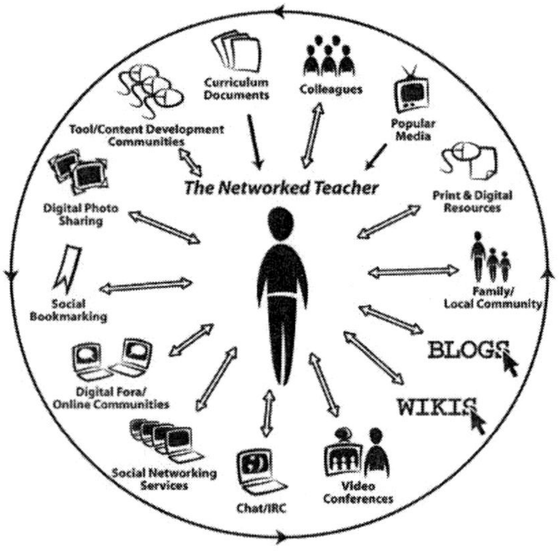

Figure 2. The networked teacher

3 Technical aspects of educational technology

Technical aspects of educational technology include education and education technology, education technology is materialized technology, is reflected in educational media technology itself. It is the use of natural science and engineering and technological achievements, membership in order to improve teaching effectiveness and teaching effectiveness. Educational technology refers to a non materialized technology refers to the choice of textbooks and teaching aids, teaching activities designed to plan, control of the teaching process, evaluation, management and other issues, it is from the perspective of education to study the problem of educational technology. Science and technology

education on the use of psychological theories of learning outcomes, research teaching content, teaching methods, membership in order to improve teaching effectiveness and teaching effectiveness.

Modern media technology and a general sense of educational technology is not essentially different, highlighting the "modern" word is more attention to those with modern science and technology to explore issues related to the absorption of modern scientific and technological achievements and systems thinking approach is more educational technology characteristics of the times. Consolidated results of the international community and with China's actual educational experts of many different teaching and exposition of modern technology defined, I think the modern media technology should be defined as: modern media technology is the modern media theory and the most advanced science and technology applied to the field of education, teaching and learning through the optimization process and the development of teaching and learning resources, teaching model, design, utilization, management and evaluation, in order to achieve the optimization theory and practice of teaching, improve teaching quality and cultivate high-quality talent .

The current way of educational technology applications including multimedia combination of classroom teaching, distance learning mode satellite television, interactive multimedia computer to individual learning styles, teaching Internet-based remote communications, virtual reality simulation teaching. In fact, the modern media technology has displayed its strong advantages: (1) information display diversity education; (2) hypertext Education Information Organization: (3) interactive educational process; large (4) Teaching Information storage capacity: (5) teaching transmitted information network; (6) the teaching of intelligent information outlet.

Conform to the development of modern media technology, schools need to focus on the completion of the following basic tasks: (1) the rational allocation of equipment, construction of modern media technology environment; (2) the development of educational software, building a modern textbook system; (3) to carry out teaching experiment, explore the construction modern teaching model; (4) strengthening teacher training, modernization of teachers; the use of educational technology generation, the corresponding need to change the following elements of the relationship between the teaching process: the transformation of the role of a teacher from teacher-centred to explain those changes in student learning the mentors and organizers: change the status of a student's status change from passive acceptance to active participation, found that the dominant position of inquiry and knowledge construction: the role of the media in a shift from a teacher to explain the changes in presentation tools for students cognitive tools: changing the teaching process to explain the process of transition from one note through the creation of scenarios to study the problem, consult learning, meaning construction and other student-centred process.

4 Modern English teaching in college

As a large state university college of energy is the basis for the development of the national economy, is to enhance China's comprehensive national strength, reflecting the superiority of the socialist market economy, the window, I was an important foundation for a stable ruling party, but also realize the important position of our Party's mass line. Modern English teaching of college will be directly reflected in the central role of political party organization in colleges and colleges are an important aspect of management and operation mechanism. With the oil industry's market economic internationalization, colleges have from the previous administration into a national monopoly to participate in international competition in the market economy subject. Therefore, improving the modern English teaching of college based work, for speeding up the economic development of the country's construction and reform of decisive significance, is a modern development of university important organizational guarantee. English teaching of the guiding ideology of "economic catch around English teaching, a good job of English teaching to promote economy, which indicates that the promotion of economic development is the central task and the goal of English teaching work, and English teaching but also for the economy spiritual foundation for development, promote market is economy healthy, orderly and rapid development.

Dialectical relationship between English teaching and the economy shows the English teaching an indispensable position and role, only in this dialectical relationship guidance to determine the exact ideas and methods of modern English teaching in order from a strategic height strengthen the party's base, and promote sustained colleges, stability and development. In the full international competition in modern society, we should take the modern situation and problems, "eighteen" spirit study English teaching is facing, so the modern college party organizations to maintain the advanced nature forever, purity, and full combat effectiveness and creative and cohesion, to enhance the core competitiveness of colleges to contribute to a modern era.

5 Modern media technology to optimize English teaching reform

From the above analysis we can conclude that the use of modern media technology to optimize English teaching reform and not just the senior leadership based on the overall understanding of the entire education reform, it is the theory and practice and the inevitable result of choice, especially reasonable use of computer multimedia technology to classroom teaching to bring in efficiency "exponentially" leap, has been for countless dedicated to the cause of education in the practice of the majority of teachers are confirmed. But we also clearly recognize that, with all the modern media media not conventional teaching, every class is not suitable for use, not what courses are taught in multimedia technology as well, but

not each text is suitable for use multimedia to teaching, it's just the regular teaching very important optimization tool, can never replace the traditional teaching of the teachers on the basic programming tools, techniques and methods, such as a stick figure, but can not affect the teachers play a dominant position.

Therefore, the English teachers in the use of modern media technology, especially multimedia technology to optimize both classroom teaching, to grasp the "degree" of the problem, to identify the modern media technology to optimize the best starting point in English teaching reform, we can not "distracting ', but do not "unworthy", to avoid falling into the following errors: the design of classroom teaching into multimedia courseware, courseware to teach these topics, coach's name, to the end of the display unit was sweeping, all the time classroom teaching with multimedia courseware control up with the idea to go courseware holding students to cause the entire teaching activities were streamlined procedures, the teacher becomes a "machine operator", the students have become a passive receptacle of knowledge, thinking in a rigid state, entire classroom can neither reflect the dominant position of the students, nor the guidance of teachers, became the center of media courseware. This is a serious breach of the principle of the use of multimedia assisted teaching.

Teaching activities should be teacher-student interaction, student interaction collision sparks thinking. Multimedia technology is a means to receive pre-aided teaching effectiveness and use, if all the links are displayed teaching multimedia courseware, one class down does not use the blackboard and chalk, blackboard all the contents should be displayed in the screen on, sometimes the content should not be writing on the blackboard is also presented on the screen, it will lose the exemplary teacher writing on the blackboard to some extent, thereby reducing the time students to think for themselves, a simple presentation tools become teachers on the media. Once the computer fails during use, teachers use computers are not very skilled, can lead to a loss of teachers. Language is a very practical lesson, but in order to demonstrate the main premise, students will lose the opportunity to practice the language, the teacher's activity instead of thinking of students, instead of the language of visual communication and realistic simulation exercises.

6 Conclusions

Modern media technology to break the boundaries between the real world and the virtual world, changing the way people exchanges fundamentally. In the modern media, interpersonal communication between the conditions, everyone can hide their true situation; you can speak freely with impunity, to express their views. Thus, it is conducive to the education of college students who learn about the true thoughts, so that their English teaching targeted; also conducive to a more in-depth discussion of the relevant issues, English teaching should produce some of its practical effect.

In the English teaching is the degree of trust between teachers and students how to have been an important factor in the impact and effectiveness of education and quality of education. In traditional teacher-student relationship, both teachers and students are always in a state of inequality, which makes student teachers are often reluctant to tell the truth, it prevents enhance the effect of English teaching. And with the help of SMS, blog, forums and other modern media, the exchange between education and the educated have some hidden, and thus bring a sense of equality of the two sides in the personality, rights and status, there is conducive to the formation of a relaxed and harmonious atmosphere, thereby eliminating the gap between teachers and students, thereby enhancing the degree of trust between teachers and students, English teaching to have good teaching.

Acknowledgements: Research college English translation teaching mode under the guidance of constructivism

References

1. Liu Hongjun. Several colleges and scientific development thinking. Learning and exploration, 11(2009)
2. Cold dives. Adapt to the modern situation and to explore modern ways-on the petroleum and petrochemical English teaching. Theoretical front, 254(2006)
3. Chen Li. Ways to enhance the effectiveness of grassroots English teaching in colleges and colleges. PARTY SCHOOL, 147(2006)
4. Mr. Zhao. Colleges in Modern English teaching of ideological and political work study. Sichuan People's Publishing House, 2009.
5. Jiang Tiezhu. Famous English teaching. Wenhui Press, 541(2008)
6. Sun Chuanming. English teaching Problems and Solutions. Coastal colleges and science and technology, 362(2005)
7. Xiao Xuebin, Julie. The impact of modern media on the English teaching and its response. Ideological Education Research, 234(2009)
8. Wang Huancheng. Modern trends in the modern media environment of English teaching of college students. Contemporary Education Forum (Management), 142(2010)
9. Lai Yong. English teaching in the modern media environment exploration. Net wealth, 102(2010)

MATEC Web of Conferences 44, 01078 (2016)
DOI: 10.1051/matecconf/20164401078

The Influence of Japanese Anime Language to Chinese Network Buzzwords

Jin Chang Cai

Teacher's College, Beihua University, Jilin, China

Abstract. In this paper, the influence of Japanese anime language to Chinese network buzzwords was studied, and the maturity and rigor were quoted. The Japanese anime language refined, creative can be so popular in the factors of psychologies also was analyzed. According to these studies, some suggestions were put forward that how to standardize the network buzzwords and how to raise its taste.

1 General instruction

Extensive use of modern Chinese vocabulary of Japanese origin, mainly the late Qing Dynasty in the early Ming Dynasty was introduced into China from Japan. When Japanese considerable number of translations, the introduction of advanced technology modern Western thought and science and technology, culture based on Chinese characters, foreign words through their transformation, innovation and then back to the time lag of China. Japanese loanwords source of this period are mainly three types: a Japanese transliteration or translation of Western words; Second, Japan in modern Western translation words borrowed from ancient China when Chinese vocabulary; Third, the Japanese with Chinese characters own words. Since the characteristics of the times, these three words on the source borrow mainly in political, economic and other aspects. the rapid development of the Internet, the emergence of Japanese to Chinese input on the source vocabulary of another peak. Japan's animation industry is highly developed; making the word on the source of animation into China has become the subject. They are rich in the number of Chinese vocabulary, become a new bright spot in the Chinese vocabulary.

Since the word on the source of animation through the network became popular later, not only on television, radio, newspapers and other media frequently appear, people in their daily lives are often used. Loan Words coexist with intrinsic meaning, enriching the expressive Chinese. For example, come hot word "Moe" relevant there, in November 2012, "China Daily" entertainment of a title is the "" good man "massive exposure Highlights sell Meng Song Joong-ki off screen." "Moe" comes from the Japanese anime film and television works, which means "cute" but surpasses "cute" What a little like "people pity, want to protect," the subtle emotions, this one word can express the vivid very complex a very delicate state, greatly enriched the expressiveness of Chinese. As another example, "control" is derived from the Japanese anime source, it means "extremely liked", more on a noun ending, represents something extreme like. June 2011 a headline Netease news on the "'brand control' 'spell personality' not bad money 'terrible schoolchildren high consumption", read newspapers everywhere "Royal Sister control," "Lolicon "" Uncle control ", even particularly like cats who also call themselves" cat control. " Acceptance and use of these high-frequency words unconsciously, we can see the network popular word on the source animation on the big influence of the Chinese language.

Figure 1. Japanese anime language manifestations

2 Date source of popular anime loanwords reason

China is still in the stage of gradually opening up, needs a substantial absorption of foreign things. Since the seventies the world, so that the country's reform and

opening policy to gradually open, people especially ideological emancipation of young people, they tend to be more recognition of foreign cultures and admiration. Groups of young people is desire and curiosity to explore the most exuberant of a group, they curious foreign things. ACG industry is well developed in Japan, has become Japan's third-largest industry, work another, their influence has gone beyond the young audience, the whole Japanese society have caused a huge impact. Since the vocabulary as the language most active part, the impact of culture on the language of ACG is highly concerned about Japanese linguists. ACG contemporary popular culture on Chinese youth groups also have a lot of appeal. Them by creating virtual characters and virtual environments, creating the ideal audience for our country a spiritual, so ACG fans especially curious teens become their huge consumer groups. In adolescents view, the new language phenomenon using ACG works appeared, new vocabulary is a fashion and trend, is the cool thing to satisfy their vanity. In addition, because these new words can be more aptly express their living conditions and psychological mood, it led to the ACG as the background on the source term is mainly popular among the young people in our country. Based on the source network buzzwords spread the particularity, that is, the majority of the youth groups. Through investigation and analysis, we believe that the main source of the words highlighted in popular Japanese youth groups because of the following two aspects.

Affix type buzzwords of today's popular discourse is one of the largest number, whether constituting the popular word, phrase or forms of discourse constitute popular buzzwords ways it is a very Nanchang way. For example, in Japan the source buzzwords, buzzwords affixes formula derived by the word formation produced particularly prominent, but also particularly easy to people to accept. This is due to affix class affixes the original meaning of the occurrence of a class, blur, then known by different root meaning with these affixes, affixes a combination of class, and then you can get a set of words, a group represent the same class things, words. One need only know that a group of similar meaning, structure the same words in one can guess the meaning of the other, so it is very easy to be understood and accepted, once people accepted, they have a strong diffusion capacity Their relative to other words in terms of vitality will be more powerful and will adapt to the development trend of modern Chinese. We can say that the class affixes word formation is derived in large numbers of new words and the most important and most effective way, so we can predict where there will be many similar affixes, they form new words from the derivative will continue to produce.

In the three elements of language (pronunciation, vocabulary, grammar), and vocabulary system is the most open, most sensitive to social changes in living systems. The emergence of a large number of the current date to reflect new things and new concepts of source words can easily enter the Chinese; it is precisely because of the language to meet the people's psychological innovative ideas. The domestic newspapers, magazines, television, Internet media also played a major role in fuelling that in order to attract readers, the audience's attention, use a lot of new popular language, especially advertisements that they tend to use more Borrowed words, This helps popular date source word and their penetration of the Chinese vocabulary system.

Domestic scholars said: "The emergence of new words and styling follows the principle of necessity first language, followed by word-building must comply with the basic rules and methods of the Chinese language, and reflect the efficiency of communication." Through investigation and analysis, we can see Prior to reflect new things, new concepts generated daily source buzzwords, Chinese original is no word to express this new thing, or existing words can not express new concepts and new things, new concepts accurately, For example, "seiyuu, dry woman, otaku, doujinshi, character set" and other Japanese animation industry to bring new things, and the resulting words reflecting these concepts, so they can be spread popular in contemporary youth groups .

To avoid dull repetition is verbal communication, and thus be vivid. Use foreign words sometimes can better achieve this aim. For example, "disappeared" intent to suddenly disappear, only for the Japanese people and not for things, it first appeared by Imamura Lu Ping in 1967 Japanese film director's name. "Disappeared" is made out of words to use metaphors, lively and expressive. At that time the Chinese, there is no such a word, and therefore the introduction comes. There are other similar such "home -, - family, - control, - Moe, into chaos, Cannian, seiyuu, colleagues," and so on, they are new, interesting, can add a lot of fun as the language of life.

China and Japan on the geography, culture are close to, and use of Chinese characters in both countries long ago. After some characters were introduced in Japan in the past followed the ancient Chinese original meaning, but the meaning of the word in modern Chinese changes; some were they given a new meaning, has become a new word. Date source buzzwords are basically Chinese Words on the source, the Chinese people friendly, easy to understand, easy to use, easier to absorb than the foreign words in other languages. Humanities and social science aspects of vocabulary we use today have 70 percent input from Japan, these are Japanese translation of words corresponding to the West, came to China after the Chinese took root. Although 70 percent of the data needs to be further research, but at least show the influence of the large Japanese to Chinese. This phenomenon is mainly because both countries use Chinese characters, but also because of this, in the process of entering the Chinese words on the source, the borrowing glyph is the highest proportion of borrowed Kanji font that is used directly.

3 ACG background

With the rapid development of computer, networking and electronic technology in today's world we have entered

the era of the ACG. This is not only reflected in the ACG booming industry itself, but also in the ACG basic necessities to people and other non-electronic industries occupation. The rapid development of the ACG make derivative products are no longer limited to text, pictures and games and other entertainment industry, but beyond the entertainment itself, throughout all aspects of daily life, such as clothing, food, stationery and so on, and in the very land of degree Vocabulary affected country. For example, the current buzzwords in the Japanese source words and animation-related proportion accounted for a large part, such as is currently popular "Lolita, is too, royal sister, natural stay, transsexuals, girl, faithful dog attack, soft sister glasses mother "they represent a class of distinctive characteristics of the avatar. In addition there are many words in the animation on the source network and everyday life are teenagers who frequent use of, this phenomenon reflects the characteristics of the times contemporary teenagers interested in animation.

Date source buzzwords in addition to most of the impact generated by the animation industry, and partly from the Japanese daily buzzwords, such as "up, Kara OK, discount, popular, old lady," and so on, as these words in society each class is used, but is not limited to youth groups. In the youth groups reflected more prominent, or buzzwords in recent years from Japanese anime.

As a new media network, with fast and instant delivery functions mass duplication of information, speed of its spread, the spread of a wide range of benefits unmatched by traditional media. Therefore, the network can best reflect the latest changes in the language and direction of development of language. Date source buzzwords on the network by means of this convenient and efficient newborn media pop up quickly. For example, ACG fans online exchanges frequently use the "sell Meng things, Meng pet" and other words, the impact of other Internet users, "Moe" was soon a popular network.

Date source buzzwords in vogue among young people by a variety of causes, partly because the Internet population is mainly young people; the other hand, youth groups or because of their own characteristics caused. In summary, we believe that second genesis mainly in the following three points: First, the closed state of adolescent life; Second, teenager's individuality and spirit of the times; Third, adolescent special cultural state of mind.

The information age has changed the way people live and work in today's way, especially contemporary teen life. It caused a lot of teenager's over-reliance on networks and electronic products, with little contact with other people and society, living in their own virtual world, avoiding the real world. For example, the words of the living conditions of the expression "otaku, house woman, otaku, dry female" and other popular teen to reveal contemporary special living conditions, "home" has become a trend. Sometimes, indeed, the virtual world than the real world seem more freedom and better, so that teenagers are more willing to stay home and soak in the network, animation, games and other virtual world, greatly reducing the chance of their exchanges and contacts with the outside world, and online communication is not face to face, but through the Internet, text messaging, voice, video, etc., such a long-term life of the particular state is bound to affect the cultural and psychological status of adolescents.

4 Teen individuality zeitgeists

This is a show themselves, individuality era. Especially contemporary teenagers, their pursuit of self-personality and distinctive style, outstanding performance for the following two characteristics: First, some young people challenge the traditional, self-advertised, there is an urgent need to do "non-mainstream" rebellious thoughts and find their own sense of presence psychological needs. This makes them the time to put some new buzzwords mention as their symbol, seen as one kind of distinctive way to express themselves. , Youth groups like the Japanese source buzzwords are derived from animation, online games and other virtual fields that interest them, these words are very strange virtual realm, such as "positive too, into chaos, colleagues" and look at the literal is difficult to know their meaning, it is difficult for adults to understand, which help youth groups to some extent between themselves and the adult world drew a boundary, highlighting their existence, highlighting its own unique personality; Second, some young people good fun of his own to keep up with the mainstream, but also to strive for the traditional mainstream of life is full of longing. For example, "Tucao" popular term, it reflects their spirit is good at self-deprecating, but also reflects their say, the courage to face their own shortcomings characteristics. Another example is the "blood" is the popular term embodies a "cheer, the goal of forging ahead," the mood, reflecting the kind of people they are excited, who worked hard to aspire to but more unreal life.

Network buzzwords to reflect the psychological state of contemporary youth highlighted in the following two aspects: First, the psychological refuse to grow, young technology, habitual act cute and evade social responsibility. For example, the very popular "Lolita, is too," the property is "Moe", and this "Moe" word generated from the time since it was labeled "play cute" label. Earlier, "Lolita, is too" cute girl is about 9-14 years old, boy, over time, gradually expanded the meaning to be used to refer to psychological naive, looks cute young twenties , so "sell Moe" has become a ages and gender "play cute" behavior. This fully demonstrates the contemporary teenagers generally have refused to grow up attitude; Second, aesthetic diversity, gender perspectives blur. Be able to demonstrate this feature contemporary adolescents have the word on the source animation, such as "transsexuals, slash, rot, attack by, BL (Boys 'Love), GL (Girls' Love)". The "pseudo-mother" means the same good looks, tall and weak, are often mistaken for girls males. The term "pseudo-mother" does not necessarily imply that men are the same as the traditional aesthetic concepts to be tall, powerful, strong and have to play. ACG and many works are "pseudo-

mother" image, and today's real life there have been many feminine men, they can confidently beauty, makeup, dress, become the representative of "the influx of people, range of children", gradually It also accepted the existence of such an image. In addition, like "slash, rot, attack by, royal sister" and other words also subvert the traditional concept of understanding in men, women and intercourse between status modes.

5 Standardization of network buzzwords

People enjoy the convenience of a modern and efficient network of life, but also bound to pursue the modernization of the network language. Modernization will bring endless stream of fresh vocabulary, if these terms are not regulated and properly guide will cause confusion network language. Therefore, standardized network language is multifaceted system engineering, in addition to Internet-related institutions management personnel, language, educators, especially media workers, which are entrusted with a very important responsibility.

Ideal network language life should be like this: not only colourful, but also methodical; both can well reflect the era of style, but also rational tradition; both accepted by the community, it also enabled the network to obtain pure language itself maintain. Even the language of self-regulation can work, but in order to faster and better achieve this goal, we need to correct social network language intervention. How to intervene is intervene in what areas, this has yet to be linguists to further research and discussion. In addition to the efforts of professionals, each Internet users on the network language specification also has an inescapable responsibility, should consciously regulate their own network terms. The pursuit of modern life makes people have in their daily lives at the expense of Chinese learning opportunities for the price. Due to increased foreign language, computer and other courses keeping with the times, our primary and secondary schools now time for language education less and less. And the method of language teaching seems there are a lot of problems. Therefore, the whole society should re-recognize the importance of language learning, renewed interest in and importance of language learning and education, the only way to promote the improvement of the quality of national languages, in order to make a real standardization network language be achieved.

The fastest network buzzwords reflect social life of the state language phenomenon closely integrated with the times. We should adopt a dialectical perspective to view the new era of Chinese network buzzwords. We should fully recognize that a new era of Chinese Internet buzzwords in the vast majority can remain worthy of praise because they are in modern society the collective wisdom of the people. Chinese network buzzwords leading the trend of Chinese vocabulary development, reflecting the trend of the future development of Chinese vocabulary. It enables the modern Chinese language more lively, more modern at the same time, also continue to integrate into the Chinese vocabulary, rich and expanding the vocabulary of modern Chinese family. Of course, we must also see many shortcomings that exist in the network buzzwords. For example, many expressions unreasonable, non-standard or even unhealthy; many buzzwords, there are some vague concept, ideographic unclear, to cause trouble understanding our language, so the phenomenon burden. After all, only a minor aspect of the lack of contradiction, we can not deny the main aspects of conflict. So we can not because of lack of network buzzwords and negated network buzzwords. Only to see the shortcomings of the kind of network is considered buzzwords network buzzwords "unrefined", there is no research value of speech is one-sided and unscientific, but also we have to be abandoned. We should dialectical view network buzzwords that only a comprehensive and objective understanding of the network buzzwords can truly guide scientific and standardized network buzzwords.

References

1. Chen Dandan, Chen Lin. Students analyze "otaku house female" phenomenon of Neijiang Normal University, 12 (2010)
2. Peng Yubo. Some Features of Network Language. Rhetorical study, 4 (2001)
3. Lin Gang. Types and characteristics of the network terminology. Rhetorical study, 26 (2002)
4. Li Li. The nature and characteristics of the network words. Language Studies, 21 (2005)
5. Cao Guojun Comics • Animation • Cartoon • animation. Language knowledge, 7 (2006)
6. Chu animation as a language in contemporary cinema, 3 (2010)
7. Feng. Foreign Language Teaching hear the application of multimedia teaching methods. Chinese education technology and equipment, 20, (2008)
8. Gu Jiangping. Analysis of contemporary Japanese Loan Words on Chinese penetration. Kanji culture, 1 (2000)
9. Luo Yixian, party Wei Ying. On the influence of Japanese animation culture of our young people. Science garden, 6 (2008)
10. TURAL multimedia technology on Foreign Language Listening Course of Modern Languages (late), 05 (2006)

MATEC Web of Conferences **44**, 01079 (2016)
DOI: 10.1051/matecconf/20164401079

Study on Multimedia Art Teaching Resources Management System based on Internet Technology

Bao Quan Pan

College of Fine Arts, Beihua University, Jilin City, China

Abstract. The main technical architecture of art teaching management system was developed on B/S model in order to help implement the network to share teaching resources. System page of Dreamweaver web page was design software, the background for using SQL Server 2000 database design, the use of ASP, ADO data combined with multimedia data transmission technology for art teaching resources system was realized.

1 General instruction

With the popularization and development of computer technology and the Internet, network teaching, especially web-based distance learning current government or institutions are very concerned, and is increasing its investment in research and development. The most important part of the network of teaching in the information age is the network teaching information resource management. This paper analyzes the current situation of online teaching, the status of the characteristics of network information resources and network information resources construction, proposed multimedia art information resource system design, the use of database technology, Active Directory technology, www technology, and video-on-demand technology to achieve complete multimedia art information Resource System. The system uses a distributed design, using SQL Serve: large database systems to ensure the performance of the system. At the same time integrated video-on-demand capabilities to watch online video clips; implements WWW client system C/S mode server management system, B / S model, in line with the current popular software operating modes, it is conducive to a network of information resources sharing.

Multimedia art information resource management system is only one of the multimedia subsystems. Multimedia art information resource system consists of Fine Arts Library and art materials. Library manager is variety of multimedia material, the use of buffer architecture; multimedia teaching materials database management, direct audit storage architecture. For multimedia video clips, video-on-demand systems integration capabilities, these video clips can be viewed online. The system provides users with a Web browser-based query system, the user can browse through the Web, query, and call the system resources. Meanwhile, the system provides the material library and textbook library management software; you can easily to the Library and manage library materials. Therefore, the development of multimedia art school teaching information resource system is of great significance.

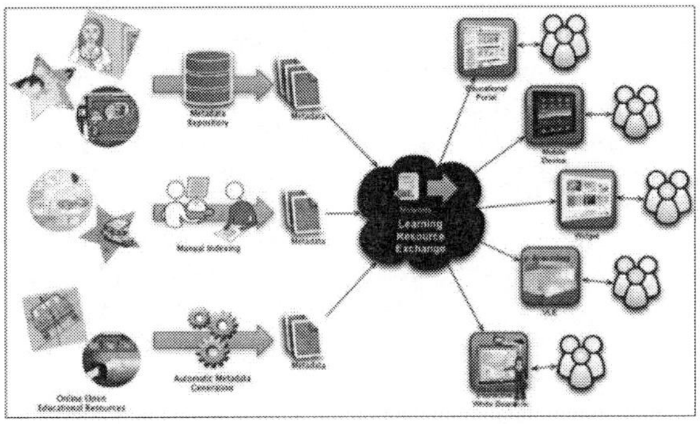

Figure 1: Overview of the Learning Resource Exchange Infrastructure

Figure 1. Architecture of art teaching management system

2 Research status and development trends

At present, many domestic university teachers according to their teaching needs, develop teaching system has given practical value. Colink After ten years of development, has become well-known domestic and foreign enterprises in the field of education, the product brand "NewClass" known continents, so that millions of teachers and learners to benefit from high-tech products Colink . Based on more than ten years of professional experience in the development and production of teaching equipment accumulated, conform to the needs of foreign language teaching mode continuous reform and development, NewClass new products constantly every year. The company main products are divided into three

categories: NewClass digital language learning system, NewClass simultaneous interpretation, training systems, NewClass multimedia art teaching system. Guangzhou Jia Hong Electronics Co., Ltd. developed which enables remote control based on the campus network, batch control, remote monitoring (as) intercom, live broadcast, streaming media and other powerful features. Multimedia control system since its launch, users get the praise and praise, and with domestic and foreign companies purchasing agent. With the development of science and technology, multimedia, teaching, online teaching, distance learning, etc. have sprung up across the country.

Guangzhou City, Guangzhou Radio and Television University is facing, the use of computer networks, satellite television networks and telecommunications networks, based on digital technology, multimedia, interactive teaching platform, municipal colleges and universities to carry out modern distance and open education, founded in September 1961, during the Cultural Revolution closed, in January 1979 re-run, in 1985, 4 menstrual approved by the Ministry of Education as a separate provincial TV. The strong support of the Guangzhou municipal government, the City Board of Education, the schools and government information technology investment and modernization of education, have been built with 3000 information points Gigabit backbone campus network system, the coupling distance education broadband network systems 13 campuses digital satellite IP access system, remote two-way video teaching system, electronic examination room network monitoring system and security monitoring systems, online classroom broadcast system, IP courseware production systems, paperless examination centres', remote reception centre, courseware on-demand systems, distance learning platform e-mail system, enrolment management system, student achievement query system, digital library, office automation system

Systems, real-time video and voice interactive system is more than 30 hardware and software applications. Guangzhou TV has become the leading Guangzhou Modern Distance Education of the main force, has become the backbone of the Guangzhou public higher education.

From the above case we can not find more extensive use of multimedia teaching system to the major schools, education is a new round of information technology in education reform appreciation.

In Britain, for example, since 1989, the United Kingdom as a developed country, in the information field of education has a pragmatic visionary and innovative strategic policy on. Over the years, the British use strong comprehensive national strength, give full play to advantages of the parties, and vigorously strengthen the information infrastructure, and actively play to the advantages of information technology education personnel, efforts to develop the use of rich information resources, contributed greatly to the entire community a comprehensive level of information upgrade, British National Learning Network has become Europe's largest education portal, but with powerful search capabilities. It is worth mentioning that the construction of the learning society in the United Kingdom by means of information technology has taken a substantial step. 2000 British "University for Industry „ the operation of government use of information technology is to enable people to learn the way of revolutionary change, it is through a modern network and communication technology, to supply the needs of learners and various educational resources in a timely manner effectively connected. Industry University Learning Network is made throughout the country, the distribution of the various learning centres constitute reasonable, all kinds of workplaces, colleges, universities, libraries, residential areas, shopping centres, football clubs, leisure centres and so on to be incorporated, it is an open to all, helping individuals and organizations understand their learning needs and to provide the most appropriate learning resources learners new organization, operation and development of the industry has made the University of British Lifelong Learning Society entered a new phase covering Australian National Australian Education Network includes not only all universities, but also cover all primary and secondary schools across Australia, it helps teachers and teaching departments at all levels to share information across Australia and around the world through strong education network, the Australian government for foreign students of the school received a rigorous curriculum and teaching quality control, and management of the curriculum and assessment in the form of legislation. If a school in the assessment or examination unqualified, will be ordered for rectification or even cancelled recruit qualified foreign students. This whole process of quality management and control relies heavily on Australian investment in education network, which ensures the quality of their education, so that it enjoys a good reputation in the international community.

3 ASP technology introductions

ASP (full name is the Active Server Pages, meaning: Active Server Pages). When the information needed for Web client sends an instruction by the server-side application requests through a Web server, generate a web page based on information in the database and passed back to the client. ASP is running on the server side, implementation of the results generated dynamically generated pages explain sent to the client browser, and scripting language is interpreted by a Web browser to perform. Because ASP is a server-side interpretation, developers do not have to consider whether the client browser supports ASP, and developers do not have to worry about other people stealing to download the program code, ASP common data link is ADO, ADO (ActiveX Data Object ActiveX Data Objects) technology refers generally be completed in several different programming methods with a specific task.

ADO connection objects can store information in a single session. OLEDB session connection Data Source objects and combinations of objects connection object has a method execution. In addition, the connection may be in

the command object, and the object is recorded dependency sets.

On JavaScript scripting language instructions is to adapt to create dynamic Web pages, a scripting language, can also apply to the client (browser) can also be used on the server side. JavaScript language created in the beginning to help change the tag on the page to development, so that the client is more abundant, because the page can be used as the target, and DOM structure of the page by using the Java script DOM operation, to interactive web pages, make Web pages and users to achieve real-time interaction, so that the page contains more active elements.

4 Multimedia art teaching resources management system requirements analysis

With the continuous development of computer technology, multimedia art teaching has become a new revolution in the field of art education, pay attention to the world. Meanwhile, people on multimedia art teaching requirements are getting higher and higher, audio, video, multimedia teaching has become an indispensable part.

In the traditional art teaching, student learning resources, mainly by teachers prepare learning materials and textbooks composition, slightly less compared to the same learning resources on the network, and since most of these data along with the completion of teaching time and the end, which triggered the student can not re-organization of knowledge at the completion of the job also rely mainly on the brain image storage, knowledge professional art teaching resources website can provide a relatively wide, and most of the teachers through careful organization, also provides links to other related learning resources, students can more easily find the right learning resources, greatly enriched the art of teaching content for the training of students' innovative ability to provide a new way, we can say, building art curriculum resources for classroom teaching art provides rich support knowledge resources, although students are in the classroom, but the network resources gave students the opportunity to transcend the boundaries of time and space, spanning ancient and modern, flying in space history and imagination. Give full play to the role of the outstanding quality of multimedia art teaching resources, teaching resources to ensure the submission of using enough multimedia materials should be submitted to meet the following requirements:

1. Submit all relevant procedures, documentation and materials.

2. The software first needs to go through the installation. Such teaching resources in advance to lie before the downloaded package upload, at the time of submission of resources relevant attributes need to be described.

3. User module using C/S mode, after teaching submissions, should pay attention to where the directory structure of the B/S mode, the online submission of materials, the same changes in the relative directory structure should be noted. "Flow,, technology to manage video data and control solutions to high-speed network transmission congestion caused by dynamic video playback problems can not successfully, to ensure quality and continuous playback, the need for application software VOD service following major technical requirements and aims.

5 Systems development goals

Construction art multimedia teaching resources is to show the form of student teaching, better enable students to understand and learn Chinese and foreign art resources, students of art proper aesthetic ideas. The system art resources include: 1 describes the different historical periods and foreign, different genres, different styles of art works of art for students to further study; 2 in chronological order to show the different historical periods, different genres, and different kinds of work. Related multimedia resources are on the one hand to deepen students' understanding of the text description, the other students the right aesthetic ideas to improve the aesthetic ability of students. Students learn to enhance their knowledge. Students and teachers through online communication to increase the interaction of student learning stimulate students 'enthusiasm and interest, through communication between teachers and students, students and students communicate, make it easier for the teacher to understand students' learning progress, learning level and learning ability and so on. We can also discuss works of art, works of art so that students can freely discuss their views on the masterpieces of play, or the lack of information related to teaching resources can be shared; works of art for the moment to discuss the main works of art such as advertising design works or a strong artistic movies, or a certain design competitions freedom to express their views, share their own arguments. Thus, multimedia plays an important role in teaching resources, the network teaching system and its important role in the teaching system play in the design of the system should achieve the following objectives.

Resource classification system enables administrators to efficiently manage the media category management and end-user repository, reasonable or not directly affect the system administrator and end-user management efficiency of resources utilization of resources, so that both are important factor. The system should provide as flexible classification management measures to meet different application of different types of materials and objects classification requirements.

6 System testing

System testing is an important stage in the lifetime of the software, is a key step in software quality assurance. More simply, software testing before the software is put into operation, the software requirements analysis, and design specifications and coding of the final review activities. Software Engineering IEEE 1983 proposed term is defined in software testing to the next is: "Use

manual or automatic means to run or determination process of a software system, which aims to verify that it meets specified needs or understand the expected results difference "between actual results. This definition clearly states: The purpose of software testing is to test the software system meets the needs is to find errors and execution process, in order to prove that the procedure is wrong, rather than proof of program error, a successful test is found so far not Wrong test found. The purpose of software testing determines how to organize the testing. If the purpose of the test, Shandong University, a master's degree thesis was to find errors as much as possible, then the test should be directed towards the more complex part of the software or more before the error location. If the test purpose is to give end users with a certain confidence quality evaluation, then the test should be directly aimed at practical applications often used in commercial assumptions.

Test is mainly based on the mission statement is to develop technical specifications and test system, is testing the principles of integrated test and evaluation software overall functionality and performance is the theoretical basis of software testing activities, test method is to test the practical application of the principles of and access to the side again It means the data. Software-based common for software testing should follow the general principles and methods to test the software. Meanwhile, for the characteristics of the software, you must find the appropriate test methods. Reasonableness test cases for testing and evaluation software plays a key role, and how to make the design of use cases fair, reasonable and typical effectively is not easy. So it should be with the software development staff and end users together, targeted research and described the actual operating environment, the formation of rational methods and techniques of software testing test suite is varied. For software testing technology, can be classified from a different angle: if you need to perform from the perspective of the software under test, the test can be divided into static and dynamic testing. From the internal structure of the test is for a system and the specific algorithm point of view, can be divided into white box and black box testing network. Static testing is the general term for methods of characterization of the test program, the main characteristic of this method is being tested without using a computer running a program, instead of using other means to achieve the purpose of detection. Dynamic testing is actually running the test program, enter the appropriate test, the results of determination to meet the requirements, so that the accuracy of testing procedures, reliability and effectiveness.

References

1. Zhang filing multimedia technology in teaching applications on the network due to remote Education Supplement, 153 (2000)
2. Pool cloud computer multimedia network technology in the teaching of Liaoning Administration College, 90 (2000)
3. Han Jing. Confront contemporary art education principal institutions of higher art China Forum on -- 2010. Art Watch, 78(2010)
4. Zhang Jun to stay. On Chinese painting teaching traditional culture. Arts education research, 47(2011)
5. Li Si Hui. On Myth and Art Education of College Students Comprehensive. Heilongjiang Science and Technology Information. 25(2008)
6. Liangtai Sheng. Reform of university teaching of Chinese painting Rethinking. Zong Tai'an College of Education Science, 45(2003)
7. Reflections by Lisa Shuai. Contemporary art trends in China. "Industry and Technology Forum." 2012.
8. Zhang Bing. Explore the aesthetic perspective of Art Education. China-school education, 15(2010)

MATEC Web of Conferences 44, 01080 (2016)
DOI: 10.1051/matecconf/20164401080

Research on Chinese Foreign Teaching based on Multimedia Aids

Jie Lu

Teacher's College, Beihua University, Jilin, China

Abstract. With rapid development of multimedia aids; Chinese foreign teaching based on the multimedia tools, as a new instructional mode has become a hot topic in online teaching. In this paper, the teaching situation and existing problems by multimedia aids was analyzed by comparing the difference between network teaching platform and traditional classroom teaching. Then the strategy of modernized teaching management and the case, which is focusing on the characteristics of electronic media was present.

1 General instruction

As China's economic strength and foreign trade, science and technology, cultural exchanges frequently, Chinese as a communication tool, it plays an important role as a bridge in the exchanges between China and the world, the Chinese learning and therefore more and more countries in the world attention. British linguist Mr. David Grando has been published in 1997, "The Future of English" a book predicted that: "the pattern of the world's languages will be restructuring, the Chinese language will be ranked as the world heads strong in the 21st century, have become language learning."In response to this trend, Chinese Foreign workers actively explore teaching methods, enrich classroom teaching.

Mr. Lv Bisong said: "the language teaching should continue to study teaching methods, produce sound or new teaching methods for each teaching methods are designed to better solve the contradiction between teachings actually exist." Therefore, in order to adapt to the times Development of the new requirements of teaching Chinese Foreign proposed by means of modern technology is used to Foreign Language Classroom Teaching. Among them, the multimedia equipment for the carrier widely used adjunct to classroom teaching middle ,, and slowly develop into a mature modern teaching model has become the mainstream of contemporary university language teaching hand of foreign language teaching classroom teaching to mature. Research on the use of multimedia in teaching Chinese Foreign very wide, involving classroom teaching as the overall design of classroom teaching methods, HSK test and management courses, but also to teaching, distance learning, multimedia technologies hear, Chinese Application vocabulary, reading, culture and other specific courses based on. The author is in a different class type is mainly the perspective of research on multimedia usage.

Author of Teaching Chinese as a classroom University of Wisconsin summer camp, Shandong University, Shandong Normal University, Tianjin Normal University, Tianjin University of Traditional Chinese Medicine survey found that in a Foreign Language classroom different class of multimedia aids have different practical and applicability. Character education is unique difficulty of making foreign language teaching, and teaching is because of the importance of oral communication level and become the focus of foreign language teaching, the author of both teaching, for example, analyzes the advantages of multimedia teaching and produced problem, and try to come to a solution.

Figure 1. Foreign Language classroom different class of multimedia aids

This study of literature, investigation, case law, interdisciplinary studies, comparative studies and other research methods, analysis application status multimedia assisted teaching methods in teaching Chinese Foreign, trying to find a meeting of traditional teaching and multimedia assisted teaching methods point, improving the quality of classroom teaching Chinese as a Foreign.

Article available at http://www.matec-conferences.org or http://dx.doi.org/10.1051/matecconf/20164401080

2 Learning theory and multimedia foreign language teaching

Humans are primarily to get outside information by vision, hearing, touch, smell and taste five different ways, the famous experimental psychologist Rui Tela confirmed by a large number of psychological experiments, five ways in which, 83 per cent of information visual acquisition, 11% comes from hearing, 3.5% from the smell, l. 5% from the tactile, 1% from the palate. Psychology multidimensional symbol stimulation theory: the amount of information passed multidimensional symbol stimulate greater than the amount of information delivered straight symbol. Chinese characters are two-dimensional, ideographic writing system is sound, form, meaning a combination of alphabetic writing is much greater, it presents information than linear line structure. This suggests that when learners of Chinese characters, when the amount of information received, psychological resource consumption is also great, mobilize more neurons. Sheen universe had compared the situation when English reading eye movement, he believes that the differences in English reading space allocation when different eye gaze. Single square structure and a plurality of kanji characters combined square combination line, so that each row of Chinese characters reading at times when you want to watch more English to read the number. Due to the special nature of the characters themselves, which determines the learner in the learning of Chinese characters in the process, the energy and stamina to pay more than ideographic writing system to pay for energy, environment and therefore need outside help, from various angles on them sensory stimulation, so that they can more easily and effectively learn Chinese characters.

As psychologists study of human learning process Cognitive Law deepening awareness of people continue to strengthen self-learning, constructivist theory became popular. Constructivism is a branch of cognitive learning theory, which emphasizes the cognitive subject of internal psychological processes, and the learner is seen as the main body of information processing, it is very different and behavioural learning theory. Behavioural learning theory emphasizes "stimulus-response", and the learner regarded as passive response to external stimuli, that is, as knowledge instil object. The constructivist theory holds that learning is situational, social and constructive, knowledge is not obtained by the teachers teach, but learners in certain situations namely social and cultural background, with its outside help, such as a teacher or a friend, use the necessary learning materials, through the construction of ways to get the sense, constructivist learning theory is a further development of cognitive learning theory, mainly the development of cognitive learning theory has some of the "construction" of thought, more emphasis on the students themselves in learning meaning active construction of knowledge, namely that the world is an objective reality, but understanding of the world and give meaning, but it is decided by each person themselves. Students are subject cognition, is the knowledge of the builders. In the process of cognition, the students already have experience on the basis of external information through processing, handling, active construction of meaning external knowledge, to acquire knowledge. Moreover, knowledge is not unique, but development and change, as people know it in-depth and constantly updated, sublimation. Therefore, when the foreign language teachers during the teaching of Chinese characters, not self-centred, but should fully understand the basis of the students' interest and students have some Kanji structure, focused, difficulty properly, individualized, targeted Chinese characters teaching, helping students construct internal character system, so that students in the learning process, and give full play the main role in this active participation on the learner's initiative, enthusiasm to play to create good conditions, that can really reflect the role of the learner's cognitive subject, so that students truly become masters of learning.

3 External Chinese character teaching multimedia condition

Character is a kind of form to express the Chinese written language symbol transfer and exchange of information, is an extremely important part of the Chinese, and therefore can not be divorced learning Chinese characters to learn. For foreign students in terms of learning Chinese characters has been adopted by the storm must learn Chinese, European and American countries for the students, the Chinese character is not only a way of writing a different language, or learning from one-dimensional linear structure to a two-dimensional block structure symbol symbolic learning change, this learning process is very complicated. Multimedia technology has been widely applied to the Chinese Foreign teaching them and gradually by the people's attention. Multimedia has a storage memory, high-speed computing, logic, automatic operation and other functions, with text, sound, graphics, animation, video and other media information in one, with strong interactivity. Multimedia students through these means, according to the individual learning needs, obtain vivid and intuitive learning materials; you can get rid of the constraints of time past the classroom, and more easily communicate with teachers, get help; you can always assess learning outcomes, optimize learning program, learning to adjust the focus. Thus, the multimedia technology and teaching Chinese Characters combined, enabling Chinese Characters Teaching achieve a multiplier effect.

Non-Chinese students feel difficult to learn Chinese characters, hard one to remember, difficult to recognize, study the fundamental reason, which with the foreign student's mother tongue habits, but this is due to the characteristics of the decision by Chinese characters themselves. Chinese characters are ideographic system, unlike the phonogram; a large number of Chinese characters, complex forms, writing difficult; there are lots of homophones, multi-tone words, words form the past, and most characters can not both phonetic and semantic. The complexity of the characters is information, its

processing procedures more complex than the phonograph. Single traditional teaching methods, it is difficult to stimulate student interest; ignore the students 'subjective needs, constraints to improve students' ability; lack of input information, for one is not strong. As the traditional way of teaching itself one way or another deficiency, affecting the efficiency of foreign students to recognize and read Chinese characters, so we need to introduce new teaching methods to promote our Chinese Foreign Teaching.

Chinese Characters as a Foreign Language teaching and traditional teaching of Chinese characters the same way, is a teaching means and methods, but the means and methods of teaching and traditional teaching, such as flip charts, compared to the projector, etc., have their own special place. Because it can sound, pictures, animation and other forms of organically combined output at the same time, by way of human-computer interaction to achieve the purpose of teaching. It's an important feature is the ability to maximize stimulate learners senses, attracting the attention of learners, develop their ability to self-learning, thus improving the efficiency of the learner to learn Chinese characters to meet their needs from different levels. Comparison of multimedia teaching of Chinese characters and traditional Chinese characters teaching methods, there are differences between them is obvious.

Learners need to autonomously determine their own learning goals, select appropriate materials, to observe, to think, to imagine, creating a series of activities in order to control the learning process, to become masters of the learning process. Learning to play the main interest is the cognitive power, traditional Chinese Foreign Teaching Since teaching methods and single way, it is easy for students to produce fatigue, and little autonomy of student learning in the classroom passively accept input information, learning Chinese characters interest and potential has not been fully exploited, and multimedia teaching methods due to the comprehensive strengths of the slide projector and other equipment, will be maps, text, sound and Mao, static and dynamic combination of sound and colour, to a greater extent stimulated the students' interest, so that students have a strong desire to learn, so that students in a happy relaxed learning environment to understand the characters of word processing. For example, in explaining the structure of strokes of Chinese characters, can explain the structure of strokes and special treatment, which is, through slow motion, quick release, static display of Chinese characters written order and display the trajectory of strokes of Chinese characters, the direction of movement. After class, since teaching software has many forms of expression, students can help these software, entirely according to their own needs very easily on this information for research and learning, and will not feel dull and boring, always maintained a lot of interest, not the learning of Chinese characters felt a fear, but a positive self-challenge, full of a sense of accomplishment.

4 Status of Multimedia Foreign Language Teaching Chinese Characters

At present, many domestic scholars multimedia technology in the teaching of Chinese Characters conducted in-depth studies, such as Lin Hua raised the importance of technical support and multimedia teaching of Chinese character stroke; Wuying Cheng discusses how to use the Chinese character handwriting recognition technology for teaching Chinese characters; Yanghao Liang It discusses the multimedia technology in the teaching of writing Chinese characters, cultural education and strengthen memory teaching three advantages; Liu Yu analysis of the characteristics of Chinese characters, summarizes the main idea to write Chinese characters font library generation system design and the main algorithm is used. Their articles have pointed out the advantages of multimedia teaching of Chinese characters, and proposed to seize the Chinese character font, etc. to teaching. When we put multimedia technology into the teaching of Chinese Characters, and achieved certain results, it should be noted that some of the problems which arise. Because things are having two sides, multimedia teaching has certain advantages, but improper use can also affect the effectiveness of teaching. Therefore, when we emphasize the application of multimedia technology in the teaching of Chinese Characters when a record can not forget the multimedia technology can not completely replace the traditional teaching role. For example, in the use of multimedia in teaching Chinese characters, ignoring the relevance and moderation, the blind pursuit of visually and trendy, it will have a negative impact on student learning. Therefore, in order to effectively learn Chinese characters, the Chinese Foreign Teaching how reasonable application of multimedia technology, to handle its relations with traditional teaching methods is a new problem that we face.

Emphasis on student-centred teaching philosophy, not to ignore the leading role of teachers in learning; outstanding multimedia many advantages, it is not to deny the teaching of teachers in the Chinese Foreign importance. Multimedia is a teaching tool, the application of multimedia in teaching Chinese as a Foreign Characters, does not mean blindly rely on multimedia and lose instructor in the classroom. Because any kind of teaching activities are inseparable participation and completion of the Teaching of Chinese teachers and students are no exception, and it requires investment in teachers and students together. So, in learning Chinese as a foreign classroom, teachers should give full play to the guiding role, motherhood; students should give full play to the initiative and cultivate awareness of independent learning. Only the two combine, blend, characters can effectively carry out teaching activities. Viewed another way, if the teachers in the use of multimedia techniques, pay attention to train students to analyze problems, problem-solving skills, blind pursuit of visual and auditory stimuli, then, the students had not masters of the classroom, while It is become images, audio, video viewers, ignoring the main classroom content, free

beyond learning activities. Therefore, the relationship between teachers and multimedia processing, should grasp the "Multimedia is an auxiliary tool, teachers are leading," this principle. Courseware design should focus on the content of classroom teaching, teachers can not be subject to the courseware display, but should be based on the content of teaching and student level, corresponding to demonstrate mastery of courseware content. In the classroom teaching of Chinese characters, according to the students' reaction, the speed of a good grasp of teaching, a good grasp of teaching objectives and teaching content, keeping in mind and student interaction and communication, timely adjustment of classroom content, so good for teaching multimedia services.

5 Conclusion

There are many multimedia features, but not each function are suitable for the needs of teaching, the use of multimedia teaching should be consistent with the purpose and content of teaching needs, not simply for the use of multimedia and the use of multimedia. As a foreign language teacher, not only from the students' attention and attract attention, increase interest in this perspective to the classroom use of multimedia. Teachers must clear various functions and various forms of multimedia content is Chinese character teaching services, regardless of whether or not if the form and teaching content related blindly to the pursuit of new ideas, in order to achieve some kind of entertainment at the expense of grandstanding, then, so will bartering distracted the attention of students, so that students because too complex content and loss, thus affecting the efficiency of students learning Chinese characters. Multimedia courseware design should pay attention to targeted, should focus on strengthening students 'visual perception and handwriting capabilities, from the reality of Chinese characters teaching and students, it is necessary to take into account the content of the teaching of Chinese characters, objectives and students' cognitive level, but also consider whether in the classroom to ease of use, but there is no need for picture, sound and playback method used should be no or little use, should try not to be too fancy, make a service to the content.

Students of different levels of hierarchy, different teaching content, teaching different objects, multimedia should be different levels of use. For example, in the high-end conversation class, good multimedia courseware can provide a dialogue scene, guide students to learn, to play the role of go-between; and in the primary listening class, multimedia will not play a big role, but only for audio playback device. Therefore, the use of multimedia teaching should be combined with other teaching methods, without neglecting traditional teaching methods, different teaching methods will be applied to foreign language teaching integrated, seek more reasonable teaching mode to achieve a multiplier effect, which adapt to the current as a Foreign Language teaching. In short, as foreign language teachers, we should be good at thinking and observation, diligent hands, an effective combination of traditional teaching methods in essence with modern multimedia tools applied to teaching practice, in order to achieve the best results of classroom teaching.

References

1. WANG Xin-wen as a foreign language news to listen to the principles and methods of teaching reading. Applied Linguistics, 56 (2000)
2. Liu Songhao. Listening Teaching Chinese as a Foreign Review World Chinese Language Teaching, 21 (2007)
3. Yang Yuan. Retrospect and Prospect of hearing theoretical research training. World Chinese Language Teaching, 35 (2014)
4. Yu Na. Teaching Chinese as a review hearing. Educational Research, 12, (2007)
5. Lu station, segment rather expensive. Teaching of Chinese-based multimedia technology. China Educational Technology and Equipment, 84 (2008)
6. Zheng Yanqun research practice a foreign language computer-assisted instruction. Commercial Press, 13 (2006)
7. TURAL multimedia technology on Foreign Language Listening Course of Modern Languages (late), 05 (2006)
8. Feng. Foreign Language Teaching hear the application of multimedia teaching methods. Chinese education technology and equipment, 20, (2008)
9. Chen Zuohong multimedia use Advanced Speaking in Foreign Language Teaching. Research of National Education, 3 (2006)
10. Tang Fuyuan, Xu Lihua Based on Blackboard Teaching Information Technology Discussion Education information, 94 (2005)
11. Han Joan personal knowledge management theory and research. DETAILED DESCRIPTION Jiangsu Nanjing Normal University, 25 (2007)
12. Zhenghan Wen. Cooperative learning classroom management strategies. Wuhan University of Science and Technology, 12 (2006)

MATEC Web of Conferences 44, 01081 (2016)
DOI: 10.1051/matecconf/20164401081

Research on Japanese-original Anime Words based on Chinese Network Catchword Sphere

Jin Chang Cai

Teacher's College, Beihua University, Jilin, China

Abstract. In this paper, the phenomenon of Japanese-original anime language's spreading in Chinese network language was discussed, and some theory of lexicology, semantics, grammar, and cultural linguistics was proposed. The characters of its different types and its influence on Chinese and the reason why the anime language can be so popular in the factors of psychologies, social also was analyzed. According to these studies, some suggestions were put forward that how to standardize the network language and how to raise its taste.

1 General instruction

Sino-Japanese cultural exchanges have become increasingly frequent prompting a large number of Japanese cultural products into China via the internet; the most important is the Japanese animation products. Recently, the Chinese government also attaches great importance to this emerging cultural industries animation, because at this stage of China's animation industry is still in the emerging stage, and there is a big gap between Japan and other developed countries, the animation industry. Japan started in Asian culture industry is the earliest, especially the development of the animation industry with considerable strong local characteristics, the various aspects of Japanese film and television animation are touted by our young people, and gradually integrated into Chinese society. Based on Japanese television anime phenomenon spreading in our country, not only to investigate the Japanese film and television animation and its impact on the enjoyment of visual, auditory and other sensory aesthetic of the economy, the social dimension of our country, more in-depth from linguistics It analyzes the impact of its linguistic phenomena intercultural communication on Chinese.

Japanese anime buzzwords as a new source of social language, recently touted by the majority of youth groups, and gradually be brought into their daily lives. Japanese animation on the source language, our predecessors have done research, but mostly from the artistic angles anime carried out. Few based vocabulary, semantics, grammar and cultural linguistics and other related theories on the source animation on the network environment systematically study the language from the linguistic point of view, in order to strengthen the academic study of Chinese language network language animation, this article will use knowledge source for the popular Japanese animation words were, multi-angle analysis of decency. Finally, the emergence of this phenomenon and put forward their own thinking.

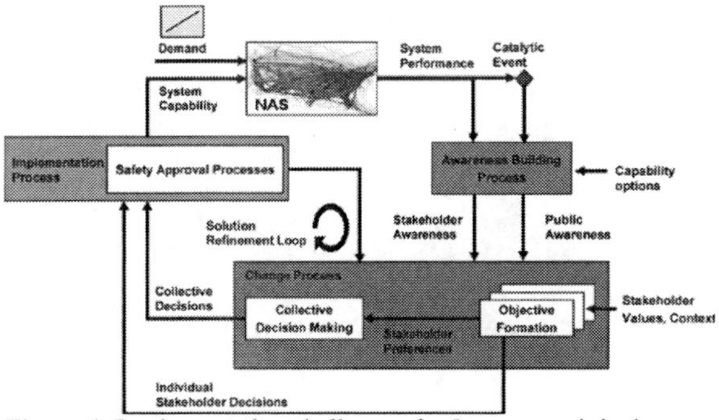

Figure 1. Implementation challenges for Japanese-original anime words systems

The text is written symbols of language recording system; it is the most important auxiliary communicative tool. It helps people to break through the language restrictions in time and space, so to expand the communicative function of language. With the development of human society, improve the technological level of long-distance communication and information exchange only in the form of letters already can not meet people's needs. The emergence is the Internet, to bring a new way of communicating, a new variant of the language - the language network. Largely solve the people exchanges require efficient, simple and so on, to meet the communication needs of people fast.

Internet language has broad and narrow sense; we put some new language phenomenon around computer technology and network exchange and the formation of, collectively known as the Internet language, which is a broad network language. It can be broken down into three

categories: one is the network-related terminology, such as a mouse, hardware, software, browser, firewall; second category is network-related special terms, such as login, Internet cafes, users, hackers, broadband; the third category is the language and symbols of Internet users in chat or blog, forums, and paste it frequently use, such as top, sofa, bench, sell Meng, fans, 4U, ^ _ ^ and so on. The first class of network language and jargon on the same jargon are used in a professional field, while the second and third categories of network language is the language of life related to the Internet, it is a narrow network language. We need to study is the third type of network language, these words is that people in the network exchanges frequently used fresh, emerging a class of languages, and thus is called a network buzzwords.

2 Network buzzwords features

Network buzzwords used in the form of a keyboard input characters, numbers, letters, Roman letters, Japanese kana, punctuation, symbols, and other symbols of operation appears that Internet technology as the basis, the Internet as a medium to express some semantics, network communication for the purpose of language. Therefore, it has with the written, spoken different and unique place.

Network buzzwords also buzzwords in one, so its essential characteristic is "pop." "Pop" is "real time" and "dynamic". Therefore, there is a network buzzwords development process: to produce pop, pop to unpopular. In line with people's social communication requires a period of buzzwords to have a strong vitality, not in line with the will gradually be eliminated. It would appear promising buzzwords have two: one is to be absorbed, be absorbed into the general vocabulary Chinese. One is the disappearance of the course they will gradually be eliminated. This shows that the buzzword is "real-time", was eliminated just buzzwords history vocabulary. Network buzzwords as is "dynamic", it then disappeared from generation to popular or accepted, there is a long or short process; generally this popular procedure is relatively short-lived, because it has real-time, that is, in rapid Under the Internet, driven by some of the new, popular term on the Internet can be immediately spread of Internet users go. When it is used after a period of time, it will disappear. If it does not, its popular frequency reaches a certain level; people will lose their freshness, which eventually evolved into fairly generic common words. For example earlier "rookie" "Dinosaur," "white collar" "blue collar" "wage earners" and other network buzzwords, have now had their glory days, become a common word. Old things will always be replaced by new, older network buzzwords same will be replaced by new, as times change, the subjective and objective conditions for the survival of the old buzzwords will disappear, he lost the popular soil, and naturally they would cease to exist. At this era can reflect the new features of the new buzzwords too will produce, this is a dynamic process of development buzzwords transition from the old. For example, network language to describe a person lovely time, from "cute" to "kawaii," the popular earliest use to the current popular "Moe" is a very typical example.

Buzzwords is a highly creative language, is a modern human wisdom. Appears at the beginning, it always gives a new look, the feeling shines, this is one important reason for the popular buzzwords, especially network buzzwords. China's Internet user's mainly young people mainly, aged mainly between 21-35 years old. Features such groups of Internet users are quick-witted, curious, creative, attention to social popular things, flaunt personality, "has a very strong sense of anti-traditional, advocating innovation, from the traditional language syntax, semantics norms, standards constraints." Therefore, they dare to break the inertia of thinking style, form their own unique insights. Coupled may be published in the virtual space to conceal the identity of their own opinions and views, have a full right to speak, they are continuing to create a rich, vivid image words and expressions to express themselves, such as "God horses (what) are the clouds, "" ginseng (life) cup (tragedy) "and other words such networks would highly infectious. In addition to the characteristics of Internet users among themselves, due to the progress of the times, people thought of liberation, the pursuit of individuality and efficiency of modern man seems unwilling to make the idea of the network so bland speak. They want to use the most simple words to express the time-saving richest, most vivid sense, but also highlights their personality and different, which reflects the contemporary creative network buzzwords.

The first need is communication: simple and quick, easy effort. With the rapid development of networks, the arrival of the information age, people increasingly prefer to use simple and clear language to express themselves, such as letters, numbers, etc. to convey information, common international letters, numbers can be expressed with a minimum of convey the wealth of information, so in this particular era was born of a number of lettered words, numbers, words. Online communication is actually in writing, spoken exchange rate. Oral communication course is the best, most concise communication tool, but the lack of specificity of the visual. Currently the network communication, we mainly keyboard input tool, according to certain input procedures. Keyboard input pinyin to input Chinese characters not only have this one form, also contains letters, numbers, the arithmetic symbols, each symbol in different languages have different sounds, such as "8" as a figure in the Chinese and English have different pronunciation, and even differences in Mandarin and dialects, such as people in some areas to read it as "fat" meaning "fortune."This gave us a simple symbol provides a rich voice material for quick and easy communication provided sufficient condition. In order to achieve writing speeds spoken, so some of the netizens will use shorthand symbols or acronyms, or create some new vocabulary. For example, "3KS (thanks abbreviations)" only need to type three times, but in the original word thanks input when you need to type 6; "OIC (oh, I see homonym

representation I understand)," when in input only need to type three times, the original sentence is not punctuation, but also need to type 6; Again Pinyin input "Jiang Zi (" like this "homonym acronym)" To type 7, type the original phrase will have 9 times. Some networks such buzzwords not only impressive, but also reflect the characteristics of its simple and easy to write, greatly reducing the communication speed.

Language network has a large number of the biggest feature is the use of symbols to communicate. Or with a combination of symbols representative of expression, such as, (* ^ __ ^ *), ^ _ ^, O (∩ _∩) O ...... and other means "happy smile"; (@ __ @) ~ X__X ~ ~ o (> _ <) o ~~ ...... such as performance, "sad, sad" facial expression; or using symbols words, such as "5201314" stands for "I love you for life" "+ U" means "Go" meaning: they represent an object or symbol combination, such as, (• •) nnn represents a caterpillar, - <- <- <@ is a flat flower roses. We are very vivid glance. In addition, there is the ancient Chinese writing enabled or borrow foreign words, and so on the way. For example, nowadays very fire of network buzzwords "embarrassing" was originally an ancient Chinese word, and now being touted users, because it is very intuitive showed a man embarrassing, embarrassing the way, and as "Mei" presence in the ancient Chinese, "Kangxi": "stay with 槑 province, or a, pass for plum Herbal: stay, plum apricot class."But in today's buzzwords in network, it also has a new meaning, Internet users look directly shape pronunciation, read "foolishly, or double-stay" means "silly, stay, very naive" means. Like body with a source vocabulary to express abstract semantics, or other circumstances also need to use a lot of words to explain and describe, the network popular word sometimes can be more simple image but also no shortage of humor render out, and has a strong visual effect to the virtual network life adds some angry and realism.

3 Dissemination in Japanese animation in China

There is "anime Kingdom," said Japan, currently the world's largest exporter of animation production. Japanese animation film and television work in China spread of 30 years, with a gradual increase in the spread of technology, showing distinct stage characteristics: release from the official Internet TV to DVD and then released.

For the general audience in terms of Japanese anime is not yet a need for psychological, mass media (mass media mainly refers to the traditional forms of media, such as movies, television, newspapers and magazines, best-selling book, etc.) to provide animation film and television works must extent to meet their common needs. But for that loyal audience of Japanese anime film and television works in terms of the mass media to provide animation film has been completely unable to meet their needs, they strongly want to look for another way to solve this problem.

Officially entered China from the Internet to millions of households starting, the number of Internet users in China since 1997 after doubling every six months remained growth. Today, China's Internet users have reached a very large number, more than 400 million people. At the same time, with the development of mobile phones, mobile services, the Internet is more ubiquitous, deep into the lives of ordinary people into make people read online and online viewing more convenient, easy, and more without spending expensive cost far Japan to seek anime crossing. And it also includes all the way showing the animation film of this cultural product: text, pictures, audio and video. Thus, in the network's convenient, fast and cheap sexual attraction, the anime fans will choose the internet of course. Thus, downloading via a network or online to watch Japanese anime number of visitors also increased significantly.

4 Network popular Japanese anime loanwords source classification

With the popularity of the Internet, Japanese animation film to do a lot of influx in China. For the first time via the Internet to translate these incoming Japanese anime into Chinese available to the majority of Chinese animation fans, partially proficient in Chinese and Japanese anime fans spontaneously established online subtitle group, in the translation process, in order to pursue efficiency, they sometimes use the Japanese kanji homology characteristics of the Japanese kanji words copied from or slightly modified, thus creating a large number of Chinese and Japanese Loan Word. Only the pursuit of translation efficiency is not enough, in order to ensure the quality of translation, they will use transliteration, translation and other means to translate. Then these forms special, innovative Japanese loanwords can easily meet contemporary animation fans novelty, difference of mentality, as their common language. Anime in Japanese language borrowed words include two forms: Loan Word and transliterated words.

The relationship between language and society very closely, language can not be separated from social and independent existence. Stalin said: "To understand the language and its development law, we must take the history of language with social development, with the creation of the language, use the language of the people closely linked to the history of research." Language with human society is interdependent influenced. Whatever the language, will be affected by other different kinds of languages, even among its own internal dialects will influence each other, penetration. Thus, the famous American linguist Bloomfield once said: "Unlike traditional features called mainstream adoption, called the language of borrowing in the range borrow, borrow and borrow our cultural differences between the dialects, the former borrowed features come. to the same language area, which features borrowed from different languages. "From the lineage of view, belongs to the Sino-Tibetan Chinese, and Japanese belong to Altaic. Therefore, Chinese with Japanese vocabulary belongs cultural

borrowing between borrowings. Now academics tend to the Chinese cultural definitions of words borrowed from other languages are: borrowing and varying degrees of "finished," the word from the alien language.

5 Network popular Japanese anime loanwords source of inspiration to us

Japanese animation culture through their own success enhance their influence in the international arena, we can also learn from them, we strive to improve the international influence of Chinese to improve China's comprehensive national strength. At any stage of a society, to improve the social cohesion of the country and the whole nation, language planning to do is to increase the frequency of the national language exchanges or the whole nation. In the previous stage of agricultural civilization, because each nation, each country link exchanges between each other is not close enough, so at that time just in terms of language planning issues in relation to a country. This will develop into modern humans, especially the era of economic globalization, any nation; any country can not rest on its laurels, and can not stay out of the tide of globalization. Therefore, an important task at this stage of language planning is to improve the country's national or native language influence.

In the context of today's globalization, cultural and ideological content has also become an important part of a national interest, and culture between the countries, comprehensive national strength has increasingly become an important parameter for the balance of interests and power. Cultural penetration and reverse osmosis are becoming an important part of the context of globalization of contention between the national interests. Currently English is rapidly expanding, linguistic hegemony prospects if you do not see this phenomenon later and blindly praise their guide language unified trend, welcomed it as the arrival of the world's common language, that this idea would be naive and harmful. States in order to enhance their own language in the international community's influence all have vigorously pursued a variety of language policy, mainly to improve the economic strength of the language. Economic power of language is a language refers to the percentage of gross national product in the region or country of the world's gross national product to use.

According to the data show that in 1977, the English-language economic power 34.6%, Japanese economic power is only 8.2%, in 2000, when English was 34.9%, 11.4% for the rapid increase in Japanese. In these 23 years, the English language economic force grew only 0.3 percent; the Japanese grew by 3.4%. This phenomenon can be seen, although the social status of English as an international language has not changed, but as a small Japanese language to enhance the international influence is enormous. This is thanks to the Japanese government's language promotion policy. Before World War II, the Japanese language promotion policy for war service, the purpose is to make the Japanese to become the lingua franca in Asia and become one of the tools of aggression. After World War II, the Japanese government aims to promote Japanese Japanese become an important means to make them with the world of cultural and economic cooperation. This policy relies on Japanese animation industry developed, strong economic strength and advanced technologies, has achieved remarkable results. In recent years, with the popularity of the Internet and youth groups love for Japanese animation, Japanese language economic strength will be further improved.

References

1. Peng Yubo. Some Features of Network Language. Rhetorical study, 4 (2001)
2. Lin Gang. Types and characteristics of the network terminology. Rhetorical study, 26 (2002)
3. Li Li. The nature and characteristics of the network words. Language Studies, 21 (2005)
4. Cao Guojun Comics • Animation • Cartoon • animation. Language knowledge, 7 (2006)
5. Chen Dandan, Chen Lin. Students analyze "otaku house female" phenomenon of Neijiang Normal University, 12 (2010)
6. Chu animation as a language in contemporary cinema, 3 (2010)
7. Gu Jiangping. Analysis of contemporary Japanese Loan Words on Chinese penetration. Kanji culture, 1 (2000)
8. Luo Yixian, party Wei Ying. On the influence of Japanese animation culture of our young people. Science garden, 6 (2008)
9. TURAL multimedia technology on Foreign Language Listening Course of Modern Languages (late), 05 (2006)
10. Feng. Foreign Language Teaching hear the application of multimedia teaching methods. Chinese education technology and equipment, 20, (2008)

MATEC Web of Conferences 44, 01082 (2016)
DOI: 10.1051/matecconf/20164401082

One Kind of Routing Algorithm Modified in Wireless Sensor Network

Ni Ni Wei[1,a], Yi Song[2]

[1]Department of computer science& Information Engineering, Wuhan Bioengineering Institute, Wuhan 430415, China

[2]Department of computer science& Information Engineering, Wuhan Bioengineering Institute, Wuhan 430415, China

Abstract. The wireless sensor networks are the emerging next generation sensor networks, Routing technology is the wireless sensor network communication layer of the core technology. To build reliable paths in wireless sensor networks, we can consider two ways: providing multiple paths utilizing the redundancy to assure the communication reliability or constructing transmission reliability mechanism to assure the reliability of every hop. Braid multipath algorithm and ReInforM routing algorithm are the realizations of these two mechanisms. After the analysis of these two algorithms, this paper proposes a ReInforM routing algorithm based braid multipath routing algorithm.

Key words: wireless sensor network; routing protocol; braid multipath; ReInforM routing

1 INTRODUCTION

Wireless sensor networks are the emerging next generation networks, which develop on the basis of the new network in the digital circuitry, wireless communications, micro-electromechanical systems and other technologies has become a hot research field.Hundreds of low cost, low power, small size, multi-functional sensor nodes in sensor networks, in the military and national defense, environmental monitoring, biomedical, smart homes, remote monitoring and other dangerous areas of the region has potentialuse value and broad application prospects [1].

For many sensor network applications with high reliability of data transmission requirements, its implementation depends mainly on the route chosen and reliable, so reliable routing protocol is particularly important.Wireless sensor network routing technology is the core technology of communications layer [2-3].Responsible for routing protocol data packets transmitted from the source node to destination node through the network to achieve in the sink node and sensor nodes transmit data reliably.

2 sensor network architecture

Wireless sensor network is deployed in the monitoring area by the large number of low-cost micro sensor nodes,which is the formation of a multi-hop ad hoc networks through wireless communication.Sensor networks is the integration of monitoring, control and wireless communication network system, its structure is shown in Figure 1, sensor network consists of sensor nodes, aggregation nodes, task management nodes and other components.Sensor nodes deployed in the designated monitoring area, the sensor nodes to monitor the data along to other sensor nodes hop by hop transmission, transmission of monitoring data in multiple nodes can be handled through the multi-hop routing to the sink node after, and finally through the Internetand satellite to reach management node, the user through the management node sensor network configuration and management, releases monitoring mission and the collection of monitoring data.

Wireless sensor network has the following characteristics: dense, and the large number of nodes; the location of sensor nodes is basically fixed; due to their own environmental impact of energy depletion and prone to failure node; environmental interference and node failures likely to cause changes in network topology;

[a] email: wnn19821024@163.com

Article available at http://www.matec-conferences.org or http://dx.doi.org/10.1051/matecconf/20164401082

sensor node energy, processing power, storage capacity and communication bandwidth are very limited.Wireless sensor networks for these characteristics, the network protocol must be able to efficiently use energy and the local network information to be able to choose the right based on the path.This article does not intersect the path based on multi-path routing mechanism described, and put forward their views.

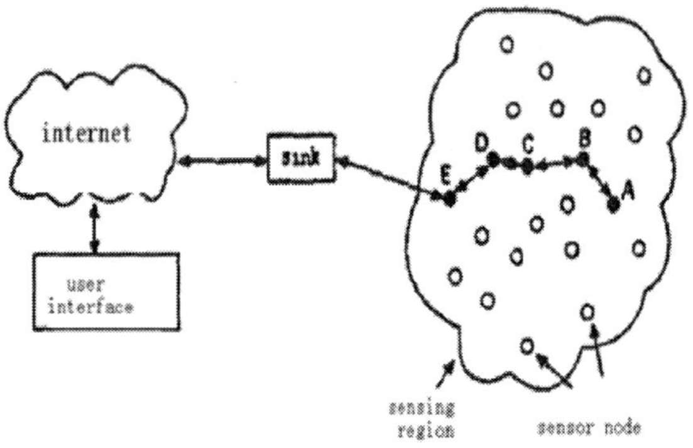

Figure 1 The network structure

3 Multi-path based on the RelnforM winding route

3.1 Multi-path routing mechanism for winding

In sensor networks, the introduction of multi-path routing is to increase the reliability of data transmission and implementation of network load balancing .In disjoint multipath, the alternate path may be much longer than the main path, for the introduction of spiral multi-path (braid multipath) concept.Multi-path winding path to overcome the main problem of single node failure.The winding path is the ideal multi-winding path by the formation of a group.A winding path that corresponds to a node on the main path, not including the nodes in the network, the formation of the source node to destination node from the optimized backup path.Winding path as the primary path of a backup path.The main path, each node has a corresponding winding path, which constitutes a winding path from the source node to destination node more than the winding path. Obviously, such an alternate path by intersecting with the main path. Proposed a multi-path routing mechanism that pre-establishment and maintenance of a path, do not need periodic flooding to be able to recover the data source node to sink node of the transmission path [3]. The basic idea is :First, build from the data source to the sink node of the main path, and then create a number of alternate paths; data transmission through the main path, while low-speed data transmission using alternate path to maintain the effectiveness of the path; When the primary path fails .When the path from the alternate path selected as the new sub-optimal path.

For the establishment of multiple paths method [4] proposed a multi-path disjoint (disjoint multipath) and wound multi-path (braid multipath) two algorithms is disjoint from the source node to destination node of any two pathsnodes do not intersect.Build process: first through the main path of convergence node enhanced information to establish the primary path; and then send the second best path to enhance the information to sub-optimal node A, node A and then choose their own optimal node B, the second-best path to enhance the information passed on.If the primary path B, B sends back information to enhance the negative A, A node to the second-best second-best path to enhance information transfer; if B is not the main path, then the B sub-optimal path to pass on increased information, until the construction of a secondoptimal path, according to the same methods, It may continue to construct a sub-optimal path to the next.

In disjoint multipath, the alternate path may be much longer than the main path, for the introduction of spiral multi-path (braid multipath) concept.Multi-path winding path to overcome the main problem of single node failure.The winding path is the ideal multi-winding path by the formation of a group.A winding path that corresponds to a node on the main path, not including the nodes in the network, the formation of the source node to destination node from the optimized backup path.Winding path as the primary path of a backup path.The main path, each node has a corresponding winding path, which constitutes a winding path from the source node to destination node more than the winding path.Obviously, such an alternate path by intersecting with the main path.

In ideal winding path, the nodes need to know the global network topology.A local multi-path generation algorithm winding as follows: the establishment of the main path, the primary path for each node (except the source node and the nodes near the source) should be enhanced alternate path to send information to their sub-optimal node (denoted as A), the second best again to find the optimal node node (denoted as B) increased dissemination of information on the alternate path.If the node B is not the main path,It will continue to spread its optimal node, until the intersection with the main path to a new backup path.

In the two multi-path generation algorithm, the alternate paths have different priorities.When the primary path fails, the second best path will be activated to become the new primary path.

3.2 RelnForM the routing mechanism

In the sensor network, sensor nodes is the data source, the monitoring data sent to the sink node.RelnForM (Reliable Information Forwarding Using Multiple Paths) route starting from the data source node,

consider the reliability, quality of communication and sensor node to sink node hop count to determine the number of required transmission path, and the number of nodes and the corresponding next hop nodeto achieve data transmission to meet reliability requirements.

In ReInForM routing, defines a reliability parameters, wit h a positive number r_s indicates less than one. The argum ent that the system requirements for the data source to sen d data packets to the sink node probability of success.Eac h node knows its neighbor nodes to the channel quality, u sing the channel error rate e_s that is less than one positive. Suppose each node to all neighbors of quality is the same. Sensor nodes through the following mechanisms to the s ink node knows the number of hops hs: the sink nod e periodically broadcast routing updates, which includes a number of hops to the sink node dom ain, node routing update information, the infor mation in the number of hops to the sink node.

According to the data source node r_s 、 e_s and h_s three parameters, we need to decide how many paths to forward data packets to ensure reliability.As e_s to a link error rate, for the data source node, After h_s the jump node packet arrival probability of convergence $(1\text{-}e_s)^{h_s}$,After p after the packet path can not reach the probability of convergence node $[1\text{-}(1\text{-}e_s)^{h_s}]^p$, so the success of the source node needsnumber of transmission path p can be calculated by the following formula:

$$p(r_s,e_s,h_s)=\frac{\lg(1-r_s)}{\lg(1-\ 1\text{-}(1\text{-}e_s)^{h_s})} \quad (1)$$

Note: The following formula, P represents the source of all nodes required the number of successful transmission path; r_s represents the system requirements for the data source to send data packets to the sink node probability of success; e_s represents the channel error rate; h_s represents the said he hops to the sink node of the h_s.

If p is greater than the number of successful data transmission path to the neighbor data source node number, you need to send multiple copies of some neighbors to copy data to meet the reliability requirements.

Data source node needs to calculate the number of forwarding path after selecting the next hop neighbor nodes, and assign the appropriate path forward.According to a sink node hops, the source node to neighbor nodes into three categories [5-7]: with their hops to the same cluster node, the node, than their less number of hops to the sink node one, node, and to the sink node than theirmore than one node.These three nodes were used. First, select the source node of a next hop node as the default, the default next hop to forward data probability data node is one. Since the source node to the default next hop node sends a success rate of the data, this path is equivalent to the success of Article forwarding path.If greater than or equal to the equation (1) calculated the number of paths, indicating that the source node only need to default the next hop node can forward data to meet the reliability requirements.Otherwise, it requires additional forwarding nodes required number of additional paths:

$$p(r_s,e_s,h_s)=\frac{\lg(1-r_s)}{\lg(1-\ 1\text{-}(1\text{-}e_s)^{h_s})}-(1-e_s) \quad (2)$$

First select additional nodes from the path of the H^-, Only when the value of p is calculated greater than the number of nodes H^- in time accordance with the formula (2), need to select nodes from H^0; If the p value is greater than the sum of the number of nodes H^- and H^0,At this point need to select nodes from H^+. Each node in the collection have been selected as the source node to create a certain number of paths, To ensure that the path of all selected nodes to provide the sum of p. Use p_{H^-}, p_{H^0}, p_{H^+} set that collection H^-, H^0, H^+, was selected as the next hop node need to create a number of paths the source node, Set H^-, H^0, H^+, in the order of selected nodes N_{H^-}, N_{H^0}, N_{H^+}, There have the formula (3)

$$N_H^- \cdot p_H^- + N_H^0 \cdot p_H^0 + N_H^+ \cdot p_H^+ = p \quad (3)$$

According to the following Proportion with p_H^-, p_H^0, p_H^+:

$$p_H^- = \frac{p_H^0}{1\text{-}e_s} = \frac{p_H^+}{(1\text{-}e_s)^2} \quad (4)$$

Select H^0 or H^+ node as the next hop node; rather than repeat the selection H^- nodes in order to maintain the balance network load.

3.3 Multi-path algorithm to improve the winding

From the above detailed description we can see: many winding paths and disjoint multipath compared to the advantage of reducing the length of the alternate paths to improve the efficiency of data transmission, but the reliability is decreased.For more winding path, if the primary path and alternate path exists for a certain period of intersecting paths, when the intersecting paths fails, after their main path and alternate path will fail, if all paths have been intersecting with a path, andthis side of the path fails, the transmission will be terminated, only

to re-establish a good network until the new primary path and alternate path can continue to transmit data.However, disjoint multipath algorithm, data transmission failure occurs only in the main path and a number of alternate paths at the same time fails.ReInForM routing mechanism has the advantage of the quality of communication channel through the transmission path and the path calculation of the number distribution, improve the reliability of data transmission and network load balancing, the energy limited by shortcomings in the face of such a routing mechanism for sensor networks toP path while transmission, energy will be costly.Therefore, it can improve the way we propose a route and wound ReInForM and combine multi-path algorithm: multi-path based on the ReInforM winding route, specifically described as follows:

Step 1: the first to use multi-pass algorithm winding aggregation node and between the source node n be a main path and alternate paths.

steset up $r_s = 1$, $e_s = 0$, Primary path used for data transmission.

Step 2: When the primary path fails, data transmission using ReInForM routing,set up r_s The reliability of the system parameter values themselves, e_s The channel error rate,

Step 3: At the same time, by priority level of the n bar, choose an alternate path as a new path connecting the main path, if there is no such path, you need to use step 1 to re-establish the primary path and alternate path, and run step 2.

4 Conclusion

In this paper, two multi-path routing algorithm and ReInforM described and analyzed, and on this basis, considering the advantages and disadvantages of each proposed a multi-winding path ReInforM based routing mechanism, this improved use of wound multi-path routing mechanismalgorithm for establishing a primary path and a number of alternate paths, when the main path in a normal state, only one main path used for data transmission, more than ReInforM multi-path routing algorithm to transfer data at the same time save a lot of energy, which energy Shousensor network is very limited sense.Failure at the main path routing to transfer data using ReInforM ensure the reliability of wireless sensor networks.Equations should be centred and should be numbered with the number on the right-hand side.

Acknowledgments. This paper is supported by Hubei Provincial Education projects (No.B2014160) and Wuhan Education Projects Foundation(No.2014217) and Wuhan Education Projects Foundation(No.2009k101)

References

1.Cui Li, Ju Hailing. And so on. Progress in wireless sensor networks [J]. Computer Research and Development, 2005 (1) :163-174.

2.Yaping LI.Analyze and Implementation of a New Route Protocol Based on MSAODV[J]. Microcomputer Information2007(8-2): 225-22

3.Qiangli Zhao, Ming Xu.Analysis and Comparison of Routing Protocols for Wireless Sensor Networks[J] Computer Science 2009.2(36):35-41.

4. D.Y Zhang, G.Q Ji. "Research on DSR-Based Energy Routing Protocols for Ad Hoc Networks". Computer Technology and Development. Vol.19,No.8,pp.15-19,2009.

5. C.X Wu, L.Z Song, J.B Wang."DSR ProtocolBased on Congestion Control and EnergyBalance Strategy".Contro l Engineering of China.VOL.17, NO 2,PP.260-263,2010.

6.Ahmad.S,Awan.I,Waqqas.A,et al. "Performance analys is of DSR& extended DSR protocols". Proc.Kuala Lump ur: the Second Asia InternationalConference on Modeling & Simulation, 2008.

7.weinini,songyi.A Reputation of Node Computation Mo del-based EXCHANG Inquiry Scheme in Ad Hoc Net wo rks[J].Experimental Technology and Management,2013 (4):96-98

MATEC Web of Conferences 44, 01083 (2016)
DOI: 10.1051/matecconf/20164401083

Effectiveness and Discussion of Ventilation Design with Automatic Revolving Window

Jing Yi Chang[1*], Yean Der Kuan[2], Chun Ching Lan[2], Hsing Ju Li[2], Yu Kun Hsu[2], Chih Yao Chen[2], En Ting Shen[2], Chih Yen Chen[1]

[1] *Department of Marine Engineering, Taipei College of Maritime Technology, Taipei, Taiwan*
[2] *Department of Refrigeration, Air-Conditioning and Energy Engineering, National Chi-Yi University of Technology, Taichung, Taiwan*

Abstract. This paper aims to improve and discuss the effectiveness of automatic revolving window ventilation on human comfort, where the temperature sensor mounted indoors gives the signal to start the stepping motor of the revolving window. There is a controller for automatic regulation according to the difference between the preset temperature and indoor temperature, where the air flow of ventilating fan imports outside air to take excess heat away from the room, in order to reduce the indoor temperature. The revolving window opening angle is simulated and analyzed, and the impact of different air rates on the indoor temperature is analyzed. This system can regulate the indoor temperature to effectively reach the optimal human comfort temperature, and can reduce the frequency of using air conditioning, in order to attain the goals of energy saving, carbon reduction, and environmental protection.

1. Introduction

This study starts with "energy saving starts with everybody", and joins the modern trend of regulating the optimum thermal comfort environment. The thermal comfort environment means the physical factors of temperature, humidity, and air flow acting synthetically on the human body, and the human body is comforted when in the optimum combination state [1]. The temperature is the key to human comfort. The human body temperature is mostly kept at 37℃ ,and if the environmental conditions are favorable for evaporating sweat, the human skin surface is kept dry. Therefore, the regulation of body temperature is very important for health and comfort [2]. When human body surface skin is exposed to the external environment, the skin transfers heat to the external environment for temperature regulation. The higher the air velocity is, the faster the skin temperature falls, and the closer the skin temperature is to the air temperature. Therefore, in addition to air temperature difference, the air velocity is closely related to human comfort in a low temperature environment [3].

Modern people mostly live in confined spaces for 90% of their life; however, indoor comfort conditions are neglected, and the environmental quality directly influences human health, thus, indoor thermal comfort and air quality are major topics [4]. Taiwan has actively advocated building energy saving in recent years, and established the system of "nine major indices of green buildings", which is devoted to ecology, energy saving, waste reduction, and health [5]. This study uses an automatic temperature sensing revolving window and an exhaust fan to adjust the indoor air flow to carry hot air away, and improve indoor air quality. The air consists of multiple gases, in addition to vapor, it consists of 78.10% nitrogen, 20.93% oxygen, and 0.03% CO2. It is obvious that oxygen accounts for a considerable proportion of the air. An excess of CO2 content in the space can cause risk to the human body by losing consciousness. Generally, the arrangement of air inlet/outlet shall avoid a short circulation flow path. This study uses a diagonal path, where the window and fan are separated at 90°, and imported fresh air is kept indoors moderately, in order that cool air can effectively flow to various corners, and exchange with hot air to eliminate human discomfort.

Energy saving must be started from the air conditioning, and the room temperature determines the operation of air conditioning. It is indicated that, the comfortable temperature is 27.17℃ when the relative humidity is 60~70% and the air velocity is 0.2 m/s; the comfortable temperature is 28.30℃ when the air velocity is 0.5m/s. According to the relative humidity and the information of the energy label, "air conditioning power consumption can be reduced by 6% as the air conditioning temperature is increased by 1℃". Outside air is imported for forced ventilation, which reduces the room temperature in advance, and the heat of indoor air is completely exchanged. In order to improve indoor air quality and human comfort, if the outside fresh air is imported by appropriate forced convection at ambient temperature without air conditioning to take indoor heat away and continuously improve the indoor air quality [6],

[a] Corresponding author: author@e-mail.org

Article available at http://www.matec-conferences.org or http://dx.doi.org/10.1051/matecconf/20164401083

the consumption of air conditioning can be reduced greatly for energy saving. The automatic system has become the present trend for improving life quality, which is also one of our goals, thus, the concept of automatic control is used in windows in order to meet humanistic demands while saving energy.

2. Research Procedures

This study discusses the overall operation of revolving windows and its effect on indoor ventilation. The temperature sensor, which is mainly a non-contact temperature sensor, detects the room temperature without contacting the test medium; the temperature is transmitted by thermal radiation or convection to the temperature sensor for temperature measurement, and the temperature data are transferred as signals to the control circuit for subsequent analysis and processing, in order to determine whether or not to adjust the room temperature, and the corrected signal is sent to the stepping motor.

As shown in Figure 1, the upper stepping motor drives the glass window to revolve, the angle is controlled according to the signal when the stepping motor is running, and the ball bearing under the window not only reduces the resistance to pivoting friction, but also reduces the noise resulted from the friction of the bearing surface, and thus, effectively prolongs the service life of the window. Finally, air is imported to reduce the room temperature, and improve the indoor air quality and human comfort. The temperature sensor again detects whether the room temperature has reached the preset temperature, then maintains control and adjustments. The aforesaid control path forms a cycle, as shown in Figure 2.

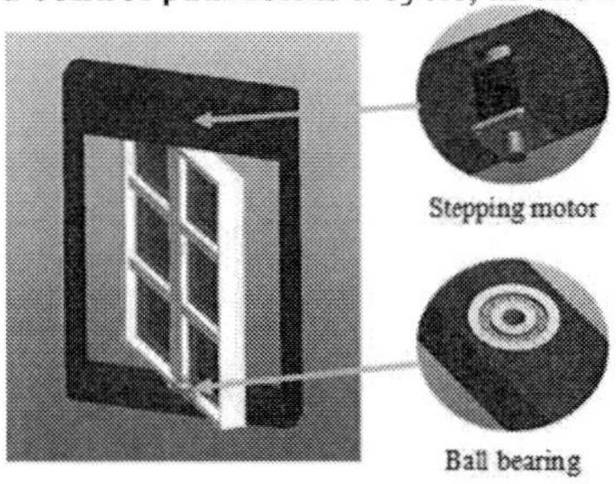

Figure 1. Schematic diagram of revolving window and assemblies

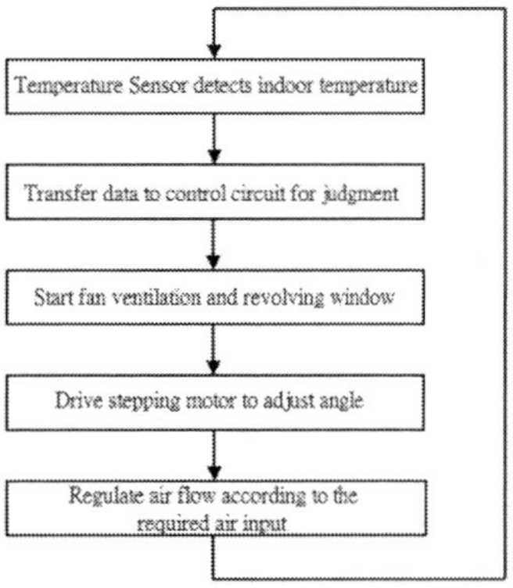

Figure 2. System control flow

2.1 Design of revolving window angle for air flow

Forced ventilation is the power generated by ventilating machinery (fan, blower, exhaust fan), and contributes to the exchange and flow of indoor and outdoor air. Mechanical ventilation is applicable to an insufficient natural air rate or a room with harmful or combustible gas. It is characterized by stable air flow, and the air rate can be controlled as required.

The ventilating fan imports the outside air into the room, the indoor air is exhausted by the ventilating fan, a low pressure field is formed in the room, the indoor heat and human exhaled CO2 are carried away by the pressure difference, and the revolving window opening is adjusted by the automatic control system, where the angles are 30, 60, and 90°, as shown in Figure 3, and the rotation speed of the fan is controlled by a variable frequency for energy saving.

Figure 3. Revolving window rotation angle

2.2 CFD software simulated fluid flow field analysis

The Ansys Fluent software uses different discrete formats and numerical methods for different complex flows and physical phenomena, and uses computing speed, stability, and accuracy in a specific domain to solve the computational problem of complex flow in various domains. The ventilation system uses heat flow field analysis software to build model parameters in a computer, the model region is defined, the mesh is designed and divided, the model uses geometrical mesh to imitate the actual state, thus, simulating the actual fluid flow and heat transfer property. There are different area solutions in the software: structured grid computation, unstructured grid computation, fluid-solid coupling, viscous and elastic flow, mixing, and thermal control analysis. Different modules are calculated according to the simulation requirements, and the simulated data results are visualized to determine the ideal analysis, as shown in Figure 4.

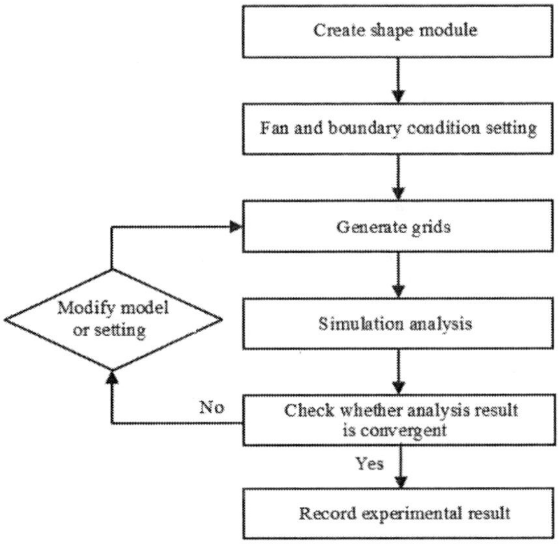

Figure 4. Simulation analysis flow chart

2.2.1 Software simulated exterior and assembly setting

The model is built according to the actual geometry and size of the analytic. The size of the simulated room is 4m×4m×3m, and Figure 5 shows the Ansys Icepak modeling. The calculation region is defined, in order to obtain accurate and rapid analysis results, the physical conditions of the problem and the complexity of the model are analyzed, and the required object and boundary condition setting are simplified or maintained, in order to build the model rapidly, and analyze the reasonable physical results. The number of grids of this house model is about 100 thousand, and the Ansys Icepak mesh generation is as shown in Figure 6. The number of grids can be reduced by simplifying the model and setting appropriate boundary conditions, in order to shorten the computing time and increase the efficiency of numerical analysis. The number of grids of mesh generation represents the accuracy of calculation, where smaller and more grids represent longer computing time, but the accuracy of the results is higher.

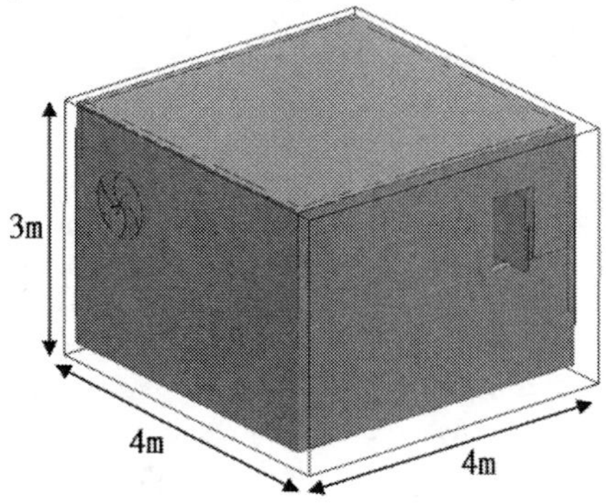

Figure 5. Ansys Icepak modeling

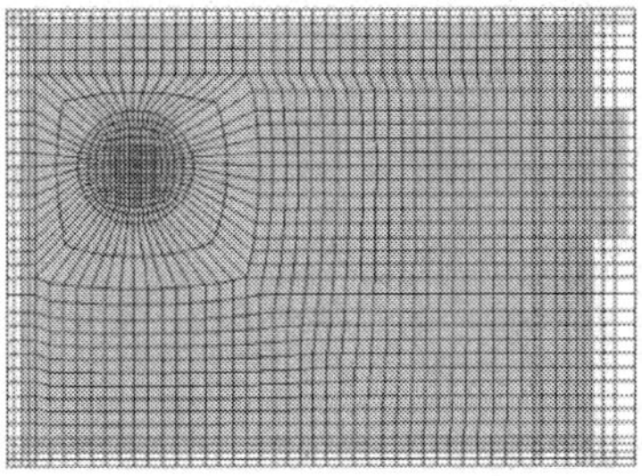

Figure 6. Front view of Ansys Icepak mesh generation

Finally, the heat source and ventilating fan are set up. The heat source simulates the human body in the room, the fan exhausts the excess heat from the room, and imports outside air to form convection. It is adjusted to the best convective section in order to observe whether the indoor air convection can effectively carry the excess heat away, and the effects of different angles on the temperature are discussed and recorded to determine the optimum conditions meeting indoor requirements, as shown in Figure 7.

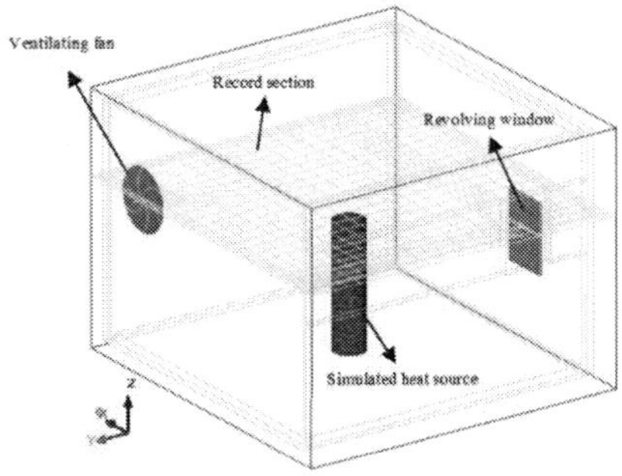

Figure 7. Icepak assembly setup diagram

2.2.2 Software simulation analysis and calculation

The analytic modeling and boundary condition settings are followed by computation. The solver plays the key role in numerical analysis, while the user evaluates the type of problem, and then selects the numerical calculation mode, which calculates the target value of convergence and the quantity of computer processor units, where the computer uses simple mathematical forms and mathematical equations for iterative computation, and the result is displayed by a convergence curve to check whether the target value of convergence is reached.

3. Results and Discussion

3.1 Ventilation and air exchange of window at various openings

This study uses Ansys Icepak software to simulate the interaction of a ventilating fan and a revolving window, and uses different angles of the revolving window to simulate the air flow and temperature distribution in the room. In the simulation of a ventilation system, the simulation data are compared with the

thermal comfort of literature to determine the optimum inhabited environment.

3.1.1 Simulated ventilation and air exchange of window at 90° opening

Figure 8 is the air flow vector diagram of a simulated revolving window at 90°. It is observed that a great deal of air is imported by the exhaust fan into the room. The maximum air velocity nearby the revolving window is 3.53011 m/s, the average air velocity in the room is 1.76506 m/s. As mentioned above, the comfortable temperature is 33.47℃ when the relative humidity is 50~80% and the air velocity is 2 m/s. According to the flow line vector arrowheads, the indoor air flow is helical, and a large volume of outside air rushes in the room. However, the number of vector lines leaving the exhaust fan is small, meaning the outside air is still flowing into the room, and the indoor air temperature is maintained at 24~25℃.

Figure 9 shows the temperature profile of a revolving window at 90°, and a 30℃ heat source is placed in the room. It is observed in the temperature profile that the temperature has not reached 30℃. The heat is dissipated by this system, in order that the indoor space is kept comfortable without air conditioning.

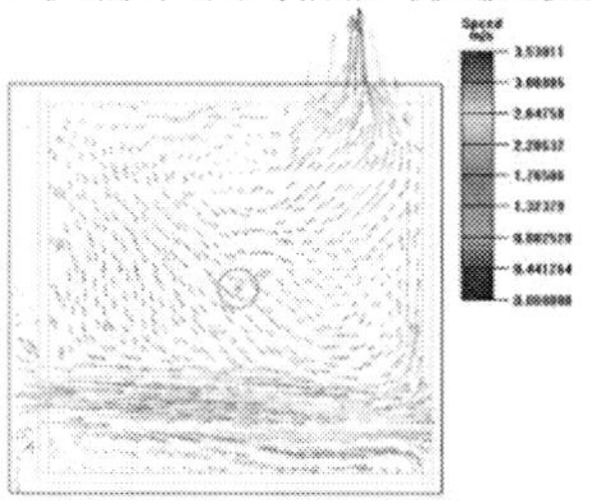

Figure 8. Top view of air flow vector of revolving window at 90°

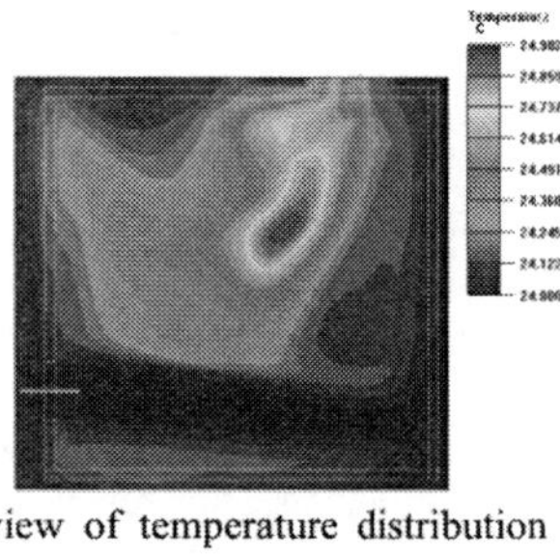

Figure 9. Top view of temperature distribution of revolving window at 90°

3.1.2 Simulated ventilation and air exchange of window at 60° opening

Figure 10 shows the air flow vector of a simulated revolving window at 60°. It is observed that much outside air enters the room through the exhaust fan. The maximum air velocity nearby the 60° revolving window is 3.29069 m/s, and the average air velocity in the room is 1.23401 m/s. The air flow imported through the window at 60° opening must be lower than that through the window at 90° opening. In order to enlarge the temperature range of this system, in the 60° opening mode, when the indoor temperature is higher than 28℃ and lower than 30℃ (included), the air exchange is actuated. According to the vector arrowheads, the indoor air flow lines are also helical, as compared with the simulation of 90° opening, the location collocation of the revolving window and ventilating fan has significant effect, and the circulating air maintains the indoor temperature at 24~25℃, as shown in Figure 11. A 30℃ heat source is placed in the room, and the temperature profile shows the peak temperature is 27.66℃, proving that this system can maintain the space at 26℃ with a 30℃ heat source.

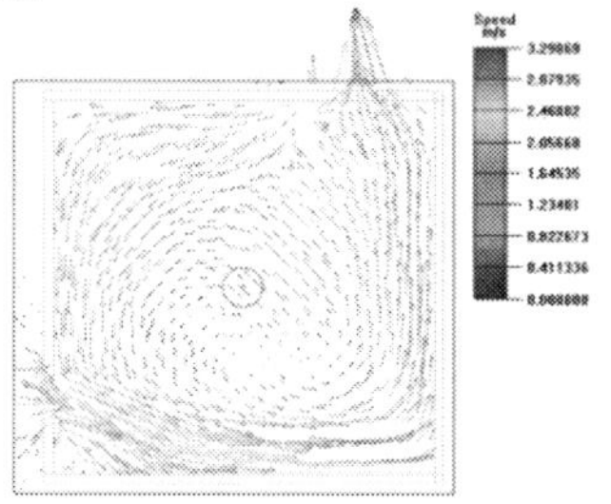

Figure 10. Top view of air flow vector of revolving window at 60°

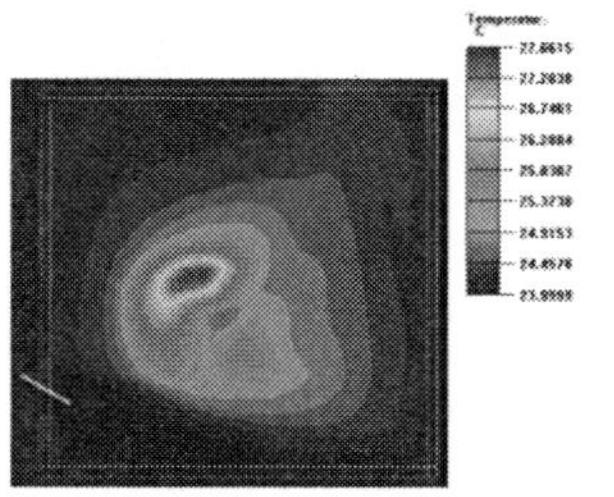

Figure 11. Top view of temperature distribution of revolving window at 60°

3.1.3 Simulated ventilation and air exchange of window at 30° opening

Figure 12 shows the air flow vector of a simulated revolving window at 30°. The imported outside air flow is lower than the 60° opening. However, in order to make this system applicable to different temperature ranges, this 30° opening mode deals with the indoor space temperature condition above 26℃ and below 28℃ (included), the outside air is imported by the exhaust fan into the room, the maximum air velocity nearby the 30° revolving window is 2.71231 m/s, the average air velocity in the room is 1.01712 m/s, the air flow input through the window at a 30° opening is the lowest among the three modes of this system, and in the temperature range of 26℃ to 28℃, thus, provided there is a little ventilation and air exchange, a comfortable temperature can be maintained. According to the vector arrowheads, the indoor air flow lines are also helical. The circulating air spreads to all corners of the room, and the temperature is maintained at 24~25℃, as shown in Figure 13; a 30℃ heat source is placed in the room, the temperature profile shows the temperature is reduced to 28.64℃, proving that when a 30℃ heat source equivalent to human body temperature is in this system, the body surface temperature can be reduced to 28℃, and the indoor ambient temperature is maintained at 26℃.

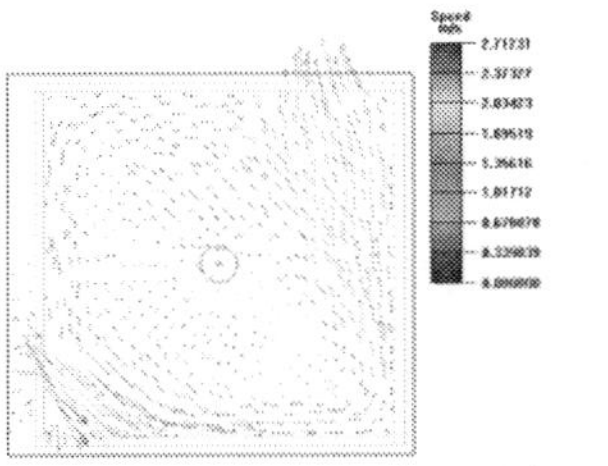

Figure 12. Top view of air flow vector of revolving window at 90°

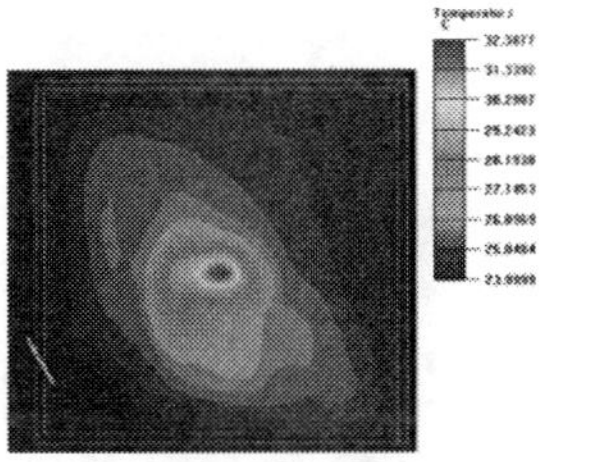

Figure 13. Top view of temperature distribution of revolving window at 90°

3.2 Air Velocity and thermal comfort of revolving window in three modes

In the simulation of three states of a revolving window, the indoor average air velocity is 1.0-1.8m/s, as shown in Table 1. Taiwan is in an insular climate, the average humidity is mostly 50-80%, as compared with literature, the comfortable temperature is 30℃ when the relative humidity is 50~80% and the air velocity is 1 m/s; the comfortable temperature increases to 31℃ when the air velocity is 1.5m/s; and the comfortable temperature is as high as 33.47℃ when the air velocity is 2 m/s. Table 1 shows that the difference between this ventilation system and the corresponding human thermal comfort is 6~7℃. Therefore, provided the room is equipped with this system device, and provides air flow in the room, the human tolerable thermal comfort temperature can rise, and the service hours of air conditioning can be greatly reduced. According to "the air conditioning power consumption can be reduced by 6% as the air conditioning temperature is increased by 1 ℃ ", this system uses air conditioning only if the indoor temperature exceeds 33.47 ℃ , thus, the energy consumption is reduced by 36~42% for the temperature difference, which saves energy.

Table 1. Simulation data compilation of three modes

Angle (°)	Average indoor temperature (℃)	Average indoor air velocity (m/s)	Human thermal comfort (℃)
30	24.8091	1.01712	30
60	24.9153	1.23401	30
90	24.3685	1.76506	31

4. Conclusion

When the indoor temperature is 26~28 ℃ , the ventilating fan is actuated, and the revolving window is opened to 30°. When the room temperature is 28~30℃, the revolving window is opened to 60°. When the room temperature is higher than 30℃, but below 33℃, the revolving window is opened to the maximum 90°. The temperature range of this ventilation system is 26~33℃, in this temperature interval, the indoor temperature can be effectively reduced to 24~25℃. According to the statistical data of the Central Weather Bureau, the monthly mean temperature of July and August is 28~30 ℃ since 2011. Therefore, this ventilation system is sufficient for the various districts of Taiwan, the consumption of air conditioning can be greatly reduced, the spending rate of fossil fuel can be reduced, and civil diseases caused by long-term application of air-conditioning systems can be relatively reduced. Future research of this system may determine the optimal position relation between the revolving window and ventilating fan, design more uniform air flow, and more significant cooling effects; moreover, as some fitments can be put in the simulation space to approximate the actual state, this ventilation system can be applied to the actual environment, and dwelling quality may be further improved.

Acknowledgements

This paper is the project NSC 102-2622-E-167-018-CC3 of Ministry of Science and Technology. Thanks to the Ministry of Science and Technology for supporting this project.

References

[1]R. J. de Deara, G. S. Bragerb, "Thermal confort in naturally ventilated buildings: revisions to ASHRAE standard 55," Energy and Buildings, Vol.**34**, pp.549-561, 2002.

[2]A.P. Gagge, J.A.J. Stolwijk, J.D. Hardy, "Comfort and thermal sensations and associated physiological responses various ambient temperatures, " Environmental Research, Vol.**1**, pp.1-20, 1967.

[3]H. Mayer, P. Höppe, "Thermal comfort of man in different urban environments," Theoretical and Applied Climatology, Vol.**38**, pp.43-49, 1987.

[4]S. Atthajariyakul, T. Leephakpreeda, "Real-time determination of optimal indoor-air condition for thermal comfort, air quality and efficient energy usage," Energy and Buildings, Vol.**36**, pp.720-733, 2004.

[5]C. L. Cheng, "Evaluating water conservation measures for Green Building in Taiwan" Building and Environment, Vol.**38**, pp.369-379, 2003.

[6]Guohui Gan, "Evaluation of room air distribution systems using computational fluid dynamics" Energy and Buildings, Vol.**23**, pp.83-93, 1995.

MATEC Web of Conferences **44**, 01084 (2016)
DOI: 10.1051/matecconf/20164401084

A Runway Incursion Detection Approach Based on Multiple Protected Area and Flight Status Machine for A-SMGCS

Jing Li[1,a], Guo Qiang Wang[1], Pan Zhu[1], Xin Lu[2] and Jian Su[2]

[1]*R&D Centre, the Second Research Institute of Civil Aviation Administration of China (CAAC), Chengdu, China*

[2]*Guilin Air Traffic Management Station of Civil Aviation of China, Guilin, Guangxi Zhuang Autonomous Region, China*

Abstract. A-SMGCS is a modular system defined in the ICAO (International Civil Aviation Organization) Manual on Advanced Surface Movement Guidance and Control System (A-SMGCS) .One of A-SMGCS goals is to provide enhanced safety and protection of the runway. This paper presents a novel runway incursion detection approach for A-SMGCS, in which a multiple protected area is proposed to decrease complexity of pre-treatment for incursion judgment, and a flight status machine is designed to specify the transitions of one flight from one target status to another. Additionally, an HMI (Human Machine Interface) independently developed by the Second Research Institute of CAAC (Civil Aviation Administration of China) was designed in order to validate the runway incursion detection approach, the result shows that the algorithm has the potential to significantly improve runway safety by early detection and alerting of runway incursions.
Keywords: runway incursion; multiple protected area; flight status machine; A-SMGCS; ICAO

1 Introduction

With the increasing demand for air transport all over the world, pressure is growing for airport systems to safely handle greater capacity in all weather conditions, improve traffic distribution and management, maximize use of existing infrastructure and so on [1].The number of accidents and incidents during airport surface movements, including runway incursions, is increasing. The hazards and risks associated with runway operations need to be managed in order to prevent runway incursions that may lead to accidents. Runway incursions have sometimes led to serious accidents with significant loss of life. Although they are not a new problem, with increasing air traffic, runway incursions have been on the rise. To improve the situation with respect to runway incursions, research on Runway Incursion Prevention System (RIPS) by NASA(National Aeronautics and Space Administration) form 2002 [2] and Manual on the Prevention of Runway Incursions by ICAO from 2006 [3,4] have been established. However, due to specific characteristics of different runways on different airports, it is too difficult to set up a model with the potential to be used at airports worldwide.

2 ICAO definition for runway incursion in A-SMGCS

ICAO Doc 9830 defines A-SMGCS as follows: Advanced surface movement guidance and control system (A-SMGCS). A-SMGCS providing routing, guidance and surveillance for the control of aircraft and vehicles in order to maintain the declared surface movement rate under all weather conditions within the aerodrome visibility operational level while maintaining the required level of safety. A-SMGCS provides for enhanced safety and protection of the runway as one means for avoiding runway incursions [5].As described in the ICAO Doc 9830, A-SMGCS consists of four basic functions:Surveillance,Control,Planning/Routing,Guidance.Implementation of A-SMGCS defines 4 levels, the second level provides for an alerting function to Air Traffic Controllers (ATC controllers) in case of intrusion of aircraft or vehicles in a pre-defined protected area around the runway system. The third level involves the detection of all conflicts on the movement area as well as improved guidance and planning for use by controllers.

Runway Incursion defined in A-SMGCS is as follows: Any occurrence at an aerodrome involving the incorrect presence of an aircraft, vehicle or person on the protected area of a surface designated for the landing and take-off of aircraft [5].

3 Runway incursion detection approach

3.1. Runway incursion area

A major concept of the runway incursion detection algorithm is the use of incursion areas, which will help to determine the position relation of target and runway. For

[a] Corresponding author: casri148@163.com

each runway, the algorithm will investigate conflicts if a track is in one of the incursion areas, depending on the type of conflict.

A runway incursion area is a software-derived three-dimensional virtual area. There are multiple incursion areas for one runway. To decrease complexity about pre-treatment of incursion judgment and take into account the error of surveillance data, a multiple protected area is proposed, which consists of approach area, line-up area, runway area and departed area. Figure 1 shows the layout of the multiple protected area.

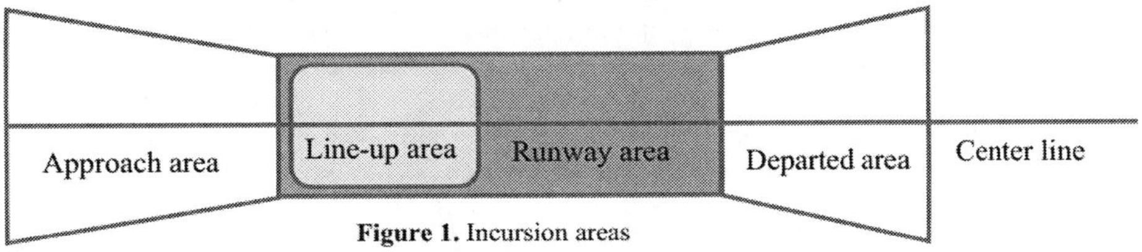

Figure 1. Incursion areas

3.2 Conflict alert

Every aerodrome has site-specific parameters and situations to be addressed. The following list provides some of the possible conflict alert scenarios that should be detectable on the runway by the A-SMGCS:

- Aircraft arriving to, or departing aircraft on, a closed runway;
- Arriving or departing aircraft with traffic on the runway (including aircraft beyond the runway-holding positions);
- Arriving or departing aircraft with moving traffic to or on a converging or intersecting runway;
- Arriving or departing aircraft with opposite direction arrival to the runway;
- Arriving or departing aircraft with traffic crossing the runway;
- Arriving or departing aircraft with taxiing traffic approaching the runway (predicted to cross the runway-holding position);
- Arriving aircraft exiting runway at high speed with converging taxiway traffic;
- Arriving aircraft with traffic in the sensitive area(when protected);
- Aircraft exiting the runway at unintended or non-approved locations;
- Unauthorized traffic approaching the runway;
- Unidentified traffic approaching the runway.

3.3 Flight target status and flight status machine

Because there are so many possible conflict scenarios, every flight target is classified as being one and only one target status to simplify the detection of complex conflict situations. Therefore, a flight status machine is designed, in which nine flight statuses or flight phases are defined for the traffic in the incursion area:

- Approaching status: track is airborne and inside approach of used runway;
- Landing status: track is runway aligned and is airborne and on final approach;
- Landed status: track is on runway;
- Taxiing status: track is on runway and is not airborne and speed is below a certain speed, or not moving;
- Line-up status: track is on runway and is in line-up area and speed is below a certain speed, or not moving;
- Rolling status: track is not airborne and ground takeoff roll is in progress;
- Departing status: track is inside runway area and speed is above a certain speed;
- Departed status: track is airborne or speed is above a certain speed;
- Unknown status: unknown intent.

A flight status machine specifies the transitions from one target status to another, figure 2 illustrates the typical transitions between statuses for arrival and departure.

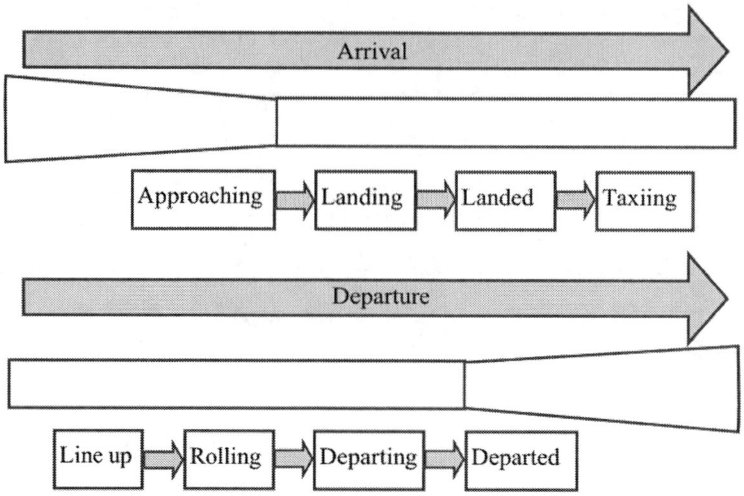

Figure 2. Typical target status transitions of one flight

There are two advantages to the flight status machine. Firstly, it avoids the possibility that a target might end up in a situation for which no target status has been defined. With a flight status machine, a target will always have a defined target status. Secondly, the flight status machine incorporates hysteresis, a technique for avoiding the problem of jumping back and forth between statuses due to surveillance errors. Figure 3 shows all the possible transitions.

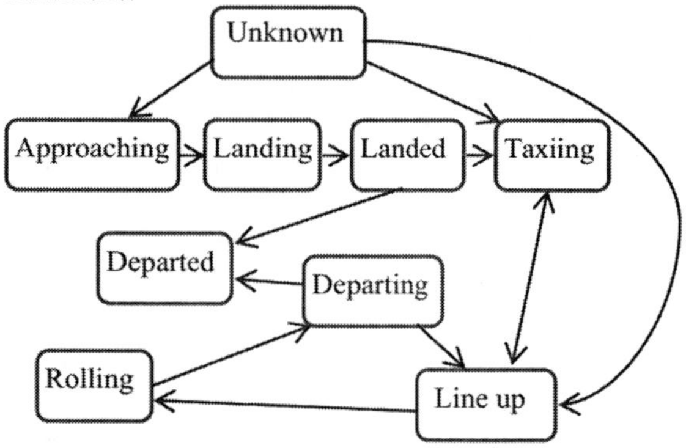

Figure 3. Possible target status transitions

3.4 Algorithm logic and process flow

In the present design, the alert function is event driven. The event, in this context, is the arrival of new surveillance data. When the new surveillance data is available, the alert function starts to run the detection. The alert function is based on a few steps below, and the process flow of the algorithm is shown as figure 4:

a) Step1: Decode the traffic data and initiate the target object;
b) Step2: Store flight target in a runway list if it enters one of the runway incursion areas;
c) Step3: Scan the targets in the runway list based on the pre-defined rules to detect runway incursion conflict;
d) Step4: Send alert if there is one.

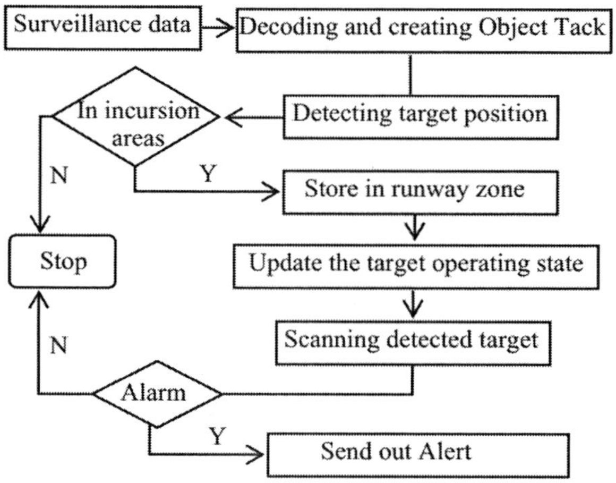

Figure 4. Process flow of the algorithm

The runway incursion detection algorithm is based on rules that define either a procedural or a physical conflict. An analysis of the nature of runway physical and procedural conflicts suggests that the conflict detection is based on four basic rules:

- Whether a movement has entered the one of the defined runway incursion areas;
- The flight target intent(target status of the target pair fits the conflict scenarios);
- Whether the two targets involved in the conflict are approaching each other;
- Whether the separation of targets is acceptable.

4 Simulation and validation of runway incursion detection approach

An HMI has been designed based on the runway incursion detection approach. The algorithm has been tested at Chengdu Shuangliu International Airport by real-time surveillance and simulation system independently developed by the Second Research

Institute of CAAC, real-time data of aircraft come from Automatic Dependent Surveillance–Broadcast(ADS-B) independently developed by the Second Research Institute of CAAC as well. ATC controllers are alerted through a pop up window and labels of the aircraft concerned displayed in yellow or red, which correspond to different type of conflicts. Controllers can acknowledge conflicts by clicking on the label so that these are displayed in their normal color again. The pop up window remains active as long as the conflict is valid. In figure 5 below, a detail of the HMI is shown, which shows an aircraft has just landed at runway 02L, another one is lining up behind it for a take-off, as soon as the departing aircraft starts accelerating, a runway incursion alert is given. A large number of different incursion scenarios were designed by the real-time surveillance and simulation system according to ATC controllers' experience. Compared with the experiment on real data, the algorithm could detect common runway incursion timely and correctly. Analysis of recorded data shows that the primary performance indicators have reached the requirements on conflict detection form ICAO Doc 9830, such as:

- PADS(Probability of Detection of an Alert Situation) > 99%
- PFA(Probability of False Alert)$<10^{-3}$
- ART(Alert Response Time)<0.5s

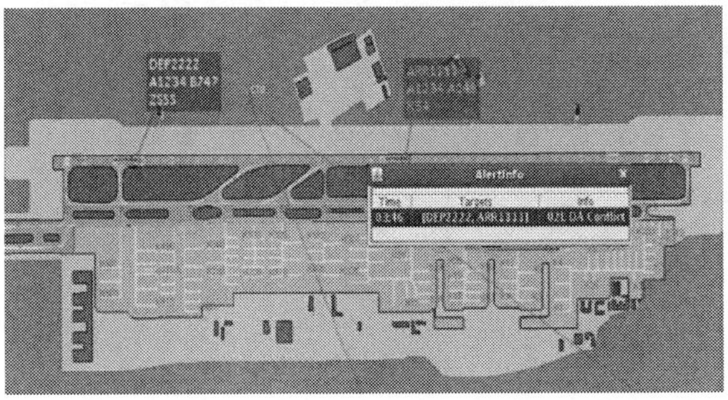

Figure 5. HMI for runway incursion detection approach

5 Conclusion

The runway incursion detection approach has been constructed in this article, and Chengdu Shuangliu International Airport has been chosen for simulation and validation, combing the local operational procedure, aerodrome layout, ADS-B surveillance data. Performance results and analyses from Shuangliu International Airport flight test verify that the algorithm has the potential to significantly improve runway safety by early detection and alerting of runway incursions. Although algorithm performance was highly successful, the system was not tested under all possible incursion scenarios, or in all weather and visibility conditions. More work is needed to test and fine tune the system under all conditions. Future research and development will focus on enhancement of the runway incursion detection approach, and explore taxiway incursion detection and apron incursion detection algorithm.

Acknowledgement

This paper is supported by the Technology and Innovation Fund Program of CAAC(MHRD20140218).

References

1. Qingchuan Feng. Aerodrome Control,Southwest Jiaotong University Press,2004:15-16.
2. David F. Green. Runway Safety Monitor Algorithm for Runway Incursion Detection and Alerting, NASA (2002) .
3. International Civil Aviation Organization. Manual on the Prevention of Runway Incursions, Doc9870. International Civil Aviation Organization (2006) .
4. International Civil Aviation Organization. Annex 10 to the Convention on International Civil Aviation(Volume I–Radio Navigation Aids). 6th ed. International Civil Aviation Organization(2006).
5. ICAO Doc 9830: Advanced Surface Movement Guidance and Control Systems (A-SMGCS) Manual(2004).

MATEC Web of Conferences **44**, 01085 (2016)
DOI: 10.1051/matecconf/20164401085

Research on routing algorithm based on the VANET

Li AN [1], Yong Mei ZHAO [1], Peng XIE and Qiong WANG [1]

Science College of Air Force Engineering University

Abstract: For the characteristics of high speed mobility of nodes, frequent changes of dynamic topology and frequent interrupts of the communication links in the VANET , this paper analyzed the defect of the current mobile ad-hoc network routing protocol, and carried on the simulation analysis on the adaptability of AODV, DSR and DSDV routing protocols in VANET applications in the VANET. Through the above research, this paper obtained the conclusion that the AODV routing protocol is more suitable for vehicular ad hoc network environment

1 INTRODUCTION

In recent years, on the account of the rapid development of wireless communication technology and the urgent need in the information technology of transportation field, the VANET(vehicular Ad Hoc Networks), one important foundation concept of intelligent transportation systems, was spawned. VANET is a type of special mobile ad hoc network, which creatively applies Ad hoc network in inter-vehicle communications, allows the drivers to obtain status information of other vehicles over the horizon (such as speed, direction, position, pressure of brakes plate, etc.) and real-time traffic information. Its main characteristic is the network nodes can move arbitrarily, frequent changes in network topology, and each node has the function of both host and router. Besides, VANET does not need the support of fixed infrastructure, can quickly set up a mobile communication network at any time and any place, which can not only increase the transportation efficiency, also the other facilities such as the safety and the reliability. Due to the high mobility of VANET, the unpredictable nature of road and the uncertainty of driving behavior, it is difficult to provide effective routing mechanism in such a complex situation.

VANET applications are very extensive, in civil in daily life or military, such as transport fleet, combat command team and the most popular of the "self driving tour" nowadays, which can solve the inter communication of the whole vehicles, also can ensure the consistency about getting the important information in the march of the whole vehicles.

For the characteristics of high speed mobility of nodes, frequent changes of dynamic topology and frequent interrupts of the communication links in the VANET, this paper analyzed whether the current routing protocol of mobile ad hoc network can meet the communication requirements of VANET or not.

2 OVERVIEW OF ROUTING PROTOCOLS IN THE MOBILE AD HOC NETWORKS

The function of routing is implemented in the network layer, which is mainly to specify the path from the source node to the destination node for the packet transmission data in the communication system. Mobile ad hoc routing protocol for inter vehicles packet transmission data is used to provide path information t. It is that the main goal is to meet practical need, at the same time to minimize the network overhead and achieve the maximization of overall utilization of resources, improve the network throughput.

The mobile ad hoc routing protocol has been widely studied. And it has different classification based on different standards. According to the routing strategy to divide, it is mainly divided into the proactive routing protocol and the on-demand routing protocol. The proactive routing protocol requires that each node should maintain a routing table that contains the routing information of all other nodes in real time, also known as the table driven routing protocol.

Corresponding author: ghxgbx@163.com

Article available at http://www.matec-conferences.org or http://dx.doi.org/10.1051/matecconf/20164401085

For example, the Destination-Sequenced Distance-Vector Routing protocol (DSDV) , regardless of whether the nodes need to send data or not, regularly broadcast updates. In an environment with large scale and fast topology changes, the continuous updating information can lead to excessive channel occupancy, which greatly reduces the performance of the system. The On-demand routing protocols is on the basis of data transmission request, passively searches routes from the source node to the destination node. If there is no data transmission request, it does not need to exchange routing information, also known as passive routing protocols. For example, the Ad hoc On-demand Distance Vector routing (AODV)protocol, is improved on the basis of the DSDV protocol, a combination of DSDV protocol and Dynamic Source Routing(DSR) protocol, broadcasts routing information only when it is needed, which reduces the total amount of broadcast. The on-demand routing protocol is a special type of routing protocols in the mobile ad hoc networks, which has the advantage of reducing overhead and improving network throughput. However, whether the route can reach the destination node each time and the delay of the route establishment can not be certain. For vehicular ad hoc networks, it is very difficult to maintain the routing table in real time, and the on-demand routing protocol is more suitable for vehicular ad hoc networks.

3 THE ANALYSIS ON VEHICLES MODEL

Considering the influence of road environment and traffic facilities, and the limitation of the safety distance between the vehicles, the simulation model of vehicular ad hoc network is different from the general model of mobile ad hoc network, and has its own unique characteristics.

Based on the analysis of vehicular ad hoc network routing protocol, we choose the AODV routing protocol which has been used widely as the protocol model. While needed to be improved in safety, the AODV routing protocol is also not entirely designed in accordance with the characteristics of vehicular ad hoc networks and is not the most suitable protocols either, but the AODV Routing Protocol is able to quickly adapt to the dynamic changes of network topology. At the same time, the storage overhead and network utilization of the AODV Routing Protocol are relatively small. In addition, the vehicular ad hoc networks have a symmetrical bidirectional connectivity. For instance, there are two adjacent vehicle nodes A and B. If A can monitor the communication content of B, then B can also monitor the communication content of A. So this paper chose the AODV routing protocol as the routing protocol model. It could be verified by simulation: The speed of each vehicle node was stable, and the structure of the linear vehicles would not change. The free communication between adjacent two nodes could be guaranteed under normal operating conditions, and the communication link would not be interrupted.

4 THE SIMULATION EVALUATION OF VEHICLES MODEL PERFORMANCE

There are several key indicators to measure the advantages and disadvantages of a VANET routing protocol performance, which include throughput, average end-to-end delay, average packet transmission rate, routing overhead, routing request time and energy consumption etc. In order to evaluate the applicability of AODV, DSR and DSDV routing protocols in VANET, this paper set the number of different communication source nodes , did the simulation contrast experiments on the average delay of end to end, the loss rate of packet and other indicators, to determine which kind of routing protocol is the most suitable for linear vehicles model.

4.1 Average end-to-end delay

Average end to end delay for data packets is the sum of all the possible delays, such as cache delay, interface queue delay, MAC layer retransmission delay, packet air propagation delay, and transformation time. The expression looks like the following:

$$\text{average end}-\text{to}-\text{end delay}=\frac{\text{the sum of the packets received delay of the destination node}}{\text{the number of packets received by the destination node}}$$

In this paper, 20 mobile nodes made up the vehicular ad hoc network, with the node speed maintained uniform 18m/s and the source node packet rate set to 3 packets /s. In the scene of 5, 10, 15 and 20 communication source nodes, through the simulation contrast experiment, the average end-to-end delay performance was obtained as shown in Table 1and Figure 1

Table 1. the average end-to-end delay performanceof AODV、DSR、DSDV

pausa / verage delay / Source node	50s			100s			200s			400s			600s		
	AODV	DSR	DSDV	AODV	DSR	DSDV	AODV	DSR	DSDV	AODV	DSR	DSDV	AODV	DSR	DSDV
5	0.065	0.039	0	0.060	0.039	0	0.057	0.038	0.041	0.056	0.038	0.050	0.056	0.038	0.053
10	0.071	0.035	0	0.060	0.033	0.029	0.077	0.035	0.026	0.062	0.030	0.040	0.057	0.029	0.043
15	0.071	0.035	0	0.060	0.033	0.020	0.088	0.028	0.020	0.059	0.023	0.027	0.064	0.022	0.027
20	0.071	0.035	0	0.058	0.030	0.005	0.094	0.021	0.016	0.067	0.019	0.024	0.059	0.018	0.031

As could be seen from Figure 1.1, with the increase of the pause time, the average end-to-end delay of AODV and DSR routing protocols had different degrees of decline, while the average end to end delay of DSDV routing protocol had a certain degree of increase. But with the increase of the communication link and the number of source nodes, the three types of protocols showed different trends. Further analysis could be concluded as follows: In the case of short pause time, the average end-to-end delay of DSDV was the smallest. The average end-to-end delay of DSR was the more and the average end-to-end delay of AODV was the maximum. With the extension of the pause time, the three routing protocols showed different trends: the delay of DSDV increase was relatively large and more than DSR. The delay of DSR slightly decreased, remaining flat basically, and the delay of AODV also had a certain degree of decline. The delay variation range of the three routing protocols was 0.05s or so, and the difference between the two was not more than 0.08s. At the same time, with the increase of the number of source nodes, the overall change trend of DSR and DSDV routing protocols would increased. It was that the delay time would be much smaller, and the delay of AODV protocol increased slightly. But generally speaking, the delay performance of the three protocols was almost the same, and the biggest difference would be less than 0.08s.

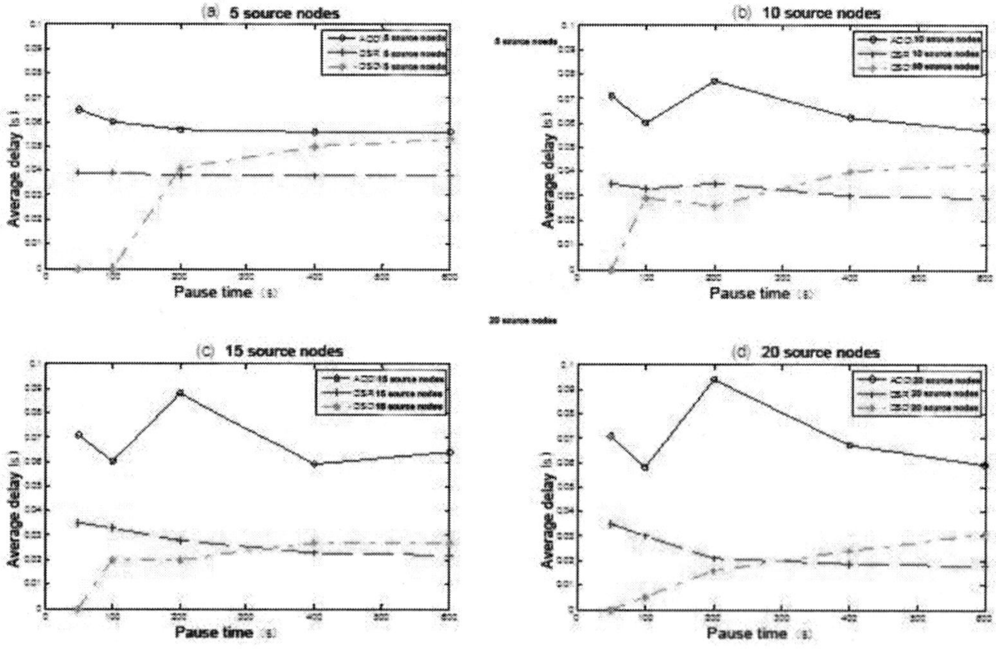

Figure 1.the average end-to-end delay performance of AODV、DSR、DSDV

4.2 Packet loss rate

Packet loss rate refers to the ratio of the packet loss and the total amount of data packets. In the same scene, the packet loss rate of the vehicular ad hoc networks with AODV, DSR and DSDV routing protocols are simulated. In the scene of 5, 10, 15 and 20 communication source nodes, through the simulation contrast experiment, the packet loss rate could be obtained with the increase of pause time and source nodes of the three routing protocols. The statistical results were shown in Table 1 and figure 1.

Table 2. the packet loss rate of AODV、DSR、DSDV

pause time / packet loss rate / source node	50s			100s			200s			400s			600s		
	AODV	DSR	DSDV	AODV	DSR	DSDV	AODV	DSR	DSDV	AODV	DSR	DSDV	AODV	DSR	DSDV
5	0.1602	0.7607	1	0.1649	0.7552	1	0.1574	0.7584	0.9368	0.1608	0.7558	0.6537	0.1630	0.7549	0.4967
10	0.2407	0.7341	1	0.2860	0.7410	0.9984	0.3980	0.7215	0.8343	0.4410	0.7129	0.6765	0.4558	0.7131	0.6154
15	0.2407	0.7341	1	0.2817	0.7306	0.9962	0.4451	0.6722	0.7666	0.4917	0.6404	0.671	0.5108	0.6227	0.671
20	0.2407	0.7341	1	0.3143	0.7410	0.9759	0.4712	0.6752	0.7568	0.5410	0.6473	0.6835	0.5698	0.6404	0.6725

As can be seen from Figure 2, the packet loss rate of AODV was kept at a relatively low level. With the increase of the number of source nodes, packet loss rate of AODV presented an upward trend, which was mainly due to a large number of traffic flow leading to network congestion, but the packet loss rate was still lower than DSR and DSDV. With the increase of the pause time and the number of source nodes, the packet loss rate of DSR changed less, maintaining at about 70%. In the case of short pause time, packet loss rate of DSDV was almost 100%. With the increase of the pause time, packet loss rate of DSDV reduced to some extent. In addition, with the increase of the number of source nodes, the downward trend tended to relief. However, when the number of source nodes was more than 15, packet loss rate of DSDV was always greater than AODV and DSR.

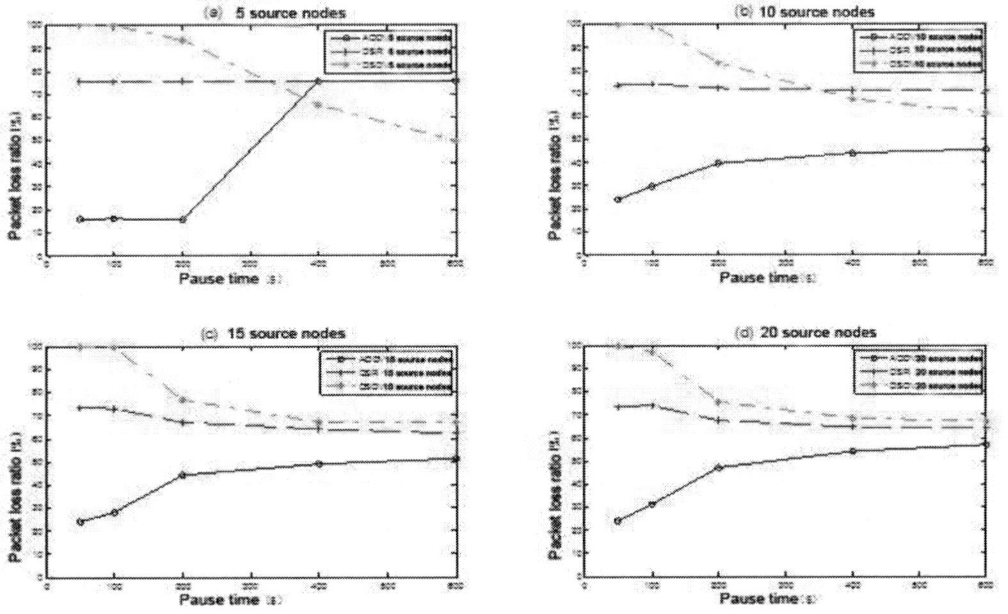

Figure 2 the packet loss rate of AODV、DSR、DSDV

Through the above simulation results on the end-to-end delay and packet loss rate of the vehicular ad hoc network, the conclusion could be summarized: With the increase of the pause time and the number of source nodes, the delay of the AODV protocol was higher than the other two protocols at the same speed, but the maximum difference was not more than 0.08s. In terms of packet loss rate, packet loss rate of AODV was significantly lower than DSR and DSDV, showing a better ability to deal with network congestion. In the process of the moving vehicles, because of the high security requirements of the linear vehicles model, the information and the instructions should be transmitted to an optimal degree, and the delay did not need to be too harsh. Based on the performance of the end-to-end delay and packet loss rate of the vehicles linear model, the AODV routing protocol was suitable for the vehicular ad hoc network which maintained at a steady cruising speed.

5 SUMMARY

VANET was known for the characteristics of autonomy, non-fixed structure, multi-hop routing, dynamic change of network topology, limited network capacity and so on. Meanwhile the application environment of VANET is very easy to meet the special circumstances, such as the narrow road, high density node distribution, high speed mobile of node and so on. For the above reasons, the transmission capacity of VANET would reduce, which makes the packet loss increases and the delay increases. The simulation experiments showed that with the increase of the pause time and the number of source nodes, the delay of AODV was a little higher than DSR and DSDV. But the biggest difference would be less than 0.08s. And AODV packet loss rate is significantly lower than DSR and DSDV, showing a better ability to deal with network congestion.

References

[1] DUAN Yunfei, ZHOULiqiong , YANGLei. Simulation and analysis of several typical hoc Ad routing protocols [J] .]communication of electric power system , 2009,30(200): 59-63.

[2] CHENLinxin , ZENGXi , CAOYi . Mobile Hoc Ad network: self organizing packet radio network technology [M] . Beijing : Publishing House of Electronics Industry, 2012.

[3] Luo Pei'en, Huang Hongyu, Shu Wei, Li Minglu, Wu Minyou. Performance Evaluation of Vehicular DTN Routing under Realistic Mobility Models [C]. In: Proceedings of IEEE Wireless Communications and Networking Conference, 2008: 2206–2211.

[4] Ali S, Bilal S. An Intelligent Routing Protocol for VANETs in City Environments [C]. Proceedings of 2nd International Conference on Computer, Control and Communication (IC42009), Karachi, Pakistan, 2009.

[5] Okada H, Takano A, Mase K. A Proposal of Linkmetric for Next-hop Forwarding Methods in Vehicular Ad Hoc Networks [C]. Proceedings of 6th IEEE Consumer Communication Sand Networking Conference, CCNC, Las Vegas, USA, 2009.

[6] Sommer C , Dressler F. Progressing Towards Realistic Mobility Models in VANET Simulations [J]. IEEE Communications Magazine, 2008, 46(11): 132-137.

[7] Hartenstein H, Laberteaux KP. A Tutorial Survey on Vehicular Ad Hoc Networks [J]. IEEE Communications Magazine, 2008, 46(6): 164-171.

MATEC Web of Conferences **44**, 01086 (2016)
DOI: 10.1051/matecconf/20164401086

Image processing and feature extraction of microscopic

Chun Hua Shi

Langfang Health Vocational College, Hebei, China, Email:545682864@qq.com

Abstract. This paper analyzes the characteristics of white blood cells, diseased cells during feature extraction, the introduction of anti-corrosion factor for microscopic image processing, experiments show that the method of classification and extraction of diseased cells have better results.

1 Introduction

In order to identify blood cells, and analyzed and classified, it is necessary to find the blood cells can be distinguished from the image feature, in order to describe the blood cells, a process called feature extraction. Reflect the characteristics of a lot of blood cell images, in addition to blood cells can be extracted directly from the segmentation feature image, but also can get more specific blood cells characterized by transformation. Commonly used in blood cell analysis and classification features are morphological features, especially the optical density, color, texture characteristics.

Because the computer automatically detect leukemia has been a problem of image processing and pattern recognition, although there are some automated blood cell morphology analysis system, but the accuracy of its analysis is not very high. We hope that from the simplest and most easily recognizable type of white blood cells begin to analyze.

2 Effective features leukemia detected

Characteristics described in the previous section is used to identify the type of white blood cell, not all effective. In this trial, considering three types of cells, segmented neutrophils granulocyte cell line, rod-shaped blood granulocytes and in dealing with the film being damaged cells.

In the study of these three leukocyte classification problems, if we do not use the optical density and texture information, only it uses geometric features. But in the feature geometry, since the cytoplasm is not much impact on the sub-classification, some features are not available. Through repeated comparison test, we finally chose the four characteristics: Area nucleus, roundness nucleus, representing the number of nuclei nucleus and nucleus of convex ratio.

The nucleus area S(1)

$$S(1)=\sum_{(i,j)\in R_c} f(i,j),\quad 其中 f(i,j)=\begin{cases}1 & (i,j)\in R_c\\ 0 & (i,j)\notin R_c\end{cases}$$

(2-1)

Formula Rc is nucleated blood cell nucleus region. S (1) is the sum of all the number of pixels Rc, which reflect the different cell nuclei size difference in the two-dimensional plane.

2. Roundness nucleus S(2)

$$S(2)=P^2/S(1) \tag{2-2}$$

P is the perimeter of the nucleus in the formula, which is calculated as

$$P=N_e+\sqrt{2}N_o \tag{2-3}$$

Formula E is the sum of the even number of nuclei area boundary chain code, No digital sum is an odd number.

Roundness is close to 1, the region is approximately circular, the greater the roundness otherwise explain the irregular shape of the nucleus. It is to a certain extent, describes the compactness of the nuclear region.

3. Nuclear accounted convex S(3):

$$S(3)=S(1)/Co(S(1)) \tag{2-4}$$

Formula Co (S (1)) to be able to just contain the nucleus area of a circle. Solving the circle area, first find the center position nucleus (that is the nucleus of the center of gravity), in the center and gradually increase the radius of the circle, the circle can have exactly know where to find the nucleus, and the nucleus is tangent to the circle.

Accounting projections reflect the depressed level than the nucleus. The higher the value of S (3), indicating the extent of the smaller nuclei depression. In general, the smaller the cells the more naive depressed, the greater the value; otherwise the value is smaller. In our experiment, the cells and the degree of nuclear recessed rod-shaped leaf granulocyte granulocytes are large and small degree of damaged cells nucleus depression.

The number of nucleus nucleus S(4):

[a] yuanquanbo@126.com

Article available at http://www.matec-conferences.org or http://dx.doi.org/10.1051/matecconf/20164401086

$$S(4)=\sum_i N(i) \quad 其中N(i)=\begin{cases}1 & NR_i \in R_c \\ 0 & NR_i \notin R_c\end{cases}$$

(2-5)

Formula NRi different cell nucleus area under one area, S (4) reflects the number of different cell nucleus area of the same region, which is divided leaf cells with other cells is an important feature of the difference between core granules.

3 Effective features access

3.1. Analyzing nucleus affiliations - merge and cut the cell nucleus

In order to make the computer to find a number of small cells from a large figure, and acquires the cell characteristics, we must find out with some policy contains several images in a blood cell, and determine their location. But contains neutrophils and segmented neutrophils rod-shaped, even relatively large degree of aggregation of blood cells in the image, the resulting image after segmentation are often found in more than one nucleus together, which belong to several nuclear zone several cells. Several nuclear area which belong to the same cell, which constitutes a problem. While the human eye which for us is very easy to judge things, but by the computer to recognize, you need a certain strategy.

As illustrated, one image is included in the two cells 3-1, wherein a cell nucleus region composed of three, and the other consists of a single cell nucleus region.

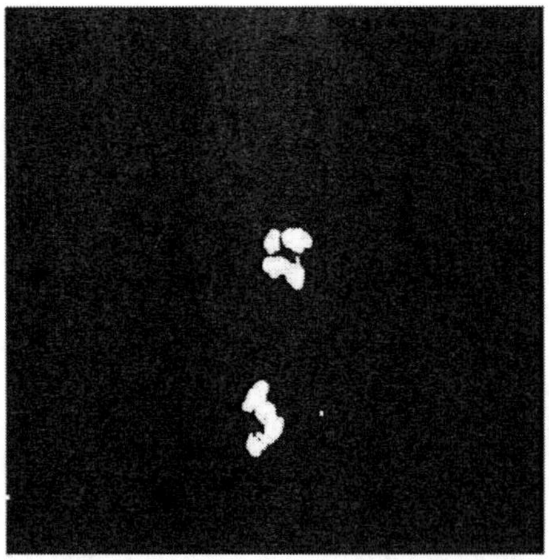

Figure 3-1 before the merger Images

Merger process:

1. image mark merge before the connected regions 1, ..., n.

2. Calculate the size of each connected region A1, ..., An.

3. For the communication area of less than a certain value of As, considered to be noise, omitted to consider (As represents the area of the noise threshold point).

4. For each of the remaining regional connectivity i, if the area is less than a certain value inf (Ac) gradually outward to search along the outer boundary of the communication area. If a limited number of steps, find another connected region j, and Aj in this area together with the communication area Ai area itself does not exceed sup (Ac), and the two connected regions circumscribed circle of diameter not exceeding D, on own mark to j; if not find another one connected region in a limited number of steps, and to give up the search. (Inf (Ac) as a nucleus area of the lower bound, sup (Ac) is the upper bound nucleus area, D is the diameter of the circumscribed circle of the upper bound nuclei.)

5. The cycle above search process until each connected region have been treated once.

6. The re-tagged images, the cells were cut to give each cell contains only a small map.

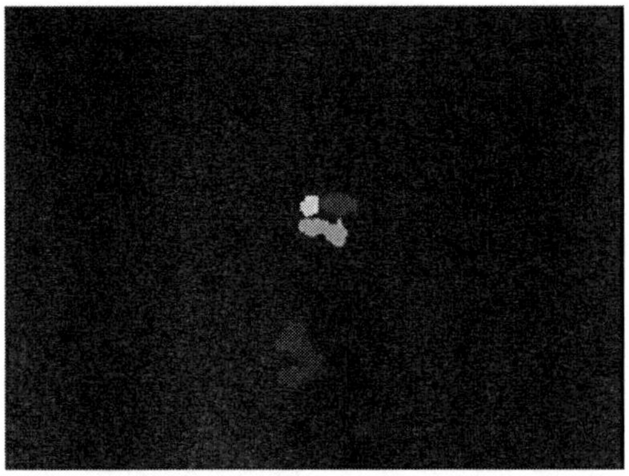

(a) Mark image pre-merger

(b) Mark images merged

Figure 3-2 is an image processing of Figure 3-1, in which Fig (a) is the result of Step 1 above labeled, and Fig. (B) is the result of re-marked. From the figure we can see that each cell in addition to being a very well-marked, can also be found in Figure 4-1 small particles are also filtered out the noise.

The image after the above steps, will give a few of each cell contains only a small diagram. Small figure characteristics of each cell extract.

3.2. Feature Extraction and problems of encountered

The article mentions four kinds of characteristics in the use of this test: Area nucleus, roundness nucleus, the nucleus and the nucleus than the number of accounts convex nuclear area. Leukocytes has been cut out small image, each graph contains only one white blood cells, so it is easy to calculate its nuclear area, perimeter nucleus, and the circumscribed circle, then, the first three features can be easily extracted.

But the number of nucleus nucleus fourth feature is not capable of very accurate extraction. Many literature [1] mentioned to use this feature to do split, but did not specify how to obtain this feature.

4 Introduction of new features - corrosion factor

Since the number of nuclei nucleus area is difficult to accurately extract the feature, but we try to extract the feature process found that although the number of nucleus can not be accurately calculated, but we found that if the nucleus in multiple etching process very characteristic changes.

For example, leaf neutrophils after 1-5 times corrosion may be disconnected; the rod neutrophils may disconnect after 3-7 times the corrosion, but may continue to open; damaged cells (the basic nucleus on spherical) through a limited number of corrosion will not be disconnected. We call this feature called anti-corrosion properties.

Calculation against corrosion characteristics are: checking cell nucleus now the number, if the number of nuclear area greater than or equal to 2, anti-corrosion factor is defined as the number of current nuclear area, otherwise start the following procedures.

Etching nuclei judge has several regional connectivity. After the 1st of corrosion, which communicates region into two, so it will be an anti-corrosion factor as 2-k, and jump out; if communication is still a number of regions, the corrosion factor is 1-k, and continue corrosion; after the i-th corrosion, if the number of regional connectivity to 2, then the corrosion factor becomes 2-ki, if the number of connected region is still 1, then the corrosion factor is the current value minus ki. (K is the penalty factor, select their own.)

We use the above method of leukocyte nuclei were analyzed to obtain the results of the analysis of: segmented neutrophils corrosion resistance characteristics substantially between 1-2, rod-shaped granulocytes corrosion resistance between 0-1, and corrosion damaged cells are basically below zero. Table 4-1 shows the characteristics of leukocytes 30, wherein the first to 10 for the leaf neutrophils, mark it as a Class 1; Article 11 and Article 20 of the rod neutrophils, which is labeled 2 category; first 21-30 of damaged cells, which marked three categories.

		area	Roundness	Accounting for more than projections
1	Segmented neutrophils	3316	36.103	0.57281
2		2980	31.834	0.41137
3		2431	38.016	0.5089
4		1875	34.68	0.55001
5		3571	33.913	0.48094
6		3243	34.399	0.40665
7		2401	40.284	0.46218
8		3047	31.947	0.62708
9		2527	42.315	0.45912
10		3765	54.987	0.51315
11	Rod-shaped granulocytes	2451	27.369	0.44981
12		2699	37.94	0.52054
13		2426	26.176	0.53756
14		2926	18.395	0.53896
15		3105	24.89	0.69092
16		2453	40.708	0.5541
17		2781	19.354	0.50518
18		3129	23.645	0.62269
19		2744	17.799	0.4749
20		2763	30.859	0.5784
21	Damaged cells	2761	11.997	0.86039
22		3247	16.577	0.52363
23		2738	10.805	0.81952
24		3878	15.988	0.86756
25		4247	13.789	0.69886
26		5288	14.932	0.65592
27		3442	12.329	0.84925
28		4362	13.315	0.60066
29		2476	12.653	0.7668
30		2575	12.304	0.76455

Corrosion resistance	Actual category	Predicted category
2	1	1
2	1	1
2	1	1
2	1	1
1.25	1	2
2	1	1
2	1	1
2	1	1
2	1	1
1.5	1	1
1	2	2

0.75	2	2
1.25	2	2
0	2	2
0.5	2	3
1	2	2
-0.25	2	2
0.75	2	2
-0.5	2	2
0.5	2	2
-1.75	3	3
-1.75	3	3
-1.75	3	3
-1.75	3	3
-1.75	3	3
-1.75	3	3
-1.75	3	3
-1.75	3	3
-1.75	3	3
-1.75	3	3

Table 4-1 Characteristics and Classification of three cells

5 Summary

We see that the nucleus of corrosion resistance between the three cells have different values, for classification, will play a good role.

References

[1] Wang Haojun Blood Cells automatic identification and classification methods. Xi'an Jiaotong University doctoral thesis, 2002.
[2] G. H. Landerweerd, B. S. Gelsema, J. F. Brenner, et al. Pattern recognition of nucleated cells from the peripheral blood. Pattern Recognition, 1983, 16(2): 131-140.
[3] D. Seigneurin, C. Gauvain, G. Brugal. A semi-quantitative analysis of human bone marrow granulocytic linage using the SAMBA 200 cell image processor: I. The normal maturation sequence. Analyt Quant Cytol, 1984, 6(3): 168-178.
[4] M. Beksac, V. B. Tipi et al. An artificial intelligent diagnostic system on differential recognition of Hematopoietic cells from microscopic images. Cytometry, 1997, 30: 145-150.
[5] P. E. Pavlova, K. P. Cyrrilov, I. N. Moumdjiev. Application of HSV colour system in identification by colour of biological objects on the basis of microscopic images. Computerized medical imaging and Graphics, 1996, 20(5): 357-364.

1. Luigi T.De Luca, *Propulsion physics* (EDP Sciences, Les Ulis, 2009)
2. F. De Lillo, F. Cecconi, G. Lacorata, A. Vulpiani, EPL, **84** (2008)

MATEC Web of Conferences 44, 01087 (2016)
DOI: 10.1051/matecconf/20164401087

Invoking Device Driver from .NET Managed Code

Peng XIE [1,a], Li AN [1] and Hong Mei ZHANG[1]

[1]College of Science, Air Force Engineering University, Xi'an, China

Abstract. It's a real problem to visit a low-level device driver from a high-level application based on the .NET platform managed code in software developing practice .This paper concerns how to solve it by a runtime interoperation services provided by Microsoft .NET Common Language Runtime（CLR） . A real world example is given in the end .

1. INTRODUCTION

The .NET is a set of software circumstance used for development and deployment of enterprise application, which introduced by Microsoft for fight with Java. we also realized .NET deeply in the process of developing a information system. But it is a fact that .NET is inferior to unmanaged native code on visiting low-level system. However, not all enterprise applications are running on high-lever virtual machine instead of low-level system. Whether .NET can visit low-level device or not, and how to vist, that is a problem we encountered in developing a information system, the resolving methods as follows:

The system we developed is a typical high-level manage application. However ,if realized to show clients' information base on telephone voice box in the Customer Relationship Management system (CRM), it requires to visit device driver provided by virtual machine, so as to set in the way of hardware work models, and extract the Caller's ID when the phone rang. How to complete it? After queried VS and MSDN, we found that use the runtime interoperation services provided by .NET Common Language Runtime (CLR) with that the .NET managed code can realize unmanaged function in visiting Dynamic Linking Library (DLL), which for Microsoft could visit Windows API under .NET circumstance.

2. VIST UNMANAGED CODE SYSTEM THROUGH .NET RUNTIME INTEROPERATION SERVICE

The runtime interoperation service provided by the .NET will contribute to look for management Code. In detail, when unmanaged function is operated by runtime interoperation services, the performing operations as following steps:

To Look for DLL including the function.

To load the DLL into memory

To locate the address of function in memory and pushes its arguments onto the stack, marshling date as required.

To transfer the control right to unmanaged function

The runtime interoperation services will introduce for managed invoking caller abnormal that generated by unmanaged function

[a] Corresponding author: xpf68@163.com

Article available at http://www.matec-conferences.org or http://dx.doi.org/10.1051/matecconf/20164401087

As Figure 1:

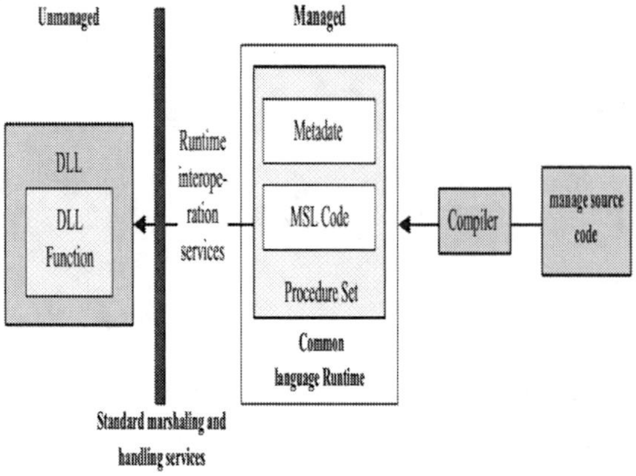

Figure 1.unmanaged and managed

3. THE METHOD OF C# VISITING THE FUNCTION FROM UNMANAGED DLL

a. Identity function of DLL

DLL function identification contains the name or serial number of function, as well as realizes the DLL file's name. For example: Specify MessageBox function in User32.dll, we need identify it (the MessageBox function)and the position (User32.dll, User 32 or user 32.)

If not specified, all character set showed by Charset field will default to ANSI.

The programmer could rename the unmanaged function in code to any required name, which need to map to DLL initial entry point.

b. Create managed-class for holding DLL function.

In order to encapsulate, it always packs the DLL function into managed-clas . Although not always do like this in every situation, the providing managed-class is very convenient method. The programmer could:

To declare DLL function in existing class.

To create a class for every DLL function, in case to find easily by isolating function from each other.

To create a class for a group of related DLL function, in case to form logical grouping and reduce system overhead.

c . Create DLL function prototype in managed-class.

In this situation, it is need to define the static method for every DLL function in managed-class, and pay special attention to substitute unmanaged date types to managed date types. The Corresponding relationship between date types in C function and Wtypes.h definition and unmanaged date types as Table 1:

Table 1. definition and unmanaged date types.

Unmanaged type of Wtypes.h	Unman-aged C Langua-ge type	Managed-class Name	C# date type
HANDLE	void*	System.IntPtr	No internal
BYTE	unsigned char	System.Byte	byte
SHORT	short	System.Int16	short
WORD	unsigned short	System.UInt16	ushort
INT	int	System.Int32	Integer
UINT	unsigned int	System.UInt32	uint
LONG	long	System.Int32	Integer
BOOL	long	System.Int32	Integer
DWORD	unsigned long	System.UInt32	uint
ULONG	unsigned long	System.UInt32	uint
CHAR	char	System.Char	char
LPSTR	char*	System.String or System.StringBuilder	String or StringBuil-der
LPCSTR	Const char*	System.String or System.String-	String or String-

		Builder	Builder
LPWSTR	wchar_t*	System.String or System.StringBuil-der	String or StringBuil-der
LPCWSTRI	Const wchar_t*	System.String or System.StringBuil-der	String or StringBuil-der
FLOAT	Float	System.Single	float
DOUBLE	Double	System.Double	double

d. Set property field

The managed prototype declaration in function can show setting property field, so as to define the behavior of managed code. For example, the character sets and calling conventions used in passing method arguments. There are related property fields and defaults related with platform runtime interoperation services in table 2:

Table2. Fields and Explanation

Fields	Explanation
BestFitMapping	To switch the most appropriate mapping
EntryPoint	To assign the invoking DLL entry point
ExactSpelling	To modify entries to maintain corresponding with character set. Different programming language, different default.
PreserveSig	To control managed method signature : switch to back HRESULT or not,s with unmanaged signature of additional parameters[out, retval]. The default is true (should not transform signature)
SetLastError	To make invoking party confirm there was an error or not in using Marshal.GetLastWin32Error API function.

e. Invoking DLL Function

4. VISIT TELEPHONE VOICE BOX DRIVER FORM C#

According to method above, we realized visiting of telephone box driver. The example as following:

a. The C++ invoking interface provided by SDK

```
bool WINAPI SW_Init();
bool WINAPI SW_Free();
void WINAPI SW_SetType(int DeviceType);
int WINAPI SW_GetCount();
int WINAPI SW_GetSN(int nIndex);
int WINAPI SW_ReceiveCID(int nIndex, char *lpBuf);
```

b. The C# packing to meet requirement of platform runtime services

```
using System.Runtime.InteropServices;
public class CCIDFun
{ [DllImport("SWind.dll", EntryPoint="SW_Init")]
public static extern int SW_Init();
[DllImport("SWind.dll", EntryPoint="SW_Free")]
public static extern int SW_Free();
[DllImport("SWind.dll", EntryPoint="SW_SetType")]
public static extern void SW_SetType(int DeviceType);
[DllImport("SWind.dll", EntryPoint="SW_GetCount")]
public static extern int SW_GetCount();
[DllImport("SWind.dll", EntryPoint="SW_GetSN")]
public static extern int SW_GetSN(int nIndex);
[DllImport("SWind.dll", EntryPoint="SW_ReceiveCID")]
public unsafe static extern int SW_ReceiveCID(int nIndex, StringBuilder lpBuf);
}
```

c. Test code

```
............
CCIDFun.SW_Init();
```

```
CCIDFun.SW_SetType(2);
int lineCount = CCIDFun.SW_GetCount();
if ( lineCount!=2 )
MessageBox.Show("Initialization failed!","Message",MessageBoxButtons.OK ,MessageBoxIcon.Information);
else
MessageBox.Show("Initialsuccess!lineCount==2" ,"Message",MessageBoxButtons.OK ,MessageBoxIcon.Information);
............
```

5. CONCLUSION

The direct way is completed in the Visual C++ NET for the mixed programming of managed code and unmanaged code. However, the runtime interoperation service is appropriate in the case of plenty of manage code occasionally invoke unmanaged code, which is proved in practice.

REFERENCES

1. Charles Petzold . Microsoft C# Windows Programming (Part I; Party II). Beijing: Peking University Press(2012)
2. Jeremy Greenwood, Boyan Jovanovic. Financial Development , Growth, and The Distribution of Income[J]. Journal Economy,2013,98:1076-1107.
3. Oded Golor, Joseph Zeira. Income Distribution and Macroeconomics[J]. The Reviews of Economic Sduies,2012, 60(1):35-52.
4. Clark, George, Lixin Colin Xu, Heng Zou. Finance and Income in Inequality: Test of Alternative Theories[C]. 2013, NO.2984.

AUTHOR: Peng XIE, Male, Born in Zhumadian City, Henan Province. Master degree, University Lecturer. Electronic science teaching and research department of science college, Air Force Engineering University.

Research Fields: Network and date integration.

MATEC Web of Conferences 44, 01088 (2016)
DOI: 10.1051/matecconf/20164401088

Kinematic Analysis on the Serve Technique of Elite Tennis Player Grigor•Dimitrov Based on 3D Virtual Reality Technology

Chuan Jia Du[1*], Ji He Zhou[2] and Shuai Wang[3]
Chengdu sport university
Chengdu, Sichuan, China
E-mail:549828421@qq.com*

Abstract: By using three-dimensional video analysis, we made a kinematic analysis on Grigor Dimitrov's Serve technique, aiming at finding the kinematic characteristics of his serve technique during various stages. The results showed that: (1) During the stage of tossing the ball and lifting the racket, the tossing height of the ball was at minimum appropriately, while the elbow extension of the tossing arm was stright, and the angle of his left knee was 95.4°, which is beneficial to making greater kicking power; (2) At the back-swing stage, Dimitrov's both feet made a great range of pedal and stretch quickly, and the "scratch-back" posture is obvious, and momentum caused by the kicking and coxae-turning was rather large; (3) When hitting the ball, the contact point was accurate and the speed of the racket head was high, which passed a relatively large initial momentum to the ball; (4) Dimitrov's entire service action was integral and coordinate, smooth and powerful, which was in accordance relatedly with kinematic characteristics.

In recent 30 years, the tennis competition has made an earth-shaking change, especially in the tennis serve, ground stoke and the strategic arrangement. As the start of every score of tennis, serve technique plays a vital role. A strong, consistent, well-placed serve is the first step toward taking the offensive. It can set up to win points, games, and matches with your other stokes [1].With fiercer tennis competition today, many elite athletes will use serve techniques as their stunts.

This paper use three-dimensional video analysis method to make corresponding exploration and analysis on the serve technique of the 2014 China Open men's tennis player Grigor•Dimitrov, so as to reveal the serve technique mode of the world's excellent potential tennis players, which can provide reference for coaches and athletes, strengthen serve training and improve serve techniques as well as enrich theoretical knowledge of the serve techniques.

Keywords: Tennis serves, kinematics analysis, 3D video analysis

1 Subject and methods

1.1 Subject

Bulgarian tennis player, Grigor•Dimitrov,the 2014 China Open men's single's player.

Table 1. Basic information of Grigor•Dimitrov

Name	Height (cm)	Weight (kg)	Birth date	Dominate hand	Highest Ranking
Grigor Dimitrov	188	77	1991.5	Right	22

1.2 Methods

1.2.1 Three-dimensional video analysis: At the game site of the 2014 China open,we used two JVC9800 cameras (made in Japan) shooting frequency:50*fpS*, to shoot the entire serve techniques of Grigor•Dimitrov.Camera 1 was right behind the side line of the tennis court, camera 2 right in front of the base line, showing an included angle about 45° between main optical axes of the two cameras(as is shown in Figure 1).Then the exertion videos were analyzed by the 3D Signal TEC V3.2HDC software, frame by frame. Europe Dempster(16 links, 21 joints parameter) was chosen as the mannequin. In the need of study, two test points (the racket's head and the ball) were added when we did the analysis. The available original data was processed smoothly by low-pass digital filtering method and the cutting frequency is 8*Hz*.

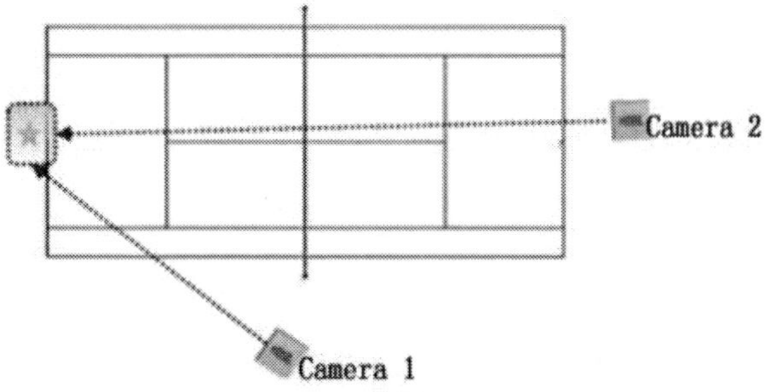

Figure 1: Diagram of camera position

1.2.2 Three-dimensional virtual reality technology method: based on the kinematics data gained by Three-dimensional video analysis, we made a more accurate diagnosis and analysis on the technical movements of the athlete. The parameters of Dimitrov's serving technology were reproducibly observed 360 ° virtual rotation in the three-dimensional virtual reality system.

2. Results

2.1 Division of the technique

Grigor Dimitrov used Foot-Back serve technique. According to the need of the research, we divided his serve techniques into the following four stages:

1) The tossing ball and lifting racket stage (S_{tl}): the moment when ball and racket were separated (BR_{sep}) to the moment when knee flexion reaches the maximum (KF_{max});

2) The backward-swing stage (S_{bs}): the moment when knee flexion reaches the maximum to the moment when racket reaches the lowest position behind (R_{lowest});

3) The swing upward at the ball stage (S_{su}): the moment when racket reaches the lowest position behind ("scratching-back" position) to the moment when hitting the ball(H_{ball});

4)The following-through stage (S_{ft}): the moment when hitting the ball to the moment when his left foot touch the ground.

2.2The tossing ball and lifting the racket stage

Tossing ball and lifting the racket stage refers to the moment when ball and racket were separated to the moment when knee flexion reaches the maximum (the height of gravity reaches lowest). During this stage, Dimitrov ' s holding-hand put the ball near to the throat area of the racket, then the ball and racket moved back while the center of gravity moved to the right foot, and when holding-hand moved near to the left hip, the racket was separated from the ball. His knee bend forward gradually,and the holding-arm straightened and put upward gradually, and his holding hand remain low position. Then making shoulder as the axis, he lifted the racket from low to high and stretched to the right side, eventually.

Table 2. Kinematic parameters of the S_{tl} (°)

moment	Left knee angle	Right knee angle	Shoulder-hip angle	Right elbow angle
BR_{sepd}	171.0	165.3	9.6	167.7
KF_{max}	95.4	123.7	31.5	78.0

The moment when ball and racket were separated, the knee angles of Dimitrov's left and right were 171.0° and 165.3° respectively, shoulder hip angle was 9.6° , the right elbow angle was 167.7° . The moment when the ball and racket separated, the right shoulder angle gradually increased from 12.5° to 83.8° . When the ball and the racket were separated, the right elbow angle decreased to 125.9° , the height of the ball was 1.91*m*. Related studies suggest that: the position of the ball when separating from hand should be at the head level[5]. If the position is too low or too high, the tossing hand would not be fully extended and the ball would be very unstable. Thus the ball could not to the batting position accurately.

The ball to the highest point moment, his knees bent to the maximum, hold the racket get-back. In this process, Dimitrov tossed the ball to the height 3.24*m*,the left and right knee angle were 95.4° and 123.7° , his right elbow angle decrease to 78.0° . Studies show that: when the center of gravity decreases to the lowest point, the knee angle of excellent tennis player was about 100° [6]. Observing through a virtual reproduction of the rotation, combined with the curve of the height of his center of gravity, we can see his knee bent fully, which lower the height of center of gravity. At the maximum knee flexion moment, his shoulder-hip angle is 31.5° , which showed that he pulled shoulder fully, which can prepare well for the next stage.

2.3 The backward-swing stage

Backward-swing stage refers to the moment when knee flexion reaches the maximum to the moment when racket reaches the lowest position behind. During this stage, Dimitrov of lower extremity joint force kicking, front hip rotation axis, chest and shoulder portion to form a larger bow back because of lower limb inertia force kicking, holding clapping effective force form a" scratching-back" posture ,racket head down.

Table 3. Kinematic parameters of the S_{bs} (°)

moment	Knee angle		Squatting knee extension amplitude		Right elbow angle
	Left	right	left	right	
KF_{max}	95.4	123.7	81.9	44.5	78.0
R_{lowest}	177.3	168.2			69.5

As is shown above,Dimitrov's at the moment when racket reaches the lowest position,his left, right knee angle were 177.3° and 168.2° .The range of his left and right knee angle were respectively 81.9° and 44.5° .The total time of the stage was 0.28 seconds,maximum kicking angular velocity was 230.7° /*s*, which showed he had a fast speed, and generated large momentum. The minimum angle of right elbow was 69.5° , which means a larger the magnitude of his elbow.

2.4 The swing-upward at the ball stage

Swing-upward at the ball stage refers to the moment when racket reaches the lowest position behind to the moment when hitting the ball. His right wrist forearm form an inward rotation of "whipping" action, which is the key action of serve technique,his shoulder trunk rotation axis on the basis of accelerated forward rotation, elbow flexion should be maintained stance against the trunk, to reduce the moment of inertia of the body, while the balance of the body play a regulatory role.

Table 4. Kinematic parameters of the S_{su}

Toss height（m）	Starting point height（m）	The distance of the highest point to the starting point（m）	Starting point height / body height
3.24	2.82	0.42	1.50

During this stage, the height of centre of gravity increased,when hitting the ball, the ball's height was 2.82*m*, the velocity of the ball was 2.84*m/s*.Related research shows that: the gap between the highest point of the ball and the starting point should be around 0.5*m*, if the peak point of the ball is too low, it will lead an insufficient "scratch back" action; if too high, will enlarge the velocity when hitting the ball[5][6], which both have a bad influence on the quality of serve technique. The appropriate ratio of spot height and body height is 1.50[6].The gap between height if peak point

and the starting height is 0.42*m*, the ratio is nearly 1.50,which showed his contact height was suitable.

Table 5. Maximum velocity of joints in the H_{ball} (m/s)

Right shoulder speed	Right elbow speed	Right wrist speed	Racket head speed
3.45	3.82	6.48	25.83

Changes of shoulder, elbow and knee hip are also an important factor affecting on the serve.When hit the ball,his right shoulder and elbow angle were 161.4° , 178.0° . His legs straight, feet off the ground, the left hip joint angle was 189.5° . The speed of right shoulder, elbow, wrist, racket head was 3.45 *m/s*, 3.82 *m/s*, 6.48 *m/s*, 25.83 *m/s*, respecting the speed increase gradually, which explained his action in line with the principle of whipping action.

2.5 The follow-through stage

Following-through stage means the moment when hitting the ball to the moment when left foot touch the ground.Follow-through stage is an indispensable part of the action.The equation $Ft = m * v$ shows that the initial speed of the ball is closely related to the total contact time and strength. The longer the contact time, the faster of the ball. After touching the ball, Dimitrov quickly rotated his forearm, at the same time of the pressure, his step forward, left foot steps onto the floor, stretching right foot to maintain balance. Racket is still in the direction of movement of the ball after ball, which is to increase the contact time. When his left foot touches the ground, his left knee angle was 162.4° , the right knee was 165.5° , leaning forward center of gravity in the left hip joint. Racket head forward across the circular path described the batting wrapped solid, and showed an aggressive serve gap.

3 Conclusions

Through 3D virtual realty technology analysis Dimitrov's serve technique, we can make conclusions as follows:

1) For the tossing ball and lifting racket stage, Dimitrov ball from hand height is 1.91*m*, and peak height is 3.24m, starting point height appropriate for the fast kicking knee is fully prepared and capable of subsequent processes cohesion appropriate. The maximum time shoulder hip knee flexion angle is 31.5° , the left and right knee angles were 95.4° ,123.7° , appropriate bent knees, lower center of gravity.

2)The backward-swing stage: Dimitrov's left and right knees kicking rate were 81.9 ° and 44.5 ° , kicking maximum angular velocity is 230.7° */s*, had huge and rapid kicking amplitude, making the virtual reality technology we can see the longer distances of the head movement trajectory.

3)The swing upward at the ball stage: starting point height was 2.82*m*, speed of the ball was 2.84*m/s*, his right shoulder, elbow, wrist and racket head speed were increasing in turn, which passed a large initial momentum to the ball.

4) With the following-through stage: Dimitrov had a good control of the center of his gravity, and wrapped the ball well, which made his serve technique more aggressive.

References

1. David Whiteside, Bruce Clifford Elliott. *Coordination and variability in the elite female tennis serve*[J].Journal of Sports Sciences; 2015, **33** (7): 675-686.
2. Zhilei Wang,ShanfeiZhang. *Kinematic Analysis on the Serve Technique of lower limbs*[J]. Journal of ningbo university of technology. 2009,**21**(3):77-80.
3. Xiping Ren. *Mechanical factor analysis of tennis serve*[J].Journal of Zhejiang Normal University, 2012,**35**(2):226-230.
4. Qiang Chen. *Affect the level of tennis serve technology for a number of factors*[J]. Journal of competitive sport,2011,28:15-16.
5. Botao Yan,Yanxi Wu. *Biomechanical analysis of the tennis serve*[J]. Journal of Sports science. 2000, **20** (4): 80-84.
6. Kai Hu,Yun Wang. *Serve action analysis of the Elite male tennis players*[J].Journal of Sports research and education: 104-106.

MATEC Web of Conferences **44**, 01089 (2016)
DOI: 10.1051/matecconf/20164401089

A Generalized Order-restricted Inference Methodology for Selecting and Clustering Genes

Rui Yin Liu[a]
College of Mathematics and System Science, Shenyang Normal University, Shenyang, 110034, P.R. China

Abstract. There are many methods for selecting and clustering genes according to their time-course or dose–response profiles. These methods all necessitate the assumption of a constant variance through time or among dosages. This homoscedasticity assumption is, however, seldom satisfied in practice. In this paper, via the application of Shi's (1994,1998) algorithms and a modified bootstrap procedure, we proposed a generalized order-restricted inference methodology for the same task without the homoscedasticity restriction. Simulation results show that our procedure can control the false positive rate and have some good qualities.
Keywords: level probability; $\bar{E}^2$ test; bootstrap sampling; PAVA algorithm

1 INTRODUCTION

In microarray experiments and dose-response studies, experimental conditions usually have some inherent orderings. The performance of statistical inference can be improved significantly if these information can be appropriately utilized in the inferencial procedure . Order restricted statistical inference is an efficient tool to use these ordering information. Depending on the particular practical situation, one can use different order restricted methodologies. The problem under consideration in this present paper, namely clustering and selection of genes, is one example of such method.

Suppose there are T time points denoted by $1,2,...,T$, and at each time point there are n_t observations, for each of G genes. Let Y_{igt} denote the *ith* expression measurement taken on gene g at time point t, $\bar{Y}_{gt}$ denote the sample mean of gene g at time point t and $\bar{Y}_g=(\bar{Y}_{g1},\bar{Y}_{g2},...,\bar{Y}_{gT})'$. The unknown true mean expression level of gene g is $(\mu_{g1},...,\mu_{gT})'$ which is restricted by some partial ordering, where $E(\bar{Y}_{gt})=\mu_{gt}$. Inequalities between the components of $\mu_g=(\mu_{g1},\mu_{g2},...,\mu_{gT})'$ define the true profile for gene g.

We adopt the following examples of inequality profiles according to Peddada et al. [1]. For notational convenience, the subscript g is dropped.

- Null profile: $C_0=\{\mu\in R^T:\mu_1=\mu_2=\cdots=\mu_T\}$.
- Monotone increasing profile (simple order):

$$C_1=\{\mu\in R^T:\mu_1\le\mu_2\le\cdots\le\mu_T\} \quad (1)$$

(with at least one strict inequality). One may similarly define a monotone decreasing profile by replacing $\le$ by $\ge$ in Equation (1).

- Up-down profile with maximum at i (umbrella order):

$$C_2=\{\mu\in R^T:\mu_1\le\mu_2\le\cdots\le\mu_i\ge\mu_{i+1}\ge\cdots\ge\mu_T\} \quad (2)$$

(with at least one strict inequality among $\mu_1\le\mu_2\le\cdots\mu_i$ and one among $\mu_i\ge\mu_{i+1}\ge\cdots\ge\mu_T$. Genes satisfying this profile have mean expression values non-decreasing in time up to time point i and non-increasing thereafter. One may similarly define a down-up profile with minimum at i.

- Cyclical profile with minima at $1,j,T$ and maxima at i,k:

$$C_3=\{\mu\in R^T:\mu_1\le\cdots\le\mu_i\ge\mu_{i+1}\ge\cdots\ge\mu_j\le\mu_{j+1}\le\cdots\le\mu_k \ge\mu_{k+1}\ge\cdots\ge\mu_T\} \quad (3)$$

(with at least one strict inequality among each monotone sub-profile). Cyclical profiles may be important in long time-course experiments where the mean expression value could oscillate.

Our objective is to match the true profile of a gene, estimated from the observed data, to one of a specified set of candidate profiles. Peddada et al. [1] proposed a powerful method based on order-restricted inference, where the estimation procedure uses the known inequalities among parameters. They called the algorithm as ORIOGEN (Order Restricted Inference for Ordered Gene ExpressioN). But, their method necessitates the assumption of a constant variance through time. This homoscedasticity assumption is seldom satisfied in practice.

In fact, Simmons and Peddada [2] applied Hartley's test for heteroscedasticity of variances for the same microarray data of Lobehofer et al. [3]. As the Hartley's test is sensitive to normality assumption, and the gene expression data are not necessarily normally distributed, Simmons and Peddada [2] computed the P-values for the Hartley's test statistic by bootstrapping the residuals. A total of 367 (610) genes out of 1900 were heteroscedastic at a level of significance 0.05 (0.10).

Under the heterogeneous set up, Simmons and Peddada [2] provided a modified method, called ORIOG EN-Hetero. This algorithm allows heteroscedasticity by boot-strapping the residuals, that is, for each gene g and time point t obtain the residuals $e_{igt}=y_{igt}-\bar{y}_{gt}, i=1,...,n_t, t=1,...,T$. Next within the tth time point draw a simple random sample of size n_t (with replacement) from $\{e_{1gt},...,e_{n_tgt}\}$. Denote the resampled residuals by $\{e^*_{1gt},...,e^*_{n_tgt}\}$. Then the bootstrap data y^*_{igt} are obtained by $y^*_{igt}=\bar{y}_g+e^*_{igt}$, where $\bar{y}_g=\sum_{t=1}^{T}n_t\bar{y}_{gt}\Big/\sum_{t=1}^{T}n_t$. They compared its performance with the ORIOGEN whereas resampling was performed by mixing samples from all time points for a given gene, under the presence of heterogeneity, through a simulation study. They analyzed the microarray data of Lobehofer et

[a] Corresponding author: liury683@126.com

al. [3] using both ORIOGEN and ORIOGEN-Hetero, and observed that 197 out of 1900 genes were statistically significant at a level of significance $\alpha = 0.05$ using ORIOGEN, whereas 140 out of 1900 were significant by ORIOGEN-Hetero at the same level of significance, 115 being significant by both the methods.

In this present paper, we propose an alternative methodology to select and cluster genes, also by using the idea of order-restricted inference. For a given candidate profile, we estimate the mean expression level using the pool-adjacent-violators algorithm (PAVA), first publishe-d by Ayer et al. [4], see also Robertson et al. [5]. See the appendix for a brief description of this algorithm. The best fitting profile for a given gene is then selected using the goodness-of-fit criterion and the $\bar{E}^2$ test statistics (the likelihood ratio test statistics under unknown variance) under homoscedastic situation (see, Robertson, et al. [5]). This algorithm lead to a substantial gain of selection and clustering correction under monotone situation.

Also we propose another method based on the algorithm proposed by Shi [6] and Shi and Jiang [7] to deal with the heteroscedastic situation where a bootstrap technology is utilized to get samples under heteroscedast-ic situation.

The rest of the paper is organized as follows. In Section 2, we describe the proposed methodologies. Results from the simulation studies are presented in Section 3. In Section 4, an illustration of the proposed methodologies and a comparison with the existing methods are made using the real microarray experiment data of Lobenhofer et al. [3]. Section 5 concludes.

2 PROPOSED METHODOLOGY

2.1 Methodology under homoscedastic situation

For $t = 1,\dots,T$ and $i = 1,\dots,n_t$, suppose Y_{it} is a normally distributed random variable with unknown mean μ_t and variance of the form $\sigma_t^2 = a_t\sigma^2$, where $a_1,\dots,a_T$ be positive and known, and σ^2 be unknown. Also assume that Y_{it}'s are independent. The likelihood function is $(2\pi\sigma^2)^{-N/2}$ $\cdot\prod_{t=1}^{T} a_t^{-n_t/2}\exp\left[-\frac{1}{2\sigma^2}\sum_{t=1}^{T} a_t^{-1}\sum_{i=1}^{n_t}(y_{it}-\mu_t)^2\right]$ with $N=\sum_{t=1}^{T} n_t$.

It is well known that the vector $\bar{Y} = (\bar{Y}_1,\dots,\bar{Y}_T)'$ is the un-restricted maximum likelihood estimator (MLE) of $\mu = (\mu_1,\dots,\mu_T)'$, the population mean vector. Suppose, however, that it is known that $\mu \in C, C = \{C_j, j = 1,\dots,p\}$, a collection of candidate profiles, is defined as like in Sec-tion 1. Then one may want the estimate also satisfying that constraint, but due to sampling variability the sample means $\bar{Y}_1,\dots,\bar{Y}_T$ may not be ordered in this way. We obtain estimates satisfying this restriction by the isotonic regre-ssion Y^*. If Y^* minimizes $\sum_{t=1}^{T}[\bar{Y}_t-\mu_t]^2\frac{n_t}{a_t}$ subject to $\mu \in C$, we call the restricted MLE Y^* the isotonic regression of $\bar{Y}$ with weights $w_t = \frac{n_t}{a_t}$. In the following we use $\hat{\mu}_C$ representing the isotonic regression of $\bar{Y}$ with respect to some order restriction defined in C. More specifically, $\hat{\mu}_{C_j}$ represents the isotonic regression of $\bar{Y}$ with respect to the order restriction C_j. For fixed $\sigma >$ 0, the isotonic regression $\hat{\mu}_C = (\hat{\mu}_{C_1},\dots,\hat{\mu}_{C_T})' \in C$ that maxi-mizes $L(y;\mu,\sigma)$ is the same for each σ. For a fixed vector $\hat{\mu}_C$, the $\hat{\sigma}^2$ that maximizes $L(y;\mu,\sigma)$ is given by $\hat{\sigma}^2 = \sum_{t=1}^{T} a_t^{-1}\sum_{t=1}^{n_t}(y_{it}-\hat{\mu}_{C_t})^2 / N$.

Denoting the estimate of σ^2 given above (with $C = C_j$) by $\hat{\sigma}^2_{C_j}$, the likelihood ratio test (LRT) rejects C_0 against C_j for small values of $\Lambda = (\hat{\sigma}^2_{C_j}/\hat{\sigma}^2_{C_0})^{N/2}$. Equivalently, the LRT rejects C_0 for large values of $\bar{E}^2_{0j} = \frac{\sum_{t=1}^{T} w_t(\hat{\mu}_{C_j t}-\hat{\mu})^2}{\sum_{t=1}^{T} a_{it}^{-1}\sum_{i=1}^{M}(Y_{it}-\hat{\mu})^2}$, where $\hat{\mu} = \bar{y} = \frac{1}{N}\sum_{t=1}^{T}\sum_{i=1}^{n_t} y_{it}$ is the maximum likelihood estimate (MLE) of $\mu_t, t = 1,\dots,T$ under C_0, and $w_t = n_t / a_t$. Here $\hat{\mu}_{C_j} = (\hat{\mu}_{C_j 1},\dots,\hat{\mu}_{C_j T})'$ is the vector of the MLEs under C_j.

2.2 Algorithm I

First, let we rewrite some definitions given in Peddada et al. [1] in order to compare with their method.

Definition 1. Two parameters in a given profile are said to be linked if the inequality between them is specified *a priori*.

Definition 2. For a given profile, a parameter is said to be *nodal* if it is linked with every other parameter in the pro-file. For example, μ_i is the only nodal parameter in *profi-le* (2) while there are no nodal parameters in *profile* (3).

Definition 3. Define the l_∞ norm of an estimated profile as the maximum difference between the estimates of two linked parameters.

Definition 4. An inequality *sub-profile* C_i within a profile C is described by the inequalities between the compone-nts of the sub-vector $\mu_i = (\mu_{i_1},\dots,\mu_{i_s})$, where $\{i_1,\dots,i_s\} \subseteq \{1,\dots,T\}$.

In view of the above definitions, Algorithm I consists of the following five steps:

Step 1. Pre-specify a collection of p candidate profiles. Denote these profiles by $C_1,\dots,C_p$.

Example 2.1 Suppose an experiment consists of four time points at 1, 2, 3, 4 hours, and we are interested in identif-ying genes belonging to either of the following profiles: $C_1 = \{\mu_1 \le \mu_2 \le \mu_3 \ge \mu_4\}$, $C_2 = \{\mu_1 \le \mu_2 \ge \mu_3 \ge \mu_4\}$.

For each gene $g, g = 1,\dots,G$, perform the following steps.

Step 2. Obtain the estimates of $\mu_{g1},\dots,\mu_{gT}$ under each of the candidate profiles $C_1,\dots,C_p$ using the PAVA algorit-hm (Barlow et al. [8] and Robertson et al. [5]).

Example 2.1 (continued). Suppose the sample mean expr-ession levels of a gene at the four time points are 1.8890, 2.8899, 1.8755, and 0.7342, respectively.

Estimation under C_1: Using the PAVA algorithm, we obtain $\hat{\mu}_1$ = 1.8890, $\hat{\mu}_2$ =2.3827, $\hat{\mu}_3$ = 2.3827, and $\hat{\mu}_4$ = 0.7324:

Estimation under C_2: In this case, $\hat{\mu}_1$ = 1.8890, $\hat{\mu}_2$ = 2.8899, $\hat{\mu}_3$ = 1.8755, and $\hat{\mu}_4$ = 0.7324.

Step 3. For each C_j, j = 1, 2,…, p, compute $\bar{e}_j^2$, where

$$\bar{e}_j^2 = \frac{\sum_{t=1}^{T} \frac{n_t}{a_t}(\hat{\mu}_{C_j t} - \bar{y})^2}{\sum_{t=1}^{T} a_t^{-1} \sum_{i=1}^{n_t} (y_{it} - \bar{y})^2}.$$ Compute $\max_j \bar{e}_j^2$.

Example 2.1 (continued). Here $\bar{e}_1^2$ = 0.3530, $\bar{e}_2^2$ = 0.4529, hence $\max(\bar{e}_1^2, \bar{e}_2^2)$=0.4529.

Step 4 (BOOTSTRAP NULL DISTRIBUTION). Let the y_{it}'s be the observations at time t, t = $1,\ldots, T$. We draw N bootstrap samples. Each bootstrap sample is obtained as follows. Combine the y_{it} observations from all the time points into a vector of length $\sum_{t=1}^{T} n_t$ and draw T simple random samples y_{it}^* with replacement, each of size n_t. Repeat Steps 2 and 3 for each bootstrap sample y_{it}^*. This results in a bootstrap distribution for $\max_j \bar{e}_j^2$, which is used for testing $H_0 : \mu \in C_0, H_a : \mu \in \bigcup_{j=1}^{p} C_j$ (4)

Step 5. Assign gene g to profile C_r if $\bar{e}_r^2 = \max_j \bar{e}_j^2 \ge z_\alpha^*$, where z_α^* is the upper α th percentile of the bootstrap distribution derived in Step 4. If $\max_j \bar{e}_j^2 \le z_\alpha^*$ or if two Profiles are tied then do not classify g into any of the p profiles.

Step 6. Repeat Steps 2-5 with every gene.

2.3 Methodology under heteroscedastic situation

The procedure described above is designed for genes with a constant variance over time or the situation where the unknown variances are in proportion. But it can not deal with situation where the unknown variances are subject to an order restriction or there are no conditions imposed on them (that is unrestricted and (possibly) unequal variances). Under this situation, we extend Peddada [1]'s method in two aspects. First, we obtain the estimates of the mean and variance using the algorithms proposed by Shi [6] and Shi and Jiang [7]. Second, we utilize a bootstrap technique to get samples under heteroscedastic situation.

2.4 Algorithm II

Step 1. Pre-specify a collection of candidate profiles. Denote these profiles by $C_1, C_2, \ldots, C_p$.

For each gene g, g = 1, 2,…, G, perform the following steps.

Step 2. Obtain the estimates of $\mu_{g1},\ldots,\mu_{gT}$ and $\sigma_{g1},\ldots,\sigma_{gT}$ under each of the candidate profiles $C_1,\ldots, C_p$ using Shi's algorithms [5, 6].

Step 3. For each C_j, $j = 1,\ldots, p$, compute $1_\infty^{g(j)}$. Let r be such that $1_\infty^{g(r)} = \max_j 1_\infty^{g(j)}$.

Step 4 (bootstrap null distribution). Let the y_{it}'s be the o-bservations at time t, t = 1,…, T, $\bar{y}_t$ and $s(y_t)^2$ the sample mean and the sample variance of y_{it}, respectively.

We standardize y_{it} to $z_{it} = \frac{y_{it} - \bar{y}_t}{s(y_t)}$. Now the means and variances are same at every time point with respect to z_{it}. We draw N bootstrap samples. Each bootstrap sample is obtained as follows. Combine the z_{it} observations from all the time points into a vector of length $\sum_{t=1}^{T} n_t$ and draw T simple random samples z_{it}^* with replacement, each of size n_t. Then we transform z_{it}^* to $y_{it}^* : y_{it}^* = z_{it}^* s(y_t) + \bar{y}$,where $\bar{y}$ represents the sample mean of all observations. Repeat Steps 2 and 3 for each bootstrap sample y_{it}^*. This results in a bootstrap distribution for $\max_j 1_\infty^{r(j)}$, which is used for testing $H_0 : \mu \in C_0, H_a : \mu \in \bigcup_{j=1}^{p} C_j$ (4)

Step 5. Assign gene g to profile C_r if $1_\infty^{g(r)} \ge z_\alpha^*$, where z_α^* is the upper α th percentile of the bootstrap distribution derived in Step 4. If ` $1_\infty^{g(r)} \le z_\alpha^*$ or if two profiles are tied then do not classify g into any of the p profiles.

Step 6. Repeat Steps 2-5 for every gene.

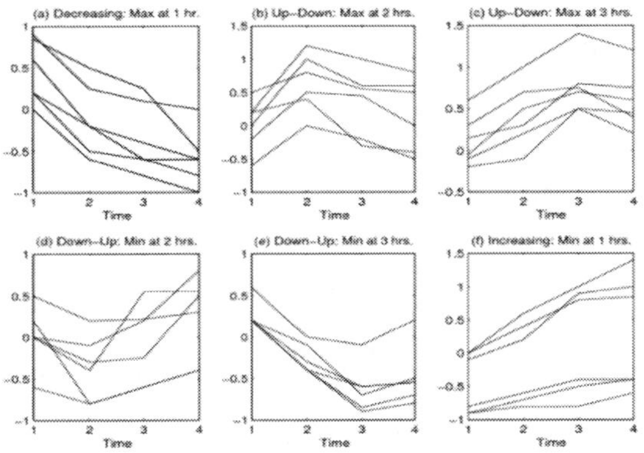

Figure1:Profiles of the simulated genes

3. SIMULATION RESULTS

We illustrate the proposed methodology, and compare the results with the results of Peddada et al. [1] and Simmons and Peddada [2], using gene expression data simulated from normal distributions. Suppose samples were harvested at 1, 2, 3, 4 hours. At each time point there are M= 15 observations. For each gene, we first assume that the variance of the expression was homoscedastic over time. For each gene g, we carry out the test procedure (4) where the alternative hypothesis is the union of the following six profiles: monotone decreasing C_1, monotone increasing C_6, two up-down profiles with maxima at 2, 3 hours C_2, C_3, respectively; and two down-up profiles with minima at 2, 3 hours C_4, C_5, respectively.

We generate two groups of data, from the same six types of profiles in Figure 1 with common variance 0.25 and 1 respectively. For every group we simulated *50* genes from every profile in Figure 1, in all *1800* genes. Assuming that the profiles of the genes are unknown, we wanted to select and cluster them to the six types of profiles using the above methodology.

Table 1(a). Selection and clustering results for data set 1.

l	ORIOGEN		Algorithm I		ORIOGEN-Hetero		Algorithm II	
	Selecting	Clustering	Selecting	Clustering	Selecting	Clustering	Selecting	Clustering
a	197	125	300	165	17	0	13	0
b	127	85	300	172	15	4	21	1
c	91	58	299	173	16	4	19	6
d	126	76	300	150	20	3	12	3
e	189	102	300	153	17	1	20	3
f	149	93	299	132	16	1	14	1

Using Algorithm I for the two groups of data with N = 10000, we selected 1798 (1800) genes with the test level α = 0.05, 300 (300) from genes simulated from Figure 1(a), 300 (300) from Figure 1(b), 299 (300) from Figure 1(c), 300 (300) from Figure 1(d), 300 (300) from Figure 1(e), 299 (300) from Figure 1(f), for the two variances. Of these, 165 (235) were clustered into C_1, 172 (238) into C_2, 173 (224) into C_3, 150 (220) into C_4, 153 (202) into C_5, 132 (180) into C_6.

We used the same data set with ORIOGEN algorithm with N = 10000 again. This time we selected 879 (1580) genes with the test level α =0.05, 197 (299) from genes simulated from Figure 1(a), 127 (248) from Figure 1(b), 91 (265) from Figure 1(c), 126 (233) from Figure 1(d), 189 (299) from Figure 1(e), 149 (236) from Figure 1(f). Of these, 125 (234) were clustered into C_1, 85 (195) into C_2, 58 (203) into C_3, 76 (182) into C_4, 102 (202) into C_5, 93 (156) into C_6.

Table 1(b). Selection and clustering results for data set 2.

l	ORIOGEN		Algorithm I		ORIOGEN-Hetero		Algorithm II	
	Selecting	Clustering	Selecting	Clustering	Selecting	Clustering	Selecting	Clustering
a	299	234	300	235	21	0	11	0
b	248	195	300	238	17	6	19	5
c	265	203	300	224	10	1	13	4
d	233	182	300	220	20	5	20	5
e	299	202	300	202	16	5	9	1
f	236	156	300	180	14	1	15	0

Using ORIOGEN-*Hetero* with N=10000, we selected 101 (98) genes with the test level α =0.05, 17 (21) from genes simulated from Figure 1(a), 15 (17) from Figure 1(b), 16 (10) from Figure 1(c), 20 (20) from Figure 1(d), 17 (16) from Figure 1(e), 16 (14) from Figure 1(f). Of these, 0 (0) were clustered into C_1, 4 (6) into C_2, 4 (1) into C_3, 3(5) into C_4, 1(5) into C_5, 1 (1) into C_6. See Tables 1(a) and 1(b) for these simulation results.

Using Algorithm II with N = 10000, we selected 99 (87) genes with the test level α =0.05, 13 (11) from genes simulated from Figure 1(a), 21 (19) from Figure 1(b), 19 (13) from Figure 1(c), 12 (20) from Figure 1(d), 20 (9) from Figure 1(e), 14 (15) from Figure 1(f). Of these, 0 (0) were clustered into C_1, 1 (5) into C_2, 6 (4) into C_3, 3 (5) into C_4, 3(1) into C_5, 1 (0) into C_6. See Tables 1(a) and 1(b) for these simulation results.

Clearly under all the situations from the results, ORIOGEN is inferior to our Algorithm I. Also we can see that Algorithm II and ORIOGEN-Hetero is inferior to both Algorithm I and ORIOGEN. The reason is obvious, because the simulated data is from homoscedastic variance, the weights ω in the algorithm obtaining the MLE estimate is fixed. But in Algorithm II and ORIOGEN-*Hetero*, the weight is computed with bootstrap samples in every iteration steps.

Table2. False positive rate of our procedure.

α	Case 1			Case 2			Case 3		Case 4
	Sc. 1	Sc. 2	Sc. 3	Sc. 1	Sc. 2	Sc. 3	Sc. 1	Sc. 2	Sc. 1
.06	.0547	.0572	.0512	.0531	.0559	.0510	.0668	.0557	.0610
.05	.0469	.0411	.0439	.0466	.0497	.0439	.0565	.0513	.0523
.03	.0227	.0247	.0216	.0208	.0249	.0219	.0326	.0285	.0392
.02	.0156	.0163	.0157	.0145	.0166	.0133	.0204	.0187	.0229
.01	.0087	.0090	.0075	.0073	.0081	.0065	.0118	.0094	.0131
.009	.0069	.0070	.0064	.0068	.0075	.0066	.0103	.0085	.0185
.006	.0046	.0044	.0047	.0041	.0049	.0044	.0076	.0056	.0056
.003	.0020	.0022	.0024	.0024	.0025	.0020	.0033	.0029	.0031

Also we generated 2000 genes from a profile with the common mean 0 across all the time points for both groups. We note that using Algorithm I and ORIOGEN with the test level α =0.05, we selected 94 and 104 genes, respectively, from the 1840 genes of the first group, 102 and 114 genes of the other group. Obviously, ORIOGEN resulted in more false positives.

We also investigated the false positive rate of our procedures. To generate unpatterned null data, we created 60 observations from four standard normal populations, each with 15 observations. Our simulations suggest that our methodology provides fairly accurate type I error rates.

Table 2 reports the false positive rates. We explored four cases. For both the Case 1 and Case 2, the null hypo thesis is, H_0: $\mu_1 = \mathrm{L} = \mu_4$, the alternative H_c is taken as the following scenarios respectively. Scenario 1: $\mu_1 \le \mu_2 \le \mu_3 \ge \mu_4$ or $\mu_1 \le \mu_2 \ge \mu_3 \ge \mu_4$;Scenario 2: $\mu_1 \le \mu_2 \le \mu_3 \le \mu_4$ or $\mu_1 \le \mu_2 \le \mu_3 \ge \mu_4$; Scenario 3: $\mu_1 \le \mu_2 \le \mu_3 \le \mu_4$ or $\mu_1 \le \mu_2 \le \mu_3 \ge \mu_4$ or $\mu_1 \le \mu_2 \ge \mu_3 \ge \mu_4$.

We assume the variances are equal in Case 1, that is $\sigma_1^2 = \mathrm{L} = \sigma_4^2 \mathrm{A} \sigma^2$, and the data in simulation are from $N_4(0, I_4)$. In Case 2 the variances are in proportion $(\sigma_1^2, \ldots, \sigma_4^2)$

$=(a_1,...,a_2)\sigma^2$, the data in simulation are from $N(0, \text{diag}(1, 3.24, 4, 2.25))$. In Case 3, the variances are subject to some order restriction. In Scenario 1 the null hypothesis $H_0: \mu_1 = \text{L} = \mu_4, \sigma_1 = \text{L} = \sigma_4$, the alternative $H_a: \mu_1 \le \mu_2 \le \mu_3 \ge \mu_4$, $\sigma_1 \ge \sigma_2 \ge \sigma_3 \le \sigma_4$ or $\mu_1 \le \mu_2 \ge \mu_3 \ge \mu_4, \sigma_1 \ge \sigma_2 \le \sigma_3 \le \sigma_4$. In Scenario 2 we assume the variances are subject to a simple order $\sigma_1 \ge \sigma_2 \ge \sigma_3 \le \sigma_4$ whatever be the null or alternative hypo theses. For this case, we discussed H_0: $\mu_1 = \mu_2 = \mu_3 = \mu_4$ vs. H_a: $\mu_1 \le \mu_2 \ge \mu_3 \ge \mu_4$ or $\mu_1 \le \mu_2 \le \mu_3 \ge \mu_4$. In Case 4, we have no idea of the variances. Here the null hypothesis H_0 is $\mu_1 = \mu_2 = \mu_3 = \mu_4$, the alternative $H_a: \mu_1 \le \mu_2 \ge \mu_3 \ge \mu_4$ or $\mu_1 \le \mu_2 \le \mu_3 \ge \mu_4$.

Table 3. False positive rate of Peddada's method.

α	.06	.05	.03	.02	.01	.009	.006	.003
Sc. 1	.0608	.0521	.0261	.0203	.0106	.0082	.0050	.0034
Sc. 2	.0624	.0536	.0314	.0177	.0097	.0084	.0077	.0020
Sc. 3	.0601	.0530	.0326	.0189	.0093	.0088	.0052	.0030

In contrast, we also investigated the false positive rate of the ORIOGEN method using bootstrap sampling under a constant variance through time. Only a small portion of the results are presented in Table 3, for the sake of brevity. Here the null hypothesis for all the cases is H_0: $\mu_1 = \mu_2 = \mu_3 = \mu_4$, the alternative H_a is also taken as Scenarios 1, 2, and 3, respectively. It is necessary to point out that ORIOGEN based on bootstrap sampling is very sensitive to the observations themselves and the number of observations.

Table 4. False positive rates of Algorithm II and the ORIOGEN-Hetero method with 6 time points.

Pattern (i=1,…,6)			Algorithm II	ORIOGEN-*Hetero*
1	$\mu_i = 0$	$\sigma_i^2 = 16$	0.033	0.034
2	$\mu_i = 0$	$\sigma_i^2 = i^2$	0.037	0.044
3	$\mu_i = 0$	$\sigma_i^2 = i^3$	0.040	0.032
4	$\mu_i = i$	$\sigma_i^2 = 16$	0.289	0.330
5	$\mu_i = i$	$\sigma_i^2 = i^2$	0.717	0.740
6	$\mu_i = i$	$\sigma_i^2 = i^3$	0.291	0.307
7	$\mu_i = 0, i = 1,2,4$ $5,6, \mu_3 = 3$	$\sigma_i^2 = 16, i = 1,2,4$ $5,6, \sigma_3^2 = 9$	0.605	0.602

We also carry out a simulation study based on 10,000 bootstrap samples and 1000 genes, at a significance level of 0.05. We compare the performances of false positive rates of the proposed method under heteroscedastic model in our paper (Algorithm II) and the ORIOGEN-Hetero algorithm of Simmons and Peddada [2]. The results are given in Table 4.

4. ANALYSIS OF REAL DATA USING DIFFERENT MRTHODOLOGIES

We consider the microarray experiment data set of Lobenhofer et al. [2] for illustration and comparison of different methodologies.

First we use Algorithm I and ORIOGEN to deal with the data assuming the homoscedasticity. At the significance level 0.005, we selected 223 out of 1900 genes using Alg-orithm I. From the selected genes, we obtained 15 genes belonging to the profile 1, 51 genes belonging to profile 2. Compared to Peddada et al. [1], there they selected 197 out of 1900 genes using ORIOGEN, there are 161 common genes. Because Algorithm I is sensitive to monotonic situation, and both 1 and 2 profile are monotonic, so Algorithm I selected 26 more genes than ORIGEN. This result tallies with the simulation.

Under heteroscedastic situation, we selected 132 genes using Algorithm II. Compared to ORIOGEN-Hetero, there are 108 genes in common. In ORIOGEN-Hetero the bootstrap sampling is restricted to one time point' residual, that is, we resample from only 8 observations at every time point t respectively. But in Algorithm II, we resample from all the observations at all the time points, that is 48 observations. There are 123 common genes between Algorithm I and ORIOGEN-Hetero. Between ORIOGEN and Algorithm II, there are 108 genes in common.

5. DISCUSSION

In this article, our research is mainly focused on two aspects of the selection and clustering algorithm. The first relates to the test method. Here we use an accurate test (i.e., LRT) to judge whether a gene should be rejected or accepted.

The second emphasis in our research is to explore the bootstrap sampling under heteroscedastic situation. We obtain samples from the standardized observations, and then take a transform to revert the samples so that they are from the null hypothesis. The simulation results show that this technique works well, and even works better than the ORIOGEN-Hetero algorithm of Simmons and Peddada [2].

Because this article focuses on the method for selection and clustering, we have not concentrated much on the analysis of the data. It should be pointed out, however, that our methodology enjoys several desirable properties. For example, the estimated mean expression levels in all cases, subject to an inequality profile, are MLEs.

In studies where experimental conditions have an inherent ordering, making use of ordering information can improve inference. In microarray experiments, the ability to exploit ordering information may be especially valuable as the genes whose expression levels change in concert through time may be components of the same cellular process or may share regulatory elements. Peddada et al. [1] have recognized the importance of time-course information and developed procedures based

on the statistical theory of order-restricted inference that makes explicit use of ordering information when selecting differentially expressed genes. Here we proposed a new selection and clustering method based on LRT under homoscedastic situation, and generalized Peddada's method to heteroscedastic situation. It is expected that methods of analysis that exploit the ordering of treatments to improve estimation will become increasingly valuable for time-course and dose-response micro-array experiments.

ACKNOWLEDGEMENTS

This work is supported by NSFC (Grant Numbers 11401393) and Liaoning Province Doctoral Startup Fund (Grant Number 20131107).

REFERENCES

1. Peddada S, Lobenhofer E, Li L, Afshari C, Weinberg C, Umbach D. Gene selection and clustering for time-course and dose-response microarray experiments using order-restricted inference. Bioinformatics, **19**: 834-841. (2003)
2. Simmons S, Peddada S, Order-restricted inference for ordered gene expression (ORIOGEN) data under heteroscedastic variances. Bioinformatics, **1(10)**: 414-419. (2007)
3. Lobenhofer E, Bennett L, Cable P, Li L, Afshari C. Regulation of DNA replication for k-genes by 17- β estradiol. *Molec.* Endocrin, **16**: 1215-1229. (2002)
4. Ayer M, Brunk HD, Ewing GM, Reid WT, Silverman E. An empirical distribution function for sampling with incomplete information. Ann. Math. Statist.,**26**: 641-647. (1955)
5. Robertson T, Wright FT, Dykstra RL. Order Restricted Statistical Inference. Wiley: New York, (1988).
6. Shi NZ. Maximum likelihood estimation of means and variances from normal populations under simultaneous order restrictions. J. Mult. Anal.; **50**: 282-293. (1994)
7. Shi NZ, Jiang H. Maximum likelihood estimation of isotonic normal means with unknown variances. J. Mult. Anal.; **64**: 183-195. (1998)
8. Barlow RE, Bartholomew DJ, Bremner JM, Brunk HD. Statistical Inference under Order Restrictions. Wiley: New York, (1972).

MATEC Web of Conferences 44, 01090 (2016)
DOI: 10.1051/matecconf/20164401090

Abnormal traffic flow data detection based on wavelet analysis

Qian Xiao[1,a], Dong Jian Wang[1] and Dan Liu[1]

[1] Institute of Information Engineering, Shenyang University, Shenyang 110044, China

Abstract. In view of the traffic flow data of non-stationary, the abnormal data detection is difficult.proposed basing on the wavelet analysis and least squares method of abnormal traffic flow data detection in this paper.First using wavelet analysis to make the traffic flow data of high frequency and low frequency component and separation, and then, combined with least square method to find abnormal points in the reconstructed signal data.Wavelet analysis and least square method, the simulation results show that using wavelet analysis of abnormal traffic flow data detection, effectively reduce the detection results of misjudgment rate and false negative rate.

1 Introduction

At present, the supply of the existing urban transportation infrastructure cannot meet the needs of the current urban development on the road, which is he main reason that caused by traffic congestion in the great cities of the world, traffic safety, and environmental pollution. Therefore, in today's rapid economic development and science and technology innovation, will have to take a new urban traffic management technology. At present, more advanced, more widely used a traffic management technology is intelligent transportation system (ITS). It through the use of advanced electronic, information, sensor and system engineering, and other technology integration and application based on relatively perfect road facilities to satisfy the actual demand of ground transportation. Traffic monitoring is through many data to rely on, general conditions have been monitor to collect traffic data. But the weather situation, equipment failure, traffic control and other reasons will often cause the lack of data acquisition and error phenomenon. Therefore, the abnormal traffic flow data detection is an essential work.

Traditional data monitoring method has regression forecast method and the Kalman filter, etc. [1,2].These methods assume that the process is stable, the system is linear, the interference of the system is white noise, thus can obtain satisfactory result in linear system steady random time series predictions. However, the problem of urban road traffic flow is someone involved in the active system, has the characteristics of nonlinear and strong disturbance. Therefore, a nonlinear system model is more in line with the actual situation. Least squares abnormal data detection suitable for normal distribution characteristics of abnormal data, but is not suitable for direct application in the abnormal data of traffic flow detection. Therefore, directly using the least-square method, there will be a large amount of data was wrongfully convicted. The current detection method of suitable for the unstable signal is wavelet analysis, this article uses the wavelet analysis method combined with least square method, make the ability to detect abnormal traffic flow data get great improvement.

2 The principle of wavelet denoising

2.1 The wavelet transform

The meaning of the wavelet transform is: call a basic wavelet function $\psi(t)$ to do after displacement τ , again under different scales a and the inner product of signal $x(t)$ to be analysed:

$$WT_x(A,\tau)=\frac{1}{\sqrt{a}}\int_{-\infty}^{+\infty}x(t)\psi^*(\frac{t-\tau}{a})dt \quad a>0 \tag{1}$$

The equivalent frequency domain of formula (1) can be said such as:

$$WT_x(a,\tau)=\frac{\sqrt{a}}{2\pi}\int_{-\infty}^{+\infty}X(\omega)\psi^*(a\omega)e^{j\omega\tau}d\omega \tag{2}$$

In formula (2), $X(\omega)$ and $\psi(\omega)$ are respectively $x(t)$ and $\psi(t)$ Fourier transform.

Has the characteristics of multi-scale wavelet transform, the signal can be observed from coarse to fine gradually, and regard it as with basic frequency characteristic $\psi(\omega)$ for bandpass filter for signal filtering under different scales a .The choice of appropriate basic wavelet, making $\psi(t)$ in time domain is a limited support, $\psi(\omega)$ are more concentrated in the frequency domain, can make the wavelet transform in time domain and frequency domain has the ability of local signal

[a] Xiao Qian: xiaoqian_neu@163.com

characteristics, which is beneficial to detect signal singularity or eliminate noise.

2.2 Wavelet decomposition and reconstruction

In 1986, S.Mallat and Y.Meyer put forward the concept of multi-resolution analysis, and give the fast algorithm of wavelet decomposition and reconstruction, namely the Mallet algorithm.According to this algorithm,if f_k is the discrete sampling data of signal $f(t)$, $f_k = c_{0,k}$, the signal $f(t)$ decomposition formula for orthogonal wavelet transform is:

$$\begin{cases} c_{j,k} = \sum_n c_{j-1,n} h_{n-2k} \\ d_{j,k} = \sum d_{j-1,n} g_{n-2k} \end{cases} \quad (3)$$

Among them, $c_{j,k}$ ----scale coefficient;

$d_{j,k}$ ----wavelet coefficients;

h, g ---- a pair of quadrature mirror filter group (QMF);

j ----decomposition layers;

N ----discrete sampling point

Wavelet reconstruction process is the inverse operation of decomposition, the corresponding reconstruction formula is:

$$c_{j-1,n} = \sum_n c_{j,n} h_{k-2n} + \sum_n d_{j,n} g_{k-2n} \quad (4)$$

Wavelet multi-resolution analysis feature to signal under the different scales of multiresolution decomposition, and intertwined in different frequency of mixed signal is decomposed into different frequency band signal, so the signal has the ability of press band processing.

3 Least-square method based on wavelet analysis

Least squares method is a kind of mathematical optimization techniques, its data by minimizing the error sum of squares to find the best match function.Can be easily obtained by means of least square method of the unknown data, and make the the sum of the squares of the error between actual data and calculated data to a minimum.Least squares calculation process is as follows:

(1) Calculate the updated sequence of arithmetic average:

$$\overline{x} = \frac{1}{n}\sum_{i=1}^{n} x_i \quad (5)$$

(2) Calculate each value of the residual error:

$$v_i = x_i - \overline{x} \quad (6)$$

(3) Using a sequence of standard error:

$$\sigma = \sqrt{\sum_{i=1}^{n} v_i^2 \Big/ (n-1)} \quad (7)$$

(4) According to the following formula, use La Yida of criteria to find abnormal data:

$$|v_i|_{\max} \le 3\sigma \quad (8)$$

Using the least square method can directly analyze the abnormal traffic flow data.Using the least square method, finding new sequence of arithmetic mean and then the residual error of individual values, using the residual error sequence of standard deviation, finally judge La Yida criterion and find the abnormal data. Least squares method is suitable for normal distribution characteristics of abnormal data detection, but is not suitable for direct application in the abnormal data of traffic flow detection. In this paper, firstly do wavelet analysis for traffic abnormal data to reconstruct the low frequency signal data, and then analyze the difference between the reconstructed sequence sequence x by the least squares method. Find abnormal data appear in the new position in the sequence, the sequence of abnormal data traffic at the corresponding position.

4 Abnormal traffic flow data simulation

4.1 Traffic data simulation based on least square method

In this paper, the simulation model of chongqing easyblog digital technology co., LTD. Production of GJK - 7 b a group of traffic flow data from the vehicle detector, each signal cycle record at a time (flow units: vehicle/cycle). In this paper, the simulation out a set of simulation data, and close to real data recorded 450 set of data, and according to the actual situation of artificial added four abnormal data points: 110 212.247.414.Using the least squares method for traffic signal data processing, be able to get the residual error, traffic signal and the residual error is shown in figure 1.

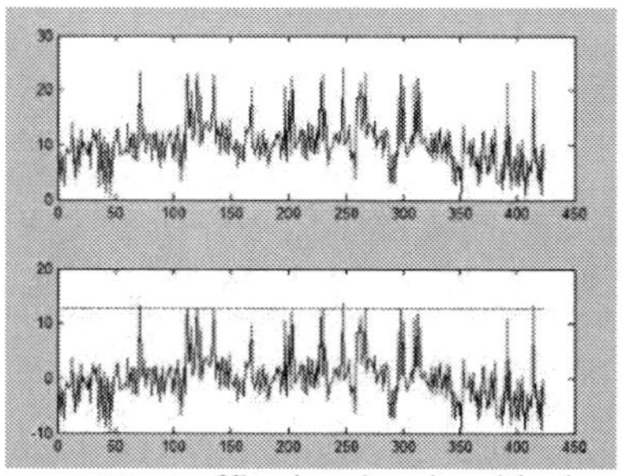

Figure 1 The traffic signal and residual error

4.2 traffic data simulation based on wavelet analysis

Selection based on the least square method of wavelet analysis to analyze traffic signal, choose db3 wavelet as the wavelet basis function, the traffic signal 2 layers wavelet decomposition scale, and then after wavelet decomposition of the low frequency part of the refactoring, the original traffic signal and reconstructing low frequency signal is shown in figure 2:

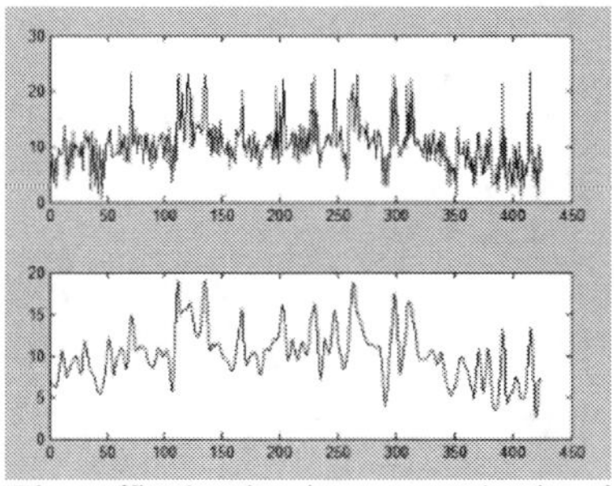

Figure 2 The traffic signal and reconstructing low frequency part

The refactoring least squares of low frequency part, reconstruct the difference sequences and residual error as shown in figure 3:

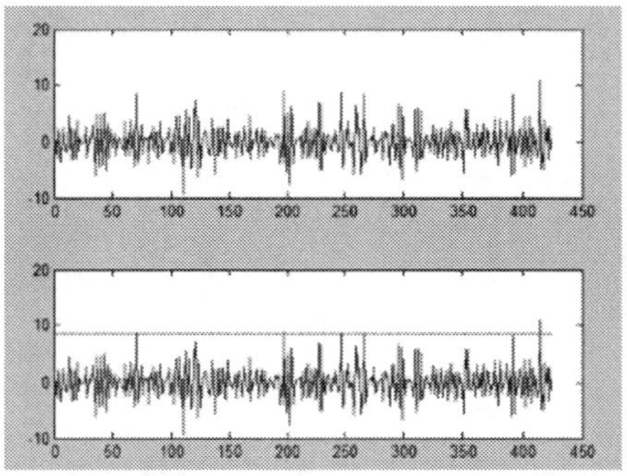

Figure 3 The difference sequences and residual error

4.3 the result analysis

In this paper, in the original traffic data added four abnormal data is as follows: 110 212.247.414, from figure 1 shows, using the least square method of traffic flow data detection, can find the abnormal data for 71.113.247.267.414, 247 and 414 of them are correct abnormal data points, and 71.113.267 is misjudgment, 110.212 is false negatives. Figure 3 shows, using wavelet analysis to detect the amount of traffic flow, you can find the abnormal data for 110.197.247.414, including 110.247.414 is correct, 197 is misjudgment, 212 is false negatives.

Table 1 abnormal data detection results contrast

The least square method	Least squares method based on wavelet analysis
Misjudgment rate of 60%	Misjudgment rate of 25%
False negative rate of 40%	False negative rate of 25%

The table 1 shows that the abnormal data by the least-square method to monitor the misjudgment rate was 60%, false negative rate was 40%. The least-square method based on wavelet analysis misjudgment rate was 25%, the false negative rate was 25%, higher than the least square method of accurate performance, so it can be seen that the least-square method based on wavelet analysis of abnormal traffic flow data detection more accurate and effective.

5 Conclusion

In order to effectively manage the traffic planning and traffic control, need to be accurate and timely collection and traffic flow data, and detect the abnormal data.This article uses wavelet analysis combined with the traditional least squares method, so as to find abnormal point in the reconstructed signal data, for detecting abnormal data of non-stationary signal.Based on wavelet analysis and least square method to simulation experiment, the results show that the wavelet analysis has good precision.

References

1. Lei Shaolan, Sun Caixin, Zhou Quan, Zhang Xiaoxing. The Reserch of Local Linear Model of Short-Term Electrical Load on Multivariate Time Series[J]. Proceedings of the CSEE. 2006.26(2):25-28.
2. Zhang Jiangshan, Zhu Guangxi. Kalman Filter for Video Object Segmentation and Tracking[J]. Journal of Image and Graphics. 2002.7(6): 606-609.
3. Li Zhimin, Yi Liangyou, Xue Ping, Dai Gao, Xie Xianbao. Short-term traffic flow detection based on wavelet[J]. Application Research of Computers, 2011.18(5):1677-1678
4. Xiao ZhiXin , Yang YueXiang , Yang Lin. Anomaly Detection and Implementation Based on Wavelet[J]. Computer Science:2006.33(10):116-118
5. Xiong Wei. Synergetic phase transition detection method for network traffic anomolies based on wavelet[J]. Journal of Computer Applications. 2012.32(8):2271-2274
6. Song Yanbo, Peng Xiaoqi. Approach Based on Wavelet Analysis for Detecting and Amending Anomalous Samples in Data Set[J]. Mini-micro Systems.2011.2： 325-329

MATEC Web of Conferences 44, 01091 (2016)
DOI: 10.1051/matecconf/20164401091

An new method to collaborative filtering recommendation based on DBN and HMM

Yong Mei Zhao[1],Hai Rong Wan[2],Zheng Xin Guo

[1] *Department of Electric and Science, College of Science, Air Force Engineering University, China*

[2] *Department of Urban and Regional Planning, College of Urban and Environmental Sciences, Peking University, China*

[3] *Department of Civil Engineering, Hunan University,China*

Abstract: The main problems of collaborative filtering are initial rating, data sparsity and recommendation in time. A recommendation approach based on HMM model, which creates nearest neighbour set by simulating the user behaviours of web browsing, is a good way to solve the above problems. However, the HMM or model parameters constantly vary with customer's changing preference. When there is a new type of data to join, the HMM can only be discovered by relearn, which will affect real time of recommendation. Therefore a recommendation approach based on DBN and HMM is proposed. The approach will improve real time recommendation, and experiments shows that it has high recommendation quality.

Key words: hidden markov model(HMM), dynamic bayes network(DBN), collaborative filtering recommendation

1 Introduction

The main problems of collaborative filtering [1] are data sparsity, initial rating, recommendation in time and the expansion of data space. In order to solve these problems, an approach to collaborative filtering recommendation based on HMM is one of the good solution [2].User behaviour changes constantly with the diversity of online consumer products, by which model or model parameters should be modified. Previous recommendation model once formed, model parameters cannot be changed arbitrarily, thus when there is a new type of data to join, the HMM can only be discovered by relearn, which will affect real time of user behaviour recommendation. It is necessary to study how to improve the adaptive capability of recommend model on the basis of using previous model by updating its structure.

Short for dynamic Bayesian networks model (DBN), because of its flexibility of modelling, is widely used in many fusion algorithms. We can create recommendation model based on DBN to implement network structure learning--adding new features on the basis of previous collaborative filtering recommendation

Article available at http://www.matec-conferences.org or http://dx.doi.org/10.1051/matecconf/20164401091

technology, and combining all previous training set and new sample for leaning, which will both save time and optimize the network structure, then makes recommendation model meets user's needs well.

2 A collaborative filtering prediction model based on HMM [3]

The HMM collaborative filtering model with users preference makes great improvements both in efficiency and accuracy recommendation results. The HMM collaborative filtering model is defined as following

$$P_{aj} = \frac{1}{n}\sum_{i=1}^{n} P_i(O \mid \lambda) \times A_{ij} \qquad (1)$$

Where , A_{ij} is the preferences of usr i for commodity j; Commodity j is what the path j represents; P_{aj} is the references probability of target user a for commodity j;. $P_i(O|\lambda)$ is the similarity of the nearest user i.

3 A collaborative filtering recommendation model based on DBN

3.1 Definition of DBN model[5,6]

The probability equation of observation variable:

$$p(X_t, A_t|Y_t) = \sum_{m=1}^{M} p(M_t = m|Y_t) p(X_t, A_t|Y_t, M_t = m) \qquad (2)$$

Where, $p(A_t|Y_t,M_t=m)$ is expressed in a simple distribution like passion distribution;

$p(X_t|A_t,Y_t,M_t=m)$

is expressed in conditional Gaussian model as following

$$p(X_t|A_t,Y_t,M_t=m)=N(X_t;u_m^u+BA_t,\textstyle\sum_m^u) \qquad (3)$$

Equation of state:

$$\theta_t = G_t\theta_{t-1} + w_t \text{, } w_t \sim N[0, W_t] \qquad (4)$$

The initial prior: $(\theta_0 \mid D_0) \sim N[m_0, C_0]$ (5)

Where θ_t is the state parameter at time t, which is a $n\times1$ matrix; G_t is $n \times n$ state transition matrix; v_t is observation error and w_t is state variables, they are independent.

W_{t_i} can hardly be determined in practice, in order to solve the faults, the discount factor δ $0<\delta<1$ is incorporated into the model. A first order polynomial model with the discount factor is called a first order polynomial discount model, the specific implementation is as follows:

$$\mu_{t_i} = \alpha + \beta_{t_i} = \alpha + \beta_{t_{i-1}} + \beta_{r_i} = \mu_{t_{i-1}} + \beta_{r_i}$$

$\beta_{t_i} = \beta_{r_i} = (r_i / r_{i-1})\beta_{t_{i-1}}$ .Where, μ_{t_i} is the level of the sequence at time t_i, β_{t_i} is the growth of sequence level from time t_{i-1} to t_i.

The state equation:

$$\begin{cases} \mu_{t_i} = \mu_{t_{i-1}} + (r_i / r_{i-1})\beta_{t_{i-1}} + w_{t_i,1} \\ \beta_{t_i} = (r_i / r_{i-1})\beta_{t_{i-1}} + w_{t_i,2} \end{cases} \qquad (6)$$

Where

$$w_{t_i} = \begin{bmatrix} w_{t_i,1} \\ w_{t_i,2} \end{bmatrix}$$

The initial information:

$$\left(\begin{bmatrix} \mu_{t_0} \\ \beta_{t_0} \end{bmatrix} | D_{t_0}\right) \quad N\left[m_{t_0}, C_{t_0}\right] \qquad (7)$$

Where

$$m_{t_0} = \begin{bmatrix} m_{t_0} \\ b_{t_0} \end{bmatrix}, C_{t_0} = \begin{bmatrix} C_{t_{0.1}} & C_{t_{0.3}} \\ C_{t_{0.3}} & C_{t_{0.2}} \end{bmatrix}$$

v_{t_i} is a term of observation error, which follows normal distribution with zero mean and variances of V_{t_i}. D_{t_i} is the information collection about system before time t_i.

$$W_{t_i} = (\delta^{-r_i} - 1) G_{t_i} G_{t_{i-1}} G_{t_i}^T$$

$$F = \begin{pmatrix} 0 \\ 1 \end{pmatrix}, G_{t_i} = \begin{bmatrix} 1 & r_i / r_{i-1} \\ 0 & r_i / r_{i-1} \end{bmatrix}, \theta_{t_i} = \begin{pmatrix} \mu_{t_i} \\ \beta_{t_i} \end{pmatrix}$$

3.2 The model of reasoning and learning algorithm

1) Model reasoning algorithm[7]

In the process of model reasoning, we mainly calculate two parameters: $\lambda$and π, which are αserved as β and in HMM.

Parameter λ and π can be calculated by the following formula:(assume the observation vector is e)

$$P(e)=\sum_{j}\lambda_j^i*\pi_j^i\ ,\forall\, i \qquad (8)$$

$$P(X_i=j|e)=\frac{\lambda_j^i*\pi_j^i}{\sum_j\lambda_j^i*\pi_j^i}\ ,\forall\, i \qquad (9)$$

The specific reasoning algorithm is as follows(algorithm 1):

For each variable X_i(poster order traversal)

If X_i is a leaf node,

If $\forall$ j are the values of observation vectors, $\lambda_j^i=1$,

Else $\lambda_j^i=0$,

Else

If $\forall\, j$ are the values of observation vectors,

$$\lambda_j^i=\prod_{c\in children(x_i)}\sum_f\lambda_f^c*P(X_c=f|X_i=j)$$

Else $\lambda_j^i=0$

For each variable Xi(preordering traverse)

If X_i is a root node,

$$\pi_j^i=P(X_i=j)$$

Else

$$\pi_j^i=\sum_{v\in CON(P)}P(X_i=j\mid X_P=v)*\pi_v^P *\prod_{s\in silbings(X_i)}\sum_f\lambda_f^s*P(X_s=f\mid X_P=v)$$

(where X_p is the father of X_i)

2) Model learning algorithm[8,9]

When the observation vector is incomplete with any given network structure, the classical EM algorithm is suitable. The training process of the algorithm is:(Algorithm 2)

Step E:

Assume the observation vector is e, the conditional probability of node C_i will be shown in equation (10):

$$P(C_i=w\mid e)=\frac{\lambda_w^i*\pi_w^i}{\sum_w\lambda_w^i*\pi_w^i} \qquad (10)$$

The probability of every solidification node can be calculated according to equation(10), using the derived algorithm based on connected-tree algorithm.

Then calculate N_{ijk}--the number of times each variable X_i appeared, assuming X_i=k, parents(X_i)=j. First choose one solidification node, which contains both X_i and its father node.

Let V_{jk}^i be the collection of solidification nodes which satisfy X_i=k and parents (X_i)=j, then

$$N_{ijk}=\sum_{w\in V_{jk}^i}P(C_i=w\mid e) \qquad (11)$$

N_{ijk} increases with the addition of the training sample.

Step M:

After calculating N_{ijk}, the conditional probability of each variable can be reevaluate as shown in formula (12):

$$P(X_i=k\mid parents(X_i)=j)=\frac{N_{ijk}}{\sum_k N_{ijk}}=\frac{N_{ijk}}{N_{ij}} \qquad (12)$$

3.3 Collaborative filtering recommendation algorithm based on DBN (algorithm 3)

Step 1: Initialize the X_0;

Step 2: Perform the collaborative filtering prediction model based on HMM (Model 1), training model based on the standard characteristics;

Step 3: Perform algorithm 1, algorithm 2 and establish DBN;

Step 4: Calculate $P(X_T|Y_{1:T})$, chose X_T maximizing $P(X_T|Y_{1:T})$.

3.4 The update model based on DBN

Combining the previous model with the nearest neighbour similarity recommended by HMM, the original forecast model of collaborative filtering updating for formula:

$$P_{aj} = \frac{1}{n}\sum_{i=1}^{n} S_i \times A_{ij} \quad (13)$$

$$S_i = \psi * P_i(O \mid \lambda) + \zeta * P_i(X_T^i \mid Y_{1:T}) \quad (14)$$

Where, A_{ij} is the preference of user i for commodity j; Commodity j is what the path j represents. P_{aj} is the probability of which target user a like commodity j. S_i is the similarity of the nearest user i. ψ and ζ are balance index which are used to define how HMM and DBN training results influence the model.

3.5 Nearest neighbour collaborative filtering method after updating

There are three parts of the updated collaborative filtering recommendation model: data pre-processing, HMM filtration, DBN updating model, collaborative filtering prediction model. Figure 1 depicts its structure:

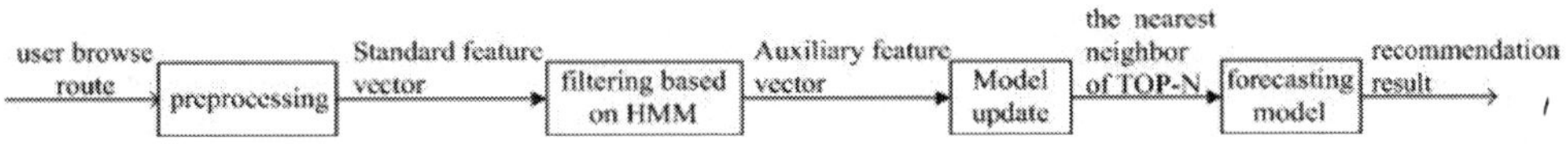

Figure 1. The updated collaborative filtering process

In nearest neighbour recommended phase, obviously, calculate $P_i(O|\lambda)$ and $P_i(X_T|Y_{1:T})$ separately, and choose X_T to maximize $P(X_T|Y_{1:T})$ and $P_i(O|\lambda)$. S_i can be considered as the similarity between user i and the target user, wherever λ is HMM parameter for a target user. N uers of the most similarity will join the nearest neighbor set.

4 Evaluation of experiment

Experimental process is: (1) Calculate the similarity between the users by training set, and find the nearest neighbours of users in various scenarios.(2) Predict all of the items of the whole users, then figure out the collection of recommended results.(3) Using recommendation results and real record in test set, calculate recommended efficiency according to the evaluation standards.

Five parameters are used in the experiment, the access time of queries, IP address, URL, browse number and page load time. We take experiment with five users(for user1, user2, and user3, user5) data. User1 is a target user randomly generated the original 20000 feature vectors(the feature vector has been treated, so there was little obvious mistake in the random data), 10000 of which are used for training network, the format is as follows:(2012-01-2222 : 10 : 15 , 192. 168. 1. 23, http://www.haoting.com/, 15 , 24)(2015-06-0212 : 02 : 15 , 192 . 168 . 1 . 21 , http://www.haoting.com/zhangjie/ , 15 , 122)……

The left 10000 of feature vectors are used for the experiment data of the nearest set recommendation. The same as user1, other users also randomly generate 20000 feature vectors for the recommendation experiment.

First of all, training the nearest set after model updating:

Perform algorithm 3, and calculate the similarity between users (Calculate $P_i(X_T|Y_{1:T})$, and choose X_T to maximize $P_i(X_T|Y_{1:T})$).When $\psi = \xi = 0.5$, new similarity S_i shows in table 1:

Table 1. The similarity of users after model updating

user	State number	Similarity based on HMM	Similarity after model updating

user1	153	0.993	0.996
user2	90	0.647	0.641
user3	145	0.975	0.985
user4	76	0.296	0.287
user5	69	0.188	0.218

This figure shows S_i--the similarity of different users in different states. Predict similarity between user1 and itself is 0.996. It is very intuitive from the figure that user3 is closest to target user1,which can be classified as nearest neighbour set.

Second, the recommendation process of user preference commodities after updating model:

We find the commodity 1001 meets the greatest degree of preferences of user3, and the recommend probability of target users is: $P_{user1, 1001} = 0.9894$.

Add user2 to the nearest neighbour set, calculate formula (14), we still find the commodity 1001 meets the greatest degree of preferences of user3.

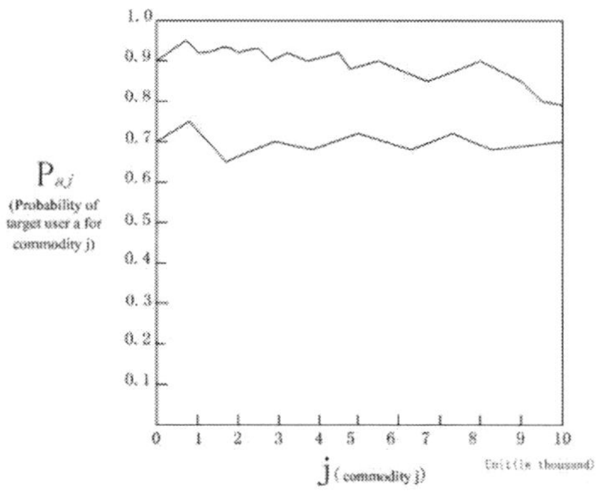

Figure 2. Results of experiment

Experiment result is shown in figure 2.The top curve providing a forecast of preferences probability of target user1 for commodity j with the nearest neighbour set (user3) while the bottom curve providing the results with the nearest neighbour (user3, user2).

5 Conclusion

We mainly introduces the method of updating the model of collaborative filtering recommendation based on access path of users, which takes user's other characteristics into consideration, such as the user's static ratings, by using the high integration of dynamic Bayesian. In this way, we update the model, and achieve the dynamic behaviour data combined with static characteristics of the data, then acquire a more accurate recommendation.

References

1.You Wen, Ye Shui-sheng. A Survey of Collaborative Filtering Algorithm Applied in E -commerce Recommender System[J]. Computer Technology and Development, 2006, 16(9): 57-61.

2.Wang Xia, Liu Qin. Research on Application of Collaborative Filtering in Recommender Systems [J].Applications of The Computer Systems, 2005, 4: 23-27.

3.Huang Guang-qiu, Zhao Yong-mei, Approach to collaborative filtering recommendation based on HMM [J]. Journal of Computer Applications, 2008.28(6)：1601-1604.

4.ZHANG Zi-li, LIU Wei-yi, State prediction based on the dynamic Bayesian network [J]. 2007, 29(1): 35-39.

5.LI Xiao-yi, XU Zhao-di, SUN Xiao-wei. Study on Parameter Learning of Bayesian Network [J].Journal of Shenyang Agricultural University,2007-02,38(1):125-128

6.Wei Fang, Discovering User Interests Based on Bayesian Network [D]. Xi'an: Xi'an University of Architecture and Technology, 2007: 25-29.

7.Liu Jie, Chinese Proper Names Recognition Based on Dynamic Bayesian Network [D], Shanxi: Shanxi University, 2006: 11-13.

8.Sun A-li, Research on Dynamic Bayesian Network Models for Audio-Visual Specch Recognition [D].Xi'an: Northwestern Polytechnical University, 2007: 28-40.

9.Wang Xing-bin, Research on Application of Bayesian Net in Robust Speech Recognition [D]. Henan: The PLA Information Engineering University, 2006:17.

MATEC Web of Conferences 44, 01092 (2016)
DOI: 10.1051/matecconf/20164401092

The Study and Application of "Trinity System" Based on Multi-living Agent Method

Dong Zhong[1,a], Zhong Ming Li[1], Chun Chen[2], Ruo Lin Ruan[3]

[1] *College of electronic and information, Hubei University of Science and Technology, Xianning, China*

[2] *College of Physical Education, Hubei University of Science and Technology, Xianning, China*

[3] *College of biomedical engineering, Hubei University of Science and Technology, Xianning, China*

Abstract—"Trinity System", which is consisted of "110,122,119" three police command stations merging into a police command center, the system is to achieve a unified alarm, unified command, joint action and to provide emergency services and urban public security. Multi-living Agent Method is a new method to analysis the complex system. This paper proposes to use a new method of multi-living agent to design "Trinity System" based on analyzing the traditional "Trinity System", according to the guiding theory of the system. The paper designs the whole framework and system software architecture of "Trinity System". It provides a good research direction to enhance the capabilities of emergency response for "Trinity System".

1 Introduction

With the rapid development of the economy and society, the city public security has become an increasing important issue. Because urban disasters and emergencies can not be avoided completely and a single sector of the government subordinate agencies is difficult to deal with the disasters and emergencies, meanwhile solving the memory and distinguish of special service code, we need to build emergency response mechanism. The key problem is to achieve "110,122,119" three police command units merging into a police command center, this is the "Trinity System". It can achieve a unified alarm, unified command, joint action to ensure emergency services and city public security. "Trinity System" [1] is an integrated system, which is consists of several subsystems. Meanwhile, "Trinity System" is a complex information system. This paper proposes to use a new method of multi-living agent to design "Trinity System" based on analyzing the traditional "Trinity System", according to the guiding theory of the system. The paper designs the whole framework and system software architecture of "Trinity System", it provides a good research direction to enhance the capabilities of emergency response for "Trinity System".

[a] e-mail: zongdong0129@163.com

2 The basic discussion of "Trinity System", the interposing of "Multi-living Agent" method

2.1 "Trinity System" is Related closely to and

Article available at http://www.matec-conferences.org or http://dx.doi.org/10.1051/matecconf/20164401092

System Theory

In addition to the general system characteristics, "Trinity System" has the characteristic of modular hierarchical system architecture design, the system software core is based on a unified messaging service platform, it merges independent species (110, 119,122) departments, multiple data, various business into a system, it can select the number of subsystems according to the actual need[2].

The core principles of system theories, such as the movement of the formation about open dissipative system layer self-organizing mechanism, evolution of the system and environment, and so on. These system theories summarized highly the trend of the dynamic development. They have practical significance for the study of "Trinity System" [3]. For example, the improving of the police efficiency is related with the response alarm systems, the environment of command and control system, a unified monitoring and management platform. It requires the system and environment co-evolution to achieve our expected requirements. In this case, In this case, this paper proposes the new method of multi-living agent to analyze and study the whole framework and system software architecture. It has important significance to improve the emergency response capacity of "Trinity System".

2.2 The basic Idea of "Multi-living Agent"

In the first, the "living" in "Multi-living agent" only comes from the word of the function (action), then it became a specific technical word by re-define the specific examples after the application[4] [5]. It can be divided into three cases:

1) The word can be used only in a qualitative sense, which is corresponding with resting state or non-live (moving) of (inactivity);

2) The word has been defined as a measure of activity intensity. If it has been given the meaning of the activity, we should use the activation in the general; if the activity meaning has been removed, then we should use the non-activation or inactivation and other words;

3) To the physiological processes occurring in the organism or in active state or property; "Living" means a nature of activity for the vitality which is going on a tenacious.

"Living" gives the vigor to the system. It has showed the character of the survival and development for "Trinity System", it plays a important role in various functions. The "more" in "Multi-active agent" reflects the multiple functions in "Trinity System" [6] [7], it has the essential attributes of multiple location, multiple levels and a number of related subsystems, the "proxy " in "multi-living agent" integrated the tendency of the human, the system function, the system's basic structure and operation of the system based on" living "sense, mapping the future vision into reality system or a representative system, it also can be mapped to a specific system, namely "Trinity System", this system has the man-machine integration, scheduling on-site emergency response center and the combination of characteristics[8]. This paper proposes the whole framework and system software architecture based on the above basic characteristics of multi-active agent.

3The design of the whole framework and system software architecture for "trinity system" based on multi-living agent method

3.1 The Design of the whole Framework for "Trinity System" based on Multi-living Agent

This paper designs the whole framework for "Trinity System" based on multi-living agent, the system is constituted of a unified monitoring and management platform, the shared platform of the plans for management, GIS/GPS sharing platform, the exchange platform for information sharing, communication integration services platform, database sharing platform. This multi-agent system is mainly to provide daily communication support for the activity of the Public Order (110) Patrol (122), Fire (119) emergency services. In addition, it is to avoid duplication investment of the government, it also can provide daily scheduling tool for urban management, forest fire, flood and other government departments. Figure1 has shown the whole framework:

For the whole framework of "Trinity System", this paper has a preliminary study based on multi-living agent approach, it is equivalent to using the multi-living agent approach to study a complex information system. For the "Trinity System", from the point of system theory, this is a complex information system and it is associated with assistant scheduling decision function, meanwhile it is a further high-level decision problem of remote dispatching. In this complex information system, "living" means in the top can be understood to make great effort to protect the network management and remote dispatching center to take the most efficient way to provide daily services for emergency communications support. At the same time, "living" also represents the timeliness and effectiveness measures of the communication when a problem comes from the system or communication handicaps occurs. "Multi-living" represents the functioning coordination among the various business systems platform agent layer (for example, response alarm system, information distribution system, a unified monitoring and management platform, GIS/GPS sharing platform, the exchange platform for information sharing, communication integration services platform, database, and various sub-sharing platform system). Meanwhile, under the construction of each "living agent", the agents can be divided into various sub-agents, such multi-level decomposition until a layer of specific hardware and software agents.

3.2 The design of system software architecture for "Trinity System" based on Multi-living Agent

The work model of "Trinity System" is a combined of unified alarm, unity and reunification alarm response alarm, the United Source police combination. The alarm command center dispatches directly to the fire command center, traffic police, patrol, police station and other police. Alarming unified platform is one of the main objectives of system implementation, Alarming platform software components are divided according to application level, we design the multi-living agent software system block diagram of "Trinity System" shown in Figure2:

The software system has been design in modular idea, the alarm system is consists of a unified platform services layer, support layer, the operating system layer, networking layer. The system should guarantee the access of the underlying, business processes and business systems are independent interfaces each other. From the viewpoint of system theories, this multi-living agent software architecture is also a complex information system. The system is mainly to achieve a unified response alarm, "110,122,119" merging into a unified response alarm platform. The paper divides the basic modules of the software system in accordance with the application of the software. It can ensure the independence among each module. The meaning of "living" in the multi-living agent software system can be understood to achieve the unity of response alarm, it can ensure the scheduling decision. At the same time, "living" also represents the business in case of alarm, the police intelligence information access interface, and police issued the interface, alarm forwarding interfaces and the external application interface are to ensure a unify platform software alarm information exchanging with the outside timeliness and effectiveness of the entire system to ensure data security. "Multi-living" represents the coordination and support of each business layer proxy of multi-agent software architecture (such as the access layer, interface layer, unified alarm platform services layer, unified platform support layer, the operating system level, network interconnection system layer, and so on.). The multi-living agent software architecture has the basic functions and features of following: Network connectivity layer proxy and the operating system layer proxy are the underlying software architecture of multi-living agent. It can ensure the system's security, stability and versatility. Support system layer proxy is running for the underlying application.

4 Conclusions

This paper proposes to use a new method of multi-living agent to design "Trinity System" based on analyzing the traditional "Trinity System", according to the guiding theory of the system. "Multi-living" represents the

functioning coordination among the various business systems platform agent layer and system, through this , the whole framework has been designed in the paper. Meanwhile, software architecture of "Trinity System" including a unified platform services layer, support layer, the operating system layer, networking layer has been use the same method to research. It provides a good research direction to enhance the capabilities of emergency response for "Trinity System".

Acknowledgements

The authors gratefully acknowledge the financial support for this work provided by the education department of Hubei Province Science and technology research project, No. B2015077; the colleges and universities of Hubei Province in 2014 the Provincial College Students' innovation and entrepreneurship training plan, No. 201410927025 and 201410927029; The school educational reform key projects of Hubei University of Science and Technology, No. 2014-XA-007 and 2014-XC-025;The National Natural Science Foundation of China (NSFC) under the Grant No. 61271256 and 61575148; the Team Plans Program of the Outstanding Young Science and Technology Innovation of Colleges and Universities in Hubei Province, Grant No.T201513, the Program of the Natural Science Foundation of Hubei Province, Grant No. 2014BAA315 and No. 2015CFB452.

References

[1]. Arun Jotshi, Qiang Gong and Rajan Batta. Dispatching and Routing of Emergency Vehicles in Disaster Mitigation Using Data Fusion. Socio-Economic Planning Sciences, 43 pp 1-24, 2009

[2]. Ryan D. Murphy, Ben Torralva, Steven M and Yalisove. "The role of an interface on Ni film removal and surface roughness after irradiation by femtosecond laser pulses," Appl. Phys. Lett. 2014,102, 181602-181606

[3]. Yuanming Sun. "Solutions to the problems of urban emergency response system in China" (in Chinese), Chongqing Administration, No.5 2006,pp:75-77.

[4]. Haifeng Deng.Clean Development Mechanism right object of Energy Resources Law. Tsinghua University Research Center Web site . 2014.

[5]. Zhou Xie. Analysis on the Legal Property of the Certified Emission Reductions(CERs) in the project of CDM. 2014 International Conference on Education Reform and Management Innovation.

[6]. Yue Wang. The new method for the construction of complex information system - multiple active agents [J]. China engineer science, 2006, 8(5): 30—34.

[7]. ZhongDong, Chen chun. The study of scheduling function optimization for trunking communication system in CERS[J]. Science, technology and engineering, 2011, 18(3): 211-213.

[8]. Lin P,Lo S M,Ng W C.A GIS-Queue Model and Its Application to Regional Evacuation. Journal of Basic Science and Engineer- ing . 2015.

[9]. Atkey.D.A. Practical methodology for the measurement of screening effectiveness of trunking. IEEE Conference Publication n 464, 2008, pp: 77-83.

[10]. G L Stüber. Principles of Mobile Communication[M] . Kluwer Academic Publishers , Second Edition 2001.

[11]. Thompdon P A,Marchant E W.A computer model for the evacuation of large building populations. Fire Safety Journal . 2014.

[12]. Lai Hong Xiao, Cui Yingan, Cui Duwu. Call center architecture based on generic sound card [J]. Computer Engineering, 2007, 22 (33):73-75.

[13]. Atkey.D.A. Practical methodology for the measurement of screening effectiveness of trunking.IEEE Conference Publication n 464, 2008, pp: 77-83.

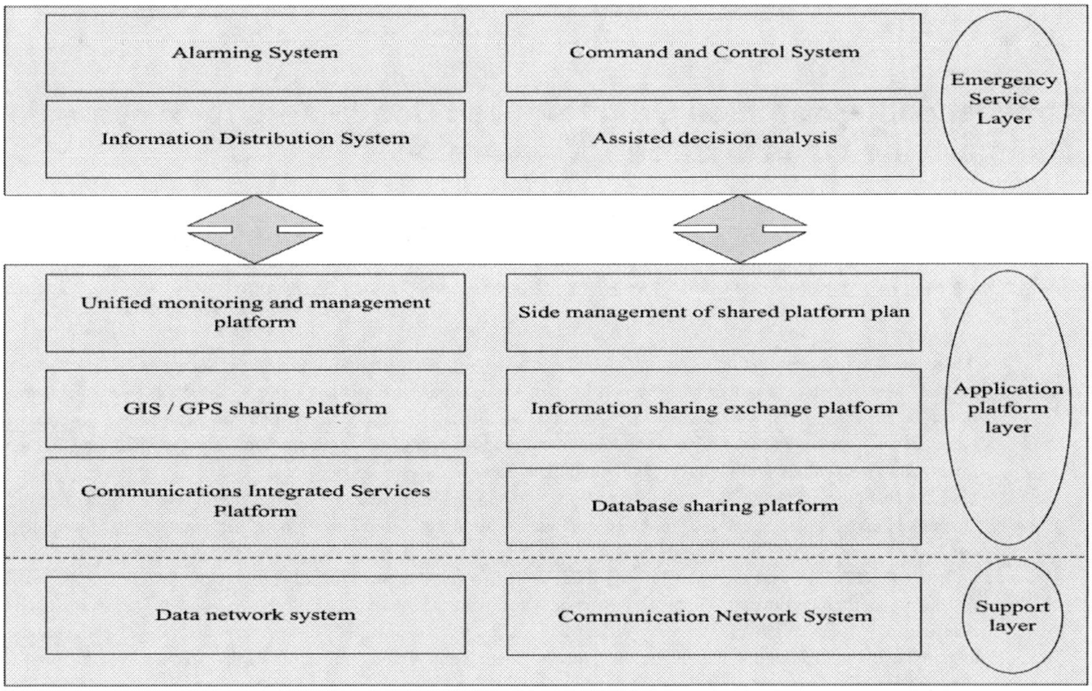

Figure1 Three more than one active agent system block diagram of the overall framework

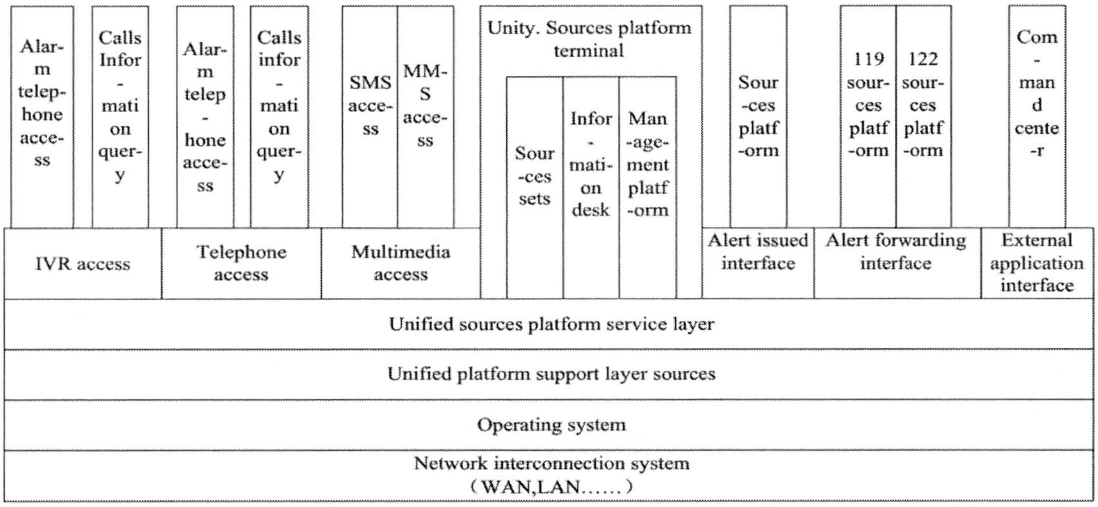

Figure2 Three more than one active agent software system block diagram

The first Author Introduction: Dong Zhong (1980--), Ph. D. His current research area is signal and communication system.

MATEC Web of Conferences 44, 01093 (2016)
DOI: 10.1051/matecconf/20164401093

Application Research on Drag Reduced Conductors for Electric Power Transmission Lines in Strong Wind Areas

Dong Qing Li[1,a], Zhen Li[1], Zhen Liu[1], Long Liu[1], Chang Long Yang[2], Wei Fan[2], Lu Yu Yang[2] and Jia Jun Si[1]

[1]*China Electric Power Research Institute, Beijing 102401, China*
[2]*Electric Power Research Institute, State Grid Liaoning Electric Power Supply Co. Ltd., Shenyang 110006, China*

Abstract. The breeze vibration duration of conductors is long, the vibration amplitude is strong and the frequency range is wide for electric power transmission lines in strong wind areas, which seriously affects the safe and stable operation of transmission lines. There are two design schemes of conductors which can achieve the purpose of reducing wind-induced disaster. One is enhancing the structural strength of conductors to withstand wind load, but the investment is enormous and the effect is limited. The other is developing drag reduced conductors to reduce wind load by changing conductor structure. This paper started from application feasibility analysis of drag reduced conductors and designed four drag reduced conductors by structure optimization of the conventional aluminium conductor steel reinforced JL/G1A-630/45-45/7, denoted as DFY630/45(45°)-R3.5, DFY630/45(60°)-R3.5, DFY630/45(45°)-R3.2 and DFY630/45(60°)-R3.2, respectively. The wind tunnel test was performed and the wind resistance coefficients in unit length of five conductors were compared. Result showed that the wind resistance coefficients in unit length of four drag reduced conductors were obviously lower than that of the conventional conductor. By controlling the manufacturing process, popularization and application of drag reduced conductors for transmission lines in strong wind areas can be realized.

1 Introduction

With the development of China's economy and the improvement of people's living standard, the power demand of whole society increases sharply. Since the energy bases are mostly located in the western region but the electric load centres are mainly concentrated in the eastern region, building power bases in the western region and transmitting power to the eastern region is an important channel for meeting power demand and resolving resource conflict. The north-western region in China, especially Xinjiang, Gansu and Ningxia Province belong to strong wind areas, the duration of strong wind is long and the wind speed is even and stable. Electric power transmission lines passing through the above areas will be greatly influenced by the strong wind climate. Under wind excitation conditions, different types of static or dynamic response will occur on the conductor [1]. Operation experience of current transmission lines indicates that the breeze vibration duration of conductors is longer, the vibration amplitude is stronger and the frequency range is wider under continuous strong wind conditions in the north-western region, which seriously affects the safe and stable operation of transmission lines and causes enormous economic losses.

Under strong wind conditions, enormous investment is often required to withstand wind load only by improving the structure strength of conductors, and the effect has certain limitation. In contrast to this, developing drag reduced conductors based on structure optimization of conventional conductors is an effective way to realize wind load reduction. The popularization and application of drag reduced conductors in strong wind areas can substantially reduce the design load of conductor structure and consequently save the construction investment, which has significant economic benefit and brilliant application prospect.

2 Application status of drag reduced conductors

The drag reduced conductor is a dedicated conductor for overhead transmission lines which can reduce wind load when applied in strong wind areas. Based on comprehensive consideration of conductor structure and surrounded flow field, the characteristics of flow field can be changed by changing the conductor structure, and finally the reduction of wind load can be realized [2].

In the 1970s, researchers in Japan began to study the drag reduced conductors. Some test results were obtained, but associated achievements were rarely applied in practical engineering. From the 1990s, intensive study on drag reduced conductors was continuously performed by Japanese researchers, and obvious advancements were obtained in mechanism study of wind load reduction and practical application of drag reduced conductors [2]. In

[a]Corresponding author: lidongqing1016@163.com (D. Li)

2006, the DR-HAL-type 820 mm^2 drag reduced conductor manufactured by Japan Furukawa Electric Company was used in the 330kV transmission line constructed by Australia Western Power Company. In 2009, the DR-ACSR/AC-type 410 mm^2 drag reduced conductor manufactured by Japan Furukawa Electric Company was used in the 275 kV transmission line constructed by Japan Kansai Electric Power Company. In addition, the DR-ACSPUAC-type 680 mm^2 drag reduced conductor manufactured by Japan Furukawa Electric Company will be used in the 154 kV transmission line constructed by Japan Shikoku Electric Power Company.

In recent years, some domestic research institutes such as China Electric Power Research Institute and Jiangsu Zhongtian Technology Co. Ltd. also made an effort on the development of drag reduced conductors, but systematic study was lacked and products cannot be directly applied in practical engineering.

3 Structure design of drag reduced conductors

The reducing effect of wind load, the constructability and corona characteristics of conductors should be comprehensively considered during conductor design. Previous studies suggested that the aerodynamic drag coefficient corresponding to the critical Reynolds number of the conductor decreased with the increase of surface roughness of the conductor, and the wind load withstood by the conductor consequently decreased [3]. In addition, as compared to the conductor with round section, aerodynamic drag distribution along the conductor with elliptic section was uneven, which made the conductor have combined characteristics of low wind load and low noise [4]. Based on the above results, the drag reduced conductors were designed as follows at the early stage: one was that several wires with larger size were applied in the outer layer of the conductor to form protrusions and increase surface roughness. The other was that several wires with different section were applied in the outer layer of the conductor to obtain elliptic section. Wind tunnel test results showed that these two conductors had lower wind resistance coefficient in unit length than conventional conductors. However, there existed great difficulty during stringing construction process for these two conductors. When tension stringing was employed, the structure of conductors would be seriously destructed after passing through the pulley. Besides, the corona excitation voltage of these two conductors decreased sharply as compared to conventional conductors.

Based on the above analysis, a slotting way on the outside surface of the conductor with round section was employed for structure design to realize a good balance between reducing wind load and increasing construction difficulty as well as decreasing corona excitation voltage. Table 1 lists main technical parameters of the conventional aluminium conductor steel reinforced JL/G1A-630/45-45/7. Fig. 1 shows the schematic sections of the conventional conductor and four designed drag reduced conductors, denoted as DFY630/45(45°)-R3.5, DFY630/45(60°)-R3.5, DFY630/45(45°)-R3.2 and DFY630/45(60°)-R3.2, respectively. As compared to the conventional conductor, shaped wires were applied in the outer layer of drag reduced conductors instead of round wires, and the outside surface was slotted. For four drag reduced conductors, the open-angle and arc radius of the outside surface were different from each other.

Table 1. Main technical parameters of conventional aluminium conductor steel reinforced JL/G1A-630/45-45/7.

Item name	Item contents
Type of conductor	JL/G1A-630/45-45/7
Name of conductor	Aluminium conductor steel reinforced
Strand number/diameter of aluminium single wire (piece/mm)	45/4.22
Strand number/diameter of galvanized steel wire (piece/mm)	7/2.81
Sectional area of conductor (mm^2)	674.0
Outer diameter (mm)	33.8
Rated tensile force (kN)	≥150.45
Elastic module of conductor (GPa)	63.0
Thermal expansion coefficient of conductor (10^{-6}/°C)	20.9×10^{-6}
DC resistance at 20 °C (Ω/km)	≤0.0459

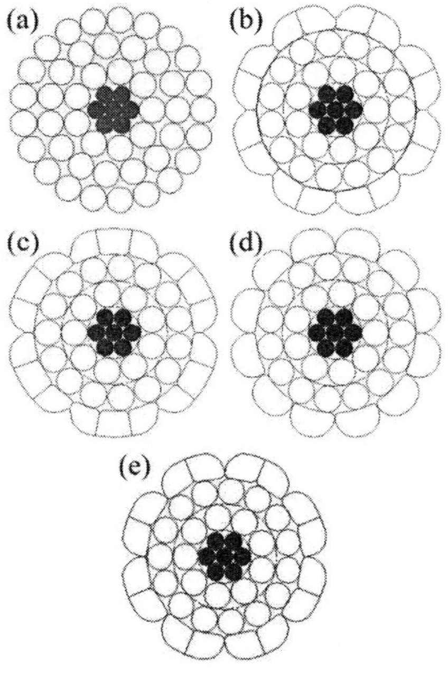

Figure 1. Schematic sections of the conventional conductor and four designed drag reduced conductors: (a) conventional conductor JL/G1A-630/45-45/7, (b) DFY630/45(45°)-R3.5, (c) DFY630/45(60°)-R3.5, (d) DFY630/45(45°)-R3.2 and (e) DFY630/45(60°)-R3.2.

4 Wind tunnel test results and discussion

In order to investigate the wind load reducing effect of drag reduced conductors, wind tunnel test was carried out to obtain the wind resistance coefficient in unit length. The wind tunnel test was completed in the low speed aerodynamics lab of China Aerodynamics Research and Development Centre. The size of test section was 1.4 m×1.4 m×2.8 m, and continuous wind speed at 10~70 m/s can be generated in the wind tunnel. Considering the wind speed range in strong wind areas, six wind speed scales including 20 m/s, 30 m/s, 40 m/s, 50 m/s, 60 m/s and 70 m/s were employed in the test. During testing, the data collection frequency of the force measurement balance was 1000 Hz and the collecting time was 1 min. Figure 2 shows the arrangement of conductor samples during wind tunnel testing. Two working conditions including the angle between the conductor and the incoming flow at 90° and 60° were considered.

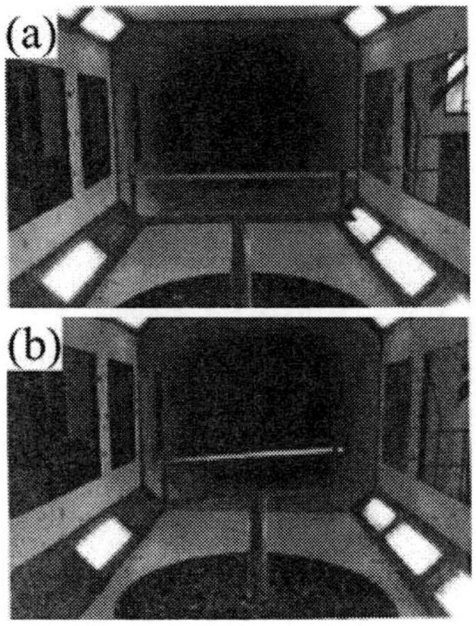

Figure 2. Arrangement of conductor samples during wind tunnel testing: (a) angle between conductor and incoming flow was 90° and (b) angle between conductor and incoming flow was 60°.

The wind resistance coefficient in unit length of the conductor can be calculated by the following equation [5]:

$$C_d = \frac{F_d}{\frac{1}{2}\rho u^2 Ld} \tag{1}$$

where C_d represents wind resistance coefficient in unit length of the conductor, F_d represents wind resistance of the conductor (N), ρ represents air density (kg/m^3), u represents wind speed (m/s), L represents length of the conductor (m) and d represents diameter of the conductor (m). The value of F_d can be directly measured by the force measurement balance. Introduce the value of F_d and other parameters into equation (1) and the value of C_d can be obtained. Table 2 and table 3 list the calculation results, in which 1# represents the conventional conductor JL/G1A-630/45-45/7, 2# represents the drag reduced conductor DFY630/45(45°)-R3.5, 3# represents the drag reduced conductor DFY630/45(60°)-R3.5, 4# represents the drag reduced conductor DFY630/45(45°)-R3.2 and 5# represents the drag reduced conductor DFY630/45(60°)-R3.2. Figure 3 shows the corresponding relationship curves between the wind resistance coefficient in unit length of the conductor and the wind speed. In can be seen from the figure that the wind resistance coefficients in unit length of four drag reduced conductors were obviously lower than that of the conventional conductor when the wind speed was larger than 30 m/s. This indicates that the slotting way on the outside surface of the conductors with round section significantly decreased the wind load withstood by the conductors and the wind load reducing effect was more obvious under strong wind conditions. Furthermore, it can also be seen from the figure that the wind resistance coefficients in unit length of four drag reduced conductors were close to each other, but slight difference also existed. Among the conductors, DFY630/45(45°)-R3.2 showed the lowest wind resistance coefficient in unit length, followed by DFY630/45(60°)-R3.2. This suggests that the wind load reducing effect of the conductor became more obvious with the reduction of open angle and arc radius of the outside surface of the conductor.

5 Manufacturing process of drag reduced conductors

The manufacturing process of the drag reduced conductor is basically consistent with that of the conventional conductor, which mainly includes aluminium ingot melting, insulating, casting, continuous rolling, wire drawing, wire twisting, packaging and transporting. But as compared to the conventional conductor, the following key points should be noted during manufacturing process of the drag reduced conductor:

(1) High-quality aluminium ingots should be used as raw materials and the composition of aluminium liquid should be effectively controlled by trace element treatment technology to guarantee the tensile strength and resistance rate of aluminium wires.

(2) Strengthen uniformity of aluminium wires should be effectively controlled by keeping aluminium liquid temperature uniform during continuous casting and rolling process, and emulsification liquid should be employed in the climbing pipe to eliminate self-annealing effect.

(3) Impurity level of aluminium wires should be effectively controlled. High-efficient and nontoxic refinery agent should be employed to remove hydrogen and alumina impurities in the aluminium liquid, and ceramic filter board should be placed in the casting drum to remove the slag in the aluminium liquid during casting process.

(4) Quality of wire drawing should be effectively controlled. High-quality wire drawing oil should be applied to guarantee the cleanness and surface quality of aluminium wires, and polycrystalline mould should be applied to improve production efficiency and guarantee product quality.

Table 2. Wind resistance coefficients in unit length of conductors under different wind speeds (angle between conductor and incoming flow was 90°)

Wind speed (m/s)	1#	2#	3#	4#	5#
20	0.98386	1.12814	1.07772	1.08130	1.08941
30	1.06949	0.94017	0.95439	0.93193	0.90630
40	0.94393	0.81939	0.84519	0.82518	0.83458
50	0.98091	0.87536	0.90226	0.83663	0.88052
60	0.96887	0.89281	0.90255	0.85423	0.86761
70	0.99009	0.90991	0.92066	0.87914	0.88313

Table 3. Wind resistance coefficients in unit length of conductors under different wind speeds (angle between conductor and incoming flow was 60°)

Wind speed (m/s)	1#	2#	3#	4#	5#
20	0.62228	0.57902	0.56156	0.62025	0.52541
30	0.64171	0.62129	0.62112	0.58154	0.57319
40	0.64860	0.58368	0.59606	0.57329	0.59369
50	0.66019	0.59569	0.62192	0.56689	0.61654
60	0.62887	0.61036	0.61578	0.56229	0.60266
70	0.65989	0.63868	0.62902	0.56640	0.62348

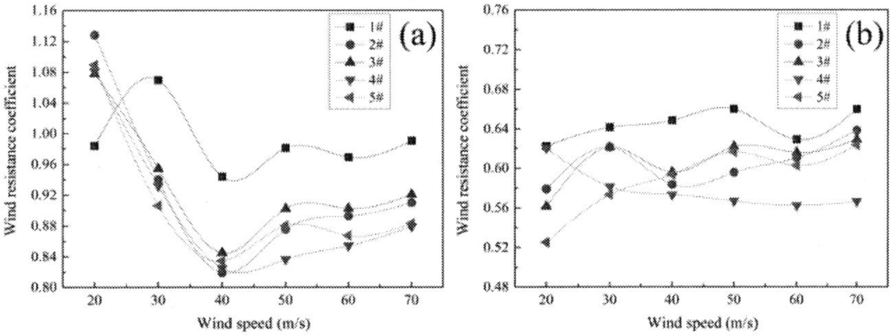

Figure 3. Relationship curves between wind resistance coefficient in unit length of conductors and wind speed: (a) angle between conductor and incoming flow was 90° and (b) angle between conductor and incoming flow was 60°.

(5) The pre-twisted device and the wire tension adjustment device should be reasonably designed to guarantee twisting quality of conductors.

6 Conclusions

In this paper, four drag reduced conductors were designed based on the structure optimization of the conventional aluminium conductor steel reinforced. The wind tunnel test was performed and the manufacturing process of drag reduced conductors was analyzed. Conclusions can be drawn as follows:

(1) The wind resistance coefficients in unit length of four drag reduced conductors were obviously lower than the conventional conductor. The slotting way on the outside surface of the conductors with round section

significantly decreased the wind load withstood by the conductor.

(2) The reducing effect of wind load was related to opening angle and arc radius of the outside surface of the conductor.

(3) The manufacturing process of drag reduced conductors was basically consistent with the conventional conductor. And the popularization and application of drag reduced conductors for electric power transmission lines in strong wind areas can be realized by finely controlling the manufacturing process to guarantee product quality.

References

1. D.Y. Kong, L. Li, X.H. Long, Z.P. Liang, Journal of Vibration and Shock **26**, 64 (2007)
2. C.Y. You, Electric Power Construction **31**, 1 (2010)
3. S. Zheno, Sumitomo electrics **122**, 61 (1983)
4. C.Y. You, Electric Power Construction **26**, 1 (2005)
5. P.Dang, X.M. Wu, B. Liu, L. Wang, W. Zeng, Q. Zheng, C.H. Li, Electric Wire & Cable **4**, 30 (2014)

MATEC Web of Conferences 44, 01094 (2016)
DOI: 10.1051/matecconf/20164401094

Structure Design and Service Performance Study of Low Wind-pressure Conductor

Zhao Lin Wang[1], Dong Qing Li[1,a], Hong Yu Zhang[2], Pei Xian Cong[2], Wei Li[2], Zhen Liu[1], Long Liu[1] and Jia Jun Si[1]

[1]*China Electric Power Research Institute, Beijing 102401, China*
[2]*Electric Power Research Institute, State Grid Liaoning Electric Power Supply Co. Ltd., Shenyang 110006, China*

Abstract. The low wind-pressure conductor is a dedicated conductor which obtains low wind resistance coefficient by changing the sectional shape of the conductor and has extensive application prospect in electric power transmission lines in strong wind areas. Previous wind tunnel testing results showed that the wind resistance coefficient in unit length of the low wind-pressure aluminium conductor steel reinforced was obviously lower than that of the conventional aluminium conductor steel reinforced, and the control factors of manufacturing process of the low wind-pressure conductor were proposed. In this paper, the low wind-pressure aluminium conductor steel reinforced JLX1/G1A(DFY)-680/45-338 was designed based on the structure optimization of the conventional aluminium conductor steel reinforced JL/G1A-630/45-45/7, and the service performance study of the conductor was carried out. Results showed that the mechanical properties, electrical properties and construction properties of the low wind-pressure conductor fully satisfied service requirements, and the conductor can be popularized and applied for transmission lines in strong wind areas.

1 Introduction

Different types of static or dynamic response will occur on the conductor under wind excitation conditions [1]. Since the 21st century, with the rapid enlargement of power grid scale and continuous evolution of climate and environment in our country, wind-induced disasters of the conductors become more serious. The typical disasters caused by wind on the conductors mainly include breeze vibration, windage yaw, gallop and subspan oscillation. Statistic data indicate that destructions caused by wind load occurred in nearly one thousand electric power transmission lines in our country in recent years, which resulted in serious economic losses and social influence. Furthermore, with the development of west to east power transmission strategy in our country, more transmission lines pass through the strong wind areas in the north-western region. The strong wind environment in the north-western region proposes higher requirements on the operational safety and reliability of transmission lines, especially Xinjiang, Gansu and Ningxia Province, in which the duration of strong wind is long and the wind speed is even and stable. The operation experience of existed transmission lines shows that the breeze vibration duration of conductors is longer, the vibration amplitude is stronger and the frequency range is wider under continuous strong wind conditions in the north-western region, and the windage yaw and subspan oscillation also frequently occur.

Vast investment is often required to realize the purpose of withstanding wind load only by improving the structure strength of conductors under strong wind conditions, and the wind load withstanding effect has certain limitation. In contrast to this, developing low wind-pressure conductors based on structure optimization of conventional conductors is an effective way to realize wind load reduction, which has brilliant application prospect. In addition, the popularization and application of low wind-pressure conductors in the regular region can substantially reduce the design load of conductor structure and consequently save the construction investment, which can realize enormous economic benefit.

Early in the 1970s, researchers in Japan began to study the low wind-pressure conductors. Some testing results were obtained, but associated research achievements were rarely applied in practical engineering. From the 1990s, Japanese researchers continued to conduct further study of low wind-pressure conductors and obtained obvious advancement in mechanism study of wind-pressure reduction and practical application of low wind-pressure conductors [2]. In this paper, the service performance study of low wind-pressure conductors was carried out, aiming to promote the application of low wind-pressure conductors for transmission lines in strong wind areas.

[a]Corresponding author: lidongqing1016@163.com (D. Li)

2 Structure design of low wind-pressure conductor

During conductor design, the reducing effect of wind load and the constructability and corona characteristics of conductors should be comprehensively considered. In this paper, the design work was carried out based on the structure optimization of the conventional aluminium conductor steel reinforced JL/G1A-630/45-45/7, and the low wind-pressure aluminium conductor steel reinforced JLX1/G1A(DFY)-630/45-338 was consequently obtained. Structures of the above two conductors are shown in Figure 1, and technical parameters are listed in Table 1.

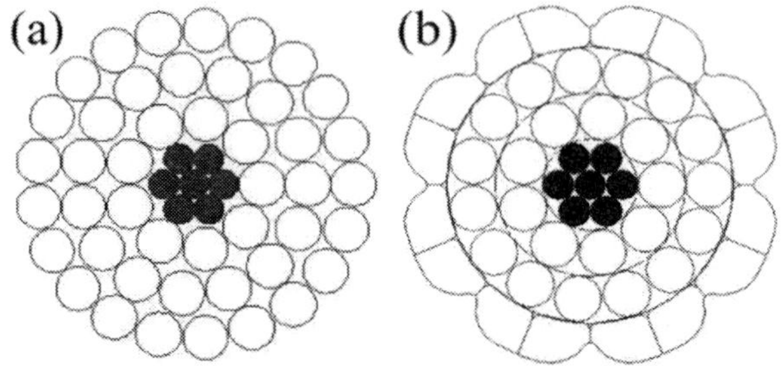

Figure 1. Structures of conductors: (a) Conventional aluminium conductor steel reinforced JL/G1A-630/45-45/7 and (b) low wind-pressure aluminium conductor steel reinforced JLX1/G1A(DFY)-630/45-338.

Table 1. Technical parameters of conductors.

Item name	Item content	
Conductor mould	JL/G1A-630/45-45/7	JLX1/G1A(DFY)-630/45-338
Conductor name	Aluminium conductor steel reinforced	Low wind-pressure aluminium conductor steel reinforced
Strand number/diameter of single aluminium wire (piece/mm)	45/4.22	45/4.22
Strand number/diameter of galvanized steel wire (piece/mm)	7/2.81	7/2.81
Sectional area of conductor (mm^2)	674.00	727.52
Outer diameter (mm)	33.80	33.75
Quality in unit length (kg/km)	2079.20	2235.44
Rated tensile force (kN)	≥150.45	≥151.00
Elastic module of conductor (GPa)	63.0	63.6
Thermal expansion coefficient of conductor (10^{-6}/°C)	20.9×10^{-6}	20.9×10^{-6}
DC resistance at 20 °C (Ω/km)	≤0.0459	≤0.0423

3 Tensile strength of single aluminium wires

Figure 2 shows the tensile strength curves of single aluminium wires of the conventional conductor and the low wind-pressure conductor after twisting. It can be seen from the figure that the change rate of tensile strength for these two conductors ranged between -6.96 % and 9.61 %. The numerical dispersion of tensile strength was small, implying that the manufacturing and twisting processes of these two conductors were controlled well. The average value of tensile strength for the conventional conductor after twisting was 191 MPa, and the value specified in technical documents was 150.45 MPa. The average value of tensile strength for the low wind-pressure conductor after twisting was 189 MPa, and the value specified in technical documents was 151 MPa. It can be found that the average values of tensile strength of single aluminium wires for these two conductors after twisting were close to each other and both of them were higher than the value specified in technical documents, indicating that the tensile strength of single aluminium

wires for these two conductors satisfied service requirements.

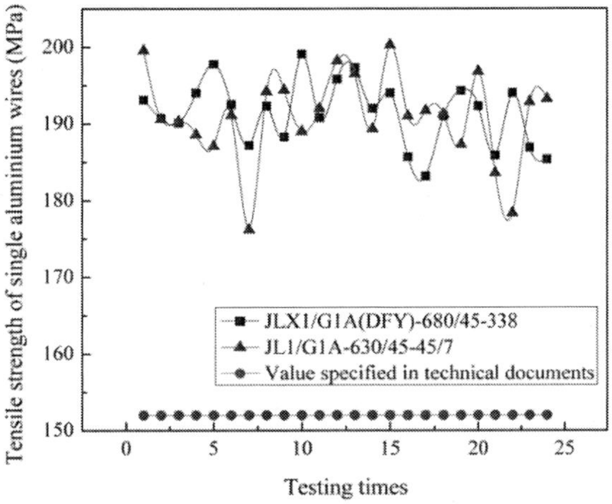

Figure 2. Tensile strength curves of single aluminium wires of the conventional conductor and the low wind-pressure conductor after twisting.

4 Vibration fatigue performance of low wind-pressure conductor

The vibration fatigue test of the low wind-pressure conductor was carried out according to enterprise standard Q/FSDYS 007-2007 'Vibration fatigue testing method of overhead conductors', and the testing tension applied to the conductor was 25 %RTS.

Figure 3. Arrangement of the vibration fatigue test of the low wind-pressure conductor.

During testing, opened the conductor clamp and checked the surface layer of the conductor carefully when the vibration time reached 2×10^7. Results showed that no strand breakage phenomenon was found in the surface layer of the conductor. After the vibration time of the conductor reached 3×10^7, opened the conductor clamp and peeled off the surface layer to check the inner layer of the conductor. Results showed that also no strand breakage occurred on the aluminium wires and galvanized steel wires. This indicates that the vibration fatigue performance of the low wind-pressure conductor satisfied the application requirement according to the enterprise standard.

5 Creep performance of low wind-pressure conductor

Creep test of the low wind-pressure conductor was carried out according to IEC standard 61395-1998 'Creep testing method of overhead naked conductor', and the testing duration was 1000 h. The testing tensions applied to the conductor were 15 %RTS, 25 %RTS and 40 %RTS, respectively. The creep rates and associated equations can be obtained according to testing results by numerical fitting as shown in Table 2. In the table, T means testing duration (unit in h). It can be seen from the table that the creep performance of the low wind-pressure conductor was in consistent with the service requirement in the IEC standard.

Table 2. Creep rates and associated equations of the low wind-pressure conductor.

Strain (kN)	Creep rate equation	Creep rate (%)		
		1000 hours	10 years	30 years
23.84 (15%RTS)	$0.0044T^{0.1965}$	0.0144	0.0346	0.0430
39.74 (25%RTS)	$0.0074T^{0.1957}$	0.0240	0.0575	0.0713
63.58 (40%RTS)	$0.0137T^{0.1939}$	0.0450	0.1072	0.1327

6 Corona and radio interference performance of low wind-pressure conductor

Corona and radio interference test of the low wind-pressure conductor was carried out according to national standard GB/T 2317.2-2008 'Testing method of electric power fittings Part 2: Corona and radio interference test'. One piece of the low wind-pressure conductor with the length of 12 m was prepared and one smooth grading ring with the diameter of 1.2 m was installed on each end of the conductor. For the grading rings, no visible corona can be found when the voltage was 1000 kV or below. After installing the grading rings, the conductor was installed on two strain hoisting points with nylon wires to keep horizontal. The height of the conductor above ground was 10 m.

During corona testing, first boosted the voltage until visible corona was detected by the ultraviolet imager on the conductor and maintained 5 min, and then reduced the voltage slowly until corona disappeared and also maintained 5 min. Recorded the corresponding voltage as the corona extinction voltage [3]. Repeated the above process 5 times and calculated the average value as testing results. Previous studies showed that the corona extinction voltage of the sample under positive DC voltage was higher than that of the sample under negative DC voltage [4]. Therefore, the negative DC voltage was employed during testing.

During radio interference testing, first boosted the voltage to specified value (0.9 times of the corona extinction voltage value of the smooth stainless pipe), and then determined the radio interference voltage RIV at 1 MHz generated in the testing circuit by the radio interferometer. Results of the corona and radio interference test of the low wind-pressure conductor are listed in Table 3. It can be seen from the table that all of the testing results satisfied the service requirement.

Table 3. Corona and radio interference testing results of the low wind-pressure conductor.

Test name	1st time	2nd time	3rd time	4th time	5th time
Corona voltage of smooth steel pipe (kV)	718	717	719	717	716
Corona voltage of conductor (kV)	659	653	661	659	654
Conductor value/steel pipe value	0.916	0.916	0.916	0.916	0.916
Specified value of RIV (μV)	≤1000	≤1000	≤1000	≤1000	≤1000
RIV(μV) actual measured value	645.7	645.7	645.7	645.7	645.7

7 Pulley passing performance of low wind-pressure conductor

The pulley passing test of the low wind-pressure conductor was carried out according to enterprise standard Q/FSDYS 008-2007 'Pulley passing testing method of conductors and ground wires in overhead transmission lines'. The arrangement of testing system is shown in Figure 4 and the testing parameters are listed in Table 4. The testing results are shown as follows: (1) no damage, strand looseness or bulge phenomena were observed on the surface of the conductor after passing through the pulley under the tension of 20 %RTS, (2) the average value of tensile strength of single aluminium wires was 188.1 MPa after passing through the pulley under the tension of 20 %RTS and the specified value in technical requirements was 152 MPa, indicating that the pulley passing performance of the low wind-pressure conductor satisfied the service requirement.

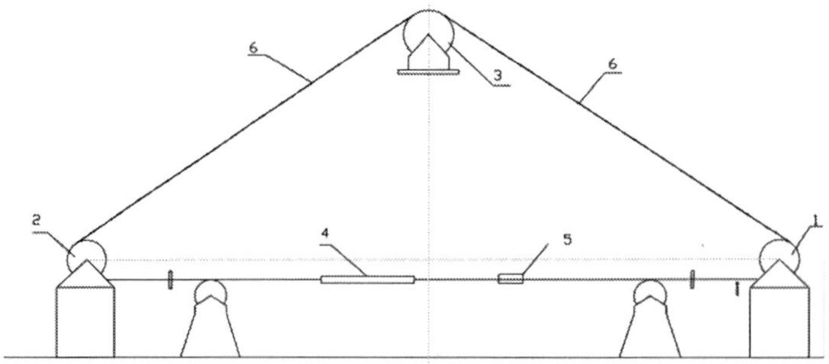

Figure 4. Arrangement of pulley passing testing system of the low wind-pressure conductor: 1-driving pulley block at the bottom, 2-driven pulley block at the bottom, 3-top pulley, 4-loading device, 5-force sensor and 6-sample conductor.

Table 4. Technical parameters of the pulley passing test of the low wind-pressure conductor.

Technical parameters	Value
Tension	30.09 kN (20 %RTS)
Wrap angle	30°
Maximum distance of linear movement of steel wire	6 m
Maximum speed of linear movement of steel wire	0.5 m/s
Reciprocating times of linear movement	10 times
Diameter of pulley	0.7 m

8 Conclusions

In this paper, the low wind-pressure aluminium conductor steel reinforced JLX1/G1A(DFY)-680/45-338 was designed based on the structure optimization of the conventional aluminium conductor steel reinforced JL/G1A-630/45-45/7, and the service performance of the conductors was investigated. Conclusions can be drawn as follows:

(1) The tensile strength of single aluminium wires of the low wind-pressure conductor was close to that of the conventional conductor and satisfied service requirements.

(2) Strand breakage phenomenon did not occur on the aluminium wires and galvanized steel wires of the low wind-pressure conductor after vibration for 3×10^7 times, which satisfied the application requirement.

(3) Both of the corona and radio interference testing results satisfied the service requirement.

(4) No damage was observed on the surface of the conductor after passing through the pulley under the tension of 20 %RTS, and the tensile strength of single aluminium wires satisfied the service requirement.

(5) All of the service performance of the low wind-pressure conductor satisfied the technical requirements, and the conductor can be popularized and applied for transmission lines in strong wind areas.

References

1. D.Y. Kong, L. Li, X.H. Long, Z.P. Liang, Journal of Vibration and Shock **26**, 64 (2007)
2. C.Y. You, Electric Power Construction **31**, 1 (2010)
3. K. Wang, Y.L. Liao, L.M. Wang, Z.C. Guan, F. Huo, W. Hu, High Voltage Engineering 36, 862 (2010)
4. J.B. Fan, Z.X. Li, C. Gu, Y. Yin, Z.Y. Su, Transactions of China Electrotechnical Society 23, 100 (2008)

MATEC Web of Conferences 44, 02001 (2016)
DOI: 10.1051/matecconf/20164402001

Research on Supporting Functions of the Information Technology on Electronic medical record

Sheng Li Hu [1,a] Jin Qing Chi [1] and Zhi Guo [2]

[1] Central Hospital of Cangzhou, Information Center , Hebei Province, China
[2] Central Hospital of Cangzhou, Human Resources Department, Hebei Province,, China

Abstract. Objective: Promote further utilization of information technology in quality control of the electronic medical record and provide forceful technological supports for medical quality control. Method: research existing problems in quality control of electronic medical record at present, put forward that the information technology should be used sufficiently, integration with other systems should be completed, quality control rules should be built and quality control time should be set and finally point out the key construction element of information technology to provide supports. Result: the article points out that further utilization of information technology in quality control of EMR should start from the standard, structuralized and paperless electronic medical record, construction of the communication platform and application of high technology. Conclusion: it is of great significance to promote improvement of quality control level of the electronic medical record and improve continuously medical quality.

1 Introduction

Along with gradually further reform of the health care system, competition in medical market becomes fiercer and fiercer. Among that, medical quality and technology level are the core of the medical market competition. Meanwhile, along with the further development of hospital informatization centering on electronic medical record, the health care industry depends more and more on informatization. The medical quality can be monitored in real time with information technology. It is the important means to improve continuously the medical quality and provide forceful technology guarantee for strengthening monitoring. The application level of information technology directly impacts the medical quality control level of hospitals.

The Basic Norms of Electronic medical record (Trial Implementation) printed and issued by The Ministry of Health also points out that: the electronic medical record system should provide technological support for quality monitoring of medical history, health care service information, data statistic analysis and medical insurance premium audit, take advantages of the system to build medical quality assessment system, improve work efficiency, guarantee medical quality, regularize diagnosis and treatment behavior and improve management level of hospitals. Therefore, it is the essential requirements of realizing intelligence and informatization of medical quality monitoring to build the quality management system of the electronic medical record centering on pre-event reminding, post-event quality control and in-event management.

2 Technology adopted at present by quality control of the electronic medical record

The traditional method of spot check of medical history cannot cover all the medical history, the time is difficult to be grasped accurately, the efficiency is lower and it is hard to improve the quality of medical history. Presently, most hospitals have started to use the electronic medical record and carry out quality control on problems existing in the medical history in an all-round way by adopting the quality control function of the system.

Quality control of the medical history mainly includes three aspects of pre-event reminding, in-event management and post-event quality control. Presently, post-event quality control is adopted by most hospitals, which targets at checking the medical history filed to check the completeness of the writing form of the medical history. When problems are found, the doctor will be informed to modify, however, the patient has left the hospital and it's hard for the doctor to remember the specific condition of the patient, so it will be difficult to guarantee the authenticity and accuracy of the medical history modified, which needs unlocking beforehand. Moreover, because of the limited knowledge of the medical history manager, the manager cannot grasp professional knowledge in each field accurately and it's hard for the manager to find the underlying problems hidden in the medical history. Therefore, hospitals should strive to control the medical quality strictly from the

[a] Corresponding author: Hu Shengli hushenglihsl@139.com

source, change the mode centering on post-event quality control, control the quality of the medical history strictly, find problems, remind the doctor timely, solve problems timely, replace the post-event management with pre-event control and guarantee to accomplish the medical history timely with certain quality.

3 Issues should be paid attention to in construction of the electronic medical record quality control system

3.1. Integration of the electronic medical record with other systems

The electronic medical record system should be integrated with the HIS, PACS, LIS, ECG and operative anesthesia system seamlessly to realize interaction and share of information and avoid occurrence of information isolated island. For example, the hospital can acquire the critical value situation of K, Ca, Na and Cr via the interface with LIS so that the patient can be treated timely in the critical time and saved to a maximum extent. Some hospitals have built data interaction platform and acquire data needed from all sorts of systems [1-3]. This kind of transmission via interchange of XML has great superiority. However, this XML language can only provide syntax norms and cannot realize standardization of syntactic structure and semantics. The use of HIL7 CDA can well realize semantic description of clinical documents of electronic medical record.

It can be seen from the present situation that information systems in most hospitals lack unified and normative interface standard, don't conform to the HL7 standard basically and the standard is not unified, which impact the medical quality control of hospitals and bring difficulties for the development of regional medical informatization.

3.2 Construction of quality control rules.

In the quality control system, the hospital should build quality control points, build various quality control rules and carry out intelligent judgment on quality control rules. Taking the time-bound control of medical history writing for an example, time-bound control is an important means to improve the medical history quality. The electronic medical record can record the creator, the creation time and component names of the template automatically backstage, save all modification trace in the past and mark accurate modification time and information of the person who modifies the medical history. The times are all read-only and the medical workers cannot modify the time. Even though the doctor records an earlier time in the medical history, the quality control is subjected to the backstage record so that the accuracy of quality control can be guaranteed. In addition, the quality control system will check the completeness of the template contents, for example, the resident admission record should include the history of the present illness and the history of the past illness. In the main complaints, there must be the position, symptom and time of duration. The check is subjected to successful save in the data base, so the doctor should develop the habit of saving the template timely.

To acquire relevant information in the electronic medical record via the quality control rules, such as node elements of the position and the symptom in the complaint, the whole structure of these node elements must be disposed. The system will carry out statistic analysis on the standard and structural extracted elements in the value range to provide forceful data support for scientific research and management of medical science.

3.3 Confirmation of the quality control time.

After the confirmation of quality control rules, the following important work is to confirm the quality control time. Taking the confirmation of the time for quality control with time limit for an example, the resident admission record should be accomplished within 24 hours after the patient is admitted to the hospital, which needs to accurately confirm the beginning and stop time of quality control. In the information system of hospitals, there are three choices of hospital admission time, namely the time when the doctor fills in the electronic hospital admission receipt in the outpatient service department, the time when the patient handles hospital admission procedures in the HIS hospital admission office and the time when the doctor gives the first doctor's advice in the resident physician department. Under this situation, it should be taken into consideration that it needs some time for the patient to arrive at the ward to receive treatment of the doctor. Therefore, it is more appropriate to take the time when the doctor gives the first doctor's advice as the hospital admission time.

For quality control with time limit of the medical history, if problem happens, the doctor will be reminded in the form of message and SMS. If the time is forced to be controlled, it will definitely bring unnecessary burden for the doctor. Therefore, it is also an important issue to strengthen communication among the quality control section, medical history room and medical workers.

3.4 Sufficient use of information technology.

In the information system of hospitals centering on the electronic medical record, the information technology should be used sufficiently, for example, the doctor can identify the stupid mistake such as that a male has a menstrual history by virtue of the automatic grading function in the system. To avoid similar medical history and guarantee the quality, technology means should be used to restrict the copy and paste functions, including shortcut keys of CTRL+C and CTRL+V. Same information of one patient can be copied; the copied contents should be checked and information of different patients should not be copied. Outer contents should not be copied to the electronic system and personalized modes should not be introduced. It must be realized that the information technology is not omnipotent. Hospitals should complete the management system; formulate

corresponding rewards and punishment measures depending on the problems existing in the quality control system to improve the enthusiasm of medical workers in writing the medical history.

Hospitals should carry out pre-event monitoring to the greatest extent via informationized means, for example, the surgery grading management can be carried out for doctors and corresponding rights and limits can be set up as per the professional title and the operational qualification of doctors. Hospitals can set up the usage rights of antibiotics in the system as per the qualification and training situation of doctor to make doctors operate within the rights and limits, reduce medical risks and guarantee medical quality.

The electronic medical record quality control system should collect system data in real time and operations such as saving, modification and deleting of data base should be carried out in real time when the doctor writing a medical history. Therefore, it has a high requirement for the server performance, the quality control server should be set up alone and it is more appropriate to choose a high-grade server.

4 The information technology provides key supporting construction elements for quality control of electronic medical record

4.1. Standardization and structuring of electronic medical record system.

The Standardization and structuring of electronic medical record data are critical to realize quality control of electronic medical record. It can be seen from the construction situation of electronic medical record in China that unified data standard has not realized truly. Although many manufacturers claim that their own system is standardized and structured electronic medical record, few of electronic medical record can conform to the Basic Architecture and Data Standard of Electronic medical record, Basic Template Data Set Standard of Electronic medical record Clinic Document, Data Array and Data Element of Electronic medical record Clinic Document and other information data standards or adopt HL7 message standard and CDA [4]. The Implementation Rules for Review Standards of Three-level General Hospitals (2011 Version) of the Ministry of Health explicitly regulates that clinic document presentation should be standardized and CDA is supported. Data standards of electronic medical record include four contents: the data structure of electronic medical record, clinic document information template of electronic medical record, data array and data element standard of clinic documents of electronic medical record and basic template and data set standard of clinic documents of electronic medical record. International and domestic standards with generally mature application should be adopted to practice to the greatest extent. Taking the international classification of diseases code ICD10 for an example, the birth place should not be a text to make doctors input arbitrarily, and a standard national code table of provinces and cities should be provided for the medical workers to conduct standard choice.

For the quality control of medical history, the structural data entry problem should be solved and the structural medical history editor should be adopted to solve the structural data collection problem of medical history writing [5-8]. To guarantee the accuracy of the data collection source, the value range of date elements should also be standardized so that required value range information can be abstracted from the data elements. Presently, the medical history quality control system in some hospitals can abstract relevant structural elements, but these structural elements cannot completely conform to the standard of the Ministry of Health. Along with the continuous improvement of knowledge of the medical science and each social field, the value range of data elements should be updated synchronously to adapt to the continuous improvement of the society.

Along with the coming of the big data times, to efficiently take advantage of the massive amounts of clinic data information, standardized and structural electronic medical record should be realized objectively to exert the use value of medical record to a maximum extent and provide important data supports for clinic scientific research, teaching and management.

The first page of the medical history is the essence, the accuracy and completeness of which must be guaranteed via information technology. Phenomena such as lacunas, omission and incomplete record should be controlled via the information technology and the key quality control points such as the main diagnosis, metastasis and progression, physician's signature, conformity of diagnosis must be filled in. Verification should be carried out as per validation rules, for example, the time of leaving the hospital should not be earlier than the hospital admission time, the time of successful salvage should not be more than the time of salvage and if surgery information has been filled in, the surgery type should be filled in as well.

4.2. Paperless electronic medical record.

To realize automatic and intelligent quality control of electronic medical record, the paperless electronic medical record must be realized firstly, because the quality control system cannot carry out efficient quality control on the paper medical history. Presently, most hospitals in China have adopted the electronic medical record system, but basically they filled in and print the electronic medical record, sign with hand and file the paper medical history in the medical history room, which is a condition that the paper medical history coexists with the electronic medical record and the true paperless electronic medical record has not been realized. If the system has a function defect or the medical workers print the medical history without timely saving the medical history, system data losses will be caused. Medical history quality control under this condition will definitely be impacted significantly. To realize the paperless electronic medical record, it is critical to apply the

electronic signature and the trusted time stamp, which can guarantee the legal enforcement of the electronic medical record and improve the accuracy of medical history quality control as well. Therefore, realization of paperless storage of electronic medical record and establishment of supporting management system are effective ways to improve the quality control level of electronic medical record.

4.3. Construction of the communication platform .

It is of significance to build the information communication platform among quality control managers and medical workers in the system to feed back the quality control result to the corresponding doctor timely, for example, the first time of course of disease should not be more than eight hours and the remaining time should be sent in the system to remind the doctor. If the doctor is only informed in the form of a message window, it will work only when the medical worker log in the electronic medical record and the form is monotonous, so the doctor is informed by the message while being informed in the form of a message window to remind the medical worker to finish the writing of the medical history. For special quality control, for example, the emergent consultation requires that the consultant should arrive at the site within ten minutes after the application of consultation is sent out. It is insufficient only with messages and news, so the telephone needs to be used to send the emergent notice.

Construct the medical history quality control tracking system and trace each problem existing in quality control. If the doctor has written the medical history or modified some problem, the problem will be showed as having been solved in the tracking system. The outstanding problems should be marked with red, which can remind the medical worker again and provide effective evidence when impose implement penalty and punishment on the quality control personnel.

4.4. Application of high and new technology.

Application of high and new technology such as the internet of Things, artificial intelligence and information mobile technology in electronic medical record can effectively improve the quality control level of the medical history, for example, the mobile workstation is used to effectively improve the nursing quality control [9]. The knowledge base provides important support for the writing of structural electronic medical record via artificial intelligent technology. In terms of construction of intelligent knowledge base, some hospitals have carried out useful exploration in knowledge collection and arrangement, knowledge creation and presentation and maintenance and application of knowledge base[10-12].

5 Conclusions

Information technology plays an irreplaceable role in quality control of electronic medical record, decrease of hidden danger of medical treatment, improvement of medical history quality, realization of refined management of hospitals, etc. However, the information technology is not omnipotent. People say that it depends on 30% technology and 70% management. Only they integrate closely can hospitals continuously improve the medical quality and promote continuous improvement of management level.

References

1. Qin Zhizhong, Li Meihua, Wang Wei. Electron Application of Screenshot in the Links Q uality Cotrolof Electronic Medical Records. Chinese Medical Record,7, (2015).
2. SHI Jun—feng, LI Qian—qian, BI Jian—xin. Electronic Medical Records Integrated Management Based on Cloud Computing. Chinese Hospital Management,35,2, (2015).
3. Li Shunfei, Tang Xiaodong, Liu Shunan etal. Design and application of medical record quality management system based on new electronic medical record. Chongqing Medicine,43,19, (2014).
4. Zhang Lei, TYe Zhou, Tuo Kuanqian et al. Development and Application of Intelligent Electronic Medical Record System with Quality and Safety as the Core. China Digital Medicine,9,5, (2014).
5. Chen Dapeng, Chen Jinxiong, Guo Zhixu. Quality Control System of New Type Electronic Medical Record. Hospital Administration Journal of Chinese People's Liberation Army,20,7, (2013).
6. Xiao Qiang, Wu Weibin, Wang Shuyan et al. Research on the Input Method of Semi-structured Electronic Medical Records Based on XML, China Digital Medicine,,10,1, (2015).
7. Qiu Sheng. On the application of structured electronic medical records. Straits Science, 9, (2013).
8. Liu Peng. Research and System Improvement of Structured Electronic Medical Record Storage Retrieval Based on Hadoop. China Digital Medicine,10,20, (2015).
9. Zhu Guojun, Lang Liwei, Lu Weishi et al. Clinical Application of Mobile Nursing Quality Control Information System. China Digital Medicine,8,10, (2014).
10. Pu Xiaoying, Zhao Guangyu, Li Ailing et al. Construction of Informatization Platform to Improve Medical Quality Management. Chinese Health Quality Mangement,20,6, (2013).
11. WANG Wei-min, ZHANG Xue-yan. Problems in electronic medical records of Beijing hospitals and their solutions. Chinese Journal of Medical Library and Information Science,8, (2015).
12. Chen Li, Dai Ziqing, Rong Xia et al. Electronic Medical Record Archiving and Clinical Demands. Chinese Medical Record,8, (2015).

MATEC Web of Conferences 44, 02002 (2016)
DOI: 10.1051/matecconf/20164402002

The Dry-filling System for the Shock Absorber of Car Engine

Rong Du, Li Wen Zhang , Xiao Yan Liu[1]

[1]*Hebei Jiaotong Vocational & Technical College, China*

Abstract. The shock absorber is considered as an important component of the suspension system. In its production process, the liquid filling for the shock absorber is a very important part. This paper introduced one kind of shock absorber stem -filling system, which achieved liquid dry -filling in the shock absorber for the car engine. The results showed that this system is stable and reliable.

1 Introduction

As an important component of the suspension system, the shock absorber of car engine[1] plays a significant role on the passenger comfort, stability and safety. In its production process, the perfusion for the shock absorber is a very important part.
Perfusion is generally divided into wet-filling and dry-filling .Wet-filling means that the artificial materials will be filled into the liquid storage tank. Although providing the products with the vacuum environment, it causes damages to people due to the low production efficiency, the high production cost, and the direct contact with the liquid (ethylene glycol) . At the same time the shell of the product will inevitably cause the liquid residues which influence the stability and security of the vehicles. The development and the manufacture of the shock absorber dry- filling equipment are introduced in the paper. The operation of the equipment is simple, improving the artificial operating environment. At the same time it can improve the production efficiency and the filling precision.

2 The introduction of the system

Dry-filling machine is used to extract the air from the cavity of shock absorber before the vacuum degree reach a certain requirement. Then it infuse the cavity with ethylene glycol, sealing it to ensure that there will be no bubbles in it. The equipment is shown in figure 1.

3 The design of the mechanical parts[3]

The mechanical parts of the system is mainly composed of a station indexing system, a vacuum system, infusion liquid, a residue recovery system and a pressure steel ball system.

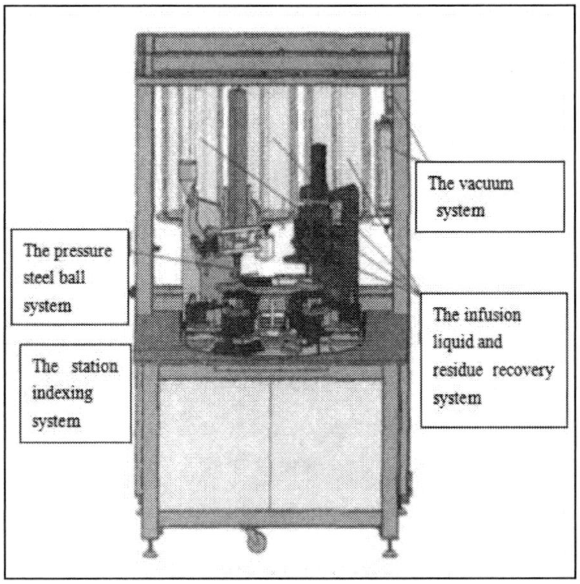

Figure 1. Dry-filling machine system structure.

3.1 The station indexing system

The dry-filling machine station indexing system is shown in figure 2.There are six stations in this part running by clockwise rotation. Each station reserves an interface for the series connection. When a product finishes its work in a certain station, the indexing plate rotating 1/6 circle will make the products into the next station for processing. The control of the stepping motor makes the back wheel intermittent regular motion. The index plate rotation is driven by the cylindrical indexing cam mechanism. When the cam rotates, the dividing section contour will rotate the roller to make the indexing plate rotate. When the cam turn in, the rest period of the

15802285470@126.com

contour, the two adjacent rollers on the torus of the cam will make the rotary plate stop.

The dry-filling machine is in the automatic state. Each station has a memory function on whether there is a material (the feeding station have artifacts into), whether the artifacts are qualified (including the twice vacuumizing and the encapsulation of the pressure steel balls). So if the indexing plate rotates automatically one time, it will send the data to the workstation in turn.

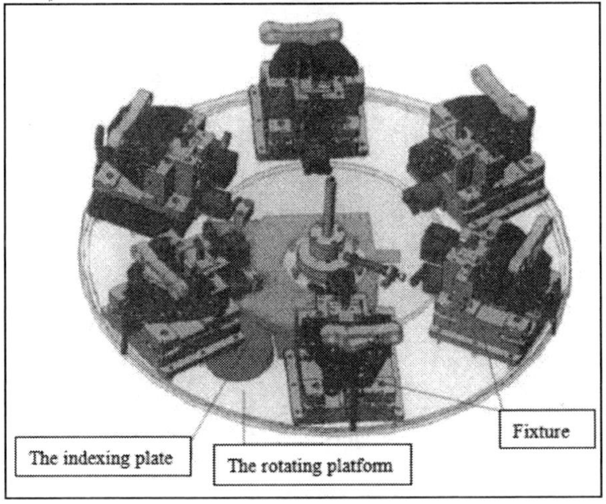

Figure 2. The station indexing system

3.2 The vacuum, infusion liquid and the residue recovery system

Above all, during the whole process of fluid infusion, we should ensure the vacuum degree[3] to meet the requirements.The vacuum requirement refers to the best vacuum optimal value before the infusion vacuumizes the cavity of the product. Generally speaking, the higher the vacuum degree is,the less air bubbles inside the cavity there will be. At the same time, the function of the product will be better. But the high vacuum degree means the high cost of the filling machine. So our design manages to balance the three comprehensive optimal goals---the cost, the efficiency and the function.

The process of the vacuum uses the negative pressure.The exhaust tube controlled by the vacuum system begins to extract air, making the cavity of the product reach the certain vacuum degree.It forms a pressure difference between the cavity and the atmosphere. As a result ,the liquid in the storage tank is filled into the cavity by its gravity caused by the atmospheric pressure inside. According to the requirement of the product specification, the first suction pipe of the system should achieve the vacuum degree for 800 Pa or less while the second suction pipe should reach the vacuum degree for Pa 200 or less. After meeting the vacuum degree requirements, the ethylene glycol from both A and B liquid tanks will be infused into the cavity of the product.The excess liquid around the pipe mouth will be pumped into the residual liquid tank, and then returns to the A/B tanks.The vacuum, the infusion liquid and the residue recovery system are shown in figure 3.

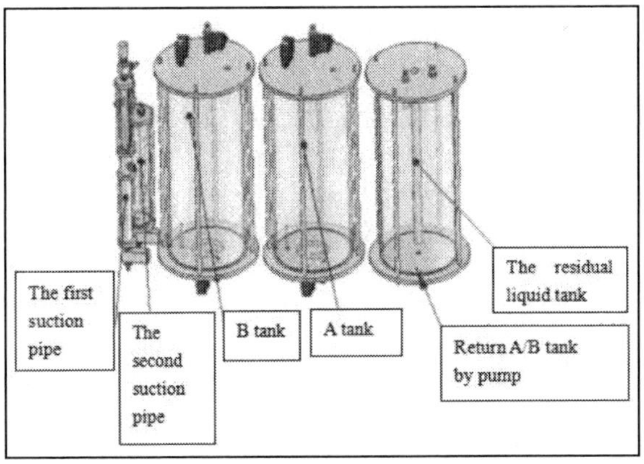

Figure 3. The vacuum, infusion liquid and the residue.

3.3 The pressure steel ball system

The structure diagram of the pressure steel ball system is shown in figure 4. After filling with the ethylene glycol and waiting for the workpiece in place, the TOX cylinder will seal it with the steel ball. The residual ethylene glycol around the steel ball will be recycled to the residual liquid tank at the instant of the movement of the pressure steel ball. The seal must be safe in this section to ensure that there will be no leakage and no escape of the steel balls. The riveting depth of the steel ball should meet the requirements . The depth can be also displayed by the displacement sensor. In this station, the steel ball is automatic feeding through the steel ball pipe to the filter base, ensuring that just one steel ball can go through every time. With the use of the optical fiber sensor ,we can detect the existence of the steel balls. The PLC will alarm when there are no balls.

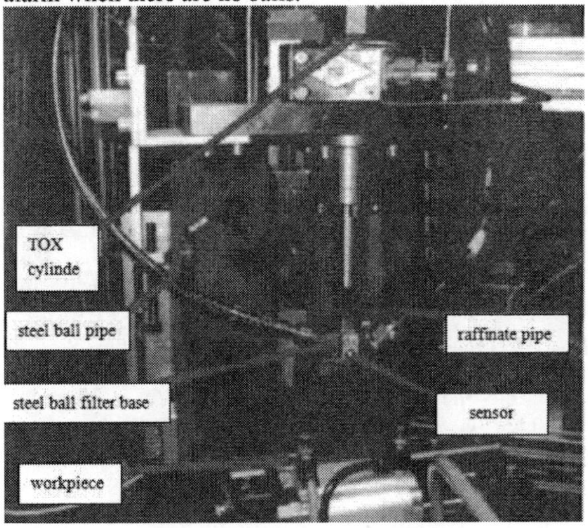

Figure 4. Pressure steel ball system.

4 The design of the control section

Due to the complicated control process and the various data,this equipment uses the IPC + PLC (industrial personal computer + programmable logic controller) to

control the model of the upper and lower place machine. The PLC can control the station motions. And the industrial computer charges the whole course of the monitoring information to achieve the actions in the process of production control, field monitoring and data processing.

4.1 The hardware design of the control part

As the core part of the control part hardware,the Mitsubishi FX2N-80MT is a programmable controller, which has low cost, high efficiency and powerful functions.The industrial personal computer is used by an ADVANTECH PCI-1711L bus data acquisition card.It is a powerful low cost, multifunction PCI bus data acquisition card,using programmable single-ended channel input mode.The sensor can change the non-electric signals such as the displacement,the pressure,the temperature and the vacuum degree into the electric signal and PCI-1711L converts the input analog voltage into a digital signal and then gives it to the industrial personal computer to process. (figure 5).

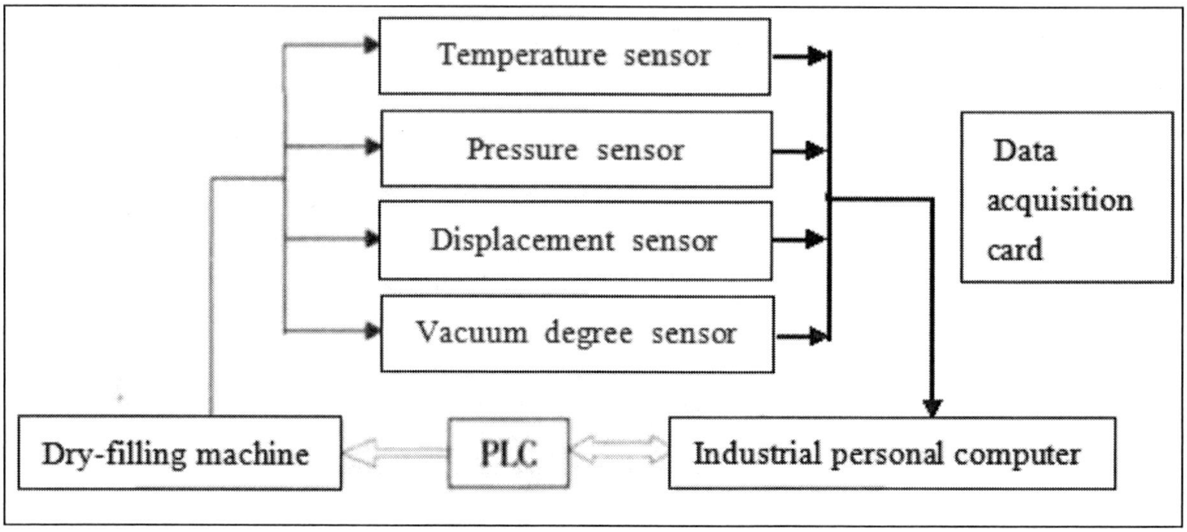

Figure 5. The hardware structure of the control part

4.2 The software design of control part

4.2.1 The system process

The flow chart of the whole system is shown in figure 6.When the equipment starts,the system will be initialized.Various parameters set up by the automatic mode feeding station begin to feed.With material in the process of the vacuum system and the infusion liquid twice vacuumize the cavity of the product,it ensures that there is no bubbles after the infusion liquid fills into cavity.When the vacuum degree meets the requirements,the infuse quantitative ethylene glycol will fill into the cavity.After filling the infusion liquid,the residue on the surface of the product will be extracted back in residual liquid tank and seal the product pouring mouth with equal diameter steel ball. When the product meets the requirement,the setting parameters will be qualified,otherwise the system will alarm and the detailed information will be shown in the master control page.

4.2.2 The design of the interface

The equipment control interface uses LabVIEW[4] software design .LabVIEW is a general programming system, with powerful database, including the serial instrument control, the data acquisition, the data analysis, the data display and the data storage. System monitoring interface of the device is mainly composed of the vacuum and infusion station monitoring, the pressure steel ball station monitoring pressure, the discharge station monitoring, the liquid level monitoring, the fault information system, the system status display, and the system operation control (figure 7). The interface can see visually dynamic vacuum degree online after the shock absorber in the vacuum process. It can also see the curve of reflected changes about the shock absorber vacuum degree .

4.2.3 Data processing

The LabVIEW software provides a variety of ways to data storage and reading. In addition to save the data, the test data file can generate the data produced by the information such as the date, the time and the parameters of each product, making the users check the data at a certain moment easily. Figure 8 is a data query interface, we can get the information of the product by entering a query condition.

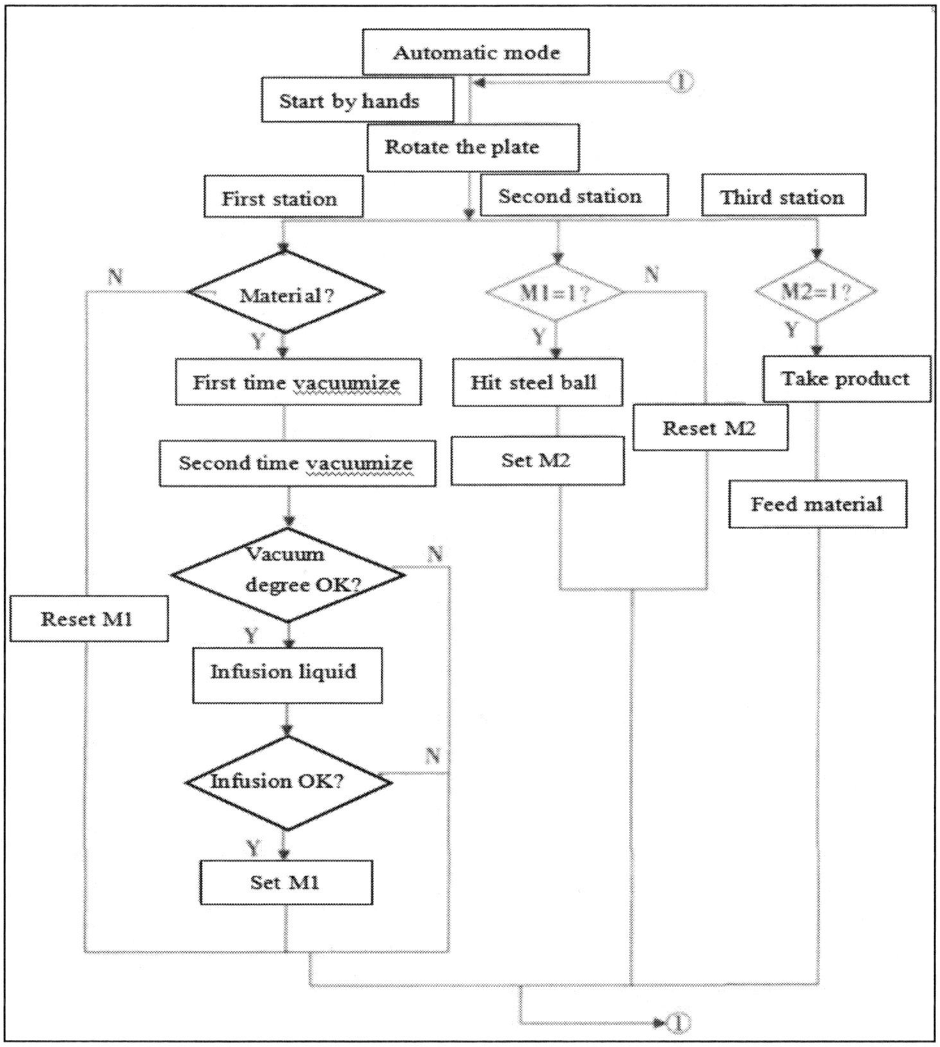

Figure 6. The flow chart of the system.

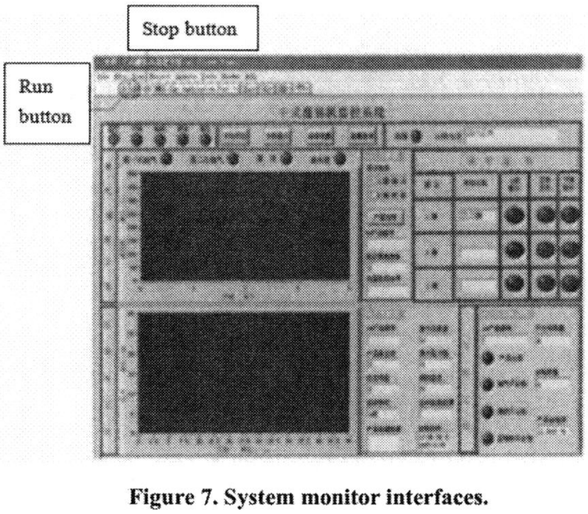

Figure 7. System monitor interfaces.

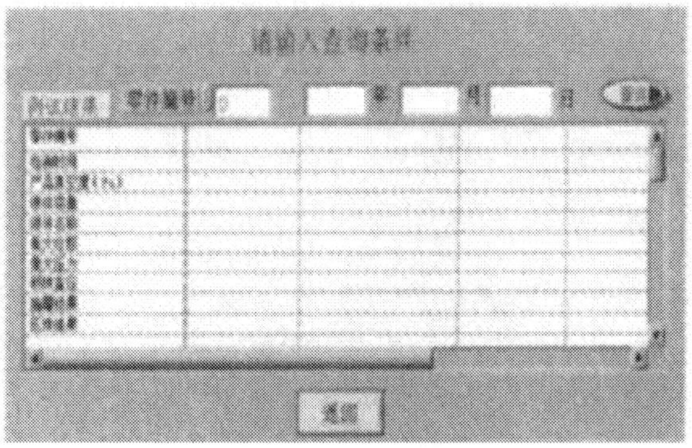

Figure 8. Data inquiry interface.

5 Conclusion

The shock absorber[5],as an important vehicle part, has high technical content.Its technical level reflects the development level of China's auto parts to some extent.The engine suspension shock absorber dry filling equipment introduced in this paper has been put into use in a suspension system co.,LTD.The design and the process of the equipment have fully considered the influence of various factors on the quality of the shock absorber filling.Thus,not only does it improve the work efficiency in the actual production,but also improve the operating environment of the workers.At the same time,the filling precision of the products has also reached a higher level.

References

1. Deqing Zhang,Modeling and Simulation Design of Vehicle Shock Absorber. Zhenjiang: Jiangsu University(2003).
2. Hao Xu,Chunyuan Cai,Junqi Yan,etc.Mechanical Design Handbook.Beijing: Mechanical Industry Press(2001).
3. Zuotong Liu.Vacuum Technology and Equipment.Nanjing:Southeast University Press(1991).
4. 4.Zhenshan Lei.LabVIEW7 Express Practical Technology Course. Beijing: China Railway Press(2005).
5. Xuemei Feng, Zuomin Liu. Development and Current Situation of Automotive Hydraulic Shock Absorber Technology .Journal of Wuhan University of Technology,2003(6):340-342

MATEC Web of Conferences 44, 02003 (2016)
DOI: 10.1051/matecconf/20164402003

The Analysis of The Fault of Electrical Power Steering

Li Wen Zhang, Rong Du and Yan Cheng[1]

[1]*Hebei Jiaotong Vocational & Technical College*

Abstract. This paper analysis the common fault types of primary Electrical Power Steering system, meanwhile classify every fault. It provides the basis for further troubleshooting and maintenance. At the same time this paper propose a practical working principle of fault-tolerant, in order to make the EPS system more security and durability.

1 Introduction

Electrical Power Steering system (EPS) System compareing to traditional mechanical hydraulic steering system has good steering agility, steering stability, low-temperature resistance and low power consumption. Moreover it has the advantages of easy integration of secondary development. Thus it shows strong vitality in the power steering systems of automobile, and will gradually replace the conventional steering system. EPS had entered the stage of mass production in some other countries, and had become the vehicle parts of high-tech products.

As a new technology, EPS is not as mature as traditional technology. However, the output of traditional steering is not independent of the input, and EPS can do this depending on the motors. Comparing to the hydraulic power steering, EPS may has different failure modes, it is very necessary to identify and research the potential failure modes.

This paper analyzes the most common fault conditions such as fault in torque sensor the vehicle speed sensor, and proposes fault tolerant method combined with the corresponding technical, and make the adaptability of troubleshooting. Structure and

2 The structure and working principle of ESP

The structure and working principle of ESP is shown in Figure 1.

ESP system consists of speed sensors, steering wheel torque sensors, speed sensors, controllers, power driver circuit, flash memory, clutch and DC motor and other components. The controller determines the rotational direction and best assist torque of the motor according to the output signal of each sensor, and send control signals to the motor and clutch, and control the rotation of the DC motor by the power driving circuit.

The output of motor drive gear and rack mechanism to produce steering power after the effect of decelerating the rotation speed to multiply the torque by the reduction mechanism.

By precise control algorithm, the motor torque can be discretionarily changed, so that the transmission mechanism can get any required value.

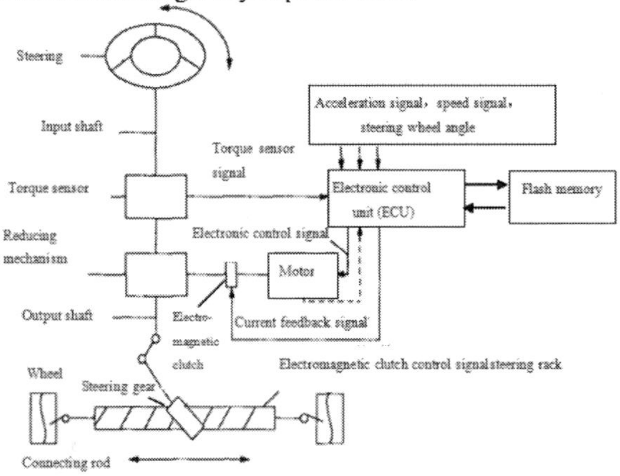

Figure 1. The structure and working principle of ESP

3 The principle and common failure modes of sensor

3.1. Torque sensor

Torque sensor measures the torque between the steering wheel and steering output shaft, and converts its value to a voltage signal to the ECU, which is an important determinant.to control the value of the power steering. Therefore, the validity of the output signal directly affects the manipulation safety of vehicles, especially high-speed of moving vehicles. Currently used torque sensors can be divided into contact sensor and non-contact sensor. The contact sensor is always swing-arm-type. The non-

15802285470@126.com

Article available at http://www.matec-conferences.org or http://dx.doi.org/10.1051/matecconf/20164402003

contact sensor is always inductance-type. This paper mainly analyses the failure modes of these two kinds of mainstream torque sensors

Figure 2 is typical structure of contact torque sensor. There is a torsion bar on the steering shaft. This device which using a potentiometer to output two independent primary signal and secondary signal by the deformation of the torsion bar, get torque and direction signal. Relatively speaking, contact structure is complex, because of that the wear of mechanical components it is easy to cause the sensor errors. For those sensors which use potentiometer to measure displacement, the wearing out of the potentiometer element also may cause the sensor errors. This kind of sensor always uses 5V power supply. Its output signal has 5 ways. P1, P2, P3 are used to provide information of angle, while T1, T2 are used to provide information of torque. Actually The signal P1 and P3 can provide sufficient information for calculate angle and the signal P2 was not necessary for the calculation of angle, it is a redundant communication channel. The signal T1 and T2 both have sufficient information for calculate torque, so they are redundant communication channels for each other. This design is facilitate not only for fault detection, but also for playing a backup role after a signal failure, in order to do fault tolerance and troubleshooting.

Figure 3 is typical structure of non-contact torque sensor. Leakage magnetic ring is riveted on the input shaft rotating with the input shaft. There is rack on the input shaft. Leakage magnetic ring has two rows of windows, respectively corresponding to sensor coil L1 and L2. The two coils are assembled in shell of the sensor, as shown in Figure 3. The working principle is based on the electromagnetic induction, and realize measurement by the change of coil inductance or mutual inductance.

After several experimental research and data analysis, and combining with relevant literature, we come to the conclusion of their failure modes, which is shown as table 1.

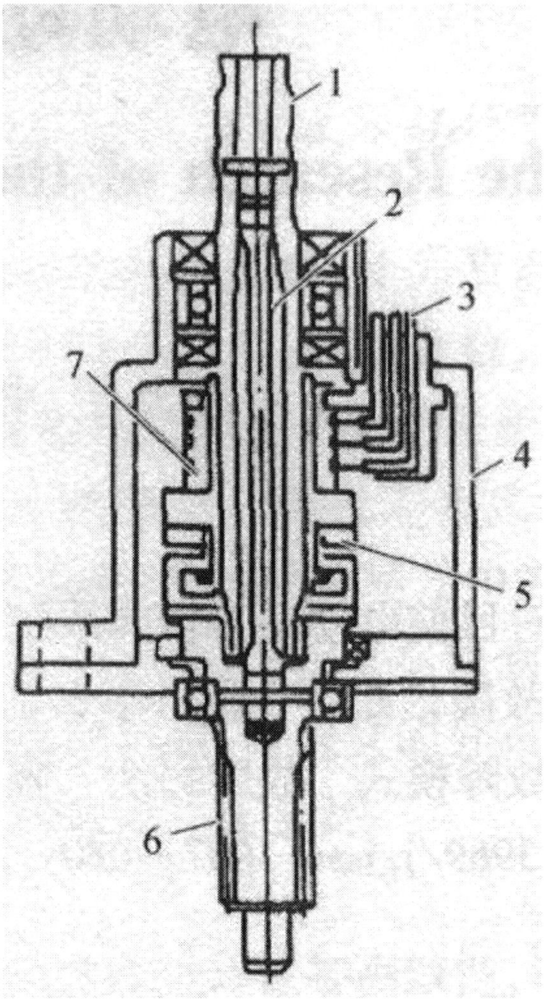

Figure 2. Contact torque sensor

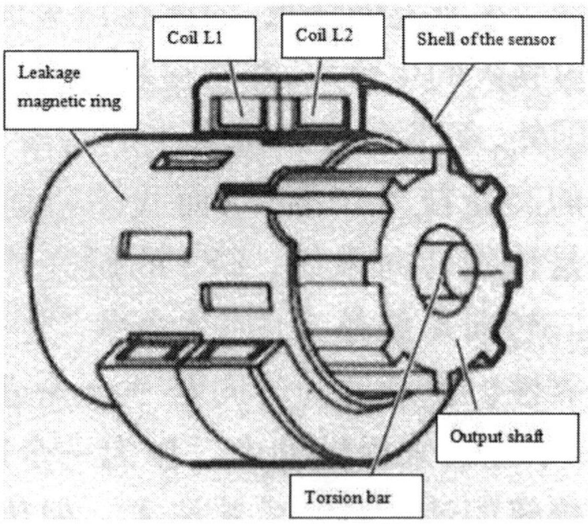

Figure 3. Non-contact torque sensor

Table 1. Failure modes of torque sensors.

Sensor type	Failure event	Failure reason
Contact torque sensor.	Primary signal and secondary signal inconsistencies.	Mechanical structural failure or wear.
	Power supply voltage is too high or too low.	Battery power is low.
	Auxiliary line open circuit	Corrosion or Foreign body
	Mechanical failure	Crashing, Design defects
	Signal mixing	Noise circumstances, poor road condition
Non-contact torque sensor.	Short circuit	pencil of lines short circuit
	Open circuit	Lead-out wire is fault soldered joint
	The voltage difference between coil L1 and L2 is higher than 30mV	Bad contact of coil L1 or L2
	String makes noise, stagnates or jitters.	Motor connector parts contact are loose, and bad contact.

3.2. Speed sensor

Speed sensor of ESP system is used for detecting the rotating speed of tire, and generate the proportional signal base on the rotating speed. Figure 4 is typical structure of speed sensor.

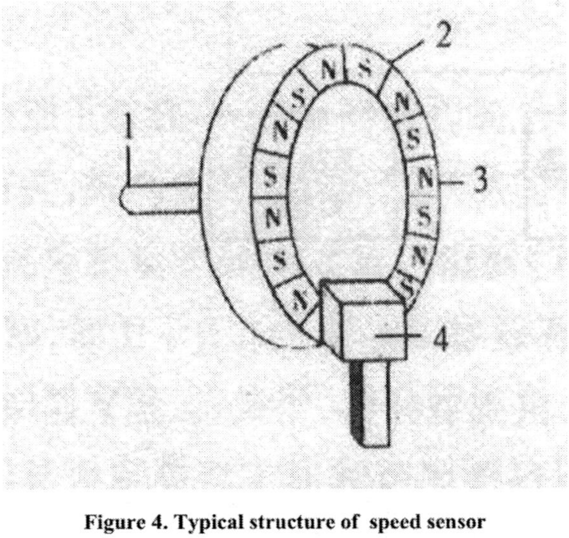

Figure 4. Typical structure of speed sensor

The working principle of speed sensor is that when the input shaft is rotating, the Hall switch integrated sensor fixed near magnetic turntable can produce a corresponding pulse in each place passed by small magnets. By detecting the number of pulses generated per unit time, we can measure the rotating speed of the input shaft. It can generate a sine pulse which has a frequency that proportional to the speed. This sine pulse change to a square wave signal by the circuit of the odometer. This square wave signal is used by odometer, and at the same time it is transmitted to ESP controller by wire for providing speed signal. Base on the speed signal, ESP provide corresponding auxiliary force. Commonly it provide a larger force at low speed so as to make steering lightly while it provide a smaller force at high speed so as to increase road feeling and operational stability. Likewise, we come to the conclusion of it failure modes, which is shown as table 2.

4 EPS working principle of fault-tolerant

Base on the above research and analysis of failure modes of sensors, we have found a new design for troubleshooting. To improve the reliability and safety of the vehicle, we add a flash memory in the ESP system and control by database. When the sensor malfunctions, the system may get the correct sensor data signal combination directly from the database in the flash memory. ECU use this dependable data signal to control the motor to provide correct auxiliary force sequentially, in order to make the ESP system subject to the minimum extent affect and work unceasingly and steadily.

Figure 5 is the logic work flow fault-tolerant principle. The primary work flow of the system is that firstly system analyses the data signal from every sensor, if the signal is regular, corresponding memory space stores this regular signal, and if the signal show that the sensor malfunctions, the system will do some appropriate treatment by fault-tolerant principle, the system will work unceasingly and steadily as well as the fault indicator lights in order to remind the driver that the sensor malfunctions and need to be repaired or be changed. When the torque sensor and speed sensor malfunction at the same time. ECU will disconnect the clutch and make the ESP system stop doing the wrong operation and switch to mechanical steering system.

Table 2. Failure modes of speed sensors.

Sensor type	Failure event	Failure reason
	Open circuit.	Mildew or corrosion.
	Can't connect to ECU.	Splice damage.
	Short circuit	Pencil of lines short circuit.
	Internal fault.	From a high speed drop into a low speed.
	Bad contact.	Splice falls off.

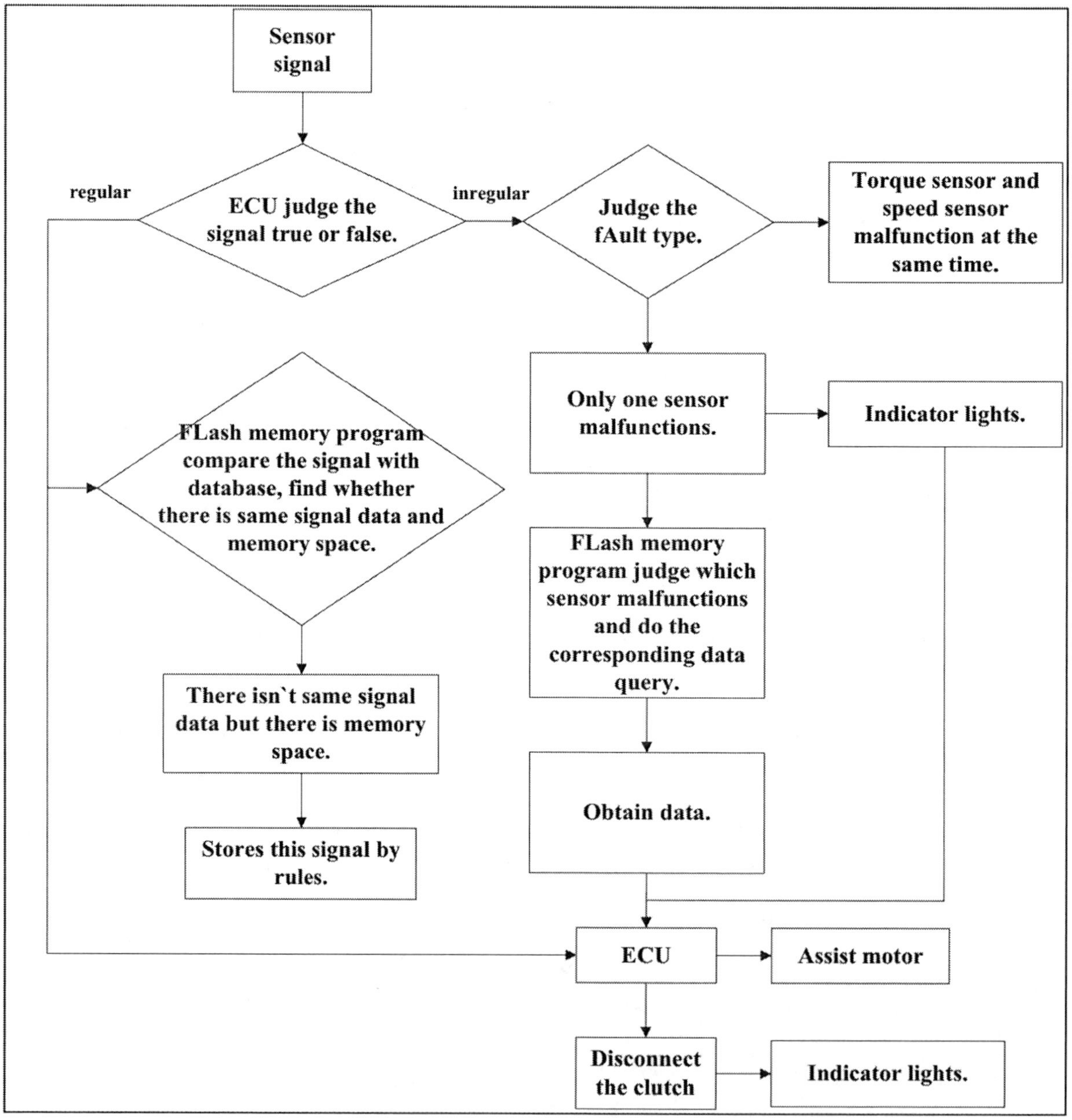

Figure 5. Logic work flow fault-tolerant principle

5 Conclusion

(1) Whether the ESP system reliable or not, that is rely on the sensor signal, so that the analysis of the common faults of the sensor is very important. This article analysis the common fault types and provides the basis for further troubleshooting and maintenance.
(2) This article use the fault-tolerant principle found a new design for ESP system. When the sensor malfunctions, the fault indicator lights, the program judges the signal and do the corresponding data query, so as to obtain the correct data and sent it to ECU. This design make the ESP system can work unceasingly and steadily during a period of time and can keep the assistant performance when the sensor malfunctions.

References

1. Osuka A, Mastuoka Y, Tsustui T, et al. Development of Pinion-Assisted Type Electric power Steering.KOYO Engineering Journal English Ediiton No.161E (2002)
2. Aly Badawy, Dieter Fehlings. Development of a New Concept of Electrically Powered Hydraulic Steering [J] . SAE transactions, 2004, 113(6) : 1074 — 1081
3. Wolfgang KemmetmüllerModeling and Nonlinear Control of an Electro-hydraulic Closed center Power-steering System [C] //Proceeding of the 44th IEEE Conference on Decision and Control. [S. l.] : [s. n.] , 2005: 5077-5082
4. Guo Xiaolin, Ji Xuewu, Liu Yahui, et al. Study on Dynamic R esponses of the vehicle Handing Models with a Speed-sensitive Hydraulic Power Steering System [J] Training, 2013: 10-11.

MATEC Web of Conferences 44, 02004 (2016)
DOI: 10.1051/matecconf/20164402004

One kind of wind energy storage pattern and corresponding equipment

Zhong Ying Yuan[1,a], Yan Ping Li[2,b]

[1,2]Liaoning Institute of Science and Mechanical Engineering, Liaoning Institute of Science and Engineering Practice Center, 117004 Benxi City, Liaoning Province, China

Abstract: This paper introduced one kind of energy transformation pattern, which can be applied to oceans and their peripheral area. With this pattern, nature wind energy can be collected, transformed and stored in order to be released continuously and turned into productivity. We described the implementation plan and corresponding equipment in detail, and gave out the results of experiment system.

Keywords: Wind energy transformation; Water level promoting; Storing pattern

1 Introduction

Natural wind power generation is one of the main forms of wind power utilization. Though wind energy has high conversion efficiency, it is difficult to be stored in long-term or large capacity and has limitations in application. This paper describes a long-term, large capacity storage pattern of natural wind energy which can release the energy intensively and continuously in order to make full use of natural resources and promote productivity development.

Wind energy storage is consisted of wind energy collection, conversion and storage. In the surrounding areas of rivers, lakes and seas, we can use wind as power and put multi-level wind pumps and reservoirs in series on the same tower to form a multi-stage water hoist tower. Then we can transfer raised level water to higher reservoirs through pipes in order to realize the energy transformation from wind energy to water potential energy and store the energy in the form of water potential energy. We can define this process as one kind of wind energy storage pattern. The advantage of this pattern is that it can store natural wind power in long-term and large capacity, and procedures don't need electricity support, working staff. It can operate automatically and make full use of wind energy and natural resources such as rivers, lakes and seas.

2 System equipment

2.1 Wind energy collection device

Wind energy collection device is consisted of the wind deflector (Figure 1) which is rotated to be mounted on the side fixed axis of the wind dump. Wind deflector can tracking wind direction and collecting wind energy. It can receive wind energy effectively and is consisted of symmetrical flared duct is rotating with fixed axis. Wind deflector is made of thin-wall materials and is in the

[a] Zhongying Yuan: lkyyzy@126.com
[b] Yanping Li: liyanping_1962@sina.com

Article available at http://www.matec-conferences.org or http://dx.doi.org/10.1051/matecconf/20164402004

shape of a symmetrical duct which is intermediate thin and gradually turning thicker on both sides. The axis section of deflector is a symmetrical flaring curve which contains collecting energy segment and diffusion segment. The air flow can come in from the collecting energy segment and come out from diffusion segment via orifice.

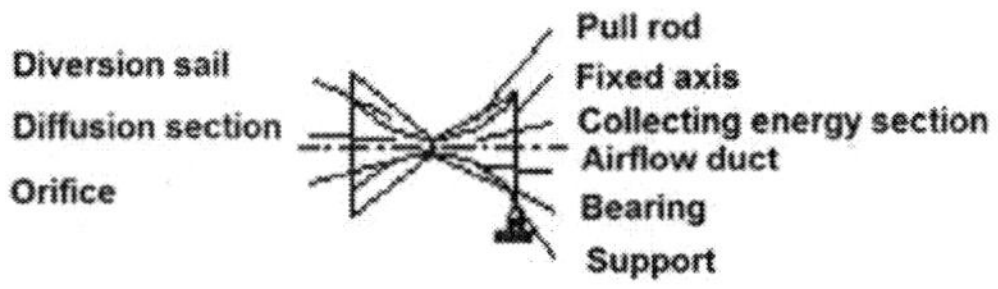

Figure 1. The cutaway view of wind deflector device

Since the pore size of the orifice is the smallest, flow rate of the fluid at the orifice is high with a small pressure and at the ends of both funnels, flow rate of the fluid is low with strong pressure. The airflow introduced into funnel sucks air flow into funnel, lets it flow towards orifice and keep it circulating. In this way, funnel can increase the flow rate and collect wind energy. Let us define the diameter of orifice is d, then the diameter of the end of funnels is 2d~3d, the distance between orifice and the end of funnels is 2d~4d, the flow rate at orifice is 2~3 times as that at the ends of funnels and acceptance ratio of wind energy is increased 3~5 times. We set a fixed axis through the circle point of the ends of funnels and vertically to the ground. The axis is connected with the rotating part of funnels and its bottom is connected with main support. In order to guarantee the intensity, stiffness and stability of funnels, we set a pair of pull rods in the vertical direction on the surface of funnels. One side of the pull rods is connected with funnels and the other side is connected with the outer edges of each bearings. Apart from the function that it can support funnels, the axis also has the function to track wind direction in order to guarantee that the ends of funnels are always towards the direction of airflow and keep the funnels always work on the perfect direction. In order to make the funnels can track wind direction more reliable, we set a pair of contra-vanes in the vertical direction on the surface of the diffusion segment of funnels. Then we put wind wheel for wind energy acceptance device near the orifice of diffusion segment. Hence, we can decrease both radial dimension of the rotating part of wind wheel and manufacturing costs of wind energy machines. What's more, It can track wind direction automatically, collect wind energy and always keep the wind acceptance device towards the right direction in order to accept and collect wind energy more effectively.

2.2 Wind energy conversion devices

Usage of a multi-stage wind pump and an impounding reservoir in series so as to constitute a high-stand hoist tower, can realize the transformation from wind energy to high-stand potential energy. Wind pumps take usage of wind energy guiding device, and take natural wind as driving force. Wind pumps consist of reciprocating pumps driven by wind wheels and mechanical drive group. A wind pump can be divided into three parts: wind receiver, transmission mechanism and reciprocating pumps.

Wind receiver: With the wind energy guiding device, the three-wing wind turbine is installed in the orifices of the wind energy guiding device which is near diffuser segment side, and the wind wheel is connected by the rotation of the horizontal drive shaft coupled with the duct. The combination of a duct and a wind wheel consist of the wind receiver, which can transform wind energy into rotational mechanical energy of the wind wheel.

Transmission mechanism: the output of the horizontal drive shaft is connected idly with the vertical drive shaft which is covered by the fixed axis. And the vertical drive shaft, the lower end of the wind duct as well as the fixed axis connected rigidly are rotatably connected, while the output of the vertical drive shaft is mounted on the main stand by horizontally rotating the other bevel gear and axis and the output of the vertical drive shaft as well meshing transmitted with driving bevel gear set in the vertical plane. There is a hinge axis fixed off center in the drive shaft. One side of connecting rod is rotatably connected with drive shaft via hinge axis and the other side is connected with the piston which can reciprocate in vertical direction in the reciprocating pump. The axis is rotatably connected with vertical drive shaft on the same axis and permalink to the main support which is fixed on the ground.

Reciprocating pumps: It is installed under the water level and is consisted of cylinder block, piston which can reciprocate in vertical direction and one-way flow tubes

for influent and effluent, which is set at the bottom of cylinder block and connected with lower plenum. Reciprocating pumps is rotatably connected with drivers via connecting rods and use the driving forces from connecting rods to change the water pressure in the sealed lower plenum which is under the piston. The change can make water flowing and rise the water level and finish the pumping operation.

Because of the combination of wind pumps and wind deflector, wind wheel is always in the best direction and can efficiently receive and utilize wind energy.

2.3 Reservoir water level automatic control device (Figure 2)

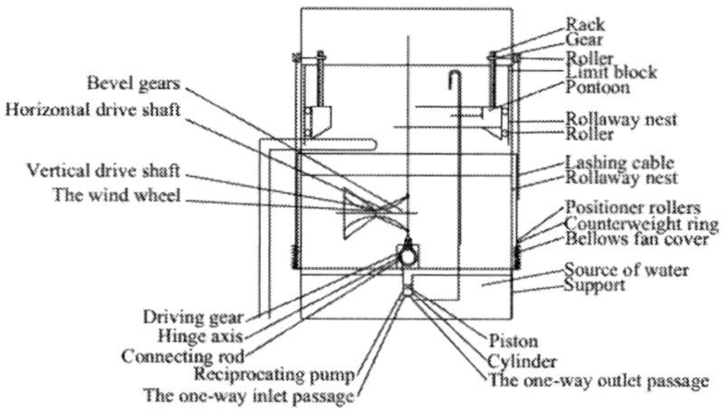

Figure 2. The operating principle diagram of the wind power water pump and the automatic control device of reservoir water level

Water level automatic control device is a feedback signal equipment which uses a hollow box in reservoir, which can produce buoyancy to drive workload or lock executive devices. It is consisted of the support, reservoir, pontoon, transmission components and air bellows covers. Top bracket is mounted with reservoir, central is installed with wind pumps and the lowermost part is water supply sources. Support is a cylindrical building which is vertical to horizon ground and has four uprights uniformly set on the surface. The water level in the reservoir is relied on the water flow from the inlet and outlet. This equipment can limit the water level by controlling the water flow from inlet. The water flow from inlet is relied on working condition of wind pump which is under the reservoir. And the working condition of wind pump is relied on the current airflow in the wind deflector. If the airflow is small, the displacement is small; If the airflow is large, the displacement is large. Hence, the displacement is proportional to airflow in the wind deflector. In this way, the water level of reservoir can be controlled by controlling the airflow in the wind deflector. The current water level can be defined as a feedback signal and transferred to the executive devices. Then we can build a closed feedback system[1].

The detail plan is: We put a sealed hollow ring buoyancy tank which has idler wheels and is defined as that it can only move on vertical direction. Top bracket is fixed symmetrically with four groups of racks in the vertical direction. The racks are meshing with wheel gears which is horizontal radial installed and is on the idler wheel which is rotatably connected with support via the same axis. The digging line of the idler wheel is fixed with heavy ring which is fixed with top bracket of bellow wind covers. There are four positioner rollers rotatably connected with heavy ring. Part of positioner rollers are in the rollway nest of support in the vertical direction. The idler wheel and rollway nest form the vertical track of bellow wind covers. The water level of reservoir is controlled within the scales which are decided by the stop blocks on the support. When the water level is higher than the lower stop block, buoyancy tank can make bellow wind cover moving upward by drivers in order to decrease effective airflow in wind deflector and also displacement of wind pump. When the water level is up to the upper stop block, the bellow wind cover will block air vent of the pump and the pump will stop working. Then the water level can be raised. Reservoir water level automatic control device is realized by mechanical linkage without electricity. The structure is quite easy and has safety in operation. It is also easy to install and repair[2].

2.4 Water potential energy storage device

Water potential energy storage device is consisted of high reservoirs which have the same height or are higher than the multi-stage hoist tower. High reservoirs(Figure 3) have large capacity. Based on theory of communicating vessels, the water flow can automatically move from high-level hoist tower to high reservoirs. In this way, the energy can be stored as water potential energy and released continuously and turned into productivity for

better society. The high water flow from high reservoir can be used to generate electricity heating, irrigation or build urban and rural water pipe network. The stage of high-level hoist tower are set based on the needed water level and the maximum water lift[3].

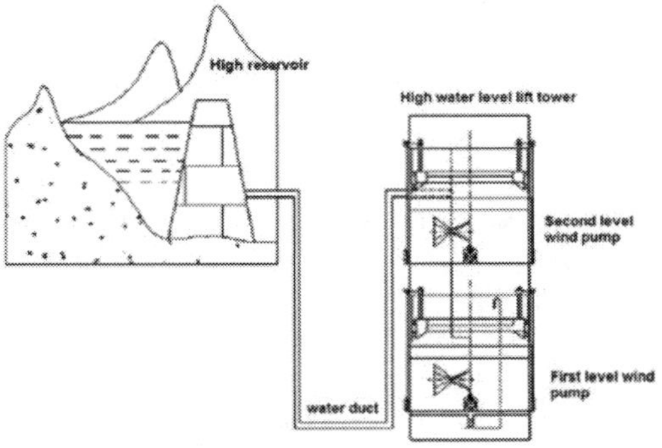

Figure 3. Wind energy storage model and corresponding operating principle diagram

3 Epilogue

Wind deflector can automatically set the inlet in the right direction in real time and effectively gather wind energy to orifice. The wind wheels in the orifice can receive wind energy and transform it to mechanical energy by making reciprocating pumps working with drivers. Then the mechanical energy can be transformed to water pressure to push the water flow to each reservoirs and water pressure can be transformed to water potential energy and stored in reservoir. Each wind pumps moves the water flow towards the highest reservoir for storage, then the tubes transfer the water flow to high reservoir and the energy can be stored in the form of high water potential energy[4].

In the spring, we put two wind pumps in series as a 2-stage hoist tower for experiment at the waterfront of Donggang City. After thirty days operation, the experiment can raise 3600m^3 sea water to 36m height under the condition that the average wind force is level four, the area of wind mouth of the wind pumps is 32 m^2 and the height of the hoist tower is 36m. The experiment system can work automatically without staff and the process is stable and reliable.

References

[1] J.Sheng. *Hydro-mechanics* , China Machine Press, (1980)

[2] M.Shi. EST,**5**,18-22(2000)

[3] X.Yong, JAP,**13**,49-52(1998)

[4] Z.Du, AESS, **21**, 364-370(2000)

MATEC Web of Conferences 44, 02005 (2016)
DOI: 10.1051/matecconf/20164402005

The research and development of the automatic solar power tracker

Yan Ping Li[1,a], Zhong Ying Yuan[2,b]

[1,2]*Liaoning Institute of Science and Mechanical Engineering, Liaoning Institute of Science and Engineering Practice Center, 117004 Benxi City, Liaoning Province, China*

Abstract: The article describes a kind of automatic tracker using solar power. It depends on two important parts which are servo system and adjusting mechanism system to keep the tracker operating normally. The article focuses on describing the characteristics and functions of two systems and the operating details of the automatic solar power tracker.

Keywords: automatic; solar tracking; saturated steam.

1. Introduction

The technology of solar power tracking is not only the basis and precondition of using solar power efficiently, but also the supporting element which can improve the solar power equipment' revenue. Nowadays, most existing solar power equipment need external electrical energy to make sure them running normally. Even if some of them have mature solar technology, there still is the limitation of operating locations such as the areas without electrical power; the high alpine areas and so on. So it is necessary to develop a kind of solar automatic tracking device which is economic, practical and safe[1].

2. The function of saturated steam pressure of NH_3

NH_3 has the certain saturated steam pressure states under the certain temperature which are showed in the table1. when the saturated vapor of NH_3 absorbs heat, the temperature and air pressure will rise; if the temperature of the saturated vapor remains unchanged, saturated vapor will be liquefaction and the heat release.

[a] Yanping Li: liyanping_1962@sina.com
[b] Zhongying Yuan: lkyyzy@126.com

Article available at http://www.matec-conferences.org or http://dx.doi.org/10.1051/matecconf/20164402005

Table1.NH_3's saturated vapor pressures and the deviations under different temperature

Temperature t_i (°C)	-35	-30	-25	-20	-15	-10	-5	0	5
Actual measurement p_i (MPa)	0.09329	0.11955	0.15161	0.19022	0.23631	0.29085	0.35486	0.42944	0.51574
Calculate result p(t)(MPa)	-0.179313	-0.07018	0.038953	0.148086	0.257219	0.366352	0.475485	0.584618	0.693751
Deviation MPa	0.272603	0.18973	0.112657	0.042134	-0.020909	-0.075502	-0.120625	-0.155178	-0.178011
Temperature t_i (°C)	10	15	20	25	30	35	40	45	50
Actual measurement p_i (MPa)	0.61495	0.72831	0.85712	1.00273	1.16650	1.34989	1.55435	1.78138	2.03262
Calculate result p(t)(MPa)	0.802884	0.912017	1.02115	1.130283	1.239416	1.348549	1.457682	1.566815	1.675948
Deviation MPa	-0.187934	-0.183707	-0.16403	-0.127553	-0.072916	0.001341	0.096668	0.214565	0.356672

Suppose to there is the linear relation between the saturated vapor of NH_3 and the temperature,

$$p=at+b \tag{1}$$

, a and b are the undetermined constants, so the objective function of least square method:

$$M=\sum[p_i-(at_i+b)]^2 \tag{2}$$

,to minimize M, the partial derivative of a and b should be equaled to 0, and then

$$a\sum t_i^2+b\sum t_i=\sum p_i t_i \tag{3}$$

$$a\sum t_i+18b=\sum p_i \text{ ,i=1-18} \tag{4}$$

in that formula, all the data are showed in the table.2: the results are a=0.0218266 and b=-0.584618. The function relationship of the saturated vapor of NH_3 and air pressure:

$$p=0.0218266t+0.584618 \tag{5}$$

, it derives $\Delta p=0.0218266\Delta t$ which means if the saturated vapor of NH_3 rises 10°C, the air pressure will rise 0.218266 Mpa. The mean square error by using least square method is:

$$M^{1/2}=0.7080906 \text{ Mpa} \tag{6}$$

Table2. the result data from the above formula

	t_i	t_i^2	p_i	$p_i t_i$
	-35	1225	0.09329	-3.26515
	-30	900	0.11955	-3.5865
	-25	625	0.15161	-3.79025
	-20	400	0.19022	-3.8044
	-15	225	0.23631	-3.54465
	-10	100	0.29085	-2.9085
	-5	25	0.35486	-1.7743
	0	0	0.42944	0
	5	25	0.51574	2.5787
	10	100	0.61495	6.1495
	15	225	0.72831	10.92465
	20	400	0.85712	17.1424
	25	625	1.00273	25.06825
	30	900	1.16650	34.995
	35	1225	1.34989	47.24615
	40	1600	1.55435	62.174
	45	2025	1.78138	80.1621
	50	2500	2.03262	101.631
∑	135	13125	13.46972	365.398

3. The structure of the automatic solar tracker

The automatic solar tracker consists of two parts which are the servo system and adjusting mechanism system. The following diagram shows the details of these two parts.

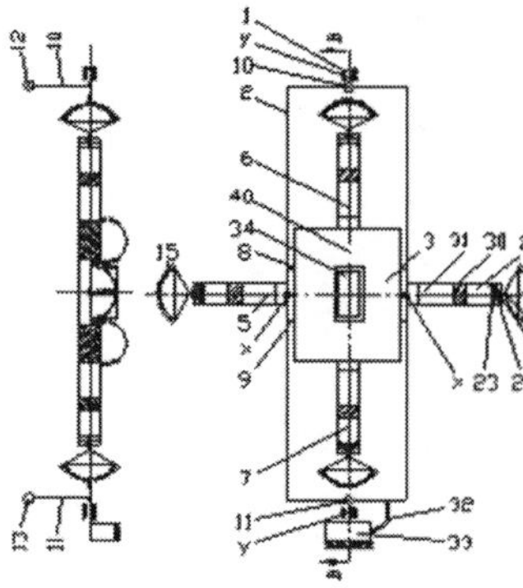

Figure1.The structure of the automatic solar tracker

3.1 Adjusting mechanism system

The adjusting mechanism system is the supporter and executive component of the automatic solar tracker. There are x-x and y-y half shafts which are mutually perpendicular and coplanar symmetric on the two symmetry axis in the rectangular frame2. And at the same time, y-y half shaft is connected with base1 which can relative rotation. The platform3 can relative rotation to the frame2, so as the frame2 can relative rotation to the frame1.The gas cylinder 30 built on the coaxial overhanging rod4 and rod5.The two ends of the axis40 are symmetry to the overhanging rod6 and rod7 which are set up on the platform3. A pair of symmetric u-shaped frame8 and frame9 set up on the frame2. And the upright tubes which are 10 and 11 perpendicular above the plane which the concurrent point between the frame2 and the half shaft y-y. The around half shaft y-y is built on the top of the upright tube which can turn balance block12 and 13.

3.2 The servo system

The four same servo systems should be set up on the four overhanging rods of the half shafts x-x and y-y. The function of servo system is working as a sensor, feedback the location of the sun, controlling and driving the adjusting mechanism to maintain the working platform3 perpendicular to the sun. The right side servo system on the half shaft x-x can be an example. A pair of concave mirrors should be set up symmetrically on the tops of the overhanging rod4 and rod5. They can adjust the sunlight in front of them into its optical focus point. There is a blackening of copper ball 18 which works as the heat collector on the optical focus point of the concave mirror. The copper ball18 is connected with heatsink23 through the oil cylinder30 and heat conducting bar. And at the same time, the heat conducting bar22 is connected with the adiabatic component24 which is on the oil cylinder30. There are two cavities in the oil cylinder30. A suitable amount of NH_3 which is the saturated steam working medium should be injected the cavity26 to against vaporizing pressurization before the system operating. The amount of saturated vapor which inject into cylinder steam should keep two phases of gas and liquid which in the state of saturated steam in it. The soft hermetic oil conduit32 on the nozzle of oil cylinder30 is connected with the nozzle of the swing hydraulic cylinder33 which on the half shaft y-y. The angle of incidence between the direction of the sun and platform3 which is the execution unit is the sense signal of servo system.

4. Operating process of automatic solar power tracker

The automatic solar tracker uses energy conversion among luminous energy, heat, air pressure, hydraulic pressure and mechanical energy in servo system to drive and adjust the system in order to track motive orbit of sun. The projected area on the apertures' plane of each concave mirror is zero when the direction of sunlight perpendicular to the working platform3. So the lighting coverage concave mirror should be zero. And at the same time, the position of the working platform3 unchanged and servo system stop operating because the blacked copper ball18 which was on the optically focal point could not collect luminous energy and absorb heat. When there is an included angle between the normal of the working platform3 and the direction of sunlight which is not perpendicular to the working platform3, at least one concave mirror is illuminated by the sunlight[2]. In order to show this problem, if the sun illuminates left skewed and above half shaft x-x, there should be some irradiated areas on the right side concave mirror14 of the tracking machine. The concave mirror absorbs solar energy on the focal point of the blacked copper ball18, and the heat transfers to the saturated steam refrigerant through heat

conducting bar22 and fin23 in the air chamber26. The saturated steam pressure increases because it absorbs heat. And then it pushes oil and gas cylinder30 to the left. Furthermore, oil pressure in the hydraulic cylinder31 increases, the shaft in the swinging hydraulic oil cylinder33 which is through oil conduit32 and the working platform3 can counterclockwise whose shaft was half shaft y-y. It is a complete tracking cycle until the working platform3 is perpendicular to the direction of sunlight and the lighting coverage on the concave mirror14 is zero. At the same time, during the process of working platform3 turning, the hydraulic pressure increases of the hydraulic circuit in the servo system which is on the left side of half shaft y-y. And the air pressure increased because the piston pushed the saturated steam under the condition of the temperature and the environment is constant. Moreover, the saturated steam would be liquidation and release of heat. And the air pressure fell back until the balance of the air pressure between the left side servo system and the right side servo system[3]. In the process of adjusting and tracking, the working platform3 moves around the half shaft y-y with an angle which is same as the angle between the direction of sunlight and the normal of the working platform3 before it moved around the half shaft y-y. During the process of the working platform3 moving around, the servo system on the left side of the half shaft x-x moved back to the original place to prepare the next tracking cycle.

5. Conclusion

This new kind of tracking device which uses solar energy without electric power is suitable for the areas without electrical power; the high alpine areas and so on. It is practical and has simple structure. It also can be horizontal floating installed which is suitable for horizontal floating solar water heaters, generators, dryers and so on. The working platform3 can use solar power effectively and track sun automatically when the symmetrical angle is in the range of +-60° between the horizontal plane and the working platform3.

References

[1] E.Li, etc. JSE, **24**, 330-333(2003)

[2] B. Wang., *SP*, (1993)

[3] X.W. , *PEP*, (1981)

MATEC Web of Conferences 44, 02006 (2016)
DOI: 10.1051/matecconf/20164402006

Analysis of Kirk effect of an innovated high side Side-Isolated N-LDMOS device

Ciou Jhong Lai[1,a], Gene Sheu[2], Ting Yao Chien[1],Chieh Chih Wu[1], Tzu Chieh Lee[1], Ravi Deivasigamani[2], Ching Yuan Wu[2], Chandrashekhar[2] and Shao Ming Yang[2]

[1]*School of Software and Microelectronics, Peking University, Beijing, China*

[2]*Department of Computer Science and Information Engineering, Asia University 500, Lioufeng Rd., Taichung 41354, Taiwan.*

Abstract. An ESOA of LDMOS device is very critical for power device performance. Kirk effect is the one of the major problem which leads to poor ESOA performance. The cause of the problem mainly due to the high beta value of parasitic NPN transistor in the p-body. In this study, we proposed a new 3D high side Side-Isolated N-Channel LDMOS which we have obtained not only benchmark Ron and breakdown performance, but also better ESOA without Kirk effect. We have compared the analysis of Kirk effect between the new device and the conventional N-LDMOS structure with LATID technique for the formation of the p-body of both device structures.

1 INTRODUCTION

LDMOS transistors are widely used in smart power technologies; Applications are in display drivers, digital audio and power management, Power switching devices etc. Because of its low channel resistance, favourable increase in Transconductance, compatibility and efficient use of silicon area of industrial, consumer electronics and automotive electronic control systems. It requires good robustness and ESOA performance against ESD damage, high temperature operation. One of the problems for On-state I-V curves is Kirk effect and we optimized beta of the parasitic NPN transistor for reducing the Kirk effect [3].

The current gain drops at high collector currents due to yet another mechanism known as the Kirk effect. Kirk effect is an important phenomenon in bipolar junction transistors at the high current condition in Figure1, especially for the HV devices with light-doped concentration, it is necessary to take the Kirk effect into consideration because most of ESD protections operate in the parasitic BJT mode. Kirk effect leads to the base extension and the peak electric field migration which greatly affect the device characteristics. Besides, the peak electric field shifted in the highly doped collector region can results in higher impact ionization rates, which promote the increase of avalanched electron-hole pairs [1] [2].

In this study we studied Tilt angle implantation and we found tilt 30 ° is the best solution for impact ionization performance. The optimization of high side lateral double-diffused Metal Oxide Semiconductor (LDMOS) With Side-Isolated 3D device replaced for the conventional 2D RESURF LDMOS device. Because, the conventional 2D RESURF LDMOS device is always suspected ably as it has Kirk effect and high leakage current problems. These will cause poor reliability and also robustness problems in the devices. So, we studied LATID process and heavier P-body doping concentration.

We found optimization the process and this design is implemented by conventional 2D RESURF LDMOS device and 3D high side Side-Isolated LDMOS structures. We found better choices for tilt 30 ° to achieve good Breakdown voltage, Low On-State Resistance and it indicates a good choice for Impact ionization.

In this work, we developed a new innovated high side Side-Isolation N-channel LDMOS 3D device on both front and back edges of the extended drift region. First, we developed the conventional 2D RESURF LDMOS and when we analyzed the electrical characteristics we noticed the high leakage current and Kirk effect problems in On-state characteristics. We innovate that one of the best solution is replaced by the 3D high side Side-Isolated device with thermo-oxide deposition and the leakage current is substantially decreased and Kirk effect problems also solved as compared to the conventional 2D RESURF LDMOS device. We demonstrated these phenomena's by using N-LDMOS device we developed by using Sentaurus simulation (3D) in Figure 2.

[a] Corresponding author: cjlai0909@gmail.com

Article available at http://www.matec-conferences.org or http://dx.doi.org/10.1051/matecconf/20164402006

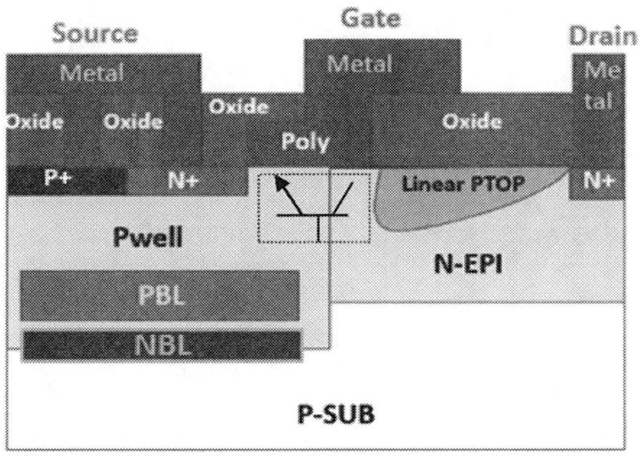

Figure 1. The High side device Under study using N-LDMOS with linear p-top. The parasitic NPN transistor is shown.

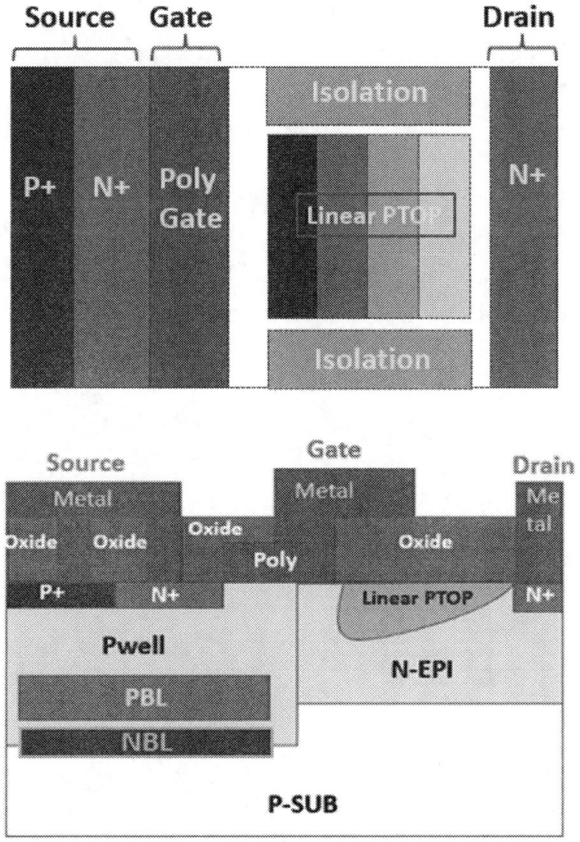

Figure 2. Schematic of 3D high side Side-Isolated N-LDMOS Structure (3D) (a) top view (b) cross section.

2 SIMULATION RESULTS AND DISCUSSION

We demonstrate the leakage current and Kirk effect problems in conventional 2D RESURF LDMOS structure and thereby affecting very important ESOA performance of the device. So, we designed 3D high side Side-Isolated techniques to reduce the beta of the parasitic NPN transistor thereby to avoid the Kirk effect and reduce the leakage current. With our new 3D High side Side-Isolation structure had 0.71um p-body width and conventional 2D structure had 0.57um p-body width. It indicates longer channel width is used to reduce the beta of the parasitic NPN transistor, In Figure 3 as we show the comparisons of the channel width between 3D high side Side-Isolated and conventional RESURF LDMOS devices.

We found the heavier p - body doping concentration average (10^^{17} atoms/cm-3) in 3D side isolation structure and conventional 2D isolation device found less average p-body doping concentrations (10^^{16} atoms/cm-3) as shown in Figure 4 and Figure 5. We simulated the on-state curves to analysis the Kirk effectively as we can see in Figure 6 and Figure 7.

The heavier doping concentration and longer channel make the Kirk minimize. We optimize the LATID process with different tilt angle implantation(7 °, 30 °, 45 ° and 60 °) and we found 7° showing the severe Kirk effect and Tilt 30° also found the best solution for Kirk effect problems in 3D high side Side-Isolated device. [4][5]

The 3D structure is showing higher p-body concentration and longer channel length as compared to the conventional 2D RESURF LDMOS device. The comparison of Off-state leakage current between 3D high side Side-Isolated N-LDMOS and conventional 2D RESURF LDMOS device at room temperature, there we can see the leakage current in a 3D Side-Isolated device is substantially reduced as compared with conventional 2D structure and it is around 10 times lesser than conventional 2D RESURF LDMOS device. The electrical characteristics comparison between 3D high side Side-Isolation device and conventional 2D RESURF LDMOS device shown in Table 1.

The Kirk is one of the most consider as N-LDMOS power device. We found LATID is one of the solutions for 2D.However the Kirk is disappearing in new innovated 3D high side Side-Isolated N-LDMOS structure because of side isolation techniques. Hence side isolation technique is one of the best solutions to solve Kirk effect problems and enhance the leakage current in smart power devices.

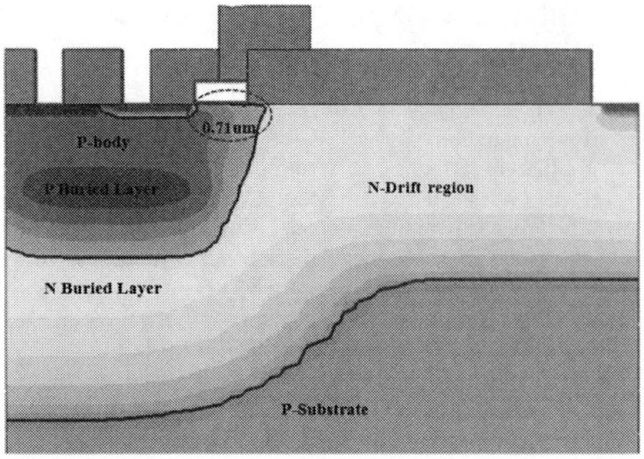

(a)

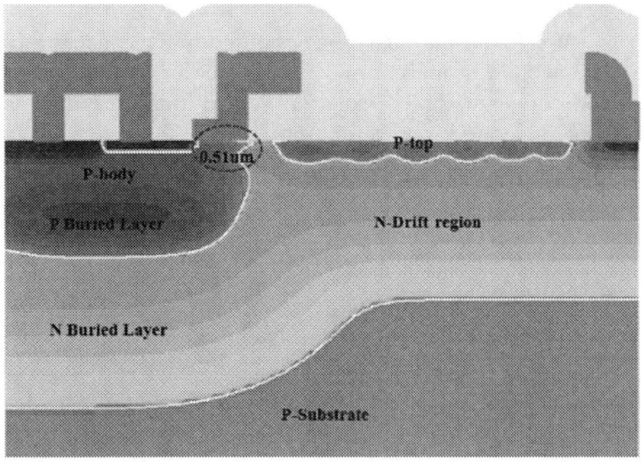

(b)

Figure 3. Device comparison between (a) 3D high side Side-Isolated with p-body and (b) Conventional 2D RESURF LDMOS Structure.

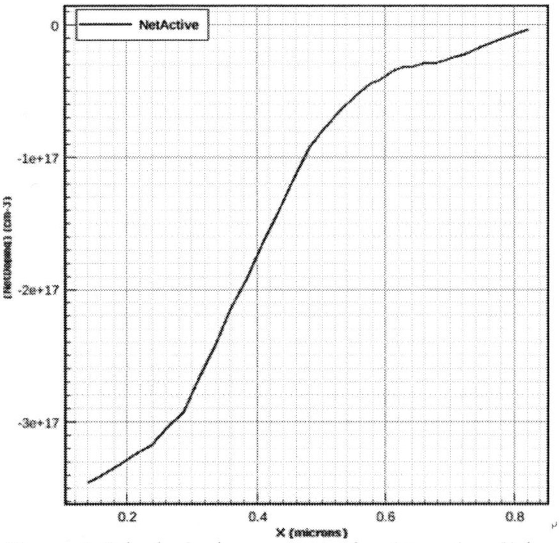

Figure 4. P-body doping concentration (atoms/cm-3) in 3D High Side Side-Isolated device.

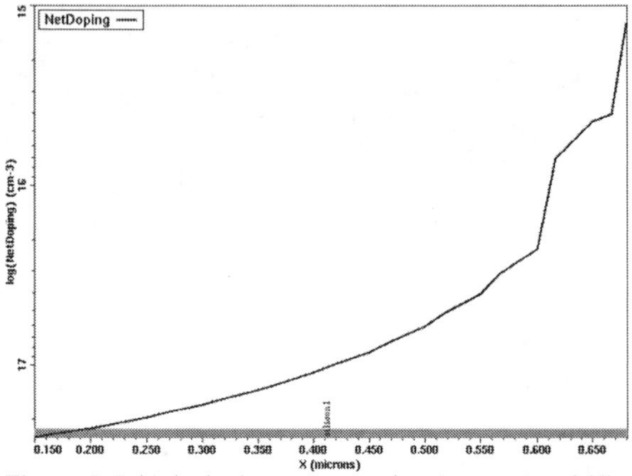

Figure 5. P-body doping concentration Conventional 2D RESURF LDMOS structure.

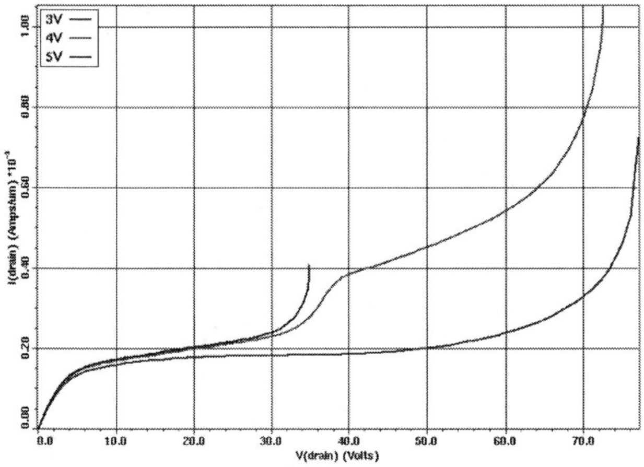

(a)

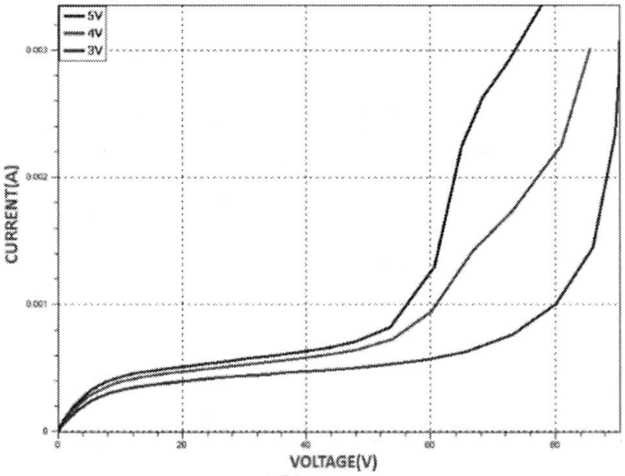

(b)

Figure 6. N-channel LDMOS On-state I-V curves comparison between 3D high side Side-Isolated with linear p-top and Conventional 2D RESURF LDMOS device.

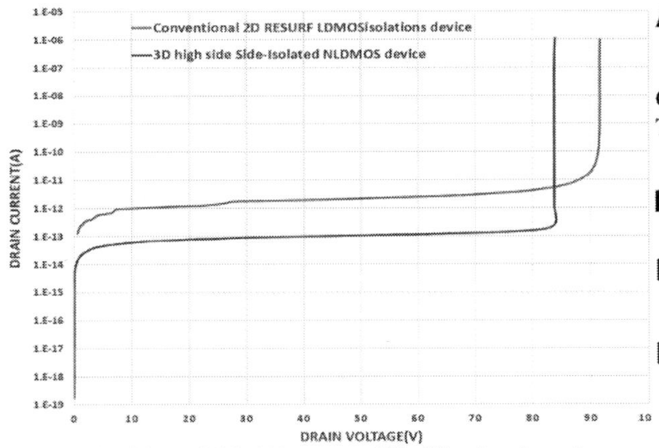

Figure 7. Plot of Id (A) verses Vd (V) showing the leakage current comparison between 3D high side Side-Isolated device and conventional 2D RESURF LDMOS device.

Table 1. Electrical characteristics comparison between 3D high side Side-Isolated N-LDMOS and 2D conventional RESURF LDMOS device.

Electrical Characteristics	Conventional 2D RESURF LDMOS device	3D high side Side-Isolated N-LDMOS device
Lateral BVD(V) at 1e-6	91.6	83.9
Vertical BVD(V) at 1e-6	482.3	109.4
Ron (mohm-mm2)	90	45.1
P-Body width(um)	0.51	0.71
BVD(V) for vg=3v	77	90.3
BVD(V) for vg=4v	72.5	85.6
BVD(V) for vg=5v	35	77.9
Kirk Effect	Yes	No

3 CONCLUSION

We have studied 3D high side Sided-Isolated N-LDMOS and conventional 2D RESURF LDMOS device and we found a Kirk effect in On-State I-V curves and this Kirk effect depends on P-body doping concentration and channel length and these interns depend on LATID. We proved this new 3D high side Side-Isolated structure can increase p-body concentration and channel as well. This device design will solve Kirk effect problems. So it shows better ESOA performance and also improved Off-state leakage current. It will boost UIS performance as well. Even the process and timing same, but the structure only different. It is one of the better solutions for smart power applications.

ACKNOWLEDGEMENT

The authors would like to thank the Taiwan National Computer Centre for providing license of the Sentaurus TCAD software for high performance computing.

REFERENCES

[1] Zhilin Sun, Weifeng Sun, Longxing Shi, Solid-State Electronics 49 (2005)

[2] Ben G. Streetman, Sanjay Kumar Banerjee, SOLID STATE ELECTRONIC DEVICES (2006)

[3] S. K. Lee, Y. C. Choi, J. H. Kim, C. J. Kim, H. S. Kang, and C. S. Song, IEEE, (2001)

[4] Tsai Minchin, Sheu Gene, Tsai Jung Ruey, Yang Shaoming ICEMI, (2011)

[5] Nie Weidong, Yi Fayou, Yu Zongguang, J.S, (2013)

MATEC Web of Conferences 44, 02007 (2016)
DOI: 10.1051/matecconf/20164402007

Study of impact of LATID on HCI reliability for LDMOS devices

Chandrashekhar[1,a], Gene Sheu[1], Shao Ming Yang[1], Ting Yao Chien[2], Yun Jung Lin[1], Chieh Chih Wu[2] and Tzu Chieh Lee[2]

[1]*Department of Computer Science and Information Engineering, Asia University 500, Lioufeng Rd., Taichung 41354, Taiwan*
[2]*School of Software and Microelectronics, Peking University, Beijing, China*

Abstract. This paper demonstrates electrical degradation due to Hot Carrier Injection (HCI) stress for nLDMOS devices with different Large Angle Tilted Implantation Doping (LATID) techniques for p-body. It seems that optimization of the device with LATID angle for p-body in nLDMOS is important to achieve improved HCI performance and observed that HCI degradation is minimum for 30^0 LATID for p-body. We observed Si/SiO2 interface trap under various stress conditions, were evaluation based on our Sentaurus simulation, and we compare trapped charge density and distribution for various LATID angles and it was less for 30^0 tilt. Trap-related models were employed to perform Ron and Id,sat degradations during the HCI stress test. So nLDMOS device with 30^0 tilt angle for p-body shows better HCI performance compared to other LATID. Also our new proposed device structure shows less HCI degradations when compared with silicon data of HCI degradations for other nLDMOS structure.

1 Introduction

Lateral DMOS transistors are widely used as integrated high-voltage switches and drivers in mixed-signal integrated circuits. The extended drain structure with isolation either by STI or Thermo-oxide and "RESURF" technology [1] are widely used to obtain high-voltage capability while keeping low on resistance so to optimize the specific resistance versus breakdown voltage trade-off. In past, a rugged LDMOS for a 0.35μm Linear BiCMOS technology, which achieves a strongly enhanced electrical SOA, has been presented [2-3]. A buried body implant was added to suppress the parasitic bipolar transistor; hence no snapback was observed in the I-V characteristics: this important feature enables an extension of the current curves to higher drain voltages, when impact ionization at the drain side of the drift region becomes dominant. Thus, an unusual current "enhancement" is reported at large gate voltages with a subsequent saturation of the current at high drain biases.
High operational drain and gate biases make the LDMOS device vulnerable to the damage caused by hot-carrier injection (HCI), and the reliability characterization in STI based LDMOS devices have recently drawn much attention [2-6]. However, very little is known on the hot-carrier injection effects in the rugged LDMOS device when it is operated in the high impact-ionization regime. Mechanism of this reliability issue was not well understood.
High kinetic energy of carriers is gained under the influence of high lateral fields in MOSFET channel and pinch-off region of the transistor. Hot carrier will be generated when non-equilibrium energy distribution is reached and impact ionization will be triggered. Sufficient energy, approximately 3.6eV for electrons and 5.0eV for holes in silicon can be acquired by hot carriers to surmount the energy barrier at Si/SiO2 interface or tunnel into the oxide and the effect will be raised when injected carriers interact with the oxide. This instability may appears and cause a device parameter shift in a long term operation of the device [3-5].
In this paper, the HCI-induced degradation of the double diffused LDMOS has been investigated for different tilt angle implantations i.e., Large Angle Tilted Implantation Doping (LATID). Special attention has been given to the impact of the current "enhancement" on the ¨ΔId,sat and ¨ΔRon and their dependence on the LATID and self-heating due to the power dissipation.

2 Experimental setup

The experimental setup was designed as flowchart in Fig. 2. Practically, the comparisons of the device degradation are performed by confrontment of IV curve before and after stress time on the device structures. Thus, degradation trend for on state resistance (RON) and drain current saturation (Id,sat) were calculated for different stress time (0s, 100s, 1000 s, 10,000 s and 100,000 s) but for 100s we didn't get any shift in HCI or may be very less shift and thus we not presented HCI results for this case but we analysed remaining stress times. On-state resistances (RON) were calculated at drain and gate voltage equals to 0.1V and 5V respectively while drain current saturation calculated at 40V of drain and 5V of gate voltage.
Degradation, thermionic HCI and classical lucky electron models were invoked in the device simulation to perform

[a] Corresponding author: chandru.3ag@gmail.com

Article available at http://www.matec-conferences.org or http://dx.doi.org/10.1051/matecconf/20164402007

the interface trap generation due to HCI. A process of electrons tunnel through a barrier in the presence of a high electric field was taken into account by using Fowler-Nordheim model. While, the lucky-electron model provides an estimate of the probability that some carriers in silicon will be transmitted to the oxide by overcoming the local energy barrier at the Si-SiO2 interface [7-9].

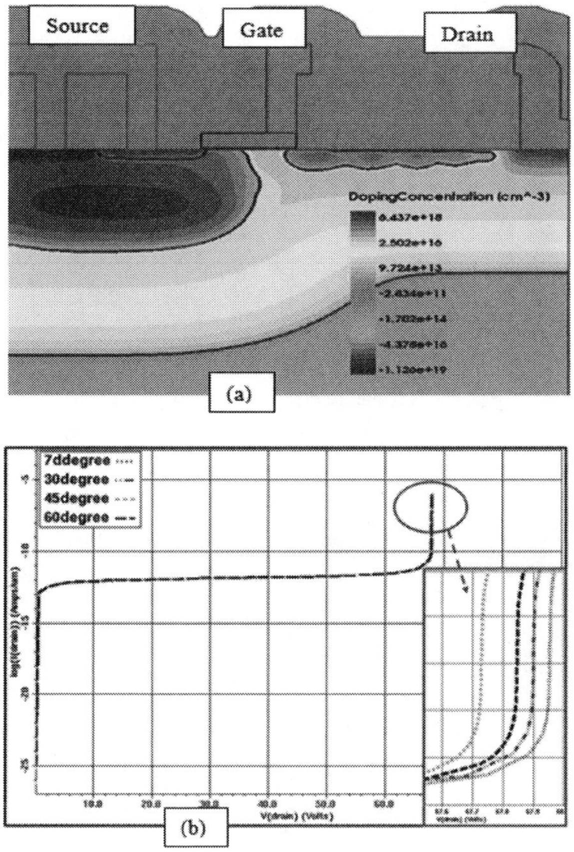

Figure 1. (a) Simulated structure of new proposed 60V nldmos and (b) Off-state bvd curves for proposed nldmos with different tilt angles (latid technique).

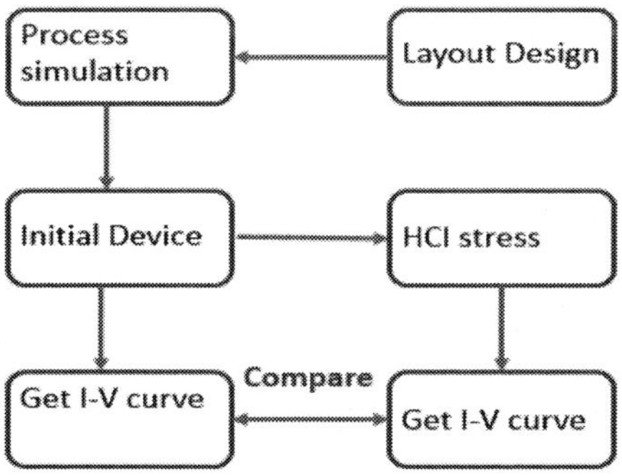

Figure 2. Flowchart of the experimental design

We also compared HCI results of our proposed nLDMOS structure with silicon HCI results for other nLDMOS device and we achieved better HCI results as compared to Silicon HCI results. This comparison with silicon HCI data we provide in next section of Results and discussion.

3 Results and discussion

As we shown in Figure 3, Trapped charges at Si/Sio2 interface are different for different LATID angle implantations. From Table 1. and Figure 3, It is clearly shows that trapped charge is least for 30^0 tilt and worst for 60^0 tilt implant. Further trapped charges for 7^0 and 30^0 seems to be equal in numerical value from Table 1 but area of trapped charges for 7^0 tilt is more than compared to 30^0 tilt. So as we know HCI degradations is because of trapped charges into the oxide region of Si/Sio2 interface and HCI degradation will be more with more traps that occurs in oxide regions. Hence we got good HCI performance for 30^0 tilt and least for 60^0 tilt implant technique. We performed HCI stress test for time 0s, 1e3s, 1e4s and 1e5s and measured on-resistance shift/degrade (ΔRon) and drain saturation current shift (ΔId,sat) and we summarize all HCI results with different LATID angles in Table 1. When we analyse the results we can explain that our new nLDMOS structure shows very good HCI performance. For instance Ron shift for 1e5 seconds HCI stress is 0.057%, which is best and Id,sat shift for HCI 1e5 seconds is 0.398% both for 30^0 tilt angle. So these results very good for HCI stress test concern. It is possible for us to achieve this HCI performance because we put lot of effort to redesign the device so that impact-ionization hotspot should happen at location away from gate and below the surface so that the hot carriers that generate and experience high lateral applied field should not reach or overcome the Si/Sio2 potential barrier and become trapped into gate-oxide region. So we kept this in mind and re-designed our device which helps to get better HCI performance and device can pass HCI life time reliability test.

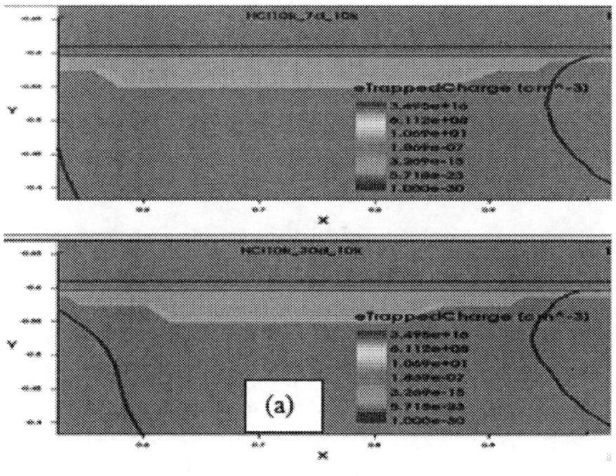

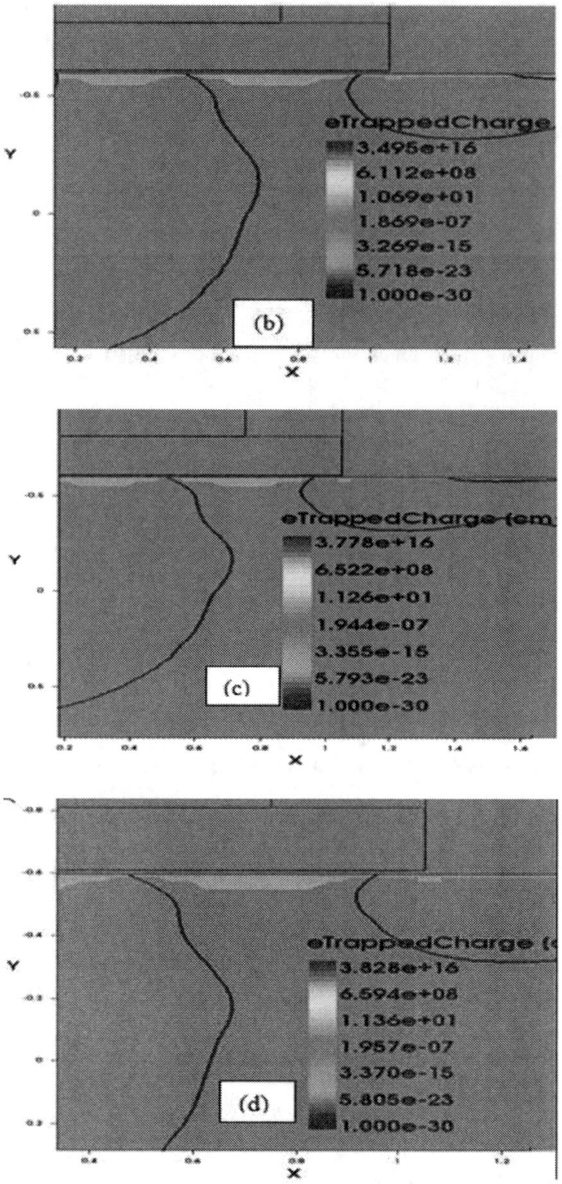

Figure 3. etrapped charge distribution for proposed n-ldmos with various latid angles after 10,000 seconds of hci stress; (a) etrapped charge comparison between 30^0 and 7^0 angle (b) etrapped charge for 30^0 angle (c) etrapped charge for 45^0 angle and (d) etrapped charge for 60^0 angle.

Additionally it can see clearly or can be referred from figure 5, our proposed new nLDMOS structure shows better HCI performance compared to silicon HCI results as ΔRon% and ΔId,sat% curves of proposed structure are more flat compared to silicon data of reference structure and further from figure 5, one can notice that ΔRon% is more severe than ΔIdsat% when compared between proposed and referred structures. So that shows less trap-charges are going into oxide that is gate-oxide and it is because impact ionization rate at offstate bvd is less than referred structure as silicon data. It indicates our device design is good for ensuring long term reliability.

Table 1. Summary of eTrapped charge distribution and hci results of proposed n-ldmos structure for different latid techniques.

		Stress=0 sec	Stress=1e3 sec	Stress=1e4 sec	Stress=1e5 sec
eTrapped Charge (cm-3)	7°	2.078e'16	2.236e'16	3.495e'16	7.459e'16
	30°	2.078e^16	2.276e^16	3.495e^16	7.473e^16
	45°	2.078e^16	2.328e^16	3.778e^16	9.005e^16
	60°	2.078e^16	2.338e^16	3.828e^16	9.15e^16
Ron shift	7°	-	0.015%	0.015%	0.061%
	30°	-	0%	0.018%	0.054%
	45°	-	0%	0.022%	0.067%
	60°	-	0.02%	0.02%	0.062%
Idsat shift (degradation)	7°	-	-0.013%	-0.1%	-0.446%
	30°	-	-0.015%	-0.092%	-0.398%
	45°	-	-0.0175%	-0.087%	-0.4%
	60°	-	-0.016%	-0.078%	-0.35%

Table 2. Comparison of HCI results between proposed nLDMOS structure and reference silicon results.

Stress time(s)	Silicon HCI results for 40V nLDMOS device (reference)		HCI results for our proposed nLDMOS structure	
	ΔRon	ΔId,sat	ΔRon	ΔId,sat
1e3	0.1%	0.09%	0~0.02%	0.013~0.017%
1e4	0.75%	0.5%	0.015~0.022%	0.077~0.1%

And we provided silicon HCI results for reference 40V nLDMOS device and to analyse clearly we put comparison table between HCI results of our new device structure and silicon HCI results of reference structure in Table 2. It can be easily understood that HCI performance of our proposed nLDMOS structure is very good as compared to silicon HCI results.

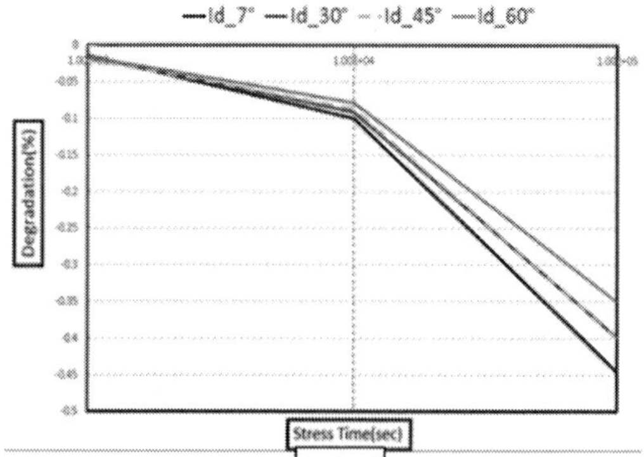

(a)

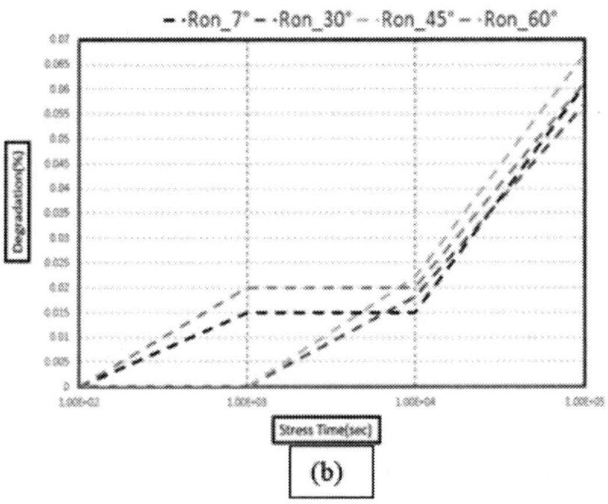

Figure 4. Plot of percentage HCI degradation Vs stress time for different latid (a) Plot of drain-current saturation (ΔId,sat) degradation Vs stress time and (b) Plot of on-resistance (ΔRon) degradation Vs stress time.

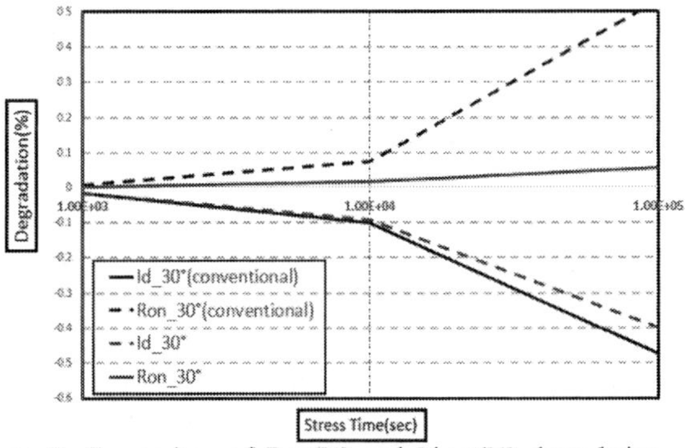

Figure 5. Comparison of Ron(%) and Id,sat(%) degradation between silicon data of reference nLDMOS and proposed nLDMOS structure

3.1 Conclusion

We have studied HCI performance in related to trapped charges at Si/Sio2 interface and that can be optimized by implementing LATID technique for p-body. We also observe that in our proposed n-LDMOS device and may be possible for any nLDMOS devices, the 30^0 tilt angle implantation for p-body shows less traps thereby achieving better HCI results. Therefore the device life time reliability is improved. Hence it's one of the better solution for the devices to be optimized in such a way that impact-ionization hotspot at off-state bvd should be away from gate and below the silicon interface and this type of device design helps to achieve less trap-charges and therefore improve HCI performance.

Acknowledgement

Authors would like to thank Taiwan National Computer Centre for providing licence of Sentaurus TCAD software for high performance computing.

References

1. A.W. Ludikhize, "A review of RESURF Technology", in Proc. Of ISPSD'00, Toulouse (France), May 22-25, 2000, pp. 11-18.
2. J.F. Chen, S.-Y. Chen, K.-S. Tian, K.-M. Wu, C.M. Liu, "On-Resistance Degradation induced by Hot-Carrier Injection in LDMOS Transistors with STI in the Drift Region", in IEEE electron dev. Lett, 29(9), PP. 1071-1073, 2008.
3. Woosung Lee and Hyunsang Hwang, "Hot Carrier Reliability Characteristics of a Bend-gate MOSFET," Solid-State Electronics, vol. **44**, pp. 1117-1119. 2000.
4. P. Moens, G. Van den bosch, and G. Groeseneken, "Hot-Carrier degradation phenomena in lateral and vertical DMOS transistors", IEEE Trans. Electron devices, Vol.**51**.no.4 PP. 623-628, Apr.2004
5. P. Heremans, R. Bellens, G. Groeseneken, and H. Maes, "Consistent Model for the Hot-carrier Degradation in N-channel and P-channel MOSFET's," IEEE Transactions on Electron Devices, vol. **35**, no. 12, p. 2194, December 1988.
6. K.M.Wu, J.F.Chen, Y.K.Su, J.R. Lee, K.W.Lin, J.R.Shih and S.L.Hsu,"Effect of gate bias on hot-carrier reliability in drain extended metal-oxide-semiconductor transistors", Appl.phys.Lett.vol.**89**, no.18, P.183 522.Nov 2006
7. Stewart E. Rauch, III, and Giuseppe La Rosa, "The energy-driven paradigm of NMOSFET hot-carrier effects," IEEE Transactions on Device and Materials Reliability, pp. 701-705, December 2005.
8. P.A. Cosmin, M. Badila, T. Dunca, "Characterization of the Thin Oxides Degradation through Fowler-Nordheim Current," International Semiconductor Conference, vol. **2**. 2003.
9. O. Penzin, A. Haggag, W. McMahon, E. Lyumkis, K. Hess, "MOSFET Degradation Kinetics and its Simulation," IEEE Transactions on Electron Devices, vol.**50**, pp. 1445 - 1450, June 2003.

MATEC Web of Conferences **44**, 02008 (2016)
DOI: 10.1051/matecconf/20164402008

The Foreign Labor Increase Impact on the Wages of Local Residents: From the Perspective of City Scale

Hui Pang[1] and Mi Zhou[2]
[1] *College of Economics; Shenyang University, Shenyang China*
[2] *College of Economics and Management; Shenyang Agricultural University, Shenyang China*

Abstract. we used CGSS2008 data and found that the influence was not significant for the local residents on migrant labors flowing, while the migrant workers increased by 1%, the annual wage income of residents in provincial city increase 1.46%, but fell 0.83% in small and medium-sized city. Therefore, the relationship between migrants and local residents is complementary effect and substitution effect coexist at the same time in mega-cities, the complementary effect is stronger than substitution effect in big city (like Provincial capital) and the substitution effect is stronger than the complementary effect in small and medium-sized city.

1 Introduction

The floating population of the city bring what kind of influence to the local labor market in China, which plays an important role in the formulation and management policy of floating population and has been the government and academic's focuses. With the development of our economy and the accelerated process of industrialization, city needs a large number of migrant workers to improve the level of city in China. However, some scholars believe that the big city is easy to realize economic agglomeration that have priority to the development (Wang and Xia , 1999).Others think that giving priority to the development of small towns can make a large number of farmers to become rapidly non-agricultural rural labors, reducing the settlement city psychological cost and the construction funds that are more in line with the Chinese conditions (Xiao, 2009). Especially the government introduced the relevant measures in the February 23, 2012.The statement is "small and medium-sized city in the future requirements of regulations on employment, education, skills training and other policy measures, and do not account for the nature of the Hukou. Continue to explore the establishment of a unified urban and rural household registration system". This suggests settlement cost of the rural labor force in small and medium-sized city will reduce. Furthermore, do immigration city scale on different rank affect the labor consistent? This study has very important realistic significance, which will help building of new towns in China and promote the orderly transfer of population urbanization.

2 Theories and Methods

We assumes that under different scales cities, Labour supply rate of floating population on different levels of education and work experience can be used as follows:

$$p_{ijt} = M_{ijt} / (M_{ijt} + N_{ijt}) \qquad (1)$$

Among them, M_{ijt} means foreign population, i level of education and work experience is j under the conditions of the t level urban size, N_{ijt} is local population, i level of education and work experience is j under the conditions of the t level urban size. The following model is constructed to measure elastic wages:

$$y_{ijt} = \theta p_{ijt} + s_i + x_j + \pi_t + (s_i \times x_j) + (s_i \times \pi_t) + (x_j \times \pi_t) + \varphi_{ijt} \qquad (2)$$

Among them, s_i says the factors related to education level of labor force, x_j says experience factors associated with the migrant population, π_t means city scale related factors. According to Borjas (2003) , we can get wage flexibility is derived as:

$$\frac{\partial \log w_{ijt}}{\partial m_{ijt}} = \frac{\theta}{(1+m_{ijt})^2} \qquad (3)$$

In addition, $m_{ijt} = M_{ijt} / N_{ijt}$

3 Data

In this paper, the data we use are from China General Social Survey 2008 open database (CGSS2008).The data

Corresponding author: dhtzor@gmail.com

Article available at http://www.matec-conferences.org or http://dx.doi.org/10.1051/matecconf/20164402008

are ranged by adopting stratified four stages unequal probability sampling: the district (county), the streets (town), residents' committees, temporary residents and residents, the district (county), street (town), the residents' committees/village, the three levels data have completed sampling based on "the fifth national population census data" (2000 census).Before the survey, temporary residents and residents (respondents) are sampled, and we get the sample of 6000, the city samples are 3982, 2018 rural samples. The data used in the study is the laborer sample data group by the education and experience from city to city.Therefore, we need to make some important concepts be defined, and select and process the samples, after processing the sample size are of 2452.

4 Model and Results

According to the calculation formula of wage elasticity, we using the weighted OLS to analyze the floating population's influence on local residents incomes under different size cities.The results of the analysis as shown in table 1.

Table 1 The floating population wage replacement of local residents under different urban size

lwagen	(1)	(2)	(3)	(4)
	city	City=1	City=2	City=3
pi	0.537*	-0.221	2.672***	-1.609**
	(0.311)	(0.435)	(0.465)	(0.590)
wage elasticity	0.27	-0.08	1.46	-0.83

Note: (1) in parentheses are standard deviations, ***p<0.01, **p<0.05, *p<0.1;(2) due to the limitation of space, there is no report all regression variables as a result, other explanatory variables including edu, exp_1, city, edu * exp_1, edu * city, exp_1* city;(3) the regression results reported in the table for different cities under each type of level of education and work experience (i, j) set of sample size for the results of the weight.

According to the salary elasticity formula $\frac{\partial \log w_{ijt}}{\partial m_{ijt}} = \frac{\theta}{(1+m_{ijt})^2}$, we can calculate the wage elasticity of substitution of local citizens about 0.27 (0.537 * 0.5), suggest that a 10% increase in labor supply can make local people salary increase 2.7%.In different cities this effect is not consistent, in the three largest cities, floating population has no significant impact on local people wage replacement, and the elasticity of substitution is very small, a 10% increase in labor supply, the salary of local residents reduce only 0.8%;Level in the provincial capital cities, floating population has significant positive influence on improving the salary for local citizens , a 10% increase in Labour supply, the local people salary will increase 14.6%;In small and medium-sized cities, the labor supply increase 10% will make local people salary decline 8.3%.Therefore, the relationship between the migrants and local residents are complementary. In order to further investigate whether wages substitution effect is from a particular group or not, this article analyzes the different levels of education and work experience, and get wage elasticity between different education - experience - city group of floating population and the citizens (as shown in table 2).

Table 2 shows, all floating workers in city group with college degree and high school diploma of have significantly improved the level of wages, although the workers who have a junior high school degree and higher vocational education reduces the local citizens incomes, but the impact is not significant. In different size cities, the effect are the most obvious in the provincial capital city, There have no significant impact on urban and small and medium-sized cities.In table 2 the column from (5)to- (8) means the impact on wages from differences of experience.Overall, the floating population have more than 10 years working experience in the cities will significantly increase the wages of local residents, the effect no matter in any city size is consistent, and are only more obvious in the provincial capital cities. For part-time experiences less than 10 years is a negative influence on local residents income. Especially in urban, the increase of floating population will significantly reduce the wages of local residents, and form a trade-off among local residents.

Table 2 Education difference、experience difference、and wage elasticity

	(1)	(2)	(3)	(4)
	Edu=1	Edu=2	Edu=3	Edu=4
city	-0.466	1.220**	-0.131	1.561**
	(0.283)	(0.509)	(0.299)	(0.723)
City=1	-1.625	0.825	-0.250	-0.336
	(1.035)	(1.059)	(0.286)	(1.619)
City=2	-2.369**	-0.177	-0.263	3.906***
	(0.687)	(0.486)	(0.496)	(0.765)
City=3	-1.993	-1.403	-2.299	-1.731
	(1.880)	(1.427)	(1.939)	(1.018)
	(5)	(6)	(7)	(8)
	Exp_1=1, 2	Exp_1=3, 4	Exp_1= 5,6	Exp_1=7, 8
	-0.494**	0.851**	1.731**	0.00955
	(0.230)	(0.310)	(0.677)	(0.783)
	-0.734**	0.770*	1.704*	0.0561
	(0.305)	(0.368)	(0.864)	(0.860)
	0.402	1.056***	2.585***	0.538
	(0.375)	(0.342)	(0.722)	(0.770)
	0.388	0.999***	2.104**	0.193
	(0.405)	(0.318)	(0.845)	(0.850)

Note: (1) that in parentheses are standard deviations,***p<0.01, **p<0.05, *p<0.1;(2)the regression results in the table above

reports for different cities take the sample size of different levels of education and the different working experience as the weight.

5 Conclusion and Discussion

In this paper, the research found that Labour mobility under different urban size have different effects on the local Labour market.In the three largest cities, flow labor have no significant impact on local residents incomer;In the other provincial capital cities, the increase of foreign labor will significantly increase the wages of local residents;While in small and medium-sized cities, will reduce the wages of the local people.The reason is that the extra large city scale expanding, the floating labors' alternative cause labor consumption, and ease the citizens' wage changes;And in the provincial capital cities, floating population promote the regional industrial division, strengthen the foreign labor cooperation with local citizens, at the same time, also improve the wage level of the local people;But, in small and medium-sized cities, because of the low labor heterogeneity degree, the competitive relationship between migrants and local residents reduce the wages of the local residents.

Acknowledgements

This work was supported by the National Science Foundation of China(NO.71203146; NO.71273179; NO.71373163; NO.71273177), the program for excellent talents in Liaoning province(NO.WJQ2014016); and agriculture youth science and technology innovation talent training plan in Liaoning province(NO.2014055).

References

1. Xue-jun Liu, Yao-hui Zhao. Labor flow's influence on urban labor market [J]. Economics (quarterly), 2(2009)
2. Ming Lu, Hong Gao, Hong Sato . Urban scale and inclusive employment [J]. Chinese academy of social sciences, 10(2012).
3. Xiao-han Zhong . Labour mobility and wage differences [J]. Chinese academy of social sciences, 1 (2006).
4. Aydemir A.,Borjas G.J. Cross - country Variation in the Impact of International Migration: Canada, Mexico, and the United States[J],Journal of the European Economic Association,5(4)(2007):663-708.
5. Borjas G.J. The Labor Demand Curve Is Downward Sloping: Reexamining the Impact of Immigration on the Labor Market[J],The Quarterly Journal of Economics, 118(4)(2003):1335-1374.

MATEC Web of Conferences 44, 02009 (2016)
DOI: 10.1051/matecconf/20164402009

Research on pipe welding information management system based on RFID

Xun Liu [1,a]

[1] Chengdu Qianjia technology Co.,Ltd, Institute of Technology, China

Abstract. This paper introduces the construction background, construction target and construction principle of the pipe welding management system based on RFID. Then, describes the specific requirements of the system. The basic principle and key technology of the system are introduced. The structure of the system (including the system design, the selections of handheld devices and high frequency passive RFID tags) is described .Then the system management software designs (including software structure, the main functions of the management center system and the main functions of the handheld detection system) are described in detail. Finally, the management system is implemented, and it is deployed to several Gas Co, which has chieved good results.

1 Introduction

With the construction of gas pipeline network, different welding parameters are different. For pipe welding, supervision, maintenance and management personnel, how to quickly know the pipe welding parameters, pipe fittings, welding inspection results and other information, is an important issue to be solved in the current management of gas pipeline network. With the continuous development of the refinement, centralization, standardization and informatization of the management of Gas Co., the information management of the pipe welding based on RFID[1] radio frequency tag technology has become the development trend of the tube information management of the Gas Co.

The specific objectives of the management system are as follows:

a.the establishment of a set of pipe welding information management system to ensure that the welding information is comprehensive, standardized, accurate, and real-time.

b.the implementation of the initialization, the sending sign and changing sign of the RFID tag , writing into and reading out the welding parameters.

c.the implementation of writing into and reading out the pipe welding inspection information

d.the implementation of the dynamic monitoring and management of the whole network pipe fitting and welding information.

e.the implementation of the electron of the tube inspection and maintenance, in order to facilitate the maintenance data management

f. the implementation of a complete and powerful report, statistical analysis and query functions, to provide the decision-making basis for the relevant departments.

The construction principles of the management system are as follows:

a. stability

Because it is a very important system of pipe network construction and daily maintenance, it must be able to run continuously.The system is based on economic and practical, cost-effective design principles. Comprehensive considering system structure, design scheme and technical support, the B/S[2] structure is adopted.The establishment of a separate database and application server, ensure the stability and reliability of the system.

Hardware must be fully considered according to the environment, and use the industrial grade RFID read and write equipment to ensure the stability of the system.

b. progressiveness

The system uses full WEB pages and advanced WEB GIS[3]technology.

RFID read and write devices integrated with RFID, GPRS and WiFi functions, better meet the actual needs of the maintenance management personnel, and lay a good foundation for the system to increase the field repair and maintenance functions.

c. maintenance convenience

Use free Baidu MAP or GIS to provide information for the pipeline maintenance management, and provide the handheld equipment for the supervision, pipe fittings maintenance and management personnel to read the pipe welding parameters.

d openness, compatibility

All kinds of design specifications, technical indicators and products are in line with international and industrial standards. All the products used in the system must are open and compatible systems, can be compatible with the products of different manufacturers, and could effectively protect the investment of the Gas Co..

[a] Xun liu: 1538768111@qq.com

e. operation convenience

The system is simple, with friendly interface, easy to install and debug, meet the requirements of different people.

2 REQUIREMENT ANALYSIS

After the completion of the pipe welding and detection, pipeline maintenance management personnel will write welding parameters, welding, testing and other information into RFID tags through the handheld device, and then insert the RFID tag into the RFID tab and do a fixed processing. Specific requirements are as follows:

a. can input the information complied with ISO 12176-4: 2003[4] standard requirements, including production date, batch of raw materials, production processes and all other production-related information into the chip, and achieve permanent traceability function.

b. the library information, including order number, number of shipments, shipping customer name, shipping date and other information can be entered into RFID tag, also saved to pipe welding information management system.

c. the information including the actual pipe welding parameters, welding date, time, ambient temperature, welders work number and other information is read by a hand held device connected to the welder, and is uploaded to the pipe welding information management system. Welding parameter file is created to facilitate the supervision personnel to inspect the welding parameters, at the same time, it can be used as a reason to find the problem and as the basis for determining the responsibility if there is a leak in the future.

d. product tracking and recognition,that is, after the completion of the project, in line operation, through the handheld reader, management and maintenance personnel can detect the specific location of the target tube, and quickly identify the specific information of the product. In the case of no more than 20 cm of soil covering, effective detection distance is within 3m.

3 SYSTEM SURVEY

3.1. Basic principles of the system

According to the project requirements, the system is designed for the installation of RFID electronic tags for welding, pipe fittings and other information preservation, as well as tracking and identifying the fittings. Engineering supervision and pipeline maintenance and management personnel read welding, pipe fittings and other information saved on the RFID tags, and by combining with wireless network (WIFI or GPRS network) and pipe welding information management system complete the welding-related information query and fittings position tracing and identification.

a. fittings archives information management

After the pipe out of the library and the completion of the welding, pipe engineering management personnel need to establish a pipe information file for each welding pipe. At the same time, the information of pipe fitting and welding parameters in demand is saved to a central management system, and alse is written to the RFID tag.

b. pipe welding information check

Engineering supervision and pipeline maintenance and management personnel can read the information in the RFID tag buried in the pipe through handheld devices, and combining with central management system, check the pipe fitting and welding information file.

c. pipe tracing and identification

In the process of the pipeline maintenance management, when the tube is in the case of no more than 20 cm cement and soil buried, pipeline maintenance managers can read the information in RFID tag embedded in the fittings through a handheld device, and combing with the GIS map find the fitting, and identify the relevant information.

d pipe line visualization management

Through the establishment of GIS system of the pipe line and terrain of the corresponding area, and electronic account of fittings, combining with geographical position and surrounding environment of the pipeline and energy facilities in the GIS platform, pipeline managers can view basic properties, maintenance records, working status, welding parameters, and so on, to achieve visualization of pipe line management. At the same time, the electronic accounting information and location information are downloaded to the handheld device for the maintenance and management personnel to check at the scene, and provide strong information support for field maintenance and maintenance.

3.2 System key technology

3.2.1 RFID radio frequency data storage and communication

Each RFID tags can provide a unique serial number encoding, and can be stored for a long time to write the data information, and with a variety of packaging methods, suitable for use in the field environment. The RFID electronic tag is powered by a handheld device in a wireless way, and the data communication between handheld device and the electronic tag is realized in the RF mode.

3.2.2 GPRS network communication

GPRS (General Packet Radio Service) is compared with the traditional GSM transmission mode, with "high speed transmission", "on-line forever", "charge according to quantity" and "freely switch" advantages, to enhance the quality of mobile communication.

3.2.3 GIS geographic information system

GIS is a new technology which has developed rapidly in recent years. GIS is a product of the interdisciplinary use of cartography, computer science,

geography, remote sensing, statistics, surveying and mapping, communication, planning and management, and widely used in various fields. In this system, it is mainly used in the computer system to display and manage the map and the pipe line information.

4 System Components

4.1 System composition

Pipe welding information management system is made up of three parts, that is, the handheld device, electronic information tag and system management center.

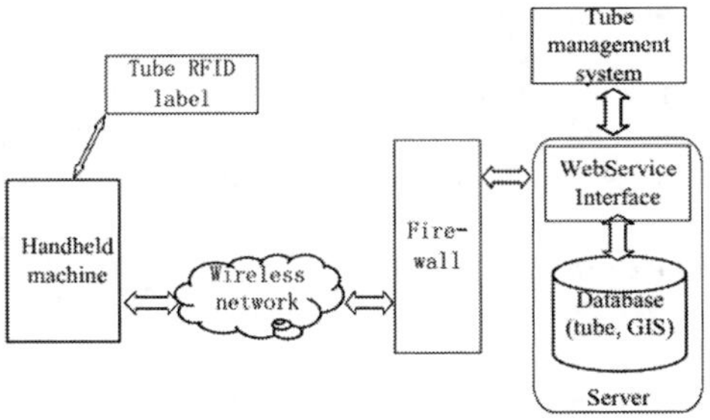

Figure.1 Overall system design

According to the requirements of the project and the use environment, the hand-held device uses a IP64 industrial grade hand-held inspection instrument, while the electronic tags of passive type and full seal design are used, the software uses B/S structure (web browsing mode) design.

A RFID tag is installed on each of the welded joints of the pipe fitting, each pipe welding management personnel holds an industrial PDA, and each project supervisor or pipeline maintenance administrator holds an industrial PDA.

4.2 Hardware introduction

4.2.1 hand-held inspection instrument GRT-PDA

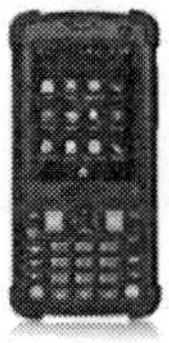

Figure.2 GRT-PDA

The main features are as follows:

a. industrial grade three proof design, fall proof,water proof and dust proof.

b. integrate RFID, GPRS, GPS and other modules.

c. built-in camera.

d. built in CE WIN operating system and powerful inspection software.

e. with a touch screen and the full function 32 key keyboard, can input information and operate software by hand written or keyboard.

f. large storage memory, place the massive information database of the electronic account, photos, maintenance records of all pipeline and energy facilities.

g. through the inspection software based on WIN CE platform, can easily query electronic account, inspection plan, find the facility near the current location, and can fill in and declare a complex inspection work content, and upload the photos.

4.2.2 High frequency passive RFID Tags

Figure.3 passive RFID Tags

Label shape: can be customized according to the design of pipe fittings, form is be shown in the Figure 3 above.

Storage capacity: 8Kbit, 16 partitions, each partition has two passwords.

Working frequency: 13.56MHZ

Communication speed：106Kboud

Read and write distance：5—10CM

Erasing times：>100000 times

Data preservation：>10 years

Packaging Materials：PVC、PET

Packaging technology：ultrasonic automatic wire and auto touch welding.

Production standard：ISO14443[5][6].

4.2.3 Installation scheme of passive RFID tag

In order to ensure that the RFID tag is installed at the fitting interface, and the communication distance is not affected by the handheld device to read the RFID tags, in manufacturing the tube, a RFID tag slot (can be rectangular, square, circles, etc.) with 2.5mm concave section in the interface is reserved. In this way, after the completion of the pipe welding, pipe welding engineering management personnel will write welded information written into RFID tags, and insert the tag into the slot, and then seal the slot with the sealing glue.

5 Design and implementation of system management software

5.1 Software structure

The software use the advanced B/S structure, the SQLSERVER, WEBGIS and other core development technology, and the terrain road map uses Baidu MAP.（Baidu GIS is free road terrain MAP information, will do some updates every year，when the user has not set up or purchase mapping road terrain data, it is the ideal choice, can provide more accurate road terrain information, and can save a lot cost of buying maps and annual renewal for users, also avoid the possible occurrence of map information copyright law disputes.）

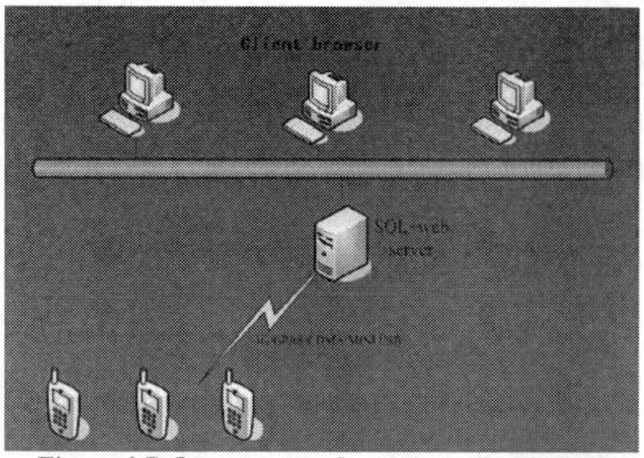

Figure.4 Software network structure sketch map

Fittings information, welding information, the welding parameters, weld inspection data and other management information are unified sent to and stored in a single database server, and through the server the software is published in Web page. Users can directly use the software with the browser in any computer by local area networks or network, do not need to install any client software. This not only greatly improve the convenience of the user of the software, but also strengthen the stability of the system, ensure the safety and reliability of the system data, and avoid the instability of the system caused by the client software, while the maintenance workload greatly is reduced.

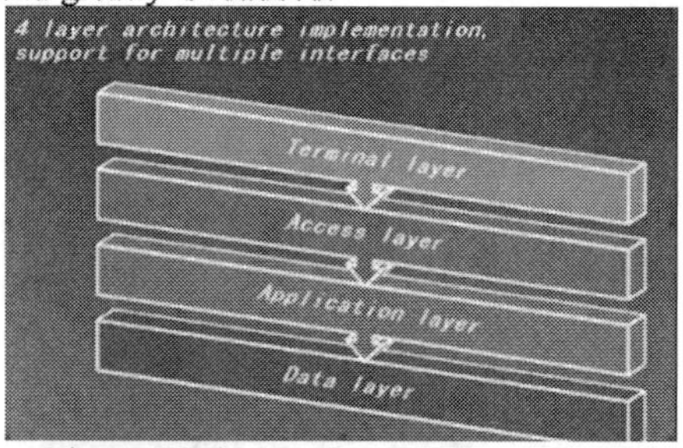

Figure.5 Software structure sketch map 1

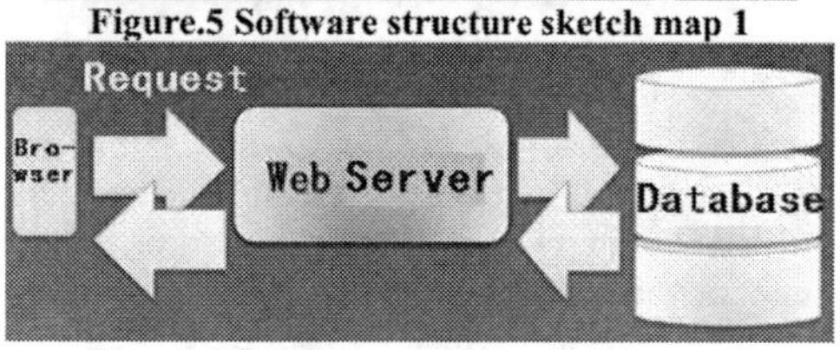

Figure.6 Software structure sketch map 2

5.2 Software main function

5.2.1 Management center system function

The main functions of the center system are as follows:

Fittings archives information management: support for tube production, procurement, storage, welding, welding parameters, testing, use and maintenance of information management.

Pipe welding and tracing GIS management: support for the map display of the deployment of the pipe and the welding distribution, also through GIS providing the fittings geographic information for pipeline maintenance and management personnel.

Sending sign: bind the RFID tag with the tube, and write the fitting information to the RFID tag.

Handheld device data download: via WIFI or GPRS the pipe welding information, sending note information, fittings geographic information and other relevant information are download to the handheld devices.

Statistical Analysis: support for a multi dimensional analysis on the installation, use, maintenance and welding related information of the fittings of the Gas Co.

5.2.2 hand-held inspection system function

The main functions of the handheld system are as follows:

Data upload and download: via WIFI or GPRS upload and download the pipe welding information, send note information, fittings geographic information and other relevant information from center management system.

Send sign: bind the RFID tag with the tube, and write the fitting information to the RFID tag.

Welding information inspection: by reading the RFID tag to obtain the information of the welding information, welding parameters and so on.

Pipe tracing: by downloading the GIS information of the location fitting, and using the RFID tag reading detection function to find the pipe within 3 meters.

Welding parameters upload and download: through data exchange with the welder, the welding parameters of the welder are downloaded, and the welding parameters of the specified tube is also uploaded to the welder in order to set the welding parameters of welder.

6 Conclusion

The construction background, needs, principles and key techniques of the pipe welding information management system based on RFID are analyzed, The overall structure design of the system is carried out. The corresponding hardware devices are selected. The design and the implementation of the system are carried out. At present, the system has been used in some Gas Co, and has achieved good economic and social benefits.

References

1. Y.F. Dan, C.G. Dan, L. Yao, *Radio Frequency Identification (RFID) Principles and Applications*,(Electronics Industry Press,2013).
2. J.N.Wang,*Software B/S development*,(Tsinghua University press,2012).
3. P. A. Longley, M. F. Goodchild, D. J. Maguire, D. W. Rhind,*Geographic Information Science and Systems 4th Edition*,(VILEY,2011).
4. ISO12176-4:2003:Plastics pipes and fittings--Equipment for fusion jointing polyethylene systems --Part 4: Traceability coding.
5. ISO/IEC 14443-1:2008 Identification cards--Contactless integrated circuit cards--Proximity cards--Part 1: Physical characteristics.
6. ISO/IEC 14443-2:2010 Identification cards--Contactless integrated circuit cards--Proximity cards--Part 2:Radio frequency power and signal interface.

MATEC Web of Conferences 44, 02010 (2016)
DOI: 10.1051/matecconf/20164402010

Analysis of space payload operation modes based on divide-and-conquer clustering

Feng Si[1,2,a], Bao Jun Lin[1] and Shan Cong Zhang[3]

[1]Academy of Opto-Electronics, Chinese Academy of Sciences, Beijing, China;
[2]University of Chinese Academy of Sciences, Beijing, China;
[3]Technology and Engineering Center for Space Utilization, Chinese Academy of Sciences, Beijing, China

Abstract. With the development of space electronic technology, the space payload operation modes are more and more complex, and manual interpretation is prone to errors for much workload. Generally the space payload's operation modes are reflected by its telemetry data. By analysing the characteristics of the payload telemetry data, it is proposed an automatic analysis method of payload operation modes based on divide-and-conquer clustering. The clustering method combines division and incremental clustering. The principle of the method is introduced and the method is validated using the actual payload telemetry data. Furthermore the improved method is proposed to the problems encountered. Experimental results show that divide-and-conquer clustering method has the feature of calculation simple and classification accurate, when applied to the classification of payload operation modes. Furthermore this method can be applied to the other areas of payload data processing by extending the method.

1 Introduction

The operation modes of space payload are much more complex, as the system size becomes larger [1]. It can be identified by the telemetry data related to the payload in orbit. The mass telemetry data will be produced every day and has large differences between different kinds of payloads in general. Traditional methods either depend on the manual judgment, or the rules according to the prior knowledge of the designer. The rules are more complex to design in the transient between operation modes. Furthermore the rules designed for specific payloads are often difficult to expand to other payloads. In order to reduce the error rate of manual interpretation and complexity of rule-based method, we present a novel method based on data mining technology to find system structure hidden in telemetry data and the operation modes of payload automatically.

There are many kinds of technology in data mining field [2-3]. According to the characteristics of the payload telemetry data, we choose data clustering method to identify the payload operation modes. Data clustering [4-7] belongs to the category of unsupervised learning, which is a discovery process that groups data set such that the intracluster similarity is maximized and the intercluster similarity is minimized. In the absence of any prior knowledge, we don't know the payloads how to work and how many operation modes do they have. In this case, the method of data clustering can help us to find the patterns in the underlying telemetry data.

In this paper, we present a novel clustering algorithm called divide-and-conquer clustering that applies group method and incremental clustering to classify payload telemetry data [8-11]. We demonstrate the effectiveness of divide-and-conquer algorithm in huge actual telemetry data of payloads. Experimental results show that this algorithm can discover the payload operation modes simply and effectively. Finally, we apply this algorithm to other fields of payload data processing.

2 Divide-and-Conquer Algorithm

According to the payload's prior work rule in orbit, much more telemetry data was generated every day (some greater than one hundred thousand records). There will be great amount of calculation if we do data clustering using one day's records directly. In order to solve this problem, we adapt the divide-and-conquer clustering algorithm. Firstly, the telemetry data will be grouped in order and then we calculate the similarity of the records in the group, complete the clustering intra-group. Secondly, within groups after clustering, eigenvector is calculated for each category. Thirdly, the similarity between groups will be calculated using eigenvectors of each category. The process will be iterative until all records are classified.

The process of clustering is as follows:

(1) Data pre-processing

Scan all the parameters in the data set and find out the characteristics of each type of data parameters, such as the parameter's data range, discrete or continuous values,

[a] Corresponding author: sifeng04@126.com

or variation of the parameter. For the voltage telemetry, temperature telemetry, or some count values of payload, it can be applied to calculate directly. But for some state variables, the numerical value only represents a different state and these state variables can't be applied for calculation directly. These data should be pre-processed for calculation [12-13].

(2) Normalization

All data will be normalized using the following formula and they will be limited in the range of [0, 1] after normalization.

$$x'_{ik} = \frac{x_{ik} - \min\limits_{1\le i\le n}\{x_{ik}\}}{\max\limits_{1\le i\le n}\{x_{ik}\} - \min\limits_{1\le i\le n}\{x_{ik}\}} \left(k = 1,2,...,m\right) \quad (1)$$

(3) Grouping

All the records in the data set will be grouped. In general, the space payload operation modes are continuous and consistent unless in fault condition. The process of grouping can be operated in the sequence of data in the data set.

(4) Clustering intra-group

Calculate the similarity between any two records in the group. We'll cluster the records according to the similarity results. After clustering intra-group, we'll calculate the eigenvector of each category, which represents the category's centroid. The similarity between two records can be analysed in the fractional distance metrics [14]. The formula is as follows:

$$dist_d^f(x,y) = \sum_{i=1}^{d}\left[(x_i - y_i)^f\right]^{1/f}, f \in (0,1) \quad (2)$$

(5) Clustering inter-group

After clustering in the groups, we'll cluster between groups using the selected eigenvectors of each category. It may be grouped continually if we have many more categories after clustering inter-group. Cluster until the terminal conditions.

(6) Evaluation of clustering result

In order to evaluate the performance of the classification, many other methods may be applied for contrast, such as manual inspection of payload operation modes, rule-based method etc.

3 Experimental Results and Discussion

3.1 The original clustering

In this section, we validate our divide-and-conquer algorithm with an actual telemetry data set of one earth observation payload. The data set contains several thousand telemetry records and we choose 300 records for test. Each record includes 206 parameters. Then we'll do the data set clustering in the algorithm above.

We do data pre-processing, normalization and divide the data records into three groups and each group has 100 records. Then we calculate the similarity of records between each other in each group. According to the similarity result, we can find records with the highest similarity to each record. But we can't classify the records only by the similarity result. Figure 1 shows the first group's 100 records and their partner records with highest similarity.

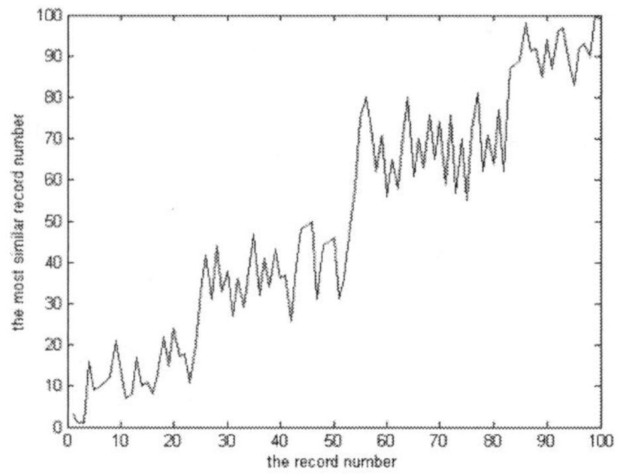

Figure 1. The record and its partner record with highest similarity

3.2 Analysis of clustering failure

By analysis the original records in the first group, we have found two main reasons for clustering failure.

The first reason is disturbance of some irrelevant parameters. Searching all parameters in the record manually, we can find some parameters which have drastic changes between different records. But the drastic changes don't reflect the system operation modes in macroscopic view. For example, the payload heartbeat signal, reversed once between adjacent records, reflects only the normal state not the operation modes change.

The second reason is parameter multiplexing problem. Some parameters are multiplexed in system design, and each cycle represent different physical meanings. Sometimes there is great numerical difference in different cycle, but this difference can't reflect the switch of system mode.

3.3 Modified clustering method

In order to solve the above problems, we'll take the following measures. Firstly, we'll apply weighted parameters instead of original parameters in similarity calculation. According to the characteristics of the parameters distribution, we'll dispatch different weights of parameters. Secondly, we can avoid the parameter multiplexing problem in system planning and design phase. Alternatively we'll use parametric subdivision for the parameters of multiplexing in the original system architecture. The subdivision parameters will reflect the system operation modes.

By taking the above two measures, we re-calculate the similarity of 100 records in the first group. The similarity calculation results show that the similarity of the same mode records is very high and mostly greater than 0.999. By manual analysis of 100 records in the first group, the group can be divided into four clusters, the 1~24 records for the compression-and-storage mode, the 25~50 records for the compression system power-off mode, the 51~82 records for the transmit system power-on mode, the 83~100 records for the system idle mode. The calculation result of modified clustering algorithm is consistent with

manual analysis. Figure 2 shows the first group's 100 records and their partner records with highest similarity.

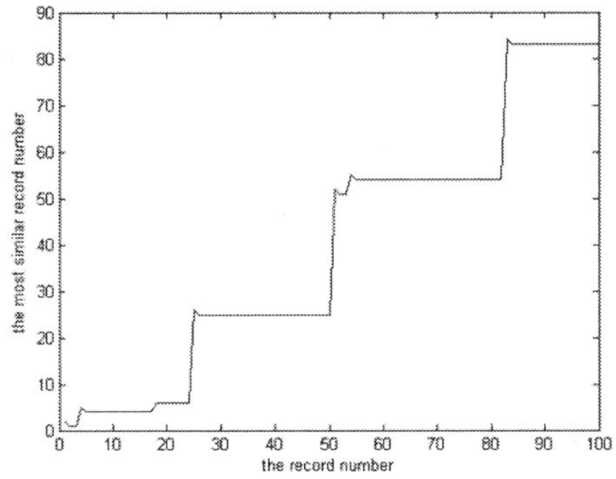

Figure 2. The record and its partner record with highest similarity (using modified clustering algorithm).

Following the same algorithm, we get the other two group records' intra-group similarity. Figure 3 shows the three group records' intra-group similarity. In the figure, we can see that the first group is divided into four clusters, the second group has two clusters and the third group has three clusters.

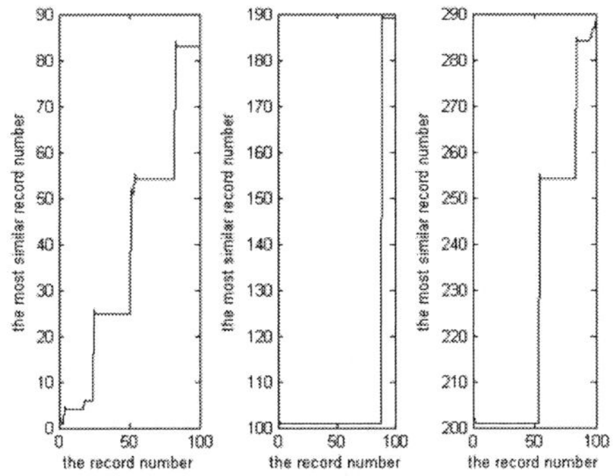

Figure 3. Clustering of every group

After completing the intra-group clustering, we'll calculate the centroid of each category. Using the selected centroid of each category, we'll calculate the similarity between categories. The result shows that the fourth category and fifth category can be merged into one cluster, sixth category and seventh category can be merged into one category. Thus the original nine categories can be combined into seven categories. Figure 4 shows the result of second round calculation.

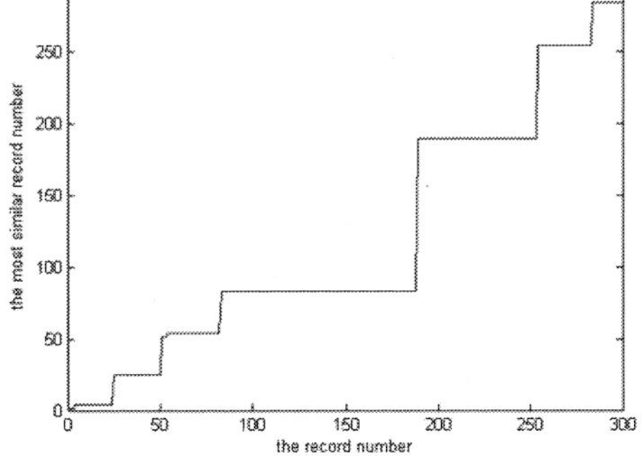

Figure 4. Clustering of three groups

Contrast to the result of the clustering algorithm, the result of manual analysis is basically the same. The following table shows the results obtained by manual analysis.

Table 1. The Result of Manual Analysis

Clustering Number	Record Number	Operation modes
1	1~3	Data Download from Channel 1
2	4~24	Channel 1 Close
3	25~50	Compression Stop
4	51~53	Compression Power Off
5	54~82	Transmission Close
6	83~188	Camera 1 Power Off
7	189~253	Compression and Storage
8	254~283	Idle
9	284~300	Data Download from Channel 2

When the clustering algorithm above is applied to the rest of the data set, we can also obtain a good classification and get the accurate payload operation modes.

3.4 Discussion on how to divide data set

In the above chapter, we have discovered that the payload operation modes can be automatically analysed using divide-and-conquer clustering to the payload telemetry data. But how to choose the best dividing method is still a problem. We'll discuss the best group method below.

We'll take into account the processing time and the clustering accuracy as the evaluation criterion. Using the data set above, we get the result of different dividing method. Figure 5 shows the calculation result. In the figure, the relative processing time is calculated by the ratio of the spending time of all dividing methods and the un-dividing method. The clustering accuracy is got by the ratio of successful clustering records and all the records.

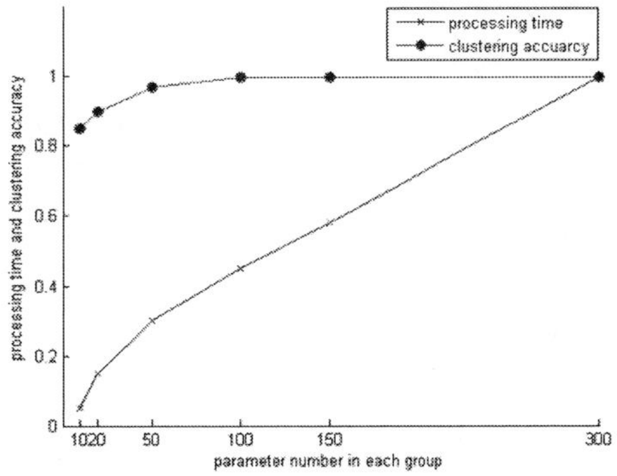

Figure 5. Relative processing time and clustering accuracy

From the figure, we can see that with the increasing records number in each group, the processing time is dramatically increased, but with the more clustering accuracy. Furthermore, the increase of the processing time is synchronous with increase of the records number in each group. But the clustering accuracy is no longer

increased when the clustering accuracy reaches a balance point. So we can get the transition point by the balance of the processing time and clustering accuracy. From figure 5, we can see that when the data set is divided into 3 groups and each group includes 100 records, the clustering accuracy will reach 100% and the processing time is only half of the un-divided method. It's a better choice for the payload operation modes clustering.

4 Conclusions

In this paper, we have presented a divide-and-conquer clustering algorithm for analysing the payload operation modes. The algorithm takes into account the group method, weighted parameter and parametric subdivision, which successfully solves the mass data, disturbance parameter and parameter multiplexing problem. Experimental results on actual telemetry data set show that the modified algorithm can successfully identify the payload's operation modes automatically. The method may be extended to the real-time processing of payload by creating the payload characteristics library. Furthermore when we have acquired all the operation modes and characteristics of payload, we can do some fault detection and fault diagnosis for the payload.

References

1. Y.F. He, G.H. Zhao, C.M. Lv, Journal of University of Chinese Academy of Science, **28**, 4(2011)
2. J. Han, M. Kamber, *Data mining: concepts and techniques*, 187~198(2006)
3. A.K. Jain, M.N. Murty, P.J. Flynn, ACM Computing Surveys, **31**, 3(1999)
4. P. Hansen, B. Jaumard, Math. Program., **79**, 1-3(1997)
5. A.K. Jain, R.C. Dubes, Englewood Cliffs Prentice Hall, **32**, 2(1988)
6. L. Kaufman, P. Rousseeuw, *Finding groups in data:An introduction to cluster analysis,* 1990
7. C.H. Cheng, IEEE Transactions on computers, **24**, 9(1975)
8. M.N. Murty, G. Krishna, Pattern Recognition, **12**(1980)
9. W.F. Eddy, A. Mockus, S. Oue, Computational Statistics & Data Analysis, **23**, 1(1996)
10. G.A. Carpenter, S. Grossberg, Neur Netw, **3**, 2(1990)
11. S. Asharaf, M.N. Murty, Pattern Recognition, **36**, 12(2003)
12. H.L. Chen, K.T. Chuang, M.S. Chen, ICDM, 2005
13. H.L. Chen, M.S. Chen, S.C. Lin, IEEE Transaction Knowledge and Data Engineering, **21**, 5(2009)
14. G. Karypis, E.H. Han, V. Kumar, IEEE Computer, **32**, 8(1999)

MATEC Web of Conferences **44**, 02011 (2016)
DOI: 10.1051/matecconf/20164402011

Development of a Health Care Information System for the Elderly at Home

Dong Wang [1, 2, a], Wan Cheng Ge[1] and Yun Guang Wang[2]

[1] *School of Electrical and Information Engineering, Tongji University, Shanghai, China*
[2] *Shanghai University Of Medicine & Health Sciences, Shanghai, China*

Abstract. The growing population aging is a serious social problem in the world today. Accidental death at home is increasing because abnormal conditions can not be discovered in time, especially to the elderly who live alone. Besides, according to statistics, over 80 percent of the elderly need the service of home care in China. A health care information system for the elderly at home is developed to monitor the real-time state of the elderly remotely in this thesis. The system can show the current positions of the elderly in the house and judge whether they are in dangerous locations or have dangerous activities. In the case of emergency, the elderly can press the emergency button. The system also provides some help for the elderly's daily life. The system offers the advantage for living at home more safely and more comfortably, and has better application prospect.

1 Introduction

With the arrival of the aging society, more and more attention is drawn to the aging problems. In China, population of labour force is thinning down, while the number of aging people is growing steadily now. Caring for the elderly becomes difficult. The children or relatives of the elderly usually can not provide enough care. Therefore, the elderly who need social services are increasing continuously. It leads to increasing the medical and welfare costs, and prevents social independence of the elderly people. Moreover, according to statistics, over 85 percent of the elderly people wish to live in their own houses. Only 6% to 8% of the elderly people accept to be taken care of in the nursing home. Because the elderly feel comfortable and warm in familiar surroundings, when he sees many acquaintances[1-3].

As the measure, a new health care information system for the elderly at home has been developed to help the elderly people to maintain their independence and enhance their quality of life. The System is composed of a server with a database and a monitoring software, smartphones with RFID cards, RFID readers and GSM base stations, and etc. This system can monitor to judge whether the elderly are in dangerous locations or has dangerous activities. The system also can offer some help services for the elderly.

2 System Configuration

2.1 System configuration

Fig. 1 shows a basic system configuration. The old person always carries a smartphone binding a RFID card with him. The RFID readers are installed in the places of the house where need detection. In the monitoring center of the community, there are working staffs keeping a 24-hour surveillance.

When the old person is moving in the house, the RFID readers will scan the card and make sure the location of the old person. Then the workstation sends the position message to the monitoring center of the community. The message will be processed by the monitoring software in the center. For example, the system will produce an alarm when the old person has been in the balcony for too long.

If the old person has a dangerous action, such as falling to the ground, the sensor in the smartphone can detect it and the smartphone sends an alarm to the monitoring center of the community. The message will be received and processed.

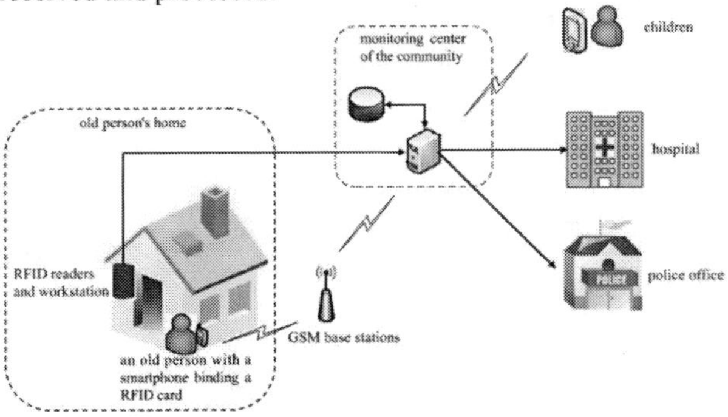

Fig.1 system configuration

2.2 System function

Based the system configuration, a new system is developed. Some hardware has been bought, such as

[a] Corresponding author: wd_lulu@163.com

RFID readers, smartphones and etc. Some software has been used, such as C#, Java and database management system. The system is consist of two sections: the monitoring software and the smartphone system[4].

The function of the monitoring software is shown as follows:

① Input the users' information such as basic information of the elderly, family information, medical records, emergency communication, and etc.

② Input the Communities' information.

③ Reminding settings for the elderly, such as medicine reminding settings and treatment reminding settings.

④ Real-time monitoring to show the elderly's current positions and alarm.

⑤ Query statistics

The function of the smartphone system includes: input the users' base information, detect the falling, detect the press of the emergency button, remind the elderly to take medicines or go to hospital, and etc.

3 Realization of RFID Indoor Positioning

3.1. Centroid localization algorithm based on RSSI

When the old person with the RFID tag in a dangerous area, the position message will be read by RFID readers and transmitted to the monitoring center. The message will be processed by the monitoring software in the center to judge whether to raise an alarm or not. This system adopts a method of RSSI to locate the old person.

RSSI(Received Signal Strength Indicator) ,is a value to indicate the electromagnetic wave energy in some medium. Because the signal strength will be reduced as it travels, the distance between signal point and receiving point can be determined by the received signal strength. According to the corresponding data, the current position of the test target will be calculated. From experience, we can have

$$PL(d) = PL(d_0) - 10\gamma \log_{10}\left(\frac{d}{d_0}\right) + X_\sigma \tag{1}$$

The equation 1 is known as signal transmission model. PL(d) is the received RSSI value, d away from the signal point. PL(d0) is the received RSSI value, d0 away from the signal point. X_σ is a Gaussian random variable, whose mean value is zero and variance is $\sigma^2(dB)$. according to the equation 1:

$$d = d_0 10^{\left(\frac{PL(d_0)-PL(d)+X_\sigma}{10\gamma}\right)} \tag{2}$$

Suppose that there are three RFID readers named A, B and C, whose coordinates are (xa, ya), (xb, yb) and (xc , yc). The current coordinate of the old person is (x, y). According to the equation 1, the distances between the current position of the old person and the RFID readers A, B and C are calculated, which are da , db and dc. The equation in terms of x and y can be obtained as follows.

$$\begin{aligned} \sqrt{(x-x_a)^2+(y-y_a)^2} &= d_a \\ \sqrt{(x-x_b)^2+(y-y_b)^2} &= d_b \\ \sqrt{(x-x_c)^2+(y-y_c)^2} &= d_c \end{aligned} \tag{3}$$

The current coordinate of the old person is obtained by solving these equations as shown above. But in actual condition it is difficult to calculate the current position of the test target precisely, for random component exists when the RSSI value is in a decay process. A centroid method is adopted to improve the positioning accuracy. Some triangles for ranging will be generated when the RFID readers read the data of the current position for many times, so the current coordinate can be obtained by many times. The centroid of these coordinates will be marked as the current coordinate of the old person. For the centroid of a triangle, it should be calculated as follows:

$$\left(\frac{x_1+x_2+x_3}{3}, \frac{y_1+y_2+y_3}{3}\right) \tag{4}$$

3.2. Realization of Positioning

① Detect signals by the RFID readers

Long-distance RFID readers are used in this system. The reading distance should be changed by adjusting the power of the RFID reader. These readers which connect with the workstation are placed in the elderly person's rooms. By polling method, the workstation detects which readers can read the card at a certain power and records the current power message which is relating to the distance. After completing the all readers' polling, the workstation begins to calculate to locate the old man's position. Polling interval is no more than 50 ms.

② Calculate the current position of the old person

The process of locating the person is shown in Fig. 2.

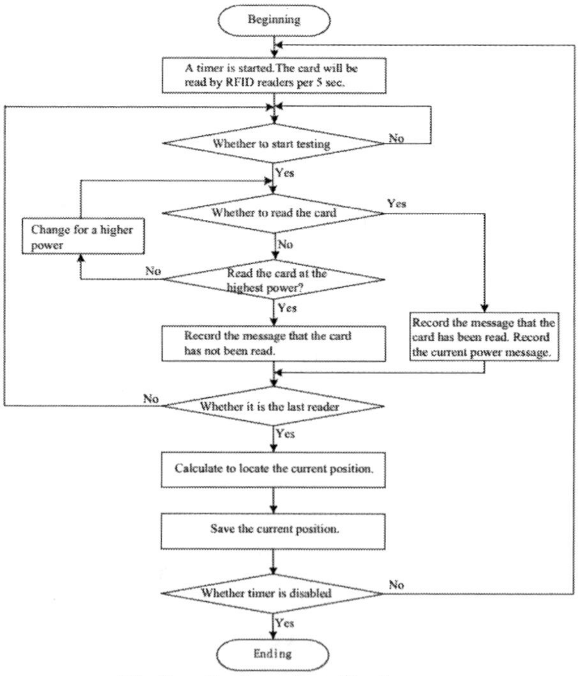

Fig.2 realization of positioning

4 Monitor a fall and process the emergency button

The smartphone in the system acts as the carrier of a RFID card, as well as the tool of detecting an old man's current motion to judge whether to alarm or not. The changes in his motion can be measured by the acceleration sensor in the smartphone.

4.1 Process the fall

The action of the old man can arguably be seen as a state of rest or an uniform motion. When the old man is falling down, he is usually in accelerated motion. And the acceleration is increased along the direction of the acceleration of gravity. The main algorithms are described below.

① Keep waiting, with monitoring the changes of the tri-axial accelerometer's square. If the square exceeds the threshold value, then proceed to next step.

② Give a loud sound for alarming, and wait for an external input.

③ If there is no external input, it should be considered that a fall occurs. And a real alarm will be send to the monitoring center. Otherwise, if there is an external input, the loud sound will be stopped. And go back to the first step to keep waiting.

4.2 Process the emergency button

It can be considered that the old man is pressing the emergency button by himself when the system detects a long press on one or more keys of the smartphone. It should be detected that the keys must be released after being pressed for a while.

4.3 The main process of the Smartphone system

The main process of the Smartphone system can be divided into several sections as shown below.

① Complete system initialization to get the configuration information. One of the main functions is to get the contact numbers stored in the Smartphone. Another is to search the linking information of the acceleration sensor in the Smartphone. In the first five seconds of system initialization, the system configuration interface can be entered if the command button is pressed.

② Start a thread and open the sensor, so the pressed key and the value of the sensor can be detected.

③ Get the tri-axial accelerometer's current values for the acceleration sensor and evaluate their square. If the square exceeds the threshold value, a loud alarm sound will be given. It is possible that a fall may have occurred, so if the cancel button is pressed in the next ten minutes, this loud noise will be stopped. Otherwise a warning message will be sent to the monitoring center by the Smartphone.

④ When the system detects a long press, a warning will be sent to the monitoring center by the Smartphone.

5 System application

At the monitoring center, the current position of the old person is showed as fig. 3, Fig.4. If necessary, the working staff in the center will phone to the old person, or go to his home to offer help, or phone to the hospital or police office.

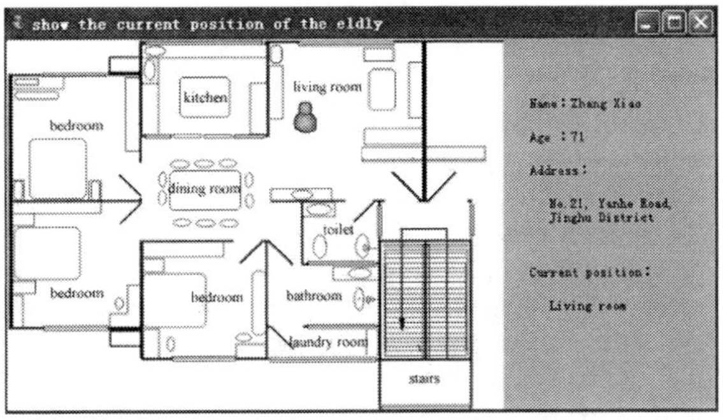

Fig.3 showing the current position of the elderly

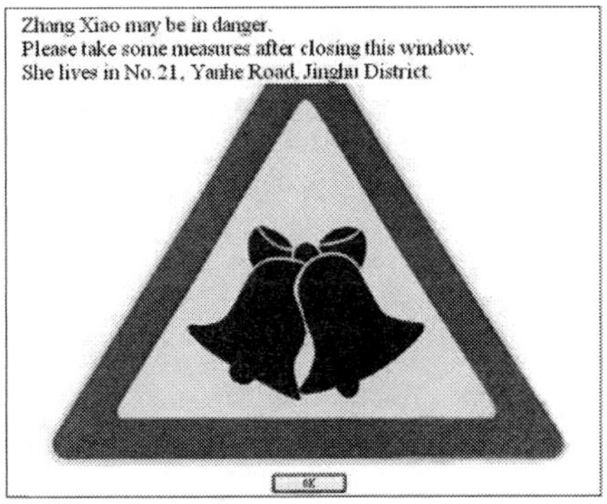

Fig.4 the alarming window

In case of asking for help owing to emergency, the old man can press the emergency button in the panel of Smartphone for three seconds and the system will enter the emergency state at once.

An RFID card uniquely identifies an elderly person in the healthcare information system. With the RFID card, data of the elderly person which are stored on the server can be accessed, such as their name, age, health information, house information, etc. There should be a defined procedure on the RFID card for the issue, cancellation, and alteration of authorisation to enter and amend data, including the changing of personal passwords. Especially, medical records of the old person should only be read by someone who has right to do that, such as his children and doctors. Hence, it protects the elderly person's privacy efficiently. With an RFID card, medical information of the elderly person in the system plays an important role in community health record. Benefits include carrying out the work of community healthcare, which can provide more protection for the quality of elderly life.

Many old people are so forgetful that the system offers a timely reminder service according to the requests of them or their children. For example, time to take medicine or hospital appointments can be set in the

system in accordance with specific conditions. When it is the correct date and time, the system will provide a reminder for them.The system also provides old people with some healthy recipes via the Smartphone or remind him not to eat certain kinds of food.

6 Discussion

The analysis of the elderly satisfaction about the various services provided by the system is shown in Fig.5. Most of them are satisfied with five services as follows, such as monitoring service in a dangerous area, monitoring service when a problem occurs, active alarm service when an emergency happens, timely reminder service (reminders to take medicines or reminders about appointments, etc), and notification service for leaving the house. As for the service providing the elderly with healthy recipes or basic nursing knowledge and skills, and the service for storing of medical records, they are not very satisfied. It shows that the basic functions of the system are, in the main, satisfactory. Compared with some other systems in which people are monitored by cameras, there is better acceptance and less fear for the elderly, because this system only sacrifices part, not all, of their privacy. They also feel that it is necessary and effective to send an active alarm by pressing the emergency button themselves in emergency circumstances.

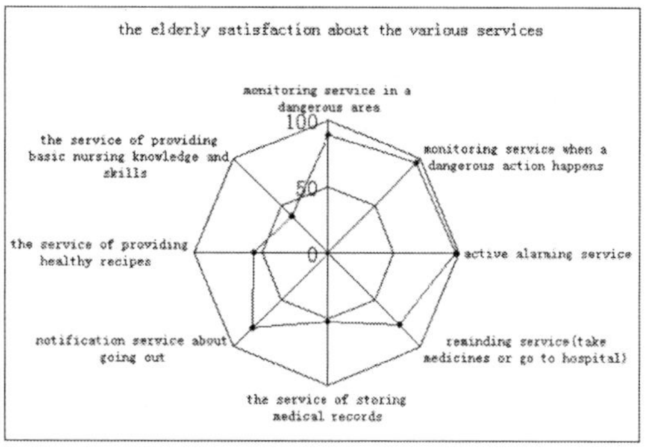

Fig.5 the elderly satisfaction about the various services

CONCLUSION

In summary, this thesis presents a scheme of a health care information system for the elderly at home based on radio-frequency identification technology and sensor technology. For the elderly, the system greatly reduces their risk of being severely injured if they are in an accident. At the same time the elderly's privacy has not been invaded [5-7]. The system has been developed to solve the social problem that there is nobody to look after the elderly in some families. The improved healthcare information system for the elderly may achieve reasonably good social and economic benefits.

ACKNOWLEDGEMENT

This research is sponsored by the Rohde & Schwarz Ltd., Munich in Germany.

References

1. ZHANG Xue-qin, WU Hong-mei, JIA Xi , Effect of the Systematic Management on the Health Status of the Empty-nest Elders in Urban Area, CHINESE GENERAL PRACTICE, 13(07):712-718, 2010(in Chinese)

2. Hou Xiaoli .Research on the Social Support System of the Urban Family Endowment. Wuhan: Central China Normal University,2009(in Chinese)

3. Zhangrui, aging: Chinese population crisis, ECOLOGICAL ECONOMY. 10:14-19, 2011(in Chinese)

4. Antonio J. Jara, Miguel A. Zamora, Antonio F. G. Skarmeta, An internet of things–based personal device for diabetes therapy management in ambient assisted living (AAL), Pers Ubiquit Comput, 15: 431–440, 2011

5. Scherr, Daniel, and Peter Kastner. Effect of Home-Based Telemonitoring Using Mobile Phone Technology on the Outcome of Heart Failure Patients After an Episode of Acute Decompensation: Randomized Controlled Trial. Journal of Medical Internet Research, 11(3):e34, 2009

6. Andre ´s Mun ˜oz, Juan Carlos Augusto, Ana Villa, Juan Antonio Botı ´a , Design and evaluation of an ambient assisted living system based on an argumentative multi-agent system, Pers Ubiquit Comput, 15:377–387, 2011

7. AAL Association. Ambient Assisted Living (AAL) Joint Programme, http://www.aal-europe.eu/ (accessed September 08, 2009).

MATEC Web of Conferences 44, 02012 (2016)
DOI: 10.1051/matecconf/20164402012

Guided Waves in a Solid Rod Embedded in Infinite Medium with Weak Interface

Zi Wei Tong[1], Qing Bang Han[1,2,*], Cheng Yin[1], Li Hua Qi[1], Yu Zhang[1] and Chang Ping Zhu[1]

[1] *College of IOT Engineering, Hohai University, Changzhou 213022, China*

[2] *Huaian Research Institute, Hohai University, Huaian 223001, China*

Abstract. The dispersion relation of the infinite long rod model with a weak interface has been deduced via wave equation of the guided waves and boundary spring interface model. The dispersion characteristics of the rigid interface and the slip interface are calculated, while the effect of different axial stiffness coefficient is also discussed. The results suggest that the phase velocity of the slip interface decreases slowly with increasing frequency at the low frequency of the L (0,1) mode. As for the weak interface, when the axial coefficient Kt is in the particular range of $[10^{10},10^{14}]$pa/m, the interface turns from the slip interface to the rigid interface. That shows the value of axial coefficient Kt is an essential prerequisite for the non-destructive evaluation to evaluate the interface cementation degree.

1 Introduction

Propagation of guided waves in a solid rod embedded in infinite medium with weak interface is an interesting research topic of practical importance. For example, it is urgent to apply Non-destructive evaluation (NDE) for the rock bolts in the mixture of rock and concrete, which are inserted to ensure the stability of the groundwork. One key issue in the above mentioned NDE process is how to evaluate bonding state between rock bolt and concrete by guided ultrasonic waves[1-4].

The propagation of guided wave in solid cylindrical media has already been widely studied, but most work is based on a model of a multilayered columnar structure with continuous interface[5-8], few attention has been focused on the semi-infinite space structure with discontinuous interface[9-10].

In this paper, we study the propagation characteristics of guided waves in a solid rod embedded in infinite medium with weak interface. This paper is arranged as follows. First, the dispersion equation using spring interface model is deduced. Second, the dispersion characteristics of guided waves in the structure under the rigid interface and slip interface are discussed, respectively. Third, we investigated the effects of different axial coefficient on the guided waves under the weak interface.

2 Theory

2.1 Weak Interface

The interface between different solid media of the layered structure is inevitable, and can be divided into two

* Corresponding author: hqb0092@163.com

categories, i.e., the rigid interface and the slip interface. The rigid interface can be presented as an interface that usually satisfies the boundary conditions of continuous stress and displacement of elastic waves while two solid medium components are well cemented. And the slip interface [7] is such an interface that can withstand the normal (or radial) stress perpendicular to the interface while the tangential (or axial) stress is identical to zero. That is, the normal (or radial) stress and displacement are continuous; the tangential (or axial) displacement is discontinuity[11].

In the procedure of using complex media or composite material, the micro-cracks occur at the interface, and the mechanical strength is reduced to form a weak boundary layer. The spring model can describe the physical characteristics of a weak interface, thus the boundary conditions of mechanical quantity at the interface is available[11].

2.2 Dispersion Equation

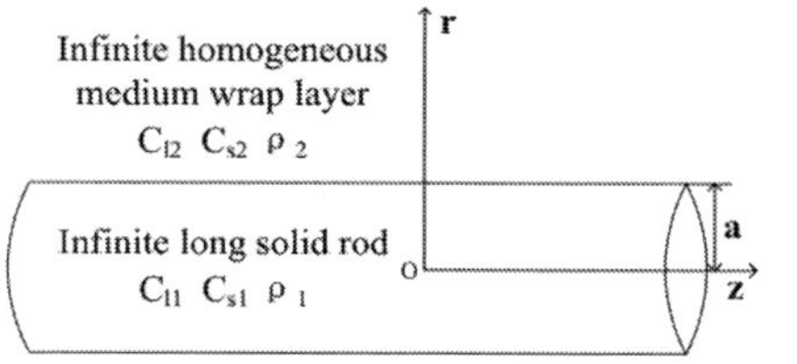

Figure 1. The schematic of infinite long solid rod embedded in infinite homogeneous medium

The system of this paper is modelled as an infinite long solid rod embedded in an infinite homogeneous isotropic medium as shown in Fig.1. It is convenient to solve this problem using cylindrical coordinate, where the z axis of the coordinate is the central axis of the solid rod. In this paper, only longitudinal modes are taken into consideration. φ1, ψ1, χ1 and φ2, ψ2, χ2 are used to represent the potential function of solid rod and wrap layer. The potential function can be expressed as

$$\begin{cases} \varphi_1 = A_1 I_n(\alpha_1 r) + K_n(\alpha_1 r) \\ \psi_1 = C_1 I_n(\beta_1 r) \end{cases} \quad (1)$$

$$\begin{cases} \varphi_2 = B_2 K_n(\alpha_2 r) \\ \psi_2 = D_2 K_n(\beta_2 r) \end{cases} \quad (2)$$

The potential function satisfies the wave equation, and can be described as

$$\nabla^2 \Phi = \frac{1}{C_l^2}\frac{\partial^2 \Phi}{\partial t^2} \quad (3)$$

$$\nabla^2 \Psi = \frac{1}{C_s^2}\frac{\partial^2 \Psi}{\partial t^2} \quad (4)$$

where, Cl and Cs are the P-wave velocity and S-wave velocity, respectively. t is time, and ∇^2 is Laplace operator.

$$C_l^2 = \frac{\lambda + 2\mu}{\rho} \quad (5)$$

$$C_s^2 = \frac{\mu}{\rho} \quad (6)$$

$$\nabla^2 = \frac{\partial^2}{\partial r^2} + \frac{1}{r}\frac{\partial}{\partial r} + \frac{\partial^2}{\partial z^2} \quad (7)$$

Here, λ and μ are both Lame parameters, ρ is the density.

It is convenient to introduce displacement potentials.

$$\begin{cases} u_r = \dfrac{\partial \Phi}{\partial r} + \dfrac{\partial^2 \Psi}{\partial r \partial z} \\ u_z = \dfrac{\partial \Phi}{\partial z} - \dfrac{\partial^2 \Psi}{\partial r^2} - \dfrac{1}{r}\dfrac{\partial \Psi}{\partial r} \end{cases} \quad (8)$$

The normal and tangential stress tractions are related to displacements using the Hooke's law.

$$\begin{cases} \sigma_{rr} = 2\mu\dfrac{\partial u_r}{\partial r} + \lambda\left(\dfrac{u_r}{r} + \dfrac{\partial u_r}{\partial r} + \dfrac{\partial u_z}{\partial z}\right) \\ \sigma_{rz} = \mu\left(\dfrac{\partial u_r}{\partial z} + \dfrac{\partial u_z}{\partial r}\right) \end{cases} \quad (9)$$

The radial and axial displacement components ur and uz can be expressed by substituting Eqs.(1) and (2) into Eq.(8).The stress components σ_{rr} and σ_{rz} in Eq. (9) also can be obtained.

A spring interface model is established in cylindrical interface (r = a). Based on the model, the boundary conditions can be written as

$$\begin{cases} \sigma_{rr}^{(1)} = \mathrm{Kn}(u_r^{(1)} - u_r^{(2)}) \\ \sigma_{rz}^{(1)} = \mathrm{Kt}(u_z^{(1)} - u_z^{(2)}) \\ \sigma_{rr}^{(1)} = \sigma_{rr}^{(2)} \\ \sigma_{rz}^{(1)} = \sigma_{rz}^{(2)} \end{cases} \quad (10)$$

where, Kn and Kt are the radial stiffness coefficient, and the axial stiffness coefficient, respectively. The functions of Kn and Kt are composed of the interface layer thickness h, equivalent bulk modulus K0 and shear modulus G0[11]. They are expressed as

$$\mathrm{Kn} = \left(\mathrm{K}_0 + \tfrac{4}{3}\mathrm{G}_0\right)/h \quad (11)$$

$$\mathrm{Kt} = \mathrm{G}_0 / h \quad (12)$$

The boundary condition of rigid interface and slip interface can be deduced from the Eq.(10). When $Kn, Kt \to \infty$, the stress is finite, so $u_r^{(1)} = u_r^{(2)}$, $u_z^{(1)} = u_z^{(2)}$, equivalent to the continuous boundary condition of rigid interface. When $Kn \to \infty$, $Kt = 0$, the boundary condition is $u_r^{(1)} = u_r^{(2)}$, $\sigma_{rz}^{(1)} = \sigma_{rz}^{(2)} = 0$,which is equivalent to the boundary condition of slip interface. It can be seen that the axial elasticity coefficient is used as a measuring metric of the axial stress tolerance level as well as an essential parameter describing a weak interface.

By substituting displacement and stress components into Eq.(10), the equations can be written as,

$$\begin{bmatrix} m_{11} & m_{12} & m_{13} & m_{14} \\ m_{21} & m_{22} & m_{23} & m_{24} \\ m_{31} & m_{32} & m_{33} & m_{34} \\ m_{41} & m_{42} & m_{43} & m_{44} \end{bmatrix} \begin{bmatrix} A_1 \\ C_1 \\ B_2 \\ D_2 \end{bmatrix} = \begin{bmatrix} b_1 \\ b_2 \\ b_3 \\ b_4 \end{bmatrix} \tag{13}$$

When the right-hand side of Eq.(13) is zero matrix, the necessary and sufficient condition for the non-zero solutions of the equation is the coefficient determinant $\Delta = 0$. It is the dispersion equation whose solution corresponds to the guided wave.

For given different values of Kn and Kt, solutions for this dispersion equation can be got which yield the correspondence between the phase velocity and frequency under the rigid interface, slip interface and weak interface.

3 Numerical results

Since our work aims at the rock bolt detection, our simulation selects concrete as material of infinite medium, and steel as the solid rod. By setting the radius of solid rod to be 10mm so that the dispersion characteristics of the structure under rigid interface, slip interface and different axial stiffness coefficient are analysed.

3.1 Rigid Interface

As the stiffness coefficient $Kn, Kt \to \infty$, the interface is the rigid interface, i.e., the stress and displacement are continuous.

The phase velocity dispersion curves are shown in the Fig.2. As can be seen, the phase velocity of the lowest mode gradually approaches to the shear-wave velocity (3260m / s) of the steel with increasing frequency. In each mode, the phase velocity decreases as the frequency gradually increases. Another feature is that each higher-order mode has a cut off frequency.

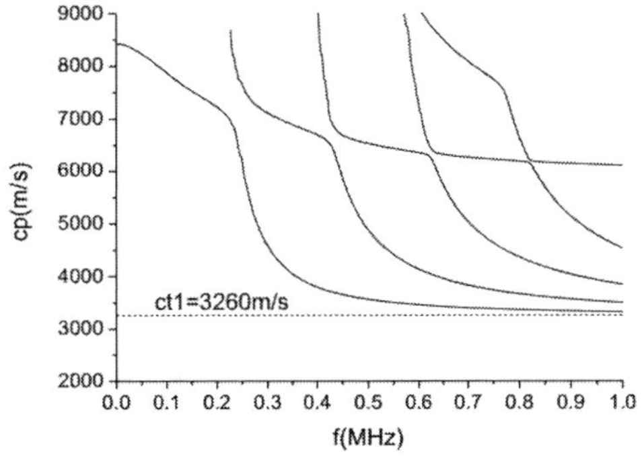

Figure2. Phase velocity dispersion curve under rigid interface

3.2 Slip Interface

When the stiffness coefficient $Kn \to \infty$, $Kt=0$, the radial displacement and axial stress are continuous. The boundary conditions are $u_r^{(1)} = u_r^{(2)}$, $\sigma_{rz}^{(1)} = \sigma_{rz}^{(2)} = 0$, which is slip interface.

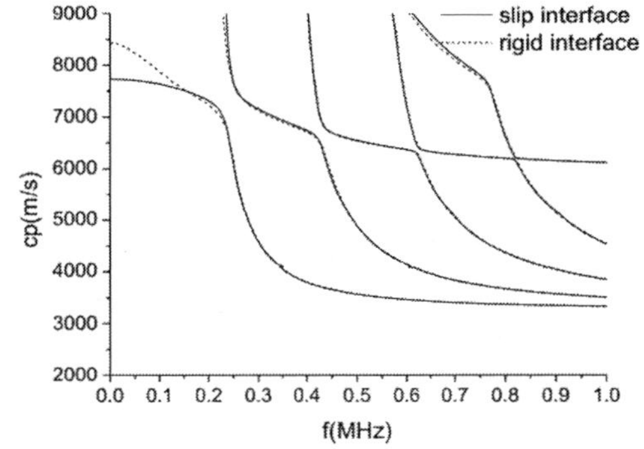

Figure 3. Dispersion curves under slip interface and rigid interface

In Fig.3, we show the phase velocity dispersion curves obtained under these boundary conditions. Several features of these results that different from rigid interface and slip interface deserve comment, especially in the low frequency of the first mode. When the frequency of the L(0,1) mode is in[0, 0.2]MHz, the phase velocity of the slip interface decreases more slowly than that in the rigid interface as the frequency increases. However, in the high-order modes, there is no significant difference between the two dispersion curves.

3.3 Weak Interface

As for the spring model, the axial elasticity coefficient is a measure of weak interface to withstand axial stress. Therefore, the dispersion curves under different axial stiffness coefficient are calculated to evaluate the weak interface.

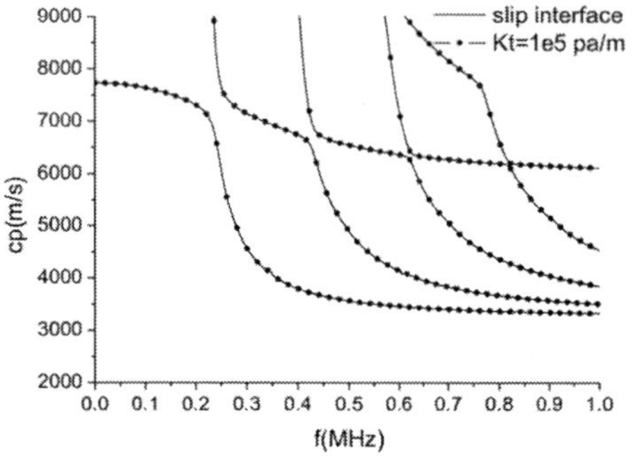

Figure 4. Dispersion curves under slip interface and $Kn \to \infty$, Kt=10^5 pa/m

Fig.4 shows the dispersion curves achieved by deducing the dispersion equation under the boundary condition $Kn \to \infty$, Kt=10^5 pa/m. It can be found that the phase velocity dispersion curves are consistent with the dispersion curves under slip interface.

In Figure 5, we show the dispersion curves under the boundary conditions $Kn \to \infty$, Kt=10^{19} pa/m. Phase velocity dispersion curves under this case are similar with the dispersion curves under rigid interface.

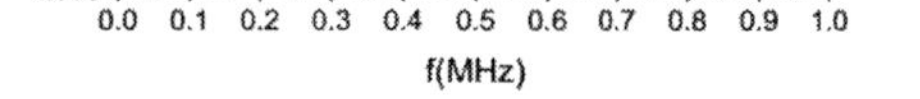

Figure 5. Dispersion curves under rigid interface a $Kn \to \infty$, Kt=10^{19} pa/m

Since only two cases concerned, it's not accurate to explain the impact brought by the axial stiffness coefficient on the guided waves. By setting f=0.1MHz, $Kn \to \infty$, the phase velocity of L(0,1) mode respect to the axial stiffness coefficient are shown in Fig.6. When Kt is in [10^5,10^{10}] pa/m and [10^{14},10^{19}] pa/m, the phase velocity remains unchanged. While Kt is in the particular value range of [10^{10},10^{14}] pa/m, the interface turns from the slip interface to the rigid interface, and the phase velocity is sensitive to the changes of Kt as well. When Kt is higher than 10^{10} pa/m, the phase velocity starts decreasing gradually as Kt increases, and stays at a minimum value when Kt approaches 10^{12} pa / m.

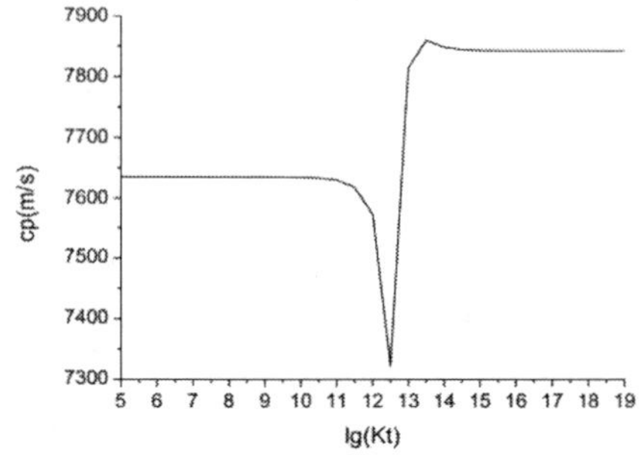

Figure 6. Guided wave phase velocity curve with Kt when f=0.1MHz

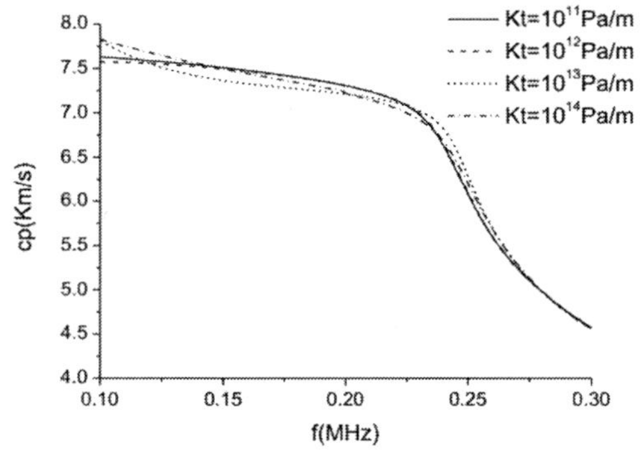

Figure 7. Guided wave phase velocity curve of L(0,1) mode with different Kt

The dispersion curves of L (0,1) mode with Kt = 10^{11}pa/m,10^{12}pa/m,10^{13}pa/m,10^{14}pa/m are shown in Fig.7. The main reason for choosing is that the phase velocity of L(0,1) mode varies greatly when the axial coefficient Kt is in the range of [10^{10},10^{14}]pa/m. Fig.7 shows that the dispersion curves for Kt=10^{13}pa/m and Kt=10^{14}pa/m have more obvious fluctuations than the dispersion curves for Kt=10^{11}pa/m and Kt=10^{12}pa/m when the frequency is smaller than 0.3MHz. As the axial coefficient increases, the phase velocity decreases faster with the frequency increasing.

From the above analysis, the dispersion curves on the L(0,1) mode of this structure have much more significant changes in a certain range of Kt. Therefore, in non-destructive evaluation, the interface cementation degree can be fully evaluated through measuring the

phase velocity of the guided wave propagating in the structure and calculating the value of Kt by inversion.

4 Conclusions

Based on the analysis, the phase velocity of the lowest mode converges to the shear-wave velocity of the solid rod with increasing frequency. Numerical results validate that, compared to rigid interface, the phase velocity of the slip interface decreases slowly with increasing frequency at the low frequency of the L (0,1) mode. As for the weak interface, when the axial coefficient Kt is in the particular range of $[10^{10},10^{14}]$pa/m, the interface transfers from the slip interface to the rigid interface and the phase velocity shows sensitivity to any slight change of the axial coefficient Kt. The value of axial coefficient Kt is an essential prerequisite for the non-destructive evaluation to evaluate the interface cementation degree.

There are still a lot of works to do in the future. One scope is the simulation of guided wave propagation in such structure model. We can establish the model with different level of split at the interface, research the propagation characteristic of the guided wave, and calculate the value of Kt by inversion according to the numerical results of simulation. Finally, the result of simulation would be useful to the non-destructive evaluation.

Acknowledgements

This work is supported by the Natural Science foundation of China Grant No. 11274091, 11574072 and the Fundamental Research Funds for the Central Universities of Hohai University No:2011B11014.

References

[1] Ivanovic A, Neilson R D, "Influence of geometry and material properties on the axial vibration of a rock bolt," Int. J. Rock Mech. Mining Sci.,**45**:941-951(2008).

[2] Madenga V, Zou D H, Zhang C., "Effects of curing time and frequency on ultrasonic wave velocity in grouted rock bolts ,"J. Appl.Geophys.,**59**:79-87(2006).

[3] M. D. Beard and M. J. S. Lowe, "Non-destructive testing of rock bolts using guided ultrasonic waves," Int. J. Rock Mech. Min. Sci. **40**, 527–536(2003).

[4] M. D. Beard, M. J. S. Lowe, and P. Cawley, "Inspection of rock bolts using guided ultrasonic waves," in Review of Progress in QNDE, edited by D.O.Thompson and D. E. Chimenti, **20**, pp.1156–1163(2001).

[5] B. X. Zhang and H. Y. Cui, "Guided waves in a multi-layered cylindrical elastic solid medium," 1. Chin. Phys. Lett.,**24(10)**: pp. 2883-2886(2007).

[6] H. Y. Cui and B. X. Zhang, Sherri Johnstone and Jon Trevelyan, "Excitation mechanisms and dispersion characteristics of guided waves in multilayered cylindrical solid media," J. Acoust. Soc. Am.,**131 (3)**:pp.2048-2062(2012).

[7] L. Laguerre and A. Grimault, "Ultrasonic transient bounded-beam propagation a solid cylinder waveguide embedded in a solid medium,"J.Acoust.Soc.Am.,**121(4)**,1924-1934 (2007).

[8] A.D. Puckett and M. L. Peterson, "A semi-analytical model for predicting multiple propagating axially symmetric modes in cylindrical waveguides,"Ultrasonics,**43**, 197–207(2005).

[9] Elena Maeva, Inna Severina, Sergiy Bondarenko, et al. "Acoustical methods for the investigation of adhesively bonded structures," A Review. Can J Phys., **82**:981-1025(2004).

[10] A.Baltazar, L.Wang, B.Xie, et al. "Inverse ultrasonic determination of imperfect interfaces and bulk properties of a layer between two solids," J.Acoust.Soc.Am,**114(3)**:1424-1434(2003).

[11] Zhang Rui, Wang Mingxi, Cao Wenwu,"Guided Wave in ultra-thin layered composite structure with weak and slip interface in different depth," Chin .Phys .Soc., **49(7)**:1297-1302(2000).

MATEC Web of Conferences 44, 02013 (2016)
DOI: 10.1051/matecconf/20164402013

The Application of the Exhaustive Polling Theory in Intelligent Traffic System

Meng Yao Wang[1,a], Hong Wei Ding[1,b], Yi Fan Zhao[1], Zhu Guan Liang[1], Long Zheng Zhu[1]
[1] School of Informatics, Yunnan University, China
[a]yakazo@163.com, [b] dhw1964@163.com

Abstract: *This paper presents a new use of exhaustive service polling system in the intelligent traffic light control system.Vehicles arrival rate is measured in the system. Through the relationship between arrival rate and mean waiting time ,mean queue length in exhaustive service polling system, achieved an technology that intelligent adjust the length of traffic light time according to the arrive rate.The more arrive rate the longer green light time. With the intelligent control, the road capacity is more.*

Keywords: polling system, exhaustive service, mean waiting time, mean queue length, intelligent traffic

1. Introduction

Intelligent transportation come into sight as one of the main solution to modern traffic pressure, gradually.Since 1868 the first traffic lights[1], traffic lights development has the changes of the red and blue traffic lights, red and green traffic lights, red, yellow and green traffic lights, and now, the intelligent traffic lights .The main rule of red yellow and green traffic light which is widely used now is the vehicles can go straight and turn left when the light is green except there is a mandatory forbidding sign in front of the intersection. And the vehicles that turn left or right must let the straight road vehicles and pedestrians go first.The vehicles which in the motorway is not allowed to over the sidewalk when the light is red. Yellow light mean to wait,vehicles must slow down when the light is yellow, but the vehicle which is very close to stop line and can't park safely can enter the intersection. And the main function is through the different colors of light indicates the specification that vehicles and pedestrians through the intersection, to ensure the safe passage of vehicles and pedestrians.

Intelligent traffic light[2] theory is not only focus on ensure the orderly safe passage of vehicles and pedestrians with the same rules of ordinary traffic lights, more is control the waiting time intelligently in order to improve the traffic efficiency under the background of increasing traffic pressure,.

According to this principle,the main task of this paper is to design a intelligent traffic lights system which use the exhaustive service polling model. This system can adjust the mean time delay according to the arrive rate .To alleviate traffic pressure, and can save transportation resources.Through reasonable design the system function, the conversion of the red, yellow, green light have an accurate time interval which requires an automated and secure system to control .

2. Specific design

we design a traffic lights system which the timekeeping time during light can be adjusted intellectually according to the change of the traffic volume.Initial idea is to install photoelectric counter in all directions at the crossroads to count the vehicles, and then enter data into the computer central control system

to analyze the data.The intersection traffic lights to ensure the safe passage of pedestrians and vehicles.There are red, green and yellow lights set up in each side .Red light means no thoroughfare, and green light means vehicles can thorough the intersection.There is yellow light for a few seconds when green to red , so that the vehicles could stop .

In this system,the exhaustive service[3] be used in the two directions of the intersection.Means that the length of green light time in any road should conforms with the result which is calculated by the exhaustive service polling theory.On other word ,the length of red light time depend on anther direction's length of green light time.And there is one would never change over the traffic volume that is length of yellow light time.

3. The exhaustive service polling model of traffic lights intelligent control system

This traffic lights intelligent control system[8] is seem as a double queues single servers polling system. For practical purposes ,suppose, the direction of North and South is seen as a queue1 with the arrival rate of vehicles which is λ_1, so as the direction of East and West.The β means the service rate[9] of the traffic light system. In this intelligent system β is 0.5,mean there are one vehicle though the intersection during the 2s.The conversion rate[10] of traffic light system is the length of yellow light time in this system,and there $\gamma=1$ means that there are 4s yellow light. The mean time delay and the mean queue length of each queues is figured out by the exhaustive service polling model which is N=2.

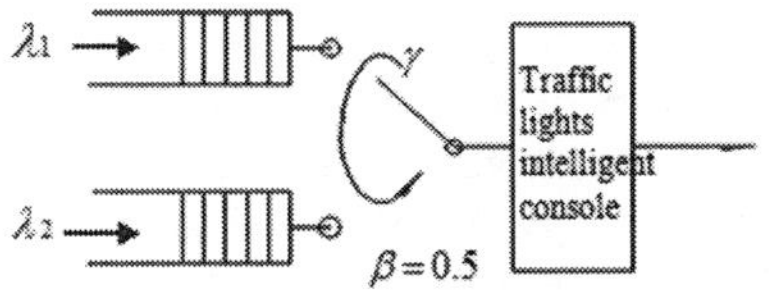

β: The service rate of the traffice light system
γ: The conversion rate of the traffice light system
λ_1: The arrival rate of queue1
λ_2: The arrival rate of queue2

Figure 1. The exhaustive service polling model of intelligent traffic lights control system

Apply this model to intelligent traffic lights control system,the mean time delay[11] of queue1 is the time of each vehicles waiting in North and South , can be calculated by the exhaustive service polling system under N=2.In order to keep the roads clear ,the road which has the more mean time delay need the longer green light time. So,the mean time delay in north and south ,we calculate, equal the time of green light in north and south. So as West and East .

Whenever the mean time delay were calculated greater than 100 seconds, we set the green light time as 100 seconds. Whenever the mean time delay less than 100 seconds but longer than 10 seconds,the traffic lights would be controlled with the calculation results. The minimal green light time is 10 seconds.

4. Queuing model and operation mode

Assume that there are 2 roads in this intelligent traffic lights control system that using the exhaustive service polling system. And those 2 roads be serviced by the one traffic lights under the rules of exhaustive service polling system .System's logic loop service queuing model is shown in figure 1.Because of the queuing system is discussed in this paper is under the discrete time state , so the time line divided according to the time slot $\tau=1$ as the unit (concise analysis into consideration, take τ as unit time)

4.1. parametric hypothesis

(1)Each queues has the vehicles arrived into their queue space with independent and identically probability distribution at any time slot the distribution of probability generating function,the mean and variance are $A(Z)$、 $\lambda = A'(1)$ and $\delta_\lambda^2 = A''(1) + \lambda - \lambda^2$ respectively.

(2)The random variable of query conversion time between the two queues is subject to a probability distribution which is mutually independent and identically distributed,the distribution of probability generating function,the mean and variance are $R(Z)$、 $\gamma = R'(1)$ and $\delta_\gamma^2 = R''(1) + \gamma - \gamma^2$ respectively.

(3)The random variable of the time that each vehicles pass the crossroads is subject to a probability distribution which is mutually independent and identically distributed, the distribution of probability generating function,

the mean and variance are $B(Z)$, $\beta = B'(1)$ and $\delta_\beta^2 = B''(1) + \beta - \beta^2$ respectively.

(4)The queue space is big enough .The number of vehicles would not more than the queue space.

(5)For the vehicles that in the each queue, according to the principle of first-in-first-out.

4.2.calculate of $\prod(x_1, x_2, \ldots x_i, \ldots x_N)$

Assuming that i road (i=1, 2) accept service of intelligent traffic lights at t_n (It' s multiple of τ), the intelligent traffic lights would turn to service $i+1$road after i road send all of its information packets by the way of exhaustive service $i+1$ road is serviced at t_{n+1} (It' s multiple of τ).

Random variable $\xi_i(n)$ is defined as the number of vehicles in i road at t_n ,so the state of the queuing system at t_n can be represented as $\xi_1(n), \xi_2(n), \ldots \xi_i(n), \ldots \xi_N(n)$.

Here: ,

The probability generating function of $\Pi_i(x_1, x_2)$:

$$G_i(z_1, z_2) = \sum_{x_1=0}^{\infty} \sum_{x_2=0}^{\infty} \Pi_i(x_1, x_2) \bullet z_1^{x_1} z_2^{x_2}$$

i =1, 2; (1)

4.3. calculate of $g_{i,s}(i, i)$

If the road i turn the green light and the vehicles in the road i begin to pass the intersection at the t_n ,and the all vehicles pass at the t_{n_1} .Because the exhaustive service ,there are $\xi_i(n_1)$ number of vehicles arrive in the road i at the t_{n_1} ,all of those vehicles pass the intersection at t_{n_2} ($t_n \le t_{n_1}$) . This process show as fig2.

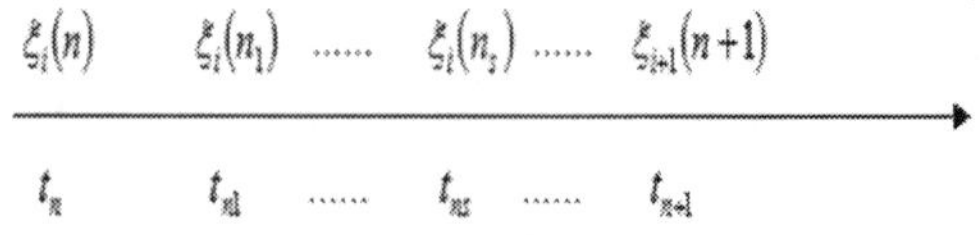

Figure 2. The process that pass all vehicles in road i

The generating function of system state equation at t_n, t_{n_1} can be defined as before :

$$g_{i,n_s}(i,i) = \rho^{2s} g_i(i,i) + \frac{\rho^{s-1}(1-\rho^s)(\beta A''(1) + \lambda^2 B''(1))}{1-\rho} g_i(i)$$

i =1,2 s =1,2 (2)

4.4. calculate of $\overline{W}_E$

We can get the mean waiting time:

$$\overline{W}_E = \overline{W}_{i1} + \overline{W}_{i2} = \frac{1}{2}\left\{\frac{R''(1)}{\gamma} + \frac{1}{1-2\rho}\left[\gamma + \rho + 2\lambda B''(1)\right] + \frac{\rho A''(1)}{\lambda(1-2\rho)}\right\}$$

(3)

5. The simulation

The simulation calculation and theoretical calculation take the same parameters . And in those simulation diagrams,we set the vertical axis narrows 10 times.

the horizontal axis load is ρ=βλ ,and ρ is proportional to the arrival rate λ.In this paper, we set the service rate β=0.5,means there are one vehicle though the intersection during the 2s.

In theory,whenever ρ=1 means this system would be on the brink of collapse.But in this paper, we set the maximum waiting time is 100s, so the ρ have to less than 0.4 .On other words ,the λ have to less than 0.8 means there are 8 vehicles though the intersection during the 10s.

The Fig3 and Fig4 reflect the theoretical value and the simulation values are the same.In those two diagrams we can find that the mean queue length and the mean time delay are proportional to load.Compare exhaustive service and gate service we can find that the mean queue length and the mean time delay of exhaustive service is shorter than the mean queue length and the mean time delay of gate service with the same system load or the same arrive rate (Because ρ is proportional to the λ),.The shorter mean queue length and the shorter mean time delay mean that the shorter green light time be needed with the same

vehicles arrive rate.So the intelligent traffic lights control system which use the exhaustive service polling system is better than the system which use gate service.

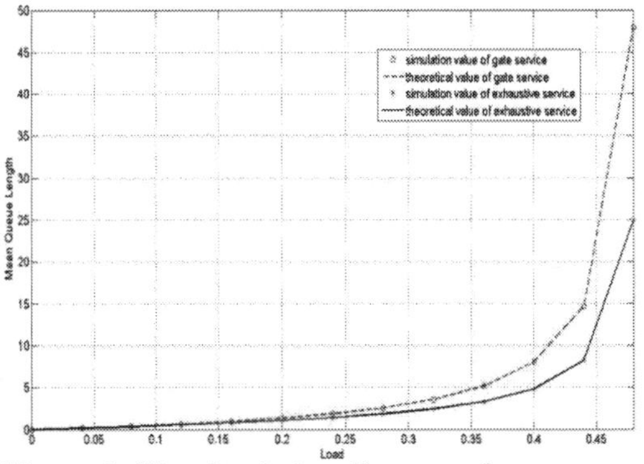

Figure 3. The simulation diagram of mean time delay

6. Conclusions

Different road has different arrival rate .In order to improve the road capacity, a intelligent control system is necessary in today.Though the exhaustive service polling system,we find the relationship that the the longer mean time delay because of the higher arrive rate.In the intelligent traffic light control system ,the longer mean time delay means should set longer green light time to keep the road open.Different time has different arrive rate ,in order to improve the road capacity,the time of traffic light has to adjust intellectually according to the arrive rate. The intelligent traffic light control system which use the exhaustive service polling system can keep the shorter waiting time with the same arrive rate.So this system can relieve the traffic congestion,improve the capacity of intersectio ns.

References

[1] Ding Hongwei, Zhao Dongfeng, Zhao Yifan. Packet delay analysis of continuous-time polling system with M-gated services[A]. Chengdu, P.R.China, August, 2010, Page(s):408-411.

[2] Qianlin Liu, Dongfeng Zhao, Dongming Zhou. An analytic model for enhancing IEEE 802.11 coordination function media access control protocol[J]. European Transactions on Telecommunications, 2011, 22(6):332-338.

[3] Jan-Pieter Dorsman, S. Borst, O. Boxma, Maria Vlasiou,Markovian polling systems with an application to wireless random-access networks[J].IEEE Trans. Eurandom Prepront Series, 2014, 5(6):1389-2355.

[4] Zhao Dongfeng, Ding Hongwei, Zhao Yifan, Wang Mingui. An Analytical Model of a Discrete-Time Polling MAC Protocol for Wireless LANs Using M-Gated Services[J]. Acta. Electronica Sinica, 2010, 38(7): 1495-1499. (in Chinese)

[5] Giambene, G.,Hadzic-Puzovic, S. Nonsaturated Performance Analysis for WiMAX Broadcast Polling Access[J]. IEEE Transactions on Vehicular Technology, 2013, 62(1):306-325.

[6] Qianlin Liu, Dongfeng Zhao, Dongming Zhou. An analytic model for enhancing IEEE 802.11 coordination function media access control protocol[J]. European Transactions on Telecommunications, 2011, 22(6):332-338.

[7] Liu Qianlin, Zhao Dongfeng，Zhao Yifan. An efficient priority service model with two-level-polling scheme[J]. High Technology Letters, 2011, 17(3): 245-251.

[8] Khoshnevis, B., Wei Yu, Lostanlen, Y. Two-Stage Channel Quantization for Scheduling and Beamforming in Network MIMO Systems: Feedback Design and Scaling Laws[J]. IEEE Journal on Selected Areas in Communications, 2013, 31(10): 2028-2042.

[8] Yang Zhijun;Ding Hongwei;Chen Chuanglong.Exhaustive service and gated service polling system with two levels of E(x) characteristics analysis[J]; Acta Electronica Sinica ,2014,04:774-778.

[9] A.S. Salama, B.K. Saleh, M.M. Eassa, Intelligent cross road traffic management system (ICRTMS), in: 2nd International Conference on Computer Technology and Development, ICCTD, Cairo, Egypt, November 2010: 27 – 31.

[10]Dimitrakopoulos, G. (2011) Intelligent transportation systems based on internet-connected vehicles: Fundamental research areas and challenges. 11th International Conference on ITS Telecommunications (ITST), Saint Peterburg, 23-25 August 2011, 145-1

MATEC Web of Conferences 44, 02014 (2016)
DOI: 10.1051/matecconf/20164402014

Interaction model of steel ladle of continuous caster in steel works

Bang Fu HUANG [1,a], Zhi Wei MA[1], Nai Yuan TIAN [2], Zhe SHI [1], Xiao Lei ZHOU [1], Jun CAI [3]

[1]*Faculty of Metallurgical and Energy Engineering, Kunming University of Science and Technology, Kunming 650093, China.*

[2]*School of Metallurgical and Ecological Engineering, University of Science and Technology Beijing, Beijing 100083, China*

[3]*Sinosteel Jinxin Consulting Company Co Ltd, Beijing 100080, China.*

Abstract. For further research on the precondition and interoperability model of interaction ladles among continuous caster, this article takes steel ladle of Y steel works as the object of research. On the basis of turnover number calculation model of single cast steel ladle, the relationship between cast number and the turnover number and turnover times and last turnover number are further analyzed. The simulation of steel ladle turnover rules was taken on the 2 continuous casters with Gantt chart. After that, the relationships between turnover number and last turnover number and non-turnover number are researched deeply. Combining with the Gantt chart, the expressions of start casting time and empty ladle ending time and heavy ladle starting time were put forward. The precondition of steel ladle interaction is obtained, which means the exchange ladle should not undertaking transport task in first stop continuous caster, and the empty ladle end time of exchange ladle of first stop continuous caster should early than the heavy ladle start time of last stop continuous caster. After applying the model to practice, 3 steel ladles of No.2 continuous caster can be reduced. This research results is supplying theoretical basis for steel ladle controlling and production organization optimization, and enriches the theory and method of metallurgical process integration.

1 Forward

As the interface technique between blast furnace and basic oxygen furnace continuous improvement, steel ladle is the vessel of liquid steel transporting between basic oxygen furnace(BOF) and continuous caster(CC) interface, and is the main tool of control steel temperature and production rhythm[1-2]. Besides, steel ladle is the buffer[3] of production rhythm. Its turnover number and operation efficiency and buffer capability are the key factors of control production and matching procedures. In a certain period of time, the less turnover number of steel ladle represents the higher turnover ratio and hot tapping ratio. At the same time, reducing turnover number has practical significance for reducing tapping temperature and keeping stabilization casting in CC[4]. However, how to reduce turnover number of steel ladle? Reducing number is the hot and difficult of production scheduling in steel works. Studies have shown that steel ladle interaction is an effective way to reduce the turnover number. What is the precondition and model of steel ladle interaction? Nowadays, the existing research results of steel ladle interaction is rare in reference.

Among the existing research results, the number of steel ladle is focused on calculation method, such as production method, time calculation method and turnover period matching method[5]. The result of the study is only applicable to the ideal state of single equipment and has more limited conditions. The turnover rule of steel ladle is simulated by Gantt chart under the condition of single-cast and multi-casts[6]. Furthermore, the calculation

[a] kmusthbf@163.com

model under different overlap heats is put forward, this method only consider overlap heat number, without the other factors on the influence of the ladle interaction among continuous casters. The author has done the ladle number calculation model of 2 and 3 continuous casters. The model is under the different overlapping time of casts[7-9]. Moreover, the revolving model under the condition of saving ladle of steel also carried on through research[10-11]. The ladle number calculation model was also put forward based on smelting cycle of basic oxygen furnace single heat bigger than or less than the casting time of continuous caster single heat. From the existing research, we can see that the precondition and influence factor of steel ladle interaction are not discussed. Therefore, using existing theory or method of ladle interaction, the application effect is apparently not good.

For further research on the precondition and interoperability model of steel ladles interaction among continuous casters, this article takes steel ladle of Y steel works as the object of research. The operation process and time is analyzed. The relationship among various parameters of single cast in CC is deeply researched. The relational expression of turnover times and turnover number and last turnover number is proposed. The turnover rules of steel ladle were simulated by using Gantt chart. Based on time expression of empty ladle finish and heavy ladle start, the precondition and interoperability model of steel ladles interaction is proposed.

2 Operation process analysis of steel ladle

In order to research the model of steel ladle interaction between CCs, the operation process and time should be controlled firstly[12]. There has 3 basic oxygen furnaces(BOF) of 100t, 2 ladle furnace(LF), 1 RH and 2 continuous casters(CC) of slab in Y steel works. Besides, Y steel works has 3 online baking positions(ONBP), 2 offline baking positions(OFBP), 1 hot repair position(HRP) and 2 de-slagging positions(DP). Through analyzing the operation process of steel ladle, the operation phase includes heavy operation and CC casting and empty operation. Operation phase of heavy ladle has 2 operation routes, which includes BOF-LF-CC and BOF-LF-RH-CC. The liquid steel of BOF-LF-CC route can supply to No.1 CC and No.2 CC. The liquid steel of BOF-LF-RH-CC route is just supply to No.2 CC. Operation phase of empty ladle has 2 operation routes, which includes DP-HRP-ONBP-BOF and DP-HRP-OFBP–BOF.

All the above operation time can be measured and statistics and inductive. As shown in Table 1.

Table 1. Operation time of steel ladle.

Time	Time term	Average value /min	Remark
Operation time of heavy steel ladle	Tapping time+Refining time+Transportation time+Waiting time	78	"BOF-LF-CC"refining route of No.1 CC's liquid steel
		74	"BOF-LF-CC"refining route of No.2 CC's liquid steel
		115	"BOF-LF-RH-CC"refining route of No.1 CC's liquid steel
Casting time of single heat	Single heat casting time of No.1 CC	32	Steel ladle of No.1 CC
	Single heat casting time of No.2 CC	27	Steel ladle of No.2 CC
Operation time of empty steel ladle	Deslagging time+Repairing time+Baking time+Transportation time+ Waiting time	63	"DP-HRP-ONBP-BOF"operation route of No.1 CC's steel ladle

Based on Table 1, turnover cycle of steel ladle can be calculated by follows equation:

$$T_{cycle}^{ladle} = T_{heavy}^{ladle} + T_{cast}^{CC} + T_{empty}^{ladle} \tag{1}$$

Where T_{cycle}^{ladle} represents turnover cycle of steel ladle, min. T_{heavy}^{ladle} represents operation time of heavy ladle, min. T_{cast}^{CC} represents single heat casting time of CC, min. T_{empty}^{ladle} represents operation time of empty ladle, min.

According to table 1, by using Eq. (1), the steel ladle turnover cycle of No.1 CC can be calculated, which equals 173 min. The steel ladle turnover cycle of No.2 CC equals 164 min under the operation route of BOF-LF-CC. The steel ladle turnover cycle of No.2 CC equals 205 min under the operation route of BOF-LF-RH-CC.

3 Number calculation model of single cast steel ladle

In order to research the precondition of steel ladle interaction, the ladle turnover number of single cast need to be confirmed. The existing research has mature research results of number calculation model [6-8]. As shown in formula (2) and (3).

$$n_{ladle}^{CC}=\left\lceil \frac{T_{cycle}^{ladle}}{T_{cast}^{CC}} \right\rceil \tag{2}$$

$$n_{ladle}^{CC}=\left\lceil 1+\frac{T_{heavy}^{ladle}+T_{empty}^{ladle}}{T_{cast}^{CC}} \right\rceil \tag{3}$$

Where n_{ladle}^{CC} represents steel ladle turnover number of single cast; $\lceil\ \rceil$ represents the symbol of round up to an integer.

According to formula (2) and (3), the number calculation model of single cast turnover ladle means that CC can cast number of liquid steel during turnover cycle. According to single heat casting time equals 32 min and turnover cycle equals 173 min, by applying Eq. (2), the No.1 CC needs 5.4 steel ladles for single casting, the number is 6 for round up to an integer. According to single heat casting time equals 27 min and turnover cycle equals 164 min, by applying Eq. (2), the No.2 CC needs 6.1 steel ladles for single casting under the operation route of BOF-LF-CC, the number is 7 for round up to an integer. This works choose the heavy ladle of "BOF-LF-CC" route as the object of research. At the same time, empty ladle choose "DP-HRP-ONBP-BOF" route.

4 Model of steel ladle interaction

The steel ladle will be exchange to other continuous caster for new transportation task once it has finished turnover, which means the interoperability among different continuous casters are realized. In some cases, the turnover number of steel ladle in steel works can reduce under some condition.

The casting heats of CC's single cast can be expressed by turnover time and turnover number and last turnover number, which is shown in formula (4).

$$N_{heat}^{CC}=i^{CC}\times n_{ladle}^{CC}+h_{ladle}^{CC} \tag{4}$$

In the equation, N_{heat}^{CC} represents casting heats of CC's single cast, i^{CC} represents complete turnover times of steel ladle, time. h_{ladle}^{CC} represents the number of steel ladle which needs turnover again after n_{ladle}^{CC} turnovers i^{CC} times, $0\le h_{ladle}^{CC}<n_{ladle}^{CC}$.

By the research, the single cast of No.1 CC needs 21 heats, it can be shown in the expression of 21=3×6+3 by using Eq.(4), the 21 heats of single cast needs 6 steel ladles turnover 3 times and the first 3 steel ladles turnover one more time again. Meanwhile, the single cast of No.2 CC needs 25 heats, the expression of 25=3×7+4 can be obtained, the 25 heats of single cast needs 7 steel ladles turnover 3 times and the first 4 steel ladles turnover one more time again.

Gantt chart is an effective tool for planning production scheduling, and the relationship between production plan and each procedure can be vivid shown[13]. The Gantt chart of operation rules of 2 CC's steel ladle are simulated, the operation process of steel ladle in various segment of time process can be shown. Based on the results above, the precondition and model of steel ladle interaction can be in-depth studied. Gantt chart is a set of lines chart, which horizontal axis represents time and vertical axis represents activities and lines represents project performance [14-16].

The Gantt chart sets No.1 CC first start and stopping casting, and No.2 CC last start casting. The overlapping time between 2 CCs is 46 min. According to the calculation results of Eq.(4), the Gantt chart is just simulated steel ladle turnover rules of No.1 CC's last 9 heats and No.2 CC's first 7 heats, the feasibility of steel

ladle interaction between CCs can be analyzed. As shown in Fig.1.

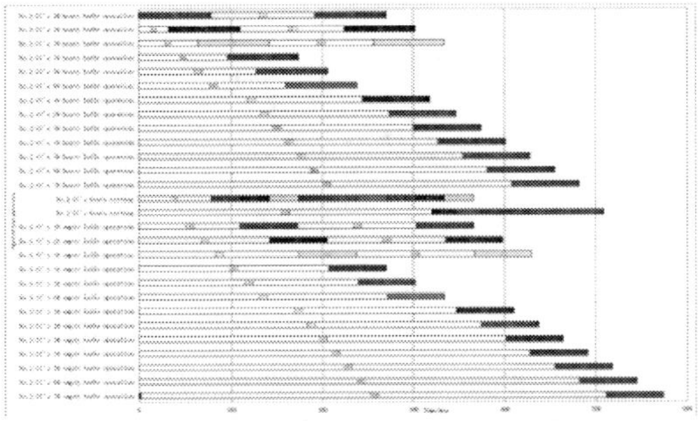

Figure 1. Gantt chart of 2 CCs' steel ladle.

As show in Fig.1, a color of line section represents the same steel ladle of CC. The last 9 steel ladles of No.1 CC need the red ladle and black ladle and yellow ladle turnover one more time again after all of ladles turnover 3 times. However, the violet ladle and brown ladle and gray ladle are finished transport task after turnover 3 times. This simulation results is consistent to the calculation results by Eq.(4).

For No.2 CC last casting, it is need to observe the 7 steel ladles, whether some ladle can exchange to No.1 for replacing 4#/5#/6# steel ladle. After that, the turnover number of No.2 CC's steel ladles can reduce.

The relationship between last need turnover number and non turnover ladle is expressed by Eq.(5) and Eq.(6) and Eq.(7).

$$g = n_{ladle}^{CC} - h \tag{5}$$

$$g = n_{ladle}^{CC} - (N_{heat}^{CC} - i \times n_{ladle}^{CC}) \tag{6}$$

$$g = n_{ladle}^{CC} \times (1+i) - N_{heat}^{CC} \tag{7}$$

Where g represents the last non turnover ladle of CC's cast.

According to Eq.(5) and Eq.(6) and Eq.(7), the serial number of last non turnover and exchange ladle can express by Eq.(8).

$$k_r^{CC} = N_{heat}^{CC} - n_{ladle}^{CC} + r \tag{8}$$

Where k_r^{CC} represents serial number of non turnover ladle of CC's cast, r represents the serial number of exchang ladle in non turnover ladle, $1 \le r \le g$.

Through analyzing single cast's steel ladle, the start casting time can express by Eq.(9).

$$T_{ks}^{CC} = t_{1s}^{CC} + (k-1) \times T_{cast}^{CC} \tag{9}$$

Where T_{ks}^{CC} represents the start casting time of No. k steel ladle, min. t_{1s}^{CC} represents the start casting time of No.1 steel ladle, min. k represents the order number of continuous casting heats.

Based on Eq.(1) and Eq.(9), the end time of No. k empty steel ladle can be expressed as shown in Eq.(10).

$$T_{ke\text{-}e}^{CC} = t_{1s}^{CC} + k \times T_{cast}^{CC} + T_{empty}^{ladle} \tag{10}$$

Where T_{ke-e}^{CC} represents the end time of No. k empty steel ladle, min。

Based on Eq.(8) and Eq.(10), the end time of No.1 CC's empty steel ladle can be expressed as shown in Eq.(11) and Eq.(12).

$$T_{ke\text{-}e}^{CC1} = t_{1s}^{CC1} + k_r^{CC1} \times T_{cast}^{CC1} + T_{empty}^{CC1-ladle} \tag{11}$$

$$T_{ke\text{-}e}^{CC1} = t_{1s}^{CC1} + (N_{heat}^{CC1} - n_{ladle}^{CC1} + r) \times T_{cast}^{CC1} + T_{empty}^{CC1-ladle} \tag{12}$$

With similar to Eq.(10), the start time of No. k heavy ladle can be expressed by Eq.(13).

$$T_{kh-s}^{CC} = t_{1s}^{CC} + (k-1) \times T_{cast}^{CC} - T_{heavy}^{ladle} \tag{13}$$

Where T_{kh-s}^{CC} represents the start time of No. k heavy steel ladle, min。

In term of No.2 CC, the start time of No. k heavy ladle can be expressed by Eq.(14).

$$T_{kh-s}^{CC2} = t_{1s}^{CC2} + (k^{CC2} - 1) \times T_{cast}^{CC2} - T_{heavy}^{CC2-ladle} \tag{14}$$

Though analyzing Fig.1 and Eq.(11) and Eq.(14), steel ladle interaction from No.1 CC to No.2 CC need to satisfy the precondition as shown below.

① The exchange ladle should not undertaking transport task of liquid steel in No.1 CC.

② The empty ladle end time of No.1 CC's exchange ladle should early than the heavy ladle start time of No.2 CC's steel ladle.

Based on above condition, the exchange time can be expressed by Eq.(15).

$$T_{ke\text{-}e}^{CC1} - T_{kh-s}^{CC2} \leq 0 \quad (15)$$

Taking Eq.(11) and Eq.(14) into Eq.(15), it can be gained Eq.(16).

$$[t_{1s}^{CC1} + k_r^{CC1} \times T_{cast}^{CC1} + T_{empty}^{CC1-ladle}] - [t_{1s}^{CC2} + (k^{CC2} - 1) \times T_{cast}^{CC2} - T_{heavy}^{CC2-ladle}] \leq 0 \quad (16)$$

By applying Eq.(15) and Eq.(16), the feasibility of steel ladle interaction between No.1 CC and No.2 CC can be analyzed. This interaction condition can supply scientific basis for reducing turnover number of steel ladle.

5 Model applying

The interaction feasibility of steel ladle under the condition of Fig.1 is analyzed by applying interaction model. Based on analyzing result of Eq.(4), the 4# and 5# and 6# ladle of No.1 CC is finished transport task after turnover 3 times. The t_{1s}^{CC1} sets 0min. The end time of 4# and 5# and 6# empty ladle is calculated from Eq.(5) to Eq.(12). The result is shown in Table 2.

Table 2. Empty ladle's ending time of 4# and 5# and 6# steel ladle of No.1 CC.

N_{heat}^{CC1} /heat	n_{lad}^{CC}	h	g	T_{cast}^{CC1} /min	$T_{empty}^{CC1-lad}$ /min	No.	r	k_r^{CC} /个	$T_{ke\text{-}e}^{CC1}$ /min
21	6	3	3	32	63	4#	1	16	575
						5#	2	17	607
						6#	3	18	639

The overlapping time between 2 CCs equals 46min. the start casting time of No.2 CC's first heat is calculated and equals 626 min by using Eq.(9). The start time of No.2 CC's 7 heavy ladles is calculated by using Eq.(14). As shown in Table 3.

Table 3. Heavy ladle's start time of No.2 CC's steel ladle.

No.	t_{1s}^{CC2} / min	k^{CC2} /heat	T_{cast}^{CC2} / min	$T_{heavy}^{CC2-ladle}$ /min	$T_{kh\text{-}s}^{CC2}$ / min
1#	626	1	27	63	563
2#		2			590
3#		3			617
4#		4			644
5#		5			671
6#		6			698
7#		7			725

By using judging condition of steel ladle interaction, $T_{ke\text{-}e}^{CC1}$ contrast to $T_{kh\text{-}s}^{CC2}$, the comparison result is shown in Table 4.

Table 4. Steel ladle interaction between No.1 CC and No.2 CC.

No.1 CC's steel ladle	Judging condition	Be replaced ladle of No.2 CC	Optimal replaced plan of No.2 CC's steel ladle
4#	$T_{ke\text{-}e}^{CC1}$ - $T_{kh-s}^{CC2} \leq 0$	2#、3#、4#、5#、6#、7#	2#
5#		3#、4#、5#、6#、7#	3#
6#		4#、5#、6#、7#	4#

In Table 4, the optimal replaced plan means the minimum temperature drop loss and quickly start next turnover. No.2 CC has 3 steel ladles that can be replaced by No.1 CC's ladle under the condition of optimal replaced plan, which means No.2 CC less investment 3 steel ladles.

From what has been discussed above, the analyzing interaction feasibility of steel ladle between CCs should control the turnover rules and cycle and number firstly, and analyze the relationship between empty ladle end time and heavy ladle start time, and propose the optimal replaced plan. Studies have shown that the cast plan and casting time of rational control and matching can raise the non-turnover number and probability of steel ladle interaction.

6 Figures and tables

(1) The turnover cycle and number of steel ladle is described under the condition of single CC. The relationship between turnover number and heavy ladle operation time and empty ladle operation time and casting time is analyzed.

(2) The operation rules of 2 CCs steel ladle is simulated under the condition of 46 min overlapping time by using Gantt chart. The relationship between heat number and turnover number and turnover times and non turnover number is analyzed. Based on start casting time and casting time of No.1 heat, the expression of empty ladle end time and heavy ladle start time is proposed by analyzing empty ladle and heavy ladle operation time.

(3) The precondition of steel ladle interaction is obtained, which means the exchange ladle has no need of

undertaking transport task in first stop CC, and the empty ladle end time of exchange ladle of first stop CC should early than the heavy ladle start time of last stop CC.

(4) The model is applied to practice. There has 3 steel ladles of No.2 CC that can be replaced by 4# and 5# and 6# ladle of No.1 CC. the optimal replaced plan is 2# and 3# and 4# ladle of No.1 CC replaced by No.2 CC's steel ladle. Besides, this research results is supplying theoretical basis for steel ladle controlling and production organization optimization. At the same time, it enriches the theory and method of metallurgical process integration.

References

1.Y Ruiyu. Metallurgical Process Engineering. the 2st Edition (2009)
2.H Bangfu, S Zhe, D Yuehua. Journal of Kunming University of Science and Technology(Natural Science Edition), 38(3),(2013)
3. Y Ruiyu. Theory and Method of Metallurgical Process Integration. the 1st Edition (2013)
4. Y Ruiyu. Acta Metall Sin, (1993).
5. L Qing, Z Ping, W Xiaodong. Journal of University of Science and Technology Beijing, , 27(2),(2005)
6. C Jun, H Dongfeng, W Hongbing. Journal of Chongqing University,,36(11),(2013)
7. H Bangfu,W Jianjun,Z Daofei. Journal of Iron and Steel Research ,26(5),(2014)
8. H Bangfu, S Zhe, Z Hongbo. Journal of Central South University (Science and Technology), 45(7),(2014)
9. H Bangfu, Z Xiaolei, Z Guifang. Applied Mechanics and Materials, (2014)
10. H Bangfu, F Bo, W Jianjun. Iron and Steel, 49(4),(2014)
11. H Bangfu, Z Xiaolei, Z Guifang. Advanced Materials Research, 1015, (2014)
12. H Bangfu. University of Science and Technology Beijing,(2011)
13. C Jun. University of Science and Technology Beijing,(2015)
14. H Dongfeng, Y Gang, X Anjun. Journal of University of Science and Technology Beijing, 32(12),(2010)
15. W Jinming , Z Kun,L Shenghui. Shandong Metellury, 31(5),(2009)
16.Maylor H. Beyond the Gantt chart Project management moving on EurManage. 19(1),(2001)

Acknowledgements

This work is supported by China Postdoctoral Science Foundation No.57 (No.2015M572647XB) and the Science Research Program of Yunnan Province Education Department(No.2014Y069).

MATEC Web of Conferences 44, 02015 (2016)
DOI: 10.1051/matecconf/20164402015

Open Knowledge Representation Techniques and Its Application in Precision Forming Design

Ping Wang [1,a], Xiao Gui Tang [2] and Bin Wang [1]

[1] *School of Mechanical Engineering, Yancheng Institute of Technology, 224051 Yancheng Jiangsu, China*
[2] *School of Mechanical Engineering, Jianghsu University, 212013 Zhenjiang Jiangsu, China*

Abstract. Precision forming knowledge of precision forging parts can be acquired from various sources and generally requires an effective representation for its efficient reuse. According to the specific characteristics of the precision forming of car forging parts, the precision forming engineering knowledge has been classified into several kinds with the method of the open knowledge representation techniques for the different kinds of knowledge proposed. The open representation techniques of precision forming knowledge and its application are described in detail, and combined with the development of the precision forming design system of the automotive starter guiding cylinder based on knowledge. The results show that the precision forming knowledge is represented in an effective way will solve the problem of fusion of precision forming knowledge and precision forming manufacturing, and improve greatly the utilization efficiency of the precision forming knowledge.

1 Introduction

Knowledge-based Engineering (KBE) has been used widely, which integrates artificial intelligence with CAX system and connects engineering design without interruption [1]. KBE application has become pivotal for enhancing manufacturing enterprises competitiveness. Product design is a highly involved, often ill-defined, complex and iterative process [2]. An effective Knowledge driven design tool requires efficient knowledge representation schemes. Therefore, many scholars have carried out the research of knowledge representation. Lee and Jeong[3] developed a distributed and flexible knowledge representation model, and tested a prototype. Edy Portmann, Patrick Kaltenrieder and Witold Pedrycz[4] put forward knowledge representation through graphs and provided an overview of different types of graphs stressing their relationships and their essential features. Haining Yao and Letha Etzkorn[5] introduced a semantic converter which converts knowledge representation in Conceptual Graphs into representation in Resource Description Framework. W.M. Wang, X. Peng[6] presented a dynamic representation of fuzzy knowledge (DRFK) method. Chen, W.L[7] put forward a knowledge representation approach based on Parameter Flow Chart. Xi P[8] studied the open representation of design knowledge in the form of formaluas, 2D mapping graphs, procedures and rules.

The problem with these researchers is that few papers have addressed the open knowledge representation in intelligent precision forming design. In this paper, we provided an open knowledge representation and its application in precision forming design system. This paper is organized as follows: Section 2 describes the precision forming design process based on knowledge. Section 3 puts forward the open representation of precision forming knowledge. Section 4 presents an application implementation of the knowledge driven precision forming design combined with the automotive starter guiding cylinder. The conclusion and future work are discussed in Section 5.

2 The precision forming design process based on knowledge

Based on the characteristics of precision forming design, the precision forming design process based on knowledge is shown in Fig. 1.

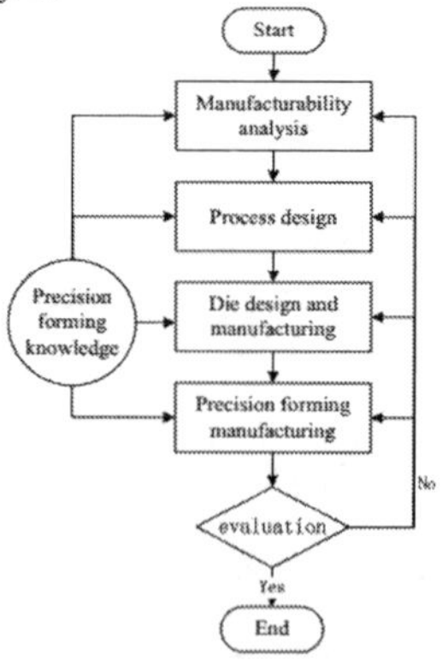

Figure 1. Precision forming design process based on knowledge.

[a] Corresponding author: wp_ycit@163.com

Article available at http://www.matec-conferences.org or http://dx.doi.org/10.1051/matecconf/20164402015

Precision forming design, especially the precision forming design of complex product is a highly involved, often ill-defined, complex process in which design engineers perform a large number of activities related to creating and evaluating solutions. Most of these activities depend upon the design knowledge obtained in previous projects. In order to improve the efficiency and quality of the precision forming design of car forging parts, precision forming knowledge should be properly fused with forming design process.

3 The open representation of precision forming knowledge

According to characteristics of the precision forming of car cold/warm forging parts, the precision forming knowledge is usually classified into four categories, namely, process design knowledge, die design knowledge, numerical simulation knowledge and forming processing knowledge. As shown in Fig.2.

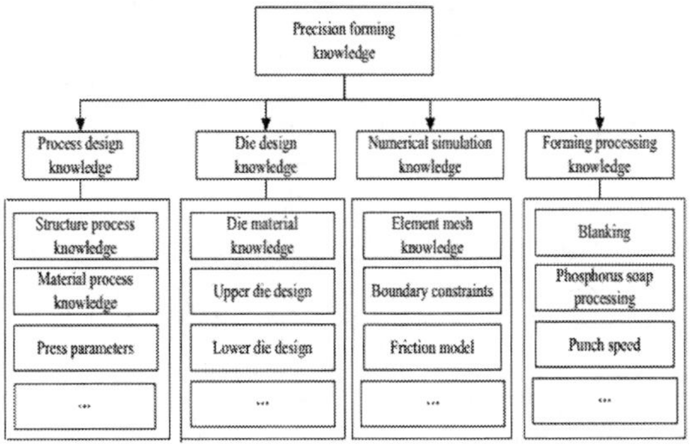

Figure 2. The classification of precision forming knowledge.

3.1 The open representation of formulas knowledge

There are many formula requires an effective representation for its efficient reuse in the process of precision forming design. The BNF (Backus Naur Form) representation is usually used to represent the knowledge. The paradigm is as following:

<formula knowledge>::=< variable > < expressions >
<variable>::=<variable name>
<variable type>
<variable value>
<expressions>::=<item>|
(<item><the operator>)

3.2 The open representation of graphs knowledge

Engineering graphs are common forms of precision forming knowledge. The BNF representation of graphs knowledge is described as following:

<graph knowledge>::=<query statement ><graph data >
<query statement >::=<graph X>|<graph Y>
<graph data >::=<graph name>
<original data>
<X data> <Y data>

3.3 The open representation of table knowledge

Engineering table knowledge is usually stored in relational database, and the designers can easily query some parameter values with the help of query statements. The BNF representation of table knowledge can be described as following:

<table knowledge>::=<query statement> <table data >
<query statement>::=<query parameter>
<table name>
<parameter field >
<conditions>
<table data >::=<table name><fields> <records>

3.4 The open representation of rule knowledge

In the process of precision forming design, process rules are usually used to represent the empirical domain knowledge. The BNF representation of process rules is as follows:

<rules>::=IF{<conditions>}THEN{<conclusions>}
<conditions>::=<variable><predicate>
< attribute value >|<facts>
<conclusions>::={<statements>|<operations>}
<statements>::={<statement items>}
<operations>::={<operation functions>}

3.5 The open representation of process knowledge based on fuzzy logic

The fuzzy sets and membership function in fuzzy mathematics can be used to represent the uncertainty process knowledge in the precision forming design development.

If U domain is numerical domain, and the process knowledge can be described by numerical values, the membership function of U domain fuzzy subset can be defined as a linear function with parameters, namely:

$$\mu_A(x,a,b,c,d)=\begin{cases} 0 & x \le a \\ \dfrac{x-a}{b-a} & a < x \le b \\ 1 & b < x \le c \\ \dfrac{d-x}{d-c} & c < x \le d \\ 0 & d < x \end{cases} \tag{1}$$

Where, a, b, c and d denote respectively design parameters, and a value is less than b value, b value is less than or equals to c value, c value is less than d value.

3.6 The open representation of case knowledge

In the process of precision forming design, there are much forming design support knowledge, such as part name, part material, part shape and similar parts forming design etc., the open representation of case knowledge is as follows:

CASE INSTANCE: Case_No
Name_of_part:
Material _of _Part:
MaterialType_of_part:
Shapetype_of_part:
...

SOLUTION
    Process_file_Name:
    Part_file_Name:
    Part_file_path:
    ...
END

3.7 The open representation of object-oriented precision forming knowledge

The method of object-oriented knowledge representation provides the approach of integrating forming process knowledge into forming design. These methods include abstraction, encapsulation, inheritance and polymorphism. The open representation of object-oriented precision forming process knowledge is as follows:

Object::=(object name, data structure, the method sets, message interface)

3.8 The open representation of precision forming knowledge based on artificial neural network

For the open knowledge representation of multiple inputs and multiple outputs precision forming process knowledge, the BP neural network is usually adopted, as shown in Fig. 3.

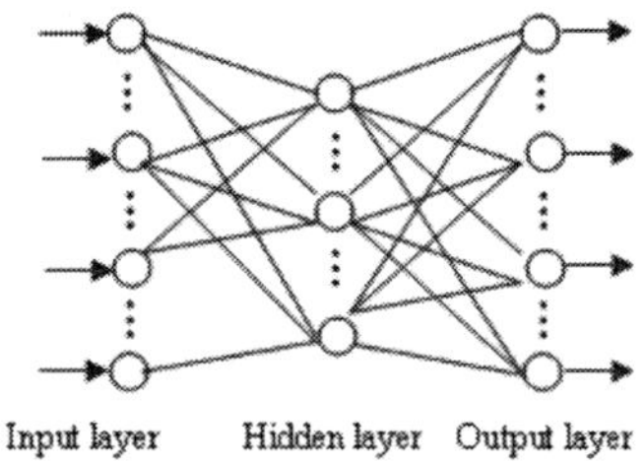

Figure 3. The BP neural network.

4 Application case

Automotive starter guiding cylinder (as shown in Fig.4) is the critical part of automotive starter transmission system, it works in a complex condition, and it has to meet the requirements for the excellent mechanical properties. At present, most automotive starter guiding cylinders are manufactured by precision forming, in which is characterized by low cost, high productivity, high precision and excellent mechanical properties. As there is so much design knowledge involved in the forming process, therefore, it can greatly improve the efficiency of the precision forming technology and die design to incorporate design knowledge and forming process, and realize the reuse and sharing of knowledge.

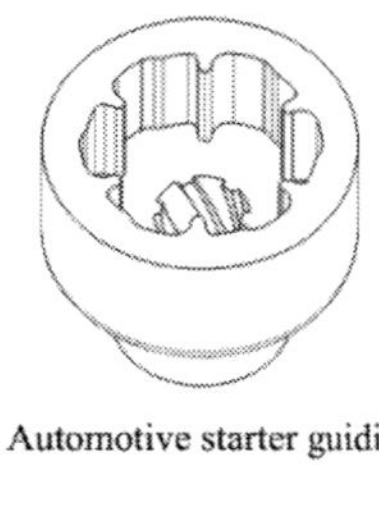

Figure 4. Automotive starter guiding cylinder.

This study proposes an open knowledge representation of the automotive starter guiding cylinder precision forming based on NX 7.5 software platforms with the help of NX/OPEN API tools, and realize the integration of precision forming design knowledge and precision forming design process. NXOPEN API is open programming interfaces of NX software. NX/OPEN API consists of C++ API, C# API, VB.NET API and Java API. Fig. 5 shows the interface of the automotive starter guiding cylinder precision forming design system based on KBE.

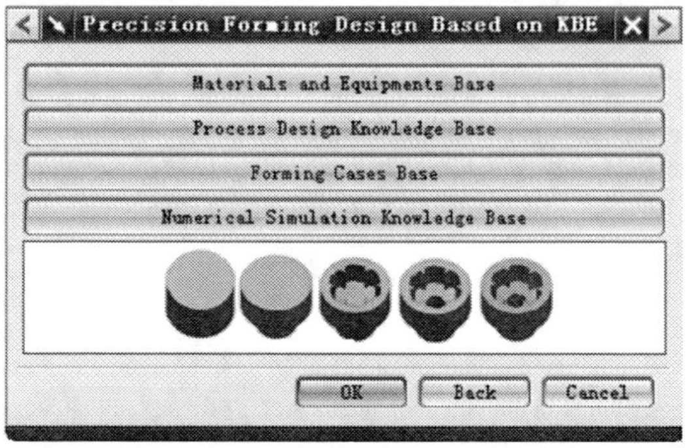

Figure 5. The interface of precision forming design based on KBE

4.1 The open representation of precision forming design formula

The complicated shape coefficient of extrusion F_k is often checked in the precision forming design, and the formula of the complicated shape coefficient of extrusion is as follows:

$$F_K = \frac{V_0}{V_1} \tag{2}$$

Where, V0 is the preformed blank volume, V1 is the volume of final forming part.

The knowledge representation of formula (2) is as follows:

FK= (V0)/ (V1)

4.2 The open representation of graphs in the precision forming design

Engineering graphs are common forms of precision forming design knowledge. Fig. 6 is the Z-versus-stroke graph for the automotive starter guiding cylinder precision forming, where Z is the forming load, stroke is the extrusion displacement.

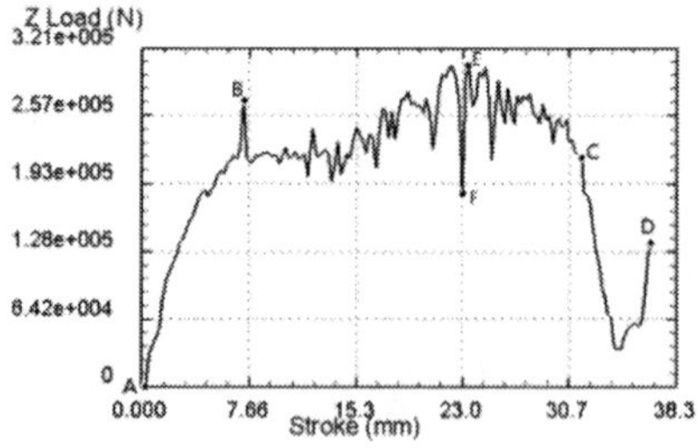

Figure 6. The Z-versus-stroke curve.

The BNF representation of graphs knowledge is described as following:

<graph knowledge>::=<query statement ><graph data >

<query statement >::=<graph X>|<graph Y>

<graph data >::=<Z_load_curve>

<original data><0.0> <0.0>

4.3 The open representation of table knowledge in the precision forming design

Table 1 is the parameters of the final forged part and the billet for the automotive starter guiding cylinder precision forming.

Table 1. The parameters of the final formed part and the billet.

Parameter	Unit	Value
The diameter of billet guiding hole	mm	16
The height of billet guiding hole	mm	34±0.5
Teeth number of helical involute spline		6
The lead of helical involute spline	mm	120
Helical angle	degree	25.6611
Normal module	mm	1.37846
Direction of turning		right
Pitch diameter	mm	16.609
Circumferential module	mm	1.52929
root diameter	mm	20.635± 0.075
outside diameter	mm	16.949±0.15
standard pitch diameter	mm	18.351
Pressure angle	degree	30

The open representation of table 1 knowledge is as follows:

The_forming_parameters=Table ("The parameters of the final formed part and the billet", the forming parameters, the value of the parameter)

4.4 The open representation of case knowledge in the precision forming design

The case knowledge of automotive starter guiding cylinder mainly includes parts name, parts material, the extrusion speed of the punch, forming temperature, friction coefficient and the stress and strain distribution in the forming process. The open representation of case knowledge is as follows:

CASE INSTANCE: Case_No. ASGC

Name_of_part: ASGC

Material _of _Part: 20CrMo

MaterialType_of_part: Metal

Shapetype_of_part: Axially Symmetrical Parts

Punch_speed: 12

Forming_temperature:20

...

SOLUTION ASGC

Process_file_Name:ASGC_process_file

Part_file_Name:ASGC.stl

Part_file_path:D:\ASGC

...

END

Fig. 7 shows the stress distribution of forming process in the forming case base.

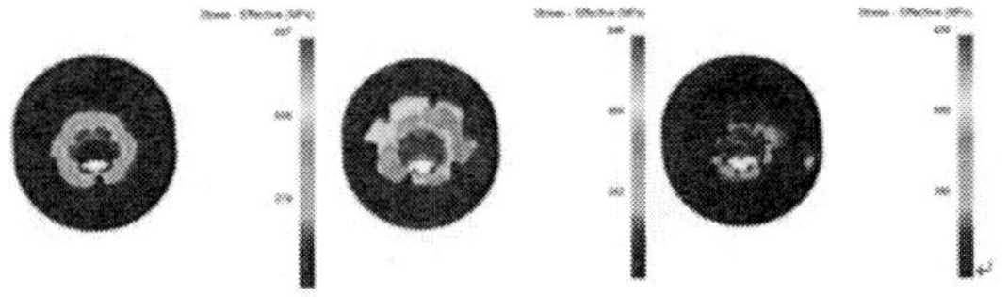

Figure 7. The stress distribution of forming process.

5 Conclusions

In this study, an open representation of precision forming design knowledge is proposed, and it can help capture design knowledge from various sources in the precision forming design process, and can effectively realize the fusion of precision forming design knowledge and precision forming process. The methods proposed are shown to be useful for precision forming knowledge reuse. In our future work, we will study how to enable designers to formulate complex knowledge queries so that relevant precision forming design knowledge can be recommended automatically.

Acknowledgment

The project was supported by joint innovation project of Jiangsu Province under Grant BY2015057-28.

References

1. J. Hu, Y.H. Peng, D.Y. Li, J.L.Yin, Robust optimization based on knowledge discovery from metal forming simulation, Journal of Materials Processing Technology, 187-188, 698–701(2007)
2. Chandrasegaran, Senthil K., et al. , The Evolution, Challenges, and Future of Knowledge Representation in Product Design Systems, Computer-Aided Design, 45,204–228(2013)
3. Lee, J. and Y. Jeong, User-centric Knowledge Representations Based on Ontology for AEC Design Collaboration",Computer-Aided Design 44,735–748(2012)
4. Edy Portmann, Patrick Kaltenrieder and Witold Pedrycz, "Knowledge representation through graphs", Procedia Computer Science 62 ,245–248(2015)
5. Haining Yao, Letha Etzkorn, "Automated conversion between different knowledge representation formats", Knowledge-Based Systems, 19,404–412,(2015)
6. W.M Wang,W.M. Wang, X. Peng, Dynamic representation of fuzzy knowledge based on fuzzy

petri net and genetic-particle swarm optimization, 41,1369–1376(2014)

7. Chen, W.L, A New Process Knowledge Representation Approach Using Parameter Flow Chart, Computers in industry, 62,9–22(2011)
8. Xi P et al., Intelligent Product Design Based on Open Knowledge Representation. Acta Aeronautica et Astronautics Sinica, 33,1746-1754(2012)

MATEC Web of Conferences **44**, 02016 (2016)
DOI: 10.1051/matecconf/20164402016

Study of Coal Mine Ventilation System Optimization based on Ventsim

Jing Gang ZHANG [1,2] , Cheng Yu SUO [1]

[1]College of Safety Engineering, North China Institute of Science & Technology, Beijing 101601,China [2]School of Resource and Safety Engineering, China University of Mining and Technology(Beijing) , Beijing 100083, China

Abstract: This article is based on the situation of too large coal mine ventilation resistance in the Majiagou coal mine. According to Majiagou coal mine late production plans, it measures resistance comprehensively, analyses the resistance distributions and the problems exist in the ventilation systems and comes up with targeted optimization programs. By studying the ventilation system model, as well as adjusting the system parameters, Ventsim software is applied to study ventilation system in Majiagou coal mine. Design of mine ventilation is proved practical in the mine ventilation system optimizations, thus Ventsim software can not only be used in the ventilation network calculation and merry-demand simulation and dynamic of wind flow, but also can be used to assist in the short-term and long-term planning for ventilation system, it is of a certain significance of guidance to find the problems in the mine management and optimizations of the ventilation network.

Keywords: Ventsim; three-dimensional ventilation; ventilation calculation; optimizations

1 Ventsim three-dimensional ventilation simulation system

Ventsim is based on independent platform mine ventilation implement software, the system has very good compatibility, 3-d model is generated by putting basis data from other mine design software or the ventilation software into the system conveniently. The real 3-D artwork technology is adopted by building a model, complicated mine ventilation process will be shown directly with 3-D by the consumers. By coloring different data in different colors, ventilation process key data and weak link are clear at a glance. By building 3-d ventilation system model , network ventilation is resolved and wind machine is selected preferably , thereby, ventilation effect is detected and controlled to satisfy the shaft design and management requests.

2 Situation of the coal mine

Single wing diagonal drawer-type is adopted in the mine ventilation. New wind of shaft enters 2nd , 3rd, 4th to 5th horizontal shaft bottom car parks, then to the 11th dark shaft ,eighth horizontal bottom, 13th dark shaft and10th horizontal transportation roadway one by one. Part of wind flow from 0005 the into the wind after washing face to 0005 return air duct by 9905 return air up to 8905 blind shaft, the 7905 blind shaft to 5 level crosscutting back in 5605 up to 3 level alleys finally to 2505 a return air lane in the west wind well back into the ground. The present type 62 A13-N024 is a main ventilating machine , whose power is 1000 kW, angle of the ventilating machine blade installation is 45 degree .

3 3-d model building and ventilation system evaluation analysis

3.1 Resistance measurement and basic data acquisition

Base point measuring method of precise barometer are adopted to measure main mine ventilation line, more than 150 points. Both measurement methods and instruments meet the requirements, besides, the data obtained by measuring are reliable and error precision is not

beyond the demand.

3.2 Building the 3-d

According to the actual situation of the mine design, with the help of AutoCAD graphic software, ventilation systematic diagram is drawn as the latest one, then every roadway centerline is traced, and AutoCAD graph is saved in the form of DXF. Then the entity roadway is generated when DXF file is imported into Ventsim system. Node level data are used to model the node fu elevation. Initial three-dimensional model is completed.

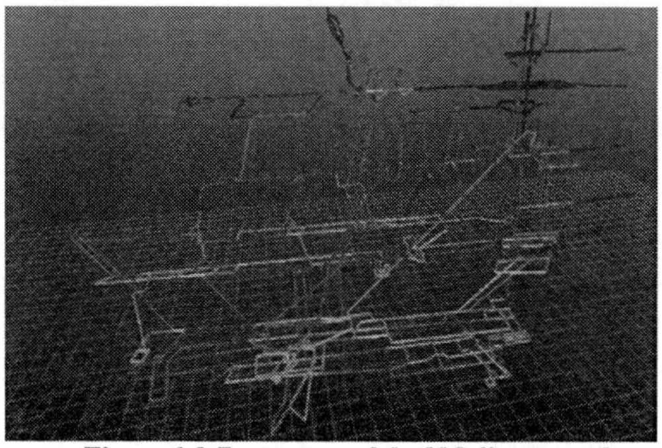

Figure 1 3-D stereo model of Majiagou coal mine

3.3 Input the main data and conduct ventilation status simulation

Basic data and material are measured based on the mine ventilation resistance. The tunnel section shape, area, the type of support and parameter of wind resistance are assigned to the corresponding roadway. The present situation of Majiagou mine ventilation system is simulated to be resolved and the condition of the underground is simulated actually. By regulating wind resistance of some branches, the wind speed, air volume and temperature of 3-d stereo model are basically consistent with practical tunnels. The results are shown in the table 1.

Table 1 The main tunnel calculating results of current situation simulation

Branch	Phrase	Tunnel name	Resistance(pa)	Air volume (m^3/s)	wind resistance (Kg/m^7)
1	1-2	Third well	74.781	69.69	0.0154
5	2-3	5 horizontal shaft bottom	91.88	39.92	0.0577
8	3-98	11th of mine 1	51.849	39.2	0.0337
9	4-98	11th of mine 2	94.113	90.84	0.0114
12	4-102	13th of mine 1	65.345	72.33	0.0125
13	102-5	13th of mine 2	15.216	38.54	0.0102
41	23-24	Westerly Wells	65.351	155.5	0.0027
42	24-105	Well westerly wind tunnel	142.971	160.44	0.0059

3.4 Mine ventilation system evaluation analysis

The division of three sections is based on: from the inlet air head into the wind alleys for inlet air section; From the inlet air cross to return for cross wind section; From the return air cross to exhaust wellhead for return air section. Resistance ratio is a measurement of air quality as one of the important signs. There are ten routes for measuring, we take 0423 a ventilation system, 0721,, 0091, all ventilation system all ventilation system, 0523 2 surfaces ventilation system. The resistance distribution of four ventilation lines is as follows in the table 2.

Table 2 Resistance distribution of Ventilation system

System Name	Section	Segment	ventilating resistance (Pa)	The percentage of the total resistance of system (%)
0423 one surface ventilation system	Air inlet section	1_9	634.627	22.68
		9-13	177.261	6.33
	Air retuning	13-105	1986.412	70.99

	section			
	Total		2798.3	100
0721 four surfaces ventilation system	Air inlet section	1-38	738.179	26.42
		38-41	406.012	14.53
	Air retuning section	41-105	1649.78	59.05
	Total		2793.971	100

4 Simulation of mine ventilation system optimization and transformation plan

4. 1 Putting forward the optimization schemes

After multiple communications and discussions with the field engineering and technical personnel, we put forward the two optimization scheme and simulate them as follow:

1) Scheme 1: Renovation project for all of the tunnels: a comprehensive renovation was conducted to wind eyes and 13 tunnels whose wind resistance is larger than others, ventilation ability is improved by expanding lane engineering and regulating system. (Wind resistance after repairing the tunnels can be got according to the similar tunnel experience values. They are shown in the Table 3)

2) Scheme 2: Based on the scheme 1, scheme 2 adopts high power fan: after implementations of expanding lane project, a great power counter-rotating fan of the west wind well BDK - 8 - No. 26 is simulated.

Table 3 the tunnels needing cleaning

Branch	Tunnel name	Initial wind resistance (kg/m^7)	Wind resistance after cleaning (kg/m^7)	Tunnel length(m)
19-21	3205C	0.0449	0.023	186
54-19	3west13Shimen	4.6949	2.4049	3000
53-54	5405	1.2293	0.3738	416
53-55	7905	30.4183	0.3738	416
104-53	8905	1.0909	0.5588	276
42-53		3.3426	1.7122	276

4.2 Simulation of data

In 3-D model directly modify tunnel attribute value of resistance dismissing then simulate.

4.3 Simulation effect analysis and determination of the optimization scheme

In terms of technology, We can analyze as follows after comprehensively comparing the simulation results of every scheme.

Table 3 Comparison of simulation results

Parameters	Westerly Wells				Central system on the 2nd Air Shaft			
Status	**Fans negative** (Pa)	**Fan flow** (m^3/s)	**change value of air volume** (m^3/s)	**change value of Pressure changes** (Pa)	**Fans negative** (Pa)	**Fan flow** (m^3/s)	**change value of air volume** (m^3/s)	**change value of Pressure changes** (Pa)
Status	2815.34	155.5						
One	2637.18	166.44	10.94	-214.154				
Two	3252.38	185.34	29.84	437.041				
Three	2972.96	151.88	-3.62	157.621	2667.66	96.73		

The scheme one: west fan air pressure value decreases to 2637.186 Pa, air volume increases to 166.44 m^3/ s. Both have no obvious effects to the ventilation system, thus not achieving the desired results. It can be adopted as a basically scheme.

The scheme two: after simulating west ventilating shaft air volume increases to 185.34 m ³ / which is close to the anticipated goal; Though the air pressure increases to 3252.381 Pa, it is still difficult to accept this result.

The scheme three: Air volume of west

ventilating shaft is calculated 151.88 m3 / s, air pressure is 2972.961 Pa, air volume of ventilating shaft 2 is 96.73 m3 / s, air pressure is 2667.660 Pa. The air down hole wind points meet the requirements, in order to achieve the desired effect; this can be used as the best solution.

To sum up, the scheme three of Majiagou coal mine ventilation system optimization is the best choice.

5 Comparisons with two-dimension ventilation calculating software in the practical application

According to the measurement of the system parameters, we also use 2 d ventilation calculating software to simulate. We can get a result of similarities and differences by comparing and analyzing:

Simulations from Ventsim and two-dimension software are basically the same. Precision and accuracy have been up to the standard.

With the advance of the work, roadway changes and entire mine ventilation network diagram need repainting, and then every branch is reassign and finally calculation to simulate the current state. Workload is very big, and very easy to make a mistake. Use Ventsim 3 d ventilation simulation system, has been established because of 3 d model and actual mine is a one-to-one relationship, solution is directly in the 3 d models, do not need painting ventilation network diagram. Roadway change, directly on the 3 d model modification roadway. In additions and deletions or modify roadway attribute, the model will be automatic inspection to change, thus automatic to calculating and the current data display in the tunnel.

In 2-d, it is difficult to show the real stratified tunnel coordinates within one drawing , and the connection among layers can not be shown. In 3-d, the system can provide rich layer management tools to hide unimportant data in the complex ventilation network and will focus on shown data.

6. Conclusion

(1)According to the actual situation and optimization and transformation objectives and requirements, we pertinently put forward three optimization schemes. Based on analysis of these simulations and optimizations, scheme three becomes the best solution.

(2) According to comparisons with two-dimension ventilation calculating software in the practical application, it is concluded that the Ventsim system takes advantages over 2d.

(3)Ventsim is applied to the simulations of Majiagou coal mine ventilation system by building ventilation system models and adjusting parameters, the mine ventilation system optimization scheme. Thus showing that applying Ventsim to ventilation design is practical. It is of some guiding significance for management researchers to find problems and optimize ventilation network.

References

[1]LUO Zhen-jiang, etc. The application of Ventsim in mine ventilation [J].Journal of nonferrous metallurgy design and research, 2009, 21 (3).

[2]DENG Hong-wei, etc. Ventilation optimization study of YunXi new mountain ore block based on Ventsim [J].Journal of mining technology, 2010, (4).

[3]WANG Ying-min, etc. Mine ventilation and safety [M]. Beijing: metallurgical industry press, 1978.

[4] LI Chun-min. The application of OpenGL in mine engineering 3 d visual simulation system [J]. Journal of Beijing science and technology university, 2004 (5) : 457 458.

[5] WEI Lian-jiang, WANG De-ming, WANG Qi, etc. the key research on building visualization of mine ventilation system [J]. Safety of coal mine, 2007, 6 (4) - 9.

[6] TIAN Hong-jian, WANG Shu-gang. Mine ventilation network multi-function simulation visualization [J]. Coal mine safety, 2008 (4) : -.

[7] JIA Peng-tao, CHANG Xin-tan. Mine ventilation visual system based on the MapObjects [J]. Coal science and technology, 2002, (12) : 50- 52.

Supported by"the Fundamental Research Funds for the Central Universities" （3142013103）（3142012029）

Introduction of author: ZHANG Jing-gang (1981.10-), male, born in Yantai of Shandong, Graduated from China mining university (Beijing) security technology and engineering doctor, a safety engineering lecturer of north China institute of science and technology, engaged in the coal mine safety, safety management and safety evaluation. E-mail：xagn@163.com Telephone:13463612776

MATEC Web of Conferences **44**, 02017 (2016)
DOI: 10.1051/matecconf/20164402017

Improvement of an Eliptic Curve Based Threshold Proxy Signature Scheme

Xiao Yu Miao

Zhejiang University of Media and Communications, Hangzhou 310018, China

Abstract. In 2006, Pomykala et al. proposed an elliptic curve based threshold proxy signature scheme as well as a proxy-protected version. They claimed their scheme had the properties of secrecy, unforgeability, non-repudiation and signer's identification. In this study, we showed inter conspiracy attack on the basic scheme and gave another attack on the proxy-protected version. We pointed out that even if the central authority is engaged, the basic model is not a proxy-protected one. We also proposed an improved scheme that can resist the known attacks to achieve higher security, and gave the security analysis of the improved scheme in detail.

1. INTRODUCTION

The concept of proxy signature was first introduced by Mambo et al. in 1996[1]. Proxy signature schemes have been suggested to be used in many applications. The concept of threshold proxy signature was proposed in 1997[2,3] , from then on it has been widely studied[4-7]. The threshold proxy signature scheme is a variant of the proxy signature scheme that the signing power is delegated to a proxy group. In a (t,n) threshold proxy signature scheme, the proxy signature key is shared among a group of n proxy signers delegated by the original signer. Any t or more proxy signers can opperatively sign a message on behalf of the original proxy signer, but t-1 or fewer proxy signers can not.

In 2006, Pomykala et al. proposed an elliptic curve based threshold proxy signature scheme as well as a proxy-protected version[6]. They claimed their scheme had the properties of secrecy, unforgeability, non-repudiation and signer's identification. They ponited out that the proxy-protected version could assure the proxy-protection property.

In this paper, we give attacks on Pomykala et al.'s scheme in detail and we also point out that even if the central authority is engaged, the basic model is not proxy-protected, and gave an improved scheme that can resist the known attacks.

2. Brief Review of Pomykala et al.'s Scheme

The scheme is based on the elliptic curve cryptosystem whose security is based on the elliptic curve discrete logarithm problem(ECDLP) in the finite Abel group $E(F_p)$, where P is a prime power. Q (on the elliptic curve E) is a point of order divisible by a large prime number.

Let P_0 be the original signer， and a set $P=\{P_1,\cdots,P_n\}$ be the proxy group of n proxy signers, H and H' be two one-way hash functions.

Each proxy signer P_i has a private key $a_i \in F_p$ and the corresponding public key $A_i = a_i Q$ ($i=0,1,\cdots,n$). The original proxy signer P_0 composes a message ω called proxy warrant that contains the valid time of the delegation, the identities of the original signer and the proxy signers, etc.

2.1 Group Secret Key Generation Phase

The original proxy signer P_0 prepares a warrant ω, chooses a random integer $r < ordQ$, computes $R = rQ$.

Then P_0 computes the group secret key $d = a_0 H + r$, which satisfies $dQ = HA_0 + R$, where $H = H(\omega, R)$.

2.2 Group Secret Key Share Phase

The original proxy signer P_0 selects a polynomial $f_0(x) = c_{0,t-1}x^{t-1} + \cdots + c_{0,1}x + d$, where each $c_{0,i}$ is a random integer.

Next the original proxy signer P_0 computes $C_{0,i} = c_{0,i}Q$, i=1,...,t-1 as his obligations, and broadcasts them to the proxy group.

Xiao-Yu Miao: miaoxiaoyu.1987@163.com

The original proxy signer P_0 computes P_i's group secret key share as $y_{i0}=f_0(x_i)$, where x_i denotes P_i's public identity. Then P_0 sends y_{i0} to each P_i via a secure channel.

With the obligations, each proxy signer P_i verifies the validity of y_{i0} by checking whether or not $y_{i0}Q=HA_0+R+\sum_{j=1}^{t-1}C_{0,j}x_i^j$, accepts the group secret key share if and only if the verification equation holds.

2.3 Proxy Signature Generation Phase

Without loss of generality, let $B=\{P_1,\cdots,P_t\}$ be the subset of t proxy signers from the group $P=\{P_1,\cdots,P_n\}$.

(1) Each proxy signer $P_i\in B$ selects a secret polynomial $f_i(x)=c_{i,t-1}x^{t-1}+\cdots+c_{i,1}x+c_{i,0}+a_i$, where $c_{i,k}$ is a random integer $<ordQ$ in F_p, for $k=0,1,\cdots,t-1$, and a_i is the secret key of P_i for i=1,…,t.

(2) Then each proxy signer P_i computes and broadcast $C_{i,k}=c_{i,k}Q$ as his obligations, for $k=0,1,\cdots,t-1$.

(3) Each P_i computes $H'=H'(\omega,R,M,B)$, $y_{ji}=H'f_i(x_j)$, and sends y_{ji} to P_j by a secret channels, for j=1,…,t-1, $i\neq j$.

(4) Each proxy signer P_j verifies the t-1 values from other proxy signers by checking the equtions

$$y_{ji}Q=H'\left(A_i+\sum_{k=0}^{t-1}x_j^kC_{j,k}\right),\ i=1,2,\cdots,t,\ i\neq j.$$

If all of the above equations hold, each proxy signer P_j computes $s_j=\sum_{i=1}^{t}y_{ji}$, for j=1,…,t.

In fact,

$$s_j=\sum_{i=1}^{t}y_{ji}=H'f(x_j)$$
$$=H'\left(x_j^{t-1}\sum_{i=1}^{t}c_{i,t-1}+\cdots+\sum_{i=1}^{t}c_{i,0}+\sum_{i=1}^{t}a_i\right)$$

Then

$$F(x)=f(x)Q$$
$$=x^{t-1}\sum_{i=1}^{t}C_{i,t-1}+\cdots+x\sum_{i=1}^{t}C_{i,1}+\sum_{i=1}^{t}C_{i,0}+\sum_{i=1}^{t}A_i$$

Let $C_k'=\sum_{i=1}^{t}C_{i,k}$, $k=0,1,\cdots,t-1$, $A'=\sum_{i=1}^{t}A_i$.

(5) Each proxy signer P_j computes his partial proxy signature on M as

$$\sigma_j=y_{j0}+\sum_{i=1}^{t}y_{ji}=y_{j0}+s_j,\ \text{j=1,…,t.}$$

Then each proxy signer P_j sends his partial proxy signature σ_j to other proxy signers via secret channels.

The shares can be verified by checking the equations

$$\sigma_jQ=HA_0+R+\sum_{k=1}^{t-1}x_j^kC_{0,k}$$
$$+\sum_{P_j\in B}\left[H'\left(A_j+\sum_{k=0}^{t-1}x_j^kC_{j,k}\right)\right],\ j=1,2,\cdots,t$$

(6) If all of the above equations hold, the threshold proxy signature on M is $(M,C_0',A',\sigma,\omega,B,R)$, where $\sigma=\sum_{j=1}^{t}\sigma_j\lambda_j^B(0)$, $\lambda_j^B(0)=\prod_{k\neq j}^{k=1,\cdots,t}\frac{-x_k}{x_j-x_k}$.

2.4 Verification of the Signature

To verify the threshold proxy signature (M,C_0',A',σ,w,B,R), firstly, the verifier checks the warrant ω. If the validity has expired, the signature is invalid.

Otherwise, the verifier computes $H=H(\omega,R)$ and $H'=H'(\omega,R,M,B)$, checks the verification equation $\sigma Q=HA_0+R+H'(C_0'+A')$. The verifier accepts the signature if and only if the verification equation holds.

3. Crptanalysis of Pomykala et al.'s Scheme

3.1 Inter Conspiracy Attack on Pomykala et al.'s Scheme

Firstly, we ponit out that the Pomykala et al.'s scheme is vulnerable to the inter conspiracy attack as following.

Let $T=\{P_{i_1},\cdots,P_{i_t}\}$ be an arbitrary subset of t proxy signers from $P=\{P_1,\cdots,P_n\}$, and (M,C_0',A',σ,w,B,R) be a valid signature by $B=\{P_1,\cdots,P_t\}$.

Then the proxy signers in T can reconstruct the proxy signature key using Lagrange interpolation formula

$$d=\sum_{j=1}^{t}f_0(x_j)\lambda_j^B(0),\ \lambda_j^B(0)=\prod_{k\neq j}^{k=1,\cdots,t}\frac{-x_k}{x_j-x_k}.$$

Then any user $P_c\in T$ can generate a forged threshold proxy signature of any message M' on behalf of the original signer P_0 as $(M',C_0',A',\sigma',\omega,B,R)$, where

$$\sigma'=d+\frac{H_C'(\sigma-d)}{H'},\ H_C'=H'(\omega,R,M',B),$$

$H'=H'(\omega,R,M,B)$. The forged signature

$(M', C_0', A', \sigma', \omega, M', B, R)$ can pass the certification in the valid delegation period, because

$$\sigma' Q = dQ + \frac{H_c'(\sigma - d)}{H'} Q$$
$$= HA_0 + R + H_c' F(0)$$
$$= H(\omega, R)A_0 + R + H'(\omega, R, M', B)(C_0' + A')$$

3.2 Attack on the Proxy-protected Version

Pomykala et al. claimed that if the central authority is not engaged, the basic model is not a proxy protect one. In the following part we'll show that the Pomykala et al.'s scheme doesn't satisfy the proxy-protected property even if a central authority is engaged.

The original proxy signer P_0 can forge a signature using a previous signature $(M, C_0', A', \sigma, w, B, R)$ and the corresponding group secret key d, on behalf of B as follows.

The original signer P_0 computes a valid warrant ω' of any message M', chooses $r' < ordQ$, computes $R' = r'Q$, $H_1 = H(\omega', R')$. Let $d' = a_0 H_1 + r'$ be the group secret key.

The forged threshold proxy signature is $(M', C_0', A', \sigma', \omega', B, R')$, where

$$\sigma' = d' + \frac{H_2(\sigma - d)}{H'}, \quad H_2 = H'(\omega', R', M', B),$$
$$H' = H'(\omega, R, M, B).$$

Then we show that the forged signature $(M', C_0', A', \sigma', \omega', B, R')$ can pass the certification. Obviously, the warrant ω' can always pass the verification because it is generated validly by the original signer. And by computing $H_1 = H(\omega', R')$ and $H_2 = H'(\omega', R', M', B)$, the forged signature satisfies the verification equations

$$\sigma' Q = d' Q + \frac{H_2(\sigma - d)}{H'} Q$$
$$= H_1 A_0 + R' + H_2(C_0' + A')$$

4. The improved threshold proxy signature scheme

The group secret key generation phase and group secret key share key share phase are the same as those in Pomykala et al.'s Scheme.

The proxy signature generation phase is as following.

Let C be an appointed clerk, who is one of the proxy signers in P, and $B = \{P_1, \cdots, P_t\}$ be the subset of proxy signers from $P = \{P_1, \cdots, P_n\}$, who actually make the threshold proxy signature on behalf of P_0.

(1) The t proxy signers of B cooperate to reconstruct the proxy signature key using the Lagrange Interpolation Formula:

$$d = \sum_{j=1}^{t} f_0(x_j)\lambda_j^B(0), \quad \lambda_j^B(0) = \prod_{k \neq j}^{k=1,\cdots,t} \frac{-x_k}{x_j - x_k}.$$

(2) Each proxy signer $P_i \in B$ chooses a random integer $k_i < ordQ$ as his secret information. Then P_i computes and broadcast $K_i = k_i Q$, let $K = \sum_{i=1}^{t} K_i$.

P_i computes $\delta_i = d + a_i + k_i H(K_i, M)$, let δ_i be his partial secret key.

(3) Each proxy signer $P_i \in B$ chooses a polynomial

$$f_i(x) = c_{i,t-1}x^{t-1} + \cdots + c_{i,1}x + c_{i,0} + \delta_i,$$

where $c_{i,k} < ordQ$, $k = 0, 1, \cdots, t-1$, is a random integer. Computes and broadcasts $C_{i,k} = c_{i,k}Q$ for $k = 0, 1, \cdots, t-1$.

P_i computes $H' = H'(\omega, K, M, B)$ and $y_{ji} = H' f_i(x_j)$, sents y_{ji} to P_j via secret channels, where j=1,...,t-1, $i \neq j$.

(4) Each P_j verifies t-1 values by checking the equations

$$y_{ji} Q = H'\left(\sum_{k=0}^{t-1} x_j^k C_{i,k} + HA_0 + R + A_i + K_i H(K_i, M)\right)$$

If all of the equations hold, P_j computes $s_j = \sum_{i=1}^{t} y_{ji} = H' f(x_j)$, and his partial signature $\sigma_j = k_j + s_j \lambda_j^B(0)$, where

$$f(x) = x^{t-1}\sum_{i=1}^{t} c_{i,t-1} + \cdots + \sum_{i=1}^{t} c_{i,0} + \sum_{i=1}^{t} \delta_i.$$

Then P_j sends δ_j to the clerk C.

(5) The clerk verifies these partial signatures by checking the equations

$$\sigma_j Q = K_j + H'[x_j^{t-1} C_{t-1}' + \ldots + x_j C_1' + t(HA_0 + R)$$
$$+ A' + \sum_{i=1}^{t} K_i H(K_i, M)]\lambda_j^B(0)$$

where $C_k' = \sum_{i=1}^{t} C_{i,k}$, $A' = \sum_{i=1}^{t} A_i$

(6) If all equations hold, the clerk computes $\sigma = \sum_{j=1}^{t} \sigma_j$.

Then the threshold proxy signature on M is $(M, C_0', A', \sigma, \omega, B, \{K_i\}_B, R)$.

To verify the signature, firstly, the verifier checks the warrant ω, if the validity has expired, the signature is invalid.Otherwise, accept the signature if and only if

$$\sigma Q = K + H'[C_0' + A' + t(HA_0 + R) + \sum_{i=1}^{t} K_i H(K_i, M)]$$

5. Security analysis of the improved scheme

(1) The secrecy of the improved scheme refers to the elliptic curve discrete logarithm problem in the finite Abel group $E(F_p)$. If an attacker attempts to obtain the secret information of the signers, he must solve the elliptic curve discrete logarithm problem, which is more difficult than solving the discrete logarithm problem. Hence all the secret information is secure. And even if t out of n proxy signers conspire to obtain the group secret key d using the Lagrange Interpolation Formula, they cannot get the secret value k from the public value K, then cannot obtain the secret key a_0 of the original signer. Similarly, no one can get the secret k_i from K_i.

(2) Our proposal assures the proxy-protected. In the improved scheme, the original signer knows the group secret key d and the previous valid signature σ, but he cannot obtain the value $\sum_{i=1}^{t} k_i$ or $f(0)$ from K and σ, because the value $\sum_{i=1}^{t} k_i$ and $H'[\sum_{i=1}^{t} c_{i,0} + td + \sum_{i=1}^{t} a_i + \sum_{i=1}^{t} k_i H(K_i, M)]$ are undistinguishable to P_0. So he cannot forge a signature which can pass the verification on behalf of the proxy group B.

(3) The improved scheme is resistant against the inter conspiracy attack mentioned in section 3.

Now consider a proxy group T wants to forge a signature on another message M' on behalf of B. They select a previous signature σ, and obtain the group secret key d. But they cannot distinguish between $\sum_{j=1}^{t} k_j$ and $f(0)$, so they cannot change the message M for M' without being detected as presented in section 3. Consequently the inter conspiracy attack is also infeasible.

(4) The improved scheme has the properties of unforgeability and non-repudiation. From the above analysis we can see that the malicious users cannot forge a valid signature. Because only the original signer can generate the group secret and delegate the shares to the proxy signers, so he cannot deny having made it. Similarly, the proxy signers cannot deny their work either. Without the secret information of the proxy signers, the clerk cannot change the proxy signer's shares or generates a partial proxy signature on behalf of P_i.

Moreover, the valid time of the proxy delegation contained in the warrant ω stipulates the life time of the proxy shares. And from a valid signature $(M, C_0', A', \sigma, \omega, B, R_B, R)$ any users may confirm the actual proxy signers who generated the proxy signature.

6. Conclusion

In this paper, we showed two attacks on the Pomykala et al.'s scheme in detail, and we also showd that the Pomykala et al.'s scheme doesn't satisfy the proxy-protected property even if a central authority is engaged. We also proposed a new scheme that can resist the known attacks to achieve higher security.

Acknowledgement

This research was the concluding achievement of the research project of Zhejiang University of Media and Communications (ZC15XJ030), and was financially supported of research project of the State Press and Publication Administration of radio and television 《Research on key technology of digital television security monitoring and alarming system based on digital watermarking》(NO.2014-42).

References

1. M. Mambo, K. Usuda and E. Okamoto: IEICE Transactions on Fundamentals, E79-A(9), 1996, 1338-1353.
2. S. Kim, S. Park, and D. Won: Proc.Information and Communications Security-ICIS'97, LNCS1334, Spring-Verlag, Berlin, 1997, 223-232.
3. K. Zhang: Proc.Information Security Workshop-ISW'97, LNCS1396, Spring-Verlag, Berlin, 1997,191-197.
4. Q. Xie: Applied Mathematics and Computeation, Vol.168(2),2005,776-782.
5. Z. H. Shao: Fundamenta Informaticae, Vol.104(4), 2010,385-392.
6. J. Pomykala, S. Barabasz: Fundamenta Informaticae, Vol.69(4),2006,411-425.
7. R. B. Lu, D. K. He, C. J. Wang: Cryptanalysis of an identity-based threshold proxy signature scheme with known signers, Journal of Electronics &Information Technology, Vol.30(1), 2008, 100-103.

MATEC Web of Conferences 44, 02018 (2016)
DOI: 10.1051/matecconf/20164402018

AutoGPA-Based 3D-QSAR Modeling and Molecular Docking Study on Factor Xa Inhibitors as Anticoagulant Agents

Fang Yuan Guo[1], Qing Yin Yan[1], Keni Lin[1], Wei Yong Hong[2], Gen Sheng Yang[1]

[1] Country College of Pharmaceutical Sciences, Zhejiang University of Technology, 310014 Hangzhou, China

[2] Taizhou Municipal Hospital of Zhejiang Province, 318000 Taizhou, China

Abstract. The three-dimensional-quantitative structure activity relationship (3D-QSAR) studies were performed on a series of direct factor Xa (FXa) inhibitors using AutoGPA-based modeling method in this paper. A training set of 38 molecules and a test set containing 10 molecules were used to build the 3D-QSAR model and validate the derived model, respectively. The developed model with correlation coefficients (r^2) of 0.8564 and cross-validated correlation coefficients (q^2) of 0.6721 were validated by an external test set of 10 molecules with predicted correlation coefficient (r_{pred}^2) of 0.6077. Docking study of FXa inhibitors and FXa active site was performed to check the induced pharmacophore query and comparative molecular field analysis (CoMFA) contour maps using MOE2012.10. It was proved to be coincidence with the interaction information between ligand and FXa active site and was rendered to provide a useful tool to improve FXa inhibitors.

1 Introduction

Thrombosis can occur in the arterial and the venous or arise from the heart and lead to most cardiovascular events. The pathological mechanisms and risk factors that may lead to arterial thrombosis and venous thrombosis ware reported and approaches for antithrombotic therapy were described.[1] Vitamin K antagonists (VKAs) and heparin are most widely used anticoagulants to date. VKAs are the only available orally active anticoagulants for long-term use which function by reducing the synthesis of the vitamin K-dependent coagulation factors while heparin is used for surgery because the ability to bind to the protein antithrombin and increase the capacity of it to inhibit factor Xa and thrombin.[2] However, both of them shared same disadvantages such as narrow therapeutic window, slow onset of action, uncontrollable therapeutic level and food and drug interaction.[3, 4] Therefore drugs that can be given in fixed doses without coagulation monitoring are a mainstay of cardiovascular therapy.[5] As alternatives to VKAs, direct thrombin inhibitors (DTI) and direct factor Xa inhibitors ware proved to be effective at reducing arterial and venous thrombosis in patients with cardiovascular disease because it has become evident that inhibition of factor IIa (FIIa, or thrombin) and factor Xa (FXa) is expected to reduce or prevent clotting.[6] Thrombin is a serine protease, which converts fibrinogen to fibrin and activates factor V, factor VIII and factor IX.[7] FXa belongs to a family of trypsin-like serine proteases, and plays a central role in the production of thrombin and the activation cascade of the blood coagulation system, linking the extrinsic and intrinsic activation pathways.[8] Since the pivotal position of FXa in the coagulation cascade, direct FXa inhibitors are supposed to be efficacious and safe compared with thrombin inhibitors.[9] Hence, the FXa inhibitors gradually become the largest family of new anticoagulants for long-term use. FXa inhibitors has become direct focus by most pharmaceutical companies resulting in the exploration of a number of small molecules, orally active FXa inhibitors, such as rivaroxaban and apixaban.[10, 11].

Although FXa inhibitors have been synthesized up in different structures to the present.[12-15] it is time consuming to synthesis and assay every compound to find some initial hits. In the last decade, Computer-aided drug design (CADD) method including dock and pharmacophore search has been applied on search and design new FXa inhibitors. Recently, 3D-QSAR has been applied on the FXa inhibitors discovery in order to reveal the binding information between the 3D structure of the molecules and biological activity values. Currently, comparative molecular field analysis (CoMFA)[16] and comparative molecular similarity indices analysis (CoMSIA)[17] are the most successful and widely used 3D-QSAR techniques in ligand-based drug design (LBDD). Steric and electrostatic requirements of a biologically active molecule are revealed in both CoMFA and CoMSIA, Additionally, CoMSIA also gives hydrogen bonding and hydrophobic fields. Besides, 3D pharmacophore query[18] was reported as an alternative modeling method using compounds containing different molecular scaffolds, and compounds with different

[a] Corresponding author: author@e-mail.org

Article available at http://www.matec-conferences.org or http://dx.doi.org/10.1051/matecconf/20164402018

structures and common chemical features can be found by ligand pharmacophore map while CoMFA and CoMSIA methods were restricted to use compounds based on common molecular scafflods. Several models[19, 20] derived by CoMFA and pharmacophore query method were reported to understand the relationship between structures and FXa protein, but information was still in urgent need.

2 Materials and methods

A dataset of 48 structures reported by Chuen Chan, Nigel S. Watson, Robert J. Young, Savvas Kleanthous et al.[21-24] The Ki values were converted to pKi(-lgKi). The Ki values which were used to build 3D-QSAR model cover wide range from 0.3nm to 285nm.

In this paper, an AutoGPA-based 3D-QSAR model was developed, which combined pharmacophore, QSAR equation (electrostatic coefficient and steric coefficient) and allowable space, using known FXa inhibitors in MOE 2012.10. The AutoGPA module in MOE2012.10 was firstly reported in 2012 and proved to be more accurate and predictive than CoMFA. The information revealed by AutoGPA was believed to be more comprehensive than that by CoMFA method.[25] Since the biological activity of compounds synthesized by chemists was measured by different methods, it was advisable to build our 3D-QSAR model with biological data assayed by same method. The inhibitor activities of these compounds were measured by using Rhodamine 110, bis-(CBZ-glycylglycyl)-L-arginine amide as the fluorogenic substrate. The selected compounds were divided into training set (38 molecules) and test set (10 molecules), the former is to generate 3D-QSAR model and the latter to valid the derived model. Structures and corresponding pKi of training set and test set are shown in Table 1 and Table 2.

Table 1 Structures and pKi of Compounds of Training Set and Predicted pKi of the Model

No.	Structure	pKi(nM)	Predicted pKi(nM)
1	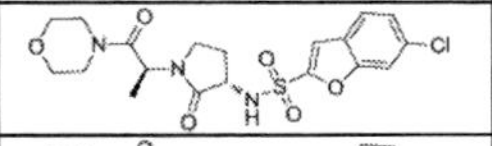	-2.454845	-2.2489986
2	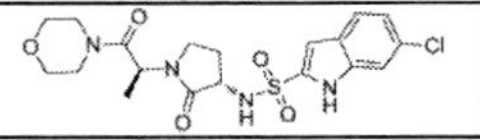	-2.230449	-2.5659335
3	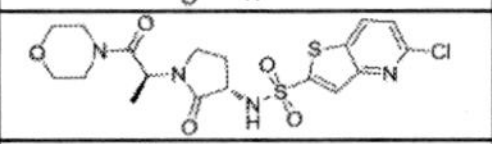	-2.2121875	-1.7590916
4	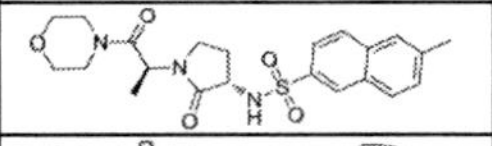	-2.0374265	-0.85005558
5	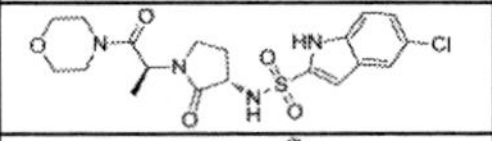	-1.9542425	-1.5657493
6	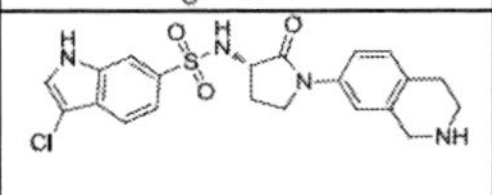	-1.1760913	-0.32048795
7	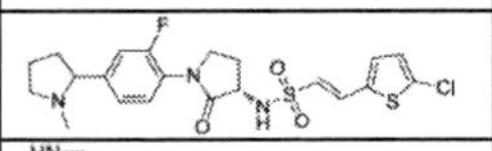	-1.1760913	-0.2353029
8	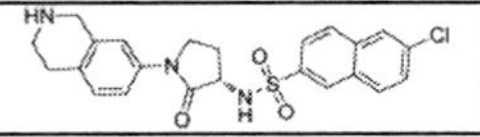	-1	-1.0271591
9	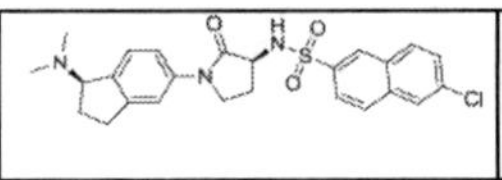	-0.95424253	-0.49813575
10	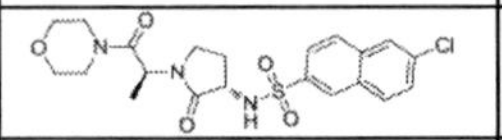	-0.77815127	-1.0598429
11	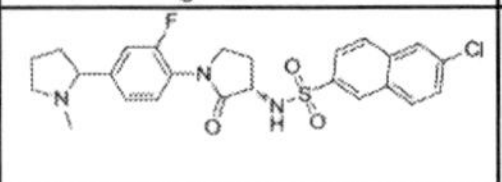	-0.77815127	-0.25860012
12	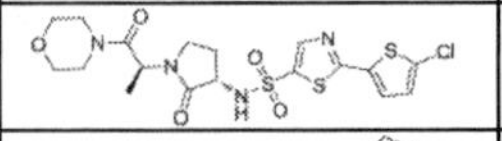	-0.69897002	-0.89788717
13	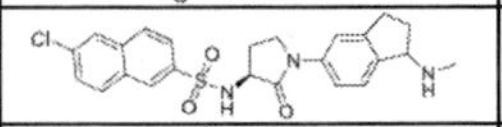	-0.69897002	-0.55868977
14	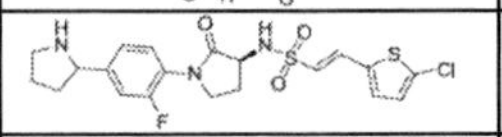	-0.69897002	-0.59239662
15	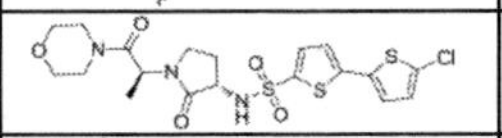	-0.60206002	-0.57396263
16	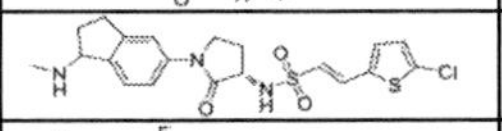	-0.60206002	-0.21306448
17	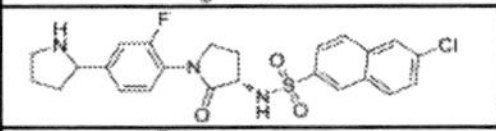	-0.60206002	-0.71907371
18	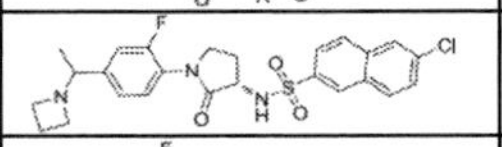	-0.60206002	-0.39323789
19	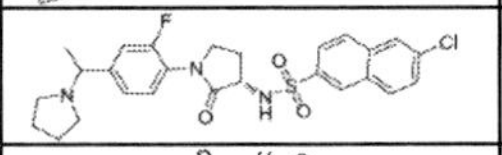	-0.60206002	-0.378041
20	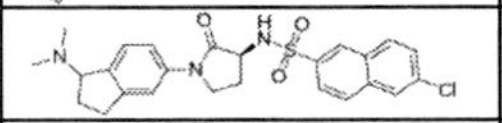	-0.47712126	-0.60638762
21	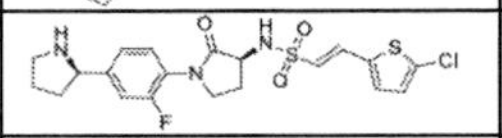	-0.47712126	-0.74732602
22	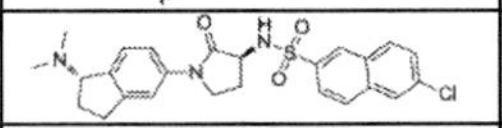	-0.30103001	-0.67790717
23	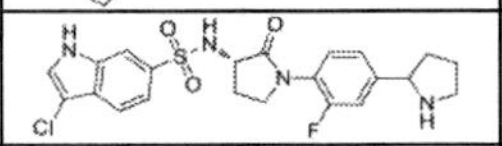	-0.30103001	-0.81083852
24	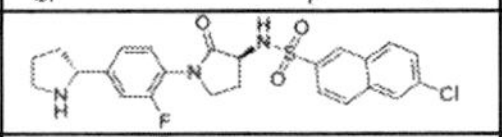	-0.30103001	-0.37835535
25	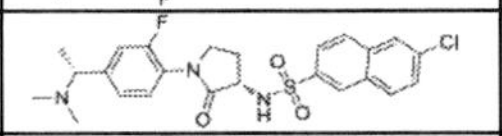	-0.30103001	-0.33332729
26	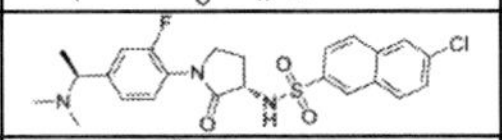	-0.30103001	-0.75211126
27	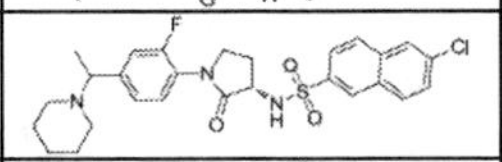	-0.30103001	-0.62196755
28	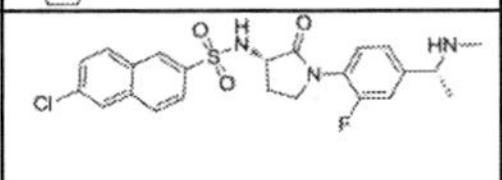	-0.30103001	-0.35713589
29	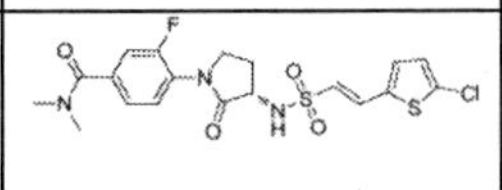	-0.17609125	-0.5085603
30	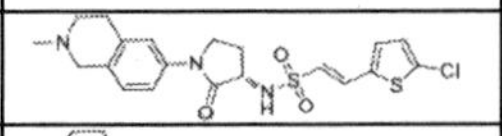	0	-0.19374266
31	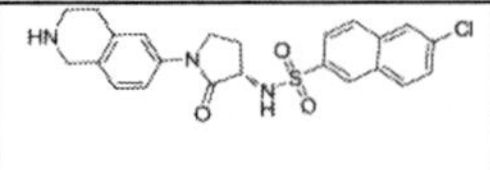	0	-0.12959768
32	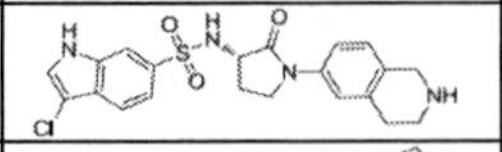	0	-0.11511542
33	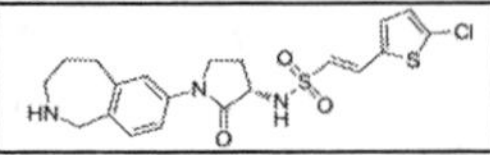	0	-0.26223373

34	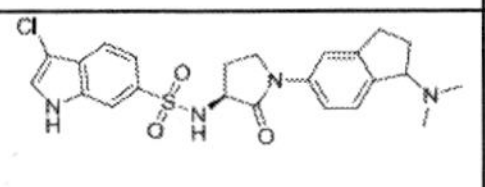	0	0.19423778
35	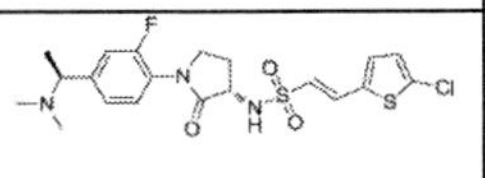	0	-0.20721151
36	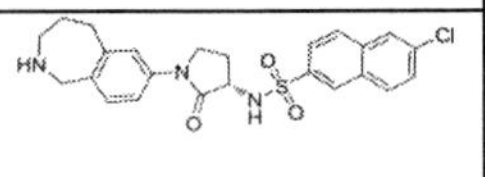	0.096910007	-0.19934152
37	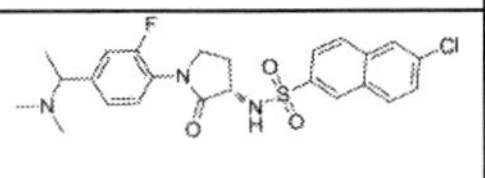	0.096910007	-0.39182049
38	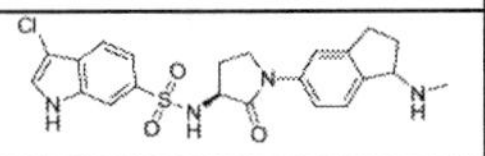	0.52287871	-0.0036566246

Table 2 Structures and pKi of Compounds of Test Set and the Predicted pKi of the Model

No.	Structure	pKi(nM)	Predicted pKi(nM)
1	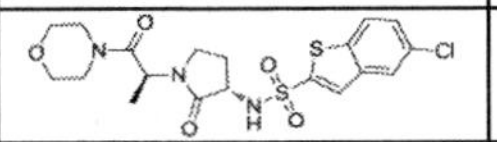	-1.6720978	-2.7134387
2	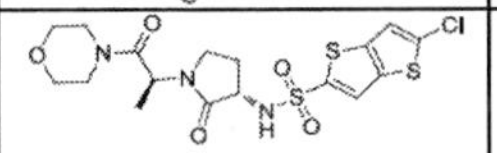	-2.217484	-1.7056421
3	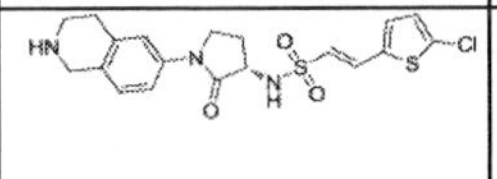	0.22184873	-0.43879896
4	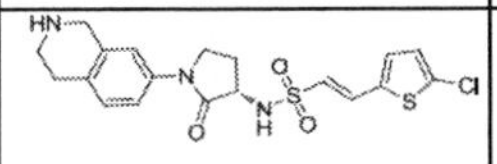	-0.90309	-0.32596833
5	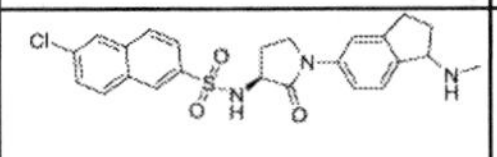	-0.69897002	-0.58388305
6	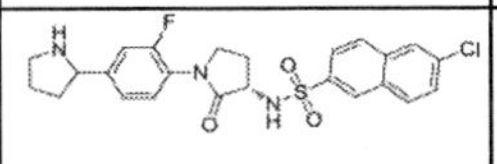	-0.30103001	-0.54039317
7	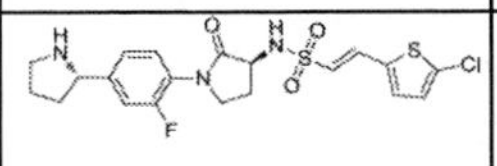	-0.77815127	-0.51108813
8	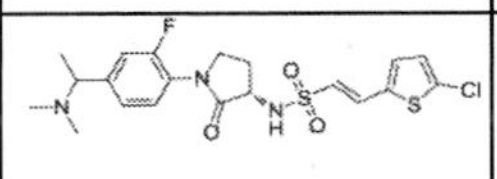	0.096910007	-0.24139532
9	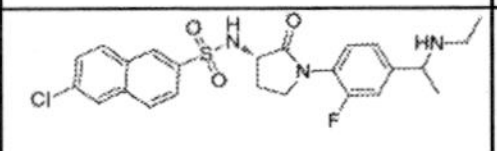	-0.47712126	-0.49380451
10	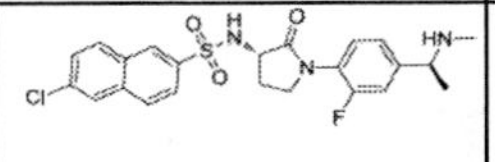	-0.60206002	-0.77911842

In order to improve the quality of the model, it was necessary to consider that the training set should consist of highly active, moderately active and less active and the activities of test set should also in a wild range. The process of the model is shown in Figure 1.

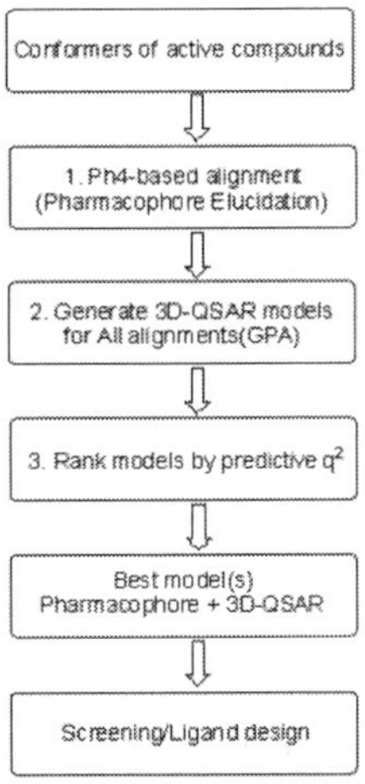

Figure 1. The process of AutoGPA model.

All of our studies including energy minimization, conformational searching and 3D-QSAR modeling were performed by MOE 2012.10 on windows 7 operating system. All structures of compounds were built and energy minimized under Merck molecular force field 94x (MMFF94x). Conformational searching for each compound was generated by conformation import method, which calculates low-energy conformations of molecules by decomposing each ligand into constituent overlapping fragment, performing stochastic conformational search on each fragment, and then assembling the fragments into unique conformers. Finally, a total of 5909 and 2454 conformations for training set and test set were generated respectively, and stored in respective database. The each generated conformation of training set was assigned to the typical pharmacophoric features such as hydrogen bond acceptor, hydrogen bond donor, positively and negatively ionized areas and aromatic center. Common pharmacophore queries were extracted from training set, in which some or most compounds were satisfied the queries, and most of conformers of compounds satisfied the four-point or five-point queries, resulting in a total of 33 pharmacophore queries, then all of these compounds were aligned to the generated pharmacophore queries above and the database contained the pharmacophore query information was stored for further AutoGPA-based 3D-QSAR model construction. Moreover, AutoGPA module improved 3D-QSAR model with allowance space around the aligned compounds makes it convenient to screen large molecule library. The AutoGPA-based 3D-QSAR model employed the algorithm of the CoMFA, as a consequence, all aligned molecules were placed in 3D grid box with a 2.0Å separation, following the calculation of electrostatic and steric interaction energies between the molecule and a series of probe atom (an sp3 carbon atom with charge +1.0) at each grip point which was to evaluated molecular fields. After all the grid potential fields were calculated, the partial-least-squares (PLS) analysis was introduced to study the relationship between grid potential fields and biological values to develop AutoGPA-based 3D-QSAR model. The optimal number of compounds up to ten is identified by leave-one-out

(LOO) cross-validation and ranked by q2. The calculation method of q2 is shown below:

$$q^2 = 1\text{-MSE/YVAR} \qquad (1)$$

where: MSE means mean squared error, YVAR is the variance of experimental data.

The best q^2 value was saved as an AutoGPA model. In order to check the robustness, accuracy, reliability and predictability of the developed model, internal validation and external validation were employed. The LOO cross-validation is used as internal validation while the prediction of test set as external validation. The validation was judged by r^2 and was calculated by a following equation:

$$r^2 = (\text{SD-PRESS})/\text{SD} \qquad (2)$$

where: SD is the sum of squared deviations of biological activity from their mean, and predictive sum of squares (PRESS) is the sum of the squared differences between the actual and predicted biological activity.

The MOE's dock application workflow begins with a prepared receptor and ligand loaded in MOE. The algorithm is divided into five stages: 1) conformational analysis; 2) placement: Triangle matcher as default; 3) rescoring (1): London dG scoring method; 4) refinement: molecular mechanics forcefield method; 5) rescoring (2): GBVI/WSA dG scoring method.

3 Results

Ten different AutoGPA models were generated and the results were summarized in the Table 3. It was ranked by q^2 and q^2>0.5 suggested that this model is reasonable and should have a good predictive ability. Thus model 1 was considered as the best model as it has highest q^2 (0.6721) value. Moreover, the correlation coefficient r^2 between observed and predicted activity was recommended to be another criteria for a given QSAR model. In this model, the r^2 of training set calculated by non cross-validation and LOO cross-validation was 0.8564 and 0.6726 respectively. External validation of test set was employed to test the predictability of this model, and the r^2 was 0.6077 which proved that the derived QSAR model is acceptable.

Table 3 Ten AutoGPA models based on the training set.

Model	PH4	Overlap	Grids	MSE	r^2	q^2
1	HHHA	31.02	38	0.0710	0.8564	0.6721
2	RHHA	30.98	70	0.1250	0.7475	0.5874
3	HDAA	30.97	34	0.1261	0.7451	0.5863
4	HHHAA	31.10	50	0.1165	0.7645	0.5792
5	HHHA	31.06	65	0.0864	0.8254	0.5679
6	RHAA	31.14	44	0.0957	0.8065	0.5575
7	RHHA	30.91	55	0.1268	0.7438	0.5357
8	RHHA	31.01	52	0.1264	0.7446	0.5229
9	HDAA	30.95	65	0.1070	0.7838	0.5164
10	RHAA	30.87	58	0.0772	0.8439	0.5002

PH4: pharmacophore feature labels; H: hydrophobic, A: projected acceptor, R: aromatic or π-ring center.
Overlap: atomic overlapping score in pharmacophore-based alignment.
Grids: number of grid point for QSAR model.
MSE: mean squared error.
r^2: correlation coefficient.
q^2: predictive coefficient in leave-one-out cross-validation.

Result of the most satisfying pharmacophore query and corresponding allowance space is shown in Figure 2. Four pharmacophores have been generated with three hydrophobiccentroids (green) and one projected acceptor (blue). The projected acceptor was located along implicit hydrogen direction and were used to annotate the location of possible hydrogen bond. Namely, an H-bond donor might located here and could form an H-bond with the ligand in a special direction. The three hydrophobic centroids indicated that the corresponding portions of ligand should decorated with hydrophobic ring or atom. The allowance space was introduced as a portion of 3D-QSAR model for the first time and helped to reject dropped conformers and evaluate the activity value in ligand screen procedure cooperating with pharmacophore query. An allowable space was suggested to be coincidence with sharp of active pocket and actually the allowance space derived by model was coincidence with the sharp of active pocket described in references. However, it was noted that no pharmacophore was generated in the p4 motif of the ligands.

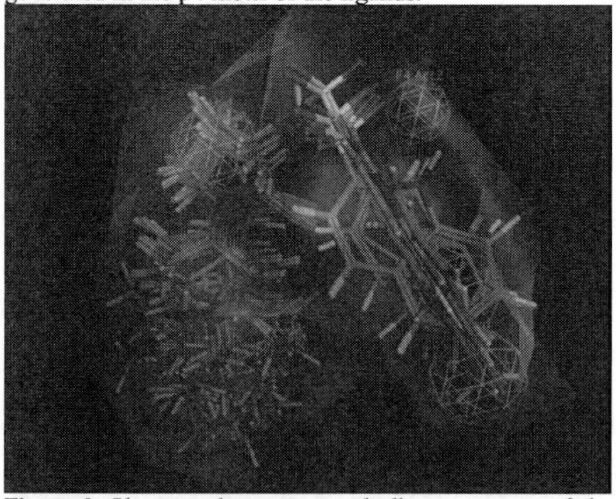

Figure 2. Pharmacophore query and allowance space of the developed model. Green ball means hydrophobic centroid (Hyd) indicating that a hydrophobic ring or atom may exist. Projected acceptor (Acc2) is represented by blue ball and stands for an acceptor forming an H-bond with ligand.

Figure 3a shows the electrostatic contour map in the developed model, as indicated by red and blue contours

representing electron donating and electron withdrawing groups would be favorable respectively. A large region of red contours around the p4 motif of the ligand indicated that the presence of an electronegative substituent such as oxygen is very important for decreasing activity (pKi) while an electropositive substituent such as nitrogen increases activity. For example, the activity value of compound 1 with morpholino amide orienting to the red region is -0.7782 while compound 33 with benzylic amine having a nitrogen atom pointed to the red region shows an enhanced activity of -0.3010.

In the steric contour map as shown in Figure 3b, green contours showed well tolerance to bulky groups, whereas yellow contours implied regions of unfavorable steric effects. The two larger green contours around p1 motif of the ligand indicated that steric features have a positive effect on activity. For example, compound 13 with 6-indoly converted to compound 12 with 6-chloronaphthyl, meanwhile, the activity value increased

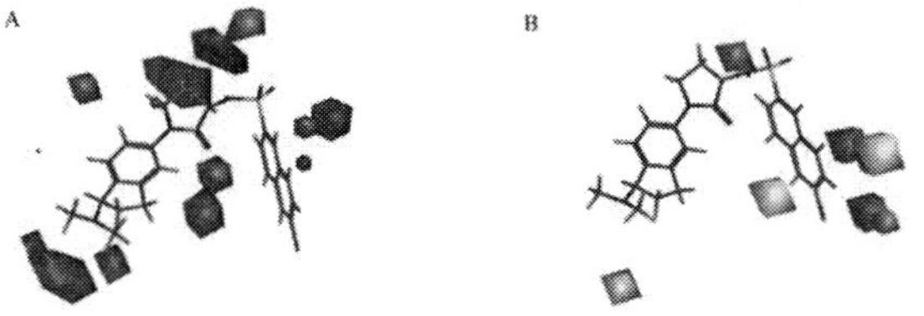

Figure 3. Electrostatic and steric contours map from AutoGPA-based model, compound 12 is shown as reference (A) Electrostatic contour map, red contour suggests electropositive charge and red contour electronegative charge. (B) Steric contour map, green represents bulky groups are favorable to increase activity and yellow indicates decrease activity.

4 Discussion

Docking study was carried out to better understand the developed model. 2y7x.pdb was downloaded via www.rcsb.org and loaded into MOE2012.10. Structure preparation was performed to correct errors in the PDB file, followed by protonate 3D to assign ionization states and position hydrogens in a macromolecular structure. Water molecules have been retained because of its possibility of binding the ligand and imparting the binding affinity. The ligand of 2y7x.pdb was separated, stored in database file and went through conformation import procedure to generate conformations. Redocking was performed with default options to verify whether the position of ligand in pdb file is right and the docked conformation in the active pocket of FXa protein and ligand interactions were shown in Figure 4a and Figure 4b respectively.

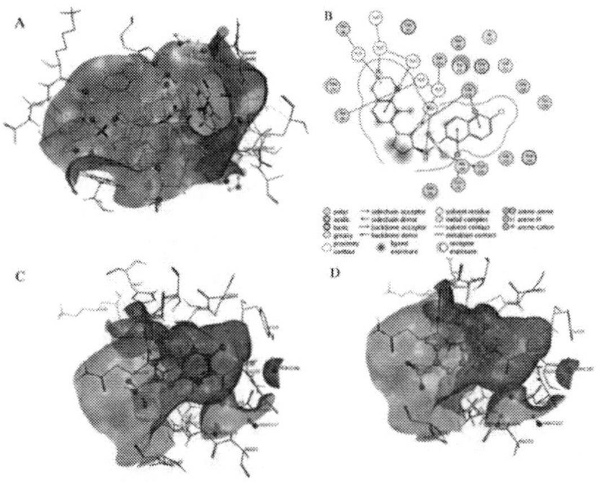

Figure 4. Docking study of active pocket in 2y7x.pdb. (A) Redocked conformation of ligand separated from 2y7x.pdb showing a well fitness for active pocket, colored by blue. (B) Ligand interactions graph drawn with MOE2012.10. (C) P1 motif of compound 24 colored by purple from side aspect. Chlorine was pointed to the center of the Tyr228 aromatic ring. (D) P1 motif of compound 23 colored by blue from side aspect cannot well fitted into S1 pocket with 6-indoly.

The active site of FXa protein is comprised of S1 pocket and S4 pocket. S1 pocket is deep, narrow and mainly formed by Tyr228 on the bottom, Asp189 and Gly226 on the side. S4 pocket is aromatic box which lined by aromatic side chains of Tyr99, Phe174 and Trp215. Present research has proved that when a p4 motif embodies a cation atom, commonly nitrogen atom under protonation state, can form an arene-cation interaction to improve binding affinity,[26, 27] thus the p4 motif interacted with any aromatic side chain of Tyr99, Phe174 and Trp215 can improve binding affinity resulted in the increase of Ki value. Therefore, it made the p4 motif to be various, which explained the reason why there is no pharmacophore generated in the p4 motif. Furthermore, two water molecules existed in S4 pocket were bind to the nitrogen atom with charge +1 of p4 motif to form two strong H-bonds, where corresponded to the large region of red contours in the electrostatic contour map of the model. As we all see, three blue sections were placed around the 3-aminopyrrolidin-2-one means ligand exposure, so a hydrophobic scaffold was needed to enhance the binding affinity. Therefore, a hydrophobic center was emerged in the pharmacophore query. Moreover, an H-bond between oxygen of the ligand and Cys220 was observed which further corroborated the evidence that a projected acceptor in active site exists and interacts with ligand through an H-bond indicated by pharmacophore query. In addition, steric contours of the model was also proved referring to the docked conformations of compound 24 and 23 by the above docking method in Figure 4c and 4d. Chlorine was well pointed towards the center of the Tyr228 aromatic ring in compound 24 owing to the replacement of 6-indoly(compound 23) by 6-chloronaphthyl, which is the so-called chloro binding mode.[28]

5 Conclusion

In conclusion, despite that different types of 3D-QSAR models of FXa inhibitors have been reported by using SYBYL and Discovery Studio, a new type of 3D-QSAR model has developed by using AutoGPA module in MOE2012.10, which was based on CoMFA method and combined pharmacophore and allowance space in our study. The model showed good prediction and reliability with q2 (0.6721) and r2 (0.8564). In addition, docking study was carried out to check the reliability of the electrostatic and steric contour map. The results of docking and the developed 3D-QSAR model were complementarity. Thus this model provided a reliable tool for screening lead compound and guiding the design of novel and potent FXa inhibitors.

References

1. N. Mackman, Nature. **451**, 914 (2008).
2. M.L. van Montfoort,J.C.M. Meijers, Thromb Haemostasis. **110**, 223 (2013).
3. A. Mochizuki, Y. Nakamoto, H. Naito, K. Uoto, T. Ohta, Bioorg Med Chem Lett. **18**, 782 (2008).
4. J.W. Eikelboom,J.I. Weitz, Circulation. **121**, 1523 (2010).
5. R. De Caterina, S. Husted, L. Wallentin, F. Andreotti, H. Arnesen, F. Bachmann, C. Baigent, K. Huber, J. Jespersen, S.D. Kristensen, G.Y.H. Lip, J. Morais, L.H. Rasmussen, A. Siegbahn, F.W.A. Verheugt, J.I. Weitz, J Am Coll Cardiol. **59**, 1413 (2012).
6. T. Kadokura, M. Kashiwa, D. Groenendaal, M. Heeringa, R. Mol, F. Verheggen, A. Garcia-Hernandez, H. Onkels, Biopharm Drug Dispos. **34**, 431 (2013).
7. M. Popovic, K. Smiljanic, B. Dobutovic, T. Syrovets, T. Simmet, E.R. Isenovic, Mol Cell Biochem. **359**, 301 (2012).
8. S. Butenas,K.G. Mann, Biochemistry-Moscow+. **67**, 3 (2002).
9. A. Bukowska, I. Zacharias, S. Weinert, K. Skopp, C. Hartmann, C. Huth, A. Goette, Eur J Pharmacol. **718**, 114 (2013).
10. D.J.P. Pinto, M.J. Orwat, S. Koch, K.A. Rossi, R.S. Alexander, A. Smallwood, P.C. Wong, A.R. Rendina, J.M. Luettgen, R.M. Knabb, K. He, B.M. Xin, R.R. Wexler, P.Y.S. Lam, J Med Chem. **50**, 5339 (2007).
11. E. Perzborn, S. Roehrig, A. Straub, D. Kubitza, F. Misselwitz, Nat Rev Drug Discov. **10**, 61 (2011).
12. T. Fujimoto, Y. Imaeda, N. Konishi, K. Hiroe, M. Kawamura, G.P. Textor, K. Aertgeerts, K. Kubo, J Med Chem. **53**, 3517 (2010).
13. A. Mochizuki, T. Nagata, H. Kanno, M. Suzuki, T. Ohta, Bioorgan Med Chem. **19**, 1623 (2011).
14. Y. Shi, S.P. O'Connor, D. Sitkoff, J. Zhang, M.X. Shi, S.N. Bisaha, Y. Wang, C. Li, Z.M. Ruan, R.M. Lawrence, H.E. Klei, K. Kish, E.C.K. Liu, S.M. Seiler, L. Schweizer, T.E. Steinbacher, W.A. Schumacher, J.A. Robl, J.E. Macor, K.S. Atwal, P.D. Stein, Bioorg Med Chem Lett. **21**, 7516 (2011).
15. G. Lopopolo, F. Fiorella, M. de Candia, O. Nicolotti, S. Martel, P.A. Carrupt, C. Altomare, Eur J Pharm Sci. **42**, 180 (2011).
16. R.D. Cramer, D.E. Patterson, J.D. Bunce, Journal of the American Chemical Society. **110**, 5959 (1988).
17. G. Klebe, Perspect Drug Discov. **12**, 87 (1998).
18. Y.L. Wang, C.Y. Lin, K.C. Shih, J.W. Huang, C.Y. Tang, Bioorg Med Chem Lett. **23**, 6286 (2013).
19. M. Chandrasekaran, S. Sakkiah, K.W. Lee, Med Chem Res. **21**, 4083 (2012).
20. J.B. Ghasemi,S. Hooshmand, Mol Simulat. **39**, 453 (2013).
21. C. Chan, A.D. Borthwick, D. Brown, C.L. Burns-Kurtis, M. Campbell, L. Chaudry, C.W. Chung, M.A. Convery, J.N. Hamblin, L. Johnstone, H.A. Kelly, S. Kleanthous, A. Patikis, C. Patel, A.J. Pateman, S. Senger, G.P. Shah, J.R. Toomey, N.S. Watson, H.E. Weston, C. Whitworth, R.J. Young, P. Zhou, J Med Chem. **50**, 1546 (2007).
22. N.S. Watson, C. Adams, D. Belton, D. Brown, C.L. Burns-Kurtis, L. Chaudry, C.E. Chan, M.A. Convery, D.E. Davies, A.M. Exall, J.D. Harling, S. Irvine, W.R. Irving, S. Kleanthous, I.M. McLay, A.J. Pateman, A.N. Patikis, T.J. Roethke, S. Senger, G.J. Stelman, J.R. Toomey, R.I. West, C. Whittaker, P. Zhou, R.J. Young, Bioorg Med Chem Lett. **21**, 1588 (2011).
23. R.J. Young, C. Adams, M. Blows, D. Brown, C.L. Burns-Kurtis, C.E. Chan, L. Chaudry, M.A. Convery, D.E. Davies, A.M. Exall, G. Foster, J.D. Harling, E. Hortense, S. Irvine, W.R. Irving, S. Jackson, S. Kleanthous, A.J. Pateman, A.N. Patikis, T.J. Roethka, S. Senger, G.J. Stelman, J.R. Toomey, R.I. West, C. Whittaker, P. Zhou, N.S. Watson, Bioorg Med Chem Lett. **21**, 1582 (2011).
24. S. Kleanthous, A.D. Borthwick, D. Brown, C.L. Burns-Kurtis, M. Campbell, L. Chaudry, C. Chan, M.O. Clarte, M.A. Convery, J.D. Harling, E. Hortense, W.R. Irving, S. Irvine, A.J. Pateman, A.N. Patikis, I.L. Pinto, D.R. Pollard, T.J. Roethka, S. Senger, G.P. Shah, G.J. Stelman, J.R. Toomey, N.S. Watson, R.I. West, C. Whittaker, P. Zhou, R.J. Young, Bioorg Med Chem Lett. **20**, 618 (2010).
25. S. Kumar,M. Tiwari, J Chemometr. **27**, 143 (2013).
26. V. Pandya, M. Jain, G. Chakrabarti, H. Soni, B. Parmar, B. Chaugule, J. Patel, T. Jarag, J. Joshi, N. Joshi, A. Rath, V. Unadkat, B. Sharma, H. Ajani, J. Kumar, K.V.V.M. Sairam, H. Patel, P. Patel, Eur J Med Chem. **58**, 136 (2012).
27. J.R. Pruitt, D.J.P. Pinto, R.A. Galemmo, R.S. Alexander, K.A. Rossi, B.L. Wells, S. Drummond, L.L. Bostrom, D. Burdick, R. Bruckner, H.Y. Chen, A. Smallwood, P.C. Wong, M.R. Wright, S. Bai, J.M. Luettgen, R.M. Knabb, P.Y.S. Lam, R.R. Wexler, J Med Chem. **46**, 5298 (2003).
28. K. Yoshikawa, T. Yoshino, Y. Yokomizo, K. Uoto, H. Naito, K. Kawakami, A. Mochizuki, T. Nagata, M. Suzuki, H. Kanno, M. Takemura, T. Ohta, Bioorg Med Chem Lett. **21**, 2133 (2011)

MATEC Web of Conferences **44**, 02019 (2016)
DOI: 10.1051/matecconf/20164402019

Continual Energy Management System of Proton Exchange Membrane Fuel Cell Hybrid Power Electric Vehicles

Yuan Ren[a], Zhi Dan Zhong, Zhi Wen Zhang, Tian Yu Luo
School of Mechatronics Engineering, Henan University of Science and Technology, Luoyang 471003, Henan Province, China

Abstract. Current research status in energy management of Proton Exchange Membrane (PEM) fuel cell hybrid power electric vehicles are first described in this paper, and then build the PEMFC/ lithium-ion battery/ ultra-capacitor hybrid system model. The paper analysis the key factors of the continuous power available in PEM fuel cell hybrid power electric vehicle and hybrid power system working status under different driving modes. In the end this paper gives the working flow chart of the hybrid power system and concludes the three items of the system performance analysis.

1 Introduction

Fuel cell hybrid power electric vehicles mean one or two auxiliary storage device(s) applied to the fuel cell electric vehicles [1]. Then the key technology of the power control is to coordinate the fuel cell system and auxiliary storage device and the electric-drive system according to the rapidly changing load. The goal of the power management is to improve the vehicle efficiency while maintaining the power balance of the vehicle under different working conditions. In this work, we just study the energy management of the Proton Exchange Membrane (PEM) fuel cell hybrid power electric vehicle.

There are different approaches in the literatures to analysis the power management in the PEM fuel cell hybrid power systems. Ref. [2] discusses the impact of the different power management strategies on the PEM fuel cell vehicles and concludes that the serial power train is shown to be more efficient than the parallel one. Diego Feroldi[3] uses the concept of the preceding horizon with the predictions of a PEM fuel cell hybrid power system (PEM fuel cell, renewable sources and batteries) with the future generation from the renewable sources(wind and solar),the future load and the state of charge(SOC) in the battery. The results show that a reduction in the loss of power supply probability (LPSP) is up to 88% which compared with the case without predictions. Rupendra Kumar Pachauri[4] compares different types of fuel cells and power management schemes. In reference [5], the author proposes a original control algorithm of the distributed generation supplied by a PEM fuel cell main sources, and the storage devices: super capacitor and batteries. Qi Li [6] adopts the power sharing strategy for a PEM Fuel cell hybrid power systems (combined with Li-ion battery and super capacitor) based on a combination of fuzzy logic control (FLC) and Haar wavelet transform (Haar-WT).The proposed the energy management system is able to ensure the low frequency of the power demand can be deals with the PEMFC and the super capacitor can supply all the high frequency components which could damage the PEMFC membrane.

This paper analyses the current research status in the energy management of Proton Exchange Membrane (PEM) fuel cell hybrid power electric vehicles. Then build the PEMFC/ lithium-ion battery/ ultra-capacitor Simulink model and gives the working flow chart of the hybrid power system under different driving mode, concludes the three items of the system performance analysis.

2 Modeling of the Energy management of the PEMFC Hybrid Power System

The basic configuration of the PEMFC powered hybrid system is shown in Fig.1. The hybrid system is composed of the PEMFC , Energy Store System (ESS) include the batteries and the ultra-capacitor, the uni-directional DC/DC converter ,the bi--directional DC/DC converter, the Power management system[6].

The main source of the hybrid system is the PEMFC which is connected to the uni-directional DC/DC converter that can raise the low voltage delivered by the PEMFC to DC bus. The batteries and the ultra-capacitor are used as ESS to supply the output power during the acceleration or for the energy recovery during braking. The Energy Store System is connected to the bi-directional DC/DC converter which allows the charge and discharge of the batteries and the ultra-capacitor.

In order to distribute the demand power, the PMS determines the reference power signals for the energy generation unit and the energy storage unit by regulating the unidirectional and bidirectional DC/DC converters.

[a] Corresponding author: ryemailcn@163.com

Article available at http://www.matec-conferences.org or http://dx.doi.org/10.1051/matecconf/20164402019

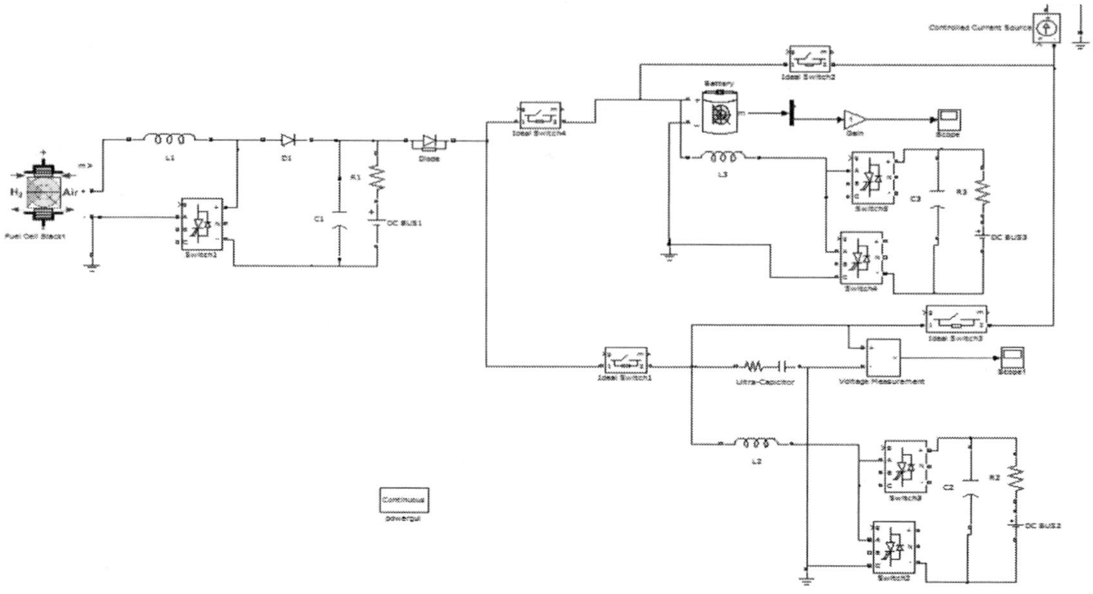

Figure 1. Power management of the PEMFC/Battery/UC powered hybrid systems

2.1 Modelling of the PEMFC

In our study, we choose PEMFC as the generation unit. The simulated model of the PEMFC is shown as Fig.2.The inputs are the voltage of the stack and stack current.

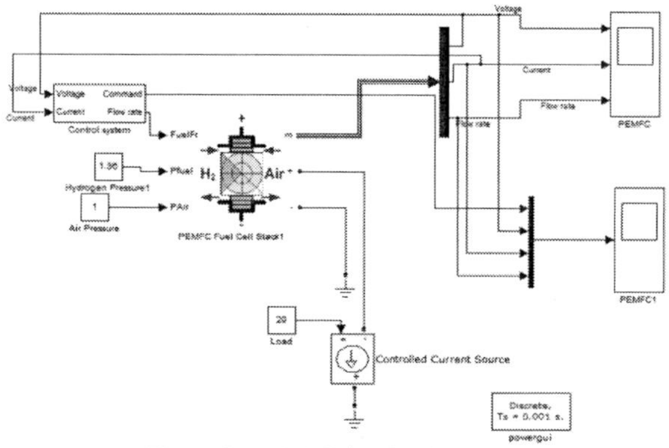

Figure 2. PEMFC simulated model

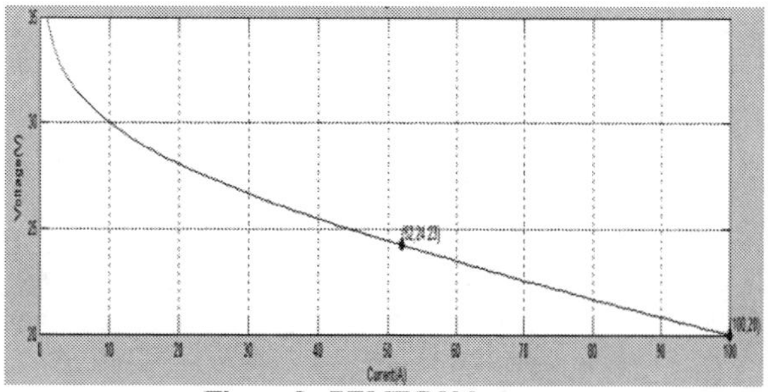

Figure 3. PEMFC V-I curve

2.2 Modelling of energy storage unit (Batteries and the ultra-capacitor)

The simulated values of the lithium-ion battery parameters are shown as the Table1, the lithium-ion battery discharge characteristic is shown as Fig.4. The equivalent circuit of the ultra-capacitor is shown as Fig.5.

Table 1. Values of lithium-ion battery parameters

Parameters	Values
Nominal voltage	23.1(V)
Rated Capacity	11.5(Ah)
Initial State-Of-Charge	75%

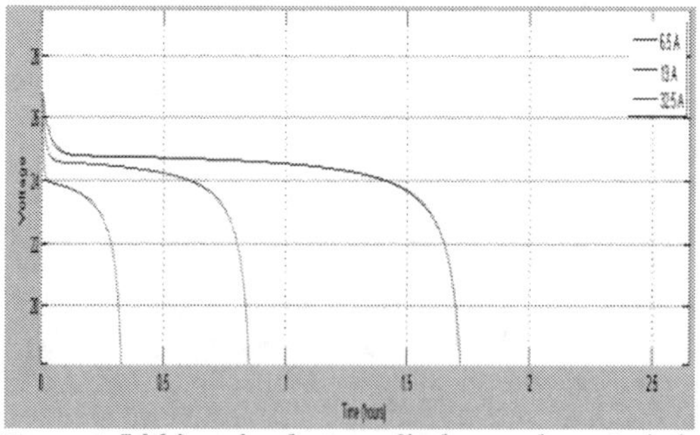

Figure 4. Lithium-ion battery discharge characteristic

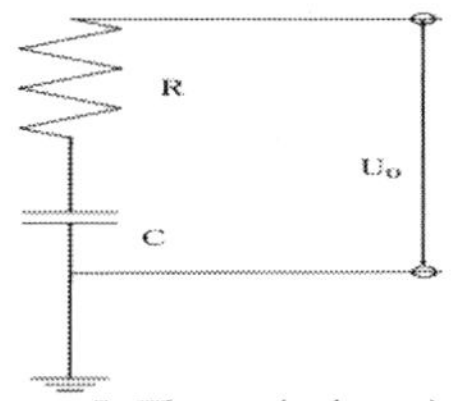

Figure 5. The equivalent circuit of the ultra-capacitor

2.3 Modelling of DC/DC converters

The unidirectional DC/DC converter for the PEMFC and the bidirectional DC/DC converter for lithium-ion battery and ultra-capacitor are shown in Fig.6 and Fig.7.

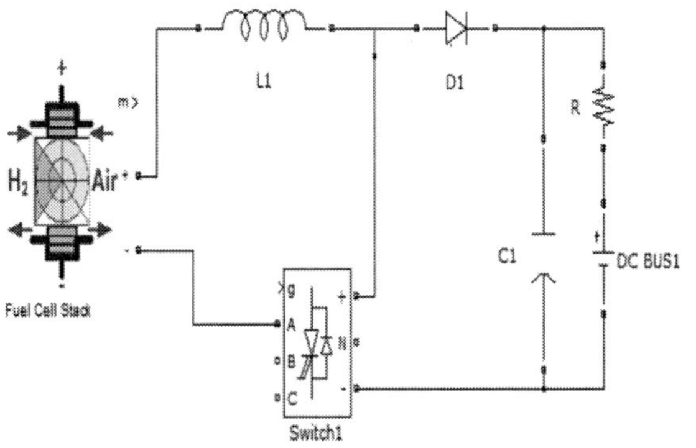

Figure6. Unidirectional DC/DC converter topology for PEMFC

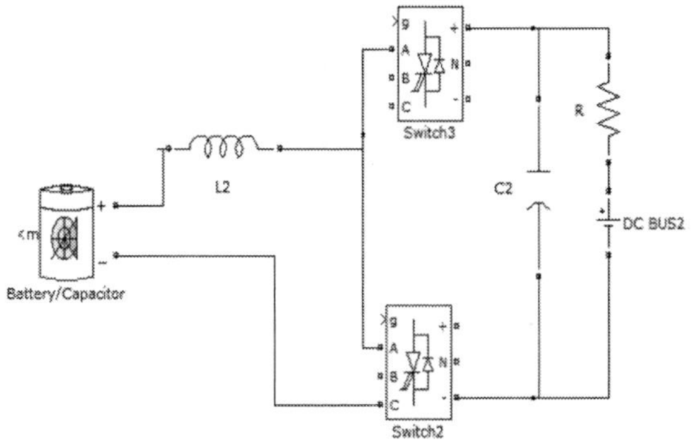

Figure 7. Bidirectional DC/DC converter topology for lithium-ion battery and ultra-capacitor

3 Power management schemes and Performance analysis

3.1. Power management schemes

The hybrid power system works at different status under different driving conditions. The Fig.8 shows the PEM FC, lithium-ion battery and ultra-capacitor working flow chart under different driving modes.

(1)At the start up mode, the whole vehicle electrical energy comes from the lithium-ion battery and then it starts PEMFC up.

(2)At the accelerate or climbing mode, the vehicle electrical energy is provided by the PEM FC , lithium-ion battery and the ultra-capacitor(UC) .

(3)When the vehicle is at the even speed driving mode, the main power is provided by the PEM FC, and if the SOC of the lithium-ion battery and UC are low, the PEMFC may charge to the lithium-ion battery and UC.

(4)At the abrupt accelerate mode, the PEM FC stops work because it couldn't bear the wave load, at this time the lithium-ion battery and UC starts undertake the change, and the UC undertake the high frequency parts.

(5)During the braking mode, the output of PEM FC is single direction, so it can't absorb the feedback current, then the lithium-ion battery and UC are composed of the brake energy regeneration.

3.2 Performance analysis

3.2.1Continuous power available

The hybrid power system must be consistently supplied during the operation. To be safe guard, it is necessary to prepare a backup power source to prevent the primary power source to be interrupted. Then the backup power source can support the power demand when critical power load required.

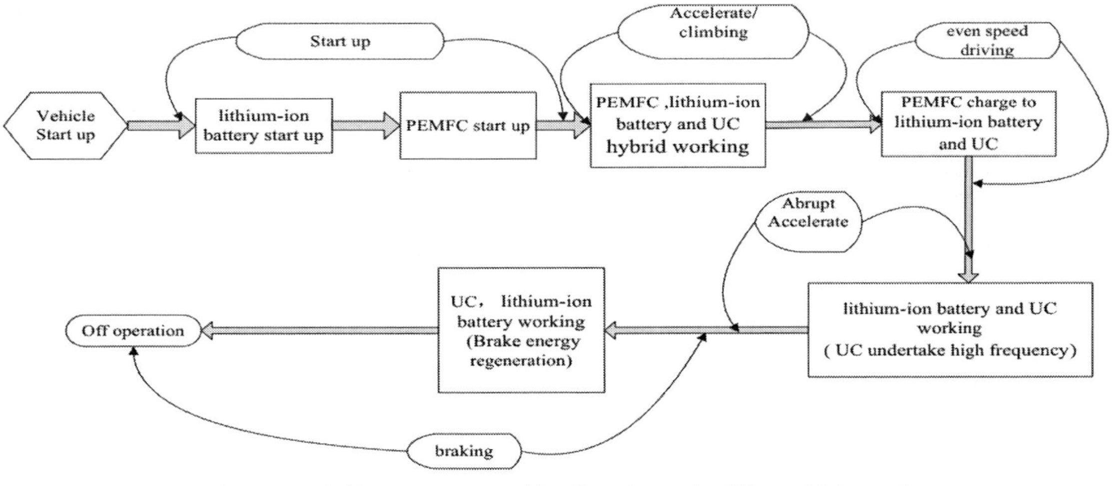

Figure 8. Hybrid power system working flow chart under different driving modes

3.2.2 Hybrid system stability

The hybrid power electric vehicles are consists of energy generation unit, storage unit and converters, which are affected by the temperature and load variation. The change of the power demand may cause instability of the power system as all units are interconnected. So the management system must be well designed to ensure the system operates at its nominal power.

3.2.3 On-board energy management

In the PEM fuel cell hybrid power electric vehicles, the transient changes in load demand may occur frequently which may be have damage to the PEMFC membrane due to oscillated pressure and the oxygen starvation, and that may reduce the lifetime of the PEMFC system. Thus, to ensure PEMFC lifetime prolongation by preventing the FC system from load changes with high frequencies, it is necessary to optimize the three power sources on-board and to meet the requirement load.

4 Conclusions

The paper analyses the current research status in the energy management of Proton Exchange Membrane (PEM) fuel cell hybrid power electric vehicles. Then build the PEMFC/ lithium-ion battery/ ultra-capacitor Simulink model including the three parts and the converters model. Then the paper gives the working flow chart of the hybrid power system under different driving mode. In the end, the paper concludes the three items of the system performance analysis.

References

1. H. Yun, S. Liu , Y. Zhao , J. Xie , C. Liu , Z. Hou , K. Wang, Int J Hydrogrn Engergy **40**, 633-641 (2015).
2. F.-C. Wang, C. Gao, S. Li, Int J Hydrogen Energy **39**,17336-17346(2014).
3. D. Feroldi, P. Rullo, D. Zumoffen, Renewable Energy **75** ,550-559(2015) .
4. R.K. Pachauri, Y.K.Chauhan, J.rser, **43**, 1301-1319(2015).
5. P. Thounthong, S. Rael, B. Davat, J.pow.sour.,**193**,376-385(2009).
6. Q. Li, W. Chen, Z.Liu , M. Li, L. Ma, J.pow.sour.,**279**,267-280(2015).
7. D. Guilbert, A. Gaillard, A. Mohammadi, A. N'Diaye, A. Djerdir, Int J Hydrogrn Engergy **40**,519-537(2015)
8. F.-C Wang, C.-H Peng, Int J Hydrogen Energy, 1-13(2014).
9. M.A.Hannan, F.A.Azidin, A.Mohamed, J.rser. **29**, 135-150(2014).
10. H. Aouzellag, K. Ghedamsi, D. Aouzellag, Int J Hydrogen Energy, **40**,7204-7213(2014).

MATEC Web of Conferences 44, 02020 (2016)
DOI: 10.1051/matecconf/20164402020

The Ergonomics Analysis In the Process of Reversed Loader Cylinder Virtual Assembly Based on CATIA and DELMIA

Di Liang[1,a], Gui Zhi Sun[1,c], Shuang Wu[1,b]

[1]*School of Mechanical Engineering, Shenyang University, Shenyang, Liaoning Province, China*

Abstract. Health and work efficiency of staff of the enterprise gradually attracted people's attention. The human factor was crucial in the manufacturing process. First establish virtual assembly model through CATIA software. Second use DELMIA software to make the rapid upper limb assessment of human body posture, lifting equation NIOSH to lift frequent location analysis, etc. Improve the unreasonable location for the improvement of human factors engineering to reduce the probability of enterprise staff occupational disease and injury, and eventually improve production efficiency.

1 Introduction

Currently, various large-scale machinery manufacturing industry continues to develop. Among them, the people and systems closely is particularly important, Accident hazards and personnel injury caused by the human factor is more cause for concern[1]. Domestic and foreign scholars conducted in-depth research of ergonomics analysis under virtual assembly, Washington State University integrated a fast upper assessment algorithm in VADE system, the study of ergonomics and virtual assembly made simple binding[2,3]. US State University system raised JIGORO system, the system made two-dimensional model of the product model import a virtual assembly under requirement environmental, to made modeling and simulation of virtual assembly process[4]. Yining Zheng and Xin Ru carried on the interaction techniques research under the virtual assembly environment human-computer[5]. Qian Sun put forward the virtual assembly technology based on DELMIA in aircraft assembly applications[6].

This paper researched virtual assembly machine cylinder production process, it carried on the cylinders three-dimensional modeling and simulation combined the CATIA software and DELMIA software.Do the man-machine operation modeling and simulation of production plant based on human factors engineering, and conduct ergonomics analysis and improvement. Better solve the problem of personnel injuries and occupational diseases, and have co-benefits with enterprise.

2 Enterprise production status

Company A newly introduced reproduced oil cylinder production workshop, new model oil cylinder put into production. Production line stuck in the past on the basis of the product, poor management of production personnel, production site confusion, efficiency and production quality has been lacking. The introduction of new products to achieve better promote enterprise development purposes, the production plant is particularly important to improve.

In this paper, introduction of the oil cylinder as the main object, 3D model of each member, as shown in Figure 1..

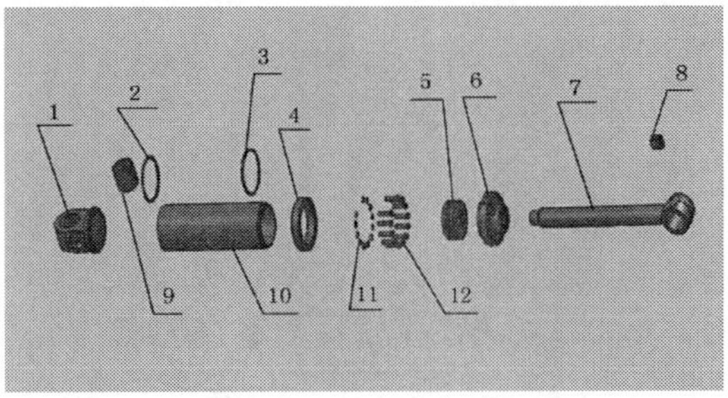

1-bottom, 2-bottom weld, 3-flange welds, 4-flanges, 5-pistons, 6-guide sleeve, 7-rod, 8-seat, 9-bushing, 10-cylinder, 11-washers, 12-screws

3 Oil cylinder Model and Virtual Assembly

This paper modeling the main components of the hydraulic oil cylinder with CATIA, as shown in Figure 2.

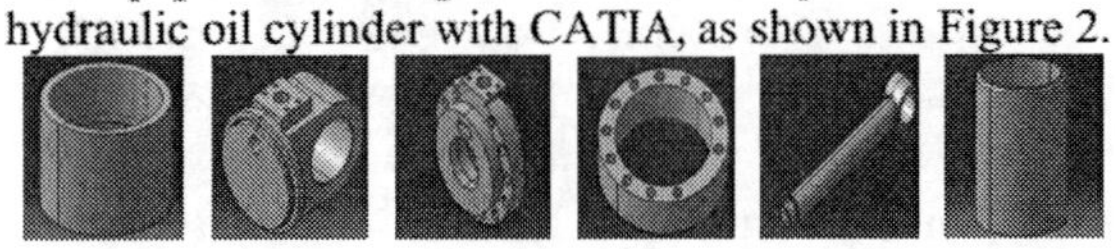

(1) (2) (3) (4) (5) (6)

[a] Corresponding author: author@e-mail.org

Article available at http://www.matec-conferences.org or http://dx.doi.org/10.1051/matecconf/20164402020

(1)—bushing (2)—bottom (3)—guide sleeve (4)—flanges(5)—rod (6)—cylinder

Figure2. The main components

Virtual assembly simulation of hydraulic cylinders, specifically including tracking command activation, compass for disassembly of parts and paths recorded.Use recorder records the assembly tree to generate the corresponding sequence, further editing the obtained three-dimensional animation of virtual simulation cylinders, as shown in Figure 3.

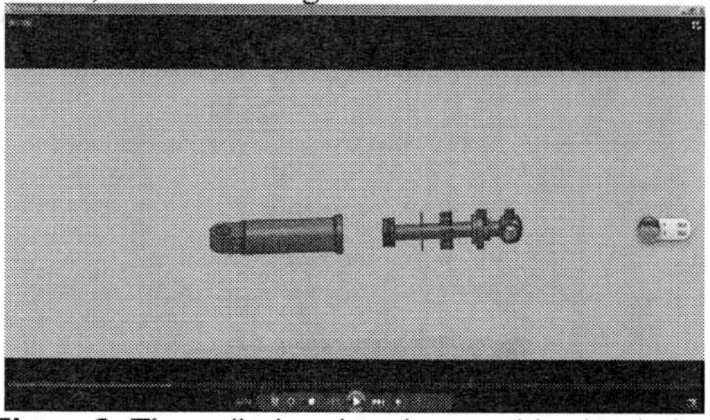

Figure3. The cylinder virtual assembly simulation animation

4 Human factors analysis of key stations based on DELMIA

4.1 Create mannequins and mannequin task

Mannequin libraries created based on the actual working conditions of staff of cylinder production plant, as shown in Figure 4.

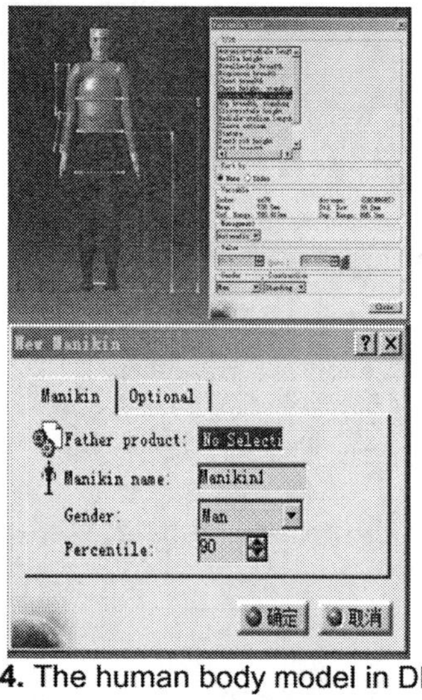

Figure4. The human body model in DELMIA

After the human body model, loading the movement to the process of the task within the human body model.

4.2 Human Factors Analysis of key station based on DELMIA

4.2.1 The analysis that can reach envelope

In virtual simulation, mannequin simulation action running, hand, eye area can be achieved by a spherical region indicates, as shown in Figure 5. If it can well cover parts or tools needed, described assembling good physical reachability, human factors analysis can be carried out. If it can not cover, the reachability is not ideal, make improvements. This paper studied stations were analyzed under the premise of good reachability, improvement for bad reachability stations, increase carts or pulley platform, better selection means or tools within reachability of range.

Figure5. The hand can reach envelope range

4.2.2 RULA rapid analysis of upper limb

Rapid upper limb Assessment used to assess the state of human upper limb in the job. For operations personnel to quickly assess the upper limb in the module of DELMIA, specifically as shown in Figure 6 and 7.

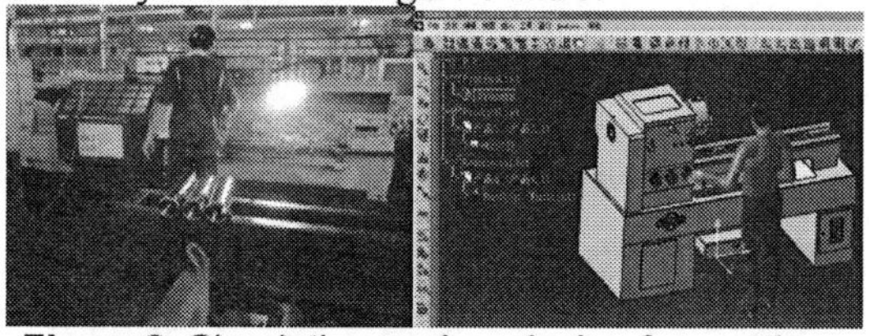

Figure6. Simulation and analysis of operations

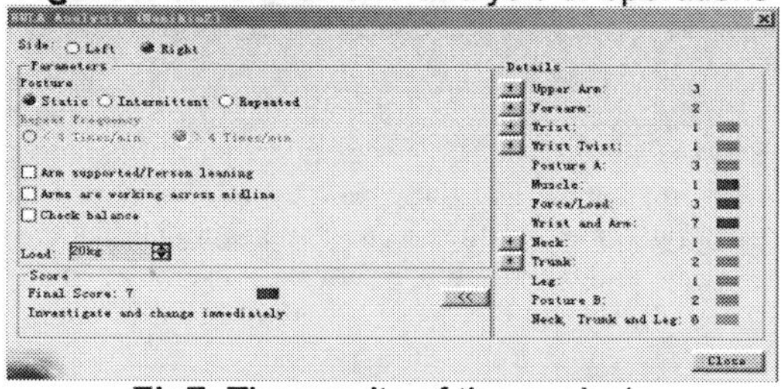

Fig7. The results of the analysis

The figure shows, 50th percentile for employee location for analysis, staff right arm comfort simulation analysis. When statically job, arm support, load 20kg. To maintain this position, RULA analysis of the resulting score of 7. Posture require immediate research and changes in posture, specific improvements and analysis are shown in Table 1.

Table1. The evaluation analysis of upper limb

Place	Scores	Improvement
Upper arm	3	Upper arm, forearm etc within an appropriate range, wrist twist reasonable range, wrist and arm projects were scores of 7, harm to Ⅳ, it should be immediately improved, here can increase the mechanical arm, reduce static time of staff handheld parts, the score of legs was 6, recommend personnel frequently changed in the squat position the center of gravity foot, to alleviate accumulated fatigue.
Forearm	2	
Wrist twist	1	
Wrist muscles	1	
Wrist and forearm	7	
Wrist	1	
Neck	1	
Trunk	2	
Legs	6	
Total	7	

4.2.3 NIOSH analysis of human body

The personnel job activity analysis module of DELMIA software can carriy on upright row analysis, lifting analysis of job activities, as shown in figure 8 and 9.

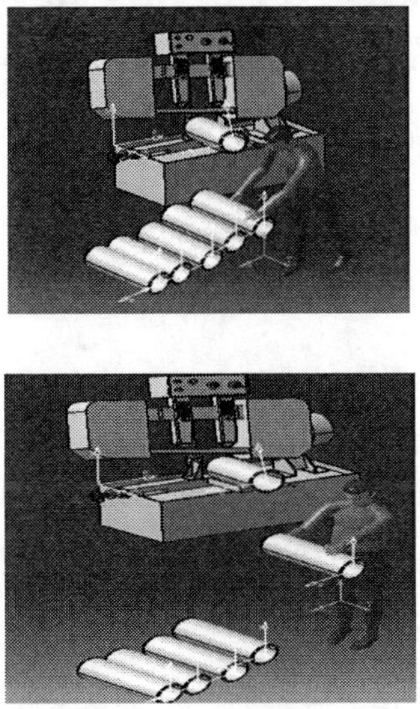

Fig8. Simulation and analysis of operations

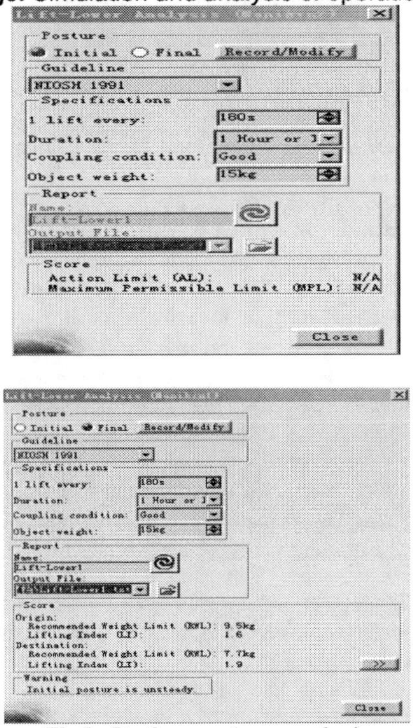

Fig9. Station posture analysis

Staff set the choice theory NIOSH1991 at the initial posture, upgrade once every 180s. Complete the work One hour a day, the results obtained in figure. Recommended the initial attitude of the limit weight was 9.5kg. This value represented, In the absence of dangerous situations, health workers lifted this limit weight and maintained for a period of time. The Lifting Index described the level of physical stress related parameters. When A was greater than 1, it would lead increasing probability of workers lower back muscle injury. The station should be adjusted, and increased robot or freighter platform, instead of the labor, reduced fatigue, improved production efficiency.

4.2.4 Analysis of human handling

Carrying Analysis Module is human factors design analysis module DELMIA software. This analysis gave two kinds of transport height. Male: the height of the ground to hand was set to 787.4 and 1117.6. Female: the height of the ground to the hand was set to 711.2 and 1041.4.Workstation analysis results were shown in Figure 10:

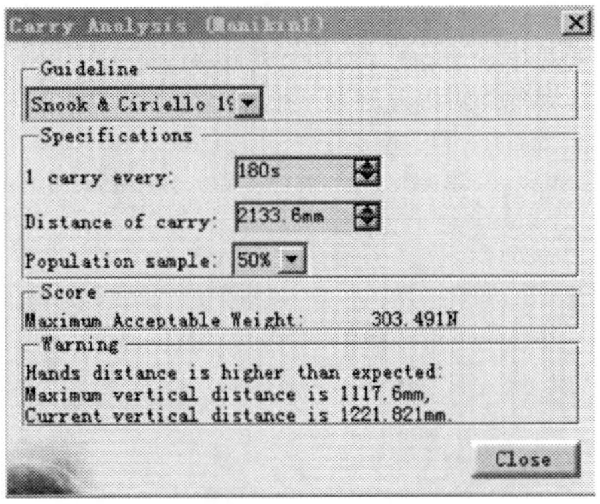

Fig10. Handling analysis results

Handling once every 180s, transport distance set 2133.6mm, 50th percentile manikin, on this basis, people in the security situation, the acceptable maximum carrying weight was 303.491N. Cylinder production plant portion station exceeds the standard, to make the appropriate improvements. For example, companies should outsource the handling device, to reduce injury and improve efficiency

4.2.5 Body sliding analysis

Under push forward working conditions, hand height was defined as three kinds, respectively, 635mm, 889mm, and 1346.2mm. Driven distance previously set six kinds, respectively 2133.6mm, 7620mm, 15240mm, 30480mm, 45720mm and 60960mm. According to the above setting distance, Analyze the sliding body force of sawing work, it was shown in figure 11. Station sliding analysis: Push once every 600s, the distance of push and pull was 2133.6mm, fifty percent of people able to complete the task, this station maximum acceptable initial thrust was 423.103N, the maximum initial tension was 323.291N, The maximum acceptable thrust termination was 314.163 N, The maximum pulling force termination was 262.287N. It is based on this data in the actual production process, to improve overload the station.

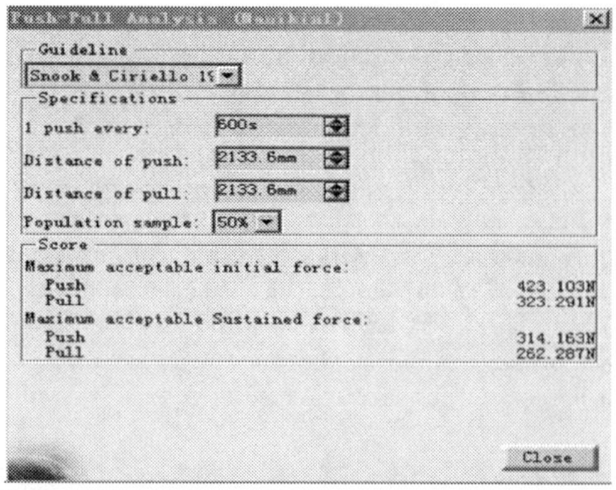

Fig11. The push and pull the analysis results

4.2.6 Biomechanical analysis of human

In this paper, make biomechanical analysis of part station in cylinder production plant and get biomechanical report results, summary analysis of its. As shown in Figure 12 analyzes the content of the specific.

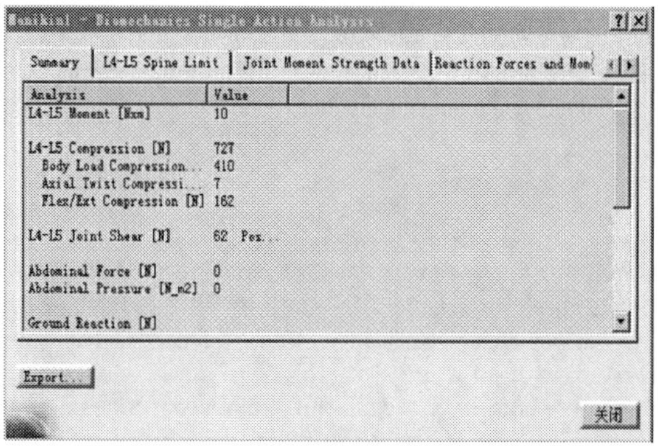

Fig12. Biomechanical analysis results of single action

The results show that the stress analysis of human body of the station, section 4-5 of the spine torque is 10N • m and pressure is 727N and other data provide data to support the production process stress on the joints. Improve the stations of greater force on the joints and against the larger, provide valid data for the production.

4.2.7 Analysis of human handling

OWAS code staff working posture, including back coded, coded legs, shoulders coded, neck coded and loading coded, these five elements are combined, determining a working posture with the code. In order to better differentiate work posture degree, using different colors to distinguish different grades, as shown in Table 2.

Table2. OWAS working posture classification table

Grade	Meaning	color
I	Not harmful to health, without improvements	green
II	Harm is not obvious, suggested improvements	yellow
III	Greater dangers, recommend short-term improvements	orange
IV	Great danger, stop job to adjust	red

OWAS analysis of the human body through different colors show up, as shown in Figure 13.

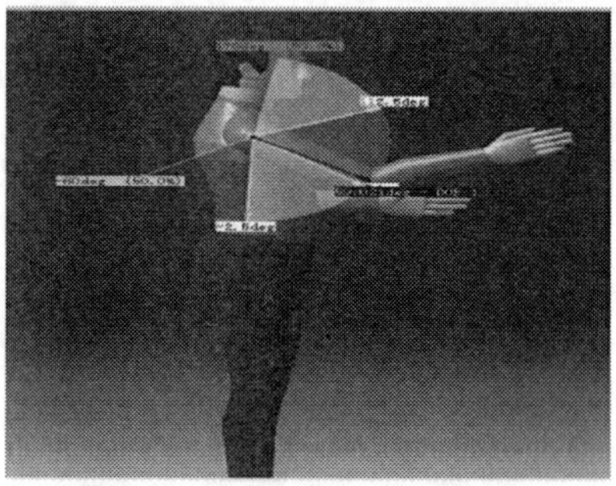

Fig13. OWAS analysis of right upper arm different comfort zones

Conclusion

First, use CATIA virtual to conduct cylinders assembly modeling analysis, stand up to demonstrate intuitively for cylinder process, lay the foundation of human factors engineering analysis. Second, carry on simulation for man-machine operation of cylinder production plant part station on based DELMIA software. Use simulation to get human factors engineering analysis results of each stage of production workers related operation. Further improve the unreasonable stations, to reduce worker injuries and occupational diseases related to the probability of the process

References

[1] Chenhui Jia. Digital factory manufacturing information integration platform based on [J].Management technology,2006,(7):103-106.

[2] Macatamney L, Corlett E N. RULA: a survey method for the investigation of work - related upper limb disorders [J]. Applied Ergonomics, 1993, 24(2): 91-99.

[3] Shaikh I, Kim Y J, Jayaram S, et al. Integration of immersive environment and rula for real - time study of workplace related musculoskeletal disorders in the upper limb. Proceedings of DETC ' 03 ASME, Chicago, Illinois, 2003.

[4] Rajan V N, Sivasubramanian K , Fernandez J E. Accessibility and ergonomic analysis of assembly product and jig designs [J] .International Journal of Industrial Ergonomics, 1999, 23(5-6): 473-487.

[5] Yining Zheng, Xin Ru,Chengtong Tang.Human-computer interaction research techniques under virtual assembly environment[J].Journal of Beijing institute of technology.2006,(26).

[6] Hui Zhang,Qian Sun,XiaoYu Wu.The virtual assembly technology based on DELMIA in aircraft assembly applications[J].Aeronautical Manufacturing Technology,2012,21:89-91.

MATEC Web of Conferences 44, 02021 (2016)
DOI: 10.1051/matecconf/20164402021

The Simulation and Study of the Operating System Efficiency Improvement of a Container Terminal

Di Liang[1,a], Shuang Wu[1,b], Gui Zhi Sun[1,c]

[1]School of Mechanical Engineering, Shenyang University, Shenyang, Liaoning Province, China

Abstract. With the rapid expansion of Chinese container terminal throughput, each container terminal increasingly pays attention to the operational efficiency of storage yard. In this paper, aim at the problem of excessive containers relocation assignments to establish the slotting optimization allocation model, and verify the validity of the model by using Matlab; Using tandem queuing network modeling to build model of the container terminal operating system,and simulate the container terminal logistics system by Witness. It can provide a reference for efficiency improvement of the container terminal operating system.

1 introduction

The large scale ship of container terminal brings all kinds of pressure to the container terminals. How to solve the problem of the construction and planning of container berths has become the scholars' key focus. Kim and Hong[1] used the heuristic methods and branch and bound method simultaneously to study containers relocation problems. K.H. Kim[2] considered some of the nature of export containers, he mainly used a dynamic programming method to determined the result. Yuewen Gao and Yousan Ji[3] analyzed the weight factor, and used the search technology to show that this method of container terminals had reference value to reduce the number of containers relocation. Jumin Hao[4] builded an optimization model about an inner shell of the container terminal yard, it improved the utilization of terminal yard effectively. Jianfeng Shen[5] proposed palletizing models, including matching rules, most preferred, and the region partition.

The main object of the study is a container terminal logistics system, for containers relocation assignment, mechanical resource configuration issues, a terminal operation system is optimized. Research ideas and methods can provide reference for related wharf optimized operating system.

2 The study of container terminal containers relocation problem

2.1 Model assumptions

It assumed that the zone and the bay of zone had been allocated in container terminal yard; According to container-delivering information, basic information of all containers have been identified, including the box weight, port of destination, etc; The containers relocation assignments just were operated during the bay. It assumed that all prepared assigned container are the same type.

2.2 The establishment and analysis of stockpiling mathematical model

2.1.1 Model parameters

J expressed the number of stacked inside each Bay; K represented the number of Bay inside per segment; I expressed the number of stack height inside each Bay. M is represented as a large positive values; N represented the total number of planned container terminal yard; d_n expressed as a destination of the n-th container; w_n was expressed as an n-th grade container carrier; c_n expressed as the n-th container property value; v_k expressed as k-th Bay carrying capacity.

S_{nkj} noted that the i-layer box position of j of k-th Bay, which can occupied by the n-th container, With 1 said it had been allocated, with 0 expressing others:

$$S_{nkji}=\begin{cases}1 & \text{If the n-th container is allocated to } slot(k,j,i)\\ 0 & \text{Others}\end{cases}$$

k = 1,2, ... K; j = 1, 2, ... J; i = 1,2, ... n = 1, 2, ... N.

$R_{kj(i-z)}$ indicated that if there had containers relocation at $slot(k,j,i)$ and $slot(k,j,i-z)$:

a Corresponding author: author@e-mail.org

$$R_{kj(i-z)}=\begin{cases}1 & \text{If containerA put on } slot(k,j,i),\\ & \text{and } slot(k,j,i\text{-}z) \text{ of container b had: } c_a<c_b \\ 0 & \text{Others}\end{cases}$$

k=1, 2, ···K, j=1, 2, ···J, i=2, 3, ···I,

z=1, 2, ···i-1。

2.1.2 Establish the model

Minimizing the number of containers relocation during the Bay is the goal of container allocation problem.

The objective function:

$$P=\min\sum_{J=1}^{J}\sum_{i=2}^{I}\sum_{z=1}^{i-1}R_{kj(i-z)} \qquad (1)$$

Restrictions:

$$\sum_{j=1}^{J}\sum_{i=1}^{I}\sum_{n=1}^{N}S_{nkji}\le V_k \qquad (2)$$

k=1, 2, ...K。

$$\sum_{n=1}^{N}S_{nkji}\le\sum_{n=1}^{N}S_{nkj(i-1)} \qquad (3)$$

i=2, 3, ...I; j=1, 2, ...J; k=1, 2, ...K。

$$\sum_{n=1}^{N}n\cdot S_{nkji}+\left(1-\sum_{n=1}^{N}S_{nkji}\right)\cdot M>\sum_{n=1}^{N}n\cdot S_{nkj(i-1)} \qquad (4)$$

i=2, 3, ...I; j=1, 2, ...J; k=1, 2, ...K。

Constraints (2) ensured that the container can not be more than the amount of energy they carry large; The constraints (3) expressed that if it is on the second layer container, others should be placed beneath the corresponding container. Constraints (4) ensured that a entering the sequence number of second layer containers was greater than its corresponding approach below the serial number.

This paper used a heuristic to calculate. It was thought as a two-dimensional coordinate system, longitudinal explained to give the container two integer , lengthways explained achieving sequential, the so-called container properties.

The destination A and the weight grade B could be determined site adopted container . Clear the level six weight classes, with a 1-6 six digital representation, w_n=1, 2, ..., 6。In a route in accordance with the order of the ports of call were numbered, d_n =1 , 2, ..., 7。If the level was set by weight w_n (w_n=1, 2, ..., 6) , n is the destination d_n (d_n=1, 2, ..., 7) , so explained that. $c_n=(d_n, w_n, x_n, y_n)$. y_n represented container n ordinate in a cartesian coordinate system, indicating the size of the container transversely value n in the cartesian coordinate system. The last generation of stacking diagram must simultaneously satisfied the formula (5) and (6).

$$\begin{cases}x_n<x_{n+l}\\ y_n=y_{n+l}\end{cases}\text{时，}\ d_n\ge d_{(n+l)} \qquad (5)$$

$$\begin{cases}x_n=x_{n+l}\\ y_n<y_{n+l}\end{cases}\text{时，}\ w_n\le w_{n+l} \qquad (6)$$

l=1, 2, ···-1。

A terminal yard, stacking number J = 6, the number of stack I = 5, $V_K=30$

Specific steps of the algorithm is: First, choose the number of columns in the order of the first data, the data in the coordinate system of the lower-left corner, select the second point on the top right of the first point. Then the new endpoint of this line as a starting point to repeat the above operation until the condition was not satisfied so far, this would give poly-line one. Secondly, from the remaining points, select the leftmost point between repeated operation of this step, poly-line could be calculated; Then, repeat the above measures, to calculate a set of poly-lines, allowing all the points were arranged in a line of group.

Taking a route Case sequentially port of call as follows: a port - Qingshui - Pusan - Lianyungang - Nagoya - Hong Kong - Yokohama. Admission container had six grades weight. Supposing a sequence of random arrival of containers was {13, 25, 16, 42, 34, 32, 54, 64, 23, 42, 51, 26, 35, 51, 14, 63, 45, 22, 64, 52, 34, 26, 34, 54, 63, 65}; Follow the proposed algorithm ,It could be get the poly-line, it was shown in Figure 1:

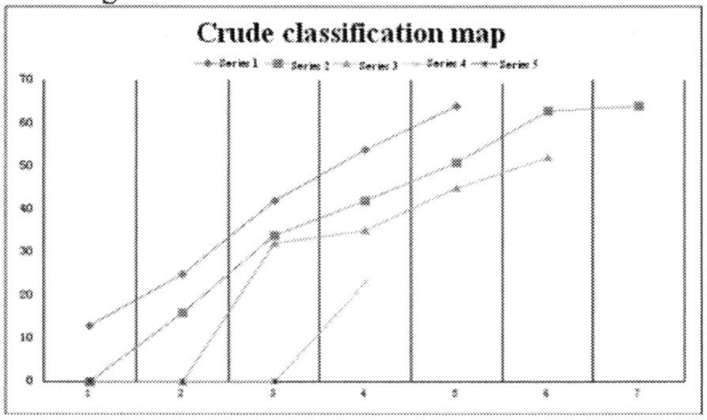

Fig1. Rough classification

According to the poly-line to know the initial state of container , it is shown in Figure 2. As can be seen from this figure, the second and third columns belonged to the long column; the first column, the fourth column and the fifth column were moderate; the sixth column belonged short columns.Over four boxes under ultrahigh column forms obtained were stacked in order with short column by column, the first step was amended, and formed Figure 3:

	65 (26)				
	64 (19)				
	63 (16)	63 (25)			
64 (8)	51 (14)	54 (24)			
54 (7)	51 (11)	52 (20)	34 (23)		
42 (4)	42 (10)	45 (17)	34 (21)	26 (22)	
25 (2)	34 (5)	35 (13)	26 (12)	22 (18)	
13 (1)	16 (3)	32 (6)	23 (9)	14 (15)	No

Fig2. Rough classification

		63 (25)			
64 (8)	65 (26)	54 (24)	34 (23)	26 (22)	
54 (7)	64 (19)	52 (20)	34 (21)	22 (18)	
42 (4)	63 (16)	45 (17)	26 (12)	14 (15)	
25 (2)	51 (14)	35 (13)	23 (9)	42 (10)	
13 (1)	51 (11)	32 (6)	16 (3)	34 (5)	No

Fig3. The first correction

According to the above method, the Pareto chart was corrected once again , the results was shown in Figure 4.

64 (8)	65 (26)	63 (25)	34 (23)	26 (22)	
54 (7)	64 (19)	54 (24)	34 (21)	22 (18)	
42 (4)	63 (16)	52 (20)	26 (12)	14 (15)	
25 (2)	51 (14)	45 (17)	23 (9)	42 (10)	
13 (1)	51 (11)	35 (13)	16 (3)	34 (5)	32 (6)

Fig4. The last correction

3 Container terminal queuing network systems analysis

3.1. Determine the container terminal tandem queuing network model

The relationship between several logistics nodes configuration of the container terminal was shown in Figure 5:

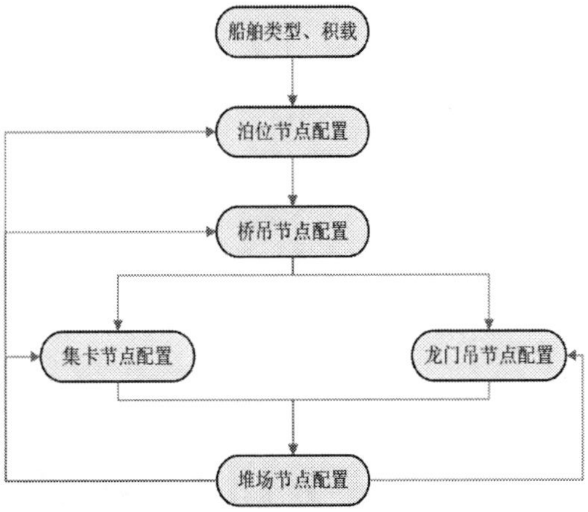

Fig5. Node configure of container terminals system

3.2 Container Terminal series line network multi-node configuration analysis

The job level of container terminal logistics network was made up of a plurality of unipolar queue subsystem. Container flows between each node formed a queuing network. According to production of operating line, a series queuing network analytic model was established. Container series line network structure of operating line production was shown in Figure 6 and Figure 7.

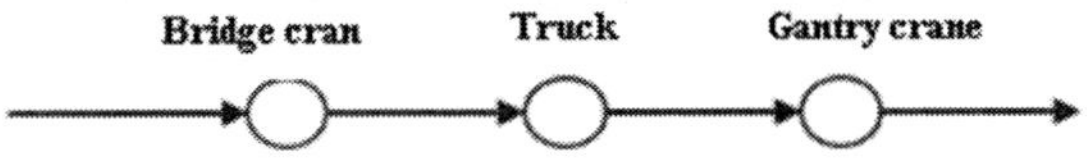

Fig6. Import container terminals system of tandem open queuing network

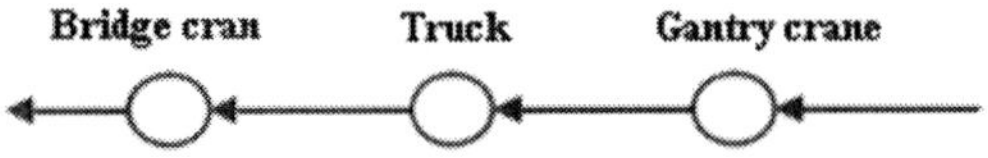

Fig7. Export Container Terminals System of Tandem Open Queuing Network

4 Container terminal modeling and simulation based on witness

4.1. Establish the model

In this paper, simulate the existing container terminal processes. The main application was the open-loop series multistage queuing network. In the process of import container loading and unloading, First Container loaded onto the truck by crane, Transport the containers shipped under the gantry by the truck, Then place container onto the yard prearranged location by gantry crane. In this paper, the based on container terminal network queuing structure system, Create a system simulation model, and use witness system make the practical operation, summary statistical indicators.

4.2. Set basic parameters

The cranes node was the import containers beginning serving node, the gantry crane node was the ending service node, while exports container was opposite. Network can be considered as only one type of customer (container). It was shown in Figure 8:

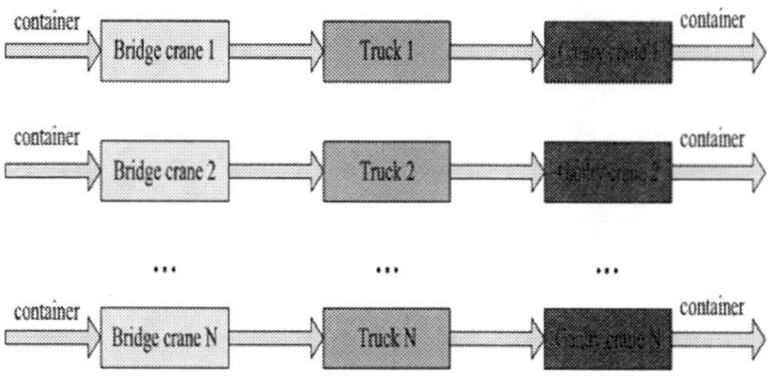

Fig8. Container Terminals System of Tandem Open Queuing Network

The truck arrived the quay crane service center, quay crane was idle, but it might not be able to receive services directly. It was carried out equipping in accordance with the relevant information received in advance of the container ship dock. If one of trucks was matching, the truck was responsible for the work of this operating line .

If the job line was idle, the containers could be set loaded onto the truck. If there were other trucks to went on the loading operation, the truck was set to enter the system waits.

4.3. The simulation process of witness

During operation of the model system simulation, container automatically entered the system, when it arrived the bridge node, which obeyed Poisson distribution, it was shown in Figure 9. 1.7 represented that a boat was removed every 1.7 minutes. The containers were transported to the yar to stacking by using the truck. In the simulation, the truck obeyed second-Ireland distribution (2.0,2,2). The simulation time was set at 2 months (60 days).

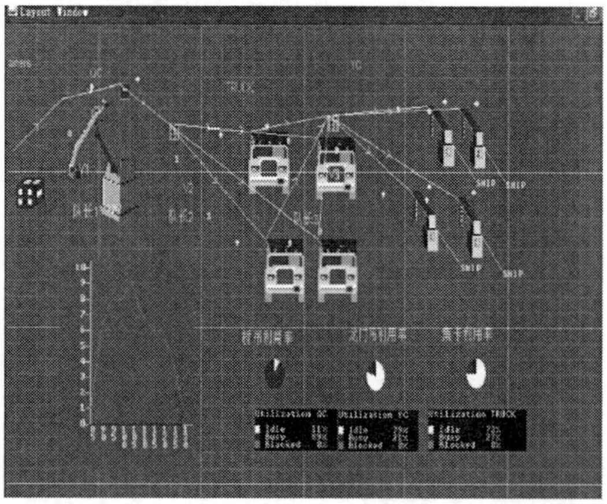

Fig9. Simulation model of mechanism configuration of container terminal

In this paper, choose four ratio to analyze the various indicators, as shown in Table 1, and then from the the average wait time and utilization of equipment to evaluate. Select the most appropriate configuration to improve the efficiency of container terminals.

Table1. Number of Container Terminals Mechanism Configuration

Crane: Truck: gantry crane	(1:4:4)	(1:5:5)	(1:5:4)	(1:4:5)
Crane utilization	85%	85%	83%	84%
Truck utilization	25%	20%	20%	25%
Gantry crane utilization	19%	15%	19%	15%
Buffers01	211455	202103	215442	206365
Buffers02	77	4	4	87
Buffers03	28	2	42	0

4.4. Analysis of test results

It could be observed from simulation, when different ratios, through objective analysis option 1: 5: 5 was the best configuration, the equipment utilization was higher, queue length was relatively short.

Conclusion

First, the optimization stockpiling mathematical model was established. Using MATLAB to select a randomly data, Use optimized model to stacking containers, Simulate the process of shipment suitcase, and get the most optimal stockpiling mathematical model.Second, the paper created a container terminal simulation model based on series line network. Based on the historical operating data of a container terminal, the model was established according to the reasonable options of this paper, and use WITNESS to make simulation experiments. The test effectively demonstrated the effectiveness of the proposed methods, there had a good reference for the scheduling of container handling equipment.

References

[1] Zhao Dan.Review and Analysis on Institutional Management for Global Ports[J]. JOURNAL OFNINGBO UNIVERSITY,2006.3(2):36-46.

[2] E.mcdowilll,gmartind.cho,west. A study of maritime container handing Oregon state university. [J]Sea grant college program ads Coregon.2011.2(2):3-6.

[3]Peter Preston, Erhan Kozan. An approach to determine storage locations of containers at seaport terminals[J]. Computers&Operations Research. 2013,27(1):13-32.

[4]Ying Xie. Port container yard stacking optimization model and algorithm[J].Journal of Central South University,2011 30(2): 78-119.

[5]Jumin Hao, Zhuoshang Ji, Yan lin. The order of mixing job Yard BAY Optimization Model[J]. Advancesin Systems Science and Applications,2000, 40(1): 102-105.

MATEC Web of Conferences **44**, 02022 (2016)
DOI: 10.1051/matecconf/20164402022

Research on Multi Position and Parallel Detection Device for Universal Circuit Breaker Controller

Xiang Fei Meng[1a], Qi Xie[1], Hui Gang Xu[1]

[1] *Changshu Institute of Technology, School of Electrical and Automation Engineering, Changshu 215500, China*

Abstract. This paper introduces a design scheme of the residual current electrical fire monitoring detector performance test system based on virtual instrument technology. In order to test different current specifications monitor detector compatiblly,the system combines virtual instrument technology and computer control technology to improve the accuracy of output current of the current generator with electric voltage compensation technology and the way of closed-loop control ,and designs two sets of different size and the same type of pneumatic fixture to solve the connection of different specifications monitoring detector, software design adopts layered structure and the method based on configuration files, to better satisfy all kinds of test requirements for different products. Practical application shows that the system has the testing results of accurate, high efficiency and convenient operation.

1 Introduction

Universal circuit breaker is a kind of switch device which is used to protect and control various kinds of faults such as the power system. the power system and the equipment overload, under voltage, short circuit and ground fault. Its core is its internal controller unit, the Universal circuit breaker protection control is achieved through its internal core unit - controller.

The multi station parallel test system described in this paper is a system designed to test the controller before assembling the circuit breaker. Can improve the efficiency of testing equipment, reduce the testing cost of the whole system, and solve the problem of rapid product testing in mass production.

2 System function analysis

Universal circuit breaker controller mainly includes control and execution. The function of control part is to measure the input signal size and according to the signal size, according to the requirements of the action to protect the performance of the signal, and to promote the implementation of the action. so as to achieve a variety of circuit breakers. As a result, the Universal circuit breaker controller testing system should have the following test function.

(1) Measurement function test. The universal circuit breaker controller can measure the electric parameters such as current, voltage, power, frequency, power and so on. It has high measurement accuracy, and its multi character protection function is based on the measurement function. So the testing function of circuit breaker is the foundation of the whole test. The test system can test the function of the controller in accordance with the error type and size according to the product specification.

(2) Multi feature protection function test. It Can carry out the three section of circuit breaker protection, grounding protection, reverse power protection, protection, over frequency, under voltage protection, over voltage protection, current imbalance protection, ZSI protection and other protection functions of the test. The test system can control the signal source to output a given signal according to the different specifications and different testing items of the controller, and test whether the protection function is correct and the action time is within the specified error range. The key to the testing of the multi characteristics protection function is to provide accurate, high accuracy and high voltage test signal.

(3) Communication function test. The "four remote" function of the circuit breaker can be realized by using the Modbus-RTU mode on the RS485 interface.

3 Comparison of test plan

There is only one station in the traditional test bench, and it is tested by the equipment and instruments, and the single test equipment is used to test the product. The resource utilization is low and the production efficiency is not ideal. For the testing of large quantities of products, the use of multi station testing method is more and more people's recognition and gets more promotion. But there are some limitations to increase the number of stations, must be in the appropriate number of cases to take other techniques to further improve efficiency.

In multi station testing, there are many kinds of technologies, such as serial test, pipeline test, parallel test.

[a] Xiangfei Meng: mxf0316@163.com

Article available at http://www.matec-conferences.org or http://dx.doi.org/10.1051/matecconf/20164402022

In this system, we use the parallel test and it can complete the same test tasks at the same time of five stations. Such arrangement is advantageous to reduce the difficulty and complexity of the software design. Through the use of multi station parallel testing technology can significantly improve the throughput of the test system, and further improve the utilization of resources and production efficiency.

Take five test system as an example, if the test Project is 3, the serial test (Table 1), the assembly line test (Table 2), and the parallel test (Table 3) are described in table three. Through observation, it is easy to draw the conclusion that in the multi station test, the test time is the longest, and the time of parallel test is the shortest, the efficiency of parallel test is the highest.

Table 1. Serial test

time slice	Station 1	Station 2	Station 3	Station 4	Station 5
1	Project 1				
2	Project 2				
3	Project 3				
4		Project 1			
5		Project 2			
6		Project 3			
7			Project 1		
8			Project 2		
9			Project 3		
10				Project 1	
11				Project 2	
12				Project 3	
13					Project 1
14					Project 2
15					Project 3

Table 2. Pipeline testing

time slice	Station 1	Station 2	Station 3	Station 4	Station 5
1	Project 1				
2	Project 2	Project 1			
3	Project 3	Project 2	Project 1		
4		Project 3	Project 2	Project 1	
5			Project 3	Project 2	Project 1
6				Project 3	Project 2
7					Project 3

Table 3. Parallel test

time slice	Station 1	Station 2	Station 3	Station 4	Station 5
1	Project 1	Project 1	Project 1	Project 1	Project 1
2	Project 2	Project 2	Project 2	Project 2	Project 2
3	Project 3	Project 3	Project 3	Project 3	Project 3

But from the point of view of resources, not all tasks can be tested in parallel, such as the use of the same test resource tasks can only be serial test. So it is necessary to solve the problem of resource allocation in the multi station test system.

4 Test task decomposition and resource allocation

Test task decomposition is the precondition and foundation of the parallel test, which affects the execution efficiency and execution time of the parallel test. It Should be based on task decomposition and normalization, the strong correlation of relative independence as the basic principle, and considering the resource usage and production enterprises of task decomposition, the decomposition of coarse and fine testing are not conducive to the project management and scheduling.

5 Test system design

The overall structure diagram of Universal control unit inspection device is shown in Figure 1. The main industrial control computer, NI data acquisition card based on PCI bus, three phase standard signal source, single station test interface circuit, current, voltage monitoring module, communication module and test stand, etc.. Circuit breaker controller can be conveniently placed in the test station of the station, through a variety of terminal connection. Power parameter measurement module WB1831B35 is used to measure the electric parameters of the three phase standard signal source.

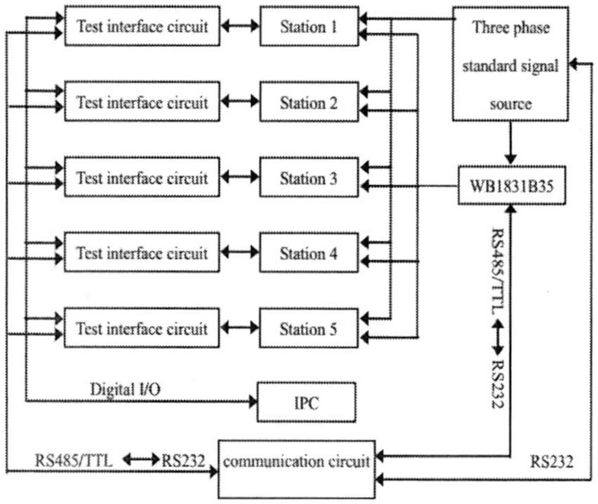

Figure 1. The test system block diagram

5.1 Three phase current and voltage signal generating circuit

The three-phase current signal generator used to produce various specifications of Universal and Universal series control components of the current test signal, the three-phase current signal generator can generate three-phase 0~4.2V voltage to current signal simulation 0~82000A. through computer control can realize phase modulation, frequency modulation and amplitude modulation function.

Three phase voltage signal generating circuit for generating voltage test signals of various specifications of UNIVERSAL and Universal series control components. The voltage generator can generate 0~1000V three-phase voltage (line voltage). the computer control can realize phase modulation, frequency modulation and amplitude modulation function. Three phase current and voltage signal generation principle is shown in figure 2.

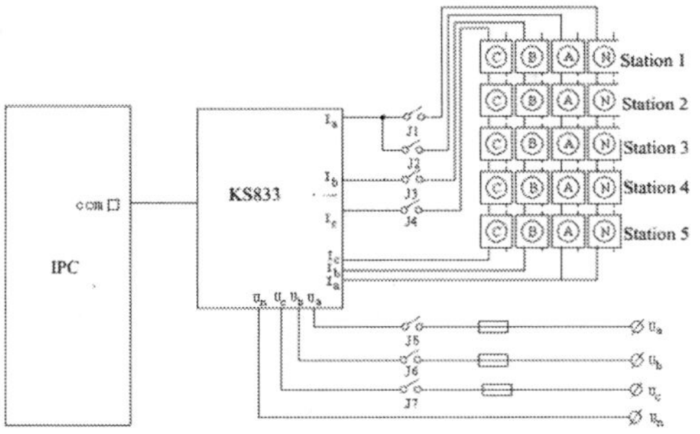

Figure 2. Three phase current and voltage signal generation principle

5.2 System software design

LabVIEW is one of the most widely used virtual instrument software to development platform, which is used in the field of instrument control, data acquisition, data analysis and data display. It is a powerful and convenient integrated development environment. Test system software is designed and developed in the LabVIEW environment. it can better reflect the hierarchical and modular, and enhance the maintainability and scalability of the system software. The key to execute the parallel test system of multi station parallel test system is to write the test program, and the design of the test software should be considered together with the hardware design of the system.

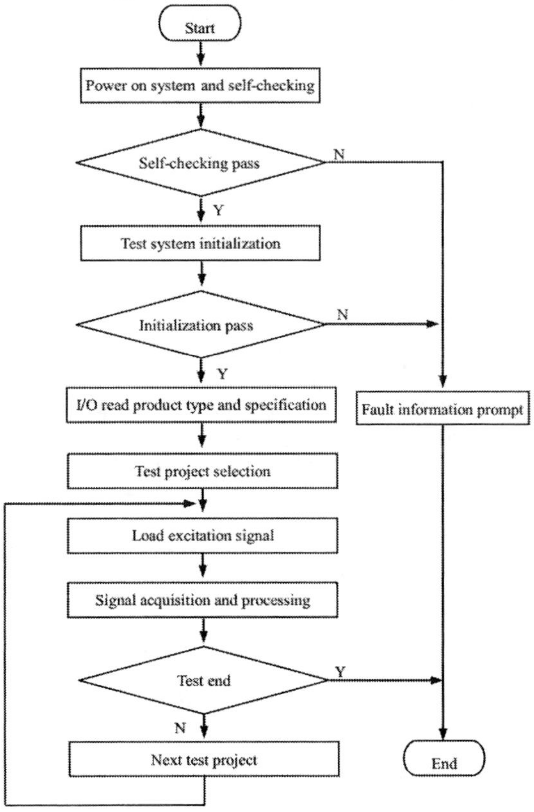

Figure 3. Test system software work flow chart

Universal circuit breaker controller testing system software adopts hierarchical structure and modular design ideas, for easy management and scheduling, each test project as a separate module, all test items can be selected according to the actual situation to do or not do, and stored in the system configuration file, so that the use of the test system becomes more flexible and convenient. System software mainly includes testing the main program, the system initialization program, the program control voltage source control program, the program controlled current source control program, the test program module, the report generation program, etc.. Test system main program for the whole system scheduling, coordination role. System work flow chart is shown in figure 3.

6 Conclusion

This paper introduces the automatic test system of Universal circuit breaker controller which combines the virtual instrument technology and computer control technology. Through the design of the array type three-phase current source and the three-phase voltage source, it can realize multi position test and parallel test. Compared with the traditional automatic test system, the test system has the advantages of high efficiency, high resource utilization and high efficiency. Practice shows that this method has high practical value and good prospect of promotion, it is a practical and feasible solution.

Acknowledgements

This paper is supported by the Jiangsu Province research joint innovation fund project (NO. BY2014075)

References

1. Feng Guanshui. Reasonable selection and application of intelligent CW3 series circuit breaker [J]. Jiangsu electric, 2008, (3):34-36.
2. Xu Ming, Hu Leigang, Zhou Yuewin. Parallel test task parallelism analysis [J]. computer engineering, 2009.35 (4): 56-60.
3. Hao Hongwu, Zhang Jun. Multilateral Detecting Optimum Design in Industrial Automatic Production. [J]. Journal of Xi' an Aerotechnical College, 2004, 22(5):32-34.

MATEC Web of Conferences 44, 02023 (2016)
DOI: 10.1051/matecconf/20164402023

Development of Wireless Dimming Control System for LED Stage Light

Hui Qin Wang[1,a] , Shi Lei Bai[2]

[1,a]School of Information Engineering , Communication University of China , Beijing,China
[2]Beijing Key Laboratory of Modern Entertainment Technology , Beijing, China

Abstract .Compared with the existing wire dimming system of LED stage light which uses the heavy light operating console to adjust the brightness of stage light, a portable wireless dimming control system for LED stage lighting is proposed, fabricated and tested in this paper. The scheme with the core of ATmega16L microcontroller is composed of wireless transmission and reception units, constant current driving circuit of LED, and the control circuit between this two modules. Through the system presented here the dimming signals are transmitted from transmission unit to reception unit, and the brightness of the LED stage light varies consequently. The experiment results show the feasibility and convenience of the proposed wireless LED dimming system for LED stage light.

1 Introduction

As a new generation of environmental light source, LED has been widely used in many areas because of high efficiency, low driving voltage, low power consumption, long life and other characteristics; a variety of colored lights based on the LED is used everywhere. It becomes possible applications to replace the incandescent bulb and fluorescent lamp in residential, industrial as well as commercial performance, stage lighting. As to LED stage light, the brightness of it should be varied as different scenes. So the dimming system for LED stage light is indispensable [1].

The common dimming system consists of light operating console, dimming controller and other auxiliary components. The dimming signal is transferred through communication lines between components. This system not only has the complex construction and bad flexibility, but also influences the application in outdoor performance. For this reason a portable wireless dimming control system with a dimming handle to take place of the heavy operating console is put forward in this paper. The dimming system is made up of wireless transmit unit, receive unit, and constant current driving circuit of LED. These two units communicate through nRF2401 wireless RF module so as to realize short distance brightness transformation of LED stage lights.

2 Overall design of system

The structure diagram of dimming control system for stage light is shown in Figure.1. The dimming system is mainly composed of a wireless transmission unit, a wireless reception unit, and the constant current driving circuit of LED. As to the transmission unit, it includes a LED manipulator and a wireless RF module. Compared with the traditional dimming system, the LED manipulator proposed here use a dimming handle instead of the heavy operating console to improve the portability of the system. With pulling the dimming handle, the output voltage of the handle is changing consequently, moreover, the voltage is converted into a 10- bits digital signal by the analog / digital convert unit of single-chip microcomputer (SCM). Subsequently, the digital signal is packaged according to the DMX512 data transmission protocol and sent to the SCM's output port. Through the part of LED manipulator the signal converts for analog into data segment meeting DMX512 protocol format[2]. Then the data is sent to the reception module through NRF24L01 wireless communication module .As far as the reception unit is concerned, it involves a wireless RF module and ATmega16L microcontroller. This unit along with the constant current driving circuit constitute the LED stage lighting dimming control circuit. According to the circuit, after collecting the dimming signal transmitted by RF module, the SCM of the dimming circuit generates a Pulse-Width Modulation (PWM) control signal to drive constant current source circuit according to the dimming signal received. Finally, the constant current driving system dims the LED lights based on the PWM signal. Because the luminance is mainly affected by LED driving current, so the selection of LED driving mode will directly influence the effect of light dimming. In a word, the LED stage light can be dimmed wirelessly in a short distance by the system proposed here [3].

3 System hardware design

[a] Corresponding author: hqwang@cuc.edu.cn

Article available at http://www.matec-conferences.org or http://dx.doi.org/10.1051/matecconf/20164402023

3.1 Wireless transmission unit

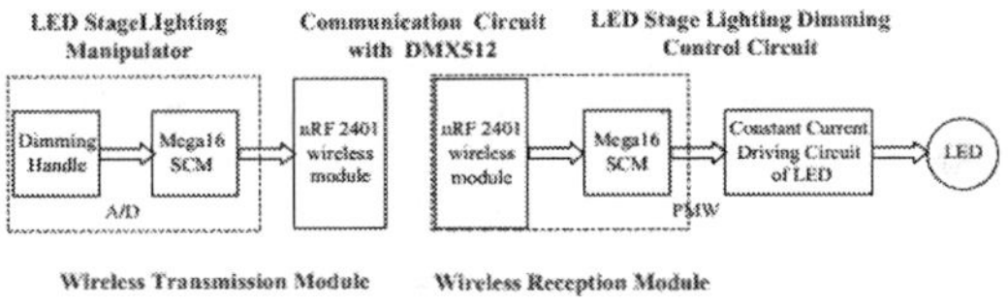

Figure 1. Diagram of wireless dimming control system

Wireless transmission unit is made up of dimming handle, ATmega16 SCM, nRF2401 wireless RF module. The SCM processes the dimming signal generated by the dimming handle and then sends the signal to the receiving part through nRF2401 wireless RF module.

3.1.1 Dimming handle

The dimming handle is essentially a continuously variable potentiometer, which is used to adjust the dimming signal so as to change the brightness of the LED stage light. With turning the knob of this element, its output voltage alters simultaneously, it subsequently is sent to the port PA0 of the SCM.

3.1.2 Micro control unit (MCU)

MCU should convert the signal gathered through PA0 into a 10- bits digital signal ,and packaged it according to the DMX512 data transmission protocol, i.e. data segment meeting DMX512 protocol format. Additional, the transmission unit employs nRF2401 for wireless communications, MCU should also has a SPI interface. Integrating above needs as well as the demands of low cost and low power, ATmega16L is selected as the MCU. ATmega16L made by ATMEL is a high performance, low power consumption of 8 bit CMOS microprocessor. it is also provided with rich resources on chip: 16K bytes of programmable Flash in system, 32 general I/O lines, three PWM output interfaces, programmable serial USART, 8 10-bit ADC, a SPI serial port.

3.1.3 nRF2401 wireless RF module

nRF2401 is an industrial-level wireless transceiver with built-in hardware link layer protocol[4]. The device works within 2.4 GHz ISM band, internally installed frequency synthesizer, power amplifier, crystal oscillator, and modulator, also fused with enhanced ShockBurst technology, its output power and communication channels could be configured by the program. Additional, it possesses two data transmission mode and the built-in SPI interface; so, MCU could control it through the SPI interface. The nRF2401 module used in transmission unit is controlled through port PB.

3.2 Wireless reception unit

Wireless reception unit is composed of nRF2401 wireless RF module, ATmega16 SCM. The DMX512 data received by nRF2401from transmitting module is processed by the microcontroller to produce PWM signal; PWM signal is output through port PD4 to control the driving circuit so as to realize the effect of brightness changing.

3.3 Constant current driving circuit of LED

According to the electrical characteristic of high-power LED array, there are two major driving methods, constant voltage driving method and constant current driving method. Most of the high power LED drivers nowadays, adopt constant current driving mode. As to choice of the high power LED stage light designed here, we use the constant current drive method. Fig.2. shows the proposed constant current driving circuit.

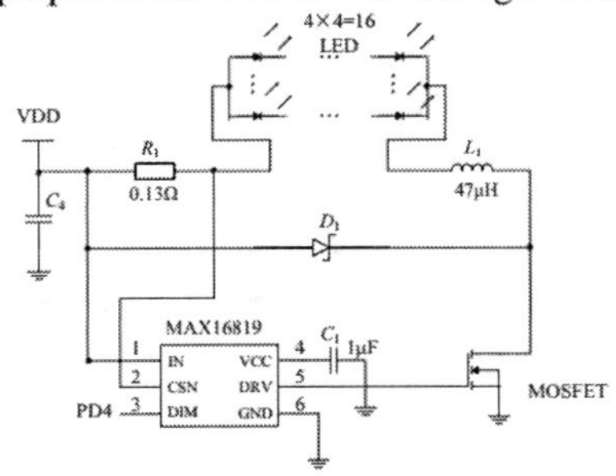

Figure 2. The constant current driving circuit on chip MAX16819

The high-power LED stage light constant current drive circuit designed here is basically constructed by one current detection resistor R_1, one inductor L_1,two capacitors C_1 and C_4,one MOSFET, one freewheeling diode D_1 which can provides a continuing loop for the current flowing through the inductor L_1 during the MOSFET closes, and step-down constant-current high-brightness LED (HB LED) driver --MAX16819. The chip is a buck converter. It operates from a 4.5V to 28V input voltage range and features a 5V/10mA on-board regulator. The output current is regulated by high side current sensing resistor R_1, adjustable pulse brightness achieve wide range. The hysteretic on-time controller and an external resistor allow the converter output voltage to adjust as needed to deliver a constant current to a series-parallel connected LED arrays. This chip used here to provide an adjustable constant forward current four strings of four series connected 5W LEDs[5].

The PWM signal output through the PD4 port of the SCM is sent into DIM. A logic level below 0.6V at DIM forces DRV output low, turning off the external MOSFET. When the logic level at DIM is more than 2.8V, the MOSFET turns on. With the MOSFET being on, the freewheeling diode-- D_1 cuts off, VDD began to power supply the inductor L_1, the high current ripples to the peak value linearly in the loop of VDD- R_1-LEDs- L_1-MOSFET-GND.When the MOSFET is off, D1 turns on, providing a continuous path for the inductor current, then the high current circulates through R_1-LEDs- L_1- D_1. Its value ripples down for the peak value. The dedicated PWM input DIM enables a wide range of pulsed dimming which is available for the need of the brightness variety for high-power LED stage light.

4 System software design

Software design of the system includes the program design of wireless transmission unit and program design of wireless reception unit, and DMX512 data package .The design of transmission unit program includes the dimming signal processing and nRF24L01 wireless communication program, the design of reception unit program mainly involves the data receiving, data processing and the output of PWM signal.

4.1 Program design of transmission unit

After the transmitting unit starts, firstly it will complete initialization of the system, including the I/O port initialization and nRF2401 initialization. Then the analog diming voltage is acquired and processed to the data segment meeting DMX512 protocol format. This data segment is transmitted though to reception unit. If the reception unit doesn't receive the data in a certain while, the segment will be sent repeatedly until receive the reply of receiver. Its flow chart is shown in Figure.3.

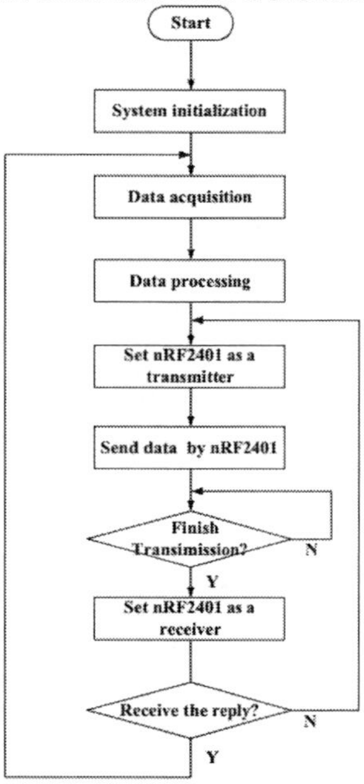

Figure 3. The program flow chart of wireless transmission unit

4.2 Program design of reception unit

After the Reception unit starts, firstly it will complete initialization of the system too. The main function need the reception unit to realize is to use PWM technology to control the brightness of LED stage light after the data information received from the transmitting unit is processed , its flow chart is shown in Figure 4.

4.3 DMX-512 protocol

DMX512 Protocol specified by the Technology Association of America Theater in 1987, it is an entertainment industry standard based on RS485, which is mainly used to control stage lighting. It covers electrical characteristics (based on EIA/TIA–485 standard), data format, data protocol, and connector type. Meanwhile, it is an Asynchronous Serial Digital Data Transmission Standard for controlling lighting equipments and accessories [6].

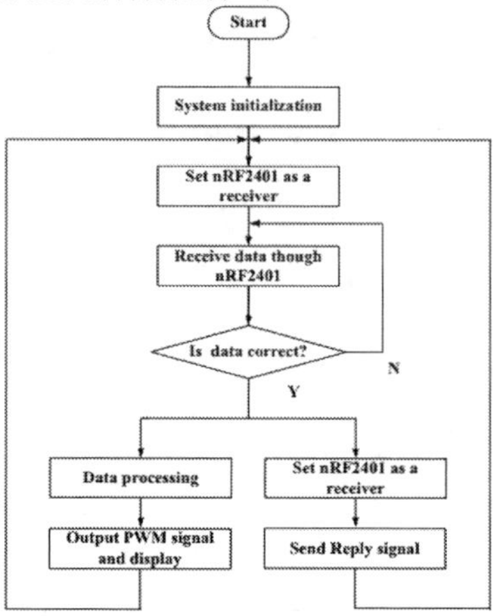

Figure 4. The program flow chart of wireless reception unit

DMX512 controller transmits data package to dim the stage lighting. The data transmitted shall be in asynchronous serial format and must meet the format and the timing of DMX512 protocol. That is fixed at one start bit, eight data bits, two stop bits and no parity. Prior to the first level transmitted, a RESET signal shall be transmitted followed by a NULL START code. Valid dimmer levels shall be to 255 decimal (00 to FF hexadecimal) representing dimmer control input levels of OFF to FULL in a linear relationship. Fig.5 shows the timing diagram of the data package in detail [7].

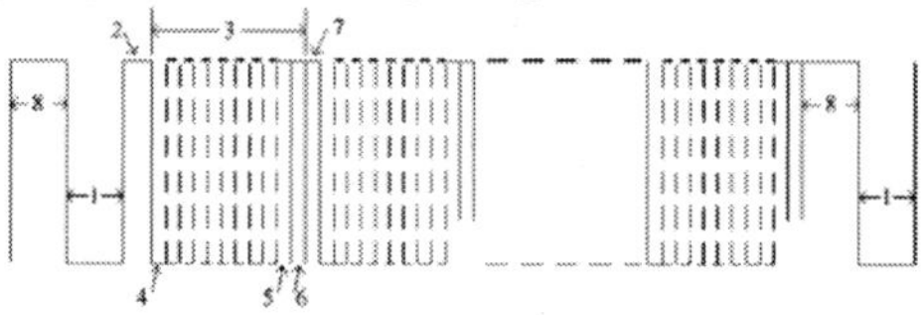

Figure 5. Timing diagram of the data package

5 Experiment and results

After the wireless dimming control system is set up, it could be debugged and the operating results also could be observed, the actual operating results are shown in Fig.6. When the dimming handle slide from turn off to fully open, the dimming signal of Transmission unit alters from 00(H) to FF (H),and the signal of reception unit changes equally.

Output the dimming signal to the constant current driving circuit, the brightness of the LED stage light will vary with the signal. Fig .7 illustrates the dimming effect of the dimming control system for LED stage light.

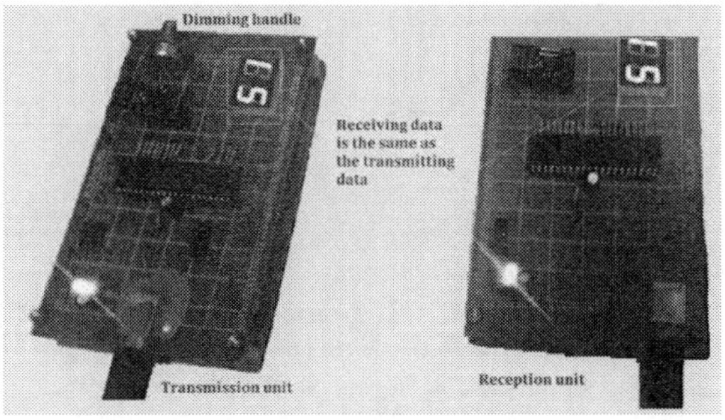

Figure.6 The actual operating results of the wireless dimming system

6 Conclusion

In this paper, we present a wireless dimming control system for LED stage light, which can realizes short distance brightness transformation of LED stage lights through wireless communication module nRF2401. The experiment results show the feasibility and convenience of the proposed wireless LED dimming system for LED stage light.

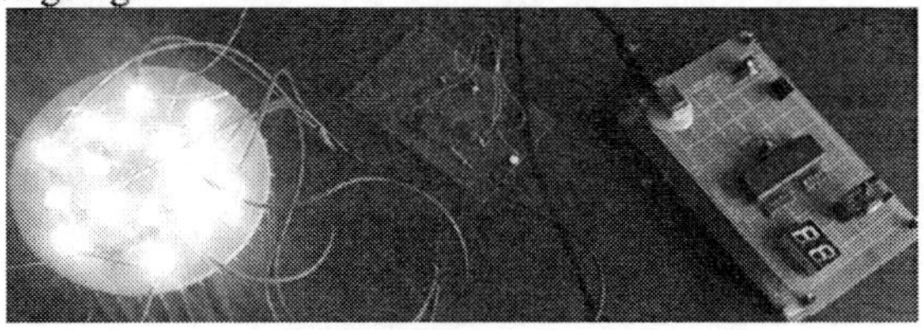

Figure .7 The dimming results of the wireless control system for LED stage light

References

1. Yushan.Cheng, Jinghsiao .Chen, Yihua. Liu,etc, Development of Wireless RGB LED Dimming Control Technology Using Smart phone, International Conference on Intelligent Green Building & Smart Grid, 1-4(2014)
2. Huiqin. Wang, Zhen .Li, Design of Portable LED Stage Lighting Dimming System, ESCA 2015, 158-161(2015)
3. Zhiliang. Chen, Liguo. Tian, Meng Li, LED Toning System Based on NRF24L01 Wireless Control, 24th Chinese Control and Decision Conference, 656-660 (2012)
4. Zhiyun. Shi, Jianping. Gai , Daihua. Wang, New high-speed wireless RF device NRF24L01 and its application,International Electronic Elements, **8**, 42-45(2007)
5. Can. Zhang, Huibin. Qin, Liyang .Qu, LED Dimming System of Wireless Remote Controller, IEEE JOURNAL ON SELECTED AREASIN COMMUNICATIONS, **28**, No. 3, APRIL 2010
6. Wei. Jiang ,Yujian. Jiang, Hui.Ren, Analysis and Prospect of Control System for StageLighting,3rd International Congress on Image and Signal Processing, 3923-3929(2010)
7. E1.11-2004 USITT_DMX521A, 15-20(2004)

MATEC Web of Conferences 44, 02024 (2016)
DOI: 10.1051/matecconf/20164402024

A Somatosensory Interaction System based on Kinect

Xiu Bo Liang[1,a], Chao Wang[1] and Zhen Wang[2]

[1]School of Software Technology, Zhejiang University, Ningbo, China
[2]College of Computer Science and Technology, Zhejiang University, Hangzhou, China

Abstract. The somatosensory interaction technique is one form of the perceptual user interface which is used in video game and virtual reality more and more widly. In this paper, a somatosensory interaction system based on Kinect is presented. Firstly, the user performances his action in front of a kinect, the sensing data from kinect is preprocessed and the main features of the action are extracted. Secondly, the performaced action is recognized by the matching algorithm based on Dynamic Time Warping Hidden Markov Model. Finally, the recognized motion is employed to interact with the virtual human and virtual environment. A series of experiments have been done to test the availablity of our system. Results show that the recognition rate is high enough to be used in virtual reality applications.

1 Introduction

Somatosensory interaction is a kind of technology, referring that the user interacts with the machine through their body movements directly. This technology aims to build a more natural interaction environment, which simulates the user's scene to create a 3D virtual model. At the same time, it combines with the character recognition, gesture recognition technology, to identify the user's actions. The set of processes makes users seem to feel the real sense in the process of the use of somatosensory interaction. In recent years, with the rapid development of information technologies such as image processing and gesture recognition, somatosensory interaction gradually appears in the research and business field, which promotes the development of the somatosensory input devices. In this paper, we employ Kinect as the input device to develop a somatosensory interaction system. With our system, the user can interact with the virtual human by his body motion.

2 Related work

In recent years, new input device (e.g. Kinect) is used to implement the virtual human control interface based on the somatosensory interaction, which makes full use of the human perception ability to express the control intention in a natural way [1, 2]. Action recognition refers to the process that computers cognizing user's motion state by certain means over a period of time. The process of action recognition generally comprises two aspects: firstly extracting the features of motion, and secondly recognizing actions using the extracted motion features. After extraction to motion features, the next job is to identify corresponding actions which contains characteristics of these movements. In order to satisfy the visual rationality, the system can generate the action which conforms to the physical law [3-5]. Sequence of actions can be considered as trajectory in the model parameter space, and each different action category can be grouped into a subset of the model parameter space. Action recognition, is the process to classify the sequence of actions to be identified into a subset of the space. Common action recognition technologies are: action recognition based on template matching, action recognition based on statistics and so on. Action recognition based on template matching often uses the algorithm of dynamic time warping (DTW). Indexing uses lower-bounding functions to prune out the number of times DTW needs to be run for certain tasks such as clustering a set of time series or finding the time series that is most similar to a given time series [6][7].

Action recognition based on statistics usually applies statistical based approach to modelling the action sequence of common probability statistical models, and the common statistical probability models are known as Hidden Markov Model (HMM) [8], etc. HMM have been widely used in many fields, such as speech recognition, activity recognition from video, gene finding, gesture tracking [9]. There are two key reasons. First the models are very rich in mathematical structure and hence can form the theoretical basis for use in a wide range of applications. Second the models, when applied properly, work very well in practice for several important applications.

3 System overview

Kinect is a sensor based on the theory on optics, through the device, we can get a sequence of actions to the system. Kinect somatosensory input device can provide human skeleton data of the 20 joint point, the skeletal data including the space position about the joint points in the coordinate system of the Kinect. Thus, obtaining the skeletal data for a continuous period of time can reflect the movement trajectory of the joints in this time. Action recognition is based on these bone data, through a certain pretreatment process, the action data is normalized. The feature of these trajectories is extracted by using motion matching algorithm. After obtaining the characteristic, we need to match the real time data at first, and then analyse and process the acquired samples to generate the model and template which need to be used in the matching stage. Motion classification modeling is to model the action feature sample in order to provide the following feature matching process. The feature matching recognition

[a] Corresponding author: liangxb@cst.zju.edu.cn

requires the use of Dynamic Time Warping and Hidden Markov Model to identify these characteristics. Finally we get the recognition result which is used to interact with the virtual human.

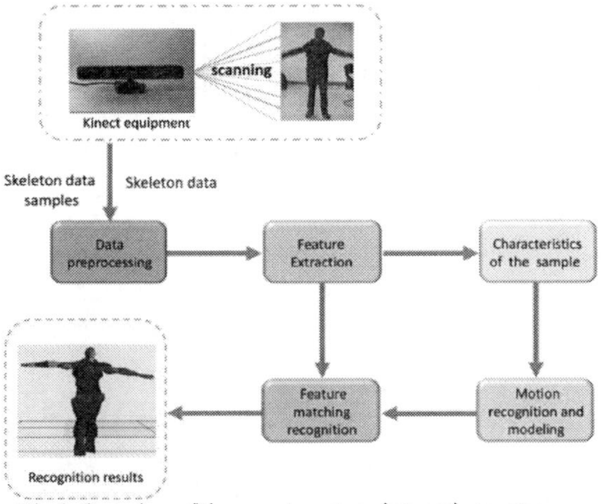

Fig 1. Overview of the somatosensory interaction system.

4 Data pre-processing and feature extraction

4.1 Data pre-processing

Action data is collected in accordance with the number of frames, and therefore we can not guarantee to collect these data at the time of the action started, and stop when the operation is completed. In this situation, we need to pre-process the data to ensure that the action data is correct.

There are two common situations when we collect the motion data: user has not started action in the starting frames of data; users has completed the action before the end of the motion data. The start and end of the action of the motion data is useless, therefore, it can be removed.

After removal of the useless part of motion data, the length of the sequence has changed. In order to ensure the consistency of the input data, it should be interpolated and sampled according to the specified length. By interpolation, we can obtain a continuous curve with all the known points, and the continuous curve is the fitting function of these data points.

4.2 Feature extraction

Feature to be replaced the action sequences. Features include the direction vector of the motion sequences, the distance, the speed of movement and so on. The process of extracting motion feature comprises calculating characteristic values from the original data, then the characteristic value de-noising processing.

4.2.1 Extraction speed feature

The data extracted from the Kinect device is coordinate data about the key points of the spatial position. The data is relative to each person's range of motion, not universal. It cannot represent a sequence of actions accurately. Therefore we need to extract location-independent features from these position sequences to represent this set of actions. Kinect samples data in a fixed time interval (30 frames per second), so the difference between each two frames can represent the speed of this action. That can be considered $v_t = P_{t+1} - P_t$. Applying the above formula, it can be considered to obtain the instantaneous velocity action. The characteristics is not relative with spatial location, so you can use the feature value in the subsequent process.

4.2.2 Extraction direction feature

In order to further simplify the input data, we can consider the motion direction of the corresponding motion from the instantaneous velocity of motion. For a set of coordinate data sequences, from the first data, the vector is calculated by the coordinates of the front and rear two points. We need to define an array of pre-set directions, multiply the vector with the direction of the various directions, take the maximum value, and put the value into the corresponding position of the array. Finally, the new array is added to the feature array. There are also some noise in the direction of the extracted features, the result is not good enough. In order to deal with this situation, we can choose the direction of the characteristic sequence of linear filter. The method is to scan the directional feature sequence, which will be all less than three consecutive equal points, and then replace it with the data in front of these points.

4.2.3 Feature extraction based on principal component analysis

Analysing principal component is a multivariate statistical method for representing the original variable sequence by using the linear transformation to select several major variables.

The process of principal component analysis [10] of data pre-processing is to subtract the mean number from each dimension and then divided by its standard deviation to achieve standardization, that is, set X is the $n \times m$ sample matrix, the result matrix is Y, each line represents a sample, and each column is a dimension of the sample. Set i as the line number, j for the column number. Then the result matrix of each Y is given by the formula (1):

$$Y_{ij} = \frac{X_{ij} - \overline{X}_j}{S_j} \quad (1)$$

Where $\overline{X}_j$ is the mean value of the j dimension, and S_j^2 is the variance of the j dimension. Next, the covariance matrix is solved by the standard matrix, and the covariance matrix method can be given by formula (2):

$$C = \frac{Y^T Y}{(n-1)} \quad (2)$$

After solving the covariance matrix, we can decompose the eigenvalues of c, get the feature vector matrix and orthogonal, then take the dimension of the corresponding dimension of the k eigenvalues, and the new feature vector p which is the projection matrix. In the end, the sample can be obtained by the dimension reduction matrix, which is projected by the projection matrix p.

5 Action recognition

5.1 Action recognition based on DTW

Template matching is a common method in pattern recognition. In the process of template matching, we calculate the similarity of the two sequences. And the similarity is generally measured by the distance between the feature vectors in feature space. Several commonly used distance, Euclidean distance, square and distance, absolute distance, weighted distance, etc.
Two n-dimensional feature vector X_1 and X_2,

$$X_1 = [x_{11}, x_{12}, \dots, x_{1n}]^T, X_2 = [x_{21}, x_{22}, \dots, x_{2n}]^T.$$

The Euclidean distance of the two vectors is defined as:

$$\|X\| = \|X_1 - X_2\| = \sqrt{(x_{11} - x_{21})^2 + (x_{12} - x_{22})^2 + \cdots + (x_{1n} - x_{2n})^2} \quad (3)$$

Square and distance defined as:

$$\|X\|^2 = (x_{11} - x_{21})^2 + (x_{12} - x_{22})^2 + \cdots + (x_{1n} - x_{2n})^2 \quad (4)$$

Absolute value distance is defined as:

$$|X| = |x_{11} - x_{21}| + |x_{12} - x_{22}| + \cdots + |x_{1n} - x_{2n}| \quad (5)$$

Weighted distance is defined as:

$$D = \alpha_1 |x_{11} - x_{21}| + \alpha_2 |x_{12} - x_{22}| + \cdots + \alpha_n |x_{1n} - x_{2n}| \quad (6)$$

Which $\alpha_1, \alpha_2, \dots, \alpha_n$ are the corresponding eigenvalues of the weighted parameters. According to the characteristics of data preprocessing process, we can have the motion rate, directional vector characteristic value and the characteristic value of PCA dimension. When using the speed of motion for identification, the distance between the two motion sequences can be measured by Euclidean distance.

It can't achieve a high recognition rate that comparing and matching the action sequence and template directly. Because even for the same action, on the one hand, in the different time, made by different people, its duration can't often be ensure, on the other hand, with one action of each fragment, everyone duration also tend to be long or short, and the template cannot keep consistent. If the sequence of the template is used to match the template using Euclidean distance directly, it often leads to a low recognition rate. DTW is a nonlinear time alignment algorithm, which will be extended or shortened to a better matching template to calculate the correlation between the two time series. DTW to match the pattern as shown in figure 2.

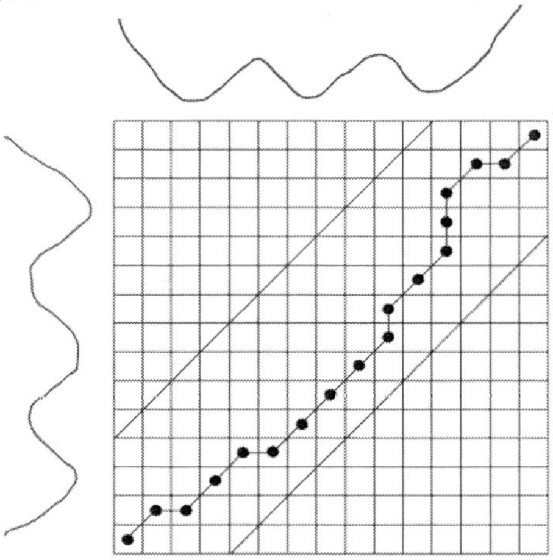

Fig 2. Dynamic time warping to match two sequences

After calculating the similarity between the sequence to be detected and the template using DTM, it can determine whether the sequence belongs to the same category with the test sequence according to the pre-set threshold. So the choice of the template has a great influence on the recognition. If the template cannot reflect all the characteristics of a type of action well, the recognition rate of the action will be reduced. In order to reduce the impact of template selection on the recognition rate, the same category of multiple templates are selected to compare when we decide the category of the test sequence at last, and the nearest neighbour algorithm[10] is introduced to classify the test sequences.

5.2 Action recognition based on HMM

Hidden Markov model is a recognition model used in the filed involved speech signal recognition based on statistics widely. When analysing the time-varying non-stationary sequence, the model can yield good results. As the action sequence is also the time variant signal, so the use of HMM to identify the action sequence, the sample size is large enough, can also achieve a high recognition rate. HMM practical application of the process need to solve the following three issues: [11]: assessment of the problem, decoding and learning problems. Forward-backward algorithm can calculate the probability of a given observation sequence in a particular model. So it can be used to solve the problem of HMM's assessment. By dynamic programming, the Viterbi algorithm can be used to determine the global optimal path, which can be used to solve the decoding problem. HMM model parameters selection and optimization problems are usually solved by Baum-Welch algorithm, Baum-Welch

algorithm is an iterative algorithm, the initial parameters of the model are given by the user, the algorithm through continuous iteration, these parameters will gradually tend to be more reasonable value.

6 Experimental Results

In order to verify the validity of the system, we carried out some experiments. The process of action matching is to classify the motion data calling the action matching module. First, the real-time motion data is pre-processed to obtain the feature vector. Then the feature vector is used as the input to classify the action matching module. The final action matching module will give the classification results. In the experiment, we draw the digital 1-9 as a test case using the right hand gesture, and test the dynamic time warping and the action matching module of Hidden Markov model. Test case of the action form, as shown in figure 3.

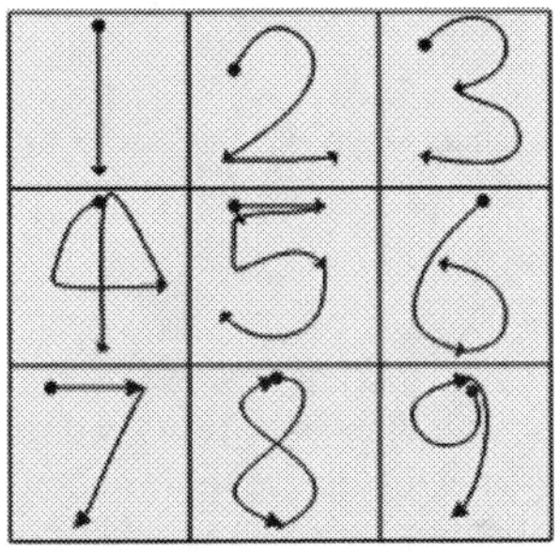

Fig 3. Test action pattern.

The test operation is carried by the user waving the right hand in the space, and the trajectory is shown in Figure 4. The solid points represent the position of the action at the beginning of the movement, and the movement of the arrow and line represents the trajectory of the movement. Each of the 20 sets of tests are used for testing. HMM and DTW were used to identify these tests, and the results are shown in figure 4:

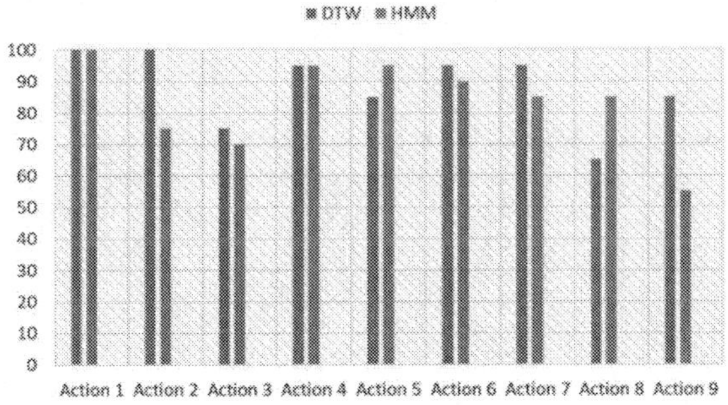

Fig 4. The test results.

Using cross validation test method, all the collected data samples are divided into test set and training set, the test set contains 20 samples, the training set contains 80 samples. From the results, we know whether the use of HMM for recognition or the use of DTW recognition, most of the action can achieve more than 75% of the recognition rate. If there are some context constraints, such as the type of action that may appear in a restricted scene, increase the morphological differences between the actions, or restrict the action of the front and back, you can also continue to improve the recognition rate of these gestures.

7 Conclusion

In this paper, we develop a somatosensory interaction system using Kinect. The captured motion should be pre-processed and feature-extracted before using for recognition. DTW and HMM are selected as the motion matching algorithm. Experimental results show that the recognition rate is high enough to be used in virtual reality applications. However, the system still exists several problems. The way of interaction is simple and rough, and it does not present an exclusive interface of somatosensory interaction well. In the feature, we will try to overcome these shortcomings.

Acknowledgement:
This work was partly supported by Ningbo Natural Science Foundation (Grant no: 2013A610064) and intelligence industry talent base of Ningbo.

References:

1. A. SHIRATORI T, HODGINS J K. Accelerometer-based user interfaces for the control of a physically simulated character [J]. ACM Transactions on Graphics, 2008, 27(5): 1-9.
2. H. SHUM, E. HO, Y. JIANG, et al. Real-time posture reconstruction for Microsoft Kinect[J]. IEEE Transactions on Cybernetics, 2013, 43(5): 1357–1369.
3. Luigi T.De Luca, *Propulsion physics* (EDP Sciences, Les Ulis, 2009) .
4. W. ZHAO, J. ZHANG, J. MIN, et al. Robust realtime physics-based motion control for human grasping[J]. ACM Transactions on Graphics, 2013, 32(6): 1–12.
5. F. HAHN, S. MARTIN, B. THOMASZEWSKI, et al. Rig-space physics [J]. ACM Transactions on Graphics, 2012, 31(4): 1–8.
6. P. HÄMÄLÄINEN, S. ERIKSSON, E. TANSKANEN et al. Online Motion Synthesis Using Sequential Monte Carlo [J]. ACM Transactions on Graphics, 2014, 33(4).
7. E. Keogh, Exact Indexing of Dynamic Time Warping. In VLDB, pp. 406-417. Hong Kong, China, 2002.
8. S. Kim, S. Park & W. Chu. An Index-based Approach for Similarity Search Supporting Time Warping in Large Sequence Databases. In Proc. 17th Intl. Conf. on Data Engineering, pp. 607-614. Heidelberg, Germany, 2001.
9. Elliott R J, L. Aggoun,Moore J B.Hidden Markov Models[M].Springer,1995.
10. T. Cover, P. Hart, Nearest neighbor pattern classification[J]. Information Theory, IEEE Transactions on,1967,13(1):21-27.
11. I. Jolliffe, Principal component analysis[M].John Wiley & Sons, Ltd,2005

MATEC Web of Conferences 44, 02025 (2016)
DOI: 10.1051/matecconf/20164402025

Double evolutional artificial bee colony algorithm for multiple traveling salesman problem

Ming Hao Xue[1], Tie Zhu Wang[2] and Sheng Mao[3]

[1] *Materiel Management & Safety Engineering College, Air Force Engineering University,* Xi'an 710043, *China*
[2] *Information Management Centre, Air Force Engineering University,* Xi'an 710043, *China*
[3] *Aeronautics and Astronautics Engineering College, Air Force Engineering University,* Xi'an 710043, *China*

Abstract: The double evolutional artificial bee colony algorithm (DEABC) is proposed for solving the single depot multiple traveling salesman problem (MTSP). The proposed DEABC algorithm, which takes advantage of the strength of the upgraded operators, is characterized by its guidance in exploitation search and diversity in exploration search. The double evolutional process for exploitation search is composed of two phases of half stochastic optimal search, and the diversity generating operator for exploration search is used for solutions which cannot be improved after limited times. The computational results demonstrated the superiority of our algorithm over previous state-of-the-art methods.

Key words: double evolutional artificial bee colony algorithm; optimization; multiple travelling salesman problem

1 Introduction

The multiple travelling salesman problem (MTSP) is a generalization of traveling salesman problem (TSP), which is a well-known NP-hard problem [1]. A new variation of artificial bee colony (ABC) algorithm, called double evolutional artificial bee colony (DEABC) algorithm is presented by taking advantage of the strength of different operations to improve the exploitation search ability and increase the convergence speed when solving MTSP. The current local search operators are characterized by different variation they can cause to the original solution, but a single operation has actually been wasted most of the time, because the process can neither create a better solution nor generate the best solution it can possibly search.

Evolutionary algorithms (EAs) and Swarm Intelligence (SI) based algorithms are two major branches of population-based optimization algorithms [2]. The ABC algorithm is one of most recently population-based methods [3] which imitates the intelligent behaviour of honey bee swarm for seeking nectar. The robust search process consists of exploration search and exploitation search, the former aims at finding promising new solutions, and the latter is to find the optimum in the neighbourhood of a good solution [4]. However, ABC is good at exploration but poor at exploitation and its convergence speed is also an issue in some cases [5,6]. Moreover, literature addressing ABC algorithm and MTSP is quite rare.

The ABC algorithm is a simulation of the swarm intelligence of honey bees for searching nectar. The artificial bee colony includes three kinds of artificial bees: employed bees, onlooker bees and scout bees. Each kind of bees corresponds to a phase in this algorithm.

After initialization, each employed bee is associated to a known food source. In employed bee phase, each employed bee performs searching in the neighborhood of its current food source, and the better ones are reserved according to fitness. In onlooker bee phase, onlooker bees first follow employed bees proportionally to the probability value, which is determined by the fitness of the food source; and then seeking a solution in the neighborhood of the food source found by the followed employed bee; finally, a better food source is reserved. In the scout bee phase, a scout bee searches a food source without the help of colony's memory.

In general, the number of employed bees and onlooker bees are equal to half of the colony size. An employed bee becomes a scout bee when its food source is abandoned; the abandonment happens when the food source cannot be improved after limited times of searching (the food source has been fully exploited).

In ABC algorithm each food source represents a possible solution for the problem and the fitness value of the solution corresponds to the nectar amount of this food source. Basic steps of the ABC algorithm are given below:

1. Initialization: randomly generate a set of solutions; a solution represents a currently known food source, and each employed bee is assigned to a food source.

2. Calculate and memorize the fitness of each food source:

[1] Corresponding author: qweilm@163.com

Article available at http://www.matec-conferences.org or http://dx.doi.org/10.1051/matecconf/20164402025

$$fitness_i = \begin{cases} \frac{1}{fit_i}, fit_i \geqslant 0 \\ 1 + abs(fit_i), fit_i < 0 \end{cases} \quad (1)$$

where fit_i is the cost value (value of objective function),

3. For each employed bee:

a. Perform local search in the neighborhood of her assigned food source

b. Calculate the fitness of the detected food source

c. Memorize the better food source

4. For each onlooker bee:

a. Choose a food source from the current found ones depending on the roulette wheel using the probability p_i, which is calculated as follows:

$$p_i = \frac{fitness_i}{\sum_{j=1}^{SN} fitness_i} \quad (2)$$

where SN is the number of solutions

b. Repeat the searching process in step 3

5. If a food source hasn't been improved after limited times, the corresponding employed bee becomes a scout bee and randomly generate a solution.

6. Repeat the step 3-6 until the maximum cycle times are completed

7. Output the optimal result.

2 Improvements for local search operators

The operators can be upgraded for two objectives: one is to obtain guidance by optimal searching mechanism; the other is to obtain greater diversity by expanding searching space. The former has an advantage over exploitation search and convergence speed, the latter can be used to further improve exploration search.

2.1 Half-stochastic optimal searching operators

Using the operators which are inspired by [7] for local search, the operations can be actually wasted most of the time, because a single searching process can neither create a better solution nor generate the best solution it can possibly search. For the first objective, we propose a new searching method, which aims to find the optimal solution in the searching space of an operator.

Taking the swap points operation as an example, the optimal searching strategy is to calculate the fitness for all possible swaps, finally swap the position of a pair of cities with the optimal fitness. However, the searching space of swap points is C_n^2, the convergence speed would be greatly compromised if we want to obtain the optimal solution.

After comprehensively considering the value of coefficient α, optimal searching space and convergence speed, an approach called half-stochastic optimal searching is proposed, and only three initial operators are qualified to be modified, they are swap points, insert point and reverse subsequence.

The procedures for half-stochastic optimal swap points (insert point or reverse subsequence) operator are as follows:

1.Generate a positive integer r randomly, the city in position r acts as a swap point (insert point or an edge of a subsequence), the value of r can't exceed n.

2.Calculate the fitness for generated solutions of all possible swaps of points (all insert positions or all subsequences can be reversed).

3.Reserve the optimal solution.

Different values of α can affect their local search ability, but they are the ones can be realized by the idea of half-stochastic optimal searching.

Obviously, the searching range can not only be the whole sequence, but also one or several tours, which is suitable to be modified for different optimizing objectives.

2.2 The diversity generating operators

The second upgrading objective takes advantage of operators with bigger value of α, which can generate new solutions with greater diversity. The α value of swap points, swap subsequences and swap-reverse subsequences are all 4, and they can all be suitable for this generating diversity.

The operation of swap can be put into two categories: one is the operated points (sequences) are within the same tour, another are located in different tours. They are named after inner-tour swap and cross-tour swap respectively. We set the times to perform the two kinds of swap operations in linear correlation with m (the number of salesman); so the need for more diversified solutions can be met when m varies.

The procedures for diversity generating operator are as follows:

1.Generate a positive integer $r1$ randomly, where the value of $r1$ can't exceed $m-1$(m is the number of salesman); define $r2=m-r1$.

2.Perform $r1$ times of inner-tour swap operations; the tour is chosen randomly each time

3.Perform $r2$ times of cross-tour swap operations; the two tours and the cities are chosen randomly each time

This sort of operators can be effective when a solution doesn't improve after certain times of iteration (a food source is fully exploited).

3 Double evolutional artificial bee colony algorithm

This section proposes a double evolutional artificial bee colony algorithm (DEABC) for solving the single depot multiple traveling salesman problem (MTSP).

3.1 Initialization

Firstly, we send all bees to find food sources, then the 50% bees finding the better solutions become employed bees; the rest become onlooker bees and return to the hive. Food sources are evaluated by their fitness. The number

of employed bees and onlooker bees are the same, both equal to the half of the colony size.

The process to find food sources generally consists of two procedures: firstly, randomly generate a permutation of n cities; secondly, randomly divide the sequence into m tours. The m is the number of salesman, and at least one city is supposed to be included in a tour.

3.2 Fitness

We adopt the function (1) to calculate fitness, and the cost function used is the same as the objective function. Since the two classic test objectives are minimizing the total distance (objective 1) and minimizing the longest tour (objective 2), we have two different cost functions. We need to maximize the fitness in both cases.

3.3 Selection

After the employed bee phase, the onlooker bees choose the food sources found by the employed bees based on probability p_i expressed as follows:

$$p_i = \frac{fitness_i}{\sum_{j=1}^{SN} fitness_j} \quad (3)$$

Where $fitness_i$ is the fitness of the food source i.

3.4 The double evolutional process

The key to this algorithm is the double evolutional process, which is specially designed for exploitation search. The exploitation search is performed in both employed bee phase and onlooker bee phase, and two evolutional approaches are proposed to enhance the search ability. For both objectives, the insert point operator and reverse subsequence operator are adopted and modified to constitute the process. The double evolutional procedures are as follows:

1.Conduct the half-stochastic optimal reverse subsequence operator for the whole sequence

2.Calculate the fitness of the generated solution and reserve the better one

3.Conduct the half-stochastic optimal insert point operator for the whole sequence generated in step 2.

4.Calculate the fitness of the generated solution and reserve the better one

The procedures of the operators can be referred to in section 2.1. The half-stochastic optimal reverse subsequence operator has the minimum α value, which has an edge over convergence, calculation and selection; it also has minimum searching space, which further increases the convergence speed. The α value of half-stochastic optimal insert operator is medium, but its searching space is minimum, which enhances the exploitation searching ability in a greater range.

This process is fit for both objectives, because the results of double evolutional process turn out to be fitness-oriented.

3.5 The exploration search

If a food source hasn't been updated after certain times (limit) of exploitation search, it will be abandoned and replaced by a new solution. The new solution is found around the abandoned solution and implemented by the diversity generating operator described in 2.2.

For objective 1, the swap subsequence operation is applied to generate a new solution; for objective 2, we choose a city randomly from a tour other than the longest tour and swap it with the city in longest tour which obtains the minimizing longest tour. For both objectives, we reserve the current optimal solution in case it is abandoned.

The number of scout bee in an iteration is set as 1, and the number of swap operation in an exploration search is set as 1. The reason for not increase the number of them is the same results can be obtained by decreasing the value of limit.

The framework of DEABC is illustrated in figure 1.

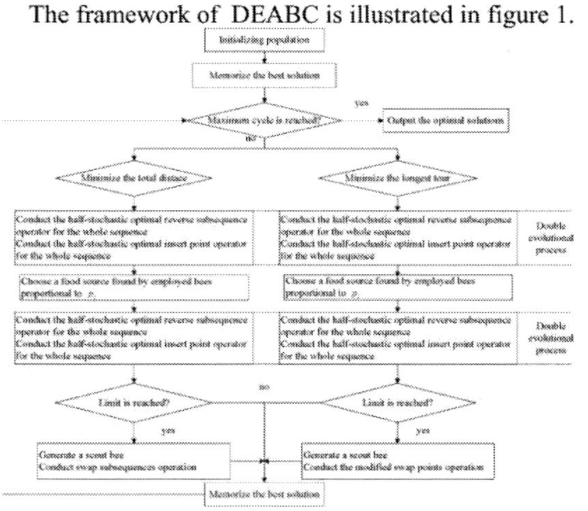

Figure.1 The framework of DEABC

4 Computational results

To evaluate the performance of DEABC, test problems in [8] is used to compare the computational results. The data are Euclidean, two dimensional symmetric problems, and the first city is always used as depot. The experimental instances with different problem size and salesmen combinations are listed in table 1. For the problem, the two objectives are optimized separately.

The results of previous algorithms are also shown for comparison. The genetic algorithm with one chromosome representation and the genetic algorithm with two chromosomes used in [8]; the two-part chromosome representation based on genetic algorithm proposed in [8] is referred to as GA2PC, the steady state grouping genetic algorithm proposed in [9] is referred to as GGA-SS; the ant colony algorithm proposed in [10] is referred to as ACO.

Table.1 Benchmark instances

Name	Cities (n)	Salesmen (m)	Origin
MTSP-1-51	51	3,5,10	[8]

MTSP-1-100	100	3,5,10,20	[8]
MTSP-1-150	150	3,5,10,20,30	[8]

The values of parameters are shown in the table 2, which are chosen empirically.

Table.2 Parameter settings in DEABC

parameters	value
Colony size	100
Maximum cycle number	1000
Limit	5
Number of employed bees	50
Number of onlooker bees	50
Number of scout bees	1

4.1 Comparison of proposed operators

First of all, a test problem is chosen for several operators proposed in this paper to compare their performance. The improved operators can be put to two categories--half stochastic optimal searching and generating diversity, we run this test because no theoretically prove has been given to determine their capabilities.

The test problem is to reveal the abilities of different operators, and prove the rationality of the design of the double evolutional process for minimizing total distance. The double evolutional process for minimizing longest tour is the same, and the exploration search for it is especially designed, so we only run test for the first objective.

We chose the MTSP-1-51 as test data, and the number of salesman is set as 3, 30 independent runs are tested for each different combination. The results are shown in table 3, where "1" represents the half-stochastic optimal swap points operator, "2" means the half-stochastic insert point operator, "3" represents the half-stochastic reverse subsequence operator, and the short line connecting different numbers means the combination of the operators; S.D. stands for standard deviation of objective values of 30 runs, time is the average time cost in seconds for each run. Considering the scale of test data, the diversity generating operators only conduct swap operation for one time in each scout bee phase.

Table.3 Experimental results of different operators

operator		1	2	3	1-2	1-3	2-3	1-2-3
Swap points	Max	580	556	471	511	466	454	454
	Min	517	468	446	452	447	446	446
	Mean	548	514	457	478	456	450	450
	S.D.	17	23	6	14	5	2	2
	Time	2.07	2.30	2.63	4.03	4.40	4.67	6.51
Swap subse-quence	Max	613	573	474	493	462	453	454
	Min	510	456	452	449	448	446	446
	Mean	545	517	459	471	454	450	450
	S.D.	20	23	5	10	4	2	2
	Time (s)	2.12	2.37	2.71	4.07	4.50	4.67	6.40
Swap-reverse	Max	580	532	465	494	458	454	454
	Min	504	463	447	452	447	446	446
	Mean	534	495	458	471	454	449	450
	S.D.	21	21	5	12	3	2	2
	Time	2.07	2.33	2.67	4.07	4.40	4.67	6.43

As can be concluded from table 3, for half-stochastic optimal searching operators, the reverse operator works best, while the swap operator is the worst; when combining the half-stochastic optimal insert and reverse operators, the results are the best; when combining all the operators, the results aren't been improved, but the time cost is the most. Based on the fact that the half-stochastic optimal reverse and insert operators can be fully capable of obtaining ideal results, the double evolutional process for minimizing total distance are designed to be the combination of the two operators.

For diversity generating operators, the swap subsequence operator works best with the double evolutional process, thus been chosen as the operator to perform exploration search.

4.2 Comparison of approaches on test problems in [8]

Table 4 and 5 compare the performance of DEABC with GA1C, GA2C, GA2PC, GGA-SS, ACO and TCX of average solution quality for objective 1 and objective2 on test problems used in [8]. The results of GA1C, GA2C, GA2PC are taken from [8], the results of GGA-SS, ACO and TCX are taken from [9], [10]. The S.D. is short for standard deviation of objective values.

As can be seen from table 4, the DEABC can obtain the best results for test problems1-7and 9-12, but it doesn't outperform ACO and GGA-SS on the 8th test problem.

For minimizing the longest tour, the superiority of DEABC is not as obvious as that of objective 1. Basically, it works well on small scale test data or the test data with more salesmen. When the number of city is relative big and the number of salesmen is relatively few, the results cannot outperform ACO and GGA-SS.

Table.4 Results for optimizing the total distance on test problems from [8]

Instances			GA1C	GA2C	GA2PC	GGA-SS	ACO	DEABC		
	n	m						Mean	S.D.	Best
1	51	3	529	570	543	449	448	450	2	446
2	51	5	564	627	586	479	478	477	3	471
3	51	10	801	879	723	584	584	584	3	579
4	100	3	27036	30972	26653	22051	22619	22979	530	21878
5	100	5	29753	44062	30408	23678	24166	24433	454	23666
6	100	10	36890	65116	31227	28488	27890	28110	565	27375
7	100	20	62471	95568	54700	40892	39949	39304	400	38377
8	150	3	46111	48108	47418	38434	39247	39900	344	39283
9	150	5	49443	51101	49947	39962	40647	40643	430	40032
10	150	10	59341	64893	54958	44274	44436	44213	420	43464
11	150	20	94291	100037	73934	56412	55980	55605	545	54617
12	150	30	131503	143476	99547	72783	71266	70824	497	69433

Table.5 Results for minimizing the longest tour on test problems from [8]

Instances			GA1C	GA2C	GA2PC	GGA-SS	ACO	DEABC		
	n	m						Mean	S.D.	Best
1	51	3	234	275	203	161	160	168	5	160
2	51	5	173	220	164	119	118	125	3	119
3	51	10	140	165	123	112	108	112	0	112
4	100	3	14722	16229	13556	8542	8817	9337	412	8755
5	100	5	11193	11606	10589	6852	6964	7561	397	7056
6	100	10	9960	10200	9463	6370	6363	6482	62	6363
7	100	20	9235	9470	8388	6359	6356	6358	0	6358
8	15	3	19875	21067	19687	1326	1388	1490	786	1372

	0					8	5	5		2
9	15	5	15229	15450	14748	8660	9270	1020	508	9553
	0							3		
1	15	1	12154	12382	11158	5875	6132	6721	229	6232
0	0	0								
1	15	2	10206	10338	10044	5252	5250	5387	94	5246
1	0	0								
1	15	3	9626	9683	8775	5247	5246	5246	0	5246
2	0	0								

5 Conclusions

This paper proposed a double evolutional artificial bee colony algorithm for solving the MTSP. The operators are then modified as half-stochastic optimal searching operators and diversity generating operators, which lay the foundation for the double evolutional process and the exploration search. Further improvements are made to the operators for different optimizing objectives. The computational results showed the competitiveness of DEABC for other algorithms.

The future work can be focused on three aspects. The first is to improve the searching ability over large scale test data. DEABC cannot outperform ACO and GGA-SS over a few test problems, so we wish to improve the algorithm by dividing the large scale test data into several relatively groups, then establish a communication mechanism to obtain better results. The second is to develop the special operators for minimizing the longest tour of all salesmen. The third is to extend the DEABC to solve MTSP with multiple depots, because the situation with multiple depots can be applied to a wider range of practical situations.

References

[1] Gorenstein S. Printing press scheduling for multi-edition periodicals. Management Science 1970;16(6):B373-83.

[2] Szeto,W., Wu,Y., &Ho,S.C.(2011). An artificial bee colony algorithm for the capacitated vehicle routing problem. European Journal of Operational Research,215(1),126-135.

[3] D. Karaboga, B. Akay. A comparative study of Artificial Bee Colony algorithm. Appl. Math. Comput.214 (2009) 108-132.

[4] Karaboga, D. (2005). An idea based on honey bee swarm for numerical optimization. Technical report-tr06, Erciyes university, engineering faculty, computer engineering department.

[5] B.Akay, D.Karaboga, A modified Artificial Bee Colony (ABC) algorithm for real-parameter optimization, Inf. Sci 192 (2012) 120-142.

[6] W. Xiang, M. An. An efficient and robust Artificial Bee Colony algorithm for numerical optimization. Comput. Oper. Res. 40 (2013) 1256-1265.

[7] S. Biswas, S. Das, S. Debchoudhury, S. Kundu, Co-evolving bee colonies by forager migration: A multi-swarm based Artificial Bee Colony algorithm for global search space, Appl. Math. Comput. 232 (2014) 216-234.

[8] A. E. Carter, C. T. Ragsdale, A new approach to solving the multiple traveling salesperson problem using genetic algorithms, Eur. J. Oper. Res. 175 (2006)245-257.

[9] A.Singh,A.S. Baghel, A new grouping genetic algorithm approach to the multiple traveling salesperson problem, Soft Comput. 13 (2009)95-101.

[10] W. Liu, S. Li, F. Zhao, A. Zheng, An ant colony optimization algorithm for the multiple traveling salesmen problem, in: 4th IEEE Industrial Conference on Industrial Electronics and Applications (ICIEA 2009), IEEE, 2009, pp. 1533–1537.

MATEC Web of Conferences 44, 02026 (2016)
DOI: 10.1051/matecconf/20164402026

Study on disruption management scheduling problem of flow shop under supply chain environment

Hong Guang Bo [1], Long Long Li[1], Yu Liu[2,3], Jia Heng Wang[1]
[1]Institute of Production Operation and Logistics Management, Dalian University of Technology, Dalian 116023, China
[2]CSR Qingdao Sifang Co., Ltd. Qingdao 266111, China
[3]Crrc Central Research Institute Qingdao 266111, China

Abstract. This paper presents a disruption scheduling model for an environment of proportional two-machine no-wait flow shop. To achieve the objects of minimization of weighted sum of makespan and minimization of weighted sum of tardiness, we introduce a revised PSO algorithm which is designed with a neighborhood search structure. According to the experiment, the effectivity of the method proposed is proven.

1 Introduction

In reality, unexpected events are often inevitable to cause disruption to flow shop system. They lead to failure of system control. Therefore, we need to carry out a scheduling recovery plan to minimize the lost.

Scheduling recovery problem is practically useful in production and processing. Many of them are proven NP-hard problems [1] and the problem in this research is one of them. There are abundant researches about the global static scheduling and periodic rolling scheduling [2]. However, random disruption is more common in production and processing practical environment. In disruption management problem, we should pay more attention to the combination of the initial scheduling objective and the new scheduling plan instead of global optimization. Lee [3] proposes two methods for unfinished jobs: one is to arrange them to other machines with extra cost and another is to wait till the recovery. Liou[4] have studied the disruption management problem in a single machine. Bo [5] establishes the scheduling model based on SPT rule.

This paper studies the disruption management recovery problem in the environment of proportional two-machine no-wait flow shop. We propose a disruption management model pred-mgt, and solve it with the HDPSO algorithm. A case study has been done to testify our research.

2 Problem description

In this research, we assume that that in the supply chain, there is a supplier known as M1 and a manufacturer known as M2. A job is processed only once at either M1 or M2, and it must be processed continuously in the supply chain. M1 or M2 can process only one job at a time, and a job's process time at M1 is proportional to that at M2. The process time of any job at M2 is longer than that at M1. The job being disrupted has to be reprocessed from the start of the supply chain. The processing environment can be named as proportional two-machine no-wait flow shop environment. The following notations are used : $J=\{1,2,\ldots,j,\ldots n\}$ ($n>1$) means job set to be processed, $W=\{\omega_1,\omega_2,\ldots,\omega_j,\ldots\omega_n\}$ ($n>1$) means job weight of priority $M=\{M_1,M_2\}$ supply chain member set, v_i means the speed of the jobs processed at M_i, p_{ij} means process time of job j at M_i, s_{ij} means start time of job j at M_i, C_{ij} means finish time of job j at M_i, C_j means finish time of job j at the whole supply chain(i.e. C_{2j}), π means feasible process schedule, $\prod$ means the set of feasible process schedule.

2.1 The initial scheduling scheme

The objective of the initial scheduling scheme is the minimization of weighted sum of makespan, which is shown as $\sum_{j=1}^{n}\omega_j C_j$. It has been proven that with the *WSPT* rule, the objective can be accomplished. Therefore, the initial scheduling can be described as $F|nwt|F(\pi)$, in which the best process schedule is $\bar{\pi}$, and the objective value is $F(\bar{\pi})=\sum_{j=1}^{n}\omega_j C_j$.

2.2 Disruption

In reality, unexpected events may cause disruption in supply chain. Some of them like power outages can impact all the members of the supply chain. Under this

Li Longlong: Lee_dlut@163.com

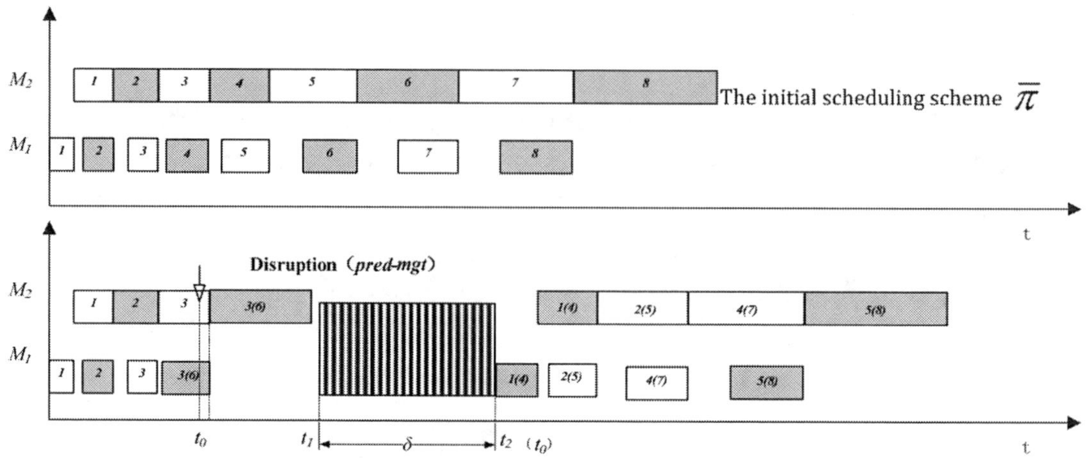

Figure.1. Disruption schematic diagram in supply chain

circumstance, in this research, the best process schedule $\overline{\pi}$ for the initial scheduling scheme will be not the best even infeasible. Hence, we need to reschedule the remaining jobs $J'=\{1,2,\cdots,j,\cdots,n'\}$ ($1\le n'\le n$).

In figure 1, the first half shows the initial scheduling scheme $\overline{\pi}$, while the second half shows the disruption management strategy with the interference of disruption. The disruption $\Delta M\,|\,[t_1,t_2]$ (briefly notated as ΔM) occurs during $t_1\sim t_2$, and the duration is notated as $\delta=t_2-t_1$. The start time after the disruption is set as t_0. We can see that job 4 and the jobs after are divided into two parts, one is processed before the disruption while the other after. Obviously, the condition $t_1>min\{t_0+p_{1j}+p_{2j}\,|\,j\in J'\}$ should be met, so that certain job or jobs can be scheduled in the window between job 3 and the disruption. The remaining jobs defined as a job set J' are renumbered from 1 to n' according to the *WSPT* rule.

In this situation, two objectives are taken consideration. One is the initial objective, the minimization of weighted sum of makespan $F_I(\pi')=\sum_{j=1}^{n}\omega_j C_j$, and the other is the recovery objective, the minimization of weighted sum of tardiness $F_{II}(\pi')=\sum_{j=1}^{n'}\omega_j T_j$.

In summary, the scheduling problem with disruption can be shown as following with three-parametric method:

$$F_2\left|nwt-sc,uni-dif,\Delta M,prep-mgt\right|F_I(\pi'),F_{II}(\pi')$$

3 Modeling and solution

3.1. Problem Model

The remaining jobs influenced by the disruption should be divided into two parts. Therefore, we define J^{t_1} and J^{t_2} as job set of jobs which are processed before t_1 and after t_2 respectively. Obviously we know $J^{t_1}\in J', J^{t_2}\in J'$. We define $C_j^{t_1}$ and $C_j^{t_2}$ as completion time of job j if it's scheduled before t_1 or after t_2. As a result, the problem is translated into a problem aiming to allocate job j before t_1 or after t_2. The problem's disruption management model $pred\text{-}mgt$ is presented below:

$$pred-mgt:\ \min_{i\in\{1,2\},j\in J'}\{F_I(\pi')=\sum\nolimits_{j=1}^{n}\omega_j C_j, F_{II}(\pi')=\sum\nolimits_{j=1}^{n'}\omega_j T_j\}$$

$$s.t.\quad C_j=C_j^{t_1}\cdot x_j+C_j^{t_2}\cdot(1-x_j),\quad C_j^{t_1}\le t_1$$

$$s_{2j}\ge C_{1(j-1)}+p_{1j},\quad \forall j\ge 2$$

$$C_{ij}=s_{ij}+p_{ij}$$

$$(s_{ij_1}\ge C_{ij_2})\vee(s_{ij_2}\ge C_{ij_1})$$

$$p_{1(j-1)}\le p_{1j},\quad \forall j\ge 2,\quad j\in J^{t_1}\ or\ j\in J^{t_2}$$

$$p_{1x}/p_{2x}=p_{1y}/p_{2y}, p_{1x}\le p_{2y}, \forall x,y\in N'$$

$$x_j=\begin{cases}1 & j\in J^{t_1}\\ 0 & j\in J^{t_2}\end{cases},\quad j=1,2,\cdots,n'$$

3.2 A solution based on HDPSO algorithm

In this research, we propose the Hybrid Discrete Particle Swarm Optimization (HDPSO) algorithm to solve the $pred\text{-}mgt$ model. The basic thought of the HDPSO algorithm is described as follow:

Initialization: The position of every particle in the population is represented by a n'-dimensional vector $X_i^{(R)}=[x'_{i,1},x'_{i,2},\cdots,x'_{i,n'}]$. $x'_{i,k}$ ($k\in\{1,2,\cdots,n'\}$) is

randomly initialized with an even-distributed random number in (0,1).

Particle evolution: The update formula of particle position consists of $\overline{P}_i(t)$ (pbest), $\overline{P}_g(t)$ (gbest) and f_N (neighborhood search strategy). The particle evolution strategy is designed as follow:

$$X_i(t+1)=f_N\left(\overline{M}_{best}\oplus\left(f_C\left(c_{p3}\otimes\left(f_M\left(c_{p1}\otimes\overline{P}_i(t)\right),f_M\left(c_{p2}\otimes\overline{P}_g(t)\right)\right)\right)\right)\right)$$

In the evolution strategy:

① $f_M\left(c_{p1}\otimes\overline{P}_i(t)\right)$ means that $\overline{P}_i(t)$ mutates with a probability of $0\le c_{p1}\le 0.5$: A random number *rand* is generated at first, and if $rand<c_{p1}$, we choose two random elements of $\overline{P}_i(t)$ and swap them with each other, otherwise, the position of particle remains unchanged $f_M\left(c_{p1}\otimes\overline{P}_i(t)\right)=\overline{P}_i(t)$.

② $f_M\left(c_{p2}\otimes\overline{P}_g(t)\right)$ means that $\overline{P}_g(t)$ mutates with a probability of $0\le c_{p2}\le 0.5$: A random number *rand* is generated at first, and if $rand<c_{p2}$, we choose two random elements of $\overline{P}_g(t)$ and swap them with each other, otherwise, the position of particle remains unchanged $f_M\left(c_{p2}\otimes\overline{P}_g(t)\right)=\overline{P}_g(t)$.

③ $f_C\left(c_{p3}\otimes\left(f_M\left(c_{p1}\otimes\overline{P}_i(t)\right),f_M\left(c_{p2}\otimes\overline{P}_g(t)\right)\right)\right)$ means that $f_M\left(c_{p1}\otimes\overline{P}_i(t)\right)$ and $f_M\left(c_{p2}\otimes\overline{P}_g(t)\right)$ crossovers with a probability of $0.5\le c_{p3}\le 1.0$: A random number *rand* is generated at first, and if $rand<c_{p3}$, we choose an random interval $[\sigma,\delta]$ ($0<\sigma,\delta\le n$) as the part that they cross with each other, otherwise, the position of particle remains unchanged $f_C\left(c_{p3}\otimes\left(f_M\left(c_{p1}\otimes\overline{P}_i(t)\right),f_M\left(c_{p2}\otimes\overline{P}_g(t)\right)\right)\right)=f_M\left(c_{p1}\otimes\overline{P}_i(t)\right)$

④ f_N means local search to $f_C\left(c_{p3}\otimes\left(f_M\left(c_{p1}\otimes\overline{P}_i(t)\right),f_M\left(c_{p2}\otimes\overline{P}_g(t)\right)\right)\right)$ with a step length of $\overline{M}_{best}$, in which $\overline{M}_{best}=\beta\cdot(1/M)\cdot\sum_{k=1}^{M}d_H\left(X_i(t),\overline{P}_k(t)\right)\cdot ln(1/u)$.

3.3 Neighborhood search design

To make up the weakness of the local search of HDPSO algorithm, we propose the neighborhood search operator.

There are two neighborhood structures in this research, insert and swap.

Insert: Choose a job processed before t_1 and a job processed after t_2 randomly. Insert the latter one into the position of the former one, and the jobs between them all move afterwards for one position.

Swap: Choose a job processed before t_1 and a job processed after t_2 randomly. Swap them with each other.

After the implementation of the two neighbourhood structures, if in the new order, the completion time of jobs before t_1 is less than t_1 and the objective evaluation becomes better, the operation of insert and swap is allowed, otherwise it's prohibited.

4 Algorithm experiment

4.1. Experiment design

In this research, processing speed of M_1 and M_2 is set as $v_2=v_1/5$. The number of initial jobs ready to be processed is 50. Jobs are sorted with the WSPT rule. p_{1j} is set as a random production time array, so p_{2j} is easy to get. The weight of jobs is w set as a random weight array. During the case, six group experiments are carried out. They are differentiated with the different disruption window. For each group, 10 times of experiments are carried out. To demonstrate the usefulness of neighborhood search, we compare the HDPSO algorithm above with the HDPSO1 algorithm (a special HDPSO algorithm without neighborhood search).

The parameters of the algorithm: the number of particles in the population is 40. The probability of particle mutation is $c_{p1}=c_{p2}=0.2$, while the probability of particle crossover is $c_{p3}=0.8$. The algorithm convergence scaling factor is $\beta=1$. The number of iterations in one experiment is 60.

Algorithms are coded and performed with $C\#$ language in *VisualStudio*2012. Running environment is *Inter Core* i3−2120@3.30*GHz* /*4GDDR3*/*Windows*7 64 bit SP1.

4.2. Experiments analysis

In this study, we use six classic indicators to evaluate the performance of the algorithm. They are ONVG, CM, D_{av} and D_{max} , TS, MS and AQ. The experimental data is shown in Table.1.

For ONVG, HDPSO algorithm has more pareto solutions than HDPSO1 algorithm. For CM, the pareto solutions of HDPSO algorithm can dominate that of HDPSO1 algorithm. For D_{av} and D_{max} , HDPSO algorithm is better than HDPSO1 algorithm in terms of average distance and minimum distance. For MS, the coverage of the optimal pareto frontier of HDPSO algorithm is better than that of HDPSO1 algorithm.

Table.1 Algorithms performance indicator comparison

Indicators		(1)ONVG		(2)CM		(3)-1 D_{av}		(3)-2 D_{max}		(4)TS		(5)MS		(6)AQ	
Algorithms		HDPSO	HDPSO1	HDPSO	HDPSO1	HDPSO	HDPSO1	HDPSO	HDPSO1	HDPSO	HDPSO1	HDPSO	HDPSO1	HDPSO	HDPSO1
Experiment1 [300,350]	mean	43.5	5.7	0.9690	0	0.0125	0.0197	0.1026	0.2929	13.7558	13.6945	0.8636	0.2472	17763.4	20104.75
	best	52	7	1	0	0.0042	0.0082	0.051	0.1983	8.0766	3.2353	1.05325	0.5561	17734.15	19811.07
	worst	35	3	0.8333	0	0.0256	0.0267	0.1366	0.5064	19.4817	25.6991	0.6760	0.0619	17797.91	20424.45
Experiment 2 [300,320]	mean	45.7	6.3	0.9357	0	0.0124	0.0226	0.1003	0.2854	12.23895	15.5095	0.9507	0.2917	17466.08	19583.53
	best	50	10	1	0	0.0029	0.0096	0.0471	0.2079	9.9048	5.8462	1.1087	0.4621	17412.37	19352.88
	worst	37	4	0.5	0	0.0308	0.0329	0.1549	0.3501	15.1915	25.2460	0.7798	0.1476	17611.54	20167.61
Experiment 3 [496,530]	mean	45.6	5.7	0.8980	0.0026	0.0096	0.0114	0.0725	0.3296	13.2403	14.4857	0.7319	0.2387	16209.42	19368.17
	best	72	7	1	0.0263	0.0020	0.0039	0.0251	0.1766	7.4479	4.2795	0.9025	0.4313	15986.1	19040.85
	worst	37	3	0.6666	0	0.0440	0.0155	0.1102	0.4925	16.6139	27.3881	0.5910	0.0208	16418.6	19624.56
Experiment 4 [496,510]	mean	44.8	5.7	0.8748	0.0123	0.0124	0.0144	0.0982	0.3237	17.3647	12.4398	0.7159	0.2657	15979.77	18940.11
	best	77	9	1	0.0526	0.0520	0.0263	0.1517	0.4757	29.5629	30.1311	1	0.5659	16179.57	19496.28
	worst	37	3	0.5714	0	0.0037	0.0067	0.0492	0.1595	10.2750	1.8966	0.4803	0.0729	15753.22	17998.38
Experiment 5 [800,820]	mean	46.5	6.3	0.9421	0	0.0107	0.0195	0.0926	0.4061	18.1912	15.6393	0.7187	0.3569	15073.64	18383.1
	best	53	9	1	0	0.0066	0.0105	0.0444	0.2827	13.2861	9.4082	0.9543	0.6413	14792.15	17951.21
	worst	31	4	0.8	0	0.0150	0.0317	0.1453	0.4766	29.0093	40.5226	0.4157	0.1155	15333.57	18889.59
Experiment 6 [760,820]	mean	46.5	6.3	0.9421	0	0.0107	0.0195	0.0926	0.4061	18.1912	15.6393	0.7187	0.3569	15073.64	18383.1
	best	53	9	1	0	0.0066	0.0105	0.0444	0.2827	13.2861	9.4082	0.9543	0.6413	14792.15	17951.21
	worst	31	4	0.8	0	0.0150	0.0317	0.1453	0.4766	29.0093	40.5226	0.4157	0.1155	15333.57	18889.59

For AQ, HDPSO algorithm gives better consideration of approximation and dispersion than HDPSO1 algorithm. To sum up, HDPSO algorithm has a better comprehensive performance than HDPSO1 algorithm. In other words, neighborhood search structure has a great improvement of the algorithm to solve this problem.

5. Conclusion

In this study, a recovery model for disruption in proportional two-machine no-wait flow shop environment has been developed, in order to minimize the weighted sum of makespan and the weighted sum of tardiness. It's solved using the HDPSO algorithm which is revised from PSO algorithm. Moreover, a neighborhood search structure with insert and swap is developed to improve the performance of the algorithm.

The environment and disruption mentioned in our study is less practical than that in real life like that disruptions do occur synchronously and so on. These conditions need our further research in the future.

References

1. Pinedo M. Scheduling theory, algorithm and systems. [M]. Fourth edition, New York : Springer Science + Business Media,LLC, 2012.
2. Stefan Voß,Andreas Witt. Hybrid flow shop scheduling as a multi-mode multi-project scheduling problem with batching requirements: A real-world application[J]. International Journal of Production Economics. 2005 (2)
3. Lee C Y,Joseph Y T,Leung,Yu G. Two Machine Scheduling under Disruptions with Transportation Considerations[J].Journal of Scheduling, 2006,9(1) :35-48.
4. Liou Tian Shy,Wang Mao Jun. Ranking fuzzy numbers with integral value[J]. Computer and Mathematics with Application, 2005,49: 1731- 1753.
5. BO Hong-guang ;PAN Yu-tao ;MA Xiao-yan. Disruption Management for Production Rescheduling in Two-machine No-wait Flow Shop [J].Operation Research and Management Science.2013,04:111-119+125.

Acknowledgements

This work was supported by the National Science and Technology Support Program (2015BAF08B02),the National Natural Science Foundation of China (71172137), and the Fundamental Research Funds for the Central Universities (DUT14RW101)

MATEC Web of Conferences **44**, 02027 (2016)
DOI: 10.1051/matecconf/20164402027

A quantitative calculation approach research of tooth surface friction characteristic parameters

Shuang Xue Fu [a]

Guangzhou Civil Aviation College, Guangzhou, Guangdong, 510403, China

Abstract: A new calculation approach of tooth surface friction characteristic parameters is raised in this paper, the caclulation approach is based on gear drive test experience and finite element multi field coupling analysis method and technology.In the process of solution, friction characteristic concept of engineering oriented complex gear drive is raised, "experiment- calculation composite model" is built, tooth surface friction characteristic parameters(friction coefficients) are inversely analyzed by the composite model under different lubrication conditions. The problem of complicated tooth friction coefficients is solved. The calculation method is a new idea on solving friction characteristic parameters under complex lubrication conditions, it unites theoretical research, system modeling, numerical simulation and experimental test, so its solution is more reasonable. Exactly research friction coefficients can help to search gear friction principle and to upgrade the level of decrease noise and vibration of gear.

Key words: Friction chracteristic parameters; Quantitative calculation; Composite model; Lubrication ; Gear drive.

1 Introduction

The research of the tooth surface friction to reduce friction, increase the load capacity of gear tooth, and improve the system transmission performance has very important significance. Studies have shown that [1-5], the tooth surface friction contribute to the formation of pitting, tooth root crack initiation and extension, and increase effect of tooth fracture. Due to tooth surface friction, the formation of pitting, tooth root crack initiation and extension and tooth fracture are intensified. At the same time, the tooth surface friction affects the dynamic characteristics of gear transmission system, it is an important origin of vibration and noise excitation [6-14].The tooth surfaces friction coefficients are exact solution has positive significance on gear fatigue strength design, failure mechanism analysis, and damping and noise-reducing. on account of the gear drive characteristics of dynamic, randomness and chaos under the complex lubrication conditions, Based on the gear drive dynamic measurement experiment, finite element method(FEM) multi-field coupled analysis and inverse computation technology are used , the complex gear drive " polymorphous friction " concept was put forward.

The experiment-simulation composite model of complex gear drive is built. Based on the composite model, the friction coefficient of the upper dividing point of single contact is solved. The theory research, system modeling, numerical simulation and experimental test are applied to the composite model, the tooth face friction coefficients are quantified calculation. It can help to perfect the calculation method of tooth surface friction coefficient, provide a reference basis for building a tooth surface friction coefficient calculation theory system.

2 Polymorphous modeling of gear drive

In the process of tooth meshing, its friction mechanism is extremely complex. In the tooth meshing range, the lubrication condition and change rule of friction process are shown as followed:

(1) In lubrication gear drive: engaging-in impact friction→ transition friction (boundary friction, mixed friction) →elastic-hydrodynamic lubrication →transition friction (boundary friction, mixed friction) →engaging-out impact friction;

(2) Without lubrication or self-lubricating gear drive: engaging-in impact friction →dry friction →engaging-out impact friction.

Based on the physical process, the complex gear drive "polymorphous friction" concept was put forward. The main purpose of this study is to find out the actual meshing tooth surface complex frictional conditions and its change rules, provide key technical support for the gear drive tribology precise design

The complex gear drive "polymorphous friction" concept, is refers to the two tooth meshing contact surfaces or friction medium (such as lubricating oil slick) explicit characteristics and status in the process of the relative movement. The experiment-simulation composite model of complex gear drive polymorphous friction process analysis and quantitative research is built. (As shown in Figure 1).This model is mainly composed of experiment and simulation module. Experiment module includes: the complex gear drive test system, the data acquisition system, the characteristic parameter extraction mechanism, etc. Simulation module includes: the inverse analysis algorithms, the finite element method (FEM) analysis, and Intergeneration Projection Genetic Algorithm (IP - GA) [15], etc. The model will be used to systematically research the friction distribution characteristics and its change rules under different lubrication conditions.

[a] Corresponding author: 25272505@qq.com

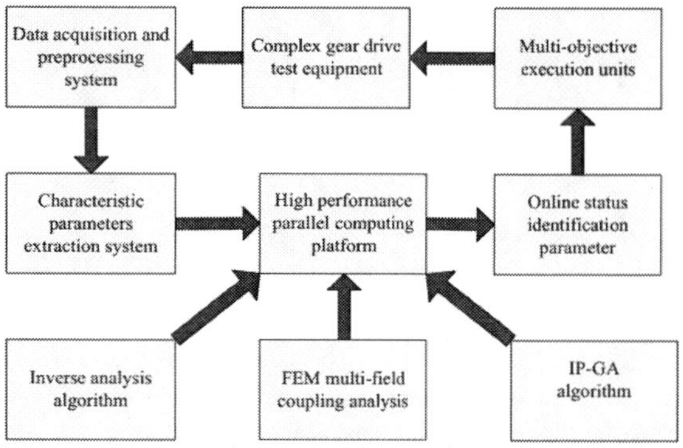

Figure 1. The complex gear drive "polymorphous friction" modeling

3 The test principle and experiment table

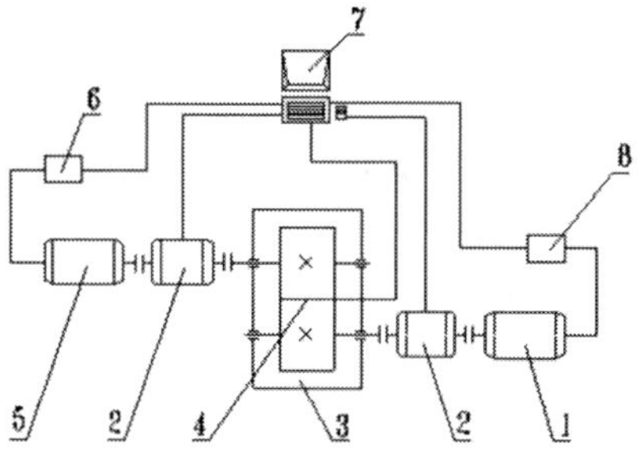

1. magnetic loader, 2. speed torque sensor, 3. gear box and gears,4. resistance strain gauge, 5. motor, 6. converter, 7.computer, 8. load controller

Figure 2. The test principle figure of acquiring key parameter

According to the mapping principle of between the force field of meshing tooth non-contact sensitive area and the tooth surface friction force, sensitive area stress and strain test scheme is designed, dynamic measurement experiment device (see Figure 2)is developed, the characteristic parameters (stress or strain of tooth root stress sensitive areas)are extracted, and the experiment table is shown in Figure 3. The location of the sensitive area can be determined by the finite element analysis of gear and photo-elastic experiment conclusion.

The system structure and working principle of extraction key characteristic parameters experiment device are expressed that:

The test gears 3 is driven by converter motor 5, the load of gear teeth will be adjusted by the magnetic loader 1 and load controller 8,the variable-speed motor and continuous variable load loaders are controlled by the computer system 7, The tooth stress and strain of sensitive area are measured by resistance strain gauge 4. The test signals are amplified by the amplifier and output to the dynamic data acquisition cards by mercury slip ring, the experimental gear box 3 temperature is controlled by the cooling system, the meshing teeth lubrication state is adjusted by the lubrication system. The extracted characteristic parameters are imported high-performance parallel computing system 7, and thus inverse analysis algorithm is run.

Figure 3. The experiment table of acquiring key parameter

4 Inverse analysis process of the meshing tooth surface friction characteristic parameters

The friction coefficient inverse analysis scheme is shown in Figure 4. In a certain lubrication condition, the Characteristic parameters (the strain sequence ε' of tooth root stress sensitive area) will be extracted by the experimental modules, the FEM multi-field coupling analysis parameter strain sequence ε in the same positions is calculated, The objective function F(μ)whose independent variable is coefficient friction μ is built, the search area of the friction coefficient is set under the lubrication condition, the IP-GA is adopted to deduced the tooth face friction coefficient μ .

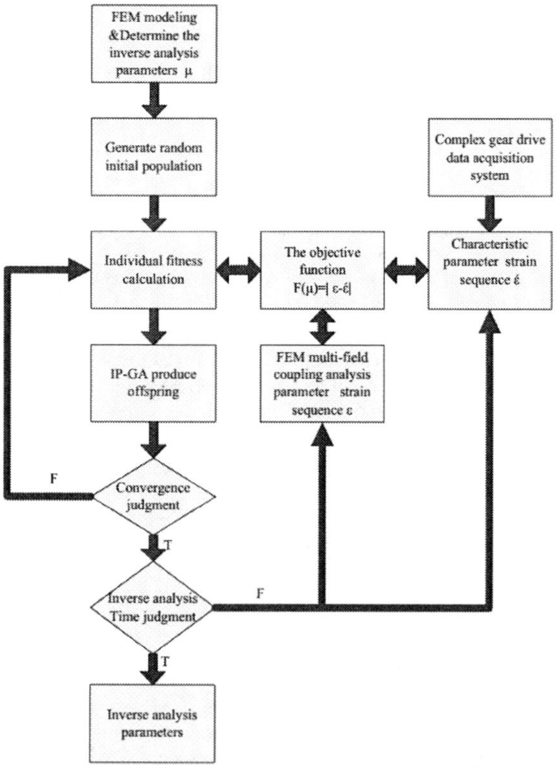

Figure 4. The flow chart of tooth friction characteristic parameters inverse analysis

5 The example of inverse analysis

5.1 Parameters of gear and material characteristic of gear

The transmission ratio of two meshing gears is 1, and the gear precision is grade 6. Tooth profile error and the deformation of axis and gearbox are ignored. Gear parameters are given in Table 1. The material of gear is 45# steel, its parameters shown in Table 2. Rotation speed n_1 is 100r/min and transmission power P is 5.6kw.

Table 1. Parameters of gear

Tooth numbers	Z	30/30
Modulus	m/mm	6
Axis diameter	d_0/mm	50
Pressure angle	α/(°)	20
Addendum coefficient	x/mm	0
Tooth width	b/mm	60

Table 2. Material characteristic of gear

Material		45#
Elastic modulus	E/GPa	204
Shearing modulus	G/GPa	79.6
Poisson's ratio	υ	0.3
Density	ρ/kg.m-3	7847

According to gear engagement curve formulas[16], the exact position coordinates of the points on tooth profile are solved in MATLAB (see Figure 5) and written into a full text date file. The file is imported as APDL (ANSYS Parametric Design Language) procedure, and then theoretical tooth profile is attained in ANSYS, the tooth profile is shown in Figure 6, and the tooth geometric model is built in ANSYS, it is shown in Figure 7.According to the analysis results of the paper [17], based on the requirements of design precision, the boundaries of gear model are reasonably determined, this paper adopts three tooth model and the gear tooth meshing model is shown in Figure 8.

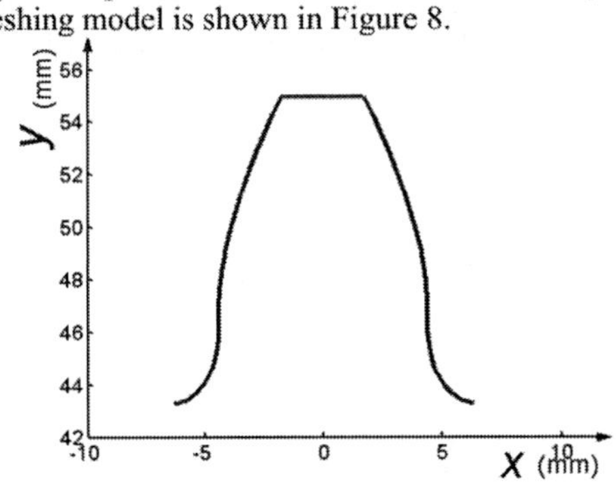

Figure 5. The tooth profile in MATLAB

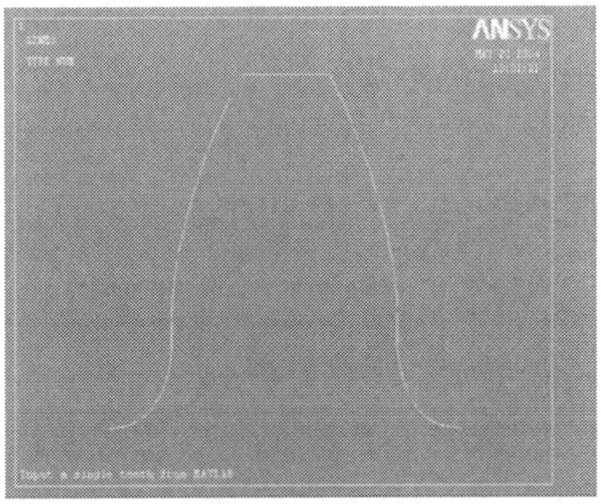

Figure 6. The tooth profile in ANSYS

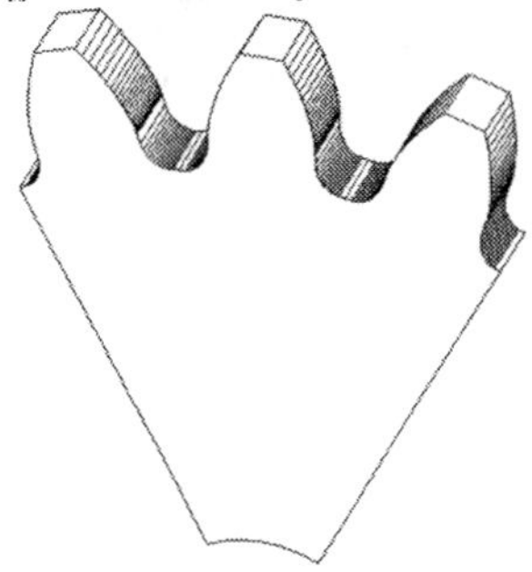

Figure 7. The tooth geometric model in ANSYS

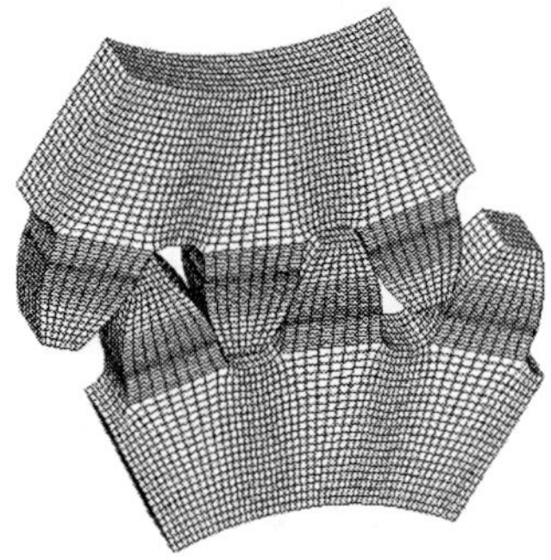

Figure 8. Gear meshing FEM model

5.2 Tooth face friction characteristic parameters inverse analysis

The input parameter sensitivity analysis must be done before inverse analysis. According to FEM analysis and the photo-elastic experiment conclusion, the maximum stress/strain section in the gear tooth root transition-curve is regarded as a sensitive area. According to study conclusion of paper[8], it is very sensitive between the tooth face friction coefficient and tooth root stress/strain.

In general, the tooth face friction coefficient is influenced by lubrication conditions. According to study conclusion of paper[18],the inverse analysis of the tooth face friction characteristic parameters (tooth face friction coefficients) are done under boundary lubrication and mixed lubrication conditions. The convergence trends of friction coefficients inverse analysis are shown in Figure 9.The inverse analysis results are shown in Table 3.

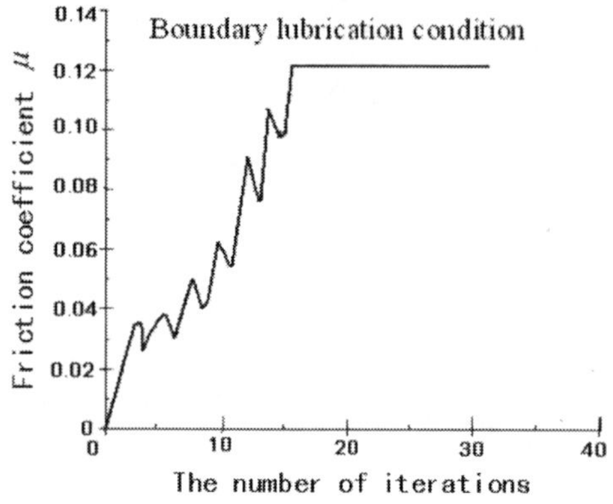

(a)

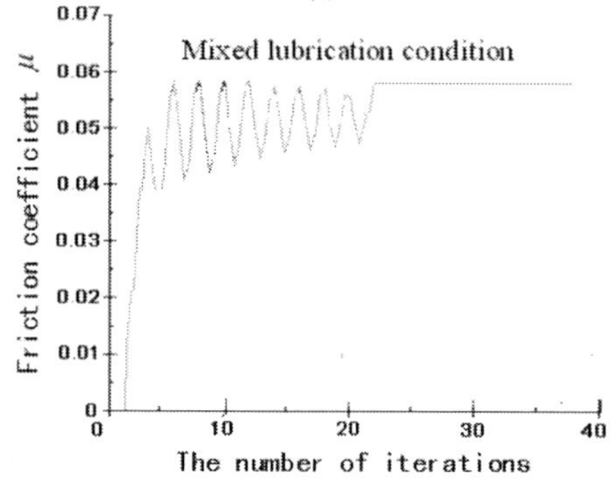

(b)

Figure 9. The convergence trends of friction coefficients inverse analysis under different lubrication conditions

Table 3. The inverse analysis results under two kinds of lubrication conditions

Lubrication conditions	Friction coefficient
Boundary lubrication condition	0.120
Mixed lubrication condition	0.060

The tooth face friction coefficient inverse analysis is based on dynamic gear drive experiment, the input parameter is tooth root strains, FEM multi-field coupled analysis is used at the same time. It can truly simulate the actual working condition, and based on the fast convergence and global optimization mechanism Properties of IP-GA , the inverse analysis values of the friction coefficients are very precise. Under boundary lubrication condition, the inverse analysis value is 0.120, under mix lubrication condition, the inverse analysis value is 0.060, and they conform to the conclusions of paper[18],the values are reliable.

6 Summary

(1)The complex gear drive " polymorphous friction " concept was put forward and the experiment—simulation composite model of complex gear drive is built.

(2)The theory research, system modeling, numerical simulation and experimental test are applied to the experiment—simulation composite model of complex gear drive, the tooth face friction coefficients can be quantified calculation.

(3)It can help to perfect the calculation method of tooth surface friction coefficient, provide a reference basis for building a tooth surface friction coefficient calculation theory system.

Acknowledgments

The authors gratefully acknowledge the support of training program of Guangdong province outstanding young teachers in colleges and universities (YQ2014178) .

References

1. Flašker J, Fajdiga G, Glodez S, et al. 2001. Numerical simulation of surface pitting due to contact loading. International Journal of Fatigue, 23(7) :599-605.
2. Lewicki D G, Handschuh R F, Spievak L E, et al. 2001. Consideration of moving tooth load in gear crack propagation predictions. ASME Journal of Mechanical Design, 123(3) :118-124.
3. Vedmar L, Henriksson B. 1998. A general approach for determining dynamic forces in spur gears. ASME Journal of Mechanical Design,120(12) :593-598.
4. Velex P, Cahouet V. 2000. Experimental and numerical investigations on the influence of tooth friction in spur and helical gear dynamics. Journal of Mechanical Design, 122(12) :515-522.
5. Aziz S M A, Seireg A. 1994. A parametric study of frictional noise in gears. Wear, 176(1) :25-28.
6. Velex P, Sainsot P. 2002. An analytical study of tooth friction excitations in errorless spur and helical gears. Mechanism and Machine Theory, 37(7) :641-658.
7. Litvin Faydor L, Fuentes Alfonso, Hayasaka Kenichi. 2006. Design, manufacture, stress analysis and experimental tests of a low-noise endurance spiral bevel gears. Mechanism and Machine Theory, 41(1):83-118.
8. Ajmi M, Velex P. 2005. A model for simulating the quasi-static and dynamic behavior of solid wide-faced spur and helical gears. Mechanism and Machine Theory, 40(2) :173–190.
9. Li S T. 2007.Finite element analyses for contact strength and bending strength of a pair of spur gears with machining errors, assembly errors and tooth modifications. Mechanism and Machine Theory, 42(1): 88-114.
10. Lewicki D G, Handschuh R F, Spievak L E, et al. 2001. Consideration of moving tooth load in gear crack propagation predictions. ASME Journal of Mechanical Design, 123(3):118-124.
11. Wang Feng,Fang Zongde,Wang Kanwei. 2014. Dynamics meshing efficiency of herringbone gears under mixed elastohydrodynamic lubrication condition. Journal Vibration and Shock, 33(16):150-154.

12. Zhang Jing, Chen Bingkui, Kang Chuanzhang, et al. 2012.Dynamic analysis for spur gears considering friction effect. Journal Vibration and Shock, 31(21):126-132.
13. Liu Changzhao,Qin Dalong,Liao Yinghua. 2014. Dynamic model for a parallel-axis helical gears transmission system based on variable friction coefficient between contact teeth. Journal Vibration and Shock, 33(24):150-157.
14. Pan Dong,Zhao Yang,Li Na,etal. 2012.The wear life prediction method of gear system. Journal of Harbin Institute of Technology, 44(9):29-33.
15. G R Liu， X Han.2003. Computational inverse techniques in nondestructive evaluation. New York: CRC Press.
16. Fu Shuangxue. 2008.Computational inverse studies of tooth friction coefficients in gear drive. Changsha: Hunan University College of Mechanical and Vehicle Engineering.
17. Zhou Changjiang, Tang Jinyuan, Zhong Zhihua et al.2005. Research on boundary of exact modeling of gear by FEM. China Mechanical Engineering, 16(22):2044-2049.
18. Editor committee of gear handbook.2006. Gear handbook. 2nd.Beijing:China Machine Press.

MATEC Web of Conferences **44**, 02028 (2016)
DOI: 10.1051/matecconf/20164402028

Research on Operation Mechanism of Civil-military Integration Equipment Support Supply Chain

Chang Feng Zhou[1,a], Yan Liu[2]

[1]National University of Defense Technology, School of Social Sciences and Humanities, Hunan Province, China
[2]National University of Defense Technology, School of Information System and Management, Hunan Province, China

Abstract. High-tech local wars under conditions of informatization is becoming increasingly dependent on the security of weapons and equipment, and civil-military integration equipment support has become a trend. Civil-military integration equipment support chain construction vigorously, must be starting from the strengthening of the top-level planning decisions, building the civil-military coordination and restraint mechanisms and establishing efficient incentives and effective oversight mechanisms to ensure the performance of various support tasks, and to enhance the equipment support ability to achieve "fast, accurate, and efficient" goals.

1 Introduction

Construction of integrated military and civilian equipment support supply-chain is a main direction and trends to adapt the development of equipment support, a long-term mechanism must be establishing to guarantee its continued stable operation. Under the conditions of market economy, it is necessary for promoting integrated military and civilian equipment support that to gradually establish and perfect the equipment support in integrated military and civilian planning and decision-making mechanisms, constraints on coordination mechanisms, incentives and supervision and evaluation mechanism, strengthening of integrated military and civilian equipment support running order.

2 Strengthen top-level planning decisions

Construction of integrated military and civilian equipment supply chain, is to break the "behind closed doors" stereotype, consider military equipment support issues in a strategic point, Overall plan military equipment support resources, and set up equipment support systems which adapt to the times.

2.1 Focused on top-tier design

Promoting the construction of integrated military and civilian equipment supply chain, is related to the country as a whole, must reflect the will of the State. Integrated military and civilian equipment support supply-chain-building involves rational allocation and use of national scientific and technological resources, involving national defense industrial base and the Foundation of national economy adjustment and harmonization of a number of important issues, such as, must stand on the national level, planning at the top, and on the basis of a unified deployment, development goals and concrete measures. Planning should be looking to the longer term, based on reality, and the development of China's market economy, enterprise level, equipment support supply chain status match, and to adjust the integrated military and civilian support supply chain development to ensure integrated military and civilian equipment support right direction and realize sustainable development of construction of equipment support supply chain.

Design at the top level, it is necessary to change the traditional military-industrial-military-separation model, must be addressed through macro-control measures, on behalf of the State and the Ministry of defence, issued a series of laws, regulations and standards. Standing at the height of the laws, regulations and standards, it is need to establish and improve the integrated military and civilian weapons research, production, support system, and then the construction of integrated military and civilian equipment supply chain is promoted.

2.2 Improve the protection implementation plan

Equipment support in accordance with the timing can be divided into the usual equipment support, emergency equipment and equipment support in wartime. Therefore, during the construction of integrated military and civilian equipment supply chain, it is need to develop appropriate equipment support processes to improve the integrated military and civilian equipment support supply chain efficiency and effectiveness.

At the time of equipment support in peacetime, its main task is to complete military training in peacetime security, military exercises and weapon experimental

[a] Corresponding author: cfzhou111@163.com

Article available at http://www.matec-conferences.org or http://dx.doi.org/10.1051/matecconf/20164402028

support, therefore, in order to comply with the laws of the market, full realization of materiel support of military, economic and social benefits. While retaining core support capacity, non-core support capacity will gradually be handed over to the local Security Department. According to the characteristics of high-tech equipment and equipment support needs, it is need to strengthen the construction of military equipment support, and comprehensive utilization of resources and Manpower, and achieve coordinated development of military resources and effective integration. Compared with traditional war under the condition of informationization war strength, because of high scientific and technological content, equipment materials consumption, the timeliness requirements of the equipment support are relatively high. Wartime or emergency equipment is mainly done during the war or State of emergency material allocate support, equipment, technical support and equipment battle damage repair services. Therefore, at the time of war or emergency, with time priority, it is need to strengthen the administrative plan, supplemented by market mechanisms, ensure equipment support translation quickly and efficiently to ensure weapons and equipment in the best tactical and technical state. While military and civilian integration during the construction of equipment support supply chain, it should pay attention to in peacetime, wartime demand peacetime construction, usually supporting wartime, peacetime and wartime, combining emergency equipment support needs.

3 Build coordination mechanism

Communication and coordination mechanism is the lubricant of integrated military and civilian equipment running smoothly, it can strengthen the correlation between organizations, strengthen the exchange of information on military and security contractors, for the implementation of integrated military and civilian equipment support supply chain provide good running condition.

3.1 Enhanced security of supply chain control

Enhancing coordination and control is a key that to ensure the integrated civilian-military equipment support running smoothly and effectively. Military-civilian coordination mechanism is the means to meet the needs of military and social logistics, from the vertical (strategic, operational and tactical levels) and horizontal (collection, storage, transportation, packaging, distribution, and so on) in two dimensions, links, military and logistics functions, tasks and link up with organizations to achieve synchronous operation, seamless connectivity. Establishment of a coordination mechanism, is the thought of modern logistics system integration, supply chain optimization, effective ways to improve safeguards effectiveness and efficiency of the military equipment, to build an integrated civilian-military essential requirements of equipment support supply chain. Both army and civilian should established exchange mechanism, regularly carried out experience exchange, and theory discussion, and business training, activities, equipment guarantees management sector to and national government procurement related sector strengthening contact, established normal coordination mechanism, and regularly joint system and situation informed system, exchange information, clear the work of points and focus of civil-military integration equipment support, consult and host daily jobs of civil-military integration equipment support system construction, Coordinate and solve major problem of civil-military integration equipment support construction.

3.2 establishing the concept of supply chain management

It is need to establish a supply chain process management concept for building military-civilian coordination mechanisms. Modern military logistics is connected to suppliers and force users, set the collection, storage, transport, distribution and other links in one equipment support supply-chain. Using the synchronous response time of supply chain management, supply chain management, demand of logistics entities of the information shared in real time makes the traditional military-logistics system, the link from "serial" to the "parallel" mode of synchronization protection activities of the Organization in order to optimize the supply chain process and shorten reaction time, improve the efficiency of logistics support. It is need to form a focus on needs of joint security forces for building a coordination mechanism. For fast to meet customer needs, the Americans proposed the concept of focusing on logistics, emphasized the integration of land and building, before and after integrated, multidimensional combination, focusing on needs of security mode. The idea is in line with the development trend of modern logistics, is the direction of military civil-military integration of military logistics support system. Building a coordination mechanism should be based on national mobilization of institutions at all levels, strategic, operational and tactical levels and coordinated logistics support force, fully coordinated air, sea and land forces logistic support forces to form focused cross-hierarchy of needs support, regional security, across services using federated security posture.

3.3 Implementation of the access and exit of private enterprises system

Establishing the system of the access and exit of private enterprises is a guide and control for army on private enterprises participating equipment support, to ensure the safe and effective operation equipment support in integrated civilian-military efforts. On one hand, it is need to set up strict access restriction mechanism, strict qualification issue. Private enterprise participates in equipment support must be in accordance with the procedure provided for critical review, in line with the National Defense Science and technology industry Council "license" system and the army's "qualification system" in order to assume control of weapon and equipment development and production qualification. Note Verify that private enterprise has ability to bear civil

liability independently, have good credit and a sound quality assurance system, and has the capacity to meet conditions and equipment development and production contract. Qualification attestation contained in qualified manufacturers list, based on preference for performance specifications for ordering objects, dynamic management mechanism. The other hand, it needs the flexible control of the companies. According to the number of companies, supply of equipment, maintenance of quality and other indicators, military can forecast enterprise development, and warn against the unqualified enterprises, and has time for re-employment qualified enterprises. It also can help enterprises make industrial transfer and exit decisions accordingly. At the same time it is need to increase the exit supervision. Underwriting companies exit the market for equipment support, first of all, it is need to be logged off license, and approved by the licensing administration office logs off before they can quit. It is need to emphasis on exit links of coordinated, timely resolve disputes on both sides to ensure a seamless transition. It is also need to perfect exit regulations, increase penalties for violations out of businesses, and earnestly safeguard the legitimate rights and interests of the military.

4 Establish an efficient incentive mechanism

In the practice of equipment support, civil-military integration relate to property rights, asset specificity, asymmetric information issues will have a complex representation. This requires from institutional settings, environments, and conditions of analysis, the choice of means of application of concrete ideas, designing effective incentive mechanisms to promote civil-military integration of equipment support supply chain.

4.1 Implementation of property right incentive

Incentive nature, remains a traditional clear property rights and reduce system cost, as it is in the present social environment institutional basis to attract collectors and private enterprises to enter the field of equipment support of the most basic and most effective approach. Our contractual system of equipment support domain is still not perfect, relationship economy occupies a certain position, only completing compact economy as soon as possible, reducing relationship economic, specific incentive measures, can clear ownership and accountability, strict protection. For any business, reasonable property and freedom of contract are prerequisites for efficient economy, so the incentive is key part of integrated military and civilian equipment support incentive mechanism.

Ownership incentive, to contract the economy is the most important economic transformation, it is a process of institutional change. In theory, the system approaches into induced institutional change and changes of compulsory system in two ways. Response induced institutional change is a group of people by the institutional imbalance caused by chance, of the spontaneous change: related groups is a spontaneous reaction to the system unbalanced, consistency of its greatest advantage is based on the agreed principles, in line with the practical environment of institutional change, so it is an effective institutional change. Changes of compulsory system refers to the system of Government by decree imposing the changes. Mandatory system changes state or Government is the owner, its biggest advantage is the ability to rely on its own force, reducing system changes cost and implementation costs, so it is a low consumption of system changes. Due to limited rationality and opportunism, relationship between them should be complementary rather than alternative. Civil-military integration equipment support of property incentive, should take combined principles including induced institutional changes and compulsory institutional changes, the specific measures should includes clear property and protection property in legal regulations, simplify application program, and reduce system cost, clear right range of the institutions and sectors to avoid property erosion, establish bid competition mechanism based on market for relies on of "public, justice, and fair", encourage enterprises to access and obtain project contractualization, standardization and scientific, reduce the costs of established information network center, messaging and information search.

4.2 Strengthening specific investment incentives

Incentive consideration is the protection of property rights, and enable enterprises to participate in equipment support initiative. Compensation for asset specificity is asset specificity to enterprises, particularly compensate for additional losses. Case of particularity in the equipment industry, it is need to help enterprises recover sunk costs which discourage companies to participate in integrated military and civilian equipment support. This is the most important private investment incentives besides of the property right motivation.

Equipment support of asset specificity will make doubts, the military and the Government should be based on the value of compensation incentives to solve this problem. Setting up incentive program is to make the private enterprises to select equipment support trades for utility no less than other options. Therefore, private asset specificity should be affected by extra costs or may in the future to compensate for losses suffered by. So-called extra costs, are sunk costs after private enterprises entering the field of equipment support. So-called loss refers to military decision making changes and other risks of asset specificity losses of enterprises. So the military not only pays for the end product--support results, but also for intermediate goods--in the process of investment and personnel training. In addition, military enterprises for the production of equipment and parts should be purchased tangible assets, for those hard to project-specific test for weapons and production equipment, the military should also invest in and, in some cases, make a commitment in the contract, if the project is cancelled, the funds paid.

Compensation may be special fund and can also be incorporated into the price. In general, with the development of China's socialist market economy, the growing maturity of the price formation mechanism and

prediction of price increase, compensation incorporated into the price is more reasonable. Equipment price incentive pricing models should be limited, which divided into the standard price and incentive price. Standard price is refers to equipment products tangible entity in military research production process, which determined through negotiations before contract signed. Incentive price is to guarantee equipment products research production and procurement task of smooth completed and need sharing of costs and should gets of profit award and compensation, which determined in contract implementation process through constantly annual negotiations. Risk compensation should be primarily determined in connection with assets dedicated risk. After assessing the expected of sunk costs and uncertainty loss because of asset specificity, risk compensation price structure can be set.

5 Establishing effective monitoring mechanisms

Oversight mechanisms are necessary constraints for integrated military and civilian equipment support chain operation, effectively guarantee the implementation of contracts for equipment support, promoting quality management contractor for equipment support. In the process of implementing equipment support, it is necessary to supervise on every step strictly, especially for equipment support services contractor in the market of rent-seeking behavior, service quality of equipment support and task completion deadlines.

5.1 Avoiding the contract of rent-seeking behavior

From the perspective of institutional economics and public choice theory, the key to harness rent-seeking behavior is to perfect institutional size and constraint to achieve resource allocation legalization, marketization and socialization. Based on the equipment contractor's cost-benefit comparison, establishing the new system by increasing rent costs and reduced rent income, rent-seeking of net income is less than the profit-seeking, thereby adjusting the contractor bias.

For equipment support services contractor in the market to give up rent-seeking behavior, consisting of a full range of supervision is set up to avoid no oversight. Headquarters based on organization structure of equipment support supply-chain complexity and number of personnel, consider setting up a level or two-level procuratorial bodies, its functions and powers, to be defined clearly, equipment support the Supreme authority. In general, procuratorial authorities are responsible for safety, production and quality management as well as the implementation of the system, monitoring, evaluation and feedback.

5.2 Overcoming moral hazard and adverse selection

So-called asymmetry is unequal information at the disposal of the parties. Prior consequences adverse selection of information asymmetry and asymmetry of information can result in moral hazard problems. Both adverse selection and moral hazard, will make the market allocation of resources loss of Pareto optimality properties. During construction process of integrated military and civilian equipment support supply chain, army private is always better to know and control for military forces, but worse for private enterprises. Contractor know its own development and production and support capabilities, management level, operator quality, preferences more clearly than in the military. Private contractors will Sign the contracts by using the advantage of the information, and intentionally concealing adverse information on the contract, which may cause problems such as adverse selection and moral hazard. In order to avoid adverse selection and effectively to avoid moral hazard, it must complete information as far as possible to overcome the asymmetry of information.

So, selecting enterprise cannot just requirements cost minimum, also to many considerations. After the bidding and before signing the contract, military should check the support enterprise for qualification review, see its quality system and confidential procedures whether in place, technology and economic strength can completed military proposed of equipment support requirements, whether has similar experience of civilian support, military also can through early demonstrates validation, and simulation test and end try, variety means active reveals enterprise information. All this contributes to good information transmission channels, enabling the military to screen different types of businesses, to overcome the harm caused by adverse selection and moral hazard risks to civil-military integration.

6 Conclusion

The construction of operation mechanism is the prerequisite and fundamental guarantee for implementing integrated operation of weapon equipment research, production, storage, and supply, and achieving supply goals of "rapid, precise and efficient" security. Only by strengthening the normal order of integrated military and civilian equipment support chain, it can promote sound and fast development of integrated military and civilian equipment support to ensure that military and civilian integration equipment support can running quickly, efficiently and smoothly.

References

1. Li Qingquan, Wang Bing, Liu Xuyang . Study on the operational mechanism of equipment material supply chain [J]. Logistics and purchasing in China, 2011,07:76-77.
2. Shuang Haijun. Weapons monitoring and incentive mechanism in procurement [D]. Chongqing University, 2010.
3. Shang Li, Dong Peng, Wu Wanqiu. Research on equipment support chain mechanism under the condition of Informationization war [J]. Logistics technology, 2009,01:148-150.

4. Straube F,Ma S H,Bohn M. Internationalization of logistics systems how Chinese and German companies enter foreign markets[M].Berlin:Springer-Verlag,2008.
5. Simatupang T M,Sandroto I V,Lubis S B H. Supply chain coordination in a fashion firm[J].Supply Chain Management:An International Journal,2004,(03):256-268.
6. Fu Y,Piplani R. Supply-side collaboration and its value in supply chains[J].European Journal of Operational Research,2004,(01):281-288.
7. Frascatore M R,Mahmoodi F. Long-term and penalty contracts in a two-stage supply chain with stochastic demand[J].European Journal of Operational Research,2008.147-156.
8. Mathur P P,Shah J. Supply chain contracts with capacity investment decision:Two-way penalties for coordination[J].International Journal of Production Economics,2008,(1):56-70.
9. Gurnani H,Gerchak Y. Coordination in decentralized assembly systems with uncertain component yields[J].European Journal of Operational Research,2007,(1):1559-1576.

MATEC Web of Conferences 44, 02029 (2016)
DOI: 10.1051/matecconf/20164402029

Study on Lubrication Theory of Orificed Throttle Based on Molecule Collision

Wei LONG, Ling GONG and Shao Hua YANG

(Faculty of mechanical and electrical engineering, Kunming University of Science and Technology, Yunnan Kunming 650500, China)

Abstract: Orifice restriction is a traditional form of throttle used in aerostatic guide way. Practically, self-excited vibration or even air hammer phenomenon will appear in gas film interior when supply gas enlarges or the film thickness decreases to micron scale. In order to analyze the process from the pressure inlet to the entrance of completely developed laminar flow, Reynolds Equation coupled with the first order velocity slip is used. Since it has rarefied property, turbulence model and molecular dynamics theory are adopted based on molecular collision theory. This paper reveals the internal cyclone law in gas chamber and the relationship between essence of the shock formation and the gas molecule velocity excitation. Further study shows that, supply pressure, film parameters and chamber parameters have important influences on cyclone phenomenon and shock wave.

Key words: orifice throttling; molecular collision; shock wave; cyclone phenomenon

1 Introduction:

Orifice restriction is a traditional type of throttle in aerostatic guide way. Lots of research reports on orifice compensated air bearing at home and abroad are available. R.R.Willis published an articles on gas pressure in orifice plate in 1828, which is the earliest literature of gas lubrication[1]. G.Belfforte derived gas flow coefficient of orifice compensated thrust bearing by experiments. And he also derived empirical formula for calculation of gas consumption and pressure distribution with a view to Reynolds number analysis and the two throttling action in 2006[2].One important phenomenon that orifice throttling is different from the inherent throttling is that the gas chamber structure will form a cyclone. In that case, there may be a shock phenomenon near gas supply hole. Carfagno S P found that through experiment: in area between the gas supply hole and the pressure gas film, the radial pressure distribution curve had a sudden drop according to laminar assumption[3].The phenomenon of gas film fluctuation in the air static pressure guide rail was studied by AOYAMA. In order to restrain the fluctuation of gas film [4-5], the structure of the throttle was reformed. Through numerical simulation; CHEN proposed that orifice gas bearing had a large vortex in the groove, so the bearing is not stable enough [6]. According to Reynolds equation, Giving appropriate initial values and boundary conditions, Meng Xian and Liu Fan used turbulence model under isothermal conditions coming to the conclusion that the gas has spiral movement along the circumferential direction of gas chamber before the gas is discharged from the gas chamber[7]. In the view of the problem of air film fluctuation in air static pressure guide, Chen Dongju found that there was a close connection between the cyclone phenomenon and the film vibration [8]. The traditional explanation of the shock in the throttle is due to the improper parameter selection, and then it produces supersonic zone near the throttle hole. Gas velocity is changed to subsonic after shock wave. These documents had no complete description of the orifice throttling process. In this paper, Reynolds Equation

coupled with the first order velocity slip was used to describe the internal cyclone law in gas chamber and the relationship between essence of the shock formation and the gas molecule velocity excitation based on molecular collision theory. A more detailed description of the orifice throttling process and flow mechanism was deduced.

2 Mathematical model and theoretical research

2.1 Modeling

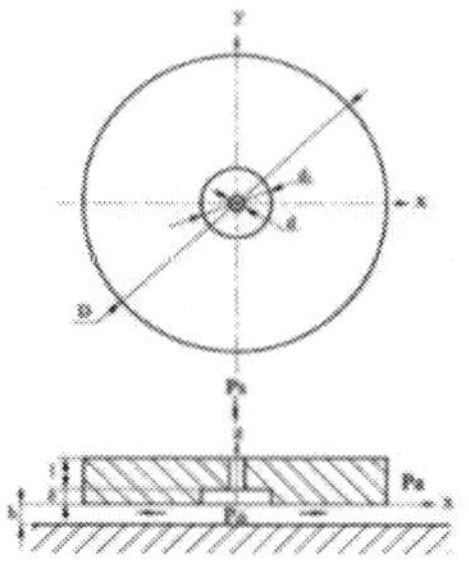

Fig 1 Diagram of orifice throttling in Descartes coordinate system

As shown in Fig.1, a single orifice compensated throttle was located in the center of a disc aerostatic thrust bearing.

Definition of effective flow sections:

$$A_{11}=\pi d^2/4, A_{12}=\pi d\left(h+\delta\right), A_{21}=\pi d_1^2/4, A_{22}=\pi d_1 h$$

Given fundamental equations of gas flow (momentum equation, continuity equation and state equation in Cartesian coordinate system), velocity slip boundary condition was taken into account:

$$\text{z=0}, u=U+l'\frac{\partial u}{\partial z}, v=l'\frac{\partial \omega}{\partial z}, \omega=0 \quad (1)$$

$$\text{z=h}, u=-l'\frac{\partial u}{\partial z}, v=-l'\frac{\partial w}{\partial z}, \omega=u\frac{\partial h}{\partial x}+v\frac{\partial h}{\partial y} \quad (2)$$

where: l' is the fluid slip length, $l'=\lambda\left(2-\sigma_v\right)/\sigma_v$. σ_v is a molecular tangential momentum regulation coefficient, which indicates the proportion of molecules that diffuse reflection at the surface of the object. λ is the average free path of gas molecules. U is the relative velocity of the slide plate and the guide rail. u , v , ω is the velocity component of x, y, z direction. u , v , ω is calculated by the momentum equation of x, y, z direction and formula (1),formula (2). ρ is eliminated through gas state equation under isothermal condition. At last get the Reynolds equation of micro scale effect by the gas continuity equation:

$$\frac{\partial}{\partial x}(ph^3\frac{\partial p}{\partial x})+\frac{\partial}{\partial y}(ph^3\frac{\partial p}{\partial y})=\frac{6\eta U}{1+6k'_n}+\frac{12\eta}{1+6k'_n}\frac{\partial(ph)}{\partial t} \quad (3)$$

where: $k'_n=\left(2-\sigma_v\right)k_n/\sigma_v$, k_n is Knudsen number. Dimensionless mathematical model was shown as Formula (3), and the Reynolds equation was obtained under micro scale:

$$\frac{\partial}{\partial \bar{x}}(\bar{h}^3\frac{\partial \bar{p}^2}{\partial \bar{x}})+\frac{\partial}{\partial \bar{y}}(\bar{h}^3\frac{\partial \bar{p}^2}{\partial \bar{y}})=\forall_x\frac{\partial(\overline{ph})}{\partial \bar{x}}+\sigma\frac{\partial(\overline{ph})}{\partial \bar{t}} \quad (4)$$

where:

$$\forall_x=\frac{12\eta lU}{(1+6k')p_0h_m^2}, \sigma=\frac{24\eta lv}{(1+6k'_n)p_0h_m^2}$$

When U=0:

$$\frac{\partial}{\partial \bar{x}}(\bar{h}^3\frac{\partial \bar{p}^2}{\partial \bar{x}})+\frac{\partial}{\partial \bar{y}}(\bar{h}^3\frac{\partial \bar{p}^2}{\partial \bar{y}})=\sigma\frac{\partial(\overline{ph})}{\partial \bar{t}} \quad (5)$$

2.2 Theoretical research

The external high pressure gas flows through the gas supply hole. Partial gas velocity vector is not change, but the others enter the gas chamber directly in form of diffusion. The molecular without speed vector changes has an impact on the bottom of the gas chamber. Molecular kinetic energy is converted into gas pressure energy, elastic deformation energy of support surface and Heat energy, etc. Hypothesis from the beginning of impact, all kinetic energy converted into pressure energy. The speed of the molecules that impact the bottom of the gas chamber is reduced. Temperature at the bottom of the gas chamber can be reduced, which makes the Heat flux in this part has instantaneous maximum. This induces fluctuation of gas film.

Assuming that the σ_v portion of the flow molecule is completely diffuse reflection, the rest $(1-\sigma_v)$ is completely specular reflection. In the case of specular reflection, normal velocity component is changed only at the impact surface. In the case of diffuse reflection, the velocity is in line with Maxwell distribution. Both specular reflection and diffuse reflection can change the movement direction of the gas molecules, which makes the angle between the two sides of the gas molecules that reflected less than 180 degrees. Through the molecular interaction and the collapse of the surface of the gas film, a small fraction of molecules get into gas film directly. Given the thickness of gas film is h, most of the molecules collide with each other and collide with the surface of the gas chamber. The molecules rise to the upper surface of gas chamber with spiral movement. Then molecules form vortex.

When h is taken from the micron level, the area of A_{22} must be less than the area of A_{21}, the area of A_{22} less than the area of A_{12}. It is clear that at least two cross section flow occurs when the external high pressure gas flows from the inlet to the gas chamber and then to the rail gap. According to the flow continuity equation, the inlet cross section area is 10 times of the area of the outlet cross section. Therefore, the external molecular velocity v_{out} of the gas chamber is 10 times of the molecular velocity v_{in} in the gas chamber. The presence of a high pressure gas chamber makes a large number of high-speed molecules near the exit of the gas chamber.

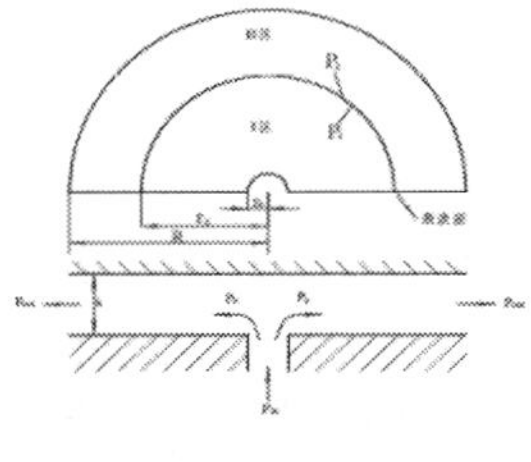

Fig 2 Diagram of supersonic zone around throttle

As shown in Figure 2: Gas flow along the radius direction, which is equivalent to the one dimensional flow of the tube whose cross-section area continues to become large. The speed of molecules in the place $r = r_0$ reaches sound speed. Obviously, it is a critical state. With speed increasing, the molecule is rapidly compressed when velocity reached supersonic. Meanwhile, shock wave generates at $r = r_s$. With the collision between each other of high speed movement, molecules become more intense, the energy consumption increases, the pressure drops, and negative pressure zone even occurs. The large pressure loss means that the bearing capacity and the static stiffness of the static pressure guide rail are decreased.

3 Simulation and analysis

Simulation of orifice compensated aero static thrust bearing with one inlet hole located in the center by ANSYS. Initial values and boundary conditions:(1)Temperature is239K.(2)Reference pressure is Pa=0.1MPa.(3) the Pressure inlet is 0.6Mpa .(4) the gas density is $1.205\,\text{kg/m}^3$ .Gas kinetic viscosity is $1.789\times10^{-5}\,\text{Ns/m}^2$.(5) The other boundaries beside inlet and oulet are all solid wall.(6) There is no heat transfer and chemical change in the whole process.

3.1 Analysis of different sizes of gas chamber cyclone

As shown in Figure 3,the results of the simulation are well matched to the lubrication theory of orifice throttle based on molecule collision. The phenomenon of cyclone is an important phenomenon of orifice throttle air static pressure guide. The presence of the cyclone can cause the fluctuation of the gas film affecting the motion accuracy of the air static pressure guide. A large number of high speed vertical movement of gas molecules have collision with gas cavity bottom. Then the speed directions of molecules change. Through the interaction between the gas molecules and the interaction between molecules and the wall surface, cyclone generates. Because of the existence of the cyclone, molecular velocity has component perpendicular to the surface of the gas chamber, which can cause the fluctuation of the gas film. As shown in Figure 3 a), b),c),gas chamber height are δ=25μm, δ=50μm, δ=80μm .With the increase of the height of the gas chamber, cyclone has a different degree of increase. This is related to the area of A and B. When A is larger, gas tends to flow in the direction of small gas resistance. A large number of molecules enter into the gas chamber after the collision with the gas film and the degree of the cyclone will become large.

a） δ=0.025mm

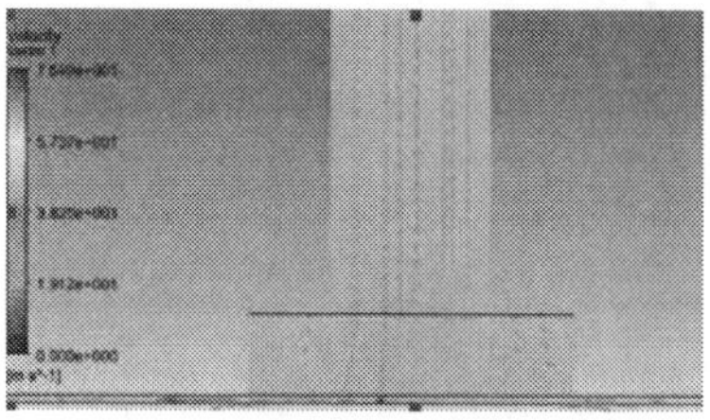

b) δ=0.05mm

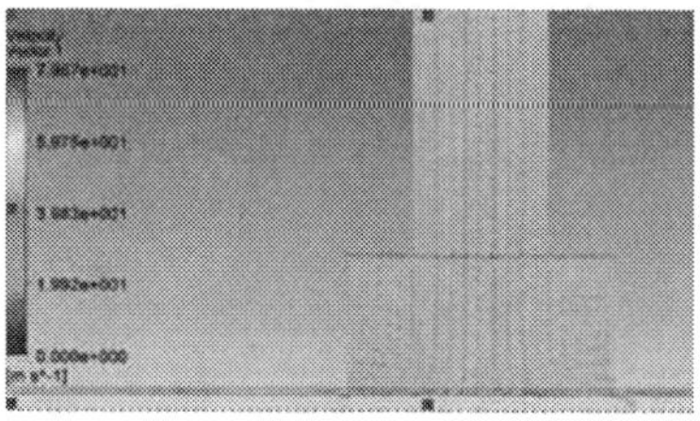

c) δ=0.1mm

Fig 3 Simulation of gas flow in feed chamber of different heights

3.2 Shock phenomenon

The system working pressure is about (0.5~0.6) MPa , generally no more than 1 MPa . The thickness of gas film is generally a few microns to a dozen microns. As shown in Figure4,Figure 5, Pressure of gas film in radial direction and radial velocity with different supply pressures that are 0.2 MPa ,0.5 MPa ,0.6 MPa ,0.7 MPa ,0.8 MPa ,1 MPa respectively and the gas film thickness is 10μm .When supply pressure suddenly increases to more than 0.8 MPa , molecular velocity in the gas chamber increase suddenly. Molecules through the gas film gap get out of the gas chamber. Velocity increases rapidly until the supersonic. The volume of a large number of high speed movement molecules is rapidly compressed and the collisions between molecules are intense. Then shock wave phenomenon occurs. The molecular kinetic energy is converted into internal energy after the impact of the collision and gas flow along the radius direction, which is equivalent to the one dimensional flow of the tube whose cross-section area continues to become large. Molecular motion velocity decreases rapidly to the subsonic speed.

Phenomenon of shock is more obvious with the increasing of supply pressure, which will bring huge fluctuations affecting the stability and rigidity of the air static pressure guide. We should try our best to avoid this phenomenon. Under the premise of ensuring the bearing capacity, the working pressure should be controlled below 0.8 MPa . As shown in Figure 5, the frontier of the velocity curve is basically coincident under different air supply pressure.

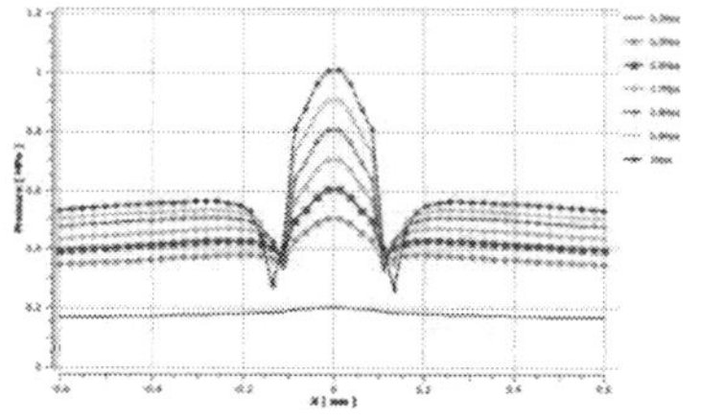

Fig 4 Pressure of gas film in radial direction with different supply pressures

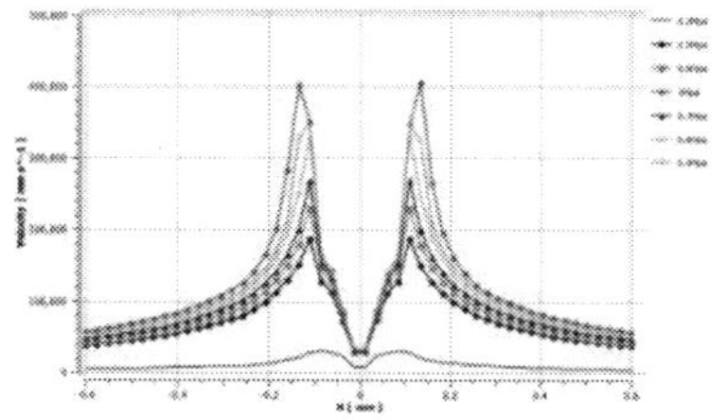

Fig 5 Radial velocity of gas flow in gas film with different supply pressures

As shown in Figure 6 and Figure 7, pressure of gas film in radial direction and radial velocity with film thickness that are 6μm,7μm,8μm,9μm,10μm respectively and the supply pressure is 0.8 MPa . Figure 7 shows that when the gas film thickness is less than 10μm , the variation tendencies of radial velocity are almost the same. When the film thickness is 10μm , the speed change is obvious. Shock wave phenomenon occurs. Figure 6 shows that, when the film thickness is 10μm , pressure in chamber change rapidly. The support ability of the high pressure gas chamber is reduced. Shock wave causes the pressure drop that causes a larger gas film wave fluctuation and the decrease of static stiffness of rail guide. Gas molecules in the gas chamber have the same speed variation trend on the condition that film thickness is not sufficient to cause a shock. There are plenty of molecules to flow out through the gas film at the same time when the film thickness increases appropriately causing shock

waves. Reducing gas film thickness appropriately can improve the bearing capacity of high pressure gas chamber.

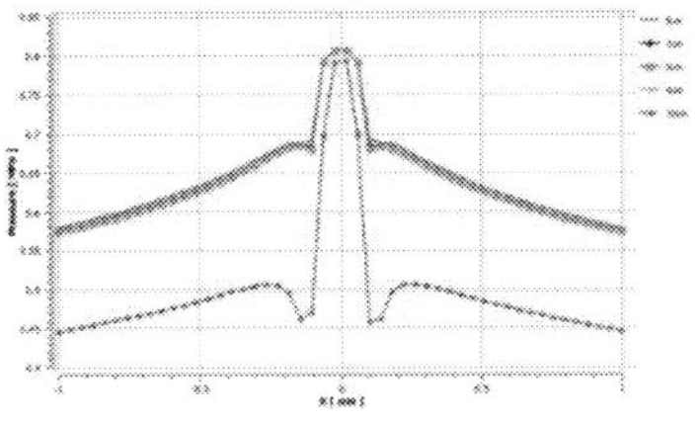

Fig 6 Pressure of gas film in radial direction with different film thickness

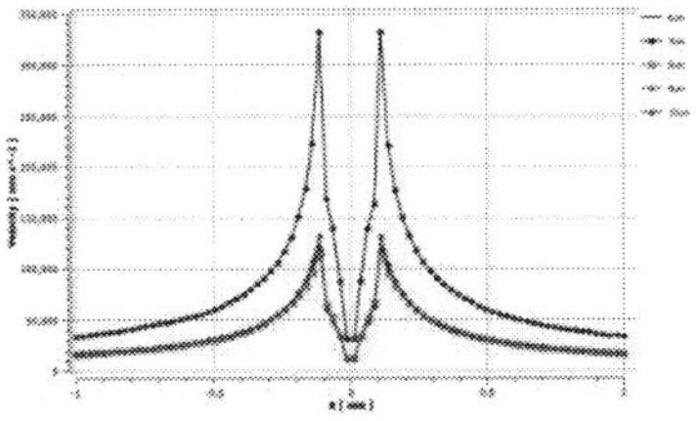

Fig 7 Radial velocity of gas flow in gas film with different film thickness

As shown in Figure 8, pressure of gas film in radial direction with different chamber height: 80μm, 90μm, 100μm, 110μm, 120μm and 200μm . The gas film thickness is h=10μm .The influence of gas chamber height on the pressure change in the gas chamber and the film is little. The position of the shock wave is not changed with the increase of the height of the gas chamber. Pressure before and after shock wave has a litter change.

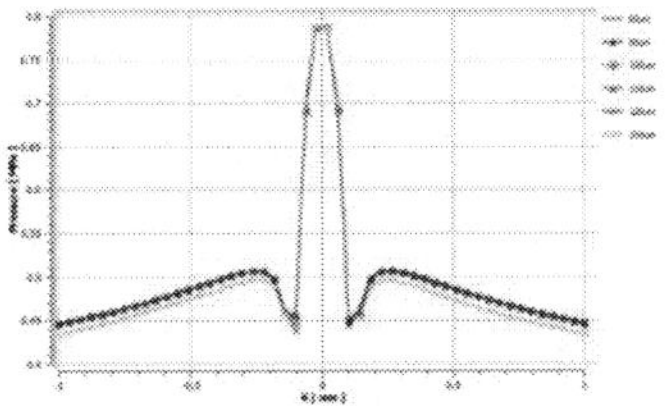

Fig 8 Pressure of gas film in radial direction with different chamber height

4 Conclusions

(1) This paper revealed the flow law from gas supply hole to gas chamber and lubrication theory of orificed throttle based on molecule collision. A new basis for the design of air static pressure guide with more stable and higher bearing capacity is put forward by analyzing the factors which influence the gas molecule collision (gas film thickness, gas chamber height, air inlet pressure).

(2)The factors that influence the stability of air static pressure guide rail are revealed. The direction of collision between the incident gas molecules and the bottom surface of the gas film change, and interaction between the gas molecules and the interaction between molecules and the wall surface causing the phenomenon of cyclone. The shock phenomenon caused by the pressure of the gas supply to the velocity of the excited molecules to the supersonic. The special structure of the orifice throttle caused the existence of the cyclone.

References

[1] G. Hirn. Sur les principaux phénomènes qui presentment les frottementes médiats[J]. Soc. Ind. Mulhouse Bull. 1854, (26): 188-277.

[2] G. Belforte, T R V V. An experimental study of high-speed rotor supported by air bearings: test RIG and first experimental results[J]. Tribol Int. 2006, 39(8): 839-845.

[3] Carfagno S P An Analysis of Experimental Data on Entrance Effect in Circular Thrust Bearings[R]. Office of Naval Research Department of the Navay Phila,1966.

[4] Aoyama T, Kakinuma Y , Kobayashi Y. Numerical and experimental analysis for the small vibratioin of aerostatic guideways[J].Annals of the CIRP ,2006, 55 [1](1):419-422.

[5] Aoyama T, Koizumi k, Kakinuma Y , et al. Numerical and experimental analysis of transient state micro-bounce of aerostatic guideways caused by small pores[J]. CIRP Annals-manufacturing Technology, 2009, 58:367-370.

[6] Chen Xuedong, He Xueming. The effect of the recess shape on performance analysis of the lubricated bearing in optical lithography[J],Tribology International, 2006,39(11):1336-1341.

[7] LIU fan, MENG xiandong. CFD study on orifice-type restrictor in aerostatic bearing[J]. 2005,32(11):21-23.

[8] CHEN dongju,BIAN yanhua,ZHOU shuai etal. Influence factor analysis for gas fluctuation of aerostatic guideway[J]. Journal of Mechanical Engineering, 2014,50(15): 97-103.

MATEC Web of Conferences 44, 02030 (2016)
DOI: 10.1051/matecconf/20164402030

Study on Bioagents or Bioaerosols standoff detection by lidar

Hui Yang[1], Yan Fei Sun[1], Tie Dong Wang[1], Xue Song Zhao[2], Yan Dong[1] and Feng Qing[1]

[1] New Star Application Technology Institute, Hefei 230031, China
[2] Key Lab. of Environmental Optics & Technology, CAS Hefei, China

Abstract. Scattering, fluorescence and polarization are the important data source for bioagent or bioaerosol time-space observation and identification. This paper stated and discussed the theory and data inversion principles for Mie scattering, laser induced fluorescence and polarization sensing Lidar. The sensing and data inversion results for bioagent/bioaerosol extinction coefficient, horizontal linear depolarization ratio were also demonstrated. The signal and SNR simulation of fluorescence lidar were also demonstrated. The sensing results revealed that the three kinds of detecting technology approaches are reasonable and potential for bioagent/bioaerosol characterization and recognition.

1 Introduction

Biological warfare agents (BWAs) or bioagents are live pathogenic microorganisms and biotoxin used in biological terrorism attack or in the battlefield, which are capable to cause mass infections or poisoning of people, animals and/or plants at reasonable economical cost. Bioagents can be sorted according to the causal agent as bacteria, viruses, rickettsiae and toxins [1, 2, 3]. Bioagents are relatively inexpensive to produce and can yield a significant impact as a terrorist weapon. Up to now, there are more than 1200 kinds of bioagents that can be produced to biological weapon. The infection of bioagents is mainly caused through absorption from respiratory tract, alimentary tract, or direct contact of skin, the deterrence will be much more awful enhanced by the recombinant DNA technique, and the death rate of un-immunized people will be nearly 100%. The World Health Organization estimated that attacking a large city with 50 kg of anthrax spores would produce 95,000 deaths and an additional 125,000 sicknesses [4]. And for viral hemorrhagic fevers, less than 10 organisms can cause decease and many of the most dangerous biological warfare agents are infectious when less than 10,000 organisms or spores are inhaled[5]. On the other hand, because of the common intrinsic fluorescence characteristics of fluorophore, such as tryptophan, tyrosine, etc., it's difficult to distinguish harmless bacteria from fatal bacteria, even genetically in some cases. Bioagents can be disseminated through at least three major ways: by vector (i.e., insects), by contaminated water or food supplies, and the most effective way of dispersion is the form of aerosol particles suspending in the air. As for the biological aerosol (bioaerosol), it includes plant and insect debris, fungal and plant spores, pollen, cells, viruses and bacteria. Abundance in the atmosphere, bioaerosol affects the cloud microphysical processes, helps to the biodiversity and disease transmission through long range transport.

Typical point detection and discrimination system based sample technique can detect bioagents/bioaerosols with a low time resolution and a relatively high false alarm rate, the bioactivity can be deteriorated during the sample procedure, and the exterior factors such as dehydration, variation of temperature will also affect the recognition result.

Early warning of a biological attack such as lidar standoff detection offers many potential capabilities not easily provided by point detection systems such as sensitivity over a wide area, easy to deploy, capability of mapping, allowing for early warning to downwind assets and population, etc. Assisted by plume modeling technique, mapping and tracking of the hazard cloud by lidar can help to determine origin, evolution of a biological attack, thus guide treatment and decontamination efforts. For example, at a condition of 20km/h wind velocity, the population on the ground can get a early warning time of about 6 minutes if the windward [6]. For these reasons the need to develop methods to remotely detect and discriminate biological aerosols from background aerosols and ultimately to discriminate biological warfare agents from naturally occurring aerosols, is paramount.

Elastic Mie scattering, laser induced fluorescence (LIF) and polarization scattering are three major bioagents/bioaerosols remote sensing techniques. In this paper, the theory, technology, ability of detection and other factors affecting detection are discussed individually.

2 Principle of Bioagents/Bioaerosols standoff detection by lidar

sanpedroman@163.com

Article available at http://www.matec-conferences.org or http://dx.doi.org/10.1051/matecconf/20164402030

Bioagents/bioaerosols remote detection is based on the interaction physical process between the laser beam and particles on the path, such as rayleigh scattering, raman scattering, Mie scattering, and the fluorescence process induced by incident ultraviolet laser beam. The fluorophores in the biological material, such as trypophan, tyrosine, Phenylalanine, and NADH(nicotinamide adenine dinucleotide) absorb the incident radiation at a ultraviolet wavelength and re-emit fluorescence at one or more longer wavelengths, and riboflavin absorbs ultraviolet and incident radiation and emits at visible wavelength.

Bioagents/bioaerosols might be non- spherical particle, the backscattering emission is not linear depolarized when illuminated by a polarized light. Through the wave plates and polarization analyzer and double-channel PMT, the received parallel and perpendicular signal can be collected and recorded individually, and finally, the bioagents/bioaerosols can be discriminated with depolarization ratio. Using depolarization ratio database for bioagents/bioaerosols and interferents, the bioagents, such as anthrax, plague, ricin, etc. and bioaerosol, such as dust, smoke, pollen, etc. can be differentiated.

So, Mie scattering lidar is used mainly for searching, positioning and space mapping of the bioagents, fluorescence lidar is used mainly to determine the fluorescence character of bioagents, and polarization lidar can be used to determine the type of bioagents cloud and provide exact early warning.

2.1 Lidar configeration

The overall schematic diagram of lidar is illustrated in Figure 1. The lidar is consisted of laser emitting sub-system, receiving sub-system and data acquisition sub-system. The returned fluorescence signal is rather weak, so the signal can be collected by photon counter, intensified CCD or PMT array. The doubled and tripled output pulse with 30mJ energy from a flash-pump Nd:YAG laser was used for Mie scattering, polarization scattering and fluorescence measurements. Beam expanders were employed to obtain outgoing laser beams with a 2-cm diameter and 0.5mrad divergence (80% of the total energy). Linear polarization purity of 1/500 for the laser beam was obtained with a polarization cube. A 300mm Cassegrain telescope with an adjustable FOV collects elastically scattered 532nm Mie, 355nm parallel and perpendicular power polarization and 355nm fluorescence signal. The scattering, polarization and fluorescence signal were accumulated for at least 60 seconds, and raman signal was accumulated for at least 30 minutes.

The main specifications of lidar are summarized in table 1.

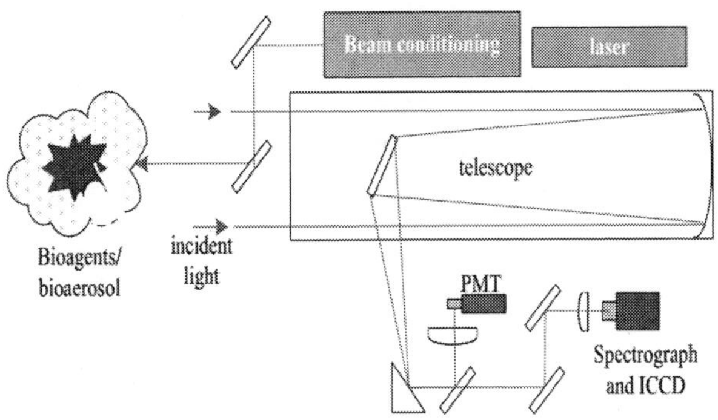

Figure. 1 Sketch of bioagent/bioaerosol sensing lidar

Table 1. Main specifications of fluorescence sensing lidar

Laser	Nd:YAG
Wavelength(nm)	532, 355, 387(Raman)
Laser pulse energy(mJ)	>40
Repetition rate(Hz)	20
Pulse width(ns)	20
Accumulated pulse counts	2000
Telescope	Schmidt-cassegrainian
Diameter(mm)	Φ300
Field of view(mrad)	1-2 adjustable
Receiver	
Filter central wavelength(nm)	465
Filter width(nm)	60
Total optical transmittance	0.16
PMT quantum yield	0.2
Range resolution(m)	15
Fluorescence central wavelength(nm)	465
NADH Quantum yield	0.1
NADH fluorescence cross section	$5e^{-12}$

2.2 Theory of mie scattering and fluorescence Llidar

The elastic lidar equation assuming single scattering and is describing the received optical power as [7]

$$P(\lambda_L,z)=P_L\cdot\frac{A_0}{z^2}\cdot\xi(\lambda_L)\cdot\beta(\lambda_L,z)\cdot\xi(z)\frac{c\cdot\tau_L}{2}\cdot T(z)(1)$$

where PL is the outgoing effect of the laser and is calculated as $P_L=E_L/\tau_L$, A_0 is the aperture area, z is the range in meter, $\xi(\lambda_L)$ is the optical efficiency of the system, $\beta(\lambda_L,z)$ is the volume backscatter coefficient for the elastic backscattering, $\xi(z)$ is the overlap function between the transmitter and the receiver field-of-view. The speed of light is c and τ_L is the pulse length of the laser, $T(z)$ is the total transmission. The laser wavelength is denoted as λ_L . The receiver noise is simulated by the detector and optical background induced noise. The total transmission at range z is in general calculated as

$$T(z) = \exp[-2\int_0^Z \alpha(\lambda_L, z)dz] \quad (2)$$

The extinction coefficient $\alpha(\lambda_L, z)$ can be divided into two terms, one for the atmospheric background and one for the bioagents/bioaerosol cloud,

$$\alpha(\lambda_L, z) = \alpha_{atm}(\lambda_L, z) + \alpha_c(\lambda_L, z) \quad (3)$$

The backscattering coefficient extinction coefficient $\beta(\lambda_L, z)$ can be also divided into two terms, one for the atmospheric background and one for the bioagents/bioaerosol cloud,

$$\beta(\lambda_L, z) = \beta_{atm}(\lambda_L, z) + \beta_c(\lambda_L, z) \quad (4)$$

The lidar ratio of atmosphere can be calculated by atmospheric mode and for the natural aerosols is set normally as $R_{atm} = \alpha / \beta$=50。

The fluorescence equation is similar to the lidar equation and is written as

$$P(\lambda, z) = P_L \cdot \frac{A_0}{z^2} \cdot K_0(\lambda_L) \cdot T(z) \cdot \xi(z) \cdot N(z) \cdot \frac{\sigma^F(\lambda_L) \cdot L^F(\lambda)}{4\pi} \cdot \frac{c_0 \cdot \tau_L}{2} \quad (5)$$

where $K_0(\lambda_L)$ is the optical filter function including the optical efficiency, N(z) is the particle concentration, $\sigma^F(\lambda_L)$ is the fluorescence cross section for the present substance and wavelength and $L^F(\lambda)$ is the fingerprint function for the present substance.

2.3 Polarization lidar equation

According to equation (1), the vertical and perpendicular backscattering signal of 355nm at distance z can be given as

$$P_\perp(z) = P_L \cdot \frac{A_0}{z^2} \cdot \xi(\lambda_L) \cdot \beta(\lambda_L, z) \cdot \xi(z) \frac{c_0 \cdot \tau_L}{2} \cdot T(z) \cdot p_\perp(z) \quad (6)$$

$$P_\parallel(z) = P_L \cdot \frac{A_0}{z^2} \cdot \xi(\lambda_L) \cdot \beta(\lambda_L, z) \cdot \xi(z) \frac{c_0 \cdot \tau_L}{2} \cdot T(z) \cdot p_\parallel(z) \quad (7)$$

Where, $p_\perp(z)$ and $p_\parallel(z)$ are the constant of two channel individually and they depend on the quantum yield of PMT and optical receiving, so the depolarization ration is given as

$$\delta(z) = \frac{P_\perp(z)/p_\perp(z)}{P_\parallel(z)/p_\parallel(z)} = \frac{P_\perp(z)}{P_\parallel(z)} \cdot \frac{p_\parallel(z)}{p_\perp(z)} \quad (8)$$

Where, $K = \frac{p_\parallel(z)}{p_\perp(z)}$ can be obtained by experimental data.

3 Data retrieval method for mie Lidar

In the hypothesis of single scattering, The Fernald method [8] was used to invert the following distributions of the aerosol extinction coefficients, the former is backward solution and the latter is forward solution

$$\alpha_c(z) = -S\alpha_{atm}(z) + \frac{X(z) \cdot \exp[2(S-1)\int_z^{z_c} \alpha_{atm}(z')dz']}{\frac{X(z_c)}{\alpha_c(z_c) + S\alpha_{atm}(z_c)} + 2\int_z^{z_c} X(z)\exp[2(S-1)\int_z^{z_c} \alpha_{atm}(z'')dz'']dz'}$$

(9)

$$\alpha_c(z) = -S\alpha_{atm}(z) + \frac{X(z) \cdot \exp[-2(S-1)\int_z^{z_c} \alpha_{atm}(z')dz']}{\frac{X(z_c)}{\alpha_c(z_c) + S\alpha_{atm}(z_c)} - 2\int_z^{z_c} X(z)\exp[-2(S-1)\int_z^{z_c} \alpha_{atm}(z'')dz'']dz'}$$

(10)

Where, $X(z) = P(z) \cdot z^2$, $S = Sc / Satm$, Sc is the aerosol extinction-to-backscattering ratio which differs with the aerosol concentration, size distribution and chemical component, its value is chosen 40~50 suggested by Sasano and Browell[9], $Satm$ is the extinction-to-backscattering ratio of atmospheric molecular valued by 8π/3, $Satm$ = 8π/3, z_c is calibration height which is selected by the calculation program automatically within the height range of 4.0~6.0km at daytime or 6.0~8.0km at nighttime. At the calibration height the content of aerosol drops to its minimized value and close to zero, so $R(z_c) = X(z_c) / \beta_{atm}(z_c)$ comes to its minimized value. So $\alpha_c(z_c)$ can be deduced by the aerosol and atmospheric molecular scattering ratio

$R(z_c) = ((\beta c(z_c) + \beta atm(z_c) / \beta atm(z_c)) = 1.01$ (11)

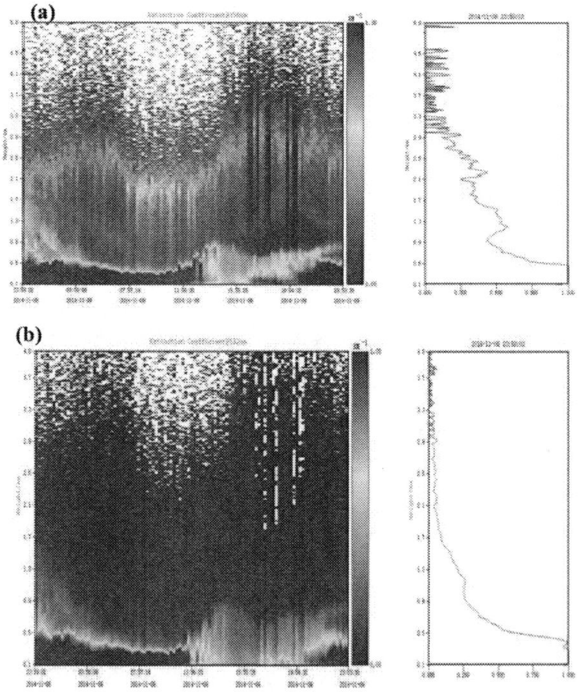

Figure. 2 Time and space distributions of bioaerosol, (a)355nm, (b)532nm

Figure 2 shows the time and space distributions of aerosol extinction coefficient measured by our multi-channel Lidar and retrieved with the Ferald method. To the right part of each diagram shows the distribution of aerosol extinction coefficient of each laser shot. The measurements were made at hefei city, china, the lidar

was laid verticallly. From figure (a) and (b), it can be easily concluded that:

At the bottom of boundary layer, the extinction coefficient distributions remained almost the same trend for the two wavelengths, the maximal value was up to $1.0km^{-1}$.

The extra aerosol cloud layer between heights from 1.7km to 2.9km were retrieved through the 355nm channel, the transmittance of 532nm channel is obviously higher, but 355nm channel is more suitable for the fine aerosol particles monitoring with a relatively high laser energy.

4 SNR of fluorescence lidar

The SNR of fluorescence signal can be described as

$$SNR(z) = \frac{N_s(z)}{\sqrt{N_s(z) + 2(N_b + N_d)}} \times \sqrt{n} \qquad (12)$$

Where, Ns (z) is photo number received at height z, Nb (z) and Nd are the photo number of background and detector dark current respectively. The more photo number received, and less background and detector noise, the SNR (z) will be higher. And also, the increased laser pulses can enhance the SNR. The simulated fluorescence signal and SNR profiles are shown in figure 3.

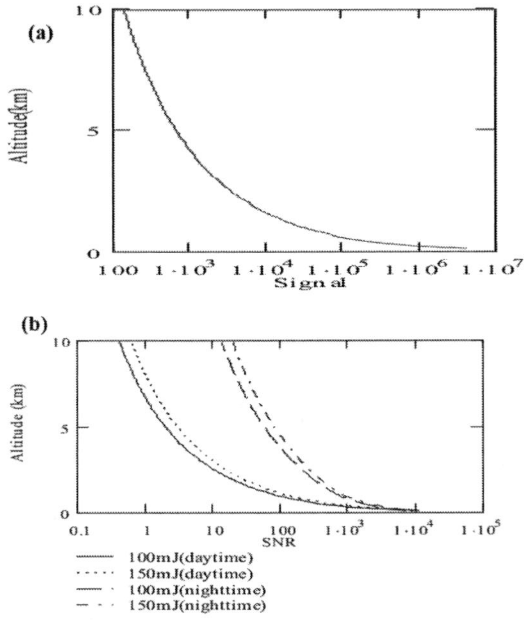

Figure. 3 profiles of simulated fluorescence signal (a) and SNR (b)

The fluorescence signal profile was simulated with standard atmospheric mode. The number of laser pulse is set as n = 2000, the night SNR is much better than that of daytime. The requirement of SNR for real lidar system is set to SNR>10.

5 Results of depolarization detection

The time and space distributions of depolarization ratio at 355nm and extinction coefficient at 532nm are shown in figure 4. The profiles were obtained by the aerosol fine particle lidar on November 27, 2014 at Hefei city. The lidar was manufactured and adjusted by AIOFM. Similarly, figure 4(a) shows the extinction coefficient profiles, and the profile on an exact single spot time is to the right. From figure 4, it can be shown that:

In the boundary layer, the height of 500m close-ground layer decreased with the time;

In the boundary layer, the complex multi-layer structured extinction coefficient distributions were observed, it means that the aerosol concentration along the laser beam path was affected seriously by the wind, humidity, press and other atmospheric condition;

The two separated vertical distributions of depolarization ratio layer were obvious, the bottom layer is ground layer and the upper layer is surface layer and boundary layer. In the ground layer of 500m height, the value of depolarization ratio remains ness than 0.01, it means that, in this layer, the aerosol particle is in the shape of fine spherical.

After 04:00pm, in the upper surface layer and boundary layer, the zigzag structured distribution of depolarization ratio was observed clearly. At some points along the path, the maximized value of depolarization ratio reached 0.3, it means that the height, the aerosol particle is not spherical caused by some complex physical and photochemistry processes, such as, coagulation, condensation, cohesion, and chemical reaction with the pollution materials released by the industrial and living activities, etc.

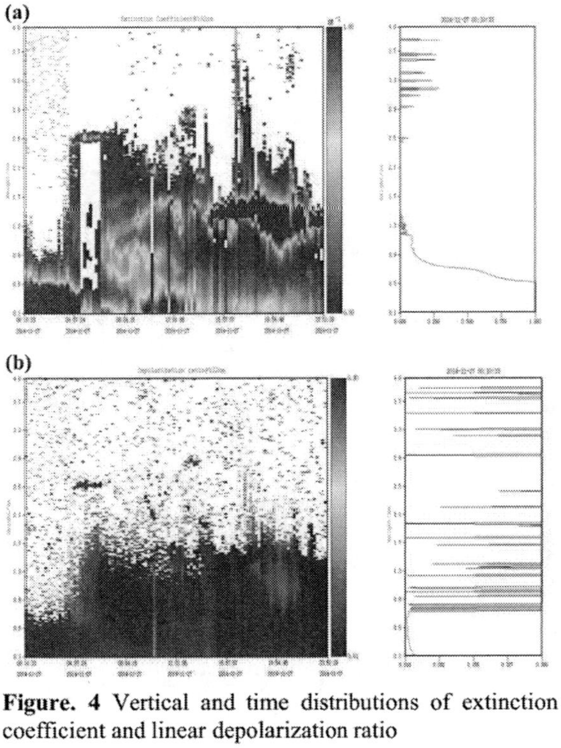

Figure. 4 Vertical and time distributions of extinction coefficient and linear depolarization ratio

6 Discussions and Conclusions

The remote sensing and recognition of bioagents/bioaserosol is the hot spot in the filed of photochemistry, biochemistry, etc. Scattering, fluorescence and polarization data are the effective data source of bioagents/bioaserosol time-space distribution monitoring and characteristics recognition. In this paper, the principle, data retrieve algorithms of Mie scattering, ultraviolet laser induced fluorescence lidar are introduced, and the results of vertical time-space evolvement, distributions of extinction coefficient, depolarization ratio observation were discussed.

With the combined multi-dimension observation data, the bioagents/bioaserosol recognition and discrimination appear feasible in principle. However, future work is required to make it reality, and the following questions must be addressed: Except the time-space distribution, how to discriminate exactly bioagents/bioaserosol with observed fluorescence data? Except 355nm wavelength, what wavelength is more effective for depolarization ration measurement, the shorter one or longer one? Does the depolarization ration is wavelength dependent? And what is effect of atmospheric factors, such as relative humidity, background aerosol fluctuation?

Acknowledgment

The work was supported by the National Natural Science Foundation of China named "Study on Technology of Ultraviolet Laser-induced Fluorescence LIDAR for Bioagent Remote Sensing" No. 41375026.

References

1. Matoušek, J.; Bendík J. & Linhart P. CBRN: (Boological weapons, 2007).
2. Klietmann, W.F. & Ruoff, K., Clin biol Rev, J. **14**, 2(2001)
3. Burger, H.A.; Solomon, W.R. Atmo Envi, J. **12**, 2(1987)
4. *Health Aspects of Chemical and Biological Weapons*(World Health Organization, Geneva, Switzerland, 1970)
5. D. R. Walt and D. R. Franz, Anal Chem, J. **A-746**(200)
6. G. M. Dougherty, D. S. Clague, and R. R. Miles, B. SPIE Opt. Photon. Global Homeland Security III, 6540(2007)
7. Measures, R. M., *Laser Remote Sensing: Fundamentals and Applications*(John Wiley & Sons, New York, 1984)
8. Fernald, F.G., Appl. Opt., J. **23**, (1984)
9. Y. Sasano and E. V. Browell, Appl. Opt. J. **28**(1989)

MATEC Web of Conferences **44**, 02031 (2016)
DOI: 10.1051/matecconf/20164402031

Analysis of starting resistance moment of direct drive wind turbine

Bin He, Quan Liu

Mechanical and Electrical Engineering School, Beijing Information Science & Technology University, Beijing, 100192, China

Abstract: Permanent magnet motor in the process of running, the permanent magnets provided the magnetic field , the core will have a strong attraction, produce the cogging torque and torque ripple, vibration and noise and other disharmony factors, seriously affect the control precision of the motor system.Therefore, in the design of permanent magnet wind turbine generator, weaken the cogging torque is very important.

Keywords: Permanent magnet motor,control precision,cogging torque

0 Preface

Wind energy is a kind of renewable energy,and it is also one of the most abund antenergy for human development and utilization.There are various ways people use wind energy, and modern society is the main way of using wind power, the wind energy is converted into easy to transport and control of power to use.Traditional doubly-fed induction generator excitation system is complex, with frequent gear transmission failure, maintenance difficulties, greatly limits the development of wind turbine applications.

The direct-drive permanent magnet wind turbine is not only remove the gear box that is easy to be damaged, also use permanent magnets to replace electric excitation, greatly improve the reliability of the system operation, efficiency is also increased.Direct-drive permanent magnet wind turbine, however, there are some technical problems need to solve.The permanent magnet make permanent magnet generator produce the cogging torque, the motor starting performance and running stability of the proposed the new challenge, as far as possible the extinction of the cogging torque, become a direct-drive major research topic of permanent magnet wind turbine .

1 The cogging torque generating mechanism and analysis method

1.1 The reason of cogging torque

The cogging torque is the inherent

Article available at http://www.matec-conferences.org or http://dx.doi.org/10.1051/matecconf/20164402031

characteristics of permanent magnet motor, especially for low speed wind power generator, the cogging torque is too large, will cause strong vibration and noise.The permanent magnet is relative to the armature winding, both the outer and the inner rotor. The armature winding in the open core with a notch, regardless of whether or not with current, will produce a magnetic force.

Once the rotor starts to rotate, the magnetic force on the formation of torque, to maintain the original state, which is the physical embodiment of cogging torque.In the process of rotation of the rotor, permanent magnet track to the region week changes greatly, which led to the magnetic field energy changes, expand the influence of cogging torque.

1.2the cogging torque analysis method

Finite element analysis method

Finite element method in electromagnetic calculation, have used the very mature, the development of commercial software such as Ansys, Ansoft has high accuracy.With finite element method can get the magnetic field distribution, the torque by the node to take.It is concluded that magnetic volume and surface force as:

$$f_i^{\Omega} = \partial_k T_{ik} \tag{1.1}$$

$$f_i^{\Gamma} = \int_1^2 T_{ik} n_k d\alpha \tag{1.2}$$

The magnetic fields of the Maxwell's tension:

$$T_{ik} = H_i B_k - \delta_{ik} \int_0^H BdH \tag{1.3}$$

The virtual displacement work as:

$$\delta W = -\int T_{ik} \partial_k N_n dv \tag{1.4}$$

Virtual displacement node shape functions:

$$\delta l_i = \sum_n N_n \delta l_{ni} \tag{1.5}$$

For the NTH node forces:

$$f_{ni} = -\int_{\Omega} T_{ik} \partial_k N_n dv \tag{1.6}$$

The effect of each node and, get the whole volume on the torque:

$$\bar{T} = \sum_{l \in V} \bar{r}_l \times \bar{f}_l \tag{1.7}$$

2 The effective methods to reduce the cogging torque

With the constant improvement of the permanent magnet material performance, remanent magnetism of magnetic steel is also attractive to alveolar, the greater the interaction between permanent magnet and slotted core, produce bigger the cogging torque.When the rotating permanent magnet direct-drive generator, produce torque ripple, vibration and noise, they will directly affect the permanent magnet direct drive wind turbine running stability and low speed startup performance.

In the design requirements through winding magnetic flux is changing, all $d\Phi / dt$ everywhere is not zero.But the magnetic flux of the total rate of change is very small, is the best way to pole magnetic flux is invariable, the cogging torque are as small as possible.To this end, we use the following methods to weaken the cogging torque.

2.1 Slit width

Under the condition of wire to make notch become smaller, the tooth and the magnetic flux become as small as possible, if necessary, can use magnetic slot wedge.

As shown in figure 1, the cogging torque amplitude increases with the slit width b0 to decrease then increase, b0 size should choose between 9 mm to 15 mm, this size range the cogging torque ripple minimum.B0, the greater the slot wedge in the assembly, the more difficult, therefore integrated magnetic properties and assembly technology, will be the best value is b0 slit width = 10 mm.

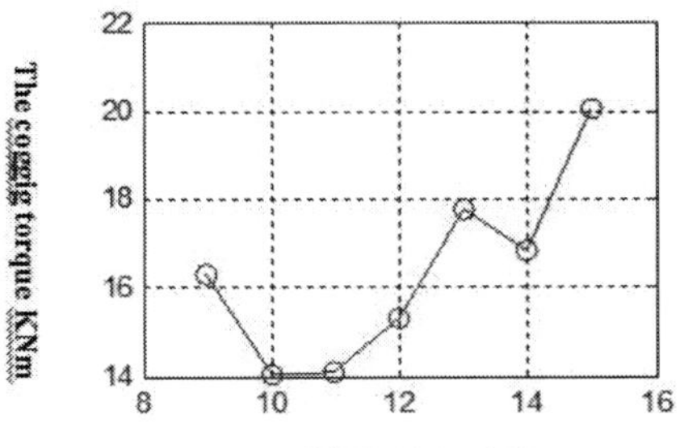

Figure 1.Different slit width the cogging torque curve peak change

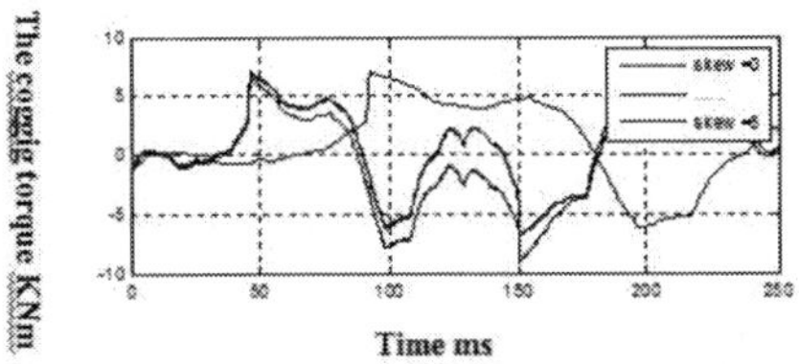

Figure 2.Different chute degree the cogging torque waveform

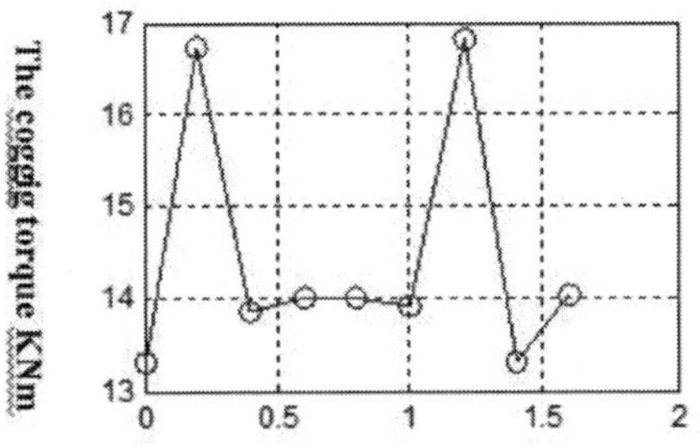

Figure 3.Different chute peak curve degree the cogging torque

2.2 Chute

USES the oblique groove and obliquepole can effectively reduce thecogging torque, but it's hard to largepermanent magnet direct-drive generator adopts chute, craft is not easy toachieve, and using inclined extremelyeasily, but the magnetic material is used up big, the price is higher.

Motor stator chute design is a common way to weaken the torque ripple, and after the chute motor as inaxial direction can be divided into multiple layers, each layer can be treated as a unit of motor, the cogging torque of each layer unit motor phasedue to the chute, added togetherto weaken the cogging torque peaks.

Because of the chute Angle is small, generally 0 ~ 5°, the cogging torque waveform trend does not produce big changes.Figure 2 ~ 3 for CAE calculation results, the cogging torque cycle after the chute and waveform trend is almost the same, less peak.Zero cogging torque ripple when the value of 21.073 kNm, chute after 0.42 degrees torque ripple value stable in 6.637 kNm, width decrease fluctuation is bigger.The size of the wind turbine is bigger, this example USES the outer rotor of the generator stator outer diameter is 4310 mm, chute to weaken the torque ripple effect is obvious.

2.3 Arc coefficient

Magnetic circuit and magnetic flux itself has asked for arc coefficient, surface generally installed magnets, arc coefficient is not less than 0.8.According to the actual notches, choose a tooth, corresponding change the minimum magnetic flux in the process of spinning area, can be determined using arc number should be greater than 0.8, even if the arc is no effect on the output coefficient is 1.

Arc coefficient is permanent magnets are arranged density parameters, evaluation for table structure, the N S pole permanent magnet arranged alternately, approximate sine is formed in the air gap flux density distribution, the technological gap between adjacent permanent magnets, adjust the gap to make magnetic induction line uniform distribution as far as possible to achieve uniform magnetic field.Permanent magnet synchronous motor rotate a fundamental wave of the cogging torque cycles and the greatest common divisor of the stator slot number and the number of the rotor

$$\gamma = \frac{N_P N_S}{N_G} = N_L \tag{2.1}$$

According to Z.Q.Z hu, the number of the best coefficient formula:

$$\alpha_p = \frac{N-1}{N} + k_2 \tag{2.2}$$

As can be seen from the figure 4, the cogging torque ripple decrease then increase first, within the range of 0.928 ~ 0.938.Considering the conducting bar permanent magnet installation to do process, will the distance between permanet magnet roundness,1 mm, the arc coefficient of 0.932.

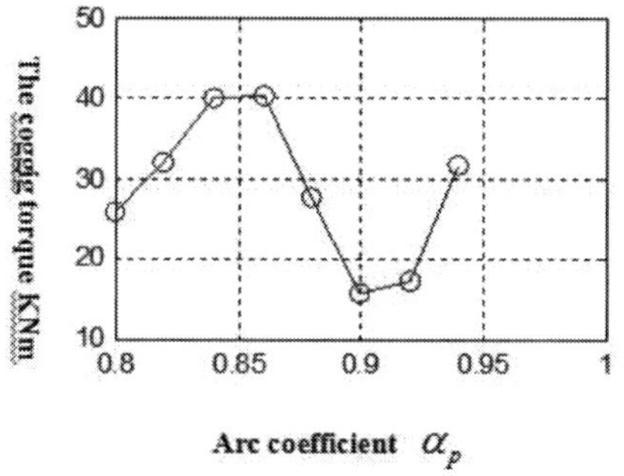

Figure 4. Different arc coefficient of the cogging torque curve peak change

2.4 The optimum parameters of the motor

According to the previous analysis, get 84 pole 84 slot motor cogging torque minimum the best parameter combination of specific parameters are shown in table 1, the rabbet width, arc coefficient,chute degree are adjusted.The cogging torque waveform comparison before and after optimization are shown, the trend of the two curves, cycle, have no obvious change, volatility is slightly different.This is due to the optimization of the parameters are not fundamentally change the motor groove structure, permanent magnet to the nonlinear attract laws of stator core did not change obviously.

Table 1.84 pole 84 slot motor cogging torque characteristics of optimal parameters

To optimize the project	The optimized parameters	Before optimization parameters
The number/slot number	84pole288	84pole288
Slot opening width(mm)	10	14
Arc coefficient	0.9	0.9
Chute degree	0	3

Can be seen from the figure 5 the cogging torque fluctuation decreased from 12.252 to 6.637KNm, reduced 47%;The motor structure design parameters of fine-tuning have played an important role in to weaken the cogging torque, effect is obvious.

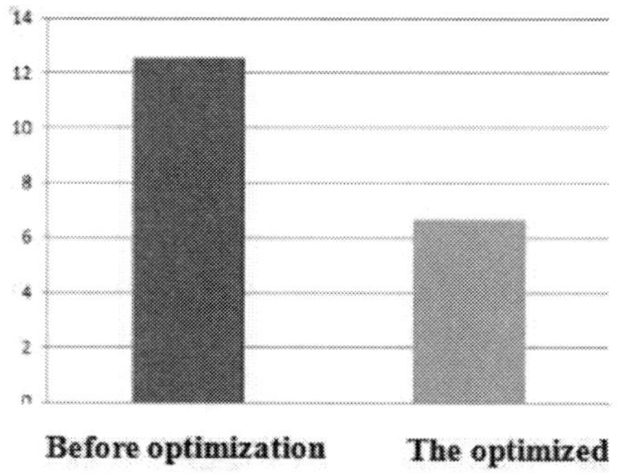

Figure 5. Peak torque contrast before and after optimization

To sum up, the local structure by adjusting the motor parameters can be found outside the wind turbine rotor cogging torque ripple minimum parameters combination, fundamentally change the motor cogging structure and size, eliminate or greatly weakened the cogging torque, so by fine-tuning the motor structure parameters is of great significance to the design of the wind turbine, improve the external rotor torque performance of wind turbines.

3 Brief summary

Starting torque of permanent magnet direct-drive generator are analyzed, and the mechanism of the cogging torque is studied.Puts forward some methods to weaken the cogging

torque, chute, slit width and the coefficient of arc generator in the aspects of optimized design, the optimum parameters of 2 MW wind turbine is obtained, and the design of this type of permanent magnet generator has played a reference.

References

1. Santiago Arnaltes, Juan Carlos Burgos. Control of Permanent-Magnet Generators Applied to Variable- Speed Wind-Energy Systems Connected to the Grid Chinchilla. IEEE Transaction on Energy Conversion, 2006,21(1): 130-135

2. Pinghua Tang, Guijie Yang, Min Luo, etal. A Current Control Scheme with Tracking Mode for PMSM System. 1st International Symposium on Systems and Control in Aerospace and Astronautics, Harbin,2006,872-876

3. R.K.Sharma,V.Sanadhya, L.Behera, etal. Vector control of a permanent magnet synchronous motor. INDICON 2008, Kanpur,India, 2008,81-86

4. Kelvin Tan,Syed Islam. Optimum control strategies in energy conversion of PMSG wind turbine system without mechanical sensors. IEEE Transactions On Energy Conversion, 2004,19(2): 392-399

5. Monica Chinchilla, Santiago Arnaltes, Juan Carlos Burgos. Control of permanent-magnet generators applied to variable-speed wind-energy systems connected to the grid. IEEE Transactions on Energy Conversion,2006,21(3)

MATEC Web of Conferences 44, 02032 (2016)
DOI: 10.1051/matecconf/20164402032

The Implementation of a Vulnerability Topology Analysis Method for ICS

Yi Lin Yang[1,2], Ji Teng Wang[1,2], Guo Ai Xu[1,2]

[1]*Beijing University of Posts and Telecommunications, Beijing, China*
[2]*NEL of Security Technology for Mobile Internet, Beijing, China*

Abstract. Nowadays Industrial Control System (ICS) is becoming more and more important in significant fields. However, the using of the general facilities in these systems makes lots of security issues exposed. Because there are a number of differences between the original IT systems and ICSs. At the same time, the traditional vulnerability scan technology lacks the ability to recognize the interactions between vulnerabilities in the network. ICSs are always in a high risk state. So, this paper focuses on the vertex polymerization of the topological vulnerability analysis. We realized a topological analysis method oriented ICSs on the basis of achievements at home and abroad. The result shows that this method can solve the problem of the complex fragility correlation among industrial control networks.

1 Review

Currently, ICSs have a wide range of applications in Chinese electric power, water conservation, sewage treatment, oil and gas, chemical, transportation, pharmaceutical and other industries. ICS has been an vital component of the national security strategy[1].

However, with the deep integration of informatization and industrialization, ICSs are increasingly using common protocol, common hardware and common software, and using a variety of ways to connect the Internet and other public network.This causes that viruses, Trojans and other threats are diffusing in the ICSs. ICSs' security issues have become increasingly prominent [2]. At the same time, since there are many differences between traditional enterprise IT systems and ICSs, the security measures of IT systems are often not well suited to ICSs. This often leads to accidents due to system failure. Many critical control systems are at high risk condition.

This paper will be based on the topological analysis techniques to study the vulnerability topological analysis techniques oriented ICSs. Compared to some related research progress, this paper makes improvement on the number of vertexes, which need to be analyzed by target topology. The advantage is reducing the cost of network administrators' exploring the industrial system vulnerabilities, as well as the time, labor and other costs.

2 Topological analysis technology oriented to ICS

Based on the existing research[3], this chapter will explain the topology analysis technology of the ICS. When analyzing the security of the ICS, the analysis flows of the topology hidden trouble analysis technology in this paper can be summarized as:

1 to read the ICS network asset allocation file provided by the user;

2 to implement the prototype system, and output the original topology vertex's and arc's information;

3 to analyze the target topology structure structured by the vertex information and the structure of the arc information in the second analysis;

4 to run vertex aggregation algorithm to execute the initial optimization and depth optimization of the target topology;

5 to get the output information of the algorithm in the fourth analysis and provide the main interface module of the tool;

6 to make topological analysis and show the results of hidden trouble analysis[4].

The overall work flow of this method is shown in Figure 1.

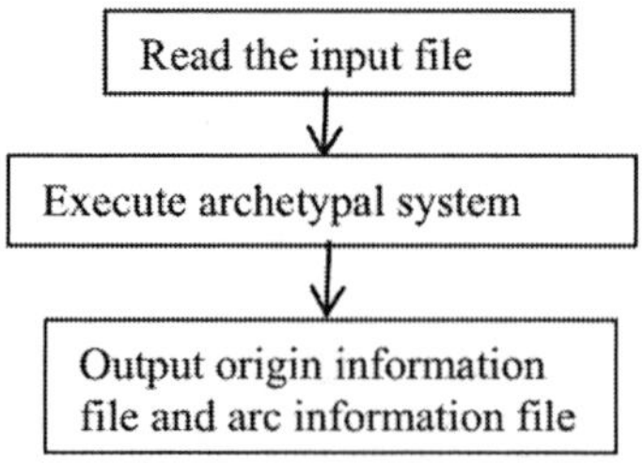

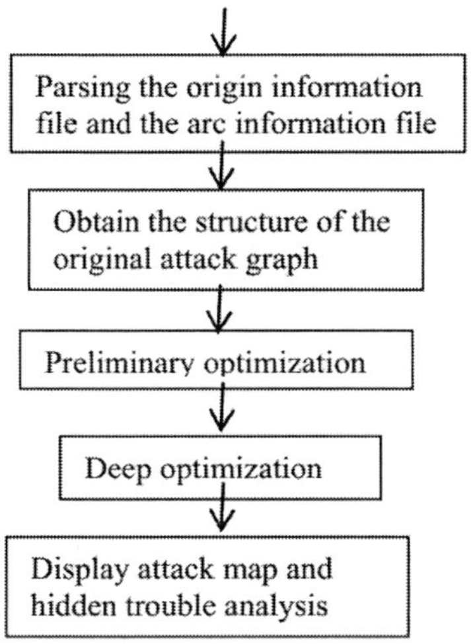

Figure 1. system's work-flow

2.1 vertex aggregation algorithm

In this paper, a simple node aggregation algorithm is designed. Through this algorithm, on the base of retaining all the vertexes' information of the prototype tool's target topology[5], we simplified all the vertexes of the original topology twice, and eventually generated a topology analysis result that the vertex number was reduced to the same number of the device in the described network. And the vertex information belonged to the same device in the original figure will be collected to corresponding device vertex in the new figure. The network device we said includes the device used by attackers. This algorithm is described as follows:

Input: The information of the target topology described by the prototype tool includes the vertex information and the arc information.

Output: An analytic topology, in which the number of vertexes is equal to the number of devices in the described network, the vertex information is not reduced. And the described attack path is consistent with the input graph.

First, we will analyze the original topology of the prototype tool. Three kinds of vertexes of the original topology are the attack steps vertex of oval, the right vertex of the diamond, which means it can obtain the right from its predecessor node, and the configuration information vertex of the rectangle. In these three kinds of vertexes, the key point is the right vertexes, because they describe the process that the attacker obtains the right to keep close to the target he wants to achieve, and they are most able to explain the attacker's attack path. The secondary vertex is the vertex of the attack's starting position described by the configuration information vertex, because it describes the origin of the attack path. We first define three classes of vertexes before the introduction of vertex aggregation algorithms.

Definition 1 (right vertex P-Node): A P-Node represents a certain level of authority derived from the derivation of the pioneer vertex.

Formal definition is:

$$\forall n2 \in P-Nodes, \exists n1 \in P-Nodes \cup C-Nodes$$

is n2's ancestor vertex,

there exists a reachable simple oriented path from n1 to n2.

Definition 2 (configuration information vertex C-Node): C-Node represents a network configuration.

Formal definition is:

$$\forall cn \in C-Nodes,$$

cn is the element of Configuration-condition.

The Configuration-condition represents a collection of network configurations.

Definition 3 (attack step vertex S-Node):

A S-Node vertex refers to a single attack will be triggered when all its preconditions(S-Node or P-Node)are satisfied.

Formal definition is:

if({pn1, pn2,...,pni} ∈ P-Nodes
or {cn1, cn2,...,cnj} ∈ C-Nodes
and {pn1, pn2,..., pni , cn1, cn2,... , cnj} ∈ Rules)
then {pn1, pn2, , pni , cn1, cn2, , cni}
sni ∈ S-Nodes

The Rules represents a collection of attack rules.

In the three kinds of vertexes, S-Node is the vertex of the logical AND type; C-Node and P-Node are the vertexes of the logical OR type[6] .

2.2 Algorithm design

Preliminary optimization

In contrast, other configuration information vertexes can be used as a supplementary information of access information, to describe the necessary conditions of obtaining a certain permission. While all the configuration information vertexes' in-degree in the original figure is 0, and their out-degree is 1. Therefore, after reserving the configuration information to permission information's subsidiary information, all the other configuration information vertexes, together with the related edges, can be removed from the original figure.

At the same time, the attack steps vertex describes the method to obtain the other permissions when the configuration information and some rights are met. So, in the original topology, the attack step vertex is the ancestor of the right information vertex. Thus, the information of the utilization method described by the attack steps vertex can be aggregated to the right vertex of their children' position. At the same time, the arc which points to it will point to the right vertex of its descendants. Then we can remove the attack steps vertex from the original figure.

After the above operation, the first step of original topological vertex aggregation algorithm is completed. Now the figure only retains the permissions vertex, the attacker's first position vertex, all arcs connected to these vertexes, and all information keeping the other vertexes in the original figure. If you do not have all information of the other vertexes to display, you can display when the users need to obtain information. After the initial

optimization of the vertex aggregation algorithm, the intermediate rendering effect of the analytic topology is shown in Figure 2.

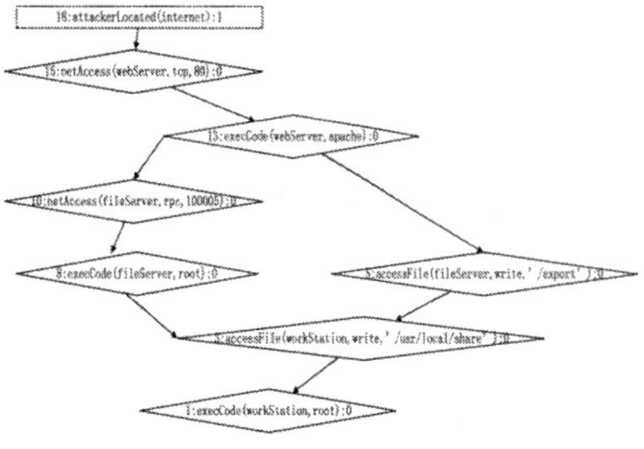

Figure 2. The intermediate rendering effect of the analytic topology after the initial optimization.

Deep optimization

After the initial optimization, the decrease of the topological vertexes' number has been extraordinarily sizable. In this case, the vertex number of the prototype tool's analytic topology, which contains 26 vertexes, has been reduced to 8, and the number of nodes has been reduced to 70%. But it has not reached the goal of the algorithm, that is, the number of vertexes is equal to the number of targets device described by the network. The reason why the number of vertexes after the initial optimization is greater than the number of devices described by the network is that multiple access behaviours occur on the same device sometimes.

In order to achieve this goal, we have to aggregate multiple permissions' acquisition behaviour that occurs on a device to the same vertex. And we describe these permissions in the order of obtaining permission in this vertex.

After the deep optimization above, the output analytic topology can be used as the final output of the algorithm. The rendering effect of the analytic topology after the deep optimization of the vertex aggregation algorithm is shown in Figure 3.

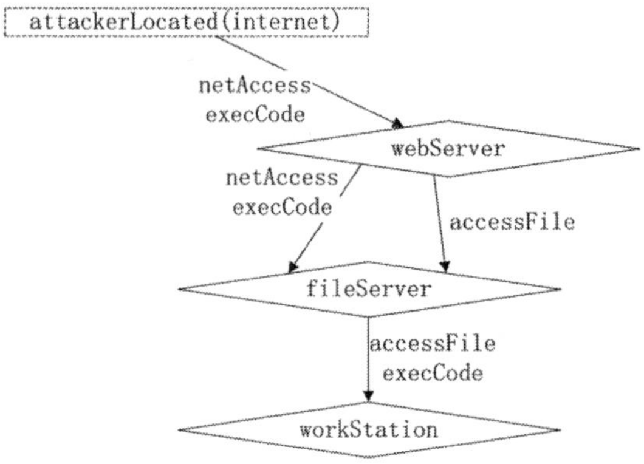

Figure 3. The rendering effect of the analytic topology after the deep optimization of this algorithm.

After gathering the multiple access happened on the same device to the same point, the attacker's attack process can be showed on the network topology of the actual ICS, and it's marked in red in the realization of the technology. This can help to identify the vulnerable hosts in the target network.

3 Technical realization and experimental analysis

After the two-step optimization of the algorithm described in the last chapter, in order to make the display effect more vivid and intuitive, we need to beautify the vertex shape of the graph in the realization of the topological analysis technology. We can use sketch map representing the corresponding equipment to describe the vertex. This has been overstepped the required work scope of the algorithm, and these work is mainly done in the technology realization boundary.

In real applications, the reduction of the vertex's scale in the analytic topology brings a shorter emergency response time for the administrator, and thus be more agile to deal with the fragile problem of the industrial control network. However, this subjective situation cannot be verified in this paper.

In order to verify the advantages of the technology described in this paper, a new approach is adopted. The implementation of the algorithm is implemented in the target network of 3, 10, 20 and 50 scales. The difference on the vertex number between the two kinds of optimization and the existing technology is compared in this paper.

Experiment 1:

The analytic topology before Ou technology's optimization is compared with the analytic topology obtained in this paper on the vertex's number. Experimental results are shown in the following diagram.

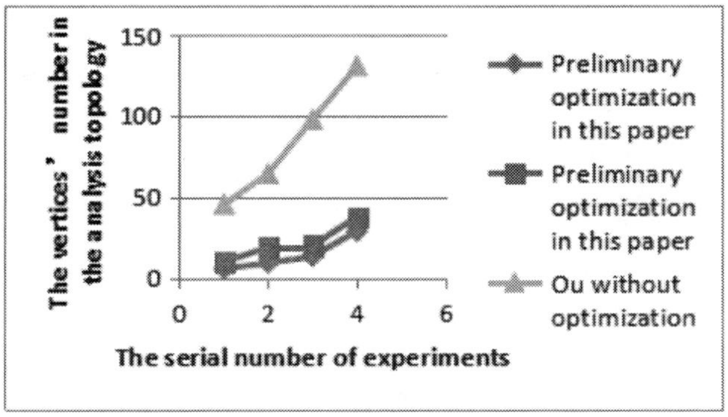

Figure 4. Experiment 1: the vertexes number's comparison in the existing technology without optimization.

What is shown in Figure 4 is that, after preliminary optimization, the vertexes scale in the topology has been significantly reduced to about 10%~30% of the existing technology. Then, after the deep optimization, the number of vertexes has been reduced in a small extent. The experimental data shows that, compared with other technologies, the number of vertexes in this paper is drastically reduced, which will lead to a lot of liberation for the vulnerable point location of topological analysis.

Experiment 2:

The vertexes number of the analytic topology with the optimization of the Ou technology is compared with the analytic topology obtained in this paper's algorithm. Experimental results are shown in the following diagram.

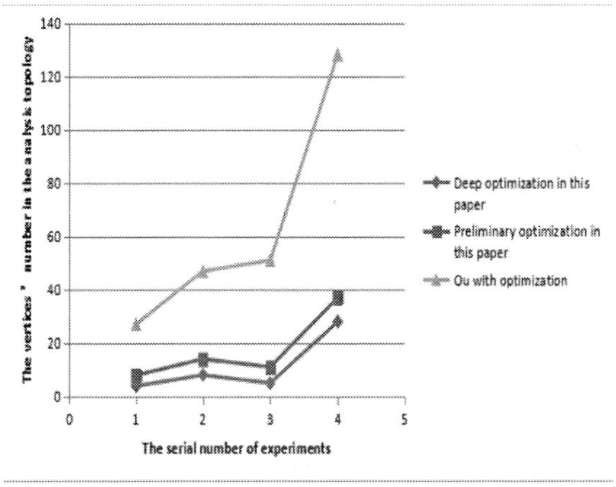

Figure 5. Experiment 2: comparison of the number of vertexes in the existing technology optimization

Ou technology itself also has the ability to optimize, we compare the analytic topology after this optimization with the technology of this paper again. After comparing Figure 4 with Figure 5, we can find that Ou technology's own optimization ability is not stable. Sometimes we can get very good optimization, sometimes cannot. But this paper can make notable optimization on the same analytic topology. This experiment shows that the optimization results of the proposed algorithm in this paper is more stable than Ou's existing technology.

4 Summary

In the field of ICS, this paper designed and implemented an ICS topology analysis technology based on graph data structure. This technology can be used in small and medium-sized industrial control network to analysis at the security hidden trouble. It also describes the attackers' might-taken attack path in compromising the network process, and highlight the fatal weakness in the network. So it can play an assistant function about forecast in the security defence of the ICS.

This technology can be used in the ICS's network security analysis. Compared to the previous research, this paper has a breakthrough in the application domain. At the same time, compared to the previous analysis, the results of this paper are more obscure and complex. After two-step optimization, the technology cooperates with the graphical interface design to show a simple, clear and intuitive topological analysis results. To some extent, the burden of network administrators on the identification of network fragility can be reduced. And the network administrator users' experience faced to ICS become friendlier.

Acknowledgment

This work is supported by National Natural Science Foundation of China Project (61302087, 61401038, U153 610079).

References

1. Peng Cheng. Information Security of Industrial Control System - China Information Security, 2014(1):31—32.
2. Qinzhi Wei. Industrial Network Control System Security and Management-Measurement& Control Technology,2013(2).
3. Shuai Zhang. Security situation and risk analysis in industrial control systems - In aspect of the risk analysis in security of ICS, 2012, 4: 46—48.
4. Ye Zhang. New focus on information security - Security of industrial control system, 2012, 4: 46—48.
5. Xinming Ou. A Logic-programming Approach to Network Security Analysis. PhD thesis, Princeton University, 2005.
6. Congli Ling. Analysis and Modeling of Vulnerability in Industrial Control System. PhD thesis, Zhejiang University, 2013.

MATEC Web of Conferences 44, 02033 (2016)
DOI: 10.1051/matecconf/20164402033

On the Adjacent Strong Equitable Edge Coloring of $P_n \vee P_n$, $P_n \vee C_n$ and $C_n \vee C_n$

Jun Liu[1,a], Chuan Cheng Zhao[1], Shu Xia Yao[2], Zhi Guo Ren[1], Qiu Ju Yue[1]

1. Lanzhou City University, School of Information Science and engineering, Lanzhou 730070, P.R.China
2. Lanzhou City University, Department of Mathematics, Lanzhou 730070, P.R.China

Abstract. A proper edge coloring of graph G is called equitable adjacent strong edge coloring if colored sets from every two adjacent vertices incident edge are different,and the number of edges in any two color classes differ by at most one,which the required minimum number of colors is called the adjacent strong equitable edge chromatic number. In this paper, we discuss the adjacent strong equitable edge coloring of join-graphs about $P_n \vee P_n$, $P_n \vee C_n$ and $C_n \vee C_n$.

1 Introduction

The coloring problem of graphs is widely applied in practice. In [1], some conditional coloring problems as introduced. Some network problem can be converted to the strong edge coloring[2–5] and adjacent strong edge coloring[6].

DEFINITION 1[2–5] For a graph G(V, E), if a proper coloring f is satisfied with $C(u) \neq C(v)$ for $\forall u, v \in V(G)(u \neq v)$, then f is called*k-strong edge coloring of* G, is abbreviated *k*-SEC, and

$$\chi'_s(G) = \min\{k \mid k-SEC\ of\ G\}$$

is called the strong edge chromatic number of G. And for $\forall u, v \in E(G), C(u) \neq C(v)$, then f is called *k-adjacent strong edge coloring of* G, is abbreviated *k*-ASEC, and

$$\chi'_{as}(G) = \min\{k \mid k-ASEC\ of\ G\}$$

is called the adjacent strong edge chromatic number of G[6].Where

$$C(u) = \{f(uv) \mid uv \in E(G)\}.$$

DEFINITION 2 Let f is a k– ASEC of Gand satisfied with $\left||E_i| - |E_j|\right| \leq 1\ i, j = 1,2,\cdots,k$

f is called *the adjacent strong equitable edge coloring of* G, and noted by *k–ASEEC*ofG, and

$$\chi'_{ase}(G) = \min\{k \mid k-ASEEC\ of\ G\}$$

is called *the adjacent strong equitable edge chromatic number of* G.Where

$$E_i = \{e \mid f(e) = i\}\ i = 1,2,\cdots,k.$$

Conjecture[6] For a connected graph with order $p \geq 3$ and $G \neq C_5$ (5-cyycle),

Where $p = |V(G)|$, $\Delta(G)$ is maximal degree of$G$.

There are many references proof this conjecture is true, for example[7-8], for $\Delta(G) \leq 3$, this conjecture is true; For a connected graph with $V(G) \geq 3$.

(1) If G is a bipartite graph with no isolate edges, then

$$\chi'_{as}(G) \leq \Delta(G) + 2$$

(2)If G is a k-chromatic graph with no isolate edges, then

$$\chi'_{as}(G) \leq \Delta(G) + O(\log k).$$

DEFINITION 3[9] For graph G and graph H, $V(G) \cap V(H) = E(G) \cap E(H) = \varnothing$, and

$$\begin{cases} V(G \cup H) = V(G) \cup V(H) \\ E(G \cup H) = E(G) \cup E(H) \cup \\ \{uv \mid u \in V(G), v \in V(H)\} \end{cases},$$

then $G \vee H$ is called join-graph of G and H.

LEMMA 1[6] If G is a connected graph with $|V(G)| \geq 3$, and $uv \in E(G), d(u) = d(v) = \Delta(G)$, then $\chi'_{as}(G) \geq \Delta(G) + 1$.

LEMMA 2[9] If $k \geq \chi'(G)$, then$k$-PEC of G has been exist

$$\left||E_i| - |E_j|\right| \leq 1 \cdot i, j = 1,2,\cdots,k$$

Where $e \in E_i$, $f(e) = i (i = 1,2,\cdots,k)$, $\chi'(G)$ is the

[a]authore-mail: 527876625@.qq.com
This studywas supported by Lanzhou City University Ph.D. Research Fund (21265099,41361013,GS[2013]GHB1084, LZCU-BS2013-09 and LZCU-BS2013-12).

chromatic number of G.

LEMMA 3 For $n \geq 3$,

$$|E(P_n \vee P_n)| = n^2 + 2n - 2$$

$$|E(P_n \vee C_n)| = n^2 + 2n - 1$$

$$|E(C_n \vee C_n)| = n^2 + 2n$$

LEMMA 4 For $n \geq 3$, then

The equation $\begin{cases} x + y = n + 3 \\ nx + (n-1)y = n^2 + 2n - 2 \end{cases}$

Have a solution $y \begin{cases} x = 1 \\ y = n - 2 \end{cases}$

The equation $\begin{cases} x + y = n + 3 \\ nx + (n-1)y = n^2 + 2n - 1 \end{cases}$

Have a solution $y \begin{cases} x = 2 \\ y = n + 1 \end{cases}$

The equation $\begin{cases} x + y = n + 3 \\ nx + (n-1)y = n^2 + 2n \end{cases}$

Have a solution $y \begin{cases} x = 3 \\ y = n \end{cases}$

For $m > n \geq 1$, there are many adjacent strong chromatic number of $P_m \vee P_n$, $P_m \vee C_n$ and $C_m \vee C_n$. In this paper we have the adjacent strong equitable chromatic number of $P_n \vee P_n$, $P_n \vee C_n$ and $C_n \vee C_n$, the others terminologies refer to [9-10].

2 Adjacent Strong Edge Coloring of $P_n \vee P_n$

THEOREM 1 For $n \geq 2$, $\chi'_{ase}(P_n \vee P_n) = n + 3$.

ProofThere are four cases to be considered.

Case1 When $n = 2$, then $P_2 \vee P_2 = K4$ (*complete graph with order* 4), it's true by [6].

When $3 \leq n \leq 6$, $\Delta(P_n \vee P_n) = n + 2$. By Lemma 1, we need to prove thatexist a $n = 3 - ASEEC$.

Let P_n and P_n be $u_1u_2 \cdots u_n$ and $v_1v_2 \cdots v_n$.

Case2 When $n = 3$, a mapping f from $E(P_3 \vee P_3)$ to{1, 2, 3, 4, 5, 6} is defined as follows:

$$f(u_2v_2) = f(u_3v_1) = 1; f(u_2v_3) = f(v_1v_2) = 2;$$

$$f(u_1v_3) = f(u_2u_3) = 3;$$

$$f(u_1u_2) = f(u_3v_2) = 4; f(u_1v_2) = f(u_2v_1) = f(u_3v_3) = 5;$$

$$f(u_1v_1) = f(v_2v_3) = 6.$$

Obviously, f is $6 - ASEEC$of $P_3 \vee P_3$.

Case3 When $n = 4$, a mapping f from $E(P_4 \vee P_4)$ to {1, 2, 3, 4, 5, 6, 7} is defined as follows:

$$f(u_1v_i) = i,\ i = 1,2,3,4;$$

$$f(u_iv_j) = i + j + 1, i = 2,3; j = 1,2,3,4;$$

$$f(u_4v_1) = 5; f(u_4v_2) = 3;$$

$$f(u_4v_3) = 7; f(u_4v_4) = 1;$$

$$f(u_1u_2) = f(v_1v_2) = 7;$$

$$f(u_2u_3) = f(v_2v_3) = 1;$$

$$f(u_3u_4) = f(v_3v_4) = 2.$$

For such f, we have:

$$C(u_1) = \{5,6\}; C(u_4) = \{3,6\};$$

$$C(v_1) = \{2,6\}; C(v_4) = \{3,5\};$$

$$C(u_2) = \{2\}; C(u_3) = \{3\};$$

$$C(v_2) = \{6\}; C(v_3) = \{4\}.$$

Where

$C(w) = \{1,2,3,4,5,6,7\} \setminus C(w)$,

$w \in \{u_1, u_2, u_3, u_4\} \cup \{v_1, v_2, v_3, v_4\}$.

So f is $7 - ASEEC$of $P_4 \vee P_4$. The conclusion is true.

Case4 When $n = 5$, a mapping f from $E(P_5 \vee P_5)$ to {1, 2, 3, 4, 5, 6, 7, 8} is given as follows:

$$f(u_1v_1) = 6; f(u_1v_j) = j, j = 2,3,4; f(u_1v_5) = 5;$$

$$f(u_iv_j) = i + j - 1, i = 2,3,4; j = 1,2,3,4,5;$$

$$f(u_5v_1) = 5; f(u_1u_2) = f(u_5v_2) = 7;$$

$$f(u_2u_3) = f(v_1v_2) = f(u_5v_3) = 8;$$

$$f(u_3u_4) = f(v_2v_3) = f(u_5v_4) = 1; f(u_5v_5) = 4;$$

$$f(u_4u_5) = f(v_3v_4) = 2; f(v_4v_5) = 3.$$

For such f, we have:

$$C(u_1) = \{1,8\}; C(u_i) = \{i-1\}, i = 2,3,4;$$

$$C(u_5) = \{3,6\}; C(v_1) = \{1,7\};$$

$$C(v_i) = \{i+4\}, i = 2,3,4; C(v_5) = \{1,2\}.$$

Where $C(w) = \{1,2,3,4,5,6,7,8\} \setminus C(w)$, $w \in \{u_i \mid i = 1,2,3,4,5\} \cup \{v_j \mid j = 1,2,3,4,5\}$.

So f is $8 - ASEEC$of $P_5 \vee P_5$. The conclusion is true.

Case5 When $n = 6$, a mapping f from $E(P_6 \vee P_6)$ to {1, 2, 3, 4, 5, 6, 7, 8, 9} is given as follows:

$$f(u_1v_1) = 5; f(u_1v_2) = 7; f(u_1v_3) = 2;$$

$$f(u_1v_4) = 9; f(u_1v_5) = 4; f(u_1v_6) = 6;$$

$$f(u_2v_1) = 9; f(u_3v_1) = 8; f(u_4v_1) = 4;$$

$$f(u_5v_1) = 3; f(u_6v_1) = 6;$$

$$f(u_iv_j) = i + j - 1, i = 2,3,4,5; j = 2,3,4,5;$$

$$f(u_6v_2) = 8; f(u_6v_3) = 3;$$

$$f(u_6v_4) = 2; f(u_6v_5) = 1; f(u_6v_6) = 7;$$

$$f(u_2v_6) = 8; f(u_3v_6) = 9;$$

$$f(u_4v_6) = 3; f(u_5v_6) = 5;$$

$$f(u_1u_2) = f(u_3u_4) = f(v_1v_2) = f(v_3v_4) = 1;$$

$$f(u_2u_3) = f(u_4u_5) = f(v_5v_6) = 2;$$

$$f(v_4v_5) = 3; f(u_5u_6) = 4; f(v_2v_3) = 9.$$

For the f, we have:

$$C(u_1) = \{3,8\}; C(u_2) = \{7\}; C(u_3) = \{3\};$$

$$C(u_4) = \{9\}; C(u_5) = \{1\}; C(u_6) = \{5,9\};$$

$$C(v_1) = \{2,7\}; C(v_2) = \{2\}; C(v_3) = \{8\};$$

$$C(v_4) = \{4\}; C(v_5) = \{5\}; C(v6) = \{1,4\}.$$

So, the f is a $9 - ASEEC$of $P_6 \vee P_6$, the Theorem 2 is true when n=6.

Case6 When $n \geq 7$.

Subcase 6.1 When $n \equiv 0 (\mathrm{mod}\ 2)$. Suppose $n = 2k, k \geq 2$.

From Lemma 5, $P_n \vee P_n$ exists a perfect matching M_1;

$(P_n \vee P_n)\setminus\{u_1,u_{k+1}\}\setminus M_1$, exist a prerfect matching M_2;

$(P_n \vee P_n)\setminus\{u_2,u_{k+2}\}\setminus\bigcup_{i=1}^{2}M_i$, exist a prerfect matching M_3;

…

$(P_n \vee P_n)\setminus\{u_k,u_n\}\setminus\bigcup_{i=1}^{k}M_i$, exist a prerfect matching M_{k+1};

$(P_n \vee P_n)\setminus\{v_1,u_{k+1}\}\setminus\bigcup_{i=1}^{k+1}M_i$, exist a prerfect matching M_{k+2};

$(P_n \vee P_n)\setminus\{v_2,u_{k+2}\}\setminus\bigcup_{i=1}^{k+2}M_i$, exist a prerfect matching M_{k+3};

…

$(P_n \vee P_n)\setminus\{v_k,u_n\}\setminus\bigcup_{i=1}^{k+1}M_i$, exist a prerfect matching M_{n+3};

Let f be as follows

$$\forall e\in M_i, f(e)=i, i=1,2,\cdots,n+3.$$

Obviously, f is a $(n+3)-ASEEC$ of $P_n \vee P_n$.

Subcase 6.2 When $n\equiv 1(\text{mod}\,2)$. Suppose $n=2k+1, k\geq 3$.

From Lemma 3, we can learn $P_n \vee P_n$ exist a perfect matching M_1;

$(P_n \vee P_n)\setminus\{u_1,u_{k+1}\}\setminus M_1$, exist a prerfect matching M_2;

$(P_n \vee P_n)\setminus\{u_2,u_{k+2}\}\setminus\bigcup_{i=1}^{2}M_i$, exist a prerfect matching M_3;

…

$(P_n \vee P_n)\setminus\{u_k,u_{n-1}\}\setminus\bigcup_{i=1}^{k}M_i$, exist a prerfect matching M_{k+1};

$(P_n \vee P_n)\setminus\{v_1,u_n\}\setminus\bigcup_{i=1}^{k+1}M_i$, exist a prerfect matching M_{k+2};

$(P_n \vee P_n)\setminus\{v_2,u_{k+1}\}\setminus\bigcup_{i=1}^{k+2}M_i$, exist a prerfect matching M_{k+3};

$(P_n \vee P_n)\setminus\{v_2,u_{k+2}\}\setminus\bigcup_{i=1}^{k+3}M_i$, exist a prerfect matching M_{k+4};

…

$(P_n \vee P_n)\setminus\{v_k,u_{n-1}\}\setminus\bigcup_{i=1}^{k+2}M_i$, exist a prerfect matching M_{n+1};

$(P_n \vee P_n)\setminus\{v_k,u_{n-1}\}\setminus\bigcup_{i=1}^{n}M_i$, exist a prerfect matching M_{n+3};

$(P_n \vee P_n)\setminus\{v_1,v_n\}\setminus\bigcup_{i=1}^{n+1}M_i$, exist a prerfect matching M_{n+2};

$(P_n \vee P_n)\setminus\{u_n,v_n\}\setminus\bigcup_{i=1}^{n+2}M_i$, exist a prerfect matching M_{n+3};

Let f be as follows

$$\forall e\in M_i, f(e)=i, i=1,2,\cdots,n+3.$$

For f we have

$$C(u_i)=C(u_{k+i})=\{i+1\}, i=2,3,\cdots,k;$$
$$C(u_1)=\{2,k+2\}, C(u_n)=\{k+2,n+3\};$$
$$C(v_i)=C(v_{k+i})=\{k+1+i\}, i=2,3,\cdots,k;$$
$$C(v_1)=\{k+3,n+2\}, C(v_n)=\{k+2,n+3\}.$$

And

$$|E_i|=\begin{cases}n, i=1\\ n-1, i=2,3,\cdots,n.\end{cases}$$

So, f is a $(n+3)-ASEEC$ of $P_n \vee P_n$.

For above reasons, the theorem 1 is true.

3 Adjacent Strong Edge Coloring of $P_n \vee C_n$

THEOREM 2 For $n\geq 3$,

$$\chi'_{ase}(P_n \vee C_n)=\begin{cases}n+3, if \quad n\equiv 0(\text{mod}2)\\ n+4, if \quad n\equiv 1(\text{mod}2)\end{cases}$$

Proof If $n\equiv 0(\text{mod}\,2)$, suppose $n=2k,\ k\geq 2$.

By lemma 1, we should only proof $P_n \vee C_n$ exist $(n+3)-ASEEC$.

By lemma 4, $P_n \vee C_n$ exists two perfect matching M_1, M_2, and $M_1\cap M_2=\varnothing$.

$(P_n \vee C_n)\setminus\{u_1,u_{k+1}\}\setminus\bigcup_{i=1}^{2}M_1$, exist a prerfect matching M_3;

$(P_n \vee C_n)\setminus\{u_2,u_{k+2}\}\setminus\bigcup_{i=1}^{3}M_1$, exist a prerfect matching M_4;

…

$(P_n \vee C_n)\setminus\{u_k,u_n\}\setminus\bigcup_{i=1}^{k+1}M_1$, exist a prerfect matching M_{n+2};

$(P_n \vee C_n)\setminus\{u_1,u_n\}\setminus\bigcup_{i=1}^{k+2}M_1$, exist a prerfect matching M_{n+3};

$(P_n \vee C_n)\setminus\{v_1,u_{k+1}\}\setminus\bigcup_{i=1}^{k+3}M_1$, exist a prerfect matching M_{n+4};

$(P_n \vee C_n)\setminus\{v_2,u_{k+2}\}\setminus\bigcup_{i=1}^{k+4}M_1$, exist a prerfect matching M_{n+5};

$(P_n \vee C_n)\setminus\{v_k,v_n\}\setminus\bigcup_{i=1}^{n+2}M_1$, exist a prerfect matching M_{n+3};

…

Let f be as follows

$$\forall e\in M_i, f(e)=i, i=1,2,\cdots,n+3.$$

For f we have

$$\bar{C}(u_i)=\bar{C}(u_{k+i})=\{i+1\}, i=1,2,\cdots,k;$$
$$\bar{C}(v_i)=\bar{C}(v_{k+i})=\{k+1+i\}, i=1,2,\cdots,k.$$

And

$$|E_i|=\begin{cases}n, i=1\\ n-1, i=2,3,\cdots,n+2.\end{cases}$$

So, f is a $(n+3)-ASEEC$ of $P_n \vee C_n$.

If $n\equiv 1(\text{mod}\,2)$, we need proof $\chi'_{ase}(P_n \vee C_n)\geq n+4$ first. By lemma 3, we have $\chi'_{ase}(P_n \vee C_n)=n+3$.

Let f is a $(n+3)-ASEEC$ of $P_n \vee C_n$. By lemma 3, $P_n \vee C_n$ must have perfect matching after dismiss two vertices they are not adjacent in $v_1v_2\cdots v_n$. For $n\equiv 1(\text{mod}\,2)$, there must have a perfect matching. Let's one vertex in $u_2u_3\cdots u_{n-1}$ and another vertex in $v_1v_2\cdots v_n$. Thus

$$C(u_{i0})=C(v_{j0}), 2\leq i_0\leq n-1, 1\leq j_0\leq n.$$

f is also a $(n+3)-ASEEC$ of $P_n \vee C_n$, It is contradictory. So $\chi'_{ase}(P_n \vee C_n)\geq n+4$, let we give a $(n+3)-ASEEC$ of $P_n \vee C_n$.

Let f be as follows

$$f(u_iv_j)=i+j-1(\text{mod}\ n+4),$$
$$i=1,2,\cdots,n-1; j=1,2,\cdots,n;$$
$$f(u_nv_i)=n+i+1(\text{mod}\ n+4),$$
$$i=1,2,\cdots,n;$$
$$f(u_iu_{i+1})=n+i+2(\text{mod}\ n+4), i=1,2,\cdots,n-2;$$
$$f(u_{n-1}u_n)=n-3; f(u_nu_1)=n+1;$$
$$f(v_iv_{i+1})=n+i+3(\text{mod}\ n+4), i=1,2,\cdots,n-1;$$

For f, we have

$\bar{C}(u_1)=\{n+2,0\};\bar{C}(u_i)=\{i-1,n+i(\mathrm{mod}(n+4))\},$
$i=2,3,\cdots,n-2;$
$\bar{C}(u_{n-1})=\{n-3,2n-1(\mathrm{mod}(n+4)\};\bar{C}(u_n)=\{n-1,n\};$
$\bar{C}(v_1)=\{n,\ n+1,n+3\};$
$\bar{C}(v_n)=\{n-1,2n-1(\mathrm{mod}(n+\ 4)),2n(\mathrm{mod}(n+\ 4))\};$
$\bar{C}(v_i)=\{n+i-1(\mathrm{mod}(n+\ 4)),$
$n+i(\mathrm{mod}(n+\ 4))\},i=2,3,\cdots,n-1.$

So f is a $(n+4)-ASEEC$ of $P_n\vee C_n$.

Hence the conclusion is true.

4 Adjacent Strong Edge Coloring of $C_n\vee C_n$

THEOREM 3 For $n\geq 3$, then

$$\chi'_{ase}(C_n\vee C_n)=\begin{cases}n+3, n=3\ \ or\ \ n\equiv 0(\mathrm{mod}2)\\ n+4, n\geq 5\ \ or\ \ n\equiv 1(\mathrm{mod}2)\end{cases}$$

Proof Supposing the two cycles are $u_1u_2\cdots u_nu_1$ and $v_1v_2\cdots v_nv_1$ with separately.

When $n=3$, $C_n\vee C_n=K_6$ (complete graph with order 6), can be seen in appendix.

Case1 $n\equiv 0(\mathrm{mod}\,2)$, by lemma 1,2,4, $C_n\vee C_n$ exist three perfect matching M_1, M_2, M_3 and $M_1\cap M_2=M_2\cap M_3=M_3\cap M_1=\varnothing$.

When $n=4$, let's f as be follows:

$f(u_1u_4)=f(u_2u_3)=f(v_1v_4)=f(v_2v_3)=7;$
$f(u_1v_4)=f(u_2v_1)=f(u_3v_3)=f(u_4v_2)=6;$
$f(u_1v_2)=f(u_2v_4)=f(u_3v_1)=f(u_4v_3)=5;$
$f(u_1v_1)=f(u_2v_3)=f(u_3u_4)=4;$
$f(u_1u_2)=f(u_3v_2)=f(u_4v_4)=3;$
$f(u_1v_3)=f(u_3v_4)=f(v_1v_2)=2;$
$f(u_2v_2)=f(u_4v_1)=f(v_3v_4)=1.$

So f is a $7-ASEEC$ of $C_4\vee C_4$.

When $n=6$,

$(C_6\vee C_6)\setminus\{u_1,u_3\}\setminus\bigcup_{i=1}^{3}M_i$, exist a prerfect matching M_4;
$(C_6\vee C_6)\setminus\{u_1,u_3\}\setminus\bigcup_{i=1}^{3}M_i$, exist a prerfect matching M_4;
$(C_6\vee C_6)\setminus\{u_2,u_5\}\setminus\bigcup_{i=1}^{4}M_i$, exist a prerfect matching M_5;
$(C_6\vee C_6)\setminus\{u_4,u_6\}\setminus\bigcup_{i=1}^{5}M_i$, exist a prerfect matching M_6;
$(C_6\vee C_6)\setminus\{v_1,v_3\}\setminus\bigcup_{i=1}^{6}M_i$, exist a prerfect matching M_7;
$(C_6\vee C_6)\setminus\{v_2,v_5\}\setminus\bigcup_{i=1}^{7}M_i$, exist a prerfect matching M_8;
$(C_6\vee C_6)\setminus\{v_4,v_6\}\setminus\bigcup_{i=1}^{8}M_i$, exist a prerfect matching M_9;

Let f be as follows

$\forall e\in M_i, f(e)=i.$

So f is a $9-ASEEC$ of $C_6\vee C_6$.

Similarly we can proof $C_n\vee C_n$ exist $(n+3)-ASEEC$ when $n\equiv 0(\mathrm{mod}\,2)$ and $n\geq 8$.

By lemma 4, $C_n\vee C_n$ exist three perfect matching M_1, M_2, M_3 and $M_1\cap M_2=M_2\cap M_3=M_3\cap M_1=\varnothing$. Suppose $n=2k,\ k\geq 2$.

$(C_n\vee C_n)\setminus\{u_1,u_{k+1}\}\setminus\bigcup_{i=1}^{3}M_i$, exist a prerfect matching M_4;
$(C_n\vee C_n)\setminus\{u_2,u_{k+2}\}\setminus\bigcup_{i=1}^{4}M_i$, exist a prerfect matching M_4;
…
$(C_n\vee C_n)\setminus\{u_k,u_n\}\setminus\bigcup_{i=1}^{k+3}M_i$, exist a prerfect matching M_{k+4};
$(C_n\vee C_n)\setminus\{v_1,v_{k+1}\}\setminus\bigcup_{i=1}^{k+1}M_i$, exist a prerfect matching M_{k+5};
…
$(C_n\vee C_n)\setminus\{v_k,v_n\}\setminus\bigcup_{i=1}^{k+4}M_i$, exist a prerfect matching M_{n+3};

Let f be as follows

$\forall e\in M_i, f(e)=i, i=1,2,\cdots,n+3.$

For f we have

$\bar{C}(u_i)=\bar{C}(u_{k+i})=\{i\}, i=1,2,\cdots,k;$
$\bar{C}(v_i)=\bar{C}(v_{k+i})=\{k+i+1\}, i=1,2,\cdots,k.$

And

$$|E_i|=\begin{cases}n, i=1,2,3;\\ n-1, i=4,5,\cdots,n+3.\end{cases}$$

So, f is a $(n+3)-ASEEC$ of $C_n\vee C_n$.

Case2 $n\equiv 1(\mathrm{mod}\,2)$ and $n\geq 5$, We proof $\chi'_{as}(C_n\vee C_n)\geq n+4$

If $\chi'_{as}(C_n\vee C_n)=n+3$, there are at least 3 colors represented at every vertex. For $|E(C_n\vee C_n)|=n^2+2n$, and each vertex lack just one color and the vertices lack the same color in a same cycle and not adjacent, and n is an odd, so it is not possible that odd number vertices lack same color. For the edge number of $C_n\vee C_n$, the number of vertices lack same color just an even. So there must have two vertices in two different cycle lack same color. It is contradictory. Thus $\chi'_{ase}(C_n\vee C_n)=n+4$ when $n\equiv 1(\mathrm{mod}\,2)$.

Let f be as follows: the edges of $u_1u_2,u_2u_3,\cdots,u_{n-1}u_n$ are coloring colors with $n+3,n+4$ rotate, the edges of $v_1v_2,v_2v_3,\cdots,v_{n-1}v_n$ are coloring colors with $n+4$, $n+3$ rotate;

$f(u_1u_n)=f(v_1v_n)=n+1; f(u_1v_j)=j, j=1,2,\cdots,n;$
$f(u_iv_j)=i+j(when\ i+j>n+2,$
$then$ mod $n+\ 2), i=2,3,\cdots,n-1; j=1,2,\cdots,n;$
$f(u_nv_1)=n+\ 2; f(u_nv_j)=j-1, j=2,3,\cdots,\ n.$

For the f, we have

$\bar{C}(u_1)=\{n+2,n+4\};\bar{C}(u_i)=\{i-1,i\},$
$i=2,3,\cdots,n-1;\bar{C}(u_n)=\{n,\ n+3\}(n\equiv 1(\mathrm{mod}\,2));$
$\bar{C}(v_1)=\{2,n+3\};\bar{C}(v_i)=\{i+1,n+i\}(when\ i+j>n+2,$
$take$ mod $n+\ 2;\bar{C}(v_n)=\{n,\ n+4\}(n\equiv 1(\mathrm{mod}\,2)).$

So, the f is a $n+4-ASEEC$ of $C_n\vee C_n$, the theorem 3 is true.

From all of above, the theorem 3 is true.

References

1. Harary F, Conditional colorability in graphs, In Graphs and Applications,Proc Graph theory Fist Colorado symp, John Wilh& Sons, New York, 1985.

2. Burris A C and Schelp R H, Vertex-distinguishing Proper Edge-colorings, J of Graph Theory, 1997, 26(2):7382.
3. Bazgan C Harkat-Benhamdine A, Li H, etc. On the Vertex-distinguishing Proper Edge-coloring of Graph, J Combin Theory Ser B, 1999, 75:288-301.
4. Balister P N, Bollob´as B, Schelp R H, Vertex distinguishing coloring of graphs with Δ(G)=2, Discrete Mathematics, 2002,252(2):17 29.
5. Balister P N,Riordan O M and Schelp R H, Vertex-distinguishing edge coloring of graphs, J. Graph Theory 42(2003)95-109.
6. Zhongfu Zhang, Linzhong Liu, Jianfang Wang, Adjacent Strong Edge Coloring of Graphs, Applied Matbhmatics Letters, 2002, 15:623-626.
7. Wang shudong, Li chongming, XuJi, et, On the adjacent strong edge coloring of some graphs, J of Mathematical Research and exposition, Vo1.22, No 4, 2002, 412-417.
8. Balister P N, Gyori and Schelp R H , On the adjacent-strong edge coloring of graphs with Δ(G) ≤ 3, J.G.T to appear.
9. Bondy J A and Marty U S R, Graph Theory with Applications, The Macmillan Press Ltd, New York, 1976.
10. Chartrand G, Linda L F, Graphs and diagraphs, Ind edition wadsirthBrokks/cole, Monterey, CA,1986

MATEC Web of Conferences 44, 02034 (2016)
DOI: 10.1051/matecconf/20164402034

Discussion of the Energy-Saving Benefits of Heat Insulating Coating for Building Windows

Jing-Yi Chang[1,a*], Yean-Der Kuan[2,b], Chun-Ching Lan[2,c], Hsing-Ju Li[2,d], Yu-Kun Hsu[2,e], Chih-Yao Chen[2,f], En-Ting Shen[2,g] and Kun-Yi Lin[1,h]

[1]*Department of Marine Engineering, Taipei College of Maritime Technology, Taipei, Taiwan*
[2]*Department of Refrigeration, Air-Conditioning and Energy Engineering, National Chi-Yi University of Technology, Taichung, Taiwan*

ABSTRACT

Nano transparent heat insulating coating is applied to window glass in this study. The heat insulating coating absorbs thermal radiation, and reduces the thermal radiation transmittance of glass, thus, preventing the building heat load from increasing in summer, or reducing the consumption of heat energy in winter. Therefore, this study will design a scaled down building model room, where heat insulating coating is coated on the inner side of the window glass of the model room, and the thermal radiation isolation effect is tested. Finally, the building energy-saving benefit of outdoor heat insulation in summer and indoor heat preservation in winter is discussed.
Keywords: Nano Transparent Heat Insulating Coating, Building Energy-Saving Benefit, Residential Energy Saving Application.

INTRODUCTION

Taiwan's green building evaluation system (EEWH) with subtropical climate characteristic is the fourth green building evaluation system in the world, as based on ecology, energy saving, waste reduction, and health, including nine major evaluation indices, which are biodiversity, greenery, on-site water retention, daily energy saving, CO2 reduction, waste reduction, indoor environment, water resource, sewage, and garbage improvement . Among the daily energy saving indices of green buildings, the energy efficient design for the major power consumption of air conditioning and lighting is the key point, and the energy saving evaluation aims at building envelopment energy efficient design, air conditioning efficiency design, and lighting efficiency design.

Generally speaking, about 95% of a building is made of reinforced concrete, and many office buildings use glass curtain walls, which are two materials of high heat capacity, and are likely to absorb and accumulate solar heat. For good airtightness, poor aeration, and high thermal storage capacity, when the outdoor heat source stops, the building materials still continuously release the accumulated radiant heat, thus, the hot air stays indoors and is unlikely to diffuse, increasing the energy consumption of air conditioning. Therefore, as Taiwan is wet and hot, and the temperature is often higher than 35℃ in summer, many buildings use all-sided glass external walls; this type of buildings is applicable to high latitude cold places for preserving solar radiation heat in winter, creating the greenhouse effect to warm the rooms. However, when this building engineering is introduced into Taiwan with its subtropical climate, indoor thermal storage increases as a result, the air conditioning load is increased, energy consumption is increased, and the indoor air conditioning power is severely wasted [1-4].

Many scholars have globally studied the thermal characteristics of building glass. Somsak [5] indicated that glass windows have considerable transmittance property, and in strong solar radiation, more radiant heat is absorbed, and thermal comfort is reduced. Ismail [6] used experiments and numerical simulation to study solar radiation heat efficiency on glass windows, and filled the phase change material and air between the double glass. The result showed the filling of phase change material could filter thermal radiation and reduce heat absorption, and the double glass reduced the absorption of radiant energy better than filling with air.

RESEARCH METHOD

2.1 MODEL ROOM DESIGN

The actual building is assumed as a single dwelling, 6m long, 5m wide, and 4m high wooden house, which is scaled down to a 30cm (L) x 25cm (W) x 12cm (H) model room constructed of 8mm plywood, as shown in Figure 1. However, if the glass thickness of the model room is scaled down, the thickness will be too small, and the model will be difficult to make and analyze. Therefore, this experiment uses the most frequently used minimum thickness of 3mm window glass on the market.

[a]dio990@gmail.com, [b]ydkuan@ncut.edu.tw, [c]as20549@yahoo.com.tw, [d]seaotter820515@yahoo.com.tw, [e]qen1112@gmail.com, [f]mark910i@yahoo.com.tw, [g]cabal02171@yahoo.com.tw, [h]kunyi0914@gmail.com

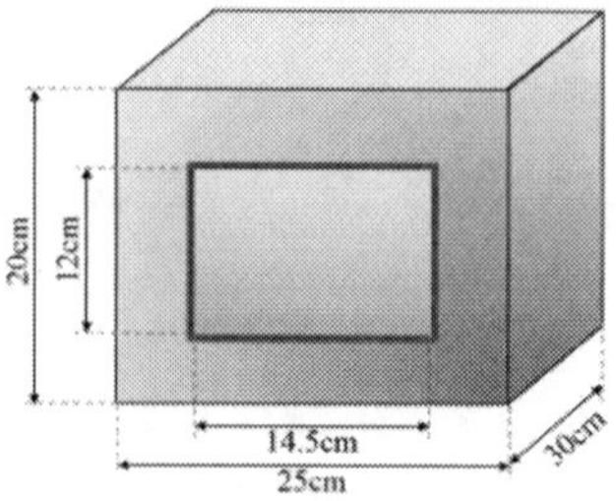

Figure 1 Structural Representation of Model Room

2.2 EXPERIMENT ON OUTDOOR HEAT INSULATION EFFICIENCY

This experiment uses a 500W halogen lamp, because the radiation wavelength of a halogen lamp is in the range of visible light and near infrared. The irradiation power of solar radiation in this wavelength range is about 90% of the total power, thus, it is the main source range of solar radiation heat. As shown in Figure 2, the halogen lamp is mounted ahead of the glass window of the model room, with an elevation angle of 30° and appropriate distance of about 55cm. The light irradiates the model room to simulate the sunlight source. The heat generated by the halogen lamp enters the room through the glass by radiation, transfer, and convection. Afterwards, the temperature is measured by T-type thermocouple wires, which are mounted on both sides of glass surface to measure the effect of radiation on the temperature of the glass surfaces with and without coating. A sensing point is mounted in the center of the room in order to detect the indoor temperature change, and estimate the energy-saving benefit of the coating.

However, the aforesaid experimental results show that the heat storage in the room may result in the greenhouse effect. Therefore, this experiment uses a forced ventilation system to import outside cool air to absorb the heat generated by radiation, in order to discharge the indoor thermal storage, and the temperature change is measured to discuss the building energy-saving benefit of outdoor heat insulation in summer, as shown in Figure 3.

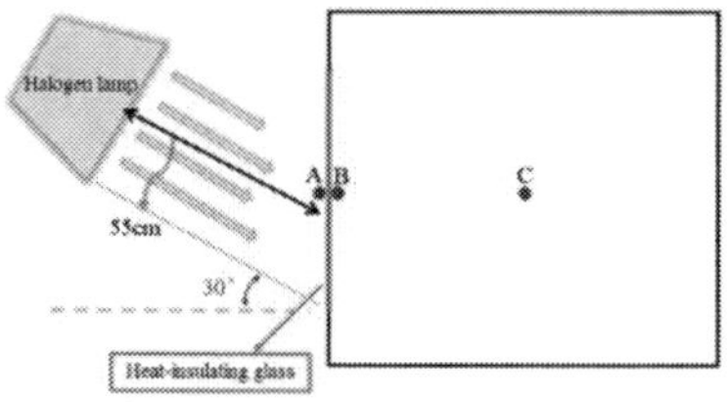

Figure 2 Outdoor Heat Insulation

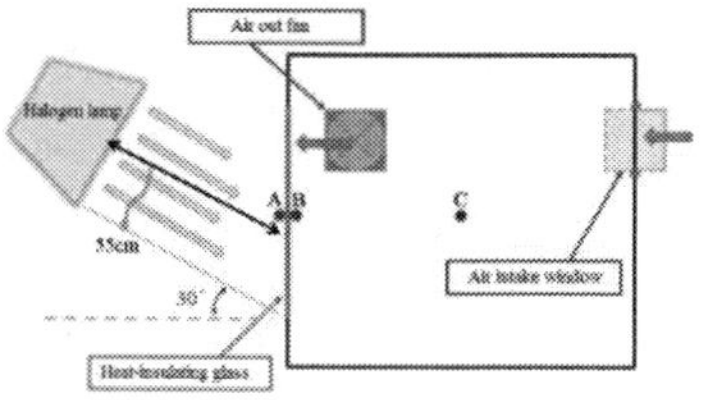

Figure 3 Outdoor Heat Insulation with Ventilation

2.3 EXPERIMENT ON INDOOR INSULATING EFFICIENCY

This experiment simulates day and night modes, respectively, in order to observe the effect of heat insulating coating on indoor thermal insulation. The night mode mounting is as shown in Figure 4. The ambient temperature is set as 23℃, and a 60W lamp is mounted in the center of model room as the indoor heating source. Finally, the temperature sensing points are mounted at the four corners of the room to observe the indoor temperature distribution. The day mode mounting is as shown in Figure 5, where the ambient temperature is 23℃, a 500W halogen lamp simulates the sunlight source, and a 60W lamp is mounted in the center of model room as the indoor heating source. The temperature sensing points are mounted at four corners of the room in order to observe the indoor temperature distribution, and discuss the insulating efficiency of glass with and without coating.

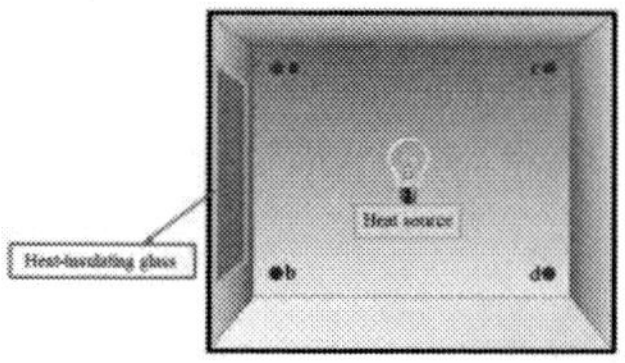

Figure 4 Indoor Insulation in Night Mode

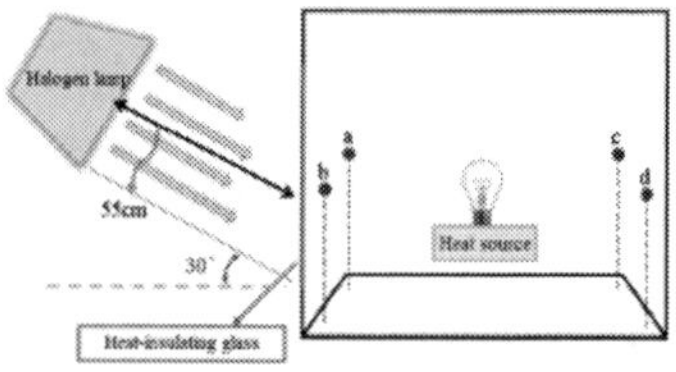

Figure 5 Indoor Insulation in Day Mode

RESULTS AND DISCUSSION

3.1 EXPERIMENTAL RESULT OF OUTDOOR HEAT INSULATION EFFICIENCY

As shown in Figure 6, according to glass surface temperature measuring points A and B, the temperature of the coated glass surface is apparently higher than the uncoated surface, the external surface temperature is 4.5 ℃ higher, and the inner surface temperature is 3.6 ℃ higher, meaning the radiant heat energy of the halogen lamp is absorbed by the heat insulating coating, the radiant heat energy is accumulated in the glass, and the temperature of the glass rises; Meanwhile the radiant heat energy is prevented from entering the room, and the radiation transmittance of glass is reduced. According to temperature measuring point C at the center of the room, the indoor temperature with coating is 0.7℃ lower than that without coating, the cooling efficiency is about 2.3%, and the air conditioning power consumption is estimated to be reduced by 4.2%.

According to temperature measuring point C at the center of the room, as shown in Figures 6 and 7, when the model room uses a ventilation mechanism, the indoor temperature is reduced by 4.3℃~4.5℃, the temperature of the glass surface without heat insulating coating is reduced by 2.2℃~5.4℃, and the temperature of the glass surface with heat insulating coating is reduced by 9.5℃ ~10.2℃, meaning this mechanism can effectively remove the thermal storage from the room and glass, and the glass surface with a coating has larger temperature drop, meaning the coating has good convection heat sinking. The heat insulating coating and ventilation mechanism can reduce the indoor temperature by 5℃, the cooling efficiency is about 16.4%, and the air conditioning power consumption can be reduced by 30%.

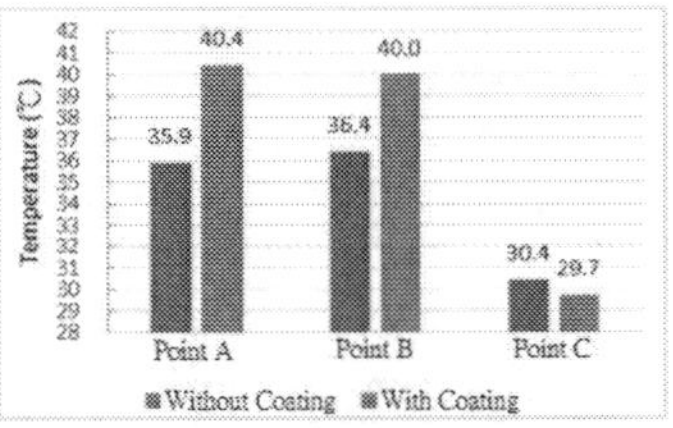

Figure 6 Temperatures Measuring Points

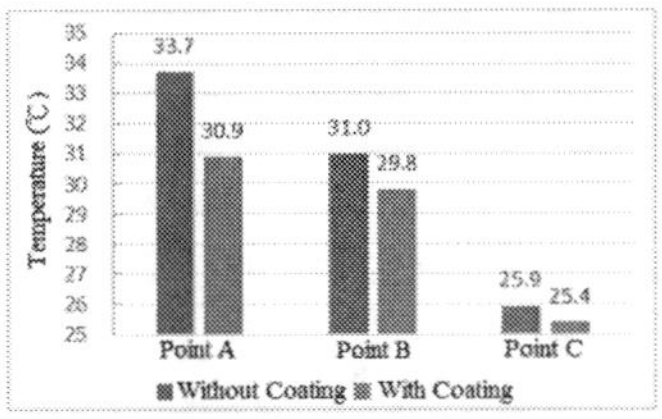

Figure 7 Temperatures Measuring Points

3.2 EXPERIMENTAL RESULT OF INDOOR INSULATING EFFICIENCY

Figure 8 shows indoor temperature night-time distribution, the temperatures at temperature measuring points a and b close to the glass window indoors are lower than the temperatures at farther temperature measuring points c and d by 0.3℃~0.7℃, meaning the glass has higher heat loss than the wood wall, and the indoor temperature falls. The temperatures at four measuring points in the room are averaged, the indoor average temperature without coating is 33.2℃, the indoor average temperature with coating is 33.7℃, meaning that the heat insulating coating can effectively reduce the heat loss of glass, and increase the indoor average temperature by 0.5 ℃. When the heating efficiency is about 1.5%, air conditioning power consumption can be reduced by 3%.

According to the aforesaid experimental results, this coating can effectively reduce the heat loss of glass. As shown in Figure 9, during the day, the temperature is higher near the glass window indoors, meaning the outdoor and indoor radiant heat is absorbed in the glass, and the glass temperature rises, thus, indirectly influencing room temperature. The temperatures at temperature measuring points a and b near the glass window indoors are higher than the temperatures at points c and d on the opposite side. As the glass window is irradiated by the halogen lamp, the temperature of the glass window with coating is higher than that without coating, because the coating absorbs radiant heat, and the loss of the indoor heat source is reduced. The temperatures at the four measuring points indoors are averaged, the indoor average temperature without coating is 34.4℃, the indoor average temperature with coating is 36.1℃, the coating increases the indoor temperature by 1.7℃, the heating efficiency is about 4.9%, and the air conditioning power consumption can be reduced by 10.2%. Therefore, the thermal insulation effect is excellent in the daytime.

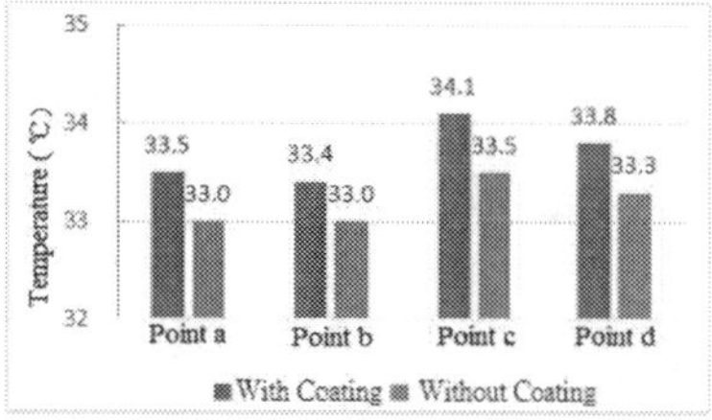

Figure 8 Indoor Temperatures at Night

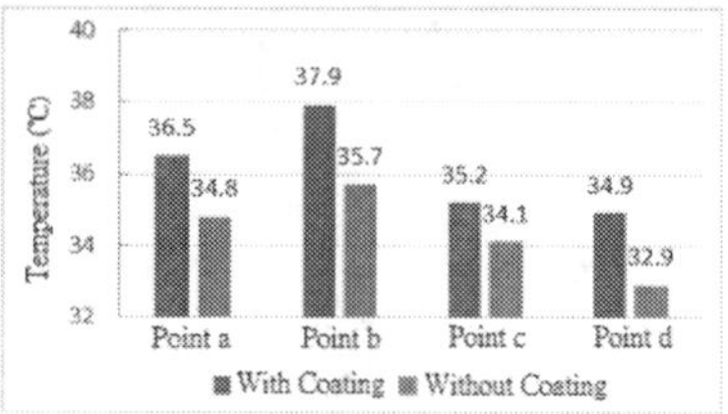

Figure 9 Indoor Temperatures at Daytime

CONCLUSION

Based on the results, the conclusions are drawn as follows:
1. The glass heat insulating coating can effectively resist radiant heat in summer, the cooling efficiency is about 2.3%, and the air conditioning power consumption is reduced by 4.2%.
2. When the heat insulating coating is combined with a ventilation mechanism, the thermal storage in the room and glass can be effectively carried away, the heat insulation efficiency is increased, the cooling efficiency is about 16.4%, and the air conditioning power consumption is reduced by 30%.
3. The glass heat insulating coating can effectively reduce indoor thermal loss in winter. The indoor temperature is increased, the heating efficiency is about 1.5% at night, and the air conditioning power consumption is reduced by 3%. The heating efficiency is about 4.9% in the daytime, the air conditioning power consumption is reduced by 10.2%; and the air conditioning power consumption is reduced by 6.6% daily.
4. As the radiation frequency of a halogen lamp is lower than the solar radiation frequency, and the glass thickness is 3mm in this study; whereas, the glass thickness for actual buildings is mostly larger than 5mm or 7mm, the actual energy-saving efficiency can be higher.

Acknowledgements

This paper is the project NSC102-2622-E-167-018-CC3 of Ministry of Science and Technology. Thanks to the Ministry of Science and Technology for supporting this project.

REFERENCES

[1] G. Alvarez, M. J. Palacios, and J. J. Flores. 1999. "A test method to evaluate the thermal performance of window glazings," Applied Thermal Engineering ., 20:803-812.

[2] A. Joudi, H. Svedung, M. Cehlin, and M. Ronnelid. 2013. "Reflective coatings for interior and exterior of buildings and improving thermal performance," Applied Energy ., 103:562-570.

[3] M. Rubin. 1982. "Solar Optical Properties of Windows," Journal of Energy Research., 6:123-133.

[4] M. Rubin. 1982. "Calculating Heat Transfer Through Windows," Journal of Energy Research., 6:341-349.

[5] S. Chaiyapinunt, and B. Phueakphongsuriya. 2005. "Performance Rating of Glass Windows and Glass Windows With Films in Aspect of Thermal Comfort and Heat Transmission," Energy and Buildings., 37:725-738.

[6] K. A. R. Ismail, and J. R. Henriquez. 2001. "Thermal Effective Windows With Moving Phase Change Material Curtains," Applied Thermal Engineering., 21:1909-1923.

[7] http:// www.daikin.co.jp

MATEC Web of Conferences 44, 02035 (2016)
DOI: 10.1051/matecconf/20164402035

The Structural and Morphology of (La0.6Sr0.4)MnO3 Thin Films Prepared by Pulsed Laser Deposition

Hai Bin Yang[1,a]

Department of Physics, college of Science Naval University of Engineering Wuhan, China

Abstract. (La0.7Sr0.3)MnO3 (LSMO) thin films were prepared on Si (100) substrate by pulsed laser deposition (PLD). Both structure and surface morphology of the films were investigated by X-ray diffraction (XRD) and atomic force microscopy (AFM). Furthermore, the chemical states and chemical composition of the films were determined by X-ray photoelectron spectroscopy (XPS) near the surface. The results indicate that the films grown on Si (100) substrates have a single pseudo cubic perovskite phase structure with a high (100) orientation. The XPS results show that La, Sr and Mn exist mainly in the forms of perovskite structure and a SrO layer was found on outermost surface.

1 Introduction

Due to the effect of colossal magnetoresistance (CMR), extensive studies have been carried out on $(La_{1-x}Sr_x)MnO_3$ (LSMO) for its interesting properties and potential application on various devices such as magnetic field sensors and memories [1-3]. LSMO shows good metallic phase with very low resistivity, moreover the electrical resistivity of LSMO can be controlled by varying the deposited oxygen pressure and remain stable against further thermal treatments in various oxygen pressure [4]. In recent years, increasing studies are being carried out on ferroelectric films and great interests have been triggered in some electronically conductive perovskite oxides [5-7]. Those conducting oxides materials showed many advantages including excellent conductivity like mental, overcoming fatigue in ferroelectric films, and with perovskite structure that is suitable for improving lattice match when they are employed as electrodes. As a material with conducting function, LSMO is also drawing more and more attention for its significant properties showing in fabrication of ferroelectric devices, in which LSMO was used as electrodes. It was reported that ferroelectric $(Pb_{0.6}Ca_{0.4})TiO_3$ and $(Ba_{0.7}Sr_{0.3})TiO_3$ thin films grown on LSMO films buffer layer showed excellent ferroelectric and fatigue properties comparing those with on other mental electrode [8-10]. There are a few reports about characters of LSMO films themselves, especially when they are employed as electrodes.

In this work, $(La_{0.7}Sr_{0.3})MnO_3$ films have been grown on single crystal substrate of Si (100) by pulsed laser deposition (PLD) process. We have used XPS and got a detailed knowledge of the surface chemical composition of $(La_{0.7}Sr_{0.3})MnO_3$ films. The purpose of the present paper is to study the crystal structure and identify the composition and chemical state of the surface of LSMO films prepared by PLD process.

2 Experimental

The LSMO thin films were grown on Si (100) substrates kept at 650°C by PLD using a KrF eximer pulsed laser (λ=248 nm), and LSMO target. The LSMO target was prepared by conventional solid state reaction [10-11]. The films were deposited at a laser repetition rate of 10 Hz and pulsed laser energy of 300 mJ. The base pressure of the system is 2 mTorr. The deposition time and rate are 10 min and 20 nm/min respectively. The oxygen pressure was kept at 200 mTorr. Finally, the LSMO films were crystallized in situ at 650 °C in 400 mTorr of oxygen for 10 min and cooled down slowly to room temperature. The thickness of the LSMO thin films measured by a Tencor P-10 surface profiler (KLA-Tencor Corporation, USA) was about 200 nm.

The crystalline structure of the LSMO thin films on Si (100) substrates were analyzed by a Philips PW3710 X-ray diffractometer. The resistivity of the LSMO thin films measured by a standard four-point method at room temperature is 6.4×10^{-4} Ω·cm. The surface morphology and

[a] Corresponding author: 8895660@qq.com

roughness were determined by AFM using tapping mode amplitude modulation. To study the film surface, XPS analyses were carried out on the ESCALab250 (VG Scientific) spectrometer by using Mg Ka (1253.6 eV) radiation.

3 Results and Discussion

3.1 Structure and Surface morphology.

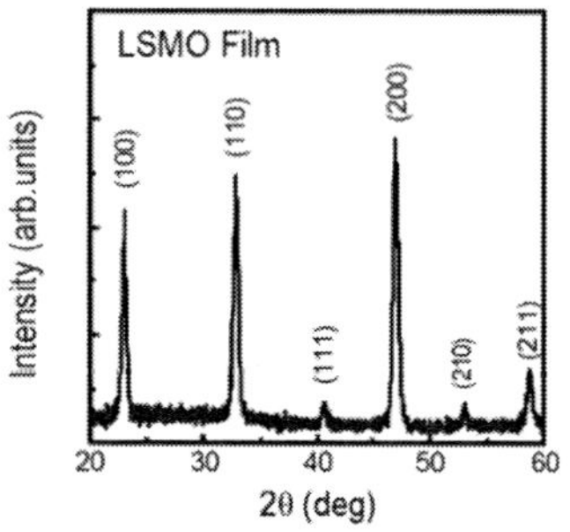

Figure. 1 XRD patterns of LSMO films

Fig. 1 shows the XD patterns of the LSMO thin films on Si (100) substrates. From the XRD analysis for the LSMO films prepared by PLD process, six-peaks (100), (110), (111), (200), (210) and (211) were observed in the XRD patterns and these diffraction peaks can be indexed to LSMO phase with pseudo cubic perovskite structure. The relative peak intensity of ΣI(h00)/ΣI(hkl) are found to be 0.588 for LSMO thin film on Si(100) substrates, indicating a remarkably strong (100) grain orientation. From the XRD data we estimated the lattice parameter to be 0.386 nm, which is equal to that of bulk (a=0.387nm). Due to large lattice mismatch between LSMO films and Si (a=0.543 nm). Therefore, the high (100)-orientation of LSMO thin films on Si (100) substrate is considered to be a self-textured growth, which is in accordance with minimum surface energy conditions.

3.2 Composition.

Fig. 2 shows the wide-scan XPS spectrum of the LSMO thin film on Si (100) substrate in the binding energy range of 0-1100 eV. All of the binding energies at various peaks were calibrated by the binding of C 1s (284.60 eV) as shown in Fig. 3, the LSMO film contains La, Sr, Mn, O and C elements near its surface, and no other impurity element was detected in the spectrum up to 1100 eV except carbon. The carbon results from surface contamination. The quantitative atomic composition near the film surface was determined from the XPS spectra of La 3d, Sr 3d, Mn 2p, and O 1s by using sensitivity factors of 10, 1.48, 2.6, and 0.66, respectively.

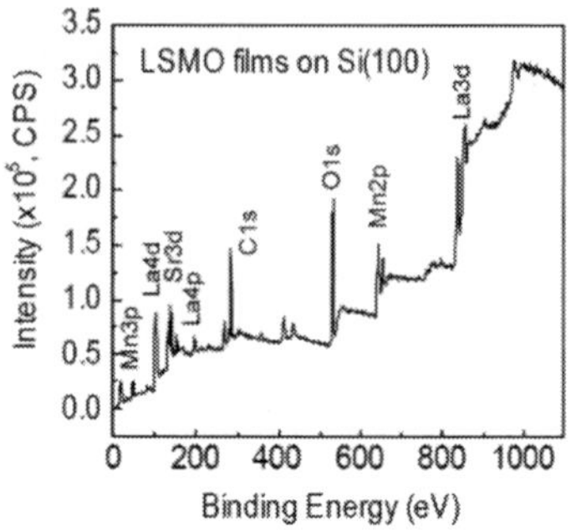

Figure. 2 Wide-scan XPS spectrum of the deposited on Si (100) substrate and LSMO thin film on Si (100) substrate crystallized in situ at 650°C for 10 min crystallized in situ at 650°C for 10 min.

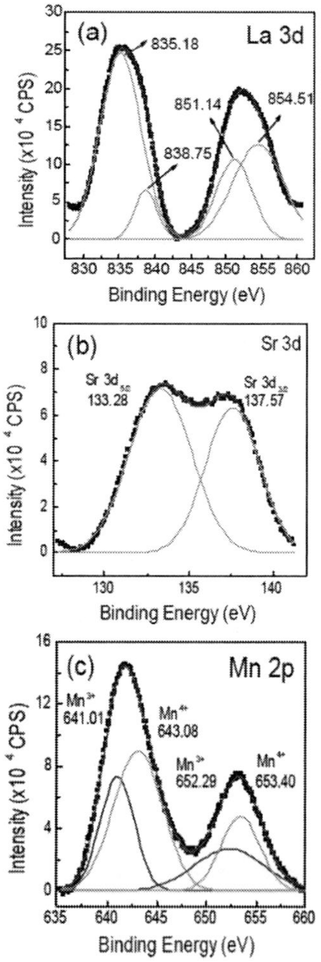

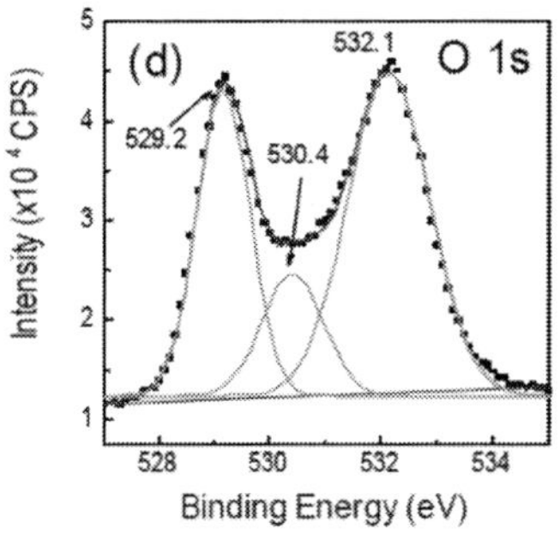

Figure. 3 Narrow-scan XPS spectra of (a) La 3d, (b) Sr 3d, (c) Mn 2p and (d) O 1s for the LSMO. The combined peaks were decomposed into individual components (red lines) on the assumption of a Gaussian line shape

Fig. 3 (b) shows the narrow-scan spectrum of Sr 3d and there are two peaks observed at 133.28 and 137.57 eV, respectively.The existing of Sr in LSMO films surface should be in the binding formation of SrO. We can infer that the main structure of LSMO surface should be perovskite structure that is able to offer suitable lattice match for preferred orientation. However, SrO is rocksalt structure with a lattice parameter of 0.516 nm that will induce so great lattice mismatch for BZT films that a preferred (100) orientation is impossible. Whereas, Bertacco et al. proved his mode with a conclusion that SrO is possible to form an epitaxial growth onto LSMO (001) with a 45o rotation of the surface square lattice of SrO with respect to that of LSMO, and the outermost SrO layer could be considered as a $La_{0.7}Sr_{0.3}O$ plane in which La has been completely substituted by Sr [12]. Therefore, It is reasonable to explain BZT films (with lattice parameter a=0.405nm) grown epitaxially on LSMO because there is a high similarity between SrO and $La_{0.7}Sr_{0.3}O$ plane that can offer a more suitable lattice parameter for BZT epitaxial growth.

Fig. 3 (c) illustrates the fine spectrum of Mn 2p core levels. After analyzed by Gaussfitted curve the spectrum are decomposed into two doublet peaks. The peak positions of Mn^{3+} and Mn^{4+} are observed at 641.01 and 643.08 eV, respectively for Mn 2p3/2 of LSMO. Also, the peak positions of Mn^{3+} and Mn^{4+} are observed at 652.29 and 653.40 eV, respectively for Mn 2p1/2 of LSMO. The value of 641.01 eV is close to the binding energy value 641.9 eV of the Mn 2p3/2 level in α-Mn_2O_3 [13]. And the binding energies of Mn^{3+} and Mn^{4+} at 641.01 and 643.08 and close to that the value 641.3 and 642.8 eV of the Mn 2p3/2 level in $La_{2/3}Sr_{1/3}MnO_3$ composites [14]. As we known that La and Sr in LSMO compounds control and cause the mixed valence of Mn^{3+} and Mn^{4+} irons and CMR effect is attributed to the itinerant electrons via Mn^{3+}-O-Mn^{4+}. In order to describe this mixed Mn^{3+}/Mn^{4+} system.

Fig. 3 (d) represents an asymmetric peak of the O1s spectra and a doublet peaks were founded. The doublet peak agrees well with the reported data on alkaline earth substituted and unsubstituted ABO_3 type perovskites [15]. The asymmetric peak indicated that existing oxygen had more than one state. Analyzing with Gauss curve-fitting process, we can find the existence of three components at the O 1s spectra with three binding energies positions at 529.2, 530.4 and 532.1 eV, respectively. The lower binding energy (BE) 529.2 and 530.4 eV is always accepted as weakly bound oxygen-mental bonds in crystal lattice such as the presence of La-O and Mn-O oxide [16]. Similar O 1s XPS with shoulder, two peaks at 529.5 and 531.0 eV, were observed on $La_{0.5}Sr_{0.5}MnO_3$ powder compounded in literature [17], in which the 529.5 eV components was attributed to O^{2-} iron of mental oxide. It is reasonable to attribute the O 1s banding energy 532.1 eV to Sr-O bond for the existence of SrO_2 layer on the outermost surface of LSMO films.

4 Conclusions

In this paper LSMO film on Si (100) substrate was prepared by PLD process. The films show pseudo cubic perovskite structure with an orientation in (100) plane. Through AFM, the surface of LSMO films deposited on Si (100) was found to be smooth and dense. Based on the analysis of the XPS, elements like La, Sr, Mn and O that showed different states that respond to the perovskite structure and an outermost SrO layer was found. Simultaneity, C contamination was observed in the films.

References

1. N.TSUDA, K.NASU, A.FUJIMORI, K.SIRATORI: Electronic Conduction in Oxides, Springer, Berlin(2012)
2. H.TANAKA, T.KAWAI: Solid State Commun Vol. **112** (1999), p. 201-205
3. M.SIRENA,N.HABERKORN, L.B.STEREN and J.GUIMPEL: J. Appl. Phys Vol. **103** (2013), p. 6177-6181
4. W.B.WU, K.U. WONG, X.G. LI, C.L. CHOY and ZHANG YH: J. Appl. Phys Vol. **97**(2010),p. 3006-3010
5. X.G. TANG, H.F. XIONG, L.L. JIANG and H.L. CHAN: Cryst. Growth Vol.**305**(2015), p. 613-619
6. I.D. KIM and H.G. KIM: Jpn.J. Appl .Phys. Part 1 Vol. **50**(2011), p. 2357-2362

7. B. CHEN, H. YANG, J. MIAO, L. ZHAO, L.X. CAO, B. XU, X.G. QIU and B.R. ZHAO: J. Appl. Phys Vol. **107**(2015), 024106-1(4)
8. C.C. CHOU, C.S. HOU, G.C. CHANG and H.F. CHENG: Appl. Surf. Sci Vol. **1449**(2013), p. 413-417
9. J. MIAO, L. CAO, J. YUAN, W. CHEN, H. YANG, B. XU, X. QIU and B. ZHAO: J. Cryst. Growth Vol. **296** (2013), p. 498-506
10. S.H. Lim, M.Murakami, S.E.Lofland, A.J.Zambano, L.G.Salamanca-Riba and I.Takeuchi: Journal of Magnetism and Magnetic Materials Vol. **351**(2014), p. 1955-1958
11. S.Y. YANG, W.L. KUANG, Y. LIOU, W.S. TSE, S.F. LEE, Y.D. YAO: J. Magn. Magn. Mater Vol. **288**(2011), p. 326–331
12. R. BERTACCO, J.P. CONTOUR, A. BARTHELEMY and J. OLIVIER: Surf. Sci Vol. **511**(2002), p. 366-372
13. V.M. Petrov, M.I. Bichurin, V.V. Zibtsev, S.K. Mandal, and G. Srinivasan: JOURNAL OF APPLIED PHYSICS Vol. **116**(2014), 113901
14. Q.X. ZHOU, M.X. DAI, R.H. WANG, L. JIN, S.J. ZHU, L. QIAN, Y.M. WU and J.W. FENG: Physica B Vol. **391**(2012), p. 206-211
15. R.J. L, T.B. W, and Y.H. C: Scripta Materialia Vol. **59**(2014), p. 897-900
16. L.JING, Z. YI, L.Y. HUA, and C. W. NAN: JOURNAL OF APPLIED PHYSICS Vol. **105**(2013), 083915
17. J.P. ZHOU, W.ZHAO, Y.Y. GUO, P. LIU, and H.W. ZHANG: JOURNAL OF APPLIED PHYSICS Vol. **105**(2011), 063913

MATEC Web of Conferences 44, 02036 (2016)
DOI: 10.1051/matecconf/20164402036

A Novel Surveillance System Applied in Civil Airport

Hua Bo Sun[1], Min Zhu Zhong[1], Ling Yun Miao[1], Xin Wang[1], Hai Meng Zhao[2, a]

[1] *China Academy of Civil Aviation Science and Technology, Beijing, 100028, P.R.China*
[2] *Beijing Key Lab of Spatial Information Integration and Its Applications, Peking University, Beijing 100871, P.R.China*

Abstract. Conventional security monitoring of civil airport usually uses a fixed camera to acquire images. There are several problems with performance including difficulties introduced in the information transmission, storage, and analysis of the process. Insect compound eyes offer unique advantages for moving target capture and these have attracted the attention of many researchers in recent years. This paper contributes to this research by proposing a new surveillance system applied in civil airport. We discuss the finished bionic structure of the system, the development of the bionic control circuit, and introduce the proposed mathematical model of bionic compound eyes for data acquisition and image mosaic. Image matching for large view is also illustrated with different conditions. This mode and algorithm effectively achieve safety surveillance of airport with large field of view and high real-time processing.

1 Introduction

Moving target detection has been applied in many applications, such as video surveillance of civil airport, in recent years. Traditional fixed camera systems for surveillance dealt with the acquired images have two main questions, one is that the field of view is limited, and the other is that data storage is too large with the accumulation. During process acquired image, we must transform the three dimensional objects, which are acquired by high resolution sensors, to two dimensional images. Following this task one must then distinguish and locate the targets using signal-processing techniques. Finally we reverse the two-dimensional information to three-dimensions in order to redisplay the actual objects. The precision of detection and the amount of calculation required are positively correlated in such transformations. The higher the precision required the greater the amount of data involved. Consequently this delivers a less than real-time performance. As a result of these tradeoffs many researchers have turned their attention to a new image acquisition and processing mode called bionic compound eyes[1]. Tanida[2] et al proposed a bionic compound eyes imaging system called TOMBO (Thin Observation Module by Bound Optics) which adapted micro lens and photo detectors for the acquisition and receiving assembly of light signals. This information is then processed to restructure the targets. Duparre[3] et al proposed and manufactured the AACO (Artificial Apposition Compound Eye Objective)[4]. Insect compound eyes have many advantages in moving target detection. They can detect and recognize targets in large areas using minimal information obtained through feature outline.

Insect compound eyes have many advantages in moving target detection. Insect compound eyes have small size, light weight, large viewing fields, and are very sensitive to moving targets. They can detect and recognize targets in large areas using minimal information obtained through feature outline. Insects can maintain high-resolution views of their targets while at the same time maintaining information about other targets in the same view. The mechanism of the compound eyes provides a solution to the tradeoffs between viewing field size, resolution, and real-time processing. These are very important problems that must be addressed when developing moving target detection systems. This paper follows on our previous work on moving object detection with bionic compound eyes applied in surveillance of airport[5].

The remainder of this paper is organized as follows. In section 2 we explain our bionic compound eyes mechanism. Section 3 provides a full overview of our system composition, biometric structure, control system, and a mathematical formulation of the data acquisition and processing model. In section 4 a report on some experimental analysis is discussed. Section 5 closes the paper with some conclusions and directions for future research.

2 Bionic mechanism

Compound eyes have many advantages including a large field of view and high sensitivity for moving target detection. Reichardt[6] et al proposed that there are two independent channels in compound eyes. One is called the "large field system" and the other is called the "small field system". The large field system detects global

[a] Corresponding author: sunhb@castc.org.cn

motion and the small field detects moving targets accurately. Our proposed detection algorithm with bionic compound eyes includes two phases. During the first phase we simulate the insect's compound eyes to detect the moving object outline and extract object in the surrounding area. In the second phase of algorithm we simulate the insect's compound eye's mechanism to accurately extract the moving object.

Compound eyes, with large view field, are very sensitive to moving objects region and location and can detect moving objects quickly with little outline information even when these objects are located in large open areas. Contour detection and variable image resolution are probably the two most important characteristics of compound eyes. Based on these characteristics we shall now propose our bionic eyes mechanism which is shown in Fig. 1.

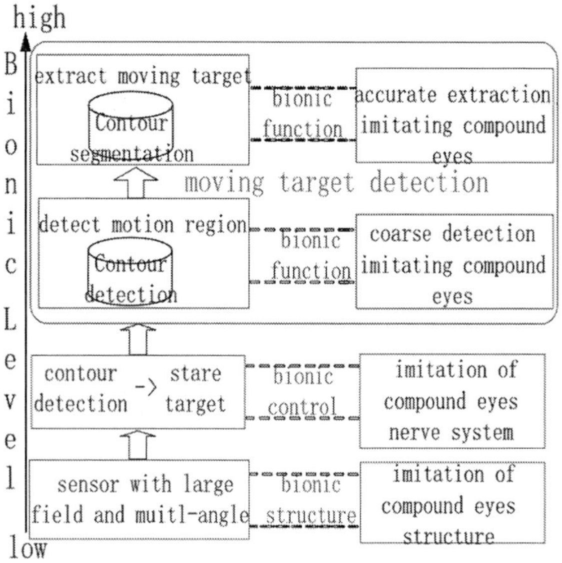

Figure 1. Schematic diagram of our bionic eyes mechanism.

Our bionic compound eyes mechanism, shown in Fig. 1, includes three components: bionic structure, bionic control, and bionic function. The biometric structure is the foundation component which acquires data using the sensors. The bionic control component then performs the contour extraction. The bionic function performs the detection of moving targets. The region of motion is computed by the bionic function. The final component of our bionic eyes mechanism is executed after contour segmentation of the remotely sensed images. The moving target is then extracted. It is clear from the structure of Fig. 1 that biometric level grows from low-level complexity to the highest level of complexity when the moving target is extracted. As commented by Corcoran et al segmentation presents a difficult problem in all object identification methodologies. Consequently segmentation is at the top of the complexity level for the biometrics in Fig. 1. In the next section we will describe, in detail, the bionic compound eyes detection system components.

3 Bionic surveillance system

In this section we describe, in detail, the bionic compound eyes detection system. The composition of the system is described in section 3.1. The biometric structure, including details of the cameras used, is described in section 3.2. Section 3.3 provides detailed information on the hardware control system. The final two sections provide the details about the data acquisition and object detection model.

3.1. Composition of the System

Based on the mechanism of insect compound eyes for detecting moving targets, we have constructed a bionic compound eyes detection system. The compound eyes structure consists of the large field of view, a multi-angle mechanical structure, a hardware control system, a data acquisition device, and an object detection model. The "electrics" component illustrates the hardware used with electrical components for control, image sensing, processing, and data storage. The mechanical components of the system are the physical components making up the compound eyes structure.

3.2 Biometric structure

According to the physical structure of insect compound eyes the mechanical structure of the bionic compound eyes is constructed using high and low resolution cameras. Our compound eyes device, which is shown in Fig. 2, consists of five cameras. Four cameras (all low resolution) surround one camera (central camera – high resolution) to form an equilateral hexagon. The fixed cameras devices are soft connected with the middle mechanical device. When detecting moving targets low resolution cameras detect the presence of moving objects while high resolution camera is responsible for target imaging. Using a servo system to control the angle of the cameras we can control the cameras to not only point to a specific position but also to monitor large areas in several directions.

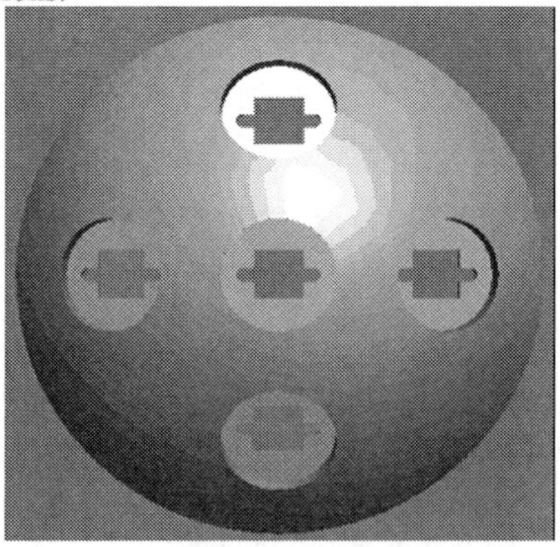

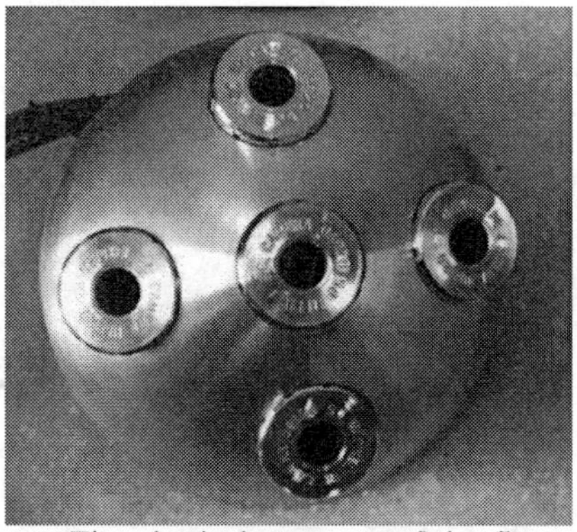

Figure 2. The physical structure of the five cameras on the compound eyes device.

As our system has a relatively large field of view the target will not quickly move out of visual range even if it is moving fast. Many authors agree with this approach such as Nanzhi et al[7] who comment that this also greatly enhances the robustness of any moving target detection systems. Subsequently this increases the detection performance.

3.3 Control System

In this section we describe the control system. The bionic compound eye's synchronous capture hardware control system consists of four parts: the DSP (Digital Signal Processor), main control unit, FPGA (Field-Programmable Gate Array) logic control unit, output unit, and the compound eyes device, physical structure is shown in Fig. 3.

Figure 3. Physical structure of control system.

The workflow of the control system is described as follows: The DSP main control core unit produces multi-channel control signals according to the combination of address bus and data bus. These signals are then transported to the FPGA controlling information source for the system. The FPGA generates synchronous sequential control units according to the combinational and sequential logic circuits. As the internal logic unit in FPGA has a precise synchronization trigger function it can generate proper multi-sync pulses whose synchronization error can be controlled in microseconds. In this way the system can fully satisfy the control function requirements. The synchronous pulses from the FPGA, after amplification, are entered into the drive output unit to drive all the shutter control circuits of the compound eyes directly.

The specific details of this are as follows: The shoot interval time can be achieved from counting the input clock and satisfying the parameters. The required waveform can be obtained by reversed phase when the count reaches the predefined value. The entire compound eyes system contains several timing controls. Three-input encoding circuits are needed at least to accomplish eight control modes with a DIP (Dual In-line Package) switch on the hardware circuit. Shoot intervals of eight different simultaneous control modes can be generated by the DIP switch while the modes can be presented by eight different display circuits.

3.4 Data acquisition model of compound eyes

Compound eyes system has the advantage that several targets within a given range can be captured simultaneously using multiple sub-eyes. However these sub-eyes can introduce many redundant images. This potential disadvantage can be minimized by re-using these redundant images to assist in reducing the random error in the targets' information.

Pengqi[8] proposed a preliminary algorithm for moving targets detection using bionic compound eyes. On the basis of this algorithm we have developed an improvement to his algorithm by proposing a bi-level contour detection model with variable resolution bionic compound eyes, as is shown in Fig. 4.

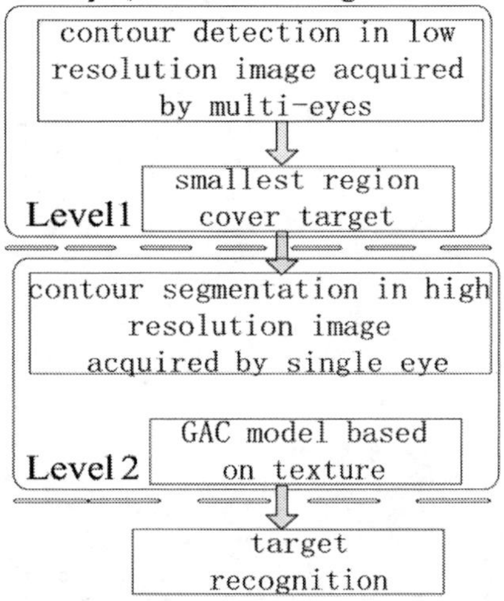

Figure 4. Flowchart diagram of the bi-level contour detection model used in our algorithm.

There are three important components of this algorithm. Firstly there is contour detection which is applied to the lowest resolution images. When this is complete the texture gradient computation is performed by conducting contour segmentation on the high resolution image(s) acquired by the single eye. Finally a Geodesic Active Contour model for texture boundary detection is applied from which the moving target is recognized.

4 Experimental and result

In this section we show an example of large view using bionic compound eyes. The example below shows the result processing the captured images using the approach SURF (Speeded-Up Robust Features) feature extraction. In this method, first of all, pre-classify the images according to the image geometric moment and the number of corner points, in order to achieve the automatic selection of image registration algorithm on the basis of the image features. SURF algorithm includes two parts: the feature detection and characterization. Feature characterization is described as

$$v = (\sum d_x, \sum d_y, \sum |d_x|, \sum |d_y|) \tag{1}$$

Wherer d_x is Haar wavelet response in the horizontal direction, d_y is Haar wavelet response in the vertical direction. Feature detection is completed by the formula (2) and (3).

$$I_{\Sigma}(x) = \sum_{i=0}^{i \le x} \sum_{j=0}^{j \le y} I(i,j) \tag{2}$$

$$H(x,\sigma) = \begin{bmatrix} L_{xx}(x,\sigma) & L_{xy}(x,\sigma) \\ L_{xy}(x,\sigma) & L_{yy}(x,\sigma) \end{bmatrix} \tag{3}$$

$I_{\Sigma}(x)$ stands for the sum of all the pixel gray values and $H_{(X,\sigma)}$ represents Hessian matrix.

The captured images are processed in the order of Fig.5.F and the result is shown as Fig.6.

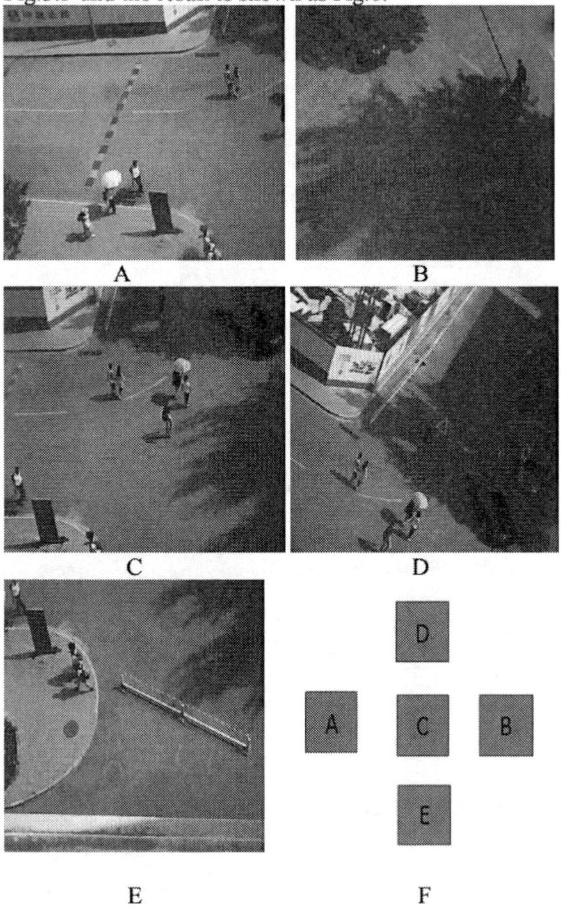

Figure 5. The experimental data captured by Bionic surveillance system.

Figure 6. The result of experimental data.

The system we have described, in this paper, for surveillance using bionic compound eyes with almost 180° field of view. This system achieves a very satisfactory tradeoff between the conflicting objects of: controlling the size of the field of view, the resolution of images captured, and the requirement to perform processing in real-time.

Acknowledgment

The work presented in this paper is supported by The Scholarship for International Young Scientists of NSFC (National Natural Science Foundation of China) (ID: U1333124 & U1433102). We thank the editor and reviewer for their contributions to improvements to this paper.

References

1. Paragious N, Deirche R. Geodesic Active Contours and Level Sets for the Detection and Tracking of Moving Objects. IEEE Transactions on Pattern Analysis and Machine Intelligence, 22, 266-280(2000).
2. Yamada K, Ishida S, Shougenji R, Tanida J. Development of three dimensional endoscope by Thin Observation by Bound Optics(TOMBO). Automation Congress, 199-205(2006).
3. Duparré J, Wippermann F, Dannberg P, Bräuer A. Artificial compound eye zoom camera. Bioinspiration biomimetics, 3, 1806-1823(2008).
4. Duparre J, Wippermann F, Darnnberg P, Schreiber P, Bräuer A, Völkel R, Scharf T. Micro-optical artificial compound eyes-from design to experimental verification of two different concepts. SPIE, 5962, 1-12(2005).
5. Huabo Sun, Haimeng Zhao and Peter Mooney et al, A Novel System for Moving Object Detection Using

Bionic Compound Eyes, Journal of Bionic Engineering, 8,313-322(2011).
6. Reichardt W. Evaluation of optical motion information by movement detectors. Journal of Comparative Physiology A: Neuroethology, Sensory, Neural, and Behavioral Physiology, 161, 533-547(1987).
7. Nanzhi Jiang, Renbiao Wu, Jian Li. Super resolution feature extraction of moving targets. IEEE Transactions on Aerospace and Electronic Systems, 37, 781-793(2001).
8. Pengqi Gao. Research on moving target detection using bionic compound eyes on UAV. Dissertation of Peking University, 21-26(2009).

MATEC Web of Conferences 44, 02037 (2016)
DOI: 10.1051/matecconf/20164402037

Gate Engineering in SOI LDMOS for Device Reliability

Aanand[1, a], Gene Sheu[1], Syed Sarwar Imam[1], Shao Wei Lu[2], Chirag Aryadeep[1], and Shao Ming Yang[1]

[1]*Department of Computer Science and Information Engineering, Asia University, 500, Lioufeng Rd., Taichung 41354, Taiwan*
[2]*School of Software and Microelectronics, Peking University, Beijing, China*

Abstract. A linearly graded doping drift region with step gate structure, used for improvement of reduced surface field (RESURF) SOI LDMOS transistor performance has been simulated with 0.35μm technology in this paper. The proposed device has one poly gate and double metal gate arranged in a stepped manner, from channel to drift region. The first gate uses n+ poly (near source) where as other two gates of aluminium. The first gate with thin gate oxide has good control over the channel charge. The third gate with thick gate oxide at drift region reduce gate to drain capacitance. The arrangement of second and third gates in a stepped manner in drift region spreads the electric field uniformly. Using two dimensional device simulations, the proposed SOI LDMOS is compared with conventional structure and the extended metal structure. We demonstrate that the proposed device exhibits significant enhancement in linearity, breakdown voltage, on-resistance and HCI. Double metal gate reduces the impact ionization area which helps to improve the Hot Carrier Injection effect.

1 Introduction

Laterally double diffused metal oxide semi-conductor (LDMOS) on SOI substrate is a promising technology for smart power transistors. Having applications in automotive, display drivers, digital audio and power management, power switching devices etc. In the recent past, developing high voltage SOI LDMOS has gained importance due to possibility of its integration with low power devices and heterogeneous microsystem.

Also in SOI LDMOS the kink appearing in the output characteristics. Though the kink can be eliminated by reducing the drift region doping concentration, [1] the increased drift region resistance degrades the other device parameter. Therefore, the motivation of this work is to explore structural modification in SOI LDMOS to enhance its high voltage capabilities and ruggedness of the device.

The SOI technology is interesting for three primary reasons. The buried oxide in the SOI structure reduces capacitive coupling to the substrate, which improves power efficiency. The SOI buried oxide also provide improved isolation between adjacent circuits, making attractive for highly integrated power amplifiers in which substrate cross talks is a concern. A third advantage is that it allows for the use of high resistivity substrates that enable the fabrication of low loss on-chip inductors.

2 Device structure

Fig. 1 shows the cross-section of our SOI double metal gate with P-top LDMOS device. The device is characterised by the double metal gate in the drift region. The first gate uses n+ poly as the gate material and the other two gates uses aluminium as the gate material. The first gate having the higher work function material (n+ poly) tries to increase the threshold voltage, but the thinner first gate oxide reduces it. Thus the design of step gate LDMOS is done in such a way that the combination of thinner and higher work function material results in the same threshold voltage as that of the conventional device.

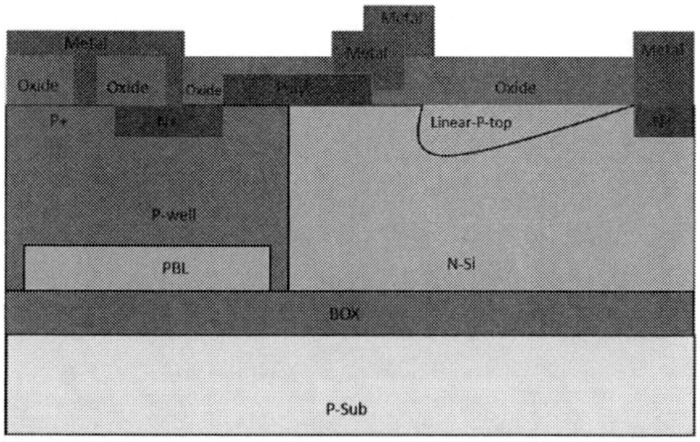

Figure. 1 Cross-section of step gate SOI LDMOS with linear P-top

[a] Corresponding author: aanand92@gmail.com

Article available at http://www.matec-conferences.org or http://dx.doi.org/10.1051/matecconf/20164402037

We developed a new innovative n-channel LDMOS device with P-top in the drift region. P-top in the drift region helps to achieves better RESURF condition, contributes to uniform electric field. [2] [5]

Table 1. Off-state characteristics

	BVDs(V)	Ron(mΩmm^2)	Vth(V)
Conventional structure	92.3	133	1.85
Single Metal Structure	100.2	119	1.5
Double Metal Structure	98.2	119	1.5

3 Kirk Effect

For lateral high voltage devices at high current density, the moving carriers influence the depleted charge, which results in high electric field near N/N+ junction. This is called Kirk effect. In the on-state significant amount of negative charge adds to the positive space charge of the N-type drift region.

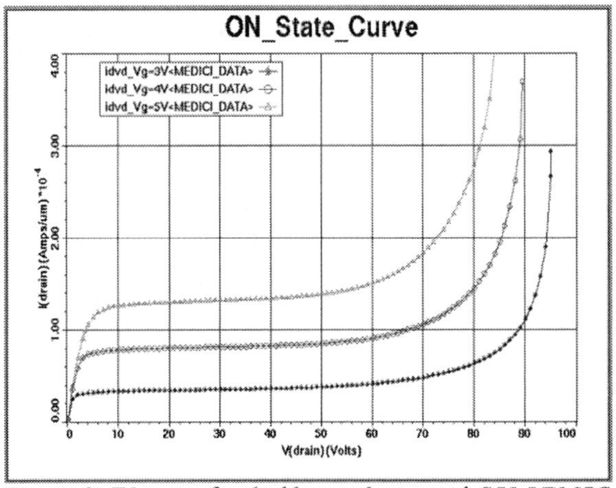

Figure 2. IV curve for double metal proposed SOI LDMOS device structure

It leads to a shift of the potential lines towards the drain. For application, the effect means the use of a longer drift region or less current per gate width.

Several methods have been proposed to alleviate Kirk effect, adding an N$^-$ buffer region, whose concentration is higher than the drift region while lighter than the drift region, has been well-known. A double RESURF technology was put forward to improve SOA. [2]

4 Hot Carrier Effect

As the electric field increases, electrons and holes traveling in the channel and drift region may gain sufficient kinetic energy to be overcome a potential barrier necessary to the SiO2 interface, and cause in the SiO2 interface charge distribution. This defines the well-known hot carrier effects (HCI), which is one of the major failure mechanisms affecting long term reliability. In the case of LDMOS applied with high voltage to the gate and drain HCI severe limitation to long term (LT-SOA). [2]

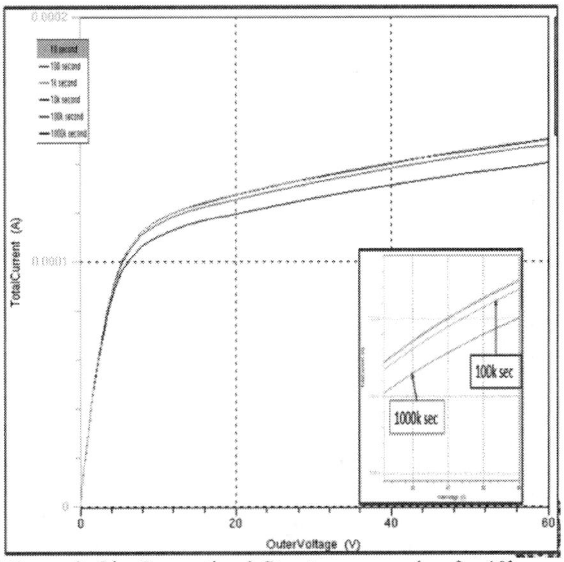

Figure 3. Id_{sat} Conventional Structure compasion for 10k sec, 100k sec, 1000k sec

As a matter of fact, HCI are induced by high electric field consequently, any action devoted to reduce the peak/plateau of the electric field in the channel and the drift region can improve the ruggedness of LDMOS and increase the corresponding LT-SOA. [2]

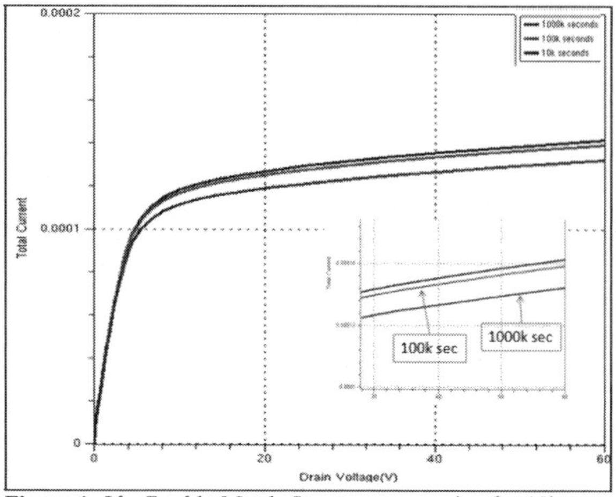

Figure 4. Id_{sat} Double Metal Structure compasion for 10k sec, 100k sec, 1000k sec

Table 2. Id_{sat} percentage change

Stress time(sec)	% shift Conventional Structure	% shift Double Metal Structure
1E4 sec	0.29 %	0.20%
1E5 sec	1.78 %	1.75%
1E6 sec	6.5 %	5.9%

5 Design Issues

A LDMOS drift region is the most important and complex part. This part has significant influence on breakdown voltage, on resistance, power consumption, device stability and reliability of SOI LDMOS. [6] Each parameter in the design of drift region will have an impact on device performance, and different process parameter has mutual influence between them. Higher breakdown voltage requires lightly doped, thick and long drift region, while low on resistance require heavily doped thin and short drift region. So the design of SOI LDMOS needs to balance between drift region doping concentration and length, maintaining certain breakdown voltage of the device and achieve the least on resistance. [7]

The main principle of the extended P-top region is to reduce the parasitic BJT effect. The hole current generated due to impact-ionization is now collected through n+ and P-top junction instead of an n+ and p-body.

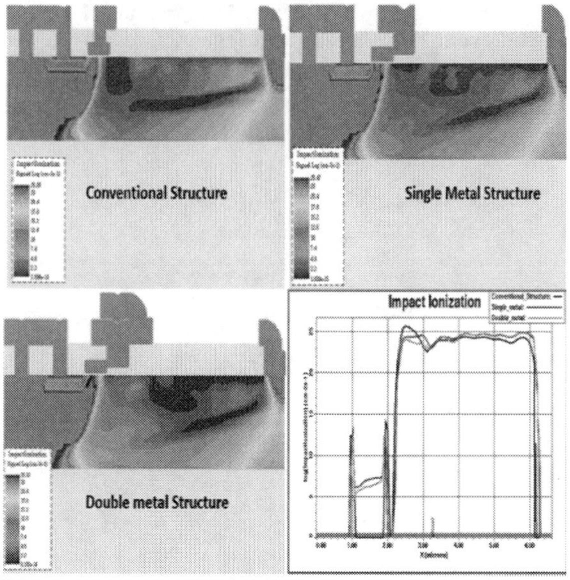

Figure 5. Impact Ionization area comparison in three different structure.

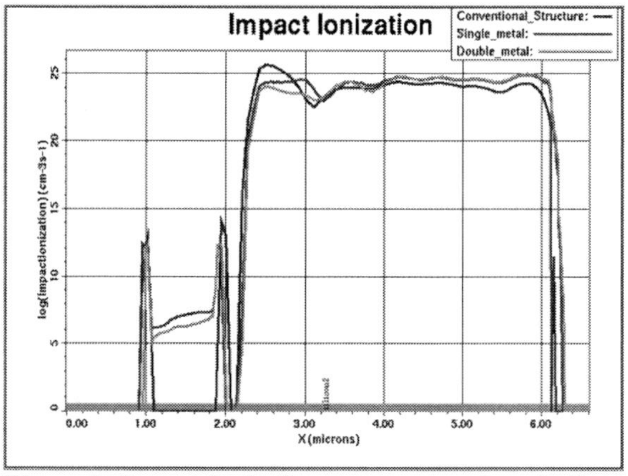

Figure 6. Impact Ionization curve comparison in three different structure.

5.1 Electric field distribution

The stepped gate structure in the drift region has three gate sections arranged with increasing gate oxide thickness from the channel side to the drain side. [3] The stepped gate structure leads to uniform electric field distribution, reduced gate-drain capacitance and facilitates the use of increased drift region doping simultaneously. [4] The gate overlap length and the stepped oxide thickness for both the devices in our simulation are designed for maximum breakdown voltage and minimum on-resistance.

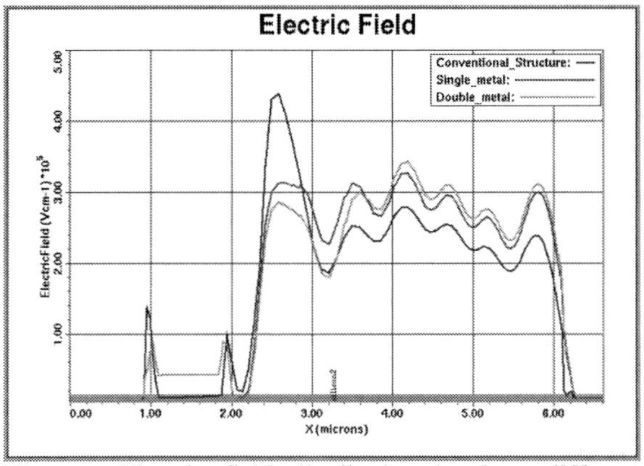

Figure 7. Electric field distribution in three different device structures.

References

1. Temple, V.A.K, "MOS-Controlled thyristors-A new class of power devices," IEEE Transactions on Electron Devices, 33(10):1609- 1618, Oct 1986.
2. P. Hower, J. Lin, S. Merchant and S. Paiva, "Using "Adaptive Resurf" to Improve the SOA of Ldmos Transistors", ISPSD 2000, pp. 345-348.
3. D. G. Lin, S. L. Tu, Y. C. See and P. Tam, "A Novel LDMOS Structure With a Step Gate Oxide," in IEDM Tech. Dig.,1995,pp.963-966.
4. R. Sithanandam and M. J. Kumar "Linearity and speed optimization in SOI LDMOS using gate engineering," Semiconductor Science and Technology, Vol.25, Article No. 015006, pp1-6, January 2010.
5. Guo Yufeng, Fang Jian, Zhang Bo, et al. A 2D analytical model of SOI double RESURF effect. Chinese Journal of Semiconductors, 2005, 26(4): 764
6. G.Toulon, I.Cortes, F.Morancho, E.Hugonnard-Bruyere, B.Villard and W.J.Toren, "Design and optimization of high voltage LDMOS transistors on 0.18µm SOI CMOS technology," Solid State Electron., vol.61, pp. 111-115, July.2011.
7. B. Zhang, Z. Li, S. Hu, and X. Luo, "Field enhancement for dielectric layer of high-voltage devices on silicon on insulator," IEEE Transactions on Electron Devices, vol. 56, no. 10, pp. 2327– 2334, 2009.

MATEC Web of Conferences 44, 02038 (2016)
DOI: 10.1051/matecconf/20164402038

Research on Mapping UML to Petri-Net in System Modeling

Chun Jian Wang[1,a], Hong Jun Fan[2] and Shuang Pan[1]

[1]Navy Submarine Academy, 266199 Qingdao, China
[2] Qingdao Branch of Naval Aeronautical Engineering Institute, 266199 Qingdao, China

Abstract. The paper analyzes the need of complex system modeling.According to the advantage and shortage of UML and Perti net, comprehensive usage of Petri net and UML can efficiently improve the comprehensiveness, consistency, accuracy and completeness of the model describing. The translation rules from UML to Petri net were proposed. So the UML model can be analyzed and verified better.

1 Submitting the manuscript

A model is the complete abstraction of a system, and the model including the comprehension and understanding that how to solve the problem and the solution of the problem. The model makes up of element and has certain system structure. The system model is the abstraction of actual system. For the huge system which has many equipments and complicated conjunction relation, how to optimize the information interaction is emphases. It has high request for the real-time communication and the cooperatively of the sub-system. The information interaction relation and type that between the system and sub-system and inner sub-system is complicated. And it has high request for real-time. Making good model for this kind of system, it can build up good foundation for development and maintenance of system.

2 The introduction of UML

Along with the advance of system's complicacy, it is more and more urgent to the need of good model language. UML develops with the object-oriented system analysis and design. It is mainly used to build the system model within the analysis and design stage, and it has scalability and commonality. Being the third generation object-oriented modeling language, it is a kind of graphical language, including demand analysis and structure and allocation.

The definition of UML includes semanteme and notation. The semantic description is based on the definition of accurate metamodel. The metamodel provides a brief and consistent and general definition elucidation for the elementses in semanteme and notation. With these, developer can obtain unanimity on semanteme.

UML includes use case diagram and collaboration diagram and interaction diagram and sequence diagram, and can also induce for the static state modeling mechanism and dynamic modeling mechanism. Figure 1 is the step of UML modeling process.

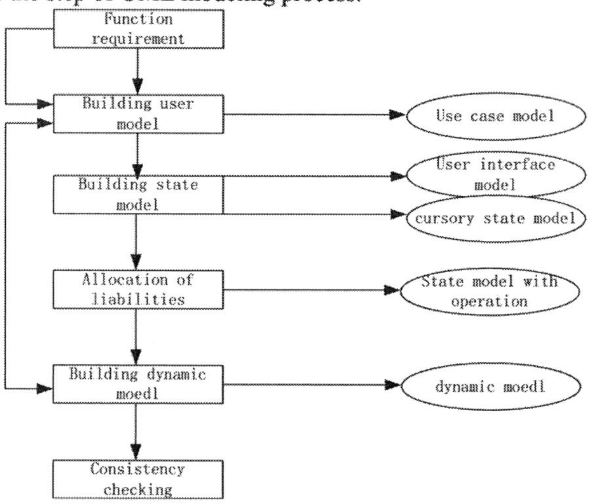

Figure 1. UML modeling process

Being an object-oriented model tool which has good definition and easy expression and direct description, UML provides effective tool for design and analysis of information system. But while constructing complicated and huge system, it is difficult to embody the cryptic concurrency between objects and the consistency of

[a] Corresponding author: zhihe_wcj@163.com
Natural Science Foundation of China(61473306)

constraint rule between objects. And it is also difficult to display the dynamic behavior character completely.
UML is applicable to describe any type of system with object-oriented technique, and is applicable to different stage of system development. From the need description to the test and maintenance after completing, UML all can be used.

3 Petri net

Petri net is put forward by Germany Carl Adam in his doctor dissertation in 1962 firstly. Petri net can not only be used to analyze the static structure, but also the dynamic behavior. And it is a kind of mathematic and graphical tool to describe and analyze. To develop the information processing system which is parallel or asynchronous or distributed or concurrent or indeterminacy, it can construct the Petri net model and analyze. Then, we can get the information about the system structure and the dynamic state behavior. According to the information, we can evaluate and improve the system.
The state element and variety element of Petri net use Place and Transition to express respectively. The function of transition is changing the state, and the function of place is to decide whether the transition can take place. The dependency relationship between transition and place uses directional-arc (arrowhead) to denote and it is a Petri net. We use circle to represent the place, and use rectangle to represent the transition, and use directional-arc to represent the input that from place to transition and output that from transition to place. During building the model, if use the concept of condition and events, then position represent the condition and transition represent the events, and all these can constitute a Petri net, such as figure 2.

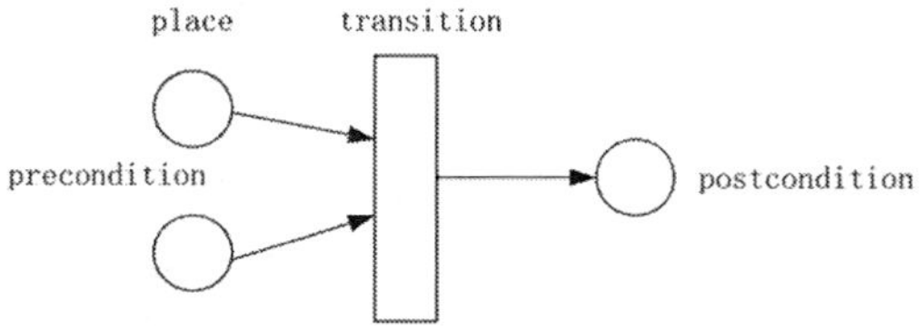

Figure 2. Petri net

Figuer 2 shows that the events are the action taking place in the system. The occurrence of these actions is controled by the state of system, while these states can be sescribed with a set of condition. Condition is the property or logic description of system and a condition can be established or not established. Because the event is an action, it probably takes place. The occurrence of an event may need a few conditions to be established at the same time, and all these conditions are called the prior condition of event. The occurrence of the event may cause the prior condition disappear and produce other conditions, and those aonditions are called subsequent condition. Petri net studies the structure and dynamic behavior of system, and pay attention to the state variety and the relation of variety that possiblly take place in the system. The Petri net can descripe the dynamic character of system laconically, such as concurrent, conflict synchronous etc. It has corresponding analysis method. So Petri net is broadly applied in building model and analysis.

4 UML mapping to Petri net

According to the different peculiarity of UML and Petri net, we can combine UML with Petri net, bringing out the best in each other. Firstly, we make use of UML's chart element to describe model and design the object in the system. Then, according to the complexity of model, mapping a part of UML model which is necessary to Petri net model based on certain rule. And then, carry on analysis and optimization. The result can amend the UML model. At last, convert those models into UML statechart and sequence diagram, and constitute an integrity UML model with other charts, such as figure 3.

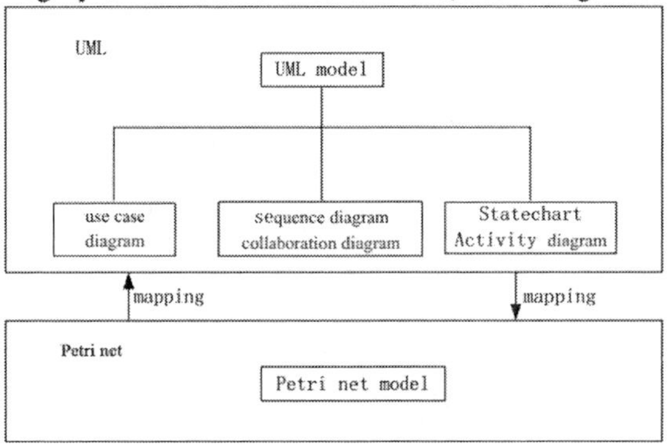

Figure 3. Model frame

The conversion of model is not to re-construct a new model, and it has to keep certain restriction. It can discover the likeness between UML and Petri net based on analysis. UML shows object accepting and sending the message and operation inside the object. Petri net shows inner place and transition. UML statechart is classic Object-Oriented variant, and it describes an object how to transfer state under events driving in its life cycle, and it gives the origin and terminus. And also it displays the detail of object's dynamic behavior, so it can convert into object's Sub-Petri net. Therefore it can withdraw information from UML statechart to construct object's Petri net model.

The mapping rule is as follows, such as Figure 4.
The place in Petri net model mapping to properties of objects in UML model.
The Subnet in Petri net model mapping to statechart of object in UML model. The place corresponds to the activity in statechart and the transition corresponds to the action in the statechart.
The transition in Petri net model mapping to activity in UML activity diagram, and the place mapping to condition.
The door transition in Petri net model mapping to the message event in UML interaction diagram (sequence diagram and collaboration diagram).

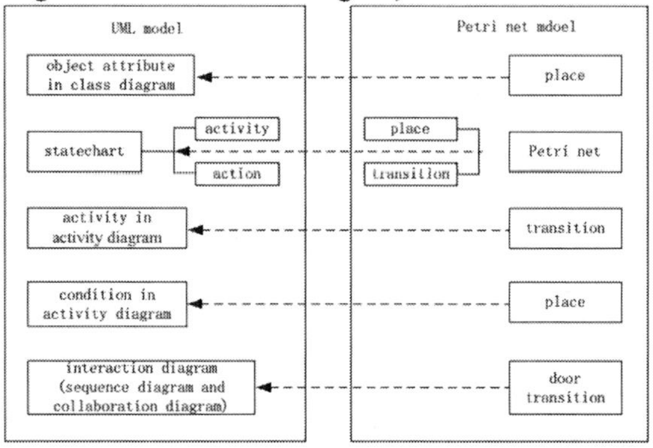

Figure 4. Petri net model mapping to UML model

UML analysis and disassemble the system from top lever bottom, and attain genus and various charts that shows the relation between the genus. Figure 5 is the statechart of UML and Figure 5 is the sequence diagram of UML. Figure 6 shows that event 1 and event 2 and event 3 and event 4 are external events. When object accepts external events, the statechart can show the operation of the object which accepts the message and the change of state under the corresponding condition.

Figure 5. State chart

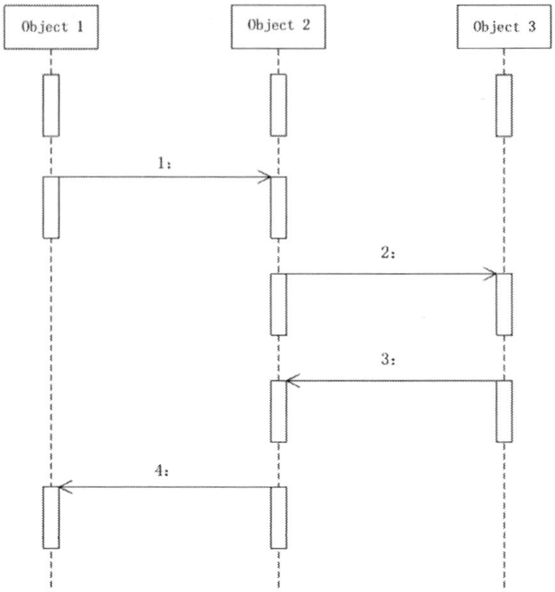

Figure 6. sequence diagram

It can abstract the mapping process from UML model to Petri net model, such as Figure 7. The mapping rule is as follows:
All properties of objects in UML model mapping to place in Petri net model.
The statechart of object in UML model mapping to Subnet in Petri net model. The activity in statechart corresponds to the place and the action in the statechart corresponds to the transition.
The activity in UML activity diagram mapping to transition in Petri net model, and the condition mapping to place.
The message event in UML interaction diagram (sequence diagram and collaboration diagram) mapping to door transition in Petri net model.

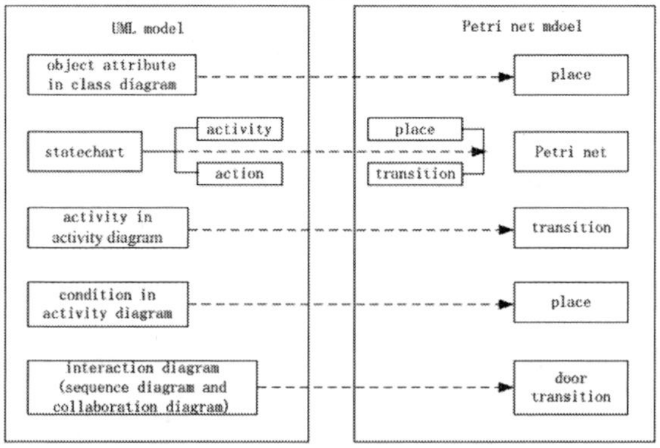

Figure 7. UML model mapping to Petri net model

According to the above rule, the triggering event of a conversion in UML statechart mapping to transition of

Subnet in Petri net model, and the source state mapping to ex-gather place of transition, and the object state mapping to behind gather place of transition, and the convertion element mapping to two arc from ex-gather place to transition and from transition to behind gather place, such as figure 8. The sequence diagram in UML model describes the delivering relation of message between objects, and mapping this relation to communication relation between Object-Oriented Petri net objects.

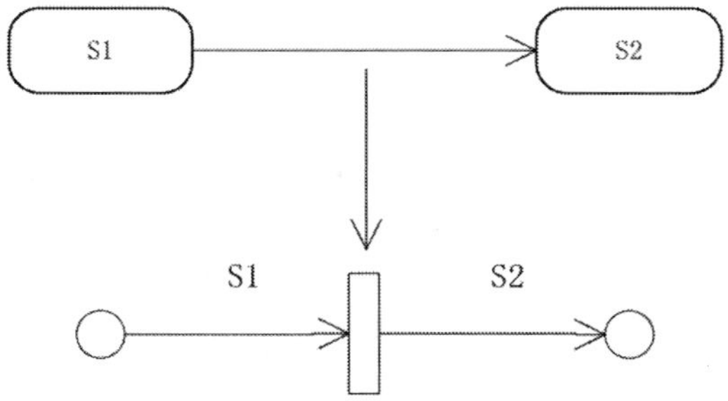

Figure 8. State chart mapping to sub Petri net

By this way, the model described by UML using class diagram and interaction diagram and collaboration diagram is mappinged to Petri net model described by place and transition and connected relation. With completing the mapping, gradual and concrete Petri net model can be established. Corresponding to UML diagram, the reflected Petri net model is also hierarchical type, and the whole Petri net model includes several Sub Petri nets. Corresponding to UML, the reflected Petri net model is also Object-Oriented. Divided into many parts, every part corresponds to one object, and the relationship between parts only pass message event. The model described with UML is reflected to Petri net model, and then it can be analyzed and optimized and described with mathematics based on Petri net theory, and carry out continuous improvement to the model.

References

1. Zhao Jun-feng, Zhou Jian-tao, Xing Guan-nan: Research of Translating UML Activity Diagram to Petri Net. Computer Science, 2014,41(7):143-147
2. Wang Yuhua, Yin Guisheng: Automatically generating a UML model from a requirement model based on ontology. Journal of Harbin Engineering University, 2012,Vol.33,No.12:735-740
3. CHAI Yu-mei,FENG Qiu-yan,WANG Li-ming: Research on Methods for Generating Test Cases of Inter-Classes Interaction Based on UML Models and OCL Constraints. Acta Electronica Sinica, 2013(6):1242-1248
4. Song A-ni, Wang Ming-zhe, Guo Fa-bin, Ni Feng: Unfolding the basic structure of colored Petri nets. SYSTEMS ENGINEERING —THEORY & PRACTICE, 2011,Vol.31,No.2:316-322
5. Wu Guo-guang, Liu Gui-xiong, Zhou Song-bin: Modeling and Dynamic Performance Evaluation of WTIM Based on Petri Nets. Journal of South China University of Technology(Natural Science Edition), 2013,Vol.41,No.9:108-112.

MATEC Web of Conferences 44, 02039 (2016)
DOI: 10.1051/matecconf/20164402039

Mapping of Force: a Process of Parametric Design from the Prototype Mechanical Mechanism to the Structural Form of a Woven HYPAR Shell

Kang Qiang Lin[1, a], Chao Hao Su[1, b]
[1,2] *Architecture Design and Research Institute, South China University of Technology, Guangzhou, 510640, China*

Abstract. From a new perspective of structural engineering, with the integration of the 1st and 3rd principal stress distribution of HYPAR shell structure into the selection of texture variation zone, this paper analyzes and demonstrates the key questions of how to establish the association between the force-flow, the texture direction and the form parameters; how to develop a dynamic, performance-optimized and adaptive iteration model of HYPAR shell structural form by setting and adjusting structurally sensitive parameters; and how to realize the process of parametric design from the mechanical mechanism of the prototype to the structural form of the woven HYPAR shell.

Introduction

In architectural parametric design, a new interdisciplinary research question has emerged as how to effectively coordinate and reconstruct the relationships between stress and form [1,2] for achieving the unification of free forms and objective constraints. To express the inner logic of structural mechanics in the form of an architectural language has created an important branch of modern architecture, that is, structure as architecture [3]. However, with the arrival of the era of digital architectural design, the "emergence" [4] of complex forms created by complex mathematical algorithms and complicated computer programs has brought severe challenges and posed a novel research topic for the integration and expression of structural mechanics. Schumacher [5, 6] . has recently declared "trying more and more to move away from the freeform play with complex curvature towards the disciplined use of structural form-finding algorithms " [7].

From yet another perspective, the mechanical prototype of a structure can be adopted as the starting point to analyze its fundamental stress mechanism and inherent relationship, and digital tools can be introduced to realize the adaptive topology of geometric forms. This paper further discusses how to establish the correlations between the mechanical mechanisms, such as stress distribution and force flow [8], and the digital geometric forms. It also demonstrates the parametric design process of the form topology of HYPAR shell structures based on the form-innovation and optimization tests of the woven texture pattern of a response mechanics mechanism.

1. Mechanical mechanism and a misunderstanding

Basis exploration: Structures play a role in form resistance, and define the relationships between stress and form, which are not so intuitive. Thus, the mechanical mechanism of a structural prototype serves as the prerequisite of the mapping of force onto form. Two mechanical logics related to the form resistance and parametric design must be clarified at this stage, they are, stress distribution and force flow.

Not merely a stress nephogram: Generally the architectural parametric design only employs the nephogram that reflects stress distribution, but has neglected force flow trace - another important factor that is fixed but hidden. Thus, there is a common misunderstanding in the integration of mechanics obtained by architectural parametric design. Consequently, a one-sided reflection of stress distribution is employed as a substitute for the reflection of the mechanical mechanism. The misunderstanding is potentially erroneous as force flow plays a very important and special role, especially in the HYPAR shells. Geometrically, a HYPAR shell is generated by revolving a straight line along another orthogonal bus. Doing this may easily lead to a mechanical misunderstanding, i.e., the force is transferred to the boundary along the orthogonal straight line direction. However, the laws of physics do not work in this way: he force transfer always searches for the most favorable form resistance path, that is, there is a superposition of suspension cable mechanism and an arch force transfer mechanism on the two diagonal directions, respectively [9] (see Fig.1).

Difference between the mathematical and physical significance: To obtain the unit form of a parametric design with an effective overall form resistance action, adapting to the path of cable plus arch seems to be both necessary and critical. Conversely, damaging this potential mechanical logic would make it impossible to construct a shell structure. Rather what would be constructed would be a shell-shaped geometric body having only a purely mathematical significance, as the force transfer mechanism would be changed.

2. Force flow and priority of mapping directivity

For brittle materials made of reinforced concrete, in line with the first strength theory(max normal stress theory), the first principal stress plays a dominant role. Therefore, the suspension cable mechanism will have a priority over the arch mechanism. Based on the mapping forms of the two forces, we can obtain a distinct data comparison through mechanical calculation (see Fig.2).

1) Arch mechanism as the priority: On the one

[a]linkangqiang0101@126.com, [b]suchaohao@scut.edu.cn

Article available at http://www.matec-conferences.org or http://dx.doi.org/10.1051/matecconf/20164402039

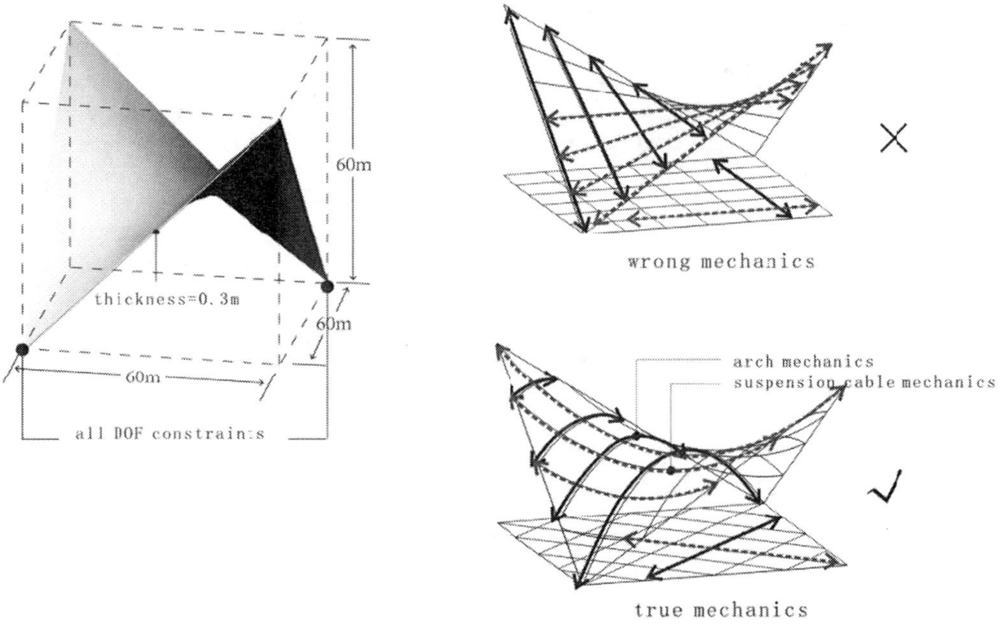

Fig. 1. Analysis of structural mechanics

hand, the tensile stress fails to be transferred along the diagonal direction. This causes the tensile stress to exceed 20 MPa at stress concentrated zones, thus necessitating a high reinforcement ratio and subsequently causing difficulty in reinforcement. On the other hand, due to the lack of a structural member in the tensile direction of the suspension cable, the overall rigidity is discounted, and the large deformation on the tensile end fails to be satisfactorily controlled (deformation value having reached as high as 1.124);

2) Suspension cable mechanism as the priority: In the second circumstance, with the directional adjustment of the mapping unit, the dominant tensile direction is cleared, the tensile stress remains fairly uniform within 13 MPa. The deformation value has recovered to 0.858, and the overall deformation is relatively uniform without any sudden variation. Although the pressure transfer path is slightly tortuous, it has not incurred any change in the prototype mechanical mechanism.

3. Iteration of the mechanical form

Following the established mechanical mechanism, the degree of spatial freedom of the structural form has a flexible range that can adapt to the architecturally significant demands such as light and shadow, air flow, thermal environment and visual interface dynamics. Thus, an iteration model can be generated between spatial form and mechanical performance by selecting or combining structurally sensitive parameters with relevant evaluation and analysis.

3.1 Structural calculation and sensitive parameters

The conventional structural mechanical calculation is usually divided into two steps: first, some fixed unit models are set to simplify complex forms; and second, the calculation results are employed for the detailed checking of the specific forms of local zones. Apparently, form parameter information, or even more sensitive parameters, have been deleted in the name of simplification. Firstly, it will result in a major error in the mechanical analysis when compared to a practical situation. Secondly, the process of adopting sensitive parameters for a dynamic regulation is suspended. Thus, as far as the woven structural form is concerned, the conventional simplified mechanical calculation has serious limitations, and hence, the structural calculation of the holo-information model seems to be more applicable and important.

The logic generated on the basis of the woven texture of the force transfer mechanism is as shown in Fig.3. Holing and warping are, respectively, conducted on the upper and lower layers, and are mutually superposed and alternated. Thus, the radius of the circle produces a correspondence with the first principal stress nephogram within its numerical interval. Accordingly it

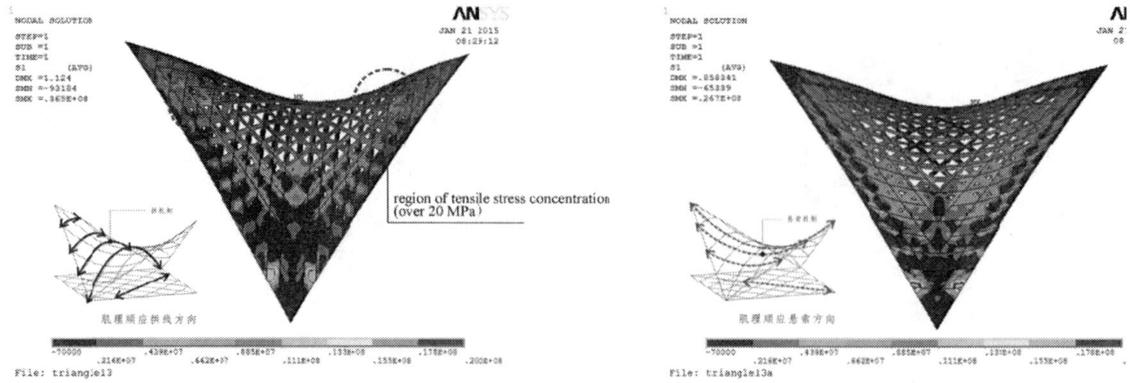

a) case1: textures along the direction of arch (archi mechanics first)

b) case2: textures along the direction of suspension cable (suspension cable mechanics first)

Fig. 2. Test of mechanical performance between two mapping ways according to arch mechanics and suspension cable mechanics

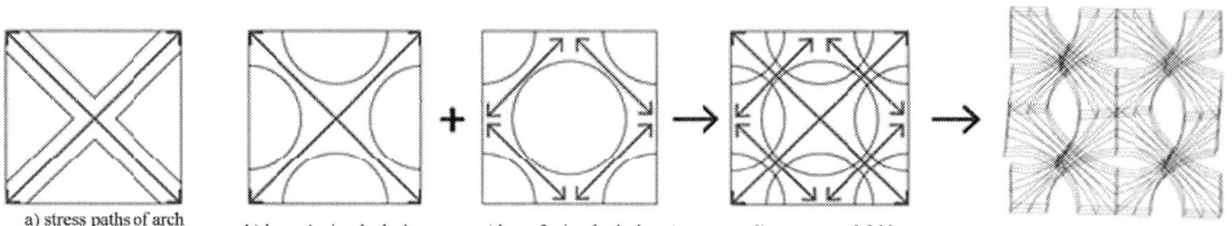

a) stress paths of arch & suspension cable direction

b) layer 1:circular holes near four edges

c) layer 2:circular holes at corners and center

d) superposed fold of two layers

e) digital model of woven units

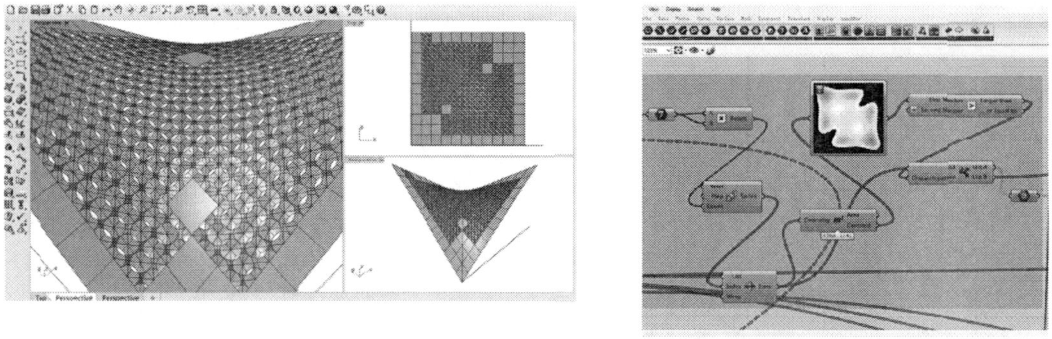

f) a woven HYPAR shell generated with Grasshopper responding to arch and suspension cable mechanics

Fig.3. Woven texture generation and its parametric design process based on prototype structural mechanics(arch + suspension cable)

reflects and regulates the distribution of the first principal stress as the first structural sensitive parameter.

The relative scale of warping not only realizes the woven form of the texture but also reflects the degree of interference with the prototype mechanical mechanism by having warping as the second structural sensitive parameter.

3.2 Iteration model between unit number and holing rate

This study conducted the iteration tests by three number scales and three holing rates (the holing rate μ is defined as the ratio of the round hole diameter d to the unit's side length L', i.e., μ=d/L'). See the results in Fig.4.

1) Small-number scale: The force transfer path of suspension cable plus arch can be determined from the principal stress vector diagram. When the holing rate μ=0.85, 0.78, there is a marked concentration of stress in the tensile zone (exceeding 20 MPa); when μ=0.70, stress concentration is eliminated and the peak displacement DMX declines from 0.734 to 0.664;

2) Medium-number scale: The principal stress vector diagram shows, relatively clearly, the force transfer path of suspension cable plus arch. When μ=0.85, there is a local concentration of stress on the edges of the round circle in the tensile zone; when μ=0.78, stress concentration gradually disappears, and declines to a level below 30 MPa; when μ=0.70, stress distribution is uniform, and the peak displacement DMX declines from 0.839 to 0.683;

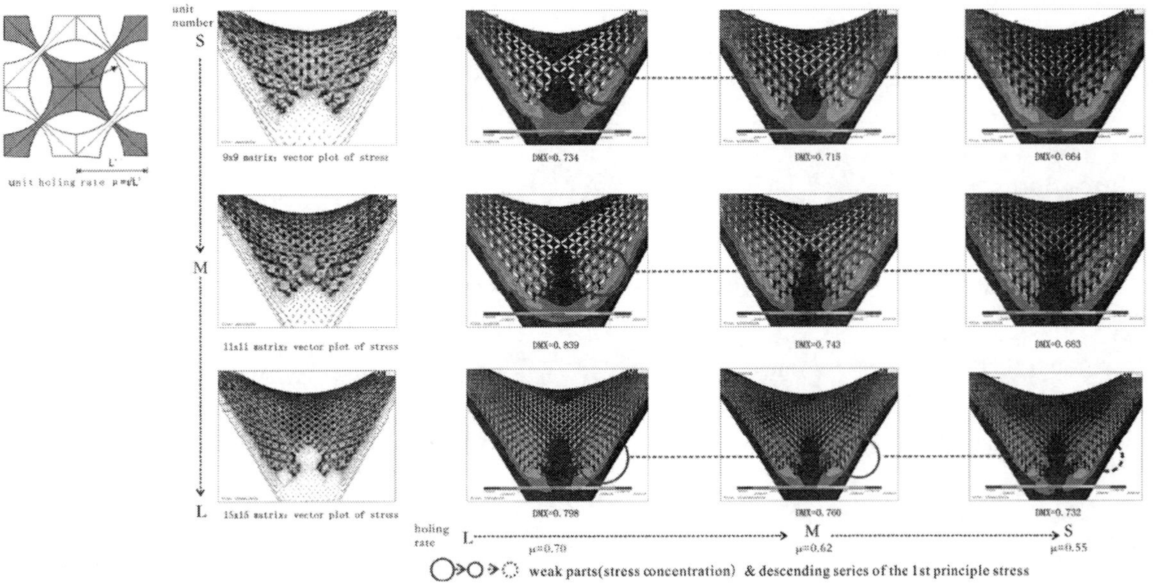

Fig.4. Structural performance in the iteration process of unit number and holing rate

3) Large-number scale: The principal stress vector diagram clearly shows the force transfer path of suspension cable plus arch. Stress distribution is uniform under the three holing rates, and there is no stress concentration zone with stress exceeding 20 MPa.

To sum up, the prototype mechanical mechanism of the shell is presented with the gradual increase in unit number. The holing rate has a relatively high structural sensitivity when the unit number is relatively small, and presents a trend of declining degree of interference with a gradual increase in unit number. When the unit number becomes relatively large, the interference of the holing rate is diminished. With a gradual increase in unit number, the peak displacement DMX shows a generally increasing trend but the overall rigidity shows a gradually decreasing trend. However, the reduction in overall rigidity can be compensated by adjusting the holing rate.

3.3 Spatial creation of mechanical form

After a series of deduction, simulation and experimental demonstration linked to the structural performance, a new combined model has been proposed for potential stress distribution, force flow trace and external building spatial forms. The performance-based structural form of the shell has provided the basis and theme for the creation of an architectural visual space. On the one hand, there exists a concentration of force potential, i.e., the counter-gravity form of shape. Considering the structural stability, the supporting area of the landing end can be appropriately enlarged to form a triangular support (when combined with the other landing points), in which case the other two suspended end points will construct a large cantilever resembling two flying wings and presenting a counter-gravity visual tension. Moreover, there is the flow of stress, i.e., the woven texture. The woven texture has essentially overturned the all-solid surface, enclosed the spatial form of the shell, and introduced the natural elements while generating a new interface form, thus creating a light and shadow-alternated spatial effect. The diversified spatial form realized through scheduling sensitive parameters can better adapt to the building functions. As far as spatial creation is concerned, the light and shadow effect and force flow rhythms, offered by the variation in the structural performance-based texture form, present a visual motivation that is not possible in the traditional enclosed shells .

4. Conclusions

A building can not change its forms randomly like sculptures, and a structure does not necessarily mean a restraint without freedom. The development of geometric forms under parametric design technology must find a new point of combination with the logic of structural mechanics. an effective technical route was proposed to unify force-driven shaping and resistance through forms , starting with a structural prototype with its inner mechanical mechanism analyzed and, then, utilized to reflect the physical law onto the geometric form. The route is also an important way of realizing the permanent rational controllability of the generation of complex forms during the whole parametric design process. As an example, a woven shell structure was discussed as a quantitative demonstration guided by the creation idea and the experimental route of "mapping of force". The key lies in how to analyze the mechanical mechanism of the structural prototype and understanding

and utilizing the force flow to avoid intuitive misunderstanding. Extension of the proposed technical route will be worthwhile to further explore and forecast the mechanical mapping of more structural prototypes.

Acknowledgment

The research described in this paper is supported by National Natural Science Foundation of China (51308218), Pearl River S&T Nova Program of Guangzhou(201506010038) and "the Fundamental Research Funds for the Central Universities" (2014ZM0012). The corresponding author is Chaohao Su.

References

[1]. Wanda J. Lewis. Modeling of Fabric Structures and Associated Design Issues [J]. Journal of Architectural Engineering, June, 2013,vol.19:81-88.

[2]. Edward Allen, Waclaw Zalewski. Form and Forces: Designing Efficient, Expressive Structures[M]. John Wiley and Sons Ltd, October 23, 2009.

[3]. Andrew Charleson. Structure As Architecture: A Source Book for Architects and Structural Engineers[M]. Routledge(2nd Revised edition). July 1, 2014.

[4]. Michael Weinstock. The Architecture of Emergence: The Evolution of Form in Nature and Civilisation[M]. Wiley, April 6, 2010.

[5]. Patrik Schumacher. The Autopoiesis of Architecture: A New Framework for Architecture[M]. Wiley(1 edition), January 18, 2011.

[6]. Patrik Schumacher. The Autopoiesis of Architecture, Volume II: A New Agenda for Architecture[M] . Wiley(1 edition), May 7, 2012.

[7]. Yang Yang, Cristopher D. Moen, James K. Guest. Three-Dimensional Force Flow Paths and Reinforcement Design in Concrete via Stress-Dependent Truss-Continuum Topology Optimization[J]. Journal of Engineering Mechanics, January 2015,vol.141: 04014106-1-10

[8]. Heino Engel, Ralph Rapson. Structure Systems[M]. Hatje Cantz, October, 2006.

[9]. AliReza Habibi. New Approximation Method for Structural Optimization[J]. Journal of Computing in Civil Engineering, 2012, vol.26:236-247.

MATEC Web of Conferences 44, 02040 (2016)
DOI: 10.1051/matecconf/20164402040

Research on Web Press Tension Control System

Sheng Jiang Chen[1], Chun Feng Zhang[1,a], Zhong You Wang[1], Qing Lin Li[2]
[1]Hubei University of Science and Technology,China
[2]Hubei Enan Xinhua Printing and Packaging Co., LTD,China

Abstract: Tension control of press is a key and difficult point of the whole machine control. The stand or fall of tension is directly related to the quality of the products. According to the characteristics of the web press tension control, this paper expounds the main factors influencing tension and the purpose of tension control, researches on the tension control principle of web tape, analyzes control rule and control circuit of tension control system, illustrates the advantages of PID control law adopted in the tension control system, and concludes the influencing factors of paper tape tension control system and the corresponding problems needed to solve in the control.

Introduction

In the process of web press work, tension control of paper is quite important. If tension control is inappropriate, fold and deformation occurs upon coil, influencing printing quality and causing waste of paper. Now most printing enterprises use traditional unit-type printer, in which power of printing unit is provided by the power source, transferred and obtained via transmission parts such as belt, mechanical shaft and gear. In this process, the shear interference transfers with the mechanical shaft, which results in the reduction of printing precision. And existing magnetic powder brake may be stuck or fail to work due to improper installation, over-speed, long time of usage, and etc. These factors directly or indirectly lead to biased printing machine tension control, which affects printing quality. So, the stability of the tension control is especially important in the field of printing production and processing, and tension control system also becomes a very important part of printing production line.

1. Purpose and influencing factors of web press tension control

Web press supplies printing material in the form of coil. Web press has very extensive application in the newspapers, books and periodicals, as well as exquisite products. In China, the web press devices currently used are mostly imported products. Both commercial paper and newspaper printing production is generally completed via a variety of brands of foreign advanced printing machine, such as WIFAG, MAN ROLAND, KBA, HEIDELBERG, GOSS, and etc. In order to achieve the work of paper printing, paper tape must keep flat and moderate degree of tension before entering the printing device, which is to keep a certain paper tension. In the process of transmission of paper tape of paper roll, the force which keeps paper tape tight is called tension. If paper tape is in an unconstrained condition in the process of printing, the tape will not be able to finish printing work. The degree of tape tension is directly related to the state of image transfer. In the process of printing, paper tape tension needs to be constant and appropriate [1]. If the degree of tension is not appropriate, a series of slips will happen, such as shifted, wrinkled, broken or torn paper tape, imprecise overprint, as well as wrong position of top/down margin, resulting in paper tape waste, affecting the machine efficiency, increasing the intensity of labor, and ultimately affecting the quality of production. When the paper tape tension is too large, it will produce certain deformation of printing network, and longitudinal folds and even transverse cuts of paper tape; when the paper tape tension is too small, it can cause imprinting fuzzy, imprecise overprint and transverse folds; when the paper tape tension is instable, it can also cause imprecise overprint, double image, longitudinal folds and other printing failures, affecting the printing production. So during the web press printing process, paper tape must have a certain tension, in order to control the movement of the tape, and the paper tape tension should be ensured constant in the process of printing. There are many reasons resulting in the change of paper tape tension and the influence of various factors has different results. The shape change of paper roll in the process of manufacture, transportation, and use will cause the paper roll to shake and skew. Unequal and oblique winding of paper roll in the process of manufacturing as well as squeezing of paper roll in transportation and storage can all result in paper roll shape changes, such as being off-center and irregular outside circle. In addition, in the use process, paper roll will be smaller and smaller in diameter. As for the same tape drive, when the paper roll diameter is not the same, the paper tape tension would be different. When the diameter of the paper roll is reduced, paper tape tension will then become bigger. In order to keep constant paper tape tension in the process of printing and satisfy the requirement of printing work, paper roll brake must be able to automatically adjust according to the paper tape tension fluctuation, to ensure that the paper tape goes into the printing device constantly and smoothly. During the steady running of the machine, paper roll brake should guarantee the stability of paper tape tension on the given value; during starting and braking, it should prevent paper roll overload and loose roll. In the process of production, as the paper roll size decreases continuously, the braking torque needed adjustment in order to keep the paper tape tension constant [2].

[a] Corresponding author: 904970780@qq.com

2. Research on intelligent fuzzy PID control of tension

2.1. Principle and characteristics of PID control

In practical engineering, the regulator control rule most widely used is the proportion/integral/differential control

or PID control (also known as PID adjustment). Having appeared in the world for nearly 70 years, the PID controller is of simple structure, high stability, reliable operation, and easy adjustment and has become one of the main techs in industrial control. When the structure and parameters of the controlled object are not fully grasped, or precise mathematical model cannot be obtained, or other technology of the control theory is difficult to use, then the structure and parameters of system controller must depend on experience and on-site commissioning, and the application of PID control technology is most convenient. In others words, when workers don't fully understand a system and the controlled object, or cannot obtain system parameters through effective measures, then PID control technology is most suitable. PID controller uses proportion, integral, differential to calculate control quantity and to accurately control, according to the system error.

2.1.1 Proportion (P) control

Proportional control is one of the simplest control methods. The controller output error signal is proportional to the input error. With only proportional control, system output will have steady-state Error.

2.1.2 Integral (I) control

In integral control, the integral of controller output error signal is proportional to that of input error signal. For an automatic control system, if there is steady-state error after entering the steady-state, this control system is then called having Steady State Error or is called system with steady-state error for short. In order to eliminate the steady-state error, the controller must introduce "integral item". Integral item depends on the time integral of error. With the increase of time, integral item will increase. In this way, even if the error is very small, integral item will also be increased with the increase of time, and promote the output of the controller, further reducing the steady state error until it is equal to zero. Therefore, with proportional and integral (PI) controllers controlling at the same time, the system could get rid of steady-state error in the steady state.

2.1.3 Differential (D) control

In the differential control, the differential of the controller output error signal (i.e., the rate of change of error) is proportional to that of input error signal. Automatic control system might vibrate or lose stability in the adjustment process of overcoming the error. This is because there is a big inertia component (link) or a lag (Delay) component which inhibits the action of the error and its change is always behind the change of the error. The solution is to advance the change of action that inhibits the error, namely when the error is close to zero, the action that inhibits the error should be zero. In short, the only introduction of "proportion" in the controller is often not enough. The role of proportional is only to amplify amplitude of error and now it needs to add the "differential" which can predict the trend of the error change. In this way, a proportional and differential (PD) controller can advance to make control function that suppresses error be zero, even negative, so as to avoid the serious overshoot of the controlled. For controlled object with large inertia or lag, proportional and differential controller can improve system dynamic characteristics in the process of adjustment.

3. Analysis of PID control

PID control algorithm, which is mature, has good control performance, high system stability and simple control algorithm. It is convenient and flexible to use and its control field is applicable to all walks of life. It has been widely used in the production process.

PID control algorithm is made up of deviation proportion (P), deviation integral (I), and deviation differential (D). In the process of research and development, if one can't fully grasp the structure and parameters of the controlled object, or can't get a more accurate mathematical model, or other control theory is hard to use, then it is particularly important to adopt PID control technology. Based on the experience and site commissioning, developers get structure and related parameters of the main system controller and do PID control calculation. In other words, when we don't have an effective measuring method for system parameter or when we have no way understand control system and the controlled object, it is most suitable for us to use PID control algorithm. PID control includes PI and PD control when applied to the actual development process [3].

PID controller calculates the controlled object mainly through proportional, integral and differential items, and on the basis of system error. The following makes a brief introduction of the three items.

When the system output error signal is proportional to the input error, this kind of control mode is proportional control, indicated by the letter P. With only proportional control, system output will have steady-state.

When the integral of system output error signal is proportional to that of input error signal, this kind of controller is integral control, namely the integral term in the PID controller, indicated by the letter I. Integral item has a role to eliminate the system steady-state error. If a control system has steady-state error after the stable operation of equipment, then the control system is called a system with error. Accordingly, it is required to introduce integral item for the system to eliminate the steady-state error. Integral item depends on the time integral of error. With the increase of time, integral will increase. Hence, even if the error is very small, integral item will also be increased with the increase of time, driving controller to increase the output and reduce steady-state error further till zero. As a result, proportional and integral items only can guarantee no steady-state error in the control system after entering the steady state. This is the commonly used PI control.

When the differential of the controller output error signal is proportional to that of input error signal, this controller is differential control, namely the differential item in the PID controller, indicated by the letter D. Because of the

large inertia or delay link, some systems present system turbulence or instability. In this case, the only introduction of proportion is not enough, because the closed-loop system makes the change of the error always faster than adjustment item, which is due to the inhibitory effect by above links or parts in the process of error control. So, we should try to make the action which inhibits error be proportional to error change. Proportion item has the effect of amplifying amplitude of system error, but now it needs to solve the problem of predicting the tendency of the error. The only solution is to introduce differential item and derive a controller with proportional and differential items at the same time so as to achieve the effect of error control in advance, to avoid excessive adjustment of the controlled, and to improve dynamic characteristics of the control system in the process of adjusting the input error. This is the commonly used PD control [4].

PID control system diagram is shown below. Error e is difference between the actual output value and the given tension. Speed n is derived after calculation. The value of tension is detected through the tension detecting device so as to form closed-loop control. The discretization of PID calculation formula and including it in programs will help to realize the tension control. And for a more accurate and stable system, the torque control module is introduced, also in the form a closed loop control, to complement PID control.

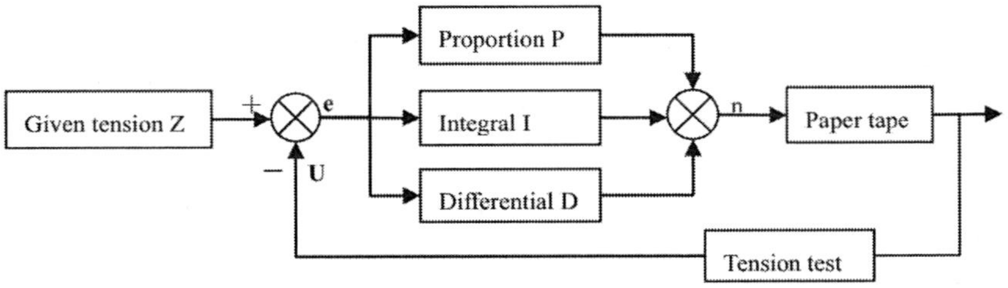

4. Conclusion

Tension control system is one of the most important parts in the printing and packaging industry. The difficulty of solving the problem of coil tension control is to reduce as far as possible the influence of speed, roll diameter and others in the process of winding. Tension control system is a system with large time-varying, strong coupling and much interference. The traditional PI control law is very difficult to get ideal control effect, so control strategy must be improved. Integral separation PID and speed change integral PID can be used in start process, automatic roll change, and parking process. Variable PID control can effectively reduce the change intensity of system damping ratio in the winding process. Compared to a single PI control law, the damping ratio changes much more slowly, so that the stability of the system can be obtained.

ACKNOWLEDGEMENT

This research was financially supported by Hubei province scientific and technological research projects （Grant NO.B2015082）

References

[1]CHEN Xubo. Discussion of Printing Machine Tension Control Device [J]. The modern industrial economy and information technology, 2012, 24: 83-84.

[2] SUN Yuqiu. Web press pneumatic tension control research [J]. Hydraulics and Pneumatics, 2008, 01:30-32.

[3] SHENG Weifeng, ZHOU Yijie & JIANG Yuewen. Tension control in the printing machinery [J]. Packaging engineering, 2001, 22(2): 4-7.

[4]WU Hongxin, SHEN Shaoping. Basis of Theory and Applications on PID Control [J]. Control Engineering, 2003, 10(1): 37-42.

MATEC Web of Conferences **44**, 02041 (2016)
DOI: 10.1051/matecconf/20164402041

A graphical feature generation approach for intrusion detection

Shi Chen [1,a], Zhen Zuo [1], Zhi Ping Huang[1] and Xiao Jun Guo [1]

[1]*Department of Instrumentation Science and Technology, National University of Defense Technology, 410073 Changsha, P.R.China*

Abstract. In order to develop a novel effective and efficient intrusion detection system, a novel hybrid method based on a graphical features-based k-nearest neighbor approach, namely GFNN, is proposed in this paper. In GFNN, k-means clustering algorithm is used to extract cluster centre of each class in the given dataset. Then, the distance between a specific data sample and each cluster centre is calculated, and a radar chart is plotted based on the new data composed of distance based features. The sub-barycentre based features for each sample are extracted from the radar chart. As a result, our proposed approach transforms the original multi-dimensional feature space into 5-dimensional sub-barycentre feature space. The experimental results of 10-fold cross-validation based on the KDDcup99 dataset show that the GFNN not only performs better than or similar to several other approaches in terms of classification accuracy, precision, and recall. It also provides high computational efficiency for the time of classifier training and testing.
Key Words: Intrusion detection; Machine learning; Graphical feature; Radar chart; k-means; k-nearest neighbors

1 Introduction

With the popularity of computer network, network security problem becomes more and more important. Although many security techniques, such as user authentication, data encryption, and firewalls, have been used to improve the security of networks, there are still many unsolved problems, which has made many researchers focus on building systems called intrusion detection systems (IDSs) [1]. Generally, IDSs can be classified into two categories: misuse detection and anomaly detection. In misuse detection, the system identifies intrusions based on known intrusion techniques and triggers alarms by detecting known exploits or attacks based on their attack signatures. Misuse detection can discover attacks with a low false positive rate, but it cannot discover novel attacks without known signatures. On the other hand, in anomaly detection, the system discovers attacks by identifying deviations from normal network activities, it can discover novel attacks but with a high false positive rate.

In order to enhance detection precision and detection stability, machine learning has been widely used to improve IDSs, such as fuzzy theory [2, 3], k-nearest neighbor (k-NN)[4, 5], support vector machine (SVM) [6, 7], artificial neural networks (ANN) [8], Naïve Bayes networks [9], decision tree [10, 11], genetic algorithm (GA) [2, 12], self-organizing maps (SOM) [13], and Markov chains [14, 15], etc. Based on the number of learning techniques used, those IDSs can be categorized as two types: IDSs using single learning techniques and IDSs with hybrid learning techniques. Prior researches have demonstrated that an ensemble of several different techniques performs better than each technique individually [2, 6, 16, 17]. However, those hybrid techniques should upgrade the computational complexity and make it hard to deal with large datasets. For classification problem with high dimensional data, feature reduction techniques are always an effective method to delete the redundancy and irrelevancy features, decrease the computation time, and finally improve the IDS system performance. In this line of research, some feature reduction techniques have been applied to improve the performance of IDSs, such as GA [12], Entropy, principal component analysis (PCA) [18], etc.

In this paper, we try to develop a novel effective and efficient intrusion detection system. The main goal of this paper is aiming to achieve feature reduction, data presentation, feature generation, and to enhance IDS with hybrid method combing k-means clustering algorithm, graphical features generation approach and k-NN classifier. Firstly, k-means clustering algorithm is used to extract cluster center of each pre-defined category in the given dataset, which contains n categories. Secondly, the distance between a specific data sample and each cluster center is calculated, and then a radar chart is applied to represent each new data sample composed of distance based features. Thirdly, new graphical features (e.g., barycenter) for each sample are extracted from the radar chart. Finally, for classification, some classifiers are used to detect attacks based on the new dataset described by graphical features to obtain the best performance.

The rest of this paper is organized as follow. Some related work on IDSs, including the use of feature reduction and representation methods, is reviewed in

[a] Corresponding author: chens_sir@163.com

Section 2. Section 3 presents a detailed description of the proposed framework, including each step of the proposed approach. The dataset, evaluation strategies, and results of a performance comparison are presented in Section 4. Finally, some conclusions are provided in Section 5.

2 Related work

Feature reduction is an important component in machine learning, especially when dealing with high dimensional data, because the use of correct features improves classification performance and reduces computational time. In the past decades, several IDSs, which use feature reduction as a preprocessing phase, have been developed.

Mukkamala and Sung [19] proposed a novel IDS based on the SVM, multivariate adaptive splines and linear genetic program. They used a new significant algorithm, which is independent of the modeling tools being applied, to select features. After an input feature being removed from the data, the remaining dataset is then used for training and testing the classifier. Then, the classifier's performance is compared to that of the original classifier in terms of relevant performance criteria. Finally, the features are ranked according to a set of rules based on the performance comparison. The performance of two feature reduction techniques, principal component analysis and linear discriminate analysis, is compared by Datti and Lakhina [20], and the back-propagation algorithm is used to test these techniques. Eesa, Orman and Brifcani [11] proposed a feature selection model based on the cuttlefish optimization algorithm (CFA) to produce the optimal subset of features. They used the decision tree as the classifier to improve the quality of the produced subsets of features. Tsai and Lin [21] proposed a hybrid approach combined k-means and k-NN to construct a triangle area-based nearest neighbor approach (TANN) for intrusion detection. In TANN, 10 triangle areas formed by the data and five class cluster centers are generated to replace the 41 original features of KDDcup99 dataset, and the approach achieved good performance. The dimensionality of data sample changed from 41 to 10. However, the dimensionality of the new features generated by TANN is based on the number of triangle areas, which is equal to $k \times (k-1)/2$ (k denotes the number of classes in the given dataset). If the classification problem contains a larger number of classes, the dimensionality of the new features will become very large. This may lead to the "curse of dimensionality" problem. To solve the problem in TANN, two improvement approaches are proposed. One is the distance sum-based hybrid method combining k-means and SVM, called DSSVM [22]. In DSSVM, the sum of distances between the data sample and k–1 of the k cluster centers is calculated to replace the original features. Then, the new k-dimensional dataset is obtained. Another approach is CANN [23] that proposed to reduce the dimensionality of features. In CANN, two distances are measured and summed, the first one based on the distance between each data sample and its cluster center, and the other is between the data and its nearest neighbor in the same cluster. As a result, a new one-dimensional distance based feature is used to represent each data sample for intrusion detection by a k-NN classifier.

With the development of network and storage capacity, multi-dimensional data representation and analysis tasks are becoming increasingly difficult and challenging. Under such circumstance, some methods of graphical representation of the multi-dimensional data have been developed in many fields. Wang and Hong [24] use a star plot, which is also called radar chart, to represent a multi-dimensional data for machine learning. In the star plot, each original feature of a data sample is represented by a line segment radiating from the central point of star plot. Then, new graphical features, such as sub-area features and sub-barycenter features, are extracted from the star plot. At last, the new dataset represented by graphical features is utilized for training and testing of k-NN classifier. For resolving a gene classification problem, Parkinson and Blaxter [25] developed a new visualization model, which is called SimiTri. By mapping a certain gene into a triangular phase space, whose three vertexes represent three selected distinct gene categories, the position of the gene within the phase space indicates its relationship to each of the three selected data sets and helps determine the category of the data. This SimiTri model can resolve 4-class classification problem. Enlightened by TANN [21] and SimiTri [25], Luo and Xia [26] proposed a novel four-angle-star based visualized feature generation approach, FASVFG, to evaluate the distance between samples in a five class classification problem for intrusion detection. In FASVFG, a four angle star is constructed by a square and four triangles. The distance between a data sample and the vertexes of four-angle-star helps determine the class the data belonging to.

Inspired by the applications of graphical representation approaches above, the radar chart, originally applied to analyze the financial situation of enterprise, is used to general new graphical features for intrusion detection in this paper. As a result, a hybrid approach is proposed to transform the original multi-dimensional feature space into low-dimensional graphical feature space. Then, the graphical features are regarded as the new feature space and used for the final classification decision.

3 The graphical features-based k-nearest neighbor (GFNN)

The proposed GFNN consists of three stages, which are cluster centers extraction, new data formation by graphical features, and training and testing k-NN based on the new data. From methods [21, 23] we learn that the distance between the data sample and each clustering center has high discriminative power, and may lead to classification algorithm (e.g., k-NN and SVM) achieving similar or better classification accuracy than the original high-dimensional feature vectors. Moreover, the graphical feature of radar chart generalization approach is a visualization strategy that enables people to identify the class to which the data belongs [24]. The experiment

results of approach in [24] show that its proposed graphical features can help achieve high classification accuracy. Specifically, GFNN intends to provide effective and efficient detection of network attacks using k-NN algorithm with low-dimensional feature vectors.

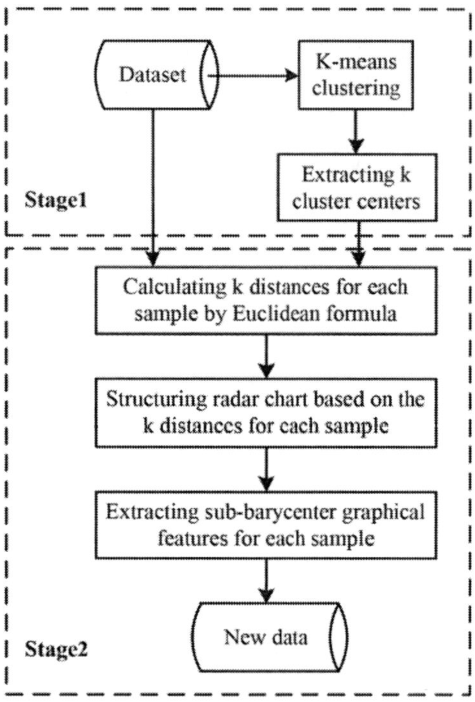

Figure 1. Process of new data formation.

3.1 Cluster centers extraction

In this paper, the KDDcup99 dataset is used, which includes five classes (four types of Internet attacks and one types of normal access). The dataset is described in detail in section 4.1. The k-means clustering algorithm is used to extract cluster centers for its simplicity and low time complexity. For five-class classification problem, the value of k is set by 5. Therefore, five cluster centers are obtained, and each cluster contain a cluster center (i.e., C_1, C_2, C_3, C_4 and C_5). The stage 1 of Figure 1 shows the process of cluster centers extraction.

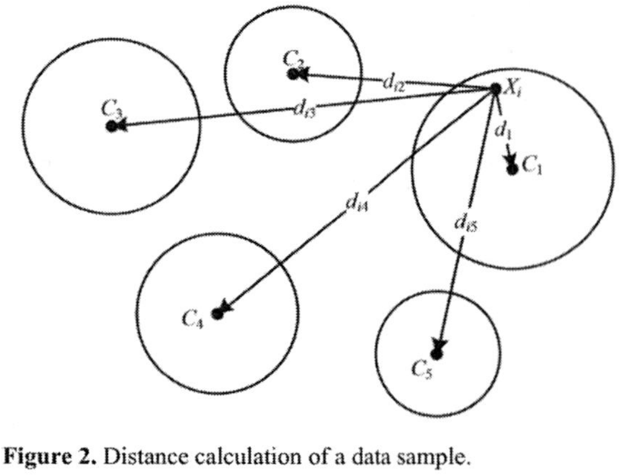

Figure 2. Distance calculation of a data sample.

3.2 New data formation by graphical features

In this stage (see stage 2 of Figure 1), first of all, the distance $d_{ij}(j=1,2,\cdots,5)$ between each n-dimensional data sample $X_i=(x_1,x_2,\cdots,x_n)$ and the five cluster centers $C_1,C_2,\cdots,C_5$ is calculated respectively based on the Euclidean distance formula. The Euclidean distance between $X_i=(x_1,x_2,\cdots,x_n)$ and each cluster center point $C_j=(c_1,c_2,\cdots,c_n)$ (see Figure 2) can be defined as

$$d_{ij}=\sqrt{\sum_{t=1}^{n}(x_t-c_t)^2} \tag{1}$$

Where $i=1,2,\cdots,m$ (m denotes the total number of the data samples), $j=1,2,\cdots,5$. Then, we can obtain five distance features for each sample, that is $D_i=(d_{i1},d_{i2},\cdots,d_{i5})$. This step transforms the n-dimensional original features vectors into the 5-dimensional distance features vectors.

To construct a radar chart, all distance data are normalized into $[a,1]$, by using the following formula:

$$d'_{ij}=a+(1-a)\frac{d_{ij}-\min_{1\le i\le m}(d_{ij})}{\max_{1\le i\le m}(d_{ij})-\min_{1\le i\le m}(d_{ij})}, \tag{2}$$
$$i=1,2,3,\cdots,m;\ j=1,2,\cdots,5.$$

Where a is the desired length of the smallest ray relative to the largest, m is the total number of the data samples, $\min_{1\le i\le m}(d_{ij})$ and $\max_{1\le i\le m}(d_{ij})$ are the minimum and maximum value of the j-th feature, respectively.

After obtaining five normalize distance features, radar chart (see Figure 3) can be plotted to represent each sample data $D'_i=(d'_{i1},d'_{i2},\cdots,d'_{i5})$.

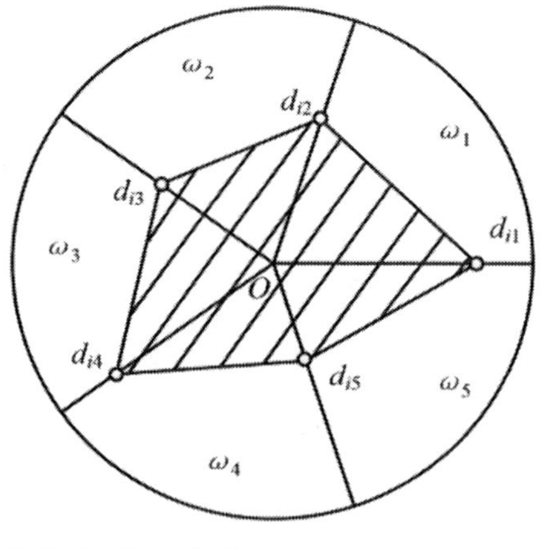

Figure 3. Radar chart of a data sample.

As shown in Figure 3, the radius of the circle is 1. Five rays, that divide the perimeter of the circle into five equal parts, represent five distance features, respectively. We can obtain a point on each ray, and the distance between the point and the center of the circle is equal to each distance data d'_{ij}. After connecting each two adjacent

points with lines, a pentagon is obtained, which is composed of five triangles. The angle formed by two adjacent rays can be calculated by $\omega_j = 2\pi / k, k = 5$ for KDDcup99 dataset.

There are several kinds of graphical features that can be extracted from the radar chart, such as area, barycenter, and perimeter of each triangle or pentagon. The work in [24] show that the performance of k-NN with sub-barycenter (the barycenter of triangle) features of radar chart is superior to that with sub-area features. Therefore, in this paper, the sub-barycenter features of radar chart are selected to form the training and testing dataset.

The sub-barycenter features of radar chart are extracted as the following. Each triangle (see Figure 4) in the pentagon has a barycenter $G_{ij} = (l_{ij}, \alpha_{ij})$, where l_{ij} is the distance between the barycenter of triangle and the center of radar chart, α_{ij} is the angle formed by $G_{ij}O$ (O donates the center of radar char) line and horizontal line.

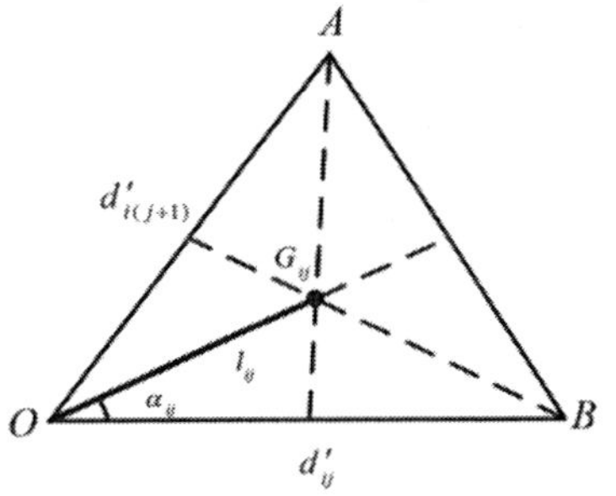

Figure 4. Barycenter of a triangle.

For simplification and dimensionality reduction, we only choose l_{ij} as the graphical features that can be obtained by

$$l_{ij} = \begin{cases} \sqrt{(\frac{d'_{ij}}{3}\sin\omega_j)^2 + [(d'_{ij}\cos\omega_j - \frac{d'_{i(j+1)}}{2})/3 + \frac{d'_{i(j+1)}}{2}]^2}, & j = 1,2,3,4 \\ \sqrt{(\frac{d'_{ij}}{3}\sin\omega_j)^2 + [(d'_{ij}\cos\omega_j - \frac{d'_{i1}}{2})/3 + \frac{d'_{i1}}{2}]^2}, & j = 5 \end{cases} \quad (3)$$

As a result, the n-dimensional original feature vectors are transformed into new five-dimensional sub-barycenter feature vectors. Finally, the new dataset D_L is used for training and testing the k-NN classifier.

3.3 Training and testing classifiers

In this stage, the new dataset $D_L = \{L_1, L_2, \cdots, L_m\}$, represented by five-dimensional feature vectors, is used to train and test k-NN classifier. Several classifiers, such as Naïve Bayes (NB), Decision Tree (J48), Random Tree (RT), and SVM, are utilized to take performance comparison with k-NN. Figure 5 shows the process of training and testing a classifier. In this stage, 10-fold cross validation is used to avoid the variability of the samples that affect the performance of model training and testing. In 10-fold cross validation, the whole dataset is divided into 10 unduplicated subsets. Nine of the 10 subsets are used as training subset and the remainder is used for testing. Then 10 classification results are obtained by 10-fold cross validation. Finally, classification accuracy is the average value of the 10 classification results.

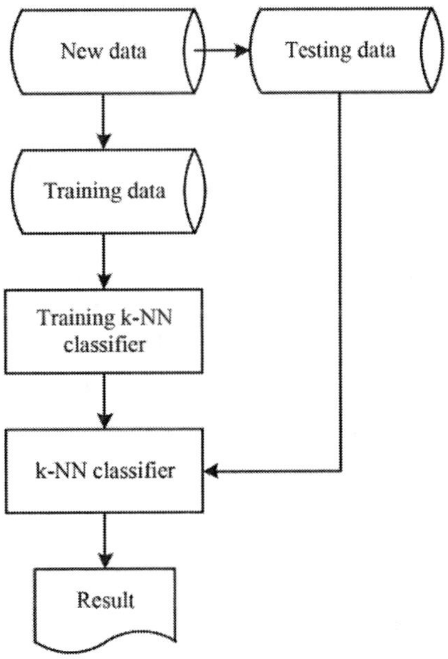

Figure 5. Training and testing k-NN with new data.

4 Experiments

4.1 The dataset

In this section, we discuss the experimental dataset: KDDcup99 dataset. KDDcup99 dataset was originally derived from the raw DARPA network traffic, which was prepared and managed by MIT Lincoln Labs in 1998. KDDcup99 dataset has become a benchmark dataset for intrusion detection. The complete dataset has almost 5 million input patterns and each record represents a TCP/IP connection. Considering the sake of simplicity, the dataset used in our study is the 10% subset, namely kddcup.data_10_percent, which contains 494,021 instances.Except normal class, the recordings in KDDcup99 dataset can be divided into four attack classes as follows:

- Denial of service (DOS): an attacker results by preventing legitimate requests to a network resource by consuming the bandwidth or by overloading computational resources, e.g., smurf;
- Probe: an attacker scans a network of computers and collect information of target system, e.g., port scanning;
- User to Root (U2R): unauthorized access to local super user privileges by a local unprivileged user, e.g., various "buffer overflow" attacks;

- Remote to Local (R2L): unauthorized access from a remote machine to a local machine, e.g., guessing password.

4.2 Dataset preprocessing

The 10% KDDcup99 dataset has a huge number of redundant records, that almost 70.5% of the records are duplicated, which cause the learning algorithm to be biased towards the most frequent records. For these duplicates, we just delete them. Then the size of the dataset changes to 145,585.

After the deletion, the dataset still have 87,832 records of class Normal and 54,572 records of class Dos. In order to reduce the experimental time, we randomly select 10% of class Normal and Dos as the final experimental Normal and Dos records, while the other three classes remain unchanged. As a result, the size of the final experimental dataset is reduced from 145,585 to 17,421.The final size of each class is shown in Table 1.

In the KDDcup99 dataset, there are several nominal features. Before extracting cluster centers based on k-means, the nominal features are mapped into binary numeric features. Note that "service type" has 67 different values, which would heavily increase the dimensionality if mapped into binary features. Specially, for comparing with DSSVM [22], the "service type" feature is not used in this paper. After mapping nominal features into binary values, 52 numeric features are constructed.

Table 1. Final size of each class.

Class	Normal	Dos	Probe	U2R	R2L
The final dataset	8,783	5,457	2,130	52	999

Because the scales of some numerical features in the KDDcup99 dataset are different, for instance, "logged in" has binary value, whereas "source bytes" has a range from 0 to 693,375,640, normalization is required that it can avoid attributes with greater values dominating these attributes with smaller values. In this paper, the numerical attributes are scaled into the interval [0, 1] by dividing every attribute value by its own maximum value.

4.3 Evaluation criteria

We choose the confusion matrix as the performance measures to estimate the efficiency of classifier. The following measures are derived from the confusion matrix, and will be used for evaluating the proposed scheme:

$$Accuracy = \frac{TP+TN}{TP+TN+FN+FP}$$

$$Pricision = \frac{TP}{TP+FP}$$

$$Recall = \frac{TP}{TP+FN}$$

Where *TP*, true positive is the number of attack test samples correctly classified as attack. *TN*, true negative is the number of normal test samples correctly classified as normal. *FP*, false positive is the number of normal test samples falsely classified as attack. *FN*, false negative is the number of attack test samples falsely classified as normal.

Moreover, we use the area under the Receiver Operating Characteristic curve (AUC) to measure the performance of the proposed method for IDS. Usually, the AUC value ranges from 0.5 to 1.0, with larger AUC values representing better performance of the classifier.

4.4 Experimental results and analysis

The experiments are carried on an Intel Core 2.90 GHz computer with 4 GB RAM running Windows 7. We use a data mining software Weka to build classifiers in the experiment. Weka is a collection of machine learning programs for data mining tasks written in Java. The version used is Weka 3.7.

4.4.1 Classification results

The performances comparison of intrusion detection model based on NB, J48, RT, SVM and k-NN with the new dataset is given in Table 2. The comparative results allow us to see the performance of each classifier and identify the best one for intrusion detection.

Table 2. Performances of NB, J48, RT, SVM, and k-NN with the new graphical features.

	Normal (%)	Dos (%)	Probe (%)	U2R (%)	R2L (%)	$Accuracy_{total}$ (%)	For the normal and attack classes		AUC_{avg}
							Precision (%)	Recall (%)	
NB	88.45	77.66	81.69	0.00	32.63	80.78	88.39	89.40	0.965
J48	**98.67**	98.55	96.38	30.77	93.59	97.86	98.60	97.90	**0.991**
RT	98.43	98.81	96.62	36.54	93.29	97.85	98.40	98.19	0.984
SVM	97.59	95.58	91.83	0.00	92.79	95.69	97.49	95.15	0.965
k-NN	98.63	**99.38**	**98.26**	**57.69**	**95.80**	**98.54**	**98.62**	**98.96**	0.990

Table 3. Performances of TANN, DSSVM and GFNN over the 52-dimentional pre-processing dataset.

	Normal (%)	Dos (%)	Probe (%)	U2R (%)	R2L (%)	Accuracy$_{total}$ (%)	For the normal and attack classes		AUC$_{avg}$
							Precision (%)	Recall (%)	
TANN(k=1)	98.75	99.24	**98.31**	55.77	95.60	**98.542**	98.73	98.85	0.990
DSSVM	**99.50**	98.09	96.34	25.00	92.29	98.037	**99.48**	96.96	0.982
GFNN(k=1)	98.63	**99.38**	98.26	**57.69**	**95.80**	98.536	98.62	**98.96**	**0.990**

The result in Table 2 indicate that, with the new graphical features, the accuracy of k-NN (k=1) is 98.54% which outperforms that of NB (80.78%), J48 (97.86%), RT (98.40%), and SVM (97.49%). In addition, for the normal and attack classes, the graphical features-based k-NN (GFNN) also provides the higher precision rate (98.62%) and recall rate (98.96%) than NB, J48, RT, and SVM. Moreover, the accuracy for class normal and the average AUC value of GFNN is only slightly lower than that of J48. As shown in Table 2, the class U2r is not well detected by any of the classifiers, since the KDD dataset is rather unbalanced. In fact, fifty-two samples of U2R represent only 0.003% of the training samples.

For evaluating the performance of GFNN, two recently proposed approaches are reproduced to compare with GFNN. These approaches are trained and tested over the 52-dimentional preprocessing dataset. One approach is distance sum-based support vector machine (DSSVM) [22]. We examine several kernel function (such as Polynomial kernel, RBF kernel) and different degree in order to obtain the best performance for comparison. Another is triangle area-based nearest neighbors (TANN) [21], in which different k values are examined for getting the best k-NN classifier for comparison.

Table 3 shows the performances of these approaches over the 52-dimentional preprocessing dataset. As illustrated in Table 3, the total classification accuracy of GFNN is 98.536%, which is slightly lower than that of TANN (98.542%) and higher than that of DSSVM (98.037%). In addition, the GFNN also works the best for class DOS, U2R and R2L among the three classifiers with an accuracy of 99.38%, 57.69% and 95.80%. Although GFNN does not perform the best for class normal and probe, accuracy and detection rates of GFNN is very similar to the ones of TANN. This indicates that there is no significant difference in their performances.

4.4.2 Efficiency evaluation

Besides the quality of the classification results obtained by GFNN, it is important to consider the efficiency of the method. We evaluate the CPU time of GFNN by comparing against the baseline k-NN, TANN, and DSSVM. We divide CPU time into feature generating, training and testing. The feature generating for TANN, DSSVM and GFNN contain three parts: (i) dataset preprocessing; (ii) cluster centers extraction with k-means; (iii) dataset transformation.

Table 4 shows a comparison of the CPU time taken by each approach. Looking at Table 4, although k-NN, with 41 original features, doesn't need to take CPU time to do feature generating, it requires greatest training and testing time. Meanwhile, the training and testing time and the total CPU time taken by GFNN is the least among these approaches. Overall, GFNN's new low-dimensional feature vectors composed of the sub-barycenter can provide relatively high efficiency for intrusion detection.

Table 4. CPU time of k-NN, TANN, DSSVM, and GFNN.

Method	Feature generating (s)	Training and testing (s)	Total (s)
k-NN (41 features)	-	51	51
TANN (10 features)	9	17	26
DSSVM (5 features)	8	46	54
GFNN (5 features)	10	11	21

5. Conclusion

In this paper, we propose a novel hybrid method based on a graphical features-based k-nearest neighbors approach, namely GFNN, for intrusion detection. The proposed approach tests intrusion detection over the KDDcup99 dataset. Firstly, the k-means clustering algorithm and radar chart are used as feature generation tools. Then, this new and 5-dimensional sub-barycenter based feature is used to represent each data sample for intrusion detection by a k-NN classifier. From simulation results, the performance of the proposed algorithm outperforms other existing approaches for class DOS, U2R and R2L. It also provides high computational efficiency for the time of classifier training and testing.

In future work, some issues will be considered. Firstly, we plan to extract other graphical features from radar chart to construct low-dimensional feature space. Secondly, different clustering algorithms and classification techniques can be applied during the cluster center extraction and classifier training stages, respectively. Finally, our proposed feature generation methods will be used as a preprocessing step over other

datasets which contain different numbers of classes and also do a thorough comparison of our proposed feature generation methods with other ones.

Acknowledgments

This work is supported by the National Natural Science Foundation of China (Grant No. 61374008).

References

1. H.J. Liao, C.H.R. Lin, Y.C. Lin, K.Y. Tung, Intrusion detection system: A comprehensive review, JOURNAL OF NETWORK AND COMPUTER APPLICATIONS, **36**,1:16-24 (2013)
2. M.S. Abadeh, J. Habibi, C. Lucas, Intrusion detection using a fuzzy genetics-based learning algorithm, Journal of Network and Computer Applications, **30**,1:414-428 (2007)
3. A. Tajbakhsh, M. Rahmati, A. Mirzaei, Intrusion detection using fuzzy association rules, Applied Soft Computing Journal, **9**,2:462-469 (2009)
4. Y.H. Liao, V.R. Vemuri, Use of k-nearest neighbor classifier for intrusion detection, COMPUTERS & SECURITY, **21**,5:439-448 (2002)
5. M.-Y. Su, Real-time anomaly detection systems for denial-of-service attacks by weighted k-nearest-neighbor classifiers, Expert Systems With Applications, **38**,4:3492-3498 (2011)
6. S. Mukkamala, A.H. Sung, A. Abraham, Intrusion detection using an ensemble of intelligent paradigms, Journal of Network and Computer Applications, **28**,2:167-182 (2005)
7. S. Mukkamala, A.H. Sung, Feature ranking and selection for intrusion detection systems using support vector machines. *In International conference on information and knowledge engineering (ICIKE)*. 503–509 (2002)
8. D. Fisch, A. Hofmann, B. Sick, On the versatility of radial basis function neural networks: A case study in the field of intrusion detection, Information Sciences, **180**,12:2421-2439 (2010)
9. Z.A. Baig, S.M. Sait, A. Shaheen, Gmdh-based networks for intelligent intrusion detection, ENGINEERING APPLICATIONS OF ARTIFICIAL INTELLIGENCE, **26**,7:1731-1740 (2013)
10. S.S.S. Sindhu, S. Geetha, A. Kannan, Decision tree based light weight intrusion detection using a wrapper approach, EXPERT SYSTEMS WITH APPLICATIONS, **39**,1:129-141 (2012)
11. A.S. Eesa, Z. Orman, A.M.A. Brifcani, A novel feature-selection approach based on the cuttlefish optimization algorithm for intrusion detection systems, EXPERT SYSTEMS WITH APPLICATIONS, **42**,5:2670-2679 (2015)
12. T. Shon, X. Kovah, J. Moon, Applying genetic algorithm for classifying anomalous tcp/ip packets, Neurocomputing, **69**,16:2429-2433 (2006)
13. D. Ippoliti, X.B. Zhou, A-ghsom: An adaptive growing hierarchical self organizing map for network anomaly detection, JOURNAL OF PARALLEL AND DISTRIBUTED COMPUTING, **72**,12:1576-1590 (2012)
14. N. Ye, Y. Zhang, C.M. Borror, Robustness of the markov-chain model for cyber-attack detection, IEEE Transactions on Reliability, **53**,1:116-123 (2004)
15. S. Shin, S. Lee, H. Kim, S. Kim, Advanced probabilistic approach for network intrusion forecasting and detection, EXPERT SYSTEMS WITH APPLICATIONS, **40**,1:315-322 (2013)
16. T. Shon, J. Moon, A hybrid machine learning approach to network anomaly detection, Information Sciences, **177**,18:3799-3821 (2007)
17. R.M. Elbasiony, E.A. Sallam, T.E. Eltobely, M.M. Fahmy, A hybrid network intrusion detection framework based on random forests and weighted k-means, Ain Shams Engineering Journal, **4**,4:753–762 (2013)
18. G. Liu, Z. Yi, S. Yang, A hierarchical intrusion detection model based on the pca neural networks, Neurocomputing, **70**,7:1561-1568 (2007)
19. Significant feature selection using computational intelligent techniques for intrusion detection. London: Springer London. 285-306 (2005)
20. R. Datti, S. Lakhina, Performance comparison of features reduction techniques for intrusion detection system, International Journal of Compute Science and Technology, **3**,1:332–335 (2012)
21. C.-F. Tsai, C.-Y. Lin, A triangle area based nearest neighbors approach to intrusion detection, Pattern Recognition, **43**,1:222-229 (2010)
22. C. Guo, Y. Zhou, Y. Ping, Z. Zhang, G. Liu, Y. Yang, A distance sum-based hybrid method for intrusion detection, Applied Intelligence, **40**,1:178-188 (2014)
23. W.C. Lin, S.W. Ke, C.F. Tsai, Cann: An intrusion detection system based on combining cluster centers and nearest neighbors, KNOWLEDGE-BASED SYSTEMS, **78**:13-21 (2015)
24. W. Hong, X. Li, The new graphical features of star plot for k nearest neighbor classifier.4682, Berlin, Heidelberg: Springer Berlin Heidelberg. 926-933 (2007)
25. J. Parkinson, M. Blaxter, Simitri - visualizing similarity relationships for groups of sequences, BIOINFORMATICS, **19**,3:390-395 (2003)
26. B. Luo, J.B. Xia, A novel intrusion detection system based on feature generation with visualization strategy, EXPERT SYSTEMS WITH APPLICATIONS, **41**,9:4139-4147 (2014)

MATEC Web of Conferences **44**, 02042 (2016)
DOI: 10.1051/matecconf/20164402042

Signal Simulation on Static Test of Guidance Station of One Antiaircraft Missile

Ke LI, Lian Yan SHI, Xin HE, Jin LUO

4th department, Shijiazhuang Mechanic Engineering College, Shijiazhuang, HEBEI, CHINA, 050003

Abstract: In order to improve trainees' operational quality of static test of guidance station of one antiaircraft missile, a static testing simulator is necessary to gain the goal. It is obvious that the key problem of developing the simulator is how to generate the static testing signals of the simulator. Aiming to solve the problem, at first, the paper adopts a standard called signal testing definition(STD), which is applied to describe simulating signals used for static testing simulation of guidance station of one antiaircraft missile; then those simulating signals for the static testing simulation are implemented based on the platform Labwindows/CVI, and D/A converters are employed for generating physical static testing signals, which are outputted through operational panels or interfaces of the static testing simulator. So the mentioned process could be helpful to realize the static testing simulator of guidance station of one antiaircraft missile.

1 Introduction

People said the more training, the high operational quality. In order to improve trainees' operational quality of static test of the guidance station of one antiaircraft missile, a static testing simulator is necessary to gain the goal. It is obvious that the key problem of developing the simulator is how to generate the static testing signals of the simulator. The paper tries to solve the key problem to help develop the simulator.

2 Simulating requirements analysis

The static test of the guidance station of one antiaircraft missile has a number of 320 plus test project, it is one of the equipment daily maintenance project in order to test whether working state of the equipment is normal, The method is to apply incentives in different testing points of the equipment, then to measure corresponding outputs to judge state of the equipment. Therefore, the realization of the static testing simulator or test simulating function is to produce the various all kinds of response signals of the equipment. According to the characteristics of the static testing training and requirements of the guidance station of one antiaircraft missile, analysis on simulation requirements would be on the following three facets for developing the static testing simulator of one antiaircraft missile.

2.1 Classification of simulating signals

(1) Transient voltages and currents: the initial voltage and current for the equipment;

(2) The DC voltages and currents: the stable voltage and current for the equipment;

(3) AC voltages: output information, noise and other signals;

(4) Controlled voltages: the equipment controlled voltage;

(5) Resistance parameters: circuit's resistance of the equipment, breakover resistance, etc.

(6) Complex waveform signals: the rectangular wave with adjustable width or frequency modulation etc. controlled by the incentive voltage or power time, as well as various instruction outputting, signals such as pulse front and back edge etc.;

(7) Sound and light signals: sound and light output when the equipment works;

(8) The state signals: they are controlled by frequency, voltage, time, or other inventive signals, in other words, they are changing signals of controlled state or time;

(9) Visual signals: focus changing, target, capture line, self-check lamp, etc.

(10) Other signals: output signals of the signal generator without power, self-check signal of voltage stabilizer circuit, etc.

2.2 Analysis on signal relationship

The static testing operation of the equipment is not only to achieve the simulation of various signals or parameters, but also to simulate logical function of the actual system, signal control relationship, etc., and analysis and identification on various incentives.

(1) Relationship among the launching control program and the control instructions;

(2) Relationship among information signals, serial data and instructions;

(3) Visual signals and detecting states;

(4) Relationship between serial commands and instructions;

(5) Control relationship among other signals.

2.3 Signal stability

(1) AC voltage: 2.5% of the nominal value;

(2) DC voltage: 2% of the nominal value;

(3) DC current: 1.5% of the nominal value;

(4) Frequency/time: 0.1% of the nominal value;

(5) Insulating resistance: 1% of the nominal value;

(6) Coefficient of instructions: 1% of the nominal value.

3 signal description and modeling

One signal of static test of the guidance station of one antiaircraft missile is selected as an example, with which the method of signal modeling and generating in the paper is depicted in detail. The selected signal waveform is shown as Figure 1.

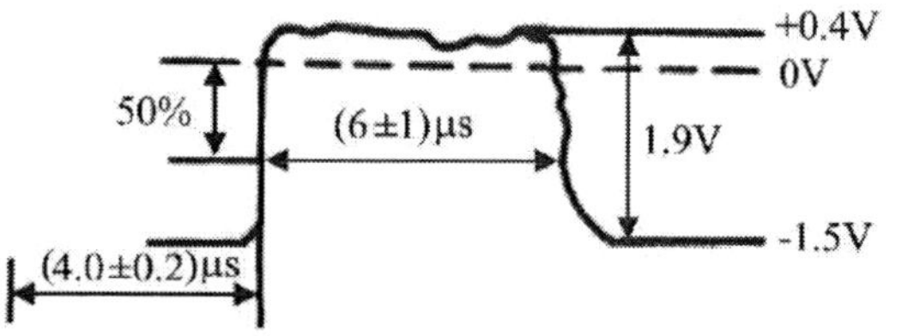

Figure 1. Selected irregular waveform

3.1 Signal simulating model based on signal testing definition [1]

The characteristics of signal testing definition (STD, IEEE1641) include:(1)it provides unique definition for all kinds of signals;(2)it provides mathematical basis for defining various signals, which would facilitate signal accurate output, recreating and usage in other testing system;(3)it provides a structure for signal combination to construct the complex signals;(4)it supports to build the scalable signal set library for more than one similar application field;(5)it offers a method of signal definition, usage and control, which could be applied by a few various programming languages;(6)the test program in accordance with STD could be applied to any test system with the same STD signal.

STD signals defined structure is shown as figure 2. Signal test and definition of STD standard are divided into signal modeling language (SML), basic signal components (BSC), test signal framework (TSF) and test procedure language (TPL). BSC layer provides the basic structure modules to build the complex signals, but its basic class components are simple signals, and unit under test (UUT) measurement signals are often more complex than what one basic class component of BSC could represent. So STD standard provides a mechanism to construct complex signals with several basic class components of BSC.

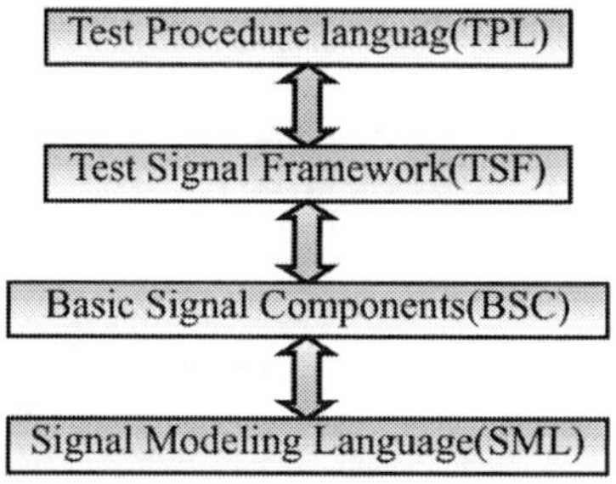

Figure 2. STD layered structure

3.2 Construction of signal model

The model structure of a selected irregular signal (its waveform is shown as fig.1), which is constructed based on a basic class component of BSC, is shown as Figure 3.

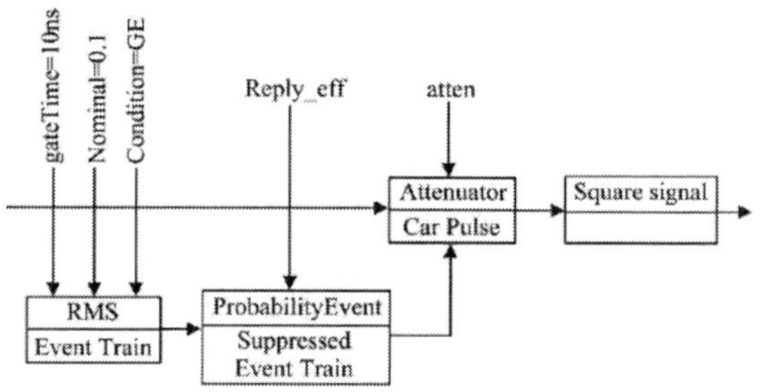

Figure 3. Block diagram of an irregular signal based on BSC of STD standard

Each module of the signal structure (RMS, probability event, attenuator, Signal delay) is one of BSC components. The small amplitude sinusoidal signal is the input signal; RMS calculates whether the root mean square value of the transmitted signal is greater than 0.1V in an assumed 10ns time, an output event would be generated while the root mean square value of the transmitted signal is over 0.1V. The reply_eff (effective rate of a response) of probability event component determines the response efficiency of one event by a value selected from 0 to 100%, then one selective generated event that produces a random disturbance signal would be sent to one gate of the attenuator; When the transmitted signal is attenuated by "atten" times, its amplitude value would be in the required range, the signal is loaded on the square wave signal, and the output is the required signal waveform.

4 Simulating signal generation of static test

The platform LabWindows/CVI is adopted to generate simulating signals of static test, which are described by XLM [2, 3].

4.1 LabWindows/CVI code

The main () function is the entrance to the program; its function is to initialize and display program, to load user panels. The codes are as follows:

```
    SineWave( 1000, 4, 30.8125e-3, &phase, sin1 );
SineWave( 1000, 0. 5, 50.8125e-3, &phase, sin2 );
WhiteNoise( 1000, 0. 05, 100, noise1 );
    WhiteNoise ( 1000, 0. 15, 100, noise2 );
    Ramp( 6, 0.4, -0.95, xiepo1 );
    fo r( i=0; i<8000; i++)
    data[i]=0;
    fo r( i= 0; i<38; i++ )
    data[i] =-1.5;
    for( i=38; i<41; i++ ) data[i]=sin1[ i-14 ] + 2.5;
    for( i=41; i<45; i++ ) data[i]=sin1[i-3]-3.6; for( i=45;
i<107; i++ ) data[i] = 0.4+noise1[i];
    for( i=107; i<113; i++ )
    data[i] = xiepo1[ i-107] +noise1[i];
    for( i=113; i<119; i++ ) data[i] =sin2[i-1]-0.95;
for( i=119; i<151; i++ ) data[i]=-1.5;
    SetCtrlAttribute( pane,l PANEL_GRAPH,
ATTR_XAX IS_GA IN, 1.0/10000 );
    SetCtrlAttribute (pane,l PANEL_GRAPH,
ATTR_XPREC ISION, 5 ); PlotY( pane Hl and le,
PANEL_GRAPH, data, 150, VAL_DOUBLE, VAL
    _THIN_LINE, VAL_EM PTY_SQUAR E,
VAL_SOL ID, 1, VAL_RED ) ;
```

The result of the program to be run is shown as Figure 4. Based on the principle introduced as section 2.2, a random small amplitude sinusoidal signal is loaded on a basic square wave to form small amplitude waveforms, and carries on the other processing technology, as shown in figure 4 wave charts, as can be seen from the diagram, using LabWindows/CVI waveform to get the waveform is similar to the original waveform (figure 1).

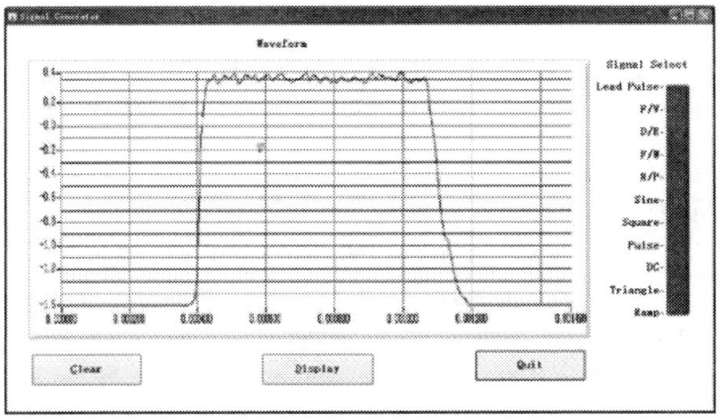

Figure 4. Irregular waveform

4.2 Simulating signal output of static test

In the oscilloscope based on the LabWindows/CVI, the waveform file generated in terms of above method is loaded to drive the oscilloscope to produce physical waveform [4, 5].

5 Conclusions

Aiming at implement of a static test training simulator of one antiaircraft missile, the paper firstly commences the system requirement analysis; secondly, the simulated waveforms of the simulator are depicted and modeled with XML language, specifically all of signal simulation models are established on STD standard. At last, the physical signals are outputted with LabWindows/CVI and D/A. The relevant experiments proved the idea of the paper is feasible, and conclusions of the paper could help to realize a static test training simulator of one antiaircraft missile.

References

1. Yang Sen, Meng Chen, Wang. ChengResearch and Application of ATS Test Description Language Based on STD Standard. Computer Measurement & Control, 2010, 3(25).
2. LIU Junhua. VISUAL INSTRUMENT PROGRAM LabWindows/CVI COURSE [M]. BEIJING: ELECTRONIC INDUSTORY PRESS, 2001.
3. QIAN Neng. C++ PROGRAM DESIGN COURSE [M]. BEIJIN:TSINGHAU PRESS, 2001.
4. YAN Bo. Research and Development of the General LFM Signals Generating System Based on DDS Technology [D]. CHENGDU: UNIVERSITY of ELECTRONIC SCIENCE AND TECHNOLOGY OF CHINA
5. TENG Xu, HU Zhiang. COUNTERMEASURE PRACTICAL TECHNOLOGY OF ELECTRIC SYSTEM [M]. BEIJIN: NATIONAL DEFENCE INDUSTORY PRESS, 2004.

MATEC Web of Conferences 44, 02043 (2016)
DOI: 10.1051/matecconf/20164402043

Research of the Technology and Application of 3D Model Based Assembly Structural Process Design for Spacecraft

Bi Le Wan [1], Wen Xing He [1,a], and Chang Yu Chen [1]

[1] 1Beijing Institute of Spacecraft Environment Engineering, Beijing 100094, China

Abstract. In order to implement spacecraft assembly based on MBD, this article proposes a method of structural process design based on 3D model. First, an Assembly Digital Mock-up (ADMU) is constructed. Second, we propose the way of assembly process design based on 3D structural process design scheme. Finally, the paper describes the application of the technology, and analyses the effect of the scheme during a satellite development. The technology and systems should be applied on other sophisticated products development, with some essential modifications.

1 Introduction

Assembly, Integrated and Test (AIT) is critical for spacecraft development. During an AIT process, Computer Aided Process Planning (CAPP) system and Kanban system are widely used for editing process files. As traditional process files consist of only texts and pictures, it is difficult for process designers to deliver product model, Bill of Material (BOM), product property and inner relationship between these information. Furthermore, based on traditional method, it is impossible to integrate and manage assembly process plan with 3D CAD model, and make alteration and data-package automatically. With the development of Model Based Definition (MBD), potential solutions to above problems are proposed [1-4].

Researchers described much technology, such as data definition based model [5-6], digital mock-up construction [7-8], process planning and tools design based 3D models [9-11]. And they didn't describe automatic construction of assembly data-package, which is based on 3D structural process design.

In order to fulfill the requirement of the spacecraft assembly, this article proposes a design method for 3D structural process scheme, which is based on the Assembly Digital Mock-up (ADMU) defined in [7]. Three keys of designing the scheme are presented. In order to construct assembly data-package, this article then describe integration method of Manufacture Executing System (MES) and 3D Structural Process Design System (3DSPDS). At last, effects of an application are discussed.

2 Development of Satellite Digitization

2.1 Model of satellite development.

For the characteristic of satellite production primarily comes about small scale production or single-piece production. Even if custom orders two satellites belonged to the same load platform, each satellite is manufactured in its unique way according to specific requirements. In other words, satellite is essentially produced in single-piece way.

Usually, Satellite product organizations consist of three departments: design department, manufacturing department and AIT department. AIT department dedicates to assembly and integrated test including final assembly process design, assembly implementation, test and so on.

2.2 Design of Three-Dimensional.

As design department design satellite, they need to use both software Pro/E and CATIA. In the area of data management, four data management are used by design department to be employed in 3D modeling, technical file, 2D drawing and so on; In the area of digitization of development research and manufacturing, some satellite adopt full-specialty 3D development research and manufacturing, a few others adopt semi-specialty 3D development research and manufacturing; In the area of digitization standard system of development research and manufacturing, design standards following by different design departments are not identical.

In addition, 2D design data include technical text-formatted files, word-formatted files, 2D CAD drawing and so on. There are other design data, for instance design update files, technical notes and troubleshooting file.

2.3 Digitization of satellite assembly.

In development research and manufacturing of spacecraft AIT, assembly department had already built digitization mock-up and created specialized process for spacecraft assembly. On the one hand it inherit Engineering Bill of Material (EBOM). On the other hand adjustment and complement would be added on EBOM. Process assembly, tools and process protection parts are

[a] Corresponding author: hewenxing@163.com

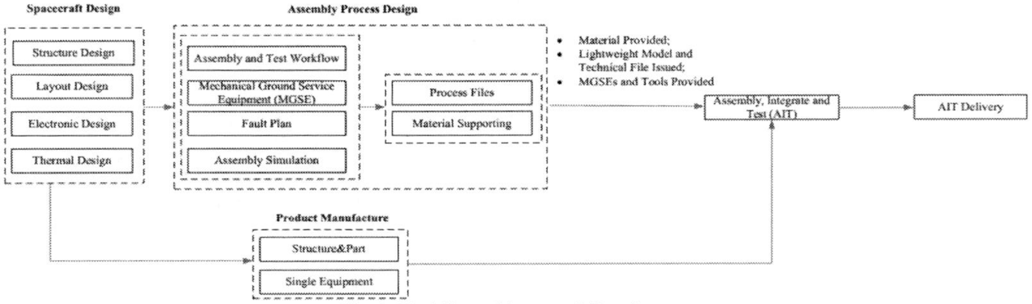

Fig. 1. Workflow of Spacecraft Development

added on base of EBOM. Same as EBOM, process digital mock-up include three components: Bill of Material, Model and Products attributes. Bill of Materiel use for delivery material information. Assembling relationship between parts and main object use for assembly technical conditions control. Model including layout, label and PMI is obtained after design lightweight. It mainly offer a good guidance field production and data sources of process design. For instance, assembly operation simulation and added process requirement. Process design depends on products attributes that had recorded assembly technology requirements, administrative information and so on.

3 Analysis of 3D Structural Process

Building bidirectional relationship between process design and production implementation is the prime condition of successful assembly for spacecraft using 3D structured process design. The core condition of bidirectional relationship is 3D structured process control of technology condition and collection of production parameters automatically.

3.1 Bidirectional relationship between process design and production implementation

Building bidirectional relationship between process design and production implementation depends on communication with information which include design requirements, design model, simulation videos, picture and so on. Using development research and manufacturing mode, 3D process files are regarded as carrier for communication. In other words, compared with traditional two-dimensional process files, 3D process files not only disseminate information by text, but also disseminate information which include design requirements, design model, simulation videos, picture and so on. Consequently, production implementation would be completed better.

From time to time, process conditions need to be updated frequently. As a consequence, in order to avoid the wrong operation, bidirectional communication between process design system and production implementation system should be built and achieve the objective that process change and production implementation bidirectional lock and unlock synchronously.

Collection the production data automatically is key point for 3D spacecraft assembly. To achieve the goal nothing but building bidirectional relationship is feasible. Such a process is meant to prevent inaccurate data getting published to live production systems which may lead to wrong decisions.

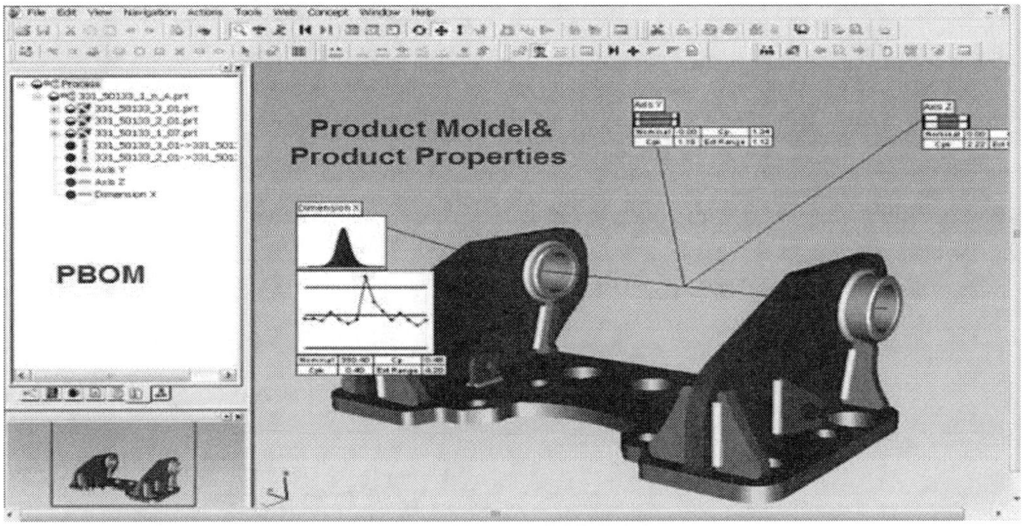

Fig.2. Assembly Process Digital Mock-up

3.2 Structured control technical conditions

Traditional 3D spacecraft assembly was simple digitization by system which could produce digit data (such as CAPP, kanban system). Data package can't be produced automatically. Performs root cause analysis, non-structural control like text hinder progress for 3D spacecraft assembly. Using 3D spacecraft assembly mode, combination of design data, process data and production data offers an efficient means of controlling and building 3D spacecraft assembly data packets. Such combinations can be tuned and optimized to match 3D spacecraft assembly. Building structured parameters which explains the assembly production condition control production condition (for example, instrument XX is installed, grounding resistance value). Therefore, on the basis of analyses of various type structured parameters on process files, structure of technical conditional controls would be built. At the same time, relevance between technical conditional controls and 3D process files is committed to build relevance between 3D process files and production data. Sequentially, it is possible to collect production data automatically.

4 Design of 3D structured process planning

Design of 3D structured process planning as illustrated in the following figure. General research approach as following: Inheritance and reconstruction of process digital mock-up of prototype design is only data source. Firstly, design and simulation for process planning should be carried out. Secondly, technological process that had been verified by simulation would be designed and compiled minutely. Information about material like manufacturing resources, assembly relationship and engineering requirements can be obtained from process digital mock-up. Then, relevant process file, including product model, video, picture and so on, would be examined, approved and sent to MES system as foundation of production and decision-making. Finally, after instruction, material and staves had been signed and recorded by MES system, relevant manufacturing information would be sent back to process design system as assembly data packets.

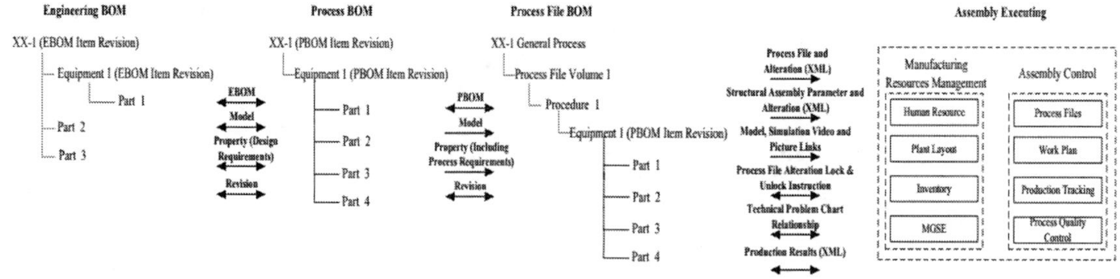

Fig.3. Scheme of 3D Structural Process Design

4.1 3D assembly process planning

According to[7],process digital mock-up not only include information about spacecraft, but also include implement, tools and process protecting parts which had been added by process itself. Meanwhile, combination with requirements of design, technological analysis and process planning can be accomplished.

First of all, using implement, tools, visual virtual human and visual virtual factory as data source, we can build all elements in the assembly simulation environment by 3D model of spacecraft. Simulation software use for design and verify technological process. Video simulation can be used for production and decision-making.

Then, Detailed process include grouping of process planning and the detailed design process route. It would be accomplished according to verified technological process or it may intersect with the verified technological process. Consequently, a better process planning was obtained.

4.2 3D assembly process compiling

3D assembly process compile many aspects include proposing manufacturing resource requirements, process requirement description by text or reference process knowledge base, defining the implementation records, adding multimedia process information and accessories, processing method and so on. Working process is as follows:

- Reference process BOM, ensure Loading parts for current process are available.
- Reference process BOM or process knowledge library, ensure tools and auxiliary material for current process are available.
- Process attribute judgment, add text "critical process" to corresponding process.
- Reference process knowledge library(for example SOP, standard operation procedure),according to process planning and technical requirements compile assembly operation process text, and add marks about corresponding key inspection points and Compulsory inspection points.
- Defined a structured implementation records
- Adding multimedia(production model, video, picture and so on) process information to process accessories
- Automatic dispatch information to MES system after process documents had been signed and controlled.

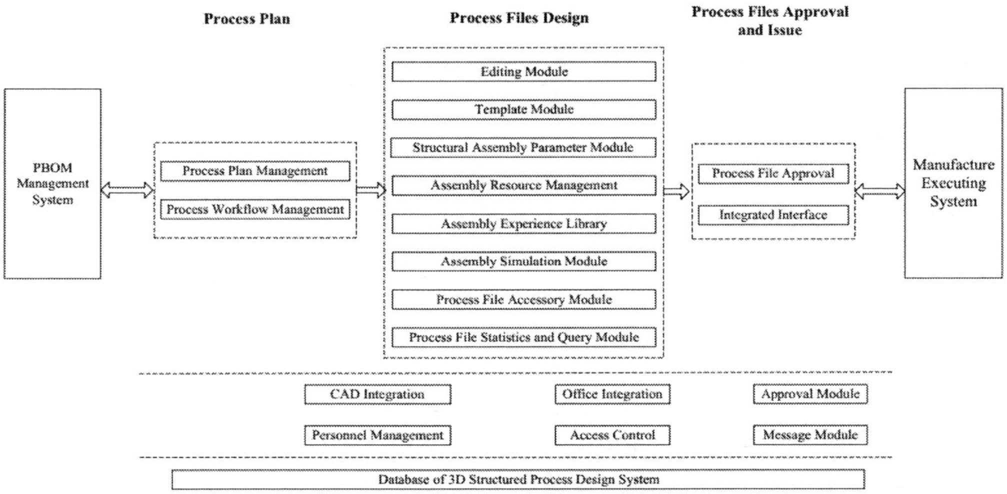

Fig.4. Framework of 3D Structured Process Design System

4.3 Bidirectional integration with MES system

3D process system send MES system information include the following: resources demanding information about materials, tools and so on; process requirement information such as PMI; multimedia(production model, video, picture and so on) process information.

In MES system, assembly production process for spacecraft as following:

• The starting point for distributed in 3D process, according to the process of form a complete set table warehouse operator start to collect and give out materials.

• According to the production plan, dispatcher distribute production task base on the module process and dynamic regulate of the control of the practical situation,

• After receiving the production task, production team start to assembly implementation and inspection based on the module process by means of checking the MES system of 3D process, and records the production condition and parameters before completion.

• After operation completed, inspector sign and record relevance process which include feedback implementation parameters of executive logging (for instance, the ground resistance) by means of checking the Real-time online MES system. Then system would sent process file with sign records and implementation parameters to 3D process system as whole satellite assembly data source by means of bidirectional integration interface.

• For sign records and implementation parameters produce on mobile termination, before 3D process system get relevant data, it would be collected by the real-time online MES system.

While the process is changing, 3D process system send lock instruction to the real-time online MES system and reminder users in relevant process. After the process change is completed, 3D process system send unlock instruction to the real-time online MES system and reminder users in relevant process and change the state of executable.

5 Framework

For system described above, you can count process digital mock-up system as data input interface of 3D structured process system mentioned in this paper. Data output interface can be regard as MES system including process planning module, process documentation, process of examination and approval and so on.

Process digital mock-up and its affiliated product are cited by association relationship between 3D structured process system and process digital mock-up system. However bidirectional communicate synchronously using website service between 3D structured process system and MES system by process, process update and executive logging.

According to technical solution as is mentioned above, a peculiar 3D structured process system for spacecraft was designed using Teamcenter from Siemens as a tool, and it was applied to several application about satellite development. In the meantime, we get 3D structured process based on uniform data source from assembly digital mock-up. Assembly process planning, assembly process documentation and distribution and coordinate closely with MES system had been researched and manufactured for spacecraft model XX. Consequently, completed assembled and production for spacecraft model XX, we generate data packets for whole satellite assembly.

6 Conclusion

In this paper we presented a concept of assembling of spacecraft. We focuses on designing a peculiar 3D assembly method meeting the demands of spacecraft. Current situation about digitization assembling for spacecraft development is explained. Furthermore, using uniform data source from assembly digital mock-up and analyzing two essential criteria about digitization assembling spacecraft, the solution was proposed for structured process design, working process and system framework about assembling spacecraft. Combined with

the actual case demonstrates it has good application outcome.

Acknowledgement

This research is supported by Natural Science Foundation of China (51405025).

References

1. Lian Ding, Dannie Davies, Christopher A. McMahon. The integration of lightweight representation and annotation for collaborative design representation. Res Eng Design. 2009,20:185-200.
2. Zorriassatine F, Wykes C, Parkin R, et al. A survey of virtual prototyping techniques for mechanical product development [J]. Proceedings of the Institution of Mechanical Engineers, Part B (Journal of Engingeering Manufacture). 2003, 217(B4):513-530.
3. Lihong Qiao, Jin Zhang. Some Key Issues in Three-Dimensional Digital Process Planning and Their Research. Aerospace Manufacturing Technology. 2010(1):29-32.
4. Tao Yang, Zhongyi Mei. Aircraft Full Three-Dimensional Implementation Technology Based on Mbd. Aerospace Manufacturing Technology. 2013(08):26-31.
5. Yuqing Fan, Yan Liang, Guocheng Feng. Data Organization of MBD-Based Assembly and Its Implementation, Aviation Maintenance & Engineering .6(2010)56-59.
6. Sebastien Gagne, Clement Fortin. Application of the CMII Model to an integrated engineering and manufacturing development environment. Ingt J Ineract Des Manuf. 2007(1):5-13.
7. Wenxing He, Bile Wan, Bin Zhang, Xinghui Wu. Research of the technology and application of process digital mock-up for spacecraft assembly. Advanced Materials Research. 2014(1037):447-452.
8. In-Ho Song, Sung-Chong Chung. Synthesis of the digital mock-up system for heterogeneous CAD assembly. Computers in Industry. 2009(60):285-295.
9. Haiyan Wang. The MBD-based Final Assembly Process Planning Data Semantic Modeling Technology Research of Civil Aircraft [D]. Shanghai Jiao Tong University. 2013.
10. Yigguang Li, Zhiyi Pan, Ruijie Yan, Wenhe Liao. APDM-based framework for collaborative aircraft tooling design. International Journal of Production Research. 2008(46):2413-2431.
11. Yingguang Li, Zhiyi Pan, Ruijie Yan, Jianbang Jian. A semantics-based approach for collaborative aircraft tooling design. Advanced Engineering Informatics. 2010(24):149-158.

MATEC Web of Conferences 44, 02044 (2016)
DOI: 10.1051/matecconf/20164402044

Three-dimensional Animation Technology in Showing the Application of the Art of Design

Cun Fu Xu[1], Xiao Cheng Zhou[2]

{College of Animation,Anhui Xinhua University,Wangjiang Road no. 555, Shushan District, Hefei, 230088}

Abstract. The three dimensional animation technology is a new technology in recent years with the development of computer hardware and software technology and produce; exhibition design art is accompanied by stages in the development of human society politics, economy and the gradual formation of art. This paper mainly studies animation how to promote and enhance the artistic design and industrial product design from the technical means of 3D, architectural exhibition as a starting point, to integration and innovation between the two studies, which reflects the perfect combination of technology and art.

1 3D Animation Technology

Three-dimensional animation animation, also known as 3D animation. Its work principle and method are to create a virtual world in the computer platform, and then in the virtual 3D world, according to the shape size of the object to display the model and the design of the scene, and then according to the need to set up the model of motion track, virtual camera movement and other animation parameters, and finally to the design intent to give a specific material and lighting effects. When this is done, it can be set up and output, through the post editing and synthesis, and ultimately generate three-dimensional animation [1].

Three dimensional animation technology, which can simulate the simple industrial products and display of art, can simulate the complex role and scene model, from the static, single model to dynamic, complex scenes can rely on powerful animation technology to achieve. Three dimensional animation relies on the design and performance of real and perfect virtual reality technology, which has a very high accuracy, authenticity and unlimited operability, and has been widely used in many fields such as business, science, technology, military, education, medicine, entertainment, etc. For example, some of the animation, character animation, architectural roaming, film and television advertising, special effects production and other works to bring an unprecedented visual feast.

With the continuous development of computer 3D animation technology and innovation, and now has been more and more valued. Because it is more intuitive, image and vivid, more intuitive, more intuitive, more able to enjoy the immersive feeling, especially for those who have not yet achieved or ready to implement the project, you can make the audience enjoy the wonderful results and display in advance after the implementation of the design scheme.

2 Display Design Art

Display design is a comprehensive discipline based on the design of art. It is through the use of certain tools and equipment, the use of certain tools and equipment, the use of certain visual communication means, in the established time and space, the use of art design language, to create a unique space and artistic conception, and the content of certain information and content in the public, and to produce a significant impact on the audience's psychological, ideological and behavior. Its core is how to efficiently transfer information to the audience, so as to achieve the purpose of perfect communication.

In the display design, the "space" is the critical factor, the need to convey the information must be displayed in public, it is a platform for people to perceive activities. Therefore, the essence of the design is how to properly handle the space form. Its premise and foundation is to understand the relationship between the spatial form and the display design. Display design art, through the form, color, lighting, video, audio, materials, text illustrations and models and other aspects of the full use of new technologies, new results, can fully mobilize the audience's vision, hearing, touch and even smell and taste, and all the ability to form a benign interaction between people and environmental science [2].

With the years of development, scientific and technological progress has now formed a "show art". In

[a] Corresponding author: Cun fu Xu[1], Xiao cheng Zhou[2] 729334333@qq.com
Anhui Province, the provincial quality project "animation professional comprehensive reform pilot", the project number: 2015zy072

Article available at http://www.matec-conferences.org or http://dx.doi.org/10.1051/matecconf/20164402044

the business activities of its display means is highly effective and direct characteristics; the function of the literary and artistic display is self-evident. Museum, science museum, art exhibition hall, Folk Museum, etc. are important part of social civilization and cultural resources, which plays an important role in inheriting civilization, enlightening wisdom, showing science and promoting the construction of spiritual civilization. This new field of display design not only enriches the contents of the exhibition, but also updates the artistic conception of the exhibition. Through the introduction of some new decoration technology and materials, it is a subject of systematic, scientific and artistic integration.

3Commercial Buildings Display Design Art Based on the Three-dimensional Animation Technology

The art of commercial architecture design includes: the design and production of urban construction and planning, city image display, city digital project, park landscape construction, municipal planning, commercial buildings, residential, public place design, virtual city and so on. Before the commencement of these projects, we must have a complete pre design and planning process, comprehensive analysis and induction of various factors, first of all to develop a detailed project objectives and plans, and then determine the rationality and feasibility of the program. In order to get the final results in the previous work, the use of virtual reality technology can easily achieve this process, through the construction roaming animation, 3D animation, animation, project bidding animation. The concept of architectural animation and other techniques for the corresponding art processing and performance, can be in the future development direction has a general understanding so as to improve working efficiency, effectively reduce the risk.

The 3D animation technology on the one hand makes the range of display design time and space and depth to expand and extend. The number of messages and effectively enhance the amount and quality of the change; on the other hand, because of the virtual display of flexibility and diversity, can make some objects in the real environment can not be displayed get dripping every performance, let a person feel personally on the scene and intimacy, so that the display design is more popular and comprehensive. Three dimensional animation technology in the commercial building display design art in the main solution to the development of the project's virtual reality performance and to develop the project promotion and publicity. In the commercial building planning and design of roaming animation can be in the display process, with the help of virtual reality technology to build a virtual three-dimensional scene, so that visitors to participate in, experience the sense of interaction and immersion [3].

With the development and progress of 3D animation technology, the typical visual image and artistic characteristics of the commercial buildings are also widely used and studied. VRP-MUSEUM (network virtual Pavilion) is a museum experience, for all kinds of large-scale exhibition center, and other industries, the exhibition hall, exhibition and temporary exhibits transplanted to the Internet 3D interactive display, publicity and education experience solutions. VRP-MUSEUM can be used to combine the traditional pavilion with the Internet and three-dimensional virtual technology to break the time and space constraints, so that a wider range of users on the network platform can truly feel the pavilion and exhibits, with online interactive experience, enjoy the search, immersive online exhibition! Compared with the traditional physical exhibition hall, the performance characteristics of the exhibition are essentially different in Table 1.

Table 1. Comparison of the characteristics of the network virtual exhibition hall and the entity Pavilion

	Online virtual exhibition hall	Entity Pavilion
Features	In a digital way to display,education, collection,researc h	In a entity mode to display,education ,collection,resear ch
Autonomy	User initiative	User passive
Convenience	Use the Internet, anywhere at any time you can access the browse	Tickets to the destination is required to enter the exhibition
Interactiveness	Interaction, games, expansion of information	such as individual interaction
Environmental control	Can be a window interactive control environme nt	The environment can not control or change
Display mode	All round, digital	Close range, entity
Presentation mode	Diversity, according to personal habits have different classification	Single fixed display mode
Extension	Extremely	Finite
Space quantity	Limited to broadband, server and hardware devices, but can be expanded and improved	Confined to buildings, it is difficult to expand, access is limited
Spatial scale	Can be reduced and enlarged, 360 degree full range of viewing	Limited by the distance between the viewer and the object
Resource saving	Environmental protection and energy saving, low carbon life	Commercial venues borrow fees, exhibition fees and further exhibits transportation

Three dimensional animation technology can be carried out in the computer platform. The 3D model of virtual object is stored in the computer, and all kinds of information in computer program. In the project, the project design in its role is obvious, through three-dimensional animation display can find out the defects in the design, so that can effectively reduce the difficulty of production, shorten the design cycle, increase the design personnel's interest, so as to reduce the cost of production. Along with the development of virtual reality technology, the application of 3D animation technology in the commercial building display design will be widely spread and applied.

4Industrial Product Display Design Base d on 3D Animation Technology

Industrial design is a discipline which follows nature and objective law. It is a combination of technology and art, function and form. It is influenced by social form, natural environment, cultural ideas and economic factors, which is based on the harmonious relationship between "function" and "beauty".

Product design is a kind of imagining and planning, the use of digital, line, color, symbol, etc. to find ways to solve the problem, through the creation of comprehensive information processing and specific carrier, the people of a certain purpose or needs to be expressed in a good form of the process, it is reflected in a certain level of economic, technological and cultural development level. Industrial products display design art is an orderly design system, which is based on a variety of media from the structure of the form, function, application of the special design to complete the transmission of information. Finally realize the function of the product, which brings people a more realistic aesthetic experience.

Product animation is a branch of animation field,it uses computer graphics (CG) technology and multimedia design software, the product structure, features, functions, working principle, using method, attention to matters such as three-dimensional animation through three-dimensional rendering, so that people's direct view, detailed and full range of dynamic understanding of product features and characteristics. Product animation has been widely used in industrial product development, testing, publicity, display and other aspects, such as the car as a representative of the means of transport animation, mobile phone as the representative of the electronic products, machinery products parts assembly animation, engineering application animation, production process, production process and other three-dimensional animation design and production. Using virtual reality technology to provide interactive, the product is placed in a certain environment or in the story, the network can use Cult3D technology on the product's work environment or the performance of the product is a dynamic display [4].

With the development of virtual reality (Reality Virtual) technology and multimedia technology, virtual reality technology and multimedia technology are used in the new product development process. At present, the virtual reality technology is introduced into the CAD environment, which will be convenient for the simulation of some properties of the new product development, and also to facilitate the design of the product changes. When the technology conditions of the company, in the virtual product design, designers can use the existing CAD system modeling, and then converted to the VR environment, so that the design staff or prospective customers to perceive products. Designers can also use the VR-CAD system, directly in the virtual environment for design and modification. For example, in the design of the car, the design personnel in a fully interactive design environment, the use of helmet display, with tactile feedback functions of data gloves, joystick, three-dimensional position tracking device, the visual, auditory, tactile and virtual product model, not only can carry out virtual cooperation, produce an immersive feeling, but also to the entire virtual product (Product Virtual) design process inspection, assessment, field address design decisions, so that the design idea is integrated. In the interactive virtual environment rapid prototyping equipment, the design of the virtual product design model of the direct design, improve the design of the initiative and creativity of the design. With the rapid development of multimedia technology, especially the combination of virtual reality and multimedia technology, the speed of the design has been accelerated by the designers from the keyboard and the mouse. Although it is only the initial stage, in the aspects of the interaction between the various sensors and multi-dimensional information environment, and realize the full range of understanding, but also to be further improved, but in the new product development and design application has great potential, and the application prospect is broad. It should be further developed and studied, so that the virtual design technology is better to help designers in the new product development to enhance the design of innovative thinking ability and product design level [5].

Through the three-dimensional animation technology to the industrial product display design art convey and performance, can the product appearance, structure and function of creative and construction, so as to determine the layout of the whole production system, through product animation and interactive, intuitive understanding of the structure and working principle. It not only shows the superiority of the function, but also is easy to manufacture, low production cost, so that the comprehensive competitiveness of products can be enhanced. Product animation in the realization of the product is more detailed, complete and comprehensive, can effectively make the target audience more conscious, active acceptance of enterprise products; on the other hand for the image of the enterprise and corporate culture, the concept of propaganda, also has great potential value.

5Three-dimensional Animation Technology and Display Design of the Integration of Innovation and Development Trends

Three-dimensional animation and display design is the combination of science and art, the design of the

realization of the need to rely on technical support, through the design of the form of beauty and technology pursuit of the function of the United States for integration and innovation, and ultimately form, function and aesthetic perfect fusion. Display design is the pursuit of a seek and create emotional and rational exploration and discovery of wisdom, looking at a higher level is to show the aesthetic design, function, environment and human factors such as harmony, intertwined with each other, through the dissemination and exhibition of 3D animation technology, will bring a unique the creative and new experience of the exhibition.

Architectural animation design for the project plan approval of the intuitive carrier, reduce communication costs between the government departments and improve the efficiency of communication. Developers can also be in the virtual reality technology, through the animation of arbitrary interception of pictures or fragments of advertising, so as to reduce the cost of advertising investment. Application of virtual reality technology, the target customers can freely walk in real estate roaming virtual reality demonstration system, free to watch, the impact of strong, can make the customer feel immersive, greatly promote the speed of the contract signing. According to the United States, the famous real estate website realtor data show that there is a virtual reality technology display real estate roaming real estate, real estate, than did not show the real estate, access rate increased by 40%, the purchase effect increased by 28.5%. Real estate can make roaming scheme has multifunction, real estate can also be used for roaming online advertising sales promotion, brand promotion, sales site display, company website and real estate website display, as the company's historical data for permanent preservation, long-term investment, leasing, commercial projects for various assessment activities. One-time investment, can be applied in all aspects of project approval, construction, sales, investment leasing, and can be used permanently.The construction of roaming animation allows buyers to choose to see the model of the image on the computer. In the sales department the use of VR technology allows buyers to see the house which will be built in the area after a few years, to see beautiful residential environment design through real estate roaming.

The VRP-PHYSICS system in the code of digital technology in the industry pioneered the application of professional industrial simulation field, is currently the only one suitable for high-end industrial simulation virtual reality system physics engine. Since the birth of the day, VRP-PHYSICS system with its powerful physical real-time computing capabilities to support the real simulation of gravity, environment, simulation of rigid body dynamics and other environmental characteristics, support for a variety of dynamic interactive means, support for a variety of high speed calculation of the impact of a variety of high speed calculation of the method, a simple and easy to be used for the majority of industrial simulation needs of excellent interactive simulation creative solutions is perfect, for the vast number of domestic industrial simulation tools and technology to achieve the level of revolutionary progress. VRP-PHYSICS system is widely used in many industries of virtual simulation: the simulation of large-scale machinery and equipment operation principle, for training and product electronic sample demonstration; production line process simulation, for skills training teaching and production line simulation monitoring; all kinds of virtual scene and real industrial facilities of interactive operation application [6].

With the development of digital technology and network technology, the application of digital technology will be more and more. The 3D display effect of virtual reality technology in digital technology has brought a wealth of ideas and immersive feeling. Through 3D animation design and production, people can be integrated into the virtual scene.

References

1. Code in digital technology. Digital City, industrial simulation.Http://www.vrp3d.com. 2012
2. Digital 3D animation creation foundation [M]. Beijing: Tsinghua University press.2010 (7, 10)
3. Qin Huaiyu. The application of virtual design in the development of new products. Visual alliance [J]. 2007.15 (1-2).Willian R Sherman Alan, B Craig
4. Virtual reality system - interface, application and design of [M]. Electronics Industry Press. 2004 (15)
5. Wei Wenshan. The design and Realization of three-dimensional animation of the network [J]. China's scientific and technological information.2006.8 (1-2)
6. Zhao Yunchuan. Display design [M]. China Light Industry Press.2001 (1)

MATEC Web of Conferences **44**, 02045 (2016)
DOI: 10.1051/matecconf/20164402045

The Undergraduate Scientific and Technological Innovation and Entrepreneurship Education Platform

Jin Bao Song[1,a]

[1] *Information Engineering School, Communication University of China, Beijing, China*

Abstract. Along with the development of innovation and entrepreneurship nowadays, how to promote the undergraduate scientific and technological innovation and entrepreneurship during the period of university education is more and more discussed by the people. How to organize and manage effectively for the undergraduate scientific and technological innovation and entrepreneurship, how to give the undergraduate scientific and technological innovation and entrepreneurship some pointed guide and cultivation, how to form an organic quality training mechanism together with class education and social education are important problems which effect undergraduate scientific and technological innovation and entrepreneurship. Firstly, the undergraduate scientific and technological innovation and entrepreneurship service platform is introduced in this paper to solve these above problems. Secondly, the new mode of scientific and technological innovation and entrepreneurship ability training for the undergraduates is analyzed. At last, a new way of thinking for the scientific and technological innovation and entrepreneurship service is provided the talent training in this paper which will play an important role on the development of innovation and entrepreneurship education.

1 Introduction

The undergraduate ability of scientific and technological innovation and entrepreneurship is one of the important contents of China's higher education talent training. It is also an important educational factor to improve the comprehensive quality of the undergraduates. It plays an important role on the cultivation of the students' competence, cooperation ability, even the leadership and the ability to make decisions. And it is the important means to meet the social demand and promote the undergraduate employment. Constructing the scientific and technological innovation country and the scientific and technological and innovative city has become a national and Beijing's important planning construction goal [1]. The Communication University of China is a famous university in the field of information transmission in China, which has outstanding contribution and the important position in media content and form innovation research, media high technology research and development and the unit decision consultation service for the enterprise or business and so on. It is an important source of the media science and technology innovation. A lot of the media realm student's innovation achievements become productive forces to promote the scientific and technological achievements through guide and cultivation, which will greatly promote the economic growth of the country [2].

2 The significance of undergraduate science and technology innovation and entrepreneurship service platform

The construction of undergraduate science and technology innovation and entrepreneurship service platform is based on the science and technology innovation park of the Communication University of China, which provides service to the full-time undergraduate and graduate students. This platform is an important part of the professional incubation service project in the modern service industry. This platform plays an important role in driving the whole environmental construction of the country's science and technology.

How to organize and manage effectively for the undergraduate scientific and technological innovation and entrepreneurship, how to give the undergraduate scientific and technological innovation and entrepreneurship some pointed guide and cultivation, how to form an organic quality training mechanism together with class education and social education are important problems which effect undergraduate scientific and technological innovation and entrepreneurship. And we must put forward the effective solution. The undergraduate science and technology innovation and entrepreneurship services platform construction is to solve these problems. The core of the platform is the

[a] Corresponding author: songjinbao@cuc.edu.cn

innovation and entrepreneurship quality ability training. The goal of the platform is to promote science and technology innovation incubation and achievements of the media. The platform provides effective information management and service, innovation and entrepreneurship training and guidance, coordination and mutual communication platform for college students with the aid of new media network, modern means of science and technology. The construction and implementation of undergraduate science and technology innovation and entrepreneurship service platform has important significance to improve enthusiasm of undergraduate innovation and enterprise, promote the produce and accelerate conversion of the university students' scientific and technological achievements, improve the success rate of entrepreneurship, regulate the college students' innovative and enterprising organization and management and form the innovation and interactive environment including university students, experts, enterprises and departments of government.

3 The construction goal of undergraduate science and technology innovation and entrepreneurship service platform

The science and technology innovation and entrepreneurship service platform is to support undergraduate innovative and enterprising work as the core target and put public welfare, demonstration, profession as the main characteristics. The specific goals are as follow:

1) The B/S interactive network is as the foundation platform, combined with the new media, virtualization and other modern means of science and technology [3]. It is for the technical integration and demonstration of information management and service, innovation and entrepreneurship training and guidance, coordination and mutual communication platform construction around undergraduate science and technology innovation and entrepreneurship activities. The Communication University of China undergraduate science and technology innovation activities comprehensive service demonstration system is established including organization, management, training, promotion, resources sharing, the information communication. And the employment and entrepreneurship comprehensive service demonstration system of Communication University of China science and technology park is also set up including entrepreneurship dynamic and hotspots tracking, employment guidance, business training, achievement presentation and investment hatch, project tracking and coordination and communication.

2) The establishment of Communication University of China undergraduate science and technology innovation and entrepreneurship service platform software and hardware test environment and operating system environment will be completed, including undergraduate science and technology innovation and entrepreneurship information service platform internal network, central server, video server, cooperation and sharing resources server, data information server, user authentication server and browser based client software and security plug-ins, etc [4].

3) Based on the platform, for the Communication University of China and its science and technology park, a group of outstanding entrepreneurs of college students are cultivated. A coaching professional team is formed. A group of college students' successful entrepreneurship models are set up. All kinds of relevant information of the enterprises and projects for college students are provided. The business consulting and training are organized in order to improve all kinds of the entrepreneurs' skills. And enterprise fast growth and independent business are promoted [5].

4) Based on the platform, the university science park industry chain is effectively extended. The new pattern of "complementary advantages and linkage development" is gradually formed with other industries inside and outside the park. The multiplication effect of entrepreneurship is realized in order to create more employment opportunities, ease Beijing and radiation regional employment pressure and promote the regional economic growth.

The Communication University of China undergraduate science and technology innovation and entrepreneurship service platform is divided into two parts:

1) Communication University of China science and technology park undergraduate science and technology innovation activities comprehensive service system:

a) A media organization management system of science and technology innovation team is established, including team building system, the daily operation management system, the reward system, coordination mechanism. The objectives and tasks of the innovative team are specified.

b) The online training and technical guidance environment are provided, focused on training management of the service around university students media science and technology training and innovation technical guidance.

c) The project results display platform is established for media science and technology innovation team project intermediary and display needs. The innovation and organization management platform is provided for the media project application and competition of national and municipal science and technology innovation.

d) The equipment and experimental environment information management platform is established in order to provide the necessary experiment and development conditions for media science and technology innovation team, including equipment and laboratory management, status enquiry, appointment management and necessary training.

e) A scientific and technological innovation BBS and media team communication space are established. The teams BBS plate and communication space are built according to professional direction. The online interactive innovation environment is formed.

2) Communication University of China science and technology park undergraduate entrepreneurship comprehensive service system:

a) The interactive college students' employment information release and online recruitment platform is established in order to provide bridge for college students' employment and the enterprises and recruitment direct to innovative team and the outstanding students.

b)The entrepreneurship policy guidance, business dynamic and hot tracking, entrepreneurship case analysis, online entrepreneurship training, science and technology resources service, innovation service navigation and so on are provided focusing on career guidance and training.

c) The results show and hatch investment link is provided and the hatch and entrepreneurial tracking information management mechanism is set up according to the needs of the entrepreneurship development.

d) The online collaboration and mutual communication platform is created, implementing online meeting and cooperation project development, white board data synchronization, audio interaction, the resource exchange and sharing function.

e) A media technology entrepreneurship BBS is established [6].

4 The overview of undergraduate science and technology innovation and entrepreneurship service platform

The Communication University of China undergraduate science and technology innovation and entrepreneurship service platform is divided into two systems. One is undergraduate science and technology innovation activities comprehensive service system. The other is undergraduate entrepreneurship comprehensive service system.

4.1. Science and technology innovation service system

The software system frame of science and technology innovation service system is shown as Figure 1. This system is mainly divided into six big modules including user login module, the project application and management module, the innovation achievements exhibit module, online training and technical guidance module, equipment and the experiment environment module and team communication BBS module. The modules specific functions are shown below.

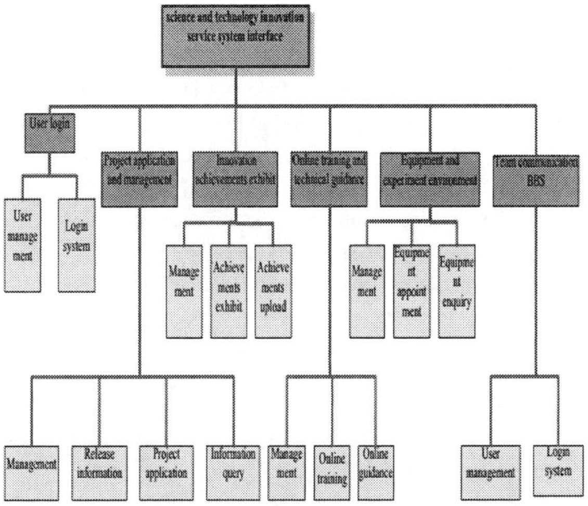

Figure 1. Science and technology innovation service system diagram

4.2. Entrepreneurship service system

The software system frame of entrepreneurship service system is shown as Figure 2. This system is mainly divided into six big modules including user login module, employment information and online recruitment module, training and policy guidance module, business incubation and entrepreneurial track module, the online collaboration and mutual communication module, team communication BBS module. Among them except employment information and online recruitment module and online collaboration and mutual communication outside module, other modules are similar to innovation service system corresponding modules. The modules specific functions are shown below.

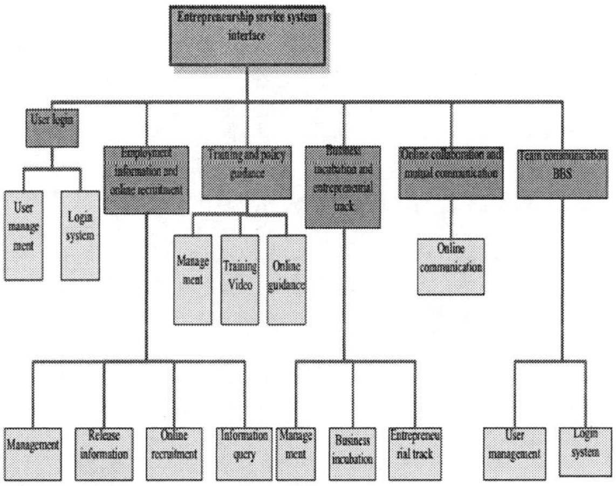

Figure 2. Entrepreneurship service system diagram

5 Development environment

5.1. Software environment summary

- server system: Windows server 2003
- database: mysql 5.1 above
- database graphic interface: navicat more than 9.0
- IDE: myeclipse 8.6 and above
- development of the main language: Java
- JDK version: JDK 1.6 above
- Java web containers: tomcat 6.0 above
- development framework: SSH
- the browser: firefox or chrome

5.2. Software environment introduction

(1) JDK:

Java SE6 software development kit, is a Java applications foundation. The J2EE is based on Java technology, so installation JDK must be configuration of J2EE environment.

(2)Tomcat:

Tomcat is a JSP engine developed by Apache organization. It has the function of the Web server, and could be used as independent Web server. But, as a Web server, Tomcat doesn't process static HTML pages more quickly and strongly than Apache. So the Apache and Tomcat is used together by letting the Apache provides processing for the Web static page services and Tomcat JSP engine provides JSP analysis in order to get better performance. Tomcat itself is a sub-project Apache, so that Tomcat provides powerful support to Apache.

(3)MySQL:

MySQL database system uses the most commonly used database management language-structured query language (SQL) for database management. Using the database graphical interface Navicat can directly add data.

(4)MyEclipse:

MyEclipse is a free IDE integrated development environment tool which supports the development of language and installing plugins can make its function more powerful.

5.3. Struts 2, Spring, Hibernate

SSH is the abbreviation of Struts2, Spring, Hibernate. It is a very popular Java Web development framework in the current Java world. Also it is a kind of the MVC. MVC is Model, View, Controller layered structure. The three parts should as far as possibly reduce coupling to improve application expansibility and maintainability, shown as Figure 3. Struts2 is mainly as a control layer, shown as Figure 4. Spring is mainly used for business layer, shown as Figure 5. Hibernate is database lasting layer, shown as Figure 6.

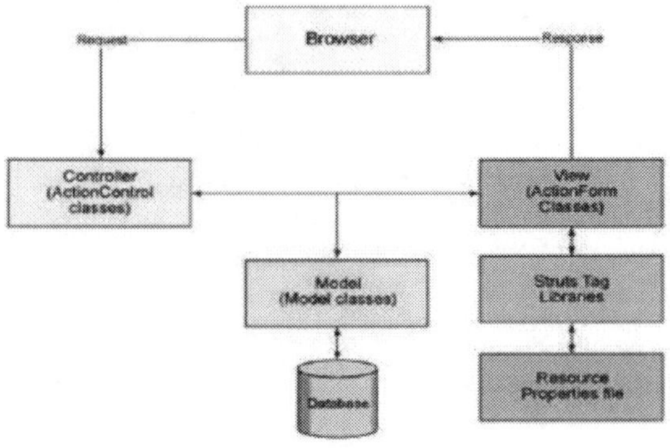

Figure 3. MVC schematic framework

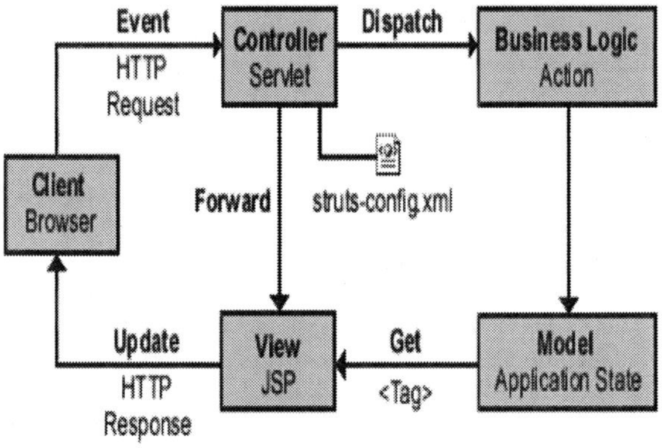

Figure 4. Structs schematic framework

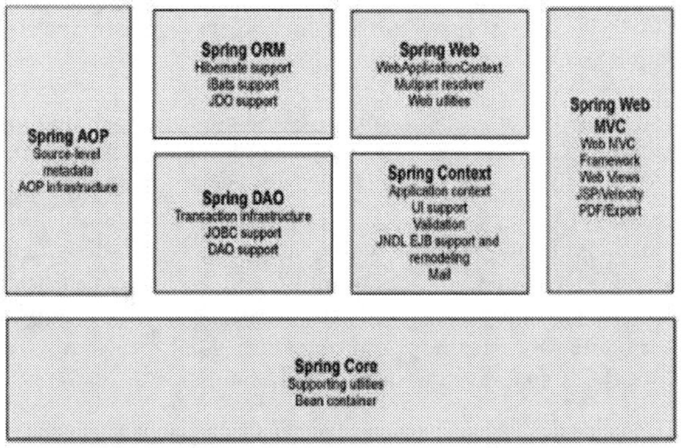

Figure 5. Spring schematic framework

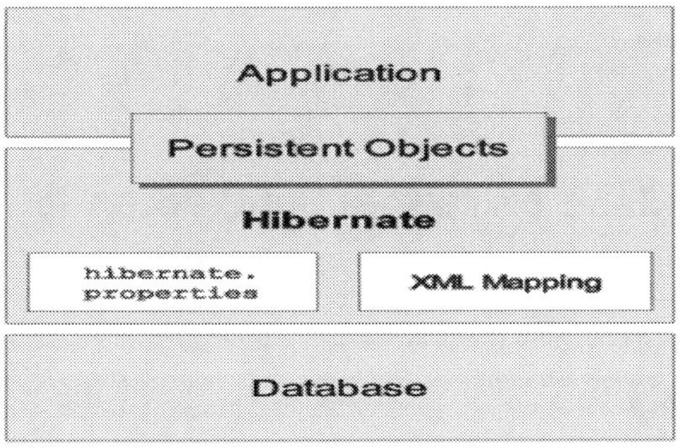

Figure 6. Hibernate schematic framework

6 Summary

In the undergraduate science and technology innovation and entrepreneurship services platform construction, we use the technical route of "architecture design" → "technical model research" → "prototype system construction" → "demonstration application and perfect system ".

1) We have deeply researched the general framework of undergraduate innovation and business information service platform. In view of the specific requirements of the college students' extracurricular scientific research and science and engineering practice activities, employment, business aspects, and organizational management, innovative and undertaking training, policy guidance, project investment promotion, hatch, equipment resources sharing, online meeting and cooperation, we have done further discussion and demand function analysis, which determines the undergraduate science and technology innovation and entrepreneurship information service platform constraint condition and basic mode.

2) According to the demand analysis and the overall framework of undergraduate science and technology innovation and entrepreneurship information services platform, we have designed the internal structure of the system and researched the Ajax, XMPP, MVC technology[7-9], established technical model that meets demand and architecture requirement, realized the relevant function module, and at the same time synchronously carried on technological verification to ensure the feasibility, reliability and scalability of the technology and the business standard.

3) We have further integrated the software and hardware resources of the undergraduate science and technology innovation and entrepreneurship information service platform, finished a practical integration development, designed and established undergraduate extracurricular technological innovation activities information service demonstration system and undergraduate employment venture information service demonstration system prototype and integrated and tested system to test system function, performance requirements.

4) We have established a practical application of the hardware and software environment. Through actual application verification and testing system at the park of science and innovation and related universities, we have gotten through technology difficult points, realized the fusion penetration and general test of the technology, and verified the feasibility and reliability of the overall scheme. Also, according to validation and evaluating the effect of the system, we have adjusted and optimized system solutions and perfected the system platform.

References

1. J. B. Song. (2012, June). The Communication University of China undergraduate science and technology innovation and entrepreneurship services platform research report. Communication University of China, Beijing, China.
2. H. Y. Ma. (2012, June). The Communication University of China undergraduate science and technology innovation and entrepreneurship services platform work report. Communication University of China, Beijing, China.
3. Z. B. Liu, Java WEB core framework. Beijing: Posts & Telecom Press, 2008, pp. 123–135.
4. W. Q. Sun, Proficient Hibernate JAVA object persistent mass media technology, Beijing: Posts & Telecom Press, 2007, pp. 212–236.
5. R. Johnson, J. Hoeller, Expert one-on-one J2EE Development without EJB, 2005.
6. C. Bauer, G. King, JAVA Persistence with hibernate, 2008.
7. J. Sack, sql server 2008 transact-sql recipes, 2010.
8. R. Stephens, Beginning database design solutions,2010
9. M. Fowler, Patterns of Enterprise Application Architecture, 2011.

MATEC Web of Conferences 44, 02046 (2016)
DOI: 10.1051/matecconf/20164402046

A hierarchical layout design method based on rubber band potential-energy descending

Cheng Yi Ou[1], Hai Hua Xiao[1], Jun Yan Ma[1,a] and Xiao Ping Liao[2]
[1]Mechancal manufacturing & automation, college of mechanical & engineering, Guangxi University, Nanning, Guangxi, China
[2]Mechancal manufacturing & automation, science and technology department, Guangxi University, Nanning, Guangxi, China

Abstract. Strip packing problems is one important sub-problem of the Cutting stock problems. Its application domains include sheet metal, ship making, wood, furniture, garment, shoes and glass. In this paper, a hierarchical layout design method based on rubber band potential-energy descending was proposed. The basic concept of the rubber band enclosing model was described in detail. We divided the layout process into three different stages: initial layout stage, rubber band enclosing stage and local adjustment stage. In different stages, the most efficient strategies were employed for further improving the layout solution. Computational results show that the proposed method performed better than the GLSHA algorithm for three out of nine instances in utilization.

1 Introduction

Strip packing problems(SPP) is one of the Cutting stock problems(CSP) which presented by R.C. Art[1] early in 1996. SPP aimed at maximizing the utilization of materials with optimal stock layout design. Because of its potential application and theoretical research value, a large number of researchers are devoted to this field from different industry, such as sheet metal, ship making, wood, furniture, garment, shoes and glass.

According to the latest classification rules from Wäscher[2], SPP is defined as an open-dimensional optimal problem, in which the given strip material has fixed width but its length is infinite. So the target of SPP is finding the most compact layout solution with minimal length for a set of layout objects.

Algorithms for solving SPP can be classified into three categories: deterministic algorithms, indeterministic algorithms and algorithms in between. Deterministic algorithms, in general, would reach an deterministic layout solution on a low time consumption, such as mathematical programming[3]. However, solutions from deterministic algorithm are relatively optimal. It can't meet actual application need. On the other hand, indeterministic algorithms own strong capability of global search, such as genetic algorithm(GA)[4], particle swarm algorithm(PSO)[5] and neural network algorithm[6]. But these algorithms usually consume a large amount of calculation time in their iteration operation. So algorithms between deterministic algorithms and indeterministic algorithms are a balance of both. They try to balance the relationship between time consumption and final optimal solution through combining specific heuristic rules and other intelligence algorithms, such as bottom-left placement algorithm(BL)[7].

However, the popular algorithms at present are still time consuming. In this paper, we introduce a hierarchical layout design method based on potential-energy descending of rubber band. The inspiration of this method is from physical phenomena. When a rubber band enclosed several objects, these objects will move close to each other until forming a compact layout solution. The proposed hierarchical conception is to divide layout process into three stages for employing efficient strategies.

The remainder of the paper is organized as follows. Section 2 describes the SPP optimization model for irregular polygons. Section 3 introduces the rubber band enclosing model and describes some essential analysis methods. Section 4 describes the proposed hierarchical layout design model in detail. Section 5 presents the computer test results and compares the proposed method with others. Section 6 is summary and prospect of this paper.

2 SPP optimization model

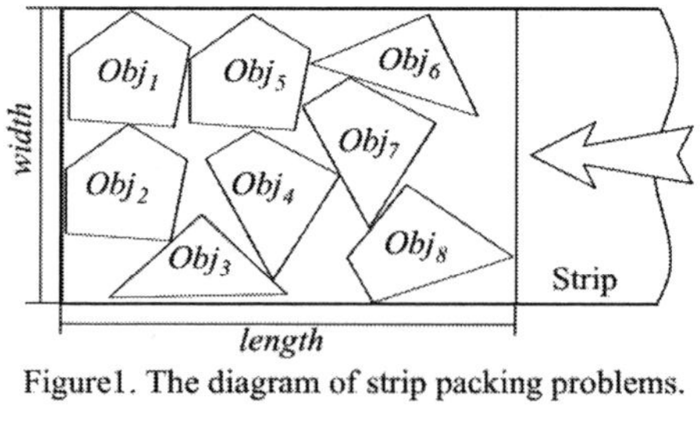

Figure1. The diagram of strip packing problems.

[a] Corresponding author: ouyi3427@126.com.

As shown in Fig.1, given a set of layout objects $Obj_1, Obj_2..Obj_n$ and a strip Str with specific width w, find a group of proper positions and angles $p_1(x_1, y_1, ang_1)..p_n(x_n, y_n, ang_n)$ for every objects so as to place them into the strip minimizing the length of utilized strip without any overlap. It can be expressed by the optimization model shown below.

$$\begin{aligned} &Find \quad p_i(x_i, y_i, ang_i) \\ &Min \quad l \\ &S.T. \quad Obj_i \subseteq Str \\ &\qquad Obj_i \cap Obj_j = \phi(i, j = 1,2..n) \end{aligned} \tag{1}$$

In other words, finding the minimal l is equivalent to maximize the material utilization of the rectangular region used. The utilization u can be expressed by equation (2).

$$u = \frac{\sum Area(Obj_i)}{w \times l} \times 100\% \tag{2}$$

Moreover, we only concentrate on irregular polygon layout problems because that any 2D objects can be instead of polygon approximately.

3 Rubber band enclosing model

Assume that several objects are enclosed by a stretched rubber band shown in Fig.2. Under the impact of elastic force from rubber band, all objects will move to each other as close as possible forming a compact layout in the end. In addition, potential energy of rubber band reaches to minimum. This layout process is the proposed rubber band potential-energy descending model(RPD).

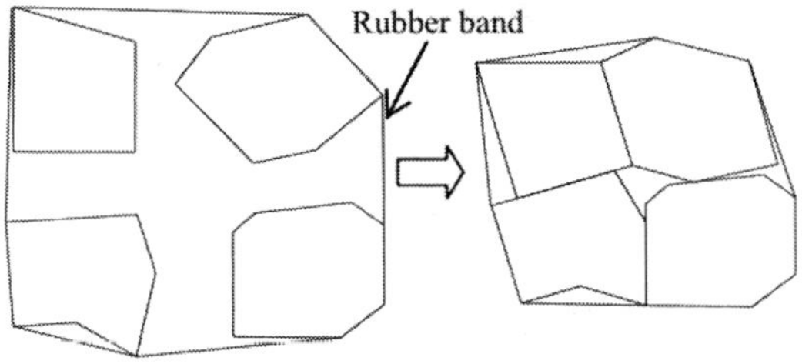

Figure 2. Rubber band enclosing model.

Some problems must be settled before constructing RPD model:

1. The construction of rubber band.
2. Force analysis and motion analysis for objects.
3. Convergence condition.

3.1 Construction of rubber band

The problem of rubber band's construction is equivalent to construct the convex hull of the vertices set of all polygons. Here we utilize Graham algorithm[8] to produce the convex hull. Graham algorithm is a classical convex hull algorithm which performs effectively when the scale of the given point set is small.

3.2 Force analysis

An object would get forces from rubber band or other objects. Force from rubber band is called elastic force denoted by $\vec{F}_{R_i}$, and force from other objects is called collision force denoted by $\vec{F}_{Obj}$.

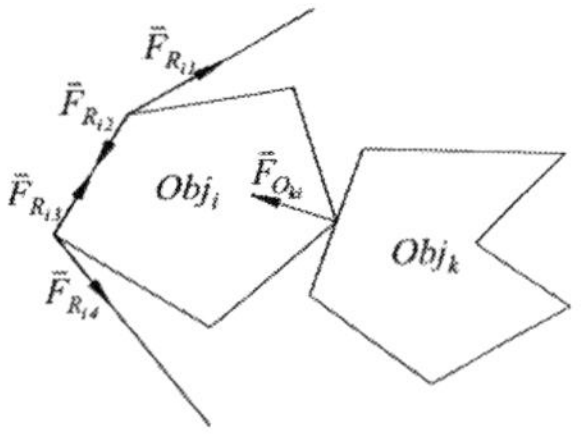

Figure 3. Force analysis.

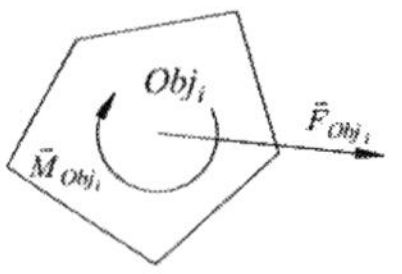

Figure 4. Resultant force and moment.

Firstly, as shown in Fig.3, calculate all elastic forces $\vec{F}_{R_{i1}}, \vec{F}_{R_{i2}}..\vec{F}_{R_{in}}$. Then utilize ray scan method[9] to check which object is under collision. Calculate all collision forces $\vec{F}_{O_{i1}}, \vec{F}_{O_{i2}}..\vec{F}_{O_{in}}$.

Secondly, calculate the resultant force with equation (3) shown as follow.

$$\vec{F}'_{Obj_i} = \sum \vec{F}_{R_{in}} + \sum \vec{F}_{O_{in}} \tag{3}$$

Finally, replace $\vec{F}'_{Obj_i}$ with a force $\vec{F}_{Obj_i}$ through the centroid and a moment $\vec{M}_{Obj_i}$ which can be calculate with the follow equation. Fig.4 shows the consequence of force analysis.

$$\vec{M}_{Obj_i} = \vec{F}_{Obj_i} \cdot d \tag{4}$$

3.3 Motion analysis

The continuous layout process is transformed into discrete time $t(t_1, t_2..t_\infty)$ for motion analysis. An assumption has been made in which the force and moment applied to objects are invariable in each time step. That is to say objects only do uniformly accelerated motion. Then let $P^{(k)}_{Obj_i}(x_i, y_i, ang_i)$ denotes present displacement vector of i-th object in k-th time step. $\vec{V}^{(k)}_{Obj_i}(vx_i, vy_i, v\omega_i)$ denotes present velocity vector. $\vec{a}^{(k)}_{Obj_i}(\alpha_i, \beta_i, \gamma_i)$ denotes present acceleration vector. According to the Newton's laws, $P^{(k)}_{Obj_i}$, $\vec{V}^{(k)}_{Obj_i}$ and $\vec{a}^{(k)}_{Obj_i}$ can be easily calculated by the following equation. Here we use area A_{Obj_i} instead of object's mass and J_{Obj_i} denotes the moment of inertia .

$$\begin{aligned} &\vec{a}^{(k)}_{Obj_i} \cdot (\alpha_i, \beta_i) = \frac{\vec{F}^{(k)}_{Obj_i}}{A_{Obj_i}} \quad \vec{a}^{(k)}_{Obj_i} \cdot \gamma_i = \frac{\vec{M}^{(k)}_{Obj_i}}{J_{Obj_i}} \\ &\vec{V}^{(k)}_{Obj_i} = \vec{V}^{(k-1)}_{Obj_i} + \vec{a}^{(k)}_{Obj_i} \cdot t^{(k)} \\ &\vec{P}^{(k)}_{Obj_i} = \vec{V}^{(k-1)}_{Obj_i} \cdot t^{(k)} + \frac{1}{2} \vec{a}^{(k)}_{Obj_i} \cdot (t^{(k)})^2 \end{aligned} \tag{5}$$

The new solution can be calculated by the following equation.

$$S^{(k)} = S^{(k-1)} + \left[\vec{P}^{(k)}_{Obj_1}, \vec{P}^{(k)}_{Obj_2} .. \vec{P}^{(k)}_{Obj_n}\right] \tag{6}$$

3.4 Convergence condition

Potential-energy of rubber band denoted by e is descending all the time until layout process get the local minimal. When the rate of change Δe reduces very close to zero, we will consider the minimal has been found. And Δe can be calculated by equation (7).

$$
\begin{aligned}
e^{(k)} &= \frac{1}{2} K \cdot (\Delta x^{(k)})^2 \\
\Delta e &= \left| e^{(k)} - e^{(k-1)} \right| \le \varepsilon
\end{aligned}
\tag{7}
$$

K denotes stiffness of rubber band and Δx denotes shape variable. ε is a very small positive number.

4 Hierarchical layout design model

Most of popular hybrid algorithms place objects following a certain sequence one by one until all objects are placed in. And the duty of intelligence algorithm is to produce more potential sequence by iteration. These algorithms are time consuming. Actually, the layout process can be divided into different stages. A better choice is to employ the most suitable strategy in corresponding stages. That is the hierarchical layout design method(HLD).

In this paper we divide layout process into three stages: initial layout stage, rubber band enclosing stage and local adjustment stage. The flow chart of HLD method has been shown in Fig.6.

4.1 Initial layout stage

In HLD, rubber band enclosing contributes a lot to layout solution. Initial layout position of each object is the key to rubber band enclosing model. Different initial layout will lead to variable solutions as shown in Fig.5. So the target in initial layout stage is to find a relatively compact solution for further layout design. A rectangle placement strategy based on exhaustive search is proposed here.

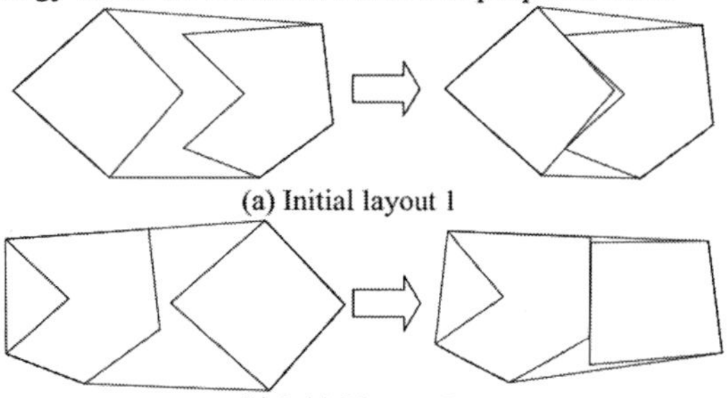

(a) Initial layout 1

(b) Initial layout 2.

Figure 5. Different initial layouts lead to different consequence.

4.1.1 Minimum rectangle bounding box

Here a minimum rectangle bounding box is utilized to replace polygons for initial layout. The following describes the basic procedure for the construction of minimum rectangle.

(1)Produce the convex hull of polygon.

(2)Rotate convex hull in a counter clockwise direction until one edge parallels to the horizontal direction.

(3)Find $x_{min}, x_{max}, y_{min}, y_{max}$ from all vertices of convex hull. Use the value $x_{max} - x_{min}$ as length and $y_{max} - y_{min}$ as width of rectangle.

(4)Record the present rotation angle and area of rectangle.

(5)Repeat the above four steps until every edge is calculated. Then choose the rectangle with minimum area as minimum rectangle bounding box.

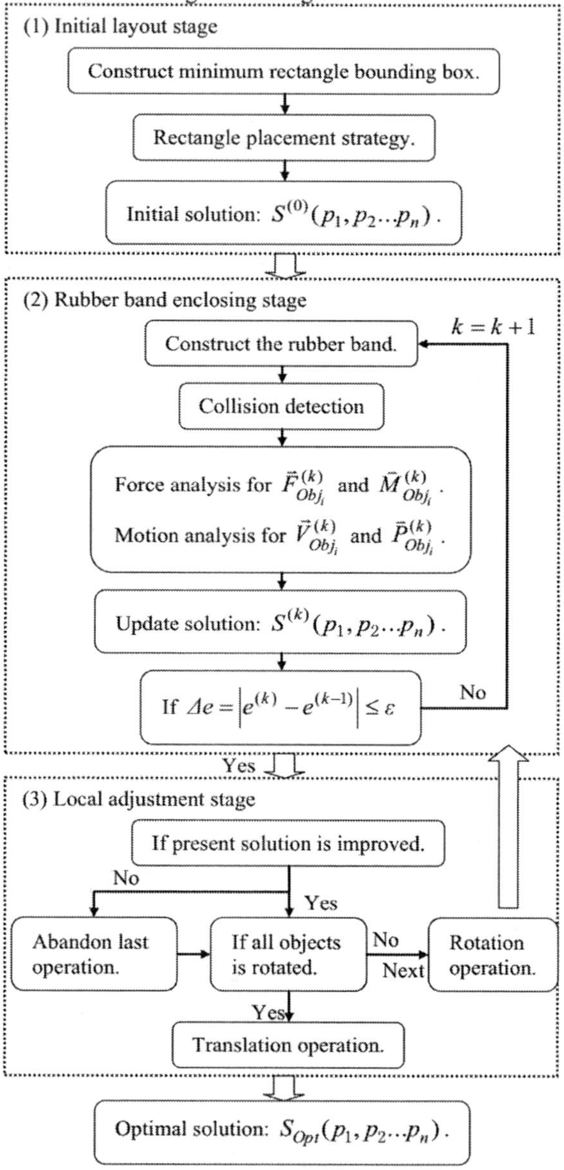

Figure 6. The flow chart of HLD method.

4.1.2 Rectangle placement strategy

Classical algorithms for rectangle packing include BL algorithm and lowest horizontal search algorithm[10]. These algorithms usually spend much computation time on their iteration. However, a relatively optimal solution

not the most is expected to be found on a reasonable time. So iteration is unnecessary. The rectangle placement strategy is described in the following.

(1)Sort all rectangle bounding boxes from large to small according to the area size.

(2)Implement lowest horizontal search for each rectangle and their 90° rotation version.

(3) Compare the utilization after one rectangle is packed in.

(4)Choose the case in which the highest utilization is got from all cases.

(5)Remove the packed rectangle from the list and return to step (2).

As shown in Fig.7, rectangle is allowed to rotate 90° and each time the case with highest utilization would be chosen for next placement operation. Obviously, the proposed strategy needn not optimize its packing sequence by time-consuming iteration.

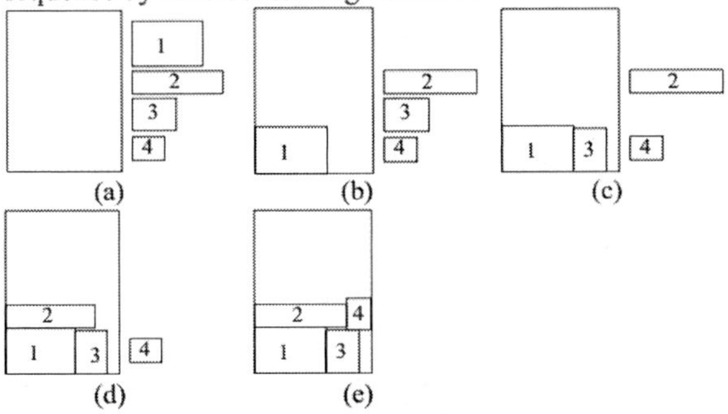

Figure 7. Diagram of rectangle placement strategy.

4.2 Rubber band enclosing stage

An initial solution $S^{(0)}(p_1,p_2..p_n)$ has been acquired after initial layout. The rubber band enclosing model will be employed here to improve the present layout. We assume that the rubber band is fixed to the bottom of the given strip so that it can drag all objects to the direction leading to a minimum length of strip. This procedure is described in the following.

(1)Set $k=0$, stiffness K and convergence precision ε.

(2)Construct the rubber band utilizing Graham algorithm and calculate the potential-energy $e^{(0)}$.

(3)Implement the ray scan method for collision detection.

(4)FOR $i=1$ TO n DO

BEGIN

Calculate the elastic force $\vec{F}^{(k)}_{R_m}$ and collision force $\vec{F}^{(k)}_{O_m}$.

Calculate the resultant force $\vec{F}^{(k)}_{Obj_i}$ and moment $\vec{M}^{(k)}_{Obj_i}$.

Calculate the velocity vector $\vec{V}^{(k)}_{Obj_i}$ and displacement vector $P^{(k)}_{Obj_i}$ at present time step $t^{(k)}$.

END

(5)Update the present solution $S^{(k)}(p_1,p_2..p_n)$ with $\left[P^{(k)}_{Obj_1},P^{(k)}_{Obj_2}..P^{(k)}_{Obj_n}\right]$. Then construct the rubber band and calculate the potential-energy $e^{(k)}$.

(6)if $\Delta e=\left|e^{(k)}-e^{(k-1)}\right|\le\varepsilon$, let $k=k+1$ and return to step(3). Otherwise output the optimal solution.

4.3 Local adjustment stage

Through the RPD operation, the solution is still relatively optimal and some operations are essential to improve it. Many factors can become obstacles to RPD's operation. The most common reason is that several objects get obstructed preventing themselves from moving close to each other further more. As a result, RPD would terminate in advance with an undesirable solution.

Here we employ rotation and translation strategy to adjust the RPD process so as to make rubber band can surround all objects more compactly.

4.3.1 Compactness of different districts

As shown in Fig.8, the rectangular region used of the strip is divided into four districts D_1,D_2,D_3,D_4 just like Cartesian coordinate is built at the centroid of this region. Assume that use object's area to denote its mass. So if the utilization reaches to 100%, the centroid and the center of mass of all objects are on the same position. Thus, through checking the relative position of the two points, the district with low compactness can be easily distinguished.

Let point (x_m,y_m) denotes center of mass of all objects, point (x_c,y_c) denotes the centroid of the rectangle region, point (x_i,y_i) denotes center of mass of Obj_i. So the relative position vector can be calculated according to the following equation.

$$(x_r,y_r)=(x_m,y_m)-(x_c,y_c) \tag{8}$$

Point (x_m,y_m) can be calculated by equation (9).

$$(x_m,y_m)=\left(\sum\frac{Area(Obj_i)}{\sum Area(Obj_n)}\cdot x_i,\sum\frac{Area(Obj_i)}{\sum Area(Obj_n)}\cdot y_i\right) \tag{9}$$

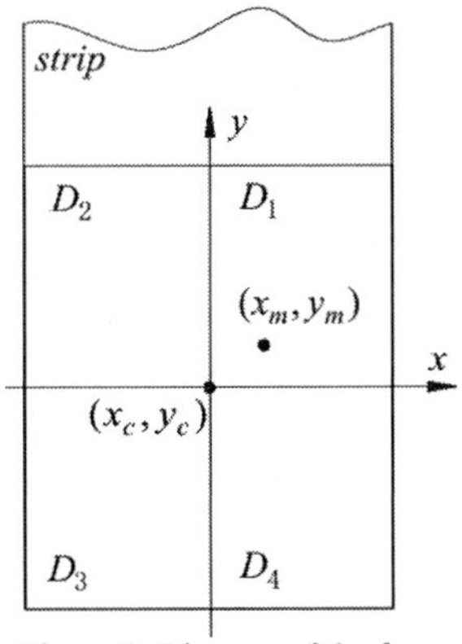

Figure 8. Diagram of the four districts.

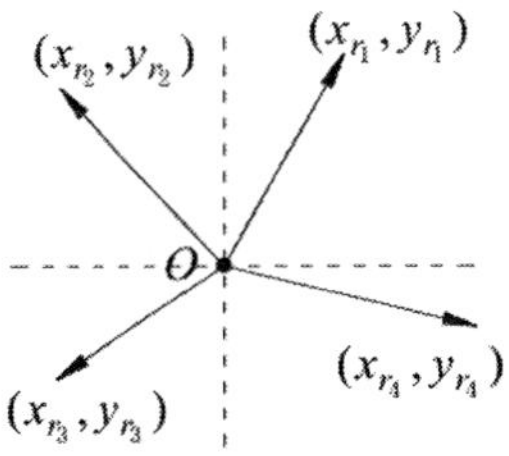

Figure 9. Relative position vector.

If $(x_r, y_r) \in D_1$ shown in Fig.9, it reveals that its opposite region D_3 owns a low compactness. That means obstruction would most possibly occur in this district. And if $(x_r, y_r) \in D_2$, D_4 owns a low compactness. Similarly, it also goes for both cases $(x_r, y_r) \in D_3$ and $(x_r, y_r) \in D_4$.

4.3.2 Rotation and translation strategy

The target of rotation and translation strategy employed in this stage is to eliminate the influence of object's obstruction. Through rotation and translation operations, make the modulus of relative position vector reduce gradually to zero.

Firstly, select out all objects which is located in the district got by calculating relative position vector. Rotate them on a certain angle one by one. Then execute the rubber band enclosing operation after one object is rotated. Check whether the new solution owns a higher utilization than before. If so, accept the new solution and calculate the relative position vector again. Otherwise, give up the rotation operation to the present object and rotate next one. If all rotation operations applied to objects made no improvement, try to translate little objects artificially from other districts to fill the space non-utilized in this district. Translation operation must obey the basic principle that each operation would help to make the relative position vector go to (0,0).

5 Experiments

HLD method was implemented in C++ on a PC with an i3 dual-core 2.53 GHz CPU and 2 GB of RAM. And a few famous benchmark instances from the ESICUP website were used to test the performance of our layout method (http://www.apdio.pt/esicup). These instances were listed in table 1. The computational results were compared with the GLSHA algorithm and the SAHA algorithm[11].

In table 1, the first four columns summaries the basic information of these instances. But it's worth noting that all objects is allowed to rotate in any angle which is different from the original instances. The last three columns present the computational results of the proposed method and other two algorithms.

Comparing the computational results of 9 benchmark instances with other two algorithms, the proposed method obtained a better result than GLSHA algorithm for three instances out of 9 instances in the utilization. And each result was very close to the one come from SAHA algorithm. The appendix presents the optimal placements obtained by HLD method for these instances.

6 Conclusions

In this paper, a hierarchical layout design method was proposed. This HLD method is used for solving the strip packing problems. The layout process of HLD method is based on rubber band potential-energy descending. It includes three stages and corresponding strategies are employed to improve the optimal solution gradually. 9 benchmark instances were used for testing the performance of the proposed method. And the results show that the HLD method is quite promising with high utilization compared with other algorithms.

Acknowledgments

We sincerely acknowledge the support of National Nature Science Foundation of China (NO. 51265002).

References

1. R.C. Art. *IBM Cambridge Scientific Centre* (1966).
2. G. Wäsche, H. Haußner, H. Schumann. EUR J OPER RES, **183**, 1109–1130 (2007).
3. J.E. Beasley. Operations Research, **33**, 49-64 (1985).
4. J.H. Holland. De Luca, *Control & Artificial Intelligence University of Michigan* (1975).
5. K. James, R. Eberhart. IEEE, **4**, 1942-1948 (1995).
6. C. Wee Liew. IEEE, **12**, 67-73 (1997).
7. S. Jakobs. EJOR, **88**, 165-181 (1996).
8. R.L. Graham. Inf. Proc. Lett, **72**, 132-133 (1972).
9. L. Xiangsha, L. Fengying, M. Junyan, L. Xiaoping. Machinery Design & Manufacture. 185-188 (2015).
10. W. Zhuting, L. Lin, C. Hao, L. Xinbao. J ENG DESIGN, **16**, 98-102 (2009).
11. A.M. Gomes, J.F. Oliveira. EJOR, **171**, 811-829 (2006).

Table 1. Benchmark instances and computational results.

Data sets	number of polygon types	Total number of polygons	Width of strip	GLSHA	SAHA	HLD
Albano	8	24	4900	0.8641	0.8742	0.8584
Blaz1	7	28	15	0.8182	0.8359	0.7513
Dagli	10	30	60	0.8549	0.8714	0.86.71
Dighe1	16	16	100	0.8267	1	0.8463
Dighe2	10	10	100	1	1	0.8248
Fu	12	12	38	0.8757	0.9095	0.8731
Jakobs1	25	25	40	0.8166	0.7888	0.7780
Jakobs2	25	25	70	0.7423	0.7728	0.7652
Mao	9	20	2550	0.8101	0.7999	0.7970

MATEC Web of Conferences 44, 02047 (2016)
DOI: 10.1051/matecconf/20164402047

The effects of urbanization on the environment pollution in China (2002-2012)

Mi Zhou [1], Xiao Lin Zhao [1] and Li Huang [2,a]

[1] College of Economics; Shenyang University, Shenyang China
[2] Information Center of Liaoning Province Commission of Rural Economy

Abstract. This paper provides an analytical framework to evaluate whether urbanization could lead to environment pollution or not. This study uses STIRPAT model and recently developed panel regression techniques that allow for heterogeneous slope coefficients and cross-section dependence to model the impact that urbanization has on SO_2 emissions for a panel of 28 provinces in China from 2002 to 2012. The estimated contemporaneous coefficients on the urbanization variables are reverse U-shape. The corresponding policy suggestion is that the government should accelerate the urbanization to transfer the economy from a manufacturing based economy to a service based economy.

1 Introduction

Rapid urbanization in China is having increasing impact on the environment of the growing urban population. More than 450 million of China's 1.3 billion population are now living in urban area where over 70 percent of China's gross domestic product(GDP) are generated, and where the environmental impacts of concentrated human activities are felt the most. Air pollution is one of the most visible environment problems in China's urban life. Especially, the ambient concentrations of sulfate, a fine particulate most damaging to human health, can lead to unsustainable development in China. If urbanization has a significant impact on sulfurs emission(SO_2) then this will have implications for sustainable development and urbanization policies.

If urbanization is found to have a positive and statistically significant impact on SO_2 emissions then this can affect forecasting models and urbanization policy. Forecasting models of SO_2 emissions that fail to take into account the impact of urbanization on SO_2 emissions will under forecast sulfur dioxide emissions. Energy and environmental policies that omit the impact of urbanization on SO_2 emissions will likely lead to inaccurate outcomes making sustainable development objectives. If urbanization is found to have a negative and statistically significant impact on SO_2 emissions then this will make sustainable development objectives easier to achieve. And if urbanization is found to have positive and statistically significant impact on SO_2 emissions and then have negative and statistically significant impact on SO_2 emissions, then we will make urbanization develop faster to span the period of negative influence stage.

This paper makes several important contributions to the literature. Firstly, the relationship between urbanization and SO_2 emissions has been studied by a number of authors, but most of this research uses a static model applied to a panel data set. A panel data set is believed to be better than cross-sectional data or time series data by including both time and cross-section dimension. However, static models cannot capture dynamic relationships. This paper uses a static and dynamic framework to model the impact of urbanization on SO_2 emissions in order to compare the results obtained by the two different models. Secondly, previous studies have mostly assumed that the impact of SO_2 emissions is homogeneous across time-series. This is a very strong assumption to make and one that is unlikely to hold across a large grouping of times. In this paper panel regression models are estimated using recent developed techniques that allow for panel unit root test. If panel data exhibits time-series dependence, estimating models with homogeneous slope coefficients may yield estimated coefficients that are biased(Andrew, 2005). In order to solve these problems, this paper use unit root tests and panel cointegration analysis.

2 A brief review of literature

According to Poumanyvong and Kaneko (2010), the existing literature points to three theories (ecological modernization, urban environmental transition and compact city theories) that are useful for explaining how urbanization can impact the natural environment.

The theory of ecological modernization details how urbanization is a process of social transformation that is an important indicator of modernization. As societies move from low to middle stages of development, environmental problems may increase because in these stages of development, economic growth takes priority

[a] Corresponding author:84123430@qq.com

Article available at http://www.matec-conferences.org or http://dx.doi.org/10.1051/matecconf/20164402047

over environmental sustainability. As societies continue to evolve to higher stages of development, environmental damages become more important and societies seek ways to make their societies more environmentally sustainable. The damaging impact of economic growth on the environment may be reduced by technological innovation, urbanization, and a shift from a manufacturing based economy to a service based economy (Crenshaw and Jenkins, 1996; Gouldson and Murphy, 1997; Mol and Spaargaren, 2000).The compact city theory believes that higher urban density can enhance the use of public infrastructure and lead to lower environmental damages(Buron,2000; Capello and Camagni,2000).

3 Data and Model

3.1 model

Following other authors, a Stochastic Impacts by Regression on Population, Affluence and Technology (STIRPAT)model is used to investigate the relationship between urbanization and SO2 emissions (eg. Liddle and Lung, 2010; Martinez-Zarzoso and Maruotti, 2011; Poumanyvong and Kaneko, 2010). The STIRPATmodel is based on the Influence, Population, Affluence, and Technology (IPAT) model developed by Ehrlich and Holdren (1971). The IPAT model relates environmental impact to population, affluence (consumption per capita), and technology.

$$I = P \times A \times T \qquad (1)$$

The IPAT model has been criticized as 1) being primarily a mathematical equation or an accounting identity which is not suitable for hypothesis testing, and 2) assuming a rigid proportionality between the variables. In response, Dietz and Rosa (1997) proposed a stochastic version of IPAT.

$$I_{it} = a_{it} P_{it}^{b} A_{it}^{c} T_{it}^{d} e_{it} \qquad (2)$$

In Eq.(2), counties are denoted by the subscript i (i=1,2...,N) and the subscript t (t=1,2,...,T) denotes the time period. Country specific effects are included through ai and eit represents the random error term. And we use this model to analysis the urbanization on the environment of each provinces in China. Taking natural logarithms of Eq.(2) provides a convenient linear specification for panel estimation.

$$\ln(I_{it}) = b\ln(P_{it}) + c\ln(A_{it}) + d\ln(T_{it}) + v_i + \varepsilon_{it} \qquad (3)$$

Country specify effects are included through v_i and ε_{it} represents the random error term. The STIRPAT model can easily accommodate additional explanatory variables and in this paper, model(3) is augmented with urbanization(U). The augmented model is

$$\ln(I_{it}) = b\ln(P_{it}) + c\ln(A_{it}) + d\ln(T_{it}) + f\ln(U_{it}) + v_i + \varepsilon_{it}$$
(4)

When it comes to estimating Eq.(4), a distinction can be made between models with homogeneous slope coefficients and models with heterogeneous slope coefficients. If the assumption of homogeneous slope coefficients is made then these models can be estimated using standard panel regression techniques like pooled OLS (POLS) and various fixed effects (FE), random effects (RE), or GMM specifications. Models with heterogeneous slope coefficients can be estimated using mean group (MG) estimators (eg. Pesaran and Smith, 1995; Pesaran, 1997) or variants onmean group estimators. Estimating panel models with heterogeneous slope coefficients is currently an active area of econometrics (eg. Eberhardt et. al., 2013).

3.2 Data and resources

The empirical analysis is based on a panel of 29 provinces in China over the period of 2002-2012 because China government had implemented the policy of urbanization reforming from 2002. Due to a lack of data, Tibet is not included and Chongqing is combined to Sichuan. These samples are restricted to those provinces for which the data on the urbanization level denoted as the proportion of the Chinese population living in urban areas(yit), and the data was abstracted from China Statistical Yearbook 2003-2013(the National Statistics Bureau of China, 2003-2013). The dependent variable environment pollution index is measured by SO2 emission value(xit), which was also from various issues of China Statistics Yearbook 2003-2013(the National Statistics Bureau of China, 2003-2013). Table 1 presents the definition of the variables and the corresponding summary statistics.

Table 1. variable definitions and descriptive statistics.

variable	definition	method	mean	min	max
u	ration of citizen to total population	$y=urban_{it}/population_{it}$	0.48	0.24	0.89
s	the amount of so2 emission	s=Sulphur Dioxideit	78.13	2.2	200.3
s^2	the square of s	s^2=s^2	8575.48	4.84	40120.09
ls	logarithmic form of s	ls=s^2	4.06	0.79	5.3
Ds	the difference of s	Ds=st-st-1	4.06	0.79	5.3

3.3 Unit root tests

The possible non-stationary property of the data is investigated by applying Bai and Carrion-i-Silvestre(2009) allowing for the structural breaks and cross-sectional dependence. The tests of belong to the so-called "second-generation" of panel unit root tests and have the important advantage to overcome the main limitation of previous tests. Although the tests show that we can reject the null hypothesis that there is a unit root, we can't still confirm that every variable does not have a unit root. Table2 shows that we can find a unit root in lag(3) for SO2, but we can find a unit root for u. So we must use the lag of u to solve the non-stationary problem.

Table 2. tests of unit root.

	coefficient	t-value	t-star	P
so2				
lag(2)	-0.6531	-15.57	-11.7192	0.0000
lag(3)	-0.2389	-6.74	0.0560	0.5223
u				
lag(2)	-0.2602	-6.27	-1.5222	0.0640
lag(3)	-0.1753	-4.16	0.2029	0.5804

4 Results

Table 3 presents empirical results for static models with heterogeneous slope coefficients. The estimated coefficient on the urbanization variable is between 0.617 and statistically significant at the 5%. The column(3) in table3 shows that the relationship between urbanization and environment pollution is reverse U shape. That means the environment can damage in the process of urbanization firstly, but as population density in city increase and the public infrastructure can facilitate migrant worker. Hence, The damaging impact of economic growth on the environment reduces by urbanization, and a shift from a manufacturing based economy to a service based economy. The column(4) and column(5) in table3 report the results of the panel cointegration tests by Westerlund and Edgerton(2008), and we can get the same conclusions as original panel regression.

Heterogeneous parameter estimates from the dynamic panel model are reported in Table 4. Looking first at the contemporaneous variables, the estimated coefficient on the affluence variable is positive and statistically significant at the 1% level. The values is -0.59 indicating a negative effect. And we can also get reverse U shape adding lagged dependent variable.

Table3. the results of panel data regression(static).

	(1)	(2)	(3)	(4)	(5)
	m1	m2	m3	m4	m5
VARIABLES	so2	lso2	lso2	lso2	lso2
u	10.14	0.617**	5.713***		
	(15.16)	(0.257)	(0.928)		
u2			-5.435***		
			(0.957)		
D.u				1.566	2.843**
				(0.972)	(1.297)
D2.u					-1.563*
					(0.905)
Constant	73.26***	3.763***	2.687***	4.065***	4.061***
	(11.54)	(0.210)	(0.280)	(0.162)	(0.162)
Observations	319	319	319	290	261
Number of n	29	29	29	29	29

Table4. the results of panel data regression(dynamic).

	(1)	(2)	(3)	(4)	(5)
	m1	m2	m3	m4	m5
VARIABLES	so2	lso2	lso2	lso2	lso2
u	-12.29***	-0.590***	-0.680***	2.278***	
	(3.457)	(0.196)	(0.197)	(0.777)	
D.u			2.183***		2.835***
			(0.817)		(1.090)
L.so2	0.970***	0.00916***	0.00924***	0.00856***	0.00986***
	(0.0100)	(0.000681)	(0.000674)	(0.000680)	(0.000757)
u2				-2.987***	
				(0.786)	
D2.u					-1.214
					(0.761)
Constant	9.248***	3.651***	3.662***	3.073***	3.271***
	(2.091)	(0.139)	(0.136)	(0.206)	(0.107)
Observations	290	290	290	290	261
Number of n	29	29	29	29	29

5 Concluding

This paper uses a STIRPAT model to explore the impact that urbanization has on sulfur dioxide emissions in China. It is expected that urbanization will continue rising in China and understanding how urbanization affects SO2 emissions is an important and timely topic to study. A better understanding of how urbanization affects SO2 emissions is necessary from a sustainable development perspective. For static specifications estimated and dynamic specifications estimated, we both get the same conclusion that the relationship between urbanization and SO2 emissions is reverse U-shape. The corresponding policy suggestion is that the government should accelerate the urbanization to transfer the economy from a manufacturing based economy to a service based economy.

Acknowledgements

This work was supported by the National Science Foundation of China(NO.71203146; NO. 71573179), the program for excellent talents in Liaoning province (NO.WJQ2014016); and agriculture youth science and technology innovation talent training plan in Liaoning province(NO.2014055).

References

1. Andrews, D.W.K., Cross-section regression with common shocks. Econometrica **73**, 1551–1585 (2005)
2. Burton, E., The compact city: just or just compact? A preliminary analysis. Urban Stud. **37**, 1969–2001 (2000)
3. Pesaran, M.H., Tosetti, E., Large panels with common factors and spatial correlations. J. Econ. **161**, 182–202 (2011)
4. Qiang Wang, Effects of urbanization on energy consumption in China, Energy Policy **65**, 332–339 (2014)

MATEC Web of Conferences **44**, 02048 (2016)
DOI: 10.1051/matecconf/20164402048

Consistently Semicontinuous Dcpo

Di Wang, Tao Lu
School of Mathematical Science, Huaibei Normal University, Huaibei 235000, Anhui,China

Abstract: In this paper, the concept of consistently semicontinuous dcpo is given,then some properties of them are discussed, especially, equivalent characterizations between consistently semicontinuous dcpo and the smallest consistently semi-prime set is given. Finally the concept of consistently semicontinuous mapping is given, and the connection between consistently dcpo and consistently semicontinuous dcpo on the base of consistently semicontinuous mapping is given.

Key words: Consistently Semi-prime set; Consistently Semicontinuous Dcpo; Consistently Semicontinuous mapping

0 Instruction

Because of the double background of computer science and mathematics in the continuous lattices theory [1], Since it has been widely concerned, one of the important aspect is to promote continuous lattices theory to more general order structure.In the literature [2], a new two - element relation "$\Leftarrow$"and a semi - continuous lattices are defined on a complete lattice, and some properties of continuous lattices are extended to the semi-continuous lattices.At present, there are many reports on the research of semi-continuous lattices. The related properties of semi-continuous lattices are discussed in the literature [3],[4],[5]and [6].Since the semi-continuous lattice is defined in the complete lattice, the semi- continuous study has some limitations. In order to get rid of the limitations, such as literature[7] dealing with continuous posets as the directed completion of general order structure of semi-continuous and semi-continuous lattices.in the literature [8], the lattice of semi-prime ideal is extended to partially ordered sets of semi-prime concept and in dcpo definition semi-continuity and give semi- continuous dcpo characterizations and properties, at the same time, many properties of semi-continuous lattices is extended to semi-continuous lattices. In this paper,the concept of consistently semicontinuous dcpo is given,then some properties and equivalent characterizations of them are discussed.

1 Preparatory knowledge

Definition 1 [7] Let L be a poset, $\emptyset \neq D \subseteq L$ .We say that D is a consistently directed set in a poset L ,if D is directed and for some $x \in L$ with $D \subseteq \downarrow x$.

Definition 2 [7] Let L be a poset, We say that P is a consistent ideal, if P is a consistently directed lower set in a poset L .

Definition 3 [9] Let L be a poset, $x \in L$, We write $X\downarrow = \{x \in P \mid x \leq y, \forall y \in S\}$, we say that is a lower bound set , $X\uparrow = \{x \in P \mid y \leq x, \forall y \in S\}$, we say that is a upper bound set.

Definition 4 [9] Let L be a poset, I is a ideal in a poset L ,we say that I is a prime ideal if $\forall x, y \in L, \exists a \in \{x, y\}\downarrow\uparrow \cap I$ with $x \in I$ or $y \in I$.

Definition 5 [7] Let L be a poset, we say that L is a consistently dcpo if every consistently directed set has the sup of in a poset L .

Definition 6 [9] Let L be a consistently dcpo, $I \subseteq L$ and I is a consistently ideal, we say that I is a **consistently** prime ideal if I is prime. We write it $CRd(L)$.

2. Consistently Semicontinuous Dcpo

Definition 7 Let L be a poset, $S \subseteq L$,we say that S is a consistently semi-prime set if consistently prime ideals $\{P_i\}_{i\in I}$ with $S = \bigcap_{i\in I} P_i$.

Remark A consistently prime ideal must be a consistently semi-prime set, not the other way. It is shown in the example.

Example Let $L = \{x_1, x_2, x_3 ...\} \cup \{a, b\}$, we define relationship "$\leq$" with $\forall i \leq j, x_i \leq x_j, a, b \leq x_i$, $\forall i \in Z^+, \bigcap\{\downarrow x_i\} = \{a, b\}$ is a consistently semi-prime set, but $\bigcap\{\downarrow x_i\} = \{a, b\}$ is not directed, so is not a consistently prime ideal.

---

[a] Corresponding author: author@e-mail.org

Definition 8 Let L be a poset, $x, y \in L$, for every consistently semi-prime set S in a poset L, if it has $\vee S$ and $y \le \vee S$ with $x \in S$, we say that $x \Leftarrow_c y$. We write it

$\Downarrow_c x = \{y \in L \mid y \Leftarrow_c x\}, \Uparrow_c x = \{y \in L \mid x \Leftarrow_c y\}$.

Definition 9 Let L a consistently dcpo. We say that L is a consistently semi-continuous dcpo if $\forall x \in L$, we have $x \in (\Downarrow_c x)\uparrow\downarrow$.

Theorem 1 Let L be a consistently dcpo, then $\Downarrow_c x = \cap\{S\} = \cap\{P\}$, there S is a consistently semi-prime set always implies the existence of $\vee S$ and $x \le \vee S$, P is a consistently prime ideal and $x \le \vee P$.

Proof It is immediate from the definition 7, definition 8 and the remark.

Corollary 1 Let L a consistently dcpo, $x, y \in L$ then $x \Leftarrow_c y$ iff for every $I \in CRd(L)$, $y \le \vee I$ always implies $x \in I$.

Lemma 1 Let A, B be subsets of a poset P. If $A \subseteq B$, we have $A\uparrow\downarrow \subseteq B\uparrow\downarrow$ and $A\downarrow\uparrow \subseteq B\downarrow\uparrow$.

Proof If $A \subseteq B$, then $B\uparrow \subseteq A\uparrow$, $B\downarrow \subseteq A\downarrow$, therefore, $A\uparrow\downarrow \subseteq B\uparrow\downarrow$ and $A\downarrow\uparrow \subseteq B\downarrow\uparrow$.

Theorem 2 Let L be a consistently dcpo, if for every $x \in L$ has consistently semi-prime set $P \subseteq \Downarrow_c x$ and $x \in P\uparrow\downarrow$, we have L is a consistently semi-continuous dcpo.

Proof For every $x \in L$, it has a consistently semi-prime set $P \subseteq \Downarrow_c x$ by conditional knowledge and $x \in P\uparrow\downarrow$. We have $P\uparrow\downarrow \subseteq (\Downarrow_c x)\uparrow\downarrow$ by lemma 1, therefore we have L is a consistently semi-continuous dcpo by definition 9.

Theorem 3 Let L be a consistently dcpo. The following are equivalent:

(1) L is a consistently semi-continuous dcpo;

(2) For every $x \in L$, $\Downarrow_c x$ is to

(3) For every $x \in L$, there exists the smallest consistently semi-prime set $S \subseteq \Downarrow_c x$ such that $x \in S\uparrow\downarrow$.

Proof $(1) \Rightarrow (2)$ For every $x \in L$, $\Downarrow_c x$ is a consistently semi-prime set by theorem 1. Since L is a consistently semi-continuous dcpo, then for every $x \in L$, we have $x \in (\Downarrow_c x)\uparrow\downarrow$. Conversely, for every $x \in L$, when S is a consistently semi-prime set and $x \in S\uparrow\downarrow$. Next, we proof that $\Downarrow_c x \subseteq S$. Let $y \in \Downarrow_c x$, since S is a consistently semi-prime set, we have a family of consistently prime ideal $\{P_i\}_{i \in I}$ with $S = \cap_{i \in I} P_i$. For every $i \in I$, we have $x \in S\uparrow\downarrow \subseteq (P_i)\uparrow\downarrow = \downarrow(\vee P_i)$ by lemma 1. Therefore $x \le \vee P_i$, and we have $y \in P_i$ following from $y \in \Downarrow_c x$. Finally we have $y \in \cap_{i \in I} P_i = S$ by any sex $i \in I$. Hence $\Downarrow_c x \subseteq S$. This (2) follows.

$(2) \Rightarrow (3)$ By Condition (2), we have the smallest consistently semi-prime set $S = \Downarrow_c x$ such that for every $x \in L$ with $x \in S\uparrow\downarrow$.

$(3) \Rightarrow (1)$ Immediate from the theorem 2.

3 Consistently Semicontinuous mapping

Definition 10 Let L, M be consistently dcpo. We we say that $f : L \to M$ is consistently prime preserving if f is order preserving and every $P \in CRd(L)$ with $\downarrow f(P) \in CRd(L)$.

Definition 11 Let L, M be consistently dcpo. We say that $f : L \to M$ is the preservation of sups about consistently ideal if f is order preserving and every $P \in CRd(L)$ with $f(\vee P) \in \vee f(P)$.

Definition 12 Let L, M be consistently dcpo. We say that $f : L \to M$ is a consistently semicontinuous mapping if for every $P \in CRd(L)$ always implies that $f(\vee P) \in \vee f(P)$ and $\downarrow f(P) \in CRd(M)$.

Theorem 4 Let L, M be consistently dcpo, a pair (g,d) is a *Galois connection* from L to M. If g is a consistently semicontinuous mapping, then d preservate relationship "$\Leftarrow_c$". In other words, for every $x,y\in M$, $x\Leftarrow_c y$ implies that $d(x)\Leftarrow_c d(y)$。

Proof Let $x,y\in M$, $x\Leftarrow_c y$, $I\in CRd(L)$ meets $d(y)\le\vee I$, we can know that $y\le g(\vee I)$ following from a pair (g,d) is a *Galois connection* from L to M. Since g is a consistently semicontinuous mapping, we have $y\le g(\vee I)=\vee g(I)=\vee\downarrow g(I)$, then $x\in\downarrow g(L)$. Therefore, there exists $z\in I$ with $x\le g(z)$, and then $d(x)\le dg(z)\le z$. Finally $d(x)\in I$ and $d(x)\Leftarrow_c d(y)$.

Theorem 5 Let L be a consistently dcpo, M is a consistently semi-continuous dcpo, a pair (g,d) is a *Galois connection* from L to M and for every $x\in M$, $\Downarrow_c x$ is a consistent ideal. If g is a consistently semicontinuous mapping even a injection, we have that L is a consistently semi-continuous dcpo.

Proof Since a pair (g,d) is a *Galois connection* from L to M, g is a injection, then d is a surjection; we can have that for every $x\in L$, there exists $y\in M$ with $d(y)=x$. Since M is a consistently semi-continuous dcpo, and for every $x\in M$, $\Downarrow_c x$ is a consistent ideal, and then $y\le\vee\Downarrow_c y$. Thus d is a lower adjoint and preserving of sups, we can see that $x=d(y)\le d(\vee\Downarrow_c y)=\vee d(\Downarrow_c y)$, then we have $x\in\downarrow\vee d(\Downarrow_c y)$. For every $z\in M$, if $z\in\Downarrow_c y$ then $z\Leftarrow_c y$. We can know that $d(z)\Leftarrow_c d(y)$ by theorem 4, that is to say $d(z)\in\Downarrow_c d(y)$, therefore, $d(\Downarrow_c y)\subseteq\Downarrow_c d(y)$, even more we have $x\in\downarrow\vee d(\Downarrow_c y)\subseteq(\Downarrow_c d(y))\uparrow\downarrow=(\Downarrow_c x)\uparrow\downarrow$. Finally, for every $x\in L$, we have $x\in(\Downarrow_c x)\uparrow\downarrow$ and so L is a consistently semi-continuous dcpo.

References

[1] GIERZ G, HOFMANN K H, KEIMEL K, et al.Continuous lattices and domain [M]. Cambridge: Cambridge University Press, 2003:1-263.

[2] ZHAO Dong-sheng Semibasis and Semibasis on Semicontinuous Lattices [J], Algebra Univers,(37)4 (1997), 458-476.

[3] BI Han-yu, XU Xiao-quan. Semi-Scott topogy and Semi-Lawson topology on Semicontinuous Lattices [J], Fuzzy Systems and Mathematics,22(2) (2008),654-658.

[4] WU Xiu-hua, LI Qing-guo. Characterizations and Function of Semicontinuous Lattices [J], JOURNAL OF MATHEMATICAL RESEARCH AND EXPOSITION, 27(3) (2007), 75-81

[5]LI Gao-lin,XU Luo-shan, CHEN Yu. Semibasis and Semibasis on Semicontinuous Lattices[J],Fuzzy Systems and Mathematics, 24(1)(2010), 51-55

[6] JIANG Guang-hao ,A Note on Semicontinuous Lattices[J],Fuzzy Systems and Mathematics, 22(1)(2008), 15-17.

[7] XU Luo-shan CONSISTENTLY CONTINUOUS POSETS AND THEIRDIRECTED COMPLETIONS [J], JOURNAL OF YANGZHOU UNIVERSITY3(1)(2000), 1-6,10

[8]LIU Yu-lian,LI Gao-lin,XU Luo-shan Semicontinuous dcpos[J] ,Fuzzy Systems and Mathematics, 5(2) (2012), 1-5

[9]GUO Zhi-lian,ZHAO Bin Consistently Semicontinuous Domaiins[J], Fuzzy Systems and Mathematics,2(1)(2012), 131-136

MATEC Web of Conferences 44, 02049 (2016)
DOI: 10.1051/matecconf/20164402049

Gray Comprehensive Evaluation Method on Coal Seam Water Injection in Order of Difficulty

Xiao Li Liu[1a,2], Zhi Ye Zhang[2,3], Meng Qian Li[2]

[1]College of Resources & Safety Engineering, China University of Mining & Thchnology, Beijing, China

[2]College of Mining Engineering, North China University of Science and Technology, China

[3]Safety department, Tangshan Stainless Stell CO.,LTD, Hebei, China

Abstract: In order to evaluate the coal mine water injection accurately, the gray comprehensive evaluation is applied in this paper, the depth of coal seam, the development degree of coal seam crack, porosity, gas pressure in coal seam, wetting edge of coal, firmness coefficient of coal are chosen as the main index to evaluate the method of water injection into coal mine. The results show that the gray comprehensive evaluation model has a relatively high reliability and accuracy, which can be used to predict the difficulty degree of water injection.

Key words: coal seam water injection, gray comprehensive evaluation, influence factors, evaluation method

0 Introduction

Coal seam water injection method, which is widely used in coal mine production, is applied to prevention of rock burst, coal dust, coal and gas outburst. The effect of water injection in some places is good, while in other places is less effective, even is hard to be injected for some coal seams, so it is important to scientifically evaluate whether the coal seam can be injected into or the difficulty degree of water injection, which provides important references for the way and parameters of water injection.

There have been considerable studies about prediction of coal seam water injection in recent years, for example, the back-propagation artificial neural network method, the fisher discrimination method, which have gotten some achievements and have become hot spot in predicting coal seam water injection in order of difficulty, however these methods also have some shortcomings.

On the basis of expert judgment, gray comprehensive evaluation method is guided by gray correlation analysis theory. In order to predict the difficulty degree of water injection into coal seam accurately, gray comprehensive evaluation model is applied in the paper on the basis of gray system theory. Provided with 8 groups of related data instances of coal seam to predict, the results can be used as references for water injection parameters.

1. Evaluation index of difficulty degree of water injection into coal seam

The difficulty degree of water injection into coal seam

[a] Corresponding author: liuxiaoli996@163.com

refers to the ability of coal adsorbing water: whether the water is easy to get into the porosity and cracks structure of coal, and in some cases which may contain whether the water is easy to run off from some cracks. In the course of water injection, if the water is hard to get into the pores and cracks structure of coal, or is easy to run off from the cracks, the effect of water injection will be influenced, even no effect, so the index of difficulty degree of water injection into coal seam is crucial to evaluate water injection.

With reference to the existing research results at home and abroad, the index′s accessible and universality in location prediction, the actual situation of typical mine at home and abroad where water injection is adopted in coal seams, the main index in this paper contains the buried depth, the development degree of coal seam crack, porosity, gas pressure in coal seam, wetting edge of coal, firmness coefficient of coal.

(1) The buried depth

The compression levels of pores and cracks are related to the formation pressure which is influenced by the buried depth. The water permeability coefficient decreased as the cracks are compressed and the pore volume decreased while the buried depth increases.

(2) The development degree of coal seam crack

The development degree of coal seam crack is an important factor affecting the coal seam water injection. In general, water is easy to be injected in high permeability coal seam.

(3) The porosity

The porosity has a direct effect on water injection. Whether the water is easy to be injected and the wetting effect are closely concerned with the nature water filling degree of coal seam and water permeability of crack which has a certain function with porosity.

(4) The gas pressure in coal seam

The gas pressure in coal seam is resistance to water injection, the effective pressure of water injection is that the water injection pressure minus the gas pressure. So in the high pressure coal seam, in order to get the same water injection volume, the water injection pressure should be improved, which increases the difficulty of water injection.

(5) The wetting edge of coal

The smaller the wetting edge of coal is, the more the capillary force is, which enhances the water injection and causes the water easily be injected.

(6) The firmness coefficient of coal

The firmness coefficient of coal comprehensively reflects the breakage degree of coal under a variety of ways. Practices show that if other conditions are similar, the less the firmness coefficient is, the easily the water is injected.

2 Gray comprehensive evaluation method on coal seam water injection method in order of difficulty

2.1 Gray system evaluation model

The basic idea of gray system evaluation is: confirming the correlation degree between comparative sequence and reference sequence according to the geometric similarity degree of family of curves composed of comparative sequence and family of curves composed by reference sequence. The more similarity of geometric between the curves composed by comparative sequence and the curves composed by reference sequence is the bigger the correlation degree is. For gray system evaluation of coal seam water injection, the comparative sequence is composed by all index value of one project.

$$C_i(j)=\{C_i(1), C_i(2),\cdots, C_i(\mathrm{m})\}, \quad (1)$$

In the formular1,i=1,2,...,n, n represents the number of the project; m represents index number of each project.

The paper chooses 8 different sites in coal mine to evaluate the coal mine water injection. The evaluation indexes of the sites is presented in Table 1.

Table 1. The evaluation indexes of coal mine water injection in different sites of coal mine

Number	Buried depth (m)	Development degree of coal seam crack(number/50 m)	Porosity(%)	Gas pressure in coal seam(MPa)	Wetting edge of coal (°)	Firmness coefficient of coal(kg/cm^2)
1	410	23	9.6	0.46	89	0.55
2	360	33	12.8	0.38	26	0.65
3	320	55	15.9	0.3	44	0.58
4	365	26	39.2	0.32	31	0.90
5	255	38	23.8	0.28	39	0.78
6	635	21	7.8	0.51	68	0.76
7	460	46	8.9	0.49	56	0.55
8	365	38	16.5	0.32	75	0.65

The matrix constructs according to the evaluation indexes of table 1:

$$\begin{bmatrix} 410 & 23 & 9.6 & 0.36 & 89 & 0.55 \\ 360 & 33 & 12.8 & 0.38 & 26 & 0.65 \\ 320 & 55 & 15.9 & 0.3 & 44 & 0.58 \\ 365 & 26 & 39.2 & 0.32 & 31 & 0.90 \\ 255 & 38 & 23.8 & 0.28 & 39 & 0.78 \\ 635 & 21 & 7.8 & 0.51 & 68 & 0.76 \\ 460 & 46 & 8.9 & 0.49 & 56 & 0.55 \\ 365 & 38 & 16.5 & 0.32 & 75 & 0.65 \end{bmatrix} \quad (2)$$

2.2 Confirming the reference sequence

When different locations in coal mine were made to be evaluated, the criterion should be made in accordance with the comparability and advanced principle which is the optimal value of each index. The optimal value is chosen in the light of the criterion which benefits the coal mine water injection. For example, the more the crack is developed, the bigger the porosity which benefits the coal mine water injection is, so the maximum value is chosen as the optimal value; where the gas pressure goes against the coal mine water injection, the minimum value was chosen as the optimal value. The optimal index set is:

$$C_0(j)=\{C_0(1), C_0(2), \cdots, C_0(m)\} = \{255,55,39.2,0.28,26,0.55\}. \quad (3)$$

When the optimal index set is chosen, the matrix D was made as follows:

$$D=\begin{bmatrix} 255 & 55 & 39.2 & 0.28 & 26 & 0.55 \\ 410 & 23 & 9.6 & 0.36 & 89 & 0.55 \\ 360 & 33 & 12.8 & 0.38 & 26 & 0.65 \\ 320 & 55 & 15.9 & 0.3 & 44 & 0.58 \\ 365 & 26 & 39.2 & 0.32 & 31 & 0.90 \\ 255 & 38 & 23.8 & 0.28 & 39 & 0.78 \\ 635 & 21 & 7.8 & 0.51 & 68 & 0.76 \\ 460 & 46 & 8.9 & 0.49 & 56 & 0.55 \\ 365 & 38 & 16.5 & 0.32 & 75 & 0.65 \end{bmatrix} \quad (4)$$

2.3 Standardization processing of the index value

As the dimension and the magnitude of the evaluation index are different, so the evaluation index cannot be compared directly, the original index value should be standard handled in formula 5:

$$X_i(j)=\frac{C_i(j)}{C_j}, \quad (5)$$

In the above formula, $C_j=\frac{1}{n}\sum_{i=0}^{n}C_i(j)$, $j=1,2,\cdots,m$.

Nondimensionalize the table 1 we can get the following matrix:

$$D' = \begin{bmatrix} 0.0744 & 0.1642 & 0.2257 & 0.0864 & 0.0573 & 0.0921 \\ 0.1197 & 0.0687 & 0.0553 & 0.1111 & 0.1960 & 0.0921 \\ 0.1051 & 0.0985 & 0.0737 & 0.1173 & 0.0573 & 0.1089 \\ 0.0934 & 0.1642 & 0.0915 & 0.0926 & 0.0969 & 0.0972 \\ 0.1066 & 0.0776 & 0.2257 & 0.0988 & 0.683 & 0.1508 \\ 0.0745 & 0.1134 & 0.1370 & 0.0864 & 0.0859 & 0.1307 \\ 0.1854 & 0.0627 & 0.0449 & 0.1574 & 0.1498 & 0.1273 \\ 0.1343 & 0.1373 & 0.0512 & 0.1512 & 0.1233 & 0.0921 \\ 0.1066 & 0.1134 & 0.0950 & 0.0988 & 0.1620 & 0.1089 \end{bmatrix} \quad (6)$$

$|x_0(j)-x_i(j)|$ is used in matrix 6, we can get the matrix 7:

$$D'' = \begin{bmatrix} 0.0321 & 0.0507 & 0.1307 & 0.0123 & 0.1079 & 0.0168 \\ 0.0307 & 0.0657 & 0.1520 & 0.0309 & 0 & 0.0168 \\ 0.0190 & 0 & 0.1341 & 0.0062 & 0.0396 & 0.0050 \\ 0.0321 & 0.0866 & 0 & 0.0123 & 0.011 & 0.0586 \\ 0 & 0.0507 & 0.0887 & 0 & 0.0286 & 0.0385 \\ 0.1109 & 0.1015 & 0.1808 & 0.071 & 0.0925 & 0.0352 \\ 0.0599 & 0.0269 & 0.1744 & 0.0648 & 0.6608 & 0 \\ 0.0321 & 0.0507 & 0.1307 & 0.0123 & 0.1079 & 0.0168 \end{bmatrix} \quad (7)$$

2.4 Confirming the weight of each evaluation index

the weight obtained by Delphi method is presented an formula 8:

$W=[w_1,w_2,\cdots,w_n]=[0.15,0.25,0.18,0.23,0.08,0.11]$. (8)

2.5 Confirming the correlation degree

According to gray system theory, when comparing sequence C_i comparing to reference sequence C_0, we can get the correlation coefficient $\xi_i(j)$ of index $C_i(j)$ by formula 9:

$$\xi_i(j) = \frac{\min_i \min_j |x_0(j)-x_i(j)| + \rho \max_i \max_j |x_0(j)-x_i(j)|}{|x_0(j)-x_i(j)| + \rho \max_i \max_j |x_0(j)-x_i(j)|},$$

$i=1,2,\cdots,n; j=1,2,\cdots,m.$ (9)

In above formula, ρ is the discrimination coefficient, which effect is to improve the significant difference between correlation coefficients. ρ is selected usually from 0 to 1, generally $\rho=0.5$. So we can get the evaluation matrix of coal mine water injection as follows:

$$\varepsilon = \begin{bmatrix} 0.9114 & 0.8670 & 0.7165 & 0.9641 & 0.7538 & 0.9516 \\ 0.9150 & 0.8341 & 0.6849 & 0.9145 & 1 & 0.9516 \\ 0.9456 & 1 & 0.7113 & 0.9816 & 0.8930 & 0.9851 \\ 0.9114 & 0.7923 & 1 & 0.9641 & 0.9678 & 0.8494 \\ 1 & 0.8670 & 0.7884 & 1 & 0.9203 & 0.8956 \\ 0.7487 & 0.7650 & 0.6463 & 0.8231 & 0.7813 & 0.9037 \\ 0.8465 & 0.9247 & 0.6545 & 0.8360 & 0.3333 & 1 \\ 0.9114 & 0.8670 & 0.7165 & 0.9641 & 0.7538 & 0.9516 \end{bmatrix} \quad (10)$$

In order to compare in general, the correlation coefficient of each index is expressed in one value which is obtained in formula 11:

$$\gamma_i = \sum_{j=1}^{n} \varepsilon_i(j) W_j \quad (11)$$

Obviously, the bigger the value of γ_i is, the better effect of coal mine water injection the site is.

$$\gamma_1 = \sum_{j=1}^{n} \varepsilon_i(j) W_j = 0.8692$$

$$\gamma_2 = \sum_{j=1}^{n} \varepsilon_i(j) W_j = 0.8641$$

$$\gamma_3 = \sum_{j=1}^{n} \varepsilon_i(j) W_j = 0.9254$$

$$\gamma_4 = \sum_{j=1}^{n} \varepsilon_i(j) W_j = 0.9074$$

$$\gamma_5 = \sum_{j=1}^{n} \varepsilon_i(j) W_j = 0.9108$$

$$\gamma_6 = \sum_{j=1}^{n} \varepsilon_i(j) W_j = 0.7711$$

$$\gamma_7 = \sum_{j=1}^{n} \varepsilon_i(j) W_j = 0.8049$$

$$\gamma_8 = \sum_{j=1}^{n} \varepsilon_i(j) W_j = 0.8692$$

From the above calculation, we can get the conclusion that:

(1) The sites from which are hard to be injected to

which are easy to be injected are: site 6, site7, site2, site1, site8, site4, site5, site3, where site 1and site 8 are in the same difficulty when water is injected.

(2) In the paper, the biggest of the correlation degree is site 3 which is closest to the optimal value, so site 3 is the best site for coal mine water injection. When the 8 sites were compared, we can find that the development degree of coal seam crack and the porosity in site 3 is high and the gas pressure in coal mine in site 3 is small, so site 3 is the best site for water injection into coal seam.

(3) In the paper, site 6 is the worst place for water injection, where buried depth is large, the porosity is small, and the gas pressu1re in coal seam is high relatively.

3 Conclusion

(1) The paper analyzed the main indexes which can best reflects the coal mine water injection in order of difficulty, the buried depth, the development degree of coal seam crack, the porosity, the gas pressure in coal seam, the wetting edge of coal and the firmness coefficient of coal were chosen as the main indexes for coal mine water injection evaluation.

(2) The gray comprehensive evaluation model of coal seam water injection was constructed by gray system theory, which achieved good results by coal seam water injection evaluation of 8 different sites in coal mine.

(3) The conclusion presents important references for selection of process and parameters.

References

[1] Yuan Zhigang, Wang Hongtu, Hu Guozhong, Liu Nianping, Fan Xiaogang. Fisher discriminant analysis model and application of classifying difficulty degree of water infusion for coal seam, Journal of China Coal Society, 2011,34(4):638-642

[2] Guo Hongyu, Su Xianbo. Research on the mechanism of gas emmission inhibition in water-flooding coal seam[J] Journal of China Coal Society, 2010,35(6):928-931

[3] Qin Shuyu, Qin Wei, Zhao Jingfu. BP neural network method application in feasibility evaluation of water infusion for coal seam[J]. Chinese Journal of Geological Hazard and Control, 2006,17(3):87-90

[4] Hai Guozhi, Li Zongxiang, Qin Shuyu. Fuzzy classification analysis method for classifying difficulty degree of water infusion for coal seam[J]. Coal Science and Technology, 1993, 21(4):18-21

MATEC Web of Conferences **44**, 02050 (2016)
DOI: 10.1051/matecconf/20164402050

Pattern of Ownership and Income Distribution:In View of "Middle-Income Trap"

Rui Na Liu
The People's Bank Of China ZhengZhou Training Institute

Abstact: China comes into the ranks of middle-income countries, "middle-income trap" problem become highly attention. Income inequality is the most important factor of fall into this trap. By analyzing the actual information and data, finds out that the main reason for this widening gap between income distributions is the vigorous developments of the private owned company, led to the big gap of the income between owner of the company and normal workers. Then by analyzing and validating the actual mathematical model, and turns out the same result. To solve the problem of "middle-income trap", we must deal with the income inequality, need to strengthen the guidance and supervision while encourage the development of the private economy. Unswervingly adhere to the public sector of the economy's dominant position, and continue to develop and perfect the public sector of the economy, along with the corresponding supporting measures.

With Over 60 years development, at present, China's per capita gross domestic product has exceeded $4000, entered the ranks of middle-income countries. Whether China can successfully avoid middle-income trap and how to avoid the trap problem become the focus of scholars attention. However, learn from the lessons of that fact that those countries,which failed to achieve the transformation of the middle-income shows that income inequality, wealth disparity is the important factors of leading to many developing countries falling into the middle-income trap. Warning by World bank report 《Revival of the east asia》, to prevent east Asia economy falling into the middle-income trap, need to solve the problem of widespread income inequality . Many scholars tried to find the reasons from the industry, the gap between the state-owned enterprise managers and worker, corruption, system problems, to some extent these are reasonable. However very few relating to the root of the actual pattern of ownership. This paper combines the actual conditions of China, guided by the Marxist distribution theory and using the mathematical model, as a trial for the analysis of the root of the unfair distribution in China.

1 Distribution relationship essentially depends on the ownership

Since reform and opening up, China's economy has continued rapid growth, from 1978 to 2010, China's gross domestic product (GDP) grew by an average of 9.8% a year. China's GDP in 1978 is $147.3 billion, and 2010 is 5.8786 trillion, increased by 40 times, Per capita GDP in 1980 is $173, $4000 in 2010,

increased by 23 times, become the world's second-largest economy only after US. China's economy accounted for the proportion of the world economy from the late 1970's less than 1% to over 9% in 2010, become the fastest growing economies in the world at this period. But the social welfare created is not spread by revenue and let all people equally share the results. We found that gini coefficient of the internal of urban residents and the entire residents is in the growing. Gini coefficient of urban residents increased from 0.161 in 1981 to 0.323 in 2007.the entire residents gini coefficient, up from 0.297 in 1981 to 0.454 in 2007. Both gini coefficients of the internal of urban residents and the entire residents, in addition to individual years slightly smaller, are growing. This suggests that the phenomenon of unfair distribution in deteriorating.

This to show that along with the rapid economic growth is not synchronized growth in people's income, but the field of distribution and widening the gap between rich and poor, polarization trend. The study found that the widening gap between income distribution in our country also is the main source of the private enterprise to develop. Of course, from the point of view of economic development, we must fully recognized great contribution of the private enterprises to the development of social productivity in the primary stage of socialism. But on the other hand, the income distribution gap is widening. The causes of unfair distribution in our country and the disparity between the rich and the poor is to lead the capitalist private ownership and poor regulation, is the inevitable result of the excessive exploitation.

2 Model Analyze and Verificate

The ownership allocation relationship and the principle of distribution, the mathematical model can be used to represent. Using mathematical language to describe the scientific principles of economics, can more clearly explain economic problems, enhance the explanatory power of the article. So, now we will build and analyze model from the perspective of ownership, and specifically explains the relationship between ownership and the distribution of income.

2.1 Necessity of private ownership economy caused by the gap between rich and poor.

Within the private ownership economy, the enterprise owners to produce the biggest purpose and motivation is unlimited pursuit of surplus value created by workers. We use m stands for the surplus value, use k stands for value of the labor force, with $\frac{m}{v}$ the degree of average Labour exploited, n for the number of workers with said use, we can conclude:

$$M = k \times \frac{m}{v} \times n$$

2.1.1At constant capital formation, the demand for workers increases with the increase of the accumulation of growth.

$$M_1 = k \times \frac{m}{v} \times n_1 ,$$

$$M_2 = k \times \frac{m}{v} \times n_2$$

Here assumes an average labor value k remains the same, and the degree of an average labor exploited $\frac{m}{v}$ also remains the same. M_1 On behalf of the original residual value,

M_2 on behalf of growth after the surplus value created by workers.

So, when $n_2 > n_1$, then $\Rightarrow M_2 > M_1$

This show, with the accumulation of capital and growth, the capitalists will gain more surplus value.

2.1.2Variable part of the capital reduction and relative surplus population, lead to the exploitation of workers degree is more and more strong.

In the process of capital accumulation, "once the capitalist system of the general foundation laid down, will appear in the process of accumulating a moment, then the development of social labor productivity become the accumulation of the most powerful levers", "Social productivity level is characterized by a worker in a certain period of time, in the same labor intensity make it into a product of the relative amounts of means of production", "the growth of labor productivity, will show that the amount of labor will be relative reduction than the quantity of production data it promote ". So to say, n is reduced in $M = k \times \frac{m}{v} \times n$.

However, the production of surplus value or to make money, is the absolute rule of private ownership economy mode of production. With n reduced, will cause the existence of relative surplus population.This creates two aspects of the consequences.

On the one hand, makes the enterprise owners do all we can to strengthen the exploitation of workers. Because, if you want to add a certain amount of surplus value production, a kind of factors can reduce by another factor increases to compensate. So $n_2 < n_1$,and $\frac{m_2}{v_2} > \frac{m_1}{v_1}$, but, the capitalists in order to achieve the goal of their own money, will inevitably make the change of the number of workers less than the variation of surplus value, so it is $\Delta n < \Delta \frac{m}{v}$, and so it must be $M_2 > M_1$.

On the other hand, makes the enterprise owners try to hold down wages. Because, capital accumulation and the relationship between the wage rate, population "in the final analysis is the same workers provide the unpaid and paid labor relations" . As long as it impact to the business owners to make money or production of surplus value, they will surely try best to hold down wages and make $k_1 > k_2$. Because $n_2 < n_1$,and the change of the number of workers is less than wages, $\Delta n < \Delta k$, so it must be $M_2 > M_1$.

So will see, In a private ownership economy, with the accumulation of capital and growth, the enterprise owners will occupy more and more surplus value and capital.Brought by the accumulation of capital "is the accumulation of wealth, and in the other, in their own products as capital to production of class, is poverty, torture, slavery, ignorance, rough, and the accumulation of moral corruption."of Marx's on capital accumulation in private ownership economy law is a scientific principles of economics, the private economy in the primary stage of socialism is applicable.

2.2 The influence of income gap for the

changes of the public sector of the economy and private ownership economy

In the primary stage of socialism, distribution according to work is the fundamental principle of the public sector of the economy.Although there are different laborer itself the individual talent, there is a difference on the physical and mental, and social labor provided by different workers in quality and quantity must be different, that cause the difference of their personal income.But the relative inequality, it is the primary stage of socialism is inevitable, and the private ownership economy in the capitalist free possession of workers' surplus value that inequality with characteristics of exploitation is fundamentally different.

Assuming that urban industrial enterprises in the public ownership and private ownership economy and other economic elements of the population function be $f(x)$、$g(y)$、$h(z)$, $f(x)$、$g(y)$ and $h(z)$ are the continuous function of a random variable x、y、z. Eliminate the effects of various factors such as population reproduction, assuming $f(x)+g(y)+h(z)=M$.

2.3. According to the weighted average, the inequality of the whole society can be as $\frac{mf(x)+ng(y)+lh(z)}{f(x)+g(y)+h(z)}=J$, and m,n,l be the gini coefficient of public sector of the

economy and private economy and other economic elements. Here mainly considering the changes of the gini coefficient of public sector of the economy and private economy, so in the process of analysis it is assumed l and $h(z)$ as invariant and $m<n$.

2.3.1 $g(y)$ increase, $f(x)$ decrease.

That is $g(y_1)<g(y_2)$, $f(x_1)>f(x_2)$

Because $f(x)+g(y)+h(z)$ is invariant,

so $|\Delta f(x)|=|\Delta g(y)|$,That is $f(x_1)-f(x_2)=g(y_2)-g(y_1)$。

Setup $\frac{mf(x_1)+ng(y_1)+lh(z_1)}{f(x_1)+g(y_1)+h(z_1)}=J_1$,

$\frac{mf(x_2)+ng(y_2)+lh(z_2)}{f(x_2)+g(y_2)+h(z_2)}=J_2$, among

$f(x_1)+g(y_1)+h(z_1)=M=f(x_2)+g(y_2)+h(z_2)$

。

From $m<n$

$\Rightarrow$

$m(f(x_1)-f(x_2))<n(g(y_2)-g(y_1))$

$\Rightarrow$

$mf(x_1)+ng(y_1)<mf(x_2)+ng(y_2)$

Because $lh(z_1)=lh(z_2)$, so

$\Rightarrow$

$mf(x_1)+ng(y_1)+lh(z_1)<mf(x_2)+ng(y_2)+lh(z_2)$

$\Rightarrow$

$\frac{mf(x_1)+ng(y_1)+lh(z_1)}{M}<\frac{mf(x_2)+ng(y_2)+lh(z_2)}{M}$

That is $J_1<J_2$;

2.3.2 $g(y)$ decrease, $f(x)$ increase.

That is $g(y_1)>g(y_2)$, $f(x_1)<f(x_2)$.

So this show that in the primary stage of

socialism, when the component proportion of private ownership economy increase, thus when the increased number of private ownership economy in the enterprise, the degree of inequality, When the increased number of the public sector of the economy in the enterprise, reduce inequality. Distribution relations, it seems, is only a performance and ownership structure as a result, the relationship between ownership structure determines the distribution and allocation.Income distribution inequality is inevitable outcome of the development of private economy energetically. Private ownership to expand once more than a certain "degree", "let the development benefit of all people" can not be truly implemented.

3 The countermeasure and suggestions for unfair distribution

The above facts and modeling study revealed that the development of private economy of our country has important influence on the change of the income gap, to effectively resolve and narrow the income gap and a polarization phenomenon, the construction of a harmonious society, make the reform results benefit to all the people, we must find the clues to solve the problem and countermeasures from the ownership level.

3.1 Continue to develop and perfect the public sector of the economy.

Because the public sector of the economy is to realize the common prosperity of the economy foundation, loss or weaken the foundation would be impossible to achieve social justice people expected. It needs to take concrete measures from the practice, continue to develop and improve the state-owned economy and collective economy and strengthen the control and guidance force. Specific measures include: (1) deepen reform of the existing management system of the public sector of the economy.(2) develop the new public ownership enterprises.

3.2 Formulate and perfect relevant law, and earnestly implement and learning.

In the labor market, the norm is oversupply situation, so business owners with its dominant position, hold down wages, reduce the welfare of workers, ignore the workers work environment, etc., laborer is in absolute disadvantage in the market. Now have to pay more attention to the protection of laborers .It requires, in areas such as labor, wages and social security and improve the relevant laws, and then carefully propaganda and carry out the legislation, Also take certain way to organize workers learn the legislation, guidance and education, make laborer know when to use law to protect their legitimate rights and interests.

3.3 Adjust the taxes, strictly enforce the tax system.

Here, the adjustment of tax burden is not general tax cuts, because the general tax cuts can not solve the problem of disparity between the rich and the poor [1]. Should distinguish between different classes, adjust the tax burden, increase a decreases, strict tax system. For the rich, should be moderate tax increases, prevent the defect of tax "reverse adjustment", and modest gift tax levy inheritance tax, property tax, etc. For broad laborer stratum, should further improve the income tax threshold, reduce the tax ordinary working-class, cancel the tax of the low-income group. In addition, also intensify tax regulation, strict enforcement of tax law, avoid tax evasion.

3.4 Play the role of trade unions and federation of industry and commerce.

As defend workers' rights organization, Unions and the federation of industry and commerce, should play their proper role. In our country, on the contrary, the unions tend to lack independence and autonomy, even too much curry favor with the management. This state of affairs should be changed. Give full play to its care help worker and its worker, supervision, and promote enterprise strictly enforce the labor law, etc. Federation should actively cooperate with related departments, guide and education business owners law-abiding, to improve the operation and management, so as to promote the development of industry and commerce.

3.5 To strengthen the theoretical education and propaganda.

Influenced by the thoughts of all kinds of "westernization", Marxism has been marginalized, and the tendency of weakening, this time more to strengthen the theoretical education and propaganda, let the sinicization of Marxism occupy the ideological position, enhance people's consciousness. Formally, should adopt flexible and varied ways, enhance persuasion. Through education and publicity, not only to improve the leadership and cadres of socialist consciousness, good and evil, also should go deep among the masses, improve discrimination, so as to keep a clear head, in front of the right and wrong, choose rational decisions.

References

1. Wu Xuangong,2010: 《The principal contradiction, cause and solution of Unfair distribution of》, 《Economic Perspectives》, No.11 Issue.

2.The national development and reform commission macroeconomic research subject，200 《Promote a reasonable residents income distribution mechanism》, 《Macroeconomic Study》 No. 5 Issue.

3. Pan Yue,2012：《The national private enterprise up to more than 9 million in the first three quarters of last year》，《Communist》 No. 3 Issue.

4. Society proceedings.2005-4-14.

5. Li Chengrui，2007：《 Big Change———Analysis of China's current social and economic structure change and its complexity》，《Discovery》 No. 5 Issue.

6. Li Chengrui，2006：《Preliminary estimates about the proportion of private economy in China at present》，《Chinese Spirit》 No. 8 Issue.

7. He Ganqiang，2005：《Basic guidelines of let the development benefit all the people _ allocate the relationship_ perfect distribution system》，《Guizhou institute of finance and economics journals》 No. 8 Issue.

8. Liu Guoguang，2007：《Several problems about distribution and property relations》，《The open herald》 No. 10 Issue.

9. 1995：《Marx and Engels anthology》 vol.2，People's Publishing House

10. 《Marx and Engels corpora》 [M]. vol.3.Beijing: People's Publishing House，1974：995.

MATEC Web of Conferences **44**, 02051 (2016)
DOI: 10.1051/matecconf/20164402051

New method for solving the bending problem of rectangular plates with mixed boundary conditions

Xin Min Liu, Zhou Lei and Jing Yao Wu
College of Civil Engineering and Mechanics, Yanshan University, Qinhuangdao, China

Abstract. A new method is used to solve the rectangular plate bending problem with mixed boundary conditions. The method overcomes the complicated derivation of the classical solution by Fourth-order differential problem into integrating question. Under uniform loading rectangular plate bending problem with one side fixed the opposite side half simply supported half fixed the other two sides free rectangular plate, one side simply supported the opposite side half simply supported half fixed the other two sides free rectangular plate is systematically solved. According to the actual boundary conditions of the rectangular plate, the corresponding characteristic equation can easily be set up. It is presented deflection curve equation and the numerical calculation. By compared the results of the equation to the finite element program, we are able to demonstrate the correctness of the method. So the method not only has certain theoretical value, but also can be directly applied to engineering practice.

1 Introduction

With the development of the construction industry, the diversity of building is in high demand. It is more and more important to calculate plates under various constraint conditions. So in this paper, applying a new method to solve the bending problem of rectangular plates with mixed boundary conditions .The method provides a simple and practical calculation method for engineering calculation of rectangular plates with mixed boundary conditions, and it has certain theoretical and engineering significance. The method is no need to consider the hypothesis of complex displacement function, which can be very easy to write the total potential energy of rectangular plate on mixed boundary conditions. According to the actual boundary conditions of rectangular plate, corresponding characteristic equation can be easily established, thereby to overcome the cumbersome derivation process in classic solution. Because this method is simple and program characteristics, especially which is more efficient to solve the other methods are not easy to solve problems.

2 Theoretical basis for the new method

Static equilibrium equation of bending plates [1-2]

$$\frac{\partial^4 w}{\partial x^4}+2\frac{\partial^4 w}{\partial x^2\partial y^2}+\frac{\partial^4 w}{\partial y^4}=\frac{q}{D} \tag{1}$$

Fourth-order differential problem is converted to integrating question due to the complicated derivation of the classical solution.

Zhou Lei: 604167145@qq.com

According to the generalized virtual work principle [3], there is

$$\iiint_V \sigma_{ij}\delta e_{ij}dV=\iiint_V F_i\delta u_i dV+\iint_{S_p}\overline{p_i}\delta u_i dS+\iint_{S_u}p_i\delta\overline{u_i}dS \tag{2}$$

Or according to the known boundary displacement variation potential energy principle [4]

$$\iiint_V \delta A(e)dV=\iiint_V F_i\delta u_i dV+\iint_{S_p}\overline{p_i}\delta u_i dS+\iint_{S_u}p_i\delta\overline{u_i}dS \tag{3}$$

Outside surface Yu Gong zero variation principle [5-7]

$$\iint_{S_u}p_i\delta\overline{u_i}\mathrm{d}S=-\iint_{S_u}\overline{u_i}\delta p_i\mathrm{d}S \tag{4}$$

Substituting (3), then

$$\iiint_V \delta A(e)dV=\iiint_V F_i\delta u_i dV+\iint_{S_p}\overline{p_i}\delta u_i dS-\iint_{S_u}\overline{u_i}\delta p_i dS \tag{5}$$

According to formula (5) can be obtained

$$\Pi_{mp}=\iiint_V \delta A(e)\mathrm{d}V-\iiint_V F_i\delta u_i\mathrm{d}V-\iint_{S_p}\overline{p_i}\delta u_i\mathrm{d}S+\iint_{S_u}\overline{u_i}\delta p_i\mathrm{d}S \tag{6}$$

Type (6) is called total potential energy of mixed variable potential energy principle [8], or simply mixed total potential energy.

Take extreme variation for u_i and p_i in the formula (6), then we have

$$\delta\Pi_{mp} = \iiint_V \delta A(e)\mathrm{d}V - \iiint_V F_i\delta u_i\mathrm{d}V - \iint_{S_p} \overline{p_i}\delta u_i\mathrm{d}S + \iint_{S_u} \bar{u}_i\delta p_i\mathrm{d}S = 0 \quad (7)$$

Pay attention to

$$\iiint_V \delta A(e)dV = \iiint_V \frac{\delta A(e)}{\partial e_{ij}}\delta e_{ij}dV = \iiint_V \sigma_{ij}\delta e_{ij}dV$$

$$= \iiint_V \sigma_{ij}\delta u_{i,j}dV = \iiint_V\left[\left(\sigma_{ij}\delta u_i\right)_{,j} - \sigma_{ij,j}\delta u_i\right]dV$$

$$= \iint_S \sigma_{ij}n_j\delta u_i dS - \iiint_V \sigma_{ij,j}\delta u_i dV$$

$$= \iint_{S_p} \sigma_{ij}n_j\delta u_i dS + \iint_{S_U} \sigma_{ij}n_j\delta u_i dS$$

$$- \iint_V \sigma_{ij,j}n_j\delta u_i dS \quad (8)$$

Mixed total potential energy is required that the displacement is weakly allowed and the boundary force is coordination allowed [9]. According to this definition, the δu_i is not zero on S_u. Type formula (8) into (7), then

$$\delta\Pi_{mp} = -\iiint_V\left(\sigma_{ij,j} + F_i\right)\delta u_i\mathrm{d}V + \iint_{S_p}\left(\sigma_{ij}n_j - \bar{p}_i\right)_i\delta u_i\mathrm{d}S + \iint_{S_u}\sigma_{ij}n_j\delta u_i\mathrm{d}S + \iint_{S_u}\bar{u}_i\delta p_i\mathrm{d}S = 0 \quad (9)$$

According to the inner surface Yu Gong zero variation principle

$$\iint_{S_u}\sigma_{ij}n_j\delta u_i\mathrm{d}S = -\iint_{S_u}u_i\delta\left(\sigma_{ij}n_j\right)\mathrm{d}S \quad (10)$$

Formula (9) becomes

$$\delta\Pi_{mp} = -\iiint_V\left(\sigma_{ij,j} + F_i\right)\delta u_i\mathrm{d}V + \iint_{S_p}\left(\sigma_{ij}n_j - \bar{p}_i\right)_i\delta u_i\mathrm{d}S - \iint_{S_u}\left(u_i - \bar{u}_i\right)\delta p_i\mathrm{d}S = 0 \quad (11)$$

Taking extreme variation on the displacement and force can obtain the corresponding deflection curve equation.

3 One side fixed the opposite side half simply supported half fixed the other two sides free rectangular plate

Take only by the unit concentrated force simply supported rectangular plate as a basic system, as shown in Fig.1. To calculate the curved rectangular plate, taking one side fixed the opposite side half simply supported half fixed the other two sides free under uniform loads rectangular plate as the actual system, as shown in Fig.2.

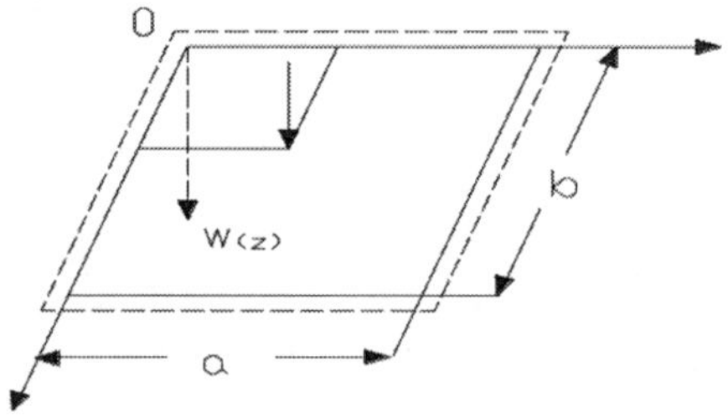

Figure 1. Virtual basic system for thin plate

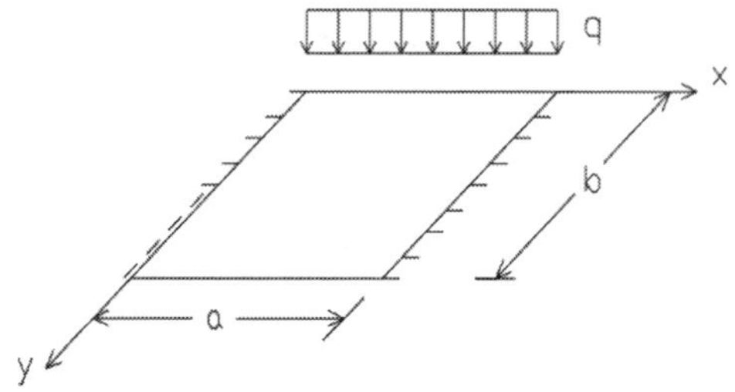

Figure 2. Actual system

3.1 Deflection surface equation

For the actual system Fig 2, fixed side bending constraint is released and this constraint is replaced by distributed moments, as shown in Fig 3.

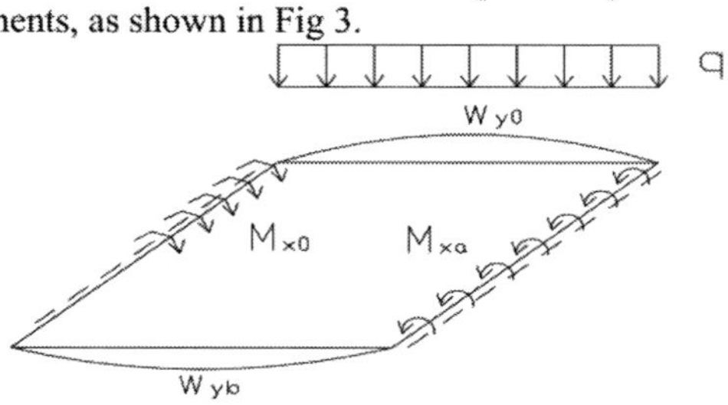

Figure 3. Actual system of fixed side bending constraints relesed

$$M_{x0} = \sum_{n=1,2}^{\infty} A_n \sin\beta_n y \qquad 0<y<b \quad (12)$$

$$M_{xa} = \sum_{n=1,2}^{\infty} B_n \sin\beta_n y \qquad 0<y<b/2 \quad (13)$$

y=0, y=b side deflection is:

$$W_{y0} = \sum_{n=1,2}^{\infty} C_m \sin\alpha_m x \quad (14)$$

$$W_{yb} = \sum_{m=1,2}^{\infty} d_m \sin\alpha_m x \quad (15)$$

The new method can get one side fixed the opposite side half simply supported half fixed the other two sides free rectangular plate total potential energy of minimum potential energy principle, such as type (16)

$$\prod_{mp}=\int_0^a\int_0^b\frac{1}{2}D\left(\frac{\partial^2 w}{\partial x^2}+\frac{\partial^2 w}{\partial y^2}\right)^2 dxdy-$$

$$\int_0^a\int_0^b\frac{2D(1-\nu)}{2}\left[\frac{\partial^2 w}{\partial x^2}\frac{\partial^2 w}{\partial y^2}-\left(\frac{\partial^2 w}{\partial x\partial y}\right)^2\right]dxdy$$

$$-\int_0^a\int_0^b qwdxdy-\int_0^{\frac{b}{2}}\overline{M}_{x0}\left(\frac{\partial w}{\partial x}\right)_{x0}dy+$$

$$\int_0^b\overline{M}_{xa}\left(\frac{\partial w}{\partial y}\right)_{xa}dy+\int_0^a w_{yb}V_{yb}dx-\int_0^a w_{y0}V_{y0}dx \quad (16)$$

The formula (12) - (15) into equation (16), where taking $\prod_{mp}$ extreme variation to get deflection surface equation:

$$W(\xi,\eta)=\int_0^a\int_0^b qw_1\,dxdy+\int_0^{\frac{b}{2}}M_{x0}w_{1x0}dy-$$

$$\int_0^b M_{xa}w_{1xa}dy+\int_0^a V_{1y0}w_{y0}dy-\int_0^a V_{1yb}w_{yb}dx+R_{1ab}k_3$$

$$=w_1+w_2+w_3+w_4+w_5 \quad (17)$$

Among them:

$$w_1=\frac{4q}{Da}\sum_{m=1,3}^{\infty}\{1+\frac{1}{2ch\frac{1}{2}\alpha_m b}[\alpha_m(\eta-\frac{b}{2})sh\alpha_m(\eta-\frac{b}{2})$$

$$-(2+\frac{1}{2}\alpha_m bth\frac{1}{2}\alpha_m b)ch\alpha_m(\eta-\frac{b}{2})]\ \}\cdot\frac{1}{\alpha_m^5}\sin\alpha_m\xi$$

$$=\frac{4q}{Da}\sum_{n=1,3}^{\infty}\{1+\frac{1}{2ch\frac{1}{2}\beta_n a}[\beta_n(\zeta-\frac{a}{2})sh\beta_n(\zeta-\frac{a}{2})-$$

$$(2+\frac{1}{2}\beta_n ath\frac{1}{2}\beta_n a)ch\beta_n(\zeta-\frac{a}{2})]\ \}\cdot\frac{1}{\beta_n^5}\sin\beta_n\eta \quad (18)$$

$$w_2=\frac{1}{4D}\sum_{n=1,2}^{\infty}\left(-\frac{\beta_n a}{sh^2\beta_n a}sh\beta_n\xi+cth\beta_n a\beta_n\xi ch\beta_n\xi\right)$$

$$\cdot\frac{A_n}{\beta_n^2}\sin\beta_n\eta-\frac{1}{4D}\sum_{n=1,2}^{\infty}\beta_n\xi sh\beta_n\xi\frac{A_n}{\beta_n^2}\sin\beta_n\eta \quad (19)$$

$$w_3=-\int_0^b M_{xa}w_{1xa}dy\frac{1}{2}\sum_{n=1,2}^{\infty}\left(\beta_n acth\beta_n a-\beta_n\xi cth\beta_n\xi\right)\cdot$$

$$\frac{B_n}{\beta_n^2 sh\beta_n a}sh\beta_n\xi\cdot\sin\beta_n\eta \quad (20)$$

$$w_4=\frac{1}{2}\sum_{n=1,2}^{\infty}2\frac{C_m}{sh\alpha_m b}sh\alpha_m(b-\eta)\sin\alpha_m\xi+$$

$$\frac{1}{2}\sum_{n=1,2}^{\infty}(1+\nu)\left[\alpha_m bcth\alpha_m b-\alpha_m(b-\eta)cth\alpha_m(b-\eta)\right]\cdot$$

$$\frac{C_m}{sh\alpha_m b}sh\alpha_m(b-\eta)\sin\alpha_m\xi \quad (21)$$

$$w_5=\frac{1}{2}\sum_{m=1,2}^{\infty}\left[2+(1-\nu)\left(\alpha_m bcth\alpha_m b-\alpha_m\eta cth\alpha_m\eta\right)\right]$$

$$\frac{d_m}{sh\alpha_m b}sh\alpha_m\eta\sin\alpha_m\xi \quad (22)$$

3.2 Boundary conditions

Deflection surface equation (18) must satisfy the following boundary conditions

$$\left(\frac{\partial w}{\partial \xi}\right)_{\xi=0}=0 \quad (23)$$

$$(w'_{1\xi}+w'_{2\xi}+w'_{3\xi}+w'_{4\xi}+w'_{5\xi})_{\xi=0}=0 \quad (24)$$

$$\left(\frac{\partial w}{\partial \xi}\right)_{\xi=a}=0 \quad (25)$$

$$(w'_{1\xi}+w'_{2\xi}+w'_{3\xi}+w'_{4\xi}+w'_{5\xi})_{\xi=a}=0 \quad (26)$$

$$-D\left[\frac{\partial^3 w}{\partial\eta^3}+(2-\nu)\frac{\partial^3 w}{\partial^2\xi\partial\eta}\right]_{\eta=0}=0 \quad (27)$$

$$-D[\omega'''_{1\eta\eta\eta}+\omega'''_{2\eta\eta\eta}+\omega'''_{3\eta\eta\eta}+\omega'''_{4\eta\eta\eta}+\omega'''_{5\eta\eta\eta}+(2-\nu)$$

$$.(\omega'''_{1\xi\xi\eta}+\omega'''_{2\xi\xi\eta}+\omega'''_{3\xi\xi\eta}+\omega'''_{4\xi\xi\eta}+\omega'''_{5\xi\xi\eta})]_{\eta=0}=0 \quad (28)$$

$$-D\left[\frac{\partial^3 w}{\partial\eta^3}+(2-\nu)\frac{\partial^3 w}{\partial^2\xi\partial\eta}\right]_{\eta=b}=0 \quad (29)$$

$$-D[\omega'''_{1\eta\eta\eta}+\omega'''_{2\eta\eta\eta}+\omega'''_{3\eta\eta\eta}+\omega'''_{4\eta\eta\eta}+\omega'''_{5\eta\eta\eta}+(2-\nu)$$

$$.(\omega'''_{1\xi\xi\eta}+\omega'''_{2\xi\xi\eta}+\omega'''_{3\xi\xi\eta}+\omega'''_{4\xi\xi\eta}+\omega'''_{5\xi\xi\eta})]_{\eta=b}=0 \quad (30)$$

Infinite equations are derived through taking the deflection surface equation into the corresponding boundary conditions of the formula (23) to formula (30) .It is obtained unknown number through assigning for equations.

3.3 Numerical calculation

Calculation parameters were taken as a=b=1m , q=100N/m^2, E=200GPa，h/a=0.005、0.1、0.2、0.3，v=0.3. Since the trigonometric convert to hyperbolic

functions makes infinite series converges issue is resolved so m=n=1， 2， 3...50. By using MATLAB software programming for the A_n， C_m， B_n ，d_m and deflection expression. For example, h/a=0.3 compared with the calculation results of ANSYS, both tend to be consistent, the error is less than 5%.

Table 1. Under uniform loading for one side fixed the opposite side half simply supported half fixed the other two sides free rectangular plate deflection value

X	y=0.00	y=0.00	y=0.25	y=0.25	y=0.5	y=0.5	y=0.75	y=0.75	y=1	y=1
	Article	ANSYS	Article	ANSYS	Article	ANSYS	Article	ANSYS	Article	ANSYS
0.0	0.000000	0.000000	0.000000	0.000000	0.000000	0.000000	0.000000	0.000000	0.000000	0.000000
0.1	0.000340	0.000331	0.000396	0.000376	0.000672	0.000666	0.001426	0.001390	0.001501	0.001591
0.2	0.001115	0.001171	0.001234	0.001194	0.001563	0.001685	0.002538	0.002629	0.002796	0.002787
0.3	0.001956	0.001985	0.002122	0.002047	0.002487	0.002598	0.003469	0.003559	0.003886	0.003879
0.4	0.002582	0.002813	0.002773	0.002651	0.003079	0.003084	0.003978	0.004042	0.004197	0.004180
0.5	0.002895	0.002934	0.003082	0.002986	0.003289	0.003269	0.004186	0.004150	0.004365	0.004299
0.6	0.002581	0.002550	0.002699	0.002600	0.003036	0.002918	0.003896	0.003868	0.004162	0.004165
0.7	0.001897	0.001916	0.002054	0.001972	0.002465	0.002373	0.003419	0.003537	0.003836	0.003848
0.8	0.000997	0.001054	0.001196	0.001137	0.001585	0.001533	0.002491	0.002423	0.002787	0.002719
0.9	0.000328	0.000324	0.000428	0.000456	0.000679	0.000682	0.000139	0.000143	0.001569	0.001501
1.0	0.000000	0.000000	0.000000	0.000000	0.000000	0.000000	0.000000	0.000000	0.000000	0.000000

4 One side simply supported the opposite side half simply supported half fixed the other two sides free rectangular plate

To calculate the curved rectangular plate, taking one side simply supported the opposite side half simply supported half fixed the other two sides free under uniform loads rectangular plate as the actual system, shown in Fig.4.

4.1 Deflection surface equation

For the actual system Fig 4, fixed side bending constraint is released and this constraint is replaced by distributed moment, as shown in Fig 5.

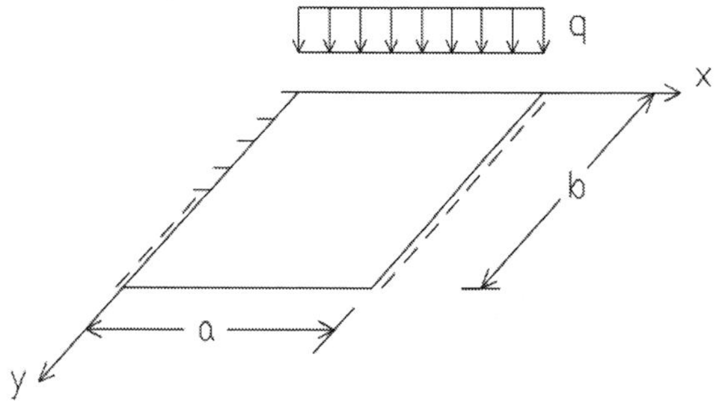

Figure 4. Actual system

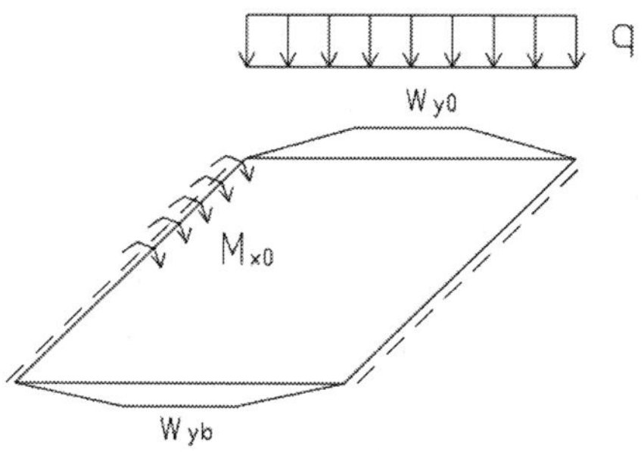

Figure 5. Actual system of fixed side bending constraints relesed

$$M_{x0} = \sum_{n=1,2}^{\infty} A_n \sin \beta_n y \tag{31}$$

y=0，y=b side deflection is:

$$w_{y0} = \sum_{,m=1,2}^{\infty} C_m \sin \alpha_m x \tag{32}$$

$$w_{yb} = \sum_{m=1,2}^{\infty} d_m \sin \alpha_m x \tag{33}$$

The new method can get one side simply supported the opposite side half simply supported half fixed the other two sides free rectangular plate total potential energy of minimum potential energy principle, such as type (34)

$$\prod_{mp}=\int_0^a\int_0^b \frac{1}{2}D\left(\frac{\partial^2 w}{\partial x^2}+\frac{\partial^2 w}{\partial y^2}\right)^2 dxdy-$$

$$\int_0^a\int_0^b \frac{2D(1-\nu)}{2}\left[\frac{\partial^2 w}{\partial x^2}\frac{\partial^2 w}{\partial y^2}-\left(\frac{\partial^2 w}{\partial x\partial y}\right)^2\right]dxdy$$

$$-\int_0^a\int_0^b qwdxdy-\int_0^{\frac{b}{2}}\overline{M}_{x0}\left(\frac{\partial w}{\partial x}\right)_{x0}dy+$$

$$\int_0^a w_{yb}V_{yb}dx-\int_0^a w_{y0}V_{y0}dx \qquad (34)$$

The formula (31) - (33) into equation (34), where taking $\prod_{mp}$ extreme variation to get deflection surface equation:

$$W(\xi,\eta)=\int_0^a\int_0^b qw_1dxdy+\int_0^{\frac{b}{2}}M_{x0}w_{1x0}dy+$$

$$\int_0^a V_{1y0}\omega_{y0}dx-\int_0^a V_{1yb}w_{yb}dx$$

$$=w_1+w_2+w_4+w_5 \qquad (35)$$

w_1 is the same as type (18); w_2 is the same as type (19); w_4 is the same as type (21); w_5 is the same as the type (22).

4.2 Boundary conditions

Deflection surface equation (35) must satisfy the following boundary conditions

$$\left(\frac{\partial w}{\partial \xi}\right)_{\xi=0}=0 \qquad (36)$$

$$-D\left[\frac{\partial^3 w}{\partial \eta^3}+(2-\nu)\frac{\partial^3 w}{\partial \eta\partial \xi^2}\right]_{\eta=0}=0 \qquad (37)$$

$$-D\left[\frac{\partial^3 w}{\partial \eta^3}+(2-\nu)\frac{\partial^3 w}{\partial \eta\partial \xi^2}\right]_{\eta=b}=0 \qquad (38)$$

Infinite equations are derived through taking the deflection surface equation into the corresponding boundary conditions of the formula (36) to formula (38) .It is obtained unknown number through assigning for equations.

4.3 Numerical calculation

Calculation parameters were taken a=b=1m， q=100N/m2, E=200GPa， h/a=0.005 、 0.1 、 0.2 、 0.3 ， v=0.3 。 m=n=1 ， 2 ， 3…50, by using MATLAB software programming for the An， Cm ,dm and deflection expression. For example, h/a=0.3 compared with the calculation results of ANSYS, both tend to be consistent, the error is less than 5%. The deflection curves of plate are showed in Fig.6.

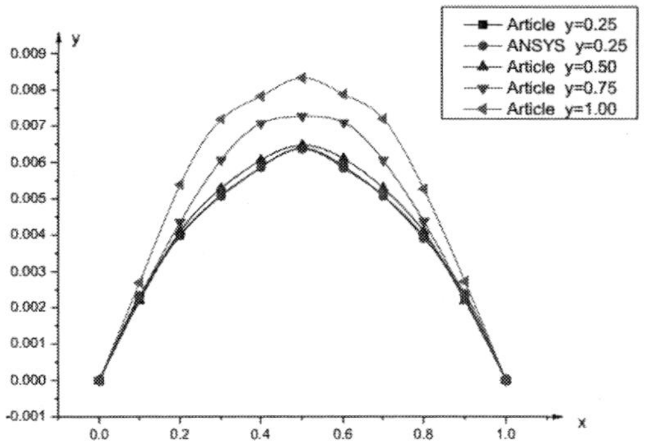

Figure 6. Virtual basic system for thin plate

5 Conclusion

In this paper, the new method is applied to solve the bending problem of rectangular plate with mixed boundary conditions under uniform loads. In the MATLAB platform, it is conducted numerical calculation for different issues. In addition, computational analysis of the rectangular plate is carried out using finite element software ANSYS. It is verified the accuracy of the numerical results by comparison, so that the new method is correct.

References

1. M. A. Leitao. A Meshless Method for Kirchhoff Plate Bending Problems. European Journal of Mechanics Solids, 2001, 52(10): 1107-1130.
2. Sewell, m.j. on Dual Approximation Principles and Optimization in Continuum Mechanics, phill. Trans. R. soc. London, 1969, (a-1162): 319-350.
3. FU BL, Energy principle and its application in elastic mechanics [M]. Beijing: Science Press, 2004:366-401,498-582.
4. Luo JX, Li Q, Research on the relationship between the Ritz method and Galerkin method [J], Shanxi Architecture, 2007,33(10): 96-97.
5. Yu F, X. B. Liu. New Exact Solutions for Free Vibrations of Rectangular Thin Plates by Symplectic Dual Method. Acta Mechanica Sinica, 2009, (2): 265-270.
6. Hu XG, Su TJ. The minimum excess principle used in dynamic analysis of elastic circular plate. Jilin Normal University Newspaper (NATURAL SCIENCE EDITION), 2005, (2): 11-16.
7. Fu BL, Variational principle of extremum value with mixed variable in elasticity[J]. Journal of Xingtai Vocational and Technical College, 2003:1-9.
8. Fu BL, Principle of minimum potential energy with mixed variables and its application [J]. Journal of Yanshan University, 2011:1-8.
9. Zhang L, Bending beam alternative method for calculating internal forces [J], Journal of Jingdezhen College, 2008, 23(2): 6-7.

MATEC Web of Conferences **44**, 02052 (2016)
DOI: 10.1051/matecconf/20164402052

Applying the Principle of Variables to Solve the Problems of Forced Vibration of the plate with three clamped and the other free with concentrated load

Ying Jie Chen ,Jing Yao Wu
YanShan University QinHuangDao 066004

Abstract. In this paper, with the principle of least action with variables to solve the problems of forced vibration of the Rectangular plate with three clamped and the other free with concentrated load, and the stable solution can be worked out. We can compare the results with the literate; it also can be proved to be true. So the results by calculating not only it have important academic value, but also it can be directly referred in the actual work.

1 Introduction

Curved rectangular sheet has been widely used in engineering practice. when calculating the stability vibration and bending of the sheet based on sheet classical theory, there will be some errors. In the previous solution, it is difficult to find an easy displacement functions to solve it. The principle of least action mixed variables applied in article[1] requires only weak displacement, that is, displacement should meet the requirements of the strain-displacement in advance, instead of boundary conditions. This eliminates the need to make displacement hypothesis. the total potential energy of mixed variables can be set up according to the actual boundary condition of the curved rectangular sheet, thus obtained the steady-state solution of forced vibration can be obtained. This solution overcomes the classical solution of the complex calculation process and the difficulty to solve certain issues and other limitations[2-5].

2 The basic equation

Figure 1 (a) is a rectangular plate with three fixed and one free, undock side $x=0,\ y=0,\ y=a$ bending moment amplitude constraint substituting $\overline{M}_{xo}$, $\overline{M}_{xa}$, $\overline{M}_{yo}$ as the Figure 1 (b) shows, also assume that the free edge of $y=b$ of deflection magnitude $\overline{w}_{yb}$

$$\overline{M}_{xo} = \sum_{n=1,2}^{\infty} A_n \sin\beta_n y \tag{1}$$

$$\overline{M}_{xa} = \sum_{n=1,2}^{\infty} B_n \sin\beta_n y \tag{2}$$

$$\overline{M}_{yo} = \sum_{m=1,2}^{\infty} C_m \sin\frac{m\pi x}{a} \tag{3}$$

$$\overline{w}_{yb} = \sum_{m=1,2}^{\infty} d_m \sin\frac{m\pi x}{a} \tag{4}$$

Wherein $\beta_n = \dfrac{n\pi}{b}$, A_n, B_n, c_m, d_m coefficients to be determined.

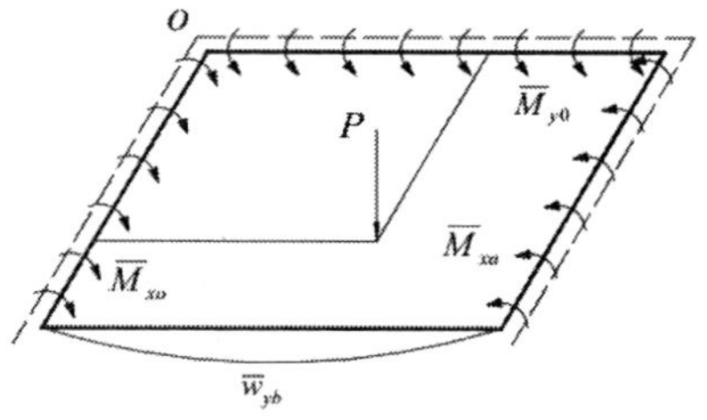

Figure 1(a). The rectangular plate with three clamped and the other free with concentrated load

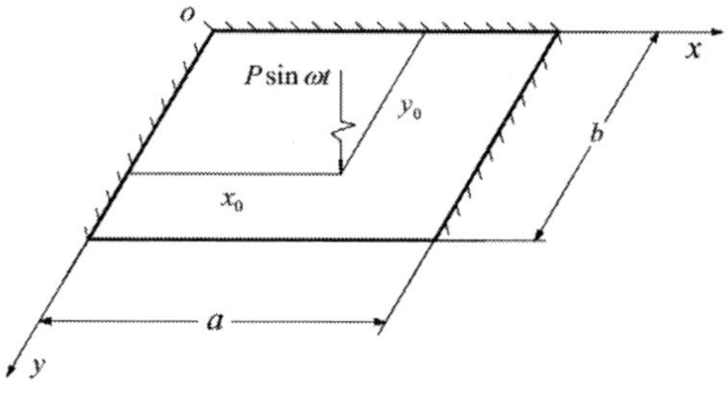

Figure 1(b). The actual system of amplitude

Let any concentrated load

$$F(x,y,t) = P\delta(x-x_0, y-y_0)\sin\omega t$$

Boundary conditions

---

[a] Corresponding author: Jingyao Wu, Email:1509369632@qq.com

$$\left.\begin{array}{l}\left(\frac{\partial w}{\partial y}\right)_{y=0}=0,\left(\frac{\partial w}{\partial x}\right)_{x=0,a=0}\\ \left[\frac{\partial^3 w}{\partial y^3}+(2-\nu)\frac{\partial^3 w}{\partial x^2\partial y}\right]_{y=0}=0\end{array}\right\} \quad (5)$$

$$\left.\begin{array}{l}w_{x=0}=w_{x=a}=w_{y=0}=0\\ \left(\frac{\partial^2 w}{\partial y^2}+\nu\frac{\partial^2 w}{\partial x^2}\right)_{y=b}=0\end{array}\right\} \quad (6)$$

3 solving any concentrated harmonic forced vibration under loads with three fixed side of rectangular plates

The total potential energy mix variable assignment

$$\Pi_{mp}=\int_0^a\int_0^b\frac{1}{2}D\left\{\left(\frac{\partial^2 w}{\partial x^2}+\frac{\partial^2 w}{\partial y^2}\right)^2 -2(1-\nu)\left[\frac{\partial^2 w}{\partial x^2}\frac{\partial^2 w}{\partial y^2}-\left(\frac{\partial^2 w}{\partial x\partial y}\right)^2\right]\right\}dxdy$$
$$\int_0^a\int_0^b\left(Pw+\frac{1}{2}\rho\omega^2 w^2\right)dxdy+$$
$$\int_0^a\overline{w}_{yb}(V_y)_{y=b}dx-\int_0^b\overline{M}_{x0}\left(\frac{dw}{dx}\right)_{x=0}dy+$$
$$\int_0^b\overline{M}_{xa}\left(\frac{dw}{dx}\right)_{x=a}dy-\int_0^a\overline{M}_{y0}\left(\frac{dw}{dy}\right)_{y=0}dy \quad (7)$$

Suppose deflection curve equation for curved rectangular plate

$$w(x,y)=\sum_{m=1,2}^{\infty}\sum_{n=1,2}^{\infty}A_{mn}\sin\alpha_m x\sin\beta_n y$$
$$(0\le x\le a\quad 0\le y<b) \quad (8)$$

Among them $\alpha_m=\frac{m\pi}{a}$

The magnitude of the deflection surface equation (8) into (7) take variational extremum formula calculated, then there are

$$\delta\Pi_{mp}=\frac{Dab}{4}\sum_{m=1,2}^{\infty}\sum_{n=1,2}^{\infty}A_{mn}\delta A_{mn}K_{dmn}^2-$$
$$q\sum_{m=1,2}^{\infty}\sum_{n=1,2}^{\infty}\delta A_{mn}\frac{ab}{\pi^2 mn}\left[1-(-1)^m\right]\cdot$$
$$\left[1-(-1)^n\right]-\sum_{m=1,2}^{\infty}\sum_{n=1,2}^{\infty}\frac{b}{2}A_n\alpha_m\delta A_{mn}$$
$$-\sum_{m=1,2}^{\infty}\sum_{n=1,2}^{\infty}(-1)^m\frac{b}{2}A_n\alpha_m\delta A_{mn}+$$
$$\sum_{m=1,2}^{\infty}\sum_{n=1,2}^{\infty}\frac{a}{2}C_m\beta_n\delta A_{mn}+(-1)^n\frac{Da}{2}$$
$$\left[\sum_{m=1,2}^{\infty}\sum_{n=1,2}^{\infty}\delta A_{mn}d_m\beta_n^3+(2-\nu)\cdot\sum_{m=1,2}^{\infty}\sum_{n=1,2}^{\infty}\delta A_{mn}d_m\alpha_m^2\beta_n\right]=0 \quad (9)$$

Among them $\lambda^2\equiv\frac{1}{D}\rho\omega^2$ $K_{dmn}^2\equiv\left(\alpha_m^2+\beta_n^2\right)^2-\lambda^2$,

From (9) can be obtained

$$A_{mn}=\sum_{m=1,2}^{\infty}\sum_{n=1,2}^{\infty}\frac{4q}{D\pi^2}\frac{1}{mn}\frac{1}{K_{dmn}^2}\left[1-(-1)^m\right]\cdot\left[1-(-1)^n\right]+$$
$$\sum_{m=1,2}^{\infty}\sum_{n=1,2}^{\infty}\frac{2}{Da}\frac{\alpha_m}{K_{dmn}^2}(A_n)+\sum_{m=1,2}^{\infty}\sum_{n=1,2}^{\infty}\frac{(-1)^m 2}{Da}\frac{\alpha_m}{K_{dmn}^2}(B_n)$$
$$+\sum_{m=1,2}^{\infty}\sum_{n=1,2}^{\infty}\frac{2}{Db}\frac{\beta_n}{K_{dmn}^2}(C_m)-\sum_{m=1,2}^{\infty}\sum_{n=1,2}^{\infty}\frac{2}{b}\frac{(-1)^n}{K_{dmn}^2}\beta_n\cdot$$
$$\left[\beta_n^2+\alpha_m^2(2-\nu)\right](d_m)=0 \quad (10)$$

The magnitude of the deflection surface equation points (10) into (8) represented by triangular series are:

$$w_1=\frac{4P}{Dab}\sum_{m=1.2}^{\infty}\sum_{n=1.2}^{\infty}\frac{\sin\alpha_m x_0\sin\beta_n y_0}{K_{dmn}^2}\cdot\sin\alpha_m x\sin\beta_n y \quad (11)$$

$$w_2=\frac{2}{Da}\sum_{m=1.2}^{\infty}\sum_{n=1.2}^{\infty}\frac{\alpha_m}{K_{dmn}^2}\sin\alpha_m x\cdot\sin\beta_n y(A_n) \quad (12)$$

$$w_3=-\frac{2}{Da}\sum_{m=1.2}^{\infty}\sum_{n=1.2}^{\infty}\frac{(-1)^m\alpha_m}{K_{dmn}^2}\cdot\sin\alpha_m x\sin\beta_n y(B_n) \quad (13)$$

$$w_5=-\frac{2}{b}\sum_{m=1.2}^{\infty}\sum_{n=1.2}^{\infty}\frac{(-1)^n}{K_{dmn}^2}\left[\beta_n^3+\alpha_m^2\beta_n(2-\nu)\right]\sin\alpha_m x\sin\beta_n y(d_m) \quad (14)$$

To speed up the convergence rate and eliminate deflection and moment magnitude of the triangular series representation of the boundary that appears in the first category discontinuity, it also must points deflection surface equation for the amplitude of the triangular series and hyperbolic functions expressed mixed form.

In the case of $\alpha_m^2<\lambda$ and $\beta_n^2<\lambda$, then there are

$$w_1=\frac{2P}{Db}\sum_{n=1,2}^{\infty}\frac{1}{\alpha_n^{'2}-\beta_n^{'2}}\left[-\frac{sh\alpha_n^{'}(a-x_0)sh\alpha_n^{''}x}{\alpha_n^{'}sh\alpha_n^{'}\alpha}+\frac{sh\beta_n^{'}(a-x_0)sh\beta_n^{'}x}{\beta_n^{'}sh\beta_n^{'}a}\right]\cdot \tag{15}$$

$$\sin\beta_n y_0\sin\beta_n y \quad (0\le x\le x_0)$$

$$w_1=\frac{2P}{Db}\sum_{n=1,2}^{\infty}\frac{1}{\alpha_n^{'2}-\beta_n^{'2}}\left[-\frac{sh\alpha_n^{'}x_0 sh\alpha_n^{'}(a-x)}{\alpha_n^{'}sh\alpha_n^{'}\alpha}+\frac{sh\beta_n^{'}x_0 sh\beta_n^{'}(a-x)}{\beta_n^{'}sh\beta_n^{'}a}\right]\cdot\sin\beta_n y_0\sin\beta_n t$$

$$x_0\le x\le a \tag{16}$$

$$w_1=\frac{2P}{Da}\sum_{m=1,2}^{\infty}\frac{1}{\alpha_m^{'2}-\beta_m^{'2}}\left[-\frac{sh\alpha_m^{'}(b-y_0)sha_m^{'}y}{\alpha_m^{'}sh\alpha_m^{'}b}+\frac{sh\beta_m^{'}(b-y_0)sh\beta_m^{'}y}{\beta_m^{'}sh\beta_m^{'}b}\right]\cdot\sin\alpha_m x_0\sin\alpha_m x$$

$$0\le y\le y_0 \tag{17}$$

$$w_1=\frac{2P}{Da}\sum_{m=1,2}^{\infty}\frac{1}{\alpha_m^{'2}-\beta_m^{'2}}\left[-\frac{sh\alpha_m^{'}y_0 sha_m^{'}(b-y)}{\alpha_m^{'}sh\alpha_m^{'}b}+\frac{sh\beta_m^{'}y_0 sh\beta_m^{'}(b-y)}{\beta_m^{'}sh\beta_m^{'}b}\right]\cdot\sin\alpha_m x_0\sin\alpha_m x$$

$$y_0\le y\le b \tag{18}$$

Among them $\alpha_n^{'2}=\sqrt{\beta_n^2+\lambda}$, $\beta_n^{'2}=\sqrt{\beta_n^2-\lambda}$

$\alpha_m^{'2}=\sqrt{\alpha_m^2+\lambda}$, $\beta_m^{'2}=\sqrt{\alpha_m^2-\lambda}$

$$w_2=\frac{1}{D}\sum_{n=1,2}^{\infty}\frac{1}{\alpha_n^{'2}-\beta_n^{'2}}\left[-\frac{sh\alpha_n^{'}(a-x)}{sh\alpha_n^{'}\alpha}+\frac{sh\beta_n^{'}(a-x)}{sh\beta_n^{'}a}\right]\sin\beta_n y(A_n) \tag{19}$$

$$w_3=\frac{1}{D}\sum_{m=1,2}^{\infty}\frac{1}{\alpha_m^{'2}-\beta_m^{'2}}\left[\frac{sha_n^{'}x}{sh\alpha_m^{'}a}-\frac{sh\beta_m^{'}x}{sh\beta_m^{'}a}\right]\sin\beta_n y(B_n) \tag{20}$$

$$w_4=\frac{1}{D}\sum_{m=1,2}^{\infty}\frac{1}{\alpha_m^{'2}-\beta_m^{'2}}\left[-\frac{sha_m^{'}(b-y)}{sh\alpha_m^{'}b}+\frac{{}_0sh\beta_m^{'}(b-y)}{sh\beta_m^{'}b}\right]\sin\alpha_m x(C_m) \tag{21}$$

$$w_5=\sum_{m=1,2}^{\infty}\frac{1}{\alpha_m^{'2}-\beta_m^{'2}}\left\{\left[\alpha_m^{'2}-\alpha_m^2(2-\nu)\right]\frac{sh\alpha_m^{'}y}{sh\alpha_m^{'}b}-\left[\beta_m^{'2}-\alpha_m^2(2-\nu)\right]\frac{sh\beta_m^{'}y}{sh\beta_m^{'}b}\right\}\cdot\sin\alpha_m x(d_m) \tag{22}$$

When $\alpha_m^2<\lambda$ and $\beta_n^2<\lambda$, easy to get the corresponding points deflection surface amplitude equation, due to limited space no longer given.

Investigation boundary conditions.

Boundary condition formula (5) is automatically satisfied, the following boundary condition investigated formula (6).When $\alpha_m^2>\lambda$ and $\beta_n^2>\lambda$, executive boundary condition $\left(\frac{\partial w}{\partial y}\right)_{y=0}=0$, then get

$$\frac{2P}{Da}\left[-\frac{sh\alpha_m^{'}(b-y_0)}{sh\alpha_m^{'}b}+\frac{sh\beta_m^{'}(b-y_0)}{sh\beta_m^{'}b}\right]\cdot\sin\alpha_m x_0+\frac{4\lambda}{Da}\sum_{n=1,2}^{\infty}\frac{\alpha_m\beta_n}{K_{dmn}^2}(A_n)-\frac{4\lambda}{Da}\sum_{n=1,2}^{\infty}\frac{(-1)^m\alpha_m\beta_n}{K_{dmn}^2}(B_n)+\frac{1}{D}(\alpha_m^{'}cth\alpha_m^{'}b-\beta_m cth\beta_m^{'}b)(C_m)+\left\{\left[\alpha_m^{'2}-\alpha_m^2(2-\nu)\right]\frac{\alpha_m^{'}}{sh\alpha_m^{'}b}\left[\beta_m^{'2}-\alpha_m^2(2-\nu)\right]\frac{\beta_m^{'}}{sh\beta_m^{'}b}\right\}(d_m)=0 \tag{23}$$

Executive boundary condition $\left(\frac{\partial w}{\partial x}\right)_{x=a}=0$, then get

$$\frac{2P}{Db}\left(-\frac{sh\alpha_n^{'}(a-x_0)}{sh\alpha_n^{'}a}+\frac{sh\beta_n^{'}(a-x_0)}{sh\beta_n^{'}a}\right)\sin\beta_m y_0+\frac{1}{D}\left(\alpha_n^{'}cth\alpha_n^{'}a-\beta_n^{'}cth\beta_n^{'}a\right)(A_n)-\frac{1}{D}\left(\frac{\alpha_n^{'}}{sh\alpha_n^{'}a}-\frac{\beta_n^{'}}{sh\beta_n^{'}a}\right)(B_n)+\frac{4\lambda}{Db}\cdot\sum_{m=1,2}^{\infty}\frac{\alpha_m\beta_n}{K_{dmn}^2}(C_n)-\frac{4\lambda}{b}\sum_{m=1,2}^{\infty}\frac{(-1)^n\alpha_m\beta_n}{K_{dmn}^2}\left[\beta_n^2+\alpha_m^2(2-\nu)\right](d_m)=0 \tag{24}$$

Executive boundary condition

$$\left[\frac{\partial^3 w}{\partial y^3}+(2-\nu)\frac{\partial^3 w}{\partial x^2\partial y}\right]_{y=b}=0,$$

then get

$$\frac{2P}{Da}\left\{\left[\alpha_m^{'2}-\alpha_m^2(2-\nu)\right]\frac{sh\alpha_m^{'}}{sh\alpha_m^{'}b}-\right.$$

$$\left.\left[\beta_m^{'2}-\alpha_m^2(2-\nu)\right]\frac{sh\beta_m^{'}y_0}{sh\beta_m^{'}b}\right\}\sin\alpha_m x_0-$$

$$\frac{4\lambda}{Da}\sum_{n=1,2}^{\infty}\frac{(-1)^n\alpha_m\beta_n}{K_{dmn}^2}\left[\alpha_m^2+\beta_n^2(2-\nu)\right](A_n)+$$

$$\frac{4\lambda}{Da}\sum_{n=1,2}^{\infty}\frac{(-1)^{m+n}\alpha_m\beta_n}{K_{dmn}^2}\left[\alpha_m^2+\beta_n^2(2-\nu)\right](B_n)+$$

$$\frac{1}{D}\left\{\left[\alpha_m^{'2}-\alpha_m^2(2-\nu)\right]\frac{\alpha_m^{'}}{sh\alpha_m^{'}b}-\right.$$

$$\left.\left[\beta_m^{'2}-\alpha_m^2(2-\nu)\right]\frac{\beta_m^{'}}{sh\beta_m^{'}b}\right\}(C_m)+$$

$$\left\{\left[\alpha_m^{'2}-\alpha_m^2(2-\nu)\right]^2\alpha_m^{'}cth\alpha_m^{'}b-\left[\beta_m^{'2}-\alpha_m^{'2}(2-\nu)\right]^2\right.$$

$$\left.\beta_m^{'}cth\beta_m^{'}b\right\}=0 \tag{25}$$

When $\alpha_m^2<\lambda$ and $\beta_n^{'}<\lambda$, the boundary condition (27) - (29)

$$\frac{2P}{Da}\left[-\frac{sh\alpha_m^{'}(b-y_0)}{sh\alpha_m^{'}b}+\frac{sh\beta_m^{''}(b-y_0)}{sh\beta_m^{'}b}\right]\cdot\sin\alpha_m x_0$$

$$+\frac{4\lambda}{Da}\sum_{n=1,2}^{\infty}\frac{\alpha_m\beta_n}{K_{dmn}^2}(A_n)-\frac{4\lambda}{Da}\sum_{n=1,2}^{\infty}\frac{(-1)^m\alpha_m\beta_n}{K_{dmn}^2}(B_n)$$

$$+\frac{1}{D}(\alpha_m^{'}cth\alpha_m^{'}b-\beta_m^{''}ctg\beta_m^{''}b)(C_m)+$$

$$\left\{\left[\alpha_m^{'2}-\alpha_m^2(2-\nu)\right]\frac{\alpha_m^{'}}{sh\alpha_m^{'}b}+\right.$$

$$\left.\left[\beta_m^{''2}-\alpha_m^2(2-\nu)\right]\frac{\beta_m^{''}}{sh\beta_m^{''}b}\right\}(d_m)=0 \tag{26}$$

$$\frac{2P}{Db}\left(-\frac{sh\alpha_n^{'}(a-x_0)}{sh\alpha_n^{'}a}+\frac{sh\beta_n^{''}(a-x_0)}{sh\beta_n^{'}a}\right)\cdot$$

$$\sin\beta_n y_0+\frac{1}{D}\left(\alpha_n^{'}cth\alpha_n^{'}a-\beta_n^{''}cth\beta_n^{''}a\right)(A_n)-$$

$$\frac{1}{D}\left(\frac{\alpha_n^{'}}{sh\alpha_n^{'}a}-\frac{\beta_n^{''}}{sh\beta_n^{'}a}\right)(B_n)+\frac{4\lambda}{Db}\cdot$$

$$\sum_{m=1,2}^{\infty}\frac{\alpha_m\beta_n}{K_{dmn}^2}(C_n)-\frac{4\lambda}{b}\sum_{m=1,2}^{\infty}\frac{(-1)^n\alpha_m\beta_n}{K_{dmn}^{'2}}$$

$$\left[\beta_n^2+\alpha_m^2(2-\nu)\right](d_m)=0 \tag{27}$$

$$\frac{2P}{Da}\left\{\left[\alpha_m^{'2}-\alpha_m^2(2-\nu)\right]\frac{sh\alpha_m^{'}y_0}{sh\alpha_m^{'}b}-\right.$$

$$\left.\left[\beta_m^{''2}-\alpha_m^2(2-\nu)\frac{sh\beta_m^{''}y_0}{sh\beta_m^{''}b}\right]\right\}\sin\alpha_m x_0-$$

$$\frac{4\lambda}{Da}\sum_{n=1,2}^{\infty}\frac{(-1)^n\alpha_m\beta_n}{K_{dmn}^2}\left[\alpha_m^2+\beta_n^2(2-\nu)\right](A_n)+$$

$$\frac{4\lambda}{Da}\sum_{n=1,2}^{\infty}\frac{(-1)^{m+n}\alpha_m\beta_n}{K_{dmn}^2}\left[\alpha_m^2+\beta_n^2(2-\nu)\right](B_n)+$$

$$\frac{1}{D}\left\{\left[\alpha_m^{'2}-\alpha_m^2(2-\nu)\right]\frac{\alpha_m^{'}}{sh\alpha_m^{'}b}-\right.$$

$$\left.\left[\beta_m^{''2}-\alpha_m^2(2-\nu)\right]\frac{\beta_m^{''}}{sh\beta_m^{''}b}\right\}(C_m)+$$

$$\left\{\left[\alpha_m^{'2}-\alpha_m^2(2-\nu)\right]^2cth\alpha_m^{'}b-\right.$$

$$\left.\left[\beta_m^{''2}-\alpha_m^2(2-\nu)\right]^2cth\beta_m^{''}b\right\}(d_m)=0 \tag{28}$$

4 Numerical Analysis

So we get four sets of infinite simultaneous equations (23)-(25) or (26)-(28). Remove restricted item, Solutions for the A_n, B_n, C_m and d_m. And then according to the formula (1) to (4) to obtain the moment and deflection magnitude of the amplitude. In particular, take each items of A_n, B_n,C_m and d_m, and assuming harmonic loads concentrated on midpoint board programming calculated for different values obtained are shown in table 1 deflection magnitude of moment magnitude and fixed side edge moment , and as shown in Figure 2 and Figure 3.

Discuss:

(1) The issue of convergence coefficient. Since the load and structural balance in the direction axis for symmetric, so there are $A_n=B_n$, $C_m=d_m=0(m=2,4...)$, C_m and d_m that is actually only take eight. And calculated that, An convergence of magnitude from 10^0 to 10^{-2} magnitude, C_m magnitude from 10^0 to converge to 10^{-4} magnitude, d_m magnitude from 10^{-2} to 10^{-5} convergence of magnitude, than the uniform load harmonic convergence is better.

(2) With regard to the distribution of M_{x0}. It is found, When $\omega/\omega_{11}=0.8$, M_{x0} larger value of the free edges will appear near the end. This suggests that, as the load frequency close to the natural frequency and a significant increase in the magnitude of the impact on its adjacent sides of the free edge of the moment.

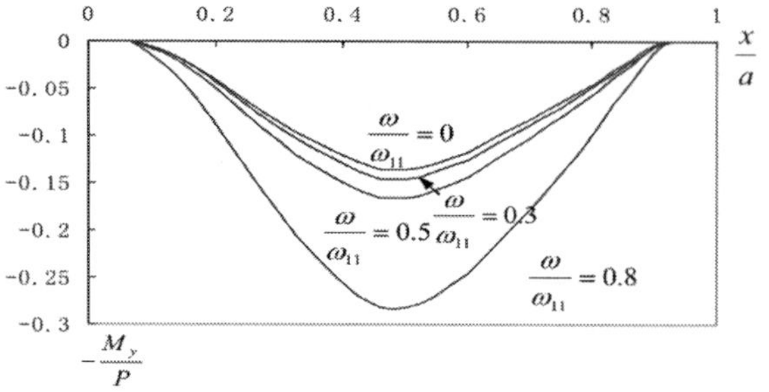

Figure 2. The amplitudes a/b=1 of the moment of clamped edge y=0

(3) With regard to the distribution of M_{x0}.When the ω/ω_{11} value is not the same,When the value is not the same, M_{y0} along $y=0$ edge was smooth symmetrical, and at both ends of a slight reverse moment appear.

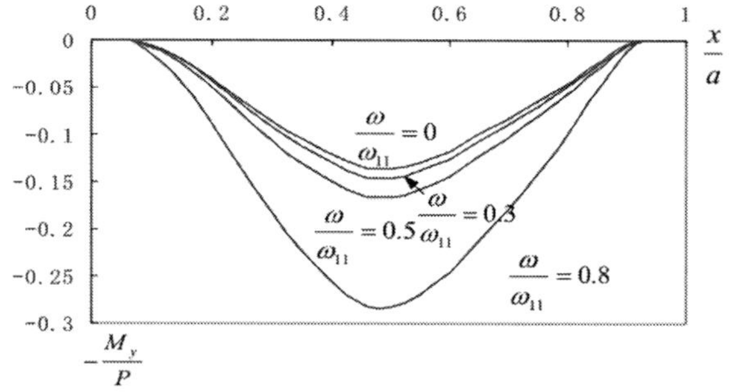

Figure 3. The amplitudes a/b=1 of the moment of clamped edge y=b

(4) The impact of load frequency. When the ω/ω_{11} from 0.0 to 0.8, the free side of the midpoint deflection of about 4.46 times the amplitude increases, y=0 along the side of the midpoint fixed maximum moment magnitude approximately double.

Table 1. The amplitudes (P) of the moment and the maximum deflection (Pa2/D) a/b=1at the clamped ends

ω/ω_{11}	$x/a(y/b)$ / $M(w)$	0.05	0.15	0.35
0.0	M_{x0}	0.000647	-0.02006	-0.1066
	M_{y0}	0.001470	-0.01934	-0.1045
	w_{yb}	0.000044	0.000508	0.002086
0.3	M_{x0}	0.000359	0.022110	-0.1142
	M_{y0}	0.001633	-0.02097	-0.1122
	w_{yb}	0.000062	0.000634	0.002515
0.5	M_{x0}	-0.000416	-0.02682	-0.13110
	M_{y0}	0.002043	-0.02459	-0.12920
	w_{yb}	0.000106	0.000957	0.003601
0.8	M_{x0}	-0.00697	-.05466	-0.22210
	M_{y0}	0.00512	-0.04353	-.2211
	w_{yb}	0.000457	0.003413	0.01171

continued

ω/ω_{11}	$x/a(y/b)$ / $M(w)$	0.5	0.7	0.9	0.95
0.0	M_{x0}	-0.1497	-0.13490	-0.08149	-0.06926
	M_{y0}	-0.1355	-0.08397	-0.00485	0.00147
	w_{yb}	0.002634	0.001712	0.000216	0.000044
0.3	M_{x0}	-0.16140	-0.14970	-0.09592	-0.08865
	M_{y0}	-0.1451	-0.09023	-0.00534	0.001633
	w_{yb}	0.00316	0.002074	0.000278	0.000062
0.5	M_{x0}	-0.1879	-0.18500	-0.13200	-0.13840
	M_{y0}	-0.1664	-0.1042	-0.00641	0.002043
	w_{yb}	0.004489	0.002989	0.000435	0.000106
0.8	M_{x0}	-0.34180	-0.4176	-0.3949	-0.5209
	M_{y0}	-0.2824	-0.17911	-0.01179	0.00512
	w_{yb}	0.01438	0.009844	0.001648	0.000457

5 Conclusion

(1) In this paper, mixed variables method for solving a rectangular plate with three fixed and one free vibration in any concentrated harmonic loads obtain the steady-state solution by forced vibration.

(2) Mix variables method is a simple vibration, universal, effective method to solve problem of forced vibration of bending a rectangular sheet.

(3) The results obtained by mixed variables method is correct, it may be practical engineering directly.

References

1. BaoLian Fu. Elasticity energy principle and its application. Beijing: Science Press, 2004: 6-56
2. BaoLian Fu. Bent sheet reciprocal new theory. Beijing: Science Press, 2003
3. FuFan Zhang. Bending under harmonic load cantilever rectangular plate. Applied Mathematics and Mechanics, 1980,1 (3): 349-362
4. FuFan Zhang. The elastic sheet (second edition) Beijing: Science Press, 1984
5. DeJian Shu, ZhengDong Shi. The elastic sheet generalized variational principle and its application [J], Beijing Aviation College, 1957, (1): 27-3

MATEC Web of Conferences 44, 02053 (2016)
DOI: 10.1051/matecconf/20164402053

The stability analysis of a rectangular plate supported at points of the corners

Yu Hong Bian[a], Chen Zhang

Key Laboratory of Mechanical Reliability for Heavy Equipments and Large Structures of Hebei Province, College of Civil Engineering and Mechanics, Yanshan University, Qinhuangdao, China

Abstract. The stability problem of a rectangular plate supported at points of corners under uniform pressures in its median plane is studied by using the reciprocal theorem. At first, according to the differential equation of transversal buckling displacement function for a thin rectangular plate, dual trigonometric series, and the reciprocal theorem, the equation of the deflection surface for a rectangular plate with four simple supported edges under uniform pressures in its median plane and a transversal concentrated unit load is established. Secondly, using the reciprocal theorem, the buckling equation for a rectangular plate supported at points of corners is derived. The unknowns here can be determined by the boundary conditions. The exact solution of critical load is given. Finally, as an example, a square plate has been calculated. The results show that the method is accurate and effective to solve the stability problem of rectangular plates. It can serve as technical reference for engineering designs.

1 Introduction

Applications of thin elastic plate are broad in many fields of aerospace industry, civil engineering, and chemical engineering and so on. However, fulsome pressures imposed upon the edges of plates can cause the breakage because of instability, even causing harm. Therefore, the stability analysis for thin elastic plate is both theoretically and practically an important topic.

Research methods about the stability problem of thin elastic rectangular plates are abundant [1-5]. However, there aren't many studies of the exact solution for the stability problem of rectangular plates with complex boundary conditions. This is because the formulas of the stability problem are generally listed according to the boundary conditions at the stability analysis for the plate. The more complex the boundary condition, the greater the difficulty of solving. In this paper, the reciprocal theorem is applied to research on the stability problem of a rectangular plate supported at points of corners under uniform pressures in its median plane. The exact solution of critical load is given. The results show that the method can solve the stability problem of rectangular plates with various boundary conditions. It is effective to solve the stability problem of thin elastic plates.

2 Buckling equation for a rectangular plate supported at points of corners

A rectangular plate with four simple supported edges under uniform pressure p_x and p_y in its median plane on the boundaries and a transversal concentrated unit load $\delta(x-\xi; y-\eta)$ at a moving point (ξ, η) is shown in Fig. 1, where

$$\delta(x-\xi; y-\eta) = \begin{cases} 1 & x=\xi, y=\eta \\ 0 & \text{otherlocations} \end{cases} \quad (1)$$

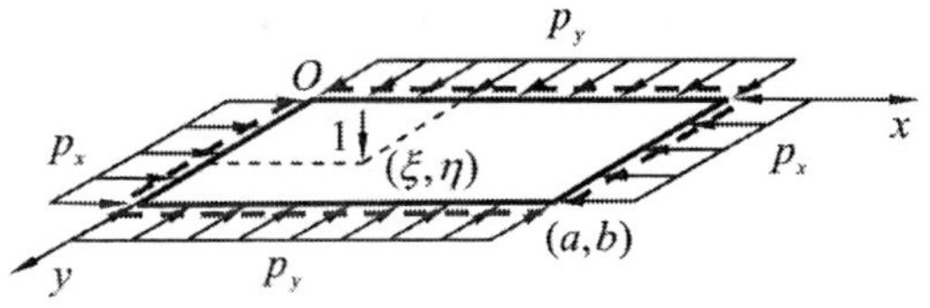

Figure 1. A rectangular plate with four simple supported edges.

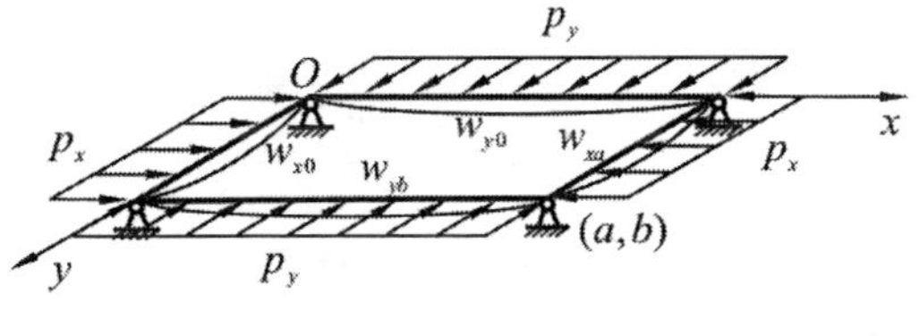

Figure 2. A rectangular plate supported at points of the corners.

The equation of the deflection surface can be easily obtained as

---

[a] Corresponding author: bianyuhong@163.com

$$w(x, y; \xi, \eta) = \sum_{m=1}^{\infty}\sum_{n=1}^{\infty} \frac{4}{abDK_{mn}} \sin\frac{m\pi\xi}{a} \sin\frac{n\pi\eta}{b} \cdot$$

$$\sin\frac{m\pi x}{a} \sin\frac{n\pi y}{b} \tag{2}$$

where D is the bending rigidity of the rectangular plate, and

$$K_{mn} = \left(\frac{m^2\pi^2}{a^2} + \frac{n^2\pi^2}{b^2}\right)^2 - \frac{p_x}{D}\frac{m^2\pi^2}{a^2} - \frac{p_y}{D}\frac{n^2\pi^2}{b^2} \tag{3}$$

Considering a rectangular plate supported at points of the corners shown in Fig. 2, the plate is in a critical condition under the pressure p_x and p_y in its median plane. The deflection equations of four free edges are respectively assumed as

$$w_{x0} = \sum_{n=1}^{\infty} a_n \sin\frac{n\pi y}{b} \tag{4}$$

$$w_{xa} = \sum_{n=1}^{\infty} b_n \sin\frac{n\pi y}{b} \tag{5}$$

$$w_{y0} = \sum_{m=1}^{\infty} c_m \sin\frac{m\pi x}{a} \tag{6}$$

$$w_{yb} = \sum_{m=1}^{\infty} d_m \sin\frac{m\pi x}{a} \tag{7}$$

The rectangular plate with four simple supported edges shown in Fig. 1 is taken as the first system; the rectangular plate supported at points of corners shown in Fig. 2 is taken as the second system. Without regard to manual action, between the first system and the second system, the reciprocal theorem is applied, there are

$$w(\xi, \eta) = \int_0^b V_{1x0} w_{x0}\, dy - \int_0^b V_{1xa} w_{xa}\, dy +$$
$$\int_0^a V_{1y0} w_{y0}\, dx - \int_0^a V_{1yb} w_{yb}\, dx \tag{8}$$

where V_{1x0}, V_{1xa}, V_{1y0}, and V_{1yb} are equivalent shearing forces on boundaries for the first system.

The Eqs. (2)-(7) are substituted into the Eq. (8), the buckling equation for a rectangular plate supported at points of corners can be obtained as

$$w(\xi, \eta) = \sum_{n=1}^{\infty} \frac{1}{\alpha_n^2 - \beta_n^2}\left\{\left[\alpha_n^2 - (2-\nu)\left(\frac{n\pi}{b}\right)^2 + \right.\right.$$
$$\left.\frac{p_x}{D}\right]\frac{\operatorname{sh}\alpha_n(a-\xi)}{\operatorname{sh}\alpha_n a} - \left[\beta_n^2 - (2-\nu)\left(\frac{n\pi}{b}\right)^2 + \right.$$
$$\left.\left.\frac{p_x}{D}\right]\frac{\operatorname{sh}\beta_n(a-\xi)}{\operatorname{sh}\beta_n a}\right\}\sin\frac{n\pi\eta}{b}(a_n) +$$

$$\sum_{n=1}^{\infty} \frac{1}{\alpha_n^2 - \beta_n^2}\left\{\left[\alpha_n^2 - (2-\nu)\left(\frac{n\pi}{b}\right)^2 + \frac{p_x}{D}\right]\frac{\operatorname{sh}\alpha_n\xi}{\operatorname{sh}\alpha_n a} - \right.$$
$$\left.\left[\beta_n^2 - (2-\nu)\left(\frac{n\pi}{b}\right)^2 + \frac{p_x}{D}\right]\frac{\operatorname{sh}\beta_n\xi}{\operatorname{sh}\beta_n a}\right\}\sin\frac{n\pi\eta}{b}(b_n) +$$

$$\sum_{m=1}^{\infty} \frac{1}{\alpha_m^2 - \beta_m^2}\left\{\left[\alpha_m^2 - (2-\nu)\left(\frac{m\pi}{a}\right)^2 + \right.\right.$$
$$\left.\frac{p_y}{D}\right]\frac{\operatorname{sh}\alpha_m(b-\eta)}{\operatorname{sh}\alpha_m b} - \left[\beta_m^2 - (2-\nu)\left(\frac{m\pi}{a}\right)^2 + \right.$$
$$\left.\left.\frac{p_y}{D}\right]\frac{\operatorname{sh}\beta_m(b-\eta)}{\operatorname{sh}\beta_m b}\right\}\sin\frac{m\pi\xi}{a}(c_m) +$$

$$\sum_{m=1}^{\infty} \frac{1}{\alpha_m^2 - \beta_m^2}\left\{\left[\alpha_m^2 - (2-\nu)\left(\frac{m\pi}{a}\right)^2 + \frac{p_y}{D}\right]\frac{\operatorname{sh}\alpha_m\eta}{\operatorname{sh}\alpha_m b} - \right.$$
$$\left.\left[\beta_m^2 - (2-\nu)\left(\frac{m\pi}{a}\right)^2 + \frac{p_y}{D}\right]\frac{\operatorname{sh}\beta_m\eta}{\operatorname{sh}\beta_m b}\right\}\sin\frac{m\pi\xi}{a}(d_m) \tag{9}$$

where ν is Poisson's ratio of the plate, and

$$\alpha_n = \sqrt{\eta_n + \sqrt{\eta_n^2 - p_n^2}},\ \beta_n = \sqrt{\eta_n - \sqrt{\eta_n^2 - p_n^2}} \tag{10}$$

$$\eta_n = \left(\frac{n\pi}{b}\right)^2 - \frac{p_x}{2D},\ p_n^2 = \left(\frac{n\pi}{b}\right)^4 - \frac{p_y}{D}\left(\frac{n\pi}{b}\right)^2 \tag{11}$$

$$\alpha_m = \sqrt{\eta_m + \sqrt{\eta_m^2 - p_m^2}},\ \beta_m = \sqrt{\eta_m - \sqrt{\eta_m^2 - p_m^2}} \tag{12}$$

$$\eta_m = \left(\frac{m\pi}{a}\right)^2 - \frac{p_y}{2D},\ p_m^2 = \left(\frac{m\pi}{a}\right)^4 - \frac{p_x}{D}\left(\frac{m\pi}{a}\right)^2 \tag{13}$$

3 Characteristic equation of critical load

The Eq. (9) should satisfy the following boundary conditions:

$$\left\{-D\left[\frac{\partial^3 w}{\partial\xi^3} + (2-\nu)\frac{\partial^3 w}{\partial\xi\partial\eta^2}\right] - p_x\frac{\partial w}{\partial\xi}\right\}_{\xi=0} = 0 \tag{14}$$

$$\left\{-D\left[\frac{\partial^3 w}{\partial\xi^3} + (2-\nu)\frac{\partial^3 w}{\partial\xi\partial\eta^2}\right] - p_x\frac{\partial w}{\partial\xi}\right\}_{\xi=a} = 0 \tag{15}$$

$$\left\{-D\left[\frac{\partial^3 w}{\partial\eta^3} + (2-\nu)\frac{\partial^3 w}{\partial\eta\partial\xi^2}\right] - p_y\frac{\partial w}{\partial\eta}\right\}_{\eta=0} = 0 \tag{16}$$

$$\left\{-D\left[\frac{\partial^3 w}{\partial\eta^3}+(2-\nu)\frac{\partial^3 w}{\partial\eta\partial\xi^2}\right]-p_y\frac{\partial w}{\partial\eta}\right\}_{\eta=b}=0 \quad (17)$$

The Eq. (9) is substituted into the Eqs. (14)-(17), after simplified and arranged, the executing equations for above boundary conditions can be respectively obtained as

$$\frac{1}{\alpha_n^2-\beta_n^2}\left\{\left[\alpha_n^2-(2-\nu)\frac{n^2\pi^2}{b^2}+\frac{p_x}{D}\right]^2\alpha_n\mathrm{cth}\alpha_n a-\left[\beta_n^2-(2-\nu)\frac{n^2\pi^2}{b^2}+\frac{p_x}{D}\right]^2\beta_n\mathrm{cth}\beta_n a\right\}(a_n)-$$
$$\frac{1}{\alpha_n^2-\beta_n^2}\left\{\left[\alpha_n^2-(2-\nu)\frac{n^2\pi^2}{b^2}+\frac{p_x}{D}\right]^2\frac{\alpha_n}{\mathrm{sh}\alpha_n a}-\left[\beta_n^2-(2-\nu)\frac{n^2\pi^2}{b^2}+\frac{p_x}{D}\right]^2\frac{\beta_n}{\mathrm{sh}\beta_n a}\right\}(b_n)+$$
$$\frac{2}{b}\sum_{m=1}^{\infty}\frac{1}{K_{mn}}\frac{m\pi}{a}\frac{n\pi}{b}\left[(1-\nu)^2\frac{m^2\pi^2}{a^2}\frac{n^2\pi^2}{b^2}-\frac{p_y}{D}\frac{m^2\pi^2}{a^2}-\frac{p_x}{D}\frac{n^2\pi^2}{b^2}+\frac{p_x p_y}{D^2}\right](c_m)-$$
$$\frac{2}{b}\sum_{m=1}^{\infty}\frac{(-1)^n}{K_{mn}}\frac{m\pi}{a}\frac{n\pi}{b}\left[(1-\nu)^2\frac{m^2\pi^2}{a^2}\frac{n^2\pi^2}{b^2}-\frac{p_y}{D}\frac{m^2\pi^2}{a^2}-\frac{p_x}{D}\frac{n^2\pi^2}{b^2}+\frac{p_x p_y}{D^2}\right](d_m)=0$$

(18)

$$\frac{1}{\alpha_n^2-\beta_n^2}\left\{\left[\alpha_n^2-(2-\nu)\frac{n^2\pi^2}{b^2}+\frac{p_x}{D}\right]^2\frac{\alpha_n}{\mathrm{sh}\alpha_n a}-\left[\beta_n^2-(2-\nu)\frac{n^2\pi^2}{b^2}+\frac{p_x}{D}\right]^2\frac{\beta_n}{\mathrm{sh}\beta_n a}\right\}(a_n)-$$
$$\frac{1}{\alpha_n^2-\beta_n^2}\left\{\left[\alpha_n^2-(2-\nu)\frac{n^2\pi^2}{b^2}+\frac{p_x}{D}\right]^2\alpha_n\mathrm{cth}\alpha_n a-\left[\beta_n^2-(2-\nu)\frac{n^2\pi^2}{b^2}+\frac{p_x}{D}\right]^2\beta_n\mathrm{cth}\beta_n a\right\}(b_n)+$$
$$\frac{2}{b}\sum_{m=1}^{\infty}\frac{(-1)^m}{K_{mn}}\frac{m\pi}{a}\frac{n\pi}{b}\left[(1-\nu)^2\frac{m^2\pi^2}{a^2}\frac{n^2\pi^2}{b^2}-\frac{p_y}{D}\frac{m^2\pi^2}{a^2}-\frac{p_x}{D}\frac{n^2\pi^2}{b^2}+\frac{p_x p_y}{D^2}\right](c_m)-$$
$$\frac{2}{b}\sum_{m=1}^{\infty}\frac{(-1)^{m+n}}{K_{mn}}\frac{m\pi}{a}\frac{n\pi}{b}\left[(1-\nu)^2\frac{m^2\pi^2}{a^2}\frac{n^2\pi^2}{b^2}-\frac{p_y}{D}\frac{m^2\pi^2}{a^2}-\frac{p_x}{D}\frac{n^2\pi^2}{b^2}+\frac{p_x p_y}{D^2}\right](d_m)=0$$

(19)

$$\frac{2}{a}\sum_{n=1}^{\infty}\frac{1}{K_{mn}}\frac{m\pi}{a}\frac{n\pi}{b}\left[(1-\nu)^2\frac{m^2\pi^2}{a^2}\frac{n^2\pi^2}{b^2}-\frac{p_y}{D}\frac{m^2\pi^2}{a^2}-\frac{p_x}{D}\frac{n^2\pi^2}{b^2}+\frac{p_x p_y}{D^2}\right](a_n)-$$
$$\frac{2}{a}\sum_{n=1}^{\infty}\frac{(-1)^m}{K_{mn}}\frac{m\pi}{a}\frac{n\pi}{b}\left[(1-\nu)^2\frac{m^2\pi^2}{a^2}\frac{n^2\pi^2}{b^2}-\frac{p_y}{D}\frac{m^2\pi^2}{a^2}-\frac{p_x}{D}\frac{n^2\pi^2}{b^2}+\frac{p_x p_y}{D^2}\right](b_n)+$$
$$\frac{1}{\alpha_m^2-\beta_m^2}\left\{\left[\alpha_m^2-(2-\nu)\frac{m^2\pi^2}{a^2}+\frac{p_y}{D}\right]^2\alpha_m\mathrm{cth}\alpha_m b-\left[\beta_m^2-(2-\nu)\frac{m^2\pi^2}{a^2}+\frac{p_y}{D}\right]^2\beta_m\mathrm{cth}\beta_m b\right\}(c_m)-$$
$$\frac{1}{\alpha_m^2-\beta_m^2}\left\{\left[\alpha_m^2-(2-\nu)\frac{m^2\pi^2}{a^2}+\frac{p_y}{D}\right]^2\frac{\alpha_m}{\mathrm{sh}\alpha_m b}-\left[\beta_m^2-(2-\nu)\frac{m^2\pi^2}{a^2}+\frac{p_y}{D}\right]^2\frac{\beta_m}{\mathrm{sh}\beta_m b}\right\}(d_m)=0$$

(20)

$$\frac{2}{a}\sum_{n=1}^{\infty}\frac{(-1)^n}{K_{mn}}\frac{m\pi}{a}\frac{n\pi}{b}\left[(1-\nu)^2\frac{m^2\pi^2}{a^2}\frac{n^2\pi^2}{b^2}-\frac{p_y}{D}\frac{m^2\pi^2}{a^2}-\frac{p_x}{D}\frac{n^2\pi^2}{b^2}+\frac{p_x p_y}{D^2}\right](a_n)-$$
$$\frac{2}{a}\sum_{n=1}^{\infty}\frac{(-1)^{m+n}}{K_{mn}}\frac{m\pi}{a}\frac{n\pi}{b}\left[(1-\nu)^2\frac{m^2\pi^2}{a^2}\frac{n^2\pi^2}{b^2}-\frac{p_y}{D}\frac{m^2\pi^2}{a^2}-\frac{p_x}{D}\frac{n^2\pi^2}{b^2}+\frac{p_x p_y}{D^2}\right](b_n)+$$
$$\frac{1}{\alpha_m^2-\beta_m^2}\left\{\left[\alpha_m^2-(2-\nu)\frac{m^2\pi^2}{a^2}+\frac{p_y}{D}\right]^2\frac{\alpha_m}{\mathrm{sh}\alpha_m b}-\left[\beta_m^2-(2-\nu)\frac{m^2\pi^2}{a^2}+\frac{p_y}{D}\right]^2\frac{\beta_m}{\mathrm{sh}\beta_m b}\right\}(c_m)-$$
$$\frac{1}{\alpha_m^2-\beta_m^2}\left\{\left[\alpha_m^2-(2-\nu)\frac{m^2\pi^2}{a^2}+\frac{p_y}{D}\right]^2\alpha_m\mathrm{cth}\alpha_m b-\left[\beta_m^2-(2-\nu)\frac{m^2\pi^2}{a^2}+\frac{p_y}{D}\right]^2\beta_m\mathrm{cth}\beta_m b\right\}(d_m)=0$$

(21)

The Eqs. (18)-(21) form a set of the homogeneous linear equations, which include the unknowns a_n, b_n, c_m, and d_m in all. Setting the determinant of the coefficients equal to zero is the characteristic equation for the stability problem.

4 Numerical example

The buckling surface of the plate is symmetrical or antisymmetric about $x = a/2$ and $y = b/2$. Four forms of the instability may exist by $a_n = b_n$, $a_n = -b_n$, $c_m = d_m$, and $c_m = -d_m$. Because symmetrical wave form corresponds to the minimum of critical load, it is reasonable to think about the Eq. (18) and (20) only. A square plate is used as an example. Let $a = b$, $\nu = 0.3$, $p_x = p_y = p$. The $p_{cr} = pa^2/D\pi^2$ is introduced as the coefficient of critical load. The Eqs. (10)-(13) are respectively substituted into the Eq. (18) and (20), there are

$$\frac{1}{p_{cr}}\left\{\left[p_{cr}-(1-\nu)n^2\right]^2 n\pi\,\mathrm{th}\frac{n\pi}{2}-\right.$$
$$\left.(1-\nu)^2 n^4\sqrt{n^2-p_{cr}}\,\pi\,\mathrm{th}\frac{\sqrt{n^2-p_{cr}}}{2}\pi\right\}(a_n)+$$
$$\sum_{m=1}^{\infty}\frac{4[n^2+(2-\nu)m^2-p_{cr}]}{mn\left[\left(\frac{m}{n}+\frac{n}{m}\right)^2-\left(\frac{1}{m^2}+\frac{1}{n^2}\right)p_{cr}\right]}\cdot$$
$$[m^2+(2-\nu)n^2-p_{cr}](c_m)=0 \tag{22}$$

$$\frac{1}{p_{cr}}\left\{\left[p_{cr}-(1-\nu)m^2\right]^2 m\pi\,\mathrm{th}\frac{m\pi}{2}-\right.$$
$$\left.(1-\nu)^2 m^4\sqrt{m^2-p_{cr}}\,\pi\,\mathrm{th}\frac{\sqrt{m^2-p_{cr}}}{2}\pi\right\}(c_m)+$$
$$\sum_{n=1}^{\infty}\frac{4[m^2+(2-\nu)n^2-p_{cr}]}{mn\left[\left(\frac{n}{m}+\frac{m}{n}\right)^2-\left(\frac{1}{m^2}+\frac{1}{n^2}\right)p_{cr}\right]}\cdot$$
$$[n^2+(2-\nu)m^2-p_{cr}](a_n)=0 \tag{23}$$

The corresponding critical load can be obtained by the determinant of the coefficients for above homogeneous linear equations equal to zero. Considering the symmetry of the plate, let $m = 1,3,5,\cdots$, $n = 1,3,5,\cdots$. Using the method of progressive searching root and programming the characteristic equation of the Eq. (22) and (23), the results are shown in Table 1.

Table 1. Critical load coefficients p_{cr} of the rectangular plate supported at points of corners.

k	8	12	16	20
p_{cr}	1.4079	1.3268	1.3004	1.2589
k	24	32	50	64
p_{cr}	1.2177	1.1826	1.1168	1.1151

where k is ranks of the determinant, i.e. the sums of the m and n. The $p_{cr} = 1.1151$ can be selected as the exact solution of critical load for the rectangular plate supported at points of corners.

5 Conclusions

By analyzing the stability of a rectangular plate supported at points of corners under uniform pressures in its median plane, the exact solution of critical load is given. The results show that the method is accurate and effective to solve the stability problem of thin elastic plates. The results of this paper will overcome errors of various approximate solutions. It provides reliable basis for the security and reliability design of engineering structures.

References

1. I. E. Harik, R. Ekambaram, Seminumerical solution for buckling of rectangular plates, Computers and Structures, **23**, 649-655 (1986)
2. F. F. Zhang, *Elastic thin plates*, 2nd ed, Beijing: Science Press (1984)
3. J. Purbolaksono, M. H. Aliabadi, Buckling analysis of shear deformable plates by boundary element method, International Journal for Numerical Methods in Engineering, **62**, 537-563 (2005)
4. C. W. Bert, K. K. Devarakonda, Buckling of rectangular plates subjected to nonlinearly distributed in-plane loading, Int. J. Solids Struct., **40**, 4097-4106 (2003)
5. X. W. Wang, X. F. Wang, X. D. Shi, Accurate buckling loads of thin rectangular plates under parabolic edge compressions by the differential quadrature method, International Journal of Mechanical Sciences, **49**, 447-453 (2007)
6. M. L. Tan, J. L. Dong, Buckling analysis of thin rectangular plates under cosine-distributed compressive loads, Engineering Mechanics, **27**, 32-35 (2010)

MATEC Web of Conferences **44**, 02054 (2016)
DOI: 10.1051/matecconf/20164402054

The Design of Folio Shielding Door

Lan Mi[1]

[1]*Environmental Management College of China, No. 8 Golden Harbor Road,Beidaihe District,Qinhuangdao City,Hebei province, China*

Abstract. Through analyzing a case of the design of a folio shielding door, the design and key technology of the equipment are shown.
KEYWORD: a folio shielding door; the design

An auto-opening electromagnetism-shield wave-absorbing door is needed by a dark room program, whose net opening size is 4m×5m(W×H),and 700mm wave-absorbing material is needed to be pasted on the door leaf.

1 The Confirmation of the Designing Project

At the beginning, it was considered to put in use the mature pneumatic flat-pressing electric translating wave-absorbing door, which had been examined reliable by various projects. Due to the fact that the net width of shield containing room was 8.5m and winding lines were needed by the sides of the room, the door did not enjoy enough space. The second option was vertical-lift wave-absorbing door. After calculating, it was figured that the net height of the containing room was merely 9.5m, that of the doorway was 5m, the minimum height of the lift door was 10m, and installing the leaf door frame needed some space as well. Therefore, the space was not enough for the vertical-lift wave-absorbing door too. Eventually, the door was expected to be a auto-rotating folio one. While the further calculation found when the door was 90°-opened, the actual net open size of the door was 2.6m, but the maximum width of transporting car was 3.2m . When the door was 145°-opened, the figure was 3.6m. It was sufficient for the equipment and car to enter, getting into the shield room. However, new problem occurred, which was the interference of door leaf and winding lines. After negotiating with the general engineer and process designers , the positions of the wind lines were adjusted, and the require was met.It was calculated when either the high end or the low end of the door leaf was pressed, the volume of deformation was approximately 10mm. When the door switch was put in the middle of the door leaf, none of the structure considered were able to meet the demand of power for switching the door. Single-spot pressing would increase the deformation of the door leaf, which would influence the function shielding. A pressing equipment was needed to meet the standard.

2 The Specifications and Parameters of the Door

Specification: 4m×5m(W×H)
Time for Opening : about 110s×2
Time for shutting : about 110s +125s
Way of Switching: auto-control
Opened Door Leaf : 145°
Screen Index: 100MHz～10GHz ≥100dB
10GHz～18GHz ≥90dB

3 Operating Principle and Structure

The size of the entrance is 4m(width)×5m(height). As shown in the figure 1, the operating time of each door leaf is 110s.The door is made up of door frame(1-0),door leaf (2-0),door leaf(3-0),hinge(4-0), chain wheel, lower part pressing system, chain installing frame, installing gantry, reduction box, trundle and chains. Chain wheel, driven by reduction box, rotates on the chains, motivating the door to open and close. As shown in the figure 2, lower part pressing structure is hidden beneath the ground at the entrance when it does not work. When the door is closed, it presses the lower part of the door tightly, making sure the door is closed well. Thus the electric continuity between door leaves and that of door leaf and door frame is ensured, and the shielding function of the door thus improved. A standard small shielding door is installed on the door leaf(2-0) for operators to go through. There is a trundle installed on the low part of the door

[a] Corresponding author: author@e-mail.org

leaf to reduce the burden of hinge on it, enlightening door leaf's deformation.

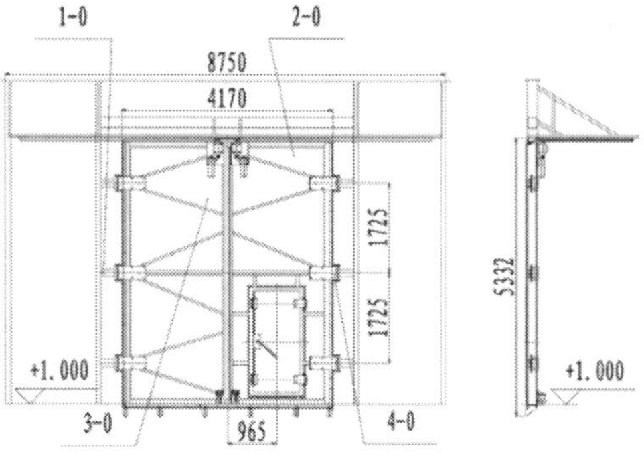

Figure 1. diagrammatic drawing of the door

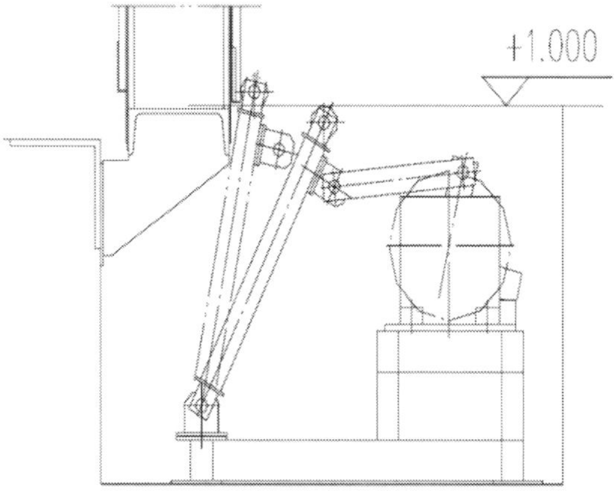

Figure 2. Lower compression mechanism

While designing the door leaf, it is examined that most power is needed when the door is opened at the first stage. Therefore, cants are arranged to put face-to-face for the gaps between door leaf and door frame and door leaves.In this way, the finer-shaped spring piece will provide a divided power vertical to the door, reducing the power needed when the door is opened. The door leaves are welded, so it is hard to remain the gaps between the leaves and frame balanced and unchanged. A adjusting board is added to make it possible to adjust the gaps on the spot, making the shielding function achievable. As shown in the Figure 3, Bronze boards are pasted on the leaves and frame, two finger-shaped beryllium -bronze springs and a electric foam are fixed on the bronze board which is on the door leaves. When the door is closed , the finger-shaped spring will shrink because of inertia, ensuring good electric continuity between door frame and leaves and improving the shielding ability of the door. The structure is shown in the figure 4. The gap is made with a certain angle between the door frame and leaves to reduce the resistance while opening it.

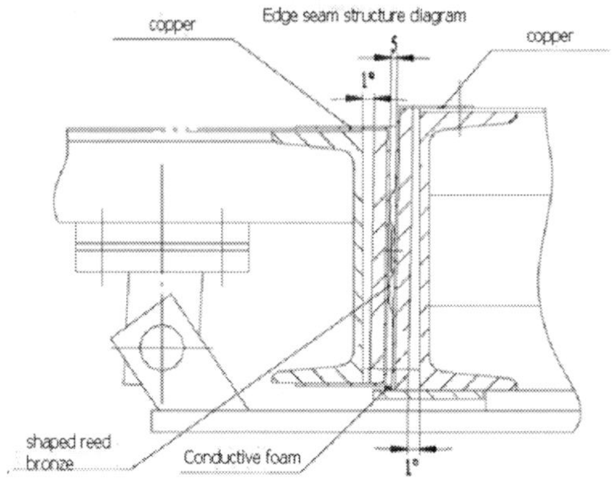

Figure 3. edge seam structure

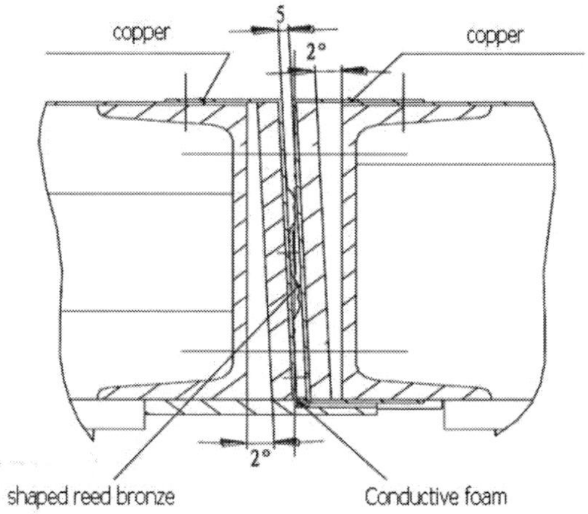

Figure 4. Structure of raphe

4 Conclusion

For shielding project, higher screen standard is easily realized in single-leaf door , and various mature products have been made. However, for, folio-shield door, a T-shape gap will from between the door leaves and frame, the shielding ability will reduce after times of switching. About 80dB of shielding doors have the effort above 10GHZ after being operated by general measures. This project is a successful exploration of folio-shield door for it is able to reach 103dB based on 10GHZ's effort and meet other ranges of dark room demand.

References

1. R.O.Duad,P.E.Hart. Use of Hough Transformation to Detect Lines and Curves in Pictures.Communications of the ACM,14,9(1972)
2. I.Mikic,P.Cosman,G.Kogut,andM.M.Trivedi.Moving shadow and object detection in traffic scenes.[J]Proceedings of International Conference on Pattern Recognition,(2000)
3. Johnson J P.Ehsani M.Guzelgunler Y Review of sensorless methods for brushlessDG.Industry Applications Conference,38(1999)

4. Yoshida M.Murai YTakada M Noise reduction by t orque ripp lesupperssion in brushless DC motor (1 998)

MATEC Web of Conferences 44, 02055 (2016)
DOI: 10.1051/matecconf/20164402055

The Outline Design of Students' Schedule Management System Based on B / S Mode

Lan Mi[1]
[1]Environmental Management College of China, No. 8 Golden Harbor Road,Beidaihe District,Qinhuangdao City,Hebei province, China

Abstract: This study is based on a preliminary outline design involved in the development of B / S mode of student schedule management system. It can provide the foundation and basis for the Panel's later detailed design and coding, and also standardize the team development. Documents will be divided into various modules, and the functional requirements of corresponding module are raised; total class diagrams, class function definitions and the function of functions are obtained for reference of the later design

1 Purpose of compiling

This document is a comprehensive and systematic presentation of the students' agenda management software architecture, and it describes the main aspects of the student program management software from different angles by using a variety of views, in order to meet the different focus and demand of relevant stakeholders of the software of the system's. This article expresses the important decision-making software architecture design staff has made the software architecture. Software Group will develop structural frame member as defined in accordance with project development plans; accordingly programmer will take detailed design of each member; test designers will test framework in accordance with the general design of the system architecture; another architecture document is also used to guide the member implementation, integration and testing.

2 System Structure Analysis

2.1 The basic structure

The system will eventually face student users, who is not familiar with knowledge of related fields, but completely familiar with the operation of the computer; on the other hand, the difference between each user's computer configuration is also larger, so the system uses B / S structure .

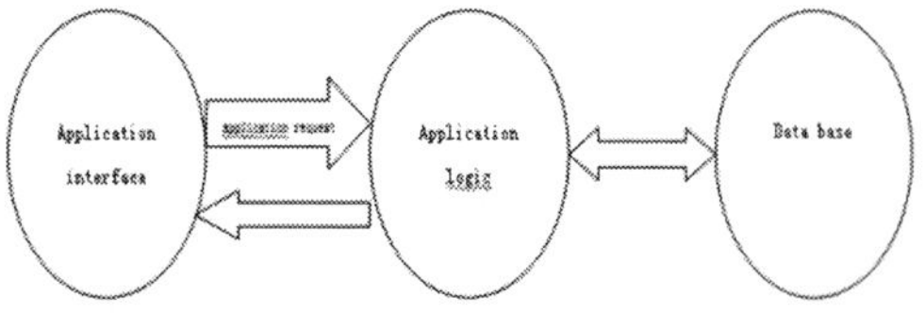

Figure 1 the three-layer B/Sstructure

[a] Corresponding author: author@e-mail.org

2.2 Module and System Architecture

Based on the user needs analysis, it designs login module, UI module, the weather module, time module, log module, course module, etc. Thus the system structure can be designed.

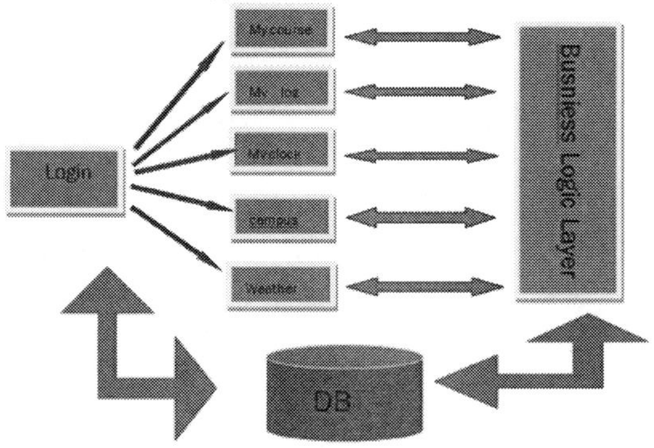

Figure 2 System Structure

3 Module Design

3.1 UI module Overview

The interface module is responsible for the preparation of the entire process, and it provides interactive interface. The general category of UI module is as follows:

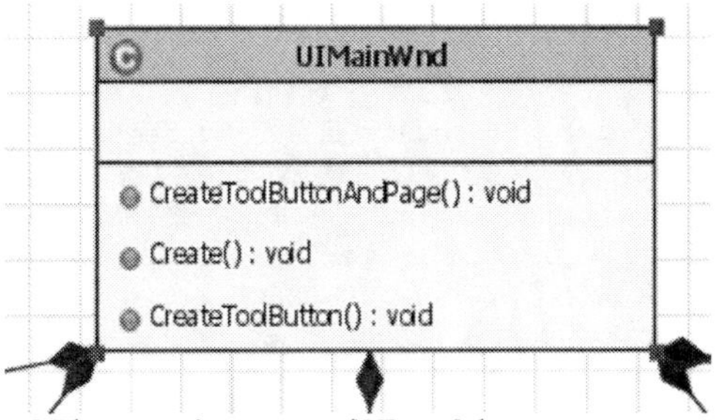

Figure 3 The general category of UI module

The definition of category is as figure 1

Number	*Function*	*Detailed Contents of Function*
1	Create()	*Create and display windows and buttons*
2	CreateToolButton ()	*Create a tool button on the main interface*
3	OnEventBtnClick_ChangeSkin *()*	*Change the skin*

3.2 Login Module Overview

This module is the first event entering into the system. The module is divided into four events: 1, user login: users who have been properly registered can log in to this system; 2, user registration: users who haven't registered yet get an account; 3, users logs out: users exit the system; 4, users' offline use: allowing users to use the system without having to log in, but the user can not manipulate the data.

Functional point design of related classes:

Checkin, users log in through comparison between the information recorded and data. If the user's information exists, he can log in, or the account or password will be warned wrong.

SetUserAccount(), set current user account。

CompareSsid(), compare users account, if it appears FLASE, it points the wrong input.

CompareKey(), compare user passwords, if it returns FALSE, it means the user input is incorrect

IsUserExist(), User's existence is checked through a user account id (primary key in the database).

Checkout, User logs off. In the main interface, when the user wants to switch accounts he can use this function. The user logs out the current account and the interface will go to the login screen.

ExitCurrentUI(), end the current interface。

GetLoginUI (), jump login interface。

Register, User registration. Users can enter their registration information, including the account password. This account password will be entered into the database.

IsUserExist(), Check if the user exists, if it does not exist, it will return TRUE, if it exists, it will return FLASE.

SetUserAccount(), Enter the user's account into the database.

UseByOffline (), It enables users to work offline (ie, Registration is not required).

GetMainUI(), Jump to the main interface.

ExitCurrentUI(), exit。

3.3 Weather Module Design Overview

This module provides weather information to the user, the user can use this module to understand weather information on the current location, or to obtain weather information of other location by typing a different location (city). The total class diagram is shown in Figure 4:

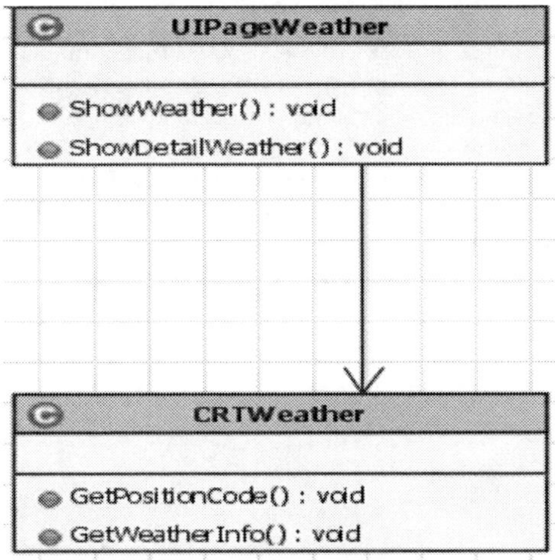

Figure 4 Weather module type diagram

3.4 Time Module Design Overview

This module displays the current time, a calendar function and date information. Total class diagram is shown in Figure 5:

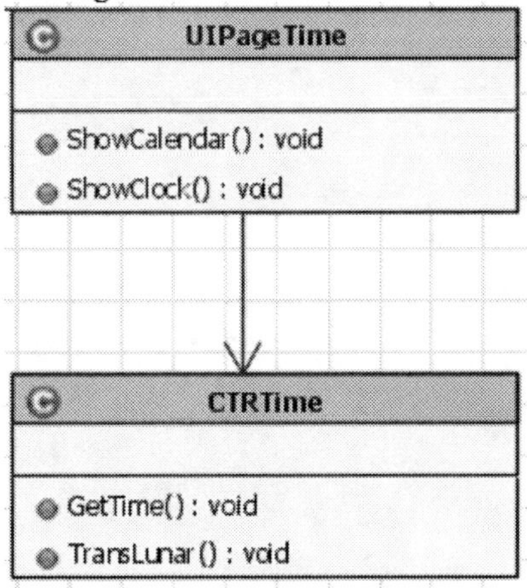

Figure 5 Time module type diagram

3.5 Log module Design Overview

The module provides log function for users. Users can make a record for a number of things worth recording during the day and store them in a database.

Users can add logs, change logs, delete the logs, view the log list, and set the log reminder.

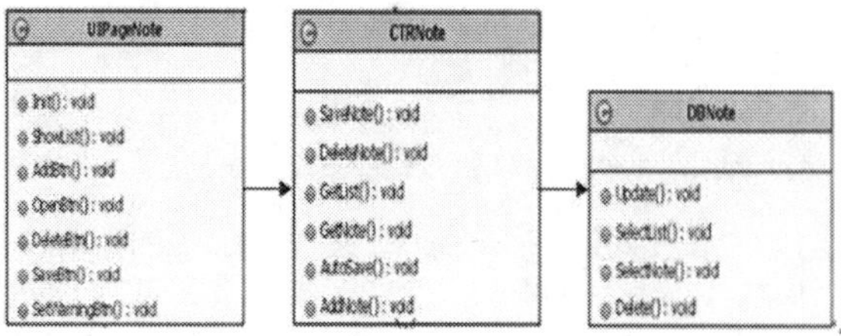

Figure 6 Log module type diagram

3.6 Course Module Overview

Course module provides users a maintainable curriculum. Users can fill in their own course information on the inside, and can choose to display real-time information about the current course of time on the desktop. By reading and writing database DBSchedule, one semester course information is stored and can be read according to user requirements. Its function processing logic is shown in Figure 7.

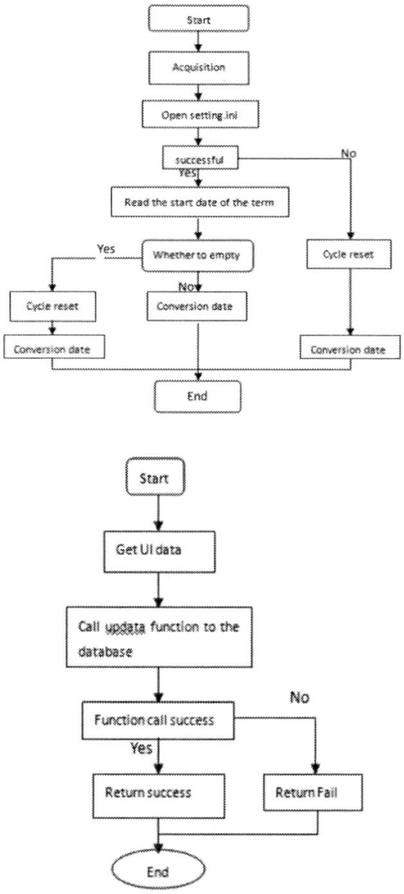

Figure 7 function logic processing diagram

4 Conclusion

This project is mainly designed for college students in general, with a higher use frequency. Besides meeting the needs of key software features, it also asks to consider security architecture design. There should be a more reliable security performance and fast response interactive features. In short, it requires stability, safety, convenience, and ease to operate and manage.

References

1. Barabba, V.P. (1991). "Through a Glass Less Darkly," Journal of the American Statistical Association, Vol. 86, No. 413, pp. 1-8.
2. Harsh, Stephen B., L. J. Connor, and G. D. Schwab. (1981). Managing The Farm Business. Prentice-Hall, Inc., Englewood Cliffs, New Jersey.
3. House, William C. (1983). Decision Support Systems – A Data-Based, Model-Oriented UserDeveloped Discipline. Petrocelli Books, Inc. New York, NY.
4. Paul T. Jaeger, Kim M.Thompson, E-government around the world: Lessons, challenges, and future directions, Government Information Quarterly, Vol. 20, 2003, pp.389-394.
5. B. Azad and S. Faraj, E-Government institutionalizing practices of a land registration mapping system, Government Information Quarterly, vol. 26, pp. 5-14, 2009.

MATEC Web of Conferences **44**, 02056 (2016)
DOI: 10.1051/matecconf/20164402056

A Novel Motor-Speed-Regulation Method

Zhou Huang[1,2], Zheng Wang Xu[1,2,a]

[1]*School of Electrical and Electronic Engineering, Hubei University of Technology, Wuhan, China*
[2]*Hubei Collaborative Innovation Center for High-efficiency Utilization of Solar Energy, Hubei University of technology, Wuhan, China*

Abstract. The traditional doubly-fed motor has less reliability because it needs carbon brushes and sliding rings which are not highly reliable. The brushless doubly-fed machine costs a lot for its framework requires special designing and processing. To overcome the disadvantages of the two kinds of motors, this paper focuses on a novel method of motor speed regulation which is based on rotating feeding. The motor speed changing around its rated speed can be realized based on the method without any carbon brush or sliding ring on the prosaic electrical motors. On the basis of the full controlled thyristor rectifying bridge structure, the basic idea is introduced; the advantages and disadvantages of this method are analyzed. This kind of systems can replace the brushed or brushless double-fed systems. They are very suitable for driving fans or pumps, or power-generating systems with variable speed constant frequency such as wind power or water power generating systems.

1 Introduction

At present, high voltage motors with high-capacity are widely used. Since the high voltage power transducers with high-capacity are quite expensive, most motors have to act in their rated speed. That will waste a great deal of energy. Some of them even could not work because their rated speed is not suitable in certain condition. For example, some factories supply water with high-capacity motors, and the demand for water varies according to the factory production conditions. When water consumption is stepping down, the water flow can only be regulated by valves because the motor can not regulate its speed. That causes energy waste and water waste. Another example is the drainage and irrigation station. There, low-head water is necessary for water and energy saving in the irrigation working condition, and on the other hand high-head water is beneficial to the rapid waterlogging drainage. If the motor can not regulate its speed, which will result in water wasting and energy wasting in irrigation, and will cause too slow drainage or even close down because the water head is not high enough to overcome the waterlogging pressure.

Since the doubly-fed motor is known, because it has a lot of advantages, such as, its speed can be regulated around its rated speed, a high-capacity motor can be controlled by a small-capacity transducer, the energy can be transmitted by a two-way duplex, it is very suitable for driving fans or pumps, or power-generating systems with variable speed constant frequency such as wind power or water power generating. A lot of scholars have been studying the doubly-fed machine and make a large number of achievements, such as improvements on the structure of rotor or stator structure, making a sane choice of transducers and power devices, the design of topology, the closed loop control strategy, vector controlling method, power allocation, reactive power controlling, motor starting, etc [1-5].

The traditional doubly-fed motor has a transducer which is connected to the motor's rotor. The motor speed can be regulated by adjusting the output frequency of the transducer. Because the transducer processes only the slip power, its capacity is usually much smaller than that of the controlled motor. When the motor speed is adjusted around its rated speed, it only demands a transducer with 1/2~1/5 of the motor capacity to realize the control. This kind of speed regulation system has come true in various fields, such as driving fans or pumps, or wind power-generating systems.

However, the traditional doubly-fed motor needs carbon brushes and sliding rings linking output of the transducer to the rotor which degrade the reliability of the system badly. We had to take into consideration the actual conditions for inspection and repair of the carbon brushes and sliding rings. In order to overcome this defect, Hunt broached a new idea about doubly-fed motor without any carbon brush and sliding ring. This kind of motor, named brushless doubly-fed motor, is studied deeply [6-10]. This type of motor is characterized by putting a control winding in the stator together with the power winding. A frequency

[a]Corresponding author: xuzw72@163.com

adjustable power is fed to the control winding by a transducer. This type of motor does not only maintain the advantage that the traditional doubly-fed motor needs a small-capacity transducer to regulate speed in a little pond, but also overcome the disadvantage that the traditional doubly-fed motor needs carbon brushes and sliding rings. But the brushless doubly-fed motor has a complicated framework, which is needed for special design and treating. So it can't be used in the normal motors. That is the reason that this kind of system has not been widely used in practice.

2 The idea of rotating feeding

Because the two kinds of doubly-fed systems have disadvantages mentioned before, if a new doubly-fed method is found for normal electrical motor, it will have a cheerful prospect. We analyzed the principle of the brushless doubly-fed motor carefully . And we found that there are two suits of stator windings in a brushless doubly-fed motor. The windings are fed by two sinusoidal currents with different frequencies separately. So, there are two rotating magnetic field established in the stator air gap with different speed. Both of them couple with the rotor and exchange energy with it. Then the output frequency of the transducer, which is connected to the controlling winding in the stator, can affect the rotating speed of the rotor.

According to the working principle of electrical motors [11], the motor working state is the interactive result of the rotating magnetic fields in the stator air gap produced by the stator current and the rotor current separately. It has only relationship with the magnetic fields, and it has no relationship with how the fields produced. That is to say, the rotating fields produced by different means have the same effect. If two stator rotating magnetic fields with different frequency can be produced in normal electrical motor which has only one stator winding, the working state in the brushless doubly-fed motor is imitated, and then doubly-fed speed regulation can be realized in the normal motors.

Because there is only one stator winding in the normal electrical motor, a short circuit accident will appear when the power source and the source outputted by the transducer are fed simply parallel to the stator by a hard connection. So the speed regulation can not be realized by that method. In order to solve the problem, we think an idea of rotating feeding. On the basis of rotating the motor on its rating speed by fed a line-frequency power source to it, the line-frequency source is "rotated" with a certain frequency. The motor speed will step upper than the rated speed if the rotating direction of the source is the same of the direction the rotor. Otherwise, the motor speed will step lower than the rated speed. And the variation of the motor speed is proportional to the rotating frequency of the source. The idea can be explained vividly. First, the stator is fed by a line-frequency power source, and the rotor rotates on the rated speed. Second, to imagine we can rotate the motor wholly on the basis of the condition in the first step, then the rotor will rotate on a different speed, and the direction and the quantity of the variation have relationship with the direction and the speed by which we rotate the whole motor. Last, because the stator can not be rotated actually, if the fed source is rotating on a certain frequency then the effect will be the same as rotating the whole motor.

3 The structure and the voltage waveforms of the example system

In order to reduce the production cost, we planed to develop the project on the basis of thyristor. The circuit analyzed below is consists of three-phase full controlled rectifying thyristor bridges. The circuit structure is shown in Figure 1. The three-phase AC power is fed to three same transformers. They output 3 three-phase AC powers with same voltage and same phase. The 3 powers are fed to the stator by an inverter consisted of thyristors.

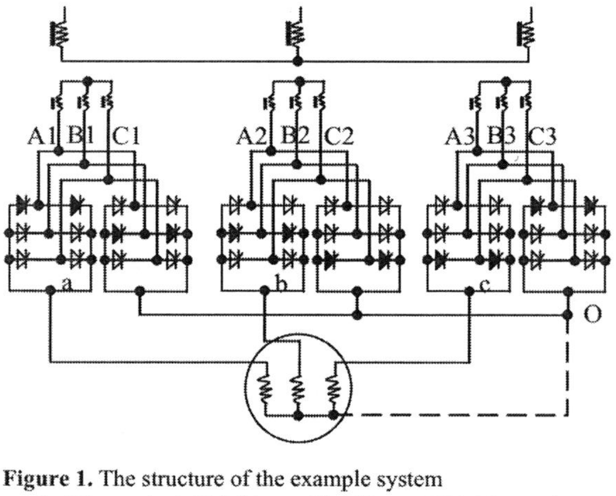

Figure 1. The structure of the example system

In Figure 1, A1B1C1、A2B2C2、A3B3C3 are the 3 three-phase AC powers. The same phases of the three powers (for instance A1、A2、A3) have same voltage and same phase with each other. Because the three AC powers come from different transformers, the direct connection of different phases causes no short current. The illustration of the connection of the neutral point (O point) is shown in Figure 2. In the figure, the B phase of the first transformer, the C phase of the second transformer and the A phase of the third transformer are connected directly, there is no short current because there is no current loop.

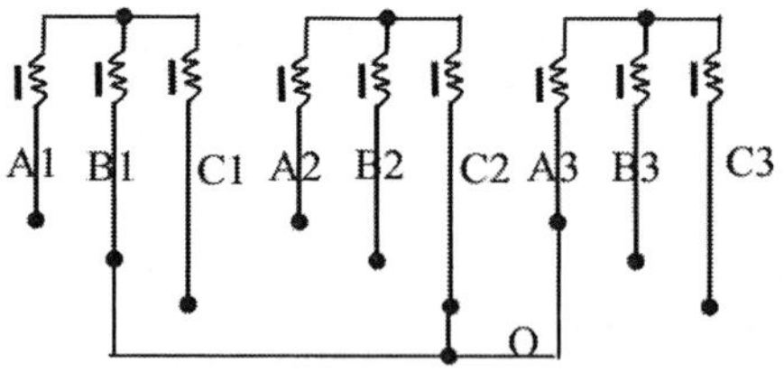

Figure 2. The illustration of the connection of the neutral point

But the three phase voltage and phase relationships are maintained in A1B1C1、A2B2C2、A3B3C3. If misunderstanding will not be caused, the indexes 1, 2, 3 will not be marked below. That is, A1B1C1、A2B2C2、A3B3C3 are represented by the same as ABC. Their voltage waveforms are shown in Figure 3.

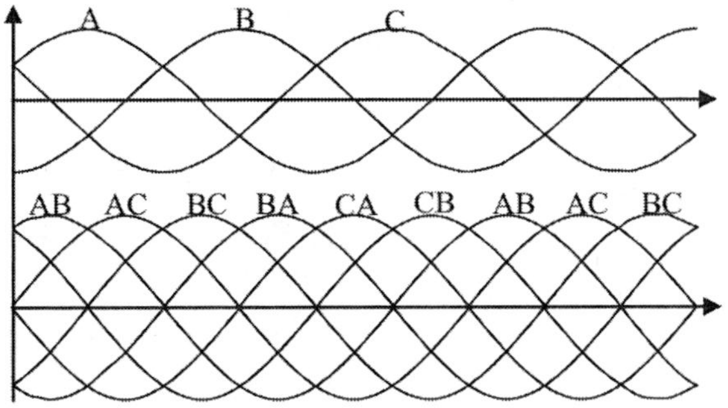

Figure 3. The waveforms of 3 three-phase AC phase voltages and line voltages

4 The working procedure of the rotating-fed system

We can see in the Figure 1, if the black thyristors conduct (the two thyristors connected in every phase work half of cycle alternately), and the other thyristors are cut off all the time, then O=B1=C2=A3, a=A1, b=B2, c=C3. Because the neutral point of the motor is also O, the phase voltage on the three stator windings are A1B1, B2C2 and C3A3 separately, or AB, BC and CA (their waveforms are shown in the left side of the moment t_1 in Figure 4). They form a three phase balance AC power with a frequency of line-frequency. So a rotating magnetic field with synchronous speed will be established in the motor air gap. The motor will work on the rated speed if the state is maintained all the time.

However, at a certain required moment, for example, at the moment t_1 in Figure 4, if the neutral point is changed from B1=C2=A3 to C1=A2=B3, that is realized by changing the thyristors connection of the neutral point, then the phase voltages on the motor stator windings change to AC, BA and CB (their waveforms are shown in Figure 4 between the moments t_1 and t_2). That is equivalent to there is a 60° phase lag shift appearing in the phase voltages, and that reduce the motor's speed from its rated speed.

If it is necessary, at another moment, for example, at the moment t_2 in Figure 4, the inputs of the motor a, b and c are changed to B1, C2 and A3 by changing the thyristors connection, and the neural point O is kept, then the phase voltages of the motor are changed to BC, CA and AB (their waveforms are shown in Figure after the moment t_2). There is a 60° phase lag shift further appearing in the phase voltages.

So there is a 60° phase lag shift at every time of changing, the phase voltages change back to the original state of AB, BC and CA after six times of changing to finish a whole cycle. If the intervals between two times of changing are equal to each other, represented by Δ t, then the period of a whole cycle can be written as T_2=6* Δ t. The rotating speed of the rotor can be written as:

$$n = n_e * (f_1 - f_2) / f_1 \quad (1)$$

Here, n_e is the rated rotating speed, f_1 is the line-frequency, and $f_2=1/T_2$ is the rotating frequency of the feeding.

If the direction of the changing is changed, for example, at the moment t_1 in Figure 5, the neutral point O is not changed and the inputs of the motor a, b and c are changed to C1, A2and B3, then the phase voltages are changed to CB, AC and BA (their waveforms are shown in Figure 5 after the moment t_1). That is equivalent to there is a 60° phase leading shift appearing in the phase voltages, and that increase the motor's speed from its rated speed. If the intervals between the changing moments are also Δ t, then the rotor speed can be written as:

$$n = n_e * (f_1 + f_2) / f_1 \quad (2)$$

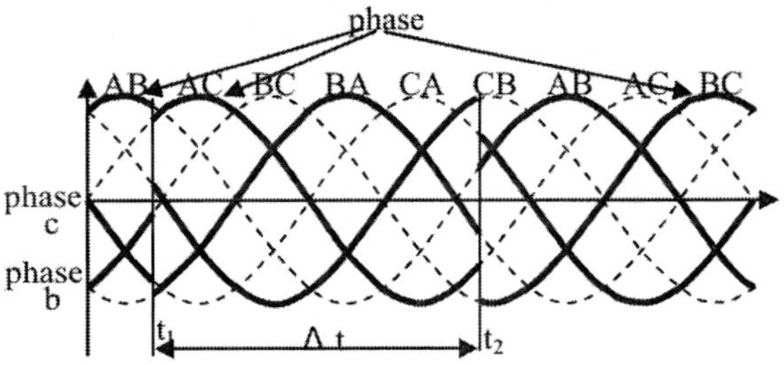

Figure 4. The illustration of rotating-fed

Here, n_e, f_1 and f_2 have the same meanings as in (1).

According to (1) and (2), the motor's speed can be adjusted upper or lower than the rated speed by the rotating feeding to achieve the same speed regulation results as the doubly-fed motors.

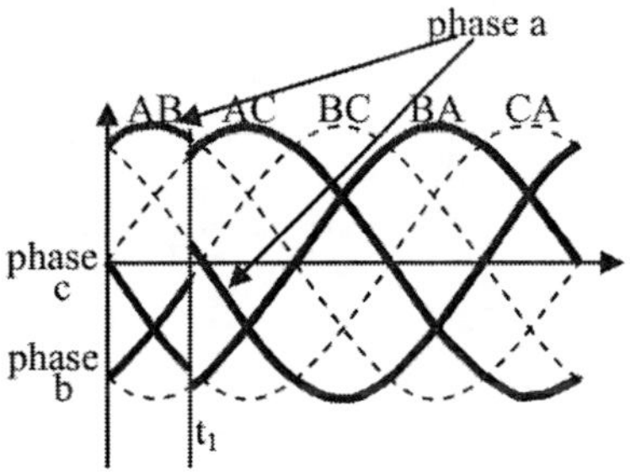

Figure 5. The illustration of rotating-fed with an exceeding rated speed

5 Conclusions

In the analyzing before, it is not taken into account that the voltages fed to the motor should be changed together with the frequency. We can realize that by conduct the other side thyristor a certain time after every time of phase current changing to zero. But that causes some problems such as reducing the output voltages,

degrading the waveforms, producing harmonics. For high-capacity motors, these effects can be reduced by using a multiple structure for the transducer.

However, there still is a problem to bring the method true. Because the inverter consisted of three phase full controlled rectifying bridges is mounted between the power grid and the motor, the whole power that is fed to the motor should pass through the transducer entirely, so the capacity of the transducer should be equal to or even larger than the capacity of the motor. It can not be realized that using a small-capacity transducer to control a high-capacity motor. For this problem, the solving method is in thinking. We prepare to feed two sinusoidal AC power with different frequencies into the stator windings by a different manner to realize the doubly-fed speed regulation for the normal motors.

Acknowledgment

This work was supported by the Key Project of Hubei Provincial Science and Technology Department, under grant 2009AA413C. We thank Professor Liu Qun for his researching on the speed regulation of doubly-fed motors.

References

1. H. Liu, Q. Tang, L. Zhu, D. Zhao, C. Li, L. Shi, power system protection and control system, **24,** 79-85 (2014)
2. S. Li, Z. Yang, Z. Liu, S. Sun, power system protection and control system, **4**, 8-13(2012)
3. L. Zhan, X. Jin, L. Zhang, Electrical Technology, **1**, 130-135 (2012)
4. Y. Li, F. Zhu, X. Zhu, H. Xu, Electrical Technology, **7**, 161-166 (2011)
5. M. Tian, C. He, Xi'an University of Science and Technology, **1**, 107-111 (2013)
6. Y. Chong, X. Wang, F. Xiong, Y. He, Chinese Society for Electrical Engineering, **S1**, 203-210 (2013)
7. C. Kan, J. Zhang, G. Chu, B. Ma, Hefei University of Technology (Natural Science), **12**, 1436-1440 (2014)
8. L. Han, H. Wang, N. Ma, H. Liu, Electric Machines and Control, **3**, 22-29 (2012)
9. S. Gong, X. Yang, L. ji, Electric Power Automation Equipment, **8**, 60-65 (2012)
10. R. Zhao, X. Wang, A. Zhang, micro motor, **7**, 18-23 (2013)
11. J. Keljik, Electric Motors & Motor Controls, (2011)

MATEC Web of Conferences **44**, 02057 (2016)
DOI: 10.1051/matecconf/20164402057

Non-contact wafer thickness measurement of capacitance sensor circuit based on CAV424

You Jun Yan[1] Dan Zhao [2] Yu Chen[3]
(1 Suzhou Vocational College Electron and communication engineering department, Suzhou, 215104)
(2.3. Risun Technology CO.,LTD, Suzhou,215121)

Abstract: Non-contact wafer thickness measurement with the CAV424 capacitance sensor special integrated circuit and arc pole plate capacitor sensor has good stability and linearity under low capacity of the bottom of sensor and low ⊿C condition. This method has a high technical advantages and practical value.Two capacitance sensors Cb, Ca measurement spacing 4mm install at the same axis which constitutes the size condition for measuring thickness. The static capacity of Ca and Cb is a constant value. The capacity of Cb and Ca will change when the silicon wafer is involved. This change is checked by the CAV424 capacitive sensor which has better linearity and higher thickness resolution.

Key words: Circular planar capacitance sensors; CAV424 application-specific integrated circuit for capacitance sensor; Application design and non-contact thickness test.

INTRODUCTION

Semiconductor silicon non-contact thickness measurement has higher difficulty and practical value. Since the silicon ingot cutting with a silicon wafer has the thickness difference even after polishing. At present it is hard to measure the thickness from several points of the silicon using the mechanical method which has a large error. Also, the force is not easy to control and it will damage the silicon easily. The application of capacitor non-contact measurement is one of the nondestructive technique [1].

1. FUNDAMENTAL

There are many kinds of measuring circuit for capacitance sensor[1] such as Tightly coupled inductor arm bridge, transformer bridge,double T bridge circuit, differential pulse width modulation circuit, frequency modulation circuit. In this paper, the principle of non contact thickness measurement of capacitance sensor is shown in Figure 1. Two capacitive sensors a and b are spaced at a fixed distance D. At this point the capacitance of a and b is a based static value Ca and Cb. The thickness of the silicon wafer in the D interval is T. It raises the capacitance of Ca and Cb which is processed by the CAV424 capacitance sensor analog circuit and gets an voltage output signal Vb out and Va out.The difference of voltage indicates the difference of capacity Ca and Cb which is related to the thickness T. Since the CAV424 circuit is the differential input and Vc constant current integral form, its linearity is excellent and the resolution can reach 0.1um.

D is a fixed interval. To obtain the thickness T of the silicon wafer:

$$T = D - (a + b) \qquad (1)$$

The a and b in the formula are the distance from the capacitance sensor a or b to the silicon wafer.

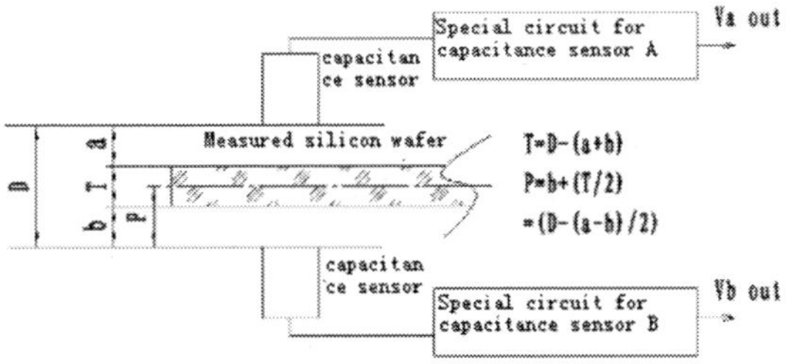

Figure 1

Corresponding author: 6211280@163.com

2. PRINCIPLE OF CAPACITANCE SENSOR

2.1 BRIEF INTRODUCTION OF CAPACITIVE SENSOR

Capacitance sensor is a cylindrical, and the shell is made by su304 stainless steel which is in order to achieve better temperature characteristics of the capacitance plate using titanium alloy material. Annular gap is filled with 0.1mm polyester film, cavity with epoxy resin potting. Capacitance sensor test surfaces are polished to a mirror which is in order to meet the anti-interference requirements of internal wires of each string with a 1K~10K resistance。

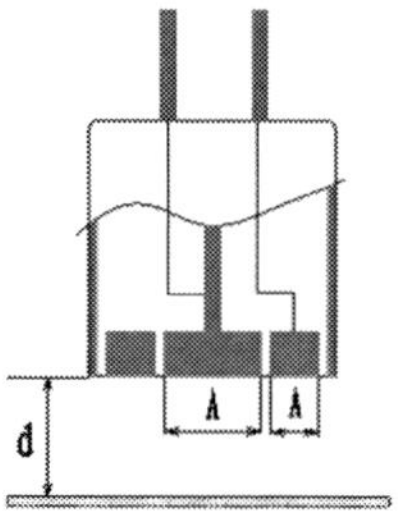

Figure 2 the structure of the single chip capacitance sensor

2.2 CALCULATION METHOD OF INITIAL CAPACITANCE VALUE OF SINGLE CHIP CAPACITANCE SENSOR[2]

$$C=\frac{\varepsilon A}{d}=\frac{\varepsilon_0 \varepsilon_r A}{d} \quad (2)$$

Among: $\varepsilon_0 = 8.85\cdot 10^{-12} F\cdot m^{-1}$, ε_r =Relative dielectric constant,

A= plate area, d= plate distance.

According to the formula, the capacitance C of sensor is changed by the distance, dielectric constant and area. When the dielectric constant and the area of the plate are fixed, the distance is the single value function of capacitance variable C. The characteristic capacitance sensor applications can measure effectively. [9] [10]

3. BRIEF INTRODUCTION OF CAV424 CAPACITANCE SENSOR CIRCUIT [4]

In Figure 3, almost all of the capacitance sensors use differential capacitance method to obtain a linear degree and a larger signal since the capacity of the capacitance sensor varies in a range of pF or up to several hundred Pf. In some applications, the unit of ⊿C is also several pF. In general, a fixed capacitor is chosen as a reference, and the other one is used to measure and amplify the differential signal.

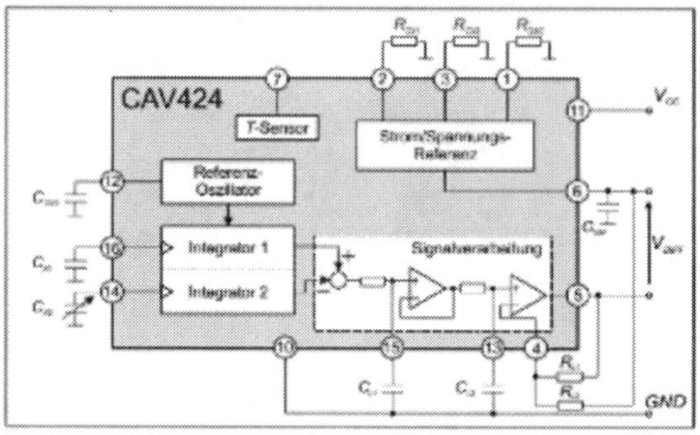

Figure 3 the internal structure of capacitance sensor circuit

3.1 CAPACITANCE INTEGRATOR [4]

Principle of two symmetrical structure built-in capacitor integrator is similar to the reference oscillator above. The difference is that discharge time is half of the charging time. Secondly, the minimum discharge voltage is limited in a built-in fixed voltage vclamp = 1.2 V. (Figure 4).

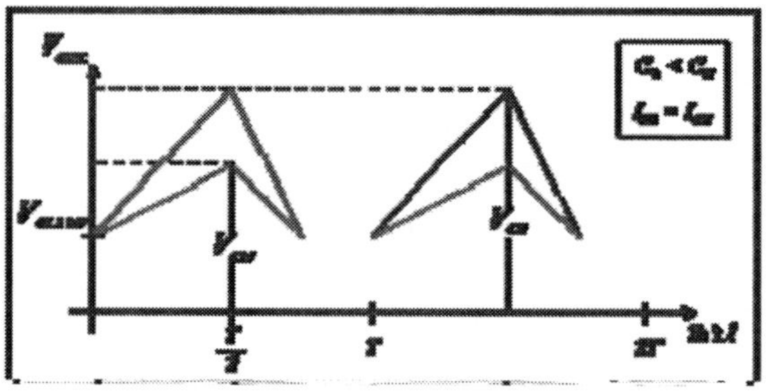

Figure 4 the output voltage of Zeit= two integrator

The capacitive current of ICR integrator and ICM are determined by external resistor RCM, RCR and reference voltage VM:

$$I_{CM}=\frac{V_M}{R_{CM}} \text{ and } I_{CR}=\frac{V_M}{R_{CR}} \quad (3),\ (4)$$

* Formula (3) and (4) do not contain the RCX. At this time the RCX value is zero. To made a good thermal coupling of the resistance, the resistance RCX = 0. Its value can be obtained by calibration software application Kali1_cav424.exc Kali1_cav424.exc and Kali2_cavV424.xls Kali2_cavV424.xls.

Capacitors CM and CR are charged to the maximum value VCM and VCR, which can be calculated by theoretical formula as follows:

$$V_{CM} = \frac{I_{CM}}{2 \cdot f_{OSC} \cdot C_M} + V_{CLAMP} \qquad (5)$$

$$V_{CR} = \frac{I_{CR}}{2 \cdot f_{OSC} \cdot C_R} + V_{CLAMP} \qquad (6)$$

First, the voltage (VCM) and VCR of two capacitors Cm and Cr are subtracted through the signal processing circuit. Adder-subtractor with the function of rectification also eliminated clamp fixed voltage VCLAMP. A DC voltage signal VTPAS is generated at the output end after filtering.

3.2 THE WORKING PRINCIPLE OF CAV424 [4]

A reference oscillator with adjustable capacitor COSC frequency drives two symmetric structure of integrator and synchronizes in the same time and phase. (Figure 3). The amplitude of two controlled integrator is determined by the result ICR/CR and ICM/CM from current and capacitance value division. CR is used as a reference capacitor and CM is used as a measuring capacitor. The integrator has a high common mode rejection ratio and resolution, so the difference between the two amplitude signal reflects the difference between the two capacitors Cr and Cm.

The voltage difference is filtered by the active power filter and transferred to the DC power source signal. (rectifier effect) And then the signal is sent to the adjustable amplifier to adjust to the desired output voltage value.

If the two current and capacitor division result ICM/CM is same as ICR/CR, the DC voltage signal is zero after rectifying and filtering(Figure 4). If the measured capacitance cm changes Δ CM, the output voltage is proportional to the 1 / Δ CM .

If the second capacitor Cr and cm values are not the same, the output end is a bias value when the Δ CM = 0. It is always superimposed on the DC voltage signal. CAV424 is a multi-purpose and can deal with almost all capacitive sensor signal. It is a complete conversion interface integrated circuit. It also has (relative change of capacitance) signal acquisition, processing and differential voltage output function. CAV424 uses a fixed reference capacitor Cr to get relative change amount Δ CM = CM,max − CM,min of a measured capacitance Cm capacitance.

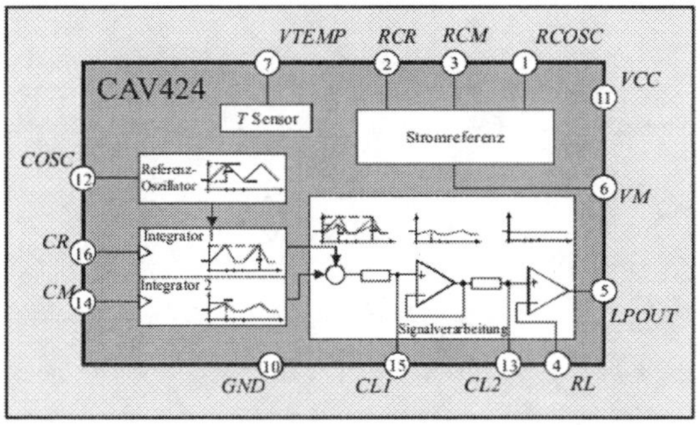

Fig. 5 current block diagram with signal processing

The reference capacitance CR value is set between the 10PF and 1NF with CAV424 design. So that the change of measured capacitance cm Δ CM can be 5% to 100% of based capacitor CR . Differential voltage output can be directly connected to the A / D conversion circuit. A digital calibration circuit system consists of integrated circuit temperature sensor and MCU.

4. APPLICATION OF CAV424

4.1. APPLICATION DESIGN OF CAV424

The circuit is shown in Figure 6. The test circuit is composed of 5 parts. CAV424 is special integrated circuit for capacitive sensor. LPOUT output has a 2.5V DC component which is amplified at the first level by a single chip microcomputer to control the programmable zero point correction circuit and a 2.5V voltage is added at the reverse side so that the output of the first stage is 1V, which is defined as the relative zero point. Programmable zero point correction application

/50K/256 ISL95810 tap digital potentiometer and MCU application STC12C5604AD use the 10 bit AD converter in the circuit to monitor and adjust the zero point of the first stage DC amplifier.The first stage of the DC amplifier is fixed, and the second stage is a variable gain amplifier which is controlled by MCU /50K/256 ISL95810 tap digital potentiometer to achieve gain adjustable.This adjustment is allowed to operate in standard sample calibration.

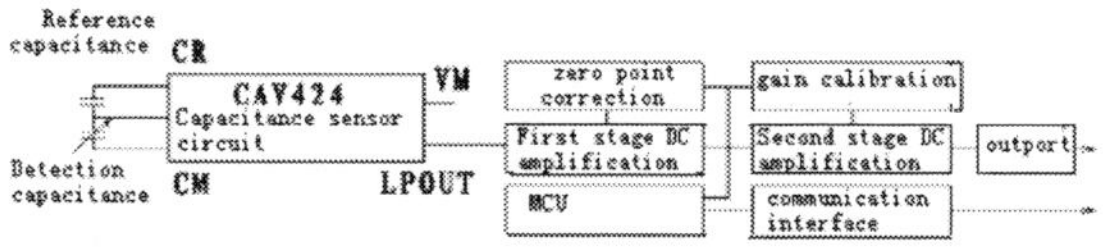

Figure 6 application circuit diagram

Application circuit CAV424 in silicon wafer thickness testing system is used in pair. The test system can be a point or several points of the form of architecture. Start and idle status of test points are controlled by a PC operating system software in real time. The second stage DC amplifier output is the final analog output for the modulus of PC-ADC conversion to calculate the thickness of the test point [6] [7] [8] [11]。 CAV424 application schematic diagram is shown in Figure 7; PCB application CAV424 diagram shown in Figure 6.

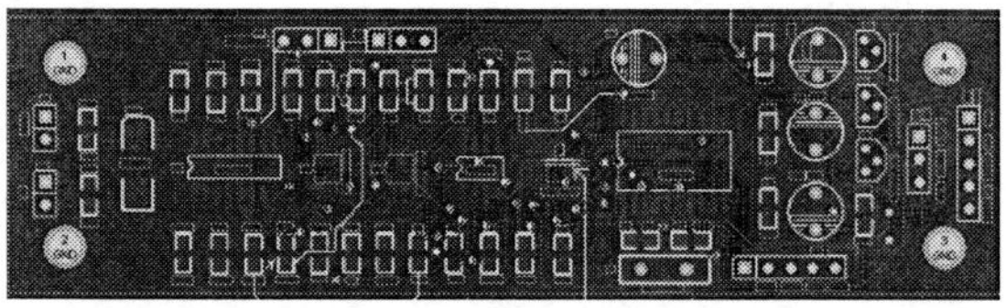

Figure 7 CAV424 application PCB diagram

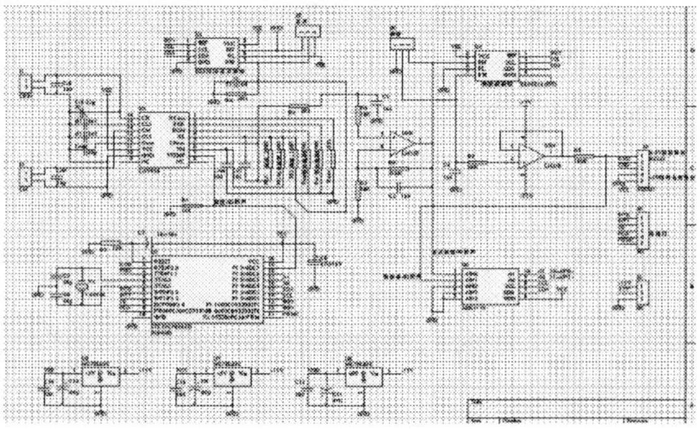

Figure 8 Schematic diagram of CAV424 application

4.2. CAV424 LINEAR RANGE AND TEST DATA ANALYSIS

CAV424 working voltage is 5V. The test sensor face to face coaxial installation distance is 4mm. Designed test wafer thickness range is 0 ~ 1 mm. CAV424 output voltage is 2.5V~4V. The absolute value of once signal voltage is 1.5V. After zero point correction, the first stage amplifier gain is Vout1=Ipout(1+Rf1/Rb1)=1.5V(1+1)=3V and the second gain stage is depend on the IPC-9112ADC sampling card benchmark 10V, which is 1mm output voltage maximum 10V, and the gain is Vout2=10/3=3.33333 times.

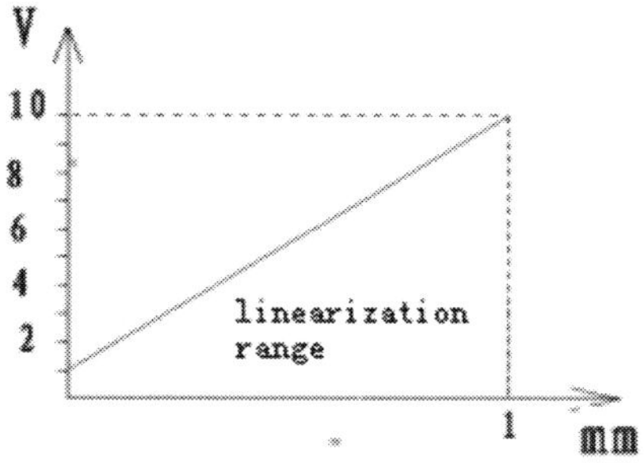

Figure 9 linear regions of test data

Figure 9 shows the test data linear region which contains an important zero point concept.

The output of the two capacitance sensors in the absence of silicon wafer should be 0V and the pitch size is D=4mm. Since the silicon chip's intervention has changed the dielectric constant to increase the capacity of the sensor, at this time, the initial value of zero adjustment of its critical values are 1V.In the 1/2 D as the interface line, when a sensor and the silicon wafer surface is 1mm, the output of the second amplifier is adjusted to 10V, The actual thickness of the linear variable ranges 0~1mm, and the voltage variable ranges 1~10V, and the resolution is 1mm /9=0.11111 um/V.In the D interval 0~1mm is Va, a is 1~10V; B is 0~1mm, Vb is 1~10V; VD=Va+Vb=18V. The measured data are shown in Table 1.

Table -1 test data table of two kinds of silicon wafers

No	Standard thickness	Measured thickness	Measured voltage	Measured thickness	error
1	0.242 (mm)	2.178 (V)	0.011 (V)	0.243 (mm)	0.001(mm)
2	0.247	1.223	1.009	0.248	0.001
3	0.245	2.205	0.013	0.246	0.001
4	0.603	4.427	1.003	0.603	0
5	0.606	5.454	0.007	0.607	0.001
6	0.606	4.451	1.010	0.607	0.001

According to the formula（1）

T = D – (a + b). Converted to voltage representation algorithm：

Thickness

T(mm)=VD-(Va+Vb)=18v-((9V-Va+(9v-Vb))*0.1111

T(mm)=18V-((9v(1-Va)+(1-Vb))*0.1111 (7)

Example: according to table 1 serial number 1 in the input data type（7）

T(mm)=-((9V(1-2.178)+(1-0.011)*0.1111=
(18-15.811)*0.1111=2.189*0.1111=0.24319mm。

After the decimal point is retained 3, the thickness of the test is 0.243mm, which is 0.001mm larger than the sample.

According to formula (7) test results show that silicon in the D timeline does not affect the accuracy of the test data. Therefore, the method based on CAV424 capacitance sensor circuit of non-contact wafer thickness measurement has high technical feasibility and practical value.

5. Conclusion

After practical application, CAV424 capacitance sensor application specific integrated circuit of non-contact wafer thickness testing system design and test device structure has high precision, simple circuit, convenient adjustment, and extremely high performance price ratio. The design has been applied in non-contact thickness measurement function of multifunctional solar silicon wafer tester.

REFERENCES

[1] W. C. Heerens. Application of capacitance technique sinsensors. [J]. Phys. Sci. instrum. No. 19: 897006

[2] Yan Youjun. Based on the virtual instrument, the.[J]. sensor and the micro system of the dynamic non-contact type silicon wafer tester，2010.(29)3:59-61

[3] Yan Zhonghao, Tan Zugen. Non electrical measurement technology [M]. Shenyang: Shenyang University of Technology, Zhejiang University. ISBN 7-111-01803-6/TM.233

[4] Shanghai Yunsheng Microelectronics Co., Ltd., < capacitance signal conversion ratio of voltage output interface integrated circuit CAV424>,[M]

[5] Cao Xiaohua et al. Journal of Hebei Institute of science and technology based on the dynamic thickness measurement technology based on single chip capacitance sensor [J]., 2007,(01):69-71

[6] Wang Xinhua, Ma Yuzhen et al. Research on plastic film thickness measurement system based on capacitance sensor [J]. Journal of sensing technology,2005,3(18-1):116-119

[7] Bian Xiaona, Liu Jing, Zhao Lizhi. Circuit design of capacitance sensor [J]. instrument technique and sensor.2008,(6):104-106

[8] Zhang Honggang, Wang Xinhang, Zheng Yizhong. Capacitance plate on-line thickness measuring instrument [J]. instrument and meter.2000.4:13-14

[9] Meng Fanwen, Zhang Yuxiang, Liang Haixia. High LJ, high precision capacitive displacement sensor design of [J]. sensor world.2007,(3):16-17,31

[10] Jia Min ye, Zhang Tao, Zhou Lipu. Both inside and outside the ring capacitance sensor sensitivity simulation [J]. Days Tianjin University School Newspaper (Natural Science and engineering and Technology Edition).2008,41(11):1309-1311

[11] Cao Xiaohua, Yang Yinbao, Yin Zhitian. Dynamic thickness measurement based on single chip capacitor sensor [J]. Journal of Hebei Institute of Technology.2007,29(1):69-71

MATEC Web of Conferences 44, 02058 (2016)
DOI: 10.1051/matecconf/20164402058

Study on ventilation and noise reduction in the main transformer room in indoor substation

Sheng Hu[a], Shao Yi Chen and Tie Nan Li

State Grid Hunan Electric Power Corporation Research Institute, 410007Changsha, Hunan Province, China

Abstract. The noise emission should be considered in the ventilation and cooling design for the main transformer room of indoor substation. In this study, based on Soundplan software, effects of four common ventilation and cooling schemes on the cooling and sound insulation were compared. The research showed that the region with low noise requirement, the ventilation could be set on the outer wall or on the door of the main transformer room, while the region with high noise requirement, air inlet muffler or ventilation through the cable interlayer under the main transformer room must be used. All of the four kinds of ventilation schemes, ventilation through the cable interlayer is the best in cooling and noise reduction.

1 Introduction

The transformer noise is one of main causes that the substation boundary noise exceeded the environment standard[1]. Compared with the outdoor-transformer substation, for indoor-transformer substation, the influence of the substation noise to the surrounding environment can be reduced because the spreading of noise could be better controlled. However, air inlets and outlets have to be set in the main transfermer rooms which cannot be full closed because there is a need of ventilation to cool the heat generated during the operation of transformers.

Currently, there's no perfect solution to consider the mutual effects between the ventilation and noise controlling for the substation, leading to unreasonable set of the air inlets and outlets and overproof noise spread of the ourdoor-transformer substation[2]. In this study, effects of four common ventilation and cooling schemes on the cooling and sound insulation effects are compared and analyzed, which will provide a good reference for future noise reduction design in the indoor substation.

2 Theoretical ventilation calculation

The ventitation temperature in the transformer room in the summer should not be higher than 45 ℃[3]. Not only air exchange rate, but also power loss of the main transformer should be considered in the main transformer room. Generally the power loss of transformer around is 1-3% and for some fine-making ones, it could be 1% or even less. In South China, the highest monthly average temperature in summer is about 34 ℃ and the indoor temperature in the transformer room is about 45 ℃. Generally speaking, the air flow rate calculated according to the heat generation is greater than that by air exchange rate. Accordingly, the air flow rate should be calculated by the heat generation multiplied by a margin coefficient.

The calculating method of the ventilation rate in the transformer room is as follows[4]:

$$V = \frac{3600Q}{(t_n - t_w)C\rho}$$

In which,

V is the air flow rate, m^3/h;

Q is heat, kW. 200 kW, according to Table 2;

P is air density, kg/m^3, generally 1.11;

C is the specific heat of air, kJ/(kg.K), generally 1;

tn is the maximum permissible temperature indoors.℃

tw is the local ventilation temperature outdoors.℃

3 The simulation model of the main transformer room

3.1. The physical and acoustic parameters

The model of the main transformer room is 10m×10m × 10m, and the door is 6m × 5m. The cable interlayer under the main transformer room is 10m×10m ×3m, which is 1.5m deeper than surface ground The sound power of the transformer is 80 dB(A), which is 5m × 5m × 5m. The transformer in the main transformer room was simplified as five area noise sources. The Sound Transmission Loss of the door is 15dB(A). The noise elimination dose of the Silencing shutter is 5dB(A). The noise elimination dose of the muffler is 20dB(A).

[a]Sheng Hu: hbhusheng@163.com

Article available at http://www.matec-conferences.org or http://dx.doi.org/10.1051/matecconf/20164402058

3.2. The model based on Soundplan software

As shown in Fig. 1, the model of four ventilation-cooling systems were build based on Soundplan software.

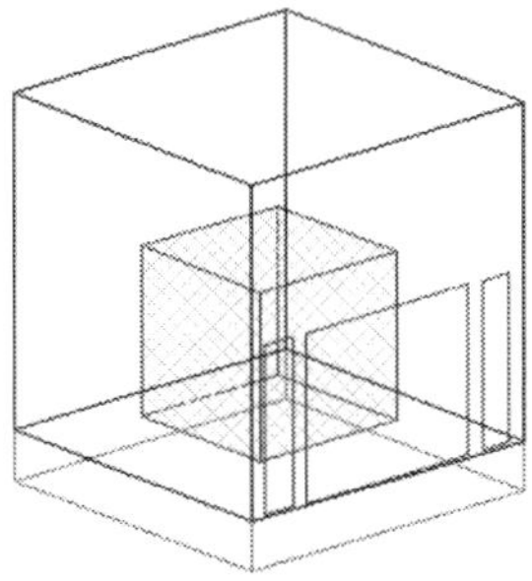

Figure 1. The simulation model of the main transformer room

4 Design of the ventilation and noise reduction system

Design of ventilation-cooling system is not only for organization of cooling air flow to ensure an appropriate ventilation rate, but also for sound insulation and noise reduction. At present natural ventilation and mechanical ventilation are employed in indoor type substations. In order to ensure the ventilation effect and efficiency of the fans, generally the natural ventilation velocity should not be greater than 5 m/s and low noise fans should be used in mechanical ventilation.

4.1. Design of cold air inlets

4.1.1 Air inlets set in the outer walls of the main transformer room

Shutter as the air inlet in the outer walls of the main transformer room is a relatively simple design. As shown in Fig. 2 and Fig. 3, the gate of the main transformer room is sound proof and intake silencing shutters are used in the outer walls of both sides of the door. The width of the shutter is in the range of 100-200 mm. Adequate ventilation area could be provided in this design, but sound insulation of the shutter is relatively small, especially for those transformers with low frequency. The sound transmission loss is smaller than 10 dB, therefore the design is applicable only to areas with low noise requirement.

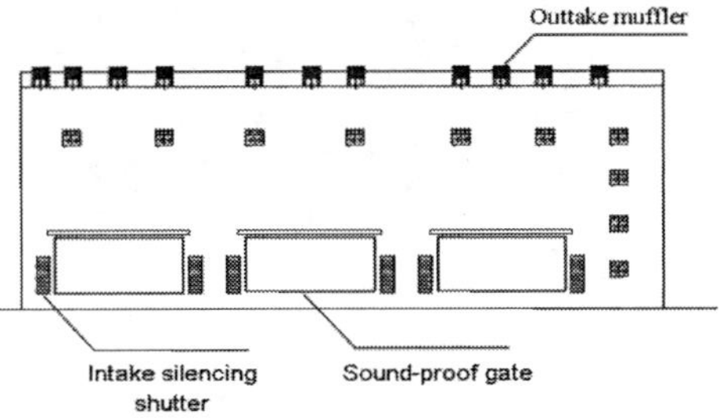

Figure 2. Schematic of the shutter on the outer wall of the main transformer room

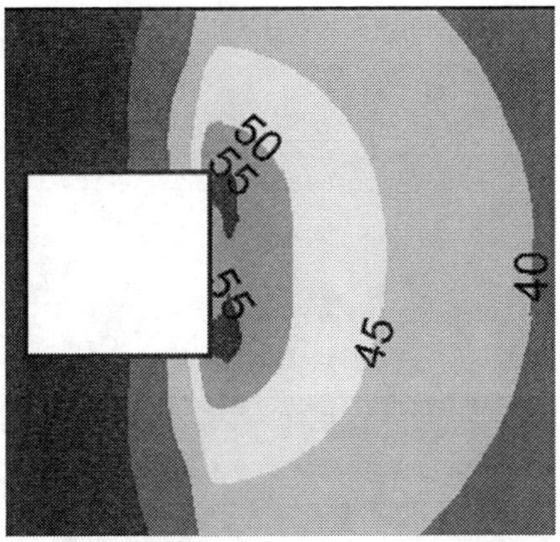

(a)

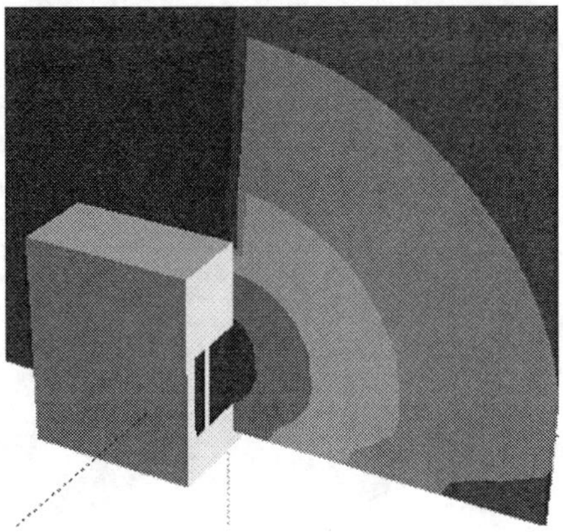

(b)

Fig.3 Sound field distribution of the inlets in the outer wall of the main transformer

4.1.2 Inlets set on the gate

Sound-proof gate with intake silencing shutters is also a common ventilation design. As shown in Fig. 4 and Fig. 5, four sound-proof gates of the main transformer room are two-way open and a certain area of silencing shutter is set below each door. The width of the shutter is consistent with the thickness of the soundproof gate. For this design the civil construction load could be saved and it is convenient to construction. Due to the limitation of the soundproof gates, the inlets area and with of the shutters are limited and the sound transmission loss is generally lower than 15 db.

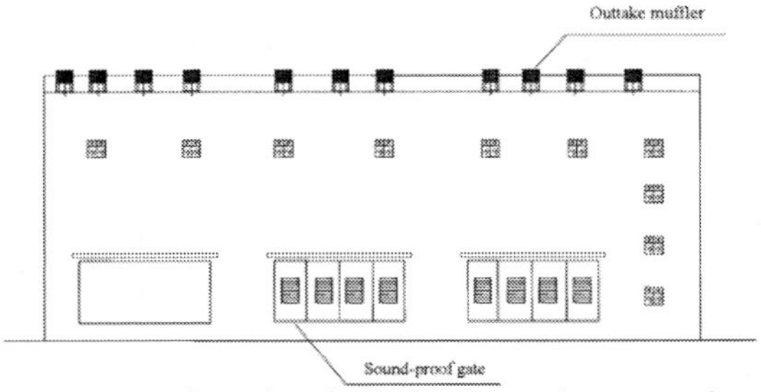

Figure 4. Schematic of the inlets on the gate of main transformer room

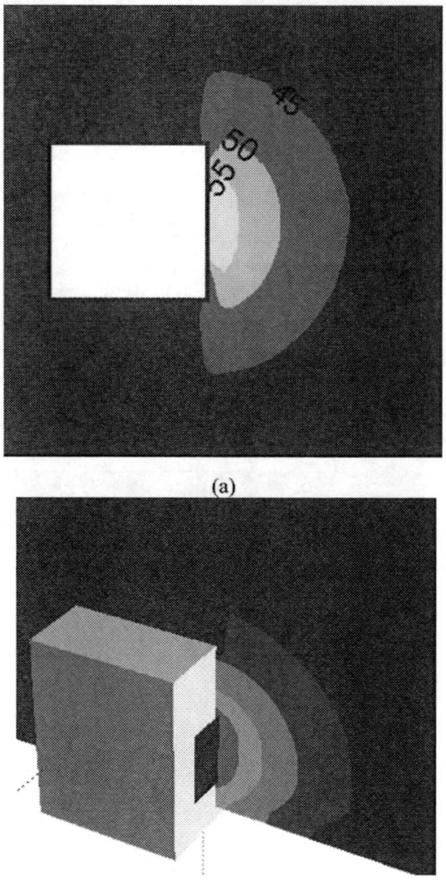

(a)

(b)

Fig.5 Sound field distribution of the inlets in the outer wall of the main transformer

4.1.3 The intake muffler

Intake mufflers are set in case of high moise requirement which cannot be satisfied with silencing shutters. As shown in Fig. 6 and Fig. 7, intake mufflers are set at the bottom of the outer wall of the main transformer room. The noise reducing effects are well related with the length of the muffle when the circumference and the area of the muffle is limited. The sound transmission loss of this scheme is up to 20-30dB. However, the size of the muffler is relatively big and the muffler will take up more space, which would influence the overall appearance.

4.1.4 Ventilation through the lower cable interlayer of the main transformer room

As shown in Fig. 8 and Fig. 9, the advantages of ventilation through the lower cable interlayer of the main transformer room are, (1) The noise would not be spread outdoors through ventilation holes, for the noise source is not directly facing the inlet;(2)The cooling effect is good, for the cold air is flowing into indoor through the bottom of the room, forming a natrual convection and ,a reasonable air distribution. (3)No extra space would be taken up and it has a good appearance.

The sound transmission loss of this scheme is up to 20-30 dB. However, it should be applied in the initial construction stage of the transformer substation and it's hard to rebuild once the construction is finished, because of the stress issue, the fire safety and rain-proof.

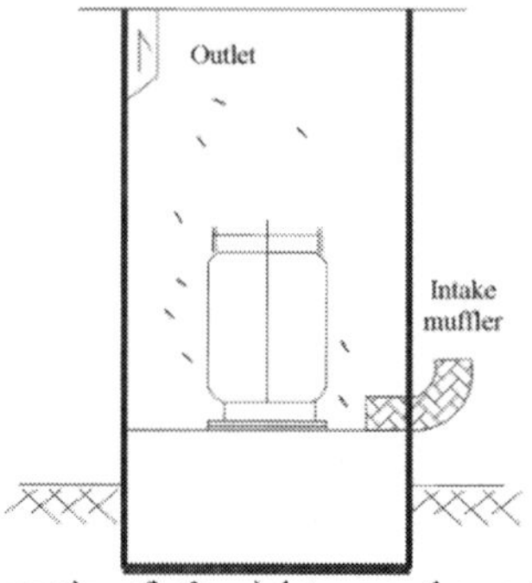

Figure 6. Schematic of the inlets on the gate of main transformer room

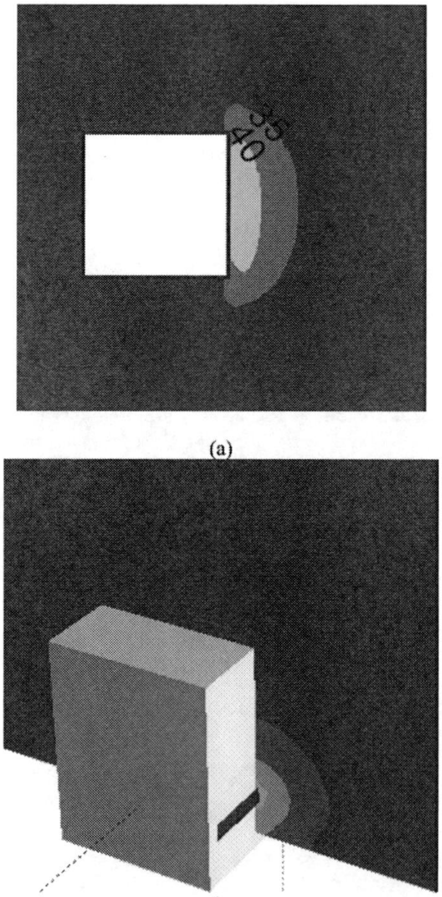

(a)

(b)

Figure 7. Sound field distribution of the inlets in the outer wall of the main transformer

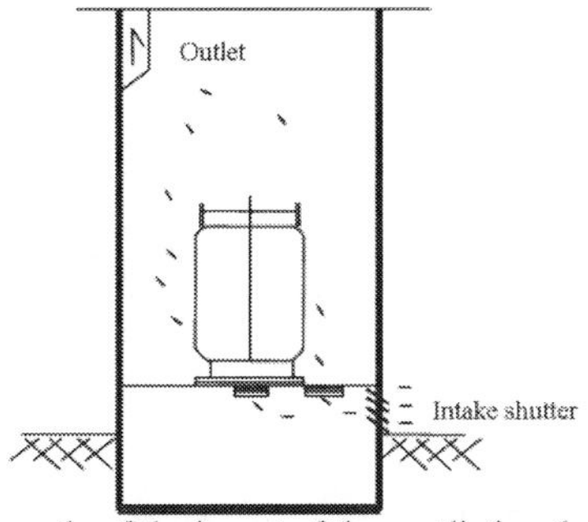

Figure 8. Schematic of the layout of the ventilation through the lower cable interlayer of the main transformer room

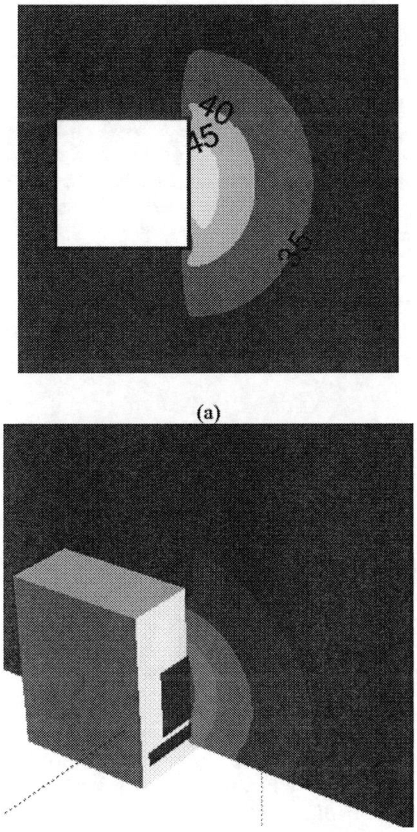

Figure 9. Sound field distribution of the inlets in the outer wall of the main transformer

4.2 Design of hot air outlets

Generally ventilation holes are set in the upper part of roof of the main transformer room, connected with the fans discharging hot air. The air volume of the fan should be greater than the calculated theoretical ventilation cooling capacity. Automatic control of the fan can be employed, so that when the temperature in the main transformer room exceeds the preset temperature the fan would automatically run. In ordinary cases cooling can be achieved by natural ventilation, which can save energy and reduce emissions. Considering the effects of fan noise, muffler can be added or fan room could be used in the design to reduce the fan noise.

5 Comparison of four ventilation and noise reduction designs

Comparison of four ventilation and noise reduction designs is shown in Table 1. In places with low noise requirements, the scheme of ventilation set in the outer wall or gates of the main transformer room can be used. In places with high noise requirements, intake mufflers must be used or ventilation through the interlayer of the lower cable layer of main transformer room could be used. Of the four kinds of ventilation schemes, the scheme of ventilation through the interlayer of the lower cable layer has the best cooling and noise reduction effects, with a moderate cost, which should be adopted when needed.

Table 1. Comparison of different ventilation and noise reduction systems

NO.	Ventilation scheme	Sound transmission loss	Cooling effect	Cost
1	Ventilation at the outer wall of the main transformer room	<10dB	good	low
2	Ventilation at the gates of the main transformer room	<15dB	fair	Low
3	Intake muffler	20-30 dB	good	High
4	ventilation through the lower cable interlayer	20-30 dB	Very good	Middle

6 Conclusions

(1)The ventilation cooling system design is not only for reasonable organization of the air flow to ensure that the appropriate ventilation rate, but also for noise reduction. (2)Different cooling schemes have different cooling and noise reduction effects, which should be adopted according to the practical needs. In places with low noise requirements, the scheme of ventilation set in the outer wall or gates of the main transformer room can be used. In places with high noise requirements, intake mufflers must be used or ventilation through the interlayer of the lower cable layer of main transformer room could be used (3)By comparing the four kinds of ventilation schemes, the scheme of ventilation through the interlayer of the lower cable layer has the best cooling and noise reduction effects with a moderate cost, which should be adopted when needed.

References

1. Jiang Chuan, Shandong power technology, 125, 3 (2002)
2. Jin Linfang, Power supply and consumption, 27, 2 (2010)
3. Design code for 30～110kV substations (GB50059-92)
4. Sun Yijian, Concise Ventilation Design Handbook.M, (1997)

MATEC Web of Conferences 44, 02059 (2016)
DOI: 10.1051/matecconf/20164402059

Research on the application of active sound barriers for the transformer noise abatement

Sheng Hu[1,a], Shao Yi Chen[1], Hai Shan Zou[2] and Tie Nan Li[1]

[1]State Grid Hunan Electric Power Corporation Research Institute, 410007Changsha, Hunan Province, China

[2]Key Laboratory of Modern Acoustics, Institute of Acoustics, Nanjing University, 210093Nanjing, Jiangsu Province, China

Abstract. Sound barriers are a type of measure most commonly used in the noise abatement of transformers. In the noise abatement project of substations, the design of sound barriers is restrained by the portal frames which are used to hold up outgoing lines from the main transformers, which impacts the noise reduction effect. If active sound barriers are utilized in these places, the noise diffraction of sound barriers can be effectively reduced. At a 110kV Substation, an experiment using a 15-channel active sound barrier has been carried out. The result of the experiment shows that the mean noise reduction value (MNRV) of the noise measuring points at the substation boundary are 1.5 dB (A). The effect of the active noise control system is impacted by the layout of the active noise control system, the acoustic environment on site and the spectral characteristic of the target area.

1 Introduction

Back in 1956, W.B.Convor from General Electric Company tried to utilize the active sound attenuation technology in controlling transformer noise. As the sound field of transformers is a free sound field in three dimensions, the fulfilment of the task back then, under premature conditions, was much too difficult, whether in sound field analysis or system implementation; therefore, the plan was abandoned, and was replaced by the passive noise control method[1]. In 1980, the American Angevine Company successfully developed an active sound attenuation method for transformers, and conditions for the commercial application of active sound attenuation became mature gradually since 1996. The electric power sector of the United States has installed active sound attenuation system for 10 transformers, and countries such as Germany, Britain and Japan have adopted the active sound attenuation method to reduce the running noises of transformers, which turned out to be obviously effective[2~4]. Sound barriers are a type of measure most commonly used in the noise abatement of transformers. In the noise abatement project of substations, the design of sound barriers is restrained by the portal frames which are used to hold up outgoing lines from the main transformer, which impacts the noise reduction effect. In recent years, many scholars have paid attention to the utilization of combing active sound attenuation technology and sound barriers to reduce noises with a wide range of frequencies. If active sound barriers are used in these places, the noise diffraction of sound barriers can be effectively reduced[5]. This paper has explored a type of vertical active sound barrier to avoid the interference of the outgoing lines of transformers, so as to reinforce the low-frequency noise attenuation effect of sound barriers.

[a]Sheng Hu: hbhusheng@163.com

2 Design of the active sound barrier system

Control objectives of the controller are closely related to the properties of noise sources, which are mainly spectral characteristic and propagation characteristic. The control system of the project adopts a distributed type of feed-forward controlled active control system, the structure diagram of which is shown in Fig. 1 and Fig. 2, including passive sound barrier 2 and distributed type of feed-forward controller array 4. The cascade system is adopted to connect controllers in order to control the extension of the system to a multiple secondary path. Each active controller consists of reference sensor 5, error sensor 6, digital signal processing module 7 and secondary loudspeaker 8. Moreover, a horizontal support 3 is installed at the top of the passive barrier with the height of h_b, and there is a equal spacing between controller units of the active controller array on the support, as shown in Figure 1; the distance between the centres of two control units is d, in order to achieve a better noise reduction effect, d should be less than half of the corresponding wave length of the maximum control frequency[6]. When the primary sound source 1 radiates noises, reference sensor would collect the information of the primary sound field, and error sensor 6 would collect the information of the total sound field of the target controlling area, and the two signals

would then be transferred to the digital signal processing module 7, which adopts the single channel feed-forward adaptive algorithms, and the result is used to regulate the output of the secondary loudspeaker to minimize the amplitude square of sound pressure at the error sensor.

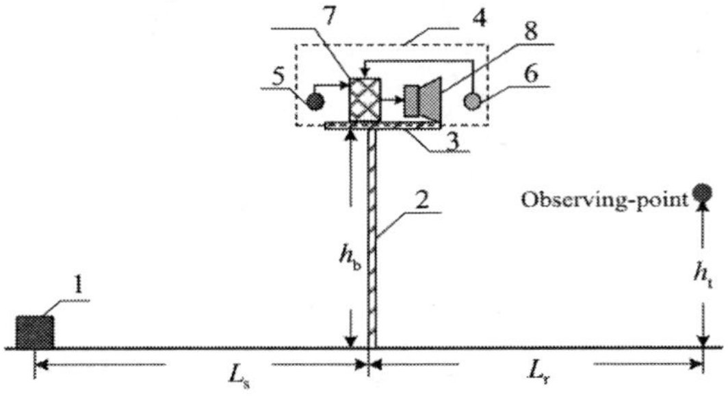

Figure 1. Structure diagram of the active sound barrier

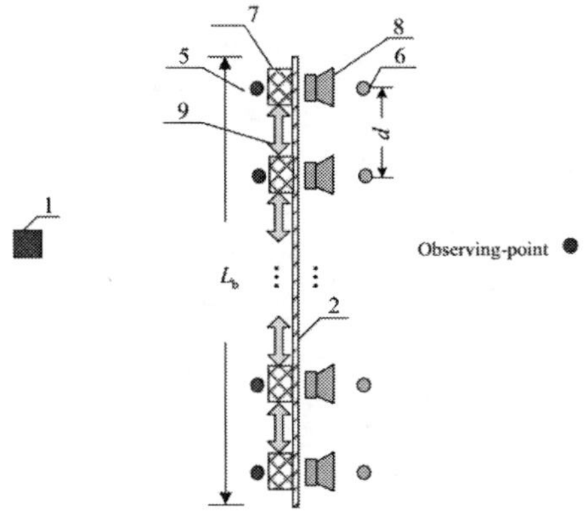

Figure 2. Structure diagram of the active sound barrier

2.1. Hardware design of the controller

The type of controller used in this project is a cascadable single-channel active controller, the schematic diagram of which is shown in Fig. 3. The quantity of the cascadable single-channel active controllers that form the controller can be changed as per the actual need. All the cascadable single-channel active controllers that form the controller are serially concatenated. The first unit is connected with the computer via a serial port communication module, and the computer sends out operating commands to any or all units via the computer's serial port, the serial port communication module of the first unit and the cascading communication module of each unit, or receives status information from any or all units. Thus the manipulation, commissioning and supervision of any unit can be performed in a more convenient and flexible way.

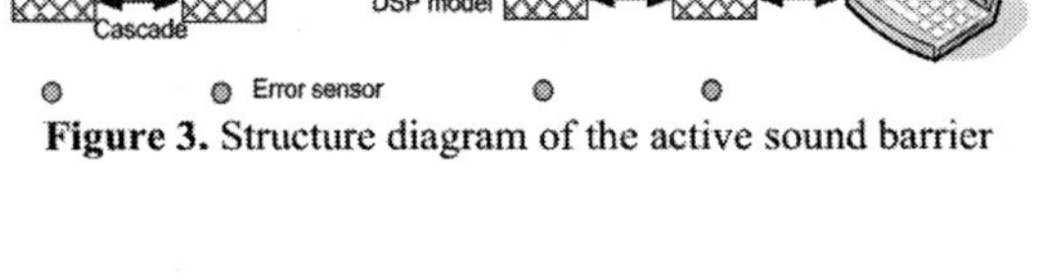

Figure 3. Structure diagram of the active sound barrier

The schematic diagram of an individual active sound controller is shown in Fig. 4. Reference sensors and error sensors would collect information from the noise source and the total sound field respectively, and then input them into the Digital Signal Processor (DSP) via a signal conditioner and A/D converter. The output signal from DSP would go through a D/A converter, filter circuit and power amplificatory circuit to drive the control source. The communication between DSP and the computer is conducted via the RS232 serial port (utilized in commissioning; only one unit uses the serial port in normal operation, and the communication of the other units is conducted via the cascading serial port). Moreover, system control can be realized by operating the interface of control software in the computer.

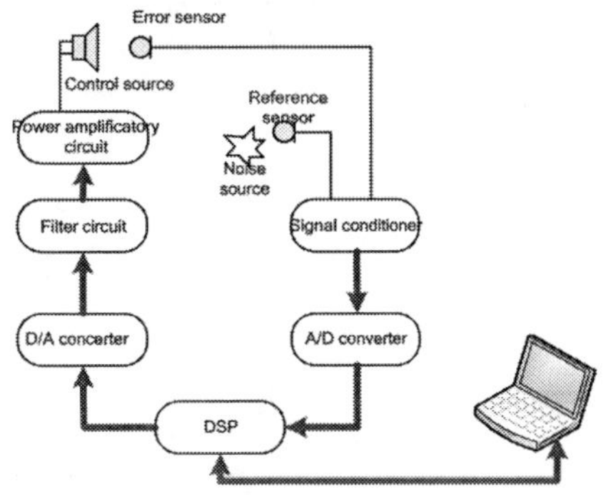

Figure 4. Structure diagram of the active sound barrier

2.2. Layout of the active sound barriers

In general, the software design of the controller can be divided into two parts, namely algorithm and auxiliary service. Algorithm, among which, is the core of the controller, which realizes the controller's basic functions, namely modeling and controlling, and auxiliary service includes operation maintenance, communication and User Interface (UI), etc. The software of this project is expected to be divided into five parts, as shown in Figure 5-9.(1) Feed-forward control algorithm software modules: include a modeling software module for the physical field between the secondary source and error sensors, a real-time signal control software module, and a filter updating control software module. These modules are performed on the real-time data processing chip contained in the DSP module of each unit.(2) Operation maintenance software modules: include an operation command processing software module and a status information reporting software module. These modules are performed on the real-time data processing chip contained in the DSP module of each unit.(3) Cascading communication software modules: performed on the real-time data processing chip contained in the DSP module of each unit.(4) Serial port communication software modules: include two parts; one part is performed on the real-time data processing chip contained in the DSP module of each unit, and the other is performed on the computer.(5) UI software modules: performed on the computer.The software modules on the data processing chip adopt the

assembly language and C language programming, and the software modules on the computer adopt the LabWindows/CVI software programming by National Instruments (NI).

3 Simulation result and analysis

The effect of active noise reduction has been simulated by using a simple model. In the simulation process, suppose the noise source is mainly composed of sounds with mono-frequencies and the harmonic waves (such as 100Hz, 200Hz and 300Hz, which is a reasonable assumption for transformer noises), the acoustic centre of the noise source is 2 meters above the ground, and there is a sound barrier, with 3 meters in height and 8 meters in width, locating at 2 meters away from the acoustic centre. Moreover, 20 sets of single channel active noise control system are installed at the top of the active sound barrier (with the sensors and controlled sound source designed at the same level), and the extra insertion loss for noises with different frequencies can be obtained by numerical simulation, as shown in Fig. 5 to Fig. 8. It is thus evident that the extra insertion loss of the mono-frequencies ranges from approximately 5 to 15dB in the acoustic shadow area, and has a slightly decrease in the other area, but still showing positive values; besides, there is extra insertion loss of 1 to 6dB even at a height of 10 meters. In the meantime, the amount of noise reduction in the error sensors of each single channel control system should be higher than 12dB.

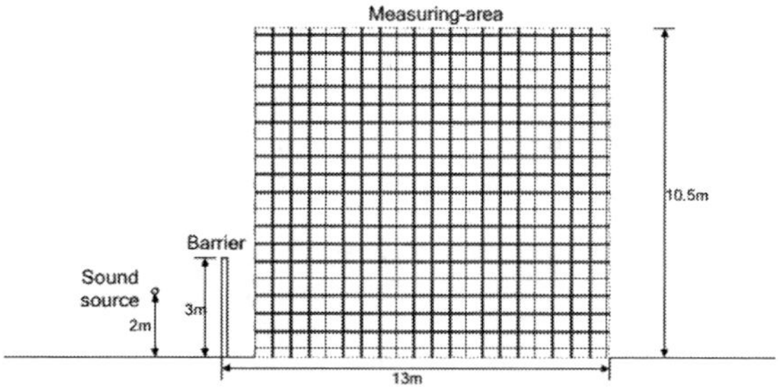

Figure 5. System location

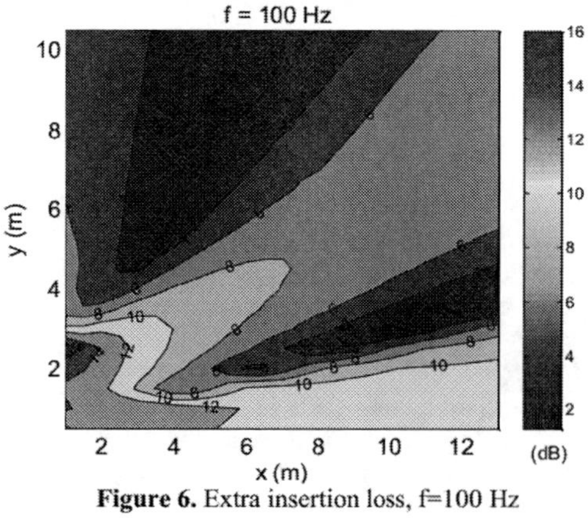

Figure 6. Extra insertion loss, f=100 Hz

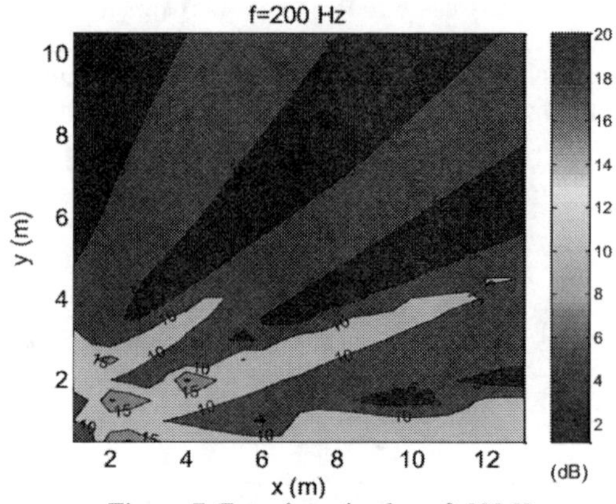

Figure 7. Extra insertion loss, f=200 Hz

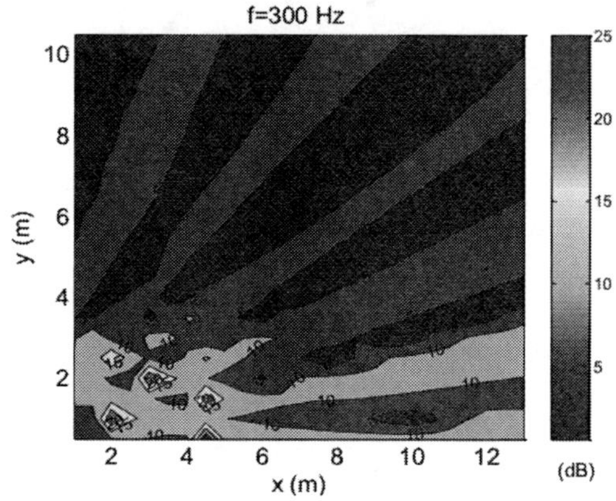

Figure 8. Extra insertion loss, f=300 Hz

4 On-site experiment

4.1. Layout of the active sound barriers

The plan view of the substation is shown in Figure 6. There are three main transformers equipped in the substation, with 110KV power distribution unit to the west, and reception office, 10KV high voltage room and control room surrounding the east. The substation itself is surrounded by residential areas, with its north bounding wall 2.0 meters away from a property management building, and east bounding wall 4.8 meters away from a 6-storey residential building and 7.0 meters away from a 16-storey residential building, and south bounding wall 32.0 meters away from a 14-storey residential building. In order to suppress the noise impact of the main transformers to their surrounding residential areas, a 12-meter high sound barrier has been set up in three sides of the main transformers, as shown in the red parts of Figure 7. The barrier has a length of 16 meters in the north and south, and 51 meters in the east. For the convenience of maintaining transformers, 1-meter long and 6-meter wide barriers have been set up only at the two corners of the west of transformers, as shown in the blue parts of the figure.7, No.1 main transformer has the highest noise level, so the active noise control system is applied in the

barrier abut No.1 main transformer in order to form an active sound barrier. Due to the restrictions of installation condition, active noise control system cannot be installed at the top of the existing barrier; therefore, a 15-channel active noise control system is set up vertically along the edge of the 1-meter long barrier in the southwest of No.1 main transformer, as shown in Fig. 9 and Fig. 10.

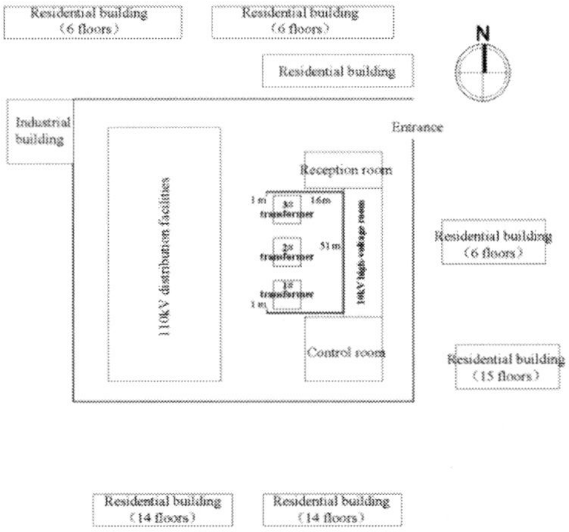

Figure 9. Plan layout of the substation

Figure 10. Picture of the active sound barriers at the substation

4.2 Experimental result and analysis

Seen from Table 1, active control has changed the sound field distribution in the space. The test result indicates that the active system has a certain effect in controlling noises with a frequency of less than 400 Hz at the factory boundary, and the decrease of A-weighted sound pressure level ranges from 0.3 to 4.3 dB. The effect of the active noise control system is impacted by the layout of the active noise reduction system, the acoustic environment on site and the spectral characteristic of the target area.

Table 1. A-weighted sound pressure level of measuring points.

Measuring Point No.	active control on	active control off	Noise Reduction Amount (dB(A))
1	55.0	55.3	-0.3
2	55.7	53.6	2.1
3	57.9	55.8	2.1
4	57.2	56.7	0.5
5	59.2	58.1	1.1
6	58.0	54.6	3.4
MNRV (dB(A))			1.5

5 Conclusions

(1) According to the spectral characteristic and propagation characteristic of transformers, the essay has developed a distributed type of feed-forward controlled active sound barrier that can be applied to the noise control of transformers.(2) The simulation result of active sound barriers shows that the extra insertion loss of the mono-frequencies (100 Hz, 200 Hz and 300 Hz to be specific) ranges from approximately 5 to 15dB in the acoustic shadow area, and has a slightly decrease in the other area, but still showing positive values; besides, there is extra insertion loss of 1 to 6dB even at a height of 10 meters.(3) An experiment using a 15-channel active sound barrier has been carried out in a 110kV substation. The result of the experiment shows that the MNRV are 1.5 dB and 1.8 dB (A) respectively for the overall SPL and A-weighted SPL of the noise measuring points at the substation boundary. The effect of the active noise control system is impacted by the layout of the active noise control system, the acoustic environment on site and the spectral characteristic of the target area.

References

1. W. B. Conver, Noise Control, 2(1956)

2. N. Hesselmann, Appl. Acoust,11(1978)

3. O. L. Angevine, Pro. Inter. Noise1992.

4. K.A. Chen, Active Noise Control(book), (2003)

5. H.S. Hai, X.F. Huang, S. Hu, X.J. Qiu, Pro. Inter. Noise 2014.

6. A. Omoto, K. Fujiwara, J. Acoust. Soc. Am., 94(1993)

MATEC Web of Conferences 44, 02060 (2016)
DOI: 10.1051/matecconf/20164402060

Research on Normal Human Plantar Pressure Test

Xi Yang Liu[1], Ren Jie Gao[2a], Si Ling Feng [1], Xian Mei Chen[1] and Yao Chi Zhao[1]

[1]School of College of Information Science and Technology, Hainan university,Hainan Haikou 570228,China

[2]Haikou People's Hospital, Hainan Haikou 570228,China

Abstract: FSR400 pressure sensor, nRF905 wireless transceiver and MSP40 SCM are used to design the insole pressure collection system, LabVIEW is used to make HMI of data acquisition, collecting a certain amount of normal human foot pressure data, statistical analysis of pressure distribution relations about five stages of swing phase during walking, using the grid closeness degree to identify plantar pressure distribution pattern recognition, and the algorithm simulation, experimental results demonstrated this method feasible.

1 Introduction

When the body in accordance with normal gait, plantar only directly contact with the ground, gait would have plantar pressure. The various factors of human physiology, diseases, etc. will affect the person's gait, it studies the body's normal plantar pressure when walking, that have important reference value for researching gait analysis, medical rehabilitation, clinical and smart shoes, and so on[1].

Based on the physical structure and division of the human foot plantar anatomical region, In accordance with the left and right foot insoles heel, arch, first metatarsal, the second metatarsal, metatarsal 3rd, 4th metatarsal, 5th metatarsal and the first toe area, each placed a film pressure sensor FSR400, each foot collects eight points force[2]. Distribution of plantar pressure sensor shown in Figure 1.

aCorresponding author: Liujinrong98@163.com

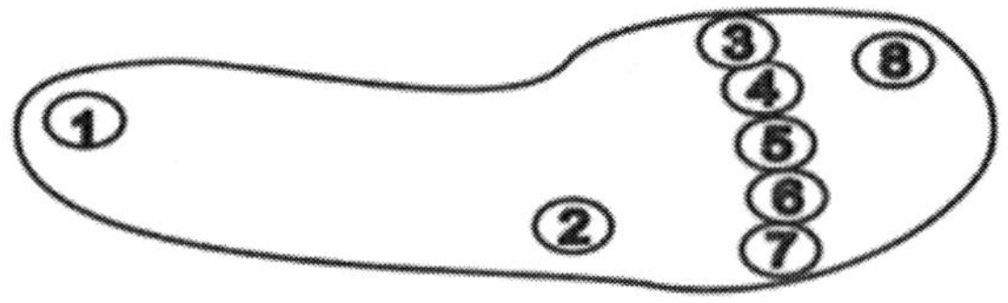

①. Heel ②. Arch ③. 1st metatarsal
④. Second metatarsal ⑤. 3rd metatarsal
⑥. 4th metatarsal ⑦. 1st metatarsal
⑧. 1st toe

Figure 1. The distribution of plantar pressure sensor

2 Insole Plantar Pressure Measurement System

2.1 Hardware Design of Insole Plantar Pressure Measurement System

The FSR400 pressure sensor converted the pressure of FSR sensor film region into a change in resistance value, thereby to obtain pressure information, and the greater the pressure, the lower the resistance. The voltage signals of 8 sensors were what we wanted to measure. Because the human body 98% of plantar pressure signal

frequencies below 10Hz, 99% of plantar pressure signal frequencies below 15Hz, so the need to design a low-pass filter circuit to filter mixed in plantar pressure signal clutter and noise. The 8-channel sensor signal were sent to the eight voltage selector switch CD4051, then separately voltage amplified and low-pass filtering process, The signals were sent the microprocessor MSP430 with A / D interface to A / D conversion, and the data was stored in the buffer zone, Then the every full 8-channel signal acquisition by nRF905 radio transmission, and by nRF905 radio reception, after MSP430 microprocessor treatment, These 8-channel signal was from the TTL level to USB level by FT232RL, Via USB interface to transfer to the PC, Application of LabVIEW virtual instrument development tools wrote software to achieve the signal display, storage and analysis. Insole plantar pressure measurement system hardware block diagram shown in Figure 2.

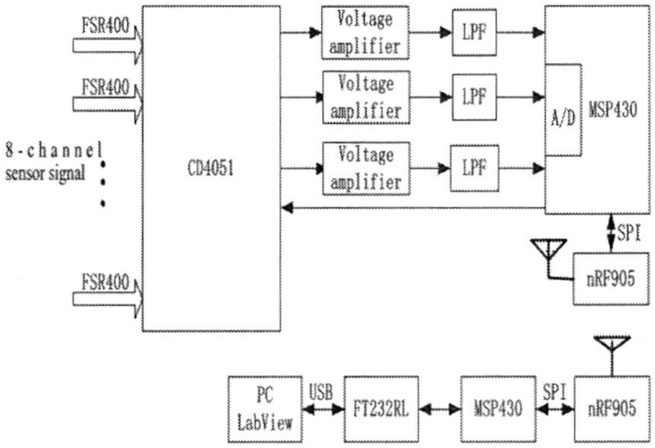

Figure 2. Insole plantar pressure measurement system hardware block diagram

Wireless transceiver module nRF905 built a complete communication protocol and CRC check circuit, and from on-board hardware automatically Manchester encoding / decoding, Just to complete all of the radio transmission through the SPI interface. Use of wireless communications technology, the collected signal was transmitted to the computer for processing, The sets of the system is easy to carry, flexible, saving transmission wire and avoiding the interference wire leaving the data transmission errors occur.

2.2 Data Acquisition HMI

Data Acquisition HMI was made by LabVIEW software. LabVIEW is virtual instrument integration environment in laboratory, It uses the structure of the graphics mode to build the program code, taking full advantage of developers familiar icons, terms and concepts, providing a portable way to test equipment programming and data acquisition systems, making the program preparation process intuitive.

First, according to the design requirements, the serial port was initialized, set the serial port was set and the baud rate was set to 9600b/s, 8 data bits, 1 stop bit, no parity. Second, the control system was set to start/pause/resume/stop/sampling interval frequency; Setting pressure threshold, when the pressure is greater than this value, the corresponding channel curve becomes green, setting the display area Y-axis display range; Setting data save path, note that the file must be in ".txt" as suffix.

PC sends a start command to the microprocessor "Start", After the microprocessor receives, sends a signal "DSR" of "ready to send" to the PC, and wait for the PC feedback signal "R" of "ready to receive", and then start to send a frame of data, the transmission is completed, return to the initial point , waiting for the next start command. After the PC receives the data, first by "String to Byte Array" command to convert the string into an array, and by measuring the file command data to the "pressure data .txt" file is saved in the appropriate folder while displaying real-time data 8 channels, each channel can display the current value of the measured data. Data Acquisition HMI shown in Figure 3.

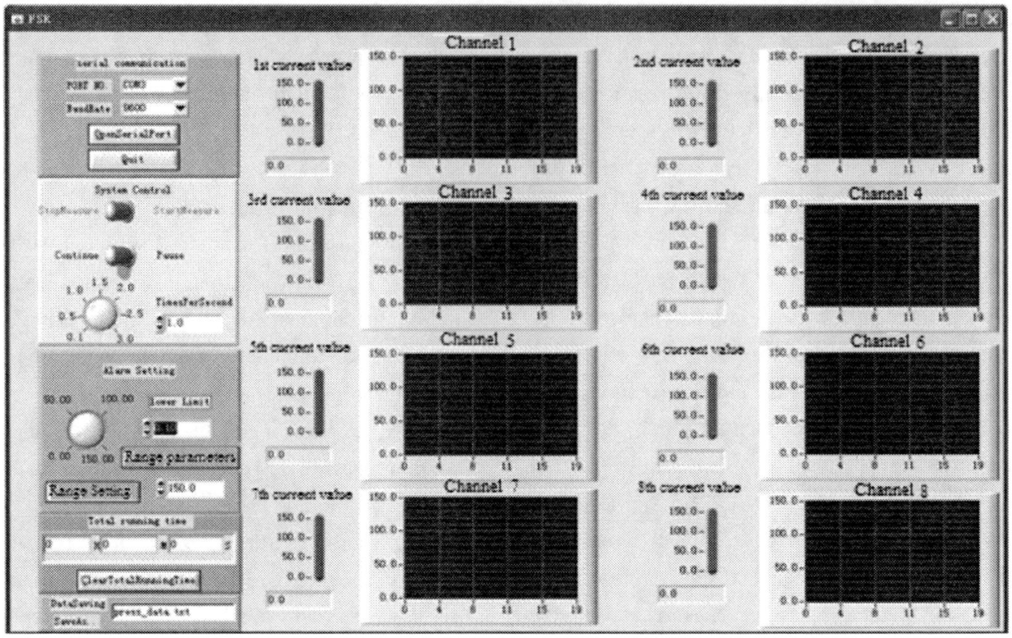

Figure 3. Data Acquisition HMI

3. Data Analysis and Processing

3.1 Membership Function

Using the insole plantar pressure gathering system above to process 67 cases of each normal walking gait cycle corresponding to pressure sensor values, statistical analysis obtain correspondence between each gait cycle and pressure sensor values relative size distribution patterns. The average peak experimentally measured 67 cases of normal walking process pressure sensor as shown in Table 1.

Table 1. The normal district average peak plantar pressure data $\left(\bar{x} \pm s\right) N/cm^2$

District	Data
Heel	35.85 ± 1.23
Arch	5.50 ± 0.45
1st metatarsal	0.93 ± 0.48
Second metatarsal	12.24 ± 0.63
3rd metatarsal	30.67 ± 1.68
4th metatarsal	31.44 ± 1.13
5th metatarsal	12.87 ± 0.74
1st toe	25.42 ± 0.57

The process of between twice land of the same foot heel is a gait cycle. A gait cycle can be divided into the swing phase and the stance phase. When the swing phase, leg off the ground and in the air, swinging forward. The stance phase with the lower limbs in contact with the ground to withstand the ground reaction force and a role in stabilizing the body. In the stance phase, can be divided into five stages (five kinds of distribution patterns):(1) Initial Contact, (2) Loading Response, (3) Mid Stance, (4) Heel Rise, (5) Toe Contact[3][4].

Due to the experimental subject's weight, height and other differences, the sensor data for the individual differences in subjects is different, so if only thinking of the specific sensor measurements, it is difficult to judge the subjects in which stance phase, so using fuzzy mathematical to process the experimental data, and using the membership function to represent the relative size of the measured sensor data. For each measurement sensor, the corresponding membership functions such as formula (1):

$$\mu = \frac{1}{\pi}\arctan[a(x - x_0)] + \frac{1}{2} \qquad (1)$$

Where x_0 is the sensor values subject standing still, a is as the adjustment factor, the value of a is the greater, the membership function μ corresponding to the curve is steeper.

3.2 Plantar Pressure Distribution Pattern Recognition

Fuzzy Recognition is often used in two ways: one is the maximum membership degree principle, also called direct method, which is mainly used to identify a single target; The other is closeness principle, also known as the indirect method, which is generally used for the cluster target identification. Closeness is the proximity of two fuzzy sets of metrics. In this paper, the principle of elective near close degree of grid to identify the subjects in which the stance phase (distribution mode).

Let $A_i(i=1,2,\cdots,n)$ be a fuzzy set of theory domain, constitutes a standard model library, it is to be a recognized fuzzy subset of domain U. If there is Closeness

$$N(B,A_j)=\max\{N(B,A_1),N(B,A_2),...,N(B,A_n)\}$$

, Called B and A_j are the most close, That is considered B to be A_j models. The grid closeness between A_i and B is $N(A_i,B)=\frac{1}{2}[A_i\bullet B+(1-A_i\odot B)]$,

Among them, $A_i\bullet B$ is called the inner product of A_i and B, $A\bullet B=\vee[u_A\wedge u_B]$; $A_i\odot B$ is called outer product of A_i and B, $A\odot B=\wedge[u_A\vee u_B]$.

The 5 stages of the stance phase are corresponding to five pressure distribution patterns. According to these five kinds of distribution patterns, the plantar pressure data of the 67 cases subjects are divided into five categories, fuzzy them and getting five sample sets, each element of these sample sets is 8-dimensional, is corresponding to fuzzy membership of 8 sensors. Each sample set is statistical and averaging, obtaining 5 standard distribution model $\{A_1,A_2,A_3,A_4,A_5\}$.

During walking, 8 sensor is placed on the foot to collect of the plantar pressure data, these data can be converted into membership, characterizing pressure value relative size. Let $B=\{b_1,b_2,\bullet\bullet\bullet,b_n\}$ represent a sample set of sample, b_i is a element of set, each element consists of eight data, to the ith element there has $b_i=\{\mu_1,\mu_2,\bullet\bullet\bullet,\mu_8\}$, μ_i is pressure sensor corresponding membership value after conversion. Specific distribution pattern is determined as follows:(1) Collect data plantar pressure during walking, get to $b_i=\{\mu_1,\mu_2,\bullet\bullet\bullet,\mu_8\}$, determine the tolerance ε; (2) Calculate $N_j(A_j,b_i)=\frac{1}{2}[A_j\circ b_i+(1-A_j\otimes b_i)]$, $A_j\in\{A_1,A_2,A_3,A_4,A_5\}$; (3) If $N_j\le\varepsilon$, then $b_i=A_j$.

4 Simulation and Analysis

In order to verify the effectiveness of this method, we have compiled a handler in Matlab platform, added 15 new subjects, collected in plantar pressure data when they were five kinds of stance phase, substituted the data to the program and got automatic recognition results as shown in Table 2.

Table 2. The algorithm identifies results

Identification Number	Initial Contact	13
	Loading Response	12
	Mid Stance	13
	Heel Rise	11
	Toe Contact	13
Number 15	The average recognition rate	82.6%

From the experiment, an average recognition rate was 82.6%, we can see the method on human plantar pressure distribution pattern has better recognition performance.

Because plantar pressure distribution pattern and the calculation of five standard distribution models $\{A_1,A_2,A_3,A_4,A_5\}$ are on the basis of statistical data, sample number is insufficient that affects to increase the recognition rate. It is necessary to improve sample

number and increase the sample diversity in the follow-up study.

References

[1].Meng Chen, Bufu Huang, ka Keung Lee, etal. An Intelligent Shoe-Intergrated System for Plantar Pressure Measurement. Processings of the 2006 IEEE International Conference on Robotics and Biomimetics, 2006:416-421.

[2].Godi M, Turcato A M, Schieppati M, et al. Test-retest reliability of an insole plantar pressure system to assess gait along linear and curved trajectories[J]. Journal of Neuroengineering & Rehabilitation, 2014, 11(1):1-8.

[3].Pauk J, Daunoraviciene K, Ihnatouski M, et al. Analysis of the plantar pressure distribution in children with foot deformities.[J]. Acta of Bioengineering & Biomechanics, 2010, 12(1):29-34.

[4]. Mao B Y, Jia X W, Zheng F R. Research on the Human Foot Pressure Distribution of Walking and Standing[J]. Orthopedic Journal of China, 2002.

Fund Project

1.Hainan social development science and technology projects: Research of the human plantar pressure characteristics Identification based on fuzzy theory(Item Number: 2015SF33）.

2.Hainan Natural Science Fund: Biogeography Optimization Algorithm Based on Multi-objective to Solve Biological Motif and Discovery Problem(Item Number: 20156226）.

3.Hainan Natural Science Fund: Key Technology Research of Smart Video Object Segmentation and Tracking Based on DRLSE(Item Number: 20156228）.

MATEC Web of Conferences **44**, 02061 (2016)
DOI: 10.1051/matecconf/20164402061

Research on Inferring ELECTRE-III's Parameters with Fuzzy information and A Case on Naval Gun Weapon System Integration

Shi Yan Sun[1], Hui Min Zhu[2]

[1] *Institute of Weaponry Engineering, Wuhan Navy University of Engineering, China*
[2] *College of Electronics Engineering, Wuhan Naval University of Engineering, China*

Abstract. Multiple attributes decision making (MADM) method is an important measure for system integration. Robustness analysis on MADM is a hotspot in these years which wins academe's great attention, and is supposed to be an effective way when countering imperfect information. Setting parameters in ELECTRE-III is a vital and difficult step. In this paper, a method of inferring ELECTRE-III' s parameters with fuzzy information based on robustness analysis is presented. First, ELECTRE-III is transformed into a continuous smooth function of each parameter vector. Then, robustness analysis structure and a parameters inferring algorithm are provided by maximizing robustness margin based on mathematics programming. Moreover, how to resolve the programming problem is also discussed. At last, a illustrative example of Naval Gun Weapon System Integration is put forward.
Key words. Robustness analysis; Multiple attributes decision making; ELECTRE-III; naval gun weapon system

1. Introduction

The shipborne weapon system has became more enormous, more complex and more expensive to cope with increasing surface and air threat, which will conflict with relatively skimpy military budget and limited loadage capability. As a subsystem of warship combat system, naval gun weapon system plays an important role and takes on many missions. How to obtain an optimal system integration plan, which will make the efficiency, cost, rate of progress, life force, reliability, maintainability, percent of tonnage to be a suited level generally, is always a pivotal problem for weapon system analysis expert and warship design department. MADM methods have been applied in the integration of many weapon system. Classical parameters (such as weights, cut or threshold) setting methods in MADM methods usually base on decision makers' common sense or intuition, and result is often rigid. Due to human experience's uncertainty, this way is more or less arbitrary which may minify the decision making's creditability. There are two approaches that acknowledge this difficulty and try to remedy it: sensitivity analysis and robustness analysis.

Sensitivity analysis is a way to estimate how much the parameters vary when leading to a constant result, or to find which is the most sensitive parameter and which is a substitute action for the optimal. The studies about sensitivity analysis are numerous: Zuoprovided a sensitivity analysis way for simple additive weighting method (a kind of classical MADM method) [1]; Rios Inusu presented a studying framework on sensitivity analysis, which included the concepts of possible optimal alternative, neighboring possible optimal alternative and sensitivity index[2]. But sensitivity analysis has its disadvantage of requiring an 'estimated' center value for each parameter and only considering the corresponding solution. It is also often performed on a single parameter at a time, and ignores the possible interdependencies between parameters. Furthermore, sensitivity analysis is theoretic rather than practical.

Robustness analysis is a hotspot in recent years

which wins academe's great attention, and is supposed to be an effective way replacing sensitivity analysis on processing imperfect information in MADM. Compared to sensitivity analysis, robustness analysis considers parameters combination rather than a single parameter at a time. It tries to know whether the conclusion changes (or not) when the parameter values vary, rather than how the parameters vary without changing conclusions. Moreover, it has a more extensive consideration, including environment parameters, method models and model parameters. There some representative contribution including the studies of Roy, Vincke, Kouvelis and Yu, Dias, etc., which exploited our scope on robustness analysis. Vincke proposed a formalism to define the concepts of robust solution and robust method. His concept of robustness is that no solution contradicts the first one [3-5]; Kouvelis and Yudefine robust solution as a rank with the best worst-case behavior in the context of discrete optimization problems[6]; Dias defines robust solution as a scenarios combination that holds the rank unchanged with fuzzy information[7], which is also the background concept of this paper. In sum, Robustness analysis is a new direction in MADM, which emphasizes that uncertain factors should be considered, and the optimal solution must be also robust and neutral.

ELECTRE-Ⅲ is one kind of important MADM methods based on valued outranking relation. How to set parameters is an important step for ELECTRE-Ⅲ. In the second section , the problem to be discussed is formulized, including ELECTRE-Ⅲ method, it's transform and the fuzzy information's denotation. In the third section, a frame of robustness analysis method based on classical optimization theory is presented, which is applied in inferring ELECTRE-Ⅲ's parameters in the fourth section. First, the constraints are transformed into continuous smooth functions of parameters vector. Then an inferring algorithm of parameters is provided by maximizing robustness margin based on mathematics programming. The fifth section provides an illustrative example of naval gun weapon system integration as a case study on the method of inferring ELECTRE-Ⅲ's parameters. Furthermore, it is discussed that this method can also be applied to other MADM methods in the last section.This paper is also an extension of a previous work of the authors. The Ref.[8] only provided a frame work on inferring ELECTRE-Ⅲ's parameters and didn't discuss how to solve it. In this paper, it is completed.

2. Formulation

2.1 ELECTRE-Ⅲ method

The outranking relation construction is based on the alternatives set $A=\{a_1,a_2,\ldots,a_n\}$. To obtain the outranking relation between the alternatives a_i and a_k ($a_i,a_k \in A$), concordance test and disconcordance test proceed as follows:

1) Basic information

Let $J=\{j\in J: j=1,2,\cdots,m\}$ denote the set of attribute indices. $y_j(a_i)$ denotes the evaluation of an alternative $a_i \in A$ on the attribute j. All the attributes are assumed to be benefit type, namely the higher the value, the better it is. Let $w=\{w_1,w_2,\cdots,w_m\}$ denote the set of weights proposed by decision makers. q_j is preference indifference threshold between alternatives on the j-th attribute, p_j denote strictly preference threshold ,and v_j denote veto threshold. Namely when the preference attribute value between $y_j(a_i)$ and $y_j(a_k)$ exceeds v_j, the judgment that alternative a_i generally outranks a_k is no longer accepted.

2) Define concordance indices and disconcordance indices

$C(a_i,a_k)$ is defined as concordance indices of alternative couples (a_i , a_k) $\in A^2$ in ELECTRE-Ⅲ method:

$$C(a_i,a_k)=\sum_{j=1}^{m} w_j \cdot c_j(a_i,a_k)\Big/\sum_{j=1}^{m} w_j \tag{1}$$

where

$$c_j(a_i,a_k)=\begin{cases}0 & \text{if } y_j(a_i)-y_j(a_k)\le q_j\\ 1 & \text{if } y_j(a_i)-y_j(a_k)\ge p_j\\ \dfrac{y_j(a_i)-y_j(a_k)-q_j}{p_j-q_j} & \text{otherwise}\end{cases} \tag{2}$$

Index $c_j(a_i,a_k)$ denotes the degree of preference a_i over a_k on the j-th attribute, and $C(a_i,a_k)$ denotes the measurement that sustains the judgment "a_i outrank a_k".

Disconcordance indices is $d_j(a_i,a_k)$:

$$d_j(a_i,a_k)=\begin{cases}0 & \text{if } y_j(a_k)-y_j(a_i)\le p_j\\ 1 & \text{if } y_j(a_k)-y_j(a_i)\ge v_j\\ \dfrac{y_j(a_k)-y_j(a_i)-p_j}{v_j-p_j} & \text{otherwise}\end{cases} \tag{3}$$

$d_j(a_i,a_k)$ denotes the measurement that rejects the judgment "a_i outrank a_k".

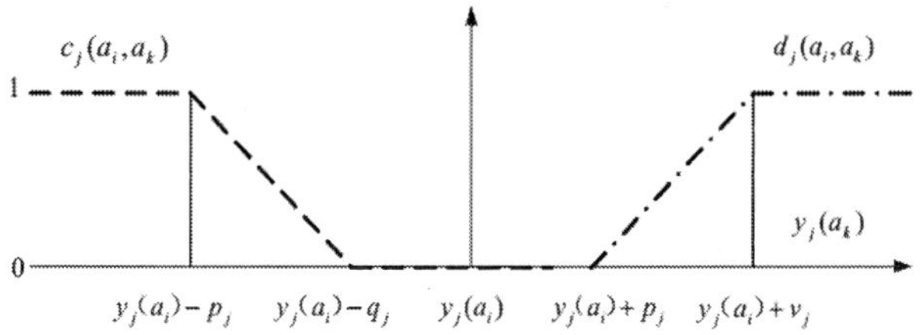

Figure 1. Definition of $c_j(a_i,a_k)$ and $d_j(a_i,a_k)$ functions

In Figure 1, horizontal axis denotes $y_j(a_k)$, vertical axis denotes the function values of $c_j(a_i,a_k)$ and $d_j(a_i,a_k)$, in which broken line is $c_j(a_i,a_k)$ function, and dashdotted line is $d_j(a_i,a_k)$ function.

Suppose

$$J^+ = \{j \in J \mid d_j(a_i,a_k) \le C(a_i,a_k)\}$$
$$J^- = \{j \in J \mid d_j(a_i,a_k) > C(a_i,a_k)\} \quad (4)$$

$J^+(a_i,a_k)$ denotes the subset of J that $d_j(a_i,a_k) \ge C(a_i,a_k)$, $J^-(a_i,a_k)$ denotes the subset that $d_j(a_i,a_k) < C(a_i,a_k)$.

3) Define valued outranking relationship

Define valued outranking relationship between alternative couple (a_i, a_k) as $S(a_i,a_k)$:

$$S(a_i,a_k) = \begin{cases} C(a_i,a_k) & \text{if } \forall j \in J^+ \\ C(a_i,a_k) \prod_{j \in J^-(a_i,a_k)} \dfrac{1-d_j(a_i,a_k)}{1-C(a_i,a_k)} & \text{if } \forall j \in J^- \end{cases} \quad (5)$$

$S(a_i,a_k)$ denotes the measurement that sustains the judgment "a_i generally outrank a_k".

Suppose

$$D_j(a_i,a_k) = \begin{cases} 1 & \text{if } \forall j \in J^+ \\ \dfrac{1-d_j(a_i,a_k)}{1-C(a_i,a_k)} & \text{if } \forall j \in J^- \end{cases} \quad (6)$$

Then

$$D(a_i,a_k) = \prod_{j \in J} D_j(a_i,a_k) \quad (7)$$

Then

$$S(a_i,a_k) = C(a_i,a_k) \cdot D(a_i,a_k) \quad (8)$$

By the valued outranking relation $S(a_i,a_k)$, it is possible to define a family of nested crisp outranking relations S_λ:

$$S_\lambda = \{(a_i,a_k) \in A \times A : S(a_i,a_k) \ge \lambda\}, \lambda \in [0.5,1] \quad (9)$$

λ is belief level that $S(a_i,a_k)$ satisfies S_λ.

2.2 Transformed ELECTRE-III

From the formulas (6)~(8), there is a nonlinear relationship between $S(a_i,a_k)$ and w, which is difficult to be solved. Furthermore the subset of attributes J^- can't be integrated into programming function. The Ref. [9] had studied the weights and veto thresholds in $S(a_i,a_k)$, and also considered that $S(a_i,a_k)$ is a continuous undifferentiable nonlinear concave function of w.

To make classical optimization methods applied easily, $S(a_i,a_k)$ is transformed as follows.

Transformed disconcordance index $d'_j(a_i,a_k)$ is:

$$d'_j(a_i,a_k) = \begin{cases} 0 & \text{if } y_j(a_k) - y_j(a_i) \le u_j \\ 1 & \text{if } y_j(a_k) - y_j(a_i) \ge v_j \\ \dfrac{y_j(a_k) - y_j(a_i) - u_j}{v_j - u_j} & \text{otherwise} \end{cases} \quad (10)$$

u_j is veto indifference threshold, $p_j \le u_j \le v_j$.

Transformed $d'_j(a_i,a_k)$ is shown as Figure 2:

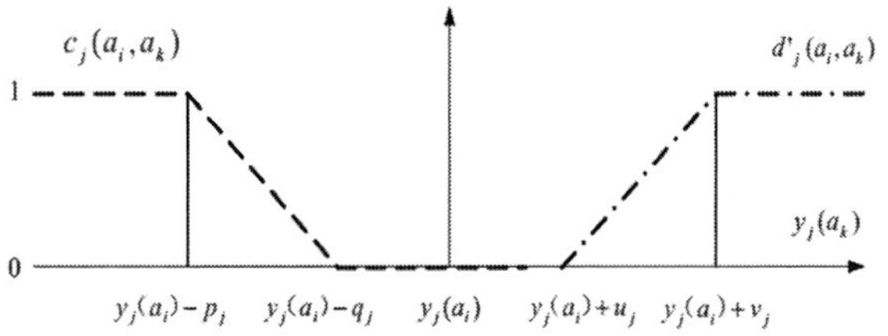

Figure 2. Functions of $c_j(a_i,a_k)$ and $d'_j(a_i,a_k)$

Transformed $D'_j(a_i,a_k)$ is:

$$D'_j(a_i,a_k) = \begin{cases} 1 & \text{if } \forall j \in J^+ \\ 1 - d'_j(a_i,a_k) & \text{if } \forall j \in J^- \end{cases} \quad (11)$$

Then

$$D'_j(a_i,a_k) = \text{Min}\{1, 1 - d'_j(a_i,a_k)\} \quad (12)$$

$$D'(a_i,a_k) = \prod_j D'_j(a_i,a_k) \quad (13)$$

The transformed $S(a_i,a_k)$ is:

$$S'(a_i,a_k) = C(a_i,a_k) \cdot D'(a_i,a_k) \quad (14)$$

$$S'_\lambda = \{(a_i,a_k) \in A \times A : S'(a_i,a_k) \ge \lambda\} \quad (15)$$

2.3 Fuzzy information's denotation

Usually, decision maker is difficult to provide exact parameters, but may present some linear constraints easily, by which an fuzzy information space can be constructed. It is formed as follows:

1) Weights space

(a) $w^l{}_j \le w_j \le w^u{}_j$;

(b) $\alpha_1 w_1 + \alpha_2 w_2 + \ldots + \alpha_m w_m \ge 0$;

(c) $\beta_0 + \beta_1 w_1 + \beta_2 w_2 + \ldots + \beta_m w_m = 0$.

All these constraints can be denoted as the space W :

$$w = (w_1, w_2, \ldots, w_m) \in W \subset \mathrm{R}^m$$

2) Cutting level space

$$\lambda^l \le \lambda \le \lambda^u$$

Denoted as the space Λ :

$$\lambda \in \Lambda \subset \mathrm{R}$$

3) Preference threshold space

$$p^l{}_j \le p_j \le p^u{}_j, j \in J$$

Denoted as :

$$p = (p_1, p_2, \ldots, p_m) \in P \subset \mathrm{R}^m$$

4) Preference indifference threshold space

$$q^l{}_j \le q_j \le q^u{}_j, j \in J$$

Denoted as :

$$q = (q_1, q_2, \ldots, q_m) \in Q \subset \mathrm{R}^m.$$

5) Veto threshold space

(a) $v^l{}_j \le v_j \le v^u{}_j, j \in J$;

(b) $v_j \ge p_j \ge q_j$;

(c) $v_j = p_j + \beta_j \cdot w_j$.

Denoted as :

$$v = (v_1, v_2, \ldots, v_m) \in V \subset \mathrm{R}^m$$

6) Veto indifference threshold space

(a) $u^l{}_j \le u_j \le u^u{}_j,\ j \in J$;

(b) $v_j \ge u_j \ge p_j$;

(c) $u_j = p_j + \gamma_j \cdot (v_j - p_j)$.

Denoted as :

$$u = (u_1, u_2, \ldots, u_m) \in U \subset \mathrm{R}^m$$

Suppose

$$\delta = \{w, \lambda, p, q, v, u\}$$

The parameters space Δ

$$\Delta = W \otimes \Lambda \otimes P \otimes Q \otimes V \otimes U$$

Then

$$\delta \in \Delta$$

3. A frame of robustness analysis

A formalized definition of robustness is provided in the Ref. [10]:

Definition 1: A conclusion C^r, is said to be robust with respect to a domain Δ, of possible values for the preference and technical parameters, if there is no a particular set of parameters, $\delta \in \Delta$, which invalidates the conclusion C^r.

The problem of inferring parameters in ELECTRE-Ⅲ is solved by maximizing robustness margin based on mathematics programming.

Let

$$\begin{aligned} S^+ &= \{(a_i, a_k) \mid S'(a_i, a_k) \ge \lambda\} \\ S^- &= \{(a_i, a_k) \mid S'(a_i, a_k) < \lambda + \varepsilon\} \end{aligned} \tag{16}$$

ε is a tiny positive number.

To keep the rank constant, the set S^+ and S^- must be unchanged. So, the optimal parameters vectors can also be got by maximizing robustness margin with the constraint conditions S^+ and S^-.

$$\begin{cases} \text{Max } \alpha(\delta) \\ \text{s.t. } \ \alpha \le S(a_i, a_k) - \lambda \ \ \forall (a_i, a_k) \in S^+ \\ \quad\ \ \alpha \le \lambda - S(a_i, a_k) + \varepsilon \ \ \forall (a_i, a_k) \in S^- \\ \quad\ \ \delta \in \Delta, j \in J \end{cases} \tag{17}$$

δ denotes every parameters in the section 2.3, and Δ denotes constrained domain.

Definition 2: Let

$$\alpha = S'(a_i, a_k) - \lambda$$

α is Robustness Margin of alternative a_i outranking a_k, $0 \le \alpha \le 1$.

The rank is more robust when α is larger.

Definition 3: If the programming (17) have solution, the maximum of α ($\alpha_{\max}$) can be obtained which is called 'maximum robustness margin', and the solution is 'optimal parameter vector' δ_{opt}.

ELECTRE-Ⅲ's parameters inferring algorithm:

1) Problem formulation: Define alternatives set A and attributes set J; Experts assign evaluation values $y_j(a_i)$.

2) Set initial parameters : Set initial parameters δ_0, parameters constraints, and other ELECTRE- Ⅲ 's parameters;

3) S^+ and S^- : Obtain S^+ and S^- by ELECTRE-Ⅲ;

4) $\alpha_{\max}$ and δ_{opt}: Solve the programming (17) to obtain maximum robustness margin $\alpha_{\max}$ and optimal parameter vector δ_{opt};

5) $S'(a_i, a_k)$: Obtain the indices $S'(a_i, a_k)$ by ELECTRE-Ⅲ with δ_{opt}, $\forall a_i, a_k \in A$;

6) Rank : Obtain the rank of set A by $S'(a_i, a_k)$.

4. Inferring ELECTRE-Ⅲ's parameters

The parameters structure of ELECTRE-Ⅲ is listed in Figure 3. The parameters to be inferred based on robustness analysis include local parameters and global parameters. When local parameters are studied, the others are fixed. In this paper, weights, cutting level, thresholds and other local parameters will be studied respectively. (The parameters to be discussed are at the left half of the Figure 3.) It is more difficult to infer global parameters, which will be discussed in later papers.

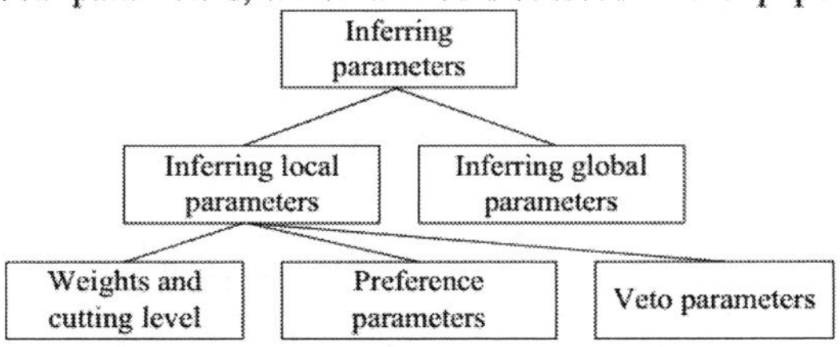

Figure. 3. Parameters structure to be Inferred

4.1 Inferring Weights and cutting level

When the parameters weights and the cutting level are analyzed, others parameters are fixed. The constraints of (17) can be embodied as follow:

$$\begin{cases} \text{Max } \alpha(w,\lambda) \\ \text{s.t. } \alpha \le \sum_{j=1}^{m} w_j \cdot c_j(a_i,a_k)\cdot D'(a_i,a_k) \Big/ \sum_{j=1}^{m} w_j - \lambda \ \forall (a_i,a_k)\in S^+ \\ \alpha \le \lambda - \sum_{j=1}^{m} w_j \cdot c_j(a_i,a_k)\cdot D'(a_i,a_k) \Big/ \sum_{j=1}^{m} w_j + \varepsilon \ \forall (a_i,a_k)\in S^- \\ \sum_{j=1}^{m} w_j = 1, w_j \ge \varepsilon, w\in W, \forall j\in J, \lambda\in\Lambda \end{cases} \quad (18)$$

The programming (18) is a linear programming of weights w and cutting level λ. The optimal estimation of w and λ can be obtained by simplex method.

4.2 Inferring Preference parameters

1) Inferring preference threshold q_j and preference indifference threshold p_j

When inferring preference threshold q_j and preference indifference threshold p_j at single attribute j, other parameters are fixed. The programming (17) is segmented and concave is difficult to solved. A eclectic method is to smooth the segmented function $c_j(a_i,a_k)$:

$$c_j(a_i,a_k) = \begin{cases} 0 & \text{if } \Delta_j(a_i,a_k) \le q^u{}_j \\ 1 & \text{if } \Delta_j(a_i,a_k) \ge p^l{}_j \\ (\Delta_j(a_i,a_k) - q_j)/(p_j - q_j) & \text{otherwise} \end{cases} \quad (19)$$

Then the constraints of (17) can be embodied as follow:

$$\begin{cases} \text{Max } \alpha(p_j,q_j) \\ \text{s.t. } (\frac{\alpha+\lambda}{D'} - C_{-j})\cdot \sum_{j=1}^{m} w_j / w_j \le c_j(a_i,a_k) \ \forall (a_i,a_k)\in S^+ \\ -(\frac{\alpha+\lambda+\varepsilon}{D'} - C_{-j})\cdot \sum_{j=1}^{m} w_j / w_j \le -c_j(a_i,a_k) \forall (a_i,a_k)\in S^- \\ p^l{}_j \le p_j \le p^u{}_j, q^l{}_j \le q_j \le q^u{}_j, j\in J \end{cases} \quad (20)$$

$$C_{-j}(a_i,a_k) = C(a_i,a_k) - w_j \cdot c_j(a_i,a_k) \Big/ \sum_{j=1}^{m} w_j \text{ 。}$$

If the programming (20) has solution, the optimal preference threshold p_j^{opt} and optimal preference indifference threshold vector q_j^{opt} can be obtained.

2) Inferring preference threshold vector q *and preference indifference threshold vector* p

The segmented function $c_j(a_i,a_k)$ is smoothed in the same way as above. If the programming problem has solution, the optimal preference threshold vector p_{opt} and optimal preference indifference threshold vector q_{opt} can be obtained.

4.3 Inferring Veto parameters

1) Inferring veto threshold v_j *and veto indifference threshold* u_j

Other parameters are fixed when veto threshold v_j and veto indifference threshold u_j of single attribute j of single attribute j are inferred. The programming (17) is also is segmented and concave. The smoothed function $d'_j(a_i,a_k)$ is:

$$d'_j(a_i,a_k) = \begin{cases} 0 & \text{if } \Delta_j(a_k,a_i) \le u^l{}_j \\ 1 & \text{if } \Delta_j(a_k,a_i) \ge v^u{}_j \\ (\Delta_j(a_i,a_k) - u_j)/(v_j - u_j) & \text{otherwise} \end{cases} \quad (21)$$

Then:

$$\begin{cases} \text{Max } \alpha(u_j,v_j) \\ \text{s.t. } (\alpha+\lambda)/C\cdot D_{-j}' \le d'_j(a_i,a_k) \ \forall (a_i,a_k)\in S^+ \\ -(\alpha+\lambda+\varepsilon)/C\cdot D_{-j}' \le -d'_j(a_i,a_k) \forall (a_i,a_k)\in S^- \\ u^l{}_j \le u_j \le u^u{}_j, v^l{}_j \le v_j \le v^u{}_j, j\in J \end{cases} \quad (22)$$

$$D_{-j}' = D'/d'_j(a_i,a_k) \text{ 。}$$

If the programming MP3 has solution, the optimal veto threshold v_j^{opt} and optimal veto indifference threshold vector u_j^{opt} can be obtained.

2) Inferring veto threshold vector q *and veto indifference threshold vector* p

The segmented function $d'_j(a_i,a_k)$ is smoothed in the same way as above. If the programming problem has solution, the optimal veto threshold vector v_{opt} and optimal veto indifference threshold vector u_{opt} can be obtained.

5. A case study of naval gun weapon system integration

As the first step of the process to obtain an optimal integration plan of naval gun weapon system, it is to design some systems that satisfy basis sea battle need and other constrain conditions, namely feasible integration alternatives. Classical system structure of feasible integration alternatives is expressed as below:

(Main sensor)∩(Spare sensor)+(Director) +(Naval gun firepower system)

Main sensor is track radar; Spare sensor is photoelectric device; Director includes some fire control equipments; Naval gun firepower system include some types of naval guns such as AK630, 37F, AK76 or their combination. Three feasible configuration alternatives on certain type warship are listed as Table 1.

Table 1. Three Feasible Integration Alternatives

	Sensor	Spare Sensor	Director	Naval gun firepower system
a_1	344 radar	GD-2	ZPJ-2B	1×AK76 1×AK630
a_2	347G radar	JM-83	ZPJ-2B	3×37F
a_3	TR47 radar	OFD-b30	CC24	2×37F 1×AK76

Decision makers attach different regard on every attribute in terms of special integration problem. Weights reflect decision maker's preference. Suppose attributes set of naval gun weapon system is w,

w ={efficiency; cost; risk; applicability; compatibility; life force} = $\{y_1, y_2, y_3, y_4, y_5, y_6\}$

According to the algorithm of section 3, the process of naval gun weapon system integration is listed as bellow:

1) Standardized attributes values of three feasible integration alternatives are provided in Table 2, initial weights vector w_0 is listed in Tab. 3. Parameters constraints are set as follows, which are more or less simple but has it's generality:

$0.3 \le w_1 \le 0.5$, $0.1 \le w_2 \le 0.2$, $w_1 \ge 2w_2$, $0.1 \le w_3 \le 0.2$, $0.1 \le w_4 \le 0.2$, $\varepsilon \le w_5 \le 0.1$, $0.1 \le w_6 \le 0.2$, $\varepsilon = 0.001$, $0.4 \le \lambda \le 0.6$, $0.5 \le m_j \le 0.7$, $0.5 \le p_j \le 0.7$, $0 \le q_j \le 0.2$, $0.5 \le \sigma_j \le 0.7$.

Table 2. Standardized Attributes Values

	y_1	y_2	y_3	y_4	y_5	y_6
a_1	0.4103	0.3529	0.1389	0.6038	0.0153	0.9318
a_2	0.8936	0.8132	0.2028	0.2722	0.7468	0.4660
a_3	0.0579	0.0099	0.1987	0.1988	0.4451	0.4186

2) The result of ELECTRE- Ⅲ with initial parameters:

$$a_2 \succ a_1 , a_2 \succ a_3$$

3) Resolve programming (18). The optimal weights vector w_{opt} are listed in Table 3, $\lambda_{\text{opt}} = 0.4$.

Table 3. Initial and optimal weights vector w_{opt}

	w_1	w_2	w_3	w_4	w_5	w_6
w_0	0.4	0.14	0.1	0.13	0.08	0.15
w_{opt}	0.40	0.15	0.10	0.20	0.001	0.149

4) Resolve programming (20) and (22). The optimal threshold vectors are listed in Table 4:

Table 4. The optimal threshold vectors

Attribute	1	2	3	4	5	6
$(p_{\text{opt}}, q_{\text{opt}})$	(0.7,02)	(0.5,0.2)	(0.5,0.2)	(0.6,0.1)	(0.7,02)	(0.7,0.2)
$(u_{\text{opt}}, v_{\text{opt}})$	(0.7,02)	(0.6,0.1)	(0.6,0.1)	(0.6,0.1)	(0.7,0.2)	(0.7,02)

5) The final result of ELECTRE-Ⅲ with optimal parameters:

$$a_2 \succ a_3 \succ a_1$$

6. Summary and conclusions

In this paper, a robustness analysis method is presented in terms of inferring ELECTRE- Ⅲ 's parameters. The programming (18) is linear, convex, and can be solved by simplex method easily; but the programming (20) and (22) are nonlinear, concave and difficult to be solved, which need further study to find more proper way.

On the other hand, this method can also be applied to infer parameters in other MADM methods. For example, for AHP method or TOPSIS method, which are based on the utility theory , the $S(a_i,a_k)$ can be defined as :

$$S(a_i,a_k) = \phi(a_i) - \phi(a_k) \tag{23}$$

$\phi(a_i), \phi(a_k)$ is the evaluation of alternative a_i , a_k respectively. The optimal parameters can also be obtained by solving the programming (17).

Acknowledgment

The author is very grateful to Doctor Xie Jun for his insightful and constructive comments and suggestions that led to an improved version of this article.

References

[1] J. Zuo, The Discussion on Sensitivity Analysis in Methods Multiple Criteria Decision Making, System Engineering Theory and Application, 1987, 7(3): 1-11.

[2] R. Inusu, S. French. A Framework for Sensitivity Analysis in Discrete Multi-objective Decision-making, European Journal of Operational Research, 1991, 54(1): 176–190..

[3] B. Roy, A Missing Link in OR-DA: Robustness Analysis, Foundations of Computing and Decision Sciences, 1998, 23(1): 141-160.

[4] Ph. Vincke, Robust Solutions And Methods in Decision Aid, Journal of Multi-Criteria Decision Analysis 1999, 8(1):181-187.

[5] Ph. Vincke, Robust and Neutral Methods for Aggregating Preferences into an Outranking Relation, European Journal of Operational Research, 1999, 112(2): 405-412.

[6] Ph. Vincke, About the Application of MCDM to Some Robustness Problems, European Journal of Operational Research, 2006. 176(3): 645-658.

[7] P. Kouvelis, G. Yu, Robust Discrete Optimization and Its Application, New York: Kluwer Academic Publishers, 1997.

[8] S.Y.,Sun, Z.M.,Qiu, H.Y.,Wang ELECTRE-III's Parameters Inferring Method Based on Robustness Analysis, Command Control & Simulation, 2006, 28(6):14-18.

[9] L. C. Dias, J. N. Climaco, On Computing ELECTRE's Credibility Indices under Partial Information , Journal of Multi-Criteria Decision Analysis 1999, 8(1):74-92.

[10]J. Figueira(Ed.), Multiple Criteria Decision Analysis: State of the Art Surveys, New York: Kluwer Academic Publishers, 2005: 346

MATEC Web of Conferences 44, 02062 (2016)
DOI: 10.1051/matecconf/20164402062

Trading strategies of institutional investors in a limit order book market

Naiwei Chen[1,2] and Mingxu Peng[1,3,a]
[1]Center of Management Decision Valuation Research, Jiangxi Normal University, Nanchang, China
[2]International Institute for Financial Research, Jiangxi Normal University, Nanchang, China
[3]College of Finance, Jiangxi Normal University, Nanchang, China

Abstract. The study aims to examine the trading strategies of institutional investors in the limit order book market. The study modifies the assumptions of prior studies [1,2] to match actual situations or to facilitate calculations. First, the investors' objective in the study is profit maximization rather than minimization of trading costs. Second, time is continuous rather than discrete. Third, price impact functions are non-linear and take the quadratic form that features increasing prices. Study results indicate that institutional investors adopt the increasing trading strategy if the permanent price impact dominates whereas they adopt the decreasing trading strategy if the transient price impact dominates. In addition, the average trading strategy is adopted if and only if the permanent and transient price impacts are combined in some fixed proportions.

1 Introduction

Most research on traditional microstructure mainly focuses on the market-maker market. However, the electronic trading system has been gradually accepted by many financial markets and has become increasingly common in real-life securities trading. Unlike the traditional dealership market, the electronic trading system is a new type of trading method in the sense that it mainly adopts the form of limit orders. Research on limit order book market can be dated back to 1960s. However, it is not until 1990s that this kind of research sees a big progress [3]. Prior studies mostly deal with the development of trading strategies and can be divided into two kinds, including studies that consider the risk of adverse selection [3-6] and those without considering such a feature [7-12].

Research on the limit order book market in China is relatively scarce. Empirical research mainly focuses on the limit order from the perspective of information asymmetry [13]. Shanghai and Shenzhen stock market and three major commodities futures market in China all adopt the limit order quotation system. Hence, it is worthwhile to study such a system in the sense that study results will provide important theoretical and empirical implications for understanding and improving the microstructure of securities market in China characterized by the limit order book quotation system.

In the limit order book market, institutional investors can easily affect the market price since their trading volume is large. Hence, it is essential and meaningful to examine the trading strategies of institutional investors and how they influence the prices and stability in the market. In fact, many studies have been devoted to this research area. For example, it is found that the average trading strategy is optimal for institutional investors from the cost minimization perspective [2]. However, it is also found that adopting the large-volume trading strategy in the beginning and the end as well as taking the average trading strategy in between is optimal based the same perspective [1]. In addition, another kind of research uses the methodology related to physical economics to study the function that deals with the impact of trading volume on prices. In particular, such research analyzes the characteristics of physical statistics for the limit order book market [13,14-20].

The study aims to examine the trading strategies of institutional investors in the limit order book market. The study modifies three assumptions of prior studies [1,2] to match actual situations or to facilitate calculations. First, the investors' objective in the study is profit maximization rather than minimization of trading costs. Second, time is continuous rather than discrete. Third, based on the research of physical economists, price impact functions are non-linear and take the quadratic form that features increasing prices.

Study results indicate that investors adopt the strategy of increasing trading volume if the permanent price impact dominates. That is, investors initially trade less to reduce the price impact and then increase trading volume gradually as time goes by. By contrast, if the transient price impact dominates, investors adopt the strategy of decreasing trading volume. That is, if large trading volume does not result in big change in long-term prices,

[a]Corresponding author: pengmingxu@gmail.com

Article available at http://www.matec-conferences.org or http://dx.doi.org/10.1051/matecconf/20164402062

investors will choose to engage in large-volume trading at the early stage and then decrease trading volume over time. In addition, if and only if the permanent and transient price impact functions are combined in some fixed proportions, investors will adopt the average trading strategy. Such a conclusion is inconsistent with the findings of prior studies [1,2]. However, our finding is more consistent with intuition and realities. Furthermore, the study finds that security price changes depend on the final value of securities rather than the initial value, consistent with the finding of prior research [21].

The remainder of the paper is structured as follows. The assumptions of the model are first provided in section 2. It should be noted that the study considers one-sided market only, where sellers provide limit orders and buyers provide market orders. Based on the assumptions, section 3 proposes the investors' objective function and solve for the profit maximization for institutional investors. The study solves for the objective function using dynamic programming and conduct static analysis based on the results. Section 4 concludes the paper.

2 Hypotheses

Limit order is an order to trade a certain number of shares at a given price or better. For the buyers, the limit orders placed below the best bid price can be considered as the total demand. For the sellers, the limit orders placed above the best ask price can be considered as the total supply. In addition, market orders will arrive continually in the limit order market, where market order is an order to trade a certain number of securities at the best bid price for sellers or at the best ask price for the buyers. Since buyers' and sellers' limit orders and their corresponding market orders are symmetric, the study considers the sellers' limit orders and the corresponding buyers' market orders to facilitate analysis.

Suppose traders need to buy some security during the continuous time period $[0,T]$ and $x(t)$ is the number of securities bought at time t. The cumulative number of securities bought by investors during the period $[t,T]$ is Q_t, which can be expressed as $Q_t = \int_t^T x(\tau)d\tau$. That is, Q_t is the number of securities yet to be traded but needed to be traded by institutional investors during the period $[t,T]$. We then have $\partial Q_t/\partial t = -x_t$. After a given time T, institutional investors cannot and will not engage in securities trading. At the same time, suppose institutional investors are well informed such that they know that the settlement value of some security at a given time in the future is V. It follows that the investors 'objective is to make sure that securities are traded at prices not greater than the future settlement value (i.e., $p_t \le V, t \le T$) in the period $[0,T]$ and that the price at time T equals the settlement value (i.e., $p_T = V$). The collection of optimal strategies for institutional investors can then be expressed as: $\varphi = \{(t, x(t)): t \in [0,T], \forall x(t) \ge 0, p_T = V\}$.

In addition, suppose investors are risk-neutral and trade a certain amount of securities $x(t)$ at a price p_t. The trading volume has impact on the price, which can be divided into two kinds, i.e., transient and permanent price impacts. Based on the conclusions drawn by physical economists, the price impact function is non-linear. More specifically, the larger the trading volume, the larger the price impact and the larger the variation of the price impact function, and vice versa. That is, $p'(x) > 0$, $p''(x) > 0$. Based on this, the price impact function can be expressed as gx^2 , meaning that the variation of the price impact function is increasing as the trading volume increases. The permanent and transient impacts account for α and *1-α*, respectively, where $\alpha \in [0,1]$. Accordingly, the permanent and transient price impact functions can be expressed as $\alpha g x^2$ and $(1-\alpha)gx^2$ respectively. To trade securities with the amount of $x(t)$, traders are required to submit the quotations below:

$$p + gx^2 \tag{1}$$

The transient price impact function $(1\text{-}\alpha)gx^2$can only affect prices for the current period and ceases to exist in the next period. By contrast, the permanent price impact function can influence the prices in the future. Hence, the speed of price variation is $dp/dt = \alpha g x^2$, where $p = p_0$, when $t = 0$ and $p = V$ when $t = T$

3 Model and analysis

Based on the above assumptions, the trading volume provided by institutional investors can influence trading prices. That is, there is a function where trading volume affects prices. The solution for the optimal strategy of institutional investors therefore depends on how institutional investors deal with the relationship between the price impact function and trading volume to maximize their profits. The objective function of institutional investors is assumed as follows:

$$J(t,p,x) = \max_x E\left[\int_0^T [V-(p+gx^2)]xdt\right] \\ s.t.\ \frac{dp}{dt} = \alpha g x,\ x \ge 0,\ p_T = V. \tag{2}$$

Solving for the trading strategy of institutional investors yields the following:

$$x = \frac{1}{3}\left[\sqrt{\alpha^2 Q_t^2 + \frac{3(V-p)}{g}} - \alpha Q_t\right] \tag{3}$$

Proposition 1: In the limit order book market, if the impact of trading volume on prices satisfies equation (1) and the objective function of institutional investors satisfies equation (2), then the optimal strategy is for the trading volume to satisfy equation (3).

From equation (3) in Proposition 1, the price movement can be derived as: $p = V - g[2\alpha x Q + 3x^2]$. This indicates that in a limit order book market where there are institutional investors, if the settlement value V at some time in the future is known and institutional investors' objective is to maximize their returns at time T, then the price movement depends on the future settlement value, permanent price impact function, intended trading volume and the current trading volume of institutional

investors. More specifically, the security price is negatively related to the permanent price impact function, current trading volume, and remaining trading volume. In addition, the security price is positively related to final settlement value. Furthermore, the security price will converge to V eventually and has no relationship with the initial value.

We then conduct comparative statics for the trading strategy. Based on equation (3), the following equation is derived:

$$\frac{\partial x}{\partial t} = \frac{(2\alpha\text{-}3g)x_t^{\ 2}}{2\sqrt{\alpha^2 Q_t^2 + \dfrac{3(V-p)}{g}}} \quad (4)$$

Equation (4) describes how the trading volume of institutional investors evolves over time. There are three scenarios.

First, when $2\alpha > 3g$, $\partial x/\partial t > 0$, This means that when the proportion of the permanent price impact is sufficiently high, institutional investors choose the strategy of increasing trading volume. That is, if the impact of trading volume on prices is permanent, institutional investors will initially trade fewer securities to avoid excessive price increases in the future and then trade increasingly more over time. Second, when $2\alpha < 3g$, $\partial x/\partial t < 0$. This means that when the proportion of the permanent price impact is smaller, institutional investors choose the strategy of decreasing trading volume. That is, if the transient price impact dominates such that the impact of trading volume on prices is temporary rather than long-lasting, institutional investors will trade more securities initially and then decreases trading volume over time. Although the price can increase dramatically in response to increased trading volume, such a price increase is mostly a transient effect such that it does not take long for the price to revert to the original level. Third, when $2\alpha = 3g$, $\partial x/\partial t = 0$. This means that when the permanent and transient price impacts are combined in some fixed proportions, institutional investors choose the average trading strategy. That is, the average trading strategy documented in prior studies [1,2] will only be adopted by institutional investors under a particular circumstance. The average trading strategy is mere a special case among all trading strategies of institutional investors and its feasibility depends on the presence of a special market structure.

Taking the partial derivative with respective to g, we have:

$$\frac{\partial x}{\partial g} = -\frac{(V-p)}{2g^2\sqrt{\alpha^2 Q_t^2 + \dfrac{3(V-p)}{g}}} \leq 0 \quad (5)$$

Equation (5) indicates that the trading volume of institutional investors at time t is inversely related to the coefficient of the price impact function. That is, if the coefficient of the price impact function increases, institutional investors will choose smaller trading volume at time t to minimize the price impact.

Taking the partial derivative with respective to α, we have:

$$\frac{\partial x}{\partial \alpha} = \frac{Q_t}{3}\left[\frac{\alpha Q_t}{\sqrt{\alpha^2 Q_t^2 + \dfrac{3(V-p)}{g}}} - 1\right] < 0 \quad (6)$$

Equation (6) indicates that investors will trade increasingly less as the permanent price impact increases. Given constant total trading volume, investors are inclined to trade as fast as possible rather than postponing their trading. As a result, investors will surely choose to trade more initially and trade less in the future. This is because when the permanent price impact dominates and becomes increasingly large, quick transactions can avoid higher payment for future trading.

Combining equations (3) to (6), it can be inferred that in general, the impact of trading volume on prices can cause institutional investors to choose different trading strategies, further influencing the movement of security prices. In the price impact function, if the proportion of the permanent price impact (α) is relatively high, meaning that the majority of the price impact will continue to affect future trading, investors will surely opt for quick and large-volume transactions. By contrast, if the proportion of the permanent price impact (α) is relatively low, meaning that the transient price impact dominates, most price impacts will vanish quickly. Investors will surely opt to trade slowly in order not to affect future prices too much.

The permanent price impact function deals with the extent to which institutional investors disclose information to the market. Stronger permanent price impact suggests that more information contained in trading can be disclosed to the market in the form of price changes. If investors disclose more information, they should trade as soon as possible and the trading volume should be as large as possible. By contrast, the transient price impact function is like a one-time shock. It does not contain any information and prices will revert to the original level immediately after any shock. When the transient price impact dominates, investors will opt for slow trading to prevent from excessive disclosure of information, which is good for profit maximization. Such inferences concur with the conclusions of prior research [21] and the realities of securities markets.

Taking the partial derivative with respective to Q, we have:

$$\frac{\partial x}{\partial Q_t} = \frac{\alpha}{3}\left[\frac{\alpha Q_t}{\sqrt{\alpha^2 Q_t^2 + \dfrac{3(V-p)}{g}}} - 1\right] < 0 \quad (7)$$

Equation (7) indicates that the trading volume at some point in time is positively related to the total volume that investors are willing to trade in the future. That is, if there are still many securities yet to be traded, the current trading volume has to increase.

In sum, trading strategies of institutional investors

depend on the price impact function and the structure of permanent and transient impacts. Results are inconsistent with those of some studies [1,2]. However, results are consistent with the real situations and the finding of another study [21]. That is, if information can be hidden effectively, inside traders will not engage in large-volume trading to reveal their information. Instead, they will disclose their information gradually.

4 Conclusions

The paper studies the trading strategies of institutional investors in a limit order book market. We modify the assumptions and the objective function in existing literature [1,2] and use different methods to solve for optimal trading strategies.

Institutional investors have been the major traders in the securities markets. The trading strategies of institutional investors have also been the major concern of institutional investors as well as regulators, other institutions, and private investors. Based on the assumption of profit maximization, the study finds that the average trading strategy is optimal for institutional investors, concurring with the finding of prior research based on the assumption of cost minimization [2]. In behavioral finance, it is difficult to derive consistent results based on cost minimization and profit maximization [22,23]. However, the study shows that the average trading strategy is optimal for institutional investors based on profit maximization, concurring with the finding based on cost minimization.

Appendix: Solution for Proposition 1

Objective function:

$$J(t,p,x) = \max_x E_0 \left[\int_0^T [V-(p+gx^2)]x\,dt \right] \quad (8)$$

$$s.t.\ \frac{dp}{dt} = \alpha g x,\ x \geq 0,\ p_T = V.$$

A Hamilton function can then be generated as follows:

$$H = (V-p)x - gx^3 + \lambda \alpha g x^2 \quad (9)$$

Taking the partial derivative with respective to x, we have:

$$\frac{\partial H}{\partial x} = (V-p) - 3gx^2 + 2\alpha g \lambda x = 0$$

$$\lambda' = -\frac{\partial H}{\partial p} = x$$

With $\lambda(T) = 0$, we have $\lambda(t) = -Q_t$.

Substituting the above into equation (9), we have:

$$x = \frac{\sqrt{\alpha^2 g^2 Q_t^2 + 3g(V-p)} - \alpha g Q_t}{3g} = \frac{1}{3}\left[\sqrt{\alpha^2 Q_t^2 + \frac{3(V-p)}{g}} - \alpha Q_t\right] \quad (10)$$

Taking the partial derivatives with respective to α, g, Q_t, and t, we have:

$$\frac{\partial x}{\partial \alpha} = \frac{Q_t}{3}\left[\frac{\alpha Q_t}{\sqrt{\alpha^2 Q_t^2 + \frac{3(V-p)}{g}}} - 1\right] < 0$$

$$\frac{\partial x}{\partial g} = -\frac{(V-p)}{2g^2\sqrt{\alpha^2 Q_t^2 + \frac{3(V-p)}{g}}} < 0$$

$$\frac{\partial x}{\partial Q_t} = \frac{\alpha}{3}\left[\frac{\alpha Q_t}{\sqrt{\alpha^2 Q_t^2 + \frac{3(V-p)}{g}}} - 1\right] < 0$$

$$\frac{\partial x}{\partial t} = \frac{3gx + \alpha\sqrt{\alpha^2 Q_t^2 + \frac{3(V-p)}{g}} - 2\alpha^2 Q_t}{6\sqrt{\alpha^2 Q_t^2 + \frac{3(V-p)}{g}}}x$$

References

1. L.R. Glosten, J Financ **49**, 1127-1161 (1994)
2. B. Biais, D. Martimort, J.-C. Rochet, Econometrica **68**, 799-837 (2000)
3. S. Chakravarty, C.W. Holden, J Financ Intermed **4**, 213-241 (1995)
4. T. Foucault, Journal Financ Mark **2**, 99-134 (1999)
5. D.J. Seppi, Rev Financ Stud **10**, 103-150 (1997)
6. C.A. Parlour, D.J. Seppi, Rev Financ Stud **16**, 301-343 (2003)
7. S. Viswanathan, J.J.D. Wang, J Financ Mark **5**, 127-167 (2002)
8. C.A. Parlour, Rev Financ Stud **11**, 789-816 (1998)
9. T. Foucault, O. Kadan, E. Kandel, Rev Financ Stud **18**, 1171-1217 (2005)
10. A.A. Obizhaeva, J. Wang, J Financ Mark **16**, 1-32 (2013)
11. I. Rosu, Working paper, University of Chicago (2004)
12. W.-X. Zhou, Quant Financ **12**, 1253-1263 (2012)
13. R. Almgren, N. Chriss, J Risk **3**, 5-40 (2001)
14. J.P. Bouchaud, M. Mézard, M. Potters, Quant Financ **2**, 251-256 (2002)
15. M. Potters, J.-P. Bouchaud, Physica A **324**, 133-140 (2003)
16. E. Smith, J.D. Farmer, L.S. Gillemot, S. Krishnamurthy, Quant Financ **3**, 481-514 (2003)
17. H. Luckock, Quant Financ **3**, 385-404 (2003)
18. P. Gopikrishnan, V. Plerou, H.E. Stanley, working paper, Massachusetts Institute of Technology, Department of Economics (2003)
19. S. Maslov, M. Mills, Physica A **299**, 234-246 (2001)
20. P. Weber, B. Rosenow*, Quant Financ **5**, 357-364 (2005)
21. A.S. Kyle, Econometrica, 1315-1335 (1985)
22. M. Kritzman, Financ Anal J **50**, 14-18 (1994)
23. M. Kritzman, Economics and Portfolio Strategy, New York: Peter L. Bernstein, Inc. (September 1997)

MATEC Web of Conferences 44, 02063 (2016)
DOI: 10.1051/matecconf/20164402063

Applications of Fuzzy adaptive PID control in the thermal power plant denitration liquid ammonia evaporation

Jing Li[1], Guo Qing Zhang[2] , Huan Xin Cheng [3,a],Li Cheng[4,a]

[1,2,3]*College of Automation and Electrical Engineering.Qingdao University of Science and Technology.Qingdao 266042.china*
[4]*Xinjiang Technical Institute of Physics and Chemistry.CAS,Urumuqi,Xinjiang,830011,China*
[a]*Urumqi Xiaming Innovation Electronic Technology Co.,Ltd,Urumuqi,Xinjiang,830011,China*

Abstract. For the control of the liquid level of liquid ammonia in thermal power plant's ammonia vaporization room, traditional PID controller parameter tuning is difficult to adapt to complex control systems, the setting of the traditional PID controller parameters is difficult to adapt to the complex control system. For the disadvantage of bad parameter setting, poor performance and so on, the fuzzy adaptive PID control is proposed. Fuzzy adaptive PID control combines the advantages of traditional PID technology and fuzzy control. By using the fuzzy controller to intelligent control the object, the performance of the PID controller is further improved, and the control precision of the system is improved[1]. The simulation results show that the fuzzy adaptive PID controller not only has the advantages of high accuracy of PID controller, but also has the characteristics of fast and strong adaptability of fuzzy controller. It realizes the optimization of PID parameters which are in the optimal state, and the maximum increase production efficiency, so that are more suitable for nonlinear dynamic system.

1 Introduction

Coal is the main energy source of our country nowadays and the future. When coal is burned in the boiler, sulfur and nitrogen oxide waste gas can be generated. Nitrogen oxides are one of the key reasons for the regional air pollution. It is not only the cause of acid rain and fog, but also causes the other mixed chemical air pollution, which is harmful to human survival and destruction of the ecological environment[2]. At present, although the vast majority of the thermal power plant is equipped with low nitrogen combustion technology in our country, but the denitration efficiency is low. The SCR technology combined with low nitrogen combustion technology using, out of stock will greatly increase the efficiency. Thermal power plant SCR device includes: flue gas system, ammonia injection system, liquid ammonia storage evaporation system, blowing ash system, SCR catalyst, and safety auxiliary equipment.

Liquid ammonia gasification is an important part of the thermal power plant denitration process hat[3]. It is also the first condition of ensure the normal operation of denitration. The safe operation of the liquid ammonia gasification directly affects the safety of the whole thermal power plant. Therefore to study advanced the application of DCS to control the denitration liquid ammonia vapors, improve the stability of the system is running safety is even more necessary, at the same time there is a growing concern of atmospheric pollution control is of great significance. So we put fuzzy adaptive PID control in the process of liquid ammonia, improve the efficiency of liquid ammonia vaporization and to meet the requirements of safety and process constraints, making the key points of each control to achieve the optimization and for the denitration follow-up work well enough ammonia gas supply, ultimately achieve the denitration efficiency maximization.

2 The design of fuzzy adaptive PID controller

2.1 PID control

PID controller is a linear controller. As shown in figure 1,

$$u(t) = k_p e(t) + k_i \int_0^t e(\tau)d\tau + \frac{de(t)}{dt}$$

In the formula, k_p is the scale factor. T_i is the integral time constant. T_d is the differential time constant.

At present, the incremental PID control algorithm is widely used, and its output $\Delta u(k)$ is the increment of the control quantity. Its formula is as follows.

$$\Delta u(k) = k_p \Delta e(k) + k_i e(k) + k_d [e(k) - \Delta e(k-1)]$$

Corresponding author: 317842602@qq.com

Article available at http://www.matec-conferences.org or http://dx.doi.org/10.1051/matecconf/20164402063

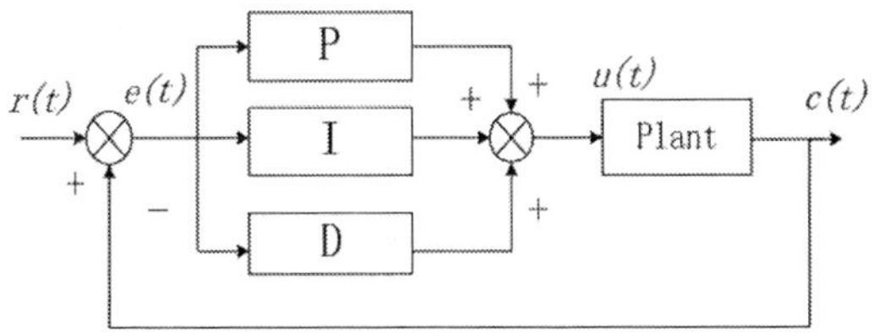

Figure 1. Block diagram of PID system

Among them, K_p is the proportion coefficient; $K_i = K_p T / T_i$ is the integral coefficient; $K_d = K_p T_d / T$ is the differential coefficient.

In the PID control process, first determine the mathematical model based on the controlled object PID, and then use the deviation e as input to calculate the amount of control and drive the appropriate enforcement agency to reduce the error until the controlled object stabilized within the allowable range.

2.2 The control principle of Fuzzy adaptive PID controller

The control principle of fuzzy adaptive PID control is to identify the fuzzy relationship with PID three parameters K_p, K_i, K_d between e and e_c, through continuous testing e and e_c in the operation, based on fuzzy control theory to online modification of the three parameters in order to satisfy different e and e_c for different requirements of the control parameters and leave the controlled object has a good dynamic and static performance[4]. The whole structure of fuzzy adaptive PID controller is as shown in figure 2.

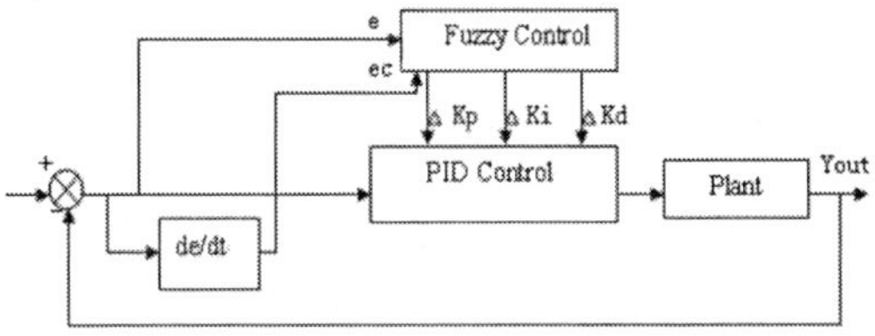

Figure 2. Block diagram of Fuzzy adaptive PID controller

2.3 The design of fuzzy adaptive PID controller

2.3.1 The determination of membership function of linguistic variables

We put the deviation e and the change rate deviation e_c as the input fuzzy controller and the three parameters of PID controller Δk_p , Δk_i , Δk_d as the output. According to the project of the actual situation, fuzzy subset of the input variables e and e_c are {negative big, negative middle, negative small, zero, positive small, positive middle, positive big}, denoted as {NB, NM, NS, ZO, PS, PM, PB}. The deviation e and deviation change rate e_c were quantified into the region of (-3, 3). Meanwhile, the fuzzy subset of the output variable KP, KI, KD are {negative big, negative middle, the negative small, zero, positive small, positive middle, positive big} denoted as {NB, NM, NS, ZO, PS, PM, PB}, respectively, to be quantified into the region of (-3, 3) (0.06, 0.06) (0, 3). These membership function curves are shown in figure 3, figure 4.

According to the membership assignment table of each fuzzy subset and the fuzzy control model of each parameter, using fuzzy synthesis reasoning design the fuzzy matrix table of PID parameters to realize online correction PID parameters. Computation formula is as follows:

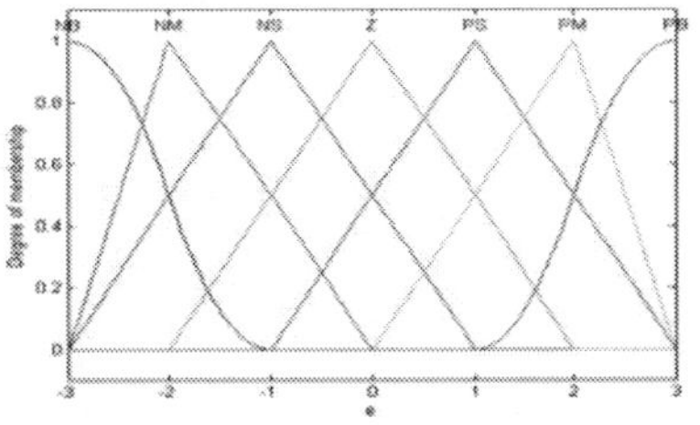

Figure 3. The membership function of input variable e e_c curve

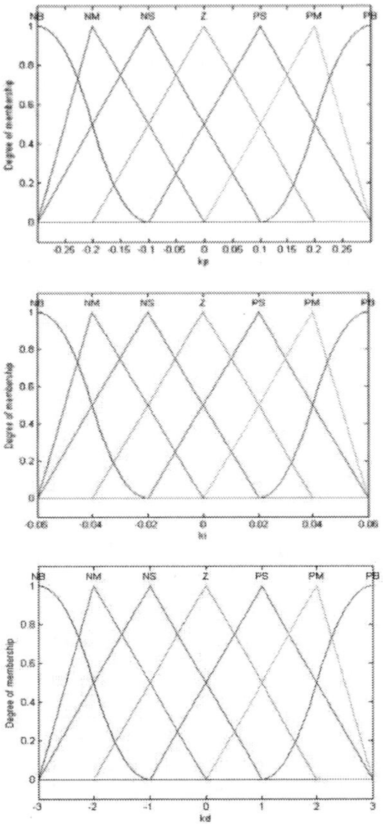

Figure 4. The membership function of output variable Δk_p Δk_i Δk_d

$$k_p = k_p^{'} + \Delta k_p$$

$$k_i = k_i^{'} + \Delta k_i$$

$$k_d = k_d^{'} + \Delta k_d$$

In the above formula $k_p^{'}, k_i^{'}, k_d^{'}$ is original PID parameter that have been setted .

2.3.2 Control rule table of fuzzy controller

Here's to establish the fuzzy rules with fuzzy adaptive PID control. First we need to judge the knowledge library based on expert knowledge and determine the three parameters in PID and fuzzy relationship between the deviation e and deviation change rate e_c.And then through continuous detection of the operation of e and e_c, according to the fuzzy control rules to determine the three parameters to online adaptive in order to meet the different requirements of the two parameters of different e and e_c, leaving the controlled object has good dynamic and static performance.

According to the parameters $K_p, K_{,i} K_d$ affect the output characteristics of the system, we can summarize the self-tuning principles of the system in the controlled process for different deviation e and deviation change rate e_c and parameters $K_p, K_{,i} K_d$ as follows:

1) When the deviation e is larger, in order to speed up the response speed of system and prevent deviation e at the beginning of the instant greatens may cause differential supersaturated and make the control action is beyond the scope of, we should take the larger KP and smaller KD, usually take $K_i = 0$.

2) When the deviation e and deviation change rate e_c are at medium size, in order to make the overshoot of system respond to reduce and guarantee a certain response speed, K_p should take smaller. In this case, the value of K_d has a great influence on the system, so we should also take a small number. The value of K_i should be appropriate.

3) When the deviation e is smaller, in order to make the system have better steady-state performance, we should increase the value of K_p KP and K_i. At the same time in order to avoid output response's oscillation around the set value, and to consider anti-jamming capability of system, K_d should be properly selected. Its principle is: when the deviation rate e_c is smaller, the value of K_d is larger, When the deviation rate e_c is larger, K_d take smaller values; Usually K_d for medium size.

Control rules table of output variable Δk_p、Δk_i、Δk_d as shown in table 1, 2, 3.

Table 1. The fuzzy rule table of Δk_p

Δk_p (e \ e_c)	NB	NM	NS	ZO	PS	PM	PB
NB	PB	PB	PM	PM	PS	ZO	ZO
NM	PB	PB	PM	PS	PS	ZO	NS
NS	PM	PM	PM	PS	ZO	NS	NS
ZO	PM	PM	PS	ZO	NS	NM	NM
PS	PS	PS	ZO	NS	NS	NM	NM
PM	PS	ZO	NS	NM	NM	NM	NB
PB	ZO	ZO	NM	NM	NM	NB	NB

Table 2. The fuzzy rule table of Δk_i

Δk_i (e \ e_c)	NB	NM	NS	ZO	PS	PM	PB
NB	NB	NB	NM	NM	NS	ZO	ZO
NM	NB	NB	NM	NS	NS	ZO	ZO
NS	NB	NM	NS	NS	ZO	PS	PS
ZO	NM	NM	NS	ZO	PS	PM	PM
PS	NM	NS	ZO	PS	PS	PM	PB
PM	ZO	ZO	PS	PS	PM	PB	PB
PB	ZO	ZO	PS	PM	PM	PB	PB

Table 3. The fuzzy rule table of Δk_d

Δk_d (e \ e_c)	NB	NM	NS	ZO	PS	PM	PB
NB	PS	NS	NB	NB	NB	NM	PS
NM	PS	NS	NB	NM	NM	NS	ZO
NS	ZO	NS	NM	NM	NS	NS	ZO
ZO	ZO	NS	NS	NS	NS	NS	ZO
PS	ZO	ZO	ZO	ZO	ZO	ZO	ZO
PM	PB	NS	PS	PS	PS	PS	PB
PB	PB	PM	PM	PM	PS	PS	PB

2.3.3 Control rule table of fuzzy controller

Mamdani inference method is a common method used in fuzzy control. Using a fuzzy relation by X to Y to represent a fuzzy conditional statement: if A then B, When the input is A*, B* can be obtained from the output.

$$B^{*} = A^{*} \circ R_{a \to b}$$

It represents the synthesis operation of fuzzy relations.

Mamdani fuzzy relationship definition of $R_a \to \varepsilon$ based on

$$u_{R_{A \to B}}(x, y) = [u_A(x) \wedge u_B(y)]$$

Therefore, according to the membership function of controller's output B * is

$$\mu_{B^*}(y) = \sup_{x \in X} \{\mu_{A^*}(x) \wedge [\mu_A(x) \wedge \mu_B(y)]\}$$

2.3.4 Defuzzification

The process of converting the fuzzy quantity into the precise quantity is called as the clarity, also known as the fuzzy, or called the fuzzy judgment. In order to obtain the accurate controlled variable, the fuzzy method is required to be able to output the accurate calculation results of the membership function. In this paper, we use the fuzzy method widely used in industrial control,

weighted average method, is taking a weighted average of the membership degree of output value clearly. Assuming that the output fuzzy sets can be represented as $U=\sum u_U(x_i)/(x_i)$, according to the following formula, we can clear quantity as follows:

$$u_c=\frac{\int_U x u_U(x)dx}{\int_U u_U(x)dx}$$

3 System simulation using Simulink

The fuzzy adaptive PID controller is used for liquid ammonia buffer tank level control. Simulink program of Fuzzy PID liquid ammonia buffer tank liquid level adaptive control is as shown below. Pay attention to the deviation e and its change size when the controlled object is in the actual passing ammonia. After the fuzzification we need check out the $\Delta k_p,\Delta k_i,\Delta k_d$ on the above should be in line, and then multiplied by the formula according to the respective ratio coefficient. Then use the formula to calculate the dynamic online PID parameters.

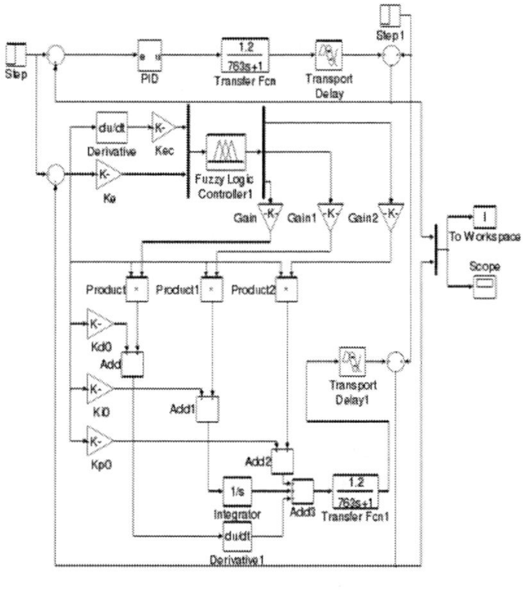

Figure 5. Fuzzy Adaptive PID Liquid Ammonia Buffer Tank Liquid Level Control System Simulation

Figures and tables, as originals of good quality and well contrasted, are to be in their final form, ready for reproduction, pasted in the appropriate place in the text. Try to ensure that the size of the text in your figures is approximately the same size as the main text (10 point). Try to ensure that lines are no thinner than 0.25 point.

At the beginning of setting parameters we use the experience of the actual project, assuming that the initial level is 1. When the simulation time is 5000 seconds, the step disturbance that value is 0.2 was added. The total simulation time is 10,000 seconds. Simulation type selects ode5 fixed step size and step length value is 1. In the fuzzy adaptive liquid ammonia buffer tank liquid level control system, deviation value K_e is 0.1, deviation change values K_{ec} is 20, object Online proportional gain quantization factor is 4.5, integral gain quantization factor is 0.0045, the initial values of proportional, integral, differential are 0.8,0.0012,50[5]. According to the formula, it can be concluded that the values of actual control ratio coefficient, the integral time and the differential time. The step response curve of fuzzy adaptive PID liquid ammonia buffer tank control system is obtained according to the simulation program. As shown in the figure below[6].

The transfer function of the liquid ammonia buffer tank level control is as follow.

$$G_{(S)}=\frac{7.3118}{500s+1}$$

Step response curve of fuzzy PID ammonia buffer tank level control system is shown below.

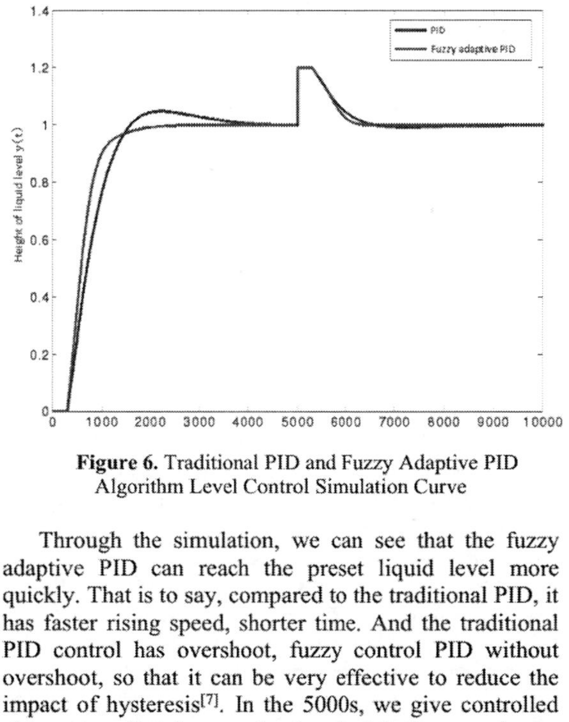

Figure 6. Traditional PID and Fuzzy Adaptive PID Algorithm Level Control Simulation Curve

Through the simulation, we can see that the fuzzy adaptive PID can reach the preset liquid level more quickly. That is to say, compared to the traditional PID, it has faster rising speed, shorter time. And the traditional PID control has overshoot, fuzzy control PID without overshoot, so that it can be very effective to reduce the impact of hysteresis[7]. In the 5000s, we give controlled object step disturbance of value is 0.2. Because in the actual engineering projects the collected signal is often affected by human being unable to control the interference signal, so when adding disturbance we observed will be more in line with the real situation. We can also see that the fuzzy control PID has better robustness and anti- disturbance ability compared with the traditional PID control[8]. This is because the control algorithm can adjust the PID parameters according to the deviation and deviation change rate and make the proportional, integral and differential parameters in

algorithm were within reasonable range. As seen in the simulation, the response can more quickly return to the set value, so that the fuzzy adaptive PID control has better effect[9].

4 Conclusions

In this paper, through the establishment of fuzzy adaptive PID controller to control the liquid ammonia system, and simulation was carried out using Simulink[10]. The simulation results show that the fuzzy adaptive PID control compared with the traditional PID control has great superiority. It possesses the advantages of both PID control and fuzzy control, which shortened the time stability and reduce the overshoot. Fuzzy adaptive PID control has strong robustness and adaptive ability. When there is an outside interference, its control effect is satisfactory.

References

1. A.S. Hodel, C.E.Hall.Variable-structure PID Control to prevent integrator windup[J]. *IEEE Transactions on Industrial Electronics*, 2001, 48(2): 442~451.
2. F.De Lillo, F.Cecconi, G.Lacorata, A.Vulpiani, EPL, **84** (2008)
3. Kennedy J, Eberhart R C, Particle swarm optimization[J], *Proc. IEEE International Conf. on Neural Networks, Perth*, (8): IEEE Piscataway, 1995: 1942-1948.
4. Zhongcai Li, Wushan Cheng, Application of fuzzy PID control algorithm in ground source heat pump air conditioning control[J], *Journal of Shanghai University of Engineering Science*, 2012, 44(3): 215-218.
5. Runyu Ye, A fuzzy adaptive PID control system computer simulation[J]. *Information technology*, 2007, (1): 801—521.
6. Ming Su, et al. Fuzzy PID control and its MATLAB simulation[J]. *computer applications*, 2004,(4).
7. Dingyu Xue, Yangquan Cheng, System simulation technology and application based on MATLAB/Simulink[M] 2 version, Beijing: Tsinghua university press, 2011.
8. Wei Lou, Xiangdong Liu. Application of fuzzy control in the boiler drum water level control system[J]. *Boiler Technology*. 2010, 41(1): 27-30.
9. Dong Yang, Experimental study on the formation of nitrogen oxides in coal combustion [D], [master's thesis] Shandong: Shan Dong university, 2004.
10. Guoguang Tian, Online self-learning of fuzzy controller rules[D], [master's thesis] Beijing, Beijing University of Chemical Technology, 2003.

MATEC Web of Conferences **44**, 02064 (2016)
DOI: 10.1051/matecconf/20164402064

Optimal Control for Single Inverted Pendulum Based on Linear Quadratic Regulator

Huan Xin Cheng[1,a], Jun Xi Chen[2], Jing Li[3], Li Cheng[4,a]

[1,2,3]*College of Automation and Electrical Engineering.Qingdao University of Science and Technology.Qingdao 266042.china*
[4]*Xinjiang Technical Institute of Physics and Chemistry.CAS,Urumuqi,Xinjiang,830011,China*
[a]*Urumqi Xiaming Innovation Electronic Technology Co.,Ltd,Urumuqi,Xinjiang,830011,China*

Abstract. This paper mainly analyzes the structure and mathematic model of the single rotation inverted pendulum, and presents a state expression. It analyzes controllability and substantial of the system with Matlab, and designs optional control. Simulation with Matlab shows that the system has good performance. At last it carries on experimental research and analysis for Q and R.

1 Introduction

Inverted pendulum system is a typical multivariable nonlinear strong coupling unstable system[1].In the process of control, such as it can effectively reflect the theory of controlling system stability, controllable, robustness, convergence rate, follow-up and tracking. Its control method in military industry, aerospace, robot and in the field of general industrial process has a wide range of uses, such as the balance in the process of the robot control, verticality control of rocket and satellite attitude control in flight, etc[1,2].Inverted pendulum system which is more ideal experimental apparatus control theory is often used to test the effect of the control strategy.

In recent years,LQR(Linear Quadratic Regulator) is the dynamic controller based on state space method.It is the development of the earliest and most mature a state space design method in the modern control theory.LQR performance index is easy to analysis, processing and calculation,the optimal solution with uniform analytic expression is convenience to form a simple linear state feedback control law, is advantageous for the project implementation[3].So the LQR control strategy is widely used in robot control, electro-hydraulic servo system, aviation engine, electric power steering system, missile control, such as structural vibration control engineering field.

This article aims at single stage linear inverted pendulum control problem, the design has realized the single inverted pendulum with LQR optimal control based on linear quadratic form, and starting from the actual control effect[2], discussed the selection of the weighted matrix Q and R will effect the features of the system.

2 The mathematical model of single stage inverted pendulum

The balance of the single-stage inverted pendulum control problem can be described as follows, an external force to the car base which makes the car stop at a predetermined position, and make the swinging rod is not down[4] so that no more than a predefined vertical deviation Angle range.

Ignore air resistance and the outside world after friction single-stage inverted pendulum system can be turned into the car and uniform quality of rod system, as shown in figure 1. M for the quality of car, l is the length of the beam centroid to the axis of rotation, displacement of x for cars, θ as the Angle of swinging rod and vertical direction, F for the role of external forces on the car, m for the beam quality[6].

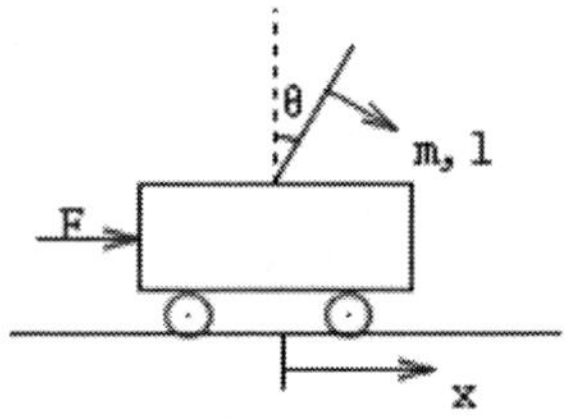

Figure 1. Structure of single level inverted pendulum systerm.

The initial conditions of the system is $\theta = 0, x = 0$.

Using Newtonian dynamics method we can find.

Corresponding author: cjx789@qq.com

Article available at http://www.matec-conferences.org or http://dx.doi.org/10.1051/matecconf/20164402064

$$\left.\begin{aligned} &M\ddot{x}+N=F \\ &N=m\ddot{x}+ml\ddot{\theta}\cos\theta-ml\dot{\theta}^2\sin\theta \\ &P-mg=-ml\ddot{\theta}\sin\theta-ml\dot{\theta}^2-ml\dot{\theta}^2\cos\theta \\ &Pl\sin\theta-Nl\cos\theta=\frac{1}{3}ml^2\ddot{\theta} \end{aligned}\right\} \quad (1)$$

In the formula, $\ddot{x},\ddot{\theta}$ is the car's acceleration respectively and the Angle of the pendulum rod acceleration respectively[9]. $\dot{x},\dot{\theta}$ is the speed of the car and swinging rod of angular velocity respectively. g is the acceleration of gravity.

For organising the type can be inverted pendulum motion equation.

$$\left.\begin{aligned} &(M+m)\ddot{x}+ml\ddot{\theta}\cos\theta-ml\dot{\theta}^2\sin\theta=F \\ &\frac{4}{3}ml^2\ddot{\theta}+ml\ddot{x}\cos\theta-mgl\sin\theta=0 \end{aligned}\right\} \quad (2)$$

Considering the swinging rod do tiny vibration near the set point $\theta=0$, to localize the type linearization which means $\cos\theta\approx1,\sin\theta\approx\theta$ .When $\theta=0$, $\dot{\theta}^2$ as the higher order infinitesimal to make approximate treatment available.We can get these formulas.

$$\left.\begin{aligned} &(M+m)\ddot{x}+ml\ddot{\theta}=F \\ &\frac{4}{3}ml^2\ddot{\theta}+ml\ddot{x}-mgl\theta=0 \end{aligned}\right\} \quad (3)$$

Equation of state of inverted pendulum are as follows:

$$\left.\begin{aligned} &\ddot{\theta}=\frac{3g(M+m)}{l(4M+m)}\theta+\frac{-3}{l(4M+m)}F \\ &\ddot{x}=\frac{-3mg}{4M+m}\theta+\frac{4}{4M+m}F \end{aligned}\right\} \quad (4)$$

This article selects four state variables are respectively the displacement of the car the car x, the speed the car $\dot{x}$,the Angle of the swinging rod and vertical direction θ, swinging rod Angle of angular $\dot{\theta}$, and state variables $x_1=x,x_2=\dot{x}$, $x_3=\theta,x_4=\dot{\theta}$, $u=F$ to establish a system state space equation[5] as follows:

$$\left.\begin{aligned} &\begin{bmatrix}\dot{x}\\ \ddot{x}\\ \dot{\theta}\\ \ddot{\theta}\end{bmatrix}=\begin{bmatrix}0&1&0&0\\0&0&\frac{-3mg}{4M+m}&0\\0&0&0&1\\0&0&\frac{3g(M+m)}{l(4M+m)}&0\end{bmatrix}\begin{bmatrix}x\\ \dot{x}\\ \theta\\ \dot{\theta}\end{bmatrix}+\begin{bmatrix}0\\ \frac{4}{4M+m}\\ 0\\ \frac{-3}{l(4M+m)}\end{bmatrix}u \\ &y=\begin{bmatrix}1000\\0010\end{bmatrix}\begin{bmatrix}x\\ \dot{x}\\ \theta\\ \dot{\theta}\end{bmatrix} \end{aligned}\right\} \quad (5)$$

3 LQR CONTROLLER DESIGN

3.1 Analysis of the stability of the inverted pendulum

Optimal control is the core of the modern control theory.The design idea is to establish the mathematical model of controlled object, choose an admissible control rule which makes the controlled object according to the predetermined requirement operation, and makes a certain performance index peaked at the last[3].Due to the optimal solution of the linear quadratic control problem can be written as a unified analytical expression and to realize the standardization of the solving process, and can form a simple linear state feedback control law is easy to form closed-loop optimal feedback control[7], easy to project implementation, has become a hot research topic of modern control theory and practice.

This article chooses the inverted pendulum Numbers are as follows:

$$M=2Kg,m=0.1kg,l=0.25,g=9.8m/s^2$$

The inverted pendulum equation of state for:

$$\left.\begin{aligned} &\dot{X}=AX+Bu \\ &y=CX \end{aligned}\right\} \quad (6)$$

And

$$A=\begin{bmatrix}0&1&0&0\\0&0&-0.363&0\\0&0&0&1\\0&0&30.489&0\end{bmatrix} \quad B=\begin{bmatrix}0\\0.494\\0\\-1.482\end{bmatrix} \quad C=\begin{bmatrix}1000\\0010\end{bmatrix}$$

Controllability of system is the precondition of controller design, controllability matrix $M=[B\ AB\ \dots\ A^{n-1}B]$, observability matrix $N=[C\ CA\ \dots\ CA^{n-1}]^T$ using MATLAB software to be calculated.System will be achieved from $Rank(M)=4$, $Rank(N)=4$ is controllable and observable.So we can add a optimal controller to the system, therefore, makes the closed-loop stability, and satisfy the transient performance indicators.

3.2 optimizing control theory of linear quadratic type

The following is the LQR control principle.

For a given state equations of linear time-invariant systems are as follows:

$$\left.\begin{aligned} &\dot{X}=AX+Bu \\ &y=CX+Du \end{aligned}\right\} \quad (7)$$

Performance of the quadratic function:

$$J=\frac{1}{2}\int_{-\infty}^{+\infty}(x^TQx+u^TRu)d_t \quad (8)$$

We need to achieve the minimum J to reach the optimal[6].

The type of the first integral system in the process of control[8], the dynamic tracking error weighted average and the integral requirements of system movement is in the process of dynamic tracking error of the measurement; The second integral item said control in the process of control of the system after the weighted total energy consumption measurement.

The Q is positive semi-definite matrix, R is positive definite matrix in the formula.

The optimal control:

$$u^{*} = -R^{-1}B^{T}Px = -Kx \qquad (9)$$

Which is suitable for the optimal feedback gain K for the solution of Riccati matrix.

We can work out the P from the Riccati matrix equation.

$$A^{T}P + PA - PBR^{-1}B^{T}P + Q = 0 \qquad (10)$$

So $K = -R^{-1}B^{T}P$. (11)

When Q and R take different values, the resulting control parameters are also different.

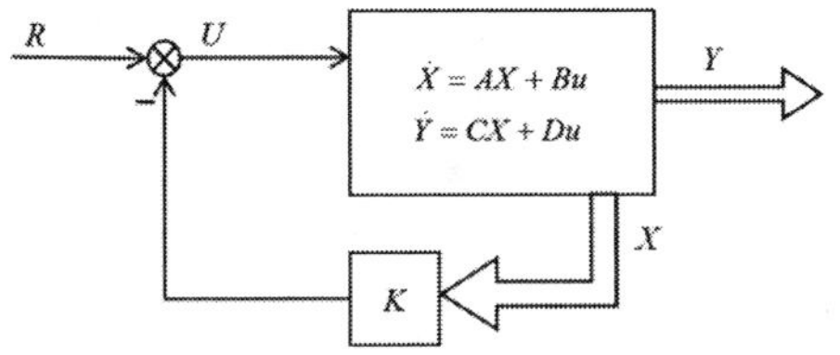

Figure 2. Schematic diagram of LQR method used in inverted pendulum

4 Simulation Results & Analysis

According to the front and the mathematical model of inverted pendulum using simulink to build a single stage inverted pendulum system model, and encapsulation.

Q and R response the relative important degree between error and energy loss respectively, usually Q and R take all diagonal matrix, single-stage inverted pendulum system is only one input, so we should take R as a scalar.Q and R show the weighted values of state variables and input variables respectively .

Using Matlab to solve $K = lqr(A,B,Q,R)$ can calculate the optimal feedback value of the coefficient matrix K.

(1) $R = 0.1, Q = \begin{bmatrix} 100\ 0\ 0\ 0 \\ 0\ 0\ 0\ 0 \\ 0\ 0\ 10\ 0 \\ 0\ 0\ 0\ 0 \end{bmatrix}$.

We can get K from $K = lqr(A,B,Q,R)$.

$K = \lfloor -31.62\ \ -23.22\ \ -104.12\ \ -18.97 \rfloor$

The simulation graphics as shown:

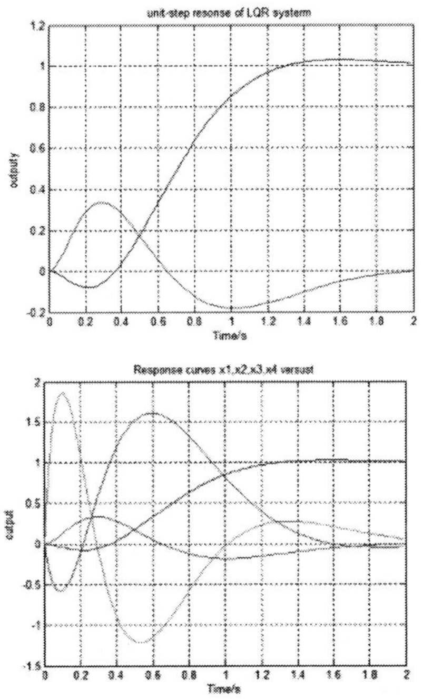

Figure 3. The simulation of R=0.1,Q=diag (100,0,10,0).

(2) $R = 1, Q = \begin{bmatrix} 100\ 0\ 0\ 0 \\ 0\ 0\ 0\ 0 \\ 0\ 0\ 10\ 0 \\ 0\ 0\ 0\ 0 \end{bmatrix}$.

We can get K from $K = lqr(A,B,Q,R)$.

$K = \lfloor -10.00\ \ -10.13\ \ -70.90\ \ -12.92 \rfloor$

The simulation graphics as shown:

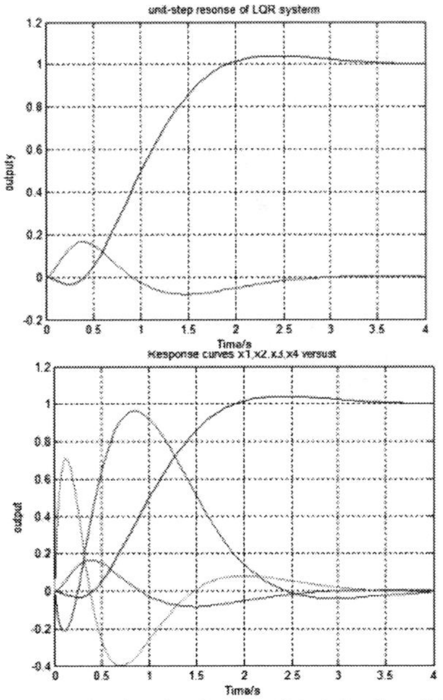

Figure 4. The simulation of R=1,Q=diag (100,0,10,0).

(3) $R = 0.1, Q = \begin{bmatrix} 100\ 0\ 0\ 0 \\ 0\ 10\ 0\ 0 \\ 0\ 0\ 10\ 0 \\ 0\ 0\ 0\ 0 \end{bmatrix}$.

We can get K from $K = lqr(A,B,Q,R)$.

$K = \lfloor -36.62\ \ -26.92\ \ -117.40\ \ -21.43 \rfloor$

The simulation graphics as shown:

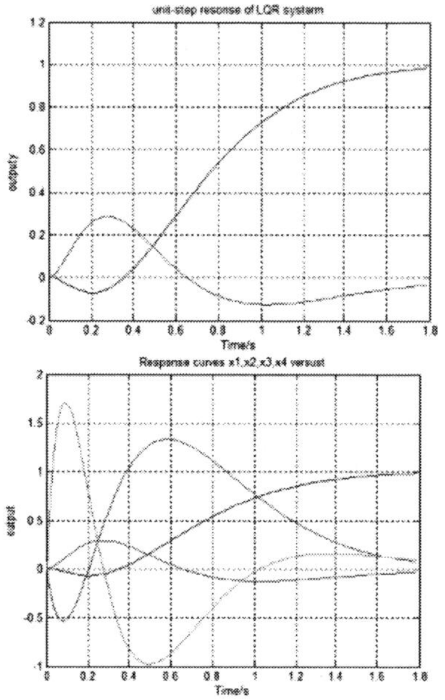

Figure 5. The simulation of R=0.1,Q=diag (100,10,10,0).

(4) $R = 1, Q = \begin{bmatrix} 100\ 0\ 0\ 0 \\ 0\ 10\ 0\ 0 \\ 0\ 0\ 10\ 0 \\ 0\ 0\ 0\ 0 \end{bmatrix}$.

We can get K from $K = lqr(A,B,Q,R)$.

$K = \lfloor -10.00\ \ -1089\ \ -73.53\ \ -13.41 \rfloor$

The simulation graphics as shown:

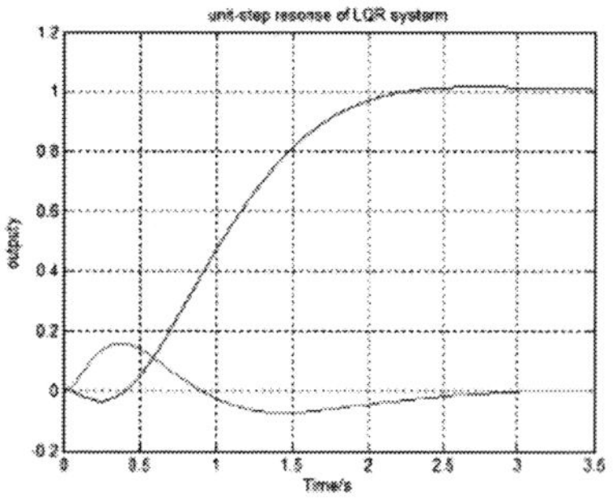

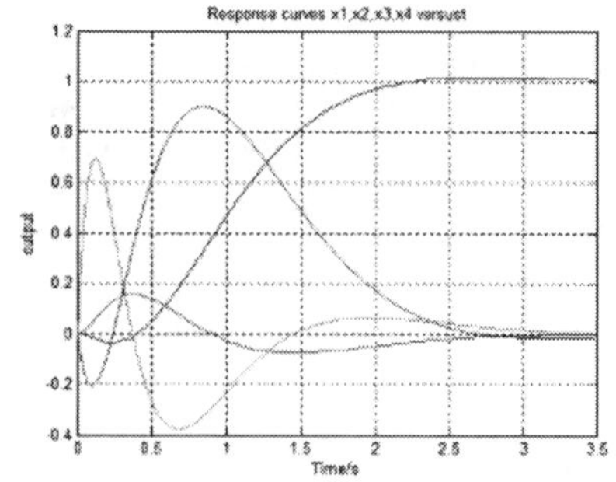

Figure 6. The simulation of R=1,Q=diag (100,10,10,0).

In the first environment corresponding results and inverted pendulum controller output below.

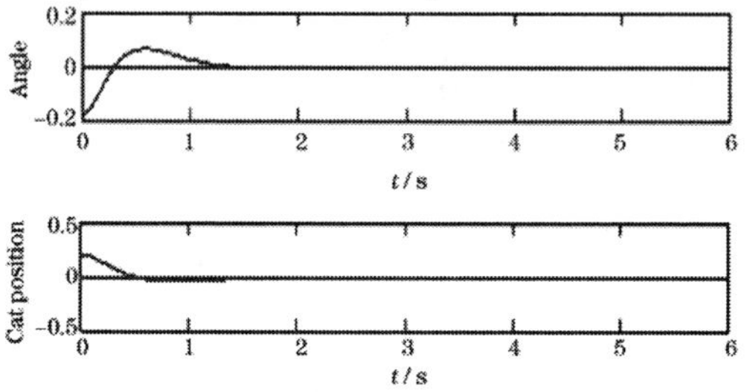

Figure 7. Inverted pendulum response chart of LQR controller.

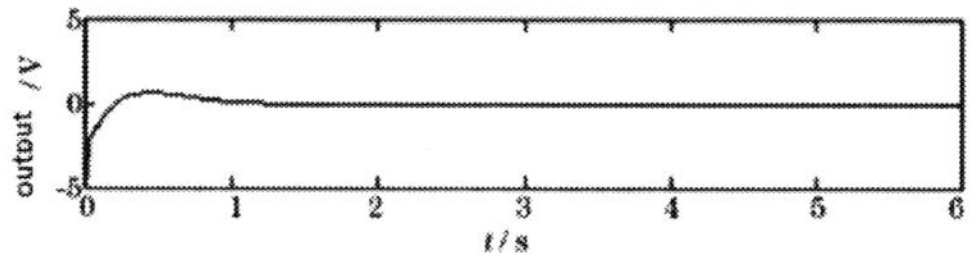

Figure 8. Output curve of LQR controller.

By the control result shows, LQR theory is adopted to control mode, the car position can accurately track the input signal, swinging rod overshoot volume is small enough, steady-state error, rise time and adjust time is basically conform to the requirements of the design index.

The simulation graph can be seen by the above increase the value of R can reduce overshoot amount of swinging rod, adjust time increased, at the same time also make car displacement changes in increasing; Increase the value of Q can make reduce the amount of regulating time and overshoot the swinging rod, the displacement of the car changes in decreasing.

5 Conclusion

LQR controller, robustness and transient characteristics of the poor, but the LQR controller has a better steady state characteristics, accurately track the input signal, the swinging rod and the overshoot of the car is small enough.

Based on the mathematical model of single stage inverted pendulum, established the state space description, and design of the single inverted pendulum with LQR controller, using MATLAB simulation and experiment results show that the system has good stability and rapidity, finally discussed the LQR matrix Q and R in the effect of the system.

References

1. Pujol G, Acho L. Stabilization of the furuta pendulum with backlash using HLMI technique: experimental validation[J]. *Asian Journal of Control*, **12**(2010)
2. Noh J S, Lee G H, Jung S. Position control of a mobile inverted pendulum system using radial basis function network[J]. *International Journal of Control, Automation, and Systems*, **8**(2010)
3. Park M, Kim Y J,Lee J J. Swing-up and LQR stabilization of a rotary inverted pendulum[J]. *Artificial Life and Robotics*, **16**(2011)
4. HUANG Mei, ZHANG He. Study on stability control for single link rotary inverted pendulum[C].Mechanic Automation and Control Engineering(MACE).2010 International Conference. Wuhan, (2010)
5. WANG Qing.*Control theory, method and application*[M]. Higher Education Press. Beijing, **104**(2011)
6. GUO Xiao Yu.Handstand for swinging pendulum control research[D].Qingdao University,Qingdao, **8**(2009)
7. XIE Li Rong. The linear quadratic optimal control in the application of the inverted pendulum[J]. J*ournal of chongqing institute of technology*, **22**(2008)
8. XU Guo Lin.Single-stage inverted pendulum system simulation research[J].*Journal of Sichuan University*,**44**(2007)
9. HUANG Xiao Ping,NIU Qin Chuan.In linear quadratic optimal control of inverted pendulum system implementation[J].*Computer Measurement & Control*,**14**(2006)

MATEC Web of Conferences 44, 02065 (2016)
DOI: 10.1051/matecconf/20164402065

The Design Of The Ultrasonic Nondestructive Testing System Based On The EMAT

Huan Xin Cheng[1,a], Xiang Yong Meng[2], Jing Li[3], Li Cheng[4,a]

[1,2,3]College of Automation and Electrical Engineering.Qingdao University of Science and Technology.Qingdao 266042.china
[4]Xinjiang Technical Institute of Physics and Chemistry.CAS,Urumuqi,Xinjiang,830011,China
[a]Urumqi Xiaming Innovation Electronic Technology Co.,Ltd,Urumuqi,Xinjiang,830011,China

Abstract. This paper introduces a kind of based on the electromagnetic acoustic transducer (EMAT) metal pipeline detection system, fusion of two dimensional orientation, shape unique technological innovation, implementation of various metal pipe wall corrosion situation of rapid, accurate, fully automated non-destructive testing.In the aspect of hardware design, single-chip microcomputer control was achieved by C language programming the launch of the pulse signal. Pulse signal was sent to launch circuit, ultrasonic signal. Design of preamplifier, controllable gain amplifier two-stage amplifier circuit for receiving signal is amplified. Including data acquisition circuit detection circuit and A/D conversion circuit, single chip microcomputer and the LabVIEW platform via A serial port communication agreement. In the aspect of software design, the design of the EMAT pipe nondestructive testing system based on LabVIEW human-computer interaction interface.

Key words: EMAT; Ultrasound; Non-destructive testing; Pipeline detection;

1 Introduction

In petroleum, chemical industry, urban water supply industry, pipeline transport network is an essential part of, and most of the pipeline facilities, is fast approaching its design life.Due to pipe used for a long time in all kinds of high temperature and high pressure medium, the corrosion of pipeline corrosion and fatigue, creep, hydrogen and other aging damage and degradation problems are more serious.This means that in view of the pipe nondestructive flaw detection is very important. Conventional NDT techniques are a serious deficiencies: detection for point by point scanning process, thus cannot be effectively used in the current industrial scale. And based on the pipeline cleaning robot, the pipeline internal detection system in operation and cost and expensive equipment complex, only applies to large trunk pipeline detection.Vehicular electromagnetic acoustic transducer (EMAT) metal pipeline detection system design from the outer wall of pipeline, make the whole equipment simple structure[1,2].And run in the pipe trunk pipeline detection equipment, compared to the system of manufacture and running cost low, easy to operate. For various types of enterprises, therefore, various grades of pipeline, provide low cost, reliable pipeline testing services.

[a] Corresponding author: author@e-mail.org

2 System design

The basic principle of ultrasonic detection is through ultrasonic wave ACTS on the detected object, according to the ultrasonic propagation in the medium of sound velocity, attenuation, impedance, reflection, transmission, scattering and other physical properties test. And test equipment, such as work piece to make defect evaluation. Design a set of EMAT[5,6] nondestructive testing system based on virtual instrument, in addition to the necessary hardware, such as the EMAT transducer, control circuit, ultrasonic emitting circuit, ultrasonic receiving circuit, data acquisition circuit, power circuit, all through the computer software is used to realize the function, achieve the greatest degree of saving hardware resource, reduce cost[3].

2.1 Design of the hardware in the system

2.1.1 EMAT transducer design

EMAT transducer design is the core component of detection system, it can realize the conversion of electrical energy into mechanical energy, the stand or fall of transducer design directly affects the stability of detection system.EMAT transducer mainly has three parts: coil, magnets, the tested parts.By changing the excitation coil in the direction of current or change the coil relative to the position of the magnet magnetic field which is formed by the formation of different types of waveform, such as longitudinal wave and transverse wave, surface wave, Lamb wave and SH wave, etc.

2.1.2 Control circuit design.

Using model AT89C52[7]single chip microcomputer as the core controller of the system.The smallest circuit of single-chip computer work, namely the center MCU control module and a clock circuit and reset circuit.Choose internal clock design, through the button to reset circuit design, the work of the single chip microcomputer minimum circuit.Take EA can make the high level + 5 v, namely let EA = 1, the program starting from the internal ROM.As shown in figure 1 is the normal work of the single chip microcomputer minimum circuit design.

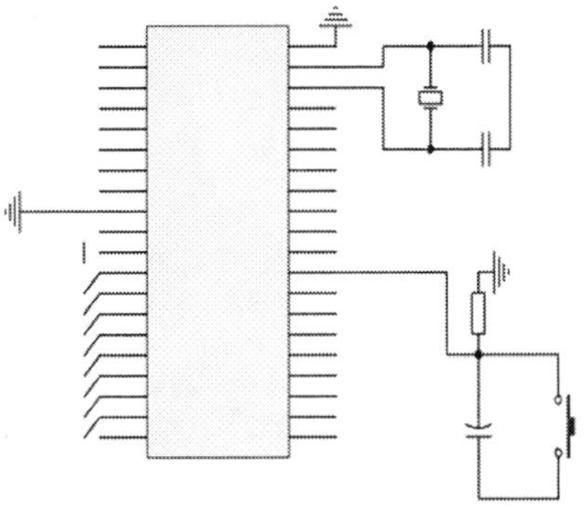

Figure 1. Minimum Working Circuit of Single Chip Unit

Crystal oscillation circuit, single chip microcomputer to normal work, is in accordance with the unified clock pulse in the sequence of operation. To produce the clock pulse, the need for oscillator and clock circuit.Internal oscillator, microcontroller through an external crystal vibration circuit, constitute the internal clock of self-excited oscillation circuit. The pulse frequency is determined by the external crystals, it is to determine the work speed of the single chip microcomputer, but crystal frequency could not choose too high, too high will reduce the stability of single chip microcomputer.In general, the MCU crystal frequency cannot be more than 25 MHZ. In order to improve the stability of the crystal oscillation circuit, eliminate higher harmonic oscillation circuit produced affect the normal work of the single chip microcomputer, in even a pin connected to two capacitance between XTAL1 and XTAL2 C16 and C17. The design selected 30 pf as C16 and C17 capacitance values.

Reset circuit, through the reset, the CPU and other components in the system are in the same initial state then SCM from the initial state began to work. From figure 1, you can see, this topic design using the key level reset circuit, through the reset button to press to make it through the resistor connected with power supply. To finish the RST pin 1, reset.

2.1.3 Ultrasonic signal transmission circuit design

Launch circuit by the host control pulse signal through the photoelectric isolation, via the transistor Q1 and Q2, Q3 after push-pull amplifier circuit to drive, in order to improve the transient response of Q4.Control pulse signal to Q4 after push-pull amplifier circuit drive control.In order to reduce the excitation pulse width, it is necessary to shorten the pulse signal along the falling edge and the rising time, selects the superior performance of MOS devices to meet the requirements.Choose high power field effect MOS tube APT10050B2VR, It is a new generation of high voltage n-channel enhancement field effect tube.It provides faster switching speed, low leakage, up to 1000 v drain-source voltage, pulse drain current of 84 a, maximum allowable by constant current for 21 a, can satisfy the fastest high-power output high frequency pulse signal of the high strength requirement.As shown in figure 2, Q4 drain by R6 by high pressure.Used in the design of 600 v high voltage dc power supply.When Q4 deadline, capacitor C4 in under the action of high voltage power supply, the R6 charge to 600 v;Q4 is conduction, C4 by Q4, R7 discharge, produced in the R8 excitation probe of high voltage pulse signal.R8 is the biggest variable resistance of 10000 ohms.We can change the R8 resistance of the resistance to alter the strength of the high voltage pulse signal.The greater the resistance, the voltage, the greater the load on the R8 produced by high voltage pulse intensity.

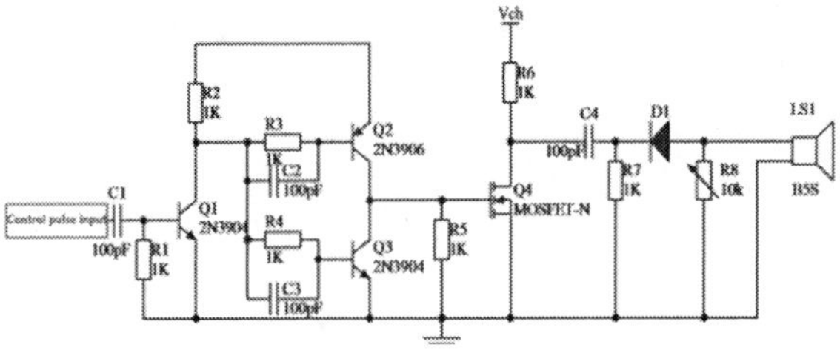

Figure 2. Launch Circuit

2.1.4 Ultrasonic signal receiving circuit design

Design using diode switch characteristics, using a diode [8]in parallel circuit of signal amplitude limit, to filter out high voltage pulse signal.Selection of resistance value of 50 KΩR9, greater than the launch R8, adjustable resistance in the circuit to avoid receiving circuit loading effect on transmission circuit.Choose has larger forward current diode D2 and D3 two-way limiter circuit,

eliminate transmission circuit of high voltage pulse, avoid its receiving into the back-end receiving circuit interference, the experimental results show that the output of this limiter circuit can achieve the anticipated effect of this design.

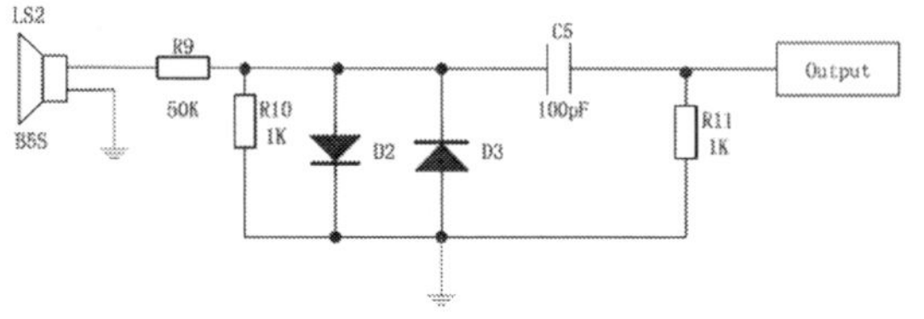

Figure 3. Ultrasonic Amplitude Limit Circuit

2.1.5 Preamplifier circuit

In this system design of the preamplifier circuit, J2 ultrasonic echo signals AD797 in-phase input terminal 3, C3, R3, R1, R2 constitute a negative feedback network and C3 capacitance value depends on the size of the signal gain.This time we design, R1 resistance of 10 ohms, R2 resistance is 400 ohms, R3 resistance of 100 ohms, C3 capacitance value of 33pF.Through calculating amplifier gain for 39 times, can be drawn from the noise of 0.98 nV/Hz.Pin 4 and pin 7-5 v and + 5 v power supply, through the two capacitor C1 and C2 in parallel, can expand the dynamic bandwidth, pin 4 can all use the same multiple shunt capacitor technology.The voltage signal preamplifier AD797 after output via pin 6 to the back of the controllable amplifier circuit.

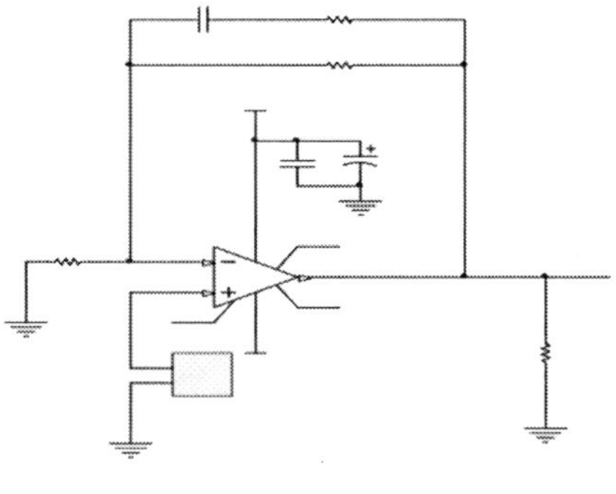

Figure 4. Diagram of Pre-amplication

2.1.6 Controllable amplifying circuit

As shown in figure 5, the 3rd pin EMAT ultrasonic echo signal received through the pre-amplifier chip AD797 amplified, the output signal which is amplifying by the AD603 chip will be output from the pin VOUT.The VOUT pin and FDBK pin connection with variable resistor R13, by changing the resistance of R13,They can be easily to choose the appropriate gain range.By adjusting the R14 variable resistance of the resistance to change the size of the gain control voltage, so as to achieve the aim of the magnification fine-tuning.

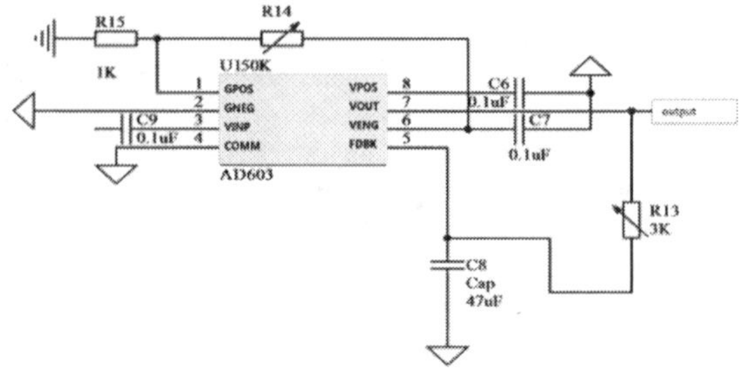

Figure 5. Controlled Amplifier Circuit

2.1.7 Ultrasonic signal acquisition circuit design

As shown in figure 6, the circuit is mainly composed of AD810, AD8036, LH033, AD810 of four integrated op-amp.Among them, the detection before in-phase amplifier composed of AD810 chip for buffer.AD810 was initially developed for multimedia an operational amplifier.It has high conversion rate, wide band, the signal distortion is small, low noise very many superior performance, so is especially suitable for as a buffer amplifier of buffer ultrasonic signal detection circuit.Finally complete the detection process of EMAT ultrasonic echo signal through AD810 chip pin 6 output to A/D conversion circuit.

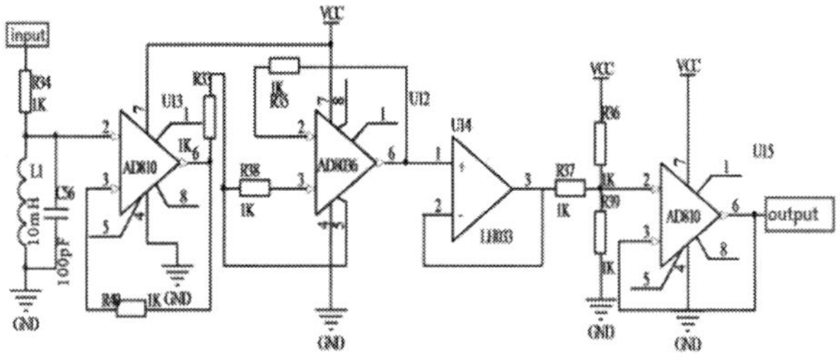

Figure 6. Buffer Detection Circuit

2.1.8 A/D conversion circuit

The design of A/D conversion[9] circuit using classic ADC0809 as A/D conversion chip.Connection with ADC0809 AT89C52 as shown in figure 7.

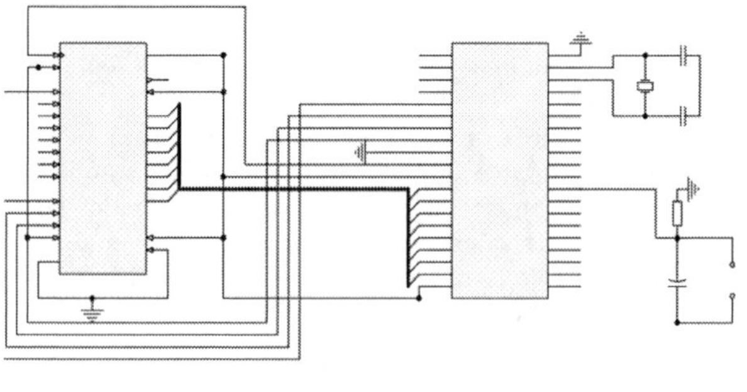

Figure 7. Analog/Digital Conversion Circuit

Process: first enter three address, and 1, will be ALE to address in the address latch;This address decoding strobe road one of the analog input to the comparator;Start up along the reset the successive approximation register;After the falling edge start A/D conversion, EOC output signals become low, indicating conversion is ongoing, until to complete A/D conversion, EOC is A high level, the result data have been deposited in the latch.When the OE input high electricity at ordinary times, output three states door open, convert the result of digital output onto the data bus。

2.1.9 Serial communication circuit

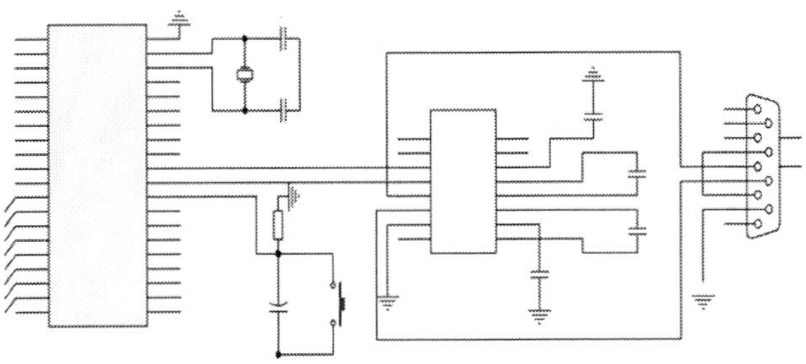

Figure 8. Serial Port Transmission Circuit

EMAT electromagnetic ultrasonic nondestructive testing system commonly used RS232 and MAX232 chip is used to realize serial transmission.RS232 is set by the American electronics industry association of asynchronous transmission standard interface.Because RS232 compatible with TTL level does not need to use the level conversion circuit to realize high and low level transformation.This design chooses MAX232 chip.MAX232 chip connection with AT89C52 single-chip computer as shown in figure 8.

2.2 PC software design of the system

In the design of serial port communication LabVIEW and microcomputer.VISA first call a Serial Port communication configuration node function Configure Serial Port to a Serial Port parameters Settings, including Serial Port resource allocation, set the baud rate for 9600, setting no check, 8 data bits, 1 stop bit, software and hardware such as shaking hands is prohibited.Initialization is completed, the use of VISA Read child nodes of the Write, VISA function to send and receive data.But at the time of receiving data, note that before calling VISA Read function, you need to use the VISA Bytes at Serial Port to query the number of Bytes of data in the data buffer, if does not accord with to Read number of Bytes, then wait.Until the TimeOut or buffer in bytes is equal to the number of bytes to Read.In addition, you can through the VISA, the Set I/O Buffer Size to Set the Size of the Buffer.Under special circumstances, can through the VISA Flush the I/O Buffer child nodes to empty Buffer data.To send and receive data, through the VISA Close function over a serial port communication.

System software, on the whole, including data acquisition, DAC spectrum analysis and waveform display, defect parameters measurement[10], record keeping and reading and so on five big modules, specific steps are as follows:

• Repeat option Controls > > Numeric > > Digital Control eight times, amend the name led by wave position respectively, the first wave amplitude, faults and defects the amplitude, frequency of filter type, filter, filter order and wave velocity.

• Repeat option Controls > > Numeric > > Digital Indicator twice, will name change for defect location, defect rate, respectively.

• Select Controls > > Boolean > > Stop Button and amend the name to Stop.

• Select Controls > > Graph > > XY Graph.XY Graph can draw out the non-uniform sampling data, and some plane curve.In view of the advantages of using XY Graph as defects in the design curve display.

• On the Graph popup menu Visible Items > > Cursor Legend, display vernier Legend plate.The default cursor legend plate have two cursors, can use the positioning tool to drag it any corner of the make it expand or narrow, needs to show the number of cursors.

Program flowchart is mainly composed of the following parts: the ultrasonic signal acquisition, filter module, wave detection module and data analysis module.Among them, the ultrasonic signal acquisition module by calling StartVI and Con - FIG VI, AI StartVI and AI ReadVI node implementation;Butterworth filter selected FilterVI child nodes to achieve;Wave detection module by calling the Peak Detector VI function;Defect analysis module according to the calculation formula of choosing appropriate arithmetic unit functions to achieve.Defect location calculation formula, which represents the ultrasonic wave velocity.First of all, subtracter function called, will launch wave and defect location code as input, the corresponding time difference.It then calls the multiplier function, will be on the output and 0.5.Then call the multiplier, will output a result with ultrasonic speed by code.Finally will output operation and display the results of pipeline defect location code is linked together, defect position can be calculated and displayed in the interface.Defect rate = defect amplitude value/first amplitude value, called divider, a defect amplitude value, amplitude value of the corresponding code as input, the output sent to the front panel display.

3 Conclusion

Choose single chip microcomputer as the core controller, using C language programming.Single chip microcomputer as a series of square wave pulse through driving circuit to produce high strength of the pulse signal of ultrasonic transducer.Receiving circuit design of

the preamplifier and controllable amplifier two-stage amplifier circuit for receiving of weak ultrasonic signal is amplified.Including data acquisition circuit detection circuit, A/D conversion circuit design.LabVIEW graphical programming based development platform, to achieve a PC and single-chip serial communication, PC via serial control microcontroller, the microcontroller serial transmission of data collected by the host computer for processing.After the relevant tests, the system design with high performance, scalability, maintainability, and other characteristics.It also has a strong practical.

References

1. Guangchun Zhang, Jingqi Zhao: Electromagnetic ultrasonic flaw detection technology research[J], the Chinese society of metal in 1979 a 1950 outstanding papers anthology.
2. Joseph Kristan: EMAT device is used to inspect railway wheels, locomotive vehicle technology [D]1999
3. Chao Meng . Ultrasonic testing system research and design [D]. Shandong, shandong university of science and technology, 2006
4. Youheng Tao. Design and implementation of the control system of digital ultrasonic flaw detector [D]. Chongqing: chongqing university, 2009
5. Jian-ping Peng, Wang Li, xiao-rong gao, ze-yong wang, chao-yong peng, Zhang Yu. Based on the wheel tread of EMAT technology flaw detector [J]. 2009 (01) instrument technique and sensor.
6. Hongxiu Zhu. Best magnetic induction intensity of the electromagnetic ultrasonic transducer (EMAT) research [J]. Journal of coal. 2005 (04)
7. Xiao-xin Liu. Based on AT89C52 single chip microcomputer remote control electric fan [J] electronic design engineering. 2012. (1).
8. Yu-ying An. Photoelectric detection and signal processing [M]. Science press, 2010.
9. Tsinghua university research Yang Suhang editor. Analog electronic technology foundation introductory tutorial [M]. Higher education press, 1998.
10. Weapon industrial nondestructive testing personnel qualification examination committee. Commonly used steel magnetic characteristic curve of quick manual [M]. Mechanical industry publishing house, 2003.
11. Xie Kai JiJianWei, Yan-guang Yu. Design of virtual oscilloscope based on LabVIEW 6 I [J]. Journal of henan science. 2003 (01).

MATEC Web of Conferences 44, 02066 (2016)
DOI: 10.1051/matecconf/20164402066

Peer Feedback in Computer Aided College English Writing Instruction

Zhuo Ma

Foreign Languages and Cultures Department, 10049 Beijing Wuzi University, China

Abstract. This study is to examine the acceptability of peer feedback in computer aided college English writing instruction. For the whole writing procedure, subjects in language labs were to take preparation, writing and evaluation stages, undergoing three editions suggested by peer feedbacks. For the first time reading, peers would comment on such general scale as subject and content of drafts, and the second focuses on specific items, for example the morphological, lexical and syntactical aspects, etc. To compare students' attitudes towards the trial, before and after the experiment, Pre-Questionnaire and Post-Questionnaire were adopted to analyze differences. From the frequency of students' views on ten statements, it is drawn that majority of subjects accept and enjoy the innovative writing process, since peer feedback is an essential and encouraging part for writing.

1 Introduction

With the development of computer technology in scientific era, computer-based teaching methodology is popularly advocated. Students under computer and net environment, can process information online, learn to construct, and communicate smoothly with peers and teachers. Network puts an inspiring set of tools within reach of the mass of computer users. According to College English Curriculum Requirements (2007), the new teaching reform should emphasize on computer applications, which may provide an updated solution to traditionally ineffective teaching techniques, soothing students' writing anxiety in classrooms, and boosting their confidence and motivation in learning.

Writing has been the weakest aspect in college English teaching, since teachers spend considerable time and energy to improve students' writing ability, yet the effects prove less fruitful. Basically speaking, this unpromising condition is to great extent attributed to the prevailing Product Writing Approach. This teaching mode is to have students write and teachers respond individually and separately, with teachers' written comments as the only feedback. Teachers' correction is the terminal and judgment of whole process of composing, therefore the majority of students either neglect comments or care little about grades, instead of perfecting.

With appearance of computer-assisted foreign language learning mode, writing instructions have been converted, from focus on result to process, from teachers' single reading and correcting to such collaborative learning activities by students as group discussion, presenting suggestions and feedbacks, cooperatively editing compositions, etc. Feedback in teaching writing refers to "the inputs to writers by readers, aiming at providing editing information for writers" [1]. Yet for feedback from teachers and peers, the latter outdo the former, as "peer feedback conform to the cognitive principle that concepts are internalized into individual knowledge through social communication" [2]. Contacts by peers with same cognitive level is more helpful in stimulating cognitive development than those from others. Reading others' papers may raise one's own sense of readers, who tend to recognize more clearly problems in their own compositions, by way of reading others, giving and accepting others' feedbacks. Besides, group discussions push students to learn from each other, and mutual correction build up their sense of responsibility so as to rely less upon teachers [3].

2 Peer feedback in NHCE based writing mode

NHCE (New Horizon College English) Online Learning System is devised as companion to NHCE Textbooks and advantageous for computer-aided writing instruction, which is presented as the follows.

2.1 Preparation stage

After the first unit in NHCE is learned, teachers release writing requirements on *Class Notice* in *Teaching Interaction* on the page of NHCE learning system. Once students log onto the NHCE system and notice the assignment, the distribution of workload within one group is carried out. Students bearing different duties begin to surf online, gathering whatever they need for this writing assignment, including writing samples, relevant grammars and reading passages, or any necessary

[a] Corresponding author: mazhuo@bwu.edu.cn

Article available at http://www.matec-conferences.org or http://dx.doi.org/10.1051/matecconf/20164402066

materials in video, audio and text forms. Then each donator sends their findings to the teacher by campus email, which being assorted and classified, are uploaded by the teacher on *Teaching Handouts* in NHCE system for students to read and internalize. Being brainstormed, students are stimulated and turn to communicate with teacher and partners. Online group discussing and questioning through *Interactive Tool* on NHCE ensue for writers to compare, delete and borrow ideas, and finally their own outline is generated.

2.2 Writing stage

Once definite thoughts are set, each student type their thinking flow onto *Teacher-Student Discussion* in *Online Class* part in NHCE system for both the teacher and students to read, evaluate and learn. Realizing that their product would be examined by audience, writers may purposefully avoid making mistakes, rack brains to improve and better the quality of drafts. When every essay appears online, mutual evaluation follows. Students edit others' passages, underline improper lines and paragraphs, and write down comments as well as suggestions below the version. Since it is the first draft evaluation, the teacher need to set rules of focusing reading perspective on aspects of subject and content. For example, students are supposed to answer the following questions while evaluating others' first draft.

- What is the best and strongest point of the article?
- Where does the shortcoming lie?
- What subject and idea does this essay convey?
- Which points of view need further explaining and stating?
- Which parts of the draft are to be added with more examples and details?
- What questions are unanswered?
- On what aspects cannot the draft attract readers and why?
- Which part of the article is loosely structured and disordered?
- Which parts are confusing and ambiguous in points?

Taking all suggestions into consideration, each subject accordingly begins to rewrite and revise the first draft, which no doubt can prove a better version. When the version is submitted online, the second round of peer reading follows. During this makeup period, the teacher specially notify editors of certain rules, such as language accuracy of grammar, spelling, expressions, and punctuations in morphological, lexical and syntactical aspects, in contrast to concentration on content in the first draft revision. The followings are some tips to refer.

- Is the Verbal Tense used properly?
- Is the verbal form accurate?
- Does the predicate agree with the subject?
- Are the prepositions used precisely?
- Are the necessary articles lost?
- Is the pronoun definitely referred? Do person and number agree?
- Are adjectives and adverbs properly used?
- Is the sentence structure complete?

2.3 Evaluation stage

As the final draft is composed, students once more come to read others' new editions, judge and vote for Excellency. Likewise, 4-5 best papers and 9-10 better ones are chosen and kept by the teacher on *Sample Writings Column* on NHCE system. The teacher's generalization marks the final step. The whole-scale summary covers students' mastery of syntax, discourse, subject, the quality of peers' feedbacks, etc. Meanwhile, students' performances in whole stages are commentated and graded, namely the extent of fulfilling duties, the degree of donation in communications, and how serious the attitude in peers' feedback, etc.

3 Questionnaires and discussions

In order to examine students' attitudes and adaptation towards the new teaching method and peer feedback, 120 students of four classes in Beijing Wuzi University were selected as subjects. Before the experiment was carried out, they took a Pre-Questionnaire. When one-term writing practice drew to end, the other Post-Questionnaire was filled. It is believed that with those voting for or disagreeing with similar statements in two questionnaires, effects of peer feedback could be generally shown.

Table 1. Frequencies of students' views on feedback in NHCE based writing mode in Pre-Questionnaire and Post-Questionnaire

Statements		SA&A		Neutral		SD&D	
		N	%	N	%	N	%
1. I like to have English writing class	Pre-Q	27	23	37	31	57	48
	Post-Q	75	63	19	16	26	22
2. While writing, I realize there will be readers for my paper.	Pre-Q	5	4	14	12	101	84
	Post-Q	84	70	23	19	13	11
3. I would rather write independently than work with peers.	Pre-Q	83	69	18	15	19	16
	Post-Q	11	9	14	12	95	79
4. I would accept teachers' feedback instead of peers.	Pre-Q	77	64	21	18	22	18
	Post-Q	21	18	31	25	68	57
5. I like to have peers read and evaluate my compositions.	Pre-Q	11	9	26	22	83	69
	Post-Q	79	66	24	20	17	14

6. Writing is a difficulty task to fulfill.	Pre-Q	97	81	16	13	7	6
	Post-Q	28	23	36	30	56	47
7. Writing is an important competence.	Pre-Q	104	87	12	10	4	3
	Post-Q	108	90	9	8	3	3
8. I read and correct my paper before it is submitted.	Pre-Q	26	22	37	31	57	48
	Post-Q	83	69	17	14	20	17
9. I rewrite the paper with teachers' comments.	Pre-Q	13	11	23	19	84	70
	Post-Q	92	77	17	14	11	9
10. I would rather write another paper than rewrite and edit.	Pre-Q	102	85	13	11	5	4
	Post-Q	24	20	35	29	61	51

Note: N=120, Pre-Q=Pre-Questionnaire, Post-Q=Post-Questionnaire, SA=Strongly Agree, A=Agree, N=Neutral, SD=Strongly Disagree, D=Disagree

From the frequencies of Students' Views on Feedback in NHCE Based Writing Mode in Pre-Questionnaire and Post-Questionnaire, the comparisons of ten items are listed. Before the research, nearly half (48%) of subjects did not like writing classes, with 31% students holding indifferent views, while after the training, 63% students began to favor the new writing course. Specifically speaking, for Pre-Questionnaire, only 4% subjects realized the existence of readers while writing, while 84% of them bore no sense of readers. However, after the study, 70% students raised the consciousness of readers, which enhanced their sense of writers. For collaborative study, 69% students refused to work with partners on writing beforehand, while experiencing group discussions and distributions of duties, only 9% students stuck to this attitude, and the frequency of those willing to accept collaborative work rose from 16% to 79%. As for feedback, most of students (64%) initially took teacher as authority and their evaluation convincing, yet once peer feedback was employed in computer based writing instruction, 57% students no longer regarded teacher as absolute authority. Accordingly, only 9% students had some idea about peer evaluation at outset of the trial; instead, afterwards 66% of them showed interest and preference for peers' comments. When asked whether writing is difficulty or not, of students instructed by traditional teaching mode, 81% of them reported their sufferance, while undergoing the innovative instruction, the number drops to 23%. However, no matter when questioned about significance of writing ability, overwhelmingly students vote for its importance. As writing is conducted by Product oriented approach, nearly half students (48%) never edit original versions, but for Post-Questionnaire, the frequency of those tending to rewrite rise to 69%. Previously, 11% students would like to reshape their papers by following teachers' comments, and 70% would not even take a look, 85% students would rather compose another than rewrite, however as the new strategy was put to end, 77% subjects began to realize the value of feedback, tend to work for better version, and half of them (51%) got rid of former attitude.

So far from the statistics presented above, it is drawn that peer feedback in NHCE writing instruction is beneficial to English learners in the following aspects. First, since students will reconsider and edit their own language output while sending out feedback to others, to guarantee accuracy of information, they are more likely to center on language itself, thus their writing skill and competence can be enhanced. Secondly, under the online environment where messages are frequently exchanged, teachers can perform their role of monitors by keeping students' communications under control so as to guide timely and specifically. Lastly, students connected online may find themselves more relaxed and less nervous in discussing, evaluating, giving suggestion and feedback, which helps to ease worries and tension. Therefore, this computer based writing approach prove more attractive, in which students are more willing to speak out one's own ideas and comments including criticisms, and either part tends to share the other's true opinions. Consequently, peer feedback is effective in editing papers and improving writing competence.

4 Conclusion

In China, most of college teachers are still employing traditional techniques, with little achievements and accomplishments. Teachers bear heavy workload and could hardly instruct students individually. Basically the sense of application of computer technology to English teaching hasn't been aroused. Or teachers may have borrowed and tried certain Computer Aided Writing Instruction strategies as QQ, Email, or Blog into writing class, however, instructors have touched rather limited tools and functions in their textbooks related learning systems, which under campus environment, is more convenient and economical. To utilize school based online learning system to teach in writing course, and emphasize peer feedback as evaluation in the midst of writing, is where this study suggests. With peer feedback proving effective and acceptable, the new approach in writing instruction is highly advocated so as to fully benefit both learners and teachers.

References

1. L. KEHC. Feedback in the writing process: A model and methods for implication. *ELT Journal*. 44(1990).
2. Y. Xianhai, et W. Yuehui. The Application of Collaborative Learning Principle in English Teaching. *Foreign Language Education*. 5(2003).

3. G. Cuihong et Q. Xiaoqing. The study on written feedback of compositions by foreign second language learners——The perspective of study and its implication on college English writing evaluation. *Journal of PLA University of Foreign Languages*. 9(2006).

MATEC Web of Conferences **44**, 02067 (2016)
DOI: 10.1051/matecconf/20164402067

The Design and Implementation of College Volunteers Task Management Platform based on Dynamic Collaborative

Xiang Li, Lin Zhe Wang[a]

College of Mathematics, Beihua University, Jilin City, China

Abstract. College volunteer's activities are currently linkages between societies and effective way. But the management of the university's volunteer is more difficulty. In order to effectively address these issues, it is necessary to construct volunteer's management platform system based on dynamic collaborative task according to the characteristics of volunteers and volunteer characteristics of scientific tasks assigned tasks, and task execution in the entire life cycle of the actual dynamic management, can effectively improve the work efficiency.

1 General instruction

Student volunteers are the main part of our youth volunteers, is an important carrier of ideological and moral education, but also to build a socialist core value system of the new carrier. In the social role theory perspective, in order to carry out clinical medical school "smoke-free hospitals, harmonious society," the volunteer activities, for example, investigate the source of motivation for college students volunteer service to study the "power source" mechanism, "intensity" mechanism, "force "mechanism system constitutes, in order to establish long-term mechanism Students volunteer work, volunteer college students to form a scientific and standardized service management model to promote the development of college students volunteer action in the socialist core value system in our country. The term was later introduced mechanisms of social science research, which originated from the Greek, originally referred to the construction and operation principle of the machine. After the introduction of social science research, its meaning is interrelated and each part of the social organism, the way of interaction. Dynamic mechanism is an important part of the mechanism, the mechanism of the system configuration and operation of the power of the group. This system consists of "power source" mechanism, "intensity" mechanism, "force fit" (together) constitute a mechanism.

Power source is to stimulate the development of the various needs of the people, and they need guidance, portrayed as reasonably necessary, the use of incentives, means the interests of science and culture means to achieve a fair and reasonable incentives. Social practice of student volunteers with full respect for the sense of participation of college students, advocates of the "dedication, friendship, mutual aid, and progress" volunteer spirit, reflecting the improvement in the relationship between people and mutual harmony between people and society and the harmonious coexistence between man and nature.

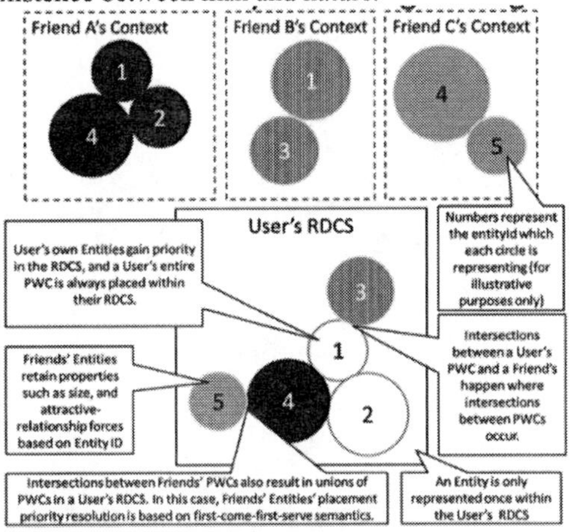

Figure 1. Collaborative dynamic neighbouring

2 Incentive motivation "power source" mechanism

Sense of participation, motivation is affecting young students volunteer to become an important factor, but also to maintain the ideological pillars of volunteers in the volunteer service organization in volunteer activities. Volunteers in volunteer service through honest labor to meet people's needs, so as to stimulate the enthusiasm of their volunteer service, make this an external driving force transformed into a self-powered hard work, full human potential.

As organizers of the Communist Youth League School of Mathematics and Student Management Office Ban first understand the motivation of volunteers participate

[a] Corresponding author: Linzhewang@126.com

Article available at http://www.matec-conferences.org or http://dx.doi.org/10.1051/matecconf/20164402067

through questionnaires, interviews, training and other means. You can see from the interview, the main motivation for college students to participate in activities there are two aspects of social motivation benefits, such as they referred to "responsibility", "helping others", "to do something good for society," and so on; the second is personal motivation of development, such as they talk about the professional skills learned in theory can be applied to social practice, exercise their abilities, develop social interaction skills. Students understand the motivation for volunteers to participate in the service, we need to know what they are, and to take effective way to mobilize and train volunteer service activities. In the whole process of voluntary service, and for changing their psychological needs, take the corresponding excitation methods to enhance the degree of their psychological satisfaction, using the means assessment, appraisal, supervision, incentives, etc., to form a reasonable incentive to provide them social interaction between people and a platform for social interaction, forming a close interaction between people and care. Students' volunteer service through contact with objects, between people, between social groups set up mutual friendship and mutual help bridge understanding of the needs of the service object, a better understanding of the needs of society.

Figure 2. Communication between Volunteers with each system diagram

Harmonious society is the essence of all parts of society as a whole, the various elements of a balanced and orderly development. Thus equilibrium is a mechanism from the perspective of social governance, that is, the coordination of social equilibrium various interactions, co-ordination, adaptation, with its key interactions "degree" of the problem.

Therefore, a balanced and harmonious society efforts mechanism refers in particular to grasp hold of forces from all levels of social interaction with the start of the driving force behind the force, effectively resolve various contradictions problems. According to the structure of China's social development, college students volunteer service organization system, is relying on the Communist Youth League organized grassroots volunteer service organization system, take a variety of forms of student volunteers to strengthen universal knowledge and expertise in training, a rich personal life experience and life experience broaden the circle of life of individuals, society and life deep experience. Students involved in volunteer work in process, in addition to skills can play, the more you can develop self-organization and leadership skills, learn new knowledge and new skills, meet and feel a sense of accomplishment from work. The student volunteers activities on society: in the care to the community, but also passed the love, spread of civilization, this "love" and "civilization" from one person to another person who uploaded eventually converging to a powerful social warmth, help build a harmonious society, to promote social progress and have some positive effect.

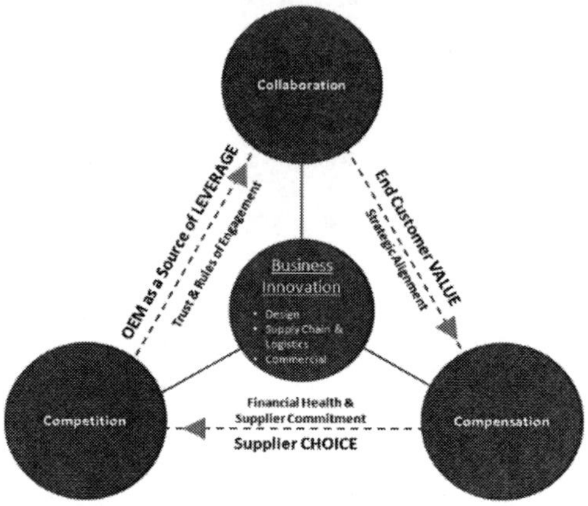

Figure 3. Competition and cooperation between volunteers

3 The same mechanism to force

Systems theory believes that the relationship between the whole and the parts of the system elements, and the elements interact together to form a system of external information and energy output. To meet the needs of most people's interests, the various combinations of positive force in the same direction, to gather and inspire them to build a harmonious society dynamic mechanism. The student volunteers practice; it is a process of construction of the system force mechanism. Meanwhile, according to the integrity of the system theory, dynamic, contact viewpoint, the integration of college students volunteer service organization resources, and concerted efforts of volunteer work. In practice, education and college students are to serve the community through practice, to understand the needs of society, and society interaction. To enjoy the social practice of advanced thinking and the pace of modernization, and to provide feedback on the social issues, these feedback and questions back to campus, back to the lab, targeted to improve their research methods and results, eliminate the absolute limits of the campus and the community.

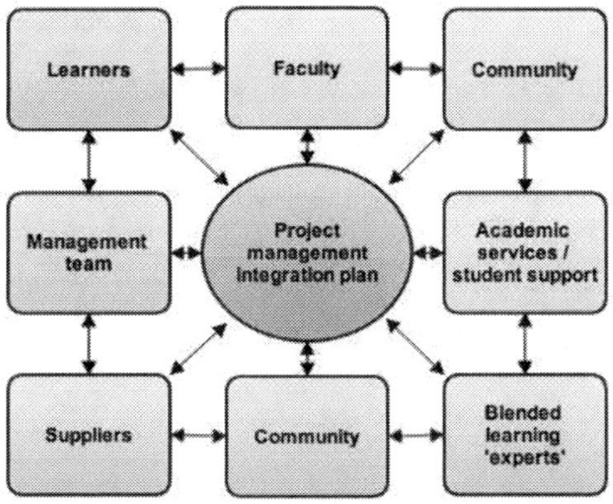

Figure 4. Project management integration plan

At present, the domestic academic research on volunteer service, and more focused on the general youth volunteer activities, while the student volunteers are a special group of young people, the less relevant research. This paper is based on the mathematical College student volunteers practice, for example, through the mechanism of power service to carry out the obligations of the student volunteers guide patient service activities, medical and social practice. Especially in the face of emergencies, emergency rescue volunteer service organizations, to enhance the campus emergency rescue service system construction, the establishment of a comprehensive emergency volunteer team to achieve a scientific, professional and community volunteer service mechanism. Standardized practice etiquette guide for diagnosis, specially invited professional etiquette teacher student volunteers related etiquette training and guidance to the student volunteers a better grasp of activity responsibilities. For example: In the process of smoking cessation advice, volunteers flexible, patient persuasion, to take a lot of humane measures, to each smoker made of sugar, to narrow the distance between each other, to facilitate the activities of. In practice, the spirited volunteers not only won the trust and support of patients and their families, has also been doctors, students' praise and affirmation.

4 College students' socialist core values

Research on college students' socialist core values recognized academics in a common theoretical studies, uncommon connotation and implementation research pathways. In fact, in order to be targeted to strengthen the college students socialist core values of education, exploration and research by ought to real natural state transition is necessary. The party's report is the socialist core values scouring the 24-word latest summarize marks party highly conscious in theory, but the spirit of volunteerism is included in the spiritual dimension of socialist core value system. Volunteering is as a new career study of its field relative later than in other Western countries. After twenty years of academic research and discussion, has now entered a rising phase. Peking University Political Development and Government Management Institute Ding bamboo that "volunteerism is a voluntary, not for remuneration and income involved in human development, promote social progress and improve the spirit of community work, a public participation in social life is very important way, is the essence of civil society and civil society organizations. Since then, the domestic scholars continue to explore the theoretical system of voluntary service study proposed a new theory, producing a wealth of research results. Throughout the study in-depth development of voluntary service, volunteer service for their country and their organizations operating and regulating aspects of research, mostly around voluntary service connotation, theory, research and analysis, problems and countermeasures to cultivate volunteers and other aspects of operations. For voluntary service and research subject, content, organization development characteristics, reasons for volunteering flourishing lagging behind other aspects, the lack of these theories restricted the development of voluntary service. In addition, the volunteer organization is not mature enough. CPC Central Committee and the State in the new situation formally proposed strategic guidelines and requirements of the socialist core values, and to participate in volunteer activities is the best mode of practicing the socialist core values. The current theory is no specific depth study of how to play the spirit of volunteerism to promote and improve students on issues related to the socialist core values.

First, build the dynamic mechanism of volunteer service system for university students. Social practice of student volunteers, it contains a rich and deep ideological and moral education content, not only has the "service to others, self-education, and optimize the social environment," the function of the Trinity, also built up a scientific and standardized service management model to achieve a stable volunteer service team, has standardized management system, unique volunteer service brand, a fixed volunteer service system. The students volunteer service activities, an increase of double the capital of self and society, volunteering motivation, self-interest and altruism factors combined with each other. Students' volunteer altruistic volunteerism embodied in echoes that reflect voluntary personal love, not for remuneration to promote social development and promote social harmony and perfection; and reflected in the student volunteers selfish personal interests tend to exercise their social practice capacity. Therefore, for a long time college students volunteer service activities to develop, we must adhere to the needs of society at the same time, considering the inherent individual student volunteers reasonable demand, so that the two combine, win-win. Student volunteers in activities to instil knowledge of perception transformed into independent thinking, in order to achieve the ultimate goal of moral education, moral education to become self-sublimation quality and promote the effectiveness of ideological and moral education.

Next, the student volunteers more mature social psychology. In a correct understanding of the psychological development of the law of the premise, to

strengthen the efforts of volunteers specifically for mental training. Organized centralized training and decentralized training combined; the universality of training and individual training combine; so that students vibrant volunteer work. Volunteer actions are enthusiastic social welfare services; they adhere to the democratic principles and respect for assistance objects, and have some expertise in their spare time, free to participate in community volunteer work. Their service activities actually fit individual needs and the reality provided opportunities for college students to experience the process of citizen volunteers to role change, but also an effective way of self-development, practice and training opportunities for volunteers to get involved in volunteer service activities more accelerated social and psychological maturity.

American sociologist David (Darvill) and Mundy (Mundy), they think volunteers "voluntarily to one or more non-relative, so who provide direct services pro bono," and "is not usually an informal neighbourhoods association, but rather to provide some kind of formal structure through his / her service. This definition is the crown for the most classic interpretation of volunteer's connotation. Richard • Pound (Richard Pound) believes that volunteers refers to the law and not subject to any other form of coercion, voluntary service person. Maria (Maria) to define the free and voluntary aspects that volunteers will contribute their spare time or knowledge to the service of others in useful activities. Without expecting anything in return the American people, "Red Cross" provides: "Red Cross volunteer is any one from beyond the usual salary and work responsibilities, to help achieve the mission of the Red Cross and donated their time and human service organizations to provide services not accepted by the people from the Red Cross paid. Penne: The spirit of volunteerism (volunteerism) is defined as: a long-term, planned, socially beneficial behaviour by the individual will decide, it makes the benefit of strangers, and occurs in the context of the organization. Potential changes in society, the voluntary sector in order to give the personal responsibility and location, provides both a people united coagulant, but also to promote social change dissolving agent. Voluntary sector is the use of government, but also to shape the government.

References

1. Qin Hui government and outside the modern enterprise - Western welfare comparative study. Hangzhou: Zhejiang People's Publishing House, 132(2009)
2. Ding Yuan Bamboo Chinese Volunteer Services Research [m] Beijing: Peking University Press,15(2007)
3. Liu Shan, Feng Xiaotian Students Volunteer Service: motivation, and problem type. Shaanxi Youth Administrative Cadres College, 55(2005)
4. Tan Jianguang, Ling Chong, Zhu Liling modern city volunteer mentality analysis. China Youth Research, 101(2005)
5. Liu Min activities and student volunteers to build a harmonious campus.New West: half [m] Peking University Press,21(2007)
6. Ding Yuan Bamboo volunteerism function in building a socialist core value system. Beijing: Peking University Press, 67(2008)

MATEC Web of Conferences 44, 02068 (2016)
DOI: 10.1051/matecconf/20164402068

Research on Singing Mechanism Application to College Music Teaching based on Intelligent Electronic Assistant

Cheng Gui Song

Teacher's College, Beihua University, Jilin City, China

Abstract. Music is one of disciplines with special arts, because under the constraints of objective factors people can derive from the physical feeling, either the acquisition of knowledge or grasp of skills. This paper reveals the issues met more easily in music teaching and nature behind the phenomenon through the research on the mechanism characteristics of three most critical and basic elements.

1 General instruction

Any construction and development of a discipline or an art categories, not just experience or just stay in the morphological level, only to find and exploit their experience or morphological diversity of the nature of the housing, and put them up to the scientific nature of contact systematic theoretical level, in order to bring about a qualitative change, and to promote their better development. And promote the construction and development of any one discipline or art categories ultimate factors, usually not only from the discipline or disciplines of the arts itself. But by the latest scientific research into the knowledge or discipline or other kinds of art in order to constantly improve, and even innovation. Throughout the history of vocal music from the heritage point of view, in fact, is the history of vocal music teaching development. "Oral teaching" is the main mode of traditional vocal music teaching; experience, feel, experience is the main theoretical basis of traditional vocal music teaching mode granted knowledge. So are bound to make an analogy, inspired imitation become the main means of teaching. Admittedly, vocal arts as a music category has the particularity of a discipline, the teaching mode and teaching methods irreplaceable leading role in the long history of traditional vocal music teaching development, so far it is still our the main mode and means of vocal teaching on. But the same can not be avoided, rely mainly on experience as a theoretical basis for the grant of knowledge and inspiration as a way to mimic the main learning and teaching methods are bound to exist its limitations and shortcomings.

This deficiency also embodied in both the grasp of vocal technique and tradition, and the vocal interpretation of the phenomenon is from their own personal experience. Thus a so-called blind men feeling the elephant, touch what like result. Vocal learning and teaching can bring some obstacles. In recent centuries, with the development of scientific and technological level of exploration and study of human anatomy in humans, acoustics, aerodynamics, etc. have made considerable progress. Many people many of whom are non-vocal music professionals in these areas will be thinking and research theory is applied to the exploration and study vocal learning occurs in various phenomena, for the traditional vocal music teaching philosophy injection of fresh blood, the traditional way of teaching vocal music and means full of new vitality.

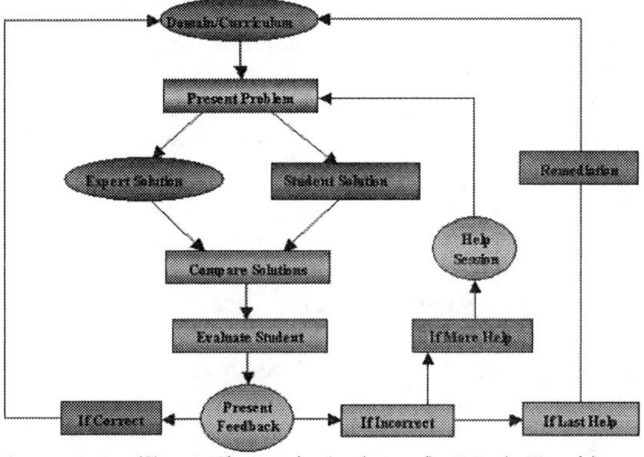

Figure 1. Intelligent Electronic Assistant for Music Teaching

2 Incentive motivation "power source" mechanism singing in touch with the difference between breathing and respiratory

As the physiological needs, the purpose of breathing human organism activity is to provide the necessary oxygen. As for the singing, the breathing is to provide a sound source of power. So, Breath and breathing our natural state of physical contact in essence they both have a difference on the purpose and methods. The perspective

Article available at http://www.matec-conferences.org or http://dx.doi.org/10.1051/matecconf/20164402068

of contact is the main organs involved in singing breathing consistent with the natural breathing time. Lung is still stored gas exchange and organs involved in the expansion and contraction of the chest organs are still the main intercostals' muscles, diaphragm, abdominal, etc., from this point of view, which is essentially the physiological breathing is consistent.

But for singing breath, its main purpose is to give the vibration of the vibrator (vocal) provide energy. This makes breathing singing are essentially different in purpose and physiological breathing. Secondly, singing respiratory system must meet the requirements can control air pressure changes, and the whole story of this pressure output, the size, the length of duration must meet specific requirements when singing, and this requirement is by controlling the aspiratory muscles and breathing together with the active participation of the respiratory muscles while the movement to achieve, which makes breathing and singing breathe a certain physiological differences in the way. Finally, due to the complex structure of human organs and tissues and among inextricably linked, so consider how to better control of breathing while singing does not affect the normal operation of the vocal cords. So, what kind of breathing control can be achieved either arbitrarily controlled air pressure without affecting the normal operation of the vocal cords.

To better understand the singing breath control process and the principle of operation of this mechanism, we can also be inspired by observing the daily life of certain phenomena. For example, many people have seen or played in a child made of elastic rubber squeezes can be issued when the whistle toys. This toy is hollow, one end of the toy has a hole, the hole can cause vibration inlaid with reeds. When you squeezes it, the toy will be through the air vent whistle, whistle hole in the air due to the role of the reed vibrate and make noise. You squeeze force, the more rapidly, and its sound is bigger and shorter, whereas the smaller sound, the longer duration. This is our reason for respiratory control when singing is roughly the same. Specific play like elastic body from our aspiratory muscles holding function, and if pressing it by hand muscles our breath when we extradited, the air is squeezed toys after by whistle vent and cause the reed (as vocal cords) vibration. Under other conditions the same conditions, the greater the pressure, the reed vibrations are more severe, the sound will be. By doing a little toy testing, may make it easier for you to understand that we control the breathing process characteristics at the time of the singing mechanism.

Figure 2. Singing Mechanism bionic agency

3 The point of view mainly vocal mechanism muscle

Larynx is located in the anterior middle, under the upper end of the trachea, hyoid; on through the hypo pharynx, below the lungs through the trachea connectivity. And we usually refer to it through a series of vocal ligaments, cartilage and other tissue attachment in the throat, and the throat is divided into several areas. First, the next vocal structure itself. Also the sound of vocal folds is lips and other sound.

There are two folds sound, so each one and the same at a level surface. Each sound folds itself divided down into two parts, the upper part is called the plicate, also called false vocal cords, the following section is called the lower folds, folds under what we call the usual sense of the vocal cords. False vocal cord in the normal pronunciation is not closed; it does not have a real sense of sound effects. The main role is to assist the true vocal cords false vocal cord closure.

Control the position of the larynx down and relatively moderate stability is necessary for vocal music. This requirement is in singing has its practical significance. Larynx bit down and remained stable from the point of view mainly vocal mechanism muscle affects the thyroid cartilage down and remain stable. The thyroid cartilage causing the vocal cords to expand longitudinally elongated tension. When the vocal tension expanding, we control the breath through to its greater pressure, the frequency of vibration of the vocal cords will increase, so that the vocal cords can be issued with the necessary conditions for a higher tone. The singing, the ability to sing has a good high and low quality sound, good or bad throat decisive position control. On the other hand, from the human voice classification analysis, the level and type of voice when singing larynx position has a great contact. Different voice types must have swallowed a certain length of pipe as a variable corresponding to the resonance pipe. The variable resonance tube shape has a direct and throat "proper position" display relevant. Essential meaning of the above is actually a good control of throat singing bits of lies.

If there is some sort of principle can prove, using only breath can make glottal vibration, or even be able to breath through the glottis partially closed, then I believe that makes learning to sing students believe should not be excessive use of throat singing muscle strength will be easier. Bell Noli effect is such a principle. Implications of this principle to bring vocal music and teaching will be very positive. Bell Noli aerodynamic effect is an important principle, its use in today's everyday life everywhere. The lifting force aircraft, sprayer required suction force, are a manifestation of this principle. At the same time it is also an element of wind instruments vibrating body vibration. To better understand the singing breath control process and the principle of operation of this mechanism, we can also be inspired by observing the daily life of certain phenomena. For example, many people have seen or played in a child made of elastic rubber squeezes can be issued when the whistle toys. This toy is hollow, one end of the toy has a hole, the hole can cause vibration inlaid with reeds. When you squeezes it, the toy will be through the air vent whistle, whistle hole in the air due to the role of the reed vibrate and make noise. You squeeze force, the more rapidly, and its sound is bigger and shorter, whereas the smaller sound, the longer duration. This is our reason for respiratory control when singing is roughly the same. Specific play like elastic body from our aspiratory muscles holding function, and if pressing it by hand muscles our breath when we extradited, the air is squeezed toys after by whistle vent and cause the reed (as vocal cords) vibration. Under other conditions the same conditions, the greater the pressure, the reed vibrations are more severe, the sound will be. By doing a little toy testing, may make it easier for you to understand that we control the breathing process characteristics at the time of the singing mechanism.

In fact, we pass a simple test can demonstrate that this principle characteristics. We'll twin vertical piece of paper each hand holding, when we put two sheets of paper on the lips, blowing when the two pieces of paper in the middle, perhaps you will think these two sheets of paper will be blown away from each other. In fact, just the opposite result, but by not separate two pieces of paper together, and began to vibrate. This phenomenon is caused by the Bell Noli effect. Its principle is as follows: before blowing, the air pressure and the air pressure in the middle of two sheets of paper the two sides of the same, in the absence of external forces, the paper original state. And when the middle of the two pieces of paper blowing in the middle of two paper because air pressure is reduced reasons, so the pressure on both sides of two pieces of paper began to push the two pieces of paper together. Two pieces of paper each squeeze of the extent and time will also change by the middle, when you stop blowing, two pieces of paper and re-open. Until next time blowing, this phenomenon will begin the process of circulation.

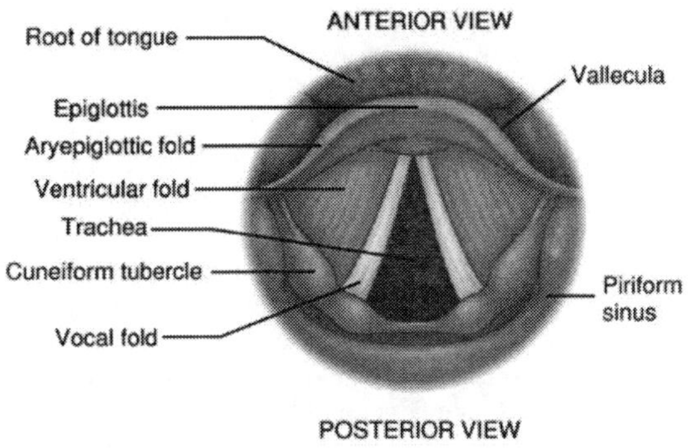

Figure 3. Vocal sound institutions and principles

4 The same mechanism to force

Prior to the structural characteristics of human resonance cavity and their effects on the sound emitted by the vocal cords to be concerned about, I think we should have the necessary knowledge of the relevant acoustic certain understanding. Because it will help us to a better understanding of "human acoustic instruments," the resonance body for sound effects.

The reason why the sound is generated and transmitted, because the vibration of a vibrating body under the action of some kind of energy, and this disturbed vibration between the vibrating body in the surrounding air molecules and molecules of the original balance of the pitch, so that the vibrating body is disrupting molecules lost like lake ripples like a stone into the sky to form a peripheral compression wave is formed. This wave is our auditory system has become a voice message is received after the treatment. Therefore, the sound waves transmitted in the form. For the size of the sound is concerned, the objective is to depend on the size of the vibrating body vibration amplitude, while the pitch is from the vibrating body vibration speed (frequency) of the decision.

For the "resonance" meaning, from the physical interpretation is: a physical cause another vibrating body vibration on the same or similar frequency vibration phenomenon. And when the same or very close to the resonance frequency of the vibration between the vibrating body and the bodies are forced, the forced vibration causes the vibrating body and the combined energy of the body itself to produce more than the vibration energy. This phenomenon is called the acoustic "resonance." When the two vibrating the vibrating body is not the same frequency, mutual interference between the two may even conflict with the energy and quickly disappears.

For singing is concerned, we want to do is to be issued after the sound of the vocal cords in the body resonates with our body resonance effect through amplification and modification of maximum efficiency, making it a beautiful, touching song. For the vocal sound experiments, humans have very clear sound to confirm the basis of the vocal cords in the body from the volume

is very weak; from the tone, the resonance effect after modification and songs have a single multi-comparison. So, if in the singing voice in order to have a more perfect, we must effectively resonate with the aid of this tool will be expanded vocal sound in volume, embellished on the sound. This is a subjective desire of the singer. But also in the production of any musical instrument makers, the need to pursue the reason resonance effect resonance body. This requirement is in singing has its practical significance. Larynx bit down and remained stable from the point of view mainly vocal mechanism muscle affects the thyroid cartilage down and remain stable. The thyroid cartilage causing the vocal cords to expand longitudinally elongated tension. When the vocal tension expanding, we control the breath through to its greater pressure, the frequency of vibration of the vocal cords will increase, so that the vocal cords can be issued with the necessary conditions for a higher tone. The singing, the ability to sing has a good high and low quality sound, good or bad throat decisive position control. On the other hand, from the human voice classification analysis, the level and type of voice when singing larynx position has a great contact. Different voice types must have swallowed a certain length of pipe as a variable corresponding to the resonance pipe.

The resonance is not the source of all the wonderful sounds of it? If you put this guiding ideology into singing practice, you will find just blindly through the pursuit of sound resonance effect to achieve the perfect idea is not practical. Even if your mouths do well, you are also in accordance with the respective cavity resonance teacher asked to do very well. The actual effect is not the person singing wishful. Do not forget, singing is a process of mutual cooperation and efforts between the various structural elements of the vocal instrument. First, in order to let the resonance effect in singing to achieve better results, you have to make your vibrating body - the vocal cords (first vibrating body) itself play better results. For singing, the resonance effect is just an effect of feeling rather than a groundless effect. In other words, the first vibrating body - the vocal cords themselves, though not the last beautiful singing only the founder, but its role is first and foremost, can not be ignored. There are two folds sound, so each one and the same at a level surface. Each sound folds itself divided down into two parts, the upper part is called the plicate, also called false vocal cords, the following section is called the lower folds, folds under what we call the usual sense of the vocal cords.

Perhaps no other discipline would like vocal, as the presence of so many of the divergent, even opposing views on the grasp of skills and knowledge. "Miss is as good of a thousand miles," the phrase used in vocal learning might be fitting. Vocal music is an art, but it is first gate technology. Good and bad judgment on the level of technology that we may be able to simply use the "yes" and "none" to a conclusion. But for technology, learning and heritage, it must reach the "know, but also know why" requirements.

In my ten years of vocal learning process, have experienced a lot of hardships, but also through a lot of detours, the reason, in addition to the constraints of objective factors, but mainly because of their lack of contact on the back of the most essential understanding of vocal phenomenon; and precisely this understanding is based on cognitive mechanisms singing on.

References

1. Liu Jiusi. On the Italian bel canto vocal performance. Qiqihar Teachers College School Newspaper, 1989.
2. Qiao Ailing Discussion and Practice of Vocal Music Teaching. Xinghai Conservatory of Music 26(2002)
3. YAN Jing-yu regulate its use singing resonance. Qilu Art Gallery, 58(2002)
4. Zhang Xian sound technical and artistic resolve singing. People's Music, 154(2005)
5. Cuiquan Xin Singing resonance cavity resonance and three practical exercises. Xinghai Conservatory of Music School Newspaper, 25(2001)
6. Xia Xianping vocal cords, glottis and vocal. Biology Bulletin, 198(2012)
7. Zhu Jiming, Rick Chan, Lubbe real larynx anatomical study. Shanxi: Anatomy, 213(2009)

MATEC Web of Conferences 44, 02069 (2016)
DOI: 10.1051/matecconf/20164402069

The Design and Application of Computer Assisted Language Learning System in Business English Writing course

Xi Wen Zhang[1], Da Peng Wang[2]

[1] *Foreign Languages' College, Beihua University, Jilin City, China*
[2] *Financial Information Center, Jilin City, China*

Abstract. The CALL (Computer Assisted Language Learning) system is an effective method in business English writing teaching, particularly for students which are non-speaking countries. The CALLS is suited to self-learning because of the Rich scenario module design. Application results are examined by using the methods of group experiments, questionnaires, examinations and others. The CALLS is especially suited to creating a better studying atmosphere among students in the process of business English writing teaching than other methods.

1 General instruction

With the deepening of China's reform and opening up, the gradual improvement of the market economic system and successfully joined the WTO, the 2008 Olympic Games and other world language-which highlights the importance of English is already self-evident. Especially in recent years the talent market feedback information indicates that the sharp increase in demand for high-quality whole society foreign trade personnel, where universities have graduate business English knowledge background of much foreign trade enterprises welcome. This makes the college and students are increasingly attach importance to business English courses are and learning to meet the social demand for complex English talents.

English as a compulsory course important universities, has long been seen as an important but isolated public basic courses, taught content is difficult to effectively combine with students future career, it is difficult to meet the different jobs actual needs. The Business English development and late in the development of English for a long time, so in the realization of the "service for the purpose of employment-oriented" use "of engineering combined with" training mode, to achieve culture technology, production, management and service the first line target process senior skilled personnel in the higher vocational education, with a big gap between the current situation and the training objectives. The reason, first of all is to limit classroom teachers professional background knowledge, in general, a high level of English teachers, but the lack of specific business practices; secondly, for themselves as well as teaching materials for classroom teaching content, are primarily text based materials, even if equipped with audio-visual materials are also part of the older or divorced from reality, which makes it difficult to truly feel the situation of students, it cannot effectively participate, cannot achieve interactive teaching.

Figure 1. Computer assisted language learning system

2 Computer-aided instructions (CAI) of manifestations

The use of multimedia technology is computer-aided instruction (CAI) of manifestations, but also the traditional teaching of the application process and form a comprehensive and creative. Multimedia for its interactive, good visibility, broad content, interesting and other distinctive features, to the education sector has brought new changes, creating a new era of teaching methods. Many suitable for the teaching of multimedia authoring software, such as Authorware, PowerPoint, Director, Flash, etc., beautifully produced courseware for teachers to provide a guarantee, it can greatly increase students' interest in learning and teaching. Especially the

multimedia courseware show integration, the selection of hypertext links, operational human-computer interaction, the richness of a large capacity storage, high-speed transmission of convenience, Macros communication sharing and other advantages can be achieved classroom teaching holistic, scientific, artistic and technical unity binding, for the "business English" This door requires a lot of interaction and practice course has a very important significance.

Figure 2. Classroom management software and interactive interface

3 Application Status Multimedia Technology in Teaching

Multimedia is accompanied by the development of computer hardware and software technology to produce and mature. It refers to the audio-visual and other graphic information conveyed in the form of synthesis. Can be summarized as understanding on the computer platform of the information carrier, including graphic images, audio, video, text, collection, processing, handling and reproduction, so that the expression of a more comprehensive information and expression.

Multimedia technology in the process of development of modern education, the first is the introduction of projection, slides, audio, video and other technologies, resulting in audio-visual education. Then with the rapid development in recent years, computer communication technology, modern education also applied computer computer-assisted instruction, that CAI (Computer-Aided Instruction) instruction. We can say that modern education is an ongoing achievement of modern science and technology applied to education practice process. Visual Education's strengths lie in its audio-visual nature. The downside is that one-way information dissemination. The CAI teaching on the contrary, interactive communication teaching information, but the lack of audio-visual teaching functions. The 1980s and the emergence are the CAI Trial VTR teaching a combination of modes, an interactive audio-visual teaching (Interactive Video) prototype, which is talking about multimedia teaching herein.

Multimedia technology, through the computer using text, text, voice, music, graphics, images, animation and other media information are digitized, and integrate it in a certain interactive interface that enables a computer to interact with the ability to show different forms of media, complete Some traditional teaching methods can not be achieved easily or teaching tasks, particularly reflected in the image of the teaching and the simulation shows: the electronic lesson plans, the image of teaching, interactive process simulation, network multimedia teaching, simulation processes are all multimedia technology in teaching practical results reflect . It combines illustrations, sensual taste, lively as a whole, rich teaching in music, visual content. It can not only be teaching, counseling, self-test, consolidate, review, assessment integration, but also in the students learning ability and mobilize the enthusiasm of students, improve learning outcomes, abilities and other aspects also play a huge role.

Multimedia technology assisted teaching can make learning interactive integrated information see illustrations, audio-visual integration, especially the formation of multimedia courseware, both teaching of reading in multimedia courseware content, you can also get sound or video-related information associated with classroom teaching watch the sequence of development of things, the sequence of events in order to observe the laws and principles summarized. This new form of access to information greatly changed the traditional mode of boring single teaching method, so that learners can intuitively vividly to obtain and understand information, to produce learning and fun-loving, active and timely access to information stimulate expression Desire, which naturally form teacher-student interaction.

Multimedia technology assisted teaching enables students to integrate information see interactive illustrations, audio-visual one, you can read in the multimedia courseware teaching content, you can also hear from the classroom associated with sound information, procedures, and laws and principles viewing event. This new form of information has changed the boring single teaching mode, so that students can understand more image information, producing learning and fun-loving, active and timely access to information stimulate the expression of desire, which naturally form teacher-student interaction.

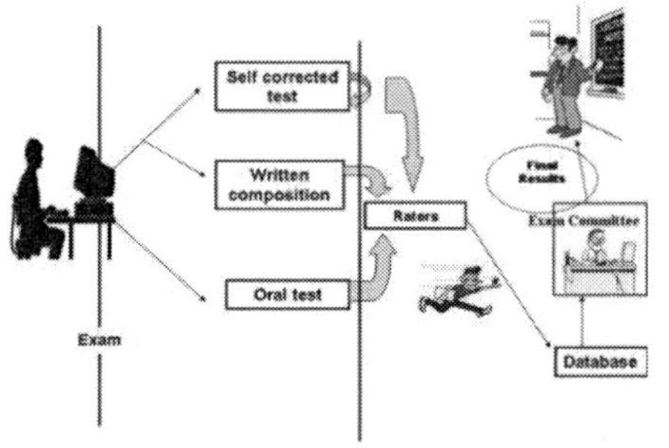

Figure 3. European association for computer assisted language learning

4 Universities Business English Course Features

Business English is a functional variant of English, is a special kind of use of English, it is in a particular

situation - that is, business occasions communicative English language, so it is a manifestation of a form of communicative competence, both with business activities professional, closely related to the ordinary people use basic English. Basic English is to learn business English the premise that there is no solid foundation of knowledge and skills in English; they would not learn business English. With the economic globalization and China to accelerate the development process of internationalization, the major institutions of higher learning should be required to have a professional business English and now. As an independent professional, including Business English, international business, financial English, foreign correspondence, marketing, English, Business Writing, foreign trade practices, business negotiations, foreign trade business practical operation of other major programs have been carefully divided and were opened, achieve a professor of English as a media student business knowledge, so as to nurture both fluent in English and familiar with international business practices talent goals. But as the world labour market continues to heat up the international business demand for talent, it had just opened in the major colleges of Business English professional "Business English" course, gradually being touted in many of our universities. Colleges and universities under the principle of "employment-oriented", in order to adapt to life in the workplace language requirements for the purpose, according to the characteristics of the actual situation of their institutions and students to different modes creation of "Business English" course, teaching content related to all aspects of business activities, but tend to pay more attention to students' language skills and communication skills. Courses are fundamental purpose is to make students English language skills and business practice, and effective combination of knowledge and students' future career, to meet the actual needs of the future for the English students in different jobs.

Therefore, the required English language skills and business expertise has become a close combination of Business English Courses greatest feature. This particularity is also being decided teachers in the "Business English" Teaching should not only pay attention to the basic training of students' English language skills, but also to strengthen the training of students and business expertise. Business English because English is more focused than the average on the application, so in teaching should not follow the traditional language teaching methods to minimize the proportion of basic knowledge of the language taught, expand the proportion of training in order to train students' language proficiency for the purpose of increasing the yield Right out of the number and weight. In the course of business English teaching, teachers teaching and students' self-learning must be combined with each other, to establish and implement a student-centered teaching self-learning mode, in order to communicate meaning for the purpose of requiring students in cognitive learning process to master professional business knowledge, to consolidate and strengthen its expertise in business practice and simulation application, and internalized cognitive learning. After learning and training, students with English as the media can really properly understood, handled and answered questions in a variety of business activities, and to establish and to maintain business ties with business partners, to improve the business communication skills. Also because of the special nature of this course, the effect evaluation criteria Business English course should be students' language communicative effectiveness and accuracy using business knowledge.

5 Interactive Teaching Business English

In the traditional classroom, there is a scene typical of teaching very common scenario: A teacher asked the students after school finished: "There are questions you do not understand the students please raise your hands?!" But often this time no people raised their hands. Are students really doing not have any doubt? There are several possible answers, perhaps some students did not think to mention the issue, perhaps introverted students did not dare show in front of the class of this class have not understood place, perhaps some students want to go back again after review relating to supplementary questions, perhaps there is no doubt that we indeed, it may just come across in the course of doing homework, in fact, such teachers in teaching and received no effective teaching subject - students, feedback information, and their level of understanding. Even if only a few people to ask questions, because of the relationship between classrooms forty minutes of class time, the teacher can only answer these questions, or simply left to the individual school and then answer. It can be seen, between teachers and students did not play an effective information feedback, the lack of communication between teachers and students interact.

Business English and general English comparison more difficult, mainly because the former includes not only the use of everyday language, but there are many technical terms, polite language to communicate with people, liturgical language, etc., and the need to finance, finance, e-commerce and domestic and international trade and the Anglo-American culture and other various disciplines, so the teachers and students, in the process of teaching and learning has a certain degree of difficulty, not the students lack of interest is that teachers lack teaching situations. Or, although students recognize the importance of business English, teachers also do everything possible to create the appropriate language to go with the situation, but the separation of limited hours, learning and practicing, or reach, "so that students will be in English language skills and business practices combined, and the mastery of knowledge and students' future career effectively combine to meet the actual needs of different jobs, "this goal. Center interactive teaching mode is "exchange", the classroom is the most wanted in the form of exchange, no classroom exchange, and there would be no conditions for implementation of classroom teaching. Effective classroom teaching to achieve the

purpose of the exchange is the prerequisite. From the perspective of exchange of information, the exchange of information between teachers and students is two-way; there is a lot of exchange of information between them. Therefore, the implementation of interactive teaching method based Business English Teaching is very necessary.

6 Interactive multimedia technologies in the sense of teaching

Meaning for the development of multimedia technology previously described characteristics and business English courses and interactive teaching, interactive multimedia technology in teaching business English is imperative. Concrete can be summarized as the following aspects:

First, students can take the initiative to learn. Through the use of multimedia technology to enhance teaching content rich and interesting, interactive teaching model to encourage students to participate, learn to enjoy the fun by participating in cattle, and can take the initiative to identify problems, propose to ask management, or even active thinking to find solutions to problems this greatly stimulated the enthusiasm of student learning active learning.

Second, the student becomes the real subject. Interactive, multimedia courseware and interactive teaching mode using panel presentations, role play, classroom discussions and other teaching methods, changing the classroom entirely controlled by teachers, students listen to talk about the shortcomings of notes, so that students become more involved in teaching activities, even control section selects teaching content and teaching progress, thus becoming one of the teaching body.

Third, the timely exchange more. Interactive multimedia technology in teaching business English, not only reflects the two-way interaction between teachers and students, but also to achieve human-computer interaction, and thus more conducive to feedback timely and accurate.

Fourth, application is practical theory. In the traditional teaching methods, mostly for teachers to make a few specific examples to illustrate how various business activities in the English language application, which shows business activities from real life and the use of multimedia technology, interactive immersive Teaching role-playing and group discussions and exchange, to realize the practical effect of teaching theory far.

References

1. Ding Jian Ge multimedia material acquisition and production of Beijing Higher Education Press, 23(2000)
2. Wang Yue Design and Research of interactive multimedia courseware, Tsinghua University master's thesis 34(1999)
3. Wang Wei "Direetor7.0 application and production instances" Science Press, 123,(2008)
4. Qing Han computer studio "Director7.0 multimedia production examples of" Machinery Industry Press, 120(2000)
5. Zhang Xian sound technical and artistic resolve singing. People's Music, 154(2005)
6. Cuiquan Xin Singing resonance cavity resonance and three practical exercises. Xinghai Conservatory of Music School Newspaper, 25(2001)
7. Xia Xianping vocal cords, glottis and vocal. Biology Bulletin, 198(2012)
8. Zhu Jiming, Rick Chan, Lubbe real larynx anatomical study. Shanxi: Anatomy, 213(2009)

MATEC Web of Conferences 44, 02070 (2016)
DOI: 10.1051/matecconf/20164402070

Research on University Network Teaching Platform (Blackboard) in Teaching Management

Zhao Xia Gou

Teacher's College, Beihua University, Jilin, China

Abstract. With rapid development of online education; teaching platform based on the network, as a new instructional mode has become a hot topic in online teaching. In this paper, the he teaching situation and existing problems on online was analyzed by comparing the difference between network teaching platform and traditional classroom teaching. Then the strategies of network teaching management and the case, which is focusing on the characteristics of Blackboard with the application of network teaching management was presents.

1 General instruction

The 21st century is dependent on the network in the digital environment and the survival of the community. Network, as a way of life, are quietly changing us. Its powerful transfer, learning and entertainment functions are people relish. Will partially replace the network-based education and supplement traditional forms of secondary education have become a new growth point of education in the 21st century. With the breakthrough development of information technology, network teaching platform based education as an important way of education, popularization of education, education and lifelong learning of social provides a good technical platform, the extension of the development of online education and improve the quality of teaching provided strong support.

With the development of network technology, the traditional teaching methods can not meet the people's needs, online teaching as a new form of education and means to break the time and space limitations of traditional teaching. For some reason, online distance education in our country started late, but developed rapidly. Our colleges and universities since 1996, made use of the advantages of resources Universities conduct envisaged Teaching. The past 10 years, with the continuous change, network teaching digitization, sharing, timeliness, interactivity, individualized teaching, abundant teaching resources, etc. has become increasingly prominent, online teaching has become one of the most important teaching mode.

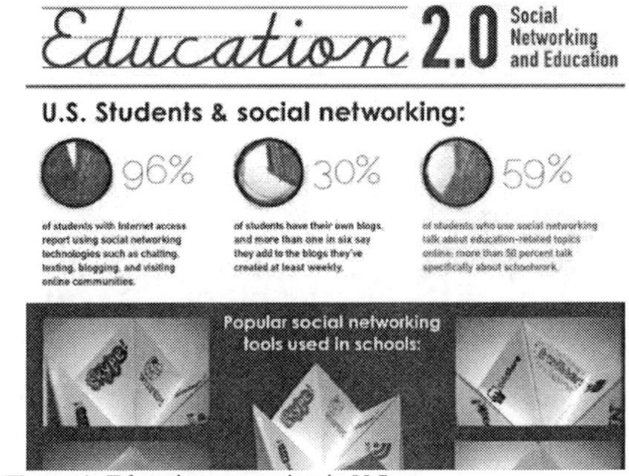

Figure 1. Education proportion in U.S

2 Major feature online teaching

First, focus on two-way exchange of teaching methods. The first major feature online teaching is a focus on two-way exchange of teaching methods. In the network of teaching methods, students can discover the one hand, in the learning process and the lack of progress, take the initiative to arrange referrals to adjust their learning to teachers to adapt teaching requirements; the other hand, teachers can understand students' learning processes through the network, The arrangements for the actual situation of teaching students to adjust according to the student. Through the exchange of teachers and students are in a timely manner, to ensure the quality and efficiency of student learning. The most obvious manifestation is the anti- "SARS" the very moment, in order to avoid its spread person-oriented or cross-infection, many schools have been closed or holiday, let students learn at school or at home on their own. If

conditions allow it (student dormitories or at home with computers with Internet access, etc.), the school can arrange for teachers and students learning through the network.

Second, students are required to learn a higher consciousness, collaboration. Another feature of the network is not only teaching students to learn a higher consciousness, also requires students to have a strong collaboration in learning. In the network teaching, students are not only to communicate with teachers, but also to communicate with other students. Students and teachers through a network of direct dialogue in order to get to the course to help students at the same time you can also get inspired by each other through the network to discuss the discussion with other students on the same course. Teaching in this communication network is regular, is necessary, which is advantageous in improving the quality and efficiency of student learning.

Third, the traditional "teacher-centred" is to the "student-centred." With the changes in the teaching and learning environment, online teaching has changed the traditional teaching concept "teacher-centred" and establish a "student-centred" new teaching concept, teachers and students in teaching roles change, students master learning The initiative, in earth moving, active learning the position, and then play the mentor teacher, mentor role. Teaching performance concept "student-centred" are: in the teaching process, students are around this centre, students enjoy the right to choose a course of clay, teachers, learning progress, learning time and so on. For example, students can query the network, want to choose their own course of study; call white already required in the teaching learning materials database: When you encounter a problem, you can request guidance or assistance to teachers through the network; also can network with other learners to discuss issues, exchange ideas; the problem can also participate in various discussions, etc. online. In short, the whole teaching activities are around to help students learn the subject, study the initiative entirely to the students, of course, which requires students to have a high learning consciousness, consciously use the network with the adjustment of learning.

Fourth, the teaching unity is personalized and collaborative learning models. Network teaching height reflects the individualized instruction and collaborative learning mode unity. Traditional classroom teaching for different students using the same textbooks, teaching methods, the "injection" type of knowledge indoctrination, this teaching is not conducive to play the potential of student's personality, is not conducive to the cultivation of innovative talents. Interactive learning, very suitable for student's individual learning, that is, from students to choose courses, discipline, progress, learning, etc., truly individualized, each student receives a "tailored" type of teaching, student's individual potential into full play.

Collaborative learning theory can be said online teaching constructivist learning theory. Constructivism holds that learning is learner with others, learners and the external environment; learners interact with the outside world produced. The theory emphasizes learner-centred, on the one hand requires the learner to the subject of information processing, knowledge of the significance of the transition from the active builders instil objects passive recipients of external stimuli and knowledge; it also requires teachers from the simple knowledge imparting, instilling active learners who construct meaning helper and facilitator transformation. Therefore, teaching students in both networks with other learners of ideas, but also with teachers learn to solve problems on a network.

3 The advantages of network teaching platform Teaching

On the Internet organized by hyperlink construct knowledge, vast information base to become the world's largest information resources to enable learners to share teaching resources different countries or log on to another educational network covered the required information, enrich the teaching content, broaden their horizons learners. This is not only conducive to the development of associative thinking and establishes links between old and new knowledge, but also for the formation and development of students' cognitive structure, namely the promotion of students to construct knowledge about the current is very advantageous.

With modern society people live, work accelerated pace of learning time for service personnel only relatively small, but also more and more fragmented, difficult for them out of a long and stable time to continue learning. Openness of the Internet so that people realize the sharing of information resources, from the traditional teaching strict requirements of time and place for learning, learners anytime, anywhere, with remote teaching system, VCD VOD system, according to their own needs flexible learning time arrangements and learning progress also can rely on teaching information retrieval system or public multimedia communication network, remote share educational resources and teacher guidance. And the network so that education has undergone profound changes, the whole process can be achieved in the online education, including Registration, study and practice, exams and scores, diploma and degree, etc., through the online school, so that more people round the university dream, rather than desperately to get into the college entrance examination this difficult path. This will not only help the implementation of quality education, but also to cultivate more knowledge economy requires adaptation of new talent.

Quality and quantity of traditional teaching is largely restricted level of teachers and school facilities and other conditions, online education is different, not only the number of students in the virtual classroom is no longer restricted, and can be combined in different school teachers taught the course content with graphics, sound, video and other multimedia forms, has greatly improved the school conditions and the environment. From the Java language online courses, practice basic computer literacy

courses teaching website, the network teaching methods in solving the popular courses of teachers, classrooms and other restrictions can play a significant role, it is worth further exploration and push) 'one. Also, the job and the exam is very heavy teaching, but the traditional way of work and exam burden on teachers too, so that teachers can not effectively use these two teaching methods. If you use the Internet will be able to solve this problem, the teacher will be able to get a lot of students learning first-hand materials, which have targeted for teachers to guide students to learn a lot of good.

Only network courseware platform online is teaching to be able to really only across time, space constraints, the breakthrough 40 minutes of constraint, the application of courseware from curricular and extra-curricular extension to allow our teachers to re-understanding as a whole, on the Course integration. Only with the network teaching platform, it may not need to produce their own teachers difficult courseware, interactive dynamic web pages written in script, we only need a simple text editor similar to Word can have fully functional network courseware, leaving out more time to focus on teaching itself. It can be said that only with the support of network teaching platform, the curriculum integration will truly become "open, resource-centred curriculum integration" powerful interactive information technology to be available to better reflect the traditional classroom teaching You can gradually expand to extracurricular theme explored in order to achieve effective, real inquiry.

4 Comparative analysis of network teaching platform ordinary classroom

Manage network teaching platform Teaching compared with ordinary classroom teaching management, in the end what is the difference? Recognize this, is the basis for teaching management network teaching platform, which requires the network teaching platform Teaching Management and ordinary classroom teaching management analysis Compare. The so-called ordinary classroom teaching management is in school, college or university campus in the general level of non-networked classroom teaching management, in fact, the management of network teaching platform Teaching ordinary classroom management and teaching there in some respects great similarities, the two are not completely separate, but after teaching online teaching platform is a new educational model, there is a big difference compared to the teaching environment and general education, therefore, teaching both conducted management inevitably vary.

Management body: Bodies of teaching management means are management science knowledge and skills have appropriate authority, engaged in teaching and management activities. In teaching management, each person can be both management body, it could be managed object, in different teaching administration, or at different times in the same teaching administration, people often play different roles, changing his identity, performance for the conversion of teaching management subjects and objects. Network teaching platform is teaching management, the body managing teachers, curriculum content administrators, and assistants and student performance evaluation. Work organization and daily management of the teacher is not only responsible for learning this course, there are FAQs and classroom teachers to provide students with the case administrator course content, even in the page, CAI courseware preparation of technical personnel, they all belong to the network teaching subjects teaching management platform. Subject ordinary classroom teaching management is relatively simple, the manager basically limited to teach instructors, teachers often several roles, both in charge of the course, marking students' work, is also responsible for the student's Tutor and even computer-aided instruction software design.

Management Object: The object of teaching management means for teaching management subjects of understanding and transforming objects with teaching management associated soil. About managing objects, including what elements exist in management science in different views: Some people, financial, and material, "said the three factors"; someone, financial, material, time and information, "said the five-factor", someone, financial, material, time Information, ten gas, the method "a seven said," and so on. On the management of network teaching platform in terms of teaching, this paper argues people, goods, information the three factors are essential elements of teaching management object. People mainly refer to the object of teaching, knowledge of the recipient, the following class focuses on lobbyists and informational material object.

(1) Material class object. Substance class object network teaching platform teaching management are: the Internet, video conferencing systems, virtual laboratories, virtual classroom, e-learning studio and so on. To manage these products, to ensure the normal operation of teaching work, which is difficult to manage quite large? The substance class object ordinary classroom teaching soils have classroom management and so on, of course, including the management of said network management platform for teaching in the teaching material class objects, but they are not yet dominant in ordinary teaching.

(2) Information objects class. In the network teaching platform in teaching, teaching is mainly carried out through the network; therefore, the information object class teaching management is primarily a network of educational information resources. As the network environment, complex and diverse sources of information, generous, produce and disseminate information without screening and validation, information object class classroom teaching soils common management if the print media, of course, also includes part of non-print media, its management the difficulty is clearly not the former.

Management Model: clues from history teaching management development, the teaching management mode can be divided into empirical management, administration management mode and science-based

management are three basic types, including science-based teaching management mode can be divided into deterministic, random, fuzzy type, system management mode. These management modes used in practice are not mutually exclusive, but mutually intersect, complement each other, but in a different mode of teaching, managers will mainly using one or several teaching management mode for teaching management.

This paper argues that the teaching management network teaching platform, should mainly stochastic and fuzzy type teaching management mode of teaching management. The so-called random type of teaching management pattern is to randomness science as guidance, acknowledge the complexity of the object, chance, mutation, using statistical regularity and randomness of mathematical models for analysis, forecasting, and then plan to implement a science teaching management. In teaching management network teaching platform, there are a lot of random phenomena, such as, teaching content, teaching methods with the rapid development of modern science and technology exhibit uncertainty. Also, the teaching process is affected network operation status, computer performance and other factors; the possibility of teaching interrupt is random. The so-called fuzzy type of teaching management is fuzzy thinking and fuzzy theory, complexity sure the object, fuzziness and fuzzy theory and fuzzy mathematical models for analysis, decision-making and evaluation, and then the implementation of a new management Science-based teaching management model. This model is concerned that the daily work of the Organization of instability and complexity. Furthermore, in the era of rapid social change, schools may be difficult to interpret a variety of information and demand signals from the external environment, it is difficult to deal with the many contradictions arising there from, this exotic uncertain information, and will certainly increase fuzziness decision-making process within the school, at the same time, the rapid development of network technology, knowledge updated accelerating teaching management have increased randomness and fuzziness.

5 Conclusion

In common classroom management, the main use of administrative type and determine the type of teaching management mode of teaching management. Teaching administrative management emphasizes the authority of administrative rule-based and regulatory organizations at all levels, the use of administrative measures and administrative means mandatory, in accordance with procedures established norms, promoting and teaching management. This teaching management model reflects the organization leadership authority. Determine the type of teaching management mode, making full use of past experience, to develop a series of plans on the basis of past experience, organization, rules and regulations, in accordance with a defined path, methodically, step by step forward.

Management tools: network teaching platform management tools in teaching computer and network technology-based, computer-based form of teaching management information system, through high-speed computing and mass storage functions of the computer, teaching management information collection, transmission, storage and processing, timely and accurately provide useful information to management, to support managers to achieve the training objectives and scientific decision-making and effective control. Education Management Information System is suitable for almost the entire range of teaching management, which includes: the teaching plan management, teaching management, teaching quality management, teacher management. The general education teaching management currently in use is still largely manual management methods, at least for now is still in the stage of development of the computer network direction.

From the viewpoint of the system point of view, any organization is a system; it exists in a more human system. The larger system is the existence and development of the environment, the organization is always inseparable from the environment. Management of the environment can be divided into two human beings: one is the general environment, including natural and social environment; the other is a special environment, mainly refers to the environment within the organization, also known as the working environment, which includes the physical environment, spiritual environment and information environment three aspects. The following face on special education and general education environment network teaching management to do a comparison.

References

1. Karl Engkvist. Digital Learning Application and Development of the global user experience - Blackboard articles .Chief Operating Officer
2. CERNET-Blackboard Technology Ltd., 230 (2005)
3. Like Dong sharing online resources to build Internet interactive learning environment Guangdong: South China Normal Science, 11 (2005)
4. John Fritz Bob Armstrong. Using Blackboard Communities for Student Government Elections and Orientation.45 (2005)
5. Tang Fuyuan, Xu Lihua Based on Blackboard Teaching Information Technology Discussion Education information, 94 (2005)
6. Han Joan personal knowledge management theory and research. DETAILED DESCRIPTION Jiangsu Nanjing Normal University, 25 (2007)
7. Zhenghan Wen. Cooperative learning classroom management strategies. Wuhan University of Science and Technology, 12 (2006)
8. Yao Castle. Xie broad-based network platform exchange of teachers and students. Zhengzhou Management + Department of University of Economics, 9 (2006)

9. Zhujie Lan research and model of college classroom knowledge management system to build. China Distance Education, 61 (2006)

MATEC Web of Conferences 44, 02071 (2016)
DOI: 10.1051/matecconf/20164402071

Research on Translation Strategy of English Subtitle Television Drama for College Students based on Cultural Differences

Gang Zhou

College of Foreign Language Education, Beihua University, Jilin City, China

Abstract. Translation strategy is closely-tied with the translation of ESTD (English Subtitle Television Drama). The research of translation strategy is to serve translations of ESTD in earlier days. The 21 S` century is the information times. The development of science and technology is quick. Quantities of ESTD grow explosively. Translations of English Subtitle Television Dramas play a significant role in the progress of Chinese science and technology. Although the quality of traditional manual translations is very good, the speed of translation is too slow. Traditional manual translations can not meet the need of translations of ESTD day by day. It is a new topic to face the new stern challenge and follow the development's steps of the times for technical translators. The paper will discuss the transformation of translation idea, and suggest carrying on translation strategy, web page translation and software translation. Finally, the author states her views on the implementation of computer assistant translation, the managements of translation projects and information-shared platform.

1 General instruction

Modern science and technology provides us with access to information in a variety of ways and channels, satellite communications and the Internet has further deepened ties between the peoples of the world, people desire to understand each other more and more intense. British and American movies, TV influx of Chinese, Chinese audiences are entertainment but also feel the exotic culture. Because of language barriers, mostly by domestic audience dubbing or subtitles are provided to specific worker information. Anglo-American drama, film development update faster, retain the original sound of the subtitle translation version is more welcomed by the public. However, since these Subtitling completed mostly by English fans, there are many aspects of the quality of the translation. This paper attempts to explore the English subtitles translated from the perspective of relevance theory commonly used techniques, hoping to give Subtitling provide some help.

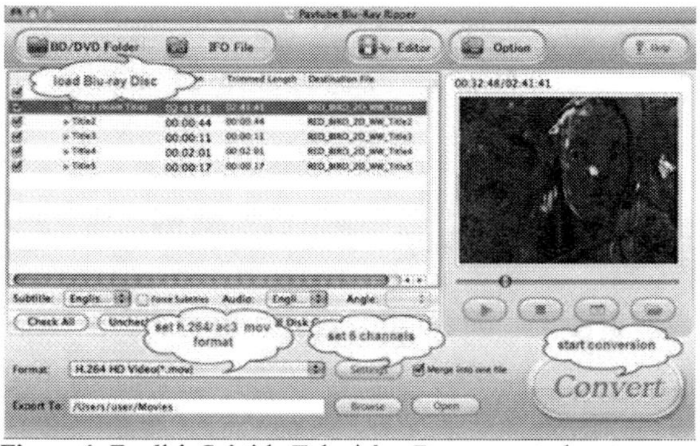

Figure 1. English Subtitle Television Drama control system

2 Western cognitive linguist sparer

Relevance Theory is the language of Western cognitive linguist sparer and Wilson Grice-based association guidelines proposed by the theory. In their view, the language of communication is an ostensive-inferential process, rather than the traditional communication theory believes encoding -decoding process. In a successful communication, the speaker's task is to put his message and communicative intentions are passed to the hearer, the hearer's task is to infer the speaker's intention speaker from the information provided. An important factor in successful communication is clear mutual communication, that speaker and hearer have the same cognitive environment. People's communicative behaviours will produce an optimal correlation expect the recipient to

accurately understand the communicative intent, it must be associated with each other to find the best words and context in communication between the two sides co-known cognitive environment, by inference was contextual knowledge implied meaning, to obtain contextual effects to achieve the purpose of communication. The so-called optimal relevance is the speaker's words can generate enough contextual effects for the hearer, without the need for further unnecessary processing.

Subtitling purpose is to help viewers get to use the target language as the primary language of the audience the same information, the purpose of bringing the audience and the same communicative language affect the original language audience. Translation is a communicative, namely communicative language translator with the original cast and translator with the target language audience. According to theory, the letters translator has a dual identity, first of all, he is the original language of a movie or TV audience, he wants to understand the true intentions of the speaker's words passed; secondly, he is a translation, it is necessary to understand his words through another language transmitted through subtitles to understand the Chinese audience. Translators must successfully complete the task of these two roles, in order to ensure the target language audience gets the same contextual effects. Optimal relevance principle is always to follow the guidelines translator. When the translator is experiencing difficulties sophisticated target language, audience gets the best translation strategy. One can make the target language audience with minimal effort you can get the original language processing intent translation is the best choice. If the target language so that viewers get the best correlation, then the translation is successful; if not, you need to be improved.

3 The original language and communicative intent of real information

Because culture of different countries, in most cases overlap, so the original language and the target language audience viewers have the same or similar cognitive environment. In case of no cultural differences, the literal translation of the target language audience enough to help get the best correlation. According to statistics, a movie or a TV series, at least seventy percent of the content can be used literally to deal with.

English and Chinese, after all, are two different languages, cultural backgrounds in different circumstances; the original language in the context of the effect will be lost in the target language. This time, literally can not speak the original language and communicative intent of real information is passed to the target language audience, the target language audience and therefore not optimal relevance. So, we need to find a language capable of producing the same original contextual effects of alternative expression in the target language. Alternative methods of translation are widely used in film and television drama appeared proverbs, idioms, and slang occasions.

Such as: You know the old saying, do not you "In for an inch, in for a mile." (You know the old saying it "insatiable."?) The answer here is an English proverb, expressed in? I do not know when you receive the benefits of the foot, and there are more demands. If the literal translation, the audience will not understand the target language to express the speaker's meaning, the translator with the Chinese idiom "insatiable" to replace, not only to convey the meaning of the original language, but also the greatest extent from the language structure retains the characteristics of the original language target language audience so get optimal relevance. Another example is "You can still put the brakes on this thing", which "put the brakes on this thing" is used to express in English, said that a person did something wrong, there are opportunities for its remedy. If the original meaning of the target language is to convey to the audience, but the structure of the English language to express this habit of it lost. Chinese idioms idiom translator has chosen a function of "too late, too late" to replace, so that viewers get the best relevance of the target language.

Translated by the translator is to add some information on the basis of the literal translation, the target language in order to help the audience understand the meaning of the original language. Because of cultural differences, when the original language is lost each other out in the target language, translated by the target language audience can help each other out to get lost, efforts to reduce handling, resulting in optimal relevance. Cultural connotation of the original language is in the target language to find relevant information, but the majority of this audience is not familiar with the target language, and then adds translation is the best solution. For example: "Link-Which means we've got to get him on board" (which means that we have to pull him into the water) "Sucre-Forget it the guy's a boy scout." (Come on, he was a Boy Scout - Italy refers to the obedient, disciplined). "A boy scout" is the meaning of the Boy Scouts, the Boy Scouts of most people know, but do not know the true meaning of its representatives. Translator added some information (meaning obedient, disciplined), to help the audience understand the information of the target language and communicative intent of the original language. Sucre-a cell phone in here" (the phone hidden in here?) "That's cardinal sin Number 1" (What are you guilty of the first seven deadly sins - meaning arrogant). For the "cardinal sin Number 1", can be found in Chinese-related information, which means the seven deadly sins in the first sin, but most people in this first sin is not clear what, then, was the original language of the audience mutual out in the target language audience is likely to be lost. In this case, the translator uses by translation, can help viewers understand the true intent of the target language speaker.

Subtitling, for words, and the space occupied and the emergence of the time, there are stringent restrictions. Studies have shown that the lower end of the subtitle to put most of the screen, a maximum of two lines, two lines of subtitles time best kept within 6 seconds, the line between subtitles retention time of 3 to 4 seconds, shall

not exceed 35 words. Thus, when the speaker speech rate faster express the content is higher, it is necessary translation information was concentrated; leaving only the important information, important information is omitted. For example: "I'm coming along on this endeavours whether you like it or not." (I will follow you). If the literal translation is "Whatever you happy or not happy, I'll follow you." However, due to a faster rate of speech speaker, a relatively long target language subtitle will affect the viewing audience, the use of concentrated translation method to solve this problem. Another example: “He’s beginning to get the idea that anybody he attaches himself to be going to end up in prison" literal translation would be: "He began to have had such a view that is dependent on anyone he will be in prison end. Words over the limit caption width. Concentrated translated as "he had thought all his people will rely on jail," omitted "beginning to get the idea that" the translation of the original meaning there is no loss, while ensuring the quality and efficiency of viewers.

4 Modern English teaching in college

Every translation has its certain constraints, subtitle translation is no exception. Nedergaard-Larsen thinks that the subtitle translation is a special type of language conversion: concentrated written translation soundtrack spoken; it appears in Luyken et al., subtitle translation including separate in theory and the three layers of meaning in fact inseparable: interlinguas transfer information, discourse Jane or concentration, and speaking into the written language. Subtitle translation after two layers of meaning to make it different from other types of translation. The original cuts in other types of translation in although have, but never reached this breadth and intensity did not change in subtitle translation; textual interpretation and translation in the way, not the existence of spoken and written language of the conversion, and the subtitle translation experiences from oral to text conversion.

Cathy: Isabella, don’t you see what he’s been doing? He’s been using you, to be near me, to smile at me behind your back, to try to rouse something in my heart that’s dead!

The characteristics of the film and television media itself will subtitle placed under the control of the operation of various scholars and translators, corresponding to different strategy are also slightly different. Understand any of the source language people will adopt a critical attitude toward captions. A not trust not immediately cause the audience, the impact of information communication. On subtitle translation, the restriction factors first have the following two aspects: the special time and space. Subtitle synchronous though not dubbing so strict, at present also not to Chinese subtitles clear time limit, but one thing is certain, that is, subtitles and sound must be synchronized. This requires the translator must use common words, with short, flexible patterns; realize the information transmission in the limited time and space. Howe. However, the author thinks that to achieve complete synchronization is almost impossible, because the movie actors lines need to finish a few seconds, and the caption usually is from the speaker's mouth began a sentence, as the audience to browse the subtitle faster than sound transmission speed, this to a certain extent disclosed on the back word, did not meet the "and" effect, inevitably reduce the pleasure of film appreciation. On the other hand, caption is flashed on the screen of text, one is fleeting, like text books, readers can cross reference, this is another kind of constraints on subtitle translation on time. So take the subtitles corresponding translation strategies should be use common words, words and phrases; sentence should concise, avoid cumbersome and lengthy, cherish with long insert component, participle structure and clause. In the regulation of the structure of sentences, passive sentences can bring some negative sentences into active sentences and affirmative; the long sentences into sentence, complex sentence into simple sentences. As in "Wuthering Heights" in 1 cases: Source: Cathy: Isabella, don’t you see what he’s been he’s been using doing? You, to be near me, to smile at me behind your back, to try to rouse something in my heart that’s dead!

Translation: Casey: Isabella, don't you understand what he's been doing? He has been using you, use you to get close to me, he was carrying you laugh at me, trying to rouse something in my heart that's dying affection! “to be near me”,” to smile at me behind your back” “to try to rouse something in my heart that’ s dead” 。

The dialogue has a long complex sentences, it contains three infinitive phrases and an attributive clause, namely: "to be near me", "to smile at me behind your back" and "to try to rouse something in my heart that’s dead". The long and complex infinitives and a subordinate clause is difficult to translate into a short and refining, complete semantic Chinese sentence, because each phrase contains different semantic information, such as hard up a long and complicated sentences, it is bound to cause a subtitle of sound and picture are not synchronized, so that not only affect the audience understanding of the subtitles, but also undermines the movie the wonderful scene. But the translator has skilfully used segmentation method to resolve this problem, that is, to resolve a long sentence into four independent Chinese phrase.

Translation: Casey: Isabella, don't you understand what he's been doing? He has been using you, use you to get close to me, he was carrying you laugh at me, trying to rouse something in my heart that's dying affection!

Subtitle translation was by way of media discourse, namely, the characteristics of their own created many restricting factors, but on the other hand, the multimedia nature film also provides many favourable conditions for cross cultural communication. As mentioned above, since restricted by time and space in the subtitle translation, translation can be cut greatly on the original text. In addition, in written translation the translator can only rely on text symbols to convey information, use words to describe the dynamic and static objects, and the subtitle

will to a large extent due to synchronization occurs, accompanied by music, pictures of natural sounds, people speak (although the audience may not understand the contents of the intonation language) information, provides many favourable conditions to overcome the cultural differences. In short, subtitle translation is restricted by factors such as time and space factors, cross-cultural factors, the subtitle translator in the translation process according to the specific situation, make the corresponding translation strategies, we must conscientiously, carefully before.

5 Conclusions

Subtitling, for words, and the space occupied and the emergence of the time, there are stringent restrictions. Studies have shown that the lower end of the subtitle to put most of the screen, a maximum of two lines, two lines of subtitles time best kept within 6 seconds, the line between subtitles retention time of 3 to 4 seconds, shall not exceed 35 words. Thus, when the speaker speech rate faster express the content is higher, it is necessary translation information was concentrated; leaving only the important information, important information is omitted. For example: "I'm coming along on this endeavours whether you like it or not." (I will follow you). If the literal translation is "Whatever you happy or not happy, I'll follow you." However, due to a faster rate of speech speaker, a relatively long target language subtitle will affect the viewing audience, the use of concentrated translation method to solve this problem. Another example: "He's beginning to get the idea that anybody he attaches himself to be going to end up in prison" literal translation would be: "He began to have had such a view that is dependent on anyone he will be in prison end." Words over the limit caption width. Concentrated translated as "he had thought all his people will rely on jail," omitted "beginning to get the idea that" the translation of the original meaning there is no loss, while ensuring the quality and efficiency of viewers.

Acknowledgements: Research college English translation teaching mode under the guidance of constructivism

References

1. Money Shaochang Film Translation-increasingly important area of parkland. Chinese translation, 12(2000)
2. Wang Rong Relevance Theory Subtitling Strategy-"Gone with the Wind" Subtitling case analysis. Beijing International Studies University, 59(2007)
3. Xing Lijuan of international film translation. Nanjing University of Technology: Social Sciences, 71(2005)
4. Xue cool. From the perspective of functional translation theory movie subtitle translation. Liaoning Normal University, 45(2006)
5. Yang Min Functional Translation Theory and sitcom "six" in the subtitle translatio. Xiangtan University, 12(2005)
6. Yang Yang film subtitling Review. Southwest Jiaotong University: Social Sciences, 97(2006)
7. Chen Li. Ways to enhance the effectiveness of grassroots English teaching in colleges and colleges. PARTY SCHOOL, 147(2006)
8. Mr. Zhao. Colleges in Modern English teaching of ideological and political work study. Sichuan People's Publishing House, 2009.
9. Jiang Tiezhu. Famous English teaching. Wenhui Press, 541(2008)
10. Sun Chuanming. English teaching Problems and Solutions. Coastal colleges and science and technology, 362(2005)
11. Xiao Xuebin, Julie. The impact of modern media on the English teaching and its response. Ideological Education Research, 234(2009)
12. Wang Huancheng. Modern trends in the modern media environment of English teaching of college students. Contemporary Education Forum (Management), 142(2010)
13. Lai Yong. English teaching in the modern media environment exploration. Net wealth, 102(2010)

MATEC Web of Conferences 44, 02072 (2016)
DOI: 10.1051/matecconf/20164402072

The Application of Computer Music Technology to College Students

Na Wang

College of Music, Beihua University, Jilin City, China

Abstract. Contemporary music education started late in China on the basis of western teaching theories formed its own unique system, which has a great influence on present computer music technology. This paper explores that contemporary music education is analyzed advantages and disadvantages of the influence on the development of Chinese class music, and the solutions are found out to the existing problems, summed up the reality enlightenment of that the contemporary music on the impact of education.

1 General instruction

Mid-20th century to the early 21st century, with the computer music technology swept through Europe and Japan and other developed countries, the development of computer technology, more and more with each passing day the music. Today, every music lover can take advantage of a complete computer music platform for music learning and creation. Musicians can be computer via MIDI (Musical Instrument Digital Interface) interface to connect electronic musical instruments constituting the system, so as to receive, control and adjust the level of sound, such as, length, timbre, dynamics, etc., through the different sources of reality "sampling" and then use the ever-changing variety of methods for processing sound, creating one can not imagine the sound. With MIDI standards, the traditional acoustic music science, law school system, acoustics, musical school, orchestration school has also undergone unprecedented revolutionary change. At the same time, by MIDI technology and multimedia technology and network information technology development and maturity, MIDI equipment, computers and music software has become increasingly closely integrated, which makes traditional music, music and dramatic changes occurred in music teaching , but also it makes people's awareness of computer music technology gradually deepened.

Now, with a highly developed computer music technology, the effects and benefits of computer generated music technology is constantly broaden people's understanding of music, these effects and benefits of music education, teaching film, radio, television, music recording, music, etc. areas to be widely used, and has played an important role. And computer music technology has infiltrated more and more areas of music education, teaching conception. With music and computer technologies have become increasingly closer in the field to produce a large number of excellent music.

Overall, now commonly used in computer music technology software: Encore, Final. Popular sequencer software: Cakewalk, Cubase. Common harmonies teaching software: Version50 and Musicator win30 and so on.

Figure 1. Computer music technology system

2 Computer music technologies

In China, computer music key technical points are purely artistic or purely commercial musical studies on production. In the computer music technology into the classroom music education, especially of the Normal University music theory class professional in this field, in general, it is not very common. Although the Ministry of Education in August 2001 issued the "Opinions on strengthening undergraduate teaching work to improve the quality of teaching," the document presented twelve strengthening undergraduate teaching work measures to improve the quality of teaching and the views and The Ministry of Education "2003-2007 Action Plan for Invigorating Education" an important part of the "Quality Project" in the proposed "information technology as a means to deepen education reform and personnel training mode reform," but confined to China's national conditions, almost close the file to "empty talk." This is

Article available at http://www.matec-conferences.org or http://dx.doi.org/10.1051/matecconf/20164402072

because :(a) In China, people use computer music technology research started relatively late, the computer MIDI and multimedia systems in college music teaching is still in the development stage. (B) As Chinese music system from the west, and gradually formed in the Chinese Modern specific political, economic, cultural and educational background, it is difficult to make up for its shortcomings. (C) At present normal student's computer music technology education relatively low starting point, teacher-student ratio is too large, plus an abstract theory courses, sound unstable, these factors greatly enhance the difficulty of computer music technology teaching.

Due to computer music technology teaching has its particularity, so the shortage of teachers, teaching facilities, inadequate case basis, only to study and explore the "plots" in the form, and on this basis to explore and build suitable for China Music Education. Currently, computer music technology application in China Teachers Teaching is not widespread; the reason is mainly reflected in the following three aspects:

First, in China, due to computer applications, penetration is not high, resulting in computer music technology started relatively late in Europe and other developed countries. Therefore, only a small part of the music research institutions, universities and teachers have the ability to use a computer music technology teaching;

Second, in our country, due to the traditional mode of thinking educational atmosphere, thus familiar with computers and courseware production of computer music teacher is not much;

Third, the current in Normal Colleges in China, there is no package, the use of computer music technology hardware facilities for teaching music; To sum up, the computer music technology in Normal computer music technology teaching in our country, but also in a "bottleneck" status. Teacher alone a mouth, a stereo equipment, it is difficult to approach a new orchestration, timbre colourful works thorough explanation to students, and the students also difficult to make a rational analysis of computer music technology to produce sound effects, and to be fully understanding. Therefore, only effective by music from the "visual arts" to "auditory art", a breakthrough in theory, various limitations on teaching methods, in order to ease the contradiction between "teaching" and "learning" to fundamentally improve teaching quality, make computer music technology to achieve a qualitative leap in teaching fundamental in order to better discover and cultivate excellent comprehensive quality talent.

3 The importance of computer music technology into the teaching of music in Normal

Ancient educator Confucius lifetime love of music and cool love to sing, and music as one of the six arts student compulsory proposed "Xing in poetry, stand ceremony, as with the music.

With the advent of the knowledge economy, a necessary requirement with suitable educational system, from the examination-oriented education steering train all-round development of innovative talents as the goal of quality education. We know that cultivate people's all-round development and innovation capacity must be built on all the psychological, physiological basis for the development of people's abilities above, such as human feeling, perception, understanding, insight, transform, divergent thinking and so on. And there will be conducive to art cultivating the basic quality of the human form. American University of Iowa Phillips (K Phillips) in the United States, "Music Educators Journal" published an article entitled "Music education is the basic idea of the establishment of a more powerful," the article, presents music important for human development resistance, which we fully understand the important position of music in education is very useful.

History of our country and the rest of the world of educational technology development tells us that any successful application of an advanced technology in education, first of all depend on the concepts of education educators update. Similarly, computer music technology into Music Education, but also by the trend of historical development decisions, and its importance can be summarized as four points:

First, the computer music technology education has a very important role in the successful implementation of quality education in. This is because: computer music technology education is a basic form of the new era of human and cultural exchanges, such as language and literacy, as it is, between human beings communicate thoughts, ideas and feelings, but also we learn a world cultural heritage of all ethnic groups important means it helps us understand the character and individuality of human culture, help us to know themselves, know our traditions and thinking behaviour. At the same time, through the computer music technology, we can get to know other peoples and their traditions and behaviour. Understanding of human cognition, psychological, emotional, and kinaesthetic On a deeper level, in order to develop and improve the knowledge of human beings, profoundly change people's attitudes and emotions. And learn computer music technology can develop and exercise the human imagination and thinking skills, in order to develop the broadest perspective, from the perspective of the natural sciences, social sciences and other infrastructure areas, sublimation human soul, to truth, goodness and beauty of harmony and unity.

Second, the computer music technology education in the New Chinese music education system reform in the key. This is because: China Music Education Curriculum System in the early 20th century, imported from the West, is in the Chinese Modern specific background of politics, economy, culture, art and education evolving. Today, the music education curriculum system has increasingly shown its drawbacks and defects, specific performance: 1, music relatively narrow field of vision. That is now China's music education system rarely reference value of

ancient Chinese music and traditional music, just blindly absorb Western music mode and content, while ignoring the big nations of the world music culture system development. 2, Music education is the form of relatively simple. That most school music education is closed single musical education rarely comes to integrated interdisciplinary teaching. 3, Music backward is failure to music education into major development trend of the times among the global technology. In application of computer music technology, for example, currently many domestic professional music creators use, and school education rarely use.

Third, the importance of education in computer music technology is to build a new music education mode. Innovative educational technology, especially in contemporary music technology and multimedia computer network of general application, the traditional teaching methods and teaching philosophy has changed dramatically, the use of new technologies in teaching makes teaching more obvious, more conducive to cultivating wealthy individuality and innovative students to help improve overall quality of students.

Fourth, computer music technology into music education is to help speed up the training of teachers. Comrade Jiang Zemin as early as the end of 1997 the national organization of the session, had said: "Today is a time of new things, new knowledge, new experiences emerging era, many of us want to learn something, no matter who, as long as the halt, do not learn something new, is certainly to be outdated. "So, in the face of a new era of rapid development of computer music technology, every teacher need to keep learning and training, it is necessary to do: 1, learning computer music technology, including hardware use of knowledge and common knowledge to use music software. 2, learning modern music education theory, establish the concept of quality education, educational research, computer music technology creatively applied to the school teaching, and to achieve the goal of interdisciplinary music education.

In the face of the future of education, the key is to learn the students to learn, learn to use, learn and create. Obviously, with the introduction of computer music technology classes, which will maximize the current situation improved and enhanced, and to achieve convergence and integration with the world trend of curriculum reform and international music education.

4 Computer music technologies in harmony Course

Harmony class conservatories and music faculties Normal Universities in the more important a subject, it is the basis for polyphonic, orchestration, musical and other technology Theory. Features harmony lesson is that it is a highly theoretical course, but also needs a lot of practice of course, there is not enough understanding of the practical exercises, and even if reluctantly harmony theory is difficult to apply in practice.

In Normal College music faculty, the general traditional teaching methods are still blackboard plus piano, which also has been become the primary means of acoustic and teaching, due to China's general music education foundation is weak, many high school teacher and student before do not understand what is harmony, therefore, faced with this kind of teaching situation, the teachers "teaching" and "learning", to a certain extent, it is difficult to reach a tacit understanding. While students learn very seriously, but for harmony of knowledge and awareness is still a blur. Because of this traditional mode of teaching is difficult to form in the minds of students on the harmony sound auditory association, making their ears feel harmonic sound beautiful, so in terms of ideology can not form the most general harmonic thinking habits, learn In the end, most people have lost interest in learning to harmony. In a sense, this is the key to Normal and acoustic difficult to improve teaching quality lies.

How can we effectively address the theory and practice of teaching harmony out of touch, hearing student image and visual image difficult to communicate the problem? This requires us to introduce MIDI computer technology and multimedia systems in teaching. The general mainly US Passport Designs has developed "Encore" notation software (vision4.2.1), UK Software Partners Company "Tonica" Harmony teaching software (Vision 5.0) and the United States jointly with the Norwegian Jo Brodtkord MusicatorA / S Company development "Musicator Win 3.0 (MW30)" music software, and utilization of their special features, depending on the students, listening to the integration of multimedia teaching harmony, the main approach is as follows:

(A) The use of Encore score display functions lectures.

Encore has a very intuitive score display function, use this feature, you can teach in harmony with the actual sound spectrum of cases in the classroom teaching harmony synchronized show in front of students, and can be quickly re-presentation. For example, the harmony of a specific connection, teachers can teach the basic laws while writing, through computer technology to play MIDI out its various manifestations, including different melodies position, a different arrangement position, a different sound range changes in areas such as acoustic factors. Students hear acoustic sound but also saw them score display, and according to their own auditory and visual perception, to teachers in the form of bomb various connections to make their own sound aesthetic judgment. Practice has proved that, in this manner harmony teaching lectures, students read, see, hear with, easy to stimulate students' interest in learning and aesthetic judgment of confidence.

(B) The use of MW3 score editing functions commented demonstration and job assignments.

MW3 score editing features are very good. When students analyze written assignments as well as assignments commenting demonstration in the classroom, using this feature can often achieve good results of

replication. For example, the parallel connection and the most commonly occurring spin, reverse and concealed fifty-eight degrees and other bad parts were, you can use the Score Editor of copies (COPY) function, will include the above error chords connected to the bottom off the copy phase Pro track the location of the same beats, and using editing functions on the new track will delete unnecessary parts, leaving only two parts of the constitution in parallel, depending on the students, the problem will hear a glance, without further too much explanation. In making demonstration, the teacher can make a variety of different configuration with a harmony exercises. Then, MW3 monorail playback function, the various acoustic configuration obtained through classroom discussion so that students listen to each playback, audio-visual integration, in order to develop students' hearing ability and harmony thinking ability, and develop their aesthetic taste and elegant harmony.

(C) The use of different types of harmony Tonica learning style and help with harmonies change problem.

Tonica is a harmony of four devoted to the study of multimedia educational software. Compared with other software, although Tonica interface design is not friendly, but for harmony teaching it, Tonica proprietary exercise function can still play its positive role. For example: teachers in the classroom can be done for the melody (or bass) with examples of harmony or students after school made a written exercises, use Automatic Harmonize Tonica choose a different style to do another harmony several different harmony configurations, enable students to appreciate the technical differences between the different harmony styles. In addition, students can practice harmonies Tonica import MIDI file format, and use it for the correct operation of harmony. In the current harmony teaching classes many colleges take Taipan special circumstances, the use of Tonica help with harmonies change problem is undoubtedly a more viable harmony teaching methods.

(D) The use of real-time recording function performed MW3 Encore and keyboard harmonies play guidance.

Keyboard Harmony Teachers play an important part harmony teaching. In the past, teaching, students are required to do seeing chords mark, thinking connectivity rules, playing four hands harmony, but for various reasons, students are often at a loss when you play, playing the wrong tone while he did not know. MW3 Encore and use real-time recording function, students play before the record button is pressed, the recording will be played and synchronization is complete, and instantly generate a score, so fleeting keyboard harmonies play converted into concrete existence sheet music form. Student scores generated instant play site based on its guidance, help students find their own advantages and problems. In addition, to strengthen the cohesion harmony exercises and improvisational accompaniment keyboard curriculum, teachers can play the four students evolved into a common harmony accompaniment texture (or simple accompaniment figure) in new tracks by four - part Harmony outline contrasts with the accompaniment of texture, easier to stimulate students' interest in learning.

(E) Site

Classical MIDI Connection, http:// www. midiworld. com/cmc/index.htm. This site records the West from the Baroque period to the twentieth century composer's midi main resource. Covering a wide range, MIDI files are also musicians playing pro, high artistic taste, and sound analysis is used as the repository, the site is preferred.

References

1. Lee to Beijing. On the computer music teaching. Fujian Art, 21 (2001)
2. Chen Xiangming teachers how to do qualitative research. Education Science Press, 12 (2001)
3. Fang Zhining. Enchanting Midi Mongolia Press, 11 (2003)
4. Yong division. Computer music production master. Beijing Hope Electronic Press, 05 (2000)
5. Zhang Kai Educational Psychology, Southwest Normal University Press, 21 (2000)
6. Qin Qingkun .MIDI technology in music technology theory and practice of teaching. Hebei University Institute of Adult Education College, 14 (2000)
7. Research Lijian Qin Information teaching music teaching environment. Alto network, 13 (2004)
8. Han Biao. Mention mediated teaching methods using digital music Modern Music Education Personnel Training Network alto, 02 (2004)
9. Like Dong heart of modern music technology-Construction of new forms of teaching mode China Education Daily, 07 (2010).
10. Li Jiahou. Computer music technology and audio-visual education innovation research and education, 18 (2009)

MATEC Web of Conferences 44, 02073 (2016)
DOI: 10.1051/matecconf/20164402073

Research and Part Implementation of Process Oriented Online Education Information System

Xue Mei Jiang

Teacher's College, Beihua University, Jilin, China

Abstract. In the context of internet applications, traditional learning management system has been an unprecedented challenge to the current distance education of adult students to fully understand the importance of the use of new media, necessity, and through part implementation of process oriented online education information system, which is the student population is widely popular media to develop and strengthen, so as to continuously improve the effectiveness, and improve the quality of personnel training. In this paper, the characteristics of the part implementation of process oriented online education information system, and how to use distance education of students as well as to strengthen the contemporary education.

1 General instruction

Distance education, also known as distance education, which goes beyond the barrier of time and space from the education, its principal means for teaching through television or the Internet and other media teaching as a carrier, which has a formal and traditional education sharp distinction, no longer need to school buildings and classrooms as a student must Venue. Using distance education students generally are not professional student, whose audience is mainly dominated amateur fellows. Because there is no limit class place, so the time and place of the class is not limited. Among the students in the learning process can also be aided learning through a variety of different ways a network, television broadcasting, as well as letter-face class research community and so on. modern distance education in various forms, inherent in distance education as the focus of education at the same time, also need to use a variety of media and a variety of teaching forms of action together, including correspondence and face to face, etc., while the students' self-learning can play a very important role. Modern Distance Education so that it can fully demonstrate the characteristics obtained, the characteristics of its teaching that the mutual separation between teachers and students, there is no form of face to face teaching, the system itself across the barrier between regions and between schools. Characteristics of distance education are: to achieve a mutual separation of teachers and students; and the way their teaching of information transmission can be specified transport system and the media in order to achieve; its method many forms coexist; and the biggest advantage is the freedom of choice Want regional and forms of learning. Distance education than traditional face to face in terms of time and space to break the barrier, and in expanding the teaching area while allowing more people access to the conditions of learning, not only that the process of teaching will greatly reduce the cost of inputs, and also the quality of teaching Contrary rise, not fall.

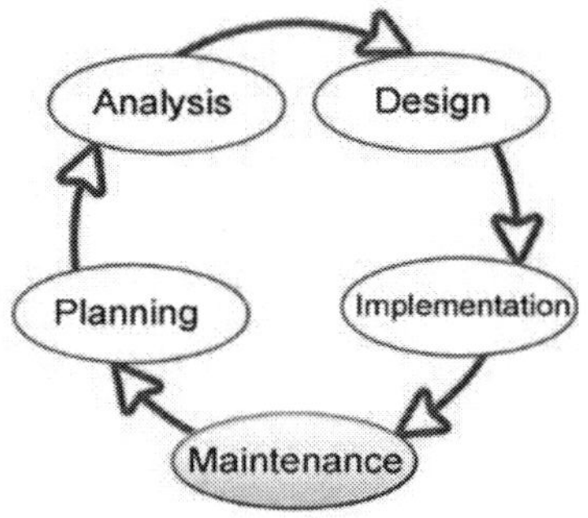

Figure 1. Part implementation of process oriented online education information system

On the development stage of distance education we can draw a conclusion very quickly in the international development of distance education, but this mode of education in our country there is a very large potential for development, to be excavated. The development of modern distance education can be said that the general trend, which is making development more quickly via the Internet as the primary carrier. As early as two thousand years of time, the world has more than one hundred countries have begun using remote education, not only that up to eighty-five percent of the world's institutions of higher learning has its own dedicated website, and in this one the most out of every four homes the school will have a pioneering online education platform as the basis

for the promotion of their programs. Online education in Europe and America because of its network technology development started earliest, and therefore has become the industry leader in today's world; the scale of its development has been relatively grown.

2 Overview of the teaching process theory

Process, from literally is a program of development of things. The teaching is mainly the result of teaching and the pursuit of contrast, it is emphasized that the directivity of learning through the learning process of the guide to make students capable of a wide range of intellectual development, rather than a single process of thinking and the pursuit of thinking not focus on results, the resulting content and the like, such as the ability to solve practical problems is an important part of the process of teaching. To sum up, the students learn to think and grasp of knowledge is the process of teaching, cognitive and generation to respect for the students in the learning process of knowledge, the formation of knowledge system among, will enhance students' personal qualities as the ultimate goal, By the way according to a certain level of education, so that students can learn the process, to understand the link between practice and results, and thus in the process of being realized gain the experience, so that students' learning ability can eventually produce. To implement the process of teaching, teachers must change their ideas, accelerate Teachers' Role, respect cognitive law, respect for the students to explore the process of listening, speaking, reading and writing teaching, fully embodies the principle of the process of teaching. In the design and implementation of online education and the use of online education should also pay attention to when reflected in the teaching process.

Concluding the process of teaching and teaching is a relative term. In the context of teaching, teaching to the conclusion that refers to after repeated demonstration for the public recognition and acceptance of knowledge. Theoretical perspective, the conclusions of the so-called teaching is teaching at the end we hope to achieve. In fact, we have been accustomed to this "know" teaching method, in fact, in terms of the students are hurt. Although reluctant to accept such students, but did not digest, do not know how to digest. People feel dull; students will show conflicting emotions, knowledge and ability to not be able to get the conversion.

The idea is to make the process of teaching students through the teaching and get a new experience that refers to the experience in the exploration and acquisition of new knowledge and experience when new knowledge. Course objectives can be distinguished only with skills, attention to process and methods, attention to emotional attitude values. Here, the goal is not the teaching of the three objectives, but rather refers to the teaching of the three aspects, three-dimensional teaching goal epitomizes the new curriculum "people-oriented" and "development of students," the core idea. Wherein both the process or method, or "attitudes and values" are focusing on experiences and insights as well as changes in the thoughts and feelings of the students on the heart, it can not be conclusive (dominance, precision, specificity, operability) way to measure, both as the "knowledge and skills" corresponding to that part of the process of the target can be referred to.

Realization of objectives depends on the process of teaching, the following from the concept of law teaching; experimental teaching, exercises, data processing and teaching evaluation results highlight the procedural aspects:

1. Concept, law teaching. Students understand new concepts, the need to go through the stage of exploration and research, rather than direct conclusion of indoctrination. A good concept teaching is beginning in the process of establishing the need to invest a lot of time and effort.

2. Experimental teaching. Whether demonstration experiment or design of experiments, guide students to treat the problem of rational thinking, cultivate rational, logical and creative ability of students to deal with things.

3. The data processing. Data processing is an important part of science, and in the course of processing the data it is very meaningful. Experimentally measured data, to enable students to conduct yourself projections and analysis, reflection source link between data and conclusions, workout data processing capabilities of students, have more general data processing methods, a deeper understanding of knowledge, so that it can form a complete set of knowledge architecture system.

4. Exercise teaching. A certain amount of exercise training is essential, it can play through training exercises to consolidate and deepen the concepts and laws of this purely theoretical understanding of knowledge and ability on how to learn and use of knowledge. Exercise training is an important part of moderation, moderation exactly how to do a basic capability through a variety of experiential activities gradually, not overnight, so in the teaching activities must be strengthened and a sufficient amount of exercise training, and in teaching activities should focus on guiding and helping students to create a variety of topics scenarios.

5. The teaching evaluation. Traditional teaching evaluation mainly depends on mastery of the high school students to the book, including the number and depth of knowledge, mainly through the students usually practice, tests, examinations, assignments and classroom answering questions orally to the results of the statistical evaluation of student achievement, such approach ignores its own evaluation of the learner in terms of non-intelligence factors.

3 Systems Business requirements analysis

Zhejiang Pharmaceutical College as a full-time colleges and universities, the traditional mode of education gradually biggest drawbacks: the lack of teacher-student interaction in the classroom, can not effectively assess teaching effectiveness and the like; and real-time remote education when students and faculty ratio disparity when the interaction effects are minimal, but by time, place and existing network hardware and bandwidth constraints conditions, can not be widely used class of non-centralized adult learning scene. System main business work flow chart is as follows:

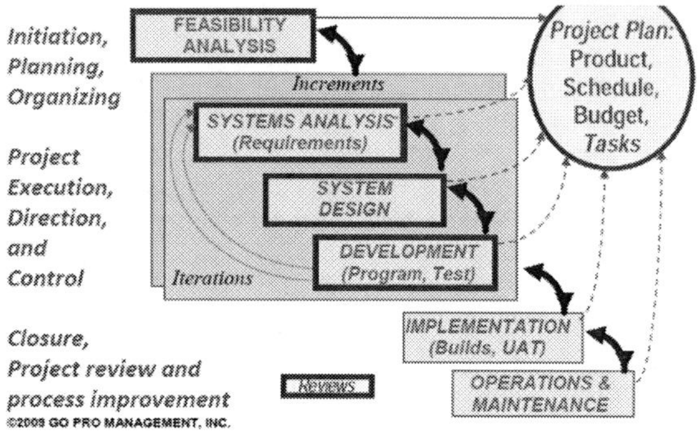

Figure 2. Project management and system development flow chart

Distance Education Information Management System workflow is as follows:

After approval by the administrator login system to learn, or to use an administrator direct the bulk registration. The system provides authorization capabilities course, the students of different major's authorization given to different courses.

Teaching is all aspects of information for maintenance and so on.

Into the teaching information resource library: including multimedia courseware, courseware material, and preparation of the course students may encounter difficult problems and answers Knowledge Learning resources and other inquiries.

Quizzes online classroom exercises, after the end of each lesson finished, completed after-school exercise test, in order to consolidate and test learning outcomes. The module automatically, in real-time scoring, all kinds of questions are used in the form of objective questions.

Online classroom is through online mock examinations system. School exercise test, the students complete a course of study, then arrange online simulation papers, upon request, in accordance with the specific requirements of the custom paper. For the sake of heavy process, light conclusions concept papers may allow students to repeat three times, and will provide the correct answer after each, take three papers of the highest points as the assessment points, simulation answers and exam papers are based on random mode.

Statistics by automatic learning outcomes: to provide fast, real-time statistics and effective learning outcomes. For example, school

When long learning, academic performance and other results.

Students or teachers or students in the class can see your learning progress situation. Flexible student learning plan based on a percentage of their course of study. The teacher will be based on the student's progress, learning the number of academic all-round understanding to facilitate the process of assessment.

Courses are classified according to provide students and teachers teaching answering specific modules, students and the lecturer here to explore more academic problem, the student common questions for everyone to share, thereby reducing the teacher to repeat answering questions, some students do not know Q. What brought the missing communication, interactive reduce the problem. According query statistics teacher student progress and found some learning behind schedule, active students are not learning, flexible to take measures, such as sending text messages or e-mail notification, urging students to learn on the platform. The level of activity will serve as one of the students answering procedural basis for assessment.

4 System design

Process of distance education system network is an important part of it, by helping with the management of the next match, and thus more reliable use of rich materials outside of the relevant disciplines, enabling multi-angle multi-level Modern Distance Education Services. The system is relatively more perfect realization of the combined visible and distance learning, making learning and exchanges between students and teachers to provide a good environment. In the analysis phase, we use object-oriented thinking and teaching methods and tools UML support system is analyzed to determine the logical structure of the system, which will be the basis for system design.

J2EE platform architecture shown on the basis of intelligence there is a further division, including the client tier, Web tier, business logic (Business Logic) layer and data access (Data Access) layer such as four further fine-grained. Among the above-mentioned various levels, the code will be different corresponding compression, and added to the different components which, in the layer and the interaction layer, components and assemblies being among obtained using, in this case the code reusability will be greatly improved. The specific role of each layer is as follows:

Client layer: its underlying application is a Web browser, and by operating in these browsers being used to achieve its purpose and function. Its main role is for the entire interface and data display, and the user can also be achieved by this layer for system maintenance and data entry.

Web layer: This layer is divided into two components being part of JSP and Servile, its core function is the Web among users sees dynamic content generation, which is typically dynamic content from the database through the business layer obtained.

Business logic layer: This layer serves huge, mainly targeted at some complex business logic to address it, most of these issues are separate properties, the layer normal work is mainly based on the conduct of the enterprise bean, its vast Most of logic are stored in the business logic layer (business Logic) in. Of course, the application server (Application Server) can automatically handle many services such as Transaction, Data Base Connection Pool and so on. The business logic is from resource management needs out, help developers to put more focus on how to build up high-quality applications.

Data Access Layer: its role in that database and information for effective control regulation, including a variety of different types of database access program management. The main work is when the business logic layer data access layer data access requests are to be made relevant data query, persistence operations to be supported when cent submit the appropriate data.

MVC (Model View Controller) that is an application depending on the division of labour is divided into three layers - model layer, view layer, control layer, is now more popular, widely used in software development and design patterns. MVC is a design pattern that emphasizes is how to separate the rational model program interface, business process logic. MVC has many advantages; it is widely used in the software industry of design patterns, help software engineering management, etc.

5 Conclusion

Paper based on the theory developed in these process-oriented teaching online teaching information systems for business requirements, functional requirements, performance requirements, security requirements analysis systems for the actual demand, and thus demand for the establishment of a corresponding functional model, given Teaching System use case analysis. System design phase are teaching management, learning management, curriculum management, communication management, system management detailed design shows a functional block diagram and IPO designing forms, ER diagrams and basic database table, and made a number of database optimization. Q through function security access control module, the main module completion process teaching and answering module implementations, and research key technical issues involved. The system uses J2EE + MVC model, the model is based on components, platform-independent system that can run on multiple operating systems such as windows, Linux, Unix, etc., using advanced architecture, ease of maintenance and development, improve efficiency but also to ensure the maintainability of the system security, scalability.

References

1. Maoyuan China popularization of higher education structures and systems. Guangzhou: Guangdong Higher Education Press, 14(2009)
2. Du to Germany, Yaoyuan Feng, Li Xing-Dong Toward Development of Adult Education. Beijing: China Renmin University Press, 267(2007)
3. He Qizong new era of education - theory and practice of lifelong education. Beijing: People's Publishing House, 23(2008)
4. Zhao new study occupational characteristics of the Adult Higher Education - Xiamen five universities, for example the status of implementation of Adult Higher Education. Xiamen University, master's thesis, 251(2007)
5. TURAL multimedia technology on Foreign Language Listening Course of Modern Languages (late), 05 (2006)
6. Feng. Foreign Language Teaching hear the application of multimedia teaching methods. Chinese education technology and equipment, 20, (2008)
7. Chen Zuohong multimedia use Advanced Speaking in Foreign Language Teaching. Research of National Education, 3 (2006)
8. Jiangde Yong. Discussion on the evaluation process implemented in the network education. Nanchang College of Education, 26 (2011)
9. Cai Jianwei. Construction of a new process of teaching evaluation platform. Xiang Chao, 84 (2011)
10. Song Jingyan distance education in the process of learning to guide the design. Business Modernization. 18 (2009)
11. Guo Yan Rui .J2EE and MVC Model in Campus Management System Development Information and Computer (Theory), 2 (2011)

MATEC Web of Conferences **44**, 02074 (2016)
DOI: 10.1051/matecconf/20164402074

Research and Design on Information Service and Management Platform based on Work Integrated Learning Mode

Qi Yuan GAO

Information engineering institute, Jilin Engineering Normal University, Jilin, Changchun 130000, China

Abstract. The work integrated learning mode is the world's more advanced kind of teaching mode, which in many countries have achieved success, but also the rapid development in China. This paper is conscientiously sum of basic school vocational college engineering student management, aimed at the exchange of services and management schools as well as schools, businesses, students communicate among emerging issues were discussed ,proposed information technology services and management, consciously to promote student learning through the application, to improve learning efficiency, can strong the service awareness of schools, businesses for the students , promote school students and the school's teaching, management form a whole, to facilitate the strengthening of students management and strengthen the contact of schools, businesses, students.

1 Introduction

Work integrated learning mode in many developed countries has achieved great success. Germany's "dual system", Australia's "new apprenticeships" in Singapore "teaching factory", South Korea's "Industry Cooperation" and other engineering education model combining the development process description, this teaching model can effectively promote economic development. In the information processing, communications technology is developed today, we explore under work-study combination mode information service approach and management tools, the use of Internet technology, wireless communication system to build a platform for students to learn, life service and help strengthen engineering regulatory alternate process, to make them happy to learn and work, to obtain higher efficiency in engineering [1].

2 Work integrated learning presentation

"Work Integrated Learning" is "theoretical classroom study and participate in social work posts on a combination of" vocational colleges and enterprises "in practice as the basis for school and comprehensive combination of relevant companies jointly established curriculum models and teaching mode, and students receive training model of paid internships. "Work Integrated Learning" vocational education in the" Industry Cooperation "targeted at the operational level of exploration and practice of the process of the concept of the" lower concept Industry Cooperation "is to implement the approach Industry Cooperation [2]. Engineering combine theoretical knowledge of the learning process and combined with practical work process. Students in vocational schools receive a general cultural knowledge, professional theory and technology education and training at the same time, take advantage of school environment and resources (typically corporate sector) to achieve the combination of work and learning, in order to get work experience, improve the overall quality of all aspects, including the students' professional skills.

Corresponding author: gqy1982@126.com

3 Establishment and application of information technology services and management platform

3.1 Information services and management platform

Four elements of engineering are schools, businesses, teachers, students. Engineering projects, these four elements interact and influence each other, establish mechanisms and management information services, combined with the implementation of the teaching mode via engineering, to achieve high-quality culture, skilled personnel [3], llustrates the associated working and learning basic elements is shown in figure 1.

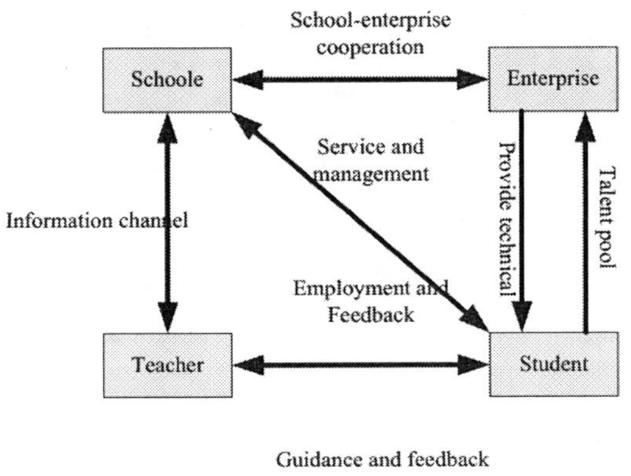

Figure 1.llustrates the associated working and learning basic elements

3.2 Information technology service management based on work integrated learning mode

School based on the actual needs, develop promotional video minutes or so, introduce school situation school, professional settings, superior resources and characteristics, the details can browse the school's website.

Through text or video information is to display business basic outlook, corporate culture, technology, and social services ability.

The most important part of resource information and management information services, in the embodiment of the combination of engineering should detail the time, place, people, jobs, operations and engineering skills, objectives and requirements, it is best to be refined to students before departure from mobilization to work and study Bouquet junction each class every day or what the thousands of teachers and students what to do, every time engineering students which targets must be met. Inform the school in advance to these students and businesses, good communication and coordination, strictly in accordance with the proposed plan for promoting the teaching mode of engineering combined [4].

3.3 Management information platform based on work integrated learning mode

Management information platform based on work integrated learning mode is shown in figure 2

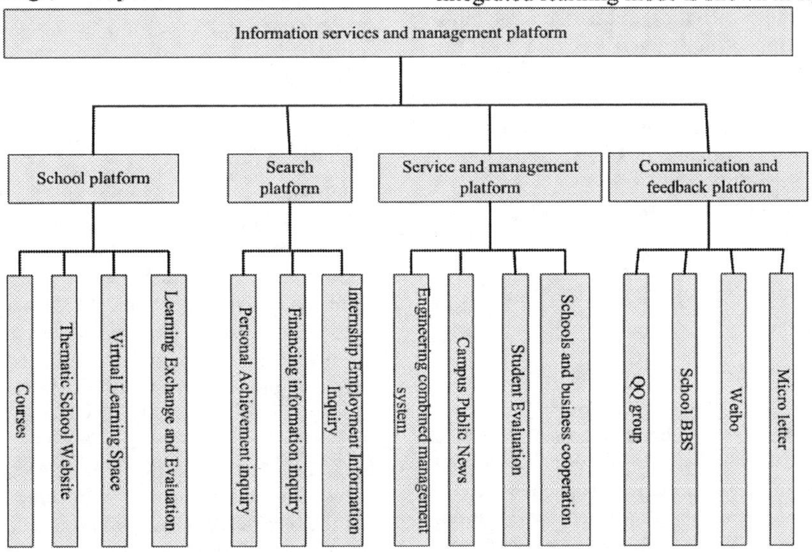

Figure 2. The frame structure and management of information services

4 Function modules and application of information services and management platform based on working integrated learning mode

Students in the teaching mode combination of engineering, because the student is not in school, the school of the student services and management barriers of space and time, must be managed and institutionalized means of information in order to eliminate the use of these effects can be obtained so that off-campus students in the same service, so that they consciously complete the learning task. Information services and management platform function module consists of four parts, each module there are specific content management services and support, to be introduced below [5].

4.1 Learning platform

Engineering work and learning processes are interwoven, mutually reinforcing process, under the guidance of engineering with the implementation of the program carried out. The main purpose is to promote science engineering work, and from work schools, promote students' skills to master. Establishment of a learning platform is assisted learning for students of engineering in more than, including courses, thematic learning website, virtual learning space, learning communication and evaluation.

Courses. Schools can combine engineering needs related to the professional development of quality courses and campus instructional video features to add a learning platform, more than students of engineering study according to their need to log in to complete the online learning platform.

Learning Website. Vocational colleges have their own portal and can easily and docking, which for the construction and application of special learning website provides a basis. By web form creating thematic network courseware, thematic resource library, thematic learning application tools, thematic learning assessment to the combination of engineering students to provide a large number of thematic learning resources and collaborative learning communication tools to make their own choices and determine the research or project design, own collection, analyze and select information, apply knowledge to solve practical problems.

Virtual learning space. On the computer network constructed using multimedia communications technology learning environment that allows teachers and students living in different places were most teaching activities. Classroom through the network, the "teaching" and "learning" environment integrated with the organization of teaching activities, online lectures, online solutions, real-time video-on-demand teaching, real-time video broadcast teaching, virtual classroom teaching monitoring, multimedia lesson planning and teaching, individualized multimedia interactive learning, synchronous tutoring, synchronous test, difficult to resolve, discuss distance learning.

Learning exchanges and evaluation. Most of the students work and study are not very clear effect of learning from the school requires much difference between students, between students and teachers, exchange training instructors and school teachers.

4.2 Query platform

Individual query results. Students landing based on personal accounts and passwords school Educational system, query subjects or printed result slips credits circumstances, be aware of learning outcomes. Funding information inquiry. While developing countries, vocational education, the introduction of a number of national student financial aid system, including a variety of ways the National Student Financial Aid scholarships, state grants, government scholarships, motivational scholarships, school scholarships. School funding information will be publicized on a regular basis, the information platform for the students concerned by querying get. internships, employment information inquiry. Employment of students in private practice at the school is very concerned about the employment information released at this stage of internships environment if not satisfied, the individual application, parental consent, after the audit report faculties school career center to reschedule new employment of internships. For the independent careers of students, the unit now dissatisfied with school there are new employment units, you can also apply for school employment recommendation. School faculty instructor authorized to inquire into this department students internships and employment status, be well aware of the whereabouts and status of each student in the school, which greatly facilitates the management of student services.

4.3 Service and management platform

During working and learning, authorities school-enterprise cooperation must be based on the relevant provisions of the necessary checks and supervision, strict examination, and to solve the problem; in order to do a good job assessing students' engineering by academic departments to develop a unified "student of engineering work in conjunction internship training assessment identification Form ", led the teachers, training instructors and business-related personnel jointly responsible for completing the assessment. Conscientiously sum up and exchange on the basis of appraisal of the work of outstanding achievements instructors, students and other concerned personnel to recognize and reward; school regularly held by the enterprise, students and parents representatives to participate in work and study experience exchange and summary We will exchange information and further promote cooperation between university and efficacy results of its work.

4.4 Communication and feedback platform

Each student has a number of teachers in the future to create engineering services group, requires that each student must be added to this group. Teachers or students can make an announcement by the group of functions, informing, various exchanges, data or file transfer. On the one hand provide for student learning life services and help the other hand, teachers and students can learn the latest information available to the other person, through point to point, point opposite the face information exchange points, to reach the student management purposes, Even if students are not online, when students have time landing can also receive the information sent by the teacher or other students, very convenient to use.

Campus BBS- like just for the university's students to build self-management by the student network system for student speech to provide information platform. Typically used to publish news, notice or announcement, also often used as chatting purposes. With the rapid development of university networks, it has become an important part of campus culture indispensable.

Micro blogging is a relationship based on user information sharing, dissemination and access platform, users can, as well as various individual components of the client community, word about text updates, and instant sharing.

AC micro message appears between people has even reached the point where more convenient. Between students and teachers can communicate with each other through the micro timely letter, to share their experiences with each other and the joy of success.

5 Information services and management practices based on working integrated learning

5.1 Factors Affecting information services and management

Combination of engineering management students, the school has a good plan for a student to leave the school, it is very difficult to implement. The use of information way for students to provide services and management, information platform builders professionalism, student consciousness and initiative put forward a very high demand.

One student factors, information services and implementation of management functions must be based on the premise of the system, so that students take the initiative to access to services and management platform for information browsing and communication, and has put forward various problems that exist in project engineering, are fed back to the instructors, schools, businesses, parties must promptly solve student problems reflected. Information services and requires students to actively manage the problems, difficulties, ideas through the platform to inform schools, school students through the coordination of the issues of concern solved, there is no reason students do not learn.

Second, the teacher factor, information services and management process, the teacher's role is to guide, managers, service providers. Before engineering, teachers need to spend a lot of time and detailed understanding of each student's basic information, work also responsible for student attendance, counseling, ideological and political education, performance assessment and evaluation of students' daily transaction processing and other work.

Three part-time technical factors counseling staff, part-time technical school counselors hired in engineering process of the students and on-site training guidance counseling, student mastery of skills primarily by their assessment and evaluation.

5.2 Role of Information Technology Services and Management

Students are the main target of school work, information technology services and management is based on the purpose of educating people at the school to take a modern way of working. Especially for students to work and study, they themselves not in school, the school has duty-bound to provide necessary assistance for their learning process, working process, the process of life, but also the use of school rules to constrain their behavior, we must implement them information technology services and management. On the one hand extended school services and management functions. Combined engineering is an important part of higher vocational teaching institutions, in this part of providing good service and management for students, to help them acquire practical skills, the successful completion of their studies. Information services and management in the benign effects of people, goods, mechanisms will form school-enterprise conspiracy, both inside and outside, all-round, multi-level service pattern.

5.3 Significance and Management Information Services

Reflect student learning initiative and efficiency. Information services and management using the restraint system and incentives to promote student initiative to acquire resource information and assistance through the platform, to keep their own learning conditions and teachers, parents, students evaluate their own learning, so that the learning process, stage learning outcomes idea.

It reflects the teaching of information management and systematic. All engineering data were transmitted, communication, storage through information technology platform. Teaching, the students do, what needs to reach a daily target requirements; instructor how to do it, to observe the state of student learning every day and do a good job guidance and records, combining learning with working embodiments are clearly defined.

Learning Assessment reflect institutionalized and impartiality of. Learning evaluation mechanisms and management of information services is the evaluation stage, after the end of a learning unit, automatically generated by the system based on feedback from objective data. After all the school units completed form summative evaluation.

6. Conclusions

Implementation of information services and management, teaching students to vocational colleges of engineering, management, service can play a certain role. In future studies, as the school-enterprise cooperation and work-study combination to change the teaching mode, schools, businesses and services to students and management will also change accordingly, management platform for application modules will be more refined, in order to truly improve teaching and management efficiency.

References

1. Zh.Q.Zhao. Understanding of some basic concepts combining engineering courses ,China Vocational and Technical Education (2008).
2. J.Zhu, Z.G.Wang. Curriculum Reform and Practice of Engineering combined mode study,Vocational Technical Institute . (2009).
3. L.ZH. Li. Engineering Practice binding mode, in vocational students vocational skills training, Sichuan Normal University . (2010).
4. T.Cheng. Vocational Campus Culture Construction Engineering Research binding mode,Hunan University . (2011).
5. J.Y.Qiu. Work-study Combination Mode Vocational School Ideological and Political Education Research ,Huaqiao University . (2014).

MATEC Web of Conferences 44, 02075 (2016)
DOI: 10.1051/matecconf/20164402075

Kinematic Analysis of a 3-dof Parallel Machine Tool with Large Workspace

Yan Shi[1, 2, a], Yan Gao[3] and Lian He Guo[4]

[1] Department of Power Engineering, Hebei Institute of Hydraulic and Electric Engineering, Cangzhou, Hebei 061001, China
[2] Water Resources Automation and Informatization Application Technology Research and Development Center of Hebei, Cangzhou, Hebei 061001, China
[3] College of Astronautics, Harbin Institute of Technology, Harbin, Heilongjiang 150000, China
[4] Unit 95927 of the PLA, Cangzhou, Hebei 061736, China

Abstract. Kinematics of a 3-dof (degree of freedom) parallel machine tool with large workspace was analyzed. The workspace volume and surface and boundary posture angles of the 3-dof parallel machine tool are relatively large. Firstly, three dimensional simulation manipulator of the 3-dof parallel machine tool was constructed, and its joint distribution was described. Secondly, kinematic models of the 3-dof parallel machine tool were fixed on, including displacement analysis, velocity analysis, and acceleration analysis. Finally, the kinematic models of the machine tool were verified by a numerical example. The study result has an important significance to the application of the parallel machine tool.

1 Introduction

Recently, parallel machine tools with limited degrees of freedom (DoF) are widely applied in many situations[1], and lots of scholars carry out research about various parallel machine tools with limited DoF. Among them, parallel machine tools with three degrees of freedom especially the 3-SPR parallel machine tool including spherical joint, prismatic joint, and revolute joint attract more attentions[2-4]. For 3-SPR parallel machine tool has less limbs, and its structure is simpler and it can be controlled more easily, it has a great application potential on many occasions no need for six degrees of freedom.

Workspace is an important influencing factor of parallel machine tool performance, it is also one of research focuses of parallel manipulator[5-7]. Determination of joint distribution among parallel machine tools with the same structure is specially important, which makes relatively larger workspace. The influence of revolute joint posture to the parallel machine tool performance about 3-SPR parallel machine tool is discussed in reference [8], and two optimum revolute joint postures were derived. On the basis of the above research, a machine tool with optimized joints is chosen as the research object, and its kinematic characteristic is mainly discussed, which lays a foundation for the application of the optimized manipulator.

2 Introduction of the manipulator

The 3-SPR manipulator is composed of a moving platform, a fixed platform and three driving limbs. The moving platform and the fixed platform are both equilateral triangle. The three driving limbs have the same structure, and from the bottom to the above is spherical joint, prismatic joint and revolute joint successively. In each limb, the prismatic joint is the driving limb. When the force from the motor is acted on the prismatic joint, the moving platform begins to move. The difference among the three driving limbs is the vector direction of the revolute joint axis. The research result shows that when axes of the three revolute joints intersect on the central point of the moving platform, the volume and the surface and the boundary posture of the manipulator are relatively larger[5]. The 3-SPR parallel manipulator studied in this paper is the above mentioned manipulator that the joint distribution is optimized. The three dimensional entity manipulator is shown as Fig. 1, and the revolute joint distribution of the moving platform is shown as Fig. 2. In Fig. 1, $A_1A_2A_3$ is the fixed platform equilateral triangle, and $a_1a_2a_3$ is the moving platform equilateral triangle. In Fig. 2, $\boldsymbol{R}_1$、$\boldsymbol{R}_2$、$\boldsymbol{R}_3$ represent the direction of the revolute vector on points a_1, a_2, a_3, the angle between which and x axis of the moving platform is 150°、90°、30°, respectively.

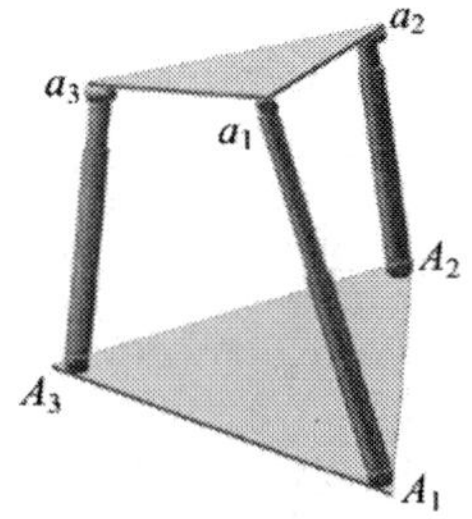

Figure 1. Three dimensional entity manipulator of 3-SPR parallel machine tool

[a] shiyanysu@163.com

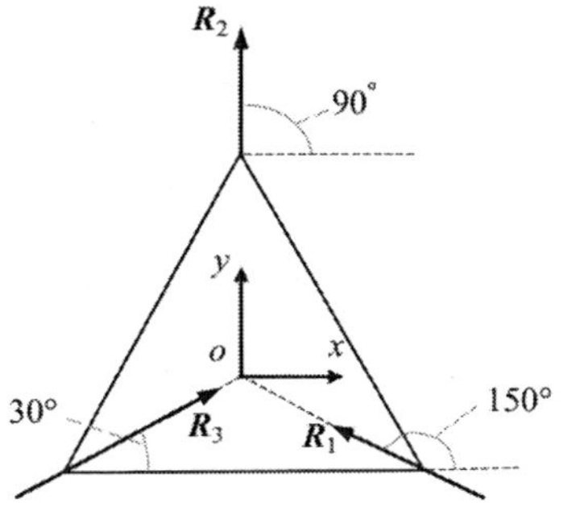

Figure 2. Revolute joint distribution of the moving platform

3 Kinematic analysis of the manipulator

3.1 Displacement analysis

Let *O-XYZ* represent the coordinate of the fixed platform, *o-xyz* represent the coordinate of the moving platform, and X_o, Y_o, Z_o represent the projection of the central point of the moving platform *o* on the fixed platform, respectively. Use *XZX* Eular angle to express the rotational matrix R_u^L, that is, the angle that the moving platform rotates around the *X* axis, the Z_1 axis and the X_2 axis is α, β, γ, respectively. Among them, Z_1 axis and X_2 axis represent the coordinate axis of the middle coordinate when the moving platform rotates for the first time and the second time, respectively. Then, R_u^L can be expressed as

$$\mathbf{R}_u^L = \begin{bmatrix} c\beta & -s\beta\cdot c\gamma & s\beta\cdot s\gamma \\ c\alpha\cdot s\beta & -s\alpha\cdot s\gamma + c\alpha\cdot c\beta\cdot c\gamma & -c\alpha\cdot c\beta\cdot s\gamma - s\alpha\cdot c\gamma \\ s\alpha\cdot s\beta & s\alpha\cdot c\beta\cdot c\gamma + c\alpha\cdot s\gamma & c\alpha\cdot c\gamma - s\alpha\cdot c\beta\cdot s\gamma \end{bmatrix} = \begin{bmatrix} x_l & y_l & z_l \\ x_m & y_m & z_m \\ x_n & y_n & z_n \end{bmatrix} \tag{1}$$

Where, *s* represents sin, *c* represents cos. It is same in the following sections.

To the studied parallel manipulator, there are the following constraint relations among variables[5]

$$\sqrt{3}\,P-Q+2e+E(\sqrt{3}\,x_m-3x_l+\sqrt{3}\,y_l-y_m)/2=0 \tag{2}$$

$$Q+e-Ey_m=0 \tag{3}$$

$$\sqrt{3}\,P+Q-2e+E(\sqrt{3}\,x_m+3x_l+\sqrt{3}\,y_l+y_m)/2=0 \tag{4}$$

Where, $P=X_ox_l+Y_ox_m+Z_ox_n$, $Q=X_oy_l+Y_oy_m+Z_oy_n$. *E* and *e* represent the circumradius of the fixed platform and the moving platform equilateral triangle, respectively. From Eq. (2) and Eq. (4), it can be derived

$$2P+E(x_m+y_l)=0 \tag{5}$$

$$2Q-4e+E(3x_l+y_m)=0 \tag{6}$$

From Eq. (3) and Eq. (6), it can be derived

$$2e-E(x_l+y_m)=0 \tag{7}$$

Substitute Eq. (1) to Eq. (3), Eq. (5) and Eq. (7), respectively, the relations between the three translational variables of the central point X_o, Y_o, Z_o and the three rotational variables of the moving platform α, β, γ can be derived

$$\begin{aligned} &-X_os\beta\cdot c\gamma+(Y_o-E)(-s\alpha\cdot s\gamma+c\alpha\cdot c\beta\cdot c\gamma)+ \\ &Z_o(s\alpha\cdot c\beta\cdot c\gamma+c\alpha\cdot s\gamma)+e=0; \\ &2X_oc\beta+(2Y_o+E)c\alpha\cdot s\beta+2Z_os\alpha\cdot s\beta-Es\beta\cdot c\gamma=0; \\ &2e-E(c\beta-s\alpha\cdot s\gamma+c\alpha\cdot c\beta\cdot c\gamma)=0 \end{aligned} \tag{8}$$

For the manipulator has three degrees of freedom, there are three independent output variables for the manipulator. Choose one translational variable X_o and two rotational variables α, γ as independent output variables, then the relation between the other two translational variables Y_o, Z_o and one rotational variable β and the independent output variables can be expressed as

$$\begin{aligned} &\beta=\arccos K; \\ &Y_o=[(3Kc\alpha\cdot c\gamma-2s\alpha\cdot s\gamma-K^2c^2\gamma)E+2X_oK(Kc\gamma+\cot\alpha\cdot s\gamma)/ \\ &\sqrt{1-K^2}+2X_o\sqrt{1-K^2}c\gamma-2e]/[s\gamma(c\alpha\cdot\cot\alpha-2s\alpha)]; \\ &Z_o=[Ec\gamma-(2Y_o+E)c\alpha]/(2s\alpha)-X_oK/(\sqrt{1-K^2}s\alpha) \end{aligned} \tag{9}$$

Where, $K=[(2e/E+s\alpha\cdot s\gamma)/(1+c\alpha\cdot c\gamma)]$.

The driving limb length of the manipulator can be expressed as

$$\begin{aligned} &r_1^2={X_o}^2+{Y_o}^2+{Z_o}^2+E^2+e^2-qEX_o+EY_o+qeP-eQ+ \\ &Ee(qy_l-3x_l+qx_m-y_m)/2; \\ &r_2^2={X_o}^2+(Y_o-E)^2+{Z_o}^2+e^2-2Eey_m+2eQ; \\ &r_3^2={X_o}^2+{Y_o}^2+{Z_o}^2+E^2+e^2+qEX_o+EY_o-qeP-eQ- \\ &Ee(qy_l+3x_l+qx_m+y_m)/2 \end{aligned} \tag{10}$$

When (X_o, α, γ) is known, the driving limb length can be derived from Eq. (1), Eq. (9) and Eq. (10).

3.2 Velocity analysis

The linear velocity of the central point of the moving platform *o* can be expressed as

$$\boldsymbol{v}=\begin{bmatrix} \dot{X}_o \\ \dot{Y}_o \\ \dot{Z}_o \end{bmatrix}=\begin{bmatrix} \partial X_o/\partial X_o & \partial X_o/\partial\alpha & \partial X_o/\partial\gamma \\ \partial Y_o/\partial X_o & \partial Y_o/\partial\alpha & \partial Y_o/\partial\gamma \\ \partial Z_o/\partial X_o & \partial Z_o/\partial\alpha & \partial Z_o/\partial\gamma \end{bmatrix}\begin{bmatrix} \dot{X}_o \\ \dot{\alpha} \\ \dot{\gamma} \end{bmatrix}=\mathbf{J}_v\boldsymbol{v}_e \tag{11}$$

Where, $\mathbf{J}_v$ represents the traslational Jacobian matrix of the manipulator[10].

When *XZX* Eular angle is adopted, the angular velocity of the moving platform can be expressed as

$$\boldsymbol{\omega}=\boldsymbol{X}\dot{\alpha}+\boldsymbol{Z}_1\dot{\beta}+\boldsymbol{x}\dot{\gamma}$$

Where,

$$\boldsymbol{Z}_1=R(X,\alpha)[0\ \ 0\ \ 1]^T=[0\ \ -s\alpha\ \ c\alpha]^T,$$

$$\boldsymbol{x}=[x_l\ \ x_m\ \ x_n]^T=[c\beta\ \ c\alpha\cdot s\beta\ \ s\alpha\cdot s\beta]^T$$

$$\begin{aligned} \boldsymbol{\omega}&=\begin{bmatrix} 1 & 0 & c\beta \\ 0 & -s\alpha & c\alpha\cdot s\beta \\ 0 & c\alpha & s\alpha\cdot s\beta \end{bmatrix}\begin{bmatrix} \dot{\alpha} \\ \dot{\beta} \\ \dot{\gamma} \end{bmatrix}= \\ &\begin{bmatrix} 1 & 0 & c\beta \\ 0 & -s\alpha & c\alpha\cdot s\beta \\ 0 & c\alpha & s\alpha\cdot s\beta \end{bmatrix}\begin{bmatrix} \partial\alpha/\partial X_o & \partial\alpha/\partial\alpha & \partial\alpha/\partial\gamma \\ \partial\beta/\partial X_o & \partial\beta/\partial\alpha & \partial\beta/\partial\gamma \\ \partial\gamma/\partial X_o & \partial\gamma/\partial\alpha & \partial\gamma/\partial\gamma \end{bmatrix}\begin{bmatrix} \dot{X}_o \\ \dot{\alpha} \\ \dot{\gamma} \end{bmatrix} \\ &=\begin{bmatrix} 1 & 0 & c\beta \\ 0 & -s\alpha & c\alpha\cdot s\beta \\ 0 & c\alpha & s\alpha\cdot s\beta \end{bmatrix}\begin{bmatrix} 0 & 1 & 0 \\ \partial\beta/\partial X_o & \partial\beta/\partial\alpha & \partial\beta/\partial\gamma \\ 0 & 0 & 1 \end{bmatrix}\begin{bmatrix} \dot{X}_o \\ \dot{\alpha} \\ \dot{\gamma} \end{bmatrix} \\ &=\mathbf{J}_\omega\boldsymbol{v}_e \end{aligned} \tag{12}$$

Where, $\mathbf{J}_\omega$ represents the rotational Jacobian matrix of the manipulator[10].

The velocity of the driving limb can be expressed as

$$\boldsymbol{v}_r = [\dot{r}_1 \quad \dot{r}_2 \quad \dot{r}_3]^T = \begin{bmatrix} \boldsymbol{\delta}_1^T & (\boldsymbol{e}_1 \times \boldsymbol{\delta}_1)^T \\ \boldsymbol{\delta}_2^T & (\boldsymbol{e}_2 \times \boldsymbol{\delta}_2)^T \\ \boldsymbol{\delta}_3^T & (\boldsymbol{e}_3 \times \boldsymbol{\delta}_3)^T \end{bmatrix}_{3\times6} \begin{bmatrix} \boldsymbol{v} \\ \boldsymbol{\omega} \end{bmatrix} \quad (13)$$

Where, $\boldsymbol{e}_i$ represents the vector from the central point to the vertex of the moving platform, $\boldsymbol{\delta}_i$ represents the unit vector of the moving platform (i =1, 2, 3). When (X_o, α, γ) and ($\dot{X}_o$、$\dot{\alpha}$、$\dot{\gamma}$) are known, the velocity of the driving limbs can be derived from Eq. (11) to Eq. (13).

3.3 Acceleration analysis

The acceleration of the driving limbs can be expressed as

$$\boldsymbol{a}_r = \begin{bmatrix} \ddot{r}_1 \\ \ddot{r}_2 \\ \ddot{r}_3 \end{bmatrix} = \begin{bmatrix} \boldsymbol{\delta}_1^T & (\boldsymbol{e}_1 \times \boldsymbol{\delta}_1)^T \\ \boldsymbol{\delta}_2^T & (\boldsymbol{e}_2 \times \boldsymbol{\delta}_2)^T \\ \boldsymbol{\delta}_3^T & (\boldsymbol{e}_3 \times \boldsymbol{\delta}_3)^T \end{bmatrix}_{3\times6} \boldsymbol{A} + \boldsymbol{V}^T \begin{bmatrix} \boldsymbol{H}_1 \\ \boldsymbol{H}_2 \\ \boldsymbol{H}_3 \end{bmatrix} \boldsymbol{V} \quad (14)$$

Where, $\boldsymbol{A} = [\boldsymbol{a} \quad \boldsymbol{\varepsilon}]^T$, $\boldsymbol{a} = [a_x \quad a_y \quad a_z]^T$ represents the linear acceleration of the central point of the moving platform, $\boldsymbol{\varepsilon} = [\varepsilon_x \quad \varepsilon_y \quad \varepsilon_z]^T$ represents the angular acceleration of the moving platform, and $\boldsymbol{V} = [\boldsymbol{v} \quad \boldsymbol{\omega}]^T$, $\boldsymbol{v} = [v_x \quad v_y \quad v_z]^T$ represents the linear velocity of the central point of the moving platform, $\boldsymbol{\omega} = [\omega_x \quad \omega_y \quad \omega_z]^T$ represents the angular velocity of the moving platform.

$$\boldsymbol{H}_i = \frac{1}{r_i}\begin{bmatrix} \boldsymbol{E}_{3\times3} & -\hat{\boldsymbol{e}}_i \\ \hat{\boldsymbol{e}}_i & -\hat{\boldsymbol{e}}_i^2 \end{bmatrix}_{6\times6} - \frac{1}{r_i}\begin{bmatrix} \boldsymbol{\delta}_i \\ \boldsymbol{e}_i \times \boldsymbol{\delta}_i \end{bmatrix}\begin{bmatrix} \boldsymbol{\delta}_i^T & (\boldsymbol{e}_i \times \boldsymbol{\delta}_i)^T \end{bmatrix} + \begin{bmatrix} \boldsymbol{0}_{3\times3} & \boldsymbol{0}_{3\times3} \\ \boldsymbol{0}_{3\times3} & \hat{\boldsymbol{e}}_i \hat{\boldsymbol{\delta}}_i \end{bmatrix}_{6\times6}, \quad (i = 1,\ 2,\ 3) \quad (15)$$

$$\hat{\boldsymbol{e}}_i = \begin{bmatrix} 0 & -e_{iz} & e_{iy} \\ e_{iz} & 0 & -e_{ix} \\ -e_{iy} & e_{ix} & 0 \end{bmatrix}, \quad \hat{\boldsymbol{\delta}}_i = \begin{bmatrix} 0 & -\delta_{iz} & \delta_{iy} \\ \delta_{iz} & 0 & -\delta_{ix} \\ -\delta_{iy} & \delta_{ix} & 0 \end{bmatrix}$$

The relation of the acceleration of the moving platform $\boldsymbol{A}$ and the acceleration of the independent variables ($\ddot{X}_o$、$\ddot{\alpha}$、$\ddot{\gamma}$) can be expressed as

$$\boldsymbol{A} = \begin{bmatrix} \boldsymbol{J}_v \\ \boldsymbol{J}_\omega \end{bmatrix}\begin{bmatrix} \ddot{X}_o \\ \ddot{\alpha} \\ \ddot{\gamma} \end{bmatrix} + \begin{bmatrix} \dot{X}_o & \dot{\alpha} & \dot{\gamma} \end{bmatrix}^T \begin{bmatrix} \boldsymbol{H}_v \\ \boldsymbol{H}_\omega \end{bmatrix}\begin{bmatrix} \dot{X}_o \\ \dot{\alpha} \\ \dot{\gamma} \end{bmatrix} \quad (16)$$

$$\boldsymbol{H}_{vi} = \begin{bmatrix} \partial \boldsymbol{J}_{vi1}/\partial X_o & \partial \boldsymbol{J}_{vi2}/\partial X_o & \partial \boldsymbol{J}_{vi3}/\partial X_o \\ \partial \boldsymbol{J}_{vi1}/\partial \alpha & \partial \boldsymbol{J}_{vi2}/\partial \alpha & \partial \boldsymbol{J}_{vi3}/\partial \alpha \\ \partial \boldsymbol{J}_{vi1}/\partial \gamma & \partial \boldsymbol{J}_{vi2}/\partial \gamma & \partial \boldsymbol{J}_{vi3}/\partial \gamma \end{bmatrix},$$

Where, $$\boldsymbol{H}_{\omega i} = \begin{bmatrix} \partial \boldsymbol{J}_{\omega i1}/\partial X_o & \partial \boldsymbol{J}_{\omega i2}/\partial X_o & \partial \boldsymbol{J}_{\omega i3}/\partial X_o \\ \partial \boldsymbol{J}_{\omega i1}/\partial \alpha & \partial \boldsymbol{J}_{\omega i2}/\partial \alpha & \partial \boldsymbol{J}_{\omega i3}/\partial \alpha \\ \partial \boldsymbol{J}_{\omega i1}/\partial \gamma & \partial \boldsymbol{J}_{\omega i2}/\partial \gamma & \partial \boldsymbol{J}_{\omega i3}/\partial \gamma \end{bmatrix}$$

$(i = 1,\ 2,\ 3)$

When (X_o, α, γ), ($\dot{X}_o$、$\dot{\alpha}$、$\dot{\gamma}$) and ($\ddot{X}_o$、$\ddot{\alpha}$、$\ddot{\gamma}$) are known, the acceleration of the driving limbs can be derived from Eq. (16) to Eq. (18).

4 Numerical experiment

Suppose the side length of the moving platform equilateral triangle is 50cm, the side length of the fixed platform equilateral triangle is 100cm, and the initial displacement of the independent output variables X_{os}=10cm, α_s= -5°, γ_s= 15°, the initial velocity of the independent output variables v_{Xos}=1cm/s, v_{as}= -0.5°/s, $v_{\gamma s}$= 0.2°/s, the initial acceleration of the independent output variables a_{Xos}=0.1cm/s², a_{as}= -0.01°/s², $a_{\gamma s}$= 0.01°/s².

Under the above conditions, the velocity of the moving platform is shown as Fig. 3, and the linear velocity of the central point of the moving platform is shown as Fig. 3a, the angular velocity of the moving platform is shown as Fig. 3b. The acceleration of the moving platform is shown as Fig. 4, and the linear acceleration of the central point of the moving platform is shown as Fig. 4a, the angular acceleration of the moving platform is shown as Fig. 4b. The kinematic solving results are shown as Fig. 5, and the displacement curve of the driving limbs is shown as Fig. 5a, the velocity curve of the driving limbs is shown as Fig. 5b, the acceleration curve of the driving limbs is shown as Fig. 5c.

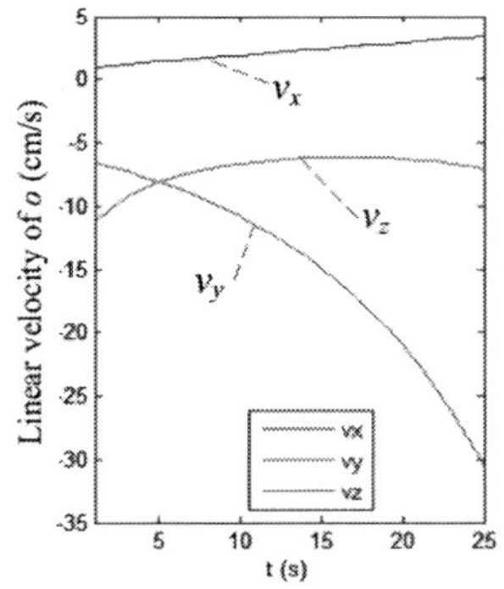

Figure 3a. Linear velocity of the central point of the moving platform

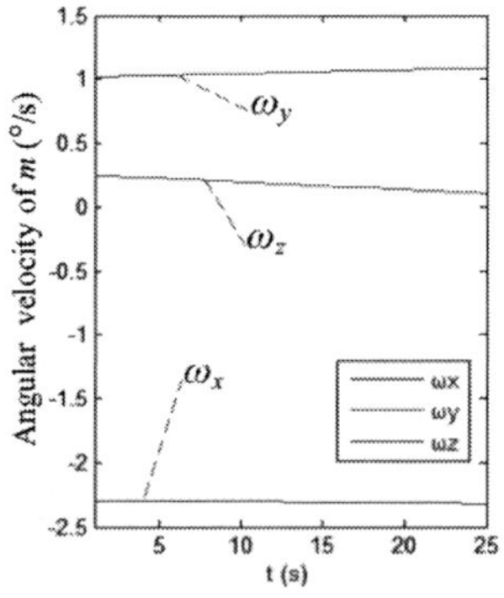

Figure 3b. Angular velocity of the moving platform

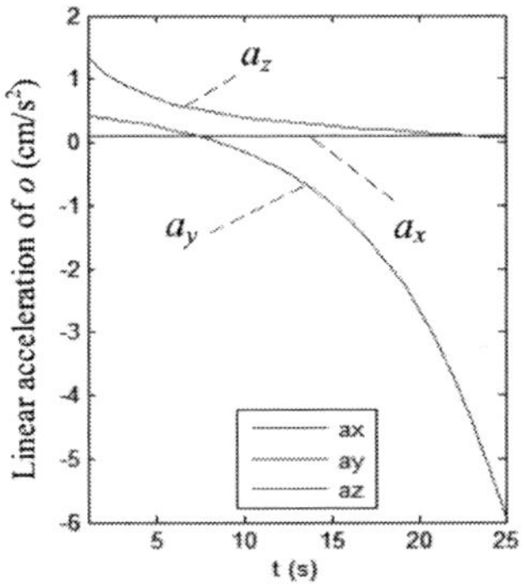

Figure 4a. Linear acceleration of the central point of the moving platform

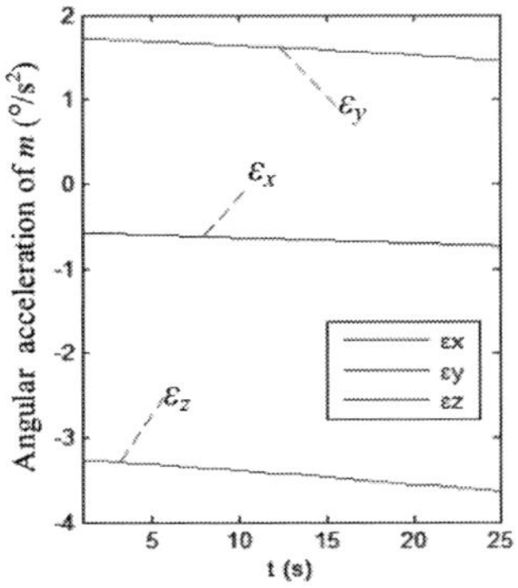

Figure 4b. Angular acceleration of the moving platform

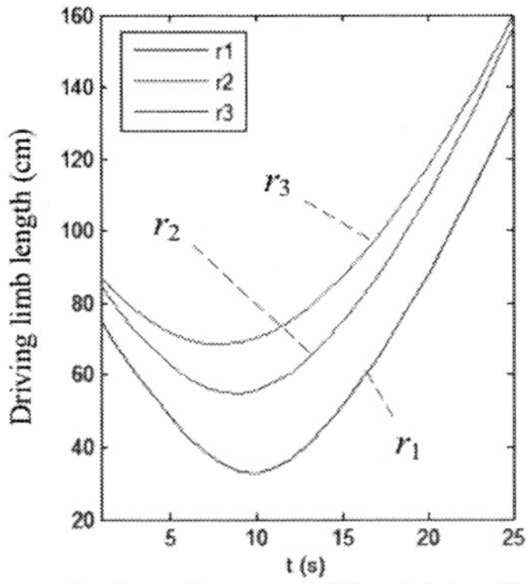

Figure 5a. Length curve of the driving limbs

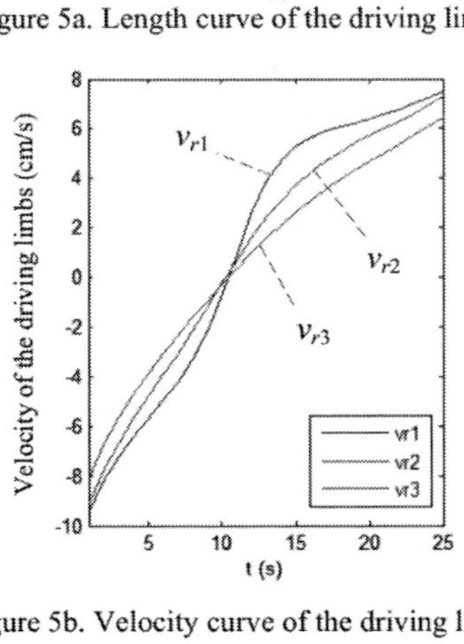

Figure 5b. Velocity curve of the driving limbs

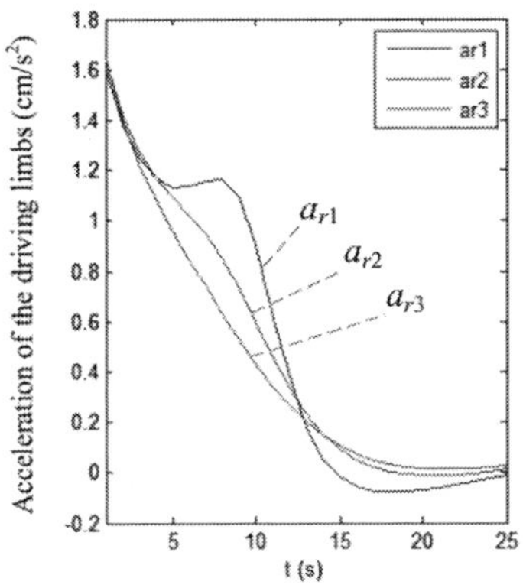

Figure 5c. Acceleration curve of the driving limbs

5 Conclusion

For the 3-SPR parallel manipulator, when axes of the three revolute joints intersect on the central point of the moving platform, the volume and the surface and the boundary posture of the manipulator are not only relatively larger, the kinematic model is also not complex. Therefore, the 3-SPR parallel manipulator with this joint distribution has more practical value. The constructed kinematic model lays the foundation for the statics, dynamics and stiffness analysis of this parallel machine tool, it also provides the instruction for the displacement control, velocity control and acceleration control during the application of the parallel machine tool.

Acknowledgement

This research was financially supported by Higher Education Institution Science and Technology Research Project of Hebei Province (QN2015158).

References

1. Y. Lu, B. Hu. Development evaluation of limited-DOF parallel manipulators [J]. Journal of Yanshan University, 2011, 35(5): 377-384.
2. N. M. Rao, K. M. Rao. Multi-position dimensional synthesis of a spatial 3-RPS parallel manipulator [J]. ASME Journal of Mechanical Design, 2006, 128(4): 815-819.
3. X. J. Liu, J. S. Wang, G. Pritschow. A new family of spatial 3-DoF fully-parallel manipulators with high rotational capability [J]. Mechanism and Machine Theory, 2005, 40(4): 475-494.
4. R. Sellaouti, F. B. Ouezdou. Design and control of a 3DOFs parallel actuated mechanism for biped application [J]. Mechanism and Machine Theory, 2005, 40(12): 1367-1393.
5. X. P. Hu, B. Li, W. S. Zhao. Research on workspace analysis of a 3-PRS-PP based parallel kinematic machine [J]. Combined Machine Tool and Automatic Machining Technology, 2005, (5):12-13.
6. Y. Lu, Y. Shi, B. Hu. Solving Reachable Workspace of Some Parallel Manipulators by CAD Variation Geometry [J]. Proceedings of the Institution of

Mechanical Engineers, Part C, Journal of Mechanical Engineering Science, 2008, 222(9):1773-1781

7. H. Li, Y. R. Zhang, D. X. Wang. Comparative analysis of optimization algorithms in workspace optimization of parallel mechanisms [J]. Journal of Mechanical Engineering, 2010, 46(13): 61-67.
8. Y. Shi, Y. Lu. Analysis about workspace of 3-SPR parallel manipulator influenced by the joints' distribution [J]. Journal of Yanshan University, 2008, 32(4): 304-310.
9. Z. Huang, Y. S. Zhao, T. S. Zhao. Advanced Spatial Mechanism [M]. Beijing: Higher Education Press, 2006: 119.
10. Y. Lu, Y. Shi, J. P. Yu. Kinematic analysis of limited-DOF parallel manipulators based on translational/rotational Jacobian and Hessian Matrices [J]. Robotica, 2009, 27(7): 971-980.

MATEC Web of Conferences **44**, 02076 (2016)
DOI: 10.1051/matecconf/20164402076

Study on the Development of Industry of Internet of Things Based on Competitive GEM Model in Fujian Province

Jun An Di[1,a], Hao Li [2,b]

[1] Department of Electronic Information Engineering, Minjiang University, Fuzhou, Fujian China 350121
[2] Straits Institute, Minjiang University, Fuzhou, Fujian China 350121

Abstract. Firstly, the basic theories of internet of things, competitive GEM model and industrial development in Fujian Province were studied in this paper. Then, the factors influencing the cultivation of industrial competitiveness of the internet of things was observed and finally the suggestions on enhancing the competitiveness of internet of things and strengthening the cultivation of talents of internet of things were put forward.

Key words:. internet of things, industrial development, Fujian, GEM model

I. Current Situations of the Development of Internet of Things in Fujian Province

As the third tide of the world information technology reform after the computer, internet and mobile communication networks, the internet of things has been included in national strategic emerging industries and begun to take shape. For example, Fujian Province has a basically completed industrial chain in sensor, network transmission and data processing and lots of enterprises with national advanced product R&D and application promotion appear in some field. According to the preliminary statistics, the annual sales revenue of the industry of internet of things was about RMB 10 billion Yuan in 2014, of which the revenue from sensor was RMB 2 billion Yuan, the revenue from transmission network was RMB 1 billion Yuan and the revenue from application software and system integration was RMB 7 billion Yuan. So far there have been more than 100 institutions and enterprises working on R&D, production, application and service of internet of things in Fujian Province and parts of technical research and development is advanced in China. For example, Fujian Province is leading in the R&D of the field below: sensors, automatic control, electronic receipt, radio card reader, self-service terminal, middleware platform of operating system of internet of things and home network system. It has established three RFID application research centers and achieved preliminary results in the transformation of scientific and technological achievement. Besides, the application market is expanded continuously. The products of Fujian Province are widely used in China in the aspect of urban management, intelligent monitoring, food trace and water quality monitoring and its sensors have been exported to foreign markets. The 2D intelligent reading machine, various labels, smart cards, RFID reading equipment and network terminals have been widely used domestically. Since 2002, the communication

Notes: this project is funded by 2015 Fujian Provincial Science and Technology Planning Project (Project No. 2015R0067)
About the author: Di Jun-an（1960-）, male, Professor of the Department of electronics Minjiang University）, Research direction: information processing.E-mail: dmieorg@163.com
Li Hao (1980-), male, lecturer and engineer of Minjiang University, doctoral graduate on information and communication engineering major in Wuhan University of Technology. Research direction: mobile information, electronic commerce, information communication. E-mail:eastlihao@163.com

operators have started to customize the solutions to the internet of things, which integrate the data collection, transmission, processing and business management for industrial customers, such as "Megaeye", "Location Service" and security monitoring, and have accumulated rich experience in the operation of internet of things. Additionally, the technology of internet of things, such as RFID has been applied perfectly in the charge for entering the island and operation of express way. The communication network equipment is advanced. Fujian has constructed a domestically advanced information network system approaching the world advanced technology level. The high-speed wired and wireless broadband have spread all over the whole province, and 97% and 100% of villages have realized the wired and wireless internet, and the relevant indicators, such as popularizing rate of mobile phone and total number of wired broadband, website, netizen and domain name has ranked the fourth to sixth in China. Fujian is one of provinces to construct TD-SCDMA firstly in China, and has basically perfect third-generation of mobile communication infrastructures and has the foundations and conditions to promote the application of extensive information network and wireless information technology more highly, deeply and largely along with the 3G network transformation construction of telecom CDMA2000 and Unicom WCDMA.

II. Empirical Study on the Competitiveness of the Industrial Cluster of Internet of Things Based on Gray Incidence Assessment Method

In the opinion of Porter, the industrial cluster refers to the gathering of the enterprises, research institutes and colleges which influence and interact mutually in certain industry. The industrial cluster is a kind of organization and management mode for regional economy. In the wake of the success of the Silicon Valley in the United States, Bangalore in India, Emilia-Romagna in Italy, Hsinchu in Taiwan, Tsukuba in Japan and Zhongguancun in China, lots of states and regions have great expectations for the industrial cluster as a successful mode to development local economy. The industrial cluster can bring about a large number of competitive advantages for enterprises in the cluster, such as the direct competitive advantage in economy of cost advantage, product difference advantage, marketing advantage and competitive advantage in market, as well as bring about the formal and informal network forming the information of communicated enterprises in order to promote the non-direct economic competitive advantage of technical innovation and provide conditions for implicit and non-coding knowledge transfer and distribution inside the region. Studies show that enterprises in the cluster have stronger competitiveness than enterprises of the same kind and at the same stage outside the cluster, which attracts more scholars to study the competitiveness of industrial cluster. There are two methods: qualitative method and quantitative method in the "GEM" model to evaluate the competitiveness of the industrial cluster. Quantitatively, a kind of model to evaluate the competitiveness of industrial cluster, GEM model is concluded based on "groundings-enterprises-markets" by two Canadian scholars: Padma and Gibson on the basis of "Diamond Model" through many years of research. GEM model consists of "three elements and six factors", namely basic elements (including resource and facility), enterprise element (including supplier/relevant enterprises and manufacturer structure/strategic factor), market element (including local market and foreign market) (see Figure 1). GEM model is based on "three elements and six factors" mentioned above. In GEM model, the three elements are respectively groundings, market and enterprises and every element consists of two factors. The groundings contain facility factor and resource factor and the enterprise contains manufacturer structure/strategy and supplier and relevant enterprises. The market contains local market and foreign market, which is the demand element of industrial cluster. For the detailed meanings of "three elements and six factors", please refer to Table 1. The quantitative evaluation of GEM model is divided into three steps:

I. Factor evaluation. Every factor in every element will be given ten points in accordance

with the world standard. 1 point indicates that the cluster develops badly in this aspect and in a similar fashion, 10 points indicates that the industrial cluster develops excellently in this aspect, has a world-class competitiveness and ranks the first in the world. For the detailed evaluation standard, please refer to Table 2.

II. Calculation of the point of "factor pair". In GEM model, factors in every element are believed to be replaceable. Thus the point of "factor pair" is the average value of the points of two factors, namely, PS (Pair Score) = (D2i-i+D2i)/2. In the formula above, PS (Pair Score) represents the "points of factor pair", D2M represents 1st factor corresponding to the ith element while D2i represents 2nd factor corresponding to the ith element. i in the formula is 1, 2 and 3.

III. Calculation of the total point of competitiveness of industrial cluster. This step is divided into two small steps. Firstly, the point of three "factor pairs" is transferred into linear score of industrial cluster. The formula is: LCS=ni=1...3(PS)= ni=1...3(D2i-l+ D2i)/2 and in the formula LCS is short for Linear Cluster Score. It can be seen from the formula above that the linear score of the industrial cluster is the product of score of three factors and the score of six factors influencing the competitiveness of industrial cluster has equal effect on the score of the competitiveness of total industrial cluster. The low score of any factor will lead to low total score. Secondly, the score of LCS is transformed to make the final score 1000 scores (indicating the status that the score of each factor will be 10 score). The calculation formula is GEM=2.5 (n.=i...3(D2i-i+D2i)/2)$^{2/3.}$

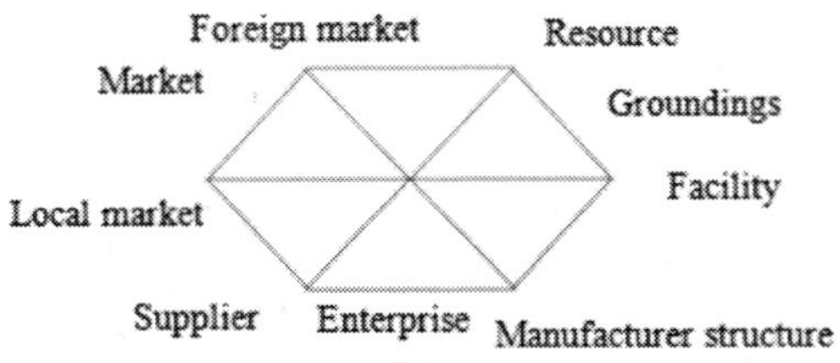

Figure 1 GEM model

Table Meaning of Elements and Factors of GEM Model

Factor	Element	Meaning
Groundings	Resource	Refers to the resources inherent locally and formed later, such as geographical position, natural resources, patent technology, financial capital
	Facility	Refers to the hardware and software, such as road, port, pipe and communication facility, software facility includes system arrangement, tax policy, training institution, commercial environment, etc.
Enterprise	Supplier/relevant enterprise	Refers to the articles and services purchased by enterprises in the cluster in the industrial cluster.
	Manufacturer structure/strategy	Refers to the number, scale of enterprises in the industrial cluster, production mode between enterprises, management mode and ownership structure, etc.
Market	Local market	Refers to the local market of industrial cluster, or a provincial or regional market, or a national market
	Foreign market	Refers to the market except fro local market, such as market outside the province and foreign market, etc.

Table 2 Grade and Scoring Standard of Factors

Grade of factor	Scoring	Scoring standard
Grade one	10 scores	Very excellent and has world-class competitiveness
Grade two	9 scores	Excellent and has world-class competitiveness
Grade three	8 scores	Unique nationally
Grade four	7 scores	Has national competitiveness
Grade five	6 scores	Exceeds national average level
Grade six	5 scores	National average level
Grade seven	4 scores	Lower than national average level
Grade eight	3 scores	Has a certain gap with national average level
Grade nine	2 scores	Has a great gap with national average level
Grade ten	1 score	Has the greatest gap with national average level and seriously influences the enhancement of industrial cluster

Evaluation of the factors influencing the competitiveness of industrial cluster of internet of things in Zhongguancun, Wuhan Donghu, Wuxi New Zone and Fuzhou Hi-tech Zone

1. Data source and evaluation method

The original data of this evaluation is from "2014 Chinese Torch Statistical Yearbook", "2014 Chinese Statistical Yearbook", "Statistical Report of the 32nd Chinese Internet Development Status", "2014 Zhongguancun Indicators", official website of Beijing Zhongguancun National Independent Innovative Demonstration Area (www.zgc.gov.cn), official website of Wuxi New Zone (www.wnd.gov.cn), government website of Wuhan Donghu Hi-tech Industrial Development Zone (www.wnd.gov.cn) and Fuzhou National Hi-tech Industrial Development Zone after sorting and calculation of the author.

It will be evaluated in gray incidence assessment method. The competitiveness of the industrial cluster of internet of things is affected by various factors. Because the data and information used for evaluation is limited, especially the extreme shortage of local data, the local industrial cluster of internet of things can be regarded as a gray system and the gray

incidence assessment method can be used to evaluate its competitiveness with limited information, and then the competitiveness of industrial cluster will become clearer and clearer and is turned from gray to white through limited information. During the evaluation, as the representative variables of the competitiveness of industrial cluster, the net profit and total income of the industrial cluster will be the reference sequence and the factors of G2EM-CI, such as groundings, enterprise, markets, value chains, governments and interactions will be the comparison sequence for evaluation. For the detailed evaluation indicator and original value of indicator, please refer to Table 3 and Table 4.

Table 3 Factors, elements and indicators for evaluation

Enterprise	Supplier and relevant supporting enterprises	Total number of incubator and productivity promoting center (unit: PCS)
	Enterprise structure strategy and competition	Number of hi-tech enterprise (Unit: PCS), hi-tech enterprise scale (total revenue/number of enterprise) (Unit: RMB ten thousand Yuan/enterprise)
Market	Local market	Total of turnover of technical output and technical input (Unit: RMB ten hundred)
	Foreign market	Turnover of domestic technical contract
Value chain	High end	Number of adopted technical standard (including national, international and industrial standard) (Unit: PCS)
Government	Planning	Planning or not (10 for yes and 1 for no)
Interaction	Production-university-research Production-supply-marketing	Number of R&D institutes in the cluster (including colleges and universities, research institutes, R&D center of company, etc.) Number of industrial association/alliance in the cluster
Competitiveness of industrial cluster	Net profit of cluster	Net profit amount
	Total revenue of cluster	Total revenue amount

Table 4 Original data of evaluation indicator based on G2EM-CI model (2014)

Industrial cluster	Technical talent	Authorized patent	Incubator	Number of enterprise	Enterprise scale	Local market	Domestic market
Zhongguancun	307370	5.7188	29	15720	1013910	2077	3906
Wuhan Donghu	83755	0.360	17	2468	118563	277	3906
Wuxi New Zone	33956	0.917	13	1021	297672	577	3906
Fuzhou Hi-tech Zone	18987	0.092	9	288	291619	54	3906

	Technical standard	Planning	R&D institute	Association/alliance	Total revenue	Net profit
Zhongguancun	1096	10	323	65	1593866575	110637253
Wuhan Donghu	10	1	131	11	292614195	17667077
Wuxi New Zone	101	10	87	8	303923610	20743716
Fuzhou Hi-tech Zone	5	1	48	3	83986381	3002729

Notes: 1. the number of incubator is the total number of incubator of national technical enterprises and productivity promotion center. 2. Enterprise scale=total revenue/number of enterprise. 3. It is supposed that each of the industrial clusters is faced with the same domestic market, and the turnover of each of the industrial cluster in domestic market is the same. 4. Technical standard includes customized international, national and industrial standards. 5. If the industrial planning about the development of internet of things is set, the score will be 10, or the score will be 1.

2. Based on the evaluation of the main factors (the net profit will be the reference sequence) influencing the competitiveness of the industrial cluster of internet of things in Zhongguancun, Wuhan Donghu, Wuxi New Zone and Fuzhou Hi-tech Zone, the initial value will be calculated. On the basis of the original data above, the various values of Zhongguancun shall be the reference value 100, thus getting the value of other industrial clusters in Table 5.

Table 5 Initial value of factors influencing the competitiveness of industrial cluster based on G2EM-CI model

Industrial cluster	Technical talent	Authorized patent	Incubator	Number of enterprise	Enterprise scale	Local market	Domestic market
Zhongguancun	100.00	100.00	100.00	100.00	100.00	100.00	100.00
Wuhan Donghu	7.24	6.29	58.62	15.69	11.69	10.92	100.00
Wuxi New Zone	11.04	16.03	44.82	6.49	29.35	27.78	100.00
Fuzhou Hi-tech Zone	6.17	1.60	31.03	1.83	28.76	2.59	100.00

	Technical standard	Planning	R&D institute	Total revenue	Association/alliance	Net profit
Zhongguancun	100.00	100.00	100.00	100.00	100.00	100.00
Wuhan Donghu	0.91	10.00	40.55	18.35	16.92	15.96
Wuxi New Zone	9.21	100.00	26.93	19.06	12.30	18.74
Fuzhou Hi-tech Zone	0.45	10.00	14.86	5.26	4.61	2.71

The gray correlation tree between factors influencing the competitiveness of industrial cluster based on G2EM-CI model and net profit. The correlation coefficient of the factors for the total revenue is calculated. The absolute value of the maximum value in difference sequence above is 94.74 while the absolute value of the minimum value is 0, the difference is great so 0.3 is collected to calculate the correlation coefficient to reduce the influence of the great difference on the evaluation. Please refer to Table 5.12.

Table 6 Correlation coefficient between factors influencing the competitiveness of industrial cluster based on G2EM-CI model and total revenue

Industrial cluster	Technical talent	Authorized patent	Incubator	Number of enterprise	Enterprise scale	Local market
Zhongguancun	1	1	1	1	1	1
Wuhan Donghu	0.761	0.702	0.413	0.914	0.810	0.792
Wuxi New Zone	0.779	0.895	0.524	0.693	0.734	0.765
Fuzhou Hi-tech Zone	0.968	0.885	0.524	0.685	0.547	0.914
	Domestic market	Technical standard	Planning	R&D institute	Association/alliance	
Zhongguancun	1	1	1	1	1	
Wuhan Donghu	0.258	0.619	0.772	0.561	0.952	
Wuxi New Zone	0.259	0.742	0.259	0.783	0.807	
Fuzhou Hi-tech Zone	0.230	0.855	0.857	0.747	0.977	

For the calculation of the correlation of factors, please refer to Table 7.

Table 7 Correlation between the factors influencing the competitiveness of industrial cluster based on G2EM-CI model and total revenue

Factors	Technical talent	Patent	Incubator	Number of enterprise	Enterprise scale	Local market	Foreign market	Technical standard	Planning	R&D institute	Association/alliance
Correlation	0.877	0.870	0.615	0.823	0.772	0.867	0.436	0.804	0.722	0.772	0.934

Order of factors influencing the net profit and total revenue of the industrial cluster based on G2EM-a model

For net profit: Groundings(0.879) → Interaction(0.844)→ Value chain(0.835)→ Enterprise(0.769)→ Government(0.723) → Market(0.670)
For total revenue: Groundings(0.873) → Interaction(0.853)→ Value chain(0.804)→ Government(0.7772) → Enterprise(0.736) → Market(0.651)

Table 5.14b Order of factors influencing the net profit and total revenue of the industrial cluster based on G2EM-a model

For net profit: Association/alliance(0.931) → Enterprise number(0.916)→ Parent(0.907)→ Market(0.902) → Technical talent(0.851) → Technical standard(0.835)→ Enterprise scale(0.783)→ R&D institute(0.757)→ Planning(0.723)→ Foreign market(0.437)
For total revenue: Association/alliance(0.934) → Technical talent(0.877) → Parent(0.870)→ Market(0.867)→ Enterprise number(0.823)→ Technical standard(0.804)→ Enterprise scale(0.772)→ R&D institute(0.772)→ Planning(0.722)→ Foreign market(0.436)

It can be seen from the evaluation above that the factors influencing the industrial cluster of internet of things are basically the same no matter the net profit or total revenue of the industrial cluster of internet of things are evaluated as the parent sequence of the evaluation of competitiveness of industrial cluster. Three factors: groundings, interaction and value chain are top three, which is of guiding significance to the cultivation of actual competitiveness of industrial cluster of internet of things.

1. Groundings are the first factor to influence the competitiveness and it shows that the knowledge resources, especially the patent and technical talents are the most critical elements to cultivate and improve the competitiveness of industrial cluster for the industrial cluster of internet of things as a hi-tech industrial cluster. Therefore, the quantity and quality of the technical talent and technical patent of internet of things should be enhanced with efforts in the process of cultivation of the competitiveness of industrial cluster of internet of things.

2. Improving the value chain of internet of things is the basic way to cultivating the competitiveness of the industrial cluster and governing the industrial cluster of internet of things. The industries in China, especially hi-tech industry have been locked in the lower end of value chain for a long time and located in the bottom of "smiling curve", and therefore, Chinese enterprises can just earn a few profits and most of values are carved up by R&D and design enterprises on both sides of the value chain. It is the only choice to walk out of the "lock" to try to improve the R&D and design ability of Chinese enterprises and adopts the high-end technology.

3. Pay attention to the expansion of local market and further improve the volume of local market. The larger the local market is in the industrial cluster and the more the manufacturers communicate and cooperate, the more intensive the corresponding technical innovation network is. Therefore, the local market has a geological advantage over the foreign market in the cultivation and improvement of the competitiveness of industrial cluster. The industrial chain of internet of thing is long and the involved industries are more, thus the government can guide the enterprises of internet of things to gather together in location through preferential policy, subsidy and special funds, etc. on the basis of existing industrial cluster of internet of things or prepared cluster, thus making the local market of internet of things stronger.

References

[1] Zou Xianhong and Yang Tao, Research on Hi-tech Industrial Competitiveness Based on Effect of Industrial Cluster [J], Technical Progress and Countermeasure, 2012 (4): 65-69

[2] Ma Xiangyang, Yin Xinyue and Chen Weidong, Research on Evaluation of Hi-tech Industrial Competitiveness Based on Passive Coordinative Mechanism- In the Case of Tianjin [J], Science & Technology and Economy, 2013 (10): 42-47

[3] Chen Hongchuan, Empirical Research on Evaluation of Hi-tech Industrial Competitiveness [J], 2012 (8): 21-29

[4] Zhang Xianfu, Liu Dengyu and Zhou Binggen, Research on Hi-tech Industrial Competitiveness Based on the Theory of Dissipative Structure-In the Case of Anhui Province in Central China [J], Resource Development and Market, 2013(6): 517-520
[5] Fang Yi and Xu Guangrui, Evaluation on Hi-tech Industrial Competitiveness in Chinese Regions [J], Science and Technology Forum of China, 2012 (5): 69-73
[6] Xu Guangrui, Hi-tech Industrial Cluster and Industrial Competitiveness in China [J], 2013 (8): 47-52

MATEC Web of Conferences 44, 02077 (2016)
DOI: 10.1051/matecconf/20164402077

Comparison and Reference of the Talent Cultivation System in Vocational Education Based on Cultural Creation and Information Industry between Fujian and Taiwan

Jun An Di[1,a], Hao Li[2,b]

[1] Department of Electronic Information Engineering, Minjiang University, Fuzhou, Fujian China 350121
[2] Straits Institute, Minjiang University, Fuzhou, Fujian China 350121

Abstract. firstly, the current situation of the cultural creation and information industry in Fujian and Taiwan is investigated and compared in this paper. Secondly, the characteristics and advantages of the talent cultivation system in the cultural creation and information industry of Taiwan are investigated. Finally, the advantages of Taiwanese cultural creation and information industry in talent cultivation are referred to greatly cultivate the talents of cultural creation and information industry in Fujian Province.

Key words:. Education in Fujian and Taiwan, cultural creation, information industry, talent cultivation

During the twelfth five-year plan, the average growth rate of the value added of cultural creation and information industry in Fujian province was 29.8% per year, 12.8% higher than average growth rate per annum, of which the value added was 4.2% of GDP in 2010. In the aspect of cultural trade, it was accumulated that the exported cultural and information products reached 1.52 dollars in Fujian Province from January to October of 2011, 57.1% higher than 2010. It was also 25.6 higher than the general growth rate of the foreign export in Fujian Province in the corresponding period. The proportion of the cultural creation and information industry is increasing year by year and it is becoming a new hot of economic growth in Fujian Province and an important support to promote the development of the west bank of Taiwan. With the characteristics of high human capital, high technical content, high additional value, low energy consumption, low materials, low pollution, the cultural creation and information industry determines the human resource to be the first resource and a bottleneck to restraint this industry. Thus, it is critical for the development and cultivation of talents of this industry, especially the managers to develop this industry. However, the shortage of talents of this industry is serious increasingly with the increasing development of the cultural creation and information industry in Fujian Province.

I. Current situation of cultural industry in Fujian Province

The cultural industry starts late in Fujian Province, thus the talents of cultural creation, cultural management and technical innovation of cultural industry are quite lack. It cannot adapt to the rapid development of cultural industry and has become a bottleneck to

Notes: this project is funded by 2013 Fujian Branch Institute of National Vocational Education Institute (Project No. GZM13003)

About the author: Di Jun-an (1960-), male, Professor of the Department of electronics Minjiang University), Research direction: information processing.E-mail: dmieorg@163.com

Li Hao (1980-), male, lecturer and engineer of Minjiang University, doctoral graduate on information and communication engineering major in Wuhan University of Technology. Research direction: mobile information, electronic commerce, information communication. E-mail:eastlihao@163.com

restraint the development of cultural industry in Fujian Province. At present, the problems, which are faced in the management and cultivation of talents of cultural industry in Fujian Province, are mainly: shortage of talent, improper talent level and structure, uncompetitive remuneration structure, imperfect talent flow market, extensive management mode, enterprises pay more attention to short-term economic benefit instead of talent cultivation, sole talent cultivation method, shortage of policy, capital and labor, etc.

1. Improper talent level and structure
In recent years, the colleges and universities of Fujian have set relevant majors to cultural industry, and also formed some special training institutions to cultivate the talents for cultural industry. However, the gap in the talent of cultural industry is large, such as the employees of cultural industry are lack and the talent level and structure are not proper. For example, there were 30 thousand enterprises working on cultural industry in 2014 and the employees were more than 300 thousand, but the proportion of design is 45.4%, the proportion of planning is 19.4%, the proportion of edition is 18.5% while the proportion of non-professional post is just 20.7%, such as finance, management and administration [3]. It is closely related to the emphasis of cultural industry on professional development direction. Besides, graduates learn theories mostly and are lack of practical experience in colleges and universities although they are delivered by talent training institutions, such as universities, vocational colleges and training base of universities, so it is hard for them to input into the development and production of the cultural creation industry. For example, 17 thousand talents were lack in animation industry of Fujian Province and it was expected that there would be 43 thousand in 2015. It is hard to change the shortage of creative talent. Besides, the employee level and structure is not proper. At present, 80% of employees working on the cultural creation industry are primary practitioners ageing from 20 to 25 but only 10% has worked for more than 8 years in this industry, and over 70% of employees work for less than two years in this industry. Among them, the proportion of employees who have received technical secondary education is 54.1%, the proportion of employees who has received junior college education is 24.4% and the proportion of employees who has received bachelor' s degree is just 23.4% 4]. Thus their quality needs to be improved further wholly.

2. Talent shortage and phenomenon of job-hopping
The cultural industry in Fujian Province is just at the initial stage, and lots of employees are from other industries, so they are lack of the systematic knowledge for cultural industry. Additionally, as a comprehensive industry, the cultural industry integrates finance, law, marketing, manufacture and so on and so it is urgent to need trans-boundary talents. However, the management system and remuneration system of cultural industry are not perfect, thus the cultivation of trans-boundary talents and free flow of high-end talents are restricted, which limits the introduction of talents to cultural enterprises. In such circumstances, lots of cultural enterprises cannot employ the professional talents, so they always pay high for the professional talents, which tend to the loss of the whole team in an enterprise, and it is a great loss for an enterprise.

The cultural industry develops early in Taiwan, so it has a relatively perfect market mechanism and talent cultivation mechanism for the development of cultural industry. The policy of cultural industry in Taiwan is always based on "how to cultivate creative talent" , "how to construct a talent cultivation system adapting to the demand of era" , etc. After more than ten years of development, Taiwan has preliminarily constructed a unique talent cultivation system for cultural industry from the general education to specialization of subject of cultural industry, from basic education to vocational education and from promotion of management authority to participation of non-government institutions. Now, the cultivation of creative talents has become an important path to facilitate the development of cultural industry in Taiwan. All is worth reference for employees and policy-makers of cultural industry in Fujian Province.

(1) Cultivate professional talents by combining the international and local knowledge

According to the course content of cultural industry, the cultural creation education in Taiwan pays more attention to the development situation of the creative industry in international developed regions as well as the local culture of Taiwan. The cultivation mode of relevant majors to cultural industry in Taiwan adopts the mode of 3 + 1 or 2 + 2, namely they will study for two years in Taiwan and then will study for two years in those countries with developed cultural industry. Combined with the international and local knowledge, the cultivated talents can not only adapt to the demand of local market, but have a greater development space.

(2) Combination of introduced teachers and self-trained teachers

Teachers will guide the cultivation of talents of cultural industry significantly and the education of cultural creation industry in Taiwan pays more attention to the cultivation of teachers. As they cultivate the local teachers, they will also introduce foreign teachers actively to drive the development of local teachers. Besides, some teachers will also be selected to study further abroad to make the teachers of cultural industry have the advantage in international educational background and make them adapt to the international development trend.

(3) Normalization of cultural creation talent cultivation

The basic education attaches great importance to the cultural creation education in Taiwan. The philosophy of cultural creation is imported to the basic education, especially the diversified cultural creation education, such as the exploration and practice of "Nine-year System in Art & Humanities" and construction of creative campus. The idea of cultural creation industry is used to reconsider and locate the construction of Art & Humanities in basic education. At the same time, the general education center in Taiwanese colleges and universities also pays attention to the development of the theory and practice of cultural creation industry. As early as 2005 the General Education Center of Feng Chia University of Taiwan held "Salon of General Education" which was featured by "Getting on the train of digital industry and cultural creation industry and becoming a winner of knowledge economy" ; the General Education Center and Creative Integration Design and Research Center of Union University and Taiwan Xiaoqu Peili Association jointly held 2008 Cultural Creation Industrial Academic Forum and Summit Forum "Global Dialogue on Earth" [12]. All these general education make the cultural creation talent cultivation normalization in Taiwan.

(4) Management department and non-government organization jointly cultivate the talents for industrial industry [13]

Since Taiwan government set the cultural creation industry as an important policy for regional development in 2002, the cultural construction association has been set under the promotion team of cultural creation industry of Ministry of Economy and has been responsible for the talent cultivation of cultural industry, environmental government and support of cultural industry. Some non-government profit institutions found the commercial change and actively entered the field of talent cultivation of cultural industry; some non-profit non-government organizations organize the cultural creation foundation and hold some lecture and courses of cultural creation. Taiwan government also transformed the government function and adjusted the governing mode as well as held the training class of cultural creation with the non-profit organizations to train the creators, operators, managers of cultural industry. And they also injected lots of fresh air to the development of cultural industrial development.

III. Learn from the advantage of talent cultivation of cultural industry and greatly cultivate the talents for industrial industry in Fujian Province

(1) Cultivate the cultural creation talents with the cooperation of colleges and universities in Fujian and Taiwan

At present the talent cultivation of the cultural industry still relies on education, and thus it is

extremely important to improve the teaching quality. Fujian Province has a backward cultural industry higher education, so they can cooperate with Taiwanese colleges and universities and select exchange student to study in Taiwan; or employ excellent teachers from Taiwan to teach in Fujian, introduce relevant training institutions and schools to found schools or training bases related to the cultural creation and give some preference or convenient measures in tax in order to make Fujian a bass of cultural creation education and cultivate various talents for the development of cultural creation industry. In May 2009, the colleges and universities and enterprises of both sides of the Taiwan Straits signed four cooperative agreements in Creative Talent Cultivation and Industrial Cooperation Forum on both Sides of the Taiwan Straits, which greatly promoted the cultivation and communication of talents of creative industry on both sides of the Taiwan Straits, especially the cultivation and introduction of hi-end talents. On April 20, 2011 Straits Institute signed a cooperative agreement with Fujian Shaoyuan No. 1 Cultural Creation Industrial Park and held the ceremony for the production-study cooperative base. Both sides would introduce Taiwanese excellent teachers and mutually cultivate the talents for cultural creation industry through the industry-university-research system construction. This action guided the promotion of joint talent cultivation for cultural creation industry by Fujian and Taiwan.

(2) The colleges and universities combines with the enterprises to achieve the professional and scale cultivation of cultural creation talents. In colleges and universities, the professional teacher team generally works at school and is lack of enterprise practice, thus they are out of line with the enterprise application. It is urgent to change this situation but there is still a long way to go. It cannot be changed in short time. The vocational training can be combined with colleges and universities or higher education in the form of 2+2 mode, namely two years of higher education are combined with two years of vocational education. The philosophy of vocational education, specific operating method, developed course system, teaching software and teaching courseware are combined with the higher education and upgraded constantly or a major is set by both sides to achieve the resource sharing and complementation at most and realize the scale cultivation of cultural creation talents. However, the talent training for cultural industry is professional and deep to some details, such as the network game development industry is involved in the training of game designer and developers and the game developers are also divided into game designer, planner and operator, especially the art staff and program developers are also refined in the market. The specialization should be resolved better in the process of such education. Without professional training, the trained talent will not adapt to and cannot meet the demand of enterprises, or they will have difficulty in employment. As a result, during the cooperation between school and enterprise, the personnel can enter enterprises for professional training based on their own major and habit as well as the market demand after learning basic theories and foundations to realize the complete connection between the talents cultivated by colleges and universities and demanded by enterprises.

(3) Keep pace with the times to cultivate and keep the cultural industry talent

The most important in cultural industry is the constant upgrading of the technology and course, because this industry develops fast and the technology upgrades fast. If teachers cannot develop at the same time and cannot catch up with the technical development, they will be eliminated and the cultivated students will also be unpopular. The talent education of cultural industry is geared to the needs of vocation and they will be undertake the research and development in the enterprise and create values for enterprises. If they learn some outdated technology, the enterprise will not be popular either. To ensure the teaching synchronization and improve the level of teachers, the source setting and teaching content must be upgraded timely in accordance with the actual situation of the development of cultural industry during teaching so that the cultivated students can adapt to the demand of enterprise. Besides, the government departments can learn from the

areas with developed cultural industry and issue some relevant policies to provide preferential policy for talents of cultural industry and resolve the worries of employees, especially the senior employees to make them threw into the construction of cultural industry contently with heart and soul.

References

[1] CCID Consulting, Great Gap in the Planning and Creating Talents at Early Stage of Chinese Animation Industry [EB /OL], Shihua Finance Website, 2014-05-21

[2] Du Guangzhong, Development and Research of Talents of Cultural Industry in Fujian Province [J], Southeast Communication, 2013 (12)

[3] Zhang Huarong, Exploration to the New Idea of the Development of Cultural Industry [J], Open Tide, 2014 (Z1)

[4] Wei Ran, Preliminary Exploration for the Talent Cultivation System of Cultural Industry in Taiwan [J], Taiwan Research, 2013 (3)

[5] Zheng Changling and Shen Jing, Colleges and Universities and Enterprises Signed a Cooperative Agreement on Creative Talent Cultivation and Industry-study Association [EB/OL], China News, 2009-05-17

[6] Miao Yuexia, Research on Constructing the Talent Communication Cooperative Experimental Plot of Both Sides of Taiwan Straits [J], Chinese Public Administration, 2014 (5)

[7] You Xiaobo, Thoughts about Strengthening the Communication and Cooperation of Both Sides of Taiwan Straits [EB/OL], http://tw.people. com cn/GB/21879.htm

MATEC Web of Conferences 44, 02078 (2016)
DOI: 10.1051/matecconf/20164402078

Research on Basis and Method of Fujian-Taiwan Cultural Creative Industry Connection

Hao Li[1,a], Jun An Di[2,b]

[1] Straits Institute, Minjiang University, Fuzhou, Fujian China 350121
[2] Department of Electronic Information Engineering, Minjiang University, Fuzhou, Fujian China 350121

Abstract. deepening Fujian-Taiwan cultural creative industry connection cooperation is of great importance to close Fujian-Taiwan relationship, forge new economic growth points, optimize and adjust industrial structure. In this paper, the opportunities, potential, basis and conditions for Fujian-Taiwan cultural creative industry connection cooperation are analyzed, and countermeasures and suggestions to deepen the connection cooperation are proposed.

Key words:. Fujian-Taiwan, cultural creative industry, connection cooperation

I. Fujian-Taiwan Cultural Creative Industry Connection Cooperation Has a Brilliant Future

i. Opportunities and potential of Fujian-Taiwan cultural creative industry connection cooperation

Firstly, the industry at these two places has much room for upgrading and transformation, and cultural creative industry has been regarded as an emerging industry in the future by the government. There is relatively complete market mechanism for the development of cultural industry in Taiwan, and there is a large cultural industry market in Fujian and even the Mainland. When the two are combined together, it can burst out great vigor and aftereffect. Secondly, the effect of overseas Chinese culture is promoted in the global scale, the corresponding derivatives are attracting more and more attention in the world, there are broad markets in the Mainland, and the global market can also be expanded constantly. Thirdly, various countries in the world face up to the development of cultural creative industry generally, and especially because of the development of Korea and Japan in aspect of cultural creative industry, the development of Taiwan is extruded. Meanwhile, the rapid rise of the Mainland imposes great impact on the economy of Taiwan, which has great influences on the manufacturers that take the Mainland as market, and they are badly in need of seeking for development in the Mainland. Fourthly, the resource endowment of the cultural creative industry at Taiwan requires to strengthen the cooperation with the Mainland. Taiwan does not have great comparative advantages in the aspect of corresponding policies for the development of cultural creative industry at Taiwan. In aspect of quantity of talents, it cannot come up to the Mainland China, Japan or Korea, but only equals Hong Kong. In aspect of technology, it obviously falls behind Japan and Korea, but is slightly superior to the Mainland and Hong Kong. Besides, its fund abundance is also obviously inferior to other countries and regions. The native market of Taiwan is too small, while the Mainland China has huge market. In aspect of internationalization competence and access commanding, Taiwan is not prominent, and the export of brand, access and service industry is always a weaker link for Taiwan. Thus, only by actively taking advantage of the market in the Mainland, and strengthening the scale economy benefits and internationalization competence of cultural creative industry of Taiwan, can Taiwan get the development prospect in the future. Especially, the cultures at Fujian and Taiwan come from the same root, and the cultural creative industries at these two places are greatly complementary. If Fujian and Taiwan can implement in-depth cooperation and complement each other's advantages, they can obtain great achievements.

Notes: this topic is subsidized by 2013 research project of Fujian branch institute of National Institute of Vocational Education (project No.: GZM13012).

About the author: Li Hao (1980-), male, lecturer and engineer of Minjiang University, doctoral graduate on information and communication engineering major in Wuhan University of Technology. Research direction: mobile information, electronic commerce, information communication. E-mail:eastlihao@163.com

Di Jun-an（1960-）, male, Professor of the Department of electronics Minjiang University）. Research direction: information processing.E-mail: dmieorg@163.com

ii. Fujian has good conditions and basis to develop cultural creative industry

Firstly, it has supporting economic development level. Generally speaking, the development of cultural creative industry is basically of the same form as economic development, and the two have certain synchronism. Currently, per capital GDP at Fujian province exceeds 4000 dollars, of which, per capital GDP for permanent population at Xiamen is 62651 yuan, and that of Fuzhou is 33492 yuan. It is proved by the experience of developed countries that when per capital GDP is between 1000-5000 dollars, the major impetuses to stimulate economic growth are manufacturing, processing and traditional service industry; when per capital GDP is between 5000-10000 dollars, they are technological innovation, creative industry, high-tech industry and service industry. Secondly, it has proper geographical and cultural advantages. Fujian and Taiwan have common cultural origins, and their cultural resources waiting to be developed are abundant. In aspect of the creativity of some local distinctive cultural products, only the ordinary people at these two places can empathize with each other. For example, the worship for Mazu is an important advantage for Fujian-Taiwan cultural creative industry cooperation. It is pointed out by experts that Fujian and Taiwan can hold activities together to create "Activity Economy" business opportunity, for example, they can hold relevant activities for urban marketing jointly on the basis of historic culture or folk property at Two Shores. The can generalize and organize industry-academy cooperation via the joint cultural creative industry. As for animation and game industry, Fujian-Taiwan dealers can start from people, issues and objects that lay the foundation for the Chinese culture, seek for the animation and game theme for their cooperation by mean of the promotion center of the cultural creative industry that they jointly support, and then join hands together to enter the international market, and seize the commanding height of Sinomania on a global scale. Thirdly, in recent years, Fujian-Taiwan cultural creative industry cooperation has certain basis. If the development thoughts can be further combed up and a batch of specific carriers and projects can be planned and generated, a batch of cultural industry brands can be forged.

II. Countermeasures and Suggestions for Strengthening Fujian-Taiwan Cultural Creative Industry Connection Cooperation

i. It requires intense crisis awareness and sense of urgency

For Fujian, how to plan to develop cultural creative industry and how to accomplish Fujian-Taiwan cultural creative industry cooperation so that Fujian can remain invincible in the new economic competition is a serious issue that needs to be solved urgently at present. For various reasons, the development of cultural creative industry at Fujian Province is not satisfactory, and the problems of inadequate total quantity, small scale, weak basis, lack of creativity, and insufficient talents coexist, which are distinctively manifested at three aspects: firstly, it starts late; secondly, it develops slow; thirdly, its features are not obvious enough, it does not have an influential brand; fourthly, its ideas are not innovative enough, and measures are not powerful enough. Since the reform and opening-up policy, Fujian that has "Wuyuan" advantages with Taiwan has not obtained optimistic achievements in aspect of obtaining investment from Taiwan. Currently, it cannot fall behind any more in aspect of Fujian-Taiwan cultural creative industry cooperation. To achieve the effect that the latercomers surpass the formers, it must introduce Taiwan cultural industry and cultural creative industry projects as it values the introduction of manufacturing industry, turn cultural creative industry into main stream, upgrade "Creative Fujian" into Fujian strategy and strategy for Western Taiwan Straits, and actually change the situation that it is important when talking about it, and it is unimportant when doing it.

ii. Planning needs to achieve high starting point and overwhelming strategies

1. Make scheming and planning for the development of cultural creative industry of the whole province by means of international bid ding. Development of cultural creative industry belongs to soft power, it cannot attract attention and form "image" as easily as infrastructural projects and manufacturing projects. But once it is completed and achievement is obtained, it can also get a great influence and a good image.

2. Set up the authentic concept of "Great Creative Province", and strive heard to demonstrate the pattern of "Creative Secretary", "Creative Provincial Governor", "Creative Mayor", "Creative District Mayor" all over the province. Consult the practice of "Cultural Oriented Country" of Japan in 1980s, highlight "Creative Fujian". List specific development thoughts and measures into *Development Plan of Western Taiwan Straits Economic Zone*. The State Council supports *Opinion* of Western Taiwan Straits, and clearly points out that it needs to promote the cultural and economic integration, strive to develop cultural creative industry, set up cross-strait cultural industry cooperation center, strengthen to cultivate special, refined, characteristic and new culture enterprises, and try hard to change Western Taiwan Straits Economic Zone into an important cultural industry base in our country (Article 25 of *Opinion*); continue to complete Taiwan-related great economic, trade and cultural activities. Establish cross-strait cultural industry park, and built a batch of cultural communication and cooperation basis towards Taiwan (Article 31 of *Opinion*). Combine with *Development Plan of Western Taiwan Straits Economic Zone,* further deepen the content of *Opinion* related to Fujian-Taiwan cultural industry cooperation, and transform it into specific operating contents, of which, cultural creative industry is one of the contents to be deepened and refined. Meanwhile, this content shall be reflected in thick and heavy color in "the Twelve Five-Year Plan" to be formulated.

iii. Policies and measures need to be more powerful

As a high-growth sunrise industry, cultural creative industry still remains at the stage that it needs to be cultivated elaborately, and the support and promotion of the government are of great importance. Although Fujian has issued the policy to speed up cultural industry, the pertinence for the development of cultural creative industry is still not powerful enough, thus, it is suggested to issue specific policy to promote cultural creative industry.

On one hand, Fujian needs to actively study weighty policies and measures, including revenue supporting policy, land policy, exhibition and meeting participation subsidy policy, talent policy, etc. Such as, broaden admittance field, lower access threshold, connect Taiwan cultural creative industry comprehensively; enjoy the same preferential policies as local enterprises of Fujian in aspect of financing, land and house resources use, and government subsidy of Fujian-

Taiwan cultural creative industry; learn from the example that Changsha Government implements the policy to return cultural undertaking construction funds in full amount towards Guangdong Electric Power Group, Press Group, Cartoon Group, and other cultural enterprises, with the purpose to solve the financial problem for enterprise development, etc. On the other hand, strive for policy positively, and try hard to get support and help of related department of our country.

iv. Establish and perfect systems and mechanisms that promote development

1. Support various cities and regions to establish the mechanism to speed up development as per their characteristics. Learn from the practice of other provinces, and support various regions to make policy innovation. For example, support to positive Xiamen as cross-strait IC design talent training base, provide enterprises and training institutions with certain subsidies by referring to service outsourcing talent subsidy policy; provide office space rent subsidy, software platform and testing platform expenses subsidy for IC design enterprises that are established in Xiamen; individual income tax can be used for first car and house purchase for the staff of IC design enterprises that are established in Xiamen; provide the treatment of local registered population for Taiwan staff of IC design enterprises that are established in Xiamen in aspect of both life and work. For example, support to set up Straits cultural creative industry investment fund and risk fund, undertake some high-risk cultural investments or share some financing risks with banks. Fund can be used for loan with discounted interest, entrusting bank for syndicated loans, and strategic equity investment, etc.

2. Strengthen intellectual property protection of cultural products and services

Intensify intellectual property communication and cooperation towards Taiwan. "Father of creative industry in the world", John Hawkins, pointed out that, if intellectual property is "currency" in creative economy, people promoting the establishment of intellectual property system are people issuing "currency". It needs to encourage cultural enterprises to apply and register related rights, strike a severe blow to various behaviors violating intellectual property, and create a favorable environment for the healthy development of cultural industry. Shanghai has established intellectual property park which can provide certain reference for us. Deepen the communication with Taiwan in aspect of intellectual property protection, publicity, information, training, education, research and application for registration, constantly improve the cooperation mechanism, expand cooperation field, improve cooperation effectiveness, and construct Fujian into an important base for the intellectual property communication and cooperation between the Mainland China and Taiwan. Explore and set up dispose coordination mechanism and early warning emergency mechanism for Fujian-Taiwan intellectual property cases, as well as Fujian-Taiwan intellectual property information sharing platform to serve Taiwan-Funded enterprises in Fujian Province. Explore to set up Fujian-Taiwan intellectual property alliance, establish intellectual property same trade industry (association) protection and service mechanism at Taiwan and China, and expand cooperation influence.

3. Encourage private capital to enter cultural industry. Lower access threshold of private enterprises, encourage and support private capital to invest and manage cultural facilities, and construct cultural undertakings or public cultural facilities that are advocated by the country; encourage and support private capital to participate reorganization and system reform of cultural institutions, set up film and television production, distribution, projection, art performance, entertainment, management in the form of holding, participation, cooperation, merger, purchase, contracting, lease, and trusteeship, and enjoy equivalent treatment as state-owned cultural enterprises; encourage and support private capital to invest and set up non-business organizations of arts and entertainment, such as culture and art intermediary, artwork collection museum, etc. Currently, it needs to try hard to set up the pilot at Fujian for private cultural studio to participate publication. At the national press and publication director conference at the beginning of 2009, it was clearly pointed out to actively study the access problem for private cultural studio to participate publication. It is suggested that Fujian take the lead to initiate this work, and strive to have one or two private cultural studios to participate. Meanwhile, it also needs to speed up the cultivation and supporting of private cultural studio.

4. Set up investment information service platform of cultural creative industry, attract various capitals

Include the entrance of overseas investment from Taiwan. Nowadays, a lot of large-scale enterprises, strategic investors and private capital are interested in investment for cultural creative industry, including capital of overseas Chinese, a large part of which belongs to substantial Taiwanese overseas Chinese, but a lot people just cannot completely understand relevant trend of the industry. It is suggested to release project, relevant information and dynamic data by means of some important introduction and marketing events, such as "9.8" fair for investment and trade, "6.18" project connection conference, cultural fair, and oversea trade fair, etc., to provide necessary conditions for qualified enterprises.

References

[1] 2009 Chinese Cultural Industry Development Report (cultural blue book) [R]. Social Sciences Academic Press, published in April of 2009.

[2] Several Opinions of the State Council to Support Fujian Province to Speed Up the Construction of Western Taiwan Straits Economic Zone. Implementation suggestions for Fujian Province to implement Several Opinions of the State Council to Support Fujian Province to Speed Up the Construction of Western Taiwan Straits Economic Zone. Fujian Comes out Ten Policies and Measures that shall Benefit Taiwan [N]. Fujian Daily, August 12, 2009.

[3] Yin Hong. Research on Creative Economy at Modern City [M]. China Economic Publishing House, edition of June of 2009.

[4] Li Wuwei. Industrialization and Industrial Innovation of Cultural Creativity [J]. Journal of Tongji University, 2014 (01).

[5] Wang Yaojie. Develop Cultural Creative Industry, Innovate Development Thoughts of Fujian [J]. Journal of Party School at Fujian Special Zone, 2014(03).

MATEC Web of Conferences 44, 02079 (2016)
DOI: 10.1051/matecconf/20164402079

The Research of Detection and Treatment of Tunnel Lining Cavity

Mei Ling Guo[1], Shui Ping Huang[2,a]

[1]Continuing Education College, Guangdong University of Science and Technology, 523083, Dongguan, China
[2]International Education College, Guangdong University of Science and Technology, 523083, Dongguan, China

Abstract. It was a threat that the lining cavity had a many risk of the tunnel operation, thus detection and prevention was particularly important. The general causes of tunnel lining cavity and corresponding prevention measures will be summarized, and methods which includes detect lining cavity and processing data were given. Last, a real engineering was given for illustrating the practical method of tunnel lining cavity detection process. The proposed method has a great significance to ensure the safety of the tunnel operation.

1 Introduction

Different kinds of tunnels in China have damages of varying degrees, ranging from the hazard of water leaking, the crack of tunnel lining, the void of tunnel lining, the problem of frost, the danger of earthquake, to the pollution of inner air, and the risk of fire, among which the void of the tunnel lining causes more subtle damage to the tunnel.

Table 1. Causes and solutions of the void of tunnel lining [1, 2].

Causes	Solutions
Void caused by concrete shrinkage.	Improve the flow of concrete by adding the water reducer or reducing the water-cement ratio.
Void caused by insufficient pressure of the pumping or inadequate flow of the concrete.	Ensure sufficient pumping pressure before construction.
Void caused by inappropriate place or wrong choice of the pumping.	Use skew pumping mouth, if there is slope, a high pumping mouth is needed for the pouring.
Void caused by inadequate loose paving of the waterproofing layer	i) The flatness of the primary support should be checked, and the unqualified one should be leveled. ii) Ensure adequate coefficient of loose paving material.
Void caused by improper sealing	Adopt the valve for the sealing.

Such problems are seen as follows: Falling rocks caused by the collapse of the void lead to bend, squeeze and destroy the tunnel, which causes the primary support damage; the joint action of the structure-rock system based on the mechanism of mechanics cannot be formed, making the force undependable and the surrounding rock unsteady; it also leaves space for water storage, adverse to waterproof and drainage, and may cause the pressure of frost heaving. Here are some causes of the void of the tunnel lining (Table 1).

It is necessary to inspect whether there is such void of the tunnel lining and accordingly deal with it appropriately, in order to ensure the safety of the tunnel work. Two specifications are consulted to direct the inspection: *The Technology of Testing the Tunnel Engineering* and *Nondestructive Testing Procedures of the Quality of the Railway Tunnel Lining.*

Now, it is to discuss the testing principles of the void of the tunnel lining, and to give a specific project case on the inspection and post-construction of the tunnel lining, which renders certain reference value to similar cases.

2 Inspection of the tunnel lining void

2.1 Testing principle [3-5]

Geological radar is usually applied for the inspection of the void of the tunnel lining. Based on the principle of the propagation characteristics of electromagnetic waves in lossy media, the transmitting antenna transmits high-frequency electromagnetic pulses to the measured media, when encountering uneven body (or interface), it will reflect part of the electromagnetic waves, the reflection coefficient of which mainly depends on the dielectric constant of the measured media. By timely receiving and processing the reflected waves of this part, the radar host achieves the purpose of inspecting and identifying the target object.

[a] Corresponding author: hsp0121@126.com

Table 2. Testing principle.

Ground Penetrating Radar (GPR) mainly uses the reflection of broadband high-frequency time domain electromagnetic pulse wave to probe the target body.	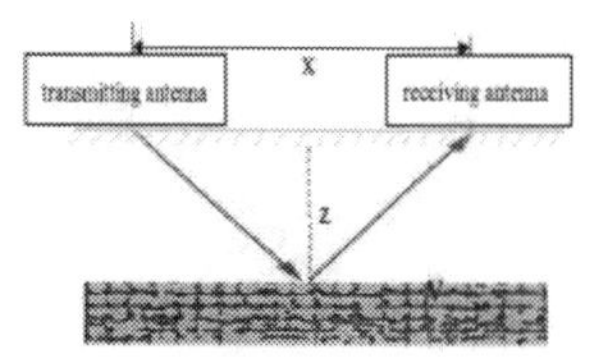
According to the formula, the radar, based on the measured $t = \sqrt{4z^2 + x^2} / v$ radar travel time, automatically calculates the depth z and scope of the reflector.	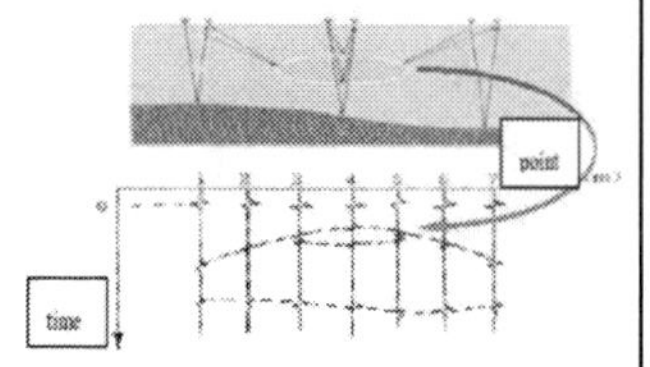

Radar antenna transmits electromagnetic waves to the concrete. As concrete, steel, hole and the density of concrete are different, their dielectric constant differentiate from each other, which makes electromagnetic waves reflecting at the interface of different media possible, received by the receiving antenna on the surface of the concrete. According to the time difference of electromagnetic wave transmitter and the reflected wave and the propagation speed of electromagnetic waves in the concrete, the reflector's distance from the surface is determined to detect the steel, the defect location and depth within the concrete.

According to the principle above, radar can be used to detect the location of the steel in the concrete, the thickness of the protective layer and the location, depth and scope of void, porosity and other defects. Table 2 shows the working principle of radar and its detection methods. 500 MB antenna, which can reach out to the depth of 3 to 4 meters, is commonly used for GPR to detect the void of the tunnel lining. [6-10].

2.2 Testing procedure

Table 3. Testing procedure.

Preparation phase	Learn designing information of the tunnel, determine detection scheme, and collect data of surrounding rock.
	Tell the construction team to conduct the traffic in the tunnel and clean the on-site facilities to ensure a smooth and safe testing work.
Implement-ation phase	Check the equipment
	Lay out the measuring point. Generally the on-site measuring line is longitudinal-centered, with survey line 3, 5 and 7, and circumferential-auxiliary, based on point measurement.
	Detect radar and calibrate medium parameter. i) Knowing the thickness of certain part or material, measure the precast object similar to the tunnel; ii) Use dual antenna to measure where no car is available in the tunnel; iii) Drill holes to measure.
	Analyze images and process datum.
	Write the testing report.

3 Project case study

3.1. General introduction

Guowan Tunnel lies in DK276+937.5 from the beginning to the end, the total length of which is 135 meters, with the V-level surrounding rock. The entrance of the tunnel is of chamfered type, while the exit adopts single pressure type. The grass slope protection of concrete skeleton is adopted on the entrance slope, while the anchor frame beam protection is adopted on the exit slope. DK276+870-DK276+895 is of chamfered type, DK276+895-DK276+920 uses I type composite lining, DK276+920-DK276+990 uses II type composite lining, and open-cut construction is available for DK276+990-DK277+005. The entrance and the exit chooses 30m, 35m respectively of φ 108 large steel pipe as advance support, with the middle section using φ 42 small steel pipe as fore poling.

3.2 Detection of the implementation situation

Field testing is conducted in accordance with the requirements of the construction side and the regulations. Radar survey lines are set longitudinally for the detection on the left arch lumbar, vault, the right arch lumbar in each of the tunnel as far as possible.

In actual field testing, as the site constraint of some tunnel construction sites and out of safety considerations of equipment and person, datum are not collected from some positions unqualified for testing conditions.

The data of GPR reflects the electrical distribution of subsurface medium, and transforms it into geological distribution. Such information as geology, construction, and GPR must be combined to get an overall picture of the target object. Lack of density and void appear in the tunnel lining. Air in the void of surrounding rock or concrete distinctively differentiates in permittivity from mold-built concrete, shotcrete, and surrounding rock. Therefore on the time profile, the same phase radar wave fractures, bents upward, and draws a clear boundary within void, concrete, and surrounding rock. If steel or steel grille exists during the process, its impact should be taken into consideration.

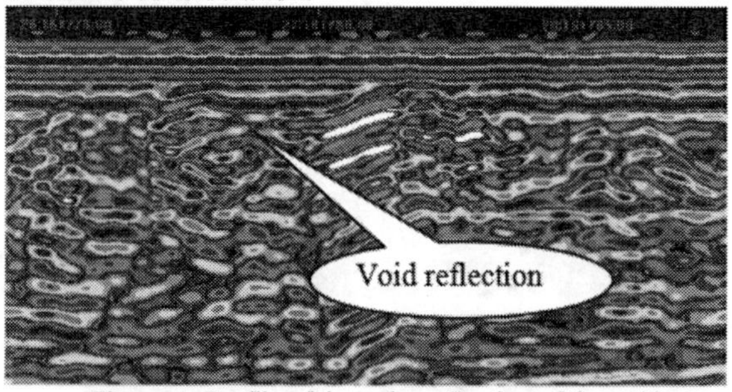

Figure 1. Profile of the radar reflection of the void.

Figure 1. is the depth profile deriving from the processed original data, and testing result (Table 4) is achieved after being analyzed. The void is characterized by strong reflection signal in the lining interface, and obvious vibration phase, at which lower interface there is

still strong reflection signal. These two sets of signal differentiate largely in time interval.

Table 4. Testing results.

Name	Position	Mileage	Depth (cm)
Guowan Tunnel	vault	DK276+909-DK276+913	24-51
		DK276+947-DK276+952	26-52
		DK276+925-DK276+929	33-60
		DK276+967-DK276+970	28-50
		DK276+982-DK276+985	29-57
	right arch lumbar	DK276+912-DK276+915	55-70

3.3 Treatment program

Table 5. Requirements on backfill material.

No.	Content
1	Be of self-stability and space -filling
2	Backfill material is liable to deform, and can be filled into void.
3	segregating from water and diluting with it
4	Be of small proportion and taking little load on the lining.

Table 6. Designing of the treatment program.

Treatment program	Content
Designing parameter of the lining drilling	Drill hole diameter:3cm
	Vent setting: 30cm-50cm above the drilling hole
	Inclination angle: 3° downward
Designing parameter of the grouting	Either is OK.
	Water-cement ratio to single pipe of cement grouting is 0.5:1 to 1:1, and 42.5R early strength portland cement is available
	Blend in proportion superplasticizer, accelerating agents and other additives through test; the additive quality should conforms to regulation GB8076. Effect should be tested before usage, initial setting time should be controlled within 5min, and final setting time within10min
Setting of the grouting pressure and grout tube	Initial pressure of grouting pressure is 0.2-0.5MPa, while final pressure is 0.5-1.2MPa. Either the method of gradual pressurized grouting or constant pressurized grouting can be adopted. Install the grouting core tube on the embedded grout pipe. Control the grouting speed within 30-60 L/min.
	Avoid the damage of waterproof board of the embedded grout pipe. Put anti-blocking facility on the top end of the grout pipe, and seal the hole firmly after grouting.

During the construction:

i) According to the mileage showed in the testing report, confirm and locate the position of the void.

ii) Accurately drill holes with rock drill in the lining void, and install grout pipe in the two ends of the void so that it can be fixed in the lining. The space around the grout pipe can be filled with the anchoring agent, and a valve should be set to avoid a secondary grouting.

iii) Clean the pipe hole before grouting and reasonable order should be taken when grouting.

iv) If the pressure rises rapidly but the slurry is hard to be injected or infused a little, the water-cement ratio should be increased, and the slurry concentration be lowered. In the meanwhile, check whether the grouting pipe is blocked, when it does, clear it.

v) Whether to stop grouting depends on the grouting pressure, grouting time, and grouting volume. One should often check the slurry quality, control the water-cement ratio, the grouting pressure, and the grouting volume of the slurry and fill in the grouting record pipe by pipe during the process.

3.4 Treatment effect

After the construction process, drill hole for coring in the grouting area when the slurry solidifies to get a better effect.

Figure 2. The grouting process of the lining void.

4 Conclusion

i) Causes of the tunnel lining void includes as follows, void caused by concrete shrinkage, insufficient pressure of the pumping or inadequate flow of the concrete, inappropriate place or wrong choice of the pumping, inadequate loose paving of the waterproofing layer. Corresponding solutions are: improve the flow of concrete by adding the water reducer or reducing the water-cement ratio, ensure sufficient pumping pressure before construction, use skew pumping mouth, and if there is slope, a high pumping mouth is needed for the pouring, the flatness of the primary support should be checked, and the unqualified one should be leveled, ensure adequate coefficient of loose paving material, and adopt the valve for the sealing.

ii) Geological radar is usually applied for the tunnel inspection. This paper summaries the testing principle and data processing method of the geological radar.

iii) This paper, taking Guowan Tunnel as an example, tells in details testing methods of the tunnel lining void and the treatment program on on-site construction.

iv) What covers in this paper renders great value to the inspection and treatment of the tunnel lining void, which in turn ensures the tunnel safety.

References

1. Ministry of Railways of the People's Republic of China, Acceptance Criteria on the Quality of Railway Tunnel Construction, Beijing: *China Railway Publishing House*, 2003.
2. Liu Yong-hua, Numerical Simulation of Secondary Lining Void or Crack in Vault. *Highway Tunnel*, (3), pp.11-13, 2006.
3. Peng Yue, Wang Gui-lin, Zhang Yongxing. Study on Impact of Lining Void on Safety of the In-service Tunnel Structure. *Underground Space and Engineering Journal*, 4(6), pp.1101-1104, 2008.
4. Zhang Zheng-guo. Application of GPR New Technology in the NDT of Tunnel Defect. *Chengdu University Journal*, (4), pp.6-10, 2003.
5. Liu Hai-jing, Zheng Jia-yan, Luo Xin, Liu Yuan-ming. Classification of Tunnel Defect and Parameter Quantitative Research Method. *Modern Tunnelling Technology*, (suppl), pp.619-623, 2006.
6. Fu Wei, Zhou Hong-feng, Fan Jin-jia. Analysis and Prevention of Concrete Crack of Tunnel secondary lining. *Communications Standardization*, (7), pp.53-55, 2005.
7. Zhou Tao, Dang Hai-yan, Wang Guo-xin. Analysis and Treatment of Collapse Caused by Tunnel Lining Void. *Shanghai Geology*, (2), pp.11-12, 2007.
8. Ding Xiao-xin, Su Hui. Management of Construction Contract, Beijing: *Chemical Industry Press*, 2005.
9. Liu Chang-ming, Song Hui-lian. Management of Project Bidding, Beijing: *Peking University Press*, 2006.

MATEC Web of Conferences 44, 02080 (2016)
DOI: 10.1051/matecconf/20164402080

Design and Implementation of Computer Hardware Monitoring System Based on Cloud Computing

Ming Liu, Ping Guo
Kunming University of Science and Technology

Abstract: From the perspective of customer service and on the basis of network, this paper proposes a computer hardware monitoring system based on cloud platform, which separates the data acquisition, storage, and analysis based on cloud computing hardware monitoring system. The computer hardware monitoring system based on cloud platform separates data storage and access. The cloud platform unifies modeling analysis of storage hardware parameters for huge amounts of data, in order to provide users with complete hardware maintenance information. This paper introduces the overall design of the hardware monitoring system, and then gives the system structure and related key technologies of implementation instance.

Key word: computer hardware monitoring system; cloud computing;

1 Introduction

Monitoring computer hardware running parameters is very important to hardware maintenance. During hardware temperature monitoring, the high temperature leads to unstable running of the computer system, and even affecting the service life of the equipment. Therefore, hardware parameters monitoring is particularly important in unattended server rooms, cluster servers and massive cloud server platforms. Desktop computers, notebook computers, smart phones, tablets or a intelligent terminal that can run program are often produced by different manufacturers having very different hardware composition and production process. It is difficult to analyze effectively the health status of the hardware device. We can assess more effectively the health status of the hardware and do timely maintenance if we can do horizontal and vertical modeling analysis of the historical data of the various parameters of hardware, and the health status data of the similar hardware equipment.

In addition, most of the existing enterprises or schools establish computer room environment monitoring systems to build computer hardware parameters such as temperature monitoring. The defect is that a considerable investment of hardware is required to run and cannot directly detect the temperature of the computer and various states and parameters. At the same time it can't make full use of the resources of existing computer system itself. All sorts of computing device and intelligent terminal maintenance often is unable to browse the user's history of hardware running parameters. This also brings great inconvenience for the hardware maintenance.

In this paper, from the user service point of view and on the basis of network monitoring parameters, we propose a computer hardware monitoring system based on cloud platform. It is a cloud computing hardware monitoring system that separates the data acquisition and storage management. The computer hardware monitoring system based on cloud platform separates data storage and access. Based on the platform it unifies modeling analysis of storage hardware parameters of huge amounts of data, so as to provide users with good hardware maintenance information. This paper introduces the overall design of the hardware monitoring system, and then gives the system structure and related key technologies of implementation instance.

Corresponding author: kgliuming@qq.com

2 System composition

Through the monitoring software to obtain the effective parameters by monitoring operating parameters of a variety of computer hardware, operating parameters and related software and through the network timing to the monitoring server to send all available; monitoring server in the cloud gets and statistics, analysis and processing all kinds of parameter information, unified algorithm, based on information of various parameters determined by monitoring computer hardware health state and save the parameter and state, promptly notify the users of health status. The client component can be composed of three parts: the client component, the cloud service module and the communication network. The client component is run on a monitored computer or intelligent terminal, and the server component is deployed on the monitor server cluster.

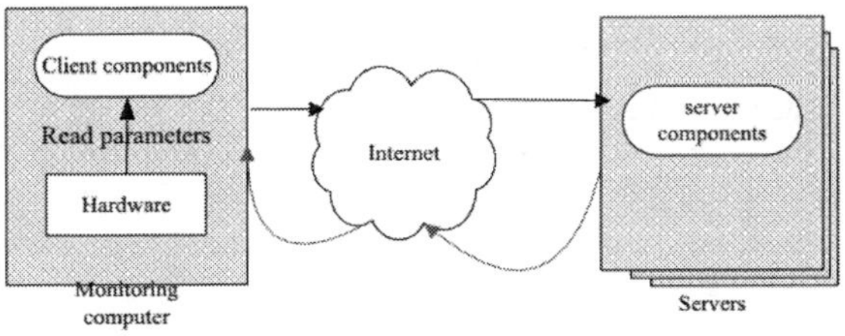

Figure 1

As shown in Figure 1, the entire system consists of three parts: client components, server components and communication networks.

3.Communication protocol design

The basic work process is that the client components read all kinds of hardware and operating parameters of the machine, and the parameters are transmitted to the monitoring server, and the running parameters are processed by the monitoring server in the cloud. The UDP/IP protocol is used as the basic communication protocol between the client and the server. When it is transmitted in the network, the communication protocol layer is as follows:

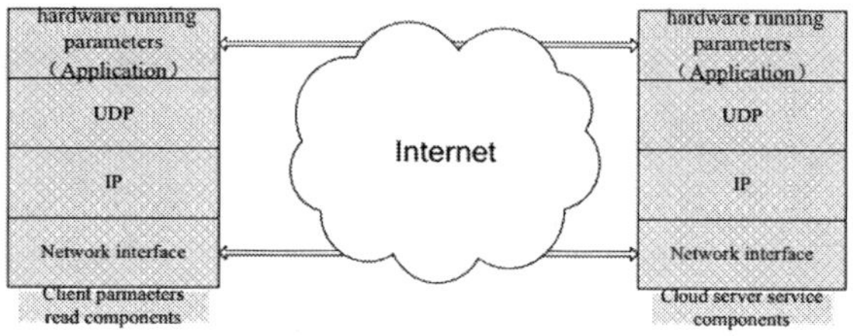

Figure 2

Monitoring information data packet format is as follows: the underlying data unit is 8 bytes, a data unit that represents a parameter value of a hardware device. The hardware device number is 1 bytes, the value range of 0~255, it can express 256 kinds of hardware, such as the agreement in the provisions of 1, express CPU, 2 express the memory, 3, said the hard disk, etc. The parameter type is a byte, range is from 0 to 255, can be expressed 256 types of parameters, such as agreement provisions 1 represent temperature 2 said fan speed, three voltage and 4 represents the frequency and 5 representing CPU utilization. The parameter value is 6 bytes, the first 4 bytes represent the integer part of the parameter, and the next two bytes represent the decimal part of the parameter. The communication protocol to UDP/IP protocol data transmission

4. Process design

The process design of computer client components

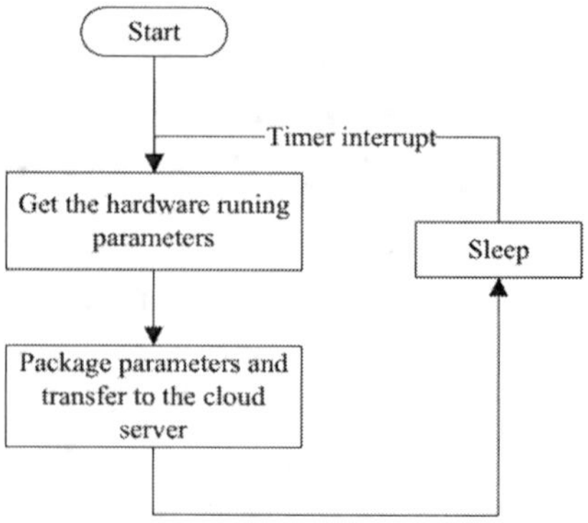

Figure 3

Set the relevant operating parameters, including the server IP address, port number and the time interval to send data to the server. Port number must be consistent with the server, usually set the server port number, and then according to the port number of the server, to set the port number of the reading software. Start the software, the software is set to start with the operating system to start. Read the storage server IP address and timer time interval. IP address can be set in the program and do not have to set. The default timer interval is 60s, can be changed according to the actual situation.

Client components to wait for the timer time to. When the timer time, read the relevant hardware sensor parameters and other operating parameters. Send the read data to the server through the UDP/IP protocol.

The process design of cloud server's service component

The cloud service component process is first set up a listener port number on the server side, and the step is only carried out when the first operation is carried out. After setting, this step can be ignored. Service software can set a default port number, if you do not manually set, then the software automatically takes the default port number. After starting the cloud service component, the service component gets the port number of the set listening port. The cloud server's service component listening the port. When there are new data packets, analysis of the data package, mainly including: validity verification, access to each other's IP address, access to the other side of the host name and hardware operating parameters. According to the host name and IP address to determine whether the client has been listening in the host library, if there is no increase in the host information, if there is to update the host state and saving

5. Parameter reading

Currently computer system motherboards, CPU and hard drive and other hardware devices are equipped with sensors, can provides CPU temperature, CPU voltage, CPU fan speed, the temperature inside the host and hard disk also provides the hard disk parameters such as temperature and hardware vendors provide the read sensor data access interface parameters can be provided

by the operating system I / O interface function read out the motherboard BIOS stored in a variety of sensors, real-time data, important parameters are: temperature of CPU, CPU voltage, CPU fan speed, the temperature inside the host, hard disk temperature. According to the need, you can also read the operating system to provide the CPU usage and other parameters.

Currently client system motherboard, CPU and hard drive and other hardware devices are integrated sensors, can provides CPU temperature, CPU voltage, CPU fan speed, mainframe temperature, as well as the hard disk also provides the hard disk parameters such as temperature and hardware vendors provide read related sensor data access interface. The basic method is to read the real time parameters of various sensors stored in the hardware through the API functions provided by the operating system. Such as in the windows system can first call API function CreateFile to open the device and returns a handle to a device associated with. Then, and then call the API function DeviceIoControl function and driving communication program, and then read the various parameters of the equipment. The basic method to obtain the operating parameters of the operating system is to call the interface functions provided by the operating system to complete the.

In the client components, in addition to reading the hardware sensor parameters, but also can easily read the operating system to provide a variety of parameters, such as the use of CPU and other important parameters. According to the actual demand, you can also read some important services, such as Windows system software, including Server SQL and other running state parameters for these servers to monitor.

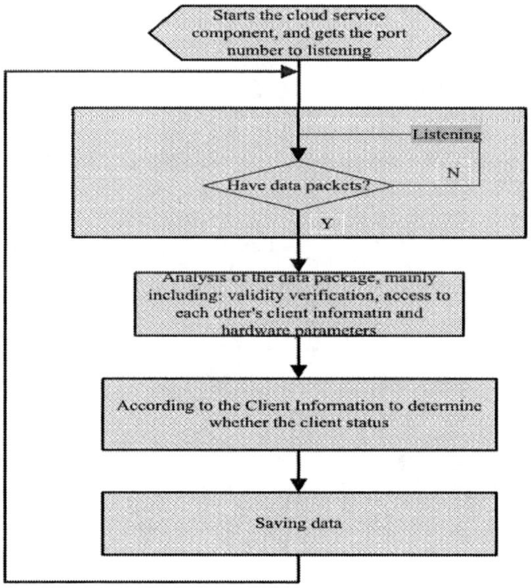

The core function of the server component is on the network resource management and scheduling, i.e. resource scheduling, allocation and recovery work. This is the resource management and scheduling module to realize the function of this layer, the kernel function is similar to the traditional stand-alone operating system. The requirements for scheduling and management of network resources to meet the needs of different the need for different attributes of different resources, strategies and methods of scheduling, allocation and recovery algorithm based on the realization of resources on demand elasticity flow. The server component also has interface with the interface module is used to realize the interaction with the user, receive and complete from the upper application and user requests. The server has two special the module, network communication and optimization module and network communication and service protocol module. The client network communication and optimization module mainly completes Interrupt start terminal interception, and the signal is transmitted to the web server, by the server to deal with. Network communication and optimization module of the server end will respond to requests from the client. The first is a network address assigned to the client, to facilitate the subsequent communication; secondly, it will on the user's identity authentication and will return to support network autonomous system example list of operating systems to carry on a choice to the user; after users choose what you want to run an operating system instance, and then call the relevant transmission protocol will part of the data to the terminal, client interaction.

Virtual resource server component driver module, is the network based on interrupt management, complete the driver and the management of virtual resources. Including the following three functions: (1) on the physical hardware, such as graphics card, such as driving, driving after all hardware devices autonomous network system in (2) in the real hardware drive based on the further formation of virtual resources, such as the virtual CPU, virtual memory, virtual memory, virtual equipment resources construction, driving and management; (3) implementation of large-scale data storage, network storage and retrieval of large data. Resource storage and management module is based on virtual network storage, further examples of the operating system, applications and data organization, storage and management for users efficiently Visit. Based on cloud computing hardware monitoring system hardware resources are divided into three categories: the first is composed of terminal, server and network hardware platform resources. Therefore, with the traditional operating system only management and scheduling applications

6. The analysis of communication efficiency

Monitoring system is often run on the existing network, in order not to affect the current system of CPU usage, and the characteristics of the variation of parameters such

as temperature, the timing of the client components can be as long as possible, the default is 10s. General recommendations are set to 30s.

At the same time, as far as possible to reduce network traffic. For the monitoring system, the amount of information is small. In order to reduce the impact of the current network traffic, the invention adopts the UDP/IP protocol between the host and the server. IP protocol related standards documents, the host or network device IP data reported length shall not be less than 576 bytes, the first 20 bytes of IP, the maximum length of 40 bytes. That is to say, IP net charge at least 516 bytes length, and then deduct the UDP protocol header 8 bytes, 508 bytes. It can be estimated that the basic data unit of each transmission monitoring information can be completed in a data packet in the network when no more than 56 units are available. Generally can be read in the BIOS hardware operating parameters have 30 or so, which is an important CPU temperature, CPU fan speed, chassis system temperature and other key parameters. Therefore, it can ensure the monitoring information in a packet to complete the transmission, there is no case of split data packets. Data does not exist in the case of sub packets, you can consider the use of the UDP protocol such a shortcut to reduce the impact of the current network traffic as much as possible.

7. Conclusion

The hardware monitoring system based on cloud computing is proposed in this paper. Through regularly reading all kinds of parameters of the sensor computing devices, and then transmitted to the cloud to store and analyze data, it can determine the health status of computer equipments. It has a good expansibility. It can monitor more detailed computer operation parameters. It can better and more effectively define computer running states. It is convenient for monitoring, management and analysis of hardware faults,. It can more effectively maintain equipment. In this paper, the hardware parameters monitoring system based on cloud computing can effectively reduce the cost of equipment maintenance.

References

1. Michael Armbrust, Armando Fox , Rean Griffith, Anthony D.Joseph, Randy Katz, Andy Konwinski, Gunho Lee, David Patterson, Ariel Rabkin, Ion Stoica, Matei Zaharia. A view of cloud computing [J] . Communications of the ACM, 2010, 53(4) : 50- 58.
2. Fay Chang, Jeffrey Dean, Sanjay Ghemawat, et al. Bigtable: A distributed storage system for structured data[A] . Proc of the Seventh Sympo sium on Operating System Design and Implementation (OSDIT06) [C] . Seattle,WA : USENIX, 2006. 205-218.
3. David Chappell. Introducing the Azure Services Platform[EB/OL] . http: //download. microsoft. com/ . . . / e/ . . . / Azure-Services- Platform. docx, 2011-03-18.
4. [4] Dhruba Borthakur . The Hadoop Distributed File System: Architecture and Design[EB/ OL] . http: / / hadoop. apache. org/

MATEC Web of Conferences 44, 02081 (2016)
DOI: 10.1051/matecconf/20164402081

Classification of leukemia diseased cells

Chun Hua Shi

Langfang Health Vocational College, Hebei, China, Email:545682864@qq.com

Abstract. In this paper, the characteristics of leukemia diseased cells, diseased cells existing classification methods were studied and analyzed, in order to solve classification categories leukemia diseased cells more characteristic dimensions of the problem of high, finite automata and kernel methods, and experimental verification the advantages of this method.

1 Introduction

Leukemia (Leukemia) is a malignant tumor of the hematopoietic system, currently in the country is a threat to children and young adults leukemia life and health of the most common malignancies. Blood disease occurs in modern society, how to properly detect blood disease and propose effective and reliable treatment options based on the detection result, it has become a major issue in today's medicine. Blood disease is due to human hematopoietic dysfunction caused by blood cells in quantity, shape, proportion and other aspects have changed, so the correct identification of blood cells are correctly detected blood disease premise. At present, for the analysis of microscopic images of leukemia also not much hope to design a blood-based leukemia microscopic image identification and classification system.

2 Blood diseases and typing

According to current international combined cell morphology, tissue staining, flow cytometry and immunohistochemistry leukemia typing will be divided into:

1. Acute leukemia: acute non-lymphocytic leukemia and acute lymphocytic leukemia:

2、Chronic leukemia:

1) chronic myelogenous leukemia (CML): bone marrow myeloid hyperplasia, intermediate stage cell hyperplasia.

2) chronic lymphocytic leukemia (CLL): bone marrow mature lymphocytes ⩾40%.

The test sample is collected from chronic myelogenous leukemia (also known as chronic myeloid leukemia) of the blood film. Chronic myeloid leukemia blood film will appear segmented neutrophils and rod-shaped granulocytes, which is cell category this test to study.

3 Existing classification

By selecting features will be recognized classification objects merge, confirm their category is called classification process. The process is based on the appropriate decision rule, the feature space is divided into different types of samples. In some practical process, the pre-given condition, the category attribute is considered often have similarities, classification error is inevitable, therefore, the classification process can only be done in a certain error rate. Obviously, the smaller the better classification error rate. However, the classification error rate and is subject to many conditions, such as classification, classifier design and selection of samples and extracted characteristics and other factors will affect the classification results.

method	characteristic	Pros and cons
Recently mean classifier	Assigned to the category average of the most recent sample category	Rapid detection of the dependent measures taken
Nearest Neighbor Classifier	Assign samples to a class of its nearest training samples category	Robust performance, testing is slow, for dependent measures taken
Bayes classifier based law (minimum risk)	Assigned to the type of sample maximum a posteriori estimate the probability of	Based on a simple Gaussian distribution assumption classifier (linear or quadratic), density estimation error sensitive
Fisher linear classifier	Using the mean square error (MSE) criterion linear classifier	Quick and easy one-class classification, similar laws Bayes classifier, classification criterion function using a covariance matrix
Binary decision tree classifier	Achieve classification by finding a series of samples based on	Iterative training process, overtraining sensitive, we need to have a termination

[a] Corresponding author: yuanquanbo@126.com

	pattern features Lanna value	condition is detected quickly
sensor	An iterative optimization of linear classifiers	Sensitive training parameters
Multilayer Perceptron Neural Network	Based iterative minimum mean square error for the Priority 2 layer or multi-layer perceptron (neurons) using a transfer function Sigmoid	Parameter sensitivity training, training is slow, non-linear classification function, overtraining sensitive, need to be adjusted

Table 3-1 several commonly used classification methods

It can be divided into statistical decision method, syntactic structure, fuzzy judgment method and artificial intelligence four categories according to their method. Former two methods is the classic pattern recognition technology, the introduction of fuzzy mathematics research in these two methods, greatly improving the classification results. Artificial Neural Network 1980 years revival, more globally relevant feature in the field of pattern recognition has made many using traditional methods difficult to achieve success. Table 3-1 lists commonly used in blood cell classification method.

As can be seen from the above discussion and the work of their predecessors, in the blood cell classification category more due to the classification, feature dimension is high, so the problem classifier selection, structural design, and classification speed, accuracy, etc. are required considering the research prospects.

4 Support vector machine kernel function method of classification of blood cells

In order to solve the multi-category classification, characteristic dimension of the problem of high blood cell classification in the above, we use support vector machine classification. Support vector machine can solve high-dimensional feature of classification.

4.1. Linearly separable support vector machine

Support vector machine can be further divided into linear separable support vector machine, kernel function vector machines. We first examine the classification question whether linear classification problems, whether to use linear support vector machine method can be solved.

Using linear support vector machine plus soft margin optimization method, using 120 samples for training, with 30 samples were tested and the results are shown in Table 4-1.

C	The total number of SV	The number of Class 1 SV	The number of Class 2 SV	The number of Class 3 SV	Accuracy
1	62	21	30	11	91.057
2	57	21	26	10	91.057
3	47	17	23	9	91.87

Table 4-1 classification linear SVM

The first column in Table 4-1 interval optimization soft penalty factor, from the above table, we found that the greater the penalty factor, the fewer number of support vectors obtained, it means that the promotion of learning machines get better. Moreover, the penalty factor, the higher the accuracy of the test. This reflects that the system is approximately linear separable, but linear classifier and can not get the best results.

4.2 Kernel Methods

If you want to use the kernel function method, then choose what kind of non-linear classifiers have the best effect? Select nonlinear classifier, in fact, it is to choose the type of kernel function and its parameters. Present research kernel is not very thorough, it has not been studied all possible kernel function and its advantages when classification. Now people can only prove out several common kernels on classification issues have a better effect. These core functions are:

1. polynomial kernel

$$K(\mathbf{x}_i,\mathbf{x}_j)=[(\mathbf{x}_i\cdot\mathbf{x}_j)+1]^d \quad d=1,2,... \tag{5-1}$$

2. Sigmoid Kernel

$$K(\mathbf{x}_i,\mathbf{x}_j)=\tanh[v(\mathbf{x}_i\cdot\mathbf{x}_j)+c] \tag{5-2}$$

3. Gauss radial basis kernel function

$$K(\mathbf{x}_i, \mathbf{x}_j) = \exp\left\{-\frac{\| \mathbf{x}_i \cdot \mathbf{x}_j \|^2}{2\sigma^2}\right\} \quad (5\text{-}3)$$

We experiment with polynomial kernel and a Gaussian kernel to do a test classification, respectively, and have chosen a few parameters for each kernel. Still 120 training samples, 30 test samples. The results are shown in Table 4-2.

Table 4-2 and Table 4-1 comparison, it can be seen, with the kernel function improved classification accuracy than the method of linear classification soft interval. Moreover, the radial basis function better than polynomial kernel function results. After you have selected the radial basis function, we choose RBF kernel function of several parameters. Gamma is where RBF kernel function parameters, C is the soft margin optimization penalty factor. After testing a number of parameters, we found that when the Gamma = 2, C = 2 - delivering up to the maximum classification accuracy, when Gamma and C and then increase, not in the correct classification rate increases. So learning machine obtained at this time is the most suitable machine learning WBC we can get.

	Degree	C	Gamma	nSV	The number of Class 1 SV	The number of Class 2 SV	The number of Class 3 SV	Correct rate
Polynomial	2	1	1	47	17	21	9	91.87
	2	2	1	42	15	19	8	92.683
	3	1	1	42	13	21	8	92.683
	2	1	2	41	14	19	8	92.683
RBF		3	3	68	23	28	17	93.333
		2	2	51	21	22	16	93.333
		1	2	67	25	27	15	92.683
		1	1	61	20	27	14	90.244
		2	1	54	19	22	13	91.87

Table 4-2 polynomial kernel and RBF kernel of the classification results

When the prediction of a learning machine with the best forecast of 93.496% accuracy rate. Its confusion matrix (Confusion Matrix) as shown in Table 4-3, where the i-th row j-th column represents the first i kind of cells into the wrong kind of probability j cells.

	Lobulated nucleus	The rod	Damaged
Lobulated nucleus	0.95	0.05	0
The rod	0.075	0.9	0.025
Damaged	0	0.05	0.95

Table 4-3 predicted confusion matrix

5 summary

By support vector machines and kernel methods on cell sorting experiments, the results illustrate the applicability of using support vector machine kernel function method on blood cell, indicating that it has a good prospect in leukemia classification pattern recognition .

References

[1] Lijing Qin blood cytology Beijing: Chinese Medicine Press, 2001.

. [2] Lin Fengru, Ren Jinhai World Health Organization on the classification and diagnosis of acute leukemia clinical meta, 2004, 19 (22): 1315 - 1318.

MATEC Web of Conferences **44**, 02082 (2016)
DOI: 10.1051/matecconf/20164402082

Online Learning Community and its Application in the Occupational Training of College Teachers

Xiu Guo Huang

School of Interpretation & Translation, Shandong University at Weihai. Weihai, Shandong Province, PRC,264209

Email:xiuguohuang@126.com

Abstract: Object: The analysis of established online learning community, and its structural elements and creation strategies can shed light on the effect of the application of online learning community in the occupational training of college teachers. **Methods:** detailed analysis of the existing successful online Teacher learning communities like the Wired for Learning and the online learning community established by Beijing Normal University. **Conclusion:** Traditional learning community took place in a specific physical environment, whose members and resources are limited by the physical environment. Online learning community can help solve many of the existing problems in traditional training and opened new possibilities for occupational training

1 Introduction

At present wireless network technology has covered our whole country, and mobile intelligent terminal has been widely used and popularized. This tremendous change has exerted its influence on every facets of our life. Considering the rapid development of information technology and the reform in every respects of our society that it has brought about, we realized that the traditional occupational training for college teachers was destined to be changed. And the internet innovation has already had a profound influence on the traditional way of learning and the training mode.

The online teacher learning community assisted by the network technology enabled teachers to circumvent the limitation and restriction of time and space that dominated the traditional learning environment. In the online teacher learning community, the teachers were offered more chances of participation and resource sharing. They can also have more accesses to interaction in various forms and at different time. The construction of online teacher learning community contributed to the depth and breadth of the study and research in the information era. Through the network environment, online teacher learning community is bound to play a great role in promoting the development of teachers' professional development.

2 Literature Review

The “community” of the online learning community was originally a sociological term, which referred to a kind of organic collective existence and the integration of the people inside it. Later it was introduced to the field of education and therefore the concept of “learning community” emerged. Now, the paradigm of teacher's professional development has changed from passive training into active learning, whose

Article available at http://www.matec-conferences.org or http://dx.doi.org/10.1051/matecconf/20164402082

core include the "teacher's knowledge of teaching, the cognitive process of teachers, teachers' acquisition of knowledge, and how to understand and apply knowledge to the classroom situation"[1]. Avalos pointed out that the cooperative learning community of teachers was to assist and stimulate teachers' acquisition of knowledge and became an important intermediary of teachers learning. Learning community refers to a community composed of learners and learning helpers. The members in learning community frequently communicate and exchange information between them, share all sorts of study resource, and fulfill some learning tasks. Thus the mutual influence and interpersonal connection among its members are formed and can contribute to the development of teachers' profession [2]. As to what kind of situation is most appropriate for teachers to update knowledge, increase knowledge and put into class practice, "community" has become an ideal place for teachers' learning and the mainstream discourse in teachers' occupational training. The goal of learning community is through the growth of collective knowledge; an increase in the individual knowledge can be achieved.

Dewey in his work *Democracy and Education* first introduced the term "community" into the field of education, whose goal is through exemplary demonstration and mutual encouragement, to create a mutual learning atmosphere for learners. In this way it can improve the learners' enthusiasm for study. Bruner in its research also pointed out in the process of learning the importance of the creation of a "community". The concept of "learning community" reflected the belief that "education is a way of life", whose purpose is to break the fixed boundaries of education, realize the lifelong development of the individual. After Giovanni studied different types of schools, he believed that schools should be reformed into community. Through a commitment to community, concept, intention, values, feelings and beliefs in Community, a link among members can be established, which emphasizes the formation and identification of the common identity of learners.

The concept of "community" stressed that through participation, cooperation and dependence on each other, support and negotiations throughout these processes, gradually a common goal, memory, communication ability, toolkit, and specification can be established. Ultimately, the identity characterized by community membership was consolidated"[3]. For members of a specific learning community, the mutual communication, sharing of learning experience and learning materials, with the other members of the community can positively influence each other and make each learner get the support and nurture. At present, the concept of "learning community" has taken root in education and teaching situation, the related research and practice of "learning community" has become a kind of "international movement".

3 Analysis and Evaluation of Online Learning Community in Occupational Training of College Teachers

The analysis of established online learning community, and its structural elements and creation strategies can shed light on the effect of the application of online learning community. At present the most successful of online learning community of this type include the Lab.net that aimed to help middle school teachers' career development, and Wired for Learning, a collaborative Learning community built by IBM to help students and teachers to form a meaningful connection in the process of communication and through collaborative tools to help teachers improve teaching. Besides inside China, the influential and successful example is the virtual learning community, an intelligent network teaching support platform,

built by the Capital Normal University, to provide the support for the sharing of learning resources, offer a variety of teaching and learning tools, and ease the burden of teachers to conduct online classes and students' cognitive load. Their improvement in teaching efficiency and quality has been proved in the empirical research.

Traditional learning community took place in a physical environment, whose members and resources are limited by the physical environment. While the online learning community is formed in the digital and virtual space, members and the resources enjoyed great flexibility. Online learning community realized the sharing of resource in the true sense and changed their way of learning and collaboration, which really enhanced the learning effect of the members of the community. The development of information technology makes it possible for the wide employment of E-learning and M-learning. Now we are moving toward U-learning, where learning can happen in any forms and at any time. These new learning concepts broke the pattern of traditional learning and made learning merge naturally into our lives. This new type of learning, a truly personalized learning, was no longer restricted by time and place. Learning resources don't just refer to traditional learning materials, such as books, notes, but all the the bits of information on the Internet, such as text, audio, video, images, and so on.

The online learning community can play a major role in the college teachers' career development. The main advantage of online learning community derives from the support of information technology that specially focused on the activity of community members, resource sharing, technology tools and relations between them. This can definitely promote the technical level of teachers' professional development. Online learning community can also strengthen the collaboration of the teachers. It is highly flexible in time and space and is suitable for the synchronous learning, asynchronous learning and group learning activities. In addition, the online learning community will help to optimize the spread of practical knowledge and thus improve teachers' occupation development. Aided by the tools, the resources and activities on the community platform, tacit knowledge can be innovated and practical knowledge can be transmitted outward. The collective sharing and internal absorption of useful information can be achieved.

The online learning community made it possible to solve many of the existing problems in the teachers' occupational development. First, in traditional teaching occupational training, in most cases, the learners are isolated from each other and therefore limited to one's own development. There are certain interactive learning activities among each other but the number is small and the effect is quite limited. Online learning community is able to strengthen mutual cooperation. Based on the digital technology, it is highly flexible in time and space and is suitable for the synchronous learning, asynchronous learning and group learning activities. Through mutual cooperation, the common professional development can be achieved. Second, the current knowledge sharing is still in a state of disorder and cannot realize effective sharing with others. For example, by cloud technology, computer can meet the demand of large data and information processing, where "the cloud" resource is accessible anywhere any time. But it is still necessary, through the appropriate construction of facilities, to separate the function of the resource from its entity, and to realize the integration and flexible configuration of resources. Only through this can the advantage of the congregation, sharing and update of resources be achieved [4]. Through the integration of the resources on the internet community platform, we can best share and absorb the collective resources.

According to Gattiker et al. (2000) research,

online learning community should possess a few essential elements, which include a social network based on personal relations, a simple and open communication channel inside the community that is accessible to all interested groups, private meetings and mutual understanding, dialogue, feedback, a common experience and a common history. We can analyze these elements in a detailed way. The primal factor in the online learning community is the community members that are the various participants of an online learning community, such as various kinds of ordinary members and team leaders. As for the occupational training of college English teachers, any online learning community of this kind must have enough interested members. Secondly, the online learning community should also be equipped with the appropriate technical tools, such as those that are used to support a variety of community learning activities such as efficient search engines, management tools, communication tools, collaboration tools, and the like. Besides, the online learning community also should have a central subject. This is initiated by the community organizer or by some members of the community and it should be of mutual interest, it is the focus of the target community activities. In the case of college English teachers occupational development, the topics would better include but not limited to the following topics like big classroom teaching, lesson preparation, choice of teaching resources, the academic development and so on. The online learning community should possess enough resources, various resources like multimedia and interactive digital resources, and also human resources in a broader sense. For example, the online learning community for college English teachers, there should be a balance of the number of inexperienced young teachers and experienced teachers to achieve the desirable effect. In a word, online learning community is a condensed experience of all the community members, which can turn a traditional "resource distribution center" into an "interactive platform" in a true sense.

4 Findings and Suggestions

After the analysis and evaluation, we can say that in the construction of online learning community, special attention must be paid to the following factors.

4.1 A clear and precise definition of the theme of the online learning community.

The theme must be pertinent to the promotion of the teachers' professional development, resources improvement and the teaching of a particular major. It also should give enough consideration to the needs of teachers and the requirements of curriculum reform. The purpose of the choice of the subject is to continuously inject confidence and motivation into new members of the learning community and to enable them to communicate in an atmosphere of equality, democracy, freedom. Therefore, we can make an organic combination of teachers' professional development and course resources construction.

4.2 The establishment of a reward mechanism in the construction of teaching resources

The implementation of the reward system on the one hand, can help teachers maintain the enthusiasm for resource construction and updating, and on the other hand, enhance the teachers' sense of the identity as being a member of the learning community. It can also prompt teachers to have a positive competition and thus realize common development for all those involved.

4.3The support of powerful learning tools and the collection of rich resources

A rich variety of resources are the essential nutrients for teachers' teaching and researching activities.

4.4 Online and offline activities should complement each other.

The focus of our efforts is the construction

of the online learning atmosphere based on the internet technique. Most of the activities are designed to be held on the online learning community platform, such as the discussion and exchange of information and other activities. Attention should also be paid to the organization of various research groups to carry out a large number of offline activities, including collective lesson preparation, the public class, expert lectures observation and etc. For the college English teachers, the online learning community should also organize the experienced teachers to conduct public classes. Other kinds of gathering and collective activities are also needed to deepen the emotional tie among community members. These activities are beneficial and can arouse the enthusiasm of members of the community, and enhance their sense of belonging.

Conclusion

The research and construction of the online learning community has important academic importance and practical significance, because the online learning community will definitely be an important tool in digital technology for the talent training work, such as the occupational training of college teachers, in the era of information. Online learning community can provide specific operating mode for the application of this new media. It can also help solve many of the existing problems in traditional training and opened new possibilities for occupational training. In the internet environment the online learning community made it possible for teachers' professional learning and teaching practice, individual learning and cooperative learning as a group to be syncretized. It is possible to break through the limit of time and space. "The internet makes the cooperative learning community in the wide area possible. Through the interactive learning technology platform, real-time and non-real -time communication and cooperation between education experts can become reality."[5]

Acknowledgements

This work was financially supported by the Research Project of Shandong University at Weihai.

References

[1]. Cohran-Smith, M., & Fries, K.. Researching Teacher Education in Changing Times: Politics and Paradigms. In C. Cochran-Smith & K.M. Zeichner (Eds), Studying Teacher Education: The Report of the AERA Panel on Research and Teacher Education (PP.69-109). New Jersey: Lawrence Erlbaum Associates. (2005)

[2]. Xue Huanyu. An Initiative Investigation into the Theory and Practice of the Learning Community. Journalof University of Geosciences, 1 (2007)

[3]. Wang Xiaofang. From Community to Partnership: the Expansion and Reform of Teachers' Learning Situation. Journal of East China Normal University. 3. (2015)

[4]. Zhu Zhiting. Opportunities and Challenges brought by Cloud technology to the Informationization of Education in China. Chinese Audio-visual Education, 10. (2012).

[5]. Zhou Su. The Teacher Learning Community in the Internet Environment as a Support to Teachers' Professional Development. Electrochemical Education Research. 6. (2007)

MATEC Web of Conferences 44, 02083 (2016)
DOI: 10.1051/matecconf/20164402083

Application of 3 kinds of practical electromagnetic spiders in electromagnetic spider web

Min Jiang

Ningbo Polytechnic; Zhejiang Ningbo 315800

Abstract: Electromagnetic spider web the launch circuit has introduced a lot , but in the center position of the utility of the spider generally have 3 kinds of circuits respectively, the use of single-chip microcomputer circuit of the low energy consumption spider by multi-channel transmission, single circuit receiver circuit. Direct use of the 3 channels of the spider and the use of PLC circuit spider, depending on the actual situation were placed.

Key words: earthquake prediction; PLC circuit; Super heterodyne receiver module; Electromagnetic spider web; GPRS switch

1 THE USE OF PLC CIRCUIT ELECTROMAGNETIC SPIDER

Our design is based on the theory of Maxwell's equations, making cloth discharging principle is in earthquake prone areas placed 6 to 8 groups (amplitude modulation 3 Road, frequency modulation 3 Road) wireless emission module (frequency by 27Mhz~49Mhz~315Mhz), (distance from near to far) using the corresponding super heterodyne, super reflex circuit receiving device receives a signal, usually 3 Road in within the range of measurement, the other 3 road at the outside of the range can be determined. Determination of abnormal signal of the earth's electric field with multiple electronic compass. A log spiral gradient is commonly used, and the eight point is placed in a similar thermometer. Spider speed is generally curl, detecting the magnetic field should be carefully not say bitter. Under the strong pressure of the seismic plate, the electromagnetic wave is usually described by divergence, which measures the change of the electric field to be taken care. PLC industrial control board FX2N-20MT does not need to convert, direct online download ladder diagram, online monitoring, power to maintain, support text and touch screen, the power supply and power supply with the power source, is no longer a common input and output isolation, the power supply ground with the board of the other ground completely isolated, in strong magnetic and other harsh environment, running stable and reliable part of the communication, made a perfect optical isolation, single output 50MA current.

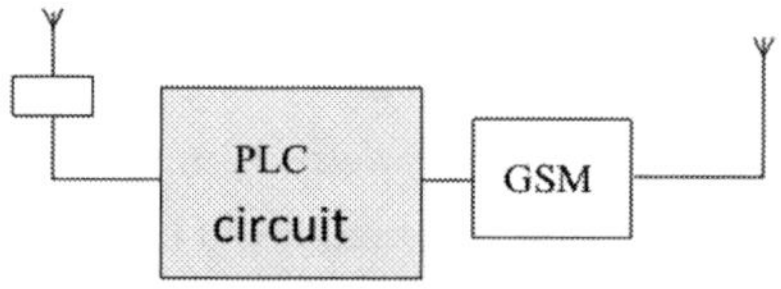

Fig.1, The use of the PLC circuit electromagnetic spider block diagram

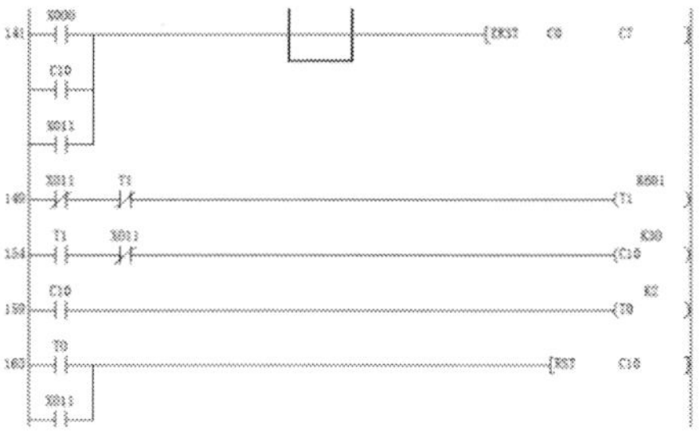

Fig.2, half an hour to receive a PLC part of the program

PLC FX-TRN-BEG-C is generally used in the introduction of basic teaching software to learn general ladder logic programming. With PLC software to determine the earth electromagnetic field anomaly and alarm, with the home thermometer indicator of the earth temperature as well as by the LED indicator of the earth electromagnetic field, can also be combined with GPRS network for remote monitoring, multiple electromagnetic spider network composed of GPRS network to determine the local electromagnetic field changes before a week before the earthquake.

2 THE USE OF SINGLE CHIP CIRCUIT OF LOW ENERGY CONSUMPTION ELECTROMAGNETIC SPIDER

This kind of spider use of single-chip microcomputer circuit of low energy consumption electromagnetic spider equipment low cost, outdoor power consumption is low, in the field can normally use more than 1 years. Use (30 m ~900 m) distance wireless remote control by multi channel transmitter, multi channel receiver circuit composition of electromagnetic fields in the range of 100 square kilometers, the main principle is: the use of electromagnetic spider network produced by the main principle is: the device is located in a dormant state micro power standby, found that the abnormal frequency of electromagnetic field, and more than a single detection system to detect the use of single chip microcomputer.

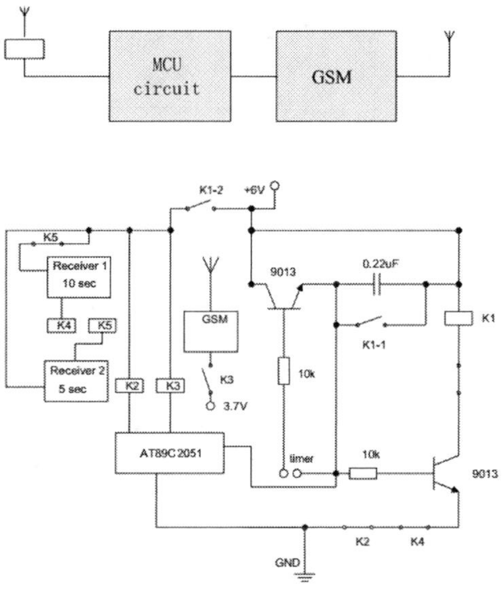

Fig.3, The use of single-chip microcomputer circuit of low energy consumption electromagnetic spider

```
         ORG            0000H
         AJMP    START1
         ORG            0030H
SAME     EQU            4EH
START1:  MOV            P1,#001
START:   MOV            A,P3
         ANL            A,#1FH
         CJNE    A,#1FH,SHIY
         AJMP    START1
SHIY:    MOV            SAME,A
         LCALL   YS
         MOV            A,P3
         ANL            A,#1FH
         CJNE    A,#1FH,SHIY1
         AJMP    START1
SHIY1:   CJNE    A,SAME,START1
         CJNE    A,#17H,NEXT1
         AJMP    LEFT
NEXT1:   CJNE    A,#0FH,NEXT2
         AJMP    RIGHT
NEXT2:   CJNE    A,#1DH,NEXT3
         AJMP    EARGE
NEXT3:   CJNE    A,#1EH,NEXT4
         AJMP    BRAKE
```

Fig.4, part of the program

The electromagnetic spider e-group and GPRS or GSM network remote control is by multiple transmitting and receiving circuit of the relay circuit can greatly increase the detection distance, which are composed of electromagnetic spider e-group and computer networking, by the specialized software to judge can accurate determination of the location of the epicenter of the earthquake. Electromagnetic spider e-group's principle is self multiplex emission, receiver with computer software judgment electromagnetic anomaly range, determine the type of earthquake, the epicenter location and alarm. GPRS network remote

control block diagram. The most simple GPRS control we chose the second generation GSM remote control, GSM is the full name of the System for Mobile Communications Global. A series of electrodynamics equations Maxwell equations which is the basis of our design theory and distributed transmitter. Electronic stopwatch with single-chip circuit is the core of the design of the receiving system, the long-term timing transmitting circuit. 6~8 group is generally required for the actual installation. Half the other half of the receiving area is in an area of the reception area. Remote alarm circuit in the normal electromagnetic do not start GSM, the exception of the remote automatic alarm when the alarm, the alarm after the alarm to be released from the remote control of the output off. Once the alarm can be more than 200 times, very convenient. Electromagnetic spider web in the use of if the alarm once every 72 hours, adjust the 72 hours after the alarm that the earthquake will occur within 72 hours. If the alarm once every 48 hours, adjust the alarm once again after 48 hours, said the earthquake will occur in about 48 hours. If every time 15 minutes alarm once, adjust the alarm once again after 15 minutes, said the earthquake will occur after 15 minutes. And so on. The accurate time of the earthquake magnitude and the earthquake occurrence can be analyzed by remote GPRS device. Usually do not need manual intervention. Ordinary household, as long as the choice of more than 2 can be early warning. When the abnormal electromagnetic generation, the remote automatic alarm, the alarm after the self - lock to be released from the remote control to launch the "output off" command. Commonly used instructions have the "output", "output", "open", "point", "memory", "point", "reply", "reply" and so on, very convenient

3 THE USE OF THREE REMOTE SWITCH OF THE ELECTROMAGNETIC SPIDER

Families in the use of low power long time magnetic field offset detector (earthquake predictor) by electronic compass, the compass. The use of specialized timing device for 5 seconds per minute. Magnetoelectric effect of pre earthquake electromagnetic anomaly is caused by the earthquake is one of the main factors, before the earthquake electromagnetic anomaly by a large number of examples confirmed. In today's world, earthquakes are frequent and destructive. If a few hours before the earthquake, when the earthquake occurred, can avoid many terrible things. The earth is a complex giant system, the establishment of a very precise kinetic equation is not achieved. Use of space electric field and the magnetic field of the earth changes in design of impending earthquake prediction device, the electric field, magnetic field parameter measurement is not necessary to enter the interior of the earth, easy realization of the technology, one of the major advantages of low power consumption for a long time the earth magnetic field offset detector is without debugging can work normally.

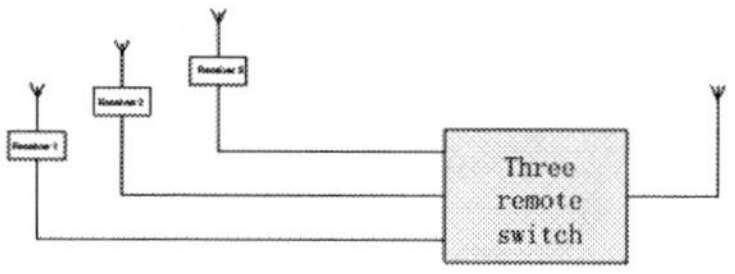

Fig.5 the use of 3 remote switch spider

Due to the static circuit power consumption is only 0.1~-0.3mA, 5 seconds per minute, when the current is generally less than 150mA, it is very economical to use electric power, No.5 batteries generally available for 1 years or so. Limited to the current level of science and technology, it is impossible to predict the magnitude of the earthquake occurrence time and place 100% accurately. But it is certain that the study of some abnormal phenomena can reduce the damage caused by the earthquake, especially the loss of human life. Using earthquake geomagnetic field before the design parameters of low power consumption for a long time earth magnetic field offset detector, can be

used for actual industrial measurements need not be carried into the interior of the earth, can be easily implemented on technology, and is suitable for large-scale low-cost cloth. Very suitable for the vast rural areas of china. Also should be extended to many families in china. Electronic compass to do the early warning circuit: the main components of the DN6851 Hall components, and now use it to monitor the earth's magnetic field, the basic principle is the use of switch type Hall sensor (Hall switch) is a new non-contact integrated circuit switch, DN6851 has a simple structure, plastic shell, small size. The combined use of two ferrite body bar to increase the magnetic field of the earth is the switch element, open collector output without contact and long service life. Fast switching speed and frequency band (direct current to 100kHz). Because the earth's magnetic field is very weak so about two ferrite rod enhanced, and achieved good results. DN6851 Hall components through the T1, T2 amplification directly driving the music integrated circuit, the circuit is connected once a minute, about 5 seconds,. When the magnetic field changes in the earthquake before the alarm. A circuit design scheme is proposed, which is simple and practical, and it is hoped to protect human's life and property in earthquake prediction. It can be predicted if they can successfully find the shock of abnormal electromagnetic field and electromagnetic wave alarm method, and then the formation of a comprehensive global monitoring system will promote the earthquake the emergence and development of before impending earthquake prediction for scientific research and earthquake prediction. Electromagnetic spider webs make up for the shortcomings of previous studies, and people are going through a powerful electromagnetic field. Human beings are higher than all animals, than any animal progress. But the dialectics tells us that every step is a step backward. When human beings are divided from the animal kingdom, many of the animals are lost. People can learn from animals. It is only from the individual animals that the abnormal performance of the natural can not come to the conclusion of the earthquake. If we in the Earth spread a electromagnetic spider web, the electromagnetic changes in the law to collect with local animal abnormal collection of comprehensive analysis, it can be animals can't come to the conclusion. This is where we humans are higher than animals. After painstaking research, we design the electromagnetic spider web was born. Why do some scientists appear to have many difficulties in seismic research? I think mainly in the three-dimensional appearance of earthquake precursor they often in point and line in the study, these are very difficult to measure the three elements of earthquake. Electromagnetic spider web is a method of area and solid, which is more advanced than the point and line method. The struggle against natural disasters must have the ability to transcend nature, and the scientific invention should be the crystallization of human wisdom. Ex seismic workers of course have an indelible contribution, but it is difficult to understand why Tangshan earthquake has not predicted success. I think that the main method of improper use of sensor.

4 DETERMINE THE EARTHQUAKE THREE ELEMENTS

The electromagnetic spider is the core of the whole device. The basic principle is that the single chip computer software is used to determine the range of electromagnetic anomalies, and to determine the type of earthquake, the location of the epicenter and the remote alarm. The earthquake, the epicenter of the earthquake, the earthquake level, known as the three elements of the earthquake. It can be predicted if they can successfully find the shock of abnormal electromagnetic field and electromagnetic wave alarm method, and then the formation of a comprehensive global

monitoring system will promote the earthquake the emergence and development of before impending earthquake prediction for scientific research and earthquake prediction. Three electromagnetic spiders in the electromagnetic spider web make up for the shortcomings of previous studies. I believe in the future we can cast a electromagnetic spider web on the earth, the electromagnetic changes were collected. It is possible to solve the difficulties in earthquake prediction.

5 SUMMARY

Pre earthquake prediction with many scientists conducting research there. For example Dr. S Kato of Hokkaido University in Japan also has a research in this area, some scientists why there appear many difficulties? I think the main reason is in stereoscopic emergence of earthquake precursor they often in point and line in the research, drilling deep wells placed one instrument, some experts put a line test resistance change, these are very difficult to measure the three elements of earthquake. Electromagnetic spider web is to the area, three-dimensional method to detect the earthquake, it should be advanced. Einstein once said: "imagination is more important than knowledge in the creation of inventions". Heaven should not negative observant and conscientious person, 1966 April 1, at 3 o'clock in the afternoon, Premier Zhou Enlai in Xingtai area of earthquake science and technology university students said: "I hope in your generation can solve the problem of earthquake prediction." Electromagnetic spider web is possible to realize this wish, and its theoretical calculation has been published in EI, SCI and ISTP. With natural disasters as a struggle must have the perseverance and ability to transcend nature, in the East China Sea in November 14, 2015 6.0 earthquake occurred before half an hour, the home of the six groups of spider web have two groups of successful prediction. It's very good. A simple saying as follows: Electromagnetic spider is not deep, Maxwell must to be learn. Log Spiral gradient, Eight point placement. Knitting speed of rotation Influence magnetic field not afraid of suffering. Divergence of plate motion change care for the electric field.

REFERENCES

1、Jiang Min. Multi point timing control circuit [J]. Electric world fourth, 1992 (4): 42-42

2、Jiang Min. Sound and light indicator of electronic compass [J].Electric world, second 1996 (2)：33

3、Jiang Min. Earthquake prediction micro integrated measurement recorder [J] Technology Innovation Herald 2010, (29): 22-23

4、Min Jiang,2013.11 How to weave the electromagnetic spider web to predict earthquakes，2013 3rd International Conference on Education and Education Management(EEM 2013)，p546-551

5、Min Jiang,2014.1 Electromagnetic spider web Application in earthquake prediction, International Core Journal of Scientific Research & Engineering Index,pp111-114

Min Jiang,2014.11 The Group of Electromagnetic spider web, Economic, Business Management and Education Innovation(EBMEI 2014),pp287-291

6、Min Jiang,2014.12 Low Power Consumption Electromagnetic spider web, 2014 4th International Conference on Education and Education Management(EEM 2014), pp74-78

7、Min Jiang, Ping Yao Wang 2015.9 Simple space electric field and earth magnetic anomaly remote alarm system,2015 International Conference on Frontiers of Manufacturing Science and Measuring Technology, pp452-458

MATEC Web of Conferences 44, 02084 (2016)
DOI: 10.1051/matecconf/20164402084

Regional differences of urban construction land in Jiangsu province, China

Xiu Lu[1], Jia Li[1,a], Fei Tao[2] and Ping Duan[1]

[1]School of Tourism and Geographical Sciences of Yunnan Normal University Yunnan, China
[2]School of Geographical Sciences of Nantong University Jiangsu, China

Abstract. Jiangsu province is a typical area of the urban extension problems. Urban construction land has been the major area of city research. And more and more people pay attention to this matter. In this paper, regional differences of urban construction land in Jiangsu province, China were analyzed. Firstly, this work is based on remote sensing images as the main data source in 2010. The spectral differences of soil cover type of waters, forest land, construction land, unused land, cultivated land were explored. Secondly, three kinds of index methods (soil adjusted vegetation index, modified normalized difference water index and the ratio resident-area index) were used to extract the information of urban construction land. Finally, urban construction land was segmented by administrative boundary information of Jiangsu Province, China. And, different areas of the urban construction land, non-urban construction land and cultivated land were compared and analyzed. The experimental results from the urban construction scale show that, in 2010, the south of Jiangsu is greater than the north of Jiangsu, and the north of Jiangsu is greater than the central of Jiangsu. From the point of proportion of cultivated land: the central of Jiangsu is greater than the north of Jiangsu, and the north of Jiangsu is greater than the south of Jiangsu.

1 Introduction

The increasing urban construction land is the significant identification of the changes of landscape structure of the rapid development. The dynamic process not only significantly changed the l overall landscape layout of city zone. At the same time it also has a significant impact on the edge of the city's agricultural distribution and the layout of natural humanities' landscape. Our country is in the stage of rapid urbanization. And Jiangsu province is the typical area of urban expansion in our country [1]. Urban land has been the main direction of urban studies. With the development of remote sensing and GIS technology, the scholars in domestic and abroad have done a lot of research on some cities in Jiangsu province and the improvement of the research methods in recent years. Ran Jiang etc (2007) adopted the method of supervised classification and visual interpretation to analyse Lianyungang city's extension and encroach on the surrounding land from 1978 to 2005 [2]. Wang lei (2008) based on the data of urban construction land area in the past years of Jiangsu province, analysing the change of time and space of the construction land expansion and exploring its effect mechanism. Zhang Xuefeng etc (2011) used TM3 and TM2 two bands transplanting in normalized construction index (NDBI) method and he combined it with NDBI to extract the urban construction land. He set a define method to be suitable for the remote sensing classification establishment and which can acquire three cities built up area of Suzhou, Wuxi and Changzhou [3]. Wu XIU (2012) used RS and GIS spatial information extraction, spatial analysis technology and theory of cellular automata to analyse and study the strength, scale and direction of urban spatial extension characteristics, dynamic mechanism. Xu Hanqiu (2005) chosen Fuzhou city thematic enhanced images as the research data, and he selected the Normalized difference construction index, soil vegetation index adjustment and correction normalized difference water index and so on to analyse the spectral characteristics. And then extract the information of urban construction land area, the main method is the rules of logic criterion [4]. Wu Hongan(2006) proposed a new method of extracting information, and he used the ratio resident index method (RRI). This method is collecting the sampling points of images of the study area and using the DN value of the image to be able to quickly extract urban building land information [5].

This paper is using remote sensing images and it is based on remote sensing and GIS to analyse the land used for urban construction in 2010 of the whole Jiangsu province. This paper is also combined with Jiangsu province administrative boundary data to obtain the

[a]Corresponding author: Li Jia (✉)
School of Tourism and Geographical Science, Yunnan Normal University, Kunming, China
e-mail: keguigiser@163.com

partition of land used for urban construction and it is accessed to different parts of the area, distribution features of urban construction land.

2 Research area and data

2.1 Research area

Jiangsu province is simply called "Su". Its location is in the eastern coastal center of mainland China. Its latitude and longitude is: 116°18 '~ 121 ° 57' 116 ° east longitude, 30 ° 45 '~ 35 ° 20' north latitude. In Jiangsu province, its area is 102600 square kilometers and its area occupies 1.06% of the territory of China. Its per capita land area is the least of all the provinces in China. Jiangsu is near the ocean and near the sea, adjoining the yellow sea in the east and the Pacific Ocean. It is geographically across north and south and its climate and vegetation also has the characteristics of the south and the north. Its border is adjacent to Shandong, Zhejiang, close to the Anhui province and Shanghai City. To 2015, Jiangsu province has administered a deputy provincial city (Nanjing), 12 district cities (Wuxi, Xuzhou, Changzhou, Suzhou, Nantong, Lianyungang, Huaian, Yancheng, Yangzhou, Zhenjiang, Yangzhou, Taizhou and Suqian).

2.2 Data source

2.2.1 Remote sensing image data

Because LANDSAT7 ETM + airborne scanning line corrector occurred major fault after May 2003. This paper selects the LANDSAT5 TM data as data sources. The 23 remote sensing images are selected for Mosaic. Due to the much image data of Jiangsu province, cloud cover, vegetation growth, some data loss and so on, some 2010 cannot use the image data, 2009 image data instead with the same region. Finally 23 images are used for mosaic which respectively including 10 images of 2009 and 13 images of 2010.

2.2.2 Administrative division data

Political map of Jiangsu province and reference in 2009 and 2010 yearbook data of Jiangsu province and other relevant information.

2.2.3 Data pre-processing

The 23 images are downloaded from Geospatial data cloud and to conduct band combination, image correction, image matching, image of administrative boundary cutting and so on in the data preprocessing.

3 Research method

3.1 Analysis of spectral information data

Because different land types have different spectral brightness values, this paper is based on predecessor-Che Feng [6] to analyse the characteristic of the spectral difference which can extract the construction land information. Choose a number of sampling points of forest land, water land, unused land, urban land and the cultivated land and so on, five land-cover types. Draw the curve between the average Digital Number and the land type class band. The general image is shown in Fig.1.

Fig.1 showing the construction land and unused land has the same change trend. Cultivated land and forest land have a similar spectral curve trend. Water has its unique spectral curve. According to the spectrum analysis of DN values, therefore, it can be simply concluded 5 classes into 3 classes: vegetation, water, and land for construction.

Secondly, it has clearly seen that in Fig.1, various classes of each band spectrum intensity is not completely consistent to another one. So we can find the gap between the other classes and the construction land and we can clearly distinguish the construction land from the information of the other classes. Now order different wave bands of different classes and the result is as follows:

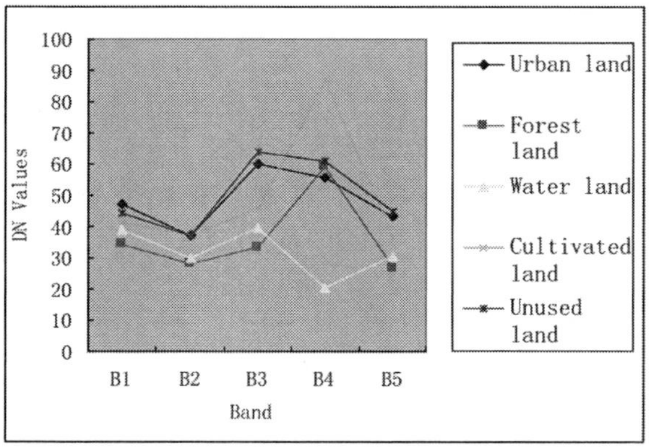

Figure1. Land type of spectrum curve

Cultivated land: band6 > band1 > band4 > band5 > band3 > band2 > band7

Forest land: band6 > band1 > band4 > band5 > band3 > band2 > band7

Water land: band6>band1>band3>band2> band4> band5> band7

Unused land: band6 > band5 > band1 > band7 > band3 > band4 > band2

Construction land: band6 > band1 > band5 > band3 > band4 > band2 > band7

After sorting, it is found that the cultivated land and the forest land satisfying: band4 > band3. Unused land and construction have a relatively similar spectrum curve of the change trend. The values of their band5 are greater than band4. According to the spectral characteristics, we adopt previous information extraction and classification model. It is a method of SAVI, MNDWI and RRI. The three-index exactly play a role of extracting the most critical urban land use types: vegetation, construction and water. Introduction of Soil Adjusting Vegetation Index can be used to distinguish between vegetation and urban construction land. And then introduction of Modified

Normalized Difference Water Index can distinguish between water and urban construction land. But because the spectral characteristics of the unused land and the urban construction land are very similar, the information of extracting contains the construction land information. Therefore it has to remove unused information in the end. From that we can obtain the complete and accurate information of the construction land.

3.2 Extraction of vegetation information

To reduce the interference of background object, on the basis of NDVI, Huete proposed a SAVI index namely soil adjusting vegetation index [7]. Its formula is:

$$SAVI= [(TM4-TM3)\,(1+L)] / (TM4+TM3+L) \quad (1)$$

In the formula, L is a factor to adjust the soil. 0 is used for high vegetation coverage and the high richness. L is used for low vegetation coverage and the low richness. In general, when L takes 0.5, it can better decrease the difference of soil.

3.3 Extraction of water information

Xu Hanqiu in 2005 put forward the Modified Normalized Difference Water Index. Operating the ratio between the band 2 and the band 5 and then to extract water body information. Its formula is [8]:

$$MNDWI = (TM2-TM5)/(TM+TM5) \quad (2)$$

It can be concluded, Modified Normalized Difference Water Index (MNDWI) extraction effect is superior to the Normalized Difference Water Index (NDWI). Using MNDWI extracts the scope of the water whose effect to the actual situation is superior to NDWI.

3.4 Extraction of the construction land information

Yang Shan in 2000 put forward a Normalized Difference Vegetation Index [9], it is a precursor to NDBI index. Later Zha Yong and others later changed it to the Normalized Difference Construction Index. Its formula is:

$$NDBI= (TM5-TM4) / (TM5+TM4) \quad (3)$$

Band5 and band4 are possibly all zero in this formula, so we need to add 0.001 in the denominator. Analysing again, construction land near-infrared wave band is less than the infrared wave band. The same applies to unused land and forest land. So the extraction of the construction land information also contains a certain amount of unused land information and forest land information.

3.5 Division of unused land and urban construction land information

The above extraction of construction land inside contains a lot of unused land information. So we must remove unused land information. We can use RRI = B1 / B4 to conduct the band calculation [5].

4 The extraction results and the analysis of regional differences

4.1 The extraction results

Use the SAVI to extract the vegetation information. Use the MNDWI to extract the water information. Use the RRI to apart the construction land from the unused land. It can generate three images including SAVI, MNDWI and RRI in the above process. Now we respectively merge the images as three new bands. It can be used to separate water, urban construction land and unused land and it can reduce data redundancy. The result is shown in Fig.2.Using the maximum likelihood method to pick up the urban land, like Fig.3.Through calculation, the area of urban land and non-urban land use situation in the following Table1.

Overall, the urban construction land in Jiangsu province occupies 1/5 of the total area of Jiangsu province. The remaining four categories: forest land, unused land, water and cultivated land accounts for 4/5. And then divide the Jiangsu province into 13 cities. Then analyse each prefecture level city construction land and preliminarily analyse the rationality of urban planning.

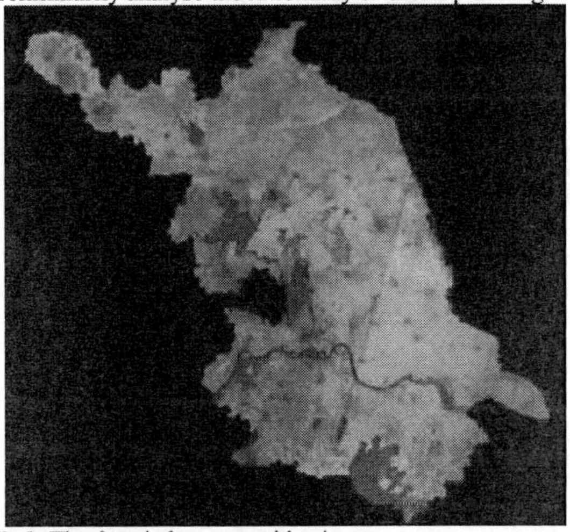

Fig 2. The three index composition image

Fig 3. Urban land extraction results in Jiangsu province

Table1. Land use type area in Jiangsu province

Land use types	Area/km²
Urban construction land	20060.699
Non-urban construction land	84038.707
Regional land use in Jiangsu province	104099.406

4.2 Regional difference analysis

Crop the land use type picture in Jiangsu province. And divide the figure into 13 cities, namely: Zhenjiang, Changzhou, Wuxi, Nanjing, Suzhou (southern area of Jiangsu), Nantong, Taizhou, Yangzhou (middle area of Jiangsu), Xuzhou, Lianyungang, Suqian, Yancheng, Huaian (northern area of Jiangsu). Use three-index method to extract 13 cities information such as the urban construction land. In software arcgis10.0, we can compute area. It can draw various land types area of the cities (including urban construction land area, cultivated land area and so on). The result shows in Table 2.

Table 2. Land type area of 13 cities in Jiangsu province

Prefecture-level city	Urban construction land area (Unit:km²)	Cultivated land area (Unit:km²)	Total area (Unit: km2)
Xuzhou	2514.8899	7632.8198	11102.03
Lianyungang	1864.0601	4670.0801	7309.387
Suqian	2005.4301	5058.0898	8567.689
Huaian	1951.53	5714.6099	9972.295
Yancheng	1994.9301	11664.9	15334.89
Yangzhou	1051.14	4211.0298	6609.79
Taizhou	995.82898	4197.9302	5783.223
Nantong	976.66803	7373.96	8901.446
Zhenjiang	728.70001	2358.0901	3826.502
Changzhou	926.98999	2506.02	4384.301
Wuxi	1215.36	1946	4602.012
Suzhou	2206.54	2949.6101	8405.863
Nanjing	1551.78	3490.46	6535.961

To sum up, Xuzhou, Huaian, Yancheng, Suzhou and Suqian cities' land area are the largest all over the 13 cities' urban construction land area in Jiangsu province. Five cities have four cities are northern regions. According to related statistics, all over the Jiangsu province, the north of Jiangsu economy is relatively less than middle and southern area of Jiangsu. Urban land area is large, does not represent the whole area proportion is large too (As shown in Fig. 4). The data shows in figure 5, Suzhou and Wuxi urban land area of total area proportion are the most. Southern area of urban land proportion ranges between 19% ~ 26% and there is not big difference among them. Yancheng's urban land area is large, but the urban land area only t account for 13% of all over the whole area.

Overall, the construction land is the largest proportion of southern region of Jiangsu. Secondly, northern region, middle region is the lowest. In contrast to the urban construction land proportion, larger proportion is the middle region, northern regions secondly, followed by a relatively low proportion is southern region in the 13 cities. (As is shown in Fig.5).

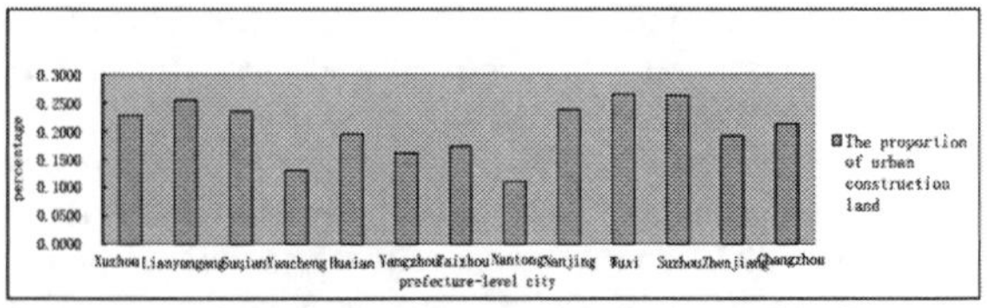

Fig 4. Proportion of urban construction land use of prefecture-level cities in Jiangsu province

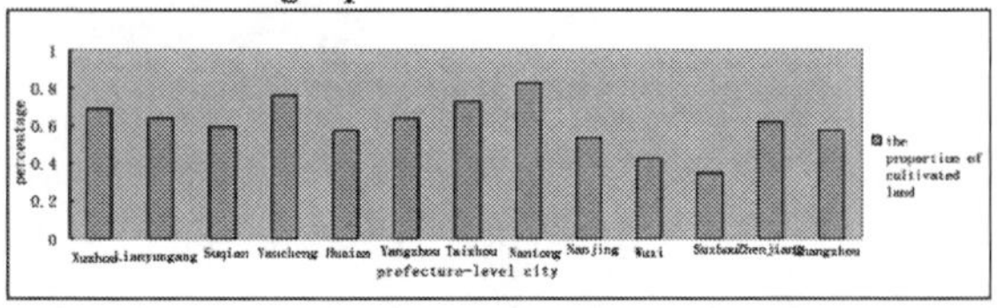

Fig 5. Proportion of cultivated land use of prefecture-level cities in Jiangsu province

Therefore, throughout the proportion of the level city in Jiangsu province and under the other land classes share a similar situation, proportion of cultivated land area is opposite to urban construction land. So, from this point, it laterally reflects the city's expansion and development based on the loss of arable land and transformation. The geographic space main present a characteristic of middle area is greater than the southern Jiangsu and greater than the northern Jiangsu area from the overall coordination between the level of economic development in Jiangsu province and the city level of intensive land use type.

5 Conclusions

This paper is based on the multiphase LANDSAT TM data as the data source. Select appropriate extraction method to extract the information of urban construction land through exploring water areas, forest land, construction land, unused land and cultivated land and so on five spectral differences of soil cover types. Make use of Jiangsu province administrative boundary information to partition for the urban construction land. Compare different parts of the city construction land area, difference of distribution characteristics. It can reveal the area of urban construction land in Jiangsu province, morphological differentiation and the pattern of the spatial distribution characteristics. The specific conclusions are as follows:

1. This paper uses SAVI, MNDWI, RRI three indices for urban construction land information extraction. The result shows that the method to extract the area size is similar to the known area of the city planning of the cities. It can be illustrated that the three index extraction method is a high extraction precision and it is a kind of relatively accurate urban land information extraction technology.

2. Jiangsu province has a total area of 104099.406 square kilometers, of which the urban construction land area of 20060.699 square kilometers, accounting for 1/5 of the total area. Divide Jiangsu province into three regions: northern area, middle area and southern Jiangsu. Southern area five regional average proportion of urban land is: 0.208281. Southern Jiangsu five regional average proportion of urban land is: 0.233177. Middle region of the five regional average proportion of urban land is: 0.14698. The south of Jiangsu is greater than northern

region and is greater than the middle region. But from the perspective of cultivated land, north Jiangsu five regional cultivated land proportion is 0.6501 on average. Five regional average proportion of cultivated land in the south of Jiangsu is 0.49913. Middle five regional average proportion of cultivated land is 0.73046. The middle region is greater than the northern region and is greater than the southern region.

All in all, the government should grasp the coordination of urban development and land use types. And we need to give full play to regional advantages and to improve land use efficiency. At the same time, giving play to the role of the government's macroeconomic regulation and control and to promote coordinated development of regional economy orderly is an extremely urgency.

References

1. Q.M. Wu and Lv H, "Jiangsu province for nearly 30 years of land use change analysis of the regional differences," The Earth Information Science Journal, 05:5670-5676, 2009.
2. Q. Ran and C.Q. Ke, "Lianyungang urban expansion and its driving force analysis," Anhui Agricultural Science, 03:725-727, 2007.
3. X.F. Zhang, Z.W. He, R. Wang and D.H. Zhang, "Su, Xi, Chang built up area used remote sensing method to extract and the analysis of urban expansion," Science of Surveying and Mapping, 02:113-115, 2011.
4. H.Q. Xu, "It is based on the spectral characteristics and normalized index to the urban building land information extraction," Geographical Research, 24(2):311-320, 2005.
5. H.A. Wu, J.J. Jiang and H.L. Zhang, "Residents ratio index apply in the information extraction in cities and towns," Journal of Nanjing Normal University (Natural Science Edition), 118-121, 2006.
6. F. Che and H. Lin, "Urban construction land remote sensing information extraction method research," Science of Surveying and Mapping, 04:97-99, 2010.
7. A.R. Huete, "A soil adjusted vegetation index (SAVI)," [J]Remote Sensing of Environment, 25(3): 295-309, 1988.
8. H.Q. Xu, "Using the modified normalized difference water index (MNDWI) to extract water body information research," Journal of Remoting Sensing, 9(5):589-585, 2005.
9. S. Yang, "Developed areas of urban and rural human settlements of information extraction and fractal research - in Wuxi city as an example," Journal of Geographical, 55(6):671-678, 2000.

MATEC Web of Conferences 44, 02085 (2016)
DOI: 10.1051/matecconf/20164402085

The Office Software Learning and Examination System Design Based on Fragmented Learning Idea

Ling Xu[1], Wei He[2]

[1]College of Computer Science, Sichuan Normal University, Chengdu, China
[2]College of Physics and Electronic Engineering, Sichuan Normal University, Chengdu, China

Abstract. Fragmented learning is that through the segmentation of learning content or learning time, make learners can use the fragmented time for learning fragmentated content, have the characteristics of time flexibility, learning targeted and high learning efficiency. Based on the fragmented learning ideas, combined with the teaching idea of micro class and interactive teaching, comprehensive utilization of flash animation design software, .NET development platform, VSTO technology, multimedia development technology and so on, design and develop a system integrated with learning, practice and examination of the Office software, which is not only conducive to the effective and personalized learning of students, but also conducive to the understanding the students' situation of teachers, and liberate teachers from the heavy labor of mechanical, focus on promoting the formation of students' knowledge system.
Keyword: fragmented thought, Office software, micro class, operating practice system

1 Fragmented learning

Fragmented learning is that through the segmentation of learning content or learning time, make learners can use the fragmented time for learning fragmentated content. Because the learning content has been divided, the learning time of each fragment becomes more controllable, which improves the flexibility to learners to control the learning time; learners can also according to their own situation, choose to learning the helpful or intrested learning content, improve the pertinence of learning; due to the learning content is divided, the learning time of a individual pieces of content is short, can protect the learner's learning interest, improve the absorption rate of knowledge, improve the learning efficiency of students.[1][2]

2 The present situation of Office software teaching

Computer application ability is the basic skill that everyone should have in the information age. So, freshmen of college will offer computer application basis or computer culture basis courses, help students know the concepts, principles and daily maintenance and grasp the use of the computer. Office software is the main component of this course.

Office software learning has the following characteristics: 1. the main content is operational content, the proportion of concept and theory is small; 2. students' computer application ability are differences due to the information technology learning conditions in middle school and family; 3. the relevance of each knowledge point is small, which is suitable for the fragmented study; 4. as college students, can not only meet the learning of simple functions, but should master more advanced applications and skills to solve practical problems; 5. because it is the operation learning content, need to use strengthen means to enhance memory and understanding,

At present, this part of teaching content mainly uses the teaching method: teachers teach and students practice. In practice, this teaching method exposes the following problems: 1. because of the less of teaching hours, more learning content, students can understand when teacher explanation, but when practice, don't know how to do; 2. because students' practice mainly in the after-school, often can not get the teacher's guidance in time, 3. in order to take care of poor students, teachers no time to introduce more valuable advanced application content in the classroom.

About the examination, the current forms are the three as bellow: First, the written examination. In this type of examination, the operation type of content are examed by fill in the blanks, select and simple answer, this examination form is too rigid, and can not really test students operation and application ability on software. Second, free work examination form. Students are required to use the software to create a work to show their ability of learning and application of the software. This form is good at testing of the students' ability of using and innovating of the software, is a good way to qualitative assessment. But is weak of comprehensive examinate the

grasp of software function of the students, and is not easy to do quantitative evaluation and give points; in addition, this form is need to provide more time to the students to complete their creation work after-class, therefore, the supervision of examination is difficult. Third, sampling work examination form. In this form of examination, the teacher produce a good sample use of the software before examination, requiring students complete the production according to the sample in limited time. The advantage of this form of examination is to facilitate the teacher to quantitative evaluation the situation of students' study of the software function. The disadvantage is that the marking workload is very large.

3 Learning and examination system design

Based on the thought of fragmentation, operation strengthening and reducing the unnecessary mechanical repetition of the teacher, we designed the Office software learning and examination system to solve the problems existing in the current teaching and examination. The system is composed of three parts, shown in figure 1.

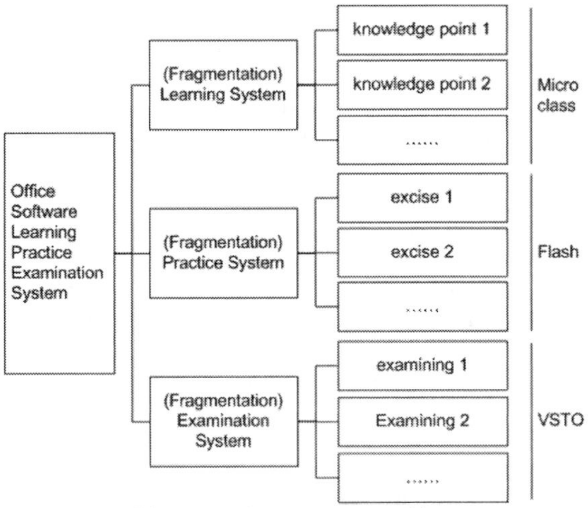

Figure 1 System composition

3.1 Learning system module

The learning system module mainly contains the teaching videos, are presented in the form of micro class, to facilitate the students to learn the related concepts, terminology and application operation. The realization of this module first needs to decompose the teaching content to knowledge points. Take the chapter of "the usage of graphic objects" in Word software as an example, the knowledges decomposition and micro classes setting as shown in figure 2.

Each knowledge point is made into one or more micro class according to the content. According to the characteristics of the content of knowledge point, the different forms of micro lesson can be selected. For example, overview, concept and principle content, can choose the teacher record form; the operation content can choose screen recording mode; principle animation demo

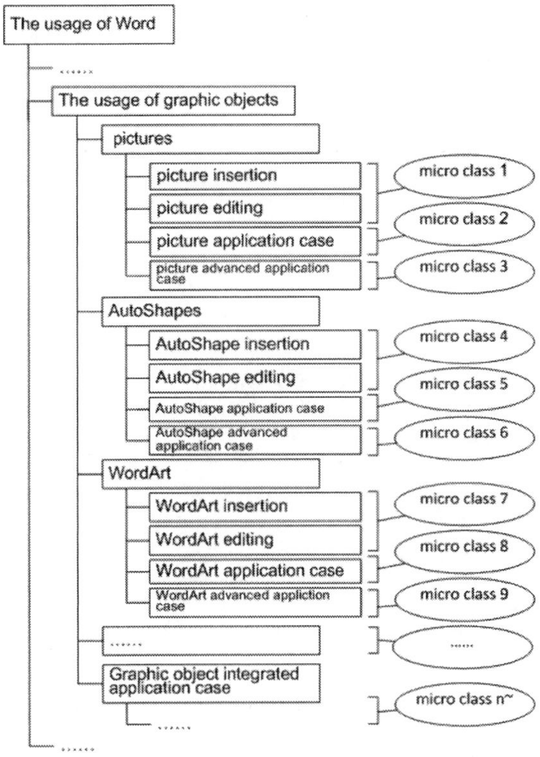

Figure 2 knowledges decomposition and micro classes setting example

content, can be directly translate animation courseware into micro lesson video; and so on. Taking into account the convenience of student learning, the time of micro classes are controled in 5-10 minutes. Finally, organize all the micro class according to the content, all the micro class according to the difficulty is divided into different levels, the first level for students with weak basis to learning the basic content, the second level for students with a certain basis to further study, the third level for students to expand and enhance the advanced application. Clearly identifies each micro class corresponding knowledge points, so, when students learning, they can according to their own situation, quickly choose their own unfamiliar content to focus on learning, so as to reduce the repeated learning time spent on the familiared content. Due to the use of the form of micro class, students can repeat study the content they did not grasp or interested in whenever and wherever possible, thus can get help at any time or place, to avoid the phenomenon of no guidance when encounter problem.

In terms of production, according to the type of the micro lesson, using different production method. For example, for the memoir micro class, in the recording chamber using a camera equipment for recording is a good method; for the demonstration of the operation type of micro class, use screen recording software, record the process of operation and demonstration, and do appropriate post editing, such as increase key annotation, tips emphasize, scene transition, interactive test, etc. finally, in the form of video rendering. This kind of micro class can be produced using Studio Camstia software.

Camstia Studio software powerful on recording screen and post editing, can record screen action easily in any color mode, including the cursor movement, menu selection, pop-up window, etc. all visible content on the screen; it also can to add markers, increase system icon, add title, add sound effects, increase the effect of mouse etc. in video post-editing. It is a very good tool for making screen recording type of micro classes. For the animation type of micro class, can use animation making software, such as flash or Powerpoint software, generate file to video files format directly after make the animation done.

3.2 Practice system module

Practice system module simulate the real software environment to help students carry out the operation exercises, strengthen students' grasp of the operation method and memory, and promote students to quickly and effectively carry out software learning. In the learning process, students often occured such situation: for a given problem, knows what or which function can be used to achieve, but do not know the specific operating methods. The reason is often because the software function is very powerful, students can not find the location of the desired function in so many menu, and don't know how to combined use of multiple functions. So, if we can provide a real software interface, and can be limited to the functional areas of the operation, to help students to quickly grasp the software is very useful. Students' comprehensive application ability of software is built on the independent function of the software. Therefore, the overall realization of this module is still using the idea of fragmentation, according to the decomposition of knowledge points, writing related issues and small tasks to allow students to practice the operation, and give prompt when students encounter problems. The operation of each small problem or task practice idea is: Through screen capture get the real interface of the software - Set the operation areas of the problem (menus, buttons, edit, etc.) to interactive area - Enter the next operation interface if operation right, otherwise, wait for correct operation or get help - Until the last step operation is completed. The implementation process is shown as figure 3.

Implementation method can be used with the visual programming language (such as VB, C#, etc.) or interactive multimedia development tools (Authorware, Flash, etc.). Among them, Flash software has the advantages of agility and flexibility, good integration capabilities and so on, so it is better to use Flash to make operation practice of each small problem or small task. [3][4][5]

So, the operation practices of a software are composed of a series of flash file, all flash files are organized according to the classification of knowledge point prepared in advance, and the related information, such as file name, file location, the corresponding knowledge are writed into database, integrate all flash files by VB.NET,

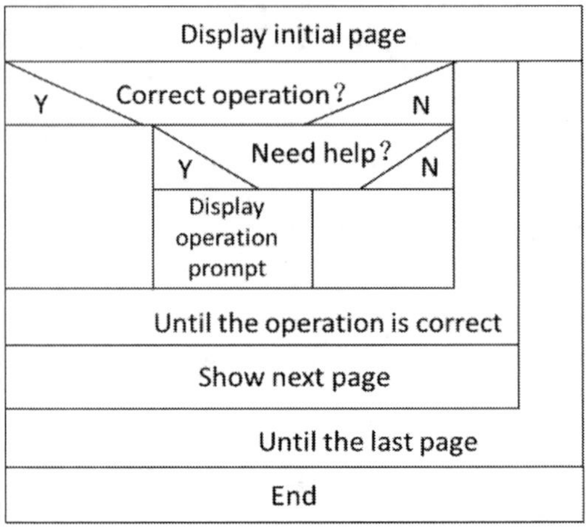

Figure 3. Practice system Implementation process

according to the operator's choice to call and display the corresponding flash file. At the same time, record the situation of seeking help during students doing exercises, in order to do targeted weaknesses training later, to help students to do reinforcement learning on the weak link, so as to quickly master the software usage. Practice system is not only conducive to students quickly become familiar with the software environment, master the operation of software, at the same time, also can make students to get help in the learning process at any time.

3.3 Examination system module

The use of software should be in the real software environment, so the final examination should be carried out in a real software environment. In order to fully assess the students' mastery of software function, it is better to use the sample test form, but the shortcoming is the workload of manual marking and the objectivity of the paper. Computer automatic scoring can solve this problem well. Using VSTO technology can realize the automatic reading of Office documents. VSTO's full name is Visual Studio Tools for Office, it added the support of .NET to Word or Excel and other software into the Studio Visual. VSTO convert Word or Excel documents into a .NET class which can be programmed, so that they become control with data binding function, we can encode it like handle the Forms Windows control and other .NET features. VSTO provides a set of Office application object model, use of these object models, we can access the various attributes of the Office document, which can be used to determine the various attributes of the document, to achieve automatic document reading. For example, for the Word document, we can use the Range object to obtain the specific text in the document, read the text format and other information to achieve automatic marking; the use of Document objects, we can get the document level information, to realize the automatic document level marking. The realize framework is shown in figure 4:

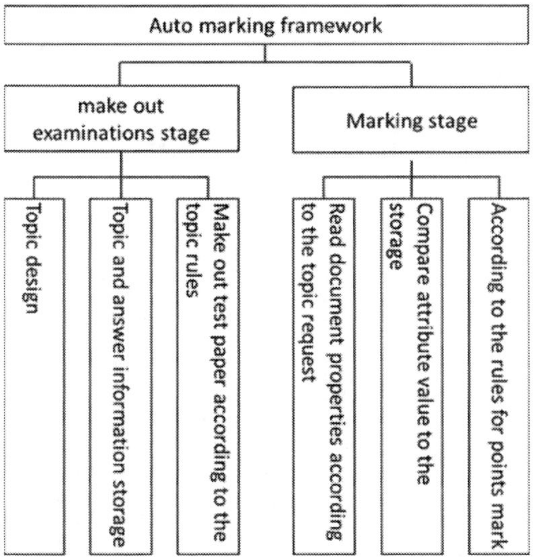

Figure 4. Examination system realize framework

Examination system composed of two parts, exam paper-generating and marking, in the stage of exam paper-generating, the teacher design questions according to the syllabus and the requirements of examination, questions and corresponding answers are written into database, form of item bank. Then, before the examination, select topics from the item band according to the rules of question-making to form the exam paper, be one person one paper. In the marking phase, the system read the students exam information, according to the questions asked, read the related property values of the document, and compare with the answer in library, according to the judgment rules to realize automatic judgment. Examination system ensures comprehensive and randomness of questions through the questions-design and paper-make rules, so as to avoid plagiarism phenomenon. At the same time, auto marking function greatly reduces the workload of teacher manual marking and more impersonal.

4 Conclusion

Based on the fragmented learning thought, using micro-class, solved the problem of basic differences between students and autonomous study in Office software teaching; using simulate actual operating environment but limit operation solve the students' study efficiency in students' autonomous operation practice; use the VSTO technology to achieve the examination papers automatic marking. Such a system is not only conducive to the students' personalized and effective learning, but also for the teacher to master the students' learning situation provides a wealth of data information, and liberate teacher from the mechanical duplication of Labor, can be more energy for teaching itself, should be the future teaching-mode of the software learning. Of course, fragmented learning is not the ultimate goal, the ultimate goal is to achieve the integration and construction of knowledge, to form knowlednage system. Therefore, in the teaching, in addition to help students to learn knowledge more effective with learning system, the teacher should guide students to carry out the processing of knowledge debris integration and migration applications, and promote the formation of students' knowledge system.

References

1.http://baike.baidu.com/link?url=UzcGD6FQiSrqhHQMG1EDunkFfuQIwiNGW-Yf_GbLVfWEcnfc8FWEwq_idFoSfUj362JHWxY5C4B4tQYQp9d20qBaidu Encyclopedia
2. J.J. Lu, China Medical Education Technology, **10**, 508 (2014)
3. W.H.Liu, *Development and production technology of micro lesson* (Higher Education Press, 2015)
4. P.Z. Gong, *Visual Basic.NET programming tutorial* (Higher Education Press, 2010)
5. Ch.M. Si, Z.J. Xu, *Adobe Flash CS6 courseware production case teaching classic tutorial* (Electronic Industry Publishing House, 2015)
6. R. Braunstein, X.M. Tao, Ch. Wang, R.R. Cao, *ActionScript 3.0 treasury* (Tsinghua University Press, 2012)
7. E. Carter, E. Lippert, *Visual Studio Tools for Office 2007: VSTO for Excel, Word, and Outlook* (Addison-Wesley Professional, 2009)
8. E. Carter, E. Lippert, *VSTO Developer's Guide* (Electronic Industry Publishing House, 2008)

MATEC Web of Conferences **44**, 02086 (2016)
DOI: 10.1051/matecconf/20164402086

Design and simulation of a novel circularly polarized antenna with polarization reconfigurable characteristics

Hai ZHANG [a], Wei Guo ZHANG, Yue He GE and Shan Ce LV

College of Information Science and Engineering, Huaqiao University, Xiamen 361021, China

Abstract. A novel circularly polarized antenna with polarization reconfigurable characteristics was designed using co-simulation of Ansoft HFSS and Designer software. It consists of a dual-polarized antenna and phase switching network which act as the feed network for the dual-polarized antenna. The phase switching network was designed based on a Wilkinson power divider, where the output port was connected with SPDT to form a switching network. By controlling the SPDT state-off / on, the phase difference of the two ports could be alternated, which generated the orthogonal modes between the two ports of dual-polarized antenna. So that Left-hand circular polarization (LHCP) and Right-hand circular polarization (RHCP) could be achieved. The simulation shown that reflection coefficient was less than -12 dB and the axial ratio was below 3 dB between 1.8 GHz and 2.4 GHz with polarization reconfigurable characteristics.

1 Introduction

Re-configurable antenna has a lot of advantages. It has been widely used in both military and civilian fields. Re-configurable antenna can be divided to frequency re-configurable antennas, pattern re-configurable antennas, polarized re-configurable antennas and now hybrid re-configurable antennas have been developed [1-3]. Polarized re-configurable antennas have anti-multipath fading effect and have the advantages of improving frequency reuse[4,5]. This reference uses slot structure and uses the PIN as a switch to control the current flow path and become the orthogonal polarization modes[6]. But the band of 3DB axial ratio is relatively narrow and opening slots will have impact on the stability of entire antenna. This reference uses MEMS as a switch and toggle polarization by controlling two corners of rectangular micro-strip antenna[7-9]. However, the reaction time of MEMS is very slow and it is unsuitable for high speed data communication applications. Besides, traditional re-configurable antennas use diode as a switch and they require sophisticated complex of DC bias circuit. Based on the dual-polarized antenna, the paper shows a novel circularly polarized antenna with polarization re-configurable characteristics[10,11]. It consists of a dual-polarized antenna and phase switching network which act as the feed network for the dual-polarized antenna. The phase switching network was designed based on a power divider, where the output port was connected with SPDT to form a switching network. A novel circularly polarized antenna with switched polarization direction can be made in this method.

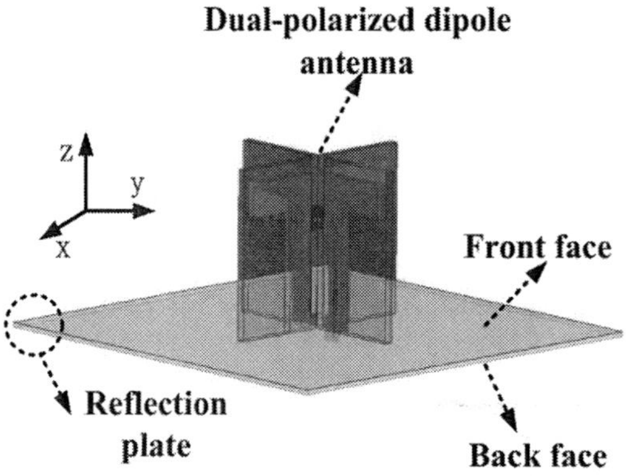

Figure 1. Structure of polarized re-configurable antenna.

2 Operating principle

Dual-polarized antenna including vertical polarization and horizontal polarization, which have two orthogonal field components, when the two orthogonal field components obey formula (1), the polarization of the radiation field is a circular polarization. The polarization will be left-hand circular polarization (LHCP) if $\sigma = \pi / 2$ while it will be right-hand circular polarization (RHCP) if $\sigma = -\pi / 2$, under the condition of $|E_1| = |E_2|$.

$$\vec{E} = E_x \vec{x} + E_y \vec{y} = E_1 \cos \varpi t \vec{x} + E_2 \cos(\varpi t + \sigma)\vec{y} \qquad (1)$$

So we can change the polarization between LHCP and RHCP by controlling the difference between the phase polarization.

[a] Author to whom correspondence should be addressed. Electronic mail: xjtuzhanghai@163.com.

Article available at http://www.matec-conferences.org or http://dx.doi.org/10.1051/matecconf/20164402086

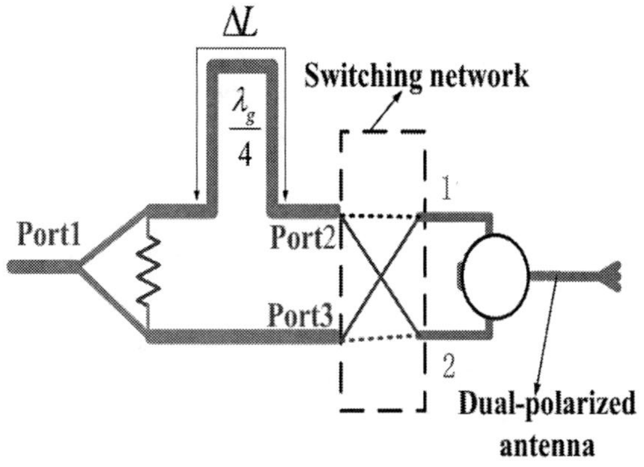

Figure 2. Principle diagram of feeding network.

The circular polarization reconfigurable antenna designed in this article is shown in figure 1, which is consisted by a dual-polarized antenna and a phase switching network. The dual-polarized antenna is consisted by a dual-polarized dipole antenna and a reflector, the function of phase switching network is to make the signal amplitude of two ports of the antenna equal and let the parameter σ switch between positive and negative polarity capable. The phase switching network using micro-strip structures and was designed in the back of the reflector so that it has the same shape with the antenna.

According to the analysis above, the phase switching network is shown in figure2, due to the micro-strip structure of the feed network, the electromagnetic wave in this antenna is Quasi-TEM mode[12-14]. So the electric field is orthogonal when radiated by the dual-polarization antenna. we use a bisection Wilkinson divider as the power network,port2 and port3 are connected with the two feed ports by the switching network, and port2 is $\lambda_g/4$ longer than port3, that is $\beta\times\Delta L=\pi/2$ degree different, which means the phase of port2 is $\pi/2$ degree slower than that of port3.When switch the network, turn on the solid line and turn off the dotted line, the signal amplitude of port1 and port2 of the antenna is equal while the phase of signal from port1 is $\pi/2$ degree faster than that of port2, the radiation field is left-hand circular polarized.

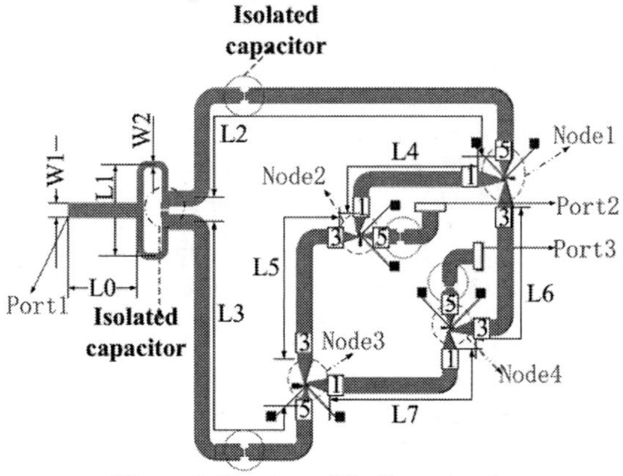

Figure 3. Structure of feeding network.

Otherwise, we will get a right-hand circular polarization field. That means we can change the polarization of the antenna by controlling the working state of the switching network.

3 Simulation Study

The dual-polarized antenna designed of cross type of printed dipole is shown in figure3, the material of the substrate is FR4, and the parameters are $\varepsilon_r=4.4$, $h=1.6\,\mathrm{mm}$ .The specific principle and procedure can be referred to document [15-17]. The main introduction here is about the design of the phase switching network. According to the theory above, the phase switching network is as what as shown in figure 3, to make the network the same shape of the antenna, the locations of port2 and port3 are designed steady. In order to prevent the RF ports from been destroyed by the overload DC voltage, a capacitance is used in the antenna. The node in figure3 is the location of switch SPDT, the function of the switch is to turn the circuit on or turn it off. The dimensions of the phase switching network L2-L7 are as follows[18-20]:

$$L_5=L_7,L_4=L_6 \tag{2}$$

$$\Delta L=(L_2+L_4)-(L_3+L_5)=\lambda_g/4 \tag{3}$$

$$\beta\times\Delta L=\pi/2 \tag{4}$$

Setting the VCTL1 = 0， VCTL2=1 （control site of SPDT） to be the first control state， the VCTL1=1， VCTL2=0 to be the second control state.

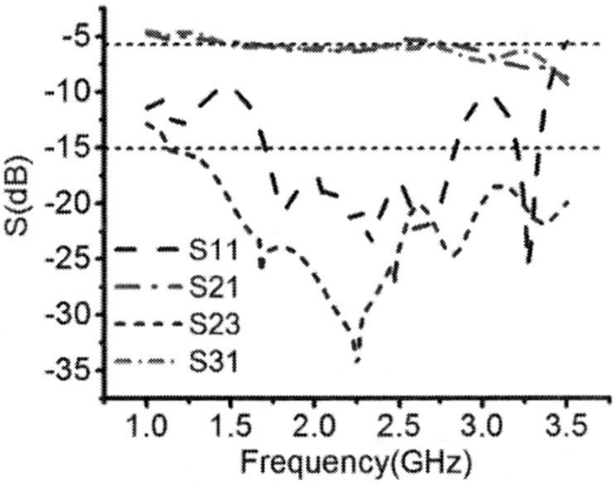

Figure 4. Simulation result of S parameter in state 1

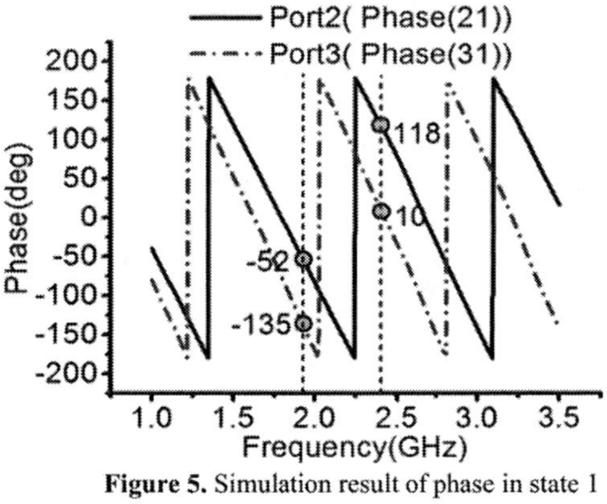

Figure 5. Simulation result of phase in state 1

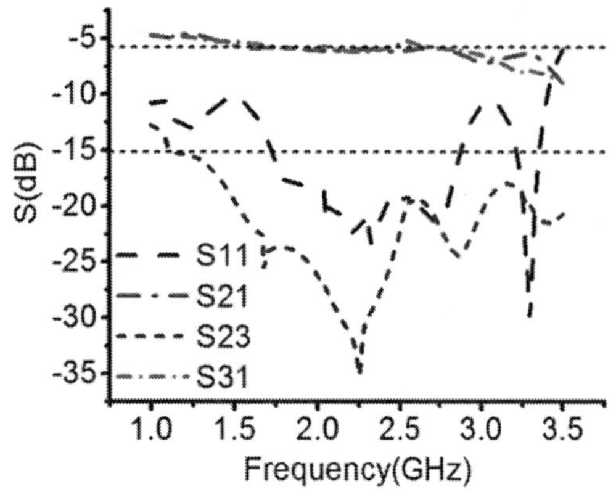

Figure 6. Simulation result of S parameter in state 2

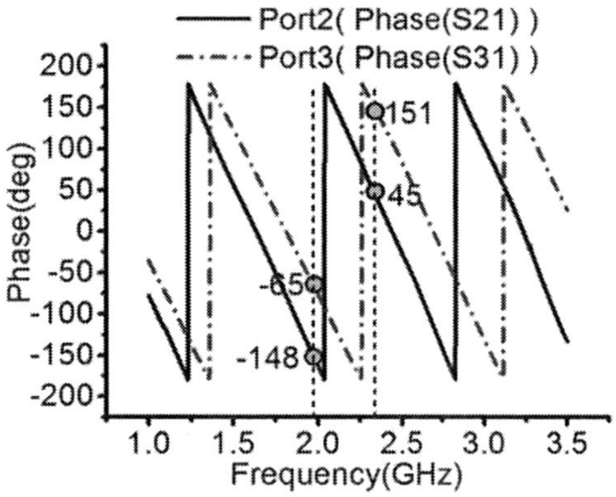

Figure 7. Simulation result of phase in state 2

when on the first control state, the node of 1 and 5 is connected and the node of 3 and 5 is cutting off. The routes of the two signals from power divider to the port 2 and port 3 are L2→L4→port2 and L3→L7→port3. So the phase of port 2 lags to port 3 about $\pi/2$.When on the second control state, the node of 3 and 5 is connected and the node of 1 and 5 is cutting off. The routes of the two signals from power divider to the port 2 and port 3 are L2→L6→port3 and L3→L5→port2. So the phase of port 2 runs ahead of port 3 about $\pi/2$.Because of the equal power division network, the amplitude of the two output ports in the two control states are equality[21].

According to the above analysis, accomplishing the simulation of the feed network in the Ansoft Designer. Adjusting the length of L2、L3 to make the phase of port 2 and port 3 differ $\pi/2$ when centre frequency is 2.25 GHz. In the simulation, I have used the S parameter from the SPDT manufacturer and considered the actual packaging of all components. The result of the simulation is shown in the figures 4 to 7.

According to the simulation, when the phase switch network is in the 1.8～2.4 GHz, the insertion loss S21、S31 of port 2 and port 3 are both about -6dB,the reflection coefficient S11 is less than -15 dB, the isolation S23 is less than -20 dB, the skewing of phase is $90^0 \pm 10^0$.In addition, when on the first control state, the phase of port 2 lags to port 3 about $\pi/2$. When on the second control state, the phase of port 2 runs ahead of port 3 about $\pi/2$ .So we can switch the phase by controlling the state of SPDT. By using dynamic united simulation function of the HFSS and Ansoft Designer to accomplished the united simulation of dual polarized antenna and phase switching network. The result of the simulation is shown by figures 8-11. Finally, according to the result of united simulation which in the frequency band from 1.8 GHz to 2.4 GHz, the antenna work in the left-hand circular polarization and right-hand circular polarization under the two control states, and the axial ratio of it is less than 3dB.

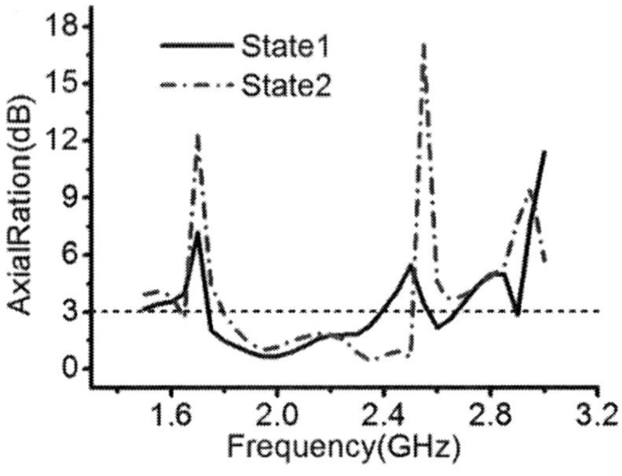

Figure 8. Simulation result of AR in state 1,2

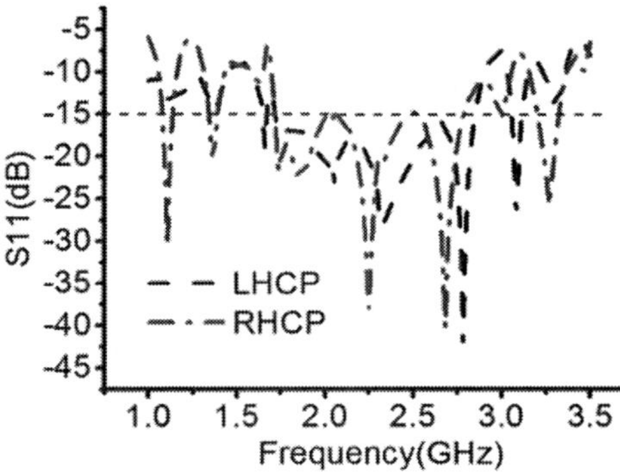

Figure 9. Simulation result of reflection coefficient in state 1,2

4 Conclusions

This paper combines the SPDT with a Wilkinson power divider to build a novel phase switching network. The switching network acts as the feed network for circularly polarized antenna. By controlling the levels between port VCTL1 and port VCTL2 of SPDT, left/right hand circular polarization direction can be switched fast. The co-simulation of Ansoft HFSS and Designer software shown that reflection coefficient was less than -12 dB and the axial ratio below 3 dB between 1.8 GHz and 2.4 GHz with polarization re-configurable characteristics. All the results shown that the performance of proposed circularly polarized antenna is fine.

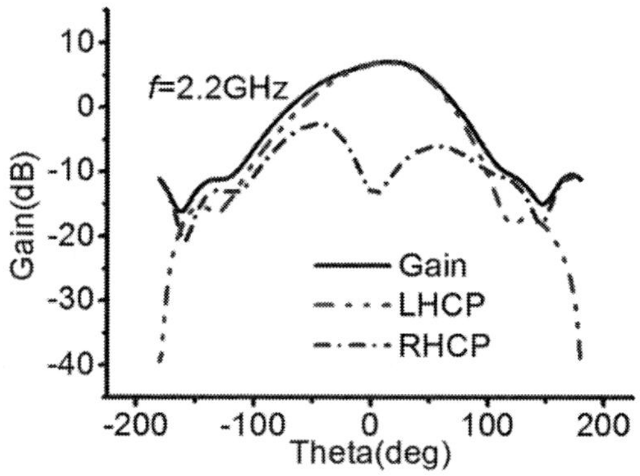

Figure 10. Simulation result of gain in state 1

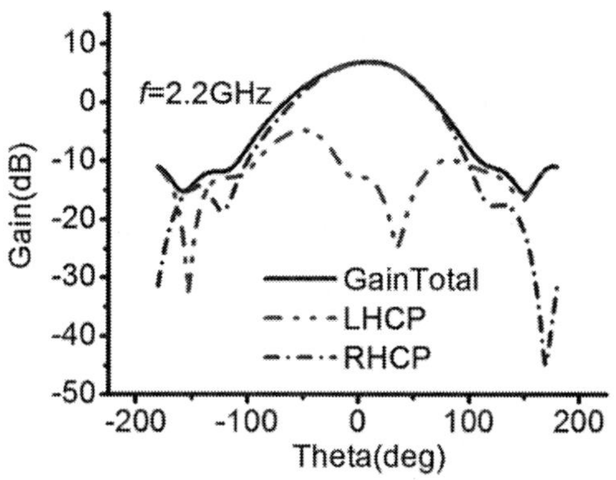

Figure 11. Simulation result of gain in state 2

Acknowledgments

This work was financially supported by the Project of Education Department of Fujian Province, China (Grant No. JA14022), and the Undergraduate Education & Teaching Reform Project of Huaqiao University, China (Grant No.2013JGYB36), Xiamen, Fujian province, China. The authors also want to thank the professor Ge and professor Tang for their kindly discussions.

References

1. Tian Yubo, Tian Guannan. Overview of researches on reconfigureabe antennas, Journal of Jiangsu University of Science and Technology, 2012, 03:271-275.

2. Z-Y Zhang, N-W Liu, J-Y Zhao, Wideband circularly polarized antenna with gain improvement, Antennas and Wireless Propagation Letters, Vol.12, 2013,pp:456-459.

3. M-J Li, K. M. Luk, A wideband dual-fed circularly polarized antenna, Electromagnetics, 2003,pp:112-114.

4. Fa-Shian Chang, Kin-Lu Wong, Tzung-Wern Chiou. Low-Cost Broadband Circularly Polarized Patch Antenna. IEEE Transactions on Antennas And Propagation, 2003, 51(10):3006-3009.

5. Y-J Hu, Z-M Qiu, B Yang, S-J,Shi, Design of novel wideband circularly polarized antenna based on Vivaldi Antenna structure, Antennas and Wireless Propagation Letters,2015,pp.1.

6. Fan Yang, Yahya Rahmat-Samii. A Reconfigurable Patch Antenna Using Switchable Slots for Circular Polarization Diversity[J]. IEEE Microwave And Wireless Components Letters, 2002, 12(3):96-98.

7. Shih-Hsun Hsu, Kai Chang. A Novel Reconfigurable Microstrip Antenna with Switchable Circular Polarization. IEEE Antennas And Wireless Propagation Letters, 2007,6:160-162.

8. E-C Wang, Y-C Liu, S-J,Fang, P, Cheng, Wideband circularly polarized antenna for GPS/Glonass,2010, pp.2511-2513.

9. L Chen, T-L Zhang, C Wang, X-W Shi, Wideband circularly polarized microstrip antenna with wide beamwidth, Antennas and Wireless Propagation Letters, Vol.13,2014,pp:1577-1590.

10. Jeen-Sheen Row, Chuang-Jiashih Shih. Polarization-Diversity Ring Slot Antenna With Frequency Agility. IEEE Transactions On Antennas And Propagation, 2012, 60(8):3953-3957.

11. Hu Yue,Yang Xuexiao,Lu Zhongliang,and Zheng Guoxin. A novel polarized reconfigurable microstrip, Journal of microwave, 2014, 24 (3): 5-8.

12. Wang Kewei, Wang Junhong. Study on the transmission and reflection properties of the microstrip line bend, Journal of microwave, 2006, 22(3):32-35.

13. A. Khalajmehrabadi, M. K. A. Rahim, and N. A. Murad: Planar Wideband Circularly Polarized Dielectric Resonator Antenna, European Conference on Antennas and Propagation (EUCAP) (2012).

14. W. Liu, K. Wei, Z. Zhang, and J. Zheng: A circularly polarized antenna with conical beam, IEEE EDAPS (2004).

15. Wang Can, Ge Yuehe. A novel design of broadband dual-polarized printed dipole antenna for base stations, Journal of Huaqiao University, 2014, 35(2):132-135.

16. C.Wang, Y.H. Ge: Journal of Huaqiao university (Natural science), Vol.35,2014, pp.132-135.

17. C.Wang, Y.H. Ge: A Novel Broadband Printed Dipole Antenna and Its Application for TD-LTE Communications, International Journal of Antennas and Propagation(2014).

18. Wang Anguo, Dong Jiawei, and Wang Peng. Design of printed dipole antenna with reconfiguration radiation pattern, Journal of Radio Science, 2010, 25(1):190-193.

19. Mak A C K, Rowell C R, Murch R D. Low cost reconfiguration land restorer planar antenna array, IEEE transactions on antennas and propagation, 2009, 57(10): 3051-3061.

20. Raj.R, Poussot B, Laheurte J M, et al. Pattern reconfiguration of micro strip antenna using flip-clip mounted package MEMS, Microwave and Optical Technology Letters, 2010,52(3):574-577.

21. Bai Yangying, Wang Bingzhong, et al. Applying weighted thinned linear array and pattern re-configurable elements to extend pattern scanning range of millimeter wave microstrip phase array, Journal of Inferred, Millimeter, and Terahertz Waves,2010,31(1):1-6.

MATEC Web of Conferences 44, 02087 (2016)
DOI: 10.1051/matecconf/20164402087

Recognition of the smart card iconic numbers

Xue Shi Xin[1,a], Qing Song[1], Lu Yang[1] and Wen He Jia[1]

[1]Automation School, Beijing University of Posts and Telecommunications, Beijing, China

Abstract. Manual way of recognizing and inputting the smart card iconic numbers leads to much time consuming, high resources consuming and low accuracy. This paper presents a new automatic method based on the technology of computer vision, including Harr operator for face detection, Fast operator for number location, image binarization, character segmentation and BP neural network for number recognition. Experimental results on 100 ID cards show that by adjusting the parameters of the BP neural network properly, the recognition accuracy is more than 99%, and the recognition time for each ID card is within 0.05 seconds.

1 Instruction

As information technology brought up the onset of intelligence age, smart cards play a significant role in our daily life. Commonly used smart cards like ID cards, credit cards play a significant role in our daily life, each smart card is distinguished by a series of unique numbers information (signature). These iconic numbers is widely used in public places like banks and airports, which calls for a high accuracy of identification and recording. Aimed at identifying and recording the numbers iconic effectively and efficiently we study the identification of Chinese ID cards.

Based on the highly developed computer vision technology, the identification and recording of ID cards are now solved by computer recognition. Yet there exists several difficulties in the process of recognition:

• Complex context. ID card's context usually consists of text in colour pattern counterfeit labels, thus a fliter of useless information is necessary during the identification.

•Abrasion and besmirch. A robust algorithm is needed to ensure accuracy.

• Various illumination environments. The identification system needs to adapt to different lighting situation.

To solve these problems, we handled the ID card image according to the computer vision techniques. We first locate the face position on the ID card by Haar face detection. Then target the ID card number area by considering the positions of text, number, face and FAST detectors. Next, we segment this target area into single characters and normalized them one by one. Finally, recognise each character with BP neural network recognition algorism.

2 Scheme

In order to realize the ID card digitization, we take pictures of ID card and upload it to computer.

2.1 Image pre-process

Pre-process is necessary for all collected images. We mainly deal with noises and tilts in this essay, which are commonly caused by some inevitable factors like light or camera issues during the image collection. We effectively solve the noise by filtering and the tilt with Hough-Transform [1] method.

2.2 Image locating

As one of the most important characteristics, facial image has fixed size and position in an ID card, which benefits the ID card numbers locating. Based on Adaboost algorithm and Haar-like feature, the ID card number position can be inferred roughly by the fixed facial image position.

By using FAST detector [2], all the corners in the image can be found. Than a filter algorithm is used to all the corners to find the position of all words and numbers in the ID cards .Combine the result of face detect, the area of ID card numbers can be determined.

Segment the image of numerical strings into 18 independent character images after the area of numbers is inferred. To be used for the recognition, each of segmented images must be normalized.

2.3 Image recognition

A dataset including 5500 images is created to recognition the printed numbers.

In the process of printed numbers recognition, the printed number recognition is presented by neural

[a] Corresponding author: songqing512@126.com

network based on BP [3]. Statistical test results of BP neural network in different parameters.

Figure 1 is a flow chart of scheme.

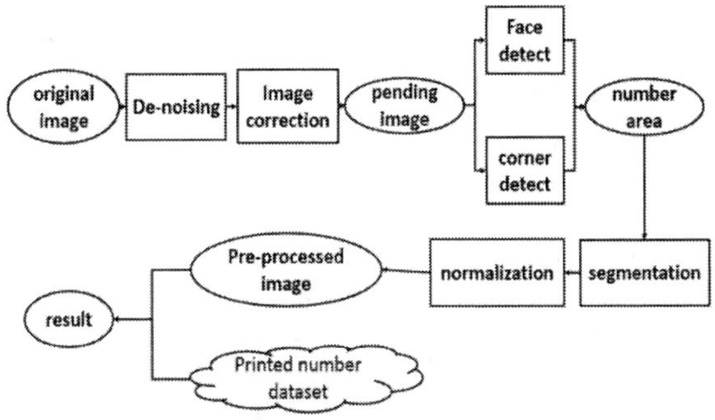

Figure 1. Flow chart of scheme.

3 Implementation

3.1 Image pre-process

3.1.1 Denoising

In order to make the image of the ID card smoother, the first processing is Gaussian filtering, which helps eliminate the noise and interference.

Two-dimension Gauss function:

$$G(x, y) = \frac{1}{2\pi\sigma^2} e^{-\frac{x^2+y^2}{2\sigma^2}} \quad (1)$$

Image of two-dimension Gauss function:

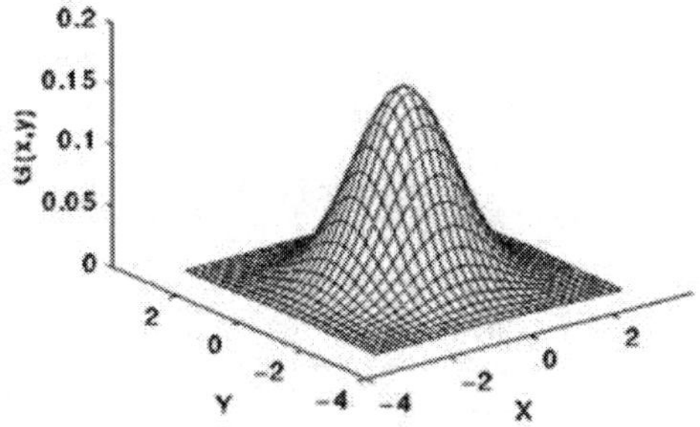

Figure 2. Image of two-dimension Gauss function.

Images in a computer are stored in the form of a two-dimension matrix. Gauss filtering makes use of two-dimension convolution operators of Gaussian kernel to convolve with the whole image successively. Therefore eliminate the noise and interference.

3.1.2 Image correction

Hough transform [1] can be applied to detection of objects of any shape. This method works well when being used to detect straight lines. The correction has high precision. The edges of ID cards have high linearity. We can figure out the angle of inclination of the photo by using the straight line on the edge and then calibrate the photo.

3.2 Image locating

3.2.1 Face localization

ID cards have uniform size and style. Every ID card has a full-faced photo, which is 32mm*26mm, in the right side of the card. The position and size of the images are fixed. According to this characteristic, the position of other text messages can be roughly determined by using the relative position of the image.

This article locate the image by using face detection technology based on Adaboost and Haar-like [4] feature.

Haar-like feature includes central feature, line feature and edge feature. They are shown below:

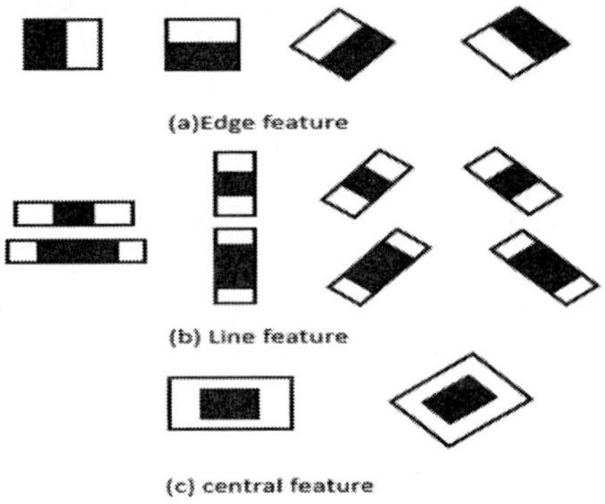

Figure 3. Haar-like feature.

In the process of faces detection, place random feature rectangles on the image in turn. The difference between sum of pixel of the white region and sum of pixel of the black region serves as a feature. If the rectangle contains faces, this eigenvalue serves as a face feature. Otherwise, this eigenvalue serves as a non-face feature. Different sizes of rectangles on different positions of the image provide large amounts of features. With Adaboost algorithm, several strong classifiers are trained by these features. After input images are detected by multiple strong classifiers, it can be confirmed that the image is a face. The effect of ID card images being detected by Haar-like tech:

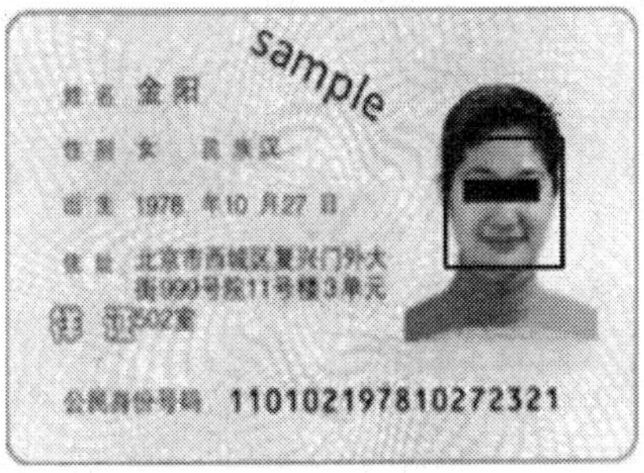

Figure 4. The result of the face detect.

3.2.2 Corner detection

Corner detection, which is in the computer vision system, is a method used to acquire the feature of images. It's widely used in fields like motion detection, image matching, video tracking, 3-D modeling and target recognition. It's also called feature points detection. In the ID card's image, corner points focus on the edge of characters, figures and faces. Characters and figures' position can be detected by analyzing the distribution of corner points.

There are various kinds of method to detect corner points. This article adopts optimized fast corner detection algorithm to locate characters and figures in the image.

FAST was put forward by Edward Rosten and Tom Drummond in 1996. It's a simple and fast method to detect corners. According to this algorithm, a pixel is defined as a corner point if it has plenty of pixels, which are in different regions in its neighbourhood.

When directly using FAST detector, it generate many FAST detector around colour textures and stains so as to cause interference. Therefore, this paper intends to optimize the corner detection.

After detection by FAST, record location information of all corners. These corners includes large amount of noise points. A position pattern of corner can be got after inputting all the positions into a blank image. With image convolution method, convolve with the whole corner image. Then employ binarization to process the image and get a new image of corner position. New positions of corners correspond to the positions of characters and figures after denoising. Comparison chart of effect before and after optimizing in Figure 5.

(a) Before optimization

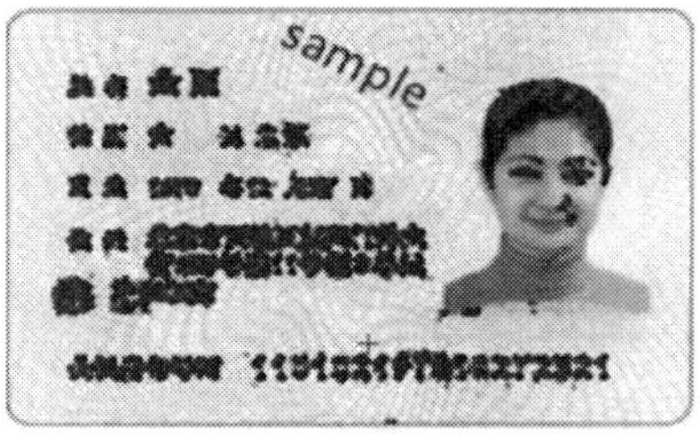

(b) After optimization

Figure 5. Figures before and after optimization.

3.2.3 Locating and segmentation of ID number

• Locating:

By locating the face and detecting corners, positions of faces, characters and figures in the image can be obtained. According to the positional relation between ID numbers and the face, we can accurately conclude that the image to the bottom left of head (bottom left of the ID card), where corners are dense, is the image of ID number. Based on steps above, location of ID numbers can be acquired.

• Segmentation:

After accurately locate the ID number and extract its region, segmentation of figures shall be conducted. Conduct binarization with the extracted image first. Due to the uneven light, it does not work well by using fixed threshold method(Figure 6 (b)). This paper employs the adaptitave local threshold(Figure 6 (c)) to achieve binarization of the image with different threshold values at different positions.

(a) original image

(b) Fixed threshold

(c) Adaptive threshold

Figure 6. The images before and after binarization

After binarization, projecting the image vertically. Count up the number of dark spot of every row and get the figure 7.

Figure 7. The vertical projection of the image

Select the centre of each blank area as segmentation point. The number segment is divided into 18 independent character images.

3.3 Recognition of ID card numbers

3.3.1 Image normalization

Pre-process always be used before the features of the numbers image are extracted. The pretreatment mainly refers to the normalization process. The process of the normalization include size normalization and position normalization.

• Position normalization:

Normalization method based the border positions is used for position normalization, find the position and center of

the border by calculation in the image of single number, than move the center to a specified position of a new blank iamge , position normalization is implemened by above processes.

• Position normalization:

The process of transforming the images of different size to the same size is the size normalization. first, calculate the length of minimum external positive square of the image , then change the length of the image by scale. Size normalization is implemened by above processes.

The result after the normalization is shown in Figure 8.

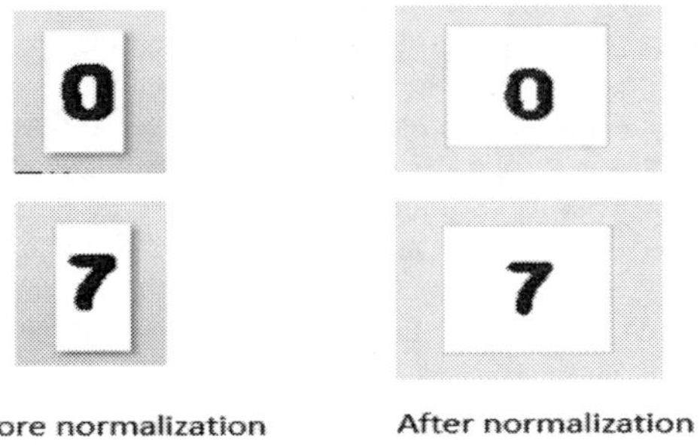

Figure 8. The normalization of the image

3.3.2 Dataset : Printed Number-11

In order to solve the problem of ID card numbers recognition, the methods of machine learning were used. In the processes of recognition, a dataset is needed to support the experiment. A dataset named NMIST was created by Corinna Cortes who works in Google Labs and Christopher J.C. Burges who works in Microsoft Research as shown in Figure 9 (a). The NMIST database is publicly available, has a training set of 60,000 examples, and a test set of 10,000 examples. It is a good database for people who want to try learning techniques and pattern recognition methods on real-world data while spending minimal efforts on preprocessing and formatting. However NMIST dataset is unsuited to printed numbers. Printed numbers has fixed font, and we need a high accuracy in the process of recognition, so this dataset is created for the printed numbers recognition.

The new dataset named Printed Number-11 as shown in Figure 9 (b) include the common fonts that the printed numbers used. Not only is the accuracy improved by using Printed Number-11, but also the situation that the numbers with wear and tear can be improved.

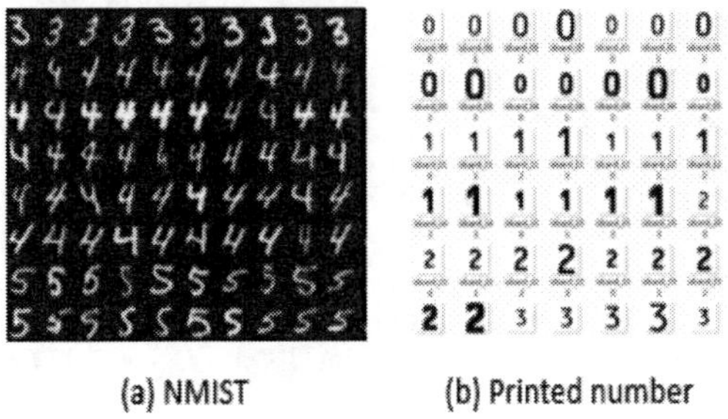

Figure 9. Datasets.

Printed Number-11 include 10 kinds of common fonts ,such as FARRINGTON-7B-Qiqi , Times New Raman , Arial etc. In each kind of font, ten numbers and a capital character "X" are included, each character saved in an image, resized to 100*100 pixels. In the process of creating dataset, different size and position of a same character are saved as different image as is shown in Figure 10 (a), (b), (c), then different degree of covering are used in each image which is to simulate the number with wear as is shown in Figure 10 (d). Eventually each character generated 500 images, a dataset include 5500 images is created to recognition the printed numbers.

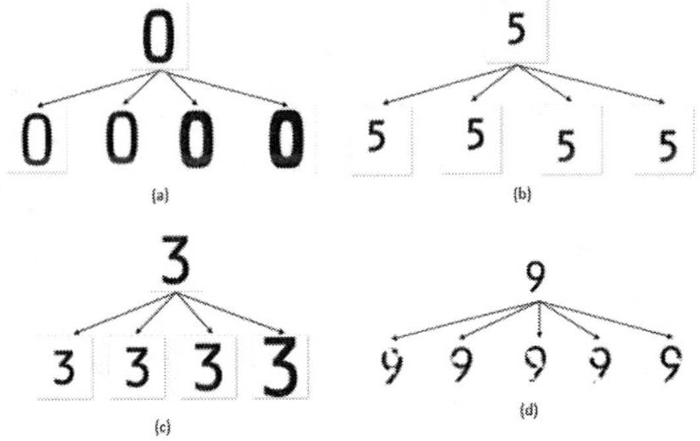

Figure 10. The process of creating dataset.

3.3.3 Recognition

In the section of printed numbers recognition, the printed number recognition is presented by neural network based on BP. As one of the important feed-forward neural network models, BP (Back-propagation) neural network is a kind of multilayer feed forward network with the nature of error back propagation.

In training stage, NMIST and Printed Number-11 is used to train different classifier, the highest accuracy used the NMIST is 95% and the highest accuracy used Printed Number-11 is more than 99%.The result show that Printed Number-11 is more suitable for printed numbers because the examples in Printed Number-11 is more similar to the printed numbers.

Recognition accuracy is affected by using different activation functions during training the neural network. For a high accuracy, this paper try to use 3 kinds of activation functions, logistic sigmoid, Tanh (hyperbolic tangent) and ReLu(rectified linear units). The plots of the functions is shown in Figure 11.

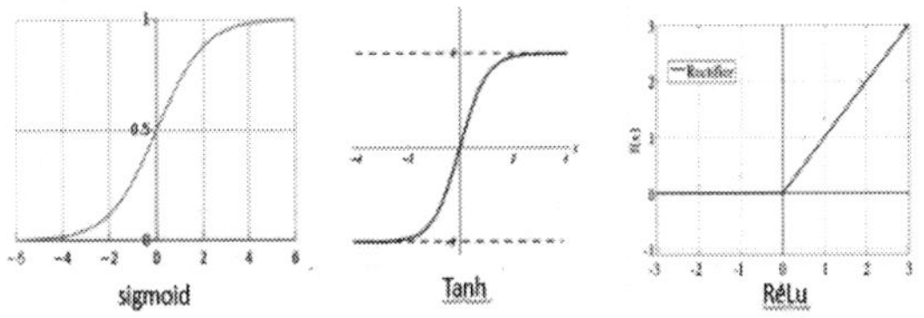

Figure 11. The plots of the activation functions.

Three kinds of different activation functions were selected for training different classifier in Single hidden layer neural network, then we use 100 ID cards to test, the result of recognition as shown in table 1.

Table 1. The performance by the different activation functions.

activation functions	correct /sum	accuracy
Sigmoid	2570/2700	95.2%
ReLu	2595/2700	96.1%
Tanh	2546/2700	94.3%

Recognition accuracy is affected by using different activation functions. The performance of Sigmoid and Tanh are unsatisfactory, the recognition results are 95.2% and 94.3%. ReLu has the best performance, the accuracy is 96.1%.The reason is that without pre-training, Sigmoid and Tanh can't reach the global optimum because the gradient vanishing problem, ReLu doesn't has this problem. Besides, the sparsity of the ReLu is can be adjusted, this is similar to the human' brain.

The neural network is composed of input layer, hidden layer and output layer. Input layer is the image we input, output layer is the recognition result. The hidden layer can be one or multi hidden layers. The result can be influenced by the number of hidden layer and the number of hidden layer nodes. This paper uses 2700 characters in 100 ID cards for validation set, test the accuracy in different number of hidden layers and different number of hidden layer nodes. The result was shown in table 2.

Table 2. The performance by different parameters.

Number of hidden layers	Number of hidden layer nodes.	correct /sum	accuracy
1	30	2591/2700	96.0%
	50	2622/2700	97.1%
	70	2635/2700	97.6%
2	30	2667/2700	98.78%
	50	2670/2700	98.89%
	70	2673/2700	99.00%
3	30	2687/2700	99.52%
	50	2692/2700	99.70%
	70	2690/2700	99.63%
4	30	2580/2700	95.56%
	50	2576/2700	95.41%
	70	25752700	95.37%

Analysis table data we can know that increasing the number of hidden layers and the number of hidden layer nodes does not necessarily gain a better accuracy. The results are best when the number of hidden layers is 3, the number of hidden layer nodes is 50 in the experiment. When the number of hidden layer is too much, over-fitting occurs frequently, resulting in reduced accuracy recognition. The number of hidden layer nodes can influence the result, but not greatly.

According to the results, select the appropriate number of hidden layers and number of hidden layer nodes in the process of recognition can improve the correct rate of recognition. When the number of hidden layers is 3, the number of hidden layer nodes is 50, the accuracy of ID card numbers recognition can reach 99.70%.

The speed of recognition can be influenced by complexity of the BP neural network. It takes more time if the network is more complex. This research uses 3 layers of hidden layers (50 nodes in each layers) BP neural network to recognition 100 ID cards in turn and records the time required by system clock in program. It take 4.57 seconds to recognition 100 ID cards, and the time for each ID card is within 0.05 seconds.

4 Conclusion

This paper introduces an algorithm of locating and recognition for the printed numbers. A new dataset named Printed Number-11 was created for printed numbers. In the process of printed numbers locating, FAST detector and image convolution are combined. In the process of printed numbers recognition, by adjusting parameters in BP neural network, the final accuracy is better than 99%, the time for each ID card is within 0.05 seconds.

Acknowledgments

Especial thanks to The Natural Science Foundation of China (NSFC) and Beijing Higher Education Young Elite Teacher Project for the financial support.

References

1. Ballard D.H.Generalizing. The Hough Transform to detect arbitrary shapes [J]. Pattern Recognition **13**, 111-122 (1981)
2. Rosten E, Drummond T. Machine learning for high-speed corner detection [M]. Computer Vision-ECCV 2006. Graz: Springer Berlin Heidelberg. 430-443 (2006)
3. Rowley H A, Baluja S, Kanade T.Neural network-based face detection [J]. Pattern Analysis and Machine Intelligence, IEEE Transactions on, **20**, 23-38 (1998)
4. Lienhart Process R, Maydt J.An extended set of haar-like features for rapid object detection [J]. 2002 International Conference on. IEEE. **1**, 900-903 (2002)

MATEC Web of Conferences 44, 02088 (2016)
DOI: 10.1051/matecconf/20164402088

Modular Design of NC Program in Multi-varieties and Small-batch Production Mode

Hong Liu[1,a], Yong Qiang Fan[1], Cheng Zhang[1] and Li Li Luo[1]

Institute of Machinery Manufacturing Technology, China Academy of Engineering Physics, Mianyang, 621900, China

Abstract. Aiming at design efficiency and quality problems of NC program in multi-varieties and small-batch production mode, this paper applied the concept of product modular design into NC program design, and presented the modular design method of NC program and its implementation techniques. By design the module NC program structure and build the database of basic module, provided technical support for the modular design of NC program. The practical application shows those: the constructed module database can be reused and can be combined, using the modular design method can effectively improve the design efficiency and quality of NC program, especially for multi-varieties and small-batch parts, provides an optimal way for NC program to quickly meet the individual demands.

1 Introduction

Today, the rapid development of economy and industrialization and the rapid upgrading of products make the production mode of mass production be gradually replaced by the production mode of multi-varieties and small-batch. In the current manufacturing industry, how to improve the quick response capability of companies to market, how to achieve the production of high efficiency, high quality and low cost, is an urgent need to solve practical problems. The NC machining is an important part of the product development. Its efficiency and ability is directly related to the efficiency of product development. And the efficiency and quality of NC programming directly determine NC machining efficiency. How to improve the efficiency of NC programming is a problem in multi-varieties and small-batch production mode [1-3].

The traditional programming method of NC program is to write program according to the parts one by one. In this way, there are many shortcomings, such as that the amount of labor is very large, that repeated programming is inevitable, that the optimized programs which are verified by practice cannot be reused and so on[4-7]. In this paper, the modular technology is applied in NC programming, and by a way of the selection and combination of modules achieves the purpose of rapid design of NC program. That solves the contradiction between the efficiency of NC programming and the individuation of products, between the repeated programming and repeated debugging of NC program, and solves the technical problem of mature NC program reused. How to set up machining program module in high level manufacturing is not currently clearly defined. The process mainly depends on the professional knowledge. In this paper, the methods and techniques in the production mode of multi-varieties and small-batch are studied, how to realize the modular program design, such as module partition, module creation, module combination and so on. That provides an optimal way for NC program to quickly meet the individual demands.

2 Technical ideas of modular NC programming

The application of modular design in product development and large-scale software development has been very mature. The design method is, firstly to analyzing the products function of a certain range including with different functions, or with the same functions and different performances, or with different specifications, on this basis to divide and design out a series of functional modules, and to constitute different products by the selection and combination of modules to meet the different market needs [8]. The Basic guiding ideology of modular design is, to combination into a variety of products with some specific function module, not only to ensure the basic functional requirements of product, but also to promote mass production, and so as to achieve the purpose of reducing the production cost. Modular design method of NC program uses the technology and ideas of modular design for product development and by creating the standard NC module database with different functions provides to the user. In the program design process, the method of the combination of different modules and matching is used to generate a large number of variants NC machining

[a] Corresponding author: scliuhong@sina.com

programs in order to improve the efficiency of NC programming.

Therefore, the technique thought of modular NC programming is to combination the modules which have already created, carries on the highly efficient preparation of NC machining program. The module is the basic component of the modular design. In order to make the NC program have a unique processing function, structure characteristic and processing level, the module function partition and the program structure are the key to the modular NC programming.

2.1 Module function partition

The principle of NC program module partition is based on the function of NC program. A complete NC program usually contains the control of machine tool, the control of motion cutting control and other functions. According to the function of NC program, the module can be divided into four kinds of function modules, namely, the main program module, the processing preparation module, the cutting condition control module and the cutting motion control module. The specific function name and implementation contents are shown in Table 1.

Table 1. The function table of program module.

Module name	Function name	Implementation content
Main program module	NC program subject	Start or stop of NC program. Program cycle times. Processing area protection. …
Processing preparation module	Processing preparation	Open or close of machine tool door. Automatic tool changing. Automatic loading or unloading workpiece. …
Cutting condition control module	Cutting condition control	Cutting fluid on or off
Cutting motion control module	tool path	Cutting parameter. Path planning. Cutting motion. …

2.2 Modular NC program composition structure

The modular NC program is composed of relatively independent basic function modules. It is responsible for a relatively independent work in the process of NC machining. Each module can be replaced by other modules. This makes the modular programming reconfigurable and efficient. When new products need to be processed, the new NC program can be programmed by module combination of some existing modules

A complete module NC program is based on the main program module as the main line. It is composed of a number of modules, including processing preparation module, cutting condition control module and cutting motion control module, to achieve the processing of multiple geometric features. The composition structure is shown in Figure 1.

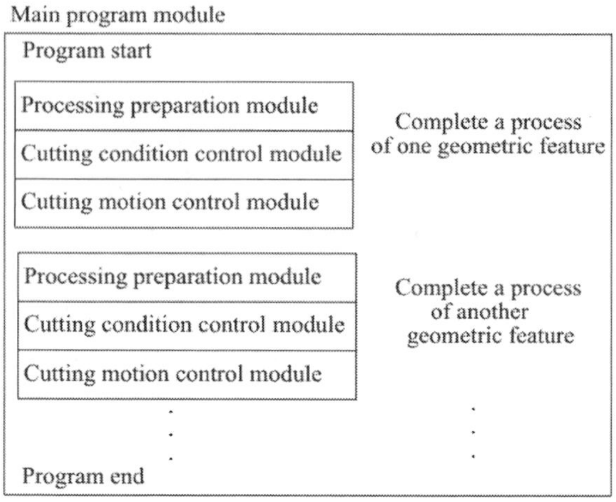

Figure 1. Modular NC program structure diagram.

3 Creating module database

3.1 Structure and function of database

The higher the standardization degree of a module is, the higher the efficiency of modular program design for product structure. When creating the module database, the module is need which has standardized to help the standardization of processing technology, which has reusability to be repeated calls for programming a new NC program and which has openness to support for the increase of new module resources or for the modify of existing modules. The structure and function of the database is shown in Figure 2.

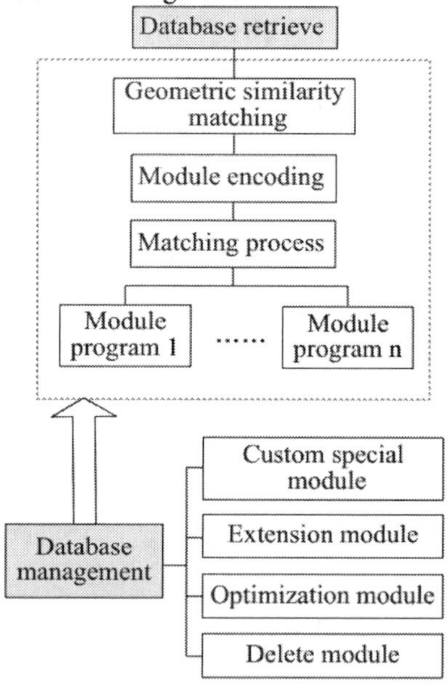

Figure 2. The structure and function of module database.

3.2 Modular program design

Because of the requirement of the module program is universal, the parameter variable is adopted in the design of module program. In the four module program, the cutting motion control module determines the modular programming diversity of NC program, and the design technique is the key. The cutting motion control module is designed as two parts. One is the geometric feature model with the geometric parameters as the variable, and the other is the machining model with the machining parameters as the variable.

The geometric feature model is a description of the shape structure and the position properties of the workpiece, including the shape feature parameter variable and the position parameter variable. Commonly used geometric feature model can be divided into the holes category, plane contour category and three-dimensional surface category and so on [9, 10]. Subordinate categories of each can have a variety of geometric features, see Figure 3.

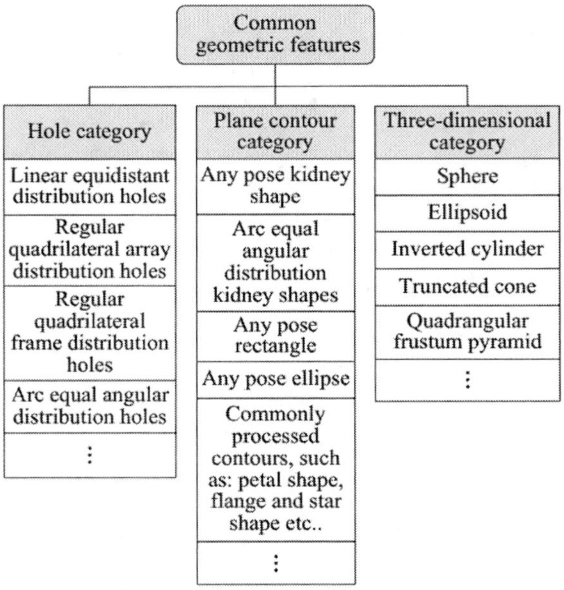

Figure 3. Common geometric feature categories map.

The similarity of geometric features determines that the parts can be processed by a similar NC program. The geometric feature belonging to the same geometry properties may have different processing parameters determined by the different material used. But the route planning of NC program is the same. So, the cutting motion control module is designed to determine the program trajectory by geometric feature model and the processing parameters by processing parameter model.

The processing model is based on the processing parameters as variables. It describes the processing methods and processing parameters. The machining parameters are determined by the machining method, which mainly includes the variables of the machining method, the tool variables, the machining strategy and the process parameters. Table 2 shows an example of a processing model variable for a surface [11].

Table 2. An example of processing model variable for a surface

Variable	Meaning
U	Surface remaining
D	Surface residual height
F	Cutting speed
R	Tool radius
C	Spare travel
B	Approaching / Retraction length value
V	Cutting direction: 1. From top to bottom 2. From bottom to up

4 Design flow of modular NC program

The process of using modular NC program design is, to decompose geometric features needed to be processed according to the processing procedure and combined with the geometric feature database, then to match the tool, to instantiate the process model parameters and the geometric model parameters of geometric features needed to be processed. At last, the NC program is generated by combination various modules. The details of the process are shown in Figure 4.

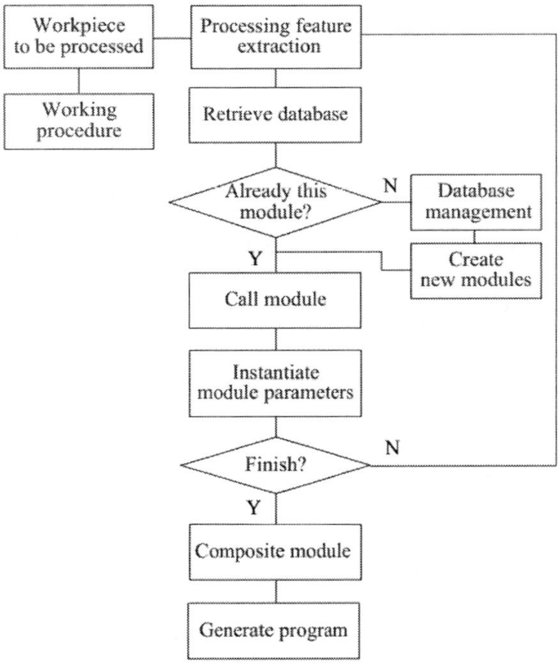

Figure 4. Design flow chart of modular program.

5 Application examples of modular programming

5.1 Applications in products

In production practice, modular NC programming technology has been applied in the processing of a number of products, including the disk type, three-dimensional space type, plane curve type, space curve type and hole type. Figure 5 shows a part of the parts programmed by the method of modular NC program design.

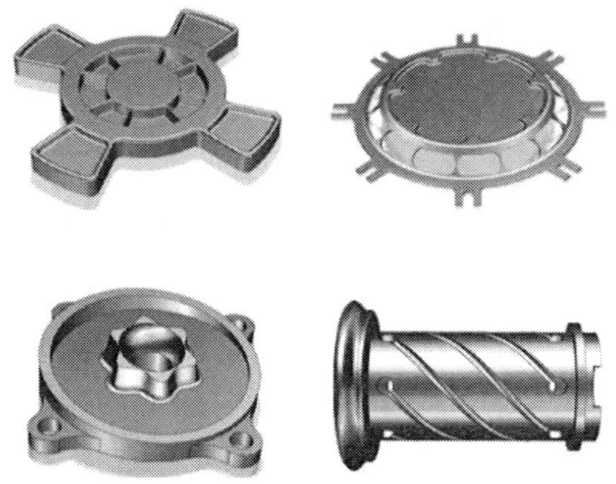

Figure 5. Part application cases of modular programming.

5.2 Analysis on Effect of Application

For a variety of products in Figure 5, the quality and efficiency of the application of modular programming are analysed.

5.2.1 Efficiency comparison

To the structure similar parts, the general programming method is each kind of different structure size corresponding one program. The number of programs will continue to increase with the increase of product types. However, modular programming only needs to select the corresponding geometric features, to combine the modules and then to complete the programming. For the workpiece with the same structure and the size difference, to complete programming only need to modify the corresponding geometric parameters and processing parameters. Efficient programming is realized through the combination of the module and the instantiation of geometric parameters and process parameters.

5.2.2 Quality assurance of modular programming

Because the modular database is designed to the structure which be able to be continuously improved and managed. On the hand, the mature modules of parts that has been processed provides effective quality assurance for parts with the same structure and different size, on the other hand, for the modules of parts that has not been processed, the design and planning are carried out by NC programming engineers with extensive experience, at the same time, they are constantly improved and perfected in the practice to ensure the quality of reliability.

6 Conclusions

The modular NC programming technology is applied in the production mode of multi-varieties and small-batch,, and the conclusion is as follows:

The created basic module unit database of common geometric features provides a technical support for the modular NC program design.

The modular NC programming method solves the contradiction between the product individuation and programming efficiency and the reuse technologies of mature NC program. It is the best way for NC program to quickly meet the individual demands.

References

1. Xuejie Fan. Brief Discussion on Business Management of Multi-varieties and Small Batch. Sci-tech Innovation and Productivity.243,P52-53(2014)
2. Gu K, Jia X, You H. A T-chart for monitoring Multi-variety and Small Batch Production Run. Quality and Reliability Engineering International. 30,P287-299(2013)
3. Cao Jun, Yin Chao, Liu Fei. Research and Application on Dynamic Statistical Process Control of Key Process in Multi-varieties and Small-batch Machining workshop. China Mechanical Engineering.22,P2822-2827(2011)
4. Haijun Jia. Research and application in NC machining Technics standardization. Aviation Precision Manufacturing Technology. 44,P59-61(2008)
5. Jun Zhan. Study on NC Programming Based on Group Technology. Electromechanical Components. 25,P29-34(2005)
6. Jia Haijun. Research and application in NC machining Technics standardization. Aviation Precision Manufacturing Technology. 44,P59-61(2008)
7. Zhanqiang Liu, Feng Qian. An Approach of CNC Parametric Programming Based on Group Technology. Journal of Shandong University of Technology. 32,P469-472(2002)
8. Baozu Yin.NC Parameter Programming Technology and Its Application. ,Electro-mechanical Engineering. 21,P60-64(2005)
9. M. Kovacic, M. Brezocnik. Evolutionary programming of CNC machines. Journal of Materials Processing Technology, P 1379–1387(2005)
10. Yanlin Jia. *Modular design*(China Machine Press,1993)
11. Hong Liu, Lili Luo, Yongqiang Fan. CNC Dual Instruction Milling Technology of Precision Surfaces of Triaxial Ellipsoid. Manufacturing Automation. 37,P21-23(2015)

MATEC Web of Conferences **44**, 02089 (2016)
DOI: 10.1051/matecconf/20164402089

A Qos Routing protocol based on AODV

Yong Qiang Li[1] , Yun Jie Zhu[1] , Qing Gang Fan[1], Yu Bin Wu[1]

[1] *Computer Staff Room, Xian Research Institute of High Technology, Xian 710025,China*

Abstract. A Qos Routing protocol based on AODV (QOSAODV) is proposed aiming at the problem of the traditional QoS routing protocol which can not be applied perfectly in VANET. The weakness of the AODV routing protocol mechanism and the protocol itself are represented. By the simulation, the effectiveness and feasibility were completely verified. QOSAODV shows the superior performances in effectively lowering the routing broke ratio as well as packet drop ratio significantly, meanwhile, increasing the network throughput and scale.
Key Words. VANET,QoS, AODV,QOSAODV,NS2, routing broke ratio

1 introduction

At present ,Routing protocol for vehicular ad hoc networks[1] has being hotspot at home and abroad. in order to improve its performance, many routing protocols has been proposed. Most of them concentrated on the use of geographic information system (GIS) vehicle routing protocol research. However, the routing protocol algorithm based on geographical location information complexity is high, the node real-time computation load is bigger, and abnormal GPS devices, protocol cannot work at all. And in terms of QoS[2]security, almost follows the traditional QoS Ad Hoc network routing protocol mechanism, unable to reflect the characteristics of vehicular ad hoc networks. Based on the above situation, this paper proposes is not based on the geographic location information of the o vehicular ad hoc networks routing protocol strategy, introducing QoS safeguard mechanism of AODV routing protocol, and make it adapted to the vehicle mobile environment.

In the AODV protocol[3], each node maintains a neighbor list inside, which only save IP address and sequence number of the neighbor, so data forwarding do not know and the link between the neighbor node which is more suitable for data forwarding, and blind selection and forwarding. But the actual link is much different from the ideal situation, especially in the road between the link status of the vehicle is more obvious. Because of its direction are different for several vehicles in the one hop range, so it can maintain effective communication mobile distance difference is great, which shows do not consider the link state and random neighbor selection as forwarding nodes of AODV strategy will often lead to link the frequent fracture.

If the node can know the state of the link between itself and the neighbor node in real time, it can effectively carry out the selective forwarding, which can improve the effective maintenance time of the link. And in single frequency wireless channel environment, each node are and the neighbor nodes share the limited wireless bandwidth resources, so through the method of monitoring the idle channel, channel access can use the degree of bandwidth[4], can be in accordance with the task transmission bandwidth requires the selection of bandwidth wider links. In this way, it can improve the performance of the AODV protocol, and also can achieve the classification of QoS tasks. Here is a reflection of this idea, a QoS strategy is proposed: (1) when the source node sends RREQ to control the message, the bandwidth requirement of the task and the link stability are written into RREQ and broadcast. (2)when the intermediate

nodes receive the RREQ packet, it first to compare their bandwidth ability and RREQ packet demands the bandwidth of the value, if not satisfied without forwarding, it discarded directly. If meet, then compare the previous radio RREQ neighbor nodes and their link-state values and RREQ packet request link stability value, if meet the forwarding, if does not meet the discarded directly, not to deal with. (3) when the destination node receives RREQ packet, they also compare their bandwidth capacity and link stability. by comparison, they embed the minimum RREP message and reply to the source node. (4) when the source node received the corresponding RREP message ,they extract its bandwidth value and stability of the link, update the routing tables, and data forwarding.

This QoS routing forwarding mechanism can effectively avoid the lack of poor condition of node and poor bandwidth link, choose a more stable and sufficient bandwidth of the link. But also some deficiencies, for example, if the intermediate node through the comparison, they will lost RREQ packet, they unable to find a satisfactory routing and lead to the routing request packet radio invalid, consumption of network bandwidth[5]. Also, if the source node find the routing path of failure for the first time, because of the change of the unpredictable link-state, the link disconnected, until received RRER message to re-launch the routing request ,they operation. Through repeated experiment and simulation, the mechanism does not significantly improve performance of routing vehicular ad hoc networks protocol.

How to accurately obtain the node itself available bandwidth capacity and link between neighbor nodes is the key of the routing protocol design performance, which influence QoS mechanism of state . Due to considering the portability of mobile terminals and CPU capacity, extract QoS index and the index of compare and select the operation and routing algorithm is not too complicated. This article take the simple and effective mathematical expectation and mathematical statistical methods to calculate the variance QoS parameter values.

(1) the available bandwidth values for:

When each node needs to know its own bandwidth available, it will access the MAC layer, and obtained value of the available bandwidth by the method of mathematical expectation. The formula is as follows:

$$\text{Bandwidth}=\frac{1}{n}\sum_{i=1}^{n} Isidle(i) \text{，} \quad (1)$$

$1 \geq \text{Bandwidth} \geq 0$

(2) Link stability degree of access:

$$\text{Link\_Stability}=\frac{1}{m}\sum_{i=1}^{m}\left(\Delta T_i-\sum \Delta T_i\right)^2 \quad (2)$$

In formula, ΔT_i As type of HELLO message of twice arrival interval time. In this paper, m was set to 10, Link _ Stability set to 100; if the calculation result more than this value, it is set to 100. 10≥Stability_Link≥0 ,if the interval of the HELLO information received are the same, it is very ideal link-state; stability degree is 0, for the best. Actual comparing with the inside of the RREQ packet link stability degree, they need a conversion function, depending on the environment Settings.

2 The QOSAODV Protocol

QOSAODV routing protocol divided into the following three steps:

(1) routing request initiated: When node receives from the upper after sending a data packet, they first check for efficient reach the destination node routing. if there are, the data packet are direct forwarded; if there are not , request is routed. Before the data was cache, message protocol extract the data packet header QoS mission requirements to carry value, and record in the routing table. Protocol use the extracted Qo S demand value do a RREQ packets and send to the neighbor node, in the form of broadcast at the same time open expansion in search and TTL increase mechanism. After waiting for a period of time, if the node have not received the corresponding RREP message, then it resend RREQ packets, if it still no response after several attempts, think this node is inaccessible, and this node sending RREQ operation is prohibited within a period of time. (2) request of routing forwarding: After intermediate node received RREQ message ,the node view check RREQ packet that have received the same source node in the recent period of time, if there are, they give up directly, if not they cache the RREQ packet and compare Qo S index. Node obtain its own bandwidth available capacity value and Link

stability value that node forward the RREQ[6] packet between a node and myself, and compare with value of QoS of RREQ packet required .

Min_Bandwidth=min(BW_node ,BW_rreq) BW_node as the available bandwidth value of the node itself, BW_rreq RREQ packet for the specified minimum bandwidth requirements.

Min_LinkStability=min(LS_node↔prenode,LS_rreq)

LS_node↔prenode is degree of stability between the node itself with neighbor node, LS_rreq RREQ is stability degree value, which were specified for packet. Intermediate nodes update routing table (create a reverse routing, record the minimum in routing table) with the minimum, and the minimum cover RREQ packet QoS value, forward. This mechanism ensure that the QoS value of RREQ packet records is always the optimal bandwidth value and best link stability.

(3) respond routing: Receiving RREQ packets, destination node, as well as the operation of the intermediate nodes, update the routing table, and concluded minimum value of QoS. In order to respond to the source node , destination node make a RREP message, QoS minimum value are written into the RREP message of destination node, and sent to the source node. RREP reply according to the RREQ packet forwarding generated in the process of reverse routing, the source node to unicast.

3 Simulation

This article uses the Manhattan model[7], The specific parameters of the simulation environment such as the following Table3-1. The proposed QOSAODV protocol's performance is analyzed using NS2 simulator.

Table 3.1 The results of simulation analysis

application layer	CBR
Transport Laye	UDP
Routing Layer	QOSADOV 、AODV
MAC Layer	802.11DCF
Wireless transmission model	shadowing mode β =2.4
Wireless transmission frequency	2.4GH
Number of nodes	20，40，60，80，100，120，140，160，180，200
Scene size	1000m×1000m
simulation time	100 s.

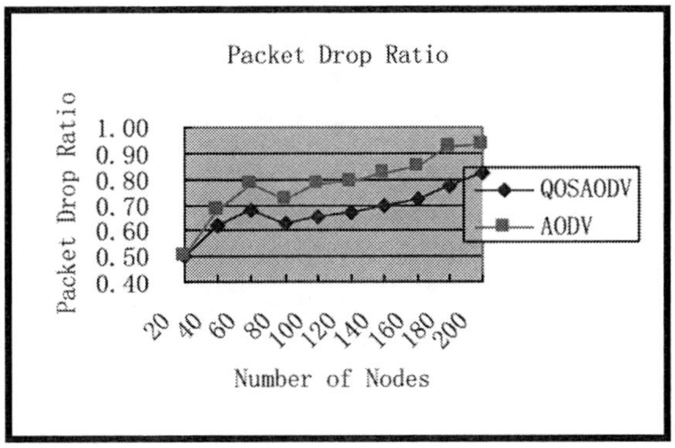

Figure 3.1 The comparison of packet loss rate

As you can see from figure 3.1, QOSAODV routing protocol AODV routing protocol and because of the increase of the number of nodes, the packet loss rate also will increase. But QOSAODV routing protocols due to its QoS safeguard mechanism, not because the number of nodes increases with the increase of packet loss rate, the number of nodes is long can reduce the packet loss rate of 11% on average, the node number once due to reach the destination node can be found with path is limited, so the two protocols performance are similar, but the number of nodes for QOSAODV routing protocol can effectively avoid the link to bedevil node and choose the forward routing path as the data is more stable, can effectively restrain the increase of the packet loss rate, intuitive proved the feasibility and effectiveness of the QOSAODV routing protocols.

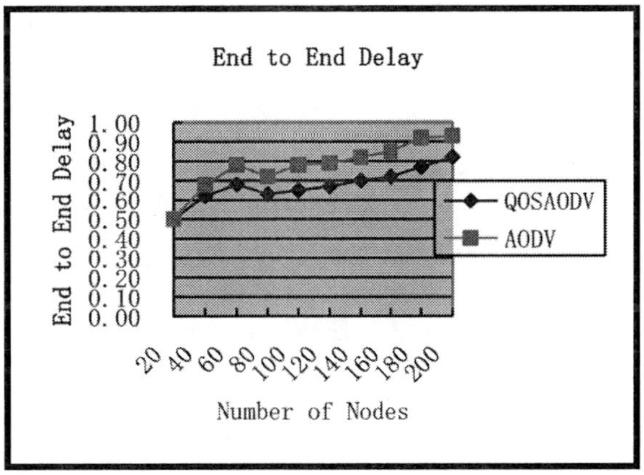

Figure 3.2 end-to-end delay

Figure 3.2 said QOSAODV routing protocol of the average end-to-end delay slightly greater than AODV, because QOSAODV routing protocols to choose the least path is not necessarily the hop. The index compared with packet loss rate and the number of routing chain scission,

for users is acceptable. Also indicated in the Figure 3.2 QOSAODV routing protocol because of increased HELLO information exchange mechanism and the active routing update mechanism regularly, so in theory is bound to increase the routing overhead. But the main communication ability for on-board wireless ad-hoc network bottleneck is not network physical channel capacity, but within the prescribed period of time how to find the path of the routing to maintain longer greater bandwidth, so add some routing overhead will not affect the larger network of physical communication ability.

4 Result

By simulation results, this paper puts forward the correctness of the theory for analyzing the stability of the link, proved QOSADOV routing protocol is better than AODV routing protocol is more suitable for mobile, nodes densely[8] vehicular ad hoc network environment. QOSADOV routing protocol can effectively reduce the average packet loss rate and the routing number of broken chain, realize the vehicular Ad Hoc networks QoS mechanism.

References

1. Passmann C, Brenzel C, Meschenmoser R. Wireless vehicle to vehicle warning system [J]. SAE2000 World Congress, USA, 2009.

2.Luisa A, Michele P. Inter-vehicle communication and cooperative system: local dynamic safety information distributed among the infra-structure and the vehicles as virtual sensors to enhance road safety [C]. Vehicular Technology Conference, Berlin, 2012.

3. Schmitz R, Leiggener A, Festag A. Analysis of path charac- teristics and transport protocol design in vehicular Ad Hoc networks [J]. Proc of the 63rd IEEE Semiannual Vehicular Technology Conf on VTC-Spring. Melbourne, Australia, 2006.

4. Rudack M, Meincke M, Lott M. On the dynamics of Ad Hoc networks for inter vehicle communication (IVC) [J]. Proceedings of the ICWN 2002, Las Vegas, USA, 2002.

5.Yih-Chun Hu,(2003), Enabling Secure High-Performance Wireless Ad Hoc Networking, PhD Thesis, Carnegie Mellon University (CMU)

6.Ilyas M.,(2003), The Handbook Of Wireless Ad Hoc Network, CRC

7.Guoqiang Wang, Damla Turgut,Ladislau Bölöni.Improving routing performance through m-limited forwarding in power-constrained wirless ad hoc networks.ScienceDirect. 2008(68):501–514

8.Sanjay Kumar Dhurandher,Sudip Misra, Mohammad S. Obaidat. EEAODR:An energy-efficient ad hoc on-demand routing protocol for mobile ad hoc networks. INTERNATIONAL JOURNALOF COMMUNICATION SYSTEMS. 2009(22):789–817

MATEC Web of Conferences **44**, 02090 (2016)
DOI: 10.1051/matecconf/20164402090

Ad hoc on-demand Distance Vector Routing Protocol Based on Load Balance

Yun Jie Zhu[1], Yong Qiang Li[1], Qing Gang Fan[1], Zhong Wang[1]

[1]*Computer Staff Room,Xian Research Institute of High Technology, Xian 721006,China*

Abstract. The ad hoc on-demand distance vector routing protocol based on load balance (AODVLB) is proposed aiming at the jitter problem. The turbulence phenomena in on-demand route protocol is presented, the delay forwarding technology is introduced to control the route building, a load calculation function have been designed. The results of simulation using ns2 show that the method decreases 20% than AODV in jitter time, improves the networks' performance significantly.
Key Words. MANET, load balance, turbulent flow, jitter, AODV

1、 introduction

A mobile ad hoc network consists of wireless mobile nodes that can communicate with other nodes through wireless links without any fixed infrastructure. Mobile Ad Hoc network [1] is a system of wireless mobile nodes which self-organize in dynamic and temporary network topologies. Ad hoc networks are easier to organize than wired networks and used in many applications, such as virtual classrooms, military communications, emergency search, rescue operations and data acquisition in hostile.

Jitter is a important performance on wireless networks.It reflects the delay variance in data transmission speed. In ensuring Quality of Service (QoS) provisioning, a network is expected to guarantee a set of measurable pre-specified service attributes to the users in terms of end-to-end performance, the lifetime of the networks, the packets loss rate and so on[2][3] Recent Qos solutions are planned to operate on trusted environments and totally assume the participating nodes to be cooperative and well behaved.[4][5]

The major drawback of conventional on-demand routing protocols such as ad hoc on-demand distance vector protocol (AODV) is the absence of the QoS provision and consideration about load of nodes before routing. In this paper, we propose the enhanced ad hoc on-demand distance vector routing protocol which is modified to improve the networks jitter in mobile ad hoc networks. The AODVLB protocol involves the delay calculating function which can determine the delay from each node's load .When the nodes forward the RREQ packets, it helps in building a path that does not have nodes exhausted and selects a better path. It tries to establish a balance of load among the nodes.

2、 Related Work

The problem of trying to decrease the delay time of networks in MANET is not new. A number of previous works has addressed different strategies spanning different net layers.

The technique, constraining the scales of the subsets of forwarding nodes, is to reduce the cost of disseminating information by limiting the cardinality of the subset of nodes which retransmit a packet. The technique, optimizing the selecting path criterions, takes the delay、hops into the path selecting metrics. The key point of these algorithms is the designation of path assessment function aiming the different requirements. It can be classified into multi-objective optimization in math.

Article available at http://www.matec-conferences.org or http://dx.doi.org/10.1051/matecconf/20164402090

Article[6]presents the m-limited forwarding technique. In case of flooding, the number of messages increases geometrically with the distance from the source to the destination, while for m-limited forwarding the increase is only linear. It gives a forwarding fitness function which determined weather does the node forward packets. In reality it reduces the power consumption as well as the waste of the network band-width, but the defect is increasing the computational complexity, in addition, the parameter of the forwarding fitness function is difficult for determining and need an amount of experiments to be modified.

When the destination gets the first RREQ, it waits for σt time and collects all other RREQ coming in this time interval[7]. After σt time, it calls the optimization function to determine the best path to select and send RREP. The Optimization function involves the time taken, the load and the hop count in determining the path that will give more reliable results.

Article [8] proposed a path building controlling mechanism. It take the hops, the load value into the RREQ packets and could improve the route generating, but the threshold is difficult to set.

3 The AODVLB Protocol

3.1 Basic Theory

A node disseminates a RREQ when it needs a route to a destination and does not have one available. When a node receives a RREQ, it first checks whether it has received a RREQ with the same Originator IP Address and RREQ ID within the last PATH_DISCOVERY_TIME. If such a RREQ has been received, the node silently discards the newly received RREQ. If a node does not generate a RREP then it will forwarding the RREQ. The destination node will generate the RREP based on some principles and send it out.[9][10]

3.2 Algorithm Flow

We proposed the AODVLB: Ad hoc on-demand Distance Vector routing Protocol Based on Load Balance. Its theory is as the same of the standard AODV, the difference is the usage of delay forwarding technology mentioned in the forth section in forwarding packets.

When a source node wants to transmit data to the destination node, first it checks whether there is any existing valid path in the routing table. If it exists, the node uses that path, otherwise, it sends RREQ to its neighbor nodes. When a node (either destination or intermediate) receives RREQ, it ensures that the received RREQ is not a duplicate RREQ, in order to prevent looping paths. If the neighbor node is the destination, it sends RREP. Otherwise, it waits for a delay and sends new RREQ to all their neighbor nodes to find the destination. When the destination gets the first RREQ, it waits for σt time and collects all other RREQ coming in this interval. After σt time, it calls the optimization function to determine the best path to select and send RREP. It also stores some other relatively inferior paths as backup paths, which may be used if there is some network failure, thereby avoiding energy and time wastage in recalculating the path. When the source node gets the RREP, it sends the data packets.

3.3 Delay Calculation Function

According the expectation of user, the ideal node can work following this model under which the throughput、delay and so on are more important when it's energy is sufficient, but the node need to save its power to length the lifetime when its energy becomes lower.

The forwarding delay should be able to assure the stable node, whose average delay is small ,to forward packets and fight for the path, besides avoid the confliction due to concurrent communication. We call the delay calculation function Dt. It contains of two parts as the formula 1. Tc calculated by the load aims to guarantee the forwarding priority of nodes with sufficient energy, while θ is the random value for avoiding confliction.

$$Dt = T_c + \theta \quad (1)$$

The Dt's value is corresponding with the forwarding waiting time, the bigger the value the longer the waiting time.

4 Simulation

The proposed AODVLB protocol's performance is analyzed using NS2 simulator. The network is

planned and implemented using network simulator with maximum of 120 nodes .The locations of the nodes are random and other parameters based on which the network is shaped are given in Table1. The simulator is applied with traditional AODV and proposed AODVLB, the results are obtained for assessment. The proposed AODVLB protocol has shown large progress over the Qos parameters such as average delay.

Table 1

Parameter	Value	Parameter	Value
Network Size	200m*100m	Max connection	10
Number of nodes	60、80、100	Simulation time	400s
Maximum speed	18km/h	MAC layer protocol	Simple Mac
Transmission range	60 meters	Initial Energy	50J
Packet size	512kb	Tx	1.8mW
Traffic type	CBR	Rx	1.3mW
Transmission rate	20times per second	Route Protocols	AODVLB、AODV

4.1 Jitter

Jitter is the performance reflecting the latency of data packets in translating process. The paper define the average delay as the time difference from the data sending time to the data receiving time, apart from the route finding time, as formula 2.

$$AD = \sum_{i=1}^{n} \frac{ReceiveT[i] - SendT[i]}{n} \quad (2)$$

The results are showing in table 2. In the scene with 60 nodes the performance is as the same in AODVDF and AODV, but the AODVDF's performance is little less than AODV's in other scene. That is because the AODVDF is to select the stable path which contains more intermediate nodes than AODV and will use more time.

Table2 Jitter

Scene Size	AODVLB	AODV
60nodes	0.28	0.28
80nodes	0.46	0.13
120nodes	0.41	0.18

4.2 Network lifetime

Network lifetime is an important indicator in performance. The relationship between the number of exhausted nodes and the running time can reflect the state of the networks. It's easy to understand, the longer the running time with the same exhausted nodes, the longer the network lifetime. The figure 1 is the simulation results under 80 nodes.

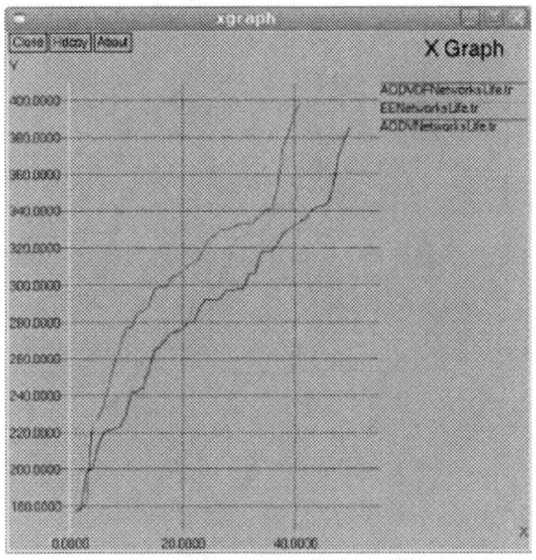

Fig.1: 80nodes

X axis denotes the number of exhausted nodes and Y axis denotes the net running time. The communicating frequency is 20 and number of link is 6.We can acknowledge that the network lifetime of AODVLB is longer than the AODV's, obviously, while the accurate value of improving is show in table 3. The traditional AODV doesn't provide reliable routing since the nodes in the network are not checked against its energy levels. While the low energy level may cause packets lost because of draining out of energy.

Table 3: The improvement on network lifetime

scene	60nodes	80nodes	120nodes
Improvement Rate	23.3%	18.1%	13.0%
Remark: $\text{Im}\,provementRate = \frac{\text{AODVLB} - AODV}{AODV}$			

4.3 Throughput Capacity

Throughput capacity is an important

performance metric reflecting the capability about the load carrying capacity of networks. The throughput is affected by the combined effects of different layers, radio channel confliction and node's cache. The proposed AODVDF can improve the throughput of networks, by selecting the stable path. The results is as table 4. The AODV is to choose the shortest path, but these paths may be unstable and failed soon. We can get the conclusion that the AODVDF can assume a greater load than the standard aodv protocol in sparse node scene.

Table 4 Received Packets Number

Scene Size	AODV	AODVLB
60	1461	3445
80	2101	2559
120	2390	2630

4.4 Result

According to the simulation results, the AODVLB is much more excellent in these metrics, balancing the average delay, extending the networks lifetime and throughput, especially in sparse nodes scene.

5 Summary and Improvement

The simulation results show that AODVLB is more efficient comparing with the AODV. We observed that there are load balancing and delay forwarding in AODVLB. All the nodes are used and the most optimized path is built and kept according to the current network state.

The AODVLB expands the improvement in route protocol to a new area, controlling the path building, but it is still imperfect and deficient in running path monitor, modifying failed path. Both of them should be considered.

References

[1] Sihai Zheng, Layuan Li, Yong Li. A QoS Routing Protocol for Mobile Ad Hoc Networks Based on Multipath. JOURNAL OF NETWORKS, VOL. 7, NO. 4, 2012:691-698

[2] Mina Masoudifar. A review and performance comparison of QoS multicast routing protocols for MANETs. Ad Hoc Networks. 2009(7):1150–1155

[3] Peter Jurcik. Real-time Communication over Cluster-tree Wire-less Sensor Networks ［R］. IPP-HURRAY Technical Report，Porto，Portugal，2010.

[4] Yih-Chun Hu,(2003), Enabling Secure High-Performance Wireless Ad Hoc Networking, PhD Thesis, Carnegie Mellon University (CMU)

[5] Ilyas M.,(2003), The Handbook Of Wireless Ad Hoc Network, CRC

[6] Guoqiang Wang, Damla Turgut,Ladislau Bölöni.Improving routing performance through m-limited forwarding in power-constrained wirless ad hoc networks.ScienceDirect. 2008(68):501–514

[7] Song JunKeun, Ryoo Jeong-dong, Kim SangCheol, et al. A Dynamic GTS Allocation Algorithm in IEEE 802.15.4 for QoS guaranteed Real-time Applications[C]// Proc of IEEE Int'l Symp on Consumer Electronics, 2007:1-6.

[8] S. Santhi,G. Sudha Sadasivam.Enhanced AOMDV for energy conservation in hybrid ad hoc networks[J]. Information and Communication Technology. 2014, Vol. 6(2):122-141.

[9] Wang Qingwen, Shi Haoshan, Qi Qian. A Cross-Layer Dynamic Probabilistic Broadcasting Strategy for Mobile Ad Hoc Networks[C]. //Proceedings of the Education Technology and Computer Science (ETCS), 2011 Third International Workshop on: vol.2: MECS, 2012:62-65.

[10] RamachandranI,Das A K,RoyS.Analysis of the contention access period of IEEE 802.15.4[J].ACM Transactions on SensorNetworks,2007,3(1)

MATEC Web of Conferences 44, 02091 (2016)
DOI: 10.1051/matecconf/20164402091

Variation function fitting method based on particle swarm optimization

Ping Duan[1], Jia Li[1a], Hai Yang Lv[2,3,4]

[1]School of Tourism and Geographical Sciences of Yunnan Normal University, Kunming, 650050, China
[2]Key Laboratory of Virtual Geographic Environment (Nanjing Normal University), Ministry of Education, Nanjing, 210023, China
[3]State Key Laboratory Cultivation Base of Geographical Environment Evolution (Jiangsu Province), Nanjing, 210023, China
[4]Jiangsu Center for Collaborative Innovation in Geographical Information Resource Development and Application, Nanjing, 210023, China

Abstract. In the Kriging interpolation method, different theory models of variation function are selected and fitted. There are many common variation function models, such as spherical model, index model, Gaussian model and so on. As these variation function models are non-linear, non-linear model are converted to linear model when these variation function models are solved. Different variation function models with different conversion methods are lack of generality in the process of Kriging interpolation. Particle swarm optimization algorithm with the advantages of global optimal solution can be directly used to solve non-linear fitting equation. In this paper, variation function model based on particle swarm optimization algorithm is fitted. Experiment shows that it is appropriate for fitting variable function based particle swarm optimization algorithm.

1 Introduction

Kriging interpolation is founded by South African geological engineer Krige. And then, Kriging interpolation theory is improved by French statisticians Matheron [1]. Kriging interpolation method as one of the common spatial interpolation has been widely used in geology, atmosphere, soil and remote sensing. Like most of the spatial interpolation method, Kriging interpolation is also based on the principle of spatial correlation. The closer distance between space objects, the greater the similarity of spatial properties. The basic principle of Kriging interpolation is that real variation function values of sampled data are firstly calculated in interpolation process. And then, theory model of variation function is constructed. Weights and Lagrange coefficient between reference points and interpolation point are calculated based on variation function model. Finally, attribute values of interpolation point are calculated by solving linear combination equations.

Variation function model is the basis of Kriging interpolation method. It is a tool to reflect the rule of regionalized variable and ultimately determines the authenticity and effectiveness of prediction results [2]. There are many common variation function models, such as linear sill model, spherical model, exponential model, Gaussian model, logarithmic model and so on[3]. These models can be divided into non-linear and linear curve fitting model. For linear curve model, variation function can be directly fitted by least squares. Compared with linear curve model, non-linear model are converted to linear model when these variation function models are solved. The difficulty of conversion increases the complexity of algorithm.

With the development of non-linear theory in recent years, non-linear curve for solving need not be converted linear curve. It can be directly solved by intelligent algorithm. Particle swarm optimization (PSO) algorithm as a kind of typical intelligent algorithm has the advantages of global optimal solution. It can not only directly solve non-linear fitting equation but also solve variation function fitting equation. In this paper, particle swarm optimization algorithm is used to fit variation function model. In order to verify the variation function theory model based on particle swarm fitting method, iron ore grade data from some region in china is tested. The fitting result of PSO algorithm is the same with the weighted least squares algorithm. As can be seen from the experimental results, the weighted least squares algorithm can be replaced by PSO algorithm. It can avoid the conversion from non-linear to linear.

2 Kriging interpolation model and method

Kriging interpolation is an optimal linear unbiased estimation method. Kriging interpolation similar with inverse distance weighted is based on sampling points around unknown points to calculate the value of unknown points. With the development of Kriging interpolation, there are many kriging interpolation methods. The basic principle of these methods are the same, so ordinary Kriging interpolation model is researched in this paper.

[a] Corresponding author: lijia8425@163.com

2.1 Kriging interpolation model

Supposed regionalized variable $Z(x)$ meet second order stationarity conditions. There are n reference points around the interpolation point x with attribute value Z (x_i). The Kriging interpolation model is [4]:

$$Z'(x)=\sum_{i=1}^{n}\lambda_i Z(x_i) \quad (1)$$

Here, λ is weight. Formula (1) need to meet the following conditions:

(1) Condition of unbiasedness:

$$\sum_{i=1}^{n}\lambda_i=1 \quad (2)$$

(2) Condition of minimum variance:

$$\sigma_E^2=E[Z'(x)\text{-}Z(x)]^2=E[Z(x)-\sum_{i=1}^{n}\lambda_i\, Z(x_i)]^2=\min \quad (3)$$

In order to minimize the estimated value of variance, according to the principle of Lagrange multipliers, let be:

$$F=\sigma_E^2-2\mu(\sum_{i=1}^{n}\lambda_i-1) \quad (4)$$

Here, μ is Lagrange multipliers.

Partial derivative of F is calculated and let be the value of partial derivative is zero. Equation set of Kriging are as follows:

$$\begin{cases}\dfrac{\partial F}{\partial\lambda_i}=2\sum_{j=1}^{n}\lambda_j c(x_i,x_j)-2c(x_i,x)-2\mu=0\\[2ex] \dfrac{\partial F}{\partial\mu}=-2\left(\sum_{i=1}^{n}\lambda_i-1\right)=0\end{cases} \quad (5)$$

Here, c is covariance. According to the relationship of covariance and variation function,

$$\gamma(h)=c(0)-c(h) \quad (6)$$

Here, h is the distance between point pairs. γ is the value of variation function.

Finally, the interpolation model can be expressed as follows:

$$\begin{bmatrix}\gamma_{11} & \cdots & \gamma_{1n} & 1\\ \vdots & \ddots & \vdots & \vdots\\ \gamma_{n1} & \cdots & \gamma_{nn} & 1\\ 1 & \cdots & 1 & 0\end{bmatrix}\cdot\begin{bmatrix}\lambda_1\\ \vdots\\ \lambda_n\\ \mu\end{bmatrix}=\begin{bmatrix}\gamma_{10}\\ \vdots\\ \gamma_{n0}\\ 1\end{bmatrix} \quad (7)$$

2.2 Kriging interpolation method

Concrete steps of Kriging interpolation are as follows [5]:

(1) Normal distribution of sampling data is determined. If sampling data not meet normal distribution, sampling data need to convert approximate normal distribution.

(2) Variation function values of sampling data are calculated. If the size of point pairs is large, variation function values with different groups are calculated.

(3) Theory model of variation function is selected and variation function curve is fitted.

(4) Weight matrix of interpolation point is calculated according to the variation function curve.

(5) The attribute value of unknown point are calculated according to linear combination of weight matrix.

In the process of Kriging interpolation, step (3) is the key step. Because the variation function curve affects the weight matrix of the interpolation point. In this paper, the particle swarm optimization algorithm is used to fit variation function curve.

3 Theory model of variation function based on particle swarm optimization algorithm

Particle swarm optimization algorithm (PSO for short) is proposed by Kennedy and Eberhart in 1995. It is a kind of swarm intelligence algorithm that simulated the search process of birds group [6]. If there is only one piece of food in some region, the most simple and effective strategy to find the food is to search the nearest area around birds.

In PSO algorithm, birds as a particle in the space, has their own position. It can be expressed by (x_i,v_i, $pbest_i$). x_i is the current position of the particle. v_i is the current speed of the particle. $pbest_i$ is the best current position that has been searched by particle. An objective function (denoted by Fitness) is given to each particle's position. The fitness of each particle can be evaluated by Fitness function. The value of Fitness function as evaluation criterion is calculated. It can update the current optimal value of the particle, denoted by $pbest_i$.

In the algorithm implementation process, some initial values are given, such as the particle position, the speed of the particles, inertia weigh of the particle w_i, randomly learning factor of the particle c_1 and c_2. Optimal solution of current particle $pbest_i$ and all particles are solved by iterative search of each particle. $gbest_i$ is the global extremum. $pbest_i$ and $gbest_i$ are velocity parameters of next updating. By n iterations, it finally can get a satisfactory result.

Mathematical expressions of update speed v and position x of particle are as follows:

$$\begin{aligned}v_{i,j}^{k+1}&=w_i v_{i,j}^{k}+c_1\cdot rand_1\cdot(pbest_{i,j}^{k}-x_{i,j}^{k})\\&+c_2\cdot rand_2\cdot(gbest_{i,j}^{k}-x_{i,j}^{k})\end{aligned} \quad (8)$$

$$x_{i,j}^{k+1}=x_{i,j}^{k}+v_{i,j}^{k+1} \quad (9)$$

Here, (i, j) is the index of the current particle. The superscript k is the k-th iteration.

The algorithm of Particle Swarm Optimization is as follows:

Table 1. The algorithm process of PSO

The algorithm of PSO
Initialize the related parameters and scope of particles
For i = 1: times of iterations
For j = 1 : sum of particles
To update the current particle velocity;
To update the current particle location;
Local optimal fitness function calculation;
Global optimal fitness function calculation;
End
End
Output optimal particle location (optimal parameters)

The flow chart is as follows :

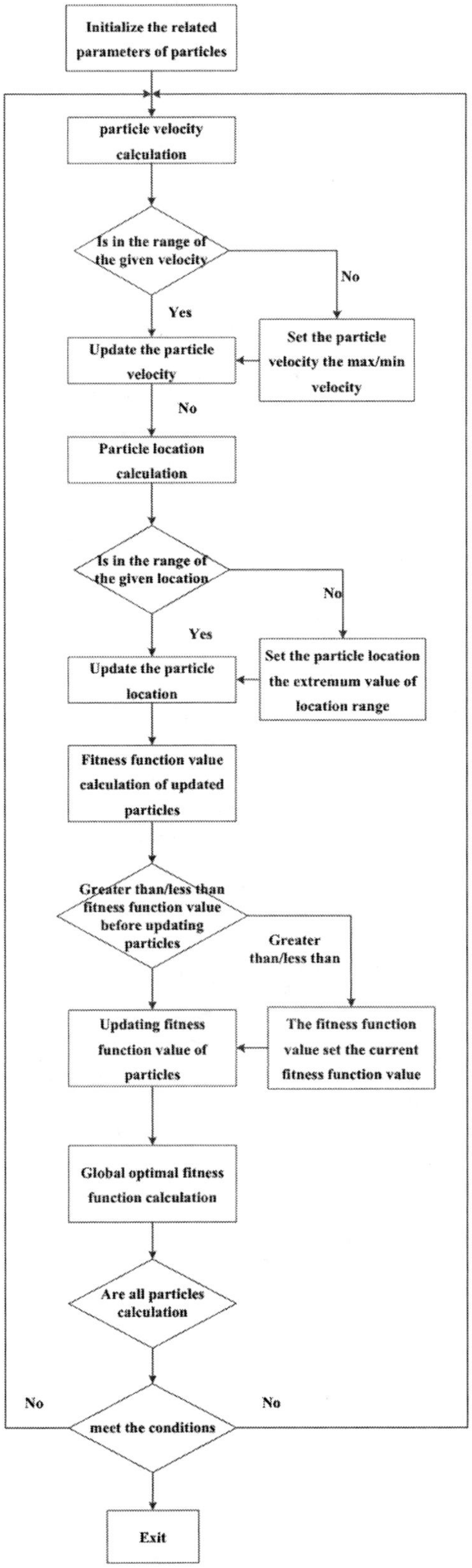

Figure 1. The flow chart of PSO algorithm

The purpose of variation function model fitting is to minimize error of curve fitting. Error corresponds to the Fitness function in PSO algorithm when curve is fitted. The mathematical expression is:

$$Fitness = \sum_{j=1}^{n} [\gamma(h_j) - \gamma'(h_j)]^2 \qquad (10)$$

Here, h_j is separation distance of variation function. $\gamma(h_j)$ is an actual value of variation function of separation distance h_j. $\gamma'(h_j)$ is the theory model value of current variation function.

In the actual process of variation function fitting, weight value is large when the distance of two points are closer in variation function diagram and vice versa. Therefore, with distance as the weight, the definition of Fitness function is:

$$Fitness = \sum_{j=1}^{n} w_j \cdot [\gamma(h_j) - \gamma'(h_j)]^2 \qquad (11)$$

Here,

$$w_j = w_i / \sum_{i=1}^{n} w_i \qquad (12)$$

$$w_i = h_j / h_{all} \qquad (13)$$

Here, h_{all} is the sum of all the separation distance h_j.

The number of unknown in variation function theory model and particle in PSO algorithm are the same. The position of particle represents the unknown in variation function theory model. The particle position of minimum Fitness function value is searched by PSO algorithm, which is the expression of curve fitting.

4 The experiment and conclusion

In order to verify the variation function theory model based on particle swarm fitting method, iron ore grade data from some region in china is tested. Iron ore grade in 3D space presents anisotropic characteristics. Variation function values of three orientations are calculated and fitted by spherical model.

Supposed the range of three particles' positions is [0, 20]. The number of particle is 15. The iteration times are 30. Spherical theory model of variation function is fitted and solved by PSO algorithm. Fitting parameters of three orientations are shown in table 2.

Table 2. Fitting parameters of spherical model of variation function on three orientations

Orientation	Nugget (c0)	High arch (c)	Range (a)
x	1.3753E-02	2.5131E-02	5.4387E+02
y	1.2412E-02	1.7804E-02	4.4146E+02
z	2.2286E-04	5.2774E-02	5.2431E+02

The fitting results of three orientations are shown in Figure 2.

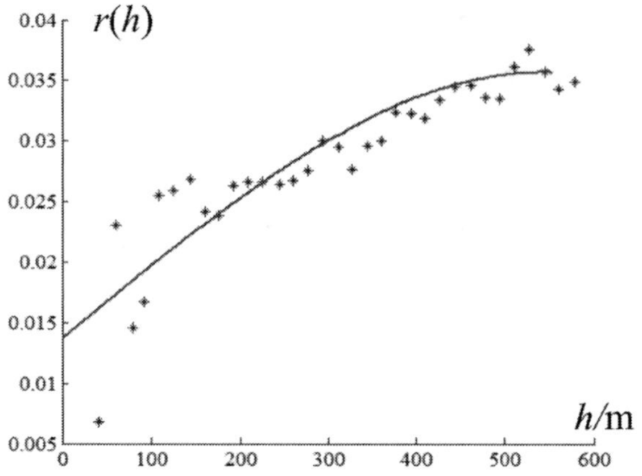

(a) Fitting curve of variation function on x orientation

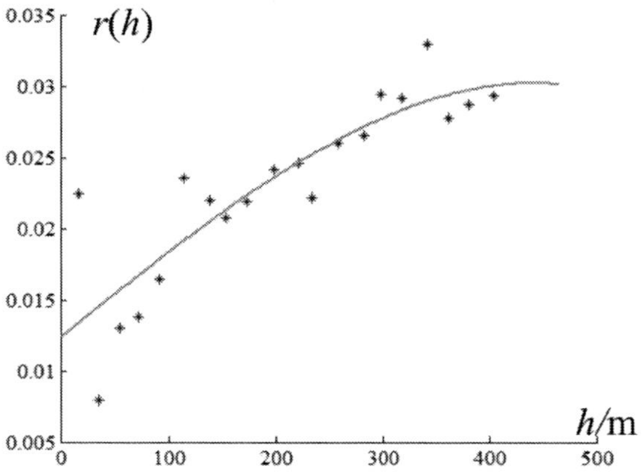

(b) Fitting curve of variation function on y orientation

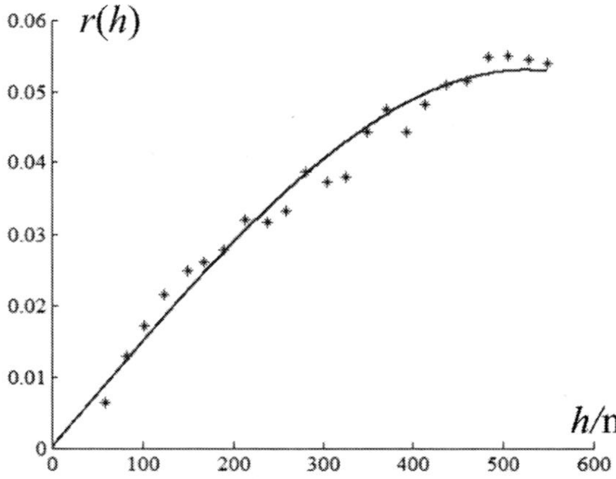

(c) Fitting curve of variation function on z orientation

Figure 2. Fitting parameters of spherical model of variation function on three orientations

Distance weighted fitting is adopted by Fitness function of PSO algorithm. The fitting result of PSO algorithm is the same with the weighted least squares algorithm. As can be seen from the experimental results, the weighted least squares algorithm can be replaced by PSO algorithm. It can avoid the conversion from non-linear to linear. Therefore, PSO algorithm is an effective method for variation function fitting.

Acknowledgements

This work has been Supported by Youths Foundation of School of Tourism and Geographical Sciences of YunNan Normal University, Doctoral Fund of YunNan Normal University (No. 0130020502050311З) and the National Natural ScienceFoundation of China (No.41271383).

References

1. G. Matheron, Principles of geostatistics. Economic Geology, **58**, 8(1963)
2. Y. Jin, M. Pan, C. Ma, Principles and Validation of unified Approach for Nested Overlap of Geological Variable Variograms. Journal of China University of Mining & Technolo, **39**, 3(2010)
3. A. L. Liu, P. F. Wang, Y. Y. Ding, Introduction to Geostatistics, Science Press in China, (2012)
4. J. P. Yue, Z. K. Zhen, Application of Particle Swarm Optimization Based Kriging Interpolation Method in Regional Land Subsidence. Surveying and mapping, 3,(2012)
5. H. Q. Sun, Geostatistics and its application, China University of Mining and Technology press, (1990)
6. L. Q. Yao, M. Pan, Q. M. Cheng, Nested Overlap of Variograms in 3D Kriging, Earth Science-Journal of China University of Geosciences, **34**,2(2009).
7. J. H. Qiao, M. Pan,Y.Jin, 3D modeling and Analysis of Natural Foundation Beating Capacity Based on Kriging Method, Acta Scientiarum Naturalium Universitatis Pekinensis, **47**, 5 (2011)
8. X. C. Mao, F. Cao, Y. H. Zou, Y. Zhao, Construction and application of variation ellipsoid for analysis of mineralization structure, Journal of Central South University(Science and Technology), **45**, 9(2014)
9. F. GAO, Research on Intelligent Particle Swarm Optimization Algorithm, Harbin Institute of Technology, (2008)
10. R. C. Eberhart, J. Kennedy, A New Optimizer Using Particle Swarm Theory. Proceedings of the Sixth International Symposium on Micro Machine and Human Science, Nagoya(1995)
11. J. Kennedy, R. C. Eberhart. Particle Swarm Optimization. Proceeding of IEEE International Conference on Neural Networks. Piscataway, (1995)
12. X. H. Shi, Y. C. Liang, H. P. Lee, C. Lu, Q. X. Wang, Particle swarm optimization-based algorithms for TSP and generalized TSP. Information Processing Letters, (2007)

MATEC Web of Conferences 44, 02092 (2016)
DOI: 10.1051/matecconf/20164402092

A Method for Cyber-Physical System Behavior Modeling and Safety Verification Based on Extended Hybrid System Description Language

Ming Fu Tuo[1,2], Xing She Zhou [1] ,Zheng Xin Guo [3] and Li Jun Shan [1]

[1] Northwestern Polytechnical University, Xi'An, China
[2] Air Force Engineering University, Xi'An, China
[3] Hunan University, Changsha, China

Abstract. The safety of Cyber-physical system(CPS) is up to its behavior, and it is a key property for CPS to be applied in critical application fields. A method for CPS behavior modeling and safety verification is put forward in this paper. The behavior model of CPS is described by extended hybrid system description language(E-HYSDEL).The formal definition of hybrid program(HP) is given, and the behavior model is transformed to HP based on the definition. The safety of CPS is verified by inputting the HP to KeYmarea. The advantage of the approach is that it models CPS intuitively and verify it's safety strictly avoiding the state space explosion

1 Introduction

Cyber Physical System(CPS) are new type of hybrid systems which characterized by deeper integrations of computation with physical processes[1].Application fields of CPS are very wide, such as Intelligent transportation, telemedicine, the smart-grid, aeronautics and astronautics, and so on[2].

Safety is a key property for CPS to be applied in critical application fields. Whether the properties of CPS can satisfies the requirements can be analyzed in the system design stage by model verification technology. This helps to find the defects of deign as early as possible, so it can reduce the risk of system development effectively.

2 Studies of CPS analysis and verification

With the widely used of CPS,the study for CPS analysis and verification becomes more and more deeply.To extend the classical verification methods is one of the ways,such as extention of FSM,optimization of fault tree,etc[3][4].There are also researchers use colored petri nets(CPN) to model and verify CPS.

Formal verification methods,such as model checking and theorem proving,are used to verify safety and other properties of CPS recently[5].Model checking technology determines the authenticity of a proposition by traversing the state space.it's main advantage is a high degree of automation. Furthermore,it can generate counterexample. However, It is difficult to overcome the sate space explosion problem. Cyber-physical systems usually are hybrid systems. They include both discrete states transitions and dynamic continuous variation processes, that is to say the sates of most CPS are infinite.

From the practical point of view, theorem proving method is more suitable for safety verification of CPS[6]. Differential dynamic logic(dL), put forward by Platzer, is one of theorem proving methods. It has been successfully used in fields such as the air traffic control system, European train control system because of its rigorous syntax and clear semantics. The operational model of dL is hybrid program(HP). dL is well supported by KeYmarea, a famous theorem prover.

[a] Corresponding author:mftuo@163.com

3 The framework of the method for CPS behaviour modelling and safety verification

In this paper,We extend HYSDEL, a traditional hybrid system description language, and name it E-HYSDEL. Furthermore, we use it to model the behavior of CPS. Based on this, the safety of CPS is verified. The framework of this new method for CPS behavior modeling and safety verification can be depicted as figure 1.

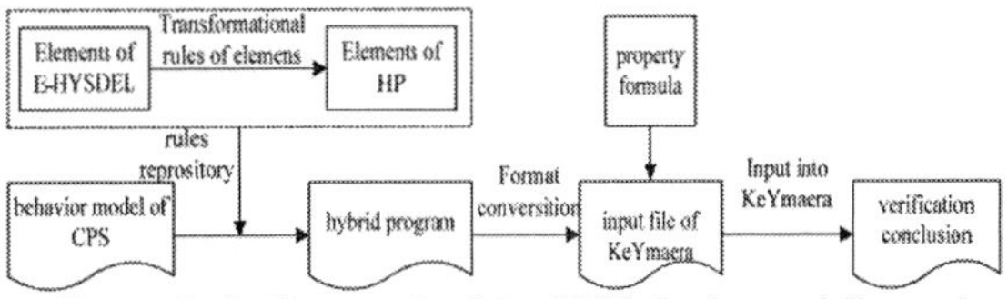

Figure 1. the framework of the CPS behavior modeling and safety verification

According to this framework, the process for CPS behavior modeling and safety verification can be divided into four steps. In the first, the transformation rules between meta-model of E-HYSDEL and meta-model of HP are established. Then, the behavior model of a specific CPS is described by E-HYSDEL code. Next, the behavior model is transformed to the corresponding HP based on the transformation rules. Finally, the formula that describes the constraints of variables affecting safety of system and the HP are inputted into KeYmarea to verify whether the safety related constraints are met.

4 The formal definition of HP

The formal definition of HP is given as follows.

HPM=(PD，VD，PC，SHPS)

PD represents parameter declaration.

VD represents dynamic variables declaration.

PC represents precondition, in other word, the constraints of variables before system runs.

SHPS represent the set of sub hybrid program. Each SHP is defined as follows.

SHP=(MS, DTS, CTS)

MS represents set of discrete states.

DTS represents set of transitions of discrete states, that is transitions between modes.

CTS represents set of dynamic processes, it describes the continuous change in a single mode.

Some transformational rules are set up based on this formal definition.

5 Application case

Room temperature control system is one of typical CPS(Fig 2).There two persons, a heater, a air conditioning, a window in room. These equipments can affect the room temperature.T1 represents the temperature of place where person 1 stay.T2 represents the temperature of place where person 2 stay. Tamb represents the temperature outside the window. Uhot represents heater power flow when it is on. Ucold represents air conditioning power flow when it is on.

The person 1 turns the heater(air conditioning) on whenever he is cold(heat).If person 2 is cold he turns the heater on unless person 1 is heat. If person 2 is heat he turns the air conditioning on unless person 1 is cold. Otherwise, heater and air conditioning are off.

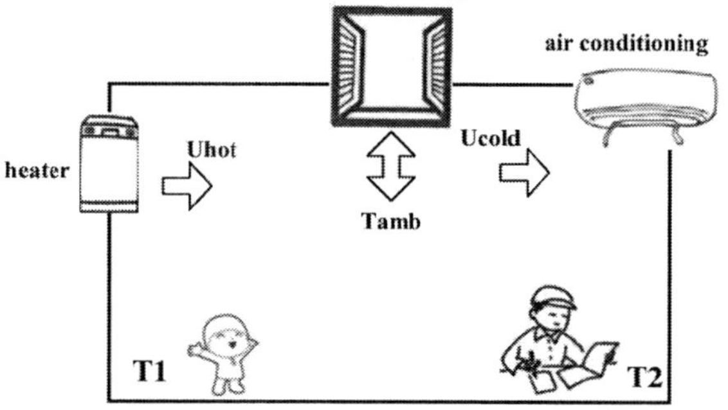

Figure 2. the room temperature system

The changes of T1 and T2 can be expressed by the following equations.

$T1' = -alpha1*(T1-Tamb)+k1*(uhot-ucold)$

$T2' = -alpha2*(T2-Tamb)+k2*(uhot-ucold)$

In these equations, Ts=0.5, alpha1 = 1, alpha2 = 0.5, k1 = 0.8, k2 = 0.4, Thot1 = 30, Tcold1 = 15, Thot2 = 35, Tcold2 = 10, Uc = 2, Uh = 2.

We will verify the conclusion that state $10 \leqslant T1,T2 \leqslant 15$ is not reachable on condition that $10 \leqslant Tamb \leqslant 30$ and the initial state is $35 \leqslant T1,T2 \leqslant 40$.

The behavior model of temperature control system is described by the following E-HYSDEL codes.

```
SYSTEM heatcool {
INTERFACE {
    STATE {
            REAL T1 [-10,50];
            REAL T2 [-10,50];
        }
    INPUT { REAL Tamb [-10,50]; }
    OUTPUT {
            REAL y1;
            REAL y2;
    }
    PARAMETER
    {
        REAL Ts=0.5, alpha1=1, alpha2=0.5, k1=0.8, k2=0.4;
        REAL Thot1=30, Tcold1=15, Thot2=35, Tcold2=10, Uc=2, Uh=2;
    }
}
IMPLEMENTATION {
    AUX {
        REAL uhot, ucold,t;
        BOOL hot1, hot2, cold1, cold2;
    }
    AD { hot1 = T1>=Thot1;
         hot2 = T2>=Thot2;
         cold1 = T1<=Tcold1;
         cold2 = T2<=Tcold2;
    }
DA { uhot = {IF cold1 | (cold2 & ~hot1) THEN Uh ELSE 0
};
     ucold = {IF hot1 | (hot2 & ~cold1) THEN Uc ELSE 0}; }
    CONTINUOUS {
        T1 = T1+Ts*(-alpha1*(T1-Tamb) +k1*(uhot-ucold));
        T2 = T2+Ts*(-alpha2*(T2-Tamb) +k2*(uhot-ucold)); }
    OUTPUT {y1=T1;
            y2=T2;
    }
    }
}
```

The behavior model is transformed to the following HP based on the former transformational rules.

```
heatcool≡ (S1∪S2) *
S1≡(
Tamb=*;?(Tamb≥10∧Tamb≤30);
if((T1≤Tcold1)∨(T2≤Tcold2∧¬T1≥Thot1))
uhot:=Uh;
else
uhot:=0;
if((T1≥Thot1)∨(T2≥Thot2∧¬T1≤Tcold1))
ucold:=Uc;
else
ucold:=0;
T1' = -alpha1*(T1-Tamb)+k1*(uhot-ucold),t' =1 ;
)
S2≡(
Tamb=*;?(Tamb≥10∧Tamb≤30);
if((T1≤Tcold1)∨(T2≤Tcold2∧¬T1≥Thot1))
uhot:=Uh;
else
uhot:=0;
if((T1≥Thot1)∨(T2≥Thot2∧¬T1≤Tcold1))
ucold:=Uc;
else
```

ucold:=0;
T2′ = -alpha2*(T2-Tamb)+k2*(uhot-ucold),t′ =1 ;
)

Finally, the safety of the system is specified by the formulation $\omega \rightarrow [\,heatcool^*\,]\,\Phi$, where ω is initial condition, and Φ is the conclusion to be verified.

verification used less steps and avoid the state space explosion.

6 Conclusion

The main idea of the given method for behavior modeling and safety verification of CPS is that modeling the behavior of CPS by hybrid automata, which is described by E-HYSDEL language, then transform this model to a corresponding dL model, described by HP, and verify the safety of the dL model by means of KeYmaera.

The advantage of this method is that it models CPS intuitively and verifies it's safety strictly. The method can also be used to verify other property of CPS, such as real-time, reliability.

References

1. Lee, E. *CPS foundations*. Proceedings of the 47th ACM/IEEE Design Automation Conference., 2010. 737–742

$\omega \equiv (Tamb \geq 10 \wedge Tamb \leq 30) \wedge (T1 \geq 35 \wedge T1 \leq 40) \wedge T2 \geq 35 \wedge T2 \leq 40)$

$\Phi \equiv \neg(\,(T1 \geq 10 \wedge T1 \leq 15) \vee (T2 \geq 10 \wedge T2 \leq 15))$

The conclusion is verified in KeYmaera after many steps. The results shows that this method for safety

2. He, J. F. *Cyber-physical systems*. Communications of the China Computer Federation, 2010, 6(1): 25–29
3. Leonardi, F., Pinto, A., and Carloni, L. P. *Synthesis of distributed execution platforms for cyber-physical systems with applications to high-performance buildings*. In: Proceedings of the IEEE/ACM International Conference on Cyber-Physical Systems. Chicago, USA: IEEE, 2011. 215–224.
4. Jha, S., Gulwani, S., Sanjit, A., and Seshia, A. *Synthesizing Switching Logic for Safety and Dwell-Time Requirements*. EECS Department, University of California, Berkeley, Technical Report No. UCB/EECS-2010-28, 2010.
5. Zhu, M., Li, B. X., and Chen, Q. Q., *transforming hybridUML to hybrid program for CPS property verification*. Electronic journals, 2012，40（6）: 1126-1132.
6. Platzer，*A Logical Analysis of Hybrid Systems: Proving Theorems for Complex Dynamics*. Heidelberg: Springer, 2010.Luigi T.De Luca, *Propulsion physics* (EDP Sciences, Les Ulis, 2009)

MATEC Web of Conferences 44, 02093 (2016)
DOI: 10.1051/matecconf/20164402093

Research into Financial Position of Listed Companies following Classification via Extreme Learning Machine Based upon DE Optimization

Yu Fu[1], Jiong Mu[1,a] and Xu Liang Duan[1]
[1] College of Information Engineering and Technology Sichuan Agricultural University, Ya'an, China

Abstract. By means of the model of extreme learning machine based upon DE optimization, this article particularly centers on the optimization thinking of such a model as well as its application effect in the field of listed company's financial position classification. It proves that the improved extreme learning machine algorithm based upon DE optimization eclipses the traditional extreme learning machine algorithm following comparison. Meanwhile, this article also intends to introduce certain research thinking concerning extreme learning machine into the economics classification area so as to fulfill the purpose of computerizing the speedy but effective evaluation of massive financial statements of listed companies pertain to different classes

1 Introduction

For investors, the financial statements of listed companies constitute an important source of information from which they can understand the current financial status of those listed companies and reasonably predict their development tendency. Unfortunately, due to the financial statements containing lots of hidden information and parameters of various indicators, it is hard to analyze them and therefore, classifying listed company's financial position via directly observing their financial statements becomes more and more tough.

The purpose of this article is to put forth a model of extreme learning machine based upon DE optimization that is capable of modeling the financial status of a listed company after learning and analyzing its financial statement samples in a given quantity and then classifying the enormous financial data of other listed companies imported later on so as to save the time spent on classification and optimize the classification effect. What's special about this article is to rest the extreme learning machine algorithm on DE optimization in the first place and then apply it to classifying listed company's financial position. By the way, there are several classification algorithms having been precedentedly proposed, for example, the Five-Class Determination Method suggested by Lv Changjiang[2] and others, which suggests to group the financial situation of listed companies into the following 5 classes: financial idleness, financial adequacy, financial balance, financial difficulty and financial bankruptcy, the Support Vector Machine (SVM) Classification Algorithm recommended by Song Jiao[3] that establishes a SVM-based financial crisis pre-warning model for listed companies to effectively prevent financial crisis, and the BP Neural Network Pre-warning Model brought forth by Yang Shu'e[4] and others, which similarly aims to help listed companies evade financial crisis. Nevertheless, articles focusing upon utilizing intelligent algorithm to quickly classify the financial statements of numerous listed companies are rather insufficient.

2 DE(Differential Evolution)optimization

As an emerging evolutionary computation technology initiated by Storn[5]-[7] and others in 1995, DE, short for Differential Evolution, is, just like many other evolutionary algorithms, a random model simulating biological evolution through which individuals more adaptive to the surroundings finally survive via repeated iteration. Thanks to its powerful global convergence ability, robustness and independence to the characteristic information of issues, DE can be employed to solve the optimization question in a tough environment that is impossible to be cracked by means of common digital planning method. The following is the algorithm thinking of DE:

First of all, randomly initiate the population in the issue's feasible region $X^0=[x_1^0,x_2^0,...,x_{Np}^0]$, Np is population scale. This individual $x_i^0=[x_{i,1}^0,x_{i,2}^0,...,x_{i,D}^0]$ is used to solve characteristic issues and D is dimension of the optimization issue. The basic idea of the algorithm is as follows: Generate a new population through mutating and intersecting the current population and subsequently, choose both populations one-on-one via the fundamental greedy thinking to ultimately give birth to a new population. To be more exact, mutate each individual x_i^t at the time of t by Formula (1) to obtain the corresponding mutated individual x_i^{t+1}, i.e.:

$$v_i^{t+1}=x_{r_1}^t+k(x_{r_2}^t-x_{r_3}^t) \qquad (1)$$

Wherein $r_1,r_2,r_3\in\{1,2,...,N_P\}$ are distinguished from each other as well as i; $x_{r_1}^t$ is father basic vector, $(x_{r_2}^t-x_{r_3}^t)$ is father differential vector and K is scaling factor. Intersect x_i^t and the mutated individual v_i^{t+1} derived from Formula (1) by Formula (2) to generate the experimental individual u_i^{t+1}, i.e.:

[a] Corresponding author: scmjmj@163.com

$$u_{i,j}^{t+1} = \begin{cases} v_{i,j}^{t+1}, If(rand(j) \le CR) \text{ or } j = rnbr(i); \\ x_{i,j}^{t}, Otherwise. \end{cases} \quad (2)$$

Wherein $rand(j)$ is evenly distributed in [0, 1] at random, CR is crossover probability within the range of [0, 1] and $rnbr(i)$ is random quantity in $\{1,2,...,D\}$. Compare the target function of the experimental individuals u_i^{t+1} and x_i^t via Formula (3). Regarding the minimization issue, accept the individuals with low target function value as the individual of new population x_i^{t+1}, i.e.:

$$x_i^{t+1} = \begin{cases} u_i^{t+1}, If\ f(u_i^{t+1}) < f(x_i^t); \\ x_{i,j}^t, Otherwise. \end{cases} \quad (3)$$

Wherein f is target function. The algorithm mentioned before is the DE algorithm model discussed in this article[8].

The general thinking of this article is to carry out data optimization in the DE algorithm model and then import the optimized data into the extreme learning machine model for the purpose of classification.

3 ELM (Extreme Learning Machine) classification

Introduced in 2004 by Huang Guangbin, an associate professor of Nanyang Technological University, the extreme learning machine mentioned herein is a Single-Hidden Layer Feedforward Neural Networks (SLFNs) learning algorithm[9]-[12] that is characterized by fast learning speed and excellent generalization[13],[16] and [17]. As for its algorithm thinking, please refer to as follows:

For a single-hidden layer neural network, assume there are N random samples (X_i, t_i), wherein:

$$X_i = [x_{i_1}, x_{i_2}, ..., x_{i_n}]^T \in R^n,$$
$$t_i = [t_{i_1}, t_{i_2}, ..., t_{i_m}]^T \in R^m. \quad (4)$$

A single-hidden neural network containing $\tilde{N}$ hidden layer nodes can be expressed as follows:

$$\sum_{i=1}^{\tilde{N}} \beta_i g(W_i \cdot X_j + b_i) = o_j,\ j = 1,...,N \quad (5)$$

In Formula (5), $g(x)$ is activation function, $W_i = [w_{i,1}, w_{i,2}, ..., w_{i,n}]^T$ is input weight, β_1 is output weight, and b_i is offset of the i hidden layer unit. $W_i \cdot X_j$ represents the inner product of W_i and X_j.

The purpose the single-hidden neural network learning intends to serve is to minimize the tolerance of output, which can be expressed in Formula (6):

$$\sum_{j=1}^{\tilde{N}} \|o_j - t_j\| = 0 \quad (6)$$

Namely, it is β_i, W_i and b_i that make Formula (7) established:

$$\sum_{i=1}^{\tilde{N}} \beta_i g(W_i \cdot X_j + b_i) = t_j,\ j = 1,...,N \quad (7)$$

Expressed via matrix: $H\beta = T$ (8)

In Formula (8), H is output of hidden layer node, β is output weight and T is expected output, i.e. there are three Formulas (9), (10) and (11) given below:

$$H(W_1,...,W_{\tilde{N}}, b_1,...,b_{\tilde{N}}, X_1,...,X_{\tilde{N}}) = \begin{bmatrix} g(W_1 \cdot X_1 + b_1) & \cdots & g(W_1 \cdot X_1 + b_{\tilde{N}}) \\ \vdots & \ddots & \vdots \\ g(W_1 \cdot X_N + b_1) & \cdots & g(W_1 \cdot X_1 + b_{\tilde{N}}) \end{bmatrix}_{N \times \tilde{N}}$$
(9)

$$\beta = \begin{bmatrix} \beta_1^T \\ . \\ . \\ . \\ \beta_{\tilde{N}}^T \end{bmatrix}_{\tilde{N} \times m} (10),\ T = \begin{bmatrix} T_1^T \\ . \\ . \\ . \\ T_{\tilde{N}}^T \end{bmatrix}_{\tilde{N} \times m} (11)$$

In order to train the single-hidden layer neural network, we hope to obtain $\hat{W}_i$, $\hat{b}_i$ and $\hat{\beta}$ to make Formula (12) established:

$$\|H(\hat{W}_i, \hat{b}_i)\hat{\beta} - T\| = \min_{W,b,\beta} \|H(W_i, b_i)\beta - T\| \quad (12)$$

In Formula (12), $i = 1,...,\tilde{N}$ means that the loss minimization function (13) is established.

$$E = \sum_{j=1}^{N} \left(\sum_{i=1}^{\tilde{N}} \beta_i g(W_i \cdot X_j + b_i) - t_j \right)^2 \quad (13)$$

In the ELM algorithm, once the input weight W_i and the hidden layer offset b_i have been determined randomly, the output matrix in the hidden layer H will be solely decided. Meanwhile, training a single-hidden neural network can be converted into the process of solving a linear system: $H\beta = T$ and the output weight β can be confirmed as $\hat{\beta} = H^{\tau}T$, wherein H^{τ} is the Moore-Penrose generalized inverse of the matrix H and the solution $\hat{\beta}$ proves to be mere and minimum.

4 Data collection

In order to better explain the model mentioned in this article and back up the actual application effect of such a model, we have extracted the financial statements of 200 listed companies from the annual report of Chinese listed companies as samples [14]. Among those companies, 87 and 113 companies are respectively listed in Shenzhen Stock Exchange and Shanghai Stock Exchange. Total 49 financial indicators [15] such as Earnings per Share, Net Profit and Debt to Assets Ratio etc. included in the financial statements are adopted as characteristic information to comprehensively assess the financial position of those companies and then classify them into the following five different levels: Excellent, Good, Normal, Unsatisfactory and Terrible. For the foregoing financial indicators, please refer to the table below:

Table 1. Financial Indicators Chosen as Characteristic Values

49 Indicators	
Primary Earnings per Share (EPS)	Current Liabilities /Liabilities in Total
Book value per Share	Asset Fixation Ratio
Total Operating Revenue per Share	Liquidity Ratio
Operating Revenue per Share	Quick Ratio
Capital Reserve per Share	Conservative Quick Ratio
Surplus Reserve per Share	Cash Ratio
Undistributed Profits per Share	Equity Belonging to Parent Company's Shareholders /Total Liabilities
Retained Earnings per Share	Tangible Assets/ Total Liabilities
Net Cash Flow per Share	Debt to Tangible Assets Ratio
Earnings before Interest and Tax per Share	Primary Earnings per Share (Year-on-Year Growth Rate)
Return on Total Assets (ROA) Ratio	Net Cash Flow Generated by Operating Activities per Share (Year-on-Year Growth Rate)
Net Return on Total Assets (ROA) Ratio	Total Operating Revenue (Year-on-Year Growth Rate)
Annualized Return on Total Assets (ROA) Ratio	Operating Revenue (Year-on-Year Growth Rate)
Annualized Net Return on Total Assets (ROA) Ratio	Operating Profit (Year-on-Year Growth Rate) 1
Net Profit Margin on Sales	Operating Profit (Year-on-Year Growth Rate) 2
Gross Profit Margin on Sales	Net Profit (Year-on-Year Growth Rate)
Ratio of Sales to Cost	Net Profit Belonging to Parent Company's Shareholders (Year-on-Year Growth Rate)
Expense Ratio in Sales Period	Net Profit Belonging to Parent Company's Shareholders Minus Extraordinary Gain or Loss (Year-on-Year Growth Rate)
Main Business Ratio	Net Cash Flow Generated by Operating Activities (Year-on-Year Growth Rate)
Debt to Assets Ratio	Monetary Fund Growth Rate
Long-term Assets Suitability Ratio	Fixed Assets Investment Expansion Ratio
Current Assets/Total Assets	Net Assets (Year-on-Year Growth Rate)
Current Debt-to-Equity Ratio	Total Liabilities (Year-on-Year Growth Rate)
Non-current Assets/Total Assets	Total Assets (Year-on-Year Growth Rate)
Tangible Assets/ Total Assets	

5 Comparison between Extreme Learning Machine Classification Algorithm Based-upon DE Optimization and Traditional Extreme Learning Machine Classification Algorithm

We divided those 200 listed companies into the following 2 parts, one is made up of 140 companies that have been respectively imported into the traditional extreme learning machine and the extreme learning machine based upon DE optimization in the Matlab environment, and the other is the remaining 60 companies whose financial statements are utilized as test samples to observe the classification situation. Regarding the first part, the above-mentioned 49 financial indicators are considered algorithm characteristic information and the corresponding extreme learning machine models have been established and trained. Finally, compare the classification conditions of both algorithms and the related results are shown below:

5.1. Results of both classification algorithms

Through MATLAB simulation, we can observe the results of both classification algorithms as shown below:

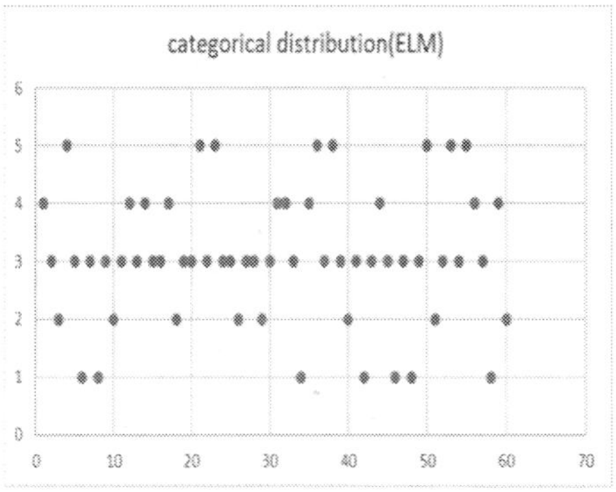

Figure 1. Classification results of the ELM algorithm

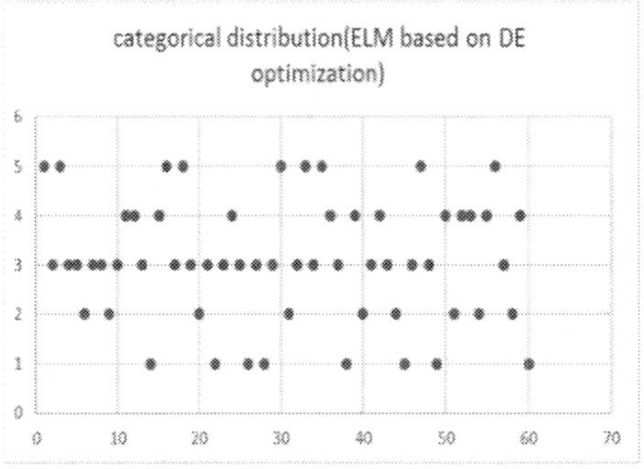

Figure 2. Classification results of the DE optimization-related ELM algorithm

The vertical coordinates shown in Figures 1 and 2 suggest that 1 denotes terrible financial situation, 2 unsatisfactory situation, 3 normal financial situation, 4 good financial situation and 5 excellent financial situation.

The classification results delineated in Figure 1 are generated by the traditional extreme learning machine classification algorithm, to be exact, the financial situation of 7 listed companies is regarded as terrible (Class 1), 8 unsatisfactory (Class 2), 27 normal (Class 3) and 10 good (Class 4) and 8 excellent (class 5). The general classification error in connection with the algorithm mentioned before is 12.7% when comparing with the actual financial situation of those listed companies, namely, 7 out of 60 listed companies are incorrectly classified, which renders the correct recognition rate of such an algorithm reach 88% more or less.

The classification results delineated in Figure 2 are generated by the DE optimization-related extreme learning machine classification algorithm, to be exact, the financial situation of 8 listed companies is regarded as terrible (Class 1), 9 unsatisfactory (Class 2), 22 normal (Class 3) and 12 good (Class 4) and 9 excellent (class 5). There are 4 out of 60 listed companies incorrectly classified, thus making the incorrect recognition rate of such an algorithm reach 6.7% that is rather less than the traditional extreme learning machine classification algorithm.

5.2 The training performance of both algorithm models is presented below

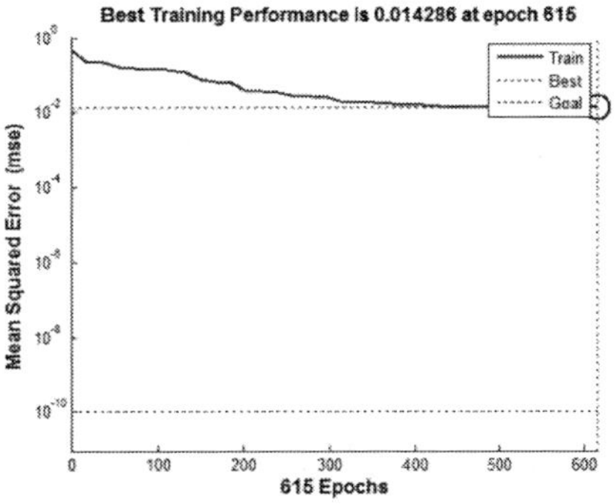

Figure 3. Training performance of the ELM algorithm

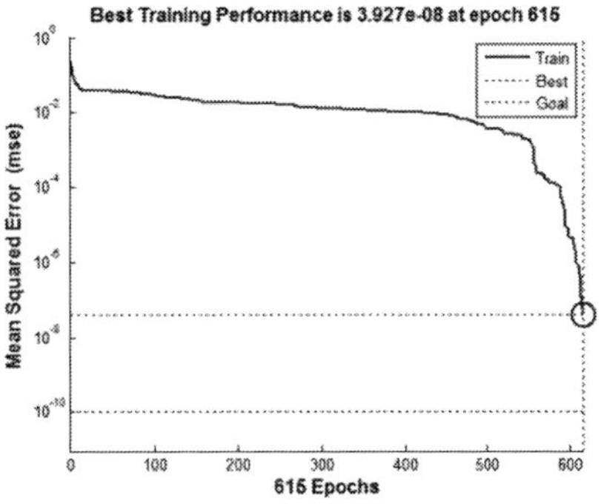

Figure 4. Training performance of the DE optimization-related ELM algorithm

In order to facilitate comparison, we have iterated both algorithms 615 times to see their error performance. Judging by Figure 3, for the traditional extreme learning machine, the Mean Square Error infinitely approaches 10^{-2} following 615 times of iteration. On the other hand, as revealed in Figure 4, for the DE optimization-related extreme learning machine, the Mean Square Error is able to reach 10^{-8} also following 615 times of iteration, which is slightly different from the target error we anticipated, i.e. 10^{-10}. To judge from what's described before, the DE optimization-related extreme learning machine algorithm is capable of effectively reducing the tolerance of data classification when comparing with the traditional extreme learning machine algorithm, accordingly elevating the accuracy in connection with data classification to an ideal status.

5.3 Comparison between sample data and ideal output results in terms of fitting degree

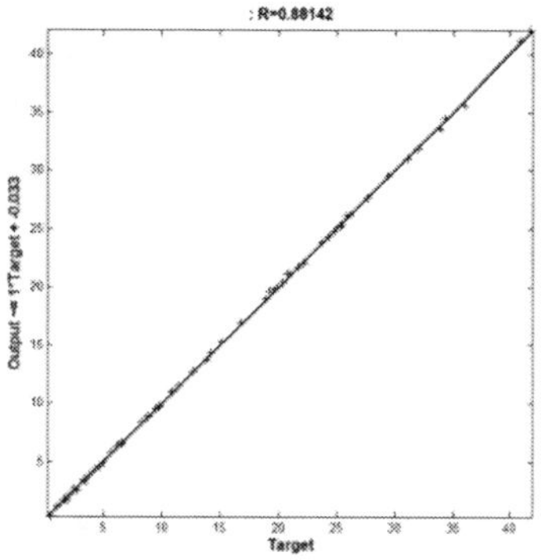

Figure 5. Comparison between sample output by the ELM algorithm and ideal output in terms of fitting degree

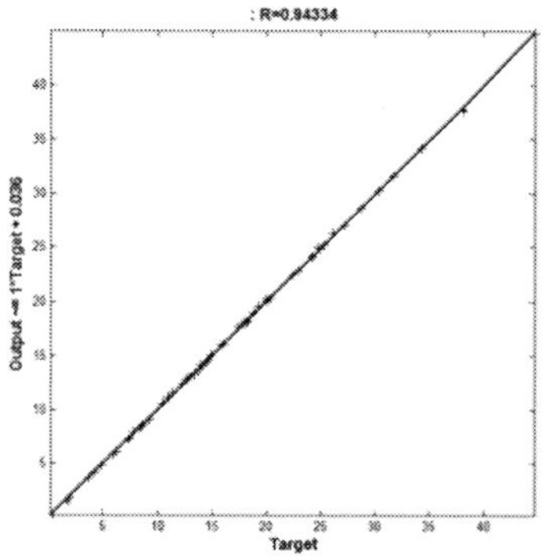

Figure 6. Comparison between sample output by the DE optimization-related ELM algorithm and ideal output in terms of fitting degree

In Figures 5 and 6, a corresponding idealized output model is built by putting the financial data of those 140 listed companies into the 2 different algorithm models so as to generate the Slope k=1 (vertical cordinate/horizontal cordinate=1), an ideal output straight line, i.e. this line entirely complies with the ideal output. In the left upper part and the right lower part of such a straight line, there are discrete intervals, namely, the further away the mark + in Figures 5 and 6 is from such a straight line, the bigger the difference between the output results of the experimental data and the ideal reults becomes. On contrary, the closer the mark + approaches the ideal output line K=1, the smaller difference between the output results of the experimental data and the ideal reults becomes, i.e. the higher the fitting degree turns. The mark + in Figures 5 and 6 represents that the actual classification results of financial data in connection with those 60 listed companies are in positive correlation with the fitting degree of the output samples, which means the higher the sample's output fitting degree is, the more accurate the classification results become.

For the traditional extreme learning machine model in Figure 5, its output fitting degree (R=0.88142) doesn't satisfactorily approach the ideal output results as we hoped since the fitting degree tolerance is as follows: Δ=1-0.88142=0.11858. For the DE optimization-related extreme learning machine model in Figure 6, the output fitting degree (R=0.94334) is obviously close to the ideal output results as the fitting degree tolerance is below: Δ=1-0.94334=0.05666.

Additionally, it is predictable that as the training sample quantity and the time of iteration continously increase, the DE optimization-related extreme learning machine algorithm is capable of making the expermental sample's fitting degree tolerance further close to ideal output, which can be seen from the training performance under the condition of same iteration times.

6 Conclusion

In this article we have proposed a DE optimization-based extreme learning machine algorithm that can be deployed to classify the financial position of different listed companies. After classifying and analyzing the financial data of those 200 listed companies and comparing with the traditional extreme learning machine algorithm, the algorithm described in this article, i.e. the DE optimization-based extreme learning machine algorithm, proves to be improved in terms of accuracy and superiority. At the same time, this article also attempted to introduce a new analysis thinking into the economic field, in other words, freeing humans from tedious and repetitive labor via a highly-efficient smart algorithm catering for a great deal of data and applying the multi-characteristic classification method to solving economic analysis issues so as to considerably cut down the time spent on financial information classification. However, this article is restricted by inadequate training and test samples. The test sample recognition rate would be higher if the training samples increased in amount.

References

1. Altman , E. , 1968 , Financial Ratios , Discriminate Analysis and the Prediction of Corporate Bankruptcy , Journal of Finance 23(Sept .)
2. Changjiang Lv, Yan Zhao, Classification of financial status of listed companies. J. Accounting Research, 11(2004).
3. Song Jiao,Corporate Financial Distress on support vector machine .J, Harbin University of Commerce (Natural Science), 23(2007)
4. .Shue Yang, Li Huang, financial early warning model of listed companies BP neural network .J, Based on System Engineering Theory and Practice, 25(2005)
5. Storn R, Price K,.Differential evolution ---- A simple and efficient adaptive scheme for global optimization over continuous spaces,R, Berkeley: University of California,(2006).
6. Storn R, Price K. Minimizing the real functions of the ICEC'96 contest by differential evolution.C, Proc of IEEE Int Conf on Evolutionary Computation. Nagoya,(1996).

7. Bo Liu, Ling Wang, Yihui Jin, Research differential evolution algorithm.J, Control and Decision, 22(2007)
8. Shengshuang Chen, based on XML documents ultimate learning machine classification .J, Computer Engineering, 37(2011).
9. G.-B. Huang, et al.,Universal Approximation Using Incremental Networks with Random Hidden Computational Nodes, IEEE Transactions on Neural Networks, 4(2006).
10. G.-B. Huang, et al.,Extreme Learning Machine: Theory and Applications, Neurocomputing, (2006).
11. N.-Y. Liang, et al., A Fast and Accurate On-line Sequential Learning Algorithm for Feedforward Networks,IEEE Transactions on Neural Networks, 6,17(2006).
12. G.-B. Huang, et al., Can Threshold Networks Be Trained Directly?, IEEE Transactions on Circuits and Systems II, 3,53(2006).
13. K. Hornik, M. Stinchcombe, and H. White, Multilayer feedforward networks are universal approximators, *Neural Netw.*, 5,2(1989).
14. H. jun Rong, Y.-S. Ong, A.-W. Tan, and Z. Zhu, A fast pruned-extreme learning machine for classification problem, *Neurocomputing*,1,72(2008).
15. G. Bontempi, M. Birattari, and H. Bersini, Recursive lazy learning for modeling and control, in *Proc. Eur. Conf. Mach. Learn.*, (1998).
16. Shizhong Liao,Chang Feng.Meta-ELM: ELM with ELM hidden nodes,J,Neurocomputing, (Mar.27) (2014).
17. Extreme Learning Machines (Trends & Controversies).J,IEEE intelligent systems, 28(2013).

Acknowledgment

This paper was funded by Sichuan Provincial Education Department ,project name: Building Agricultural Internet of Things hierarchical storage model(15ZB0017).

MATEC Web of Conferences 44, 02094 (2016)
DOI: 10.1051/matecconf/20164402094

Analysis of the impact of economic growth factors to resources and environment in Jiangsu Province -- Based on Commoner model

Min Zhang[a]

Department of Management, Jincheng College, Nanjing University of Aeronautics & Astronautics ,China

Abstract. In order to response to the increasingly polluted environment, maintain sustainable economic and social development in Jiangsu province, the author calculated the index of the resource environment in Jiangsu, using LMDI(logarithmic-mean Divisia index) decomposition method based on the Commoner model(we can see from formula(2),(5),(6)&(7)), to reflect the three major influencing factors of cumulative effects. In table 2 and figure 3, the research results show the expansion of the size of economy and growth of population make resources consumption increase and environmental pollution aggravate, while technological progress reduce the pressure of resources and environment. According to the findings, the paper proposes the policy recommendations, such as develop circular economy, promote technological innovation and strengthen regional cooperation mechanism and so on to reduce the environmental pollution while economic developing. These will be useful to the policymakers.
Keywords. Economic growth factors; Resources and environment; Commoner model; LMDI（logarithmic-mean Divisia index）

1 Introduction

In the book *Process Of Economic Growth* [1], American economist Rostow divided the economic growth into six stages: traditional society, create precondition for fast developing phase, fast developing phase, to mature, the phase of high mass consumption and the pursuit of quality of life. The fast developing stage is one of the most important mutations, there are three conditions: high accumulation rate and set up a leading department and appropriate system guarantee. When meets the three conditions, the economy will develop fast, then the economic departments gradually become strong, enter into the phase of mature. The mature stage is the period of a society to use the modern science and technology effectively to allocate resources.

More than 20 years of development in Jiangsu generally experienced the stage Rostow had described, which is in the transitional period being pushed off from the fast developing to the mature stage. Jiangsu is a major economic province; its economic development occupies an important position in the whole country. Jiangsu province' GDP in 2014 [2] reached 6.50883 trillion yuan, accounting for 10.2% of national GDP, ranks second following Guangdong province. Per capita GDP is 81874 yuan, total retail sales of social consumer goods are 2.3209 trillion yuan, accounting for 8.8% of the country. The rapid economic growth in Jiangsu is established on the basis of a large number of resources such as land,

[a] Corresponding author:jshalf@163.com

water, minerals and energy resources. Economic development consume large resources, at the same time, it can also damage the natural resources and ecological environment.

Through the studies of Jiangsu economy, population, environment pollution and so on, the paper will explore the coordinate, sustainable development path of economic, ecological and social.

2 Analysis of resources and environment in Jiangsu province

After more than 20 years of rapid development, marked by per capita GDP reaching $3000, economic and social development in Jiangsu province's has entered a new stage. During this period, development is facing many opportunities meanwhile severe resource constraints and environmental pressure. Jiangsu has created accounting for more than 10% of the country's economy with about 1.1% of the country's land area, 5.7% of the population. The speeding up of industrialization has brought the increase of energy consumption for production of coal, natural gas, crude oil, more than 90% of these resources rely on outsourcing, which makes the energy cost be larger [3].

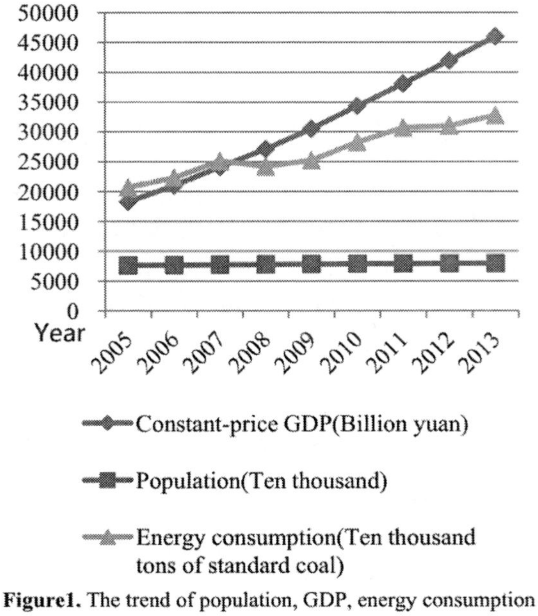

Figure1. The trend of population, GDP, energy consumption in Jiangsu Province from 2005 to 2013

As can be seen from the figure 1, during the eight years, GDP shows growth trend in Jiangsu province from 1.827212 trillion yuan to 4.596518 trillion yuan, the annual average growth rate is 12.5%. Accompanying With the development of economy, energy consumption is also growing from 207.2374 million tons to 327.5661

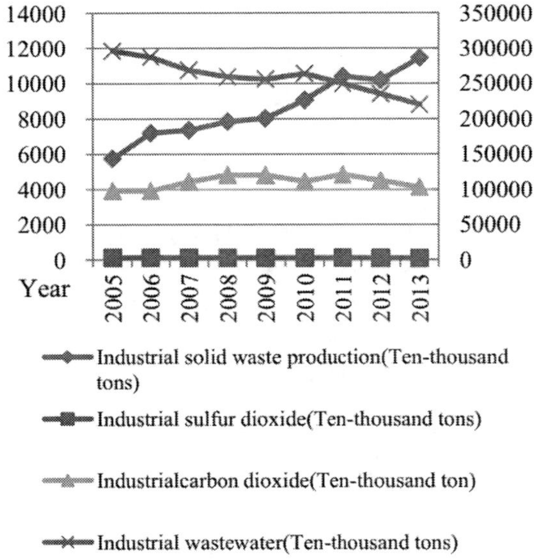

Figure2. The trend of Three Industrial Wastes and the industrial carbon emissions in Jiangsu province

million tons of standard coal, 1.58 times higher than in 2005, the average annual growth rate is 6%. While population growth in Jiangsu province is slow, increasing by only 1.05 times.

Along with the economic development, energy consumption brings environmental pollution. From the figure 2 we can see, in addition to the emissions of industrial waste water is decreasing; the other three indicators are all increasing. Among them, the most significant growth is the industrial solid waste emissions, from 57.57 million tons to 109.165 million tons, increased nearly 90%.

3 Introduction of Commoner Model and the data sources

3.1 Introduction of Commoner Model

Commoner[4,5]believed that environmental quality is mainly influenced by three factors: (1) Population growth factor, which is mainly reflected by population size; (2) Economic growth factor, it is mainly reflected by per capita output; (3) Technical progress factor, mainly

reflected by pollution emissions of the unit production value .

I.e., the emissions of pollutants quantity = population * (production/population) * (emissions/production), specifically expressed as:

$$I = \frac{G}{P} \times P \times \frac{I}{G} \tag{1}$$

In the equation, I indicates pollution emissions, P shows total population, G indicates GDP. On the right side of the equation, the first one means economic size effect, the second indicates effect of population growth, the third one shows effect of technological progress.

Based on factorization analysis type(1), there will be three results: if the effect of some factor to the environment is positive number, it shows the elements will increase the environmental stress; If the effect of some factor to the environment is negative number, it indicates the factor reducing the pressure of environment, conducive to the coordinated development; If the effect of some factor to the environment is zero, then it indicates that the elements do not produce environmental pressures.

On the basis of The Commoner Model, using logarithmic-mean Divisia index (LMDI) [6,7] to analyze these three elements. LMDI decomposition method is one complete decomposition method[8], won't produce residual, and easy to be transformed between multiplication and addition decomposition form, any kind of selection is no difference. This paper uses the additive form. Specific as follows:

$$I = E \times P \times C \tag{2}$$

Among them, E=G/P indicates the size of the economy, P shows population growth effect, C=I/G indicates technical progress effect.

$$\Delta I = I^T - I^0 = \Delta I_E + \Delta I_P + \Delta I_C \tag{3}$$

$$\Delta I_X = \sum \frac{I_i^t - I_0^t}{\ln I_i^t - \ln I_0^t} \ln \frac{X_i^t}{X_0^t} \tag{4}$$

In formula (3), ΔI means emissions change from 0~t years, I^Tmeans the pollution emissions of t year, I^0means the pollution emissions of 0 year. ΔI_E Shows the impact of economic size on pollution emissions; ΔI_P means the influence of population growth on pollution emission; ΔI_Cshows the influence of technology progress on pollution emission. In formula (4), ΔI_X indicates the effect value that change of various factors on pollution emissions.

According to Ang's [9]LMDI decomposition method, the right side of type (3) can be expressed as:

$$\Delta I_E = \sum \frac{I_i^t - I_0^t}{\ln I_i^t - \ln I_0^t} \ln \frac{E_i^t}{E_0^t} \tag{5}$$

$$\Delta I_P = \sum \frac{I_i^t - I_0^t}{\ln I_i^t - \ln I_0^t} \ln \frac{P_i^t}{P_0^t} \tag{6}$$

$$\Delta I_C = \sum \frac{I_i^t - I_0^t}{\ln I_i^t - \ln I_0^t} \ln \frac{C_i^t}{C_0^t} \tag{7}$$

3.2 Date sources

We choose the data of Jiangsu Province from year 2005 to 2013 to study. Among them, the data about GDP, population, energy consumption, industrial three wastes are derived from the corresponding year of Jiangsu Statistical Yearbook [10], and the industrial carbon emissions data are from the balance of energy terminal consumption data which are in the China Energy Statistical Yearbook [11], calculating according to coefficient of the carbon conversion of various energy consumption from table 1 [3]. And GDP is transformed by the conversion coefficient into constant price GDP in 2005 according to Jiangsu Statistical Yearbook.

Table 1 .The carbon conversion coefficient of three energy consumption

Data sources	Coal consumption coefficient of carbon emissions	Oil consumption coefficient of carbon emissions	Natural gas consumption coefficient of carbon emissions
DOE/EIA	0.702	0.478	0.389
IEEJ	0.756	0.586	0.449
CNSTI	0.728	0.583	0.409
mean value	0.728	0.549	0.416

4 Analysis of the influence factors of resources and environment

It's calculated according to the data obtained above for each influence factor's contribution to the pollution emissions, the results are shown in table 2.

Table 2. The cumulative effects of various factors from 2005 to 2013(units, ten thousand tons)

Year	Effect of economic size	Effect of population growth	Effect of technology progress
2005	—	—	—
2006	39287.16	2672.25	-49327.20
2007	75965.15	5162.14	-106423.05
2008	107361.83	6552.12	-147634.00
2009	138534.62	8276.16	-183682.05
2010	173047.75	10598.86	-212022.73
2011	197856.54	11427.12	-250134.77
2012	218256.27	11850.71	-285919.67
2013	236115.24	12178.93	-318539.20
mean value	148303.07	8589.79	-194210.34

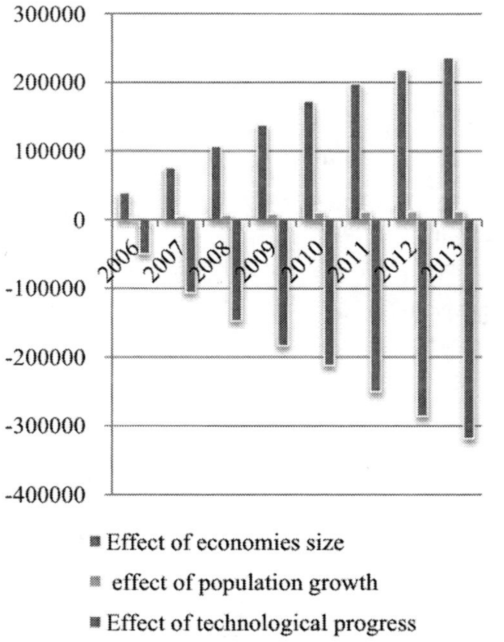

Figure3. The cumulative effects of various factors of each year

It can be seen from table 2 and figure 3, the decomposition results show that among the three influence factors in the study, the effect of economic size and population growth in 2006-2013 is positive, these two factors have made the environmental pressure increased heavily, and the effect of technical progress during this period is negative, indicating this factor reducing the pressure on resources and environment, that is, this factor has inhibition effects on resources and environment.

4.1 Analysis of influence of economic size to resources and environment

Panayotou [12,13]put forward Environmental Kuznets Theory in 1993, he thought that the environment pollution will experience from high to low along with the development of a country's economy, deteriorating at first and then gradually improving, it will appear in the form of inverted u-shaped. It also means that: on the one hand, economic development would lead to pollution emissions, but on the other hand, the development of economy makes people's living standards improve, the requirements for environmental quality increase, investment of protection money by the state is becoming more and more abundant. Therefore, economic development will benefit to improve the environment.

The table 2 shows that the effect of economic size in Jiangsu province from 2006 to 2013 is positive, rising year by year, it also indicates the expansion of economic size has increased the resource consumption and caused the increase of environmental pollution. The effect of economic size plays a leading role.

4.2 Analysis of influence of population scale to resources and environment

Population growth will inevitably require the expansion of the size of economic activity to keep increasing requirements of material and spiritual products. Under the condition of existing resources, there is also a sustainable population limits. Shown in Figure 1, the total population in Jiangsu Province is slow growth, and the growth of population contributed averages 85.8979 million tons of environment pollution. The increase of population size brings high pressure of resources, ecological environment, but it' s not a leading role.

4.3 Analysis of influence of technical progress to resources and environment

Simon [4] proposed that, technological progress can develop a new industry, increase the ability of conversion from raw material to product. The transformation of old industrial chain and improve the energy efficiency. Therefore, it must rely on technological progress to reduce resource consumption and improve the ecological environment.

We generally think that technological progress is helpful for us to achieve the sustainable development; it is key point to overcome the shortage of resources and environmental pollution problems by economic development. In fact, the relevant data analysis of Jiangsu province can also prove that the calculation results of technology progress effect are negative, indicating technological progress reduce the pressure on the environment and promote the coordinated development of economy and environment.

5. Conclusion

In this paper, by the calculation of GDP, pollution emissions and etc. of Jiangsu province, we find that from 2005 to 2013, both expanded economies of scale and population growth brought pressure to environmental resources, while technological progress decreased pressure of environment. In order to realize the sustainable development of economic and society of Jiangsu province, we need do as these if we want to reduce environmental pollution accompany with rapid economic development [14,15]:

(1)Make known the concept of cleaner production, reduce the waste and pollutants from fundamental source and encourage enterprises to produce green products, set up and promote ecological economic demonstration area; (2) Develop circular economy, transform the mode of economic growth. Promote further measures on the strategic adjustment of industrial structure, achieve the economic growth by manufacturing and services; Increase investment in new energy and environmental protection and energy saving products. (3) Promote technological innovation, increase investment in regional environmental protection, encourage enterprises to improve product process or assembly line, make the enterprise reduce pollution levels at the same time achieve a win-win economic and ecological environment benefits. (4) Strengthen the regional cooperation and promote the pollution prevention actively. Jiangsu province should strengthen the regional cooperation mechanism to achieve the greatest degree of economic green growth.

References

1.Jiangsu province bureau's Web site, http://www.jssb.gov.cn/goveinfo/xxgkml/ywgz/dtyw/200606/t20060626_8015.html

2.Jiangsu Statistical Yearbook, http://www.jssb.gov.cn/2015nj/indexc.htm

3. S.S.Lin, S&T Management Research, **13**:62-65(2013)

4. H.A.Hu. Liaoning Normal University,(2013)

5. G.Z.Lee, China Economic Publishing House,(2007)

6. H.J. Yang, M.Y.Lee, H.Q.Liu, **02**:125-129,(2014)

7. P. Fernández González,M. Landajo,M.J. Presno. Energy, **73**(2014)

8. M.Sun, Jilin University,(2010)

9. B. W. Ang, Energy Policy, **32**(9):1131-1139,(2004)

10. Jiangsu Statistical Yearbook. http://www.jssb.gov.cn/tjxxgk/tjsj/tjnq/jstjnj2015/index_212.html

11. China Energy Statistical Yearbook. http://epub.cnki.net/kns/brief/default_result.aspx

12. T. Wang, Yangzhou University, (2014)

13. Panayoutou. Working Paper WP238, Technoloty and Employment Programme, Geneva, (1993)

14. J. Bollen, Corjan Brink. Energy Economics, **46**(2014)

15. J.Bollen.Technological Forecasting & Social Change, **90**(2015)

Sources of funds: Excellent course of statistics of Jingcheng college,(2014-J-10)

MATEC Web of Conferences 44, 02095 (2016)
DOI: 10.1051/matecconf/20164402095

The Study of Application System for Small and Medium CTI Based on Voice Card

Dong Zhong[1] , Zhong Ming Li[1], Chun Chen[2], Ruo Lin Ruan[3]

[1] *College of electronic and information, Hubei University of Science and Technology, Xianning, China*

[2]*College of Physical Education, Hubei University of Science and Technology, Xianning, China*

[3]*College of biomedical engineering, Hubei University of Science and Technology, Xianning, China*

Abstract. With the rapid development of computer telecommunications integration (CTI) technology, the development of application system for small and medium CTI are updated constantly, but the study of application system for small and medium CTI, we are lack of a stability and unified model. In this paper, the author analyzes the unified structure platform of application system for small and medium CTI based on voice card. Meanwhile, the author introduces a suitable software architecture model and general procedural framework for application system for small and medium CTI based on voice card by using the idea of hierarchical design, which shows the versatility of the architecture. It provided an efficient channel for the development of small and medium CTI.

1 Introduction

As the rapid development of communication and computer technology in China, it makes that the state intelligence process continues to speed up, so computer Telecommunication integration (CTI) came into being. CTI technology has came to overcome the single drawback of the traditional telecommunications and computer services, it has been used widely in telecommunications, mobile, China Unicom, transportation, postal, banking and other industries, it improved greatly the operational level of the corresponding industries. In the paper the author studies application system for small and medium CTI based on voice card and introduces a suitable software architecture model and general procedural framework for application system for small and medium CTI based on voice card. This voice card as the core of small and medium-scale system is to study CTI application. It is convenient to the research and development of CTI application.

2 A unified structure of small and medium CTI application platform

CTI technology makes use of the advantages of computer information processing, it embodies the characteristics of traffic handling capability for the communication system. The CTI technology can realize the control and comprehensive applications for the voice, fax and data communications, it also offers value-added communication through using telephone communications and computer information processing to make software interface, hardware interface and control equipment integrated[1].The existing application system for small and medium CTI program is convenient to the switch, the advantages of this program is that the system is stable and

it can support large-scale applications, but the design of such systems is complex, meanwhile a unified interface standard is difficult [2], but the use of voice Calgary IPC program, application systems for medium and small CTI can overcome these shortcomings and meet the basic business need.

It is the system unified structure platform of small and medium CTI for all kinds of business needs, the application platform is based on the voice card of CTI applications platform in figure 1.There are some equipments in the enterprise LAN, including CTI server, business server, WEB server, central database, Internet gateways, agents, and some computer peripherals (seat phones, headsets) [3]. The voice card server is the core of the whole system for the small and medium CTI systems which is emphasis on cost. The software systems of servers are installed in this server. Now the CTI application platform not only supports the access of traditional telephone voice, but also including the website construction of B / S [4].

The voice card is the core of the system hardware including the simulation resource cards, digital resource cards, IP resource cards, fax resource cards and other resource cards[5]. The voice card can be used as any single resource card according to the different services in Figure 1, which can also be integrated with several voice resource cards. All kinds of voice cards can be used as PCI / CPCI bus peripherals. There are H.100/H.110 bus connections in these voice cards.

3 Software structure of small and medium CTI application system

In this paper, the author used hierarchical design ideas to shorten the cycle of the application system for small and medium CTI and improve software development efficiency, which has been showed in figure 2. The system software structure is divided into four layers, including the business functions layer, the control layer, the unified interface layer, the physical resource layer. It provides a reference model for the small and medium CTI application system.

3.1 The business function layser

The layer is mainly to achieve a variety of business needs for the system, it loads the appropriate modules and business management modules which is based on the interface layer and control layer, such as artificial agent management, TTS / voice document management, record management, the basic functions of data management and system expansion of other businesses.

3.2 The control layser

The control layer is the core of the system, which is responsible for handling the call control process. The layer is respond to inputting events of the user according to the requests of the user, researching voice process files, routing automatically to the business function module, controlling and scheduling the resources.

3.3 The unified interface layser

The unified interface layer packs further the function of the physical resource layer, meanwhile, it provides users with the relative standard API or a COM object interface. This layer is responsible for providing the state detection (signal tone detection, etc.), receiving double-audio code (dual tone multi-frequency, DTMF), call admission, call control (call setup / disconnect, caller ID extraction, etc.) and digital sound recording and other basic functions.

3.4 The physics resources

The physical resource layer provides mainly the hardware environment of the system, such as analog trunk cards, digital trunk cards, IP resource cards, fax resource cards and other resources cards. The system software is divided into four layers by using the hierarchical idea, which can improve software development efficiency.

4 General program architecture design of small and medium CTI application system

With the exception of telecommunications and other large enterprises, all sectors of society, the demands for CTI applications are mostly small scale, these systems are appropriate to adopt the voice card program. The requirements of application systems for small and

medium CTI are very similar and most of the call center industry is the single application development, so the duplication work is exist, software reuse rate is low, product development cycle is long, feature upgrades is difficult, the stability of the scale is not easy protection. In order to overcome these handicaps, the article presents a general procedural framework. It provides a convenient model for the development of the application system for small and medium CTI. It has been showed in figure 3.

The main program is the core of this program framework, each module is associated with the outside. The reason for this program framework is general is that the developers need only to do one main program for application system for small and medium CTI, then depending on the different needs of CTI application systems, the main work for developers is the business / functional module development, it is no longer need to spend much effort to develop the main program. In addition, this architecture can be used as the application reference model for secondary development of small and medium CTI, and this architecture is suitable for different operating systems and databases.

The process of the main program in the framework is: (1) initializing the device driver and the related resources card; (2) waiting for the accessing of the phone call, recording the number of the time calling, distributing reasonably a channel according to the voice channel of the boards; (3) detecting the call is on-hook or not in time, if it is not on-hook, this call will automatically release the channel resources of the sharing sound cards.

5 Conclusion

The core of the application system for small and medium CTI based on voice card is computer telecommunications integration technology, the author uses the design ideas of hierarchical structure in this paper, the software structure is divided into four layers, separating layers, they are closely related to each other, On this basis, the author design a general structure of program development for the small and medium CTI. The platform has been used the object-oriented technology and increased new features by increasing a collection of objects. We have designed and implemented a public security system and the three-one phone system in a prison by using the above architecture, the designed program structure of the two systems are exactly the same, the current two systems have been applied successfully in the community, the system is stable, practical value is high.

Acknowledgements

The authors gratefully acknowledge the financial support for this work provided by the education department of Hubei Province Science and technology research project, No. B2015077; the colleges and universities of Hubei Province in 2014 the Provincial College Students' innovation and entrepreneurship training plan, No. 201410927025 and 201410927029; The school educational reform key projects of Hubei University of Science and Technology, No. 2014-XA-007 and 2014-XC-025;The National Natural Science Foundation of China (NSFC) under the Grant No. 61271256 and 61575148; the Team Plans Program of the Outstanding Young Science and Technology Innovation of Colleges and Universities in Hubei Province, Grant No.T201513, the Program of the Natural Science Foundation of Hubei Province, Grant No. 2014BAA315 and No. 2015CFB452.

References

[1] Sun Bin. Call center based on CTI technology, design and implementation of [D]. Beijing: Beijing University of Posts and .2014:136-140.

[2] Lin Xiaoyong, Lu Jun. Enterprise CTI application platform-level research and development [J]. Communication Technology .2014,3 (10) :19-23.

[3] Lu Chun. call center voice-based board design [J]. Communication Technology .2015,01 (42) :48-50.

[4] Cui Yingan. call center architecture based on generic sound card [J]. Computer Engineering .2013,11,22 (33) :73-75.

[5] Brendan. Designing the Best Call Center for Your Business Puhlication Date [M]. New York: Harner Row, 2004:231-238.

[6] Thompdon P A,Marchant E W.A computer model for the evacuation of large building populations. Fire Safety Journal . 2014.

[7] SamShanmuganK.EECS862Simulationprojectber analysisofrayleighfadingchannel[J].IEEECommunica

tionsMagazine, 2013:1- 15.

[8] Charlie C. L. Wang，YuWang，Matthew M. F. Yuen. Feature based 3D garment designThrough ZD sketches[J]. Computer_aided Design, 2012 (35):659-672.

[9] Byung-Gyu and Dong-Jo Park,Adaptive image normalisation based on block processing for enhancement of fingerprint image,Electronic Letters,2014,38(14):696-698.

[10] HongL, WanY, A.K.Jain:Figer print image enhancement:algorithm and performance evaluation, IEEE Transactions on Pattenr Analysis and Machine Intelligence,1998, 20(8): 777-789.

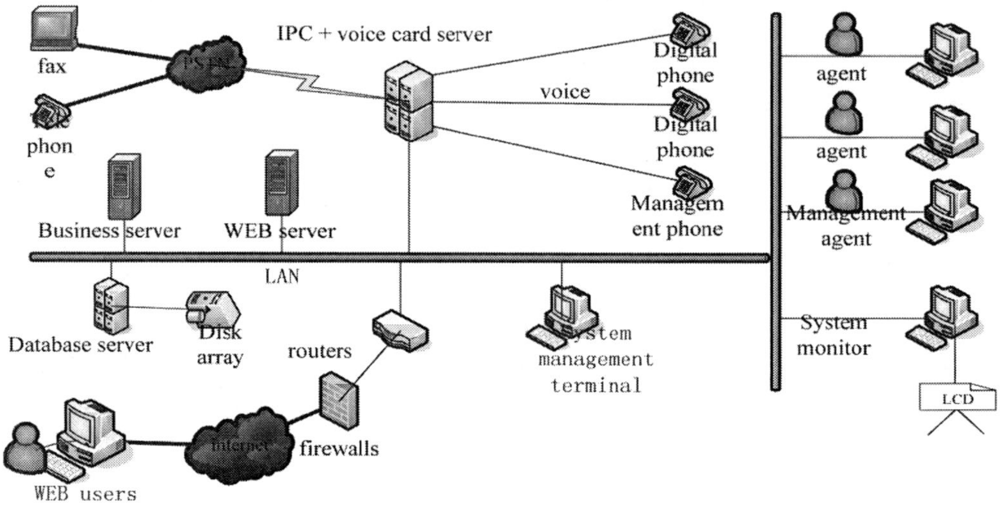

Figure 1. The system Unified Structure Platform of Small and Medium CTI

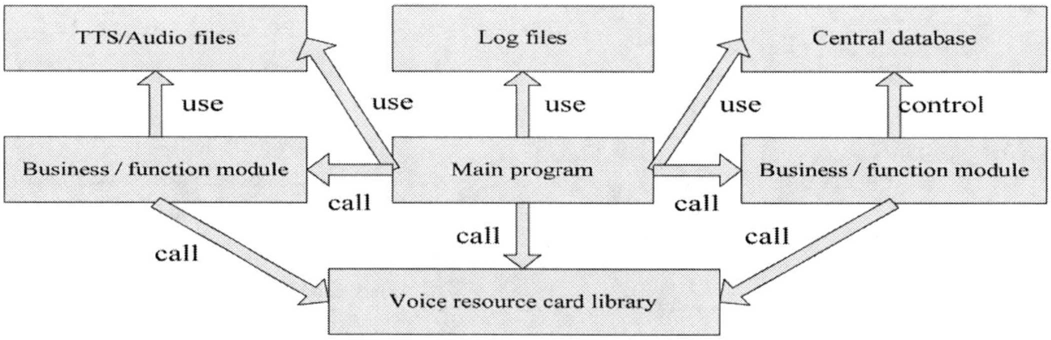

Figure 3. The Program Framework

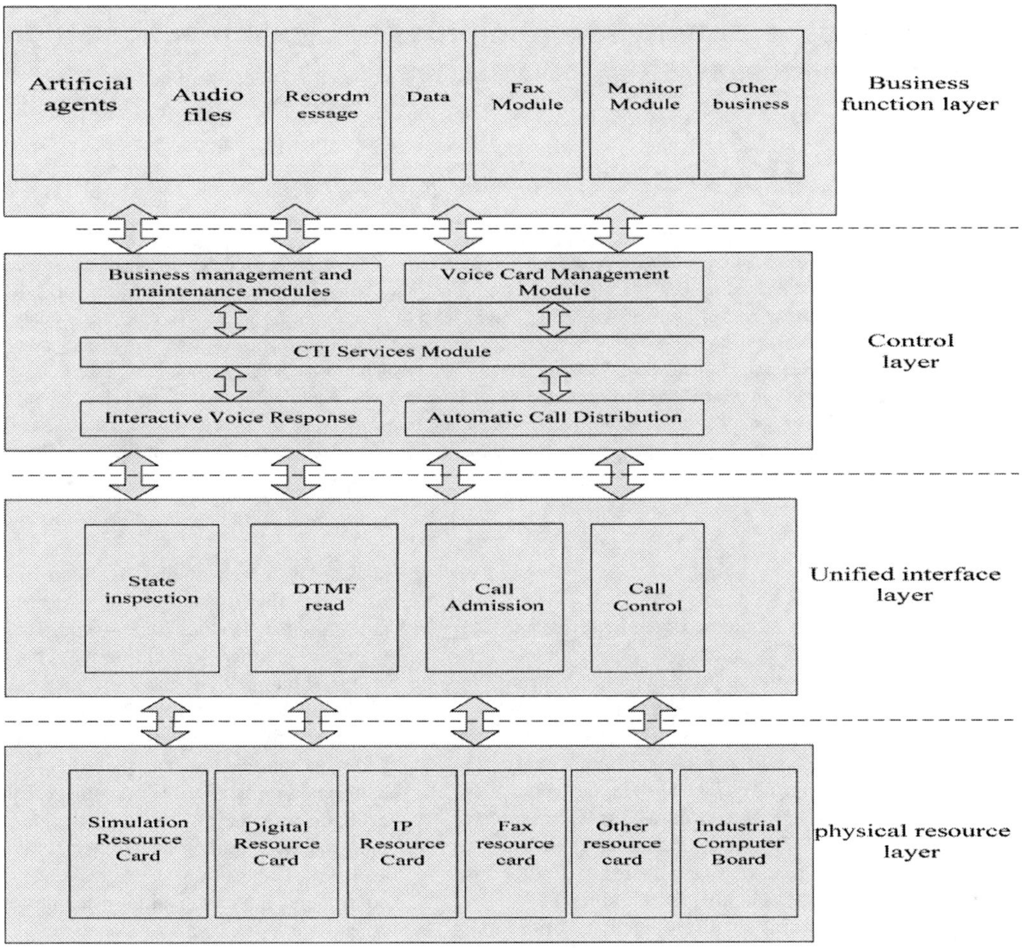

Figure 2. The Hierarchical Structure of System Software

MATEC Web of Conferences 44, 02096 (2016)
DOI: 10.1051/matecconf/20164402096

Novel, low-cost alternative technologies to tackle practical, industrial conundrums – a case study of batteries

Victor K. Y. Chan[1,a] and Sok Lei Leong[1]

[1]Macao Polytechnic Institute, School of Business, Rua de Luís Gonzaga Gomes, Macao, China.

Abstract. Whereas batteries in comparison with most other means of energy storage are more environmentally friendly and economical in their operation, they are beset by low energy replenishment rates, low energy storage density, high capital cost of themselves, and high capital cost of energy replenishment infrastructures. Mainly based on ergonomics, this paper proposes a novel, low-cost alternative technology to practically and industrially make these weaknesses irrelevant to some extent without calling for revolutionary technological breakthroughs in material science, batteries' microstructures, or battery manufacturing technologies. The technology takes advantage of modularization of battery systems, prioritization of charging and discharging of battery module(s) according to ease of unloading and/or loading the battery module(s) and/or ease of loading replacement battery module(s) of the battery module(s).

1 Introduction

Through discharging energy stored, charged batteries can power electrical and/or electronic instruments, equipment, devices, and/or machineries, which comprise and/or are connected to housings where such batteries are usually installed.

On the one hand, as particularly but not exclusively manifested by battery-powered electrical vehicles versus internal combustion vehicles, battery power is far more environmentally friendly [1] and economical in its operation in terms of the recurrent cost than most other means of energy storage [2]. The former is vulnerable to a range of vexed conundrums on the other hand. Such conundrums are ascribable to the weaknesses of battery power vis-à-vis other means of energy storage in respect of the former's fundamental and practical properties as elucidated below as well as the compromise between such properties:

1. <u>Low energy replenishment rates</u>: As far as energy replenishment through charging is concerned, the current, non-experimental battery charging technologies permit an energy delivery rate in kilowatts (kW) [3] in contrast with, for example, thousands of kW in the case of a typical gas pump for replenishing energy stored in internal combustion vehicles. In fact, such rates are limited not only by the charging technologies but also the capacity of and compatibility with the local electric power grid [3]. Low charging rates result in prolonged charging durations.
2. <u>Low energy storage density</u>: Energy storage density refers to the energy stored per unit weight of the storage system, which is over ten times lower for batteries than gasoline, for example [3]. A consequence in the case of vehicles is electric vehicles' shorter vehicle ranges between energy replenishments than those of internal combustion vehicles [1, 4]. Another concomitant consequence is the relatively large sizes and heavy weights of batteries themselves and their housings where the batteries are installed. Worst still, for the same type of batteries, their sizes and weights perceivably increase with their total energy storable. As such, especially but not exclusively, instruments, equipment, devices, and/or machineries consuming considerable power and/or energy necessitate batteries of commensurately considerable sizes and weights. Typical examples of instruments, equipment, devices, and/or machineries consuming considerable power and/or energy include electric vehicles, which usually comprise housings where battery systems are installed, so quite many aspects of electric vehicle design are usually sacrificed in order to accommodate sizable and heavy-weight batteries.
3. <u>High capital cost of energy replenishment infrastructures</u>: Such infrastructures usually involve not only standardized and inter-operable charging facilities but also upgrade of the local electric power grid [3] and thus may sometimes call for mega-projects at the national or even international level to implement. The odds are also that such implementation is exceptionally political and prone to obstinate resistance, especially, when

[a] Corresponding author: vkychan@ipm.edu.mo

standardization or other kinds of vested interests are concerned [3].

4. High capital cost of batteries: The higher capital cost of batteries than that of other means of energy storage render the overall capital cost of electrical and/or electronic instruments, equipment, devices, and/or machineries with batteries as the means of energy storage higher than that of comparable products adopting other means of energy storage [1, 3]. Such a difference is obvious when it comes to electric vehicles versus internal combustion vehicles [1, 3].

For the sake of tackling these four weaknesses, effort of current research in both academia and industry is highly focussed on material science and battery microstructures to discover and/or synthesize ameliorated battery chemistry and anode/cathode materials that in combination can give rise to higher charging rates and energy storage density and on inventing more ingenious manufacturing technologies to lower the production cost of batteries of a particular chemistry, anode/cathode materials, and battery microstructures [5]. Both nature scientists and social scientists have also researched into ways to construct charging infrastructures at minimal cost and incentivize investment in such infrastructures [3]. It is true that all such research has borne fruit [3, 5]. Nonetheless, much less accentuation has been accorded to leveraging ergonomics of battery usage to make the four aforesaid weaknesses irrelevant to some extent, enabling even batteries based on current technologies of material science and battery microstructures to practically and industrially power a broader range of electrical and/or electronic instruments, equipment, devices, and/or machineries and thus replace other means of energy storage prevailing in such applications.

This paper proposes an ergonomics-based, novel, low-cost alternative technology, which is now a patent pending of the authors, to fill this gap. The paper further illustrates why and how such a technology may be able to practically and industrially make the four aforementioned weaknesses irrelevant to some extent and thus pave the way for batteries powering such electrical and/or electronic instruments, equipment, devices, and/or machineries as electrical vehicles without revolutionary technological breakthroughs in material science and battery microstructures and/or heavy investment in the invention of improved battery manufacturing technologies being a prerequisite for the technology's deployment in such real-life applications.

2 The ergonomics of battery energy replenishment

The four weaknesses of battery power as enumerated in the last section are manifested in the replenishment of energy stored in battery systems. There are two obvious approaches to replenish the energy stored in a partially or fully discharged battery system installed in a housing, namely,

1. charging (or recharging) the discharged battery system and
2. replacing the discharged battery system with a replacement battery system storing more energy than the discharged battery system whilst the discharged battery system is optionally to be charged (or recharged) with some charging facilities and to replace another discharged battery system subsequently.

In view of weakness 2 expounded in the last section, especially, if not exclusively, for aforementioned instruments, equipment, devices, and/or machineries consuming considerable power and/or energy, both these two approaches are practically beset by a fundamental difficulty to unload such battery systems of considerable sizes and weights from the housings and load (or reload) such battery systems after charging or load replacement battery systems, resulting in the following scenarios for the aforesaid approaches 1 and 2.

In approach 1, either the discharged battery systems must be charged when still remaining installed in the housings (i.e. in situ) or the discharged battery systems must be unloaded from the housings with appreciable effort before the discharged battery systems can be charged (or recharged) somewhere else with charging facilities and subsequently loaded (or reloaded) into the housings again with appreciable effort.

Charging the discharged battery systems when still remaining installed in the housings implies the necessary availability of charging facilities in the vicinity of the housings. For example, in the case of electric vehicles, this in turn implies immense infrastructures of charging facilities in a large number of parking spaces where the electric vehicles park and thus their discharged battery systems are optionally charged concurrently given that weakness 1 detailed in the last section confines charging to electric vehicles parking for protracted durations. SAE J1772 [6], IEC 62196 [7], and CHAdeMO [8] concern typical standards of such charging facilities. Weakness 3 as explained in the last section renders extensive availability of parking spaces with such immense infrastructures rather economically infeasible.

Alternatively, unloading discharged battery systems from their housings before charging and subsequent loading (or reloading) the charged battery systems implies the necessary availability of trained personnel and/or specialized loading and/or unloading facilities in the vicinity of the housings. For example, in the case of electric vehicles, this in turn implies immense infrastructures of trained personnel and/or specialized loading and/or unloading facilities in parking spaces or designated service stations where electric vehicles park or stop over and thus the electric vehicles' discharged battery systems are optionally unloaded for charging somewhere else and subsequently loaded (or reloaded) back into housings. Moreover, this also implies immense infrastructures to transport the discharged battery systems between such parking spaces or service stations and where there are charging facilities to charge the discharged battery systems. All these immense infrastructures aggravate weakness 3 delineated in the last section.

In approach 2, the discharged battery systems must be unloaded from the housings with appreciable effort, and

the replacement battery systems must be loaded into the housings again with appreciable effort. For example, in the case of electric vehicles, this in turn calls for immense infrastructures of trained personnel and/or specialized loading and/or unloading facilities at designated service stations where discharged battery systems are unloaded and replacement battery systems loaded. This again exacerbates weakness 3 elaborated in the last section.

Worst still, as with most engineering optimizations where cost poses constraints on the optimization of and the compromise between system properties, the capital cost of batteries (to which weakness 4 of the last section relates) surges when attempting to increase charging rates (to which weakness 1 above relates) and energy storage density (to which weakness 2 above relates) [9]. In summary, both approaches 1 and 2 are plagued by some or all of the four weaknesses of the last section.

3 The proposed technology

The proposed technology aims at a solution to the aforementioned fundamental difficulty to unload and/or load battery systems, especially but not exclusively, those of considerable sizes and weights, based on the following principles:

1. Each battery system in a housing is modularized such that it is composed of a number of battery modules, each (or at least each of some of them) being individually unloadable from and loadable into the housing with substantially less effort than unloading and loading the battery system as a whole and each (or at least each of some of them) being optionally, individually chargeable and/or dischargeable.
2. Prioritization of battery module(s) to be charged and/or prioritization of battery module(s) to be discharged depends on ease of unloading and/or loading the battery module(s) to be charged and/or ease of loading replacement battery module(s) of the battery module(s) to be charged and/or depend on ease of unloading and/or loading the battery module(s) to be discharged and/or ease of loading replacement battery module(s) of the battery module(s) to be discharged. The ease of unloading and loading of particular battery module(s) may be due to, inter alia, the geographical location(s) of the battery module(s) in the housing.
3. Optionally, when the battery system is charged as a whole, additional charging priority is accorded to battery module(s) that are less easily unloadable and/or less easily loadable and/or battery module(s) of which replacement battery module(s) are less easily loadable vis-à-vis battery module(s) that are more easily unloadable and/or more easily loadable and/or battery module(s) of which replacement battery module(s) are more easily loadable. Highness and lowness of such charging priority are realized respectively by high and low relative intensity of electric current for charging where relative intensity of electric current for charging battery module(s) is the ratio of the intensity of electric current for charging the battery module(s) to the energy storage capacity of the battery module(s), and low relative intensity of electric current for charging may but does not necessarily mean not charging at all, i.e., zero intensity of electric current for charging.
4. Optionally, when the battery system is discharged, whether or not to power instrument(s), equipment, device(s), and/or machinery(ies), additional discharging priority is accorded to battery module(s) that are more easily unloadable and/or more easily loadable and/or battery module(s) of which replacement battery module(s) are more easily loadable vis-à-vis battery module(s) that are less easily unloadable and/or less easily loadable and/or battery module(s) of which replacement battery module(s) are less easily loadable. Highness and lowness of such discharging priority are realized respectively by high and low relative intensity of electric current for discharging where relative intensity of electric current for discharging battery module(s) is the ratio of the intensity of electric current for discharging the battery module(s) to the energy storage capacity of the battery module(s), and low relative intensity of electric current for discharging may but does not necessarily mean not discharging at all, i.e., zero intensity of electric current for discharging.
5. Optionally, battery module(s) that are more easily unloadable and/or more easily loadable and/or battery module(s) of which replacement battery module(s) are more easily loadable are accorded additional discharging priority for being discharged whereas battery module(s) that are less easily unloadable and/or less easily loadable and/or battery module(s) of which replacement battery module(s) are less easily loadable are accorded additional charging priority for being charged such that the battery module(s) being discharged charge(s) the battery module(s) being charged.

In essence, this proposed technology is to keep, to a possible extent, battery module(s) that are more easily unloadable and/or more easily loadable and/or battery module(s) of which replacement battery module(s) are more easily loadable at a lower state of charge than battery module(s) that are less easily unloadable and/or less easily loadable and/or battery module(s) of which replacement battery module(s) are less easily loadable. This way, battery module(s) that are more easily unloadable and/or more easily loadable and/or battery module(s) of which replacement battery module(s) are more easily loadable are more likely in more need of energy replenishment than battery module(s) that are less easily unloadable and/or less easily loadable and/or battery module(s) of which replacement battery module(s) are less easily loadable. To replenish the energy stored in the battery system, users can choose, inter alia, either one of the following options:

1. unloading battery module(s) that are more easily unloadable and/or more easily loadable, charging the unloaded battery modules(s), and loading (or reloading) the charged battery module(s) with less

effort and less specialized facilities than analogously unloading, charging, and loading (or reloading) battery module(s) that are less easily unloadable and/or less easily loadable and with substantially less effort and less specialized facilities than analogously unloading, charging, and loading (or reloading) the battery system as a whole.

2. unloading battery module(s) that are more easily unloadable and/or battery module(s) of which replacement battery module(s) are more easily loadable and loading charged replacement battery module(s) with less effort and less specialized facilities than analogously unloading battery module(s) that are less easily unloadable and/or battery module(s) of which replacement battery module(s) are less easily loadable and loading charged replacement battery module(s) with substantially less effort and specialized facilities than unloading the battery system as a whole and loading a charged replacement battery system as a whole.

Both these options 1 and 2 concomitantly replenish the energy stored in battery module(s) more in need of stored energy replenishment.

For option 1, it is noteworthy that unloading, charging, and loading (or reloading) battery modules(s) that are more easily unloadable and/or more easily loadable need less specialized facilities than analogously unloading, charging, and loading (or reloading) battery module(s) that are less easily unloadable and/or less easily loadable because the former situation obviously involves less sophistication in disassembling, conveyance, assembling, etc. Likewise, unloading, charging, and loading (or reloading) battery modules(s) that are more easily unloadable and/or more easily loadable need substantially less specialized facilities than analogously unloading, charging, and loading (or reloading) the battery system as a whole because the former situation involves handling of smaller size(s) and weight(s) of battery module(s) than those of the battery system as a whole in the latter situation, the former situation involves smaller charging power than the latter situation, and the smaller size(s) and weight(s) of battery module(s) in the former situation allow minimal facilities to convey the battery module(s) between the housing and where charging facilities are located. For example, in the case of electric vehicles, unloading and loading (or reloading) battery modules(s) that are more easily unloadable and/or more easily loadable and conveyance of such unloaded battery module(s) between where the electric vehicles are parked and where charging facilities are located may be practically be performed manually by the users without specialized facilities whatsoever whilst charging may be performed with domestic and mains-based charging facilities or the like at homes, offices, etc.

For option 2, unloading battery module(s) that are more easily unloadable and/or battery module(s) of which replacement battery module(s) are more easily loadable and loading charged replacement battery module(s) need less specialized facilities than analogously unloading battery module(s) that are less easily unloadable and/or battery module(s) of which replacement battery module(s) are less easily loadable and loading charged replacement battery module(s) because the former situation obviously involves less sophistication in disassembling, conveyance, assembling, etc. Likewise, unloading battery module(s) that are more easily unloadable and/or battery module(s) of which replacement battery module(s) are more easily loadable and loading charged replacement battery module(s) need substantially less specialized facilities than unloading the battery system as a whole and loading a replacement battery system as a whole because the former situation involves handling of smaller size(s) and weight(s) of battery module(s) than those of the battery system as a whole in the latter situation. Also, for this option 2, charging may be performed with domestic and mains-based charging facilities or the like at homes, offices, etc.

In short, both options 1 and 2 reduce the use of specialized facilities and thus the cost of energy replenishment infrastructures (to which weakness 3 above relates). Better still, charging rates (to which weakness 1 above relates) are rendered by either of these two options somewhat irrelevant to the users' convenience and operational cost in that these two options' charging may be performed with domestic and mains-based charging facilities or the like at homes, offices, etc., obviating employment of specialized charging facilities, which are presumably expensive and relatively less readily accessible, for extended time periods. Likewise, with either options 1 or 2, although low energy storage density (to which weakness 2 above relates) of battery systems still leads to their considerable sizes and weights, the use of expensive, specialized charging facilities to handle large battery sizes and weights is no longer necessitated thanks to the proposed technology's modularization of battery systems and thus their energy replenishment. As a final result, with the proposed technology, there may be room for reducing the capital cost of batteries (to which weakness 4 above relates) given the less need to increase the charging rates (to which weakness 1 above relates) and the energy storage density (to which weakness 2 above relates), relaxing quite some capital cost optimization constraints.

4 Conclusion

Mainly based on the ergonomics of battery energy replenishment, this paper proposes a novel, low-cost alternative technology that may be able to practically and industrially make irrelevant to some extent the four major weaknesses of battery power vis-à-vis other means of energy storage and thus pave the way for batteries powering such electrical and/or electronic instruments, equipment, devices, and/or machineries as electrical vehicle without revolutionary technological breakthroughs in material science and battery microstructures and/or heavy investment in the invention of improved battery manufacturing technologies being a prerequisite for the technology's deployment in such real-life applications.

The proposed technology takes advantage of modularization of battery systems, prioritization of charging and discharging of battery module(s) according to ease of unloading and/or loading the battery module(s) and/or ease of loading replacement battery module(s) of the battery module(s). This proposed technology may be able to eradicate the need for specialized charging facilities altogether and thus is particularly fit for densely populated metropolitans where space for such facilities (for example, private garages in the case of electric vehicle battery systems) is not only hardly available but also costly.

Acknowledgments

This article was supported by Grant (004/2013/A) of the Science and Technology Development Fund, the Government of Macao Special Administrative Region.

References

1. M. Hülsmann, D. Fornahl (eds.), *Evolutionary Paths Towards the Mobility Patterns of the Future*, Lecture Notes in Mobility (2014)
2. C.-S. N. Shiau, C. Samaras, R. Hauffe, J.J. Michalek, Impact of battery weight and charging patterns on the economic and environmental benefits of plug-in hybrid vehicles, *2009 Annual Meeting of the Transportation Research Board* (2009)
3. M. Ralston, N. Nigro, *Plug-In Electric Vehicles: Literature Review* (2011)
4. L. Raykin, H.L. MacLean, M.J. Roorda, Implications of driving patterns on well-to-wheel performance of plug-in hybrid electric vehicles, *Environ. Sci. Technol.* **46**, 6363–6370 (2012)
5. M.-C. Lin, M. Gong, B. Lu, Y. Wu, D.-Y. Wang, M. Guan, M. Angell, C. Chen, J. Yang, B.-J. Hwang, H. Dai, An ultrafast rechargeable aluminium-ion battery, *Nature* **520**, 324–328 (2015)
6. SAE International, *J1772_201210: SAE Electric Vehicle and Plug in Hybrid Electric Vehicle Conductive Charge Coupler* (2012)
7. International Electrotechnical Commission, *IEC 62196-3:2014: Plugs, Socket-Outlets, Vehicle Connectors and Vehicle Inlets - Conductive Charging of Electric Vehicles* (2014)
8. CHAdeMO, Technological details, http://www.chademo.com/wp/technology/details/ (Accessed 14/01/2016)
9. Texas Instruments Incorporated, *Characteristics of Rechargeable Batteries* (2011)

AUTHOR INDEX

AUTHOR INDEX

AUTHOR INDEX

AUTHOR INDEX

AUTHOR INDEX